VICTORIAN LITERATURE

POETRY

VICTORIAN LITERATURE

POETRY

Donald J. Gray

INDIANA UNIVERSITY

G. B. Tennyson

UNIVERSITY OF CALIFORNIA, LOS ANGELES

MACMILLAN PUBLISHING CO., INC.

New York

Macmillan Publishing Co., Inc.
866 Third Avenue, New York, New York 10022

Library of Congress Cataloging in Publication Data

Gray, Donald J
  Victorian literature.

  Bibliography: p.
  Includes index.
  1. English poetry—19th century. I. Tennyson,
G. B., joint author. II. Title.
PR1223.G73 1976   821'.8'08   75-11623
ISBN 0-02-346130-6

Printing 1 2 3 4 5 6 7 8   Year 6 7 8 9 0 1 2

ACKNOWLEDGMENTS

COLUMBIA UNIVERSITY PRESS. *Emily Brontë:* Selections from Emily Brontë are reprinted from *The Complete Poems of Emily Jane Brontë,* edited by C. W. Hatfield (1941).

MACMILLAN PUBLISHING CO., INC. *William Butler Yeats:* Excerpt, "The Trembling of the Veil" from *Autobiography* by William Butler Yeats. Copyright 1924 by Macmillan Publishing Co., Inc., renewed 1952 by Bertha Georgie Yeats.

OXFORD UNIVERSITY PRESS. *Arthur Hugh Clough:* Excerpts from Scenes V, VI, XII, XIV of *Dipsychus* by Arthur Hugh Clough; "Is it true, ye gods, who treat us"; "Easter Day I, Naples, 1849"; "Easter Day II"; "The Latest Decalogue"; "Resignation —To Faustus"; reprinted from *The Poems of Arthur Hugh*

Clough, edited by H. F. Lowry, A. L. P. Norrington, and F. L. Mulhauser (1951), by permission of Oxford University Press, Oxford. *Gerard Manley Hopkins:* Excerpt from *Journal* 1864 from *Journals and Papers of Gerard Manley Hopkins,* edited by Humphry House and Graham Storey (1967); Letter to Alexander Baillie from *Further Letters of Hopkins,* 2nd ed., edited by Claude Colleer Abbott (1956); Letters to Richard Watson Dixon from *Correspondence of Gerard Manley Hopkins and R. W. Dixon,* 2nd ed., edited by Claude Colleer Abbott (1956); "I am like a slip of comet"; "The Beginning of the End"; "Let me be to Thee as the circling bird"; reprinted from *Poems of Gerard Manley Hopkins,* 4th ed., edited by W. H. Gardner and H. H. Mackenzie (1967); published by Oxford University Press by arrangement with the Society of Jesus.

PREFACE

My FUNDAMENTAL intention in selecting the poems of this anthology was to illustrate the central canon of poetry published in Great Britain between 1830 and 1900. This canon is represented here in selections from twenty-six poets, beginning with some of the poems Wordsworth published in the 1830s and ending with selections from Thomas Hardy's first volumes of verse. Wordsworth was established as a major poet during the early Victorian decades in which he published his last poems; most of the others were recognized by 1900 as the principal poets of the period. A few—notably John Clare, Gerard Manley Hopkins, Thomas Hardy, and perhaps Emily Brontë—were not added to the roll of important poets until many of the poems they wrote during the nineteenth century were published in the twentieth. There have also been shifts in judgment, and in the grounds of judgment, since 1900. Some poets are more (Matthew Arnold and Arthur Hugh Clough) or less (Elizabeth Barrett Browning and Rudyard Kipling) esteemed today than in their lifetimes. The two dominant poets of the period, Tennyson and Robert Browning, are now admired not as sages or ethical teachers, as they once were, but as poets of exceptional lyric and dramatic gifts who attained a remarkable moral authority in their culture. Swinburne, both admired and dispraised during and after his lifetime, seems now to be attaining a secure stature as a similarly powerful cultural figure whose intensity made his writing important to mid- and late-century readers in their decisions about who they were, what they were for, and what they were against.

I have tried to reflect the premises and consequences of nineteenth- as well as twentieth-century estimates in my choice and arrangement of the writings of these poets. I have included some of the poems by which they were best known in their century. With a few exceptions (Hopkins again) I have arranged the poets in an order determined by the dates of their first significant publication. Poems by each author are also usually arranged by date of publication, with the date of composition, when it is known, in parentheses. (When a poem has two significant dates of publication, in earlier and later versions, say, or in a magazine and then in a volume, both dates are cited.) The chronological arrangement is intended to reveal the development of individual poets and of Victorian poetry as a nineteenth-century reader might have perceived them. At the same time, my decisions about the kind and number of poems to be included have been influenced by my own mid-twentieth-century sensibility. I have included, for example, more poems by William Barnes, Emily Brontë, and Thomas Hood than a mid-Victorian reader would have expected. I have probably selected more of the enigmatic, deeply ambivalent lyric and dramatic poems of Tennyson and Robert Browning than would have been approved by those many contemporaries who liked the firm resolutions of their longer poems. I have included these latter selections in order to suggest what Victorian poetry is to our perception as well as what it was in the perception of its contemporary readers, and to demonstrate how and why its achievement still attracts, moves, and pleases.

The poems I have selected as representative of styles and themes common in early-, mid-, and late-Victorian poetry establish a literary context for the writing of the principal poets. They also suggest the variety and frequent excellence of Victorian poetry. Some of these poems are interesting because they are fine poems, some because they were once very popular, and some because they are good and were popular. Along with the writing of better-known poets, they record some of the ways in which writers influence one another, how themes, styles, and conventions are set and changed. These representative poems also intimate something of the dense mesh of expectations and associations with which Victorian readers received a poem. Sometimes they testify to the prevalence of certain features of style and statement in the period. Sometimes they remind us that Victorian literary taste and standards were not simple and that earlier forms and conceptions of poetry persisted all through the period.

The selections of comic poems, religious poems, and hymns, and of popular and political songs, are intended to enlarge the usual idea of Victorian literature. Except for some of the religious poems, the verse I have included in these sections was not usually thought to be literature, even by the Victorians who used and enjoyed it. But in their use and enjoyment these poems and songs served two ancient functions of literature. Their writers used the sound and forms of words, meter, and rhyme to give pleasure—sometimes also to give point to moral and political statements, but always to give pleasure. Further, these poems brought the people they pleased together in a recognition and affirmation of the shared ideas and feelings that constitute a culture. Many of these poems are related to conventional poetry of the period in their imitation or travesty of its prevalent themes, language, and forms. Other familiar poems, especially hymns and street ballads, gave their forms and rhythms to some conventionally literary poems. But the principal reason for regarding familiar verse itself as literature is not its relationship to the established poetry of high Victorian culture. It is literature because of the power or wit with which it articulated ideas and feelings important to the many Victorians it pleased, even though its sounds and sentiments were so familiar a part of their lives that they themselves did not think these poems to be anything so remarkable as poetry.

Of the several, necessary limitations of this anthology I wish to specify three. It is not possible within the bounds of this collection to suggest the number and quality of long narrative and dramatic poems that were a central part and expression of Victorian ideas about poetry. The dominant idea of poetry all through the nineteenth century in Britain was enacted in the lyric: a poem that was intense, telling, melodious, and short; often a rendering of particular or personal experience; and always, fundamentally, an expression of feeling addressed to feeling. But the grand, prophetic ambitions of Victorian poets often took them to long forms—to epic, versions of Greek and Elizabethan tragedy, collections of narrative and dramatic episodes like *The Idylls of the King* and *The Ring and the Book,* connected narratives in verse like Elizabeth Barrett Browning's *Aurora Leigh* and Patmore's *The Angel in the House,* and extended self-dramatizations of sensibility like Browning's *Sordello,* Philip James Bailey's *Festus,* and Alexander Smith's *A Life-Drama.* The intentions and effects of these poems are apparent only when they are read whole, or at least read in parts long enough to suggest the scale and design of the whole. This anthology of shorter poems does represent the strong narrative and dramatic traditions that flourished along with the lyric tradition in the poetry of the period. These shorter poems should be read, however, in the knowledge that a tradition of long poems also flourished continuously in the literature of nineteenth-century Britain.

Second, the inclusion of some familiar and popular verse is a small recognition that almost all the poetry we habitually think of as part of Victorian literature was written and read by no more than a minority of that minority that was economically, politically, and socially dominant in Victorian Britain. Scores of volumes of poems were published each year during the period, and poems were very often printed in the hundreds of newspapers, magazines, and annuals published in the century. The normal printing of an edition of poems, however, was only about 500 copies. The sales of a few poems were extraordinary, for poetry; for example, the first episodes of Tennyson's *The Idylls of the King* sold 10,000 copies of its first edition of 40,000 copies in the first week of publication in 1859, and 60,000 copies were printed of the first edition of his *Enoch Arden* volume in 1864. These figures, impressive as they are, must be seen against other statistics of literacy and readership. In 1860 the literate population of England and Scotland was perhaps 16 million. In 1864 the daily circulation of London newspapers was over half a million, and in the same year it was estimated that the weekly sales of penny and half-penny magazines of fiction directed to working-class audiences were over a million copies. Victorian poems and poets did act, directly and indirectly, on the consciousness and will of people who, whether they read them or not, lived in a society that publicly honored poets. But even the best-known and most-honored poets managed their influence literally from an eminence. From the beginning of the period poets who took themselves seriously knew they were set apart by the very craft and power by which the most ambitious of them wanted to change the lives of their contemporaries.

Finally, it is not possible in this anthology to suggest how its poems were related to and shaped by, how they expressed and whether they altered, the other components of Victorian lives. The great intellectual, religious, scientific, and political conceptions and controversies that rolled through the period cannot be responsibly described in a brief space. I have not tried to do more than identify them sparsely in notes and introductions when references to them seemed necessary. Essentially, I have put these

Victorian poems only in the company of one another. Their relationships with one another, and with the larger history of British romanticism that is suggested at one end of the period in selections from Wordsworth and at the other in selections from Yeats and Hardy, do answer the important question of what these poems are. How they functioned in the cultures in which they were written and read is another question. Its answer lies in the relationships not between poems but between poems and other articulations of idea and feeling. How, for example, is the matter of science or politics transformed when it is taken into a poem? Why do some readers desire such transformations? Why, when most people living in the Victorian period did not buy or presumably enjoy what they took to be serious poetry, did some of the structures of their society nonetheless assure that (even as now) such poems were encountered in schools, and that (unlike now) state funerals, battles, and other national events were celebrated by the Poet Laureate and in street ballads alike? The study of poetry that will engage such questions will move through the poems to a study of how science and politics were known by the readers of Tennyson and Browning, what these readers said they wanted from poetry, what the differences were between the audiences of the laureate and the street singer, how these differences fit with the forms and effects of social structures and institutions, and how, finally, the poems themselves fit in this matrix of knowledge, need, and social circumstance that presses in on them and on which they press. A study of Victorian poetry, in short, cannot end with the poems. But it must begin and return there. The poems of this anthology are chosen to illuminate the manifold character and development of Victorian poetry so that questions about its social, cultural, and psychological functions, in its time and ours, can be accurately founded and pointedly framed.

I have learned to ask questions about Victorian poetry and culture from the books of Raymond Williams, M. H. Abrams, Frank Kermode, Morse Peckham, and Robert Langbaum, among others listed in the general bibliography given at the end of this anthology. I wish also to thank Martha Vicinus, who has taught me a great deal about Victorian popular songs and working-class poetry; Anthony Shipps of the Indiana University Library, who has been unfailingly helpful in identifying quotations in the poems; William Cagle of the Lilly Library at Indiana and the staffs of the Lilly and University Libraries, who helped me to find and borrow many hard-to-find texts; Georg Tennyson for his advice and example; and D. Anthony English of Macmillan for many assistances, for being patient, and, finally and yet more usefully, for not being patient. Above all, I recall with affection the conversations and friendships with Philip Appleman and with George Levine, William Madden, and Michael Wolff in which this anthology, and a great deal more, began.

A NOTE ON THE TEXTS AND BIBLIOGRAPHIES

The source of the text of each selection is identified in annotations or in the introduction to the selection. With a few exceptions—poems published from manuscript after the author's death, for example, or some hymns and popular songs, where it is more interesting to know the version most people were singing than to know the sometimes different version the author originally published—the texts are those of the last edition pub-

lished with the author's oversight. The bibliographies appended to each
set of selections are intended to list only books and essays fundamental and
preliminary to further study. The sources of more extensive bibliographies
in Victorian poetry and literature are listed in the general bibliography
at the end of the text.

A Note on Editorial Responsibility

Although *Victorian Literature: Poetry* and its companion work, *Victorian Literature: Prose,* were conceived and undertaken together, Georg
Tennyson and I divided our editorial task between the volumes. Professor
Tennyson assumed principal responsibility for the prose. I am responsible
for the anthology of poetry.

Donald J. Gray

CONTENTS

William Barnes

337

Emily Brontë

351

PART TWO

EARLY VICTORIAN
POEMS 1830–1850

Walter Savage Landor
362

Winthrop Mackworth Praed
363

Ebenezer Elliott
365

Felicia Hemans
367

Letitia Elizabeth Landon
368

Hartley Coleridge
369

James Clarence Mangan
371

Samuel Ferguson
373

Ebenezer Jones
375

Thomas Babington Macaulay
376

William Edmondstoune Aytoun
380

Richard Hengist Horne
383

PART FOUR
MID-VICTORIAN
POEMS 1850–1880

Robert Stephen Hawker
735

Alexander Smith
737

Sydney Dobell
738

William Johnson Cory
740

Charles Tennyson Turner
741

John Byrne Leicester Warren, Third Baron de Tabley
742

PART SIX

LATE-VICTORIAN POEMS 1880–1900

PART NINE

RELIGIOUS POEMS
AND HYMNS

John Keble
951

Robert Montgomery
954

John Henry Newman
956

Reginald Heber
959

James Montgomery
960

Bernard Barton
963

Josiah Conder
963

Charlotte Elliott
964

Sarah Flower Adams
965

Henry Francis Lyte
966

PART ONE

Principal Victorian
Poets 1830-1850

William Wordsworth
1770–1850

In the preface to the first collected edition of his poems in 1815 Wordsworth wrote that a great and original poet must create the taste by which he is to be enjoyed. He seems always to have been confident that he was a great poet. But it was not until the last decades of his life, which were also the first decades of the Victorian era, that he was sure his poems had found and made their proper readers. It had taken several years to sell the relatively few copies of the collected editions published in 1815, 1820, and 1827, and there was a time in the mid-1820s when all or almost all of Wordsworth's books were out of print. But the collected edition he published in 1832 was modestly successful, and by the mid-1830s Wordsworth, for the first time in his life, was making a significant and steady income from the writing of poetry. After 1835 until his death in 1850 there was hardly a year in which he did not put a volume or edition of new or old poems before his increasing audience.

Reviewers of Wordsworth's poems early in the century had ridiculed his simplicity or professed to be mystified by poems celebrating a transcendent union between humans and nature. By 1830, however, students in the universities and young men in London were gathering to read and discuss these poems as important testaments of emotional, intellectual, and religious experience. Reviewers of the volumes containing new poems he published in 1835 and 1842 usually, and sometimes reverentially, wrote about him as the most distinguished living British writer. There were other marks of fame as well as eminence: honorary degrees from Oxford and Cambridge, election to the Irish Academy, the poet laureateship in 1843. Tourists came just to look at his house in the Lake District, and young writers came to visit him there. When he came to London he met Tennyson and Thomas Carlyle, and in London and from Rydal Mount he wrote and talked about such current matters as copyright law, capital punishment, the law regulating public assistance to the poor, and the impact of towns and machinery on the affective and imaginative lives of humans. In short, Wordsworth in the last decades of his life was a large presence in the literary scene in which writers of the generation of Tennyson and Browning were coming into their identities as poets.

The foundation of Wordsworth's eminence was that he had helped to invent the dominant idea of nineteenth-century British poetry and to establish in his practice one of its principal languages. The idea is a complex one whose center is a belief that there is an energy in things which bespeaks a profoundly unifying order, and that there is an energy in man which in moments of high feeling and perception joins with the life in things. The human agency of this perception and union is the imagination, which cooperates with the life and order of natural creation to make forms that express a harmony between the life within and the life without. Among these forms are poems that hold the memory of or reenact those moments in which humans know and feel the high pleasure of existing within an order whose ultimate source and meaning are divine. In Wordsworth's practice such poems are typically lyric and narrative. Their action is often that of the poet making a meaning of what he sees or remembers, affirming and preserving the harmony as he shapes the form of the poem which will hold it. The idiom of his poems is typically one in which the poet moves from precise descriptions of particular natural objects and ordinary events to an elevated (but also precise) rhetoric of reflection and exclamation at the meaning and feeling he has helped to create. The effect of these poems, or at least their intention, is not only to alleviate the states of alienation and emotional deadness or hysteria into which humans are likely to fall when they regard a world that seems to be made of discrete, disordered, and ugly objects. The effect is also to rectify intellectual, moral, and even social and political disorder by lit-

4

4

WILLIAM WORDSWORTH

erally creating order and, more important, the pleasure of order in the lives of humans.

Wordsworth knew that in his latter years he could no longer consistently write poems that created and held the experience of communion with a life and order beyond the self, beyond even the material and mortal. He thought the "Ode on the Power of Sound," which he wrote in 1828 and published in his 1835 volume of poems, was such a poem; in subsequent editions of his poetry he placed it among the "Poems of Imagination," the most important class of his poems. Whatever one may think of that judgment, the "Power of Sound," along with poems such as "Steamboats, Viaducts, and Railways" and his poem on a drawing of the bird of paradise, may fairly represent the language and ambitions of poems in which Wordsworth exercises a poet's imagination to try to invest the temporal and mundane with the meaning of the eternal and divine. Sometimes too in his late poems he displays his remarkable ability to describe objects in a landscape in a rounded, resonant series of images which manifestly is the harmony to which it testifies. More often he is less ambitious in his late poems, content (as in "Yarrow Revisited") to appropriate the historical or conventional associations of the places he writes about and to reflect on these meanings in discursive language rather than to dramatize his discovery of them.

But no matter how greatly his powers as a poet had diminished in his latter years, he was absolutely sure of their high purposes. Whether he is writing deliberately argumentative sonnets endorsing capital punishment or demonstrating how the impalpable power of sound might be an agency of divine grace, he wrote his poems to make a difference in the life of his time. In the "Prelude" to the volume of new and old poems he published in 1842, he sends his poems as consolation and exhortation into the wind of social, political, and moral distress, and one of the reasons he can hope that his poems will have an effect is that they will join "with thy Forerunners that through many a year / Have faithfully prepared each other's way." The continuity and integrity of the achievement he calls upon here are important. In the 1830s and 1840s Wordsworth performed the office of a great poet by pressing his entire canon upon an increasing audience, by continually sending new and old poems to nourish a sensibility he had helped to create and which

he thought must flourish if society was to be sound. It is this insistence that a poet must be so continually and centrally present in his culture, must work so hard and long to affect, however gradually, how people live with the life in things, that makes Wordsworth an important example and measure for the poets who in the last decades of his life were entering upon his calling.

CHRONOLOGY

1770 Born in Westmorland in the north of England. Wordsworth's father was a steward and law agent for the estates of a local titled landholder; his mother was the daughter of a merchant.

1778–87 After the death of his mother (1778) Wordsworth attended school as a boarder; after his father's death (1783) he was placed in the guardianship of two uncles. He entered Cambridge University in 1787.

1791–92 After graduation from Cambridge (1791), he visited France and was attracted by the promise of the Revolution. He met Annette Villon (1791); their daughter was born in the following year.

1793 First volumes of poems, *An Evening Walk* and *Descriptive Sketches,* published.

1795 A small legacy from a friend enabled Wordsworth to continue his exclusive attention to the writing of poetry.

1798–1801 First edition of *Lyrical Ballads* (1798) published; second edition, with Wordsworth's "Preface," published 1801. After a winter in Germany (1798–99), Wordsworth settled with his sister Dorothy in the Lake District in the north of England.

1802–05 Married Mary Hutchinson (1802); their first child (of five children) was born in 1803. Wordsworth began writing the first version of his long autobiographical poem, *The Prelude,* which he completed in 1805.

1807 *Poems in Two Volumes* published.

1813 Wordsworth was appointed Stamp Distributor for Westmorland; his duties were to oversee the collection of duties levied on licenses, legal documents, pamphlets, etc.; his income was usually between £100 and £200 a year. He moved to Rydal Mount in the Lake District, his home for the rest of his life.

1814 *The Excursion,* a long reflective poem, published.

1815 First collected edition of poems, in two

volumes with a preface, published; *The White Doe of Rylstone,* a kind of fanciful romance on a religious theme, was also published.

1819 *Peter Bell* and *The Waggoner* published, both narrative poems.

1820 Four-volume collected edition of poems published; *The River Duddon,* a series of sonnets describing landscape and meditating on its historical and moral associations, was also published.

1822 *Memorials of a Tour on the Continent* and *Ecclesiastical Sketches,* the latter a series of sonnets on topics in the history of the Church of England, published.

1827 Five-volume collected edition of poems published.

1831 With Wordsworth's editorial advice, a selection from his poems "chiefly for the use of schools and young persons" published.

1832 Another collected edition of his poems— the fourth—published.

1835 *Yarrow Revisited and Other Poems* published.

1836–37 Six-volume collected edition of poems published; with some corrections and additions, this edition was reprinted eight times by 1851.

1838 A collection of Wordsworth's sonnets published.

1842 *Poems, Chiefly of Early and Late Years* published. Wordsworth received a pension from the government to honor his services to literature, and he resigned the Stamp Distributorship.

1843 Wordsworth appointed poet laureate.

1845 One-volume collected edition of poems published.

1849 A new collected edition of his poems, including Wordsworth's final revisions, published.

1850 Wordsworth died in April. In July *The Prelude* was published, in a revised version he had prepared in the 1830s.

EDITIONS

The standard edition of Wordsworth's poetry is that edited by Ernest de Selincourt and Helen Darbishire, *The Poetical Works of William Wordsworth, Edited from the Manuscripts, with Textual and Critical Notes,* 5 volumes, revised edition (1952–59). The texts of the poems printed below are those of nineteenth-century editions which are consistent with those of the standard edition. *The Prelude* has also been edited by Ernest de Selincourt; a revised edition, by Helen Darbishire, was published in 1959.

Paul M. Zall has collected and edited *The Literary Criticism of William Wordsworth* (1966). W. J. B. Owen and J. W. Smyser have edited *The Prose Works* in three volumes (1974). *The Letters of William and Dorothy Wordsworth,* edited by Ernest de Selincourt, 6 volumes (1935–39), are being reedited and added to: the letters from 1787 to 1805 have been edited by Chester L. Shaver (1967), and those from 1806 to 1820 have been edited by Mary Moorman and Alan G. Hill (2 volumes, 1969–70). L. N. Broughton's edition of the correspondence between Wordsworth and one of his American editors, *Wordsworth and Reed:*
. . . 1836–1850 (1933), is informative about Wordsworth's ideas of himself and his poetry during these years.

BIOGRAPHY AND CRITICISM

The standard biography is Mary Moorman, *William Wordsworth: A Biography* (1957, 1965).

Bateson, F. W. *Wordsworth: A Re-interpretation* (1954; 1956).

Batho, Edith C. *The Later Wordsworth* (1933).

Darbishire, Helen. *The Poet Wordsworth* (1950).

Groom, Bernard. *The Unity of Wordsworth's Poetry* (1966).

Hartman, Geoffrey. *Wordsworth's Poetry, 1787–1814* (1964).

Jones, John. *The Egotistical Sublime* (1954). Includes a discussion of Wordsworth's religious poems of the 1820s.

Lindenberger, Herbert. *On Wordsworth's* Prelude (1963). Includes a discussion of the reception of the poem.

Logan, James V. *Wordsworthian Criticism: A Guide and Bibliography* (1947). A bibliography of the commentary on Wordsworth's writing from 1850 to 1944. Elton F. Henley and David H. Stam continue this bibliography in *Wordsworthian Criticism 1945–1964* (revised edition, 1965).

Lyon, Judson Stanley. *The Excursion: A Study* (1950). Includes a discussion of the reception and fourteenth-century reputation of the poem.

Peek, Katherine. *Wordsworth in England: Studies in the History of His Fame* (1943).

Perkins, David. *Wordsworth and the Poetry of Sincerity* (1964). Includes a discussion of Wordsworth's changing sense of his audience.

Scoggins, James. *Imagination and Fancy: Complementary Modes in the Poetry of Wordsworth* (1967). Discusses Wordsworth's arrangements of his poems in his 1815 and later collected editions.

Sperry, Willard. *Wordsworth's Anti-Climax* (1935).

Woodring, Carl. *Wordsworth* (1965).

"If thou indeed derive thy light from Heaven"[1]

If thou indeed derive thy light from Heaven,
Then, to the measure of that heaven-born light,
Shine, Poet! in thy place, and be content:—
The stars pre-eminent in magnitude,
And they that from the zenith dart their beams,
(Visible though they be to half the earth,
Though half a sphere be conscious of their
     brightness)
Are yet of no diviner origin,
No purer essence, than the one that burns,   10
Like an untended watch-fire, on the ridge
Of some dark mountain; or than those which
     seem
Humbly to hang, like twinkling winter lamps,
Among the branches of the leafless trees;
All are the undying offspring of one Sire:
Then, to the measure of the light vouchsafed,
Shine, Poet! in thy place, and be content.
                      (After 1813) 1827; 1837

On the Power of Sound

The Ear addressed, as occupied by a spiritual functionary, in communion with sounds, individual, or combined in studied harmony.—Sources and effects of those sounds (to the close of 6th Stanza).—The power of music, whence proceeding, exemplified in the idiot.—Origin of music, and its effect in early ages—how produced (to the middle of 10th Stanza).—The mind recalled to sounds acting casually and severally.—Wish uttered (11th Stanza) that these could be united into a scheme or system for moral interests and intellectual contemplation.—(Stanza 12th.)—The Pythagorean theory of numbers and music, with their supposed power over the motions of the universe—imaginations consonant with such a theory.—Wish expressed (in 11th Stanza) realized, in some degree, by the representation of all sounds under the form of thanksgiving to the Creator.—(Last Stanza) the destruction of earth and the planetary system —the survival of audible harmony, and its support in the Divine Nature, as revealed in Holy Writ.

I

Thy functions are ethereal,
As if within thee dwelt a glancing mind,
Organ of vision! And a Spirit aërial
Informs the cell of Hearing, dark and blind;
Intricate labyrinth, more dread for thought
To enter than oracular cave;[1]
Strict passage, through which sighs are brought,
And whispers for the heart, their slave;
And shrieks, that revel in abuse
Of shivering flesh; and warbled air,   10
Whose piercing sweetness can unloose
The chains of frenzy, or entice a smile
Into the ambush of despair;
Hosannas pealing down the long-drawn aisle,
And requiems answered by the pulse that beats
Devoutly, in life's last retreats!

II

The headlong streams and fountains
Serve Thee, invisible Spirit, with untired
     powers;
Cheering the wakeful tent on Syrian mountains,
They lull perchance ten thousand thousand
     flowers.   20
That roar, the prowling lion's *Here I am,*
How fearful to the desert wide!
That bleat, how tender! of the dam
Calling a straggler to her side.
Shout, cuckoo!—let the vernal soul
Go with thee to the frozen zone;
Toll from thy loftiest perch, lone bell-bird, toll!
At the still hour to Mercy dear,
Mercy from her twilight throne
Listening to nun's faint throb of holy fear,   30
To sailor's prayer breathed from a darkening
     sea
Or widow's cottage-lullaby.

---

[1] Wordsworth placed this poem at the beginning of the collected edition of his poetry he prepared in 1845. The poem was written after he moved to Rydal Mount in 1813, first published in the collected edition of 1827, and revised (lines 2 and 14–16 being added) in 1837.

[1] Oracular cave: an allusion to natural topographical features associated with prophecy, such as the cleft in the earth at the shrine at Delphi at which Greek priestesses prophesied.

III

Ye Voices, and ye Shadows
And Images of voice—to hound and horn
From rocky steep[2] and rock-bestudded meadows
Flung back, and, in the sky's blue caves,
     reborn—
On with your pastime! till the church-tower
     bells
A greeting give of measured glee;
And milder echoes from their cells
Repeat the bridal symphony.
Then, or far earlier, let us rove
Where mists are breaking up or gone,
And from aloft look down into a cove
Besprinkled with a careless quire,[3]
Happy milk-maids, one by one
Scattering a ditty each to her desire,
A liquid concert matchless by nice Art,
A stream as if from one full heart.

IV

Blest be the song that brightens
The blind man's gloom, exalts the veteran's
     mirth;
Unscorned the peasant's whistling breath, that
     lightens
His duteous toil of furrowing the green earth.
For the tired slave, Song lifts the languid oar,
And bids it aptly fall, with chime
That beautifies the fairest shore,
And mitigates the harshest clime.
Yon pilgrims see—in lagging file
They move; but soon the appointed way
A choral *Ave Marie* shall beguile,
And to their hope the distant shrine
Glisten with a livelier ray:
Nor friendless he, the prisoner of the mine,
Who from the well-spring of his own clear breast
Can draw, and sing his griefs to rest.

V

When civic renovation
Dawns on a kingdom, and for needful haste
Best eloquence avails not, Inspiration
Mounts with a tune, that travels like a blast
Piping through cave and battlemented tower;
Then starts the sluggard, pleased to meet
That voice of Freedom, in its power
Of promises, shrill, wild, and sweet!

Who, from a martial *pageant*, spreads
Incitements of a battle-day,
Thrilling the unweaponed crowd with plume-
     less heads?—
Even She whose Lydian airs inspire[4]
Peaceful striving, gentle play
Of timid hope and innocent desire
Shot from the dancing Graces, as they move
Fanned by the plausive[5] wings of Love.   80

VI

How oft along thy mazes,
Regent[6] of sound, have dangerous Passions trod!
O Thou, through whom the temple rings with
     praises,
And blackening clouds in thunder speak of God,
Betray not by the cozenage of sense
Thy votaries, wooingly resigned
To a voluptuous influence
That taints the purer, better, mind;
But lead sick Fancy to a harp
That hath in noble tasks been tried;   90
And, if the virtuous feel a pang too sharp,
Soothe it into patience—stay
The uplifted arm of Suicide;
And let some mood of thine in firm array
Knit every thought the impending issue needs,
Ere martyr burns, or patriot bleeds!

VII

As Conscience, to the centre
Of being, smites with irresistible pain,
So shall a solemn cadence, if it enter
The mouldy vaults of the dull idiot's brain,   100
Transmute him to a wretch from quiet hurled—
Convulsed as by a jarring din;
And then aghast, as at the world
Of reason partially let in
By concords winding with a sway
Terrible for sense and soul!
Or, awed he weeps, struggling to quell dismay.
Point not these mysteries to an Art
Lodged above the starry pole;
Pure modulations flowing from the heart   110
Of divine Love, where Wisdom, Beauty, Truth
With Order dwell, in endless youth?

VIII

Oblivion may not cover
All treasures hoarded by the miser, Time.

---

[2] Steep: precipice.   [3] Quire: choir.
[4] She: Aphrodite, the classical goddess of love, on whom the three Graces of refinement and beauty attended. Lydian: one of the modes of Greek music, characterized as soft and effeminate.
[5] Plausive: applauding.   [6] Regent: ruling principle or power.

Orphean[7] Insight! truth's undaunted lover,
To the first leagues of tutored passion climb,
When Music deigned within this grosser sphere
Her subtle essence to enfold,
And voice and shell drew forth a tear
120 Softer than Nature's self could mould.
Yet *strenuous* was the infant Age:
Art, daring because souls could feel,
Stirred nowhere but an urgent equipage
Of rapt imagination sped her march
Through the realms of woe and weal:
Hell to the lyre bowed low; the upper arch
Rejoiced that clamorous spell and magic verse
Her wan disasters could disperse.

IX

The GIFT to king Amphion[8]
130 That walled a city with its melody
Was for belief no dream:—thy skill, Arion![9]
Could humanize the creatures of the sea,
Where men were monsters. A last grace he craves,
Leave for one chant;—the dulcet sound
Steals from the deck o'er willing waves,
And listening dolphins gather round.
Self-cast, as with a desperate course,
'Mid that strange audience, he bestrides
A proud One docile as a managed horse;
And singing, while the accordant hand
140 Sweeps his harp, the Master rides;
So shall he touch at length a friendly strand,
And he, with his preserver, shine starbright
In memory, through silent night.

X

The pipe of Pan,[10] to shepherds
Couched in the shadow of Mænalian pines,
Was passing sweet; the eyeballs of the leopards,

That in high triumph drew the Lord of vines,[11]
How did they sparkle to the cymbal's clang!
While Fauns and Satyrs beat the ground   150
In cadence,—and Silenus swang
This way and that, with wild-flowers crowned.
To life, to *life* give back thine ear:
Ye who are longing to be rid
Of fable, though to truth subservient, hear
The little sprinkling of cold earth that fell
Echoed from the coffin-lid;
The convict's summons in the steeple's knell;
"The vain distress-gun", from a leeward shore,
Repeated—heard, and heard no more!   160

XI

For terror, joy, or pity,
Vast is the compass and the swell of notes:
From the babe's first cry to voice of regal city,
Rolling a solemn sea-like bass, that floats
Far as the woodlands—with the trill to blend
Of that shy songstress, whose love-tale
Might tempt an angel to descend,
While hovering o'er the moonlight vale.
Ye wandering Utterances, has earth no scheme,
No scale of moral music—to unite   170
Powers that survive but in the faintest dream
Of memory?—O that ye might stoop to bear
Chains, such precious chains of sight
As laboured minstrelsies through ages wear!
O for a balance fit the truth to tell
Of the Unsubstantial, pondered well!

XII

By one pervading spirit
Of tones and numbers all things are controlled,
As sages[12] taught, where faith was found to merit

---

[7] Orphean: Orpheus was a musician, poet, religious teacher, and mystic of classical Greek myth. Apollo, the god of poetry, was his teacher, perhaps his father. The music of Orpheus quieted the beasts and made even the rocks and trees move, and when in mourning for his wife he stopped playing, the natural world reverted to disorder and the rule of force. Orpheus descended to the underworld to find his wife, charmed its inhabitants by his music, and won permission for his wife's return to the upper world, only to lose her again because he violated one of the conditions for her release and looked back at her before they stepped into the light.

[8] Amphion: a king of the city of Thebes in classical Greek myth whose music charmed into their places the stones that made the walls of his city.

[9] Arion: another musician of Greek myth. Threatened with robbery on a ship, he asked to play one last song, and then threw himself into the sea, where he was rescued by one of the dolphins who had been attracted by his music. A bronze statue of Arion astride a dolphin was a famous piece of classical Greek art (see lines 143–144).

[10] Pan: the god of herds and shepherds in classical Greek mythology.

[11] Lord of vines: Dionysus, god of revelry and wine in Greek mythology. He rides in a chariot drawn by leopards and is attended by fauns and satyrs, wild creatures with the torsos of men and the legs, horns, and ears of goats. Silenus is another of the familiars of Dionysus; he is usually depicted as a fat, drunken middle-aged man.

[12] Sages: as Wordsworth indicates in his headnote to this poem, he refers here to the theories of the sixth-century B.C. Greek philosopher and mathematician Pythagoras and his followers, who worked out the mathematical ratios of the intervals of music, and then extended their perception to the idea that number is the basis of the harmony and order of the entire cosmos.

80 Initiation in that mystery old.
The heavens, whose aspect makes our minds as
    still
As they themselves appear to be,
Innumerable voices fill
With everlasting harmony;
The towering headlands, crowned with mist,
Their feet among the billows, know
That Ocean is a mighty harmonist;
Thy pinions, universal Air,
Ever waving to and fro,
90 Are delegates of harmony, and bear
Strains that support the Seasons in their round;
Stern Winter loves a dirge-like sound.

XIII

Break forth into thanksgiving,
Ye banded instruments of wind and chords;
Unite, to magnify the Ever-living,
Your inarticulate notes with the voice of words!
Nor hushed be service from the lowing mead,[13]
Nor mute the forest hum of noon;
Thou too be heard, lone eagle! freed
00 From snowy peak and cloud, attune
Thy hungry barkings to the hymn
Of joy, that from her utmost walls
The six-days' Work by flaming Seraphim[14]
Transmits to Heaven! As Deep to Deep
Shouting through one valley calls,
All worlds, all natures, mood and measure keep
For praise and ceaseless gratulation, poured
Into the ear of God, their Lord!

XIV

A Voice to Light gave Being;[15]
10 To Time, and Man his earth-born chronicler;
A Voice shall finish doubt and dim foreseeing,
And sweep away life's visionary stir;
The trumpet (we, intoxicate with pride,
Arm at its blast for deadly wars)
To archangelic lips applied,
The grave shall open, quench the stars.[16]

O Silence! are Man's noisy years
No more than moments of thy life?
Is Harmony, blest queen of smiles and tears,
With her smooth tones and discords just,   220
Tempered into rapturous strife,
Thy destined bond-slave? No! though earth be
    dust
And vanish, though the heavens dissolve, her
    stay
Is in the WORD, that shall not pass away.

                         (1828) 1835

Yarrow Revisited

The following Stanzas are a memorial of a day
    passed with Sir Walter Scott and other Friends
    visiting the Banks of the Yarrow under his
    guidance, immediately before his departure from
    Abbotsford, for Naples.
The title "Yarrow Revisited" will stand in no need
    of explanation for Readers acquainted with the
    Author's previous poems suggested by that cele-
    brated Stream.[1]

I

The gallant Youth, who may have gained,
    Or seeks, a "winsome Marrow,"[2]
Was but an Infant in the lap
    When first I looked on Yarrow;
Once more, by Newark's Castle-gate
    Long left without a warder,
I stood, looked, listened, and with Thee,
    Great Minstrel of the Border!

Grave thoughts ruled wide on that sweet day,
    Their dignity installing
In gentle bosoms, while sere leaves   10
    Were on the bough, or falling;
But breezes played, and sunshine gleamed—
    The forest to embolden;
Reddened the fiery hues, and shot
    Transparence through the golden.

---

[13] Mead: meadow.

[14] Six-days' Work: the universe, made in six days by God. Seraphim are the highest order of
angels: the figure here is of a continuous amplification and harmony of sound from the earth
to the ends of the created universe and then into eternal, infinite reality.

[15] "And God said, Let there be light" (Genesis 1:3).

[16] "And I heard a great voice out of heaven saying, Behold, the tabernacle of God is with
men, and he will dwell with them" (Revelation 21:3). See also Revelation 21:4–7; and Chap-
ters 8–10.

[1] The previous poems are "Yarrow Unvisited" (composed 1803, published 1807) and "Yarrow
Visited" (1814; 1815). In the notes Wordsworth dictated to Isabella Fenwick in 1842–43, he is
quoted as saying, "There is too much pressure of fact for these verses to harmonize as much as
I could wish with the two preceding poems."

[2] Winsome Marrow: fair spouse. The phrase is used by William Hamilton, an eighteenth-
century poet, in his imitation Scots ballad, "The Braes of Yarrow."

For busy thoughts the Stream flowed on
  In foamy agitation;
20   And slept in many a crystal pool
  For quiet contemplation:
No public and no private care
  The freeborn mind enthralling,
We made a day of happy hours,
  Our happy days recalling.

Brisk Youth appeared, the Morn of Youth,
  With freaks of graceful folly,—
Life's temperate Noon, her sober Eve,
  Her Night not melancholy;
Past, present, future, all appeared
30   In harmony united,
Like guests that meet, and some from far,
  By cordial love invited.

And if, as Yarrow, through the woods
  And down the meadow ranging,
Did meet us with unaltered face,
  Though we were changed and changing;
If, *then,* some natural shadows spread
  Our inward prospect over,
The soul's deep valley was not slow
40   Its brightness to recover.

Eternal blessings on the Muse,
  And her divine employment!
The blameless Muse, who trains her Sons
  For hope and calm enjoyment;
Albeit sickness, lingering yet,
  Has o'er their pillow brooded;
And Care waylays their steps—a Sprite
  Not easily eluded.

For thee, O SCOTT! compelled to change
50   Green Eildon-hill and Cheviot
For warm Vesuvio's vine-clad slopes;
  And leave thy Tweed and Tiviot[3]
For mild Sorento's breezy waves;
  May classic Fancy, linking
With native Fancy her fresh aid,
  Preserve thy heart from sinking!

Oh! while they minister to thee,
  Each vying with the other,
May Health return to mellow Age,
60   With Strength, her venturous brother;
And Tiber, and each brook and rill
  Renowned in song and story,

With unimagined beauty shine,
  Nor lose one ray of glory!

For Thou, upon a hundred streams,
  By tales of love and sorrow,
Of faithful love, undaunted truth,
  Hast shed the power of Yarrow;
And streams unknown, hills yet unseen,
  Wherever they invite Thee,   70
At parent Nature's grateful call,
  With gladness must requite Thee.

A gracious welcome shall be thine,
  Such looks of love and honour
As thy own Yarrow gave to me
  When first I gazed upon her;
Beheld what I had feared to see,
  Unwilling to surrender
Dreams treasured up from early days,
  The holy and the tender.   80

And what, for this frail world, were all
  That mortals do or suffer,
Did no responsive harp, no pen,
  Memorial tribute offer?
Yea, what were mighty Nature's self?
  Her features, could they win us,
Unhelped by the poetic voice
  That hourly speaks within us?

Nor deem that localised Romance
  Plays false with our affections;   90
Unsanctifies our tears—made sport
  For fanciful dejections:
Ah, no! the visions of the past
  Sustain the heart in feeling
Life as she is—our changeful Life,
  With friends and kindred dealing.

Bear witness, Ye, whose thoughts that day
  In Yarrow's groves were centred;
Who through the silent portal arch
  Of mouldering Newark enter'd;   100
And clomb the winding stair that once
  Too timidly was mounted
By the "last Minstrel," (not the last!)
  Ere he his Tale recounted.[4]

Flow on for ever, Yarrow Stream!
  Fulfil thy pensive duty,
Well pleased that future Bards should chant
  For simple hearts thy beauty;

[3] Eildon and Cheviot are names of hills in Scotland; Tweed and Tiviot are names of rivers.
[4] Scott's *The Lay of the Last Minstrel* (1805) begins with the minstrel entering Newark castle to beg his dinner and sing the story that is the narrative of the poem.

To dream-light dear while yet unseen,
110   Dear to the common sunshine,
And dearer still, as now I feel,
    To memory's shadowy moonshine!

                 (1831) 1835

A Place of Burial in the South of Scotland

Part fenced by man, part by a rugged steep
That curbs a foaming brook, a Graveyard lies;
The hare's best couching-place for fearless sleep;
Which moonlit elves, far seen by credulous eyes,
Enter in dance. Of church, or sabbath ties,
No vestige now remains; yet thither creep
Bereft Ones, and in lowly anguish weep
Their prayers out to the wind and naked skies.
Proud tomb is none; but rudely-sculptured
    knights,
10 By humble choice of plain old times, are seen
Level with earth, among the hillocks green:
Union not sad, when sunny daybreak smites
The spangled turf, and neighbouring thickets
    ring
With *jubilate* from the choirs of spring!

                 (1831) 1835

Cave of Staffa [I][1]

We saw, but surely, in the motley crowd,
Not One of us has felt the far-famed sight;
How *could* we feel it? each the other's blight,
Hurried and hurrying, volatile and loud.
O for those motions only that invite
The Ghost of Fingal to his tuneful Cave
By the breeze entered, and wave after wave
Softly embosoming the timid light!
And by *one* Votary who at will might stand
10 Gazing and take into his mind and heart,
With undistracted reverence, the effect
Of those proportions where the almighty hand
That made the worlds, the sovereign Architect,
Has deigned to work as if with human Art!

                 (1833) 1835

Cave of Staffa [II]

   The reader may be tempted to exclaim, "How came this . . . , after the dissatisfaction expressed in the preceding one?" In fact, at the risk of incurring the reasonable displeasure of the master of the steamboat, I returned to the cave, and explored it under circumstances more favorable to those imaginative impressions which it is so wonderfully fitted to make upon the mind. [Wordsworth's note]

Ye shadowy Beings, that have rights and claims
In every cell of Fingal's mystic Grot,
Where are ye? Driven or venturing to the spot,
Our fathers glimpses caught of your thin
    Frames,
And, by your mien and bearing knew your
    names;
And they could hear *his* ghostly song who trod
Earth, till the flesh lay on him like a load,
While he struck his desolate harp without hopes
    or aims.
Vanished ye are, but subject to recall;
Why keep *we* else the instincts whose dread law   10
Ruled here of yore, till what men felt they saw,
Not by black arts but magic natural!
If eyes be still sworn vassals of belief,
Yon light shapes forth a Bard, that shade a
    Chief.

                 (1833) 1835

Steamboats, Viaducts, and Railways

Motions and Means, on land and sea at war
With old poetic feeling, not for this,
Shall ye, by Poets even, be judged amiss!
Nor shall your presence, howsoe'er it mar
The loveliness of Nature, prove a bar
To the Mind's gaining that prophetic sense
Of future change, that point of vision, whence
May be discovered what in soul ye are.
In spite of all that beauty may disown
In your harsh features, Nature doth embrace   10
Her lawful offspring in Man's art; and Time,
Pleased with your triumphs o'er his brother
    Space,
Accepts from your bold hands the proffered
    crown
Of hope, and smiles on you with cheer sublime.

                 (1833) 1835

"Most sweet it is with unuplifted eyes"

Most sweet it is with unuplifted eyes
To pace the ground, if path be there or none,

---

[1] The Cave of Staffa, also called Fingal's Cave, is on an island in Scotland. Fingal is one of the heroes of James Macpherson's fabricated Ossianic epic poems, first published in 1762.

While a fair region round the traveller lies
Which he forbears again to look upon;
Pleased rather with some soft ideal scene,
The work of Fancy, or some happy tone
Of meditation, slipping in between
The beauty coming and the beauty gone.
If Thought and Love desert us, from that day
10 Let us break off all commerce with the Muse:
With Thought and Love companions of our
    way,
Whate'er the senses take or may refuse,
The Mind's internal heaven shall shed her dews
Of inspiration on the humblest lay.

                              (1833) 1835

"The leaves that rustled on this oak-crowned hill"

The leaves that rustled on this oak-crowned hill,
And sky that danced among those leaves, are
    still;
Rest smooths the way for sleep; in field and
    bower
Soft shades and dews have shed their blended
    power
On drooping eyelid and the closing flower;
Sound is there none at which the faintest heart
Might leap, the weakest nerve of superstition
    start;
Save when the Owlet's unexpected scream
Pierces the ethereal vault; and ('mid the gleam
10 Of unsubstantial imagery, the dream,
From the hushed vale's realities, transferred
To the still lake) the imaginative[1] Bird
Seems, 'mid inverted mountains, not unheard.

    Grave Creature!—whether, while the moon
        shines bright
On thy wings opened wide for smoothest flight,
Thou art discovered in a roofless tower,
Rising from what may once have been a lady's
    bower;
Or spied where thou sitt'st moping in thy mew
At the dim centre of a churchyard yew;
20 Or, from a rifted crag or ivy tod[2]
Deep in a forest, thy secure abode,
Thou giv'st, for pastime's sake, by shriek or
    shout,
A puzzling notice of thy whereabout—
May the night never come, nor day be seen,
When I shall scorn thy voice or mock thy mien!

In classic ages men perceived a soul
Of sapience in thy aspect, headless Owl!
Thee Athens reverenced in the studious grove;
And, near the golden sceptre grasped by Jove,
His Eagle's favourite perch, while round him
    sate   30
The Gods revolving the decrees of Fate,
Thou, too, wert present at Minerva's side:
Hark to that second larum![3]—far and wide
The elements have heard, and rock and cave
    replied.

                              (1834) 1835

"Blest Statesman He, whose Mind's unselfish will"

Blest Statesman He, whose Mind's unselfish will
Leaves him at ease among grand thoughts:
    whose eye
Sees that, apart from magnanimity,
Wisdom exists not; nor the humbler skill
Of Prudence, disentangling good and ill
With patient care. What tho' assaults run high,
They daunt not him who holds his ministry,
Resolute, at all hazards, to fulfil
Its duties;— prompt to move, but firm to wait,—
Knowing, things rashly sought are rarely found;   1[
That, for the functions of an ancient State—
Strong by her charters, free because imbound,
Servant of Providence, not slave of Fate—
Perilous is sweeping change, all chance unsound.

                              (1838) 1838

First published in the Quarterly Review *in 1841,
when it was quoted by Henry Taylor in an essay on
Wordsworth's sonnets. The fourteen "Sonnets upon
the Punishment of Death," of which this poem is the
last, were written in response to a debate in Parlia-
ment in 1836 over a proposal to reduce the number
of crimes for which the death penalty could be
imposed. Wordsworth opposed the then extreme
argument that capital punishment be abolished for
all crimes except treason and murder.*

Apology

from *Sonnets upon the Punishment of Death*

The formal World relaxes her cold chain
For One who speaks in numbers; ampler scope

---

[1] Imaginative: imagined.   [2] Tod: clump.   [3] Larum: literally, alarm, a warning call.

His utterance finds; and, conscious of the gain,
Imagination works with bolder hope
The cause of grateful reason to sustain;
And, serving Truth, the heart more strongly
    beats
Against all barriers which his labour meets
In lofty place, or humble Life's domain.
Enough;—before us lay a painful road,
10   And guidance have I sought in duteous love
From Wisdom's heavenly Father. Hence hath
    flowed
Patience, with trust that, whatsoe'er the way
Each takes in this high matter, all may move
Cheered with the prospect of a brighter day.
                                    1841

Prelude

Prefixed to the Volume Entitled Poems
Chiefly of Early and Late Years

In desultory walk through orchard grounds,
Or some deep chestnut grove, oft have I paused
The while a Thrush, urged rather than
    restrained
By gusts of vernal storm, attuned his song
To his own genial instincts; and was heard
(Though not without some plaintive tones
    between)
To utter, above showers of blossom swept
From tossing boughs, the promise of a calm,
Which the unsheltered traveller might receive
10   With thankful spirit. The descant, and the wind
That seemed to play with it in love or scorn,
Encouraged and endeared the strain of words
That haply flowed from me, by fits of silence
Impelled to livelier pace. But now, my Book!
Charged with those lays, and others of like
    mood,
Or loftier pitch if higher rose the theme,
Go, single—yet aspiring to be joined
With thy Forerunners that through many a year
Have faithfully prepared each other's way—
20   Go forth upon a mission best fulfilled
When and wherever, in this changeful world,
Power hath been given to please for higher ends
Than pleasure only; gladdening to prepare
For wholesome sadness, troubling to refine,
Calming to raise; and, by a sapient Art

Diffused through all the mysteries of our Being,
Softening the toils and pains that have not
    ceased
To cast their shadows on our mother Earth
Since the primeval doom. Such is the grace
Which, though unsued for, fails not to descend   30
With heavenly inspiration; such the aim
That Reason dictates; and, as even the wish
Has virtue in it, why should hope to me
Be wanting that sometimes, where fancied ills
Harrass the mind and strip from off the bowers
Of private life their natural pleasantness,
A Voice—devoted to the love whose seeds
Are sown in every human breast, to beauty
Lodged within compass of the humblest sight,
To cheerful intercourse with wood and field,   40
And sympathy with man's substantial griefs—
Will not be heard in vain? And in those days
When unforeseen distress[1] spreads far and wide
Among a People mournfully cast down,
Or into anger roused by venal words
In recklessness flung out to overturn
The judgment, and divert the general heart
From mutual good—some strain of thine, my
    Book!
Caught at propitious intervals, may win
Listeners who not unwillingly admit   50
Kindly emotion tending to console
And reconcile; and both with young and old
Exalt the sense of thoughtful gratitude
For benefits that still survive, by faith
In progress, under laws divine, maintained.
                                    1842

"*A Poet!*—He hath put his heart to school"

I was impelled to write this Sonnet by the dis-
gusting frequency with which the word *artistical*,
imported with other impertinences from the Ger-
mans, is employed by writers of the present day:
for artistical let them substitute artificial, and the
poetry written on this system, both at home and
abroad, will be for the most part much better char-
acterised. [From the Fenwick notes]

A POET!—He hath put his heart to school,
Nor dares to move unpropped upon the staff
Which Art hath lodged within his hand—must
    laugh

---

[1] The lines toward the conclusion allude to the discontents then [1842] fomented through the
country by the Anti-Corn-Law League: the particular causes of such troubles are transitory, but
disposition to excite and liability to be excited are nevertheless permanent, and therefore proper
objects for the poet's regard. [From the Fenwick notes]

By precept only, and shed tears by rule.
Thy Art be Nature; the live current quaff,
And let the groveller sip his stagnant pool,
In fear that else, when Critics grave and cool
Have killed him, Scorn should write his epitaph.
How does the Meadow-flower its bloom unfold?
10   Because the lovely little flower is free
Down to its root, and, in that freedom, bold;
And so the grandeur of the Forest-tree
Comes not by casting in a formal mould,
But from its *own* divine vitality.

                                                1842

Airey-Force Valley

        —— Not a breath of air
Ruffles the bosom of this leafy glen.
From the brook's margin, wide around, the
    trees
Are steadfast as the rocks; the brook itself,
Old as the hills that feed it from afar,
Doth rather deepen than disturb the calm
Where all things else are still and motionless.
And yet, even now, a little breeze, perchance
Escaped from boisterous winds that rage
    without,
10   Has entered, by the sturdy oaks unfelt,
But to its gentle touch how sensitive
Is the light ash! that, pendent from the brow
Of yon dim cave, in seeming silence makes
A soft eye-music of slow-waving boughs,
Powerful almost as vocal harmony
To stay the wanderer's steps and soothe his
    thoughts.

                                      (1835) 1842

"Lyre! though such power do in thy magic live"

Lyre! though such power do in thy magic live
    As might from India's farthest plain
    Recall the not unwilling Maid,
        Assist me to detain
        The lovely Fugitive:
Check with thy notes the impulse which,
        betrayed
By her sweet farewell looks, I longed to aid.
Here let me gaze enrapt upon that eye,
10   The impregnable and awe-inspiring fort
Of contemplation, the calm port

By reason fenced from winds that sigh
Among the restless sails of vanity.
But if no wish be hers that we should part,
A humbler bliss would satisfy my heart.
        Where all things are so fair,
Enough by her dear side to breathe the air
        Of this Elysian weather;
And, on or in, or near, the brook, espy
    Shade upon the sunshine lying
        Faint and somewhat pensively;   20
    And downward Image gaily vying
        With its upright living tree
'Mid silver clouds, and openings of blue sky
As soft almost and deep as her cerulean eye.
Nor less the joy with many a glance
Cast up the Stream or down at her beseeching,
To mark its eddying foam-balls prettily distrest
By ever-changing shape and want of rest;
        Or watch, with mutual teaching,
        The current as it plays   30
        In flashing leaps and stealthy creeps
        Adown a rocky maze;
Or note (translucent summer's happiest
        chance!)
In the slope-channel floored with pebbles
        bright,
Stones of all hues, gem emulous of gem,
So vivid that they take from keenest sight
The liquid veil that seeks not to hide them.

                                                1842

Suggested by a Picture of the Bird of Paradise

    This subject has been treated of in another note.
I will here only by way of comment direct attention
to the fact that pictures of animals and other pro-
ductions of nature as seen in conservatories, menag-
eries, museums, etc., would do little for the national
mind, nay they would be rather injurious to it, if
the imagination were excluded by the presence of
the object, more or less out of a state of nature. If it
were not that we learn to talk and think of the lion
and the eagle, the palm-tree and even the cedar,
from the impassioned introduction of them so fre-
quently into Holy Scripture and by great poets, and
divines who write as poets, the spiritual part of our
nature, and therefore the higher part of it, would
derive no benefit from such intercourse with such
objects. [From the Fenwick notes]

The gentlest Poet, with free thoughts endowed,
And a true master of the glowing strain,
Might scan the narrow province with disdain

That to the Painter's skill is here allowed.
This, this the Bird of Paradise! disclaim
The daring thought, forget the name;
This the Sun's Bird, whom Glendoveers[1] might
    own
As no unworthy Partner in their flight
Through seas of ether, where the ruffling sway
Of nether air's rude billows is unknown;
Whom Sylphs, if e'er for casual pastime they
Through India's spicy regions wing their way,
Might bow to as their Lord. What character,
O sovereign Nature! I appeal to thee,
Of all thy feathered progeny
Is so unearthly, and what shape so fair?
So richly decked in variegated down,
Green, sable, shining yellow, shadowy brown,
Tints softly with each other blended,
Hues doubtfully begun and ended;
Or intershooting, and to sight
Lost and recovered, as the rays of light
Glance on the conscious plumes touched here
    and there?
Full surely, when with such proud gifts of life
Began the pencil's strife,
O'erweening Art was caught as in a snare.

  A sense of seemingly presumptuous wrong
Gave the first impulse to the Poet's song;
But, of his scorn repenting soon, he drew
A juster judgment from a calmer view;
And, with a spirit freed from discontent,
Thankfully took an effort that was meant
Not with God's bounty, Nature's love to vie,
Or made with hope to please that inward eye
Which ever strives in vain itself to satisfy,
But to recall the truth by some faint trace
Of power ethereal and celestial grace,
That in the living Creature find on earth a
    place.

                                        1842

This poem was published in Poems, Chiefly of
Early and Late Years *(1842) as one of a group of
poems which bore the title "Memorials of a Tour in
Italy. 1837." According to Henry Crabb Robinson,*
*who accompanied Wordsworth on the tour, the
poem was probably not written during the tour.*

At Florence

Under the shadow of a stately Pile,
The dome of Florence, pensive and alone,
Nor giving heed to aught that passed the while,
I stood, and gazed upon a marble stone,
The laurelled Dante's favourite seat. A throne,
In just esteem, it rivals; though no style
Be there of decoration to beguile
The mind, depressed by thought of greatness
    flown.
As a true man, who long had served the lyre,
I gazed with earnestness, and dared no more.   10
But in his breast the mighty Poet bore
A Patriot's heart, warm with undying fire.
Bold with the thought, in reverence I sate down,
And, for a moment, filled that empty Throne.
                                        1842

On the Projected Kendal and Windermere Railway

Is then no nook of English ground secure
From rash assault? Schemes of retirement sown
In youth, and 'mid the busy world kept pure
As when their earliest flowers of hope were
    blown,
Must perish;—how can they this blight endure?
And must he too the ruthless change bemoan
Who scorns a false utilitarian lure
'Mid his paternal fields at random thrown?
Baffle the threat, bright Scene, from Orrest-head
Given to the pausing traveller's rapturous
    glance: 10
Plead for thy peace, thou beautiful romance
Of nature; and, if human hearts be dead,
Speak, passing winds; ye torrents, with your
    strong
And constant voice, protest against the wrong.
                              (1844) 1844

[1] Glendoveers: a race of beautiful sprites in Robert Southey's poem *The Curse of Kehama*
(1810).

John Clare
1793-1864

JOHN CLARE'S FATHER, himself the illegitimate son of a village woman and an itinerant Scots fiddler and schoolmaster, was a farm laborer; Clare's mother was the daughter of a shepherd. Both were illiterate. At one time there were plans that Clare, whose unusual abilities were recognized by the masters of the schools he attended when he was not working in the fields, would be placed as an assistant teacher in a school. But the hard circumstances of agricultural labor required that he leave school when he was fourteen years old to work variously in his native Northamptonshire as a ploughman, gardener, lime-burner, and ordinary day laborer. He continued to read—books on botany, mathematics, travel, and farming as well as eighteenth-century novels, James Thomson's literary pastoral *The Seasons* (the first book he bought), Milton, and other seventeenth- and eighteenth-century poets. There was, as he later wrote, "a feeling of ambition about me, that wishes to gain notice or to rise above my fellows." He started to write in the ballad forms he had heard from his father and read in the penny broadsides sold by peddlers, and in the literary forms of his reading. In 1817 he tried without success to put together a list of subscribers to subsidize the publication of a collection of his poems. Through the offices of a local bookseller, the volume was eventually published in London in 1820 as *Poems Descriptive of Rural Life and Scenery*. It attracted a good deal of favorable if sometimes condescending attention, and it sold well, about 3000 copies, a good sale for its time. In 1821 he published a second collection of poems, *The Village Minstrel*.

Clare continued to live in Northamptonshire. He married in 1820, worked in the fields during the seasons of planting and harvest, wrote poems mostly in a conventionally pastoral style, and kept a notebook full of close observations of birds, flowers, and snakes. A fund was created by subscription from his London publisher and other literary friends which assured him a small annual income, and he published poems and some prose sketches in magazines and annuals. During his visits to London in the 1820s he met writers, editors, and painters. He greatly extended his reading to include Keats, Wordsworth, Byron, Blake, and other contemporary writers. His second collection of poems had not sold well, and he fretted through frustrating delays before *A Shepherd's Calendar*, a description of the events and look of the countryside in each of the twelve months, was published in 1827. It too was a financial failure and was received only indifferently by reviewers. Clare kept on writing, and by 1832 he was again trying to publish a collection of 300 poems by subscription. Again, a friend found a London publisher for a selection from these poems, and what turned out to be Clare's final volume of verse, *The Rural Muse*, was published in 1835.

Only a few more of his poems were to be published or reprinted during the remainder of the century, principally in biographies prepared by Frederick Martin (1865) and J. L. Cherry (1873) after his death in 1864. From his young manhood Clare had suffered from epilepticlike seizures. In the 1830s he suffered as well from bouts of depression and some probably associated physical disabilities. He was lonely during his visits to London, felt isolated in Northamptonshire, was still ambitious for fame as a poet but had won little recognition for a talent that had developed from his early literary pastoralism to the taut style of poems like "Badger." Early in the 1830s he began to act under the first of several delusions, all having to do with unrealized possibility, that were to persist until his death: that he had two wives, the first a woman he had not seen since 1816; that he was a prizefighter deprived of a chance to win a championship; that he was Byron. In 1837 he was placed in a private asylum for the mentally disordered, from which he simply walked away in 1841. After a short stay with his wife and children, he was committed in the same year as a pauper farmer to the General Lunatic Asylum of Northampton, where he remained until his death.

The treatment in both these institutions was, for the time, humane, and he was encouraged to write. He did, voluminously; in 1845 a superintendent of the Northampton asylum who transcribed his poems found that there were over 800 of them. Sometimes Clare wrote in return for a gift of tobacco or drink, sometimes to ease himself in memories of landscape and women or in satiric outbursts in the manner of Byron, and at least once, between 1844 and 1850, in the hope of publishing another volume of verse.

Even though Clare was still writing poems at mid-century, and still thought of himself as a poet who wrote for publication, he is not in the usual description a Victorian poet. Few mid-Victorian readers knew his poetry, and he did not know much about the generation that had succeeded Byron and Keats. On the other hand, many of the poems he published in his 1835 volume had moved out of the ballad and pastoral modes that were his first models, and they are also different from the characteristic poems of the first generations of romantic poets against whom he came in the 1820s to measure himself—from the poems of Keats, for example, whose descriptions of nature he thought fanciful, and from Wordsworth's landscape poems, in which Clare was put off by an intrusive "godliness." Clare's later poems are interesting, and they belong in this anthology, because in his isolation in the first decades of the Victorian period he worked out in a telling way one of the possibilities of nineteenth-century romanticism.

Remembering in the asylum his early efforts at verse, he wrote, "as I found nature then so I made her." The terms of the transaction, even then, were nature and self, an accurate but individual perception and then a creation, a concern not with poetic language, forms, and attitudes to be brought to the life out there, but rather with what can be seen, who is seeing, and what is to be made of this junction of self and the nature he finds. Increasingly Clare used unelaborated lyric forms and a strongly particular idiom to record, not the moods in which he regarded nature, but the different realities he found in it and made of it: its settled harmonies and its violences, its threats to annihilate his identity, its existence in his memory as a place of solace and joy. In some of his later poems he renders what he sees in a landscape with a rigorous particularity that makes no overt motion to leave its scene. In others he insists on his presence as an identity who out of his own needs has made the scene he remembers, or who simply stands in a creation he finds so powerful that he fears it will overwhelm him. Clare's later poems are important because in them he preserved in an original purity the impulse on which other poets throughout the century were to venture more elaborate poetic structures. In these poems he cut down to one of the nerves which run through nineteenth-century British poetry: the premise that a poem gives meaning and pleasure by authentically making and holding a particular moment in which humans find a place, a reposeful or dangerous sense and assertion of self, among and without falsifying the enormous and various life in things.

EDITIONS

Not all of Clare's poems have been published from the manuscripts in which they were composed or transcribed, and from the beginning those who have transcribed or prepared Clare's poems for the press have in different ways and degrees altered his texts. The most complete edition is J. W. Tibble's two-volume *The Poems of John Clare* (1935), which includes most of the poems published in Clare's lifetime and about 300 other poems from manuscript. Tibble modernizes and regularizes Clare's spelling and punctuation. His edition is supplemented by *Poems of John Clare's Madness* (1949), edited by Geoffrey Grigson, and *The Later Poems of John Clare* (1964), edited by Eric Robinson and Geoffrey Summerfield. The later edition remarks the inaccuracy of some of Grigson's texts and offers a more literal transcription from the manuscripts of the poems. Except where otherwise noted, the texts printed here are those of Tibble's edition.

BIOGRAPHY AND CRITICISM

The standard biography of Clare is by J. W. and Anne Tibble, *John Clare: A Life* (new edition, 1972). Edmund Blunden has edited *Sketches in the Life of John Clare Written by Himself* (1931), which includes a memoir Clare wrote in 1821. The Tibbles have also edited Clare's letters (1951) and prose (1951). There are chapters on Clare's poetry in John Heath-Stubbs' *The Darkling Plain* (1950) and Raymond Williams' *The Country and the City*

(1973). See also J. W. and Anne Tibble, *John
Clare: His Life and Poetry* (1956); John Bar-
rell, *The Idea of Landscape and the Sense of
Place, 1730–1840: An Approach to the Poetry
of John Clare* (1972); and Mark Storey, *The
Poetry of John Clare* (1974). Mark Storey has
also edited *John Clare: The Critical Heritage*
(1973).

The Missel-Thrush's Nest

In early March, before the lark
Dare start, beside the huge oak tree,
Close fixed agen the powdered bark,
The mavis' nest I often see;
And mark, as wont, the bits of wool
Hang round about its early bed;
She lays six eggs in colours dull,
Blotched thick with spots of burning red.

(1824–32)

Schoolboys in Winter

The schoolboys still their morning rambles take
To neighbouring village school with playing
 speed,
Loitering with pastime's leisure till they quake,
Oft looking up the wild-geese droves to heed,
Watching the letters which their journeys make;
Or plucking haws on which the fieldfares feed,
And hips, and sloes;[1] and on each shallow lake
Making glib[2] slides, where they like shadows go
Till some fresh pastimes in their minds awake.
Then off they start anew and hasty blow
Their numbed and clumpsing[3] fingers till they
 glow;
Then races with their shadows wildly run
That stride huge giants o'er the shining snow
In the pale splendour of the winter sun.

(1824–32)

A Faithless Shepherd

A faithless shepherd courted me,
He stole away my liberty.
When my poor heart was strange to men,
He came and smiled and stole it then.

When my apron would hang low,
Me he sought through frost and snow.

When it puckered up with shame,
And I sought him, he never came.

When summer brought no fears to fright,
He came to guard me every night.
When winter nights did darkly prove,
None came to guard me or to love.

I wish, I wish, but all in vain,
I wish I was a maid again.
A maid again I cannot be,
Oh, when will green grass cover me?

I wish my babe had ne'er been born,
I've made its pillow on a thorn,
I wish my sorrows all away,
My soul with God, my body clay.

He promised beds as fine as silk
And sheets for love as white as milk,
But when he'd won my heart away
Left me to want a bed of clay.

He kept his sheep on yonder hill,
His heart seemed soft but it was steel;
I ran with love and was undone,
Oh, had I walked ere I did run!

He has two hearts and I have none,
He'll be a rogue, when I am gone,
To thee my baby, unto thee,
As he has been too long to me.

I weep the past, I dread the gloom
Of sorrows in the time to come,
When thou without a friend shalt be,
Weeping on a stranger's knee.

I wish, my child, thou'dst ne'er been born,
I've made thy pillow on a thorn,
I wish our sorrows both away,
Our souls with God, our bodies clay.

(1824–32)

Nature's Hymn to the Deity

All nature owns with one accord
The great and universal Lord:
The sun proclaims him through the day,
The moon when daylight drops away,
The very darkness smiles to wear

---

[1] Haws: hawthorn berries; hips: the false fruit of roses; sloes: the fruit of the blackthorn tree.
[2] Glib: smooth.   [3] Clumpsing: benumbed.

The stars that show us God is there,
On moonlight seas soft gleams the sky,
And, "God is with us," waves reply.

Winds breathe from God's abode, "We come,"
10 Storms louder own God is their home,
And thunder yet with louder call,
Sounds, "God is mightiest over all";
Till earth, right loath the proof to miss,
Echoes triumphantly, "He is,"
And air and ocean makes reply,
"God reigns on earth, in air and sky."

All nature owns with one accord
The great and universal Lord:
Insect and bird and tree and flower—
20 The witnesses of every hour—
Are pregnant with his prophecy
And, "God is with us," all reply.
The first link in the mighty plan
Is still—and all upbraideth man.
(1824–32) 1835

The Hailstorm in June 1831

Darkness came o'er like chaos; and the sun,
As startled with the terror, seemed to run
With quickened dread behind the beetling
  cloud;
The old wood groaned, like nature in her
  shroud;
And each old rifted oak-tree's mossy arm
Seemed shrinking from the presence of the
  storm.
As it still nearer came, they shook beyond
Their former fears, as if to burst the bond
Of earth, that bound them to that ancient place,
Where danger seemed to threaten all their race.
They had withstood all tempests since their
  birth,
Yet now seemed bowing to the very earth;
Like reeds they bent, like drunken men they
  reeled,
And man for safety ran and sought the open
  field.
(1824–32) 1835

The Milking Shed

Good God! and can it be that such a nook
  As this can raise such sudden rapture up?
  Two dotterel[1] trees, an oak and ash, that stoop

Their aged bodies o'er a little brook,
  And raise their sheltering heads above and
  o'er
A little hovel, raised on four old props
  Old as themselves to look on—and what
  more?
Naught but a hawthorn hedge!—and yet one
  stops
  In admiration and in joy, to gaze
Upon these objects, feeling, as I stand,   10
  That naught in all this wide world's thorny
  ways
Can match this bit of feeling's fairyland.
  How can it be? Time owns the potent spell
  I've known it from a boy, and love it well.
(1824–32) 1835

Beans in Blossom

The south-west wind, how pleasant in the face
It breathes! while, sauntering in a musing pace,
I roam these new-ploughed fields; or by the side
Of this old wood, where happy birds abide,
And the rich blackbird, through his golden bill,
Utters wild music when the rest are still.
Now luscious comes the scent of blossomed bean,
As o'er the path in rich disorder lean
Its stalks; whence bees, in busy songs and toils,
Load home luxuriantly their yellow spoils.   10
The herd-cows toss the mole-hills in their play;
And often stand the stranger's steps at bay,
Mid clover blossoms red and tawny white,
Strong scented with the summer's warm delight.
(1824–32) 1835

Badger

When midnight comes a host of dogs and men
Go out and track the badger to his den,
And put a sack within the hole, and lie
Till the old grunting badger passes by.
He comes and hears—they let the strongest
  loose.
The old fox hears the noise and drops the goose.
The poacher shoots and hurries from the cry,
And the old hare half wounded buzzes by.
They get a forkèd stick to bear him down   10
And clap[1] the dogs and take him to the town,
And bait him all the day with many dogs,
And laugh and shout and fright the scampering
  hogs.

[1] Dotterel: trees that have been pollarded—their branches cut back to the trunk to promote a dense growth.
[1] Clap: set on.

He runs along and bites at all he meets:
They shout and hollo down the noisy streets.

He turns about to face the loud uproar
And drives the rebels to their very door.
The frequent stone is hurled where'er they go;
When badgers fight, then every one's a foe.
20   The dogs are clapt and urged to join the fray;
The badger turns and drives them all away.
Though scarcely half as big, demure and small,
He fights with dogs for hours and beats them all.
The heavy mastiff, savage in the fray,
Lies down and licks his feet and turns away.
The bulldog knows his match and waxes cold,
The badger grins and never leaves his hold.
He drives the crowd and follows at their heels
And bites them through—the drunkard swears
    and reels.

The frighted women take the boys away,
30   The blackguard laughs and hurries on the fray.
He tries to reach the woods, an awkward race,
But sticks and cudgels quickly stop the chase.
He turns agen and drives the noisy crowd
And beats the many dogs in noises loud.
He drives away and beats them every one,
And then they loose them all and set them on.
He falls as dead and kicked by boys and men,
Then starts and grins and drives the crowd agen;
Till kicked and torn and beaten out he lies
And leaves his hold and cackles, groans, and
40   dies.
                                        (1835–37)

Mouse's Nest

I found a ball of grass among the hay
And progged[1] it as I passed and went away;
And when I looked I fancied something stirred,
And turned agen and hoped to catch the bird—
When out an old mouse bolted in the wheats
With all her young ones hanging at her teats;
She looked so odd and so grotesque to me,
I ran and wondered what the thing could be,
And pushed the knapweed bunches where I
    stood;
Then the mouse hurried from the craking
10   brood.
The young ones squeaked, and as I went away
She found her nest again among the hay.

[1] Progged: prodded.
[1] Text from Robinson and Summerfield's edition.

The water o'er the pebbles scarce could run
And broad old cesspools glittered in the sun.
                                        (1835–37)

Written in a Thunder Storm
July 15th 1841[1]

The heavens are wrath—the thunders rattling
    peal
Rolls like a vast volcano in the sky
Yet nothing starts the apathy I feel
Nor chills with fear eternal destiny

My soul is apathy—a ruin vast
Time cannot clear the ruined mass away
My life is hell—the hopeless die is cast
And manhoods prime is premature decay

Roll on ye wrath of thunders—peal on peal
Till worlds are ruins and myself alone   10
Melt heart and soul cased in obdurate steel
Till I can feel that nature is my throne

I live in love sun of undying light
And fathom my own heart for ways of good
In its pure atmosphere day without night
Smiles on the plains the forest and the flood

Smile on ye elements of earth and sky
Or frown in thunders as ye frown on me
Bid earth and its delusions pass away
But leave the mind as its creator free   20
                                        (1841)

Child Harold *is the title Clare gave to a collection
of songs, ballads, and stanzas in the Spenserian
form in which Byron wrote* Childe Harold's Pil-
grimage *(1812–18). The two poems reprinted here
exist in manuscripts written about 1841. The text
is that of Robinson and Summerfield's edition of
Clare's later poems.*

"The blackbird startles from the homestead hedge"

from *Child Harold*

The blackbird startles from the homestead
    hedge

Raindrops and leaves fall yellow as he springs
Such images are natures sweetest pledge
To me there's music in his rustling wings
"Prink prink" he cries and loud the robin sings
The small hawk like a shot drops from the sky
Close to my feet for mice and creeping things
Then swift as thought again he suthers[1] bye
And hides among the clouds from the pursue-
ing eye

Ballad

from *Child Harold*

The Blackbird Has Built In The Pasture Agen
And The Thorn Oer The Pond Shows A
  Delicate Green
Where I Strolled With Patty[1] Adown In The
  Glen
And Spent Summer Evenings And Sundays
  Unseen
How Sweet The Hill Brow
And The Low Of The Cow
And The Sunshine That Gilded The Bushes
  So Green
When Evening Brought Dews Natures Thirst
  To Allay
And Clouds Seemed To Nestle Round Hamlets
  And Farms
While In The Green Bushes We Spent The
  Sweet Day
And Patty Sweet Patty Was Still in My Arms

The Love Bloom That Redded Upon Her
  Sweet Lips
The Love Light That Glistened Within Her
  Sweet Eye
The Singing Bees There That The Wild
  Honey Sips
From Wild Blossoms Seemed Not So Happy
  As I
How Sweet Her Smile Seemed
While The Summer Sun Gleamed
And The Laugh Of The Spring Shadowed Joys
  From On High
While The Birds Sung About Us and Cattle
  Grazed Round
And Beauty Was Blooming On Hamlets and
  Farms
How Sweet Steamed The Inscence Of Dew
  From The Ground

While Patty Sweet Patty Sat Locked In My
  Arms

I Am

I am: yet what I am none cares or knows,
  My friends forsake me like a memory lost;
I am the self-consumer of my woes,
  They rise and vanish in oblivious host,
Like shades in love and death's oblivion lost;
And yet I am, and live with shadows tost
Into the nothingness of scorn and noise,
  Into the living sea of waking dreams,
Where there is neither sense of life nor joys,
  But the vast shipwreck of my life's esteems; 10
And e'en the dearest—that I loved the best—
Are strange—nay, rather stranger than the rest.

I long for scenes where man has never trod,
  A place where woman never smiled or wept;
There to abide with my Creator, God,
  And sleep as I in childhood sweetly slept:
Untroubling and untroubled where I lie,
The grass below—above the vaulted sky.

(1844–45) 1865

Where She Told Her Love

I saw her crop a rose
  Right early in the day,
And I went to kiss the place
  Where she broke the rose away,
And I saw the patten[1] rings
  Where she o'er the stile had gone,
And I love all other things
  Her bright eyes look upon.
If she looks upon the hedge or up the leafing
tree,
The whitethorn or the brown oak are made
dearer things to me.   10

I have a pleasant hill
  Which I sit upon for hours,
Where she cropt some sprigs of thyme
  And other little flowers;
And she muttered as she did it
  As does beauty in a dream,
And I loved her when she hid it
  On her breast, so like to cream,

---

[1] Suthers: to make a rushing noise.
[1] Patty was the name of Clare's wife.
[1] Patten: a clog or sandal.

Near the brown mole on her neck that to me a
    diamond shone;
Then my eye was like to fire, and my heart was
20 like to stone.

    There is a small green place
        Where cowslips early curled,
    Which on sabbath day I trace,
        The dearest in the world.
    A little oak spreads o'er it,
        And throws a shadow round,
    A green sward close before it,
        The greenest ever found:
There is not a woodland nigh nor is there a
    green grove,
Yet stood the fair maid nigh me and told me all
30 her love.

                              (1844–45) 1873

Secret Love

I hid my love when young till I
Couldn't bear the buzzing of a fly;
I hid my love to my despite
Till I could not bear to look at light:
I dare not gaze upon her face
But left her memory in each place;
Where'er I saw a wild flower lie
I kissed and bade my love good-bye.

I met her in the greenest dells,
10 Where dewdrops pearl the wood bluebells;
The lost breeze kissed her bright blue eye,
The bee kissed and went singing by,
A sunbeam found a passage there,
A gold chain round her neck so fair;
As secret as the wild bee's song
She lay there all the summer long.

I hid my love in field and town
Till e'en the breeze would knock me down;
20 The bees seemed singing ballads o'er,
The fly's bass turned a lion's roar;
And even silence found a tongue,
To haunt me all the summer long;
The riddle nature could not prove
Was nothing else but secret love.

                              (1844–45)

Dewdrops

The dewdrops on every blade of grass are so
much like silver drops that I am obliged to
stoop down as I walk to see if they are pearls,
and those sprinkled on the ivy-woven beds of
primroses underneath the hazels, whitethorns,
and maples are so like gold beads that I stooped
down to feel if they were hard, but they melted
from my finger. And where the dew lies on the
primrose, the violet and whitethorn leaves,
they are emerald and beryl, yet nothing more
than the dews of the morning on the budding
leaves; nay, the road grasses are covered with
gold and silver beads, and the further we go the
brighter they seem to shine, like solid gold and
silver. It is nothing more than the sun's light
and shade upon them in the dewy morning;
every thorn-point and every bramble-spear has
its trembling ornament: till the wind gets a
little brisker, and then all is shaken off, and all
the shining jewelry passes away into a common
spring morning full of budding leaves, prim-
roses, violets, vernal speedwell, bluebell and
orchis, and commonplace objects.

                              (1844–45)

Clock-a-Clay[1]

In the cowslip pips[2] I lie,
Hidden from the buzzing fly,
While green grass beneath me lies,
Pearled with dew like fishes' eyes,
Here I lie, a clock-a-clay,
Waiting for the time of day.

While grassy forest quakes surprise,
And the wild wind sobs and sighs,
My gold home rocks as like to fall,
On its pillar green and tall;   10
When the pattering rain drives by
Clock-a-clay keeps warm and dry.

Day by day and night by night,
All the week I hide from sight;
In the cowslip pips I lie,
In rain and dew still warm and dry;
Day and night, and night and day,
Red, black-spotted clock-a-clay.

My home shakes in wind and showers,
Pale green pillar topped with flowers,   20
Bending at the wild wind's breath,
Till I touch the grass beneath;
Here I live, lone clock-a-clay,
Watching for the time of day.

                              (1844–50) 1873

---

[1] Clock-a-clay: the insect familiarly known as a ladybird, or ladybug.   [2] Pips: seeds.

[Fragment]

FOUND ON A BIT OF BLANK
PAPER IN CLARE'S POCKET
AUGUST 27TH, 1848[1]

Some pretty face remembered in our youth
Seems ever with us whispering love and truth.

Evening

'Tis evening: the black snail has got on his
    track,
    And gone to its nest is the wren,
And the packman snail, too, with his home on
    his back,
    Clings to the bowed bents[1] like a wen.

The shepherd has made a rude mark with his
    foot
    Where his shadow reached when he
    first came,
And it just touched the tree where his secret
    love cut
    Two letters that stand for love's name.

The evening comes in with the wishes of love,
    And the shepherd he looks on the
    flowers,
And thinks who would praise the soft song of
    the dove,
    And meet joy in these dew-falling
    hours.

For nature is love, and finds haunts for true
    love,[2]
    Where nothing can hear or intrude;
It hides from the eagle and joins with the dove,
    In beautiful green solitude.

               (1842–64) 1873

Autumn Change

The leaves of autumn drop by twos and threes,
And the black cloud hung o'er the old low
    church
Is fixed as is a rock that never stirs.
But look again and you may well perceive
The weathercock is in another sky,
And the cloud passing leaves the blue behind.

Crimson and yellow, blotched with iron-brown,
The autumn tans and variegates the leaves;
The nuts are ripe in woods about the town;
Russet the cleared fields where the bindweed
    weaves
Round stubbles and still flowers; the trefoil[1]
    seeds
And troubles all the lands. From rig[2] to furrow
There's nothing left but rubbish and foul
    weeds.
I love to see the rabbits' snug-made burrow
Under the old hedge-bank or huge mossed oak
Claspt fast with ivy—there the rabbit breeds
Where the kite peelews and the ravens croak
And hares and rabbits at their leisure feed,
As varying autumn through her changes runs,
Season of sudden storms and brilliant suns.

               (1842–64)

The Crow Sat on the Willow

The crow sat on the willow-tree
    A-lifting up his wings,
And glossy was his coat to see,
    And loud the ploughman sings,
"I love my love because I know
    The milkmaid she loves me";
And hoarsely croaked the glossy crow
    Upon the willow-tree.
"I love my love," the ploughman sung,
And all the fields with music rung.

"I love my love, a bonny lass,
    She keeps her pails so bright,
And blithe she trips the dewy grass
    At morning and at night.
A cotton dress her morning gown,
    Her face was rosy health;
She traced the pastures up and down,
    And nature was her wealth."
He sung, and turned each furrow down,
His sweetheart's love in cotton gown.

"My love is young and handsome
    As any in the town,
She's worth a ploughman's ransom
    In the drab cotton gown."
He sang and turned his furrow o'er
    And urged his team along,

---

[1] Printed in Grigson's edition of Clare's later poems.   [1] Bents: coarse grass.

[2] In the edition prepared by Robinson and Summerfield, the second half of this line is given from a transcription of Clare's manuscript: "and the wishers [mistress? wishes?] of love."

[1] Trefoil: clover.   [2] Rig: the ridge made by the plow as it turns up the earth.

While on the willow as before
  The old crow croaked his song:
The ploughman sung his rustic lay
30 And sung of Phoebe all the day.

The crow he was in love, no doubt,
  And [so were] many things:
The ploughman finished many a bout,
  And lustily he sings,
"My love she is a milking-maid
  With red rosy cheek;
Of cotton drab her gown was made,
  I loved her many a week."
His milking-maid the ploughman sung
40 Till all the fields around him rung.

                (1842–64)

The Lover's Invitation

Now the wheat is in the ear, and the rose is on
    the brere,[1]
And bluecaps[2] so divinely blue, with poppies of
    bright scarlet hue,
Maiden, at the close o' eve, wilt thou, dear, thy
    cottage leave,
    And walk with one that loves thee?

When the even's tiny tears bead upon the
    grassy spears,
And the spider's lace is wet with its pinhead
    blebs[3] of dew,
Wilt thou lay thy work aside and walk by
    brooklets dim descried,
    Where I delight to love thee?

While thy footfall lightly prest tramples by the
    skylark's nest,
And the cockle's streaky eyes mark the snug
10   place where it lies,
Mary, put thy work away, and walk at dewy
    close o' day
    With me to kiss and love thee.

There's something in the time so sweet, when
    lovers in the evening meet,
The air so still, the sky so mild, like slumbers
    of the cradled child,
The moon looks over fields of love, among the
    ivy sleeps the dove:
    To see thee is to love thee.

So come, my Mary, now's the hour to feel the
    evening's soothing power,
The ladybird has sought repose on golden
    pillows in the rose,
The white moth's round the hawthorn bush,
    on its blue eggs sits the thrush: 20
    And I'll ever after love thee.[4]
           (1842–64) 1873

Song

I peeled bits of straw and I got switches too
From the grey peeling willow as idlers do,
And I switched at the flies as I sat all alone
Till my flesh, blood, and marrow was turned to
  dry bone.
My illness was love, though I knew not the
  smart,
But the beauty of love was the blood of my
  heart.[1]
Crowded places, I shunned them as noises too
  rude
And fled to the silence of sweet solitude,
Where the flower in green darkness buds,
  blossoms, and fades,
Unseen of all shepherds and flower-loving   10
  maids—
The hermit bees find them but once and away;
There I'll bury alive and in silence decay.

I looked on the eyes of fair woman too long,
Till silence and shame stole the use of my
  tongue:
When I tried to speak to her I'd nothing to say,
So I turned myself round and she wandered
  away.
When she got too far off, why, I'd something
  to tell,
So I sent sighs behind her and walked to my
  cell.
Willow switches I broke and peeled bits of
  straws,
Ever lonely in crowds, in nature's own laws—   20
My ball-room the pasture, my music the bees,
My drink was the fountain, my church the tall
  trees.
Who ever would love or be tied to a wife
When it makes a man mad all the days of his
  life?
            (1842–64)

---

[1] Brere: briar.   [2] Bluecaps: the bird also named the blue titmouse.
[3] Blebs: drops of liquid.   [4] This poem was published in 1873 lacking this final stanza.
[1] In their edition of Clare's later poetry, Robinson and Summerfield divide this poem into
four stanzas of six lines each.

We Passed by Green Closes[1]

The path crossed green closes and went down
    the lane
Where the black snail reposes and the slime
    marks remain
The hook prickle bramble Arch's[2] over the
    grass
And tears in her ramble The gown o' the lass

The Wind in her ribbons green Wantoned and
    played
And danced round as they'd been i' love wi'
    the maid
Fine straw was her bonnet her cheek was the
    rose
Passing bee settled on it by mistake I suppose

Blue skippers[3] in sunny hours open and shut
Where wormwood and grunsel[4] flowers by the
    cart ruts
Where bees while birds whistle Sung all the
    lane down

And passes the thistle For the flowers on her
    gown

The footpath all noon day We paced i' the
    lane
The day it was Sunday The bells rung again
The bare[5] Mare was snorting Beside of her foal
Love from that days courting Burns my heart
    to a coal

                 (1842–64)

Birds' Nests

'Tis spring, warm glows the south,
Chaffinch carries the moss in his mouth
To filbert hedges all day long,
And charms the poet with his beautiful song;
The wind blows bleak o'er the sedgy fen,
But warm the sun shines by the little wood,
Where the old cow at her leisure chews her cud.

                 (1863)

Thomas Hood
1799-1845

THOMAS HOOD WAS, to use a phrase that his conduct of his occupation helped to make honorable, an entirely professional literary man. He was born in London, and literally born into his trade: his father was a bookseller and publisher, and his mother was the daughter of an engraver. After an indifferent education in a series of schools, he went to work in 1813 or 1814 as a clerk and then as an apprentice engraver of illustrations on woodblocks, a craft in which he became proficient. In 1821 he became a subeditor of the recently founded *London Magazine*, mostly reading copy and helping with the production of the journal. The monthly *London Magazine* was to become one of the principal literary journals of the 1820s, and Hood soon joined Charles Lamb, Thomas DeQuincey, John Clare, and other writers of similar distinction as a contributor to the journal. In 1825 he collaborated with John Hamilton Reynolds, a poet and journalist who had been a friend of Keats, in a collection of comic poems, *Odes and Addresses to Great People*. In the next year he collected in the first series of *Whims and Oddities* some of the writings and drawings he had published in magazines. A second series was published in 1827, and the two series were

---

[1] The text of this poem is that printed in Robinson and Summerfield's edition. Closes: enclosed fields.
[2] Arch's: arches.   [3] Skippers: butterflies.   [4] Grunsel: a common weed.
[5] In his edition of Clare's later poems, Grigson reads this word as "bay."

combined in 1832 and frequently republished during the rest of the century. In these early years of his career Hood also wrote farces and sketches for comic actors and monologists, edited one of the then popular annuals of literary pieces and engravings, and served as a drama critic.

Most of Hood's work in these early years was comic, and almost all of it was journalism of one kind or another. In 1827 he also published a volume of conventionally earnest poems, *The Plea of the Midsummer Fairies,* whose character is epitomized in his "Ode: Autumn": fanciful, graceful, pleasantly melancholy, derivative from Keats. He occasionally published other verse that was not comic, including "The Dream of Eugene Aram" (separately published in 1831), a poem about the reveries of a murderer, and his most famous poem, "The Song of the Shirt" (1843). He also published a three-volume novel, *Tylney Hall* (1834), and a series of travel sketches, *Up the Rhine* (1840). But by 1830 it was clear that his reputation, livelihood, and most remarkable talent lay in comic verse and its illustration. In that year he published the first *Comic Annual,* a series he continued until 1842, missing volumes only in 1840 and 1841. Each *Annual* was a book-length miscellany for which Hood, after the first number, wrote all the prose and verse and furnished fifty full-page drawings.

The annuals were popular, but Hood's hospitable ways and some failed investments got him in financial trouble in the mid-1830s. Rather than relieve his debts by declaring bankruptcy, he moved to the Continent in 1835 until he could pay his creditors. He returned to London in 1840, and he immediately resumed the busy journalism now habitual to him. In addition to publishing the last volume of the *Comic Annual* in 1842, he edited and wrote for the *New Monthly Magazine* (in which he published "Miss Kilmansegg and Her Golden Leg"), contributed to the comic weekly *Punch,* and conducted his own magazine in 1844–45 (Robert Browning was one of his contributors). In 1844 he published yet another collection of his comic prose and verse, *Whimsicalities.* In the same year he received an annual government pension of £100 for his services to literature, which mitigated the financial difficulties of which he was never entirely free. For most of his life he had been physically frail and in poor health, probably as a result of rheumatic fever in his adolescence. After his return from the Continent his health began to deteriorate, and after a long illness in which he continued to work hard as a writer and editor, he died in 1845.

Hood's gifts as a poet were an unusual metrical skill, a facility in a range of poetic forms, from street ballads and mock-odes to real odes and narratives like "The Last Man," an audacity which was ready to mix the language of the streets and newspapers with the tones and words of elevated poetry, and a comedian's timing which knew when to deploy the incongruities and dissonances of puns, parody, topical allusions, and shifts to the vernacular. His humor and his sentimentality were at once defenses against and expressions of a complex sensibility moved by pain. His comic and, less frequently, his sentimental verse, tens of thousands of lines written against the deadlines of magazines and annuals, is often mechanical in its formulas and obscure or quaint in its allusions to events and attitudes no longer remembered or important. But at his best he converted one of the major themes of nineteenth-century British poetry, a sense of an exhausted, spiritless material creation full of accident and malevolence, into a fundamentally serious, hard-edged grotesquerie which runs from poems like "The Last Man" through his parodies of pathetic ballads to the social mockery of "Miss Kilmansegg."

The topicality of his verse, especially in his poems of the 1840s, also helped to keep moving in nineteenth-century British poetry the idea that a poem might alter contemporary actualities by putting them, exaggerated but undisguised, into poems, just as Dickens at the same time was putting them into novels. "The Song of the Shirt," for example, came directly out of journalistic accounts of the plight of exploited seamstresses. Its immediate popularity—it was made into a street ballad, printed on pocket handkerchiefs, turned into a play—took it quickly back into and further excited the public consciousness out of which it came. If the poem did not help settle the social issue, which was certainly Hood's hope for it, it at least announced that poetry had something to do with such issues. In less evident ways Hood's comic verse worked similarly to keep poetry open to contemporary life, and life open to poetry. His abilities helped to make the language of nineteenth-century British poetry more supple by bringing into it words, rhythms, images, forms, and tones that described some of the ordinary content of contemporary lives, especially urban lives, lived without heroism and heavy-breathing portentousness, sustained in a wiry humor and by quick releases of sharply focused tears and anger. In turn, his comic poems, in part because they were taken in so easily by contemporary readers, touched their concerns with such intelligent pleasures as a steady suspicion of grand postures, a wry accommodation to disappointments, losses, irrationalities, and destructions that cannot be helped, and a simple humanitarian outrage at the plain, needless, and foolish facts of human and social error that can be put right.

EDITIONS

The standard edition of Hood's poems is *The Complete Poetical Works of Thomas Hood,* edited by Walter Jerrold (1906). The texts printed below are those of the original publications of Hood's poems in his books and annuals; these texts are usually but not always consistent with those in Jerrold's edition. John Clubbe has edited the *Selected Poems of Thomas Hood* (1970); his edition includes full, useful, and often necessary annotations. Peter F. Morgan has edited *The Letters of Thomas Hood* (1973).

BIOGRAPHY AND CRITICISM

Hood's daughter and son compiled a two-volume *Memorials of Thomas Hood,* by F. F. Broderip and Tom Hood, Jr. (1860). The best biography and study is J. C. Reid's *Thomas Hood* (1963). Walter Jerrold's *Hood: His Life and Times* (1907), and John Clubbe's *Victorian Forerunner: The Later Career of Thomas Hood* (1968) are also useful. John Heath Stubb's *The Darkling Plain* (1950) contains a chapter on Hood's poetry. Laurence Bander's *Thomas Hood,* a pamphlet in the Writers and Work series (1963), and Lloyd Jeffrey's short study, *Thomas Hood* (1973), contain select bibliographies of writing about Hood.

Ode: Autumn

I

I saw old Autumn in the misty morn
Stand shadowless like Silence, listening
To silence, for no lonely bird would sing
Into his hollow ear from woods forlorn,
Nor lowly hedge nor solitary thorn;
Shaking his languid locks all dewy bright
With tangled gossamer that fell by night,
    Pearling his coronet of golden corn.

II

Where are the songs of Summer?—With the sun,
Oping the dusky eyelids of the south,   10
Till shade and silence waken up as one,
And Morning sings with a warm odorous mouth.
Where are the merry birds?—Away, away,
On panting wings through the inclement skies,
    Lest owls should prey
    Undazzled at noon-day,
And tear with horny beak their lustrous eyes.

III

Where are the blooms of Summer?—In the west,
Blushing their last to the last sunny hours,
When the mild Eve by sudden Night is prest   20
Like tearful Proserpine,[1] snatch'd from her flow'rs
    To a most gloomy breast.
Where is the pride of Summer,—the green prime,—
The many, many leaves all twinkling?—Three
    On the moss'd elm; three on the naked lime
Trembling,—and one upon the old oak tree!
    Where is the Dryads'[2] immortality?—
Gone into mournful cypress and dark yew,
Or wearing the long gloomy Winter through
    In the smooth holly's green eternity.   30

IV

The squirrel gloats on his accomplish'd hoard,
The ants have brimm'd their garners with ripe grain,
    And honey bees have stor'd
The sweets of Summer in their luscious cells;
The swallows all have wing'd across the main;
But here the Autumn melancholy dwells,
    And sighs her tearful spells
Amongst the sunless shadows of the plain.
    Alone, alone,
    Upon a mossy stone,   40
She sits and reckons up the dead and gone

---

[1] Proserpine: in classical mythology Proserpine (or Persephone) is the daughter of Ceres (Demeter), the goddess of the fertility of growing things. Proserpine was abducted to the underworld by Pluto, and allowed to return to the surface and sunlight of the earth only for half the year.
[2] Dryads: wood nymphs.

With the last leaves for a love-rosary;
Whilst all the wither'd world looks drearily,
Like a dim picture of the drowned past
In the hush'd mind's mysterious far-away,
Doubtful what ghostly thing will steal the last
Into that distance, grey upon the grey.

V

O go and sit with her, and be o'ershaded
Under the languid downfall of her hair;
50 She wears a coronal of flowers faded
Upon her forehead, and a face of care;—
There is enough of wither'd everywhere
To make her bower,—and enough of gloom;
There is enough of sadness to invite,
If only for the rose that died, whose doom
Is Beauty's,—she that with the living bloom
Of conscious cheeks most beautifies the light:
There is enough of sorrowing, and quite
Enough of bitter fruits the earth doth bear,—
60 Enough of chilly droppings for her bowl;
Enough of fear and shadowy despair,
To frame her cloudy prison for the soul!
                                        1823; 1827

The Last Man[1]

'Twas in the year two thousand and one,
A pleasant morning of May,
I sat on the gallows-tree all alone,
A-chaunting a merry lay,—
To think how the pest[2] had spared my life,
To sing with the larks that day!—

When up the heath came a jolly knave,
Like a scarecrow, all in rags:
It made me crow to see his old duds
10 All aboard in the wind, like flags:—
So up he came to the timbers' foot
And pitch'd down his greasy bags.—

Good Lord! how blythe the old beggar was!
At pulling out his scraps,—
The very sight of his broken orts[3]
Made a work in his wrinkled chaps:[4]
"Come down," says he, "you Newgate bird,[5]
And have a taste of my snaps!"[6]——

Then down the rope, like a tar from the mast,
I slided, and by him stood;   20
But I wished myself on the gallows again
When I smelt that beggar's food,—
A foul beef-bone and a mouldy crust;—
"Oh!" quoth he, "the heavens are good!"

Then after this grace he cast him down:
Says I, "You'll get sweeter air
A pace or two off, on the windward side,"—
For the felons' bones lay there—
But he only laugh'd at the empty skulls,
And offered them part of his fare.   30

"I never harm'd *them*, and they won't
    harm me;
Let the proud and the rich be cravens!"
I did not like that strange beggar man,
He look'd so up at the heavens.
Anon he shook out his empty old poke;[7]
"There's the crumbs," saith he, "for the
    ravens!"

It made me angry to see his face,
It had such a jesting look;
But which I made up my mind to speak,   40
A small case-bottle[8] he took:
Quoth he, "Though I gather the green
    watercress,
My drink is not of the brook!"

Full manners-like he tender'd the dram;
Oh, it came of a dainty cask!
But, whenever it came to his turn to pull,
"Your leave, good Sir, I must ask;
But I always wipe the brim with my sleeve,
When a hangman sups at my flask!"

And then he laugh'd so loudly and long,   50
The churl was quite out of breath;
I thought the very Old One was come
To mock me before my death,
And wish'd I had buried the dead men's bones
That were lying about the heath!

But the beggar gave me a jolly clap—
"Come, let us pledge each other,
For all the wide world is dead beside,

---

[1] Thomas Campbell (1777–1844) had published a poem on this theme and with this title in 1823, and Mary Shelley (1797–1851) published a novel with the same theme and title in 1826.
[2] Pest: pestilence.   [3] Orts: leftover bits of food.   [4] Chaps: jaw.
[5] Newgate bird: Newgate was the name of a London prison in which criminals condemned to be hanged were jailed.
[6] Snaps: bits of food; snacks.   [7] Poke: bag or sack.
[8] Case-bottle: a flask protected by a covering.

And we are brother and brother—
60 I've a yearning for thee in my heart,
As if we had come of one mother.

"I've a yearning for thee in my heart
That almost makes me weep,
For as I pass'd from town to town
The folks were all stone-asleep,—
But when I saw thee sitting aloft,
It made me both laugh and leap!"

Now a curse (I thought) be on his love,
And a curse upon his mirth,—
70 An' if it were not for that beggar man
I'd be the King of the earth,—
But I promised myself, an hour should come
To make him rue his birth!—

So down we sat and bous'd⁹ again
Till the sun was in mid-sky,
When, just when the gentle west-wind came,
We hearken'd a dismal cry;
"Up, up, on the tree,"¹⁰ quoth the beggar man,
'Till these horrible dogs go by!'

80 And, lo! from the forest's far-off skirts,
They came all yelling for gore,
A hundred hounds pursuing at once,
And a panting hart before,
Till he sunk down at the gallows' foot
And there his haunches they tore!

His haunches they tore, without a horn
To tell when the chase was done;
And there was not a single scarlet coat
To flaunt it in the sun!—
90 I turn'd, and look'd at the beggar man,
And his tears dropt one by one!

And with curses sore he chid at the hounds,
Till the last dropt out of sight,
Anon, saith he, "let's down again,
And ramble for our delight,
For the world's all free, and we may choose
A right cozie barn for to-night!"

With that, he set up his staff on end,
And it fell with the point due West;
So we far'd that way to a city great,
100 Where the folks had died of the pest—
It was fine to enter in house and hall
Wherever it liked me best;—

For the porters all were stiff and cold,
And could not lift their heads;
And when we came where their masters lay,
The rats leapt out of the beds:—
The grandest palaces in the land
Were as free as workhouse¹¹ sheds.

But the beggar man made a mumping¹² face,
And knocked at every gate: 110
It made me curse to hear how he whined,
So our fellowship turn'd to hate,
And I bade him walk the world by himself,
For I scorn'd so humble a mate!

So *he* turn'd right, and *I* turn'd left,
As if we had never met;
And I chose a fair stone house for myself,
For the city was all to let;
And for three brave holidays drank my fill
Of the choicest that I could get. 120

And because my jerkin was coarse and worn,
I got me a properer vest;
It was purple velvet, stitch'd o'er with gold,
And a shining star at the breast,—
'Twas enough to fetch old Joan from her grave
To see me so purely drest!—

But Joan was dead and under the mould,
And every buxom lass;
In vain I watch'd, at the window pane
For a Christian soul to pass;— 130
But sheep and kine wander'd up the street,
And browsed on the new-come grass.—

When lo! I spied the old beggar man,
And lustily he did sing!—
His rags were lapp'd in a scarlet cloak,
And a crown he had like a King;
So he stept right up before my gate
And danc'd me a saucy fling!

Heaven mend us all!—but, within my mind,
I had kill'd him then and there; 140
To see him lording so braggart-like
That was born to his beggar's fare,
And how he had stolen the royal crown
His betters were meant to wear.

But God forbid that a thief should die
Without his share of the laws!
So I nimbly whipt my tackle¹³ out,

---

⁹ Bous'd: drank excessively.   ¹⁰ Tree: gallows.
¹¹ Workhouse sheds: the outbuildings of the institutions in which paupers were housed.
¹² Mumping: begging.   ¹³ Tackle: equipment.

And soon tied up his claws,—
I was judge myself, and jury, and all,
150   And solemnly tried the cause.

But the beggar man would not plead, but cried
Like a babe without its corals,[14]
For he knew how hard it is apt to go
When the law and a thief have quarrels,—
There was not a Christian soul alive
To speak a word for his morals.

Oh, how gaily I doff'd my costly gear,
And put on my work-day clothes;
I was tired of such a long Sunday life,—
160   And never was one of the sloths;
But the beggar man grumbled a weary deal,
And made many crooked mouths.

So I haul'd him off to the gallows' foot,
And blinded him in his bags;[15]
'Twas a weary job to heave him up,
For a doom'd man always lags;
But by ten of the clock he was off his legs
In the wind and airing his rags!

So there he hung and there I stood,
170   The LAST MAN left alive,
To have my own will of all the earth:
Quoth I, now I shall thrive!
But when was ever honey made
With one bee in a hive?

My conscience began to gnaw my heart,
Before the day was done,
For other men's lives had all gone out,
Like candles in the sun!—
But it seem'd as if I had broke, at last,
180   A thousand necks in one!

So I went and cut his body down
To bury it decentlie;—
God send there were any good soul alive
To do the like by me!
But the wild dogs came with terrible speed,
And bay'd me up the tree!

My sight was like a drunkard's sight,
And my head began to swim,
To see their jaws all white with foam,

Like the ravenous ocean brim;—   190
But when the wild dogs trotted away
Their jaws were bloody and grim!

Their jaws were bloody and grim, good Lord!
But the beggar man, where was he?—
There was nought of him but some ribbons of
   rags
Below the gallows tree!—
I know the Devil, when I am dead,
Will send his hounds for me!—

I've buried my babies one by one,
And dug the deep hole for Joan,   200
And cover'd the faces of kith and kin,
And felt the old churchyard stone
Go cold to my heart, full many a time,
But I never felt so lone!

For the lion and Adam were company,
And the tiger him beguiled:
But the simple kine are foes to my life,
And the household brutes are wild.
If the veriest cur would lick my hand,
I could love it like a child!   210

And the beggar man's ghost besets my dream,
At night to make me madder,—
And my wretched conscience within my breast,
Is like a stinging adder;—
I sigh when I pass the gallows' foot,
And look at the rope and ladder!

For hanging looks sweet,—but, alas! in vain
My desperate fancy begs,—
I must turn my cup of sorrows quite up,
And drink it to the dregs,—   220
For there is not another man alive,
In the world, to pull my legs![16]

                                            1826

Faithless Nelly Gray

A Pathetic Ballad

Ben Battle was a soldier bold,
   And used to war's alarms:
But a cannon-ball took off his legs,
   So he laid down his arms!

---

[14] Corals: pieces of coral were used as teething rings for children.
[15] Blinded him in his bags: used his trousers as a blindfold.
[16] To pull my legs: the agonies of a hanged man were shortened by pulling his legs to assure
that his neck was broken.

Now as they bore him off the field,
  Said he, "Let others shoot,
For here I leave my second leg,
  And the Forty-second Foot!"

The army-surgeons made him limbs:
  Said he,—"They're only pegs:
But there's as wooden Members[1] quite
  As represent my legs!"

Now Ben loved a pretty maid,
  Her name was Nelly Gray;
So he went to pay her his devours[2]
  When he'd devoured his pay!

But when he called on Nelly Gray,
  She made him quite a scoff;
And when she saw his wooden legs,
  Began to take them off![3]

"Oh, Nelly Gray! Oh, Nelly Gray!
  Is this your love so warm?
The love that loves a scarlet coat
  Should be more uniform!"

Said she, "I loved a soldier once,
  For he was blythe and brave;
But I will never have a man
  With both legs in the grave!

"Before you had those timber toes,
  Your love I did allow,
But then, you know, you stand upon
  Another footing now!"

"O, Nelly Gray! O, Nelly Gray!
  For all your jeering speeches,
At duty's call, I left my legs
  In Badajos's *breaches!*"[4]

"Why, then," said she, "you've lost the feet
  Of legs in war's alarms,
And now you cannot wear your shoes
  Upon your feats of arms!"

"O, false and fickle Nelly Gray!
  I know why you refuse:—
Though I've no feet—some other man
  Is standing in my shoes!

I wish I ne'er had seen your face;
  But, now, a long farewell!

For you will be my death:—alas!
  You will not be my *Nell!*"

Now when he went from Nelly Gray,
  His heart so heavy got—
And life was such a burthen grown,
  It made him take a knot!

So round his melancholy neck,
  A rope he did entwine,
And, for his second time in life,
  Enlisted in the Line![5]

One end he tied around a beam,
  And then removed his pegs,
And, as his legs were off,—of course,
  He soon was off his legs!

And there he hung, till he was dead
  As any nail[6] in town,—
For though distress had cut him up,
  It could not cut him down!

A dozen men sat on his corpse,
  To find out why he died—
And they buried Ben in four cross-roads,
  With a *stake* in his inside![7]

1826

The Carelesse Nurse Mayd

I sawe a Mayd sitte on a Bank,
Beguiled by Wooer fayne and fond;
And whiles His flatterynge Vowes She drank,
Her Nurselynge slipt within a Pond!

All Even Tide they Talkde and Kist,
For She was fayre and He was Kinde;
The Sunne went down before She wist
Another Sonne had sett behinde!

With angrie Hands and frownynge Browe,
That deemd Her owne the Urchine's Sinne,   10
She pluckt Him out, but he was nowe
Past being Whipt for fallynge in.

She then beginnes to wayle the Ladde
With Shrikes that Echo answerde round—
O! foolishe Mayd to be soe sadde
The Momente that her Care was drownd!

1830

---

[1] Members: members of Parliament.   [2] Devours: devoirs: a formal call.
[3] Take them off: mock them.
[4] Badajos: city in Spain taken by Wellington and British troops during the Peninsular campaign in 1812.
[5] The Line: regular infantry.   [6] Nail: a weight.   [7] A traditional mode of burial for suicides.

Domestic Didactics by an Old Servant

The Broken Dish

What's life but full of care and doubt,
  With all its fine humanities,
With parasols we walk about,
  Long pigtails and such vanities.

We plant pomegranite trees and things,
  And go in gardens sporting,
With toys and fans of peacocks' wings
  To painted ladies courting.

10

We gather flowers of every hue,
  And fish in boats for fishes,
Build summer-houses painted blue,—
  But life's as frail as dishes.

Walking about their groves of trees,
  Blue bridges and blue rivers,
How little thought them two Chinese,
  They'd both be smash'd to shivers.

1839

from Miss Kilmansegg and Her Precious Leg: Her Fancy Ball

"Miss Kilmansegg and Her Precious Leg" was published in two installments in the New Monthly Magazine *in 1840–41. The heroine is a wealthy young lady who loses a leg in an accident and has it replaced with one of gold. Eventually she is married to a mercenary adventurer, is brained by him with her own leg, and judged to be a suicide, "Be-*

cause her own Leg had killed her!" Clubbe in his edition of selections from Hood's poetry notes (pp. 362–363) that the Kilmanseggs were a noble family of Hanover who retained connections with the Hanoverian line of British kings which began with George I in 1714; members of the family were prominent in London society during the regency and reign of George IV (1811–30), and their name carried for Hood and probably for at least some of his readers connotations of a vulgarly spectacular world of money and pleasure.

'Tis Curiosity's Benefit Night—
And perchance 'tis the English-Second-Sight;
  But whatever it be, so be it—
As the friends and guests of Miss Kilmansegg
Crowd in to look at her Golden Leg,
    As many more
    Mob round the door,
  To see them going to see it!

In they go—in jackets and cloaks,
Plumes and bonnets, turbans and toques,   1010
  As if to a Congress of Nations:
Greeks and Malays, with daggers and dirks,
Spaniards, Jews, Chinese, and Turks—
Some like original foreign works,
  But mostly like bad translations.

In they go, and to work like a pack,
Juan, Moses, and Shacabac,[1]
Tom, and Jerry,[2] and Springheel'd Jack,[3]
  For some of low Fancy are lovers—
Skirting, zigzagging, casting about,   1020
Here and there, and in and out,
With a crush, and a rush, for a full-bodied rout[4]
  Is one of the stiffest of covers.[5]

In they went, and hunted about,
Open-mouth'd like chub and trout,
And some with the upper lip thrust out,
  Like that fish for routing, a barbel[6]—
While Sir Jacob stood to welcome the crowd,
And rubbed his hands, and smiled aloud,

[1] Shacabac is a beggar in the *Arabian Nights* who is tricked by illusory feasts before he wins a real one.
[2] Tom and Jerry are the names of the heroes of Pierce Egan's *Life in London* (1821), a very popular fiction of life among the "fancy"—the fast, sporting set—in London.
[3] Springheel'd Jack: in 1838 the London newspapers carried accounts of a man who came to be referred to as "Springheel'd Jack," who terrorized women by leaping at them and then bounding away. Increasingly fanciful accounts were published in pamphlets, and the phrase remained current until the end of the century, when it provided the name of a naval rocket.
[4] Rout: a fashionable gathering.
[5] Covers: a hunting term: the vegetation in which the quarry is hunted.
[6] Barbel: a fish of the carp tribe which has fleshy filaments (barbs) hanging from its mouth.

1030 And bow'd, and bow'd, and bow'd, and bow'd,
   Like a man who is sawing marble.

For Princes were there, and Noble Peers;
Dukes descended from Norman spears;
Earls that dated from early years;
   And Lords in vast variety—
Besides the Gentry both new and old—
For people who stand on legs of gold,
   Are sure to stand well with society.

"But where—where—where?" with one accord
1040 Cried Moses and Mufti, Jack and my Lord,
   Wang-fong and Il Bondocani[7]—
When slow, and heavy, and dead as a dump,[8]
They heard a foot begin to stump,
    Thump! lump!
    Lump! thump!
   Like the Spectre[9] in "Don Giovanni!"

And lo! the Heiress, Miss Kilmansegg,
With her splendid, brilliant, beautiful leg,
   In the garb of a Goddess olden—
1050 Like chaste Diana[10] going to hunt,
With a golden spear—which of course was
   blunt,
And a tunic loop'd up to a gem in front,
   To show the Leg that was Golden!

Gold! still gold; her Crescent behold,
That should be silver, but would be gold;
   And her robe's auriferous spangles!
Her golden stomacher—how she would melt!
Her golden quiver, and golden belt,
   Where a golden bugle dangles!

1060 And her jewelled Garter? Oh, sin! oh, shame!
Let Pride and Vanity bear the blame,
That bring such blots on female fame!
   But to be a true recorder,
Besides its thin transparent stuff,
The tunic was loop'd quite high enough
   To give a glimpse of the Order![11]

But what have sin or shame to do
With a Golden Leg—and a stout one too?
   Away with all Prudery's panics!
That the precious metal, by thick and thin,   1070
Will cover square acres of land or sin,
   Is a fact made plain
   Again and again,
   In Morals as well as Mechanics.

A few, indeed, of her proper sex,
Who seem'd to feel her foot on their necks,
And fear'd their charms would meet with
   checks
   From so rare and splendid a blazon—
A few cried "fie!"—and "forward"—and
   "bold!"
And said of the Leg it might be gold,   1080
   But to them it look'd like brazen!

'Twas hard they hinted for flesh and blood,
Virtue and Beauty, and all that's good,
   To strike to mere dross their top-gallants—
But what were Beauty, or Virtue, or Worth,
Gentle manners, or gentle birth,
Nay, what the most talented head on earth
   To a Leg worth fifty Talents![12]

But the men sang quite another hymn
Of glory and praise to the precious Limb—   1090
Age, sordid Age, admir'd the whim,
   And its indecorum pardon'd—
While half of the young—ay, more than half—
Bow'd down and worshipp'd the Golden Calf,
Like the Jews when their hearts were
   harden'd.[13]

     .   .   .

Nor yet did the Heiress herself omit
The arts that help to make a hit,   1130
   And preserve a prominent station,
She talk'd and laugh'd far more than her share;
And took a part in "Rich and Rare

---

[7] Wang-fong and Il Bondocani: the first is the hero of a pantomime by Charles Dibdin the Younger performed first in 1812; the second is the hero of a comic opera by Thomas Dibdin, performed first in 1802.

[8] Dump: a leaden piece used in games.

[9] Spectre: the ghost of the Commandante who comes to take Don Juan to hell in Mozart's opera, which was first performed in 1787.

[10] Diana: the goddess of the moon as well as of the hunt; thus the reference to a crescent that ought to be silver below (line 1055).

[11] Order: the emblem of the Order of the Garter, a chivalric order founded in the mid-fourteenth century, was worn by men tied below the knee, and by women on the arm.

[12] Talent: a unit of weight used in the ancient Mediterranean world, referred to in the parable of the talents in Matthew 25:14–30.

[13] Exodus 32.

Were the gems she wore"—and the gems were
    there,[14]
    Like a Song with an Illustration.

She even stood up with a Count of France
To dance—alas! the measures we dance
    When Vanity plays the Piper!
Vanity, Vanity, apt to betray,
1140 And lead all sorts of legs astray,
Wood, or metal, or human clay,—
    Since Satan first play'd the Viper!

But first she doff'd her hunting gear,
And favour'd Tom Tug[15] with her golden spear
    To row with down the river—
A Bonze[16] had her golden bow to hold;
A Hermit her belt and bugle of gold;
    And an Abbot her golden quiver.

1150 And then a space was clear'd on the floor,
And she walk'd the Minuet de la Cour,
With all the pomp of a Pompadour,[17]
    But although she began *andante,*
Conceive the faces of all the Rout,
When she finished off with a whirligig bout,
And the Precious Leg stuck stiffly out
    Like the leg of a *Figuranté.*[18]

So the courtly dance was goldenly done,
And golden opinions, of course, it won
    From all different sorts of people—
1160 Chiming, ding-dong, with flattering phrase,
In one vociferous peal of praise,
Like the peal that rings on Royal days
    From Loyalty's parish-steeple.

And yet, had the leg been one of those
That dance for bread in flesh-colour'd hose,

With Rosina's pastoral bevy,[19]
The jeers it had met,—the shouts! the scoff!
The cutting advice to "take itself off,"
    For sounding but half so heavy.

Had it been a leg like those, perchance,   1170
That teach little girls and boys to dance,
To set, poussette,[20] recede, and advance,
    With the steps and figures most proper,—
Had it hopp'd for a weekly or quarterly sum,
How little of praise or grist would have come
    To a mill with such a hopper![21]

But the Leg was none of those limbs forlorn—
Bartering capers and hops for corn—
That meet with public hisses and scorn,
    Or the morning journal denounces—   1180
Had it pleased to caper from morn till dusk,
There was all the music of "Money Musk,"[22]
    In its ponderous bangs and bounces.

But, hark;—as slow as the strokes of a pump,
    Lump, thump!
    Thump, lump!
As the Giant of Castle Otranto[23] might stump
    To a lower room from an upper—
Down she goes with a noisy dint,
For taking the crimson turban's hint,   1190
A noble Lord at the Head of the Mint
    Is leading the Leg to supper!

But the supper, alas! must rest untold,
With its blaze of light, and its glitter of gold,
    For to paint that scene of glamour,
It would need the Great Enchanter's[24] charm,
Who waves over Palace, and Cot, and Farm,
An arm like the Goldbeater's Golden Arm
    That wields a Golden Hammer.[25]

[14] "Rich and Rare": the first words of a song by Thomas Moore (1779–1852), collected in *Irish Melodies,* first published in 1820 and frequently republished.
[15] Tom Tug: the name of a character in a play by Charles Dibdin, *The Waterman* (1774).
[16] Bonze: Buddhist monk.
[17] Pompadour: the Marquise de Pompadour (1721–64), the mistress of Louis XV of France.
[18] *Figuranté:* a dancer in the ballet chorus used in most of the London theaters. Ballet girls were popularly imagined to be sexually promiscuous.
[19] *Rosina* is a musical play by Frances Brooke (1724–89) which uses pastoral settings; it was first performed in 1782, and like the other plays Hood names was performed throughout the early nineteenth century.
[20] Pousette: to dance with hands joined in a circle.
[21] Hopper: a receptable that holds grain and feeds it to the stones that grind it.
[22] Money Musk: a country dance tune.
[23] Castle Otranto: the setting of Horace Walpole's *The Castle of Otranto* (1764) is haunted by a spectral giant.
[24] Great Enchanter: George Henry Robins, a famous auctioneer in the first half of the nineteenth century, was so described.
[25] Goldbeater's Golden Arm: most likely a London shop sign advertising a goldsmith: the same sign appears in Dickens' *A Tale of Two Cities* (1859), which is set in late-eighteenth-century London and Paris (Book II, Chapter 6).

He—only HE could fitly state
THE MASSIVE SERVICE OF GOLDEN PLATE,
With the proper phrase and expansion—
The rare selection of FOREIGN WINES—
The ALPS OF ICE and MOUNTAINS OF PINES,
The punch in OCEANS and sugary shrines,
The TEMPLE OF TASTE from GUNTER'S DESIGNS—[26]
In short, all that WEALTH with a FEAST combines,
In a SPLENDID FAMILY MANSION.

Suffice it each mask'd outlandish guest,
Ate and drank of the very best,
According to critical conners—
And then they pledg'd the Hostess and Host,
But the Golden Leg was the standing toast,
And as somebody swore,
Walk'd off with more
Than its share of the "Hips!" and honours!

"Miss Kilmansegg!—
Full glasses I beg!—
Miss Kilmansegg and her Precious Leg!"
And away went the bottle careering!
Wine in bumpers! and shouts in peals!
Till the Clown didn't know his head from his heels,
The Mussulman's eyes danced two-some reels,
And the Quaker was hoarse with cheering!

1840–41

from A Black Job

No doubt the pleasure is as great,
Of being cheated as to cheat.

—HUDIBRAS[1]

The history of human-kind to trace,
Since Eve—the first of dupes—our doom unriddled,
A certain portion of the human race
Has certainly a taste for being diddled.
Witness the famous Mississippi dreams![2]
A rage that time seems only to redouble—
The Banks, Joint-Stocks, and all the flimsy schemes,
For rolling in Pactolian[3] streams,
That cost our modern rogues so little trouble.
No matter what,—to pasture cows on stubble,
To twist sea-sand into a solid rope,
To make the French bricks and fancy bread of rubble,
Or light with gas the whole celestial cope—
Only propose to blow a bubble,
And Lord! what hundreds will subscribe for soap!

Soap!—it reminds me of a little tale,
Tho' not a pig's, the hawbuck's[4] glory,
When rustic games and merriment prevail—
But here's my story:
Once on a time—no matter when—
A knot of very charitable men
Set up a Philanthropical Society,
Professing on a certain plan,
To benefit the race of man,
And in particular that dark variety,
Which some suppose inferior—as in vermin,
The sable is to ermine,
As smut[5] to flour, as coal to alabaster,
As crows to swans, as soot to driven snow,
As blacking, or as ink to "milk below,"[6]
Or yet a better simile to show,
As ragman's dolls to images in plaster!

However, as is usual in our city,
They had a sort of managing Commitee,
A board of grave responsible Directors—
A Secretary, good at pen and ink—
A Treasurer, of course, to keep the chink,
And quite an army of Collectors!
Not merely male, but female duns,
Young, old, and middle-aged—of all degrees—
With many of those persevering ones,
Who mite by mite would beg a cheese!

[26] Gunter's designs: William Gunter conducted a fashionable confectioner's shop in the early Victorian period and wrote a well-known pastry cookbook. Ices are a name for any of a number of frozen confections; pines are pineapples. The style and typography of this stanza are parodies of the handbills with which auctions were advertised.

[1] Samuel Butler's (1612–80) *Hudibras*, a picaresque satire on puritanism, was published in several parts between 1663 and 1678.

[2] Several banks in Mississippi issued bonds in the 1830s in which speculators in England invested, and lost, heavily.

[3] Pactolian: golden; from the river in Lydia famous for its golden sands.

[4] Hawbuck: country bumpkin. [5] Smut: Soot.

[6] "Milk below": the cry of street vendors of milk.

And what might be their aim?
 To rescue Afric's sable sons from fetters—
To save their bodies from the burning shame
 Of branding with hot letters—
Their shoulders from the cowhide's bloody
 strokes,
 Their necks from iron yokes?
To end or mitigate the ills of slavery,
50 The Planter's avarice, the Driver's knavery?
To school the heathen Negroes and enlighten
 'em,
 To polish up and brighten 'em,
And make them worthy of eternal bliss?
Why, no—the simple end and aim was this—
Reading a well-known proverb much amiss—
 To wash and whiten 'em!

They look'd so ugly in their sable hides:
 So dark, so dingy, like a grubby lot
60 Of sooty sweeps, or colliers, and besides,
 However the poor elves
 Might wash themselves
Nobody knew if they were clean or not—
On Nature's fairness they were quite a blot!
Not to forget more serious complaints
That even while they join'd in pious hymn,
 So black they were and grim,
 In face and limb,
They look'd like Devils, tho' they sang like
 Saints!
 The thing was undeniable!
70 They wanted washing! not that slight ablution
 To which the skin of the White Man is
 liable,
Merely removing transient pollution—
 But good, hard, honest, energetic rubbing
 And scrubbing,
Sousing each sooty frame from heels to head
 With stiff, strong, saponaceous lather,
 And pails of water—hottish rather,
But not so boiling as to turn 'em red!

So spoke the philanthropic man
80 Who laid, and hatch'd, and nursed the plan—
 And oh! to view its glorious consummation!
 The brooms and mops,
 The tubs and slops,
 The baths and brushes in full operation!
To see each Crow, or Jim, or John,[7]
Go in a raven and come out a swan.
 While fair as Cavendishes, Vanes, and
 Russells,

Black Venus rises from the soapy surge,
And all the little Niggerlings emerge
 As lily-white as mussels.   90

Sweet was the vision—but alas!
 However in prospectus bright and sunny,
To bring such visionary scenes to pass
 One thing was requisite, and that was—
 money!
Money, that pays the laundress and her bills,
For socks and collars, shirts and frills,
Cravats and kerchiefs—money, without which
The negroes must remain as dark as pitch;
 A thing to make all Christians sad and shiv-
 ery,
To think of millions of immortal souls   100
Dwelling in bodies black as coals,
 And living—so to speak—in Satan's livery!

Money—the root of evil,—dross, and stuff!
 But oh! how happy ought the rich to feel,
Whose means enable them to give enough
 To blanch an African from head to heel!
How blessed—yea thrice blessed—to subscribe
 Enough to scour a tribe!
 While he whose fortune was at best a brittle
 one,
Although he gave but pence, how sweet to
 know   110
He helped to bleach a Hottentot's great toe,
 Or little one!

Moved by this logic (or appall'd)
 To persons of a certain turn so proper,
The money came when call'd,
 In silver, gold, and copper,
Presents from "Friends to blacks," or foes to
 whites,
"Trifles," and "offerings," and "widows' mites,"
Plump legacies, and yearly benefactions,
 With other gifts   120
 And charitable lifts,
Printed in lists and quarterly transactions.
 As thus—Elisha Brettel,
 An iron kettle.
 The Dowager Lady Scannel,
 A piece of flannel.
 Rebecca Pope,
 A bar of soap.
 The Misses Howels,
 Half-a-dozen towels.   130
 The Master Rush's

---

[7] Jim Crow: from a minstrel song whose refrain contains the lines, "Jump, Jim Crow." Ameri-
can minstrel troupes were very popular in England in the late 1830s and 1840s.

Two scrubbing brushes.
Mr. T. Groom,
A stable broom,
And Mrs. Grubb,
A tub.

Great were the sums collected!
And great results in consequence expected.
140   But somehow, in the teeth of all endeavour,
      According to reports
      At yearly courts,
    The Blacks, confound them! were as black as
      ever!

Yes! spite of all the water sous'd aloft,
Soap, plain and mottled, hard and soft,
Soda and pearlash, huckaback[8] and sand,
Brooms, brushes, palm of hand,
And scourers in the office strong and clever,
    In spite of all the tubbing, rubbing, scrub-
      bing,
    The routing and the grubbing,
150   The Blacks, confound them! were as black as
      ever!

.   .   .

    However, nothing dashed
By such repeated failures, or abash'd,
The Court still met;—the Chairman and
      Directors,
    The Secretary, good at pen and ink,
    The worthy Treasurer, who kept the chink,
      And all the cash Collectors;
With hundreds of that class, so kindly
      credulous,
90   Without whose help, no charlatan alive,
    Or Bubble Company could hope to thrive,
Or busy Chevalier, however sedulous—
Those good and easy innocents in fact,
    Who willingly receiving chaff for corn,
As pointed out by Butler's tact,
Still find a secret pleasure in the act
    Of being pluck'd and shorn!

However, in long hundreds there they were,
    Thronging the hot, and close, and dusty
      court,
00 To hear once more addresses from the Chair,
    And regular Report.
Alas! concluding in the usual strain,
    That what with everlasting wear and tear,
    The scrubbing-brushes hadn't got a hair—

      [8] Huckabuck: a rough linen fabric.

The brooms—mere stumps—would never serve
    again—
The soap was gone, the flannels all in shreds,
    The towels worn to threads,
The tubs and pails too shatter'd to be
    mended—
    And what was added with a deal of pain,
    But as accounts correctly would explain,   210
Tho' thirty thousand pounds had been
    expended—
    The Blackamoors had still been wash'd in
    vain!

"In fact, the negroes were as black as ink,
Yet, still as the Committee dared to think,
And hoped the proposition was not rash,
A rather free expenditure of cash—"
But ere the prospect could be made more
    sunny—
    Up jump'd a little, lemon-coloured man,
    And with an eager stammer, thus began,
In angry earnest, though it sounded funny: 220
"What! More subscriptions! No—no—no,—
    not I!
You have had time—time—time enough to try!
They won't come white! then why—why—why
    —why—why,
    More money?"

"Why!" said the Chairman, with an accent
    bland,
And gentle waving of his dexter hand,
"Why must we have more dross, and dirt, and
    dust,
    More filthy lucre, in a word, more gold—
    The why, sir, very easily is told,
Because Humanity declares we must!   230
We've scrubb'd the negroes till we've nearly
    killed 'em,
    And finding that we cannot wash them white,
    But still their nigritude offends the sight,
    We mean to gild 'em!"
                1844

The Song of the Shirt

With fingers weary and worn,
  With eyelids heavy and red,
A Woman sat, in unwomanly rags,
  Plying her needle and thread—
    Stitch! stitch! stitch!
In poverty, hunger, and dirt,

And still with a voice of dolorous pitch
She sang the "Song of the Shirt!"

"Work! work! work!
10 While the cock is crowing aloof!
    And work—work—work,
Till the stars shine through the roof!
It's Oh! to be a slave
    Along with the barbarous Turk,
Where woman has never a soul to save,
    If this is Christian work!

"Work—work—work
Till the brain begins to swim;
    Work—work—work
20 Till the eyes are heavy and dim!
Seam, and gusset, and band,
    Band, and gusset, and seam,
Till over the buttons I fall asleep,
    And sew them on in a dream!

"Oh, Men with Sisters dear!
    Oh Men! with Mothers and Wives!
It is not linen you're wearing out,
    But human creatures' lives!
        Stitch—stitch—stitch,
30   In poverty, hunger and dirt,
Sewing at once, with a double thread,
    A Shroud as well as a Shirt.

"But why do I talk of Death?
    That Phantom of grisly bone,
I hardly fear his terrible shape,
    It seems so like my own—
    It seems so like my own,
Because of the fasts I keep;
Oh, God! that bread should be so dear,
40   And flesh and blood so cheap!

"Work—work—work!
    My labour never flags;
And what are its wages? A bed of straw,
    A crust of bread—and rags.
That shatter'd roof,—and this naked floor—
    A table—a broken chair—
And a wall so blank, my shadow I thank
    For sometimes falling there!

"Work—work—work!
50 From weary chime to chime,
    Work—work—work—
As prisoners work for crime!

Band, and gusset, and seam,
    Seam, and gusset, and band,
Till the heart is sick, and the brain benumb'd,
    As well as the weary hand.

"Work—work—work,
In the dull December light,
    And work—work—work,
When the weather is warm and bright—   60
While underneath the eaves
    The brooding swallows cling
As if to show me their sunny backs
    And twit me with the spring.

"Oh! but to breathe the breath
Of the cowslip and primrose sweet—
    With the sky above my head,
And the grass beneath my feet,
For only one short hour
    To feel as I used to feel,   70
Before I knew the woes of want
    And the walk that costs a meal!

"Seam, and gusset, and band,
Band, and gusset, and seam,
    Work, work, work,
Like the Engine that works by Steam!
A mere machine of iron and wood
    That toils for Mammon's sake
Without a brain to ponder and craze
    Or a heart to feel—and break![1]   80

"Oh! but for one short hour!
    A respite however brief!
No blessed leisure for Love or Hope,
    But only time for Grief!
A little weeping would ease my heart,
    But in their briny bed
My tears must stop, for every drop
    Hinders needle and thread!"

With fingers weary and worn,
    With eyelids heavy and red,   90
A Woman sate in unwomanly rags,
    Plying her needle and thread—
        Stitch! stitch! stitch!
    In poverty, hunger, and dirt,
And still with a voice of dolorous pitch,—
Would that its tone could reach the Rich!—
    She sang this "Song of the Shirt!"
                                                    1843

[1] This stanza was not included when the poem was first printed in *Punch* in 1843.

Elizabeth Barrett Browning
1806-61

ELIZABETH BARRETT was born and spent her early years in the north of England, near Durham, where her family lived on a small estate. She was intellectually voracious, precocious, and highly competitive, desiring the classical education offered as a matter of course to her brothers but rarely even aspired to by young women of her time. She studied French, Latin, and Greek, sometimes with the tutors of her brothers, and she read philosophy, history, and poetry on her own. Her first poem, *The Battle of Marathon,* written in 1818 or 1819 and published anonymously in 1820, was a narrative in the manner of Pope's translation of Homer. In 1821, when she was fifteen, she published some poems in a London literary magazine on the political repression of Greece, one of the themes of Byron's poetry, and she later published verses on the death of Byron. A second volume of poems, *An Essay on Mind and Other Poems,* was published in 1826, and she included some of her poems in a translation of Aeschylus' *Prometheus Unbound* which she published, again anonymously, in 1833.

Elizabeth Barrett's father had inherited property in Jamaica, and when in 1832 the abolition of slavery in British possessions required some rearrangements of the family's finances, the Barretts moved, finally settling in London in 1835. Elizabeth Barrett was already living in the periodic seclusion of a semi-invalid. Her illnesses are sometimes described as beginning with a spinal injury when she was fifteen years old, sometimes more vaguely attributed to nervous disorders. It is certain that their effects were compounded by injudicious but then customary prescriptions of opiates, by depression and self-recrimination which followed the drowning of her favorite brother in 1835, and by the rigorous protectiveness of her father, who refused his permission to her marriage, never acknowledged it or saw his daughter after she married, and never opened the letters she wrote to him.

But especially after she moved to London, she continued a vigorous intellectual and literary life. She contributed poems and reviews to magazines and annuals, met some writers and literary critics in her room in her father's house, and corresponded with other writers and painters. In 1838 she published *The Seraphim and Other Poems,* the first volume to appear bearing her name. The favorable reviews of these poems started the growth of a steadily increasing reputation as a poet of fervent religious and moral statement and forceful, if occasionally strained, poetic conceptions and language. By 1844, when she published a collection of old and new *Poems* in two volumes, she was probably the best-known and most-read poet of earnest pretensions in England.

It was his high opinion of the 1844 volume that prompted Robert Browning to write to Elizabeth Barrett early in 1845, saying even before he met her that he loved her as well as her poems. He was brought to her room to meet her four months later, and they began a series of visits and an almost daily correspondence which culminated in the adventure of their marriage and elopement to Italy in 1846. Elizabeth Barrett Browning spent the rest of her life in Italy, mostly in Florence, where the Brownings' son and only child was born in 1849. Mrs. Browning became a fierce partisan of Italian independence from the political domination of Austria and France, and she wrote of her conviction in *Casa Guidi Windows* (1851) and in the political poems of the last volume of verse she published before her death, *Poems Before Congress* (1860). She maintained her popularity in England, especially through the successively enlarged editions of her 1844 *Poems* which she published in 1850 (this collection included the love poems she wrote for her husband, *Sonnets from the Portuguese*), 1853, and 1856. In 1857 she published *Aurora Leigh,* a long novel in verse which was immediately and persistently popular. In 1850, when Wordsworth died, Elizabeth Barrett Browning was suggested as his successor as poet laureate, and at the time of her death in 1861 her reputation, now overshadowed by that of Tennyson, was still greater than that of her husband.

Elizabeth Barrett's contemporary readers usually admired poems like *Aurora Leigh,* "The Seraphim," "A Drama of Exile," "The Romaunt of Margaret," "Lady Geraldine's Courtship"—long poems, often weighted with the machinery of romance, allegory, and appropriated myth, in which large themes were brought to reassuringly conventional resolutions in forms associated with highly literary discourse. It is not possible in this selection to display the ambitions and effects of such poems. But something of their quality is represented in "The Dead Pan," one of her most admired poems, and in her habit in other poems of turning from descriptions of objects and episodes into elucidations of their parabolic meanings. It is easier to represent another characteristic that pleased nineteenth-century readers —a still attractive energy of restlessness and engagement with a range of concerns, from topical political and social issues to questions of religious belief. All through her life, from her early poems on Greece and Byron to her late poems on Italian politics, she took topical matter into her poems. She was also always ready to try various forms and dictions, from the conceits and allegories of poems like "My Doves" through the measured turns of her sonnets to the sentimental conventions and excited polemics of "The Cry of the Children." In one way, her restlessness was a substitute for a poetic voice of her own. Like other poets whose popularity has not survived their moment, she sometimes seems to have been herself moved and carried by then current literary devices and tastes rather than moving into them and making them her own. But if her popularity has not survived, some of her poetry has and should. It is, even the best of it, sometimes gaudy and overstated. But these qualities are the faults of a reach and commitment that to her contemporaries were the signs of a serious poet doing a serious task. The signs still mean what they once did, and while they help to explain the exceptional esteem and attention her poetry won in her own time, the purpose and will she invested in her poetry also still give some of it a striking color and pressure.

EDITIONS

The texts of the poems reprinted below, except where otherwise noted, are those of the fourth edition of the poems of Elizabeth Barrett Browning, published in 1856. This edition was the last prepared by her for the press. The principal collections of her letters are *The Letters of Robert Browning and Elizabeth Barrett,* edited by Elvan Kintner (1969), and *The Letters of Elizabeth Barrett Browning,* edited by F. G. Kenyon (1897). Michael Timko's essay in *The Victorian Poets* (second edition, 1968) lists and describes other published collections of letters. Willard Bissell Pope has recently edited *Invisible Friends: The Correspondence of Elizabeth Barrett Browning and Benjamin Robert Haydon, 1842–1845* (1972). Philip Kelley and Ronald Hudson have edited a previously unpublished diary written by Elizabeth Barrett in 1831–32 (1969).

BIOGRAPHY AND CRITICISM

The definitive biography is Gardner Taplin's *The Life of Elizabeth Barrett Browning* (1957). Alethea Hayter's *Mrs. Browning: A Poet's Work and Its Setting* (1962) is a study of her life and work; Hayter's *A Sultry Month: Scenes of London Life in 1846* (1965) also describes Elizabeth Barrett's place and activities in London intellectual and artistic circles in an account that centers on events leading to the suicide of the painter Benjamin Haydon. Hayter's *Elizabeth Barrett Browning* in the Writers and Their Work series (1965) contains a short bibliography of commentary on her writing; see also Ehrsam, Deily, and Smith (General Bibliography); L. N. Broughton, C. S. Northup, and R. B. Pearsall, *Robert Browning: A Bibliography* (1953); and William S. Peterson, *Robert and Elizabeth Barrett Browning: An Annotated Bibliography, 1951–1970* (1974). Warner Barnes' *A Bibliography of Elizabeth Barrett Browning* (1967) lists, among other matters, her contributions to periodicals and annuals.

My Doves

O Weisheit! Du red'st wie eine Taube!

—GOETHE[1]

My little doves have left a nest
  Upon an Indian tree,
Whose leaves fantastic take their rest
  Or motion from the sea;
For ever there, the sea-winds go
With sunlit paces to and fro.

The tropic flowers looked up to it,
  The tropic stars looked down,
And there my little doves did sit,
  With feathers softly brown,
And glittering eyes that showed their right
To general Nature's deep delight.

And God them taught, at every close
  Of murmuring waves beyond
And green leaves round, to interpose
  Their choral voices fond,
Interpreting that love must be
The meaning of the earth and sea.

Fit ministers! Of living loves,
  Theirs hath the calmest fashion,
Their living voice the likest moves
  To lifeless intonation,
The lovely monotone of springs
And winds and such insensate things.

My little doves were ta'en away
  From that glad nest of theirs,
Across an ocean rolling grey,
  And tempest-clouded airs.
My little doves, who lately knew
The sky and wave by warmth and blue!

And now, within the city prison,
  In mist and chillness pent,
With sudden upward look they listen
  For sounds of past content—
For lapse of water, swell of breeze,
Or nut-fruit falling from the trees.

The stir without the glow of passion,
  The triumph of the mart,
The gold and silver as they clash on
  Man's cold metallic heart—   40
The roar of wheels, the cry for bread,—
These only sounds are heard instead.

Yet still, as on my human hand
  Their fearless heads they lean,
And almost seem to understand
  What human musings mean,
(Their eyes, with such a plaintive shine
Are fastened upwardly to mine!)

Soft falls their chant as on the nest
  Beneath the sunny zone;   50
For love that stirred it in their breast
  Has not aweary grown,
And 'neath the city's shade can keep
The well of music clear and deep.

And love that keeps the music, fills
  With pastoral memories,
All echoings from out the hills,
  All droppings from the skies,
All flowings from the wave and wind,
Remembered in their chant, I find.   60

So teach ye me the wisest part,
  My little doves! to move
Along the city-ways with heart
  Assured by holy love,
And vocal with such songs as own
A fountain to the world unknown.

'Twas hard to sing by Babel's[2] stream—
  More hard, in Babel's street!
But if the soulless creatures deem
  Their music not unmeet   70
For sunless walls—let *us* begin,
Who wear immortal wings within!

To me, fair memories belong
  Of scenes that used to bless,
For no regret, but present song
  And lasting thankfulness,
And very soon to break away,
Like types, in purer things than they.

I will have hopes that cannot fade,
  For flowers the valley yields!   80

[1] "O Wisdom, you speak as a dove." From Goethe's lyric fable, "The Eagle and the Dove" (*Adler und Taube*), written about 1774, in which a dove consoles a stricken eagle by speaking of humble pleasures and achievements.

[2] Babel: probably a play on Babylon, the city of Babylonia to which the Jews of the Old Testament were exiled; and Babel, the city whose inhabitants found themselves speaking different languages when they tried to build a tower that would reach to heaven.

I will have humble thoughts instead
  Of silent, dewy fields!
My spirit and my God shall be
My seaward hill, my boundless sea.

1838

The Sea-Mew

Affectionately Inscribed to M. E. H.[1]

I

How joyously the young sea-mew
Lay dreaming on the waters blue,
Whereon our little bark had thrown
A little shade, the only one,—
But shadows ever man pursue.

II

Familiar with the waves and free
As if their own white foam were he,
His heart upon the heart of ocean
Lay learning all its mystic motion,
And throbbing to the throbbing sea.

III

And such a brightness in his eye,
As if the ocean and the sky
Within him had lit up and nurst
A soul God gave him not at first,
To comprehend their majesty.

IV

We were not cruel, yet did sunder
His white wing from the blue waves under,
And bound it, while his fearless eyes
Shone up to ours in calm surprise,
As deeming us some ocean wonder!

V

We bore our ocean bird unto
A grassy place, where he might view
The flowers that curtsey to the bees,
The waving of the tall green trees,
The falling of the silver dew.

VI

But flowers of earth were pale to him
Who had seen the rainbow fishes swim;

And when earth's dew around him lay
He thought of ocean's wingèd spray,
And his eye waxèd sad and dim.

VII

The green trees round him only made
A prison with their darksome shade;
And dropped his wing, and mournèd he
For his own boundless glittering sea—
Albeit he knew not they could fade.

VIII

Then One her gladsome face did bring,
Her gentle voice's murmuring,
In ocean's stead his heart to move
And teach him what was human love—
He thought it a strange, mournful thing.

IX

He lay down in his grief to die,
  (First looking to the sea-like sky
That hath no waves!) because, alas!
Our human touch did on him pass,
And with our touch, our agony.

1838

The Soul's Expression

With stammering lips and insufficient sound
I strive and struggle to deliver right
That music of my nature, day and night
With dream and thought and feeling inter-
  wound,

And inly answering all the senses round
With octaves of a mystic depth and height
Which step out grandly to the infinite
From the dark edges of the sensual ground!
This song of soul I struggle to outbear
Through portals of the sense, sublime and
  whole,
And utter all myself into the air.
But if I did it,—as the thunder-roll
Breaks its own cloud, my flesh would perish
  there,
Before that dread apocalypse of soul.

1843

[1] M. E. H.: Mary Hunter, the daughter of George Barrett Hunter, a clergyman and close
friend of Elizabeth Barrett in the 1830s when the Barretts were living at Sidmouth, on the south-
western coast of England. A sea mew is a gull.

The Cry of the Children

'Φεῦ, φεῦ, τί προσδέρκεσθέ μ' ὄμμασιν, τέκνα;¹

—MEDEA

I

Do ye hear the children weeping, O my
    brothers,
    Ere the sorrow comes with years?
They are leaning their young heads against
    their mothers,
    And *that* cannot stop their tears.
The young lambs are bleating in the meadows,
    The young birds are chirping in the nest,
The young fawns are playing with the shadows,
    The young flowers are blowing toward the
        west—
But the young, young children, O my brothers,
    They are weeping bitterly!
They are weeping in the playtime of the others,
    In the country of the free.

II

Do you question the young children in the
    sorrow
    Why their tears are falling so?
The old man may weep for his to-morrow
    Which is lost in Long Ago.
The old tree is leafless in the forest,
    The old year is ending in the frost,
The old wound, if stricken, is the sorest,
    The old hope is hardest to be lost:
But the young, young children, O my brothers,
    Do you ask them why they stand
Weeping sore before the bosoms of their
    mothers,
    In our happy Fatherland?

III

They look up with their pale and sunken
    faces,
    And their looks are sad to see,
For the man's hoary anguish draws and presses
    Down the cheeks of infancy;
"Your old earth," they say, "is very dreary,
    Our young feet," they say, "are very weak!
Few paces have we taken, yet are weary—
    Our grave-rest is very far to seek.
Ask the aged why they weep, and not the
    children;
    For the outside earth is cold;

And we young ones stand without, in our
    bewildering,
    And the graves are for the old."

IV

"True," say the children, "it may happen
    That we die before our time.
Little Alice died last year—her grave is shapen
    Like a snowball, in the rime.
We looked into the pit prepared to take her.
    Was no room for any work in the close clay!
From the sleep wherein she lieth none will
    wake her,
    Crying, 'Get up, little Alice! it is day.'
If you listen by that grave, in sun and shower,
    With your ear down, little Alice never cries.
Could we see her face, be sure we should not
    know her,
    For the smile has time for growing in her
        eyes.
And merry go her moments, lulled and stilled
    in
    The shroud by the kirk-chime!
It is good when it happens," say the children,
    "That we die before our time."

V

Alas, alas, the children! they are seeking
    Death in life, as best to have.
They are binding up their hearts away from
    breaking,
    With a cerement from the grave.
Go out, children, from the mine and from the
    city,
    Sing out, children, as the little thrushes do.
Pluck your handfuls of the meadow-cowslips
    pretty.
    Laugh aloud, to feel your fingers let them
        through!
But they answer, "Are your cowslips of the
    meadows
    Like our weeds anear the mine?
Leave us quiet in the dark of the coal-shadows,
    From your pleasures fair and fine!

VI

"For oh," say the children, "we are weary,
    And we cannot run or leap.
If we cared for any meadows, it were merely
    To drop down in them and sleep.
Our knees tremble sorely in the stooping,
    We fall upon our faces, trying to go;

---

¹ "Alas, my children, why do you look at me": from the *Medea* of Euripedes (c. 480–406 B.C.).
Spoken by Medea before she slaughtered her children in vengeance.

And, underneath our heavy eyelids drooping,
   The reddest flower would look as pale as
      snow.
For, all day, we drag our burden tiring
   Through the coal-dark, underground—
Or, all day, we drive the wheels of iron
   In the factories, round and round.

VII

"For all day the wheels are droning, turning,—
   Their wind comes in our faces,—
Till our hearts turn,—our heads with pulses
      burning,
80   And the walls turn in their places.
Turns the sky in the high window blank and
      reeling,
   Turns the long light that drops adown the
      wall,
Turn the black flies that crawl along the
      ceiling,
   All are turning, all the day, and we with all.
And all day the iron wheels are droning,
   And sometimes we could pray,
"O ye wheels" (breaking out in a mad
      moaning)
   'Stop! be silent for to-day!' "

VIII

Ay! be silent! Let them hear each other breath-
      ing
90   For a moment, mouth to mouth!
Let them touch each other's hands, in a fresh
      wreathing
   Of their tender human youth!
Let them feel that this cold metallic motion
   Is not all the life God fashions or reveals.
Let them prove their living souls against the
      notion
   That they live in you, or under you, O
      wheels!—
Still, all day, the iron wheels go onward,
   Grinding life down from its mark;
And the children's souls, which God is calling
      sunward,
100   Spin on blindly in the dark.

IX

Now tell the poor young children, O my
      brothers,
   To look up to Him and pray;
So the blessèd One who blesseth all the others,
   Will bless them another day.
They answer, "Who is God that He should
      hear us,
   While the rushing of the iron wheels is
      stirred?
When we sob aloud, the human creatures near
      us
   Pass by, hearing not, or answer not a word.
And *we* hear not (for the wheels in their re-
      sounding)
   Strangers speaking at the door.   110
Is it likely God, with angels singing round Him,
   Hears our weeping any more?

X

"Two words, indeed, of praying we remember,
   And at midnight's hour of harm,
'Our Father,' looking upward in the chamber,
   We say softly for a charm.[2]
We know no other words except 'Our Father,' "
   And we think that, in some pause of angels'
      song,
God may pluck them with the silence sweet to
      gather,
   And hold both within His right hand which   120
      is strong.
" 'Our Father!' If He heard us, He would
      surely
   (For they call Him good and mild)
Answer, smiling down the steep world very
      purely,
   'Come and rest with me, my child.' "

XI

"But, no!" say the children, weeping faster,
   "He is speechless as a stone.
And they tell us, of His image is the master
   Who commands us to work on.
Go to!" say children,—"up in Heaven,

---

[2] Elizabeth Barrett Browning's note: "A fact rendered pathetically historical by Mr. Horne's report of his commission. The name of the poet of 'Orion' and 'Cosmo de'Medici' has, however, a change of associations, and comes in time to remind me that we have some noble poetic heat of literature still,—however open to the reproach of being somewhat gelid in our humanity." Richard Hengist Horne (1803–84) was a member of the Parliamentary commission which investigated the conditions of the employment of children in factories in 1842 and 1843. Many of the details of Browning's poem are taken from the report of the commission, and her excited indignation reflects the strong public response the report elicited. Horne's *Orion* (1843), a verse epic, and *Cosmo de'Medici* (1837), a tragedy in verse, were his most popular poems. Elizabeth Barrett was closely associated with him in the preparation of *The New Spirit of the Age* (1844), a collection of essays (some of them by her) on the literature of the 1830s and 1840s.

Dark, wheel-like, turning clouds are all we
130   find.
Do not mock us; grief has made us unbeliev-
     ing—
     We look up for God, but tears have made us
     blind."
Do you hear the children weeping and
     disproving,
     O my brothers, what ye preach?
For God's possible is taught by His world's
     loving,
     And the children doubt of each.

XII

And well may the children weep before you!
     They are weary ere they run.
They have never seen the sunshine, nor the
     glory
140   Which is brighter than the sun.
They know the grief of man, without his
     wisdom.
     They sink in man's despair, without his calm;
Are slaves, without the liberty in Christdom,
     Are martyrs, by the pang without the palm,—
Are worn, as if with age, yet unretrievingly
     The harvest of its memories cannot reap,—
Are orphans of the earthly love and heavenly.
     Let them weep! let them weep!

XIII

They look up with their pale and sunken faces,
150   And their look is dread to see,
For they mind you of their angels in high
     places,
     With eyes turned on Deity!—
"How long," they say, "how long, O cruel
     nation,
     Will you stand, to move the world, on a
     child's heart,—
Stifle down with a mailed heel its palpitation,
     And tread onward to your throne amid the
     mart?
Our blood splashes upward, O gold-heaper,
     And your purple shows your path!
But the child's sob in the silence curses deeper
160   Than the strong man in his wrath."
                        1843

*"The Gods of Greece," by Frederich von Schiller
(1759–1805), is a lament for the departed world of
Greek mythology, bright and quick with the life of
the gods incorporate in material things. The poem
had been paraphrased in English by John Kenyon,
a friend of both Elizabeth Barrett and Robert
Browning, in an annual published in 1843.*

The Dead Pan

Excited by Schiller's "Gotter Griechenlands," and
partly founded on a well-known tradition men-
tioned in a treatise of Plutarch ("De Oraculorum
Defectu"), according to which, at the hour of the
Saviour's agony, a cry of "Great Pan is dead!" swept
across the waves in the hearing of certain mariners,
—and the oracles ceased.
    It is in all veneration to the memory of the death-
less Schiller, that I oppose a doctrine still more dis-
honouring to poetry than to Christianity.
    As Mr. Kenyon's graceful and harmonious para-
phrase of the German poem was the first occasion of
the turning of my thoughts in this direction, I take
advantage of the pretence to indulge my feelings
(which overflow on other grounds) by inscribing my
lyric to that dear friend and relative, with the ear-
nestness of appreciating esteem as well as of affec-
tionate gratitude. [Elizabeth Barrett's note]

I

Gods of Hellas, gods of Hellas,
Can ye listen in your silence?
Can your mystic voices tell us
Where ye hide? In floating islands,
With a wind that evermore
Keeps you out of sight of shore?
             Pan, Pan is dead.

II

In what revels are ye sunken,
In old Æthiopia?
Have the Pygmies made you drunken,   10
Bathing in mandragora[1]
Your divine pale lips, that shiver
Like the lotus in the river?
             Pan, Pan is dead.

III

Do ye sit there still in slumber,
In gigantic Alpine rows?
The black poppies out of number
Nodding, dripping from your brows
To the red lees of your wine,
And so kept alive and fine?   20
             Pan, Pan is dead.

[1] Mandragora: the herb also known as mandrake, whose root was used as a narcotic and to
promote conception.

IV

Or lie crushed your stagnant corses[2]
Where the silver spheres roll on,
Stung to life by centric forces
Thrown like rays out from the sun?—
While the smoke of your old altars
Is the shroud that round you welters?
                    Great Pan is dead.

V

"Gods of Hellas, gods of Hellas,"
30   Said the old Hellenic tongue!
Said the hero-oaths, as well as
Poets' songs the sweetest sung!
Have ye grown deaf in a day?
Can ye speak not yea or nay—
                    Since Pan is dead?

VI

Do ye leave your rivers flowing
All alone, O Naiades,[3]
While your drenchèd locks dry slow in
This cold feeble sun and breeze?—
40   Not a word the Naiads say,
Though the rivers sun for aye.
                    For Pan is dead.

VII

From the gloaming of the oak-wood,
O ye Dryads, could ye flee?
At the rushing thunderstroke, would
No sob tremble through the tree?—
Not a word the Dryads say,
Though the forests wave for aye.
                    For Pan is dead.

VIII

50   Have ye left the mountain places,
Oreads wild, for other tryst?
Shall we see no sudden faces

Strike a glory through the mist?
Not a sound the silence thrills
Of the everlasting hills.
                    Pan, Pan is dead.

IX

O twelve gods of Plato's vision,
Crowned to starry wanderings,—[4]
With your chariots in procession,
And your silver clash of wings!   60
Very pale ye seem to rise,
Ghosts of Grecian deities,—
                    Now Pan is dead!

X

Jove,[5] that right hand is unloaded,
Whence the thunder did prevail,
While in idiocy of godhead
Thou art staring the stars pale!
And thine eagle, blind and old,
Roughs his feathers in the cold.   70
                    Pan, Pan is dead.

XI

Where, O Juno, is the glory
Of thy regal look and tread?
Will they lay, for evermore, thee,
On thy dim, straight, golden bed?
Will thy queendom all lie hid
Meekly under either lid?
                    Pan, Pan is dead.

XII

Ha, Apollo! floats his golden
Hair all mist-like where he stands,   80
While the Muses hang enfolding
Knee and foot with faint wild hands?
'Neath the clanging of thy bow,
Niobe[6] looked lost as thou!
                    Pan, Pan is dead.

---

[2] Corses: corpses.

[3] Naiades: nymphs of rivers and streams, as Dryads are the nymphs or spirits of trees, and Oreads the nymphs of hills and mountains.

[4] In the dialogues *Timaeus* and *Laws* Plato describes myths in which the gods become the spirits of the stars, imparting to them their motion.

[5] Jove: Jupiter, or Zeus, the chief of the gods in classical mythology. In the following stanzas the Roman names of the gods are used more often than their Greek names: Juno (Hera), Jove's consort; Apollo, the god of music; Pallas Athene, the goddess of wisdom; Bacchus (Dionysus), the god of revels and wine; Neptune (Poseidon), the god of the sea; Pluto (Hades), the god of the underworld; Ceres (Demeter), the goddess of vegetation and growing things; Aphrodite, the goddess of beauty; Hermes, the messenger of the gods known for his trickery; Cybele (Rhea, or Ops), the wife of Saturn, chief of the gods before Zeus (Cybele's crown depicts turrets and battlements); Vesta (Hestia), the goddess of the hearth.

[6] Niobe: a queen of Thebes whose children were killed by Apollo in punishment for her boast that her family ought to be worshipped as gods.

XIII

Shall the casque with its brown iron,
Pallas' broad blue eyes, eclipse,
And no hero take inspiring
From the god-Greek of her lips?
'Neath her olive dost thou sit,
Mars the mighty cursing it?
    Pan, Pan is dead.

XIV

Bacchus, Bacchus! on the panther
He swoons,—bound with his own vines.
And his Mænads[7] slowly saunter,
Head aside, among the pines,
While they murmur dreamingly,
"Evohe—ah—evohe—!"
    Ah, Pan is dead!

XV

Neptune lies beside the trident,
Dull and senseless as a stone;
And old Pluto deaf and silent
Is cast out into the sun.
Ceres smileth stern thereat,
"We *all* now are desolate—
    Now Pan is dead."

XVI

Aphrodite! dead and driven
As thy native foam, thou art;
With the cestus[8] long done heaving
On the white calm of thine heart!
Ai Adonis! at that shriek,
Not a tear runs down her cheek—
    Pan, Pan is dead.

XVII

And the Loves, we used to know from
One another, huddled lie,
Frore[9] as taken in a snow-storm,
Close beside her tenderly,—
As if each had weakly tried
Once to kiss her as he died.
    Pan, Pan is dead.

XVIII

What, and Hermes? Time enthralleth
All thy cunning, Hermes, thus,—

And the ivy blindly crawleth
Round thy brave caduceus?[10]
Hast thou no new message for us,
Full of thunder and Jove-glories?
    Nay, Pan is dead.

XIX

Crownèd Cybele's great turret
Rocks and crumbles on her head.
Roar the lions of her chariot
Toward the wilderness, unfed.   130
Scornful children are not mute,—
"Mother, mother, walk a-foot—
    Since Pan is dead."

XX

In the fiery-hearted centre
Of the solemn universe,
Ancient Vesta,—who could enter
To consume thee with this curse?
Drop thy grey chin on thy knee,
O thou palsied Mystery!
    For Pan is dead.   140

XXI

Gods, we vainly do adjure you,—
Ye return nor voice nor sign!
Not a votary could secure you
Even a grave for your Divine!
Not a grave, to show thereby,
Here these grey old gods do lie.
    Pan, Pan is dead.

XXII

Even that Greece who took your wages,
Calls the obolus[11] outworn.
And the hoarse deep-throated ages   150
Laugh your godships unto scorn.
And the poets do disclaim you,
Or grow colder if they name you—
    And Pan is dead.

XXIII

Gods bereavèd, gods belated,
With your purples rent asunder!
Gods discrowned and desecrated,
Disinherited of thunder!

[7] Maenads: women who participate in the orgiastic rites of Bacchus. "Evohe" is the cry of these rites.
[8] Cestus: a belt possessed by Aphrodite which had the power of inspiring love. Adonis was a mortal with whom Aphrodite (Venus) was in love; he was killed while hunting.
[9] Frore: an obsolete form of frozen.
[10] Caduceus: the emblem of Hermes—two snakes entwined on a staff.
[11] Obolus: an ancient Greek coin.

Now, the goats may climb and crop
160   The soft grass on Ida's[12] top—
                              Now, Pan is dead.

          XXIV

Calm, of old, the bark went onward,
When a cry more loud than wind,
Rose up, deepened, and swept sunward,
From the pilèd Dark behind;
And the sun shrank and grew pale,
Breathed against by the great wail—
                              "Pan, Pan is dead."

          XXV

And the rowers from the benches
170   Fell,—each shuddering on his face—
While departing Influences[13]
Struck a cold back through the place;
And the shadow of the ship
Reeled along the passive deep—
                              "Pan, Pan is dead."

          XXVI

And that dismal cry rose slowly
And sank slowly through the air,
Full of spirit's melancholy
And eternity's despair!
180   And they heard the words it said—
PAN IS DEAD—GREAT PAN IS DEAD—
                              PAN, PAN IS DEAD.

          XXVII

'Twas the hour when One in Sion
Hung for love's sake on a cross;
When His brow was chill with dying,
And His soul was faint with loss;
When his priestly blood dropped downward,
And His kingly eyes looked throneward—
                              Then, Pan was dead.

          XXVIII

190   By the love He stood alone in,
His sole Godhead rose complete,
And the false gods fell down moaning,
Each from off his golden seat;
All the false gods with a cry
Rendered up their deity—
                              Pan, Pan was dead.

          XXIX

Wailing wide across the islands,
They rent, vest-like, their Divine!
And a darkness and a silence
Quenched the light of every shrine;   200
And Dodona's[14] oak swang lonely
Henceforth, to the tempest only,
                              Pan, Pan was dead.

          XXX

Pythia[15] staggered,—feeling o'er her,
Her lost god's forsaking look.
Straight her eyeballs filmed with horror,
And her crispy fillets shook,
And her lips gasped through their foam,
For a word that did not come.
                              Pan, Pan was dead.   210

          XXXI

O ye vain false gods of Hellas,
Ye are silent evermore!
And I dash down this old chalice,
Whence libations ran of yore.
See, the wine crawls in the dust
Wormlike—as your glories must,
                              Since Pan is dead.

          XXXII

Get to dust, as common mortals,
By a common doom and track!
Let no Schiller from the portals   220
Of that Hades, call you back,
Or instruct us to weep all
At your antique funeral.
                              Pan, Pan is dead.

          XXXIII

By your beauty, which confesses
Some chief Beauty conquering you,—
By our grand heroic guesses,
Through your falsehood, at the True,—
We will weep *not* . . . ! earth shall roll
Heir to each god's aureole—   230
                              And Pan is dead.

          XXXIV

Earth outgrows the mythic fancies
Sung beside her in her youth;

---

[12] Ida: a hill near ancient Troy; it was the site of several episodes in classical mythology, such as the choice by Paris of Aphrodite as the most fair of the gods, the consequence of which was the outbreak of the Trojan war.
   [13] Influences: used in the sense of spirits that stream into mortal life.
   [14] Dodona: site of an oracle of Zeus.   [15] Pythia: priestess of the oracle of Apollo at Delphi.

And those debonaire[16] romances
Sound but dull beside the truth.
Phœbus'[17] chariot-course is run.
Look up, poets, to the sun!
           Pan, Pan is dead.

XXXV

Christ hath sent us down the angels;
240 And the whole earth and the skies
Are illumed by altar-candles
Lit for blessèd mysteries;
And a Priest's hand, through creation,
Waveth calm and consecration—
           And Pan is dead.

XXXVI

Truth is fair: should we forego it?
Can we sigh right for a wrong?
God himself is the best Poet,
And the Real is his song.
250 Sing his truth out fair and full,
And secure his beautiful.
           Let Pan be dead.

XXXVII

Truth is large. Our aspiration
Scarce embraces half we be.
Shame, to stand in His creation,
And doubt truth's sufficiency!—
To think God's song unexcelling
The poor tales of our own telling—
           When Pan is dead.

XXXVIII

260 What is true and just and honest,
What is lovely, what is pure—
All of praise that hath admonisht,
All of virtue, shall endure,—
These are themes for poets' uses,
Stirring nobler than the Muses,
           Ere Pan was dead.

XXXIX

O brave poets, keep back nothing,
Nor mix falsehood with the whole.
Look up Godward; speak the truth in
270 Worthy song from earnest soul!
Hold, in high poetic duty,
Truest Truth the fairest Beauty.
           Pan, Pan is dead.
                1844

Grief

I tell you, hopeless grief is passionless;
That only men incredulous of despair,
Half-taught in anguish, through the mid-night
    air
Beat upward to God's throne in loud access
Of shrieking and reproach. Full desertness,
In souls as countries, lieth silent-bare
Under the blanching, vertical eye-glare
Of the absolute Heavens. Deep-hearted man,
    express
Grief for thy Dead in silence like to death:—
Most like a monumental statue set   10
In everlasting watch and moveless woe,
Till itself crumble to the dust beneath.
Touch it: the marble eyelids are not wet.
If it could weep, it could arise and go.
                1844

The Poet

The poet hath the child's sight in his breast,
And sees all *new*. What oftenest he has viewed,
He views with the first glory. Fair and good
Pall never on him, at the fairest best,
But stand before him holy and undressed
In week-day false conventions, such as would
Drag other men down from the altitude
Of primal types, too early dispossessed.
Why, God would tire of all his heavens, as soon
As thou, O godlike, childlike poet, didst,   10
Of daily and nightly sights of sun and moon!
And therefore hath He set thee in the midst,
Where men may hear thy wonder's ceaseless
    tune,
And praise his world for ever, as thou bidst.
                1847

Hiram Powers' *Greek Slave*[1]

They say Ideal beauty cannot enter
The house of anguish. On the threshold stands
An alien Image with enshackled hands,
Called the Greek Slave! as if the artist meant
    her
(That passionless perfection which he lent her,

---

[16] Debonaire: not a common word in the nineteenth century; used here, somewhat scornfully,
in its old sense of refined, gentle manner.
   [17] Phœbus: a name of Apollo when he is associated with the sun.
   [1] Hiram Powers (1805–73) was an American sculptor who lived much of his mature profes-
sional life in Florence, where the Brownings knew him. His extremely popular statue *Greek
Slave* was completed in 1843.

Shadowed not darkened where the sill
    expands)
To, so, confront man's crimes in different lands
With man's ideal sense. Pierce to the centre,
Art's fiery finger, and break up ere long
10 The serfdom of this world! Appeal, fair stone,
From God's pure heights of beauty against
    man's wrong!
Catch up in thy divine face, not alone
East griefs but west,—and strike and shame the
    strong,
By thunders of white silence, overthrown.

                                                  1850

*Hugh Stuart Boyd (1781–1848) published several
translations of the writings of the Greek fathers
of the Church, including Gregory of Nazianus, a
translation of Aeschylus' Agamemnon, and some
religious tracts. He moved near the Barretts when
they were living at Hope End in 1826, and Eliza-
beth Barrett began reading to him (he had been
blind since the age of thirty) in Greek, and learn-
ing from him much of her considerable knowledge
of Greek language and literature. By the 1840s,
when both she and Boyd were living in London,
their relationship was no longer close, partly be-
cause Boyd had little knowledge of contemporary
letters.*

Hugh Stuart Boyd

His Blindness

God would not let the spheric Lights accost
This God-loved man, and bade the earth stand
    off
With all her beckoning hills, whose golden stuff
Under the feet of the royal sun is crossed.
Yet such things were to him not wholly lost,—
Permitted, with his wandering eyes light-proof,
To catch fair visions, rendered full enough
By many a ministrant accomplished ghost,—
Still seeing, to sounds of softly-turned book-
    leaves,
10 Sappho's[1] crown-rose, and Meleager's[2] spring,
And Gregory's starlight on Greek-burnished
    eves![3]
Till Sensuous and Unsensuous seemed one
    thing,
Viewed from one level,—earth's reapers at the
    sheaves

Scarce plainer than Heaven's angels on the
    wing!

                                                  1850

from Sonnets from the Portuguese

*Elizabeth Barrett composed the first draft of the
forty-four* Sonnets from the Portuguese *in the
months before her marriage in 1846. She showed
them to Browning first in 1849, and published them
in an edition of her poems in 1850. She chose the
title of the sequence, which suggests a translation or
adaptation, in part to veil the intensely personal
circumstances of which she writes in the sonnets.
The title itself also carried a private meaning; after
reading "Catarina to Camoens," one of Elizabeth
Barrett's early poems about the woman with whom
the sixteenth-century Portuguese poet Camoens was
supposed to be in love, Browning associated the
woman who was to become his wife with Catarina,
or, "the Portuguese."*

VII

The face of all the world is changed, I think,
Since first I heard the footsteps of thy soul
Move still, oh still, beside me, as they stole
Betwixt me and the dreadful outer brink
Of obvious death, where I, who thought to sink,
Was caught up into love, and taught the whole
Of life in a new rhythm. The cup of dole
God gave for baptism, I am fain to drink,
And praise its sweetness, Sweet, with thee anear.
The names of country, heaven, are changed
    away   10
For where thou art or shalt be, there or here;
And this . . . this lute and song . . . loved
    yesterday,
(The singing angels know) are only dear,
Because thy name moves right in what they say.

X

Yet, love, mere love, is beautiful indeed
And worthy of acceptation. Fire is bright,
Let temple burn, or flax; an equal light
Leaps in the flame from cedar-plank or weed;
And love is fire; and when I say at need

---

[1] Sappho was a Greek lyric poet of the seventh century before Christ.
[2] Meleager was a Greek epigrammist of the first century before Christ.
[3] St. Gregory of Nazianus was a fourth-century bishop and theologian who wrote in Greek.

I love thee . . . mark! . . . I love thee;—in
10   thy sight
I stand transfigured, glorified aright,
With conscience of the new rays that proceed
Out of my face toward thine. There's nothing
    low
In love, when love the lowest: meanest
    creatures
Who love God, God accepts while loving so.
And what I *feel,* across the inferior features
Of what I *am,* doth flash itself, and show
How that great work of Love enhances
    Nature's.

XVII

My poet, thou canst touch on all the notes
God set between His After and Before,
And strike up and strike off the general roar
Of the rushing worlds a melody that floats
In a serene air purely. Antidotes
Of medicated music, answering for
Mankind's forlornest uses, thou canst pour
From thence into their ears. God's will devotes
Thine to such ends, and mine to wait on thine.
10 How, Dearest, wilt thou have me for most use?
A hope, to sing by gladly?—or a fine
Sad memory, with thy songs to interfuse?
A shade, in which to sing . . . of palm or
    pine?
A grave, on which to rest from singing? . . .
    Choose.

XXII

When our two souls stand up erect and strong,
Face to face, silent, drawing nigh and nigher,
Until the lengthening wings break into fire
At either curvèd point,—what bitter wrong
Can the earth do to us, that we should not
    long
Be here contented? Think. In mounting higher,
The angels would press on us and aspire
To drop some golden orb of perfect song
Into our deep, dear silence. Let us stay
10 Rather on earth, Belovèd,—where the unfit
Contrarious moods of men recoil away
And isolate pure spirits, and permit
A place to stand and love in for a day,
With darkness and the death-hour rounding it.

XXIV

Let the world's sharpness like a clasping knife
Shut in upon itself and do no harm
In this close hand of Love, now soft and warm,
And let us hear no sound of human strife
After the click of the shutting. Life to life—
I lean upon thee, Dear, without alarm,
And feel as safe as guarded by a charm
Against the stab of worldlings, who if rife
Are weak to injure. Very whitely still
The lilies of our lives may reassure   10
Their blossoms from their roots, accessible
Alone to heavenly dews that drop not fewer;
Growing straight, out of man's reach, on the
    hill.
God only, who made us rich, can make us poor.
    1850

Summing Up in Italy

(Inscribed to Intelligent Publics Out of It)

I

Observe how it will be at last,
    When our Italy stands at full stature,
A year ago tied down so fast[1]
    That the cord cut the quick of her nature!
You'll honor the deed and its scope,
    Then, in logical sequence upon it,
Will use up the remnants of rope
    By hanging the men who have done it.

II

The speech in the Commons, which hits you
    A sketch off, how dungeons must feel,—   10
The official despatch, which commits you
    From stamping out groans with your heel,—
Suggestions in journal or book for
    Good efforts,—are praised as is meet:
But what in this world can men look for,
    Who only achieve and complete?

III

True, you've praise for the fireman who sets his
    Brave face to the axe of the flame,
Disappears in the smoke, and then fetches
    A babe down, or idiot that's lame,—   20

[1] With the temporary assistance of France, in 1859 some of the states into which Italy was then divided joined to declare war on Austria, which effectively controlled large parts of Italy. The armistice negotiated in the same year left the actual unification of Italy some distance away, and did not even finally settle the question of the power foreign governments exercised in Italy. But the fact that several states had taken concerted action gave properly founded hope to such partisans of Italian unity and independence as Elizabeth Barrett Browning.

For the boor even, who rescues through pity
　　A sheep from the brute who would kick it:
But saviours of nations!—'t is pretty,
　　And doubtful: they *may* be so wicked:

IV

Azeglio, Farini, Mamiani,
　　Ricasoli,—doubt by the dozen!—here's
Pepoli too, and Cipriani,
　　Imperial cousins and cozeners—
Arese, Laiatico,[2]—courtly
30　　Of manners, if stringent of mouth:
Garibaldi![3] we'll come to him shortly
　　(As soon as he *ends* in the South).

V

Napoleon[4]—as strong as ten armies,
　　Corrupt as seven devils—a fact
You accede to, then seek where the harm is
　　Drained off from the man to his act,
And find—a free nation! Suppose
　　Some hell-brood in Eden's sweet greenery,
Convoked for creating—a rose!
40　　Would it suit the infernal machinery?

VI

Cavour,[5]—to the despot's desire,
　　Who his own thought so craftily marries—
What is he but just a thin wire
　　For conducting the lightning from Paris?
Yes, write down the two as compeers,
　　Confessing (you would not permit a lie)

He bore up his Piedmont ten years
　　Till she suddenly smiled and was Italy.

VII

And the King,[6] with that "stain on his
　　scutcheon,"
　　Savoy—as the calumny runs;   50
(If it be not his blood,—with his clutch on
　　The sword, and his face to the guns.)
O first, where the battle-storm gathers,
　　O loyal of heart on the throne,
Let those keep the "graves of their fathers"
　　Who quail, in a nerve, from their own!

VIII

For *thee*—through the dim Hades-portal
　　The dream of a voice—"Blessed thou
Who hast made all thy race twice immortal!
　　No need of the sepulchres now!   60
—Left to Bourbons and Hapsburgs, who fester
　　Above-ground with worm-eaten souls,
While the ghost of some pale feudal jester
　　Before them strews treaties in holes."

IX

But hush!—am I dreaming a poem
　　Of Hades, Heaven, Justice? Not I;
I began too far off, in my proem,
　　With what men believe and deny:
And on earth, whatsoever the need is
　　(To sum up as thoughtful reviewers),   70
The moral of every great deed is—
　　The virtue of slandering the doers.

　　　　　　　　　　　　　　　　　　　　　　　　　1860

[2] Massimo d'Azeglio, Count Terenzio Mamiana della Rovere, Baron Bettino Ricasoli, Count Arese, and Count Gioacchino Pepoli were all noblemen active in the politics that moved the states of Italy away from the domination of the Austrian empire and toward concert with one another. Luigi Carlo Farini and Lionetto Cipriani, the first a doctor and the second a military commander, were also active. "Laiatico" is perhaps Giacomo Lacaita, for a time in exile in England, who returned to England on a diplomatic mission in 1860.

[3] Giuseppe Garibaldi (1807–82), one of the great heroes of Italian nationhood, fled to South America in 1834 to escape execution for his revolutionary actions, returned in 1848 to engage in the uprisings of that year, was exiled again, to return again in 1854. In 1860 he led forces that freed Sicily from the control of the Bourbon dynasty, and then crossed the straits to enter Naples, where he met and pledged obedience to Victor Emmanuel II, who was proclaimed the king of a united Italy in 1861.

[4] Louis Napoleon, or Napoleon III (1808–73), son of a brother of Napoleon Bonaparte, was elected to the presidency of France in 1848, and assumed the title of emperor in 1852. He agreed to assist some of the Italian states in the war against Austria in 1859, and then withdrew his support and led the way to an armistice.

[5] Count Camillo Benso di Cavour (1810–61) was a dominant figure in the government of Piedmont, the strongest and central state in the confederation that opposed Austria. He conducted the negotiations that brought Napoleon into an alliance, although one of the prices of this assistance was an agreement that France would hold authority in Nice and Savoy.

[6] Victor Emmanuel II (1820–78), son of the ruler of Piedmont, became the figure around whom the several currents moving toward independence and unification began to collect in the 1840s and 1850s. He was proclaimed king of Italy in 1861, but it was another decade before Rome was added to the kingdom. The "stain on the scutcheon" presumably is the agreement in 1859 to cede Savoy to the French.

Alfred Lord Tennyson
1809–1892

LIKE WORDSWORTH and Robert Browning, Tennyson practiced no other profession during a long life than that of poet. Except for one late play in prose, he wrote and published nothing but verse, and he began writing that very early. In addition to *The Devil and the Lady*, his imitation of an early seventeenth-century drama, before he was fifteen years old he had written an epic poem in imitation of Walter Scott, which does not survive. By the end of 1832, in which year he turned twenty-three, he had published three volumes of verse, and the poem with which he had won a prize at Cambridge had also been published. But he then entered a troubled and very important passage in his life of about ten or twelve years during which, until the publication of *Poems* in 1842, Tennyson steadily wrote and revised many poems but published almost none of them.

The death of his friend Arthur Hallam in 1833 was the first of a series of events that unsettled Tennyson's personal life. An early romance in 1834–35 came to nothing, or, worse than nothing, to disillusionment about a young woman of a superior financial and social station whom Tennyson apparently idealized. His engagement in 1838 to the woman who would eventually become his wife was temporarily broken off in 1840. In 1837 Tennyson, his mother, and his family left the house in which he had grown up, and then moved twice more in the next four years. The health and fortunes of his six brothers were unsteady and worrisome all through these years. By 1840 his own health, physical and mental, began to suffer, and in 1843 he was ill enough to subject himself to a curious course of therapy that required that he be wrapped in wet sheets between immersions in hot and cold baths.

But for all the uncertainty of these years about money, love, health, and home, he continued to think of himself entirely as a poet, and he wrote a great deal of poetry, some of it the finest he ever wrote. The reviews of his 1832 volume of verse were sometimes severe, occasionally derisive. But throughout the 1830s his poems, his oddly powerful person and personality, and a kind of rumor of his promise won him the attention of a growing number of readers, critics, and other poets. The poems of his 1842 volume, one of the most remarkable collections of poetry published in England in the nineteenth century, confirmed this reputation and were the first vehicle by which it was slowly—the reviews of the 1842 volume were favorable, but its sales were not exceptional—transmitted to a larger public. The lyrics of *In Memoriam*, which went into three editions in the year of its publication, finally brought Tennyson the large and national audience he believed necessary to the fully effective practice of the office of poet. After the publication of the first of the *Idylls of the King* in 1859, the means, purposes, and stature of his practice were firmly established. He was after 1860 the preeminent poet of his country and time. Volumes of his poetry sold like novels: 10,000 copies of the first four episodes of the *Idylls* in the first week of their publication (800 copies of the first edition of the 1842 *Poems* had been printed, and they were not sold out for several years); 40,000 copies of the *Enoch Arden* volume in the first few weeks of its publication in 1864. Some of Tennyson's contemporaries continued to find him obscure and fanciful in his language and morbid in his obsession with states of doubt and personal desolation. Especially as successive *Idylls* appeared in the 1860s and after, Robert Browning and younger poets such as Meredith and Swinburne complained about the want of vigor and bite in the ornate surfaces and finely modulated music of his verse. But from the 1860s on Tennyson was recognized, by most of his contemporaries who tendered such recognition, as the writer somehow elected to express and educate their feelings, to certify and buttress their beliefs, to celebrate their national and moral worth, and to tell them stories of their aspirations and of the dark troubles of human fallibility that might defeat them.

The shape and achievements of Tennyson's career before and after 1850 make plausible certain distinctions, conventional in accounts of his poetry, between the lyric and the laureate Tennyson, the private poet of melancholy, doubt, and fragile certitude, and the public poet who confidently explicates and endorses the civic and moral meanings of the Duke of Wellington, the International Exhibition of 1861, and the great, gleaming mystery on the horizon of human perception. It is true that after *In Memoriam* most of Tennyson's poems are in narrative and dramatic forms, including his late, persistent interest in writing for the stage. It is also true that when he did write poems of direct address in the years of his laureateship, the address was often oratorical rather than lyrical, straight-out pronouncements on political, social, and even philosophical topics rather than expressions of the state of one sensibility in a particular situation. He is also less ready in his latter poems than he had been in his earlier years to end poems in the enigmatic resonances of "The Kraken," for example, or of "Walking to the Mail." His later poems, "Rizpah," say, and "The Higher Pantheism," characteristically consider the incomprehensible and aberrant in a frame and from a vantage which offer assurances that it all finally makes sense, and that the sense it makes is good. Tennyson in his poetry after *In Memoriam* simply seems in the confident exercise of his talent to have settled the concern he expressed in "The Palace of Art" and some of the lyrics of *In Memoriam* that the personal, troubled sources of his poetry may deprive it of public uses. Wherever poetry may come from, however mysterious and private its sources in the memory, knowledge, and feelings of the poet, Tennyson usually seems sure in his later poems that the ultimate residence of his poems is in the public life and sensibility of his time, and he seems equally sure that he knows how to move his poems into their proper residence and make them effective there.

But the increasing explicitness and self-consciousness with which Tennyson after 1850 performed his public responsibilities as a poet ought not to disguise important continuities in his practice. Except for *In Memoriam*, Tennyson never wrote very much in the personal address of lyric (and even in *In Memoriam* he insisted, according to his son Hallam, that the speaker was not always the poet). Tennyson's lyricism is in large part a matter of the melody of his verse, and he continued to attend to this music, especially in the sonorities of his laureate poems for public occasions. From the beginning to the end of his career he wrote dramatic and narrative poems about persons in perilous situations (the Second-Rate Mind, Oenone, Arthur and Bedivere, Lucretius) which figure larger moral and social difficulties. He had always thought it proper for a poet to speak out directly in verse on the topics and in the discursive language he uses, for example, in both an early poem like "You Ask Me Why" and in the concluding address "To the Queen" of the *Idylls*. Perhaps most important, Tennyson never lost his sometimes fearful conviction that the source of poetry was indeed mysterious, intuitive, and utterly private, a flash and gleam of high feeling and knowledge that came unwilled, a visitation from a finally inexpressible reality. Nor did he ever lose a sense of himself as a poet who, in the late poem "Milton" as in "The Palace of Art," was obligated both to acknowledge and to leave the quiet, secluded places he associated with the fundamental impulse of his poetry. In sum, when Tennyson moved out from his reclusive first decades as a poet to enact an idea about poetry that served the rest of the century as a model, he brought with him and made part of that idea some of the tonalities and premises of the already masterful poems in which he tried out the difficult imperatives of a private and mysterious gift he had decided to enlist in the highest duties he could imagine for a poet.

The selection offered here is intended to represent the most important kinds, matter, styles, and purposes of Tennyson's poetry. Because the *Idylls of the King*, available now in several separate editions, is represented only by the "Morte d'Arthur," the selection does not accurately measure the high proportion of narrative verse in Tennyson's canon. Like most nineteenth-century British poets who aspired to achieve fully their idea of a major poet, Tennyson was frequently a teller of tales, and the matter of his stories was various: Arthurian; domestic and topical ("Alymer's Field," "Despair"); fanciful and fabulistic ("The Palace of Art," "Merlin and the Gleam"); sometimes, as in "The Vision of Sin" and a late ballad like "Rizpah," eerie and preternatural; and occasionally classical, although he most often used the events of classical mythology as premises on which to found dramatic monologues by speakers poised in a moment of or after the action. Even as a narrative poet he is a poet of episodes; the narrative line of his longest and most ambitious poems, the *Idylls, Maud, In Memoriam,* is moved through discrete but related episodes. In another principal kind of his poetry—"Mariana," for example, "The Lotos-Eaters," and especially his dramatic monologues—Tennyson entirely subordinates story to become a poet of isolated moments of mood, trance, and climactic decision or revelation. The events behind and in all these narrative and dramatic poems are often vivid, even sensational: wars, betrayals, abandonments, insanities, murder, suicides, execution. Their themes are those of Tennyson's poetry from beginning to end: isolation, paralysis, destruction, the necessary losses and uncertainties of mortality, the necessity and will to transcend these dangerous mental and moral states. Again, it is worth noting that this last theme is enunciated throughout Tennyson's poetry, although it is more consistent in his later verse, the sign and source of his place as the poet of the feelings, beliefs, wishes, and needs of many of his contemporaries.

In addition to suggesting the differences and continuities in the dominant kinds and themes of Tennyson's poetry, this selection is intended to demonstrate something of the exceptional variety of technical means Tennyson used in his poetry. The registers of his diction vary, for example, from the colloquial line of "Will Waterproof" and the dialect of the "Northern Farmer" poems to the elevated diction of "Ulysses" and "Lucretius." He used conventional forms of lyric, ode, ballad, and the verse of explicit political or social statement. He also experimented with the "monodrama" of *Maud,* the idyllic forms he adapted from classical sources, the conventions of elegy he incorporated into the medley of lyric and discursive poems which make up *In Memoriam,* and the curious kind of poem he devised in "Mariana," neither exactly narrative nor lyric, its evocative descriptive details suggesting a speaker who is not defined and a story that is not told. He used a wide range of English meters, experimented with classical meters, and liked to point out how artfully he had arranged the consonants of his lines to work subtle and precise effects. Its high moral and social purposes were essential to Tennyson's

idea of poetry. But their attainment began in craft, and one of the most important and consistent characteristics of his entire life as a poet is the great care he expended in the craft of poetry, and the pleasure he took and gave in his unusual technical skills.

CHRONOLOGY

1809 Born in Lincolnshire; his father was a clergyman in the Church of England, the rector of Somersby, who had been required to take clerical orders when his own father passed over him and settled an inheritance upon a younger brother; his mother was the daughter of a clergyman, the rector of a nearby parish.

1815–20 Tennyson was educated in a local grammar school, and, after 1820, at home by his father.

1823–24 Tennyson wrote *The Devil and the Lady,* an imitation of a Jacobean grotesque comedy.

1827 *Poems by Two Brothers,* which included poems by his brother Charles (see Part Four) and a few by another brother, Frederick, published; Tennyson entered Cambridge.

1829 Met Arthur Henry Hallam, the son of an eminent historian; Tennyson was elected to the Apostles, an undergraduate debating and essay club, and he won a university prize for his poem, *Timbuctoo.*

1830 *Poems, Chiefly Lyrical* published.

1831 Tennyson's father died, after a physical and mental illness of about seven years which sometimes issued in drunken violence and once caused a separation between his mother and father. Tennyson returned to Somersby without taking his degree from Cambridge.

1832 *Poems* published.

1833 Hallam, engaged this year to marry Tennyson's sister, died while visiting Europe. A narrative poem, *The Lover's Tale,* was prepared for publication but withdrawn by Tennyson. He began to write the lyrics of *In Memoriam* and to revise his earlier poems, enterprises he continued all through the 1830s. Except for two contributions to periodicals, he published no poetry until 1842.

1838–40 Tennyson was engaged in 1838 to marry Emily Sellwood; the engagement was broken in 1840 because of Tennyson's uncertain prospects and unorthodox religious beliefs.

1842 *Poems* published in two volumes, the first of selections, many of them revised, from the 1830 and 1832 volumes, and the second of new poems.

1843 After losing the little money he had in a commercial venture, Tennyson entered a private hospital for treatment of physical and mental disabilities.

1845 Granted a government pension of £200 annually because of his literary distinction.

1847 *The Princess* published: a sometimes philosophical, sometimes burlesque, fanciful and topical narrative poem about the status and education of women.

1850 *In Memoriam,* an elegy for Hallam, published. Tennyson's engagement to Emily Sellwood was revived and they were married. He was appointed poet laureate after the death of Wordsworth.

1852–53 First son born (a second son was born in 1854). Tennyson's first major laureate poem, "Ode on the Death of the Duke of Wellington," published (1852). Tennyson and his family moved to the Isle of Wight in the south of England.

1855 *Maud and Other Poems* published.

1859 First narratives of the *Idylls of the King* published; the sequence of twelve idylls was eventually completed in 1885.

1864 *Enoch Arden and Other Poems* published.

1865 Tennyson refused an offer of a baronetcy.

1869–70 *The Holy Grail and Other Poems* published at the end of 1869 (dated 1870). First collected edition of poems published, in ten volumes (1870).

1872 *Gareth and Lynette* published. *Idylls of the King* were now virtually complete, lacking only one of the twelve episodes.

1875–79 *Queen Mary,* the first of Tennyson's plays, published; it was produced in 1876. *Harold,* a second play also on an historical subject, was published in 1876; another play, *The Falcon,* was produced in 1879. *The Lover's Tale,* an early poem omitted from editions of his poems, was published in 1879 to frustrate unauthorized publication.

1880 *Ballads and Other Poems* published.

1881–83 Two more of Tennyson's plays performed: *The Cup* in 1881, and *The Promise of May,* a play in prose, in 1882. Tennyson accepted a baronetcy in 1883 and took his seat in the House of Lords.

1884 *The Cup* and *The Falcon* published; another play, *Becket,* also published; it was not performed until 1893. One-volume edition of collected poems, with some revisions, published; it was the ninth separate collected edition issued, including the first in 1870.

1885 *Tiresias and Other Poems* published.

1886 *Locksley Hall Sixty Years After and Other Poems* published.

1889 *Demeter and Other Poems* published.

1892 *The Foresters,* a play, published and performed in New York. Tennyson died in October. *The Death of Œnone, Akbar's Dream and Other Poems* was published three weeks after his death.

EDITIONS

The texts below are those of the "Eversley" edition of Tennyson's poems (1907–8; American edition 1908). This edition, long standard, has now been supplemented by Christopher Ricks' edition of *The Poems of Tennyson* (1969), which includes some poems not included in the Eversley edition, and some others not previously published at all. *The Devil and the Lady,* Tennyson's juvenile play, and some of his other early poems were published in separate editions in 1930 and 1931, and in one volume in 1964. John Pfordresher has edited *A Variorum Edition of Tennyson's Idylls of the King* (1973). The correspondence between Tennyson and Queen Victoria has been edited and published by Hope Dyson and Charles Tennyson in *Dear and Honoured Lady* (1969). James O. Hoge has edited *The Letters of Emily Lady Tennyson* (1974).

BIOGRAPHY AND CRITICISM

Tennyson's son Hallam published *Alfred Lord Tennyson: A Memoir* in 1897, and another volume of reminiscences, *Tennyson and His Friends* in 1911. Tennyson's grandson, Charles Tennyson, published a new biography, *Alfred Tennyson,* in 1949. Charles Tennyson has also published an account of Tennyson's early years in "The Somersby Tennysons" (*Victorian Studies,* Christmas Supplement, 1963); and, with Hope Dyson, *The Tennysons* (1974), a history of the family. Ralph Rader's *Maud: The Biographical Genesis* (1963) is also in effect a biography of Tennyson in the 1830s and 1840s.

Other Useful Books

Berry, Francis. *Poetry and the Physical Voice* (1962). Includes a discussion of the physical characteristics of Tennyson's voice and their effect on his poetry.

Bradley, A. C. *A Commentary on Tennyson's* In Memoriam (3rd edition, 1910).

Buckley, Jerome. *Tennyson: The Growth of a Poet* (1960).

Bush, Douglas. *Mythology and the Romantic Tradition* (revised edition, 1963). Includes a chapter on Tennyson's knowledge and use of classical poetry.

Eggers, J. Philip. *King Arthur's Laureate: A Study of Tennyson's* Idylls of the King (1971).

Groom, Bernard. *The Diction of Poetry from Spenser to Bridges* (1955). Includes his study of the diction of the poetry of Tennyson, Browning, and Arnold, published separately in 1939.

Killham, John. *Tennyson and the Princess: Reflections of an Age* (1958).

Killham, John, ed. *Critical Essays on the Poetry of Tennyson* (1960).

Lounsbury, Thomas. *The Life and Times of Tennyson* (1915). An account of only the first decades of his life and career.

Nicolson, Harold. *Tennyson* (1923). An early and influential argument that the public Tennyson was different from and less than the private Tennyson.

Paden, W. D. *Tennyson in Egypt: A Study of the Imagery in His Earlier Work* (1942).

Palmer, D. J., ed. *Tennyson.* Writers and Their Background series (1973). Includes essays on his laureate poems, plays, and his audience.

Pitt, Valerie. *Tennyson Laureate* (1962).

Priestley, F. E. L. *Language and Structure in Tennyson's Poetry* (1973).

Pyre, J. F. A. *The Formation of Tennyson's Style* (1921).

Richardson, Joanna. *The Preeminent Victorian* (1962).

Ricks, Christopher. *Tennyson* (1972).

Rosenberg, John D. *The Fall of Camelot: A Study of Tennyson's* Idylls of the King (1973).

Shannon, Edgar, Jr. *Tennyson and the Reviewers . . . 1827–51* (1952).

Sinfield, Alan. *The Language of Tennyson's* In Memoriam (1973).

Richard H. Shepherd's *Tennysoniana: Notes Bibliographical and Critical* (2nd edition revised 1879) includes a list of reviews of Tennyson's poems. Charles Tennyson and Christine Fall have compiled *Alfred Tennyson, An Annotated Bibliography* of publications concerning the poet through 1964 (1967). B. C. Southam's *Tennyson* (1971), in the series Writers and Their Work, contains a selected bibliography. John D. Jump has edited *Tennyson: The Critical Heritage* (1967).

Midnight[1]

'Tis midnight o'er the dim mere's lonely bosom,
  Dark, dusky, windy midnight: swift are driven
The swelling vapours onward: every blossom
  Bathes its bright petals in the tears of heaven.
Imperfect, half-seen objects meet the sight,
  The other half our fancy must pourtray;
A wan, dull, lengthen'd sheet of swimming light
  Lies the broad lake: the moon conceals her ray,
Sketch'd faintly by a pale and lurid gleam
  Shot thro' the glimmering clouds: the lovely planet   10
Is shrouded in obscurity; the scream
  Of owl is silenc'd; and the rocks of granite
Rise tall and drearily, while damp and dank
Hang the thick willows on the reedy bank.
Beneath, the gurgling eddies slowly creep,
  Blacken'd by foliage; and the glutting wave,
That saps eternally the cold grey steep,
  Sounds heavily within the hollow cave.
All earth is restless—from his glossy wing[2]
  The heath-fowl lifts his head at intervals;   20
  Wet, driving, rainy, come the bursting squalls;
All nature wears her dun dead covering.
Tempest is gather'd, and the brooding storm
Spreads its black mantle o'er the mountain's form;
And, mingled with the rising roar, is swelling,
From the far hunter's booth, the blood hound's yelling.
The water-falls in various cadence chiming,
  Or in one loud unbroken sheet descending,

[1] Published in *Poems by Two Brothers* (1827); not reprinted until Hallam Tennyson reprinted an edition of this volume in 1893. The text is that of 1827 and 1893 printings.
[2] Tennyson's note in 1827: "The succeeding lines are a paraphrase of Ossian." James Macpherson's Ossianic poems were first published in 1762.

Salute each other thro' the night's dark
   womb;
The moaning pine-trees to the wild blast
30   bending,
Are pictured faintly thro' the chequer'd
   gloom;
The forests, half-way up the mountain
   climbing,
Resound with crash of falling branches;
   quiver
Their aged mossy trunks: the startled doe
Leaps from her leafy lair: the swelling river
   Winds his broad stream majestic, deep, and
   slow.

                 1827

To Poesy[1]

O God, make this age great that we may be
   As giants in Thy praise! and raise up Mind,
Whose trumpet-tongued, aerial melody
   May blow alarum loud to every wind,
And startle the dull ears of human kind!
Methinks I see the world's renewed youth
   A long day's dawn, when Poesy shall bind
Falsehood beneath the altar of great Truth:
The clouds are sunder'd toward the morning-
   rise;
10   Slumber not now, gird up thy loins for fight,
And get thee forth to conquer. I, even I,
Am large in hope that these expectant eyes
Shall drink the fullness of thy victory,
   Tho' thou art all unconscious of thy Might.

                (1828)

Mariana

Mariana in the moated grange.
              MEASURE FOR MEASURE[1]

With blackest moss the flower-plots
   Were thickly crusted, one and all:
The rusted nails fell from the knots
   That held the pear[2] to the gable-wall.

The broken sheds look'd sad and strange:
   Unlifted was the clinking latch;
   Weeded and worn the ancient thatch
Upon the lonely moated grange.
   She only said, "My life is dreary,
      He cometh not," she said;   10
   She said, "I am aweary, aweary,
      I would that I were dead!"

Her tears fell with the dews at even;
   Her tears fell ere the dews were dried;
She could not look on the sweet heaven,
   Either at morn or eventide.
After the flitting of the bats,
   When thickest dark did trance the sky,
   She drew her casement-curtain by,
And glanced athwart the glooming flats.   20
   She only said, "The night is dreary,
      He cometh not," she said;
   She said, "I am aweary, aweary,
      I would that I were dead!"

Upon the middle of the night,
   Waking she heard the night-fowl crow:
The cock sung out an hour ere light:
   From the dark fen the oxen's low
Came to her: without hope of change,
   In sleep she seem'd to walk forlorn,   30
   Till cold winds woke the gray-eyed morn
About the lonely moated grange.
   She only said, "The day is dreary,
      He cometh not," she said;
   She said, "I am aweary, aweary,
      I would that I were dead!"

About a stone-cast from the wall
   A sluice with blacken'd waters slept,
And o'er it many, round and small,
   The cluster'd marish-mosses[3] crept.   40
Hard by a poplar shook alway,
   All silver-green with gnarlèd bark:
   For leagues no other tree did mark
The level waste, the rounding gray.

[1] Written in 1828. Not printed in Tennyson's lifetime or in the standard edition of his poetry. The text is that printed in Hallam Tennyson's *Memoir* (I, 60). Ricks in his edition (p. 168) changes "Tho'" in the last line to "For."
[1] Tennyson's note in the standard edition of his poetry: "The *moated grange* was no particular grange, but one which rose to the music of Shakespeare's words: 'There, at the moated grange, resides this dejected Mariana' (*Measure for Measure*, III, i)" (I, 665).
[2] Tennyson's note: "Altered from 'peach' [in the 1830 volume], because 'peach' spoils the desolation of the picture. It is not a characteristic of the scenery I had in mind" (I, 666). The revision was made in 1865; the poem was not much revised from its first publication in 1830.
[3] Tennyson's note: "*marish-mosses,* the little march-moss lumps that float on the surface of the water" (I, 666).

She only said, "My life is dreary,
  He cometh not," she said;
She said, "I am aweary, aweary,
  I would that I were dead!"

And ever when the moon was low,
  And the shrill winds were up and away,
In the white curtain, to and fro,
  She saw the gusty shadow sway.
But when the moon was very low,
  And wild winds bound within their cell,
The shadow of the poplar fell
Upon her bed, across her brow.
  She only said, "The night is dreary,
    He cometh not," she said;
  She said, "I am aweary, aweary,
    I would that I were dead!"

All day within the dreamy house,
  The doors upon their hinges creak'd;
The blue fly sung in the pane; the mouse
  Behind the mouldering wainscot shriek'd,
Or from the crevice peer'd about.
  Old faces glimmer'd thro' the doors,
  Old footsteps trod the upper floors,
Old voices called her from without.
  She only said, "My life is dreary,
    He cometh not," she said;
  She said, "I am aweary, aweary,
    I would that I were dead!"

The sparrow's chirrup on the roof,
  The slow clock ticking, and the sound
Which to the wooing wind aloof
  The poplar made, did all confound
Her sense; but most she loathed the hour
  When the thick-moted sunbeam lay
  Athwart the chambers, and the day
Was sloping toward his western bower.
  Then, said she, "I am very dreary,
    He will not come," she said;
  She wept, "I am aweary, aweary,
    Oh God, that I were dead!"

1830

Supposed Confessions Of a Second-Rate Sensitive Mind[1]

O God! my God! have mercy now.
I faint, I fall. Men say that Thou
Didst die for me, for such as *me*,
Patient of ill, and death, and scorn,
And that my sin was as a thorn
Among the thorns that girt Thy brow,
Wounding Thy soul.—That even now,
In this extremest misery
Of ignorance, I should require
A sign! and if a bolt of fire   10
Would rive the slumbrous summer noon
While I do pray to Thee alone,
Think my belief would stronger grow!
Is not my human pride brought low?
The boastings of my spirit still?
The joy I had in my freewill
All cold, and dead, and corpse-like grown?
And what is left to me, but Thou,
And faith in Thee? Men pass me by;
Christians with happy countenances—   20
And children all seem full of Thee!
And women smile with saint-like glances
Like Thine own mother's when she bow'd
Above Thee, on that happy morn
When angels spake to men aloud,
And Thou and peace to earth were born.
Goodwill to me as well as all—
I one of them: my brothers they:
Brothers in Christ—a world of peace
And confidence, day after day;   30
And trust and hope till things should cease,
And then one Heaven receive us all.

How sweet to have a common faith!
To hold a common scorn of death!
And at a burial to hear
The creaking cords which wound and eat
Into my human heart, whene'er
Earth goes to earth, with grief, not fear,
With hopeful grief, were passing sweet![2]

[1] *In Poems, Chiefly Lyrical* (1830), in which this poem was first printed, its title was "Supposed Confessions of A Second-Rate Mind Not in Unity with Itself." It was not reprinted until 1884.

[2] In the 1830 volume, these lines followed:

A grief not uninformed, and dull,
Hearted with hope, of hope as full
As is the blood with life, or night
And a dark cloud with rich moonlight.
To stand beside a grave, and see
The red small atoms wherewith we
Are built, and smile in calm, and say
"These little motes and grains shall be
"Clothed on with immortality

"More glorious than the noon of day.
"All that is pass'd into the flowers,
"And into beasts and other men,
"And all the Norland whirlwind showers
"From open vaults, and all the sea
"O'erwashes with sharp salts, again
"Shall fleet together all, and be
"Indued with immortality."

40 Thrice happy state again to be
   The trustful infant on the knee!
   Who lets his rosy fingers play
   About his mother's neck, and knows
   Nothing beyond his mother's eyes.
   They comfort him by night and day;
   They light his little life alway;
   He hath no thought of coming woes;
   He hath no care of life or death;
   Scarce outward signs of joy arise,
50 Because the Spirit of happiness
   And perfect rest so inward is;
   And loveth so his innocent heart,
   Her temple and her place of birth,
   Where she would ever wish to dwell,
   Life of the fountan there, beneath
   Its salient springs, and far apart,
   Hating to wander out on earth,
   Or breathe into the hollow air,
   Whose chillness would make visible
60 Her subtil, warm, and golden breath,
   Which mixing with the infant's blood,
   Fulfils him with beatitude.
   Oh! sure it is a special care
   Of God, to fortify from doubt,
   To arm in proof, and guard about
   With triple-mailèd trust, and clear
   Delight, the infant's dawning year.

   Would that my gloomed fancy were
   As thine, my mother, when with brows
70 Propt on thy knees, my hands upheld
   In thine, I listen'd to thy vows,
   For me outpour'd in holiest prayer—
   For me unworthy!—and beheld
   Thy mild deep eyes upraised, that knew
   The beauty and repose of faith,
   And the clear spirit shining thro'.
   Oh! wherefore do we grow awry
   From roots which strike so deep? why dare
   Paths in the desert? Could not I
80 Bow myself down, where thou hast knelt,
   To the earth—until the ice would melt
   Here, and I feel as thou hast felt?
   What Devil had the heart to scathe
   Flowers thou hadst rear'd—to brush the dew
   From thine own lily, when thy grave
   Was deep, my mother, in the clay?
   Myself? Is it thus? Myself? Had I
   So little love for thee? But why
   Prevail'd not thy pure prayers? Why pray
90 To one who heeds not, who can save
   But will not? Great in faith, and strong
   Against the grief of circumstance

Wert thou, and yet unheard. What if
Thou pleadest still, and seest me drive
Thro' utter dark a full-sail'd skiff,
Unpiloted i' the echoing dance
Of reboant whirlwinds, stooping low
Unto the death, not sunk! I know
At matins and at evensong,
That thou, if thou wert yet alive,   10
In deep and daily prayers would'st strive
To reconcile me with thy God.
Albeit, my hope is gray, and cold
At heart, thou wouldest murmur still—
"Bring this lamb back into Thy fold,
My Lord, if so it be Thy will."
Would'st tell me I must brook the rod
And chastisement of human pride;
That pride, the sin of devils, stood
Betwixt me and the light of God!   11
That hitherto I had defied
And had rejected God—that grace
Would drop from his o'er-brimming love,
As manna on my wilderness,
If I would pray—that God would move
And strike the hard, hard rock, and thence,
Sweet in their utmost bitterness,
Would issue tears of penitence
Which would keep green hope's life. Alas!
I think that pride hath now no place   12
Nor sojourn in me. I am void,
Dark, formless, utterly destroyed.
Why not believe then? Why not yet
Anchor thy frailty there, where man
Hath moor'd and rested? Ask the sea
At midnight, when the crisp slope waves
After a tempest, rib and fret
The broad-imbased beach, why he
Slumbers not like a mountain tarn?
Wherefore his ridges are not curls   1
And ripples of an inland mere?
Wherefore he moaneth thus, nor can
Draw down into his vexed pools
All that blue heaven which hues and paves
The other? I am too forlorn,
Too shaken: my own weakness fools
My judgment, and my spirit whirls,
Moved from beneath with doubt and fear.

"Yet," said I, in my morn of youth,
The unsunn'd freshness of my strength,   1
When I went forth in quest of truth,
"It is man's privilege to doubt,
If so be that from doubt at length,
Truth may stand forth unmoved of change,
An image with profulgent brows,

And perfect limbs, as from the storm
Of running fires and fluid range
Of lawless airs, at last stood out
This excellence and solid form
50 Of constant beauty. For the Ox
Feeds in the herb, and sleeps, or fills
The horned valleys all about,
And hollows of the fringed hills
In summer heats, with placid lows
Unfearing, till his own blood flows
About his hoof. And in the flocks
The lamb rejoiceth in the year,
And raceth freely with his fere,[3]
And answers to his mother's calls
60 From the flower'd furrow. In a time,
Of which he wots not, run short pains
Thro' his warm heart; and then, from whence
He knows not, on his light there falls
A shadow; and his native slope,
Where he was wont to leap and climb,
Floats from his sick and filmed eyes,
And something in the darkness draws
His forehead earthward, and he dies.
Shall man live thus, in joy and hope
70 As a young lamb, who cannot dream,
Living, but that he shall live on?
Shall we not look into the laws
Of life and death, and things that seem,
And things that be, and analyse
Our double nature, and compare
All creeds till we have found the one,
If one there be?" Ay me! I fear
All may not doubt, but everywhere
Some must clasp Idols. Yet, my God,
80 Whom call I Idol? Let Thy dove
Shadow me over, and my sins
Be unremember'd, and Thy love
Enlighten me. Oh teach me yet
Somewhat before the heavy clod
Weighs on me, and the busy fret
Of that sharp-headed worm begins
In the gross blackness underneath.

O weary life! O weary death!
O spirit and heart made desolate!
90 O damned vacillating state!

1830

The Mystic[1]

Angels have talked with him, and showed him
   thrones:
Ye knew him not: he was not one of ye,
Ye scorned him with an undiscerning scorn:
Ye could not read the marvel in his eye,
The still serene abstraction: he hath felt
The vanities of after and before;
Albeit, his spirit and his secret heart
The stern experiences of converse lives,
The linkèd woes of many a fiery change
Had purified, and chastened, and made free. 10
Always there stood before him, night and day,
Of wayward varycolored circumstance
The imperishable presences serene
Colossal, without form, or sense, or sound,
Dim shadows but unwaning presences
Fourfacèd to four corners of the sky:
And yet again, three shadows, fronting one,
One forward, one respectant,[2] three but one;
And yet again, again and evermore,
For the two first were not, but only seemed, 20
One shadow in the midst of a great light,
One reflex from eternity on time,
One mighty countenance of perfect calm,
Awful with most invariable eyes.
For him the silent congregated hours,
Daughters of time, divinely tall, beneath
Severe and youthful brows, with shining eyes
Smiling a godlike smile (the innocent light
Of earliest youth pierced through and through
   with all
Keen knowledges of low-embowèd eld[3]) 30
Upheld, and ever hold aloft the cloud
Which droops lowhung on either gate of life,
Both birth and death: he in the centre fixt,
Saw far on each side through the grated gates
Most pale and clear and lovely distances.
He often lying broad awake, and yet
Remaining from the body, and apart
In intellect and power and will, hath heard
Time flowing in the middle of the night,
And all things creeping to a day of doom. 40
How could ye know him? Ye were yet within
The narrower circle; he had wellnigh reached
The last, which with a region of white flame,

---

[3] Fere: companion.
[1] This poem was not reprinted in Tennyson's lifetime or in the standard edition of his poetry. The text is that of the 1830 volume.
[2] Looking backward, and thus facing the previous figure.
[3] Bowed-over age.

Pure without heat, into a larger air
Upburning, and an ether of black blue,
Investeth and ingirds all other lives.

                                                    1830

The Kraken

Below the thunders of the upper deep;
Far, far beneath in the abysmal sea,
His ancient, dreamless, uninvaded sleep
The Kraken[1] sleepeth: faintest sunlights flee
About his shadowy sides: above him swell
Huge sponges of millennial growth and height;
And far away into the sickly light,
From many a wondrous grot and secret cell
Unnumber'd and enormous polypi
10 Winnow with giant arms the slumbering green.
There hath he lain for ages and will lie
Battening upon huge seaworms in his sleep,
Until the latter fire shall heat the deep;
Then once by man and angels to be seen,
In roaring he shall rise and on the surface die.[2]

                                                    1830

Ode to Memory

                    Addressed To ——[1]

            I

            Thou who stealest fire,
        From the fountains of the past,
        To glorify the present; oh, haste,
            Visit my low desire!
        Strengthen me, enlighten me!
        I faint in this obscurity,
        Thou dewy dawn of memory.

            II

        Come not as thou camest of late,
        Flinging the gloom of yesternight
10 On the white day; but robed in soften'd light
            Of orient state.
    Whilome thou camest with the morning mist,
        Even as a maid, whose stately brow
    The dew-impearled winds of dawn have kiss'd,
            When, she, as thou,
    Stays on her floating locks the lovely freight

Of overflowing blooms, and earliest shoots
Of orient green, giving safe pledge of fruits,
        Which in wintertide shall star
    The black earth with brilliance rare.   20

            III
Whilome thou camest with the morning mist,
        And with the evening cloud,
Showering thy gleaned wealth into my open
                breast
    (Those peerless flowers which in the rudest
                wind
            Never grow sere,
When rooted in the garden of the mind,
        Because they are the earliest of the year).
            Nor was the night thy shroud.
In sweet dreams softer than unbroken rest
Thou leddest by the hand thine infant Hope.   30
The eddying of her garments caught from thee
The light of thy great presence; and the cope[2]
        Of the half-attain'd futurity,
        Tho' deep not fathomless,
Was cloven with the million stars which tremble
O'er the deep mind of dauntless infancy.
Small thought was there of life's distress;
For sure she deem'd no mist of earth could dull
Those spirit-thrilling eyes so keen and beauti-
                ful:
Sure she was nigher to heaven's spheres,   40
Listening the lordly music flowing from
                The illimitable years.
        O strengthen me, enlighten me!
        I faint in this obscurity,
        Thou dewy dawn of memory.

            IV
Come forth, I charge thee, arise,
Thou of the many tongues, the myriad eyes!
Thou comest not with shows of flaunting vines
            Unto mine inner eye,
            Divinest Memory!   50
    Thou wert not nursed by the waterfall
Which ever sounds and shines
        A pillar of white light upon the wall
Of purple cliffs, aloof descried:
Come from the woods that belt the gray hill-
                side,

[1] The kraken is a fabulous sea monster; in the notes to the standard edition of his poetry, Tennyson says that he learned of the kraken in an account in the *Biographie Universelle* (1823) (I, 665).
[2] According to Revelation, at the end of the world the sea will become blood and all its creatures will die (8:8–9).
[1] In the 1830 volume the subtitle was "Written Very Early in Life."
[2] Cope: vault or cover, as in vault of heaven.

The seven elms, the poplars four
That stand beside my father's door,[3]
And chiefly from the brook that loves
To purl o'er matted cress and ribbed sand,
60   Or dimple in the dark of rushy coves,
Drawing into his narrow earthen urn,
          In every elbow and turn,
The filter'd tribute of the rough woodland,
          O! hither lead thy feet!
Pour round mine ears the livelong bleat
Of the thick-fleeced sheep from wattled folds,
          Upon the ridged wolds,
When the first matin-song hath waken'd loud
Over the dark dewy earth forlorn,
70   What time the amber morn
Forth gushes from beneath a low-hung cloud.

          V
Large dowries doth the raptured eye
     To the young spirit present
          When first she is wed;
               And like a bride of old
          In triumph led,
               With music and sweet showers
               Of festal flowers,
          Unto the dwelling she must sway.
80   Well hast thou done, great artist Memory,
          In setting round thy first experiment
               With royal frame-work of wrought gold;
Needs must thou dearly love thy first essay,
And foremost in thy various gallery
          Place it, where sweetest sunlight falls
          Upon the storied walls;
               For the discovery
And newness of thine art so pleased thee,
That all which thou hast drawn of fairest
90   Or boldest since, but lightly weighs
With thee unto the love thou bearest
The first-born of thy genius. Artist-like,
Ever retiring thou dost gaze
On the prime labour of thine early days:
No matter what the sketch might be;
Whether the high field on the bushless Pike,[4]
Or even a sand-built ridge
Of heaped hills that mound the sea,
Overblown with murmurs harsh,
100 Or even a lowly cottage whence we see
Stretch'd wide and wild the waste enormous
          marsh,

Where from the frequent bridge,
Like emblems of infinity,
The trenched waters run from sky to sky;
Or a garden bower'd close
With plaited alleys of the trailing rose,
Long alleys falling down to twilight grots,
Or opening upon level plots
Of crowned lilies, standing near
Purple-spiked lavender: 110
Whither in after life retired
From brawling storms,
From weary wind,
With youthful fancy re-inspired,
     We may hold converse with all forms
Of the many-sided mind,
And those whom passion hath not blinded,
Subtle-thoughted, myriad-minded.

My friend,[5] with you to live alone,
Were how much better than to own   120
A crown, a sceptre, and a throne!

O strengthen me, enlighten me!
I faint in this obscurity,
Thou dewy dawn of memory.
                                        1830; 1842

The Poet

The poet in a golden clime was born,
     With golden stars above;
Dower'd with the hate of hate, the scorn of
          scorn,
     The love of love.

He saw thro' life and death, thro' good and ill,
     He saw thro' his own soul.
The marvel of the everlasting will,
     An open scroll,

Before him lay: with echoing feet he threaded
     The secretest walks of fame: 10
The viewless arrows of his thoughts were headed
     And wing'd with flame,

Like Indian reeds blown from his silver tongue,
     And of so fierce a flight,

---

[3] In his note in the standard edition of his poetry Tennyson identifies this scene as the rectory at Somersby (I, 670).
[4] Tennyson's note: "Cumberland word for peak" (I, 671).
[5] In his note Tennyson remarked that these lines were added to an early version of this poem before it was published in 1830; they are addressed to Arthur Hallam (I, 669).

From Calpe[1] unto Caucasus they sung,
 Filling with light

And vagrant melodies the winds which bore
 Them earthward till they lit;
Then, like the arrow-seeds of the field flower,[2]
20 The fruitful wit

Cleaving, took root, and springing forth anew
 Where'er they fell, behold,
Like to the mother plant in semblance, grew
 A flower all gold,

And bravely furnish'd all abroad to fling
 The winged shafts of truth,
To throng with stately blooms the breathing
  spring
 Of Hope and Youth.

So many minds did gird their orbs with beams,
30 Tho' one did fling the fire.
Heaven flow'd upon the soul in many dreams
 Of high desire.

Thus truth was multiplied on truth, the world
 Like one great garden show'd,
And thro' the wreaths of floating dark upcurl'd,
 Rare sunrise flow'd.

And Freedom rear'd in that august sunrise
 Her beautiful bold brow,
When rites and forms before his burning eyes
40 Melted like snow.

There was no blood upon her maiden robes
 Sunn'd by those orient skies;
But round about the circles of the globes
 Of her keen eyes

And in her raiment's hem was traced in flame
 WISDOM, a name to shake
All evil dreams of power—a sacred name.
 And when she spake,

Her words did gather thunder as they ran,
50 And as the lightning to the thunder
Which follows it, riving the spirit of man,
 Making earth wonder,

So was their meaning to her words. No sword
 Of wrath her right arm whirl'd,

But one poor poet's scroll, and with *his* word
 She shook the world.

       1830; 1842

 *Tennyson's note in the standard edition of his
poetry: "Haroun Alraschid lived at the time of
Charlemagne, and was renowned for his splendour
and his patronage of literary men. I had only the
translation—from the French of Galland—of the
Arabian Nights when this was written, so I talked
of sofas, etc." (I, 668). Antonine Galland's transla-
tion was first translated into English in 1705–8; it
was often reprinted. This poem was also published,
slightly revised, in the 1842 Poems in Two Volumes.*

Recollections of the Arabian Nights

When the breeze of a joyful dawn blew free
In the silken sail of infancy,
The tide of time flow'd back with me,
 The forward-flowing tide of time;
And many a sheeny summer-morn,
Adown the Tigris I was borne,
By Bagdat's shrines of fretted gold,
High-walled gardens green and old;
True Mussulman was I and sworn,
 For it was in the golden prime
 Of good Haroun Alraschid.

Anight my shallop, rustling thro'
The low and bloomed foliage, drove
The fragrant, glistening deeps,[1] and clove
The citron-shadows in the blue:
By garden porches on the brim,
The costly doors flung open wide,
Gold glittering thro' lamplight dim,
And broider'd sofas on each side:
 In sooth it was a goodly time,
 For it was in the golden prime
 Of good Haroun Alraschid.

Often, where clear-stemm'd platans[2] guard
The outlet, did I turn away
The boat-head down a broad canal
From the main river sluiced, where all
The sloping of the moon-lit sward
Was damask-work, and deep inlay
Of braided blooms unmown, which crept

---

[1] Calpe: Gibraltar. [2] Field flower: dandelion.
[1] Tennyson's note: ". . . the passage means that the deeps were driven before the prow"
(I, 668).
[2] Platans: plane trees.

30 Adown to where the water slept.
     A goodly place, a goodly time,
       For it was in the golden prime
       Of good Haroun Alraschid.

   A motion from the river won
   Ridged the smooth level, bearing on
   My shallop thro' the star-strown calm,
   Until another night in night
   I enter'd, from the clearer light,
   Imbower'd vaults of pillar'd palm,
40 Imprisoning sweets, which, as they clomb
   Heavenward, were stay'd beneath the dome
     Of hollow boughs.—A goodly time,
       For it was in the golden prime
       Of good Haroun Alraschid.

   Still onward; and the clear canal
   Is rounded to as clear a lake.
   From the green rivage[3] many a fall
   Of diamond rillets musical,
   Thro' little crystal arches low
50 Down from the central fountain's flow
   Fall'n silver-chiming, seemed to shake
   The sparkling flints beneath the prow.
     A goodly place, a goodly time,
       For it was in the golden prime
       Of good Haroun Alraschid.

   Above thro' many a bowery turn
   A walk with vary-colour'd shells
   Wander'd engrain'd.[4] On either side
   All round about the fragrant marge
60 From fluted vase, and brazen urn
   In order, eastern flowers large,
   Some dropping low their crimson bells
   Half-closed, and others studded wide
     With disks and tiars, fed the time
     With odour in the golden prime
       Of good Haroun Alraschid.

   Far off, and where the lemon grove
   In closest coverture upsprung,
   The living airs of middle night
70 Died round the bulbul[5] as he sung;
   Not he: but something which possess'd
   The darkness of the world, delight,
   Life, anguish, death, immortal love,
   Ceasing not, mingled, unrepress'd,
     Apart from place, withholding time,
     But flattering the golden prime
       Of good Haroun Alraschid.

   Black the garden-bowers and grots
   Slumber'd: the solemn palms were ranged
   Above, unwoo'd of summer wind: 80
   A sudden splendour from behind
   Flush'd all the leaves with rich gold-green,
   And, flowing rapidly between
   Their interspaces, counterchanged
   The level lake with diamond-plots
     Of dark and bright. A lovely time,
       For it was in the golden prime
       Of good Haroun Alraschid.

   Dark-blue the deep sphere overhead,
   Distinct with vivid stars inlaid,   90
   Grew darker from that under-flame:
   So, leaping lightly from the boat,
   With silver anchor left afloat,
   In marvel whence that glory came
   Upon me, as in sleep I sank
   In cool soft turf upon the bank,
     Entranced with that place and time,
     So worthy of the golden prime
       Of good Haroun Alraschid.

   Thence thro' the garden I was drawn—   100
   A realm of pleasance, many a mound,
   And many a shadow-chequer'd lawn
   Full of the city's stilly sound,
   And deep myrrh-thickets blowing round
   The stately cedar, tamarisks,[6]
   Thick rosaries of scented thorn,
   Tall orient shrubs, and obelisks
     Graven with emblems of the time,
     In honour of the golden prime
       Of good Haroun Alraschid.   110

   With dazed vision unawares
   From the long alley's latticed shade
   Emerged, I came upon the great
   Pavilion of the Caliphat.
   Right to the carven cedarn doors,
   Flung inward over spangled floors,
   Broad-based flights of marble stairs
   Ran up with golden balustrade,
     After the fashion of the time,
     And humour of the golden prime
       Of good Haroun Alraschid.   120

   The fourscore windows all alight
   As with the quintessence of flame,
   A million tapers flaring bright
   From twisted silvers[7] look'd to shame

---

[3] Rivage: bank.   [4] The walk is as if dyed into the fabric of the landscape.
[5] Bulbul: nightingale.   [6] Tamarisks: a family of desert trees and shrubs.
[7] Silvers: candelabra.

The hollow-vaulted dark, and stream'd
Upon the mooned[8] domes aloof
In inmost Bagdat, till there seem'd
Hundreds of crescents on the roof
130   Of night new-risen, that marvellous time
    To celebrate the golden prime
      Of good Haroun Alraschid.

Then stole I up, and trancedly
Gazed on the Persian girl alone,
Serene with argent-lidded eyes
Amorous, and lashes like to rays
Of darkness, and a brow of pearl
Tressed with redolent ebony,
In many a dark delicious curl,
140   Flowing beneath her rose-hued zone;
    The sweetest lady of the time,
    Well worthy of the golden prime
      Of good Haroun Alraschid.

Six columns, three on either side,
Pure silver, underpropt a rich
Throne of the massive ore, from which
Down-droop'd, in many a floating fold,
Engarlanded and diaper'd[9]
With inwrought flowers, a cloth of gold.
150   Thereon, his deep eye laughter-stirr'd
With merriment of kingly pride,
    Sole star of all that place and time,
    I saw him—in his golden prime,
      THE GOOD HAROUN ALRASCHID.

                          1830; 1842

Tennyson's note in the standard edition: "Taken from an Italian novellette, Donna di Scalotta *[Ricks gives the full title of the story and the source, a fourteenth-century collection,* Cento Novelle Antiche, *p. 354]. Shalott and Astolat are the same words. The Lady of Shalott is evidently the Elaine of the* Morte *d'Arthur, but I do not think that I had ever heard of the latter when I wrote the former. Shalott was a softer sound than 'Scalott'" (I, 680). Tennyson added the entire matter of the weaving and the curse.*

The Lady of Shalott (1832)

PART I
On either side the river lie
Long fields of barley and of rye,

That clothe the wold and meet the sky;
And thro' the field the road runs by
    To many-tower'd Camelot;
The yellowleavèd waterlily,
The greensheathèd daffodilly,
Tremble in the water chilly,
    Round about Shalott.

Willows whiten, aspens shiver,   10
The sunbeam-showers break and quiver
In the stream that runneth ever
By the island in the river
    Flowing down to Camelot.
Four gray walls, and four gray towers,
Overlook a space of flowers,
And the silent isle imbowers
    The Lady of Shalott.

Underneath the bearded barley,
The reaper, reaping late and early,   20
Hears her ever chanting cheerly,
Like an angel, singing clearly,
    O'er the stream of Camelot.
Piling the sheaves in furrows airy,
Beneath the moon, the reaper weary
Listening whispers, " 'tis the fairy
    Lady of Shalott."

The little isle is all inrailed
With a rose-fence, and overtrailed
With roses: by the marge unhailed   30
The shallop flitteth silkensailed,
    Skimming down to Camelot.
A pearlgarland winds her head:
She leaneth on a velvet bed,
Fully royally apparelled,
    The Lady of Shalott.

PART II
No time hath she to sport and play:
A charmèd web she weaves alway.
A curse is on her, if she stay
Her weaving, either night or day,   40
    To look down to Camelot.
She knows not what the curse may be;
Therefore she weaveth steadily,
Therefore no other care hath she,
    The Lady of Shalott.

She lives with little joy or fear,
Over the water, running near,

---

[8] Tennyson's note: "*mooned,* crowned with the Mohammedan crescent moon. The crescent is Ottoman, not Arabian, an anachronism pardonable in a boy's vision" (I, 669).

[9] Diaper'd: in a pattern in which geometric figures flow into one another, making a continuous line and design.

The sheepbell tinkles in her ear,
Before her hangs a mirror[1] clear,
    Reflecting tower'd Camelot.
And as the mazy web she whirls,
She sees the surly village churls,
And the red cloaks of market girls,
    Pass onward from Shalott.

Sometimes a troop of damsels glad,
An abbot on an ambling pad,[2]
Sometimes a curly shepherd lad,
Or long-hair'd page in crimson clad,
    Goes by to tower'd Camelot;
And sometimes thro' the mirror blue
The knights come riding two and two:
She hath no loyal knight and true,
    The Lady of Shalott.

But in her web she still delights
To weave the mirror's magic sights,
For often thro' the silent nights
A funeral, with plumes and lights
    And music, came from Camelot:
Or when the moon was overhead,
Came two lovers lately wed:
"I am half sick of shadows," said
    The Lady of Shalott.

PART III

A bow-shot from her bower-eaves,
He rode between the barley-sheaves,
The sun came dazzling thro' the leaves,
And flamed upon the brazen greaves
    Of bold Sir Lancelot.
A red-cross knight for ever kneel'd
To a lady in his shield,
That sparkled on the yellow field,
    Beside remote Shalott.

The gemmy bridle glitter'd free,
Like to some branch of stars we see
Hung in the golden Galaxy.
The bridle bells rang merrily
    As he rode down from Camelot:
And from his blazon'd baldric slung
A mighty silver bugle hung,
And as he rode his armor rung,
    Beside remote Shalott.

All in the blue unclouded weather
Thick-jewell'd shone the saddle-leather,

The helmet and the helmet-feather
Burned like one burning flame together,
    As he rode down from Camelot.
As often thro' the purple night,
Below the starry clusters bright,
Some bearded meteor, trailing light,
    Moves over green Shalott.

His broad clear brow in sunlight glow'd;   100
On burnish'd hooves his war-horse trode;
From underneath his helmet flow'd
His coal-black curls as on he rode,
    As he rode down from Camelot.
From the bank and from the river
He flash'd into the crystal mirror,
"Tirra lirra, tirra lirra,"
    Sang Sir Lancelot.

She left the web, she left the loom,
She made three paces thro' the room,   110
She saw the water-flower bloom,
She saw the helmet and the plume,
    She look'd down to Camelot.
Out flew the web and floated wide;
The mirror crack'd from side to side;
"The curse is come upon me," cried
    The Lady of Shalott.

PART IV

In the stormy east-wind straining,
The pale yellow woods were waning,
The broad stream in his banks complaining,   120
Heavily the low sky raining
    Over tower'd Camelot:
Outside the isle a shallow boat
Beneath a willow lay afloat,
Below the carven stern she wrote,
    The Lady of Shalott.

A cloudwhite crown of pearl she dight.
All raimented in snowy white
That loosely flew (her zone in sight,
Clasped with one blinding diamond bright)   130
    Her wide eyes fixed on Camelot,
Though the squally eastwind keenly
Blew, with folded arms serenely
By the water stood the queenly
    Lady of Shalott.

With a steady stony glance—
Like some bold seer in a trance,

[1] Tapestry is woven from the reverse side; the mirror enables the weaver to see the design being woven.

[2] Pad: easy-gaited horse.

Beholding all his own mischance,
Mute, with a glassy countenance—
140   She looked down to Camelot.
It was the closing of the day,
She loosed the chain, and down she lay;
The broad stream bore her far away,
      The Lady of Shalott.

As when to sailors while they roam,
By creeks and outfalls far from home,
Rising and dropping with the foam,
From dying swans wild warblings come,
      Blown shoreward; so to Camelot
150 Still as the boathead wound along
The willowy hills and fields among,
They heard her chanting her deathsong,
      The Lady of Shalott.

A longdrawn carol, mournful, holy,
She chanted loudly, chanted lowly,
Till her eyes were darkened wholly,
And her smooth face sharpened slowly,
      Turned to tower'd Camelot:
For ere she reach'd upon the tide
160 The first house by the water-side,
Singing in her song she died,
      The Lady of Shalott.

Under tower and balcony,
By gardenwall and gallery,
A pale, pale corpse she floated by,
Deadcold, between the houses high,
      Dead into tower'd Camelot.
Knight and burgher, lord and dame,
To the planked wharfage came:
170 Below the stern they read her name,
      "The Lady of Shalott."

They crossed themselves, their stars they blest,
Knight, minstrel, abbot, squire, and guest.
There lay a parchment on her breast,
That puzzled more than all the rest,
      The wellfed wits at Camelot.
"The web was woven curiously,
The charm is broken utterly,
Draw near and fear not—this is I,
180   *The Lady of Shalott."*

1832

The Lady of Shalott (1842)

PART I
On either side the river lie
Long fields of barley and of rye,
That clothe the wold and meet the sky;
And thro' the field the road runs by
      To many-tower'd Camelot;
And up and down the people go,
Gazing where the lilies blow
Round an island there below,
      The island of Shalott.

Willows whiten, aspens quiver,
Little breezes dusk and shiver
Thro' the wave that runs for ever
By the island in the river
      Flowing down to Camelot.
Four gray walls, and four gray towers,
Overlook a space of flowers,
And the silent isle imbowers
      The Lady of Shalott.

By the margin, willow-veil'd,
Slide the heavy barges trail'd
By slow horses; and unhail'd
The shallop flitteth silken-sail'd
      Skimming down to Camelot:
But who hath seen her wave her hand?
Or at the casement seen her stand?
Or is she known in all the land,
      The Lady of Shalott?

Only reapers, reaping early
In among the bearded barley,
Hear a song that echoes cheerly
From the river winding clearly,
      Down to tower'd Camelot;
And by the moon the reaper weary,
Piling sheaves in uplands airy,
Listening, whispers "'T is the fairy
      Lady of Shalott."

PART II
There she weaves by night and day
A magic web with colours gay.
She has heard a whisper say,
A curse is on her if she stay
      To look down to Camelot.
She knows not what the curse may be,
And so she weaveth steadily,
And little other care hath she,
      The Lady of Shalott.

And moving thro' a mirror clear
That hangs before her all the year,
Shadows of the world appear.
There she sees the highway near
      Winding down to Camelot:
There the river eddy whirls,

And there the surly village-churls,
And the red cloaks of market girls,
     Pass onward from Shalott.

Sometimes a troop of damsels glad,
An abbot on an ambling pad,
Sometimes a curly shepherd-lad,
Or long-hair'd page in crimson clad,
     Goes by to tower'd Camelot;
And sometimes thro' the mirror blue
The knights come riding two and two:
She hath no loyal knight and true,
     The Lady of Shalott.

But in her web she still delights
To weave the mirror's magic sights,
For often thro' the silent nights
A funeral, with plumes and lights
     And music, went to Camelot;
Or when the moon was overhead,
Came two young lovers lately wed;
"I am half sick of shadows," said
     The Lady of Shalott.

PART III
A bow-shot from her bower-eaves,
He rode between the barley-sheaves,
The sun came dazzling thro' the leaves,
And flamed upon the brazen greaves
     Of bold Sir Lancelot.
A red-cross knight for ever kneel'd
To a lady in his shield,
That sparkled on the yellow field,
     Beside remote Shalott.

The gemmy bridle glitter'd free,
Like to some branch of stars we see
Hung in the golden Galaxy.
The bridle bells rang merrily
     As he rode down to Camelot:
And from his blazon'd baldric slung
A mighty silver bugle hung,
And as he rode his armor rung,
     Beside remote Shalott.

All in the blue unclouded weather
Thick-jewell'd shone the saddle-leather,
The helmet and the helmet-feather
Burn'd like one burning flame together,
     As he rode down to Camelot;
As often thro' the purple night,
Below the starry clusters bright,
Some bearded meteor, trailing light,
     Moves over still Shalott.

His broad clear brow in sunlight glow'd;   100
On burnish'd hooves his war-horse trode;
From underneath his helmet flow'd
His coal-black curls as on he rode,
     As he rode down to Camelot.
From the bank and from the river
He flash'd into the crystal mirror,
"Tirra lirra," by the river
     Sang Sir Lancelot.

She left the web, she left the loom,
She made three paces thro' the room,   110
She saw the water-lily bloom,
She saw the helmet and the plume,
     She look'd down to Camelot.
Out flew the web and floated wide;
The mirror crack'd from side to side;
"The curse is come upon me," cried
     The Lady of Shalott.

PART IV
In the stormy east-wind straining,
The pale yellow woods were waning,
The broad stream in his banks complaining,   120
Heavily the low sky raining
     Over tower'd Camelot;
Down she came and found a boat
Beneath a willow left afloat.
And round about the prow she wrote
     The Lady of Shalott.

And down the river's dim expanse
Like some bold seër in a trance,
Seeing all his own mischance—
With a glassy countenance   130
     Did she look to Camelot.
And at the closing of the day
She loosed the chain, and down she lay;
The broad stream bore her far away,
     The Lady of Shalott.

Lying, robed in snowy white
That loosely flew to left and right—
The leaves upon her falling light—
Thro' the noises of the night
     She floated down to Camelot: 140
And as the boat-head wound along
The willowy hills and fields among,
They heard her singing her last song,
     The Lady of Shalott.

Heard a carol, mournful, holy,
Chanted loudly, chanted lowly,
Till her blood was frozen slowly,

And her eyes were darken'd wholly,
   Turn'd to tower'd Camelot.
150 For ere she reach'd upon the tide
The first house by the water-side,
Singing in her song she died,
   The Lady of Shalott.

Under tower and balcony,
By garden-wall and gallery,
A gleaming shape she floated by,
Dead-pale between the houses high,
   Silent into Camelot.
Out upon the wharfs they came,
160 Knight and burgher, lord and dame,
And round the prow they read her name,
   The Lady of Shalott.

Who is this? and what is here?
And in the lighted palace near
Died the sound of royal cheer;
And they cross'd themselves for fear,
   All the knights at Camelot:
But Lancelot mused a little space;
He said, "She has a lovely face;
170 God in his mercy lend her grace,
   The Lady of Shalott."

                      1842

Mariana in the South

With one black shadow at its feet,
   The house thro' all the level shines,
Close-latticed to the brooding heat,
   And silent in its dusty vines:
A faint-blue ridge upon the right,
   An empty river-bed before,
   And shallows on a distant shore,
In glaring sand and inlets bright.
     But "Ave Mary," made she moan,
10   And "Ave Mary," night and morn,
     And "Ah," she sang, "to be all alone,
      To live forgotten, and love forlorn."

She, as her carol sadder grew,
   From brow and bosom slowly down
Thro' rosy taper fingers drew
   Her streaming curls of deepest brown
To left and right, and made appear
   Still-lighted in a secret shrine,
   Her melancholy eyes divine,
20 The home of woe without a tear.
     And "Ave Mary," was her moan,
      "Madonna, sad is night and morn,"

And "Ah," she sang, "to be all alone,
   To live forgotten, and love forlorn."

Till all the crimson changed, and past
   Into deep orange o'er the sea,
Low on her knees herself she cast,
   Before Our Lady murmur'd she;
Complaining, "Mother, give me grace
   To help me of my weary load."
   And on the liquid mirror glow'd
The clear perfection of her face.
     "Is this the form," she made her moan,
      "That won his praises night and morn?"
     And "Ah," she said, "but I wake alone,
      I sleep forgotten, I wake forlorn."

Nor bird would sing, nor lamb would bleat,
   Nor any cloud would cross the vault,
But day increased from heat to heat,
   On stony drought and steaming salt;
Till now at noon she slept again,
   And seem'd knee-deep in mountain grass,
   And heard her native breezes pass,
And runlets babbling down the glen.
     She breathed in sleep a lower moan,
      And murmuring, as at night and morn,
     She thought, "My spirit is here alone,
      Walks forgotten, and is forlorn."

Dreaming, she knew it was a dream:
   She felt he was and was not there.
She woke: the babble of the stream
   Fell, and, without, the steady glare
Shrank one sick willow sere and small.
   The river-bed was dusty-white;
   And all the furnace of the light
Struck up against the blinding wall.
     She whisper'd, with a stifled moan
      More inward than at night or morn,
     "Sweet Mother, let me not here alone
      Live forgotten and die forlorn."

And, rising, from her bosom drew[1]
   Old letters, breathing of her worth,
For "Love," they said, "must needs be true,
   To what is loveliest upon earth."
An image seem'd to pass the door,
   To look at her with slight, and say
   "But now thy beauty flows away,
So be alone for evermore."
     "O cruel heart," she changed her tone,
      "And cruel love, whose end is scorn,

---

[1] This stanza and the one following were added, along with some extensive revisions of the other stanzas, between the first publication of this poem in 1832 and its publication in 1842.

Is this the end to be left alone,
    To live forgotten, and die forlorn?"

But sometimes in the falling day
    An image seem'd to pass the door,
To look into her eyes and say,
    "But thou shalt be alone no more."
And flaming downward over all
    From heat to heat the day decreased,
    And slowly rounded to the east
The one black shadow from the wall.
    "The day to night," she made her moan,
      "The day to night, the night to morn,
    And day and night I am left alone
      To live forgotten, and love forlorn."

At eve a dry cicala sung,[2]
    There came a sound as of the sea;
Backward the lattice-blind she flung,
    And lean'd upon the balcony.
There all in spaces rosy-bright
    Large Hesper glitter'd on her tears,
    And deepening thro' the silent spheres
Heaven over Heaven rose the night.
    And weeping then she made her moan,
    "The night comes on that knows not morn,
    When I shall cease to be all alone,
      To live forgotten, and love forlorn."

                  1832; revised 1842

The Miller's Daughter

I see the wealthy miller yet,
    His double chin, his portly size,
And who that knew him could forget
    The busy wrinkles round his eyes?
The slow wise smile that, round about
    His dusty forehead drily curl'd,
Seem'd half-within and half-without,
    And full of dealings with the world?

In yonder chair I see him sit,
    Three fingers round the old silver cup—
I see his gray eyes twinkle yet
    At his own jest—gray eyes lit up

With summer lightnings of a soul
    So full of summer warmth, so glad,
So healthy, sound, and clear and whole,
    His memory scarce can make me sad.

Yet fill my glass: give me one kiss:
    My own sweet Alice, we must die.
There's somewhat in this world amiss
    Shall be unriddled by and by.   20
There's somewhat flows to us in life,
    But more is taken quite away.
Pray, Alice, pray, my darling wife,
    That we may die the self-same day.

Have I not found a happy earth?
    I least should breathe a thought of pain
Would God renew me from my birth
    I'd almost live my life again.
So sweet it seems with thee to walk,
    And once again to woo thee mine—   30
It seems in after-dinner talk
    Across the walnuts and the wine—

To be the long and listless boy
    Late-left an orphan of the squire,
Where this old mansion mounted high
    Looks down upon the village spire:
For even here, where I and you
    Have lived and loved alone so long,
Each morn my sleep was broken thro'
    By some wild skylark's matin song.   40

And oft I heard the tender dove
    In firry woodlands making moan;
But ere I saw your eyes, my love,
    I had no motion of my own.
For scarce my life with fancy play'd
    Before I dream'd that pleasant dream—
Still hither thither idly sway'd
    Like those long mosses in the stream.

Or from the bridge I lean'd to hear
    The milldam rushing down with noise,   50
And see the minnows everywhere
    In crystal eddies glance and poise,

---

[2] In the 1832 version, the final stanza was:

One dry cicala's summer song
    At night filled all the gallery,
Backward the latticeblind she flung,
    And leaned upon the balcony.
Ever the low wave seemed to roll
    Up to the coast: far on, alone
    In the East, large Hesper overshone
The mourning gulf, and on her soul

Poured divine solace, or the rise
Of moonlight from the margin gleamed,
Volcano-like, afar, and streamed
    On her white arm, and heavenward eyes.
    Not all alone she made her moan,
    Yet ever sang she, night and morn,
    "Madonna! lo! I am all alone,
    Love-forgotten and love-forlorn."

The tall flag-flowers when they sprung
  Below the range of stepping-stones,
Or those three chestnuts near, that hung
  In masses thick with milky cones.

But, Alice, what an hour was that,
  When after roving in the woods
('Twas April then), I came and sat
60 Below the chestnuts, when their buds
Were glistening to the breezy blue;
  And on the slope, an absent fool,
I cast me down, nor thought of you,
  But angled in the higher pool.[1]

A love-song I had somewhere read,
  An echo from a measured strain,
Beat time to nothing in my head
  From some odd corner of the brain.
It haunted me, the morning long,
70 With weary sameness in the rhymes,
The phantom of a silent song,
  That went and came a thousand times.

Then leapt a trout. In lazy mood
  I watch'd the little circles die;
They past into the level flood,
  And there a vision caught my eye;
The reflex of a beauteous form,
  A glowing arm, a gleaming neck,
As when a sunbeam wavers warm
80 Within the dark and dimpled beck.[2]

For you remember, you had set,
  That morning, on the casement-edge
A long green box of mignonette,
  And you were leaning from the ledge:
And when I raised my eyes, above
  They met with two so full and bright—
Such eyes! I swear to you, my love,
  That these have never lost their light.

I loved, and love dispell'd the fear
90 That I should die an early death:
For love possess'd the atmosphere,
  And fill'd the breast with purer breath.
My mother thought, What ails the boy?
  For I was alter'd, and began
To move about the house with joy,
  And with the certain step of man.

I loved the brimming wave that swam
  Thro' quiet meadows round the mill,

The sleepy pool above the dam,
  The pool beneath it never still,   10
The meal-sacks on the whiten'd floor,
  The dark round of the dripping wheel,
The very air about the door
  Made misty with the floating meal.

And oft in ramblings on the wold,
  When April nights began to blow,
And April's crescent glimmer'd cold,
  I saw the village lights below;
I knew your taper far away,
  And full at heart of trembling hope,   11
From off the wold I came, and lay
  Upon the freshly-flower'd slope.

The deep brook groan'd beneath the mill;
  And "by that lamp," I thought, "she sits!"
The white chalk-quarry from the hill
  Gleam'd to the flying moon by fits.
"O that I were beside her now!
  O will she answer if I call?
O would she give me vow for vow,
  Sweet Alice, if I told her all?"   12

Sometimes I saw you sit and spin;
  And, in the pauses of the wind,
Sometimes I heard you sing within;
  Sometimes your shadow cross'd the blind.
At last you rose and moved the light,
  And the long shadow of the chair
Flitted across into the night,
  And all the casement darken'd there.

But when at last I dared to speak,
  The lanes, you know, were white with may,[3] 13
Your ripe lips moved not, but your cheek
  Flush'd like the coming of the day;
And so it was—half-sly, half-shy,
  You would, and would not, little one!
Although I pleaded tenderly,
  And you and I were all alone.

And slowly was my mother brought
  To yield consent to my desire:
She wish'd me happy, but she thought
  I might have look'd a little higher; 14
And I was young—too young to wed:
  "Yet must I love her for your sake;
Go fetch your Alice here," she said:
  Her eyelid quiver'd as she spake.

[1] Higher pool: "The sleepy pool above the dam," (line 99).   [2] Beck: small brook.
[3] May: hawthorn in blossom.

And down I went to fetch my bride:
   But, Alice, you were ill at ease;
This dress and that by turns you tried,
   Too fearful that you should not please.
I loved you better for your fears,
   I knew you could not look but well;
And dews, that would have fall'n in tears,
   I kiss'd away before they fell.

I watch'd the little flutterings,
   The doubt my mother would not see;
She spoke at large of many things,
   And at the last she spoke of me;
And turning look'd upon your face,
   As near this door you sat apart,
And rose, and, with a silent grace
   Approaching, press'd you heart to heart.

Ah, well—but sing the foolish song
   I gave you, Alice, on the day
When, arm in arm, we went along,
   A pensive pair, and you were gay
With bridal flowers—that I may seem,
   As in the nights of old, to lie
Beside the mill-wheel in the stream,
   While those full chestnuts whisper by.

It is the miller's daughter,
   And she is grown so dear, so dear,
That I would be the jewel
   That trembles in her ear:
For hid in ringlets day and night,
I'd touch her neck so warm and white.

And I would be the girdle
   About her dainty dainty waist,
And her heart would beat against me,
   In sorrow and in rest:
And I should know if it beat right,
I'd clasp it round so close and tight.

And I would be the necklace,
   And all day long to fall and rise
Upon her balmy bosom,
   With her laughter or her sighs,
And I would lie so light, so light,
I scarce should be unclasp'd at night.

A trifle, sweet! which true love spells—
   True love interprets—right alone.
His light upon the letter dwells,
   For all the spirit is his own.
So, if I waste words now, in truth
   You must blame Love. His early rage
Had force to make me rhyme in youth,
   And makes me talk too much in age.

And now those vivid hours are gone,
   Like mine own life to me thou art,
Where Past and Present, wound in one,
   Do make a garland for the heart:
So sing that other song I made,
   Half-anger'd with my happy lot,
The day, when in the chestnut shade
   I found the blue Forget-me-not.

Love that hath us in the net,[4]
Can he pass, and we forget?
Many suns arise and set.
Many a chance the years beget.
Love the gift is Love the debt.
     Even so.
Love is hurt with jar and fret.
Love is made a vague regret.
Eyes with idle tears are wet.
Idle habit links us yet.
What is love? for we forget:
     Ah, no! no!

Look thro' mine eyes with thine. True wife,
   Round my true heart thine arms entwine
My other dearer life in life,
   Look thro' my very soul with thine!
Untouch'd with any shade of years,
   May those kind eyes for ever dwell!
They have not shed a many tears,
   Dear eyes, since first I knew them well.

Yet tears they shed: they had their part
   Of sorrow: for when time was ripe,
The still affection of the heart
   Became an outward breathing type,
That into stillness past again,
   And left a want unknown before;

50

60

70

80

190

200

210

220

---

[4] This poem was thoroughly revised from its version printed in the 1832 volume. In 1832, the lover remembers this song:

All yesternight you met me not.
My ladylove, forget me not.
When I am gone, regret me not,
But, here or there, forget me not.
With your arched eyebrow threat me not,
   And tremulous eyes, like April skies,
   That seem to say, "forget me not."
I pray you, love, forget me not.

In idle sorrow set me not;
Regret me not: forget me not:
Oh! leave me not; oh, let me not
Wear quite away;—forget me not.
With rougish laughter fret me not
   From dewy eyes, like April skies,
   That ever *look,* "forget me not."
Blue as the blue forget-me-not.

Although the loss had brought us pain,
230   That loss but made us love the more,

With farther lookings on. The kiss,
    The woven arms, seem but to be
Weak symbols of the settled bliss,
    The comfort, I have found in thee:
But that God bless thee, dear—who wrought
    Two spirits to one equal mind—
With blessings beyond hope or thought,
    With blessings which no words can find.

Arise, and let us wander forth,
240   To yon old mill across the wolds;
For look, the sunset, south and north,
    Winds all the vale in rosy folds,
And fires your narrow casement glass,
    Touching the sullen pool below:
On the chalk-hill the bearded grass
    Is dry and dewless. Let us go.
                    1832; revised 1842

Œnone was a river nymph and prophet. She was married to Paris, son of Priam, ruler of Troy. While tending his flock of sheep on Mount Ida, near Troy, Paris was asked by Here, wife of Zeus, and Pallas Athena and Aphrodite, the goddesses of wisdom and of love, to decide the award of an apple which Eris (Discord) had thrown into a gathering of the gods, saying that it was to be given to the most fair. After Paris awarded the prize to Aphrodite, he goes to Sparta and returns with Helen, the most beautiful woman in the world. This act issues in the Trojan War and the eventual destruction of Troy, which Œnone dimly foresees at the end of this poem. In a part of the story that Tennyson does not recount, Paris is wounded in the war and returns to Mount Ida to ask Œnone to heal him. She refuses, later repents of her refusal, and hangs herself when she learns that he has died.

Œnone (1832)

There is a dale in Ida, lovelier
Than any in old Ionia, beautiful
With emerald slopes of sunny sward, that lean
Above the loud glenriver,[1] which hath worn
A path thro' steepdown granite walls below
Mantled with flowering tendriltwine. In front
The cedarshadowy valleys open wide.

Far-seen, high over all the Godbuilt wall
And many a snowycolumned range divine,
Mounted with awful sculptures—men and
    Gods,
The work of Gods—bright on the darkblue sky
The windy citadel of Ilion
Shone, like the crown of Troas.[2] Hither came
Mournful Œnone, wandering forlorn
Of Paris, once her playmate. Round her neck,
Her neck all marblewhite and marblecold,
Floated her hair or seemed to float in rest.
She, leaning on a vine-entwinèd stone,
Sang to the stillness, till the mountain-shadow
Sloped downward to her seat from the upper
    cliff.

"O mother Ida, manyfountained Ida,
Dear mother Ida, hearken ere I die.
The grasshopper is silent in the grass,
The lizard with his shadow on the stone
Sleeps like a shadow, and the scarlet winged
Cicala in the noonday leapeth not.
Along the water-rounded granite-rock
The purple flower droops: the golden bee
Is lily-cradled: I alone awake.
My eyes are full of tears, my heart of love,
My heart is breaking, and my eyes are dim,
And I am all aweary of my life.

"O mother Ida, many-fountain'd Ida,
Dear mother Ida, hearken ere I die.
Hear me, O Earth, hear me, O Hills, O Caves
That house the cold crown'd snake! O moun-
    tain brooks,
I am the daughter of a River-God,
Hear me, for I will speak, and build up all
My sorrow with my song, as yonder walls
Rose slowly to a music slowly breathed,
A cloud that gather'd shape; for it may be
That, while I speak of it, a little while
My heart may wander from its deeper woe.

"O mother Ida, many-fountain'd Ida,
Dear mother Ida, hearken ere I die.
Aloft the mountain lawn was dewy-dark,
And dewy dark aloft the mountain pine.
Beautiful Paris, evil-hearted Paris,
Leading a jet-black goat white-horn'd, white-
    hooved,
Came up from reedy Simois[3] all alone.

---

[1] Tennyson's note in standard edition: "I had an idiotic hatred of hyphens in those days, but though I printed such words as "glénríver," "téndriltwíne" I always gave them in reading their full two accents. Coleridge thought because of these hyphenated words that I could not scan" (I, 686–687).

[2] Ilion: Troy; Troas—the region of which Troy was the capital.   [3] Simois: a river.

"O mother Ida, hearken ere I die.
I sate alone: the goldensandalled morn
Rosehued the scornful hills: I sate alone
With downdrop eyes: whitebreasted like a star
Fronting the dawn he came: a leopard skin
From his white shoulder drooped: his sunny
    hair
Clustered about his temples like a God's:
And his cheek brightened, as the foambow
    brightens
When the wind blows the foam; and I called
    out,
'Welcome, Apollo, welcome home, Apollo,
Apollo, my Apollo, loved Apollo.'

"Dear mother Ida, hearken ere I die.
He, mildly smiling, in his milkwhite palm
Close-held a golden apple, lightningbright
With changeful flashes, dropt with dew of
    Heaven
Ambrosially smelling. From his lip,
Curved crimson, the fullflowing river of speech
Came down upon my heart.
                    'My own Œnone,
Beautifulbrowed Œnone, mine own soul,
Behold this fruit, whose gleaming rind ingrav'n
"For the most fair" in aftertime may breed
Deep evilwilledness of heaven and sere
Heartburning toward hallowed Ilion;
And all the colour of my afterlife
Will be the shadow of today. Today
Here and Pallas and the floating grace
Of laughterloving Aphrodite meet
In manyfolded Ida to receive
This meed of beauty, she to whom my hand
Award the palm. Within the green hillside,
Under yon whispering tuft of oldest pine,
Is an ingoing grotto, strown with spar[4]
And ivymatted at the mouth, wherein
Thou unbeholden may'st behold, unheard
Hear all, and see thy Paris judge of Gods.'

Dear mother Ida, hearken ere I die.
It was the deep midnoon: one silvery cloud
Had lost his way between the piney hills.
They came—all three—the Olympian god-
    desses:
Naked they came to the smoothswarded bower,
Lustrous with lilyflower, violeteyed
Both white and blue, with lotetree-fruit[5] thick-
    set,
Shadowed with singing pine: and all the while,
Above, the overwandering ivy and vine

This way and that in many a wild festoon
Ran riot, garlanding the gnarlèd boughs
With bunch and berry and flower thro' and
    thro'.
On the treetops a golden glorious cloud
Leaned, slowly dropping down ambrosial dew.
How beautiful they were, too beautiful   100
To look upon! but Paris was to me
More lovelier than all the world beside.

"O mother Ida, hearken ere I die.
First spake the imperial Olympian
With archèd eyebrow smiling sovranly,
Fulleyèd Here. She to Paris made
Proffer of royal power, ample rule
Unquestioned, overflowing revenue
Wherewith to embellish state 'from many a
    vale
And riversundered champaign clothed with
    corn,   110
Or upland glebe wealthy in oil and wine—
Honour and homage, tribute, tax and toll
From many an inland town, and haven large,
Mast-thronged below her shadowing citadel
In glassy bays among her tallest towers.'

O mother Ida, hearken ere I die.
Still she spake on and still she spake of power
'Which in all action is the end of all.
Power fitted to the season, measured by
The height of the general feeling, wisdomborn   120
And throned of wisdom—from all neighbour
    crowns
Alliance and allegiance evermore.
Such boon from me Heaven's Queen to thee
    kingborn,
A shepherd all thy life but yet kingborn,
Should come most welcome, seeing men, in
    power
Only, are likest Gods, who have attain'd
Rest in a happy place and quiet seats
Above the thunder, with undying bliss
In knowledge of their own supremacy,
The changeless calm of undisputed right,   130
The highest height and topmost strength of
    power.'

"Dear mother Ida, hearken ere I die.
She ceased, and Paris held the costly fruit
Out at arm's-length, so much the thought of
    power
Flatter'd his spirit; but Pallas where she stood
Somewhat apart, her clear and bared limbs

---

[4] Spar: crystalline minerals.   [5] Lote-tree: lotus tree.

O'erthwarted with the brazen-head'd spear
Upon her pearly shoulder leaning cold,
The while, above, her full and earnest eye
140 Over her snow-cold breast and angry cheek
Kept watch, waiting decision, made reply.

" 'Selfreverence, selfknowledge, selfcontrol
Are the three hinges of the gates of Life,
That open into power, everyway
Without horizon, bound or shadow or cloud.
Yet not for power (power of herself
Will come uncalled-for) but to live by law,
Acting the law we live by without fear,
And because right is right, to follow right
Were wisdom, in the scorn of consequence.
150 (Dear mother Ida, hearken ere I die.)
Not as men value gold because it tricks
And blazons outward Life with ornament,
But rather as the miser, for itself.
Good for selfgood doth half destroy selfgood.
The means and end, like two coiled snakes,
    infect
Each other, bound in one with hateful love.
So both into the fountain and the stream
A drop of poison falls. Come hearken to me,
160 And look upon me and consider me,
So shalt thou find me fairest, so endurance,
Like to an athlete's arm, shall still become
Sinew'd with motion, till thine active will
(As the dark body of the Sun robed round
With his own ever-emanating lights)
Be flooded o'er with her own effluences,
And thereby grow to freedom.'
             "Here she ceas'd,
And Paris ponder'd, and I cried, 'O Paris,
Give it to Pallas!' but he heard me not,
170 Or hearing would not hear me, woe is me!

"O mother Ida, many-fountain'd Ida,
Dear mother Ida, hearken ere I die.
Idalian Aphrodite oceanborn,
Fresh as the foam, newbathed in Paphian[6]
    wells,
With rosy slender fingers upward drew
From her warm brow and bosom her dark hair
Fragrant and thick, and on her head upbound
In a purple band: below her lucid neck
Shone ivorylike, and from the ground her foot
180 Gleamed rosywhite, and o'er her rounded form
Between the shadows of the vinebunches
Floated the glowing sunlights, as she moved.

"Dear mother Ida, hearken ere I die.
She with a subtle smile in her mild eyes,
The herald of her triumph, drawing nigh
Half-whisper'd in his ear, 'I promise thee
The fairest and most loving wife in Greece,'
I only saw my Paris raise his arm:
I only saw great Here's angry eyes,
As she withdrew into the golden cloud,   19
And I was left alone within the bower;
And from that time to this I am alone,
And I shall be alone until I die.

"Yet, mother Ida, hearken ere I die.
Fairest—why fairest wife? am I not fair?
My love hath told me so a thousand times.
Methinks I must be fair, for yesterday,
When I past by, a wild and wanton pard,[7]
Eyed like the evening star, with playful tail
Crouch'd fawning in the weed. Most loving is
    she?   20
Ah me, my mountain shepherd, that my arms
Were wound about thee, and my hot lips prest
Close, close to thine in that quick-falling dew
Of fruitful kisses, thick as Autumn rains
Flash in the pools of whirling Simois.

Dear mother Ida, hearken ere I die.
They came, they cut away my tallest pines,[8]
My dark tall pines, that plumed the craggy
    ledge
High over the blue gorge, or lower down
Filling greengulphèd Ida, all between   21
The snowy peak and snow-white cataract
Foster'd the callow eaglet—from beneath
Whose thick mysterious boughs in the dark
    morn
The panther's roar came muffled, while I sat
Low in the valley. Never, never more
Shall lone Œnone see the morning mist
Sweep thro' them; never see them overlaid
With narrow moon-lit slips of silver cloud,
Between the loud stream and the trembling
    stars.

"Oh! mother Ida, hearken ere I die.   2
Hath he not sworn his love a thousand times,
In this green valley, under this green hill,
Ev'n on this hand, and sitting on this stone?
Seal'd it with kisses? water'd it with tears?
O happy tears, and how unlike to these!
O happy Heaven, how canst thou see my face?
O happy earth, how canst thou bear my weight?

[6] Idalia and Paphos were cities in Cyprus associated with the worship of Aphrodite.
[7] Pard: leopard.   [8] To build the ships in which Paris was to sail for Helen.

O death, death, death, thou ever-floating cloud,
There are enough unhappy on this earth,
230 Pass by the happy souls, that love to live:
I pray thee, pass before my light of life,
And shadow all my soul, that I may die.
Thou weighest heavy on the heart within,
Weigh heavy on my eyelids: let me die.

"Yet, mother Ida, hear me ere I die.
I will not die alone, for fiery thoughts
Do shape themselves within me, more and
    more,
Whereof I catch the issue, as I hear
Dead sounds at night come from the inmost
    hills,
240 Like footsteps upon wool. I dimly see
My far-off doubtful purpose, as a mother
Conjectures of the features of her child
Ere it is born. I will not die alone.

Dear mother Ida, hearken ere I die.
Hear me, O earth. I will not die alone,
Lest their shrill happy laughter come to me
Walking the cold and starless road of Death
Uncomforted, leaving my ancient love
With the Greek woman. I will rise and go
250 Down into Troy, and ere the stars come forth
Talk with the wild Cassandra,[9] for she says
A fire dances before her, and a sound
Rings ever in her ears of armed men.
What this may be I know not, but I know
That, wheresoe'er I am by night and day,
All earth and air seem only burning fire."
                                        1832

Œnone (1842)

There lies a vale in Ida, lovelier
Than all the valleys of Ionian hills.
The swimming vapour slopes athwart the glen,
Puts forth an arm, and creeps from pine to
    pine,
And loiters, slowly drawn. On either hand
The lawns and meadow-ledges midway down
Hang rich in flowers, and far below them roars
The long brook falling thro' the clov'n ravine
In cataract after cataract to the sea.
0 Behind the valley topmost Gargarus
Stands up and takes the morning; but in front
The gorges, opening wide apart, reveal

Troas and Ilion's column'd citadel,
The crown of Troas.
                    Hither came at noon
Mournful Œnone, wandering forlorn
Of Paris, once her playmate on the hills.
Her cheek had lost the rose, and round her
    neck
Floated her hair or seem'd to float in rest.
She, leaning on a fragment twined with vine,
Sang to the stillness, till the mountain-shade   20
Sloped downward to her seat from the upper
    cliff.

"O mother Ida, many-fountain'd Ida,
Dear mother Ida, harken ere I die.
For now the noonday quiet holds the hill:
The grasshopper is silent in the grass:
The lizard, with his shadow on the stone,
Rests like a shadow, and the winds are dead.[1]
The purple flower droops, the golden bee
Is lily-cradled; I alone awake.
My eyes are full of tears, my heart of love,   30
My heart is breaking, and my eyes are dim,
And I am all aweary of my life.

"O mother Ida, many-fountain'd Ida,
Dear mother Ida, harken ere I die.
Hear me, O Earth, hear me, O Hills, O Caves
That house the cold crown'd snake! O moun-
    tain brooks,
I am the daughter of a River-God,
Hear me, for I will speak, and build up all
My sorrow with my song, as yonder walls
Rose slowly to a music slowly breathed,   40
A cloud that gather'd shape; for it may be
That, while I speak of it, a little while
My heart may wander from its deeper woe.

"O mother Ida, many-fountain'd Ida,
Dear mother Ida, harken ere I die.
I waited underneath the dawning hills,
Aloft the mountain lawn was dewy-dark,
And dewy-dark aloft the mountain pine:
Beautiful Paris, evil-hearted Paris,
Leading a jet-black goat white-horn'd, white-
    hooved,   50
Came up from reedy Simois all alone.

"O mother Ida, harken ere I die.
Far-off the torrent call'd me from the cleft:

[9] Paris' sister, also a prophet, who foretold (as Œnone also seems to foretell) the Trojan War.
[1] In the 1842 volume this line read: ". . . and the cicala sleeps." Tennyson's note: "I did not like the jump, 'Rests like a shadow—and the cicala sleeps.' Moreover, in the heat of noon the cicala is generally at its loudest, though I have read that, in extreme heat, it is silent" (I, 688) .

Far up the solitary morning smote
The streaks of virgin snow. With down-dropt
      eyes
I sat alone; white-breasted like a star
Fronting the dawn he moved; a leopard skin
Droop'd from his shoulder, but his sunny hair
Cluster'd about his temples like a God's:
60   And his cheek brighten'd as the foam-bow
      brightens
When the wind blows the foam, and all my
      heart
Went forth to embrace him coming ere he
      came.

      "Dear mother Ida, harken ere I die.
He smiled, and opening out his milk-white
      palm
Disclosed a fruit of pure Hesperian[2] gold,
That smelt ambrosially, and while I look'd
And listen'd, the full-flowing river of speech
Came down upon my heart.
                          " 'My own Œnone,
Beautiful-brow'd Œnone, my own soul,
Behold this fruit, whose gleaming rind
70   ingraven
"For the most fair," would seem to award it
      thine,
As lovelier than whatever Oread[3] haunt
The knolls of Ida, loveliest in all grace
Of movement, and the charm of married
      brows.'

      "Dear mother Ida, harken ere I die.
He prest the blossom of his lips to mine,
And added, 'This was cast upon the board,
When all the full-faced presence of the Gods
Ranged in the halls of Peleus; whereupon
Rose feud, with question unto whom 'twere
80   due:
But light-foot Iris[4] brought it yester-eve,
Delivering, that to me, by common voice
Elected umpire, Herè comes to-day,
Pallas and Aphroditè, claiming each
This meed of fairest. Thou, within the cave
Behind yon whispering tuft of oldest pine,
Mayst well behold them unbeheld, unheard
Hear all, and see thy Paris judge of Gods.'

      "Dear mother Ida, harken ere I die.
90   It was the deep midnoon: one silvery cloud

Had lost his way between the piney sides
Of this long glen. Then to the bower they came,
Naked they came to that smooth-swarded
      bower,
And at their feet the crocus brake like fire,
Violet, amaracus, and asphodel,
Lotos and lilies; and a wind arose,
And overhead the wandering ivy and vine,
This way and that, in many a wild festoon
Ran riot, garlanding the gnarled boughs
With bunch and berry and flower thro' and
      thro'.   100

      "O mother Ida, harken ere I die.
On the tree-tops a crested peacock lit,
And o'er him flow'd a golden cloud, and lean'd
Upon him, slowly dropping fragrant dew.
Then first I heard the voice of her, to whom
Coming thro' Heaven, like a light that grows
Larger and clearer, with one mind the Gods
Rise up for reverence. She to Paris made
Proffer of royal power, ample rule
Unquestion'd, overflowing revenue   110
Wherewith to embellish state, 'from many a
      vale
And river-sunder'd champaign clothed with
      corn,
Or labour'd mine undrainable of ore.
Honour,' she said, 'and homage, tax and toll,
From many an inland town and haven large,
Mast-throng'd beneath her shadowing citadel
In glassy bays among her tallest towers.'

      "O mother Ida, harken ere I die.
Still she spake on and still she spake of power,
'Which in all action is the end of all;   120
Power fitted to the season; wisdom-bred
And throned of wisdom—from all neighbor
      crowns
Alliance and allegiance, till thy hand
Fail from the sceptre-staff. Such boon from me,
From me, Heaven's Queen, Paris, to thee king-
      born,
A shepherd all thy life but yet king-born,
Should come most welcome, seeing men, in
      power
Only, are likest Gods, who have attain'd
Rest in a happy place and quiet seats
Above the thunder, with undying bliss   130
In knowledge of their own supremacy.'

---

[2] The golden apples of the garden of Hesperus, guarded by a dragon, were gifts of the Earth
to Here.
[3] Oread: mountain nymph.
[4] Iris, goddess of the rainbow, was the messenger used by the gods when they intended discord.

"Dear mother Ida, harken ere I die.
She ceased, and Paris held the costly fruit
Out at arm's-length, so much the thought of
    power
Flatter'd his spirit; but Pallas where she stood
Somewhat apart, her clear and bared limbs
O'erthwarted with the brazen-headed spear
Upon her pearly shoulder leaning cold,
The while, above, her full and earnest eye
40 Over her snow-cold breast and angry cheek
Kept watch, waiting decision, made reply.

    " 'Self-reverence, self-knowledge, self-control,
These three alone lead life to sovereign power.
Yet not for power (power of herself
Would come uncall'd for) but to live by law,
Acting the law we live by without fear;
And, because right is right, to follow right
Were wisdom in the scorn of consequence.'

    "Dear mother Ida, harken ere I die.
50 Again she said: 'I woo thee not with gifts.
Sequel of guerdon[5] could not alter me
To fairer. Judge thou me by what I am,
So shalt thou find me fairest.
                Yet, indeed,
If gazing on divinity disrobed
Thy mortal eyes are frail to judge of fair,
Unbias'd by self-profit, oh! rest thee sure
That I shall love thee well and cleave to thee,
So that my vigour, wedded to thy blood,
Shall strike within thy pulses, like a God's,
60 To push thee forward thro' a life of shocks,
Dangers, and deeds, until endurance grow
Sinew'd with action, and the full-grown will,
Circled thro' all experiences, pure law,
Commeasure perfect freedom.'
                "Here she ceas'd,
And Paris ponder'd, and I cried, 'O Paris,
Give it to Pallas!' but he heard me not,
Or hearing would not hear me, woe is me!

    "O mother Ida, many-fountain'd Ida,
Dear mother Ida, harken ere I die.
70 Idalian Aphroditè beautiful,
Fresh as the foam, new-bathed in Paphian
    wells,
With rosy slender fingers backward drew
From her warm brows and bosom her deep hair
Ambrosial, golden round her lucid throat
And shoulder: from the violets her light foot
Shone rosy-white, and o'er her rounded form

Between the shadows of the vine-bunches
Floated the glowing sunlights, as she moved.

    "Dear mother Ida, harken ere I die.   180
She with a subtle smile in her mild eyes,
The herald of her triumph, drawing nigh
Half-whisper'd in his ear, 'I promise thee
The fairest and most loving wife in Greece,'
She spoke and laugh'd; I shut my sight for fear;
But when I look'd, Paris had raised his arm,
And I beheld great Herè's angry eyes,
As she withdrew into the golden cloud,
And I was left alone within the bower;
And from that time to this I am alone,
And I shall be alone until I die.   190

    "Yet, mother Ida, harken ere I die.
Fairest—why fairest wife? am I not fair?
My love hath told me so a thousand times.
Methinks I must be fair, for yesterday,
When I past by, a wild and wanton pard,
Eyed like the evening star, with playful tail
Crouch'd fawning in the weed. Most loving is
    she?
Ah me, my mountain shepherd, that my arms
Were wound about thee, and my hot lips prest
Close, close to thine in that quick-falling dew   200
Of fruitful kisses, thick as Autumn rains
Flash in the pools of whirling Simois!

    "O mother, hear me yet before I die.
They came, they cut away my tallest pines,
My tall dark pines, that plumed the craggy
    ledge
High over the blue gorge, and all between
The snowy peak and snow-white cataract
Foster'd the callow eaglet—from beneath
Whose thick mysterious boughs in the dark
    morn
The panther's roar came muffled, while I sat   210
Low in the valley. Never, never more
Shall lone Œnone see the morning mist
Sweep thro' them; never see them overlaid
With narrow moon-lit slips of silver cloud,
Between the loud stream and the trembling
    stars.

    "O mother, hear me yet before I die.
I wish that somewhere in the ruin'd folds,
Among the fragments tumbled from the glens,
Or the dry thickets, I could meet with her
The Abominable,[6] that uninvited came   220

---

[5] Tennyson's note: "addition of reward."   [6] Eris.

Into the fair Peleïan banquet-hall,
And cast the golden fruit upon the board,
And bred this change; that I might speak my
      mind,
And tell her to her face how much I hate
Her presence, hated both of Gods and men.

"O mother, hear me yet before I die.
Hath he not sworn his love a thousand times,
In this green valley, under this green hill,
Ev'n on this hand, and sitting on this stone?
230   Seal'd it with kisses? water'd it with tears?
O happy tears, and how unlike to these!
O happy Heaven, how canst thou see my face?
O happy earth, how canst thou bear my weight?
O death, death, death, thou ever-floating cloud,
There are enough unhappy on this earth,
Pass by the happy souls, that love to live:
I pray thee, pass before my light of life,
And shadow all my soul, that I may die.
Thou weighest heavy on the heart within,
240   Weigh heavy on my eyelids: let me die.

"O mother, hear me yet before I die.
I will not die alone, for fiery thoughts
Do shape themselves within me, more and
      more,
Whereof I catch the issue, as I hear
Dead sounds at night come from the inmost
      hills,
Like footsteps upon wool. I dimly see
My far-off doubtful purpose, as a mother
Conjectures of the features of her child
Ere it is born: her child!—a shudder comes
250   Across me: never child be born of me,
Unblest, to vex me with his father's eyes!

"O mother, hear me yet before I die.
Hear me, O earth. I will not die alone,
Lest their shrill happy laughter come to me
Walking the cold and starless road of Death
Uncomforted, leaving my ancient love
With the Greek woman. I will rise and go
Down into Troy, and ere the stars come forth
Talk with the wild Cassandra, for she says
260   A fire dances before her, and a sound
Rings ever in her ears of armed men.
What this may be I know not, but I know
That, wheresoe'er I am by night and day,
All earth and air seem only burning fire."
                                        1842

*This poem preceded "The Palace of Art" in both
the 1832 and 1842 volumes. Although "The Palace
of Art" was thoroughly revised between 1832 and
1842, its prefatory poem was only slightly changed.
It is addressed to R. C. Trench. Tennyson's note in
the standard edition: "Trench (afterwards Arch-
bishop of Dublin) said, when we were at Trinity
(Cambridge) together, 'Tennyson, we cannot live
in Art.' This poem is the embodiment of my own
belief that the Godlike life is with man and for
man" (I, 691–692).*

To ————

With the Following Poem

I send you here a sort of allegory,
  (For you will understand it) of a soul,
A sinful soul possess'd of many gifts,
A spacious garden full of flowering weeds,
A glorious Devil, large in heart and brain,
That did love Beauty only, (Beauty seen
In all varieties of mould and mind)
And Knowledge for its beauty; or if Good,
Good only for its beauty, seeing not
That Beauty, Good, and Knowledge are three
      sisters   10
That doat upon each other, friends to man,
Living together under the same roof,
And never can be sunder'd without tears.
And he that shuts Love out, in turn shall be
Shut out from Love, and on her threshold lie
Howling in outer darkness. Not for this
Was common clay ta'en from the common
      earth
Moulded by God, and temper'd with the tears
Of angels to the perfect shape of man.
                                   1832; 1842

The Palace of Art

I built my soul a lordly pleasure-house,
  Wherein at ease for aye to dwell.
I said, "O Soul, make merry and carouse,
  Dear soul, for all is well."

A huge crag-platform, smooth as burnish'd
      brass,
  I chose. The ranged ramparts bright
From level meadow-bases of deep grass
  Suddenly scaled the light.

Thereon I built it firm. Of ledge or shelf
  The rock rose clear, or winding stair.   10
My soul would live alone unto herself
  In her high palace there.

And "while the world runs round and round,"
    I said,
"Reign thou apart, a quiet king,
Still as, while Saturn whirls, his stedfast shade
    Sleeps on his luminous ring."[1]

To which my soul made answer readily:
    "Trust me, in bliss I shall abide
In this great mansion, that is built for me,
    So royal-rich and wide."
           *   *   *   *
            *   *   *   *[2]

Four courts I made, East, West and South and
    North,
    In each a squared lawn, wherefrom
The golden gorge of dragons spouted forth
    A flood of fountain-foam.

And round the cool green courts there ran a
    row
    Of cloisters, branch'd like mighty woods,
Echoing all night to that sonorous flow
    Of spouted fountain-floods.

And round the roofs a gilded gallery
    That lent broad verge to distant lands,
Far as the wild swan wings, to where the sky
    Dipt down to sea and sands.

From those four jets four currents in one swell
    Across the mountain stream'd below
In misty folds, that floating as they fell
    Lit up a torrent-bow.

And high on every peak a statue seem'd
    To hang on tiptoe, tossing up
A cloud of incense of all odour steam'd
    From out a golden cup.

So that she thought, "And who shall gaze upon
    My palace with unblinded eyes,
While this great bow will waver in the sun,
    And that sweet incense rise?"

For that sweet incense rose and never fail'd,
    And, while day sank or mounted higher,
The light äerial gallery, golden-rail'd,
    Burnt like a fringe of fire.

Likewise the deep-set windows, stain'd and
    traced,
    Would seem slow-flaming crimson fires   50
From shadow'd grots of arches interlaced,
    And tipt with frost-like spires.
           *   *   *   *
           *   *   *   *

Full of long-sounding corridors it was,
    That over-vaulted grateful gloom,
Thro' which the livelong day my soul did pass,
    Well-pleased, from room to room.

Full of great rooms and small the palace stood,
    All various, each a perfect whole
From living Nature, fit for every mood
    And change of my still soul.   60

For some were hung with arras green and blue,
    Showing a gaudy summer-morn,
Where with puff'd cheek the belted hunter
    blew
    His wreathed bugle-horn.

One seem'd all dark and red—a tract of sand,
    And some one pacing there alone,
Who paced for ever in a glimmering land,
    Lit with a low large moon.

One show'd an iron coast and angry waves
    You seem'd to hear them climb and call   70
And roar rock-thwarted under bellowing caves,
    Beneath the windy wall.

And one, a full-fed river winding slow
    By herds upon an endless plain,
The ragged rims of thunder brooding low,
    With shadow-streaks of rain.

And one, the reapers at their sultry toil.
    In front they bound the sheaves. Behind
Were realms of upland, prodigal in oil,
    And hoary[3] to the wind.   80

And one a foreground black with stones and
    slags,
    Beyond, a line of heights, and higher
All barr'd with long white cloud the scornful
    crags,
    And highest, snow and fire.

---

[1] Hallam Tennyson's note in the standard edition: "The shadow of Saturn thrown on the luminous ring, though the planet revolves in ten and a half hours, appears to be motionless" (I, 693).

[2] Tennyson marked the divisions of the poem by asterisks.

[3] Hoary: the underside of the olive leaf, which shows in the wind, is white.

And one, an English home—gray twilight
        pour'd
    On dewy pastures, dewy trees,
Softer than sleep—all things in order stored,
    A haunt of ancient Peace.

Nor these alone, but every landscape fair,
90   As fit for every mood of mind,
Or gay, or grave, or sweet, or stern, was there,
    Not less than truth design'd.
                *   *   *   *
                *   *   *   *
Or the maid-mother by a crucifix.
    In tracts of pasture sunny-warm.
Beneath branch-work of costly sardonyx⁴
    Sat smiling, babe in arm.

Or in a clear-wall'd city on the sea,
    Near gilded organ-pipes, her hair
Wound with white roses, slept Saint Cecily;⁵
100   An angel look'd at her.

Or thronging all one porch of Paradise
    A group of Houris⁶ bow'd to see
The dying Islamite, with hands and eyes
    That said, We wait for thee.

Or mythic Uther's deeply-wounded son⁷
    In some fair space of sloping greens
Lay, dozing in the vale of Avalon,
    And watch'd by weeping queens.

Or hollowing one hand against his ear,
110   To list a foot-fall, ere he saw
The wood-nymph, stay'd the Ausonian king⁸ to
        hear
    Of wisdom and of law.

Or over hills with peaky tops engrail'd,⁹
    And many a tract of palm and rice,

The throne of Indian Cama¹⁰ slowly sail'd
    A summer fann'd with spice.

Or sweet Europa's¹¹ mantle blew unclasp'd,
    From off her shoulder backward borne:
From one hand droop'd a crocus: one hand
        grasp'd
    The mild bull's golden horn.   120

Or else flush'd Ganymede,¹² his rosy thigh
    Half-buried in the Eagle's down,
Sole as a flying star shot thro' the sky
    Above the pillar'd town.

Nor these alone: but every legend fair
    Which the supreme Caucasian mind¹³
Carved out of Nature for itself was there,
    Not less than life design'd.
                *   *   *   *
                *   *   *   *
Then in the towers I placed great bells that
        swung,
    Moved of themselves, with silver sound;   130
And with choice paintings of wise men I hung
    The royal dais round.

For there was Milton like a seraph strong,
    Beside him Shakespeare bland and mild;
And there the world-worn Dante grasp'd his
        song,
    And somewhat grimly smiled.

And there the Ionian father¹⁴ of the rest;
    A million wrinkles carved his skin;
A hundred winters snow'd upon his breast,
    From cheek and throat and chin.   140

Above, the fair hall-ceiling stately-set
    Many an arch high up did lift,
And angels rising and descending met
    With interchange of gift.

---

⁴ Sardonyx: the color of this mineral can be changed by heat so that it can be carved to imitate, as Tennyson says in his note in the standard edition, "among other things, bunches of grapes with green tendrils" (I, 693).
⁵ St. Cecilia was a virgin martyr of the early Church; she is the patron saint of church music.
⁶ Houris: nymphs of Mohammedean paradise.   ⁷ Uther's son: Arthur.
⁸ Ausonian king: Numa Pompilius, second king of Rome, instructed in the laws of his kingdom by the nymph Egeria.
⁹ Engrailed: indented at the edge with small concave curves.
¹⁰ Cama: Tennyson's note: "the Hindu God of young love, son of Brahma" (I, 695).
¹¹ Europa was abducted by Zeus, in the form of a bull.
¹² Ganymede: a beautiful young man also admired by Zeus, and carried off by one of Zeus' eagles to serve as cupbearer to the gods.
¹³ Hallam Tennyson's note in the standard edition: "The Caucasian range was thought to form the N. W. border of Western Asia, from which the races who peopled Europe originally came" (I, 695).
¹⁴ Ionian father: Homer.

Below was all mosaic choicely plann'd
  With cycles of the human tale
Of this wide world, the times of every land
  So wrought they will not fail.

The people here, a beast of burden slow,
  Toil'd onward, prick'd with goads and
    stings;
Here play'd, a tiger, rolling to and fro
  The heads and crowns of kings;

Here rose, an athlete, strong to break or bind
  All force in bonds that might endure,
And here once more like some sick man
    declined,
  And trusted any cure.

But over these she trod: and those great bells
  Began to chime. She took her throne:
She sat betwixt the shining Oriels,[15]
  To sing her songs alone.

And thro' the topmost Oriels' coloured flame
  Two godlike faces gazed below;
Plato the wise, and large-brow'd Verulam,
  The first of those who know.

And all those names that in their motion were
  Full-welling fountain-heads of change,
Betwixt the slender shafts were blazon'd fair
  In diverse raiment strange:

Thro' which the lights, rose, amber, emerald,
    blue,
  Flush'd in her temples and her eyes,
And from her lips, as morn from Memnon,[16]
    drew
  Rivers of melodies.

No nightingale delighteth to prolong
  Her low preamble all alone,
More than my soul to hear her echo'd song
  Throb thro' the ribbed stone;

Singing and murmuring in her feastful mirth,
  Joying to feel herself alive,
Lord over Nature, Lord of the visible earth,
  Lord of the senses five;

Communing with herself: "All these are mine,
  And let the world have peace or wars,
'T is one to me." She—when young night
    divine
  Crown'd dying day with stars,

Making sweet close of his delicious toils—
  Lit light in wreaths and anadems,[17]
And pure quintessences of precious oils
  In hollow'd moons of gems,

To mimic heaven; and clapt her hands and
    cried,
  "I marvel if my still delight   190
In this great house so royal-rich, and wide,
  Be flatter'd to the height.

"O all things fair to sate my various eyes!
  O shapes and hues that please me well!
O silent faces of the Great and Wise,
  My Gods, with whom I dwell!

"O God-like isolation which art mine,
  I can but count thee perfect gain,
What time I watch the darkening droves of
    swine
  That range on yonder plain.   200

"In filthy sloughs they roll a prurient[18] skin,
  They graze and wallow, breed and sleep;
And oft some brainless devil enters in,
  And drives them to the deep."

Then of the moral instinct would she prate
  And of the rising from the dead,
As hers by right of full-accomplish'd Fate;
  And at the last she said:

"I take possession of man's mind and deed.
  I care not what the sects may brawl.   210
I sit as God holding no form of creed,
  But contemplating all."

* * * *
* * * *

Full oft the riddle of the painful earth
  Flash'd thro' her as she sat alone,
Yet not the less held she her solemn mirth,
  And intellectual throne.

---

[15] Oriels: recessed, or bay, windows, here ornamented with colored glass to make likenesses of Plato and Francis Bacon (Verulam).
[16] Memnon: an Ethiopian king whose statue gave forth musical notes when it was struck by the rays of the rising sun.
[17] Anadems: crowns. Hollow'd moons of gems: jewels hollowed to be used as lamps.
[18] Prurient: itching.

And so she throve and prosper'd: so three years
  She prosper'd; on the fourth she fell,
Like Herod,[19] when the shout was in his ears,
    Struck thro' with pangs of hell.   220

Lest she should fail and perish utterly,
  God, before whom ever lie bare
The abysmal deeps of Personality,
    Plagued her with sore despair.

When she would think, where'er she turn'd her
      sight
  The airy hand confusion wrought,
Wrote, "Mene, mene,"[20] and divided quite
    The kingdom of her thought.

Deep dread and loathing of her solitude   230
  Fell on her, from which mood was born
Scorn of herself; again, from out that mood
    Laughter at her self-scorn.

"What! is not this my place of strength," she
      said,
  "My spacious mansion built for me,
Whereof the strong foundation-stones were
      laid
    Since my first memory?"

But in dark corners of her palace stood
  Uncertain shapes; and unawares
On white-eyed phantasms weeping tears of
      blood,   240
    And horrible nightmares,

And hollow shades enclosing hearts of flame,
  And, with dim fretted[21] foreheads all,
On corpses three-months-old at noon she came,
    That stood against the wall.

A spot of dull stagnation, without light
  Or power of movement, seem'd my soul,
'Mid onward-sloping motions infinite
    Making for one sure goal.

A still salt pool, lock'd in with bars of sand,   250
  Left on the shore; that hears all night
The plunging seas draw backward from the
      land
    Their moon-led waters white.

A star that with the choral starry dance
  Join'd not, but stood, and standing saw
The hollow orb of moving Circumstance[22]
    Roll'd round by one fix'd law.

Back on herself her serpent pride had curl'd
  "No voice," she shriek'd in that lone hall,
"No voice breaks thro' the stillness of this
      world:
    One deep, deep silence all!"   260

She, mouldering with the dull earth's moulder-
      ing sod,
  Inwrapt tenfold in slothful shame,
Lay there exiled from eternal God,
    Lost to her place and name;

And death and life she hated equally,
  And nothing saw, for her despair,
But dreadful time, dreadful eternity,
    No comfort anywhere;

Remaining utterly confused with fears,
  And ever worse with growing time,   270
And ever unrelieved by dismal tears,
    And all alone in crime:

Shut up as in a crumbling tomb, girt round
  With blackness as a solid wall,
Far off she seem'd to hear the dully sound
    Of human footsteps fall.

As in strange lands a traveller walking slow,
  In doubt and great perplexity,
A little before moon-rise hears the low
    Moan of an unknown sea;   280

And knows not if it be thunder, or a sound
  Of rocks thrown down, or one deep cry
Of great wild beasts; then thinketh, "I have
      found
    A new land, but I die."

She howl'd aloud, "I am on fire within.
  There comes no murmur of reply.
What is it that will take away my sin,
    And save me lest I die?"

[19] Herod was struck dead as crowds proclaimed that he was not a man but a god.
[20] Mene, mene: the first word of the message dooming the kingdom of Belshazzar, written mysteriously on a wall during a banquet. Daniel 5:25–26.
[21] Tennyson's note: "Not wrinkled, but worm-fretted" (I, 698).
[22] Tennyson's note: "Some old writer calls the Heavens 'the Circumstance.' . . . Here it is more or less a play on the word" (I, 698).

So when four years were wholly finished,
   She threw her royal robes away.
"Make me a cottage in the vale," she said,
   "Where I may mourn and pray.

"Yet pull not down my palace towers, that are
   So lightly, beautifully built.
Perchance I may return with others there
   When I have purged my guilt."
                          1832; revised 1842

The Lotos-Eaters[1]

"Courage!" he said, and pointed toward the
   land,
"This mounting wave will roll us shoreward
   soon."
In the afternoon they came unto a land
In which it seemed always afternoon.
All round the coast the languid air did swoon,
Breathing like one that hath a weary dream.
Full-faced above the valley stood the moon;
And like a downward smoke, the slender
   stream
Along the cliff to fall and pause and fall did
   seem.

A land of streams! some, like a downward
   smoke,
Slow-dropping veils of thinnest lawn, did go;
And some thro' wavering lights and shadows
   broke,
Rolling a slumbrous sheet of foam below.
They saw the gleaming river seaward flow
From the inner land; far off, three mountain-
   tops,
Three silent pinnacles of aged snow,
Stood sunset-flush'd: and, dew'd with showery
   drops,
Up-clomb the shadowy pine above the woven
   copse.

The charmed sunset linger'd low adown
In the red West: thro' mountain clefts the dale
Was seen far inland, and the yellow down
Border'd with palm, and many a winding vale
And meadow, set with slender galingale;[2]

A land where all things always seem'd the same!
And round about the keel with faces pale,
Dark faces pale against that rosy flame,
The mild-eyed melancholy Lotos-eaters came.

Branches they bore of that enchanted stem,
Laden with flower and fruit, whereof they gave
To each, but whoso did receive of them,   30
And taste, to him the gushing of the wave
Far far away did seem to mourn and rave
On alien shores; and if his fellow spake,
His voice was thin, as voices from the grave;
And deep-asleep he seem'd, yet all awake,
And music in his ears his beating heart did
   make.

They sat them down upon the yellow sand,
Between the sun and moon upon the shore;
And sweet it was to dream of Fatherland,
Of child, and wife, and slave; but evermore   40
Most weary seem'd the sea, weary the oar,
Weary the wandering fields of barren foam.
Then some one said, "We will return no
   more;"
And all at once they sang, "Our island home
Is far beyond the wave; we will no longer
   roam."

Choric Song

I

There is sweet music here that softer falls
Than petals from blown roses on the grass,
Or night-dews on still waters between walls
Of shadowy granite, in a gleaming pass;
Music that gentlier on the spirit lies,   50
Than tir'd eyelids upon tir'd[3] eyes;
Music that brings sweet sleep down from the
   blissful skies.
Here are cool mosses deep,
And thro' the moss the ivies creep,
And in the stream the long-leaved flowers weep,
And from the craggy ledge the poppy hangs in
   sleep.

II

Why are we weigh'd upon with heaviness,
And utterly consumed with sharp distress,

---

[1] In the ninth book of *The Odyssey*, early in their journey homeward to Ithaca from the Trojan War, Odysseus and his crew land on the island of the Lotos-eaters, where some of his men are tempted to remain and must be bound and returned to the ships to continue the journey.

[2] Galingale: the aromatic root of certain East Indian plants.

[3] Tennyson's note in the standard edition: "I printed, contrary to my custom, 'tir'd,' not 'tired,' for fear that readers might pronounce the word 'tirèd,' whereas I wished them to read it 'tiërd,' prolonging as much as might be the dipthhongic *i*" (I, 701).

While all things else have rest from weariness?
60 All things have rest: why should we toil alone,
We only toil, who are the first of things,
And make perpetual moan,
Still from one sorrow to another thrown:
Nor ever fold our wings,
And cease from wanderings,
Nor steep our brows in slumber's holy balm;
Nor harken what the inner spirit sings,
"There is no joy but calm!"
Why should we only toil, the roof and crown
of things?

III

70 Lo! in the middle of the wood,
The folded leaf is woo'd from out the bud
With winds upon the branch, and there
Grows green and broad, and takes no care,
Sun-steep'd at noon, and in the moon
Nightly dew-fed; and turning yellow
Falls, and floats adown the air.
Lo! sweeten'd with the summer light,
The full-juiced apple, waxing over-mellow,
Drops in a silent autumn night.
80 All its allotted length of days,
The flower ripens in its place,
Ripens and fades, and falls, and hath no toil,
Fast-rooted in the fruitful soil.

IV

Hateful is the dark-blue sky,
Vaulted o'er the dark-blue sea.
Death is the end of life; ah, why
Should life all labour be?
Let us alone. Time driveth onward fast,
And in a little while our lips are dumb.
90 Let us alone. What is it that will last?
All things are taken from us, and become
Portions and parcels of the dreadful Past.
Let us alone. What pleasure can we have
To war with evil? Is there any peace
In ever climbing up the climbing wave?
All things have rest, and ripen toward the grave
In silence; ripen, fall, and cease:
Give us long rest or death, dark death, or
dreamful ease.

V

How sweet it were, hearing the downward
stream,

With half-shut eyes ever to seem   100
Falling asleep in a half-dream!
To dream and dream, like yonder amber light,
Which will not leave the myrrh-bush on the
height;
To hear each other's whisper'd speech;
Eating the Lotos day by day,
To watch the crisping ripples on the beach,
And tender curving lines of creamy spray;
To lend our hearts and spirits wholly
To the influence of mild-minded melancholy;
To muse and brood and live again in memory,   110
With those old faces of our infancy
Heap'd over with a mound of grass,
Two handfuls of white dust, shut in an urn of
brass!

VI[4]

Dear is the memory of our wedded lives,
And dear the last embraces of our wives
And their warm tears: but all hath suffer'd
change:
For surely now our household hearths are cold:
Our sons inherit us: our looks are strange:
And we should come like ghosts to trouble joy.
Or else the island princes over-bold   120
Have eat our substance, and the minstrel sings
Before them of the ten years' war in Troy,
And our great deeds, as half-forgotten things.
Is there confusion in the little isle?
Let what is broken so remain.
The Gods are hard to reconcile:
'Tis hard to settle order once again.
There *is* confusion worse than death,
Trouble on trouble, pain on pain,
Long labour unto aged breath,   130
Sore task to hearts worn out by many wars
And eyes grown dim with gazing on the pilot-
stars.

VII

But, propt on beds of amaranth and moly,[5]
How sweet (while warm airs lull us, blowing
lowly)
With half-dropt eyelid still,
Beneath a heaven dark and holy,
To watch the long bright river drawing slowly
His waters from the purple hill—

[4] All of the sixth section of the "Choric Song" was added by Tennyson when he revised for
the 1842 volume the version of this poem which appeared in 1832.
[5] Amaranth is a fabled plant that never fades; moly is described in Tennyson's note as "the
sacred herb of mystical power, used as a charm by Odysseus against Circe," a sorceress who later
in his journey turns some of his men into pigs (I, 702).

To hear the dewy echoes calling
From cave to cave thro' the thick-twined vine—
To watch the emerald-colour'd water falling
Thro' many a woven acanthus-wreath divine!
Only to hear and see the far-off sparkling brine,
Only to hear were sweet, stretch'd out beneath
   the pine.

VIII

The Lotos blooms below the barren peak:
The Lotos blows by every winding creek:
All day the wind breathes low with mellower
   tone:
Thro' every hollow cave and alley lone
Round and round the spicy downs the yellow
   Lotos-dust is blown.
We have had enough of action, and of mo-
   tion we,[6]
Roll'd to starboard, roll'd to larboard, when
   the surge was seething free,
Where the wallowing monster spouted his
   foam-fountains in the sea.
Let us swear an oath, and keep it with an equal
   mind,
In the hollow Lotos-land to live and lie
   reclined
On the hills like Gods together, careless of
   mankind.
For they lie beside their nectar, and the bolts
   are hurl'd
Far below them in the valleys, and the clouds
   are lightly curl'd

Round their golden houses, girdled with the
   gleaming world:
Where they smile in secret, looking over wasted
   lands,
Blight and famine, plague and earthquake,
   roaring deeps and fiery sands,
Clanging fights, and flaming towns, and sinking
   ships, and praying hands.
But they smile, they find a music centred in a
   doleful song
Steaming up, a lamentation and an ancient tale
   of wrong,
Like a tale of little meaning tho' the words are
   strong;
Chanted from an ill-used race of men that
   cleave the soil,
Sow the seed, and reap the harvest with
   enduring toil,
Storing yearly little dues of wheat, and wine
   and oil;
Till they perish and they suffer—some, 'tis
   whisper'd—down in hell
Suffer endless anguish, others in Elysian valleys
   dwell,
Resting weary limbs at last on beds of
   asphodel.
Surely, surely, slumber is more sweet than toil,
   the shore
Than labour in the deep mid-ocean, wind and
   wave and oar;
Oh rest ye, brother mariners, we will not
   wander more.

                         1832; revised 1842

---

[6] In the 1832 volume the poem ended with this passage:

We have had enough of motion,
Weariness and wild alarm,
Tossing on the tossing ocean,
Where the tuskèd seahorse walloweth
In a stripe of grassgreen calm,
At noon tide beneath the lee;
And the monstrous narwhale swalloweth
His foamfountains in the sea.
Long enough the winedark wave our weary
   bark did carry.
This is lovelier and sweeter,
Men of Ithaca, this is meeter,
In the hollow rosy vale to tarry,
Like a dreamy Lotos-eater, a delirious Lotos-
   eater
We will eat the Lotos, sweet
As the yellow honeycomb,
In the valley some, and some
On the ancient heights divine;
And no more roam,
On the loud hoar foam,
To the melancholy home
At the limit of the brine,

The little isle of Ithaca, beneath the day's
   decline.
We'll lift no more the shattered oar,
No more unfurl the straining sail;
With the blissful Lotos-eaters pale
We will abide in the golden vale
Of the Lotos-land, till the Lotos fail;
We will not wander more.
Hark! how sweet the horned ewes bleat
On the solitary steeps,
And the merry lizard leaps,
And the foamwhite waters pour;
And the dark pine weeps,
And the lithe vine creeps,
And the heavy melon sleeps
On the level of the shore:
Oh! islanders of Ithaca, we will not wander
   more.
Surely, surely slumber is more sweet than toil,
   the shore
Than labour in the ocean, and rowing with
   the oar.
Oh! islanders of Ithaca, we will return no more.

"You ask me, why, tho' ill at ease"[1]

You ask me, why, tho' ill at ease,
    Within this region I subsist,
    Whose spirits falter in the mist,
And languish for the purple seas.

It is the land that freemen till,
    That sober-suited Freedom chose,
    The land, where girt with friends or foes
A man may speak the thing he will;

A land of settled government,
10   A land of just and old renown,
    Where Freedom slowly broadens down
From precedent to precedent:

Where faction seldom gathers head,
    But by degrees to fullness wrought,
    The strength of some diffusive thought
Hath time and space to work and spread.

Should banded unions persecute
    Opinion, and induce a time
    When single thought is civil crime,
20 And individual freedom mute;

Tho' Power should make from land to land
    The name of Britain trebly great—
    Tho' every channel of the State
Should fill and choke with golden sand—

Yet waft me from the harbour-mouth,
    Wild wind! I seek a warmer sky,
    And I will see before I die
The palms and temples of the South.

                 (1833)   1842

The Epic[1]

At Francis Allen's on the Christmas-eve,—
The game of forfeits done—the girls all kiss'd
Beneath the sacred bush[2] and past away—
The parson Holmes, the poet Everard Hall,
The host, and I sat round the wassail-bowl,
Then half-way ebb'd: and there we held a talk,
How all the old honour had from Christmas gone,
Or gone, or dwindled down to some odd games
In some odd nooks like this; till I, tired out
With cutting eights that day upon the pond,   10
Where, three times slipping from the outer edge,
I bump'd the ice into three several stars,
Fell in a doze; and half-awake I heard
The parson taking wide and wider sweeps,
Now harping on the church-commissioners,
Now hawking at Geology and schism;[3]
Until I woke, and found him settled down
Upon the general decay of faith
Right thro' the world, "at home was little left,
And none abroad: there was no anchor, none,   20
To hold by." Francis, laughing, clapt his hand
On Everard's shoulder, with "I hold by him."
"And I," quoth Everard, "by the wassail-bowl."
"Why yes," I said, "we knew your gift that way
At college: but another which you had,
I mean of verse (for so we held it then),
What came of that?" "You know," said Frank, "he burnt
His epic, his King Arthur, some twelve books"—
And then to me demanding why? "Oh, sir,   30
He thought that nothing new was said, or else
Something so said 'twas nothing—that a truth
Looks freshest in the fashion of the day:
God knows: he has a mint of reasons: ask.
It pleased me well enough." "Nay, nay," said Hall,
"Why take the style of those heroic times?

---

[1] In a note in the standard edition, Hallam Tennyson writes that this poem was written "about 1833." Tennyson adds that with two other poems on political themes—"Of Old Sat Freedom on the Heights" and "Love Thou the Land"—the poem was shown to Wordsworth: "they were the first poems of mine which he read" (I, 710).

[1] In a note in the standard edition Hallam Tennyson quotes his father's friend, Edward FitzGerald: "Morte d'Arthur when read to us from manuscript in 1835 had no introduction or epilogue; which were added to anticipate or excuse the 'faint Homeric echoes,' etc." (I, 712).

[2] Forfeits: any game in which players must surrender some personal item for making a mistake, and redeem it by performing some ludicrous penalty. Sacred bush: mistletoe.

[3] A commission had been established in 1836 to administer the revenues of the church. The commissioners, geological evidence which called into question conventional theological accounts of how and when the earth and its creatures were created, and divisions within the church like those which were to send some of its members into Roman Catholicism, were current topics of controversy in the 1830s.

For nature brings not back the Mastodon,
Nor we those times; and why should any man
Remodel models? these twelve books of mine
Were faint Homeric echoes, nothing-worth,
Mere chaff and draff, much better burnt."
      "But I,"
Said Francis, "pick'd the eleventh from this
      hearth
And have it: keep a thing, its use will come.
I hoard it as a sugar-plum for Holmes."
He laugh'd, and I, tho' sleepy, like a horse
That hears the corn-bin open, prick'd my ears;
For I remember'd Everard's college fame
When we were Freshmen: then at my request
He brought it; and the poet little urged,
But with some prelude of disparagement,
Read, mouthing out his hollow oes and aes,[4]
Deep-chested music, and to this result.

Morte d'Arthur[1]

So all day long the noise of battle roll'd
Among the mountains by the winter sea;
Until King Arthur's table, man by man,
Had fallen in Lyonnesse[2] about their Lord,
King Arthur: then, because his wound was
      deep,
The bold Sir Bedivere uplifted him,
Sir Bedivere the last of all his knights,
And bore him to a chapel nigh the field,
A broken chancel with a broken cross,
That stood on a dark strait of barren land.
On one side lay the Ocean, and on one
Lay a great water, and the moon was full.

Then spake King Arthur to Sir Bedivere:
"The sequel of to-day unsolders all
The goodliest fellowship of famous knights
Whereof this world holds record. Such a sleep
They sleep—the men I loved. I think that we
Shall never more, at any future time,
Delight our souls with talk of knightly deeds,
Walking about the gardens and the halls

Of Camelot, as in the days that were.
I perish by this people which I made,—
Tho' Merlin sware that I should come again
To rule once more—but let what will be, be,
I am so deeply smitten thro' the helm
That without help I cannot last till morn.
Thou therefore take my brand Excalibur,
Which was my pride: for thou rememberest
      how
In those old days, one summer noon, an arm
Rose up from out the bosom of the lake,   30
Clothed in white samite,[3] mystic, wonderful,
Holding the sword—and how I row'd across
And took it, and have worn it, like a king:
And, wheresoever I am sung or told
In aftertime, this also shall be known:
But now delay not: take Excalibur,
And fling him far into the middle mere:
Watch what thou seëst, and lightly bring me
      word."

To him replied the bold Sir Bedivere:
"It is not meet, Sir King, to leave thee thus,   40
Aidless, alone, and smitten thro' the helm.
A little thing may harm a wounded man.
Yet I thy hest will all perform at full,
Watch what I see, and lightly bring thee word."

So saying, from the ruin'd shrine he stept
And in the moon athwart the place of tombs,
Where lay the mighty bones of ancient men,
Old knights, and over them the sea-wind sang
Shrill, chill, with flakes of foam. He, stepping
      down
By zig-zag paths, and juts of pointed rock,   50
Came on the shining levels of the lake.

There drew he forth the brand Excalibur,
And o'er him, drawing it, the winter moon,
Brightening the skirts of a long cloud, ran forth
And sparkled keen with frost against the hilt:
For all the haft twinkled with diamond sparks,
Myriads of topaz-lights, and jacinth-work[4]
Of subtlest jewellery. He gazed so long

[4] In a note in the stardard edition, Hallam Tennyson quotes Edward FitzGerald's remark that this description "is something as A. T. read, with a broad north country vowel. . . . His voice, very deep and deep-chested, but rather murmuring than mouthing, like the sound of a far sea or of a pine-wood" (I, 712).
[1] Except that he changes the time of Arthur's last battle from summer to winter, and has the king attended only by Sir Bedivere rather than by Sir Bedivere and one other knight, Tennyson follows the account of Thomas Malory's fifteenth-century *Morte d'Arthur* (XXI).
[2] Tennyson's note in the standard edition: "*Lyonnesse*. The country of legend that lay between Cornwall and the Scilly Islands and included part of Cornwall" (I, 715).
[3] Samite: heavy silk, interwoven with gold and silver.
[4] Tennyson's note: "Jacinth is the hyacinth stone, blue and purple" (I, 715).

That both his eyes were dazzled, as he stood,
60 This way and that dividing the swift mind,
In act to throw: but at the last it seem'd
Better to leave Excalibur conceal'd
There in the many-knotted waterflags,
That whistled stiff and dry about the marge.
So strode he back slow to the wounded King.

Then spake King Arthur to Sir Bedivere:
"Hast thou perform'd my mission which I gave?
What is it thou hast seen? or what hast heard?"

And answer made the bold Sir Bedivere:
70 "I heard the ripple washing in the reeds,
And the wild water lapping on the crag."

To whom replied King Arthur, faint and
        pale:
"Thou hast betray'd thy nature and thy name,
Not rendering true answer, as beseem'd
Thy fëalty, nor like a noble knight:
For surer sign had follow'd, either hand,
Or voice, or else a motion of the mere.
This is a shameful thing for men to lie.
Yet now, I charge thee, quickly go again
80 As thou art lief and dear, and do the thing
I bad thee, watch, and lightly bring me word."

Then went Sir Bedivere the second time
Across the ridge, and paced beside the mere,
Counting the dewy pebbles, fix'd in thought;
But when he saw the wonder of the hilt,
How curiously and strangely chased, he smote
His palms together, and he cried aloud,

"And if indeed I cast the brand away,
Surely a precious thing, one worthy note,
90 Should thus be lost for ever from the earth,
Which might have pleased the eyes of many
        men.
What good should follow this, if this were
        done?
What harm, undone? deep harm to disobey,
Seeing obedience is the bond of rule.
Were it well to obey then, if a king demand
An act unprofitable, against himself?
The King is sick, and knows not what he does.
What record, or what relic of my lord
Should be to aftertime, but empty breath
100 And rumours of a doubt? but were this kept,
Stored in some treasure-house of mighty kings,
Some one might show it at a joust of arms,

Saying, 'King Arthur's sword, Excalibur,
Wrought by the lonely maiden of the Lake.
Nine years she wrought it, sitting in the deeps
Upon the hidden bases of the hills.'
So might some old man speak in the aftertime
To all the people, winning reverence.
But now much honour and much fame were
        lost."

So spake he, clouded with his own conceit,[5]   110
And hid Excalibur the second time,
And so strode back slow to the wounded King.

Then spoke King Arthur, breathing heavily:
"What is it thou hast seen? or what hast
        heard?"

And answer made the bold Sir Bedivere:
"I heard the water lapping on the crag,
And the long ripple washing in the reeds."

To whom replied King Arthur, much in
        wrath:
"Ah, miserable and unkind, untrue,
Unknightly, traitor-hearted! Woe is me!   120
Authority forgets a dying king,
Laid widow'd of the power in his eye
That bow'd the will. I see thee what thou art,
For thou, the latest-left of all my knights,
In whom should meet the offices of all,
Thou wouldst betray me for the precious hilt;
Either from lust of gold, or like a girl
Valuing the giddy pleasure of the eyes.
Yet, for a man may fail in duty twice,
And the third time may prosper, get thee
        hence: 130
But, if thou spare to fling Excalibur,
I will arise and slay thee with my hands."

Then quickly rose Sir Bedivere, and ran,
And, leaping down the ridges lightly, plunged
Among the bulrush-beds, and clutch'd the
        sword,
And strongly wheel'd and threw it. The great
        brand
Made lightnings in the splendour of the
        moon,
And flashing round and round, and whirl'd in
        an arch,
Shot like a streamer of the northern morn,[6]
Seen where the moving isles of winter[7] shock   140

---

[5] Conceit: elaborate argument.   [6] Streamer of the northern morn: the aurora borealis.
[7] Moving isles of winter: icebergs.

By night, with noises of the northern sea.
So flash'd and fell the brand Excalibur:
But ere he dipt the surface, rose an arm
Clothed in white samite, mystic, wonderful,
And caught him by the hilt, and brandish'd
   him
Three times, and drew him under in the mere.
And lightly went the other to the King.

Then spoke King Arthur, drawing thicker
   breath:
"Now see I by thine eyes that this is done.
50 Speak out: what is it thou hast heard, or seen?"

And answer made the bold Sir Bedivere:
"Sir King, I closed mine eyelids, lest the gems
Should blind my purpose, for I never saw,
Nor shall see, here or elsewhere, till I die,
Not tho' I live three lives of mortal men,
So great a miracle as yonder hilt.
Then with both hands I flung him, wheeling
   him;
But when I look'd again, behold an arm,
Clothed in white samite, mystic, wonderful,
That caught him by the hilt, and brandish'd
60   him
Three times, and drew him under in the mere."

And answer made King Arthur, breathing
   hard:
"My end draws nigh; 'tis time that I were gone.
Make broad thy shoulders to receive my weight,
And bear me to the margin; yet I fear
My wound hath taken cold, and I shall die."

So saying, from the pavement he half rose,
Slowly, with pain, reclining on his arm,
And looking wistfully with wide blue eyes
70 As in a picture. Him Sir Bedivere
Remorsefully regarded thro' his tears,
And would have spoken, but he found not
   words,
Then took with care, and kneeling on one
   knee,
O'er both his shoulders drew the languid
   hands,
And rising bore him thro' the place of tombs.

But, as he walk'd, King Arthur panted hard,
Like one that feels a nightmare on his bed
When all the house is mute. So sigh'd the King,
Muttering and murmuring at his ear, "Quick,
   quick!
I fear it is too late, and I shall die."   180
But the other swiftly strode from ridge to ridge,
Clothed with his breath, and looking, as he
   walk'd,
Larger than human on the frozen hills.
He heard the deep behind him, and a cry
Before. His own thought drove him, like a
   goad.
Dry clash'd his harness in the icy caves
And barren chasms, and all to left and right
The bare black cliff clang'd round him, as he
   based
His feet on juts of slippery crag that rang
Sharp-smitten with the dint of armed heels—   190
And on a sudden, lo! the level lake,
And the long glories of the winter moon.

Then saw they how there hove a dusky barge,
Dark as a funeral scarf from stem to stern,
Beneath them; and descending they were ware
That all the decks were dense with stately
   forms
Black-stoled, black-hooded, like a dream—by
   these
Three Queens with crowns of gold[8]—and from
   them rose
A cry that shiver'd to the tingling stars,
And, as it were one voice, an agony   200
Of lamentation, like a wind, that shrills
All night in a waste land, where no one comes,
Or hath come, since the making of the world.

Then murmur'd Arthur, "Place me in the
   barge,"
And to the barge they came. There those three
   Queens
Put forth their hands, and took the King, and
   wept.
But she, that rose the tallest of them all
And fairest, laid his head upon her lap,
And loosed the shatter'd casque, and chafed his
   hands,

[8] Tennyson's note: "In the original *Morte d'Arthur* one was King Arthur's sister, Queen Morgan le Fay; the other was the Queen of Northgalis; the third was the Queen of the Waste Lands. Some say that the three Queens are Faith, Hope, and Charity." Hallam Tennyson goes on to quote his father's opinion about critics who put forward the latter interpretation: "They are right, and they are not right. They mean that, and they do not. They are three of the noblest of women. They are also those three Graces, but they are much more. I hate to be tied down to say, '*This* means *that*,' because the thought within the image is much more than any one interpretation" (I, 716).

210 And call'd him by his name, complaining loud,
And dropping bitter tears against his brow
Striped with dark blood: for all his face was
    white
And colourless, and like the wither'd moon
Smote by the fresh beam of the springing east;
And all his greaves and cuisses[9] dash'd with
    drops
Of onset;[10] and the light and lustrous curls—
That made his forehead like a rising sun
High from the daïs-throne—were parch'd with
    dust;
Or, clotted into points and hanging loose,
Mix'd with the knightly growth that fringed
220 his lips.
So like a shatter'd column lay the King;
Not like that Arthur who, with lance in rest,
From spur to plume a star of tournament,
Shot thro' the lists at Camelot, and charged
Before the eyes of ladies and of kings.

    Then loudly cried the bold Sir Bedivere,
"Ah! my Lord Arthur, whither shall I go?
Where shall I hide my forehead and my eyes?
For now I see the true old times are dead,
230 When every morning brought a noble chance,
And every chance brought out a noble knight.
Such times have been not since the light that
    led
The holy Elders with the gift of myrrh.
But now the whole ROUND TABLE is dissolved
Which was an image of the mighty world;
And I, the last, go forth companionless,
And the days darken round me, and the years,
Among new men, strange faces, other minds."

    And slowly answered Arthur from the barge:
"The old order changeth, yielding place to
240 new,
And God fulfils Himself in many ways,
Lest one good custom should corrupt the
    world.
Comfort thyself: what comfort is in me?
I have lived my life, and that which I have
    done
May He within Himself make pure! but thou,
If thou shouldst never see my face again,
Pray for my soul. More things are wrought by
    prayer
Than this world dreams of. Wherefore, let thy
    voice
Rise like a fountain for me night and day.
250 For what are men better than sheep or goats

That nourish a blind life within the brain,
If, knowing God, they lift not hands of prayer
Both for themselves and those who call them
    friend?
For so the whole round earth is every way
Bound by gold chains about the feet of God.
But now farewell. I am going a long way
With these thou seëst—if indeed I go—
(For all my mind is clouded with a doubt)
To the island-valley of Avilion;
Where falls not hail, or rain, or any snow,   260
Nor ever wind blows loudly; but it lies
Deep-meadow'd, happy, fair with orchard-
    lawns
And bowery hollows crown'd with summer sea,
Where I will heal me of my grievous wound."

    So said he, and the barge with oar and sail
Moved from the brink, like some full-breasted
    swan
That, fluting a wild carol ere her death,
Ruffles her pure cold plume, and takes the
    flood
With swarthy webs. Long stood Sir Bedivere
Revolving many memories, till the hull   270
Look'd one black dot against the verge of
    dawn,
And on the mere the wailing died away.

Here ended Hall, and our last light, that long
Had wink'd and threaten'd darkness, flared and
    fell:
At which the Parson, sent to sleep with sound,
And waked with silence, grunted "Good!"
    but we
Sat rapt: it was the tone with which he read—
Perhaps some modern touches here and there
Redeem'd it from the charge of nothingness—
Or else we loved the man, and prized his work; 280
I know not: but we sitting, as I said,
The cock crew loud; as at that time of year
The lusty bird takes every hour for dawn:
Then Francis, muttering, like a man ill-used,
"There now—that's nothing!" drew a little
    back,
And drove his heel into the smoulder'd log,
That sent a blast of sparkles up the flue:
And so to bed; where yet in sleep I seem'd
To sail with Arthur under looming shores,
Point after point; till on to dawn, when dreams 290
Begin to feel the truth and stir of day,
To me, methought, who waited with a crowd,
There came a bark that, blowing forward, bore

_____

[9] Greaves and cuisses: leg and thigh armor.   [10] Drops of onset: marks of battle.

King Arthur, like a modern gentleman
Of stateliest port; and all the people cried,
"Arthur is come again: he cannot die."
Then those that stood upon the hills behind
Repeated—"Come again, and thrice as fair;"
And, further inland, voices echo'd—"Come
With all good things, and war shall be no
    more."
At this a hundred bells began to peal,
That with the sound I woke, and heard indeed
The clear church-bells ring in the Christmas-
    morn.

                    (1833–34) 1842

*Tennyson said, in his notes in the standard edi-
tion, that "Ulysses" was written in 1833, "soon after
Arthur Hallam's death, and it gives the feeling
about the need of going forward and braving the
struggle of life perhaps more simply than anything
in* In Memoriam" *(I, 726). The* Odyssey *ends with
Odysseus' triumphant return to Ithaca, but even
before his return he learns that after his triumph
he must again undertake a mysterious voyage. In
Canto XXVI of* The Inferno, *Dante tells the story
of that voyage, in which Odysseus (Ulysses) and all
his crew are lost at sea in sight of the mountain of
Purgatory. Tennyson refers to both these sources in
his notes.*

Ulysses

It little profits that an idle king,
By this still hearth, among these barren crags,
Match'd with an aged wife, I mete and dole
Unequal laws unto a savage race,
That hoard, and sleep, and feed, and know not
    me.

I cannot rest from travel; I will drink
Life to the lees: all times I have enjoy'd
Greatly, have suffer'd greatly, both with those
That loved me, and alone; on shore, and when
Thro' scudding drifts the rainy Hyades[1]
Vext the dim sea: I am become a name;
For always roaming with a hungry heart
Much have I seen and known; cities of men
And manners, climates, councils, governments,
Myself not least, but honour'd of them all;
And drunk delight of battle with my peers,
Far on the ringing plains of windy Troy.
I am a part of all that I have met;

Yet all experience is an arch wherethro'
Gleams that untravell'd world, whose margin
    fades   20
For ever and for ever when I move.
How dull it is to pause, to make an end,
To rust unburnish'd, not to shine in use!
As tho' to breathe were life. Life piled on life
Were all too little, and of one to me
Little remains: but every hour is saved
From that eternal silence, something more,
A bringer of new things; and vile it were
For some three suns to store and hoard myself,
And this gray spirit yearning in desire   30
To follow knowledge like a sinking star,
Beyond the utmost bound of human thought.

This is my son, mine own Telemachus,
To whom I leave the sceptre and the isle—
Well-loved of me, discerning to fulfil
This labour, by slow prudence to make mild
A rugged people, and thro' soft degrees
Subdue them to the useful and the good.
Most blameless is he, centred in the sphere
Of common duties, decent not to fail   40
In offices of tenderness, and pay
Meet adoration to my household gods,
When I am gone. He works his work, I mine.

There lies the port; the vessel puffs her sail:
There gloom the dark broad seas. My mariners,
Souls that have toil'd, and wrought, and
    thought with me—
That ever with a frolic welcome took
The thunder and the sunshine, and opposed
Free hearts, free foreheads—you and I are old;
Old age hath yet his honour and his toil;   50
Death closes all: but something ere the end,
Some work of noble note, may yet be done,
Not unbecoming men that strove with Gods.
The lights begin to twinkle from the rocks:
The long day wanes: the slow moon climbs: the
    deep
Moans round with many voices. Come, my
    friends.
'Tis not too late to seek a newer world.
Push off, and sitting well in order smite
The sounding furrows; for my purpose holds
To sail beyond the sunset, and the baths   60
Of all the western stars, until I die.
It may be that the gulfs will wash us down:
It may be we shall touch the Happy Isles,
And see the great Achilles, whom we knew.

[1] Rainy Hyades: stars whose rising was thought to portend storm.

Tho' much is taken, much abides; and tho'
We are not now that strength which in old days
Moved earth and heaven, that which we are,
    we are;
One equal temper of heroic hearts,
Made weak by time and fate, but strong in will
70 To strive, to seek, to find, and not to yield.

                                (1833) 1842

Walking to the Mail

JOHN. I'm glad I walk'd. How fresh the
meadows look
Above the river, and, but a month ago,
The whole hill-side was redder than a fox.
Is yon plantation where this byway joins
The turnpike?
    JAMES. Yes.
    JOHN.   And when does this come by?
    JAMES. The mail?[1] At one o'clock.
    JOHN.   What is it now?
    JAMES. A quarter to.
    JOHN.   Whose house is that I see?
No, not the County Member's with the vane:
Up higher with the yew-tree by it, and half
A score of gables.
10 JAMES.   That? Sir Edward Head's:
But he's abroad: the place is to be sold.
    JOHN. O, his. He was not broken.
    JAMES.   No, sir, he,
Vex'd with a morbid devil in his blood
That veil'd the world with jaundice, hid his
    face
From all men, and commercing with himself,
He lost the sense that handles daily life—
That keeps us all in order more or less—
And sick of home went overseas for change.
    JOHN. And whither?
    JAMES.   Nay, who knows? he's here
and there.
20 But let him go; his devil goes with him,
As well as with his tenant, Jocky Dawes.
    JOHN. What's that?
    JAMES. You saw the man—on Monday,
was it?—
There by the humpback'd willow; half stands
    up

And bristles, half has fall'n and made a bridge;
And there he caught the younker tickling
    trout—
Caught in flagrante—what's the Latin word?—
Delicto:[2] but his house, for so they say.
Was haunted with a jolly ghost, that shook
The curtains, whined in lobbies, tapt at doors,
And rummaged like a rat: no servant stay'd: 30
The farmer vext packs up his beds and chairs,
And all his household stuff; and with his boy
Betwixt his knees, his wife upon the tilt,[3]
Sets out, and meets a friend who hails him,
    "What!
You're flitting!" "Yes, we're flitting," says the
    ghost—
(For they had pack'd the thing among the
    beds,)
"Oh well," says he, "you flitting with us too—
Jack, turn the horses' heads and home again."
    JOHN. He left his wife behind; for so I
heard.
    JAMES. He left her, yes. I met my lady once: 40
A woman like a butt,[4] and harsh as crabs.
    JOHN. Oh yet but I remember, ten years
back—
'Tis now at least ten years—and then she was—
You could not light upon a sweeter thing:
A body slight and round, and like a pear
In growing, modest eyes, a hand, a foot
Lessening in perfect cadence, and a skin
As clean and white as privet when it flowers.
    JAMES. Ay, ay, the blossom fades, and they
that loved
At first like dove and dove were cat and dog.   50
She was the daughter of a cottager,[5]
Out of her sphere. What betwixt shame and
    pride,
New things and old, himself and her, she sour'd
To what she is: a nature never kind!
Like men, like manners: like breeds like, they
    say:
Kind nature is the best: those manners next
That fit us like a nature second-hand;
Which are indeed the manners of the great.
    JOHN. But I had heard it was this bill[6] that
past,
And fear of change at home, that drove him
    hence.   60

---

    [1] Mail: mail coach.
    [2] Younker: young man, caught fishing on Sir Edward's property; in flagrante delicto: in the
offending act.
    [3] Tilt: coarse canvas cover.   [4] Butt: barrel.   [5] Cottager: rural laborer.
    [6] The Reform Bill of 1832, which extended the franchise and diluted the political power of
landholders like Sir Edward.

JAMES.   That was the last drop in the cup of gall.
I once was near him, when his bailiff brought
A Chartist[7] pike. You should have seen him wince
As from a venomous thing: he thought himself
A mark for all, and shudder'd, lest a cry
Should break his sleep by night, and his nice eyes
Should see the raw mechanic's bloody thumbs
Sweat on his blazon'd chairs; but, sir, you know
That these two parties still divide the world—
Of those that want, and those that have: and still
The same old sore breaks out from age to age
With much the same result. Now I myself,
A Tory to the quick, was as a boy
Destructive, when I had not what I would.
I was at school—a college in the South:
There lived a flayflint[8] near; we stole his fruit,
His hens, his eggs; but there was law for *us;*
We paid in person. He had a sow, sir. She,
With meditative grunts of much content,
Lay great with pig, wallowing in sun and mud.
By night we dragg'd her to the college tower
From her warm bed, and up the cork-screw stair
With hand and rope we haled the groaning sow,
And on the leads[9] we kept her till she pigg'd.
Large range of prospect had the mother sow,
And but for daily loss of one she loved
As one by one we took them—but for this—
As never sow was higher in this world—
Might have been happy: but what lot is pure?
We took them all, till she was left alone
Upon her tower, the Niobe[10] of swine,
And so return'd unfarrow'd to her sty.
     JOHN.   They found you out?
     JAMES.   Not they.
     JOHN.   Well—after all—
What know we of the secret of a man?
His nerves were wrong. What ails us who are sound,
That we should mimic this raw fool the world,
Which charts us all in its coarse blacks or whites,

As ruthless as a baby with a worm,
As cruel as a schoolboy ere he grows
To Pity—more from ignorance than will.   100

But put your best foot forward, or I fear
That we shall miss the mail: and here it comes
With five at top: as quaint a four-in-hand
As you shall see—three pyebalds and a roan.

                                        1842

Hallam Tennyson, in a note in the standard edition, writes that the idea of this poem came from a translation (1783) by William Jones of the Moâl-lakât, *seven Arabic poems, in one of which a poet stops at the site of the tent of a former mistress and grieves over his loss. Hallam Tennyson goes on to quote his father: "The mistake that people make is that they think the poet's poems are a kind of 'catalogue raisonne' of his very own self, and of all the facts of his life, not seeing that they often only express a poetic instinct, or judgment on character real or imagined, and on the facts of lives real or imagined." In a later note in the standard edition Tennyson said of the speaker of this poem: "He is a passionate young man. . . . The whole poem represents young life, its good side, its deficiencies, and its yearnings" (I, 728, 729).*

Locksley Hall

Comrades, leave me here a little, while as yet
     'tis early morn;
Leave me here, and when you want me, sound
     upon the bugle-horn.

'Tis the place, and all around it, as of old, the
     curlews call,
Dreary gleams about the moorland flying over
     Locksley Hall:[1]

Locksley Hall, that in the distance overlooks
     the sandy tracts,
And the hollow ocean-ridges roaring into
     cataracts.

Many a night from yonder ivied casement, ere
     I went to rest,

---

[7] Among the other demands of their Charter, the Chartists asked for universal male suffrage and payment for members of Parliament (which would permit men of modest means to serve). Some of their political agitation threatened violence in the late 1830s and 1840s.
     [8] Tennyson's note: "*flayflint,* a skinflint" (I, 721).   [9] Leads: roof.
     [10] The children of Niobe, queen of Thebes, were killed by the gods in punishment for her boasts that she and her family were worthy of the homage paid to gods.
     [1] Tennyson's note in standard edition: "*I.e.* while dreary gleams of light are flying across a dreary moorland, . . . (not referring to the curlews, as some commentators insist)" (I, 728).

Did I look on great Orion sloping slowly to the
  West.

Many a night I saw the Pleiads, rising thro' the
  mellow shade,
Glitter like a swarm of fire-flies tangled in a
10 silver braid.

Here about the beach I wander'd, nourishing a
  youth sublime
With the fairy tales of science, and the long
  result of Time;

When the centuries behind me like a fruitful
  land reposed;
When I clung to all the present for the promise
  that it closed:

When I dipt into the future far as human eye
  could see;
Saw the Vision of the world, and all the wonder
  that would be.—

In the Spring a fuller crimson comes upon the
  robin's breast;
In the Spring the wanton lapwing gets himself
  another crest;

In the Spring a livelier iris changes on the
  burnish'd dove;
In the Spring a young man's fancy lightly turns
20 to thoughts of love.

Then her cheek was pale and thinner than
  should be for one so young,
And her eyes on all my motions with a mute
  observance hung.

And I said, "My cousin Amy, speak, and speak
  the truth to me,
Trust me, cousin, all the current of my being
  sets to thee."

On her pallid cheek and forehead came a
  colour and a light,
As I have seen the rosy red flushing in the
  northern night.

And she turn'd—her bosom shaken with a
  sudden storm of sighs—
All the spirit deeply dawning in the dark of
  hazel eyes—

Saying, "I have hid my feelings, fearing they
  should do me wrong;"

Saying, "Dost thou love me, cousin?" weeping.
  "I have loved thee long."   3

Love took up the glass of Time, and turn'd it
  in his glowing hands;
Every moment, lightly shaken, ran itself in
  golden sands.

Love took up the harp of Life, and smote on
  all the chords with might;
Smote the chord of Self, that, trembling, pass'd
  in music out of sight.

Many a morning on the moorland did we hear
  the copses ring,
And her whisper throng'd my pulses with the
  fulness of the Spring.

Many an evening by the waters did we watch
  the stately ships,
And our spirits rush'd together at the touching
  of the lips.

O my cousin, shallow-hearted! O my Amy,
  mine no more!
O the dreary, dreary moorland! O the barren,
  barren shore!   4

Falser than all fancy fathoms, falser than all
  songs have sung,
Puppet to a father's threat, and servile to a
  shrewish tongue!

Is it well to wish thee happy?—having known
  me—to decline
On a range of lower feelings and a narrower
  heart than mine!

Yet it shall be: thou shalt lower to his level
  day by day,
What is fine within thee growing coarse to
  sympathise with clay.

As the husband is, the wife is: thou art mated
  with a clown,
And the grossness of his nature will have
  weight to drag thee down.

He will hold thee, when his passion shall have
  spent its novel force,
Something better than his dog, a little dearer
  than his horse.   5

What is this? his eyes are heavy: think not they
  are glazed with wine.

Go to him: it is thy duty: kiss him: take his
  hand in thine.

It may be my lord is weary, that his brain is
  overwrought:
Soothe him with thy finer fancies, touch him
  with thy lighter thought.

He will answer to the purpose, easy things to
  understand—
Better thou wert dead before me, tho' I slew
  thee with my hand!

Better thou and I were lying, hidden from the
  heart's disgrace,
Roll'd in one another's arms, and silent in a
  last embrace.

Cursed be the social wants that sin against the
  strength of youth!
Cursed be the social lies that warp us from the
  living truth!

Cursed be the sickly forms that err from honest
  Nature's rule!
Cursed be the gold that gilds the straiten'd
  forehead of the fool!

Well—'tis well that I should bluster!—Hadst
  thou less unworthy proved—
Would to God—for I had loved thee more than
  ever wife was loved.

Am I mad, that I should cherish that which
  bears but bitter fruit?
I will pluck it from my bosom, tho' my heart
  be at the root.

Never, tho' my mortal summers to such length
  of years should come
As the many-winter'd crow that leads the
  clanging rookery home.

Where is comfort? in division of the records of
  the mind?
Can I part her from herself, and love her, as
  I knew her, kind?

I remember one that perish'd: sweetly did she
  speak and move:
Such a one do I remember, whom to look at
  was to love.

Can I think of her as dead, and love her for the
  love she bore?

No—she never loved me truly: love is love for
  evermore.

Comfort? comfort scorn'd of devils! this is truth
  the poet sings,
That a sorrow's crown of sorrow is remember-
  ing happier things.

Drug thy memories, lest thou learn it, lest thy
  heart be put to proof,
In the dead unhappy night, and when the rain
  is on the roof.

Like a dog, he hunts in dreams, and thou art
  staring at the wall,
Where the dying night-lamp flickers, and the
  shadows rise and fall.   80

Then a hand shall pass before thee, pointing
  to his drunken sleep,
To thy widow'd marriage-pillows, to the tears
  that thou wilt weep.

Thou shalt hear the "Never, never," whisper'd
  by the phantom years,
And a song from out the distance in the
  ringing of thine ears;

And an eye shall vex thee, looking ancient
  kindness on thy pain.
Turn thee, turn thee on thy pillow: get thee
  to thy rest again.

Nay, but Nature brings thee solace; for a tender
  voice will cry.
'Tis a purer life than thine; a lip to drain thy
  trouble dry.

Baby lips will laugh me down: my latest rival
  brings thee rest.
Baby fingers, waxen touches, press me from the
  mother's breast.   90

O, the child too clothes the father with a
  dearness not his due.
Half is thine and half is his: it will be worthy
  of the two.

O, I see thee old and formal, fitted to thy petty
  part,
With a little board of maxims preaching down
  a daughter's heart.

"They were dangerous guides the feelings—she
  herself was not exempt—

Truly, she herself had suffer'd"—Perish in thy
    self-contempt!

Overlive it—lower yet—be happy! wherefore
    should I care?
I myself must mix with action, lest I wither by
    despair.

What is that which I should turn to, lighting
    upon days like these?
Every door is barr'd with gold, and opens but
100   to golden keys.

Every gate is throng'd with suitors, all the
    markets overflow.
I have but an angry fancy: what is that which
    I should do?

I had been content to perish, falling on the
    foeman's ground,
When the ranks are roll'd in vapour, and the
    winds are laid with sound.

But the jingling of the guinea helps the hurt
    that Honour feels,
And the nations do but murmur, snarling at
    each other's heels.

Can I but relive in sadness? I will turn that
    earlier page.
Hide me from my deep emotion, O thou
    wondrous Mother-Age!

Make me feel the wild pulsation that I felt
    before the strife,
When I heard my days before me, and the
110   tumult of my life;

Yearning for the large excitement that the
    coming years would yield,
Eager-hearted as a boy when first he leaves his
    father's field,

And at night along the dusky highway near
    and nearer drawn,
Sees in heaven the light of London flaring like
    a dreary dawn;

And his spirit leaps within him to be gone
    before him then,
Underneath the light he looks at, in among the
    throngs of men:

Men, my brothers, men the workers, ever
    reaping something new:
That which they have done but earnest of the
    things that they shall do.

For I dipt into the future, far as human eye
    could see,
Saw the Vision of the world, and all the wonder
    that would be;   120

Saw the heavens fill with commerce, argosies of
    magic sails,
Pilots of the purple twilight, dropping down
    with costly bales;

Heard the heavens fill with shouting, and there
    rain'd a ghastly dew
From the nations' airy navies grappling in the
    central blue;

Far along the world-wide whisper of the south-
    wind rushing warm,
With the standards of the peoples plunging
    thro' the thunderstorm;

Till the war-drum throbb'd no longer, and the
    battle-flags were furl'd
In the Parliament of man, the Federation of
    the world.

There the common sense of most shall hold a
    fretful realm in awe,
And the kindly earth shall slumber, lapt in
    universal law.   13

So I triumph'd ere my passion sweeping thro'
    me left me dry,
Left me with the palsied heart, and left me
    with the jaundiced eye;

Eye, to which all order festers, all things here
    are out of joint:
Science moves, but slowly slowly, creeping on
    from point to point:

Slowly comes a hungry people, as a lion,
    creeping nigher,
Glares at one that nods and winks behind a
    slowly-dying fire.

Yet I doubt not thro' the ages one increasing
    purpose runs,

And the thoughts of men are widen'd with the
    process[2] of the suns.

What is that to him that reaps not harvest of
    his youthful joys,
Tho' the deep heart of existence beat for ever
    like a boy's?

Knowledge comes, but wisdom lingers, and I
    linger on the shore,
And the individual withers, and the world is
    more and more.

Knowledge comes, but wisdom lingers, and he
    bears a laden breast,
Full of sad experience, moving toward the
    stillness of his rest.

Hark, my merry comrades call me, sounding on
    the bugle-horn,
They to whom my foolish passion were a target
    for their scorn:

Shall it not be scorn to me to harp on such a
    moulder'd string?
I am shamed thro' all my nature to have loved
    so slight a thing.

Weakness to be wroth with weakness! woman's
    pleasure, woman's pain—
Nature made them blinder motions bounded
    in a shallower brain:

Woman is the lesser man, and all thy passions,
    match'd with mine,
Are as moonlight unto sunlight, and as water
    unto wine—

Here at least, where nature sickens, nothing.
    Ah, for some retreat
Deep in yonder shining Orient, where my life
    began to beat;

Where in wild Mahratta-battle[3] fell my father
    evil-starr'd;—
I was left a trampled orphan, and a selfish
    uncle's ward.

Or to burst all links of habit—there to wander
    far away,
On from island unto island at the gateways of
    the day.

Larger constellations burning, mellow moons
    and happy skies,
Breadths of tropic shade and palms in cluster,
    knots of Paradise.   160

Never comes the trader, never floats an
    European flag,
Slides the bird o'er lustrous woodland, swings
    the trailer from the crag;

Droops the heavy-blossom'd bower, hangs the
    heavy-fruited tree—
Summer isles of Eden lying in dark-purple
    spheres of sea.

There methinks would be enjoyment more
    than in this march of mind,
In the steamship, in the railway, in the
    thoughts that shake mankind.

There the passions cramp'd no longer shall
    have scope and breathing space;
I will take some savage woman, she shall rear
    my dusky race.

Iron-jointed, supple-sinew'd, they shall dive,
    and they shall run,
Catch the wild goat by the hair, and hurl their
    lances in the sun;   170

Whistle back the parrot's call, and leap the
    rainbows of the brooks,
Not with blinded eyesight poring over misera-
    ble books—

Fool, again the dream, the fancy! but I *know*
    my words are wild,
But I count the gray barbarian lower than the
    Christian child.

I, to herd with narrow foreheads, vacant of our
    glorious gains,
Like a beast with lower pleasures, like a beast
    with lower pains!

Mated with a squalid savage—what to me were
    sun or clime?
I the heir of all the ages, in the foremost files
    of time—

I that rather held it better men should perish
    one by one,

[2] Process of the suns: Tennyson's note: "progress of years" (I, 730).
[3] Mahratta-battle: the Mahratta were defeated at Bombay early in the nineteenth century.

180   Than that earth should stand at gaze like
     Joshua's[4] moon in Ajalon!

Not in vain the distance beacons. Forward,
    forward let us range,
Let the great world spin for ever down the
    ringing grooves of change.[5]

Thro' the shadow of the globe we sweep into
    the younger day:
Better fifty years of Europe than a cycle of
    Cathay.

Mother-Age (for mine I knew not) help me as
    when life begun:
Rift the hills, and roll the waters, flash the
    lightnings, weigh the Sun.

O, I see the crescent promise of my spirit hath
    not set.
Ancient founts of inspiration well thro' all my
    fancy yet.

Howsoever these things be, a long farewell to
    Locksley Hall!
Now for me the woods may wither, now for me
190   the roof-tree fall.

Comes a vapour from the margin, blackening
    over heath and holt,
Cramming all the blast before it, in its breast
    a thunderbolt.

Let it fall on Locksley Hall, with rain or hail,
    or fire or snow;
For the mighty wind arises, roaring seaward,
    and I go.

                        1842

Will Waterproof's Lyrical Monologue

Made at the Cock[1]

O plump head-waiter at The Cock,
    To which I most resort,
How goes the time? 'Tis five o'clock.
    Go fetch a pint of port:

But let it not be such as that
    You set before chance-comers,
But such whose father-grape grew fat
    On Lusitanian[2] summers.

No vain libation to the Muse,
    But may she still be kind,
And whisper lovely words, and use
    Her influence on the mind,
To make me write my random rhymes,
    Ere they be half-forgotten;
Nor add and alter, many times,
    Till all be ripe and rotten.

I pledge her, and she comes and dips
    Her laurel in the wine,
And lays it thrice upon my lips,
    These favour'd lips of mine;
Until the charm have power to make
    New lifeblood warm the bosom,
And barren commonplaces break
    In full and kindly blossom.

I pledge her silent at the board;
    Her gradual fingers steal
And touch upon the master-chord
    Of all I felt and feel.
Old wishes, ghosts of broken plans,
    And phantom hopes assemble;
And that child's heart within the man's
    Begins to move and tremble.

Thro' many an hour of summer suns,
    By many pleasant ways,
Against its fountain upward runs
    The current of my days:
I kiss the lips I once have kiss'd;
    The gas-light wavers dimmer;
And softly, thro' a vinous mist,
    My college friendships glimmer.

I grow in worth, and wit, and sense,
    Unboding critic-pen,
Or that eternal want of pence
    Which vexes public men,
Who hold their hands to all, and cry
    For that which all deny them—

---

[4] The Biblical hero Joshua commanded the moon and sun to stand still during one of his battles (Joshua 10).

[5] Tennyson's note: "When I went by the first train from Liverpool to Manchester (1830) I thought that the wheels ran in a groove" (I, 731).

[1] The Cock Tavern, by Temple Bar in London.

[2] Lusitania is an old name for the region that is now the country of Portugal.

Who sweep the crossings,[3] wet or dry,
  And all the world go by them.

Ah yet, tho' all the world forsake,
  Tho' fortune clip my wings,
I will not cramp my heart, nor take
  Half-views of men and things.
Let Whig and Tory stir their blood;
  There must be stormy weather;
But for some true result of good
  All parties work together.

Let there be thistles, there are grapes;
  If old things, there are new;
Ten thousand broken lights and shapes,
  Yet glimpses of the true.
Let raffs[4] be rife in prose and rhyme,
  We lack not rhymes and reasons,
As on this whirligig of Time
  We circle with the seasons.

This earth is rich in man and maid,
  With fair horizons bound:
This whole wide earth of light and shade
  Comes out a perfect round.
High over roaring Temple-bar,
  And set in Heaven's third story,
I look at all things as they are,
  But thro' a kind of glory.

———

Head-waiter, honour'd by the guest
  Half-mused, or reeling ripe,
The pint, you brought me, was the best
  That ever came from pipe.
But tho' the port surpasses praise,
  My nerves have dealt with stiffer.
Is there some magic in the place?
  Or do my peptics differ?

For since I came to live and learn,
  No pint of white or red
Had ever half the power to turn
  This wheel within my head,
Which bears a season'd brain about,
  Unsubject to confusion,
Tho' soak'd and saturate, out and out,
  Thro' every convolution.

For I am of a numerous house,
  With many kinsmen gay,   90
Where long and largely we carouse
  As who shall say me nay:
Each month, a birth-day coming on,
  We drink defying trouble,
Or sometimes two would meet in one,
  And then we drank it double;

Whether the vintage, yet unkept,
  Had relish fiery-new,
Or elbow-deep in sawdust, slept,
  As old as Waterloo;   100
Or, stow'd when classic Canning[5] died,
  In musty bins and chambers,
Had cast upon its crusty side
  The gloom of ten Decembers.

The Muse, the jolly Muse, it is!
  She answer'd to my call,
She changes with that mood or this,
  Is all-in-all to all;
She lit the spark within my throat,
  To make my blood run quicker,   110
Used all her fiery will, and smote
  Her life into the liquor.

And hence this halo lives about
  The waiter's hands, that reach
To each his perfect pint of stout,
  His proper chop to each.
He looks not like the common breed
  That with the napkin dally;
I think he came like Ganymede,[6]
  From some delightful valley.   120

The Cock was of a larger egg
  Than modern poultry drop,
Stept forward on a firmer leg,
  And cramm'd a plumper crop;
Upon an ampler dunghill trod,
  Crow'd lustier late and early,
Sipt wine from silver, praising God,[7]
  And raked in golden barley.

A private life was all his joy,
  Till in a court he saw   130

[3] Sweep the crossings: a mode of begging in London, by asking money of someone after sweeping a clean passage across a street for him or her.

[4] Raffs: crude writing in which sound is more important than sense.

[5] George Canning, prime minister and a famous parliamentarian and orator in an eighteenth-century style, died in 1827.

[6] Ganymede was a young mortal kidnapped by Zeus to serve as cupbearer to the gods.

[7] Tennyson's note in standard edition: "As the bird drinks he holds up his neck. There is accordingly an old English saying about the cock 'praising God' when he drinks" (I, 736).

A something-pottle-bodied boy
    That knuckled at the taw:[8]
He stoop'd and clutch'd him, fair and good,
    Flew over roof and casement:
His brothers of the weather stood
    Stock-still for sheer amazement.

But he, by farmstead, thorpe, and spire,
    And follow'd with acclaims,
A sign to many a staring shire,
140   Came crowing over Thames.
Right down by smoky Paul's they bore,
    Till, where the street grows straiter,
One fix'd for ever at the door,
    And one became head-waiter.

———————

But whither would my fancy go?
    How out of place she makes
The violet of a legend blow
    Among the chops and steaks!
'Tis but a steward of the can,
150   One shade more plump than common;
As just and mere a serving-man
    As any born of woman.

I ranged too high: what draws me down
    Into the common day?
Is it the weight of that half-crown
    Which I shall have to pay?
For, something duller than at first,
    Nor wholly comfortable,
I sit, my empty glass reversed,
160   And thrumming on the table:

Half fearful that, with self at strife,
    I take myself to task;
Lest of the fulness of my life
    I leave an empty flask:
For I had hope, by something rare,
    To prove myself a poet:
But, while I plan and plan, my hair
    Is gray before I know it.

So fares it since the years began,
170   Till they be gather'd up;
The truth, that flies the flowing can,
    Will haunt the vacant cup:
And others' follies teach us not,
    Nor much their wisdom teaches;

And most, of sterling worth, is what
    Our own experience preaches.

Ah, let the rusty theme alone!
    We know not what we know.
But for my pleasant hour, 'tis gone;
    'Tis gone, and let it go.   180
'Tis gone: a thousand such have slipt
    Away from my embraces,
And fallen into the dusty crypt
    Of darken'd forms and faces.

Go, therefore, thou! thy betters went
    Long since, and came no more;
With peals of genial clamour sent
    From many a tavern-door,
With twisted quirks and happy hits,
    From misty men of letters;   190
The tavern-hours of mighty wits—
    Thine elders and thy betters.

Hours, when the Poet's words and looks
    Had yet their native glow:
Nor yet the fear of little books
    Had made him talk for show;
But, all his vast heart sherris-warm'd,[9]
    He flash'd his random speeches,
Ere days, that deal in ana swarm'd,[10]
    His literary leeches.

So mix for ever with the past,
    Like all good things on earth!
For should I prize thee, couldst thou last,
    At half thy real worth?
I hold it good, good things should pass:
    With time I will not quarrel:
It is but yonder empty glass
    That makes me maudlin-moral.

———————

Head-waiter of the chop-house here,
    To which I most resort,   210
I too must part: I hold thee dear
    For this good pint of port.
For this, thou shalt from all things suck
    Marrow of mirth and laughter;
And wheresoe'er thou move, good luck
    Shall fling her old shoe after.

But thou wilt never move from hence,
    The sphere thy fate allots:

———

    [8] Pottle-bodied boy/That knuckled at the taw: pot-bellied boy playing marbles.
    [9] Sherris: sherry.
    [10] Ana: sayings of, and anecdotes and information about, literary figures. "Swarm'd" here
means "give birth to."

Thy latter days increased with pence
    Go down among the pots:
Thou battenest by the greasy gleam
    In haunts of hungry sinners,
Old boxes,[11] larded with the steam
    Of thirty thousand dinners.

We fret, we fume, would shift our skins,
    Would quarrel with our lot;
Thy care is, under polish'd tins,
    To serve the hot-and-hot;[12]
To come and go, and come again,
    Returning like the pewit,
And watch'd by silent gentlemen,
    That trifle with the cruet.

Live long, ere from thy topmost head
    The thick-set hazel dies;
Long, ere the hateful crow shall tread
    The corners of thine eyes:
Live long, nor feel in head or chest
    Our changeful equinoxes,
Till mellow Death, like some late guest,
    Shall call thee from the boxes.

But when he calls, and thou shalt cease
    To pace the gritted floor,
And, laying down an unctuous lease
    Of life, shalt earn no more;
No carved cross-bones, the types of Death,
    Shall show thee past to Heaven:
But carved cross-pipes, and, underneath,
    A pint-pot neatly graven.

                         1842

"This describes the soul of a youth who has given himself up to pleasure and Epicureanism. He at length is worn out and wrapt in the mists of satiety. Afterwards he grows into a cynical old man afflicted with the 'curse of nature,' and joining in the Feast of Death. Then we see the landscape which symbolizes God, Law and the future life" (I, 740–741). [*Tennyson's note in the standard edition*]

The Vision of Sin

I

I had a vision when the night was late:
A youth came riding toward a palace-gate.
He rode a horse with wings, that would have
    flown,
But that his heavy rider kept him down.

And from the palace came a child of sin,
And took him by the curls, and led him in,
Where sat a company with heated eyes,
Expecting when a fountain should arise:
A sleepy light upon their brows and lips—
As when the sun, a crescent of eclipse,   10
Dreams over lake and lawn, and isles and
    capes—
Suffused them, sitting, lying, languid shapes,
By heaps of gourds, and skins of wine, and
    piles of grapes.

II

Then methought I heard a mellow sound,
Gathering up from all the lower ground;
Narrowing in to where they sat assembled
Low voluptuous music winding trembled,
Wov'n in circles: they that heard it sigh'd,
Panted hand-in-hand with faces pale,
Swung themselves, and in low tones replied;   20
Till the fountain spouted, showering wide
Sleet of diamond-drift and pearly hail;
Then the music touch'd the gates and died;
Rose again from where it seem'd to fail,
Storm'd in orbs of song, a growing gale;
Till thronging in and in, to where they waited,
As 'twere a hundred-throated nightingale,
The strong tempestuous treble throbb'd and
    palpitated;
Ran into its giddiest whirl of sound,
Caught the sparkles, and in circles,   30
Purple gauzes, golden hazes, liquid mazes,
Flung the torrent rainbow round:
Then they started from their places,
Moved with violence, changed in hue,
Caught each other with wild grimaces,
Half-invisible to the view,
Wheeling with precipitate paces
To the melody, till they flew,
Hair, and eyes, and limbs, and faces,
Twisted hard in fierce embraces,   40
Like to Furies, like to Graces,
Dash'd together in blinding dew:
Till, kill'd with some luxurious agony,
The nerve-dissolving melody
Flutter'd headlong from the sky.

III

And then I look'd up toward a mountain-tract,
That girt the region with high cliff and lawn:
I saw that every morning, far withdrawn
Beyond the darkness and the cataract,
God made Himself an awful rose of dawn,   50

[11] Boxes: Tennyson's note: "The pews where the diners sit" (I, 736).
[12] Hot-and-hot: hot dishes served in succession.

Unheeded: and detaching, fold by fold,
From those still heights, and, slowly drawing
   near,
A vapour heavy, hueless, formless, cold,
Came floating on for many a month and year,
Unheeded: and I thought I would have spoken,
And warn'd that madman ere it grew too late:
But, as in dreams, I could not. Mine was
   broken,
When that cold vapour touch'd the palace gate,
And link'd again. I saw within my head
A gray and gap-tooth'd man as lean as death,
Who slowly rode across a wither'd heath,
And lighted at a ruin'd inn, and said:

60

           IV
"Wrinkled ostler, grim and thin!
   Here is custom come your way;
Take my brute, and lead him in,
   Stuff his ribs with mouldy hay.

"Bitter barmaid, waning fast!
   See that sheets are on my bed;
What! the flower of life is past:
   It is long before you wed.

70

"Slip-shod waiter, lank and sour,
   At the Dragon on the heath!
Let us have a quiet hour,
   Let us hob-and-nob with Death.

"I am old, but let me drink;
   Bring me spices, bring me wine;
I remember, when I think,
   That my youth was half divine.

"Wine is good for shrivell'd lips,
   When a blanket wraps the day,
When the rotten woodland drips,
   And the leaf is stamp'd in clay.

80

"Sit thee down, and have no shame,
   Cheek by jowl, and knee by knee:
What care I for any name?
   What for order or degree?

"Let me screw thee up a peg:
   Let me loose thy tongue with wine:
Callest thou that thing a leg?
   Which is thinnest? thine or mine?

90

"Thou shalt not be saved by works:
   Thou hast been a sinner too:
Ruin'd trunks on wither'd forks,
   Empty scarecrows, I and you!

"Fill the cup, and fill the can:
   Have a rouse before the morn:
Every moment dies a man,
   Every moment one is born.

"We are men of ruin'd blood;
   Therefore comes it we are wise.
Fish are we that love the mud,
   Rising to no fancy-flies.

"Name and fame! to fly sublime
   Thro' the courts, the camps, the schools,
Is to be the ball of Time,
   Bandied by the hands of fools.

"Friendship!—to be two in one—
   Let the canting liar pack!
Well I know, when I am gone,
   How she mouths behind my back.

"Virtue!—to be good and just—
   Every heart, when sifted well,
Is a clot of warmer dust,
   Mix'd with cunning sparks of hell.

"O! we two as well can look
   Whited thought and cleanly life
As the priest, above his book
   Leering at his neighbour's wife.

"Fill the cup, and fill the can:
   Have a rouse before the morn:
Every moment dies a man,
   Every moment one is born.

"Drink, and let the parties rave:
   They are fill'd with idle spleen;
Rising, falling, like a wave,
   For they know not what they mean.

"He that roars for liberty
   Faster binds a tyrant's power;
And the tyrant's cruel glee
   Forces on the freer hour.

"Fill the can, and fill the cup:
   All the windy ways of men
Are but dust that rises up,
   And is lightly laid again.

"Greet her with applausive breath,
   Freedom, gaily doth she tread;
In her right a civic wreath,
   In her left a human head.

100

110

120

130

"No, I love not what is new;
  She is of an ancient house:
And I think we know the hue
  Of that cap upon her brows.

"Let her go! her thirst she slakes
  Where the bloody conduit runs,
Then her sweetest meal she makes
  On the first-born of her sons.[1]

"Drink to lofty hopes that cool—
  Visions of a perfect State:
Drink we, last, the public fool,
  Frantic love and frantic hate.

"Chant me now some wicked stave,
  Till thy drooping courage rise,
And the glow-worm of the grave
  Glimmer in thy rheumy eyes.

"Fear not thou to loose thy tongue;
  Set thy hoary fancies free;
What is loathsome to the young
  Savours well to thee and me.

"Change reverting to the years,
  When thy nerves could understand
What there is in loving tears,
  And the warmth of hand in hand.

"Tell me tales of thy first love—
  April hopes, the fools of chance;
Till the graves begin to move,
  And the dead begin to dance.

"Fill the can, and fill the cup:
  All the windy ways of men
Are but dust that rises up,
  And is lightly laid again.

"Trooping from their mouldy dens
  The chap-fallen[2] circle spreads:
Welcome, fellow-citizens,
  Hollow hearts and empty heads!

"You are bones, and what of that?
  Every face, however full,
Padded round with flesh and fat,
  Is but modell'd on a skull.

"Death is king, and Vivat Rex!
  Tread a measure on the stones,   180
Madam—if I know your sex,
  From the fashion of your bones.

"No, I cannot praise the fire
  In your eye—nor yet your lip:
All the more do I admire
  Joints of cunning workmanship.

"Lo! God's likeness—the ground-plan—
  Neither modell'd, glazed, nor framed:
Buss[3] me, thou rough sketch of man,
  Far too naked to be shamed!   190

"Drink to Fortune, drink to Chance,
  While we keep a little breath!
Drink to heavy Ignorance!
  Hob-and-nob with brother Death!

"Thou art mazed, the night is long,
  And the longer night is near:
What! I am not all as wrong
  As a bitter jest is dear.

"Youthful hopes, by scores, to all,
  When the locks are crisp and curl'd;   200
Unto me my maudlin gall
  And my mockeries of the world.

"Fill the cup, and fill the can:
  Mingle madness, mingle scorn!
Dregs of life, and lees of man:
  Yet we will not die forlorn."

V
The voice grew faint: there came a further
    change:
Once more uprose the mystic mountain-range:
Below were men and horses pierced with
    worms,
And slowly quickening into lower forms;   210
By shards and scurf of salt, and scum of dross,
Old plash of rains, and refuse patch'd with
    moss.
Then some one spake: "Behold! it was a crime
Of sense avenged by sense that wore with
    time."[4]

[1] An allusion to the course of the French Revolution, which moved to the Reign of Terror in which some of the leaders of the Revolution were executed.

[2] Chap-fallen: literally, with lower jaw hanging, as in death.

[3] Buss: kiss.

[4] Tennyson's note: "The sensualist becomes worn out by his senses." In an edition of his poems published in 1865, Tennyson restored two lines which had been in an early version of the poem, and which, according to Hallam Tennyson, "were intended by my father to make the thought clearer":

> "Another answer'd: 'But a crime of sense?
> Give him new nerves with old experience.'" (I, 741)

Another said: "The crime of sense became
The crime of malice, and is equal blame."
And one: "He had not wholly quench'd his
    power;
A little grain of conscience made him sour."
At last I heard a voice upon the slope
220 Cry to the summit, "Is there any hope?"
To which an answer peal'd from that high
    land,
But in a tongue no man could understand;
And on the glimmering limit far withdrawn
God made Himself an awful rose of dawn.

                              1842

The Poet's Song[1]

The rain had fallen, the Poet arose,
  He pass'd by the town and out of the street,
A light wind blew from the gates of the sun,
  And waves of shadow went over the wheat,
And he sat him down in a lonely place,
  And chanted a melody loud and sweet,
That made the wild-swan pause in her cloud,
  And the lark drop down at his feet.

The swallow stopt as he hunted the fly,
  The snake slipt under a spray,
10 The wild hawk stood with the down on his
    beak,
  And stared, with one foot on the prey,
And the nightingale thought, "I have sung
  many songs,
  But never a one so gay,
For he sings of what the world will be
  When the years have died away."

                              1842

Arthur Henry Hallam died in Vienna in September 1833, at the age of twenty-two. He had been Tennyson's closest friend at Cambridge, was engaged to be married to Tennyson's sister Emily, had written an early and important assessment of Tennyson's poetry in a review of his volume of 1830, and was thought by his friends to be destined to play a large role in the intellectual and political life of his time. The quality of this friendship, and some of its other circumstances, are described in the poem itself.

Tennyson began writing sections of the poem in 1833. In the 1840s he frequently recited some of the lyrics to friends, or let them read them in manuscript. In 1850 he printed a small private edition of
the poem. Later in the same year it was published, with some further revisions, anonymously.

Tennyson said of the poem, in remarks quoted in the standard edition of his poetry: "It was meant to be a kind of Divine Commedia, ending with happiness. The sections were written at many different places, and as the phases of our intercourse came to my memory and suggested them. I did not write them with any view of weaving them into a whole, or for publication, until I found that I had written so many. The different moods of sorrow as in a drama are dramatically given, and my conviction that fear, doubts, and suffering will find answer and relief only through Faith in a God of Love. 'I' is not always the author speaking of himself, but the voice of the human race speaking thro' him. After the death of A. H. H., the divisions of the poem are made by First Xmas Eve (Section XXVIII), Second Xmas (LXXVIII), Third Xmas Eve (CIV and CV, etc.)" (II, 525).

In Memoriam A. H. H.

Obit MDCCCXXXIII

Strong Son of God, immortal Love,
  Whom we, that have not seen thy face,
  By faith, and faith alone, embrace,
Believing where we cannot prove;

Thine are these orbs of light and shade;[1]
  Thou madest Life in man and brute;
  Thou madest Death; and lo, thy foot
Is on the skull which thou hast made.

Thou wilt not leave us in the dust:
  Thou madest man, he knows not why,
  He thinks he was not made to die;
And thou hast made him: thou art just.

Thou seemest human and divine,
  The highest, holiest manhood, thou:
  Our wills are ours, we know not how;
Our wills are ours, to make them thine.

Our little systems have their day;
  They have their day and cease to be:
  They are but broken lights of thee,
And thou, O Lord, art more than they.

We have but faith: we cannot know;
  For knowledge is of things we see;
  And yet we trust it comes from thee,
A beam in darkness: let it grow.

---

[1] Printed as the last poem in *Poems in Two Volumes*, 1842.
[1] Tennyson's note: ". . . *orbs of light and shade*. Sun and moon" (II, 545).

Let knowledge grow from more to more,
    But more of reverence in us dwell;
    That mind and soul, according well,
May make one music as before,

But vaster. We are fools and slight;
    We mock thee when we do not fear:
    But help thy foolish ones to bear;
Help thy vain worlds to bear thy light.

Forgive what seem'd my sin in me;
    What seem'd my worth since I began;
    For merit lives from man to man,
And not from man, O Lord, to thee.

Forgive my grief for one removed,
    Thy creature, whom I found so fair.
    I trust he lives in thee, and there
I find him worthier to be loved.

Forgive these wild and wandering cries,
    Confusions of a wasted[2] youth;
    Forgive them where they fail in truth,
And in thy wisdom make me wise.

                                    (1849)

I

I held it truth, with him who sings
    To one clear harp in divers tones,
    That men may rise on stepping-stones
Of their dead selves to higher things.[3]

But who shall so forecast the years
    And find in loss a gain to match?
    Or reach a hand thro' time to catch
The far-off interest of tears?

Let Love clasp Grief lest both be drown'd,
    Let darkness keep her raven gloss:
    Ah, sweeter to be drunk with loss,
To dance with death, to beat the ground,

Than that the victor Hours should scorn
    The long result of love, and boast,
    "Behold the man that loved and lost,
But all he was is overworn."

II

Old Yew, which graspest at the stones
    That name the under-lying dead,
    Thy fibres net the dreamless head,
Thy roots are wrapt about the bones.

The seasons bring the flower again,
    And bring the firstling to the flock;
    And in the dusk of thee, the clock
Beats out the little lives of men.

O not for thee the glow, the bloom,
    Who changest not in any gale,
    Nor branding summer suns avail
To touch thy thousand years of gloom:

And gazing on thee, sullen tree,
    Sick for thy stubborn hardihood,
    I seem to fail from out my blood
And grow incorporate into thee.

III[4]

O Sorrow, cruel fellowship,
    O Priestess in the vaults of Death,
    O sweet and bitter in a breath,
What whispers from thy lying lip?

"The stars," she whispers, "blindly run;
    A web is wov'n across the sky;
    From out waste places comes a cry,
And murmurs from the dying sun:

"And all the phantom, Nature, stands—
    With all the music in her tone,
    A hollow echo of my own,—
A hollow form with empty hands."

And shall I take a thing so blind,
    Embrace her as my natural good;
    Or crush her, like a vice of blood,
Upon the threshold of the mind?

IV

To Sleep I give my powers away;
    My will is bondsman to the dark;
    I sit within a helmless bark,
And with my heart I muse and say:

70

80

90

---

[2] Wasted: made desolate.
[3] Tennyson's note: "I alluded to Goethe's creed." Hallam Tennyson adds, referring to the phrase "divers tones," "My father would often say, 'Goethe is consummate in so many different styles" (II, 546).
[4] A version of this section written in 1833 is quoted in Ricks' edition of Tennyson's poems (p. 866). The section is one of the earliest conceived of the poem.

O heart, how fares it with thee now,
 That thou should'st fail from thy desire,
 Who scarcely darest to inquire,
100 "What is it makes me beat so low?"

Something it is which thou hast lost,
 Some pleasure from thine early years.
 Break, thou deep vase of chilling tears,
That grief hath shaken into frost![5]

Such clouds of nameless trouble cross
 All night below the darken'd eyes;
 With morning wakes the will, and cries,
"Thou shalt not be the fool of loss."

  V
I sometimes hold it half a sin
110   To put in words the grief I feel;
 For words, like Nature, half reveal
And half conceal the Soul within.

But, for the unquiet heart and brain,
 A use in measured language lies;
 The sad mechanic exercise,
Like dull narcotics, numbing pain.

In words, like weeds,[6] I'll wrap me o'er,
 Like coarsest clothes against the cold:
 But that large grief which these enfold
120 Is given in outline and no more.

  VI
One writes, that "Other friends remain,"
 That "Loss is common to the race"—
 And common is the commonplace,
And vacant chaff well meant for grain.

That loss is common would not make
 My own less bitter, rather more:
 Too common! Never morning wore
To evening, but some heart did break.

O father, wheresoe'er thou be,
130   Who pledgest now thy gallant son;
 A shot, ere half thy draught be done,
Hath still'd the life that beat from thee.

O mother, praying God will save
 Thy sailor,—while thy head is bow'd,
 His heavy-shotted hammock-shroud
Drops in his vast and wandering grave.

Ye know no more than I who wrought
 At that last hour to please him well;
 Who mused on all I had to tell,
And something written, something thought;[7] 14

Expecting still his advent home;
 And ever met him on his way
 With wishes, thinking, "here to-day,"
Or "here to-morrow will he come."

O somewhere, meek, the unconscious dove,
 That sittest ranging golden hair;
 And glad to find thyself so fair,
Poor child, that waitest for thy love!

For now her father's chimney glows
 In expectation of a guest;
 And thinking "this will please him best,"
She takes a riband or a rose;

For he will see them on to-night;
 And with the thought her colour burns;
 And, having left the glass, she turns
Once more to set a ringlet right;

And, even when she turn'd, the curse
 Had fallen, and her future Lord
 Was drown'd in passing thro' the ford,
Or kill'd in falling from his horse. 16

O what to her shall be the end?
 And what to me remains of good?
 To her, perpetual maidenhood,
And unto me no second friend.

  VII[8]
Dark house, by which once more I stand
 Here in the long unlovely street,
 Doors, where my heart was used to beat
So quickly, waiting for a hand,

---

[5] Tennyson's note: "Water can be brought below freezing point and not turn into ice—if it be kept still; but if it be moved suddenly it turns into ice and may break the vase" (II, 547).

[6] Weeds: clothing, as in widow's weeds.

[7] Hallam Tennyson's note: "My father was writing to Arthur Hallam in the hour that he died" (II, 548).

[8] This section and the next were apparently written late in the composition of the poem; they are not in the manuscripts in which many of the poems written in the 1830s and early 1840s appear, and they were not printed in the private edition of the poem in 1850 (Ricks, p. 870). The "dark house" is the London residence of Hallam's father.

170
A hand that can be clasp'd no more—
    Behold me, for I cannot sleep,
    And like a guilty thing I creep
At earliest morning to the door.

He is not here; but far away
    The noise of life begins again,
    And ghastly thro' the drizzling rain
On the bald street breaks the blank day.

VIII

A happy lover who has come
    To look on her that loves him well,
    Who 'lights and rings the gateway bell,
180 And learns her gone and far from home;

He saddens, all the magic light
    Dies off at once from bower and hall,
    And all the place is dark, and all
The chambers emptied of delight:

So find I every pleasant spot
    In which we two were wont to meet,
    The field, the chamber and the street,
For all is dark where thou art not.

190
Yet as that other, wandering there
    In those deserted walks, may find
    A flower beat with rain and wind,
Which once she foster'd up with care;

So seems it in my deep regret,
    O my forsaken heart, with thee
    And this poor flower of poesy
Which little cared for fades not yet.

But since it pleased a vanish'd eye,
    I go to plant it on his tomb,
    That if it can it there may bloom,
200 Or dying, there at least may die.

IX[9]

Fair ship, that from the Italian shore
    Sailest the placid ocean-plains
    With my lost Arthur's loved remains,
Spread thy full wings, and waft him o'er.

So draw him home to those that mourn
    In vain; a favourable speed
    Ruffle thy mirror'd mast, and lead
Thro' prosperous floods[10] his holy urn.

All night no ruder air perplex
    Thy sliding keel, till Phosphor,[11] bright   210
    As our pure love, thro' early light
Shall glimmer on the dewy decks.

Sphere all your lights around, above;
    Sleep, gentle heavens, before the prow;
    Sleep, gentle winds, as he sleeps now,
My friend, the brother of my love;

My Arthur, whom I shall not see
    Till all my widow'd race be run;
    Dear as the mother to the son,
More than my brothers are to me.   220

X

I hear the noise about thy keel;
    I hear the bell struck in the night:
    I see the cabin-window bright;
I see the sailor at the wheel.

Thou bring'st the sailor to his wife,
    And travell'd men from foreign lands;
    And letters unto trembling hands;
And, thy dark freight, a vanish'd life.

So bring him: we have idle dreams:
    This look of quiet flatters thus   230
    Our home-bred fancies: O to us,
The fools of habit, sweeter seems

To rest beneath the clover sod,
    That takes the sunshine and the rains,
    Or where the kneeling hamlet drains
The chalice of the grapes of God;

Than if with thee the roaring wells
    Should gulf him fathom-deep in brine;
    And hands so often clasp'd in mine,
Should toss with tangle[12] and with shells.   240

XI

Calm is the morn without a sound,
    Calm as to suit a calmer grief,
    And only thro' the faded leaf
The chestnut pattering to the ground:

Calm and deep peace on this high wold,[13]
    And on these dews that drench the furze,
    And all the silvery gossamers
That twinkle into green and gold:

---

[9] Written in 1833 (Ricks, p. 872). The ship is that carrying Hallam's body to England.
[10] Prosperous floods: favorable tides.   [11] Tennyson's note: "*Phosphor,* star of dawn." (II, 548)
[12] Tennyson's note: "*tangle,* or 'oar-weed'" (II, 549).
[13] In this section and the next the speaker is standing, as Tennyson describes it in his note, on "A Lincolnshire wold or upland from which the whole range of marsh to the sea is visible" (II, 549).

Calm and still light on yon great plain
  250   That sweeps with all its autumn bowers,
          And crowded farms and lessening towers,
To mingle with the bounding main:

Calm and deep peace in this wide air,
        These leaves that redden to the fall;
        And in my heart, if calm at all,
If any calm, a calm despair:

Calm on the seas, and silver sleep,
        And waves that sway themselves in rest,
        And dead calm in that noble breast
  260 Which heaves but with the heaving deep.

        XII
Lo, as a dove when up she springs
        To bear thro' Heaven a tale of woe,
        Some dolorous message knit below
The wild pulsation of her wings;

Like her I go; I cannot stay;
        I leave this mortal ark behind,[14]
        A weight of nerves without a mind,
And leave the cliffs, and haste away

O'er ocean-mirrors rounded large,
  270   And reach the glow of southern skies,
          And see the sails at distance rise,
And linger weeping on the marge,

And saying; "Comes he thus, my friend?
        Is this the end of all my care?"
        And circle moaning in the air:
"Is this the end? Is this the end?"

And forward dart again, and play
        About the prow, and back return
        To where the body sits, and learn
  280 That I have been an hour away.

        XIII
Tears of the widower, when he sees
        A late-lost form that sleep reveals,
        And moves his doubtful arms, and feels
Her place is empty, fall like these;

Which weep a loss for ever new,
        A void where heart on heart reposed;
        And, where warm hands have prest and
            closed,
Silence, till I be silent too.

Which weep the comrade of my choice,
        An awful thought, a life removed,   290
        The human-hearted man I loved,
A Spirit, not a breathing voice.

Come Time, and teach me, many years,
        I do not suffer in a dream;
        For now so strange do these things seem,
Mine eyes have leisure for their tears;

My fancies time to rise on wing,
        And glance about the approaching sails,
        As tho' they brought but merchants' bales,
And not the burthen that they bring.   300

        XIV
If one should bring me this report,
        That thou[15] hadst touch'd the land to-day,
        And I went down unto the quay,
And found thee lying in the port;

And standing, muffled round with woe,
        Should see thy passengers in rank
        Come stepping lightly down the plank,
And beckoning unto those they know;

And if along with these should come
        The man I held as half-divine;   310
        Should strike a sudden hand in mine,
And ask a thousand things of home;

And I should tell him all my pain,
        And how my life had droop'd of late,
        And he should sorrow o'er my state
And marvel what possess'd my brain;

And I perceived no touch of change,
        No hint of death in all his frame,
        But found him all in all the same,
I should not feel it to be strange.   320

        XV
To-night the winds begin to rise
        And roar from yonder dropping day:
        The last red leaf is whirl'd away,
The rooks are blown about the skies;

The forest crack'd, the waters curl'd,
        The cattle huddled on the lea;
        And wildly dash'd on tower and tree
The sunbeam strikes along the world:

---

[14] Tennyson's note: "My spirit flies from out my material self" (II, 549).   [15] Thou: the ship.

And but for fancies, which aver
    That all thy motions gently pass
    Athwart a plane of molten glass,[16]
I scarce could brook the strain and stir

That makes the barren branches loud;
    And but for fear it is not so,[17]
    The wild unrest that lives in woe
Would dote and pore on yonder cloud

That rises upward always higher,
    And onward drags a labouring breast,
    And topples round the dreary west,
A looming bastion fringed with fire.

XVI

What words are these have fall'n from me?
    Can calm despair and wild unrest
    Be tenants of a single breast,
Or sorrow such a changeling be?

Or doth she only seem to take
    The touch of change in calm or storm;
    But knows no more of transient form
In her deep self, than some dead lake

That holds the shadow of a lark
    Hung in the shadow of a heaven?
    Or has the shock, so harshly given,
Confused me like the unhappy bark

That strikes by night a craggy shelf,
    And staggers blindly ere she sink?
    And stunn'd me from my power to think
And all my knowledge of myself;

And made me that delirious man
    Whose fancy fuses old and new,
    And flashes into false and true,
And mingles all without a plan?

XVII[18]

Thou comest, much wept for: such a breeze
    Compell'd thy canvas, and my prayer
    Was as the whisper of an air
To breathe thee over lonely seas.

For I in spirit saw thee move
    Thro' circles of the bounding sky,
    Week after week: the days go by:
Come quick, thou bringest all I love.

Henceforth, wherever thou may'st roam,
    My blessing, like a line of light,
    Is on the waters day and night,
And like a beacon guards thee home.

So may whatever tempest mars
    Mid-ocean, spare thee, sacred bark;
    And balmy drops in summer dark
Slide from the bosom of the stars.

So kind an office hath been done,
    Such precious relics brought by thee;
    The dust of him I shall not see
Till all my widow'd race be run.

XVIII

'Tis well; 'tis something; we may stand
    Where he in English earth is laid,
    And from his ashes may be made
The violet of his native land.

'Tis little; but it looks in truth
    As if the quiet bones were blest
    Among familiar names to rest
And in the places of his youth.

Come then, pure hands, and bear the head
    That sleeps or wears the mask of sleep,
    And come, whatever loves to weep,
And hear the ritual of the dead.

Ah yet, ev'n yet, if this might be,
    I, falling on his faithful heart,
    Would breathing thro' his lips impart
The life that almost dies in me;

That dies not, but endures with pain,
    And slowly forms the firmer mind,
    Treasuring the look it cannot find,
The words that are not heard again.

XIX

The Danube to the Severn gave[19]
    The darken'd heart that beat no more;
    They laid him by the pleasant shore,
And in the hearing of the wave.

There twice a day the Severn fills;
    The salt sea-water passes by,
    And hushes half the babbling Wye,
And makes a silence in the hills.

---

[16] His fancy is that the ship carrying Hallam's body sails on a sea calm as glass.

[17] Hallam Tennyson's note: "The stormy night, except it were for my fear for the 'sacred bark,' would be in sympathy with me" (II, 550).

[18] According to Ricks (pp. 879–881) this and the following two sections were written in 1833–34.

[19] Hallam was buried at Clevedon, in the west of England, near the Bristol Channel. The Channel's tides flow into the Severn River; the Wye flows into the Severn.

The Wye is hush'd nor moved along,
410   And hush'd my deepest grief of all,
          When fill'd with tears that cannot fall,
I brim with sorrow drowning song.

The tide flows down, the wave again
          Is vocal in its wooded walls;
          My deeper anguish also falls,
And I can speak a little then.

XX

The lesser griefs that may be said,
          That breathe a thousand tender vows,
          Are but as servants in a house
420 Where lies the master newly dead;

Who speak their feeling as it is,
          And weep the fulness from the mind:
          "It will be hard," they say, "to find
Another service such as this."

My lighter moods are like to these,
          That out of words a comfort win;
          But there are other griefs within,
And tears that at their fountain freeze;

For by the hearth the children sit
430   Cold in that atmosphere of Death,
          And scarce endure to draw the breath,
Or like to noiseless phantoms flit:

But open converse is there none,
          So much the vital spirits sink
          To see the vacant chair, and think,
"How good! how kind! and he is gone."

XXI

I sing to him that rests below,
          And, since the grasses round me wave,
          I take the grasses of the grave,
440 And make them pipes whereon to blow.

The traveller hears me now and then,
          And sometimes harshly will he speak:
          "This fellow would make weakness weak,
And melt the waxen hearts of men."

Another answers, "Let him be,
          He loves to make parade of pain,
          That with his piping he may gain
The praise that comes to constancy."

A third is wroth: "Is this an hour
          For private sorrow's barren song,   450
          When more and more the people throng
The chairs and thrones of civil power?

"A time to sicken and to swoon,
          When Science reaches forth her arms
          To feel from world to world, and charms
Her secret from the latest moon?"

Behold, ye speak an idle thing:
          Ye never knew the sacred dust:
          I do but sing because I must,
And pipe but as the linnets sing: 460

And one is glad; her note is gay,
          For now her little ones have ranged;
          And one is sad; her note is changed,
Because her brood is stol'n away.

XXII

The path by which we twain did go,
          Which led by tracts that pleased us well,
          Thro' four sweet years[20] arose and fell,
From flower to flower, from snow to snow:

And we with singing cheer'd the way,
          And, crown'd with all the season lent,   470
          From April on to April went,
And glad at heart from May to May:

But where the path we walk'd began
          To slant the fifth autumnal slope,
          As we descended following Hope,
There sat the Shadow fear'd of man;

Who broke our fair companionship,
          And spread his mantle dark and cold,
          And wrapt thee formless in the fold,
And dull'd the murmur on thy lip,   480

And bore thee where I could not see
          Nor follow, tho' I walk in haste,
          And think, that somewhere in the waste
The Shadow sits and waits for me.

XXIII

Now, sometimes in my sorrow shut,
          Or breaking into song by fits,
          Alone, alone, to where he sits,
The Shadow cloak'd from head to foot,

---

[20] Four sweet years: Tennyson met Hallam in 1829.

Who keeps the keys of all the creeds,[21]
490   I wander, often falling lame,
    And looking back to whence I came,
Or on to where the pathway leads;

And crying, How changed from where it ran
    Thro' lands where not a leaf was dumb;
    But all the lavish hills would hum
The murmur of a happy Pan:[22]

When each by turns was guide to each,
    And Fancy light from Fancy caught,
    And Thought leapt out to wed with
        Thought
500 Ere Thought could wed itself with Speech;

And all we met was fair and good,
    And all was good that Time could bring,
    And all the secret of the Spring
Moved in the chambers of the blood;

And many an old philosophy
    On Argive[23] heights divinely sang,
    And round us all the thicket rang
To many a flute of Arcady.[24]

    XXIV
And was the day of my delight
510   As pure and perfect as I say?
    The very source and fount of Day
Is dash'd with wandering isles of night.[25]

If all was good and fair we met,
    This earth had been the Paradise
    It never look'd to human eyes
Since our first Sun arose and set.

And is it that the haze of grief
    Makes former gladness loom so great?
    The lowness of the present state,
520 That sets the past in this relief?

Or that the past will always win
    A glory from its being far;
    And orb into the perfect star
We saw not, when we moved therein?

    XXV
I know that this was Life,—the track
    Whereon with equal feet we fared;
    And then, as now, the day prepared
The daily burden for the back.

But this it was that made me move
    As light as carrier-birds in air; 530
    I loved the weight I had to bear,
Because it needed help of Love:

Nor could I weary, heart or limb,
    When mighty Love would cleave in twain
    The lading of a single pain,
And part it, giving half to him.

    XXVI
Still onward winds the dreary way;
    I with it; for I long to prove
    No lapse of moons can canker Love,
Whatever fickle tongues may say. 540

And if that eye which watches guilt
    And goodness, and hath power to see
    Within the green the moulder'd tree,
And towers fall'n as soon as built—

Oh, if indeed that eye foresee
    Or see (in Him is no before)
    In more of life true life no more
And Love the indifference to be,

Then might I find, ere yet the morn 550
    Breaks hither over Indian seas,
    That Shadow waiting with the keys,
To shroud me from my proper scorn.[26]

    XXVII
I envy not in any moods
    The captive void of noble rage,
    The linnet born within the cage,
That never knew the summer woods:

I envy not the beast that takes
    His license in the field of time,
    Unfetter'd by the sense of crime,
To whom a conscience never wakes; 560

[21] Tennyson's note: "After death we shall learn the truth of all beliefs" (II, 551).
[22] Pan: Greek emblem of pastoral nature; the god of forests and pastures.
[23] Argive: Greek, from Argos, a city especially known for its musicians.
[24] Arcady: mountainous region of Greece, associated with pastoral poets.
[25] Tennyson's note: ". . . isles of night, sun-spots" (II, 551).
[26] Tennyson's note: "*my proper scorn*, scorn of myself" (II, 552).

Nor, what may count itself as blest,
    The heart that never plighted troth
    But stagnates in the weeds of sloth;
Nor any want-begotten rest.

I hold it true, whate'er befall;
    I feel it, when I sorrow most;
    'Tis better to have loved and lost
Then never to have loved at all.

XXVIII[27]

The time draws near the birth of Christ:
570   The moon is hid; the night is still;
    The Christmas bells from hill to hill
Answer each other in the mist.

Four voices of four hamlets round,
    From far and near, on mead and moor,
    Swell out and fail, as if a door
Were shut between me and the sound:

Each voice four changes on the wind,
    That now dilate, and now decrease,
    Peace and goodwill, goodwill and peace,
580 Peace and goodwill, to all mankind.

This year I slept and woke with pain,
    I almost wish'd no more to wake,
    And that my hold on life would break
Before I heard those bells again:

But they my troubled spirit rule,
    For they controll'd me when a boy;
    They bring me sorrow touch'd with joy,
The merry merry bells of Yule.

XXIX

With such compelling cause to grieve
590   As daily vexes household peace,
    And chains regret to his decease,
How dare we keep our Christmas-eve;

Which brings no more a welcome guest
    To enrich the threshold of the night
    With shower'd largess of delight
In dance and song and game and jest?

Yet go, and while the holly boughs
    Entwine the cold baptismal font,
    Make one wreath more for Use and Wont,
600 That guard the portals of the house;

Old sisters of a day gone by,
    Gray nurses, loving nothing new;
    Why should they miss their yearly due
Before their time? They too will die.

XXX[28]

With trembling fingers did we weave
    The holly round the Christmas hearth;
    A rainy cloud possess'd the earth,
And sadly fell our Christmas-eve.

At our old pastimes in the hall
    We gambol'd, making vain pretence   610
    Of gladness, with an awful sense
Of one mute Shadow watching all.

We paused: the winds were in the beech:
    We heard them sweep the winter land;
    And in a circle hand-in-hand
Sat silent, looking each at each.

Then echo-like our voices rang;
    We sung, tho' every eye was dim,
    A merry song we sang with him
Last year: impetuously we sang: 620

We ceased: a gentler feeling crept
    Upon us: surely rest is meet:
    "They rest," we said, "their sleep is sweet,"
And silence follow'd, and we wept.

Our voices took a higher range;
    Once more we sang: "They do not die
    Nor lose their mortal sympathy,
Nor change to us, although they change;

"Rapt from the fickle and the frail
    With gather'd power, yet the same,   630
    Pierces the keen seraphic flame
From orb to orb, from veil to veil."

Rise, happy morn, rise, holy morn,
    Draw forth the cheerful day from night:
    O Father, touch the east, and light
The light that shone when Hope was born.

XXXI

When Lazarus[29] left his charnel-cave,
    And home to Mary's house return'd,
    Was this demanded—if he yearn'd
To hear her weeping by his grave?   640

[27] One of the first-written sections of the poem, begun in 1833 (*Memoir*, I, 109).
[28] This section, and the two following, were also first written in 1833 (Ricks, pp. 889–891).
[29] Lazarus was raised from the dead by Christ (John 11–12).

"Where wert thou, brother, those four days?"
    There lives no record of reply,
    Which telling what it is to die
Had surely added praise to praise.

From every house the neighbours met,
    The streets were fill'd with joyful sound,
    A solemn gladness even crown'd
The purple brows of Olivet.[30]

Behold a man raised up by Christ!
650   The rest remaineth unreveal'd;
    He told it not; or something seal'd
The lips of that Evangelist.

XXXII

Her eyes are homes of silent prayer,
    Nor other thought her mind admits
    But, he was dead, and there he sits,
And he that brought him back is there.

Then one deep love doth supersede
    All other, when her ardent gaze
    Roves from the living brother's face,
660 And rests upon the Life indeed.

All subtle thought, all curious fears,
    Borne down by gladness so complete,
    She bows, she bathes the Saviour's feet
With costly spikenard[31] and with tears.

Thrice blest whose lives are faithful prayers,
    Whose loves in higher love endure;
    What souls possess themselves so pure,
Or is there blessedness like theirs?

XXXIII

O thou that after toil and storm
670   Mayst seem to have reach'd a purer air,
    Whose faith has centre everywhere,
Nor cares to fix itself to form,

Leave thou thy sister when she prays,
    Her early Heaven, her happy views;
    Nor thou with shadow'd hint confuse
A life that leads melodious days.

Her faith thro' form is pure as thine,
    Her hands are quicker unto good:
    Oh, sacred be the flesh and blood
680 To which she links a truth divine!

See thou, that countest reason ripe
    In holding by the law within,
    Thou fail not in a world of sin,
And ev'n for want of such a type.

XXXIV

My own dim life should teach me this,
    That life shall live for evermore,
    Else earth is darkness at the core,
And dust and ashes all that is;

This round of green, this orb of flame,
    Fantastic beauty; such as lurks   690
    In some wild Poet, when he works
Without a conscience or an aim.

What then were God to such as I?
    'Twere hardly worth my while to choose
    Of things all mortal, or to use
A little patience ere I die;

'Twere best at once to sink to peace,
    Like birds the charming serpent draws,
    To drop head-foremost in the jaws
Of vacant darkness and to cease.   700

XXXV

Yet if some voice that man could trust
    Should murmur from the narrow house,
    "The cheeks drop in; the body bows;
Man dies: nor is there hope in dust:"

Might I not say? "Yet even here,
    But for one hour, O Love, I strive
    To keep so sweet a thing alive:"
But I should turn mine ears and hear

The moanings of the homeless sea,
    The sound of streams that swift or slow   710
    Draw down Æonian hills,[32] and sow
The dust of continents to be;

And Love would answer with a sigh,
    "The sound of that forgetful shore[33]
    Will change my sweetness more and more,
Half-dead to know that I shall die."

O me, what profits it to put
    An idle case? If Death were seen
    At first as Death, Love had not been,
Or been in narrowest working shut,   720

---

[30] Olivet: the Mount of Olives in Jerusalem, one of the scenes of Christ's passion.
[31] Spikenard: a fragrant ointment.
[32] Tennyson's note: "*Æonian hills,* the everlasting hills" (II, 555).
[33] Tennyson's note: "The land where all things are forgotten" (II, 555).

Mere fellowship of sluggish moods,
 Or in his coarsest Satyr-shape
 Had bruised the herb and crush'd the
  grape,
And bask'd and batten'd in the woods.

XXXVI
Tho' truths in manhood darkly join,
 Deep-seated in our mystic frame,
 We yield all blessing to the name
Of Him that made them current coin;

730   For Wisdom dealt with mortal powers,
 Where truth in closest words shall fail,
 When truth embodied in a tale
Shall enter in at lowly doors.[34]

And so the Word had breath, and wrought
 With human hands the creed of creeds
 In loveliness of perfect deeds,
More strong than all poetic thought;

Which he may read that binds the sheaf,
 Or builds the house, or digs the grave,
 And those wild[35] eyes that watch the wave
740 In roarings round the coral reef.

XXXVII
Urania[36] speaks with darken'd brow:
 "Thou pratest here where thou art least;
 This faith has many a purer priest,
And many an abler voice than thou.

"Go down beside thy native rill,
 On thy Parnassus[37] set thy feet,
 And hear thy laurel whisper sweet
About the ledges of the hill."

And my Melpomene replies,
750   A touch of shame upon her cheek:
 "I am not worthy ev'n to speak
Of thy prevailing mysteries;

"For I am but an earthly Muse,
 And owning but a little art
 To lull with song an aching heart,
And render human love his dues;

"But brooding on the dear one dead,
 And all he said of things divine,
 (And dear to me as sacred wine
To dying lips is all he said),   760

"I murmur'd, as I came along,
 Of comfort clasp'd in truth reveal'd;
 And loiter'd in the master's field,
And darken'd sanctities with song."

XXXVIII
With weary steps I loiter on,
 Tho' always under alter'd skies
 The purple from the distance dies,
My prospect and horizon gone.

No joy the blowing season[38] gives,
 The herald melodies of spring,   770
 But in the songs I love to sing
A doubtful gleam of solace lives.

If any care for what is here
 Survive in spirits render'd free,
 Then are these songs I sing of thee
Not all ungrateful to thine ear.

XXXIX[39]
Old warder of these buried bones,
 And answering now my random stroke
 With fruitful cloud and living smoke,[40]
Dark yew, that graspest at the stones   780

And dippest toward the dreamless head,
 To thee too comes the golden hour
 When flower is feeling after flower;[41]
But Sorrow—fixt upon the dead,

---

[34] In his note in the standard edition Tennyson remarks that "truth logically argued out" will not persuade mortally limited humanity, "whereas truth coming in the story of the Gospel can influence the poorest" (II, 555).

[35] Tennyson's note: ". . . the Pacific Islanders, 'wild' having a sense of 'barbarian' in it" (II, 555).

[36] Urania is the muse of astronomy; and in Milton's *Paradise Lost*, of heavenly poetry; Melpomene (line 749) is the muse of tragedy, and here, of elegy.

[37] Parnassus: a mountain in Greece fabled to be the haunt of Apollo and the muses of poetry.

[38] Tennyson's note: "*the blowing season,* the blossoming season" (II, 556).

[39] This section was written in 1868, and first published in 1869.

[40] Tennyson's note: "The yew, when flowering, in a wind or when struck sends up its pollen like smoke" (II, 556).

[41] Hallam Tennyson notes that the yew is dioecious, its single-sexed flowers on separate plants (II, 556).

And darkening the dark graves of men,—
    What whisper'd from her lying lips?
    Thy gloom is kindled at the tips,
And passes into gloom again.

XL

Could we forget the widow'd hour
    And look on Spirits breathed away,
    As on a maiden in the day
When first she wears her orange-flower!

When crown'd with blessing she doth rise
    To take her latest leave of home,
    And hopes and light regrets that come
Make April of her tender eyes;

And doubtful joys the father move,
    And tears are on the mother's face,
    As parting with a long embrace
She enters other realms of love;

Her office there to rear, to teach,
    Becoming as is meet and fit
    A link among the days, to knit
The generations each with each;

And, doubtless, unto thee is given
    A life that bears immortal fruit
    In those great offices that suit
The full-grown energies of heaven.

Ay me, the difference I discern!
    How often shall her old fireside
    Be cheer'd with tidings of the bride,
How often she herself return,

And tell them all they would have told,
    And bring her babe, and make her boast,
    Till even those that miss'd her most
Shall count new things as dear as old:

But thou and I have shaken hands,
    Till growing winters lay me low;
    My paths are in the fields I know
And thine in undiscover'd lands.

XLI

Thy spirit ere our fatal loss
    Did ever rise from high to higher;
    As mounts the heavenward altar-fire,
As flies the lighter thro' the gross.

But thou art turn'd to something strange,
    And I have lost the links that bound
    Thy changes; here upon the ground,
No more partaker of thy change.

Deep folly! yet that this could be—
    That I could wing my will with might   830
    To leap the grades of life and light,
And flash at once, my friend, to thee.

For tho' my nature rarely yields
    To that vague fear implied in death;
    Nor shudders at the gulfs beneath,
The howlings from forgotten fields;[42]

Yet oft when sundown skirts the moor
    An inner trouble I behold,
    A spectral doubt which makes me cold,
That I shall be thy mate no more,   840

Tho' following with an upward mind
    The wonders that have come to thee,
    Thro' all the secular to-be,[43]
But evermore a life behind.

XLII

I vex my heart with fancies dim:
    He still outstript me in the race;
    It was but unity of place
That made me dream I rank'd with him.

And so may Place retain us still,
    And he the much-beloved again,   850
    A lord of large experience, train
To riper growth the mind and will:

And what delights can equal those
    That stir the spirit's inner deeps,
    When one that loves but knows not, reaps
A truth from one that loves and knows?

XLIII

If Sleep and Death be truly one,
    And every spirit's folded bloom
    Thro' all its intervital[44] gloom
In some long trance should slumber on;   860

Unconscious of the sliding hour,
    Bare of the body, might it last,
    And silent traces of the past
Be all the colour of the flower:

---

[42] Tennyson's note: "The eternal miseries of the Inferno" (II, 557).
[43] Tennyson's note: "aeons of the future" (II, 558).
[44] Intervital: between this life and the next.

So then were nothing lost to man;
　　So that still garden of the souls
　　In many a figured leaf enrolls
The total world since life began;[45]

And love will last as pure and whole
870　　As when he loved me here in Time,
　　And at the spiritual prime[46]
Rewaken with the dawning soul.

XLIV

How fares it with the happy dead?
　　For here the man is more and more;
　　But he forgets the days before
God shut the doorways of his head.[47]

The days have vanish'd, tone and tint,
　　And yet perhaps the hoarding sense
　　Gives out at times (he knows not whence)
880　A little flash, a mystic hint;

And in the long harmonious years
　　(If Death so taste Lethean springs[48]) ,
　　May some dim touch of earthly things
Surprise thee ranging with thy peers.

If such a dreamy touch should fall,
　　O turn thee round, resolve the doubt;
　　My guardian angel will speak out
In that high place, and tell thee all.

XLV

The baby new to earth and sky,
890　　What time his tender palm is prest
　　Against the circle of the breast,
Has never thought that "this is I":

But as he grows he gathers much,
　　And learns the use of "I," and "me,"
　　And finds "I am not what I see,
And other than the things I touch."

So rounds he to a separate mind
　　From whence clear memory may begin,
　　As thro' the frame that binds him in
900　His isolation grows defined.

This use may lie in blood and breath,
　　Which else were fruitless of their due,
　　Had man to learn himself anew
Beyond the second birth of Death.

XLVI

We ranging down this lower track,
　　The path we came by, thorn and flower,
　　Is shadow'd by the growing hour,
Lest life should fail in looking back.

So be it: there no shade can last
　　In that deep dawn behind the tomb,
　　But clear from marge to marge shall bloom
The eternal landscape of the past;

A lifelong tract of time reveal'd;
　　The fruitful hours of still increase;
　　Days order'd in a wealthy peace,
And those five years its richest field.

O Love, thy province were not large,
　　A bounded field, nor stretching far;
　　Look also, Love, a brooding star,[49]
A rosy warmth from marge to marge.

XLVII

That each, who seems a separate whole,
　　Should move his rounds, and fusing all
　　The skirts of self again, should fall
Remerging in the general Soul,

Is faith as vague as all unsweet:
　　Eternal form shall still divide
　　The eternal soul from all beside;
And I shall know him when we meet:

And we shall sit at endless feast,
　　Enjoying each the other's good:
　　What vaster dream can hit the mood
Of Love on earth? He seeks at least

Upon the last and sharpest height,
　　Before the spirits fade away,
　　Some landing-place, to clasp and say,
"Farewell! We lose ourselves in light."[50]

[45] Tennyson here imagines the dead as sleeping flowers, the whole history of the world collectively stored in their markings, waiting their awakening at the last judgment.

[46] Tennyson's note: "Dawn of the spiritual life hereafter" (II, 558) .

[47] Tennyson's note: "Closing of the skull after babyhood" (II, 558) .

[48] Lethean springs: in classical mythology, the water of the river Lethe causes amnesia.

[49] Tennyson's note: "As if Lord of the whole life"; Hallam Tennyson adds, " (not merely of those five years of friendship) ,—the wider landscape aglow with the sunrise of 'that deep dawn behind the tomb' " (II, 559–560) .

[50] Tennyson's note: "If we are to be finally merged in the Universal Soul, Love asks to have at least one more parting before we lose ourselves" (II, 560) .

XLVIII

If these brief lays, of Sorrow born,
    Were taken to be such as closed
    Grave doubts and answers here proposed,
Then these were such as men might scorn:

Her care is not to part and prove;
    She takes, when harsher moods remit,
    What slender shade of doubt may flit,
And makes it vassal unto love:

And hence, indeed, she sports with words,
    But better serves a wholesome law,
    And holds it sin and shame to draw
The deepest measure from the chords:

Nor dare she trust a larger lay,
    But rather loosens from the lip
    Short swallow-flights of song, that dip
Their wings in tears, and skim away.

XLIX

From art, from nature, from the schools,
    Let random influences glance,
    Like light in many a shiver'd lance
That breaks about the dapple pools:

The lightest wave of thought shall lisp,
    The fancy's tenderest eddy wreathe,
    The slightest air of song shall breathe
To make the sullen surface crisp.[51]

And look thy look, and go thy way,
    But blame not thou the winds that make
    The seeming-wanton ripple break,
The tender-pencil'd shadow play.

Beneath all fancied hopes and fears
    Ay me, the sorrow deepens down,
    Whose muffled motions blindly drown
The bases of my life in tears.

L

Be near me when my light is low,
    When the blood creeps, and the nerves
        prick
    And tingle; and the heart is sick,
And all the wheels of Being slow.

Be near me when the sensuous frame
    Is rack'd with pangs that conquer trust;
    And Time, a maniac scattering dust,
And Life, a Fury slinging flame.

Be near me when my faith is dry,
    And men the flies of latter spring,
    That lay their eggs, and sting and sing
And weave their petty cells and die.   980

Be near me when I fade away,
    To point the term of human strife,
    And on the low dark verge of life
The twilight of eternal day.

LI

Do we indeed desire the dead
    Should still be near us at our side?
    Is there no baseness we would hide?
No inner vileness that we dread?

Shall he for whose applause I strove,
    I had such reverence for his blame,   990
    See with clear eye some hidden shame
And I be lessen'd in his love?

I wrong the grave with fears untrue:
    Shall love be blamed for want of faith?
    There must be wisdom with great Death:
The dead shall look me thro' and thro'.

Be near us when we climb or fall:
    Ye watch, like God, the rolling hours
    With larger other eyes than ours,
To make allowance for us all.   1000

LII

I cannot love thee as I ought,
    For love reflects the thing beloved;
    My words are only words, and moved
Upon the topmost froth of thought.

"Yet blame not thou thy plaintive song,"
    The Spirit of true love replied;
    "Thou canst not move me from thy side,
Nor human frailty do me wrong.

"What keeps a spirit wholly true
    To that ideal which he bears?   1010
    What record? not the sinless years
That breathed beneath the Syrian blue:[52]

"So fret not, like an idle girl,
    That life is dash'd with flecks of sin.
    Abide:[53] thy wealth is gather'd in,
When Time hath sunder'd shell from pearl."

---

[51] Hallam Tennyson's note: "*crisp,* curl, ripple" (II, 560).
[52] The Gospel record of Christ's life.
[53] Tennyson's note: "*Abide,* wait without wearying" (II, 561).

LIII

How many a father have I seen,
   A sober man, among his boys,
   Whose youth was full of foolish noise,
1020 Who wears his manhood hale and green:

And dare we to this fancy give,
   That had the wild oat not been sown,
   The soil, left barren, scarce had grown
The grain by which a man may live?

Or, if we held the doctrine sound
   For life outliving heats of youth,
   Yet who would preach it as a truth
To those that eddy round and round?

Hold thou the good: define it well:
1030   For fear divine Philosophy
   Should push beyond her mark, and be
Procuress to the Lords of Hell.

LIV

Oh yet we trust that somehow good
   Will be the final goal of ill,
   To pangs of nature, sins of will,
Defects of doubt, and taints of blood;

That nothing walks with aimless feet;
   That not one life shall be destroy'd,
   Or cast as rubbish to the void,
1040 When God hath made the pile[54] complete;

That not a worm is cloven in vain;
   That not a moth with vain desire
   Is shrivell'd in a fruitless fire,
Or but subserves another's gain.

Behold, we know not anything;
   I can but trust that good shall fall
   At last—far off—at last, to all,
And every winter change to spring.

So runs my dream: but what am I?
1050   An infant crying in the night:
   An infant crying for the light:
And with no language but a cry.

LV[55]

The wish, that of the living whole
   No life may fail beyond the grave,
   Derives it not from what we have
The likest God within the soul?[56]

Are God and Nature then at strife,
   That Nature lends such evil dreams?
   So careful of the type she seems,
So careless of the single life;   106

That I, considering everywhere
   Her secret meaning in her deeds,
   And finding that of fifty seeds[57]
She often brings but one to bear,

I falter where I firmly trod,
   And falling with my weight of cares
   Upon the great world's altar-stairs
That slope thro' darkness up to God,

I stretch lame hands of faith, and grope,
   And gather dust and chaff, and call   10'
   To what I feel is Lord of all,
And faintly trust the larger hope.

LVI

"So careful of the type?" but no.
   From scarped cliff and quarried stone
   She cries, "A thousand types are gone:
I care for nothing, all shall go.

"Thou makest thine appeal to me:
   I bring to life, I bring to death:
   The spirit does but mean the breath:
I know no more." And he, shall he,   10:

Man, her last work, who seem'd so fair,
   Such splendid purpose in his eyes,
   Who roll'd the psalm to wintry skies,
Who built him fanes[58] of fruitless prayer,

Who trusted God was love indeed
   And love Creation's final law—
   Tho' Nature, red in tooth and claw
With ravine, shriek'd against his creed—

---

[54] Pile: building or tower.

[55] In his memoir of his father's life Hallam Tennyson claims that this section, and the others confronting evidence that species have evolved and become extinct, were written before 1844, the year in which Robert Chambers' *Vestiges of Creation,* a study of the geological evidence of evolution, was published. Tennyson learned of similar evidence in Charles Lyell's *Principles of Geology* (1830–33) , which he read in 1837 (*Memoir,* I, 223, 162) .

[56] Tennyson's note: "The inner consciousness—the divine in man" (II, 561) .

[57] Tennyson's note: " 'Fifty' should be 'myriad' " (II, 561) .

[58] Fanes: temples.

Who loved, who suffer'd countless ills,
    Who battled for the True, the Just,
    Be blown about the desert dust,
Or seal'd within the iron hills?[59]

No more? A monster then, a dream,
    A discord. Dragons of the prime,[60]
    That tare each other in their slime,
Were mellow music match'd with him.

O life as futile, then, as frail!
    O for thy voice to soothe and bless!
    What hope of answer, or redress?
Behind the veil, behind the veil.

LVII

Peace; come away: the song of woe
    Is after all an earthly song:
    Peace; come away: we do him wrong
To sing so wildly: let us go.

Come; let us go: your cheeks are pale;
    But half my life I leave behind:
    Methinks my friend is richly shrined;
But I shall pass; my work will fail.[61]

Yet in these ears, till hearing dies,
    One set slow bell will seem to toll
    The passing of the sweetest soul
That ever look'd with human eyes.

I hear it now, and o'er and o'er,
    Eternal greetings to the dead;
    And "Ave, Ave, Ave," said,
"Adieu, adieu" for evermore.

LVIII

In those sad words I took farewell:
    Like echoes in sepulchral halls,
    As drop by drop the water falls
In vaults and catacombs, they fell;

And, falling, idly broke the peace
    Of hearts that beat from day to day,
    Half-conscious of their dying clay,
And those cold crypts where they shall cease.

The high Muse answer'd: "Wherefore grieve
    Thy brethren with a fruitless tear?
    Abide a little longer here,
And thou shalt take a nobler leave."

LIX[62]

O Sorrow, wilt thou live with me
    No casual mistress, but a wife,
    My bosom-friend and half of life;
As I confess it needs must be;

O Sorrow, wilt thou rule my blood,
    Be sometimes lovely like a bride,
    And put thy harsher moods aside,
If thou wilt have me wise and good.

My centred passion cannot move,
    Nor will it lessen from to-day;
    But I'll have leave at times to play
As with the creature of my love;

And set thee forth, for thou art mine,
    With so much hope for years to come,
    That, howsoe'er I know thee, some
Could hardly tell what name were thine.

LX

He past; a soul of nobler tone:
    My spirit loved and loves him yet,
    Like some poor girl whose heart is set
On one whose rank exceeds her own.

He mixing with his proper sphere,
    She finds the baseness of her lot,
    Half jealous of she knows not what,
And envying all that meet him there.

The little village looks forlorn;
    She sighs amid her narrow days,
    Moving about the household ways,
In that dark house where she was born.

The foolish neighbours come and go,
    And tease her till the day draws by:
    At night she weeps, "How vain am I!
How should he love a thing so low?"

LXI

If, in thy second state sublime,
    Thy ransom'd reason change replies
    With all the circle of the wise,
The perfect flower of human time;

And if thou cast thine eyes below,
    How dimly character'd and slight,
    How dwarf'd a growth of cold and night,
How blanch'd with darkness must I grow!

[59] Fossilized.   [60] Prime: dawn of time.

[61] Tennyson's note: "The poet speaks of these poems. Methinks I have built a rich shrine to my friend, but it will not last" (II, 562).

[62] Hallam Tennyson's note: "Inserted in 1851 [in the fourth edition of the poem] as a pendant to Section III" (II, 563).

Yet turn thee to the doubtful shore,
1170   Where thy first form was made a man;
      I loved thee, Spirit, and love, nor can
The soul of Shakspeare love thee more.

LXII

Tho' if an eye that's downward cast
      Could make thee somewhat blench or fail,
      Then be my love an idle tale,
And fading legend of the past;

And thou, as one that once declined,
      When he was little more than boy,
      On some unworthy heart with joy,
1180 But lives to wed an equal mind;

And breathes a novel world, the while
      His other passion wholly dies,
      Or in the light of deeper eyes
Is matter for a flying smile.

LXIII

Yet pity for a horse o'er-driven,
      And love in which my hound has part,
      Can hang no weight upon my heart
In its assumptions up to heaven;

And I am so much more than these,
1190   As thou, perchance, art more than I,
      And yet I spare them sympathy,
And I would set their pains at ease.

So mayst thou watch me where I weep,
      As, unto vaster motions bound,
      The circuits of thine orbit round
A higher height, a deeper deep.

LXIV

Dost thou look back on what hath been,
      As some divinely gifted man,
      Whose life in low estate began
1200 And on a simple village green;

Who breaks his birth's invidious bar,
      And grasps the skirts of happy chance,
      And breasts the blows of circumstance,
And grapples with his evil star;

Who makes by force his merit known
      And lives to clutch the golden keys,
      To mould a mighty state's decrees,
And shape the whisper of the throne;

And moving up from high to higher,
      Becomes on Fortune's crowning slope   121
      The pillar of a people's hope,
The centre of a world's desire;

Yet feels, as in a pensive dream,
      When all his active powers are still,
      A distant dearness in the hill,
A secret sweetness in the stream,

The limit of his narrower fate,
      While yet beside its vocal springs
      He play'd at counsellors and kings,
With one that was his earliest mate;   122

Who ploughs with pain his native lea
      And reaps the labour of his hands,
      Or in the furrow musing stands;
"Does my old friend remember me?"

LXV

Sweet soul, do with me as thou wilt;
      I lull a fancy trouble-tost
      With "Love's too precious to be lost,
A little grain shall not be spilt."

And in that solace can I sing,
      Till out of painful phases wrought   123
      There flutters up a happy thought,
Self-balanced on a lightsome wing:

Since we deserved the name of friends,
      And thine effect so lives in me,
      A part of mine may live in thee
And move thee on to noble ends.

LXVI

You thought my heart too far diseased;
      You wonder when my fancies play
      To find me gay among the gay,
Like one with any trifle pleased.   124

The shade by which my life was crost,
      Which makes a desert in the mind,
      Has made me kindly with my kind,
And like to him whose sight is lost;

Whose feet are guided thro' the land,
      Whose jest among his friends is free,
      Who takes the children on his knee,
And winds their curls about his hand:

He plays with threads, he beats his chair
      For pastime, dreaming of the sky;   125
      His inner day can never die,
His night of loss is always there.

LXVII

When on my bed the moonlight falls,
    I know that in thy place of rest
    By that broad water of the west,[63]
There comes a glory on the walls;

Thy marble bright in dark appears,
    As slowly steals a silver flame
    Along the letters of thy name,
And o'er the number of thy years.

The mystic glory swims away;
    From off my bed the moonlight dies;
    And closing eaves of wearied eyes
I sleep till dusk is dipt in gray:

And then I know the mist is drawn
    A lucid veil from coast to coast,
    And in the dark church like a ghost
Thy tablet glimmers to the dawn.

LXVIII

When in the down I sink my head,
    Sleep, Death's twin-brother, times my
        breath;
    Sleep, Death's twin-brother, knows not
        Death,
Nor can I dream of thee as dead:

I walk as ere I walk'd forlorn,
    When all our path was fresh with dew,
    And all the bugle breezes blew
Reveillée to the breaking morn.

But what is this? I turn about,
    I find a trouble in thine eye,
    Which makes me sad I know not why,
Nor can my dream resolve the doubt:

But ere the lark hath left the lea
    I wake, and I discern the truth;
    It is the trouble of my youth
That foolish sleep transfers to thee.

LXIX

I dream'd there would be Spring no more,
    That Nature's ancient power was lost:
    The streets were black with smoke and
        frost,
They chatter'd trifles at the door:

I wander'd from the noisy town,
    I found a wood with thorny boughs: 1290
    I took the thorns to bind my brows,
I wore them like a civic crown:

I met with scoffs, I met with scorns
    From youth and babe and hoary hairs:
    They call'd me in the public squares
The fool that wears a crown of thorns:[64]

They call'd me fool, they call'd me child:
    I found an angel of the night;
    The voice was low, the look was bright;
He look'd upon my crown and smiled: 1300

He reach'd the glory of a hand,
    That seem'd to touch it into leaf:
    The voice was not the voice of grief,
The words were hard to understand.

LXX

I cannot see the features right,
    When on the gloom I strive to paint
    The face I know; the hues are faint
And mix with hollow masks of night;

Cloud-towers by ghostly masons wrought,
    A gulf that ever shuts and gapes,   1310
    A hand that points, and palled shapes
In shadowy thoroughfares of thought;

And crowds that stream from yawning doors,
    And shoals of pucker'd faces drive;
    Dark bulks that tumble half alive,
And lazy lengths on boundless shores;

Till all at once beyond the will
    I hear a wizard music roll,
    And thro' a lattice on the soul
Looks thy fair face and makes it still.   1320

LXXI

Sleep, kinsman thou to death and trance
    And madness, thou hast forged at last
    A night-long Present of the Past
In which we went thro' summer France.[65]

Hadst thou such credit with the soul?
    Then bring an opiate trebly strong,
    Drug down the blindfold sense of wrong
That so my pleasure may be whole;

---

[63] Tennyson's note: "The Severn" (II, 563). In another note he adds: "I myself did not see Clevedon till years after the burial of A. H. H. (Jan. 3, 1834), and then in later editions of *In Memoriam* I altered [in line 1267] the word 'chancel' . . . to 'dark church'" (II, 563–564).

[64] Tennyson's note: "To write poems about death and grief is 'to wear a crown of thorns,' which the people say ought to be laid aside" (II, 564).

[65] Tennyson and Hallam traveled together through France in 1830.

While now we talk as once we talk'd
1330   Of men and minds, the dust of change,
     The days that grow to something strange,
In walking as of old we walk'd

Beside the river's wooded reach,
     The fortress, and the mountain ridge,
     The cataract flashing from the bridge,
The breaker breaking on the beach.

LXXII

Risest thou thus, dim dawn, again,
     And howlest, issuing out of night,
     With blasts that blow the poplar white,
1340   And lash with storm the streaming pane?

Day, when my crown'd estate begun
     To pine in that reverse of doom,
     Which sicken'd every living bloom,
And blurr'd the splendour of the sun;

Who usherest in the dolorous hour
     With thy quick tears that make the rose
     Pull sideways, and the daisy close
Her crimson fringes to the shower;

Who might'st have heaved a windless flame
1350   Up the deep East, or, whispering, play'd
     A chequer-work of beam and shade
Along the hills, yet look'd the same.

As wan, as chill, as wild as now;
     Day, mark'd as with some hideous crime,
     When the dark hand struck down thro'
       time,
And cancell'd nature's best: but thou,

Lift as thou may'st thy burthen'd brows
     Thro' clouds that drench the morning star,
     And whirl the ungarner'd sheaf afar,
1360   And sow the sky with flying boughs,

And up thy vault with roaring sound
     Climb thy thick noon, disastrous day;
     Touch thy dull goal of joyless gray,
And hide thy shame beneath the ground.

LXXIII

So many worlds, so much to do,
     So little done, such things to be,
     How know I what had need of thee,
For thou wert strong as thou wert true?

The fame is quench'd that I foresaw,
1370   The head hath miss'd an earthly wreath:
     I curse not nature, no, nor death;
For nothing is that errs from law.

We pass; the path that each man trod
     Is dim, or will be dim, with weeds:
     What fame is left for human deeds
In endless age? It rests with God.

O hollow wraith of dying fame,
     Fade wholly, while the soul exults,
     And self-infolds the large results
Of force that would have forged a name.   13

LXXIV

As sometimes in a dead man's face,
     To those that watch it more and more,
     A likeness, hardly seen before,
Comes out—to some one of his race:

So, dearest, now thy brows are cold,
     I see thee what thou art, and know
     Thy likeness to the wise below,
Thy kindred with the great of old.

But there is more than I can see,
     And what I see I leave unsaid,   13
     Nor speak it, knowing Death has made
His darkness beautiful with thee.

LXXV

I leave thy praises unexpress'd
     In verse that brings myself relief,
     And by the measure of my grief
I leave thy greatness to be guess'd;

What practice howsoe'er expert
     In fitting aptest words to things,
     Or voice the richest-toned that sings,
Hath power to give thee as thou wert?   14

I care not in these fading days
     To raise a cry that lasts not long,
     And round thee with the breeze of song
To stir a little dust of praise.

Thy leaf has perish'd in the green,
     And, while we breathe beneath the sun,
     The world which credits what is done
Is cold to all that might have been.

So here shall silence guard thy fame;
     But somewhere, out of human view,   14
     Whate'er thy hands are set to do
Is wrought with tumult of acclaim.

LXXVI

Take wings of fancy, and ascend,
     And in a moment set thy face
     Where all the starry heavens of space
Are sharpen'd to a needle's end;

Take wings of foresight; lighten thro'
    The secular abyss[66] to come,
    And lo, thy deepest lays are dumb
420 Before the mouldering of a yew;

And if the matin songs,[67] that woke
    The darkness of our planet, last,
    Thine own shall wither in the vast,
Ere half the lifetime of an oak.

Ere these have clothed their branchy bowers
    With fifty Mays, thy songs are vain;
    And what are they when these remain
The ruin'd shells of hollow towers?

LXXVII

What hope is here for modern rhyme
430   To him, who turns a musing eye
    On songs, and deeds, and lives, that lie
Foreshorten'd in the tract of time?

These mortal lullabies of pain
    May bind a book, may line a box,
    May serve to curl a maiden's locks;
Or when a thousand moons shall wane

A man upon a stall may find,
    And, passing, turn the page that tells
    A grief, then changed to something else,
440 Sung by a long-forgotten mind.

But what of that? My darken'd ways
    Shall ring with music all the same;
    To breathe my loss is more than fame,
To utter love more sweet than praise.

LXXVIII

Again at Christmas did we weave
    The holly round the Christmas hearth;
    The silent snow possess'd the earth,
And calmly fell our Christmas-eve:

The yule-clog[68] sparkled keen with frost,
450   No wing of wind the region swept,
    But over all things brooding slept
The quiet sense of something lost.

As in the winters left behind,
    Again our ancient games had place,
    The mimic picture's breathing grace,
And dance and song and hoodman-blind.[69]

Who show'd a token of distress?
    No single tear, no mark of pain:
    O sorrow, then can sorrow wane?
O grief, can grief be changed to less?   1460

O last regret, regret can die!
    No—mixt with all this mystic frame,
    Her deep relations are the same,
But with long use her tears are dry.

LXXIX

"More than my brothers are to me,"[70]—
    Let this not vex thee, noble heart!
    I know thee of what force thou art
To hold the costliest love in fee.[71]

But thou and I are one in kind,
    As moulded like in Nature's mint;   1470
    And hill and wood and field did print
The same sweet forms in either mind.

For us the same cold streamlet curl'd
    Thro' all his eddying coves; the same
    All winds that roam the twilight came
In whispers of the beauteous world.

At one dear knee we proffer'd vows,
    One lesson from one book we learn'd,
    Ere childhood's flaxen ringlet turn'd
To black and brown on kindred brows.   1480

And so my wealth resembles thine,
    But he was rich where I was poor,
    And he supplied my want the more
As his unlikeness fitted mine.

LXXX

If any vague desire should rise,
    That holy Death ere Arthur died
    Had moved me kindly from his side,
And dropt the dust on tearless eyes;

---

[66] Tennyson's note: "the ages upon ages to be" (II, 566).
[67] Tennyson's note: "The great early poets" (II, 566).
[68] Clog: Northern and Scottish dialect for log.
[69] Tennyson's notes: *"The mimic picture's breathing grace. Tableaux vivants."* "Hoodman-blind, blind man's bluff" (II, 566–567).
[70] Tennyson's note: "This section is addressed to my brother Charles (Tennyson Turner)" (II, 567). See Section IX.
[71] In fee: possession.

Then fancy shapes, as fancy can,
1490   The grief my loss in him had wrought,
        A grief as deep as life or thought,
But stay'd in peace with God and man.

I make a picture in the brain;
        I hear the sentence that he speaks;
        He bears the burthen of the weeks
But turns his burthen into gain.

His credit thus shall set me free;
        And, influence-rich to soothe and save,
        Unused example from the grave
1500 Reach out dead hands to comfort me.

LXXXI

Could I have said while he was here,[72]
        "My love shall now no further range;
        There cannot come a mellower change,
For now is love mature in ear."

Love, then, had hope of richer store:
        What end is here to my complaint?
        This haunting whisper makes me faint,
"More years had made me love thee more."

But Death returns an answer sweet:
1510   "My sudden frost was sudden gain,
        And gave all ripeness to the grain,
It might have drawn from after-heat."

LXXXII

I wage not any feud with Death
        For changes wrought on form and face;
        No lower life that earth's embrace
May breed with him, can fright my faith.

Eternal process moving on,
        From state to state the spirit walks;
        And these are but the shatter'd stalks,
1520 Or ruin'd chrysalis of one.

Nor blame I Death, because he bare
        The use of virtue out of earth:
        I know transplanted human worth
Will bloom to profit, otherwhere.

For this alone on Death I wreak
        The wrath that garners in my heart;
        He put our lives so far apart
We cannot hear each other speak.

LXXXIII

Dip down upon the northern shore,
        O sweet new-year delaying long;   152
        Thou doest expectant nature wrong;
Delaying long, delay no more.

What stays thee from the clouded noons,
        Thy sweetness from its proper place?
        Can trouble live with April days,
Or sadness in the summer moons?

Bring orchis, bring the foxglove spire,
        The little speedwell's darling blue,
        Deep tulips dash'd with fiery dew,
Laburnums, dropping-wells of fire.   154

O thou, new-year, delaying long,
        Delayest the sorrow in my blood,
        That longs to burst a frozen bud
And flood a fresher throat with song.

LXXXIV

When I contemplate all alone
        The life that had been thine below,
        And fix my thoughts on all the glow
To which thy crescent would have grown;

I see thee sitting crown'd with good,
        A central warmth diffusing bliss   155
        In glance and smile, and clasp and kiss,
On all the branches of thy blood;

Thy blood, my friend, and partly mine;
        For now the day was drawing on,
        When thou should'st link thy life with
                one[73]
Of mine own house, and boys of thine

Had babbled "Uncle" on my knee;
        But that remorseless iron hour
        Made cypress of her orange flower,
Despair of Hope, and earth of thee.   156

I seem to meet their least desire,
        To clap their cheeks, to call them mine.
        I see their unborn faces shine
Beside the never-lighted fire.

I see myself an honour'd guest,
        Thy partner in the flowery walk
        Of letters, genial table-talk,
Or deep dispute, and graceful jest;

[72] Tennyson's note: "Would that I could have said, etc." (II, 567).
[73] One: Tennyson's sister Emily, to whom Hallam was engaged to be married.

While now thy prosperous labour fills
570   The lips of men with honest praise,
      And sun by sun the happy days
Descend below the golden hills

With promise of a morn as fair;
      And all the train of bounteous hours
      Conduct by paths of growing powers,
To reverence and the silver hair;

Till slowly worn her earthly robe,
      Her lavish mission richly wrought,
      Leaving great legacies of thought,
580 Thy spirit should fail from off the globe;

What time mine own might also flee,
      As link'd with thine in love and fate,
      And, hovering o'er the dolorous strait
To the other shore, involved in thee,

Arrive at last the blessed goal,
      And He that died in Holy Land
      Would reach us out the shining hand
And take us as a single soul.

What reed was that on which I leant?
590   Ah, backward fancy, wherefore wake
      The old bitterness again, and break
The low beginnings of content.

     LXXXV[74]
Thus truth came borne with bier and pall,
      I felt it, when I sorrow'd most,
      'Tis better to have loved and lost,
Than never to have loved at all—

O true in word, and tried in deed,
      Demanding, so to bring relief
      To this which is our common grief,
600 What kind of life is that I lead;

And whether trust in things above
      Be dimm'd of sorrow, or sustain'd;
      And whether love for him have drain'd
My capabilities of love;

Your words have virtue such as draws
      A faithful answer from the breast,
      Thro' light reproaches, half exprest,
And loyal unto kindly laws.

My blood an even tenor kept,
      Till on mine ear this message falls,   1610
      That in Vienna's fatal walls
God's finger touch'd him, and he slept.

The great Intelligences fair
      That range above our mortal state,
      In circle round the blessed gate,
Received and gave him welcome there;

And led him thro' the blissful climes,
      And show'd him in the fountain fresh
      All knowledge that the sons of flesh
Shall gather in the cycled times.   1620

But I remain'd, whose hopes were dim,
      Whose life, whose thoughts were little
         worth,
      To wander on a darken'd earth,
Where all things round me breathed of him.

O friendship, equal-poised control,
      O heart, with kindliest motion warm,
      O sacred essence, other form,
O solemn ghost, O crowned soul!

Yet none could better know than I,
      How much of act at human hands   1630
      The sense of human will demands[75]
By which we dare to live or die.

Whatever way my days decline,
      I felt and feel, tho' left alone,
      His being working in mine own,
The footsteps of his life in mine;

A life that all the Muses deck'd
      With gifts of grace, that might express
      All-comprehensive tenderness,
All-subtilising intellect: 1640

---

    [74] A part of this section was written as early as 1833. In the earliest editions of the standard edition of the poems, Hallam Tennyson remarked that this entire section was addressed to Edmund Lushington, who became a close friend of Tennyson in the 1830s and married his sister Cecilia in 1842. But Hallam withdrew this note after 1913, possibly because he discovered the early version of the poem (Ricks, p. 932). But then he added a note that lines 1707 f. refer to Emily Sellwood, to whom Tennyson became engaged to marry in 1838. If these lines refer to Emily, the concluding lines of the poem (1693–96 and 1709 f.) surely refer to Lushington.
    [75] Tennyson's note: ". . . the knowledge that we have free will demands from us action" (II, 569).

And so my passion hath not swerved
    To works of weakness, but I find
    An image comforting the mind,
And in my grief a strength reserved.

Likewise the imaginative woe,
    That loved to handle spiritual strife,
    Diffused the shock thro' all my life,
But in the present broke the blow.

My pulses therefore beat again
1650   For other friends that once I met;
    Nor can it suit me to forget
The mighty hopes that make us men.

I woo your love: I count it crime
    To mourn for any overmuch;
    I, the divided half of such
A friendship as had master'd Time;

Which masters Time indeed, and is
    Eternal, separate from fears:
    The all-assuming months and years
1660 Can take no part away from this:

But Summer on the steaming floods,
    And Spring that swells the narrow brooks,
    And Autumn, with a noise of rooks,
That gather in the waning woods,

And every pulse of wind and wave
    Recalls, in change of light or gloom,
    My old affection of the tomb,
And my prime passion in the grave:

My old affection of the tomb,
1670   A part of stillness, yearns to speak:
    "Arise, and get thee forth and seek
A friendship for the years to come.

"I watch thee from the quiet shore;
    Thy spirit up to mine can reach;
    But in dear words of human speech
We two communicate no more."

And I, "Can clouds of nature stain
    The starry clearness of the free?
    How is it? Canst thou feel for me
1680 Some painless sympathy with pain?"

And lightly does the whisper fall;
    " 'Tis hard for thee to fathom this;
    I triumph in conclusive bliss,
And that serene result of all."

So hold I commerce with the dead;
    Or so methinks the dead would say;
    Or so shall grief with symbols play
And pining life be fancy-fed.

Now looking to some settled end,
    That these things pass, and I shall prove   169
    A meeting somewhere, love with love,
I crave your pardon, O my friend;

If not so fresh, with love as true,
    I, clasping brother-hands, aver
    I could not, if I would, transfer
The whole I felt for him to you.

For which be they that hold apart
    The promise of the golden hours?
    First love, first friendship, equal powers,
That marry with the virgin heart.   170

Still mine, that cannot but deplore,
    That beats within a lonely place,
    That yet remembers his embrace,
But at his footstep leaps no more,

My heart, tho' widow'd, may not rest
    Quiet in the love of what is gone,
    But seeks to beat in time with one
That warms another living breast.

Ah, take the imperfect gift I bring,
    Knowing the primrose yet is dear,   171
    The primrose of the later year,
As not unlike to that of Spring.

LXXXVI
Sweet after showers, ambrosial air,
    That rollest from the gorgeous gloom
    Of evening over brake and bloom
And meadow, slowly breathing bare

The round of space, and rapt below
    Thro' all the dewy-tassell'd wood,
    And shadowing down the horned flood[76]
In ripples, fan my brows and blow   172

[76] In his notes in the standard edition Tennyson places the occasion of this poem in a particular evening at Barmouth, when the wind was from the west off fields of fern (brake) and flowers (and thus "ambrosial") and he looked out at the ocean "Between two promontories" (II, 570).

The fever from my cheek, and sigh
    The full new life that feeds thy breath
    Throughout my frame, till Doubt and
      Death,
Ill brethren, let the fancy fly

From belt to belt of crimson seas
    On leagues of odour streaming far,
    To where in yonder orient star
A hundred spirits whisper "Peace."

LXXXVII

I past beside the reverend walls[77]
    In which of old I wore the gown;
    I roved at random thro' the town,
And saw the tumult of the halls;

And heard once more in college fanes[78]
    The storm their high-built organs make,
    And thunder-music, rolling, shake
The prophet blazon'd on the panes;

And caught once more the distant shout,
    The measured pulse of racing oars
    Among the willows; paced the shores
And many a bridge, and all about

The same gray flats again, and felt
    The same, but not the same; and last
    Up that long walk of limes I past
To see the rooms in which he dwelt.

Another name was on the door:
    I linger'd; all within was noise
    Of songs, and clapping hands, and boys
That crash'd the glass and beat the floor;

Where once we held debate, a band
    Of youthful friends, on mind and art,
    And labour, and the changing mart,
And all the framework of the land;

When one would aim an arrow fair,
    But send it slackly from the string;
    And one would pierce an outer ring,
And one an inner, here and there;

And last the master-bowman, he,
    Would cleave the mark. A willing ear
    We lent him. Who, but hung to hear
The rapt oration flowing free

From point to point, with power and grace
    And music in the bounds of law,
    To those conclusions when we saw
The God within him light his face,

And seem to lift the form, and glow
    In azure orbits heavenly-wise;
    And over those ethereal eyes
The bar of Michael Angelo.[79]

LXXXVIII

Wild bird,[80] whose warble, liquid sweet,
    Rings Eden thro' the budded quicks,[81]
    O tell me where the senses mix,
O tell me where the passions meet,

Whence radiate: fierce extremes employ
    Thy spirits in the darkening leaf,
    And in the midmost heart of grief
Thy passion clasps a secret joy:

And I—my harp would prelude woe—
    I cannot all command the strings;
    The glory of the sum of things
Will flash along the chords and go.

LXXXIX

Witch-elms that counterchange the floor
    Of this flat lawn with dusk and bright;[82]
    And thou, with all thy breadth and height
Of foliage, towering sycamore;

How often, hither wandering down,
    My Arthur found your shadows fair,
    And shook to all the liberal air
The dust and din and steam of town:

He brought an eye for all he saw;
    He mixt in all our simple sports;
    They pleased him, fresh from brawling
      courts
And dusty purlieus of the law.

O joy to him in this retreat,
    Immantled in ambrosial dark,
    To drink the cooler air, and mark
The landscape winking thro' the heat:

O sound to rout the brood of cares,
    The sweep of scythe in morning dew,
    The gust that round the garden flew,
And tumbled half the mellowing pears!

[77] Tennyson's note: "Trinity College, Cambridge" (II, 570).   [78] Fanes: chapels.
[79] Tennyson's note: "The broad bar of frontal bone over the eyes of Michael Angelo" (II, 570).
[80] Wild bird: nightingale.
[81] Hallam Tennyson's note: "quickset thorn" (II, 570); more generally, hedgerows.
[82] The scene is Tennyson's family home, the rectory at Somersby.

O bliss, when all in circle drawn
    About him, heart and ear were fed
    To hear him, as he lay and read
The Tuscan poets on the lawn:

Or in the all-golden afternoon
    A guest, or happy sister, sung,
    Or here she brought the harp and flung
A ballad to the brightening moon:

Nor less it pleased in livelier moods,
1810   Beyond the bounding hill to stray,
    And break the livelong summer day
With banquet in the distant woods;

Whereat we glanced from theme to theme,
    Discuss'd the books to love or hate,
    Or touch'd the changes of the state,
Or threaded some Socratic dream;

But if I praised the busy town,
    He loved to rail against it still,
    For "ground in yonder social mill
1820 We rub each other's angles down,

"And merge" he said "in form and gloss
    The picturesque of man and man."
    We talk'd: the stream beneath us ran,
The wine-flask lying couch'd in moss,

Or cool'd within the glooming wave;
    And last, returning from afar,
    Before the crimson-circled star
Had fall'n into her father's grave,[83]

And brushing ankle-deep in flowers,
1830   We heard behind the woodbine vcil
    The milk that bubbled in the pail,
And buzzings of the honied hours.

    XC
He tasted love with half his mind,
    Nor ever drank the inviolate spring
    Where nighest heaven, who first could fling
This bitter seed among mankind;

That could the dead, whose dying eyes
    Were closed with wail, resume their life,
    They would but find in child and wife
1840 An iron welcome when they rise:

'Twas well, indeed, when warm with wine,
    To pledge them with a kindly tear,
    To talk them o'er, to wish them here,
To count their memories half divine;

But if they came who past away,
    Behold their brides in other hands;
    The hard heir strides about their lands,
And will not yield them for a day.

Yea, tho' their sons were none of these,
    Not less the yet-loved sire would make   185
    Confusion worse than death, and shake
The pillars of domestic peace.

Ah dear, but come thou back to me:
    Whatever change the years have wrought,
    I find not yet one lonely thought
That cries against my wish for thee.

    XCI
When rosy plumelets tuft the larch,
    And rarely pipes the mounted thrush;
    Or underneath the barren bush
Flits by the sea-blue bird of March;   186

Come, wear the form by which I know
    Thy spirit in time among thy peers;
    The hope of unaccomplish'd years
Be large and lucid round thy brow.

When summer's hourly-mellowing change
    May breathe, with many roses sweet,
    Upon the thousand waves of wheat,
That ripple round the lonely grange;

Come: not in watches of the night,
    But where the sunbeam broodeth warm,   187
    Come, beauteous in thine after form,
And like a finer light in light.

    XCII
If any vision should reveal
    Thy likeness, I might count it vain
    As but the canker of the brain;
Yea, tho' it spake and made appeal

To chances where our lots were cast
    Together in the days behind,
    I might but say, I hear a wind
Of memory murmuring the past.   188

---

[83] Tennyson's note: "Before Venus, the evening star, had dipt into the sunset. The planets, according to Laplace, were evolved from the sun" (II, 571).

Yea, tho' it spake and bared to view
    A fact within the coming year;
    And tho' the months, revolving near,
Should prove the phantom-warning true,

They might not seem thy prophecies,
    But spiritual presentiments,
    And such refraction of events
As often rises ere they rise.[84]

XCIII

I shall not see thee. Dare I say
    No spirit ever brake the band
    That stays him from the native land
Where first he walk'd when claspt in clay?

No visual shade of some one lost,
    But he, the Spirit himself, may come
    Where all the nerve of sense is numb;
Spirit to Spirit, Ghost to Ghost.

O, therefore from thy sightless[85] range
    With gods in unconjectured bliss,
    O, from the distance of the abyss
Of tenfold-complicated change,[86]

Descend, and touch, and enter; hear
    The wish too strong for words to name;
    That in this blindness of the frame
My Ghost may feel that thine is near.

XCIV

How pure at heart and sound in head,
    With what divine affections bold
    Should be the man whose thought would
        hold
An hour's communion with the dead.

In vain shalt thou, or any, call
    The spirits from their golden day,
    Except, like them, thou too canst say,
My spirit is at peace with all.

They haunt the silence of the breast,
    Imaginations calm and fair,
    The memory like a cloudless air,
The conscience as a sea at rest:

But when the heart is full of din,
    And doubt beside the portal waits,
    They can but listen at the gates,
And hear the household jar within.

XCV

By night we linger'd on the lawn,
    For underfoot the herb was dry;
    And genial warmth; and o'er the sky
The silvery haze of summer drawn;

And calm that let the tapers burn
    Unwavering: not a cricket chirr'd:
    The brook alone far-off was heard,
And on the board the fluttering urn:[87]

And bats went round in fragrant skies,
    And wheel'd or lit the filmy shapes[88]
    That haunt the dusk, with ermine capes
And woolly breasts and beaded eyes;

While now we sang old songs that peal'd
    From knoll to knoll, where, couch'd at
       ease,
    The white kine glimmer'd, and the trees
Laid their dark arms about the field.

But when those others, one by one,
    Withdrew themselves from me and night,
    And in the house light after light
Went out, and I was all alone,

A hunger seized my heart; I read
    Of that glad year which once had been,
    In those fall'n leaves which kept their
       green,
The noble letters of the dead:

And strangely on the silence broke
    The silent-speaking words, and strange
    Was love's dumb cry defying change
To test his worth; and strangely spoke

The faith, the vigour, bold to dwell
    On doubts that drive the coward back,
    And keen thro' wordy snares to track
Suggestion to her inmost cell.

[84] Tennyson's note: "The heavenly bodies are seen above the horizon, by refraction, before they actually rise" (II, 571).

[85] Sightless: beyond sight.

[86] Hallam Tennyson's note: "Refers to the ten heavens of Dante [*Paradiso*, XXVIII]" (II, 572).

[87] In his note Tennyson places this section in a particular occasion at Somersby: "It was a marvellously still night, and I asked my brother Charles to listen to the brook, which we had never heard so far off before" (II, 572). The urn is a tea-urn with a flame under it.

[88] Tennyson's note: "Moths" (II, 572).

So word by word, and line by line,
  The dead man touch'd me from the past,
  And all at once it seem'd at last
The living soul[89] was flash'd on mine,

And mine in this[90] was wound, and whirl'd
  About empyreal heights of thought,
  And came on that which is, and caught
1960 The deep pulsations of the world,

Æonian[91] music measuring out
  The steps of Time—the shocks of
    Chance—
  The blows of Death. At length my trance
Was cancell'd, stricken thro' with doubt.

Vague words! but ah, how hard to frame
  In matter-moulded forms of speech,
  Or ev'n for intellect to reach
Thro' memory that which I became:

Till now the doubtful dusk reveal'd
  The knolls once more where, couch'd at
1970   ease,
  The white kine glimmer'd, and the trees
Laid their dark arms about the field:

And suck'd from out the distant gloom
  A breeze began to tremble o'er
  The large leaves of the sycamore,
And fluctuate all the still perfume,

And gathering freshlier overhead,
  Rock'd the full-foliaged elms, and swung
  The heavy-folded rose, and flung
1980 The lilies to and fro, and said

"The dawn, the dawn," and died away;
  And East and West, without a breath,
  Mixt their dim lights, like life and death,
To broaden into boundless day.

XCVI

You say, but with no touch of scorn,
  Sweet-hearted, you, whose light-blue eyes
  Are tender over drowning flies,
You tell me, doubt is Devil-born.[92]

I know not: one indeed I knew
  In many a subtle question versed,   199
  Who touch'd a jarring lyre at first,
But ever strove to make it true:

Perplext in faith, but pure in deeds,
  At last he beat his music out.
  There lives more faith in honest doubt,
Believe me, than in half the creeds.

He fought his doubts and gather'd strength,
  He would not make his judgment blind,
  He faced the spectres of the mind
And laid them: thus he came at length   200

To find a stronger faith his own;
  And Power was with him in the night,
  Which makes the darkness and the light,
And dwells not in the light alone,

But in the darkness and the cloud,
  As over Sinaï's peaks of old,
  While Israel made their gods of gold,
Altho' the trumpet blew so loud.[93]

XCVII

My love has talk'd with rocks and trees;
  He finds on misty mountain-ground   20
  His own vast shadow glory-crown'd;
He sees himself in all he sees.

Two partners of a married life—
  I look'd on these and thought of thee
  In vastness and in mystery,
And of my spirit as of a wife.

These two—they dwelt with eye on eye,
  Their hearts of old have beat in tune,
  Their meetings made December June,
Their every parting was to die.   20

Their love has never past away;
  The days she never can forget
  Are earnest that he loves her yet,
Whate'er the faithless people say.

---

[89] Tennyson's note: "*The living soul.* The Deity, maybe. The first reading [until 1872] 'his living soul' troubled me, as perhaps giving a wrong impression." Hallam Tennyson goes on to quote his father as saying, "Of course the greater Soul may include the less. . . . I have often had that feeling of being whirled up and rapt into the Great Soul" (II, 573).
[90] Until 1872, "mine in his was wound."   [91] Æonian: of the ages.
[92] You: possibly Emily Sellwood, who was troubled by Tennyson's (to her) unorthodox religious beliefs and questionings.
[93] In his note Tennyson quotes the passage from Exodus (19:16) in which Moses communes with God in the cloud on the top of the mountain while his people made idols below (II, 573-574).

Her life is lone, he sits apart,
   He loves her yet, she will not weep,
   Tho' rapt in matters dark and deep
He seems to slight her simple heart.

He thrids the labyrinth of the mind,
   He reads the secret of the star,
   He seems so near and yet so far,
He looks so cold: she thinks him kind.

She keeps the gift of years before,
   A wither'd violet is her bliss:
   She knows not what his greatness is,
For that, for all, she loves him more.

For him she plays, to him she sings
   Of early faith and plighted vows;
   She knows but matters of the house,
And he, he knows a thousand things.

Her faith is fixt and cannot move,
   She darkly feels him great and wise,
   She dwells on him with faithful eyes,
"I cannot understand: I love."

XCVIII

You[94] leave us: you will see the Rhine,
   And those fair hills I sail'd below,
   When I was there with him; and go
By summer belts of wheat and vine

To where he breathed his latest breath,
   That City. All her splendour seems
   No livelier than the wisp that gleams
On Lethe in the eyes of Death.

Let her great Danube rolling fair
   Enwind her isles, unmark'd of me:
   I have not seen, I will not see
Vienna; rather dream that there,

A treble darkness, Evil haunts
   The birth, the bridal; friend from friend
   Is oftener parted, fathers bend
Above more graves, a thousand wants

Gnarr at the heels of men, and prey
   By each cold hearth, and sadness flings
   Her shadow on the blaze of kings:
And yet myself have heard him say,

That not in any mother town[95]
   With statelier progress to and fro
   The double tides of chariots flow
By park and suburb under brown

Of lustier leaves; nor more content,
   He told me, lives in any crowd,
   When all is gay with lamps, and loud
With sport and song, in booth and tent,

Imperial halls, or open plain;
   And wheels the circled dance, and breaks
   The rocket molten into flakes
Of crimson or in emerald rain.

XCIX

Risest thou thus, dim dawn, again,
   So loud with voices of the birds,
   So thick with lowings of the herds,
Day, when I lost the flower of men;

Who tremblest thro' thy darkling red
   On yon swoll'n brook that bubbles fast
   By meadows breathing of the past,
And woodlands holy to the dead;

Who murmurest in the foliaged eaves
   A song that slights the coming care,
   And Autumn laying here and there
A fiery finger on the leaves;

Who wakenest with thy balmy breath
   To myriads on the genial earth,
   Memories of bridal, or of birth,
And unto myriads more, of death.

O wheresoever those may be,
   Betwixt the slumber of the poles,
   To-day they count as kindred souls;
They know me not, but mourn with me.

C

I climb the hill:[96] from end to end
   Of all the landscape underneath,
   I find no place that does not breathe
Some gracious memory of my friend;

No gray old grange, or lonely fold,
   Or low morass and whispering reed,
   Or simple stile from mead to mead,
Or sheepwalk up the windy wold;

---

[94] Tennyson's note: "'You' is imaginary" (II, 574). Tennyson traveled to Germany with Hallam in 1832.
[95] Tennyson's note: "*mother town*, metropolis" (II, 575).
[96] Tennyson's note: "Hill above Somersby" (II, 575).

Nor hoary knoll of ash and haw
 That hears the latest linnet trill,
 Nor quarry trench'd along the hill
And haunted by the wrangling daw;

Nor runlet tinkling from the rock;
2110 Nor pastoral rivulet that swerves
 To left and right thro' meadowy curves,
That feed the mothers of the flock;

But each has pleased a kindred eye,
 And each reflects a kindlier day;
 And, leaving these, to pass away,[97]
I think once more he seems to die.

CI

Unwatch'd, the garden bough shall sway,
 The tender blossom flutter down,
 Unloved, that beech will gather brown,
2120 This maple burn itself away;

Unloved, the sun-flower, shining fair,
 Ray round with flames her disk of seed,
 And many a rose-carnation feed
With summer spice the humming air;

Unloved, by many a sandy bar,
 The brook shall babble down the plain,
 At noon or when the lesser wain[98]
Is twisting round the polar star;

Uncared for, gird the windy grove,
2130 And flood the haunts of hern and crake;
 Or into silver arrows break
The sailing moon in creek and cove;

Till from the garden and the wild
 A fresh association blow,
 And year by year the landscape grow
Familiar to the stranger's child;

As year by year the labourer tills
 His wonted glebe, or lops the glades;[99]
 And year by year our memory fades
2140 From all the circle of the hills.

CII

We leave the well-beloved place
 Where first we gazed upon the sky;
 The roofs, that heard our earliest cry,
Will shelter one of stranger race.

We go, but ere we go from home,
 As down the garden-walks I move,
 Two spirits of a diverse love
Contend for loving masterdom.

One whispers, "Here thy boyhood sung
 Long since its matin song, and heard 2150
 The low love-language of the bird
In native hazels tassel-hung."

The other answers, "Yea, but here
 Thy feet have stray'd in after hours
 With thy lost friend among the bowers,
And this hath made them trebly dear."

These two have striven half the day,
 And each prefers his separate claim,
 Poor rivals in a losing game,
That will not yield each other way. 2160

I turn to go: my feet are set
 To leave the pleasant fields and farms;
 They mix in one another's arms
To one pure image of regret.

CIII

On that last night before we went
 From out the doors where I was bred,
 I dream'd a vision of the dead,
Which left my after-morn content.

Methought I dwelt within a hall,
 And maidens[100] with me: distant hills 2170
 From hidden summits fed with rills
A river sliding by the wall.

The hall with harp and carol rang.
 They sang of what is wise and good
 And graceful. In the centre stood
A statue veil'd, to which they sang;

---

[97] This section, and the three following, describe the poet's feelings when Tennyson and the other members of his family moved from Somersby in 1837.
[98] Lesser wain: the constellation Ursa minor.
[99] Wonted glebe: usual field; lops the glades: trims clearings in the forests.
[100] Tennyson's note: "They are the muses, poetry, arts—all that made life beautiful here." He goes on to identify the "hidden summits" with the divine, and the "river" with life (II, 576).

And which, tho' veil'd, was known to me,
    The shape of him I loved, and love
    For ever: then flew in a dove
180 And brought a summons from the sea:[101]

And when they learnt that I must go
    They wept and wail'd, but led the way
    To where a little shallop lay
At anchor in the flood below;

And on by many a level mead,
    And shadowing bluff that made the banks,
    We glided winding under ranks
Of iris, and the golden reed;

And still as vaster grew the shore
190   And roll'd the floods in grander space,
    The maidens gather'd strength and grace
And presence, lordlier than before;[102]

And I myself, who sat apart
    And watch'd them, wax'd in every limb;
    I felt the thews of Anakim,[103]
The pulses of a Titan's heart;

As one would sing the death of war,
    And one would chant the history
    Of that great race, which is to be,
200 And one the shaping of a star;

Until the forward-creeping tides
    Began to foam, and we to draw
    From deep to deep, to where we saw
A great ship lift her shining sides.

The man we loved was there on deck,
    But thrice as large as man he bent
    To greet us. Up the side I went,
And fell in silence on his neck:

Whereat those maidens with one mind
10   Bewail'd their lot; I did them wrong:
    "We served thee here," they said, "so long,
And wilt thou leave us now behind?"

So rapt I was, they could not win
    An answer from my lips, but he
    Replying, "Enter likewise ye
And go with us:" they enter'd in.

And while the wind began to sweep
    A music out of sheet and shroud,
    We steer'd her toward a crimson cloud
That landlike slept along the deep.   2220

CIV

The time draws near the birth of Christ;
    The moon is hid, the night is still;
    A single church below the hill
Is pealing, folded in the mist.

A single peal of bells below,
    That wakens at this hour of rest
    A single murmur in the breast,
That these are not the bells I know.

Like strangers' voices here they sound,
    In lands where not a memory strays,   2230
    Nor landmark breathes of other days,
But all is new unhallow'd ground.[104]

CV

To-night ungather'd let us leave
    This laurel, let this holly stand:
    We live within the stranger's land,
And strangely falls our Christmas-eve.

Our father's dust is left alone
    And silent under other snows:
    There in due time the woodbine blows,
The violet comes, but we are gone.   2240

No more shall wayward grief abuse
    The genial hour with mask and mime;
    For change of place, like growth of time,
Has broke the bond of dying use.

Let cares that petty shadows cast,
    By which our lives are chiefly proved,
    A little spare the night I loved,
And hold it solemn to the past.

But let no footstep beat the floor,
    Nor bowl of wassail mantle[105] warm;   2250
    For who would keep an ancient form
Thro' which the spirit breathes no more?

Be neither song, nor game, nor feast;
    Nor harp be touch'd, nor flute be blown;
    No dance, no motion, save alone
What lightens in the lucid east

---

[101] Tennyson's note: *"sea,* eternity" (II, 576).
[102] Tennyson's note: "The progress of the Age" (II, 576).
[103] Anakim: Biblical giants (Deuteronomy); the Titans are the giant divinities of classical mythology.
[104] Tennyson's note: "High Beech, Epping Forest (where we were living)" (II, 577).
[105] Mantle: become frothy.

Of rising worlds by yonder wood.
　　Long sleeps the summer in the seed;
　　Run out your measured arcs, and lead
2260　The closing cycle rich in good.

CVI

Ring out, wild bells, to the wild sky,
　　The flying cloud, the frosty light:
　　The year is dying in the night;
Ring out, wild bells, and let him die.

Ring out the old, ring in the new,
　　Ring, happy bells, across the snow:
　　The year is going, let him go;
Ring out the false, ring in the true.

Ring out the grief that saps the mind,
2270　For those that here we see no more;
　　Ring out the feud of rich and poor,
Ring in redress to all mankind.

Ring out a slowly dying cause,
　　And ancient forms of party strife;
　　Ring in the nobler modes of life,
With sweeter manners, purer laws.

Ring out the want, the care, the sin,
　　The faithless coldness of the times;
　　Ring out, ring out my mournful rhymes,
2280　But ring the fuller minstrel in.

Ring out false pride in place and blood,
　　The civic slander and the spite;
　　Ring in the love of truth and right,
Ring in the common love of good.

Ring out old shapes of foul disease;
　　Ring out the narrowing lust of gold;
　　Ring out the thousand wars of old,
Ring in the thousand years of peace.

Ring in the valiant man and free,
2290　The larger heart, the kindlier hand;
　　Ring out the darkness of the land,
Ring in the Christ that is to be.[106]

CVII

It is the day when he[107] was born,
　　A bitter day that early sank
　　Behind a purple-frosty bank
Of vapour, leaving night forlorn.

The time admits not flowers or leaves
　　To deck the banquet. Fiercely flies
　　The blast of North and East, and ice
Makes daggers at the sharpen'd eaves,　　2300

And bristles all the brakes and thorns
　　To yon hard crescent, as she hangs
　　Above the wood which grides[108] and clangs
Its leafless ribs and iron horns

Together, in the drifts that pass
　　To darken on the rolling brine
　　That breaks the coast. But fetch the wine,
Arrange the board and brim the glass;

Bring in great logs and let them lie,
　　To make a solid core of heat;　　　　231
　　Be cheerful-minded, talk and treat
Of all things ev'n as he were by;

We keep the day. With festal cheer,
　　With books and music, surely we
　　Will drink to him, whate'er he be,
And sing the songs he loved to hear.

CVIII

I will not shut me from my kind,
　　And, lest I stiffen into stone,
　　I will not eat my heart alone,
Nor feed with sighs a passing wind:　　232

What profit lies in barren faith,
　　And vacant yearning, tho' with might
　　To scale the heaven's highest height,
Or dive below the wells of Death?

What find I in the highest place,
　　But mine own phantom chanting hymns?
　　And on the depths of death there swims
The reflex of a human face.[109]

I'll rather take what fruit may be
　　Of sorrow under human skies:　　　　23
　　'Tis held that sorrow makes us wise,
Whatever wisdom sleep with thee.

CIX

Heart-affluence in discursive talk
　　From household fountains never dry;
　　The critic clearness of an eye,
That saw thro' all the Muses' walk;

---

[106] Tennyson's note: "The broader Christianity of the future" (II, 577).
[107] He: Hallam.
[108] Tennyson's note: "grides, grates" (II, 578).
[109] In a note paraphrasing this section Tennyson wrote: ". . . it is useless trying to find him in the other worlds—I find nothing but the reflections of myself" (II, 578).

Seraphic intellect and force
    To seize and throw the doubts of man;
    Impassion'd logic, which outran
340 The hearer in its fiery course;

High nature amorous of the good,
    But touch'd with no ascetic gloom;
    And passion pure in snowy bloom
Thro' all the years of April blood;

A love of freedom rarely felt,
    Of freedom in her regal seat
    Of England; not the schoolboy heat,
The blind hysterics of the Celt;

And manhood fused with female grace
350   In such a sort, the child would twine
    A trustful hand, unask'd, in thine,
And find his comfort in thy face;

All these have been, and thee mine eyes
    Have look'd on: if they look'd in vain,
    My shame is greater who remain,
Nor let thy wisdom make me wise.[110]

    CX
Thy converse drew us with delight,
    The men of rathe[111] and riper years:
    The feeble soul, a haunt of fears,
360 Forgot his weakness in thy sight.

On thee the loyal-hearted hung,
    The proud was half disarm'd of pride,
    Nor cared the serpent at thy side
To flicker with his double tongue.

The stern were mild when thou wert by,
    The flippant put himself to school
    And heard thee, and the brazen fool
Was soften'd, and he knew not why;

While I, thy nearest, sat apart,
370   And felt thy triumph was as mine;
    And loved them more, that they were thine,
The graceful tact, the Christian art;

Nor mine the sweetness or the skill,
    But mine the love that will not tire,
    And, born of love, the vague desire
That spurs an imitative will.

    CXI
The churl in spirit, up or down
    Along the scale of ranks, thro' all,
    To him who grasps a golden ball,
By blood a king, at heart a clown;   2380

The churl in spirit, howe'er he veil
    His want in forms for fashion's sake,
    Will let his coltish nature break
At seasons thro' the gilded pale:

For who can always act? but he,
    To whom a thousand memories call,
    Not being less but more than all
The gentleness he seem'd to be,

Best seem'd the thing he was, and join'd
    Each office of the social hour   2390
    To noble manners, as the flower
And native growth of noble mind;

Nor ever narrowness or spite,
    Or villain fancy fleeting by,
    Drew in the expression of an eye,
Where God and Nature met in light;

And thus he bore without abuse
    The grand old name of gentleman,
    Defamed by every charlatan,
And soil'd with all ignoble use.   2400

    CXII
High wisdom[112] holds my wisdom less,
    That I, who gaze with temperate eyes
    On glorious insufficiencies,
Set light by narrower perfectness.

But thou, that fillest all the room
    Of all my love, art reason why
    I seem to cast a careless eye
On souls, the lesser lords of doom.[113]

For what wert thou? some novel power
    Sprang up for ever at a touch,   2410
    And hope could never hope too much,
In watching thee from hour to hour,

---

[110] Tennyson's note: "If I do not let thy wisdom make me wise" (II, 580).
[111] Rathe: early.
[112] Hallam Tennyson's note: "*High wisdom* is ironical. 'High wisdom' has been twitting the poet that although he gazes with calm and indulgent eyes on unaccomplished greatness ["glorious insufficiencies"] yet he makes light of ["Set light by"] narrower natures more perfect in their own small way" (II, 581).
[113] Tennyson's note: "Those that have free-will, but less intellect" (II, 581).

Large elements in order brought,
   And tracts of calm from tempest made,
   And world-wide fluctuation sway'd
In vassal tides that follow'd thought.

CXIII

'Tis held that sorrow makes us wise;
   Yet how much wisdom sleeps with thee
   Which not alone had guided me,
2420 But served the seasons that may rise;

For can I doubt, who knew thee keen
   In intellect, with force and skill
   To strive, to fashion, to fulfil—
I doubt not what thou wouldst have been:

A life in civic action warm,
   A soul on highest mission sent,
   A potent voice of Parliament,
A pillar steadfast in the storm,

Should licensed boldness gather force,
2430 Becoming, when the time has birth,
   A lever to uplift the earth
And roll it in another course,

With thousand shocks that come and go,
   With agonies, with energies,
   With overthrowings, and with cries,
And undulations to and fro.

CXIV

Who loves not Knowledge? Who shall rail
   Against her beauty? May she mix
   With men and prosper! Who shall fix
2440 Her pillars?[114] Let her work prevail.

But on her forehead sits a fire:
   She sets her forward countenance
   And leaps into the future chance,
Submitting all things to desire.

Half-grown as yet, a child, and vain—
   She cannot fight the fear of death.
   What is she, cut from love and faith,
But some wild Pallas[115] from the brain

Of Demons? fiery-hot to burst
   All barriers in her onward race   2455
   For power. Let her know her place;
She is the second, not the first.

A higher hand must make her mild,
   If all be not in vain; and guide
   Her footsteps, moving side by side
With wisdom, like the younger child:

For she is earthly of the mind,
   But Wisdom heavenly of the soul.
   O, friend, who camest to thy goal
So early, leaving me behind,   2460

I would the great world grew like thee,
   Who grewest not alone in power
   And knowledge, but by year and hour
In reverence and in charity.

CXV

Now fades the last long streak of snow,
   Now burgeons every maze of quick[116]
   About the flowering squares,[117] and thick
By ashen roots[118] the violets blow.

Now rings the woodland loud and long,
   The distance takes a lovelier hue,   2475
   And drown'd in yonder living blue
The lark becomes a sightless song.

Now dance the lights on lawn and lea,
   The flocks are whiter down the vale,
   And milkier every milky sail
On winding stream or distant sea;

Where new the seamew pipes, or dives
   In yonder greening gleam, and fly
   The happy birds, that change their sky
To build and brood; that live their lives   2485

From land to land; and in my breast
   Spring wakens too; and my regret
   Becomes an April violet,
And buds and blossoms like the rest.

---

[114] Tennyson's note refers to Proverbs 9:1—"Wisdom hath builded her house, she hath hewn out her seven pillars" (II, 581).

[115] Pallas: Pallas Athena, Greek goddess of wisdom, born from the forehead of the ruler of the gods.

[116] Maze of quick: quickset, a hedgerow.   [117] Squares: fields.

[118] Ashen roots: roots of ash trees.

CXVI

Is it, then, regret for buried time
That keenlier in sweet April wakes,
And meets the year, and gives and takes
The colours of the crescent prime?[119]

490 Not all: the songs, the stirring air,
The life re-orient out of dust,
Cry thro' the sense to hearten trust
In that which made the world so fair.

Not all regret: the face will shine
Upon me, while I must alone;
And that dear voice, I once have known,
Still speak to me of me and mine:

Yet less of sorrow lives in me
For days of happy commune dead;
Less yearning for the friendship fled,
500 Than some strong bond which is to be.

CXVII

O days and hours, your work is this
To hold me from my proper place,
A little while from his embrace,
For fuller gain of after bliss:

That out of distance might ensue
Desire of nearness doubly sweet;
And unto meeting when we meet,
Delight a hundredfold accrue,

For every grain of sand that runs,
10 And every span of shade that steals,
And every kiss of toothed wheels,[120]
And all the courses of the suns.

CXVIII

Contemplate all this work of Time,
The giant labouring in his youth;
Nor dream of human love and truth,
As dying Nature's earth and lime;

But trust that those we call the dead
Are breathers of an ampler day
For ever nobler ends. They say,
20 The solid earth whereon we tread

In tracts of fluent heat began,
And grew to seeming-random forms,
The seeming prey of cyclic storms,
Till at the last arose the man;

Who throve and branch'd from clime to clime,
The herald of a higher race,
And of himself in higher place,
If so he type this work of time

Within himself, from more to more;
Or, crown'd with attributes of woe   2530
Like glories, move his course, and show
That life is not as idle ore,

But iron dug from central gloom,
And heated hot with burning fears,
And dipt in baths of hissing tears,
And batter'd with the shocks of doom

To shape and use. Arise and fly
The reeling Faun,[121] the sensual feast;
Move upward, working out the beast,
And let the ape and tiger die.   2540

CXIX[122]

Doors, where my heart was used to beat
So quickly, not as one that weeps
I come once more; the city sleeps;
I smell the meadow in the street;

I hear a chirp of birds; I see
Betwixt the black fronts long-withdrawn
A light-blue lane of early dawn,
And think of early days and thee,

And bless thee, for thy lips are bland,
And bright the friendship of thine eye;   2550
And in my thoughts with scarce a sigh
I take the pressure of thine hand.

CXX

I trust I have not wasted breath:
I think we are not wholly brain,
Magnetic mockeries; not in vain,
Like Paul with beasts, I fought with Death;[123]

---

[119] Tennyson's note: "*crescent prime*, growing spring" (II, 582).
[120] Tennyson's note: ". . . *span of shade*. . . . The sun-dial. . . . *toothed wheels*. The clock"
(II, 582).
[121] Faun: half-man, half-goat; a mythological figure of sensuality.
[122] See note to Section VII.
[123] In his note Tennyson cites a verse from 1 Corinthians 15:32—"If after the manner of men
I have fought with beasts at Ephesus, what advantageth it me?" (II, 582).

Not only cunning casts in clay:
    Let Science prove we are, and then
    What matters Science unto men,
2560 At least to me? I would not stay.

Let him, the wiser man who springs
    Hereafter, up from childhood shape
    His action like the greater ape,
But I was *born* to other things.[124]

CXXI

Sad Hesper o'er the buried sun
    And ready, thou, to die with him,
    Thou watchest all things ever dim
And dimmer, and a glory done:

The team is loosen'd from the wain,[125]
2570   The boat is drawn upon the shore;
    Thou listenest to the closing door,
And life is darken'd in the brain.

Bright Phosphor, fresher for the night,
    By thee the world's great work is heard
    Beginning, and the wakeful bird;
Behind thee comes the greater light:

The market boat is on the stream,
    And voices hail it from the brink;
    Thou hear'st the village hammer clink,
2580 And see'st the moving of the team.

Sweet Hesper-Phosphor,[126] double name
    For what is one, the first, the last,
    Thou, like my present and my past,
Thy place is changed; thou art the same.

CXXII

Oh, wast thou with me, dearest, then,
    While I rose up against my doom,[127]
    And yearn'd to burst the folded gloom,
To bare the eternal Heavens again,

To feel once more, in placid awe,
2590   The strong imagination roll
    A sphere of stars about my soul,
In all her motion one with law;

If thou wert with me, and the grave
    Divide us not, be with me now,
    And enter in at breast and brow,
Till all my blood, a fuller wave,

Be quicken'd with a livelier breath,
    And like an inconsiderate boy,
    As in the former flash of joy,
I slip the thoughts of life and death;   260

And all the breeze of Fancy blows,
    And every dew-drop paints a bow,[128]
    The wizard lightnings deeply glow,
And every thought breaks out a rose.

CXXIII

There rolls the deep where grew the tree.
    O earth, what changes hast thou seen!
    There where the long street roars, hath
        been
The stillness of the central sea.

The hills are shadows, and they flow
    From form to form, and nothing stands;   261
    They melt like mist, the solid lands,
Like clouds they shape themselves and go.

But in my spirit will I dwell,
    And dream my dream, and hold it true;
    For tho' my lips may breathe adieu,
I cannot think the thing farewell.

CXXIV

That which we dare invoke to bless;
    Our dearest faith; our ghastliest doubt;
    He, They, One, All; within, without;
The Power in darkness whom we guess;   262

I found Him not in world or sun,
    Or eagle's wing, or insect's eye;
    Nor thro' the questions men may try,
The petty cobwebs we have spun:

If e'er when faith had fall'n asleep,
    I heard a voice "believe no more"
    And heard an ever-breaking shore
That tumbled in the Godless deep;

[124] Tennyson's note: "Spoken ironically against mere materialism, not against evolution" (II, 583).
[125] Wain: wagon.
[126] Tennyson's note: "The evening star is also the morning star, death and sorrow brighten into death and hope" (II, 583).
[127] Tennyson's note: "*doom*—that of grief" (II, 583).
[128] Tennyson's note: "Every dew-drop turns into a miniature rainbow" (II, 583).

A warmth within the breast would melt
 The freezing reason's colder part,
 And like a man in wrath the heart
Stood up and answer'd "I have felt."

No, like a child in doubt and fear:
 But that blind clamour made me wise;
 Then was I as a child that cries,
But, crying, knows his father near;

And what I am beheld again
 What is, and no man understands;
 And out of darkness came the hands
That reach thro' nature, moulding men.

CXXV

Whatever I have said or sung,
 Some bitter notes my harp would give,
 Yea, tho' there often seem'd to live
A contradiction on the tongue,

Yet Hope had never lost her youth;
 She did but look through dimmer eyes;
 Or Love but play'd with gracious lies,
Because he felt so fix'd in truth:

And if the song were full of care,
 He breathed the spirit of the song;
 And if the words were sweet and strong
He set his royal signet there;

Abiding with me till I sail
 To seek thee on the mystic deeps,
 And this electric force, that keeps
A thousand pulses dancing, fail.

CXXVI

Love is and was my Lord and King,
 And in his presence I attend
 To hear the tidings of my friend,
Which every hour his couriers bring.

Love is and was my King and Lord,
 And will be, tho' as yet I keep
 Within his court on earth, and sleep
Encompass'd by his faithful guard,

And hear at times a sentinel
 Who moves about from place to place,
 And whispers to the worlds of space,
In the deep night, that all is well.

CXXVII

And all is well, tho' faith and form
 Be sunder'd in the night of fear;
 Well roars the storm to those that hear
A deeper voice across the storm,

Proclaiming social truth shall spread,
 And justice, ev'n tho' thrice again
 The red fool-fury of the Seine[129]
Should pile her barricades with dead.

But ill for him that wears a crown,
 And him, the lazar, in his rags:
 They tremble, the sustaining crags;
The spires of ice are toppled down,

And molten up, and roar in flood;
 The fortress crashes from on high,
 The brute earth lightens to the sky,
And the great Æon sinks in blood,

And compass'd by the fires of Hell;
 While thou, dear spirit, happy star,
 O'erlook'st the tumult from afar,
And smilest, knowing all is well.

CXXVIII

The love that rose on stronger wings,
 Unpalsied when he met with Death,
 Is comrade of the lesser faith
That sees the course of human things.

No doubt vast eddies in the flood
 Of onward time shall yet be made,
 And throned races may degrade;
Yet O ye mysteries of good,

Wild Hours that fly with Hope and Fear,
 If all your office had to do
 With old results that look like new;
If this were all your mission here,

To draw, to sheathe a useless sword,
 To fool the crowd with glorious lies,
 To cleave a creed in sects and cries,
To change the bearing of a word,

To shift an arbitrary power,
 To cramp the student at his desk,
 To make old bareness picturesque
And tuft with grass a feudal tower;

[129] The French Revolution, here used as the type of political and social revolution.

Why then my scorn might well descend
2710   On you and yours. I see in part
     That all, as in some piece of art,
Is toil cöoperant to an end.

CXXIX

Dear friend, far off, my lost desire,
     So far, so near in woe and weal;
     O loved the most, when most I feel
There is a lower and a higher;

Known and unknown; human, divine;
     Sweet human hand and lips and eye;
     Dear heavenly friend that canst not die,
2720 Mine, mine, for ever, ever mine;

Strange friend, past, present, and to be;
     Loved deeplier, darklier understood;
     Behold, I dream a dream of good,
And mingle all the world with thee.

CXXX

Thy voice is on the rolling air;
     I hear thee where the waters run;
     Thou standest in the rising sun,
And in the setting thou art fair.

What art thou then? I cannot guess;
2730   But tho' I seem in star and flower
     To feel thee some diffusive power,
I do not therefore love thee less:

My love involves the love before;
     My love is vaster passion now;
     Tho' mix'd with God and Nature thou,
I seem to love thee more and more.

Far off thou art, but ever nigh;
     I have thee still, and I rejoice;
     I prosper, circled with thy voice;
2740 I shall not lose thee tho' I die.

CXXXI

O living will[130] that shalt endure
     When all that seems shall suffer shock,
     Rise in the spiritual rock,
Flow thro' our deeds and make them pure,

That we may lift from out of dust
     A voice as unto him that hears,
     A cry above the conquer'd years
To one that with us works, and trust,

With faith that comes of self-control,
     The truths that never can be proved   2750
     Until we close with all we loved,
And all we flow from, soul in soul.[131]

O true and tried, so well and long,
     Demand not thou a marriage lay;[132]
     In that it is thy marriage day
Is music more than any song.

Nor have I felt so much of bliss
     Since first he told me that he loved
     A daughter of our house; nor proved[133]
Since that dark day a day like this;   2760

Tho' I since then have number'd o'er
     Some thrice three years: they went and came,
     Remade the blood and changed the frame,
And yet is love not less, but more;

No longer caring to embalm
     In dying songs a dead regret,
     But like a statue solid-set,
And moulded in colossal calm.

Regret is dead, but love is more
     Than in the summers that are flown,   2770
     For I myself with these have grown
To something greater than before;

[130] Tennyson's note: "*O living will*. That which we know as Free-will in man" (II, 586).

[131] In a note on this section in the standard edition, Hallam Tennyson quotes his father: "Yes, it is true that there are moments when the flesh is nothing to me, when I feel and know the flesh to be the vision, God and the Spiritual the only real and true. Depend upon it, the Spiritual *is* the real: it belongs to one more than the hand and the foot. You may tell me that my hand and foot are only imaginary symbols of my existence, I could believe you; but you never, never can convince me that the *I* is not an eternal Reality, and that the Spiritual is not the true and real part of me" (II, 585–586).

[132] The marriage celebrated in the epilogue to *In Memoriam* is that of Edmund Lushington to Tennyson's sister Cecilia in 1842. It is probable, however, that the poem was not completely written until 1845 (Ricks, p. 981).

[133] Proved: experienced.

Which makes appear the songs I made
  As echoes out of weaker times,
  As half but idle brawling rhymes,
The sport of random sun and shade.

But where is she, the bridal flower,
  That must be made a wife ere noon?
  She enters, glowing like the moon
780 Of Eden on its bridal bower:

On me she bends her blissful eyes
  And then on thee; they meet thy look
  And brighten like the star that shook
Betwixt the palms of paradise.

O when her life was yet in bud,
  He too foretold the perfect rose.
  For thee she grew, for thee she grows
For ever, and as fair as good.

And thou art worthy; full of power;
90   As gentle; liberal-minded, great,
  Consistent;[134] wearing all that weight
Of learning lightly like a flower.

But now set out: the noon is near,
  And I must give away the bride;
  She fears not, or with thee beside
And me behind her, will not fear.

For I that danced her on my knee,
  That watch'd her on her nurse's arm,
  That shielded all her life from harm
00 At last must part with her to thee;

Now waiting to be made a wife,
  Her feet, my darling, on the dead;
  Their pensive tablets round her head,
And the most living words of life

Breathed in her ear. The ring is on,
  The "wilt thou" answer'd, and again
  The "wilt thou" ask'd, till out of twain
Her sweet "I will" has made you one.

Now sign your names, which shall be read,
10   Mute symbols of a joyful morn,
  By village eyes as yet unborn;
The names are sign'd, and overhead

Begins the clash and clang that tells
  The joy to every wandering breeze;
  The blind wall rocks, and on the trees
The dead leaf trembles to the bells.

O happy hour, and happier hours
  Await them. Many a merry face
  Salutes them—maidens of the place,
That pelt us in the porch with flowers.   2820

O happy hour, behold the bride
  With him to whom her hand I gave.
  They leave the porch, they pass the grave
That has to-day its sunny side.

To-day the grave is bright for me,
  For them the light of life increased,
  Who stay to share the morning feast,
Who rest to-night beside the sea.

Let all my genial spirits advance
  To meet and greet a whiter sun;   2830
  My drooping memory will not shun
The foaming grape of eastern France.

It circles round, and fancy plays,
  And hearts are warm'd and faces bloom,
  As drinking health to bride and groom
We wish them store of happy days.

Nor count me all to blame if I
  Conjecture of a stiller guest,
  Perchance, perchance, among the rest,
And, tho' in silence, wishing joy.   2840

But they must go, the time draws on,
  And those white-favour'd horses wait;
  They rise, but linger; it is late;
Farewell, we kiss, and they are gone.

A shade falls on us like the dark
  From little cloudlets on the grass,
  But sweeps away as out we pass
To range the woods, to roam the park,

Discussing how their courtship grew,
  And talk of others that are wed,   2850
  And how she look'd, and what he said,
And back we come at fall of dew.

Again the feast, the speech, the glee,
  The shade of passing thought, the wealth
  Of words and wit, the double health,
The crowning cup, the three-times-three,

And last the dance;—till I retire:
  Dumb is that tower which spake so loud,
  And high in heaven the streaming cloud,
And on the downs a rising fire: 2860

[134] Consistent: of qualities well-knit, harmonious.

And rise, O moon, from yonder down,
    Till over down and over dale
    All night the shining vapour sail
And pass the silent-lighted town,

The white-faced halls, the glancing rills,
    And catch at every mountain head,
    And o'er the friths that branch and spread
Their sleeping silver thro' the hills;

And touch with shade the bridal doors,
2870   With tender gloom the roof, the wall;
    And breaking let the splendour fall
To spangle all the happy shores

By which they rest, and ocean sounds,
    And, star and system rolling past,
    A soul shall draw from out the vast
And strike his being into bounds,

And, moved thro' life of lower phase,
    Result in man, be born and think,
    And act and love, a closer link
2880 Betwixt us and the crowning race

Of those that, eye to eye, shall look
    On knowledge; under whose command
    Is Earth and Earth's, and in their hand
Is Nature like an open book;

No longer half-akin to brute,
    For all we thought and loved and did,
    And hoped, and suffer'd, is but seed
Of what in them is flower and fruit;

Whereof the man, that with me trod
2890   This planet, was a noble type
    Appearing ere the times were ripe,
That friend of mine who lives in God,

That God, which ever lives and loves,
    One God, one law, one element,
    And one far-off divine event,
To which the whole creation moves.
                 (1833–49) 1850

Arthur Wellesley, Duke of Wellington, died on September 14, 1852, and was buried with great pageantry on November 18. He had defeated Napoleon's armies in Spain and Portugal in 1809–14, and defeated Napoleon himself at the decisive battle of Waterloo in 1815. Later he served as a cabinet minister (he was prime minister from 1828 to 1830) and commander-in-chief, and in the last years of his life he was a secure and revered national hero. The poem was Tennyson's first major work as poet laureate; he published it as a pamphlet shortly before Wellington's funeral, and in a revised version in 1853. As he always was, Tennyson was uneasy that readers might take a poem written for a public occasion as somehow poetically inauthentic. His son quotes him as saying, late in his life, "They call the 'Ode on the Duke of Wellington' a Laureate Ode; nothing of the kind! it was written from a genuine admiration of the man" (Memoir, II, 403).

Ode on the Death of the Duke of Wellington

I

Bury the Great Duke
    With an empire's lamentation,
Let us bury the Great Duke
    To the noise of the mourning of a mighty
        nation,
Mourning when their leaders fall,
Warriors carry the warrior's pall,
And sorrow darkens hamlet and hall.

II

Where shall we lay the man whom we deplore?
Here, in streaming London's central roar.[1]
Let the sound of those he wrought for,
And the feet of those he fought for,
Echo round his bones for evermore.

III

Lead out the pageant: sad and slow,
As fits an universal woe,
Let the long, long procession go,
And let the sorrowing crowd about it grow,
And let the mournful martial music blow;
The last great Englishman is low.

IV

Mourn, for to us he seems the last,
Remembering all his greatness in the Past.
No more in soldier fashion will he greet
With lifted hand the gazer in the street.
O friends, our chief state-oracle is mute:
Mourn for the man of long-enduring blood,
The statesman-warrior, moderate, resolute,
Whole in himself, a common good.
Mourn for the man of amplest influence,
Yet clearest of ambitious crime,

---

[1] Wellington was buried in St. Paul's Cathedral.

Our greatest yet with least pretence,
Great in council and great in war,
Foremost captain of his time,
Rich in saving common-sense,
And, as the greatest only are,
In his simplicity sublime.
O good gray head which all men knew,
O voice from which their omens all men drew,
O iron nerves to true occasion true,
O fall'n at length that tower of strength
Which stood four-square to all the winds that
   blew!
Such was he whom we deplore.
The long self-sacrifice of life is o'er.
The great World-victor's[2] victor will be seen
   no more.

V

All is over and done:
Render thanks to the Giver,
England, for thy son.
Let the bell be toll'd.
Render thanks to the Giver,
And render him to the mould.
Under the cross of gold
That shines over city and river,
There he shall rest for ever
Among the wise and the bold.
Let the bell be toll'd:
And a reverent people behold
The towering car, the sable steeds:
Bright let it be with its blazon'd deeds,[3]
Dark in its funeral fold.
Let the bell be toll'd:
And a deeper knell in the heart be knoll'd;
And the sound of the sorrowing anthem roll'd
Thro' the dome of the golden cross;
And the volleying cannon thunder his loss;
He knew their voices of old.
For many a time in many a clime
His captain's-ear has heard them boom
Bellowing victory, bellowing doom:
When he with those deep voices wrought,
Guarding realms and kings from shame;
With those deep voices our dead captain taught
The tyrant, and asserts his claim

In that dread sound to the great name,
Which he has worn so pure of blame,
In praise and in dispraise the same,
A man of well-attemper'd frame.
O civic muse, to such a name,
To such a name for ages long,
To such a name,
Preserve a broad approach of fame,
And ever-echoing avenues of song.

VI

Who is he that cometh, like an honour'd guest,   80
With banner and with music, with soldier and
   with priest,
With a nation weeping, and breaking on my
   rest?[4]
Mighty Seaman, this is he
Was great by land as thou by sea.
Thine island loves thee well, thou famous man,
The greatest sailor since our world began.
Now, to the roll of muffled drums,
To thee the greatest soldier comes;
For this is he
Was great by land as thou by sea;   90
His foes were thine; he kept us free;
O give him welcome, this is he
Worthy of our gorgeous rites,
And worthy to be laid by thee;
For this is England's greatest son,
He that gain'd a hundred fights,
Nor ever lost an English gun;
This is he that far away
Against the myriads of Assaye[5]
Clash'd with his fiery few and won;   100
And underneath another sun,
Warring on a later day,
Round affrighted Lisbon drew
The treble works, the vast designs
Of his labour'd rampart-lines,[6]
Where he greatly stood at bay,
Whence he issued forth anew,
And ever great and greater grew,
Beating from the wasted vines
Back to France her banded swarms,   110
Back to France with countless blows,
Till o'er the hills her eagles flew

---

[2] World-victor: Napoleon.

[3] Blazon'd deeds: the names of Wellington's military victories were inscribed on the funeral car.

[4] These words are spoken by Horatio Nelson, England's great naval hero of the Napoleonic wars, whose victories in the Baltic and at the mouth of the Nile are named below.

[5] Assaye: the place of a victory Wellington won in India in 1803.

[6] During his campaigns in Spain and Portugal, Wellington defended Lisbon by building extensive defensive lines.

Beyond the Pyrenean pines,[7]
Follow'd up in valley and glen
With blare of bugle, clamour of men,
Roll of cannon and clash of arms,
And England pouring on her foes.
Such a war had such a close.
Again their ravening eagle rose
120 In anger, wheel'd on Europe-shadowing wings,
And barking for the thrones of kings;
Till one that sought but Duty's iron crown
On that loud sabbath[8] shook the spoiler down;
A day of onsets[9] of despair!
Dash'd on every rocky square
Their surging charges foam'd themselves away;
Last, the Prussian trumpet blew;
Thro' the long-tormented air
Heaven flash'd a sudden jubilant ray,[10]
And down we swept and charged and over-
130   threw.
So great a soldier taught us there,
What long-enduring hearts could do
In that world-earthquake, Waterloo!
Mighty Seaman, tender and true,
And pure as he from taint of craven guile,
O saviour of the silver-coasted isle,
O shaker of the Baltic and the Nile,
If aught of things that here befall
Touch a spirit among things divine,[11]
140 If love of country move thee there at all,
Be glad, because his bones are laid by thine!
And thro' the centuries let a people's voice
In full acclaim,
A people's voice,
The proof and echo of all human fame,
A people's voice, when they rejoice
At civic revel and pomp and game,
Attest their great commander's claim
With honour, honour, honour, honour to him,
150 Eternal honour to his name.

        VII
A people's voice! we are a people yet.
Tho' all men else their nobler dreams forget,

Confused by brainless mobs and lawless Powers;
Thank Him who isled us here, and roughly set
His Briton in blown seas and storming
    showers,
We have a voice, with which to pay the debt
Of boundless love and reverence and regret
To those great men who fought, and kept it
    ours.
And keep it ours, O God, from brute control;
O Statesmen, guard us, guard the eye, the soul   16
Of Europe, keep our noble England whole,
Ar.d save the one true seed of freedom sown
Betwixt a people and their ancient throne,
That sober freedom out of which there springs
Our loyal passion for our temperate kings;
For, saving that, ye help to save mankind
Till public wrong be crumpled into dust,
And drill the raw world for the march of mind,
Till crowds at length be sane and crowns be
    just.
But wink no more in slothful overtrust.   17
Remember him who led your hosts;
He bad you guard the sacred coasts.
Your cannons moulder on the seaward wall;[12]
His voice is silent in your council-hall
For ever; and whatever tempests lour
For ever silent; even if they broke
In thunder, silent; yet remember all
He spoke among you, and the Man who spoke;
Who never sold the truth to serve the hour,
Nor palter'd with Eternal God for power;   1
Who let the turbid streams of rumour flow
Thro' either babbling world of high and low;
Whose life was work, whose language rife
With rugged maxims hewn from life;
Who never spoke against a foe;
Whose eighty winters freeze with one rebuke
All great self-seekers trampling on the right:
Truth-teller was our England's Alfred[13] named;
Truth-lover was our English Duke;
Whatever record leap to light   1
He never shall be shamed.

---

[7] In 1813 the French armies in Spain and Portugal retreated over the Pyrenees into France, pursued by Wellington.
[8] Loud Sabbath: the battle of Waterloo, in which British and Prussian troops defeated Napoleon's army, was fought on Sunday, 18 June, 1815.
[9] Onsets: battles.
[10] Tennyson's note in the standard edition of his poetry: "The setting sun glanced on this last charge of the English and Prussians" (I, 754).
[11] Tennyson's note: "Dwell upon the word 'touch' and make it as long as 'can touch'" (I, 755).
[12] In the 1840s Wellington insistently warned that Great Britain was neglecting its military and was vulnerable to invasion.
[13] Alfred: ninth-century Saxon king.

VIII

Lo! the leader in these glorious wars
Now to glorious burial slowly borne,
Follow'd by the brave of other lands,
He, on whom from both her open hands
Lavish Honour shower'd all her stars,
And affluent Fortune emptied all her horn.
Yet, let all good things await
Him who cares not to be great,
But as he saves or serves the state.
Not once or twice in our rough island-story,
The path of duty was the way to glory:
He that walks it, only thirsting
For the right, and learns to deaden
Love of self, before his journey closes,
He shall find the stubborn thistle bursting
Into glossy purples, which outredden
All voluptuous garden-roses.
Not once or twice in our fair island-story,
The path of duty was the way to glory:
He, that ever following her commands,
On with toil of heart and knees and hands,
Thro' the long gorge to the far light has won
His path upward, and prevail'd,
Shall find the toppling crags of Duty scaled
Are close upon the shining table-lands
To which our God Himself is moon and sun.
Such was he: his work is done.
But while the races of mankind endure
Let his great example stand
Colossal, seen of every land,
And keep the soldier firm, the statesman pure:
Till in all lands and thro' all human story
The path of duty be the way to glory:
And let the land whose hearths he saved from
    shame
For many and many an age proclaim
At civic revel and pomp and game,
And when the long-illumined cities flame,
Their ever-loyal iron leader's fame,
With honour, honour, honour, honour to him,
Eternal honor to his name.

IX

Peace, his triumph will be sung
By some yet unmoulded tongue
Far on in summers that we shall not see:
Peace, it is a day of pain
For one about whose patriarchal knee
Late the little children clung:
O peace, it is a day of pain
For one upon whose hand and heart and brain
Once the weight and fate of Europe hung.

[14] Fane: Temple.

Ours the pain, be his the gain!
More than is of man's degree
Must be with us, watching here
At this, our great solemnity.
Whom we see not we revere;
We revere, and we refrain
From talk of battles loud and vain,
And brawling memories all too free
For such a wise humility
As befits a solemn fane:[14]   250
We revere, and while we hear
The tides of Music's golden sea
Setting toward eternity,
Uplifted high in heart and hope are we,
Until we doubt not that for one so true
There must be other nobler work to do
Than when he fought at Waterloo,
And Victor he must ever be.
For tho' the Giant Ages heave the hill
And break the shore, and evermore   260
Make and break, and work their will;
Tho' world on world in myriad myriads roll
Round us, each with different powers,
And other forms of life than ours,
What know we greater than the soul?
On God and Godlike men we build our trust.
Hush, the Dead March wails in the people's
    ears:
The dark crowd moves, and there are sobs and
    tears:
The black earth yawns: the mortal disappears;
Ashes to ashes, dust to dust;   270
He is gone who seem'd so great.—
Gone; but nothing can bereave him
Of the force he made his own
Being here, and we believe him
Something far advanced in State,
And that he wears a truer crown
Than any wreath that man can weave him.
Speak no more of his renown,
Lay your earthly fancies down,
And in the vast cathedral leave him.   280
God accept him, Christ receive him.

1852; revised 1853

*"Maud" is one of several poems—"Locksley Hall"
is another—in which Tennyson dramatizes the
theme of love frustrated by the crass prejudices of
rank and money. Ralph Rader in* The Biographical
Genesis of Tennyson's "Maud" *(1963) recounts the
circumstances of Tennyson's relationship with Rosa
Baring, the wealthy stepdaughter of an admiral,
who lived near Somersby and whom Tennyson met*

*in 1834. He was both discouraged and disillusioned
in his love for her (in 1838 she married somebody
else), and Rader plausibly argues that this experi-
ence was part of the impetus which went into
"Maud" and other poems on the same theme.*

*Tennyson himself, in notes included in the stand-
ard edition of his poetry, said of the poem: "This
poem of 'Maud or the Madness' [the original title
of the poem in manuscript] is a little* Hamlet, *the
history of a morbid, poetic soul, under the blighting
influence of a recklessly speculative age. He is the
heir of madness, an egoist with the makings of a
cynic, raised to a pure and holy love which elevates
his whole nature, passing from the height of triumph
to the lowest depth of misery, driven into madness
by the loss of her whom he has loved, and, when he
has at length passed through the fiery furnace, and
has recovered his reason, giving himself up to work
for the good of mankind through the unselfishness
born of a great passion. The peculiarity of this poem
is that different phases of passion in one person take
the place of different characters" (II, 502–503).*

*Most of the poem was written shortly before its
publication in 1855, although two of the lyrics (see
subsequent notes) were written in the 1830s. Tenny-
son added some passages for a second edition of the
poem in 1856; the most important additions are
noted. In 1859 he divided the poem, originally or-
ganized as twenty-six continuously numbered sec-
tions, into Parts I and II; in 1865, Part III was made
separate as well. The subtitle, "A Monodrama," was
added in 1875.*

Maud: A Monodrama

PART I

I

I

I hate the dreadful hollow behind the little
  wood,
Its lips in the field above are dabbled with
  blood-red heath,
The red-ribb'd ledges drip with a silent horror
  of blood,
And Echo there, whatever is ask'd her, answers
  "Death."

II

For there in the ghastly pit long since a body
  was found,
His who had given me life—O father! O God!
  was it well?—
Mangled, and flatten'd, and crush'd, and dinted
  into the ground:

There yet lies the rock that fell with him when
  he fell.

III

Did he fling himself down? who knows? for a
  vast speculation had fail'd,
And ever he mutter'd and madden'd, and ever
  wann'd with despair,
And out he walk'd when the wind like a broken
  worldling wail'd,
And the flying gold of the ruin'd woodlands
  drove thro' the air.

IV

I remember the time, for the roots of my hair
  were stirr'd
By a shuffled step, by a dead weight trail'd, by
  a whisper'd fright,
And my pulses closed their gates with a shock
  on my heart as I heard
The shrill-edged shriek of a mother divide the
  shuddering night.

V

Villainy somewhere! whose? One says, we are
  villains all.
Not he: his honest fame should at least by me
  be maintained:
But that old man, now lord of the broad estate
  and the Hall,
Dropt off gorged from a scheme that had left
  us flaccid and drain'd.

VI

Why do they prate of the blessings of Peace?
  we have made them a curse,
Pickpockets, each hand lusting for all that is
  not its own;
And lust of gain, in the spirit of Cain, is it
  better or worse
Than the heart of the citizen hissing in war on
  his own hearthstone?

VII

But these are the days of advance, the works of
  the men of mind,
When who but a fool would have faith in a
  tradesman's ware or his word?
Is it peace or war? Civil war, as I think, and
  that of a kind
The viler, as underhand, not openly bearing
  the sword.

VIII

Sooner or later I too may passively take the
  print

Of the golden age—why not? I have neither
  hope nor trust;
May make my heart as a millstone, set my face
  as a flint,
Cheat and be cheated, and die: who knows?
  we are ashes and dust.

IX

Peace sitting under her olive, and slurring the
  days gone by,
When the poor are hovell'd and hustled
  together, each sex, like swine,[1]
When only the ledger lives, and when only not
  all men lie;
Peach in her vineyard—yes!—but a company
  forges the wine.

X

And the vitriol madness flushes up in the
  ruffian's head,
Till the filthy by-lane rings to the yell of the
  trampled wife,
And chalk and alum and plaster are sold to the
  poor for bread,[2]
And the spirit of murder works in the very
  means of life,

XI

And Sleep must lie down arm'd, for the
  villainous centre-bits[3]
Grind on the wakeful ear in the hush of the
  moonless nights,
While another is cheating the sick of a few
  last gasps, as he sits
To pestle a poison'd poison behind his
  crimson lights.

XII

When a Mammonite mother kills her babe for
  a burial fee,
And Timour-Mammon[4] grins on a pile of
  children's bones,

Is it peace or war? better, war! loud war by
  land and by sea,
War with a thousand battles, and shaking a
  hundred thrones!

XIII

For I trust if an enemy's fleet came yonder
  round by the hill,
And the rushing battle-bolt sang from the
  three-decker[5] out of the foam, 50
That the smooth-faced snubnosed rogue would
  leap from his counter and till,
And strike, if he could, were it but with his
  cheating yardwand,[6] home.—

XIV[7]

What! am I raging alone as my father raged in
  his mood?
Must *I* too creep to the hollow and dash myself
  down and die
Rather than hold by the law that I made,
  nevermore to brood
On a horror of shatter'd limbs and a wretched
  swindler's lie?

XV

Would there be sorrow for *me?* there was *love*
  in the passionate shriek,
Love for the silent thing that had made false
  haste to the grave—
Wrapt in a cloak, as I saw him, and thought
  he would rise and speak
And rave at the lie and the liar, ah God, as he
  used to rave. 60

XVI

I am sick of the Hall and the hill, I am sick of
  the moor and the main.
Why should I stay? can a sweeter chance ever
  come to me here?
O, having the nerves of motion as well as the
  nerves of pain,
Were it not wise if I fled from the place and
  the pit and the fear?

---

[1] Perhaps an allusion to the workhouses established under the Poor Law of 1834, in which poor relief was made as unpalatable as possible and the sexes were segregated (until 1847, when a husband and wife over sixty years of age could ask to live together).
  [2] This allusion, like that to adulterated wine in line 36, is a topical reference to scandalous revelations about the substances used to adulterate bread.
  [3] Villainous centre-bits: drills used by burglars.
  [4] Timour-Mammon: Timour is a name of Tamerlane, a fourteenth-century Oriental tyrant. Mammon is the god of wealth. The Mammonite mother is another topical reference, this one probably to an incident reported in Carlyle's *Past and Present* (1843) in which the parents of three children were found guilty of poisoning them in order to collect a fee for their burial from a burial society.
  [5] Three-decker: warship.   [6] Cheating yardwand: inaccurate measure.
  [7] Sections xiv, xv, and xvi were added in 1856.

XVII

Workmen up at the Hall!—they are coming
  back from abroad;
The dark old place will be gilt by the touch of
  a millionaire:
I have heard, I know not whence, of the
  singular beauty of Maud;
I play'd with the girl when a child; she
  promised then to be fair.

XVIII

Maud with her venturous climbings and
  tumbles and childish escapes,
Maud the delight of the village, the ringing
70   joy of the Hall,
Maud with her sweet purse-mouth when my
  father dangled the grapes,
Maud the beloved of my mother, the moon-
  faced darling of all,—

XIX

What is she now? My dreams are bad. She may
  bring me a curse.
No, there is fatter game on the moor; she will
  let me alone.
Thanks, for the fiend best knows whether
  woman or man be the worse.
I will bury myself in myself, and the Devil may
  pipe to his own.

II

Long have I sigh'd for a calm: God grant I
  may find it at last!
It will never be broken by Maud, she has
  neither savour nor salt,
But a cold and clear-cut face, as I found when
  her carriage past,
Perfectly beautiful: let it be granted her: where
80   is the fault?
All that I saw (for her eyes were downcast,
  not to be seen)
Faultily faultless, icily regular, splendidly null,
Dead perfection, no more; nothing more, if it
  had not been
For a chance of travel, a paleness, an hour's
  defect of the rose,
Or an underlip, you may call it a little too
  ripe, too full,
Or the least little delicate aquiline curve in a
  sensitive nose,
From which I escaped heart-free, with the least
  little touch of spleen.

8 Orion: the constellation called the Hunter.

III

Cold and clear-cut face, why come you so
  cruelly meek,
Breaking a slumber in which all spleenful folly
  was drown'd,
Pale with the golden beam of an eyelash dead
  on the cheek,   9*
Passionless, pale, cold face, star-sweet on a
  gloom profound;
Womanlike, taking revenge too deep for a
  transient wrong
Done but in thought to your beauty, and ever
  as pale as before
Growing and fading and growing upon me
  without a sound,
Luminous, gemlike, ghostlike, deathlike, half
  the night long
Growing and fading and growing, till I could
  bear it no more,
But arose, and all by myself in my own dark
  garden ground,
Listening now to the tide in its broad-flung
  shipwrecking roar,
Now to the scream of a madden'd beach dragg'd
  down by the wave,
Walk'd in a wintry wind by a ghastly glimmer,
  and found   10
The shining daffodil dead, and Orion[8] low in
  his grave.

IV

I

A million emeralds break from the ruby-budded
  lime
In the little grove where I sit—ah, wherefore
  cannot I be
Like things of the season gay, like the bountiful
  season bland,
When the far-off sail is blown by the breeze of
  a softer clime,
Half-lost in the liquid azure bloom of a
  crescent of sea,
The silent sapphire-spangled marriage ring of
  the land?

II

Below me, there, is the village, and looks how
  quiet and small!
And yet bubbles o'er like a city, with gossip,
  scandal, and spite;

And Jack on his ale-house bench has as many
  lies as a Czar;
10 And here on the landward side, by a red rock,
  glimmers the Hall;
And up in the high Hall-garden I see her pass
  like a light;
But sorrow seize me if ever that light be my
  leading star!

III

When have I bow'd to her father, the wrinkled
  head of the race?
I met her to-day with her brother, but not to
  her brother I bow'd:
I bow'd to his lady-sister as she rode by on the
  moor;
But the fire of a foolish pride flash'd over her
  beautiful face.
O child, you wrong your beauty, believe it, in
  being so proud;
Your father has wealth well-gotten, and I am
  nameless and poor.

IV

I keep but a man and a maid, ever ready to
20 slander and steal;
I know it, and smile a hard-set smile, like a
  stoic, or like
A wiser epicurean, and let the world have its
  way:
For nature is one with rapine, a harm no
  preacher can heal;
The Mayfly is torn by the swallow, the sparrow
  spear'd by the shrike,
And the whole little wood where I sit is a world
  of plunder and prey.

V

We are puppets, Man in his pride, and Beauty
  fair in her flower;
Do we move ourselves, or are moved by an
  unseen hand at a game
That pushes us off from the board, and others
  ever succeed?
Ah yet, we cannot be kind to each other here
  for an hour;
We whisper, and hint, and chuckle, and grin
30 at a brother's shame;

However we brave it out, we men are a little
  breed.

VI

A monstrous eft[9] was of old the Lord and
  Master of Earth,
For him did his high sun flame, and his river
  billowing ran,
And he felt himself in his force to be Nature's
  crowning race.
As nine months go to the shaping an infant
  ripe for his birth,
So many a million of ages have gone to the
  making of man:
He now is first, but is he the last? is he not too
  base?

VII

The man of science himself is fonder of glory,
  and vain,
An eye well-practised in nature, a spirit bounded
  and poor;
The passionate heart of the poet is whirl'd into
  folly and vice.   140
I would not marvel at either, but keep a
  temperate brain;
For not to desire or admire, if a man could
  learn it, were more
Than to walk all day like the sultan of old in
  a garden of spice.

VIII

For the drift of the Maker is dark, an Isis[10] hid
  by the veil.
Who knows the ways of the world, how God
  will bring them about?
Our planet is one, the suns are many, the world
  is wide.
Shall I weep if a Poland fall? shall I shriek if a
  Hungary fail?
Or an infant civilization be ruled with rod or
  with knout?[11]
I have not made the world, and He that made
  it will guide.

IX

Be mine a philosopher's life in the quiet wood-
  land ways,   150

---

[9] Tennyson's note: "*A monstrous eft,* the great old lizards of geology" (II, 506).
[10] Isis: Egyptian goddess of motherhood and fertility.
[11] Parts of Poland were occupied by Russia and Austria in the 1840s, and a revolt of the Hungarians against Austria was put down in 1849. The *knout,* a heavy whip used for flogging, was a popular emblem in the 1840s and 1850s to signify the tyranny of the Russian czars; Ricks points out (p. 1051) that in a poem written in 1852 ("Hands All Round!") Tennyson refers to "Russian whips and Austrian rods."

Where if I cannot be gay let a passionless peace
    be my lot,
Far-off from the clamour of liars belied in the
    hubbub of lies;
From the long-neck'd geese of the world that
    are ever hissing dispraise
Because their natures are little, and, whether
    he heed it or not,
Where each man walks with his head in a cloud
    of poisonous flies.

X

And most of all would I flee from the cruel
    madness of love,
The honey of poison-flowers and all the meas-
    ureless ill.
Ah Maud, you milkwhite fawn, you are all
    unmeet for a wife.
Your mother is mute in her grave as her image
    in marble above;
Your father is ever in London, you wander
160   about at your will;
You have but fed on the roses and lain in the
    lilies of life.

V

I

A voice by the cedar tree
In the meadow under the Hall!
She is singing an air that is known to me,
A passionate ballad gallant and gay,
A martial song like a trumpet's call!
Singing alone in the morning of life,
In the happy morning of life and of May,
Singing of men that in battle array,
170 Ready in heart and ready in hand,
March with banner and bugle and fife
To the death, for their native land.

II

Maud with her exquisite face,
And wild voice pealing up to the sunny sky,
And feet like sunny gems on an English
    green,
Maud in the light of her youth and her grace,
Singing of Death, and of Honour that cannot
    die,
Till I well could weep for a time so sordid
    and mean,
And myself so languid and base.

III

180 Silence, beautiful voice!
Be still, for you only trouble the mind

With a joy in which I cannot rejoice,
A glory I shall not find.
Still! I will hear you no more,
For your sweetness hardly leaves me a choice
But to move to the meadow and fall before
Her feet on the meadow grass, and adore,
Not her, who is neither courtly nor kind,
Not her, not her, but a voice.

VI

I

Morning arises stormy and pale,   19
No sun, but a wannish glare
In fold upon fold of hueless cloud,
And the budded peaks of the wood, are
    bow'd
Caught and cuff'd by the gale:
I had fancied it would be fair.

II

Whom but Maud should I meet
Last night, when the sunset burn'd
On the blossom'd gable-ends
At the head of the village street,
Whom but Maud should I meet?   20
And she touch'd my hand with a smile so
    sweet,
She made me divine amends
For a courtesy not return'd.

III

And thus a delicate spark
Of glowing and growing light
Thro' the livelong hours of the dark
Kept itself warm in the heart of my dreams,
Till at last when the morning came
Ready to burst in a colour'd flame;
In a cloud, it faded, and seems   21
But an ashen-gray delight.

IV

What if with her sunny hair,
And smile as sunny as cold,
She meant to weave me a snare
Of some coquettish deceit,
Cleopatra-like as of old
To entangle me when we met,
To have her lion roll in a silken net
And fawn at a victor's feet.

V

Ah, what shall I be at fifty   22
Should Nature keep me alive,

If I find the world so bitter
When I am but twenty-five?
Yet, if she were not a cheat,
If Maud were all that she seem'd,
And her smile were all that I dream'd,
Then the world were not so bitter
But a smile could make it sweet.

VI

What if tho' her eye seem'd full
Of a kind intent to me,
What if that dandy-despot, he,
That jewell'd mass of millinery,
That oil'd and curl'd Assyrian bull[12]
Smelling of musk[13] and of insolence,
Her brother, from whom I keep aloof,
Who wants the finer politic sense
To mask, tho' but in his own behoof,
With a glassy smile his brutal scorn—
What if he had told her yestermorn
How prettily for his own sweet sake
A face of tenderness might be feign'd,
And a moist mirage in desert eyes,
That so, when the rotten hustings[14] shake
In another month to his brazen lies,
A wretched vote may be gain'd.

VII

For a raven ever croaks, at my side,
Keep watch and ward, keep watch and
    ward,[15]
Or thou wilt prove their tool.
Yea, too, myself from myself I guard,
For often a man's own angry pride
Is cap and bells for a fool.

VIII

Perhaps the smile and tender tone
Came out of her pitying womanhood,
For am I not, am I not, here alone
So many a summer since she died,
My mother, who was so gentle and good?
Living alone in an empty house,
Here half-hid in the gleaming wood,
Where I hear the dead at midday moan,
And the shrieking rush of the wainscot
    mouse,

And my own sad name in corners cried,
When the shiver of dancing leaves is
    thrown
About its echoing chambers wide,
Till a morbid hate and horror have grown
Of a world in which I have hardly mixt,
And a morbid eating lichen fixt
On a heart half-turn'd to stone.

IX

O heart of stone, are you flesh, and caught
By that you swore to withstand?
For what was it else within me wrought
But, I fear, the new strong wine of love,
That made my tongue so stammer and trip
When I saw the treasured splendour, her
    hand,
Come sliding out of her sacred glove,
And the sunlight broke from her lip?

X

I have play'd with her when a child;
She remembers it now we meet.
Ah, well, well, well, I *may* be beguiled
By some coquettish deceit.
Yet, if she were not a cheat,
If Maud were all that she seem'd,
And her smile had all that I dream'd,
Then the world were not so bitter
But a smile could make it sweet.

VII

I

Did I hear it half in a doze
    Long since, I know not where?
Did I dream it an hour ago,
    When asleep in this arm-chair?

II

Men were drinking together,
    Drinking and talking of me;
"Well, if it prove a girl, the boy
    Will have plenty: so let it be."

III

Is it an echo of something
    Read with a boy's delight,

---

[12] Tennyson's note: "*Assyrian Bull.* With hair curled like that of the bulls on Assyrian sculpture" (II, 507). In 1853 the British Museum had acquired a large sculpture of a bull from excavations at Nineveh.

[13] Musk: perfume.

[14] Hustings: literally, the temporary platform from which a political candidate is nominated, and on which he stands to make his address to the electors; by extension, the entire electoral process.

[15] Ward: the action of a lookout.

Viziers[16] nodding together
    In some Arabian night?

IV

Strange, that I hear two men,
    Somewhere, talking of me;
"Well, if it prove a girl, my boy
300   Will have plenty: so let it be."

VIII

She came to the village church,
And sat by a pillar alone;
An angel watching an urn
Wept over her, carved in stone;
And once, but once, she lifted her eyes,
And suddenly, sweetly, strangely blush'd
To find they were met by my own;
And suddenly, sweetly, my heart beat stronger
And thicker, until I heard no longer
310 The snowy-banded,[17] dilettante,
Delicate-handed priest intone;
And thought, is it pride? and mused and sigh'd,
"No surely, now it cannot be pride."

IX

I was walking a mile,
More than a mile from the shore,
The sun look'd out with a smile
Betwixt the cloud and the moor,
And riding at set of day
Over the dark moor land,
320 Rapidly riding far away,
She waved to me with her hand.
There were two at her side,
Something flash'd in the sun,
Down by the hill I saw them ride,
In a moment they were gone:
Like a sudden spark
Struck vainly in the night,
Then returns the dark
With no more hope of light.

X

I

330 Sick, am I sick of a jealous dread?
Was not one of the two at her side

This new-made lord, whose splendour plucks
The slavish hat from the villager's head?
Whose old grandfather has lately died,
Gone to a blacker pit, for whom
Grimy nakedness dragging his trucks
And laying his trams[18] in a poison'd gloom
Wrought, till he crept from a gutted mine
Master of half a servile shire,
And left his coal all turn'd into gold   34
To a grandson, first of his noble line,
Rich in the grace all women desire,
Strong in the power that all men adore,
And simper and set their voices lower,
And soften as if to a girl, and hold
Awe-stricken breaths at a work divine,
Seeing his gewgaw castle shine,
New as his title, built last year,
There amid perky[19] larches and pine,
And over the sullen-purple moor   35
(Look at it) pricking a cockney ear.

II

What, has he found my jewel out?
For one of the two that rode at her side
Bound for the Hall, I am sure was he:
Bound for the Hall, and I think for a bride.
Blithe would her brother's acceptance be.
Maud could be gracious too, no doubt
To a lord, a captain, a padded shape,
A bought commission, a waxen face,
A rabbit mouth that is ever agape—   36
Bought? what is it he cannot buy?
And therefore splenetic, personal, base,
A wounded thing with a rancorous cry,
At war with myself and a wretched race,
Sick, sick to the heart of life, am I.

III

Last week came one to the county town,
To preach our poor little army down,
And play the game of the despot kings,
Tho' the state has done it and thrice as well.
This broad-brimm'd hawker of holy things,[20]   37
Whose ear is cramm'd with his cotton, and
        rings
Even in dreams to the chink of his pence,
This huckster put down war! can he tell
Whether war be a cause or a consequence?

---

[16] Viziers: councillors.
[17] Snowy-banded: bands are the strips of cloth worn at the neck of clerical dress.
[18] Trucks and trams: vehicles used in mining coal   [19] Perky: self-assertive.
[20] The broad-brimmed hat suggests that the pacifist speaker was a Quaker. John Bright, a Quaker, a member of Parliament who was opposed to the Crimean War, and the son of a father who had made money in cotton, was suggested as the model of this figure. Tennyson's note: "I did not even know at the time that he was a Quaker" (II, 507).

Put down the passions that make earth Hell!
Down with ambition, avarice, pride,
Jealousy, down! cut off from the mind
The bitter springs of anger and fear;
80 Down too, down at your own fireside,
With the evil tongue and the evil ear,
For each is at war with mankind.

IV[21]

I wish I could hear again
The chivalrous battle-song
That she warbled alone in her joy!
I might persuade myself then
She would not do herself this great wrong,
To take a wanton dissolute boy
For a man and leader of men.

V

Ah God, for a man with heart, head, hand,
90 Like some of the simple great ones gone
For ever and ever by,
One still strong man in a blatant[22] land,
Whatever they call him, what care I,
Aristocrat, democrat, autocrat—one
Who can rule and dare not lie.

VI

And ah for a man to arise in me,
That the man I am may cease to be!

XI

I

O let the solid ground
Not fail beneath my feet
00 Before my life has found
What some have found so sweet;
Then let come what come may,
What matter if I go mad,
I shall have had my day.

II

Let the sweet heavens endure,
Not close and darken above me
Before I am quite quite sure
That there is one to love me;

Then let come what come may
To a life that has been so sad,   410
I shall have had my day.

XII

I

Birds in the high Hall-garden
When twilight was falling,
Maud, Maud, Maud, Maud,[23]
They were crying and calling.

II

Where was Maud? in our wood;
And I, who else?, was with her,
Gathering woodland lilies,
Myriads blow together.

III

Birds in our wood sang   420
Ringing thro' the valleys,
Maud is here, here, here[24]
In among the lilies.

IV

I kiss'd her slender hand,
She took the kiss sedately;
Maud is not seventeen,
But she is tall and stately.

V

I to cry out on pride
Who have won her favour!
O Maud were sure of heaven   430
If lowliness[25] could save her.

VI

I know the way she went
Home with her maiden posy,
For her feet have touch'd the meadows
And left the daisies rosy.[26]

VII

Birds in the high Hall-garden
Were crying and calling to her,
Where is Maud, Maud, Maud?
One is come to woo her.

---

[21] This section, and section vi below, were added in 1856.   [22] Blatant: brawling, clamorous.
[23] Tennyson's note: "Like the rooks' caw" (II, 508).
[24] Tennyson's note: "Like the call of the little birds" (II, 508).
[25] Lowliness: meekness.
[26] Tennyson's note: "Because if you tread on the daisy, it turns up a rosy underside" (II, 508).

VIII

440
    Look, a horse at the door,
      And little King Charley[27] snarling!
    Go back, my lord, across the moor,
      You are not her darling.

XIII

I

Scorn'd, to be scorn'd by one that I scorn,
Is that a matter to make me fret?
That a calamity hard to be borne?
Well, he may live to hate me yet.
Fool that I am to be vext with his pride!
I past him, I was crossing his lands;
450 He stood on the path a little aside;
His face, as I grant, in spite of spite,
Has a broad-blown comeliness, red and white,
And six feet two, as I think, he stands;
But his essences[28] turn'd the live air sick,
And barbarous opulence jewel-thick
Sunn'd itself on his breast and his hands.

II

Who shall call me ungentle, unfair?
I long'd so heartily then and there
To give him the grasp of fellowship;
460 But while I past he was humming an air,
Stopt, and then with a riding whip
Leisurely tapping a glossy boot,
And curving a contumelious lip,
Gorgonized[29] me from head to foot
With a stony British stare.

III

Why sits he here in his father's chair?
That old man never comes to his place:
Shall I believe him ashamed to be seen?
For only once, in the village street,
470 Last year, I caught a glimpse of his face,
A gray old wolf and a lean.
Scarcely, now, would I call him a cheat;
For then, perhaps, as a child of deceit,
She might by a true descent be untrue;
And Maud is as true as Maud is sweet:
Tho' I fancy her sweetness only due
To the sweeter blood by the other side;
Her mother has been a thing complete,
However she came to be so allied.
480 And fair without, faithful within,
Maud to him is nothing akin:

Some peculiar mystic grace
Made her only the child of her mother,
And heap'd the whole inherited sin
On that huge scapegoat of the race,
All, all upon the brother.

IV

Peace, angry spirit, and let him be!
Has not his sister smiled on me?

XIV

I

Maud has a garden of roses
And lilies fair on a lawn;   4
There she walks in her state
And tends upon bed and bower,
And thither I climb'd at dawn
And stood by her garden-gate;
A lion ramps[30] at the top,
He is claspt by a passion-flower.

II

Maud's own little oak-room
(Which Maud, like a precious stone
Set in the heart of the carven gloom,
Lights with herself, when alone   5
She sits by her music and books
And her brother lingers late
With a roystering company) looks
Upon Maud's own garden-gate:
And I thought as I stood, if a hand, as white
As ocean-foam in the moon, were laid
On the hasp of the window, and my Delight
Had a sudden desire, like a glorious ghost, to
    glide,
Like a beam of the seventh Heaven, down to
    my side,
There were but a step to be made.   5

III

The fancy flatter'd my mind,
And again seem'd overbold;
Now I thought that she cared for me,
Now I thought she was kind
Only because she was cold.

IV

I heard no sound where I stood
But the rivulet on from the lawn

---

[27] King Charley: her spaniel.   [28] Essences: perfume.
[29] Gorgonized: in classical mythology, the gaze of the Gorgon Medusa turned humans to stone.
[30] Ramps: as in rampant, with forelegs raised.

Running down to my own dark wood;
Or the voice of the long sea-wave as it swell'd
Now and then in the dim-gray dawn;
But I look'd, and round, all round the house I
    beheld
The death-white curtain drawn;[31]
Felt a horror over me creep,
Prickle my skin and catch my breath,
Knew that the death-white curtain meant but
    sleep,
Yet I shudder'd and thought like a fool of the
    sleep of death.

XV

So dark a mind within me dwells,
    And I make myself such evil cheer,
That if *I* be dear to some one else,
    Then some one else may have much to fear;
But if *I* be dear to some one else,
    Then I should be to myself more dear.
Shall I not take care of all that I think,
Yea even of wretched meat and drink,
If I be dear,
If I be dear to some one else.

XVI

I

This lump of earth has left his estate
The lighter by the loss of his weight;
And so that he find what he went to seek,
And fulsome Pleasure clog him, and drown
His heart in the gross mud-honey[32] of town,
He may stay for a year who has gone for a
    week:
But this is the day when I must speak,
And I see my Oread[33] coming down,
O this is the day!
O beautiful creature, what am I
That I dare to look her way;
Think I may hold dominion sweet,
Lord of the pulse that is lord of her breast,
And dream of her beauty with tender dread,
From the delicate Arab arch[34] of her feet
To the grace that, bright and light as the crest
Of a peacock, sits on her shining head,
And she knows it not: O, if she knew it,
To know her beauty might half undo it.

I know it the one bright thing to save
My yet young life in the wilds of Time,
Perhaps from madness, perhaps from crime,
Perhaps from a selfish grave.[35]

II

What, if she be fasten'd to this fool lord,
Dare I bid her abide by her word?
Should I love her so well if she
Had given her word to a thing so low?
Shall I love her as well if she
Can break her word were it even for me?
I trust that it is not so.

III

Catch not my breath, O clamorous heart,
Let not my tongue be a thrall to my eye,
For I must tell her before we part,
I must tell her, or die.

XVII

Go not, happy day,
    From the shining fields,
Go not, happy day,
    Till the maiden yields.
Rosy is the West,
    Rosy is the South,
Roses are her cheeks,
    And a rose her mouth
When the happy Yes
    Falters from her lips,
Pass and blush the news
    Over glowing ships;
Over blowing seas,
    Over seas at rest,
Pass the happy news,
    Blush it thro' the West;
Till the red man dance
    By his red cedar-tree,
And the red man's babe
    Leap, beyond the sea.
Blush from West to East,
    Blush from East to West,
Till the West is East,
    Blush it thro' the West.
Rosy is the West,
    Rosy is the South,
Roses are her cheeks,
    And a rose her mouth.

[31] That is, curtains are drawn at every window of the house.
[32] Mud-honey: degrading pleasures; sweet, cloying mud.
[33] Oread: nymph of mountains and hills.
[34] Arab arch: arched like the neck of a graceful horse.
[35] Selfish grave: self-willed grave, by suicide.

XVIII

I

I have led her home, my love, my only friend.
600   There is none like her, none.
And never yet so warmly ran my blood
And sweetly, on and on
Calming itself to the long-wish'd-for end,
Full to the banks, close on the promised good.

II

None like her, none.
Just now the dry-tongued laurels' pattering talk
Seem'd her light foot along the garden walk,
And shook my heart to think she comes once
        more;
But even then I heard her close the door,
610   The gates of heaven are closed, and she is gone.

III

There is none like her, none,
Nor will be when our summers have deceased.
O, art thou sighing for Lebanon[36]
In the long breeze that streams to thy delicious
        East,
Sighing for Lebanon,
Dark cedar, tho' thy limbs have here increased,
Upon a pastoral slope as fair,
And looking to the South, and fed
With honey'd rain and delicate air,
620   And haunted by the starry head
Of her whose gentle will has changed my fate,
And made my life a perfumed altar-flame;
And over whom thy darkness must have spread
With such delight as theirs of old, thy great
Forefathers of the thornless garden, there
Shadowing the snow-limb'd Eve from whom she
        came.

IV

Here will I lie, while these long branches sway,
And you fair stars that crown a happy day
Go in and out as if at merry play,
630   Who am no more so all forlorn
As when it seem'd far better to be born
To labour and the mattock-harden'd hand,
Than nursed at ease and brought to understand
A sad astrology,[37] the boundless plan
That makes you tyrants in your iron skies,
Innumerable, pitiless, passionless eyes,

Cold fires, yet with power to burn and brand
His nothingness into man.

V

But now shine on, and what care I,
Who in this stormy gulf have found a pearl   6‹
The countercharm of space and hollow sky,
And do accept my madness, and would die
To save from some slight shame one simple girl.

VI

Would die; for sullen-seeming Death may give
More life to Love than is or ever was
In our low world, where yet 'tis sweet to live.
Let no one ask me how it came to pass;
It seems that I am happy, that to me
A livelier emerald twinkles in the grass,
A purer sapphire melts into the sea.   6‹

VII

Not die; but live a life of truest breath,[38]
And teach true life to fight with mortal wrongs.
O, why should Love, like men in drinking-
        songs,
Spice his fair banquet with the dust of death?
Make answer, Maud my bliss,
Maud made my Maud by that long loving kiss,
Life of my life, wilt thou not answer this?
"The dusky strand of Death inwoven here
With dear Love's tie, makes Love himself more
        dear."

VIII

Is that enchanted moan only the swell   6‹
Of the long waves that roll in yonder bay?
And hark the clock within, the silver knell
Of twelve sweet hours that past in bridal white,
And died to live, long as my pulses play;
But now by this my love has closed her sight
And given false death her hand, and stol'n away
To dreamful wastes where footless fancies dwell
Among the fragments of the golden day.
May nothing there her maiden grace affright!
Dear heart, I feel with thee the drowsy spell.   6‹
My bride to be, my evermore delight,
My own heart's heart, my ownest own, farewell;
It is but for a little space I go:
And ye[39] meanwhile far over moor and fell

---

[36] Lebanon: a mountain in Syria, famous in Biblical times for cedars.
[37] Tennyson's note: "The *sad astrology* is modern astronomy, for of old astrology was thought
to sympathise with and rule man's fate" (II, 509).
[38] Tennyson's note: "This is the central idea—the holy power of Love" (II, 509).
[39] Ye: stars. Tennyson's note: "His newer astrology describes them [not as 'cold Fires' but as]
'soft splendours' " (II, 509).

Beat to the noiseless music of the night!
Has our whole earth gone nearer to the glow
Of your soft splendours that you look so bright?
I have climb'd nearer out of lonely Hell.
Beat, happy stars, timing with things below,
Beat with my heart more blest than heart can
    tell,
Blest, but for some dark undercurrent woe
That seems to draw—but it shall not be so:
Let all be well, be well.

            XIX[40]

   I

Her brother is coming back to-night,
Breaking up my dream of delight.

   II

My dream? do I dream of bliss?
I have walk'd awake with Truth.
O when did a morning shine
So rich in atonement as this
For my dark-dawning youth,
Darken'd watching a mother decline
And that dead man at her heart and mine:
For who was left to watch her but I?
Yet so did I let my freshness die.

   III

I trust that I did not talk
To gentle Maud in our walk
(For often in lonely wanderings
I have cursed him even to lifeless things)
But I trust that I did not talk,
Not touch on her father's sin:
I am sure I did but speak
Of my mother's faded cheek
When it slowly grew so thin
That I felt she was slowly dying
Vext with lawyers and harass'd with debt:
For how often I caught her with eyes all wet,
Shaking her head at her son and sighing
A world of trouble within!

   IV

And Maud too, Maud was moved
To speak of the mother she loved
As one scarce less forlorn,
Dying abroad and it seems apart
From him who had ceased to share her heart,
And ever mourning over the feud,
The household Fury sprinkled with blood

40 All of Section XIX was added in 1856.

By which our houses are torn:
How strange was what she said,
When only Maud and the brother
Hung over her dying bed—
That Maud's dark father and mine   720
Had bound us one to the other,
Betrothed us over their wine,
On the day when Maud was born;
Seal'd her mine from her first sweet breath.
Mine, mine by a right, from birth till death.
Mine, mine—our fathers have sworn.

   V

But the true blood spilt had in it a heat
To dissolve the precious seal on a bond,
That, if left uncancell'd, had been so sweet:
And none of us thought of a something
    beyond,   730
A desire that awoke in the heart of the child,
As it were a duty done to the tomb,
To be friends for her sake, to be reconciled;
And I was cursing them and my doom,
And letting a dangerous thought run wild
While often abroad in the fragrant gloom
Of foreign churches—I see her there,
Bright English lily, breathing a prayer
To be friends, to be reconciled!

   VI

But then what a flint is he!   740
Abroad, at Florence, at Rome,
I find whenever she touch'd on me
This brother had laugh'd her down,
And at last, when each came home,
He had darken'd into a frown,
Chid her, and forbid her to speak
To me, her friend of the years before;
And this was what had redden'd her cheek
When I bow'd to her on the moor.

   VII

Yet Maud, altho' not blind   750
To the faults of his heart and mind,
I see she cannot but love him,
And says he is rough but kind,
And wishes me to approve him,
And tells me, when she lay
Sick once, with a fear of worse,
That he left his wine and horses and play,
Sat with her, read to her, night and day,
And tended her like a nurse.

   VIII

Kind? but the deathbed desire   760
Spurn'd by this heir of the liar—

Rough but kind? yet I know
He has plotted against me in this,
That he plots against me still.
Kind to Maud? that were not amiss.
Well, rough but kind; why, let it be so:
For shall not Maud have her will?

IX

For, Maud, so tender and true,
As long as my life endures
770   I feel I shall owe you a debt,
That I never can hope to pay;
And if ever I should forget
That I owe this debt to you
And for your sweet sake to yours;
O then, what then shall I say?—
If ever I *should* forget,
May God make me more wretched
Than ever I have been yet!

X

So now I have sworn to bury
780   All this dead body of hate,
I feel so free and so clear
By the loss of that dead weight,
That I should grow light-headed, I fear,
Fantastically merry;
But that her brother comes, like a blight
On my fresh hope, to the Hall to-night.

XX

I

Strange, that I felt so gay,
Strange, that *I* tried to-day
To beguile her melancholy;
The Sultan, as we name him,—
790   She did not wish to blame him—
But he vext her and perplext her
With his worldly talk and folly:
Was it gentle to reprove her
For stealing out of view
From a little lazy lover
Who but claims her as his due?
Or for chilling his caresses
By the coldness of her manners,
800   Nay, the plainness of her dresses?
Now I know her but in two,
Nor can pronounce upon it
If one should ask me whether
The habit, hat, and feather,
Or the frock and gipsy bonnet
Be the neater and completer;
For nothing can be sweeter
Than maiden Maud in either.

II

But to-morrow, if we live,
Our ponderous squire will give   8
A grand political dinner
To half the squirelings near;
And Maud will wear her jewels,
And the bird of prey will hover,
And the titmouse hope to win her
With his chirrup at her ear.

III

A grand political dinner
To the men of many acres,
A gathering of the Tory,
A dinner and then a dance   8
For the maids and marriage-makers,
And every eye but mine will glance
At Maud in all her glory.

IV

For I am not invited,
But, with the Sultan's pardon,
I am all as well delighted,
For I know her own rose-garden,
And mean to linger in it
Till the dancing will be over;
And then, oh then, come out to me   8
For a minute, but for a minute,
Come out to your own true lover,
That your true lover may see
Your glory also, and render
All homage to his own darling,
Queen Maud in all her splendour.

XXI

Rivulet crossing my ground,
And bringing me down from the Hall
This garden-rose that I found,
Forgetful of Maud and me,
And lost in trouble and moving round   8
Here at the head of a tinkling fall,
And trying to pass to the sea;
O Rivulet, born at the Hall,
My Maud has sent it by thee
(If I read her sweet will right)
On a blushing mission to me,
Saying in odour and colour, "Ah, be
Among the roses to-night."

XXII

I

Come into the garden, Maud,
For the black bat, night, has flown,   8

Come into the garden, Maud,
   I am here at the gate alone;
And the woodbine spices are wafted abroad,
   And the musk of the rose is blown.

II
For a breeze of morning moves,
   And the planet of Love[41] is on high,
Beginning to faint in the light that she loves
   On a bed of daffodil sky,
To faint in the light of the sun she loves,
   To faint in his light, and to die.

III
All night have the roses heard
   The flute, violin, bassoon;
All night has the casement jessamine stirr'd
   To the dancers dancing in tune;
Till a silence fell with the waking bird,
   And a hush with the setting moon.

IV
I said to the lily, "There is but one
   With whom she has heart to be gay.
When will the dancers leave her alone?
   She is weary of dance and play."
Now half to the setting moon are gone,
   And half to the rising day;
Low on the sand and loud on the stone
   The last wheel echoes away.

V
I said to the rose, "The brief night goes
   In babble and revel and wine.
O young lord-lover, what sighs are those,
   For one that will never be thine?
But mine, but mine," so I sware to the rose,
   "For ever and ever, mine."

VI
And the soul of the rose went into my blood,
   As the music clash'd in the hall;
And long by the garden lake I stood,
   For I heard your rivulet fall
From the lake to the meadow and on to the
      wood,
   Our wood, that is dearer than all;

VII
From the meadow your walks have left so sweet
   That whenever a March-wind sighs

---

[41] Planet of Love: Venus.

He sets the jewel-print of your feet   890
   In violets blue as your eyes,
To the woody hollows in which we meet
   And the valleys of Paradise.

VIII
The slender acacia would not shake
   One long milk-bloom on the tree;
The white lake-blossom fell into the lake
   As the pimpernel dozed on the lea;
But the rose was awake all night for your sake,
   Knowing your promise to me;
The lilies and roses were all awake,   900
   They sigh'd for the dawn and thee.

IX
Queen rose of the rosebud garden of girls,
   Come hither, the dances are done,
In gloss of satin and glimmer of pearls,
   Queen lily and rose in one;
Shine out, little head, sunning over with curls,
   To the flowers, and be their sun.

X
There has fallen a splendid tear
   From the passion-flower at the gate.
She is coming, my dove, my dear;   910
   She is coming, my life, my fate;
The red rose cries, "She is near, she is near;"
   And the white rose weeps, "She is late;"
The larkspur listens, "I hear, I hear;"
   And the lily whispers, "I wait."

XI
She is coming, my own, my sweet;
   Were it ever so airy a tread,
My heart would hear her and beat,
   Were it earth in an earthy bed;
My dust would hear her and beat,   920
   Had I lain for a century dead;
Would start and tremble under her feet,
   And blossom in purple and red.

PART II

I

I
"The fault was mine, the fault was mine"—
Why am I sitting here so stunn'd and still,
Plucking the harmless wild-flower on the
      hill?—

It is this guilty hand!—
And there rises ever a passionate cry
From underneath in the darkening land—
What is it, that has been done?
O dawn of Eden bright over earth and sky,
The fires of Hell brake out of thy rising sun,
10   The fires of Hell and of Hate;
For she, sweet soul, had hardly spoken a word,
When her brother ran in his rage to the gate,
He came with the babe-faced lord;
Heap'd on her terms of disgrace,
And while she wept, and I strove to be cool,
He fiercely gave me the lie,[1]
Till I with as fierce an anger spoke,
And he struck me, madman, over the face,
Struck me before the languid fool,
20   Who was gaping and grinning by:
Struck for himself an evil stroke;
Wrought for his house an irredeemable woe;
For front to front[2] in an hour we stood,
And a million horrible bellowing echoes broke
From the red-ribb'd hollow behind the wood,
And thunder'd up into Heaven the Christless
      code,
That must have life for a blow.
Ever and ever afresh they seem'd to grow.
Was it he lay there with a fading eye?
30   "The fault was mine," he whisper'd, "fly!"
Then glided out of the joyous wood
The ghastly Wraith of one that I know;
And there rang on a sudden a passionate cry,
A cry for a brother's blood:
It will ring in my heart and my ears, till I die,
      till I die.

II

Is it gone? my pulses beat—
What was it? a lying trick of the brain?
Yet I thought I saw her stand,
A shadow there at my feet,
40   High over the shadowy land.
It is gone; and the heavens fall in a gentle rain,
When they should burst and drown with
      deluging storms
The feeble vassals of wine and anger and lust,
The little hearts that know not how to forgive:
Arise, my God, and strike, for we hold Thee
      just,

Strike dead the whole weak race of venomous
      worms,
That sting each other here in the dust;
We are not worthy to live.

II[3]

I

See what a lovely shell,
Small and pure as a pearl,
Lying close to my foot,
Frail, but a work divine,
Made so fairily well
With delicate spire and whorl,
How exquisitely minute,
A miracle of design!

II

What is it? a learned man
Could give it a clumsy name.
Let him name it who can,
The beauty would be the same.

III

The tiny cell is forlorn,
Void of the little living will
That made it stir on the shore.
Did he stand at the diamond door
Of his house in a rainbow frill?
Did he push, when he was uncurl'd,
A golden foot or a fairy horn
Thro' his dim water-world?

IV

Slight, to be crush'd with a tap
Of my finger-nail on the sand,
Small, but a work divine,
Frail, but of force to withstand,
Year upon year, the shock
Of cataract seas that snap
The three-decker's oaken spine
Athwart the ledges of rock,
Here on the Breton strand!

V

Breton, not Briton; here
Like a shipwreck'd man on a coast
Of ancient fable and fear—
Plagued with a flitting to and fro,
A disease, a hard mechanic ghost

[1] Gave me the lie: charged him with falsehood.

[2] Front to front: facing one another in a duel. Because duelling was illegal, the survivors often fled the country to escape prosecution.

[3] Tennyson's note: "In Brittany. The shell undestroyed amid the storm perhaps symbolises to him his own first and highest nature preserved amid the storms of passion" (II, 509). At least part of this lyric was originally written in the 1830s (Charles Tennyson, *Alfred Tennyson*, p. 281).

That never came from on high
Nor ever arose from below,
But only moves with the moving eye,
Flying along the land and the main—
Why should it look like Maud?
Am I to be overawed
By what I cannot but know
Is a juggle[4] born of the brain?

VI

Back from the Breton coast,
Sick of a nameless fear,
Back to the dark sea-line
Looking, thinking of all I have lost;
An old song vexes my ear,
But that of Lamech is mine.[5]

VII

For years, a measureless ill,
For years, for ever, to part—
But she, she would love me still;
And as long, O God, as she
Have a grain of love for me,
So long, no doubt, no doubt,
Shall I nurse in my dark heart,
However weary, a spark of will
Not to be trampled out.

VIII

Strange, that the mind, when fraught
With a passion so intense
One would think that it well
Might drown all life in the eye,—
That it should, by being so overwrought,
Suddenly strike on a sharper sense
For a shell, or a flower, little things
Which else would have been past by!
And now I remember, I,
When he lay dying there,
I noticed one of his many rings
 (For he had many, poor worm) and thought
It is his mother's hair.[6]

IX

Who knows if he be dead?
Whether I need have fled?
Am I guilty of blood?

However this may be,
Comfort her, comfort her, all things good,
While I am over the sea!
Let me and my passionate love go by,
But speak to her all things holy and high,
Whatever happen to me!
Me and my harmful love go by;
But come to her waking, find her asleep,
Powers of the height, Powers of the deep,   130
And comfort her tho' I die!

III[7]

Courage, poor heart of stone!
I will not ask thee why
Thou canst not understand
That thou art left for ever alone:
Courage, poor stupid heart of stone.—
Or if I ask thee why,
Care not thou to reply:
She is but dead, and the time is at hand
When thou shalt more than die.   140

IV[8]

I

O that 't were possible
After long grief and pain
To find the arms of my true love
Round me once again!

II

When I was wont to meet her
In the silent woody places
By the home that gave me birth,
We stood tranced in long embraces
Mixt with kisses sweeter, sweeter
Than anything on earth.   150

III

A shadow flits before me,
Not thou, but like to thee:
Ah Christ, that it were possible
For one short hour to see
The souls we loved, that they might tell us
What and where they be.

---

[4] Juggle: trick.
[5] Tennyson in his note cites Genesis 4:23, the words of Lamech to his wives: "I have slain a man to my wounding, and a young man to my hurt" (II, 510).
[6] A ring enclosing a lock of his mother's hair.
[7] This lyric was not in the first printed version of the poem in 1855; it was added in 1856.
[8] A version of this lyric was first written in 1833–34; it was published in 1837 in a collection titled *The Tribute*. In his note Tennyson says that a friend "begged me to weave a story round this poem, and so *Maud* came into being" (II, 510).

IV

It leads me forth at evening,
It lightly winds and steals
In a cold white robe before me,
160   When all my spirit reels
At the shouts, the leagues of lights,
And the roaring of the wheels.

V

Half the night I waste in sighs,
Half in dreams I sorrow after
The delight of early skies;
In a wakeful doze I sorrow
For the hand, the lips, the eyes,
For the meeting of the morrow,
The delight of happy laughter,
170   The delight of low replies.

VI

'Tis a morning pure and sweet,
And a dewy splendour falls
On the little flower that clings
To the turrets and the walls;
'Tis a morning pure and sweet,
And the light and shadow fleet;
She is walking in the meadow,
And the woodland echo rings;
In a moment we shall meet;
180   She is singing in the meadow
And the rivulet at her feet
Ripples on in light and shadow
To the ballad that she sings.

VII

Do I hear her sing as of old,
My bird with the shining head,
My own dove with the tender eye?
But there rings on a sudden a passionate cry,
There is some one dying or dead,
And a sullen thunder is roll'd;
190   For a tumult shakes the city,
And I wake, my dream is fled;
In the shuddering dawn, behold,
Without knowledge, without pity,
By the curtains of my bed
That abiding phantom cold.

VIII

Get thee hence, nor come again,
Mix not memory with doubt,
Pass, thou deathlike type of pain,
Pass and cease to move about!
200   'Tis the blot upon the brain
That *will* show itself without.

IX

Then I rise, the eavedrops fall,
And the yellow vapours choke
The great city sounding wide;
The day comes, a dull red ball
Wrapt in drifts of lurid smoke
On the misty river-tide.

X

Thro' the hubbub of the market
I steal, a wasted frame,
It crosses here, it crosses there,
Thro' all that crowd confused and loud,
The shadow still the same;
And on my heavy eyelids
My anguish hangs like shame.

XI

Alas for her that met me,
That heard me softly call,
Came glimmering thro' the laurels
At the quiet evenfall,
In the garden by the turrets
Of the old manorial hall.

XII

Would the happy spirit descend
From the realms of light and song,
In the chamber or the street,
As she looks among the blest,
Should I fear to greet my friend
Or to say "Forgive the wrong,"
Or to ask her, "Take me, sweet,
To the regions of thy rest"?

XIII

But the broad light glares and beats,
And the shadow flits and fleets
And will not let me be;
And I loathe the squares and streets,
And the faces that one meets,
Hearts with no love for me:
Always I long to creep
Into some still cavern deep,
There to weep, and weep, and weep
My whole soul out to thee.

V

I

Dead, long dead,
Long dead!
And my heart is a handful of dust,
And the wheels go over my head,

And my bones are shaken with pain,
For into a shallow grave they are thrust,
Only a yard beneath the street,
And the hoofs of the horses beat, beat,
The hoofs of the horses beat,
Beat into my scalp and my brain,
With never an end to the stream of passing feet,
Driving, hurrying, marrying, burying,
Clamour and rumble, and ringing and clatter,
And here beneath it is all as bad,
For I thought the dead had peace, but it is
    not so;
To have no peace in the grave, is that not sad?
But up and down and to and fro,
Ever about me the dead men go;
And then to hear a dead man chatter
Is enough to drive one mad.

II

Wretchedest age, since Time began,
They cannot even bury a man;
And tho' we paid our tithes in the days that are
    gone,
Not a bell was rung, not a prayer was read.
It is that which makes us loud in the world of
    the dead;
There is none that does his work, not one;
A touch of their office might have sufficed,
But the churchman fain would kill their
    church,
As the churches have kill'd their Christ.

III

See, there is one of us sobbing,
No limit to his distress;
And another, a lord of all things, praying
To his own great self, as I guess;
And another, a statesman there, betraying
His party-secret, fool, to the press;
And yonder a vile physician, blabbing
The case of his patient—all for what?
To tickle the maggot born in an empty head,
And wheedle a world that loves him not,
For it is but a world of the dead.

IV

Nothing but idiot gabble!
For the prophecy given of old
And then not understood,
Has come to pass as foretold;
Nor let any man think for the public good,
But babble, merely for babble.

For I never whisper'd a private affair
Within the hearing of cat or mouse,
No, not to myself in the closet alone,
But I heard it shouted at once from the top of
    the house;
Everything came to be known.
Who told *him* we were there?   290

V

Not that gray old wolf, for he came not back
From the wilderness, full of wolves, where he
    used to lie;
He has gather'd the bones for his o'ergrown
    whelp to crack;
Crack them now for yourself, and howl, and
    die.

VI

Prophet, curse me the blabbing lip,
And curse me the British vermin, the rat;
I know not whether he came in the Hanover
    ship,[9]
But I know that he lies and listens mute
In an ancient mansion's crannies and holes:
Arsenic, arsenic, sure, would do it,   300
Except that now we poison our babes, poor
    souls!
It is all used up for that.

VII

Tell him now: she is standing here at my head;
Not beautiful now, not even kind;
He may take her now; for she never speaks her
    mind,
But is ever the one thing silent here.
She is not *of* us, as I divine;
She comes from another stiller world of the
    dead,
Stiller, not fairer than mine.

VIII

But I know where a garden grows,   310
Fairer than aught in the world beside,
All made up of the lily and rose
That blow by night, when the season is good,
To the sound of dancing music and flutes:
It is only flowers, they had no fruits,
And I almost fear they are not roses, but blood;
For the keeper was one, so full of pride,
He linkt a dead man there to a spectral bride;
For he, if he had not been a Sultan of brutes,
Would he have that hole in his side?   320

[9] A species of rat came to England in the eighteenth century, carried, their enemies said, on the ships that brought George I and the Hanoverian line to the throne of England in 1714.

IX

But what will the old man say?[10]
He laid a cruel snare in a pit
To catch a friend of mine one stormy day;
Yet now I could even weep to think of it;
For what will the old man say
When he comes to the second corpse in the pit?

X

Friend, to be struck by the public foe,
Then to strike him and lay him low,
That were a public merit, far,
330   Whatever the Quaker holds, from sin;
But the red life spilt for a private blow—
I swear to you, lawful and lawless war
Are scarcely even akin.

XI

O me, why have they not buried me deep
      enough?
Is it kind to have made me a grave so rough,
Me, that was never a quiet sleeper?
Maybe still I am but half-dead;
Then I cannot be wholly dumb;
I will cry to the steps above my head
And somebody, surely, some kind heart will
      come
To bury me, bury me
Deeper, ever so little deeper.

PART III

I

My life has crept so long on a broken wing
Thro' cells of madness, haunts of horror and
      fear,
That I come to be grateful at last for a little
      thing:
My mood is changed, for it fell at a time of
      year
When the face of night is fair on the dewy
      downs,
And the shining daffodil dies, and the
      Charioteer
And starry Gemini hang like glorious crowns
Over Orion's grave low down in the west,
That like a silent lightning under the stars

She seem'd to divide in a dream from a band
      of the blest,
And spoke of a hope for the world in the
      coming wars—
"And in that hope, dear soul, let trouble have
      rest,
Knowing I tarry for thee," and pointed to Mars
As he glow'd like a ruddy shield on the Lion's
      breast.[1]

II

And it was but a dream, yet it yielded a dear
      delight
To have look'd, tho' but in a dream, upon eyes
      so fair,
That had been in a weary world my one thing
      bright;
And it was but a dream, yet it lighten'd my
      despair
When I thought that a war would arise in
      defence of the right,
That an iron tyranny now should bend or
      cease,
The glory of manhood stand on his ancient
      height,
Nor Britain's one sole God be the millionaire:
No more shall commerce be all in all, and
      Peace
Pipe on her pastoral hillock a languid note,
And watch her harvest ripen, her herd increase,
Nor the cannon-bullet rust on a slothful shore,
And the cobweb woven across the cannon's
      throat
Shall shake its threaded tears in the wind no
      more.

III

And as months ran on and rumour of battle
      grew,
"It is time, it is time, O passionate heart,"
      said I
(For I cleaved to a cause that I felt to be pure
      and true),
"It is time, O passionate heart and morbid eye,
That old hysterical mock-disease should die."
And I stood on a giant deck and mix'd my
      breath
With a loyal people shouting a battle cry,

[10] Tennyson's note: *"what will the old man say?* Maud's father. The second corpse is Maud's brother, the lover's father being the first corpse, whom the lover thinks that Maud's father murdered" (II, 511).
[1] The Charioteer, the Gemini, and Orion are constellations; the place of Orion, low in the west, sets this passage in early spring (see also Part I, line 101). The Lion is also a constellation, and the planet Mars has moved into it. The lion is also the emblem of Great Britain, at war with Russia in the Crimea in 1854–56.

Till I saw the dreary phantom arise and fly
Far into the North, and battle, and seas of
    death.

    IV

Let it go or stay, so I wake to the higher aims
Of a land that has lost for a little her lust of
    gold,
And love of a peace that was full of wrongs and
    shames,
Horrible, hateful, monstrous, not to be told;
And hail once more to the banner of battle
    unroll'd!
Tho' many a light shall darken, and many shall
    weep
For those that are crush'd in the clash of
    jarring claims,
Yet God's just wrath shall be wreak'd on a
    giant liar;
And many a darkness into the light shall leap,
And shine in the sudden making of splendid
    names,
And noble thought be freër under the sun,
And the heart of a people beat with one desire;
For the peace, that I deem'd no peace, is over
    and done,[2]
And now by the side of the Black and the
    Baltic[3] deep,
And deathful-grinning mouths of the fortress,
    flames
The blood-red blossom of war with a heart of
    fire.

    V

Let it flame or fade, and the war roll down like
    a wind,
We have proved we have hearts in a cause, we
    are noble still,
And myself have awaked, as it seems, to the
    better mind;
It is better to fight for the good than to rail at
    the ill;

I have felt with my native land, I am one with
    my kind,
I embrace the purpose of God, and the doom[4]
    assign'd.

            1855

To the Rev. F. D. Maurice

Come, when no graver cares employ,
Godfather, come and see your boy:[1]
    Your presence will be sun in winter,
Making the little one leap for joy.

For, being of that honest few,
Who give the Fiend himself his due,
    Should eighty-thousand college-councils
Thunder "Anathema," friend, at you;

Should all our churchmen foam in spite
At you, so careful of the right,   10
    Yet one lay-hearth would give you welcome
(Take it and come) to the Isle of Wight;[2]

Where, far from noise and smoke of town,
I watch the twilight falling brown
    All round a careless-order'd garden
Close to the ridge of a noble down.

You'll have no scandal while you dine,
But honest talk and wholesome wine,
    And only hear the magpie gossip
Garrulous under a roof of pine: 20

For groves of pine on either hand,
To break the blast of winter, stand;
    And further on, the hoary Channel
Tumbles a billow on chalk and sand;

Where, if below the milky steep
Some ship of battle slowly creep,[3]
    And on thro' zones of light and shadow
Glimmer away to the lonely deep,

---

    [2] In 1855, this line read, "For the long, long canker of peace is over and done"; and the poem ended with line 53. In 1856, line 50 was revised, and lines 54-59 added.
    [3] The Crimean peninsula is in the Black Sea.   [4] Doom: fate.
    [1] Maurice, a writer on theology, was godfather to Hallam Tennyson. In 1853 Maurice published some essays in which he argued, among other matters, that God's punishment for sins was not eternal. In consequence, he was forced to resign his fellowship in King's College of London University; Tennyson refers to this controversy in the second stanza of the poem.
    [2] In 1853 Tennyson moved to an estate, Farringford, on the Isle of Wight in the south of England.
    [3] Steep: cliff. The ships of battle would be sailing, if they sailed, to the Crimea; Russia had destroyed ships of the Turkish Ottoman empire late in 1853 ("the Northern sin"), and by the spring of the following year England was at war with Russia. Tennyson himself dated this poem "January, 1854."

30   We might discuss the Northern sin
     Which made a selfish war begin;
       Dispute the claims, arrange the chances;
     Emperor, Ottoman, which shall win:

     Or whether war's avenging rod
     Shall lash all Europe into blood;
       Till you should turn to dearer matters,
     Dear to the man that is dear to God;

     How best to help the slender store,
     How mend the dwellings, of the poor;
       How gain in life, as life advances,
40   Valour and charity more and more.

     Come, Maurice, come: the lawn as yet
     Is hoar with rime, or spongy-wet;
       But when the wreath of March has
         blossom'd,
     Crocus, anemone, violet,

     Or later, pay one visit here,
     For those are few we hold as dear;
       Nor pay but one, but come for many,
     Many and many a happy year.
                  (January 1854)   1855

Although "Tithonus" was not published until 1860, at least a version of it was written in 1833. Tennyson said that he intended the poem as a pendent to "Ulysses," which properly suggests that it too is a response to Hallam's death. Ricks in his edition of Tennyson's poems prints the earlier version under the title "Tithon" (pp. 566–568).

Tithonus was a mortal beloved of Eos, the Dawn. At her request, the gods granted him immortality, but she neglected to ask also for the gift of eternal youth. There are two endings to the legend: in one, Eos abandons Tithonus, helplessly weak with age, in her palace; in the other, she pities him and turns him into a grasshopper, supposed to live forever.

Tithonus

The woods decay, the woods decay and fall,
The vapours weep their burthen to the
    ground,
Man comes and tills the field and lies beneath,
And after many a summer dies the swan.
Me only cruel immortality
Consumes: I wither slowly in thine arms,
Here at the quiet limit of the world,
A white-hair'd shadow roaming like a dream
The ever-silent spaces of the East,
10 Far-folded mists, and gleaming halls of morn.

  Alas! for this gray shadow, once a man—
So glorious in his beauty and thy choice,
Who madest him thy chosen, that he seem'd
To his great heart none other than a God!
I ask'd thee, "Give me immortality."
Then didst thou grant mine asking with a
    smile,
Like wealthy men who care not how they give.
But thy strong Hours indignant work'd their
    wills,
And beat me down and marr'd and wasted me,
And tho' they could not end me, left me
    maim'd
To dwell in presence of immortal youth,
Immortal age beside immortal youth,
And all I was, in ashes. Can thy love,
Thy beauty, make amends, tho' even now,
Close over us, the silver star, thy guide,
Shines in those tremulous eyes that fill with
    tears
To hear me? Let me go: take back thy gift:
Why should a man desire in any way
To vary from the kindly race of men,
Or pass beyond the goal of ordinance
Where all should pause, as is most meet for
    all?

  A soft air fans the cloud apart; there comes
A glimpse of that dark world where I was born.
Once more the old mysterious glimmer steals
From thy pure brows, and from thy shoulders
    pure,
And bosom beating with a heart renew'd.
Thy cheek begins to redden thro' the gloom,
Thy sweet eyes brighten slowly close to mine,
Ere yet they blind the stars, and the wild team
Which love thee, yearning for thy yoke, arise,
And shake the darkness from their loosen'd
    manes,
And beat the twilight into flakes of fire.

  Lo! ever thus thou growest beautiful
In silence, then before thine answer given
Departest, and thy tears are on my cheek.

  Why wilt thou ever scare me with thy tears,
And make me tremble lest a saying learnt,
In days far-off, on that dark earth, be true?
"The Gods themselves cannot recall their
    gifts."

  Ay me! ay me! with what another heart
In days far-off, and with what other eyes
I used to watch—if I be he that watch'd—
The lucid outline forming round thee; saw
The dim curls kindle into sunny rings;

Changed with thy mystic change, and felt my
    blood
Glow with the glow that slowly crimson'd all
Thy presence and thy portals, while I lay,
Mouth, forehead, eyelids, growing dewy-warm
With kisses balmier than half-opening buds
Of April, and could hear the lips that kiss'd
Whispering I knew not what of wild and sweet,
Like that strange song I heard Apollo sing,
While Ilion like a mist rose into towers.[1]

Yet hold me not for ever in thine East:
How can my nature longer mix with thine?
Coldly thy rosy shadows bathe me, cold
Are all thy lights, and cold my wrinkled feet
Upon thy glimmering thresholds, when the
    steam
Floats up from those dim fields about the
    homes
Of happy men that have the power to die,
And grassy barrows of the happier dead.
Release me, and restore me to the ground;
Thou seëst all things, thou wilt see my grave:
Thou wilt renew thy beauty morn by morn;
I earth in earth forget these empty courts,
And thee returning on thy silver wheels.

1860; 1864

Ode Sung at the Opening of the International Exhibition[1]

I

Uplift a thousand voices full and sweet,
    In this wide hall with earth's invention
        stored,
        And praise the invisible universal Lord,
Who lets once more in peace the nations meet,
    Where Science, Art, and Labour have
        outpour'd
Their myriad horns of plenty at our feet.

II

O silent father of our Kings to be[2]
Mourn'd in this golden hour of jubilee,
For this, for all, we weep our thanks to thee!

III

The world-compelling[3] plan was thine,—   10
And, lo! the long laborious miles
Of Palace; lo! the giant aisles,
Rich in model and design;
Harvest-tool and husbandry,
Loom and wheel and enginery,
Secrets of the sullen mine,
Steel and gold, and corn and wine,
Fabric rough, or fairy-fine,
Sunny tokens of the Line,[4]
Polar marvels, and a feast   20
Of wonder, out of West and East,
And shapes and hues of Art divine!
All of beauty, all of use,
That one fair planet can produce,
    Brought from under every star,
Blown from over every main,
And mixt, as life is mixt with pain,
    The works of peace with works of war.

IV

    Is the goal so far away?
    Far, how far no tongue can say,   30
    Let us dream our dream to-day.

V

O ye, the wise who think, the wise who reign,
From growing commerce loose her latest chain,
And let the fair white-wing'd peacemaker fly
To happy havens under all the sky,
And mix the seasons and the golden hours;
Till each man find his own in all men's good,
And all men work in noble brotherhood,
Breaking their mailed fleets and armed towers,
And ruling by obeying Nature's powers,   40
And gathering all the fruits of earth and
        crown'd with all her flowers.

1862; 1874

Aylmer's Field

1793

Dust are our frames; and, gilded dust, our pride
Looks only for a moment whole and sound;
Like that long-buried body of the king,

---

[1] Apollo helped to build the walls of Troy.

[1] Written in 1861 and sung in October of that year, to music by W. S. Bennett. The poem was revised before its first publication in 1862, and revised again before it appeared in its final form in 1874.

[2] Albert, Prince Consort of Victoria and one of the organizers of the Exhibition, died in December 1861. These lines were added after the performance of the "Ode" but before its first publication.

[3] Compelling: bringing together.   [4] Line: the equator.

Found lying with his urns and ornaments,
Which at a touch of light, an air of heaven,
Slipt into ashes, and was found no more.[1]

Here is a story which in rougher shape
Came from a grizzled cripple, whom I saw
Sunning himself in a waste field alone—
10 Old, and a mine of memories—who had served,
Long since, a bygone Rector of the place,
And been himself a part of what he told.

Sir Aylmer Aylmer, that almighty man,
The county God—in whose capacious hall,
Hung with a hundred shields, the family tree
Sprang from the midriff of a prostrate king—
Whose blazing wyvern[2] weathercock'd the spire,
Stood from his walls and wing'd his entry-gates
And swang besides on many a windy sign—
20 Whose eyes from under a pyramidal head
Saw from his windows nothing save his own—
What lovelier of his own had he than her,
His only child, his Edith, whom he loved
As heiress and not heir regretfully?
But "he that marries her marries her name"
This fiat somewhat soothed himself and wife,
His wife a faded beauty of the Baths,[3]
Insipid as the Queen upon a card;
Her all of thought and bearing hardly more
30 Than his own shadow in a sickly sun.

A land of hops and poppy-mingled corn,
Little about it stirring save a brook!
A sleepy land, where under the same wheel
The same old rut would deepen year by year
Where almost all the village had one name;
Where Aylmer followed Aylmer at the Hall
And Averill Averill at the Rectory
Thrice over; so that Rectory and Hall,
Bound in an immemorial intimacy,
40 Were open to each other; tho' to dream
That Love could bind them closer well had
    made
The hoar hair of the Baronet bristle up
With horror, worse than had he heard his priest
Preach an inverted scripture, sons of men
Daughters of God;[4] so sleepy was the land.

And might not Averill, had he will'd it so,
Somewhere beneath his own low range of roofs,
Have also set his many-shielded tree?
There was an Aylmer-Averill marriage once.
When the red rose was redder than itself,
And York's white rose as red as Lancaster's,
With wounded peace which each had prick'd
    to death.[5]
"Not proven" Averill said, or laughingly
"Some other race of Averills"—prov'n or no,
What cared he? what, if other or the same?
He lean'd not on his fathers but himself.
But Leolin, his brother, living oft
With Averill, and a year or two before
Call'd to the bar, but ever call'd away
By one low voice to one dear neighbourhood,
Would often, in his walks with Edith, claim
A distant kinship to the gracious blood
That shook the heart of Edith hearing him.

Sanguine he was: a but less vivid hue
That of that islet in the chestnut-bloom[6]
Flamed in his cheek; and eager eyes, that still
Took joyful note of all things joyful, beam'd,
Beneath a manelike mass of rolling gold,
Their best and brightest, when they dwelt on
    hers,
Edith, whose pensive beauty, perfect else,
But subject to the season or the mood,
Shone like a mystic star between the less[7]
And greater glory varying to and fro,
We know not wherefore; bounteously made,
And yet so finely, that a troublous touch
Thinn'd, or would seem to thin her in a day,
A joyous to dilate, as toward the light.
And these had been together from the first.
Leolin's first nurse was, five years after, hers:
So much the boy foreran; but when his date
Doubled her own, for want of playmates, he
(Since Averill was a decad and a half
His elder, and their parents underground)
Had tost his ball and flown his kite, and roll'd
His hoop to pleasure Edith, with her dipt
Against the rush of the air in the prone[8] swing,
Made blossom-ball or daisy-chain, arranged

---

[1] Tennyson's note in the standard edition of his poetry: "This happened on opening an Etruscan tomb at the city of Tarquinii in Italy" (I, 744).

[2] Wyvern: winged dragon, used in heraldry.

[3] Baths: fashionable resorts, like that at Bath in the west of England.

[4] The scripture (Genesis 6:2) refers to sons of God and daughters of men.

[5] In the fifteenth century, after the "War of the Roses," the struggle between the houses of York and Lancaster for the throne of Britain.

[6] Hallam Tennyson's note: "The rosy spot in the flower" (I, 744).

[7] Tennyson's note: "The variable star of astronomy with its maximums and minimums of brightness" (I, 744).

[8] Prone: downward.

Her garden, sow'd her name and kept it green
In living letters, told her fairy-tales,
Show'd her the fairy footings[9] on the grass,
The little dells of cowslip, fairy palms,
The petty marestail[10] forest, fairy pines,
Or from the tiny pitted target blew
What look'd a flight of fairy arrows[11] aim'd
All at one mark, all hitting: make-believes
For Edith and himself: or else he forged,
But that was later, boyish histories
Of battle, bold adventure, dungeon, wreck,
Flights, terrors, sudden rescues, and true love
Crown'd after trial; sketches rude and faint,
But where a passion yet unborn perhaps
Lay hidden as the music of the moon
Sleeps in the plain eggs of the nightingale.
And thus together, save for college-times
Or Temple-eaten terms,[12] a couple, fair
As ever painter painted, poet sang,
Or Heaven in lavish bounty moulded, grew.
And more and more, the maiden woman-
grown,
He wasted hours with Averill; there, when first
The tented winter-field[13] was broken up
Into that phalanx of the summer spears
That soon should wear the garland; there again
When burr and bine[14] were gather'd; lastly
there
At Christmas; ever welcome at the Hall,
On whose dull sameness his full tide of youth
Broke with a phosphorescence charming even
My lady; and the Baronet yet had laid
No bar between them: dull and self-involved,
Tall and erect, but bending from his height
With half-allowing smiles for all the world,
And mighty courteous in the main—his pride
Lay deeper than to wear it as his ring—
He, like an Aylmer in his Aylmerism,
Would care no more for Leolin's walking with
her
Than for his old Newfoundland's, when they
ran
To loose him at the stables, for he rose

Twofooted at the limit of his chain,
Roaring to make a third: and how should Love,
Whom the cross-lightnings of four chance-met
eyes
Flash into fiery life from nothing, follow   130
Such dear familiarities of dawn?
Seldom, but when he does, Master of all.

So these young hearts not knowing that they
loved,
Not she at least, nor conscious of a bar
Between them, nor by plight or broken ring
Bound, but an immemorial intimacy,
Wander'd at will, and oft accompanied
By Averill: his, a brother's love, that hung
With wings of brooding shelter o'er her peace,
Might have been other, save for Leolin's—   140
Who knows? but so they wander'd, hour by
hour
Gather'd the blossom that rebloom'd, and
drank
The magic cup that fill'd itself anew.

A whisper half reveal'd her to herself.
For out beyond her lodges, where the brook
Vocal, with here and there a silence, ran
By sallowy rims,[15] arose the labourers' homes,
A frequent haunt of Edith, on low knolls
That dimpling died into each other, huts
At random scatter'd, each a nest in bloom.   150
Her art, her hand, her counsel all had wrought
About them: here was one that, summer-
blanch'd,
Was parcel-bearded with the traveller's-joy[16]
In Autumn, parcel ivy-clad; and here
The warm-blue breathings of a hidden hearth
Broke from a bower of vine and honeysuckle:
One look'd all rosetree, and another wore
A close-set robe of jasmine sown with stars:
This had a rosy sea of gillyflowers
About it; this, a milky-way on earth,   160
Like visions in the Northern dreamer's[17]
heavens,

---

[9] Fairy footings: a ring of mushrooms.
[10] Marestail: an aquatic plant with elongated shoots.   [11] Fairy arrows: dandelion seeds.
[12] Temple-eaten terms: a student at law in the Temple in London was required to eat a certain number of dinners in the Temple during his term of study.
[13] Tennyson's note: *"The tented winter-field.* Referring to the way in which the hop poles are stacked in the winter" (I, 745). They will be placed upright, like spears, in the summer.
[14] Tennyson's. note: *"burr and bine* refer to the hop plant. 'Burr,' the rough cone; 'bine,' the climbing stem" (I, 745).
[15] Sallowy rims: willowed banks.
[16] Parcel: part; traveller's-joy: a wild shrub, of the genus clematis.
[17] Northern dreamer: Emanuel Swedenborg (1688–1772), whose mystical doctrines about the immanence of spiritual reality in all things were founded in revelations which came to him in dreams.

A lily-avenue climbing to the doors;
One, almost to the martin-haunted eaves
A summer burial deep in hollyhocks;
Each, its own charm; and Edith's everywhere;
And Edith ever visitant with him,
He but less loved than Edith,[18] of her poor:
For she—so lowly-lovely and so loving,
Queenly responsive when the loyal hand

170 Rose from the clay it work'd in as she past,
Not sowing hedgerow texts[19] and passing by,
Nor dealing goodly counsel from a height
That makes the lowest hate it, but a voice
Of comfort and an open hand of help,
A splendid presence flattering the poor roofs
Revered as theirs, but kindlier than themselves
To ailing wife or wailing infancy
Or old bedridden palsy,—was adored;
He, loved for her and for himself. A grasp

180 Having the warmth and muscle of the heart,
A childly way with children, and a laugh
Ringing like proven golden coinage true,
Were no false passport to that easy realm,
Where once with Leolin at her side the girl,
Nursing a child, and turning to the warmth
The tender pink five-beaded baby-soles,
Heard the good mother softly whisper "Bless,
God bless 'em: marriages are made in Heaven."

A flash of semi-jealousy clear'd it to her.
190 My lady's Indian kinsman unannounced
With half a score of swarthy faces came.
His own, tho' keen and bold and soldierly,
Sear'd by the close ecliptic,[20] was not fair;
Fairer his talk, a tongue that ruled the hour,
Tho' seeming boastful: so when first he dash'd
Into the chronicle of a deedful day,
Sir Aylmer half forgot his lazy smile
Of patron "Good! my lady's kinsman! good!"
My lady with her fingers interlock'd,
200 And rotatory thumbs on silken knees,
Call'd all her vital spirits into each ear
To listen: unawares they flitted off,
Busying themselves about the flowerage
That stood from out a stiff brocade in which,
The meteor of a splendid season, she,
Once with this kinsman, ah so long ago,
Stept thro' the stately minuet of those days:
But Edith's eager fancy hurried with him
Snatch'd thro' the perilous passes of his life:

Till Leolin ever watchful of her eye,
Hated him with a momentary hate.
Wife-hunting, as the rumour ran, was he:
I know not, for he spoke not, only shower'd
His oriental gifts on everyone
And most on Edith: like a storm he came,
And shook the house, and like a storm he went.

Among the gifts he left her (possibly
He flow'd and ebb'd uncertain, to return
When others had been tested) there was one,
A dagger, in rich sheath with jewels on it
Sprinkled about in gold that branch'd itself
Fine as ice-ferns on January panes
Made by a breath. I know not whence at first,
Nor of what race, the work; but as he told
The story, storming a hill-fort of thieves
He got it; for their captain after fight,
His comrades having fought their last below,
Was climbing up the valley; at whom he shot:
Down from the beetling crag to which he clung
Tumbled the tawny rascal at his feet,
This dagger with him, which when now
    admired
By Edith whom his pleasure was to please,
At once the costly[21] Sahib yielded to her.

And Leolin, coming after he was gone,
Tost over all her presents petulantly:
And when she show'd the wealthy scabbard,
    saying
"Look what a lovely piece of workmanship!"
Slight was his answer "Well—I care not for it:"
Then playing with the blade he prick'd his
    hand,
"A gracious gift to give a lady, this!"
"But would it be more gracious" ask'd the girl
"Were I to give this gift of his to one
That is no lady?" "Gracious? No" said he.
"Me?—but I cared not for it. O pardon me,
I seem to be ungraciousness itself."
"Take it" she added sweetly, "tho' his gift;
For I am more ungracious ev'n than you,
I care not for it either;" and he said
"Why then I love it:" but Sir Aylmer past,
And neither loved nor liked the thing he heard.

The next day came a neighbour. Blues and
    reds[22]

---

[18] But less loved: only Edith is loved more.
[19] Hedgerow texts: a reference to the pious practice of calling on the poor to leave religious tracts.
[20] Tennyson's note: "close ecliptic, sun of tropics" (I, 745).
[21] Costly: lavish.   [22] Blues and reds: conservative and liberal political factions.

They talk'd of: blues were sure of it, he
    thought:
Then of the latest fox—where started—kill'd
In such a bottom: "Peter had the brush,[23]
My Peter, first:" and did Sir Aylmer know
That great pock-pitten fellow had been caught?
Then made his pleasure echo, hand to hand,
And rolling as it were the substance of it
Between his palms a moment up and down—
"The birds were warm, the birds were warm
    upon him;[24]
We have him now:" and had Sir Aylmer
    heard—
Nay, but he must—the land was ringing of it—
This blacksmith border-marriage[25]—one they
    knew—
Raw from the nursery—who could trust a
    child?
That cursed France with her egalities!
And did Sir Aylmer (deferentially
With nearing chair and lower'd accent)
    think—
For people talk'd—that it was wholly wise
To let that handsome fellow Averill walk
So freely with his daughter? people talk'd—
The boy might get a notion into him;
The girl might be entangled ere she knew.
Sir Aylmer Aylmer slowly stiffening spoke:
"The girl and boy, Sir, know their differences!"
"Good," said his friend, "but watch!" and he,
    "Enough,
More than enough, Sir! I can guard my own."
They parted, and Sir Aylmer Aylmer watch'd.

Pale, for on her the thunders of the house
Had fallen first, was Edith that same night;
Pale as the Jephtha's daughter,[26] a rough piece
Of early rigid colour, under which
Withdrawing by the counter door to that
Which Leolin open'd, she cast back upon him
A piteous glance, and vanish'd. He, as one
Caught in a burst of unexpected storm,
And pelted with outrageous epithets,
Turning beheld the Powers of the House
On either side the hearth, indignant; her,
Cooling her false cheek with a featherfan,

Him, glaring, by his own stale devil spurr'd,   290
And, like a beast hard-ridden, breathing hard.
"Ungenerous, dishonourable, base,
Presumptuous! trusted as he was with her
The sole succeeder to their wealth, their lands,
The last remaining pillar of their house,
The one transmitter of their ancient name,
Their child." "Our child!" "Our heiress!"
    "Ours!" for still,
Like echoes from beyond a hollow, came
Her sicklier iteration. Last he said,
"Boy, mark me! for your fortunes are to make.   300
I swear you shall not make them out of mine.
Now inasmuch as you have practised on her,
Perplext her, made her half forget herself,
Swerve from her duty to herself and us—
Things in an Aylmer deem'd impossible,
Far as we track ourselves—I say that this—
Else I withdraw favour and countenance
From you and yours for ever—shall you do.
Sir, when you see her—but you shall not see
    her—
No, you shall write, and not to her, but me: 310
And you shall say that having spoken with me,
And after look'd into yourself, you find
That you meant nothing—as indeed you know
That you meant nothing. Such a match as this!
Impossible, prodigious!" These were words,
As meted by his measure of himself,
Arguing boundless forbearance: after which,
And Leolin's horror-stricken answer, "I
So foul a traitor to myself and her,
Never oh never," for about as long   320
As the wind-hover[27] hangs in balance, paused
Sir Aylmer reddening from the storm within,
Then broke all bonds of courtesy, and crying
"Boy, should I find you by my doors again,
My men shall lash you from them like a dog;
Hence!" with a sudden execration drove
The footstool from before him, and arose;
So, stammering "scoundrel" out of teeth that
    ground
As in a dreadful dream, while Leolin still
Retreated half-aghast, the fierce old man   330
Follow'd, and under his own lintel stood
Storming with lifted hands, a hoary face

[23] Brush: tail of the fox, a hunting trophy.

[24] A poacher has been caught with stolen birds in his possession.

[25] Tennyson's note: "At Gretna Green [in Scotland] for many years a blacksmith married the runaway couples by Scotch law" (I, 745). In Scottish law a declaration of intention to marry constituted a legal marriage; parental consent for persons not of legal age was not required.

[26] Jephtha: a warrior in the Old Testament who vowed to sacrifice the first living being he encountered on his return home if he were granted victory. Upon entering his village, he encountered first his only daughter (Judges 11).

[27] Wind-hover: a name of the kestrel, a small falcon.

Meet for the reverence of the hearth, but now,
Beneath a pale and unimpassion'd moon,
Vext with unworthy madness, and deform'd.

    Slowly and conscious of the rageful eye
That watch'd him, till he heard the ponderous
    door
Close, crashing with long echoes thro' the land,
Went Leolin; then, his passions all in flood
340 And masters of his motion, furiously
Down thro' the bright lawns to his brother's ran
And foam'd away his heart at Averill's ear:
Whom Averill solaced as he might, amazed:
The man was his, had been his father's, friend:
He must have seen, himself had seen it long;
He must have known, himself had known:
    besides,
He never yet had set his daughter forth
Here in the woman-markets of the west,
Where our Caucasians let themselves be sold.
Some one, he thought, had slander'd Leolin to
350   him.
"Brother, for I have loved you more as son
Than brother, let me tell you: I myself—
What is their pretty saying? jilted, is it?
Jilted I was: I say it for your peace.
Pain'd, and, as bearing in myself the shame
The woman should have borne, humiliated,
I lived for years a stunted sunless life;
Till after our good parents past away
Watching your growth, I seem'd again to grow.
360 Leolin, I almost sin in envying you:
The very whitest lamb in all my fold
Loves you: I know her: the worst thought she
    has
Is whiter even than her pretty hand:
She must prove true: for, brother, where two
    fight
The strongest wins, and truth and love are
    strength,
And you are happy: let her parents be."

    But Leolin cried out the more upon them—
Insolent, brainless, heartless! heiress, wealth,
Their wealth, their heiress! wealth enough was
    theirs
370 For twenty matches. Were he lord of this,
Why twenty boys and girls should marry on it,
And forty blest ones bless him, and himself
Be wealthy still, ay wealthier. He believed

This filthy marriage-hindering Mammon[28]
    made
The harlot of the cities: nature crost
Was mother of the foul adulteries
That saturate soul with body. Name, too!
    name,
Their ancient name! they *might* be proud; its
    worth
Was being Edith's. Ah how pale she had look'd
Darling, to-night! they must have rated[29] her   3
Beyond all tolerance. These old pheasant-lords,
These partridge-breeders of a thousand years,
Who had mildew'd in their thousands, doing
    nothing
Since Egbert[30]—why, the greater their disgrace
Fall back upon a name! rest, rot in that!
Not *keep* it noble, make it nobler? fools,
With such a vantage-ground for nobleness!
He had known a man, a quintessence of man,
The life of all—who madly loved—and he,
Thwarted by one of these old father-fools,
Had rioted his life out, and made an end.
He would not do it! her sweet face and faith
Held him from that: but he had powers, he
    knew it:
Back would he to his studies, make a name,
Name, fortune too: the world should ring of
    him
To shame these mouldy Alymers in their
    graves:
Chancellor,[31] or what is greatest would he be—
"O brother, I am grieved to learn your grief—
Give me my fling, and let me say my say."

    At which, like one that sees his own excess,
And easily forgives it as his own,
He laugh'd; and then was mute; but presently
Wept like a storm: and honest Averill seeing
How low his brother's mood had fallen, fetch'd
His richest beeswing[32] from a binn reserved
For banquets, praised the waning red, and told
The vintage—when *this* Aylmer came of age—
Then drank and past it; till at length the two,
Tho' Leolin flamed and fell again, agreed
That much allowance must be made for men.
After an angry dream this kindlier glow
Faded with morning, but his purpose held.

    Yet once by night again the lovers met,
A perilous meeting under the tall pines

---

[28] Mammon: wealth.   [29] Rated: censured.   [30] Egbert: ninth-century king of West Saxons.
[31] Chancellor: the Lord Chancellor is the highest judicial officer in Great Britain.
[32] Beeswing: a crust formed in port that has been stored for a long time. Ricks (p. 1171) notes
of the phrase "the waning red" that port as it matures becomes less red.

That darken'd all the northward of her Hall.
Him, to her meek and modest bosom prest
In agony, she promised that no force,
Persuasion, no, nor death could alter her:
He, passionately hopefuller, would go,
20 Labour for his own Edith, and return
In such a sunlight of prosperity
He should not be rejected. "Write to me!
They loved me, and because I love their child
They hate me: there is war between us, dear,
Which breaks all bonds but ours; we must
    remain
Sacred to one another." So they talk'd,
Poor children, for their comfort: the wind
    blew;
The rain of heaven, and their own bitter tears,
Tears, and the careless rain of heaven, mixt
30 Upon their faces, as they kiss'd each other
In darkness, and above them roar'd the pine.

   So Leolin went; and as we task ourselves
To learn a language known but smatteringly
In phrases here and there at random, toil'd
Mastering the lawless science of our law,
That codeless myriad of precedent,
That wilderness of single instances,
Thro' which a few, by wit or fortune led,
May beat a pathway out to wealth and fame.
-0 The jests, that flash'd about the pleader's room,
Lightning of the hour, the pun, the scurrilous
    tale,—
Old scandals buried now seven decads deep
In other scandals that have lived and died,
And left the living scandal that shall die—
Were dead to him already; bent as he was
To make disproof of scorn, and strong in hopes
And prodigal of all brain-labour he,
Charier of sleep, and wine, and exercise,
Except when for a breathing-while at eve,
0 Some niggard fraction of an hour, he ran
Beside the river-bank: and then indeed
Harder the times were, and the hands of power
Were bloodier, and the according hearts of men
Seem'd harder too; but the soft river-breeze,
Which fann'd the gardens of that rival rose[33]
Yet fragrant in a heart remembering
His former talks with Edith, on him breathed
Far purelier in his rushings to and fro,

After his books, to flush his blood with air,
Then to his books again. My lady's cousin,   460
Half-sickening of his pension'd afternoon,
Drove in upon the student once or twice,
Ran a Malayan amuck against the times,[34]
Had golden hopes for France and all mankind,
Answer'd all queries touching those at home
With a heaved shoulder and a saucy smile,
And fain had haled him out into the world,
And air'd him there: his nearer friend would
    say
"Screw not the chord too sharply lest it snap."
Then left alone he pluck'd her dagger forth   470
From where his wordless heart had kept it
    warm,
Kissing his vows upon it like a knight.
And wrinkled benchers[35] often talk'd of him
Approvingly, and prophesied his rise:
For heart, I think, help'd head: her letters too,
Tho' far between, and coming fitfully
Like broken music, written as she found
Or made occasion, being strictly watch'd,
Charm'd him thro' every labyrinth till he saw
An end, a hope, a light breaking upon him.   480

   But they that cast her spirit into flesh,
Her worldly-wise begetters, plagued them-
    selves
To sell her, those good parents, for her good.
Whatever eldest-born of rank or wealth
Might lie within their compass, him they lured
Into their net made pleasant by the baits
Of gold and beauty, wooing him to woo.
So month by month the noise about their doors,
And distant blaze of those dull banquets, made
The nightly wirer of their innocent hare[36]   490
Falter before he took it. All in vain.
Sullen, defiant, pitying, wroth, return'd
Leolin's rejected rivals from their suit
So often, that the folly taking wings
Slipt o'er those lazy limits down the wind
With rumour, and became in other fields
A mockery to the yeomen over ale,
And laughter to their lords: but those at home,
As hunters round a hunted creature draw
The cordon close and closer toward the death,   500
Narrow'd her goings out and comings in;
Forbad her first the house of Averill,

[33] Tennyson's note: "The Temple garden where Somerset picked the red, Plantagenet the white roses" (I, 745), another reference to the self-destructive civil war of the Roses.
[34] Tennyson's note: "Made an attack like those Malays who rush about in a frenzy and attack their fellow-men, yelling 'Amook'" (I, 745).
[35] Benchers: senior members of the Inns of Court, of which the Temple is one. They pass on the qualifications of students at law who request admission to the bar.
[36] Wirer of the innocent hare: poacher.

Then closed her access to the wealthier farms,
Last from her own home-circle of the poor
They barr'd her: yet she bore it: yet her cheek
Kept colour: wondrous! but, O mystery!
What amulet drew her down to that old oak,
So old, that twenty years before, a part
Falling had let appear the brand of John[37]—
510 Once grovelike, each huge arm a tree, but now
The broken base of a black tower, a cave
Of touchwood,[38] with a single flourishing spray.
There the manorial lord too curiously
Raking in that millennial touchwood-dust
Found for himself a bitter treasure-trove;
Burst his own wyvern on the seal, and read
Writhing a letter from his child, for which
Came at the moment Leolin's emissary,
A crippled lad, and coming turn'd to fly,
520 But scared with threats of jail and halter[39] gave
To him that fluster'd his poor parish wits
The letter which he brought, and swore besides
To play their go-between as heretofore
Nor let them know themselves betray'd; and
    then,
Soul-stricken at their kindness to him, went
Hating his own lean heart and miserable.

Thenceforward oft from out a despot dream
The father panting woke, and oft, as dawn
Aroused the black republic[40] on his elms,
530 Sweeping the frothfly from the fescue brush'd
Thro' the dim meadow toward his treasure-
    trove,
Seized it, took home, and to my lady,—who
    made
A downward crescent of her minion mouth,
Listless in all despondence,—read; and tore,
As if the living passion symbol'd there
Were living nerves to feel the rent; and burnt,
Now chafing at his own great self defied,
Now striking on huge stumbling-blocks of scorn
In babyisms, and dear diminutives
540 Scatter'd all over the vocabulary
Of such a love as like a chidden child,
After much wailing, hush'd itself at last
Hopeless of answer: then tho' Averill wrote
And bad him with good heart sustain himself—
All would be well—the lover heeded not,
But passionately restless came and went,
And rustling once at night about the place,

There by a keeper shot at, slightly hurt,
Raging return'd: nor was it well for her
Kept to the garden now, and grove of pines,   55
Watch'd even there; and one was set to watch
The watcher, and Sir Aylmer watch'd them all,
Yet bitterer from his readings: once indeed,
Warm'd with his wines, or taking pride in her,
She look'd so sweet, he kiss'd her tenderly
Not knowing what possess'd him: that one kiss
Was Leolin's one strong rival upon earth;
Seconded, for my lady follow'd suit,
Seem'd hope's returning rose: and then ensued
A Martin's summer[41] of his faded love,   5(
Or ordeal by kindness; after this
He seldom crost his child without a sneer;
The mother flow'd in shallower acrimonies:
Never one kindly smile, one kindly word:
So that the gentle creature shut from all
Her charitable use, and face to face
With twenty months of silence, slowly lost
Nor greatly cared to lose, her hold on life.
Last, some low fever ranging round to spy   5
The weakness of a people or a house,
Like flies that haunt a wound, or deer, or men,
Or almost all that is, hurting the hurt—
Save Christ as we believe him—found the girl
And flung her down upon a couch of fire,
Where careless of the household faces near,
And crying upon the name of Leolin,
She, and with her the race of Aylmer, past.

Star to star vibrates light: may soul to soul
Strike thro' a finer element of her own?
So,—from afar,—touch as at once? or why   5
That night, that moment, when she named his
    name,
Did the keen shriek "Yes love, yes, Edith, yes,"
Shrill, till the comrade of his chambers woke,
And came upon him half-arisen from sleep,
With a weird bright eye, sweating and
    trembling,
His hair as it were crackling into flames,
His body half flung forward in pursuit,
And his long arms stretch'd as to grasp a flyer:[42]
Nor knew he wherefore he had made the cry;
And being much befool'd and idioted   5
By the rough amity of the other, sank
As into sleep again. The second day,
My lady's Indian kinsman rushing in,

---

[37] Tennyson's note: "In cutting down trees in Sherwood Forest, letters have been found in the heart of the trees, showing the brands of particular reigns. . . . King John's was eighteen inches within the bark" (I, 746). John's reign was 1199–1216.
[38] Touchwood: dry, decayed wood, used for tinder.   [39] Halter: hanging.
[40] Black republic: rooks; frothfly: a fly that lives in the fescue, a meadow grass.
[41] Martin's summer: in America, Indian summer.   [42] Flyer: fugitive.

A breaker of the bitter news from home,
Found a dead man, a letter edged with death
Beside him, and the dagger which himself
Gave Edith, redden'd with no bandit's blood:
"From Edith" was engraven on the blade.

Then Averill went and gazed upon his death.
And when he came again, his flock believed—
Beholding how the years which are not Time's
Had blasted him—that many thousand days
Were clipt by horror from his term of life.
Yet the sad mother, for the second death
Scarce touch'd her thro' that nearness of the
    first,
And being used to find her pastor texts,[43]
Sent to the harrow'd brother, praying him
To speak before the people of her child,
And fixt the Sabbath. Darkly that day rose:
Autumn's mock sunshine of the faded woods[44]
Was all the life of it; for hard on these,
A breathless burthen of low-folded heavens
Stifled and chill'd at once; but every roof
Sent out a listener: many too had known
Edith among the hamlets round, and since
The parents' harshness and the hapless loves
And double death were widely murmur'd, left
Their own gray tower, or plain-faced
    tabernacle,[45]
To hear him; all in mourning these, and those
With blots of it about them, ribbon, glove
Or kerchief; while the church,—one night,
    except
For greenish glimmerings thro' the lancets,[46]—
    made
Still paler the pale head of him, who tower'd
Above them, with his hopes in either grave.

Long o'er his bent brows linger'd Averill,
His face magnetic to the hand from which
Livid he pluck'd it forth, and labour'd thro'
His brief prayer-prelude, gave the verse
    "Behold,

Your house is left unto you desolate![47]
But lapsed into so long a pause again   630
As half amazed half frighted all his flock:
Then from his height and loneliness of grief
Bore down in flood, and dash'd his angry heart
Against the desolations of the world.

Never since our bad earth became one sea,
Which rolling o'er the palaces of the proud,
And all but those who knew the living God—
Eight that were left to make a purer world—
When since had flood, fire, earthquake, thunder
    wrought
Such waste and havock as the idolatries,   640
Which from the low light of mortality
Shot up their shadows to the Heaven of
    Heavens,
And worshipt their own darkness in the
    Highest?
"Gash thyself, priest, and honour thy brute
    Baäl,[48]
And to thy worst self sacrifice thyself,
For with thy worst self hast thou clothed thy
    God.
Then came a Lord in no wise like to Baäl.
The babe shall lead the lion. Surely now
The wilderness shall blossom as the rose.
Crown thyself, worm, and worship thine own
    lusts!—   650
No coarse and blockish God of acreage[49]
Stands at thy gate for thee to grovel to—
Thy God is far diffused in noble groves
And princely halls, and farms, and flowing
    lawns,
And heaps of living gold that daily grow,
And title-scrolls and gorgeous heraldries.
In such a shape dost thou behold thy God.
Thou wilt not gash thy flesh for *him;* for thine
Fares richly, in fine linen, not a hair
Ruffled upon the scarfskin,[50] even while   660
The deathless ruler[51] of thy dying house
Is wounded to the death that cannot die;

[43] Tennyson's note: "It is implied that she had given Averill the text upon which he preached" (I, 746).
[44] Tennyson's note: "A day without sun, the only faint resemblance to sunshine being the bright yellow of the faded autumn leaves" (I, 746).
[45] Tabernacle: a sometimes derisory name for the churches of Nonconformist sects; Averill is, of course, a clergyman of the Established Church.
[46] Lancets: narrow, arched windows.
[47] The text is from the gospel of Luke 13:35; it is Christ's lament for Jerusalem.
[48] Baäl: a name of a group of Canaanite or Phoenician gods; the name is often given to a fertility god, who was worshipped in rituals involving sacrifice, self-mutilation, and sexual practices.
[49] Tennyson's note: "The Roman god Terminus, who presided over the boundaries of private properties" (I, 746).
[50] Scarfskin: outer layer of skin.   [51] Tennyson's note: "*deathless ruler,* the soul" (I, 747).

And tho' thou numberest with the followers
Of One who cried, 'Leave all and follow me.'
Thee therefore with His light about thy feet,
Thee with His message ringing in thine ears,
Thee shall thy brother man, the Lord from
    Heaven,
Born of a village girl, carpenter's son,
Wonderful, Prince of peace, the Mighty God,
670 Count the more base idolator of the two;
Crueller: as not passing thro' the fire
Bodies, but souls—thy children's—thro' the
    smoke,
The blight of low desires—darkening thine
    own
To thine own likeness; or if one of these,
Thy better born unhappily from thee,
Should, as by miracle, grow straight and fair—
Friends, I was bid to speak of such a one
By those who most have cause to sorrow for
    her—
Fairer than Rachel[52] by the palmy well,
680 Fairer than Ruth among the fields of corn,
Fair as the Angel that said 'Hail!' she seem'd,
Who entering fill'd the house with sudden
    light.[53]
For so mine own was brighten'd: where indeed
The roof so lowly but that beam of Heaven
Dawn'd sometime thro' the doorway? whose the
    babe
Too ragged to be fondled on her lap,
Warm'd at her bosom? The poor child of shame
The common care whom no one cared for, leapt
To greet her, wasting his forgotten heart,[54]
690 As with the mother he had never known,
In gambols; for her fresh and innocent eyes
Had such a star of morning in their blue,
That all neglected places of the field
Broke into nature's music when they saw her.
Low was her voice, but won mysterious way
Thro' the seal'd ear to which a louder one
Was all but silence—free of alms her hand—
The hand that robed your cottage-walls with
    flowers
Has often toil'd to clothe your little ones;
700 How often placed upon the sick man's brow
Cool'd it, or laid his feverous pillow smooth!
Had you one sorrow and she shared it not?
One burthen and she would not lighten it?

One spiritual doubt she did not soothe?
Or when some heat of difference sparkled out,
How sweetly would she glide between your
    wraths,
And steal you from each other! for she walk'd
Wearing the light yoke of that Lord of love,
Who still'd the rolling wave of Galilee!
And one—of him I was not bid to speak— 71
Was always with her, whom you also knew.
Him too you loved, for he was worthy love.
And these had been together from the first;
They might have been together till the last.
Friends, this frail bark of ours, when sorely
    tried,
May wreck itself without the pilot's guilt,
Without the captain's knowledge: hope with
    me.
Whose shame is that, if he went hence with
    shame?
Nor mine the fault, if losing both of these
I cry to vacant chairs and widow'd walls, 72
'My house is left unto me desolate.' "

While thus he spoke, his hearers wept; but
    some,
Sons of the glebe, with other frowns than those
That knit themselves for summer shadow,
    scowl'd
At their great lord. He, when it seem'd he saw
No pale sheet-lightnings from afar, but fork'd
Of the near storm, and aiming at his head,
Sat anger-charm'd from sorrow, soldier-like,
Erect: but when the preacher's cadence flow'd
Softening thro' all the gentle attributes 73
Of his lost child, the wife, who watch'd his face,
Paled at a sudden twitch of his iron mouth;
And "O pray God that he hold up" she thought
"Or surely I shall shame myself and him."

"Nor yours the blame—for who beside your
    hearths
Can take her place—if echoing me you cry
'Our house is left unto us desolate'?
But thou O thou that killest, hadst thou known,
O thou that stonest, hadst thou understood
The things belonging to thy peace and ours! 74
Is there no prophet but the voice that calls
Doom upon kings, or in the waste 'Repent'?

[52] Rachel, the mother of Joseph, was first seen by her husband Jacob as she stood by a well.
[53] Ruth was a woman of Moab who accompanied her mother-in-law Naomi on her return to Jerusalem (Genesis 39:10; Ruth). The Angel is that which in Luke 1:28–31 announces to Mary that she will be the mother of Christ.
[54] Tennyson's note: "*Wasting his forgotten heart*, lavishing his neglected feelings of love" (I, 747).

Is not our own child on the narrow way,[55]
Who down to those that saunter in the broad
Cries 'Come up hither,' as a prophet to us?
Is there no stoning save with flint and rock?
Yes, as the dead we weep for testify—
No desolation but by sword and fire?
Yes, as your moanings witness, and myself
Am lonelier, darker, earthlier for my loss.
Give me your prayers, for he is past your
    prayers,
Not past the living fount of pity in Heaven.
But I that thought myself long-suffering, meek,
Exceeding 'poor in spirit'—how the words
Have twisted back upon themselves, and mean
Vileness, we are grown so proud—I wish'd my
    voice
A rushing tempest of the wrath of God
To blow these sacrifices thro' the world—
Sent like the twelve-divided concubine[56]
To inflame the tribes: but there—out yonder—
    earth
Lightens from her own central Hell—O there
The red fruit of an old idolatry—
The heads of chiefs and princes fall so fast,
They cling together in the ghastly sack—
The land all shambles—naked marriages[57]
Flash from the bridge, and ever-murder'd
    France,
By shores that darken with the gathering wolf,
Runs a river of blood to the sick sea.
Is this a time to madden madness then?
Was this a time for these to flaunt their pride?
May Pharaoh's darkness,[58] folds as dense as
    those
Which hid the Holiest from the people's eyes
Ere the great death, shroud this great sin from
    all!
Doubtless our narrow world must canvass it:
O rather pray for those and pity them,
Who, thro' their own desire accomplish'd, bring
Their own gray hairs with sorrow to the
    grave—

Who broke the bond which they desired to
    break,
Which else had link'd their race with times to
    come—
Who wove coarse webs to snare her purity,   780
Grossly contriving their dear daughter's
    good—
Poor souls, and knew not what they did, but
    sat
Ignorant, devising their own daughter's death!
May not that earthly chastisement suffice?
Have not our love and reverence left them
    bare?
Will not another take their heritage?
Will there be children's laughter in their hall
For ever and for ever, or one stone
Left on another, or is it a light thing
That I, their guest, their host, their ancient
    friend,   790
I made by these the last of all my race,
Must cry to these the last of theirs, as cried
Christ ere His agony to those that swore
Not by the temple but the gold, and made
Their own traditions God, and slew the Lord,
And left their memories a world's curse—
    'Behold,
Your house is left unto you desolate'?"

Ended he had not, but she brook'd no more:
Long since her heart had beat remorselessly,
Her crampt-up sorrow pain'd her, and a sense   800
Of meanness in her unresisting life.
Then their eyes vext her; for on entering
He had cast the curtains of their seat aside—
Black velvet of the costliest—she herself
Had seen to that: fain had she closed them
    now,
Yet dared not stir to do it, only near'd
Her husband inch by inch, but when she laid,
Wife-like, her hand in one of his, he veil'd
His face with the other, and at once, as falls
A creeper when the prop is broken, fell   810
The woman shrieking at his feet, and swoon'd.

[55] Narrow way: the way that leads to salvation (Matthew 7:14).
[56] Tennyson's note refers to Judges 19:29: an account of how, after the rape and murder of a concubine, a part of her body was sent to each of the twelve tribes of Israel, to rouse their vengeance.
[57] Averill in these lines refers to the French Revolution and the Reign of Terror. So does Tennyson's note: "He alludes to the report, horrible and hardly credible, that when the heads were taken out of the sack, two were sometimes found clinging together, one having bitten into the other in the momentary convulsion that followed decapitation" (I, 747). "Naked marriages" refers to the practice during the Terror of tying naked men and women together and throwing them into a river.
[58] The ninth plague sent upon the Egyptians to force the Pharaoh to permit Moses and his people to depart was a pall of darkness (Exodus 10:21).

Then her own people bore along the nave
Her pendent hands, and narrow meagre face
Seam'd with the shallow cares of fifty years:
And her the Lord of all the landscape round
Ev'n to its last horizon, and of all
Who peer'd at him so keenly, follow'd out
Tall and erect, but in the middle aisle
Reel'd, as a footsore ox in crowded ways
820   Stumbling across the market to his death,
Unpitied; for he groped as blind, and seem'd
Always about to fall, grasping the pews
And oaken finials[59] till he touch'd the door;
Yet to the lychgate,[60] where his chariot stood,
Strode from the porch, tall and erect again.

     But nevermore did either pass the gate
Save under pall with bearers. In one month,
Thro' weary and yet ever wearier hours,
The childless mother went to seek her child;
830   And when he felt the silence of his house
About him, and the change and not the
     change,
And those fixt eyes of painted ancestors
Staring for ever from their gilded walls
On him their last descendant, his own head
Began to droop, to fall; the man became
Imbecile; his one word was "desolate;"
Dead for two years before his death was he;
But when the second Christmas came, escaped
His keepers, and the silence which he felt,
840   To find a deeper in the narrow gloom
By wife and child; nor wanted at this end
The dark retinue reverencing death
At golden thresholds; nor from tender hearts,
And those who sorrow'd o'er a vanish'd race,
Pity, the violet on the tyrant's grave.
Then the great Hall was wholly broken down,
And the broad woodland parcell'd into farms;
And where the two contrived their daughter's
     good,
Lies the hawk's cast,[61] the mole has made his
     run,
850   The hedgehog underneath the plantain bores,[62]
The rabbit fondles his own harmless face,

The slow-worm[63] creeps, and the thin weasel
     there
Follows the mouse, and all is open field.

                                                                    1864

In the Valley of Cauteretz[1]

All along the valley, stream that flashest white,
Deepening thy voice with the deepening of the
     night,
All along the valley, where thy waters flow,
I walk'd with one I loved two and thirty years
     ago.
All along the valley, while I walk'd to-day,
The two and thirty years were a mist that rolls
     away;
For all along the valley, down thy rocky bed,
Thy living voice to me was as the voice of the
     dead,
And all along the valley, by rock and cave and
     tree,
The voice of the dead was a living voice to me.   1

                                                        (1861) 1864

from Experiments in Quantity

Milton

Alcaics[1]

O mighty-mouth'd inventor of harmonies,
O skill'd to sing of Time or Eternity,
     God-gifted organ-voice of England,
          Milton, a name to resound for ages;
Whose Titan angels, Gabriel, Abdiel,[2]

---

[59] Finials: ornaments on the ends of the pews.   [60] Lychgate: roofed gate.
[61] Hawk's cast: indigestible matter thrown up from the crop of the hawk.
[62] Plantain: a low, broad-leaved herb.   [63] Slow-worm: a kind of lizard.
[1] Tennyson's note in the standard edition of his poetry: "A valley in the Pyrenees, where I
had been with Arthur Hallam in former years" (in 1830) (I, 760) .
[1] An alcaic verse is customarily a four-stanza poem; each stanza has four lines, and each line
four stressed syllables. The verse is named for Alcaeus, a Greek lyric poet of the sixth century
before Christ; it was also used by the Roman poet Horace.
[2] Abdiel: an angel in *Paradise Lost* who resists Lucifer's urging to revolt against God.

Starr'd from Jehovah's gorgeous armouries,
Tower, as the deep-domed empyrëan
Rings to the roar of an angel onset[3]—
Me rather all that bowery loneliness,
The brooks of Eden mazily murmuring,
And bloom profuse and cedar arches
Charm, as a wanderer out in ocean,
Where some refulgent sunset of India
Streams o'er a rich ambrosial ocean isle,
And crimson-hued the stately palm-woods
Whisper in odorous heights of even.

Hendecasyllabics[1]

O you chorus of indolent reviewers,
Irresponsible, indolent reviewers,
Look, I come to the test, a tiny poem
All composed in a metre of Catullus,
All in quantity, careful of my motion,
Like the skater on ice that hardly bears him,
Lest I fall unawares before the people,
Waking laughter in indolent reviewers.
Should I flounder awhile without a tumble
Thro' this metrification of Catullus,
They should speak to me not without a
    welcome,
All that chorus of indolent reviewers.
Hard, hard, hard is it, only not to tumble,
So fantastical is the dainty metre.
Wherefore slight me not wholly, nor believe me
Too presumptuous, indolent reviewers.
O blatant Magazines, regard me rather—
Since I blush to belaud myself a moment—
As some rare little rose, a piece of inmost
Horticultural art, or half coquette-like
Maiden, not to be greeted unbenignly.

                                    1863; 1864

*In his note in the standard edition of his poetry,
Tennyson wrote that the two "Northern Farmer"
poems are not "photographs, . . . they are imagina-
tive. The first is founded on the dying words of a
farm-baliff, as reported to me by my old great-uncle
when he was verging upon 80: 'God A'Mighty little
knows what He's about a-taking me. An' Squire will*

*be so mad an' all.' I conjectured the man from that
one saying.*

*"The Farmer, New Style, is likewise founded on a
single sentence: 'When I canters my 'erse along the
ramper (highway), I 'ears "proputty, proputty,
proputty".' I had been told that a rich farmer in
our neighborhood was in the habit of saying this. I
never saw the man and know no more of him" (I,
757–758).*

Northern Farmer

Old Style

I[1]

Wheer 'asta beän saw long and meä liggin' 'ere
    aloän?
Noorse? thourt nowt o' a noorse: whoy,
    Doctor's abeän an' agoän:
Says that I moänt 'a naw moor aäle: but I
    beänt a fool:
Git ma my aäle, fur I beänt a-gawin' to breäk
    my rule.

II[2]

Doctors, they knaws nowt, fur a says what's
    nawways true:
Naw soort o' koind o' use to saäy the things
    that a do.
I've 'ed my point o' aäle ivry noight sin' I beän
    'ere,
An' I've 'ed my quart ivry market-noight for
    foorty year.

III[3]

Parson's a beän loikewoise, an' a sittin' 'ere o'
    my bed.
"The amoighty's a taäkin o' you to 'issén, my
    friend," a said,   10
An' a towd ma my sins, an's toithe were due,
    an' I gied it in hond;
I done moy duty boy 'um, as I 'a done boy the
    lond.

IV[4]

Larn'd a ma' beä. I reckons I 'annot sa mooch
    to larn.

[3] Onset: battle.
[1] Hendecasyllabics—an eleven-syllable verse—is one of several classical meters in which Tenny-
son experimented in the 1860s. The verse was originated by the Roman lyric poet Catullus, and
it is common in Greek and Latin poetry.
[1] Stanza I: 'asta beän: hast thou been; liggin': lying; agoän: gone.   [2] Stanza II: point: pint.
[3] Stanza III: 'issén: himself; towd: told; toithe: tithe; boy: by; lond: land.
[4] Stanza IV: Larn'd a ma' beä: learned he [the parson] may be; a cast oop: he brought up;
barne: child; hallus: always; raäte: taxes.

But a cast oop, thot a did, 'bout Bessy Marris's
   barne.
Thaw a knaws I hallus voäted wi' Squoire an'
   choorch an' staäte,
An' i' the woost o' toimes I wur niver agin the
   raäte.

*V*⁵

An' I hallus coom'd to 's chooch afoor moy
   Sally wur deäd,
An' 'eärd 'um a bummin' awaäy loike a
   buzzard-clock ower my 'eäd,
An' I niver knaw'd whot a meän'd but I thowt
   a 'ad summut to saäy,
An' I thowt a said whot a owt to 'a said an' I
20   coom'd awaäy.

*VI*⁶

Bessy Marris's barne! tha knaws she laäid it to
   meä.
Mowt a beän, mayhap, for she wur a bad un,
   sheä.
'Siver, I kep 'um, I kep 'um, my lass, tha mun
   understond;
I done moy duty boy 'um as I 'a done boy the
   lond.

*VII*⁷

But Parson a cooms an' a goäs, an' a says it eäsy
   an' freeä
"The amoighty's a taäkin o' you to 'issén, my
   friend," says 'eä.
I weänt saäy men be loiars, thaw summun said
   it in 'aäste:
But 'e reäds wonn sarmin a weeäk, an' I 'a
   stubb'd Thurnaby waäste.

*VIII*⁸

D'ya moind the waäste, my lass? naw, naw, tha
   was not born then;
Theer wur a boggle in it, I often 'eärd 'um
30   mysen;

Moäst loike a butter-bump, fur I 'eärd 'um
   about an' about,
But I stubb'd 'um oop wi' the lot, an' raäved
   an' rembled 'um out.

*IX*⁹

Keäper's it wur; fo' they fun 'um theer a-laäid
   of 'is faäce
Down i' the woild 'enemies afoor I coom'd to
   the plaäce.
Noäks or Thimbleby—toäner 'ed shot 'um as
   deäd as a naäil.
Noäks were 'ang'd for it oop at 'soize—but git
   ma my aäle.

*X*¹⁰

Dubbut looök at the waäste: theer warn't not
   feeäd for a cow;
Nowt at all but bracken an' fuzz, an' looök at
   it now—
Warn't worth nowt a haäcre, an' now theer's
   lots o' feeäd,
Fourscoor yows upon it an' some on it down i'
   seeäd.

*XI*¹¹

Nobbut a bit on it's left, an' I meän'd to 'a
   stubb'd it at fall,
Done it ta-year I meän'd, an' runn'd plow
   thruff it an' all,
If godamoighty an' parson 'ud nobbut let ma
   aloän,
Meä, wi' haäte hoonderd haäcre o' Squoire's,
   an' lond o' my oän.

*XII*¹²

Do godamoighty knaw what a's doing a-taäkin'
   o' meä?
I beänt wonn as saws 'ere a beän an' yonder a
   peä;
An' Squoire 'ull be sa mad an' all—a' dear a'
   dear!
And I 'a managed for Squoire coom Michael-
   mas thutty year.

---

⁵ Stanza V: buzzard clock: cockchafer (Tennyson's note) ; summut: something.
⁶ Stanza VI: laäid it to meä: accused me of being the father; mowt: might; 'Siver: howsoever; mun: must; boy 'um: by him.
⁷ Stanza VII: summun: some might; stubb'd: broke for cultivation.
⁸ Stanza VIII: moind: remember; boggle: spirit, bogey; butter-bump: bittern (Tennyson's note) ; lot: the waste ground; raäved an' rembled: tore up and threw away.
⁹ Stanza IX: Keäper's it wur: it was the spirit of a gamekeeper; Down i' the woild 'enemies: the keeper was found face down in the wild anemones; toäner: one or the other; oop at 'soize: at the assizes, the county court.
¹⁰ Stanza X: Dubbut: do but; fuzz: furse; yows: ewes; down i' seeäd: seeded.
¹¹ Stanza XI: Nobbut: only; ta-year: this year; thruff: through; haäte: eight.
¹² Stanza XII: wonn as saws: one who sows; Michaelmas: feast day of St. Michael the Arch-angel, September 29, used to mark one of the quarters of the year; thutty: thirty.

XIII[13]

A mowt 'a taäen owd Joänes, as 'ant not a
    'aäpoth o' sense,
Or a mowt 'a taäen young Robins—a niver
    mended a fence:
But godamoighty a moost taäke meä an' taäke
    ma now
Wi' aäf the cows to cauve an' Thurnaby hoälms
    to plow!

XIV[14]

Loook 'ow quoloty smoiles when they seeäs ma
    a passin' boy,
Says to thessén naw doubt "what a man a beä
    sewerloy!"
Fur they knaws what I beän to Squoire sin fust
    a coom'd to the 'All;
I done moy duty by Squoire an' I done moy
    duty boy hall.

XV[15]

Squoire's i' Lunnon, an' summun I reckons 'ull
    'a to wroite,
For whoä's to howd the lond ater meä thot
    muddles ma quoit;
Sartin-sewer I beä, thot a weänt niver give it to
    Joänes,
Naw, nor a moänt to Robins—a niver rembles
    the stoäns.

XVI[16]

But summun 'ull come ater meä mayhap wi' 'is
    kittle o' steäm
Huzzin' an' maäzin' the blessed feälds wi' the
    Divil's oän teäm.
Sin' I mun doy I mun doy, thaw loife they says
    is sweet,
But sin' I mun doy I mun doy, for I couldn
    abeär to see it.

XVII[17]

What atta stannin' theer fur, an' doesn bring
    ma the aäle?
Doctor's a 'toättler, lass, an a's hallus i' the
    owd taäle;

I weänt breäk rules fur Doctor, a knaws naw
    moor nor a floy;
Git ma my aäle I tell tha, an' if I mun doy I
    mun doy.

1864

Northern Farmer

New Style

I[1]

Dosn't thou 'ear my 'erse's legs, as they canters
    awaäy?
Proputty, proputty, proputty—that's what I
    'ears 'em saäy.
Proputty, proputty, proputty—Sam, thou's an
    ass for thy paäins:
Theer's moor sense i' one o' 'is legs nor in all
    thy braäins.

II[2]

Woä—theer's a craw to pluck wi' tha, Sam:
    yon's parson's 'ouse—
Dosn't thou knaw that a man mun be eäther
    a man or a mouse?
Time to think on it then; for thou'll be
    twenty to weeäk.
Proputty, proputty—woä then woä—let ma
    'ear mysén speäk.

III

Me an' thy muther, Sammy, 'as beän a-talkin'
    o' thee;
Thou's beän talkin' to muther, an' she beän a
    tellin' it me. 10
Thou'll not marry for munny—thou's sweet
    upo' parson's lass—
Noä—thou'll marry for luvv—an' we boäth
    on us thinks tha an ass.

IV[3]

Seeä'd her todaäy goä by—Saäint's-daäy—they
    was ringing the bells.

---

[13] Stanza XIII: A mowt 'a taäen: might have taken; aäpoth: halfpenny; aäf: half; cauve: calve; hoälms: holms, bottom land.

[14] Stanza XIV: quoloty: quality, the gentry; thessén: themselves; sewerloy: surely; 'All: the Squire's hall.

[15] Stanza XV: summun: someone; howd: hold; quoit: quite; Sartin-sewer: certain sure; rembles: throws away.

[16] Stanza XVI: kittle o' steäm: steam thresher; Huzzin' an' maäzin': worrying and amazing; thaw: though.

[17] Stanza XVII: atta: art thou; 'toättler: teetotaller; an a's hallus i' the owd taäle: always says the same thing; nor a floy: than a fly.

[1] Stanza I: 'erse: horse

[2] Stanza II: craw to pluck: matter to talk about; to weeäk: this week; mysén: myself.

[3] Stanza IV: Scoors o' gells: scores of girls; graws: grows.

She's a beauty thou thinks—an' soä is scoors
 o' gells,
Them as 'as munny an' all—wot's a beauty?—
 the flower as blaws.
But proputty, proputty sticks, an' proputty,
 proputty graws.

V[4]

Do'ant be stunt: taäke time: I knaws what
 maäkes tha sa mad.
Warn't I craäzed fur the lasses mysén when I
 wur a lad?
But I knaw'd a Quaäker feller as often 'as
 towd ma this:
20 "Doänt thou marry for munny, but goä wheer
 munny is!"

VI[5]

An' I went wheer munny war: an' thy muther
 coom to 'and,
Wi' lots o' munny laaïd by, an' a nicetish bit o'
 land.
Maäybe she warn't a beauty:—I niver giv it a
 thowt—
But warn't she as good to cuddle an' kiss as a
 lass as 'ant nowt?

VII[6]

Parson's lass 'ant nowt, an' she weänt 'a nowt
 when 'e's deäd,
Mun be a guvness, lad, or summut, and addle
 her breäd:
Why? fur 'e's nobbut a curate, an' weänt niver
 git hissen clear,
An' 'e maäde the bed as 'e ligs on afoor 'e
 coom'd to the shere.

VIII[7]

An thin 'e coom'd to the parish wi' lots o'
 Varsity debt,
Stook to his taaïl they did, an' 'e 'ant got shut
30 on 'em yet.
An' 'e ligs on 'is back i' the grip, wi' noän to
 lead 'im a shuvv,
Woorse nor a far-welter'd yowe: fur, Sammy, 'e
 married fur luvv.

IX

Luvv? what's luvv? thou can luvv thy lass an'
 'er munny too,
Maakin' 'em goä togither as they've good right
 to do.
Could'n I luvv thy muther by cause o' 'er
 munny laaïd by?
Naäy—fur I luvv'd 'er a vast sight moor fur
 it: reäson why.

X[8]

Ay, an' thy muther says thou wants to marry
 the lass,
Cooms of a gentleman burn: an' we boäth on
 us thinks tha an ass.
Woä then, proputty, wiltha?—an ass as near as
 mays nowt—
Woä then, wiltha? dangtha!—the bees is as fell
 as owt.

XI[9]

Breäk me a bit o' the esh for his 'eäd, lad, out
 o' the fence!
Gentleman burn! what's gentleman burn? is it
 shillins an' pence?
Proputty, proputty's ivrything 'ere, an',
 Sammy, I'm blest
If it isn't the saäme oop yonder, fur them as
 'as it's the best.

XII

Tis'n them as 'as munny as breäks into 'ouses
 an' steäls,
Them as 'as coäts to their backs an' taäkes
 their regular meäls.
Noä, but it's them as niver knaws wheer a
 meäl's to be 'ad.
Taäke my word for it, Sammy, the poor in a
 loomp is bad.

XIII[10]

Them or thir feythers, tha sees, mun 'a beän
 a laäzy lot,
Fur work mun 'a gone to the gittin' whiniver
 munny was got.

---

[4] Stanza V: Stunt: obstinate (Tennyson's note). [5] Stanza VI: 'ant nowt: has nothing.

[6] Stanza VII: addle: earn; nobbut: nothing but; clear: out of debt; ligs: lies; shere: shire.

[7] Stanza VIII: Varsity debt: college debts; grip: ditch; Woorse nor a far-welter'd yowe: worse off than a sheep lying on its back.

[8] Stanza X: as near as mays nowt: as near as can be; Woä then: spoken to the horse; the bees is as fell as owt: the flies are as fierce as anything (Tennyson's note).

[9] Stanza XI: bit o' the esh: branch of an ash tree.

[10] Stanza XIII: ammost: almost; tued an' moil'd 'issén deäd: worked himself to death.

Feyther 'ad ammost nowt; leästways 'is munny
was 'id.
But 'e tued an' moil'd 'issén deäd, an' 'e died a
good un, 'e did.

XIV[11]

Loook thou theer wheer Wrigglesby beck
cooms out by the 'ill!
Feyther run oop to the farm, an' I runs oop
to the mill;
An' I'll run oop to the brig, an' that thou'll
live to see;
And if thou marries a good un I'll leäve the
land to thee.

XV

Thim's my noätions, Sammy, wheerby I means
to stick;
But if thou marries a bad un, I'll leäve the
land to Dick.—
Coom oop, proputty, proputty—that's what I
'ears 'im saäy—
Proputty, proputty, proputty—canter an'
canter awaäy.

1869

The Higher Pantheism

The sun, the moon, the stars, the seas, the hills
and the plains—
Are not these, O Soul, the Vision of Him who
reigns?

Is not the Vision He? tho' He be not that
which He seems?
Dreams are true while they last, and do we not
live in dreams?

Earth, these solid stars, this weight of body and
limb,
Are they not sign and symbol of thy division
from Him?

Dark is the world to thee: thyself art the
reason why;
For is He not all but that which has power to
feel "I am I"?

Glory about thee, without thee; and thou
fulfillest thy doom
Making Him broken gleams, and a stifled
splendour and gloom.

Speak to Him thou for He hears, and Spirit
with Spirit can meet—
Closer is He than breathing, and nearer than
hands and feet.

God is law, say the wise; O Soul, and let us
rejoice,
For if He thunder by law the thunder is yet
His voice.

Law is God, say some: no God at all, says the
fool;
For all we have power to see is a straight staff
bent in a pool;

And the ear of man cannot hear, and the eye
of man cannot see;
But if we could see and hear, this Vision—
were it not He?

1869

*Lucretius (c. 99–55 B.C.) was a Roman poet who
argued, in his great work* De Rerum Natura, *that
nothing exists but the atoms of matter, and that hu-
man content lay in the calm acceptance of a mate-
rial universe and in the high pleasures of thought
and art. Lucretius' suicide after being driven mad
by a love potion is the subject of a legend dating
back at least to the fourth century.*

Much of Tennyson's poem paraphrases parts of
De Rerum Natura. *In his notes to the standard edi-
tion of his father's poetry, Hallam Tennyson iden-
tifies some of the passages in* Lucretius *adapted in
this poem. Tennyson asked Hugh Munro, who pub-
lished an edition of Lucretius in 1864, to read his
poem: "Munro said that everything was Lucretian
thro' the poem, and that there was no suggestion
which he could make. He, however, did suggest the
alteration of 'shepherds' to 'neat-herds' [line 87]"*
(I, 749–750).

Lucretius

Lucilia, wedded to Lucretius, found
Her master cold; for when the morning flush
Of passion and the first embrace had died
Between them, tho' he lov'd her none the less,
Yet often when the woman heard his foot
Return from pacings in the field, and ran
To greet him with a kiss, the master took
Small notice, or austerely, for—his mind
Half buried in some weightier argument,
Or fancy-borne perhaps upon the rise   10

---

[11] Stanza XIV: beck: brook; feyther run oop: my father's land ran as far as; brig: bridge.

And long roll of the Hexameter—he past
To turn and ponder those three hundred scrolls
Left by the Teacher,[1] whom he held divine.
She brook'd it not; but wrathful, petulant,
Dreaming some rival, sought and found a witch
Who brew'd the philtre which had power, they said,
To lead an errant passion home again.
And this, at times, she mingled with his drink,
And this destroy'd him; for the wicked broth
20 Confused the chemic labour of the blood,
And tickling the brute brain within the man's
Made havoc among those tender cells, and check'd
His power to shape: he loathed himself; and once
After a tempest woke upon a morn
That mock'd him with returning calm, and cried:

  "Storm in the night! for thrice I heard the rain
Rushing; and once the flash of a thunderbolt—
Methought I never saw so fierce a fork—
Struck out the streaming mountain-side, and show'd
30 A riotous confluence of watercourses
Blanching and billowing in a hollow of it,
Where all but yester-eve was dusty-dry.

  "Storm, and what dreams, ye holy Gods, what dreams!
For thrice I waken'd after dreams. Perchance
We do but recollect the dreams that come
Just ere the waking: terrible! for it seem'd
A void was made in Nature; all her bonds
Crack'd; and I saw the flaring atom-streams[2]
And torrents of her myriad universe,
40 Ruining along the illimitable inane,
Fly on to clash together again, and make
Another and another frame of things
For ever: that was mine, my dream, I knew it—
Of and belonging to me, as the dog
With inward yelp and restless forefoot plies

His function of the woodland:[3] but the next!
I thought that all the blood by Sylla[4] shed
Came driving rainlike down again on earth,
And where it dash'd the reddening meadow, sprang
No dragon warriors from Cadmean teeth,[5]
For these I thought my dream would show to me,
But girls, Hetairai,[6] curious in their art,
Hired animalisms, vile as those that made
The mulberry-faced Dictator's[7] orgies worse
Than aught they fable of the quiet Gods.
And hands they mixt, and yell'd and round me drove
In narrowing circles till I yell'd again
Half-suffocated, and sprang up, and saw—
Was it the first beam of my latest day?

  "Then, then, from utter gloom stood out the breasts,
The breasts of Helen, and hoveringly a sword
Now over and now under, now direct,
Pointed itself to pierce, but sank down shamed
At all that beauty; and as I stared, a fire,
The fire that left a roofless Ilion,[8]
Shot out of them, and scorch'd me that I woke.

  "Is this thy vengeance, holy Venus, thine,
Because I would not one of thine own doves,[9]
Not ev'n a rose, were offer'd to thee? thine,
Forgetful how my rich procœmion[10] makes
Thy glory fly along the Italian field,
In lays that will outlast thy Deity?

  "Deity? nay, thy worshippers. My tongue
Trips, or I speak profanely. Which of these
Angers thee most, or angers thee at all?
Not if thou be'st of those who, far aloof
From envy, hate and pity, and spite and scorn,
Live the great life which all our greatest fain
Would follow, center'd in eternal calm.

  "Nay, if thou canst, O Goddess, like ourselves

---

[1] The Teacher: the Greek philosopher Epicurus (c. 341–270 B.C.).
[2] In his note in the standard edition, Hallam Tennyson cites *De Rerum Natura*, i, lines 999f. (I, 750).
[3] Hallam Tennyson's note: *De Rerum Natura*, iv, lines 991f. (I, 750).
[4] Sylla: the Roman general Sulla (138–78 B.C.), who near the end of his life ruled Rome as a dictator through proscriptions and executions.
[5] Cadmean teeth: the dragon's teeth sowed by Cadmus in Greek mythology, from which armed warriors sprang.
[6] Hetairai: courtesans.   [7] Sulla died of dissipation.   [8] Ilion: Troy.
[9] Hallam Tennyson's note: *De Rerum Natura*, v, lines 1198f. (I, 751).
[10] Procœmion: the proem to Lucretius' poem, in which he celebrates Venus as a name for the generative energy of creation.

Touch, and be touch'd, then would I cry to
    thee
To kiss thy Mavors,[11] roll thy tender arms
Round him, and keep him from the lust of
    blood
That makes a steaming slaughter-house of
    Rome.

    "Ay, but I meant not thee; I meant not
    her,[12]
Whom all the pines of Ida shook to see
Slide from that quiet heaven of hers, and
    tempt
The Trojan, while his neat-herds were abroad;
Nor her that o'er her wounded hunter wept
Her Deity false in human-amorous tears;
Nor whom her beardless apple-arbiter
Decided fairest. Rather, O ye Gods,
Poet-like, as the great Sicilian[13] called
Calliope to grace his golden verse—
Ay, and this Kypris[14] also—did I take
That popular name of thine to shadow forth
The all-generating powers and genial heat
Of Nature, when she strikes thro' the thick
    blood
Of cattle, and light is large, and lambs are glad
Nosing the mother's udder, and the bird
Makes his heart voice amid the blaze of
    flowers:
Which things appear the work of mighty Gods.

    "The Gods! and if I go *my* work is left
Unfinish'd—*if* I go. The Gods, who haunt
The lucid interspace of world and world,
Where never creeps a cloud, or moves a wind,
Nor ever falls the least white star of snow,
Nor ever lowest roll of thunder moans,
Nor sound of human sorrow mounts to mar

Their sacred everlasting calm! and such,   110
Not all so fine, nor so divine a calm,
Not such, nor all unlike it, man may gain
Letting his own life go. The Gods, the Gods!
If all be atoms, how then should the Gods
Being atomic not be dissoluble,
Not follow the great law? My master held
That Gods there are, for all men so believe.
I prest my footsteps into his, and meant[15]
Surely to lead my Memmius[16] in a train
Of flowery clauses onward to the proof   120
That Gods there are, and deathless. Meant? I
    meant?
I have forgotten what I meant: my mind
Stumbles, and all my faculties are lamed.

    "Look where another of our Gods, the Sun,
Apollo, Delius, or of older use
All-seeing Hyperion[17]—what you will—
Has mounted yonder; since he never sware,
Except his wrath were wreak'd on wretched
    man,
That he would only shine among the dead
Hereafter; tales! for never yet on earth   130
Could dead flesh creep, or bits of roasting ox
Moan round the spit[18]—nor knows he what he
    sees;
King of the East altho' he seem, and girt
With song and flame and fragrance, slowly lifts
His golden feet on those empurpled stairs
That climb into the windy halls of heaven:
And here he glances on an eye new-born,
And gets for greeting but a wail of pain;
And here he stays upon a freezing orb
That fain would gaze upon him to the last;   140
And here upon a yellow eyelid fall'n
And closed by those who mourn a friend in
    vain,

[11] Mavors: Mars. Hallam Tennyson cites *De Rerum Natura,* i, lines 31f. (I, 751).

[12] Her: the Greek goddess Aphrodite, like Venus the goddess of love: she seduced Anchises while he tended his flocks on Mount Ida (the issue of this seduction was Aeneas, one of the first settlers of Rome); fell in love with Adonis, who was killed while hunting; and persuaded Paris to judge her the most fair, rewarded him with the love of Helen, and so instigated the Trojan war (see note to "Œnone," p. 74).

[13] Hallam Tennyson, in his note in the standard edition, identifies the "great Sicilian" as Theocritus, a Greek pastoral poet who refined the Doric poetry of Sicily. Other commentators think that the reference is to Empedocles, a Greek philosopher of the fourth century before Christ, who invoked Calliope, the Greek muse of eloquence and heroic poetry, in his philosophic poems.

[14] Kypris: a name of Aphrodite, from the island of Cyprus, sacred to her worship. Hallam Tennyson cites *De Rerum Natura,* i, lines 2f. (I, 751).

[15] Hallam Tennyson cites *De Rerum Natura,* v, 146–194, 1161–1291; iii, lines 1f. (I, 758).

[16] Memmius: Caius Memmius Gemellus, to whom Lucretius' poem was dedicated.

[17] Apollo, the god of song and prophecy, became identified with Hyperion, the sun. Delius, or Delos, is an island associated with his worship.

[18] When Odysseus' men kill the cattle of the Sun, the flesh crawled with worms and moaned before it could be eaten: *Odyssey,* Book XII.

Not thankful that his troubles are no more.
And me, altho' his fire is on my face
Blinding, he sees not, nor at all can tell
Whether I mean this day to end myself,
Or lend an ear to Plato where he says,
That men like soldiers may not quit the post
Allotted by the Gods:[19] but he that holds
150   The Gods are careless, wherefore need he care
Greatly for them, nor rather plunge at once,
Being troubled, wholly out of sight, and sink
Past earthquake—ay, and gout and stone, that
    break
Body toward death, and palsy, death-in-life,
And wretched age—and worst disease of all,
These prodigies of myriad nakednesses,
And twisted shapes of lust, unspeakable,
Abominable, strangers at my hearth
Not welcome, harpies miring every dish,
160   The phantom husks of something foully done,
And fleeting thro' the boundless universe,
And blasting the long quiet of my breast
With animal heat and dire insanity?

    "How should the mind, except it loved
      them, clasp
These idols[20] to herself? or do they fly
Now thinner, and now thicker, like the flakes
In a fall of snow, and so press in, perforce
Of multitude, as crowds that in an hour
Of civic tumult jam the doors, and bear
The keepers down, and throng, their rags and
170   they
The basest, far into that council-hall
Where sit the best and stateliest of the land?

    "Can I not fling this horror off me again,
Seeing with how great ease Nature can smile,
Balmier and nobler from her bath of storm,
At random ravage? and how easily
The mountain there has cast his cloudy slough,
Now towering o'er him in serenest air,
A mountain o'er a mountain,—ay, and within
180   All hollow as the hopes and fears of men?

    "But who was he, that in the garden snared
Picus and Faunus, rustic Gods?[21] a tale

To laugh at—more to laugh at in myself—
For look! what is it? there? yon arbutus
Totters; a noiseless riot underneath
Strikes through the wood, sets all the tops
    quivering—
The mountain quickens into Nymph and
    Faun;
And here an Oread[22]—how the sun delights
To glance and shift about her slippery sides,
And rosy knees and supple roundedness,   19
And budded bosom-peaks—who this way runs
Before the rest—A satyr, a satyr, see,
Follows; but him I proved impossible;[23]
Twy-natured is no nature: yet he draws
Nearer and nearer, and I scan him now
Beastlier than any phantom of his kind
That ever butted his rough brother-brute
For lust or lusty blood or provender:
I hate, abhor, spit, sicken at him; and she
Loathes him as well; such a precipitate heel,   20
Fledged as it were with Mercury's ankle-wing,
Whirls her to me: but will she fling herself,
Shameless upon me? Catch her, goat-foot: nay,
Hide, hide them, million-myrtled wilderness,
And cavern-shadowing laurels, hide! do I
    wish—
What?—that the bush were leafless? or to
    whelm
All of them in one massacre? O ye Gods,
I know you careless, yet, behold, to you
From childly wont and ancient use I call—
I thought I lived securely as yourselves—   21
No lewdness, narrowing envy, monkey-spite,
No madness of ambition, avarice, none:
No larger feast than under plane or pine
With neighbours laid along the grass, to take
Only such cups as left us friendly-warm,
Affirming each his own philosophy—
Nothing to mar the sober majesties
Of settled, sweet, Epicurean life.[24]
But now it seems some unseen monster lays
His vast and filthy hands upon my will,   22
Wrenching it backward into his; and spoils
My bliss in being; and it was not great;
For save when shutting reasons up in rhythm,

---

    [19] Socrates' words in the *Phaedo* as he confronts his execution.

    [20] Idols: images, the shapes temporarily made by the flux of atoms.

    [21] Picus and Faunus, prophetic divinities of Rome, were trapped by Numa, according to legend an early king of Rome, and made to tell the secrets of the gods.

    [22] Nymph, Faun, Oread: spirits of natural objects. Lines 189–191 were omitted when the poem was first published in a magazine in 1868; line 188 reads, "And here an Oread, and this way she runs."

    [23] Satyrs were licentious spirits, half-man and half-horse or goat. Hallam Tennyson cites *De Rerum Natura*, ii, 700; v, lines 837f., 878f. (I, 752).

    [24] For this passage, lines 211–218, Hallam Tennyson cites *De Rerum Natura*, ii, lines 29f.; ii, 66 (I, 752).

Or Heliconian honey[25] in living words,
To make a truth less harsh, I often grew
Tired of so much within our little life,
Or of so little in our little life—
Poor little life that toddles half an hour
Crown'd with a flower or two, and there an
    end—
And since the nobler pleasure seems to fade,
Why should I, beastlike as I find myself,
Not manlike end myself?—our privilege—
What beast has heart to do it? And what man,
What Roman would be dragg'd in triumph
    thus?
Not I; not he, who bears one name with her[26]
Whose death-blow struck the dateless doom of
    kings,
When, brooking not the Tarquin in her veins,
She made her blood in sight of Collatine
And all his peers, flushing the guiltless air,
Spout from the maiden fountain in her heart.
And from it sprang the Commonwealth, which
    breaks
As I am breaking now!

            "And therefore now
Let her, that is the womb and tomb of all,[27]
Great Nature, take, and forcing far apart
Those blind beginnings that have made me
    man,
Dash them anew together at her will
Thro' all her cycles—into man once more,
Or beast or bird or fish, or opulent flower:
But till this cosmic order everywhere[28]
Shatter'd into one earthquake in one day
Cracks all to pieces,—and that hour perhaps
Is not so far when momentary man
Shall seem no more a something to himself,
But he, his hopes and hates, his homes and
    fanes,[29]
And even his bones long laid within the grave,
The very sides of the grave itself shall pass,
Vanishing, atom and void, atom and void,
Into the unseen for ever,—till that hour,

My golden work in which I told a truth[30]
That stays the rolling Ixionian wheel,   260
That numbs the Fury's ringlet-snake,[31] and
    plucks
The mortal soul from out immortal hell,
Shall stand: ay, surely: then it fails at last
And perishes as I must; for O Thou,
Passionless bride, divine Tranquillity,
Yearn'd after by the wisest of the wise,
Who fail to find thee, being as thou art
Without one pleasure and without one pain,
Howbeit I know thou surely must be mine
Or soon or late, yet out of season, thus   270
I woo thee roughly, for thou carest not
How roughly men may woo thee so they win—
Thus—thus: the soul flies out and dies in the
    air."

    With that he drove the knife into his side:
She heard him raging, heard him fall; ran in,
Beat breast, tore hair, cried out upon herself
As having fail'd in duty to him, shriek'd
That she but meant to win him back, fell on
    him,
Clasp'd, kiss'd him, wail'd: he answer'd, "Care
    not thou!
Thy duty? What is duty? Fare thee well!"   280
                1868; 1869

from The Idylls of the King

Dedication

These to His Memory[1]—since he held them
    dear,
Perchance as finding there unconsciously
Some image of himself—I dedicate,

---

[25] The Helicon was a mountain in Greece sacred to Apollo and poetry. Hallam Tennyson cites *De Rerum Natura*, i, lines 936f.; iv, lines 11f. (I, 752).

[26] Her: Lucretia, or Lucrece, raped by Tarquin of the family of Collatine, killed herself; in consequence, a revolt deposed the family of Tarquin, and a republic was established in Rome.

[27] Hallam Tennyson cites *De Rerum Natura*, v, 258 (I, 752).

[28] Hallam Tennyson cites *De Rerum Natura*, v, lines 94f. (I, 752).   [29] Fanes: temples.

[30] Hallam Tennyson cites *De Rerum Natura*, iv, lines 8f; iii, 978–1023 (I, 753).

[31] Ixion is punished in the underworld by being lashed to a wheel by serpents and driven forever in the wind; the three Furies, who pursue and punish transgressors, have hair made of serpents.

[1] Albert, Prince Consort to Victoria, died in December 1861. Tennyson had published the first four (there were finally to be twelve) of *The Idylls of the King* in 1859. The dedication to Albert was first published in a new edition of these first *Idylls* in 1862.

I dedicate, I consecrate with tears—
These Idylls.

                 And indeed He seems to me
Scarce other than my king's ideal knight,
"Who reverenced his conscience as his king;
Whose glory was, redressing human wrong;
Who spake no slander, no, nor listen'd to it;
10 Who loved one only and who clave to her—"
Her—over all whose realms to their last isle,
Commingled with the gloom of imminent
    war,[2]
The shadow of His loss drew like eclipse,
Darkening the world. We have lost him; he is
    gone:
We know him now: all narrow jealousies
Are silent, and we see him as he moved,
How modest, kindly, all-accomplish'd, wise,
With what sublime repression of himself,
And in what limits, and how tenderly;
20 Not swaying to this faction or to that;
Not making his high place the lawless perch
Of wing'd ambitions, nor a vantage-ground
For pleasure; but thro' all this tract of years
Wearing the white flower of a blameless life,
Before a thousand peering littlenesses,
In that fierce light which beats upon a throne
And blackens every blot: for where is he
Who dares foreshadow for an only son
A lovelier life, a more unstain'd, than his?
30 Or how should England dreaming of *his* sons
Hope more for these than some inheritance
Of such a life, a heart, a mind as thine,
Thou noble Father of her Kings to be,
Laborious for her people and her poor—
Voice in the rich dawn of an ampler day—
Far-sighted summoner of War and Waste
To fruitful strifes and rivalries of peace[3]—
Sweet nature gilded by the gracious gleam
Of letter, dear to Science, dear to Art,
40 Dear to thy land[4] and ours, a Prince indeed,
Beyond all titles, and a household name,
Hereafter, thro' all times, Albert the Good.

Break not, O woman's-heart, but still
    endure;
Break not, for thou art Royal, but endure,
Remembering all the beauty of that star
Which shone so close beside Thee that ye made
One light together, but has past and leaves
The Crown a lonely splendor.

                May all love,
His love, unseen but felt, o'ershadow Thee,
The love of all Thy sons encompass Thee,   50
The love of all Thy daughters cherish Thee,
The love of all Thy people comfort Thee,
Till God's love set Thee at his side again!
                        1862

To the Queen[1]

O loyal to the royal in thyself,
And loyal to thy land, as this to thee—
Bear witness, that rememberable day,
When, pale as yet and fever-worn, the Prince
Who scarce had pluck'd his flickering life
    again
From halfway down the shadow of the grave,
Past with thee thro' thy people and their love,
And London roll'd one tide of joy thro' all
Her trebled millions, and loud leagues of man
And welcome![2] witness, too, the silent cry,
The prayer of many a race and creed, and
    clime—
Thunderless lightnings[3] striking under sea
From sunset and sunrise of all thy realm,
And that true North, whereof we lately heard
A strain to shame us "keep you to yourselves;
So loyal is too costly! friends—your love
Is but a burthen; loose the bond, and go."[4]
Is this the tone of empire? here the faith
That made us rulers? this, indeed, her voice
And meaning, whom the roar of Hougoumont[5]

---

[2] In the early years of the American Civil War there was a possibility that Great Britain would assist the Confederacy against the Federal forces.

[3] Albert helped to organize such international exhibitions as that for which Tennyson wrote an ode in 1861 (p. 169).

[4] Albert was the son of the Duke of Saxe-Coburg Gotha.

[1] In 1872 Tennyson published "Gareth and Lynette," which he said completed *The Idylls of the King* (he was later to add one more idyll). In 1873, in a collected edition of his poetry, *The Idylls* were published together for the first time, and this epilogue was added.

[2] The Prince of Wales, later Edward VII, was seriously ill with typhoid in 1871–72. His first public appearance with his mother (who was not often seen in public after Albert's death) to attend a thanksgiving service for his recovery was an occasion of public celebration.

[3] Thunderless lightnings: overseas telegraph.

[4] Some of Tennyson's contemporaries thought that the costs of the Empire—specifically here, Canada—were too large to justify its maintenance.

[5] Hougoumont: Waterloo.

Left mightiest of all peoples under heaven?
What shock has fool'd her since, that she
    should speak
So feebly? wealthier—wealthier—hour by hour!
The voice of Britain, or a sinking land,
Some third-rate isle half-lost among her seas?
There rang her voice, when the full city peal'd
Thee and thy Prince! The loyal to their crown
Are loyal to their own far sons, who love
Our ocean-empire with her boundless homes
For ever-broadening England, and her throne
In our vast Orient, and one isle, one isle,
That knows not her own greatness: if she
    knows
And dreads it we are fallen.—But thou, my
    Queen,
Not for itself, but thro' thy living love
For one to whom I made it o'er his grave
Sacred, accept this old imperfect tale,
New-old, and shadowing Sense at war with
    Soul
Ideal manhood closed in real man,[6]
Rather than that gray king whose name, a
    ghost,
Streams like a cloud, man-shaped, from
    mountain peak,
And cleaves to cairn and cromlech[7] still; or
    him
Of Geoffrey's book, or him of Malleor's,[8] one
Touch'd by the adulterous finger of a time
That hover'd between war and wantonness,
And crownings and dethronements: take
    withal
Thy poet's blessing, and his trust that Heaven
Will blow the tempest in the distance back
From thine and ours: for some are scared, who
    mark,
Or wisely or unwisely, signs of storm,
Waverings of every vane with every wind,
And wordy trucklings to the transient hour,
And fierce or careless looseners of the faith,
And Softness breeding scorn of simple life,
Or Cowardice, the child of lust for gold,

Or Labour, with a groan and not a voice,
Or Art with poisonous honey stol'n from
    France,
And that which knows, but careful for itself,
And that which knows not, ruling that which
    knows
To its own harm: the goal of this great world
Lies beyond sight: yet—if our slowly-grown   60
And crown'd Republic's crowning common-
    sense,
That saved her many times, not fail—their
    fears
Are morning shadows huger than the shapes
That cast them, not those gloomier which
    forego
The darkness of that battle in the West
Where all of high and holy dies away.

                                    1873

In the Garden at Swainston

Nightingales warbled without,
    Within was weeping for thee:
Shadows of three dead men[1]
    Walk'd in the walks with me,
    Shadows of three dead men and thou wast
    one of the three.

Nightingales sang in his woods:
    The Master was far away:
Nightingales warbled and sang
    Of a passion that lasts but a day;
    Still in the house in his coffin the Prince of
    courtesy lay.   10

Two dead men have I known
    In courtesy like to thee:
Two dead men have I loved
    With a love that ever will be:
    Three dead men have I loved and thou art
    last of the three.

                            (1870) 1874

---

[6] This line was inserted in 1891, to emphasize, according to Hallam Tennyson, the humanity of Arthur as well as his spirituality.

[7] A cairn is a mound of stones, a cromlech a circle of stones: both serve as memorials or land-marks.

[8] Two of Tennyson's sources for the story of Arthur were the accounts of Geoffrey of Monmouth and Thomas Malory.

[1] Tennyson's note in the standard edition of his poetry: "Sir John Simeon, Henry Lushington, and Arthur Hallam" (I, 760). Swainston Hall was Sir John Simeon's house on the Isle of Wight; he served in Parliament, managed his estate, and was Tennyson's close friend from the 1850s. Henry Lushington was the younger brother of Edmund, who married Tennyson's sister Cecilia (see note pp. 126, 142). Tennyson knew Henry when they were both at Cambridge; he died at Malta in 1855 while serving in the government there.

Rizpah[1]

17–

I

Wailing, wailing, wailing, the wind over land and sea—
And Willy's voice in the wind, "O mother, come out to me."
Why should he call me to-night, when he knows that I cannot go?
For the downs are as bright as day, and the full moon stares at the snow.

II

We should be seen, my dear; they would spy us out of the town.
The loud black nights for us, and the storm rushing over the down,
When I cannot see my own hand, but am led by the creak of the chain,
And grovel and grope for my son till I find myself drenched with the rain.

III

Anything fallen again? nay—what was there left to fall?
I have taken them home, I have number'd the bones, I have hidden them all.
What am I saying? and what are *you?* do you come as a spy?
Falls? what falls? who knows? As the tree falls so must it lie.

IV

Who let her in? how long has she been? you—what have you heard?
Why did you sit so quiet? you never have spoken a word.
O—to pray with me—yes—a lady—none of their spies—
But the night has crept into my heart, and begun to darken my eyes.

V

Ah—you, that have lived so soft, what should *you* know of the night,
The blast and the burning shame and the bitter frost and the fright?
I have done it, while you were asleep—you were only made for the day.

I have gather'd my baby together—and now you may go your way.

VI

Nay—for it's kind of you, Madam, to sit by an old dying wife.
But say nothing hard of my boy, I have only an hour of life.
I kiss'd my boy in the prison, before he went out to die.
"They dared me to do it," he said, and he never has told me a lie.
I whipt him for robbing an orchard once when he was but a child—
"The farmer dared me to do it," he said; he was always so wild—
And idle—and couldn't be idle—my Willy—he never could rest.
The King should have made him a soldier, he would have been one of his best.

VII

But he lived with a lot of wild mates, and they never would let him be good;
They swore that he dare not rob the mail, and he swore that he would;
And he took no life, but he took one purse, and when all was done
He flung it among his fellows—"I'll none of it," said my son.

VIII

I came into court to the Judge and the lawyers. I told them my tale,
God's own truth—but they kill'd him, they kill'd him for robbing the mail.
They hang'd him in chains for a show—we had always borne a good name—
To be hang'd for a thief—and then put away—isn't that enough shame?
Dust to dust—low down—let us hide! but they set him so high
That all the ships of the world could stare at him, passing by.
God 'ill pardon the hell-black raven and horrible fowls of the air,
But not the black heart of the lawyer who kill'd him and hang'd him there.

IX

And the jailer forced me away. I had bid him my last goodbye;

[1] The story is founded on an anecdote Tennyson had heard from a friend, and later read about. Rizpah was a mother in the Old Testament who guarded the bones of her hanged sons day and night (2 Samuel 21:8–10).

They had fasten'd the door of his cell. "O
mother!" I heard him cry.
I couldn't get back tho' I tried, he had some-
thing further to say,
And now I never shall know it. The jailer
forced me away.

X

Then since I couldn't but hear that cry of my
boy that was dead,
They seized me and shut me up: they fasten'd
me down on my bed.
"Mother, O mother!"—he call'd in the dark to
me year after year—
They beat me for that, they beat me—you
know that I couldn't but hear;
And then at the last they found I had grown
so stupid and still
They let me abroad again—but the creatures
had worked their will.

XI

Flesh of my flesh was gone, but bone of my
bone was left—
I stole them all from the lawyers—and you,
will you call it a theft?—
My baby, the bones that had suck'd me, the
bones that had laughed and had cried—
Theirs? O no! they are mine—not theirs—they
had moved in my side.

XII

Do you think I was scared by the bones? I
kiss'd 'em, I buried 'em all—
I can't dig deep, I am old—in the night by the
churchyard wall.
My Willy 'ill rise up whole when the trumpet
of judgment 'ill sound,
But I charge you never to say that I laid him in
holy ground.[2]

XIII

They would scratch him up—they would hang
him again on the cursed tree.
Sin? O, yes—we are sinners, I know—let all
that be,
And read me a Bible verse of the Lord's good
will toward men—
"Full of compassion and mercy, the Lord"—let
me hear it again;

"Full of compassion and mercy—long-
suffering."[3] Yes, O, yes!
For the lawyer is born but to murder—the
Saviour lives but to bless.
He 'll never put on the black cap except for
the worst of the worst,
And the first may be last—I have heard it in
church—and the last may be first.
Suffering—O long-suffering—yes, as the Lord
must know,
Year after year in the mist and the wind and
the shower and the snow.

XIV

Heard, have you? what? they have told you he
never repented his sin.
How do they know it? are *they* his mother?
are *you* of his kin? 70
Heard! have you ever heard, when the storm
on the downs began,
The wind that 'ill wail like a child and the sea
that 'ill moan like a man?

XV

Election, Election and Reprobation[4]—it 's all
very well.
But I go to-night to my boy, and I shall not
find him in Hell.
For I cared so much for my boy that the Lord
has look'd into my care,
And He means me I 'm sure to be happy with
Willy, I know not where.

XVI

And if *he* be lost—but to save *my* soul, that is
all your desire:
Do you think that I care for *my* soul if my boy
be gone to the fire?
I have been with God in the dark—go, go, you
may leave me alone—
You never have borne a child—you are just as
hard as a stone. 80

XVII

Madam, I beg your pardon! I think that you
mean to be kind,
But I cannot hear what you say for my Willy's
voice in the wind—
The snow and the sky so bright—he used but
to call in the dark,

[2] As a hanged criminal her son could not be buried in the consecrated ground of the church cemetery.
[3] Psalms 86:15.
[4] Election and reprobation, in the doctrine of Calvinism, are the predestined states of salvation or damnation.

And he calls to me now from the church and
  not from the gibbet—for hark!
Nay—you can hear it yourself—it is coming—
  shaking the walls—
Willy—the moon 's in a cloud——Good-night.
  I am going. He calls.

                                    (1878) 1880

*Tiresias, blinded because he looked on Pallas
Athene as she emerged from her bath, was given the
gift of prophecy by her in recompense. In this poem
he speaks to Menœceus, the son of Creon, later to
become ruler of Thebes. At the moment of the
poem the rulership of Thebes is being disputed by
Eteocles and Polynices, sons of Oedipus; Polynices
is laying siege to the city. Tiresias prophesies that
the invasion will be unsuccessful and Thebes will
survive if Menœceus gives himself as a voluntary
victim in battle. Hallam Tennyson, in a note in the
standard edition, writes that the poem was "partly
written" in 1833 (IV, 563).*

Tiresias

I wish I were as in the years of old,
While yet the blessed daylight made itself
Ruddy thro' both the roofs of sight, and woke
These eyes, now dull, but then so keen to seek
The meanings ambush'd under all they saw,
The flight of birds, the flame of sacrifice,
What omens may foreshadow fate to man
And woman, and the secrets of the Gods.
  My son, the Gods, despite of human prayer,
10 Are slower to forgive than human kings.
The great God, Arês[1], burns in anger still
Against the guiltless heirs of him from Tyre,
Our Cadmus,[2] out of whom thou art, who
    found
Beside the springs of Dircê, smote, and still'd
Thro' all its folds the multitudinous beast,
The dragon, which our trembling fathers call'd
The God's own son.
                    A tale, that told to me,
When but thine age, by age as winter-white
As mine is now, amazed, but made me yearn
20 For larger glimpses of that more than man
Which rolls the heavens, and lifts and lays the
    deep,

Yet loves and hates with mortal hates and
    loves,
And moves unseen among the ways of men.
  Then, in my wanderings all the lands that lie
Subjected to the Heliconian ridge[3]
Have heard this footstep fall, altho' my wont
Was more to scale the highest of the heights
With some strange hope to see the nearer God.
  One naked peak—the sister of the sun
Would climb from out the dark, and linger
    there   3
To silver all the valleys with her shafts—
There once, but long ago, five-fold thy term
Of years, I lay; the winds were dead for heat;
The noonday crag made the hand burn; and
    sick
For shadow—not one bush was near—I rose
Following a torrent till its myriad falls
Found silence in the hollows underneath.
  There is a secret olive-glade I saw
Pallas Athene climbing from the bath
In anger; yet one glittering foot disturb'd   4
The lucid well; one snowy knee was prest
Against the margin flowers; a dreadful light
Came from her golden hair, her golden helm
And all her golden armour on the grass,
And from her virgin breast, and virgin eyes
Remaining fixt on mine, till mine grew dark
For ever, and I heard a voice that said
"Henceforth be blind, for thou hast seen too
    much,
And speak the truth that no man may believe."
  Son, in the hidden world of sight, that lives   5
Behind this darkness, I behold her still,
Beyond all work of those who carve the stone,
Beyond all dreams of Godlike womanhood,
Ineffable beauty, out of whom, at a glance,
And as it were, perforce, upon me flash'd
The power of prophesying—but to me
No power—so chain'd and coupled with the
    curse
Of blindness and their unbelief, who heard
And heard not, when I spake of famine,
    plague,
Shrine-shattering earthquake, fire, flood, thun-
    derbolt,   6
And angers of the Gods for evil done
And expiation lack'd—no power on Fate,

---

[1] Arês: the god of war.
[2] Cadmus: the founder of Thebes. He killed a dragon guarding a spring, and sowed the dragon's teeth. From them armed men sprang up, who began to fight among one another. The five survivors were the first citizens of Thebes. The spring is named for Dircê, who was tied to a wild bull and dragged to her death, and her body thrown into the spring that bears her name.
[3] The Helicon is a mountain in central Greece, near Thebes.

Theirs, or mine own! for when the crowd
   would roar
For blood, for war, whose issue was their doom,
To cast wise words among the multitude
Was flinging fruit to lions; nor, in hours
Of civil outbreak, when I knew the twain
Would each waste each, and bring on both the
   yoke
Of stronger states, was mine the voice to curb
The madness of our cities and their kings.
   Who ever turn'd upon his heel to hear
My warning that the tyranny of one
Was prelude to the tyranny of all?
My counsel that the tyranny of all
Led backward to the tyranny of one?
    This power hath work'd no good to aught
    that lives,
And these blind hands were useless in their
   wars.
O therefore that the unfulfill'd desire,
The grief for ever born from griefs to be,
The boundless yearning of the Prophet's
   heart—
Could *that* stand forth, and like a statue,
   rear'd
To some great citizen, win all praise from all
Who past it, saying, "That was he!"
                    In vain!
Virtue must shape itself in deed, and those
Whom weakness or necessity have cramp'd
Within themselves, immerging, each, his urn
In his own well, draws solace as he may.
   Menœceus, thou hast eyes, and I can hear
Too plainly what full tides of onset[4] sap
Our seven high gates, and what a weight of
   war
Rides on those ringing axles! jingle of bits,
Shouts, arrows, tramp of the hornfooted horse
That grind the glebe to powder! Stony showers
Of that ear-stunning hail of Arês crash
Along the sounding walls. Above, below,
Shock after shock, the song-built towers and
   gates[5]
Reel, bruised and butted with the shuddering
War-thunder of iron rams; and from within
The city comes a murmur void of joy,
Lest she be taken captive—maidens, wives,
And mothers with their babblers of the dawn,
And oldest age in shadow from the night,

Falling about their shrines before their Gods,
And wailing "Save us."
             And they wail to thee!
These eyeless eyes, that cannot see thine own,
See this, that only in thy virtue lies
The saving of our Thebes; for, yesternight,
To me, the great God Arês, whose one bliss
Is war, and human sacrifice—himself
Blood-red from battle, spear and helmet tipt   110
With stormy light as on a mast at sea,
Stood out before a darkness, crying, "Thebes,
Thy Thebes shall fall and perish, for I loathe
The seed of Cadmus—yet if one of these
By his own hand—if one of these—"
                     My son,
No sound is breathed so potent to coerce,
And to conciliate, as their names who dare
For that sweet mother land which gave them
   birth
Nobly to do, nobly to die. Their names,
Graven on memorial columns, are a song   120
Heard in the future; few, but more than wall
And rampart, their examples reach a hand
Far thro' all years, and everywhere they meet
And kindle generous purpose, and the strength
To mould it into action pure as theirs.
   Fairer thy fate than mine, if life's best end
Be to end well! and thou refusing this.
Unvenerable will thy memory be
While men shall move the lips: but if thou
   dare—
Thou, one of these, the race of Cadmus—then   130
No stone is fitted in yon marble girth[6]
Whose echo shall not tongue thy glorious doom,
Nor in this pavement but shall ring thy name
To every hoof that clangs it, and the springs
Of Dircê laving yonder battle-plain,
Heard from the roofs by night, will murmur
   thee
To thine own Thebes, while Thebes thro' thee
   shall stand
Firm-based with all her Gods.
                  The Dragon's cave
Half hid, they tell me, now in flowing vines—
Where once he dwelt and whence he roll'd
   himself   140
At dead of night—thou knowest, and that
   smooth rock
Before it, altar-fashion'd, where of late

---

[4] Onset: battle.
[5] One legend of the founding of Thebes says that Amphion, a son of Zeus, built its walls by charming its stones into place through song.
[6] Marble girth: the walls of the city.

The woman-breasted Sphinx,[7] with wings
   drawn back,
Folded her lion paws, and look'd to Thebes.
There blanch the bones of whom she slew, and
   these
Mixt with her own, because the fierce beast
   found
A wiser than herself, and dash'd herself
Dead in her rage: but thou art wise enough,
Tho' young, to love thy wiser, blunt the curse
150 Of Pallas,[8] hear, and tho' I speak the truth
Believe I speak it, let thine own hand strike
Thy youthful pulses into rest and quench
The red God's anger, fearing not to plunge
Thy torch of life in darkness, rather—thou
Rejoicing that the sun, the moon, the stars
Send no such light upon the ways of men
As one great deed.
         Thither, my son, and there
Thou, that hast never known the embrace of
   love,
Offer thy maiden life.
             This useless hand!
160 I felt one warm tear fall upon it. Gone!
He will achieve his greatness.
               But for me,
I would that I were gather'd to my rest,
And mingled with the famous kings of old,
On whom about their ocean-islets flash
The faces of the Gods—the wise man's word,
Here trampled by the populace underfoot,
There crown'd with worship—and these eyes
   will find
The men I knew, and watch the chariot whirl
About the goal again, and hunters race
170 The shadowy lion, and the warrior-kings,
In height and prowess more than human, strive
Again for glory, while the golden lyre
Is ever sounding in heroic ears
Heroic hymns, and every way the vales
Wind, clouded with the grateful incense-fume
Of those who mix all odour to the Gods
On one far height in one far-shining fire.

———

"One height and one far-shining fire"
And while I fancied that my friend[9]

For this brief idyll would require   18
   A less diffuse and opulent end,
And would defend his judgment well,
   If I should deem it over nice—
The tolling of his funeral bell
   Broke on my Pagan Paradise,
And mixt the dream of classic times
   And all the phantoms of the dream,
With present grief, and made the rhymes,
   That miss'd his living welcome, seem
Like would-be guests an hour too late,   19
   Who down the highway moving on
With easy laughter find the gate
   Is bolted, and the master gone.
Gone into darkness, that full light
   Of friendship! past, in sleep, away
By night, into the deeper night!
   The deeper night? A clearer day
Than our poor twilight dawn on earth—
   If night, what barren toil to be!
What life, so maim'd by night, were worth   20
   Our living out? Not mine to me
Remembering all the golden hours
   Now silent, and so many dead,
And him the last; and laying flowers,
   This wreath, above his honour'd head,
And praying that, when I from hence
   Shall fade with him into the unknown,
My close of earth's experience
   May prove as peaceful as his own.
                    1885

Despair

A man and his wife having lost faith in God, and
hope of a life to come, and being utterly miserable
in this, resolve to end themselves by drowning. The
woman is drowned, but the man rescued by a minis-
ter of the sect he had abandoned.

I
Is it you, that preach'd in the chapel there
   looking over the sand?
Follow'd us too that night, and dogg'd us, and
   drew me to land?

II
What did I feel that night? You are curious.
   How should I tell?

[7] The Sphinx asked travelers a riddle (what walks on four legs in the morning, two legs at noon, and three legs at twilight?) and killed those who could not answer. Oedipus answered (man), and was proclaimed king of Thebes because he rid the land of the Sphinx.
[8] Curse of Pallas: although Pallas Athene gave Tiresias the gift of prophecy, she also said that his prophecy would not be believed.
[9] In the volume in which "Tiresias" was first published in 1885, it was preceded by a poem to Edward FitzGerald, who died before "Tiresias" itself was finished. These concluding lines are in the meter of the introductory poem to FitzGerald.

Does it matter so much what I felt? You
  rescued me—yet—was it well
That you came unwish'd for, uncall'd,
  between me and the deep and my doom,
Three days since, three more dark days of the
  Godless gloom
Of a life without sun, without health, without
  hope, without any delight
In anything here upon earth? but ah God, that
  night, that night
When the rolling eyes of the lighthouse there
  on the fatal neck
Of land running out into rock—they had
  saved many hundreds from wreck—
Glared on our way toward death, I remember
  I thought, as we past,
Does it matter how many they saved? we are
  all of us wreck'd at last—
"Do you fear?" and there came thro' the roar
  of the breaker a whisper, a breath,
"Fear? am I not with you? I am frighted at life
  not death."

III

And the suns of the limitless Universe sparkled
  and shone in the sky,
Flashing with fires as of God, but we knew
  that their light was a lie—
Bright as with deathless hope—but, however
  they sparkled and shone,
The dark little worlds running round them
  were worlds of woe like our own—
No soul in the heaven above, no soul on the
  earth below,
A fiery scroll written over with lamentation
  and woe.

IV

See, we were nursed in the drear nightfold of
  your fatalist creed,[1]
And we turn'd to the growing dawn, we had
  hoped for a dawn indeed,
When the light of a Sun that was coming
  would scatter the ghosts of the Past,
And the cramping creeds that had madden'd
  the peoples would vanish at last,
And we broke away from the Christ, our
  human brother and friend,

For He spoke, or it seem'd that He spoke, of a
  Hell without help, without end.

V

Hoped for a dawn and it came, but the
  promise had faded away;
He had past from a cheerless night to the glare
  of a drearier day;
He is only a cloud and a smoke who was once
  a pillar of fire.[2]
The guess of a worm in the dust and the
  shadow of its desire—   30
Of a worm as it writhes in a world of the weak
  trodden down by the strong,
Of a dying worm in a world, all massacre,
  murder, and wrong.

VI

O we poor orphans of nothing—alone on that
  lonely shore—
Born of the brainless Nature who knew not
  that which she bore!
Trusting no longer that earthly flower would
  be heavenly fruit—
Come from the brute, poor souls—no souls—
  and to die with the brute——

VII

Nay, but I am not claiming your pity: I know
  you of old—
Small pity for those that have ranged from the
  narrow warmth of your fold,
Where you bawl'd the dark side of your faith
  and a God of eternal rage,
Till you flung us back on ourselves, and the
  human heart, and the Age.   40

VIII

But pity—the Pagan held it a vice—was in her
  and in me,
Helpless, taking the place of the pitying God
  that should be!
Pity for all that aches in the grasp of an idiot
  power,
And pity for our own selves on an earth that
  bore not a flower;
Pity for all that suffers on land or in air or the
  deep,
And pity for our own selves till we long'd for
  eternal sleep.

---

[1] Tennyson's note in the standard edition of his poetry: "In my boyhood I came across this Calvinist creed—and assuredly, however unfathomable the mystery, if one cannot believe in the freedom of the human will as of the divine, life is hardly worth the living" (IV, 564).

[2] God led the Israelites out of Egypt by appearing by day as a cloud, and by night as a pillar of fire (Exodus 13:21).

IX

"Lightly step over the sands! the waters—you
    hear them call!
Life with its anguish, and horrors, and errors
    —away with it all!"
And she laid her hand in my own—she was
    always loyal and sweet—
Till the points of the foam in the dusk came
    playing about our feet.
There was a strong sea-current would sweep
    us out to the main.
"Ah God" tho' I felt as I spoke I was taking
    the name in vain—
"Ah God" and we turn'd to each other, we
    kiss'd, we embraced, she and I,
Knowing the Love we were used to believe
    everlasting would die:
We had read their know-nothing[3] books and
    we lean'd to the darker side—
Ah God, should we find Him, perhaps,
    perhaps, if we died, if we died;
We never had found Him on earth, this earth
    is a fatherless Hell—
"Dear Love, for ever and ever, for ever and
    ever farewell,"
Never a cry so desolate, not since the world
    began,
Never a kiss so sad, no, not since the coming
    of man!

X

But the blind wave cast me ashore, and you
    saved me, a valueless life.
Not a grain of gratitude mine! You have
    parted the man from the wife.
I am left alone on the land, she is all alone in
    the sea;
If a curse meant ought, I would curse you for
    not having let me be.

XI

Visions of youth—for my brain was drunk
    with the water, it seems;
I had past into perfect quiet at length out of
    pleasant dreams,
And the transient trouble of drowning—what
    was it when match'd with the pains
Of the hellish heat of a wretched life rushing
    back thro' the veins?

XII

Why should I live? one son had forged on his
    father and fled,

And if I believed in a God, I would thank him,
    the other is dead,
And there was a baby-girl, that had never
    look'd on the light:
Happiest she of us all, for she past from the
    night to the night.

XIII

But the crime, if a crime, of her eldest-born,
    her glory, her boast,
Struck hard at the tender heart of the mother,
    and broke it almost;
Tho', glory and shame dying out for ever in
    endless time,
Does it matter so much whether crown'd for a
    virtue, or hang'd for a crime?

XIV

And ruin'd by *him,* by *him,* I stood there,
    naked, amazed
In a world of arrogant opulence, fear'd myself
    turning crazed,
And I would not be mock'd in a madhouse!
    and she, the delicate wife,
With a grief that could only be cured, if cured,
    by the surgeon's knife,—

XV

Why should we bear with an hour of torture,
    a moment of pain,
If every man die for ever, if all his griefs are
    in vain,
And the homeless planet at length will be
    wheel'd thro' the silence of space,
Motherless evermore of an ever-vanishing race,
When the worm shall have writhed its last, and
    its last brother-worm will have fled
From the dead fossil skull that is left in the
    rocks of an earth that is dead?

XVI

Have I crazed myself over their horrible infidel
    writings? O yes,
For these are the new dark ages, you see, of the
    popular press,
When the bat comes out of his cave, and the
    owls are whooping at noon,
And Doubt is the lord of this dunghill and
    crows to the sun and the moon,
Till the Sun and the Moon of our science are
    both of them turn'd into blood,
And Hope will have broken her heart,
    running after a shadow of good;

---

[3] Agnostic, a word that came into use at the end of the 1860s.

For their knowing and know-nothing books
    are scatter'd from hand to hand—
We have knelt in your know-all chapel too
    looking over the sand.

XVII

What! I should call on that Infinite Love that
    has served us so well?
Infinite cruelty rather that made everlasting
    Hell,
Made us, foreknew us, foredoom'd us, and
    does what he will with his own;
Better our dead brute mother who never has
    heard us groan!

XVIII

Hell? if the souls of men were immortal, as
    men have been told,
The lecher would cleave to his lusts, and the
    miser would yearn for his gold,
And so there were Hell for ever! but were
    there a God as you say,
His Love would have power over Hell till it
    utterly vanish'd away.

XIX

Ah yet—I have had some glimmer, at times, in
    my gloomiest woe,
Of a God behind all—after all—the great God
    for aught that I know;
But the God of Love and of Hell together—
    they cannot be thought,
If there be such a God, may the Great God
    curse him and bring him to nought!

XX

Blasphemy! whose is the fault? is it mine? for
    why would you save
A madman to vex you with wretched words,
    who is best in his grave?
Blasphemy! ay, why not, being damn'd beyond
    hope of grace?
O would I were yonder with her, and away
    from your faith and your face!
Blasphemy! true! I have scared you pale with
    my scandalous talk,
But the blasphemy to *my* mind lies all in the
    way that you walk.

XXI

Hence! she is gone! can I stay? can I breathe
    divorced from the Past?

You needs must have good lynx-eyes if I do not
    escape you at last.
Our orthodox coroner doubtless will find it a
    felo-de-se,
And the stake and the cross-road,[4] fool, if you
    will, does it matter to me?

                          1881; 1885

Demeter was the Greek goddess of marriage and human fertility; Persephone was her daughter, the goddess of vegetation. One day while playing in the vale of Enna, near a lake around which spring was perpetual, Persephone was seen by Pluto, the god of the underworld, who fell in love with her and carried her to his kingdom. Demeter, thinking that the earth had conspired to admit her daughter, denied it its fertility, but when she learned that Pluto had taken her daughter, she appealed to Zeus for her return. Eventually, Persephone was permitted to spend part of the year on the surface of the earth, and the rest in the underworld.

In his note in the standard edition of Tennyson's poetry, Hallam Tennyson wrote: "The poem was written at my request, because I knew that my father considered Demeter one of the most beautiful types of womanhood. He said: 'I will write it, but when I write an antique like this I must put it into a frame—something modern about it.'" Tennyson cited as an example of the frame of modern relevance lines 126–136 (IV, 585–586).

Demeter and Persephone

(In Enna)

Faint as a climate-changing bird that flies
All night across the darkness, and at dawn
Falls on the threshold of her native land,
And can no more, thou camest, O my child,
Led upward by the God of ghosts and dreams,
Who laid thee at Eleusis,[1] dazed and dumb
With passing thro' at once from state to state,
Until I brought thee hither, that the day,
When here thy hands let fall the gather'd
    flower,
Might break thro' clouded memories once
    again   10
On thy lost self. A sudden nightingale
Saw thee, and flash'd into a frolic of song
And welcome; and a gleam as of the moon,
When first she peers along the tremulous deep,

---

[4] Felo-de-se: a suicide. In an old, superstitious tradition not practiced in the nineteenth century, suicides were buried at a crossroads with a stake through their hearts.
[1] Persephone was returned at Eleusis, the site of a temple to Demeter.

Fled wavering o'er thy face, and chased away
That shadow of a likeness to the king
Of shadows, thy dark mate. Persephone!
Queen of the dead no more—my child! Thine
    eyes
Again were human-godlike, and the Sun
20 Burst from a swimming fleece of winter gray,
And robed thee in his day from head to feet—
"Mother!" and I was folded in thine arms.

    Child, those imperial, disimpassion'd eyes
Awed even me at first, thy mother—eyes
That oft had seen the serpent-wanded power[2]
Draw downward into Hades with his drift
Of flickering spectres, lighted from below
By the red race of fiery Phlegethon;[3]
But when before have Gods or men beheld
30 The Life that had descended re-arise,
And lighted from above him by the Sun?
So mighty was the mother's childless cry,
A cry that rang thro' Hades, Earth, and
    Heaven!

    So in this pleasant vale we stand again,
The field of Enna, now once more ablaze
With flowers that brighten as thy footstep falls,
All flowers—but for one black blur of earth
Left by that closing chasm, thro' which the car
Of dark Aïdoneus[4] rising rapt thee hence.
40 And here, my child, tho' folded in thine arms,
I feel the deathless heart of motherhood
Within me shudder, lest the naked glebe
Should yawn once more into the gulf, and
    thence
The shrilly whinnyings of the team of Hell,
Ascending, pierce the glad and songful air,
And all at once their arch'd necks, midnight-
    maned,
Jet upward thro' the mid-day blossom. No!
For, see, thy foot has touch'd it; all the space
Of blank earth-baldness clothes itself afresh,
50 And breaks into the crocus-purple hour
That saw thee vanish.

           Child, when thou wert gone,
I envied human wives, and nested birds,
Yea, the cubb'd lioness; went in search of thee
Thro' many a palace, many a cot,[5] and gave
Thy breast to ailing infants in the night,[6]

And set the mother waking in amaze
To find her sick one whole; and forth again
Among the wail of midnight winds, and cried,
"Where is my loved one? Wherefore do ye
    wail?"
And out from all the night an answer shrill'd,
"We know not, and we know not why we
    wail."
I climb'd on all the cliffs of all the seas,
And ask'd the waves that moan about the
    world
"Where? do ye make your moaning for my
    child?"
And round from all the world the voices came
"We know not, and we know not why we
    moan."
"Where?" and I stared from every eagle-peak,
I thridded[7] the black heart of all the woods,
I peer'd thro' tomb and cave, and in the storms
Of Autumn swept across the city, and heard
The murmur of their temples chanting me,
Me, me, the desolate Mother! "Where?"—and
    turn'd,
And fled by many a waste, forlorn of man,
And grieved for man thro' all my grief for
    thee,—
The jungle rooted in his shatter'd hearth,
The serpent coil'd about his broken shaft,
The scorpion crawling over naked skulls;—
I saw the tiger in the ruin'd fane[8]
Spring from his fallen God, but trace of thee
I saw not; and far on, and, following out
A league of labyrinthine darkness, came
On three gray heads[9] beneath a gleaming rift.
"Where?" and I heard one voice from all the
    three
"We know not, for we spin the lives of men,
And not of Gods, and know not why we spin!
There is a Fate beyond us." Nothing knew.

    Last as the likeness of a dying man,
Without his knowledge, from him flits to warn
A far-off friendship that he comes no more,
So he, the God of dreams, who heard my cry,
Drew from thyself the likeness of thyself
Without thy knowledge, and thy shadow past
Before me, crying "The Bright one in the
    highest[10]
Is brother of the Dark one in the lowest,

---

[2] Mercury, whose staff is entwined with serpents, was despatched by the gods to bring Persephone from the underworld.
[3] Race of Phlegethon: the current of a river of fire in Hades.
[4] Aïdoneus: Pluto.   [5] Cot: cottage.
[6] Tennyson's note: "*gave thy breast*, the breast which had suckled thee" (IV, 586).
[7] Thridded: threaded: [8] Fane: temple.   [9] The Fates.   [10] Zeus, Pluto's brother.

And Bright and Dark have sworn that I, the
    child
Of thee, the great Earth-Mother, thee, the
    Power
That lifts her buried life from gloom to bloom,
Should be for ever and for evermore
    Bride of Darkness."

                   So the Shadow wail'd.
Then I, Earth-Goddess, cursed the Gods of
    Heaven.
I would not mingle with their feasts; to me
Their nectar smack'd of hemlock on the lips,
Their rich ambrosia tasted aconite.[11]
The man, that only lives and loves an hour,
Seem'd nobler than their hard Eternities.
My quick tears kill'd the flower, my ravings
    hush'd
The bird, and lost in utter grief I fail'd
To send my life thro' olive-yard and vine
And golden grain, my gift to helpless man.
Rain-rotten died the wheat, the barley-spears
Were hollow-husk'd, the leaf fell, and the sun,
Pale at my grief, drew down before his time
Sickening, and Ætna[12] kept her winter snow.
    Then He, the brother of this Darkness, He
Who still is highest, glancing from his height
On earth a fruitless fallow, when he miss'd
The wonted steam of sacrifice, the praise
And prayer of men, decreed that thou
    should'st dwell
For nine white moons of each whole year with
    me,
Three dark ones in the shadow with thy King.

    Once more the reaper in the gleam of dawn
Will see me by the landmark far away,
Blessing his field, or seated in the dusk
Of even, by the lonely threshing-floor,
Rejoicing in the harvest and the grange.
    Yet I, Earth-Goddess, am but ill-content
With them, who still are highest. Those gray
    heads,
What meant they by their "Fate beyond the
    Fates"
But younger kindlier Gods to bear us down,
As we bore down the Gods before us?[13] Gods,
To quench, not hurl the thunderbolt, to stay,
Not spread the plague, the famine; God indeed,

To send the noon into the night and break
The sunless halls of Hades into Heaven?
Till thy dark lord accept and love the Sun,
And all the Shadow die into the Light,
When thou shalt dwell the whole bright year
    with me,
And souls of men, who grew beyond their race,
And made themselves as Gods against the fear
Of Death and Hell; and thou that hast from
    men,
As Queen of Death, that worship which is
    Fear,   140
Henceforth, as having risen from out the dead,
Shalt ever send thy life along with mine
From buried grain thro' springing blade, and
    bless
Their garner'd Autumn also, reap with me,
Earth-mother, in the harvest hymns of Earth
The worship which is Love, and see no more
The Stone, the Wheel,[14] the dimly-glimmering
    lawns
Of that Elysium, all the hateful fires
Of torment, and the shadowy warrior glide
Along the silent field of Asphodel.[15]
                            1889   150

Vastness

I

Many a hearth upon our dark globe sighs after
    many a vanish'd face,
Many a planet by many a sun may roll with
    the dust of a vanish'd race.

II

Raving politics, never at rest—as this poor
    earth's pale history runs,—
What is it all but a trouble of ants in the
    gleam of a million million of suns?

III

Lies upon this side, lies upon that side, truth-
    less violence mourn'd by the Wise,
Thousands of voices drowning his own in a
    popular torrent of lies upon lies;

IV

Stately purposes, valour in battle, glorious
    annals of army and fleet,

[11] Aconite: a dried root, used as a sedative.   [12] Ætna: a volcano in Sicily.
    [13] The Gods before us: the Titans, overthrown to introduce the more refined reign of the gods.
    [14] The stone which Sisyphus must eternally push up a hill, and the wheel on which Ixion is eternally punished.
    [15] Asphodel: the eternal flower of the Elysian fields, where dead heroes reside.

Death for the right cause, death for the wrong
   cause, trumpets of victory, groans of defeat;

V

Innocence seethed in her mother's milk, and
   Charity setting the martyr aflame;
Thraldom who walks with the banner of
   Freedom, and recks not to ruin a realm in
10   her name.

VI

Faith at her zenith, or all but lost in the gloom
   of doubts that darken the schools;
Craft with a bunch of all-heal[1] in her hand,
   follow'd up by her vassal legion of fools;

VII[2]

Trade flying over a thousand seas with her
   spice and her vintage, her silk and her corn;
Desolate offing,[3] sailorless harbours, famishing
   populace, wharves forlorn;

VIII

Star of the morning, Hope in the sunrise;
   gloom of the evening, Life at a close;
Pleasure who flaunts on her wide down-way
   with her flying robe and her poison'd rose;

IX

Pain, that has crawl'd from the corpse of
   Pleasure, a worm which writhes all day, and
   at night
Stirs up again in the heart of the sleeper, and
   stings him back to the curse of the light;

X

Wealth with his wines and his wedded harlots;
   honest Poverty, bare to the bone;
Opulent Avarice, lean as Poverty; Flattery
20   gilding the rift in a throne;

XI

Fame blowing out from her golden trumpet a
   jubilant challenge to Time and to Fate;
Slander, her shadow, sowing the nettle on all
   the laurel'd graves of the Great;

XII

Love for the maiden, crown'd with marriage,
   no regrets for aught that has been,

Household happiness, gracious children,
   debtless competence, golden mean;

XIII

National hatreds of whole generations, and
   pigmy spites of the village spire;
Vows that will last to the last death-ruckle,[4]
   and vows that are snapt in a moment of fire;

XIV

He that has lived for the lust of the minute,
   and died in the doing it, flesh without mind;
He that has nail'd all flesh to the Cross, till
   Self died out in the love of his kind;

XV

Spring and Summer and Autumn and Winter,
   and all these old revolutions of earth;
All new-old revolutions of Empire—change of
   the tide—what is all of it worth?

XVI

What the philosophies, all the sciences, poesy,
   varying voices of prayer?
All that is noblest, all that is basest, all that
   is filthy with all that is fair?

XVII

What is it all, if we all of us end but in being
   our own corpse-coffins at last,
Swallow'd in Vastness, lost in Silence, drown'd
   in the deeps of a meaningless Past?

XVIII

What but a murmur of gnats in the gloom, or
   a moment's anger of bees in their hive?—

       *   *   *   *   *[5]

Peace, let it be! for I loved him,[6] and love him
   for ever: the dead are not dead but alive.

                           1885; 1889

*In his note in the standard edition of his poetry
Tennyson wrote that the Gleam "signifies in my
poem the higher poetic imagination" (IV, 594).
Hallam Tennyson goes on to write that his father
wrote the poem "For those who care to know about
his literary history" (IV, 594). In the* Idylls of the
King *Merlin, the magician of Arthur's court, is
finally ensnared by the sensual Vivien.*

---

[1] All-heal: any of several plants used in folk medicine.
  [2] This poem was first published in a magazine in 1885; Tennyson added stanzas vii and viii
when it was published in a volume of poetry in 1889.
  [3] Offing: the part of the deep sea visible from the shore.   [4] Death-ruckle: death rattle.
  [5] Asterisks are in the original.   [6] Him: most probably Arthur Hallam.

Merlin and the Gleam

I

O young Mariner,
You from the haven
Under the sea-cliff,
You that are watching
The gray Magician
With eyes of wonder,
I am Merlin,
And *I* am dying,
I am Merlin
Who follow The Gleam.

II

Mighty the Wizard
Who found me at sunrise
Sleeping, and woke me
And learn'd me Magic!
Great the Master,
And sweet the Magic,
When over the valley,
In early summers,
Over the mountain,
On human faces,
And all around me,
Moving to melody,
Floated The Gleam.

III

Once at the croak of a Raven[1]
 who crost it,
A barbarous people,
Blind to the magic
And deaf to the melody,
Snarl'd at and cursed me.
A demon vext me,
The light retreated,
The landskip[2] darken'd,
The melody deaden'd,
The Master whisper'd,
"Follow The Gleam."

IV

Then to the melody,
Over a wilderness
Gliding, and glancing at

Elf of the woodland,
Gnome of the cavern,
Griffin and Giant,   40
And dancing of Fairies
In desolate hollows,
And wraiths of the mountain,
And rolling of dragons
By warble of water,
Or cataract music
Of falling torrents,
Flitted The Gleam.[3]

V

Down from the mountain
And over the level,   50
And streaming and shining on
Silent river,
Silvery willow,
Pasture and plowland,
Innocent maidens,
Garrulous children,
Homestead and harvest,
Reaper and gleaner,
And rough-ruddy faces
Of lowly labour,   60
Slided The Gleam—

VI

Then, with a melody
Stronger and statelier,
Led me at length
To the city and palace
Of Arthur the king;
Touch'd at the golden
Cross of the churches,
Flash'd on the Tournament,
Flicker'd and bicker'd   70
From helmet to helmet,
And last on the forehead
Of Arthur the blameless
Rested the Gleam.

VII

Clouds and darkness
Closed upon Camelot;
Arthur had vanish'd
I knew not whither,

---

[1] Hallam Tennyson in his elaborate interpretation of the poem in the standard edition—"the reading of the poet's riddle as he gave it to me" (IV, 598) —says that the croak of the raven is "the harsh voice of those who were unsympathetic" to his early poems (IV, 595). More specifically, the raven might refer to J. W. Croker or John Wilson ("Christopher North"), who affected to write in the company of a raven: both reviewed Tennyson's early poems unfavorably.

[2] Landskip: landscape.

[3] Hallam Tennyson's reading: the poems of "his own romantic fancy," followed by "Eclogues and English Idyls" (IV, 595).

The king who loved me,
80 And cannot die;[4]
For out of the darkness
Silent and slowly
The Gleam, that had waned to a wintry
    glimmer
On icy fallow
And faded forest,
Drew to the valley
Named of the shadow,
And slowly brightening
Out of the glimmer,
90 And slowly moving again to a melody
Yearningly tender,
Fell on the shadow,
No longer a shadow,
But clothed with The Gleam.

    VIII
And broader and brighter
The Gleam flying onward,
Wed to the melody,
Sang thro' the world;
And slower and fainter,
100 Old and weary,
But eager to follow,
I saw, whenever
In passing it glanced upon
Hamlet or city,
That under the Crosses
The dead man's garden,
The mortal hillock,
Would break into blossom;
And so to the land's
110 Last limit I came—
And can no longer,
But die rejoicing,
For thro' the Magic
Of Him the Mighty,
Who taught me in childhood,
There on the border
Of boundless Ocean,
And all but in Heaven
Hovers The Gleam.

    IX
120 Not of the sunlight,
Not of the moonlight,

Not of the starlight!
O young Mariner,
Down to the haven,
Call your companions,
Launch your vessel,
And crowd your canvas,
And, ere it vanishes
Over the margin,
After it, follow it,
Follow The Gleam.

                                    1889

The Roses on the Terrace

Rose,[1] on this terrace fifty years ago,
    When I was in my June, you in your May,
Two words, "My Rose" set all your face aglow,
    And now that I am white, and you are gray,
That blush of fifty years ago, my dear,
    Blooms in the Past, but close to me to-day
As this red rose, which on our terrace here
    Glows in the blue of fifty miles away.

                                    1889

Crossing the Bar[1]

Sunset and evening star,
    And one clear call for me!
And may there be no moaning of the bar,
    When I put out to sea,

But such a tide as moving seems asleep,
    Too full for sound and foam,
When that which drew from out the boundless
        deep
    Turns again home.

Twilight and evening bell,
    And after that the dark!
And may there be no sadness of farewell,
    When I embark;

For tho' from out our bourne of Time and
        Place
    The flood may bear me far,
I hope to see my Pilot face to face
    When I have crost the bar.

                                    1889

---

[4] Hallam Tennyson's note: "Here my father united the two Arthurs, the Arthur of the Idylls and the Arthur [Hallam] 'the man he held as half divine.' He himself had fought with death, and had come out victorious to find 'a stronger faith his own,' and a hope for himself, for all those is sorrow and for universal humankind, that never forsook him through the future years" (IV, 597).
[1] Rosa Baring; see note to *Maud* (p. 147–148). Tennyson connects the terrace of Aldworth, his last house, with the distant terrace of Rosa's youthful home.
[1] Tennyson asked that this poem be placed at the end of all editions of his poetry.

Robert Browning
1812–1889

It took the young Robert Browning nearly ten years to find the short dramatic forms, especially the dramatic monologue, in which he could effectively exercise his masterful poetic talent. It required another twenty years before his talent was generally recognized as in fact masterful by mid-century readers and critics. And then in the 1860s, when the publication of the poems of *Dramatis Personae* and his long poem *The Ring and the Book* brought what he called fame, the terms of his recognition were that he was acknowledged to be the other great poet of his generation. Even in his eminence Browning was perceived against and as somehow different from the model of a poet already established in the writing and public person of Tennyson.

One source of the difference was that Browning was unusually difficult in the vocabulary and syntax of his poems, in his often recondite subject matter, and in the ambiguity permitted by his dramatic forms. His early poems, especially the long, confused narrative of *Sordello,* had given him the reputation of being nearly unintelligible, and to the end of his life even his admirers thought of themselves as having acquired a special taste and competence. When the Browning Society was formed late in his life, for example, it not only banded together readers who thought that their liking for Browning gave them a peculiar identity. Its members also tried to make a machinery of reading clubs and explications that would at last break through the perplexities and resistances of large numbers of other, as yet unconverted, readers and thus create for the master the large audience and influence proper to a great poet.

There is also in Browning's verse a particularity and privacy different from the intimacy and occasional reclusiveness of Tennyson when the poet in the poems descends to the depths of personality. The situations of the poet in *In Memoriam,* of Bedivere and Arthur in the "Morte d'Arthur," of Tennyson's Ulysses and Lucretius are particular and complex. But there is in all these poems a governing sensibility that moves them to a generalizing gesture, and it is not difficult to imagine how the figures in them move in turn into the emotional, intellectual, and moral lives of Tennyson's contemporary readers. Browning's elliptical style and dramatic forms, on the other hand, characteristically tend to emphasize the particularity of the often eccentric speakers, occasions, and circumstances of his poems. Further, Browning often withholds an informing sensibility or personality from his poems, pretending that the poet is not in them at all. "You speak out, *you,*" he wrote to Elizabeth Barrett in 1845, "—I only make men and women speak—give you the truth broken into prismatic hues, and fear the pure white light, even if it is in me." In the poetry of his latter years Browning was more ready to speak out directly in his own voice, usually to affirm, in the face of death and human error, an authentic optimism about eternity and divine rectitude. But given such broken lights as Bishop Blougram, Caliban, and Ned Bratts, and given the painful misunderstandings dramatized in a poem like "Inapprehensiveness" and in curious fables such as those of "The Cardinal and the Dog" and "Pan and Luna," it was and still is difficult to make references from Browning's poems to the normal beliefs and doubts of readers who, Browning and his admirers were sure, lived in and could learn from the deliberately flawed perspectives of these oblique witnesses to the whole pure light.

Browning came to his difficult differences from premises common in his century. Like other nineteenth-century romantic poets, he believed that natural creation extends into the supernatural, and that the poet stands at their border. As he wrote in 1852 in his essay on Shelley (see Part Ten), whose example dominated his early ideas and practice, poetry is "a sublime fragmentary essay toward the presentment of the correspondency of the universe to the Deity, of the natural to the super-natural, of the actual to the ideal." The central characters of his three early long poems, *Pauline, Paracelsus,* and *Sordello,* are young men who try to complete large intellectual and artistic designs that will display how imperfection fits with perfection. Each of them fails, but each learns the lesson enunciated by the speaker of *Pauline* after he has sadly foresworn the idealism of Shelley: the ideal cannot be imposed on but must be pursued through the concrete and actual. This theme persists in Browning's verse, along with an associated and even more important theme, that of the necessary failure of human will. It is necessary and good to act in an imperfect actuality, and wrong to surrender to imperfection. It is also inevitable that human action will fail when it tries to attain a wholeness possible only in heaven. But the heaven of wholeness is ultimately, perhaps solely, available to those who have tried and failed for it on earth.

The problem for Browning was to find a form that would testify to the perfection beyond the grasp of human will and not deny the imperfect fact of the actual world. Before and after he wrote *Sordello,* the third of his early long poems, Browning wrote *Strafford* and four other plays for the stage (only two of the four were performed), and he published them and two other dramas in *Bells and Pomegranates,* the series of pamphlets he published at his own expense from 1841 to 1846. But it was *Pippa Passes,* the first poem to be published in the series, and not the plays that predicted the form of Browning's achievement. *Pippa Passes* is a series of connected but discrete dramatic scenes that together make a statement more complex than that accessible in the experience and understanding of any character in the poem. In some of the other dramatic monologues and narratives in the *Bells and Pomegranates* series, including "My Last Duchess" and "The Flight of the Duchess," he explored more boldly the possibilities of forms in which limited and sometimes morally reprehensible persons bespeak the fallen character of human experience while the poet who does not speak maneuvers our response to suggest that there are larger and more noble possibilities to be wished and tried for. In the poems of *Men and Women,* as remarkable a collection as that published by Tennyson in 1842, Browning creates a kind of counterpoint in which different voices—the speakers of "Love Among the

Ruins" and "Evelyn Hope"; Fra Lippo Lippi and Andrea del Sarto; David in "Saul," Cleon, Karshish, and Blougram—are played against one another so that the entire round is suggested by speakers who (except for David) see but one of its arcs. In *The Ring and the Book,* his retelling of the story of a seventeenth-century Roman murder and trial through the perspectives of its participants, victims, and observers, he himself enters the poem (as, indeed, he enters at the end of "Bishop Blougram's Apology") to help make a whole, a ring, of these partial accounts. But even then the poet speaks in the presence of perceptions biased by self-interest, ignorance, villainy, and by innocence itself. At his best and most characteristic, Browning to the end of his career founded his poems in occasions and personae, and used language and forms, that acknowledged he chose to believe and celebrate where he finally could not know, and where, more important, he knows that humans will err.

Browning's most ambitious attempt to display the whole in its broken parts is *The Ring and the Book,* which is not represented in this selection because the monologues of its villains and victims do depend upon one another for their effect. Dramatic monologues such as "My Last Duchess" and "Count Gismond," which Browning paired in their original publication under the title "Italy and France," and the counterpoint of some of the monologues from *Men and Women* do at least suggest how one poem in a set may complicate and enlarge the effect and meaning of another. It is also possible to read the poems of *Men and Women* as parts of one long poem that develops a theme about the power of love in a fallen reality. Poems have been selected from *Men and Women* that preserve the line of this development, from the surrender of "Love Among the Ruins" through the stubborn celebration of "The Last Ride Together" to the triumphant assertion, even though it may finally reside in a silence beyond language, of "One Word More."

For the rest of it, this selection is chosen to represent the several themes, registers of tone and language, and forms of Browning's verse. The themes persist throughout the canon of his poetry: the necessity to act in the world; the inevitability of failure; the excitements and possibility of flesh; the existence of a spiritual reality that will reward action, retrieve failure, and redeem actuality. Browning also wrote frequently about the agency of poetry and art to reveal, in Fra Lippo Lippi's phrase, "the value and significance of flesh." Some of these poems are included: "Pictor Ignotus" and "Waring" from his early poetry; "Transcendentalism," "How It Strikes a Contemporary," "One Word More" from *Men and Women;* the epilogues and prologues to his later volumes of poems. To the end of his career Browning maintained the gnarled surfaces and surprise of his verse by mixing recondite words with topical allusions, and earnest elevations with comic deflations ("Inapprehensiveness") or startling grotesque conceits ("Pan and Luna"). He was less various in the meters and forms of his poetry. But like most Victorian poets, he was proud of his technical facility and of the fact that when he wanted to, as in "One Word More," he could summon into his repertory an unusual meter and form fit for their occasion.

In his late verse, Browning returned to narrative forms, and he came increasingly to write in the direct, discursive voice of a poem like "Prospice." But he continued to mistrust the melody and resolutions of Tennyson (especially in the *Idylls of the King*) as too readily satisfying, and measured by his practice, some of the poetic styles of the latter decades of the century are too languid and finished in the craft with which they sadly accept that art can order only small corners of experience. The point about Browning that this selection tries to enforce is that he attempts the major task of nineteenth-century romantic poetry in a way different from that of the other principal poets of the century. More than that of any other major romantic poet, his practice expresses a will to perform the highest office he could imagine for poetry, to touch the finite to the infinite, while at the same time acknowledging that human consciousness, will, and language are inadequate to his task. Like Moses in "One Word More" he tries in his poems to bring water from rock. He holds with the miracle, the divine possibility, of water. But at his most characteristic he also recalls that his medium, never to be fully transcended in this life, is rock.

CHRONOLOGY

1812 Born in a suburb of London; his father was a clerk in the Bank of England, a man of sure and independent tastes who had collected a good library of literature and history; his mother was the daughter of a ship-owner and the granddaughter of a Hamburg merchant.

1820–28 Browning was educated mostly at home by tutors and by his own use of his father's library. He completed a volume of poems in 1825–26, most of which he destroyed after his parents tried and failed to find a publisher for them. At the time of his first writing in verse Browning began reading, and was strongly moved by, the poetry of Shelley and Keats.

1828–29 Attended part of a term at the University of London.

1833–34 *Pauline* published, its expenses being paid for by Browning's aunt. Browning visited Russia.

1835 *Paracelsus* published; the expenses of this volume too, like all of his volumes of poems until *Christmas-Eve and Easter-Day,* were paid by Browning or his family.

1836–37 The actor-manager William Macready, whom Browning met along with Dickens, Carlyle, and others as he began to move in the literary and theatrical worlds of London, asked Browning to write a play. *Strafford* was published and performed (only five times) in 1837.

1840 *Sordello* published.

1841 First number of *Bells and Pomegranates,* a series of sixteen-page pamphlets containing poems and plays, published. The first number was the dramatic poem *Pippa Passes.*

1842 *Bells and Pomegranates II,* a verse play, published. The third number of the series, *Dramatic Lyrics,* was also published this year; it included "My Last Duchess" and "Waring."

1843 *Bells and Pomegranates IV* and *V,* each containing a play, published. The play published in the fifth number, *A Blot in the 'Scutcheon,* was performed (three times).

1844 *Bells and Pomegranates VI,* containing a play (*Colombe's Birthday*) performed in this year and again in 1853, published. Browning began contributing poems to a magazine.

1845 Browning began a correspondence with Elizabeth Barrett; four months later Browning was taken to meet her in the room in which she spent most of her days. *Bells and Pomegranates VII,* titled *Dramatic Romances and Lyrics,* and including "The Flight of the Duchess" and the first version of "Saul," published.

1846   *Bells and Pomegranates VIII,* contain-
ing two plays, one (*A Soul's Tragedy*) in
verse and prose, published. Browning and
Elizabeth Barrett were married. They eloped
to Italy.

1847–49   The Brownings settled in Florence;
their son (and only child) was born in 1849.
An edition of Browning's poems, including
Paracelsus and the *Bells and Pomegranates*
series, published.

1850   *Christmas-Eve and Easter-Day* pub-
lished.

1851–52   Browning wrote an essay on Shelley
for a proposed edition of some of Shelley's
letters (1852); the essay and the edition
were not published when the letters were
discovered to be spurious. The Brownings
returned to England for a short visit in 1851
and again in 1852.

1855   *Men and Women* published. The
Brownings again visited England.

1856   John Kenyon, a relative of Elizabeth
Barrett Browning, died; he had been pro-
viding the Brownings a small annual in-
come, and he left them each a legacy which
made them financially secure.

1861   Elizabeth Barrett Browning died. Rob-
ert Browning returned to England to live.

1863   Collected edition of Browning's poems
published.

1864   *Dramatis Personae* published.

1868–69   Six-volume collected edition of po-
ems published, including *Pauline* for the
first time, in a revised version (1868). *The
Ring and the Book* published in four vol-
umes, a volume each month from November
1868 to February 1869.

1871   *Balustion's Adventure* and *Prince Ho-
henstiel-Schwangen* published.

1872   *Fifine at the Fair* published.

1873   *Red Cotton Night-Cap Country* pub-
lished.

1875   *Aristophanes' Apology* and *The Inn Al-
bum* published.

1876   *Pacchiarotto and How He Worked in
Distemper, with Other Poems,* published.

1877   Translation of *The Agamemnon of
Aeschylus* published.

1878   *La Saisiaz,* and *The Two Poets of
Croisic* published. A cheap edition of Brown-
ing's poems began to be published (1878–
82); this edition was one of about a dozen
collected editions published in the 1870s
and 1880s. Browning visited Italy for first
time since the death of his wife.

1879–80   *Dramatic Idyls, First Series* (1879)
and *Second Series* (1880) published.

1881   The Browning Society founded in Lon-
don.

1883   *Jocoseria* published.

1884   *Ferishtah's Fancies* published.

1887   *Parleyings with Certain People of Im-
portance in Their Day* published.

1888   First volumes of *Poetical Works,* even-
tually to comprise seventeen volumes, pub-
lished (1888–94); Browning supervised the
text of all but one of these volumes.

1889   *Asolando* published. Browning died in
Venice on the day of its publication in Lon-
don.

EDITIONS

The standard editions of Browning's poems
and plays are still the Centenary edition, edited
by F. G. Kenyon in ten volumes in 1912, and
the Florentine edition, edited by Charlotte
Porter and Helen G. Clarke in twelve volumes
in 1910. Both editions are based on the 1888–
94 edition of Browning's verse, which (with
the exception of one volume) Browning saw
through the press. The texts published here
are those of the 1888–94 edition, which are con-
sistent with those of the Centenary edition. A
variorum edition of Browning's poems is now
being published under the general editorship of
Roma J. King, Jr. Four volumes have appeared
(1969–73) containing Browning's poems and
plays through those published in the *Bells and
Pomegranates* series. Ian Jack has also edited
a one-volume edition of *Browning: Poetical
Works: 1833–1864* (1970). Paul Turner has
edited the 1855 text of *Men and Women*
(1972), and included useful notes to the po-
ems. An essay on the Italian poet Tasso and
the British poet Thomas Chatterton which
Browning published in 1842 has been edited
and published by Donald Smalley (1948).

BIOGRAPHY AND CRITICISM

Only a part of Browning's letters have been
collected and published. The most recent edi-
tion of *The Letters of Robert Browning and
Elizabeth Barrett, 1845–46* has been edited by
Elvan Kintner (1969). T. L. Hood's edition
of the *Letters of Robert Browning, Collected
by Thomas J. Wise* (1933), and *New Letters
of Robert Browning,* edited by William C.
DeVane and Kenneth L. Knickerbocker
(1950), contain letters from Browning to vari-

ous correspondents. F. G. Kenyon's edition of the correspondence between *Robert Browning and Alfred Domett* (1906), a friend of Browning's who emigrated to New Zealand in the 1840s, includes important material concerning the early passages of Browning's career. Thomas J. Collins has edited *The Brownings to the Tennysons: Letters from Robert Browning and Elizabeth Barrett Browning to Alfred, Emily, and Hallam Tennyson, 1852–1889* (1971).

Biographies by W. H. Griffin and H. C. Minchin, *The Life of Robert Browning* (1910; revised edition, 1938), and Mrs. Sutherland Orr, *The Life and Letters of Robert Browning* (1891; revised edition, 1908) are standard sources of letters and biographical information. Betty Miller's *Robert Browning: A Portrait* (1952) considers the effects of Browning's relationship with his Evangelical mother on his life and character. Maisie Ward has published a two-volume biography, *Robert Browning and His World* (1967–69); and William Irvine and Park Honan have published *The Book, The Ring, and the Poet: A Biography of Robert Browning* (1974). E. A. Horsman's edition of *The Diary of Alfred Domett, 1872–1885* (1953) contains pertinent matter on Browning's life after Domett returned to England in the 1870s.

OTHER USEFUL BOOKS

Altick, Richard D., and Loucks, James F., Jr. *Browning's Roman Murder Story* (1968).

Blackburn, Thomas. *Robert Browning: A Study of His Poetry* (1974).

Collins, Thomas J. *Robert Browning's Moral-Esthetic Theory, 1833–1855* (1967).

Cook, Eleanor. *Browning's Lyrics* (1974).

DeVane, William C. *Browning's Parleyings: The Autobiography of a Mind* (1927).

Drew, Philip. *The Poetry of Browning* (1970).

Groom, Bernard. *The Diction of Poetry from Spenser to Bridges* (1955). Includes his study of the diction of the poetry of Tennyson, Browning, and Arnold, published separately in 1939.

Hair, Donald S. *Browning's Experiments with Genre* (1972).

Harrold, William E. *The Variance and the Unity: A Study of the Complementary Poems of Robert Browning* (1973).

Honan, Park. *Browning's Characters* (1961).

Jack, Ian. *Browning's Major Poetry* (1973).

King, Roma A., Jr. *The Bow and the Lyre:* *The Art of Robert Browning* (1957); and *The Focusing Artifice: The Poetry of Robert Browning* (1968).

Langbaum, Robert. *The Poetry of Experience* (1957). An essential summary and advance of speculation about the nature and function of the dramatic monologue.

Litzinger, Boyd. *Time's Revenges: Browning's Reputation as a Thinker, 1889–1962* (1964).

Lounsbury, T. R. *The Early Literary Career of Robert Browning* (1911).

Melchiori, Barbara. *Browning's Poetry of Reticence* (1968).

Raymond, W. O. *The Infinite Moment, and Other Essays on Robert Browning* (1950; revised edition, 1965).

Shaw, W. David. *The Dialectic Temper: The Rhetorical Art of Robert Browning* (1968).

Wenger, C. N. *The Aesthetics of Robert Browning* (1924).

William C. DeVane's *A Browning Handbook* (second edition, 1955) is a useful commentary on all of Browning's verse and on some of the scholarship and criticism concerning his life and work. L. N. Broughton, C. S. Northup, and Robert Pearsall have compiled *Robert Browning: A Bibliography, 1830–1950* (1953); this bibliography has been extended by William S. Peterson in *Robert and Elizabeth Barrett Browning: An Annotated Bibliography, 1951–70* (1974). The bibliography of commentary on Browning's poems is brought up to 1965 in *The Browning Critics*, edited by Boyd Litzinger and Kenneth L. Knickerbocker (1965), which is primarily a collection of essays on Browning's poetry. Philip Drew has also edited a useful collection of critical essays on Browning's poetry (1966). Boyd Litzinger and Donald Smalley have compiled a collection of nineteenth- and twentieth-century commentary in *Browning: The Critical Heritage* (1970).

from Pauline

A Fragment of a Confession

Pauline, *Browning's first published poem, was published anonymously in 1833. In a handwritten note in one of the copies of the poem, Browning described it as "written in pursuance of a foolish plan which occupied me mightily for a time, and which had for its object the enabling me to assume & realize I know not how many different characters;—meanwhile the world was never to guess that 'Brown, Smith, Jones & Robinson' (as the spelling books have it) the respective authors of this poem, the other novel, such an opera, such a speech, etc. etc. were no other than one and the same individual. The present abortion was the first work of the Poet of the batch, who would have been more legitimately myself than most of the others; but I surrounded him with all manner of (to my then notion) poetical accessories, and had planned quite a delightful life for him." (Quoted in DeVane, p. 41.) The poem was not reprinted until 1868, when Browning revised it slightly; he revised it again, and again slightly, before he published it in the final collected edition of 1888.*

The poem is a long monologue addressed by a poet to Pauline, a figure of no discernible identity. In his monologue the poet considers, among other matters, his failure to achieve the high, visionary certainty and song of Shelley, the "Sun-treader" whom he invokes in the first passage excerpted from the poem. Near the end of the poem the poet finds one resolution of his difficulty when he descends with Pauline into the close, concrete, and particular, and then emerges to enlarge his verse and vision, like a stream rising from a narrow and densely covered source into a broad river.

Sun-treader, life and light be thine for ever!
Thou art gone from us; years go by and spring
Gladdens and the young earth is beautiful,
Yet thy songs come not, other bards arise,
But none like thee: they stand, thy majesties,
Like mighty works which tell some spirit there
Hath sat regardless of neglect and scorn,
Till, its long task completed, it hath risen
And left us, never to return, and all
10   Rush in to peer and praise when all in vain.
The air seems bright with thy past presence yet,
But thou art still for me as thou hast been
When I have stood with thee as on a throne
With all thy dim creations gathered round
Like mountains, and I felt of mould like them,
And with them creatures of my own were
     mixed,
Like things half-lived, catching and giving life.
But thou art still for me who have adored
Tho' single, panting but to hear thy name
20   Which I believed a spell to me alone,
Scarce deeming thou wast as a star to men!
As one should worship long a sacred spring
Scarce worth a moth's flitting, which long
     grasses cross,

And one small tree embowers droopingly—
Joying to see some wandering insect won
To live in its few rushes, or some locust
To pasture on its boughs, or some wild bird
Stoop for its freshness from the trackless air:
And then should find it but the fountain-head,
Long lost, of some great river washing towns   30
And towers, and seeing old woods which will
     live
But by its banks untrod of human foot,
Which, when the great sun sinks, lie quivering
In light as some thing lieth half of life
Before God's foot, waiting a wondrous change;
Then girt with rocks which seek to turn or stay
Its course in vain, for it does ever spread
Like a sea's arm as it goes rolling on,
Being the pulse of some great country—so
Wast thou to me, and art thou to the world!   40
And I, perchance, half feel a strange regret
That I am not what I have been to thee:
Like a girl one has silently loved long
In her first loneliness in some retreat,
When, late emerged, all gaze and glow to view
Her fresh eyes and soft hair and lips which
     bloom
Like a mountain berry: doubtless it is sweet
To see her thus adored, but there have been
Moments when all the world was in our praise,
Sweeter than any pride of after hours.   50
Yet, sun-treader, all hail! From my heart's heart
I bid thee hail! E'en in my wildest dreams,
I proudly feel I would have thrown to dust
The wreaths of fame which seemed o'erhanging
     me,
To see thee for a moment as thou art.

And if thou livest, if thou lovest, spirit!
Remember me who set this final seal
To wandering thought—that one so pure as
     thou
Could never die. Remember me who flung
All honour from my soul, yet paused and said   60
"There is one spark of love remaining yet,
For I have nought in common with him, shapes
Which followed him avoid me, and foul forms
Seek me, which ne'er could fasten on his mind;
And though I feel how low I am to him,
Yet I aim not even to catch a tone
Of harmonies he called profusely up;
So, one gleam still remains, although the last."
Remember me who praise thee e'en with tears,
For never more shall I walk calm with thee;   70
Thy sweet imaginings are as an air,
A melody some wondrous singer sings,
Which, though it haunt men oft in the still eve,

They dream not to essay; yet it no less
But more is honoured. I was thine in shame,
And now when all thy proud renown is out,
I am a watcher whose eyes have grown dim
With looking for some star which breaks on
 him
Altered and worn and weak and full of tears.

.   .   .

Night, and one single ridge of narrow path
Between the sullen river and the woods
Waving and muttering, for the moonless night
Has shaped them into images of life,
Like the uprising of the giant-ghosts,
Looking on earth to know how their sons fare:
Thou art so close by me, the roughest swell
Of wind in the tree-tops hides not the panting
Of thy soft breasts. No, we will pass to
 morning—
Morning, the rocks and valleys and old woods.
How the sun brightens in the mist, and here,
Half in the air, like creatures of the place,
Trusting the element, living on high boughs
That swing in the wind—look at the silver
 spray
Flung from the foam-sheet of the cataract
Amid the broken rocks! Shall we stay here
With the wild hawks? No, ere the hot noon
 come,
Dive we down—safe! See this our new retreat
Walled in with a sloped mound of matted
 shrubs,
Dark, tangled, old and green, still sloping down
To a small pool whose waters lie asleep
Amid the trailing boughs turned water-plants:
And tall trees overarch to keep us in,
Breaking the sunbeams into emerald shafts,
And in the dreamy water one small group
Of two or three strange trees are got together
Wondering at all around, as strange beasts herd
Together far from their own land: all wildness,
No turf nor moss, for boughs and plants pave
 all,
And tongues of bank go shelving in the lymph,[1]
Where the pale-throated snake reclines his
 head,
And old grey stones lie making eddies there,
The wild-mice cross them dry-shod. Deeper in!
Shut thy soft eyes—now look—still deeper in!
This is the very heart of the woods all round
Mountain-like heaped above us; yet even here
One pond of water gleams; far off the river

Sweeps like a sea, barred out from land; but
 one—
One thin clear sheet has overleaped and wound
Into this silent depth, which gained, it lies   40
Still, as but let by sufferance; the trees bend
O'er it as wild men watch a sleeping girl,
And through their roots long creeping plants
 out-stretch
Their twined hair, steeped and sparkling;
 farther on,
Tall rushes and thick flag-knots[2] have combined
To narrow it; so, at length, a silver thread,
It winds, all noiselessly through the deep wood
Till thro' a cleft-way, thro' the moss and stone,
It joins its parent-river with a shout.

Up for the glowing day, leave the old woods!   50
See, they part, like a ruined arch: the sky!
Nothing but sky appears, so close the roots
And grass of the hill-top level with the air—
Blue sunny air, where a great cloud floats laden
With light, like a dead whale that white birds
 pick,
Floating away in the sun in some north sea.
Air, air, fresh life-blood, thin and searching air,
The clear, dear breath of God that loveth us,
Where small birds reel and winds take their
 delight!
Water is beautiful, but not like air: 60
See, where the solid azure waters lie
Made as of thickened air, and down below,
The fern-ranks like a forest spread themselves
As though each pore could feel the element;
Where the quick glancing serpent winds his
 way,
Float with me there, Pauline!—but not like air.
                                              1833

*"My Last Duchess" and "Count Gismond" were
first published, in the third number of Browning's
series of pamphlets titled* Bells and Pomegranates,
*together under the title "Italy and France": the first
poem was subtitled "I. Italy," and the second "II.
France." The poems were given their present titles
in a collected edition of his poetry Browning pub-
lished in 1849.*

My Last Duchess

Ferrara

That's my last Duchess painted on the wall,
Looking as if she were alive. I call

---

[1] Lymph: spring.   [2] Flag-knots: clumps of water plants, like cattails.

That piece a wonder, now: Frà Pandolf's[1]
  hands
Worked busily a day, and there she stands.
Will't please you sit and look at her? I said
"Frà Pandolf" by design, for never read
Strangers like you that pictured countenance,
The depth and passion of its earnest glance,
But to myself they turned (since none puts by
10 The curtain I have drawn for you, but I)
And seemed as they would ask me, if they durst,
How such a glance came there; so, not the first
Are you to turn and ask thus. Sir, 'twas not
Her husband's presence only, called that spot
Of joy into the Duchess' cheek: perhaps
Frà Pandolf chanced to say "Her mantle laps
Over my lady's wrist too much," or "Paint
Must never hope to reproduce the faint
Half-flush that dies along her throat:" such
  stuff
20 Was courtesy, she thought, and cause enough
For calling up that spot of joy. She had
A heart—how shall I say?—too soon made glad,
Too easily impressed; she liked whate'er
She looked on, and her looks went everywhere.
Sir, 't was all one! My favour[2] at her breast,
The dropping of the daylight in the West,
The bough of cherries some officious fool
Broke in the orchard for her, the white mule
She rode with round the terrace—all and each
Would draw from her alike the approving
30 speech,
Or blush, at least. She thanked men,—good!
  but thanked
Somehow—I know not how—as if she ranked
My gift of a nine-hundred-years-old name
With anybody's gift. Who'd stoop to blame
This sort of trifling? Even had you skill
In speech— (which I have not) —to make your
  will
Quite clear to such an one, and say, "Just this
Or that in you disgusts me; here you miss,
Or there exceed the mark"—and if she let
40 Herself be lessoned so, nor plainly set
Her wits to yours, forsooth, and made excuse,
—E'en then would be some stooping; and I
  choose
Never to stoop. Oh sir, she smiled, no doubt,
Whene'er I passed her; but who passed without
Much the same smile? This grew; I gave
  commands;[3]

Then all smiles stopped together. There she
  stands
As if alive. Will't please you rise? We'll meet
The company below, then. I repeat,
The Count your master's known munificence
Is ample warrant that no just pretence[4]   50
Of mine for dowry will be disallowed;
Though his fair daughter's self, as I avowed
At starting, is my object. Nay, we'll go
Together down, sir. Notice Neptune, though,
Taming a sea-horse, thought a rarity,
Which Claus of Innsbruck cast in bronze for
  me!

                         1842

Count Gismond

Aix In Provence

I

Christ God who savest man, save most
  Of men Count Gismond who saved me!
Count Gauthier, when he chose his post,
  Chose time and place and company
To suit it; when he struck at length
My honour, 't was with all his strength.

II

And doubtlessly ere he could draw
  All points to one, he must have schemed!
That miserable morning saw
  Few half so happy as I seemed,   10
While being dressed in queen's array
To give our tourney prize away.

III

I thought they loved me, did me grace
  To please themselves; 't was all their deed;
God makes, or fair or foul, our face;
  If showing mine so caused to bleed
My cousins' hearts, they should have dropped
A word, and straight the play had stopped.

IV

They, too, so beauteous! Each a queen
  By virtue of her brow and breast;   20
Not needing to be crowned, I mean,
  As I do. E'en when I was dressed,
Had either of them spoke, instead
Of glancing sideways with still head!

---

[1] Frà Pandolf, like Claus of Innsbruck (line 56), is a fictitious artist.
[2] Favour: a ribbon or some other gift accepted and worn as a token of love.
[3] Browning said of these lines that "the commands were that she should be put to death, . . .
or he might have had her shut up in a convent." (Quoted in DeVane, p. 109.)
[4] Pretence: claim.

V

But no: they let me laugh, and sing
    My birthday song quite through, adjust
The last rose in my garland, fling
    A last look on the mirror, trust
My arms to each an arm of theirs,
And so descend the castle-stairs—

VI

And come out on the morning-troop
    Of merry friends who kissed my cheek,
And called me queen, and made me stoop
    Under the canopy— (a streak
That pierced it, of the outside sun,
Powdered with gold its gloom's soft dun) —

VII

And they could let me take my state
    And foolish throne amid applause
Of all come there to celebrate
    My queen's-day—Oh I think the cause
Of much was, they forgot no crowd
Makes up for parents in their shroud!

VIII

However that be, all eyes were bent
    Upon me, when my cousins cast
Theirs down; 't was time I should present
    The victor's crown, but . . . there, 't will
        last
No long time . . . the old mist again
Blinds me as then it did. How vain!

IX

See! Gismond's at the gate, in talk
    With his two boys: I can proceed.
Well, at that moment, who should stalk
    Forth boldly—to my face, indeed—
But Gauthier, and he thundered "Stay!"
And all stayed. "Bring no crowns, I say!

X

"Bring torches! Wind the penance-sheet[1]
    About her! Let her shun the chaste,
Or lay herself before their feet!
    Shall she whose body I embraced
A night long, queen it in the day?
For honour's sake no crowns, I say!"

XI

I? What I answered? As I live,
    I never fancied such a thing

As answer possible to give.
    What says the body when they spring
Some monstrous torture-engine's whole
    Strength on it? No more says the soul.

XII

Till out strode Gismond; then I knew
    That I was saved. I never met
His face before, but, at first view,
    I felt quite sure that God had set   70
Himself to Satan; who would spend
A minute's mistrust on the end?

XIII

He strode to Gauthier, in his throat
    Gave him the lie, then struck his mouth
With one back-handed blow that wrote
    In blood men's verdict there. North, South,
East, West, I looked. The lie was dead,
And damned, and truth stood up instead.

XIV

This glads me most, that I enjoyed
    The heart of the joy, with my content   80
In watching Gismond unalloyed
    By any doubt of the event:
God took that on him—I was bid
Watch Gismond for my part: I did.

XV

Did I not watch him while he let
    His armourer just brace his greaves,[2]
Rivet his hauberk,[3] on the fret
    The while! His foot . . . my memory
        leaves
No least stamp out, nor how anon
He pulled his ringing gauntlets on.   90

XVI

And e'en before the trumpet's sound
    Was finished, prone lay the false knight,
Prone as his lie, upon the ground:
    Gismond flew at him, used no sleight
O' the sword, but open-breasted drove,
Cleaving till out the truth he clove.

XVII

Which done, he dragged him to my feet
    And said "Here die, but end thy breath
In full confession, lest thou fleet
    From my first, to God's second death!   100
Say, hast thou lied?" And, "I have lied
To God and her," he said, and died.

[1] Penance-sheet: Gauthier asks that she be disgraced as a sinner, dressed in penitential clothing and burned at the stake.
[2] Greaves: armor for the lower leg.   [3] Hauberk: a tunic of chain mail.

XVIII

Then Gismond, kneeling to me, asked
   —What safe my heart holds, though no
      word
Could I repeat now, if I tasked
   My powers for ever, to a third
Dear even as you are. Pass the rest
Until I sank upon his breast.

XIX

Over my head his arm he flung
110   Against the world; and scarce I felt
His sword (that dripped by me and swung)
   A little shifted in its belt:
For he began to say the while
How South our home lay many a mile.

XX

So 'mid the shouting multitude
   We two walked forth to never more
Return. My cousins have pursued
   Their life, untroubled as before
I vexed them. Gauthier's dwelling-place
120 God lighten! May his soul find grace!

XXI

Our elder boy has got the clear
   Great brow; tho' when his brother's black
Full eye shows scorn, it . . . Gismond here?
   And have you brought my tercel[4] back?
I just was telling Adela
How many birds it struck since May.

                         1842

Waring[1]

I

I

What's become of Waring
Since he gave us all the slip,
Chose land-travel or seafaring,
Boots and chest or staff and scrip,
Rather than pace up and down
Any longer London town?

II

Who'd have guessed it from his lip
Or his brow's accustomed bearing,
On the night he thus took ship
10 Or started landward?—little caring

For us, it seems, who supped together
  (Friends of his too, I remember)
And walked home thro' the merry weather,
  The snowiest in all December.
I left his arm that night myself
For what's-his-name's, the new prose-poet
Who wrote the book there, on the shelf—
How, forsooth, was I to know it
If Waring meant to glide away
Like a ghost at break of day?
Never looked he half so gay!

III

He was prouder than the devil:
How he must have cursed our revel!
Ay and many other meetings,
Indoor visits, outdoor greetings,
As up and down he paced this London,
With no work done, but great works undone,
Where scarce twenty knew his name.
Why not, then, have earlier spoken,
Written, bustled? Who's to blame
If your silence kept unbroken?
"True, but there were sundry jottings,
Stray-leaves, fragments, blurrs and blottings,
Certain first steps were achieved
Already which"— (is that your meaning?)
"Had well borne out whoe'er believed
In more to come!" But who goes gleaning
Hedgeside chance-blades, while full-sheaved
Stand cornfields by him? Pride, o'erweening
Pride alone, puts forth such claims
O'er the day's distinguished names.

IV

Meantime, how much I loved him,
I find out now I've lost him.
I who cared not if I moved him,
Who could so carelessly accost him,
Henceforth never shall get free
Of his ghostly company,
His eyes that just a little wink
As deep I go into the merit
Of this and that distinguished spirit—
His cheeks' raised colour, soon to sink,
As long I dwell on some stupendous
And tremendous (Heaven defend us!)
Monstr'-inform'-ingens-horrend-ous[2]
Demoniaco-seraphic

---

[4] Tercel: a male hawk, here used in the sport of falconry.
[1] Something of the character and circumstances of the central character of this poem are modeled on those of Browning's friend Alfred Domett, an ambitious man who published two volumes of verse before he emigrated to New Zealand in 1842. He later served as prime minister of New Zealand.
[2] A paraphrase of a line in Virgil's *Aeneid*, describing the Cyclops Polyphemus.

Penman's latest piece of graphic.
Nay, my very wrist grows warm
With his dragging weight of arm.
E'en so, swimmingly appears,
Through one's after-supper musings,
Some lost lady of old years
With her beauteous vain endeavour
And goodness unrepaid as ever;
The face, accustomed to refusings,
We, puppies that we were . . . Oh never
Surely, nice of conscience, scrupled
Being aught like false, forsooth, to?
Telling aught but honest truth to?
What a sin, had we centupled
Its possessor's grace and sweetness!
No! she heard in its completeness
Truth, for truth's a weighty matter,
And, truth, at issue, we can't flatter!
Well, 't is done with; she's exempt
From damning us thro' such a sally;
And so she glides, as down a valley,
Taking up with her contempt,
Past our reach; and in, the flowers
Shut her unregarded hours.

V

Oh, could I have him back once more,
This Waring, but one half-day more!
Back, with the quiet face of yore,
So hungry for acknowledgment
Like mine! I'd fool him to his bent.
Feed, should not he, to heart's content?
I'd say, "to only have conceived,
Planned your great works, apart from progress,
Surpasses little works achieved!"
I'd lie so, I should be believed.
I'd make such havoc of the claims
Of the day's distinguished names
To feast him with, as feasts an ogress
Her feverish sharp-toothed gold-crowned child!
Or as one feasts a creature rarely
Captured here, unreconciled
To capture; and completely gives
Its pettish humours license, barely
Requiring that it lives.

VI

Ichabod, Ichabod,
The glory is departed![3]   100
Travels Waring East away?
Who, of knowledge, by hearsay,
Reports a man upstarted
Somewhere as a god,
Hordes grown European-hearted,
Millions of the wild made tame
On a sudden at his fame?
In Vishnu-land what Avatar?[4]
Or who in Moscow, toward the Czar,
With the demurest of footfalls   110
Over the Kremlin's pavement bright
With serpentine and syenite,[5]
Steps, with five other Generals
That simultaneously take snuff,
For each to have pretext enough
And kerchiefwise unfold his sash
Which, softness' self, is yet the stuff
To hold fast where a steel chain snaps,
And leave the grand white neck no gash?
Waring in Moscow, to those rough   120
Cold northern natures borne perhaps,
Like the lambwhite maiden[6] dear
From the circle of mute kings
Unable to repress the tear,
Each as his sceptre down he flings,
To Dian's fane at Taurica,
Where now a captive priestess, she alway
Mingles her tender grave Hellenic speech
With theirs, tuned to the hailstone-beaten beach
As pours some pigeon, from the myrrhy lands   130
Rapt by the whirlblast to fierce Scythian strands[7]
Where breed the swallows, her melodious cry
Amid their barbarous twitter!
In Russia? Never! Spain were fitter!
Ay, most likely 't is in Spain
That we and Waring meet again
Now, while he turns down that cool narrow
    lane
Into the blackness, out of grave Madrid
All fire and shine, abrupt as when there's slid
Its stiff gold blazing pall   140
From some black coffin-lid.

---

[3] 1 Samuel 4:21: a lament upon the birth of Ichabod after the Israelites have been beaten by the Philistines, and the Ark of the Covenant taken.

[4] Vishnu-land: Vishnu is a Hindu god who is worshipped in various incarnations, each of them called an avatar of the god.

[5] Serpentine and syenite: kinds of rock, the first usually a mottled green in color, the second a crystalline rock.

[6] Lambwhite maiden: Iphigenia, the daughter of Agamemnon, was about to be sacrificed by her father in order to appease the gods when Diana spirited her away to Tauris, where she became a priestess of the goddess' temple.

[7] Scythian strands: the northern shores of the Black Sea.

Or, best of all,
I love to think
The leaving us was just a feint;
Back here to London did he slink,
And now works on without a wink
Of sleep, and we are on the brink
Of something great in fresco-paint:
Some garret's ceiling, walls and floor,
150 Up and down and o'er and o'er
He splashes, as none splashed before
Since great Caldara Polidore.[8]
Or Music means this land of ours
Some favour yet, to pity won
By Purcell from his Rosy Bowers,[9]—
"Give me my so-long promised son,
Let Waring end what I begun!"
Then down he creeps and out he steals
Only when the night conceals
160 His face; in Kent 't is cherry-time,
Or hops are picking: or at prime
Of March he wanders as, too happy,
Years ago when he was young,
Some mild eve when woods grew sappy
And the early moths had sprung
To life from many a trembling sheath
Woven the warm boughs beneath;
While small birds said to themselves
What should soon be actual song,
170 And young gnats, by tens and twelves,
Made as if they were the throng
That crowd around and carry aloft
The sound they have nursed, so sweet and pure,
Out of a myriad noises soft,
Into a tone that can endure
Amid the noise of a July noon
When all God's creatures crave their boon,
All at once and all in tune,
And get it, happy as Waring then,
180 Having first within his ken
What a man might do with men:
And far too glad, in the even-glow,
To mix with the world he meant to take
Into his hand, he told you, so—
And out of it his world to make,

To contract and to expand
As he shut or oped his hand.
Oh Waring, what's to really be?
A clear stage and a crowd to see!
Some Garrick,[10] say, out shall not he
The heart of Hamlet's mystery pluck?
Or, where most unclean beasts are rife,
Some Junius[11]—am I right?—shall tuck
His sleeve, and forth with flaying-knife!
Some Chatterton shall have the luck
Of calling Rowley into life![12]
Some one shall somehow run a muck[13]
With this old world for want of strife
Sound asleep. Contrive, contrive
To rouse us, Waring! Who's alive?
Our men scarce seem in earnest now.
Distinguished names!—but 't is, somehow,
As if they played at being names
Still more distinguished, like the games
Of children. Turn our sport to earnest
With a visage of the sternest!
Bring the real times back, confessed
Still better than our very best!

II

I
"When I last saw Waring . . ."
(How all turned to him who spoke!
You saw Waring? Truth or joke?
In land-travel or sea-faring?)

II
"We were sailing by Triest
Where a day or two we harboured:
A sunset was in the West,
When, looking over the vessel's side,
One of our company espied
A sudden speck to larboard.
And as a sea-duck flies and swims
At once, so came the light craft up,
With its sole lateen sail[14] that trims
And turns (the water round its rims
Dancing, as round a sinking cup)

[8] Caldara Polidore: a sixteenth-century Italian painter who painted the friezes in the Vatican in Rome.
[9] Henry Purcell: a seventeenth-century English composer: "From Rosy Bowers" is the name of one of his songs.
[10] David Garrick: a famous eighteenth-century English actor.
[11] Junius: the pseudonym of a political writer, not yet identified with certainty, who wrote a series of satiric letters in the English press at the end of the eighteenth century.
[12] Thomas Chatterton (1752–1770) fabricated a set of poems he attributed to a fifteenth-century monk named Thomas Rowley.
[13] Run a muck: run amok: this phrase came into the English language from Malay, where it means a murderous frenzy.
[14] Lateen sail: a triangular sail commonly used on the northern coast of Africa.

And by us like a fish it curled,
And drew itself up close beside,
Its great sail on the instant furled,
And o'er its thwarts a shrill voice cried,
(A neck as bronzed as a Lascar's) [15]
'Buy wine of us, you English Brig?
Or fruit, tobacco and cigars?
A pilot for you to Triest?
Without one, look you ne'er so big,
They'll never let you up the bay!
We natives should know best.'
I turned, and 'just those fellows' way,'
Our captain said, 'The 'long-shore thieves
Are laughing at us in their sleeves.'

III

"In truth, the boy leaned laughing back;
And one, half-hidden by his side
Under the furled sail, soon I spied,
With great grass hat and kerchief black,
Who looked up with his kingly throat,
Said somewhat, while the other shook
His hair back from his eyes to look
Their longest at us; then the boat,
I know not how, turned sharply round,
Laying her whole side on the sea
As a leaping fish does; from the lee
Into the weather, cut somehow
Her sparkling path beneath our bow
And so went off, as with a bound,
Into the rosy and golden half
O' the sky, to overtake the sun
And reach the shore, like the sea-calf
Its singing cave; yet I caught one
Glance ere away the boat quite passed,
And neither time nor toil could mar
Those features: so I saw the last
Of Waring!"—You? Oh, never star
Was lost here but it rose afar!
Look East, where whole new thousands are!
In Vishnu-land what Avatar?

1842

Thirty years after he wrote it, Browning, in letters quoted in the Centenary edition of his poetry (III, xi–xii), claimed that he did not intend specifically to attack Wordsworth in this poem, but only to use him as a kind of model for the figure of a leader who has betrayed the intensity of his earlier commitments. But the poem does clearly refer to the circumstances of Wordsworth's acceptance of a government pension in 1842 and of the laureateship in 1845, as well as to the more general

fact of his turning away in his middle and old age from the politically liberal sympathies of his young manhood.

The Lost Leader

I

Just for a handful of silver he left us,
    Just for a riband to stick in his coat—
Found the one gift of which fortune bereft us,
    Lost all the others she lets us devote;
They, with the gold to give, doled him out
        silver,
    So much was theirs who so little allowed:
How all our copper[1] had gone for his service!
    Rags—were they purple, his heart had
        been proud!
We that had loved him so, followed him,
        honoured him,
    Lived in his mild and magnificent eye,   10
Learned his great language, caught his clear
        accents,
    Made him our pattern to live and to die!
Shakespeare was of us, Milton was for us,
    Burns, Shelley, were with us,—they watch
        from their graves!
He alone breaks from the van and the freemen,
    —He alone sinks to the rear and the slaves!

II

We shall march prospering,—not thro' his
        presence;
    Songs may inspirit us,—not from his lyre;
Deeds will be done,—while he boasts his
        quiescence,
    Still bidding crouch whom the rest bade
        aspire: 20
Blot out his name, then, record one lost soul
        more,
    One task more declined, one more footpath
        untrod,
One more devils'-triumph and sorrow for
        angels,
    One wrong more to man, one more insult
        to God!
Life's night begins: let him never come back
        to us!
    There would be doubt, hesitation and
        pain,
Forced praise on our part—the glimmer of
        twilight,
    Never glad confident morning again!

[15] Lascar: Indian sailor.   [1] Copper: pennies; what little we have.

Best fight on well, for we taught him—strike
    gallantly,
30   Menace our heart ere we master his own;
Then let him receive the new knowledge and
    wait us,
      Pardoned in heaven, the first by the
      throne!

                                  1845

Garden Fancies

I—The Flower's Name

I

Here's the garden she walked across,
    Arm in my arm, such a short while since:
Hark, now I push its wicket, the moss
    Hinders the hinges and makes them wince!
She must have reached this shrub ere she
    turned,
    As back with that murmur the wicket
    swung;
For she laid the poor snail, my chance foot
    spurned,
    To feed and forget it the leaves among.

II

Down this side of the gravel-walk
    She went while her robe's edge brushed
10   the box:[1]
And here she paused in her gracious talk
    To point me a moth on the milk-white
    phlox.
Roses, ranged in valiant row,
    I will never think that she passed you by!
She loves you noble roses, I know;
    But yonder, see, where the rock-plants lie!

III

This flower she stopped at, finger on lip,
    Stooped over, in doubt, as settling its
    claim;

Till she gave me, with pride to make no slip,
    Its soft meandering Spanish name:
What a name! Was it love, or praise?
    Speech half-asleep or song half-awake?
I must learn Spanish, one of these days,
    Only for that slow sweet name's sake.

IV

Roses, if I live and do well,
    I may bring her, one of these days,
To fix you fast with as fine a spell,
    Fit you each with his Spanish phrase;
But do not detain me now; for she lingers
    There, like sunshine over the ground,
And ever I see her soft white fingers
    Searching after the bud she found.

V

Flower, you Spaniard, look that you grow not,
    Stay as you are and be loved for ever!
Bud, if I kiss you 't is that you blow not:
    Mind, the shut pink mouth opens never!
For while it pouts, her fingers wrestle,
    Twinkling the audacious leaves between,
Till round they turn and down they nestle—
    Is not the dear mark still to be seen?

VI

Where I find her not, beauties vanish;
    Whither I follow her, beauties flee;
Is there no method to tell her in Spanish
    June's twice June since she breathed it
    with me?
Come, bud, show me the least of her traces,
    Treasure my lady's lightest footfall!
—Ah, you may flout and turn up your faces—
    Roses, you are not so fair after all!

II—Sibrandus Schafnaburgensis[2]

I

Plague take all your pedants, say I!
    He who wrote what I hold in my hand,
Centuries back was so good as to die,
    Leaving this rubbish to cumber the land;
This, that was a book in its time,
    Printed on paper and bound in leather,
Last month in the white of a matin-prime[3]
    Just when the birds sang all together.

---

[1] Box: a shrub, used for hedges.
[2] The name of a character in a book Browning read in his childhood; appropriated here as a suitable name for a pedant.
[3] Matin-prime: both words refer to the hours at which certain prayers are to be said in the office of the church; while retaining these precise and somewhat recondite associations, Browning uses the phrase more loosely to refer to early morning in spring.

II

Into the garden I brought it to read,
    And under the arbute and laurustine[4]
Read it, so help me grace in my need,
    From title-page to closing line.
Chapter on chapter did I count,
    As a curious traveller counts Stonehenge;
Added up the mortal amount;
    And then proceeded to my revenge.

III

Yonder's a plum-tree with a crevice
    An owl would build in, were he but sage;
For a lap of moss, like a fine pont-levis[5]
    In a castle of the Middle Age,
Joins to a lip of gum, pure amber;
    When he'd be private, there might he
        spend
Hours alone in his lady's chamber:
    Into this crevice I dropped our friend.

IV

Splash, went he, as under he ducked,
    —At the bottom, I knew, rain-drippings
        stagnate:
Next, a handful of blossoms I plucked
    To bury him with, my bookshelf's
        magnate;
Then I went in-doors, brought out a loaf,
    Half a cheese, and a bottle of Chablis;
Lay on the grass and forgot the oaf
    Over a jolly chapter of Rabelais.

V

Now, this morning, betwixt the moss
    And gum that locked our friend in limbo,
A spider had spun his web across,
    And sat in the midst with arms akimbo:
So, I took pity, for learning's sake,
    And, *de profundis, accentibus lætis,*
Cantate![6] quoth I, as I got a rake;
    And up I fished his delectable treatise.

VI

Here you have it, dry in the sun,
    With all the binding all of a blister,

And great blue spots where the ink has run,
    And reddish streaks that wink and glister
O'er the page so beautifully yellow:
    Oh, well have the droppings played their
        tricks!
Did he guess how toadstools grow, this fellow?
    Here's one stuck in his chapter six!

VII

How did he like it when the live creatures
    Tickled and toused and browsed him all
        over,   50
And worm, slug, eft,[7] with serious features,
    Came in, each one, for his right of trover?[8]
—When the water-beetle with great blind deaf
        face
    Made her eggs the stately deposit
And the newt borrowed just so much of the
        preface
    As tiled in the top of his black wife's
        closet?

VIII

All that life and fun and romping,
    All that frisking and twisting and coupling,
While slowly our poor friend's leaves were
        swamping
    And clasps were cracking and covers
        suppling!   60
As if you had carried sour John Knox[9]
    To the play-house at Paris, Vienna or
        Munich,
Fastened him into a front-row box,
    And danced off the ballet with trousers and
        tunic.

IX

Come, old martyr! What, torment enough is it?
    Back to my room shall you take your sweet
        self.
Good-bye, mother-beetle; husband-eft, *sufficit!*
    See the snug niche I have made on my
        shelf!
A.'s book shall prop you up, B.'s shall cover
        you,
    Here's C.'s to be grave with, or D. to be
        gay,   70

---

[4] Arbute and laurustine: trees or shrubs that bear pink or white flowers.
[5] Pont levis: drawbridge.   [6] "From the depths, with joyous accents, sing!"
[7] Eft: a small semiaquatic salamander.
[8] Right of trover: a claim to the possession of property; strictly, an action at law to recover property wrongfully used.
[9] John Knox: sixteenth-century Scottish religious reformer.

And with E. on each side, and F. right over
 you,
 Dry-rot at ease till the Judgment-day!
 1844; 1845

Meeting at Night[1]

I

The gray sea and the long black land;
And the yellow half-moon large and low;
And the startled little waves that leap
In fiery ringlets from their sleep,
As I gain the cove with pushing prow,
And quench its speed i' the slushy sand.

II

Then a mile of warm sea-scented beach;
Three fields to cross till a farm appears;
A tap at the pane, the quick sharp scratch
10 And blue spurt of a lighted match,
And a voice less loud, thro' its joys and fears,
Than the two hearts beating each to each!

Parting at Morning

Round the cape of a sudden came the sea,
And the sun looked over the mountain's rim:
And straight was a path of gold for him,
And the need of a world of men for me.
1845

Pictor Ignotus[1]

Florence, 15–

I could have painted pictures like that youth's
 Ye praise so. How my soul springs up! No
 bar
Stayed me—ah, thought which saddens while it
 soothes!
 —Never did fate forbid me, star by star,
To outburst on your night with all my gift
 Of fires from God: nor would my flesh
 have shrunk
From seconding my soul, with eyes uplift
 And wide to heaven, or, straight like
 thunder, sunk
To the centre, of an instant; or around
10 Turned calmly and inquisitive, to scan
The license and the limit, space and bound,
 Allowed to truth made visible in man.

And, like that youth ye praise so, all I saw,
 Over the canvas could my hand have flung,
Each face obedient to its passion's law,
 Each passion clear proclaimed without a
 tongue;
Whether Hope rose at once in all the blood,
 A-tiptoe for the blessing of embrace,
Or Rapture drooped the eyes, as when her
 brood
 Pull down the nesting dove's heart to its
 place;
Or Confidence lit swift the forehead up,
 And locked the mouth fast, like a castle
 braved,—
O human faces, hath it spilt, my cup?
 What did ye give me that I have not saved?
Nor will I say I have not dreamed (how well!)
 Of going—I, in each new picture,—forth,
As, making new hearts beat and bosoms swell,
 To Pope or Kaiser, East, West, South, or
 North,
Bound for the calmly-satisfied great State,
 Or glad aspiring little burgh, it went,
Flowers cast upon the car which bore the
 freight,
 Through old streets named afresh from the
 event,
Till it reached home, where learned age should
 greet
 My face, and youth, the star not yet
 distinct
Above his hair, lie learning at my feet!—
 Oh, thus to live, I and my picture, linked
With love about, and praise, till life should
 end,
 And then not go to heaven, but linger
 here,
Here on my earth, earth's every man my
 friend,—
 The thought grew frightful, 't was so
 wildly dear!
But a voice changed it. Glimpses of such sights
 Have scared me, like the revels through a
 door
Of some strange house of idols at its rites!
 This world seemed not the world it was
 before:

<hr/>

[1] "Meeting at Night" and "Parting at Morning" were originally published under one title, "Night and Morning." Late in his life Browning said that both poems are spoken by a man; "him" in the third line of the second poem refers to the sun (DeVane, p. 178).
[1] Pictor Ignotus: painter unknown, a phrase Browning uses here as a name for a kind of painter who for one reason or another remains within the conventions of an established style in a period in which new styles are not only becoming popular but, at this moment in sixteenth-century Italian painting, are beginning permanently to displace the old.

Mixed with my loving trusting ones, there
    trooped
    . . . Who summoned those cold faces that
    begun
To press on me and judge me? Though I
    stooped
    Shrinking, as from the soldiery a nun,
They drew me forth, and spite of me . . .
    enough!
    These buy and sell our pictures, take and
    give,
Count them for garniture[2] and household-stuff,
    And where they live needs must our
    pictures live
And see their faces, listen to their prate,
    Partakers of their daily pettiness,
Discussed of—"This I love, or this I hate,
    This likes me more, and this affects me
    less!"
Wherefore I chose my portion. If at whiles
    My heart sinks, as monotonous I paint
These endless cloisters and eternal aisles
    With the same series, Virgin, Babe and
    Saint,
With the same cold calm beautiful regard,—
    At least no merchant traffics in my heart;
The sanctuary's gloom at least shall ward
    Vain tongues from where my pictures
    stand apart:
Only prayer breaks the silence of the shrine
    While, blackening in the daily candle-
    smoke,
They moulder on the damp wall's travertine,[3]
    'Mid echoes the light footstep never woke.
So, die my pictures! surely, gently die!
    O youth, men praise so—holds their praise
    its worth?
Blown harshly, keeps the trump its golden cry?
    Tastes sweet the water with such specks of
    earth?

                             1845

The Flight of the Duchess[1]

I

You're my friend:
    I was the man the Duke spoke to;
    I helped the Duchess to cast off his yoke, too;

So here's the tale from beginning to end,
My friend!

II

Ours is a great wild country:
    If you climb to our castle's top,
    I don't see where your eye can stop;
For when you've passed the cornfield country,
    Where vineyards leave off, flocks are packed,   10
And sheep-range leads to cattle-tract,
And cattle-tract to open-chase,
And open-chase to the very base
Of the mountain where, at a funeral pace,
Round about, solemn and slow,
One by one, row after row,
Up and up the pine-trees go,
So, like the black priests up, and so
Down the other side again
    To another greater, wilder country,   20
That's one vast red drear burnt-up plain,
Branched through and through with many a
    vein
Whence iron's dug, and copper's dealt;
    Look right, look left, look straight before,—
Beneath they mine, above they smelt,
    Copper-ore and iron-ore,
And forge and furnace mould and melt,
    And so on, more and ever more,
Till at the last, for a bounding belt,
    Comes the salt sand hoar of the great sea-
    shore,   30
—And the whole is our Duke's country.

III

I was born the day this present Duke was—
    (And O, says the song, ere I was old!) [2]
In the castle where the other Duke was—
    (When I was happy and young, not old!)
I in the kennel, he in the bower:
We are of like age to an hour.
My father was huntsman in that day;
Who has not heard my father say
That, when a boar was brought to bay,   40
Three times, four times out of five,
With his huntspear he'd contrive
To get the killing-place transfixed,
And pin him true, both eyes betwixt?
And that's why the old Duke would rather
He lost a salt-pit than my father,

---

[2] Garniture: decoration.   [3] Travertine: limestone.
[1] The germ of this poem is a Scots ballad, "The Gypsy Laddie," which Browning heard as a boy. The first nine sections of the poem were published in *Hood's Magazine* in April 1845; Browning completed the poem later in the year and published it in the seventh number of *Bells and Pomegranates* in November 1845.
[2] The "song" is Samuel Taylor Coleridge's "Youth and Age," first published in 1828.

And loved to have him ever in call;
That's why my father stood in the hall
When the old Duke brought his infant out
50   To show the people, and while they passed
The wondrous bantling round about,
    Was first to start at the outside blast
As the Kaiser's courier blew his horn
Just a month after the babe was born.
"And," quoth the Kaiser's courier, "since
The Duke has got an heir, our Prince
    Needs the Duke's self at his side:"
The Duke looked down and seemed to wince,
    But he thought of wars o'er the world wide,
60   Castles a-fire, men on their march,
The toppling tower, the crashing arch;
    And up he looked, and awhile he eyed
The row of crests and shields and banners
Of all achievements after all manners,
    And "ay," said the Duke with a surly pride.
    The more was his comfort when he died
At next year's end, in a velvet suit,
With a gilt glove on his hand, his foot
In a silken shoe for a leather boot,
70   Petticoated like a herald,
      In a chamber next to an ante-room,
      Where he breathed the breath of page and
        groom,
      What he called stink, and they, perfume:
—They should have set him on red Berold
Mad with pride, like fire to manage!
They should have got his cheek fresh tannage
Such a day as to-day in the merry sunshine!
Had they stuck on his fist a rough-foot merlin![3]
(Hark, the wind's on the heath at its game!
80   Oh for a noble falcon-lanner[4]
To flap each broad wing like a banner,
And turn in the wind, and dance like flame!)
Had they broached a white-beer[5] cask from
    Berlin
—Or if you incline to prescribe mere wine
Put to his lips, when they saw him pine,
A cup of our own Moldavia fine,
Cotnar for instance, green as May sorrel
And ropy with sweet,—we shall not quarrel.

IV

So, at home, the sick tall yellow Duchess
90   Was left with the infant in her clutches,
She being the daughter of God knows who:
    And now was the time to revisit her tribe.

Abroad and afar they went, the two,
    And let our people rail and gibe
At the empty hall and extinguished fire,
    As loud as we liked, but ever in vain,
Till after long years we had our desire,
    And back came the Duke and his mother
    again.

V

And he came back the pertest little ape
That ever affronted human shape;
Full of his travel, struck at himself.
    You'd say, he despised our bluff old ways?
—Not he! For in Paris they told the elf
    Our rough North land was the Land of Lays,
    The one good thing left in evil days;
Since the Mid-Age was the Heroic Time,
    And only in wild nooks like ours
Could you taste of it yet as in its prime,
    And see true castles, with proper towers,
Young-hearted women, old-minded men,
And manners now as manners were then.
So, all that the old Dukes had been, without
    knowing it,
This Duke would fain know he was, without
    being it;
'T was not for the joy's self, but the joy of his
    showing it,
Nor for the pride's self, but the pride of our
    seeing it,
He revived all usages thoroughly worn-out,
The souls of them fumed-forth, the hearts of
    them torn-out:
And chief in the chase his neck he perilled
On a lathy[6] horse, all legs and length,
With blood for bone, all speed, no strength;
—They should have set him on red Berold
With the red eye slow consuming in fire,
And the thin stiff ear like an abbey-spire!

VI

Well, such as he was, he must marry, we heard:
And out of a convent, at the word,
Came the lady, in time of spring.
—Oh, old thoughts they cling, they cling!
That day, I know, with a dozen oaths
I clad myself in thick hunting-clothes
Fit for the chase of urochs or buffle[7]
In winter-time when you need to muffle.

---

[3] Rough-foot merlin: a species of hawk used in hunting.
[4] Falcon-lanner: another species of hawk used in hunting.
[5] White-beer: Browning perhaps refers to a mixture of flour, milk, and ale or beer.
[6] Lathy: thin, narrow-boned   [7] Urochs or buffle: wild bulls or buffalo.

But the Duke had a mind we should cut a
    figure,
  And so we saw the lady arrive:
My friend, I have seen a white crane bigger!
  She was the smallest lady alive,
Made in a piece of nature's madness,
Too small, almost, for the life and gladness
  That over-filled her, as some hive
Out of the bears' reach on the high trees
Is crowded with its safe merry bees:
In truth, she was not hard to please!
Up she looked, down she looked, round at the
    mead,[8]
Straight at the castle, that's best indeed
To look at from outside the walls:
As for us, styled the "serfs and thralls,"
She as much thanked me as if she had said it,
  (With her eyes, do you understand?)
Because I patted her horse while I led it;
  And Max, who rode on her other hand,
Said, no bird flew past but she inquired
What its true name was, nor ever seemed
    tired—
If that was an eagle she saw hover,
And the green and grey bird on the field was
    the plover.
When suddenly appeared the Duke:
  And as down she sprung, the small foot
    pointed
On to my hand,—as with a rebuke,
  And as if his backbone were not jointed,
The Duke stepped rather aside than forward,
  And welcomed her with his grandest smile;
  And, mind you, his mother all the while
Chilled in the rear, like a wind to Nor'ward;
And up, like a weary yawn, with its pullies
Went, in a shriek, the rusty portcullis;[9]
And, like a glad sky the north-wind sullies,
The lady's face stopped its play,
As if her first hair had grown grey;
For such things must begin some one day.

VII

In a day or two she was well again;
As who should say, "You labour in vain!
This is all a jest against God, who meant
I should ever be, as I am, content
And glad in his sight; therefore, glad I will
    be."
So, smiling as at first went she.

VIII

She was active, stirring, all fire—
Could not rest, could not tire—

To a stone she might have given life!
  (I myself loved once, in my day)
—For a shepherd's, miner's, huntsman's wife,
  (I had a wife, I know what I say)
Never in all the world such an one!   180
And here was plenty to be done,
And she that could do it, great or small,
She was to do nothing at all.
There was already this man in his post,
  This in his station, and that in his office,
And the Duke's plan admitted a wife, at most,
  To meet his eye, with the other trophies,
Now outside the hall, now in it,
  To sit thus, stand thus, see and be seen,
At the proper place in the proper minute,   190
  And die away the life between.
And it was amusing enough, each infraction
  Of rule— (but for after-sadness that came)
To hear the consummate self-satisfaction
  With which the young Duke and the old
    dame
Would let her advise, and criticise,
And, being a fool, instruct the wise,
  And, child-like, parcel out praise or blame:
They bore it all in complacent guise,
As though an artificer, after contriving   200
A wheel-work image as if it were living,
Should find with delight it could motion to
    strike him!
So found the Duke, and his mother like him:
The lady hardly got a rebuff—
That had not been contemptuous enough,
With his cursed smirk, as he nodded applause,
And kept off the old mother-cat's claws.

IX

So, the little lady grew silent and thin,
  Paling and ever paling,
As the way is with a hid chagrin;   210
  And the Duke perceived that she was ailing,
And said in his heart, " 'Tis done to spite me,
But I shall find in my power to right me!"
Don't swear, friend! The old one, many a year,
Is in hell, and the Duke's self . . . you shall
    hear.

X

Well, early in autumn, at first winter-warning,
When the stag had to break with his foot, of a
    morning,
A drinking-hole out of the fresh tender ice
That covered the pond till the sun, in a trice,

---

[8] Mead: meadow.   [9] Portcullis: an iron grating over the gateway.

220 Loosening it, let out a ripple of gold,
  And another and another, and faster and
    faster,
Till, dimpling to blindness, the wide water
    rolled:
  Then it so chanced that the Duke our master
Asked himself what were the pleasures in
    season,
  And found, since the calendar bade him be
    hearty,
He should do the Middle Age no treason
  In resolving on a hunting-party.
Always provided, old books showed the way of
    it!
  What meant old poets by their strictures?
230 And when old poets had said their say of it,
  How taught old painters in their pictures?
We must revert to the proper channels,
Workings in tapestry, paintings on panels,
And gather up woodcraft's authentic
    traditions:
Here was food for our various ambitions,
As on each case, exactly stated—
  To encourage your dog, now, the properest
    chirrup,
  Or best prayer to Saint Hubert[10] on mount-
    ing your stirrup—
We of the household took thought and
    debated.
Blessed was he whose back ached with the
240   jerkin[11]
His sire was wont to do forest-work in;
Blesseder he who nobly sunk "ohs"
And "ahs" while he tugged on his grandsire's
    trunk-hose;[12]
What signified hats if they had no rims on,
  Each slouching before and behind like the
    scallop,
  And able to serve at sea for a shallop,
Loaded with lacquer and looped with crimson?
So that the deer now, to make a short rhyme
    on 't,
  What with our Venerers, Prickers and
    Verderers,[13]
  Might hope for real hunters at length and
250   not murderers,
And oh the Duke's tailor, he had a hot time
    on 't!

XI
Now you must know that when the first
    dizziness
  Of flap-hats and buff-coats and jack-boots
    subsided,
  The Duke put this question, "The Duke's
    part provided,
Had not the Duchess some share in the
    business?"
For out of the mouth of two or three witnesses
Did he establish all fit-or-unfitnesses:
And, after much laying of heads together,
Somebody's cap got a notable feather
By the announcement with proper unction
That he had discovered the lady's function;
Since ancient authors gave this tenet,
"When horns wind a mort[14] and the deer is at
    siege,
Let the dame of the castle prick forth on her
    jennet,[15]
  And, with water to wash the hands of her
    liege
In a clean ewer with a fair towelling,
Let her preside at the disemboweling."
Now, my friend, if you had so little religion
  As to catch a hawk, some falcon-lanner,
  And thrust her broad wings like a banner
Into a coop for a vulgar pigeon;
And if day by day and week by week
  You cut her claws, and sealed her eyes,
  And clipped her wings, and tied her beak,
    Would it cause you any great surprise
If, when you decided to give her an airing,
You found she needed a little preparing?
—I say, should you be such a curmudgeon,
If she clung to the perch, as to take it in
    dudgeon?
Yet when the Duke to his lady signified,
Just a day before, as he judged most dignified,
In what a pleasure she was to participate,—
  And, instead of leaping wide in flashes,
  Her eyes just lifted their long lashes,
As if pressed by fatigue even he could not
    dissipate,
And duly acknowledged the Duke's
    forethought,
But spoke of her health, if her health were
    worth aught,
Of the weight by day and the watch by night,

---

[10] Saint Hubert: the patron saint of hunters.   [11] Jerkin: a sleeveless jacket.
[12] Trunk-hose: short full breeches reaching to mid-thigh.
[13] Venerers, Prickers and Verderers: huntsmen, horsemen, and those whose task is to preserve
  the venison.
[14] Wind a mort: sound the horn when the quarry dies.
[15] Prick forth on her jennet: ride out on a small horse.

And much wrong now that used to be right,
So, thanking him, declined the hunting,—
Was conduct ever more affronting?
With all the ceremony settled—
  With the towel ready, and the sewer[16]
  Polishing up his oldest ewer,
  And the jennet pitched upon, a piebald,
  Black-barred, cream-coated and pink
    eyeballed,—
No wonder if the Duke was nettled!
And when she persisted nevertheless,—
Well, I suppose here's the time to confess
That there ran half round our lady's chamber
A balcony none of the hardest to clamber;
And that Jacynth the tire-woman,[17] ready in
  waiting,
Stayed in call outside, what need of relating?
And since Jacynth was like a June rose, why, a
  fervent
Adorer of Jacynth of course was your servant;
And if she had the habit to peep through the
  casement,
  How could I keep at any vast distance?
  And so, as I say, on the lady's persistence,
The Duke, dumb-stricken with amazement,
Stood for a while in a sultry smother,
  And then, with a smile that partook of the
    awful,
Turned her over to his yellow mother
  To learn what was held decorous and lawful;
And the mother smelt blood with a cat-like
  instinct,
As her cheek quick whitened thro' all its
  quince-tinct.[18]
Oh, but the lady heard the whole truth at
  once!
  What meant she?—Who was she?—Her duty
  and station,
The wisdom of age and the folly of youth, at
  once,
  Its decent regard and its fitting relation—
In brief, my friend, set all the devils in hell
  free
And turn them out to carouse in a belfry
And treat the priests to a fifty-part canon,[19]
And then you may guess how that tongue of
  hers ran on!
Well, somehow or other it ended at last
And, licking her whiskers, out she passed;

And after her,—making (he hoped) a face
  Like Emperor Nero or Sultan Saladin,
Stalked the Duke's self with the austere grace
  Of ancient hero or modern paladin,
From door to staircase—oh such a solemn
Unbending of the vertebral column!

XII

However, at sunrise our company mustered;
  And here was the huntsman bidding
    unkennel,
And there 'neath his bonnet the pricker
  blustered,
  With feather dank as a bough of wet fennel;
For the court-yard walls were filled with fog
You might have cut as an axe chops a log—
Like so much wool for colour and bulkiness;
And out rode the Duke in a perfect sulkiness,
Since, before breakfast, a man feels but
  queasily,
  And a sinking at the lower abdomen
  Begins the day with indifferent omen.
And lo, as he looked around uneasily,
The sun ploughed the fog up and drove it
  asunder
This way and that from the valley under;
  And, looking through the court-yard arch,
  Down in the valley, what should meet him
  But a troop of Gipsies on their march?
No doubt with the annual gifts to greet him.

XIII

Now, in your land, Gipsies reach you, only
  After reaching all lands beside;
North they go, South they go, trooping or
  loncly,
  And still, as they travel far and wide,
Catch they and keep now a trace here, a trace
  there,
That puts you in mind of place here, a place
  there.
But with us, I believe they rise out of the
  ground,
And nowhere else, I take it, are found
With the earth-tint yet so freshly embrowned:
Born, no doubt, like insects which breed on
The very fruit they are meant to feed on.
For the earth—not a use to which they don't
  turn it,

---

[16] Sewer: a member of the staff of a medieval household responsible for serving at table.
[17] Tire-woman: maid. [18] Quince-tinct: yellow tincture.
[19] Fifty-part canon: a canon is the repetition of a musical phrase in another key; a fifty-part canon would be, as Browning said in a remark on this line, "a notable peal" (E. Berdoe, *The Browning Encyclopedia* [1902], p. 180).

The ore that grows in the mountain's womb,
  Or the sand in the pits like a honeycomb,
They sift and soften it, bake it and burn it—
Whether they weld you, for instance, a snaffle[20]
With side-bars never a brute can baffle;
Or a lock that's a puzzle of wards within wards;
Or, if your colt's fore-foot inclines to curve
    inwards,
Horseshoes they hammer which turn on a
    swivel
370 And won't allow the hoof to shrivel.
Then they cast bells like the shell of the
    winkle[21]
That keep a stout heart in the ram with their
    tinkle;
But the sand—they pinch and pound it like
    otters;
Commend me to Gipsy glass-makers and
    potters!
Glasses they'll blow you, crystal-clear,
Where just a faint cloud of rose shall appear,
As if in pure water you dropped and let die
A bruised black-blooded mulberry;
And that other sort, their crowning pride,
380 With long white threads distinct inside,
Like the lake-flower's fibrous roots which
    dangle
Loose such a length and never tangle,
Where the bold sword-lily cuts the clear waters,
And the cup-lily couches with all the white
    daughters:
Such are the works they put their hand to,
The uses they turn and twist iron and sand to.
And these made the troop, which our Duke
    saw sally
Toward his castle from out of the valley,
Men and women, like new-hatched spiders,
390 Come out with the morning to greet our riders.
And up they wound till they reached the ditch,
Whereat all stopped save one, a witch
That I knew, as she hobbled from the group,
By her gait directly and her stoop,
I, whom Jacynth was used to importune
To let that same witch tell us our fortune.
The oldest Gipsy then above ground;
And, sure as the autumn season came round,
She paid us a visit for profit or pastime,
400 And every time, as she swore, for the last time.
And presently she was seen to sidle
Up to the Duke till she touched his bridle,
So that the horse of a sudden reared up
As under its nose the old witch peered up

With her worn-out eyes, or rather eye-holes
  Of no use now but to gather brine,
  And began a kind of level whine
Such as they used to sing to their viols
When their ditties they go grinding
Up and down with nobody minding:
And then, as of old, at the end of the humming
Her usual presents were forthcoming
—A dog-whistle blowing the fiercest of trebles,
(Just a sea-shore stone holding a dozen fine
    pebbles,)
Or a porcelain mouth-piece to screw on a pipe-
    end,—
And so she awaited her annual stipend.
But this time, the Duke would scarcely vouch-
    safe
  A word in reply; and in vain she felt
  With twitching fingers at her belt
  For the purse of sleek pine-martin[22] pelt,
Ready to put what he gave in her pouch
    safe,—
Till, either to quicken his apprehension,
Or possibly with an after-intention,
She was come, she said, to pay her duty
To the new Duchess, the youthful beauty.
No sooner had she named his lady,
Than a shine lit up the face so shady,
And its smirk returned with a novel
    meaning—
For it struck him, the babe just wanted
    weaning;
If one gave her a taste of what life was and
    sorrow,
She, foolish to-day, would be wiser to-morrow;
And who so fit a teacher of trouble
As this sordid crone bent well-nigh double?
So, glancing at her wolf-skin vesture,
  (If such it was, for they grow so hirsute
  That their own fleece serves for natural
    fur-suit)
He was contrasting, 't was plain from his
    gesture,
The life of the lady so flower-like and delicate
With the loathsome squalor of this helicat.[23]
I, in brief, was the man the Duke beckoned
  From out of the throng, and while I drew
    near
He told the crone—as I since have reckoned
  By the way he bent and spoke into her ear
With circumspection and mystery—
The main of the lady's history,
Her frowardness and ingratitude:

---

[20] Snaffle: bridle bit.   [21] Winkle: a marine snail.
[22] Pine-martin: marten.   [23] Helicat: hog.

And for all the crone's submissive attitude
I could see round her mouth the loose plaits
    tightening,
And her brow with assenting intelligence
    brightening,
    As though she engaged with hearty goodwill
    Whatever he now might enjoin to fulfil,
And promised the lady a thorough frightening.
And so, just giving her a glimpse
Of a purse, with the air of a man who imps[24]
The wing of the hawk that shall fetch the
    hernshaw,[25]
    He bade me take the Gipsy mother
    And set her telling some story or other
Of hill or dale, oak-wood or fernshaw,[26]
To wile away a weary hour
For the lady left alone in her bower,
Whose mind and body craved exertion
And yet shrank from all better diversion.

    XIV

Then clapping heel to his horse, the mere
    curveter,[27]
    Out rode the Duke, and after his hollo
Horses and hounds swept, huntsman and
    servitor,
    And back I turned and bade the crone
    follow.
And what makes me confident what's to be
    told you
    Had all along been of this crone's devising,
Is, that, on looking round sharply, behold you,
    There was a novelty quick as surprising:
    For first, she had shot up a full head in stature,
    And her step kept pace with mine nor
    faltered,
As if age had foregone its usurpature,
    And the ignoble mien was wholly altered,
And the face looked quite of another nature,
And the change reached too, whatever the
    change meant,
Her shaggy wolf-skin cloak's arrangement:
For where its tatters hung loose like sedges,[28]
Gold coins were glittering on the edges,
Like the band-roll strung with tomans[29]
Which proves the veil a Persian woman's:
And under her brow, like a snail's horns newly
    Come out as after the rain he paces,
Two unmistakeable eye-points duly
    Live and aware looked out of their places.

So, we went and found Jacynth at the entry
Of the lady's chamber standing sentry;
I told the command and produced my
    companion,
And Jacynth rejoiced to admit any one,
For since last night, by the same token,
Not a single word had the lady spoken:
They went in both to the presence together,
While I in the balcony watched the weather.

    XV

And now, what took place at the very first of
    all,
I cannot tell, as I never could learn it:
Jacynth constantly wished a curse to fall
On that little head of hers and burn it
If she knew how she came to drop so soundly
    Asleep of a sudden and there continue
The whole time sleeping as profoundly
    As one of the boars my father would pin you
'Twixt the eyes where life holds garrison,
—Jacynth forgive me the comparison!
But where I begin my own narration
Is a little after I took my station
To breathe the fresh air from the balcony,
And, having in those days a falcon eye,
To follow the hunt thro' the open country,
    From where the bushes thinlier crested
The hillocks, to a plain where's not one tree.
    When, in a moment, my ear was arrested
By—was it singing, or was it saying,
Or a strange musical instrument playing
In the chamber?—and to be certain,
I pushed the lattice, pulled the curtain,
And there lay Jacynth asleep,
Yet as if a watch she tried to keep,
In a rosy sleep along the floor
With her head against the door;
While in the midst, on the seat of state,
Was a queen—the Gipsy woman late,
With head and face downbent
On the lady's head and face intent:
For, coiled at her feet like a child at ease,
The lady sat between her knees,
And o'er them the lady's clasped hands met,
And on those hands her chin was set,
And her upturned face met the face of the
    crone
Wherein the eyes had grown and grown
As if she could double and quadruple

[24] Imps: grafts a feather into the wing of a hawk.
[25] Hernshaw: heron.   [26] Fernshaw: a thicket of fern.
[27] Curveter: a curvet is a leap in which momentarily all four legs of the horse are off the
ground.
[28] Sedges: marsh plants.   [29] Tomans: Persian gold coins.

At pleasure the play of either pupil
  —Very like, by her hands' slow fanning,
As up and down like a gor-crow's[30] flappers
They moved to measure, or bell-clappers.
  I said "Is it blessing, is it banning,
Do they applaud you or burlesque you—
  Those hands and fingers with no flesh on?"
But, just as I thought to spring in to the rescue,
  At once I was stopped by the lady's expression:

540 For it was life her eyes were drinking
From the crone's wide pair above unwinking,
  —Life's pure fire received without shrinking,
Into the heart and breast whose heaving
Told you no single drop they were leaving,
  —Life, that filling her, passed redundant
    Into her very hair, back swerving
Over each shoulder, loose and abundant,
    As her head thrown back showed the white
      throat curving;
And the very tresses shared in the pleasure,
550 Moving to the mystic measure,
Bounding as the bosom bounded.
I stopped short, more and more confounded,
As still her cheeks burned and eyes glistened,
As she listened and she listened:
When all at once a hand detained me,
The selfsame contagion gained me,
And I kept time to the wondrous chime,
Making out words and prose and rhyme,
Till it seemed that the music furled
560   Its wings like a task fulfilled, and dropped
  From under the words it first had propped,
And left them midway in the world:
Word took word as hand takes hand,
I could hear at last, and understand,
And when I held the unbroken thread,
The Gipsy said:—

"And so at last we find my tribe.
  And so I set thee in the midst,
And to one and all of them describe
570   What thou saidst and what thou didst,
Our long and terrible journey through,
And all thou art ready to say and do
In the trials that remain:
I trace them the vein and the other vein
That meet on thy brow and part again,
Making our rapid mystic mark;
  And I bid my people prove and probe

Each eye's profound and glorious globe
Till they detect the kindred spark
In those depths so dear and dark,   58
Like the spots that snap and burst and flee,
Circling over the midnight sea.
And on that round young cheek of thine
  I make them recognize the tinge,
As when of the costly scarlet wine
  They drip so much as will impinge
And spread in a thinnest scale afloat
One thick gold drop from the olive's coat
Over a silver plate whose sheen
Still thro' the mixture shall be seen.   59
For so I prove thee, to one and all,
  Fit, when my people ope their breast,
To see the sign, and hear the call,
  And take the vow, and stand the test
  Which adds one more child to the rest—
When the breast is bare and the arms are wide,
And the world is left outside.
For there is probation to decree,
And many and long must the trials be
Thou shalt victoriously endure,   6
If that brow is true and those eyes are sure;
Like a jewel-finder's fierce assay
  Of the prize he dug from its mountain-
    tomb—
Let once the vindicating ray
  Leap out amid the anxious gloom,
And steel and fire have done their part
And the prize falls on its finder's heart;
So, trial after trial past,
Wilt thou fall at the very last
Breathless, half in trance   6
With the thrill of the great deliverance,
  Into our arms for evermore;
And thou shalt know, those arms once curled
  About thee, what we knew before,
How love is the only good in the world.[31]
Henceforth be loved as heart can love,
Or brain devise, or hand approve!
Stand up, look below,
It is our life at thy feet we throw
To step with into light and joy;   6
Not a power of life but we employ
To satisfy thy nature's want;
Art thou the tree that props the plant,
Or the climbing plant that seeks the tree—
Canst thou help us, must we help thee?
If any two creatures grew into one,

[30] Gor-crow: carrion crow.
[31] Browning sent "The Flight of the Duchess" to Elizabeth Barrett for her criticism before
he published the poem; undoubtedly the gypsy's appeal to the duchess rehearses the urgency of
Browning's appeal, later in 1845, that Elizabeth leave her seclusion and marry him.

They would do more than the world has done:
Though each apart were never so weak,
Ye vainly through the world should seek
For the knowledge and the might
Which in such union grew their right:
So, to approach at least that end,
And blend,—as much as may be, blend
Thee with us or us with thee,—
As climbing plant or propping tree,
Shall some one deck thee, over and down
   Up and about, with blossoms and leaves?
Fix his heart's fruit for thy garland-crown,
   Cling with his soul as the gourd-vine cleaves,
Die on thy boughs and disappear
While not a leaf of thine is sere?
Or is the other fate in store,
And art thou fitted to adore,
To give thy wondrous self away,
And take a stronger nature's sway?
I foresee and could foretell
Thy future portion, sure and well:
But those passionate eyes speak true, speak
   true,
Let them say what thou shalt do!
Only be sure thy daily life,
In its peace or in its strife,
Never shall be unobserved;
   We pursue thy whole career,
   And hope for it, or doubt, or fear,—
Lo, hast thou kept thy path or swerved,
We are beside thee in all thy ways,
With our blame, with our praise,
Our shame to feel, our pride to show,
Glad, angry—but indifferent, no!
Whether it be thy lot to go,
For the good of us all, where the haters meet
In the crowded city's horrible street;
Or thou step alone through the morass
Where never sound yet was
Save the dry quick clap of the stork's bill,
For the air is still, and the water still,
When the blue breast of the dipping coot
Dives under, and all is mute.
So, at the last shall come old age,
Decrepit as befits that stage;
How else wouldst thou retire apart
With the hoarded memories of thy heart,
And gather all to the very least
Of the fragments of life's earlier feast,
Let fall through eagerness to find
The crowning dainties yet behind?
Ponder on the entire past
Laid together thus at last,
When the twilight helps to fuse
The first fresh with the faded hues,

And the outline of the whole,
As round eve's shades their framework roll,
Grandly fronts for once thy soul.
And then as, 'mid the dark, a gleam
   Of yet another morning breaks,
And like the hand which ends a dream,
Death, with the might of his sunbeam,
   Touches the flesh and the soul awakes,
Then——"
   Ay, then indeed something would happen!   690
   But what? For here her voice changed like
   a bird's;
   There grew more of the music and less of
   the words;
Had Jacynth only been by me to clap pen
To paper and put you down every syllable
   With those clever clerkly fingers,
   All I've forgotten as well as what lingers
In this old brain of mine that's but ill able
To give you even this poor version
   Of the speech I spoil, as it were, with
     stammering
   —More fault of those who had the
     hammering   700
   Of prosody into me and syntax,
   And did it, not with hobnails but tintacks!
But to return from this excursion,—
Just, do you mark, when the song was sweetest,
The peace most deep and the charm
   completest,
There came, shall I say, a snap—
   And the charm vanished!
   And my sense returned, so strangely
   banished,
And, starting as from a nap,
I knew the crone was bewitching my lady,   710
With Jacynth asleep; and but one spring
   made I
Down from the casement, round to the portal,
   Another minute and I had entered,—
When the door opened, and more than mortal
   Stood, with a face where to my mind centred
All beauties I ever saw or shall see,
The Duchess: I stopped as if struck by palsy.
She was so different, happy and beautiful,
   I felt at once that all was best,
   And that I had nothing to do, for the rest,   720
But wait her commands, obey and be dutiful.
Not that, in fact, there was any commanding;
   I saw the glory of her eye,
And the brow's height and the breast's
     expanding
   And I was hers to live or to die.
As for finding what she wanted,
You know God Almighty granted

Such little signs should serve wild creatures
    To tell one another all their desires,
730   So that each knows what its friend requires,
And does its bidding without teachers.
I preceded her; the crone
Followed silent and alone;
I spoke to her, but she merely jabbered
    In the old style; both her eyes had slunk
    Back to their pits; her stature shrunk;
    In short, the soul in its body sunk
Like a blade sent home to its scabbard.
We descended, I preceding;
740 Crossed the court with nobody heeding;
All the world was at the chase,
The courtyard like a desert-place,
The stable emptied of its small fry;
I saddled myself the very palfrey
I remember patting while it carried her,
The day she arrived and the Duke married her.
And, do you know, though it's easy deceiving
Oneself in such matters, I can't help believing
The lady had not forgotten it either,
750 And knew the poor devil so much beneath her
Would have been only too glad for her service
To dance on hot ploughshares like a Turk
    dervise,[32]
But, unable to pay proper duty where owing it,
Was reduced to that pitiful method of
    showing it:
For though the moment I began setting
His saddle on my own nag of Berold's
    begetting,
(Not that I meant to be obtrusive)
    She stopped me, while his rug was shifting,
    By a single rapid finger's lifting,
760 And, with a gesture kind but conclusive,
And a little shake of the head, refused me,—
I say, although she never used me,
Yet when she was mounted, the Gipsy behind
    her,
And I ventured to remind her,
I suppose with a voice of less steadiness
    Than usual, for my feeling exceeded me,
—Something to the effect that I was in
    readiness
    Whenever God should please she needed
    me,—
Then, do you know, her face looked down
    on me
770 With a look that placed a crown on me,
And she felt in her bosom,—mark, her bosom—

And, as a flower-tree drops its blossom,
Dropped me . . . ah, had it been a purse
Of silver, my friend, or gold that's worse,
Why, you see, as soon as I found myself
    So understood,—that a true heart so may
    gain
    Such a reward,—I should have gone home
    again,
Kissed Jacynth, and soberly drowned myself!
It was a little plait of hair
    Such as friends in a convent make
    To wear, each for the other's sake,—
This, see, which at my breast I wear,
Ever did (rather to Jacynth's grudgment),
And ever shall, till the Day of Judgment.
And then,—and then,—to cut short,—this is
    idle,
    These are feelings it is not good to foster,—
I pushed the gate wide, she shook the bridle,
    And the palfrey bounded,—and so we lost
    her.

XVI
When the liquor's out why clink the cannikin?
I did think to describe you the panic in
The redoubtable breast of our master the
    mannikin,
And what was the pitch of his mother's
    yellowness,
    How she turned as a shark to snap the
    sparerib
    Clean off, sailors say, from a pearl-diving
    Carib,
When she heard, what she called the flight of
    the feloness
—But it seems such child's play,
What they said and did with the lady away!
And to dance on, when we've lost the music,
Always made me—and no doubt makes you—
    sick.
Nay, to my mind, the world's face looked so
    stern
As that sweet form disappeared through the
    postern,[33]
She that kept it in constant good humour,
It ought to have stopped; there seemed nothing
    to do more.
But the world thought otherwise and went on,
And my head's one that its spite was spent on:
Thirty years are fled since that morning,
And with them all my head's adorning.

[32] Dervise: dervish, a member of a Muslim sect whose rituals involve dances that lead to a
trance.
[33] Postern: a back gate.

Nor did the old Duchess die outright,
As you expect, of suppressed spite,
The natural end of every adder
Not suffered to empty its poison-bladder:
But she and her son agreed, I take it,
That no one should touch on the story to wake
    it,
For the wound in the Duke's pride rankled
    fiery,
So, they made no search and small inquiry—
And when fresh Gipsies have paid us a visit,
    I've
Noticed the couple were never inquisitive,
But told them they're folks the Duke don't
    want here,
And bade them make haste and cross the
    frontier.
Brief, the Duchess was gone and the Duke was
    glad of it,
    And the old one was in the young one's
        stead,
    And took, in her place, the household's head,
And a blessed time the household had of it!
And were I not, as a man may say, cautious
How I trench,[34] more than needs, on the
    nauseous,
I could favour you with sundry touches
Of the paint-smutches with which the Duchess
Heightened the mellowness of her cheek's yel-
    lowness
(To get on faster) until at last her
Cheek grew to be one master-plaster
Of mucus and fucus from mere use of ceruse:[35]
In short, she grew from scalp to udder
Just the object to make you shudder.

XVII
You're my friend—
What a thing friendship is, world without end!
How it gives the heart and soul a stir-up
    As if somebody broached you a glorious
        runlet,
    And poured out, all lovelily, sparklingly,
        sunlit,
Our green Moldavia, the streaky syrup,
Cotnar as old as the time of the Druids—
Friendship may match with that monarch of
    fluids;
Each supples a dry brain, fills you its ins-and-
    outs,

Gives your life's hour-glass a shake when the
    thin sand doubts
Whether to run on or stop short, and
    guarantees
Age is not all made of stark sloth and arrant
    ease.
I have seen my little lady once more,
    Jacynth, the Gipsy, Berold, and the rest of it,
For to me spoke the Duke, as I told you before;
    I always wanted to make a clean breast of it:
And now it is made—why, my heart's blood,
    that went trickle,   850
    Trickle, but anon, in such muddy driblets,
Is pumped up brisk now, through the main
    ventricle,
    And genially floats me about the giblets.[36]
I'll tell you what I intend to do:
I must see this fellow his sad life through—
He is our Duke, after all,
And I, as he says, but a serf and thrall.
My father was born here, and I inherit
    His fame, a chain he bound his son with;
Could I pay in a lump I should prefer it,   860
    But there's no mine to blow up and get done
        with:
So, I must stay till the end of the chapter.
For, as to our middle-age-manners-adapter,
Be it a thing to be glad on or sorry on,
Some day or other, his head in a morion[37]
And breast in a hauberk,[38] his heels he'll kick
    up,
Slain by an onslaught fierce of hiccup.
And then, when red doth the sword of our
    Duke rust,
And its leathern sheath lie o'ergrown with a
    blue crust,
Then I shall scrape together my earnings;   870
    For, you see, in the churchyard Jacynth
        reposes,
    And our children all went the way of the
        roses:
It's a long lane that knows no turnings.
One needs but little tackle to travel in;
    So, just one stout cloak shall I indue:
And for a staff, what beats the javelin
    With which his boars my father pinned you?
And then, for a purpose you shall hear
    presently,
    Taking some Cotnar, a tight plump skinful,

---

[34] Trench: encroach.   [35] Ceruse: a cosmetic containing white lead.
[36] Giblets: entrails, specifically, the viscera of fowl.
[37] Morion: a helmet with no visor.   [38] Hauberk: a tunic of chain mail.

880   I shall go journeying, who but I, pleasantly!
   Sorrow is vain and despondency sinful.
What's a man's age? He must hurry more, that's
   all;
    Cram in a day, what his youth took a year
    to hold:
    When we mind labour, then only, we're too
    old—
What age had Methusalem when he begat
   Saul?
And at last, as its haven some buffeted ship
   sees,
   (Come all the way from the north-parts with
   sperm oil)
I hope to get safely out of the turmoil
And arrive one day at the land of the Gipsies,
890   And find my lady, or hear the last news of her
From some old thief and son of Lucifer,
His forehead chapleted green with wreathy
   hop,
Sunburned all over like an Æthiop.
And when my Cotnar begins to operate
And the tongue of the rogue to run at a proper
   rate,
And our wine-skin, tight once, shows each
   flaccid dent,
I shall drop in with—as if by accident—
"You never knew, then, how it all ended,
What fortune good or bad attended
900   The little lady your Queen befriended?"
—And when that's told me, what's remaining?
This world's too hard for my explaining.
The same wise judge of matters equine
   Who still preferred some slim four-year-old
   To the big-boned stock of mighty Berold,
And, for strong Cotnar, drank French weak
   wine,
He also must be such a lady's scorner!
   Smooth Jacob still robs homely Esau:
   Now up, now down, the world's one see-saw.
910   —So, I shall find out some snug corner
Under a hedge, like Orson[39] the wood-knight,
Turn myself round and bid the world good
   night;
And sleep a sound sleep till the trumpet's
   blowing
Wakes me (unless priests cheat us laymen)

To a world where will be no further throwing
Pearls before swine that can't value them.
   Amen!

                      1845

Love Among the Ruins[1]

I

Where the quiet-colored end of evening smiles
   Miles and miles
On the solitary pastures where our sheep
   Half-asleep
Tinkle homeward thro' the twilight, stray or
   stop
   As they crop—
Was the site once of a city great and gay,
   (So they say)
Of our country's very capital, its prince
   Ages since
Held his court in, gathered councils, wielding
   far
   Peace or war.

II

Now,—the country does not even boast a tree,
   As you see,
To distinguish slopes of verdure, certain rills
   From the hills
Intersect and give a name to, (else they run
   Into one)
Where the domed and daring palace shot its
   spires
   Up like fires
O'er the hundred-gated circuit of a wall
   Bounding all,
Made of marble, men might march on nor be
   pressed,
   Twelve abreast.

III

And such plenty and perfection, see, of grass
   Never was!
Such a carpet as, this summer-time, o'erspreads
   And embeds
Every vestige of the city, guessed alone,
   Stock or stone—

[39] The story of how Esau, a hunter and man of the field, sold his birthright to his brother Jacob for a meal of bread and lentils is in Genesis 25; Orson is one of the heroes of the early French romance *Valentine and Orson*, a story of two brothers, one of whom is sent to serve at court, and the other (Orson) is left to grow up in the wild forest.
[1] Browning placed this poem first in the volume *Men and Women* (1855). Originally, the poem was divided into fourteen stanzas of six lines each, emphasizing the division between present and past within each of the present stanzas.

Where a multitude of men breathed joy and
  woe
    Long ago;
Lust of glory pricked their hearts up, dread of
  shame
    Struck them tame;
And that glory and that shame alike, the gold
    Bought and sold.

IV

Now,—the single little turret that remains
    On the plains,
By the caper[2] overrooted, by the gourd
    Overscored,
While the patching houseleek's[3] head of
  blossom winks
    Through the chinks—
Marks the basement whence a tower in ancient
  time
    Sprang sublime,
And a burning ring, all round, the chariots
  traced
    As they raced,
And the monarch and his minions and his
  dames
    Viewed the games.

V

And I know, while thus the quiet-coloured eve
    Smiles to leave
To their folding, all our many-tinkling fleece
    In such peace,
And the slopes and rills in undistinguished grey
    Melt away—
That a girl with eager eyes and yellow hair
    Waits me there
In the turret whence the charioteers caught
  soul
    For the goal,
When the king looked, where she looks now,
  breathless, dumb
    Till I come.

VI

But he looked upon the city, every side,
    Far and wide,
All the mountains topped with temples, all the
  glades'
    Colonnades,
All the causeys,[4] bridges, aqueducts,—and then,
    All the men!

When I do come, she will speak not, she will
  stand,
    Either hand
On my shoulder, give her eyes the first embrace
    Of my face,   70
Ere we rush, ere we extinguish sight and speech
    Each on each.

VII

In one year they sent a million fighters forth
    South and North,
And they built their gods a brazen pillar high
    As the sky,
Yet reserved a thousand chariots in full force—
    Gold, of course.
Oh heart! oh blood that freezes, blood that
  burns!
    Earth's returns   80
For whole centuries of folly, noise and sin!
    Shut them in,
With their triumphs and their glories and the
  rest!
    Love is best.

                                    (1852) 1855

Evelyn Hope

I

Beautiful Evelyn Hope is dead!
    Sit and watch by her side an hour.
That is her book-shelf, this her bed;
    She plucked that piece of geranium-flower,
Beginning to die too, in the glass;
    Little has yet been changed, I think:
The shutters are shut, no light may pass
    Save two long rays thro' the hinge's chink.

II

Sixteen years old when she died!
    Perhaps she had scarcely heard my name;   10
It was not her time to love; beside,
    Her life had many a hope and aim,
Duties enough and little cares,
    And now was quiet, now astir,
Till God's hand beckoned unawares,—
    And the sweet white brow is all of her.

III

Is it too late then, Evelyn Hope?
    What, your soul was pure and true,

---

[2] Caper: a low prickly shrub. [3] Houseleek: a pink-flowered plant.
[4] Causey: a paved highway.

The good stars met in your horoscope,
20   Made you of spirit, fire and dew—
And, just because I was thrice as old
      And our paths in the world diverged so
         wide,
Each was nought to each, must I be told?
      We were fellow mortals, nought beside?

       IV

No, indeed! for God above
      Is great to grant, as mighty to make,
And creates the love to reward the love:
      I claim you still, for my own love's sake!
Delayed it may be for more lives yet,
30   Through worlds I shall traverse, not a few:
Much is to learn, much to forget
      Ere the time be come for taking you.

       V

But the time will come,—at last it will,
      When, Evelyn Hope, what meant (I shall
         say)
In the lower earth, in the years long still,
      That body and soul so pure and gay?
Why your hair was amber, I shall divine,
      And your mouth of your own geranium's
         red—
And what you would do with me, in fine,
40   In the new life come in the old one's stead.

       VI

I have lived (I shall say) so much since then,
      Given up myself so many times,
Gained me the gains of various men,
      Ransacked the ages, spoiled the climes;
Yet one thing, one, in my soul's full scope,
      Either I missed or itself missed me:
And I want and find you, Evelyn Hope!
      What is the issue? let us see!

       VII

I loved you, Evelyn, all the while.
50   My heart seemed full as it could hold?
There was place and to spare for the frank
         young smile,
      And the red young mouth, and the hair's
         young gold.
So, hush,—I will give you this leaf to keep:
      See, I shut it inside the sweet cold hand!

There, that is our secret: go to sleep!
      You will wake, and remember, and under-
         stand.

                                        1855

The details of the life of the Italian painter Fra Lippo Lippi (c. 1406–1469) are similar to those recounted in Browning's poem. He was brought up by his aunt, Mona Lapaccia, was put with the Carmelite Friars in Florence while still an adolescent, showed his talent as a painter, and was patronized by Cosimo de'Medici, a member of the great family of Florence. The anecdote about Lippi's escape from Cosimo's palace, in which he was confined in order that he would complete some paintings, appears in standard accounts of his life. So does the fact of his love of carnal pleasure: later in his life Lippi ran away with a novice in an order of nuns, and near the end of his life he and his wife were released from their religious vows and their marriage recognized.

Fra Lippo Lippi

I am poor brother Lippo, by your leave!
You need not clap your torches to my face.
Zooks, what's to blame? you think you see a
      monk!
What, 't is past midnight, and you go the
      rounds,
And here you catch me at an alley's end
Where sportive ladies leave their doors ajar?
The Carmine's[1] my cloister: hunt it up,
Do,—harry out, if you must show your zeal,
Whatever rat, there, haps on his wrong hole,
And nip each softling of a wee white mouse,
Weke, weke, that's crept to keep him company!
Aha, you know your betters! Then, you'll take
Your hand away that's fiddling on my throat,
And please to know me likewise. Who am I?
Why, one, sir, who is lodging with a friend
Three streets off—he's a certain . . . how d'ye
      call?
Master—a . . . Cosimo of the Medici,
I' the house that caps the corner. Boh! you
      were best!
Remember and tell me, the day you're hanged,
How you affected such a gullet's-gripe!
But you, sir, it concerns you that your knaves
Pick up a manner nor discredit you:
Zooks, are we pilchards,[2] that they sweep the
      streets

---

[1] Carmine: the name of the monastery of the Carmelites in Florence.
[2] Pilchards: a common kind of fish.

And count fair prize what comes into their net?
He's Judas to a tittle, that man is!
Just such a face! Why, sir, you make amends.
Lord, I'm not angry! Bid your hangdogs go
Drink out this quarter-florin[3] to the health
Of the munificent House that harbours me
(And many more beside, lads! more beside!)
And all's come square again. I'd like his face—
His, elbowing on his comrade in the door
With the pike and lantern,—for the slave that
    holds
John Baptist's head a-dangle by the hair
With one hand ("Look you, now," as who
    should say)
And his weapon in the other, yet unwiped!
It's not your chance to have a bit of chalk,
A wood-coal or the like? or you should see!
Yes, I'm the painter, since you style me so.
What, brother Lippo's doings, up and down,
You know them and they take you?[4] like
    enough!
I saw the proper twinkle in your eye—
'Tell you, I liked your looks at very first.
Let's sit and set things straight now, hip to
    haunch.
Here's spring come, and the nights one makes
    up bands
To roam the town and sing out carnival,
And I've been three weeks shut within my
    mew,
A-painting for the great man, saints and saints
And saints again. I could not paint all night—
Ouf! I leaned out of window for fresh air.
There came a hurry of feet and little feet,
A sweep of lute-strings, laughs, and whiffs of
    song,—
Flower o' the broom,
Take away love, and our earth is a tomb!
Flower o' the quince,
I let Lisa go, and what good in life since?[5]
Flower o' the thyme—and so on. Round they
    went.
Scarce had they turned the corner when a titter
Like the skipping of rabbits by moonlight,—
    three slim shapes,
And a face that looked up . . . zooks, sir, flesh
    and blood,

That's all I'm made of! Into shreds it went,
Curtain and counterpane and coverlet,
All the bed-furniture—a dozen knots,
There was a ladder! Down I let myself,
Hands and feet, scrambling somehow, and so
    dropped,
And after them. I came up with the fun
Hard by Saint Laurence,[6] hail fellow, well
    met,—
Flower o' the rose,
If I've been merry, what matter who knows?
And so as I was stealing back again   70
To get to bed and have a bit of sleep
Ere I rise up to-morrow and go work
On Jerome[7] knocking at his poor old breast
With his great round stone to subdue the flesh,
You snap me of the sudden. Ah, I see!
Though your eye twinkles still, you shake your
    head—
Mine's shaved—a monk, you say—the sting's
    in that!
If Master Cosimo announced himself,
Mum's the word naturally; but a monk!
Come, what am I a beast for? tell us, now!   80
I was a baby when my mother died
And father died and left me in the street.
I starved there, God knows how, a year or two
On fig-skins, melon-parings, rinds and shucks,
Refuse and rubbish. One fine frosty day,
My stomach being empty as your hat,
The wind doubled me up and down I went.
Old Aunt Lapaccia trussed me with one hand,
(Its fellow was a stinger as I knew)
And so along the wall, over the bridge,   90
By the straight cut to the convent. Six words
    there,
While I stood munching my first bread that
    month:
"So, boy, you're minded," quoth the good fat
    father
Wiping his own mouth, 't was refection-time,—
"To quit this very miserable world?
Will you renounce" . . . "the mouthful of
    bread?" thought I;
By no means! Brief, they made a monk of me;
I did renounce the world, its pride and greed,
Palace, farm, villa, shop and banking-house,

---

[3] Quarter-florin: a florin was a gold coin.   [4] Take you: amuse you.
[5] The interspersed songs are Browning's version of a form of Italian folk song named *stornelli,* three-line (rather than two-line) verses often sung in a kind of lyric competition in which successive singers try to cap the verses of one another.
[6] Saint Laurence: the church of San Lorenzo.
[7] Jerome: St. Jerome, one of the fathers of the early Church, a fourth-century ascetic who lived in the desert.

100 Trash, such as these poor devils of Medici
Have given their hearts to—all at eight years
    old.
Well, sir, I found in time, you may be sure,
'T was not for nothing—the good bellyful,
The warm serge and the rope that goes all
    round,
And day-long blessed idleness beside!
"Let's see what the urchin's fit for"—that came
    next.
Not overmuch their way, I must confess.
Such a to-do! They tried me with their books:
Lord, they'd have taught me Latin in pure
    waste!
110 *Flower o' the clove,*
All the Latin, I construe is, "amo" I love!
But, mind you, when a boy starves in the streets
Eight years together, as my fortune was,
Watching folk's faces to know who will fling
The bit of half-stripped grape-bunch he desires,
And who will curse or kick him for his pains,—
Which gentleman processional and fine,
Holding a candle to the Sacrament,
Will wink and let him lift a plate and catch
120 The droppings of the wax to sell again,
Or holla for the Eight[8] and have him
    whipped,—
How say I?—nay, which dog bites, which lets
    drop
His bone from the heap of offal in the street,—
Why, soul and sense of him grow sharp alike,
He learns the look of things, and none the less
For admonition from the hunger-pinch.
I had a store of such remarks, be sure,
Which, after I found leisure, turned to use.
I drew men's faces on my copy-books,
Scrawled them within the antiphonary's[9]
130   marge,
Joined legs and arms to the long music-notes,
Found eyes and nose and chin for A's and B's,
And made a string of pictures of the world
Betwixt the ins and outs of verb and noun,
On the wall, the bench, the door. The monks
    looked black.
"Nay," quoth the Prior, "turn him out, d' ye
    say?
In no wise. Lose a crow and catch a lark.
What if at last we get our man of parts,
We Carmelites, like those Camaldolese

And Preaching Friars,[10] to do our church up
    fine
And put the front on it that ought to be!"
And hereupon he bade me daub away.
Thank you! my head being crammed, the walls
    a blank,
Never was such prompt disemburdening.
First, every sort of monk, the black and white,
I drew them, fat and lean: then, folk at church,
From good old gossips waiting to confess
Their cribs[11] of barrel-droppings, candle-
    ends,—
To the breathless fellow at the altar-foot,
Fresh from his murder, safe and sitting there[12]
With the little children round him in a row
Of admiration, half for his beard and half
For that white anger of his victim's son
Shaking a fist at him with one fierce arm,
Signing himself with the other because of
    Christ
(Whose sad face on the cross sees only this
After the passion of a thousand years)
Till some poor girl, her apron o'er her head,
(Which the intense eyes looked through) came
    at eve
On tiptoe, said a word, dropped in a loaf,
Her pair of earrings and a bunch of flowers
(The brute took growling), prayed, and so
    was gone.
I painted all, then cried " 'T is ask and have;
Choose, for more's ready!"—laid the ladder
    flat,
And showed my covered bit of cloister-wall.
The monks closed in a circle and praised loud
Till checked, taught what to see and not to see,
Being simple bodies,—"That's the very man!
Look at the boy who stoops to pat the dog!
That woman's like the Prior's niece who comes
To care about his asthma: it's the life!"
But there my triumph's straw-fire flared and
    funked;
Their betters took their turn to see and say:
The Prior and the learned pulled a face
And stopped all that in no time. "How? what's
    here?
Quite from the mark of painting, bless us all!
Faces, arms, legs and bodies like the true
As much as pea and pea! it's devil's-game!
Your business is not to catch men with show,

---

[8] The Eight: the magistrates of Florence.

[9] Antiphonary: the book containing the hymns and responses sung by the choir.

[10] The monastic order of the Camaldolese maintained a monastery near Florence; the Preaching Friars was a name for the Dominican order.   [11] Cribs: thefts.

[12] The murderer has sought sanctuary from civil law in a church.

30 With homage to the perishable clay,
But lift them over it, ignore it all,
Make them forget there's such a thing as flesh.
Your business is to paint the souls of men—
Man's soul, and it's a fire, smoke . . . no, it's
  not . . .
It's vapour done up like a new-born babe—
(In that shape when you die it leaves your
  mouth)
It's . . . well, what matters talking, it's the
  soul!
Give us no more of body than shows soul!
Here's Giotto,[13] with his Saint a-praising God,
0 That sets us praising,—why not stop with him?
Why put all thoughts of praise out of our head
With wonder at lines, colours, and what not?
Paint the soul, never mind the legs and arms!
Rub all out, try at it a second time.
Oh, that white smallish female with the
  breasts,
She's just my niece . . . Herodias,[14] I would
  say,—
Who went and danced and got men's heads
  cut off!
Have it all out!" Now, is this sense, I ask?
A fine way to paint soul, by painting body
0 So ill, the eye can't stop there, must go further
And can't fare worse! Thus, yellow does for
  white
When what you put for yellow's simply black,
And any sort of meaning looks intense
When all beside itself means and looks nought.
Why can't a painter lift each foot in turn,
Left foot and right foot, go a double step,
Make his flesh liker and his soul more like,
Both in their order? Take the prettiest face,
The Prior's niece . . . patron-saint—is it so
  pretty
0 You can't discover if it means hope, fear,
Sorrow or joy? won't beauty go with these?
Suppose I've made her eyes all right and blue,
Can't I take breath and try to add life's flash,
And then add soul and heighten them three-
  fold?
Or say there's beauty with no soul at all—
(I never saw it—put the case the same—)
If you get simple beauty and nought else,
You get about the best thing God invents:

That's somewhat: and you'll find the soul you
  have missed,
Within yourself, when you return him thanks.   220
"Rub all out!" Well, well, there's my life, in
  short,
And so the thing has gone on ever since.
I'm grown a man no doubt, I've broken
  bounds:
You should not take a fellow eight years old
And make him swear to never kiss the girls.
I'm my own master, paint now as I please—
Having a friend, you see, in the Corner-house!
Lord, it's fast holding by the rings in front—
Those great rings serve more purposes than
  just
To plant a flag in, or tie up a horse!   230
And yet the old schooling sticks, the old grave
  eyes
Are peeping o'er my shoulder as I work,
The heads shake still—"It's art's decline, my
  son!
You're not of the true painters, great and old;
Brother Angelico's the man, you'll find;
Brother Lorenzo[15] stands his single peer:
Fag on at flesh, you'll never make the third!"
Flower o' the pine
You keep your mistr . . . manners, and I'll
  stick to mine!
I'm not the third, then: bless us, they must
  know!   240
Don't you think they're the likeliest to know,
They with their Latin? So, I swallow my rage,
Clench my teeth, suck my lips in tight, and
  paint
To please them—sometimes do and sometimes
  don't;
For, doing most, there's pretty sure to come
A turn, some warm eve finds me at my saints—
A laugh, a cry, the business of the world—
(*Flower o' the peach,*
Death for us all, and his own life for each!)
And my whole soul revolves, the cup runs over,   250
The world and life's too big to pass for a
  dream,
And I do these wild things in sheer despite,
And play the fooleries you catch me at,
In pure rage! The old mill-horse, out at grass
After hard years, throws up his stiff heels so,

---

[13] Giotto: Giotto di Bondone (1276–1337), a famous religious painter, sculptor, and architect.
[14] Herodias: The wife of the brother of King Herod who, when John the Baptist said that she could not lawfully marry Herod, had her daughter Salome (who actually did the dancing) ask Herod for the gift of John's head (Matthew 14:1–12).
[15] Angelico: Fra Angelico, Giovanni da Fiesole (1387–1455), painted in the conventions of medieval religious art; Lorenzo Monaco (c. 1370–c. 1425) was a monk of the order of Camaldolese who painted in the same tradition.

Although the miller does not preach to him
The only good of grass is to make chaff.
What would men have? Do they like grass or
    no—
May they or mayn't they? all I want's the thing
260 Settled for ever one way. As it is,
You tell too many lies and hurt yourself:
You don't like what you only like too much,
You do like what, if given you at your word,
You find abundantly detestable.
For me, I think I speak as I was taught;
I always see the garden and God there
A-making man's wife: and, my lesson learned,
The value and significance of flesh,
I can't unlearn ten minutes afterwards.

270   You understand me: I'm a beast, I know.
But see, now—why, I see as certainly
As that the morning-star's about to shine,
What will hap some day. We've a youngster
    here
Comes to our convent, studies what I do,
Slouches and stares and lets no atom drop:
His name is Guidi[16]—he'll not mind the
    monks—
They call him Hulking Tom, he lets them
    talk—
He picks my practice up—he'll paint apace,
I hope so—though I never live so long,
280 I know what's sure to follow. You be judge!
You speak no Latin more than I, belike;
However, you're my man, you've seen the
    world
—The beauty and the wonder and the power,
The shapes of things, their colours, lights and
    shades,
Changes, surprises,—and God made it all!
—For what? Do you feel thankful, ay or no,
For this fair town's face, yonder river's line,
The mountain round it and the sky above,
Much more the figures of man, woman, child,
290 These are the frame to? What's it all about?
To be passed over, despised? or dwelt upon,
Wondered at? oh, this last of course!—you say.
But why not do as well as say,—paint these
Just as they are, careless what comes of it?
God's works—paint anyone, and count it
    crime

To let a truth slip. Don't object, "His works
Are here already; nature is complete:
Suppose you reproduce her— (which you can't)
There's no advantage! You must beat her,
    then."
For, don't you mark? we're made so that we
    love   300
First when we see them painted, things we
    have passed
Perhaps a hundred times nor cared to see;
And so they are better, painted—better to us,
Which is the same thing. Art was given for
    that;
God uses us to help each other so,
Lending our minds out. Have you noticed,
    now,
Your cullion's[17] hanging face? A bit of chalk,
And trust me but you should, though! How
    much more,
If I drew higher things with the same truth!
That were to take the Prior's pulpit-place,   310
Interpret God to all of you! Oh, oh,
It makes me mad to see what men shall do
And we in our graves! This world's no blot for
    us,
Nor blank; it means intensely, and means
    good:
To find its meaning is my meat and drink.
"Ay, but you don't so instigate to prayer!"
Strikes in the Prior: "when your meaning's
    plain
It does not say to folk—remember matins,[18]
Or, mind you fast next Friday!" Why, for this
What need of art at all? A skull and bones,   3.
Two bits of stick nailed crosswise, or, what's
    best,
A bell to chime the hour with, does as well.
I painted a Saint Laurence[19] six months since
At Prato, splashed the fresco in fine style:
"How looks my painting, now the scaffold's
    down?"
I ask a brother: "Hugely," he returns—
"Already not one phiz[20] of your three slaves
Who turn the Deacon off his toasted side,
But's scratched and prodded to our heart's
    content,
The pious people have so eased their own   3
With coming to say prayers there in a rage:

---

[16] Guidi: Tomasso Guidi, known as Masaccio (1401–1428), was older than Lippi and not his pupil; Browning here accepts a traditional account that was questioned even in the nineteenth century.
[17] Cullion: a base fellow; the word derives from the Middle English word for testicle.
[18] Matins: morning prayers.
[19] Saint Laurence: an early Christian martyr, killed by being roasted on a gridiron. Prato is a town near Florence, whose church contains Lippi's work.   [20] Phiz: face.

We get on fast to see the bricks beneath.
Expect another job this time next year,
For pity and religion grow i' the crowd—
Your painting serves its purpose!" Hang the
    fools!

—That is—you'll not mistake an idle word
Spoke in a huff by a poor monk, God wot,
Tasting the air this spicy night which turns
The unaccustomed head like Chianti wine!
40 Oh, the church knows! don't misreport me,
    now!
It's natural a poor monk out of bounds
Should have his apt word to excuse himself:
And hearken how I plot to make amends.
I have bethought me: I shall paint a piece
. . . There's for you! Give me six months,
    then go, see
Something in Sant' Ambrogio's!²¹ Bless the
    nuns!
They want a cast o' my office. I shall paint
God in the midst. Madonna and her babe,
Ringed by a bowery flowery angel-brood,
50 Lilies and vestments and white faces, sweet
As puff on puff of grated orris-root²²
When ladies crowd to Church at midsummer.
And then i' the front, of course a saint or
    two—
Saint John,²³ because he saves the Florentines,
Saint Ambrose,²⁴ who puts down in black and
    white
The convent's friends and gives them a long
    day,
And Job, I must have him there past mistake,
The man of Uz (and Us without the z,
Painters who need his patience) . Well, all
    these
60 Secured at their devotion, up shall come
Out of a corner when you least expect,
As one by a dark stair into a great light,
Music and talking, who but Lippo! I!—
Mazed, motionless and moonstruck—I'm the
    man!
Back I shrink—what is this I see and hear?

I, caught up with my monk's things by mistake,
My old serge gown and rope that goes all
    round,
I, in this presence, this pure company!
Where's a hole, where's a corner for escape?
Then steps a sweet angelic slip of a thing   370
Forward, puts out a soft palm—"Not so fast!"
—Addresses the celestial presence, "nay—
He made you and devised you, after all,
Though he's none of you! Could Saint John
    there draw—
His camel-hair make up a painting-brush?²⁵
We come to brother Lippo for all that,
Iste perfecit opus!"²⁶ So, all smile—
I shuffle sideways with my blushing face
Under the cover of a hundred wings
Thrown like a spread of kirtles when you're
    gay   380
And play hot cockles,²⁷ all the doors being
    shut,
Till, wholly unexpected, in there pops
The hothead husband! Thus I scuttle off
To some safe bench behind, not letting go
The palm of her, the little lily thing
That spoke the good word for me in the nick,
Like the Prior's niece . . . Saint Lucy,²⁸ I
    would say.
And so all's saved for me, and for the church
A pretty picture gained. Go, six months hence!
Your hand, sir, and good-bye: no lights, no
    lights!   390
The street's hushed, and I know my own way
    back,
Don't fear me! There's the gray beginning.
    Zooks!

1855

By the Fire-Side

I

How well I know what I mean to do
    When the long dark autumn-evenings
        come:

---

²¹ Sant' Ambrogio's: the church of St. Ambrose in Florence, for which Lippi painted *The Coronation of the Virgin,* the painting he describes at the end of the poem.
²² Orris-root: the fragant root of the European iris.
²³ Saint John: John the Baptist was the patron saint of Florence.
²⁴ Saint Ambrose was a leader of the early Church in Florence.
²⁵ John is described in Mark (1:6) as being clothed in camel hair.
²⁶ Lippi did paint himself into his picture, his head near a scroll bearing the words "Iste perfecit opus": this man made the work.
²⁷ Hot cockles: a children's game in which a blindfolded person guesses who touches him or her.
²⁸ Saint Lucy: an early Christian martyr, the patron saint of the blind, and here associated with light.

And where, my soul, is thy pleasant hue?
    With the music of all thy voices, dumb
In life's November too!

II
I shall be found by the fire, suppose,
    O'er a great wise book as beseemeth age,
While the shutters flap as the cross-wind blows
    And I turn the page, and I turn the page,
10 Not verse now, only prose!

III
Till the young ones whisper, finger on lip,
    "There he is at it, deep in Greek:
Now then, or never, out we slip
    To cut from the hazels by the creek
A mainmast for our ship!"

IV
I shall be at it indeed, my friends:
    Greek puts already on either side
Such a branch-work forth as soon extends
    To a vista opening far and wide,
20 And I pass out where it ends.

V
The outside-frame, like your hazel-trees:
    But the inside-archway widens fast,
And a rarer sort succeeds to these,
    And we slope to Italy at last
And youth, by green degrees.

VI
I follow wherever I am led,
    Knowing so well the leader's hand:
Oh woman-country, wooed not wed,
    Loved all the more by earth's male-lands,
30 Laid to their hearts instead!

VII
Look at the ruined chapel again
    Half-way up in the Alpine gorge!
Is that a tower, I point you plain,
    Or is it a mill, or an iron-forge
Breaks solitude in vain?

VIII
A turn, and we stand in the heart of things;
    The woods are round us, heaped and dim;
From slab to slab how it slips and springs,
    The thread of water single and slim,
40 Through the ravage some torrent brings!

IX
Does it feed the little lake below?
    That speck of white just on its marge
Is Pella;[1] see, in the evening-glow,
    How sharp the silver spear-heads charge
When Alp meets heaven in snow!

X
On our other side is the straight-up rock;
    And a path is kept 'twixt the gorge and it
By boulder-stones where lichens mock
    The marks on a moth, and small ferns fit
Their teeth to the polished block.

XI
Oh the sense of the yellow mountain-flowers,
    And thorny balls, each three in one,
The chestnuts throw on our path in showers!
    For the drop of the woodland fruit's begun,
These early November hours,

XII
That crimson the creeper's leaf across
    Like a splash of blood, intense, abrupt,
O'er a shield else gold from rim to boss,[2]
    And lay it for show on the fairy-cupped
Elf-needled mat of moss,

XIII
By the rose-flesh mushrooms, undivulged
    Last evening—nay, in to-day's first dew
Yon sudden coral nipple bulged,
    Where a freaked fawn-coloured flaky crew
Of toadstools peep indulged.

XIV
And yonder, at foot of the fronting ridge
    That takes the turn to a range beyond,
Is the chapel reached by the one-arched bridge
    Where the water is stopped in a stagnant pond
Danced over by the midge.[3]

XV
The chapel and bridge are of stone alike,
    Blackish-gray and mostly wet;
Cut hemp-stalks steep in the narrow dyke.
    See here again, how the lichens fret
And the roots of the ivy strike!

[1] Pella: a village in northern Italy. [2] Boss: raised ornamentation. [3] Midge: a small fly.

XVI

Poor little place, where its one priest comes
    On a festa-day, if he comes at all,
To the dozen folk from their scattered homes,
    Gathered within that precinct small
By the dozen ways one roams—

XVII

To drop from the charcoal-burners' huts,
    Or climb from the hemp-dressers' low
       shed,
Leave the grange where the woodman stores
    his nuts,
    Or the wattled cote⁴ where the fowlers
       spread
Their gear on the rock's bare juts.

XVIII

It has some pretension too, this front,
    With its bit of fresco half-moon-wise
Set over the porch, Art's early wont:
    'T is John in the Desert,⁵ I surmise,
But has borne the weather's brunt—

XIX

Not from the fault of the builder, though,
    For a pent-house properly projects
Where three carved beams make a certain
    show,
    Dating—good thought of our architect's—
'Five, six, nine, he lets you know.

XX

And all day long a bird sings there,
    And a stray sheep drinks at the pond at
       times;
The place is silent and aware;
    It has had its scenes, its joys and crimes,
But that is its own affair.

XXI

My perfect wife, my Leonor,
    Oh heart, my own, oh eyes, mine too,
Whom else could I dare look backward for,
    With whom beside should I dare pursue
The path gray heads abhor?

XXII

For it leads to a crag's sheer edge with them;
    Youth, flowery all the way, there stops—

Not they; age threatens and they contemn,
    Till they reach the gulf wherein youth
       drops,
One inch from life's safe hem! 110

XXIII

With me, youth led . . . I will speak now,
    No longer watch you as you sit
Reading by fire-light, that great brow
    And the spirit-small hand propping it,
Mutely, my heart knows how—

XXIV

When, if I think but deep enough,
    You are wont to answer, prompt as rhyme;
And you, too, find without rebuff
    Response your soul seeks many a time
Piercing its fine flesh-stuff. 120

XXV

My own, confirm me! If I tread
    This path back, is it not in pride
To think how little I dreamed it led
    To an age so blest that, by its side,
Youth seems the waste instead?

XXVI

My own, see where the years conduct!
    At first, 't was something our two souls
Should mix as mists do; each is sucked
    In each now: on, the new stream rolls,
Whatever rocks obstruct.

XXVII

Think, when our one soul understands 130
    The great Word which makes all things
       new,
When earth breaks up and heaven expands,
    How will the change strike me and you
In the house not made with hands?

XXVIII

Oh I must feel your brain prompt mine,
    Your heart anticipate my heart,
You must be just before, in fine,
    See and make me see, for your part,
New depths of the divine!

XXIX

But who could have expected this 140
    When we two drew together first

---

⁴ Wattled cote: a coop made of interwoven branches.
⁵ John in the Desert: a picture of the ascetic St. John, a father of the early Church who lived
in the desert.

Just for the obvious human bliss,
    To satisfy life's daily thirst
With a thing men seldom miss?

XXX

Come back with me to the first of all,
    Let us lean and love it over again,
Let us now forget and now recall,
    Break the rosary in a pearly rain,
And gather what we let fall!

XXXI

150 What did I say?—that a small bird sings
    All day long, save when a brown pair
Of hawks from the wood float with wide wings
    Strained to a bell:[6] 'gainst noon-day glare
You count the streaks and rings.

XXXII

But at afternoon or almost eve
    'T is better; then the silence grows
To that degree, you half believe
    It must get rid of what it knows,
160 Its bosom does so heave.

XXXIII

Hither we walked then, side by side,
    Arm in arm and cheek to cheek,
And still I questioned or replied,
    While my heart, convulsed to really speak,
Lay choking in its pride.

XXXIV

Silent the crumbling bridge we cross,
    And pity and praise the chapel sweet,
And care about the fresco's loss,
    And wish for our souls a like retreat,
170 And wonder at the moss.

XXXV

Stoop and kneel on the settle[7] under,
    Look through the window's grated square:
Nothing to see! For fear of plunder,
    The cross is down and the altar bare,
As if thieves don't fear thunder.

XXXVI

We stoop and look in through the grate,
    See the little porch and rustic door,
Read duly the dead builder's date;
    Then cross the bridge that we crossed
        before,
180 Take the path again—but wait!

XXXVII

Oh moment, one and infinite!
    The water slips o'er stock[8] and stone;
The West is tender, hardly bright:
    How gray at once is the evening grown—
One star, its chrysolite![9]

XXXVIII

We two stood there with never a third,[10]
    But each by each, as each knew well:
The sights we saw and the sounds we heard,
    The lights and the shades made up a spell
Till the trouble grew and stirred.   190

XXXIX

Oh, the little more, and how much it is!
    And the little less, and what worlds away!
How a sound shall quicken content to bliss,
    Or a breath suspend the blood's best play,
And life be a proof of this!

XL

Had she willed it, still had stood the screen
    So slight, so sure, 'twixt my love and her:
I could fix her face with a guard between,
    And find her soul as when friends confer,
Friends—lovers that might have been.   20

XLI

For my heart had a touch of the woodland-
        time,
    Wanting to sleep now over its best.
Shake the whole tree in the summer-prime,
    But bring to the last leaf no such test!
"Hold the last fast!" runs the rhyme.

XLII

For a chance to make your little much,
    To gain a lover and lose a friend,
Venture the tree and a myriad such,
    When nothing you mar but the year can
        mend:
But a last leaf—fear to touch!   21

XLIII

Yet should it unfasten itself and fall
    Eddying down till it find your face
At some slight wind—best chance of all!
    Be your heart henceforth its dwelling-
        place
You trembled to forestall!

---

[6] Strained to a bell: extended out and downward.   [7] Settle: a bench under the window.
[8] Stock: stump.   [9] Chrysolite: an olive-green stone.
[10] In the letters of their courtship, Elizabeth and Robert Browning sometimes refer to how
a third person might judge their words and actions.

XLIV

Worth how well, those dark grey eyes,
  That hair so dark and dear, how worth
That a man should strive and agonize,
  And taste a veriest hell on earth
220 For the hope of such a prize!

XLV

You might have turned and tried a man,
  Set him a space to weary and wear,
And prove which suited more your plan,
  His best of hope or his worst despair,
Yet end as he began.

XLVI

But you spared me this, like the heart you are,
  And filled my empty heart at a word.
If two lives join, there is oft a scar,
  They are one and one, with a shadowy
    third;
230 One near one is too far.

XLVII

A moment after, and hands unseen
  Were hanging the night around us fast;
But we knew that a bar was broken between
  Life and life: we were mixed at last
In spite of the mortal screen.

XLVIII

The forests had done it; there they stood;
  We caught for a moment the powers at
    play:
They had mingled us so, for once and good,
  Their work was done—we might go or
    stay,
40 They relapsed to their ancient mood.

XLIX

How the world is made for each of us!
  How all we perceive and know in it
Tends to some moment's product thus,
  When a soul declares itself—to wit,
By its fruit, the thing it does!

L

Be hate that fruit or love that fruit,
  It forwards the general deed of man,
And each of the Many helps to recruit
  The life of the race by a general plan;
50 Each living his own, to boot.

LI

I am named and known by that moment's
    feat;
  There took my station and degree;

So grew my own small life complete,
  As nature obtained her best of me—
One born to love you, sweet!

LII

And to watch you sink by the fire-side now
  Back again, as you mutely sit
Musing by fire-light, that great brow
  And the spirit-small hand propping it,
Yonder, my heart knows how! 260

LIII

So, earth has gained by one man the more,
  And the gain of earth must be heaven's
    gain too;
And the whole is well worth thinking o'er
  When autumn comes: which I mean to do
One day, as I said before.

1855

Any Wife to Any Husband

I

My love, this is the bitterest, that thou—
Who art all truth, and who dost love me now
  As thine eyes say, as thy voice breaks to
    say—
Shouldst love so truly, and couldst love me
    still
A whole long life through, had but love its
    will,
  Would death that leads me from thee
    brook delay.

II

I have but to be by thee, and thy hand
Will never let mine go, nor heart withstand
  The beating of my heart to reach its place.
When shall I look for thee and feel thee gone? 10
When cry for the old comfort and find none?
  Never, I know! Thy soul is in thy face.

III

Oh, I should fade—'t is willed so! Might I save,
Gladly I would, whatever beauty gave
  Joy to thy sense, for that was precious too.
It is not to be granted. But the soul
Whence the love comes, all ravage leaves that
    whole;
  Vainly the flesh fades; soul makes all
    things new.

IV

It would not be because my eye grew dim
Thou couldst not find the love there, thanks to
    Him
  Who never is dishonoured in the spark 20

He gave us from his fire of fires, and bade
Remember whence it sprang, nor be afraid
    While that burns on, though all the rest
      grow dark.

V

So, how thou wouldst be perfect, white and
    clean
Outside as inside, soul and soul's demesne[1]
    Alike, this body given to show it by!
Oh, three-parts through the worst of life's
    abyss,
What plaudits from the next world after this,
    Couldst thou repeat a stroke and gain the
30   sky!

VI

And is it not the bitterer to think
That, disengage our hands and thou wilt sink
    Although thy love was love in very deed?
I know that nature! Pass a festive day,
Thou dost not throw its relic-flower away
    Nor bid its music's loitering echo speed.

VII

Thou let'st the stranger's glove lie where it
    fell;
If old things remain old things all is well,
    For thou art grateful as becomes man
      best:
40 And hadst thou only heard me play one tune,
Or viewed me from a window, not so soon
    With thee would such things fade as with
      the rest.

VIII

I seem to see! We meet and part; 't is brief;
The book I opened keeps a folded leaf,
    The very chair I sat on, breaks the rank;
That is a portrait of me on the wall—
Three lines, my face comes at so slight a call:
    And for all this, one little hour to thank!

IX

But now, because the hour through years was
    fixed,
50 Because our inmost beings met and mixed,
    Because thou once hast loved me—wilt
      thou dare
Say to thy soul and Who may list beside,
"Therefore she is immortally my bride;
    Chance cannot change my love, nor time
      impair.

X

"So, what if in the dusk of life that's left,
I, a tired traveller of my sun bereft,
    Look from my path when, mimicking the
      same,
The fire-fly glimpses past me, come and gone?
—Where was it till the sunset? where anon
    It will be at the sunrise! What's to
      blame?"   6

XI

Is it so helpful to thee? Canst thou take
The mimic up, nor, for the true thing's sake,
    Put gently by such efforts at a beam?
Is the remainder of the way so long,
Thou need'st the little solace, thou the strong?
    Watch out thy watch, let weak ones doze
      and dream!

XII

—Ah, but the fresher faces! "Is it true,"
Thou'lt ask, "some eyes are beautiful and new?
    Some hair,—how can one choose but grasp
      such wealth?
And if a man would press his lips to lips   7
Fresh as the wilding hedge-rose-cup there slips
    The dew-drop out of, must it be by stealth?

XIII

"It cannot change the love still kept for Her,
More than if such a picture I prefer
    Passing a day with, to a room's bare side:
The painted form takes nothing she possessed,
Yet, while the Titian's Venus[2] lies at rest,
    A man looks. Once more, what is there to
      chide?"

XIV

So must I see, from where I sit and watch,
My own self sell myself, my hand attach   8
    Its warrant to the very thefts from me—
Thy singleness of soul that made me proud,
Thy purity of heart I loved aloud,
    Thy man's-truth I was bold to bid God
      see!

XV

Love so, then, if thou wilt! Give all thou canst
Away to the new faces—disentranced,
    (Say it and think it) obdurate no more:
Re-issue looks and words from the old mint,
Pass them afresh, no matter whose the print
    Image and superscription once they bore!   9

[1] Demesne: land attached to a manor or estate.
[2] Titian: sixteenth-century Italian painter, given to exceptionally striking color and sensuous form.

XVI

Re-coin thyself and give it them to spend,—
It all comes to the same thing at the end,
    Since mine thou wast, mine art and mine
        shalt be,
Faithful or faithless, sealing up the sum
Or lavish of my treasure, thou must come
    Back to the heart's place here I keep for
        thee!

XVII

Only, why should it be with stain at all?
Why must I, 'twixt the leaves of coronal,
    Put any kiss of pardon on thy brow?
Why need the other women know so much,
And talk together, "Such the look and such
    The smile he used to love with, then as
        now!"

XVIII

Might I die last and show thee! Should I find
Such hardship in the few years left behind,
    If free to take and light my lamp, and go
Into thy tomb, and shut the door and sit,
Seeing thy face on those four sides of it
    The better that they are so blank, I know!

XIX

Why, time was what I wanted, to turn o'er
Within my mind each look, get more and more
    By heart each word, too much to learn at
        first;
And join thee all the fitter for the pause
'Neath the low doorway's lintel. That were
        cause
    For lingering, though thou calledst, if I
        durst!

XX

And yet thou art the nobler of us two:
What dare I dream of, that thou canst not do,
    Outstripping my ten small steps with one
        stride?
I'll say then, here's a trial and a task—
Is it to bear?—if easy, I'll not ask:
    Though love fail, I can trust on in thy
        pride.

XXI

Pride?—when those eyes forestall the life
        behind
The death I have to go through!—when I find,
    Now that I want thy help most, all of thee!
What did I fear? Thy love shall hold me fast
Until the little minute's sleep is past
    And I wake saved.—And yet it will not be!

1855

An Epistle

*Containing the Strange Medical
Experience of Karshish, The Arab
Physician*

Karshish, the picker-up of learning's crumbs,
The not-incurious in God's handiwork
(This man's-flesh he hath admirably made,
Blown like a bubble, kneaded like a paste,
To coop up and keep down on earth a space
That puff of vapour from his mouth, man's
        soul)
—To Abib,[1] all-sagacious in our art,
Breeder in me of what poor skill I boast,
Like me inquisitive how pricks and cracks
Befall the flesh through too much stress and
        strain,   10
Whereby the wily vapour fain would slip
Back and rejoin its source before the term,—
And aptest in contrivance (under God)
To baffle it by deftly stopping such:—
The vagrant Scholar to his Sage at home
Sends greeting (health and knowledge, fame
        with peace)
Three samples of true snakestone[2]—rarer still,
One of the other sort, the melon-shaped,
(But fitter, pounded fine, for charms than
        drugs)
And writeth now the twenty-second time.   20

    My journeyings were brought to Jericho:
Thus I resume. Who studious in our art
Shall count a little labour unrepaid?
I have shed sweat enough, left flesh and bone
On many a flinty furlong of this land.
Also, the country-side is all on fire
With rumours of a marching hitherward:

---

[1] Like Karshish, his teacher Abib is an imagined person. The word "Karshish" is a transliteration of an Arabic word which means "one who gathers."
[2] Snakestone: any stone used as a charm for snakebite.

Some say Vespasian cometh, some, his son.[3]
A black lynx snarled and pricked a tufted ear;
30 Lust of my blood inflamed his yellow balls:
I cried and threw my staff and he was gone.
Twice have the robbers stripped and beaten
        me,
And once a town declared me for a spy;
But at the end, I reach Jerusalem,
Since this poor covert where I pass the night,
This Bethany, lies scarce the distance thence
A man with plague-sores at the third degree
Runs till he drops down dead. Thou laughest
        here!
'Sooth, it elates me, thus reposed and safe,
40 To void the stuffing of my travel-scrip[4]
And share with thee whatever Jewry yields.
A viscid choler is observable
In tertians,[5] I was nearly bold to say;
And falling-sickness[6] hath a happier cure
Than our school wots of: there's a spider here
Weaves no web, watches on the ledge of tombs,
Sprinkled with mottles on an ash-gray back;
Take five and drop them . . . . but who knows
        his mind,
The Syrian runagate I trust this to?
50 His service payeth me a sublimate[7]
Blown up his nose to help the ailing eye.
Best wait: I reach Jerusalem at morn,
There set in order my experiences,
Gather what most deserves, and give thee all—
Or I might add, Judæa's gum-tragacanth[8]
Scales off in purer flakes, shines clearer-grained,
Cracks 'twixt the pestle and the porphyry,[9]
In fine exceeds our produce. Scalp-disease
Confounds me, crossing so with leprosy—
Thou hadst admired one sort I gained at
60   Zoar[10]—
But zeal outruns discretion. Here I end.

Yet stay: my Syrian blinketh gratefully,
Protesteth his devotion is my price—
Suppose I write what harms not, though he
        steal?
I half resolve to tell thee, yet I blush,

What set me off a-writing first of all.
An itch I had, a sting to write, a tang!
For, be it this town's barrenness—or else
The Man had something in the look of him—
His case has struck me far more than 't is
        worth.
So, pardon if— (lest presently I lose
In the great press of novelty at hand
The care and pains this somehow stole from
        me)
I bid thee take the thing while fresh in mind,
Almost in sight—for, wilt thou have the truth?
The very man is gone from me but now,
Whose ailment is the subject of discourse.
Thus then, and let thy better wit help all!

        'T is but a case of mania—subinduced
By epilepsy, at the turning-point
Of trance prolonged unduly some three days:
When, by the exhibition of some drug
Or spell, exorcisation, stroke of art
Unknown to me and which 't were well to
        know,
The evil thing out-breaking all at once
Left the man whole and sound of body
        indeed,—
But, flinging (so to speak) life's gates too wide,
Making a clear house of it too suddenly,
The first conceit that entered might inscribe
Whatever it was minded on the wall
So plainly at that vantage, as it were,
(First come, first served) that nothing subse-
        quent
Attaineth to erase those fancy-scrawls
The just-returned and new-established soul
Hath gotten now so thoroughly by heart
That henceforth she will read or these or none.
And first—the man's own firm conviction rests
That he was dead (in fact they buried him)
—That he was dead and then restored to life
By a Nazarene physician of his tribe:
—'Sayeth, the same bade "Rise," and he did
        rise.
"Such cases are diurnal,"[11] thou wilt cry.

---

[3] Vespasian: the Roman emperor Vespasian invaded Palestine in A.D. 66; his son destroyed
Jerusalem four years later. Lazarus at the time in which the poem is set is therefore older than
fifty (line 109), but that estimate of his age is Karshish's, and Lazarus' resurrection has worked
physical as well as mental changes in him.
[4] Travel-scrip: a bag or wallet.
[5] Viscid choler . . . tertians: a sticky bile in people afflicted with a kind of malaria.
[6] Falling-sickness: epilepsy.
[7] Sublimate: a substance derived from changing a solid to a vapor and then back to a solid.
[8] Gum-tragacanth: a substance extracted from a shrub.
[9] Porphyry: a rock; here, the ground against which a substance is pounded with a pestle.
[10] Zoar: a city near the Dead Sea.
[11] Diurnal: occur every day.

Not so this figment!—not, that such a fume,
Instead of giving way to time and health,
Should eat itself into the life of life,
As saffron tingeth flesh, blood, bones and all!
For see, how he takes up the after-life.
The man—it is one Lazarus a Jew,
Sanguine, proportioned, fifty years of age,
The body's habit wholly laudable,
As much, indeed, beyond the common health
As he were made and put aside to show.
Think, could we penetrate by any drug
And bathe the wearied soul and worried flesh,
And bring it clear and fair, by three days'
        sleep!
Whence has the man the balm that brightens
        all?
This grown man eyes the world now like a
        child.
Some elders of his tribe, I should premise,
Led in their friend, obedient as a sheep,
To bear my inquisition. While they spoke,
Now sharply, now with sorrow,—told the
        case,—
He listened not except I spoke to him,
But folded his two hands and let them talk,
Watching the flies that buzzed: and yet no fool.
And that's a sample how his years must go.
Look, if a beggar, in fixed middle-life,
Should find a treasure,—can he use the same
With straitened habits and with tastes starved
        small,
And take at once to his impoverished brain
The sudden element that changes things,
That sets the undreamed-of rapture at his hand
And puts the cheap old joy in the scorned dust?
Is he not such an one as moves to mirth—
Warily parsimonious, when no need,
Wasteful as drunkenness at undue times?
All prudent counsel as to what befits
The golden mean, is lost on such an one:
The man's fantastic will is the man's law.
So here—we call the treasure knowledge, say,
Increased beyond the fleshy faculty—
Heaven opened to a soul while yet on earth,
Earth forced on a soul's use while seeing
        heaven:
The man is witless of the size, the sum,
The value in proportion of all things,
Or whether it be little or be much.
Discourse to him of prodigious armaments
Assembled to besiege his city now,
And of the passing of a mule with gourds—

'T is one! Then take it on the other side,   150
Speak of some trifling fact,—he will gaze rapt
With stupor at its very littleness,
 (Far as I see) as if in that indeed
He caught prodigious import, whole results;
And so will turn to us the bystanders
In ever the same stupor (note this point)
That we too see not with his opened eyes.
Wonder and doubt come wrongly into play,
Preposterously, at cross purposes.
Should his child sicken unto death,—why, look   160
For scarce abatement of his cheerfulness,
Or pretermission of the daily craft!
While a word, gesture, glance from that same
        child
At play or in the school or laid asleep,
Will startle him to an agony of fear,
Exasperation, just as like. Demand
The reason why—" 't is but a word," object—
"A gesture"—he regards thee as our lord
Who lived there in the pyramid alone,
Looked at us (dost thou mind?) when, being
        young,
We both would unadvisedly recite   170
Some charm's beginning, from that book of his,
Able to bid the sun throb wide and burst
All into stars, as suns grown old are wont.
Thou and the child have each a veil alike
Thrown o'er your heads, from under which ye
        both
Stretch your blind hands and trifle with a
        match
Over a mine of Greek fire,[12] did ye know!
He holds on firmly to some thread of life—
(It is the life to lead perforcedly)
Which runs across some vast distracting orb   180
Of glory on either side that meagre thread,
Which, conscious of, he must not enter yet—
The spiritual life around the earthly life:
The law of that is known to him as this,
His heart and brain move there, his feet stay
        here.
So is the man perplext with impulses
Sudden to start off crosswise, not straight on,
Proclaiming what is right and wrong across,
And not along, this black thread through the
        blaze—
"It should be" baulked by "here it cannot be."   190
And oft the man's soul springs into his face
As if he saw again and heard again
His sage that bade him "Rise" and he did rise.
Something, a word, a tick o' the blood within

---

[12] Greek fire: a weapon composed of sulphur, naphtha, and saltpeter; not known to be used
before the seventh century A.D.

Admonishes: then back he sinks at once
To ashes, who was very fire before,
In sedulous recurrence to his trade
Whereby he earneth him the daily bread;
And studiously the humbler for that pride,
200 Professedly the faultier that he knows
God's secret, while he holds the thread of life.
Indeed the especial marking of the man
Is prone submission to the heavenly will—
Seeing it, what it is, and why it is.
'Sayeth, he will wait patient to the last
For that same death which must restore his
        being
To equilibrium, body loosening soul
Divorced even now by premature full growth:
He will live, nay, it pleaseth him to live
So long as God please, and just how God
210   please.
He even seeketh not to please God more
(Which meaneth, otherwise) than as God
        please.
Hence, I perceive not he affects to preach
The doctrine of his sect whate'er it be,
Make proselytes as madmen thirst to do:
How can he give his neighbour the real
        ground,
His own conviction? Ardent as he is—
Call his great truth a lie, why, still the old
"Be it as God please" reassureth him.
220 I probed the sore as thy disciple should:
"How, beast," said I, "this stolid carelessness
Sufficeth thee, when Rome is on her march
To stamp out like a little spark thy town,
Thy tribe, thy crazy tale and thee at once?"
He merely looked with his large eyes on me.
The man is apathetic, you deduce?
Contrariwise, he loves both old and young,
Able and weak, affects the very brutes
And birds—how say I? flowers of the field—
230 As a wise workman recognizes tools
In a master's workshop, loving what they make.
Thus is the man as harmless as a lamb:
Only impatient, let him do his best,
At ignorance and carelessness and sin—
An indignation which is promptly curbed:
As when in certain travel I have feigned
To be an ignoramus in our art
According to some preconceived design,
And happed to hear the land's practitioners,
240 Steeped in conceit sublimed by ignorance,
Prattle fantastically on disease,

Its cause and cure—and I must hold my peace!

     Thou wilt object—Why have I not ere this
Sought out the sage himself, the Nazarene
Who wrought this cure, inquiring at the
        source,
Conferring with the frankness that befits?
Alas! it grieveth me, the learned leech
Perished in a tumult many years ago,
Accused,—our learning's fate,—of wizardry,
Rebellion, to the setting up a rule
And creed prodigious as described to me.
His death, which happened when the earth-
        quake[13] fell
(Prefiguring, as soon appeared, the loss
To occult learning in our lord the sage
Who lived there in the pyramid alone)
Was wrought by the mad people—that's their
        wont!
On vain recourse, as I conjecture it,
To his tried virtue, for miraculous help—
How could he stop the earthquake? That's
        their way!
The other imputations must be lies:
But take one, though I loathe to give it thee,
In mere respect for any good man's fame.
(And after all, our patient Lazarus
Is stark mad; should we count on what he says?
Perhaps not: though in writing to a leech
'T is well to keep back nothing of a case.)
This man so cured regards the curer, then,
As—God forgive me! who but God himself,
Creator and sustainer of the world,
That came and dwelt in flesh on it awhile!
—'Sayeth that such an one was born and lived,
Taught, healed the sick, broke bread at his
        own house,
Then died, with Lazarus by, for aught I know,
And yet was . . . what I said nor choose
        repeat,
And must have so avouched himself, in fact,
In hearing of this very Lazarus
Who saith—but why all this of what he saith?
Why write of trivial matters, things of price
Calling at every moment for remark?
I noticed on the margin of a pool
Blue-flowering borage, the Aleppo sort,[14]
Aboundeth, very nitrous. It is strange!

     Thy pardon for this long and tedious case,
Which, now that I review it, needs must seem

---

[13] In Matthew the sky darkens and the earth breaks open during the crucifixion of Christ.
[14] Borage: a plant supposed to produce an effect of exhilaration; its stem contains nitre.
Aleppo is in Syria.

Unduly dwelt on, prolixly set forth!
Nor I myself discern in what is writ
Good cause for the peculiar interest
And awe indeed this man has touched me with.
Perhaps the journey's end, the weariness
Had wrought upon me first. I met him thus:
I crossed a ridge of short sharp broken hills
Like an old lion's cheek teeth. Out there came
A moon made like a face with certain spots
Multiform, manifold and menacing:
Then a wind rose behind me. So we met
In this old sleepy town at unaware,
The man and I. I send thee what is writ.
Regard it as a chance, a matter risked
To this ambiguous Syrian—he may lose,
Or steal, or give it thee with equal good.
Jerusalem's repose shall make amends
For time this letter wastes, thy time and mine;
Till when, once more thy pardon and farewell!

    The very God! think, Abib; dost thou
       think?
So, the All-Great, were the All-Loving too—
So, through the thunder comes a human voice
Saying, "O heart I made, a heart beats here!
Face, my hands fashioned, see it in myself!
Thou hast no power nor mayst conceive of
     mine,
But love I gave thee, with myself to love,
And thou must love me who have died for
     thee!"
The madman saith He said so: it is strange.
                      1855

On the first day of the year in 1852, Browning re-
solved to write a poem a day for two weeks. This
poem was one of the products of that resolution;
"Love Among the Ruins" was another. In the third
act of King Lear, *Edgar, disguised as a madman,*
complains that a foul fiend has led him "through
fire and through flame, through ford and whirlpool,
over bog and quagmire, . . . set ratsbane by his
porridge; made him proud of heart to ride on a bay
trotting-horse over four-inched bridges, to course
his own shadow for a traitor." Edgar then sings a
part of the ballad about "Childe Rowland to the
dark tower came,/His word was still, Fie, foh, and
fum;/I smell the blood of a British man" (III, iv).
Browning took the germ of the poem from this
song, and some of its imagery from a book on land-
scape, Gerard de Lairesse's The Art of Painting in
All Its Branches *(see DeVane, p. 350). "Childe" is*
a young, unproven knight.

Childe Roland to the Dark Tower Came

(See Edgar's song in "Lear")

I

My first thought was, he lied in every word,
    That hoary cripple, with malicious eye
    Askance to watch the working of his lie
On mine, and mouth scarce able to afford
Suppression of the glee, that pursed and scored
    Its edge, at one more victim gained
      thereby.

II

What else should he be set for, with his staff?
    What, save to waylay with his lies, ensnare
    All travellers who might find him posted
      there,
And ask the road? I guessed what skull-like
    laugh   10
Would break, what crutch 'gin write my
    epitaph
    For pastime in the dusty thoroughfare,

III

If at his counsel I should turn aside
    Into that ominous tract which, all agree,
    Hides the Dark Tower. Yet acquiescingly
I did turn as he pointed: neither pride
Nor hope rekindling at the end descried,
    So much as gladness that some end might
      be.

IV

For, what with my whole world-wide
    wandering,
    What with my search drawn out thro'
    years, my hope   20
    Dwindled into a ghost not fit to cope
With that obstreperous joy success would
    bring,—
I hardly tried now to rebuke the spring
    My heart made, finding failure in its scope.

V

As when a sick man very near to death
    Seems dead indeed, and feels begin and
      end
    The tears and takes the farewell of each
      friend,
And hears one bid the other go, draw breath
Freelier outside, ("since all is o'er," he saith,
    "And the blow fallen no grieving can
      amend;")   30

VI

While some discuss if near the other graves
    Be room enough for this, and when a day
    Suits best for carrying the corpse away,
With care about the banners, scarves and
    staves:
And still the man hears all, and only craves
    He may not shame such tender love and
    stay.

VII

Thus, I had so long suffered in this quest,
    Heard failure prophesied so oft, been writ
    So many time among "The Band"—to wit,
The knights who to the Dark Tower's search
40   addressed
Their steps—that just to fail as they, seemed
    best,
    And all the doubt was now—should I be
    fit?

VIII

So, quiet as despair, I turned from him,
    That hateful cripple, out of his highway
    Into the path he pointed. All the day
Had been a dreary one at best, and dim
Was settling to its close, yet shot one grim
    Red leer to see the plain catch its estray.[1]

IX

For mark! no sooner was I fairly found
50   Pledged to the plain, after a pace or two,
    Than, pausing to throw backward a last
    view
O'er the safe road, 't was gone; gray plain all
    round:
Nothing but plain to the horizon's bound.
    I might go on; nought else remained to
    do.

X

So, on I went. I think I never saw
    Such starved ignoble nature; nothing
    throve:
    For flowers—as well expect a cedar grove!
But cockle, spurge,[2] according to their law
Might propagate their kind, with none to awe,
    You'd think; a burr had been a treasure-
60   trove.

XI

No! penury, inertness and grimace,
    In some strange sort, were the land's
    portion. "See
    Or shut your eyes," said Nature peevishly,
"It nothing skills:[3] I cannot help my case:
'T is the Last Judgment's fire must cure this
    place,
    Calcine[4] its clods and set my prisoners
    free."

XII

If there pushed any ragged thistle-stalk
    Above its mates, the head was chopped;
    the bents[5]
    Were jealous else. What made those holes
    and rents
In the dock's[6] harsh swarth leaves, bruised as
    to baulk
All hope of greenness? 't is a brute must walk
    Pashing their life out, with a brute's
    intents.

XIII

As for the grass, it grew as scant as hair
    In leprosy; thin dry blades pricked the
    mud
    Which underneath looked kneaded up
    with blood.
One stiff blind horse, his every bone a-stare,
Stood stupefied, however he came there:
    Thrust out past service from the devil's
    stud!

XIV

Alive? he might be dead for aught I know,
    With that red gaunt and colloped[7] neck
    a-strain,
    And shut eyes underneath the rusty mane;
Seldom went such grotesqueness with such
    woe;
I never saw a brute I hated so;
    He must be wicked to deserve such pain.

XV

I shut my eyes and turned them on my heart.
    As a man calls for wine before he fights,
    I asked one draught of earlier, happier
    sights,

---

[1] Estray: stray.
[2] Cockle: a plant with prickly burrs; spurge: a shrubby plant whose stem has a bitter milky juice.
[3] Skills: matters. [4] Calcine: reduce to powder. [5] Bents: coarse grasses.
[6] Dock: a coarse weedy plant. [7] Colloped: ridged.

Ere fitly I coud hope to play my part.
Think first, fight afterwards—the soldier's art:
 One taste of the old time sets all to rights.

XVI

Not it! I fancied Cuthbert's reddening face
 Beneath its garniture[8] of curly gold,
 Dear fellow, till I almost felt him fold
An arm in mine to fix me to the place,
That way he used. Alas, one night's disgrace!
 Out went my heart's new fire and left it
  cold.

XVII

Giles then, the soul of honour—there he stands
 Frank as ten years ago when knighted first.
 What honest man should dare (he said)
  he durst.
Good—but the scene shifts—faugh! what hang-
  man hands
Pin to his breast a parchment? His own bands
 Read it. Poor traitor, spit upon and curst!

XVIII

Better this present than a past like that;
 Back therefore to my darkening path
  again!
 No sound, no sight as far as eye could
  strain.
Will the night send a howlet[9] or a bat?
I asked: when something on the dismal flat
 Came to arrest my thoughts and change
  their train.

XIX

A sudden little river crossed my path
 As unexpected as a serpent comes.
 No sluggish tide congenial to the glooms;
This, as it frothed by, might have been a bath
For the fiend's glowing hoof—to see the wrath
 Of its black eddy bespate with flakes and
  spumes.

XX

So petty yet so spiteful! All along,
 Low scrubby alders kneeled down over it;
 Drenched willows flung them headlong in
  a fit
Of mute despair, a suicidal throng:
The river which had done them all the wrong,
 Whate'er that was, rolled by, deterred no
  whit.

XXI

Which, while I forded,—good saints, how I
  feared
 To set my foot upon a dead man's cheek,
 Each step, or feel the spear I thrust to
  seek
For hollows, tangled in his hair or beard!
—It may have been a water-rat I speared,
 But, ugh! it sounded like a baby's shriek.

XXII

Glad was I when I reached the other bank.
 Now for a better country. Vain presage!
 Who were the strugglers, what war did
  they wage,
Whose savage trample thus could pad the
  dank   130
Soil to a plash? Toads in a poisoned tank,
 Or wild cats in a red-hot iron cage—

XXIII

The fight must so have seemed in that fell
  cirque.[10]
 What penned them there, with all the
  plain to choose?
 No foot-print leading to that horrid
  mews,[11]
None out of it. Mad brewage set to work
Their brains, no doubt, like galley-slaves the
  Turk
 Pits for his pastime, Christians against
  Jews.

XXIV

And more than that—a furlong on—why,
  there!
 What bad use was that engine for, that
  wheel,   140
 Or brake, not wheel—that harrow fit to
  reel
Men's bodies out like silk? with all the air
Of Tophet's[12] tool, on earth left unaware,
 Or brought to sharpen its rusty teeth of
  steel.

XXV

Then came a bit of stubbed[13] ground, once a
  wood,
 Next a marsh, it would seem, and now
  mere earth
 Desperate and done with; (so a fool finds
  mirth,

---

[8] Garniture: embellishment.   [9] Howlet: owl.   [10] Cirque: circle.
[11] Mews: a cage for hawks.   [12] Tophet: hell.   [13] Stubbed: marked with stumps of trees.

Makes a thing and then mars it, till his mood
Changes and off he goes!) within a rood[14]—
150   Bog, clay and rubble, sand and stark black
        dearth.

XXVI

Now blotches rankling, coloured gay and grim,
    Now patches where some leanness of the
        soil's
    Broke into moss or substances like boils;
Then came some palsied oak, a cleft in him
Like a distorted mouth that splits its rim
    Gaping at death, and dies while it recoils.

XXVII

And just as far as ever from the end!
    Nought in the distance but the evening,
        nought
    To point my footstep further! At the
        thought,
160 A great black bird, Apollyon's[15] bosom-friend,
Sailed past, nor beat his wide wing dragon-
        penned[16]
    That brushed my cap—perchance the
        guide I sought.

XXVIII

For, looking up, aware I somehow grew,
    'Spite of the dusk, the plain had given
        place
    All round to mountains—with such name
        to grace
Mere ugly heights and heaps now stolen in
        view.
How thus they had surprised me,—solve it,
        you!
    How to get from them was no clearer case.

XXIX

Yet half I seemed to recognize some trick
    Of mischief happened to me, God knows
170   when—
    In a bad dream perhaps. Here ended,
        then,
Progress this way. When, in the very nick
Of giving up, one time more, came a click
    As when a trap shuts—you're inside the
        den!

XXX

Burningly it came on me all at once,
    This was the place! those two hills on the
        right,
    Crouched like two bulls locked horn in
        horn in fight;
While to the left, a tall scalped mountain . . .
        Dunce,
Dotard, a-dozing at the very nonce,
    After a life spent training for the sight!

XXXI

What in the midst lay but the Tower itself?
    The round squat turret, blind as the fool's
        heart,
    Built of brown stone, without a counter-
        part
In the whole world. The tempest's mocking elf
Points to the shipman thus the unseen shelf
    He strikes on, only when the timbers
        start.[17]

XXXII

Not see? because of night perhaps?—why, day
    Came back again for that! before it left,
    The dying sunset kindled through a cleft:
The hills, like giants at a hunting, lay,
Chin upon hand, to see the game at bay,—
    "Now stab and end the creature—to the
        heft!"

XXXIII

Not hear? when noise was everywhere! it tolled
    Increasing like a bell. Names in my ears
    Of all the lost adventurers my peers,—
How such a one was strong, and such was bold,
And such was fortunate, yet each of old
    Lost, lost! one moment knelled the woe of
        years.

XXXIV

There they stood, ranged along the hill-sides,
     met
    To view the last of me, a living frame
    For one more picture! in a sheet of flame
I saw them and I knew them all. And yet
Dauntless the slug-horn to my lips I set,
    And blew *"Childe Roland to the Dark
    Tower came."*

                       (1852) 1855

---

[14] Rood: a measure of area or length; about a quarter-acre or seven or eight yards.
[15] Apollyon: a name for the devil.
[16] Dragon-penned: its pinions fashioned like those of a dragon.   [17] Start: pull apart.

A Light Woman

I

So far as our story approaches the end,
    Which do you pity the most of us three?—
My friend, or the mistress of my friend
    With her wanton eyes, or me?

II

My friend was already too good to lose,
    And seemed in the way of improvement
      yet,
When she crossed his path with her hunting-
      noose
    And over him drew her net.

III

When I saw him tangled in her toils,
    A shame, said I, if she adds just him
To her nine-and-ninety other spoils,
    The hundredth for a whim!

IV

And before my friend be wholly hers,
    How easy to prove to him, I said,
An eagle's the game her pride prefers,
    Though she snaps at a wren instead!

V

So, I gave her eyes my own eyes to take,
    My hand sought hers as in earnest need,
And round she turned for my noble sake,
    And gave me herself indeed.

VI

The eagle am I, with my fame in the world,
    The wren is he, with his maiden face.
—You look away and your lip is curled?
    Patience, a moment's space!

VII

For see, my friend goes shaking and white;
    He eyes me as the basilisk:[1]
I have turned, it appears, his day to night,
    Eclipsing his sun's disk.

VIII

And I did it, he thinks, as a very thief:
    "Though I love her—that, he compre-
      hends—
One should master one's passions, (love, in
      chief)
    And be loyal to one's friends!"

IX

And she,—she lies in my hand as tame
    As a pear late basking over a wall;
Just a touch to try and off it came;
    'T is mine,—can I let it fall?

X

With no mind to eat it, that's the worst!
    Were it thrown in the road, would the case
      assist?
'T was quenching a dozen blue-flies' thirst
    When I gave its stalk a twist.   40

XI

And I,—what I seem to my friend, you see:
    What I soon shall seem to his love, you
      guess:
What I seem to myself, do you ask of me?
    No hero, I confess.

XII

'T is an awkward thing to play with souls,
    And matter enough to save one's own:
Yet think of my friend, and the burning coals
    He played with for bits of stone!

XIII

One likes to show the truth for the truth;
    That the woman was light is very true: 50
But suppose she says,—Never mind that youth!
    What wrong have I done to you?

XIV

Well, any how, here the story stays,
    So far at least as I understand;
And, Robert Browning, you writer of plays,
    Here's a subject made to your hand!

                    1855

How It Strikes a Contemporary

I only knew one poet in my life:
And this, or something like it, was his way.

    You saw go up and down Valladolid,[1]
A man of mark, to know next time you saw.
His very serviceable suit of black
Was courtly once and conscientious still,
And many might have worn it, though none
    did:
The cloak, that somewhat shone and showed
    the threads,

[1] Basilisk: a legendary reptile that could kill by looking at its victim.
[1] Valladolid: a town in north central Spain.

Had purpose, and the ruff, significance.
He walked and tapped the pavement with his
10   cane,
Scenting the world, looking it full in face,
An old dog, bald and blindish, at his heels.
They turned up, now, the alley by the church,
That leads nowhither; now, they breathed
        themselves
On the main promenade just at the wrong
        time:
You'd come upon his scrutinizing hat,
Making a peaked shade blacker than itself
Against the single window spared some house
Intact yet with its mouldered Moorish work,—
20   Or else surprise the ferrel of his stick
Trying the mortar's temper 'tween the chinks
Of some new shop a-building, French and fine.
He stood and watched the cobbler at his trade,
The man who slices lemons into drink,
The coffee-roaster's brazier, and the boys
That volunteer to help him turn its winch.
He glanced o'er books on stalls with half an
        eye,
And fly-leaf ballads[2] on the vendor's string,
And broad-edge bold-print posters by the wall.
30   He took such cognizance of men and things,
If any beat a horse, you felt he saw;
If any cursed a woman, he took note;
Yet stared at nobody,—you stared at him,
And found, less to your pleasure than surprise,
He seemed to know you and expect as much.
So, next time that a neighbor's tongue was
        loosed,
It marked the shameful and notorious fact,
We had among us, not so much a spy,
As a recording chief-inquisitor,
40   The town's true master if the town but knew!
We merely kept a governor for form,
While this man walked about and took account
Of all thought, said and acted, then went home,
And wrote it fully to our Lord the King
Who has an itch to know things, he[3] knows
        why,
And reads them in his bedroom of a night.
Oh, you might smile! there wanted not a touch,
A tang of . . . well, it was not wholly ease
As back into your mind the man's look came.
50   Stricken in years a little,—such a brow

His eyes had to live under!—clear as flint
On either side the formidable nose
Curved, cut and coloured like an eagle's claw.
Had he to do with A.'s surprising fate?
When altogether old B. disappeared
And young C. got his mistress,—was't our
        friend,
His letter to the King, that did it all?
What paid the bloodless man for so much
        pains?
Our Lord the King has favourites manifold,
And shifts his ministry some once a month;
Our city gets new governors at whiles,—
But never word or sign, that I could hear,
Notified to this man about the streets
The King's approval of those letters conned
The last thing duly at the dead of night.
Did the man love his office? Frowned our Lord,
Exhorting when none heard—"Beseech me not!
Too far above my people,—beneath me!
I set the watch,—how should the people know?
Forget them, keep me all the more in mind!"
Was some such understanding 'twixt the two?

        I found no truth in one report at least—
That if you tracked him to his home, down
        lanes
Beyond the Jewry,[4] and as clean to pace,
You found he ate his supper in a room
Blazing with lights, four Titians[5] on the wall,
And twenty naked girls to change his plate!
Poor man, he lived another kind of life
In that new stuccoed third house by the bridge,
Fresh-painted, rather smart than otherwise!
The whole street might o'erlook him as he sat,
Leg crossing leg, one foot on the dog's back,
Playing a decent cribbage with his maid
(Jacynth, you're sure her name was) o'er the
        cheese
And fruit, three red halves of starved winter-
        pears,
Or treat of radishes in April. Nine,
Ten, struck the church clock, straight to bed
        went he.

        My father, like the man of sense he was,
Would point him out to me a dozen times;
" 'St—'St," he'd whisper, "the Corregidor!"[6]

---

[2] Fly-leaf ballads: ballads printed on a single sheet of paper.
[3] When this poem was first published in *Men and Women* (1855), the pronouns referring to
"Our Lord the King" were capitalized.
[4] Jewry: the quarter of the city in which Jews lived.
[5] Titians: paintings by the sixteenth-century Italian painter, known especially for sensuous
subjects and rich color.
[6] Corregidor: the chief magistrate of the town.

I had been used to think that personage
Was one with lacquered breeches, lustrous belt,
And feathers like a forest in his hat,
Who blew a trumpet and proclaimed the news,
Announced the bull-fights, gave each church its
    turn,
And memorized the miracle in vogue!
He had a great observance from us boys;
We were in error; that was not the man.

    I'd like now, yet had haply been afraid,
To have just looked, when this man came to
    die,
And seen who lined the clean gay garret-sides
And stood about the neat low truckle-bed,
With the heavenly manner of relieving guard.
Here had been, mark, the general-in-chief,
Thro' a whole campaign of the world's life and
    death,
Doing the King's work all the dim day long,
In his old coat and up to knees in mud,
Smoked like a herring, dining on a crust,—
And, now the day was won, relieved at once!
No further show or need for that old coat,
You are sure, for one thing! Bless us, all the
    while
How sprucely we are dressed out, you and I!
A second, and the angels alter that.
Well, I could never write a verse,—could you?
Let's to the Prado[7] and make the most of time.
                      1855

The Last Ride Together

I

I said—Then, dearest, since 't is so,
Since now at length my fate I know,
Since nothing all my love avails,
Since all, my life seemed meant for, fails,
    Since this was written and needs must be—
My whole heart rises up to bless
Your name in pride and thankfulness!
Take back the hope you gave,—I claim
Only a memory of the same,
—And this beside, if you will not blame,
    Your leave for one more last ride with me.

II

My mistress bent that brow of hers;
Those deep dark eyes where pride demurs
When pity would be softening through,

[7] Prado: the promenade of the city.

Fixed me a breathing-while or two
    With life or death in the balance: right!
The blood replenished me again;
My last thought was at least not vain:
I and my mistress, side by side
Shall be together, breathe and ride,   20
So, one day more am I deified.
    Who knows but the world may end
        tonight?

III

Hush! if you saw some western cloud
All billowy-bosomed, over-bowed
By many benedictions—sun's
And moon's and evening-star's at once—
    And so, you, looking and loving best,
Conscious grew, your passion drew
Cloud, sunset, moonrise, star-shine too,
Down on you, near and yet more near,   30
Till flesh must fade for heaven was here!—
Thus leant she and lingered—joy and fear!
    Thus lay she a moment on my breast.

IV

Then we began to ride. My soul
Smoothed itself out, a long-cramped scroll
Freshening and fluttering in the wind.
Past hopes already lay behind.
    What need to strive with a life awry?
Had I said that, had I done this,
So might I gain, so might I miss.   40
Might she have loved me? just as well
She might have hated, who can tell!
Where had I been now if the worst befell?
    And here we are riding, she and I.

V

Fail I alone, in words and deeds?
Why, all men strive and who succeeds?
We rode; it seemed my spirit flew,
Saw other regions, cities new,
    As the world rushed by on either side.
I thought,—All labour, yet no less   50
Bear up beneath their unsuccess.
Look at the end of work, contrast
The petty done, the undone vast,
This present of theirs with the hopeful past!
    I hoped she would love me; here we ride.

VI

What hand and brain went ever paired?
What heart alike conceived and dared?

What act proved all its thought had been?
What will but felt the fleshy screen?
60   We ride and I see her bosom heave.
There's many a crown for who can reach.
Ten lines, a stateman's life in each!
The flag stuck on a heap of bones,
A soldier's doing! what atones?
They scratch his name on the Abbey-stones.[1]
    My riding is better, by their leave.

VII

What does it all mean, poet? Well,
Your brains beat into rhythm, you tell
What we felt only; you expressed
70 You hold things beautiful the best,
    And pace them in rhyme so, side by side.
'T is something, nay 't is much: but then,
Have you yourself what's best for men?
Are you—poor, sick, old ere your time—
Nearer one whit your own sublime
Than we who never have turned a rhyme?
    Sing, riding's a joy! For me, I ride.

VIII

And you, great sculptor—so, you gave
A score of years to Art, her slave,
80 And that's your Venus, whence we turn
To yonder girl that fords the burn![2]
    You acquiesce, and shall I repine?
What, man of music, you grown grey
With notes and nothing else to say,
Is this your sole praise from a friend,
"Greatly his opera's strains intend,
But in music we know how fashions end!"
    I gave my youth; but we ride, in fine.

IX

90 Who knows what's fit for us? Had fate
Proposed bliss here should sublimate[3]
My being—had I signed the bond—
Still one must lead some life beyond,
    Have a bliss to die with, dim-descried.
This foot once planted on the goal,
This glory-garland round my soul,

Could I descry such? Try and test!
I sink back shuddering from the quest.
Earth being so good, would Heaven seem best?
    Now, Heaven and she are beyond this ride.

X

And yet—she has not spoke so long!
What if heaven be that, fair and strong
At life's best, with our eyes upturned
Whither life's flower is first discerned,
    We, fixed so, ever should so abide?
What if we still ride on, we two
With life for ever old yet new,
Changed not in kind but in degree,
The instant made eternity,—
And heaven just prove that I and she
    Ride, ride together, for ever ride?

1855

Bishop Blougram's character and opinions are like those conventional mid-nineteenth-century opinions in England ascribed to Roman Catholic bishops in general; he is modeled yet more closely on the character and career of Nicholas Wiseman (1802–65). Until 1850 England was regarded by the Vatican as a pagan country, and Roman Catholic bishops in England were missionaries whose bishoprics took their names from places outside England. In 1850 in a proclamation that incited a great deal of anti-Roman Catholic feeling, the Vatican created English bishoprics, and Wiseman was named Archbishop of Westminster and so the principal member of the Roman Catholic hierarchy in England.

Bishop Blougram's Apology[1]

No more wine? then we 'll push back chairs
    and talk.
A final glass for me, though: cool, i' faith!
We ought to have our Abbey back,[2] you see.
It 's different, preaching in basilicas,
And doing duty in some masterpiece
Like this of brother Pugin's,[3] bless his heart!

---

[1] Abbey-stones: the walls of Westminster Abbey, in which national heroes are buried.
[2] Burn: brook.   [3] Sublimate: to elevate, refine.
[1] Browning uses the word "apology" here as it is used in the word "apologetics," systematic discourse, usually on religious topics. Blougram's apology is an argument for his beliefs and way of conducting a priestly life, formally organized to meet the objections of an opponent Blougram imagines to be secular, pragmatic, and materialist in belief and conduct. John Henry Newman was to use the word "apology" in this way in his elucidation of his religious beliefs, *Apologia pro Vita Sua* (1864).
[2] Abbey: Westminster Abbey, which would be the seat of the Roman Catholic archbishop of England, were England again to become a Roman Catholic country.
[3] A. W. N. Pugin (1812–52), an architect who helped to revive a Gothic style of architecture in England. He was a convert to Roman Catholicism.

I doubt if they're half baked, those chalk
    rosettes,
Ciphers and stucco-twiddlings everywhere;
It 's just like breathing in a lime-kiln: eh?
These hot long ceremonies of our church
Cost us a little—oh, they pay the price,
You take me—amply pay it! Now, we 'll talk.

So, you despise me, Mr. Gigadibs.
No deprecation,—nay, I beg you, sir!
Beside 't is our engagement: don't you know,
I promised, if you 'd watch a dinner out,
We 'd see truth dawn together?—truth that
    peeps
Over the glasses' edge when dinner 's done,
And body gets its sop and holds its noise
And leaves soul free a little. Now 's the time:
Truth's break of day! You do despise me then.
And if I say, "despise me,"—never fear!
I know you do not in a certain sense—
Not in my arm-chair, for example: here,
I well imagine you respect my place
(*Status, entourage,* worldly circumstance)
Quite to its value—very much indeed:
—Are up to the protesting eyes of you
In pride at being seated here for once—
You 'll turn it to such capital account!
When somebody, through years and years to
    come,
Hints of the bishop,—names me—that 's
    enough:
"Blougram? I knew him"— (into it you slide)
Dined with him once, a Corpus Christi Day,[4]
All alone, we two; he 's a clever man:
And after dinner,—why, the wine you know,—
Oh, there was wine, and good!—what with the
    wine . . .
'Faith, we began upon all sorts of talk!
He 's no bad fellow, Blougram; he had seen
Something of mine he relished, some review:
He 's quite above their humbug in his heart,
Half-said as much, indeed—the thing 's his
    trade.
I warrant, Blougram 's sceptical at times:
How otherwise? I liked him, I confess!"
Che che,[5] my dear sir, as we say at Rome,
Don't you protest now! It 's fair give and take;

You have had your turn and spoken your
    home-truths:
The hand 's mine now, and here you follow
    suit.

Thus much conceded, still the first fact
    stays—
You do despise me; your ideal of life   50
Is not the bishop's: you would not be I.
You would like better to be Goethe, now,
Or Buonaparte, or, bless me, lower still,
Count D'Orsay,[6]—so you did what you pre-
    ferred,
Spoke as you thought, and, as you cannot help,
Believed or disbelieved, no matter what,
So long as on that point, whate'er it was,
You loosed your mind, were whole and sole
    yourself.
—That, my ideal never can include,
Upon that element of truth and worth   60
Never be based! for say they make me Pope—
(They can't—suppose it for our argument!)
Why, there I 'm at my tether's end, I 've reached
My height, and not a height which pleases you:
An unbelieving Pope won't do, you say.
It 's like those eerie stories nurses tell,
Of how some actor on a stage played Death,
With pasteboard crown, sham orb and tinselled
    dart,[7]
And called himself the monarch of the world;
Then, going in the tire-room[8] afterward,   70
Because the play was done, to shift himself,
Got touched upon the sleeve familiarly,
The moment he had shut the closet door,
By Death himself. Thus God might touch a
    Pope
At unawares, ask what his baubles mean,
And whose part he presumed to play just now.
Best be yourself, imperial, plain and true!

So, drawing comfortable breath again,
You weigh and find, whatever more or less
I boast of my ideal realized   80
Is nothing in the balance when opposed
To your ideal, your grand simple life,
Of which you will not realize one jot.

---

[4] Corpus Christi Day: a feast of the Roman Catholic church, honoring the sacrament of the
Eucharist, and observed on the Thursday following the eighth Sunday after Easter.
    [5] *Che che:* what, what?
    [6] Count D'Orsay: a famous dandy and familiar of fashionable society in London in the early
Victorian decades.
    [7] Dart: spear.   [8] Tire-room: dressing room.

I am much, you are nothing; you would be all,
I would be merely much: you beat me there.

No, friend, you do not beat me: hearken why!
The common problem, yours, mine, every
     one's,
Is—not to fancy what were fair in life
Provided it could be,—but, finding first
90 What may be, then find how to make it fair
Up to our means: a very different thing!
No abstract intellectual plan of life
Quite irrespective of life's plainest laws,
But one, a man, who is man and nothing more,
May lead within a world which (by your leave)
Is Rome or London, not Fool's-paradise.
Embellish Rome, idealize away,
Make paradise of London if you can,
You 're welcome, nay, you 're wise.

                                        A simile!
100 We mortals cross the ocean of this world
Each in his average cabin of a life;
The best 's not big, the worst yields elbow-
     room.
Now for our six months' voyage—how prepare?
You come on shipboard with a landsman's list
Of things he calls convenient: so they are!
An India screen is pretty furniture,
A piano-forte is a fine resource,
All Balzac's novels occupy one shelf,
The new edition fifty volumes long;
110 And little Greek books, with the funny type
They get up well at Leipsic,[9] fill the next:
Go on! slabbed marble, what a bath it makes!
And Parma's pride, the Jerome, let us add!
'T were pleasant could Correggio's fleeting
     glow
Hang full in face of one where'er one roams,
Since he more than the others brings with him
Italy's self,—the marvellous Modenese![10]—
Yet was not on your list before, perhaps.
—Alas, friend, here 's the agent . . . is 't the
     name?
120 The captain, or whoever 's master here—
You see him screw his face up; what 's his cry
Ere you set foot on shipboard? "Six feet
     square!"
If you won't understand what six feet mean,
Compute and purchase stores accordingly—
And if, in pique because he overhauls

Your Jerome, piano, bath, you come on board
Bare—why, you cut a figure at the first
While sympathetic landsmen see you off;
Not afterward, when long ere half seas over,
You peep up from your utterly naked boards   1
Into some snug and well-appointed berth,
Like mine for instance (try the cooler jug—
Put back the other, but don't jog the ice!)
And mortified you mutter "Well and good;
He sits enjoying his sea-furniture;
'T is stout and proper, and there 's store of it:
Though I 've the better notion, all agree,
Of fitting rooms up. Hang the carpenter,
Neat ship-shape fixings and contrivances—
I would have brought my Jerome, frame and
     all!"   1
And meantime you bring nothing: never
     mind—
You 've proved your artist-nature: what you
     don't
You might bring, so despise me, as I say.

     Now come, let 's backward to the starting-
        place.
See my way: we 're two college friends, suppose.
Prepare together for our voyage, then;
Each note and check the other in his work,—
Here 's mine, a bishop's outfit; criticize!
What 's wrong? why won't you be a bishop too?

     Why first, you don't believe, you don't and
        can't,   1
(Not statedly, that is, and fixedly
And absolutely and exclusively)
In any revelation called divine.
No dogmas nail your faith; and what remains
But say so, like the honest man you are?
First, therefore, overhaul theology!
Nay, I too, not a fool, you please to think,
Must find believing every whit as hard:
And if I do not frankly say as much,
The ugly consequence is clear enough.   1

     Now wait, my friend: well, I do not believe—
If you 'll accept no faith that is not fixed,
Absolute and exclusive, as you say.
You 're wrong—I mean to prove it in due time.
Meanwhile, I know where difficulties lie
I could not, cannot solve, nor ever shall,
So give up hope accordingly to solve—

---

[9] Leipsic: the Teubner editions of classical texts were printed in Leipsic; the series began in
1849. Turner (p. 340) notes that a new edition of the novels of Honoré de Balzac (1799-1850)
was announced for publication in 1855.
[10] Parma's pride . . . the marvelous Modenese: a painting of St. Jerome, by Correggio, a
native of the Italian district of Modena; it hung in a museum at Parma.

(To you, and over the wine) . Our dogmas then
With both of us, though in unlike degree,
Missing full credence—overboard with them!
I mean to meet you on your own premise:
Good, there go mine in company with yours!

And now what are we? unbelievers both,
Calm and complete, determinately fixed
To-day, to-morrow and for ever, pray?
You 'll guarantee me that? Not so, I think!
In no wise! all we 've gained is, that belief,
As unbelief before, shakes us by fits,
Confounds us like its predecessor. Where 's
The gain? how can we guard our unbelief,
Make it bear fruit to us?—the problem here.
Just when we are safest, there 's a sunset-
	touch,
A fancy from a flower-bell, some one's death,
A chorus-ending from Euripides,—
And that 's enough for fifty hopes and fears
As old and new at once as nature's self,
To rap and knock and enter in our soul,
Take hands and dance there, a fantastic ring,
Round the ancient idol, on his base again,—
The grand Perhaps![11] We look on helplessly.
There the old misgivings, crooked questions
	are—
This good God,—what he could do, if he
	would,
Would, if he could—then must have done long
	since:
If so, when, where and how? some way must
	be,—
Once feel about, and soon or late you hit
Some sense, in which it might be, after all.
Why not, "The Way, the Truth, the Life?"

				—That way
Over the mountain, which who stands upon
Is apt to doubt if it be meant for a road;
While, if he views it from the waste itself,
Up goes the line there, plain from base to
	brow,
Not vague, mistakable! what 's a break or two
Seen from the unbroken desert either side?
And then (to bring in fresh philosophy)
What if the breaks themselves should prove at
	last
The most consummate of contrivances
To train a man's eye, teach him what is faith?
And so we stumble at truth's very test!
All we have gained then by our unbelief

Is a life of doubt diversified by faith,   210
For one of faith diversified by doubt:
We called the chess-board white,—we call it
	black.

"Well," you rejoin, "the end 's no worse, at
	least;
We 've reason for both colours on the board:
Why not confess then, where I drop the faith
And you the doubt, that I 'm as right as you?

Because, friend, in the next place, this being
	so,
And both things even,—faith and unbelief
Left to a man's choice,—we 'll proceed a step,
Returning to our image, which I like.   220

A man's choice, yes—but a cabin passen-
	ger's—
The man made for the special life o' the
	world—
Do you forget him? I remember though!
Consult our ship's conditions and you find
One and but one choice suitable to all;
The choice, that you unluckily prefer,
Turning things topsy-turvy—they or it
Going to the ground. Belief or unbelief
Bears upon life, determines its whole course,
Begins at its beginning. See the world   230
Such as it is,—you made it not, nor I;
I mean to take it as it is,—and you,
Not so you 'll take it,—though you get nought
	else.
I know the special kind of life I like,
What suits the most my idiosyncrasy,
Brings out the best of me and bears me fruit
In power, peace, pleasantness and length of
	days.
I find that positive belief does this
For me, and unbelief, no whit of this.
—For you, it does, however?—that, we 'll try!   240
'T is clear, I cannot lead my life, at least,
Induce the world to let me peaceably,
Without declaring at the outset, "Friends,
I absolutely and peremptorily
Believe!"—I say, faith is my waking life:
One sleeps, indeed, and dreams at intervals,
We know, but waking 's the main point with
	us,
And my provision 's for life's waking part.
Accordingly, I use heart, head and hand

[11] The grand Perhaps: the French writer Rabelais (1494?–1553) said on his deathbed that he was leaving to seek "un grand Peut-Être."

All day, I build, scheme, study, and make
250   friends;
And when night overtakes me, down I lie,
Sleep, dream a little, and get done with it,
The sooner the better, to begin afresh.
What 's midnight doubt before the dayspring's
       faith?
You, the philosopher, that disbelieve,
That recognize the night, give dreams their
       weight—
To be consistent you should keep your bed,
Abstain from healthy acts that prove you man,
For fear you drowse perhaps at unawares!
260   And certainly at night you 'll sleep and dream,
Live through the day and bustle as you please.
And so you live to sleep as I to wake,
To unbelieve as I to still believe?
Well, and the common sense o' the world calls
       you
Bed-ridden,—and its good things come to me.
Its estimation, which is half the fight,
That 's the first-cabin comfort I secure:
The next . . . but you perceive with half an
       eye!
Come, come, it 's best believing, if we may;
You can't but own that!

270   Next, concede again,
If once we choose belief, on all accounts
We can't be too decisive in our faith,
Conclusive and exclusive in its terms,
To suit the world which gives us the good
       things.
In every man's career are certain points
Whereon he dares not be indifferent;
The world detects him clearly, if he dare,
As baffled at the game, and losing life.
He may care little or he may care much
280   For riches, honour, pleasure, work, repose,
Since various theories of life and life's
Success are extant which might easily
Comport with either estimate of these;
And whoso chooses wealth or poverty,
Labour or quiet, is not judged a fool
Because his fellow would choose otherwise:
We let him choose upon his own account
So long as he 's consistent with his choice.
But certain points, left wholly to himself,
290   When once a man has arbitrated on,

We say he must succeed there or go hang.
Thus, he should wed the woman he loves most
Or needs most, whatsoe'er the love or need—
For he can't wed twice. Then, he must avouch,
Or follow, at the least, sufficiently,
The form of faith his conscience holds the best,
Whate'er the process of conviction was:
For nothing can compensate his mistake
On such a point, the man himself being judge:
He cannot wed twice,[12] nor twice lose his soul.   300

   Well now, there 's one great form of Chris-
       tian faith
I happened to be born in—which to teach
Was given me as I grew up, on all hands,
As best and readiest means of living by;
The same on examination being proved
The most pronounced moreover, fixed, precise
And absolute form of faith in the whole world—
Accordingly, most potent of all forms
For working on the world. Observe, my friend!
Such as you know me, I am free to say,   310
In these hard latter days which hamper one,
Myself—by no immoderate exercise
Of intellect and learning, but the tact
To let external forces work for me,
—Bid the street's stones be bread and they are
       bread;
Bid Peter's creed, or rather, Hildebrand's,[13]
Exalt me o'er my fellows in the world
And make my life an ease and joy and pride;
It does so,—which for me 's a great point
       gained,
Who have a soul and body that exact   320
A comfortable care in many ways.
There 's power in me and will to dominate
Which I must exercise, they hurt me else:
In many ways I need mankind's respect,
Obedience, and the love that 's born of fear:
While at the same time, there 's a taste I have,
A toy of soul, a titillating thing,
Refuses to digest these dainties crude.
The naked life is gross till clothed upon:
I must take what men offer, with a grace   330
As though I would not, could I help it, take!
An uniform I wear though over-rich—
Something imposed on me, no choice of mine;
No fancy-dress worn for pure fancy's sake
And despicable therefore! now folk kneel

---

[12] Cannot wed twice: divorce was difficult in nineteenth-century England, requiring an act of
Parliament; and it was of course not possible for Roman Catholics to divorce.
[13] Hildebrand: Gregory VII, an eleventh-century pope who claimed authority over temporal
rulers. The apostle Peter, whom Christ enjoined to tend his flock, was the first pope of the early
Christian Church.

And kiss my hand—of course the Church's
    hand.
Thus I am made, thus life is best for me,
And thus that it should be I have procured;
And thus it could not be another way,
I venture to imagine.

                You 'll reply,
So far my choice, no doubt, is a success;
But were I made of better elements,
With nobler instincts, purer tastes, like you,
I hardly would account the thing success
Though it did all for me I say.

                    But, friend,
We speak of what is; not of what might be,
And how 't were better if 't were otherwise.
I am the man you see here plain enough:
Grant I 'm a beast, why, beasts must lead
    beasts' lives!
Suppose I own at once to tail and claws;
The tailless man exceeds me: but being tailed
I 'll lash out lion fashion, and leave apes
To dock[14] their stump and dress their haunches
    up.
My business is not to remake myself,
But make the absolute best of what God made.
Or—our first simile—though you prove me
    doomed
To a viler berth still, to the steerage-hole,
The sheep-pen or the pig-stye, I should strive
To make what use of each were possible;
And as this cabin gets upholstery,
That hutch should rustle with sufficient straw.

    But, friend, I don't acknowledge quite so fast
I fail of all your manhood's lofty tastes
Enumerated so complacently,
On the mere ground that you forsooth can find
In this particular life I choose to lead
No fit provision for them. Can you not?
Say you, my fault is I address myself
To grosser estimators than should judge?
And that 's no way of holding up the soul,
Which, nobler, needs men's praise perhaps, yet
    knows

One wise man's verdict outweighs all the
    fools'—
Would like the two, but, forced to choose,
    takes that.
I pine among my million imbeciles
(You think) aware some dozen men of sense
Eye me and know me, whether I believe
In the last winking Virgin,[15] as I vow,
And am a fool, or disbelieve in her
And am a knave,—approve in neither case,
Withhold their voices though I look their way: 380
Like Verdi when, at his worst opera's end
(The thing they gave at Florence,—what 's its
    name?)
While the mad houseful's plaudits near
    outbang
His orchestra of salt-box, tongs and bones,
He looks through all the roaring and the
    wreaths
Where sits Rossini patient in his stall.[16]

    Nay, friend, I meet you with an answer
    here—
That even your prime men who appraise their
    kind
Are men still, catch a wheel within a wheel,
See more in a truth than the truth's simple self,   390
Confuse themselves. You see lads walk the street
Sixty the minute; what 's to note in that?
You see one lad o'erstride a chimney-stack;
Him you must watch—he 's sure to fall, yet
    stands!
Our interest 's on the dangerous edge of things.
The honest thief, the tender murderer,
The superstitious atheist, demirep[17]
That loves and saves her soul in new French
    books—
We watch while these in equilibrium keep
The giddy line midway: one step aside,   400
They 're classed and done with. I, then, keep
    the line
Before your sages,—just the men to shrink
From the gross weights, coarse scales and labels
    broad
You offer their refinement. Fool or knave?
Why needs a bishop be a fool or knave

---

[14] Dock: cut off.

[15] See also line 728. The question of a belief in miracles was a common topic of theological dispute in the nineteenth century; and Roman Catholics were often charged with being indiscriminate, especially in crediting contemporary miracles, such as statues of the Virgin whose eyes were alleged to move.

[16] An episode that occurred at the first performance of Guiseppe Verdi's (1813–1901) opera *Macbeth* in 1847. Gioacchino Rossini (1792–1868) had by that date completed his best work; Verdi's still lay ahead of him.

[17] Demirep: a woman of doubtful reputation; often a prostitute who moves on the fringes of fashionable society.

When there 's a thousand diamond weights
   between?
So, I enlist them. Your picked twelve, you 'll
   find
Profess themselves indignant, scandalized
At thus being held unable to explain
410 How a superior man who disbelieves
May not believe as well: that 's Schelling's
   way![18]
It 's through my coming in the tail of time,
Nicking the minute with a happy tact.
Had I been born three hundred years ago
They 'd say, "What 's strange? Blougram of
   course believes";
And, seventy years since, "disbelieves of course."
But now, "He may believe; and yet, and yet
How can he?" All eyes turn with interest.
Whereas, step off the line on either side—
420 You, for example, clever to a fault,
The rough and ready man who write apace,
Read somewhat seldomer, think perhaps even
   less—
You disbelieve! Who wonders and who cares?
Lord So-and-so—his coat bedropped with wax,
All Peter's chains about his waist, his back
Brave with the needlework of Noodledom[19]—
Believes! Again, who wonders and who cares?
But I, the man of sense and learning too,
The able to think yet act, the this, the that,
430 I, to believe at this late time of day!
Enough; you see, I need not fear contempt.

   —Except it 's yours! Admire me as these may,
You don't. But whom at least do you admire?
Present your own perfection, your ideal,
Your pattern man for a minute—oh, make
   haste,
Is it Napoleon you would have us grow?
Concede the means; allow his head and hand,
(A large concession, clever as you are)
Good! In our common primal element

Of unbelief (we can't believe, you know— 44
We 're still at that admission, recollect!)
Where do you find—apart from, towering o'er
The secondary temporary aims
Which satisfy the gross taste you despise—
Where do you find his star?—his crazy trust
God knows through what or in what? it 's alive
And shines and leads him, and that's all we
   want.
Have we aught in our sober night shall point
Such ends as his were, and direct the means
Of working out our purpose straight as his, 4
Nor bring a moment's trouble on success
With after-care to justify the same?
—Be a Napoleon, and yet disbelieve—
Why, the man 's mad, friend, take his light
   away!
What 's the vague good o' the world, for which
   you dare
With comfort to yourself blow millions up?
We neither of us see it! we do see
The blown-up millions—spatter of their brains
And writhing of their bowels and so forth,
In that bewildering entanglement 4
Of horrible eventualities
Past calculation to the end of time!
Can I mistake for some clear word of God
(Which were my ample warrant for it all)
His puff of hazy instinct, idle talk,
"The State, that 's I," quack-nonsense about
   crowns,
And (when one beats the man to his last hold)
A vague idea of setting things to rights,
Policing people efficaciously,
More to their profit, most of all to his own; 4
The whole to end that dismallest of ends
By an Austrian marriage,[20] cant to us the
   Church,
And resurrection of the old *régime?*
Would I, who hope to live a dozen years,
Fight Austerlitz[21] for reasons such and such?

---

[18] Friedrich Wilhelm Joseph von Schelling (1775–1854), a German idealist philosopher, was often accused of inconsistency. Blougram here perhaps refers to Schelling's insistence, in one stage of his thought, that human knowledge of external objects is limited because we cannot fully know existences distinct from our own; and to his idea, in another stage of his thought, that all existences are identical because they proceed from an absolute existence whose being we can intuit.

[19] One of the points of contention in the 1850s, both within the Church of England and between its clergy and that of the Roman Catholic church, was that involving the ritual of worship—whether vestments and churches should be elaborately decorated, for example, and whether the ceremonies themselves should be intricate. No matter what his church, Blougram's Lord So-and-so, his coat splattered with wax from church candles and fatuously ornamented, thinks that faith should be preclaimed in distinctive ritual.

[20] Napoleon divorced his wife in 1810 to marry the Archduchess Maria Louisa of Austria because he wanted an heir.

[21] Austerlitz: the site of a decisive battle in 1805, in which Napoleon defeated the Russian and Austrian armies.

No: for, concede me but the merest chance
Doubt may be wrong—there 's judgment, life
    to come!
With just that chance, I dare not. Doubt proves
    right?
This present life is all?—you offer me
Its dozen noisy years, without a chance
That wedding an archduchess, wearing lace,
And getting called by divers new-coined names,
Will drive off ugly thoughts and let me dine,
Sleep, read and chat in quiet as I like!
Therefore I will not.

          Take another case;
Fit up the cabin yet another way.
What say you to the poets? shall we write
Hamlet, Othello—make the world our own,
Without a risk to run of either sort?
I can't!—to put the strongest reason first.
"But try," you urge, "the trying shall suffice;
The aim, if reached or not, makes great the
    life:
Try to be Shakespeare, leave the rest to fate!"
Spare my self-knowledge—there 's no fooling
    me!
If I prefer remaining my poor self,
I say so not in self-dispraise but praise.
If I 'm a Shakespeare, let the well alone;
Why should I try to be what now I am?
If I 'm no Shakespeare, as too probable,—
His power and consciousness and self-delight
And all we want in common, shall I find—
Trying for ever? while on points of taste
Wherewith, to speak it humbly, he and I
Are dowered alike—I 'll ask you, I or he,
Which in our two lives realizes most?
Much, he imagined—somewhat, I possess.
He had the imagination; stick to that!
Let him say, "In the face of my soul's works
Your world is worthless and I touch it not
Lest I should wrong them"—I 'll withdraw my
    plea.
But does he say so? look upon his life!
Himself, who only can, gives judgment there.
He leaves his towers and gorgeous palaces
To build the trimmest house in Stratford town;

Saves money, spends it, owns the worth of
    things,
Giulio Romano's pictures, Dowland's lute;[22]
Enjoys a show, respects the puppets, too,
And none more, had he seen its entry once,
Than "Pandulph, of fair Milan cardinal."[23]
Why then should I who play that personage,   520
The very Pandulph Shakespeare's fancy made,
Be told that had the poet chanced to start
From where I stand now (some degree like
    mine
Being just the goal he ran his race to reach)
He would have run the whole race back,
    forsooth,
And left being Pandulph, to begin write plays?
Ah, the earth's best can be but the earth's best!
Did Shakespeare live, he could but sit at home
And get himself in dreams the Vatican,
Greek busts, Venetian paintings, Roman walls,   530
And English books, none equal to his own,
Which I read, bound in gold (he never did).
—Terni's fall, Naples' bay and Gothard's
    top[24]—
Eh, friend? I could not fancy one of these;
But, as I pour this claret, there they are:
I 've gained them—crossed St. Gothard last July
With ten mules to the carriage and a bed
Slung inside; is my hap[25] the worse for that?
We want the same things, Shakespeare and
    myself,
And what I want, I have: he, gifted more,   540
Could fancy he too had them when he liked,
But not so thoroughly that, if fate allowed,
He would not have them also in my sense.
We play one game; I send the ball aloft
No less adroitly that of fifty strokes
Scarce five go o'er the wall so wide and high
Which sends them back to me: I wish and get.
He struck balls higher and with better skill,
But at a poor fence level with his head,
And hit—his Stratford house, a coat of arms,   550
Successful dealings in his grain and wool,—
While I receive heaven's incense in my nose
And style myself the cousin of Queen Bess.[26]
Ask him, if this life's all, who wins the game?

---

[22] Giulio Romano: a sixteenth-century Italian painter; Shakespeare refers to him in *The Winter's Tale*. John Dowland: a contemporary of Shakespeare, a musician and composer.

[23] *King John*, III, i. In the play Pandulph, as papal legate, excommunicates John.

[24] Terni: a city in central Italy, famous for its waterfalls; St. Gothard: a pass in the Alps between Italy and Switzerland.

[25] Hap: fortune.

[26] Wiseman's family traced its descent from a member of the court of Henry VIII, Elizabeth's father. But it is more likely that Browning here has Blougram claim a secular authority as a bishop—that now and especially if he were Shakespeare's contemporary, he can treat with temporal rulers as the representative of a ruler who also claims secular power.

Believe—and our whole argument breaks up.
Enthusiasm 's the best thing, I repeat;
Only, we can't command it; fire and life
Are all, dead matter 's nothing, we agree:
And be it a mad dream or God's very breath,
560 The fact 's the same,—belief's fire, once in us,
Makes of all else mere stuff to show itself:
We penetrate our life with such a glow
As fire lends wood and iron—this turns steel,
That burns to ash—all 's one, fire proves its
     power
For good or ill, since men call flare success.
But paint a fire, it will not therefore burn.
Light one in me, I 'll find it food enough!
Why, to be Luther—that 's a life to lead,
Incomparably better than my own.
He comes, reclaims God's earth for God, he
570   says,
Sets up God's rule again by simple means,
Re-opens a shut book, and all is done.
He flared out in the flaring of mankind;
Such Luther's luck was: how shall such be
     mine?
If he succeeded, nothing 's left to do:
And if he did not altogether—well,
Strauss[27] is the next advance. All Strauss should
     be
I might be also. But to what result?
He looks upon no future: Luther did.
580 What can I gain on the denying side?
Ice makes no conflagration. State the facts,
Read the text right, emancipate the world—
The emancipated world enjoys itself
With scarce a thank-you: Blougram told it first
It could not owe a farthing,—not to him
More than Saint Paul! 't would press its pay,
     you think?
Then add there 's still that plaguy hundredth
     chance
Strauss may be wrong. And so a risk is run—
For what gain? not for Luther's, who secured
590 A real heaven in his heart throughout his life,
Supposing death a little altered things.

    "Ay, but since really you lack faith," you
        cry,
You run the same risk really on all sides,

In cool indifference as bold unbelief.
As well be Strauss as swing 'twixt Paul and
     him.
It 's not worth having, such imperfect faith,
No more available to do faith's work
Than unbelief like mine. Whole faith, or
     none!"

    Softly, my friend! I must dispute that point.
Once own the use of faith, I 'll find you faith.
We 're back on Christian ground. You call for
     faith:
I show you doubt, to prove that faith exists.
The more of doubt, the stronger faith, I say,
If faith o'ercomes doubt. How I know it does?
By life and man's free will, God gave for that!
To mould life as we choose it, shows our
     choice:
That 's our one act, the previous work 's his
     own.
You criticize the soul? it reared this tree—
This broad life and whatever fruit it bears!
What matter though I doubt at every pore,
Head-doubts, heart-doubts, doubts at my
     fingers' ends,
Doubts in the trivial work of every day,
Doubts at the very bases of my soul
In the grand moments when she probes her-
     self—
If finally I have a life to show,
The thing I did, brought out in evidence
Against the thing done to me underground
By hell and all its brood, for aught I know?
I say, whence sprang this? shows it faith or
     doubt?
All 's doubt in me; where 's break of faith in
     this?
It is the idea, the feeling and the love,
God means mankind should strive for and
     show forth
Whatever be the process to that end,—
And not historic knowledge, logic sound,
And metaphysical acumen, sure!
"What think ye of Christ," friend? when all 's
     done and said,
Like you this Christianity or not?
It may be false, but will you wish it true?

[27] David Friedrich Strauss (1808–74) published a life of Christ in German in 1835 (it was translated into English in 1846). Strauss's work is an advance upon Luther's, in Blougram's ironic argument, because while Luther translated the Bible and opened it to the personal interpretations of believing Christians, Strauss proposed an account of Christ's life he believed to be historically sound by analyzing the accounts of the New Testament and discarding elements he thought to be mythic. In the view of conventional theologians, Strauss denied or at least compromised claims to Christ's divinity by dismissing as inaccurate some of the events upon which these claims were founded.

Has it your vote to be so if it can?
Trust you an instinct silenced long ago
That will break silence and enjoin you love
What mortified philosophy is hoarse,
And all in vain, with bidding you despise?
If you desire faith—then you 've faith enough:
What else seeks God—nay, what else seek
    ourselves?
You form a notion of me, we 'll suppose,
On hearsay; it 's a favourable one:
"But still" (you add), "there was no such good
    man,
Because of contradiction in the facts.
One proves, for instance, he was born in
    Rome,[28]
This Blougram; yet throughout the tales of
    him
I see he figures as an Englishman."
Well, the two things are reconcileable.
But would I rather you discovered that,
Subjoining—"Still, what matter though they
    be?
Blougram concerns me nought, born here or
    there."

    Pure faith indeed—you know not what you
    ask!
Naked belief in God the Omnipotent,
Omniscient, Omnipresent, sears too much
The sense of conscious creatures to be borne.
It were the seeing him, no flesh shall dare.
Some think, Creation 's meant to show him
    forth:
I say it 's meant to hide him all it can,
And that 's what all the blessed evil 's for.
Its use in Time is to environ us,
Our breath, our drop of dew, with shield
    enough
Against that sight till we can bear its stress.
Under a vertical sun, the exposed brain
And lidless eye and disemprisoned heart
Less certainly would wither up at once
Than mind, confronted with the truth of him.
But time and earth case-harden us to live;
The feeblest sense is trusted most; the child
Feels God a moment, ichors[29] o'er the place,

Plays on and grows to be a man like us.
With me, faith means perpetual unbelief
Kept quiet like the snake 'neath Michael's[30]
    foot
Who stands calm just because he feels it
    writhe.
Or, if that 's too ambitious,—here 's my box[31]—
I need the excitation of a pinch
Threatening the torpor of the inside-nose
Nigh on the imminent sneeze that never comes.
"Leave it in peace" advise the simple folk:
Make it aware of peace by itching-fits,
Say I—let doubt occasion still more faith!

    You 'll say, once all believed, man, woman,
    child,
In that dear middle-age these noodles praise.
How you 'd exult if I could put you back
Six hundred years, blot out cosmogony,
Geology, ethnology, what not,
(Greek endings, each the little passing-bell
That signifies some faith 's about to die),
And set you square with Genesis again,[32]—
When such a traveller told you his last news,
He saw the ark a-top of Ararat[33]
But did not climb there since 't was getting
    dusk
And robber-bands infest the mountain's foot!
How should you feel, I ask, in such an age,
How act? As other people felt and did;
With soul more blank than this decanter's
    knob,
Believe—and yet lie, kill, rob, fornicate
Full in belief's face, like the beast you 'd be!

    No, when the fight begins within himself,
A man's worth something. God stoops o'er his
    head,
Satan looks up between his feet—both tug—
He 's left, himself, i' the middle: the soul
    wakes
And grows. Prolong that battle through his
    life!
Never leave growing till the life to come!
Here, we' ve got callous to the Virgin's winks
That used to puzzle people wholesomely:

[28] Wiseman was born in Spain, of British parents.

[29] Ichor: an ethereal fluid which runs in the veins of the gods of Greek mythology.

[30] Michael: one of the archangels who helped expel Satan from Paradise; he is conventionally depicted in arms with his foot on the head of a dragon.

[31] Box: snuffbox.

[32] The findings of geology and other sciences offered data inconsistent with the account of the creation of the universe given in Genesis.

[33] Ararat: a mountain in what is now Turkey on the top of which Noah's ark is supposed to have come to rest when the flood receded.

Men have outgrown the shame of being fools.
What are the laws of nature, not to bend
If the Church bid them?—brother Newman[34]
    asks.
Up with the Immaculate Conception, then—
On to the rack with faith!—is my advice.
Will not that hurry us upon our knees,
Knocking our breasts, "It can't be—yet it shall!
Who am I, the worm, to argue with my Pope?
Low things confound the high things!" and so
    forth.
710   That 's better than acquitting God with grace
As some folk do. He 's tried—no case is proved,
Philosophy is lenient—he may go!

    You 'll say, the old system 's not so obsolete
But men believe still: ay, but who and where?
King Bomba's lazzaroni[35] foster yet
The sacred flame, so Antonelli[36] writes;
But even of these, what ragamuffin-saint
Believes God watches him continually,
As he believes in fire that it will burn,
Or rain that it will drench him? Break fire's
720   law,
Sin against rain, although the penalty
Be just a singe or soaking? "No," he smiles;
Those laws are laws that can enforce them-
    selves."

    The sum of all is—yes, my doubt is great,
My faith 's still greater, then my faith 's
    enough.
I have read much, thought much, experienced
    much,
Yet would die rather than avow my fear
The Naples liquefaction may be false,[37]
When set to happen by the palace-clock
730   According to the clouds or dinner-time.

I hear you recommend, I might at least
Eliminate, decrassify my faith
Since I adopt it; keeping what I must
And leaving what I can—such points as this.
I won't—that is, I can't throw one away.
Supposing there 's no truth in what I hold
About the need of trial to man's faith,
Still, when you bid me purify the same,
To such a process I discern no end.
Clearing off one excrescence to see two,   74
There 's ever a next in size, now grown as big,
That meets the knife: I cut and cut again!
First cut the Liquefaction, what comes last
But Fichte's clever cut at God himself?[38]
Experimentalize on sacred things!
I trust nor hand nor eye nor heart nor brain
To stop betimes: they all get drunk alike.
The first step, I am master not to take.

    You 'd find the cutting-process to your taste
As much as leaving growths of lies unpruned,   7
Nor see more danger in it,—you retort.
Your taste 's worth mine; but my taste proves
    more wise
When we consider that the steadfast hold
On the extreme end of the chain of faith
Gives all the advantage, makes the difference
With the rough purblind mass we seek to rule:
We are their lords, or they are free of us,
Just as we tighten or relax our hold.
So, other matters equal, we 'll revert
To the first problem—which, if solved my way   7
And thrown into the balance, turns the scale—
How we may lead a comfortable life,
How suit our luggage to the cabin's size.

    Of course you are remarking all this time
How narrowly and grossly I view life,

[34] John Henry Newman (1801–90), one of the leaders of the Oxford Movement, which tried to connect the English church with the early Christian church, became a Roman Catholic in 1845. His argument for belief in miracles was predicated on the premise that God commands the laws of physical nature. The Immaculate Conception is the belief that the Virgin Mary was free from original sin, the sin all humans inherit from Adam. Browning may intend here to refer to another doctrine of the Roman Catholic church, that Christ was conceived without the agency of sexual intercourse, which is a suspension of the laws of nature.
[35] King Bomba: a derisive name for Ferdinand II, king of the Two Sicilies. Lazzaroni: beggars of Naples.
[36] Antonelli: a cardinal who was secretary to Pope Pius IX (1792–1878).
[37] A vial of the blood of St. Januarius was kept in a church in Naples; the blood was restored to its liquid state when, usually on the feast day of the saint, it was brought into the presence of his statue. Newman, arguing in the early 1850s for a belief in miracles, specifically cited this phenomenon as a contemporary miracle.
[38] Johann Gottlieb Fichte (1765–1814), another German idealist philosopher, maintained that consciousness formulates for itself the objects of its knowledge, that we only know our ideas of things. The "clever cut," then, may be a notion that God only exists as our idea; or Blougram may refer here more generally to Fichte's idea, sometimes regarded as atheistic by conventional nineteenth-century theologians, that God exists only in the moral order of the universe.

Respect the creature-comforts, care to rule
The masses, and regard complacently
"The cabin," in our old phrase. Well, I do.
I act for, talk for, live for this world now,
As this world prizes action, life and talk:
No prejudice to what next world may prove,
Whose new laws and requirements, my best
    pledge
To observe then, is that I observe these now,
Shall do hereafter what I do meanwhile.
Let us concede (gratuitously though)
Next life relieves the soul of body, yields
Pure spiritual enjoyment: well, my friend,
Why lose this life i' the meantime, since its use
May be to make the next life more intense?

Do you know, I have often had a dream
(Work it up in your next month's article)
Of man's poor spirit in its progress, still
Losing true life for ever and a day
Through ever trying to be and ever being—
In the evolution of successive spheres—
Before its actual sphere and place of life,
Halfway into the next, which having reached,
It shoots with corresponding foolery
Halfway into the next still, on and off!
As when a traveller, bound from North to
    South,
Scouts[39] fur in Russia: what 's its use in France?
In France spurns flannel: where 's its need in
    Spain?
In Spain drops cloth, too cumbrous for Algiers!
Linen goes next, and last the skin itself,
A superfluity at Timbuctoo.
When, through his journey, was the fool at
    ease?
I 'm at ease now, friend; worldly in this world,
I take and like its way of life; I think
My brothers, who administer the means,
Live better for my comfort—that 's good too;
And God, if he pronounce upon such life,
Approves my service, which is better still.
If he keep silence,—why, for you or me
Or that brute beast pulled-up in to-day's
    "Times,"
What odds is 't, save to ourselves, what life we
    lead?

You meet me at this issue: you declare,—
All special-pleading done with—truth is truth,
And justifies itself by undreamed ways.
You don't fear but it's better, if we doubt,

To say so, act up to our truth perceived   810
However feebly. Do then,—act away!
'T is there I 'm on the watch for you. How one
    acts
Is, both of us agree, our chief concern:
And how you 'll act is what I fain would see
If, like the candid person you appear,
You dare to make the most of your life's
    scheme
As I of mine, live up to its full law
Since there 's no higher law that counterchecks.
Put natural religion to the test
You've just demolished the revealed with—
    quick,   820
Down to the root of all that checks your will,
All prohibition to lie, kill and thieve,
Or even to be an atheistic priest!
Suppose a pricking to incontinence—
Philosophers deduce you chastity
Or shame, from just the fact that at the first
Whoso embraced a woman in the field,
Threw club down and forewent his brains
    beside,
So, stood a ready victim in the reach
Of any brother savage, club in hand;   830
Hence saw the use of going out of sight
In wood or cave to prosecute his loves:
I read this in a French book t' other day.
Does law so analysed coerce you much?
Oh, men spin clouds of fuzz where matters end,
But you who reach where the first thread
    begins,
You 'll soon cut that!—which means you can,
    but won't,
Through certain instincts, blind, unreasoned-
    out,
You dare not set aside, you can't tell why,
But there they are, and so you let them rule.   840
Then, friend, you seem as much a slave as I,
A liar, conscious coward and hypocrite,
Without the good the slave expects to get,
In case he has a master after all!
You own your instincts? why, what else do I,
Who want, am made for, and must have a God
Ere I can be aught, do aught?—no mere name
Want, but the true thing with what proves its
    truth,
To wit, a relation from that thing to me,
Touching from head to foot—which touch I
    feel,   850
And with it take the rest, this life of ours!
I live my life here; yours you dare not live.

[39] Scouts: rejects.

Not as I state it, who (you please subjoin)
Disfigure such a life and call it names,
While, to your mind, remains another way
For simple men: knowledge and power have
     rights,
But ignorance and weakness have rights too.
There needs no crucial effort to find truth
If here or there or anywhere about:
860 We ought to turn each side, try hard and see,
And if we can't, be glad we 've earned at least
The right, by one laborious proof the more,
To graze in peace earth's pleasant pasturage.
Men are not angels, neither are they brutes:
Something we may see, all we cannot see.
What need of lying? I say, I see all,
And swear to each detail the most minute
In what I think a Pan's face—you, mere cloud:
I swear I hear him speak and see him wink,
870 For fear, if once I drop the emphasis,
Mankind may doubt there 's any cloud at all.
You take the simple life—ready to see,
Willing to see (for no cloud 's worth a face) —
And leaving quiet what no strength can move,
And which, who bids you move? who has the
     right?
I bid you; but you are God's sheep, not mine:
"Pastor est tui Dominus."[40] You find
In this the pleasant pasture of our life
Much you may eat without the least offence,
880 Much you don't eat because your maw objects,
Much you would eat but that your fellow-flock
Open great eyes at you and even butt,
And thereupon you like your mates so well
You cannot please yourself, offending them;
Though when they seem exorbitantly sheep,
You weigh your pleasure with their butts and
     bleats
And strike the balance. Sometimes certain fears
Restrain you, real checks since you find them
     so;
Sometimes you please yourself and nothing
     checks:
And thus you graze through life with not one
890   lie,
And like it best.

                          But do you, in truth's name?
If so, you beat—which means you are not I—

Who needs must make each mine and feed my
     fill
Not simply unbutted at, unbickered with,
But motioned to the velvet of the sward
By those obsequious wethers' very selves.
Look at me, sir; my age is double yours:
At yours, I knew beforehand, so enjoyed,
What now I should be—as, permit the word,
I pretty well imagine your whole range   90
And stretch of tether twenty years to come.
We both have minds and bodies much alike:
In truth's name, don't you want my bishopric,
My daily bread, my influence and my state?
You 're young. I 'm old; you must be old one
     day;
Will you find then, as I do hour by hour;
Women their lovers kneel to, who cut curls
From your fat lap-dog's ear to grace a brooch—
Dukes, who petition just to kiss your ring—
With much beside you know or may conceive?   9.
Suppose we die to-night: well, here am I,
Such were my gains, life bore this fruit to me,
While writing all the same my articles
On music, poetry, the fictile vase
Found at Albano, chess, Anacreon's[41] Greek.
But you—the highest honour in your life,
The thing you 'll crown yourself with, all your
     days,
Is—dining here and drinking this last glass
I pour you out in sign of amity
Before we part for ever. Of your power   9.
And social influence, worldly worth in short,
Judge what 's my estimation by the fact,
I do not condescend to enjoin, beseech,
Hint secrecy on one of all these words!
You're shrewd and know that should you
     publish one
The world would brand the lie—my enemies
     first,
Who 'd sneer—"the bishop 's an arch-hypocrite
And knave perhaps, but not so frank a fool."
Whereas I should not dare for both my ears
Breathe one such syllable, smile one such smile, 9:
Before the chaplain who reflects myself—
My shade 's so much more potent than your
     flesh.
What 's your reward, self-abnegating friend?
Stood you confessed of those exceptional
And privileged great natures that dwarf mine—

---

[40] The Lord is your shepherd.
[41] Fictile: made of clay; Albano: a lake in an extinct volcano in Italy; Anacreon: a Greek lyric
poet of the sixth century B.C. who wrote on sensual pleasures. Wiseman wrote and lectured on
art, literature, and science, had recently (1854) published a novel (Fabiola, or The Church of
the Catacombs), and founded (1836) a cultural quarterly, the Dublin Review.

A zealot with a mad ideal in reach,
A poet just about to print his ode,
A statesman with a scheme to stop this war,[42]
An artist whose religion is his art—
40 I should have nothing to object: such men
Carry the fire, all things grow warm to them,
Their drugget 's[43] worth my purple, they beat
	me.
But you,—you 're just as little those as I—
You, Gigadibs, who, thirty years of age,
Write statedly for Blackwood's Magazine,[44]
Believe you see two points in Hamlet's soul
Unseized by the Germans yet—which view you
	'll print—
Meantime the best you have to show being still
That lively lightsome article we took
50 Almost for the true Dickens,—what 's its name?
"The Slum and Cellar, or Whitechapel life
Limned after dark!" it made me laugh, I know,
And pleased a month, and brought you in ten
	pounds.
—Success I recognize and compliment,
And therefore give you, if you choose, three
	words
(The card and pencil-scratch is quite enough)
Which whether here, in Dublin or New York,
Will get you, prompt as at my eyebrow's wink,
Such terms as never you aspired to get
60 In all our own reviews and some not ours.
Go write your lively sketches! be the first
"Blougram, or The Eccentric Confidence"—
Or better simply say, "The Outward-bound."
Why, men as soon would throw it in my teeth
As copy and quote the infamy chalked broad
About me on the church-door opposite.
You will not wait for that experience though,
I fancy, howsoever you decide,
To discontinue—not detesting, not
70 Defaming, but at least—despising me!

———————

Over his wine so smiled and talked his hour
Sylvester Blougram, styled *in partibus
Episcopus, nec non*[45]— (the deuce knows what
It 's changed to by our novel hierarchy)
With Gigadibs the literary man,

Who played with spoons, explored his plate's
	design,
And ranged the olive-stones about its edge,
While the great bishop rolled him out a mind
Long crumpled, till creased consciousness lay
	smooth.[46]

For Blougram, he believed, say, half he
	spoke.					980
The other portion, as he shaped it thus
For argumentatory purposes,
He felt his foe was foolish to dispute.
Some arbitrary accidental thoughts
That crossed his mind, amusing because new,
He chose to represent as fixtures there,
Invariable convictions (such they seemed
Beside his interlocutor's loose cards
Flung daily down, and not the same way twice)
While certain hell-deep instincts, man's weak
	tongue					990
Is never bold to utter in their truth
Because styled hell-deep ('t is an old mistake
To place hell at the bottom of the earth)
He ignored these,—not having in readiness
Their nomenclature and philosophy:
He said true things, but called them by wrong
	names.
"On the whole," he thought, "I justify myself
On every point where cavillers like this
Oppugn my life: he tries one kind of fence,
I close, he 's worsted, that 's enough for him.	1000
He 's on the ground: if ground should break
	away
I take my stand on, there 's a firmer yet
Beneath it, both of us may sink and reach.
His ground was over mine and broke the first:
So, let him sit with me this many a year!"

He did not sit five minutes. Just a week
Sufficed his sudden healthy vehemence.
Something had struck him in the "Outward-
	bound"
Another way than Blougram's purpose was:
And having bought, not cabin-furniture	1010
But settler's-implements (enough for three)
And started for Australia—there, I hope,

---

[42] This war: presumably the Crimean War, which began in 1854.
[43] Drugget: a coarse cloth.
[44] *Blackwood's Magazine:* a popular, middle-class monthly magazine.
[45] *In partibus* . . . : before England was divided by the Vatican into Roman Catholic episcopal sees, Blougram's title would have been *in partibus infidelium:* a bishop in a pagan country; *nec non:* and also (a bishop of a see outside England) .
[46] Line 979 was added after the poem first appeared in *Men and Women* in 1855.

By this time he has tested his first plough,
And studied his last chapter of St. John.[47]
1855

Andrea del Sarto, the son of a tailor, was born in Florence in 1486. In 1518 he went to Paris to paint under the patronage of Francis I, who gave him some money to return to Italy and buy paintings for the king's own collection. According to the story Browning used, Andrea was persuaded by his wife, Lucrezia, to remain in Florence and to use the king's money to build a house. Browning's principal source for the circumstances of Andrea's life was Giorgio Vasari's Lives of the Painters *(1550), in which Lucrezia is described as artful, and Andrea's paintings are characterized as showing great technical facility, but as lacking in boldness, animation, and force. Andrea died in 1531.*

Andrea del Sarto

(*Called "The Faultless Painter"*)

But do not let us quarrel any more,
No, my Lucrezia; bear with me for once:
Sit down and all shall happen as you wish.
You turn your face, but does it bring your
    heart?
I'll work then for your friend's friend, never
    fear,
Treat his own subject after his own way,
Fix his own time, accept too his own price,
And shut the money into this small hand
When next it takes mine. Will it? tenderly?
Oh, I'll content him,—but to-morrow, Love!
I often am much wearier than you think,
This evening more than usual, and it seems
As if—forgive now—should you let me sit
Here by the window with your hand in mine
And look a half-hour forth on Fiesole,[1]
Both of one mind, as married people use,
Quietly, quietly the evening through,
I might get up to-morrow to my work
Cheerful and fresh as ever. Let us try.
To-morrow, how you shall be glad for this!
Your soft hand is a woman of itself,
And mine the man's bared breast she curls
    inside.
Don't count the time lost, neither; you must
    serve

For each of the five pictures we require:
It saves a model. So! keep looking so—
My serpentining beauty, rounds on rounds!
—How could you ever prick those perfect ears,
Even to put the pearl there! oh, so sweet—
My face, my moon, my everybody's moon,
Which everybody looks on and calls his,
And, I suppose, is looked on by in turn,
While she looks—no one's: very dear, no less.
You smile? why, there's my picture ready made,
There's what we painters call our harmony!
A common greyness silvers everything,—
All in a twilight, you and I alike
—You, at the point of your first pride in me
(That's gone you know),—but I, at every
    point;
My youth, my hope, my art, being all toned
    down
To yonder sober pleasant Fiesole.
There's the bell clinking from the chapel-top;
That length of convent-wall across the way
Holds the trees safer, huddled more inside;
The last monk leaves the garden; days decrease,
And autumn grows, autumn in everything.
Eh? the whole seems to fall into a shape
As if I saw alike my work and self
And all that I was born to be and do,
A twilight-piece. Love, we are in God's hand.
How strange now, looks the life he makes us
    lead;
So free we seem, so fettered fast we are!
I feel he laid the fetter: let it lie!
This chamber for example—turn your head—
All that's behind us! You don't understand
Nor care to understand about my art,
But you can hear at least when people speak:
And that cartoon,[2] the second from the door
—It is the thing, Love! so such things should
    be—
Behold Madonna!—I am bold to say.
I can do with my pencil what I know,
What I see, what at bottom of my heart
I wish for, if I ever wish so deep—
Do easily, too—when I say, perfectly,
I do not boast, perhaps: yourself are judge,
Who listened to the Legate's talk last week,
And just as much they used to say in France.
At any rate 't is easy, all of it!
No sketches first, no studies, that's long past:
I do what many dream of, all their lives,

—Dream? strive to do, and agonize to do,
And fail in doing. I could count twenty such
On twice your fingers, and not leave this town,
Who strive—you don't know how the others
    strive
To paint a little thing like that you smeared
Carelessly passing with your robes afloat,—
Yet do much less, so much less, Someone says,
(I know his name, no matter) —so much less!
Well, less is more, Lucrezia: I am judged.
There burns a truer light of God in them,
In their vexed beating stuffed and stopped-up
    brain,
Heart, or whate'er else, than goes on to prompt
This low-pulsed forthright craftsman's hand of
    mine.
Their works drop groundward, but themselves,
    I know,
Reach many a time a heaven that's shut to me,
Enter and take their place there sure enough,
Though they come back and cannot tell the
    world.
My works are nearer heaven, but I sit here.
The sudden blood of these men! at a word—
Praise them, it boils, or blame them, it boils
    too.
I, painting from myself and to myself,
Know what I do, am unmoved by men's blame
Or their praise either. Somebody remarks
Morello's[3] outline there is wrongly traced,
His hue mistaken; what of that? or else,
Rightly traced and well ordered; what of that?
Speak as they please, what does the mountain
    care?
Ah, but a man's reach should exceed his grasp,
Or what's a heaven for? All is silver-grey
Placid and perfect with my art: the worse!
I know both what I want and what might gain,
And yet how profitless to know, to sigh
"Had I been two, another and myself,
Our head would have o'erlooked the world!"
    No doubt.
Yonder's a work now, of that famous youth
The Urbinate who died five years ago.[4]
('T is copied, George Vasari[5] sent it me.)
Well, I can fancy how he did it all,
Pouring his soul, with kings and popes to see,
Reaching, that heaven might so replenish him,

Above and through his art—for it gives way;   110
That arm is wrongly put—and there again—
A fault to pardon in the drawing's lines,
Its body, so to speak: its soul is right,
He means right—that, a child may understand.
Still, what an arm! and I could alter it:
But all the play, the insight and the stretch—
Out of me, out of me! And wherefore out?
Had you enjoined them on me, given me soul,
We might have risen to Rafael, I and you!
Nay, Love, you did give all I asked, I think—   120
More than I merit, yes, by many times.
But had you—oh, with the same perfect brow,
And perfect eyes, and more than perfect
    mouth,
And the low voice my soul hears, as a bird
The fowler's pipe, and follows to the snare—
Had you, with these the same, but brought a
    mind!
Some women do so. Had the mouth there urged
"God and the glory! never care for gain.
The present by the future, what is that?
Live for fame, side by side with Agnolo![6]   130
Rafael is waiting: up to God, all three!"
I might have done it for you. So it seems:
Perhaps not. All is as God over-rules.
Beside, incentives come from the soul's self;
The rest avail not. Why do I need you?
What wife had Rafael, or has Agnolo?
In this world, who can do a thing, will not;
And who would do it, cannot, I perceive:
Yet the will's somewhat—somewhat, too, the
    power—
And thus we half-men struggle. At the end,   140
God, I conclude, compensates, punishes.
'T is safer for me, if the award be strict,
That I am something underrated here,
Poor this long while, despised, to speak the
    truth.
I dared not, do you know, leave home all day,
For fear of chancing on the Paris lords.
The best is when they pass and look aside;
But they speak sometimes; I must bear it all.
Well may they speak! That Francis, that first
    time,
And that long festal year at Fontainebleau![7]   150
I surely then could sometimes leave the
    ground,

---

[3] Morello: a mountain in the Apennines north of Florence.
[4] Urbinate: Raphael (1483–1520), one of the several great contemporaries to whom Andrea refers in his monologue, was born in Urbino.
[5] Vasari, who was born in 1511, was once an apprentice to Andrea.
[6] Agnolo: Michaelangelo (1475–1564), another of Andrea's great contemporaries, and also born in Florence.
[7] Fontainebleau: a royal seat outside Paris.

Put on the glory, Rafael's daily wear,
In that humane great monarch's golden look,—
One finger in his beard or twisted curl
Over his mouth's good mark that made the
    smile,
One arm about my shoulder, round my neck,
The jingle of his gold chain in my ear,
I painting proudly with his breath on me,
All his court round him, seeing with his eyes,
160 Such frank French eyes, and such a fire of souls
Profuse, my hand kept plying by those
    hearts,—
And, best of all, this, this, this face beyond,
This in the background, waiting on my work,
To crown the issue with a last reward!
A good time, was it not, my kingly days?
And had you not grown restless . . . but I
    know—
'T is done and past; 't was right, my instinct
    said;
Too live the life grew, golden and not grey,
And I'm the weak-eyed bat no sun should
    tempt
Out of the grange whose four walls make his
170   world.
How could it end in any other way?
You called me, and I came home to your heart.
The triumph was—to reach and stay there;
    since
I reached it ere the triumph, what is lost?
Let my hands frame your face in your hair's
    gold,
You beautiful Lucrezia that are mine!
"Rafael did this, Andrea painted that;
The Roman's[8] is the better when you pray,
But still the other's Virgin was his wife—"
180 Men will excuse me. I am glad to judge
Both pictures in your presence; clearer grows
My better fortune, I resolve to think.
For, do you know, Lucrezia, as God lives,
Said one day Agnolo, his very self,
To Rafael . . . I have known it all these
    years . . .
(When the young man was flaming out his
    thoughts
Upon a palace-wall for Rome to see,
Too lifted up in heart because of it)
"Friend, there's a certain sorry little scrub
Goes up and down our Florence, none cares
190   how,
Who, were he set to plan and execute

As you are, pricked on by your popes and
    kings,
Would bring the sweat into that brow of
    yours!"
To Rafael's!—And indeed the arm is wrong.
I hardly dare . . . yet, only you to see,
Give the chalk here—quick, thus the line
    should go!
Ay, but the soul! he's Rafael! rub it out!
Still, all I care for, if he spoke the truth,
 (What he? why, who but Michel Agnolo?
Do you forget already words like those?)   20
If really there was such a chance, so lost,—
Is, whether you're—not grateful—but more
    pleased.
Well, let me think so. And you smile indeed!
This hour has been an hour! Another smile?
If you would sit thus by me every night
I should work better, do you comprehend?
I mean that I should earn more, give you more.
See, it is settled dusk now; there's a star;
Morello's gone, the watch-lights show the wall,
The cue-owls speak the name we call them by.   2
Come from the window, love,—come in, at last,
Inside the melancholy little house
We built to be so gay with. God is just.
King Francis may forgive me: oft at nights
When I look up from painting, eyes tired out,
The walls become illumined, brick from brick
Distinct, instead of mortar, fierce bright gold,
That gold of his I did cement them with!
Let us but love each other. Must you go?
That Cousin here again? he waits outside?   2
Must see you—you, and not with me? Those
    loans?
More gaming debts to pay? you smiled for that?
Well, let smiles buy me! have you more to
    spend?
While hand and eye and something of a heart
Are left me, work's my ware, and what's it
    worth?
I'll pay my fancy. Only let me sit
The grey remainder of the evening out,
Idle, you call it, and muse perfectly
How I could paint, were I but back in France,
One picture, just one more—the Virgin's face,   2
Not yours this time! I want you at my side
To hear them—that is, Michel Agnolo—
Judge all I do and tell you of its worth.
Will you? To-morrow, satisfy your friend.
I take the subjects for his corridor,

_____

[8] The Roman: Raphael went to Rome in 1508, where he helped design and execute the paint-
ings and tapestries of St. Peter's.

Finish the portrait out of hand—there, there,
And throw him in another thing or two
If he demurs; the whole should prove enough
To pay for this same Cousin's freak. Beside,
40   What's better and what's all I care about,
Get you the thirteen scudi for the ruff!
Love, does that please you? Ah, but what does
    he,
The Cousin! What does he to please you more?

    I am grown peaceful as old age to-night.
I regret little, I would change still less.
Since there my past life lies, why alter it?
The very wrong to Francis!—it is true
I took his coin, was tempted and complied,
And built this house and sinned, and all is said.
50   My father and my mother died of want.
Well, had I riches of my own?[9] you see
How one gets rich! Let each one bear his lot.
They were born poor, lived poor, and poor
    they died:
And I have laboured somewhat in my time
And not been paid profusely. Some good son
Paint my two hundred pictures—let him try!
No doubt, there's something strikes a balance.
    Yes,
You loved me quite enough, it seems to-night.
This must suffice me here. What would one
    have?
In heaven, perhaps, new chances, one more
    chance—
60   Four great walls in the New Jerusalem,[10]
Meted on each side by the angel's reed,
For Leonard,[11] Rafael, Agnolo and me
To cover—the three first without a wife,
While I have mine! So—still they overcome
Because there's still Lucrezia,—as I choose.

Again the Cousin's whistle! Go, my Love.
                    1855

Old Pictures in Florence

I

The morn when first it thunders in March,
  The eel in the pond gives a leap, they say:

As I leaned and looked over the aloed[1] arch
  Of the villa-gate this warm March day,
No flash snapped, no dumb thunder rolled
  In the valley beneath where, white and
    wide
And washed by the morning water-gold,
  Florence lay out on the mountain-side.

II

River and bridge and street and square
  Lay mine, as much at my beck and call,   10
Through the live translucent bath of air,
  As the sights in a magic crystal ball.
And of all I saw and of all I praised,
  The most to praise and the best to see
Was the startling bell-tower Giotto[2] raised:
  But why did it more than startle me?

III

Giotto, how, with that soul of yours,
  Could you play me false who love you so?
Some slights if a certain heart endures
  Yet it feels, I would have your fellows
    know!   20
I' faith, I perceive not why I should care
  To break a silence that suits them best,
But the thing grows somewhat hard to bear
  When I find a Giotto join the rest.

IV

On the arch where olives overhead
  Print the blue sky with twig and leaf,
(That sharp-curled leaf which they never
    shed)
  'Twixt the aloes, I used to lean in chief,
And mark through the winter afternoons,
  By a gift God grants me now and then,   30
In the mild decline of those suns like moons,
  Who walked in Florence, besides her men.

V

They might chirp and chaffer, come and go
  For pleasure or profit, her men alive—
My business was hardly with them, I trow,
  But with empty cells of the human hive;
—With the chapter-room, the cloister-porch,
  The church's apsis,[3] aisle or nave,

---

[9] Vasari in his account of Andrea's life accused him of neglecting the want of his parents.
[10] New Jerusalem: the glorified city after the apocalypse. (Revelation 21).
[11] Leonard: Leonardo da Vinci (1452–1519).
[1] Aloe: a plant of the lily family.
[2] Bell-tower: the campanile of the cathedral in Florence, built from the designs of Giotto di Bondone (1276–1337).
[3] Apsis: apse, the semicircular, vaulted part of a church.

Its crypt, one fingers along with a torch,
40   Its face set full for the sun to shave.

VI

Wherever a fresco peels and drops,
      Wherever an outline weakens and wanes
Till the latest life in the painting stops,
      Stands One whom each fainter pulse-tick
        pains:
One, wishful each scrap should clutch the
      brick,
      Each tinge not wholly escape the plaster,
—A lion who dies of an ass's kick,
      The wronged great soul of an ancient
       Master.

VII

For oh, this world, and the wrong it does!
      They are safe in heaven with their backs
50   to it,
The Michaels and Rafaels,[4] you hum and buzz
      Round the works of, you of the little wit!
Do their eyes contract to the earth's old scope,
      Now that they see God face to face,
And have all attained to be poets, I hope?
      'T is their holiday now, in any case.

VIII

Much they reck of your praise and you!
      But the wronged great souls—can they be
       quit
Of a world where their work is all to do,
60   Where you style them, you of the little wit,
Old Master This and Early the Other,
      Not dreaming that Old and New are
       fellows:
A younger succeeds to an elder brother,
      Da Vincis derive in good time from
       Dellos.[5]

IX

And here where your praise might yield
       returns,
      And a handsome word or two give help,
Here, after your kind, the mastiff girns[6]
      And the puppy pack of poodles yelp.
What, not a word for Stefano there,
70   Of brow once prominent and starry,

Called Nature's Ape and the world's despair
      For his peerless painting? (See Vasari.) [7]

X

There stands the Master. Study, my friends,
      What a man's work comes to! So he plans
       it,
Performs it, perfects it, makes amends
      For the toiling and moiling, and then, *sic
       transit!*[8]
Happier the thrifty blind-folk labour,
      With upturned eye while the hand is busy,
Not sidling a glance at the coin of their
       neighbor!
      'T is looking downward that makes one
       dizzy.

XI

"If you knew their work you would deal your
       dole."
      May I take upon me to instruct you?
When Greek Art ran and reached the goal,
      Thus much had the world to boast *in
       fructu*[9]—
The Truth of Man, as by God first spoken,
      Which the actual generations garble,
Was re-uttered, and Soul (which Limbs
       betoken)
      And Limbs (Soul informs) made new in
       marble.

XII

So, you saw yourself as you wished you were,
      As you might have been, as you cannot be;
Earth here, rebuked by Olympus there:
      And grew content in your poor degree
With your little power, by those statues' god-
      head,
      And your little scope, by their eyes' full
       sway,
And your little grace, by their grace embodied,
      And your little date, by their forms that
       stay.

XIII

You would fain be kinglier, say, than I am?
      Even so, you will not sit like Theseus.

---

[4] Michaels and Rafaels: paintings by Michaelangelo (1475–1564) and Raphael (1483–1520).
[5] Da Vincis . . . Dellos: Niccolo Dello was a minor Italian painter of the fifteenth century whose modest, accomplished works are of another order of achievement from that of da Vinci.
[6] Girns: snarls.
[7] Stefano: a pupil of Giotto, called the "Ape of Nature" for the fidelity of his painting. Giorgio Vasari's *The Lives of Painters* (1550) was Browning's usual source of information about the painters of the Italian Renaissance.
[8] *Sic transit:* so it passes.   [9] *In fructu:* as fruit.

You would prove a model? The Son of Priam
    Has yet the advantage in arms' and knees'
100   use.
You're wroth—can you slay your snake like
    Apollo?
    You're grieved—still Niobe's the grander!
You live—there's the Racer's frieze to follow:
    You die—there's the dying Alexander.[10]

XIV

So, testing your weakness by their strength,
    Your meagre charms by their rounded
        beauty,
Measured by Art in your breadth and length,
    You learned—to submit is a mortal's duty.
—When I say "you" 't is the common soul,
110   The collective, I mean: the race of Man
That receives life in parts to live in a whole,
    And grow here according to God's clear
        plan.

XV

Growth came when, looking your last on them
    all,
    You turned your eyes inwardly one fine
        day
And cried with a start—What if we so small
    Be greater and grander the while than
        they?
Are they perfect of lineament, perfect of
    stature?
    In both, of such lower types are we
Precisely because of our wider nature;
120   For time, theirs—ours, for eternity.

XVI

To-day's brief passion limits their range;
    It seethes with the morrow for us and
        more.
They are perfect—how else? they shall never
    change:
    We are faulty—why not? we have time in
        store.
The Artificer's hand is not arrested
    With us; we are rough-hewn, nowise
        polished:

They stand for our copy, and, once invested
    With all they can teach, we shall see them
        abolished.

XVII

'T is a life-long toil till our lump be leaven—
    The better! What's come to perfection
        perishes.   130
Things learned on earth, we shall practise in
    heaven:
    Works done least rapidly, Art most
        cherishes.
Thyself shalt afford the example, Giotto!
    Thy one work, not to decrease or diminish,
Done at a stroke, was just (was it not?) "O?"[11]
    Thy great Campanile is still to finish.

XVIII

Is it true that we are now, and shall be here-
    after,
    But what and where depend on life's
        minute?
Hails heavenly cheer or infernal laughter
    Our first step out of the gulf or in it?   140
Shall Man, such step within his endeavour,
    Man's face, have no more play and action
Than joy which is crystallized for ever,
    Or grief, an eternal petrifaction?

XIX

On which I conclude, that the early painters,
    To cries of "Greek Art and what more
        wish you?"—
Replied, "To become now self-acquainters,
    And paint man man, whatever the issue!
Make new hopes shine through the flesh they
    fray,
    New fears aggrandize the rags and tatters: 150
To bring the invisible full into play!
    Let the visible go to the dogs—what
        matters?"

XX

Give these, I exhort you, their guerdon and
    glory

[10] In this stanza Browning names some of the subjects of great classical sculptures: Theseus, a hero of Greek mythology, represented in the statuary of the frieze of the Parthenon; Paris, son of Priam, the ruler of Troy, represented in the sculptures of the island of Aegina as drawing a bow; the god Apollo, who killed the python at the oracle at Delphi; Niobe, whose children were killed by the gods after she boasted that her family ought also to be honored in ceremonies like those dedicated to the gods; Alexander, the great conqueror, who died in his thirty-third year. The Racer's Frieze (of horsemen) is also a part of the frieze of the Parthenon.

[11] According to legend, when Giotto was asked to send examples of his skill to a prospective patron, he placed his elbow on his hip and with his arm so pivoted drew freehand a perfect circle.

For daring so much, before they well did
    it.
The first of the new, in our race's story,
    Beats the last of the old; 't is no idle
        quiddit.
The worthies began a revolution,
    Which if on earth you intend to acknowl-
        edge,
Why, honour them now! (ends my allocution)
160   Nor confer your degree when the folk leave
    college.

XXI

There's a fancy some lean to and others hate—
    That, when this life is ended, begins
New work for the soul in another state,
    Where it strives and gets weary, loses and
        wins:
Where the strong and the weak, this world's
    congeries,
    Repeat in large what they practised in
        small,
Through life after life in unlimited series;
    Only the scale's to be changed, that's all.

XXII

Yet I hardly know. When a soul has seen
170   By the means of Evil that Good is best,
And, through earth and its noise, what is
    heaven's serene,—
    When our faith in the same has stood the
        test—
Why, the child grown man, you burn the rod,
    The uses of labour are surely done;
There remaineth a rest for the people of God:
    And I have had troubles enough, for one.

XXIII

But at any rate I have loved the season
    Of Art's spring-birth so dim and dewy;
My sculptor is Nicolo the Pisan,
180   My painter—who but Cimabue?

Nor ever was man of them all indeed,
    From these to Ghiberti and Ghirlandajo,[12]
Could say that he missed my critic-meed.
    So, now to my special grievance—heigh
        ho!

XXIV

Their ghosts still stand, as I said before,
    Watching each fresco flaked and rasped,
Blocked up, knocked out, or whitewashed o'er:
    —No getting again what the church has
        grasped!
The works on the wall must take their chance;
    "Works never conceded to England's thick
    clime!"   19
(I hope they prefer their inheritance
    Of a bucketful of Italian quick-lime.)

XXV

When they go at length, with such a shaking
    Of heads o'er the old delusion, sadly
Each master his way through the black streets
    taking,
    Where many a lost work breathes though
        badly—
Why don't they bethink them of who has
    merited?
    Why not reveal, while their pictures dree[13]
Such doom, how a captive might be out-fer-
    reted?
    Why is it they never remember me?   2(

XXVI

Not that I expect the great Bigordi,
    Nor Sandro to hear me, chivalric, bellicose;
Nor the wronged Lippino; and not a word I
    Say of a scrap of Frà Angelico's:
But are you too fine, Taddeo Gaddi,
    To grant me a taste of your intonaco,[14]
Some Jerome that seeks the heaven with a sad
    eye?
    Not a churlish saint, Lorenzo Monaco?[15]

---

[12] Nicolo the Pisan was a thirteenth-century Italian painter and sculptor; Giovanni Cimabue (1240–1302) was the first of the great Italian painters of the Renaissance, and by legend the teacher of Giotto. Lorenzo Ghiberti (1381–1455) and Domenico Bigordi, or Ghirlandajo (1449–1494), followed in this tradition of naturalistic painting and sculpture: Ghirlandajo was Michaelangelo's teacher.

[13] Dree: endure.

[14] Intonaco: rough plaster used as a base for fresco painting.

[15] Lorenzo Monaco was a painter of the early fifteenth century. The other painters named in this stanza are Ghirlandajo, whose family name was Bigordi; Sandro Botticelli (1457–1515); Filippino Lippi (1460–1505), the son of Fra Lippo Lippi; Fra Angelico, or Giovanni da Fiesole (1387–1455); Taddeo Gaddi (1300–1366). Monaco and Fra Angelico are relatively austere monastic painters; Gaddi was a pupil of Giotto who worked on his master's campanile after Giotto's death.

XXVII

Could not the ghost with the close red cap,
    My Pollajolo,[16] the twice a craftsman,
Save me a sample, give me the hap
    Of a muscular Christ that shows the
        draughtsman?
No Virgin by him the somewhat petty,
    Of finical touch and tempera crumbly—
Could not Alesso Baldovinetti[17]
    Contribute so much, I ask him humbly?

XXVIII

Margheritone of Arezzo,[18]
    With the grave-clothes garb and swaddling
        barret[19]
(Why purse up mouth and beak in a pet so,
    You bald old saturnine poll-clawed
        parrot?)
Not a poor glimmering Crucifixion,
    Where in the foreground kneels the donor?
If such remain, as is my conviction,
    The hoarding it does you but little
        honour.

XXIX

They pass; for them the panels may thrill,
    The tempera grow alive and tinglish;
Their pictures are left to the mercies still
    Of dealers and stealers, Jews and the
        English,
Who, seeing mere money's worth in their prize,
    Will sell it to somebody calm as Zeno[20]
At naked High Art, and in ecstasies
    Before some clay-cold vile Carlino![21]

XXX

No matter for these! But Giotto, you,
    Have you allowed, as the town-tongues
        babble it,—
Oh, never! it shall not be counted true—
    That a certain precious little tablet
Which Buonarotti eyed like a lover,[22]—
    Was buried so long in oblivion's womb
And, left for another than I to discover,
    Turns up at last! and to whom?—to
        whom? 240

XXXI

I, that have haunted the dim San Spirito,
    (Or was it rather the Ognissanti?) [23]
Patient on altar-step planting a weary toe!
    Nay, I shall have it yet! *Detur amanti!*[24]
My Koh-i-noor[25]—or (if that's a platitude)
    Jewel of Giamschid,[26] the Persian Sofi's
        eye;
So, in anticipative gratitude,
    What if I take up my hope and prophesy?

XXXII

When the hour grows ripe, and a certain
    dotard
    Is pitched, no parcel that needs invoicing, 250
To the worse side of the Mont Saint Gothard,[27]
    We shall begin by way of rejoicing;
None of that shooting the sky (blank
    cartridge),
    Nor a civic guard, all plumes and lacquer,
Hunting Radetzky's soul like a partridge
    Over Morello with squib and cracker.[28]

---

[16] Antonio Pollajolo (1430–98) was especially known for the anatomical accuracy of his figures.

[17] Alesso Baldovinetti (1422–99), worked in mosaic as well as fresco, and was known for his minutely executed designs.

[18] Margheritone of Arezzo (1236–1313) was an early innovator from the manner of early fourteenth-century Italian painters.

[19] Barret: a flat cap.

[20] Zeno: a Greek philosopher who founded the school of the Stoics.

[21] Carlino: Carlo Dolci (1616–86), used here as an example of lifelessly smooth painting.

[22] A certain precious little tablet: during his residence in Italy Browning sought out and bought many Italian paintings. He refers here to a painting of the Last Supper, supposed to be that painted by Giotto and admired by Michaelangelo (Buonarotti), which had recently been found and purchased while Browning was living in Florence.

[23] San Spirito; Ognissanti: churches in Florence.

[24] *Detur amanti:* let it be given to the one who loves it.

[25] Koh-i-noor: a diamond from India, given to Queen Victoria in 1850, and much commented upon subsequently.

[26] Jewel of Giamschid: a ruby, belonging to the sultan of Persia.

[27] A certain dotard: Ferdinand, Grand-Duke of Tuscany, who because of his collaboration with the Austrians who at this time ruled Italy, ought to be pitched over the Gothard pass and into Switzerland.

[28] Radetzky: Joseph Wenzel Radetzky, an Austrian general who served as governor of Italy, and who ought also be chased past Morello, a mountain north of Florence.

XXXIII

This time we'll shoot better game and bag 'em
    hot—
    No mere display at the stone of Dante,[29]
But a kind of sober Witanagemot
260   (Ex: "Casa Guidi," *quod videas ante*) [30]
Shall ponder, once Freedom restored tò
    Florence,
    How Art may return that departed with
    her.
Go, hated house, go each trace of the Loraine's,
    And bring us the days of Orgagna hither![31]

XXXIV

How we shall prologize, how we shall perorate,
    Utter fit things upon art and history,
Feel truth at blood-heat and falsehood at zero
    rate,
    Make of the want of the age no mystery;
Contrast the fructuous and sterile eras,
    Show—monarchy ever its uncouth cub
270   licks
Out of the bear's shape into Chimæra's,[32]
    While Pure Art's birth is still the repub-
    lic's.

XXXV

Then one shall propose in a speech (curt
    Tuscan,[33]
    Expurgate and sober, with scarcely an
    "issimo,"[34])
To end now our half-told tale of Cambuscan,[35]
    And turn the bell-tower's *alt* to *altissimo:*
And fine as the beak of a young beccaccia[36]
    The Campanile, the Duomo's fit ally,[37]
Shall soar up in gold full fifty braccia,[38]
280   Completing Florence, as Florence Italy.

XXXVI

Shall I be alive that morning the scaffold
    Is broken away, and the long-pent fire,
Like the golden hope of the world, unbaffled
    Springs from its sleep, and up goes the
    spire
While "God and the People"[39] plain for its
    motto,
    Thence the new tricolour[40] flaps at the
    sky?
At least to foresee that glory of Giotto
    And Florence together, the first am I!

                        1855

*The story of David playing to Saul is in 1 Samuel
16:14–23. Browning considerably elaborates the
Old Testament account, which states only that "the
Spirit of the Lord departed from Saul, and an evil
spirit from the Lord troubled him." David, a young
shepherd who had just been anointed by Samuel as
the next king because Saul has disobeyed a com-
mand of the Lord, is sent for, is loved by Saul, and
becomes his armor bearer. "And it came to pass,
when the evil spirit from God was upon Saul, that
David took an harp, and played with his hand: so
Saul was refreshed, and was well, and the evil spirit
departed from him."*

Saul

I

Said Abner,[1] "At last thou art come! Ere I tell,
    ere thou speak,
Kiss my cheek, wish me well!" Then I wished
    it, and did kiss his cheek.
And he, "Since the King, O my friend, for thy
    countenance sent,

---

[29] The stone of Dante: a stone outside Florence, by legend Dante's favorite seat.

[30] In *Casa Guidi Windows* (1851), a poem pleading for the liberty of Italy, Elizabeth Barrett Browning imagines a Witanagemot—a great national council like that held by the Anglo-Saxon kings—at which all lovers of Italy will convene. *Quod videas ante:* which you have seen before.

[31] Hated house. . . Orgagna: the hated house is the house of Loraine, which had won control of Tuscany and Florence in the eighteenth century; Orgagna is the name of Andrea di Cione, a fourteenth-century painter who here represents the achievement of Florence in the years of her freedom.

[32] Chimæra: a three-headed monster.

[33] Curt Tuscan: Dante's use of the Tuscan dialect in his writing made it the literary language of Italy.

[34] *issimo:* superlative.

[35] Cambuscan: Cambuscan was a king of Tartary, the hero of the Squire's Tale in *The Canterbury Tales*, left unfinished by Chaucer.

[36] Beccaccia: woodcock.

[37] Duomo: the cathedral, a structure literally fitted to Giotto's bell-tower.

[38] Braccia: cubit (about eighteen inches).

[39] "God and the People" was the motto of Guiseppe Mazzini (1805–72), the great leader of Italian national autonomy.

[40] The tricolor is the Italian flag of red, green, and white.

[1] Abner: an officer in Saul's army.

Neither drunken nor eaten have we; nor until from his tent
Thou return with the joyful assurance the King liveth yet,
Shall our lip with the honey be bright, with the water be wet.
For out of the black mid-tent's silence, a space of three days,
Not a sound hath escaped to thy servants, of prayer nor of praise,
To betoken that Saul and the Spirit have ended their strife,
And that, faint in his triumph, the monarch sinks back upon life.

II

"Yet now my heart leaps, O beloved! God's child with his dew
On thy gracious gold hair, and those lilies still living and blue
Just broken to twine round thy harp-strings, as if no wild heat
Were now raging to torture the desert!"

III

Then I, as was meet,
Knelt down to the God of my fathers, and rose on my feet,
And ran o'er the sand burnt to powder. The tent was unlooped;
I pulled up the spear that obstructed, and under I stooped;
Hands and knees on the slippery grass-patch, all withered and gone,
That extends to the second enclosure, I groped my way on
Till I felt where the foldskirts fly open. Then once more I prayed,
And opened the foldskirts and entered, and was not afraid
But spoke, "Here is David, thy servant!" And no voice replied.
At the first I saw nought but the blackness; but soon I descried
A something more black than the blackness—the vast, the upright
Main prop which sustains the pavilion: and slow into sight
Grew a figure against it, gigantic and blackest of all.
Then a sunbeam, that burst thro' the tent-roof, showed Saul.

² Jerboa: a leaping hare.

IV

He stood as erect as that tent-prop, both arms stretched out wide
On the great cross-support in the centre, that goes to each side;
He relaxed not a muscle, but hung there as, caught in his pangs   30
And waiting his change, the king-serpent all heavily hangs,
Far away from his kind, in the pine, till deliverance come
With the spring-time,—so agonized Saul, drear and stark, blind and dumb.

V

Then I tuned my harp,—took off the lilies we twine round its chords
Lest they snap 'neath the stress of the noon-tide—those sunbeams like swords!
And I first played the tune all our sheep know, as, one after one,
So docile they come to the pen-door till folding be done.
They are white and untorn by the bushes, for lo, they have fed
Where the long grasses stifle the water within the stream's bed;
And now one after one seeks its lodging, as star follows star   40
Into eve and the blue far above us,—so blue and so far!

VI

—Then the tune, for which quails on the corn-land will each leave his mate
To fly after the player; then, what makes the crickets elate
Till for boldness they fight one another: and then, what has weight
To set the quick jerboa² a-musing outside his sand house—
There are none such as he for a wonder, half bird and half mouse!
God made all the creatures and gave them our love and our fear,
To give sign, we and they are his children, one family here.

VII

Then I played the help-tune of our reapers, their wine-song, when hand

Grasps at hand, eye lights eye in good friend-
50   ship, and great hearts expand
And grow one in the sense of this world's life.
        —And then, the last song
When the dead man is praised on his journey
        —"Bear, bear him along
With his few faults shut up like dead flowerets!
        Are balm-seeds not here
To console us? The land has none left such as
        he on the bier.
Oh, would we might keep thee, my brother!"
        —And then, the glad chaunt
Of the marriage,—first go the young maidens,
        next, she whom we vaunt
As the beauty, the pride of our dwelling.—
        And then, the great march
Wherein man runs to man to assist him and
        buttress an arch[3]
Nought can break; who shall harm them, our
        friends?—Then, the chorus intoned
As the Levites[4] go up to the altar in glory
60   enthroned.
But I stopped here: for here in the darkness
        Saul groaned.

VIII

And I paused, held my breath in such silence,
        and listened apart;
And the tent shook, for mighty Saul shuddered:
        and sparkles 'gan dart
From the jewels that woke in his turban, at
        once with a start,
All its lordly male-sapphires,[5] and rubies coura-
        geous at heart.
So the head: but the body still moved not, still
        hung there erect.
And I bent once again to my playing, pursued
        it unchecked,
As I sang,—

IX

                "Oh, our manhood's prime vigour!
        No spirit feels waste,
Not a muscle is stopped in its playing nor
        sinew unbraced.
Oh, the wild joys of living! the leaping from
70   rock up to rock,
The strong rending of boughs from the fir-tree,
        the cool silver shock

Of the plunge in a pool's living water, the hunt
        of the bear,
And the sultriness showing the lion is couched
        in his lair.
And the meal, the rich dates yellowed over
        with gold dust divine,
And the locust-flesh steeped in the pitcher, the
        full draught of wine,
And the sleep in the dried river-channel where
        bulrushes tell
That the water was wont to go warbling so
        softly and well.
How good is man's life, the mere living! how
        fit to employ
All the heart and the soul and the senses for
        ever in joy!
Hast thou loved the white locks of thy father,
        whose sword thou didst guard
When he trusted thee forth with the armies,
        for glorious reward?
Didst thou see the thin hands of thy mother,
        held up as men sung
The low song of the nearly-departed, and hear
        her faint tongue
Joining in while it could to the witness, 'Let
        one more attest,
I have lived, seen God's hand thro' a lifetime,
        and all was for best'?
Then they sung thro' their tears in strong
        triumph, not much, but the rest.
And thy brothers, the help and the contest, the
        working whence grew
Such result as, from seething grape-bundles, the
        spirit strained true:
And the friends of thy boyhood—that boyhood
        of wonder and hope,
Present promise and wealth of the future
        beyond the eye's scope,—
Till lo, thou art grown to a monarch; a people
        is thine;
And all gifts, which the world offers singly, on
        one head combine!
On one head, all the beauty and strength, love
        and rage (like the throe
That, a-work in the rock, helps its labour and
        lets the gold go)
High ambition and deeds which surpass it,
        fame crowning them,—all

---

[3] Arch: a military formation in which soldiers mass together and hold their shields over their
heads.
[4] Levites: the sons of Levi, who assisted the priests of Israel.
[5] Male-sapphire: an exceptionally brilliant blue gem.

Brought to blaze on the head of one creature—
  King Saul!"⁶

X

And lo, with that leap of my spirit,—heart,
  hand, harp and voice,
Each lifting Saul's name out of sorrow, each
  bidding rejoice
Saul's fame in the light it was made for—as
  when, dare I say,
The Lord's army, in rapture of service, strains
  through its array,
And upsoareth the cherubim-chariot—"Saul!"
  cried I, and stopped,
And waited the thing that should follow. Then
  Saul, who hung propped
By the tent's cross-support in the centre, was
  struck by his name.
Have ye seen when Spring's arrowy summons
  goes right to the aim,
And some mountain, the last to withstand her,
  that held (he alone,
While the vale laughed in freedom and
  flowers) on a broad bust of stone
A year's snow bound about for a breastplate,—
  leaves grasp of the sheet?
Fold on fold all at once it crowds thunderously
  down to his feet,
And there fronts you, stark, black, but alive
  yet, your mountain of old,
With his rents, the successive bequeathings of
  ages untold—
Yea, each harm got in fighting your battles,
  each furrow and scar
Of his head thrust 'twixt you and the tempest
  —all hail, there they are!

—Now again to be softened with verdure, again
  hold the nest
Of the dove, tempt the goat and its young to
  the green on his crest
For their food in the ardours of summer. One
  long shudder thrilled
All the tent till the very air tingled, then sank
  and was stilled
At the King's self left standing before me,
  released and aware.
What was gone, what remained? All to
  traverse, 'twixt hope and despair;
Death was past, life not come: so he waited.
  Awhile his right hand
Held the brow, helped the eyes left too vacant
  forthwith to remand   120
To their place what new objects should enter:
  't was Saul as before.
I looked up and dared gaze at those eyes, nor
  was hurt any more
Than by slow pallid sunsets in autumn, ye
  watch from the shore,
At their sad level gaze o'er the ocean—a sun's
  slow decline
Over hills which, resolved in stern silence,
  o'erlap and entwine
Base with base to knit strength more intensely:
  so, arm folded arm
O'er the chest whose slow heavings subsided.

XI
                    What spell or what charm,
(For, awhile there was trouble within me)
  what next should I urge
To sustain him where song had restored him?
  —Song filled to the verge

---

⁶ The first nine stanzas of "Saul" were completed in 1845, and published in that year as one of
the *Dramatic Romances and Lyrics* in the *Bells and Pomegranates* series. In 1845 the long line of
the final version of the poem was broken into half lines, and the final lines of the ninth stanza
read:

> And the friends of thy boyhood—that boyhood
>   With wonder and hope,
> And the promise and wealth in the future,—
>   The eye's eagle scope,—
> Till lo, thou art grown to a monarch,
>   A people is thine!
> Oh all, all the world offers singly,
>   On one head combine,
> On one head the joy and the pride,
>   Even rage like the throe
> That opes the rock, helps its glad labour,
>   And lets the gold go—
> And ambition that sees a sun lead it
>   Oh, all of these—all
> Combine to unite in one creature
>   —Saul!

His cup with the wine of this life, pressing all
130   that it yields
Of mere fruitage, the strength and the beauty:
    beyond, on what fields,
Glean a vintage more potent and perfect to
    brighten the eye
And bring blood to the lip, and commend
    them the cup they put by?
He saith, "It is good"; still he drinks not: he
    lets me praise life,
Gives assent, yet would die for his own part.

XII

            Then fancies grew rife
Which had come long ago on the pasture, when
    round me the sheep
Fed in silence—above, the one eagle wheeled
    slow as in sleep;
And I lay in my hollow and mused on the
    world that might lie
'Neath his ken, though I saw but the strip
    'twixt the hill and the sky:
And I laughed—"Since my days are ordained
140   to be passed with my flocks,
Let me people at least, with my fancies, the
    plains and the rocks,
Dream the life I am never to mix with, and
    image the show
Of mankind as they live in those fashions I
    hardly shall know!
Schemes of life, its best rules and right uses,
    the courage that gains,
And the prudence that keeps what men strive
    for." And now these old trains
Of vague thought came again; I grew surer;
    so, once more the string
Of my harp made response to my spirit, as
    thus—

XIII

            "Yea, my King,"
I began—"thou dost well in rejecting mere
    comforts that spring
From the mere mortal life held in common by
    man and by brute:
In our flesh grows the branch of this life, in
150   our soul it bears fruit.
Thou hast marked the slow rise of the tree,—
    how its stem trembled first
Till it passed the kid's lip, the stag's antler;
    then safely outburst
The fan-branches all round; and thou mindest
    when these too, in turn
Broke a-bloom and the palm-tree seemed
    perfect: yet more was to learn,

E'en the good that comes in with the palm-
    fruit. Our dates shall we slight,
When their juice brings a cure for all sorrow?
    or care for the plight
Of the palm's self whose slow growth produced
    them? Not so! stem and branch
Shall decay, nor be known in their place, while
    the palm-wine shall staunch
Every wound of man's spirit in winter. I pour
    thee such wine.
Leave the flesh to the fate it was fit for! the
    spirit be thine!   16
By the spirit, when age shall o'ercome thee,
    thou still shalt enjoy
More indeed, than at first when inconscious,
    the life of a boy.
Crush that life, and behold its wine running!
    Each deed thou hast done
Dies, revives, goes to work in the world; until
    e'en as the sun
Looking down on the earth, though clouds
    spoil him, though tempests efface,
Can find nothing his own deed produced not,
    must everywhere trace
The results of his past summer-prime,—so,
    each ray of thy will,
Every flash of thy passion and prowess, long
    over, shall thrill
Thy whole people, the countless, with ardour,
    till they too give forth
A like cheer to their sons, who in turn fill the
    South and the North   1
With the radiance thy deed was the germ of.
    Carouse in the past!
But the license of age has its limit; thou diest
    at last:
As the lion when age dims his eyeball, the
    rose at her height,
So with man—so his power and his beauty
    forever take flight.
No! Again a long draught of my soul-wine!
    Look forth o'er the years!
Thou hast done now with eyes for the actual;
    begin with the seer's!
Is Saul dead? In the depth of the vale make
    his tomb—bid arise
A gray mountain of marble heaped four-
    square till, built to the skies,
Let it mark where the great First King
    slumbers: whose fame would ye know?
Up above see the rock's naked face, where the
    record shall go   18
In great characters cut by the scribe,—Such
    was Saul, so he did;

With the sages directing the work, by the
  populace chid,—
For not half, they'll affirm, is comprised there!
  Which fault to amend,
In the grove with his kind grows the cedar,
  whereon they shall spend
(See, in tablets 't is level before them) their
  praise, and record
With the gold of the graver,[7] Saul's story,—
  the statesman's great word
Side by side with the poet's sweet comment.
  The river's a-wave
With smooth paper-reeds grazing each other
  when prophet-winds rave:
So the pen gives unborn generations their due
  and their part
In thy being! Then, first of the mighty, thank
  God that thou art!"

XIV

And behold while I sang . . . but O Thou
  who didst grant me that day,
And before it not seldom hast granted thy
  help to essay,
Carry on and complete an adventure,—my
  shield and my sword
In that act where my soul was thy servant, thy
  word was my word,—
Still be with me, who then at the summit of
  human endeavour
And scaling the highest, man's thought could,
  gazed hopeless as ever
On the new stretch of heaven above me—till,
  mighty to save,
Just one lift of thy hand cleared that distance
  —God's throne from man's grave!
Let me tell out my tale to its ending—my voice
  to my heart
Which can scarce dare believe in what marvels
  last night I took part,
As this morning I gather the fragments, alone
  with my sheep,
And still fear lest the terrible glory evanish
  like sleep!
For I wake in the gray dewy covert, while
  Hebron[8] upheaves
The dawn struggling with night on his
  shoulder, and Kidron[9] retrieves
Slow the damage of yesterday's sunshine.

XV

I say then,—my song
While I sang thus, assuring the monarch, and
  ever more strong
Made a proffer of good to console him—he
  slowly resumed
His old motions and habitudes kingly. The
  right-hand replumed
His black locks to their wonted composure,
  adjusted the swathes
Of his turban, and see—the huge sweat that
  his countenance bathes,   210
He wipes off with the robe; and he girds now
  his loins as of yore,
And feels slow for the armlets of price, with
  the clasp set before.
He is Saul, ye remember in glory,—ere error[10]
  had bent
The broad brow from the daily communion;
  and still, though much spent
Be the life and the bearing that front you, the
  same, God did choose,
To receive what a man may waste, desecrate,
  never quite lose.
So sank he along by the tent-prop till, stayed
  by the pile
Of his armour and war-cloak and garments,
  he leaned there awhile,
And sat out my singing,—one arm round the
  tent-prop, to raise
His bent head, and the other hung slack—till
  I touched on the praise   220
I foresaw from all men in all time, to the man
  patient there;
And thus ended, the harp falling forward.
  Then first I was 'ware
That he sat, as I say, with my head just above
  his vast knees
Which were thrust out on each side around me,
  like oak-roots which please
To encircle a lamb when it slumbers. I looked
  up to know
If the best I could do had brought solace: he
  spoke not, but slow
Lifted up the hand slack at his side, till he
  laid it with care
Soft and grave, but in mild settled will, on my
  brow: thro' my hair
The large fingers were pushed, and he bent
  back my head, with kind power—

---

[7] Graver: engraver.   [8] Hebron: the name of a mountain and a city in Judea.
[9] Kidron: a brook near Jerusalem.
[10] Error: Saul had disobeyed the Lord's command to destroy utterly the property and population of a nation with which the Israelites were at war.

All my face back, intent to peruse it, as men
230   do a flower.
Thus held he me there with his great eyes that
      scrutinized mine—
And oh, all my heart how it loved him! but
      where was the sign?
I yearned—"Could I help thee, my father,
      inventing a bliss,
I would add, to that life of the past, both the
      future and this;
I would give thee new life altogether, as good,
      ages hence,
As this moment,—had love but the warrant,
      love's heart to dispense!"

XVI

Then the truth came upon me. No harp more
—no song more! out-broke—

XVII

"I have gone the whole round of creation: I
      saw and I spoke:
I, a work of God's hand for that purpose,
      received in my brain
And pronounced on the rest of his handwork
240   —returned him again
His creation's approval or censure: I spoke as
      I saw:
I report, as a man may of God's work—all's
      love, yet all's law.
Now I lay down the judgeship he lent me.
      Each faculty tasked
To perceive him, has gained an abyss, where a
      dewdrop was asked.
Have I knowledge? confounded it shrivels at
      Wisdom laid bare.
Have I forethought? how purblind, how blank,
      to the Infinite Care!
Do I task any faculty highest, to image success?
I but open my eyes,—and perfection. no more
      and no less,
In the kind I imagined, full-fronts me, and God
      is seen God
In the star, in the stone, in the flesh, in the
250   soul and the clod.
And thus looking within and around me, I ever
      renew
(With that stoop of the soul which in bending
      upraises it too)
The submission of man's nothing-perfect to
      God's all-complete,
As by each new obeisance in spirit, I climb to
      his feet.
Yet with all this abounding experience, this
      deity known,

I shall dare to discover some province, some
      gift of my own.
There's a faculty pleasant to exercise, hard to
      hoodwink,
I am fain to keep still in abeyance, (I laugh as
      I think)
Lest, insisting to claim and parade in it, wot
      ye, I worst
E'en the Giver in one gift.—Behold, I could
      love if I durst!
But I sink the pretension as fearing a man
      may o'ertake
God's own speed in the one way of love: I
      abstain for love's sake.
—What, my soul? see thus far and no farther?
      when doors great and small,
Nine-and-ninety flew ope at our touch, should
      the hundredth appal?
In the least things have faith, yet distrust in
      the greatest of all?
Do I find love so full in my nature, God's
      ultimate gift,
That I doubt his own love can compete with
      it? Here, the parts shift?
Here, the creature surpass the Creator,—the
      end, what Began?
Would I fain in my impotent yearning do all
      for this man,
And dare doubt he alone shall not help him,
      who yet alone can?
Would it ever have entered my mind, the bare
      will, much less power,
To bestow on this Saul what I sang of, the
      marvellous dower
Of the life he was gifted and filled with? to
      make such a soul,
Such a body, and then such an earth for
      insphering the whole?
And doth it not enter my mind (as my warm
      tears attest)
These good things being given, to go on, and
      give one more, the best?
Ay, to save and redeem and restore him,
      maintain at the height
This perfection,—succeed with life's dayspring,
      death's minute of night?
Interpose at the difficult minute, snatch Saul
      the mistake,
Saul the failure, the ruin he seems now,—and
      bid him awake
From the dream, the probation, the prelude,
      to find himself set
Clear and safe in new light and new life,—a
      new harmony yet

To be run, and continued, and ended—who
knows?—or endure!
The man taught enough, by life's dream, of
the rest to make sure;
By the pain-throb, triumphantly winning
intensified bliss,
And the next world's reward and repose, by
the struggles in this.

XVIII

"I believe it! 'T is thou, God, that givest, 't is
I who receive:
In the first is the last, in thy will is my power
to believe.
All's one gift: thou canst grant it moreover, as
prompt to my prayer
As I breathe out this breath, as I open these
arms to the air.
From thy will, stream the worlds, life and
nature, thy dread Sabaoth:[11]
I will?—the mere atoms despise me! Why am
I not loth
To look that, even that in the face too? Why
is it I dare
Think but lightly of such impuissance? What
stops my despair?
This;—'t is not what man Does which exalts
him, but what man Would do!
See the King—I would help him but cannot,
the wishes fall through.
Could I wrestle to raise him from sorrow, grow
poor to enrich,
To fill up his life, starve my own out, I would
—knowing which,
I know that my service is perfect. Oh, speak
through me now!
Would I suffer for him that I love? So wouldst
thou—so wilt thou!
So shall crown thee the topmost, ineffablest,
uttermost crown—
And thy love fill infinitude wholly, nor leave
up nor down
One spot for the creature to stand in! It is by
no breath,
Turn of eye, wave of hand, that salvation joins
issue with death!
As thy Love is discovered almighty, almighty
be proved
Thy power, that exists with and for it, of
being Beloved!
He who did most, shall bear most; the strong-
est shall stand the most weak.

[11] Sabaoth: armies.

'T is the weakness in strength, that I cry for!
my flesh, that I seek
In the Godhead! I seek and I find it. O Saul,
it shall be
A Face like my face that receives thee; a Man
like to me,   310
Thou shalt love and be loved by, for ever: a
Hand like this hand
Shall throw open the gates of new life to thee!
See the Christ stand!"

XIX

I know not too well how I found my way home
in the night.
There were witnesses, cohorts about me, to left
and to right,
Angels, powers, the unuttered, unseen, the
alive, the aware:
I repressed, I got through them as hardly, as
strugglingly there,
As a runner beset by the populace famished
for news—
Life or death. The whole earth was awakened,
hell loosed with her crews;
And the stars of night beat with emotion, and
tingled and shot
Out in fire the strong pain of pent knowledge:
but I fainted not,   320
For the Hand still impelled me at once and
supported, suppressed
All the tumult, and quenched it with quiet,
and holy behest,
Till the rapture was shut in itself, and the
earth sank to rest.
Anon at the dawn, all that trouble had
withered from earth—
Not so much, but I saw it die out in the day's
tender birth;
In the gathered intensity brought to the grey
of the hills;
In the shuddering forests' held breath; in the
sudden wind-thrills;
In the startled wild beasts that bore off, each
with eye sidling still
Though averted with wonder and dread; in
the birds stiff and chill
That rose heavily, as I approached them, made
stupid with awe: 330
E'en the serpent that slid away silent,—he felt
the new law.
The same stared in the white humid faces
upturned by the flowers;

The same worked in the heart of the cedar and
   moved the vine-bowers:
And the little brooks witnessing murmured,
   persistent and low,
With their obstinate, all but hushed voices—
   —"E'en so, it is so!"

                              1845; 1855

Holy-Cross Day

On Which the Jews Were Forced to Attend an Annual Christian Sermon in Rome

["*Now was come about Holy-Cross Day, and now must my lord preach his first sermon to the Jews: as it was of old cared for in the merciful bowels of the Church, that, so to speak, a crumb at least from her conspicuous table here in Rome should be, though but once yearly, cast to the famishing dogs, under-trampled and bespitten-upon beneath the feet of the guests. And a moving sight in truth, this, of so many of the besotted blind restif and ready-to-perish Hebrews! now maternally brought–nay (for He saith, 'Compel them to come in') haled, as it were, by the head and hair, and against their obstinate hearts, to partake of the heavenly grace. What awakening, what striving with tears, what working of a yeasty conscience! Nor was my lord wanting to himself on so apt an occasion; witness the abundance of conversions which did incontinently reward him: though not to my lord be altogether the glory."*
      —DIARY BY THE BISHOP'S SECRETARY, 1600.][1]

   What the Jews really said, on thus being driven to church, was rather to this effect:—

I

Fee, faw, fum! bubble and squeak!
Blessedest Thursday 's the fat of the week.
Rumble and tumble, sleek and rough,
Stinking and savoury, smug and gruff,
Take the church-road, for the bell's due chime
Gives us the summons—'t is sermon-time!

II

Boh, here 's Barnabas! Job, that 's you?
Up stumps Solomon—bustling too?
Shame, man! greedy beyond your years

To handsel[2] the bishop's shaving-shears?
Fair play 's a jewel! Leave friends in the lurch?
Stand on a line ere you start for the church!

III

Higgledy piggledy, packed we lie,
Rats in a hamper, swine in a stye,
Wasps in a bottle, frogs in a sieve,
Worms in a carcase, fleas in a sleeve.
Hist! square shoulders, settle your thumbs
And buzz for the bishop—here he comes.

IV

Bow, wow, wow—a bone for the dog!
I liken his Grace to an acorned hog.
What, a boy at his side, with the bloom of a
   lass,
To help and handle my lord's hour-glass!
Didst ever behold so lithe a chine?[3]
His cheek hath laps like a fresh-singed swine.

V

Aaron 's asleep—shove hip to haunch,
Or somebody deal him a dig in the paunch!
Look at the purse with the tassel and knob,
And the gown with the angel and thingumbob!
What 's he at, quotha? reading his text!
Now you've his curtsey—and what comes next?

VI

See to our converts—you doomed black dozen—
No stealing away—nor cog nor cozen![4]
You five, that were thieves, deserve it fairly;
You seven, that were beggars, will live less
   sparely;
You took your turn and dipped in the hat,
Got fortune—and fortune gets you; mind that!

VII

Give your first groan—compunction's at work;
And soft! from a Jew you mount to a Turk.
Lo, Micah,—the selfsame beard on chin
He was four times already converted in!
Here's a knife, clip quick—it's a sign of
   grace—
Or he ruins us all with his hanging-face.

---

[1] The custom of preaching to the Jews on Holy-Cross Day (September 14) was actually practiced. Browning invented the note of the bishop's secretary which serves as an epigraph. Turner (p. 369) points out that the allusions to the New Testament in the epigraph (the crumb cast to the dogs—Matthew 15:26–27; "Compel them to come in"—Luke 14:23; "to my lord be altogether the glory"—1 Corinthians 10:31) come from texts that predict the eventual triumph of the Jews.
[2] To be the first to be shaved by the bishop, as a sign of conversion to Christianity.
[3] Chine: a cut of meat which includes the backbone.
[4] Cog nor cozen: no cheating or deceiving.

VIII

Whom now is the bishop a-leering at?
I know a point where his text falls pat.
I 'll tell him to-morrow, a word just now
Went to my heart and made me vow
I meddle no more with the worst of trades—
Let somebody else pay his serenades.[5]

IX

Groan all together now, whee—hee—hee!
It 's a-work, it 's a-work, ah, woe is me!
It began, when a herd of us, picked and placed,
Were spurred through the Corso,[6] stripped to
    the waist;
Jew brutes, with sweat and blood well spent
To usher in worthily Christian Lent.

X

It grew, when the hangman entered our
    bounds,
Yelled, pricked us out to his church like
    hounds:
It got to a pitch, when the hand indeed
Which gutted my purse would throttle my
    creed:
And it overflows when, to even the odd,
Men I helped to their sins help me to their
    God.

XI

But now, while the scapegoats leave our flock,
And the rest sit silent and count the clock,
Since forced to muse the appointed time
On these precious facts and truths sublime,—
Let us fitly employ it, under our breath,
In saying Ben Ezra's Song of Death.[7]

XII

For Rabbi Ben Ezra, the night he died,
Called sons and sons' sons to his side,
And spoke, "This world has been harsh and
    strange;
Something is wrong: there needeth a change.
But what, or where? at the last or first?
In one point only we sinned, at worst.

XIII

"The Lord will have mercy on Jacob yet,
And again in his border see Israel set.

When Judah beholds Jerusalem,
The stranger-seed shall be joined to them:
To Jacob's House shall the Gentiles cleave.
So the Prophet saith and his sons believe.

XIV

"Ay, the children of the chosen race   80
Shall carry and bring them to their place:
In the land of the Lord shall lead the same,
Bondsmen and handmaids. Who shall blame,
When the slaves enslave, the oppressed ones
    o'er
The oppressor triumph for evermore?

XV

"God spoke, and gave us the word to keep,
Bade never fold the hands nor sleep
'Mid a faithless world,—at watch and ward,
Till Christ at the end relieve our guard.
By His servant Moses the watch was set:
Though near upon cock-crow, we keep it yet.   90

XVI

"Thou! if thou wast He, who at mid-watch
    came,
By the starlight, naming a dubious name!
And if, too heavy with sleep—too rash
With fear—O Thou, if that martyr-gash
Fell on Thee coming to take thine own,
And we gave the Cross, when we owed the
    Throne—

XVII

"Thou art the Judge. We are bruised thus.
But, the Judgment over, join sides with us!
Thine too is the cause! and not more thine
Than ours, is the work of these dogs and swine, 100
Whose life laughs through and spits at their
    creed!
Who maintain Thee in word, and defy Thee
    in deed!

XVIII

"We withstood Christ then? Be mindful how
At least we withstand Barabbas[8] now!
Was our outrage sore? But the worst we spared,
To have called these—Christians, had we
    dared!

---

[5] Pay his serenades: lend him money to conduct his love-affairs.

[6] Corso: a street in Rome in which horse races were sometimes held. The suggestion is that Jews were run like horses through the street.

[7] Rabbi Ben Ezra: an eleventh-century scholar, born in Spain, who argued that the plan of existence was divine and therefore perfect, and that doubts and failures are therefore a necessary part of the plan as it moves toward its consummation. Browning invents his "Song of Death."

[8] Barabbas: the criminal whom the populace asked Pilate to pardon instead of Christ.

Let defiance to them pay mistrust of Thee,
And Rome make amends for Calvary!

XIX

"By the torture, prolonged from age to age,
110 By the infamy, Israel's heritage,
By the Ghetto's plague, by the garb's disgrace,
By the badge of shame, by the felon's place,
By the branding-tool, the bloody whip,
And the summons to Christian fellowship,—

XX

"We boast our proof that at least the Jew
Would wrest Christ's name from the Devil's
     crew.
Thy face took never so deep a shade
But we fought them in it, God our aid!
A trophy to bear, as we march, thy band,
120 South, East, and on to the Pleasant Land!''

[Pope Gregory XVI. abolished this bad busi-
     ness of the Sermon.—R.B.]
                                        1855

Cleon

"As certain also of your own poets have said"—[1]

Cleon the poet (from the sprinkled isles,[2]
Lily on lily, that o'erlace the sea,
And laugh their pride when the light wave
     lisps "Greece") —
To Protus in his Tyranny:[3] much health!

They give thy letter to me, even now:
I read and seem as if I heard thee speak.
The master of thy galley still unlades
Gift after gift; they block my court at last
And pile themselves along its portico
10 Royal with sunset, like a thought of thee:
And one white she-slave from the group
     dispersed
Of black and white slaves (like the chequer-
     work
Pavement, at once my nation's work and gift,
Now covered with this settle-down of doves),
One lyric woman, in her crocus vest

Woven of sea-wools,[4] with her two white hands
Commends to me the strainer and the cup
Thy lip hath bettered ere it blesses mine.

Well-counselled, king, in thy munificence!
For so shall men remark, in such an act
Of love for him whose song gives life its joy,
Thy recognition of the use of life;
Nor call thy spirit barely adequate
To help on life in straight ways, broad enough
For vulgar souls, by ruling and the rest.
Thou, in the daily building of thy tower,—
Whether in fierce and sudden spasms of toil,
Or through dim lulls of unapparent growth,
Or when the general work 'mid good acclaim
Climbed with the eye to cheer the architect,—
Didst ne'er engage in work for mere work's
     sake—
Hadst ever in thy heart the luring hope
Of some eventual rest a-top of it,
Whence, all the tumult of the building hushed,
Thou first of men mightst look out to the East:
The vulgar saw thy tower, thou sawest the sun.
For this, I promise on thy festival
To pour libation, looking o'er the sea,
Making this slave narrate thy fortunes, speak
Thy great words, and describe thy royal face—
Wishing thee wholly where Zeus lives the most,
Within the eventual element of calm.

Thy letter's first requirement meets me
     here.
It is as thou hast heard: in one short life
I, Cleon, have effected all those things
Thou wonderingly dost enumerate.
That epos on thy hundred plates of gold
Is mine,—and also mine the little chant,
So sure to rise from every fishing-bark
When, lights at prow, the seamen haul their
     net.
The image of the sun-god on the phare,[5]
Men turn from the sun's self to see, is mine;
The Pœcile,[6] o'er-storied its whole length,
As thou didst hear, with painting, is mine too.
I know the true proportions of a man
And woman also, not observed before;
And I have written three books on the soul,
Proving absurd all written hitherto,
And putting us to ignorance again.

[1] From Acts 17:28; the lines are part of an address of Paul to the Athenians. Cleon and Protus are not historical persons.
[2] Sprinkled isles: usually identified as the Sporades, east of Greece, near Crete.
[3] Tyranny: an area governed by an absolute ruler.
[4] Sea-wools: wool dyed purple with murex, a marine mollusk.   [5] Phare: lighthouse.
[6] Pœcile: the Portico at Athens, decorated with paintings.

For music,—why, I have combined the moods,[7]
Inventing one. In brief, all arts are mine;
Thus much the people know and recognize,
Throughout our seventeen islands. Marvel not.
We of these latter days, with greater mind
Than our forerunners, since more composite,
Look not so great, beside their simple way,
To a judge who only sees one way at once,
One mind-point and no other at a time,—
Compares the small part of a man of us
With some whole man of the heroic age,
Great in his way—not ours, nor meant for
    ours.
And ours is greater, had we skill to know:
For, what we call this life of men on earth,
This sequence of the soul's achievements here
Being, as I find much reason to conceive,
Intended to be viewed eventually
As a great whole, not analyzed to parts,
But each part having reference to all,—
How shall a certain part, pronounced
    complete,
Endure effacement by another part?
Was the thing done?—than, what's to do
    again?
See, in the chequered pavement opposite,
Suppose the artist made a perfect rhomb,
And next a lozenge, then a trapezoid—
He did not overlay them, superimpose
The new upon the old and blot it out,
But laid them on a level in his work,
Making at last a picture; there it lies.
So, first the perfect separate forms were made,
The portions of mankind; and after, so,
Occurred the combinations of the same.
For where had been a progress, otherwise?
Mankind, made up of all the single men,—
In such a synthesis the labour ends.
Now mark me! those divine men of old time
Have reached, thou sayest well, each at one
    point
The outside verge that rounds our faculty;
And where they reached, who can do more
    than reach?
It takes but little water just to touch
At some one point the inside of a sphere,
And, as we turn the sphere, touch all the rest
In due succession: but the finer air

Which so palpably nor obviously,
Though no less universally, can touch
The whole circumference of that emptied
    sphere,
Fills it more fully than the water did;
Holds thrice the weight of water in itself
Resolved into a subtler element.
And yet the vulgar call the sphere first full
Up to the visible height—and after, void;   110
Not knowing air's more hidden properties.
And thus our soul, misknown, cries out to Zeus
To vindicate his purpose in our life:
Why stay we on the earth unless to grow?
Long since, I imaged, wrote the fiction out,
That he or other god descended here
And, once for all, showed simultaneously
What, in its nature, never can be shown,
Piecemeal or in succession;—showed, I say,
The worth both absolute and relative   120
Of all his children from the birth of time,
His instruments for all appointed work.
I now go on to image,—might we hear
The judgment which should give the due to
    each,
Show where the labour lay and where the ease,
And prove Zeus' self, the latent everywhere!
This is a dream:—but no dream, let us hope,
That years and days, the summers and the
    springs,
Follow each other with unwaning powers.
The grapes which dye thy wine are richer far,   130
Through culture, than the wild wealth of the
    rock;
The suave plum than the savage-tasted drupe;[8]
The pastured honey-bee drops choicer sweet;
The flowers turn double, and the leaves turn
    flowers;
That young and tender crescent-moon, thy
    slave,
Sleeping above her robe as buoyed by clouds,
Refines upon the women of my youth.
What, and the soul alone deteriorates?
I have not chanted verse like Homer, no—
Nor swept string like Terpander,[9] no—nor
    carved   140
And painted men like Phidias[10] and his friend:
I am not great as they are, point by point.
But I have entered into sympathy

---

[7] Moods: the moods or modes of Greek music were made by arranging the notes of an octave differently according to certain fixed patterns of their intervals.

[8] Drupe: wild plum.

[9] Terpander: a musician of the seventh century B.C., reputed to have founded Greek music.

[10] Phidias: a Greek sculptor of the fifth century B.C. whose principal work was in the decoration of the Parthenon; his friend is probably Pericles, not a painter but a patron of artists and the ruler of Athens in the great years of its political and cultural power.

With these four, running these into one soul,
Who, separate, ignored each other's art.
Say, is it nothing that I know them all?
The wild flower was the larger; I have dashed
Rose-blood upon its petals, pricked its cup's
Honey with wine, and driven its seed to fruit,
150 And show a better flower if not so large:
I stand myself. Refer this to the gods
Whose gift alone it is! which, shall I dare
(All pride apart) upon the absurd pretext
That such a gift by chance lay in my hand,
Discourse of lightly or depreciate?
It might have fallen to another's hand: what
    then?
I pass too surely: let at least truth stay!

    And next, of what thou followest on to
        ask.
This being with me as I declare, O king,
160 My works, in all these varicoloured kinds,
So done by me, accepted so by men—
Thou askest, if (my soul thus in men's hearts)
I must not be accounted to attain
The very crown and proper end of life?
Inquiring thence how, now life closeth up,
I face death with success in my right hand:
Whether I fear death less than dost thyself
The fortunate of men? "For" (writest thou)
"Thou leavest much behind, while I leave
        nought.
170 Thy life stays in the poems men shall sing,
The pictures men shall study; while my life,
Complete and whole now in its power and joy,
Dies altogether with my brain and arm,
Is lost indeed; since, what survives myself?
The brazen statue to o'erlook my grave,
Set on the promontory which I named.
And that—some supple courtier of my heir
Shall use its robed and sceptred arm, perhaps,
To fix the rope to, which best drags it down.
180 I go then: triumph thou, who dost not go!"

    Nay, thou art worthy of hearing my whole
        mind.
Is this apparent, when thou turn'st to muse
Upon the scheme of earth and man in chief,
That admiration grows as knowledge grows?
That imperfection means perfection hid,
Reserved in part, to grace the after-time?
If, in the morning of philosophy,
Ere aught had been recorded, nay perceived,
Thou, with the light now in thee, couldst have
        looked
190 On all earth's tenantry, from worm to bird,

Ere man, her last, appeared upon the stage—
Thou wouldst have seen them perfect, and
    deduced
The perfectness of others yet unseen.
Conceding which,—had Zeus then questioned
    thee
"Shall I go on a step, improve on this,
Do more for visible creatures than is done?"
Thou wouldst have answered, "Ay, by making
    each
Grow conscious in himself—by that alone.
All's perfect else: the shell sucks fast the rock,
The fish strikes through the sea, the snake both
        swims   2
And slides, forth range the beasts, the birds
        take flight,
Till life's mechanics can no further go—
And all this joy in natural life is put
Like fire from off thy finger into each,
So exquisitely perfect is the same.
But 't is pure fire, and they mere matter are;
It has them, not they it: and so I choose
For man, thy last premeditated work
 (If I might add a glory to the scheme)
That a third thing should stand apart from
        both,   2
A quality arise within his soul,
Which, intro-active, made to supervise
And feel the force it has, may view itself,
And so be happy." Man might live at first
The animal life: but is there nothing more?
In due time, let him critically learn
How he lives; and, the more he gets to know
Of his own life's adaptabilities,
The more joy-giving will his life become.
Thus man, who hath this quality, is best.   2

    But thou, king, hadst more reasonably
        said:
"Let progress end at once,—man make no step
Beyond the natural man, the better beast,
Using his senses, not the sense of sense."
In man there's failure, only since he left
The lower and inconscious forms of life.
We called it an advance, the rendering plain
Man's spirit might grow conscious of man's
        life,
And, by new lore so added to the old,
Take each step higher over the brute's head.   2
This grew the only life, the pleasure-house,
Watch-tower and treasure-fortress of the soul,
Which whole surrounding flats of natural life
Seemed only fit to yield subsistence to;
A tower that crowns a country. But alas,
The soul now climbs it just to perish there!

For thence we have discovered ('t is no
    dream—
We know this, which we had not else
    perceived)
That there's a world of capability
For joy, spread round about us, meant for us,
Inviting us; and still the soul craves all,
And still the flesh replies, "Take no jot more
Than ere thou clombst the tower to look
    abroad!
Nay, so much less as that fatigue has brought
Deduction to it." We struggle, fain to enlarge
Our bounded physical recipiency,
Increase our power, supply fresh oil to life,
Repair the waste of age and sickness: no,
It skills not! life's inadequate to joy,
As the soul sees joy, tempting life to take.
They praise a fountain in my garden here
Wherein a Naiad[11] sends the water-bow
Thin from her tube; she smiles to see it rise.
What if I told her, it is just a thread
From that great river which the hills shut up,
And mock her with my leave to take the same?
The artificer has given her one small tube
Past power to widen or exchange—what boots
To know she might spout oceans if she could?
She cannot lift beyond her first thin thread:
And so a man can use but a man's joy
While he sees God's. Is it for Zeus to boast,
"See, man, how happy I live, and despair—
That I may be still happier—for thy use!"
If this were so, we could not thank our lord,
As hearts beat on to doing; 't is not so—
Malice it is not. Is it carelessness?
Still, no. If care—where is the sign? I ask,
And get no answer, and agree in sum,
O king, with thy profound discouragement,
Who seest the wider but to sigh the more.
Most progress is most failure: thou sayest well.

    The last point now:—thou dost except a
      case—
Holding joy not impossible to one
With artist-gifts—to such a man as I
Who leave behind me living works indeed;
For, such a poem, such a painting lives.
What? dost thou verily trip upon a word,
Confound the accurate view of what joy is
(Caught somewhat clearer by my eyes than
    thine)

With feeling joy? confound the knowing how
And showing how to live (my faculty)
With actually living?—Otherwise
Where is the artist's vantage o'er the king?
Because in my great epos I display
How divers men young, strong, fair, wise, can
    act—
Is this as though I acted? if I paint,
Carve the young Phœbus,[12] am I therefore
    young?
Methinks I'm older that I bowed myself
The many years of pain that taught me art!   290
Indeed, to know is something, and to prove
How all this beauty might be enjoyed, is
    more:
But, knowing nought, to enjoy is something
    too.
Yon rower, with the moulded muscles there,
Lowering the sail, is nearer it than I.
I can write love-odes: thy fair slave's an ode.
I get to sing of love, when grown too grey
For being beloved: she turns to that young
    man,
The muscles all a-ripple on his back.
I know the joy of kingship: well, thou art king!   300

    "But," sayest thou— (and I marvel, I
      repeat,
To find thee trip on such a mere word) "what
Thou writest, paintest, stays; that does not die:
Sappho[13] survives, because we sing her songs,
And Æschylus,[14] because we read his plays!"
Why, if they live still, let them come and take
Thy slave in my despite, drink from thy cup,
Speak in my place. Thou diest while I survive?
Say rather that my fate is deadlier still,
In this, that every day my sense of joy   310
Grows more acute, my soul (intensified
By power and insight) more enlarged, more
    keen;
While every day my hairs fall more and more,
My hand shakes, and the heavy years
    increase—
The horror quickening still from year to year,
The consummation coming past escape
When I shall know most, and yet least enjoy—
When all my works wherein I prove my worth,
Being present still to mock me in men's
    mouths,
Alive still, in the praise of such as thou,   320

---

[11] Naiad: a water nymph.
[12] Phœbus: a name of Apollo, Greek god of music, prophecy, and (sometimes) the sun.
[13] Sappho, a lyric poet, was born about 600 B.C.
[14] Æschylus, the first major Greek tragedians, was born in 525 B.C.

I, I the feeling, thinking, acting man,
The man who loved his life so over-much,
Sleep in my urn. It is so horrible,
I dare at times imagine to my need
Some future state revealed to us by Zeus,
Unlimited in capability
For joy, as this is in desire for joy,
—To seek which, the joy-hunger forces us:
That, stung by straitness of our life, made
      strait
330 On purpose to make prized the life at large—
Freed by the throbbing impulse we call death,
We burst there as the worm into the fly,
Who, while a worm still, wants his wings. But
      no!
Zeus has not yet revealed it; and alas,
He must have done so, were it possible!

      Live long and happy, and in that thought
            die:
Glad for what was! Farewell. And for the rest,
I cannot tell thy messenger aright
Where to deliver what he bears of thine
To one called Paulus;[15] we have heard his
340   fame
Indeed, if Christus be not one with him—
I know not, nor am troubled much to know.
Thou canst not think a mere barbarian Jew
As Paulus proves to be, one circumcized,
Hath access to a secret shut from us?
Thou wrongest our philosophy, O king,
In stooping to inquire of such an one,
As if his answer could impose at all!
He writeth, doth he? well, and he may write.
350 Oh, the Jew findeth scholars! certain slaves
Who touched on this same isle, preached him
      and Christ;
And (as I gathered from a bystander)
Their doctrine could be held by no sane man.
                                          1855

Two in the Campagna[1]

I
I wonder do you feel to-day
      As I have felt since, hand in hand,
We sat down on the grass, to stray
      In spirit better through the land,
This morn of Rome and May?

II
For me, I touched a thought, I know,
      Has tantalized me many times,
(Like turns of thread the spiders throw
      Mocking across our path) for rhymes
To catch at and let go.

III
Help me to hold it! First it left
      The yellowing fennel, run to seed
There, branching from the brickwork's cleft,
      Some old tomb's ruin: yonder weed
Took up the floating weft,

IV
Where one small orange cup amassed
      Five beetles,—blind and green they grope
Among the honey-meal: and last,
      Everywhere on the grassy slope
I traced it. Hold it fast!

V
The champaign with its endless fleece
      Of feathery grasses everywhere!
Silence and passion, joy and peace,
      An everlasting wash of air—
Rome's ghost since her decease.

VI
Such life here, through such lengths of hours,
      Such miracles performed in play,
Such primal naked forms of flowers,
      Such letting nature have her way
While heaven looks from its towers!

VII
How say you? Let us, O my dove,
      Let us be unashamed of soul,
As earth lies bare to heaven above!
      How is it under our control
To love or not to love?

VIII
I would that you were all to me,
      You that are just so much, no more.
Nor yours nor mine, nor slave nor free!
      Where does the fault lie? What the core
O' the wound, since wound must be?

IX
I would I could adopt your will,
      See with your eyes, and set my heart

[15] Paulus: Paul of Tarsus, who was preaching in Greece around the year 50.
[1] Campagna: the area around Rome which once comprised the old district of Latium and in which were the ruins of its cities.

Beating by yours, and drink my fill
    At your soul's springs,—your part my part
In life, for good and ill.

X

No. I yearn upward, touch you close,
    Then stand away. I kiss your cheek,
Catch your soul's warmth,—I pluck the rose
    And love it more than tongue can speak—
Then the good minute goes.

XI

Already how am I so far
    Out of that minute? Must I go
Still like the thistle-ball, no bar,
    Onward, whenever light winds blow,
Fixed by no friendly star?

XII

Just when I seemed about to learn!
    Where is the thread now? Off again!
The old trick! Only I discern—
    Infinite passion, and the pain
Of finite hearts that yearn.

                            1855

A Grammarian's Funeral

Shortly after the Revival of Learning in Europe

Let us begin and carry up this corpse,
    Singing together.
Leave we the common crofts, the vulgar
    thorpes[1]
    Each in its tether
Sleeping safe on the bosom of the plain,
    Cared-for till cock-crow:
Look out if yonder be not day again
    Rimming the rock-row!
That's the appropriate country; there, man's
    thought,
    Rarer, intenser,
Self-gathered for an outbreak, as it ought,
    Chafes in the censer.
Leave we the unlettered plain its herd and
    crop;
    Seek we sepulture
On a tall mountain, citied to the top,
    Crowded with culture!

All the peaks soar, but one the rest excels;
    Clouds overcome it;
No! yonder sparkle is the citadel's
    Circling its summit.   20
Thither our path lies; wind we up the heights:
    Wait ye the warning?
Our low life was the level's and the night's;
    He's for the morning.
Step to a tune, square chests, erect each head,
    'Ware the beholders!
This is our master, famous calm and dead,
    Borne on our shoulders.

Sleep, crop and herd! sleep, darkling thorpe
    and croft,
    Safe from the weather!   30
He, whom we convoy to his grave aloft,
    Singing together,
He was a man born with thy face and throat,
    Lyric Apollo![2]
Long he lived nameless: how should spring
    take note
    Winter would follow?
Till lo, the little touch, and youth was gone!
    Cramped and diminished,
Moaned he, "New measures, other feet anon!
    My dance is finished?"   40
No, that's the world's way: (keep the moun-
    tain-side,
    Make for the city!)
He knew the signal, and stepped on with pride
    Over men's pity;
Left play for work, and grappled with the
    world
    Bent on escaping:
"What's in the scroll," quoth he, "thou keepest
    furled?
    Show me their shaping,
Theirs who most studied man, the bard and
    sage,—
    Give!"—So, he gowned[3] him.   50
Straight got by heart that book to its last page:
    Learned, we found him.
Yea, but we found him bald too, eyes like lead,
    Accents uncertain:
"Time to taste life," another would have said,
    "Up with the curtain!"
This man said rather, "Actual life comes next?
    Patience a moment!
Grant I have mastered learning's crabbed text,
    Still there's the comment.   60

[1] Crofts: enclosed fields . . . thorpes: villages.
[2] Apollo: the Greek god of music; sometimes associated with the sun.
[3] Gowned: put on a scholar's gown.

Let me know all! Prate not of most or least,
　　Painful or easy!
Even to the crumbs I'd fain eat up the feast,
　　Ay, nor feel queasy."
Oh, such a life as he resolved to live,
　　When he had learned it,
When he had gathered all books had to give!
　　Sooner, he spurned it.
Image the whole, then execute the parts—
70　　Fancy the fabric
Quite, ere you build, ere steel strike fire from
　　　quartz,
　　Ere mortar dab brick!

(Here's the town-gate reached: there's the
　　　market-place
　　Gaping before us.)
Yea, this in him was the peculiar grace
　　(Hearten our chorus!)
That before living he'd learn how to live—
　　No end to learning:
Earn the means first—God surely will contrive
80　　Use for our earning.
Others mistrust and say, "But time escapes:
　　Live now or never!"
He said, "What's time? Leave Now for dogs
　　　and apes!
　　Man has Forever."
Back to his book then: deeper drooped his
　　　head:
　　Calculus racked him:
Leaden before, his eyes grew dross of lead:
　　Tussis attacked him.[4]
90　"Now, master, take a little rest!"—not he!
　　(Caution redoubled,
Step two abreast, the way winds narrowly!)
　　Not a whit troubled
Back to his studies, fresher than at first,
　　Fierce as a dragon
He (soul-hydroptic[5] with a sacred thirst)
　　Sucked at the flagon.
Oh, if we draw a circle premature,
　　Heedless of far gain,
Greedy for quick returns of profit, sure
100　　Bad is our bargain!
Was it not great? did not he throw on God,
　　(He loves the burthen) —
God's task to make the heavenly period
　　Perfect the earthen?
Did not he magnify the mind, show clear
　　Just what it all meant?

He would not discount life, as fools do here,
　　Paid by instalment.
He ventured neck or nothing—heaven's success
　　Found, or earth's failure:　　　　　　　　　1
"Wilt thou trust death or not?" He answered
　　　"Yes:
　　Hence with life's pale lure!"
That low man seeks a little thing to do,
　　Sees it and does it:
This high man, with a great thing to pursue,
　　Dies ere he knows it.
That low man goes on adding one to one,
　　His hundred's soon hit:
This high man, aiming at a million,
　　Misses an unit.　　　　　　　　　　　　　1
That, has the world here—should he need the
　　　next,
　　Let the world mind him!
This, throws himself on God, and unperplexed
　　Seeking shall find him.
So, with the throttling hands of death at strife,
　　Ground he at grammar;
Still, thro' the rattle,[6] parts of speech were rife:
　　While he could stammer
He settled *Hoti's* business—let it be!—
　　Properly based *Oun*—　　　　　　　　　　1
Gave us the doctrine of the enclitic *De*,[7]
　　Dead from the waist down.
Well, here's the platform, here's the proper
　　　place:
　　Hail to your purlieus,
All ye highfliers of the feathered race,
　　Swallows and curlews!
Here's the top-peak; the multitude below
　　Live, for they can, there:
This man decided not to Live but Know—
　　Bury this man there?　　　　　　　　　　1
Here—here's his place, where meteors shoot,
　　　clouds form,
　　Lightnings are loosened,
Stars come and go! Let joy break with the
　　　storm,
　　Peace let the dew send!
Lofty designs must close in like effects:
　　Loftily lying,
Leave him—still loftier than the world
　　　suspects,
　　Living and dying.

　　　　　　　　　　　　　　　　　　　　1855

---

[4] Calculus: gall-stone . . . Tussis: a cough.　　[5] Hydroptic: insatiably thirsty.
[6] Rattle: death rattle.
[7] *Hoti; Oun; De:* Greek particles; the enclitic *De* is dead from the waist down because it is not emphatic, and pronounced as part of the preceding sound.

"Transcendentalism: A Poem in Twelve Books"

Stop playing, poet! May a brother speak?
'T is you speak, that's your error. Song's our
    art:
Whereas you please to speak these naked
    thoughts
Instead of draping them in sights and sounds.
—True thoughts, good thoughts, thoughts fit
    to treasure up!
But why such long prolusion and display,
Such turning and adjustment of the harp,
And taking it upon your breast, at length,
Only to speak dry words across its strings?
Stark-naked thought is in request enough:
Speak prose and hollo it till Europe hears!
The six-foot Swiss tube,[1] braced about with
    bark,
Which helps the hunter's voice from Alp to
    Alp—
Exchange our harp for that,—who hinders
    you?

    But here's your fault; grown men want
        thought, you think;
Thought's what they mean by verse, and seek
    in verse.
Boys seek for images and melody,
Men must have reason—so, you aim at men.
Quite otherwise! Objects throng our youth, 't is
    true;
We see and hear and do not wonder much:
If you could tell us what they mean, indeed!
As German Boehme[2] never cared for plants
Until it happed, a-walking in the fields,
He noticed all at once that plants could speak,
Nay, turned with loosened tongue to talk with
    him.
That day the daisy had an eye indeed—
Colloquized with the cowslip on such themes!
We find them extant yet in Jacob's prose.
But by the time youth slips a stage or two
While reading prose in that tough book he
    wrote

(Collating and emendating the same
And settling on the sense most to our mind),
We shut the clasps and find life's summer past.
Then, who helps more, pray, to repair our
    loss—
Another Boehme with a tougher book
And subtler meanings of what roses say,—
Or some stout Mage like him of Halberstadt,[3]
John, who made things Boehme wrote thoughts
    about?
He with a "look you!" vents a brace of rhymes,
And in there breaks the sudden rose herself,   40
Over us, under, round us every side,
Nay, in and out the tables and the chairs
And musty volumes, Boehme's book and all,—
Buries us with a glory, young once more,
Pouring heaven into this shut house of life.

    So come, the harp back to your heart again!
You are a poem, though your poem's naught.
The best of all you showed before, believe,
Was your own boy-face o'er the finer chords
Bent, following the cherub at the top   50
That points to God with his paired half-moon
    wings.

                  1855

One Word More[1]

To E. B. B.

I

There they are, my fifty men and women
Naming me the fifty poems finished!
Take them, Love, the book and me together:
Where the heart lies, let the brain lie also.

II

Rafael[2] made a century of sonnets,
Made and wrote them in a certain volume
Dinted with the silver-pointed pencil
Else he only used to draw Madonnas:
These, the world might view—but one, the
    volume.

---

[1] Swiss-tube: a wooden megaphone used in the Alps.

[2] German Boehme: Jacob Boehme (1575–1624) believed that he saw the fundamental structure and harmonious principles of all created things.

[3] John of Halberstadt: Johannes Teutonicus, a medieval scholar reputed to be a magician.

[1] This poem, dedicated to his wife, was placed by Browning at the end of the *Men and Women* (1855). It is written in a measure (trochaic pentameter) which Browning had not used before, and did not use again, his equivalent to the sonnets of Raphael and the portrait painted by Dante to which he refers in the poem.

[2] Rafael: according to Browning's principal source of information about the painters of the Italian Renaissance, Giorgio Vasari's *Lives of the Painters* (1550), Raphael (1483–1520) was in love with a young girl to whom he remained constant throughout his life.

Who that one, you ask? Your heart instructs
10   you.
Did she live and love it all her life-time?
Did she drop, his lady of the sonnets,
Die, and let it drop beside her pillow
Where it lay in place of Rafael's glory,
Rafael's cheek so duteous and so loving—
Cheek, the world was wont to hail a painter's,
Rafael's cheek, her love had turned a poet's?

III

You and I would rather read that volume,
  (Taken to his beating bosom by it)
20 Lean and list the bosom-beats of Rafael,
Would we not? than wonder at Madonnas—
Her, San Sisto names, and Her, Foligno,
Her, that visits Florence in a vision,
Her, that's left with lilies in the Louvre³—
Seen by us and all the world in circle.

IV

You and I will never read that volume.
Guido Reni,⁴ like his own eye's apple
Guarded long the treasure-book and loved it.
Guido Reni dying, all Bologna
Cried, and the world cried too, "Ours, the
30   treasure!"
Suddenly, as rare things will, it vanished.

V

Dante once prepared to paint an angel:
Whom to please? You whisper "Beatrice."
While he mused and traced it and retraced it,
(Peradventure with a pen corroded
Still by drops of that hot ink he dipped for,
When, his left-hand i' the hair o' the wicked,
Back he held the brow and pricked its stigma,
Bit into the live man's flesh for parchment,
40 Loosed him, laughed to see the writing rankle,
Let the wretch go festering through
    Florence) —
Dante, who loved well because he hated,
Hated wickedness that hinders loving,
Dante standing, studying his angel,—
In there broke the folk of his Inferno.
Says he—"Certain people of importance"
(Such he gave his daily dreadful line to)

"Entered and would seize, forsooth, the poet."
Says the poet—"Then I stopped my
    painting."⁵

VI

You and I would rather see that angel,
Painted by the tenderness of Dante,
Would we not?—than read a fresh Inferno.

VII

You and I will never see that picture.
While he mused on love and Beatrice,
While he softened o'er his outlined angel,
In they broke, those "people of importance."
We and Bice⁶ bear the loss forever.

VIII

What of Rafael's sonnets, Dante's picture?
This: no artist lives and loves, that longs not
Once, and only once, and for one only,
(Ah, the prize!) to find his love a language
Fit and fair and simple and sufficient—
Using nature that's an art to others,
Not, this one time, art that's turned his nature.
Ay, of all the artists living, loving,
None but would forego his proper dowry,—
Does he paint? he fain would write a poem,—
Does he write? he fain would paint a picture,
Put to proof art alien to the artist's,
Once, and only once, and for one only,
So to be the man and leave the artist,
Gain the man's joy, miss the artist's sorrow.

IX

Wherefore? Heaven's gift takes earth's
    abatement!
He⁷ who smites the rock and spreads the water,
Bidding drink and live a crowd beneath him,
Even he, the minute makes immortal,
Proves, perchance, but mortal in the minute,
Desecrates, belike, the deed in doing.
While he smites, how can he but remember,
So he smote before, in such a peril,
When they stood and mocked—"Shall smiting
    help us?"
When they drank and sneered—"A stroke is
    easy!"

³ Browning here identifies four of Raphael's paintings of the Madonna.
⁴ Guido Reni: an Italian painter, born in 1575.
⁵ Dante recounts this episode in his *Vita Nuova*, his account of his early life and of his love for
Beatrice, with whom he had also fallen in love when she was a young girl.
⁶ Bice: Beatrice.
⁷ He: Moses, who brought water from the rocks during the exodus of the Israelites from
Egypt, during which his people complained of the difficulties of their journey through the
desert.

When they wiped their mouths and went their
   journey,
Throwing him for thanks—"But drought was
   pleasant."
Thus old memories mar the actual triumph;
Thus the doing savors of disrelish;
Thus achievement lacks a gracious somewhat;
O'er-importuned brows becloud the mandate,
Carelessness or consciousness—the gesture.
For he bears an ancient wrong about him,
Sees and knows again those phalanxed faces,
Hears, yet one time more, the 'customed
   prelude—
"How shouldst thou, of all men, smite, and
   save us?"
Guesses what is like to prove the sequel—
"Egypt's flesh-pots—nay, the drought was
   better."

X

Oh, the crowd must have emphatic warrant!
Theirs, the Sinai-forehead's cloven brilliance,[8]
Right-arm's rod-sweep, tongue's imperial fiat.
Never dares the man put off the prophet.

XI

Did he love one face from out the thousands,
(Were she Jethro's daughter, white and wifely,
Were she but the Æthiopian bondslave,) [9]
He would envy yon dumb patient camel,
Keeping a reserve of scanty water
Meant to save his own life in the desert;
Ready in the desert to deliver
(Kneeling down to let his breast be opened)
Hoard and life together for his mistress.

XII

I shall never, in the years remaining,
Paint you pictures, no, nor carve you statues,
Make you music that should all-express me;
So it seems: I stand on my attainment.
This of verse alone, one life allows me;
Verse and nothing else have I to give you.
Other heights in other lives, God willing:
All the gifts from all the heights, your own,
   Love!

XIII

Yet a semblance of resource avails us—
Shade so finely touched, love's sense must seize
   it.
Take these lines, look lovingly and nearly,
Lines I write the first time and the last time.   120
He who works in fresco, steals a hair brush,[10]
Curbs the liberal hand, subservient proudly,
Cramps his spirit, crowds its all in little,
Makes a strange art of an art familiar,
Fills his lady's missal-marge with flowerets.
He who blows thro' bronze, may breathe thro'
   silver,
Fitly serenade a slumbrous princess.
He who writes, may write for once as I do.

XIV

Love, you saw me gather men and women,
Live or dead or fashioned by my fancy,   130
Enter each and all, and use their service,
Speak from every mouth,—the speech, a poem.
Hardly shall I tell my joys and sorrows,
Hopes and fears, belief and disbelieving:
I am mine and yours—the rest be all men's,
Karshish, Cleon, Norbert and the fifty.
Let me speak this once in my true person,
Not as Lippo, Roland or Andrea,
Though the fruit of speech be just this
   sentence:
Pray you, look on these my men and women,   140
Take and keep my fifty poems finished;
Where my heart lies, let my brain lie also!
Poor the speech; be how I speak, for all things.

XV

Not but that you know me! Lo, the moon's
   self!
Here in London, yonder late in Florence,
Still we find her face, the thrice-transfigured.[11]
Curving on a sky imbrued with colour,
Drifted over Fiesole by twilight,
Came she, our new crescent of a hair's-breadth.
Full she flared it, lamping Samminiato,[12]   150
Rounder 'twixt the cypresses and rounder,
Perfect till the nightingales applauded.
Now, a piece of her old self, impoverished,

---

[8] God gave Moses the commandments on Sinai, appearing in thunder and lightening.

[9] Moses married both Zipporah, the daughter of Jethro, and an Ethiopian woman.

[10] Browning here compares his poems to the usually large and ambitious subjects of fresco, painted directly on a treated wall, as opposed to the more delicate work for which a fine painter's brush is appropriate.

[11] Thrice-transfigured: the moon has moved from its new through its full to its old phase during the time that Browning and his wife have traveled from Fiesole, outside Florence, to London.

[12] Samminiato: a church near Florence.

Hard to greet, she traverses the houseroofs,
Hurries with unhandsome thrift of silver,
Goes dispiritedly, glad to finish.

XVI

What, there's nothing in the moon noteworthy?
Nay: for if that moon could love a mortal,[13]
Use, to charm him (so to fit a fancy),
160   All her magic ('t is the old sweet mythos)
She would turn a new side to her mortal,
Side unseen of herdsman, huntsman, steers-
man—
Blank to Zoroaster on his terrace,
Blind to Galileo on his turret,
Dumb to Homer,[14] dumb to Keats—him, even!
Think, the wonder of the moonstruck mortal—
When she turns round, comes again in heaven,
Opens out anew for worse or better!
Proves she like some portent of an iceberg
170   Swimming full upon the ship it founders,
Hungry with huge teeth of splintered crystals?
Proves she as the paved work of a sapphire
Seen by Moses when he climbed the mountain?
Moses, Aaron, Nadab and Abihu[15]
Climbed and saw the very God, the Highest,
Stand upon the paved work of a sapphire.
Like the bodied heaven in his clearness
Shone the stone, the sapphire of that paved
work,
When they ate and drank and saw God also!

XVII

What were seen? None knows, none ever shall
180   know.
Only this is sure—the sight were other,
Not the moon's same side, born late in
Florence,
Dying now impoverished here in London.
God be thanked, the meanest of his creatures
Boasts two soul-sides, one to face the world
with,
One to show a women when he loves her!

XVIII

This I say of me, but think of you, Love!
This to you—yourself my moon of poets!
Ah, but that's the world's side, there's the
wonder,
Thus they see you, praise you, think they know
you!
There, in turn I stand with them and praise
you—
Out of my own self, I dare to phrase it.
But the best is when I glide from out them,
Cross a step or two of dubious twilight,
Come out on the other side, the novel
Silent silver lights and darks undreamed of,
Where I hush and bless myself with silence.

XIX

Oh, their Rafael of the dear Madonnas,
Oh, their Dante of the dread Inferno,
Wrote one song—and in my brain I sing it,
Drew one angel—borne, see, on my bosom!
                                        R. B.
                                        1855

Dîs Aliter Visum; or, le Byron de nos jours[1]

I

Stop, let me have the truth of that!
   Is that all true? I say, the day
Ten years ago when both of us
   Met on a morning, friends—as thus
We meet this evening, friends or what?—

II

Did you—because I took your arm
   And sillily smiled, "A mass of brass
That sea looks, blazing underneath!"
   While up the cliff-road edged with heath,
We took the turns nor came to harm—

---

[13] Diana, the goddess of the moon, fell in love with the mortal Endymion; among others, Keats wrote a poem based on this myth.

[14] Zoroaster was the founder of an Eastern religion in which the symbolism of light and dark is central, and the sun and the stars observed and worshipped. The astronomical observations of Galileo (1564–1642) led him to conclude that the moon's light was reflected, and that its surface was punctuated with mountains. One of the so-called "Homeric hymns" is to the moon.

[15] During the sojourn in the desert, Moses and some of the leaders and elders of his people saw God, "under his feet as it were a paved work of a sapphire stone, and as it were the body of heaven in his clearness" (Exodus 24:9–10).

[1] Dîs aliter visum: a phrase from the second book of Virgil's *Aeneid*: "The gods see otherwise." The subtitle, "The Byron of our day," plays the character of the poet in the poem against the legend of the imperious Byron.

III

Did you consider "Now makes twice
   That I have seen her, walked and talked
With this poor pretty thoughtful thing,
   Whose worth I weigh: she tries to sing;
Draws, hopes in time the eye grows nice;

IV

"Reads verse and thinks she understands;
   Loves all, at any rate, that 's great,
Good, beautiful; but much as we
   Down at the bath-house love the sea,
Who breathe its salt and bruise its sands:

V

"While . . . do but follow the fishing-gull
   That flaps and floats from wave to cave!
There 's the sea-lover, fair my friend!
   What then? Be patient, mark and mend!
Had you the making of your scull?"[2]

VI

And did you, when we faced the church
   With spire and sad slate roof, aloof
From human fellowship so far,
   Where a few graveyard crosses are,
And garlands for the swallows' perch,—

VII

Did you determine, as we stepped
   O'er the lone stone fence, "Let me get
Her for myself, and what 's the earth
   With all its art, verse, music, worth—
Compared with love, found, gained, and kept?

VIII

"Schumann 's[3] our music-maker now;
   Has his march-movement youth and mouth?
Ingres 's[4] the modern man that paints;
   Which will lean on me, of his saints?
Heine[5] for songs; for kisses, how?"

IX

And did you, when we entered, reached
   The votive frigate,[6] soft aloft
Riding on air this hundred years,
   Safe-smiling at old hopes and fears,—
Did you draw profit while she preached?

X

Resolving, "Fools we wise men grow!
   Yes, I could easily blurt out curt
Some question that might find reply
   As prompt in her stopped lips, dropped eye,
And rush of red to cheek and brow: 50

XI

"Thus were a match made, sure and fast,
   'Mid the blue weed-flowers round the mound
Where, issuing, we shall stand and stay
   For one more look at baths and bay,
Sands, sea-gulls, and the old church last—

XII

"A match 'twixt me, bent, wigged and lamed,
   Famous, however, for verse and worse,
Sure of the Fortieth spare Arm-chair[7]
   When gout and glory seat me there,
So, one whose love-freaks pass unblamed,—   60

XIII

"And this young beauty, round and sound
   As a mountain-apple, youth and truth
With loves and doves, at all events
   With money in the Three per Cents;[8]
Whose choice of me would seem profound:—

XIV

She might take me as I take her.
   Perfect the hour would pass, alas!
Climb high, love high, what matter? Still,
   Feet, feelings, must descend the hill:
An hour's perfection can't recur.   70

XV

"Then follows Paris and full time
   For both to reason: 'Thus with us!'
She 'll sigh, 'Thus girls give body and soul
   At first word, think they gain the goal,
When 't is the starting-place they climb!

XVI

" 'My friend makes verse and gets renown;
   Have they all fifty years, his peers?
He knows the world, firm, quiet and gay;
   Boys will become as much one day:
They're fools; he cheats, with beard less brown.   80

[2] Scull: oar, or boat; i.e., equipment with which to move on water.

[3] Robert Schumann (1810–56).   [4] Jean August Ingres (1780–1867).

[5] Heinrich Heine (1800–56), a lyric poet.

[6] Votive frigate: a model of a ship hung in a church as an offering.

[7] Fortieth spare arm-chair: a seat in the French Academy, whose membership is limited to forty distinguished persons, usually elected in their old ages.

[8] Three per Cents: investments, thought to be unusually secure, in bonds of the British government.

XVII

" 'For boys say, *Love me or I die!*
    He did not say, *The truth is, youth*
I want, who am old and know too much;
    I'd catch youth: lend me sight and touch!
Drop heart's blood where life's wheels grate
    dry!'

XVIII

"While I should make rejoinder"— (then
    It was, no doubt, you ceased that least
Light pressure of my arm in yours)
    " 'I can conceive of cheaper cures
90 For a yawning-fit o'er books and men.

XIX

" 'What? All I am, was, and might be,
    All, books taught, art brought, life's whole
        strife,
Painful results since precious, just
    Were fitly exchanged, in wise disgust,
For two cheeks freshened by youth and sea?

XX

" 'All for a nosegay!—what came first;
    With fields on flower, untried each side;
I rally, need my books and men,
    And find a nosegay': drop it, then,
100 No match yet made for best or worst!"

XXI

That ended me. You judged the porch
    We left by, Norman;[9] took our look
At sea and sky; wondered so few
    Find out the place for air and view;
Remarked the sun began to scorch;

XXII

Descended, soon regained the baths,
    And then, good-bye! Years ten since then:
Ten years! We meet: you tell me, now,
    By a window-seat for that cliff-brow,
110 On carpet-stripes for those sand-paths.

XXIII

Now I may speak: you fool, for all
    Your lore! Who made things plain in vain?
What was the sea for? What, the grey
    Sad church, that solitary day,
Crosses and graves and swallows' call?

XXIV

Was there nought better than to enjoy?
    No feat which, done, would make time break,
And let us pent-up creatures through
    Into eternity, our due?
No forcing earth teach heaven's employ?

XXV

No wise beginning, here and now,
    What cannot grow complete (earth's feat)
And heaven must finish, there and then?
    No tasting earth's true food for men,
Its sweet in sad, its sad in sweet?

XXVI

No grasping at love, gaining a share
    O' the sole spark from God's life at strife
With death, so, sure of range above
    The limits here? For us and love,
Failure; but, when God fails, despair.

XXVII

This you call wisdom? Thus you add
    Good unto good again, in vain?
You loved, with body worn and weak;
    I loved, with faculties to seek:
Were both loves worthless since ill-clad?

XXVIII

Let the mere star-fish in his vault
    Crawl in a wash of weed, indeed,
Rose-jacynth[10] to the finger-tips:
    He, whole in body and soul, outstrips
Man, found with either in default.

XXIX

But what 's whole, can increase no more,
    Is dwarfed and dies, since here 's its sphere.
The devil laughed at you in his sleeve!
    You knew not? That I well believe;
Or you had saved two souls: nay, four.

XXX

For Stephanie sprained last night her wrist,
    Ankle or something. "Pooh," cry you?
At any rate she danced, all say,
    Vilely; her vogue has had its day.
Here comes my husband from his whist.

                                                            1864

---

[9] Norman: an architectural style of about the tenth century.
[10] Rose-jacynth: the color of a reddish-orange gem.

Abt Vogler[1]

(After he has been extemporizing upon the musical instrument of his invention)

I

Would that the structure brave, the manifold music I build,
    Bidding my organ obey, calling its keys to their work,
Claiming each slave of the sound, at a touch, as when Solomon willed
    Armies of angels that soar, legions of demons that lurk,
Man, brute, reptile, fly,—alien of end and of aim,
    Adverse, each from the other heaven-high, hell-deep removed,—
Should rush into sight at once as he named the ineffable Name,[2]
    And pile him a palace straight, to pleasure the princess he loved!

II

Would it might tarry like his, the beautiful building of mine,
    This which my keys in a crowd pressed and importuned to raise!
Ah, one and all, how they helped, would dispart now and now combine,
    Zealous to hasten the work, heighten their master his praise!
And one would bury his brow with a blind plunge down to hell,
    Burrow awhile and build, broad on the roots of things,
Then up again swim into sight, having based me my palace well,
    Founded it, fearless of flame, flat on the nether springs.

III

And another would mount and march, like the excellent minion he was,
    Ay, another and yet another, one crowd but with many a crest,
Raising my rampired[3] walls of gold as transparent as glass,
    Eager to do and die, yield each his place to the rest:
For higher still and higher (as a runner tips with fire,
    When a great illumination surprises a festal night—
Outlining round and round Rome's dome[4] from space to spire)
    Up, the pinnacled glory reached, and the pride of my soul was in sight.

IV

In sight? Not half! for it seemed, it was certain, to match man's birth,
    Nature in turn conceived, obeying an impulse as I;
And the emulous heaven yearned down, made effort to reach the earth,
    As the earth had done her best, in my passion, to scale the sky:
Novel splendours burst forth, grew familiar and dwelt with mine,
    Not a point nor peak but found and fixed its wandering star;
Meteor-moons, balls of blaze: and they did not pale nor pine,
    For earth had attained to heaven, there was no more near nor far.

V

Nay more; for there wanted not who walked in the glare and glow,
    Presences plain in the place; or, fresh from the Protoplast,[5]
Furnished for ages to come, when a kindlier wind should blow,
    Lured now to begin and live, in a house to their liking at last;
Or else the wonderful Dead who have passed through the body and gone,
    But were back once more to breathe in an old world worth their new:

20

30

[1] Georg Joseph Vogler (1749–1814) was a priest (hence Abt or Abbé) who lived as professional musician. He was well known for his talent as an extemporizer, especially on a portable organ he devised. Browning knew of Vogler through his own music teacher, who had himself studied under Vogler.

[2] Solomon, king of the Israelites in the tenth century before Christ, was supposed to possess a seal inscribed with the unspeakable, secret name of God, with which he commanded the demons of earth and air. He was also known for the luxurance of his palaces, and for his liaisons with infidel queens and princesses.

[3] Rampired: ramparted.

[4] Rome's dome: the dome of St. Peter's, which was illuminated on feast days.

[5] Protoplast: an object formed first; the type or model.

What never had been, was now; what was, as
   it shall be anon;
     And what is,—shall I say, matched both?
40   for I was made perfect too.

VI

All through my keys that gave their sounds to
   a wish of my soul,
     All through my soul that praised as its
     wish flowed visibly forth,
All through music and me! For think, had I
   painted the whole,
     Why, there it had stood, to see, nor the
     process so wonder-worth:
Had I written the same, made verse—still,
   effect proceeds from cause,
     Ye know why the forms are fair, ye hear
     how the tale is told;
It is all triumphant art, but art in obedience
   to laws,
     Painter and poet are proud in the artist-
     list enrolled:—

VII

But here is the finger of God, a flash of the will
   that can,
     Existent behind all laws, that made them
50   and, lo, they are!
And I know not if, save in this, such gift be
   allowed to man,
     That out of three sounds he frame, not a
     fourth sound, but a star.[6]
Consider it well: each tone of our scale in itself
   is nought;
     It is everywhere in the world—loud, soft,
     and all is said:
Give it to me to use! I mix it with two in my
   thought:
     And, there! Ye have heard and seen:
     consider and bow the head!

VIII

Well, it is gone at last, the palace of music I
   reared;
     Gone! and the good tears start, the praises
     that come too slow;
For one is assured at first, one scarce can say
   that he feared,
     That he even gave it a thought, the gone
60   thing was to go.

Never to be again! But many more of the kind
   As good, nay, better perchance: is this
   your comfort to me?
To me, who must be saved because I cling
   with my mind
     To the same, same self, same love, same
     God: ay, what was, shall be.

IX

Therefore to whom turn I but to thee, the
   ineffable Name?
     Builder and maker, thou, of houses not
     made with hands![7]
What, have fear of change from thee who art
   ever the same?
     Doubt that thy power can fill the heart
     that thy power expands?
There shall never be one lost good! What was,
   shall live as before;
     The evil is null, is nought, is silence
     implying sound;
What was good shall be good, with, for evil, so
   much good more;
     On the earth the broken arcs; in the
     heaven, a perfect round.

X

All we have willed or hoped or dreamed of
   good shall exist;
     Not its semblance, but itself; no beauty,
     nor good, nor power
Whose voice has gone forth, but each survives
   for the melodist
     When eternity affirms the conception of an
     hour.
The high that proved too high, the heroic for
   earth too hard,
     The passion that left the ground to lose
     itself in the sky,
Are music sent up to God by the lover and the
   bard;
     Enough that he heard it once: we shall
     hear it by-and-by.

XI

And what is our failure here but a triumph's
   evidence
     For the fullness of the days? Have we
     withered or agonized?

[6] A star: a chord: because each sound or note is distinct, the chord is not a fourth sound like
the first three, but a new sound made from its constituent notes.
[7] 2 Corinthians 5:1.

Why else was the pause prolonged but that
    singing might issue thence?
    Why rushed the discords in but that
      harmony should be prized?
Sorrow is hard to bear, and doubt is slow to
    clear,
    Each sufferer says his say, his scheme of
      the weal and woe:
But God has a few of us whom he whispers in
    the ear;
    The rest may reason and welcome: 't is we
      musicians know.

XII

Well, it is earth with me; silence resumes her
    reign:
    I will be patient and proud, and soberly
      acquiesce.
Give me the keys. I feel for the common chord
    again,
    Sliding by semitones, till I sink to the
      minor,—yes,
And I blunt it into a ninth, and I stand on
    alien ground,
    Surveying awhile the heights I rolled from
      into the deep;
Which, hark, I have dared and done, for my
    resting-place is found,
    The C Major of this life: so, now I will
      try to sleep.[8]

1864

In Shakespeare's The Tempest, *Caliban is a
monstrous being who inhabits the island to which
Prospero, a magician and the exiled duke of Milan,
and his daughter Miranda come. Through imprison-
ment and punishment, Caliban is taught to serve
Prospero, while Ariel, another inhabitant of the is-
land who had been imprisoned by Caliban's mother,
is set free by Prospero and serves him in order to
earn absolute freedom. Caliban's mother was Sy-
corax, who worshipped a god named Setebos. Shake-
speare does not mention the Quiet, a deity Brown-
ing has Caliban invent as a counter to the character
of Setebos.*
   *Browning uses the phrase "natural theology" to
mean a study in which an idea of a divine being is
formulated and demonstrated by referring to the
nature and order of material creation. In 1864,
when the poem was first published, the notion of
an imperfectly evolved creature imagining an im-*
*perfect (but perhaps evolving) divinity would
probably put many readers in mind of Charles
Darwin's* The Origin of Species *(1859) and the
controversy that followed the publication of his
argument that species evolved by adaptation from
common types of life. But arguments that material
creation manifested the attributes of God were
common in the eighteenth and nineteenth cen-
turies, and Browning, before he knew of Darwin,
was doubtful that a satisfying idea of God could
be derived from and proved in the natural order.*

Caliban upon Setebos; or, Natural Theology in the Island

*"Thou thoughtest that I was altogether such a one as
thyself."*[1]

['Will sprawl, now that the heat of day is best,
Flat on his belly in the pit's much mire,
With elbows wide, fists clenched to prop his
    chin.
And, while he kicks both feet in the cool slush,
And feels about his spine small eft-things[2]
    course,
Run in and out each arm, and make him laugh:
And while above his head a pompion-plant,[3]
Coating the cave-top as a brow its eye,
Creeps down to touch and tickle hair and
    beard,
And now a flower drops with a bee inside,   10
And now a fruit to snap at, catch and crunch,—
He looks out o'er yon sea which sunbeams cross
And recross till they weave a spider-web
(Meshes of fire, some great fish breaks at times)
And talks to his own self, howe'er he please,
Touching that other, whom his dam called
    God.
Because to talk about Him, vexes—ha,
Could He but know! and time to vex is now,
When talk is safer than in winter-time.
Moreover Prosper and Miranda sleep   20
In confidence he drudges at their task,
And it is good to cheat the pair, and gibe,
Letting the rank tongue blossom into speech.]

Setebos, Setebos, and Setebos!
'Thinketh, He dwelleth i' the cold o' the moon.

'Thinketh He made it, with the sun to match,
But not the stars; the stars came otherwise;

---

[8] Vogler's concluding modulation is from his uncommon improvisations to the natural scale of
C major, which contains no sharps or flats.
   [1] The epigraph is from Psalms 50:21—God is speaking to the wicked he has come to judge.
   [2] Eft-things: small lizards.   [3] Pompion-plant: a pumpkin vine.

Only made clouds, winds, meteors, such as that:
Also this isle, what lives and grows thereon,
30 And snaky sea which rounds and ends the same.

'Thinketh, it came of being ill at ease:
He hated that He cannot change His cold,
Nor cure its ache. 'Hath spied an icy fish
That longed to 'scape the rock-stream where
    she lived,
And thaw herself within the lukewarm brine
O' the lazy sea her stream thrusts far amid,
A crystal spike 'twixt two warm walls of wave;
Only, she ever sickened, found repulse
At the other kind of water, not her life,
(Green-dense and dim-delicious, bred o' the
40   sun)
Flounced back from bliss she was not born to
    breathe,
And in her old bounds buried her despair,
Hating and loving warmth alike: so He.

'Thinketh, He made thereat the sun, this isle,
Trees and the fowls here, beast and creeping
    thing.
Yon otter, sleek-wet, black, lithe as a leech;
Yon auk, one fire-eye in a ball of foam,
That floats and feeds; a certain badger brown
He hath watched hunt with that slant white-
    wedge eye
By moonlight; and the pie[4] with the long
50   tongue
That pricks deep into oakwarts for a worm,
And says a plain word when she finds her prize,
But will not eat the ants; the ants themselves
That build a wall of seeds and settled stalks
About their hole—He made all these and more,
Made all we see, and us, in spite: how else?
He could not, Himself, make a second self
To be His mate; as well have made Himself:
He would not make what he mislikes or slights,
60 An eyesore to Him, or not worth His pains:
But did, in envy, listlessness or sport,
Make what Himself would fain, in a manner,
    be—
Weaker in most points, stronger in a few,
Worthy, and yet mere playthings all the while,
Things He admires and mocks too,—that is it.
Because, so brave, so better though they be,
It nothing skills if He begin to plague.
Look now, I melt a gourd-fruit into mash,
Add honeycomb and pods, I have perceived,

Which bite like finches when they bill and
    kiss,—   70
Then, when froth rises bladdery,[5] drink up all,
Quick, quick, till maggots scamper through my
    brain;
Last, throw me on my back i' the seeded thyme.
And wanton, wishing I were born a bird.
Put case, unable to be what I wish,
I yet could make a live bird out of clay:
Would not I take clay, pinch my Caliban
Able to fly?—for, there, see, he hath wings,
And great comb like the hoopoe's[6] to admire,
And there, a sting to do his foes offence,   80
There, and I will that he begin to live,
Fly to yon rock-top, nip me off the horns
Of grigs[7] high up that make the merry din,
Saucy through their veined wings, and mind
    me not.
In which feat, if his leg snapped, brittle clay,
And he lay stupid-like,—why, I should laugh;
Aid if he, spying me, should fall to weep,
Beseech me to be good, repair his wrong,
Bid his poor leg smart less or grow again,—
Well, as the chance were, this might take or else 90
Not take my fancy: I might hear his cry,
And give the mankin three sound legs for one,
Or pluck the other off, leave him like an egg,
And lessoned he was mine and merely clay.
Were this no pleasure, lying in the thyme,
Drinking the mash, with brain become alive,
Making and marring clay at will? So He.

'Thinketh, such shows nor right nor wrong in
    Him,
Nor kind, nor cruel: He is strong and Lord.
'Am strong myself compared to yonder crabs   100
That march now from the mountain to the sea;
'Let twenty pass, and stone the twenty-first,
Loving not, hating not, just choosing so.
'Say, the first straggler that boasts purple spots
Shall join the file, one pincer twisted off;
'Say, this bruised fellow shall receive a worm,
And two worms he whose nippers end in red;
As it likes me each time, I do: so He.

Well then, 'supposeth He is good i' the main,
Placable if His mind and ways were guessed,   1
But rougher than His handiwork, be sure!
Oh, He hath made things worthier than Him-
    self,

4 Pie: magpie, which imitates sounds and can be taught to say words. Oakwarts are protuber-
ances on the tree.
5 Bladdery: in bubbles like bladders.   6 Hoopoe: a brightly plumaged bird.
7 Grigs: grasshoppers.

And envieth that, so helped, such things do
    more
Than He who made them! What consoles but
    this?
That they, unless through Him, do nought at
    all,
And must submit: what other use in things?
'Hath cut a pipe of pithless elder-joint
That, blown through, gives exact the scream o'
    the jay
When from her wing you twitch the feathers
    blue:
Sound this, and little birds that hate the jay   120
Flock within stone's throw, glad their foe is
    hurt:
Put case such pipe could prattle and boast
    forsooth
"I catch the birds, I am the crafty thing,
I make the cry my maker cannot make
With his great round mouth; he must blow
    through mine!"
Would not I smash it with my foot? So He.

But wherefore rough, why cold and ill at ease?
Aha, that is a question! Ask, for that,
What knows,—the something over Setebos
That made Him, or He, may be, found and   130
    fought,
Worsted, drove off and did to nothing, per-
    chance.
There may be something quiet o'er His head,
Out of His reach, that feels nor joy nor grief,
Since both derive from weakness in some way.
I joy because the quails come; would not joy
Could I bring quails here when I have a mind:
This Quiet, all it hath a mind to, doth.
'Esteemeth stars the outposts of its couch,
But never spends much thought nor care that
    way.
It may look up, work up,—the worse for those   140
It works on! 'Careth but for Setebos
The many-handed as a cuttle-fish,
Who, making Himself feared through what He
    does,
Looks up, first, and perceives he cannot soar
To what is quiet and hath happy life;
Next looks down here, and out of very spite
Makes this a bauble-world to ape yon real,
These good things to match those as hips[8] do
    grapes.
'T is solace making baubles, ay, and sport.

Himself peeped late, eyed Prosper at his books   150
Careless and lofty, lord now of the isle:
Vexed, 'stitched a book of broad leaves, arrow-
    shaped,
Wrote thereon, he knows what, prodigious
    words;
Has peeled a wand and called it by a name;
Weareth at whiles for an enchanter's robe
The eyed skin of a supple oncelot;
And hath an ounce[9] sleeker than youngling
    mole,
A four-legged serpent he makes cower and
    couch,
Now snarl, now hold its breath and mind his
    eye,
And saith she is Miranda and my wife: 160
'Keeps for his Ariel a tall pouch-bill crane
He bids go wade for fish and straight disgorge;
Also a sea-beast, lumpish, which he snared,
Blinded the eyes of, and brought somewhat
    tame,
And split its toe-webs, and now pens the drudge
In a hole o' the rock and calls him Caliban;
A bitter heart that bides its time and bites.
'Plays thus at being Prosper in a way,
Taketh his mirth with make-believes: so He.

His dam held that the Quiet made all things   170
Which Setebos vexed only: 'holds not so.
Who made them weak, meant weakness He
    might vex.
Had He meant other, while His hand was in,
Why not make horny eyes no thorn could
    prick,
Or plate my scalp with bone against the snow,
Or overscale my flesh 'neath joint and joint,
Like an orc's[10] armour? Ay,—so spoil His sport!
He is the One now: only He doth all.

'Saith, He may like, perchance, what profits
    Him.
Ay, himself loves what does him good; but why?   180
'Gets good no otherwise. This blinded beast
Loves whoso places flesh-meat on his nose,
But, had he eyes, would want no help, but hate
Or love, just as it liked him: He hath eyes.
Also it pleaseth Setebos to work,
Use all His hands, and exercise much craft,
By no means for the love of what is worked.
'Tasteth, himself, no finer good i' the world
When all goes right, in this safe summer-time,

8 Hips: the false fruit of rose bushes.
9 Ounce: like oncelot, a name for a small feline animal such as a lynx or ocelot.
10 Orc: sea monster.

190 And he wants little, hungers, aches not much,
     Than trying what to do with wit and strength.
     'Falls to make something: 'piled yon pile of
          turfs,
     And squared and stuck there squares of soft
          white chalk,
     And, with a fish-tooth, scratched a moon on
          each,
     And set up endwise certain spikes of tree,
     And crowned the whole with a sloth's skull
          a-top,
     Found dead i' the woods, too hard for one to
          kill.
     No use at all i' the work, for work's sole sake;
     'Shall some day knock it down again: so He.

200 'Saith He is terrible: watch His feats in proof!
     One hurricane will spoil six good months' hope.
     He hath a spite against me, that I know,
     Just as He favours Prosper, who knows why?
     So it is, all the same, as well I find.
     'Wove wattles half the winter, fenced them firm
     With stone and stake to stop she-tortoises
     Crawling to lay their eggs here: well, one wave,
     Feeling the foot of Him upon its neck,
     Gaped as a snake does, lolled out its large
          tongue,
     And licked the whole labour flat; so much for
210   spite.
     'Saw a ball flame down late (yonder it lies)
     Where, half an hour before, I slept i' the shade:
     Often they scatter sparkles: there is force!
     'Dug up a newt He may have envied once
     And turned to stone, shut up inside a stone.
     Please Him and hinder this?—What Prosper
          does?
     Aha, if He would tell me how! Not he!
     There is the sport: discover how or die!
     All need not die, for of the things o' the isle
220 Some flee afar, some dive, some run up trees;
     Those at His mercy,—why, they please Him
          most
     When . . . when . . . well, never try the same
          way twice!
     Repeat what act has pleased, He may grow
          wroth.
     You must not know His ways, and play Him
          off,
     Sure of the issue. 'Doth the like himself:
     'Spareth a squirrel that it nothing fears
     But steals the nut from underneath my thumb,
     And when I threat, bites stoutly in defence:
     'Spareth an urchin[11] that contrariwise,

[11] Urchin: hedgehog.

Curls up into a ball, pretending death   230
For fright at my approach: the two ways please.
But what would move my choler more than
     this,
That either creature counted on its life
To-morrow and next day and all days to come,
Saying, forsooth, in the inmost of its heart,
"Because he did so yesterday with me,
And otherwise with such another brute,
So must he do henceforth and always."—Ay?
Would teach the reasoning couple what "must"
     means!
'Doth as he likes, or wherefore Lord? So He.   240

'Conceiveth all things will continue thus,
And we shall have to live in fear of Him
So long as He lives, keeps His strength: no
     change,
If He have done His best, make no new world
To please Him more, so leave off watching
     this,—
If He surprise not even the Quiet's self
Some strange day,—or, suppose, grow into it
As grubs grow butterflies: else, here are we,
And there is He, and nowhere help at all.

'Believeth with the life, the pain shall stop.   250
His dam held different, that after death
He both plagued enemies and feasted friends:
Idly! He doth His worst in this our life,
Giving just respite lest we die through pain,
Saving last pain for worst,—with which, an
     end.
Meanwhile, the best way to escape His ire
Is, not to seem too happy. 'Sees, himself,
Yonder two flies, with purple films and pink,
Bask on the pompion-bell above: kills both.
'Sees two black painful beetles roll their ball   260
On head and tail as if to save their lives:
Moves them the stick away they strive to clear.

Even so, 'would have Him misconceive, suppose
This Caliban strives hard and ails no less,
And always, above all else, envies Him;
Wherefore he mainly dances on dark nights,
Moans in the sun, gets under holes to laugh,
And never speaks his mind save housed as now:
Outside, 'groans, curses. If He caught me here,
O'erheard this speech, and asked "What
     chucklest at?"   270
'Would, to appease Him, cut a finger off,
Or of my three kid yearlings burn the best,
Or let the toothsome apples rot on tree,

Or push my tame beast for the orc to taste:
While myself lit a fire, and made a song
And sung it, "*What I hate, be consecrate*
To celebrate Thee and Thy state, no mate
For Thee; what see for envy in poor me?"
Hoping the while, since evils sometimes mend,
280 Warts rub away and sores are cured with slime,
That some strange day, will either the Quiet
    catch
And conquer Setebos, or likelier He
Decrepit may doze, doze, as good as die.

[What, what? A curtain o'er the world at once!
Crickets stop hissing; not a bird—or, yes,
There scuds His raven that has told Him all!
It was fool's play this prattling! Ha! The wind
Shoulders the pillared dust, death's house o' the
    move,
And fast invading fires begin! White blaze—
A tree's head snaps—and there, there, there,
290   there, there,
His thunder follows! Fool to gibe at Him!
Lo! 'Lieth flat and loveth Setebos!
'Maketh his teeth meet through his upper lip,
Will let those quails fly, will not eat this month
One little mess of whelks, so he may 'scape!]
                    1864

Prospice[1]

Fear death?—to feel the fog in my throat,
    The mist in my face,
When the snows begin, and the blasts denote
    I am nearing the place,
The power of the night, the press of the storm,
    The post of the foe;
Where he stands, the Arch Fear in a visible
    form,
    Yet the strong man must go:
For the journey is done and the summit
    attained,
10   And the barriers fall,
Though a battle's to fight ere the guerdon be
    gained,
    The reward of it all.
I was ever a fighter, so—one fight more,
    The best and the last!

I would hate that death bandaged my eyes, and
    forbore,
    And bade me creep past.
No! let me taste the whole of it, fare like my
    peers
    The heroes of old,
Bear the brunt, in a minute pay glad life's
    arrears
    Of pain, darkness and cold.   20
For sudden the worst turns the best to the
    brave,
    The black minute's at end,
And the elements' rage, the fiend-voices that
    rave,
    Shall dwindle, shall blend,
Shall change, shall become first a peace out of
    pain,
    Then a light, then thy breast,
O thou soul of my soul![2] I shall clasp thee
    again,
    And with God be the rest!
                    1864

A Likeness

Some people hang portraits up
In a room where they dine or sup:
    And the wife clinks tea-things under,
And her cousin, he stirs his cup,
    Asks, "Who was the lady, I wonder?"
" 'T is a daub John bought at a sale,"
    Quoth the wife,—looks black as thunder:
"What a shade beneath her nose!
Snuff-taking, I suppose,—"
Adds the cousin, while John's corns ail.   10

Or else, there 's no wife in the case,
But the portrait 's queen of the place,
    Alone mid the other spoils
Of youth,—masks, gloves and foils,[1]
And pipe-sticks, rose, cherry-tree, jasmine,
    And the long whip, the tandem-lasher,[2]
And the cast from a fist ("not, alas! mine,
    "But my master's, the Tipton Slasher"),[3]
And the cards where pistol-balls mark ace,
And a satin shoe used for cigar-case,   20

---

[1] Prospice: "look forward."   [2] Elizabeth Barrett Browning died in 1861.
[1] The masks, gloves, and foils are used in fencing.
[2] The tandem-lasher is a whip used to drive a team of fast horses.
[3] "The Tipton Slasher" was a boxer whose name was Bill Perry. He was beaten by Tom Sayers in 1857, in a fight in which Sayers won the championship belt of England. Sayers then fought the American John C. Heenan to a draw in 1860, in perhaps the most famous boxing match of the nineteenth century.

And the chamois-horns ("shot in the
     Chablais")
   And prints—Rarey drumming on Cruiser,[4]
   And Sayers, our champion, the bruiser,
And the little edition of Rabelais:
Where a friend, with both hands in his pockets,
   May saunter up closer to examine it,
   And remark a good deal of Jane Lamb in it,
"But the eyes are half out of their sockets;
That hair 's not so bad, where the gloss is,
30 But they 've made the girl's nose a proboscis:
Jane Lamb, that we danced with at Vichy![5]
What, is not she Jane? Then, who is she?"

All that I own is a print,
An etching, a mezzotint;
'T is a study, a fancy, a fiction,
Yet a fact (take my conviction)
Because it has more than a hint
   Of a certain face, I never
Saw elsewhere touch or trace of
40 In women I 've seen the face of:
   Just an etching, and, so far, clever.

I keep my prints, an imbroglio,
Fifty in one portfolio.
When somebody tries my claret,
We turn round chairs to the fire,
Chirp over days in a garret,
   Chuckle o'er increase of salary,
Taste the good fruits of our leisure,
Talk about pencil and lyre,
50 And the National Portrait Gallery:
Then I exhibit my treasure.
After we 've turned over twenty,
   And the debt of wonder my crony owes
   Is paid to my Marc Antonios,[6]
He stops me—"Festina lentè![7]
What 's that sweet thing there, the etching?"
How my waistcoat-strings want stretching,
   How my cheeks grow red as tomatos,
How my heart leaps! But hearts, after leaps,
   ache.

60 "By the by, you must take, for a keepsake,
   That other, you praised, of Volpato's."[8]

The fool! would he try a flight further and
     say—
He never saw, never before to-day,
What was able to take his breath away,
A face to lose youth for, to occupy age
With the dream of, meet death with,—why, I'll
     not engage
But that, half in a rapture and half in a rage,
I should toss him the thing's self—"'T is only
     a duplicate,
"A thing of no value! Take it, I supplicate!"
                                                    1864

Epilogue [to *Dramatis Personae*]

FIRST SPEAKER (*as David*)[1]

I
On the first of the Feast of Feasts,
   The Dedication Day,
When the Levites joined the Priests[2]
   At the Altar in robed array,
Gave signal to sound and say,—

II
When the thousands, rear and van,
   Swarming with one accord
Became as a single man
   (Look, gesture, thought and word)
In praising and thanking the Lord,—   1

III
When the singers lift up their voice,
   And the trumpets made endeavour,
Sounding, "In God rejoice!"
   Saying, "In Him rejoice
Whose mercy endureth for ever!"—

IV
Then the Temple filled with a cloud,
   Even the House of the Lord;
Porch bent and pillar bowed:
   For the presence of the Lord,
In the glory of His cloud,   2
   Had filled the House of the Lord.

---

[4] J. S. Rarey was an American horse trainer; Cruiser is the name of a horse.
[5] Vichy: a resort area in France.
[6] Marc Antonios: engravings done by Marcantonio Raimondi, who worked in the early sixteenth century in Italy.
[7] *Festina lentè:* hasten slowly.
[8] Volpato's: an engraving by Giovanni Volpato, an eighteenth-century Italian engraver.
[1] David: the king of the Israelites to whom many of the celebratory psalms of the Old Testament were conventionally attributed, speaks here of a time when God seemed to be fully present in the rituals of religion.
[2] Feast of Feasts: the dedication of the temple in Jerusalem built by David's son Solomon. The Levites are of the tribe of Levi, who assisted priests in the performance of ritual.

SECOND SPEAKER *(as Renan)* [3]
Gone now! All gone across the dark so far,
    Sharpening fast, shuddering ever, shutting
        still,
Dwindling into the distance, dies that star
    Which came, stood, opened once! We
        gazed our fill
With upturned faces on as real a Face[4]
    That, stooping from grave music and mild
        fire,
Took in our homage, made a visible place
    Through many a depth of glory, gyre on
        gyre,[5]
For the dim human tribute. Was this true?
    Could man indeed avail, mere praise of
        his,
To help by rapture God's own rapture too,
    Thrill with a heart's red tinge that pure
        pale bliss?
Why did it end? Who failed to beat the breast,
    And shriek, and throw the arms protesting
        wide,
When a first shadow showed the star addressed
    Itself to motion, and on either side
The rims contracted as the rays retired;
    The music, like a fountain's sickening
        pulse,
Subsided on itself, awhile transpired
    Some vestige of a Face no pangs convulse,
No prayers retard; then even this was gone,
    Lost in the night at last. We, lone and left
Silent through centuries, ever and anon
    Venture to probe again the vault bereft
Of all now save the lesser lights, a mist
    Of multitudinous points, yet suns, men
       say—
And this leaps ruby, this lurks amethyst,
    But where may hide what came and loved
       our clay?
How shall the sage detect in yon expanse
    The star which chose to stoop and stay for
       us?
Unroll the records! Hailed ye such advance
    Indeed, and did your hope evanish thus?
Watchers of twilight, is the worst averred?
    We shall not look up, know ourselves are
       seen,
Speak, and be sure that we again are heard,
    Acting or suffering, have the disk's serene

Reflect our life, absorb an earthly flame,
    Nor doubt that, were mankind inert and
       numb,
Its core had never crimsoned all the same,   60
    Nor, missing ours, its music fallen dumb?
Oh, dread succession to a dizzy post,
    Sad sway of sceptre whose mere touch
       appals,
Ghastly dethronement, cursed by those the most
    On whose repugnant brow the crown next
       falls!

THIRD SPEAKER

I
Witless alike of will and way divine,
How heaven's high with earth's low should
    intertwine!
Friends, I have seen through your eyes: now
    use mine!

II
Take the least man of all mankind, as I;
Look at his head and heart, find how and why   70
He differs from his fellows utterly:

III
Then, like me, watch when nature by degrees
Grows alive round him, as in Arctic seas
(They said of old) the instinctive water flees

IV
Toward some elected point of central rock,
As though, for its sake only, roamed the flock
Of waves about the waste: awhile they mock

V
With radiance caught for the occasion,—hues
Of blackest hell now, now such reds and blues
As only heaven could fitly interfuse,—   80

VI
The mimic monarch of the whirlpool, king
O' the current for a minute: then they wring
Up by the roots and oversweep the thing,

VII
And hasten off, to play again elsewhere
The same part, choose another peak as bare,
They find and flatter, feast and finish there.

---

[3] Ernest Renan (1823–92), a French historian and scholar of Oriental languages, wrote *La Vie de Jésus* (1863), which Browning read in the year of its publication. Renan thought that an increase in a knowledge of the history of Christ's time tended to diminish the authority of the scriptural accounts of his life, and thus to compromise belief in the human, historical presence of God in the person of Christ.
[4] Face: of Christ.   [5] Gyre: a spiral.

VIII

When you see what I tell you,—nature dance
About each man of us, retire, advance,
As though the pageant's end were to enhance

IX

His worth, and—once the life, his product,
gained—
Roll away elsewhere, keep the strife sustained,
And show thus real, a thing the North but
feigned—

X

When you acknowledge that one world could
do
All the diverse work, old yet ever new,
Divide us, each from other, me from you,—

XI

Why, where's the need of Temple, when the
walls
O' the world are that? What use of swells and
falls
From Levites' choir, Priests' cries, and trumpet-
calls?

XII

That one Face, far from vanish, rather grows,
Or decomposes but to recompose,
Become my universe that feels and knows.

1864

Shop

I

So, friend, your shop was all your house!
    Its front, astonishing the street,
Invited view from man and mouse
    To what diversity of treat
    Behind its glass—the single sheet!

II

What gimcracks, genuine Japanese:
    Gape-jaw and goggle-eye, the frog;
Dragons, owls, monkeys, beetles, geese;
    Some crushed-nosed human-hearted dog:
    Queer names, too, such a catalogue!

III

I thought "And he who owns the wealth
    Which blocks the window's vastitude,
—Ah, could I peep at him by stealth
    Behind his ware, pass shop, intrude
    On house itself, what scenes were viewed!

IV

"If wide and showy thus the shop,
    What must the habitation prove?
The true house with no name a-top—
    The mansion, distant one remove
    Once get him off his traffic-groove!

V

"Pictures he likes, or books perhaps;
    And as for buying most and best,
Commend me to these City[1] chaps!
    Or else he's social, takes his rest
    On Sundays, with a Lord for guest.

VI

"Some suburb-palace, parked about
    And gated grandly, built last year:
The four-mile walk to keep off gout;
    Or big seat sold by bankrupt peer:
    But then he takes the rail,[2] that's clear.

VII

"Or, stop! I wager, taste selects
    Some out o' the way, some all-unknown
Retreat: the neighbourhood suspects
    Little that he who rambles lone
    Makes Rothschild[3] tremble on his throne!"

VIII

Nowise! Nor Mayfair[4] residence
    Fit to receive and entertain,—
Nor Hampstead[5] villa's kind defence
    From noise and crowd, from dust and
        drain,—
    Nor country-box[6] was soul's domain!

IX

Nowise! At back of all that spread
    Of merchandize, woe's me, I find
A hole i' the wall where, heels by head,
    The owner couched, his ware behind,
    —In cupboard suited to his mind.

---

[1] City: the financial district of London.
[2] Takes the rail: moves to an advantageous place in a race.
[3] Rothschild: a famous banking family.   [4] Mayfair: a fashionable district in London.
[5] Hampstead: still, in the mid-nineteenth century, a suburb of London.
[6] Country-box: country house.

X

For why? He saw no use of life
  But, while he drove a roaring trade,
To chuckle "Customers are rife!"
  To chafe "So much hard cash outlaid
  Yet zero in my profits made!

XI

"This novelty costs pains, but—takes?
  Cumbers my counter! Stock no more!
This article, no such great shakes,
  Fizzes like wildfire? Underscore
  The cheap thing—thousands to the fore!"

XII

'T was lodging best to live most nigh
  (Cramp, coffinlike as crib might be)
Receipt of Custom;[7] ear and eye
  Wanted no outworld: "Hear and see
  The bustle in the shop!" quoth he.

XIII

My fancy of a merchant-prince
  Was different. Through his wares we groped
Our darkling way to—not to mince
  The matter—no black den where moped
  The master if we interloped!

XIV

Shop was shop only: household-stuff?
  What did he want with comforts there?
"Walls, ceiling, floor, stay blank and rough,
  So goods on sale show rich and rare!
  'Sell and scud home' be shop's affair!"

XV

What might he deal in? Gems, suppose!
  Since somehow business must be done
At cost of trouble,—see, he throws
  You choice of jewels, every one,
  Good, better, best, star, moon and sun!

XVI

Which lies within your power of purse?
  This ruby that would tip aright
Solomon's sceptre? Oh, your nurse
  Wants simply coral,[8] the delight
  Of teething baby,—stuff to bite!

XVII

Howe'er your choice fell, straight you took
  Your purchase, prompt your money rang
On counter,—scarce the man forsook
  His study of the "Times," just swang
  Till-ward his hand that stopped the clang,—

XVIII

Then off made buyer with a prize,
  Then seller to his "Times" returned,
And so did day wear, wear, till eyes
  Brightened apace, for rest was earned:
  He locked door long ere candle burned.   90

XIX

And whither went he? Ask himself,
  Not me! To change of scene, I think.
Once sold the ware and pursed the pelf,
  Chaffer[9] was scarce his meat and drink,
  Nor all his music—money-chink.

XX

Because a man has shop to mind
  In time and place, since flesh must live,
Needs spirit lack all life behind,
  All stray thoughts, fancies fugitive,
  All loves except what trade can give?   100

XXI

I want to know a butcher paints,
  A baker rhymes for his pursuit,
Candlestick-maker much acquaints
  His soul with song, or, haply mute,
  Blows out his brains upon the flute!

XXII

But—shop each day and all day long!
  Friend, your good angel slept, your star
Suffered eclipse, fate did you wrong!
  From where these sorts of treasures are,
  There should our hearts be[10]—Christ, how   110
    far!

                            (1874) 1876

Natural Magic

I

All I can say is—I saw it!
The room was as bare as your hand.
I locked in the swarth little lady,—I swear,

---

[7] Custom: trade.   [8] Pieces of coral were often used as teething rings.
[9] Chaffer: haggling.
[10] "For where your treasure is, there will your heart be also" (Matthew 6:21).

From the head to the foot of her—well, quite
    as bare!
"No Nautch[1] shall cheat me," said I, "taking
    my stand
At this bolt which I draw!" And this bolt—I
    withdraw it,
And there laughs the lady, not bare, but
    embowered
With—who knows what verdure, o'erfruited,
    o'er-flowered?
      Impossible! Only—I saw it!

II

10   All I can sing is—I feel it!
This life was as blank as that room;
I let you pass in here. Precaution, indeed?
Walls, ceiling and floor,—not a chance for a
    weed!
Wide opens the entrance: where 's cold now,
    where 's gloom?
No May to sow seed here, no June to reveal it,
Behold you enshrined in these blooms of your
    bringing,
These fruits of your bearing—nay, birds of
    your winging!
      A fairy-tale! Only—I feel it!
                    1876

Magical Nature

I

Flower—I never fancied, jewel—I profess you!
    Bright I see and soft I feel the outside of a
    flower.
Save but glow inside and—jewel, I should guess
    you,
    Dim to sight and rough to touch: the glory
    is the dower.

II

You, forsooth, a flower? Nay, my love, a jewel—
    Jewel at no mercy of a moment in your
    prime!
Time may fray the flower-face: kind be time or
    cruel,
    Jewel, from each facet, flash your laugh at
    time!
                    1876

Epilogue [to *Pacchiarotto and Other Poems*]

μεστοὶ . . .
οἱ δ' ἀμφορῆς οἴνου μέλανος ἀνθοσμίου.[1]

I

"The poets pour us wine—"[2]
    Said the dearest poet I ever knew,
Dearest and greatest and best to me.
You clamour athirst for poetry—
We pour. "But when shall a vintage be"—
    You cry—"strong grape, squeezed gold from
    screw,
Yet sweet juice, flavoured flowery-fine?
That were indeed the wine!"

II

One pours your cup—stark strength,
    Meat for a man; and you eye the pulp
Strained, turbid still, from the viscous blood
Of the snaky bough: and you grumble "Good!
For it swells resolve, breeds hardihood;
    Despatch it, then, in a single gulp!"
So, down, with a wry face, goes at length
The liquor: stuff for strength.

III

One pours your cup—sheer sweet,
    The fragrant fumes of a year condensed:
Suspicion of all that 's ripe or rathe,[3]
From the bud on branch to the grass in swathe.
"We suck mere milk of the seasons," saith
    A curl of each nostril—"dew, dispensed
Nowise for nerving man to feat:
Boys sip such honeyed sweet!"

IV

And thus who wants wine strong,
    Waves each sweet smell of the year away;
Who likes to swoon as the sweets suffuse
His brain with a mixture of beams and dews[4]
Turned syrupy drink—rough strength eschews:
    "What though in our veins your wine-stock
    stay?
The lack of the bloom does our palate wrong.
Give us wine sweet, not strong!"

---

[1] Nautch: an Indian entertainment featuring dancers, or a female dancer in this entertainment. The trick described in the first stanza is a characteristic one performed by Indian conjurers.
[1] "and pitchers full of dark red wine": Aristophanes, *Plutus*.
[2] This line is from Elizabeth Barrett Browning's "The Wine of Cyprus" (1844).
[3] Rathe: early, new.   [4] Beams and dews: the sun and moisture which nurtured the grape.

V

Yet wine is—some affirm—
  Prime wine is found in the world somewhere,
Of potable strength with sweet to match.
You double your heart its dose, yet catch—
As the draught descends—a violet-smatch,[5]
  Softness—however it came there,
Through drops expressed by the fire and worm:
Strong sweet wine—some affirm.

VI

Body and bouquet both?
  'T is easy to ticket a bottle so;
But what was the case in the cask, my friends?
Cask? Nay, the vat—where the maker mends
His strong with his sweet (you suppose) and
  blends
  His rough with his smooth, till none can
  know
How it comes you may tipple, nothing loth,
Body and bouquet both.

VII

"You" being just—the world.
  No poets—who turn, themselves, the winch
Of the press; no critics—I 'll even say,
(Being flustered and easy of faith to-day)
Who for love of the work have learned the way
  Till themselves produce home-made, at a
  pinch:
No! You are the world, and wine ne'er purled
Except to please the world!

VIII

"For, oh the common heart!
  And, ah the irremissible sin
Of poets who please themselves, not us!
Strong wine yet sweet wine pouring thus,
How please still—Pindar and Æschylus![6]—
  Drink—dipt into by the bearded chin
Alike and the bloomy lip—no part
Denied the common heart!

IX

"And might we get such grace,
  And did you moderns but stock our vault
With the true half-brandy half-attar-gul,[7]
How would seniors indulge at a hearty pull

While juniors tossed off their thimbleful!
  Our Shakespeare and Milton escaped your
  fault,   70
So, they reign supreme o'er the weaker race
That wants the ancient grace!"

X

If I paid myself with words
  (As the French say well) I were dupe indeed!
I were found in belief that you quaffed and
  bowsed
At your Shakespeare the whole day long,
  caroused
In your Milton pottle-deep[8] nor drowsed
  A moment of night—toped on, took heed
Of nothing like modern cream-and-curds.
Pay me with deeds, not words!   80

XI

For—see your cellarage!
  There are forty barrels with Shakespeare's
  brand.
Some five or six are abroach: the rest
Stand spigoted, fauceted. Try and test
What yourselves call best of the very best!
  How comes it that still untouched they
  stand?
Why don't you try tap, advance a stage
With the rest in cellarage?

XII

For—see your cellarage!
  There are four big butts of Milton's brew.   90
How comes it you make old drips and drops
Do duty, and there devotion stops?
Leave such an abyss of malt and hops
  Embellied in butts which bungs still glue?
You hate your bard! A fig for your rage!
Free him from cellarage!

XIII

'T is said I brew stiff drink,
  But the deuce a flavour of grape is there.
Hardly a May-go-down,[9] 't is just
A sort of a gruff Go-down-it-must—   100
No Merry-go-down, no gracious gust
  Commingles the racy with Springtide's rare!
"What wonder," say you "that we cough, and
  blink
At Autumn's heady drink?"

---

[5] Violet-smatch: trace of violet.
[6] Pindar was a Greek lyric poet of the fifth century before Christ; Aeschuylus was his contemporary, the first great Greek tragedian. The poem by Elizabeth Barrett Browning from which Browning takes the first line of this poem is about the achievement of Greek poetry.
[7] Attar-gul: rose perfumed.   [8] Pottle: about half a gallon.
[9] May-go-down: a wine that may be easily swallowed if one wishes.

XIV

Is it a fancy, friends?
    Mighty and mellow are never mixed,
Though mighty and mellow be born at once.
Sweet for the future,—strong for the nonce!
Stuff you should stow away, ensconce
110   In the deep and dark, to be found fast-fixed
At the century's close: such time strength
        spends
A-sweetening for my friends!

XV

And then—why, what you quaff
    With a smack of lip and a cluck of tongue,
Is leakage and leavings—just what haps
From the tun some learned taster taps
With a promise "Prepare your watery chaps!
    Here 's properest wine for old and young!
Dispute its perfection—you make us laugh!
120 Have faith, give thanks, but—quaff!"

XVI

Leakage, I say, or—worse—
    Leavings suffice pot-valiant[10] souls.
Somebody, brimful, long ago,
Frothed flagon he drained to the dregs; and lo,
Down whisker and beard what an overflow!
    Lick spilth that has trickled from classic
        jowls,
Sup the single scene, sip the only verse—
Old wine, not new and worse!

XVII

I grant you: worse by much!
130   Renounce that new where you never gained
One glow at heart, one gleam at head,
And stick to the warrant of age instead!
No dwarf's-lap! Fatten, by giants fed!
    You fatten, with oceans of drink undrained?
You feed—who would choke did a cobweb
        smutch
The Age you love so much?

XVIII

A mine 's beneath a moor:
    Acres of moor roof fathoms of mine
Which diamonds dot where you please to dig;
140 Yet who plies spade for the bright and big?
Your product is—truffles, you hunt with a pig!
    Since bright-and-big, when a man would
        dine,

Suits badly: and therefore the Koh-i-noor[11]
May sleep in mine 'neath moor!

XIX

Wine, pulse in might from me!
    It may never emerge in must[12] from vat,
Never fill cask nor furnish can,
Never end sweet, which strong began—
God's gift to gladden the heart of man;
    But spirit 's at proof, I promise that!
No sparing of juice spoils what should be
Fit brewage—mine for me.

XX

Man's thoughts and loves and hates!
    Earth is my vineyard, these grew there:
From grape of the ground, I made or marred
My vintage; easy the task or hard,
Who set it—his praise be my reward!
    Earth's yield! Who yearn for the Dark Blue
        Sea's,
Let them "lay, pray, bray"[13]—the addle-pates!
Mine be Man's thoughts, loves, hates!

XXI

But someone says "Good Sir!"
    ('T is a worthy versed in what concerns
The making such labour turn out well)
"You don't suppose that the nosegay-smell
Needs always come from the grape? Each bell
    At your foot, each bud that your culture
        spurns,
The very cowslip[14] would act like myrrh
On the stiffest brew—good Sir!

XXII

"Cowslips, abundant birth
    O'er meadow and hillside, vineyard too,
—Like a schoolboy's scrawlings in and out
Distasteful lesson-book—all about
Greece and Rome, victory and rout—
    Love-verses instead of such vain ado!
So, fancies frolic it o'er the earth
Where thoughts have rightlier birth.

XXIII

"Nay, thoughtlings they themselves:
    Loves, hates—in little and less and least!
Thoughts? *'What is a man beside a mount!'*
Loves? *'Absent—poor lovers the minutes
        count!'*

---

[10] Pot-valiant: courageous when drunk.
[11] Koh-i-noor: a large diamond given to Queen Victoria in 1850.   [12] Must: mold.
[13] A gibe at Byron's grammar in a line of *Childe Harold's Pilgrimage*: "And dashest him again
to earth;—there let him lay" (IV, clxxx).
[14] Browning's original title for this poem was "Cowslip Wine."

Hates? *'Fie—Pope's letters to Martha Blount!'*[15]
  These furnish a wine for a children's-feast:
Insipid to man, they suit the elves
Like thoughts, loves, hates themselves."

XXIV

And, friends, beyond dispute
  I too have the cowslips dewy and dear.
Punctual as Springtide forth peep they:
I leave them to make my meadow gay.
But I ought to pluck and impound them, eh?
  Not let them alone, but deftly shear
And shred and reduce to—what may suit
Children, beyond dispute?

XXV

And, here's May-month, all bloom,
  All bounty: what if I sacrifice?
If I out with shears and shear, nor stop
Shearing till prostrate, lo, the crop?
And will you prefer it to ginger-pop
  When I 've made you wine of the memories
Which leave as bare as a churchyard tomb
My meadow, late all bloom?

XXVI

Nay, what ingratitude
  Should I hesitate to amuse the wits
That have pulled so long at my flask, nor
    grudged
The headache that paid their pains, nor
    budged
From bunghole before they sighed and judged
  "Too rough for our taste, to-day, befits
The racy and right when the years conclude!"
Out on ingratitude!

XXVII

Grateful or ingrate—none,
  No cowslip of all my fairy crew
Shall help to concoct what makes you wink
And goes to your head till you think you think!
I like them alive: the printer's ink
  Would sensibly tell on the perfume too.
I may use up my nettles, ere I 've done;
But of cowslips—friends get none!

XXVIII

Don't nettles make a broth
  Wholesome for blood grown lazy and thick?
Maws out of sorts make mouths out of taste.

My Thirty-four Port[16]—no need to waste
On a tongue that 's fur and a palate—paste!
  A magnum for friends who are sound! The
    sick—
I 'll posset and cosset them, nothing loth,
Henceforward with nettle-broth!

                                        1876

*Browning adapted the narrative of this poem
from an episode in John Bunyan's* The Life and
Death of Mr. Badman *(1680), which contains the
story of Old Tod, a thief who appeared one hot day
in a courtroom at Hartford, confessed to a lifetime
of thievery, and was hanged along with his wife.
Browning changes the scene to Bedford, where Bun-
yan was imprisoned between 1660 and 1672 for
preaching without a license. Browning also has his
fictional Ned Bratts converted by Bunyan's* The
Pilgrim's Progress, *which was not published until
1678; some of this book was written during another
short term in the Bedford jail in 1675.*

Ned Bratts

'T was Bedford Special Assize,[1] one daft Mid-
    summer's Day:
A broiling blasting June,—was never its like,
    men say.
Corn stood sheaf-ripe already, and trees looked
    yellow as that;
Ponds drained dust-dry, the cattle lay foaming
    around each flat.
Inside town, dogs went mad, and folk kept
    bibbing beer
While the parsons prayed for rain. 'T was
    horrible, yes—but queer:
Queer—for the sun laughed gay, yet nobody
    moved a hand
To work one stroke at his trade: as given to
    understand
That all was come to a stop, work and such
    worldly ways,
And the world's old self about to end in a merry
    blaze.   10
Midsummer's Day moreover was the first of
    Bedford Fair,
With Bedford Town's tag-rag and bobtail
    a-bowsing there.

But the Court House, Quality[2] crammed:
    through doors ope, windows wide,

---

[15] Alexander Pope wrote gossipy letters to Martha Blount (1690–1762), to whom he also dedi-
cated or addressed several poems.
[16] Thirty-four Port: an aged, mellow wine.
[1] Assize: a session of a court to hear civil and criminal cases.
[2] Quality: persons of superior social station.

High on the Bench you saw sit Lordships side
  by side.
There frowned Chief Justice Jukes, fumed
  learned Brother Small,
And fretted their fellow Judge: like threshers,
  one and all,
Of a reek with laying down the law in a
  furnace. Why?
Because their lungs breathed flame—the
  regular crowd forbye[3]—
From gentry pouring in—quite a nosegay, to
  be sure!
How else could they pass the time, six mortal
20 hours endure
Till night should extinguish day, when matters
  might haply mend?
Meanwhile no bad resource was—watching
  begin and end
Some trial for life and death, in a brisk five
  minutes' space,
And betting which knave would 'scape, which
  hang, from his sort of face.

So, their Lordships toiled and moiled, and a
  deal of work was done
 (I warrant) to justify the mirth of the crazy
  sun
As this and t' other lout, struck dumb at the
  sudden show
Of red robes and white wigs, boggled nor
  answered "Boh!"
When asked why he, Tom Styles, should not—
  because Jack Nokes
Had stolen the horse—be hanged: for Judges
30 must have their jokes,
And louts must make allowance—let 's say, for
  some blue fly
Which punctured a dewy scalp where the
  frizzles[4] stuck awry—
Else Tom had fleered scot-free, so nearly over
  and done
Was the main of the job. Full-measure, the
  gentles enjoyed their fun,
As a twenty-five were tried, rank puritans[5]
  caught at prayer
In a cow-house and laid by the heels,—have at
  'em, devil may care!—

And ten were prescribed the whip, and ten a
  brand on the cheek,
And five a slit of the nose—just leaving enough
  to tweak.

Well, things at jolly high-tide, amusement
  steeped in fire,
While noon smote fierce the roof's red tiles to
  heart's desire,
The Court a-simmer with smoke, one ferment
  of oozy flesh,
One spirituous humming musk[6] mount-mount-
  ing until its mesh
Entoiled all heads in a fluster, and Serjeant
  Postlethwayte
—Dashing the wig oblique as he mopped his
  oily pate—
Cried "Silence, or I grow grease! No loophole
  lets in air?
Jurymen,—Guilty, Death! Gainsay me if you
  dare!"
—Things at this pitch, I say,—what hubbub
  without the doors?
What laughs, shrieks, hoots and yells, what
  rudest of uproars?

Bounce through the barrier throng a bulk
  comes rolling vast!
Thumps, kicks,—no manner of use!—spite of
  them rolls at last
Into the midst a ball which, bursting, brings to
  view
Publican Black Ned Bratts and Tabby his big
  wife too:
Both in a muck-sweat,[7] both . . . were never
  such eyes uplift
At the sight of yawning hell, such nostrils—
  snouts that sniffed
Sulphur, such mouths a-gape ready to swallow
  flame!
Horrified, hideous, frank fiend-faces! yet, all
  the same,
Mixed with a certain . . . eh? how shall I
  dare style—mirth
The desperate grin of the guess that, could
  they break from earth,

---

[3] Forbye: in addition, added to.   [4] Frizzles: curls.
[5] After Charles II was returned to the throne in 1660 and the monarchy restored after the
strongly puritan dominion of the Commonwealth from 1649 to 1660, religious dissent to the
established Anglican church was decreasingly tolerated. Bunyan himself was an exceptionally
rigorous dissenter, deeply troubled by a sense of his own sinfulness and deeply suspicious of
those secular institutions and customs—like those of established religion—which permitted
people to neglect the enormous and unremitting personal efforts necessary for salvation.
[6] Musk: heavy odor.   [7] Muck-sweat: heavy sweat.

Heaven was above, and hell might rage in
  impotence
Below the saved, the saved!

           "Confound you! (no offence!)
Out of our way,—push, wife! Yonder their
  Worships be!"
Ned Bratts has reached the bar, and "Hey, my
  Lords," roars he,
"A Jury of life and death, Judges the prime of
  the land,
Constables, javelineers,[8]—all met, if I under-
  stand,
To decide so knotty a point as whether 't was
  Jack or Joan
Robbed the henroost, pinched the pig, hit the
  King's Arms with a stone,
Dropped the baby down the well, left the
  tithesman[9] in the lurch,
Or, three whole Sundays running, not once
  attended church!
What a pother—do these deserve the parish-
  stocks or whip,
More or less brow to brand, much or little
  nose to snip,—
When, in our Public, plain stand we—that 's
  we stand here,
I and my Tab, brass-bold, brick-built of beef
  and beer,
—Do not we, slut? Step forth and show your
  beauty, jade![10]
Wife of my bosom—that 's the word now!
  What a trade
We drove! None said us nay: nobody loved his
  life
So little as wag a tongue against us,—did they,
  wife?
Yet they knew us all the while, in their hearts,
  for what we are
—Worst couple, rogue and quean,[11] unhanged
  —search near and far!
Eh, Tab? The pedlar, now—o'er his noggin—
  who warned a mate
To cut and run, nor risk his pack where its
  loss of weight
Was the least to dread,—aha, how we two
  laughed a-good

As, stealing round the midden,[12] he came on
  where I stood
With billet[13] poised and raised,—you, ready
  with the rope,—
Ah, but that 's past, that 's sin repented of, we
  hope!
Men knew us for that same, yet safe and sound
  stood we!
The lily-livered knaves knew too (I 've baulked
  a d——)
Our keeping the "Pied Bull" was just a mere
  pretence:
Too slow the pounds make food, drink,
  lodging, from out the pence!
There 's not a stoppage to travel[14] has chanced,
  this ten long year,
No break into hall or grange, no lifting of nag
  or steer,   90
Not a single roguery, from the clipping[15] of a
  purse
To the cutting of a throat, but paid us toll.
  Od's curse!
When Gipsy Smouch made bold to cheat us of
  our due,
—Eh, Tab? the Squire's strong-box we helped
  the rascal to—
I think he pulled a face, next Sessions'
  swinging-time!
He danced the jig that needs no floor,—and,
  here 's the prime,
'T was Scroggs that houghed[16] the mare! Ay,
  those were busy days!

"Well, there we flourished brave, like scripture-
  trees called bays,[17]
Faring high, drinking hard, in money up to
  head
—Not to say, boots and shoes, when . . .
  Zounds, I nearly said—   100
Lord, to unlearn one's language! How shall
  we labour, wife?
Have you, fast hold, the Book?[18] Grasp, grip it,
  for your life!
See, sire, here 's life, salvation! Here 's—hold
  but out my breath—
When did I speak so long without once
  swearing? 'Sdeath,

---

[8] Javelineers: men in the retinue of a sheriff armed with javelins.
[9] Tithesman: one who collects a levy for support of the church.
[10] Slut . . . jade: used here to describe a saucy, flirtatious woman.
[11] Quean: a disreputable woman.   [12] Midden: dunghill or refuse heap.
[13] Billet: a chunky piece of wood.   [14] Stoppage to travel: highway robbery.
[15] Clipping: stealing.   [16] Houghed: to hamstring.
[17] "I have seen the wicked in great power, and spreading himself like a green bay tree"
(Psalms 37:35).
[18] The Book: Bunyan's *The Pilgrim's Progress*.

No, nor unhelped by ale since man and boy!
    And yet
All yesterday I had to keep my whistle wet
While reading Tab this Book: book? don't say
    "book"—they 're plays,
Songs, ballads and the like: here's no such
    strawy blaze,
But sky wide ope, sun, moon, and seven stars
    out full-flare!
Tab, help and tell! I 'm hoarse. A mug! or
110   —no, a prayer!
Dip for one out of the Book! Who wrote it in
    the Jail
—He plied his pen unhelped by beer, sirs, I 'll
    be bail!

"I 've got my second wind. In trundles she—
    that 's Tab.
'Why, Gammer,[19] what 's come now, that—
    bobbing like a crab[20]
On Yule-tide bowl—your head 's a-work and
    both your eyes
Break loose? Afeard, you fool? As if the dead
    can rise!
Say—Bagman Dick was found last May with
    fuddling-cap[21]
Stuffed in his mouth: to choke's a natural
    mishap!'
'Gaffer, be—blessed,' cries she, 'and Bagman
    Dick as well!
I, you, and he are damned: this Public[22] is our
120   hell:
We live in fire: live coals don't feel!—once
    quenched, they learn—
Cinders do, to what dust they moulder while
    they burn!'

" 'If you don't speak straight out,' says I—
    belike I swore—
'A knobstick, well you know the taste of, shall,
    once more,
Teach you to talk, my maid!' She ups with such
    a face,
Heart sunk inside me. 'Well, pad on, my prate-
    apace!'

" 'I 've been about those laces we need for . . .
    never mind!
If henceforth they tie hands, 't is mine they 'll
    have to bind.
You know who makes them best—the Tinker in
    our cage,
Pulled-up for gospelling, twelve years ago: no
    age
To try another trade,—yet, so he scorned to
    take
Money he did not earn, he taught himself the
    make
Of laces, tagged and tough[23]—Dick Bagman
    found them so!
Good customers were we! Well, last week, you
    must know
His girl,—the blind young chit, who hawks
    about his wares,—
She takes it in her head to come no more—
    such airs
These hussies have! Yet, since we need a
    stoutish lace,—
"I 'll to the jail-bird father, abuse her to his
    face!"
So, first I filled a jug to give me heart, and
    then,
Primed to the proper pitch, I posted to their
    den—
Patmore—they style their prison! I tip the
    turnkey, catch
My heart up, fix my face, and fearless lift the
    latch—
Both arms a-kimbo, in bounce with a good
    round oath
Ready for rapping out: no "Lawks" nor "By
    my troth!"

" 'There sat my man, the father. He looked
    up: what one feels
When heart that leapt to mouth drops down
    again to heels!
He raised his hand . . . Hast seen, when
    drinking out the night,
And in, the day, earth grow another something
    quite
Under the sun's first stare? I stood a very stone.

---

[19] Gammer: an old woman, as gaffer (line 119) is an old man.

[20] Crab: apple. One of the Christmas customs of the later seventeenth century was to drink flagons of ale and apples.

[21] Fuddling-cap: drinking cap.

[22] Public: public-house; the tavern owned by Bratts and his wife.

[23] After his imprisonment Bunyan supported his family by making long laces with tips (tags), which were sold in the streets by his blind daughter. Bunyan's father was a tinker, and tinker's sons so frequently followed their father's occupations that tinkers were regarded as something of a hereditary caste.

"'"Woman!" (a fiery tear he put in every tone),
"How should my child frequent your house where lust is sport,
Violence—trade? Too true! I trust no vague report.
Her angel's hand, which stops the sight of sin, leaves clear
The other gate of sense, lets outrage through the ear.
What has she heard!—which, heard shall never be again.
Better lack food than feast, a Dives[24] in the— wain
Or reign or train—of Charles!"[25] (His language was not ours:
'T is my belief, God spoke: no tinker has such powers).
"Bread, only bread they bring—my laces: if we broke
Your lump of leavened sin, the loaf's first crumb would choke!"

"'Down on my marrow-bones! Then all at once rose he:
His brown hair burst a-spread, his eyes were suns to see:
Up went his hands: "Through flesh, I reach, I read thy soul!
So may some stricken tree look blasted, bough and bole,
Champed by the fire-tooth, charred without, and yet, thrice-bound
With dreriment[26] about, within may life be found,
A prisoned power to branch and blossom as before,
Could but the gardener cleave the cloister, reach the core,
Loosen the vital sap: yet where shall help be found?
Who says 'How save it?'—nor 'Why cumbers it the ground?'
Woman, that tree art thou! All sloughed about with scurf,[27]

Thy stag-horns fright the sky, thy snake-roots sting the turf!
Drunkenness, wantonness, theft, murder gnash and gnarl
Thine outward, case thy soul with coating like the marle[28]
Satan stamps flat upon each head beneath his hoof!
And how deliver such? The strong men keep aloof,
Lover and friend stand far, the mocking ones pass by,
Tophet[29] gapes wide for prey: lost soul, despair and die!
What then? 'Look unto me and be ye saved!' saith God:
'I strike the rock, outstreats[30] the life-stream at my rod!
Be your sins scarlet, wool shall they seem like, —although
As crimson red, yet turn white as the driven snow!'"

"'There, there, there! All I seem to somehow understand
Is—that, if I reached home, 't was through the guiding hand
Of his blind girl which led and led me through the streets
And out of town and up to door again. What greets
First thing my eye, as limbs recover from their swoon?
A book—this Book she gave at parting. "Father's boon—
The Book he wrote: it reads as if he spoke himself:
He cannot preach in bonds, so—take it down from the shelf
When you want counsel,—think you hear his very voice!"

"'Wicked dear Husband, first despair and then rejoice!

---

[24] Dives: a rich man in a parable in Luke 16:19–31, who neglected the needs of a poor beggar, is tormented in hell, and is refused his request that the now dead beggar be sent to warn his brethren of Dives' fate: "If they hear not Moses and the prophets, neither will they be persuaded, though one rose from the dead."
[25] Charles is Charles II, restored to the English throne in 1660; Charles' Wain is a name for the constellation also known as the Big Dipper.
[26] Dreriment: dreariness.
[27] Sloughed about with scurf: a scaly deposit on the tree like a dead skin.
[28] Marle: a loose, sandy deposit.
[29] Tophet: a shrine near Jerusalem at which human sacrifices were performed.
[30] Outstreats: exudes.

Dear wicked Husband, waste no tick of
    moment more,
Be saved like me, bald trunk! There 's green-
    ness yet at core,
Sap under slough! Read, read!'

        "Let me take breath, my lords!
I 'd like to know, are these—hers, mine, or
    Bunyan's words?
I 'm 'wildered—scarce with drink,—nowise
    with drink alone!
You 'll say, with heat: but heat 's no stuff to
    split a stone
Like this black boulder—this flint heart of
    mine: the Book—
That dealt the crashing blow! Sirs, here 's the
200   fist that shook
His beard till Wrestler Jem howled like a just-
    lugged[31] bear!
You had brained me with a feather: at once I
    grew aware
Christian[32] was meant for me. A burden at your
    back,
Good Master Christian? Nay,—yours was that
    Joseph's sack,[33]
—Or whose it was,—which held the cup,—
    compared with mine!
Robbery loads my loins, perjury cracks my
    chine,[34]
Adultery . . . nay, Tab, you pitched me as I
    flung!
One word, I 'll up with fist . . . No, sweet
    spouse, hold your tongue!

"I 'm hasting to the end. The Book, sirs—take
    and read!

You have my history in a nutshell,—ay, indeed!
It must off, my burden! See,—slack straps and
    into pit,
Roll, reach the bottom, rest, rot there—a
    plague on it!
For a mountain 's sure to fall and bury
    Bedford Town,
'Destruction'[35]—that 's the name, and fire shall
    burn it down!
O 'scape the wrath in time! Time 's now, if
    not too late.
How can I pilgrimage up to the wicket-gate?
Next comes Despond the slough:[36] not that I
    fear to pull
Through mud, and dry my clothes at brave
    House Beautiful—
But it 's late in the day, I reckon: had I left
    years ago
Town, wife, and children dear . . . Well,
    Christian did, you know!—
Soon I had met in the valley and tried my
    cudgel's strength
On the enemy horned and winged,[37] a-straddle
    across its length!
Have at his horns, thwick—thwack: they snap,
    see! Hoof and hoof—
Bang, break the fetlock-bones! For love's sake,
    keep aloof
Angels! I 'm man and match,—this cudgel for
    my flail,—
To thresh him, hoofs and horns, bat's wing and
    serpent's tail!
A chance gone by! But then, what else does
    Hopeful[38] ding
Into the deafest ear except—hope, hope 's the
    thing?

---

[31] Lugged: pulled by the ears or hair.

[32] Christian: the Pilgrim of Bunyan's book. (In the first published version of the poem, Browning had Bratts refer to him as "Christmas.") Christian's burden, which he acquires upon reading the Bible, is his fear that he may fail of salvation.

[33] Joseph's sack: after his brothers sell Joseph into Egypt, where he prospers, they come to him to ask him, whom they do not recognize, to relieve their famine. He gives them grain, but secretes a cup in the sack of one of them (Benjamin), and then apprehends them as thieves (Genesis 43–44).

[34] Chine: backbone.

[35] Destruction: *The Pilgrim's Progress* begins with the conviction of Christian that he lives in the City of Destruction (a conviction learned from the reading of a book) and that he must flee to be saved.

[36] Despond the slough: the Slough of Despond is one of the first of the obstacles through which Christian passes on his journey through to the Celestial City; the House Beautiful, where he is succored by Discretion, Prudence, and other virtues, is one of the first of the places of rest and renewal he comes to in his journey. Other places on the journey are named below: Vanity Fair, a city in which Christian is imprisoned and tried; and the Delectable Mountains, near the Celestial City.

[37] The enemy horned and winged: Apollyon, a hellish monster Christian must conquer in the Valley of Humiliation.

[38] Hopeful: one of reassuring guides Christian meets on his journey.

Too late i' the day for me to thrid[39] the
   windings: but
There 's still a way to win the race by death's
   short cut!
Did Master Faithful[40] need climb the
   Delightful Mounts?
No, straight to Vanity Fair,—a fair, by all
   accounts,
Such as is held outside,—lords, ladies, grand
   and gay,—
Says he in the face of them, just what you hear
   me say.
And the Judges brought him in guilty, and
   brought him out
To die in the market-place—St. Peter's
   Green's[41] about
The same thing: there they flogged, flayed,
   buffeted, lanced with knives,
Pricked him with swords,—I 'll swear, he 'd
   full a cat's nine lives,—
So to his end at last came Faithful,—ha, ha, he!
Who holds the highest card? for there stands
   hid, you see,
Behind the rabble-rout, a chariot, pair and all:
He 's in, he 's off, he 's up, through clouds, at
   trumpet-call,
Carried the nearest way to Heaven-gate! Odds
   my life—
Has nobody a sword to spare? not even a knife?
Then hang me, draw and quarter! Tab—do
   the same by her!
O Master Worldly-Wiseman . . . that 's
   Master Interpreter,[42]
Take the will, not the deed! Our gibbet 's
   handy close:
Forestall Last Judgment-Day! Be kindly, not
   morose!
There wants no earthly judge-and-jurying:
   here we stand—
Sentence our guilty selves: so, hang us out of
   hand!
Make haste for pity's sake! A single moment's
   loss
Means—Satan 's lord once more: his whisper
   shoots across

All singing in my heart, all praying in my
   brain,
'It comes of heat and beer!'—hark how he
   guffaws plain!
To-morrow you'll wake bright, and, in a safe
   skin, hug
Your sound selves, Tab and you, over a
   foaming jug!
You 've had such qualms before, time out of
   mind!' He 's right!
Did not we kick and cuff and curse away, that
   night
When home we blindly reeled, and left poor
   humpback Joe
I' the lurch to pay for what . . . somebody
   did, you know! 260
Both of us maundered then 'Lame humpback,
   —never more
Will he come limping, drain his tankard at our
   door!
He 'll swing, while—somebody . . .' Says Tab,
   'No, for I 'll peach!'[43]
'I 'm for you, Tab,' cries I, 'there 's rope
   enough for each!'
So blubbered we, and bussed, and went to bed
   upon
The grace of Tab's good thought: by morning,
   all was gone!
We laughed—'What 's life to him, a cripple of
   no account?'
Oh, waves increase around—I feel them mount
   and mount!
Hang us! To-morrow brings Tom Bearward
   with his bears:
One new black-muzzled brute beats Sackerson,
   he swears: 270
(Sackerson, for my money!) And, baiting[44] o'er,
   the Brawl
They lead on Turner's Patch,—lads, lasses, up
   tails all,—
I 'm i' the thick o' the throng! That means the
   Iron Cage,
—Means the Lost Man[45] inside! Where 's hope
   for such as wage
War against light? Light 's left, light 's here, I
   hold light still,

---

[39] Thrid: thread.
[40] Master Faithful: another of Christian's reassuring companions; he is tried (along with Christian) in Vanity Fair, executed, and taken directly to the Celestial City.
[41] St. Peter's Green: St. Peter's is a church in Bedford.
[42] Master Worldly-Wiseman; Master Interpreter: two more of the personages Christian meets on his journey.
[43] Peach: confess.   [44] Baiting: an entertainment in which dogs are set upon a chained bear.
[45] The Lost Man in the Iron Cage: a man whom Christian sees who has despaired of being saved.

So does Tab—make but haste to hang up both!
    You will?"

I promise, when he stopped you might have
    heard a mouse
Squeak, such a death-like hush sealed up the
    old Mote House.
But when the mass of man sank meek upon his
    knees,
While Tab, alongside, wheezed a hoarse "Do
280   hang us, please!"
Why, then the waters rose, no eye but ran with
    tears,
Hearts heaved, heads thumped, until, paying
    all past arrears
Of pity and sorrow, at last a regular scream
    outbroke
Of triumph, joy and praise.

                My Lord Chief Justice spoke,
First mopping brow and cheek, where still, for
    one that budged,
Another bead broke fresh: "What Judge, that
    ever judged
Since first the world began, judged such a case
    as this?
Why, Master Bratts, long since, folk smelt you
    out, I wis!
I had my doubts, i' faith, each time you played
    the fox
Convicting geese of crime in yonder witness-
290   box—
Yea, much did I misdoubt, the thief that stole
    her eggs
Was hardly goosey's self at Reynard's[46] game, i'
    feggs![47]
Yet thus much was to praise—you spoke to
    point, direct—
Swore you heard, saw the theft: no jury could
    suspect—
Dared to suspect,—I 'll say,—a spot in white so
    clear:
Goosey was throttled, true: but thereof godly
    fear
Came of example set, much as our laws intend;
And, though a fox confessed, you proved the
    Judge's friend.
What if I had my doubts? Suppose I gave them
    breath,

Brought you to bar: what work to do, ere
    'Guilty, Death,'—
Had paid our pains! What heaps of witnesses
    to drag
From holes and corners, paid from out the
    County's bag!
Trial three dog-days long! Amicus Curiæ[48]—
    that 's
Your title, no dispute—truth-telling Master
    Bratts!
Thank you, too, Mistress Tab! Why doubt
    one word you say?
Hanging you both deserve, hanged both shall
    be this day!
The tinker needs must be a proper man. I 've
    heard
He lies in Jail long since: if Quality 's good
    word
Warrants me letting loose,—some house-
    holder,[49] I mean—
Freeholder,[50] better still,—I don't say but—
    between
Now and next Sessions . . . Well! Consider of
    his case,
I promise to, at least: we owe him so much
    grace.
Not that—no, God forbid!—I lean to think,
    as you,
The grace that such repent is any jail-bird's
    due:
I rather see the fruit of twelve years' pious
    reign—
Astræa Redux,[51] Charles restored his rights
    again!
—Of which, another time! I somehow feel a
    peace
Stealing across the world. May deeds like this
    increase!
So, Master Sheriff, stay that sentence I
    pronounced
On those two dozen odd: deserving to be
    trounced
Soundly, and yet . . . well, well, at all events
    despatch
This pair of—shall I say, sinner-saints?—ere
    we catch
Their jail-distemper too. Stop tears, or I 'll
    indite

---

[46] Reynard: the fox who is the hero of a series of French fables.   [47] I' feggs: in faith.
[48] Amicus Curiæ: friend of the court.
[49] Householder: owner of residence and thus entitled to vote.
[50] Freeholder: owner of an estate and hence entitled to vote.
[51] Astræa Redux: Justice returned; the title of a poem by John Dryden (1613–1700) celebrat-
ing the return of Charles II to the English throne.

All weeping Bedfordshire for turning Bunyan-
    ite!"

So, forms were galloped through. If Justice, on
    the spur,
Proved somewhat expeditious, would Quality
    demur?
And happily hanged were they,—why lengthen
    out my tale?—
Where Bunyan's Statue[52] stands facing where
    stood his Jail.

                    (1878) 1879

Pan and Luna

Si credere dignum est.   —GEORGIC. III. 390.[1]

O worthy of belief I hold it was,
Virgil, your legend in those strange three lines!
No question, that adventure came to pass
One black night in Arcadia: yes, the pines,
Mountains and valleys mingling made one
    mass
Of black with void black heaven: the earth's
    confines,
The sky's embrace,—below, above, around,
All hardened into black without a bound.

Fill up a swart stone chalice to the brim
With fresh-squeezed yet fast-thickening poppy-
    juice:
See how the sluggish jelly, late a-swim,
Turns marble to the touch of who would loose
The solid smooth, grown jet from rim to rim,
By turning round the bowl! So night can fuse
Earth with her all-comprising sky. No less,
Light, the least spark, shows air and emptiness.

And thus it proved when—diving into space,
Stript of all vapour, from each web of mist
Utterly film-free—entered on her race
The naked Moon, full-orbed antagonist
Of night and dark, night's dowry: peak to base,
Upstarted mountains, and each valley, kissed
To sudden life, lay silver-bright: in air
Flew she revealed, Maid-Moon with limbs all
    bare.

Still as she fled, each depth—where refuge
    seemed—
Opening a lone pale chamber, left distinct
Those limbs: mid still-retreating blue, she
    teemed
Herself with whiteness,—virginal, uncinct[2]
By any halo save what finely gleamed
To outline not disguise her: heaven was linked   30
In one accord with earth to quaff the joy,
Drain beauty to the dregs without alloy.

Whereof she grew aware. What help? When, lo,
A succourable cloud with sleep lay dense:
Some pine-tree-top had caught it sailing slow,
And tethered for a prize: in evidence
Captive lay fleece on fleece of piled-up snow
Drowsily patient: flake-heaped how or whence,
The structure of that succourable cloud,
What matter? Shamed she plunged into its
    shroud.   40

Orbed—so the woman-figure poets call
Because of rounds on rounds—that apple-
    shaped
Head which its hair binds close into a ball
Each side the curving ears—that pure
    undraped
Pout of the sister paps—that . . . Once for all,
Say—her consummate circle thus escaped
With its innumerous circlets, sank absorbed,
Safe in the cloud—O naked Moon full-orbed!

But what means this? The downy swathes com-
    bine,
Conglobe, the smothery coy-caressing stuff   50
Curdles about her! Vain each twist and twine
Those lithe limbs try, encroached on by a fluff
Fitting as close as fits the dented spine
Its flexile ivory outside-flesh: enough!
The plumy drifts contract, condense,
    constringe,[3]
Till she is swallowed by the feathery springe.[4]

As when a pearl slips lost in the thin foam
Churned on a sea-shore, and, o'er-frothed,
    conceits
Herself safe-housed in Amphitrite's[5] dome,—
If, through the bladdery[6] wave-worked yeast,
    she meets   60

---

[52] A statue of Bunyan was given to the town of Bedford in 1874.

[1] "If we may trust report." The third book of Virgil's *Georgics* contains an allusion to the legend that Pan, the god of forests and pastures, usually depicted with the horns and hooves of a goat, once captured the moon in a cloud of fleece, and the moon went into eclipse while she yielded to his desire.

[2] Uncinct: unencircled.   [3] Constringe: constrict.   [4] Springe: snare.

[5] Amphitrite: goddess of the sea.   [6] Bladdery: bubbling.

What most she loathes and leaps from,—elf
 from gnome
No gladlier,—finds that safest of retreats
Bubble about a treacherous hand wide ope
To grasp her— (divers who pick pearls so
 grope) —

So lay this Maid-Moon clasped around and
 caught
By rough red Pan, the god of all that tract:
He it was schemed the snare thus subtly
 wrought
With simulated earth-breath,—wool-tufts
 packed
Into a billowy wrappage. Sheep far-sought
70 For spotless shearings yield such: take the fact
As learned Virgil gives it,—how the breed
Whitens itself for ever: yes, indeed!

If one forefather ram, though pure as chalk
From tinge on fleece, should still display a
 tongue
Black 'neath the beast's moist palate, prompt
 men baulk
The propagating plague: he gets no young:[7]
They rather slay him,—sell his hide to caulk
Ships with, first steeped in pitch,—nor hands
 are wrung
In sorrow for his fate: protected thus,
80 The purity we love is gained for us.

So did Girl-moon, by just her attribute
Of unmatched modesty betrayed, lie trapped,
Bruised to the breast of Pan, half-god half-
 brute,
Raked by his bristly boar-sward while he
 lapped
—Never say, kissed her! that were to pollute
Love's language—which moreover proves
 unapt
To tell how she recoiled—as who finds thorns
Where she sought flowers—when, feeling, she
 touched—horns!

Then—does the legend say?—first moon-eclipse
Happened, first swooning-fit which puzzled
90 sore
The early sages? Is that why she dips

Into the dark, a minute and no more,
Only so long as serves her while she rips
The cloud's womb through and, faultless as
 before,
Pursues her way? No lesson for a maid
Left she, a maid herself thus trapped, betrayed?

Ha, Virgil? Tell the rest, you! "To the deep
Of his domain the wildwood, Pan forthwith
Called her, and so she followed"—in her sleep,
Surely?—"by no means spurning him." The
 myth   1
Explain who may! Let all else go, I keep
—As of a ruin just a monolith—
Thus much, one verse of five words, each a
 boon:
Arcadia, night, a cloud, Pan, and the moon.

———————————

"Touch him ne'er so lightly, into song he
 broke:[8]
Soil so quick-receptive,—not one feather-seed,
Not one flower-dust fell but straight its fall
 awoke
Vitalizing virtue: song would song succeed
Sudden as spontaneous—prove a poet-soul!"

                                                                      Indeed?
Rock's the song-soil rather, surface hard and
 bare:
Sun and dew their mildness, storm and frost
 their rage
Vainly both expend,—few flowers awaken
 there:
Quiet in its cleft broods—what the after age
Knows and names a pine, a nation's heritage.
                                                                      1880

*Francis Furini (c. 1600–49) was an Italian
painter, many of whose paintings include female
nudes. At the age of forty he became a priest, and
according to the account of his life Browning knew,
on his deathbed he asked that his paintings of nudes
be destroyed. The source of information about
Furini was Filippo Baldinucci's (1624–96) multi-
volumed collection of biographies of painters, pub-
lished in Italy at the end of the seventeenth cen-
tury. Baldinucci condemns Furini's painting of
nudes, and endorses his request, which was not
honored.*

---

[7] Virgil gives this advice in the third book of the *Georgics*.
 [8] Browning printed these lines, which serve as a kind of epilogue to *Dramatic Idyls: Second
Series* (1880), immediately after "Pan and Luna" in the standard collection of his poems. In a
postscript to this epilogue, written in an album of the daughter of Henry Wadsworth Long-
fellow and published in America but never included by Browning in his collected poems,
Browning disclaimed the suggestion that he had himself in mind as the type of poet who makes
a durable achievement grow slowly out of rock; he names Dante as the poet he meant. See
DeVane, pp. 457–458.

from Parleyings with Certain People of Importance in Their Day

With Francis Furini

I

Nay, *that,* Furini, never I at least
Mean to believe! What man you were I know,
While you walked Tuscan earth, a painter-
  priest,
Something about two hundred years ago.
Priest—you did duty punctual as the sun
That rose and set above Saint Sano's church,
Blessing Mugello:[1] of your flock not one
But showed a whiter fleece because of smirch,
Your kind hands wiped it clear from: were
  they poor?
Bounty broke bread apace,—did marriage lag
For just the want of moneys that ensure
Fit hearth-and-home provision?—straight your
  bag
Unplumped itself,—reached hearts by way of
  palms
Goodwill's shake had but tickled. All about
Mugello valley, felt some parish qualms
At worship offered in bare walls without
The comfort of a picture?—prompt such need
Our painter would supply, and throngs to see
Witnessed that goodness—no unholy greed
Of gain—had coaxed from Don Furini—he
Whom princes might in vain implore to toil
For worldly profit—such a masterpiece.
Brief—priest, you poured profuse God's wine
  and oil
Praiseworthily, I know: shall praising cease
When, priestly vesture put aside, mere man,
You stand for judgment? Rather—what
  acclaim
—"Good son, good brother, friend in whom we
  scan
No fault nor flaw"—salutes Furini's name,
The loving as the liberal! Enough:

Only to ope a lily, though for sake   30
Of setting free its scent, disturbs the rough
Loose gold about its anther.[2] I shall take
No blame in one more blazon, last of all—
Good painter were you: if in very deed
I styled you great—what modern art dares call
My word in question? Let who will take heed
Of what he seeks and misses in your brain
To balance that precision of the brush
Your hand could ply so deftly: all in vain
Strives poet's power for outlet when the push   40
Is lost upon a barred and bolted gate
Of painter's impotency. Agnolo[3]—
Thine were alike the head and hand, by fate
Doubly endowed! Who boasts head only—woe
To hand's presumption should brush emulate
Fancy's free passage by the pen, and show
Thought wrecked and ruined where the
  inexpert
Foolhardy fingers half grasped, half let go
Film-wings the poet's pen arrests unhurt!
No—painter such as that miraculous   50
Michael, who deems you? But the ample gift
Of gracing walls else blank of this our house
Of life with imagery, one bright drift
Poured forth by pencil,—man and woman
  mere,
Glorified till half owned for gods,—the dear
Fleshly perfection of the human shape,—
This was apportioned you whereby to praise
Heaven and bless earth. Who clumsily essays,
By slighting painter's craft, to prove the ape
Of poet's pen-creation, just betrays   60
Two-fold ineptitude.

II

                                By such sure ways
Do I return, Furini, to my first
And central confidence—that he I proved
Good priest, good man, good painter, and
  rehearsed
Praise upon praise to show—not simply loved
For virtue, but for wisdom honoured too
Needs must Furini be,—it follows—who
Shall undertake to breed in me belief
That, on his death-bed, weakness played the
  thief
With wisdom, folly ousted reason quite?   70
List to the chronicler! With main and might—
So fame runs—did the poor soul beg his friends

[1] Saint Sano, in the town of Mugello, was the name of Furini's church when he became a priest.
[2] Anther: the part of a flower's stamen that contains pollen.
[3] Agnolo: Michaelangelo (1475–1564).

To buy and burn his hand-work, make amends
For having reproduced therein— (Ah me!
Sighs fame—that 's friend Filippo) [4]—nudity!
Yes, I asure you: he would paint—not men
Merely—a pardonable fault—but when
He had to deal with—oh, not mother Eve
Alone, permissibly in Paradise
80 Naked and unashamed,—but dared achieve
Dreadful distinction, at soul-safety's price
By also painting women— (why the need?)
Just as God made them: there, you have the
        truth!
Yes, rosed from top to toe in flush of youth,
One foot upon the moss-fringe, would some
        Nymph[5]
Try, with its venturous fellow, if the lymph[6]
Were chillier than the slab-stepped fountain-
        edge;
The while a-heap her garments on its ledge
Of boulder lay within hand's easy reach,
90 —No one least kid-skin cast around her! Speech
Shrinks from enumerating case and case
Of—were it but Diana[7] at the chase,
With tunic tucked discreetly hunting-high!
No, some Queen Venus set our necks awry,
Turned faces from the painter's all-too-frank
Triumph of flesh! For—whom had he to thank
—This self-appointed nature-student? Whence
Picked he up practice? By what evidence
Did he unhandsomely become adept
100 In simulating bodies? How except
By actual sight of such? Himself confessed
The enormity: quoth Philip[8] "When I pressed
The painter to acknowledge his abuse
Of artistry else potent—what excuse
Made the infatuated man? I give
His very words: 'Did you but know, as I,
—O scruple-splitting sickly-sensitive
Mild-moral-monger, what the agony
Of Art is ere Art satisfy herself
110 In imitating Nature—(Man, poor elf,
Striving to match the finger-mark of Him
The immeasurably matchless)—gay or grim,

Pray, would your smile be? Leave mere fools to
        tax
Art's high-strung brain's intentness as so lax
That, in its mid-throe, idle fancy sees
The moment for admittance!' Pleadings
        these—
Specious, I grant." So adds, and seems to wince
Somewhat, our censor—but shall truth
        convince
Blockheads like Baldinucci?[9]

III

                                        I resume
My incredulity: your other kind   1
Of soul, Furini, never was so blind,
Even through death-mist, as to grope in gloom
For cheer beside a bonfire piled to turn
Ashes and dust all that your noble life
Did homage to life's Lord by,—bid them burn
—These Baldinucci blockheads—pictures rife
With record, in each rendered loveliness,
That one appreciative creature's debt
Of thanks to the Creator more or less,
Was paid according as heart's-will had met   1
Hand's-power in Art's endeavour to express
Heaven's most consummate of achievements,
        bless
Earth by a semblance of the seal God set
On woman his supremest work. I trust
Rather, Furini, dying breath had vent
In some fine fervour of thanksgiving just
For this—that soul and body's power you
        spent—
Agonized to adumbrate, trace in dust
That marvel which we dream the firmament
Copies in star-device when fancies stray
Outlining, orb by orb, Andromeda[10]—
God's best of beauteous and magnificent
Revealed to earth—the naked female form.
Nay, I mistake not: wrath that 's but lukewarm
Would boil indeed were such a critic styled
Himself an artist: artist! Ossa piled
Topping Olympus[11]—the absurd which crowns

---

[4] Filippo: Baldinucci.   [5] Nymph: mythological spirit of forests and waters.
[6] Lymph: water.   [7] Diana: Roman goddess of the moon and the hunt.
[8] Philip: Baldinucci again.
[9] Browning's intemperate criticism of Baldinucci is undoubtedly sponsored, as DeVane per-
suasively argues (pp. 513–514), by the hostile reception accorded to the paintings of his son
Robert Wiedemann Browning, often because they too contained figures of nude female figures.
[10] Andromeda in a Greek myth is the daughter of Cepheus, who has her chained to a rock to
be devoured by a sea monster in order to appease the anger of sea nymphs with whom his wife
has compared her beauty. Andromeda is saved by Perseus, who kills the monster and is wed to
Andromeda.
[11] In a Greek myth the giants of the earth, in their battle against the gods, pile the mountain
Ossa on top of the mountain Pelion to try to climb into Olympus, the home of the gods.

The extravagant—whereat one laughs, not
   frowns.
Paints he? One bids the poor pretender take
His sorry self, a trouble and disgrace,
From out the sacred presence, void the place
Artists claim only. What—not merely wake
Our pity that suppressed concupiscence—
A satyr masked as matron[12]—makes pretence
To the coarse blue-fly's instinct—can perceive
No better reason why she should exist—
—God's lily-limbed and blush-rose-bosomed
   Eve—
Than as a hot-bed for the sensualist
To fly-blow with his fancies, make pure stuff
Breed him back filth—this were not crime
   enough?
But further—fly to style itself—nay, more—
To steal among the sacred ones, crouch down
Though but to where their garments sweep the
   floor—
—Still catching some faint sparkle from the
   crown
Crowning transcendent Michael, Leonard,
Rafael,[13]—to sit beside the feet of such,
Unspurned because unnoticed, then reward
Their toleration—mercy overmuch—
By stealing from the throne-step to the fools
Curious outside the gateway, all-agape
To learn by what procedure, in the schools
Of Art, a merest man in outward shape
May learn to be Correggio![14] Old and young,
These learners got their lesson: Art was just
A safety-screen—(Art, which Correggio's tongue
Calls "Virtue")—for a skulking vice: mere lust
Inspired the artist when his Night and Morn
Slept and awoke in marble on that edge
Of heaven above our awestruck earth: lust-born
His Eve[15] low bending took the privilege
Of life from what our eyes saw—God's own
   palm

That put the flame forth—to the love and
   thanks
Of all creation save this recreant!

    IV

              Calm
Our phrase, Furini! Not the artist-ranks
Claim riddance of an interloper: no—
This Baldinucci did but grunt and sniff
Outside Art's pale—ay, grubbed, where pine-
   trees grow,
For pignuts[16] only.

    V

          You the Sacred! If
Indeed on you has been bestowed the dower
Of Art in fulness, graced with head and hand,   190
Head—to look up not downwards, hand—of
   power
To make head's gain the portion of a world
Where else the uninstructed ones too sure
Would take all outside beauty—film that's
   furled
About a star—for the star's self, endure
No guidance to the central glory,—nay,
(Sadder) might apprehend the film was fog,
Or (worst) wish all but vapour well away,
And sky's pure product thickened from earth's
   bog—
Since so, nor seldom, have your worthiest failed   200
To trust their own soul's insight—why? except
For warning that the head of the adept
May too much prize the hand, work unassailed
By scruple of the better sense that finds
An orb within each halo, bids gross flesh
Free the fine spirit-pattern, nor enmesh
More than is meet a marvel custom blinds
Only the vulgar eye to. Now, less fear
That you, the foremost of Art's fellowship,
Will oft—will ever so offend! But—hip   210
And thigh—smite the Philistine![17] *You*—slunk
   here—

[12] Satyr masked as matron: one of the critics who chastised the younger Browning for his painting of nudes was J. C. Horsley, sometime secretary of the Royal Academy, who wrote a letter of protest to a newspaper over the signature, "A British Matron."

[13] Michaelangelo, Leonardo da Vinci, and Raphael, all of whom worked in the late fifteenth and early sixteenth centuries.

[14] Correggio (1494–1534), another painter of the Italian renaissance, which to Browning was the great flowering of an art that celebrated the human possibilities of mankind.

[15] Night and Morn are figures in a group of statuary by Michaelangelo; his painting depicting the creation of Eve is part of the decoration of the Sistine chapel in Rome.

[16] Pignut: a bitter-flavored nut.

[17] The Philistines established hegemony in the region which was to become the Israelite kingdom around 1150 B.C.; the Israelites warred with them through the ninth century B.C. The phrase was used in the mid-nineteenth century—for example, by Matthew Arnold in *Culture and Anarchy* (1869)—to characterize a narrow, insensitive, materialistic class, enemies to the truth and its chosen agents.

Connived at, by too easy tolerance,
Not to scrape palette simply or squeeze brush,
But dub your very self an Artist? Tush—
You, of the daubings, is it, dare advance
This doctrine that the Artist-mind must needs
Own to affinity with yours—confess
Provocative acquaintance, more or less,
With each impurely-peevish worm that breeds
220 Inside your brain's receptacle?

VI

         Enough.
Who owns "I dare not look on diadems
Without an itch to pick out, purloin gems
Others contentedly leave sparkling"—gruff
Answers the guard of the regalia: "Why—
Consciously kleptomaniac—thrust yourself
Where your illicit craving after pelf
Is tempted most—in the King's treasury?
Go elsewhere! Sort with thieves, if thus you
   feel—
When folk clean-handed simply recognize
230 Treasure whereof the mere sight satisfies—
But straight your fingers are on itch to steal!
Hence with you!"
        Pray, Furini!

VII

       "Bounteous God,
Deviser and Dispenser of all gifts
To soul through sense,—in Art the soul uplifts
Man's best of thanks! What but Thy measur-
   ing-rod
Meted forth heaven and earth? more intimate,
Thy very hands were busied with the task
Of making, in this human shape, a mask—
A match for that divine. Shall love abate
Man's wonder? Nowise! True—true—all too
240   true—
No gift but, in the very plenitude
Of its perfection, goes maimed, misconstrued
By wickedness or weakness: still, some few
Have grace to see Thy purpose, strength to mar
Thy work by no admixture of their own,
—Limn truth not falsehood, bid us love alone
The type untampered with, the naked star!"

VIII

And, prayer done, painter—what if you should
   preach?
Not as of old when playing pulpiteer
250 To simple-witted country folk, but here
In actual London try your powers of speech
On us the cultured, therefore sceptical—
What would you? For, suppose he has his word

In faith's behalf, no matter how absurd,
This painter-theologian? One and all
We lend an ear—nay, Science takes thereto—
Encourages the meanest who has racked
Nature until he gains from her some fact,
To state what truth is from his point of view,
Mere pin-point though it be: since many such
Conduce to make a whole, she bids our friend
Come forward unabashed and haply lend
His little life-experience to our much
Of modern knowledge. Since she so insists,
Up stands Furini.

IX

       "Evolutionists!
At truth I glimpse from depths, you glance
   from heights,
Our stations for discovery opposites,—
How should ensue agreement? I explain:
'T is the tip-top of things to which you strain
Your vision, until atoms, protoplasm,
And what and whence and how may be the
   spasm
Which sets all going, stop you: down perforce
Needs must your observation take its course,
Since there 's no moving upwards: link by link
You drop to where the atoms somehow think,
Feel, know themselves to be: the world 's be-
   gun,
Such as we recognize it. Have you done
Descending? Here 's ourself,—Man, known
   today,
Duly evolved at last,—so far, you say,
The sum and seal of being's progress. Good!
Thus much at least is clearly understood—
Of power does Man possess no particle:
Of knowledge—just so much as shows that still
It ends in ignorance on every side:
But righteousness—ah, Man is deified
Thereby, for compensation! Make survey
Of Man's surroundings, try creation—nay,
Try emulation of the minimized
Minuteness fancy may conceive! Surprised
Reason becomes by two defeats for one—
Not only power at each phenomenon
Baffled, but knowledge also in default—
Asking what *is* minuteness—yonder vault
Speckled with suns, or this the millionth—
   thing,
How shall I call?—that on some insect's wing
Helps to make out in dyes the mimic star?
Weak, ignorant, accordingly we are:
What then? The worse for Nature! Where
   began
Righteousness, moral sense except in Man?

True, he makes nothing, understands no whit:
Had the initiator-spasm seen fit
Thus doubly to endow him, none the worse
And much the better were the universe.
What does Man see or feel or apprehend
Here, there, and everywhere, but faults to
    mend,
Omissions to supply,—one wide disease
Of things that are, which Man at once would
    ease
Had will but power and knowledge? failing
    both—
Things must take will for deed—Man, nowise
    loth,
Accepts pre-eminency: mere blind force—
Mere knowledge undirected in its course
By any care for what is made or marred
In either's operation—*these* award
The crown to? Rather let it deck thy brows,
Man, whom alone a righteousness endows
Would cure the wide world's ailing! Who
    disputes
Thy claim thereto? Had Spasm more attributes
Than power and knowledge in its gift, before
Man came to pass? The higher that we soar,[18]
The less of moral sense like Man's we find:
No sign of such before,—what comes behind,
Who guesses? But until there crown our sight
The quite new—not the old mere infinite
Of changings,—some fresh kind of sun and
    moon,—
Then, not before, shall I expect a boon
Of intuition just as strange, which turns
Evil to good, and wrong to right, unlearns
All Man's experience learned since Man was he.
Accept in Man, advanced to this degree,
The Prime Mind,[19] therefore! neither wise nor
    strong—
Whose fault? but were he both, then right, not
    wrong
As now, throughout the world were paramount
According to his will,—which I account
The qualifying faculty. He stands
Confessed supreme—the monarch whose
    commands
Could he enforce, how bettered were the world!
He 's at the height this moment—to be hurled
Next moment to the bottom by rebound
Of his own peal of laughter. All around
Ignorance wraps him,—whence and how and
    why

Things are,—yet cloud breaks and lets blink
    the sky
Just overhead, not elsewhere! What assures
His optics that the very blue which lures
Comes not of black outside it, doubly dense?
Ignorance overwraps his moral sense,
Winds him about, relaxing, as it wraps,
So much and no more than lets through
    perhaps
The murmured knowledge—'Ignorance exists.'

X

"I at the bottom, Evolutionists,
Advise beginning, rather. I profess   350
To know just one fact—my self-conscious-
    ness,—
'Twixt ignorance and ignorance enisled,—
Knowledge: before me was my Cause—that 's
    styled
God: after, in due course succeeds the rest,—
All that my knowledge comprehends—at best—
At worst, conceives about in mild despair.
Light needs must touch on either darkness:
    where?
Knowledge so far impinges on the Cause
Before me, that I know—by certain laws
Wholly unknown, whate'er I apprehend   360
Within, without me, had its rise: thus blend
I, and all things perceived, in one Effect.
How far can knowledge any ray project
On what comes after me—the universe?
Well, my attempt to make the cloud disperse
Begins—not from above but underneath:
I climb, you soar,—who soars soon loses breath
And sinks, who climbs keeps one foot firm on
    fact
Ere hazarding the next step: soul's first act
(Call consciousness the soul—some name we
    need)   370
Getting itself aware, through stuff decreed
Thereto (so call the body)—who has stept
So far, there let him stand, become adept
In body ere he shift his station thence
One single hair's breadth. Do I make pretence
To teach, myself unskilled in learning? Lo,
My life's work! Let my pictures prove I know
Somewhat of what this fleshly frame of ours
Or is or should be, how the soul empowers
The body to reveal its every mood   380
Of love and hate, pour forth its plenitude
Of passion. If my hand attained to give

---

[18] Higher that we soar: that is, the farther scientists move toward abstract, theoretical explana-
tions of how life came into matter.
[19] Prime Mind: the creator of the moral, as opposed to the material, universe.

Thus permanence to truth else fugitive,
Did not I also fix each fleeting grace
Of form and feature—save the beauteous
    face—
Arrest decay in transitory might
Of bone and muscle—cause the world to bless
For ever each transcendent nakedness
Of man and woman? Were such feats achieved
390 By sloth, or strenuous labour unrelieved,
—Yet lavished vainly? Ask that underground
(So may I speak) of all on surface found
Of flesh-perfection! Depths on depths to probe
Of all-inventive artifice, disrobe
Marvel at hiding under marvel, pluck
Veil after veil from Nature—were the luck
Ours to surprise the secret men so name,
That still eludes the searcher—all the same,
Repays his search with still fresh proof—
    'Externe,
400 Not inmost, is the Cause, fool! Look and learn!'
Thus teach my hundred pictures: firm and fast
There did I plant my first foot. And the next?
Nowhere! 'T was put forth and withdrawn,
    perplexed
At touch of what seemed stable and proved
    stuff
Such as the coloured clouds are: plain enough
There lay the outside universe: try Man—
My most immediate! and the dip began
From safe and solid into that profound
Of ignorance I tell you surges round
410 My rock-spit of self-knowledge. Well and ill,
Evil and good irreconcilable
Above, beneath, about my every side,—
How did this wild confusion far and wide
Tally with my experience when my stamp—
So far from stirring—struck out, each a lamp,
Spark after spark of truth from where I stood—
Pedestalled triumph? Evil there was good,
Want was the promise of supply, defect
Ensured completion,—where and when and
    how?
Leave that to the First Cause! Enough that
420   now,
Here where I stand, this moment's me and
    mine,
Shows me what is, permits me to divine
What shall be. Wherefore? Nay, how other-
    wise?
Look at my pictures! What so glorifies
The body that the permeating soul
Finds there no particle elude control
Direct, or fail of duty,—most obscure

When most subservient? Did that Cause ensure
The soul such raptures as its fancy stings
Body to furnish when, uplift by wings
Of passion, here and now, it leaves the earth,
Loses itself above, where bliss has birth—
(Heaven, be the phrase) —did that same Cause
    contrive
Such solace for the body, soul must dive
At drop of fancy's pinion, condescend
To bury both alike on earth, our friend
And fellow, where minutely exquisite
Low lie the pleasures, now and here—no herb
But hides its marvel, peace no doubts perturb
In each small mystery of insect life—
—Shall the soul's Cause thus gift the soul, yet
    strife
Continue still of fears with hopes,—for why?
What if the Cause, whereof we now descry
So far the wonder-working, lack at last
Will, power, benevolence—a protoplast,[20]
No consummator, sealing up the sum
Of all things,—past and present and to come
Perfection? No, I have no doubt at all!
There 's my amount of knowledge—great or
    small,
Sufficient for my needs: for see! advance
Its light now on that depth of ignorance
I shrank before from—yonder where the world
Lies wreck-strewn,—evil towering, prone good
    —hurled
From pride of place, on every side. For me
(Patience, beseech you!) knowledge can but be
Of good by knowledge of good's opposite—
Evil,—since, to distinguish wrong from right,
Both must be known in each extreme, beside—
(Or what means knowledge—to aspire or bide
Content with half-attaining? Hardly so!)
Made to know on, know ever, I must know
All to be known at any halting-stage
Of my soul's progress, such as earth, where
    wage
War, just for soul's instruction, pain with joy,
Folly with wisdom, all that works annoy
With all that quiets and contents,—in brief,
Good strives with evil.

                              "Now then for relief,
Friends, of your patience kindly curbed so
    long.
'What?' snarl you, 'Is the fool's conceit thus
    strong—
Must the whole outside world in soul and sense
Suffer, that he grow sage at its expense?'

---

[20] Protoplast: first model, from which other forms will be made.

By no means! 'T is by merest touch of toe
I try—not trench on—ignorance, just know—
And so keep steady footing: how you fare,
Caught in the whirlpool—that 's the Cause's
    care,
Strong, wise, good,—this I know at any rate
In my own self,—but how may operate
With you—strength, wisdom, goodness—no
    least blink
Of knowledge breaks the darkness round me.
    Think!
Could I see plain, be somehow certified
All was illusion,—evil far and wide
Was good disguised,—why, out with one huge
    wipe
Goes knowledge from me. Type needs anti-
    type:
As night needs day, as shine needs shade, so
    good
Needs evil: how were pity understood
Unless by pain? Make evident that pain
Permissibly masks pleasure—you abstain
From outstretch of the finger-tip that saves
A drowning fly. Who proffers help of hand
To weak Andromeda exposed on strand
At mercy of the monster? Were all true,
Help were not wanting: 'But 't is false,' cry
    you,
'Mere fancy-work of paint and brush!' No less,
Were mine the skill, the magic, to impress
Beholders with a confidence they saw
Life,—veritable flesh and blood in awe
Of just as true a sea-beast,—would they stare
Simply as now, or cry out, curse and swear,
Or call the gods to help, or catch up stick
And stone, according as their hearts were quick
Or sluggish? Well, some old artificer
Could do as much,—at least, so books aver,—
Able to make-believe, while I, poor wight,
Make-fancy, nothing more. Though wrong
    were right,
Could we but know—still wrong must needs
    seem wrong
To do right's service, prove men weak or
    strong,
Choosers of evil or of good. 'No such
Illusion possible!' Ah, friends, you touch
Just here my solid standing-place amid
The wash and welter, whence all doubts are
    bid

Back to the ledge they break against in foam,
Futility: my soul, and my soul's home
This body,—how each operates on each,
And how things outside, fact or feigning, teach
What good is and what evil,—just the same,
Be feigning or be fact the teacher,—blame
Diffidence nowise if, from this I judge
My point of vantage, not an inch I budge.
All—for myself—seems ordered wise and well
Inside it,—what reigns outside, who can tell?   520
Contrariwise, who needs be told 'The space
Which yields thee knowledge,—do its bounds
    embrace
Well-willing and wise-working, each at height?
Enough: beyond thee lies the infinite—
Back to thy circumscription!'

                                        "Back indeed!
Ending where I began—thus: retrocede,
Who will,—what comes first, take first, I
    advise!
Acquaint you with the body ere your eyes
Look upward: this Andromeda of mine—
Gaze on the beauty, Art hangs out for sign   530
There 's finer entertainment underneath.
Learn how they ministrate to life and death—
Those incommensurably marvellous
Contrivances which furnish forth the house
Where soul has sway! Though Master keep
    aloof,
Signs of His presence multiply from roof
To basement of the building. Look around,
Learn thoroughly,—no fear that you confound
Master with messuage![21] He 's away, no doubt,
But what if, all at once, you come upon   540
A startling proof—not that the Master gone
Was present lately—but that something—
    whence
Light comes—has pushed Him into residence?
Was such the symbol's meaning,—old,
    uncouth—
That circle of the serpent, tail in mouth?[22]
Only by looking low, ere looking high,
Comes penetration of the mystery."

    XI
Thanks! After sermonizing, psalmody!
Now praise with pencil, Painter! Fools attaint
Your fame, forsooth, because its power inclines   550
To livelier colours, more attractive lines
Than suit some orthodox sad sickly saint

[21] Messuage: a dwelling house and its associated buildings, as on an estate.
[22] The figure of a serpent devouring its tail is the ouroboros, an ancient symbol of eternity (as
the serpent continually renews itself in successive incarnations). In the Middle Ages the figure
also came to symbolize man's search for knowledge; and in some cosmologies it was also a figure
of the limits of the earth, encircled by a serpent.

—Grey male emaciation, haply streaked
Carmine by scourgings—or they want, far
  worse—
Some self-scathed woman, framed to bless not
  curse
Nature that loved the form whereon hate
  wreaked
The wrongs you see. No, rather paint some
  full
Benignancy, the first and foremost boon
Of youth, health, strength,—show beauty's
  May, ere June
560 Undo the bud's blush, leave a rose to cull
—No poppy, neither! yet less perfect-pure,
Divinely-precious with life's dew besprent.
Show saintliness that 's simply innocent
Of guessing sinnership exists to cure.
All in good time! In time let age advance
And teach that knowledge helps—not
  ignorance—
The healing of the nations. Let my spark
Quicken your tinder! Burn with—Joan of Arc!
Not at the end, nor midway when there grew
570 The brave delusions, when rare fancies flew
Before the eyes, and in the ears of her
Strange voices woke imperiously astir:
No,—paint the peasant girl all peasant-like,
Spirit and flesh—the hour about to strike
When this should be transfigured, that
  inflamed,
By heart's admonishing "Thy country shamed,
Thy king shut out of all his realm except
One sorry corner!" and to life forth leapt
The indubitable lightning "Can there be
Country and king's salvation—all through
580 me?"
Memorize that burst's moment, Francis!
  Tush—
None of the nonsense-writing! Fitlier brush
Shall clear off fancy's film-work and let show
Not what the foolish feign but the wise know—
Ask Sainte-Beuve else!—or better, Quicherat,[23]
The downright-digger into truth that 's—Bah,

Bettered by fiction? Well, of fact thus much
Concerns you, that "of prudishness no touch
From first to last defaced the maid; anon,
Camp-use compelling"—what says D'Alençon[24]   5
Her fast friend?—"though I saw while she un-
  dressed
How fair she was—especially her breast—
Never had I a wild thought!"—as indeed
I nowise doubt. Much less would she take
  heed—
When eve came, and the lake, the hills around
Were all one solitude and silence,—found
Barriered impenetrably safe about,—
Take heed of interloping eyes shut out,
But quietly permit the air imbibe
Her naked beauty till . . . but hear the scribe!   6
Now as she fain would bathe, one even-tide,
God's maid, this Joan, from the pool's edge she
  spied
The fair blue bird clowns call the Fisher-king:
And " 'Las," sighed she, "my Liege is such a
  thing
As thou, lord but of one poor lonely place
Out of his whole wide France: were mine the
  grace
To set my Dauphin free as thou, blue bird!"
Properly Martin-fisher—that 's the word,
Not yours nor mine: folk said the rustic oath
In common use with her was—"By my troth"?   6
No,—"By my Martin"! Paint this![25] Only, turn
Her face away—that face about to burn
Into an angel's when the time is ripe!
That task 's beyond you. Finished, Francis?
  Wipe
Pencil, scrape palette, and retire content!
"Omnia non omnibus"[26]—no harm is meant!
                                                              1887

Prologue [to *Asolando*
Fancies and Facts][1]

"The Poet's age is sad: for why?
    In youth, the natural world could show

[23] Charles Augustin Sainte-Beuve (1804–69) was a French literary critic who was especially in-
terested in the biographical circumstances of literature; Jules Joseph Etienne Quicherat
(1814–82) edited a mid-nineteenth-century edition of the proceedings of the trial of Jeanne
d'Arc.
[24] Percival de Cagny D'Alençon wrote an account of Jeanne d'Arc which is reproduced in
Quicherat's volumes.
[25] This scene was the subject of one of the paintings of Browning's son, and the painting was
one of those that was attacked for its representation of female nudity.
[26] *Omnia non omnibus:* all, not everything.
[1] Asolando is Browning's name for Asolo, a town near the Italian Alps which Browning first
visited in 1838. His last visit was in September 1889, during which the prologue to the last
volume of his poems published during his lifetime was written. *Asolando* was published in
England on the day Browning died in Venice, December 12, 1889.

No common object but his eye
   At once involved with alien glow—
His own soul's iris-bow.[2]

"And now a flower is just a flower:
   Man, bird, beast are but beast, bird, man—
Simply themselves, uncinct[3] by dower
   Of dyes which, when life's day began,
Round each in glory ran."

Friend, did you need an optic glass,
   Which were your choice? A lens to drape
In ruby, emerald, chrysopras,[4]
   Each object—or reveal its shape
Clear outlined, past escape,

The naked very thing?—so clear
   That, when you had the chance to gaze,
You found its inmost self appear
   Through outer seeming—truth ablaze,
Not falsehood's fancy-haze?

How many a year, my Asolo,
   Since—one step just from sea to land—
I found you, loved yet feared you so—
   For natural objects seemed to stand
Palpably fire-clothed! No—

No mastery of mine o'er these!
   Terror with beauty, like the Bush[5]
Burning but unconsumed. Bend knees,
   Drop eyes to earthward! Language? Tush!
Silence 't is awe decrees.

And now? The lambent flame is—where?
   Lost from the naked world: earth, sky,
Hill, vale, tree, flower,—Italia's rare
   O'er-running beauty crowds the eye—
But flame? The Bush is bare

Hill, vale, tree, flower—they stand distinct,
   Nature to know and name. What then?
A Voice spoke thence which straight unlinked
   Fancy from fact: see, all 's in ken:
Has once my eyelid winked?

No, for the purged ear apprehends
   Earth's import, not the eye late dazed:
The Voice said "Call my works thy friends!

   At Nature dost thou shrink amazed?
God is it who transcends."

   Asolo: Sept. 6, 1889.

Now

Out of your whole life give but a moment!
All of your life that has gone before,
All to come after it,—so you ignore
So you make perfect the present,—condense,
In a rapture of rage, for perfection's
   endowment,
Thought and feeling and soul and sense—
Merged in a moment whch gives me at last
You around me for once, you beneath me,
   above me—
Me—sure that despite of time future, time
   past,—
This tick of our life-time 's one moment you
   love me!   10
How long such suspension may linger? Ah,
   Sweet—
The moment eternal—just that and no more—
When ecstasy's utmost we clutch at the core
While cheeks burn, arms open, eyes shut and
   lips meet!
      1889

Bad Dreams III

This was my dream: I saw a Forest
   Old as the earth, no track nor trace
Of unmade man. Thou, Soul, explorest—
   Though in a trembling rapture—space
Immeasurable! Shrubs, turned trees,
Trees that touch heaven, support its frieze
Studded with sun and moon and star:
While—oh, the enormous growths that bar
Mine eye from penetrating past
   Their tangled twine where lurks—nay, lives   10
Royally lone, some brute-type cast
   I' the rough, time cancels, man forgives.

On, Soul! I saw a lucid City
   Of architectural device

[2] Iris-bow: rainbow.
[3] Uncinct: unencircled.
[4] Chrysopras: a green stone.
[5] The Bush: God appeared to Moses in a bush that burned but was not consumed by its flame (Exodus 3:12).

Every way perfect. Pause for pity,
　Lightning! nor leave a cicatrice[1]
On those bright marbles, dome and spire,
Structures palatial,—streets which mire
Dares not defile, paved all too fine
20　For human footstep's smirch, not thine—
Proud solitary traverser,
　My Soul, of silent lengths of way—
With what ecstatic dread, aver,
　Lest life start sanctioned by thy stay!

Ah, but the last sight was the hideous!
　A City, yes—a Forest, true,—
But each devouring each. Perfidious
Snake-plants had strangled what I knew
Was a pavilion once: each oak
30　Held on his horns some spoil he broke
By surreptitiously beneath
Upthrusting: pavements, as with teeth,
Griped huge weed widening crack and split
　In squares and circles stone-work erst.
Oh, Nature—good! Oh, Art—no whit
　Less worthy! Both in one—accurst!

1889

Inapprehensiveness

We two stood simply friend-like side by side,
Viewing a twilight country far and wide,
Till she at length broke silence. "How it towers
Yonder, the ruin o'er this vale of ours![1]
The West's faint flare behind it so relieves
Its rugged outline—sight perhaps deceives,
Or I could almost fancy that I see
A branch wave plain—belike some wind-sown
　tree
Chance-rooted where a missing turret was.
10　What would I give for the perspective glass
At home, to make out if 't is really so!

Has Ruskin[2] noticed here at Asolo
That certain weed-growths on the ravaged wall
Seem" . . . something that I could not say at
　all,
My thought being rather—as absorbed she sent
Look onward after look from eyes distent
With longing to reach Heaven's gate left ajar—
"Oh, fancies that might be, oh, facts that are!
What of a wilding? By you stands, and may
So stand unnoticed till the Judgment Day,
One who, if once aware that your regard
Claimed what his heart holds,—woke, as from
　its sward
The flower, the dormant passion, so to speak—
Then what a rush of life would startling wreak
Revenge on your inapprehensive stare
While, from the ruin and the West's faint flare,
You let your eyes meet mine, touch what you
　term
Quietude—that 's an universe in germ—
The dormant passion needing but a look
To burst into immense life!"
　　　　　　　　　"No, the book
Which noticed how the wall-growths wave,"
　said she
"Was not by Ruskin."
　　　　　　　　I said "Vernon Lee?"[3]
1889

The Cardinal and the Dog

Crescenzio, the Pope's Legate at the High
　Council, Trent,[1]
—Year Fifteen hundred twenty-two, March
　Twenty-five—intent
On writing letters to the Pope till late into the
　night,
Rose, weary, to refresh himself, and saw a
　monstrous sight:

[1] Cicatrice: a mark or scar; usually, the scar left on an organic substance when part of it is removed.
[1] The ruin is that of the palace of a member of the Cornaro family of Venice, who reigned as queen of Cyprus in the fifteenth century, and then established a court in Asolo.
[2] John Ruskin (1819–1900), whose books on gothic and renaissance architecture literally taught his mid-century contemporaries what to look for and see in the architecture of the continent.
[3] Vernon Lee: the pen name of Violet Paget (1856–1935), who published several studies of Italian and renaissance art in the latter decades of the nineteenth century.
[1] Browning first wrote this poem for the son of a friend, who asked him to provide a text for which he could draw a picture. Browning took the story from Nathaniel Wanley's *Wonders of the Little World* (1678). The Council of Trent, which met in 1551–52 (not 1522), was convened by the hierarchy of the Roman Catholic church to address the doctrinal and political questions raised by the Reformation and the growth of Protestantism. Cardinal Crescenzio was the legate of Pope Julius III at the Council, and was regarded as a foe of Protestants. Browning added the lines 5 and 15 when he revised the poem for publication in 1889 (DeVane, p. 535).

(I give mine Author's very words: he penned,
  I reindite.)

A black Dog of vast bigness, eyes flaming, ears
  that hung
Down to the very ground almost, into the
  chamber sprung
And made directly for him, and laid himself
  right under
The table where Crescenzio wrote—who called
  in fear and wonder
His servants in the ante-room, commanded
  everyone
To look for and find out the beast: but,
  looking, they found none.

The Cardinal fell melancholy, then sick, soon
  after died:
And at Verona, as he lay on his death-bed, he
  cried
Aloud to drive away the Dog that leapt on his
  bed-side.
Heaven keep us Protestants from harm: the
  rest . . . no ill betide!

                                    (1842) 1889

Development

My Father was a scholar and knew Greek.[1]
When I was five years old, I asked him once
"What do you read about?"
                              "The siege of Troy."[2]
"What is a siege and what is Troy?"
                                        Whereat
He piled up chairs and tables for a town,
Set me a-top for Priam, called our cat
—Helen, enticed away from home (he said)
By wicked Paris, who couched somewhere close
Under the footstool, being cowardly,
But whom—since she was worth the pains,
  poor puss—
Towzer and Tray,—our dogs, the Atreidai,—
  sought

By taking Troy to get possession of
—Always when great Achilles ceased to sulk,
 (My pony in the stable) —forth would prance
And put to flight Hector—our page-boy's self.
This taught me who was who and what was
  what:
So far I rightly understood the case
At five years old: a huge delight it proved
And still proves—thanks to that instructor sage
My Father, who knew better than turn straight   20
Learning's full flare on weak-eyed ignorance,
Or, worse yet, leave weak eyes to grow sand-
  blind,
Content with darkness and vacuity.

It happened, two or three years afterward,
That—I and playmates playing at Troy's
  Siege—
My Father came upon our make-believe.
"How would you like to read yourself the tale
Properly told, of which I gave you first
Merely such notion as a boy could bear?
Pope,[3] now, would give you the precise account 30
Of what, some day, by dint of scholarship,
You 'll hear—who knows?—from Homer's very
  mouth.
Learn Greek by all means, read the 'Blind Old
  Man,
Sweetest of Singers'—*tuphlos* which means
  'blind,'
Hedistos which means 'sweetest.' Time enough!
Try, anyhow, to master him some day;
Until when, take what serves for substitute,
Read Pope, by all means!"
                            So I ran through Pope,
Enjoyed the tale—what history so true?
Also attacked my Primer, duly drudged,   40
Grew fitter thus for what was promised next—
The very thing itself, the actual words,
When I could turn—say, Buttmann[4] to
  account.

Time passed, I ripened somewhat: one fine
  day,
"Quite ready for the Iliad, nothing less?

---

[1] Browning's father did know Greek, and he did play a large part in the education of his son.

[2] Siege of Troy: the story of the *Iliad,* in which Helen, the wife of Meneleus (one of the Atreidai, the sons of Atreus), is carried off to Troy by Paris, the son of Priam, king of Troy. Achilles was one of the great heroes of the forces which invested Troy in an attempt to win Helen back and revenge her seduction; at one point in the siege he withdrew from the battle because he was angered by a decision of his commanders', but he emerged to fight and kill Hector, another son of Priam and one of the heroes of the Trojan forces.

[3] The translation of the *Iliad* by Alexander Pope was first published in 1715–20.

[4] Philipp Karl Buttmann (1764–1829) was a German philologist whose Greek grammar was standard, and frequently translated into English.

There 's Heine,[5] where the big books block the
    shelf:
Don't skip a word, thumb well the Lexicon!"

I thumbed well and skipped nowise till I
    learned
Who was who, what was what, from Homer's
    tongue,
50 And there an end of learning. Had you asked
The all-accomplished scholar, twelve years old,
"Who was it wrote the Iliad?"—what a laugh!
"Why, Homer, all the world knows: of his life
Doubtless some facts exist: it 's everywhere:
We have not settled, though, his place of birth:
He begged, for certain, and was blind beside:
Seven cities claimed him—Scio, with best right,
Thinks Byron.[6] What he wrote? Those Hymns
    we have.
Then there 's the 'Battle of the Frogs and
    Mice,'
60 That 's all—unless they dig 'Margites' up
(I 'd like that) nothing more remains to
    know."

Thus did youth spend a comfortable time;
Until—"What 's this the Germans say is fact
That Wolf[7] found out first? It 's unpleasant
    work
Their chop and change, unsettling one's belief:
All the same, while we live, we learn, that 's
    sure."
So, I bent brow o'er *Prolegomena.*
And, after Wolf, a dozen of his like
Proved there was never any Troy at all,
Neither Besiegers nor Besieged,—nay,
70   worse,—
No actual Homer, no authentic text,
No warrant for the fiction I, as fact,
Had treasured in my heart and soul so long—
Ay, mark you! and as fact held still, still hold,
Spite of new knowledge, in my heart of hearts
And soul of souls, fact's essence freed and fixed
From accidental fancy's guardian sheath.
Assuredly thenceforward—thank my stars!—

However it got there, deprive who could—
Wring from the shrine my precious tenantry,
Helen, Ulysses, Hector, and his Spouse,
Achilles and his Friend?—though Wolf—ah,
    Wolf!
Why must he needs come doubting, spoil a
    dream?

But then "No dream 's worth waking"[8]—
    Browning says:
And here 's the reason why I tell thus much.
I, now mature man, you anticipate,
May blame my Father justifiably
For letting me dream out my nonage thus,
And only by such slow and sure degrees
Permitting me to sift the grain from chaff,
Get truth and falsehood known and named as
    such.
Why did he ever let me dream at all,
Not bid me taste the story in its strength?
Suppose my childhood was scarce qualified
To rightly understand mythology,
Silence at least was in his power to keep:
I might have—somehow—correspondingly—
Well, who knows by what method, gained my
    gains,
Been taught, by forthrights not meanderings,
My aim should be to loathe, like Peleus' son,[9]
A lie as Hell's Gate, love my wedded wife,
Like Hector, and so on with all the rest.
Could not I have excogitated this
Without believing such men really were?
That is—he might have put into my hand
The "Ethics"? In translation, if you please,
Exact, no pretty lying that improves,
To suit the modern taste: no more, no less—
The "Ethics":[10] 't is a treatise I find hard
To read aright now that my hair is grey,
And I can manage the original.
At five years old—how ill had fared its leaves!
Now, growing double o'er the Stagirite,
At least I soil no page with bread and milk,
Nor crumple, dogsear and deface—boys' way.
                       1889

---

[5] Heine: Christian Gottlob Heyne (1729–1812), whose text of the poem was standard, and who assumed that the received version of the *Iliad* was composed by a single author.

[6] In "The Bride of Abydos" Byron calls Homer "The blind old man of Scio's rocky isle" (Canto II, line 27).

[7] Freidrich August Wolf (1759–1824), another German philologist and scholar, who first advanced the idea, in his *Prolegomena to Homer* (1795), that Homer's poems were transmitted orally and altered by other bards in the transmission.

[8] This line does not occur in any other of Browning's poems.

[9] Peleus' son: Achilles.

[10] The Ethics: a treatise by Aristotle (384–322 B.C.). Aristotle was born at Stagira.

Epilogue [to *Asolando*]

At the midnight in the silence of the sleep-time,
  When you set your fancies free,
Will they pass to where—by death, fools think,
  imprisoned—
Low he lies who once so loved you, whom you
  loved so,
      —Pity me?

Oh to love so, be so loved, yet so mistaken!
  What had I on earth to do
With the slothful, with the mawkish, the
  unmanly?
Like the aimless, helpless, hopeless, did I drivel
  —Being—who?

One who never turned his back but marched
  breast forward,
  Never doubted clouds would break,
Never dreamed, though right were worsted,
  wrong would triumph,
Held we fall to rise, are baffled to fight better,
    Sleep to wake.

No, at noonday in the bustle of man's work-
  time
  Greet the unseen with a cheer!
Bid him forward, breast and back as either
  should be,
"Strive and thrive!" cry "Speed,—fight on, fare
  ever
      There as here!"   20

          1889

William Barnes
1801–1886

WILLIAM BARNES was born in Dorset in the south of England into a family of small landowners, somewhat reduced in means by the uncertainties of agriculture during and after the Napoleonic wars at the beginning of the nineteenth century. After his early schooling he became a clerk in a law office. He continued a course of self-directed study, learning Latin and Greek mostly on his own, and when he was twenty-three years old he started a school. He married the daughter of a local government official in 1827, and with his wife, who died in 1852, he conducted schools in Dorset for the next thirty-five years. He continued his own study, learning French, German, Italian, Persian (he kept his diaries in Italian and translated poems from both Italian and Persian), Anglo-Saxon, and Welsh. He published pamphlets and essays in local and national magazines on archeology, history, and philology; he was especially interested in the latter study. He learned wood engraving, wrote and performed music, tinkered with the invention of mechanical devices, and wrote on topics in mathematics and engineering. He also studied for ordination in the Church of England. He was ordained a priest when he was forty-eight years old, and in 1850 he received a bachelor of divinity degree from Cambridge under an arrangement by which persons who are admitted to a college and keep their names on its books for ten years are awarded a B.D. upon the payment of certain fees. Barnes served as a curate in the 1850s while he was still keeping a school. He finally received a church appointment which included an income in 1862, the same year in which he received a small government pension. He spent the rest of his life as a country priest in Dorset.

Barnes' first poems, which he published in Dorset in 1820 and 1822, were in standard English. In the 1830s he wrote some poems in a Dorset dialect and published them in local newspapers. To some of these poems, including "The Common A-Took In," he gave the name "eclogue." The combination of dialect and a name associated with Latin poetry on rural topics epitomizes the character of all of

Barnes' poetry. Although he became best known for his dialect poems, all through his life he alternated publications of poems in dialect and standard English. His first two collections of poems published outside Dorset were *Poems of Rural Life in the Dorset Dialect* (1844) and *Poems, Partly of Rural Life (in National English)* (1846). Later he published two more collections of dialect poems, *Hwomely Rhymes* (1859) and a third volume of *Poems of Rural Life* (1862), and another volume of *Poems of Rural Life in Common English* (1868). In the last years of his life Barnes wrote only in standard English. As an adult he did not speak a Dorset dialect. The dialect in which he wrote was not a transcription of the speech he heard in contemporary Dorset, but a somewhat idealized version of the dialect spoken around his birthplace in the vale of Blackmore in the early years of the nineteenth century. For in his philological studies in the 1830s and after Barnes began to work out a theory that English could be a truly national language, common or at least understood in all regions and classes, if it was divested of its Latin and Continental words and made consistent with its Anglo-Saxon origins. The dialect he used in his poetry is, therefore, not a record but a reconstruction, even a kind of literary creation. It is, in the words of Bernard Jones, the most recent editor of Barnes' poetry, "a speech which Barnes thought the Blackmore landfolk would have spoken if their speech had grown by its own laws [presumably as Barnes derived them] from the times of Alfred."

Barnes' ideas about philology, which he put forward extensively in pamphlets, books, and essays in popular and specialized journals, were those of an amateur and have now been superseded. But their effect on his poetry was very great, and the effect of his poetry on a few other poets was limited but clearly acknowledged. Through his attention to what he conceived to be the nature of English, he made a literary language, in dialect and standard English, which seemed to preserve the grain of his medium as it existed outside his poems. That quality of authenticity, as well as his rural Dorset settings and subjects, is what Thomas Hardy responded to in his admiration of Barnes as an artist who worked in and brought out the character of his medium, rather than decorated and disguised it. That is also why Gerard Manley Hopkins, who, like

Barnes, had ideas about the instress or intrinsic character and structures of things, said that Barnes' dialect poems could be translated into standard English without losing their effect, a problematic proposition that Barnes independently tested by writing his own standard English versions of some of his dialect poems.

Unquestionably, Barnes' dialect achieves a singular music and thereby enforces the effect of the particularity of his poems: they do, in line, word, image, and sound, fall solidly, satisfyingly into place. But his use of dialect is a sign rather than the source of Barnes' accomplishment as a poet. He thought that all language comes from speech, not from books, and that its rhythms and sounds were shaped to the breath. Whether he wrote in dialect or standard English he expended a conscious art to give the language of his poems not only native words but also a natural movement, beat, and sound. Barnes used other, equally artful means to these effects. He had a very strong sense of formal, pictorial composition, displayed, for example, in his use of color. Especially in his later poems, he had an equally strong sense of the form of verse paragraphs and stanzas, which he often shaped and fixed with the rhymes of monosyllabic words or through the use of refrains.

For all his art, he had none of the big bardic ambitions of the nineteenth-century poets from whom, in his modest Dorset occupations, he was isolated. "I write pictures which I see in my mind," he said, and the point of writing the pictures was to bring out the beauty, the fitness and harmony, of what he saw, and not to impose, find, or create himself in landscape and dramatic event. Like his dialect, the places and events he fixed in his poems are almost always those of rural Dorset in the early years of the nineteenth century. Memory is very important in his poetry. He wrote, he said, for the same reason he made music, as a "refreshment of mind from care or irksomeness," or, somewhat more grandly, to offer examples of the "unmistaken working of man in accordance with the beautiful in nature." Sometimes, as in "The Child and the Mowers," Barnes does attach a mild message to a poem. Poems like "The Common A-Took In" and "Leädy Day" are more subtly resonant and telling as they sharpen to an edge of social comment in their arrangement of the details of the uncertain lives of farming tenants. But most often, as Barnes makes clear in "The Young Rhymer Snubbed" and "Dock Leaves," the purpose of the poem is to give the pleasure of memory. The poem holds places and people as they were, out of time, in a composition and language intended not to strike something new out of experience but to show why we are moved by some of its contents, why we want to remember the look of "Green" and "Round Things," the events of one Whitsuntide long ago, and the look of Jenny with her new ribbons, caught forever in an image of absolutely satisfying grace as she turns her head to speak before she leaves her home.

EDITIONS

Unless otherwise noted, the texts printed below are those of the collected editions Barnes published in 1868 and 1879. The most recent edition is *The Poems of William Barnes,* edited by Bernard Jones (1962). All of the places named in Barnes' poems are in Dorset. Some of the orthographic devices by which Barnes rendered his version of the Dorset dialect which are too persistent to be individually glossed are: *v* for *f* (*vire* for fire) ; *z* for *s* (*zaid* for said) ; *eä* for *a* (*meäke* for make) ; and the *o* sound in *one* or *boat* rendered as *woone* and *bwoat*. Some common dialect words: *avore* (before), *het* (heat) ; *mead* (meadow), *mid* (might), *drough* (through), and *thik* (this).

Thomas Hardy compiled a selection of Barnes' poems for publication in 1908, and Geoffrey Grigson edited a selection in 1950. A selection of one hundred of Barnes' poems, with a preface by E. M. Forster reprinted from *Two Cheers for Democracy* (1951), was published in 1971.

BIOGRAPHY AND CRITICISM

A life of Barnes was published by his daughter, L. Baxter, in 1887. Giles Dugdale's *Barnes of Dorset* (1953) is the only recent biography. W. T. Levy's *Barnes: The Man and the Poems* (1960) is the only book-length study of his life and work. See also: Trevor W. Hearl, *William Barnes the Schoolmaster* (1966) ; Geoffrey Grigson's two essays on Barnes, in *Harp of Aeolus* (1948) and *Poems and Poets* (1969) ; and John Heath-Stubbs'

The Darkling Plain (1950). Three other useful essays: Philip Larkin, "William Barnes," in *Listener,* 16 August 1962; R. A. Forsyth, "The Conserving Myth of William Barnes," in *Romantic Mythologies,* edited by Ian Fletcher (1967) ; and Paul Zietlow, "Thomas Hardy and William Barnes: Two Dorset Poets," in *Publications of the Modern Language Association,* 84 (1969).

Leädy-Day, an' Ridden House[1]

Aye, back at Leädy-Day, you know,
I come vrom Gullybrook to Stowe;
At Leädy-Day I took my pack
O' rottletraps,[2] an' turn'd my back
Upon the weather-beäten door,
That had a-screen'd, so long avore,
The mwost that theäse zide o' the greäve,
I'd live to have, or die to seäve!
My childern, an' my vier-pleäce,[3]
Where Molly wi' her cheerful feäce,   10
When I'd a-trod my wat'ry road
Vrom night-bedarken'd vields abrode,
Wi' nimble hands, at evenen, blest
Wi' vire an' vood my hard-won rest;
The while the little woones did clim',
So sleek-skinn'd, up from lim' to lim',
Till, strugglen hard an' clingen tight,
They reach'd at last my feäce's height,
All tryen which could soonest hold
My mind wi' little teäles they twold.   20
An' ridden house is such a caddle,[4]
I shan't be over keen vor mwore o't,
Not yet a while, you mid be sure o't,—
I'd rather keep to woone wold staddle.[5]

Well, zoo, avore the east begun
To redden wi' the comen zun,
We left the beds our mossy thatch
Wer never mwore to overstratch,
An' borrow'd uncle's wold hoss *Dragon,*
To bring the slowly lumbren waggon,   30
An' when he come, we vell a-packen
The bedsteads, wi' their rwopes an' zacken;[6]
An' then put up the wold eärm-chair,
An' cwoffer[7] vull ov e'then-ware,
An' vier-dogs,[8] an' copper kittle,

---

[1] Leädy-Day: Lady Day, March 25, which marks one of the quarters of the year and thus is one of the days on which annual leases of houses expire and people move—"ridden house."

[2] Rottletraps: old household goods.   [3] Vier-pleäce: fireplace.

[4] Caddle: confusion.   [5] Staddle: foundation; often used of a hayrick.

[6] Zacken: sacking, bedding.   [7] Cwoffer: box.

[8] Vier-dogs: fire dogs, metal braces to hold logs for burning.

Wi' crocks an saucepans, big an' little;
An' fryen-pan, vor aggs to slide
40 In butter round his hissen zide,
An' gridire's even bars, to bear
The drippen steäke above the gleäre
O' brightly-glowen coals. An' then
All up o' top o' them ageän
The woaken bwoard, where we did eat
Our croust o' bread or bit o' meat,—
An' when the bwoard wer up, we tied
Upon the reäves,⁹ along the zide,
The woaken stools, his glossy meätes,¹⁰
50 Bwoth when he's beäre, or when the pleätes
Do clatter loud wi' knives, below
Our merry feäces in a row.
An' put between his lags, turn'd up'ard,
The zalt-box an' the corner cupb'ard.
An' then we laid the wold clock-ceäse,
All dumb, athirt upon his feäce,
Vor we'd a-left, I needen tell ye,
Noo works 'ithin his head or belly.
An' then we put upon the pack
60 The settle,¹¹ flat upon his back;
An' after that, a-tied in pairs
In woone another, all the chairs,
An' bits o' lumber wo'th a ride,
An' at the very top a-tied,
The childern's little stools did lie,
Wi' lags a-turn'd toward the sky:
Zoo there we lwoaded up our scroff,¹²
An' tied it vast, an' started off.
An',—as the waggon cooden car¹³ all
70 We had to teäke,—the butter-barrel
An' cheese-wring, wi' his twinen screw,
An' all the païls an' veäts, an' blue
Wold milk leads,¹⁴ and a vew things mwore,
Wer all a-carr'd the day avore.
And when the mwost ov our wold stuff
Wer brought outside o' thik brown ruf,
I rambled roun' wi' narrow looks,
In fusty holes an' darksome nooks,
To gather all I still mid vind,
80 O' rags or sticks a-left behind.
An' there the unlatch'd doors did creak,
A-swung by winds, a-streamen weak
Drough empty rooms, an' meäken sad
My heart, where me'th woonce meäde me glad.

Vor when a man do leäve the he'th
An' ruf where vu'st he drew his breath,
Or where he had his bwoyhood's fun,
An' things wer woonce a-zaid an' done
That took his mind, do touch his heart
A little bit, I'll answer vor't.
Zoo ridden house is such a caddle,
That I would rather keep my staddle.
1844

Easter Zunday¹

Last Easter Jim put on his blue
Frock cwoat, the vu'st time—vier² new;
Wi' yellow buttons all o' brass,
That glitter'd in the zun lik' glass;
An' pok'd 'ithin the button-hole
A tutty³ he'd a-begg'd or stole.
A span-new wes'co't, too, he wore,
Wi' yellow stripes all down avore;
An' tied his breeches' lags below
The knee, wi' ribbon in a bow;
An' drow'd his kitty-boots⁴ azide,
An' put his laggens on, an' tied
His shoes wi' strings two vingers wide,
    Because 'twer Easter Zunday.

An' after mornen church wer out
He come back hwome, an' stroll'd about
All down the vields, an' drough the leäne,
Wi' sister Kit an' cousin Jeäne,
A-turnen proudly to their view
His yollow breast an' back o' blue.
The lambs did play, the grounds wer green,
The trees did bud, the zun did sheen;
The lark did zing below the sky,
An' roads wer all a-blown so dry,
As if the zummer wer begun;
An' he had sich a bit o' fun!
He meäde the maïdens squeäl an' run,
    Because 'twer Easter Zunday.
1844

Dock-Leaves¹

The dock-leaves that do spread so wide
Up yonder zunny bank's green zide,
Do bring to mind what we did do

---

⁹ Reäves: wagon frame.   ¹⁰ Meätes: mates (to the oaken board).
¹¹ Settle: a high-backed wooden bench.   ¹² Scroff: odd pieces of lumber.
¹³ Car: carry.   ¹⁴ Milk leads: kettles or pails for milking.
¹ When this poem was first printed in 1844 it was the first part of a four-stanza poem titled "Easter Time": in 1879 he made the other two stanzas into a separate poem titled "Easter Monday."
² Vier: absolutely.   ³ Tutty: nosegay, small bunch of flowers.   ⁴ Kitty-boots: low boots.
¹ Dock-leaves: the leaves of a coarse, weedy plant often used in folk medicine.

At plaÿ wi' dock-leaves years agoo:
How we,—when nettles had a-stung
Our little hands, when we wer young,—
Did rub 'em wi' a dock, an' zing
"Out nettl', in dock. In dock, out sting."
An' when your feäce, in zummer's het,[2]
Did sheen wi' tricklen draps o' zweat,
How you, a-zot bezide the bank,
Didst toss your little head, an' pank,[3]
An' teäke a dock-leaf in your han',
An' whisk en lik' a leädy's fan;
While I did hunt, 'ithin your zight,
Vor streaky cockle-shells to fight.

In all our plaÿ-geämes we did bruise
The dock-leaves wi' our nimble shoes;
Bwoth where we merry chaps did fling
You maïdens in the orcha'd swing,
An' by the zaw-pit's dousty bank,
Where we did taït[4] upon a plank.
—(D'ye mind how woonce, you cou'den zit
The bwoard, an' vell off into pit?)
An' when we hunted you about
The grassy barken,[5] in an' out
Among the ricks, your vlee-en[6] frocks
An' nimble veet did strik' the docks.
An' zoo they docks, a-spread so wide
Up yonder zunny bank's green zide,
Do bring to mind what we did do
Among the dock-leaves years agoo.

1844

Jenny's Ribbons

Jeän ax'd what ribbon she should wear
'Ithin her bonnet to the feäir?
She had woone white, a-gi'ed her when
She stood at Meäry's chrissenen;
She had woone brown, she had woone red,
A keepseäke vrom her brother dead,
That she did like to wear, to goo
To zee his greäve below the yew.

She had woone green among her stock,
That I'd a-bought to match her frock;
She had woone blue to match her eyes,
The colour o' the zummer skies,
An' thik, though I do like the rest,

Is he that I do like the best,
Because she had en[1] in her heäir
When vu'st I walk'd wi' her at feäir.

The brown, I zaid, would do to deck
Thy heäir; the white would match thy neck;
The red would meäke thy red cheäk wan
A-thinken o' the gi'er gone;   20
The green would show thee to be true;
But still I'd sooner zee the blue,
Because 'twer he that deck'd thy heäir
When vu'st I walked wi' thee at feäir.

Zoo, when she had en on, I took
Her han' 'ithin my elbow's crook,
An' off we went athirt the weir[2]
An' up the meäd toward the feäir;
The while her mother, at the geäte,
Call'd out an' bid her not staÿ leäte,
An' she, a-smilen wi' her bow   30
O' blue, look'd roun' an' nodded, *No.*

1844

Whitsuntide an' Club Walken[1]

Ees, last Whit-Monday, I an' Meäry
Got up betimes to mind the deäiry;
An' gi'ed the milken païls a scrub,
An' dress'd, an' went to zee the club.
Vor up at public-house, by ten
O'clock the pleäce wer vull o' men,
A-dress'd to goo to church, an' dine,
An' walk about the pleäce in line.
Zoo off they started, two an' two,
Wi' païnted poles an' knots o' blue,   10
An' girt silk flags,—I wish my box[2]
'D a-got em all in ceäpes an' frocks,—
A-weäven wide an' flappen loud
In plaÿsome winds above the crowd;
While fifes did squeak an' drums did rumble,
An' deep beäzzoons did grunt an' grumble,
An' all the vo'k in gath'ren crowds
Kick'd up the doust in smeechy[3] clouds,
That slowly rose an' spread abrode
In streamen aïr above the road.   20
An' then at church there wer sich lots
O' hats a-hangen up wi' knots,
An' poles a-stood so thick as iver ,

2 Het: heat.   3 Pank: pant.   4 Taït: play seesaw.   5 Barken: cow yard.
6 Vlee-en: flying.   1 En: him.
2 Athirt the weir: athwart the small dam or lock.
1 Whitsuntide: the seventh Sunday after Easter. The clubs were societies formed to provide sickness or burial benefits for their members; the "club-walkens" were annual meetings.
2 Girt: great. Box: for storing clothing.   3 Smeechy: thick, smoky.

The rushes stood bezide a river.
An' Mr. Goodman gi'ed em warnen
To spend their evenen lik' their mornen;
An' not to praÿ wi' mornen tongues,
An' then to zwear wi' evenen lungs;
Nor vu'st sheäke hands, to let the wrist
30   Lift up at last a bruisen vist:
Vor clubs were all a-meän'd vor friends,
He twold em, an' vor better ends
Than twiten vo'k an' picken quarrels,
An' tipplen cups an' empten barrels,—
Vor meäken woone man do another
In need the kindness ov a brother.

An' after church they went to dine
'Ithin the long-wall'd room behine
The public-house, where you remember,
40   We had our dance back last December.
An' there they meäde sich stunnen clatters
Wi' knives an' forks, an' pleätes an' platters;
An' waïters ran, an' beer did pass
Vrom tap to jug, vrom jug to glass:
An' when they took away the dishes,
They drink'd good healths, an' wish'd good
        wishes,
To all the girt vo'k o' the land,
An' all good things vo'k took in hand;
An' woone cried *hip, hip, hip!* an' hollow'd,⁴
50   An' tothers all struck in, an' vollow'd;
An' grabb'd their drink wi' eager clutches,
An' swigg'd it wi' sich hearty glutches,
As vo'k, stark mad wi' pweison stuff,
That thought theirzelves not mad enough.

An' after that they went all out
In rank ageän, an' walk'd about,
An' gi'ed zome parish vo'k a call;
An' then went down to Narley Hall
An' had zome beer, an' danc'd between
60   The elem trees upon the green.
An' down along the road they done
All sorts o' mad-cap things vor fun;
An' danc'd, a-poken out their poles,
An' pushen bwoys down into holes:
An' Sammy Stubbs come out o' rank,
An' kiss'd me up ageän the bank,
A saucy chap; I ha'nt vorgi'ed en⁵
Not yet,—in short, I han't a-zeed en.

Zoo in the dusk ov evenen, zome
Went back to drink, an' zome went hwome.

                                                    1844

Lullaby

The rook's¹ nest do rock on the tree-top
Where vew foes can stand;
The martin's is high, an' is deep
In the steep cliff o' zand.
But thou, love, a-sleepen where vootsteps
Mid² come to thy bed,
Hast father an' mother to watch thee
An' shelter thy head.
        Lullaby, Lilibrow. Lie asleep;
        Blest be thy rest.   1

An' zome birds do keep under ruffen³
Their young vrom the storm,
An' zome wi' nest-hoodens o' moss
An' o' wool, do lie warm.
An' we wull look well to the houseruf
That o'er thee mid leäk,
An' the blast that mid beät on thy windee
Shall not smite thy cheäk.
        Lullaby, Lilibrow. Lie asleep;
        Blest be thy rest.   2
                                                    1844

Eclogue: The Common A-Took In¹

Thomas an' John

THOMAS
Good morn t'ye, John. How b'ye? how b'ye?
Zoo you be gwaïn to market, I do zee.
Why, you be quite a-lwoaded wi' your geese.

JOHN
Ees, Thomas, ees.
Why, I'm a-getten rid ov ev'ry goose
An' goslen I've a-got: an' what is woose,
I fear that I must zell my little cow.

THOMAS
How zoo, then, John? Why, what's the matter
        now?

---

⁴ Hollow'd: holloaed.   ⁵ En: him.   ¹ Rook: crow.   ² Mid: might   ³ Ruffen: roofing.
¹ The common was land around a village or town open to the inhabitants for grazing and the
cultivation of small plots. During the eighteenth century laws were passed enclosing commons—
that is, assigning ownership to the land and prohibiting its traditional open use. The passage of
a General Enclosure Act in 1801 accelerated the process of closing the commons, and by 1845
four million acres of land had been enclosed.

What, can't ye get along? B'ye run a-ground?
An' can't paÿ twenty shillens vor a pound?[2]
What, can't ye put a lwoaf on shelf?

JOHN

                Ees, now;
But I do fear I shan't 'ithout my cow.
No; they do meän to teäke the moor in, I do
    hear,
An' 'twill be soon begun upon;
Zoo I must zell my bit o' stock to-year,
Because they woon't have any groun' to run
    upon.

THOMAS

Why, what d'ye tell o'? I be very zorry
To hear what they be gwaïn about;
But yet I s'pose there'll be a 'lotment[3] vor ye,
When they do come to mark it out.

JOHN

No; not vor me, I fear. An' if there should,
Why 'twoulden be so handy as 'tis now;
Vor 'tis the common that do do me good,
The run vor my vew geese, or vor my cow.

THOMAS

Ees, that's the job; why 'tis a handy thing
To have a bit o' common, I do know,
To put a little cow upon in Spring,
The while woone's bit ov orcha'd grass[4] do
    grow.

JOHN

Aye, that's the thing, you zee. Now I do mow
My bit o' grass, an' meäke a little rick;
An' in the zummer, while do grow,
My cow do run in common vor to pick
A bleäde or two o' grass, if she can vind em,
Vor tother cattle don't leäve much behind em.
Zoo in the evenen, we do put a lock[5]
O' nice fresh grass avore the wicket;[6]
An' she do come at vive or zix o'clock,
As constant as the zun, to pick it.
An' then, bezides the cow, why we do let
Our geese run out among the emmet[7] hills;
An' then when we do pluck em, we do get
Vor zeäle[8] zome veathers an' zome quills;
An' in the winter we do fat em well,

An' car[9] em to the market vor to zell
To gentlevo'ks, vor we don't oft avvword
To put a goose a-top ov ouer bwoard;
But we do get our feäst,—vor we be eäble
To clap the giblets up a-top o' teäble.

THOMAS

An' I don't know o' many better things,
Than geese's heads and gizzards, lags an' wings.   50

JOHN

An' then, when I ha' nothen else to do,
Why I can teäke my hook[10] an' gloves, an' goo
To cut a lot o' vuzz[11] and briars
Vor heten ovens, or vor lighten viers.[12]
An' when the children be too young to eärn
A penny, they can g'out in zunny weather,
An' run about, an' get together
A bag o' cow-dung vor to burn.

THOMAS

'Tis handy to live near a common;
But I've a-zeed, an' I've a-zaid,   60
That if a poor man got a bit o' bread,
They'll try to teäke it vrom en.[13]
But I wer twold back tother day,
That they be got into a way
O' letten bits o' groun' out to the poor.

JOHN

Well, I do hope 'tis true, I'm sure;
An' I do hope that they will do it here,
Or I must goo to workhouse,[14] I do fear.
                    1834; 1844

A Witch

There's thik wold hag, Moll Brown, look zee,
    jus' past!
I wish the ugly sly wold witch
Would tumble over into ditch;
I woulden pull her out not very vast.
No, no. I don't think she's a bit belied,[1]
No, she's a witch; aye, Molly's evil-eyed.
Vor I do know o' many a withren blight
A-cast on vo'k by Molly's mutter'd spite;
She did, woone time, a dreadvul deäl o' harm
To Farmer Gruff's vo'k, down at Lower Farm.   10

---

[2] Twenty shillens: In English currency until recently, there were twenty shillings in a pound.
[3] 'Lotment: a piece of land allotted for the particular use of one person.
[4] Orcha'd grass: grass in an orchard.   [5] Lock: armful.
[6] Avore the wicket: before the gate.   [7] Emmet: ant.   [8] Zeäle: sale.   [9] Car: carry.
[10] Hook: sickle.   [11] Vuzz: furze, an evergreen shrub.   [12] Viers: fires.   [13] En: him.
[14] Workhouse: county or parish home for the indigent.   [1] Belied: lied about.

Vor there, woone day, they happened to offend
  her,
An' not a little to their sorrow,
Because they woulden gi'e or lend her
Zome'hat she come to bag or borrow;
An' zoo, they soon began to vind
That she'd a-gone an' left behind
Her evil wish, that had such pow'r
That she did meäke their milk an' eäle turn
  zour,
An' addle all the aggs their vowls did lay;
20 They coulden vetch[2] the butter in the churn,
An' all the cheese begun to turn
All back ageän to curds an' whey;
The little pigs, a-runnen wi' the zow,
Did zicken, zomehow, noobody know'd how,
An' vall, an' turn their snouts toward the sky,
An' only gi'e woone little grunt, an' die;
An' all the little ducks an' chicken
Wer death-struck out in yard a-picken
Their bits o' food, an' vell upon their head,
An' flapp'd their little wings an' drapp'd down
30 dead.
They coulden fat the calves, they woulden
  thrive;
They coulden seäve their lambs alive;
Their sheep wer all a-coath'd,[3] or gi'ed noo
  wool;
The hosses vell away to skin an' bwones,
An' got so weak they coulden pull
A half a peck o' stwones:
The dog got dead-alive an' drowsy,
The cat vell zick an' woulden mousy;
An' every time the vo'k went up to bed,
40 They wer a-hag-rod[4] till they wer half dead.
They us'd to keep her out o' house, 'tis true,
A-naïlen up at door a hosses shoe;
An' I've a-heärd the farmer's wife did try
To dawk[5] a needle or a pin
In drough her wold hard wither'd skin,
An' draw her blood, a-comen by:
But she could never vetch a drap,
For pins would ply an' needles snap
Ageän her skin; an' that, in coo'se,
50 Did meäke the hag bewitch em woo'se.

                                                1844

Slow to Come, Quick A-Gone

Ah! there's a house that I do know
Besouth o' yonder trees,

Where northern winds can hardly blow
But in a softest breeze.
An' there woonce sounded zongs an' teäles
Vrom vaïce o' maïd or youth,
An' sweeter than the nightengeäle's
Above the copses lewth.[1]

How swiftly there did run the brooks,
How swift wer winds in flight,
How swiftly to their roost the rooks[2]
Did vlee o'er head at night.
Though slow did seem to us the peäce
O' comen days a-head,
That now do seem as in a reäce
Wi' aïr-birds to ha' vled.

                                                1859

The Bean Vield

'Twer where the zun did warm the lewth,[1]
An' win' did whiver[2] in the sheäde,
The sweet-aïr'd beäns were out in blooth,[3]
Down there 'ithin the elem gleäde;
A yellow-banded bee did come,
An' softly pitch, wi' hushen hum,
Upon a beän, an' there did sip,
Upon a swaÿen blossom's lip:
An' there cried he, "Aye, I can zee,
This blossom's all a-zent vor me."

A-jilted up an' down, astride
Upon a lofty ho'se a-trot,
The meäster then come by wi' pride,
To zee the beäns that he'd a-got;
An' as he zot upon his ho'se,
The ho'se ageän did snort an' toss
His high-ear'd head, an' at the zight
Ov all the blossom, black an' white:
"Ah! ah!" thought he, the seäme's the bee,
"Theäse beäns be all a-zent vor me."

Zoo let the woorld's riches breed
A strife o' claïms, wi' weak an' strong,
Vor now what cause have I to heed
Who's in the right, or in the wrong;
Since there do come drough yonder hatch,[4]
An' bloom below the house's thatch,
The best o' maïdens, an' do own
That she is mine, an' mine alwone:
Zoo I can zee that love do gi'e
The best ov all good gifts to me.

---

[2] Vetch: fetch, make.   [3] A-coath'd: diseased from a worm in the stomach.
[4] Hag-rod: hag-ridden, bothered by evil spirits.   [5] Dawk: push.
[1] Copses lewth: shelter of a grove of trees.   [2] Rooks: crows.   [1] Lewth: shelter.
[2] Whiver: quiver.   [3] Blooth: a mass of blossom.   [4] Hatch: half door.

Vor whose be all the crops an' land
A-won an' lost, an' bought, an' zwold;
Or whose, a-roll'd vrom hand to hand,
The highest money that's a-twold?
Vrom man to man a-passen on,
'Tis here to-day, to-morrow gone.
But there's a blessen high above
It all—a soul o' stedvast love:
Zoo let it vlee, if God do gi'e
Sweet Jessie vor a gift to me.

                                        1859

The Bwoat

Where cows did slowly seek the brink
O' *Stour*,[1] drough zunburnt grass, to drink;
Wi' vishen float,[2] that there did zink
    An' rise, I zot as in a dream.
The dazzlen zun did cast his light
On hedge-row blossom, snowy white,
Though nothen yet did come in zight,
    A-stirren on the straÿen stream;

Till, out by sheädy rocks there show'd,
A bwoat along his foamy road,
Wi' thik feäir maïd at mill, a-row'd
    Wi' Jeäne behind her brother's oars.
An' steätely as a queen o' vo'k,
She zot wi' floaten scarlet cloak,
An' comen on, at ev'ry stroke,
    Between my withy-sheäded[3] shores.

The broken stream did idly try
To show her sheäpe a-riden by,
The rushes brown-bloom'd stems did ply,
    As if they bow'd to her by will.
The rings o' water, wi' a sock,
Did break upon the mossy rock,
An' gi'e my beätèn heart a shock,
    Above my float's up-leäpen quill.

Then, lik' a cloud below the skies,
A-drifted off, wi' less'nen size,
An' lost, she floated vrom my eyes,
    Where down below the stream did wind;
An' left the quiet weäves woonce mwore
To zink to rest, a sky-blue'd vloor,

Wi' all so still's the clote[4] they bore,
    Aye, all but my own ruffled mind.

                                        1859

Dobbin Dead

Thomas an' John A-Ta'ken O't

JOHN
I do veel vor ye, Thomas, vor I be afeär'd
You've a-lost your wold meäre then, by what
    I've a-heärd.

THOMAS
Ees, my meäre is a-gone, an' the cart's in the
    shed
Wi' his wheelbonds[1] a-rusten, an' I'm out o'
    bread;
Vor what be my han's vor to eärn me a croust,
Wi' noo meäre's vower[2] lags vor to trample the
    doust.

JOHN
Well, how did it happen? He vell vrom the
    brim
Ov a cliff, as the teäle is, an' broke ev'ry lim'.

THOMAS
Why, I gi'ed en his run, an' he shook his wold
    meäne,
An' he rambled a-veeden in Westergap Leäne;   10
An' there he must needs goo a-riggen, an'
    crope[3]
Vor a vew bleädes o' grass up the wost o' the
    slope;
Though I should ha' thought his wold head
    would ha' know'd
That vor stiff lags, lik' his, the best pleäce wer
    the road.

JOHN
An' you hadden a-kept en[4] so short he must
    clim',
Lik' a gwoat, vor a bleäde, at the risk ov a lim'.

THOMAS
Noo, but there, I'm a-twold, he did clim' an'
    did slide,
An' did screäpe, an' did slip, on the shelven[5]
    bank-zide,

---

[1] Stour: a river in Dorset.   [2] Vishen float: float on a fishing line.   [3] Withy: willow.
[4] Clote: yellow water lily.   [1] Wheelbonds: iron rims or tires.   [2] Vower: four.
[3] A-riggen: climbing. Crope: crept.   [4] En: him. Short: ill-fed.   [5] Shelven: sloping.

An' at langth lost his vooten, an' roll'd vrom
   the top,
Down, thump, kick, an' higgledly, piggledly,
20   flop.

JOHN

Dear me, that is bad! I do veel vor your loss,
Vor a vew years agoo, Thomas, I lost my ho'se.

THOMAS

How wer't? If I heärd it, I now ha' vorgot;
Wer the poor thing bewitch'd or a-pweison'd,
   or what?

JOHN

He wer out, an' a-meäken his way to the brink
O' the stream at the end o' Church Leäne, vor
   to drink;
An' he met wi' zome yew-twigs the men had
   a-cast
Vrom the yew-tree, in churchyard, the road that
   he past.
He wer pweison'd.

THOMAS

                O dear, 'tis a hard loss to bear,
Vor a tranter's[6] whole bread is a-lost wi' his
30   meäre;
But ov all churches' yew-trees, I never zet eyes
On a tree that would come up to thik woone
   vor size.

JOHN

Noo, 'tis long years agone, but do linger as
   clear
In my mind though as if I'd a-heärd it to year.
When King George wer in Do'set,[7] an show'd
   us his feäce
By our very own doors, at our very own pleäce,
That he look'd at thik yew-tree, an' nodded his
   head,
An' he zaid,—an' I'll tell ye the words that he
   zaid:—
"I'll be bound, if you'll sarch my dominions
   all drough,
That you woon't vind the fellow to thik there
40   wold yew."
                                        1859

The Child an' the Mowers

O, aye! they had woone child bezide,
   An' a finer your eyes never met,
'Twer a dear little fellow that died
   In the zummer that come wi' such het;[1]
By the mowers, too thoughtless in fun,
   He wer then a-zent off vrom our eyes,
Vrom the light ov the dew-dryen zun,—
   Aye! vrom days under blue-hollow'd skies.

He went out to the mowers in meäd,[2]
   When the zun wer a-rose to his height,   1
An' the men wer a-swingen the sneäd,[3]
   Wi' their eärms in white sleeves, left an'
      right;
An' out there, as they rested at noon,
   O! they drench'd en vrom eäle-horns too
      deep,
Till his thoughts wer a-drown'd in a swoon;
   Aye! his life wer a-smother'd in sleep.

Then they laid en[4] there-right on the ground,
   On a grass-heap, a-zweltren wi' het,
Wi' his heäir all a-wetted around
   His young feäce, wi' the big drops o' zweat;   2
In his little left palm he'd a-zet,
   Wi' his right hand, his vore-vinger's tip,
As vor zome'hat he woulden vorget,—
   Aye! zome thought that he woulden let
      slip.

Then they took en in hwome to his bed,
   An' he rose vrom his pillow noo mwore,
Vor the curls on his sleek little head
   To be blown by the wind out o' door.
Vor he died while the haÿ russled grey
   On the staddle[5] so leätely begun;   3
Lik' the mown-grass a-dried by the day,—
   Aye! the zwath-flow'r's a-killed by the zun.
                                        1862

Tokens

Green mwold on zummer bars[1] do show
   That they've a-dripp'd in Winter wet;
The hoof-worn ring o' groun' below
   The tree, do tell o' storms or het;[2]

---

[6] Tranter: teamster, carter.
[7] King George: George III (1738–1820) was king of England from 1760 until his death; he visited Dorset in the early years of the nineteenth century during the Napoleonic wars.
[1] Het: heat.   [2] Meäd: meadow.   [3] Sneäd: stem of a scythe.   [4] En: him.
[5] Staddle: base of a hayrick.   [1] Bars: branches.
[2] Het: heat, which causes animals to seek shade.

The trees in rank along a ledge
Do show where woonce did bloom a hedge;
An' where the vurrow-marks do stripe
The down, the wheat woonce rustled ripe.
Each mark ov things a-gone vrom view—
To eyezight's woone, to soulzight two.

The grass ageän the mwoldren door
   'S a token sad o' vo'k a-gone,
An' where the house, bwoth wall an' vloor,
   'S a-lost, the well mid[3] linger on.
What tokens, then, could Meäry gi'e
That she'd a-liv'd, an' liv'd vor me,
But things a-done vor thought an' view?
Good things that nwone ageän can do,
An' every work her love ha' wrought,
To eyezight's woone, but two to thought.

1862

Zummer Thoughts in Winter Time

Well, aye, last evenen, as I shook
My locks[1] ov haÿ by Leecombe brook,
The yollow zun did weakly glance
Upon the winter meäd[2] askance,
A-casten out my narrow sheäde
Athirt[3] the brook, an' on the meäd,
The while ageän my lwonesome ears
Did russle weatherbeäten spears,
Below the withy's[4] leafless head
That overhung the river's bed;
I there did think o' days that dried
The new-mow'd grass o' zummer-tide,
When white-sleev'd mowers' whetted bleädes
Rung sh'ill along the green-bough'd gleädes,
An' maïdens gaÿ, wi' plaÿsome chaps,
A-zot wi' dinners in their laps,
Did talk wi' merry words that rung
Around the ring, vrom tongue to tongue;
An' welcome, when the leaves ha' died,
Be zummer thoughts in winter-tide.

1862

Air an' Light[1]

Ah! look an' zee how widely free
To all the land the win' do goo;

If here a tree do swaÿ, a tree
On yon'er hill's a-swaÿen too.
How wide the light do bring to zight
The pleäce an' liven feäce o' man;
How vur the stream do run vor lip
To drink, or hand to sink and dip!

But oone mid be a-smote wi' woe
That midden pass, in wider flight,   10
To other souls, a-droopen low,
Ah' hush'd like birds at vall o' night.
But zome be sad wi' others glad;
In turn we all mid murn our lot,
An' many a day that have a-broke
Oone heart is jaÿ to other vo'k.

The mornen zun do cast abroad
His light on drops o' dewy wet,
An' down below his noontide road
The streams do gleäre below his het;[2]   20
His evenen light do sparkle bright
Across the quiv'ren gossamer;
But I, though fair he still mid glow,
Do miss a zight he cannot show.

(1864)

Round Things

A fairy ring as round's the sun
On our green meadow bends its rim,
Out where we saw the wavelings run
Across the pond with rounded brim.
And there by round-built ricks of hay,
By sun-heat burnt, by sunshine brown'd,
We met in merry ring to play,
All springing on, and wheeling round.

And there, as stones we chanc'd to fling
Swept out in flight a lofty bow,   10
And fell on water, ring by ring
Of waves bespread the pool below,
Beside the bridge's arch, that springs
Between the banks, within the brims,
Where swung the lowly-bending swings,
On elm-tree boughs, on mossy limbs.

1868

---

[3] Mid: might.   [1] Locks: armfuls.   [2] Meäd: meadow.   [3] Athirt: athwart.
[4] Withy: willow.
[1] Text from Jones' edition. Barnes published a version of this poem in standard English in 1868.
[2] Het: heat.

Rings[1]

A veäiry ring so round's the zun
    In summer leäze[2] did show his rim,
An' near, at hand, the weäves did run
    Athirt the pond wi' rounded brim:
An' there by round built ricks ov haÿ,
    By het[3] a-burn'd, by zuns a-brown'd,
We all in merry ring did plaÿ,
    A-springen on, a-wheelen round.

As there a stwone that we did fling
    Did zweep, in flight, a lofty bow,
An' vell in water, ring by ring
    O' weäves bespread the pool below,
Bezide the bridge's arch, that sprung
    Between the banks, within the brims,
Where swung the lowly benden swing,
    On elem boughs, on mossy limbs.
                (After 1868?)

Black an' White[1]

By the wall o' the geärden, a-stannen chalk
    white
In the light o' the moon, back in Maÿ,
There wer you all in black at my zide, a-come
    round
On the ground where the cypress did swaÿ:
Oh! the white an' the black! Which wer
    feäirest to view?
Why the black, a-meäde feäirest on you.

By the water, a-vallèn in many a bow
White as snow, down the rock's peaky steep,[2]
There your own petted cow wer a-showen her
    back
O' deep black, a-laid down vor her sleep:
Ah! the white an' the black! Which wer feäirest
    to view?
Why the black, a-meäde feäirest on you.

When you stroll'd down the village, a-walken
    bedight[3]
All in white, at the leäte evenen tide,
The while *Towsy*, your own loven dog, wi' his
    back
Sleeky black, did walk on at your zide:

Ah! the black an' the white! Which wer feäirest
    to view?
Why the white, a-meäde feäirest on you.

At the end o' the barken[4] the granary stood,
    O' black wood, wi' white geese at his zide,
An' the white-winged swans, on the quick-
    runnen weäve,
By the cave o' black darkness did glide:
Ah! the black an' the white! Which wer feäirest
    to view?
Why the white, a-meäde feäirest on you.
                (After 1868?)

Shellbrook [National English]

When out at Shellbrook, round by stile and
    tree,
With longer days and sunny hours come on,
With spring and all its sunny showers come on,
With May and all its shining flowers come on,
How merry young with young folk met in glee.

And there how we in merry talk went by
The foam below the river bay, all white,
And blossom on the green-leav'd may[1], all white,
And chalk beside the dusty way, all white,
Where glitt'ring water match'd with blue the
    sky.

Or else in winding paths and lanes, along
The wooded hillocks, sloping steep, we roam'd,
Or down the dells and dingles[2] deep we roam'd,
Or by the bending brook's wide sweep we
    roam'd,
On holidays, with merry laugh or song.

But now, the frozen churchyard wallings keep
The patch of tower-shaded ground all white,
Where friends can find the frosted mound, all
    white
With turfy sides upswelling round, all white,
With young offsunder'd from the young in
    sleep.
                1868

Shellbrook [Dorset][1]

Then out at Shellbrook, roun' by stile an' tree,
Wi' longer days an' zunny hours a-come,

---

[1] Text from Jones.   [2] Leäze: unmown field.   [3] Het: heat.
[1] Text from Jones. Barnes published a version of this poem in standard English in 1868.
[2] Steep: nearly sheer side.   [3] Bedight: dressed.   [4] Barken: cow yard.
[1] May: hawthorne.   [2] Dells and dingles: small hollows and ravines.
[1] Text from Jones.

Wi' spring an' all the zunny show'rs a-come,
Wi' Maÿ an' all its sheenen flow'rs a-come,
How sweet vor young wi' young to meet in glee.

An' there how we in merry talk did goo
By foam below the river baÿ, all white,
By blossom on the green-leaved Maÿ, all white,
By chalk bezide the dousty waÿ, all white,
Where glitt'ren waters match'd the sky wi' blue.

Or else in winden paths by vield or drong,[2]
We over knaps[3] a-slopen steep did wind,
Or down the dells a-zinken deep did wind,
Or where the benden brook did zweep did
  wind,
All young wi' young in merry laugh or zong.

But now the winter-vrozen churchyard wall do
  keep
The plot o' tower-sheäded ground all white,
Where friends can vind the vrosted mound, all
  white,
Wi' turf a-zwellen up so round, all white,
Wi' young a-sunder'd vrom the young in sleep.
                              (After 1868?)

Green[1]

Our zummer way to church did wind about
The cliff, where ivy on the ledge wer green.

Our zummer way to town did skirt the wood,
Where sheenen leaves in tree an' hedge wer
  green.

Our zummer way to milken in the meäd,
Wer on by brook, where fluttren zedge wer
  green.

Our hwomeward ways did all run into one,
Where moss upon the roofstwones' edge wer
  green.
                              (After 1868?)

Lowshot Light[1]

As I went eastward, while the zun did zet,
His yollow light on bough by bough did sheen.

An' there, among the gil'cups by the knap,[2]
Below the elems, cow by cow did sheen.

While after heäiry-headed horses' heels,
Wi' slowly-rollen wheels, the plough did sheen.

An' up among the vo'k upon the reäves,[3]
One lovely feäce, wi' zunny brow, did sheen.

An' bright, vor that one feäce, the bough, an'
  cow,
An' plough, in my sweet fancy, now do sheen.   10
                              (After 1868?)

The Zun A-Lighten Eyes A-Shut[1]

I zot awhile, wi' eyelids down,
Below a clouded sky; an' blind
To rick an' roof a-turnen brown,
Injaÿ'd a feäirer zight in mind.
But when ageän the zunsheen glow'd
Through meeten[2] lids, to eyes all blind
To land a-lyen round, he show'd
A brighter landsceäpe to my mind.

An' when my youthvul mind vorzook
The day's hard truth, vor zome feäir zight,   10
O' leäter years, 'twer your sweet look
Did touch my fancy's dream wi' light.
My comen days by your gaÿ feäce
Did seem so feäir as you wer feäir;
Wi' you, my fancy's ev'ry pleäce
Wer ever gaÿ, vor you wer there.
                              (After 1868?)

Come an' Meet Me wi' the Childern on the Road[1]

Well, to-day Jeäne is my set time vor to goo
To the grist-mill out at Sherbrook under Bere,
Wi' my spring-cart out in cart-house, vier new,
An' zome grist corn, to come hwomeward wi'
  en leer.[2]
Zoo's the whole day will be dry,
By the readship o' the sky,
Come to meet me, wi' the childern, on the road.

---

[2] Drong: a narrow path.   [3] Knaps: small hills.
[1] Text from Jones.   [1] Text from Jones.
[3] Reäves: ladderlike framework of a wagon.
[1] Text from Jones.   [2] En leer: him empty.

[2] Gil'cups: buttercups. Knap: small hill.
[1] Text from Jones.   [2] Meeten: closed.

Vor the zunsheen vrom the blue sky's hollow
    height
Is a-sparklen on the stream-weäve an' the
    zedge,[3]
10 An' the orchard is a broadsheet o' the white
O' new tree-blooth[4] over blossom in the hedge:
Zoo when clock-bells do ring vour,
Let em warn ye out o' door,
Come an' meet me, wi' the childern, on the
    road.

You can saunter, if I'm leätish by the clock,
To some greygles[5] vor the childern on the
    ridge,
Or can loiter in the tree-lewth,[6] on the rock
Where the stream-foam is a-shot down by the
    bridge;
The while Joe's line an' his hook
20 Mid[7] catch minnows in the brook,
Out to meet me, wi' his sister, on the road.

If you'll dawdle a vew vurlongs on ahead,
You'll be welcome at the Welldon's, on the
    knap,[8]
Where the cowslips be so clwose grown in a
    bed
That our Poll's hands will ha' soon vill'd up
    her lap,
Vor a tosty[9] up so big
As her small head's curly wig,
Out to meet me, wi' her brother, on the road.

At the time, then, I've a-twold ye, you mid hear
30 My two wheel rims come a-spinnen on the road,
An' the spring cart wi' the seat up shall be leer
To teäke you, Jeäne, an' the childern vor his
    lwoad.
Zoo come out, then, to the zun
Wi' the youngsters vor a run,
Come an' meet me, wi' the childern, on the
    road.

                  (After 1868?)

The Young Rhymer Snubbed[1]

To meäke up rhymes, my mind wer zoo a-vire
    'Twer idle work to try to keep me quiet,
O' meäken rhymes my heart did never tire;
    Though I should never be a gaïner by it.

"You meäke up rhyme!" vo'k zaid, "why who
    would buy it?
    Could you write fine enough to please a
      squire?
    An' rhyme's what plaïn vo'k woudden
      much require;
You'd vind your rhymes would eärn but scanty
    diet,
An' if I'd any cure vor it, I'm sure I'd try it."

An' father too, in learnen noo great crammer,
    Zaid rhymen wer a treäde but vew got fat
      in;
That men wi' neämes a-ringen wi' a clamour
    Did live in holes not fit to put a cat in,
An' sleep on locks o' straw, or bits o' matten;[2]
    An' mother zaid she'd sooner hear me
      stammer
Than gauk about a-gabblen rhymes an' Latin.
I'd better crack my noddle wi' her patten,[3]
She used to zay, or crack en wi' a hammer,
Than vill en up wi' rhymes, an' silly stuff o'
    grammar.

My father didden rhymy. He knew better.
    Bezides his business, an' to buy an' zell,
He only learnt to write a friend a letter,
    That always went a-hopen he wer well;
Or in a ledger, or a bill, to tell
    Vor what an' when a man became his
      debtor;
    An' mother too, I never shall vorget her,
Wer only just a-taught to read an' spell,
An' mark a teäble-cloth or napkin pretty well.

An' zoo I vound my friends think all the seäme
    o't,
    That rhyme won't vill the pocket over
      tight,
But then my heart did kindle wi' the fleäme o't,
    Whenever I did zee a touchen zight,
An' I did all but lose my wits there-right.
    'Tis likely I shall meäke a losen geäme o't,
    But still, ageän, to lighten off the bleäme
      o't,
Vor all do keep me poor, it still will bring
My heart a pleasure that do leäve noo sting.
                        1869

---

[3] Zedge: sedge, a tufted plant that grows near water.   [4] Blooth: mass of blossom.
[5] Greygles: wild hyacinth.   [6] Lewth: shelter.   [7] Mid: might.   [8] Knap: small hill.
[9] Tosty: a ball of cowslip blossoms.
[1] This poem was first printed in 1869, in the second edition of Barnes' third collection of poems
in the Dorset dialect. He dropped the poem from the one-volume collection he published in
1879.
[2] Matten: matting.   [3] Patten: clog or thick-soled shoe.

Emily Brontë
1818–1848

EMILY BRONTË lived almost all her life in her father's parsonage in the north of England. Her mother died in 1822, two years after the family moved to Haworth. Her father was a clergyman in the Church of England, educated at Cambridge, possessed of an adequate library and a conventional literary taste, without much money and anxious for the future of his children. Except for two short stays in schools in 1824–25 (when two of her sisters died within six weeks of each other) and again in 1835, Emily Brontë was educated at home, in part by her father and later by drawing and music masters who were to prepare her and her surviving sisters Charlotte and Anne for the occupation of governess. Emily went out to teach only once, for six months in 1836–37. In 1842 she went with Charlotte to Brussels, where they studied as prelude to a plan to open a school of their own. The plan failed, and while her sisters worked as governesses, Emily remained at Haworth. After 1844 she was joined by her sisters, who helped her to care for their father as his eyesight failed and for their elder brother Branwell, who returned to Haworth in 1845 to complete the ruin of his artistic and literary ambitions in addictions to alcohol and opium. Branwell died in 1848. Emily Brontë died three months later of an inflammation of the lungs which began when she caught a cold at his funeral.

In their childhood Charlotte and Branwell Brontë had begun a long narrative of the political and military adventures of the inhabitants of imaginary countries they named Glasstown and, later, Angria. After Charlotte left to go to school in 1831, Emily and Anne, who had participated in the invention of the earlier narratives, began a chronicle of their own of an island they called Gondal. It was for the Gondal story that Emily Brontë began to write poems. Her earliest surviving poem was written in 1836, and she continued to write or to revise poems about the characters and situations of Gondal until only months before her death.

In 1844 she began to transcribe her poems into two notebooks, one for Gondal poems and one for personal poems. Charlotte found the notebooks, and she persuaded Emily to include some of her poems in a collection whose publication in 1846 the sisters subsidized as *Poems, by Currer, Ellis, and Acton Bell*. Only two copies of the book were sold, but Charlotte had already begun to send around to publishers a parcel containing three novels carrying the same pseudonyms. Emily's novel was accepted and published as *Wuthering Heights,* by Ellis Bell, in 1847; so was Anne's, published as *Agnes Grey,* by Acton Bell. Charlotte's novel was not published, but its merits encouraged a publisher to invite another submission, and *Jane Eyre,* by Currer Bell, was published a few months before *Wuthering Heights* in 1847. After Emily's death, and that of Anne in 1849, Charlotte edited and published a further selection from Emily's poems in an edition of the two novels and some of the poetry of her two sisters.

For all this stir of shared invention and publication, Emily Brontë was an intensely private writer. She knew something of, responded to, and wrote within a strain of nineteenth-century romantic literature—Scott, Byron, the preternaturalism of ballads and gothic fiction—which was given to dramatizing extreme experience. The history of Gondal incorporated some of the drama of the history of her time: avatars of the powerful Duke of Wellington act in it, and when Victoria was crowned, so was Gondal's queen. Emily Brontë herself lived authentically outside the imagined interiors of her writing. She moved with decision and competence in the sad, often difficult circumstances of life at Haworth, and she preserved in her poems some of the deep pleasure she found in the feelings and landscapes of that life. But at the age of nineteen she had said, "I am the only being." She resented her sister's discovery of her poems, which she almost certainly would not have published on her own initiative. She resented even more, after the publication of *Wuthering Heights,* Charlotte Brontë's inadvertent disclosure to her publisher of the identity of Ellis Bell. She seems to have been content that her poems express and enlarge no consciousness but her own and that of the characters of Gondal.

It is not possible here responsibly to make the connections Emily Brontë neglected or resisted. There is certainly no consistently direct relationship between the events of her life and the events of her poems. Their themes and situations of imprisonment, rebellion, sexual passion, guilt, punishment, death, and release, which run through the Gondal poems especially, are undoubtedly in some degree transformations of her sense of herself and her situation in Haworth. But the terms and mechanism of these transformations are too complicated and problematical to be briefly discussed. It is possible and useful to mark the relationship between the larger history of nineteenth-century literature and one theme fundamental to Emily Brontë's personal poems and the poems of Gondal. (It is to the point that the two kinds of poems cannot always be separated; some poems that begin with the objects and emotions of her own life are converted to episodes in the Gondal story.) All through her poems she offers an idea of the manifold possibility of existence. She proposes a being larger than its available circumstances and identities, straining to be connected, absorbed, or released into other presences she could become. As the story of Gondal has been reconstructed by Fanny Ratchford and Laura Hinkley (see below), the country is eventually commanded by an imperious queen, perhaps herself the illegitimate daughter of an emperor. She has several names, plays multiple roles within the same relationship (she marries her uncle, seduces the adopted son of her stepdaughter, sacrifices her own daughter to preserve her political identity as heir to the throne), and her restless adventures in self-realization end in her assassination. Emily Brontë's personal poems also sometimes present colloquies between versions of the self ("I'll come when thou are saddest"); or they stop before the limits of identity in gestures of self-contempt or longing for the release of death; or they celebrate the moments when memory, imagination, or vision break the lim-

its of the self in the here and now and open to intimations of enormously larger, but not necessarily divine, existences.

In her poems (her novel is another matter) Emily Brontë did not try for large forms that would dramatize the conflict and resolution of these attempts to break through the constrictive forms in which one ordinarily knows life and is known in it. But in her poems she is nonetheless often in the company of writers who attempted one of the most audacious of nineteenth-century ideas about literature and the creative imagination. Unlike John Clare, whose writing her poems sometimes resemble in their directness and intense individuality, she was not so much concerned to make in poems a nature she found outside them. Her poems sometimes render or appropriate to episodes in the Gondal story what she saw in the moors and sky of the landscape around Haworth. But even in some of these poems she was fundamentally concerned to make herself. Out of her privacy and its complicated needs, out of her resistances to be named and known in the bounds of conventional identity, she wrote poems that participate in the most radical tenet of nineteenth-century romanticism. That is the idea—made into a myth in "Hertha" by Swinburne, for example, who may have learned something of the myth from William Blake—that the self entirely makes what it knows. What calls to us from beyond our present selves ("Heralds of me") are not energies waiting to be discovered and enjoyed, but capacities of being literally created by being known, and brought to increase the experience we know by being born and named in the words of a poem.

EDITIONS

The texts of the poems below which are dated "1846" are those published in that year in *Poems,* by Currer, Ellis, and Acton Bell; presumably Emily Brontë prepared or approved these poems for the press. The texts of the other poems are those of the manuscripts edited by C. W. Hatfield in *The Complete Poems of Emily Jane Brontë* (1941). Fannie E. Ratchford, in *The Brontë's Web of Childhood* (1941) and *Gondal's Queen* (1955), and Laura L. Hinkley, in *Charlotte and Emily: The Brontës* (1945), reconstruct the story of Gondal from the verses of Emily and Anne Brontë and a few remarks in their letters.

BIOGRAPHY AND CRITICISM

The Shakespeare Head Brontë, edited by Thomas J. Wise and J. A. Symington (1932–38), contains a biography of the sisters and a collection of their letters. Winifred Gerin's *Emily Brontë* (1971) is the most recent and authoritative biography; among other useful studies are Muriel Spark and Derek Stanford's *Emily Brontë: Her Life and Work* (1953), John Hewish's *Emily Brontë: A Critical and Biographical Study* (1969), and the chapter on Emily Brontë's poems and novel in J. Hillis Miller's *The Disappearance of God* (1963). Elizabeth Gaskell's *The Life of Charlotte Brontë* (1857), and a recent biography of the father of the Brontës, *A Man of Sorrows* (1965), by J. Lock and W. T. Dixon, contain information about Emily Brontë. For the commentary on Emily Brontë's writing see the chapter on the Brontës by Mildred G. Christian in *Victorian Fiction,* edited by Lionel Stevenson (1964); *Emily Brontë: Criticism 1900–1968,* prepared by Janet M. Barclay (1974); and *The Brontës: The Critical Heritage,* edited by Miriam Allott (1974).

"Tell me, tell me, smiling child"[1]

Tell me, tell me, smiling child,[2]
What the past is like to thee?
"An Autumn evening soft and mild
With a wind that sighs mournfully."

Tell me, what is the present hour?
"A green and flowery spray
Where a young bird sits gathering its power
To mount and fly away."

And what is the future, happy one?
"A sea beneath a cloudless sun;
A mighty, glorious, dazzling sea
Stretching into infinity."

(1836)

"I am the only being whose doom"

I am the only being whose doom[1]
No tongue would ask, no eye would mourn;
I never caused a thought of gloom,
A smile of joy, since I was born.

In secret pleasure, secret tears,
This changeful life has slipped away,
As friendless after eighteen years,
As lone as on my natal day.

There have been times I cannot hide,
There have been times when this was drear,   10
When my sad soul forgot its pride
And longed for one to love me here.

But those were in the early glow
Of feelings since subdued by care;
And they have died so long ago,
I hardly now believe they were.

First melted off the hope of youth,
Then fancy's rainbow fast withdrew;
And then experience told me truth
In mortal bosoms never grew.   20

'Twas grief enough to think mankind
All hollow, servile, insincere;
But worse to trust to my own mind
And find the same corruption there.

(May 17, 1837)

"I saw thee, child, one summer's day"

I saw thee, child, one summer's day[1]
Suddenly leave thy cheerful play,
And in the green grass, lowly lying,
I listened to thy mournful sighing.

I knew the wish that waked that wail;
I knew the source whence sprung those tears;
You longed for fate to raise the veil
That darkened over coming years.

[1] Titles in quotation marks are supplied by the editor.

[2] Fannie Ratchford, in a preface to Hatfield's edition of Emily Brontë's poems, classifies this poem as belonging to the Gondal story: she identifies the child as Augusta Geraldine Almeda, whom Hinkley in turn describes as the illegitimate daughter of an emperor who eventually becomes queen of Gondal.

[1] Perhaps a poem describing Augusta's father (Hinkley), or a boy, later seduced by Augusta, who is the adopted son of the daughter of Augusta's second husband (Ratchford). Emily Brontë was eighteen years old in July 1836.

[1] Both Ratchford and Hinkley think that this poem is about the adopted son of the daughter of Augusta's second husband. Hinkley speculates that the poem is spoken by the boy's grandmother.

The anxious prayer was heard, and power
10 Was given me, in that silent hour,
To open to an infant's eye
The portals of futurity.

But, child of dust, the fragrant flowers,
The bright blue sky and velvet sod
Were strange conductors to the bowers
Thy daring footsteps must have trod.

I watched my time, and summer passed,
And Autumn waning fleeted by,
And doleful winter nights at last
20 In cloudy mourning clothed the sky.

And now I'm come: this evening fell
Not stormily, but stilly drear;
A sound sweeps o'er thee like a knell
To banish joy and welcome care;

A fluttering blast that shakes the leaves,
And whistles round the gloomy wall,
And lingering long lamenting grieves,
For 'tis the spectre's call.

He hears me: what a sudden start
30 Sent the blood icy to that heart;
He wakens, and how ghastly white
That face looks in the dim lamplight.

Those tiny hands in vain essay
To thrust the shadowy fiend away;
There is a horror on his brow,
An anguish in his bosom now;

A fearful anguish in his eyes
Fixed strainedly on the vacant air;
Heavily bursts in long-drawn sighs
40 His panting breath, enchained by fear.

Poor child, if spirits such as I
Could weep o'er human misery,
A tear might flow, aye, many a tear,
To see the road that lies before,
To see the sunshine disappear,
And hear the stormy waters roar,
Breaking upon a desolate shore,
Cut off from hope in early day,
From power and glory cut away.

But it is doomed, and morning's light
Must image forth the scowl of night,
And childhood's flower must waste its bloom
Beneath the shadow of the tomb.

(July 1837)

"The sun has set, and the long grass now"

The sun has set, and the long grass now[1]
Waves drearily in the evening wind;
And the wild bird has flown from that old grey
    stone,
In some warm nook a couch to find.

In all the lonely landscape round
I see no sight and hear no sound,
Except the wind that far away
Comes sighing o'er the heathy sea.

(1837)

"I'll come when thou art saddest"

I'll come when thou art saddest,[1]
Laid alone in the darkened room;
When the mad day's mirth has vanished,
And the smile of joy is banished
From evening's chilly gloom.

I'll come when the heart's real feeling
Has entire unbiassed sway,
And my influence o'er thee stealing,
Grief deepening, joy congealing,
Shall bear thy soul away.

Listen, 'tis just the hour,
The awful time for thee;
Dost thou not feel upon thy soul
A flood of strange sensations roll,
Forerunners of a sterner power,
Heralds of me?

(1837)

"All hushed and still within the house"

All hushed and still within the house;
Without—all wind and driving rain;

[1] Spoken probably by Augusta, in the scene in which her first husband has been killed in battle.
[1] Perhaps spoken by or to Augusta after she has left her illegitimate child to die in a snow-storm because the existence of the child (fathered by the man who is later to become her first husband) would compromise her political ambitions (Hinkley).

But something whispers to my mind,
Through rain and through the wailing wind,
   Never again.
Never again? Why not again?
Memory has power as real as thine.

                   (1838)

"Why do I hate that lone green dell?"

Why do I hate that lone green dell?[1]
Buried in moors and mountains wild,
That is a spot I had loved too well
Had I but seen it when a child.

There are bones whitening there in the
   summer's heat,
But it is not for that, and none can tell;
None but one can the secret repeat
Why I hate that lone green dell.

Noble foe, I pardon thee
All thy cold and scornful pride,
For thou wast a priceless friend to me
When my sad heart had none beside.

And, leaning on thy generous arm,
A breath of old times over me came;
The earth shone round with a long-lost charm;
Alas, I forgot I was not the same.

Before a day—an hour—passed by,
My spirit knew itself once more;
I saw the gilded vapours fly
And leave me as I was before.

           (May 9, 1838)

" 'Twas one of those dark, cloudy days"

'Twas one of those dark, cloudy days
That sometimes come in summer's blaze,
When heaven drops not, when earth is still,
And deeper green is on the hill.

           (June 1838)

"How still, how happy! . . ."

How still, how happy! Those are words
That once would scarce agree together;
I loved the plashing of the surge,
The changing heaven, the breezy weather,

More than smooth seas and cloudless skies
And solemn, soothing, softened airs
That in the forest woke no sighs
And from the green spray shook no tears.

How still, how happy! Now I feel
Where silence dwells is sweeter far   10
Than laughing mirth's most joyous swell
However pure its raptures are.

Come, sit down on this sunny stone:
'Tis wintry light o'er flowerless moors—
But sit—for we are all alone
And clear expand heaven's breathless shores.

I could think in the withered grass
Spring's budding wreaths we might discern;
The violet's eye might shyly flash
And young leaves shoot among the fern.   20

It is but thought—full many a night
The snow shall clothe those hills afar
And storms shall add a drearier blight
And winds shall wage a wilder war,

Before the lark may herald in
Fresh foliage twined with blossoms fair
And summer days again begin
Their glory-haloed crown to wear.

Yet my heart loves December's smile
As much as July's golden beam;   30
Then let us sit and watch the while
The blue ice curdling on the stream.
        (December 7, 1838)

Love and Friendship[1]

Love is like the wild rose-briar,
Friendship like the holly-tree—
The holly is dark when the rose-briar blooms
But which will bloom most constantly?

---

[1] Spoken by Augusta as she revisits the glen where many years before she abandoned her illegitimate daughter to die. The "noble foe" is the wife of Augusta's father, who permits her to return to her home after the death in battle of her first husband (Hinkley).

[1] This poem was published in 1850 in a new edition of writing by Emily and Anne Brontë, prepared by Charlotte.

The wild rose-briar is sweet in spring,
Its summer blossoms scent the air;
Yet wait till winter comes again
And who will call the wild-briar fair?

Then scorn the silly rose-wreath now
10   And deck thee with the holly's sheen,
That when December blights thy brow
He still may leave thy garland green.

                                        (1839)   1850

"At such a time, in such a spot"

At such a time, in such a spot,[1]
The world seems made of light;
Our blissful hearts remember not
How surely follows night.

I cannot, Alfred, dream of aught
That casts a shade of woe;
That heaven is reigning in my thought,
Which wood and wave and earth have caught
From skies that overflow.

10   That heaven which my sweet lover's brow
Has won me to adore,
Which from his blue eyes beaming now
Reflects a still intenser glow
Than nature's heaven can pour.

I know our souls are all divine;
I know that when we die,
What seems the vilest, even like thine
A part of God himself shall shine
In perfect purity.

20   But coldly breaks November's day;
Its changes, charmless all;
Unmarked, unloved, they pass away;
We do not wish one hour to stay,
Nor sigh at evening's fall.

And glorious is the gladsome rise
Of June's rejoicing morn;
And who with unregretful eyes
Can watch the lustre leave its skies
To twilight's shade forlorn?

Then art thou not my golden June
All mist and tempest free?
As shines earth's sun in summer noon
So heaven's sun shines in thee.

Let others seek its beams divine
In cell and cloister drear;
But I have found a fairer shrine
And happier worship here.

By dismal rites they win their bliss—
By penance, fasts, and fears;
I have one rite: a gentle kiss;
One penance: tender tears.

O could it thus forever be
That I might so adore;
I'd ask for all eternity
To make a paradise for me,
My love—and nothing more!

                                        (1840, 1843)

The Night-Wind[1]

In summer's mellow midnight,
A cloudless moon shone through
Our open parlour window
And rosetrees wet with dew.

I sat in silent musing,
The soft wind waved my hair:
It told me Heaven was glorious,
And sleeping Earth was fair.

I needed not its breathing
To bring such thoughts to me,
But still it whispered lowly,
"How dark the woods will be!

"The thick leaves in my murmur
Are rustling like a dream,
And all their myriad voices
Instinct with spirit seem."

I said, "Go, gentle singer,
Thy wooing voice is kind,
But do not think its music
Has power to reach my mind.

---

[1] Titled in Emily Brontë's manuscript "A. G. A. to A. S." Spoken by Augusta to Lord Alfred, her second husband and also her uncle (Hinkley).
[1] The poem bears this title in Emily Brontë's manuscript. Charlotte Brontë made a few changes in the text of the poem when she prepared it for publication in 1850.

"Play with the scented flower,
The young tree's supple bough,
And leave my human feelings
In their own course to flow."

The wanderer would not leave me;[2]
Its kiss grew warmer still—
"O come," it sighed so sweetly,
"I'll win thee 'gainst thy will.

"Have we not been from childhood friends?[3]
Have I not loved thee long?
As long as thou hast loved the night[4]
Whose silence wakes my song.

"And when thy heart is laid at rest
Beneath the church-yard stone
I shall have time enough to mourn
And thou to be alone."[5]

         (September 11, 1840) 1850

"Aye, there it is! It wakes to-night"

Aye, there it is! It wakes to-night[1]
Sweet thoughts that will not die
And feeling's fires flash all as bright
As in the years gone by!

And I can tell by thine altered cheek
And by thy kindled gaze
And by the words thou scarce dost speak,
How wildly fancy plays.

Yes, I could swear that glorious wind
Has swept the world aside,

Has dashed its memory from thy mind
Like foam-bells from the tide—

And thou art now a spirit pouring
Thy presence into all—
The essence of the Tempest's roaring
And of the Tempest's fall—

A universal influence
From Thine own influence free;
A principle of life, intense,
Lost to mortality.   20

Thus truly when that breast is cold
Thy prisoned soul shall rise,
The dungeon mingle with the mould—
The captive with the skies.

         (July 6, 1841) 1850

A Day Dream

On a sunny brae alone I lay
One summer afternoon;
It was the marriage-time of May
With her young lover, June.

From her Mother's heart seemed loath to part
That queen of bridal charms,
But her Father smiled on the fairest child
He ever held in his arms.

The trees did wave their plumy crests,
The glad birds carolled clear;   10
And I, of all the wedding guests,
Was only sullen there.

---

[2] 1850: "The wanderer would not heed me."
[4] 1850: "As long as thou, the solemn night."
[5] 1850: "And when thy heart is resting
    Beneath the church-aisle stone,
  I shall have time for mourning,
    And *thou* for being alone."
Emily Brontë was buried in the church at Haworth.
[1] Spoken by Augusta in prison, after the death of her first husband (and the father, before their marriage, of their illegitimate child) (Hinkley). When she prepared this poem for publication in 1850 Charlotte Brontë, among other changes, changed the first stanza to read:

    Ay—there it is! it wakes to-night
    Deep feelings I thought dead
    Strong in the blast—quick gathering light—
    The heart's flame kindles red.

She also added five lines to the end of the poem:

    Nature's deep being, thine shall hold,
    Her spirit all thy spirit fold,
      Her breath absorb thy sighs.
    Mortal! though soon life's tale is told,
      Who once lives, never dies!

[3] 1850: "Were we not friends from childhood?"

There was not one but wished to shun
My aspect void of cheer;
The very grey rocks, looking on,
Asked, "What do you here?"

And I could utter no reply:
In sooth I did not know
Why I had brought a clouded eye
20   To greet the general glow.

So, resting on a heathy bank,
I took my heart to me;
And we together sadly sank
Into a reverie.

We thought, "When winter comes again,
Where will these bright things be?
All vanished, like a vision vain,
An unreal mockery!

"The birds that now so blithely sing,
30   Through deserts frozen dry,
Poor spectres of the perished Spring
In famished troops will fly.

"And why should we be glad at all?
The leaf is hardly green,
Before a token of its fall
Is on the surface seen."

Now whether it were really so
I never could be sure;
But as, in fit of peevish woe,
40   I stretched me on the moor,

A thousand thousand gleaming fires
Seemed kindling in the air;
A thousand thousand silvery lyres
Resounded far and near:

Methought the very breath I breathed
Was full of sparks divine,
And all my heather-couch was wreathed
By that celestial shine.

And, while the wide earth echoing rung
50   To that strange minstrelsy,
The little glittering spirits sung,
Or seemed to sing, to me:

"O mortal, mortal, let them die;
Let Time and Tears destroy,

That we may overflow the sky
With universal joy.

"Let Grief distract the sufferer's breast,
And Night obscure his way;
They hasten him to endless rest,
And everlasting day.

"To Thee the world is like a tomb,
A desert's naked shore;
To us, in unimagined bloom,
It brightens more and more.

"And could we lift the veil and give
One brief glimpse to thine eye
Thou would'st rejoice for those that live,
Because they live to die."

The music ceased—the noonday Dream
Like dream of night withdrew
But Fancy still will sometimes deem
Her fond creation true.
                          (March 5, 1844) 1846

"The linnet in the rocky dells"

The linnet in the rocky dells,[1]
The moor-lark in the air,
The bee among the heather-bells
That hide my lady fair:

The wild deer browse above her breast;
The wild birds raise their brood;
And they, her smiles of love caressed,
Have left her solitude!

I ween, that when the grave's dark wall
Did first her form retain,
They thought their hearts could ne'er recall
The light of joy again.

They thought the tide of grief would flow
Unchecked through future years,
But where is all their anguish now,
And where are all their tears?

Well, let them fight for Honour's breath,
Or Pleasure's shade pursue—
The Dweller in the land of Death
Is changed and careless too.

[1] Spoken by the captain of her guard after he discovers the assassinated body of Augusta. Printed in 1846 without change from the manuscript.

And if their eyes should watch and weep
Till sorrow's source were dry,
She would not, in her tranquil sleep,
Return a single sigh.

Blow, west wind, by the lonely mound,
And murmur, summer streams,
There is no need of other sound
To soothe my Lady's dreams.

E. W.
(May 1, 1844)   1846

To Imagination

When weary with the long day's care,
And earthly change from pain to pain,
And lost, and ready to despair,
Thy kind voice calls me back again—
O my true friend, I am not lone
While thou canst speak with such a tone!

So hopeless is the world without,
The world within I doubly prize;
Thy world where guile and hate and doubt
And cold suspicion never rise;
Where thou and I and Liberty
Have undisputed sovereignty.

What matters it that all around
Danger, and guilt, and darkness lie,
If but within our bosom's bound
We hold a bright, untroubled sky,
Warm with ten thousand mingled rays
Of suns that know no winter days?

Reason indeed may oft complain
For Nature's sad reality,
And tell the suffering heart how vain
Its cherished dreams must always be;
And Truth may rudely trample down
The flowers of Fancy newly blown.

But thou art ever there to bring
The hovering vision back, and breathe
New glories o'er the blighted spring
And call a lovelier life from death,
And whisper with a voice divine
Of real worlds as bright as thine.

I trust not to thy phantom bliss,
Yet still in evening's quiet hour

With never-failing thankfulness
I welcome thee, benignant power,
Sure solacer of human cares
And sweeter hope, when hope despairs.

(September 3, 1844)   1846

Remembrance[1]

Cold in the earth—and the deep snow piled
   above thee!
Far, far removed, cold in the dreary grave!
Have I forgot, my Only Love, to love thee,
Severed at last by Time's all-severing wave?

Now, when alone, do my thoughts no longer
   hover
Over the mountains on that northern shore;
Resting their wings where heath and fern-
   leaves cover
Thy noble heart for ever, ever more?

Cold in the earth, and fifteen wild Decembers
From those brown hills have melted into
   spring—
Faithful indeed is the spirit that remembers   10
After such years of change and suffering!

Sweet Love of youth, forgive if I forget thee
While the World's tide is bearing me along:
Other desires and other hopes beset me,
Hopes which obscure but cannot do thee
   wrong.

No later light has lightened up my heaven,
No second morn has ever shone for me:
All my life's bliss from thy dear life was given—
All my life's bliss is in the grave with thee.   20

But when the days of golden dreams had
   perished
And even Despair was powerless to destroy,
Then did I learn how existence could be
   cherished,
Strengthened and fed without the aid of joy;

Then did I check the tears of useless passion,
Weaned my young soul from yearning after
   thine;
Sternly denied its burning wish to hasten
Down to that tomb already more than mine!

---

[1] In Emily Brontë's manuscript the title of this poem is "R. Alcona to J. Brenzaida." Hinkley identifies Rosina of Alcona as the wife of Julius, the father of the heroine of the Gondal story, Augusta. Ratchford identifies Rosina with Augusta herself, wife but not daughter to Julius. The poem is Rosina's lament for her husband, assassinated fifteen years earlier.

And even yet, I dare not let it languish,
30 Dare not indulge in Memory's rapturous pain;
Once drinking deep of that divinest anguish,
How could I seek the empty world again?
                                  (March 3, 1845) 1846

Death[1]

Death, that struck when I was most confiding
In my certain Faith of Joy to be,
Strike again, Time's withered branch dividing
From the fresh root of Eternity!

Leaves, upon Time's branch, were growing
    brightly,
Full of sap and full of silver dew;
Birds, beneath its shelter, gathered nightly;
Daily, round its flowers, the wild bees flew.

Sorrow passed and plucked the golden blossom,
10 Guilt stripped off the foliage in its pride;
But, within its parent's kindly bosom,
Flowed forever Life's restoring tide.

Little mourned I for the parted Gladness,
For the vacant nest and silent song;
Hope was there and laughed me out of sadness,
Whispering, "Winter will not linger long."

And behold, with tenfold increase blessing
Spring adorned the beauty-burdened spray;
Wind and rain and fervent heat caressing
20 Lavished glory on that second May.

High it rose; no wingèd grief could sweep it;
Sin was scared to distance with its shine:
Love and its own life had power to keep it
From all wrong, from every blight but thine!

Cruel Death! the young leaves droop and
    languish!
Evening's gentle air may still restore—
No: the morning sunshine mocks my anguish—
Time for me must never blossom more!

Strike it down, that other boughs may flourish
Where that perished sapling used to be;
Thus, at least, its mouldering corpse will
    nourish
That from which it sprung—Eternity.
                                  (April 10, 1845) 1846

"No coward soul is mine"

No coward soul is mine
No trembler in the world's storm-troubled
    sphere
I see Heaven's glories shine
And Faith shines equal arming me from Fear

O God within my breast
Almighty ever-present Deity
Life, that in me hast rest
As I Undying Life, have power in Thee

Vain are the thousand creeds
That move men's hearts, unutterably vain,
Worthless as withered weeds
Or idlest froth amid the boundless main

To waken doubt in one
Holding so fast by thy infinity
So surely anchored on
The steadfast rock of Immortality

With wide-embracing love
Thy spirit animates eternal years
Pervades and broods above,
Changes, sustains, dissolves, creates and rears

Though Earth and moon were gone[1]
And suns and universes ceased to be
And thou wert left alone
Every Existence would exist in thee

There is not room for Death
Nor atom that his might could render void
Since thou art Being and Breath
And what thou art may never be destroyed.[2]
                                  (January 2, 1846) 1850

---

[1] Perhaps (Ratchford) a lament for Julius, by Rosina/Augusta.
[1] 1850: "Though earth and man were gone."
[2] 1850: "Thou—THOU art Being and Breath,
        And what THOU art may never be destroyed."

PART TWO

Early Victorian Poems
1830-1850

Walter Savage Landor

1775–1864

Walter Savage Landor was, like Wordsworth, a survivor from the first decades of the nineteenth century into the early decades of Victoria's reign. Landor published his first volume of verse in 1795, a moderately well-known Oriental narrative, Gebir, in 1798, and he first collected his poems in 1831 in a volume that also contained some new poems. By that time he was principally known as the author of Imaginary Conversations (1824–29), a series of invented colloquies in prose between remarkable historical personages. He lived in Italy from 1815 to 1835, and even after his return to England and the publication of volumes of verse in 1846, 1847, and 1853 he was not a large presence in the literary scene. Nor did the compression, finish, and wit of his verse seem to have markedly affected the practice of early- and mid-Victorian poets. But in a time when young poets often saw themselves as ecstatic visionaries, he helped to keep current an idea of poetry as an old and demanding craft, and of the poet as a learned, urbane sensibility who tempered joy and melancholy through insistently ordered artifice. The standard edition is The Poetical Works of Walter Savage Landor, edited by Stephen Wheeler (1937). The texts printed here are those of the original editions; Wheeler takes these texts as standard. The standard biography is Robert Super's Landor (1954).

[To Ianthe][1]

Past ruin'd Ilion Helen lives,[2]
  Alcestis[3] rises from the shades;
Verse calls them forth; 'tis verse that gives
  Immortal youth to mortal maids.

Soon shall Oblivion's deepening veil
  Hide all the peopled hills you see,
The gay, the proud, while lovers hail
  In distant ages you and me.

The tear for fading beauty check,
  For passing glory cease to sigh;
One form shall rise above the wreck,
  One name, Ianthe, shall not die.

1831

Dirce[1]

Stand close around, ye Stygian set,
  With Dirce in one boat conveyed!
Or Charon, seeing, may forget
  That he is old and she a shade.

1831

Alciphron and Leucippe

An ancient chestnut's blossoms threw
Their heavy odour over two:
Leucippe, it is said, was one,
The other then was Alciphron.
  "Come, come! why should we stand beneath
This hollow tree's unwholesome breath,"
Said Alciphron, "here's not a blade
Of grass or moss, and scanty shade.
Come; it is just the hour to rove
In the lone dingle[1] shepherds love,
There, straight and tall, the hazel twig
Divides the crooked rock-held fig,
O'er the blue pebbles where the rill
In winter runs, and may run still.
Come then, while fresh and calm the air,
And while the shepherds are not there."
  Leucippe. But I would rather go when they
Sit round about and sing and play.
Then why so hurry me? for you

---

[1] Ianthe is Landor's name for Jane Sophia Swift, whom he met and loved early in the century, and with whom he retained a friendship until her death in 1851.

[2] Ilion: Troy, to which Helen was abducted, causing the Trojan War.

[3] Alcestis: in Greek mythology she agreed to die for her husband, and was rescued from the underworld by Hercules.

[1] In Greek mythology Dirce is a queen who died violently; Charon is the boatman who conveys the dead across the river Styx into the underworld.

[1] Dingle: small wooded valley.

Like play and song and shepherds too.
ALCIPHRON.   I like the shepherds very well,
And song and play, as you can tell.
But there is play I sadly fear,
And song I would not have you hear.
  LEUCIPPE.   What can it be? what can it be?
  ALCIPHRON.   To you may none of them re-
    peat
  The play that you have played with me,
The song that made your bosom beat.
  LEUCIPPE.   Don't keep your arm about my
    waist.
  ALCIPHRON.   Might not you stumble?
  LEUCIPPE.   Well then, do.
But why are we in all this haste?
  ALCIPHRON.   To sing.
  LEUCIPPE.   Alas! and not play too?
                                        1846

[On Grey Cliffs][1]

Night airs that make tree-shadows walk, and
  sheep
Washed white in the cold moonshine on grey
  cliffs.
                                        1846

Dying Speech of an Old Philosopher

I strove with none, for none was worth my
    strife:
  Nature I loved, and, next to Nature, Art:
I warm'd both hands before the fire of Life;
  It sinks; and I am ready to depart.
                                   1849; 1853

Defiance

Catch her and hold her if you can . . .
See, she defies you with her fan,
Shuts, opens, and then holds it spred
In threat'ning guize above your head.
Ah! why did you not start before
She reacht the porch and closed the door?
Simpleton! will you never learn
That girls and time will not return;
Of each you should have made the most.
Once gone, they are for ever lost.   10
In vain your knuckles knock your brow,
In vain will you remember how
Like a slim brook the gamesome maid
Sparkled, and ran into the shade.
                                        1858

Winthrop Mackworth Praed
1802–1839

While he was a student at Eton, Winthrop Mack-worth Praed began and contributed to a literary magazine of such quality that its numbers were collected and several times reprinted. He continued to write for periodicals when he was at Cambridge and later while he looked around to establish himself in the society of comfortable people of social and political consequence into which he had been born. Eventually, he read law, was admitted to the bar in 1829, and elected to Parliament in 1830. He attracted the attention of the Tory leaders, but his health began to fail, and he died before he could fulfill the promise of his political career. He probably did realize the promise of his gifts as a poet. He seems to have thought of verse not as the substance or fundament of life, but as a means of wry and witty comment on the social manners and politics which were its substance. Except for a privately printed collection of political poems in 1835, Praed's poems were not collected until 1864. But all through the Victorian period some readers knew the deft play and point with which, firmly at home in his class and time, he practiced a minor but persistent and honorable tradition of light,

[1] These lines were added in 1846 to an *Imaginary Conversation* between Lord Brooke and Philip Sidney.

amusing verse that touched intelligently on the ways he and people like him lived and worked. The most useful collection of Praed's verse is Kenneth Allott's well-annotated Selected Poems *(1953). The standard biography is Derek Hudson's* A Poet in Parliament *(1939). The texts reprinted here are those of the original publication of the poems in periodicals.*

Ode [To Popularity]

> *Quis multà gracilis te puer in rosâ*
> *Perfusus liquidis urget odoribus*
> *Grato, Pyrrha, sub antro?*
>
>   HOR.[1]

O fondest, and O frailest fair,
That ever made a poet swear,
   Bewitching Popularity!
O patroness of songs and scents,
Of budgets and disfranchisements,
   Of treason and vulgarity—

Tell me whom now your fickle pen
Pronounces first of mortal men
   In magazine and journal?
10 For whom the golden lute you wake,
And whose renown you mean to make
   For just nine weeks eternal?

Dote you on Grey's[2] experienced brow,
Because he's quite as silly now
   As erst our fathers found him?
Or do you lead the approving cheer
When Baron Brougham,[3] the peerless peer,
   Is flinging dirt around him?

Does soft Sir James,[4] by talking big,
20 Of rope and cable, sloop and brig,
   Persuade you he's a hero?

Or does Sir Thomas[5] please you more
By telling, as he told before,
   The history of Nero?

Oh, Waterloo!—you used to say
You never would forget the day
   That cracked the French cuirasses;
But Wednesday last, at half-past ten,
You let the ragged gentlemen
   Smash all his Grace's glasses.[6]

You know you've jilted St. John Long,[7]
And bidden Southwark's noisy throng
   Send poor Sir Robert[8] packing;
You know, without a reason why,
You're burning Hunt in effigy,
   And leaving off his blacking.[9]

Happy, on whom untried you smile!
He dreams not for how short a while
   You solemnise the wedding:—
How soon you jump from wreaths to stones,
From Wellington to Colonel Jones,
   From kissing to beheading.

Such stormy waves are not for me:
As Graham says, I've seen the sea
   Suck down the struggling packet;
And I renounce the sail and oar,
And hang, to dry upon the shore,
   My trowsers and my jacket.

                         1831; 1835

Stanzas to the Speaker Asleep

Sleep, Mr. Speaker![1] it's surely fair,
If you don't in your bed, that you should in
   your chair;

---

[1] From the odes (I, v) of the Roman poet Horace (65–8 B.C.): the translation in the Loeb Classical Library reads: "What slender youth, bedewed with perfumes, embraces thee amid many a rose, O Pyrrha, in the pleasant grotto?" The poem is about inconstancy.

[2] Charles Grey (1764–1845), later the second Earl Grey, prime minister in 1831–32 during the Parliament which finally passed a bill reforming parliamentary elections.

[3] Henry Brougham (1778–1868), an energetic reforming lawyer and politician. He was created Baron Brougham and Vaux in 1830.

[4] Sir James Graham (1792–1861), first lord of the admiralty in Grey's administration.

[5] Sir Thomas Denham (1779–1854) was attorney-general in Grey's ministry. He alluded to Nero in a well-known speech early in the 1820s.

[6] The Duke of Wellington was unpopular in the early 1830s because of his refusal to support parliamentary reform. In 1831 a mob broke the windows of his London residence.

[7] St. John Long (1798–1834) was a fashionable London physician who was twice tried for manslaughter in the 1820s because of the deaths of his patients.

[8] Sir Robert Wilson (1777–1849), a member of Parliament for Southwark, a district in London. He was unpopular because of his opposition to parilamentary reform, and was threatened with opposition in his district by Colonel Leslie Jones (line 41), who attained some renown as the writer of pro-reform letters in the late 1820s.

[9] Henry Hunt (1773–1835), a radical member of Parliament who was also a manufacturer of shoeblacking.

[1] Speaker: the presiding member of the House of Commons.

Longer and longer still they grow,
Tory and Radical, Aye and No;
Talking by night, and talking by day:
Sleep, Mr. Speaker—sleep, sleep while you may!

Sleep, Mr. Speaker! slumber lies
Light and brief on a Speaker's eyes;
Fielden or Finn,[2] in a minute or two,
Some disorderly thing will do;
Riot will chase repose away:
Sleep, Mr. Speaker—sleep, sleep while you may!

Sleep, Mr. Speaker! Cobbett[3] will soon
Move to abolish the sun and moon;
Hume,[4] no doubt, will be taking the sense
Of the House on a saving of thirteen-pence;

Grattan will growl, or Baldwin bray:
Sleep, Mr. Speaker—sleep, sleep while you may!

Sleep, Mr. Speaker! dream of the time
When loyalty was not quite a crime; 20
When Grant was a pupil in Canning's[5] school;
When Palmerston fancied Wood a fool:[6]
Lord! how principles pass away!—
Sleep, Mr. Speaker—sleep, sleep while you may!

Sleep, Mr. Speaker! sweet to men
Is the sleep that comes but now and then;
Sweet to the sorrowful, sweet to the ill,
Sweet to the children that work in a mill;
You have more need of sleep than they:
Sleep, Mr. Speaker—sleep, sleep while you may! 30
                    1833; 1835

Ebenezer Elliott
1781–1849

Ebenezer Elliott, the son of a clerk, was an iron-worker and finally the master of a small foundry. His first published poem in 1801 was in an eighteenth-century tradition of pastoral poetry. He continued to write pastoral and descriptive poetry, but in The Splendid Village *(1831) he also moved to discursive or derisive attacks on the politics that were creating dispossession, unemployment, and misery in the countryside. Again and again he attacked the Corn Laws, which kept the price of domestic grain high by regulating imports, and he became best known as the author of* Corn-Law Rhymes, *published in book form in 1830 and enlarged in 1831. Elliott helped to organize the Chartist movement later in the 1830s, and he continued to agitate against the Corn Laws until their repeal in 1846. A collection of his poetry was published in 1834; the texts printed here are those of that edition.*

[2] Finn: William Francis Finn, with Henry Grattan and Herbert Baldwin (line 17), were Irish members of Parliament who supported Daniel O'Connell (1775–1847) in his campaign for repeal of the political union between England and Ireland. John Fielden (1784–1849) was a middle-class reforming member of Parliament.

[3] William Cobbett (1763–1835) published politically radical newspapers and pamphlets, especially his *Weekly Register,* all during the first three decades of the century. He was tried for sedition in 1831, and elected to Parliament the next year.

[4] Joseph Hume (1777–1855), another reforming politician who specialized in questions about the budget.

[5] Charles Grant, later Baron Glenelg (1778–1866), once followed the conservative leadership of George Canning (1770–1827) but moved in the 1830s toward liberal positions.

[6] Henry Palmerston (1784–1865) held important offices from the 1820s through the 1850s, including the office of prime minister 1855–58. He broke with the Conservative party in 1828, and served in the Whig ministry of Grey. Matthew Wood (1768–1843) was a member of Parliament who endorsed parliamentary reform.

Caged Rats[1]

Ye coop us up, and tax our bread,
  And wonder why we pine;
But ye are fat, and round, and red,
  And fill'd with tax-bought wine.
Thus, twelve rats starve while three rats thrive,
  (Like you on mine and me,)
When fifteen rats are caged alive,
  With food for nine and three.

Haste! havoc's torch begins to glow,
  The ending is begun;
Make haste; destruction thinks ye slow;
  Make haste to be undone!
Why are ye call'd "my lord," and "squire,"
  While fed by mine and me,
And wringing food, and clothes and fire
  From bread-tax'd misery?

Make haste, slow rogues! *prohibit* trade,
  Prohibit honest gain;
Turn all the good that God hath made
  To fear, and hate, and pain;
Till beggars all, assassins all,
  All cannibals we be,
And death shall have no funeral
  From shipless sea to sea.

                           1830–31

The Tree of Rivelin[1]

The lightning, like an Arab, cross'd
  The moon's dark path on high,
And wild on Rivelin writhed and toss'd
  The stars and troubled sky,
Where lone the tree of ages grew,
  With branches wide and tall;
Ah! who, when such a tempest blew,
  Could hear his stormy fall?
But now the skies, the stars are still,
  The blue wave sleeps again,

And heath and moss, by rock and rill,
  Are whispering in disdain,
That Rivelin's side is desolate,
  Her giant in the dust!
Beware, O Power! for God is great,
  O Guilt, for God is just!
And boast not, Pride! while millions pine,
  That wealth secures thy home;
The storm that shakes all hearths *but* thine
  Is *not* the storm to come.
The tremor of the stars is pale,
  The dead clod quakes with fear,
The storm slinks down, o'er hill and vale,
  When God in wroth draws near.
But if the Upas[2] *will* not bend
  Beneath the frown of Heaven,
A *whisper* cometh, which shall rend
  What thunder hath not riven.

                           1830–31

from Steam

VII

No; there he moves, the thoughtful engineer,
The soul of all this motion; rule in hand,
And coarsely apron'd—simple, plain, sincere—
An honest man; self-taught to understand
The useful wonders which he built and
  plann'd.
Self-taught to read and write—a poor man's
  son,
Though poor no more—how would he sit
  alone,
When the hard labour of the day was done,
Bent o'er his table, silent as a stone,
To make the wisdom of the wise his own!
How oft' of Brindley's deeds th' apprenticed
  boy
Would speak delighted, long ere freedom came!
And talk of Watt![1] while, shedding tears of joy,

---

[1] Elliott took this figure from one of the writings of Thomas Perronet Thompson (1783–1869): "Suppose, now that a hundred rats . . . were caged up and supplied with a limited quantity of food, and encouraged to multiply till they starved each other by the subdivision of the allowance;—and say whether this picture, ugly and disgusting as it is, is not a representation of the condition in which the country has been placed by the influence of the monopolists." Thompson was an editor, writer on economics and politics, and member of Parliament. His *Cathechism on Corn-Laws* (1827) was well known and widely used during the agitation for their repeal.

[1] Rivelin is a river near Sheffield, in which Elliott lived and worked, in the north of England.

[2] Upas: a tree that kills living creatures in its shade.

[1] James Brindley (1716–72) was an English engineer especially well known for building canals. James Watt (1736–1819) was a Scottish inventor and instrument maker best remembered for his devices to use the power of steam. Brindley was from a poor family and died illiterate.

His widow'd mother heard, and hoped the name
Of her poor boy, like theirs, would rise to fame.
Was not her love prophetic? Is he famed?
Yea; for deep foresight, and improving skill,
And patience, which might make the proud ashamed.
Built by himself, lo, yonder, from the hill
His dwelling peeps!—and she is with him still;
Happy to live, and well prepared to die!

VIII

How unlike him is Grip, the upstart sly,
Who on the dunghill, whence he lately rose,
Lost his large organ of identity,[2]
And left his sire to starve! Alas, he knows
No poor man now! But every day he goes
To visit his nine acres, pitiless
Of him who tills the road, that shoeless boor,
Who feeds his brother exile in distress.
Hark! muttering oaths, he wonders why our poor

Are not all Irish! Eyeing, then, the moor,
He swears, if he were king, what he would do!
Our corn-importing rogues should have a fall;
For he would plough the rocks, and trench them, too.
And then of bloody papists doth he bawl;—
If he were king, he'd (damn them!) shoot them all.
And then he quotes the Duke![3] and sagely thinks
That princes should be loyal to the throne.
And then he talks of privilege—and winks:
Game he can't eat, he hints; but kills his own.   40
And then he calls the land a marrow bone,
Which tradesmen suck; for he no longer trades,
But talks of traffic[4] with defensive sneer.
Full deeply is he learn'd in modes and grades,
And condescends to think my lord his peer!
Yet, lo! he noddeth at the engineer—
Grins at the fellow—grunts—and lounges on!
                                          1833

Felicia Hemans
1793–1835

Felicia Hemans published her first book of poems when she was only fifteen years old, and a popular book, The Domestic Affections *(1812), before she was twenty. After she separated from her husband in 1818, she began to write prolifically, publishing over a dozen volumes of verse before her death and contributing regularly to monthly magazines and annuals. Her name came in the 1830s to stand for a kind of sentimental poetry of natural description and plangent, conventional melody. Some of her poems that have retained their popularity, however —"The Graves of a Household," "Casabianca" ("The boy stood on the burning deck") —celebrate the gains and losses of heroism and imperial enter-prise. Her work was frequently collected and re-printed during the nineteenth century, especially in the United States, where it was very popular. The texts printed here are those of a collected edition published in Edinburgh, with a memoir by Mrs. Hemans' sister, in 1839.*

The Graves of a Household

They grew in beauty, side by side,
    They fill'd one home with glee;—
Their graves are sever'd, far and wide,
    By mount, and stream, and sea.

---

[2] Organ of identity: a phrase of the pseudoscience of phrenology, which offered to analyze character by the presence or absence of certain features, bumps, and indentations of the head.

[3] The Duke: the Duke of Wellington (1769–1852), in the 1830s a hero of conservatives because of his opposition to political reform and to the granting of certain privileges to Roman Catholics.

[4] Traffic: commerce.

The same fond mother bent at night
  O'er each fair sleeping brow;
She had each folded flower in sight—
  Where are those dreamers now?

One, 'midst the forest of the West,
10   By a dark stream is laid—
The Indian knows his place of rest,
  Far in the cedar-shade.

The sea, the blue lone sea, hath one—
  He lies where pearls lie deep;
He was the loved of all, yet none
  O'er his low bed may weep.

One sleeps where southern vines are drest,
  Above the noble slain:
He wrapt his colours round his breast
20   On a blood-red field of Spain.

And one—o'er *her* the myrtle showers
  Its leaves, by soft winds fann'd;
She faded 'midst Italian flowers—
  The last of that bright band.

And parted thus they rest, who play'd
  Beneath the same green tree;
Whose voices mingled as they pray'd
  Around one parent knee!

They that with smiles lit up the hall,
  And cheer'd with song the hearth—
Alas! for love, if *thou* wert all,
  And naught beyond, O Earth!

1828

The Orange Bough

Oh! bring me one sweet orange bough,
To fan my cheek, to cool my brow;
One bough, with pearly blossoms drest,
And bind it, mother! on my breast!

Go, seek the grove along the shore,
Whose odours I must breathe no more;
The grove where every scented tree
Thrills to the deep voice of the sea.

Oh! Love's fond sighs, and fervent prayer,
And wild farewell, are lingering there:
Each leaf's light whisper hath a tone,
My faint heart, even in death, would own.

Then bear me thence one bough, to shed
Life's parting sweetness round my head,
And bind it, mother! on my breast
When I am laid in lonely rest.

1834

Letitia Elizabeth Landon
1802–1838

Letitia Elizabeth Landon began to publish verse in magazines before she was twenty, and she published her first volume of verse in 1821. Her second volume, The Improvistorice *(1824), went through six editions before her death and established her as a well-known writer. She continued to write poems and reviews for literary journals, published several more volumes of verse and three novels, and edited a successful literary annual. She also became the topic of scandalous gossip in the London literary and political circles in which she moved. In 1838 she left for Africa as the wife of a colonial official, and she died by poison, probably accidentally self-administered, in the same year. For all the gloss of sensationalism conferred by her life and some of the historical and chivalric topics of her verse, its persistent tone and function are rightly fixed in her own statement in a preface to a volume published in 1828 that in her poetry she tries for the softening and elevating effects of "grief, disappointment, the fallen leaf, the faded flower, the broken heart, and the early grave." Her poems were collected several times during her lifetime. The text of the first poem printed here is that of an edition published in London in 1850; the text of the second poem is from Miles (see "General Bibliography").*

A Child Screening a Dove from a Hawk

By Stewardson[1]

Ay, screen thy favourite dove, fair child,
  Ay, screen it if you may,—
Yet I misdoubt thy trembling hand
  Will scare the hawk away.

That dove will die, that child will weep,—
  Is this their destinie?
Ever amid the sweets of life
  Some evil thing must be.

Ay, moralise,—is it not thus
  We've mourn'd our hope and love?
Ah! there are tears for every eye,
  A hawk for every dove!

                             1825

The Unknown Grave

There is a little lonely grave
  Which no one comes to see,
The foxglove and red orchis wave
  Their welcome to the bee.
There never falls the morning sun,
  It lies beneath the wall,
But there when weary day is done
  The lights of sunset fall,
Flushing the warm and crimson air,
As life and hope were present there.

There sleepeth one who left his heart
  Behind him in his song;
Breathing of that diviner part
  Which must to heaven belong,
The language of those spirit chords,
  But to the poet known,
Youth, love, and hope yet use his words,
  They seem to be his own:
And yet he has not left a name,
The poet died without his fame.   20

How many are the lovely lays
  That haunt our English tongue;
Defrauded of their poet's praise,
  Forgotten he who sung.
Tradition only vaguely keeps
  Sweet fancies round his tomb;
Its tears are what the wild flower weeps,
  Its record is that bloom;
Ah, surely Nature keeps with her
The memory of her worshipper.   30

One of her loveliest mysteries
  Such spirit blends at last,
With all the fairy fantasies
  Which o'er some scenes are cast:
A softer beauty fills the grove,
  A light is in the grass,
A deeper sense of truth and love
  Comes o'er us as we pass;
While lingers in the heart one line
The nameless poet hath a shrine.   40

                             1838

Hartley Coleridge
1796–1849

Hartley Coleridge, the son of Samuel Taylor Coleridge, grew up in the Lake country in the north of England. He studied at Oxford and won a fellowship after his graduation, but he was already drinking intemperately and was required to resign. For a while he worked in London as a contributor to magazines, and then he returned to the Lake country, opened a school that failed, and spent the rest of his life writing for magazines and accumulating a body of poetry, much of which was not published in his lifetime. He published a volume of poems in 1833, and a collection of memoirs of eminent North-

[1] Thomas Stewardson (1781–1859), a painter best known for his portraits.

ern personages in the same year, and an edition of the seventeenth-century playwrights Massinger and Ford in 1840. There are two biographies: E. L. Griggs' Hartley Coleridge *(1929), and Herbert Hartman's* Hartley Coleridge: Poet's Son and Poet *(1931). Coleridge's poems were collected after his death in an edition prepared by his brother Derwent (1851). The texts printed here are those of the 1851 edition.*

Address to Certain Gold Fishes

Restless forms of living light
Quivering on your lucid wings,
Cheating still the curious sight
With a thousand shadowings;—
Various as the tints of even,
Gorgeous as the hues of heaven,
Reflected on your native streams
In flitting, flashing, billowy gleams!

Harmless warriors, clad in mail
10   Of silver breastplate, golden scale;—
Mail of Nature's own bestowing,
With peaceful radiance mildly glowing,—
Fleet are ye, as fleetest galley
Or pirate rover sent from Sallee;[1]
Keener than the Tartar's arrow,
Sport ye in your sea so narrow.

Was the sun himself your sire?
Were ye born of vital fire?
Or of the shade of golden flowers,
20   Such as we fetch from eastern bowers,
To mock this murky clime of ours?
Upwards, downwards, now ye glance,
Weaving many a mazy dance;
Seeming still to grow in size
When ye would elude our eyes.
Pretty creatures! we might deem
Ye were happy as ye seem,—
As gay, as gamesome, and as blithe,
As light, as loving, and as lithe,
30   As gladly earnest in your play,
As when ye gleam'd in far Cathay;

And yet, since on this hapless earth
There's small sincerity in mirth,
And laughter oft is but an art
To drown the outcry of the heart;
It may be, that your ceaseless gambols,
Your wheelings, dartings, divings, rambles,
Your restless roving round and round

The circuit of your crystal bound,—
Is but the task of weary pain,
40   An endless labour, dull and vain;
And while your forms are gaily shining
Your little lives are inly pining!
Nay! but still I fain would dream
That ye are happy as ye seem,
Deck'd in Oriental pride,
By homely British fire-side.

                           1833

Summer Rain

Thick lay the dust, uncomfortably white,
In glaring mimicry of Arab sands.
The woods and mountains slept in hazy light;
The meadows look'd athirst and tawny tann'd;
The little rills had left their channels bare,
With scarce a pool to witness what they were;
And the shrunk river gleam'd 'mid oozy stones,
That stared like any famish'd giant's bones.

Sudden the hills grew black, and hot as stove
The air beneath; it was a toil to be.
There was a growling as of angry Jove,
Provoked by Juno's prying jealousy—
A flash—a crash—the firmament was split,
And down it came in drops—the smallest fit
To drown a bee in fox-glove bell conceal'd;
Joy fill'd the brook, and comfort cheer'd the field.

                           1851

To a Deaf and Dumb Little Girl

Like a loose island on the wide expanse,
Unconscious floating on the fickle sea,
Herself her all, she lives in privacy;
Her waking life as lonely as a trance,
Doom'd to behold the universal dance,
And never hear the music which expounds
The solemn step, coy slide, the merry bounds,
The vague, mute language of the countenance.
In vain for her I smooth my antic rhyme;
She cannot hear it; all her little being
Concentered in her solitary seeing—
What can she know of beaut[eous] or sublime?
And yet methinks she looks so calm and good,
God must be with her in her solitude.

                           1851

---

[1] Sallee: Salé, a port on the Atlantic coast of Morocco.

Rydal[1]

Nigh to the mansion of a titled dame,
A charitable lady, though recluse,
Begirt with trees too reverend for use,
A village lies, and Rydal is its name.
Its natives know not what is meant by fame:
They little know how men in future time
Will venerate the spot, where prose and rhyme

Too strong for aught but Heaven itself to tame,
Gush'd from a mighty Poet. Yet all calm,
Calm as the antique trunks whose hollow age   10
The woodman spares, sweet thoughts on every
    page
Breathe for the soul admonitory balm.
'Tis Nature teaching what she never knew;
The Beautiful is good, the good is true.

                       1851

James Clarence Mangan
1803–1849

James Clarence Mangan did not publish a volume of poems during his lifetime, and never published in a periodical outside Ireland. His translations of German poems, imitations of Oriental poems, and reworkings in verse of Irish heroic and legendary matter he learned from prose translations (he did not know the Irish language) were frequently published in Dublin newspapers and magazines and made him a principal figure in the Irish literary and nationalist movement which flourished throughout the century. The texts printed here are those from the Poems of James Clarence Mangan, *a centenary edition edited by D. J. O'Donoghue and published in Dublin and London (1903). O'Donoghue also published a biography of Mangan in 1897.*

Kathaleen Ny-Houlahan[1]

(From the Irish of William Heffernan)
Long they pine in weary woe, the nobles of our
    land,
Long they wander to and fro, proscribed, alas!
    and banned;
Feastless, houseless, altarless, they bear the
    exile's brand,
    But their hope is in the coming-to of
        Kathaleen Ny-Houlahan!

Think her not a ghostly hag, too hideous to be
    seen,
Call her not unseemly names, our matchless
    Kathaleen;
Young she is, and fair she is, and would be
    crowned a queen,
    Were the king's son at home here with
        Kathaleen Ny-Houlahan!

Sweet and mild would look her face, O, none
    so sweet and mild,
Could she crush the foes by whom her beauty
    is reviled;   10
Woollen plaids would grace herself and robes
    of silk her child,
    If the king's son were living here with
        Kathaleen Ny-Houlahan!

Sore disgrace it is to see the Arbitress of
    thrones,
Vassal to a *Saxoneen* of cold and sapless bones!
Bitter anguish wrings our souls—with heavy
    sighs and groans
    We wait the Young Deliverer of Kathaleen
        Ny-Houlahan!

Let us pray to Him who holds Life's issues in
    His hands—

---

[1] Rydal was the site of Wordsworth's house in the Lake District.
[1] One of the traditional names for Ireland. William Heffernan was an early eighteenth-century Irish poet whose songs were never collected.

Him who formed the mighty globe, with all its
 thousand lands;
Girding them with seas and mountains, rivers
 deep, and strands,
  To cast a look of pity upon Kathaleen Ny-
10   Houlahan!

He, who over sands and waves led Israël
 along—
He, who fed, with heavenly bread, that chosen
 tribe and throng—
He, who stood by Moses, when his foes were
 fierce and strong—
  May He show forth His might in saving
  Kathaleen Ny-Houlahan.

            1841

The Irish Language

(From the Irish of Philip Fitzgibbon[1])

I

The language of Erin is brilliant as gold;
It shines with a lustre unrivalled of old.
Even glanced at by strangers to whom 'tis
 unknown
It dazzles their eyes with a light all its own!

II

It is music, the sweetest of music, to hear;
No lyre ever like it enchanted your ear.
Not the lute, or the flute, or the quaint
 clarionet,
For deep richness of tone could compete with
 it yet!

III

It is fire to the mind—it is wine to the heart—
10 It is melting and bold—it is Nature and Art!
Name one other language, renowned though it
 be,
That so wakes up the soul, as the storm the
 deep sea!

IV

For its bards—there are none in cell, cottage,
 or hall,
In the climes of the haughty Iberian and Gaul,

Who despair not to match them—their marvel-
 ful tones
Might have won down the gods of old Greece
 from their thrones!

V

Then it bears back your spirit on History's
 wings
To the glories of Erin's high heroes and kings,
When the proud name of Gael swelled from
 ocean to shore,
Ere the days of the Saxon and Northman of
 yore.

VI

Is the heart of the land of this tongue
 undecayed?
Shall the Sceptre and Sword sway again as they
 swayed?
Shall our Kings ride in triumph o'er war-fields
 again,
Till the sun veils his face from the hosts of the
 slain?

VII

O, then shall our halls with the Gaelic resound,
In the notes of the harp and the *claoirseach*[2]
 half-drowned,
And the banquet be spread, and the chess-
 board all night
Test the skill of our Chiefs, and their power
 for the fight.

VIII

Then our silken-robed minstrels, a silver
 haired band,
Shall rewake the young slumbering blood of
 the land,
And our bards no more plaintive on Banba's[3]
 dark wrongs,
Shall then fill *two* worlds[4] with the fame of
 their songs.

IX

And the gates of our *Brughaidhs*[5] again shall
 stand wide,
And their *cead mile failte*[6] woo all withinside,
And the travel-tired wayfarer find by the
 hearth

---

[1] Philip Fitzgibbon is not identified in any of the standard histories or biographical dictionaries of Irish literature.
[2] *Claoirseach:* bagpipes. [3] Banba: a name for Ireland.
[4] O'Donoghue's note: America and Europe. [5] *Brughaidhs:* purveyors of food.
[6] *Cead mile failte:* a hundred thousand welcomes.

Cheery Plenty where now, alas! all is Black
  Dearth.

X

The down-trodden Poor shall meet kindness
  and care,
And the Rich be as happy to spare and to
  share!
And the Mighty shall rule unassailed in their
  might,
And all voices be blent in one choir of delight!

XI

The bright Golden Era that poets have sung
Shall revive, and be chaunted anew in our
  tongue;
The skies shall rain Love on the land's breadth
  and length,
And the grain rise like armies battalioned in
  strength.

XII

The priest and the noble, the serf and his lord,
Shall sustain one another with word and with
  sword—
The Learned shall gain more than gold by
  their lore,
And all Fate took away she shall trebly restore.

XIII

Like rays round a centre, like stars round the
  moon,
Like Ocean round Earth, when it heaves in the
  noon,   50
Shall our chiefs, a resplendent and panoplied
  ring,
In invincible valour encircle their King.

XIV

And thou, O Grand Language, please Heaven,
  shalt win
Proud release from the tomb thou art
  sepulchred in.
In palace, in shieling,[7] on highway, on hill,
Shalt thou roll as a river, or glide as a rill!

XV

The story of Eiré shall shine forth in thee;
Thou shall sound as a horn from the lips of
  the Free;
And our priests in their forefathers' temples
  once more
Shall through Thee call on men to rejoice and
  adore!

                                                              1849   60

Samuel Ferguson
1810–1886

Samuel Ferguson entered the practice of law in 1838 after his graduation from Trinity College, Dublin. His successful legal career culminated in his appointment as deputy-keeper of public records in Ireland; he was knighted in 1878 for his service in organizing the records. He knew some Irish and a great deal of antiquarian lore, and in the 1860s he began to publish poems based on Irish heroic narratives and legendary history. He was best known for these poems, and for vigorous celebrations of work and daring which he published in magazines in Dublin and Scotland. But he also articulated the vein of fairy legend and pastoral particularity in the Irish literary tradition which Yeats and others were to continue and enlarge in the last decades of the century. Ferguson's poems were collected in 1880 and again in 1918. The texts printed here are from the first edition of Lays of the Western Gael *(1865).*

[7] Shieling: rural hut.

The Fairy Thorn

"Get up, our Anna dear, from the weary
  spinning-wheel;
For your father's on the hill, and your mother
  is asleep;
Come up above the crags, and we'll dance a
  highland reel
Around the fairy thorn on the steep."[1]

At Anna Grace's door 'twas thus the maidens
  cried,
Three merry maidens fair in kirtles of the
  green;
And Anna laid the rock and the weary wheel
  aside,
The fairest of the four, I ween.

They're glancing through the glimmer of the
  quiet eve,
Away in milky wavings of neck and ancle
  bare;
The heavy-sliding stream in its sleepy song
  they leave,
And the crags in the ghostly air:

And linking hand and hand, and singing as
  they go,
The maids along the hillside have ta'en their
  fearless way,
Till they come to where the rowan trees in
  lonely beauty grow
Beside the Fairy Hawthorn grey.

The Hawthorn stands between the ashes tall
  and slim,
Like matron with her twin grand-daughters at
  her knee;
The rowan berries cluster o'er her low head
  grey and dim
In ruddy kisses sweet to see.

The merry maidens four have ranged them in
  a row,
Between each lovely couple a stately rowan
  stem,
And away in mazes wavy, like skimming birds
  they go,
Oh, never caroll'd bird like them!

But solemn is the silence on the silvery haze
That drinks away their voices in echoless
  repose,

And dreamily the evening has still'd the
  haunted braes,
And dreamier the gloaming grows.

And sinking one by one, like lark-notes from
  the sky
When the falcon's shadow saileth across the
  open shaw,[2]
Are hush'd the maidens' voices, as cowering
  down they lie
In the flutter of their sudden awe.

For, from the air above and the grassy mound
  beneath,
And from the mountain-ashes and the old
  White-thorn between,
A Power of faint enchantment doth through
  their beings breathe,
And they sink down together on the green.

They sink together silent, and stealing side to
  side,
They fling their lovely arms o'er their drooping
  necks so fair,
Then vainly strive again their naked arms to
  hide,
For their shrinking necks again are bare.

Thus clasp'd and prostrate all, with their
  heads together bow'd,
Soft o'er their bosoms beating—the only human
  sound—
They hear the silky footsteps of the silent fairy
  crowd,
Like a river in the air, gliding round.

Nor scream can any raise, nor prayer can any
  say,
But wild, wild the terror of the speechless
  three—
For they feel fair Anna Grace drawn silently
  away,
By whom they dare not look to see.

They feel their tresses twine with her parting
  locks of gold,
And the curls elastic falling, as her head with-
  draws;
They feel her sliding arms from their tranced
  arms unfold,
But they dare not look to see the cause:

For heavy on their senses the faint enchant-
  ment lies

---

[1] Steep: hill.   [2] Shaw: a wood bordering a field.

Through all that night of anguish and perilous
  amaze;
And neither fear nor wonder can ope their
  quivering eyes
Or their limbs from the cold ground raise,

Till out of night the earth has roll'd her dewy
  side,
With every haunted mountain and streamy
  vale below;
When, as the mist dissolves in the yellow
  morning-tide,
The maidens' trance dissolveth so.

Then fly the ghastly three as swiftly as they
  may,
And tell their tale of sorrow to anxious friends
  in vain—
They pined away and died within the year and
  day,
And ne'er was Anna Grace seen again.

1834; 1865

The Lapful of Nuts[1]

Whene'er I see soft hazel eyes
  And nut-brown curls

I think of those bright days I spent
  Among the Limerick girls;
When up through Cratla woods I went
  Nutting with thee;
And we pluck'd the glossy clustering fruit
  From many a bending tree.

Beneath the hazel boughs we sat,
  Thou, love, and I,   10
And the gather'd nuts lay in thy lap,
  Beneath thy downcast eye:
But little we thought of the store we'd won,
  I, love, or thou;
For our hearts were full, and we dared not own
  The love that's spoken now.

Oh, there's wars for willing hearts in Spain,
  And high Germanie!
And I'll come back, ere long, again
  With knightly fame and fee: 20
And I'll come back, if I ever come back,
  Faithful to thee,
That sat with thy white lap full of nuts,
  Beneath the hazel tree.

1865

Ebenezer Jones
1820–1860

Ebenezer Jones earned his living as a clerk in London. The son of a severely Calvinistic religious family, an admirer of Shelley and Carlyle, and a supporter of Chartist and other radical political movements in the 1830s and 1840s, he began to write poetry and some political prose marked by an intense consciousness of the overwhelming energies running through nature and society. He published one volume of verse, Studies of Sensation and Event, in 1843 at his own expense. It attracted some notice, but it was not a financial success, and he published no more volumes of verse during his lifetime. His volume was republished in 1879 and included a few poems that did not appear in its first edition. The text printed here is from Miles (see "General Bibliography").

When the World Is Burning

(Stanzas for Music)

When the world is burning,
Fired within, yet turning
  Round with face unscathed;
Ere fierce flames, uprushing,

---

[1] A translation of an Irish lyric.

O'er all lands leap, crushing,
   Till earth fall, fire-swathed;
Up amidst the meadows,
Gently through the shadows,
   Gentle flames will glide,
10 Small, and blue, and golden.
Though by bard beholden,
When in calm dreams folden,—
   Calm his dreams will bide.

Where the dance is sweeping,
Through the greensward peeping,
   Shall the soft lights start;

Laughing maids, unstaying,
Deeming it trick-playing,
High their robes upswaying,
   O'er the lights shall dart;
And the woodland haunter,
Shall not cease to saunter
   When, far down some glade,
Of the great world's burning,
One soft flame upturning
Seems, to his discerning,
   Crocus in the shade.

1879

Thomas Babington Macaulay
1800–1859

The public life of Thomas Babington Macaulay is almost entirely a chronicle of exceptional successes. Before his culminating and greatest success as a writer, the publication of the first two volumes of his History of England from the Accession of James II in 1849, he had become well known as an essayist in the Edinburgh Review, to which he began contributing in the 1820s. He had also, after his graduation from Cambridge and an unsuccessful attempt in the practice of law, been elected to Parliament in 1830 and served as a member of the governing council in India from 1834 to 1838. Thoroughly read in the writings of Roman historians and attracted by the notion that among their sources were ballads and verse narratives of early Roman history, he reworked some of this history in Lays of Ancient Rome (1842), a collection that was immediately and persistently popular. Macaulay also published a three-volume collection of his essays in 1843, and two more volumes of History of England (all he completed) in 1855. He remained a member of Parliament for most of his life, occasionally served in other political posts, and was elevated to the peerage in 1857. The classic life of Macaulay is G. O. Trevelyan's The Life and Letters of Lord Macaulay (1876), now complemented by John Clive's Macaulay: The Shaping of the Historian (1973) and by the first two volumes of a new edition of his letters, edited by Thomas Pinney (1974).

The story of Horatius, a hero of Rome in the sixth century B.C., is told in Livy and other Roman histories. In the exploit celebrated in this poem, he and two companions have volunteered to hold a bridge over the river Tiber against an invading Etruscan army until the bridge can be undermined. In a prefatory note to the poem Macaulay calls it a "ballad" that "is supposed to have been made about a hundred and twenty years after the war which it celebrates, and just before the taking of Rome by the Gauls. The author seems to have been an honest citizen, proud of the military glory of his country, sick of the disputes of factions, and much given to pining after good old times which had never really existed." The text printed here is that of The Works of Lord Macaulay, edited by his sister Lady Trevelyan, first published in 1866.

from Horatius

31

"Horatius," quoth the Consul,
   "As thou sayest, so let it be."
And straight against that great array
   Forth went the dauntless Three.
For Romans in Rome's quarrel
   Spared neither land nor gold,
Nor son nor wife, nor limb nor life,
   In the brave days of old.

32

Then none was for a party;
  Then all were for the state;
Then the great man helped the poor,
  And the poor man loved the great:
Then lands were fairly portioned;
  Then spoils were fairly sold:
The Romans were like brothers
  In the brave days of old.

33

Now Roman is to Roman
  More hateful than a foe,
And the Tribunes beard the high,
  And the Fathers grind the low.
As we wax hot in faction,
  In battle we wax cold:
Wherefore men fight not as they fought
  In the brave days of old.

34

Now while the Three were tightening
  Their harness[1] on their backs,
The Consul was the foremost man
  To take in hand an axe:
And Fathers mixed with Commons
  Seized hatchet, bar, and crow,
And smote upon the planks above,
  And loosed the props below.

35

Meanwhile the Tuscan army,
  Right glorious to behold,
Came flashing back the noonday light,
Rank behind rank, like surges bright
  Of a broad sea of gold.
Four hundred trumpets sounded
  A peal of warlike glee,
As that great host, with measured tread,
And spears advanced, and ensigns spread,
Rolled slowly towards the bridge's head,
  Where stood the dauntless Three.

36

The Three stood calm and silent
  And looked upon the foes,
And a great shout of laughter
  From all the vanguard rose:
And forth three chiefs came spurring
  Before that deep array;
To earth they sprang, their swords they drew,
And lifted high their shields, and flew
  To win the narrow way;

. . .

40

Herminius smote down Aruns:[2]
  Lartius laid Ocnus low:
Right to the heart of Lausulus
  Horatius sent a blow.
"Lie there," he cried, "fell pirate!
  No more, aghast and pale,
From Ostia's[3] walls the crowd shall mark
The track of thy destroying bark.   60
No more Campania's[4] hinds shall fly
To woods and caverns when they spy
  Thy thrice accursed sail."

41

But now no sound of laughter
  Was heard amongst the foes.
A wild and wrathful clamour
  From all the vanguard rose.
Six spears' lengths from the entrance
  Halted that deep array,
And for a space no man came forth   70
  To win the narrow way.

42

But hark! the cry is Astur:
  And lo! the ranks divide;
And the great Lord of Luna
  Comes with his stately stride.
Upon his ample shoulders
  Clangs loud the four-fold shield,
And in his hand he shakes the brand
  Which none but he can wield.

43

He smiled on those bold Romans
  A smile serene and high;   80
He eyed the flinching Tuscans,
  And scorn was in his eye.
Quoth he, "The she-wolf's litter
  Stand savagely at bay:
But will ye dare to follow,
  If Astur clears the way?"

44

Then, whirling up his broadsword
  With both hands to the height,

---

[1] Harness: armor.   [2] Aruns: the son of Lars Porsena, the leader of the Etruscan forces.
[3] Ostia: a city on the Tiber.   [4] Campania is a province in central Italy.

He rushed against Horatius,
   And smote with all his might.
90 With shield and blade Horatius
   Right deftly turned the blow.
The blow, though turned, came yet too nigh;
It missed his helm, but gashed his thigh:
The Tuscans raised a joyful cry
   To see the red blood flow.

45

He reeled, and on Herminius
   He leaned one breathing-space;
Then, like a wild cat mad with wounds,
100   Sprang right at Astur's face.
Through teeth, and skull, and helmet,
   So fierce a thrust he sped,
The good sword stood a hand-breadth out
   Behind the Tuscan's head.

46

And the great Lord of Luna
   Fell at that deadly stroke,
As falls on Mount Alvernus
   A thunder-smitten oak.
Far o'er the crashing forest
110   The giant arms lie spread;
And the pale augurs, muttering low,
   Gaze on the blasted head.

47

On Astur's throat Horatius
   Right firmly pressed his heel,
And thrice and four times tugged amain,
   Ere he wrenched out the steel.
"And see," he cried, "the welcome,
   Fair guests, that waits you here!
What noble Lucumo comes next
120   To taste our Roman cheer?"

48

But at his haughty challenge
   A sullen murmur ran,
Mingled of wrath, and shame, and dread,
   Along that glittering van.
There lacked not men of prowess,
   Nor men of lordly race;
For all Etruria's noblest
   Were round the fatal place.

49

But all Etruria's noblest
130   Felt their hearts sink to see
On the earth the bloody corpses,
   In the path the dauntless Three:

And, from the ghastly entrance
   Where those bold Romans stood,
All shrank, like boys who unaware,
Ranging the woods to start a hare,
Come to the mouth of the dark lair
Where, growling low, a fierce old bear
   Lies amidst bones and blood.

.   .   .

53

But meanwhile axe and lever
   Have manfully been plied;
And now the bridge hangs tottering
   Above the boiling tide.
"Come back, come back, Horatius!"
   Loud cried the Fathers all.
"Back, Lartius! back, Herminius!
   Back, ere the ruin fall!"

54

Back darted Spurius Lartius;
   Herminius darted back:
And, as they passed, beneath their feet
   They felt the timbers crack.
But when they turned their faces,
   And on the farther shore
Saw brave Horatius stand alone,
   They would have crossed once more.

55

But with a crash like thunder
   Fell every loosened beam,
And, like a dam, the mighty wreck
   Lay right athwart the stream:
And a long shout of triumph
   Rose from the walls of Rome,
As to the highest turret-tops
   Was splashed the yellow foam.

56

And, like a horse unbroken
   When first he feels the rein,
The furious river struggled hard,
   And tossed his tawny mane;
And burst the curb, and bounded,
   Rejoicing to be free;
And whirling down, in fierce career,
Battlement, and plank, and pier,
   Rushed headlong to the sea.

57

Alone stood brave Horatius,
   But constant still in mind;

Thrice thirty thousand foes before,
   And the broad flood behind.
"Down with him!" cried false Sextus,[5]
   With a smile on his pale face.
"Now yield thee," cried Lars Porsena,
   "Now yield thee to our grace."

58
Round turned he, as not deigning
   Those craven ranks to see;
Nought spake he to Lars Porsena,
   To Sextus nought spake he;
But he saw on Palatinus[6]
   The white porch of his home;
And he spake to the noble river
   That rolls by the towers of Rome.

59
"Oh, Tiber! father Tiber!
   To whom the Romans pray,
A Roman's life, a Roman's arms,
   Take thou in charge this day!"
So he spake, and speaking sheathed
   The good sword by his side,
And with his harness on his back,
   Plunged headlong in the tide.

60
No sound of joy or sorrow
   Was heard from either bank;
But friends and foes in dumb surprise,
   With parted lips and straining eyes,
   Stood gazing where he sank;
And when above the surges
   They saw his crest appear,
All Rome sent forth a rapturous cry,
And even the ranks of Tuscany
   Could scarce forbear to cheer.

61
But fiercely ran the current,
   Swollen high by months of rain:
And fast his blood was flowing;
   And he was sore in pain,
And heavy with his armour,
   And spent with changing blows:
And oft they thought him sinking,
   But still again he rose.

62
Never, I ween, did swimmer,
   In such an evil case,

Struggle through such a raging flood
   Safe to the landing place:
But his limbs were borne up bravely
   By the brave heart within,   220
And our good father Tiber
   Bare bravely up his chin.

63
"Curse on him!" quoth false Sextus;
   "Will not the villain drown?
But for this stay, ere close of day
   We should have sacked the town!"
"Heaven help him!" quoth Lars Porsena,
   "And bring him safe to shore;
For such a gallant feat of arms
   Was never seen before."   230

64
And now he feels the bottom;
   Now on dry earth he stands;
Now round him throng the Fathers;
   To press his gory hands;
And now with shouts and clapping,
   And noise of weeping loud,
He enters through the River-Gate,
   Borne by the joyous crowd.

65
They gave him of the corn-land,
   That was of public right,   240
As much as two strong oxen
   Could plough from morn till night;
And they made a molten image,
   And set it up on high,
And there it stands unto this day
   To witness if I lie.

66
It stands in the Comitium,[7]
   Plain for all folk to see;
Horatius in his harness,
   Halting upon one knee: 250
And underneath is written,
   In letters all of gold,
How valiantly he kept the bridge
   In the brave days of old.

67
And still his name sounds stirring
   Unto the men of Rome,
As the trumpet-blast that cries to them
   To charge the Volscian[8] home;

---

[5] Sextus: a cowardly Roman renegade with Porsena's army.
[6] The Palantine was a part of Rome near the center.
[7] Comitium: a place of assembly for one of the Roman political bodies.
[8] Volscian: an ancient people in Italy.

And wives still pray to Juno[9]
   For boys with hearts as bold
260 As his who kept the bridge so well
   In the brave days of old.

68
And in the nights of winter,
   When the cold north winds blow,
And the long howling of the wolves
   Is heard amidst the snow;
When round the lonely cottage
   Roars loud the tempest's din,
And the good logs of Algidus[10]
270   Roar louder yet within;

69
When the oldest cask is opened,
   And the largest lamp is lit,

When the chestnuts glow in the embers,
   And the kid turns on the spit;
When young and old in circle
   Around the firebrands close;
When the girls are weaving baskets,
   And the lads are shaping bows;

70
When the goodman mends his armour,
   And trims his helmet's plume;
When the goodwife's shuttle merrily
   Goes flashing through the loom;
With weeping and with laughter
   Still is the story told,
How well Horatius kept the bridge
   In the brave days of old.

1842

William Edmondstoune Aytoun
1813–1865

William Edmondstoune Aytoun practiced law and the profession of letters in Edinburgh. He published a volume of verse in 1832, shortly after his graduation from Edinburgh University. During the 1830s and 1840s he contributed translations of German poets and essays to Blackwood's, a monthly magazine published in Edinburgh. He collaborated with Theodore Martin in The Bon Gaultier Ballads (see Part Seven), published in 1845 and popular for the rest of the century. In 1845 he began lecturing as the professor of rhetoric and belles lettres in the university at Edinburgh. The Lays of the Scottish Cavaliers (1849) established him as an earnest poet in a then popular tradition of robust narrative, and like Macaulay's Lays of Ancient Rome, the volume provided pieces for declamation which became well known through frequent use. Aytoun published another poetic burlesque, Firmilian, an attack on such prolix romantic poets of self-conscious elevation as Philip James Bailey, in 1854, and a heroic poem of his own, Bothwell, in 1856. He also published (with Martin) a volume of translations from Goethe, and he continued to publish sketches and poems in Blackwood's and other magazines.

The Scots memorialized in this poem were followers of James II of England, who was driven from the throne and into France in 1688. Some of his officers volunteered their services to the king of France and fought as a company in France and Germany. The text printed here is that of the 1849 edition of the Lays. It differs slightly from that published in the standard Oxford edition of Poems of William Edmondstoune Aytoun (1921).

from The Island of the Scots

I
The Rhine is running deep and red,
   The island lies before—
"Now is there one of all the host
   Will dare to venture o'er?
For not alone the river's sweep
   Might make a brave man quail:
The foe are on the further side,
   Their shot comes fast as hail.
God help us, if the middle isle
   We may not hope to win!

[9] Juno: wife of Zeus and queen of the gods.

[10] Algidus: a range of mountains near Rome.

Now is there any of the host
  Will dare to venture in?"

II

"The ford is deep, the banks are steep,
  The island-shore lies wide:
Nor man nor horse could stem its force,
  Or reach the further side.
See there! amidst the willow-boughs
  The serried bayonets gleam;
They've flung their bridge—they've won the
    isle;
  The foe have crossed the stream!
Their volley flashes sharp and strong—
  By all the Saints! I trow
There never yet was soldier born
  Could force that passage now!"

III

So spoke the bold French Mareschal
  With him who led the van,
Whilst rough and red before their view
  The turbid river ran.
Nor bridge nor boat had they to cross
  The wild and swollen Rhine,
And thundering on the other bank
  Far stretched the German line.
Hard by there stood a swarthy man
  Was leaning on his sword,
And a saddened smile lit up his face
  As he heard the Captain's word.
"I've seen a wilder stream ere now
  Than that which rushes there;
I've stemmed a heavier torrent yet
  And never thought to dare.
If German steel be sharp and keen,
  Is ours not strong and true?
There may be danger in the deed,
  But there is honour too."

IV

The old lord in his saddle turned,
  And hastily he said—
"Hath bold Duguesclin's fiery heart
  Awakened from the dead?
Thou art the leader of the Scots—
  Now well and sure I know,
That gentle blood in dangerous hour
  Ne'er yet ran cold nor slow,
And I have seen ye in the fight
  Do all that mortal may:

If honour is the boon ye seek,
  It may be won this day—
The prize is in the middle isle,
  There lies the venturous way.
And armies twain are on the plain,
  The daring deed to see— 60
Now ask thy gallant company
  If they will follow thee!"

V

Right gladsome looked the Captain then,
  And nothing did he say,
But he turned him to his little band—
  Oh few, I ween, were they!
The relics of the bravest force
  That ever fought in fray.
No one of all that company
  But bore a gentle name, 70
Not one whose fathers had not stood
  In Scotland's fields of fame.
All they had marched with great Dundee[1]
  To where he fought and fell,
And in the deadly battle-strife
  Had venged their leader well;
And they had bent the knee to earth
  When every eye was dim,
As o'er their hero's buried corpse
  They sang the funeral hymn; 80
And they had trod the Pass once more,
  And stooped on either side
To pluck the heather from the spot
  Where he had dropped and died;
And they had bound it next their hearts,
  And ta'en a last farewell
Of Scottish earth and Scottish sky,
  Where Scotland's glory fell.
Then went they forth to foreign lands
  Like bent and broken men, 90
Who leave their dearest hope behind,
  And may not turn again.

. . .

VII

No stay—no pause. With one accord
  They grasped each other's hand,
Then plunged into the angry flood,
  That bold and dauntless band.
High flew the spray above their heads,
  Yet onward still they bore,
Midst cheer, and shout, and answering yell,
  And shot, and cannon-roar— 100

[1] Dundee: John Graham of Claverhouse, Viscount Dundee (*c.* 1649–89), was killed while leading the forces of James against those of William, who had married James' daughter and was proclaimed king of England in 1689.

"Now, by the Holy Cross! I swear,
  Since earth and sea began,
Was never such a daring deed
  Essayed by mortal man!"

VIII

Thick blew the smoke across the stream,
  And faster flashed the flame:
The water plashed in hissing jets
  As ball and bullet came.
Yet onwards pushed the Cavaliers
110 All stern and undismayed,
With thousand armèd foes before,
  And none behind to aid.
Once, as they neared the middle stream,
  So strong the torrent swept,
That scarce that long and living wall
  Their dangerous footing kept.
Then rose a warning cry behind,
  A joyous shout before:
"The current's strong—the way is long—
120 They'll never reach the shore!
See, see! they stagger in the midst,
  They waver in their line!
Fire on the madmen! break their ranks,
  And whelm them in the Rhine!"

. . .

X

The German heart is stout and true,
  The German arm is strong;
The German foot goes seldom back
  Where armèd foemen throng.
But never had they faced in field
130 So stern a charge before,
And never had they felt the sweep
  Of Scotland's broad claymore.[2]
Not fiercer pours the avalanche
  Adown the steep incline,
That rises o'er the parent-springs
  Of rough and rapid Rhine—
Scarce swifter shoots the bolt from heaven
  Than came the Scottish band
Right up against the guarded trench,
140 And o'er it sword in hand.
In vain their leaders forward press—
  They meet the deadly brand!
O lonely island of the Rhine—
  Where seed was never sown,
What harvest lay upon thy sands,
  By those strong reapers thrown?

[2] Claymore: a large two-edged sword.

What saw the winter moon that night,
  As, struggling through the rain,
She poured a wan and fitful light
  On marsh, and stream, and plain? 150
A dreary spot with corpses strewn,
  And bayonets glistening round;
A broken bridge, a stranded boat,
  A bare and battered mound;
And one huge watch-fire's kindled pile,
  That sent its quivering glare
To tell the leaders of the host
  The conquering Scots were there!

XI

And did they twine the laurel-wreath
  For those who fought so well? 160
And did they honour those who lived,
  And weep for those who fell?
What meed of thanks was given to them
  Let agèd annals tell.
Why should they twine the laurel-wreath—
  Why crown the cup with wine?
It was not Frenchmen's blood that flowed
  So freely on the Rhine—
A stranger band of beggared men
  Had done the venturous deed: 170
The glory was to France alone,
  The danger was their meed.
And what cared they for idle thanks
  From foreign prince and peer?
What virtue had such honied words
  The exiles' hearts to cheer?
What mattered it that men should vaunt
  And loud and fondly swear,
That higher feat of chivalry
  Was never wrought elsewhere? 180
They bore within their breasts the grief
  That fame can never heal—
The deep, unutterable woe
  Which none save exiles feel.
Their hearts were yearning for the land
  They ne'er might see again—
For Scotland's high and heathered hills,
  For mountain, loch, and glen—
For those who haply lay at rest
  Beyond the distant sea, 190
Beneath the green and daisied turf
  Where they would gladly be!

XII

Long years went by. The lonely isle
  In Rhine's impetuous flood

Has ta'en another name from those
  Who bought it with their blood:
And, though the legend does not live—
  For legends lightly die—
The peasant, as he sees the stream
  In winter rolling by,

And foaming o'er its channel-bed
  Between him and the spot
Won by the warriors of the sword,
Still calls that deep and dangerous ford
  The Passage of the Scot.

1849

Richard Hengist Horne
1803–1884

Richard Hengist Horne, after a military educa-
tion and adventures in Mexico and North America,
returned to London in 1826 to begin a career in lit-
erature. He wrote poems and literary and political
journalism for magazines and newspapers, edited a
monthly magazine, edited a life of Napoleon and a
modernized version of Chaucer's poems, and pub-
lished several heroic tragedies in verse. In 1843 he
decided to publish Orion at a farthing (but only
to people who possessed a proper accent and could
pronounce the title correctly) as a self-advertising
gesture of protest against the modest sales of vol-
umes of poetry in the 1830s and early 1840s. The
poem was immediately popular, going into its sixth
edition, by which time its price was over two shill-
ings, before the end of the year. Until the end of
his long life Horne continued to write and publish
prolifically, both in England and in Australia, where
he lived from 1852 to 1869. His best-known work
was The New Spirit of the Age (1844), a collection
of essays mostly written by him about the literature
of the 1840s. Two recent biographies of Horne have
been published: Cyril Pearl, Always Morning
(1960), and Ann Blainey, The Farthing Poet
(1968).

Orion is a version of the Greek myth of a giant
hunter who is loved by Diana (Artemis), the god-
dess of the moon, and finally translated into a con-
stellation. Horne makes the myth into a fable of
human, earthly strength progressing through the
refinements of love and spiritual insight to a tri-
umphantly transcendent state. His hero first loves
Artemis, who rejects him as still too full of earth;
and then Merope, whom he tries to force in a frus-
trated rage and is in consequence blinded by her
father; and finally Eos, the goddess of morning,
who restores his sight and prepares him for his
transcendence. The text printed here is that of the
original farthing edition.

from Orion

from Book 1
CANTO 2

[Orion and Artemis]

  There was a slumbrous silence in the air,
By noon-tide's sultry murmurs from without
Made more oblivious. Not a pipe was heard
From field or wood; but the grave beetle's
    drone
Passed near the entrance: once the cuckoo
    called
O'er distant meads, and once a horn began
Melodious plaint, then died away. A sound
Of murmurous music yet was in the breeze,
For silver gnats that harp on glassy strings,
And rise and fall in sparkling clouds, sustained   10
Their dizzy dances o'er the seething meads.
With brain as dizzy stood Orion now
I' the quivering bower. There rapturous he
    beheld,
As in a trance, not conscious of himself,
The perfect sculpture of that naked form,
Whose Parian whiteness and clear outline
    gleamed
In its own hue, nor from the foliage took
One tint, nor from his ample frame one shade.
Her lovely hair hung drooping, half
    unbound,—
Fair silken braids, fawn-tinted delicately,   20

That on one shoulder lodged their opening
    coil.
Her large round arms of dazzling beauty lay
In matchless symmetry and inviolate grace
Along the mossy floor. At length he dropped
Softly upon his knees, his clasped hands raised
Above his head, 'till by resistless impulse
His arms descending, were expanded wide—
Swift as a flash, erect the Goddess rose!

    Her eyes shot through Orion, and he felt
30 Within his breast an icy dart. Confronted,
Mutely they stood, but all the bower was filled
With rising mist that chilled him to the bone,
Colder, as more obscure the space became;
And ere the last collected shape he saw
Of Artemis, dispersing fast amid
Dense vapoury clouds, the aching wintriness
Had risen to his teeth, and fixed his eyes,
Like glistering stones in the congealing air.

.   .   .

from Book 3

CANTO 1

[The Herald Poet]

The man who for his race might supersede
The work of ages, dies worn out—not used,

And in his track disciples onward strive,
Some hairs'-breadths only from his starting
    point:
Yet lives he not in vain; for if his soul
Hath entered others, though imperfectly,
The circle widens as the world spins round,—
His soul works on while he sleeps 'neath the
    grass.
So, let the firm Philosopher renew
His wasted lamp—the lamp wastes not in vain,   1
Though he no mirrors for its rays may see,
Nor trace them through the darkness;—let the
    Hand
Which feels primeval impulses, direct
A forthright plough, and make his furrow
    broad,
With heart untiring while one field remains;
So, let the herald Poet shed his thoughts,
Like seeds that seem but lost upon the wind.
Work in the night, thou sage, while
    Mammon's brain
Teems with low visions on his couch of
    down;—
Break, thou, the clods while high-throned
    Vanity,   2
Midst glaring lights and trumpets, holds its
    court;—
Sing, thou, thy song amidst the stoning crowd,
Then stand apart, obscure to man, with GOD.
The poet of the future knows his place,
Though in the present shady be his seat,
And all his laurels deepening but the shade.

1843

Philip James Bailey
1816–1902

Philip James Bailey studied at Glasgow University and was admitted to the practice of law in London before retiring to his father's house in 1836 to write a long poem on the model of Goethe's Faust *in which he would ask and answer the most profound questions about man, God, and the universe. The first version of* Festus, *then a poem of about 8000 lines, was published in 1839. For the rest of his life Bailey added to and published successively*

*longer versions of the poem. The verse of three other volumes—*The Angel World *(1850),* The Mystic *(1855), and* Universal Hymn *(1867)—was eventually incorporated into the poem, which in its seventh and final version (1889) was nearly 40,000 lines in length. The poem was both admired for its gaudy fervor and finally orthodox moral and theological sentiments, and mocked for its prolixity and undiscriminating confidence that whatever a poet* *thinks to say is poetry. The popularity and notoriety of the poem sponsored a small school, called the "Spasmodics" by their detractors, of which Alexander Smith's "A Life Drama" (1853) and Sydney Dobell's uncompleted* Balder *(1853) were taken to be examples.*

Festus is strung along the terrestial and celestial travels of the hero who gives the poem its name. In his journey he converses with Lucifer, angels, and earthly representatives of beauty, art, religion, science, and the like, learning and more often instructing them in the nature of all things. At the end of the poem Lucifer admits and submits to the triumphant goodness and mercy of God. For all its discursive character and didactic intentions the poem proceeds from conventional romantic ideas that the visible world is an emblem or incarnation of transcendent reality, and that the poet's exceptional vision and metaphorical language rightly express the morally elevating truth also bespoken by the matter of God's creation. The passage printed here is from the third edition of the poem, published in London in 1848.

from Festus

Proem to the Third Edition

Poetry is itself a thing of God;
He made His prophets poets: and the more
We feel of poesie do we become
Like God in love and power,—under-makers.
And song is of the supernatural
Natural utterance; and solely can
Speak the unbounded beauty of the world,
And the premortal concords of pure mind.
All great lays, equals to the minds of men,
Deal more or less with the Divine, and have

For end some good of mind or soul of man.
The mind is this world's, but the soul is God's;
The wise man joins them here all in his power.
The high and holy works, amid lesser lays,
Stand up like churches among village cots;
And it is joy to think that in every age,
However much the world was wrong therein,
The greatest works of mind or hand have been
Done unto God. So may they ever be!
It shews the strength of wish we have to be
    great,   20
And the sublime humility of might.
  True fiction hath in it a higher end
Than fact; it is the possible compared
With what is merely positive, and gives
To the conceptive soul an inner world,
A higher, ampler, Heaven than that wherein
The nations sun themselves. In that bright
    state
Are met the mental creatures of the men
Whose names are writ highest on the rounded
    crown
Of Fame's triumphal arch; the shining shapes   30
Which star the skies of that invisible land,
Which, whosoe'er would enter, let him
    learn;—
'Tis not enough to draw forms fair and lively,
Their conduct likewise must be beautiful;
A hearty holiness must crown the work,
As a gold cross the minster-dome, and shew,
Like that instonement of divinity,
That the whole building doth belong to God.
And for the book before us, though it were,
What it is not, supremely little, like   40
The needled angle of a high church spire,
Its sole end points to God the Father's glory,
From all eternity seen; making clear
His might and love in saving sinful man.

                               1848

Martin Farquhar Tupper
1810–1889

Martin Farquhar Tupper, the son of a London physician, graduated from Oxford in 1832 and was soon after admitted to the bar. He never practiced *law, however: he had already published a volume of poems in 1832, and in 1838 he published two volumes, a continuation of Coleridge's "Christabel"*

in Geraldine and Other Poems, *and the first series
of the sententious poems of* Proverbial Philosophy.
*He published three other volumes under the same
title, the last in 1876. All were extraordinarily popu-
lar. The first series went through more than fifty
editions in Tupper's lifetime, and more than 250,-
000 copies of the volumes in the series were sold in
England (more than a million were sold in the
United States). Tupper also published other vol-
umes and pamphlets of verse, many of them on
topical issues. He published an autobiography in
1886; Derek Hudson's* Martin Tupper: His Rise
and Fall *(1949) is the most substantial twentieth-
century account of his career. The texts printed
here are those of an edition of all four series of*
Proverbial Philosophy *published in London in
1880.*

from Proverbial Philosophy, First Series

from Of Invention

. . . Behold the barren reef, which an earth-
  quake hath just left dry;
It hath no beauty to boast of, no harvest of
  fair fruits:
But soon the lichen fixeth there, and, dying,
  diggeth its own grave,
And softening suns and splitting frosts
  crumble the reluctant surface;
And cormorants roost there, and the snail
  addeth its slime,
And efts,[1] with muddy feet, bring their
  welcome tribute;
And the sea casteth out her dead, wrapped in
  a shroud of weeds;
And orderly nature arrangeth again the
  disunited atoms:
Anon, the cold smooth stone is warm with
  feathery grass,
And the light sporules of the fern are dropt by
10 the passing wind.
The wood-pigeon, on swift wing, leaveth its
  crop-full of grain;

The squirrel's jealous care planteth the
  fircone and the filbert;
Years pass, and the sterile rock is rank with
  tangled herbage;
The wild vine clingeth to the brier, and ivy
  runneth green among the corn;
Lordly beeches are studded on the down, and
  willows crowd around the rivulet;
And the tall pine and hazel thicket shade the
  rambling hunter.
Shall the rock boast of its fertility? shall it
  lift the head in pride?—
Shall the mind of man be vain of the harvest
  of its thoughts?
The savage is that rock: and a million chances
  from without,
By little and little acting on the mind, heap
  up the hotbed of society;
And the soul, fed and fattened on the thoughts
  and things around it,
Groweth to perfection, full of fruit, the fruit of
  foreign seeds.
For we learn upon a hint, we find upon a clue,
We yield an hundred-fold; but the great sower
  is Analogy.
There must be an acrid sloe before a luscious
  peach,
A boll of rotting flax before the bridal veil,
An egg before an eagle, a thought before a
  thing,
A spark struck into tinder, to light the lamp
  of knowledge,
A slight suggestive nod to guide the watching
  mind,
A half-seen hand upon the wall, pointing to
  the balance of Comparison.
By culture man may do all things, short of the
  miracle,—Creation:
Here is the limit of thy power,—here let thy
  pride be stayed:
The soil may be rich, and the mind may be
  active, but neither yield unsown
The eye cannot make light, nor the mind make
  spirit:
Therefore it is wise in man to name all novelty
  invention:
For it is to find out things that are, not to
  create the unexisting:
It is to cling to contiguities, to be keen in
  catching likeness,
And with energetic elasticity to leap the gulfs
  of contrast.

1838

from Proverbial Philosophy, Fourth Series

Of Curious Questions

This world of strange creations, so prodigal in
 wastefulness of life,
Teeming with eggs, and seeds, and germs,
 nipped by death continually,
Is it then a nursery and storehouse for other
 orbs elsewhere,
A workshop where the Maker constructeth His
 machines,
Each to live developing more gloriously here-
 after
By progress toward perfection in their natures
 and their forms?
The multitudes on multitudes here only born
 to die,
So intricately fashioned and so exquisitely
 coloured,
Have these no life beyond, wherein to worship
 God
And show to angel-minds His skill, by man too
 long unnoted?

For all are cherished darlings of their Father,
 and each might be His masterpiece,
And none were made solely for destruction,
 toys to be flung away:
Would He annihilate a creature His mercy
 once hath formed,
Nor rather let it grow to bliss, continuously
 progressing?
Can the Unchangeable be changed, or His
 purpose fail,
Or any weak caprice be mingled with His vast
 design?
There is more than room enow for all the
 generations of earth's children
In yonder shoal of suns we see, with unseen
 planets round them,—
And all we note are but a sample of the
 wondrous whole,
The many mansions waiting to be filled with
 various life; 20
For it is Infinity, not space, innumerable homes
 for happy creatures,
Every star a sun, invisibly attended by its
 system,
And each of those vast satellites, various in
 form and glory,
To be stocked from this nursery of earth, and
 perfect all her seeds:
Who knoweth? nothing shall be wasted; not
 one egg in vain;
Every kind of life immortal in its Maker!

1876

PART THREE

Principal Victorian Poets 1850-1880

Arthur Hugh Clough
1819–1861

THROUGHOUT the first passage of his life, until he was thirty years old, Arthur Hugh Clough seemed to be efficiently fulfilling the expectations of his friends and teachers that he would take a powerful part in the intellectual culture of mid-century England. Clough had won fellowships, published poems, witnessed and written about major political events on the Continent, and impressed his friends and students with the force, clarity, and honesty of a mind and character that insisted on hard tests for all opinions, including his own. Fifteen years later, after his death when he was forty-three years old, his friends began asking the question, invited by their own high estimate of him and repeated ever since by biographers who share that estimate: what went wrong? It is possible, as some of Clough's biographers have believed, that the high personal standards and moral rigor he learned from Dr. Thomas Arnold of Rugby came to cross the imperatives of Clough's intelligence, and he wore himself out trying to find an intellectually honest way to believe in a transcendent reality and to live in mid-nineteenth-century England. It is also possible, in the opinion of one of the exceptionally gifted people who were always attracted by Clough, the economist, political writer, literary critic, and journalist Walter Bagehot, that Clough simply found nothing to do commensurate with his abilities. But it is also possible to say that nothing went wrong. Clough did find one important thing to do: he wrote poetry. Although almost all his poetry was written before 1853, before it was clear that the momentum of his public career was beginning to falter, in his poetry not only did he display, he also fulfilled limited but strong and singular abilities.

Clough's resignation of his fellowship in an Oxford college in 1848 showed the exceptionally scrupulous intelligence of his religious beliefs. But it did not deprive him of a vocation. One of the conditions for continuing to hold the fellowship was eventual ordination in the Church of England, and Clough never intended to take clerical orders. Similarly one of the reasons for his resignation as principal of University Hall in the University of London was his difficulty in fitting his complicated religious opinions into the creed of an established sect. But although he enjoyed his acquaintance with Thomas Carlyle and other writers living in London, he was not entirely at home in the climate of intellectual and literary life in London, sharper and more varied than that of Oxford, and he was not a particularly effective academic administrator. After he gave up his plan to live and teach in the United States, he returned to England in 1853 to begin work in the Education Office; he had apparently decided that the occupations of teaching and writing were either closed to him or somehow unsatisfying. He wrote his friends that he enjoyed his work in the Education Office—better quill-pushing, he said, than boy-pushing. He worked very hard in useful public projects with Florence Nightingale and others, kept up a correspondence with Emerson and other American writers and intellectuals, and sustained friendships with some remarkably intelligent people in England. His duties in the Education Office gave him time to write, but not until the end of his life did he resume the writing of poetry in the narratives of the uncompleted *Mari Magno*, a set of stories about relations between men and women told to one another by the passengers on a ship. It does seem likely that Clough, like his friend Matthew Arnold, came to think that the act of writing poetry was itself an insufficiently effective mode of engagement with a confused and fallen world. It was hard to act confidently as a poet in this world, hard to be honest about its gross and clamant actuality and truthful about possibilities larger and more fruitful than those immediately discernible in the present. Again like Arnold, Clough found other means of action. But it is exactly the tension of living and acting as poet in the world that is the energy of Clough's poetry, and it was in expressing that tension that he did best and most tellingly what it was in him to do.

What he did was to make a poetry which, to appropriate two phrases from "Dipsychus," would "own the positive and the present" and speak "the Second Reverence, for things around." He was wary that the refining distances of poetry not be overwhelmed in his acknowledgment of the particular and the immediate. In his first published poem, *The Bothie of Tober-na-Vuolich,* he used his command of classical prosody to devise an English hexameter whose odd music connects and preserves a range of pleasures it stands a little apart from: talking about books, falling in love, swimming in cold water. In *Amours de Voyage* Clough used the same meter with a more trenchant irony to tell the story of a young man who watches the suppression of the Roman republic, reflects on the risks of action in love and war, and loses his chance to win the love of a young English girl: here the gain and cost of the distanced, esthetic regard of irony is at once the medium and theme of the poem. The uncompleted "Dipsychus" is yet more experimental in its junctures of the gross and refined, with its counterpoint of street songs and blank verse, and its vernacular deflations of high meditative measures and language.

In "Dipsychus" Clough seems finally unable to command his sense of himself in the world, to find and finish a poetic structure that will hold and resolve the vacillations of its protagonist as he wobbles between poles of possibility in himself and his reality. But the ambitions and experimental nature of "Dipsychus" accurately define Clough's achievement as a poet. He pressed out from the conventional poetic language of his time to find his own vocabulary, rhythms, literary forms and tones so that he could put the hard matter of the world into his poetry and ask, in an adult, complex, hard-to-deceive scrutiny, whether it answered his desires. His short poems are perhaps most effective when, as in "Natura Naturans," he threads a self-regarding wit though the declamatory rhythms and big figures and allusions he uses without irony in other poems. But even the sometimes stiff line and language of the two "Easter Day" poems are founded in a careful prosody, diction, and structure that try to render accurately the painful turnings of a principled intelligence looking directly at an experience that will not easily yield to desires that it be redeemed.

Clough's poetry was not well known during his lifetime. After the publication of a two-volume collection of his prose and poetry in 1869, the number of his readers began steadily to increase; the 1869 collection went through fifteen editions by the end of the century. Some of his readers found Clough's poetry obscure. It is not a difficult poetry. It is rarely recondite in vocabulary and allusion, and it is relatively bare of ornament. Much of its strength lies in its syntactical clarity, its frequent use of common words, and the confident use of colloquial rhythms that in the *Bothie* and parts of "Dipsychus" especially deliver elevated discourse in a facsimilie of natural talk. Other nineteenth-century readers found Clough troubling in his themes and in the indeterminacy of his resolutions. It was undoubtedly his perplexity to which readers in the last decades of the nineteenth century, themselves troubled in their religious beliefs, principally responded. His themes and the pained but strong-minded irresolution of his belief in the transcendental meaning of mortal existence are still important in any reading of Clough's poetry. But Clough is interesting as a poet because of how he wrote, and not primarily because of what he wrote about. He was ready to engage in poetry matter and questions that confused and disturbed others of his generation, and he was ready to mix various forms, meters, and registers of language unconventionally in order to articulate the particular complexity and urgency of the condition in which he found himself and the world. His condition and the questions it sponsored are still compelling. But it is the thoughtful audacity of Clough's means of talking about them in verse that makes his poetry durable.

CHRONOLOGY

1819   Born in Liverpool; his father was a not very successful cotton merchant; his mother was the daughter of a banker.

1822–23   During this winter Clough's father emigrated to South Carolina with his family.

1828–36   Clough was sent back to England for his education, entering Rugby in 1829, the year after Thomas Arnold had become the school's headmaster. Until his family returned to England in 1836, Clough sometimes stayed in the Arnolds' house.

1837–41 Clough entered Oxford after winning a scholarship. He took his degree in 1841, the year in which his father's business failed. After failing to win a fellowship, Clough served for a time as a private tutor to students at Rugby.

1842–47 Clough was elected to a fellowship in Oriel College, Oxford, where he also served as a lecturer. He and Matthew Arnold formed a close friendship in these years when Arnold was first a student and then, like his father and Clough before him, elected to a fellowship in Oriel in 1845.

1848 *The Bothie of Tober-na-Vuolich* published. Clough was in Paris during the 1848 revolution. At the end of 1848 he resigned his fellowship because he was unable to describe his subscription to the Thirty-Nine Articles of the creed of the Church of England as a conclusive declaration of his religious belief.

1849 *Ambarvalia* published, a collection of the poems of Clough and his friend Thomas Burbidge. Clough was visiting in Rome during the downfall of the Roman republic; he wrote *Amours de Voyage,* a narrative poem in letters written in the colloquial hexameters he used in *The Bothie,* during his stay in Rome. On his return he assumed the duties of the Principal of University Hall, University of London; later he added the duties of the Chair of English Literature in the University.

1850 During a visit to Venice, Clough wrote most of "Dipsychus."

1851–52 At the end of 1851, Clough resigned from the University of London, again in part because he was unwilling to describe his religious beliefs in a way that made them consistent with established forms of religious doctrine. He traveled to the United States with the idea of emigrating permanently; he lived in Boston and Cambridge, renewed a friendship with Ralph Waldo Emerson, began a translation of the Roman biographer Plutarch, wrote for American magazines, tutored, and considered beginning a school.

1853–54 Clough returned to England to take an appointment in the Education Office; his duties were to adjust the grades of those who examined candidates for degrees, and to administer some examinations himself. He married in 1854; his wife was the daughter of a government official and the cousin of Florence Nightingale, whom Clough later assisted in her several campaigns for the reform of hospital care.

1856 Clough was appointed secretary to a commission which reviewed the education of military officers.

1858 *Amours de Voyage* published serially in an American magazine. Clough was appointed private secretary to the vice-president of a government committee on education.

1859 Clough's revision of John Dryden's translation of Plutarch's *Lives* published.

1860–61 Clough took a leave from the Education Office because of poor health. After traveling to Greece and on the Continent, he died in Florence in 1861. An edition of his poems was published in 1862. An enlarged edition, including "Dipsychus," was privately published in 1865; a two-volume edition *The Poems and Prose Remains* was published in 1869, and frequently reprinted during the rest of the century.

EDITIONS

The texts of the poems reprinted below are those of *The Poems of Arthur Hough Clough,* second edition, edited by F. L. Mulhauser (1974). Mulhauser takes as his texts versions of the poems Clough prepared for an edition published in Boston in 1862. For poems not published in 1862, his texts are based on available manuscripts and printed versions. Buckner B. Trawick has edited *Selected Prose Works of Arthur Hugh Clough* (1964). Clough's *Correspondence* has been edited by F. L. Mulhauser (1957). H. F. Lowry's edition of *The Letters of Matthew Arnold to Arthur Hugh Clough* (1932) is also pertinent to an understanding of Clough's ideas about poetry in the 1840s. H. F. Lowry and Ralph L. Rusk have edited *The Emerson-Clough Letters* (1934, reprinted 1968), and Clough's letters to one of Matthew Arnold's brothers are published in *The New Zealand Letters of Thomas Arnold the Younger . . . and Letters of Arthur Hugh Clough, 1847–1851,* edited by James Bertram (1966).

BIOGRAPHY AND CRITICISM

Katherine Chorley's *Arthur Hugh Clough: The Uncommitted Mind* (1962) is the most generally informative of several biographies of Clough. Richard Gollin in "Clough Despite

Himself," *Essays in Criticism,* 12 (1962) contests some of the emphases and premises of Lady Chorley's reading of Clough's life. A. O. J. Cockshut in "Clough: The Real Doubter," in *The Unbelievers: English Agnostic Thought 1840–1890* (1964) discusses Clough's intellectual skepticism and religious belief.

OTHER USEFUL BOOKS AND
ESSAYS

Biswas, Robindra Kumar. *Arthur Hugh Clough: Towards a Reconsideration* (1972).

Greenberger, Evelyn Barish. *Arthur Hugh Clough: The Growth of a Poet's Mind* (1970).

Harris, Wendell. *Arthur Hugh Clough* (1970).

Houghton, Walter E. *The Poetry of Clough* (1963).

Timko, Michael. *Innocent Victorian: The Satiric Poetry of Clough* (1966).

Veyriras, Paul. *Arthur Hugh Clough* (1964).

Williams, David. *Too Quick Despairer: The Life and Work of Arthur Hugh Clough* (1969).

Arthur Hugh Clough: A Descriptive Catalogue, compiled by Richard M. Gollin, Walter E. Houghton, and Michael Timko (1967) is a bibliography of works by and about Clough. See also *Clough: The Critical Heritage,* edited by Michael Thorpe (1972).

Qui Laborat, Orat[1]

O only Source of all our light and life,
 Whom as our truth, our strength, we see and
  feel,
But whom the hours of mortal moral strife
 Alone aright reveal!

Mine inmost soul, before Thee inly brought,
 Thy presence owns ineffable, divine;
Chastised each rebel self-encentered thought,
 My will adoreth Thine.

With eye down-dropt, if then this earthly mind
10 Speechless remain, or speechless e'en depart,
Nor seek to see (for what of earthly kind
 Can see Thee as Thou art?) —

If sure assured 'tis profanely bold
 In thought's abstractest forms to seem to see,
It dare not dare the dread communion hold
 In ways unworthy Thee,—

[1] Who works, prays.

O not unowned, Thou shalt unnamed forgive,
 In worldly walks the prayerless heart
  prepare,
And if in work its life it seem to live,
 Shalt make that work be prayer.

Nor times shall lack, when while the work it
  plies,
 Unsummoned powers the blinding film shall
  part,
And scarce by happy tears made dim, the eyes
 In recognition start.

As wills Thy will, give or e'en forbear
 The beatific supersensual sight,
So, with Thy blessing blest, that humbler
  prayer
 Approach Thee morn and night.
                                    (1845?) 1849

"My wind is turned to bitter north"

My wind is turned to bitter north,
 That was so soft a south before;
My sky, that shone so sunny bright,
 With foggy gloom is clouded o'er:
My gay green leaves are yellow-black,
 Upon the dank autumnal floor;
For love, departed once, comes back
 No more again, no more.

A roofless ruin lies my home,
 For winds to blow and rains to pour;
One frosty night befell, and lo,
 I find my summer days are o'er:
The heart bereaved, of why and how
 Unknowing, knows that yet before
It had what e'en to Memory now
 Returns no more, no more.
                                    (1845?) 1849

"Look you, my simple friend . . ."

Look you, my simple friend, 'tis one of those,
(Alack, a common weed of our ill time),
Who, do whate'er they may, go where they will,
Must needs still carry about the looking-glass
Of vain philosophy. And if so be
That some small natural gesture shall escape
 them,

(Nature will out) straightway about they turn,
And con it duly there, and note it down,
With inward glee and much complacent chuck-
    ling,
10 Part in conceit of their superior science,
Part in forevision of the attentive look
And laughing glance that may one time
    reward them,
When the fresh ore, this day dug up, at last
Shall, thrice refined and purified, from the
    mint
Of conversation intellectual
Into the golden currency of wit
Issue—satirical or pointed sentence,
Impromptu, epigram, or it may be sonnet,
Heir undisputed to the pinkiest page
20 In the album of a literary lady.

   And can it be, you ask me, that a man,
With the strong arm, the cunning faculties,
And keenest forethought gifted, and, within,
Longings unspeakable, the lingering echoes
Responsive to the still-still-calling voice
Of God Most High,—should disregard all
    these,
And half-employ all those for such an aim
As the light sympathy of successful wit,
Vain titillation of a moment's praise?
30 Why, so is good no longer good, but crime
Our truest, best advantage, since it lifts us
Out of the stifling gas of men's opinion
Into the vital atmosphere of Truth,
Where He again is visible, tho' in anger.
                                    (1840) 1849

Qua Cursum Ventus[1]

As ships, becalmed at eve, that lay
   With canvas drooping, side by side,
Two towers of sail at dawn of day
   Are scarce long leagues apart descried;

When fell the night, upsprung the breeze,
   And all the darkling hours they plied,
Nor dreamt but each the self-same seas
   By each was cleaving, side by side:

E'en so—but why the tale reveal
   Of those, whom, year by year unchanged,
Brief absence joined anew, to feel
   Astounded, soul from soul estranged?

At dead of night their sails were filled,
   And onward each rejoicing steered—
Ah, neither blame, for neither willed,
   Or wist, what first with dawn appeared!

To veer, how vain! On, onward strain,
   Brave barks! In light, in darkness too,
Through winds and tides one compass guides:—
   To that, and your own selves, be true.   20

But O blithe breeze, and O great seas,
   Though ne'er, that earliest parting past,
On your wide plain they join again,
   Together lead them home at last!

One port, methought, alike they sought,
   One purpose hold where'er they fare,—
O bounding breeze, O rushing seas,
   At last, at last, unite them there!
                                    (1845?) 1849

Natura Naturans[1]

Beside me,—in the car,[2]—she sat,
   She spake not, no, nor looked to me:
From her to me, from me to her,
   What passed so subtly stealthily?
As rose to rose that by it blows
   Its interchanged aroma flings;
Or wake to sound of one sweet note
   The virtues of disparted strings.

Beside me, nought but this!—but this,
   That influent as within me dwelt   10
Her life, mine too within her breast,
   Her brain, her every limb she felt:
We sat; while o'er and in us, more
   And more, a power unknown prevailed,
Inhaling, and inhaled,—and still
   'Twas one, inhaling or inhaled.

Beside me, nought but this;—and passed;
   I passed; and know not to this day
If gold or jet her girlish hair,
   If black, or brown, or lucid-grey   20
Her eye's young glance: the fickle chance
   That joined us, yet may join again;
But I no face again could greet
   As hers, whose life was in me then.

---

[1] The title is a phrase from Virgil's *Aeneid;* a loose translation is, "Wherever the winds set the course."
[1] The nature of nature.   [2] Car: specified in line 27 as a second-class railway car.

As unsuspecting mere a maid
   As, fresh in maidhood's bloomiest bloom,
In casual second-class did e'er
   By casual youth her seat assume;
Or vestal, say, of saintliest clay,
30   For once by balmiest airs betrayed
Unto emotions too too sweet
   To be unlingeringly gainsaid:

Unowning then, confusing soon
   With dreamier dreams that o'er the glass
Of shyly ripening woman-sense
   Reflected, scarce reflected, pass,
A wife may-be, a mother she
   In Hymen's[3] shrine recalls not now,
She first in hour, ah, not profane,
40   With me to Hymen learnt to bow.

Ah no!—Yet owned we, fused in one,[4]
   The Power which e'en in stones and earths
By blind elections felt, in forms
   Organic breeds to myriad births;
By lichen small on granite wall
   Approved, its faintest feeblest stir
Slow-spreading, strengthening long, at last
   Vibrated full in me and her.

In me and her—sensation strange!
50   The lily grew to pendent head,
To vernal airs and mossy bank
   Its sheeny primrose spangles spread,
In roof o'er roof of shade sun-proof
   Did cedar strong itself outclimb,
And altitude of aloe proud
   Aspire in floreal crown sublime;

Flashed flickering forth fantastic flies,
   Big bees their burly bodies swung,
Rooks roused with civic din the elms,
60   And lark its wild reveillez rung;
In Libyan dell the light gazelle,
   The leopard lithe in Indian glade,
And dolphin, brightening tropic seas,
   In us were living, leapt and played:

Their shells did slow crustacea build,
   Their gilded skins did snakes renew,
While mightier spines for loftier kind
   Their types in amplest limbs outgrew;

Yea, close comprest in human breast,
   What moss, and tree, and livelier thing,   70
What Earth, Sun, Star of force possest,
   Lay budding, burgeoning forth for Spring.

Such sweet preluding sense of old
   Led on in Eden's sinless place
The hour when bodies human first
   Combined the primal prime embrace,
Such genial heat the blissful seat
   In man and woman owned unblamed,
When, naked both, its garden paths
   They walked unconscious, unashamed: 80

Ere, clouded yet in mistiest dawn,
   Above the horizon dusk and dun,
One mountain crest with light had tipped
   That Orb that is the Spirit's Sun;
Ere dreamed young flowers in vernal showers
   Of fruit to rise the flower above,
Or ever yet to young Desire
   Was told the mystic name of Love.

                (1846–47) 1849

"Is it true, ye gods, who treat us"

Is it true, ye gods, who treat us
As the gambling fool is treated,
O ye, who ever cheat us,
And let us feel we're cheated!
Is it true that poetical power,
The gift of heaven, the dower
Of Apollo and the Nine,[1]
The inborn sense, "the vision and the faculty
   divine,"
All we glorify and bless
In our rapturous exaltation,   10
All invention, and creation,
Exuberance of fancy, and sublime imagination,
All a poet's fame is built on,
The fame of Shakespeare, Milton,
Of Wordsworth, Byron, Shelley,
Is in reason's grave precision,
Nothing more, nothing less,
Than a peculiar conformation,
Constitution, and condition
Of the brain and of the belly?   20
Is it true, ye gods who cheat us?
And that's the way ye treat us?

Oh say it, all who think it,
Look straight, and never blink it!
If it is so, let it be so,
And we will all agree so;
But the plot has counterplot,
It may be, and yet be not.

(1842) 1849

from The Bothie of Tober-na-Vuolich

The Bothie of Tober-na-Vuolich *was first published in 1848 as* The Bothie of Toper-na-Fuosich. *"Bothie" is a Scots dialect word meaning "hut or cottage"; Clough changed the place name in his title when one of the reviewers of the poem suggested that the original name was a ribald Highland toast to the female sexual organ. The action of the poem takes place during an Oxford reading party in the Highlands. Adam, a tutor, has taken Philip Hewson, the hero of the poem, and a group of his fellow students (Hobbes, Arthur, Hope, Airlie, Lindsay, who is also called "the Piper," and some others) into Scotland to help them prepare for their examinations. Philip, intellectually restless and a political and social radical, meets and falls in love with Elspie Mackaye, the daughter of a farmer. He overcomes her reluctance and her father's dubiety, returns to Oxford to complete his degree, marries Elspie and sets off for New Zealand.*

In a note to the first edition of the poem Clough warned his readers "to expect every kind of irregularity in these modern hexameters." The six metrical feet of classical hexameters are measured by the amount of time required to pronounce their syllables—a quantitative measure. Clough, as is normal in English, measures his line by distributing six accented syllables through it, but he also gave it something of the looseness of spoken English, as well as moving a little toward quantitative measures, by varying the number of syllables in the line. For other examples of Clough's hexameters see his poem "Acteon" and lines 63–77 of Scene V of "Dipsychus."

from Book III

There is a stream, I name not its name, lest
 inquisitive tourist

Hunt it, and make it a lion,[1] and get it at last
 into guide-books,   20
Springing far off from a loch unexplored in
 the folds of great mountains,
Falling two miles through rowan[2] and stunted
 alder, enveloped
Then for four more in a forest of pine, where
 broad and ample
Spreads, to convey it, the glen with heathery
 slopes on both sides:
Broad and fair the stream, with occasional falls
 and narrows;
But, where the glen of its course approaches
 the vale of the river,
Met and blocked by a huge interposing mass
 of granite,
Scarce by a channel deep-cut, raging up, and
 raging onward,
Forces its flood through a passage so narrow
 a lady would step it.
There, across the great rocky wharves, a
 wooden bridge goes,   30
Carrying a path to the forest; below, three
 hundred yards, say,
Lower in level some twenty-five feet, through
 flats of shingle,[3]
Stepping-stones and a cart-track cross in the
 open valley.
 But in the interval here the boiling, pent-
 up water
Frees itself by a final descent, attaining a
 basin,
Ten feet wide and eighteen long, with white-
 ness and fury
Occupied partly, but mostly pellucid, pure, a
 mirror;
Beautiful there for the colour derived from
 green rocks under;
Beautiful, most of all, where beads of foam
 uprising
Mingle their clouds of white with the delicate
 hue of the stillness.   40
Cliff over cliff for its sides, with rowan and
 pendent birch boughs,
Here it lies, unthought of above at the bridge
 and pathway,
Still more enclosed from below by wood and
 rocky projection.
You are shut in, left alone with yourself and
 perfection of water,
Hid on all sides, left alone with yourself and
 the goddess of bathing.

[1] Lion: a celebrity; usually used of persons. [2] Rowan: a small tree that bears a red fruit.
[3] Shingle: rounded stones somewhat larger than gravel.

Here, the pride of the plunger, you stride
  the fall and clear it;
Here, the delight of the bather, you roll in
  beaded sparklings,
Here into pure green depth drop down from
  lofty ledges.
  Hither, a month agone, they had come, and
  discovered it; hither
(Long a design, but long unaccountably left
50   unaccomplished) ,
Leaving the well-known bridge and pathway
  above to the forest,
Turning below from the track of the carts over
  stone and shingle,
Piercing a wood, and skirting a narrow and
  natural causeway
Under the rocky wall that hedges the bed of
  the streamlet,
Rounded a craggy point, and saw on a sudden
  before them
Slabs of rock, and a tiny beach, and perfection
  of water,
Picture-like beauty, seclusion sublime, and the
  goddess of bathing.
There they bathed, of course, and Arthur, the
  glory of headers,[4]
Leapt from the ledges with Hope, he twenty
  feet, he thirty;
There, overbold, great Hobbes from a ten-foot
60   height descended,
Prone, as a quadruped, prone with hands and
  feet protending;
There in the sparkling champagne, ecstatic,
  they shrieked and shouted.
  "Hobbes's gutter" the Piper entitles the spot,
  profanely,
Hope "the Glory" would have, after Arthur,
  the glory of headers:
But, for before they departed, in shy and
  fugitive reflex
Here in the eddies and there did the splendour
  of Jupiter glimmer,
Adam adjudged it the name of Hesperus, star
  of the evening.

                    ·   ·   ·

from Book VII

And he continued more firmly, although
  with stronger emotion:

Elspie, why should I speak it? you cannot
  believe it, and should not:
Why should I say that I love, which I all but
  said to another?
Yet should I dare, should I say, O Elspie, you
  only I love; you,   5
First and sole in my life that has been and
  surely that shall be;
Could—O, could you believe it, O Elspie,
  believe it and spurn not!
Is it—possible,—possible, Elspie?
                    Well,—she answered,
And she was silent some time, and blushed all
  over, and answered
Quietly, after her fashion, still knitting, Maybe,
  I think of it,
Though I don't know that I did: and she
  paused again; but it may be,
Yes,—I don't know, Mr. Philip,—but only it
  feels to me strangely
Like to the high new bridge, they used to build
  at, below there,
Over the burn[1] and glen on the road. You
  won't understand me.
But I keep saying in my mind—this long time
  slowly with trouble   6
I have been building myself, up, up, and
  toilfully raising,
Just like as if the bridge were to do it itself
  without masons,
Painfully getting myself upraised one stone on
  another,
All one side I mean; and now I see on the
  other
Just such another fabric uprising, better and
  stronger,
Close to me, coming to join me: and then I
  sometimes fancy,—
Sometimes I find myself dreaming at nights
  about arches and bridges,—
Sometimes I dream of a great invisible hand
  coming down, and
Dropping the great key-stone in the middle:
  there in my dreaming,
There I feel the great key-stone coming in, and
  through it   7
Feel the other part—all the other stones of the
  archway,
Joined into mine with a strange happy sense
  of completeness. But, dear me,
This is confusion and nonsense. I mix all the
  things I can think of.

---

[4] Header: dive.   [1] Burn: brook.

And you won't understand, Mr. Philip.
                              But while she was speaking,
So it happened, a moment she paused from her
     work, and, pondering,
Laid her hand on her lap: Philip took it: she
     did not resist:
So he retained her fingers, the knitting being
     stopped. But emotion
Came all over her more and yet more, from
     his hand, from her heart, and
Most from the sweet idea and image her brain
     was renewing.
So he retained her hand, and, his tears down-
     dropping on it,
Trembling a long time, kissed it at last. And
     she ended.
And as she ended, uprose he; saying, What
     have I heard? Oh,
What have I done, that such words should be
     said to me? Oh, I see it,
See the great key-stone coming down from the
     heaven of heavens!
And he fell at her feet, and buried his face in
     her apron.
     But as under the moon and stars they went
          to the cottage,
Elspie sighed and said, Be patient, dear Mr.
     Philip,
Do not do anything hasty. It is all so soon, so
     sudden.
Do not say anything yet to any one.
                              Elspie, he answered,
Does not my friend go on Friday? I then shall
     see nothing of you:
Do not I go myself on Monday?
                              But oh, he said, Elspie;
Do as I bid you, my child; do not go on calling
     me Mr.;
Might I not just as well be calling you Miss
     Elspie?
Call me, this heavenly night, for once, for the
     first time, Philip.
     Philip, she said and laughed, and said she
          could not say it;
Philip, she said; he turned, and kissed the
     sweet lips as they said it.

     But on the morrow Elspie kept out of the
          way of Philip;
And at the evening seat, when he took her hand
     by the alders,
Drew it back, saying, almost peevishly,
                              No, Mr. Philip,
I was quite right, last night; it is too soon, too
     sudden.

What I told you before was foolish perhaps,
     was hasty.
When I think it over, I am shocked and terrified
     at it.
Not that at all I unsay it; that is, I know I
     said it,
And when I said it, felt it. But oh, we must
     wait, Mr. Philip!
We mustn't pull ourselves at the great key-
     stone of the centre;
Some one else up above must hold it, fit it, and
     fix it;
If we try ourselves, we shall only damage the
     archway,
Damage all our own work that we wrought,
     our painful up-building.
When, you remember, you took my hand last
     evening, talking,
I was all over a tremble: and as you pressed
     the fingers   110
After, and afterwards kissed it, I could not
     speak. And then, too,
As we went home, you kissed me for saying
     your name. It was dreadful.
I have been kissed before, she added, blushing
     slightly,
I have been kissed more than once by Donald
     my cousin, and others;
It is the way of the lads, and I make up my
     mind not to mind it;
But Mr. Philip, last night, and from you, it
     was different quite, Sir.
When I think of all that, I am shocked and
     terrified at it.
Yes, it is dreadful to me.
                              She paused, but quickly continued,
Smiling almost fiercely, continued, looking
     upward.
You are too strong, you see, Mr. Philip! just
     like the sea there,   120
Which *will* come, through the straits and all
     between the mountains,
Forcing its great strong tide into every nook
     and inlet,
Getting far in, up the quiet stream of sweet
     inland water,
Sucking it up, and stopping it, turning it,
     driving it backward,
Quite preventing its own quiet running: and
     then, soon after,
Back it goes off, leaving weeds on the shore,
     and wrack and uncleanness:
And the poor burn in the glen tries again its
     peaceful running,

But it is brackish and tainted, and all its banks
    in disorder.
That was what I dreamt all last night. I was
    the burnie,
Trying to get along through the tyrannous
    brine, and could not;
I was confined and squeezed in the coils of the
    great salt tide, that
Would mix-in itself with me, and change me;
    I felt myself changing;
And I struggled, and screamed, I believe, in
    my dream. It was dreadful.
You are too strong, Mr. Philip! I am but a
    poor slender burnie,
Used to the glens and the rocks, the rowan and
    birch of the woodies,
Quite unused to the great salt sea; quite afraid
    and unwilling.
    Ere she had spoken two words, had Philip
    released her fingers:
As she went on, he recoiled, fell back, and
    shook, and shivered;
There he stood, looking pale and ghastly;
    when she had ended,
Answering in hollow voice,
                It is true; oh quite true, Elspie;
Oh, you are always right; oh, what, what have
    I been doing!
I will depart to-morrow. But oh, forget me not
    wholly,
Wholly, Elspie, nor hate me, no, do not hate
    me, my Elspie.
    But a revulsion passed through the brain
    and bosom of Elspie;
And she got up from her seat on the rock,
    putting by her knitting;
Went to him, where he stood, and answered:
                No, Mr. Philip,
No, you are good, Mr. Philip, and gentle; and
    I am the foolish;
No, Mr. Philip, forgive me.
                She stepped right to him, and boldly
Took up his hand, and placed it in hers; he
    daring no movement;
Took up the cold hanging hand, up-forcing
    the heavy elbow.
I am afraid, she said, but I will! and kissed
    the fingers.
And he fell on his knees and kissed her own
    past counting.

    But a revulsion wrought in the brain and
    bosom of Elspie;

[1] A first: a degree with first-class honors.

And the passion she just had compared to the
    vehement ocean,
Urging in high spring-tide its masterful way
    through the mountains,
Forcing and flooding the silvery stream, as it
    runs from the inland;
That great power withdrawn, receding here
    and passive,
Felt she in myriad springs, her sources, far in
    the mountains,
Stirring, collecting, rising, upheaving, forth-
    outflowing,
Taking and joining, right welcome, that
    delicate rill in the valley,
Filling it, making it strong, and still descend-
    ing, seeking,
With a blind forefeeling descending ever, and
    seeking,
With a delicious forefeeling, the great still sea
    before it;
There deep into it, far, to carry, and lose in its
    bosom,
Waters that still from their sources exhaustless
    are fain to be added.
    As he was kissing her fingers, and knelt on
    the ground before her,
Yielding backward she sank to her seat, and
    of what she was doing
Ignorant, bewildered, in sweet multitudinous
    vague emotion,
Stooping, knowing not what, put her lips to
    the hair on his forehead:
And Philip, raising himself, gently, for the first
    time, round her
Passing his arms, close, close, enfolded her,
    close to his bosom.
    As they went home by the moon, Forgive me,
    Philip, she whispered;
I have so many things to think of, all of a
    sudden;
I who had never once thought a thing,—
    in my ignorant Highlands.

        .   .   .

from Book IX

Philip returned to his books, but returned
    to his Highlands after;
Got a first,[1] 'tis said; a winsome bride, 'tis
    certain.
There while courtship was ending, nor yet the
    wedding appointed,

Under her father he studied the handling of
hoe and of hatchet:
Thither that summer succeeding came Adam
and Arthur to see him
Down by the lochs from the distant
Glenmorison: Adam the tutor,
Arthur, and Hope; and the Piper anon who
was there for a visit;
He had been into the schools; plucked almost;
all but a *gone-coon;*[2]
So he declared; never once had brushed up his
hairy Aldrich;[3]
Into the great might-have-been upsoaring
sublime and ideal
Gave to historical questions a free poetical
treatment;
Leaving vocabular ghosts undisturbed in their
20 lexicon-limbo,
Took Aristophanes up at a shot; and the
whole three last weeks
Went, in his life and the sunshine rejoicing, to
Nuneham and Godstowe:[4]
What were the claims of Degree to those of
life and the sunshine?
There did the four find Philip, the poet, the
speaker, the chartist,[5]
Delving at Highland soil, and railing at High-
land landlords,
Railing, but more, as it seemed, for the fun of
the Piper's fury.
There saw they David and Elspie Mackaye,
and the Piper was almost,
Almost deeply in love with Bella the sister of
Elspie;
But the good Adam was heedful; they did not
go too often.
There in the bright October, the gorgeous
30 bright October,

When the brackens are changed, and heather
blooms are faded,
And amid russet of heather and fern green
trees are bonnie,
Alders are green, and oaks, the rowan scarlet
and yellow,
Heavy the aspen, and heavy with jewels of gold
the birch-tree,
There, when shearing had ended, and barley-
stooks[6] were garnered,
David gave Philip to wife his daughter, his
darling Elspie;
Elspie the quiet, the brave, was wedded to
Philip the poet.
So won Philip his bride. They are married
and gone—But oh, Thou
Mighty one, Muse of great Epos, and Idyll the
playful and tender,[7]
Be it recounted in song, ere we part, and thou
fly to thy Pindus,   140
(Pindus is it, O Muse, or Ætna, or even
Ben-nevis?)[8]
Be it recounted in song, O Muse of the Epos
and Idyll,
Who gave what at the wedding, the gifts and
fair gratulations.
Adam, the grave careful Adam, a medicine-
chest and tool-box,
Hope a saddle, and Arthur a plough, and the
Piper a rifle,
Airlie a necklace for Elspie, and Hobbes a
Family Bible,
Airlie a necklace, and Hobbes a Bible and iron
bedstead.
What was the letter, O Muse, sent withal by
the corpulent hero?
This is the letter of Hobbes the kilted and
corpulent hero.

[2] Schools; plucked: "Schools" was Oxford slang for the examinations for an undergraduate degree; to be "plucked" was to fail the examinations. "A gone-coon" was American slang, probably picked up from the minstrel shows popular in England in the 1840s.

[3] *Hairy* Aldrich: Henry Aldrich (1647–1710) published a handbook to logic (*Artis Logicae Compendium:* 1691) which remained a popular textbook in British schools and universities through the nineteenth century. "Hairy" was mid-century Oxford slang for "difficult"; it is also a pun on Aldrich's first name.

[4] Nuneham and Godstowe: villages near Oxford which were often the destinations of rowing parties on the river.

[5] The chartist: Chartism was a predominantly working-class political movement of the 1840s which agitated for, among other points of its Charter, universal male suffrage and parliamentary reform.

[6] Stooks: shocks.

[7] Epos and Idyll: an epos is a poem on an epic theme, an idyll one on the themes of re-clusive, pastoral life.

[8] Pindus is the name of a mountain chain in Greece; Ætna that of a volcanic mountain in Sicily; and Ben-nevis is a mountain in Scotland. The conjunction associates Scotland with the sites of classical pastoral poetry.

So the last speech and confession is made, O
  150   my eloquent speaker!
So *the good time* is *coming*,[9] or come is it? O
      my chartist!
So the Cathedral is finished at last, O my Pugin
      of Women;[10]
Finished, and now, is it true? to be taken out
      whole to New Zealand!
Well, go forth to thy field, to thy barley, with
      Ruth, O Boaz,[11]
Ruth, who for thee hath deserted her people,
      her gods, her mountains.
Go, as in Ephrath[12] of old, in the gate of
      Bethlehem said they,
Go, be the wife in thy house both Rachel and
      Leah unto thee![13]
Be thy wedding of silver, albeit of iron thy
      bedstead!
Yea, to the full golden fifty renewed be! and
      fair memoranda
Happily fill the fly-leaves duly left in the
  160   Family Bible.
Live, and when Hobbes is forgotten, may'st
      thou, an unroasted Grandsire,
See thy children's children, and Democracy
      upon New Zealand!
  This was the letter of Hobbes, and this the
      postscript after.
Wit in the letter will prate, but wisdom speaks
      in a postscript;
Listen to wisdom—*Which things*—you perhaps
      didn't know, my dear fellow,
I have reflected; *Which things are an allegory*,
      Philip.
For this Rachel-and-Leah is marriage; which,
      I have seen it,

Lo, and have known it, is always, and must be,
      bigamy only,
Even in noblest kind a duality, compound,
      and complex,
One part heavenly-ideal, the other vulgar and
      earthy: 17
For this Rachel-and-Leah is marriage, and
      Laban their father
Circumstance, chance, the world, our uncle
      and hard taskmaster.
Rachel we found as we fled from the daughters
      of Heth[14] by the desert;
Rachel we met at the well; we came, we saw,
      we kissed her;
Rachel we serve-for, long years,—that seem as
      a few days only,
E'en for the love we have to her,—and win her
      at last of Laban.
Is it not Rachel we take in our joy from the
      hand of her father?
Is it not Rachel we lead in the mystical veil
      from the altar?
Rachel we dream-of at night: in the morning,
      behold, it is Leah.
"Nay, it is custom," saith Laban, the Leah
      indeed is the elder.   18
Happy and wise who consents to redouble his
      service to Laban,
So, fulfilling her week, he may add to the
      elder the younger,
Not repudiates Leah, but wins the Rachel
      unto her!
Neither hate thou thy Leah, my Jacob, she
      also is worthy;
So, many days shall thy Rachel have joy, and
      survive her sister;

---

9 "The Good Time Coming" is a poem by Charles Mackay (1814–89) published in a newspaper and then in a volume of political poems in 1846 and popular as a Chartist song. See Part 8.

10 Pugin of Women: Augustus Welby Pugin (1812–52), most notably in his designs for the houses of Parliament in 1836–37 and his book *Contrasts Between the Architecture of the 15th and 19th Centuries* (1836), strongly advocated and advanced the early Victorian taste for Gothic architecture. Earlier in the poem Philip has been called a "Pugin of women" because of a discourse in which he argues that the beauty of women is a function of the grace with which they use their bodies in work.

11 In the Old Testament book of Ruth, Ruth leaves her own country to accompany her mother-in-law on her return to Israel, and there marries Boaz.

12 Ephrath: a name for Bethlehem.

13 Rachel and Leah: In the book of Genesis (Chapter 29) Jacob is sent to find a wife among the daughters of his uncle Laban. He chooses Laban's younger daughter Rachel, and he is promised her in marriage if he serves his uncle for seven years. But on the wedding night Laban substitutes his elder daughter Leah for the promised bride, because it is the custom that the elder daughter marry first. When Jacob discovers the deception, he is promised Rachel also as his wife if he will serve another seven years. He does and marries Rachel as well. At first, because she is hated by Jacob, God makes Leah more fruitful than Rachel, but eventually both bear Jacob sons.

14 Heth: a name for the Hittites, a people who lived in the land later populated by the Israelites. Jacob's brother, the coarse Esau, took his wives from the Hittites.

Yea, and her children—*Which things are an*
   allegory, Philip,
Aye, and by Origen's[15] with a vengeance truly,
   a long one!
    This was a note from the Tutor, the grave
    man nicknamed Adam.
I shall see you of course, my Philip, before
   your departure;
Joy be with you, my boy, with you and your
   beautiful Elspie.
Happy is he that found, and finding was not
   heedless;
Happy is he that found, and happy the friend
   that was with him.
    So won Philip his bride:—
    They are married, and gone to New Zealand.
Five hundred pounds in pocket, with books,
   and two or three pictures,
Tool-box, plough, and the rest, they rounded
   the sphere to New Zealand.
There he hewed, and dug; subdued the earth
   and his spirit;
There he built him a home; there Elspie bare
   him his children,
David and Bella; perhaps ere this too an Elspie
   or Adam;
There hath he farmstead and land, and fields
   of corn and flax fields;
And the Antipodes too have a Bothie of
   Tober-na-vuolich.

                      (1848) 1848

90

200

Resignation—To Faustus[1]

O land of Empire, art and love!
   What is it that you show me?
A sky for Gods to tread above,
   A soil for pigs below me!
O in all place and shape and kind
   Beyond all thought and thinking,
The graceful with the gross combined,
   The stately with the stinking!
Whilst words of mighty love to trace,
   Which thy great walls I see on,
Thy porch I pace or take my place
   Within thee, great Pantheon,[2]
What sights untold of contrast bold
   My ranging eyes must be on!

10

What though uprolled by young and old
   In slumbrous convolution
Neath pillared shade must lie displayed
   Bare limbs that scorn ablution,
Should husks that swine would never pick
   Bestrew that patterned paving,
And sores to make a surgeon sick
   For charity come craving?
Though oft the meditative cur
   Account it small intrusion
Through that great gate to quit the stir
   Of market-place confusion,
True brother of the bipeds there,
   If Nature's need requireth,
Lifts up his leg with tranquil air
   And tranquilly retireth:
Though priest think fit to stop and spit
   Beside the altar solemn,
Yet, boy, that nuisance why commit
   On this Corinthian column?—

20

30

O richly soiled and richly sunned,
Exuberant, fervid, and fecund!
   Are these the fixed condition
On which may Northern pilgrim come
To imbibe thine ether-air, and sum
   Thy store of old tradition?
Must we be chill, if clean, and stand
Foot-deep in dirt in classic land?

40

So is it: in all ages so,
And in all places man can know,
From homely roots unseen below
In forest-shade in woodland bower
The stem that bears the ethereal flower
Derives that emanative power;
From mixtures fetid foul and sour
Draws juices that those petals fill.

50

Ah Nature, if indeed thy will
Thou own'st it, it shall not be ill!
And truly here, in this quick clime
Where, scarcely bound by space or time,
The elements in half a day
Toss off with exquisitest play
What our cold seasons toil and grieve,
And never quite at last achieve;
Where processes, with pain and fear
Disgust and horror wrought, appear

60

---

[15] Origen: a third-century Christian scholar and theologian known for his exegetical works.
[1] The manuscript that bears the fair copy of this poem includes its present title, a reference to Matthew Arnold's "Resignation. To Fausta." The first 34 lines of the poem were not published in any nineteenth-century collection of Clough's poetry. In these collections the poem was titled "At Rome."
[2] Pantheon: a temple at Rome, dedicated to all the gods.

The quick mutations of a dance,
Wherein retiring but to advance,
Life, in brief interpause of death,
One moment sitting, taking breath,
Forth comes again as glad as e'er
In some new figure full as fair,
Where what has scarcely ceased to be,
Instinct with newer birth we see—
What dies already, look you, lives;
70 In such a clime, who thinks, forgives;
Who sees, will understand; who knows,
In calm of knowledge find repose,
And thoughtful as of glory gone,
So too of more to come anon,
Of permanent existence sure,
Brief intermediate breaks endure.
   O Nature, if indeed thy will,
Thou ownest it, it is not ill!
And e'en as oft on heathy hill,
80 On moorland black, and ferny fells,
Beside thy brooks and in thy dells,
Was welcomed erst the kindly stain
Of thy true earth, e'en so again
With resignation fair and meet
The dirt and refuse of thy street
My philosophic foot shall greet,
So leave but perfect to my eye
Thy columns set against thy sky!

                                        (1849?)

Easter Day

I

Naples, 1849[1]

Through the great sinful streets of Naples as
      I past,
With fiercer heat than flamed above my head
My heart was hot within me; till at last
My brain was lightened, when my tongue had
      said

Christ is not risen!

   Christ is not risen, no,
   He lies and moulders low;
      Christ is not risen.

What though the stone were rolled away, and
      though
      The grave found empty there!—   1
   If not there, then elsewhere;
If not where Joseph[2] laid Him first, why then
      Where other men
Translaid Him after; in some humbler clay
      Long ere to-day
Corruption that sad perfect work hath done,
Which here she scarcely, lightly had begun.
      The foul engendered worm
Feeds on the flesh of the life-giving form
Of our most Holy and Anointed One.   2

   He is not risen, no,
   He lies and moulders low;
      Christ is not risen.

   Ashes to ashes, dust to dust;[3]
As of the unjust, also of the just—
      Christ is not risen.

What if the women, ere the dawn was grey,
Saw one or more great angels, as they say,
Angels, or Him himself? Yet neither there, nor
      then,
Nor afterward, nor elsewhere, nor at all,   3
Hath He appeared to Peter or the Ten,
Nor, save in thunderous terror, to blind Saul;[4]
Save in an after-Gospel and late Creed
   He is not risen indeed,
      Christ is not risen.

Or what if e'en, as runs the tale, the Ten
Saw, heard, and touched, again and yet again?
What if at Emmaüs' inn and by Capernaum's
      lake[5]

[1] The title of this poem was added when it was first published in 1865. In Clough's manuscript it is titled "Naples, August, 1849."
[2] Joseph: Joseph of Arimathaea, who requested and buried the body of Christ after his crucifixion. The story of the women who came to the tomb to find the body gone is told in all four of the gospels (Matthew, Mark, Luke, and John).
[3] "Ashes to ashes, dust to dust; in sure and certain hope of the Resurrection unto eternal life": from the burial service of the *Book of Common Prayer* used in the Church of England. Lines 24–26 were omitted when the poem was first published in 1865.
[4] The Ten: the other apostles, minus Judas, who betrayed Christ; Saul: Saul of Tarsus, converted to Christianity by a vision while on a journey to Damascus, began his ministry under the name of Paul.
[5] In the account of Luke (Chapter 24) Christ appears after his crucifixion to some of his apostles as they walked toward Emmaus, a village outside Jerusalem. In the account of John (Chapter 21) Christ appears to the apostles as they are fishing on the sea of Galilee; Capernaum is a town on that sea.

Came One the bread that brake,
Came One that spake as never mortal spake,
And with them ate and drank and stood and
    walked about?
        Ah! "some" did well to "doubt"![6]
Ah! the true Christ, while these things came to
    pass,
Nor heard, nor spake, nor walked, nor dreamt,
    alas!
        He was not risen, no,
        He lay and mouldered low,
            Christ was not risen.

As circulates in some great city crowd
A rumour changeful, vague, importunate, and
    loud,
From no determined centre, or of fact,
        Or authorship exact,
        Which no man can deny
        Nor verify;
    So spread the wondrous fame;
        He all the same
    Lay senseless, mouldering, low.
        He was not risen, no,
            Christ was not risen!

Ashes to ashes, dust to dust;
As of the unjust, also of the just—
    Yea, of that Just One too.
This is the one sad Gospel that is true,
        Christ is not risen.

───────

Is He not risen, and shall we not rise?
        Oh, we unwise!
What did we dream, what wake we to discover?
Ye hills, fall on us, and ye mountains, cover!
        In darkness and great gloom
Come ere we thought it is *our* day of doom,
    From the cursed world which is one tomb,
            Christ is not risen!

Eat, drink, and die, for we are men deceived,
Of all the creatures under heaven's wide cope
We are most hopeless who had once most hope,
We are most wretched that had most believed.
        Christ is not risen.[7]

Eat, drink, and play, and think that this is
    bliss!

There is no Heaven but this!
    There is no Hell;—
Save Earth, which serves the purpose doubly
    well,
        Seeing it visits still
With equallest apportionments of ill   80
Both good and bad alike, and brings to one
    same dust
        The unjust and the just
        With Christ, who is not risen.

Eat, drink, and die, for we are souls bereaved,
Of all the creatures under this broad sky
We are most hopeless, that had hoped most
    high,
And most beliefless, that had most believed.
    Ashes to ashes, dust to dust;   90
    As of the unjust, also of the just—
        Yea, of that Just One too.
    It is the one sad Gospel that is true,
        Christ is not risen.

───────

        Weep not beside the Tomb,
        Ye women, unto whom
He was great solace while ye tended Him;
        Ye who with napkin o'er His head
And folds of linen round each wounded limb
        Laid out the Sacred Dead;   100
And thou that bar'st Him in thy Wondering
    Womb.
Yea, Daughters of Jerusalem, depart,
Bind up as best ye may your own sad bleeding
    heart;
Go to your homes, your living children tend,
        Your earthly spouses love;
    Set your affections *not* on things above,
Which moth and rust corrupt, which quickliest
    come to end:[8]
Or pray, if pray ye must, and pray, if pray ye
    can,
For death; since dead is He whom ye deemed
    more than man,
        Who is not risen, no,   110
        But lies and moulders low,
            Who is not risen.

    Ye men of Galilee!
Why stand ye looking up to heaven, where Him
    ye ne'er may see,

───────

[6] "And when they saw him, they worshipped him: but some doubted" (Matthew 28:17).
[7] Lines 72–76 were omitted when the poem was published in 1865.
[8] "Lay not up for yourselves treasures upon earth, where moth and rust doth corrupt. . . . : But lay up for yourselves treasures in heaven, where neither moth nor rust doth corrupt. . . . : For where your treasure is, there will be your heart also" (Matthew 6:19–21). These words are spoken by Christ during the sermon on the mount.

Neither ascending hence, nor hither returning
      again?
    Ye ignorant and idle fishermen!
Hence to your huts and boats and inland native
      shore,
    And catch not men, but fish;[9]
    Whate'er things ye might wish,
Him neither here nor there ye e'er shall meet
120   with more.
    Ye poor deluded youths, go home,
    Mend the old nets ye left to roam,
    Tie the split oar, patch the torn sail;
    It was indeed "an idle tale,"[10]
      He was not risen.

And oh, good men of ages yet to be,
Who shall believe *because* ye did not see,
    Oh, be ye warned! be wise!
    No more with pleading eyes,
130   And sobs of strong desire,
Unto the empty vacant void aspire,
Seeking another and impossible birth
That is not of your own and only Mother
      Earth.
But if there is no other life for you,
Sit down and be content, since this must even
      do:
      He is not risen.

    One look, and then depart,
    Ye humble and ye holy men of heart!
And ye! ye ministers and stewards of a word
Which ye would preach, because another
140   heard,—
    Ye worshippers of that ye do not know,
    Take these things hence and go;
      He is not risen.

    Here on our Easter Day
We rise, we come, and lo! we find Him
      not;
    Gardener nor other on the sacred spot,
Where they have laid Him is there none to say!
No sound, nor in, nor out; no word
Of where to seek the dead or meet the living
      Lord;
150 There is no glistering of an angel's wings,
There is no voice of heavenly clear behest:

Let us go hence, and think upon these things
In silence, which is best.
    Is He not risen? No—
    But lies and moulders low—
      Christ is not risen.[11]
                (1849) 1865

Easter Day

    II

So while the blear-eyed pimp beside me walked,
And talked,
For instance, of the beautiful danseuse,
And "Eccellenza sure must see, if he would
      choose"
Or of the lady in the green silk there,
Who passes by and bows with minx's air,
Or of the little thing not quite fifteen,
Sicilian-born who surely should be seen.
So while the blear-eyed pimp beside me walked
And talked, and I too with fit answer talked,[1]
So in the sinful streets, abstracted and alone,
I with my secret self held communing of my
      own.

So in the southern city spake the tongue
    Of one that somewhat overwildly sung;
    But in a later hour I sat and heard
    Another voice that spake, another graver
      word.
    Weep not, it bade, whatever hath been said,
    Though He be dead, He is not dead.
      In the true Creed
      He is yet risen indeed,
        Christ is yet risen.

      Weep not beside His tomb,
      Ye women unto whom
    He was great comfort and yet greater grief;
Nor ye faithful few that went with Him to
      roam,
Seek sadly what for Him ye left, go hopeless to
      your home;
Nor ye despair, ye sharers yet to be of their
      belief;
    Though He be dead, He is not dead,
      Not gone, though fled,

---

[9] "Fear not; from henceforth thou shalt catch men" (Luke 5:10). These words are also spoken by Christ, to the apostles.

[10] When the women returned from the tomb to tell the apostles of the resurrection, "their words seemed to them as idle tales, and they believed them not" (Luke 24:11).

[11] In one of the manuscript versions of this poem, and in the version published in 1865, the last line ends in a question mark. In another manuscript the poem ends with a dash.

[1] Lines 1–10 were omitted in 1865, and in editions of Clough's poetry until Mulhauser's 1974 edition.

Not lost, though vanished;
Though He return not, though
He lies and moulders low;
   In the true Creed
He is yet risen indeed,
   Christ is yet risen.

Sit if ye will, sit down upon the ground,
Yet not to weep and wail, but calmly look
     around.
   Whate'er befell,
   Earth is not hell;
Now, too, as when it first began,
Life yet is Life and Man is Man.
For all that breathe beneath the heaven's high
     cope,
Joy with grief mixes, with despondence hope.
Hope conquers cowardice, joy grief:
Or at the least, faith unbelief.
   Though dead, not dead;
   Not gone, though fled;
   Not lost, not vanished.
   In the great Gospel and true Creed,
   He is yet risen indeed;
     Christ is yet risen.

                (1849?)   1865

The Latest Decalogue

Thou shalt have one God only; who
Would be at the expense of two?
No graven images may be
Worshipped, except the currency:
Swear not at all; for for thy curse
Thine enemy is none the worse:
At church on Sunday to attend
Will serve to keep the world thy friend:
Honour thy parents; that is, all
From whom advancement may befall:
Thou shalt not kill; but needst not strive
Officiously to keep alive:
Do not adultery commit;
Advantage rarely comes of it:
Thou shalt not steal; an empty feat,
When it's so lucrative to cheat:
Bear not false witness; let the lie
Have time on its own wings to fly:
Thou shalt not covet; but tradition
Approves all forms of competition.

The sum of all is, thou shalt love,
If any body, God above:

       ¹ Fliers: fugitives.

At any rate shall never labour
More than thyself to love thy neighbour.

              (1849–50)   1862

"Say not the struggle nought availeth"

Say not the struggle nought availeth,
   The labour and the wounds are vain,
The enemy faints not, nor faileth,
   And as things have been, things remain.

If hopes were dupes, fears may be liars;
   It may be, in yon smoke concealed,
Your comrades chase e'en now the fliers,¹
   And, but for you, possess the field.

For while the tired waves, vainly breaking,
   Seem here no painful inch to gain,   10
Far back through creeks and inlets making
   Came, silent, flooding in, the main,

And not by eastern windows only,
   When daylight comes, comes in the light,
In front the sun climbs slow, how slowly,
   But westward, look, the land is bright.

             (1849–50)   1862

"It fortifies my soul to know"

It fortifies my soul to know
That, though I perish, Truth is so:
That, howsoe'er I stray and range,
Whate'er I do, Thou dost not change.
I steadier step when I recall
That, if I slip, Thou dost not fall.

              (1850)   1862

from Dipsychus

"Dipsychus," Clough's most ambitious poem, is a series of thirteen scenes, written in 1850 but never arranged in a final order by Clough and not published during his lifetime. Some sections of the poem, occasionally altered, were published as separate lyrics in 1862 and 1863. Most of the poem was printed for the first time in 1865 and again in the collected edition of 1869.

   The hero of the poem—Dipsychus, the two-souled or two-selved—is a young man traveling in Venice. He is ambivalent about a variety of topics which are the subjects of soliloquies or dialogues with an attendant Spirit: whether to indulge himself sexually, whether to choose a conventional profession, whether and how to enjoy the material pleasures his social station permits him, whether or not God and transcendent ethical principles and sanctions exist. None of these questions are resolved when they are proposed. But they reduce to a fundamental question Dipsychus confronts throughout the poem and settles by surrender at the end: is it necessary to act in the external world of things and other actions, or is it permissible or even possible to remain in an internal reality of ideas and constantly refining thought? The Spirit, in part a traditional Mephistophelian tempter to a fallen world, consistently counsels submission to material reality. But the Spirit is also a disillusioned sensibility who has already come to Dipsychus' final resolution. His buoyantly cynical celebration of unreflective material pleasure, therefore, and especially his cruelly clear-minded prediction of how Dipsychus will conduct an alternative life (Scene XII), also serve finally to end the poem in yet another duality, two tonalities of submission, one grudging and glum, and the other vigorous although presumably damned.

Probably about the same time that he composed "Dipsychus" Clough composed a fragment, "Dipsychus Continued," which picks up the story thirty years later. Dipsychus, famous now as the Lord Chief Justice of England, is visited by the guilt of his submission, dramatized as a woman with whom he has had an affair. He resigns his judgeship and retires from the world of action, apparently to ponder again the newly unresolved difficulties of his dilemma.

Passages from "Dipsychus" were printed in earlier collections of Clough's poetry, but the poem first appeared in print under its present title in the 1865 edition of Clough's poetry. Not all the verse in Clough's manuscript appeared in the 1865 poems, and the arrangement of scenes was somewhat different from that adopted by his twentieth-century editors. Except where noted, all the passages reprinted here were published in the 1865 and 1869 collections of Clough's verse.

FROM SCENE V

DIPSYCHUS

Yes, it is beautiful ever, let foolish men rail at
    it never.[1]
Yes, it is beautiful truly, my brothers, I grant
    it you duly.
Wise are ye others that choose it, and happy ye
    all that can use it.
Life it is beautiful wholly, and could we
    eliminate only
This interfering, enslaving, o'ermastering
    demon of craving,
This wicked tempter inside us to ruin still
    eager to guide us,
Life were beatitude, action a possible pure
    satisfaction.

SPIRIT

    (Hexameters, by all that's odious,
    Beshod with rhyme to run melodious!)

DIPSYCHUS

All as I go on my way I behold them consorting
    and coupling;
Faithful, it seemeth, and fond; very fond, very
    possibly faithful;
All as I go on my way with a pleasure sincere
    and unmingled.
Life it is beautiful truly, my brothers, I grant
    it you duly;
But for perfection attaining is one method
    only, abstaining;
Let us abstain, for we should so, if only we
    thought that we could so.

SPIRIT

    (Bravo, bravissimo! this time though
    You rather were run short for rhyme though;
    Not that on that account your verse
    Could be much better or much worse.) [2]

---

[1] In the 1865 and 1869 editions of Clough's poems lines 63–80 were placed later in the poem, so that they followed the songs by Dipsychus and the Spirit with the refrain "There is no God" (Scene VI).

[2] In 1865 and 1869 lines 78–81 were not in parentheses. Lines 82–98 were printed separately in 1863; and in the 1869 edition of Clough's poems the lines were printed both as a separate poem with the title "The Hidden Love" and as a part of "Dipsychus." In addition to capitalizing the first letter of "thee" in the first stanza, "The Hidden Love" contains these two stanzas, from a notebook written by Clough in 1849–50 and inserted between the first and second stanzas of the passage as it is printed above:

            What is it then to me
            If others are inquisitive to see?
            Why should I quit my place to go and ask
            If other men are working at their task?
            Leave my own buried roots to go
            And see that brother plants shall grow;

DIPSYCHUS
O let me love my love unto myself alone,
And know my knowledge to the world
    unknown;
No witness to the vision call,
Beholding, unbeheld of all;
And worship thee, with thee withdrawn, apart,
Whoe'er, whate'er thou art,
Within the closest veil of mine own inmost
    heart.

Better it were, thou sayest, to consent,
Feast while we may, and live ere life be spent;
Close up clear eyes, and call the unstable sure,
The unlovely lovely, and the filthy pure;
In self-belyings, self-deceivings roll,
And lose in Action, Passion, Talk, the soul.

Nay, better far to mark off thus much air
And call it heaven, place bliss and glory there;
Fix perfect homes in the unsubstantial sky,
And say, what is not, will be by-and-by;
What here exists not must exist elsewhere.
But play no tricks upon thy soul, O man;
Let fact be fact, and life the thing it can.

SPIRIT
    To these remarks so sage and clerkly,[3]
    Worthy of Malebranche or Berkeley,
    I trust it won't be deemed a sin
    If I too answer "with a grin."

These juicy meats, this flashing wine,
    May be an unreal mere appearance;

Only—for my inside, in fine,
    They have a singular coherence.

This lovely creature's glowing charms   110
    Are gross illusion, I don't doubt that;
But when I pressed her in my arms
    I somehow didn't think about that.

This world is bad enough, may-be;
    We do not comprehend it;
But in one fact can all agree
    God won't, and we can't mend it.

Being common sense, it can't be sin
    To take it as we find it;
The pleasure to take pleasure in;   120
    The pain, try not to mind it.

DIPSYCHUS
Where are the great, whom thou would'st wish
    to praise thee?
Where are the pure, whom thou would'st
    choose to love thee?
Where are the brave, to stand supreme above
    thee,
Whose high commands would rouse, whose
    chiding raise thee?[4]
    Seek, seeker, in thyself; submit to find
    In the stones, bread; and life in the blank
    mind.

    (Written in London, standing in the Park,
    An evening in July, just before dark.)

    And turn away from Thee, O Thou most Holy Light,
    To look if other orbs their orbits keep aright,
    Around their proper sun,
    Deserting Thee, and being undone.

    O let me love my love unto myself alone,
    And know my knowledge to the world unknown;
    And worship Thee, O hid One, O much sought,
    As but man can or ought,
    Within the abstracted'st shrine of my
        least breathed-on thought.

Lines 99–101 do not appear under the title "The Hidden Love."
[3] The first two stanzas of the Spirit's reply were published in 1865 and 1869. The third stanza was not published in the nineteenth century; in 1865 and 1869 a slightly different version of the last two stanzas was placed after line 81 in this scene, and two other stanzas substituted. George Berkeley (1685–1753) was a bishop of the Church of England and a philosopher who held that sensible objects do not exist until they are perceived. Nicholas Malebranche (1638–1715) was a French philosopher who held that humans do not perceive objects directly, but perceive rather the ideas of objects as these ideas exist in the mind of God. Both Berkeley and Malebranche were regarded as antimaterialist thinkers.
[4] 1865 and 1869: "Whose high commands would cheer, whose chidings rouse thee."

SPIRIT

130 As I sat at the café, I said to myself,[5]
 They may talk as they please about what
   they call pelf,
 They may sneer as they like about eating
   and drinking,
 But help it I cannot, I cannot help thinking
  How pleasant it is to have money, heigh ho!
  How pleasant it is to have money.

 I sit at my table *en grand seigneur,*[6]
 And when I have done, throw a crust to the
   poor;
 Not only the pleasure, one's self, of good
   living,
 But also the pleasure of now and then giving.
140 So pleasant it is to have money, heigh ho!
  So pleasant it is to have money.

 It was but last winter I came up to Town,[7]
 But already I'm getting a little renown;
 I make new acquaintance where'er I appear;
 I am not too shy, and have nothing to fear.
  So pleasant it is to have money, heigh ho!
  So pleasant it is to have money.

 I drive through the streets, and I care not a
   d—mn;
 The people they stare, and they ask who I
   am;
150 And if I should chance to run over a cad,[8]
 I can pay for the damage if ever so bad.
  So pleasant it is to have money, heigh ho!
  So pleasant it is to have money.

 We stroll to our box and look down on the
   pit,[9]
 And if it weren't low should be tempted to
   spit;
 We loll and we talk until people look up,
 And when it's half over we go out and sup.
  So pleasant it is to have money, heigh ho!
  So pleasant it is to have money.

160 The best of the table and best of the fare—
 And as for the others, the devil may care;
 It isn't our fault if they dare not afford

To sup like a prince and be drunk as a lord.
 So pleasant it is to have money, heigh ho!
 So pleasant it is to have money.

We sit at our tables and tipple champagne;
Ere one bottle goes, comes another again;
The waiters they skip and they scuttle about,
And the landlord attends us so civilly out.
 So pleasant it is to have money, heigh ho!
 So pleasant it is to have money.

It was but last winter I came up to town,
But already I'm getting a little renown;
I get to good houses without much ado,
Am beginning to see the nobility too.
 So pleasant it is to have money, heigh ho!
 So pleasant it is to have money.

O dear! what a pity they ever should lose it!
For they are the gentry that know how to
  use it;
So grand and so graceful, such manners,
  such dinners,
But yet, after all, it is we are the winners.
 So pleasant it is to have money, heigh ho!
 So pleasant it is to have money.

Thus I sat at my table *en grand seigneur,*
And when I had done threw a crust to the
  poor;
Not only the pleasure, one's self, of good
  eating,
But also the pleasure of now and then
  treating.
 So pleasant it is to have money, heigh ho!
 So pleasant it is to have money.

They may talk as they please about what
  they call pelf,
And how one ought never to think of one's
  self,
And how pleasures of thought surpass eating
  and drinking—
My pleasure of thought is the pleasure of
  thinking
 How pleasant it is to have money, heigh ho!
 How pleasant it is to have money.

---

[5] A version of lines 130–195 was printed separately in 1862 and 1863 under the title "Spectator ab Extra." Except for two small changes ("town" for "Town": line 142; and "d—n" for "d—mn": line 148) the text printed here is that published in 1865 and 1869 as a part of "Dipsychus."

[6] *En grand seigneur:* in the manner of a great lord.

[7] Town: the fashionable life and precincts of a metropolis.

[8] Cad: Oxford slang for a common person, a townsman.

[9] Pit: the cheap seats on the floor level of a theater.

(Written in Venice, but for all parts true,
'Twas not a crust I gave him, but a sou.[10])

A gondola here, and a gondola there,
'Tis the pleasantest fashion of taking the air.
To right and to left; stop, turn, and go
    yonder,
And let us repeat, o'er the tide as we wander,
  How pleasant it is to have money, heigh ho!
  How pleasant it is to have money.

.   .   .

From Scene VI

Spirit

What now? the Lido shall it be?[1]
That none may say we didn't see
The ground which Byron used to ride on,
And do I don't know what beside on.
Ho, *barca!*[2] here! and this light gale
Will let us run it with a sail.

Dipsychus

I dreamt a dream; till morning light
A bell rang in my head all night,
Tinkling and tinkling first, and then
Tolling; and tinkling; tolling again.
So brisk and gay, and then so slow!
O joy, and terror! mirth, and woe!
Ting, ting, there is no God; ting, ting—
Dong, there is no God; dong,
There is no God; dong, dong!

Ting, ting, there is no God; ting, ting;
Come dance and play, and merrily sing—
Ting, ting a ding; ting, ting a ding![3]
O pretty girl who trippest along,
Come to my bed—it isn't wrong.
Uncork the bottle, sing the song!
Ting, ting a ding: dong, dong.
Wine has dregs; the song an end;
A silly girl is a poor friend
And age and weakness who shall mend?
Dong, there is no God; Dong!

Ting, ting a ding! Come dance and sing!
Staid Englishmen, who toil and slave
From your first breeching[4] to your grave,
And seldom spend and always save,   30
And do your duty all your life
By your young family and wife;
Come, be't not said you ne'er had known
What earth can furnish you alone.
The Italian, Frenchman, German even,
Have given up all thoughts of heaven;
And you still linger—oh, you fool!—
Because of what you learnt at school.
You should have gone at least to college,
And got a little ampler knowledge.   40
Ah well, and yet—dong, dong, dong:
Do, if you like, as now you do;
If work's a cheat, so's pleasure too;
And nothing's new and nothing's true;
Dong, there is no God; dong!

O Rosalie, my precious maid,[5]
I think thou thinkest love is true;
And on thy fragrant bosom laid
I almost could believe it too.
O in our nook, unknown, unseen,   50
We'll hold our fancy like a screen,
Us and the dreadful fact between.
And it shall yet be long, aye, long,
The quiet notes of our low song
Shall keep us from that sad dong, dong.
Hark, hark, hark! O voice of fear!
It reaches us here, even here!
Dong, there is no God; dong!

Ring ding, ring ding, tara, tara,
To battle, to battle—haste, haste—   60
To battle, to battle—aha, aha!
On, on, to the conqueror's feast.
From east and west, and south and north,
Ye men of valour and of worth,
Ye mighty men of arms, come forth,
And work your will, for that is just;
And in your impulse put your trust,
Beneath your feet the fools are dust.
Alas, alas! O grief and wrong,
The good are weak, the wicked strong;   70

[10] Sou: coin of small value.
[1] With the exception of some omitted lines which are noted below, the songs of Dipsychus and the Spirit were published in 1865 and 1869 in versions that are different from the text printed here only in a few variations in punctuation. Lido: the stretch of land which separates the lagoon of Venice from the sea.
[2] Barca: boat.
[3] Lines 18–27 did not appear in 1865 or in later nineteenth-century editions of Clough's poems.
[4] In 1865 and 1869: for "breeching" (putting on trousers) the line had "childhood."
[5] Lines 46–49 did not appear in 1865 or 1869.

And O my God, how long, how long?[6]
Dong, there is no God; dong!

Ring, ting; to bow before the strong,
There is a rapture too in this;
Speak, outraged maiden, in thy wrong[7]
Did terror bring no secret bliss?
Were boys' shy lips worth half a song
Compared to the hot soldier's kiss?
Work for thy master, work, thou slave
80 He is not merciful, but brave.
Be't joy to serve, who free and proud
Scorns thee and all the ignoble crowd;
Take that, 'tis all thou art allowed,
Except the snaky hope that they
May some time serve, who rule to-day,
When, by hell-demons, shan't they pay?
O wickedness, O shame and grief,
And heavy load, and no relief!
O God, O God! and which is worst,
90 To be the curser or the curst,
The victim or the murderer? Dong
Dong, there is no God; dong!

Ring ding, ring ding, tara, tara,
Away, and hush that preaching—fagh!
Ye vulgar dreamers about peace,
Who offer noblest hearts, to heal
The tenderest hurts honour can feel,
Paid magistrats and the Police!
O piddling merchant justice, go,
100 Exacter rules than yours we know;
Resentment's rule, and that high law
Of whoso best the sword can draw.
Ah well, and yet—dong, dong, dong.
Go on, my friends, as now you do;
Lawyers are villains, soldiers too;
And nothing's new and nothing's true.
Dong, there is no God; dong!

O Rosalie, my lovely maid,[8]
I think thou thinkest love is true;
110 And on thy faithful bosom laid
I almost could believe it too.
The villainies, the wrongs, the alarms

Forget we in each other's arms.
No justice here, no God above;
But where we are, is there not love?
What? what? thou also go'st? For how
Should dead truth live in lover's vow?
What, thou? thou also lost? Dong
Dong, there is no God; dong!

I had a dream, from eve to light
A bell went sounding all the night.
Gay mirth, black woe, thin joys, huge pain:
I tried to stop it, but in vain.
It ran right on, and never broke;
Only when day began to stream
Through the white curtains to my bed,
And like an angel at my head
Light stood and touched me—I awoke,
And looked, and said, "It is a dream."

SPIRIT
Ah! not so bad. You've read, I see,
Your Béranger,[9] and thought of me.
But really you owe some apology
For harping thus upon theology.
I'm not a judge, I own; in short,
Religion may not be my forte.
The Church of England I belong to,
But think Dissenters not far wrong too;
They're vulgar dogs; but for his *creed*
I hold that no man will be d——d.
My Establishment I must respect,[10]
Her ordinances don't neglect;
Attend at Church on Sunday once,
And in the Prayer book am no dunce;
Baptise my babies; nay, my wife
Would be churched too once in her life.
She's taken, I regret to state,
Rather a Puseyite[11] turn of late.
To set the thing quite right, I went
At Easter to the Sacrament.
'Tis proper once a year or so
To do the civil thing and show—
But come and listen in your turn
And you shall hear and mark and learn.

[6] "My soul is also sore vexed: but thou, O Lord, how long?": Psalms 6:3—"And they cried out with a loud voice, saying, How Long, O Lord, holy and true, dost thou not judge and avenge our blood on them that dwell on the earth?"—Revelation 6:10.
[7] Lines 75–78 were not printed in 1865 or 1869.
[8] Lines 108–119 were not printed in 1865 or 1869.
[9] Béranger: Pierre Jean de Béranger (1780–1857), a writer of witty, lightly satircal verse.
[10] Lines 140–151 were not printed in 1865 or 1869.
[11] Puseyite: Edward Bouverie Pusey (1800–1882) was one of the leaders of the Oxford Movement within the Church of England which attempted to emphasize the historical connection of the English church with that of Rome. Pusey was himself accused of heresy, and his name became associated with doctrines and forms of ritual which were suspiciously Roman to conventional members of the English church.

"There is no God," the wicked saith,[12]
  "And truly it's a blessing,
For what he might have done with us
  It's better only guessing."

"There is no God," a youngster thinks,
  "Or really, if there may be,
He surely didn't mean a man
  Always to be a baby."

"There is no God, or if there is,"
  The tradesman thinks, " 'twere funny
If he should take it ill in me
  To make a little money."

"Whether there be," the rich man says,
  "It matters very little,
For I and mine, thank somebody,
  Are not in want of victual."

Some others, also, to themselves
  Who scarce so much as doubt it,
Think there is none, when they are well,
  And do not think about it.

But country folks who live beneath
  The shadow of the steeple;
The parson and the parson's wife,
  And mostly married people;

Youths green and happy in first love,
  So thankful for illusion;
And men caught out in what the world
  Calls guilt, in first confusion;

And almost every one when age,
  Disease, or sorrows strike him,
Inclines to think there is a God,
  Or something very like Him.

But *eccoci!* with our *barchetta*,
Here at the Sant' Elisabetta.[13]

DIPSYCHUS
Vineyards and maize, that's pleasant for sore
  eyes.

SPIRIT
And on the island's other side,
The place where Murray's faithful Guide[14]   190
Informs us Byron used to ride.

DIPSYCHUS
These trellised vines! enchanting! Sandhills,
  ho!
The sea, at last the sea—the real broad sea—
Beautiful! and a glorious breeze upon it.

SPIRIT
Look back; one catches at this station
Lagoon and sea in combination.

DIPSYCHUS
On her still lake the city sits,
Where bark and boat about her flits,
Nor dreams, her soft siesta taking,
Of Adriatic billows breaking.   200
I do; and see and hear them. Come! to the sea!

SPIRIT
  The wind I think is the *sirocco*.[15]
  Yonder, I take it, is Malmocco.
  Thank you! it never was my passion
  To skip o'er sand hills in that fashion.

DIPSYCHUS
Oh, a grand surge! we'll bathe; quick, quick!
  undress!
Quick, quick! in, in!
We'll take the crested billows by their backs
And shake them. Quick! in, in!
And I will taste again the old joy   210
I gloried in so when a boy.

SPIRIT
  Well; but it 's not so pleasant for the feet;
  We should have brought some towels and a
  sheet.

DIPSYCHUS
In, in! I go. Ye great winds blow,
And break, thou curly waves, upon my breast.

---

[12] Lines 154–185 were printed separately in 1862 and 1863 and as a part of "Dipsychus" in 1865 and 1869.

[13] *Eccoci!*: here we are! The Sant' Elisabetta was the location of the bathing house on the Lido.

[14] Murray: the publishing house of John Murray published a series of travelers' handbooks in the mid-nineteenth century.

[15] The Spirit's interruptions of Dipsychus' paens to the sea were not printed in 1865 or 1869. Nor were lines 228–229 and 234–235 of his concluding speech. *Sirocco*: an unpleasant hot wind. Malmocco in the mid-nineteenth century was the entrance from the sea to the port of Venice.

SPIRIT
    Hm! I'm undressing. Doubtless all is well—
    I only wish these thistles were at hell.
    By heaven, I'll stop before that bad yet
        worse is,
    And take care of our watches—and our
        purses.

DIPSYCHUS
220   Aha! come, come—great waters, roll!
    Accept me, take me, body and soul!—
    Aha!

SPIRIT
        Come, no more of that stuff,
    I'm sure you've stayed in long enough.

DIPSYCHUS
That's done me good. It grieves me though
I never came here long ago.

SPIRIT
    Pleasant perhaps. However, no offence,
    Animal spirits are not common sense.
    You think perhaps I have outworn them—
    Certainly I have learnt to scorn them;
230   They're good enough as an assistance,
    But in themselves a poor existence.
    But you—with this one bathe, no doubt,
    Have solved all questions out and out.
    'Tis Easter Day, and on the Lido
    Lo, Christ the Lord is risen indeed, O!

.   .   .

FROM SCENE XII

DIPSYCHUS
What, loitering still? Still, O foul spirit, there?
Go hence, I tell thee, go! I *will* beware.

(alone)
It must be then. I feel it in my soul;
The iron enters, sundering flesh and bone,
And sharper than the two-edged sword of God.[1]
I come into deep waters—help, O help!
The floods run over me.

Therefore, farewell! a long and last farewell,
Ye pious sweet simplicities of life,

Good books, good friends, and holy moods,
    and all
That lent rough life sweet Sunday-seeming
    rests,
Making earth heaven-like. Welcome, wicked
    world,
The hardening heart, the calculating brain
Narrowing its doors to thought, the lying lips,
The calm-dissembling eyes; the greedy flesh,
The world, the Devil—welcome, welcome,
    welcome!

from within
This stern Necessity of things[2]
On every side our being rings;
Our sallying eager actions fall
Vainly against that iron wall.
Where once her finger points the way,
The wise think only to obey;
Take life as she has ordered it,
And come what may of it, submit,
Submit, submit!

Who take implicitly her will,
For these her vassal-chances still
Bring store of joys, successes, pleasures;
But whoso ponders, weighs, and measures,
She calls her torturers up to goad
With spur and scourges on the road;
He does at last with pain whate'er
He spurned at first. Of such, beware,
Beware, beware!

DIPSYCHUS
O God, O God! The great floods of the fiend
Flow over me! I come into deep waters
Where no ground is!

SPIRIT
        Don't be the least afraid;
    There's not the slightest reason for alarm.
    I only meant by a perhaps rough shake
    To rouse you from a dreamy, unhealthy sleep.
    Up, then—up, and be going: the large world,
    The thronged life waits us.
               Come, my pretty boy,
    You have been making mows[3] to the blank
    sky

---

[1] "For the word of God is quick, and powerful, and sharper than any two-edged sword, piercing even to the dividing asunder of soul and spirit, and of the joints and marrow, and is a discerner of the thoughts and intents of the heart" (Hebrews 4:12).

[2] Lines 87–104 were printed separately in 1862 and 1863; and (along with Dipsychus' preceding soliloquy) as a part of "Dipsychus" in 1865 and 1869.

[3] Mows: derisive mouths.

Quite long enough for good. We'll put you
up
Into the higher form.[4] 'Tis time you learn
The Second Reverence, for things around.
Up, then, and go amongst them; don't be
timid;
Look at them quietly a bit: by-and-by
Respect will come, and healthy appetite.
So let us go.
             How now! not yet awake?
Oh, you will sleep yet, will you! Oh, you
shirk,
You try and slink away! You cannot, eh?
Nay now, what folly's this? Why will you
fool yourself?
Why will you walk about thus with your
eyes shut,
Treating for facts the self-made hues that
float[5]
On tight-pressed pupils, which you know are
not facts?
To use the undistorted light of the sun
Is not a crime; to look straight out upon
The big plain things that stare one in the
face
Does not contaminate; to see pollutes not
What one must feel if one won't see; what *is*,
And will be too, howe'er we blink, and must
One way or other make itself observed.
Free walking's better than being led about;
and
What will the blind man do, I wonder, if
Some one should cut the string of his dog?
Just think,
What could you do, if I should go away?
   O, you have paths of your own before you,
have you?
What shall it take to? literature, no doubt?
Novels, reviews? or poems! if you please!
The strong fresh gale of life will feel, no
doubt,
The influx of your mouthful of soft air.
Well, make the most of that small stock of
knowledge
You've condescended to receive from me;
That's your best chance. Oh, you despise
that! Oh,
Prate then of passions you have known in
dreams,

Of huge experience gathered by the eye;
Be large of aspiration, pure in hope,
Sweet in fond longings, but in all things
vague.
Breathe out your dreamy scepticism, relieved   150
By snatches of old songs. People will like
that, doubtless.
Or will you write about philosophy?
For a waste far-off *maybe* overlooking
The fruitful *is* close by, live in metaphysic,
With transcendental logic fill your stomach,
Schematise joy, effigiate meat and drink;
Or, let me see, a mighty Work, a Volume,
The Complemental of the inferior Kant,
The Critic of Pure Practic,[6] based upon
The Antinomies of the Moral Sense: for,
look you,   160
We cannot act without assuming x,
And at the same time y, its contradictory;
Ergo, to act. People will buy that, doubtless.
Or you'll perhaps teach youth (I do not
question
Some downward turn you may find, some
evasion
Of the broad highway's glaring white ascent),
Teach youth—in a small way; that is, always
So as to have much time left for yourself;
This you can't sacrifice, your leisure's
precious.
Heartily you will not take to anything;   170
Will parents like that, think you? "He
writes poems,[7]
He's odd opinions—hm!—and's not in
Orders"—
For that you won't be. Well, old college
fame,
The charity of some free-thinking merchant,
Or friendly intercession brings a first pupil;
And not a second. Oh, or if it should,
Whatever happen, don't I see you still,
Living no life at all? Even as now
An o'ergrown baby, sucking at the dugs
Of Instinct, dry long since. Come, come, you
are old enough   180
For spoon-meat surely.
                Will you go on thus
Until death end you? if indeed it does.
For what it does, none knows. Yet as for you,

[4] Higher form: a higher grade in school.   [5] 1865 and 1869: for "float" reads "flash."
[6] Kant: Immanuel Kant (1724–1804), the German idealist philosopher whose best known
work was the *Critique of Pure Reason* (1781, 1786). 1865 and 1869 read "Practice."
[7] Lines 171–176 were not printed in 1865 or 1869. Orders: ordination in the clergy of the
Church of England.

You'll hardly have the courage to die
    outright;
You'll somehow halve even it. Methinks I
    see you,
Through everlasting limbos of void time,
Twirling and twiddling ineffectively,
And indeterminately swaying for ever.
Come, come, spoon-meat at any rate.
                        Well, well,
190   I will not persecute you more, my friend.
Only do think, as I observed before,
What *can* you do, if I should go away?[8]

DIPSYCHUS
Is the hour here, then? Is the minute come—
The irreprievable instant of stern time?
O for a few, few grains in the running glass,
Or for some power to hold them! O for a few
Of all that went so wastefully before!
It must be then, e'en now.

           from within
                It must, it must.[9]
'Tis Common Sense! and human wit
200   Can claim no higher name than it.
Submit, submit!

Necessity! and who shall dare
Bring to *her* feet excuse or prayer?
Beware, beware!
We must, we must.
Howe'er we turn and pause and tremble—
Howe'er we shrink, deceive, dissemble—
Whate'er our doubting, grief, disgust,
The hand is on us, and we must,
210   We must, we must.
'Tis Common Sense! and human wit
Can find no better name than it.
Submit, submit!

Fear not, my lamb, whate'er men say,
I am the Shepherd; and the Way.[10]

        .   .   .

SCENE XIV

DIPSYCHUS
Twenty-one past, twenty-five coming on;
One third of life departed, nothing done.
Out of the Mammon of Unrighteousness
That we make friends, the Scripture is express.[1]
Mephisto,[2] come; we will agree
Content; you'll take a moiety.

SPIRIT
   A moiety, ye gods, he, he!

DIPSYCHUS
Three quarters then. One eye you close,
And lay your finger to your nose.
Seven eighths? nine tenths? O griping beast!
Leave me a decimal at least.

SPIRIT
   Oh, one of ten! to infect the nine
   And make the devil a one be mine!
   Oh, one! to jib all day, God wot,
   When all the rest would go full trot!
   One very little one, eh? to doubt with,
   Just to pause, think, and look about with?
   In course! you counted on no less—
   You thought it likely I'd say yes!

DIPSYCHUS
Be it then thus—since that it must, it seems.
Welcome, O world, henceforth; and farewell
    dreams!
Yet know, Mephisto, know, nor you nor I

---

[8] "Can" was not italicized in 1865 or 1869.

[9] Lines 199–213 were printed separately in 1862 and 1863, and as a part of "Dipsychus" in 1865 and 1869.

[10] Lines 214–215 were not printed in 1865 or 1869. "I am the good shepherd, and know my sheep, and am known of mine" (John 12:14). "I am the way, the truth, and the life: no man cometh unto the Father, but by me" (John 14:6). Both sentences are spoken by Christ.

[1] "And I say unto you, Make to yourselves friends of the mammon of unrighteousness; that, when ye fail, they may receive you into everlasting habitations" (Luke 16:9). The sentence is spoken by Christ in explication of the parable of the unjust steward who reduced the debts of his master's creditors so that he might be favorably received by them should he be turned out of his stewardship. The text continues: "He that is faithful in that which is least is faithful also in much: and he that is unjust in the least is also unjust in much. If therefore ye have not been faithful in the unrighteous mammon, who will commit to your trust the true riches? . . . No servant can serve two masters: for either he will hate the one, and love the other; or else he will hold to the one, and despise the other. Ye cannot serve God and mammon" (Luke 16:1–13).

[2] Mephisto: a variant of Mephistopheles, a traditional name of Satan, used by Goethe in his version of *Faust* (1808–1832). In 1865 and 1869 Dipsychus' tempter is addressed here as "My Spirit"; lines 8–11 are also reduced to two lines of verse.

Can in this matter either sell or buy;
For the fee simple of this trifling lot
To you or me, trust me, pertaineth not.
I can but render what is of my will,
And behind it somewhat remaineth still.
Oh, your sole chance was in the childish mind
Whose darkness dreamed that vows like this
  could bind;
Thinking all lost, it made all lost, and brought
In fact the ruin which had been but thought.
Thank Heaven (or you!) that's past these
  many years,
And we have knowledge wiser than our fears.
So your poor bargain take, my man,
And make the best of it you can.

SPIRIT

  With reservations! oh, how treasonable!
  When I had let you off so reasonable.
  However, I don't fear; be it so!
  Brutus is honourable, I know;[3]
  So mindful of the dues of others,
  So thoughtful for his poor dear brothers,
  So scrupulous, considerate, kind—
  He wouldn't leave the devil behind
  If he assured him he had claims
  For his good company to hell-flames!
  No matter, no matter, the bargain's made;
  And I for my part will not be afraid.
  Little Bo Peep, she lost her sheep[4]
  And knew not where to find them.
  He, he! With reservations, Christo!
  A child like you to cheat Mephisto!
  With reservations! oh, ho, ho!
  But time, my friend, has yet to show
  Which of us two will closest fit
  The proverb of the Biter Bit.[5]
  Little Bo Peep, she lost her sheep—

DIPSYCHUS
Tell me thy name, now it is over.

SPIRIT
              Oh!
  Why, Mephistopheles, you know—
  At least you've lately called me so;
  Belial[6] it was some days ago.
  But take your pick; I've got a score—

Never a royal baby more.
For a brass plate upon a door
What think you of *Cosmocrator?*[7]

DIPSYCHUS
Τοὺς Κοσμοκράτορας τοῦ αἰῶνος τούτου[8]
And that you are indeed, I do not doubt you.

SPIRIT
  Ephesians, ain't it? near the end
  You dropt a word to spare your friend.
  What follows, too, in application
  Would be absurd exaggeration.   70

DIPSYCHUS
The Power of this World! hateful unto God!

SPIRIT
  Cosmarchon's shorter, but sounds odd:
  One wouldn't like, even if a true devil,
  To be taken for a vulgar Jew devil.

DIPSYCHUS
Yet in all these things we—'tis Scripture too—
Are more than conquerors, even over you.

SPIRIT
  Come, come, don't maunder any longer,
  Time tests the weaker and the stronger;
  And we, without procrastination,
  Must set, you know, to our vocation.   80
  O goodness; won't you find it pleasant
  To own the positive and present;
  To see yourself like people round,
  And feel your feet upon the ground!

  Little Bo Peep, she lost her sheep![9]
  Aside
  In the Piazza di San Marco
  O won't I try him after dark, oh
  O Jesus Christ! it will be funny
  If I don't get my earnest money.

DIPSYCHUS
Peace, peace! I come.   90
            (Exeunt ambo)[9]
            (1850) 1865

---

[3] The refrain of Mark Anthony's ironic speech in Shakespeare's *Julius Caesar* (III, 2).
[4] Lines 48–51, and line 56, were not printed in 1865 or 1869.
[5] The Biter Bit: the cheater cheated.
[6] Belial: a name Milton gives to one of the fallen angels in *Paradise Lost* (1667).
[7] *Cosmocrator:* ruler of the visible universe.
[8] The full text (Ephesians 6:12) is "the rulers of the darkness of this world."
[9] Lines 85–90 were not printed in 1865 or 1869.   [10] *Exeunt ambo:* they exit together.

"It is not sweet content, be sure"

It is not sweet content, be sure,
  That moves the nobler Muse to song,
Yet when could truth come whole and pure
  From hearts that inly writhe with wrong?

It is not calm and peaceful breasts
  That see or read the problem true;
They only know on whom 't has prest
  Too hard to hope to solve it too.

Our ills are worse than at their ease
10 Mere blameless happy souls suspect;
They only study the disease,
  Alas, who live not to detect.

            (1851) 1869

"The grasses green of sweet content"

The grasses green of sweet content
That spring, no matter high or low,
Where'er a living thing can grow,
On chilly hills and rocky rent,

And by the lowly streamlet's side—
Oh! why did e'er I turn [from] these?—
The lordly tall umbrageous trees,
That stand in high aspiring pride,

With massive trunks on high sustain
10 A world of boughs with leaf and fruits,
And drive their wide-extending roots
Deep down into the subject plain.

Oh, what with these had I to do?—
That germs of things above their kind
May live, pent up and close confined
In humbler forms, it may be true;

Yet great is that which gives our lot;
High laws and powers our will transcend,
And not for this, till time do end,
20 Shall any be what he is not.

Each in its place, as each was sent,
Just nature [ranges] side by side,

Alike the oak tree's lofty pride
And grasses green of sweet content.

            (1851) 1869

Actæon[1]

Over a mountain-slope with lentisk,[2] and with
  abounding
Arbutus, and the red oak overtufted, 'mid a
  noontide
Now glowing fervidly, the Leto-born,[3] the
  divine one,
Artemis, Arcadian wood-rover, alone, hunt-
  weary,
Unto a dell cent'ring many streamlets her foot
  unerring
Had guided. Platanus[4] with fig-tree shaded a
  hollow,
Shaded a waterfall, where pellucid yet
  abundant
Streams from perpetual full-flowing sources a
  current:
Lower on either bank in sunshine flowered the'
  oleanders:
Plenteous under a rock green herbage here to
  the margin
Grew with white poplars o'ercrowning. She,
  thither arrived,
Unloosing joyfully the vest unfolded upon her,
Swift the divine shoulders discovering, swiftly
  revealing
Her maidenly bosom and all her beauty
  beneath it,
To the river waters overflowing to receive her
Yielded her ambrosial nakedness. But with an
  instant
Conscious, with the' instant the' immortal
  terrific anger
Flew to the guilty doer: that moment, where
  amid amply
Concealing plane leaves he the' opportunity,
  pursued
Long fruitlessly, possessed, unwise, Actæon, of
  hunters,
Hapless of Arcadian and most misguided of
  hunters,
Knew the divine mandate, knew fate directed
  upon him.

[1] Actæon in classical mythology was a hunter who saw Artemis, the virgin goddess of the moon and of the hunt, naked while she bathed. She turned him into a stag, and he was hunted to death by his own dogs.
[2] Lentisk: a tree or an evergreen shrub.
[3] Leto-born: Artemis was the daughter of Jupiter and Leto.   [4] Platanus: plane trees.

He, crouching, furtively, with audacious
   tremulous glance,
Espied approaching, saw descending, disarray-
   ing,
And the' unclad shoulders awestruck, awestruck
   let his eyes see
The maidenly bosom, but not—dim fear fell
   upon them—
Not more had witnessed. Not, therefore, less
   the forest through
Ranging, their master ceasing thenceforth to
   remember,

With the' instant together trooping came as to
   devour him
His dogs from the' ambush.—Transformed
   suddenly before them,   30
He fled, an antlered stag wild with terror to
   the mountain.
She, the liquid stream in, her limbs carelessly
   reclining,
The flowing waters collected grateful about
   her.

                            (1861?) 1869

Matthew Arnold
1822–1888

IN 1869, when a two-volume edition of his poetry was about to be published, Arnold wrote to his mother an estimate of what he knew by then was to be nearly the whole of his achievement as a poet. He had written almost no poetry after the mid-1860s, and even many of the poems in *New Poems* (1867) had been written before 1860. His view of his poetry, then, was summary, and his tone almost detached. "My poems represent," he wrote, "on the whole, the main movement of mind of the last quarter of a century, and thus they will probably have their day as people become conscious to themselves of what that movement of mind is, and interested in the literary productions which reflect it. It might fairly be argued that I have less poetical sentiment than Tennyson, and less intellectual vigour and abundance than Browning; yet, because I have perhaps more of a fusion of the two than either of them, and have more regularly applied that fusion to the main line of modern development, I am likely enough to have my turn, as they have had theirs."

Arnold's poetry has had, and still holds, its turn in the attention of those who read and study nineteenth-century British poetry. One of its interests, as he predicted, is its fusion of sentiment and idea which reflects one of the responses to their historical moment of a generation of writers and intellectuals who came to maturity at mid-century, half a generation younger than Tennyson and Browning, half a generation older than Swinburne, Hopkins, and Hardy. The question of that moment, the main movement of mind in it, was how to reestablish the authority of institutions that, in Arnold's opinion, civilize society. Arnold believed that he was living in a postrevolutionary epoch. In his view a man who saw things truly and whole could at mid-century neither stand against nor be exuberantly caught up in the excitement of changes wrought by industrialism, science, the long, slow passage toward democracy, the increase in knowledge and the commitment to reason which disputed traditional historical and intellectual grounds of religious belief. In such a time an effective intelligence and sensibility must rather work to assure that the new society was not cut off from the ideas, feelings, and traditions that had steadied and sweetened human experience in the past. In the formulation of Arnold's best-known prose work, he wanted to command change by culture, "the best that has been thought and said in the world" (the past tense is important), and so to prevent change from accelerating into anarchy. It is fair to say that he left the heavy work of this command to his prose. His poetry often enacted his sad anxiety that he and his fellows would not succeed, that the modern, materialistic, skeptical spirit of the time would break free from the traditional agencies of culture. But in his prose, into which he put his first energies as a writer after 1860, he aggressively strove to reform and reconstruct the institutions he thought essential to civilization: religion, education, literature, a class and political structure which enabled the leadership of the most thoughtful and right-feeling, the central, national authority of the state.

As he came to acknowledge, in his ideas about education and religion he was very much his father's son. Thomas Arnold's great achievement was to make Rugby a pattern for the education of young men destined to serve responsibly in their society. By 1837, when Matthew Arnold entered his father's school, the pattern was firmly in place: a curriculum that included mathematics, modern languages, and modern history along with classical studies; the self-government of students, supervised and sometimes checked by the headmaster; an emphasis on moral principle rather than precept as the fundament of conduct; and an insistence that talent had a duty to grow, succeed, and lead. Matthew Arnold accepted a government appointment as an inspector of schools in part because he saw it as an instrument for serious work. For more than thirty years he tried to use the power of the state to give the middle classes entering the schools an education that was humane as well as utilitarian, that did not neglect the teaching of literature, history, and modern languages in order to secure the bare necessities of literacy and computation.

Later in his life Arnold tried to affect the religious institutions of his country so that they too could help in the work of culture. His father believed in a state religion because he thought the state had a responsibility toward the spiritual life of its citizens. But for Thomas Arnold the quality and power of that life were more important than the forms of creed and ritual that expressed them, and it was more important for society that a national church gather believing Christians to itself than that it insist on differences in dogma and ritual which divide sects from one another. When in the 1870s Arnold began to write on religion, he moved beyond his father to argue that religious belief could not survive modern skepticism and historical knowledge if it was founded on a literal belief in Scripture and miraculous interventions by God in time and nature. Religion is, rather, as he wrote in the book of his which was most popular in his lifetime, *Literature and Dogma* (1873), "morality touched with emotion"; and God is not a person encumbered by now-dubious doctrines of the Trinity and the Incarnation, but simply a premise of perfection, an "enduring power, not ourselves, which makes for righteousness." A national church is preferable because it provides a center that sustains and offers communion to the righteous. But the important matter is that religion and the church be relieved of the arid and now doomed task of defending and enforcing old creeds, and instead urge people to do the right because it pleases them to be righteous, and because they love the authority of God.

Arnold's hope for literature was that it would join and perhaps lead the state, schools, and religion in civilizing, by his lights, a rationalistic and materialistic time. In his first essay in literary criticism, the preface to the 1853 edition of his poems (see Part Ten), he claimed for poetry only the benefit that it makes us enjoy what is permanent, profound, and most healthily ordered in human experience and the human psyche. Twenty years later, in *Literature and Dogma,* he gave the name of literature to the true and sustaining spirit of religious faith, as opposed to the analytic spirit that founded faith in ever more vulnerable refinements of dogma and exegeses of Scripture. By the end of his life, in essays such as "The Study of Poetry," Arnold is ready to place his hope for culture in a reciprocity between humanity and poetry: humanity will preserve poetry because poetry will save humanity. The power of poetry is not, for Arnold, a power not ourselves: it is not God or religion. Poetry rather expresses the best of ourselves. It is not so much a version of religious belief as it is another kind of church, a social and cultural institution in which people are brought together to feel the truth, to love it, and to wish to be happy by living in it with one another.

Arnold did not claim that his own poetry, or that of his British contemporaries, performed this function. The literature of the past could do it. Literary criticism, which brought the past into the present, could also help to civilize the time, and criticism manifested as well a creative joy like that of literature, if inferior to it. But the time needed to be made better before it could produce a poetry that would make it great. It is difficult, Arnold wrote in 1853, "under the circumstances amidst which we live, to think clearly, to feel nobly, and to delineate firmly," and so to write poems whose design and execution will rejoice and steady their readers. What remains to the poets of his country and time is the responsibility not to confuse and dissipate the craft of poetry. They must honor and write before the example of the past so that when changes in society made great poets again possible, they would have available to them unbroken traditions of poetic language, forms, and purposes in which great poetry had been written.

One consequence of this opinion, which Arnold did not change, was that after 1860 Arnold made himself another busy life as a writer of prose. For he wanted an instrument that would not simply reflect but would act in the main movement of mind. Another consequence is that his prose and poetry express different tonalities of his response to his time. The forms of his prose are expository and polemical, its tone urgent, its ground assumption a belief that he can change how his contemporaries think, feel, and act. The modes and tones of his poetry, on the other hand, are most often contemplative, meditative, elegiac. In his poems poets and heroes stand apart from the difficulties of their times, or, like his judgment of his friend Arthur Hugh Clough in "Thyrsis," enter them to be torn and baffled. Sometimes Arnold wrote poems, often sonnets, in which as in his prose he plainly urged what to do and how to be. Some of his meditative and elegiac poems—"Rugby Chapel," for example—end by rousing their speaker and readers to resume the march against the troubles whose casualties they have stepped aside to contemplate. In his early poem "The Strayed Reveller," and in "Sohrab and Rustum," a poem he esteemed highly (and, it might be argued, in "Empedocles on Etna" as well), Arnold achieves resolutions that suggest that to imagine a form and language for pain and loss is not just a solace but also a gain, a saving act of order within and against the shapeless whirl of the world. But it is finally true that Arnold's poems, fewer and less varied in tone than those of the major contemporary poets to whom he compared himself, are interesting not because they represent a mind moving to realize the hope of culture in the present. They are interesting because the best of his poems are singularly affecting expressions of the jeopardy in which a sensibility educated in the traditions of the past found culture and poetry itself in the middle of the nineteenth century.

This selection from Arnold's poems emphasizes his lyric, elegiac, and meditative verse. In addition to "Empedocles on Etna," he wrote one other long dramatic poem, the verse tragedy *Merope* (1858). He wrote two long narrative poems, "Tristam and Iseult" (1852) and "Balder Dead" (1855), in addition to "Sorhab and Rustum." But even part of "Tristam and Iseult" was written in lyric soliloquies and dialogue, something like the form of "The Strayed Reveller," which Arnold classified as lyric in his arrangement of his collected poems. This persistence in his poetry of a reflective, undeclamatory voice, and the recurrence of situations and themes of isolation and loss, may disguise how various Arnold could be in the language, meters, and stanzaic forms of his lyric poems. Consider, for example, the ornamented, highly conventional beginning of "The Scholar Gypsy" and the relative plainness of "Thyrsis," his elegy to Clough written in the same ten-line stanza. Or consider the differences in the accents of the four-beat rhymed lines of "Resignation," the "Memorial Verses" to Wordsworth, and the more discursive "Epilogue to Lessing's 'Laocoön'." Even within regular meters Arnold often loosens his line to a freer rhythm, and in "Philomela" and "Dover Beach" he permits the mood and statement of his line and stanza to take their own measure. The relatively small body of Arnold's verse has come in the twentieth century to claim an attention proper to a major poet in part because in his poetry he anticipates what has become a common twentieth-century apprehension of the jeopardy of his, or any, idea of high culture. In part too the very sound of his poetry is sometimes familiar to twentieth-century readers who are used to a poetry that sometimes does without the regular meters and conventional verse forms that Arnold, carefully tending to the craft of his verse, occasionally passed beyond as he strove for a poetic voice apt to the fine, complicated sentiment of his utterance.

CHRONOLOGY

1822 Born in a town on the Thames near London, where his father, later to become the famously innovating headmaster of

Rugby, conducted a school; his mother was the daughter of a Church of England clergyman.

1833–36   After a boyhood in Rugby, where his father moved the family in 1828, and in the Lake district, where the Arnolds had a house after 1833 and became acquainted with the Wordsworths, Arnold spent a year as a pupil in one of the schools which his father had attended.

1837–41   Arnold continued his education at Rugby, where he won a prize for one of his poems (1840) and a scholarship to Balliol College, Oxford (1840).

1841–44   Arnold entered Oxford, where he made a close friendship with Arthur Hugh Clough, who had lived with the Arnolds when he preceded Arnold as a student at Rugby. Arnold's father was appointed to a professorship of history at Oxford in 1841; he died the following year. After taking his degree in 1844, Arnold taught briefly at Rugby.

1845   Arnold was elected to a fellowship at Oriel College, Oxford; his father and, later, Clough were also fellows of Oriel.

1846   During a visit to France and Switzerland, he called on the French novelist George Sand.

1847–48   Appointed private secretary to Lord Lansdowne, an admirer of his father and a member of the Liberal ministry, Arnold moved to London. In 1848 and the following year he took his vacation in Switzerland, where he probably met the woman who figures in the poems to Marguerite (see pp. 450–454).

1849   *The Strayed Reveller, and Other Poems* published.

1851   Arnold appointed an Inspector of Schools through the offices of Lord Lansdowne: his duties were to travel in England and Wales, and eventually around London, to inspect schools and teacher training colleges conducted by nonconformist religious sects to assure that they met standards set by the government. In this year Arnold married Frances Lucy Wrightman, the daughter of a judge; their marriage had earlier been discouraged by her family because of Arnold's uncertain profession and income.

1852   *Empedocles on Etna, and Other Poems* published. The Arnolds' first son (of six children, eventually) born.

1853   A collection of Arnold's *Poems* pub-

lished, excluding "Empedocles on Etna" and including a preface (see Part Ten) explaining its omission.

1857   Arnold was appointed to a five-year term, later renewed, as Professor of Poetry at Oxford. His duties were to deliver three lectures annually (he retained his inspectorate); he was the first to deliver the lectures in English instead of Latin.

1858   *Merope: A Tragedy* published.

1859   *England and the Italian Question* published, Arnold's first extensive essay in prose commentary on current political and social questions.

1860–61   After traveling to learn about Continental schools, Arnold published two reports in 1860 and 1861. *On Translating Homer*, a set of his Oxford lectures, published (1861).

1865   Arnold collected some essays and some of his Oxford lectures which had also been published in periodicals into the first series of *Essays in Criticism*.

1867   *New Poems* published; most of these poems had been written in the 1850s. Arnold returned "Empedocles on Etna" to his canon in this volume. *On the Study of Celtic Literature*, a set of his Oxford lectures, also published.

1869   *Culture and Anarchy,* a series of essays on the state of British politics, society, and sensibility, published; a part of the volume had been Arnold's last lecture at Oxford in 1867, and others were published first in magazines in 1867–68. A collected edition of Arnold's poems in two volumes was also published in 1869.

1870–77   Arnold published a series of essays and discourses on religion: *St. Paul and Protestantism* (1870), *Literature and Dogma* (1873), *God and the Bible* (1875), *Last Essays on Church and Religion* (1877). In 1871 he published *Friendship's Garland,* a continuation of the social criticism he conducted in *Culture and Anarchy,* and in 1877 he published a new two-volume edition of his poems.

1878–79   *Mixed Essays* published (1879); a selection of his poems was published in 1878.

1882   *Irish Essays and Others* published.

1883–86   Arnold lectured in the United States in 1883–84; the lectures were published in 1885 as *Discourses in America*. In 1883 Arnold was awarded an annual government pension for his services to literature. In 1886 he retired from his inspectorate of schools.

1888 Arnold died. *Essays in Criticism,* Second Series was published shortly after his death.

EDITIONS

The texts printed below are those of the Library edition of Arnold's poems published in 1885. The standard edition is *The Poetical Works of Matthew Arnold,* edited by C. B. Tinker and H. F. Lowry (1950); Tinker and Lowry base their edition on the 1885 edition. Tinker and Lowry have also published *The Poetry of Matthew Arnold: A Commentary* (1940). Kenneth Allott's annotated edition of *The Poems of Matthew Arnold* (1965) contains full and useful notes, especially about the sources for the poems.

Ten volumes of *The Complete Prose Works of Matthew Arnold* (1960–), edited by R. W. Super, have been published. G. W. E. Russell edited a two-volume collection of Arnold's letters in 1895, later (1903–4) reprinted as part of an edition of Arnold's writing. H. F. Lowry has edited *The Letters of Matthew Arnold to Arthur Hugh Clough* (1932); William E. Buckler's *Matthew Arnold's Books: Toward a Publishing Diary* (1958) includes many of Arnold's letters to his publishers; and H. F. Lowry, Karl Young, and W. H. Dunn have edited Arnold's *Note-Books* (1952).

BIOGRAPHY AND CRITICISM

The best account of Arnold's professional career, and the best book on Arnold, is Lionel Trilling's *Matthew Arnold* (1949), a biography of his mind and talent. Three short lives of Arnold are useful: by J. D. Jump (1955), Fraser Neiman (1968), and Douglas Bush (1971).

OTHER USEFUL BOOKS

Alexander, Edward. *Matthew Arnold and John Stuart Mill* (1965); and, *Matthew Arnold, John Ruskin, and the Modern Temper* (1973).

Anderson, Warren D. *Matthew Arnold and the Classical Tradition* (1965).

Baum, Paull F. *Ten Studies in the Poetry of Matthew Arnold* (1958).

Brown, E. K. *Matthew Arnold: A Study in Conflict* (1948).

Culler, A. Dwight. *Imaginative Reason: The Poetry of Matthew Arnold* (1966).

Gottfried, Leon. *Matthew Arnold and the Romantics* (1963).

Groom, Bernard. *The Diction of Poetry from Spenser to Bridges* (1955). Includes his study of the diction of the poetry of Tennyson, Browning, and Arnold, published separately in 1939.

James, D. G. *Matthew Arnold and the Decline of English Romanticism* (1961).

Jamison, William A. *Arnold and the Romantics* (1958).

Madden, William A. *Matthew Arnold: A Study of the Aesthetic Temperament in Victorian England* (1967).

McCarthy, Patrick. *Matthew Arnold and the Three Classes* (1964).

Raleigh, John Henry. *Matthew Arnold and American Culture* (1957).

Robbins, William. *The Ethical Idealism of Matthew Arnold* (1959).

Roper, Alan. *Arnold's Poetic Landscapes* (1969).

Sells, Iris. *Matthew Arnold and France: The Poet* (1935).

Stange, G. Robert. *Matthew Arnold: The Poet as Humanist* (1967).

Super, R. H. *The Time-Spirit of Matthew Arnold* (1970).

Temple, Ruth Z. *The Critic's Alchemy* (1953). Includes chapters on Arnold's knowledge and use of French literature.

Carl Dawson has edited *Matthew Arnold: the Poetry; the Critical Heritage* (1973); and David DeLaura has edited *Matthew Arnold: Twentieth Century Views* (1973). Both contain bibliographies of commentary on Arnold. See also C. T. Wilkins, *The English Reputation of Arnold 1840–77* (1959); and Ehrsam, Deily, and Smith (General Bibliography).

The Strayed Reveller[1]

The Portico of Circe's Palace. Evening

A YOUTH. CIRCE

THE YOUTH
Faster, faster,

---

[1] In Book 10 of Homer's *Odyssey* some of the crew of Odysseus (Ulysses) are entertained in the house of the magician Circe, who then turns them into swine. Odysseus, possessed of an herb which makes him immune from her magic, rescues his men, delays to be entertained by Circe, but then continues his journey homeward. Arnold uses only the setting of this episode, and the identities of Circe as a magician and Odysseus as an experienced man who ultimately holds to his single purpose of returning home, in his poem about a young man who leaves

O Circe, Goddess,
Let the wild, thronging train,
The bright procession
Of eddying forms
Sweep through my soul!

Thou standest, smiling
Down on me! thy right arm,
Lean'd up against the column there,
10 Props thy soft cheek;
Thy left holds, hanging loosely,
The deep cup, ivy-cinctured,
I held but now.

Is it, then, evening
So soon? I see, the night-dews,
Cluster'd in thick beads, dim
The agate brooch-stones
On thy white shoulder;
The cool night-wind, too,
20 Blows through the portico,
Stirs thy hair, Goddess,
Waves thy white robe!

CIRCE
Whence art thou, sleeper?

THE YOUTH
When the white dawn first
Through the rough fir-planks
Of my hut, by the chestnuts,
Up at the valley-head,
Came breaking, Goddess!
I sprang up, I threw round me
30 My dappled fawn-skin;
Passing out, from the wet turf,
Where they lay, by the hut door,
I snatch'd up my vine-crown, my fir-staff,
All drench'd in dew—
Came swift down to join
The rout early gather'd
In the town, round the temple,
Iacchus' white fane[2]
On yonder hill.

40 Quick I pass'd, following
The wood-cutters' cart-track
Down the dark valley;—I saw

On my left, through the beeches,
Thy palace, Goddess,
Smokeless, empty!
Trembling, I enter'd; beheld
The court all silent,
The lions sleeping,
On the altar this bowl.
I drank, Goddess!   5
And sank down here, sleeping,
On the steps of thy portico.

CIRCE
Foolish boy! Why tremblest thou?
Thou lovest it, then, my wine?
Wouldst more of it? See, how glows,
Through the delicate, flush'd marble,
The red, creaming liquor,
Strown with dark seeds!
Drink, then! I chide thee not,
Deny thee not my bowl.   6
Come, stretch forth thy hand, then—so!
Drink—drink again!

THE YOUTH
Thanks, gracious one!
Ah, the sweet fumes again!
More soft, ah me,
More subtle-winding
Than Pan's[3] flute-music!
Faint—faint! Ah me,
Again the sweet sleep!

CIRCE
Hist! Thou—within there!   7
Come forth, Ulysses!
Art tired with hunting?
While we range the woodland,
See what the day brings.

ULYSSES
Ever new magic!
Hast thou then lured hither,
Wonderful Goddess, by thy art,
The young, languid-eyed Ampelus,[4]
Iacchus' darling—
Or some youth beloved of Pan,   8
Of Pan and the Nymphs?
That he sits, bending downward

pleasure to find in Circe's wine the imagined forms of remote places, and of great and painful deeds.
[2] Iacchus: a deity associated with Dionysus, (Bacchus), the classical god of revelry and wine, whose rites are celebrated in revels. Fane: temple.
[3] Pan: the classical god of nature.
[4] Ampelus: the son of a satyr and a nymph—and a favorite of Dionysus—who was killed in a fall from a tree and placed among the stars.

His white, delicate neck
To the ivy-wreathed marge
Of thy cup; the bright, glancing vine-leaves
That crown his hair,
Falling forward, mingling
With the dark ivy-plants—
His fawn-skin, half untied,
Smear'd with red wine-stains? Who is he,
That he sits, overweigh'd
By fumes of wine and sleep,
So late, in thy portico?
What youth, Goddess,—what guest
Of Gods or mortals?

CIRCE
Hist! he wakes!
I lured him not hither, Ulysses.
Nay, ask him!

THE YOUTH
Who speaks? Ah, who comes forth
To thy side, Goddess, from within?
How shall I name him?
This spare, dark-featured,
Quick-eyed stranger?
Ah, and I see too
His sailor's bonnet,
His short coat, travel-tarnish'd,
With one arm bare!—
Art thou not he, whom fame
This long time rumours
The favour'd guest of Circe, brought by the
    waves?
Art thou he, stranger?
The wise Ulysses,
Laertes' son?

ULYSSES
I am Ulysses.
And thou, too, sleeper?
Thy voice is sweet.
It may be thou hast follow'd
Through the islands some divine bard,
By age taught many things,
Age and the Muses;
And heard him delighting

The chiefs and people
In the banquet, and learn'd his songs,
Of Gods and Heroes,
Of war and arts,
And peopled cities,
Inland, or built
By the grey sea.—If so, then hail!
I honour and welcome thee.

THE YOUTH
The Gods are happy.
They turn on all sides
Their shining eyes,
And see below them
The earth and men.

They see Tiresias[5]
Sitting, staff in hand,
On the warm, grassy
Asopus[6] bank,
His robe drawn over
His old, sightless head,
Revolving inly
The doom of Thebes.

They see the Centaurs[7]
In the upper glens
Of Pelion, in the streams,
Where red-berried ashes fringe
The clear-brown shallow pools,
With streaming flanks, and heads
Read'd proudly, snuffing
The mountain wind.

They see the Indian
Drifting, knife in hand,
His frail boat moor'd to
A floating isle thick-matted
With large-leaved, low-creeping melon-plants,[8]
And the dark cucumber.
He reaps, and stows them,
Drifting—drifting;—round him,
Round his green harvest-plot,
Flow the cool lake-waves,
The mountains ring them.

[5] Tiresias: a blind seer who prophesied or witnessed the events that brought down the ruling house of Thebes, from his prophesy that Oedipus would kill his father, the ruler of Thebes, through his warnings that Oedipus was destroying himself, to the death of Oedipus' daughter Antigone and the fall of Thebes.
[6] The Asopus is a river in Greece.
[7] The Centaurs were a race of beings, with the upper bodies of men and the lower bodies of horses, who lived on Mount Pelion.
[8] Arnold took this account of artificial islands on which plants are cultivated from Alexander Burnes' *Travels into Bokhara* (1834).

They see the Scythian[9]
On the wide stepp, unharnessing
His wheel'd house at noon.
He tethers his beast down, and makes his
   meal—
Mares' milk, and bread
Baked on the embers;—all around
The boundless, waving grass-plains stretch,
   thick-starr'd
With saffron and the yellow hollyhock
170 And flag-leaved iris-flowers.
Sitting in his cart
He makes his meal; before him, for long miles,
Alive with bright green lizards,
And the springing bustard-fowl,
The track, a straight black line,
Furrows the rich soil; here and there
Clusters of lonely mounds
Topp'd with rough-hewn,
Grey, rain-blear'd statues, overpeer
180 The sunny waste.

They see the ferry
On the broad, clay-laden
Lone Chorasmian stream;[10]—thereon,
With snort and strain,
Two horses, strongly swimming, tow
The ferry-boat, with woven ropes
To either bow
Firm harness'd by the mane; a chief,
With shout and shaken spear,
190 Stands at the prow, and guides them; but astern
The cowering merchants, in long robes,
Sit pale beside their wealth
Of silk-bales and of balsam-drops,
Of gold and ivory,
Of turquoise-earth and amethyst,
Jasper and chalcedony,[11]
And milk-barr'd onyx-stones.
The loaded boat swings groaning

In the yellow eddies;
The Gods behold them.   20

They see the Heroes
Sitting in the dark ship
On the foamless, long-heaving
Violet sea,
At sunset nearing
The Happy Islands.[12]

   These things, Ulysses,
The wise bards also
Behold and sing.
But oh, what labour!   21
O prince, what pain!

They too can see
Tiresias;[13]—but the Gods,
Who give them vision,
Added this law:
That they should bear too
His groping blindness,
His dark foreboding,
His scorn'd white hairs;
Bear Hera's anger   22
Through a life lengthen'd
To seven ages.

They see the Centaurs
On Pelion;—then they feel,
They too, the maddening wine
Swell their large veins to bursting; in wild pain
They feel the biting spears
Of the grim Lapithæ, and Theseus, drive,
Drive crashing through their bones; they feel
High on a jutting rock in the red stream   2
Alcmena's[14] dreadful son
Ply his bow;—such a price
The Gods exact for song:
To become what we sing.

---

[9] Scythians: the people who inhabited a region north of the Black and Aral seas.

[10] Chorasmian: Chorasmia was a province of ancient Persia which bordered the river Oxus. Arnold also found the details of this passage in Burnes' *Travels into Bokhara*.

[11] Jasper and chalcedony: quartz stones, the first usually green in color, the second gray or pale blue.

[12] The Happy Isles was one of the names for the realm of the fortunate dead in classical mythology; according to some accounts, the heroic crew of Jason's ship the Argo reached them.

[13] Tiresias was once for a time changed into a woman because he killed two snakes he found coupling. When Zeus and his consort Hera argued about whether men or women took greater pleasure in sexual intercourse, they referred the question to Tiresias, who said that women had the greater pleasure. In anger Hera blinded him; in compensation, Zeus granted him a long life.

[14] The Centaurs were driven from Mount Pelion by a neighboring people, the Lapithae, when they got drunk at the wedding feast of their king and tried to carry off the bride. Theseus and Heracles, the son of Alcmena, joined in fighting the Centaurs; both were also heroes of the adventures of the Argo.

They see the Indian
On his mountain lake; but squalls
Make their skiff reel, and worms
In the unkind spring have gnawn
Their melon-harvest to the heart.—They see
40 The Scythian; but long frosts
Parch them in winter-time on the bare stepp,
Till they too fade like grass; they crawl
Like shadows forth in spring.

They see the merchants
On the Oxus stream;—but care
Must visit first them too, and make them pale.
Whether, through whirling sand,
A cloud of desert robber-horse have burst
Upon their caravan; or greedy kings,
50 In the wall'd cities the way passes through,
Crush'd them with tolls; or fever-airs,
On some great river's marge,
Mown them down, far from home.

They see the Heroes
Near harbour;—but they share
Their lives, and former violent toil in Thebes,
Seven-gated Thebes, or Troy;
Or where the echoing oars
Of Argo first
60 Startled the unknown sea.[15]

The old Silenus[16]
Came, lolling in the sunshine,
From the dewy forest-coverts,
This way, at noon.
Sitting by me, while his Fauns
Down at the water-side
Sprinkled and smoothed
His drooping garland,
He told me these things.

70 But I, Ulysses,
Sitting on the warm steps,
Looking over the valley,
All day long, have seen,
Without pain, without labour,

Sometimes a wild-hair'd Mænad[17]—
Sometimes a Faun[18] with torches—
And sometimes, for a moment,
Passing through the dark stems
Flowing-robed, the beloved,
The desired, the divine,   280
Beloved Iacchus.

Ah, cool night-wind, tremulous stars!
Ah, glimmering water,
Fitful earth-murmur,
Dreaming woods!
Ah, golden-hair'd, strangely smiling Goddess,
And thou, proved, much enduring,
Wave-toss'd Wanderer!
Who can stand still?
Ye fade, ye swim, ye waver before me—   290
The cup again!

Faster, faster,
O Circe, Goddess,
Let the wild, thronging train,
The bright procession
Of eddying forms,
Sweep through my soul!

                                                            1849

Written in Butler's Sermons[1]

Affections, Instincts, Principles, and Powers,
Impulse and Reason, Freedom and Control—
So men, unravelling God's harmonious whole,
Rend in a thousand shreds this life of ours.

Vain labour! Deep and broad, where none may
    see,
Spring the foundations of that shadowy throne
Where man's one nature, queen-like, sits alone,
Centred in a majestic unity;

And rays her powers, like sister-islands seen
Linking their coral arms under the sea,   10
Or cluster'd peaks with plunging gulfs between

---

[15] The youth refers here to three great adventures of classical legend: the siege of Troy, from which Odysseus is returning when he meets Circe; the siege of Thebes, held by one son of Oedipus and invested by another; and the journey of the Argo under the command of Jason in quest of the golden fleece.

[16] Silenus: a satyr, half-man and half-goat, and the drunken companion of Dionysus.

[17] Mænad: a frenzied female participant in Dionysian rites.

[18] Faun: a spirit of nature, usually depicted in human shape with pointed ears, horns, and a goat's tail.

[1] The *Fifteen Sermons* of Joseph Butler (1692–1752), a bishop and theologian of the Church of England, were used as a textbook during Arnold's study at Oxford. Butler carefully and confidently named the several agencies by which humans act, and then referred their right action to the supervention of conscience.

Spann'd by aërial arches all of gold,
Whereo'er the chariot wheels of life are roll'd
In cloudy circles to eternity.

1849

To a Republican Friend, 1848[1]

God knows it, I am with you. If to prize
Those virtues, prized and practised by too few,
But prized, but loved, but eminent in you,
Man's fundamental life; if to despise

The barren optimistic sophistries
Of comfortable moles, whom what they do
Teaches the limit of the just and true
(And for such doing they require not eyes) ;

10 If sadness at the long heart-wasting show
Wherein earth's great ones are disquieted;
If thoughts, not idle, while before me flow

The armies of the homeless and unfed—
If these are yours, if this is what you are,
Then am I yours, and what you feel, I share.

1849

To a Republican Friend

Continued

Yet, when I muse on what life is, I seem
Rather to patience prompted, than that proud
Prospect of hope which France proclaims so
    loud—
France, famed in all great arts, in none
    supreme;

Seeing this vale, this earth, whereon we dream,
Is on all sides o'ershadow'd by the high

Uno'erleap'd Mountains of Necessity,
Sparing us narrower margin than we deem.

Nor will that day dawn at a human nod,
When, bursting through the network super-
    posed
By selfish occupation—plot and plan,

Lust, avarice, envy—liberated man,
All difference with his fellow-mortal closed,
Shall be left standing face to face with God.

1849

A Memory-Picture[1]

Laugh, my friends, and without blame
Lightly quit what lightly came;
Rich to-morrow as to-day,
Spend as madly as you may!
I, with little land to stir,
Am the exacter labourer.
    Ere the parting hour go by,[2]
    Quick, thy tablets, Memory![3]

Once I said: "A face is gone
If too hotly mused upon;
And our best impressions are
Those that do themselves repair."
Many a face I so let flee,
Ah! is faded utterly.
    Ere the parting hour go by,
    Quick, thy tablets, Memory!

Marguerite says: "As last year went,
So the coming year'll be spent;
Some day next year, I shall be,
Entering heedless, kiss'd by thee."
Ah, I hope!—yet, once away,
What may chain us, who can say?
    Ere the parting hour go by,
    Quick, thy tablets, Memory!

---

[1] The friend is Arthur Hugh Clough, who was excited by the revolutions of 1848 on the Continent.
[1] First printed in 1849 as "To My Friends, who ridiculed a Tender Leave-Taking," and then republished in 1853 as the first poem in the "Switzerland" sequence. In 1869 Arnold deleted the present first stanza and a following stanza reprinted below; he restored the first stanza in 1877, and at the same time he took the poem out of the "Switzerland" lyrics.
[2] Until 1857 the refrain was: "Ere the parting kiss be dry."
[3] Until 1869 the first stanza was followed by this stanza:

> But my Youth reminds me—"Thou
> Hast liv'd light as these live now:
> As these are, thou too wert such:
> Much hast had, hast squander'd much."
> Fortune's now less frequent heir,
> Ah! I husband what's grown rare.
>   Ere the parting kiss be dry [1857: hour go by]
>   Quick, thy tablets, Memory!

Paint that lilac kerchief, bound
Her soft face, her hair around;
Tied under the archest chin
Mockery ever ambush'd in.
Let the fluttering fringes streak
30 All her pale, sweet-rounded cheek.
    Ere the parting hour go by,
    Quick, thy tablets, Memory!

Paint that figure's pliant grace
As she tow'rd me lean'd her face,
Half refused and half resign'd
Murmuring: "Art thou still unkind?"
Many a broken promise then
Was new made—to break again.
40   Ere the parting hour go by,
    Quick, thy tablets, Memory!

Paint those eyes, so blue, so kind,
Eager tell-tales of her mind;
Paint, with their impetuous stress
Of inquiring tenderness,
Those frank eyes, where deep I see
An angelic gravity.
    Ere the parting hour go by,
    Quick, thy tablets, Memory!

What, my friends, these feeble lines
50 Show, you say, my love declines?
To paint ill as I have done,
Proves forgetfulness begun?
Time's gay minions, pleased you see,
Time, your master, governs me;
    Pleased, you mock the fruitless cry:
    "Quick, thy tablets, Memory!"

Ah, too true! Time's current strong
Leaves us fixt to nothing long.
Yet, if little stays with man,
Ah, retain we all we can!
If the clear impression dies,
Ah, the dim remembrance prize!
    Ere the parting hour go by,
    Quick, thy tablets, Memory!

                            1849; 1869

The story of Arnold's poem is told in an old Danish folk ballad. It appears in a book by Hans Christian Andersen, The True Story of My Life, *which was translated into English in 1847, and the ballad itself had been translated in 1826 and paraphrased in a review in 1825, both by George Borrow. In Andersen's version the woman stays on the shore because she is frightened when the stat-*

ues *turn from her upon her entrance into the church; in Borrow's paraphrase the merman comes to the church to call to her, but she decides to remain with her family. The woman's name is not Margaret in any of the versions Arnold might have known, and the emphasis on the merman is also his own.*

The Forsaken Merman

Come, dear children, let us away;
Down and away below!
Now my brothers call from the bay,
Now the great winds shoreward blow,
Now the salt tides seaward flow;
Now the wild white horses play,
Champ and chafe and toss in the spray.
Children dear, let us away!
This way, this way!

Call her once before you go—   10
Call once yet!
In a voice that she will know:
"Margaret! Margaret!"
Children's voices should be dear
 (Call once more) to a mother's ear;
Children's voices, wild with pain—
Surely she will come again!
Call her once and come away;
This way, this way!
"Mother dear, we cannot stay!   20
The wild white horses foam and fret."[1]
Margaret! Margaret!

Come, dear children, come away down;
Call no more!
One last look at the white-wall'd town,
And the little grey church on the windy shore,
Then come down!
She will not come though you call all day;
Come away, come away!

Children dear, was it yesterday   30
We heard the sweet bells over the bay?
In the caverns where we lay,
Through the surf and through the swell,
The far-off sound of a silver bell?
Sand-strewn caverns, cool and deep,
Where the winds are all asleep;
Where the spent lights quiver and gleam,
Where the salt weed sways in the stream,
Where the sea-beasts, ranged all round,
Feed in the ooze of their pasture-ground;   40

---

[1] This line was added in 1869.

Where the sea-snakes coil and twine,
Dry their mail[2] and bask in the brine;
Where great whales come sailing by,
Sail and sail, with unshut eye,
Round the world for ever and aye?
When did music come this way?
Children dear, was it yesterday?

Children dear, was it yesterday
(Call yet once) that she went away?
50 Once she sate with you and me,
On a red gold throne in the heart of the sea,
And the youngest sate on her knee.
She comb'd its bright hair, and she tended it
    well,
When down swung the sound of a far-off bell.
She sigh'd, she look'd up through the clear
    green sea;
She said: "I must go, for my kinsfolk pray
In the little grey church on the shore to-day.
'Twill be Easter-time in the world—ah me!
And I lose my poor soul, Merman! here with
    thee."
60 I said: "Go up, dear heart, through the waves;
Say thy prayer, and come back to the kind sea-
    caves!"
She smiled, she went up through the surf in the
    bay.
Children dear, was it yesterday?

    Children dear, were we long alone?
"The sea grows stormy, the little ones moan;
Long prayers," I said, "in the world they say;
Come!" I said; and we rose through the surf in
    the bay.
We went up the beach, by the sandy down
Where the sea-stocks bloom, to the white-wall'd
    town;
Through the narrow paved streets, where all
70   was still,
To the little grey church on the windy hill.
From the church came a murmur of folk at
    their prayers,
But we stood without in the cold blowing airs.
We climb'd on the graves, on the stones worn
    with rains,
And we gazed up the aisle through the small
    leaded panes.
She sate by the pillar; we saw her clear:
"Margaret, hist! come quick, we are here!
Dear heart," I said, "we are long alone;
The sea grows stormy, the little ones moan."
80 But, ah, she gave me never a look,

For her eyes were seal'd to the holy book!
Loud prays the priest; shut stands the door.
Come away, children, call no more!
Come away, come away, call no more!

    Down, down, down!
Down to the depths of the sea!
She sits at her wheel in the humming town,
Singing most joyfully.
Hark what she sings: "O joy, O joy,
For the humming street, and the child with its
    toy!   90
For the priest, and the bell, and the holy well;
For the wheel where I spun,
And the blessed light of the sun!"
And so she sings her fill,
Singing most joyfully,
Till the spindle[3] drops from her hand,
And the whizzing wheel stands still.
She steals to the window, and looks at the sand,
And over the sand at the sea;
And her eyes are set in a stare;   100
And anon there breaks a sigh,
And anon there drops a tear,
From a sorrow-clouded eye,
And a heart sorrow-laden,
A long, long sigh;
For the cold strange eyes of a little Mermaiden
And the gleam of her golden hair.

    Come away, away children;
Come children, come down!
The hoarse wind blows coldly;   110
Lights shine in the town.
She will start from her slumber
When gusts shake the door;
She will hear the winds howling,
Will hear the waves roar.
We shall see, while above us
The waves roar and whirl,
A ceiling of amber,
A pavement of pearl.
Singing: "Here came a mortal,   120
But faithless was she!
And alone dwell for ever
The kings of the sea."

But, children, at midnight,
When soft the winds blow,
When clear falls the moonlight,
When spring-tides are low;
When sweet airs come seaward
From heaths starr'd with broom,[4]
And high rocks throw mildly   130

2 Mail: scales.   3 Spindle: a stick used to form and twist yarn in hand spinning.
4 Broom: a shrub with long branches and yellow flowers.

On the blanch'd sands a gloom;
Up the still, glistening beaches,
Up the creeks we will hie,
Over banks of bright seaweed
The ebb-tide leaves dry.
We will gaze, from the sand-hills,
At the white, sleeping town;
At the church on the hill-side—
And then come back down.
140 Singing: "There dwells a loved one,
But cruel is she!
She left lonely for ever
The kings of the sea."

1849

In Utrumque Paratus[1]

If, in the silent mind of One all-pure,[2]
    At first imagined lay
The sacred world; and by procession sure
From those still deeps, in form and colour drest,
Seasons alternating, and night and day,
The long-mused thought to north, south, east,
        and west,
    Took then its all-seen way;

O waking on a world which thus-wise springs!
    Whether it needs thee count
10 Betwixt thy waking and the birth of things
Ages or hours—O waking on life's stream!
By lonely pureness to the all-pure fount
(Only by this thou canst) the colour'd dream
    Of life remount!

Thin, thin the pleasant human noises grow,
    And faint the city gleams;
Rare the lone pastoral huts—marvel not thou!
The solemn peaks but to the stars are known,
But to the stars, and the cold lunar beams;
Alone the sun arises, and alone   20
    Spring the great streams.

But, if the wild unfather'd mass no birth[3]
    In divine seats hath known;
In the blank, echoing solitude if Earth,
Rocking her obscure body to and fro,
Ceases not from all time to heave and groan,
Unfruitful oft, and at her happiest throe
    Forms, what she forms, alone;

O seeming sole to awake, thy sun-bathed head
    Piercing the solemn cloud   30
Round thy still dreaming brother-world out-
        spread!
O man, whom Earth, thy long-vext mother,
        bare
Not without joy—so radiant, so endow'd
(Such happy issue crown'd her painful care) —
    Be not too proud!

Oh when most self-exalted, most alone,
    Chief dreamer, own thy dream!
Thy brother-world stirs at thy feet unknown,
Who hath a monarch's hath no brother's part;
Yet doth thine inmost soul with yearning teem.   40
—Oh, what a spasm shakes the dreamer's heart!
    "I, too, but seem."[4]

1849

Resignation

To Fausta[1]

To die be given us, or attain!
Fierce work it were, to do again.

---

[1] The title is a phrase from Virgil's *Aeneid* (2, 61): "prepared for either."

[2] The first possibility of the origin of things is taken from the idealist philosopher Plotinus (205–270), who proposed that existence proceeded from the mind of one, pure existence.

[3] The second possibility is that the present forms of life on earth emerged or evolved from matter.

[4] In 1869 Arnold substituted this stanza for the last stanza of the poem:

> Thy native world stirs at thy feet unknown,
>   Yet there thy secret lies!
> Out of this stuff, these forces, thou art grown,
> And proud self-severance from them were disease.
> O scan thy native world with pious eyes!
> High as thy life be risen, 'tis from these;
>   And these, too, rise.

In subsequent editions of his poetry Arnold returned to the original last stanza.

[1] Arnold closed *The Strayed Reveller* (1849), his first volume of poems, with this poem. "Fausta" is Arnold's elder sister Jane: Allott in his note in the annotated edition (p. 84) remarks the Latin meaning of "fortunate" of the name Arnold gives to his sister in this poem. The occasion of the poem is a walk, and memories of an earlier walk, in the Lake country in the north of England.

So pilgrims, bound for Mecca, pray'd
At burning noon; so warriors said,
Scarf'd with the cross,[2] who watch'd the miles
Of dust which wreathed their struggling files
Down Lydian mountains;[3] so, when snows
Round Alpine summits, eddying rose,
The Goth, bound Rome-wards; so the Hun,
10   Crouch'd on his saddle, while the sun
Went lurid down o'er flooded plains
Through which the groaning Danube strains
To the drear Euxine;[4]—so pray all,
Whom labours, self-ordain'd, enthrall;
Because they to themselves propose
On this side the all-common close
A goal which, gain'd, may give repose.
So pray they; and to stand again
Where they stood once, to them were pain;
20   Pain to thread back and to renew
Past straits, and currents long steer'd through.

But milder natures, and more free—
Whom an unblamed serenity
Hath freed from passions, and the state
Of struggle these necessitate;
Whom schooling of the stubborn mind
Hath made, or birth hath found, resign'd—
These mourn not, that their goings pay
Obedience to the passing day.
30   These claim not every laughing Hour
For handmaid to their striding power;
Each in her turn, with torch uprear'd,
To await their march; and when appear'd,
Through the cold gloom, with measured race,
To usher for a destined space
(Her own sweet errands all forgone)
The too imperious traveller on.
These, Fausta, ask not this; nor thou,
Time's chafing prisoner, ask it now!

40   We left, just ten years since, you say,
That wayside inn we left to-day.
Our jovial host, as forth we fare,
Shouts greeting from his easy chair.
High on a bank our leader stands,
Reviews and ranks his motley bands,
Makes clear our goal to every eye—
The valley's western boundary.
A gate swings to! our tide hath flow'd
Already from the silent road.
50   The valley-pastures, one by one,

Are threaded, quiet in the sun;
And now beyond the rude stone bridge
Slopes gracious up the western ridge.
Its woody border, and the last
Of its dark upland farms is past—
Cool farms, with open-lying stores,
Under their burnish'd sycamores;
All past! and through the trees we glide,
Emerging on the green hill-side.
There climbing hangs, a far-seen sign,   60
Our wavering, many-colour'd line;
There winds, upstreaming slowly still
Over the summit of the hill.
And now, in front, behold outspread
Those upper regions we must tread!
Mild hollows, and clear heathy swells,
The cheerful silence of the fells.
Some two hours' march with serious air,
Through the deep noontide heats we fare;
The red-grouse, springing at our sound,   70
Skims, now and then, the shining ground;
No life, save his and ours, intrudes
Upon these breathless solitudes.
O joy! again the farms appear.
Cool shade is there, and rustic cheer;
There springs the brook will guide us down,
Bright comrade, to the noisy town.
Lingering, we follow down; we gain
The town, the highway, and the plain.
And many a mile of dusty way,   80
Parch'd and road-worn, we made that day;
But, Fausta, I remember well,
That as the balmy darkness fell
We bathed our hands with speechless glee,
That night, in the wide-glimmering sea.[5]

Once more we tread this self-same road,
Fausta, which ten years since we trod;
Alone we tread it, you and I,
Ghosts of that boisterous company.
Here, where the brook shines, near its head,   90
In its clear, shallow, turf-fringed bed;
Here, whence the eye first sees, far down,
Capp'd with faint smoke, the noisy town;
Here sit we, and again unroll,
Though slowly, the familiar whole.
The solemn wastes of heathy hill
Sleep in the July sunshine still;
The self-same shadows now, as then,
Play through this grassy upland glen;

[2] Scarf'd: covered or adorned with a scarf or mantle bearing a cross.
[3] Lydian: Lydia was the name of a country in Asis Minor bordering the Aegean Sea.
[4] Euxine: a name for the Black Sea.
[5] Presumably the walkers were somehow transported another twenty miles, so that they arrived
at the Irish Sea by nightfall.

The loose dark stones on the green way
Lie strewn, it seems, where then they lay;
On this mild bank above the stream,
(You crush them!) the blue gentians gleam.
Still this wild brook, the rushes cool,
The sailing foam, the shining pool!
These are not changed; and we, you say,
Are scarce more changed, in truth, than they.

The gipsies, whom we met below,
They, too, have long roam'd to and fro;
They ramble, leaving, where they pass,
Their fragments on the cumber'd[6] grass.
And often to some kindly place
Chance guides the migratory race,
Where, though long wanderings intervene,
They recognise a former scene.
The dingy tents are pitch'd; the fires
Give to the wind their wavering spires;
In dark knots crouch round the wild flame
Their children, as when first they came;
They see their shackled beasts again
Move, browsing, up the gray-wall'd lane.
Signs are not wanting, which might raise
The ghost in them of former days—
Signs are not wanting, if they would;
Suggestions to disquietude.
For them, for all, time's busy touch,
While it mends little, troubles much.
Their joints grow stiffer—but the year
Runs his old round of dubious cheer;
Chilly they grow—yet winds in March,
Still, sharp as ever, freeze and parch;
They must live still—and yet, God knows,
Crowded and keen the country grows;
It seems as if, in their decay,
The law grew stronger every day.
So might they reason, so compare,
Fausta, times past with times that are.
But no!—they rubb'd through yesterday
In their hereditary way,
And they will rub through, if they can,
To-morrow on the self-same plan,
Till death arrive to supersede,
For them, vicissitude and need.

The poet, to whose mighty heart
Heaven doth a quicker pulse impart,
Subdues that energy to scan
Not his own course, but that of man.
Though he move mountains, though his day
Be pass'd on the proud heights of sway,
Though he hath loosed a thousand chains,
Though he hath borne immortal pains,
Action and suffering though he know—
He hath not lived, if he lives so.
He sees, in some great-historied land,
A ruler of the people stand,
Sees his strong thought in fiery flood
Roll through the heaving multitude;
Exults—yet for no moment's space
Envies the all-regarded place.
Beautiful eyes meet his—and he
Bears to admire uncravingly;
They pass—he, mingled with the crowd,
Is in their far-off triumphs proud.
From some high station he looks down,
At sunset, on a populous town;
Surveys each happy group, which fleets,
Toil ended, through the shining streets,
Each with some errand of its own—
And does not say: *I am alone.*
He sees the gentle stir of birth
When morning purifies the earth;
He leans upon a gate and sees
The pastures, and the quiet trees.
Low, woody hill, with gracious bound,
Folds the still valley almost round;
The cuckoo, loud on some high lawn,
Is answer'd from the depth of dawn;
In the hedge straggling to the stream,
Pale, dew-drench'd, half-shut roses gleam;
But, where the farther side slopes down,
He sees the drowsy new-waked clown[7]
In his white quaint-embroider'd frock
Make, whistling, tow'rd his mist-wreathed
　　flock—
Slowly, behind his heavy tread,
The wet, flower'd grass heaves up its head.
Lean'd on his gate, he gazes—tears
Are in his eyes, and in his ears
The murmur of a thousand years.
Before him he sees life unroll,
A placid and continuous whole—
That general life, which does not cease,
Whose secret is not joy, but peace;
That life, whose dumb wish is not miss'd
If birth proceeds, if things subsist;
The life of plants, and stones, and rain,
The life he craves—if not in vain
Fate gave, what chance shall not control,
His sad lucidity of soul.

You listen—but that wandering smile,
Fausta, betrays you cold the while!
Your eyes pursue the bells of foam

---

[6] Cumber'd: occupied in an obstructive manner.　　[7] Clown: farmer.

Wash'd, eddying, from this bank, their home.
Those gipsies, so your thoughts I scan,
Are less, the poet more, than man.
They feel not, though they move and see;
Deeper[8] *the poet feels; but he*
Breathes, when he will, immortal air,
Where Orpheus[9] *and where Homer are.*
In the day's life, whose iron round
210 *Hems us all in, he is not bound;*
He leaves his kind, o'erleaps their pen,
And flees the common life of men.[10]
He escapes thence, but we abide—
Not deep the poet sees, but wide.

The world in which we live and move
Outlasts aversion, outlasts love,
Outlasts each effort, interest, hope,
Remorse, grief, joy;—and were the scope
Of these affections wider made,
220 Man still would see, and see dismay'd,
Beyond his passion's widest range,
Far regions of eternal change.
Nay, and since death, which wipes out man,
Finds him with many an unsolved plan,
With much unknown, and much untried,
Wonder not dead, and thirst not dried,
Still gazing on the ever full
Eternal mundane spectacle—
This world in which we draw our breath,
230 In some sense, Fausta, outlasts death.

Blame thou not, therefore, him who dares
Judge vain beforehand human cares;
Whose natural insight can discern
What through experience others learn;
Who needs not love and power, to know
Love transient, power an unreal show;
Who treads at ease life's uncheer'd ways—
Him blame not, Fausta, rather praise!
Rather thyself for some aim pray
240 Nobler than this, to fill the day;
Rather that heart, which burns in thee,
Ask, not to amuse, but to set free;
Be passionate hopes not ill resign'd
For quiet, and a fearless mind.
And though fate grudge to thee and me
The poet's rapt security,
Yet they, believe me, who await
No gifts from chance, have conquer'd fate.
They, winning room to see and hear,

And to men's business not too near,   250
Through clouds of individual strife
Draw homeward to the general life.
Like leaves by suns not yet uncurl'd;
To the wise, foolish; to the world,
Weak;—yet not weak, I might reply,
Not foolish, Fausta, in His eye,
To whom each moment in its race,
Crowd as we will its neutral space,
Is but a quiet watershed
Whence, equally, the seas of life and death are
    fed.   260

Enough, we live!—and if a life,
With large results so little rife,
Though bearable, seem hardly worth
This pomp of worlds, this pain of birth;
Yet, Fausta, the mute turf we tread,
The solemn hills around us spread,
This stream which falls incessantly,
The strange-scrawl'd rocks,[11] the lonely sky,
If I might lend their life a voice,
Seem to bear rather than rejoice.   270
And even could the intemperate prayer
Man iterates, while these forbear,
For movement, for an ampler sphere,
Pierce Fate's impenetrable ear;
Not milder is the general lot
Because our spirits have forgot,
In action's dizzying eddy whirl'd,
The something that infects the world.

                                               1849

"Empedocles on Etna" was first published in 1852 as the title poem of the volume of poetry Arnold published in that year. Arnold excluded the poem from an edition he published in 1853, however, because as he wrote in the "Preface" to this collection, it is necessary that a poem "in-spirit and rejoice the reader: that it shall convey a charm, and infuse delight"; and no such "poeti-cal enjoyment" can be derived from a situation "in which the suffering finds no vent in action; in which a continuous state of mental distress is prolonged, unrelieved by incident, hope, or resist-ance; in which there is everything to be endured, nothing to be done." Arnold restored the poem to his canon in 1867, at the request, he wrote then, of Robert Browning. Arnold did publish one of the songs of Callicles (Act I, lines 427–460) in the 1853 edition of his poems, and in 1855 he re-

---

8 Until 1881 this word was "Deeply."   9 Orpheus: a poet and musician of Greek myth.
10 Lines 211 and 212 were added in 1881.
11 Strange-scrawl'd rocks: marked with the striations of glacial action.

published the other four songs of Callicles as well.

Empedocles was a Greek philosopher of the fifth century B.C. His thought is preserved only in fragments, and the events of his life, including his reputation as a magician and his suicide by jumping into the crater of the volcanic Mount Etna in Sicily, are partly legendary. In his notes for the poem, reproduced in Tinker and Lowry's Commentary (pp. 291–292), Arnold fashions an Empedocles who "sees things as they are—the world as it is—God as he is" without "the religious consolation of other men" and the fragments and parables by which they know. But at the end of his life "his friends are dead: the world is all against him, & incredulous of the truth: his mind is overtasked by the effort to hold fast so great & severe a truth in solitude: the atmosphere he breathes not being modified by the presence of human life, is too rare for him. He perceives still the truth of the truth [sic], but cannot be transported and rapturously agitated by his grandeur: his spring and elasticity of mind are gone: he is clouded, oppressed, dispirited, without hope & energy." He therefore chooses to die, before he becomes utterly dead to the spirit of life and the victim of "depression & overtension of mind," "to be reunited with the universe, before by exaggerating his human side he has become utterly estranged from it."

Pausanias, like Peisianax and Pantheia, who are named later in the poem, is named as a friend of Empedocles in the accounts of his life Arnold knew. Arnold invented the character Callicles, whose name is derived from the Greek word for "beauty."

Empedocles on Etna

A Dramatic Poem

PERSONS

EMPEDOCLES.
PAUSANIAS, *a Physician.*
CALLICLES, *a young Harp-player.*

The Scene of the Poem is on Mount Etna; at first in the forest region, afterwards on the summit of the mountain.

ACT I. SCENE I.
Morning. A Pass in the forest region of Etna.

CALLICLES

(Alone, resting on a rock by the path.)
The mules, I think, will not be here this hour;

They feel the cool wet turf under their feet
By the stream-side, after the dusty lanes
In which they have toil'd all night from Catana,[1]
And scarcely will they budge a yard. O Pan,[2]
How gracious is the mountain at this hour!
A thousand times have I been here alone,
Or with the revellers from the mountain-towns,
But never on so fair a morn;—the sun
Is shining on the brilliant mountain-crests,   10
And on the highest pines; but farther down,
Here in the valley, is in shade; the sward
Is dark, and on the stream the mist still hangs;
One sees one's footprints crush'd in the wet grass,
One's breath curls in the air; and on these pines
That climb from the stream's edge, the long grey tufts,
Which the goats love, are jewell'd thick with dew.
Here will I stay till the slow litter comes.
I have my harp too—that is well.—Apollo![3]
What mortal could be sick or sorry here?   20
I know not in what mind Empedocles,
Whose mules I follow'd, may be coming up,
But if, as most men say, he is half mad
With exile, and with brooding on his wrongs,
Pausanias, his sage friend, who mounts with him,
Could scarce have lighted on a lovelier cure.
The mules must be below, far down. I hear
Their tinkling bells, mix'd with the song of birds,
Rise faintly to me—now it stops!—Who's here?
Pausanias! and on foot? alone?   30

PAUSANIAS

                          And thou, then?
I left thee supping with Peisianax,
With thy head full of wine, and thy hair crown'd,
Touching thy harp as the whim came on thee,
And praised and spoil'd by master and by guests
Almost as much as the new dancing-girl.
Why hast thou follow'd us?

CALLICLES

                          The night was hot,
And the feast past its prime; so we slipp'd out,
Some of us, to the portico to breathe;—

---

[1] Catana: a town at the foot of Mt. Etna.
[3] Apollo: the god of music and song.

[2] Pan: the deity of nature.

Peisianax, thou know'st, drinks late;—and
  then,
40 As I was lifting my soil'd garland off,
I saw the mules and litter in the court,
And in the litter sate Empedocles;
Thou, too, wast with him. Straightway I sped
  home;
I saddled my white mule, and all night long
Through the cool lovely country follow'd you,
Pass'd you a little since as morning dawn'd,
And have this hour sate by the torrent here,
Till the slow mules should climb in sight again.
And now?

PAUSANIAS
            And now, back to the town with speed!
Crouch in the wood first, till the mules have
50   pass'd;
They do but halt, they will be here anon.
Thou must be viewless to Empedocles;
Save mine, he must not meet a human eye.
One of his moods is on him that thou know'st;
I think, thou wouldst not vex him.

CALLICLES
                              No—and yet
I would fain stay, and help thee tend him. Once
He knew me well, and would oft notice me;
And still, I know not how, he draws me to him,
And I could watch him with his proud sad face,
60 His flowing locks and gold-encircled brow
And kingly gait, for ever; such a spell
In his severe looks, such a majesty
As drew of old the people after him,
In Agrigentum and Olympia,[4]
When his star reign'd, before his banishment,
Is potent still on me in his decline.
But oh! Pausanias, he is changed of late;
There is a settled trouble in his air
Admits no momentary brightening now,
70 And when he comes among his friends at feasts,
'Tis as an orphan among prosperous boys.
Thou know'st of old he loved this harp of
  mine,
When first he sojourn'd with Peisianax;
He is now always moody, and I fear him;
But I would serve him, soothe him, if I could,
Dared one but try.

PAUSANIAS
                    Thou wast a kind child ever!
He loves thee, but he must not see thee now.
Thou hast indeed a rare touch on thy harp,
He loves that in thee, too;—there was a time
(But that is pass'd), he would have paid thy
  strain   80
With music to have drawn the stars from
  heaven.
He hath his harp and laurel with him still,
But he has laid the use of music by,
And all which might relax his settled gloom.
Yet thou may'st try thy playing, if thou wilt—
But thou must keep unseen; follow us on,
But at a distance! in these solitudes,
In this clear mountain-air, a voice will rise,
Though from afar, distinctly; it may soothe
  him.
Play when we halt, and, when the evening
  comes   90
And I must leave him (for his pleasure is
To be left musing these soft nights alone
In the high unfrequented mountain-spots),
Then watch him, for he ranges swift and far,
Sometimes to Etna's top, and to the cone;
But hide thee in the rocks a great way down,
And try thy noblest strains, my Callicles,
With the sweet night to help thy harmony!
Thou wilt earn my thanks sure, and perhaps
  his.

CALLICLES
More than a day and night, Pausanias,   100
Of this fair summer-weather, on these hills,
Would I bestow to help Empedocles.
That needs no thanks; one is far better here
Than in the broiling city in these heats.
But tell me, how hast thou persuaded him
In this his present fierce, man-hating mood,
To bring thee out with him alone on Etna?

PAUSANIAS
Thou hast heard all men speaking of Pantheia
The woman who at Agrigentum lay
Thirty long days in a cold trance of death,   110
And whom Empedocles call'd back to life.
Thou art too young to note it, but his power
Swells with the swelling evil of this time,

4 Agrigentum was a town in Sicily, in which Empedocles won his early fame. According to
the accounts Arnold followed, he then traveled to the east—Olympia is the name of a region
in Greece—returned to Sicily to find the aristocrats of Agrigentum hostile to him, and settled
in the house of the wealthy Peisianax of Syracuse.

And holds men mute to see where it will rise.
He could stay swift diseases in old days,
Chain madmen by the music of his lyre,
Cleanse to sweet airs the breath of poisonous
    streams,
And in the mountain-chinks inter the winds.
This he could do of old; but now, since all
Clouds and grows daily worse in Sicily,
Since broils tear us in twain, since this new
    swarm
Of sophists[5] has got empire in our schools
Where he was paramount, since he is banish'd
And lives a lonely man in triple gloom—
He grasps the very reins of life and death.
I ask'd him of Pantheia yesterday,
When we were gather'd with Peisianax,
And he made answer, I should come at night
On Etna here, and be alone with him,
And he would tell me, as his old, tried friend,
Who still was faithful, what might profit me;
That is, the secret of this miracle.

CALLICLES

Bah! Thou a doctor! Thou art superstitious.
Simple Pausanias, 'twas no miracle!
Pantheia, for I know her kinsmen well,
Was subject to these trances from a girl.
Empedocles would say so, did he deign;
But he still lets the people, whom he scorns,
Gape and cry *wizard* at him, if they list.
But thou, thou art no company for him!
Thou art as cross, as sour'd as himself!
Thou hast some wrong from thine own citizens,
And then thy friend is banish'd, and on that,
Straightway thou fallest to arraign the times,
As if the sky was impious not to fall.
The sophists are no enemies of his;
I hear, Gorgias,[6] their chief, speaks nobly of
    him,
As of his gifted master, and once friend.
He is too scornful, too high-wrought, too bitter.
'Tis not the times, 'tis not the sophists vex him;
There is some root of suffering in himself,
Some secret and unfollow'd vein of woe,
Which makes the time look black and sad to
    him.
Pester him not in this his sombre mood

With questionings about an idle tale,
But lead him through the lovely mountain-
    paths,
And keep his mind from preying on itself,
And talk to him of things at hand and
    common,
Not miracles! thou art a learned man,
But credulous of fables as a girl.   160

PAUSANIAS

And thou, a boy whose tongue outruns his
    knowledge,
And on whose lightness blame is thrown away.
Enough of this! I see the litter wind
Up by the torrent-side, under the pines.
I must rejoin Empedocles. Do thou
Crouch in the brushwood till the mules have
    pass'd;
Then play thy kind part well. Farewell till
    night!

SCENE II
*Noon. A Glen on the highest skirts of the
    woody region of Etna.*

EMPEDOCLES—PAUSANIAS

PAUSANIAS
The noon is hot. When we have cross'd the
    stream,
We shall have left the woody tract, and come
Upon the open shoulder of the hill.
See how the giant spires of yellow bloom
Of the sun-loving gentian, in the heat,
Are shining on those naked slopes like flame!
Let us rest here; and now, Empedocles,
Pantheia's history!
                    [*A harp-note below is heard.*

EMPEDOCLES
                    Hark! what sound was that
Rose from below? If it were possible,
And we were not so far from human haunt,   10
I should have said that some one touch'd a
    harp.
Hark! there again!

---

[5] Sophists: a school of philosophers and teachers who tended to explain the universe in terms
of physical phenomena. They practiced and taught a method of skeptical questioning of
established beliefs and modes of thought, which gave them a reputation of not being
interested in truth, but only in the rhetorical conduct of the argument.

[6] Gorgias: a philosopher of the fifth century B.C., born in Sicily. He taught rhetoric, and
thus his association with the fifth-century sophists; he was also interested in science, and in
questions about the relative status of external objects and human perceptions or ideas of
them.

PAUSANIAS
                              'Tis the boy Callicles,
The sweetest harp-player in Catana.
He is for ever coming on these hills,
In summer, to all country-festivals,
With a gay revelling band; he breaks from
    them
Sometimes, and wanders far among the glens.
But heed him not, he will not mount to us;
I spoke with him this morning. Once more,
    therefore,
20 Instruct me of Pantheia's story, Master,
As I have pray'd thee.

EMPEDOCLES
                              That? and to what end?

PAUSANIAS
It is enough that all men speak of it.
But I will also say, that when the Gods
Visit us as they do with sign and plague,
To know those spells of thine which stay their
    hand
Were to live free from terror.

EMPEDOCLES
                              Spells? Mistrust them!
Mind is the spell which governs earth and
    heaven.
Man has a mind with which to plan his safety;
Know that, and help thyself!

PAUSANIAS
                              But thine own words?
30 "The wit and counsel of man was never clear,
Troubles confound the little wit he has."[7]
Mind is a light which the Gods mock us with,
To lead those false who trust it.
                              [The harp sounds again.

EMPEDOCLES
                              Hist! once more!
Listen, Pausanias!—Ay, 'tis Callicles;
I know these notes among a thousand. Hark!

CALLICLES
                              (Sings unseen, from below)
The track winds down to the clear stream,
To cross the sparkling shallows; there
The cattle love to gather, on their way
To the high mountain-pastures, and to stay,
Till the rough cow-herds drive them past,
Knee-deep in the cool ford; for 'tis the last
Of all the woody, high, well-water'd dells
On Etna; and the beam
Of noon is broken there by chestnut-boughs
Down its steep verdant sides; the air
Is freshen'd by the leaping stream, which
    throws
Eternal showers of spray on the moss'd roots
Of trees, and veins of turf, and along dark
    shoots
Of ivy-plants, and fragrant hanging bells
Of hyacinths, and on late anemonies,
That muffle its wet banks; but glade,
And stream, and sward, and chestnut-trees,
End here; Etna beyond, in the broad glare
Of the hot noon, without a shade,
Slope behind slope, up to the peak, lies bare;
The peak, round which the white clouds play.

In such a glen, on such a day,
On Pelion, on the grassy ground,
Chiron, the aged Centaur lay,[8]
The young Achilles standing by.
The Centaur taught him to explore
The mountains; where the glens are dry
And the tired Centaurs come to rest,
And where the soaking springs abound
And the straight ashes grow for spears,
And where the hill-goats come to feed,
And the sea-eagles build their nest.
He show'd him Phthia far away,
And said: O boy, I taught this lore
To Peleus, in long distant years!
He told him of the Gods, the stars,
The tides;—and then of mortal wars,
And of the life which heroes lead
Before they reach the Elysian place
And rest in the immortal mead;
And all the wisdom of his race.[9]

---

[7] Allott (p. 157) notes that one of Arnold's sources of information about Empedocles, a book on Greek philosophers published by Simon Karsten in 1830, includes Empedocles' statement that men have meager means to gain knowledge, "and many evils break in to blunt the edge of careful thought."

[8] Chiron, one of the Centaurs—half-man and half-horse—who lived on Mount Pelion in Greece, was known for his knowledge of medicine, music, and hunting, and taught some of the heroes of Greek mythology, including Achilles, the son of Peleus, king of Phthia.

[9] This is the first of four of Callicles' songs printed in 1855 under the general title, "The Harp Player on Etna."

The music below ceases, and EMPEDOCLES
*speaks, accompanying himself in a solemn
manner on his harp.*[10]

The out-spread world to span
A cord the Gods first slung,
And then the soul of man
There, like a mirror, hung,
And bade the winds through space impel the
    gusty toy.

Hither and thither spins
The wind-borne, mirroring soul,
A thousand glimpses wins,
And never sees a whole;
Looks once, and drives elsewhere, and leaves
    its last employ.

The Gods laugh in their sleeve
To watch man doubt and fear,
Who knows not what to believe
Since he sees nothing clear,
And dares stamp nothing false where he finds
    nothing sure.

Is this, Pausanias, so?
And can our souls not strive,
But with the winds must go,
And hurry where they drive?
Is fate indeed so strong, man's strength indeed
    so poor?

I will not judge. That man,
Howbeit, I judge as lost,
Whose mind allows a plan,
Which would degrade it most;
And he treats doubt the best who tries to see
    least ill.

Be not, then, fear's blind slave!
Thou art my friend; to thee,
All knowledge that I have,
All skill I wield, are free.
Ask not the latest news of the last miracle,

Ask not what days and nights
In trance Pantheia lay,
But ask how thou such sights
May'st see without dismay;   110
Ask what most helps when known, thou son of
    Anchitus!

What? hate, and awe, and shame
Fill thee to see our time;
Thou feelest thy soul's frame
Shaken and out of chime?
What? life and chance go hard with thee too,
    as with us;

Thy citizens, 'tis said,
Envy thee and oppress,
Thy goodness no men aid,
All strive to make it less;   120
Tyranny, pride, and lust, fill Sicily's abodes;

Heaven is with earth at strife,
Signs make thy soul afraid,
The dead return to life,
Rivers are dried, winds stay'd;
Scarce can one think in calm, so threatening
    are the Gods;

And we feel, day and night,
The burden of ourselves—
Well, then, the wiser wight[11]
In his own bosom delves,   130
And asks what ails him so, and gets what cure
    he can.

---

[10] In one of his notes for the poem Arnold wrote that Empedocles was "one of the last of the Orpheuslike religious philosophers" (*Commentary*, p. 290), that is, one of the last to try to express religious truth in song, another distinction between him and the sophists, who used more discursive methods. Tinker and Lowry in their *Commentary* (pp. 292–301) also describe how much of Empedocles' thought as Arnold presents it in this long speech to Pausanias is drawn from that of Lucretius, a Roman philosopher of the first century B.C. who emphasized the indifference of nature to man and the necessity to moderate desire and to live rationally, and from that of Epicetus, a moralist of similar ideas and sensibility who lived in Rome and Greece in the first century A.D. In 1867, in a letter quoted in Tinker and Lowry's *Commentary* (pp. 287–288), Arnold denied that Empedocles and Obermann were "mouthpieces through which to vent my own opinion. . . . I have now, and no doubt had still more then [1852], a sympathy with the figure Empedocles presents to the imagination; but neither then nor now would my creed, if I wished or were able to draw it out in black and white, be by any means identical with that contained in the preachment of Empedocles. . . . If the creed of Empedocles were, as exhibited in my poem, a satisfying one, he ought to have lived after delivering himself of it, not died."

[11] Wight: creature.

The sophist sneers: Fool, take
Thy pleasure, right or wrong.
The pious wail: Forsake
A world these sophists throng.
Be neither saint nor sophist-led, but be a man!

These hundred doctors try
To preach thee to their school.
We have the truth! they cry;
140   And yet their oracle,
Trumpet it as they will, is but the same as
thine.

Once read thy own breast right,
And thou hast done with fears;
Man gets no other light,
Search he a thousand years.
Sink in thyself! there ask what ails thee, at that
shrine!

What makes thee struggle and rave?
Why are men ill at ease?—
'Tis that the lot they have
150   Fails their own will to please;
For man would make no murmuring, were his
will obey'd.

And why is it, that still
Man with his lot thus fights?—
'Tis that he makes this *will*
The measure of his *rights,*
And believes Nature outraged if his will's gain-
said.

Couldst thou, Pausanias, learn
How deep a fault is this;
Couldst thou but once discern
160   Thou has no *right* to bliss,
No title from the Gods to welfare and repose;

Then thou wouldst look less mazed
Whene'er of bliss debarr'd,
Nor think the Gods were crazed
When thy own lot went hard.
But we are all the same—the fools of our own
woes!

For, from the first faint morn
Of life, the thirst for bliss
Deep in man's heart is born;
170   And, sceptic as he is,
He fails not to judge clear if this be quench'd
or no.

Nor is the thirst to blame.
Man errs not that he deems
His welfare his true aim,
He errs because he dreams
The world does not exist that welfare to
bestow.

We mortals are no kings
For each of whom to sway
A new-made world up-springs,
Meant merely for his play;
No, we are strangers here; the world is from of
old.

In vain our pent wills fret,
And would the world subdue.
Limits we did not set
Condition all we do;
Born into life we are, and life must be our
mould.

Born into life!—man grows
Forth from his parents' stem,
And blends their bloods, as those
Of theirs are blent in them;
So each new man strikes root into a far fore-
time.

Born into life!—we bring
A bias with us here,
And, when here, each new thing
Affects us we come near;
To tunes we did not call our being must keep
chime.[12]

Born into life!—in vain,
Opinions, those or these,
Unalter'd to retain
The obstinate mind decrees;
Experience, like a sea, soaks all-effacing in.

Born into life!—who lists
May what is false hold dear,
And for himself make mists
Through which to see less clear;
The world is what it is, for all our dust and
din.

Born into life!—'tis we,
And not the world, are new;
Our cry for bliss, our plea,
Others have urged it too—
Our wants have all been felt, our errors made
before.

---

[12] Lines 187–196 were added in 1867. Originally, lines 197–201 followed lines 202–206.

No eye could be too sound
To observe a world so vast,
No patience too profound
To sort what's here amass'd;
How man may here best live no care too great
   to explore.

But we—as some rude guest
Would change, where'er he roam,
The manners there profess'd
To those he brings from home—
We mark not the world's course, but would
   have *it* take *ours*.

The world's course proves the terms
On which man wins content;
Reason the proof confirms—
We spurn it, and invent
A false course for the world, and for ourselves,
   false powers.

Riches we wish to get,
Yet remain spendthrifts still;
We would have health, and yet
Still use our bodies ill;
Bafflers of our own prayers, from youth to life's
   last scenes.

We would have inward peace,
Yet will not look within;
We would have misery cease,
Yet will not cease from sin;
We want all pleasant ends, but will use no
   harsh means;

We do not what we ought,
What we ought not, we do,
And lean upon the thought
That chance will bring us through;
But our own acts, for good or ill, are mightier
   powers.

Yet, even when man forsakes
All sin,—is just, is pure,
Abandons all which makes
His welfare insecure,—
Other existences there are, that clash with ours.

Like us, the lightning-fires
Love to have scope and play;
The stream, like us, desires
An unimpeded way;
Like us, the Libyan wind delights to roam at
   large.

Streams will not curb their pride
The just man not to entomb,
Nor lightnings go aside
To give his virtues room;
Nor is that wind less rough which blows a good
   man's barge.

Nature, with equal mind,
Sees all her sons at play;
Sees man control the wind,
The wind sweep man away;   260
Allows the proudly-riding and the foundering
   bark.

And, lastly, though of ours
No weakness spoil our lot,
Though the non-human powers
Of Nature harm us not,
The ill deeds of other men make often *our* life
   dark.

What were the wise man's plan?—
Through this sharp, toil-set life,
To work as best he can,
And win what's won by strife.—   270
But we an easier way to cheat our pains have
   found.

Scratch'd by a fall, with moans
As children of weak age
Lend life to the dumb stones
Whereon to vent their rage,
And bend their little fists, and rate[13] the sense-
   less ground;

So, loath to suffer mute,
We, peopling the void air,
Make Gods to whom to impute
The ills we ought to bear;   280
With God and Fate to rail at, suffering easily.

Yet grant—as sense long miss'd
Things that are now perceived,
And much may still exist
Which is not yet believed—
Grant that the world were full of Gods we can-
   not see;

All things the world which fill
Of but one stuff are spun,
That we who rail are still,
With what we rail at, one;   290
One with the o'erlabour'd Power that through
   the breadth and length

[13] Rate: berate.

Of earth, and air, and sea,
In men, and plants, and stones,
Hath toil perpetually,
And travails, pants, and moans;
Fain would do all things well, but sometimes
      fails in strength.

And patiently exact
This universal God
Alike to any act
300   Proceeds at any nod,
And quietly declaims the cursings of himself.

This is not what man hates,
Yet he can curse but this.
Harsh Gods and hostile Fates
Are dreams! this only *is*—
Is everywhere; sustains the wise, the foolish
      elf.[14]

Nor only, in the intent
To attach blame elsewhere,
Do we at will invent
310   Stern Powers who make their care
To embitter human life, malignant Deities;

But, next, we would reverse
The scheme ourselves have spun,
And what we made to curse
We now would lean upon,
And feign kind Gods who perfect what man
      vainly tries.

Look, the world tempts our eye,
And we would know it all!
We map the starry sky,
320   We mine this earthen ball,
We measure the sea-tides, we number the sea-
      sands;

We scrutinise the dates
Of long-past human things,
The bounds of effaced states,
The lines of deceased kings;
We search out dead men's words, and works of
      dead men's hands;

We shut our eyes, and muse
How our own minds are made,
What springs of thought they use,
330   How righten'd, how betray'd—
And spend our wit to name what most employ
      unnamed.

But still, as we proceed
The mass swells more and more
Of volumes yet to read,
Of secrets yet to explore.
Our hair grows grey, our eyes are dimm'd, our
      heat is tamed;

We rest our faculties,
And thus address the Gods:
"True science if there is,
It stays in your abodes!
Man's measures cannot mete[15] the immeasur-
      able All.

"You only can take in
The world's immense design.
Our desperate search was sin,
Which henceforth we resign,
Sure only that your mind sees all things which
      befal."

Fools! That in man's brief term
He cannot all things view,
Affords no ground to affirm
That there are Gods who do;
Nor does being weary prove that he has where
      to rest.

Again.—Our youthful blood
Claims rapture as its right;
The world, a rolling flood
Of newness and delight,
Draws in the enamour'd gazer to its shining
      breast;

Pleasure, to our hot grasp,
Gives flowers after flowers;
With passionate warmth we clasp
Hand after hand in ours;
Now do we soon perceive how fast our youth is
      spent.

At once our eyes grow clear!
We see, in blank dismay,
Year posting after year,
Sense after sense decay;
Our shivering heart is mined by secret discon-
      tent;

Yet still, in spite of truth,
In spite of hopes entomb'd,
That longing of our youth
Burns ever unconsumed,
Still hungrier for delight as delights grow more
      rare.

[14] Elf: mischievous person.   [15] Mete: measure.

We pause; we hush our heart,
And thus address the Gods:
"The world hath fail'd to impart
The joy our youth forebodes,
Fail'd to fill up the void which in our breasts
    we bear.

"Changeful till now, we still
Look'd on to something new;
Let us, with changeless will,
Henceforth look on to you,
To find with you the joy we in vain here
    require!"

Fools! That so often here
Happiness mock'd our prayer,
I think, might make us fear
A like event elsewhere;
Make us, not fly to dreams, but moderate
    desire.

And yet, for those who know
Themselves, who wisely take
Their way through life, and bow
To what they cannot break,
Why should I say that life need yield but
    moderate bliss?

Shall we, with temper spoil'd,
Health sapp'd by living ill,
And judgment all embroil'd
By sadness and self-will,
Shall *we* judge what for man is not true bliss or
    is?

Is it so small a thing
To have enjoy'd the sun,
To have lived light in the spring,
To have loved, to have thought, to
    have done;
To have advanced true friends, and beat down
    baffling foes—

That we must feign a bliss
Of doubtful future date,
And, while we dream on this,
Lose all our present state,
And relegate to worlds yet distant our repose?

Not much, I know, you prize
What pleasures may be had,
Who look on life with eyes
Estranged, like mine, and sad;   410
And yet the village-churl feels the truth more
    than you,

Who's loath to leave this life
Which to him little yields—
His hard-task'd sunburnt wife,
His often-labour'd fields,
The boors with whom he talk'd, the country-
    spots he knew.

But thou, because thou hear'st
Men scoff at Heaven and Fate,
Because the Gods thou fear'st
Fail to make blest thy state,   420
Tremblest, and wilt not dare to trust the joys
    there are!

I say: Fear not! Life still
Leaves human effort scope.
But, since life teems with ill,
Nurse no extravagant hope;
Because thou must not dream, thou need'st not
    then despair!

*A long pause. At the end of it the notes of a
harp below are again heard and* CALLICLES
sings:—

Far, far from here,
The Adriatic breaks in a warm bay
Among the green Illyrian[16] hills; and there
The sunshine in the happy glens is fair,   430
And by the sea, and in the brakes.[17]
The grass is cool, the sea-side air
Bouyant and fresh, the mountain flowers
More virginal and sweet than ours.
And there, they say, two bright and aged
    snakes,
Who once were Cadmus and Harmonia,[18]
Bask in the glens or on the warm sea-shore,
In breathless quiet, after all their ills;
Nor do they see their country, nor the place
Where the Sphinx lived among the frowning
    hills,   440

[16] Illyrian: Illyria was an old name for a region of the Balkan peninsula on the Adriatic.
[17] Brakes: marshy land.
[18] Cadmus was the legendary founder of Thebes who married Harmonia, the daughter of Ares, the god of war, and Aphrodite, the goddess of love. Troubled by the gods after he accidentally killed a snake sacred to them, he asked that he and his wife be changed into serpents. Arnold published this song in 1853 under the title "Cadmus and Harmonia."

Nor the unhappy palace of their race,
Nor Thebes, nor the Ismenus,[19] any more.

There those two live, far in the Illyrian
    brakes!
They had stay'd long enough to see,
In Thebes, the billow of calamity
Over their own dear children roll'd,[20]
Curse upon curse, pang upon pang,
For years, they sitting helpless in their home,
A grey old man and woman; yet of old
450   The Gods had to their marriage come,
And at the banquet all the Muses sang.

Therefore they did not end their days
In sight of blood; but were rapt, far away,
To where the west-wind plays,
And murmurs of the Adriatic come
To those untrodden mountain-lawns; and
    there
Placed safely in changed forms, the pair
Wholly forget their first sad life, and home,
And all that Theban woe, and stray
460   For ever through the glens, placid and dumb.

EMPEDOCLES
That was my harp-player again!—where is he?
Down by the stream?

PAUSANIAS
                    Yes, Master, in the wood.

EMPEDOCLES
He ever loved the Theban story well!
But the day wears. Go now, Pausanias,
For I must be alone. Leave me one mule;
Take down with thee the rest to Catana.
And for young Callicles, thank him from me;
Tell him, I never fail'd to love his lyre—
But he must follow me no more to-night.

PAUSANIAS
470   Thou wilt return to-morrow to the city?

EMPEDOCLES
Either to-morrow or some other day,
In the sure revolutions of the world,
Good friend, I shall revisit Catana.
I have seen many cities in my time,
Till mine eyes ache with the long spectacle,
And I shall doubtless see them all again;
Thou know'st me for a wanderer from of old.
Meanwhile, stay me not now. Farewell,
    Pausanias!
        He departs on his way up the mountain.

PAUSANIAS (ALONE)
I dare not urge him further—he must go;
But he is strangely wrought!—I will speed back
And bring Peisianax to him from the city;
His counsel could once soothe him. But,
    Apollo!
How his brow lighten'd as the music rose!
Callicles must wait here, and play to him;
I saw him through the chestnuts far below,
Just since, down at the stream.—Ho! Callicles!
        He descends, calling.

ACT II
Evening. The Summit of Etna.

EMPEDOCLES
                                  Alone!—
On this charr'd, blacken'd, melancholy waste,
Crown'd by the awful peak, Etna's great mouth,
Round which the sullen vapour rolls—alone!
Pausanias is far hence, and that is well,
For I must henceforth speak no more with man.
He hath his lesson too, and that debt's paid;
And the good, learned, friendly, quiet man
May bravelier front his life, and in himself
Find henceforth energy and heart. But I—
The weary man, the banish'd citizen,
Whose banishment is not his greatest ill,
Whose weariness no energy can reach,
And for whose hurt courage is not the cure—
What should I do with life and living more?

---

[19] The Ismenus: a river which runs through Thebes.
[20] The calamities of Thebes began when Oedipus unknowingly killed his father, the ruler of
Thebes, solved the riddle of the Sphinx and thus lifted a curse on the land, and then un-
knowingly married the widowed queen, his mother. Self-blinded and exiled after he dis-
covered his crimes, Oedipus left the rule of Thebes to his two sons. They quarreled and killed
each other in a war for the rule of Thebes, and their sister Antigone was buried alive in
punishment for disobeying the edict that the body of her rebellious brother remain unburied.
One of the daughters of Cadmus and Harmonia was seduced by Zeus and conceived Dionysus,
the god of wine and revelry; she died of terror when Zeus later came to her in thunder and
lightning. Another daughter raised Dionysus and was later driven mad in a Dionysian rite; yet
another daughter gave birth to Actæon, who was changed to a stag and torn to pieces by his
own dogs when he accidentally saw Aphrodite, the goddess of love, bathing.

No, thou are come too late, Empedocles!
And the world hath the day, and must break
    thee,
Not thou the world. With men thou canst not
    live,
Their thoughts, their ways, their wishes, are
    not thine;
And being lonely thou art miserable,
For something has impair'd thy spirit's
    strength,
And dried its self-sufficing fount of joy.
Thou canst not live with men nor with
    thyself—
O sage! O sage!—Take then the one way left;
And turn thee to the elements, thy friends,
Thy well-tried friends, thy willing ministers,
And say: Ye helpers, hear Empedocles,
Who asks this final service at your hands!
Before the sophist-brood hath overlaid
The last spark of man's consciousness with
    words—
Ere quite the being of man, ere quite the world
Be disarray'd of their divinity—
Before the soul lose all her solemn joys,
And awe be dead, and hope impossible,
And the soul's deep eternal night come on—
Receive me, hide me, quench me, take me
    home!

*He advances to the edge of the crater. Smoke
and fire break forth with a loud noise, and*
CALLICLES *is heard below singing:—*

The lyre's voice is lovely everywhere;
In the court of Gods, in the city of men,
And in the lonely rock-strewn mountain-glen,
In the still mountain air.

Only to Typho[1] it sounds hatefully;
To Typho only, the rebel o'erthrown,
Through whose heart Etna drives her roots of
    stone
To imbed them in the sea.

Wherefore dost thou groan so loud?
Wherefore do thy nostrils flash,
Through the dark night, suddenly,
Typho, such red jets of flame?—

Is thy tortured heart still proud?
Is thy fire-scathed arm still rash?
Still alert thy stone-crush'd frame?   50
Doth thy fierce soul still deplore
Thine ancient rout by the Cilician[2] hills,
And that curst treachery on the Mount of
    Gore?[3]
Do thy bloodshot eyes still weep
The fight which crown'd thine ills,
Thy last mischance on this Sicilian deep?
Hast thou sworn, in thy sad lair,
Where erst the strong sea-currents suck'd thee
    down,
Never to cease to writhe, and try to rest,   60
Letting the sea-stream wander through thy
    hair?
That thy groans, like thunder prest,
Begin to roll, and almost drown
The sweet notes whose lulling spell
Gods and the race of mortals love so well,
When through thy caves thou hearest music
    swell?

But an awful pleasure bland
Spreading o'er the Thunderer's[4] face,
When the sound climbs near his seat,
The Olympian council sees;   70
As he lets his lax right hand,
Which the lightnings doth embrace,
Sink upon his mighty knees.
And the eagle, at the beck
Of the appeasing, gracious harmony,
Droops all his sheeny, brown, deep-feather'd
    neck,
Nestling nearer to Jove's feet;
While o'er his sovran eye
The curtains of the blue films slowly meet
And the white Olympus-peaks   80
Rosily brighten, and the soothed Gods smile
At one another from their golden chairs,
And no one round the charmed circle speaks.
Only the loved Hebe[5] bears
The cup about, whose draughts beguile
Pain and care, with a dark store
Of fresh-pull'd violets wreathed and nodding
    o'er;
And her flushed feet glow on the marble floor.

---

[1] Typho: one of the giants who attacked the gods and is imprisoned under Mt. Etna.

[2] Cicilian: an old name for a region in Asia Minor near present-day Turkey.

[3] Mount of Gore: in a note first published in 1885 Arnold referred to a legend that a mountain was so named in the belief that Typho's blood had spilled on it during the battle in which he was vanquished. Before the battle Typho had treacherously been given fruit to sustain him which perished during the fight.

[4] Thunderer: Jove or Zeus, chief of the gods who reside on Olympus.

[5] Hebe: daughter of Juno, Jove's consort, and cupbearer to the gods.

EMPEDOCLES
He fables, yet speaks truth!
90 The brave, impetuous heart yields everywhere
To the subtle, contriving head;
Great qualities are trodden down,
And littleness united
Is become invincible.

These rumblings are not Typho's groans, I
    know!
These angry smoke-bursts
Are not the passionate breath
Of the mountain-crush'd, tortured, intractable
    Titan king—
But over all the world
100 What suffering is there not seen
Of plainness oppress'd by cunning,
As the well-counsell'd Zeus oppress'd
That self-helping son of earth!
What anguish of greatness,
Rail'd and hunted from the world,
Because its simplicity rebukes
This envious, miserable age!

I am weary of it.
—Lie there, ye ensigns
110 Of my unloved preëminence
In an age like this!
Among a people of children,
Who throng'd me in their cities,
Who worshipp'd me in their houses,
And ask'd, not wisdom,
But drugs to charm with,
But spells to mutter—
All the fool's-armoury of magic!—Lie there,
My golden circlet,
120 My purple robe!

CALLICLES (FROM BELOW)
As the sky-brightening south-wind clears the
    day,
And makes the mass'd clouds roll,
The music of the lyre blows away
The clouds which wrap the soul.

Oh! that Fate had let me see
That triumph of the sweet persuasive lyre,
That famous, final victory,
When jealous Pan with Marsyas did conspire;[6]
When, from far Parnassus' side,

Young Apollo, all the pride
Of the Phrygian flutes to tame,
To the Phrygian highlands came;
Where the long green reed-beds sway
In the rippled waters grey
Of that solitary lake
Where Mæander's springs are born;
Whence the ridged pine-wooded roots
Of Messogis westward break,
Mounting westward, high and higher.
There was held the famous strife;
There the Phrygian brought his flutes,
And Apollo brought his lyre;
And, when now the westering sun
Touch'd the hills, the strife was done,
And the attentive Muses said:
"Marsyas, thou are vanquished!"
Then Apollo's minister
Hang'd upon a branching fir
Marsyas, that unhappy Faun,
And began to whet his knife.
But the Mænads,[7] who were there,
Left their friend, and with robes flowing
In the wind, and loose dark hair
O'er their polish'd bosoms blowing,
Each her ribbon'd tambourine
Flinging on the mountain-sod,
With a lovely frighten'd mien
Came about the youthful God.
But he turn'd his beauteous face
Haughtily another way,
From the grassy sun-warm'd place
Where in proud repose he lay,
With one arm over his head,
Watching how the whetting sped.

But aloof, on the lake-strand,
Did the young Olympus[8] stand,
Weeping at his master's end;
For the Faun had been his friend.
For he taught him how to sing,
And he taught him flute-playing.
Many a morning had they gone
To the glimmering mountain-lakes,
And had torn up by the roots
The tall crested water-reeds
With long plumes and soft brown seeds,
And had carved them into flutes,
Sitting on a tabled stone

[6] Marsayas was a faun of Phrygia in Asia Minor. He was persuaded by Pan, the spirit of nature and the inventor of the shepherd's flute, to challenge Apollo and his lyre to a musical contest. Apollo won, and had Marsyas flayed: the tears of his friends made a river that flowed into the Maeander, a river that flows by Mt. Messogis toward the Aegean sea.
[7] Mænads: female celebrants in the rites of Dionysus.
[8] Olympus: here a friend and student of Marsyas; in some accounts he is his father.

Where the shoreward ripple breaks.
And he taught him how to please
The red-snooded[9] Phrygian girls,
Whom the summer evening sees
Flashing in the dance's whirls
Underneath the starlit trees
In the mountain-villages.
Therefore now Olympus stands,
At his master's piteous cries
Pressing fast with both his hands
His white garment to his eyes,
Not to see Apollo's scorn;—
Ah, poor Faun, poor Faun! ah, poor Faun!

EMPEDOCLES
And lie thou there,
My laurel bough!
Scornful Apollo's ensign, lie thou there![10]
Though thou hast been my shade in the world's
    heat—
Though I have loved thee, lived in honouring
    thee—
Yet lie thou there,
My laurel bough!

I am weary of thee.
I am weary of the solitude
Where he who bears thee must abide—
Of the rocks of Parnassus,
Of the gorge of Delphi,[11]
Of the moonlit peaks, and the caves.
Thou guardest them, Apollo!
Over the grave of the slain Pytho,
Though young, intolerably severe!
Thou keepest aloof the profane,
But the solitude oppresses thy votary!
The jars of men reach him not in thy valley—
But can life reach him?
Thou fencest him from the multitude—
Who will fence him from himself?
He hears nothing but the cry of the torrents,
And the beating of his own heart.
The air is thin, the veins swell,
The temples tighten and throb there—
Air! air!

Take thy bough, set me free from my solitude;
I have been enough alone!

Where shall thy votary fly then? back to
    men?—

But they will gladly welcome him once more,
And help him to unbend his too tense thought,
And rid him of the presence of himself,
And keep their friendly chatter at his ear,
And haunt him, till the absence from himself,
That other torment, grow unbearable;
And he will fly to solitude again,
And he will find its air too keen for him,
And so change back; and many thousand times
Be miserably bandied to and fro   230
Like a sea-wave, betwixt the world and thee,
Thou young, implacable God! and only death
Can cut his oscillations short, and so
Bring him to poise. There is no other way.

And yet what days were those, Parmenides![12]
When we were young, when we could number
    friends
In all the Italian cities like ourselves,
When with elated hearts we join'd your train,
Ye Sun-born Virgins! on the road of truth.
Then we could still enjoy, then neither thought 240
Nor outward things were closed and dead to us;
But we received the shock of mighty thoughts
On simple minds with a pure natural joy;
And if the sacred load oppress'd our brain,
We had the power to feel the pressure eased,
The brow unbound, the thoughts flow free
    again,
In the delightful commerce of the world.
We had not lost our balance then, nor grown
Thought's slaves, and dead to every natural
    joy.
The smallest thing could give us pleasure
    then—   250
The sports of the country-people,
A flute-note from the woods,
Sunset over the sea;
Seed-time and harvest,
The reapers in the corn,
The vinedresser in his vineyard,
The village-girl at her wheel.

Fulness of life and power of feeling, ye
Are for the happy, for the souls at ease,
Who dwell on a firm basis of content!   260
But he, who has outlived his prosperous days—
But he, whose youth fell on a different world
From that on which his exiled age is thrown—

---

[9] Snood: a net or fabric to tie or hold a woman's hair.
[10] Line 193 was first inserted in 1867.
[11] Delphi was the site of the shrine of Apollo, near Mt. Parnassus, also sacred to him.
Apollo had slain Pytho or Python, the dragon that guarded Delphi.
[12] Parmenides: also a Greek philosopher of the fifth century B.C. Arnold noted in the 1867
edition of his poems that line 239 is taken from the fragments of Parmenides.

Whose mind was fed on other food, was train'd
By other rules than are in vogue to-day—
Whose habit of thought is fix'd, who will not
    change,
But, in a world he loves not, must subsist
In ceaseless opposition, be the guard
Of his own breast, fetter'd to what he guards,
270 That the world win no mastery over him—
Who has no friend, no fellow left, not one;
Who has no minute's breathing space allow'd
To nurse his dwindling faculty of joy——
Joy and the outward world must die to him,
As they are dead to me.

A long pause, during which EMPEDOCLES
*remains motionless, plunged in thought. The
night deepens. He moves forward and gazes
round him, and proceeds:—*

And you, ye stars,
Who slowly begin to marshal,
As of old, in the fields of heaven,
Your distant, melancholy lines!
280 Have you, too, survived yourselves?
Are you, too, what I fear to become?
You, too, once lived;
You, too, moved joyfully
Among august companions,
In an older world, peopled by Gods,
In a mightier order,
The radiant, rejoicing, intelligent Sons of
    Heaven.
But now, ye kindle
Your lonely, cold-shining lights,
290 Unwilling lingerers
In the heavenly wilderness,
For a younger, ignoble world;
And renew, by necessity,
Night after night your courses,
In echoing, unnear'd silence,
Above a race you know not—
Uncaring and undelighted,
Without friend and without home;
Weary like us, though not
300 Weary with our weariness.[13]

No, no, ye stars! there is no death with you,
No languor, no decay! languor and death,
They are with me, not you! ye are alive—
Ye, and the pure dark ether where ye ride
Brilliant above me! And thou, fiery world,

That sapp'st the vitals of this terrible mount
Upon whose charr'd and quaking crust I
    stand—
Thou, too, brimmest with life!—the sea of
    cloud,
That heaves its white and billowy vapours up
To moat this isle of ashes from the world,   3
Lives; and that other fainter sea, far down,
O'er whose lit floor a road of moonbeams leads
To Etna's Liparëan[14] sister-fires
And the long dusky line of Italy—
That mild and luminous floor of waters lives,
With held-in joy swelling its heart; I only,
Whose spring of hope is dried, whose spirit has
    fail'd,
I, who have not, like these, in solitude
Maintain'd courage and force, and in myself
Nursed an immortal vigour—I alone   3
Am dead to life and joy, therefore I read
In all things my own deadness.
             A long silence. He continues:—

Oh, that I could glow like this mountain!
Oh, that my heart bounded with the swell of
    the sea!
Oh, that my soul were full of light as the stars!
Oh, that it brooded over the world like the air!

But no, this heart will glow no more; thou art
A living man no more, Empedocles!
Nothing but a devouring flame of thought—
But a naked, eternally restless mind!   3
             After a pause:—

To the elements it came from
Everything will return—
Our bodies to earth,
Our blood to water,
Heat to fire,
Breath to air.
They were well born, they will be well
    entomb'd—
But mind? . . .

And we might gladly share the fruitful stir
Down in our mother earth's miraculous womb; 3
Well would it be
With what roll'd of us in the stormy main;
We might have joy, blent with the all-bathing
    air,
Or with the nimble, radiant life of fire.

[13] Lines 276–300 were printed separately in 1855 under the title, "The Philosopher and the Stars."
[14] Liparëan: the Lipari islands northeast of Sicily are volcanic.

But mind, but thought—
If these have been the master part of us—
Where will *they* find their parent element?
What will receive *them,* who will call *them*
home?
But we shall still be in them, and they in us,
And we shall be the strangers of the world,
And they will be our lords, as they are now;
And keep us prisoners of our consciousness,
And never let us clasp and feel the All
But through their forms, and modes, and
stifling veils.

And we shall be unsatisfied as now;
And we shall feel the agony of thirst,
The ineffable longing for the life of life
Baffled for ever; and still thought and mind
Will hurry us with them on their homeless
march,
Over the unallied unopening earth,
Over the unrecognising sea; while air
Will blow us fiercely back to sea and earth,
And fire repel us from its living waves.
And then we shall unwillingly return
Back to this meadow of calamity,
This uncongenial place, this human life;
And in our individual human state
Go through the sad probation all again,
To see if we will poise our life at last,
To see if we will now at last be true
To our own only true, deep-buried selves,
Being one with which we are one with the
whole world;
Or whether we will once more fall away
Into some bondage of the flesh or mind,
Some slough of sense, or some fantastic maze
Forged by the imperious lonely thinking-power.
And each succeeding age in which we are born
Will have more peril for us than the last;
Will goad our senses with a sharper spur,
Will fret our minds to an intenser play,
Will make ourselves harder to be discern'd.
And we shall struggle awhile, gasp and rebel—
And we shall fly for refuge to past times,
Their soul of unworn youth, their breath of
greatness;
And the reality will pluck us back,
Knead us in its hot hand, and change our na-
ture
And we shall feel our powers of effort flag,
And rally them for one last fight—and fail;
And we shall sink in the impossible strife,
And be astray for ever.

Slave of sense   390
I have in no wise been;—but slave of
thought? . . .
And who can say: I have been always free,
Lived ever in the light of my own soul?—
I cannot; I have lived in wrath and gloom,
Fierce, disputatious, ever at war with man,
Far from my own soul, far from warmth and
light.
But I have not grown easy in these bonds—
But I have not denied what bonds these were.
Yea, I take myself to witness,
That I have loved no darkness,   400
Sophisticated no truth,
Nursed no delusion,
Allow'd no fear!

And therefore, O ye elements! I know—
Ye know it too—it hath been granted me
Not to die wholly, not to be all enslaved.
I feel it in this hour. The numbing cloud
Mounts off my soul; I feel it, I breathe free.

Is it but for a moment?
—Ah, boil up, ye vapours!   410
Leap and roar, thou sea of fire!
My soul glows to meet you.
Ere it flag, ere the mists
Of despondency and gloom
Rush over it again,
Receive me, save me!
                    [*He plunges into the crater.*

CALLICLES (FROM BELOW)
        Through the black, rushing smoke-
            bursts,
        Thick breaks the red flame;
        All Etna heaves fiercely
        Her forest-clothed frame.   420

        Not here, O Apollo!
        Are haunts meet for thee.
        But, where Helicon[15] breaks down
        In cliff to the sea,

        Where the moon-silver'd inlets
        Send far their light voice
        Up the still vale of Thisbe,
        O speed, and rejoice!

        On the sward at the cliff-top
        Lie strewn the white flocks,   430
        On the cliff-side the pigeons
        Roost deep in the rocks.

[15] Helicon: a mountain in Greece sacred to Apollo and the Muses of poetry. Thisbe (line 427) is a town between the mountain and the sea.

In the moonlight the shepherds,
Soft lull'd by the rills,
Lie wrapt in their blankets
Asleep on the hills.

—What forms are these coming
So white through the gloom?
What garments out-glistening
440   The gold-flower'd broom?

What sweet-breathing presence
Out-perfumes the thyme?
What voices enrapture
The night's balmy prime?—

'Tis Apollo comes leading
His choir, the Nine.[16]
—The leader is fairest,
But all are divine.

They are lost in the hollows!
450   They stream up again!
What seeks on this mountain
The glorified train?—

They bathe on this mountain,
In the spring by their road;
Then on to Olympus,
Their endless abode.

—Whose praise do they mention?
Of what is it told?—
What will be for ever;
460   What was from of old.

First hymn they the Father
Of all things; and then,
The rest of immortals,
The action of men.

The day in his[17] hotness,
The strife with the palm;
The night in her silence,
The stars in their calm.

                        (1849–52) 1852

from Switzerland

"Switzerland" was first used by Arnold as the
title for a group of six poems published in the
1853 edition of his poetry. One of the poems had

been first published in 1849; the others were first
published in 1852. By 1869 the number of poems in
the series increased to eight, and then was finally
established at seven when the lyric now called "A
Memory-Picture," originally the first poem in the
series, was dropped from it.

Arnold was in Switzerland in September 1848,
and again the following autumn. Later in his life
he told his children that Marguerite was an
imagined person. But in 1848 he wrote to Clough
that he had lingered a day at one hotel "for the
sake of the blue eyes of one of its inmates" (Com-
mentary, p. 153), and he returned to the same hotel
during his visit in 1849. Nothing is known about the
actual identity of the woman he calls Marguerite.
But it is certain that these lyrics, and probably
some others not included in the series (for ex-
ample, "The Forsaken Merman"), are elaborations
of events, emotions, and memories of encounters
in 1848 and 1849.

1. Meeting

Again I see my bliss at hand,
The town, the lake are here;
My Marguerite smiles upon the strand,[1]
Unalter'd with the year.

I know that graceful figure fair,
That cheek of languid hue;
I know that soft, enkerchief'd hair,
And those sweet eyes of blue.

Again I spring to make my choice;
Again in tones of ire
I hear a God's tremendous voice:
"Be counsell'd, and retire."

Ye guiding Powers who join and part,
What would ye have with me?
Ah, warn some more ambitious heart,
And let the peaceful be!

                                          1852

2. Parting

Ye storm-winds of Autumn!
Who rush by, who shake
The window, and ruffle
The gleam-lighted lake;
Who cross to the hill-side
Thin-sprinkled with farms,

---

[16] The Nine: the Muses.   [17] In 1852 the pronoun in this line and in line 467 was "its."
[1] Arnold's note in 1877: "See . . . the poem called *A Memory-Picture*."

Where the high woods strip sadly
Their yellowing arms—
Ye are bound for the mountains!
Ah! with you let me go
Where your cold, distant barrier,
The vast range of snow,
Through the loose clouds lifts dimly
Its white peaks in air—
How deep is their stillness!
Ah, would I were there!

But on the stairs what voice is this I hear,
Buoyant as morning, and as morning clear?
Say, has some wet bird-haunted English lawn
Lent it the music of its trees at dawn?
Or was it from some sun-fleck'd mountain-
              brook
That the sweet voice its upland clearness took?
        Ah! it comes nearer—
        Sweet notes, this way!

        Hark! fast by the window
        The rushing winds go,
        To the ice-cumber'd gorges,
        The vast seas of snow!
        There the torrents drive upward
        Their rock-strangled hum;
        There the avalanche thunders
        The hoarse torrent dumb.
        —I come, O ye mountains!
        Ye torrents, I come!

But who is this, by the half-open'd door,
Whose figure casts a shadow on the floor?
The sweet blue eyes—the soft, ash-colour'd
              hair—
The cheeks that still their gentle paleness
              wear—
The lovely lips, with their arch smile that tells
The unconquer'd joy in which her spirit
              dwells—
        Ah! they bend nearer—
        Sweet lips, this way!

        Hark! the wind rushes past us!
        Ah! with that let me go
        To the clear, waning hill-side,
        Unspotted by snow,
        There to watch, o'er the sunk vale,
        The frore mountain-wall,
        Where the niched snow-bed sprays down
        Its powdery fall.

There its dusky blue clusters
The aconite[2] spreads;
There the pines slope, the cloud-strips
Hung soft in their heads.
No life but, at moments,
The mountain-bee's hum.
—I come, O ye mountains!
Ye pine-woods, I come!

Forgive me! forgive me!
    Ah, Marguerite, fain   60
Would these arms reach to clasp thee!
    But see! 'tis in vain:

In the void air, towards thee,
    My stretch'd arms are cast;
But a sea rolls between us—
    Our different past!

To the lips, ah! of others
    Those lips have been prest,
And others, ere I was,
    Were strain'd to that breast;   70

Far, far from each other
    Our spirits have grown;
And what heart knows another?
    Ah! who knows his own?

Blow, ye winds! lift me with you!
    I come to the wild.
Fold closely, O Nature!
    Thine arms round thy child.

To thee only God granted
    A heart ever new—   80
To all always open,
    To all always true.

Ah! calm me, restore me;
    And dry up my tears
On thy high mountain-platforms,
    Where morn first appears;

Where the white mists, for ever,
    Are spread and upfurl'd—
In the stir of the forces
    Whence issued the world.   90
                                    1852

3. A Farewell[3]

My horse's feet beside the lake,
Where sweet the unbroken moonbeams lay,

---

[2] Aconite: a poisonous herb (monkshood) with white or purple flowers.
[3] Added to the series in 1854.

Sent echoes through the night to wake
Each glistening strand, each heath-fringed bay.

The poplar avenue was pass'd,
And the roof'd bridge that spans the stream;
Up the steep street I hurried fast,
Led by thy taper's starlike beam.

I came! I saw thee rise!—the blood
Pour'd flushing to thy languid cheek.
Lock'd in each other's arms we stood,
In tears, with hearts too full to speak.

Days flew;—ah, soon I could discern
A trouble in thine alter'd air!
Thy hand lay languidly in mine,
Thy cheek was grave, thy speech grew rare.

I blame thee not!—this heart, I know,
To be long loved was never framed;
For something in its depths doth glow
Too strange, too restless, too untamed.

And women—things that live and move
Mined by the fever of the soul—
They seek to find in those they love
Stern strength, and promise of control.

They ask not kindness, gentle ways—
These they themselves have tried and known;
They ask a soul which never sways
With the blind gusts that shake their own.

I too have felt the load I bore
In a too strong emotion's sway;
I too have wish'd, no woman more,
This starting, feverish heart away.

I too have long'd for trenchant force,
And will like a dividing spear;
Have praised the keen, unscrupulous course,
Which knows no doubt, which feels no fear.

But in the world I learnt, what there
Thou too wilt surely one day prove,
That will, that energy, though rare,
Are yet far, far less rare than love.

Go, then!—till time and fate impress
This truth on thee, be mine no more!
They will!—for thou, I feel, not less
Than I, wast destined to this lore.

4 Boon: benign.

We school our manners, act our parts—
But He, who sees us through and through,
Knows that the bent of both our hearts
Was to be gentle, tranquil, true.

And though we wear out life, alas!
Distracted as a homeless wind,
In beating where we must not pass,
In seeking what we shall not find;

Yet we shall one day gain, life past,
Clear prospect o'er our being's whole;
Shall see ourselves, and learn at last
Our true affinities of soul.

We shall not then deny a course
To every thought the mass ignore;
We shall not then call hardness force,
Nor lightness wisdom any more.

Then, in the eternal Father's smile,
Our soothed, encouraged souls will dare
To seem as free from pride and guile,
As good, as generous, as they are.

Then we shall know our friends!—though
    much
Will have been lost—the help in strife,
The thousand sweet, still joys of such
As hand in hand face earthly life—

Though these be lost, there will be yet
A sympathy august and pure;
Ennobled by a vast regret,
And by contrition seal'd thrice sure.

And we, whose ways were unlike here,
May then more neighbouring courses ply;
May to each other be brought near,
And greet across infinity.

How sweet, unreach'd by earthly jars,
My sister! to maintain with thee
The hush among the shining stars,
The calm upon the moonlit sea!

How sweet to feel, on the boon⁴ air,
All our unquiet pulses cease!
To feel that nothing can impair
The gentleness, the thirst for peace—

The gentleness too rudely hurl'd
On this wild earth of hate and fear;

The thirst for peace a raving world
Would never let us satiate here.

1852

4. Isolation: To Marguerite

We were apart; yet, day by day,
I bade my heart more constant be.
I bade it keep the world away,
And grow a home for only thee;
Nor fear'd but thy love likewise grew,
Like mine, each day, more tried, more true.

The fault was grave! I might have known,
What far too soon, alas! I learn'd—
The heart can bind itself alone,
And faith may oft be unreturn'd.
Self-sway'd our feelings ebb and swell—
Thou lov'st no more;—Farewell! Farewell!

Farewell!—and thou, thou lonely heart,
Which never yet without remorse
Even for a moment didst depart
From thy remote and spheréd course
To haunt the place where passions reign—
Back to thy solitude again!

Back! with the conscious thrill of shame
Which Luna felt, that summer-night,
Flash through her pure immortal frame,
When she forsook the starry height
To hang over Endymion's sleep
Upon the pine-grown Latmian steep.[5]

Yet she, chaste queen, had never proved
How vain a thing is mortal love,
Wandering in Heaven, far removed.
But thou hast long had place to prove
This truth—to prove, and make thine own:
"Thou hast been, shalt be, art, alone."

Or, if not quite alone, yet they
Which touch thee are unmating things—
Ocean and clouds and night and day;
Lorn autumns and triumphant springs;
And life, and others' joy and pain,
And love, if love, of happier men.

Of happier men—for they, at least,
Have *dream'd* two human hearts might blend

In one, and were through faith released
From isolation without end
Prolong'd; nor knew, although not less
Alone than thou, their loneliness.

1857

5. To Marguerite—Continued

Yes! in the sea of life enisled,
With echoing straits between us thrown,
Dotting the shoreless watery wild,
We mortal millions live *alone*.
The islands feel the enclasping flow,
And then their endless bounds they know.

But when the moon their hollows lights,
And they are swept by balms of spring,
And in their glens, on starry nights,
The nightingales divinely sing;
And lovely notes, from shore to shore,
Across the sounds and channels pour—

Oh! then a longing like despair
Is to their farthest caverns sent;
For surely once, they feel, we were
Parts of a single continent!
Now round us spreads the watery plain—
Oh might our marges meet again!

Who order'd, that their longing's fire
Should be, as soon as kindled, cool'd?
Who renders vain their deep desire?—
A God, a God their severance ruled!
And bade betwixt their shores to be
The unplumb'd, salt, estranging sea.

1852

7. The Terrace at Berne

(*Composed Ten Years After the Preceding*)[6]
Ten years!—and to my waking eye
Once more the roofs of Berne appear;
The rocky banks, the terrace high,
The stream!—and do I linger here?

The clouds are on the Oberland,
The Jungfrau snows look faint and far;

[5] Endymion, a shepherd on Mount Latmos, was seen and loved by Diana, the virgin goddess of the moon.
[6] The preceding poem is "Absence," probably written in 1848–49 but not published until 1852. "Absence" is a poem in which a "fair stranger's eyes of grey" remind the poet of Marguerite and his separation from her.

But bright are those green fields at hand,
And through those fields comes down the Aar,[7]

10
And from the blue twin-lakes it comes,
Flows by the town, the churchyard fair;
And 'neath the garden-walk it hums,
The house!—and is my Marguerite there?

Ah, shall I see thee, while a flush
Of startled pleasure floods thy brow,
Quick through the oleanders brush,
And clap thy hands, and cry: '*Tis thou!*

Or hast thou long since wander'd back,
Daughter of France! to France, thy home;
And flitted down the flowery track
20
Where feet like thine too lightly come?

Doth riotous laughter now replace
Thy smile; and rouge, with stony glare,
Thy cheek's soft hue; and fluttering lace
The kerchief that enwound thy hair?

Or is it over?—art thou dead?—
Dead!—and no warning shiver ran
Across my heart, to say thy thread
Of life was cut, and closed thy span!

Could from earth's ways that figure slight
30
Be lost, and I not feel 'twas so?
Of that fresh voice the gay delight
Fail from earth's air, and I not know?

Or shall I find thee still, but changed,
But not the Marguerite of thy prime?
With all thy being re-arranged,
Pass'd through the crucible of time;

With spirit vanish'd, beauty waned,
And hardly yet a glance, a tone,
A gesture—anything—retain'd
40
Of all that was my Marguerite's own?

I will not know! For wherefore try,
To things by mortal course that live,
A shadowy durability,
For which they were not meant, to give?

Like driftwood spars, which meet and pass
Upon the boundless ocean-plain,
So on the sea of life, alas!
Man meets man—meets, and quits again.

I knew it when my life was young;
I feel it still, now youth is o'er.
—The mists are on the mountain hung,
And Marguerite I shall see no more.

(1863)   1867

Memorial Verses[1]

Goethe in Weimar sleeps, and Greece,
Long since, saw Byron's struggle cease.[2]
But one such death remain'd to come;
The last poetic voice is dumb—
We stand to-day by Wordsworth's tomb.

When Byron's eyes were shut in death,
We bow'd our head and held our breath.
He taught us little; but our soul
Had *felt* him like the thunder's roll.
With shivering heart the strife we saw
Of passion with eternal law;
And yet with reverential awe
We watch'd the fount of fiery life
Which served for that Titantic strife.

When Goethe's death was told, we said:
Sunk, then, is Europe's sagest head.
Physician of the iron age,
Goethe has done his pilgrimage.
He took the suffering human race,
He read each wound, each weakness clear;
And struck his finger on the place,
And said: *Thou ailest here, and here!*
He look'd on Europe's dying hour
Of fitful dream and feverish power;
His eye plunged down the weltering strife,
The turmoil of expiring life—
He said: *The end is everywhere,*
Art still has truth, take refuge there!
And he was happy, if to know
Causes of things, and far below
His feet to see the lurid flow

---

[7] Oberland: a section of the Alps near the lakes of Thun and Brienz (the twin lakes of line 9). The Jungfrau is a peak in this range; the Aar is a river that flows from Switzerland into the Rhine.

[1] The Arnold family's house at Fox How in the Lake district was near Rydal Mount, Wordsworth's home. The elegy was written at the request of Edward Quillinan, the husband of Wordsworth's daughter.

[2] Goethe died in 1832, Byron in 1824, when Arnold was two years old.

Of terror, and insane distress,
And headlong fate, be happiness.

And Wordsworth!—Ah, pale ghosts, rejoice!
For never has such soothing voice
Been to your shadowy world convey'd,
Since erst, at morn, some wandering shade
Heard the clear song of Orpheus[3] come
Through Hades, and the mournful gloom.
Wordsworth has gone from us—and ye,
Ah, may ye feel his voice as we!
He too upon a wintry clime
Had fallen—on this iron time
Of doubts, disputes, distractions, fears.
He found us when the age had bound
Our souls in its benumbing round;
He spoke, and loosed our heart in tears.[4]
He laid us as we lay at birth
On the cool flowery lap of earth,
Smiles broke from us and we had ease;
The hills were round us, and the breeze
Went o'er the sun-lit fields again;
Our foreheads felt the wind and rain.
Our youth return'd; for there was shed
On spirits that had long been dead,
Spirits dried up and closely furl'd,
The freshness of the early world.

Ah! since dark days still bring to light
Man's prudence and man's fiery might,
Time may restore us in his course
Goethe's sage mind and Byron's force;
But where will Europe's latter hour
Again find Wordsworth's healing power?
Others will teach us how to dare,
And against fear our breast to steel;
Others will strengthen us to bear—
But who, ah! who, will make us feel?
The cloud of mortal destiny,
Others will front it fearlessly—
But who, like him, will put it by?

Keep fresh the grass upon his grave
O Rotha,[5] with thy living wave!

Sing him thy best! for few or none
Hears thy voice right, now he is gone.

1850; 1852

Self-Dependence

Weary of myself, and sick of asking
What I am, and what I ought to be,
At this vessel's prow I stand, which bears me
Forwards, forwards, o'er the starlit sea.

And a look of passionate desire
O'er the sea and to the stars I send:
"Ye who from my childhood up have calm'd
  me,
Calm me, ah, compose me to the end!

"Ah, once more," I cried, "ye stars, ye waters,
On my heart your mighty charm renew;   10
Still, still let me, as I gaze upon you,
Feel my soul becoming vast like you!"

From the intense, clear, star-sown vault of
  heaven,
Over the lit sea's unquiet way,
In the rustling night-air came the answer:
"Wouldst thou *be* as these are? *Live* as they.

"Unaffrighted by the silence round them,
Undistracted by the sights they see,
These demand not that the things without
  them
Yield them love, amusement, sympathy.   20

"And with joy the stars perform their shining,
And the sea its long moon-silver'd roll;
For self-poised they live, nor pine with noting
All the fever of some differing soul.

"Bounded by themselves, and unregardful
In what state God's other works may be,
In their own tasks all their powers pouring,
These attain the mighty life you see."

[3] Orpheus was a legendary Greek musician, the son of Apollo and one of the Muses, whose song persuaded the ruler of the underworld to release Orpheus' dead wife. As he was about to step onto the surface of the earth, however, Orpheus violated an injunction not to look behind him, and his wife was carried back into Hades.

[4] In its first appearance, in *Fraser's* monthly magazine in 1850, these three lines were placed between lines 47 and 48:

> He tore us from the prison-cell
> Of festering thoughts and personal fears,
> Where we had long been doom'd to dwell.

[5] Rotha: a river in the Lake District which flows near the graveyard in which Wordsworth was buried.

O air-born voice! long since, severely clear,
30 A cry like thine in mine own heart I hear:
"Resolve to be thyself; and know that he,
Who finds himself, loses his misery!"

                                                    1852

The Buried Life

Light flows our war of mocking words, and yet,
Behold, with tears mine eyes are wet!
I feel a nameless sadness o'er me roll.
Yes, yes, we know that we can jest,
We know, we know that we can smile!
But there's a something in this breast,
To which thy light words bring no rest,
And thy gay smiles no anodyne.
Give me thy hand, and hush awhile,
10 And turn those limpid eyes on mine,
And let me read there, love! thy inmost soul.

Alas! is even love too weak
To unlock the heart, and let it speak?
Are even lovers powerless to reveal
To one another what indeed they feel?
I knew the mass of men conceal'd
Their thoughts, for fear that if reveal'd
They would by other men be met
With blank indifference, or with blame
    reproved;
20 I knew they lived and moved
Trick'd in disguises, alien to the rest
Of men, and alien to themselves—and yet
The same heart beats in every human breast!

But we, my love!—doth a like spell benumb
Our hearts, our voices?—must we too be dumb?

Ah! well for us, if even we,
Even for a moment, can get free
Our heart, and have our lips unchain'd;
For that which seals them hath been deep-
    ordain'd!
30 Fate, which foresaw
How frivolous a baby man would be—
By what distractions he would be possess'd,
How he would pour himself in every strife,
And well-nigh change his own identity—
That it might keep from his capricious play
His genuine self, and force him to obey
Even in his own despite his being's law,
Bade through the deep recesses of our breast
The unregarded river of our life
40 Pursue with indiscernible flow its way;
And that we should not see

The buried stream, and seem to be
Eddying at large in blind uncertainty,
Though driving on with it eternally.

But often, in the world's most crowded streets,
But often, in the din of strife,
There rises an unspeakable desire
After the knowledge of our buried life;
A thirst to spend our fire and restless force
In tracking out our true, original course;
A longing to inquire
Into the mystery of this heart which beats
So wild, so deep in us—to know
Whence our lives come and where they go.
And many a man in his own breast then delves,
But deep enough, alas! none ever mines.
And we have been on many thousand lines,
And we have shown, on each, spirit and power;
But hardly have we, for one little hour,
Been on our own line, have we been our-
    selves—
Hardly had skill to utter one of all
The nameless feelings that course through our
    breast,
But they course on for ever unexpress'd.
And long we try in vain to speak and act
Our hidden self, and what we say and do
Is eloquent, is well—but 'tis not true!
And then we will no more be rack'd
With inward striving, and demand
Of all the thousand nothings of the hour
Their stupefying power;
Ah yes, and they benumb us at our call!
Yet still, from time to time, vague and forlorn,
From the soul's subterranean depth upborne
As from an infinitely distant land,
Come airs, and floating echoes, and convey
A melancholy into all our day.

Only—but this is rare—
When a belovéd hand is laid in ours,
When, jaded with the rush and glare
Of the interminable hours,
Our eyes can in another's eyes read clear,
When our world-deafen'd ear
Is by the tones of a loved voice caress'd—
A bolt is shot back somewhere in our breast,
And a lost pulse of feeling stirs again.
The eye sinks inward, and the heart lies plain.
And what we mean, we say, and what we
    would, we know.
A man becomes aware of his life's flow,
And hears its winding murmur; and he sees
The meadows where it glides, the sun, the
    breeze.

And there arrives a lull in the hot race
Wherein he doth for ever chase
That flying and elusive shadow, rest.
An air of coolness plays upon his face,
And an unwonted calm pervades his breast.
And then he thinks he knows
The hills where his life rose,
And the sea where it goes.

                                        1852

*Étienne Pivert de Senacour (1770–1846) was a
French writer who published a series of letters
under the title* Obermann *(1804). In a letter
quoted in Tinker and Lowry's* Commentary *(pp.
271–272) Arnold recounts the "extraordinary im-
pression" created on him by Senacour's writing
when he read it as a young man: "Senacour looked
on the old religion of Christendom much as other
enthusiasts of the French Revolution looked at it;
he was, however, profoundly religious, and when
the world consolidated itself again after the Revo-
lution without a new religion, but with a patching
up of the old in which he saw no permanence and
no sincerity, 'his heart within him', as the Psalmist
says, 'became desolate'." In a note to another poem,
"Obermann Once More" (1867), Arnold points to
"the profound inwardness, the austere sincerity, of
his principal work,* Obermann, *the delicate feeling
for nature which it exhibits, and the melancholy
eloquence of many passages of it. . . . of all writ-
ers he is the most perfectly isolated and the least
attitudinising. His chief work, too, has a value and
power of its own, apart from these merits of its
author. The stir of all the main forces, by which
modern life is and has been impelled, lives in the
letters of* Obermann; *the dissolving agencies of the
eighteenth century, the fiery storm of the French
Revolution, the first faint promise and dawn of
that new world which our own time is but now
more fully bringing to light" (Commentary, pp.
253–254).*

Stanzas in Memory of the Author of "Obermann"

November, 1849

In front the awful Alpine track
Crawls up its rocky stair;
The autumn storm-winds drive the rack,
Close o'er it, in the air.

Behind are the abandon'd baths[1]
Mute in their meadows lone;
The leaves are on the valley-paths,
The mists are on the Rhone—

The white mists rolling like a sea!
I hear the torrents roar.   10
—Yes, Obermann, all speaks of thee;
I feel thee near once more!

I turn thy leaves! I feel their breath
Once more upon me roll;
That air of languor, cold, and death,
Which brooded o'er thy soul.

Fly hence, poor wretch, whoe'er thou art,
Condemn'd to cast about,
All shipwreck in thy own weak heart,
For comfort from without!   20

A fever in these pages burns
Beneath the calm they feign;
A wounded human spirit turns,
Here, on its bed of pain.

Yes, though the virgin mountain-air
Fresh through these pages blows;
Though to these leaves the glaciers spare
The soul of their white snows;

Though here a mountain-murmur swells
Of many a dark-bough'd pine;   30
Though, as you read, you hear the bells
Of the high-pasturing kine[2]—

Yet, through the hum of torrent lone,
And brooding mountain-bee,
There sobs I know not what ground-tone
Of human agony.

Is it for this, because the sound
Is fraught too deep with pain,
That, Obermann! the world around
So little loves thy strain?   40

Some secrets may the poet tell,
For the world loves new ways;
To tell too deep ones is not well—
It knows not what he says.

[1] Arnold's note in 1869: "The Baths of Leuk. The poem was conceived, and partly com-
posed, in the valley going down from the foot of the Gemmi Pass towards the Rhone." Arnold
refers here to a visit in 1849; he had made the same journey a year earlier.
[2] Kine: cattle.

Yet, of the spirits who have reign'd
In this our troubled day,
I know but two, who have attain'd,
Save thee, to see their way.

50 By England's lakes, in grey old age,
His quiet home one keeps;[3]
And one, the strong much-toiling sage,
In German Weimar sleeps.

But Wordsworth's eyes avert their ken
From half of human fate;
And Goethe's course few sons of men
May think to emulate.

For he pursued a lonely road,
His eyes on Nature's plan;
Neither made man too much a God,
60 Nor God too much a man.

Strong was he, with a spirit free
From mists, and sane, and clear;
Clearer, how much! than ours—yet we
Have a worse course to steer.

For though his manhood bore the blast
Of a tremendous time,
Yet in a tranquil world was pass'd
His tenderer youthful prime.

But we, brought forth and rear'd in hours
70 Of change, alarm, surprise—
What shelter to grow ripe is ours?
What leisure to grow wise?

Like children bathing on the shore,
Buried a wave beneath,
The second wave succeeds, before
We have had time to breathe.

Too fast we live, too much are tried,
Too harass'd, to attain
Wordsworth's sweet calm, or Goethe's wide
80 And luminous view to gain.

And then we turn, thou sadder sage,
To thee! we feel thy spell!
—The hopeless tangle of our age,
Thou too hast scann'd it well!

Immoveable thou sittest, still
As death, composed to bear!
Thy head is clear, thy feeling chill,
And icy thy despair.

Yes, as the son of Thetis said,[4]
I hear thee saying now:
Greater by far than thou are dead;
Strive not! die also thou!

Ah! two desires toss about
The poet's feverish blood.
One drives him to the world without,
And one to solitude.

The glow, he cries, *the thrill of life,*
Where, where do these abound?—
Not in the world, not in the strife
Of men, shall they be found.

He who hath watch'd, not shared, the strife,
Knows how the day hath gone.
He only lives with the world's life,
Who hath renounced his own.

To thee we come, then! Clouds are roll'd
Where thou, O seer! art set;
Thy realm of thought is drear and cold—
The world is colder yet!

And thou hast pleasures, too, to share
With those who come to thee—
Balms floating on thy mountain-air,
And healing sights to see.

How often, where the slopes are green
On Jaman,[5] hast thou sate
By some high chalet-door, and seen
The summer-day grow late;

And darkness steal o'er the wet grass
With the pale crocus starr'd,
And reach that glimmering sheet of glass
Beneath the piny sward,

Lake Leman's waters, far below!
And watch'd the rosy light
Fade from the distant peaks of snow;
And on the air of night

---

[3] Arnold's note in 1852: "Written in November, 1849." Wordsworth died in 1850. Goethe, born in 1749 (into the "tranquil world" of line 67), died at Weimar in 1832.
[4] Thetis: the mother of the Greek hero Achilles, who speaks this sentiment in Book 21 of the *Iliad.*
[5] Jaman: a peak near the Lake of Geneva (Lake Leman).

Heard accents of the eternal tongue
Through the pine branches play—
Listen'd, and felt thyself grow young!
Listen'd and wept——Away!

30 Away the dreams that but deceive
And thou, sad guide, adieu!
I go, fate drives me; but I leave
Half of my life with you.

We, in some unknown Power's employ,
Move on a rigorous line;
Can neither, when we will, enjoy,
Nor, when we will, resign.

I in the world must live; but thou,
Thou melancholy shade!
Wilt not, if thou canst see me now,
40 Condemn me, nor upbraid.

For thou art gone away from earth,
And place with those dost claim,
The Children of the Second Birth,
Whom the world could not tame;

And with that small, transfigured band,
Whom many a different way
Conducted to their common land,
Thou learn'st to think as they.

Christian and pagan, king and slave,
50 Soldier and anchorite,
Distinctions we esteem so grave,
Are nothing in their sight.

They do not ask, who pined unseen,
Who was on action hurl'd,
Whose one bond is, that all have been
Unspotted by the world.

There without anger thou wilt see
Him who obeys thy spell
No more, so he but rest, like thee,
60 Unsoil'd!—and so, farewell.

Farewell!—Whether thou now liest near
That much-loved inland sea,
The ripples of whose blue waves cheer
Vevey and Meillerie:[6]

And in that gracious region bland,
Where with clear-rustling wave
The scented pines of Switzerland
Stand dark round thy green grave,

Between the dusty vineyard-walls
Issuing on that green place   170
The early peasant still recalls
The pensive stranger's face,

And stoops to clear thy moss-grown date
Ere he plods on again;—
Or whether, by maligner fate,
Among the swarms of men,

Where between granite terraces
The blue Seine rolls her wave,
The Capital of Pleasure sees
The hardly-heard-of grave;—   180

Farewell! Under the sky we part,
In this stern Alpine dell.
O unstrung will! O broken heart!
A last, a last farewell!

(1849) 1852

When Arnold finished "Sohrab and Rustum" in 1853, in time to include it as the first poem in the edition of his poetry published in that year (from which he excluded "Empedocles on Etna"), he thought it "by far the best thing I have yet done. . . . I have had the greatest pleasure in composing it—a rare thing with me, and, as I think, a good test of the pleasure what you write is likely to afford to others; but then the story is a very noble and excellent one" (Commentary, p. 73).

Arnold knew the story, which appears in the tenth-century Persian epic the Shah Nameh *(Book of Kings) of Firdausi, from John Malcolm's* History of Persia *(1815) and from a paraphrase in a review by the French critic Charles Sainte-Beuve of a recent translation of Firdausi's poetry (in* Causeries du Lundi, *1 [1850]). Rustum is the great hero of the Persians in their recurring battles with the Tartars, ruled by Afrasiab. According to Malcolm's paraphrase of Firdausi's narrative, Rustum had other sons, and near the end of his long life he even met in single combat the son of Sohrab, who revealed himself to his grandfather in time to prevent a misfortune like that of the death of Sohrab.*

In a note to the second edition (1854) of his 1853 poems, Arnold recounted Malcolm's version of the combat of Sohrab and Rustum, which differs from his own principally in describing three meetings which Arnold collapses into one: the first combat is broken off by mutual consent; the second is won by Sohrab, who spares Rustum; and the third ends as Arnold describes it. Allott in his edition of Arnold's poetry notes the frequent use

[6] Vevey and Meillerie: towns on the shores of the Lake of Geneva.

*of Homer, especially of the story of Achilles in the
Iliad. Arnold also drew again on Alexander Burnes'
Travels into Bokhara (1833) for many of the
names of cities, rivers, and mountains—most of
them in present-day Iran, Afghanistan, and the
Uzbeck of the Soviet Union—with which the poem
is decorated.*

Sohrab and Rustum

An Episode

And the first grey of morning fill'd the east,
And the fog rose out of the Oxus stream.
But all the Tartar camp along the stream
Was hush'd, and still the men were plunged in
    sleep;
Sohrab alone, he slept not; all night long
He had lain wakeful, tossing on his bed;
But when the grey dawn stole into his tent,
He rose, and clad himself, and girt his sword,
And took his horseman's cloak, and left his
    tent,
10 And went abroad into the cold wet fog,
Through the dim camp to Peran-Wisa's[1] tent.
   Through the black Tartar tents he pass'd,
    which stood
Clustering like bee-hives on the low flat strand
Of Oxus,[2] where the summer-floods o'erflow
When the sun melts the snows in high Pamere;
Through the black tents he pass'd, o'er that
    low strand,
And to a hillock came, a little back
From the stream's brink—the spot where first a
    boat,
Crossing the stream in summer, scrapes the
    land.
20 The men of former times had crown'd the top
With a clay fort; but that was fall'n, and now
The Tartars built there Peran-Wisa's tent,
A dome of laths, and o'er it felts were spread.
And Sohrab came there, and went in, and stood
Upon the thick piled carpets in the tent,
And found the old man sleeping on his bed
Of rugs and felts, and near him lay his arms.
And Peran-Wisa heard him, though the step
Was dull'd; for he slept light, an old man's
    sleep;
30 And he rose quickly on one arm, and said:—
   "Who art thou? for it is not yet clear dawn.
Speak! is there news, or any night alarm?"

But Sohrab came to the bedside, and said:—
   "Thou know'st me, Peran-Wisa! it is I.
The sun is not yet risen, and the foe
Sleep; but I sleep not; all night long I lie
Tossing and wakeful, and I come to thee.
For so did King Afrasiab bid me seek
Thy counsel, and to heed thee as thy son,
In Samarcand, before the army march'd;   4
And I will tell thee what my heart desires.
Thou know'st if, since from Ader-baijan first
I came among the Tartars and bore arms,
I have still served Afrasiab well, and shown,
At my boy's years, the courage of a man.
This too thou know'st, that while I still bear
    on
The conquering Tartar ensigns through the
    world,
And beat the Persians back on every field,
I seek one man, one man, and one alone—
Rustum, my father; who I hoped should greet, 5
Should one day greet, upon some well-fought
    field,
His not unworthy, not inglorious son.
So I long hoped, but him I never find.
Come then, hear now, and grant me what I ask.
Let the two armies rest to-day; but I
Will challenge forth the bravest Persian lords
To meet me, man to man; if I prevail,
Rustum will surely hear it; if I fall—
Old man, the dead need no one, claim no kin.
Dim is the rumour of a common fight,   6
Where host meets host, and many names are
    sunk;
But of a single combat fame speaks clear."
   He spoke; and Peran-Wisa took the hand
Of the young man in his, and sigh'd, and
    said:—
   "O Sohrab, an unquiet heart is thine!
Canst thou not rest among the Tartar chiefs,
And share the battle's common chance with us
Who love thee, but must press for ever first,
In single fight incurring single risk,
To find a father thou hast never seen?   7
That were far best, my son, to stay with us
Unmurmuring; in our tents, while it is war,
And when 'tis truce, then in Afrasiab's towns.[3]
But, if this one desire indeed rules all,
To seek out Rustum—seek him not through
    fight!
Seek him in peace, and carry to his arms,

---

[1] Peran-Wisa: Afrasiab's principal minister and one of his generals.
[2] The Oxus (its present name is the Amu Darya) is a major river that flows from the
Pamere plateau northwest to the Aral Sea. It was sometimes the boundary between the Persian
and Tartar kingdoms.
[3] Lines 71–73 were added in 1854.

O Sohrab, carry an unwounded son!
But far hence seek him, for he is not here.
For now it is not as when I was young,
When Rustum was in front of every fray;
But now he keeps apart, and sits at home,
In Seistan, with Zal, his father old.
Whether that his own mighty strength at last
Feels the abhorr'd approaches of old age,
Or in some quarrel with the Persian King.
There go!—Thou wilt not? Yet my heart fore-
   bodes
Danger or death awaits thee on this field.
Fain would I know thee safe and well, though
   lost
To us; fain therefore send thee hence, in peace
To seek thy father, not seek single fights
In vain;—but who can keep the lion's cub
From ravening, and who govern Rustum's son?
Go, I will grant thee what thy heart desires.''
   So said he, and dropp'd Sohrab's hand, and
      left
His bed, and the warm rugs whereon he lay;
And o'er his chilly limbs his woollen coat
He pass'd, and tied his sandals on his feet,
And threw a white cloak round him, and he
   took
In his right hand a ruler's staff, no sword;
And on his head he set his sheep-skin cap,
Black, glossy, curl'd, the fleece of Kara-Kul;
And raised the curtain of his tent, and call'd
His herald to his side, and went abroad.
   The sun by this had risen, and clear'd the
      fog
From the broad Oxus and the glittering sands.
And from their tents the Tartar horsemen filed
Into the open plain; so Haman bade—
Haman, who next to Peran-Wisa ruled
The host, and still was in his lusty prime.
From their black tents, long files of horse, they
   stream'd;
As when some grey November morn the files,
In marching order spread, of long-neck'd cranes
Stream over Casbin and the southern slopes
Of Elburz, from the Aralian estuaries,
Or some frore[4] Caspian reed-bed, southward
   bound
For the warm Persian sea-board—so they
   stream'd.
The Tartars of the Oxus, the King's guard,
First, with black sheep-skin caps and with long
   spears;

Large men, large steeds; who from Bokhara
   come
And Khiva, and ferment the milk of mares.
Next, the more temperate Toorkmuns of the
   south,
The Tukas, and the lances of Salore,
And those from Attruck and the Caspian sands;
Light men and on light steeds, who only drink
The acrid milk of camels, and their wells.
And then a swarm of wandering horse, who
   came
From far, and a more doubtful service own'd;
The Tartars of Ferghana, from the banks
Of the Jaxartes, men with scanty beards
And close-set skull-caps; and those wilder
   hordes
Who roam o'er Kipchak and the northern
   waste,
Kalmucks and unkempt Kuzzaks, tribes who
   stray
Nearest the Pole, and wandering Kirghizzes,
Who come on shaggy ponies from Pamere;
These all filed out from camp into the plain.
And on the other side the Persians form'd;—
First a light cloud of horse, Tartars they seem'd,
The Ilyats of Khorassan; and behind,
The royal troops of Persia, horse and foot,
Marshall'd battalions bright in burnish'd steel.
But Peran-Wisa with his herald came,
Threading the Tartar squadrons to the front,
And with his staff kept back the foremost
   ranks.
And when Ferood,[5] who led the Persians, saw
That Peran-Wisa kept the Tartars back,
He took his spear, and to the front he came,
And check'd his ranks, and fix'd them where
   they stood.
And the old Tartar came upon the sand
Betwixt the silent hosts, and spake, and said:—
   "Ferood, and ye, Persians and Tartars, hear!
Let there be truce between the hosts to-day.
But choose a champion from the Persian lords
To fight our champion Sohrab, man to man.''
   As, in the country, on a morn in June,
When the dew glistens on the pearled ears,
A shiver runs through the deep corn[6] for joy—
So, when they heard what Peran-Wisa said,
A thrill through all the Tartar squadrons ran
Of pride and hope for Sohrab, whom they
   loved.
   But as a troop of pedlars, from Cabool,

30
90
100
110
120
130
140
150
160

---

[4] Frore: frozen. [5] Ferood: the brother of Kai Khosroo, ruler of the Persians.
[6] Corn: grain.

Cross underneath the Indian Caucasus,
That vast sky-neighbouring mountain of milk
    snow;
Crossing so high, that, as they mount, they pass
Long flocks of travelling birds dead on the
    snow,
Choked by the air, and scarce can they them-
    selves
Slake their parch'd throats with sugar'd
    mulberries—
In single file they move, and stop their breath,
For fear they should dislodge the o'erhanging
    snows—
So the pale Persians held their breath with
    fear.

170   And to Ferood his brother chiefs came up
To counsel; Gudurz and Zoarrah[7] came,
And Feraburz, who ruled the Persian host
Second, and was the uncle of the King;
These came and counsell'd, and then Gudurz
    said:—
    "Ferood, shame bids us take their challenge
    up,
Yet champion have we none to match this
    youth.
He has the wild stag's foot, the lion's heart.
But Rustum came last night; aloof he sits
And sullen, and has pitch'd his tents apart.
180   Him will I seek, and carry to his ear
The Tartar challenge, and this young man's
    name.
Haply he will forget his wrath, and fight.
Stand forth the while, and take their challenge
    up."
    So spake he; and Ferood stood forth and
    cried:—
"Old man, be it agreed as thou hast said!
Let Sohrab arm, and we will find a man."
    He spake: and Peran-Wisa turn'd, and strode
Back through the opening squadrons to his
    tent.
But through the anxious Persians Gudurz ran,
And cross'd the camp which lay behind, and
190   reach'd,
Out on the sands beyond it, Rustum's tents.
Of scarlet cloth they were, and glittering gay,
Just pitch'd; the high pavilion in the midst
Was Rustum's, and his men lay camp'd
    around.

And Gudurz enter'd Rustum's tent, and found
Rustum; his morning meal was done, but still
The table stood before him, charged with
    food—
A side of roasted sheep, and cakes of bread,
And dark green melons; and there Rustum sate
Listless, and held a falcon on his wrist,[8]   200
And play'd with it; but Gudurz came and stood
Before him; and he look'd, and saw him stand,
And with a cry sprang up and dropp'd the
    bird,
And greeted Gudurz with both hands, and
    said:—
    "Welcome! these eyes could see no better
    sight.
What news? but sit down first, and eat and
    drink."
    But Gudurz stood in the tent-door, and
    said:—
"Not now! a time will come to eat and drink,
But not to-day; to-day has other needs.
The armies are drawn out, and stand at gaze; 210
For from the Tartars is a challenge brought
To pick a champion from the Persian lords
To fight their champion—and thou know'st his
    name—
Sohrab men call him, but his birth is hid.
O Rustum, like thy might is this young man's!
He has the wild stag's foot, the lion's heart;
And he is young, and Iran's chiefs are old,
Or else too weak; and all eyes turn to thee.
Come down and help us, Rustum, or we lose!"
    He spoke; but Rustum answer'd with a
    smile:—   220
"Go to! if Iran's chiefs are old, then I
Am older; if the young are weak, the King
Errs strangely; for the King, for Kai Khosroo,[9]
Himself is young, and honours younger men,
And lets the aged moulder to their graves.
Rustum he loves no more, but loves the
    young—
The young may rise at Sohrab's vaunts, not I.
For what care I, though all speak Sohrab's
    fame?
For would that I myself had such a son,
And not that one slight helpless girl I have— 230
A son so famed, so brave, to send to war,

---

[7] Gudurz and Zoarrah are named in Malcolm as powerful members of the court.
[8] Malcolm does not recount that Rustum was brooding in his tent; Sainte-Beuve does, and draws a parallel to Achilles' similar behavior in the *Iliad*.
[9] Kai Khosroo, the ruler of the Persians, was the great-grandson of the king whom Rustum first served with his glorious deeds.

And I to tarry with the snow-hair'd Zal,[10]
My father, whom the robber Afghans vex,
And clip his borders short, and drive his herds,
And he has none to guard his weak old age.
There would I go, and hang my armour up,
And with my great name fence that weak old man,
And spend the goodly treasures I have got,
And rest my age, and hear of Sohrab's fame,
And leave to death the hosts of thankless kings,   40
And with these slaughterous hands draw sword no more."
    He spoke, and smiled; and Gudurz made reply:—
"What then, O Rustum, will men say to this,
When Sohrab dares our bravest forth, and seeks
Thee most of all, and thou, whom most he seeks,
Hidest thy face? Take heed lest men should say:
Like some old miser, Rustum hoards his fame,
And shuns to peril it with younger men."
    And, greatly moved, then Rustum made reply:—
"O Gudurz, wherefore dost thou say such words?   50
Thou knowest better words than this to say.
What is one more, one less, obscure or famed,
Valiant or craven, young or old, to me?
Are not they mortal, am not I myself?
But who for men of nought would do great deeds?
Come, thou shalt see how Rustum hoards his fame!
But I will fight unknown, and in plain arms;
Let not men say of Rustum, he was match'd
In single fight with any mortal man."
    He spoke, and frown'd; and Gudurz turn'd, and ran   260
Back quickly through the camp in fear and joy—
Fear at his wrath, but joy that Rustum came.
But Rustum strode to his tent-door, and call'd
His followers in, and bade them bring his arms,
And clad himself in steel; the arms he chose
Were plain, and on his shield was no device,
Only his helm was rich, inlaid with gold,
And, from the fluted spine atop, a plume
Of horsehair waved, a scarlet horsehair plume.
So arm'd, he issued forth; and Ruksh, his horse,   270
Follow'd him like a faithful hound at heel—

Ruksh, whose renown was noised through all the earth,
The horse, whom Rustum on a foray once
Did in Bokhara by the river find
A colt beneath its dam, and drove him home,
And rear'd him; a bright bay, with lofty crest,
Dight with a saddle-cloth of broider'd green
Crusted with gold, and on the ground were work'd
All beasts of chase, all beasts which hunters know.
So follow'd, Rustum left his tents, and cross'd   280
The camp, and to the Persian host appear'd.
And all the Persians knew him, and with shouts
Hail'd; but the Tartars knew not who he was.
And dear as the wet diver to the eyes
Of his pale wife who waits and weeps on shore,
By sandy Bahrein, in the Persian Gulf,
Plunging all day in the blue waves, at night,
Having made up his tale of precious pearls,
Rejoins her in their hut upon the sands—
So dear to the pale Persians Rustum came.   290
    And Rustum to the Persian front advanced,
And Sohrab arm'd in Haman's tent, and came.
And as afield the reapers cut a swath
Down through the middle of a rich man's corn,
And on each side are squares of standing corn,
And in the midst a stubble, short and bare—
So on each side were squares of men, with spears
Bristling, and in the midst, the open sand.
And Rustum came upon the sand, and cast
His eyes toward the Tartar tents, and saw   300
Sohrab come forth, and eyed him as he came.
    As some rich woman, on a winter's morn,
Eyes through her silken curtains the poor drudge
Who with numb blacken'd fingers makes her fire—
At cock-crow, on a starlit winter's morn,
When the frost flowers the whiten'd window-panes—
And wonders how she lives, and what the thoughts
Of that poor drudge may be; so Rustum eyed
The unknown adventurous youth, who from afar
Came seeking Rustum, and defying forth   310
All the most valiant chiefs; long he perused
His spirited air, and wonder'd who he was.
For very young he seem'd, tenderly rear'd;

[10] Zal means "the aged": he was born with white hair, and for that reason abandoned to die, but he was saved and reared by a griffin, a fabulous creature half-eagle and half-lion (see lines 679–682).

Like some young cypress, tall, and dark, and
straight,
Which in a queen's secluded garden throws
Its slight dark shadow on the moonlit turf,
By midnight, to a bubbling fountain's sound—
So slender Sohrab seem'd, so softly rear'd.
And a deep pity enter'd Rustum's soul
320 As he beheld him coming; and he stood,
And beckon'd to him with his hand, and
said:—
     "Oh thou young man, the air of Heaven is
soft,
And warm, and pleasant; but the grave is cold!
Heaven's air is better than the cold dead grave.
Behold me! I am vast, and clad in iron,
And tried; and I have stood on many a field
Of blood, and I have fought with many a foe—
Never was that field lost, or that foe saved.
O Sohrab, wherefore wilt thou rush on death?
330 Be govern'd! quit the Tartar host, and come
To Iran, and be as my son to me,
And fight beneath my banner till I die!
There are no youths in Iran brave as thou."
     So he spake, mildly; Sohrab heard his voice,
The mighty voice of Rustum, and he saw
His giant figure planted on the sand,
Sole, like some single tower, which a chief
Hath builded on the waste in former years
Against the robbers; and he saw that head,
Streak'd with its first grey hairs;—hope filled
340   his soul,
And he ran forward and embraced his knees,
And clasp'd his hand within his own, and
said:—
     "O, by thy father's head! by thine own soul!
Art thou not Rustum? speak! art thou not he?"
     But Rustum eyed askance the kneeling
youth,
And turn'd away, and spake to his own soul:—
     "Ah me, I muse what this young fox may
mean!
False, wily, boastful, are these Tartar boys.
For if I now confess this thing he asks,
350 And hide it not, but say: *Rustum is here!*
He will not yield indeed, nor quit our foes,
But he will find some pretext not to fight,
And praise my fame, and proffer courteous gifts,
A belt or sword perhaps, and go his way.
And on a feast-tide, in Afrasiab's hall,
In Samarcand, he will arise and cry:
'I challenged once, when the two armies camp'd
Beside the Oxus, all the Persian lords
To cope with me in single fight; but they
360 Shrank, only Rustum dared; then he and I
Changed gifts, and went on equal terms away.'

So will he speak, perhaps, while men applaud;
Then were the chiefs of Iran shamed through
me."
     And then he turn'd, and sternly spake
aloud:—
"Rise! wherefore dost thou vainly question thus
Of Rustum? I am here, whom thou hast call'd
By challenge forth; make good thy vaunt, or
yield!
Is it with Rustum only thou wouldst fight?
Rash boy, men look on Rustum's face and flee!
For well I know, that did great Rustum stand   370
Before thy face this day, and were reveal'd,
There would be then no talk of fighting more.
But being what I am, I tell thee this—
Do thou record it in thine inmost soul:
Either thou shalt renounce thy vaunt and yield,
Or else thy bones shall strew this sand, till
winds
Bleach them, or Oxus with his summer-floods,
Oxus in summer wash them all away."
     He spoke; and Sohrab answer'd on his
feet:—
"Art thou so fierce? Thou wilt not fright me so!   380
I am no girl, to be made pale by words.
Yet this thou hast said well, did Rustum stand
Here on this field, there were no fighting then.
But Rustum is far hence, and we stand here.
Begin! thou art more vast, more dread than I,
And thou art proved, I know, and I am
young—
But yet success sways with the breath of
Heaven.
And though thou thinkest that thou knowest
sure
Thy victory, yet thou canst not surely know.
For we are all, like swimmers in the sea,   390
Poised on the top of a huge wave of fate,
Which hangs uncertain to which side to fall.
And whether it will heave us up to land,
Or whether it will roll us out to sea,
Back out to sea, to the deep waves of death,
We know not, and no search will make us
know;
Only the event will teach us in its hour."
     He spoke, and Rustum answer'd not, but
hurl'd
His spear; down from the shoulder, down it
came,
As on some partridge in the corn a hawk,   40
That long has tower'd in the airy clouds,
Drops like a plummet; Sohrab saw it come,
And sprang aside, quick as a flash; the spear
Hiss'd, and went quivering down into the sand,
Which it sent flying wide;—then Sohrab threw

In turn, and full struck Rustum's shield; sharp rang,
The iron plates rang sharp, but turn'd the spear.
And Rustum seized his club, which none but he
Could wield; an unlopp'd trunk it was, and huge,
Still rough—like those which men in treeless plains
410 To build them boats fish from the flooded rivers,
Hyphasis or Hydaspes, when, high up
By their dark springs, the wind in winter-time
Hath made in Himalayan forests wrack,
And strewn the channels with torn boughs—so huge
The club which Rustum lifted now, and struck
One stroke; but again Sohrab sprang aside,
Lithe as the glancing snake, and the club came
Thundering to earth, and leapt from Rustum's hand.
420 And Rustum follow'd his own blow, and fell
To his knees, and with his fingers clutch'd the sand;
And now might Sohrab have unsheathed his sword,
And pierced the mighty Rustum while he lay
Dizzy, and on his knees, and choked with sand;
But he look'd on, and smiled, nor bared his sword,
But courteously drew back, and spoke, and said:—
"Thou strik'st too hard! that club of thine will float
Upon the summer-floods, and not my bones.
But rise, and be not wroth! not wroth am I;
430 No, when I see thee, wrath forsakes my soul.
Thou say'st, thou art not Rustum; be it so!
Who art thou then, that canst so touch my soul?
Boy as I am, I have seen battles too—
Have waded foremost in their bloody waves,
And heard their hollow roar of dying men;
But never was my heart thus touch'd before.
Are they from Heaven, these softenings of the heart?
O thou old warrior, let us yield to Heaven!
Come, plant we here in earth our angry spears,
440 And make a truce, and sit upon this sand,
And pledge each other in red wine, like friends,
And thou shalt talk to me of Rustum's deeds.
There are enough foes in the Persian host,

Whom I may meet, and strike, and feel no pang;
Champions enough Afrasiab has, whom thou
Mayst fight; fight *them,* when they confront thy spear!
But oh, let there be peace 'twixt thee and me!"
He ceased, but while he spake, Rustum had risen,
And stood erect, trembling with rage; his club
He left to lie, but had regain'd his spear, 450
Whose fiery point now in his mail'd right-hand
Blazed bright and baleful, like that autumn-star,[11]
The baleful sign of fevers; dust had soil'd
His stately crest, and dimm'd his glittering arms.
His breast heaved, his lips foam'd, and twice his voice
Was choked with rage; at last these words broke way:—
"Girl! nimble with thy feet, not with thy hands!
Curl'd minion, dancer, coiner of sweet words!
Fight, let me hear thy hateful voice no more!
Thou art not in Afrasiab's gardens now 460
With Tartar girls, with whom thou art wont to dance;
But on the Oxus-sands, and in the dance
Of battle, and with me, who make no play
Of war; I fight it out, and hand to hand.
Speak not to me of truce, and pledge, and wine!
Remember all thy valour; try thy feints
And cunning! all the pity I had is gone;
Because thou hast shamed me before both the hosts
With thy light skipping tricks, and thy girl's wiles."
He spoke, and Sohrab kindled at his taunts, 470
And he too drew his sword; at once they rush'd
Together, as two eagles on one prey
Come rushing down together from the clouds,
One from the east, one from the west; their shields
Dash'd with a clang together, and a din
Rose, such as that the sinewy woodcutters
Make often in the forest's heart at morn,
Of hewing axes, crashing trees—such blows
Rustum and Sohrab on each other hail'd.
And you would say that sun and stars took part 480
In that unnatural conflict; for a cloud
Grew suddenly in Heaven, and dark'd the sun
Over the fighters' heads; and a wind rose

---

[11] Autumn-star: Sirius, the Dog Star, associated with the sultriness and fevers of late summer (the dog days).

Under their feet, and moaning swept the plain,
And in a sandy whirlwind wrapp'd the pair.
In gloom they twain were wrapp'd, and they
    alone;
For both the on-looking hosts on either hand
Stood in broad daylight, and the sky was pure,
And the sun sparkled on the Oxus stream.
But in the gloom they fought, with bloodshot
490   eyes
And labouring breath; first Rustum struck the
    shield
Which Sohrab held stiff out; the steel-spiked
    spear
Rent the tough plates, but fail'd to reach the
    skin,
And Rustum pluck'd it back with angry groan.
Then Sohrab with his sword smote Rustum's
    helm,
Nor clove its steel quite through; but all the
    crest
He shore away, and that proud horsehair
    plume,
Never till now defiled, sank to the dust;
And Rustum bow'd his head; but then the
    gloom
500 Grew blacker, thunder rumbled in the air,
And lightnings rent the cloud; and Ruksh, the
    horse,
Who stood at hand, utter'd a dreadful cry;—
No horse's cry was that, most like the roar
Of some pain'd desert-lion, who all day
Hath trail'd the hunter's javelin in his side,
And comes at night to die upon the sand.
The two hosts heard that cry, and quaked for
    fear,
And Oxus curdled as it cross'd his stream.
But Sohrab heard, and quail'd not, but rush'd
    on,
510 And struck again; and again Rustum bow'd
His head; but this time all the blade, like glass,
Sprang in a thousand shivers on the helm,
And in the hand the hilt remain'd alone.
Then Rustum raised his head; his dreadful eyes
Glared, and he shook on high his menacing
    spear,
And shouted: *Rustum!*—Sohrab heard that
    shout,
And shrank amazed; back he recoil'd one step,
And scann'd with blinking eyes the advancing
    form;
And then he stood bewilder'd; and he dropp'd
His covering shield, and the spear pierced his
520   side.
He reel'd, and staggering back, sank to the
    ground;

And then the gloom dispersed, and the wind
    fell,
And the bright sun broke forth, and melted all
The cloud; and the two armies saw the pair—
Saw Rustum standing, safe upon his feet,
And Sohrab, wounded, on the bloody sand.
    Then, with a bitter smile, Rustum began:—
"Sohrab, thou thoughtest in thy mind to kill
A Persian lord this day, and strip his corpse,
And bear thy trophies to Afrasiab's tent.   530
Or else that the great Rustum would come
    down
Himself to fight, and that thy wiles would move
His heart to take a gift, and let thee go.
And then that all the Tartar host would praise
Thy courage or thy craft, and spread thy fame,
To glad thy father in his weak old age.
Fool, thou art slain, and by an unknown man!
Dearer to the red jackals shalt thou be
Than to thy friends, and to they father old."
    And, with a fearless mien, Sohrab replied:— 540
"Unknown thou art; yet thy fierce vaunt is
    vain.
Thou dost not slay me, proud and boastful
    man!
No! Rustum slays me, and this filial heart.
For were I match'd with ten such men as thee,
And I were that which till to-day I was,
They should be lying here, I standing there.
But that belovéd name unnerved my arm—
That name, and something, I confess, in thee,
Which troubles all my heart, and made my
    shield
Fall; and thy spear transfix'd an unarm'd foe. 550
And now thou boastest, and insult'st my fate.
But hear thou this, fierce man, tremble to hear:
The mighty Rustum shall avenge my death!
My father, whom I seek through all the world,
He shall avenge my death, and punish thee!"
    As when some hunter in the spring hath
    found
A breeding eagle sitting on her nest,
Upon the craggy isle of a hill-lake,
And pierced her with an arrow as she rose,
And follow'd her to find her where she fell   560
Far off;—anon her mate comes winging back
From hunting, and a great way off descries
His huddling young left sole; at that, he checks
His pinion, and with short uneasy sweeps
Circles above his eyry, with loud screams
Chiding his mate back to her nest; but she
Lies dying, with the arrow in her side,
In some far stony gorge out of his ken,
A heap of fluttering feathers—never more
Shall the lake glass her, flying over it;   570

Never the black and dripping precipices
Echo her stormy scream as she sails by—
As that poor bird flies home, nor knows his loss,
So Rustum knew not his own loss, but stood
Over his dying son, and knew him not.

But, with a cold incredulous voice, he said:—
"What prate is this of fathers and revenge?
The mighty Rustum never had a son."

580 And, with a failing voice, Sohrab replied:—
"Ah yes, he had! and that lost son am I.
Surely the news will one day reach his ear,
Reach Rustum, where he sits, and tarries long,
Somewhere, I know not where, but far from
        here;
And pierce him like a stab, and make him leap
To arms, and cry for vengeance upon thee.
Fierce man, bethink thee, for an only son!
What will that grief, what will that vengeance
        be?
Oh, could I live, till I that grief had seen!
Yet him I pity not so much, but her,
590 My mother, who in Ader-baijan dwells
With that old king, her father, who grows grey
With age, and rules over the valiant Koords.
Her most I pity, who no more will see
Sohrab returning from the Tartar camp,
With spoils and honour, when the war is done.
But a dark rumour will be bruited up,
From tribe to tribe, until it reach her ear;
And then will that defenceless woman learn
That Sohrab will rejoice her sight no more,
600 But that in battle with a nameless foe,
By the far-distant Oxus, he is slain."

He spoke; and as he ceased, he wept aloud,
Thinking of her he left, and his own death.
He spoke; but Rustum listen'd, plunged in
        thought.
Nor did he yet believe it was his son
Who spoke, although he call'd back names he
        knew;
For he had had sure tidings that the babe,
Which was in Ader-baijan born to him,
Had been a puny girl, no boy at all—
610 So that sad mother sent him word, for fear
Rustum should seek the boy, to train in arms.
And so he deem'd that either Sohrab took,
By a false boast, the style of Rustum's son;
Or that men gave it him, to swell his fame.

So deem'd he; yet he listen'd, plunged in
        thought
And his soul set to grief, as the vast tide
Of the bright rocking Ocean sets to shore
At the full moon; tears gather'd in his eyes;
For he remember'd his own early youth,
And all its bounding rapture; as, at dawn,   620
The shepherd from his mountain-lodge descries
A far, bright city, smitten by the sun,
Through many rolling clouds—so Rustum saw
His youth; saw Sohrab's mother, in her bloom;
And that old king, her father, who loved well
His wandering guest, and gave him his fair
        child[12]
With joy; and all the pleasant life they led,
They three, in that long-distant summer-time—
The castle, and the dewy woods, and hunt
And hound, and morn on those delightful hills   630
In Ader-baijan. And he saw that youth,
Of age and looks to be his own dear son,
Piteous and lovely, lying on the sand,
Like some rich hyacinth[13] which by the scythe
Of an unskilful gardener has been cut,
Mowing the garden grass-plots near its bed,
And lies, a fragrant tower of purple bloom,
On the mown, dying grass—so Sohrab lay,
Lovely in death, upon the common sand.
And Rustum gazed on him with grief, and
        said:—   640
"O Sohrab, thou indeed art such a son
Whom Rustum, wert thou his, might well have
        loved.
Yet here thou errest, Sohrab, or else men
Have told thee false—thou art not Rustum's
        son.
For Rustum had no son; one child he had—
But one—a girl; who with her mother now
Plies some light female task, nor dreams of
        us—
Of us she dreams not, nor of wounds, nor war."
But Sohrab answer'd him in wrath; for now
The anguish of the deep-fix'd spear grew fierce,   650
And he desired to draw forth the steel,
And let the blood flow free, and so to die—
But first he would convince his stubborn foe;
And, rising sternly on one arm, he said:—
"Man, who art thou who dost deny my
        words?

[12] In Sainte-Beuve's paraphrase of the story Sohrab's mother offers herself to Rustum so that she may bear a son by so great a man. Rustum courteously marries her, but leaves after their wedding night.
[13] Hyacinth was a youth loved by Apollo, the classical god of song. Apollo accidentally killed Hyacinth during a game, and in his sorrow he promised to celebrate the youth in song, and caused a flower to grow from his blood.

Truth sits upon the lips of dying men,
And falsehood, while I lived, was far from
　　mine.
I tell thee, prick'd upon this arm I bear
That seal which Rustum to my mother gave,
660　That she might prick it on the babe she bore."
　　He spoke; and all the blood left Rustum's
　　　　cheeks,
And his knees totter'd, and he smote his hand
Against his breast, his heavy mailed hand,
That the hard iron corslet clank'd aloud;
And to his heart he press'd the other hand,
And in a hollow voice he spake, and said:—
　　"Sohrab, that were a proof which could not
　　　　lie!
If thou show this, then art thou Rustum's son."
　　Then, with weak hasty fingers, Sohrab loosed
670　His belt, and near the shoulder bared his arm,
And show'd a sign in faint vermilion points
Prick'd; as a cunning workman, in Pekin,
Pricks with vermilion some clear porcelain vase,
An emperor's gift—at early morn he paints,
And all day long, and, when night comes, the
　　　　lamp
Lights up his studious forehead and thin
　　　　hands—
So delicately prick'd the sign appear'd
On Sohrab's arm, the sign of Rustum's seal.
It was that griffin, which of old rear'd Zal,
680　Rustum's great father, whom they left to die,
A helpless babe, among the mountain-rocks;
Him that kind creature found, and rear'd, and
　　　　loved—
Then Rustum took it for his glorious sign.
And Sohrab bared that image on his arm,
And himself scann'd it long with mournful
　　　　eyes,
And then he touch'd it with his hand and
　　　　said:—
　　"How say'st thou? Is that sign the proper sign
Of Rustum's son, or of some other man's?"
　　He spoke; but Rustum gazed, and gazed, and
　　　　stood
690　Speechless; and then he utter'd one sharp cry:
O boy—thy father!—and his voice choked
　　　　there.
And then a dark cloud pass'd before his eyes,
And his head swam, and he sank down to earth.
But Sohrab crawl'd to where he lay, and cast
His arms about his neck, and kiss'd his lips,
And with fond faltering fingers stroked his
　　　　cheeks,
Trying to call him back to life; and life
Came back to Rustum, and he oped his eyes,
And they stood wide with horror; and he seized

In both his hands the dust which lay around,　700
And threw it on his head, and smirch'd his
　　　　hair,—
His hair, and face, and beard, and glittering
　　　　arms;
And strong convulsive groanings shook his
　　　　breast,
And his sobs choked him; and he clutch'd his
　　　　sword,
To draw it, and for ever let life out.
But Sohrab saw his thought, and held his
　　　　hands,
And with a soothing voice he spake, and
　　　　said:—
　　"Father, forbear! for I but meet to-day
The doom which at my birth was written down
In Heaven, and thou art Heaven's unconscious
　　　　hand.　710
Surely my heart cried out that it was thou,
When first I saw thee; and thy heart spoke too,
I know it! but fate trod those promptings down
Under its iron heel; fate, fate engaged
The strife, and hurl'd me on my father's spear.
But let us speak no more of this! I find
My father; let me feel that I have found!
Come, sit beside me on this sand, and take
My head betwixt thy hands, and kiss my
　　　　cheeks,
And wash them with thy tears, and say: My
　　　　son!　720
Quick! quick! for number'd are my sands of
　　　　life,
And swift; for like the lightning to this field
I came, and like the wind I go away—
Sudden, and swift, and like a passing wind.
But it was writ in Heaven that this should be."
　　So said he, and his voice released the heart
Of Rustum, and his tears broke forth; he cast
His arms round his son's neck, and wept aloud,
And kiss'd him. And awe fell on both the hosts,
When they saw Rustum's grief; and Ruksh, the
　　　　horse,　730
With his head bowing to the ground and mane
Sweeping the dust, came near, and in mute woe
First to the one then to the other moved
His head, as if inquiring what their grief
Might mean; and from his dark, compassionate
　　　　eyes,
The big warm tears roll'd down, and caked the
　　　　sand.
But Rustum chid him with stern voice, and
　　　　said:—
　　"Ruksh, now thou grievest; but, O Ruksh,
　　　　thy feet
Should first have rotted on their nimble joints,

40 Or ere they brought thy master to this field!"
But Sohrab look'd upon the horse and
said:—
"Is this, then, Ruksh? How often, in past days,
My mother told me of thee, thou brave steed,
My terrible father's terrible horse! and said,
That I should one day find thy lord and thee.
Come, let me lay my hand upon thy mane!
O Ruksh, thou art more fortunate than I;
For thou hast gone where I shall never go,
And snuff'd the breezes of my father's home.
50 And thou hast trod the sands of Seistan,
And seen the River of Helmund, and the Lake
Of Zirrah; and the aged Zal himself
Has often stroked thy neck, and given thee
food,
Corn in a golden platter soak'd with wine,
And said: *O Ruksh! bear Rustum well!*—but I
Have never known my grandsire's furrow'd
face,
Nor seen his lofty house in Seistan,
Nor slaked my thirst at the clear Helmund
stream;
But lodged among my father's foes, and seen
60 Afrasiab's cities only, Samarcand,
Bokhara, and lone Khiva in the waste,
And the black Toorkmun tents; and only
drunk
The desert rivers, Moorghab and Tejend,
Kohik, and where the Kalmuks feed their
sheep,
The northern Sir; and this great Oxus stream,
The yellow Oxus, by whose brink I die."
Then, with a heavy groan, Rustum
bewail'd:—
"Oh, that its waves were flowing over me!
Oh, that I saw its grains of yellow silt
70 Roll tumbling in the current o'er my head!"
But, with a grave mild voice, Sohrab
replied:—
"Desire not that, my father! thou must live.
For some are born to do great deeds, and live,
As some are born to be obscured, and die.
Do thou the deeds I die too young to do,
And reap a second glory in thine age;
Thou art my father, and thy gain is mine.
But come! thou seest this great host of men
Which follow me; I pray thee, slay not these!
80 Let me entreat for them; what have they done?
They follow'd me, my hope, my fame, my star.
Let them all cross the Oxus back in peace.
But me thou must bear hence, not send with
them,
But carry me with thee to Seistan,
And place me on a bed, and mourn for me,

Thou, and the snow-hair'd Zal, and all thy
friends.
And thou must lay me in that lovely earth,
And heap a stately mound above my bones,
And plant a far-seen pillar over all.
That so the passing horseman on the waste   790
May see my tomb a great way off, and cry:
Sohrab, the mighty Rustum's son, lies there,
Whom his great father did in ignorance kill!
And I be not forgotten in my grave."
And, with a mournful voice, Rustum
replied:—
"Fear not! as thou hast said, Sohrab, my son,
So shall it be; for I will burn my tents,
And quit the host, and bear thee hence with
me,
And carry thee away to Seistan,
And place thee on a bed, and mourn for thee,   800
With the snow-headed Zal, and all my friends.
And I will lay thee in that lovely earth,
And heap a stately mound above thy bones,
And plant a far-seen pillar over all,
And men shall not forget thee in thy grave.
And I will spare thy host; yea, let them go!
Let them all cross the Oxus back in peace!
What should I do with slaying any more?
For would that all whom I have ever slain
Might be once more alive; my bitterest foes,   810
And they who were call'd champions in their
time,
And through whose death I won that fame I
have—
And I were nothing but a common man,
A poor, mean soldier, and without renown,
So thou mightest live too, my son, my son!
Or rather would that I, even I myself,
Might now be lying on this bloody sand,
Near death, and by an ignorant stroke of thine,
Not thou of mine! and I might die, not thou;
And I, not thou, be borne to Seistan;   820
And Zal might weep above my grave, not thine;
And say: *O son, I weep thee not too sore,*
For willingly, I know, thou met'st thine end!
But now in blood and battles was my youth,
And full of blood and battles is my age,
And I shall never end this life of blood."
Then, at the point of death, Sohrab
replied:—
"A life of blood indeed, thou dreadful man!
But thou shalt yet have peace; only not now,
Not yet! but thou shalt have it on that day,   830
When thou shalt sail in a high-masted ship,
Thou and the other peers of Kai Khosroo,
Returning home over the salt blue sea,
From laying thy dear master in his grave."

And Rustum gazed in Sohrab's face, and
    said:—
"Soon be that day, my son, and deep that sea!
Till then, if fate so wills, let me endure."
    He spoke; and Sohrab smiled on him, and
    took
The spear, and drew it from his side, and eased
840 His wound's imperious anguish; but the blood
Came welling from the open gash, and life
Flow'd with the stream;—all down his cold
    white side
The crimson torrent ran, dim now and soil'd,
Like the soil'd tissue of white violets
Left, freshly gather'd, on their native bank,
By children whom their nurses call with haste
Indoors from the sun's eye; his head droop'd
    low,
His limbs grew slack; motionless, white, he
    lay—
White, with eyes closed; only when heavy gasps,
Deep heavy gasps quivering through all his
850   frame,
Convulsed him back to life, he open'd them,
And fix'd them feebly on his father's face;
Till now all strength was ebb'd, and from his
    limbs
Unwillingly the spirit fled away,
Regretting the warm mansion which it left,
And youth, and bloom, and this delightful
    world.
    So, on the bloody sand, Sohrab lay dead;
And the great Rustum drew his horseman's
    cloak
Down o'er his face, and sate by his dead son.
860 As those black granite pillars, once high-rear'd
By Jemshid in Persepolis,[14] to bear
His house, now 'mid their broken flights of
    steps
Lie prone, enormous, down the mountain
    side—
So in the sand lay Rustum by his son.
    And night came down over the solemn waste,
And the two gazing hosts, and that sole pair,
And darken'd all; and a cold fog, with night,
Crept from the Oxus. Soon a hum arose,
As of a great assembly loosed, and fires
870 Began to twinkle through the fog; for now

Both armies moved to camp, and took their
    meal;
The Persians took it on the open sands
Southward, the Tartars by the river marge;
And Rustum and his son were left alone.
    But the majestic river floated on,
Out of the mist and hum of that low land,
Into the frosty starlight, and there moved,
Rejoicing, through the hush'd Chorasmian
    waste,
Under the solitary moon;—he flow'd
Right for the polar star, past Orgunjè,   88
Brimming, and bright, and large; then sands
    begin
To hem his watery march, and dam his streams,
And split his currents; that for many a league
The shorn and parcell'd Oxus strains along
Through beds of sand and matted rushy isles—
Oxus, forgetting the bright speed he had
In his high mountain-cradle in Pamere,
A foil'd circuitous wanderer—till at last
The long'd-for dash of waves is heard, and wide
His luminous home of waters opens, bright   8
And tranquil, from whose floor the new-bathed
    stars
Emerge, and shine upon the Aral Sea.
                                          1853

Philomela[1]

Hark! ah, the nightingale—
The tawny-throated!
Hark! from that moonlit cedar what a burst!
What triumph! hark! what pain!

O wanderer from a Grecian shore,
Still, after many years, in distant lands,
Still nourishing in thy bewilder'd brain
That wild, unquench'd, deep-sunken, old-world
    pain—
Say, will it never heal?
And can this fragrant lawn
With its cool trees, and night,
And the sweet, tranquil Thames,
And moonshine, and the dew,
To thy racked heart and brain
Afford no balm?

---

[14] Jemshid: an early ruler of the Persians who founded the great Persian city of Persepolis.
[1] In the classical myth Philomela is raped by her sister's husband, a king of the city of
Daulis in Thrace, an old name for the region of the Balkan peninsula. In revenge Philomela's
sister kills her own son and serves him to her husband at a banquet. To protect the sisters
from further vengeance, they are then changed to birds: in the Latin version of the myth,
Philomela becomes a nightingale.

Dost thou to-night behold,
Here, through the moonlight on this English
    grass,
The unfriendly palace in the Thracian wild?
Dost thou again peruse
With hot cheeks and sear'd eyes
The too clear web, and thy dumb sister's
    shame?[2]
Dost thou once more assay
Thy flight, and feel come over thee,
Poor fugitive, the feathery change
Once more, and once more seem to make
    resound.
With love and hate, triumph and agony,
Lone Daulis, and the high Cephissian vale?[3]
Listen, Eugenia[4]—
How thick the bursts come crowding through
    the leaves!
Again—thou hearest?
Eternal passion!
Eternal pain!

                                        1853

Arnold prefaced this poem, in its first and subsequent publications, with an abstract of a passage in Joseph Glanvill's The Vanity of Dogmatizing *(1661). Glanvill's name for the young man, like Arnold's, is the Scholar-Gypsy. Arnold omits some other details in his condensation: that the young man is driven to the gypsies not only by poverty but by the fact that he has no friends to help him on in a world which runs by favor and preferment; that he can recount conversations at which he was not present; and that the Scholar himself emphasizes the agency of imagination in performing his mystery (in Arnold's early notes for the poem he refers to its subject as "the first mesmerist" or "the wandering mesmerist"): "what he did was by the power of* Imagination, *his* Phancy *binding theirs . . . : there were warrantable wayes of heightening the* Imagination *to that pitch, as to bind anothers"* (quoted in Commentary, *p. 206).*

The Scholar-Gipsy

Go, for they call you, shepherd, from the hill;
    Go, shepherd, and untie the wattled cotes![1]
        No longer leave thy wistful flock unfed,

Nor let thy bawling fellows rack their throats,
    Nor the cropp'd herbage shoot another
        head.[2]
        But when the fields are still,
    And the tired men and dogs all gone to rest,
    And only the white sheep are sometimes
        seen
        Cross and recross the strips of moon-
            blanch'd green,
    Come, shepherd, and again begin the quest!   10

Here, where the reaper was at work of late—
    In this high field's dark corner, where he
        leaves
        His coat, his basket, and his earthen cruse,[3]
    And in the sun all morning binds the sheaves,
        Then here, at noon, comes back his stores
            to use—
        Here will I sit and wait,
    While to my ear from uplands far away
        The bleating of the folded flocks is borne,
        With distant cries of reapers in the corn—
    All the live murmur of a summer's day.   20

Screen'd is this nook o'er the high, half-reap'd
        field,
    And here till sun-down, shepherd! will I be.
        Through the thick corn the scarlet poppies
            peep,
    And round green roots and yellowing stalks
        I see
        Pale pink convolvulus in tendrils creep;
        And air-swept lindens yield
    Their scent, and rustle down their perfumed
        showers
        Of bloom on the bent grass where I am
            laid,
        And bower me from the August sun with
            shade;
    And the eye travels down to Oxford's towers.   30

And near me on the grass lies Glanvil's book—
    Come, let me read the oft-read tale again!
        The story of the Oxford scholar poor,
        Of pregnant parts and quick inventive brain,

[2] In the Greek version of the myth Philomela's tongue is cut out by the king to prevent her from telling of the rape, and it is her sister who is changed to a nightingale; Philomela becomes a swallow.

[3] Cephissian vale: the valley of the principal river of Thrace.

[4] Eugenia: a female name with classical associations for Arnold; he early used it in an imitation of a poem of Latin poet Horace.

[1] Wattled cotes: sheds or coops made of woven branches.

[2] Shoot another head: sprout again.   [3] Cruse: jar or pot.

Who, tired of knocking at preferment's
     door,[4]
     One summer-morn forsook
His friends, and went to learn the gipsy-lore,
     And roam'd the world with that wild
          brotherhood,
     And came, as most men deem'd, to little
          good,
40   But came to Oxford and his friends no more.

But once, years after, in the country-lanes,
     Two scholars, whom at college erst he knew,
     Met him, and of his way of life enquired;
     Whereat he answer'd, that the gipsy-crew,
          His mates, had arts to rule as they desired
          The workings of men's brains,
     And they can bind them to what thoughts
          they will.
     "And I," he said, "the secret of their art,
     When fully learn'd, will to the world
          impart;
     But it needs heaven-sent moments for this
50   skill."

This said, he left them, and return'd no
          more.—
     But rumours hung about the country-side,
          That the lost Scholar long was seen to
               stray,
     Seen by rare glimpses, pensive and tongue-
          tied,
          In hat of antique shape, and cloak of grey,
          The same the gipsies wore.
Shepherds had met him on the Hurst[5] in
          spring;
          At some lone alehouse in the Berkshire
               moors,
          On the warm ingle-bench,[6] the smock-
               frock'd boors
60   Had found him seated at their entering,

But, 'mid their drink and clatter, he would fly.
     And I myself seem half to know thy looks,
          And put the shepherds, wanderer! on thy
               trace;
     And boys who in lone wheatfields scare the
          rooks

I ask if thou hast pass'd their quiet place;
     Or in my boat I lie
Moor'd to the cool bank in the summer-heats,
     'Mid wide grass meadows which the
          sunshine fills,
     And watch the warm, green-muffled
          Cumner hills,
     And wonder if thou haunt'st their shy
          retreats.

For most, I know, thou lov'st retired ground!
     Thee at the ferry Oxford riders blithe,
          Returning home on summer-nights, have
               met
     Crossing the stripling Thames at Bab-lock-
          hithe,
          Trailing in the cool stream thy fingers wet,
          As the punt's rope chops round;[7]
     And leaning backward in a pensive dream,
          And fostering in thy lap a heap of flowers
          Pluck'd in shy fields and distant Wych-
               wood bowers,
     And thine eyes resting on the moonlit stream.

And then they land, and thou are seen no
          more!—
     Maidens, who from the distant hamlets come
          To dance around the Fyfield elm in May,
     Oft through the darkening fields have seen
          thee roam,
          Or cross a stile into the public way.
          Oft thou hast given them store
     Of flowers—the frail-leaf'd, white anemony,
          Dark bluebells drench'd with dews of
               summer eves,
          And purple orchises with spotted leaves—
     But none hath words she can report of thee.

And, above Godstow Bridge, when hay-time's
          here
     In June, and many a scythe in sunshine
          flames,
          Men who through those wide fields of
               breezy grass
     Where black-wing'd swallows haunt the
          glittering Thames,

---

[4] Glanvill's words: "a Lad . . . of very pregnant and ready parts, and yet wanting the encouragement of preferment"; that is, the award of an appointment in the Church.

[5] The Hurst: a hill in the Cumner hills, near to Oxford on the southwest. The other place-names of the poem belong to this region: the villages of Bab-lock-hithe, Fyfield, and Godstow on the upper Thames; the woods of Wychwood, Bagley, and Thessaly, and finally the towers of Christ Church, one of the colleges of Oxford.

[6] Ingle-bench: bench near the hearth.

[7] Punt's rope chops round: an abrupt movement of the boat's rope.

To bathe in the abandon'd lasher[8] pass,
  Have often pass'd thee near
Sitting upon the river bank o'ergrown;
  Mark'd thine outlandish garb, thy figure
    spare,
  Thy dark vague eyes, and soft abstracted
    air—
But, when they came from bathing, thou
    wast gone!

At some lone homestead in the Cumner hills,
  Where at her open door the housewife darns,
  Thou hast been seen, or hanging on a gate
To watch the threshers in the mossy barns.
  Children, who early range these slopes and
    late
    For cresses from the rills,
  Have known thee eying, all an April-day,
  The springing pastures and the feeding
    kine;[9]
And mark'd thee, when the stars come out
    and shine,
Through the long dewy grass move slow
    away.

In autumn, on the skirts of Bagley Wood—
  Where most the gipsies by the turf-edged way
    Pitch their smoked tents, and every bush
      you see
  With scarlet patches tagg'd and shreds of
    grey,
    Above the forest-ground called Thessaly—
    The blackbird, picking food,
  Sees thee, nor stops his meal, nor fears at all;
  So often has he known thee past him stray,
  Rapt, twirling in thy hand a wither'd
    spray,
And waiting for the spark from heaven to
    fall.

And once, in winter, on the causeway chill
  Where home through flooded fields foot-
    travellers go,
  Have I not pass'd thee on the wooden
    bridge,
  Wrapt in thy cloak and battling with the
    snow,
    Thy face tow'rd Hinksey and its wintry
      ridge?
    And thou hast climb'd the hill,

And gain'd the white brow of the Cumner
    range;
  Turn'd once to watch, while thick the
    snowflakes fall,
  The line of festal light in Christ-Church
    hall—
Then sought thy straw in some sequester'd
    grange.

But what—I dream! Two hundred years are
    flown
Since first thy story ran through Oxford halls,
  And the grave Glanvil did the tale inscribe
That thou wert wander'd from the studious
    walls
    To learn strange arts, and join a gipsy-
      tribe;
    And thou from earth art gone
Long since, and in some quiet churchyard
    laid—
  Some country-nook, where o'er thy
    unknown grave
  Tall grasses and white flowering nettles
    wave,
Under a dark, red-fruited yew-tree's shade.

—No, no, thou hast not felt the lapse of hours!
  For what wears out the life of mortal men?
    'Tis that from change to change their
      being rolls;
  'Tis that repeated shocks, again, again,
    Exhaust the energy of strongest souls
    And numb the elastic powers.
  Till having used our nerves with bliss and
    teen,[10]
    And tired upon a thousand schemes our
      wit,
    To the just-pausing Genius[11] we remit
Our worn-out life, and are—what we have
    been.

Thou hast not lived, why should'st thou perish,
    so?
  Thou hadst *one* aim, *one* business, *one*
    desire;
    Else wert thou long since number'd with
      the dead!
    Else hadst thou spent, like other men, thy
      fire!

[8] Lasher: the water that rushes through the opening in a weir or lock, or the pool into which it falls.
  [9] Kine: cattle. [10] Teen: vexation.
  [11] Just-pausing Genius: either the tutelary spirit of an individual who guides him or her through life; or the spirit and character of the age itself.

The generations of thy peers are fled,
  And we ourselves shall go;
But thou possessest an immortal lot,
  And we imagine thee exempt from age
  And living as thou liv'st on Glanvil's page,
160 Because thou hadst—what we, alas! have not.

For early didst thou leave the world, with
      powers
  Fresh, undiverted to the world without,
    Firm to their mark, not spent on other
      things;
  Free from the sick fatigue, the languid doubt,
    Which much to have tried, in much been
      baffled, brings.
      O life unlike to ours!
Who fluctuate idly without term or scope,
  Of whom each strives, nor knows for what
    he strives,
    And each half lives a hundred different
      lives;
  Who wait like thee, but not, like thee, in
170   hope.

Thou waitest for the spark from heaven! and
    we,
  Light half-believers of our casual creeds,
  Who never deeply felt, nor clearly will'd,
  Whose insight never has borne fruit in deeds,
    Whose vague resolves never have been
      fulfill'd;
    For whom each year we see
  Breeds new beginnings, disappointments new;
  Who hesitate and falter life away,
  And lose to-morrow the ground won
    today—
180 Ah! do not we, wanderer! await it too?

Yes, we await it!—but it still delays,
  And then we suffer! and amongst us one,
  Who most has suffer'd, takes dejectedly
  His seat upon the intellectual throne;
  And all his store of sad experience he
    Lays bare of wretched days;
  Tells us his misery's birth and growth and
    signs,

  And how the dying spark of hope was fed,
  And how the breast was soothed, and how
    the head,
  And all his hourly varied anodynes.[12]   19

This for our wisest! and we others pine,
  And wish the long unhappy dream would
    end,
    And waive all claim to bliss, and try to
      bear;
  With close-lipp'd patience for our only
    friend,
    Sad patience, too near neighbour to
      despair—
    But none has hope like thine!
Thou through the fields and through the
    woods dost stray,
  Roaming the country-side, a truant boy,
  Nursing thy project in unclouded joy,
  And every doubt long blown by time away.   20

O born in days when wits were fresh and clear,
  And life ran gaily as the sparkling Thames;
    Before this strange disease of modern life,
  With its sick hurry, its divided aims,
    Its heads o'ertax'd, its palsied hearts, was
      rife—
    Fly hence, our contact fear!
Still fly, plunge deeper in the bowering wood!
  Averse, as Dido did with gesture stern
  From her false friend's approach in Hades
    turn,
Wave us away, and keep thy solitude![13]

Still nursing the unconquerable hope,
  Still clutching the inviolable shade,
    With a free, onward impulse brushing
      through,
  By night, the silver'd branches of the glade—
    Far on the forest-skirts, where none
      pursue.
    On some mild pastoral slope
Emerge, and resting on the moonlit pales[14]
  Freshen thy flowers as in former years
  With dew, or listen with enchanted ears,
  From the dark dingles,[15] to the nightingales!   22

---

[12] In 1883 Arnold said that these lines were written after he had read Goethe's autobiography, *Dichtung und Wahrheit* (1811–32), and referred to him. The lines seem a more apt description of Tennyson, who had succeeded Wordsworth as Poet Laureate after publishing *In Memoriam* in 1850.

[13] In Virgil's *Aeneid* Dido is the queen of Carthage who loves Aeneas. He eventually leaves her to continue the journey which will end in the founding of Rome, and she kills herself. When Aeneas later travels through the underworld he sees her shade, asks for a sign of farewell, but is left heavyhearted as she turns from him.

[14] Pales: fence posts.   [15] Dingle: small wooded valley.

But fly our paths, our feverish contact fly!
  For strong the infection of our mental strife,
    Which, though it gives no bliss, yet spoils
      for rest;
  And we should win thee from thy own fair
      life,
    Like us distracted, and like us unblest.
      Soon, soon thy cheer would die,
  Thy hopes grow timorous, and unfix'd thy
      powers,
    And thy clear aims be cross and shifting
      made;
    And then thy glad perennial youth would
      fade,
  Fade, and grow old at last, and die like ours.

Then fly our greetings, fly our speech and
      smiles!
—As some grave Tyrian trader,[16] from the
      sea,
  Descried at sunrise an emerging prow
  Lifting the cool-hair'd creepers stealthily,
    The fringes of a southward-facing brow
      Among the Ægæan isles;
  And saw the merry Grecian coaster come,
    Freighted with amber grapes, and Chian
      wine,
    Green, bursting figs, and tunnies steep'd in
      brine[17]—
  And knew the intruders on his ancient home,

The young light-hearted masters of the waves—
  And snatch'd his rudder, and shook out more
      sail;
  And day and night held on indignantly
  O'er the blue Midland waters with the gale,
    Betwixt the Syrtes and soft Sicily,
      To where the Atlantic raves
  Outside the western straits; and unbent sails
    There, where down cloudy cliffs, through
      sheets of foam,
    Shy traffickers, the dark Iberians come;
  And on the beach undid his corded bales.

1853

Persistency of Poetry[1]

Though the Muse be gone away,
Though she move not earth to-day,
Souls, erewhile who caught her word,
Ah! still harp on what they heard.

1867

Arnold did not publish this pastoral elegy to Clough until 1866, and the poem was probably not completed until shortly before its publication. Thyrsis is the name of a shepherd in one of the pastoral idylls of Theocritus, a Greek poet of the fourth century B.C. *who established many of the conventions of pastoral poetry. "Thyrsis" is in the tradition of Milton's "Lycidas" and Shelley's "Adonais," which also use the conventions of poetic shepherds and the regenerating rhythms of natural scenery in elegies for dead poets. Arnold regretted that these conventions, and his decision to recall his friend in the setting of their country walks around Oxford, required him to neglect "much in Clough (the whole prophet side, in fact). . . . I feel this so much that I do not send the poem to Mrs. Clough. Still Clough had this idyllic side, too; to deal with this suited my desire to deal again with that Cumner country: anyway, only so could I treat the matter this time" (from a letter quoted in* Commentary, *p. 216).*

Thyrsis

A Monody, to Commemorate the Author's Friend, Arthur Hugh Clough, Who Died at Florence, 1861

How changed is here each spot man makes or
      fills!
  In the two Hinkseys nothing keeps the same;
    The village street its haunted mansion
      lacks,
  And from the sign is gone Sibylla's name,[1]
    And from the roofs the twisted chimney-
      stacks—
      Are ye too changed, ye hills?
  See, 'tis no foot of unfamiliar men

---

[16] Tyre was the principal city of ancient Phoenecia, whose people were Mediterranean traders. The Aegean islands are in the Aegean, an arm of the Mediterranean between Greece and Asia Minor. The trader sails westward, between Sicily and the Syrtes, gulfs on the coast of Africa, through the Strait of Gibraltar to open trading with the inhabitants of the region now known as Spain.

[17] Chian wine: of the Aegean island of Chios. Tunnies: a large, common food fish of the Mediterranean.

[1] Without a title, this stanza served as a preface to Arnold's 1867 volume of poetry.

[1] The hostess of an inn in South Hinksey, a village near Oxford, was Sybella Curr, who died in 1860. The "haunted mansion" was in the village of North Hinksey. As in "The Scholar Gipsy" the place-names of villages, farms, hills, and locks on the upper Thames are those of the countryside around Oxford.

To-night from Oxford up your pathway
        strays!
    Here came I often, often, in old days—
10 Thyrsis and I; we still had Thyrsis then.

Runs it not here, the track by Childsworth
        Farm,
    Past the high wood, to where the elm-tree
        crowns
    The hill behind whose ridge the sunset
        flames?
The signal-elm,[2] that looks on Ilsley Downs,
    The Vale, the three lone weirs, the youth-
        ful Thames?—
        This winter-eve is warm,
    Humid the air! leafless, yet soft as spring,
    The tender purple spray on copse and
        briers!
    And that sweet city with her dreaming
        spires,
20 She needs not June for beauty's heightening,

Lovely all times she lies, lovely to-night!—
    Only, methinks, some loss of habit's power
    Befalls me wandering through this upland
        dim.
    Once pass'd I blindfold here, at any hour;
    Now seldom come I, since I came with him.
        That single elm-tree bright
    Against the west—I miss it! is it gone?
    We prized it dearly; while it stood, we said,
    Our friend, the Gipsy-Scholar, was not
        dead;
    While the tree lived, he in these fields lived
30   on.

Too rare, too rare, grow now my visits here,
    But once I knew each field, each flower, each
        stick;
    And with the country-folk acquaintance
        made
    By barn in threshing-time, by new-built rick.
    Here, too, our shepherd-pipes we first
        assay'd.
        Ah me! this many a year
    My pipe is lost, my shepherd's holiday!
    Needs must I lose them, needs with heavy
        heart
    Into the world and wave of men depart;
40 But Thyrsis of his own will went away.

It irk'd him to be here, he could not rest.
    He loved each simple joy the country yields,
        He loved his mates; but yet he could not
        keep,
    For that a shadow lour'd[3] on the fields,
        Here with the shepherds and the silly[4]
        sheep.
        Some life of men unblest
    He knew, which made him droop, and fill'd
        his head.
        He went; his piping took a troubled sound
        Of storms that rage outside our happy
        ground;
    He could not wait their passing, he is dead.

So, some tempestuous morn in early June,
    When the year's primal burst of bloom is
        o'er,
        Before the roses and the longest day—
    When garden-walks and all the grassy floor
        With blossoms red and white of fallen
        May[5]
        And chestnut-flowers are strewn—
    So have I heard the cuckoo's parting cry,
        From the wet field, through the vext
        garden-trees,
        Come with the volleying rain and tossing
        breeze:
    The bloom is gone, and with the bloom go I!

Too quick despairer, wherefore wilt thou go?
    Soon will the high Midsummer pomps come
        on,
        Soon will the musk carnations break and
        swell,
    Soon shall we have gold-dusted snapdragon,
        Sweet-William with his homely cottage-
        smell,
        And stocks[6] in fragrant blow;
    Roses that down the alleys shine afar,
        And open, jasmine-muffled lattices,
        And groups under the dreaming garden-
        trees,
    And the full moon, and the white evening-
        star.

He hearkens not! light comer, he is flown!
    What matters it? next year he will return,
        And we shall have him in the sweet spring-
        days,

---

[2] In an appendix in the *Commentary*, "The Scholar-Gipsy Country," by Sir Francis Wylie (pp. 351–373), Sir Francis identifies the tree of the poem as an oak that is visible for some distance from the path Arnold specifies in this stanza.
[3] Lour'd: frowned.   [4] Silly: helpless; a conventional epithet.
[5] May: the blossoms of the hawthorne tree.
[6] Stocks: gilly flowers, or an herb of the mustard family which bear sweet-scented flowers.

With whitening hedges, and uncrumpling
    fern,
    And blue-bells trembling by the forest-
        ways,
        And scent of hay new-mown.
But Thyrsis never more we swains shall see;
    See him come back, and cut a smoother
        reed,
        And blow a strain the world at last shall
        heed—
For Time, not Corydon, hath conquer'd
    thee![7]

Alack, for Corydon no rival now!—
    But when Sicilian shepherds lost a mate,
        Some good survivor with his flute would
        go,
    Piping a ditty sad for Bion's fate;[8]
        And cross the unpermitted ferry's flow,
        And relax Pluto's brow,
    And make leap up with joy the beauteous
        head
        Of Proserpine, among whose crowned hair
        Are flowers first open'd on Sicilian air,
    And flute his friend, like Orpheus, from the
        dead.[9]

O easy access to the hearer's grace
    When Dorian shepherds sang to Prosperine!
    For she herself had trod Sicilian fields,
She knew the Dorian water's gush divine,
    She knew each lily white which Enna[10]
        yields,
        Each rose with blushing face;
She loved the Dorian pipe, the Dorian strain.
    But ah, of our poor Thames she never
        heard!
    Her foot the Cumner cowslips never stirr'd;
And we should tease her with our plaint in
    vain!

Well! wind-dispersed and vain the words will
    be,
    Yet, Thyrsis, let me give my grief its hour
    In the old haunt, and find our tree-topp'd
        hill!
Who, if not I, for questing here hath power?
    I know the wood which hides the daffodil,
    I know the Fyfield tree,
I know what white, what purple fritillaries[11]
    The grassy harvest of the river-fields,
    Above by Ensham, down by Sandford,
        yields,
    And what sedged brooks are Thames's tribu-
    taries;   110

I know these slopes; who knows them if not
    I?—
    But many a dingle[12] on the loved hill-side,
        With thorns once studded, old, white-
        blossom'd trees,
    Where thick the cowslips grew, and far
        descried
        High tower'd the spikes of purple orchises,
        Hath since our day put by
    The coronals of that forgotten time;
        Down each green bank hath gone the
        ploughboy's team,
    And only in the hidden brookside gleam
Primroses, orphans of the flowery prime.   120

Where is the girl, who by the boatman's door,
    Above the locks, above the boating throng,
    Unmoor'd our skiff when through the
        Wytham flats,
    Red loosestrife and blond meadow-sweet[13]
        among
        And darting swallows and light water-
        gnats,
        We track'd the shy Thames shore?

[7] Corydon: another conventional name for a shepherd; in Virgil's seventh eclogue shepherds named Thyrsis and Corydon engage in a singing match.

[8] Bion was a pastoral poet of the second century B.C. who, according to legend, died of poison. Allott (pp. 501–502) remarks how closely lines 71–77 and 82–100 are modeled on the "Lament for Bion," attributed in the nineteenth century to Moscus, a contemporary of Bion. Moscus and Theocritus, like Bion, lived and wrote in Sicily, whose landscapes are the settings of their pastoral poetry.

[9] The underworld, the realm of the dead of classical mythology, is in some accounts (for example, in Virgil's *Aeneid*) entered by ferry over a river. Proserpine (Persephone), the daughter of the goddess of fertility and herself the goddess of growing things, was carried off by Pluto, the ruler of the underworld, but later permitted to spend part of the year on the surface of the earth. The song of Orpheus, a masterful musician, also persuaded the ruler of the underworld to permit Orpheus' dead wife to return to the upper world, but she returned to Hades when Orpheus disobeyed an injunction not to look behind him before he stepped onto the surface of the earth.

[10] Dorian refers to one of the races of the ancient Hellenic peoples. Enna is a vale in Sicily.

[11] Fritillaries: butterflies.   [12] Dingle: small wooded valley.

[13] Loosestrife is a kind of primrose; meadow-sweet is a plant like a rose that bears white or pink flowers.

Where are the mowers, who, as the tiny swell
  Of our boat passing heaved the river-grass,
    Stood with suspended scythe to see us
      pass?—
130 They are all gone, and thou art gone as well!

Yes, thou are gone! and round me too the night
  In ever-nearing circle weaves her shade.
    I see her veil draw soft across the day,
    I feel her slowly chilling breath invade
      The cheek grown thin, the brown hair
        sprent[14] with grey;
      I feel her finger light
  Laid pausefully upon life's headlong train;—
    The foot less prompt to meet the morning
      dew,
    The heart less bounding at emotion new,
  And hope, once crush'd, less quick to spring
140   again.

And long the way appears, which seem'd so
    short
  To the less practised eye of sanguine youth;
    And high the mountain-tops, in cloudy air,
  The mountain-tops where is the throne of
    Truth,
      Tops in life's morning-sun so bright and
        bare!
      Unbreachable the fort
  Of the long-batter'd world uplifts its wall;
    And strange and vain the earthly turmoil
      grows,
    And near and real the charm of thy repose,
150 And night as welcome as a friend would fall.

But hush! the upland hath a sudden loss
  Of quiet!—Look, adown the dusk hill-side,
    A troop of Oxford hunters going home,
    As in old days, jovial and talking, ride!
  From hunting with the Berkshire hounds
    they come.
      Quick! let me fly, and cross
  Into yon farther field!—'Tis done; and see,
    Back'd by the sunset, which doth glorify
    The orange and pale violet evening-sky,
160 Bare on its lonely ridge, the Tree! the Tree!

I take the omen! Eve lets down her veil,
  The white fog creeps from bush to bush
    about,
    The west unflushes, the high stars grow
      bright,
  And in the scatter'd farms the lights come
    out.
    I cannot reach the signal-tree to-night,
      Yet, happy omen, hail!
  Hear it from thy broad lucent Arno-vale[15]
    (For there thine earth-forgetting eyelids
    keep
    The morningless and unawakening sleep
  Under the flowery oleanders pale),   17

Hear it, O Thyrsis, still our tree is there!—
  Ah, vain! These English fields, this upland
    dim,
    These brambles pale with mist engar-
      landed,
  That lone, sky-pointing tree, are not for him;
    To a boon southern country he is fled,
      And now in happier air,
  Wandering with the great Mother's train
    divine
    (And purer or more subtle soul than thee,
    I trow, the mighty Mother doth not see)
  Within a folding of the Apennine,[16]   18

Thou hearest the immortal chants of old!—
  Putting his sickle to the perilous grain
    In the hot cornfield of the Phrygian king,
  For thee the Lityerses-song again
    Young Daphnis with his silver voice doth
      sing;
      Sings his Sicilian fold,
  His sheep, his hapless love, his blinded
    eyes—
    And how a call celestial round him rang,
    And heavenward from the fountain-brink
    he sprang,
  And all the marvel of the golden skies.[17] 19

There thou art gone, and me thou leavest here
  Sole in these fields! yet will I not despair.
    Despair I will not, while I yet descry

[14] Sprent: sprinkled.   [15] Arno: a river that flows through Florence, where Clough is buried.
[16] Great Mother: Rhea was the mother of many of the gods of classical mythology; her daughter Ceres (Demeter), the goddess of fertility, was also worshipped as the mother of Proserpine (Persephone). The Apennines are a mountain range in Italy.
[17] Arnold's note in 1869: "Daphnis, the ideal Sicilian shepherd of Greek pastoral poetry, was said to have followed into Phrygia his mistress Piplea, who had been carried off by robbers, and to have found her in the power of the king of Phrygia, Lityerses. Lityerses used to make strangers try a contest with him in reaping corn, and to put them to death if he overcame them. Hercules arrived in time to save Daphnis, took upon himself the reaping contest with Lityerses, overcame him, and slew him. The Lityerses song connected with this

'Neath the mild canopy of English air
 That lonely tree against the western sky.
  Still, still these slopes, 'tis clear,
Our Gipsy-Scholar haunts, outliving thee!
 Fields where soft sheep from cages pull the
  hay,
 Woods with anemonies in flower till May,
Know him a wanderer still; then why not
 me?   200

A fugitive and gracious light he seeks,
 Shy to illumine; and I seek it too.
  This does not come with houses or with
   gold,
 With place, with honour, and a flattering
   crew;
  'Tis not in the world's market bought and
   sold—
  But the smooth-slipping weeks
Drop by, and leave its seeker still untired;
 Out of the heed of mortals he is gone,
 He wends unfollow'd, he must house
  alone;
210 Yet on he fares, by his own heart inspired.

Thou too, O Thyrsis, on like quest wast
  bound;
 Thou wanderedst with me for a little hour!
  Men gave thee nothing; but this happy
   quest,
 If men esteem'd thee feeble, gave thee power,
  If men procured thee trouble, gave thee
   rest.
   And this rude Cumner ground,
 Its fir-topped Hurst, its farms, its quiet fields,
  Here cam'st thou in thy jocund youthful
   time,
  Here was thine height of strength, thy
   golden prime!
220 And still the haunt beloved a virtue yields.

What though the music of thy rustic flute
 Kept not for long its happy, country tone;
  Lost it too soon, and learnt a stormy note
 Of men contention-tost, of men who groan,
  Which task'd thy pipe too sore, and tired
   thy throat—
   It fail'd, and thou wast mute!

Yet hadst thou always visions of our light,
 And long with men of care thou couldst
  not stay,
 And soon thy foot resumed its wandering
  way,
 Left human haunt, and on alone till night. 230

Too rare, too rare, grow now my visits here!
 'Mid city-noise, not, as with thee of yore,
  Thyrsis! in reach of sheep-bells is my
   home.
 —Then through the great town's harsh,
   heart-wearying roar,
 Let in thy voice a whisper often come,
  To chase fatigue and fear:
 Why faintest thou? I wander'd till I died.
 Roam on! The light we sought is shining
  still.
 Dost thou ask proof? Our tree yet crowns
  the hill,
Our Scholar travels yet the loved hill-side. 240
          1866; 1867

Dover Beach

The sea is calm to-night.
The tide is full, the moon lies fair
Upon the straits;—on the French coast the
 light
Gleams and is gone; the cliffs of England stand,
Glimmering and vast, out in the tranquil bay.
Come to the window, sweet is the night-air!
Only, from the long line of spray
Where the sea meets the moon-blanch'd land,
Listen! you hear the grating roar
Of pebbles which the waves draw back, and
 fling,   10
At their return, up the high strand,
Begin, and cease, and then again begin,
With tremulous cadence slow, and bring
The eternal note of sadness in.

Sophocles long ago
Heard it on the Ægæan, and it brought
Into his mind the turbid ebb and flow
Of human misery;[1] we

---

tradition was . . . one of the early plaintive strains of Greek popular poetry, and used to be
sung by corn-reapers. Other traditions represented Daphnis as beloved by a nymph who exacted
from him an oath to love no one else. He fell in love with a princess, and was struck blind by
the jealous nymph. Mercury, who was his father, raised him to Heaven, and made a fountain
spring up in the place from which he ascended.''
 [1] It is not certain whether Arnold had in mind specific passages of the Greek tragedian
Sophocles (496?–406 B.C.) or simply cites him as emblematic of the human tragic condition.

Find also in the sound a thought,
Hearing it by this distant northern sea.

The Sea of Faith
Was once, too, at the full, and round earth's
    shore
Lay like the folds of a bright girdle furl'd.
But now I only hear
Its melancholy, long, withdrawing roar,
Retreating, to the breath
Of the night-wind, down the vast edges drear
And naked shingles[2] of the world.

Ah, love, let us be true
30 To one another! for the world, which seems
To lie before us like a land of dreams,
So various, so beautiful, so new,
Hath really neither joy, nor love, nor light,
Nor certitude, nor peace, nor help for pain;
And we are here as on a darkling plain
Swept with confused alarms of struggle and
    flight,
Where ignorant armies clash by night.[3]
                                    (1851?) 1867

Palladium[1]

Set where the upper streams of Simois[2] flow
Was the Palladium, high 'mid rock and wood;
And Hector was in Ilium, far below,[3]
And fought, and saw it not—but there it stood!

It stood, and sun and moonshine rain'd their
    light
On the pure columns of its glen-built hall.
Backward and forward roll'd the waves of fight
Round Troy—but while this stood, Troy could
    not fall.

So, in its lovely moonlight, lives the soul.
10 Mountains surround it, and sweet virgin air;
Cold plashing, past it, crystal waters roll;
We visit it by moments, ah, too rare!

We shall renew the battle in the plain
To-morrow;—red with blood with Xanthus be;
Hector and Ajax will be there again,
Helen will come upon the wall to see.

Then we shall rust in shade, or shine in strife,
And fluctuate 'twixt blind hopes and blind
    despairs,
And fancy that we put forth all our life,
And never know how with the soul it fares.

Still doth the soul, from its lone fastness high,
Upon our life a ruling effluence send.
And when it fails, fight as we will, we die;
And while it lasts, we cannot wholly end.
                                                1867

Growing Old

What is it to grow old?
Is it to lose the glory of the form,
The lustre of the eye?
Is it for beauty to forego her wreath?
—Yes, but not this alone.

Is it to feel our strength—
Not our bloom only, but our strength—decay?
Is it to feel each limb
Grow stiffer, every function less exact,
Each nerve more loosely strung?

Yes, this, and more; but not
Ah, 'tis not what in youth we dream'd 'twould
    be!
'Tis not to have our life
Mellow'd and soften'd as with sunset-glow,
A golden day's decline.

'Tis not to see the world
As from a height, with rapt prophetic eyes,
And heart profoundly stirr'd;
And weep, and feel the fulness of the past,
The years that are no more.

    [2] Shingles: beaches of coarse rounded stones.
    [3] Thucydides, a Greek historian of the fifth century B.C., describes such a battle in his history of the Peloponnesian War, which was translated by Arnold's father in 1830–35. The battle ended with soldiers in the same army fighting one another, for they mistrusted, in Thomas Arnold's translation, "their knowing who was friend and who was foe."
    [1] The Palladium was an image of the goddess Pallas Athena in the city of Troy. So long as the image remained in the city, Troy could not be taken. Eventually the image was stolen by the Greeks.
    [2] Simois: like Xanthus (line 14) a river near Troy.
    [3] Hector: the son of Priam, ruler of Troy (Ilium). He fought with Ajax, one of the Greek heroes, but was finally killed by Achilles, the great warrior of the Greeks.

It is to spend long days
And not once feel that we were ever young;
It is to add, immured
In the hot prison of the present, month
To month with weary pain.

It is to suffer this,
And feel but half, and feebly, what we feel.
Deep in our hidden heart
Festers the dull remembrance of a change,
But no emotion—none.

It is—last stage of all—
When we are frozen up within, and quite
The phantom of ourselves,
To hear the world applaud the hollow ghost
Which blamed the living man.

                                                 1867

The Progress of Poesy

A Variation[1]

Youth rambles on life's arid mount,
And strikes the rock, and finds the vein,
And brings the water from the fount,
The fount which shall not flow again.

The man mature with labour chops
For the bright stream a channel grand,
And sees not that the sacred drops
Ran off and vanish'd out of hand.

And then the old man totters nigh,
And feebly rakes among the stones.
The mount is mute, the channel dry;
And down he lays his weary bones.

                                                 1867

A Nameless Epitaph

Ask not my name, O friend!
That Being only, which hath known each man
From the beginning, can
Remember each unto the end.

                                                 1867

The Last Word

Creep into thy narrow bed,
Creep, and let no more be said!
Vain thy onset! all stands fast.
Thou thyself must break at last.

Let the long contention cease!
Geese are swans, and swans are geese.
Let them have it how they will!
Thou art tired; best be still.

They out-talk'd thee, hiss'd thee, tore thee?
Better men fared thus before thee;   10
Fired their ringing shot and pass'd,
Hotly charged—and sank at last.

Charge once more, then, and be dumb!
Let the victors, when they come,
When the forts of folly fall,
Find thy body by the wall!

                                                 1867

Epilogue to Lessing's Laocoön

One morn as through Hyde Park we walk'd,
My friend and I, by chance we talk'd
Of Lessing's famed Laocoön;[1]
And after we awhile had gone
In Lessing's track, and tried to see
What painting is, what poetry—
Diverging to another thought,
"Ah," cries my friend, "but who hath taught
Why music and the other arts
Oftener perform aright their parts   10
Than poetry? why she, than they,
Fewer fine successes can display?

"For 'tis so, surely! Even in Greece,
Where best the poet framed his piece,
Even in that Phœbus-guarded ground[2]
Pausanias[3] on his travels found
Good poems, if he look'd, more rare
(Though many) than good statues were—
For these, in truth, were everywhere.
Of bards full many a stroke divine   20
In Dante's, Petrarch's, Tasso's line,

---

[1] The variation is on the poem of the same title by Thomas Gray (1716–1771).

[1] *Laokoon* (1766), by Gotthold Ephraim Lessing (1729–1781), is a treatise in esthetics which distinguishes between the properties and effects of poetry and the plastic arts of painting and sculpture; the latter, unlike poetry, can treat only of single, fixed moments in time.

[2] Phœbus: a name of Apollo, the god of song and poetry who is with this name also associated with the sun.

[3] Pausanias: a traveler in the second century A.D. who wrote an account of Greece.

The land of Ariosto show'd;[4]
And yet, e'en there, the canvas glow'd
With triumphs, a yet ampler brood,
Of Raphael and his brotherhood.
And nobly perfect, in our day
Of haste, half-work, and disarray,
Profound yet touching, sweet yet strong,
Hath risen Goethe's, Wordsworth's song;
30 Yet even I (and none will bow
Deeper to these) must needs allow,
They yield us not, to soothe our pains,
Such multitude of heavenly strains
As from the kings of sound are blown,
Mozart, Beethoven, Mendelssohn."

While thus my friend discoursed, we pass
Out of the path, and take the grass.
The grass had still the green of May,
And still the unblacken'd elms were gay;
40 The kine[5] were resting in the shade,
The flies a summer-murmur made.
Bright was the morn and south the air;
The soft-couch'd cattle were as fair
As those which pastured by the sea,
That old-world morn, in Sicily,
When on the beach the Cyclops lay,
And Galatea from the bay
Mock'd her poor lovelorn giant's lay.[6]
"Behold," I said, "the painter's sphere!
50 The limits of his art appear.
The passing group, the summer-morn,
The grass, the elms, that blossom'd thorn—
Those cattle couch'd, or, as they rise,
Their shining flanks, their liquid eyes—
These, or much greater things, but caught
Like these, and in one aspect brought!
In outward semblance he must give
A moment's life of things that live;
Then let him choose his moment well,
60 With power divine its story tell."

Still we walk'd on, in thoughtful mood,
And now upon the bridge we stood.
Full of sweet breathings was the air,
Of sudden stirs and pauses fair.
Down o'er the stately bridge the breeze

Came rustling from the garden-trees
And on the sparkling waters play'd;
Light-plashing waves an answer made,
And mimic boats their haven near'd.
Beyond, the Abbey-towers[7] appear'd,   7
By mist and chimneys unconfined,
Free to the sweep of light and wind;
While through their earth-moor'd nave below
Another breath of wind doth blow,
Sound as of wandering breeze—but sound
In laws by human artists bound.
"The world of music!" I exclaim'd:—
"This breeze that rustles by, that famed
Abbey recall it! what a sphere
Large and profound, hath genius here!   8
The inspired musician what a range,
What power of passion, wealth of change!
Some source of feeling he must choose
And its lock'd fount of beauty use,
And through the stream of music tell
Its else unutterable spell;
To choose it rightly is his part,
And press into its inmost heart.

"*Miserere, Domine!*[8]
The words are utter'd, and they flee.   9
Deep is their penitential moan,
Mighty their pathos, but 'tis gone.
They have declared the spirit's sore
Sore load, and words can do no more.
Beethoven takes them then—those two
Poor, bounded words—and makes them new;
Infinite makes them, makes them young;
Transplants them to another tongue,
Where they can now, without constraint,
Pour all the soul of their complaint,   10
And roll adown a channel large
The wealth divine they have in charge.
Page after page of music turn,
And still they live and still they burn,
Eternal, passion-fraught, and free—
Miserere, Domine!"

Onward we moved, and reach'd the Ride[9]
Where gaily flows the human tide.
Afar, in rest the cattle lay;

[4] Ariosto: an early sixteenth-cetury Italian poet; Dante (1265–1321) and Petrarch (1304–1374) were his great predecessors, Tasso (1544–1595) his successor, and the painter Raphael (1483–1520) his contemporary.
[5] Kine: cattle.
[6] The third century B.C. pastoral poet Theocritus, who lived and wrote in Sicily and Greece, tells the story of the Cyclops, a one-eyed giant, who neglected his herds to pine futilely for the sea nymph Galatea.
[7] Abbey: Wesminster Abbey.
[8] *Miserere, Domine!:* "Lord, have mercy!": words of the Mass.
[9] The Ride: a part of the park fenced off for carriages and horsemen; it was a fashionable gathering place.

10   We heard, afar, faint music play;
But agitated, brisk, and near,
Men, with their stream of life, were here.
Some hang upon the rails, and some
On foot behind them go and come.
This through the Ride upon his steed
Goes slowly by, and this at speed.
The young, the happy, and the fair,
The old, the sad, the worn, were there;
Some vacant, and some musing went,
20   And some in talk and merriment.
Nods, smiles, and greetings, and farewells!
And now and then, perhaps, there swells
A sigh, a tear—but in the throng
All changes fast, and hies along.
Hies, ah, from whence, what native ground?
And to what goal, what ending, bound?
"Behold, at last the poet's sphere!
But who," I said, "suffices here?

"For, ah! so much he has to do;
30   Be painter and musician too!
The aspect of the moment show,
The feeling of the moment know!
The aspect not, I grant, express
Clear as the painter's art can dress;
The feeling not, I grant, explore
So deep as the musician's lore—
But clear as words can make revealing,
And deep as words can follow feeling.
But, ah! then comes his sorest spell
40   Of toil—he must life's *movement* tell!
The thread which binds it all in one,
And not its separate parts alone.
The *movement* he must tell of life,
Its pain and pleasure, rest and strife;
His eye must travel down, at full,
The long, unpausing spectacle;
With faithful unrelaxing force
Attend it from its primal source,
From change to change and year to year
50   Attend it of its mid career,
Attend it to the last repose
And solemn silence of its close.

"The cattle rising from the grass
His thought must follow where they pass;
The penitent with anguish bow'd
His thought must follow through the crowd.
Yes! all this eddying, motely throng[10]
That sparkles in the sun along,
Girl, statesman, merchant, soldier bold,
60   Master and servant, young and old,

[10] Motely throng: motley.

Grave, gay, child, parent, husband, wife,
He follows home, and lives their life.

"And many, many are the souls
Life's movement fascinates, controls;
It draws them on, they cannot save
Their feet from its alluring wave;
They cannot leave it, they must go
With its unconquerable flow.
But ah! how few, of all that try
This mighty march, do aught but die!   170
For ill-endow'd for such a way,
Ill-stored in strength, in wits, are they.
They faint, they stagger to and fro,
And wandering from the stream they go;
In pain, in terror, in distress,
They see, all round, a wilderness.
Sometimes a momentary gleam
They catch of the mysterious stream;
Sometimes, a second's space, their ear
The murmur of its waves doth hear.   180
That transient glimpse in song they say,
But not as painter can pourtray—
That transient sound in song they tell,
But not, as the musician, well.
And when at last their snatches cease,
And they are silent and at peace,
The stream of life's majestic whole
Hath ne'er been mirror'd on their soul.

"Only a few the life-stream's shore
With safe unwandering feet explore;   190
Untired its movement bright attend,
Follow its windings to the end.
Then from its brimming waves their eye
Drinks up delighted ecstasy,
And its deep-toned, melodious voice
For ever makes their ear rejoice.
They speak! the happiness divine
They feel, runs o'er in every line;
Its spell is round them like a shower—
It gives them pathos, gives them power.   200
No painter yet hath such a way,
Nor no musician made, as they,
And gather'd on immortal knolls
Such lovely flowers for cheering souls.
Beethoven, Raphael, cannot reach
The charm which Homer, Shakespeare, teach.
To these, to these, their thankful race
Gives, then, the first, the fairest place;
And brightest is their glory's sheen,
For greatest hath their labour been."   210

1867

Rugby Chapel

November 1857[1]

Coldly, sadly descends
The autumn-evening. The field
Strewn with its dank yellow drifts
Of wither'd leaves, and the elms,
Fade into dimness apace,
Silent;—hardly a shout
From a few boys late at their play!
The lights come out in the street,
In the school-room windows;—but cold,
10   Solemn, unlighted, austere,
Through the gathering darkness, arise
The chapel-walls, in whose bound
Thou, my father! art laid.

There thou dost lie, in the gloom
Of the autumn evening. But ah!
That word, *gloom,* to my mind
Brings thee back, in the light
Of thy radiant vigour, again;
In the gloom of November we pass'd
20   Days not dark at thy side;
Seasons impair'd not the ray
Of thy buoyant cheerfulness clear.
Such thou wast! and I stand
In the autumn evening, and think
Of bygone autumns with thee.

Fifteen years have gone round
Since thou arosest to tread,
In the summer-morning, the road
Of death, at a call unforeseen,
30   Sudden. For fifteen years,
We who till then in thy shade
Rested as under the boughs
Of a mighty oak, have endured
Sunshine and rain as we might,
Bare, unshaded, alone,
Lacking the shelter of thee.

O strong soul, by what shore
Tarriest thou now? For that force,
Surely, has not been left vain!
40   Somewhere, surely, afar,
In the sounding labour-house vast
Of being, is practised that strength,
Zealous, beneficent, firm!

Yes, in some far-shining sphere,
Conscious or not of the past,
Still thou performest the word
Of the Spirit in whom thou dost live—
Prompt, unwearied, as here!
Still thou upraisest with zeal
The humble good from the ground,
Sternly repressest the bad!
Still, like a trumpet, dost rouse
Those who with half-open eyes
Tread the border-land dim
'Twixt vice and virtue; reviv'st,
Succourest!—this was thy work,
This was thy life upon earth.

What is the course of the life
Of mortal men on the earth?—
Most men eddy about
Here and there—eat and drink,
Chatter and love and hate,
Gather and squander, are raised
Aloft, are hurl'd in the dust,
Striving blindly, achieving
Nothing; and then they die—
Perish;—and no one asks
Who or what they have been,
More than he asks what waves,
In the moonlit solitudes mild
Of the midmost Ocean, have swell'd,
Foam'd for a moment, and gone.

And there are some, whom a thirst
Ardent, unquenchable, fires,
Not with the crowd to be spent,
Not without aim to go round
In an eddy of purposeless dust,
Effort unmeaning and vain.
Ah yes! some of us strive
Not without action to die
Fruitless, but something to snatch
From dull oblivion, nor all
Glut the devouring grave!
We, we have chosen our path—
Path to a clear-purposed goal,
Path of advance!—but it leads
A long, steep journey, through sunk
Gorges, o'er mountains in snow.
Cheerful, with friends, we set forth—
Then, on the height, comes the storm.
Thunder crashes from rock

---

[1] Thomas Arnold died in 1842. Arnold apparently began to plan this elegy to him in 1857, when he read Thomas Hughes' *Tom Brown's Schooldays* (1857), a novel about Rugby which contains a description of Thomas Arnold's funeral. Arnold later wrote to his mother that it was an opinion expressed in 1858 by one of the reviewers of Hughes' novel, "of Papa's being a narrow bustling fanatic, which moved me first to the poem" (quoted in *Commentary,* p. 240).

To rock, the cataracts reply,
Lightnings dazzle our eyes.
Roaring torrents have breach'd
The track, the stream-bed descends
In the place where the wayfarer once
Planted his footstep—the spray
Boils o'er its borders! aloft
The unseen snow-beds dislodge
Their hanging ruin; alas,
Havoc is made in our train!
Friends, who set forth at our side,
Falter, are lost in the storm.
We, we only are left!
With frowning foreheads, with lips
Sternly compress'd, we strain on,
On—and at nightfall at last
Come to the end of our way,
To the lonely inn 'mid the rocks;
Where the gaunt and taciturn host
Stands on the threshold, the wind
Shaking his thin white hairs—
Holds his lantern to scan
Our storm-beat figures, and asks:
Whom in our party we bring?
Whom we have left in the snow?

Sadly we answer: We bring
Only ourselves! we lost
Sight of the rest in the storm.
Hardly ourselves we fought through,
Stripp'd, without friends, as we are.
Friends, companions, and train,
The avalanche swept from our side.

But thou would'st not *alone*
Be saved, my father! *alone*
Conquer and come to thy goal,
Leaving the rest in the wild.
We were weary, and we
Fearful, and we in our march
Fain to drop down and to die.
Still thou turnedst, and still
Beckonedst the trembler, and still
Gavest the weary thy hand.

If, in the paths of the world,
Stones might have wounded thy feet,
Toil or dejection have tried
Thy spirit, of that we saw

Nothing—to us thou wast still
Cheerful, and helpful, and firm!
Therefore to thee it was given   140
Many to save with thyself;
And, at the end of thy day,
O faithful shepherd! to come,
Bringing thy sheep in thy hand.[2]

And through thee I believe
In the noble and great who are gone;
Pure souls honour'd and blest
By former ages, who else—
Such, so soulless, so poor,
Is the race of men whom I see—   150
Seem'd but a dream of the heart,
Seem'd but a cry of desire.
Yes! I believe that there lived
Others like thee in the past,
Not like the men of the crowd
Who all round me to-day
Bluster or cringe, and make life
Hideous, and arid, and vile;
But souls temper'd with fire,
Fervent, heroic, and good,   160
Helpers and friends of mankind.

Servants of God!—or sons
Shall I not call you? because
Not as servants ye knew
Your Father's innermost mind,
His, who unwillingly sees
One of his little ones lost—
Yours is the praise, if mankind
Hath not as yet in its march
Fainted, and fallen, and died!   170

See! In the rocks of the world
Marches the host of mankind,
A feeble, wavering line.
Where are they tending?—A God
Marshall'd them, gave them their goal.
Ah, but the way is so long!
Years they have been in the wild!
Sore thirst plagues them, the rocks,
Rising all round, overawe;
Factions divide them, their host   180
Threatens to break, to dissolve.
—Ah, keep, keep them combined!
Else, of the myriads who fill

[2] Allott (p. 449) quotes a description of Thomas Arnold's conduct during walks in the Lake District from A. P. Stanley's *Life of Thomas Arnold* (1844): ". . . himself the guide and life of the party, always on the look out how best to break the ascent by gentle stages, comforting the little ones in their falls, and helping forward those who were tired, himself always keeping with the laggers, that none might strain their strength."

That army, not one shall arrive;
Sole they shall stray; in the rocks
Stagger for ever in vain,
Die one by one in the waste.

Then, in such hour of need
Of your fainting, dispirited race,
190 Ye, like angels, appear,
Radiant with ardour divine!
Beacons of hope, ye appear!
Languor is not in your heart,
Weakness is not in your word,
Weariness not on your brow.
Ye alight in our van! at your voice,
Panic, despair, flee away.
Ye move through the ranks, recall
The stragglers, refresh the outworn,
200 Praise, re-inspire the brave!
Order, courage, return.
Eyes rekindling, and prayers,
Follow your steps as ye go.
Ye fill up the gaps in our files,
Strengthen the wavering line,
Stablish, continue our march,
On, to the bound of the waste,
On, to the City of God.

                                                    1867

Stanzas from the Grande Chartreuse[1]

Through Alpine meadows soft-suffused
With rain, where thick the crocus blows,
Past the dark forges long disused,
The mule-track from Saint Laurent[2] goes.
The bridge is cross'd, and slow we ride,
Through forest, up the mountain-side.

The autumnal evening darkens round,
The wind is up, and drives the rain;
While, hark! far down, with strangled sound
10 Doth the Dead Guier's[3] stream complain,
Where that wet smoke, among the woods,
Over his boiling cauldron broods.

Swift rush the spectral vapours white
Past limestone scars with ragged pines,
Showing—then blotting from our sight!—
Halt—through the cloud-drift something
     shines!
High in the valley, wet and drear,
The huts of Courrerie appear.

Strike leftward! cries our guide; and higher
Mounts up the stony forest-way.
At last the encircling trees retire;
Look! through the showery twilight grey
What pointed roofs are these advance?—
A palace of the Kings of France?

Approach, for what we seek is here!
Alight, and sparely sup, and wait
For rest in this outbuilding near;
Then cross the sward and reach that gate.
Knock; pass the wicket! Thou art come
To the Carthusians' world-famed home.

The silent courts, where night and day
Into their stone-carved basins cold
The splashing icy fountains play—
The humid corridors behold!
Where, ghostlike in the deepening night,
Cowl'd forms brush by in gleaming white.

The chapel, where no organ's peal
Invests the stern and naked prayer—
With penitential cries they kneel
And wrestle; rising then, with bare
And white uplifted faces stand,
Passing the Host from hand to hand;

Each takes, and then his visage wan
Is buried in his cowl once more.
The cells!—the suffering Son of Man
Upon the wall—the knee-worn floor—
And where they sleep, that wooden bed,
Which shall their coffin be, when dead![4]

The library, where tract and tome
Not to feed priestly pride are there,

---

[1] The Grande Chartreuse, in the French Alps, was the principal monastery of the Carthusians, a monastic order founded in the eleventh century. The monastery itself was built in the seventeenth century. Arnold visited it in 1851, and published this poem in a magazine in 1855. He republished it, with a few significant changes, in 1867.
[2] Saint Laurent: a village below the monastery. Courrerie (line 18) is a village in the mountains near it.
[3] Dead Guier: The Guiers Mort is a river that begins near the monastery and flows into the Guiers Vif in the valley below it.
[4] Tinker and Lowry in their *Commentary* remark Arnold's inaccuracy in describing the practices of the monks, who did not pass the communion host from hand to hand and did not sleep in their coffins (pp. 249–252).

To hymn the conquering march of Rome,
Nor yet to amuse, as ours are!
They paint of souls the inner strife,
Their drops of blood, their death in life.

The garden, overgrown—yet mild,
See, fragrant herbs are flowering there!
Strong children of the Alpine wild
Whose culture is the brethren's care;
Of human tasks their only one,
And cheerful works beneath the sun.

Those halls, too, destined to contain
Each its own pilgrim-host of old,
From England, Germany, or Spain—
All are before me! I behold
The House, the Brotherhood austere!
—And what am I, that I am here?

For rigorous teachers seized my youth,
And purged its faith, and trimm'd its fire,
Show'd me the high, white star of Truth,[5]
There bade me gaze, and there aspire.
Even now their whispers pierce the gloom:
What dost thou in this living tomb?

Forgive me, masters of the mind!
At whose behest I long ago
So much unlearnt, so much resign'd—
I come not here to be your foe!
I seek these anchorites, not in ruth,
To curse and to deny your truth;

Not as their friend, or child, I speak!
But as, on some far northern strand,
Thinking of his own Gods, a Greek
In pity and mournful awe might stand
Before some fallen Runic stone[6]—
For both were faiths, and both are gone.

Wandering between two worlds, one dead,
The other powerless to be born,
With nowhere yet to rest my head,
Like these, on earth I wait forlorn.
Their faith, my tears, the world deride—
I come to shed them at their side.

Oh, hide me in your gloom profound,
Ye solemn seats of holy pain!
Take me, cowl'd forms, and fence me round,
Till I possess my soul again;
Till free my thoughts before me roll,
Not chafed by hourly false control!

For the world cries your faith is now
But a dead time's exploded dream;
My melancholy, sciolists[7] say,
Is a pass'd mode, an outworn theme—   100
As if the world had ever had
A faith, or sciolists been sad!

Ah, if it *be* pass'd, take away,
At least, the restlessness, the pain;
Be man henceforth no more a prey
To these out-dated stings again!
The nobleness of grief is gone—
Ah, leave us not the fret alone!

But—if you cannot give us ease—
Last of the race of them who grieve   110
Here leave us to die out with these
Last of the people who believe!
Silent, while years engrave the brow;
Silent—the best are silent now.

Achilles ponders in his tent,[8]
The kings of modern thought are dumb;
Silent they are, though not content,
And wait to see the future come.
They have the grief men had of yore,
But they contend and cry no more.   120

Our fathers water'd with their tears[9]
This sea of time whereon we sail,
Their voices were in all men's ears
Who pass'd within their puissant hail.
Still the same ocean round us raves,
But we stand mute, and watch the waves.

For what avail'd it, all the noise
And outcry of the former men?—
Say, have their sons achieved more joys,
Say, is life lighter now than then?   130

[5] In 1855 these lines read:

> "And prun'd its faith and quench'd its fire,
> Showed me the pale cold star of Truth."

[6] Runic stone: a stone inscribed with characters.
[7] Sciolists: intellectual pretenders.
[8] Achilles: in Homer's *Iliad* the great hero of the Greeks withdraws from the siege of Troy to sulk in his tent because his wishes have been frustrated.
[9] In 1855: "Their fathers"; and line 126: "They stand."

The sufferers died, they left their pain—
The pangs which tortured them remain.

What helps it now, that Byron bore,
With haughty scorn which mock'd the smart,
Through Europe to the Ætolian shore
The pageant of his bleeding heart?
That thousands counted every groan,[10]
And Europe made his woe her own?

What boots it, Shelley! that the breeze
140 Carried thy lovely wail away,
Musical through Italian trees
Which fringe thy soft blue Spezzian bay?[11]
Inheritors of thy distress
Have restless hearts one throb the less?

Or are we easier, to have read,
O Obermann! the sad, stern page,
Which tells us how thou hidd'st thy head
From the fierce tempest of thine age
In the lone brakes of Fontainebleau,
150 Or chalets near the Alpine snow?[12]

Ye slumber in your silent grave!—
The world, which for an idle day
Grace to your mood of sadness gave,
Long since hath flung her weeds away.
The eternal trifler breaks your spell;
But we—we learnt your lore too well!

Years hence, perhaps, may dawn an age,
More fortunate, alas! than we,
Which without hardness will be sage,
160 And gay without frivolity.
Sons of the world, oh, speed those years;
But, while we wait, allow our tears!

Allow them! We admire with awe
The exulting thunder of your race;
You give the universe your law,
You triumph over time and space!
Your pride of life, your tireless powers,
We laud them, but they are not ours.[13]

We are like children rear'd in shade
170 Beneath some old-world abbey wall,

Forgotten in a forest-glade,
And secret from the eyes of all.
Deep, deep the greenwood round them waves,
Their abbey, and its close of graves!

But, where the road runs near the stream,
Oft through the trees they catch a glance
Of passing troops in the sun's beam—
Pennon, and plume, and flashing lance!
Forth to the world those soldiers fare,
To life, to cities, and to war!   1

And through the wood, another way,
Faint bugle-notes from far are borne,
Where hunters gather, staghounds bay,
Round some fair forest-lodge at morn.
Gay dames are there, in sylvan green;
Laughter and cries—those notes between!

The banners flashing through the trees
Make their blood dance and chain their eyes;
That bugle-music on the breeze
Arrests them with a charm'd surprise.   1
Banner by turns and bugle woo:
Ye shy recluses, follow too!

O children, what do ye reply?—
"Action and pleasure, will ye roam
Through these secluded dells to cry
And call us?—but too late ye come!
Too late for us your call ye blow,
Whose bent was taken long ago.

"Long since we pace this shadow'd nave;
We watch those yellow tapers shine,   2
Emblems of hope over the grave,[14]
In the high altar's depth divine;
The organ carries to our ear
Its accents of another sphere.

"Fenced early in this cloistral round
Of reverie, of shade, of prayer,
How should we grow in other ground?
How should we flower in foreign air?
—Pass, banners, pass, and bugles, cease;
And leave our desert[15] to its peace!"

                                     1855; 1867 2

[10] Byron left England in 1816, in part because of the collapse of his tumultuous year-long marriage and because of slanders about his relationship with his half sister. He lived mostly in Italy, went to Greece in 1823 to assist in an insurrection against the Turks, and died the next year in the Aetolian region of Greece.
[11] Shelley was drowned in 1822 in the Gulf of Spezzia in Italy.
[12] See Arnold's note to the "Stanzas in Memory of the Author of 'Obermann'" (p. 457 above). Brakes: marshy land.
[13] In 1855: "They awe us"; later (1867) "We mark them"; then (1877) "We praise them."
[14] In 1855: "Emblems of light above the grave."
[15] 1855: "And leave our forest to its peace!"

Coventry Patmore
1823–1896

COVENTRY PATMORE enjoyed two literary reputations during his lifetime. The more prominent was as the author of *The Angel in the House,* one of the most popular books of poetry published in England in the second half of the nineteenth century; by the end of the century it had sold about a quarter of a million copies after its separately titled and published sections were published together in 1863. The second was a more select esteem among writers and painters at two different times in his life. As a young poet he was enrolled as one of the Immortals in the pantheon of the Pre-Raphaelites (see pp. 559–561 for a brief account of this group of writers and painters), and Tennyson and other poets also admired the intense, sometimes fanciful particularity of his early poems. Later in his life, after the publication of *The Angel in the House,* he began writing a series of odes whose unusual prosody and strongly metaphoric nature engaged the attention of Gerard Manley Hopkins and Robert Bridges. When he wrote *The Angel in the House* Patmore left behind the decorated fancies of his early poems and made a quiet, accessible, and reassuring poetry out of the ordinary relationships and circumstances of men and women, especially their domestic relationships in courtship and within the sanctity of marriage. In the odes he wrote late in his life he made it clear that he took that last phrase literally. He imagined the love of men and women, including its sexual expression, as a type of the love of God for humans, and in the odes of his last years he returned to a highly symbolic and emphatically measured language appropriate to his conception of the human and mundane as the vesture or sacrament of the divine.

Patmore's father was Peter George Patmore, a literary journalist, dramatic critic, and familiar of William Hazlitt, Charles Lamb, and other writers in London during the 1820s and 1830s. His mother was a Scot, with some money of her own, a woman of rigid religious views

and conduct. Patmore was born in the country near London, and until he was sixteen years old he was educated mostly at home. He was then sent to Paris for a while to study art, and he returned to London in 1840 to begin the literary or artistic career for which his father and his father's life had without much conscious will been preparing him. Patmore published his first volme of *Poems* in 1844. They were heavily influenced by Keats and the 1842 poems of Tennyson, and they were attacked and praised for their highly literary finish and extravagance. In 1845 Patmore's father lost his money in financial speculations, and Patmore went to work at literary journalism; he continued to write prose during the rest of his life, some of it collected in two volumes, *Principle in Art* and *Religio Poetae,* in 1889 and 1893. A year later he was appointed to a post in the British Museum, and in the next year he married the daughter of a Congregationalist minister. He became a friend of Tennyson (who read to him from the manuscript of *In Memoriam*), Carlyle, Ruskin, and Robert Browning. The Pre-Raphaelite journal, *The Germ,* invited his contributions, and he helped persuade Ruskin to defend the Pre-Raphaelites when their paintings were attacked in 1851. Patmore himself reviewed the frescoes Dante Gabriel Rossetti and others painted at Oxford in 1857.

He came to dislike the poems of his first volume, most of which he never reprinted in his later collected editions, and in his poetry of the 1840s and 1850s he started to work toward the contemporary detail and simple, regular, eight-beat line of *The Angel of the House,* deliberately chosen, he later said, because so much of contemporary poetry was antique and quaint. The first part of the poem was published in 1854, the second in 1856, and the two parts he entitled "The Victories of Love," the story of an unhappy marriage finally strengthened by its troubles, were published in 1860 and 1861. The four parts were published together in 1863, and the volume remained in print and popular for the rest of the century.

Patmore's wife died in 1862. Still saddened by his loss, he went to Rome in 1864, where he took a step long pendant and converted to Roman Catholicism. He also met the woman who was to become his second wife in Rome, a Roman Catholic daughter of an English landowner who herself possessed a considerable fortune. They were married in 1864, and Patmore resigned from the British Museum and moved to a country estate. He was to live out of London the rest of his life. (He was also to marry a third time after the death of his second wife in 1880.) He began reading extensively in both erotic literature and the literature of religious mysticism. He had long been interested in prosody and in sixteenth- and seventeenth-century British poetry. He had planned to continue the story of *The Angel in the House* in two more parts, but instead he began to write the odes he eventually published in *The Unknown Eros* in 1877 and (enlarged) in 1878. Patmore's odes were not popular when they were first published, although they picked up a currency when a collected edition of his poems published in 1886 went into five more editions in the next decade. He wrote only a few poems after he published the 1878 collection of his odes. Even in the last flurry of his fame in the 1890s his odes remained the work of a rather special poet whose final development was thoughtfully attended to largely by late-century Roman Catholic writers and readers and poets like Bridges and Hopkins who were working out their own experiments in prosody.

Patmore's theories about the meters of English verse are subtle and complicated. In brief, he wanted a line and verse form unbounded by the stresses and length of conventional meters but given shape by irregular rhymes and carefully calculated stresses in verse lines of varying length. He measured his lines not by the number of syllables each contained but by the time required to speak them, and he threaded short lines in and out of longer ones in order to slow the voice in these lines and emphasize their stresses. He used his liberation from conventional verse forms and prosody to write poems that are often quite direct in their language and figures, such as his poems of personal loss ("Departure"). He also used the freedom of his odes to elaborate his idea that the body and all its properties and events are emblems of a transcendental reality that makes human life holy. In all his late poems, as in his early poetry and in *The Angel in the House,* he participated in and advanced some of the major purposes of the poetry of his period. He thought that poetry was an extraordinary power that could urge his contemporaries toward truth by revealing that the objects of the material and immediate, the truly astonishing excitements of the body and of human existence, were sacraments of transcendental meaning. His talent could not sustain the long or intricate forms he thought appropriate to the size of his idea of poetry. But he often enough achieved rhythms and figures of a telling rightness that made good his persistent claim that the poet and his language were the unique bearers of a fundamental and necessary revelation.

EDITIONS

The texts reprinted below are those of the 1886 edition of Patmore's poems, which is consistent with the standard edition, *The Poems of Coventry Patmore,* edited by Frederick Page (1949). Patmore's essays were collected in an edition published in 1913; his "Essay on English Metrical Law" was republished in 1961, edited by M. A. Roth. Some of Patmore's letters to Hopkins are printed in *Further Letters of Gerard Manley Hopkins, Including His Correspondence with Patmore,* edited by C. C. Abbott (revised edition, 1956).

BIOGRAPHY AND CRITICISM

The standard biography is Derek Patmore's *The Life and Times of Coventry Patmore* (1949); Derek Patmore is the poet's greatgrandson. Basil Champneys' *Memoirs and Correspondence of Coventry Patmore* (1900) and Edmund Gosse's *Coventry Patmore* (1905) contain some personal reminiscences.

J. C. Reid's *The Mind and Art of Coventry Patmore* (1957) is the most complete and intelligent study of Patmore's poetry and esthetics, including a full exposition of Patmore's ideas about prosody and the character and sources of his ideas about mysticism. There are two earlier studies of Patmore's poetry: Frederick Page, *Patmore: A Study in Poetry* (1933), and E. J. Oliver, *Coventry Patmore* (1956). There are essays about Patmore's poetry in Herbert Read, *In Defence of Shelley and Other Essays* (1936); F. L. Lucas, *Ten Victorian Poets* (revised edition, 1948); John Heath-Stubbs,

The Darkling Plain (1950); Mario Praz, *The Hero in Eclipse in Victorian Fiction* (translated 1956); and John Holloway, *The Chartered Mirror* (1960).

from The Angel in the House

The Angel in the House *is an account of the courtship and marriage of the speaker of the poem, a young man named Felix, and Honoria, the daughter of a clergyman. The first two books of the poem, "The Betrothal" (1854) and "The Espousals" (1856), were first published together in 1856. "Faithful for Ever" (1860) and "The Victories of Love" (1861), both written in the form of letters, were published as parts of* The Angel in the House *in 1863. The first two books of the poem are divided into episodes, narrated by Felix, which are named "Cantos." Each canto is introduced by short lyrics, "Preludes," in which Patmore, not always in character as Felix, meditates more speculatively on love and the poetry of love.*

BOOK I

CANTO I

Preludes

I
The Impossibility

Lo, Love's obey'd by all. 'Tis right
   That all should know what they obey,
Lest erring conscience damp delight,
   And folly laugh our joys away.
Thou Primal Love, who grantest wings
   And voices to the woodland birds,
Grant me the power of saying things
   Too simple and too sweet for words!

II
Love's Reality

I walk, I trust, with open eyes;
   I've travell'd half my worldly course;
And in the way behind me lies
   Much vanity and some remorse;
I've lived to feel how pride may part
   Spirits, tho' match'd like hand and glove;
I've blush'd for love's abode, the heart;
   But have not disbelieved in love;
Nor unto love, sole mortal thing
   Of worth immortal, done the wrong   10
To count it, with the rest that sing,
   Unworthy of a serious song;
And love is my reward; for now,
   When most of dead'ning time complain,
The myrtle[1] blooms upon my brow,
   Its odour quickens all my brain.

III
The Poet's Confidence

The richest realm of all the earth
   Is counted still a heathen land:
Lo, I, like Joshua,[2] now go forth
   To give it into Israel's hand.
I will not hearken blame or praise;
   For so should I dishonour do
To that sweet Power by which these Lays
   Alone are lovely, good, and true;
Nor credence to the world's cries give,
   Which ever preach and still prevent   10
Pure passion's high prerogative
   To make, not follow, precedent.
From love's abysmal[3] ether rare
   If I to men have here made known
New truths, they, like new stars, were there
   Before, though not yet written down.
Moving but as the feelings move,
   I run, or loiter with delight,
Or pause to mark where gentle Love
   Persuades the soul from height to height,   20
Yet, know ye, though my words are gay
   As David's dance, which Michal scorn'd,[4]

---

[1] Myrtle: a crown of myrtle leaf, associated with triumphs in love and poetry.

[2] Joshua: after the death of Moses, Joshua led the Israelites into Canaan, the promised land: Joshua 1:7.

[3] Abysmal: of fathomless depths.

[4] David's dance: as King David brought the sacred ark of the covenant back to his city, he sang and danced before it. Michal, one of the daughters of the former king Saul, disapproved of his dancing because he "uncovered himself . . . in the eyes of the handmaids of his servants." David replied: "It was before the Lord, which chose me before thy father, and before all his house, to appoint me ruler over the people of the Lord, over Israel: therefore will I play before the Lord." Michal's punishment was that she bore no children.

If kindly you receive the Lay,
  You shall be sweetly help'd and warn'd.
                         1854

BOOK I

CANTO VI

The Dean[1]

1

The Ladies rose.[2] I held the door,
  And sigh'd, as her departing grace
Assured me that she always wore
  A heart as happy as her face;
And, jealous of the winds that blew,
  I dreaded, o'er the tasteless wine,
What fortune momently might do
  To hurt the hope that she'd be mine.

2

Towards my mark the Dean's talk set:
10 He praised my "Notes on Abury,"
Read when the Association met
  At Sarum;[3] he was pleased to see
I had not stopp'd, as some men had,
  At Wrangler[4] and Prize Poet; last,
He hoped the business was not bad
  I came about: then the wine pass'd.

3

A full glass prefaced my reply:
  I loved his daughter, Honor; I told
My estate and prospects; might I try
20 To win her? At my words so bold
My sick heart sank. Then he: He gave
  His glad consent, if I could get
Her love. A dear, good Girl! she'd have
  Only thee thousand pounds as yet;
More bye and bye. Yes, his good will
  Should go with me; he would not stir;
He and my father in old time still

Wish'd I should one day marry her;
  But God so seldom lets us take
    Our chosen pathway, when it lies
In steps that either mar or make
    Or alter others' destinies,
That, though his blessing and his pray'r
    Had help'd, should help, my suit, yet he
Left all to me, his passive share
    Consent and opportunity
My chance, he hoped, was good: I'd won
    Some name already; friends and place
Appear'd within my reach, but none
    Her mind and manners would not grace.
Girls love to see the men in whom
    They invest their vanities admired;
Besides, where goodness is, there room
    For good to work will be desired.
'Twas so with one now pass'd away;
    And what she was at twenty-two,
Honor was now; and he might say
    Mine was a choice I could not rue.

4

He ceased, and gave his hand. He had won
  (And all my heart was in my word),
From me the affection of a son,
  Whichever fortune Heaven conferr'd!
Well, well, would I take more wine? Then go
  To her; she makes tea on the lawn
These fine warm afternoons. And so
  We went whither my soul was drawn;
And her light-hearted ignorance
  Of interest in our discourse
Fill'd me with love, and seem'd to enhance
  Her beauty with pathetic force,
As, through the flowery mazes sweet,
  Fronting the wind that flutter'd blythe,
And loved her shape, and kiss'd her feet,
  Shown to their insteps proud and lithe,
She approach'd, all mildness and young trust,
  And ever her chaste and noble air
Gave to love's feast its choicest gust,
  A vague, faint augury of despair.
                         1854

[1] The Dean: an ecclesiastical title; here it describes a clergyman who supervises one of the districts of a diocese.

[2] The Ladies rose: according to the custom that after dinner the women retire from the table, leaving the men to wine.

[3] Abury, or Avebury: an ancient village in the west of England situated entirely within monolithic stones which are older than those at Stonehenge. Sarum is also a town in the west of England; the Association presumably is an historical or antiquarian society.

[4] Wrangler: the title given to students who receive the top grade on the mathematics examination at Cambridge.

BOOK II

CANTO I

Preludes

II
The Kites

I saw three Cupids (so I dream'd),
  Who made three kites, on which were drawn,
In letters that like roses gleam'd,
  "Plato," "Anacreon," and "Vaughan."[1]
The boy who held by Plato tried
  His airy venture first; all sail,
It heav'nward rush'd till scarce descried,
  Then pitch'd and dropp'd, for want of tail.
Anacreon's Love, with shouts of mirth
  That pride of spirit thus should fall,
To his kite link'd a lump of earth,
  And, lo, it would not soar at all.
Last, my disciple freighted his
  With a long streamer made of flowers,
The children of the sod, and this
  Rose in the sun, and flew for hours.

                                                    1856

BOOK II

CANTO XI

Preludes

I
Platonic Love

Right art thou who wouldst rather be
  A doorkeeper in Love's fair house,
Than lead the wretched revelry
  Where fools at swinish troughs carouse.
But do not boast of being least;
  And if to kiss thy Mistress' skirt
Amaze thy brain, scorn not the Priest
  Whom greater honours do not hurt.
Stand off and gaze, if more than this
  Be more than thou canst understand,
Revering him whose power of bliss,
  Angelic, dares to seize her hand,

Or whose seraphic love makes flight
  To the apprehension of her lips;
And think, the sun of such delight
  From thine own darkness takes eclipse.
And, wouldst thou to the same aspire,
  This is the art thou must employ,
Live greatly; so shalt thou acquire
  Unknown capacities of joy.   20

II
A Demonstration

Nature, with endless being rife,
  Parts each thing into "him" and "her,"
And, in the arithmetic of life,
  The smallest unit is a pair;
And thus, oh, strange, sweet half of me,
  If I confess a loftier flame,
If more I love high Heaven than thee,
  I more than love thee, thee I am;
And, if the world's not built of lies,
  Nor all a cheat the Gospel tells,   10
If that which from the dead shall rise
  Be I indeed, not something else,
There's no position more secure
  In reason or in faith than this,
That those conditions must endure,
  Which, wanting, I myself should miss.

IV
Constancy Rewarded

I vow'd unvarying faith, and she,
  To whom in full I pay that vow,
Rewards me with variety
  Which men who change can never know.

The Wedding

1

Life smitten with a feverish chill,
  The brain too tired to understand,
In apathy of heart and will,
  I took the woman from the hand
Of him who stood for God, and heard
  Of Christ, and of the Church his Bride;

---

[1] Plato, Anacreon, and Vaughan: the Greek philosopher Plato here represents idealistic assumptions about reality, while the sixth-century B.C. Greek poet Anacreon, known for his lyric celebrations of love and wine, represents materialistic and hedonistic attitudes. The English poet and clergyman Henry Vaughan (1622–95), who wrote religious poems and poems describing the countryside, and whose religious poems are often at once intensely spiritual and particular in their origins and metaphors, is the exemplar of poets who do not leave but spiritualize the earthly.

The Feast,[1] by presence of the Lord
   And his first Wonder, beautified;
The mystic sense to Christian men;
10   The bonds in innocency made,
And gravely to be enter'd then
   For children, godliness, and aid,
And honour'd, and kept free from smirch;
   And how a man must love his wife
No less than Christ did love His Church,
   If need be, giving her his life;
And, vowing then the mutual vow,
   The tongue spoke, but intention slept.
'Tis well for us Heaven asks not how
20   We take this oath, but how 'tis kept.

2

O, bold seal of a bashful bond,
   Which makes the marriage-day to be,
To those before it and beyond,
   An iceberg in an Indian sea!

.   .   .

4

Whirl'd off at last, for speech I sought,
   To keep shy Love in countenance;
But, whilst I vainly tax'd my thought,
   Her voice deliver'd mine from trance:
"Look, is not this a pretty shawl,
   Aunt's parting gift." "She's always kind,"
"The new wing spoils Sir John's old Hall:
   You'll see it, if you pull the blind."

5

I drew the silk: in heaven the night
10   Was dawning; lovely Venus shone,
In languishment of tearful light,
   Swathed by the red breath of the sun.
                    1856

BOOK II

CANTO XII

Preludes

I

The Married Lover

Why, having won her, do I woo?
   Because her spirit's vestal grace

Provokes me always to pursue,
   But, spirit-like, eludes embrace;
Because her womanhood is such
   That, as on court-days subjects kiss
The Queen's hand, yet so near a touch
   Affirms no mean familiarness,
Nay, rather marks more fair the height
   Which can with safety so neglect
To dread, as lower ladies might,
   That grace could meet with disrespect,
Thus she with happy favour feeds
   Allegiance from a love so high
That thence no false conceit proceeds
   Of difference bridged, or state put by;
Because, although in act and word
   As lowly as a wife can be,
Her manners, when they call me lord,
   Remind me 'tis by courtesy;
Not with her least consent of will,
   Which would my proud affection hurt,
But by the noble style that still
   Imputes an unattain'd desert;
Because her gay and lofty brows,
   When all is won which hope can ask,
Reflect a light of hopeless snows
   That bright in virgin ether bask;
Because, though free of the outer court
   I am, this Temple keeps its shrine
Sacred to Heaven; because, in short,
   She's not and never can be mine.
                    1856

Departure

   It was not like your great and gracious ways!
Do you, that have nought other to lament,
Never, my Love, repent
Of how, that July afternoon,
You went,
With sudden, unintelligible phrase,
And frighten'd eye,
Upon your journey of so many days,
Without a single kiss, or a good-bye?
I knew, indeed, that you were parting soon;
And so we sate, within the low sun's rays,
You whispering to me, for your voice was weak,
Your harrowing praise.
Well, it was well,
To hear you such things speak,
And I could tell

---

[1] Feast: the wedding at Cana, at which Christ worked his first miracle and changed water to wine (John 2:1–11).

What made your eyes a growing gloom of love,
As a warm South-wind sombres a March grove.
And it was like your great and gracious ways
To turn your talk on daily things, my Dear,
Lifting the luminous, pathetic lash
To let the laughter flash,
Whilst I drew near,
Because you spoke so low that I could scarcely
    hear.
But all at once to leave me at the last,
More at the wonder than the loss aghast,
With huddled, unintelligible phrase,
And frighten'd eye,
And go your journey of all days
With not one kiss, or a good-bye,
And the only loveless look the look with which
    you pass'd:
'Twas all unlike your great and gracious ways.
                  1877–78

Vesica Piscis[1]

  In strenuous hope I wrought,
And hope seem'd still betray'd;
Lastly I said,
"I have labour'd through the Night, nor yet
Have taken aught;
But at Thy word I will again cast forth the
    net!"[2]
And, lo, I caught
 (Oh, quite unlike and quite beyond my
    thought,)
Not the quick, shining harvest of the Sea,
For food, my wish,
But Thee!
Then, hiding even in me,
As hid was Simon's coin within the fish,[3]
Thou sigh'st, with joy, "Be dumb,
Or speak but of forgotten things to far-off times
    to come."
                  1877–78

Arbor Vitæ[1]

  With honeysuckle, over-sweet, festoon'd;
With bitter ivy bound;
Terraced with funguses unsound;
Deform'd with many a a boss
And closed scar, o'ercushion'd deep with moss;
Bunch'd all about with pagan mistletoe;[2]
And thick with nests of the hoarse bird[3]
That talks, but understands not his own word;
Stands, and so stood a thousand years ago,
A single tree.   10
Thunder has done its worst among its twigs,
Where the great crest yet blackens, never
    pruned,
But in its heart, alway
Ready to push new verdurous boughs, whene'er
The rotting saplings near it fall and leave it
    air,
Is all antiquity and no decay.
Rich, though rejected by the forest-pigs,
Its fruit, beneath whose rough, concealing rind
They that will break it find
Heart-succouring savour of each several meat,   20
And kernell'd drink of brain-renewing power,
With bitter condiment and sour,
And sweet economy of sweet,
And odours that remind
Of haunts of childhood and a different day.
Beside this tree,
Praising no Gods nor blaming, sans a wish,
Sits, Tartar-like,[4] the Time's civility,
And eats its dead-dog off a golden dish.
                  1877–78

To the Body

  Creation's and Creator's crowning good;
Wall of infinitude;
Foundation of the sky,
In Heaven forecast
And long'd for from eternity,

---

   [1] Vesica Piscis: purse of a fish.
   [2] Luke 5:1–11: the account of the miraculous draught of fishes, in which Peter and his companions, having fished all night and caught nothing, are told by Christ to lower their nets again, and find them filled.
   [3] Another miracle, this one worked when Simon Peter was asked whether Christ paid tribute money to the state: Christ told him to catch a fish, "and when thou has opened his mouth, thou shalt find a piece of money; that take, and give unto them for me and thee" (Matthew 17:24).
   [1] Arbor Vitæ: the tree of life.
   [2] Mistletoe was associated with the rituals of the Druids, priests of pagan Britain.
   [3] Hoarse bird: crow.
   [4] Tartar-like: barbarously.

Though laid the last;
Reverberating dome,
Of music cunningly built home
Against the void and indolent disgrace
10 Of unresponsive space;
Little, sequester'd pleasure-house
For God and for His Spouse;[1]
Elaborately, yea, past conceiving, fair,
Since, from the graced decorum of the hair,
Ev'n to the tingling, sweet
Soles of the simple, earth-confiding feet,
And from the inmost heart
Outwards unto the thin
Silk curtains of the skin,
20 Every least part
Astonish'd hears
And sweet replies to some like region of the
        spheres;
Form'd for a dignity prophets but darkly name,
Lest shameless men cry "Shame!"
So rich with wealth conceal'd
That Heaven and Hell fight chiefly for this
        field;
Clinging to everything that pleases thee
With indefectible fidelity;
Alas, so true
30 To all thy friendships that no grace
Thee from thy sin can wholly disembrace;
Which thus 'bides with thee as the Jebusite,[2]
That, maugre[3] all God's promises could do,
The chosen People never conquer'd quite;
Who therefore lived with them,
And that by formal truce and as of right,
In metropolitan Jerusalem.

For which false fealty
Thou needs must, for a season, lie
In the grave's arms, foul and unshriven,   4(
Albeit, in Heaven,
Thy crimson-throbbing Glow
Into its old abode aye pants to go,
And does with envy see
Enoch, Elijah, and the Lady,[4] she
Who left the roses in her body's lieu.
O, if the pleasures I have known in thee
But my poor faith's poor first-fruits be,
What quintessential, keen, ethereal bliss
Then shall be his   5(
Who has thy birth-time's consecrating dew
For death's sweet chrism retain'd,
Quick, tender, virginal, and unprofaned!
                                    1877–78

A Retrospect

I, trusting that the truly sweet
    Would still be sweetly found the true,
Sang, darkling, taught by heavenly heat,
    Songs which were wiser than I knew.
To the unintelligible dream
    That melted like a gliding star,
I said: "We part to meet, fair Gleam!
    You are eternal, for you *are*."
To Love's strange riddle, fiery writ
    In flesh and spirit of all create,
"Mocker," I said, "of mortal wit,
    Me you shall not mock. I can wait."
                                    1886

[1] His Spouse: the human soul.
[2] Jebusite: member of a tribe which for a long time resisted the authority of the Israelites who entered Canaan as the promised land.
[3] Maugre: despite.
[4] Enoch, Elijah, and the Lady: Enoch was a patriarch of the Old Testament who was taken into heaven in his coporeal body (Genesis 5:24) ; the prophet Elijah was also taken in his body into heaven in a chariot of fire and a whirlwind (II Kings 2:11) . The doctrine that Mary, the mother of Christ, was taken into heaven in her body did not become a dogma of the Roman Catholic Church until 1950, but it was advanced in the Church consistently from at least the fourth century.

Edward FitzGerald

1809–1883

A BRIEF ACCOUNT of the life and writing of Edward FitzGerald is necessarily largely an account of his version of *The Rubáiyát*. FitzGerald chose to live an uneventful, increasingly reclusive life. He was born in Suffolk, an eastern country bordering on the sea, into an old and eminent family of wealth; after her father's death, when she and her husband took her family name of FitzGerald, his mother was said to be the richest commoner in England. FitzGerald lived for a time in Paris while a child, went to school in England, and entered Cambridge in 1826. He met William Makepeace Thackeray at Cambridge, who was to be his friend for the rest of his life. Later he met Tennyson, with whom he made an equally close friendship. After his graduation in 1839, FitzGerald lived in deliberately eccentric simplicity, first in London, and after 1837 in the country. He edited in 1849 the poems of one of his neighbors, the Quaker Bernard Barton. His ideas about editing were unusual and predicted his treatment of the poems he made into *The Rubáiyát;* he thought himself licensed to truncate poems and to conflate two or more poems into one in order to make texts that pleased him. He also published anonymously a dialogue on university education (*Euphranor:* 1851) and a collection of epigrams and wise sayings (*Polonius:* 1852).

FitzGerald began to study languages in the 1840s, and he published translations of six plays of the seventeenth-century Spanish playwright Calderon in 1853, and a translation of *Salámán and Absál,* by the fifteenth-century Persian poet Jámi, in 1856. Three years later he published the first edition of *The Rubáiyát,* again anonymously. For the rest of his life FitzGerald revised this text. He also published privately translations of two more plays by Calderon, translations of some Greek plays, and a selection from the poetry of the early nineteenth-century poet George Crabbe, whose son was another of FitzGerald's neighbors and friends. In 1856 he married the daughter of Bernard Barton. This attempt to alter his quietly independent way was a mistake, and he and his wife separated a year later. He continued his friendships with Tennyson, Thackeray, Thomas Carlyle, and others, wrote letters for which he would be remembered as a minor and engaging literary figure if he had not attempted *The Rubáiyát,* indulged and then finally abandoned an addiction to boating, and gradually let his quiet, rather isolated life run down, not sorry, in the end, to see it go. FitzGerald's life, like the poems of *The Rubáiyát,* has a wistfully sad tone founded on a secure, even comfortable sense of the limits of his own identity. "I am a man of taste," he once said, "of whom there are hundreds born every year." Both the pleasing ease and control of his poems, and their melancholy, can be referred to that rarely violated sense of what he could and could not do and be.

FitzGerald learned Persian in the 1850s with Edward Byles Cowell, another of his Suffolk neighbors. He began to translate a manuscript of the poems of Omar Khayyám in the Bodleian library at Oxford, and when Cowell went out to India as a professor of British history, he sent FitzGerald copies of a second manuscript he found there. Arthur J. Arberry argues in the preface to his translation of two recently discovered manuscripts (see below) that manuscripts of the poetry of Omar Khayyám are selections from a relatively large corpus of perhaps 750 poems. The Bodleian manuscript FitzGerald used contains 158 poems. He made his own choices from this selection, and sometimes he "mashed" (his word) two or more of Omar's poems together to make a single quatrain. After he published the first edition of *The Rubáiyát,* anonymously, in 1859, he continued to revise, add to, and rearrange the quatrains of his translation in editions published in 1868, 1872, and 1879. Eventually FitzGerald made a poem whose large pattern moved from sunrise to moonrise, from young manhood to death, from the quiet pleasures of

love, wine, and natural beauty to a wish that
the "scheme of things" permitted individual
existence to survive the night, and to the
knowledge that it does not.

FitzGerald's translations from the Persian—
Arberry calls FitzGerald's poem a "paraphrase"
—were very free. Arberry's edition of the two
recently discovered manuscripts of Omar Khay-
yám's poems, and a late nineteenth-century
edition of FitzGerald's *Rubáiyát* by E. Heron-
Allen (1899), include many demonstrations of
how FitzGerald transformed or heightened one
or another of the tones of Omar's verse, usually
to emphasize the unhappy transience of the
world's pleasures and to express a pensive skep-
ticism about the good intentions of its creators.
For example, in Arberry's translation, for which
he uses an eight-line stanza form where Fitz-
Gerald used quatrains, the sources of Fitz-
Gerald's Quatrains XXXV and XCI are:

I pressed my lip against the bowl
  In an extremity of greed,
  Seeking to snatch my ardent need,
Long life for my too fleeting soul.

Soft spake the bowl and secretly,
  As lip against my lip it lay:
  "I too was once as thou to-day;
This little moment, bear with me!"

.   .   .

O let me with good wine be fed—
  My dear companions, do not fail!—
  Until my cheeks, now amber-pale,
Be changed to rubies, rich and red.

And when I die, as die I must,
  Wash my cold body all with wine;
  Carve me the timber of the vine
For coffin, to preserve my dust.

Arberry's literal translation of the verse Fitz-
Gerald made into his most famous lines
(Quatrain XII) is:

If hand should give (i.e. if there should be at
  hand) of the pith of wheat a loaf,
and of wine a two-maunder (jug), of a sheep a
  thigh,
with a little sweetheart seated in a desolation,
a pleasure it is that is not the attainment of any
  sultan.

And the source of the poem (Quatrain CI)
FitzGerald chose to end his *Rubáiyát*, as sad

as FitzGerald's version but less insistent on
absence and emptiness, is:

When ye are met in harmony,
  Beloved friends, in after days,
  And on each other's beauty gaze,
And are rejoiced by what ye see;

And when the saki, standing there,
  Takes in his hand the Magian wine,
  Think on the anguish that is mine
And O, recall me in a prayer.

FitzGerald first tried, unsuccessfully, to pub-
lish the quatrains of *The Rubáiyát* in a
monthly magazine in the mid-1850s. He then
had the first edition, consisting of seventy-five
quatrains, printed at his own expense and pub-
lished in a pamphlet in 1859. Only a few copies
were sold, and his poem did not begin to at-
tract attention until the unsold copies were
offered at a penny (later increased to two-
pence) and were found, bought, and exclaimed
over by Dante Gabriel Rossetti, Swinburne,
and other writers and critics of their circle and
generation in the early 1860s. Even then the
great popularity of *The Rubáiyát* awaited the
last two decades of the century. FitzGerald was
himself an unrepentant admirer of the early
poems of Tennyson, and he never liked the
more grand discursive and narrative modes into
which the laureate developed. His poems con-
tinued into the second half of the century
something of the remoteness, evocative symbol-
ism, and polished finish and craft of the kind
of early Victorian poetry he liked, and it was to
these qualities that Rossetti and others re-
sponded. FitzGerald also expressed a melan-
choly and skepticism, especially common in the
last decades of the century, that was not so
much an anguished condition to be resolved as
it was a mood which permitted and even itself
possessed certain pleasures. FitzGerald was not
the poet, nor the man, to delve into this mood
to its fundament. *The Rubáiyát*, unlike *In
Memoriam*, say, or even Tennyson's early "Sup-
posed Confessions of a Second-Rate Mind,"
risks no deep trouble that requires large and
conclusive consolations. In its final version
FitzGerald's poem opens in a dawn that has al-
ready surrendered to the inevitability of night.
It meets this inevitability as some poets in the
generation after Swinburne's were characteris-
tically to meet it, with limited self-assertions of
a craft which offers a shadowed joy and ease

and stands against the emptiness that denies their wishes, but which they will not wish away.

EDITIONS

The text of *The Rubáiyát* reprinted here is that of the fourth edition as it appears in *The Letters and Literary Remains of Edward Fitz-Gerald*, edited by Walter A. Wright (1902–3). *The Variorum and Definitive Edition of the Poetical and Prose Writings of FitzGerald*, edited by George Bentham (1902–3), contains versions of all of FitzGerald's writing and a bibliography of his writing and writing about him. Nathan Haskell Dole has edited *The Rubáiyát of Omar Khayyám: A Multi-Variorum Edition* (1896); and Carl J. Weber's *Fitz-Gerald's Rubáiyát: A Centennial Edition* (1959) is a usefully annotated text which includes a bibliography. Arthur J. Arberry has edited *FitzGerald's Salámán and Absál: A Study* (1956), which includes two versions of the translation by FitzGerald and a literal translation by Arberry. FitzGerald's letters comprise four volumes of Walter Wright's seven-volume *Letters and Literary Remains*.

Three studies compare FitzGerald's translation with the Persian of Omar: E. Heron-Allen, *FitzGerald's Rubáiyát of Omar Khayyám* (1899); and two books by Arthur J. Arberry, *The Romance of the Rubáiyát* (1959) and *Omar Khayyám: A New Version* (1952). Arberry's translations cited earlier in this introduction are in the latter study.

BIOGRAPHY AND CRITICISM

The standard biography is A. McKinley Terhune, *The Life of Edward FitzGerald* (1947). Joanna Richardson's *FitzGerald* (1960) is a pamphlet in the Writers and Their Work series which contains a selected bibliography. Carl J. Weber's "The Discovery of FitzGerald's *Rubáiyát*," *Library Chronicle of the University of Texas,* 7 (1963) recounts and examines the circumstances of this event. John Yohannan, "The Fin de Siècle Cult of FitzGerald's *Rubáiyát of Omar Khayyám*," *Review of National Literature,* 2 (1971), discusses Fitz-Gerald's later popularity.

W. F. Prideaux, *Notes for a Bibliography of Edward FitzGerald* (1901) includes references to writing about FitzGerald to 1900. See also Ehrsam, Deily, and Smith (General Bibliography).

Rubáiyát of Omar Khayyám of Naishápúr

I

Wake! For the Sun, who scatter'd into flight
The Stars before him from the Field of Night,
    Drives Night along with them from Heav'n, and strikes
The Sultán's Turret with a Shaft of Light.

II

Before the phantom of False morning[1] died,
Methought a Voice within the Tavern cried,
    "When all the Temple is prepared within,
"Why nods the drowsy Worshipper outside?"[2]

III

And, as the Cock crew, those who stood before
The Tavern shouted—"Open then the Door!   10
    "You know how little while we have to stay,
"And, once departed, may return no more."

IV

Now the New Year[3] reviving old Desires,
The thoughtful Soul to Solitude retires,

---

[1] FitzGerald's note: "The 'False Dawn,' . . . a transient Light on the Horizon about an hour before the . . . True Dawn; a well-known Phenomenon in the East."

[2] In the first edition of 1859 the first two quatrains read:

> "Awake! for Morning in the Bowl of Night
> Has flung the Stone that puts the Stars to Flight:
> And Lo! the Hunter of the East has caught
> The Sultán's Turret in a Noose of Light.

> "Dreaming when Dawn's Left Hand was in the Sky
> I heard a Voice within the Tavern cry,
> 'Awake, my Little ones, and fill the Cup
> 'Before Life's Liquor in its Cup be dry'."

FitzGerald noted that flinging a stone in a bowl was a traditional signal of departure in the East. "The Hunter of the East" is the sun; "Dawn's Left Hand" is FitzGerald's first figure for the false dawn.

[3] FitzGerald's note: "New Year. Beginning with the Vernal Equinox, it must be remembered."

Where the WHITE HAND OF MOSES on the
    Bough
Puts out, and Jesus from the Ground suspires.[4]

V

Iram[5] indeed is gone with all his Rose,
And Jamshyd's Sev'n-ring'd Cup[6] where no
    one knows;
    But still a Ruby kindles in the Vine,
20 And many a Garden by the Water blows.

VI

And David's lips are lockt;[7] but in divine
High-piping Pehleví,[8] with "Wine! Wine!
    Wine!
    Red Wine!"—the Nightingale cries to the
    Rose
That sallow cheek of hers to' incarnadine.

VII

Come, fill the Cup, and in the fire of Spring
Your Winter-garment of Repentance fling:
    The Bird of Time has but a little way
To flutter—and the Bird is on the Wing.[9]

VIII

Whether at Naishápúr or Babylon,
Whether the Cup with sweet or bitter run,   30
    The Wine of Life keeps oozing drop by
        drop,
    The Leaves of Life keep falling one by one.[10]

IX

Each Morn a thousand Roses brings, you say;
Yes, but where leaves the Rose of Yesterday?[11]
    And this first Summer month that brings the
        Rose
Shall take Jamshyd and Kaikobád[12] away.

X

Well, let it take them! What have we to do
With Kaikobád the Great, or Kaikhosrú?
    Let Zál and Rustum bluster as they will,
Or Hátim call to Supper—heed not you.[13]   40

XI

With me along the strip of Herbage strown
That just divides the desert from the sown,
    Where name of Slave and Sultán is forgot—
And Peace to Mahmúd on his golden
        Throne![14]

[4] In his notes FitzGerald cites Exodus 4:6–7, in which God commands Moses to put his hand in his bosom, "and when he took it out, behold, his hand was leprous as snow"; when God commands him to repeat the act, his hand is made whole again. According to the Persians, FitzGerald continues, "the Healing Power of Jesus resided in His Breath." The whole figure is of God's power issuing in flowers and healing winds and energy.

[5] Iram: a city built by an ancient Persian king; according to one tradition, it was built in imitation of Paradise, and destroyed by God as punishment for pride.

[6] Jamshyd's Sev'n-ring'd Cup: Jemshid or Jemsheed was a ninth-century B.C. Persian king who built the city of Persepolis into its commanding glory. According to FitzGerald's note, the seven-ringed cup was a divining cup whose design symbolized the seven planets, the seven seas, and other natural phenomena.

[7] David: the king and singer of the Hebrew Old Testament, frequently referred to in Persian poetry as an emblem of lyric song.

[8] Pehleví: a form of the Persian language which FitzGerald believed to be that of the old heroic poems.

[9] 1859: "To fly—and Lo! the Bird is on the Wing."

[10] Quatrain added after 1859 edition.

[11] 1859:   "And look—a thousand Blossoms with the Day
                    Woke—and a thousand scatter'd into Clay:"

[12] Kaikobád: a seventh-century B.C. Persian ruler, the founder of the dynasty in which Kaikhosrú (X), or Cyrus the Great, was the principal figure.

[13] Kaikhosrú: Cyrus the Great, a sixth-century B.C. king and warrior who conquered parts of India and founded the Persian empire. Zál and Rustum: heroes of the Persian epic poem, *The Book of Kings:* see note to Matthew Arnold's "Sohrab and Rustum." Hátim: a Persian poet legendary for his generosity. In 1859 this stanza read:

        "But come with old Khayyám, and leave the Lot
        Of Kaikobád and Kaikhosrú forgot:
            Let Rustum lay about him as he will,
            Or Hátim Tai cry Supper—heed them not."

[14] Mahmúd: a Persian ruler of the eleventh century (he died in 1030) who also invaded India and extended the Persian empire. In 1859 this line read: "And pity Sultán Mahmúd on his Throne."

XII

A Book of Verses underneath the Bough,
A Jug of Wine, a Loaf of Bread—and Thou
 Beside me singing in the Wilderness—
Oh, Wilderness were Paradise enow!

XIII

Some for the Glories of This World: and some
Sigh for the Prophet's Paradise to come;
 Ah, take the Cash, and let the Credit go,
Nor heed the rumble of a distant Drum![15]

XIV

Look to the blowing[16] Rose about us—"Lo,
Laughing," she says, "into the world I blow,
 At once the silken tassel of my Purse[17]
Tear, and its Treasure on the Garden throw."

XV

And those who husbanded the Golden grain,
And those who flung it to the winds like Rain,
 Alike to no such aureate Earth are turn'd
As, buried once, Men want dug up again.

XVI

The Worldly Hope men set their Hearts upon
Turns Ashes—or it prospers; and anon,
 Like Snow upon the Desert's dusty Face,
Lighting a little hour or two—is gone.[18]

XVII

Think, in this batter'd Caravanserai[19]
Whose Portals are alternate Night and Day,

How Sultán after Sultán with his Pomp
Abode his destined Hour, and went his way.[20]

XVIII

They say the Lion and the Lizard keep
The Courts where Jamshyd gloried and drank
 deep:
 And Bahrám, that great Hunter—the Wild
 Ass[21]
Stamps o'er his Head, but cannot break his
 Sleep.

XIX

I sometimes think that never blows so red
The Rose as where some buried Cæsar bled;
 That every Hyacinth the Garden wears
Dropt in her Lap from some once lovely
 Head.[22]

XX

And this reviving Herb whose tender Green
Fledges[23] the River-Lip on which we lean—
 Ah, lean upon it lightly! for who knows
From what once lovely Lip it springs unseen!

XXI

Ah, my Belovéd, fill the Cup that clears
To-day of past Regrets and future Fears:
 To-morrow!—why, To-morrow I may be
Myself with Yesterday's Sev'n thousand Years.[24]

---

[15] FitzGerald's note: "A Drum—beaten outside a Palace." In 1859 quatrains XII and XIII read:

> "Here with a Loaf of Bread beneath the Bough,
> A Flask of Wine, a Book of Verse—and Thou
> Beside me singing in the Wilderness—
> And Wilderness is Paradise enow.
>
> " 'How sweet is mortal Sovranty!'—think some:
> Others—'How blest the Paradise to come!'
> Ah, take the Cash in hand and wave the Rest;
> Oh, the brave Music of a *distant* Drum!"

[17] FitzGerald's note: "That is, the Rose's Golden Centre."   [16] Blowing: blooming.
[18] In 1859 quatrain XVI preceded XV.
[19] Caravanserai: an inn at which caravans stop for the night.
[20] 1859: "Abode his Hour or two, and went his way."
[21] The Courts: Persepolis. Bahrám Gur (of the Wild Ass) was a fifth-century Persian ruler who also built regally; FitzGerald in his note describes his seven castles, each a different color and each housing a different mistress.
[22] FitzGerald's note: "I am reminded of an old English Superstition, that our Anemone Pulsatilla . . . grows only where Danish Blood has been spilt." The classical myth of Hyacinth is that of a youth beloved and accidentally killed by the god Apollo, who changed his blood into a flower.
[23] Fledges: covers with a down or early feathers.
[24] FitzGerald's note: "A thousand years to each Planet."

XXII
For some we loved, the loveliest and the best
That from his Vintage rolling Time hath
    prest,[25]
  Have drunk their Cup a Round or two
    before,
And one by one crept silently to rest.

XXIII
And we, that now make merry in the Room
They left, and Summer dresses in new bloom,
  Ourselves must we beneath the Couch of
    Earth
Descend—ourselves to make a Couch—for
  whom?

XXIV
Ah, make the most of what we yet may spend,
Before we too into the Dust descend;
  Dust into Dust, and under Dust to lie,
Sans Wine, sans Song, sans Singer, and—sans
  End![26]

XXV
Alike for those who for TO-DAY prepare,
And those that after some TO-MORROW stare,
  A Muezzín[27] from the Tower of Darkness
  cries,
"Fools! your Reward is neither Here nor
    There."

XXVI
Why, all the Saints and Sages who discuss'd
Of the Two Worlds so wisely—they are thrust
  Like foolish Prophets forth; their Words to
  Scorn
Are scatter'd, and their Mouths are stopt with
  Dust.[28]

XXVII
Myself when young did eagerly frequent
Doctor and Saint, and heard great argument

About it and about: but evermore
Came out by the same door where in I went.

XXVIII
With them the seed of Wisdom did I sow,
And with mine own hand wrought to make it
  grow;
  And this was all the Harvest that I reap'd—
"I came like Water, and like Wind I go."

XXIX
Into this Universe, and *Why* not knowing
Nor *Whence*, like Water willy-nilly flowing;
  And out of it, as Wind along the Waste,
I know not *Whither*, willy-nilly blowing.

XXX
What, without asking, hither hurried *Whence?*
And, without asking, *Whither* hurried hence!
  Oh, many a Cup of this forbidden Wine
Must drown the memory of that insolence![29]

XXXI
Up from Earth's Centre through the Seventh
  Gate
I rose, and on the Throne of Saturn sate,[30]
  And many a Knot unravel'd by the Road;
But not the Master-knot of Human Fate.

XXXII
There was the Door to which I found no Key;
There was the Veil through which I might not
  see:
  Some little talk awhile of ME and THEE
There was—and then no more of THEE and
  ME.[31]

XXXIII
Earth could not answer; nor the Seas that
  mourn
In flowing Purple, of their Lord forlorn;

---

[25] 1859:   "Lo! some we loved, the loveliest and best
    That Time and Fate of all their Vintage prest,"

[26] Sans: without.   [27] Muezzín: the crier who calls the Muslim faithful to prayer.
[28] In 1859 this quatrain followed that presently numbered XXVI:

    "Oh, come with old Khayyám, and leave the Wise
    To talk; one thing is certain, that Life flies;
    One thing is certain, and the Rest is Lies;
    The Flower that once has blown for ever dies."

[29] 1859:   "Another and another Cup to drown
    The Memory of this Impertinence!"

[30] FitzGerald's note: "Saturn, Lord of the Seventh Heaven."
[31] FitzGerald's note: "some dividual Existence or Personality distinct from the Whole."

Nor rolling Heaven, with all his Signs
reveal'd
And hidden by the sleeve of Night and Morn.[32]

XXXIV

Then of the THEE IN ME who works behind
The Veil, I lifted up my hands to find
   A lamp amid the Darkness; and I heard,
As from Without—"THE ME WITHIN THEE
   BLIND!"[33]

XXXV

Then to the Lip of this poor earthen Urn
I lean'd, the Secret of my Life to learn:
   And Lip to Lip it murmur'd—"While you
   live,
"Drink!—for, once dead, you never shall
40   return."

XXXVI

I think the Vessel, that with fugitive
Articulation answer'd, once did live,
   And drink; and Ah! the passive Lip I kiss'd,
How many Kisses might it take—and give!

XXXVII

For I remember stopping by the way
To watch a Potter thumping his wet Clay:
   And with its all-obliterated Tongue
It murmur'd—"Gently, Brother, gently,
   pray!"[34]

XXXVIII

And has not such a Story from of Old
50 Down Man's successive generations roll'd
   Of such a clod of saturated Earth
Cast by the Maker into Human mould?[35]

XXXIX

And not a drop that from our Cups we throw
For Earth to drink of,[36] but may steal below
   To quench the fire of Anguish in some Eye
There hidden—far beneath, and long ago.

XL

As then the Tulip for her morning sup
Of Heav'nly Vintage from the soil looks up,
   Do you devoutly do the like, till Heav'n
To Earth invert you—like an empty Cup.   160

XLI

Perplext no more with Human or Divine,
To-morrow's tangle to the winds resign,
   And lose your fingers in the tresses of
The Cypress-slender Minister of Wine.[37]

XLII

And if the Wine you drink, the Lip you press,
End in what All begins and ends in—YES;
   Think that you are TO-DAY what YESTERDAY
You were—TO-MORROW you shall not be less.[38]

XLIII

So when the Angel of the darker Drink[39]
At last shall find you by the river-brink,   170
   And, offering his Cup, invite your Soul
Forth to your Lips to quaff—you shall not
   shrink.

XLIV

Why, if the Soul can fling the Dust aside,
And naked on the Air of Heaven ride,
   Were't not a Shame—were't not a Shame for
   him
In this clay carcase crippled to abide?

[32] Quatrain added after 1859.
[33] 1859:   "Then to the rolling Heav'n itself I cried,
   Asking, 'What Lamp had Destiny to guide
   'Her little Children stumbling in the Dark?'
   And—'A blind Understanding!' Heav'n replied."
[34] In his notes FitzGerald recounts a story of a traveler who found the water in an earthen cup bitter to the taste, and then learned that the cup had been made from the dust of a man, "and, into whatever shape renewed, can never lose the bitter flavour of Mortality."
[35] Except for earlier versions of quatrains XLII and XLVIII, quatrains XXXVIII through LIII were added after 1859.
[36] FitzGerald's note: "The custom of throwing a little Wine on the ground before drinking still continues in Persia."
[37] Minister of Wine: the woman who pours the wine.
[38] 1859:   "Ah, fill the Cup:—what boots it to repeat
   How Time is slipping underneath our Feet:
   Unborn TO-MORROW, and dead YESTERDAY,
   Why fret about them if TO-DAY be sweet!"
[39] Angel of the darker Drink: Azrael, the agent of death in Eastern mythology.

XLV

'T is but a Tent where takes his one day's rest
A Sultán to the realm of Death addrest;
  The Sultán rises, and the dark Ferrásh[40]
180 Strikes, and prepares it for another Guest.

XLVI

And fear not lest Existence closing your
Account, and mine, should know the like no
    more;
  The Eternal Sákí[41] from that Bowl has
    pour'd
Millions of Bubbles like us, and will pour.

XLVII

When You and I behind the Veil are past,
Oh, but the long, long while the World shall
    last,
  Which of our Coming and Departure heeds
As the Sea's self should heed a pebble-cast.

XLVIII

A Moment's Halt—a momentary taste
190 Of BEING from the Well amid the Waste—
  And Lo!—the phantom Caravan has reach'd
The NOTHING it set out from—Oh, make
    haste![42]

XLIX

Would you that spangle of Existence spend
About THE SECRET—quick about it, Friend!
  A Hair perhaps divides the False and True—
And upon what, prithee, may life depend?

L

A Hair perhaps divides the False and True;
Yes; and a single Alif[43] were the clue—
  Could you but find it—to the Treasure-
    house,
200 And peradventure to THE MASTER too;

LI

Whose secret Presence, through Creation's veins
Running Quicksilver-like eludes your pains;
  Taking all shapes from Máh to Máhi;[44] and
They change and perish all—but He remains;

LII

A moment guess'd—then back behind the Fold
Immerst of Darkness round the Drama roll'd
  Which, for the Pastime of Eternity,
He doth Himself contrive, enact, behold.

LIII

But if in vain, down on the stubborn floor
Of Earth, and up to Heav'n's unopening Door, 21
  You gaze TO-DAY, while You are You—how
    then
TO-MORROW, You when shall be You no more?

LIV

Waste not your Hour, nor in the vain pursuit
Of This and That endeavour and dispute;
  Better be jocund with the fruitful Grape
That sadden after none, or bitter, Fruit.[45]

LV

You know, my Friends, with what a brave
    Carouse
I made a Second Marriage in my house;
  Divorced old barren Reason from my Bed,
And took the Daughter of the Vine to Spouse. 22

LVI

For "Is" and "Is-NOT" though with Rule and
    Line,
And "UP-AND-DOWN" by Logic I define,
  Of all that one should care to fathom, I
Was never deep in anything but—Wine.[46]

LVII

Ah, but my Computations, People say,
Reduced the Year to better reckoning?—Nay,
  'Twas only striking from the Calendar
Unborn To-morrow, and dead Yesterday.[47]

LVIII

And lately, by the Tavern Door agape,
Came shining through the Dusk an Angel
    Shape   23
  Bearing a Vessel on his Shoulder; and
He bid me taste of it; and 't was—the Grape!

[40] Ferrásh: servant.   [41] Sákí: wine-bearer.
[42] 1859:   "One Moment in Annihilation's Waste,
                 One Moment, of the Well of Life to taste—
                 The Stars are setting and the Caravan
                 Starts for the Dawn of Nothing—Oh, make haste!"
[43] Alif: the first letter of the Arabic alphabet.
[44] FitzGerald's note: "From Máh to Máhi; from Fish to Moon."
[45] 1859:   "How long, how long, in infinite Pursuit
                 Of This and That endeavour and dispute?
                 Better be merry with the fruitful Grape
                 Than sadden after none, or bitter, Fruit."
[46] FitzGerald's note: "A Jest, of course, at his Studies."   [47] Added after 1859.

LIX

The Grape that can with Logic absolute
The Two-and-Seventy jarring Sects confute:[48]
  The sovereign Alchemist that in a trice
Life's leaden metal into Gold transmute:

LX

The mighty Mahmúd, Allah-breathing Lord,
That all the misbelieving and black Horde[49]
  Of Fears and Sorrows that infest the Soul
40 Scatters before him with his whirlwind Sword.

LXI

Why, be this Juice the growth of God, who
    dare
Blaspheme the twisted tendril as a Snare?
  A Blessing, we should use it, should we not?
And if a Curse—why, then, Who set it there?[50]

LXII

I must abjure the Balm of Life, I must,
Scared by some After-reckoning ta'en on trust,
  Or lured with Hope of some Diviner Drink,
To fill the Cup—when crumbled into Dust!

LXIII

Oh threats of Hell and Hopes of Paradise!
One thing at least is certain—*This* Life flies; 250
  One thing is certain and the rest is Lies;
The Flower that once has blown[51] for ever dies.

LXIV

Strange, is it not? that of the myriads who
Before us pass'd the door of Darkness through,
  Not one returns to tell us of the Road,
Which to discover we must travel too.[52]

LXV

The Revelations of Devout and Learn'd
Who rose before us, and as Prophets burn'd,
  Are all but Stories, which, awoke from
    Sleep
They told their comrades, and to Sleep
    return'd[53] 260

LXVI

I sent my Soul through the Invisible,
Some letter of that After-life to spell:
  And by and by my Soul return'd to me,
And answer'd "I Myself am Heav'n and Hell:"

---

[48] FitzGerald's note: "The Seventy-Two Religions supposed to divide the World, *including* Islamism, as some think; but others not."
[49] FitzGerald's note: "Alluding to Sultan Mahmúd's Conquest of India and its dark people."
[50] 1859: "But leave the Wise to wrangle, and with me
            The Quarrel of the Universe let be:
              And, in some corner of the Hubbub coucht,
              Make Game of that which makes as much of Thee."
[51] Blown: bloomed. [52] Quatrains LXII through LXIV were added after 1859.
[53] The passage from quatrains LXV through LXIX was thoroughly revised after 1859.
Quatrain LXVIII was added. The others originally read:

  [LXV]
  "For in and out, above, about, below,
  'Tis nothing but a Magic Shadow-show,
    Play'd in a Box whose Candle is the Sun,
  Round which we Phantom Figures come and go.

  [LXVI]
  "And if the Wine you drink, the Lip you press,
  End in the Nothing all Things end in—Yes—
    Then fancy while Thou art, Thou are but what
  Thou shalt be—Nothing—Thou shalt not be less.

  [LXVII]
  "While the Rose blows along the River Brink,
  With old Khayyám the Ruby Vintage drink:
    And when the Angel with his darker Draught
  Draws up to Thee—take that, and do not shrink.

  [LXIX]
  " 'T is all a Chequer-board of Nights and Days
  Where Destiny with Men for Pieces plays:
    Hither and thither moves, and mates, and slays,
  And one by one back in the Closet lays."

LXVII
Heav'n but the Vision of fulfill'd Desire,
And Hell the Shadow from a Soul on fire,
    Cast on the Darkness into which Ourselves,
So late emerged from, shall so soon expire.

LXVIII
We are no other than a moving row
270 Of Magic Shadow-shapes that come and go
    Round with the Sun-illumined Lantern held
In Midnight by the Master of the Show;[54]

LXIX
But helpless Pieces of the Game He plays
Upon this Chequer-board of Nights and Days;
    Hither and thither moves, and checks, and slays,
And one by one back in the Closet lays.

LXX
The Ball no question makes of Ayes and Noes,
But Here or There as strikes the Player goes;
    And He that toss'd you down into the Field,
280 *He* knows about it all—HE knows—HE knows!

LXXI
The Moving Finger writes; and, having writ,
Moves on: nor all your Piety nor Wit
    Shall lure it back to cancel half a Line,
Nor all your Tears wash out a Word of it.

LXXII
And that inverted Bowl they call the Sky,
Whereunder crawling coop'd we live and die.
    Lift not your hands to *It* for help—for It
As impotently moves as you or I.

LXXIII
With Earth's first Clay They did the Last Man knead,
290 And there of the Last Harvest sow'd the Seed:
    And the first Morning of Creation wrote
What the Last Dawn of Reckoning shall read.

LXXIV
YESTERDAY *This* Day's Madness did prepare;
TO-MORROW's Silence, Triumph, or Despair:

Drink! for you know not whence you came, nor why:
Drink! for you know not why you go, nor where.[55]

LXXV
I tell you this—When, started from the Goal,
Over the flaming shoulders of the Foal
    Of Heav'n Parwín and Mushtarí[56] they flung,
In my predestined Plot of Dust and Soul   300

LXXVI
The Vine had struck a fibre: which about
If clings my Being—let the Dervish flout;[57]
    Of my Base metal may be filed a Key,
That shall unlock the Door he howls without.

LXXVII
And this I know: whether the one True Light
Kindle to Love, or Wrath-consume me quite,
    One Flash of It within the Tavern caught
Better than in the Temple lost outright.

LXXVIII
What! out of senseless Nothing to provoke
A conscious Something to resent the yoke   310
    Of unpermitted Pleasure, under pain
Of Everlasting Penalties, if broke!

LXXIX
What! from his helpless Creature be repaid
Pure Gold for what he lent him dross-allay'd—
    Sue for a Debt we never did contract,
And cannot answer—Oh the sorry trade![58]

LXXX
Oh Thou, who didst with pitfall and with gin[59]
Beset the Road I was to wander in,
    Thou wilt not with Predestined Evil round
Enmesh, and then impute my Fall to Sin!   320

LXXXI
Oh Thou, who Man of baser Earth didst make,
And ev'n with Paradise devise the Snake:

---

[54] In his notes FitzGerald refers to a magic lantern used in the East which revolves around a lighted candle centered within it.
[55] Quatrain added after 1859.
[56] Parwín and Mushtarí: the group of stars known as the Pleiades, and the planet Jupiter. The Foal would seem to be the sun.
[57] Dervish: a member of a Muslim religious order given to extravagant dancing and chanting as forms of worship. In 1859 this line read, "Let the Súfi flout": see note to quatrain LXXXVII.
[58] Quatrains LXXVIII and LXXIX were added after 1859. Answer: be responsible for.
[59] Gin: a trap.

For all the Sin wherewith the Face of Man
Is blacken'd—Man's forgiveness give—and
      take![60]

LXXXII

As under cover of departing Day
Slunk hunger-stricken Ramazán[61] away,
    Once more within the Potter's house alone
I stood, surrounded by the Shapes of Clay.

LXXXIII

Shapes of all Sorts and Sizes, great and small,

That stood along the floor and by the wall;   330
    And some loquacious Vessels were; and some
Listen'd perhaps, but never talk'd at all.

LXXXIV

Said one among them—"Surely not in vain
"My substance of the common Earth was ta'en
    "And to this Figure moulded, to be broke,
Or trampled back to shapeless Earth again."

LXXXV

Then said a Second—"Ne'er a peevish Boy

[60] In 1859 the first part of the poem closed with quatrain now numbered LXXXI. Then fol-
lowed a separate section entitled "Kúza-Náma": the Book of Pots. This sequence—from the
quatrain now numbered LXXXII through XC—was thoroughly revised after 1859. Originally,
it read:

> [LXXXII]
> "Listen again. One Evening at the Close
> Of Ramazán, ere the better Moon arose,
>   In that old Potter's Shop I stood alone
> With the clay Population round in Rows.
>
> [LXXXIII]
> "And, strange to tell, among the Earthen Lot
> Some could articulate, while others not:
>   And suddenly one more impatient cried—
> 'Who *is* the Potter, pray, and who the Pot?'
>
> [LXXXIV]
> "Then said another—'Surely not in vain
> 'My Substance from the common Earth was ta'en,
>   'That He who subtly wrought me into Shape
> 'Should stamp me back to common Earth again.'
>
> [LXXXV]
> "Another said—Why, ne'er a peevish Boy,
> 'Would break the Bowl from which he drank in Joy;
>   'Shall He that *made* the Vessel in pure Love
> 'And Fansy, in an after Rage destroy!'
>
> [LXXXVI]
> "None answer'd this; but after Silence spake
> A Vessel of a more ungainly Make:
>   'They sneer at me for leaning all awry;
> 'What! did the Hand then of the Potter shake?'
>
> [LXXXIII absent]
>
> [LXXXIV]
> "Said one—Folks of a surly Tapster tell,
> 'And daub his Visage with the Smoke of Hell;
>   'They talk of some strict Testing of us—Pish!
> 'He's a Good Fellow, and 't will all be well.'
>
> [LXXXV]
> "Then said another with a long-drawn Sigh,
> 'My Clay with long oblivion is gone dry:
>   'But, fill me with the old familiar Juice,
> 'Methinks I might recover by-and-bye!'
>
> [LXXXVI]
> "So while the Vessels one by one were speaking,
> One spied the little Crescent all were seeking:
>   And then they jogg'd each other, 'Brother! Brother!
> 'Hark to the Porter's Shoulder-knot a-creaking!' "

[61] Ramazán: a month of fasting for Muslim believers.

"Would break the Bowl from which he drank
      in joy;
   "And He that with his hand the Vessel made
340 Will surely not in after Wrath destroy."

LXXXVI

After a momentary silence spake
Some Vessel of a more ungainly Make;
   "They sneer at me for leaning all awry:
"What! did the Hand then of the Potter
      shake?"

LXXXVII

Whereat some one of the loquacious Lot—
I think a Súfi pipkin[62]—waxing hot—
   "All this of Pot and Potter—Tell me then,
"Who is the Potter, pray, and who the Pot?"

LXXXVIII

"Why," said another, "Some there are who tell
350 "Of one who threatens he will toss to Hell
   "The luckless Pots he marr'd in making—
      Pish!
"He's a Good Fellow, and 't will all be well."

LXXXIX

"Well," murmur'd one, "Let whoso make or
      buy,
"My Clay with long Oblivion is gone dry:
   "But fill me with the old familiar Juice,
"Methinks I might recover by and by."

XC

So while the Vessels one by one were speaking,
The little Moon look'd in that all were seeking:
   And then they jogg'd each other, "Brother!
      Brother!
"Now for the Porter's shoulder-knot a-creak-
360   ing."[63]

.   .   .   .

XCI

Ah, with the Grape my fading Life provide,
And wash the Body whence the Life has died,
   And lay me, shrouded in the living Leaf,
By some not unfrequented Garden-side.[64]

XCII

That ev'n my buried Ashes such a snare
Of Vintage shall fling up into the Air
   As not a True-believer passing by
But shall be overtaken unaware.

XCIII

Indeed the Idols I have loved so long
Have done my credit in this World much
      wrong: 37(
   Have drown'd my Glory[65] in a shallow Cup,
And sold my Reputation for a Song.

XCIV

Indeed, indeed, Repentance oft before
I swore—but was I sober when I swore?
   And then and then came Spring, and Rose-
      in-hand
My thread-bare Penitence apieces tore.

XCV

And much as Wine has play'd the Infidel,
And robb'd me of my Robe of Honour—Well,
   I wonder often what the Vintners buy
One half so precious as the stuff they sell.   38(

XCVI

Yet Ah, that Spring should vanish with the
      Rose!
That Youth's sweet-scented manuscript should
      close!
   The Nightingale that in the branches sang,
Ah whence, and whither flown again, who
      knows!

XCVII

Would but the Desert of the Fountain yield
One glimpse—if dimly, yet indeed, reveal'd,
   To which the fainting Traveller might
      spring,
As springs the trampled herbage of the field!

XCVIII

Would but some wingéd Angel ere too late
Arrest the yet unfolded Roll of Fate,   390
   And make the stern Recorder otherwise
Enregister, or quite obliterate![66]

---

[62] Súfi: a Persian mystical sect whose philosophers and poets wrote speculations and allegories on abstruse questions.

[63] FitzGerald's note: "At the Close of the Fasting Month, Ramazán (which makes the Musulman unhealthy and unamiable), the first Glimpse of the New Moon . . . is looked for with the utmost Anxiety, and hailed with Acclamation. Then it is that the Porter's Knot may be heard—toward the *Cellar*": that is, coming to get the pots so that they may be used in feasting.

[64] 1859: "So bury me by some sweet Garden-side."   [65] 1859: "drown'd my Honour."

[66] Quatrains XCVII and XCVIII were added after 1859.

XCIX

Ah Love, could you and I with Him conspire
To grasp this sorry Scheme of Things entire,
    Would we not shatter it to bits—and then
Re-mould it nearer to the Heart's Desire!

.   .   .   .

C

Yon rising Moon that looks for us again—
How oft hereafter will she wax and wane;

How oft hereafter rising look for us
Through this same Garden—and for *one* in
    vain![67]   400

CI

And when like her, oh Sákí, you shall pass[68]
Among the Guests Star-scatter'd on the Grass,
    And in your joyous errand reach the spot
Where I made One—turn down an empty
    Glass!

                                    1859; revised 1879

George Meredith
1828–1909

GEORGE MEREDITH became famous in his maturity as a novelist, and then near the end of his life as a grand old man of letters, a sage and oracle who like Wordsworth, Tennyson, and Browning rose into an old age full of celebrity, honor, the homage of young writers, and the adulation of devoted readers. This status is interesting because in nineteenth-century England it was customarily poets rather than novelists who were accorded this kind of veneration. Like Thomas Hardy, Meredith wanted to make a major achievement and reputation as a poet rather than as a novelist. Unlike Hardy, he did not come close to realizing his wish: then as now it is his fiction that has first claim to attention. But he wrote poetry all through his life, and especially in the last decades of his life he performed in his poetry as if he were the seer whom major Victorian poets aspired to become. He thought that he had a philosophy, and he certainly held and argued in his poems a connected set of beliefs about human evolution, the individual self, nature, society, race, history, war, death, and how they all come together to require an ethic

of human conduct and to promise a progress of human civilization. He also had a style of his own, always quick and elliptical, at the end of his career gnomic and obscure. His style announced that he had something singular and complicated to say, deserving, he thought and demanded, of uncommonly close and serious study.

Although he described the circumstances of his childhood in one of his early novels, *Evan Harrington* (1861), Meredith was reticent about his origins, perhaps in part because he was trying to enforce his sense of being uncommon. His grandfather was a tailor and kept a naval outfitting shop in Portsmouth, on the southern coast of England. His own father studied medicine, but took over the tailoring business when Meredith's grandfather died. Meredith's mother, who died when he was five years old and left him a small legacy, was the daughter of an innkeeper. Meredith went to school in Portsmouth, and then by his own choice when he was fourteen years old he was sent to a school in Germany conducted by the Moravian Brethren, an evangelical sect whose

[67] 1859:   "Ah, Moon of my Delight who know'st no wane,
            The Moon of Heav'n is rising once again:
                How oft hereafter rising shall she look
            Through this same Garden after me—in vain!"
[68] 1859:   "And when Thyself with shining Foot shall pass"

roots were medieval. He returned to London in 1844 and went to work in a law office. His father, who had moved to London to open a tailoring shop, soon emigrated to South Africa, and Meredith was on his own in London.

He decided in the 1840s to become a writer, and in 1851 he published his first book of poems, which included the early version of "Love in the Valley," at his own expense. Two years earlier he had married Mary Ellen Nicolls, the daughter of the novelist Thomas Love Peacock. She was older than Meredith, a widow, and the mother of a child. They lived with her father and in lodgings in seaside towns during the 1850s, had a child of their own, and worked, both of them, at their ambitions to become professional writers. Meredith published some poems in periodicals, and in 1856 and 1857 he also began publishing short, fanciful fictions in magazines. In 1858 his wife left him and went to the Continent with a painter by whom she later had a son. She returned to England in 1859 and died two years later. Meredith did not visit her as she was dying, but immediately after her death he began writing the painful story of "Modern Love." He had moved by this time to London with his son, and he had published in 1859 his first substantial fiction, *The Ordeal of Richard Feverel*. He began working as a correspondent for a provincial newspaper, as a contributor to a London newspaper (he went to Italy as a war correspondent in 1866), and as a reader of manuscripts of fiction for a London publisher. He moved to the Surrey countryside outside London, married again in 1864, and in 1868 moved to his house at Box Hill, where he lived the rest of his life.

By the early 1860s Meredith was a central figure in the London literary world. He was a friend of Dante Gabriel Rossetti and Swinburne, with whom for a brief time he shared a house, and of practical, rationalist literary critics and journalists like John Morley and Leslie Stephen. Although he published *Modern Love, and Poems of the English Roadside, with Poems and Ballads* in 1862, it was by then clear that the main line of his energy and reputation was to be fiction. He published four novels in the 1860s, usually serializing them in magazines before they appeared in bound volumes. He published four more long fictions (including *The Egoist* in 1879) before the relative popularity of *Diana of the Crossways* in 1884–85, and the first volumes of a collected

edition of his novels in 1885 confirmed his distinction as a writer. Even then it took eleven years to sell out a second edition of his third volume of poems, *Poems and Lyrics of the Joy of Earth*, for which he had again to pay the expenses of publication in 1883. But Meredith persevered, and as his ability to sustain long fictions flagged, he increased the frequency with which he wrote and published poems. He published volumes of new poems in 1887, 1888, 1892 (an enlarged edition of the *Modern Love* volume was published in the same year), 1898, 1901, and a posthumous volume in 1909. A collected edition of his poems was published in 1898.

The topics and themes of Meredith's early poems are often celebrations of the corruscating and resilient energies of things immediately around—the landscapes of spring and autumn, young girls, the tough cheer of Juggling Jerry. In his early poems Meredith tried for a particularity and vigor he saw as different from the decorum and finish of what in the 1860s he called "Tennysonian green tea." He never abandoned this particularity or his willingness, as in a late poem like "Jump-to-Glory Jane," to make poetry of the contemporary, eccentric, and what to many mid-century readers and critics seemed the low and vulgar. In his later poetry, however, Meredith increasingly used myth and elaborate metaphor to state his ideas about how to live on an earth that can be made good. The later version of "Love in the Valley," for example, which appeared in *Poems and Lyrics of the Joyful Earth* (1883), Meredith's first extended articulation of his ideas about man and nature in poetry, suggests by its transformation of a young woman into something like the spirit of earth in springtime how he converted a style that was always attentive to the look of things into a highly metaphoric, mythic mode. Even "Modern Love," which is fundamentally an introspective analysis of how the love of two people for one another can go wrong, can be fit into his later emphasis. Humans go wrong, he came to say, not just because of the peculiar errors and incompatibilities of individuals. Humans are also unhappy because the enormous imperatives and habits of ego and its social forms close them within anxiously self-protective and therefore finally self-destructive refusals to live in concert with other lives.

Meredith did not fully elaborate this creed until he wrote his late novels, which often mock the suffocating rigidities of social forms, and the poems he wrote in the 1880s and after. The fundamental premise of the creed is that nature—or earth, the word he often used when he wanted to emphasize the beneficent possibilities of material creation—has no ironies and sorrows. Its recurring rhythms and displays of life and death, peace and strife, are joyous. If humans will work with earth to realize its plan, they, like its other creatures, will be happy. That happiness also depends upon a harmony within the self of the matter and impulses of human evolution, which Meredith briefly identified as blood, brain, and spirit. But the principal enemies are ego and the usual forms of human society, which confer artificial identities on people, separate them from one another and from other living things, and encourage erroneous notions of possessing the earth and other people and of passing through life into another existence in which the glorified individual ego will survive. Humans will not be happy until they transcend the limits of ego, fit themselves into the rhythms of earth, and accept struggle and death not as tests or transitions to another life but as conclusive episodes with their own joy and beauty in a beautiful plan. The happy end of individual existence is finally a willingness not to be, an ultimate identification of the self with what all humans who have ever lived have done and become in their fruitful commerce with the rest of earth.

That is rudely to simplify the complicated, sometimes obscure ideas out of which Meredith wrote poems like "Ode to the Spirit of Earth in Autumn" and "The Appeasement of Demeter." But even in their simplification the scale of Meredith's ideas is apparent. It is their scale, and the fact that they were trusted to poetry, that is the point here. Meredith's poetry is most satisfying when he uses verse forms (sonnets, short lyrics), myths ("Melampus," "King Harald's Trance"), and metaphors of landscape whose compression matches the percussive music and impacted syntax of his line. Long passages of Meredith's poetry can be trying because the architecture and dynamics of the poem sometimes disappear in the quick turns and enigmatic proofs of an argument conducted by an oracle possesssed of a larger truth than he can plainly utter. But whatever their lapses, Meredith's poems are the testament of a writer who at the end of the nineteenth century, when many poets thought of themselves in the sad twilight of a grand prophetic tradition in poetry, made poetry the vehicle of a large and complex truth he imagined to be redemptive. Without their cosmologies of a finite reality enfolded or shot through by a redeeming infinity, Meredith aspired to the prophetic office that Wordsworth, Tennyson, and Browning had helped establish for poetry. He also added to the variety of means fashioned by nineteenth-century British poets in their attempt to penetrate and exalt the meaning of ordinary experience. In some of his early poems he worked out an emphatic, concrete idiom that made poetry of the immediate and particular. Then in his later poems he extended the reach of his idiom, and sometimes succeeded in the most ambitious task imagined by the poets of his century, to make new and inspiriting myths of the visible and temporal earth.

EDITIONS

The texts reprinted here are those of an edition of the poems published in a collected edition of Meredith's works in 1896–98. The texts are consistent with the standard Memorial edition (1909–11) and with G. O. Trevelyan's usefully annotated *The Poetical Works of George Meredith* (1912). *The Letters of George Meredith* have been published in an edition prepared by C. L. Cline (1970).

BIOGRAPHY AND CRITICISM

The most useful biography of Meredith is Lionel Stevenson's *The Ordeal of George Meredith* (1953). Siegfried Sassoon's *Meredith* (1948) contains elucidations of the themes of the novels and poems. See also S. M. Ellis' *Meredith: His Life and Friends* (1919), and Jack Lindsay's *George Meredith: His Life and Work* (1956). Diane Johnson in *Lesser Lives* (1972) tells the story of Mary Ellen Nicolls, Meredith's first wife.

G. O. Trevelyan's *The Poetry and Philosophy of Meredith* (1906) is the standard and extremely useful commentary on Meredith's poems. Norman Kelvin's *A Troubled Eden: Nature and Society in the Works of Meredith* (1961) discusses the poems in explicating the topic of its subtitle. *Meredith Now*, edited by Ian Fletcher (1971), contains a strong essay by John Lucas on "Meredith as Poet." Patricia Grunden's "The Woods of Westermain," *Victorian Poetry*, 5 (1967) studies a long poem by Meredith which is one of his most important statements of his ideas about nature and society.

Maurice Buxton Forman's *Meredithiana* (1924) contains a bibliography of writings about Meredith which is supplemented by H. Lewis Sawin's "George Meredith: A Bibliography of Meredithiana 1920–53," *Bulletin of Bibliography*, 21 (1955). Forman's *Meredith: Some Early Appreciations* (1909) and J. A. Hammerton's *Meredith in Anecdote and Criticism* (1909) contain extracts from contemporary reviews of Meredith's novels and poems. Ioan Williams has edited *Meredith: The Critical Heritage* (1971). Phyllis Bartlett's pamphlet, *Meredith* (1963), in the Writers and Their Work series, contains a selected bibliography. See also the survey of commentary on Meredith by C. L. Cline in *Victorian Fiction,* edited by Lionel Stevenson (1964).

Love in the Valley (1851)

Under yonder beech-tree standing on the green
    sward,
    Couch'd with her arms behind her little
      head,
Her knees folded up, and her tresses on her
    bosom,
    Lies my young love sleeping in the shade.
Had I the heart to slide one arm beneath her!
    Press her dreaming lips as her waist I folded
      slow,
Waking on the instant she could not but
    embrace me—
Ah! would she hold me, and never let me
    go?

Shy as the squirrel, and wayward as the
    swallow;
    Swift as the swallow when athwart the
10   western flood
Circleting the surface he meets his mirror'd
    winglets,—
    Is that dear one in her maiden bud.
Shy as the squirrel whose nest is in the pine
    tops;
    Gentle—ah! that she were jealous as the
      dove!
Full of all the wildness of the woodland
    creatures,
    Happy in herself is the maiden that I love!

What can have taught her distrust of all I tell
    her?

Can she truly doubt me when looking on my
    brows?
Nature never teaches distrust of tender love-
    tales,
    What can have taught her distrust of all my
      vows?   2
No, she does not doubt me! on a dewy eve-tide
    Whispering together beneath the listening
      moon,
I pray'd till her cheek flush'd, implored till
    she faltered—
    Fluttered to my bosom—ah! to fly away so
      soon!

When her mother tends her before the
    laughing mirror,
    Tying up her laces, looping up her hair,
Often she thinks—were this wild thing wedded,
    I should have more love, and much less care.
When her mother tends her before the bashful
    mirror,
    Loosening her laces, combing down her
      curls,   3
Often she thinks—were this wild thing wedded,
    I should lose but one for so many boys and
      girls.

Clambering roses peep into her chamber,
    Jasmine and woodbine, breathe sweet, sweet,
White-necked swallows twittering of Summer,
    Fill her with balm and nested peace from
      head to feet.
Ah! will the rose-bough see her lying lonely,
    When the petals fall and fierce bloom is on
      the leaves?
Will the Autumn garners see her still
    ungathered,
    When the fickle swallows forsake the
      weeping eaves?   4

Comes a sudden question—should a strange
    hand pluck her!
    Oh! what an anguish smites me at the
      thought,
Should some idle lordling bribe her mind with
    jewels!—
    Can such beauty ever thus be bought?
Sometimes the huntsmen prancing down the
    valley
    Eye the village lasses, full of sprightly mirth;
They see as I see, mine is the fairest!
    Would she were older and could read my
      worth!

Are there not sweet maidens if she still deny
    me?
    Show the bridal Heavens but one bright star?   5

Wherefore thus then do I chase a shadow,
  Clattering one note like a brown eve-jar?[1]
So I rhyme and reason till she darts before
    me—
  Thro' the milky meadows from flower to
    flower she flies,
Sunning her sweet palms to shade her dazzled
    eyelids
  From the golden love that looks too eager in
    her eyes.

When at dawn she wakens, and her fair face
    gazes
  Out on the weather thro' the window panes,
Beauteous she looks! like a white water-lily
  Bursting out of bud on the rippled river
    plains.
When from bed she rises clothed from neck to
    ankle
  In her long nightgown, sweet as boughs of
    May,
Beauteous she looks! like a tall garden lily
  Pure from the night and perfect for the day!

Happy, happy time, when the grey star twin-
    kles
  Over the fields all fresh with bloomy dew;
When the cold-cheeked dawn grows ruddy up
    the twilight,
  And the gold sun wakes, and weds her in the
    blue.
Then when my darling tempts the early
    breezes,
  She the only star that dies not with the dark!
Powerless to speak all the ardour of my passion
  I catch her little hand as we listen to the
    lark.

Shall the birds in vain then valentine their
    sweethearts,
  Season after season tell a fruitless tale?
Will not the virgin listen to their voices,
  Take the honeyed meaning, wear the bridal
    veil?
Fears she frost of winter, fears she the bare
    branches?
  Waits she the garlands of spring for her
    dower?
Is she a nightingale that will not be nested
  Till the April woodland has built her bridal
    bower?

Then come merry April with all thy birds and
    beauties!

With thy crescent brows and thy flowery,
    showery glee;
With thy budding leafage and fresh green
    pastures;
  And may thy lustrous crescent grow a honey-
    moon for me!
Come merry month of the cuckoo and the
    violet!
  Come weeping Loveliness in all thy blue
    delight!
Lo! the nest is ready, let me not languish
    longer!
  Bring her to my arms on the first May night.
                                              1851

Love in the Valley (1878)

Under yonder beech-tree single on the green-
    sward,
  Couched with her arms behind her golden
    head,
Knees and tresses folded to slip and ripple idly,
  Lies my young love sleeping in the shade.
Had I the heart to slide an arm beneath her,
  Press her parting lips as her waist I gather
    slow,
Waking in amazement she could not but
    embrace me:
  Then would she hold me and never let me
    go?

Shy as the squirrel and wayward as the
    swallow,
  Swift as the swallow along the river's light   10
Circleting the surface to meet his mirrored
    winglets,
  Fleeter she seems in her stay than in her
    flight.
Shy as the squirrel that leaps among the pine-
    tops,
  Wayward as the swallow overhead at set of
    sun,
She whom I love is hard to catch and conquer,
  Hard, but O the glory of the winning were
    she won!

When her mother tends her before the
    laughing mirror,
  Tying up her laces, looping up her hair,
Often she thinks, were this wild thing wedded,
  More love should I have, and much less care. 20

[1] Eve-jar: a common night bird whose song is a whirring noise.

When her mother tends her before the lighted
    mirror,
    Loosening her laces, combing down her curls,
Often she thinks, were this wild thing wedded,
    I should miss but one for many boys and
    girls.

Heartless she is as the shadow in the meadows
    Flying to the hills on a blue and breezy noon.
No, she is athirst and drinking up her wonder:
    Earth to her is young as the slip of the new
    moon.
Deals she an unkindness, 'tis but her rapid
    measure,
    Even as in a dance; and her smile can heal
30   no less:
Like the swinging May-cloud that pelts the
    flowers with hailstones
    Off a sunny border, she was made to bruise
    and bless.

Lovely are the curves of the white owl
    sweeping
    Wavy in the dusk lit by one large star.
Lone on the fir-branch, his rattle-note
    unvaried,
    Brooding o'er the gloom, spins the brown
    eve-jar.[1]
Darker grows the valley, more and more
    forgetting:
    So were it with me if forgetting could be
    willed.
Tell the grassy hollow that holds the bubbling
    well-spring,
    Tell it to forget the source that keeps it
40   filled.

Stepping down the hill with her fair compan-
    ions,
    Arm in arm, all against the raying West,
Boldly she sings, to the merry tune she
    marches,
    Brave in her shape, and sweeter unpossessed.
Sweeter, for she is what my heart first awaking
    Whispered the world was; morning light is
    she.
Love that so desires would fain keep her
    changeless;
    Fain would fling the net, and fain have her
    free.

Happy happy time, when the white star hovers
50   Low over dim fields fresh with bloomy dew,

Near the face of dawn, that draws athwart the
    darkness,
    Threading it with colour, like yewberries the
    yew.
Thicker crowd the shades as the grave East
    deepens
    Glowing, and with crimson a long cloud
    swells.
Maiden still the morn is; and strange she is,
    and secret;
    Strange her eyes; her cheeks are cold as cold
    sea-shells.

Sunrays, leaning on our southern hills and
    lighting
    Wild cloud-mountains that drag the hills
    along,
Oft ends the day of your shifting brilliant
    laughter
    Chill as a dull face frowning on a song.   60
Ay, but shows the South-West a ripple-
    feathered bosom
    Blown to silver while the clouds are shaken
    and ascend
Scaling the mid-heavens as they stream, there
    comes a sunset
    Rich, deep like love in beauty without end.

When at dawn she sighs, and like an infant
    to the window
    Turns grave eyes craving light, released from
    dreams,
Beautiful she looks, like a white water-lily
    Bursting out of bud in havens of the streams.
When from bed she rises clothed from neck to
    ankle
    In her long nightgown sweet as boughs of
    May,   70
Beautiful she looks, like a tall garden lily
    Pure from the night, and splendid for the
    day.

Mother of the dews, dark eye-lashed twilight,
    Low-lidded twilight, o'er the valley's brim,
Rounding on thy breast sings the dew-
    delighted skylark,
    Clear as though the dewdrops had their voice
    in him.
Hidden where the rose-flush drinks the rayless
    planet,
    Fountain-full he pours the spraying
    fountain-showers.

[1] Eve-jar: a common night bird that makes a whirring noise.

Let me hear her laughter, I would have her
  ever
    Cool as dew in twilight, the lark above the
    flowers.

All the girls are out with their baskets for the
  primrose;
    Up lanes, woods through, they troop in
    joyful bands.
My sweet leads: she knows not why, but now
  she loiters,
    Eyes the bent anemones, and hangs her
    hands.
Such a look will tell that the violets are
  peeping,
    Coming the rose: and unaware a cry
Springs in her bosom for odours and for
  colour,
    Covert and the nightingale; she knows not
    why.

Kerchiefed head and chin she darts between
  her tulips,
    Streaming like a willow grey in arrowy rain:
Some bend beaten cheek to gravel, and their
  angel
    She will be; she lifts them, and on she
    speeds again.
Black the driving raincloud breasts the iron
  gateway:
    She is forth to cheer a neighbour lacking
    mirth.
So when sky and grass met rolling dumb for
  thunder
    Saw I once a white dove, sole light of earth.

Prim little scholars are the flowers of her
  garden,
    Trained to stand in rows, and asking if they
    please.
I might love them well but for loving more the
  wild ones:
    O my wild ones! they tell me more than
    these.
You, my wild one, you tell of honied field-rose,
    Violet, blushing eglantine in life; and even
    as they,
They by the wayside are earnest of your good-
  ness,
    You are of life's, on the banks that line the
    way.

Peering at her chamber the white crowns the
  red rose,
    Jasmine winds the porch with stars two and
    three.
Parted is the window; she sleeps; the starry
  jasmine
    Breathes a falling breath that carries
    thoughts of me.
Sweeter unpossessed, have I said of her my
  sweetest?
    Not while she sleeps: while she sleeps the
    jasmine breathes,   110
Luring her to love; she sleeps; the starry
  jasmine
    Bears me to her pillow under white rose-
    wreaths.

Yellow with birdfoot-trefoil are the grass-
  glades;
    Yellow with cinquefoil[2] of the dew-grey leaf;
Yellow with stonecrop;[3] the moss-mounds are
  yellow;
    Blue-necked the wheat sways, yellowing to
    the sheaf.
Green-yellow bursts from the copse the
  laughing yaffle;[4]
    Sharp as a sickle is the edge of shade and
    shine:
Earth in her heart laughs looking at the
  heavens,
    Thinking of the harvest: I look and think
    of mine.   120

This I may know: her dressing and undressing
    Such a change of light shows as when the
    skies in sport
Shift from cloud to moonlight; or edging over
  thunder
    Slips a ray of sun; or sweeping into port
White sails furl; or on the ocean borders
    White sails lean along the waves leaping
    green.
Visions of her shower before me, but from
  eyesight
    Guarded she would be like the sun were she
    seen.

Front door and back of the mossed old farm-
  house
    Open with the morn, and in a breezy link   130

---

[2] Birdfoot-trefoil; cinquefoil: small plants of three and five leaves.
[3] Stonecrop: a herb with yellow flowers.   [4] Yaffle: green woodpecker.

Freshly sparkles garden to stripe-shadowed
        orchard,
    Green across a rill where on sand the
        minnows wink.
Busy in the grass the early sun of summer
    Swarms, and the blackbird's mellow fluting
        notes
Call my darling up with round and roguish
        challenge:
    Quaintest, richest carol of all the singing
        throats!

Cool was the woodside; cool as her white dairy
    Keeping sweet the cream-pan; and there the
        boys from school,
Cricketing below, rushed brown and red with
        sunshine;
    O the dark translucence of the deep-eyed
140   cool!
Spying from the farm, herself she fetched a
        pitcher
    Full of milk, and tilted for each in turn the
        beak.
Then a little fellow, mouth up and on tiptoe,
    Said, "I will kiss you": she laughed and
        leaned her cheek.

Doves of the fir-wood walling high our red roof
    Through the long noon coo, crooning
        through the coo.
Loose droop the leaves, and down the sleepy
        roadway
    Sometimes pipes a chaffinch; loose droops
        the blue.
Cows flap a slow tail knee-deep in the river,
150   Breathless, given up to sun and gnat and fly.
Nowhere is she seen; and if I see her nowhere,
    Lightning may come, straight rains and tiger
        sky.

O the golden sheaf, the rustling treasure-
        armful!
    O the nutbrown tresses nodding interlaced!
O the treasure-tresses one another over
    Nodding! O the girdle slack about the waist!
Slain are the poppies that shot their random
        scarlet
    Quick amid the wheatears: wound about the
        waist,
Gathered, see these brides of Earth one blush
        of ripeness!
160   O the nutbrown tresses nodding interlaced!

Large and smoky red the sun's cold disk drops,
    Clipped by naked hills, on violet shaded
        snow:

Eastward large and still lights up a bower of
        moonrise,
    Whence at her leisure steps the moon aglow.
Nightlong on black print-branches our beech-
        tree
    Gazes in this whiteness: nightlong could I.
Here may life on death or death on life be
        painted.
    Let me clasp her soul to know she cannot
        die!

Gossips count her faults; they scour a narrow
        chamber
    Where there is no window, read not heaven
        or her.   17
"When she was a tiny," one aged woman
        quavers,
    Plucks at my heart and leads me by the ear.
Faults she had once as she learnt to run and
        tumbled:
    Faults of feature some see, beauty not
        complete.
Yet, good gossips, beauty that makes holy
    Earth and air, may have faults from head to
        feet.

Hither she comes; she comes to me; she lingers,
    Deepens her brown eyebrows, while in new
        surprise
High rise the lashes in wonder of a stranger;
    Yet am I the light and living of her eyes.   18
Something friends have told her fills her heart
        to brimming,
    Nets her in her blushes, and wounds her,
        and tames.—
Sure of her haven, O like a dove alighting,
    Arms up, she dropped: our souls were in our
        names.

Soon will she lie like a white-frost sunrise.
    Yellow oats and brown wheat, barley pale as
        rye,
Long since your sheaves have yielded to the
        thresher,
    Felt the girdle loosened, seen the tresses fly.
Soon will she lie like a blood-red sunset.
    Swift with the to-morrow, green-winged
        Spring!   19
Sing from the South-West, bring her back the
        truants,
    Nightingale and swallow, song and dipping
        wing.

Soft new beech-leaves, up to beamy April
    Spreading bough on bough a primrose
        mountain, you,

Lucid in the moon, raise lilies to the skyfields,
    Youngest green transfused in silver shining
        through:
Fairer than the lily, than the wild white
      cherry:
    Fair as in image my seraph love appears
Borne to me by dreams when dawn is at my
      eyelids:
    Fair as in the flesh she swims to me on tears.

Could I find a place to be alone with heaven,
    I would speak my heart out: heaven is my
      need.
Every woodland tree is flushing like the
      dogwood,
    Flashing like the whitebeam,[5] swaying like
      the reed.
Flushing like the dogwood crimson in
      October;
    Streaming like the flag-reed[6] South-West
      blown;
Flashing as in gusts the sudden-lighted white-
      beam:
    All seem to know what is for heaven alone.

                1878; 1883

The Promise in Disturbance[1]

How low when angels fall their black descent,
Our primal thunder tells: known is the pain
Of music, that nigh throning wisdom went,
And one false note cast wailful to the insane.
Now seems the language heard of Love as rain
To make a mire where fruitfulness was meant.
The golden harp gives out a jangled strain,
Too like revolt from heaven's Omnipotent.
But listen in the thought; so may there come
Conception of a newly-added chord,
Commanding space beyond where ear has
    home.
In labour of the trouble at its fount,
Leads Life to an intelligible Lord
The rebel discords up the sacred mount.

                1892

The story of Modern Love *is of a marriage drift-
ing toward wreck as its principals meet and act on
one another in a largely social round of dinners
and visits to country houses. The wife has a lover
(sonnets III and XV, for example); the husband
begins and abandons an affair with a golden-
haired woman (sonnets XXVII to XL); the hus-
band and wife try and fail to resume their marriage
(sonnets XLII to XLVIII); and the wife commits
suicide. The matter of the poem is the complex and
varying response of the husband to these events.
The poem undoubtedly works out some of Mere-
dith's feelings about the dissolution of his own
marriage in 1857–58. But it is a dramatic poem. Even
when the sonnets are not spoken in the first per-
son by the husband, they are spoken from within
his consciousness. Measured by the attitudes and
possibilities Meredith enacts and enunciates in
other poems, the husband is less than Meredith,
his confused response destructively limited and self-
pitying.*

*The woman addressed as "Madam" in the poem
is the wife of the marriage. The "Lady" is the
golden-haired woman with whom the husband tries
to fall in love. In those sonnets written in the first
person, "he" is often the wife's lover.*

*The form of the poem is an unconventional son-
net of sixteen lines arranged in four quatrains.
Meredith invokes and departs from other conven-
tions of love poetry (see sonnet XXX, for example,
and the pastoral conventions of sonnet XVIII) as
one of his ways of insisting on the modernity, the
new quality and meaning, of the love which is the
story and matter of the poem.*

*The text printed below includes the relatively
few and slight revisions Meredith made when he
republished the poem in 1892 and 1898.*

Modern Love

I

By this he knew she wept with waking eyes:
That, at his hand's light quiver by her head,
The strange low sobs that shook their common
    bed
Were called into her with a sharp surprise,
And strangled mute, like little gaping snakes,
Dreadfully venomous to him. She lay
Stone-still, and the long darkness flowed away
With muffled pulses. Then, as midnight makes
Her giant heart of Memory and Tears
Drink the pale drug of silence, and so beat   10
Sleep's heavy measure, they from head to feet
Were moveless, looking through their dead
    black years,

---

[5] Whitebeam: a small tree with leaves that are white on their undersides.

[6] Flag-reed: an irislike reed that grows in moist places.

[1] When Meredith reprinted "Modern Love" in a volume of poems in 1892, he added this sonnet as an introductory poem to the sequence. It was written after the original publication of "Modern Love" in 1862.

By vain regret scrawled over the blank wall.
Like sculptured effigies they might be seen
Upon their marriage-tomb, the sword between;
Each wishing for the sword that severs all.

II

It ended, and the morrow brought the task.
Her eyes were guilty gates, that let him in
By shutting all too zealous for their sin:
20   Each sucked a secret, and each wore a mask.
But, oh, the bitter taste her beauty had!
He sickened as at breath of poison-flowers:
A languid humour stole among the hours,
And if their smiles encountered, he went mad,
And raged deep inward, till the light was
      brown
Before his vision, and the world, forgot,
Looked wicked as some old dull murder-spot.
A star with lurid beams, she seemed to crown
The pit of infamy: and then again
30   He fainted on his vengefulness, and strove
To ape the magnanimity of love,
And smote himself, a shuddering heap of pain.

III

This was the woman; what now of the man?
But pass him. If he[1] comes beneath a heel,
He shall be crushed until he cannot feel,
Or, being callous, haply till he can.
But he is nothing:—nothing? Only mark
The rich light striking out from her on him!
Ha! what a sense it is when her eyes swim
40   Across the man she singles, leaving dark
All else! Lord God, who mad'st the thing so
      fair,
See that I am drawn to her even now!
It cannot be such harm on her cool brow
To put a kiss? Yet if I meet him there!
But she is mine! Ah, no! I know too well
I claim a star whose light is overcast:
I claim a phantom-woman in the Past.
The hour has struck, though I heard not the
      bell!

IV

All other joys of life he strove to warm,
50   And magnify, and catch them to his lip:
But they had suffered shipwreck with the ship,
And gazed upon him sallow from the storm.
Or if Delusion came, 'twas but to show
The coming minute mock the one that went.
Cold as a mountain in its star-pitched tent,
Stood high Philosophy, less friend than foe:

[1] He: here, the wife's lover.

Whom self-caged Passion, from its prison-bars,
Is always watching with a wondering hate.
Not till the fire is dying in the grate,
Look we for any kinship with the stars.   6
Oh, wisdom never comes when it is gold,
And the great price we pay for it full worth:
We have it only when we are half earth.
Little avails that coinage to the old!

V

A message from her set his brain aflame.
A world of household matters filled her mind,
Wherein he saw hypocrisy designed:
She treated him as something that is tame,
And but at other provocation bites.
Familiar was her shoulder in the glass,   7
Through that dark rain: yet it may come to
      pass
That a changed eye finds such familiar sights
More keenly tempting than new loveliness.
The "What has been" a moment seemed his
      own:
The splendours, mysteries, dearer because
      known,
Nor less divine: Love's inmost sacredness
Called to him, "Come!"—In his restraining
      start,
Eyes nurtured to be looked at scarce could see
A wave of the great waves of Destiny
Convulsed at a checked impulse of the heart.   8

VI

It chanced his lips did meet her forehead cool.
She had no blush, but slanted down her eye.
Shamed nature, then, confesses love can die:
And most she punishes the tender fool
Who will believe what honours her the most!
Dead! is it dead? She has a pulse, and flow
Of tears, the price of blood-drops, as I know,
For whom the midnight sobs around Love's
      ghost,
Since then I heard her, and so will sob on.
The love is here; it has but changed its aim.   9
O bitter barren woman! what's the name?
The name, the name, the new name thou hast
      won?
Behold me striking the world's coward stroke!
That will I not do, though the sting is dire.
—Beneath the surface this, while by the fire
They sat, she laughing at a quiet joke.

VII

She issues radiant from her dressing-room,
Like one prepared to scale an upper sphere:

—By stirring up a lower, much I fear!
How deftly that oiled barber lays his bloom!
That long-shanked dapper Cupid with frisked
   curls
Can make known women torturingly fair;
The gold-eyed serpent dwelling in rich hair
Awakes beneath his magic whisks and twirls.
His art can take the eyes from out my head,
Until I see with eyes of other men;
While deeper knowledge crouches in its den,
And sends a spark up:—is it true we are wed?
Yea! filthiness of body is most vile,
But faithlessness of heart I do hold worse.
The former, it were not so great a curse
To read on the steel-mirror of her smile.

VIII

Yet it was plain she struggled, and that salt
Of righteous feeling made her pitiful.
Poor twisting worm, so queenly beautiful!
Where came the cleft between us? whose the
   fault?
My tears are on thee, that have rarely dropped
As balm for any bitter wound of mine:
My breast will open for thee at a sign!
But, no: we are two reed-pipes, coarsely
   stopped:
The God once filled them with his mellow
   breath;
And they were music till he flung them down,
Used! used! Hear now the discord-loving clown
Puff his gross spirit in them, worse than death!
I do not know myself without thee more:
In this unholy battle I grow base:
If the same soul be under the same face,
Speak, and a taste of that old time restore!

IX

He felt the wild beast in him betweenwhiles
So masterfully rude, that he would grieve
To see the helpless delicate thing receive
His guardianship through certain dark defiles.
Had he not teeth to rend, and hunger too?
But still he spared her. Once: "Have you no
   fear?"
He said: 'twas dusk; she in his grasp; none
   near.
She laughed: "No, surely; am I not with you?"
And uttering that soft starry "you," she leaned
Her gentle body near him, looking up;
And from her eyes, as from a poison-cup,
He drank until the flittering eyelids screened.
Devilish malignant witch! and oh, young beam
Of heaven's circle-glory! Here thy shape

To squeeze like an intoxicating grape—
I might, and yet thou goest safe, supreme.

X

But where began the change; and what's my
   crime?
The wretch condemned, who has not been
   arraigned,
Chafes at his sentence. Shall I, unsustained,
Drag on Love's nerveless body thro' all time?
I must have slept, since now I wake. Prepare,
You lovers, to know Love a thing of moods:
Not, like hard life, of laws. In Love's deep
   woods,
I dreamt of loyal Life:—the offence is there!
Love's jealous woods about the sun are curled;
At least, the sun far brighter there did beam.—
My crime is, that the puppet of a dream,
I plotted to be worthy of the world.
Oh, had I with my darling helped to mince
The facts of life, you still had seen me go
With hindward feather and with forward toe,
Her much-adored delightful Fairy Prince!

XI

Out in the yellow meadows, where the bee
Hums by us with the honey of the Spring,
And showers of sweet notes from the larks on
   wing
Are dropping like a noon-dew, wander we.
Or is it now? or was it then? for now,
As then, the larks from running rings pour
   showers:
The golden foot of May is on the flowers,
And friendly shadows dance upon her brow.
What's this, when Nature swears there is no
   change
To challenge eyesight? Now, as then, the grace
Of heaven seems holding earth in its embrace.
Nor eyes, nor heart, has she to feel it strange?
Look, woman, in the West. There wilt thou see
An amber cradle near the sun's decline:
Within it, featured even in death divine,
Is lying a dead infant, slain by thee.

XII

Not solely that the Future she destroys,
And the fair life which in the distance lies
For all men, beckoning out from dim rich
   skies:
Nor that the passing hour's supporting joys
Have lost the keen-edged flavour, which begat
Distinction in old times, and still should breed
Sweet Memory, and Hope,—earth's modest
   seed,

And heaven's high-prompting: not that the
    world is flat
Since that soft-luring creature I embraced
Among the children of Illusion went:
Methinks with all this loss I were content,
If the mad Past, on which my foot is based,
Were firm, or might be blotted: but the whole
190 Of life is mixed: the mocking Past will stay:
And if I drink oblivion of a day,
So shorten I the stature of my soul.

XIII

"I play for Seasons; not Eternities!"
Says Nature, laughing on her way. "So must
All those whose stake is nothing more than
    dust!"
And lo, she wins, and of her harmonies
She is full sure! Upon her dying rose
She drops a look of fondness, and goes by,
Scarce any retrospection in her eye;
200 For she the laws of growth most deeply knows,
Whose hands bear, here, a seed-bag—there, an
    urn.[2]
Pledged she herself to aught, 'twould mark her
    end!
This lesson of our only visible friend
Can we not teach our foolish hearts to learn?
Yes! yes!—but, oh, our human rose is fair
Surpassingly! Lose calmly Love's great bliss,
When the renewed for ever of a kiss
Whirls life within the shower of loosened hair!

XIV

What soul would bargain for a cure that brings
210 Contempt the nobler agony to kill?
Rather let me bear on the bitter ill,
And strike this rusty bosom with new stings!
It seems there is another veering fit,
Since on a gold-haired lady's eyeballs pure
I looked with little prospect of a cure,
The while her mouth's red bow loosed shafts
    of wit.
Just heaven! can it be true that jealousy
Has decked the woman thus? and does her head
Swim somewhat for possessions forfeited?
220 Madam, you teach me many things that be.
I open an old book, and there I find
That "Women still may love whom they
    deceive."
Such love I prize not, madam: by your leave,
The game you play at is not to my mind.

XV

I think she sleeps: it must be sleep, when low
Hangs that abandoned arm toward the floor;
The face turned with it. Now make fast the
    door.
Sleep on: it is your husband, not your foe.
The Poet's black stage-lion of wronged love
Frights not our modern dames:—well if he
    did!   230
Now will I pour new light upon that lid,[3]
Full-sloping like the breasts beneath. "Sweet
    dove,
Your sleep is pure. Nay, pardon: I disturb.
I do not? good!" Her waking infant-stare
Grows woman to the burden my hands bear:
Her own handwriting to me when no curb
Was left on Passion's tongue. She trembles
    through;
A woman's tremble—the whole instrument:—
I show another letter lately sent.
The words are very like: the name is new.   240

XVI

In our old shipwrecked days there was an hour,
When in the firelight steadily aglow,
Joined slackly, we beheld the red chasm grow
Among the clicking coals. Our library-bower
That eve was left to us: and hushed we sat
As lovers to whom Time is whispering.
From sudden-opened doors we heard them
    sing:
The nodding elders mixed good wine with
    chat.
Well knew we that Life's greatest treasure lay
With us, and of it was our talk. "Ah, yes!   250
Love dies!" I said: I never thought it less.
She yearned to me that sentence to unsay.
Then when the fire domed blackening, I found
Her cheek was salt against my kiss, and swift
Up the sharp scale of sobs her breast did lift:—
Now am I haunted by that taste! that sound!

XVII

At dinner, she is hostess, I am host.
Went the feast ever cheerfuller? She keeps
The Topic over intellectual deeps
In buoyancy afloat. They see no ghost.   260
With sparkling surface-eyes we ply the ball:
It is in truth a most contagious game:
HIDING THE SKELETON, shall be its name.
Such play as this the devils might appal!
But here's the greater wonder; in that we,

---

[2] Urn: funeral urn.   [3] Lid: eyelid.

Enamoured of an acting nought can tire,
Each other, like true hypocrites, admire;
Warm-lighted looks, Love's ephemerioe,[4]
Shoot gaily o'er the dishes and the wine.
270 We waken envy of our happy lot.
Fast, sweet, and golden, shows the marriage-
knot.
Dear guests, you now have seen Love's corpse-
light shine.

XVIII

Here Jack and Tom are paired with Moll and
Meg.
Curved open to the river-reach is seen
A country merry-making on the green.
Fair space for signal shakings of the leg.
That little screwy[5] fiddler from his booth,
Whence flows one nut-brown stream,
commands the joints
Of all who caper here at various points.
280 I have known rustic revels in my youth:
The May-fly pleasures of a mind at ease.
An early goddess was a country lass:
A charmed Amphion-oak[6] she tripped the grass.
What life was that I lived? The life of these?
Heaven keep them happy! Nature they seem
near.
They must, I think, be wiser than I am;
They have the secret of the bull and lamb.
'Tis true that when we trace its source, 'tis
beer.

XIX

No state is enviable. To the luck alone
290 Of some few favoured men I would put claim.
I bleed, but her who wounds I will not blame.
Have I not felt her heart as 'twere my own
Beat thro' me? could I hurt her? heaven and
hell!
But I could hurt her cruelly! Can I let
My Love's old time-piece to another set,
Swear it can't stop, and must for ever swell?
Sure, that's one way Love drifts into the mart
Where goat-legged buyers[7] throng. I see not
plain:—
My meaning is, it must not be again.
300 Great God! the maddest gambler throws his
heart.

If any state be enviable on earth,
'Tis yon born idiot's, who, as days go by,
Still rubs his hands before him, like a fly,
In a queer sort of meditative mirth.

XX

I am not of those miserable males
Who sniff at vice and, daring not to snap,
Do therefore hope for heaven. I take the hap[8]
Of all my deeds. The wind that fills my sails
Propels; but I am helmsman. Am I wrecked,
310 I know the devil has sufficient weight
To bear: I lay it not on him, or fate.
Besides, he's damned. That man I do suspect
A coward, who would burden the poor deuce
With what ensues from his own slipperiness.
I have just found a wanton-scented tress
In an old desk, dusty for lack of use.
Of days and nights it is demonstrative,
That, like some aged star, gleam luridly.
If for those times I must ask charity,
320 Have I not any charity to give?

XXI

We three are on the cedar-shadowed lawn;
My friend being third. He who at love once
laughed
Is in the weak rib by a fatal shaft
Struck through, and tells his passion's bashful
dawn
And radiant culmination, glorious crown,
When "this" she said: went "thus": most
wondrous she.
Our eyes grow white, encountering: that we
are three,
Forgetful; then together we look down.
But he demands our blessing; is convinced
330 That words of wedded lovers must bring good.
We question; if we dare! or if we should!
And pat him, with light laugh. We have not
winced.
Next, she has fallen. Fainting points the sign
To happy things in wedlock.[9] When she wakes,
She looks the star that thro' the cedar shakes:
Her lost moist hand clings mortally to mine.

XXII

What may the woman labour to confess?
There is about her mouth a nervous twitch.

---

[4] Ephemerioe: simple, short-lived creatures.   [5] Screwy: tipsy.
[6] Amphion-oak: the powers of the musician Amphion in classical mythology were so great that his music could make trees dance.
[7] Goat-legged buyers: Satyrs, mythological creatures, half-man and half-goat, who embodied energies of carnal lust.
[8] Hap: event, consequence.   [9] The cause of the fainting is taken to be pregnancy.

'Tis something to be told, or hidden:—which?
340 I get a glimpse of hell in this mild guess.
She has desires of touch, as if to feel
That all the household things are things she
    knew.
She stops before the glass. What sight in view?
A face that seems the latest to reveal!
For she turns from it hastily, and tossed
Irresolute steals shadow-like to where
I stand; and wavering pale before me there,
Her tears fall still as oak-leaves after frost.
She will not speak. I will not ask. We are
350 League-sundered by the silent gulf between.
You burly lovers on the village green,
Yours is a lower, and a happier star!

XXIII

'Tis Christmas weather, and a country house
Receives us: rooms are full: we can but get
An attic-crib. Such lovers will not fret
At that, it is half-said. The great carouse
Knocks hard upon the midnight's hollow door,
But when I knock at hers, I see the pit.
Why did I come here in that dullard fit?
360 I enter, and lie couched upon the floor.
Passing, I caught the coverlet's quick beat:—
Come, Shame, burn to my soul! and Pride, and
    Pain—
Foul demons that have tortured me, enchain!
Out in the freezing darkness the lambs bleat.
The small bird stiffens in the low starlight.
I know not how, but shuddering as I slept,
I dreamed a banished angel to me crept:
My feet were nourished on her breasts all
    night.

XXIV

The misery is greater, as I live!
370 To know her flesh so pure, so keen her sense,
That she does penance now for no offence,
Save against Love. The less can I forgive!
The less can I forgive, though I adore
That cruel lovely pallor which surrounds
Her footsteps; and the low vibrating sounds
That come on me, as from a magic shore.
Low are they, but most subtle to find out
The shrinking soul. Madam, 'tis understood
When women play upon their womanhood,
380 It means, a Season gone. And yet I doubt
But I am duped. That nun-like look waylays
My fancy. Oh! I do but wait a sign!
Pluck out the eyes of pride! thy mouth to mine!
Never! though I die thirsting. Go thy ways!

XXV

You like not that French novel? Tell me why.
You think it quite unnatural. Let us see.
The actors are, it seems, the usual three:
Husband, and wife, and lover. She—but fie!
In England we'll not hear of it. Edmond,
The lover, her devout chagrin doth share;   390
Blanc-mange[10] and absinthe are his penitent
    fare,
Till his pale aspect makes her over-fond:
So, to preclude fresh sin, he tries rosbif.[11]
Meantime the husband is no more abused:
Auguste forgives her ere the tear is used.
Then hangeth all on one tremendous IF:—
If she will choose between them. She does
    choose;
And takes her husband, like a proper wife.
Unnatural? My dear, these things are life:
And life, some think, is worthy of the Muse.   40

XXVI

Love ere he bleeds, an eagle in high skies,
Has earth beneath his wings: from reddened
    eve
He views the rosy dawn. In vain they weave
The fatal web below while far he flies.
But when the arrow strikes him, there's a
    change.
He moves but in the track of his spent pain,
Whose red drops are the links of a harsh chain,
Binding him to the ground, with narrow range.
A subtle serpent then has Love become.
I had the eagle in my bosom erst: 41
Henceforward with the serpent I am cursed.
I can interpret where the mouth is dumb.
Speak, and I see the side-lie of a truth.
Perchance my heart may pardon you this deed:
But be no coward:—you that made Love bleed,
You must bear all the venom of his tooth!

XXVII

Distraction is the panacea, Sir!
I hear my oracle of Medicine say.
Doctor! that same specific yesterday
I tried, and the result will not deter   42
A second trial. Is the devil's line
Of golden hair, or raven black, composed?
And does a cheek, like any sea-shell rosed,
Or clear as widowed sky, seem most divine?
No matter, so I taste forgetfulness.
And if the devil snare me, body and mind,
Here gratefully I score:—he seeméd kind,
When not a soul would comfort my distress!

---

[10] Blanc-mange: a dessert made of white gelatine. [11] Rosbif: roast beef.

O sweet new world, in which I rise new made!
O Lady, once I gave love: now I take!
Lady, I must be flattered. Shouldst thou wake
The passion of a demon, be not afraid.

XXVIII

I must be flattered. The imperious
Desire speaks out. Lady, I am content
To play with you the game of Sentiment,
And with you enter on paths perilous;
But if across your beauty I throw light,
To make it threefold, it must be all mine.
First secret; then avowed. For I must shine
Envied,—I, lessened in my proper sight!
Be watchful of your beauty, Lady dear!
How much hangs on that lamp you cannot
   tell.
Most earnestly I pray you, tend it well:
And men shall see me as a burning sphere;
And men shall mark you eyeing me, and groan
To be the God of such a grand sunflower!
I feel the promptings of Satanic power,
While you do homage unto me alone.

XXIX

Am I failing? For no longer can I cast
A glory round about this head of gold.
Glory she wears, but springing from the mould;
Not like the consecration of the Past!
Is my soul beggared? Something more than
   earth
I cry for still: I cannot be at peace
In having Love upon a mortal lease.
I cannot take the woman at her worth!
Where is the ancient wealth wherewith I
   clothed
Our human nakedness, and could endow
With spiritual splendour a white brow
That else had grinned at me the fact I loathed?
A kiss is but a kiss now! and no wave
Of a great flood that whirls me to the sea.
But, as you will! we'll sit contentedly,
And eat our pot of honey on the grave.

XXX

What are we first? First, animals; and next
Intelligences at a leap; on whom
Pale lies the distant shadow of the tomb,
And all that draweth on the tomb for text.

Into which state comes Love, the crowning
   sun:
Beneath whose light the shadow loses form.
We are the lords of life, and life is warm.
Intelligence and instinct now are one.
But nature says: "My children most they seem
When they least know me: therefore I decree
That they shall suffer." Swift doth young Love
   flee,
And we stand wakened, shivering from our
   dream.
Then if we study Nature we are wise.
Thus do the few who live but with the day:
The scientific animals are they.—
Lady, this is my sonnet to your eyes.[12]

XXXI

This golden head has wit in it. I live
Again, and a far higher life, near her.
Some women like a young philosopher;
Perchance because he is diminutive.
For woman's manly god must not exceed
Proportions of the natural nursing size.
Great poets and great sages draw no prize
With women: but the little lap-dog breed,
Who can be hugged, or on a mantel-piece
Perched up for adoration, these obtain
Her homage. And of this we men are vain?
Of this! 'Tis ordered for the world's increase!
Small flattery! Yet she has that rare gift
To beauty, Common Sense. I am approved.
It is not half so nice as being loved,
And yet I do prefer it. What's my drift?

XXXII

Full faith I have she holds that rarest gift
To beauty, Common Sense. To see her lie
With her fair visage an inverted sky
Bloom-covered, while the underlids uplift,
Would almost wreck the faith; but when her
   mouth
(Can it kiss sweetly? sweetly!) would address
The inner me that thirsts for her no less,
And has so long been languishing in drouth,
I feel that I am matched; that I am man!
One restless corner of my heart or head,
That holds a dying something never dead,
Still frets, though Nature giveth all she can.
It means, that woman is not, I opine,
Her sex's antidote. Who seeks the asp

---

[12] One of the conventions of love sonnets is a poem that praises the beauty of one of the beloved's features, such as her eyes. The sketch of human evolution in this sonnet is also a reduction of Meredith's full conception, which proposed suffering not as an irony but as one of the means by which humans and nature joined to work out large, beneficial results.

For serpents' bites?[13] 'Twould calm me could
    I clasp
Shrieking Bacchantes[14] with their souls of wine!

XXXIII

"In Paris, at the Louvre, there have I seen
The sumptuously-feathered angel pierce
Prone Lucifer, descending. Looked he fierce,
Showing the fight a fair one? Too serene!
The young Pharsalians did not disarray
Less willingly their locks of floating silk:
That suckling mouth of his upon the milk
Of heaven might still be feasting through the
    fray.[15]
Oh, Raphael! when men the Fiend do fight,
They conquer not upon such easy terms.
Half serpent in the struggle grow these worms.
And does he grow half human, all is right."
This to my Lady in a distant spot,
Upon the theme: *While mind is mastering clay,*
Gross clay invades it. If the spy you play,
My wife, read this! Strange love-talk, is it not?

XXXIV

Madam would speak with me. So, now it
    comes:
The Deluge or else Fire![16] She's well; she
    thanks
My husbandship. Our chain on silence clanks.
Time leers between, above his twiddling
    thumbs.
Am I quite well? Most excellent in health!
The journals, too, I diligently peruse.
Vesuvius is expected to give news:
Niagara is no noisier. By stealth
Our eyes dart scrutinizing snakes. She's glad
I'm happy, says her quivering under-lip.
"And are not you?" "How can I be?" "Take
    ship!
For happiness is somewhere to be had."
"Nowhere for me!" Her voice is barely heard.
I am not melted, and make no pretence.
With commonplace I freeze her, tongue and
    sense.
Niagara or Vesuvius is deferred.

520

530

540

XXXV

It is no vulgar nature I have wived.
Secretive, sensitive, she takes a wound
Deep to her soul, as if the sense had swooned,
And not a thought of vengeance had survived.
No confidences has she: but relief
Must come to one whose suffering is acute.
O have a care of natures that are mute!
They punish you in acts: their steps are brief.
What is she doing? What does she demand
From Providence or me? She is not one
Long to endure this torpidly, and shun
The drugs that crowd about a woman's hand.
At Forfeits[17] during snow we played, and I
Must kiss her. "Well performed!" I said: then
    she:
"'Tis hardly worth the money, you agree?"
Save her? What for? To act this wedded lie!

55

56

XXXVI

My Lady unto Madam makes her bow.
The charm of women is, that even while
You're probed by them for tears, you yet may
    smile,
Nay, laugh outright, as I have done just now.
The interview was gracious: they anoint
(To me aside) each other with fine praise:
Discriminating compliments they raise,
That hit with wondrous aim on the weak
    point:
My Lady's nose of Nature might complain.
It is not fashioned aptly to express
Her character of large-browed steadfastness.
But Madam says: Thereof she may be vain!
Now, Madam's faulty feature is a glazed
And inaccessible eye, that has soft fires,
Wide gates, at love-time, only. This admires
My Lady. At the two I stand amazed.

5⁷

XXXVII

Along the garden terrace, under which
A purple valley (lighted at its edge
By smoky torch-flame on the long cloud-ledge
Whereunder dropped the chariot) glimmers
    rich,

5⁸

---

[13] For serpent's bites: to cure serpent's bites.

[14] Bacchantes: women celebrants of the orgiastic rites of Bacchus, classical god of wine and revelry.

[15] The painting is that of St. Michael forcing Satan into Hell, by Raphael (1483–1520). Pharsalia in the region of Thessaly in Greece was supposed to have been the site of a battle between the armies of Julius Caesar and Pompey in 48 B.C. Both armies included young aristocrats who went to war luxuriously.

[16] Deluge or Fire: means by which the world may end, echoed in references to Niagara and the volcanic mountain Vesuvius.

[17] Forfeits: any game in which trivial penalties are imposed.

A quiet company we pace, and wait
The dinner-bell in prae-digestive calm.
So sweet up violet banks the Southern balm
Breathes round, we care not if the bell be late:
Though here and there grey seniors question
    Time
In irritable coughings. With slow foot
The low rosed moon, the face of Music mute,
Begins among her silent bars to climb.
As in and out, in silvery dusk, we thread,
590   I hear the laugh of Madam, and discern
My Lady's heel before me at each turn.
Our tragedy, is it alive or dead?

XXXVIII

Give to imagination some pure light
In human form to fix it, or you shame
The devils with that hideous human game:—
Imagination urging appetite!
Thus fallen have earth's greatest Gogmagogs,[18]
Who dazzle us, whom we can not revere:
Imagination is the charioteer
500   That, in default of better, drives the hogs.
So, therefore, my dear Lady, let me love!
My soul is arrowy[19] to the light in you.
You know me that I never can renew
The bond that woman broke: what would you
    have?
'Tis Love, or Vileness! not a choice between,
Save petrifaction! What does Pity here?
She killed a thing, and now it's dead, 'tis dear.
Oh, when you counsel me, think what you
    mean!

XXXIX

She yields: my Lady in her noblest mood
510   Has yielded: she, my golden-crownëd rose!
The bride of every sense! more sweet than those
Who breathe the violet breath of maidenhood.
O visage of still music in the sky!
Soft moon! I feel thy song, my fairest friend!
True harmony within can apprehend
Dumb harmony without. And hark! 'tis nigh!
Belief has struck the note of sound: a gleam
Of living silver shows me where she shook
Her long white fingers down the shadowy
    brook,
That sings her song, half waking, half in
520   dream.

What two come here to mar this heavenly
    tune?
A man is one: the woman bears my name,
And honour. Their hands touch! Am I still
    tame?
God, what a dancing spectre seems the moon!

XL

I bade my Lady think what she might mean.
Know I my meaning, I? Can I love one,
And yet be jealous of another? None
Commits such folly. Terrible Love, I ween,
Has might, even dead, half sighing to upheave
The lightless seas of selfishness amain: 630
Seas that in a man's heart have no rain
To fall and still them. Peace can I achieve,
By turning to this fountain-source of woe,
This woman, who's to Love as fire to wood?
She breathed the violet breath of maidenhood
Against my kisses once! but I say, No!
The thing is mocked at! Helplessly afloat,
I know not what I do, whereto I strive.
The dread that my old love may be alive
Has seized my nursling new love by the throat.   640

XLI

How many a thing which we cast to the
    ground,
When others pick it up becomes a gem!
We grasp at all the wealth it is to them;
And by reflected light its worth is found.
Yet for us still 'tis nothing! and that zeal
Of false appreciation quickly fades.
This truth is little known to human shades,
How rare from their own instinct 'tis to feel!
They waste the soul with spurious desire,
That is not the ripe flame upon the bough.   650
We two have taken up a lifeless vow
To rob a living passion: dust for fire!
Madam is grave, and eyes the clock that tells
Approaching midnight. We have struck
    despair
Into two hearts. O, look we like a pair
Who for fresh nuptials joyfully yield all else?

XLII

I am to follow her. There is much grace
In women when thus bent on martyrdom.
They think that dignity of soul may come,
Perchance, with dignity of body. Base!   660

[18] Gogmagogs: Gogmagog is a British giant mentioned in the legendary history of Britain by
Geoffrey of Monmouth (c. 1100–1154). The name is derived from that of Gog, an evil prince
from the land of Magog who threatens the forces of the Hebrew God in the Old Testament
(Ezekiel 38–39); in Revelation 20:8, Magog has also become a personage, joined with Gog as
one of the forces in Armageddon, the great battle before the end of the world.
[19] Arrowy: directed like an arrow.

But I was taken by that air of cold
And statuesque sedateness, when she said
"I'm going"; lit a taper, bowed her head,
And went, as with the stride of Pallas bold.
Fleshly indifference horrible! The hands
Of Time now signal: O, she's safe from me!
Within those secret walls what do I see?
Where first she set the taper down she stands:
Not Pallas: Hebe shamed![20] Thoughts black as
  death
Like a stirred pool in sunshine break. Her
670   wrists
I catch: she faltering, as she half resists,
"You love . . . ? love . . . ? love . . . ?" all
  on an indrawn breath.

XLIII

Mark where the pressing wind shoots javelin-
  like
Its skeleton shadow on the broad-backed wave!
Here is a fitting spot to dig Love's grave;
Here where the ponderous breakers plunge and
  strike,
And dart their hissing tongues high up the
  sand:
In hearing of the ocean, and in sight
Of those ribbed wind-streaks running into
  white.
680   If I the death of Love had deeply planned,
I never could have made it half so sure,
As by the unblest kisses which upbraid
The full-waked sense; or failing that, degrade!
'Tis morning: but no morning can restore
What we have forfeited. I see no sin:
The wrong is mixed. In tragic life, God wot,
No villain need be! Passions spin the plot:
We are betrayed by what is false within.

XLIV

They say, that Pity in Love's service dwells,
690   A porter at the rosy temple's gate.
I missed him going: but it is my fate
To come upon him now beside his wells;
Whereby I know that I Love's temple leave,
And that the purple doors have closed behind.
Poor soul! if, in those early days unkind,
Thy power to sting had been but power to
  grieve,

We now might with an equal spirit meet,
And not be matched like innocence and vice.
She for the Temple's worship has paid price,
And takes the coin of Pity as a cheat.   700
She sees through simulation to the bone:
What's best in her impels her to the worst:
Never, she cries, shall Pity soothe Love's thirst,
Or foul hypocrisy for truth atone!

XLV

It is the season of the sweet wild rose,
My Lady's emblem in the heart of me!
So golden-crownëd shines she gloriously,
And with that softest dream of blood she
  glows:
Mild as an evening heaven round Hesper[21]
  bright!
I pluck the flower, and smell it, and revive   710
The time when in her eyes I stood alive.
I seem to look upon it out of Night.
Here's Madam, stepping hastily. Her whims
Bid her demand the flower, which I let drop.
As I proceed, I feel her sharply stop,
And crush it under heel with trembling limbs.
She joins me in a cat-like way, and talks
Of company, and even condescends
To utter laughing scandal of old friends.
These are the summer days, and these our
  walks.   720

XLVI

At last we parley: we so strangely dumb
In such a close communion! It befell
About the sounding of the Matin-bell,[22]
And lo! her place was vacant, and the hum
Of loneliness was round me. Then I rose,
And my disordered brain did guide my foot
To that old wood where our first love-salute
Was interchanged: the source of many throes!
There did I see her, not alone. I moved
Toward her, and made proffer of my arm.   730
She took it simply, with no rude alarm;
And that disturbing shadow passed reproved.
I felt the pained speech coming, and declared
My firm belief in her, ere she could speak.
A ghastly morning came into her cheek,
While with a widening soul on me she stared.

[20] Pallas: a name of Athena, daughter of Zeus and classical goddess of wisdom, used here to suggest an imperious self-assurance. Hebe was the daughter of Zeus and his consort Hera; she was the goddess of youth and cupbearer to the gods, from which station she was once dismissed because of a fall.
[21] Hesper: the evening star.
[22] Matin-bell: morning bell, here a bell announcing breakfast in the country house in which they are staying.

XLVII

We saw the swallows gathering in the sky,
And in the osier-isle[23] we heard them noise.
We had not to look back on summer joys,
Or forward to a summer of bright dye:
But in the largeness of the evening earth
Our spirits grew as we went side by side.
The hour became her husband and my bride.
Love, that had robbed us so, thus blessed our
  dearth!
The pilgrims of the year waxed very loud
In multitudinous chatterings, as the flood
Full brown came from the West, and like pale
  blood
Expanded to the upper crimson cloud.
Love, that had robbed us of immortal things,
This little moment mercifully gave,
Where I have seen across the twilight wave
The swan sail with her young beneath her
  wings.

XLVIII

Their sense is with their senses all mixed in,
Destroyed by subtleties these women are!
More brain, O Lord, more brain! or we shall
  mar
Utterly this fair garden we might win.
Behold! I looked for peace, and thought it
  near.
Our inmost hearts had opened, each to each.
We drank the pure daylight of honest speech.
Alas! that was the fatal draught, I fear.
For when of my lost Lady came the word,
This woman, O this agony of flesh!
Jealous devotion bade her break the mesh,
That I might seek that other like a bird.
I do adore the nobleness! despise
The act! She has gone forth, I know not where.
Will the hard world my sentience of her share?
I feel the truth; so let the world surmise.

XLIX

He found her by the ocean's moaning verge,
Nor any wicked change in her discerned;
And she believed his old love had returned,
Which was her exultation, and her scourge.
She took his hand, and walked with him, and
  seemed
The wife he sought, though shadow-like and
  dry.

She had one terror, lest her heart should sigh,
And tell her loudly she no longer dreamed.
She dared not say, "This is my breast: look in."
But there's a strength to help the desperate
  weak.
That night he learned how silence best can
  speak
The awful things when Pity pleads for Sin.
About the middle of the night her call
Was heard, and he came wondering to the bed.
"Now kiss me, dear! it may be, now!" she said.
Lethe[24] had passed those lips, and he knew all.

L

Thus piteously Love closed what he begat:
The union of this ever-diverse pair!
These two were rapid falcons in a snare,
Condemned to do the flitting of the bat.
Lovers beneath the singing sky of May,
They wandered once; clear as the dew on
  flowers:
But they fed not on the advancing hours:
Their hearts held cravings for the buried day.
Then each applied to each that fatal knife,
Deep questioning, which probes to endless
  dole.
Ah, what a dusty answer gets the soul
When hot for certainties in this our life!—
In tragic hints here see what evermore
Moves dark as yonder midnight ocean's force,
Thundering like ramping[25] hosts of warrior
  horse,
To throw that faint thin line upon the shore!

1862

Juggling Jerry

I

Pitch here the tent, while the old horse grazes:
  By the old hedge-side we'll halt a stage.
It's nigh my last above the daisies:
  My next leaf'll be man's blank page.
Yes, my old girl! and it's no use crying:
  Juggler, constable, king, must bow.
One that outjuggles all's been spying
  Long to have me, and he has me now.

II

We've travelled times to this old common:
  Often we've hung our pots in the gorse.[1]

---

[23] Osier: willow.
[24] Lethe: a river in the underworld of classical mythology whose waters when drunk cause forgetfulness.
[25] Ramping: rearing.   [1] Gorse: a prickly shrub.

We've had a stirring life, old woman,
    You, and I, and the old grey horse.
Races, and fairs, and royal occasions,
    Found us coming to their call:
Now they'll miss us at our stations:
    There's a Juggler outjuggles all!

III

Up goes the lark, as if all were jolly!
    Over the duck-pond the willow shakes.
Easy to think that grieving's folly,
20   When the hand's firm as driven stakes!
Ay, when we're strong, and braced, and man-
    ful,
    Life's a sweet fiddle: but we're a batch
Born to become the Great Juggler's han'ful:
    Balls he shies up, and is safe to catch.

IV

Here's where the lads of the village cricket:
    I was a lad not wide from here:
Couldn't I whip off the bail from the wicket?[2]
    Like an old world those days appear!
Donkey, sheep, geese, and thatched ale-house—
    I know them!
30   They are old friends of my halts, and seem,
Somehow, as if kind thanks I owe them:
    Juggling don't hinder the heart's esteem.

V

Juggling's no sin, for we must have victual:
    Nature allows us to bait for the fool.
Holding one's own makes us juggle no little;
    But, to increase it, hard juggling's the rule.
You that are sneering at my profession,
    Haven't you juggled a vast amount?
There's the Prime Minister, in one Session,
40   Juggles more games than my sins'll count.

VI

I've murdered insects with mock thunder:
    Conscience, for that, in men don't quail.
I've made bread from the bump of wonder:[3]
    That's my business, and there's my tale.
Fashion and rank all praised the professor:
    Ay! and I've had my smile from the Queen:
Bravo, Jerry! she meant: God bless her!
    Ain't this a sermon on that scene?

VII

I've studied men from my topsy-turvy
    Close,[4] and, I reckon, rather true.   50
Some are fine fellows: some, right scurvy:
    Most, a dash between the two.
But it's a woman, old girl, that makes me
    Think more kindly of the race:
And it's a woman, old girl, that shakes me
    When the Great Juggler I must face.

VIII

We two were married, due and legal:
    Honest we've lived since we've been one.
Lord! I could then jump like an eagle:
    You danced bright as a bit o' the sun.   60
Birds in a May-bush we were! right merry!
    All night we kiss'd, we juggled all day.
Joy was the heart of Juggling Jerry!
    Now from his old girl he's juggled away.

IX

It's past parsons to console us:
    No, nor no doctor fetch for me:
I can die without my bolus;[5]
    Two of a trade, lass, never agree!
Parson and Doctor!—don't they love rarely
    Fighting the devil in other men's fields!   70
Stand up yourself and match him fairly:
    Then see how the rascal yields!

X

I, lass, have lived no gipsy, flaunting
    Finery while his poor helpmate grubs:
Coin I've stored, and you won't be wanting:
    You shan't beg from the troughs and tubs.
Nobly you've stuck to me, though in his
    kitchen
    Many a Marquis would hail you Cook!
Palaces you could have ruled and grown rich
    in,
    But your old Jerry you never forsook.   80

XI

Hand up the chirper![6] ripe ale winks in it;
    Let's have comfort and be at peace.
Once a stout draught made me light as a
    linnet.
    Cheer up! the Lord must have his lease.

---

[2] Bail; wicket: in the game of cricket the wicket is made of two strips of wood (bails) placed on top of three others set into the ground. The bowler or pitcher tries to knock the bails free.

[3] Bump of wonder: the pseudoscience of phrenology, popular in the nineteenth century, attributed traits of individual personality to the relative prominence of bumps and indentations on certain parts of the surface of the head.

[4] Close: an enclosed area, especially of a church.   [5] Bolus: an oversized pill.

[6] Chirper: cheering cup or glass.

May be—for none see in that black hollow—
  It's just a place were we're held in pawn,
And, when the Great Juggler makes as to
    swallow,
  It's just the sword-trick—I ain't quite gone!

XII

Yonder came smells of the gorse, so nutty,
  Gold-like and warm: it's the prime of May.
Better than mortar, brick and putty
  Is God's house on a blowing day.
Lean me more up the mound; now I feel it:
  All the old heath-smells! Ain't it strange?
There's the world laughing, as if to conceal it,
  But He's by us, juggling the change.

XIII

I mind it well, by the sea-beach lying,
  Once—it's long gone—when two gulls we be-
    held,
Which, as the moon got up, were flying
  Down a big wave that sparked and swelled.
Crack, went a gun: one fell: the second
  Wheeled round him twice, and was off for
    new luck:
There in the dark her white wing beckon'd:—
  Drop me a kiss—I'm the bird dead-struck!

1859; 1862

Ode to the Spirit of Earth in Autumn

Fair Mother Earth lay on her back last night,
To gaze her fill on Autumn's sunset skies,
When at a waving of the fallen light
Sprang realms of rosy fruitage o'er her eyes.
A lustrous heavenly orchard hung the West,
Wherein the blood of Eden bloomed again:
Red were the myriad cherub-mouths that
    pressed,
Among the clusters, rich with song, full fain,
But dumb, because that overmastering spell
Of rapture held them dumb: then, here and
    there,
A golden harp lost strings; a crimson shell
Burnt grey; and sheaves of lustre fell to air.
The illimitable eagerness of hue
Bronzed, and the beamy winged bloom that
    flew
'Mid those bunched fruits and thronging
    figures failed.

A green-edged lake of saffron touched the blue,
With isles of fireless purple lying through:
And Fancy on that lake to seek lost treasures
    sailed.

Not long the silence followed:
  The voice that issues from thy breast,   20
    O glorious South-west,
  Along the gloom-horizon holloa'd;
Warning the valleys with a mellow roar
Through flapping wings; then sharp the wood-
    land bore
  A shudder and a noise of hands:
  A thousand horns from some far vale
  In ambush sounding on the gale.
  Forth from the cloven sky came bands
Of revel-gathering spirits; trooping down,
Some rode the tree-tops; some on torn cloud-
    strips   30
  Burst screaming thro' the lighted town:
And scudding seaward, some fell on big ships:
  Or mounting the sea-horses blew
  Bright foam-flakes on the black review
  Of heaving hulls and burying beaks.[1]

Still on the farthest line, with outpuffed cheeks,
'Twixt dark and utter dark, the great wind
    drew
From heaven that disenchanted harmony
To join earth's laughter in the midnight blind:
Booming a distant chorus to the shrieks   40
            Preluding him: then he,
His mantle streaming thunderingly behind,
Across the yellow realm of stiffened Day,
Shot thro' the woodland alleys signals three;
  And with the pressure of a sea
Plunged broad upon the vale that under lay.

  Night on the rolling foliage fell:
  But I, who love old hymning night,
  And know the Dryad[2] voices well,
  Discerned them as their leaves took flight,   50
  Like souls to wander after death:
  Great armies in imperial dyes,
  And mad to tread the air and rise,
  The savage freedom of the skies
  To taste before they rot. And here,
  Like frail white-bodied girls in fear,
  The birches swung from shrieks to sighs;
  The aspens, laughers at a breath,
  In showering spray-falls mixed their cries,
  Or raked a savage ocean-strand   60

---

[1] Beaks: projections from the prows of ships.
[2] Dryad: spirits of trees and woods in classical mythology.

With one incessant drowning screech.
Here stood a solitary beech,
That gave its gold with open hand,
And all its branches, toning chill,
Did seem to shut their teeth right fast,
To shriek more mercilessly shrill,
And match the fierceness of the blast.

But heard I a low swell that noised
Of far-off ocean, I was 'ware
Of pines upon their wide roots poised,
70   Whom never madness in the air
Can draw to more than loftier stress
Of mournfulness, not mournfulness
For melancholy, but Joy's excess,
That singing on the lap of sorrow faints:
And Peace, as in the hearts of saints
Who chant unto the Lord their God;
Deep Peace below upon the muffled sod,
The stillness of the sea's unswaying floor.
80   Could I be sole there not to see
The life within the life awake;
The spirit bursting from the tree,
And rising from the troubled lake?
Pour, let the wines of Heaven pour!
The Golden Harp is struck once more,
And all its music is for me!
Pour, let the wines of Heaven pour!
And, ho, for a night of Pagan glee!

    There is a curtain o'er us.
90   For once, good souls, we'll not pretend
To be aught better than her who bore us,
And is our only visible friend.
Hark to her laughter! who laughs like
    this,
Can she be dead, or rooted in pain?
She has been slain by the narrow brain,
But for us who love her she lives again.
    Can she die? O, take her kiss!

The crimson-footed nymph is panting up the
    glade,
With the wine-jar at her arm-pit, and the
    drunken ivy-braid
Round her forehead, breasts, and thighs: starts
100   a Satyr,[3] and they speed:
Hear the crushing of the leaves: hear the
    cracking of the bough!

And the whistling of the bramble, the piping
    of the weed!

But the bull-voiced oak is battling now:
The storm has seized him half-asleep,
And round him the wild woodland throngs
To hear the fury of his songs,
The uproar of an outraged deep.
He wakes to find a wrestling giant
Trunk to trunk and limb to limb,
And on his rooted force reliant   110
He laughs and grasps the broadened giant,
And twist and roll the Anakim;[4]
And multitudes, acclaiming to the cloud,
    Cry which is breaking, which is bowed.

    Away, for the cymbals clash aloft
In the circles of pine, on the moss-floor
    soft.
The nymphs of the woodland are
    gathering there.
They huddle the leaves, and trample, and
    toss;
They swing in the branches, they roll in
    the moss,
    They blow the seed on the air.   120
Back to back they stand and blow
The winged seed on the cradling air,
A fountain of leaves over bosom and back.
The pipe of the Faun[5] comes on their
    track,
And the weltering alleys overflow
With musical shrieks and wind-wedded
    hair.
The riotous companies melt to a pair.
    Bless them, mother of kindness!

    A star has nooded through
The depths of the flying blue.
Time only to plant the light   130
Of a memory in the blindness.
But time to show me the sight
Of my life thro' the curtain of night;
Shining a moment, and mixed
With the onward-hurrying stream,
Whose pressure is darkness to me;
Behind the curtain, fixed,
Beams with endless beam
That star on the changing sea.   140

[3] Nymph and Satyr: the ivy-braid suggests that the nymph is a celebrant of the rites of Bacchus or Dionysus, classical gods of wine and revelry; the Satyr, half-man and half-goat, is a familiar of this god.
[4] Anakim: a race of giants in the Old Testament.
[5] Faun: another embodiment of natural energies, usually depicted with pointed ears, a tail, and goat's feet.

Great Mother Nature! teach me, like thee,
To kiss the season and shun regrets.
And am I more than the mother who bore,
Mock me not with thy harmony!
    Teach me to blot regrets,
    Great Mother! me inspire
    With faith that forward sets
    But feeds the living fire,
    Faith that never frets
150   For vagueness in the form.
    In life, O keep me warm!
    For, what is human grief?
    And what do men desire?
Teach me to feel myself the tree,
    And not the withered leaf.
Fixed am I and await the dark to-be.
    And O, green bounteous Earth!
Bacchante[6] Mother! stern to those
Who live not in thy heart of mirth;
160 Death shall I shrink from, loving thee?
Into the breast that gives the rose,
    Shall I with shuddering fall?

    Earth, the mother of all,
    Moves on her stedfast way,
    Gathering, flinging, sowing.
    Mortals, we live in her day,
    She in her children is growing.

She can lead us, only she,
Unto God's footstool, whither she reaches:
170 Loved, enjoyed, her gifts must be,
Reverenced the truths she teaches,
Ere a man may hope that he
Ever can attain the glee
Of things without a destiny![7]

    She knows not loss:
    She feels but her need,
    Who the winged seed
    With the leaf doth toss.

And may not men to this attain?
That the joy of motion, the rapture of
    being,
Shall throw strong light when our season is
    fleeing,
Nor quicken aged blood in vain,
At the gates of the vault, on the verge of
    the plain?

Life thoroughly lived is a fact in the brain, 180
    While eyes are left for seeing.
Behold, in yon stripped Autumn, shiver-
    ing grey,
    Earth knows no desolation.
    She smells regeneration
    In the moist breath of decay.

Prophetic of the coming joy and strife, 190
    Like the wild western war-chief sink-
    ing
    Calm to the end he eyes unblinking,
Her voice is jubilant in ebbing life.

    He for his happy hunting-fields
    Forgets the droning chant, and yields
    His numbered breaths to exultation
    In the proud anticipation:
    Shouting the glories of his nation,
    Shouting the grandeur of his race,
    Shouting his own great deeds of
      daring: 200
    And when at last death grasps his face,
    And stiffened on the ground in peace
He lies with all his painted terrors glaring;
Hushed are the tribe to hear a threading
    cry:
    Not from the dead man;
    Not from the standers-by:
    The spirit of the red man
Is welcomed by his fathers up on high.
            1862

A Ballad of Past Meridian

I

Last night returning from my twilight walk
I met the grey mist Death, whose eyeless brow
Was bent on me, and from his hand of chalk
He reached me flowers as from a withered
    bough:
O Death, what bitter nosegays givest thou!

II

Death said, I gather, and pursued his way.
Another stood by me, a shape in stone,
Sword-hacked and iron-stained, with breasts of
    clay,

[6] Bacchante: a celebrant of rites to Bacchus.
[7] The version of this poem published in 1862 contained a 45-line passage that included a de-
scription of "the strange perversions that we are", "pious humpback mountebanks" who expect
a smile from "our Creator" when we tell him that "his prime work is vile." The passage was not
included in the 1896–98 edition; it is reprinted in Trevelyan.

And metal veins that sometimes fiery shone:
10   O Life, how naked and how hard when known!

III

Life said, As thou hast carved me, such am I.
Then memory, like the nightjar[1] on the pine,
And sightless hope, a woodlark in night sky,
Joined notes of Death and Life till night's
    decline:
Of Death, of Life, those inwound notes are
    mine.

                              1876; 1883

Melampus[1]

I

With love exceeding a simple love of the things
    That glide in grasses and rubble of woody
        wreck;
Or change their perch on a beat of quivering
        wings
    From branch to branch, only restful to pipe
        and peck;
Or, bristled, curl at a touch their snouts in a
        ball;
    Or cast their web between bramble and
        thorny hook;
The good physician Melampus, loving them
        all,
    Among them walked, as a scholar who reads
        a book.

II

For him the woods were a home and gave him
        the key
    Of knowledge, thirst for their treasures in
10   herbs and flowers.
The secrets held by the creatures nearer than
        we
    To earth he sought, and the link of their
        life with ours:
And where alike we are, unlike where, and the
        veined
    Division, veined parallel, of a blood that
        flows
In them, in us, from the source by man
        unattained
    Save marks he well what the mystical woods
        disclose.

III

And this he deemed might be boon of love to
        a breast
    Embracing tenderly each little motive shape,
The prone, the flitting, who seek their food
        whither best
    Their wits direct, whither best from their
        foes escape: 20
For closer drawn to our mother's natural milk,
    As babes they learn where her motherly help
        is great:
They know the juice for the honey, juice for
        the silk,
    And need they medical antidotes find them
        straight.

IV

Of earth and sun they are wise, they nourish
        their broods,
    Weave, build, hive, burrow and battle, take
        joy and pain
Like swimmers varying billows: never in woods
    Runs white insanity fleeing itself: all sane
The woods revolve: as the tree its shadowing
        limns
    To some resemblance in motion, the rooted
        life   30
Restrains disorder: you hear the primitive
        hymns
    Of earth in woods issue wild of the web of
        strife.

V

Now sleeping once on a day of marvellous fire,
    A brood of snakes he had cherished in grave
        regret
That death his people had dealt their dam and
        their sire,
    Through savage dread of them, crept to his
        neck, and set
Their tongues to lick him: the swift affection-
        ate tongue
    Of each ran licking the slumberer: then his
        ears
A forked red tongue tickled shrewdly: sudden
        upsprung,
    He heard a voice piping: Ay, for he has no
        fears!   4

----

[1] Nightjar: a night bird whose song is a whirring noise.
[1] Melampus in classical mythology once saved the young of a pair of snakes that had been
killed. In consequence he was given the capacity to understand the language of all creatures,
and he was enabled to effect many cures of human disease and disability.

VI

A bird said that, in the notes of birds, and the
speech
  Of men, it seemed: and another renewed:
  He moves
To learn and not to pursue, he gathers to
teach;
  He feeds his young as do we, and as we love
  loves.
No fears have I of a man who goes with his
head
  To earth, chance looking aloft at us, kind of
  hand:
I feel to him as to earth of whom we are fed;
  I pipe him much for his good could he
  understand.

VII

Melampus touched at his ears, laid finger on
wrist:
  He was not dreaming, he sensibly felt and
  heard.
Above, through leaves, where the tree-twigs
thick intertwist,
  He spied the birds and the bill of the
  speaking bird.
His cushion mosses in shades of various green,
  The lumped, the antlered, he pressed, while
  the sunny snake
Slipped under: draughts he had drunk of clear
Hippocrene,[2]
  It seemed, and sat with a gift of the Gods
  awake.

VIII

Divinely thrilled was the man, exulting full,
  As quick well-waters that come of the heart
  of earth,
Ere yet they dart in a brook are one bubble-
pool
  To light and sound, wedding both at the
  leap of birth.
The soul of light vivid shone, a stream within
stream;
  The soul of sound from a musical shell
  outflew;
Where others hear but a hum and see but a
beam,
  The tongue and eye of the fountain of life
  he knew.

IX

He knew the Hours: they were round him,
laden with seed
  Of hours bestrewn upon vapour, and one by
  one
They winged as ripened in fruit the burden
decreed
  For each to scatter; they flushed like the buds
  in sun,
Bequeathing seed to successive similar rings,
  Their sisters, bearers to men of what men
  have earned: 70
He knew them, talked with the yet unred-
dened; the stings,
  The sweets, they warmed at their bosoms
  divined, discerned.

X

Not unsolicited, sought by diligent feet,
  By riddling fingers expanded, oft watched
  in growth
With brooding deep as the noon-ray's quicken-
ing wheat,
  Ere touch'd, the pendulous flower of the
  plants of sloth,
The plants of rigidness, answered question and
squeeze,
  Revealing wherefore it bloomed uninviting,
  bent,
Yet making harmony breathe of life and
disease,
  The deeper chord of a wonderful
  instrument.   80

XI

So passed he luminous-eyed for earth and the
fates
  We arm to bruise or caress us: his ears were
  charged
With tones of love in a whirl of voluble hates,
  With music wrought of distraction his heart
  enlarged.
Celestial-shining, though mortal, singer, though
mute,
  He drew the Master of harmonies,[3] voiced or
  stilled,
To seek him; heard at the silent medicine-root
  A song, beheld in fulfillment the unfulfilled.

---

[2] Hippocrene: a fountain on the mountain of Helicon, the residence of Apollo, the classical
god of song, and the Muses of song and poetry. The waters of the fountain confer poetic
inspiration.
[3] Master of harmonies: Apollo.

XII

Him Phoebus,[4] lending to darkness colour and
  form
  Of light's excess, many lessons and counsels
90 gave;
Showed Wisdom lord of the human intricate
  swarm,
  And whence prophetic it looks on the hives
  that rave,
And how acquired, of the zeal of love to
  acquire,
  And where it stands, in the centre of life a
  sphere;
And Measure, mood of the lyre, the rapturous
  lyre,
  He said was Wisdom, and struck him the
  notes to hear.

XIII

Sweet, sweet: 'twas glory of vision, honey, the
  breeze
  In heat, the run of the river on root and
  stone,
All senses joined, as the sister Pierides
  Are one, uplifting their chorus, the Nine, his
100 own.[5]
In stately order, evolved of sound into sight,
  From sight to sound intershifting, the man
  descried
The growths of earth, his adored, like day out
  of night,
  Ascend in song, seeing nature and song
  allied.

XIV

And there vitality, there, there solely in song,
  Resides, where earth and her uses to men,
  their needs,
Their forceful cravings, the theme are: there is
  it strong,
  The Master said: and the studious eye that
  reads,
(Yea, even as earth to the crown of Gods on
  the mount),
  In links divine with the lyrical tongue is
110 bound.
Pursue thy craft: it is music drawn of a fount
  To spring perennial; well-spring is common
  ground.

XV

Melampus dwelt among men: physician and
  sage,
  He served them, loving them, healing them;
  sick or maimed
Or them that frenzied in some delirious rage
  Outran the measure, his juice of the woods
  reclaimed.
He played on men, as his master, Phoebus, on
  strings
  Melodious: as the God did he drive and
  check,
Through love exceeding a simple love of the
  things
  That glide in grasses and rubble of woody
  wreck.   12

1883

Lucifer in Starlight

On a starred night Prince Lucifer uprose.
Tired of his dark dominion swung the fiend
Above the rolling ball in cloud part screened,
Where sinners hugged their spectre of repose.
Poor prey to his hot fit of pride were those.
And now upon his western wing he leaned,
Now his huge bulk o'er Afric's sands careened,
Now the black planet shadowed Arctic snows.
Soaring through wider zones that pricked his
  scars
With memory of the old revolt from Awe,
He reached a middle height, and at the stars,
Which are the brain of heaven, he looked, and
  sank.
Around the ancient track marched, rank on
  rank,
The army of unalterable law.

1883

King Harald's Trance[1]

I

Sword in length a reaping-hook amain
Harald sheared his field, blood up to shank:
  'Mid the swathes of slain,
  First at moonrise drank.

---

[4] Phoebus: a name of Apollo, especially when he is associated with the sun.
[5] Pierides; the Nine: the Muses, who were born on the mountain of Pieria.
[1] Harald was the name of several ninth- and tenth-century kings of Norway and Denmark.
This story is not commonly told of any of them.

II

Thereof hunger, as for meats the knife,
Pricked his ribs, in one sharp spur to reach
    Home and his young wife,
    Nigh the sea-ford beach.

III

After battle keen to feed was he:
Smoking flesh the thresher washed down fast,
    Like an angry sea
    Ships from keel to mast.

IV

Name us glory, singer, name us pride
Matching Harald's in his deeds of strength;
    Chiefs, wife, sword by side,
    Foemen stretched their length!

V

Half a winter night the toasts hurrahed,
Crowned him, clothed him, trumpeted him
    high,
    Till awink he bade
    Wife to chamber fly.

VI

Twice the sun had mounted, twice had sunk,
Ere his ears took sound; he lay for dead;
    Mountain on his trunk,
    Ocean on his head.

VII

Clamped to couch, his fiery hearing sucked
Whispers that at heart made iron-clang:
    Here fool-women clucked,
    There men held harangue.

VIII

Burial to fit their lord of war
They decreed him: hailed the kingling: ha!
    Hateful! but this Thor[2]
    Failed a weak lamb's baa.

IX

King they hailed a branchlet, shaped to fare,
Weighted so, like quaking shingle spume,[3]
    When his blood's own heir
    Ripened in the womb!

X

Still he heard, and doglike, hoglike, ran
Nose of hearing till his blind sight saw:

Woman stood with man
Mouthing low, at paw.

XI

Woman, man, they mouthed; they spake a
    thing
Armed to split a mountain, sunder seas:
    Still the frozen king
    Lay and felt him freeze.

XII

Doglike, hoglike, horselike now he raced,
Riderless, in ghost across a ground
    Flint of breast, blank-faced,
    Past the fleshly bound.

XIII

Smell of brine his nostrils filled with might:
Nostrils quickened eyelids, eyelids hand:
    Hand for sword at right
    Groped, the great haft[4] spanned.

XIV

Wonder struck to ice his people's eyes:
Him they saw, the prone upon the bier,
    Sheer from backbone rise,
    Sword uplifting peer.

XV

Sitting did he breathe against the blade,
Standing kiss it for that proof of life:
    Strode, as netters wade,
    Straightway to his wife.

XVI

Her he eyed: his judgement was one word,
Foulbed! and she fell: the blow clove two.
    Fearful for the third,
    All their breath indrew.

XVII

Morning danced along the waves to beach;
Dumb his chiefs fetched breath for what might
    hap:
    Glassily on each
    Stared the iron cap.

XVIII

Sudden, as it were a monster oak
Split to yield a limb by stress of heat,
    Strained he, staggered, broke
    Doubled at their feet.

1887

[2] Thor: god of thunder in Norse mythology.
[3] Shingle spume: froth of a wave on the beach.
[4] Haft: handle.

The Appeasement of Demeter[1]

I

Demeter devastated our good land,
In blackness for her daughter snatched below.
Smoke-pillar or loose hillock was the sand,
Where soil had been to clasp warm seed and
      throw
The wheat, vine, olive, ripe to Summer's ray.
Now whether night advancing, whether day,
      Scarce did the baldness show:
The hand of man was a defeated hand.

II

Necessity, the primal goad to growth,
Stood shrunken; Youth and Age appeared as
      one;
Like Winter Summer; good as labour sloth;
Nor was there answer wherefore beamed the
      sun,
Or why men drew the breath to carry pain.
High reared the ploughshare, broken lay the
      wain,
      Idly the flax-wheel spun
Unridered: starving lords were wasp and moth.

III

Lean grassblades losing green on their bent
      flags,
Sang chilly to themselves; lone honey-bees
Pursued the flowers that were not with dry
      bags;
Sole sound aloud the snap of sapless trees,
More sharp than slingstones on hard breast-
      plates hurled.
Back to first chaos tumbled the stopped world,
      Careless to lure or please.
A nature of gaunt ribs, an Earth of crags.

IV

No smile Demeter cast: the gloom she saw,
Well draped her direful musing; for in gloom,
In thicker gloom, deep down the cavern-maw,[2]
Her sweet had vanished; liker unto whom,
And whose pale place of habitation mute,
She and all seemed where seasons, pledged for
      fruit
      Anciently, gaped for bloom:
Where hand of man was as a plucked fowl's
      claw.

V

The wrathful Queen descended on a vale,
That ere the ravished hour for richness heaved.
Iambe, maiden of the merry tale,
Beside her eyed the once red-cheeked, green-
      leaved.
It looked as if the Deluge had withdrawn.
Pity caught at her throat; her jests were gone.
      More than for her who grieved,
She could for this waste home have piped the
      wail.

VI

Iambe, her dear mountain-rivulet
To waken laughter from cold stones, beheld
A riven wheatfield cracking for the wet,
And seed like infant's teeth, that never swelled,
Apeep up flinty ridges, milkless round.
Teeth of the giants marked she where thin
      ground
      Rocky in spikes rebelled
Against the hand here slack as rotted net.

VII

The valley people up the ashen scoop[3]
She beckoned, aiming hopelessly to win
Her Mistress in compassion of yon group
So pinched and wizened; with their aged grin,
For lack of warmth to smile, on mouths of woe,
White as in chalk outlining little O
      Dumb, from a falling chin;
Young, old, alike half-bent to make the hoop.

VIII

Their tongues of birds they wagged, weak-
      voiced as when
Dark underwaters the recesses choke;
With cluck and upper quiver of a hen
In grasp, past pecking: cry before the croak.
Relentlessly their gold-haired Heaven, their
      fount
Bountiful of old days, heard them recount
      This and that cruel stroke:
Nor eye nor ear had she for piteous men.

IX

A figure of black rock by sunbeams crowned
Through stormclouds, where the volumed[4]
      shades enfold
An earth in awe before the claps resound

---

[1] Demeter in classical mythology was the goddess of fertility. Her daughter Persephone (Proserpine) was abducted to the underworld by its ruler, and in her angry mourning Demeter caused the vale of Enna in Sicily, where the abduction occurred, to cease its fertility. Demeter was finally brought to relent by a servant girl, Iambe, who caused her to laugh.
[2] Maw: stomach cavity.   [3] Scoop: valley running up the mountain.   [4] Volumed: massed.

And woods and dwellings are as billows rolled,
The barren Nourisher[5] unmelted shed
Death from the looks that wandered with the
        dead
    Out of the realms of gold,
In famine for her lost, her lost unfound.

X

Iambe from her Mistress tripped; she raised
The cattle-call above the moan of prayer;
And slowly out of fields their fancy grazed,
Among the droves, defiled[6] a horse and mare:
The wrecks of horse and mare: such ribs as
        view
Seas that have struck brave ships ashore, while
        through
    Shoots the swift foamspit: bare
They nodded, and Demeter on them gazed.

XI

Howbeit the season of the dancing blood,
Forgot was horse of mare, yea, mare of horse:
Reversed, each head at either's flank, they
        stood.
Whereat the Goddess, in a dim remorse,
Laid hand on them, and smacked; and her
        touch pricked.
Neighing within, at either's flank they licked;
    Played on a moment's force
At courtship, withering to the crazy nod.

XII

The nod was that we gather for consent;
And mournfully amid the group a dame,
Interpreting the thing in nature meant,
Her hands held out like bearers of the flame,
And nodded for the negative sideways.
Keen at her Mistress glanced Iambe: rays
      From the Great Mother came:
Her lips were opened wide; the curse was rent.

XIII

She laughed: since our first harvesting heard
      none
Like thunder of the song of heart: her face,
The dreadful darkness, shook to mounted sun,
And peal on peal across the hills held chase.
She laughed herself to water; laughed to fire;
Laughed the torrential laugh of dam and sire
      Full of the marrowy race.
Her laughter, Gods! was flesh on skeleton.

XIV

The valley people huddled, broke, afraid,
Assured, and taking lightning in the veins
They puffed, they leaped, linked hands,
        together swayed,
Unwitting happiness till golden rains
Of tears in laughter, laughter weeping, smote
Knowledge of milky mercy from that throat   110
      Pouring to heal their pains:
And one bold youth set mouth at a shy maid.

XV

Iambe clapped to see the kindly lusts
Inspire the valley people, still on seas,
Like poplar-tops relived from stress of gusts,
With rapture in their wonderment; but these,
Low homage being rendered, ran to plough,
Fed by the laugh, as by the mother cow
      Calves at the teats they tease:
Soon drove they through the yielding furrow-
        crusts.   120

XVI

Uprose the blade in green, the leaf in red,
The tree of water and the tree of wood:
And soon among the branches overhead
Gave beauty juicy issue sweet for food.
O Laughter! beauty plumped and love had
        birth.
Laughter! O thou reviver of sick Earth!
      Good for the spirit, good
For body, thou! to both art wine and bread!
            1887; 1888

Dirge in Woods[1]

A wind sways the pines,
    And below
Not a breath of wild air;
Still as the mosses that glow
On the flooring and over the lines
Of the roots here and there.
The pine-tree drops its dead;
They are quiet, as under the sea.
Overhead, overhead
Rushes life in a race,   10
As the clouds the clouds chase;
    And we go,
And we drop like the fruits of the tree,
    Even we,
    Even so.
           1870; 1888

---

[5] Nourisher: Demeter.   [6] Defiled: took out in a file.
[1] First published in a magazine in 1870 as the last stanza of a long poem which is reprinted
in the Memorial edition.

Jump-to-Glory Jane

I

A revelation came on Jane,
The widow of a labouring swain:
And first her body trembled sharp,
Then all the woman was a harp
With winds along the strings; she heard,
Though there was neither tone nor word.

II

For past our hearing was the air,
Beyond our speaking what it bare,
And she within herself had sight
Of heaven at work to cleanse outright,
To make of her a mansion fit
For angel hosts inside to sit.

III

They entered, and forthwith entranced,
Her body braced, her members danced;
Surprisingly the woman leapt;
And countenance composed she kept:
As gossip neighbours in the lane
Declared, who saw and pitied Jane.

IV

These knew she had been reading books,
The which was witnessed by her looks
Of late: she had a mania
For mad folk in America,[1]
And said for sure they led the way,
But meat and beer were meant to stay.[2]

V

That she had visited a fair,
Had seen a gauzy lady there,
Alive with tricks on legs alone,
As good as wings, was also known:
And longwhiles in a sullen mood,
Before her jumping, Jane would brood.

VI

A good knee's height, they say, she sprang;
Her arms and feet like those who hang:
As if afire the body sped,
And neither pair contributed.
She jumped in silence: she was thought
A corpse to resurrection caught.

VII

The villagers were mostly dazed;
They jeered, they wondered, and they praised.
'Twas guessed by some she was inspired,
And some would have it she had hired
An engine in her petticoats,
To turn their wits and win their votes.

VIII

Her first was Winny Earnes, a kind
Of woman not to dance inclined;
But she went up, entirely won,
Ere Jump-to-glory Jane had done;
And once a vixen wild for speech,
She found the better way to preach.

IX

No long time after, Jane was seen
Directing jumps at Daddy Green;
And that old man, to watch her fly,
Had eyebrows made of arches high;
Till homeward he likewise did hop,
Oft calling on himself to stop!

X

It was a scene when man and maid,
Abandoning all other trade,
And careless of the call to meals,
Went jumping at the woman's heels.
By dozens they were counted soon,
Without a sound to tell their tune.

XI

Along the roads they came, and crossed
The fields, and o'er the hills were lost,
And in the evening reappeared;
Then short like hobbled horses reared,
And down upon the grass they plumped:
Alone their Jane to glory jumped.

XII

At morn they rose, to see her spring
All going as an engine thing;
And lighter than the gossamer
She led the bobbers following her,
Past old acquaintances, and where
They made the stranger stupid stare.

---

[1] Several extreme evangelical religious sects in nineteenth-century Britain were connected to similar sects and movements in America.
[2] The sect espouses vegetarianism and abstinence from alcohol, as well as dancing, as a way to grace.

XIII

When turnips were a filling crop,
In scorn they jumped a butcher's shop:
Or, spite of threats to flog and souse,
They jumped for shame a public-house:
And much their legs were seized with rage
If passing by the vicarage.

XIV

The tightness of a hempen rope
Their bodies got; but laundry soap
Not handsomer can rub the skin
For token of the washed within.
Occasionally coughers cast
A leg aloft and coughed their last.

XV

The weaker maids and some old men,
Requiring rafters for the pen[3]
On rainy nights, were those who fell.
The rest were quite a miracle,
Refreshed as you may search all round
On Club-feast days[4] and cry, Not found!

XVI

For these poor innocents, that slept
Against the sky, soft women wept:
For never did they any theft;
'Twas known when they their camping left,
And jumped the cold out of their rags;
In spirit rich as money-bags.

XVII

They jumped the question, jumped reply;
And whether to insist, deny,
Reprove, persuade, they jumped in ranks
Or singly, straight the arms to flanks,
And straight the legs, with just a knee
For bending in a mild degree.

XVIII

The villagers might call them mad;
An endless holiday they had,
Of pleasure in a serious work:
They taught by leaps where perils lurk,
And with the lambkins practised sports
For 'scaping Satan's pounds and quarts.[5]

XIX

It really seemed on certain days,
When they bobbed up their Lord to praise,

And bobbing up they caught the glance
Of light, our secret is to dance,
And hold the tongue from hindering peace;
To dance out preacher and police.

XX

Those flies of boys disturbed them sore
On Sundays and when daylight wore:
With withies[6] cut from hedge or copse,
They treated them as whipping-tops,
And flung big stones with cruel aim;
Yet all the flock jumped on the same. 120

XXI

For what could persecution do
To worry such a blessed crew,
On whom it was as wind to fire,
Which set them always jumping higher?
The parson and the lawyer tried,
By meek persistency defied.

XXII

But if they bore, they could pursue
As well, and this the Bishop too;
When inner warnings proved him plain
The chase for Jump-to-glory Jane. 130
She knew it by his being sent
To bless the feasting in the tent.

XXIII

Not less than fifty years on end,
The Squire had been the Bishop's friend:
And his poor tenants, harmless ones,
With souls to save! fed not on buns,
But angry meats: she took her place
Outside to show the way to grace.

XXIV

In apron suit[7] the Bishop stood;
The crowding people kindly viewed. 140
A gaunt grey woman he saw rise
On air, with most beseeching eyes:
And evident as light in dark
It was, she set to him for mark.

XXV

Her highest leap had come: with ease
She jumped to reach the Bishop's knees:
Compressing tight her arms and lips,
She sought to jump the Bishop's hips:

---

[3] Requiring a roof under which to sleep.
[4] Club-feast: the outing of a working-class or lower-middle-class group.
[5] Trevelyan's note: "pounds of meat and quarts of ale" (p. 601).   [6] Withies: branches.
[7] Apron suit: an apron was a part of the ceremonial dress of a bishop.

Her aim flew at his apron-band,[8]
150 That he might see and understand.

XXVI

The mild inquiry of his gaze
Was altered to a peaked amaze,
At sight of thirty in ascent,
To gain his notice clearly bent:
And greatly Jane at heart was vexed
By his ploughed look of mind perplexed.

XXVII

In jumps that said, Beware the pit!
More eloquent than speaking it—
That said, Avoid the boiled, the roast;
160 The heated nose on face of ghost,
Which comes of drinking: up and o'er
The flesh with me! did Jane implore.

XXVIII

She jumped him high as huntsmen go
Across the gate; she jumped him low,
To coax him to begin and feel
His infant steps returning, peel
His mortal pride, exposing fruit,
And off with hat and apron suit.

XXIX

We need much patience, well she knew,
170 And out and out, and through and through,
When we would gentlefolk address,
However we may seek to bless:
At times they hide them like the beasts
From sacred beams; and mostly priests.

XXX

He gave no sign of making bare,
Nor she of faintness or despair.
Inflamed with hope that she might win,
If she but coaxed him to begin,
She used all arts for making fain;
180 The mother with her babe was Jane.

XXXI

Now stamped the Squire, and knowing not
Her business, waved her from the spot.
Encircled by the men of might,
The head of Jane, like flickering light,

As in a charger, they beheld
Ere she was from the park[9] expelled.

XXXII

Her grief, in jumps of earthly weight,
Did Jane around communicate:
For that the moment when began
The holy but mistaken man,   19
In view of light, to take his lift,
They cut him from her charm adrift!

XXXIII

And he was lost: a banished face
For ever from the ways of grace,
Unless pinched hard by dreams in fright.
They saw the Bishop's wavering sprite
Within her look, at come and go,
Long after he had caused her woe.

XXXIV

Her greying eyes (until she sank
At Fredsham on the wayside bank,   20
Like cinder heaps that whitened lie
From coals that shot the flame to sky)
Had glassy vacancies, which yearned
For one in memory discerned.

XXXV

May those who ply the tongue that cheats,
And those who rush to beer and meats,
And those whose mean ambition aims
At palaces and titled names,
Depart in such a cheerful strain
As did our Jump-to-glory Jane!   21

XXXVI

Her end was beautiful: one sigh.
She jumped a foot when it was nigh.
A lily in a linen clout[10]
She looked when they had laid her out.
It is a lily-light she bears
For England up the ladder-stairs.

                                        1889; 1892

Penetration and Trust[1]

I

Sleek as a lizard at round of a stone,
The look of her heart slipped out and in.

---

[8] Apron-band: the string tying the apron.   [9] Park: grounds of the squire's estate.
[10] Clout: piece of cloth.
[1] Trevelyan's note: "A lord is going to the distant war and is saying farewell to his lady. He looks in her eyes to see if she will be faithful in his absence, penetrates her innocent, inmost thought, and trusts her. She therefore cries out . . . that whatever happens in the war he will always be victor at home in her heart" (p. 604).

Sweet on her lord her soft eyes shone,
As innocents clear of a shade of sin.

II

He laid a finger under her chin,
His arm for her girdle at waist was thrown:
Now, what will happen and who will win,
With me in the fight and my lady lone?

III

He clasped her, clasping a shape of stone;
Was fire on her eyes till they let him in.
Her breast to a God of the daybeams shone,
And never a corner for serpent sin.

1892

Night of Frost in May

With splendour of a silver day,
A frosted night had opened May:
And on that plumed and armoured night,
As one close temple hove our wood,
Its border leafage virgin white.
Remote down air an owl hallooed.
The black twig dropped without a twirl;
The bud in jewelled grasp was nipped;
The brown leaf cracked a scorching curl;
A crystal off the green leaf slipped.
Across the tracks of rimy tan,
Some busy thread at whiles would shoot;
A limping minnow-rillet[1] ran,
To hang upon an icy foot.

In this shrill hush of quietude,[2]
The ear conceived a severing cry.
Almost it let the sound elude,
When chuckles three, a warble shy,
From hazels of the garden came,
Near by the crimson-windowed farm.
They laid the trance on breath and frame,
A prelude of the passion-charm.

Then soon was heard, not sooner heard
Than answered, doubled, trebled, more,
Voice of an Eden in the bird
Renewing with his pipe of four
The sob: a troubled Eden, rich
In throb of heart: unnumbered throats

Flung upward at a fountain's pitch
The fervour of the four long notes,
That on the fountain's pool subside,
Exult and ruffle and upspring:
Endless the crossing multiplied
Of silver and of golden string.
There chimed a bubbled underbrew
With witch-wild spray of vocal dew.

It seemed a single harper swept
Our wild wood's inner chords and waked
A spirit that for yearning ached
Ere men desired and joyed or wept.
Or now a legion ravishing
Musician rivals did unite
In love of sweetness high to sing
The subtle song that rivals light;
From breast of earth to breast of sky:
And they were secret, they were nigh:
A hand the magic might disperse;
The magic swung my universe.

Yet sharpened breath forbade to dream,
Where all was visionary gleam;
Where Seasons, as with cymbals, clashed;
And feelings, passing joy and woe,
Churned, gurgled, spouted, interflashed,
Nor either was the one we know:
Nor pregnant of the heart contained
In us were they, that griefless plained,
That plaining soared; and through the heart
Struck to one note the wide apart:—
A passion surgent from despair;
A paining bliss in fervid cold;
Off the last vital edge of air,
Leap heavenward of the lofty-souled,
For rapture of a wine of tears;
As had a star among the spheres
Caught up our earth to some mid-height
Of double life to ear and sight,
She giving voice to thought that shines
Keen-brilliant of her deepest mines;
While steely drips the rillet clinked,
And hoar[3] with crust the cowslip swelled.

Then was the lyre of earth beheld,
Then heard by me: it holds me linked;
Across the years to dead-ebb shores
I stand on, my blood-thrill restores.

---

[1] Minnow-rillet: small brook.
[2] In the note in his edition of Meredith's poems George Trevelyan writes: "In the second stanza . . . and following stanzas the song of the nightingales is described. First one sings alone from hazels near the farm, and then a number from the woodland" (p. 596).
[3] Hoar: frosted.

But would I conjure into me
Those issue notes, I must review
What serious breath the woodland drew;
The low throb of expectancy;
How the white mother-muteness pressed
80   On leaf and meadow-herb; how shook,
Nigh speech of mouth, the sparkle-crest
Seen spinning on the bracken-crook.[4]

                                          1892

Empedocles[1]

I
He leaped. With none to hinder,
Of Aetna's fiery scoriae[2]
In the next vomit-shower, made he
    A more peculiar cinder.

And this great Doctor, can it be,
He left no saner recipe
For men at issue with despair?
Admiring, even his poet owns,
While noting his fine lyric tones,
The last of him was heels in air!

II
Comes Reverence, her features
Amazed to see high Wisdom hear,
With glimmer of a faunish leer,
    One mock her pride of creatures.
Shall such sad incident degrade
A stature casting sunniest shade?
O Reverence! let Reason swim;
Each life its critic deed reveals;
And him reads Reason at his heels,
If heels in air the last of him!

                                          1892

Christina Rossetti
1830–1894

CHRISTINA ROSSETTI was born in London, the youngest of four children, and the second daughter, born to Gabriele and Frances Rossetti. Her father was a political exile from Italy who earned a living by teaching Italian while he wrote Italian poetry and ingenious exegeses of Dante's writing. Her mother was a member of an Anglo-Italian family (Gabriele Rossetti never became a British citizen) and a devout member of the Church of England. Like her brothers, Dante Gabriel and William Michael, Christina Rossetti became interested early in literature and painting, and she wrote enough poems in her adolescence to make up a volume that was privately printed in 1847. Like her sister, who eventually became an Anglican nun, Christina was a fervently earnest member of the Church of England, and much of her mature poetry was written for explicitly devotional occasions.

She was educated at home, mostly by her mother. When she was fifteen years old, her health was made precarious by a suspected heart disease. She was an invalid again for relatively long periods later in her life, in the late 1860s and early 1870s, and during her last illness in the 1890s. For a while in 1851 and after, when the always sparse finances of the Rossettis were strained yet further by the illness of her father, Christina Rossetti helped her mother conduct a school. In 1848 she was engaged to James Collinson, a painter and associate of her brothers in the Pre-Raphaelite Brotherhood. She at first refused his proposal because he had once converted to Roman Catholicism from the Church of England; she

[4] Bracken-crook: hooked leaf of a fern.
[1] See note to Matthew Arnold's "Empedocles on Etna."
[2] Scoriae: clinkerlike masses of cooled lava.

broke the engagement when he returned to Roman Catholicism. In the 1860s she refused to marry Charles Cayley, a translator of Dante and also an associate of the Pre-Raphaelite circle, because of the diffidence or indeterminancy of his religious beliefs. Except for her writing and the recognition it brought her, and for two trips to the Continent and visits to the houses and studios of her brothers' friends and colleagues, these were the only gestures out of a life lived at home, principally with her mother and sister.

Her poems are often personal in the sense that they express her feelings about herself and her connections with others, with the possibilities of life outside her narrow bound, and with God. But her poems were not intended to be private, and she did not think of poetry as wholly a means of self-expression. From the beginning she wrote for publication. According to a memoir written by her brother William Michael (see below), she thought that poets who published their writing bore a great responsibility, presumably to the moral states of their readers. She began publishing her poems in magazines and annuals around 1850; one of her early poems, "Dream Land," was published in the Pre-Raphaelite journal, *The Germ*. In 1862 she published her first collection of poems, *Goblin Market and Other Poems,* and she published a second volume, *The Prince's Progress and Other Poems,* four years later. She was never able to support herself by her writing. William Michael Rossetti estimated that she earned an average of £40 a year, the equivalent in the 1970s of about $1000, from her writing after 1860. Her first volumes of poetry did, however, establish her among literary critics and readers as a considerable poet in the carefully wrought verse forms, sensuous surfaces, and quaint figures which were among the features of one of the important mid-century poetic styles. "Goblin Market" in particular was immediately acknowledged as a principal poem in a nineteenth-century tradition of strongly evocative fables like Tennyson's "The Vision of Sin" and, earlier, Samuel Taylor Coleridge's "The Rime of the Ancient Mariner."

Christina Rossetti published a volume of poems for children, *Sing Song,* in 1872, a new edition containing her first two volumes of poems in 1875, and another volume of poems, *A Pageant and Other Poems,* in 1881. This last volume included the sonnet sequence "Monna Innominata." In the 1870s she began increasingly to write devotional verse and prose. Many of the poems she included in collected editions of her poetry in 1875 and later first appeared in *Annus Domini* (1874), a calendar of poems for the liturgical year, and in other books of religious reflection and scriptural commentary, some of them published by the Society for the Propagation of Christian Knowledge, a missionary agency of the Church of England.

The public responsibility Christina Rossetti placed on her talent is naturally more patent in her devotional writing than it is in lyrics and fables whose situations and purposes are not explicitly religious. Yet for all its strangeness, and for all its transfigured relevance to the psychic and emotional urgencies of her private life, "Goblin Market" is unmistakably also a moral fable about sensual temptation and the power of self-sacrificing love. On the other hand, much of the power of devotional poems such as "Long Barren" and "Ash Wednesday" resides in the forcefully particular feelings which also inform some of her more personal lyrics: a fear of being shut out from possibility which will complete her, and of being imprisoned in a temporal world whose pleasures are at best only signs of heaven and whose sorrows and aridities are preparations for it. To say that the public, common language of religious doctrine and experience gave Christina Rossetti a way to enlarge the resonance of these themes is not to discount the authenticity of her religious poems, nor is it to see them as sublimations of the desires and frustrations of her individual life. Such a discount would be obtuse, and so would a reading of her development which sees her as subsiding from the odd fancies of "Goblin Market" into conventionally religious themes and figures in her later poems.

Religious belief was always a part of her life, and if its emphasis was unusually ascetic, its vocabulary was always that of a quite orthodox Christianity. She very early found her style of concrete, lucid, often quaint and surprising figures which she fits into tightly ordered verse forms. In the recurrent pattern of her poems she lays out sequences of feeling in these clearlined figures and stanzas, each stanza or passage framing a new or heightened condition of the feeling, like notes in a musical theme. She did not really develop in this style. She rather moved within it to articulate in her later poems desires and fears about religious salvation which she now described as universal as well as particular. The taut verse forms, frequent verbs, and sharply rendered images of her religious poems sometimes recall those of seventeenth-century devotional poetry. But these qualities are also characteristic of "Goblin Market" and other poems, and it is this persistent clarity and energy of style that holds for her a place in the literary and intellectual culture of nineteenth-century Britain, from which she withheld herself but into which she conscientiously sent her personal as well as her devotional poems to deliver their truths and work their good.

EDITIONS

The texts reprinted here are those of the *Poetical Works of Christina Rossetti,* edited by William Michael Rossetti (1904); this edition also contains a memoir by William Michael Rossetti. He also published some of his sister's letters in *Ruskin: Rossetti: Pre-Raphaelitism* (1899), *Family Letters of Christina Rossetti* (1908), and *Rossetti Papers, 1862–70* (1903). Other letters are published in Mackenzie Bell's biography, *Christina Rossetti* (1898); in Janet Troxell's edition of letters by *Three Rossettis* (1937); and in Lona Packer's edition of *The Rossetti-Macmillan Letters* (1963).

BIOGRAPHY AND CRITICISM

Mackenzie Bell's biography and the memoir William Michael Rossetti included in his edition of his sister's poems have now been superseded as standard biographical sources by Lona Packer's *Christina Rossetti* (1963). The authority of Packer's biography is injured by her attempt to establish a love affair between Christina Rossetti and William Bell Scott (see Part Four); Packer's evidence and speculations are corrected by William E. Fredeman in a review in *Victorian Studies,* 8 (1964) which uses material from Scott's papers.

See also: Marya Zaturenska, *Christina Rossetti* (1949); Thomas B. Swann, *Wonder and Whimsey: The Fantastic World of Christina Rossetti* (1960); and Barbara Garlitz, "Christina Rossetti's *Sing Song* and Nineteenth-Century Children's Poetry," *Publications of the Modern Language Association,* 70 (1955).

Georgina Battiscombe's pamphlet in the Writers and Their Work series, *Christina Rossetti* (1965), contains a select bibliography. Other bibliographies of writing about Christina Rossetti are included in William E. Fredeman,

Pre-Raphaelitism: A Biblio-Critical Study (1965), and in Ehrsam, Deily, and Smith (see General Bibliography).

Song

When I am dead, my dearest,
  Sing no sad songs for me;
Plant thou no roses at my head,
  Nor shady cypress tree:
Be the green grass above me
  With showers and dewdrops wet:
And if thou wilt, remember,
  And if thou wilt, forget.

I shall not see the shadows,
  I shall not feel the rain;
I shall not hear the nightingale
  Sing on as if in pain:
And dreaming through the twilight
  That doth not rise nor set,
Haply I may remember,
  And haply may forget.

(1848) 1862

Dream Land

Where sunless rivers weep
Their waves into the deep,
She sleeps a charmèd sleep:
  Awake her not.
Led by a single star,
She came from very far
To seek where shadows are
  Her pleasant lot.

She left the rosy morn,
She left the fields of corn,
For twilight cold and lorn
  And water springs.
Through sleep, as through a veil,
She sees the sky look pale,
And hears the nightingale
  That sadly sings.

Rest, rest, a perfect rest
Shed over brow and breast;
Her face is toward the west,
  The purple land.
She cannot see the grain
Ripening on hill and plain,
She cannot feel the rain
  Upon her hand.

Rest, rest, for evermore
Upon a mossy shore;
Rest, rest at the heart's core
   Till time shall cease:
Sleep that no pain shall wake;
Night that no morn shall break,
Till joy shall overtake
   Her perfect peace.

           (1849) 1850; 1862

Symbols

I watched a rosebud very long
   Brought on by dew and sun and shower,
   Waiting to see the perfect flower:
Then, when I thought it should be strong,
   It opened at the matin hour[1]
And fell at evensong.

I watched a nest from day to day,
   A green nest full of pleasant shade,
   Wherein three speckled eggs were laid:
But when they should have hatched in May,
   The two old birds had grown afraid
Or tired, and flew away.

Then in my wrath I broke the bough
   That I had tended so with care,
   Hoping its scent should fill the air:
I crushed the eggs, not heeding how
   Their ancient promise had been fair:
I would have vengeance now.

But the dead branch spoke from the sod,
   And the eggs answered me again:
   Because we failed dost thou complain?
Is thy wrath just? And what if God,
   Who waiteth for thy fruits in vain,
Should also take the rod?

           (1849) 1862

The Three Enemies

THE FLESH
"Sweet, thou art pale."
          "More pale to see,
Christ hung upon the cruel tree
And bore His Father's wrath for me."

"Sweet, thou art sad."
          "Beneath a rod

More heavy, Christ for my sake trod
The winepress of the wrath of God."

"Sweet, thou art weary."
          "Not so Christ;
Whose mighty love of me sufficed
For Strength, Salvation, Eucharist."

"Sweet, thou art footsore."   10
          "If I bleed,
His feet have bled; yea in my need
His Heart once bled for mine indeed."

THE WORLD
"Sweet, thou art young."
          "So He was young
Who for my sake in silence hung
Upon the Cross with Passion wrung."

"Look, thou art fair."
          "He was more fair
Than men, Who deigned for me to wear
A visage marred beyond compare."

"And thou hast riches."
          "Daily bread.
All else is His: Who, living, dead,   20
For me lacked where to lay His Head."

"And life is sweet."
          "It was not so
To Him, Whose Cup did overflow
With mine unutterable woe."

THE DEVIL
"Thou drinkest deep."
          "When Christ would sup
He drained the dregs from out my cup:
So how should I be lifted up?"

"Thou shalt win Glory."
          "In the skies,
Lord Jesus, cover up mine eyes
Lest they should look on vanities."   30

"Thou shalt have Knowledge."
          "Helpless dust!
In thee, O Lord, I put my trust:
Answer Thou for me, Wise and Just."

"And Might."—
          "Get thee behind me. Lord,

[1] Matin-hour: hour of the earliest morning prayers, as evensong is an evening prayer.

Who has redeemed and not abhorred
My soul, oh keep it by Thy Word."

(1851) 1862

The World

By day she woos me, soft, exceeding fair:
    But all night as the moon so changeth she;
    Loathsome and foul with hideous leprosy,
And subtle serpents gliding in her hair.
By day she woos me to the outer air,
    Ripe fruits, sweet flowers, and full satiety:
    But thro' the night a beast she grins at me,
A very monster void of love and prayer.
By day she stands a lie: by night she stands
10   In all the naked horror of the truth,
With pushing horns and clawed and clutching
    hands.
Is this a friend indeed, that I should sell
    My soul to her, give her my life and youth,
Till my feet, cloven too, take hold on hell?

(1854) 1862

My Dream

Hear now a curious dream I dreamed last
    night,
Each word whereof is weighed and sifted truth.

I stood beside Euphrates[1] while it swelled
Like overflowing Jordan in its youth.
It waxed and coloured sensibly to sight;
Till out of myriad pregnant waves there welled
Young crocodiles, a gaunt blunt-featured crew,
Fresh-hatched perhaps and daubed with birth-
    day dew.
The rest if I should tell, I fear my friend,
10   My closest friend, would deem the facts untrue;
And therefore it were wisely left untold;
Yet if you will, why, hear it to the end.

Each crocodile was girt with massive gold
And polished stones that with their wearers
    grew:
But one there was who waxed beyond the rest,
Wore kinglier girdle and a kingly crown,

Whilst crowns and orbs and sceptres starred his
    breast.
All gleamed compact and green with scale on
    scale,
But special burnishment adorned his mail
And special terror weighed upon his frown;   2
His punier brethren quaked before his tail,
Broad as a rafter, potent as a flail.
So he grew lord and master of his kin:
But who shall tell the tale of all their woes?
An execrable appetite arose,
He battened on them, crunched, and sucked
    them in.
He knew no law, he feared no binding law,
But ground them with inexorable jaw.
The luscious fat distilled upon his chin,
Exuded from his nostrils and his eyes,   3
While still like hungry death he fed his maw;
Till, every minor crocodile being dead
And buried too, himself gorged to the full,
He slept with breath oppressed and unstrung
    claw.

Oh marvel passing strange which next I saw!
In sleep he dwindled to the common size,
And all the empire faded from his coat.
Then from far off a wingèd vessel came,
Swift as a swallow, subtle as a flame:
I know not what it bore of freight or host,   4
But white it was as an avenging ghost.
It levelled strong Euphrates in its course;
Supreme yet weightless as an idle mote
It seemed to tame the waters without force
Till not a murmur swelled or billow beat.
Lo, as the purple shadow swept the sands,
The prudent crocodile rose on his feet,
And shed appropriate tears and wrung his
    hands.

What can it mean? you ask. I answer not
For meaning, but myself much echo, What?   5
And tell it as I saw it on the spot.

(1855) 1862

A Triad[1]

Three sang of love together: one with lips
    Crimson, with cheeks and bosom in a glow,

---

[1] Euphrates: the associations of this Asian river with pagan civilizations and empires are probably intended to be counter to the Biblical associations of the Jordan River.
[1] Christina Rossetti did not republish this poem after it appeared in the volume of verse she published in 1862. In his notes to the collected edition of her poems, William Michael Rossetti writes, "I presume that my sister, with over-strained scrupulosity, considered its moral tone to be somewhat open to exception" (p. 480).

Flushed to the yellow hair and finger-tips;
  And one there sang who soft and smooth as
    snow
  Bloomed like a tinted hyacinth at a show;
And one was blue with famine after love,
  Who like a harpstring snapped rang harsh
    and low
The burden[2] of what those were singing of.
One shamed herself in love; one temperately
Grew gross in soulless love, a sluggish wife;
One famished died for love. Thus two of three
  Took death for love and won him after strife;
One droned in sweetness like a fattened bee:
  All on the threshold, yet all short of life.

                              (1856) 1862

Shut Out[1]

The door was shut. I looked between
  Its iron bars; and saw it lie,
  My garden, mine, beneath the sky,
Pied with all flowers bedewed and green.

From bough to bough the song-birds crossed,
  From flower to flower the moths and bees:
  With all its nests and stately trees
It had been mine, and it was lost.

A shadowless spirit kept the gate,
  Blank and unchanging like the grave.
  I, peering through, said; "Let me have
Some buds to cheer my outcast state."

He answered not. "Or give me, then,
  But one small twig from shrub or tree;
  And bid my home remember me
Until I come to it again."

The spirit was silent; but he took
  Mortar and stone to build a wall;
  He left no loophole great or small
Through which my straining eyes might look.

So now I sit here quite alone,
  Blinded with tears; nor grieve for that,
  For nought is left worth looking at
Since my delightful land is gone.

A violet bed is budding near,
  Wherein a lark has made her nest;

And good they are, but not the best;
And dear they are, but not so dear.

                              (1856) 1862

A Birthday

My heart is like a singing bird
  Whose nest is in a watered shoot:
My heart is like an apple-tree
  Whose boughs are bent with thickset fruit;
My heart is like a rainbow shell
  That paddles in a halcyon sea;
My heart is gladder than all these
  Because my love is come to me.

Raise me a dais of silk and down;
  Hang it with vair[1] and purple dyes;   10
Carve it in doves and pomegranates,
  And peacocks with a hundred eyes;
Work it in gold and silver grapes,
  In leaves and silver fleurs-de-lys;
Because the birthday of my life
  Is come, my love is come to me.

                          (1857) 1861; 1862

A Better Resurrection

I have no wit, no words, no tears;
  My heart within me like a stone
Is numbed too much for hopes or fears.
  Look right, look left, I dwell alone;
I lift mine eyes, but dimmed with grief
  No everlasting hills I see;
My life is in the falling leaf:
  O Jesus, quicken me.

My life is like a faded leaf,
  My harvest dwindled to a husk: 10
Truly my life is void and brief
  And tedious in the barren dusk;
My life is like a frozen thing,
  No bud nor greenness can I see;
Yet rise it shall—the sap of Spring;
  O Jesus, rise in me.

My life is like a broken bowl,
  A broken bowl that cannot hold
One drop of water for my soul
  Or cordial in the searching cold;   20

---

[2] Burden: undersong, accompaniment.
[1] In his notes to the collected edition William Michael Rossetti remarks that in manuscript this poem "bears the too significant title, *What Happened to Me?*" (p. 480).
[1] Vair: squirrel fur.

Cast in the fire the perished thing;
   Melt and remould it, till it be
A royal cup for Him, my King:
    O Jesus, drink of me.

                 (1857) 1862

Up-Hill

Does the road wind up-hill all the way?
   Yes, to the very end.
Will the day's journey take the whole long
    day?
   From morn to night, my friend.

But is there for the night a resting-place?
   A roof for when the slow dark hours begin.
May not the darkness hide it from my face?
   You cannot miss that inn.

Shall I meet other wayfarers at night?
10   Those who have gone before.
Then must I knock, or call when just in sight?
   They will not keep you standing at that
    door.

Shall I find comfort, travel-sore and weak?
   Of labour you shall find the sum.
Will there be beds for me and all who seek?
   Yea, beds for all who come.

           (1858) 1861; 1862

Goblin Market

Morning and evening
Maids heard the goblins cry:
"Come buy our orchard fruits,
Come buy, come buy:
Apples and quinces,
Lemons and oranges,
Plump unpecked cherries,
Melons and raspberries,
Bloom-down-cheeked peaches,
10 Swart-headed mulberries,
Wild free-born cranberries,
Crab-apples, dewberries,
Pine-apples, blackberries,
Apricots, strawberries;—
All ripe together
In summer weather,—
Morns that pass by,
Fair eves that fly;

Come buy, come buy:
Our grapes fresh from the vine,   2
Pomegranates full and fine,
Dates and sharp bullaces,[1]
Rare pears and greengages,
Damsons and bilberries,[2]
Taste them and try:
Currants and gooseberries,
Bright-fire-like barberries,
Figs to fill your mouth,
Citrons from the South,
Sweet to tongue and sound to eye;   3
Come buy, come buy."

Evening by evening
Among the brookside rushes,
Laura bowed her head to hear,
Lizzie veiled her blushes:
Crouching close together
In the cooling weather,
With clasping arms and cautioning lips,
With tingling cheeks and fingertips.
"Lie close," Laura said,
Pricking up her golden head:
"We must not look at goblin men,
We must not buy their fruits:
Who knows upon what soil they fed
Their hungry thirsty roots?"   4
"Come buy," call the goblins
Hobbling down the glen.
"Oh," cried Lizzie, "Laura, Laura,
You should not peep at goblin men."
Lizzie covered up her eyes,
Covered close lest they should look;   5
Laura reared her glossy head,
And whispered like the restless brook:
"Look, Lizzie, look, Lizzie,
Down the glen tramp little men.
One hauls a basket,
One bears a plate,
One lugs a golden dish
Of many pounds' weight.
How fair the vine must grow
Whose grapes are so luscious;
How warm the wind must blow
Through those fruit bushes."   6
"No," said Lizzie: "No, no, no;
Their offers should not charm us,
Their evil gifts would harm us."
She thrust a dimpled finger
In each ear, shut eyes and ran:
Curious Laura chose to linger
Wondering at each merchant man.

---

[1] Bullaces: wild plums.   [2] Bilberries: dark blue-black fruit of a shrub.

One had a cat's face,
One whisked a tail,
One tramped at a rat's pace,
One crawled like a snail,
One like a wombat[3] prowled obtuse and furry,
One like a ratel[4] tumbled hurry skurry.
She heard a voice like voice of doves
Cooing all together:
They sounded kind and full of loves
In the pleasant weather.

Laura stretched her gleaming neck
Like a rush-imbedded swan,
Like a lily from the beck,[5]
Like a moonlit poplar branch,
Like a vessel at the launch
When its last restraint is gone.

Backwards up the mossy glen
Turned and trooped the goblin men,
With their shrill repeated cry,
"Come buy, come buy."
When they reached where Laura was
They stood stock still upon the moss,
Leering at each other,
Brother with queer brother;
Signalling each other,
Brother with sly brother.
One set his basket down,
One reared his plate;
One began to weave a crown
Of tendrils, leaves, and rough nuts brown
(Men sell not such in any town);
One heaved the golden weight
Of dish and fruit to offer her:
"Come buy, come buy," was still their cry.
Laura stared but did not stir,
Longed but had no money.
The whisk-tailed merchant bade her taste
In tones as smooth as honey,
The cat-faced purr'd,
The rat-paced spoke a word
Of welcome, and the snail-paced even was
    heard;
One parrot-voiced and jolly
Cried "Pretty Goblin" still for "Pretty Polly";
One whistled like a bird.

But sweet-tooth Laura spoke in haste:
"Good Folk, I have no coin;
To take were to purloin:

I have no copper in my purse,
I have no silver either,
And all my gold is on the furze[6]   120
That shakes in windy weather
Above the rusty heather."
"You have much gold upon your head,"
They answered all together:
"Buy from us with a golden curl."
She clipped a precious golden lock.
She dropped a tear more rare than pearl,
Then sucked their fruit globes fair or red.
Sweeter than honey from the rock,
Stronger than man-rejoicing wine,   130
Clearer than water flowed that juice;
She never tasted such before,
How should it cloy with length of use?
She sucked and sucked and sucked the more
Fruits which that unknown orchard bore;
She sucked until her lips were sore;
Then flung the emptied rinds away
But gathered up one kernel stone,
And knew not was it night or day
As she turned home alone.   140

Lizzie met her at the gate
Full of wise upbraidings:
"Dear, you should not stay so late,
Twilight is not good for maidens;
Should not loiter in the glen
In the haunts of goblin men.
Do you not remember Jeanie,
How she met them in the moonlight,
Took their gifts both choice and many,
Ate their fruits and wore their flowers   150
Plucked from bowers
Where summer ripens at all hours?
But ever in the moonlight
She pined and pined away;
Sought them by night and day,
Found them no more, but dwindled and grew
    grey;
Then fell with the first snow,
While to this day no grass will grow
Where she lies low:
I planted daisies there a year ago   160
That never blow.[7]
You should not loiter so."
"Nay, hush," said Laura:
"Nay, hush, my sister:
I ate and ate my fill,
Yet my mouth waters still:

[3] Wombat: a marsupial that looks like a small bear; native to Australia.
[4] Ratel: a badgerlike quadruped; native to South Africa.   [5] Beck: creek.
[6] Furze: an evergreen shrub with yellow flowers.   [7] Blow: bloom.

To-morrow night I will
Buy more;" and kissed her.
"Have done with sorrow;
170 I'll bring you plums to-morrow
Fresh on their mother twigs,
Cherries worth getting;
You cannot think what figs
My teeth have met in,
What melons icy-cold
Piled on a dish of gold
Too huge for me to hold,
What peaches with a velvet nap,
Pellucid grapes without one seed:
180 Odorous indeed must be the mead[8]
Whereon they grow, and pure the wave they
          drink
With lilies at the brink,
And sugar-sweet their sap."

Golden head by golden head,
Like two pigeons in one nest
Folded in each other's wings,
They lay down in their curtained bed:
Like two blossoms on one stem,
Like two flakes of new-fall'n snow,
190 Like two wands of ivory
Tipped with gold for awful kings.
Moon and stars gazed in at them,
Wind sang to them lullaby,
Lumbering owls forebore to fly,
Not a bat flapped to and fro
Round their nest:
Cheek to cheek and breast to breast
Locked together in one nest.

Early in the morning
200 When the first cock crowed his warning,
Neat like bees, as sweet and busy,
Laura rose with Lizzie:
Fetched in honey, milked the cows,
Aired and set to rights the house,
Kneaded cakes of whitest wheat,
Cakes for dainty mouths to eat,
Next churned butter, whipped up cream,
Fed their poultry, sat and sewed;
Talked as modest maidens should:
210 Lizzie with an open heart,
Laura in an absent dream,
One content, one sick in part;
One warbling for the mere bright day's delight,
One longing for the night.

At length slow evening came:
They went with pitchers to the reedy brook;

Lizzie most placid in her look,
Laura most like a leaping flame.
They drew the gurgling water from its deep.
Lizzie plucked purple and rich golden flags,[9]   22
Then turning homeward said: "The sunset
          flushes
Those furthest loftiest crags;
Come, Laura, not another maiden lags.
No wilful squirrel wags,
The beasts and birds are fast asleep."
But Laura loitered still among the rushes,
And said the bank was steep.

And said the hour was early still,
The dew not fall'n, the wind not chill;
Listening ever, but not catching   23
The customary cry,
"Come buy, come buy,"
With its iterated jingle
Of sugar-baited words:
Not for all her watching
Once discerning even one goblin
Racing, whisking, tumbling, hobbling—
Let alone the herds
That used to tramp along the glen,
In groups or single,   24
Of brisk fruit-merchant men.

Till Lizzie urged, "O Laura, come;
I hear the fruit-call, but I dare not look:
You should not loiter longer at this brook:
Come with me home.
The stars rise, the moon bends her arc,
Each glow-worm winks her spark,
Let us get home before the night grows dark:
For clouds may gather
Though this is summer weather,   25
Put out the lights and drench us through;
Then if we lost our way what should we do?"

Laura turned cold as stone
To find her sister heard that cry alone,
That goblin cry,
"Come buy our fruits, come buy."
Must she then buy no more such dainty fruit?
Must she no more such succous[10] pasture find,
Gone deaf and blind?
Her tree of life drooped from the root: 26
She said not one word in her heart's sore ache:
But peering thro' the dimness, nought
          discerning,
Trudged home, her pitcher dripping all the
          way;

[8] Mead: meadow.   [9] Flags: reeds.   [10] Succous: containing juice.

So crept to bed, and lay
Silent till Lizzie slept;
Then sat up in a passionate yearning,
And gnashed her teeth for baulked desire, and
    wept
As if her heart would break.

Day after day, night after night,
Laura kept watch in vain
In sullen silence of exceeding pain.
She never caught again the goblin cry,
"Come buy, come buy;"—
She never spied the goblin men
Hawking their fruits along the glen:
But when the noon waxed bright
Her hair grew thin and grey;
She dwindled, as the fair full moon doth turn
To swift decay and burn
Her fire away.

One day remembering her kernel-stone
She set it by a wall that faced the south;
Dewed it with tears, hoped for a root,
Watched for a waxing shoot,
But there came none.
It never saw the sun,
It never felt the trickling moisture run:
While with sunk eyes and faded mouth
She dreamed of melons, as a traveller sees
False waves in desert drouth
With shade of leaf-crowned trees,
And burns the thirstier in the sandful breeze.

She no more swept the house,
Tended the fowls or cows,
Fetched honey, kneaded cakes of wheat,
Brought water from the brook:
But sat down listless in the chimney-nook
And would not eat.

Tender Lizzie could not bear
To watch her sister's cankerous care,
Yet not to share.
She night and morning
Caught the goblins' cry:
"Come buy our orchard fruits,
Come buy, come buy:"—
Beside the brook, along the glen,
She heard the tramp of goblin men,
The voice and stir
Poor Laura could not hear;
Longed to buy fruit to comfort her,
But feared to pay too dear.
She thought of Jeanie in her grave,

Who should have been a bride;
But who for joys brides hope to have
Fell sick and died
In her gay prime,
In earliest winter time,
With the first glazing rime,
With the first snow-fall of crisp winter time.

Till Laura dwindling   320
Seemed knocking at Death's door.
Then Lizzie weighed no more
Better and worse;
But put a silver penny in her purse,
Kissed Laura, crossed the heath with clumps of
    furze
At twilight, halted by the brook:
And for the first time in her life
Began to listen and look.

Laughed every goblin
When they spied her peeping: 330
Came towards her hobbling,
Flying, running, leaping,
Puffing and blowing,
Chuckling, clapping, crowing,
Clucking and gobbling,
Mopping and mowing,[11]
Full of airs and graces,
Pulling wry faces,
Demure grimaces,
Cat-like and rat-like,   340
Ratel- and wombat-like,
Snail-paced in a hurry,
Parrot-voiced and whistler,
Helter skelter, hurry skurry,
Chattering like magpies,
Fluttering like pigeons,
Gliding like fishes,—
Hugged her and kissed her:
Squeezed and caressed her:
Stretched up their dishes,   350
Panniers, and plates:
"Look at our apples
Russet and dun,
Bob at our cherries,
Bite at our peaches,
Citrons and dates,
Grapes for the asking,
Pears red with basking
Out in the sun,
Plums on their twigs;   360
Pluck them and suck them,—
Pomegranates, figs."

[11] Mopping and mowing: grimacing.

"Good folk," said Lizzie,
Mindful of Jeanie:
"Give me much and many:"
Held out her apron,
Tossed them her penny.
"Nay, take a seat with us,
Honour and eat with us,"
370 They answered grinning:
"Our feast is but beginning.
Night yet is early,
Warm and dew-pearly,
Wakeful and starry:
Such fruits as these
No man can carry;
Half their bloom would fly,
Half their dew would dry,
Half their flavour would pass by.
380 Sit down and feast with us,
Be welcome guest with us,
Cheer you and rest with us."—
"Thank you," said Lizzie: "But one waits
At home alone for me:
So without further parleying,
If you will not sell me any
Of your fruits though much and many,
Give me back my silver penny
I tossed you for a fee."—
390 They began to scratch their pates,
No longer wagging, purring,
But visibly demurring,
Grunting and snarling.
One called her proud,
Cross-grained, uncivil;
Their tones waxed loud,
Their looks were evil.
Lashing their tails
They trod and hustled her,
400 Elbowed and jostled her,
Clawed with their nails,
Barking, mewing, hissing, mocking,
Tore her gown and soiled her stocking,
Twitched her hair out by the roots,
Stamped upon her tender feet,
Held her hands and squeezed their fruits
Against her mouth to make her eat.

White and golden Lizzie stood,
Like a lily in a flood,—
410 Like a rock of blue-veined stone
Lashed by tides obstreperously,—
Like a beacon left alone
In a hoary[12] roaring sea,
Sending up a golden fire,—

Like a fruit-crowned orange-tree
White with blossoms honey-sweet
Sore beset by wasp and bee,—
Like a royal virgin town
Topped with gilded dome and spire
Close beleaguered by a fleet   42
Mad to tug her standard down.

One may lead a horse to water,
Twenty cannot make him drink.
Though the goblins cuffed and caught her,
Coaxed and fought her,
Bullied and besought her,
Scratched her, pinched her black as ink,
Kicked and knocked her,
Mauled and mocked her,
Lizzie uttered not a word;   43
Would not open lip from lip
Lest they should cram a mouthful in:
But laughed in heart to feel the drip
Of juice that syruped all her face,
And lodged in dimples of her chin,
And streaked her neck which quaked like curd.
At last the evil people,
Worn out by her resistance,
Flung back her penny, kicked their fruit
Along whichever road they took,   44
Not leaving root or stone or shoot;
Some writhed into the ground,
Some dived into the brook
With ring and ripple,
Some scudded on the gale without a sound,
Some vanished in the distance.

In a smart, ache, tingle,
Lizzie went her way;
Knew not was it night or day;
Sprang up the bank, tore thro' the furze,   4
Threaded copse and dingle,[13]
And heard her penny jingle
Bouncing in her purse,—
Its bounce was music to her ear.
She ran and ran
As if she feared some goblin man
Dogged her with gibe or curse
Or something worse:
But not one goblin skurried after,
Nor was she pricked by fear;   4
The kind heart made her windy-paced
That urged her home quite out of breath with
    haste
And inward laughter.

---

[12] Hoary: white with waves.   [13] Dingle: a cleft between hills.

She cried, "Laura," up the garden,
"Did you miss me?
Come and kiss me.
Never mind my bruises,
Hug me, kiss me, suck my juices
70 Squeezed from goblin fruits for you,
Goblin pulp and goblin dew.
Eat me, drink me, love me;
Laura, make much of me;
For your sake I have braved the glen
And had to do with goblin merchant men."

Laura started from her chair,
Flung her arms up in the air,
Clutched her hair:
"Lizzie, Lizzie, have you tasted
For my sake the fruit forbidden?
80 Must your light like mine be hidden,
Your young life like mine be wasted,
Undone in mine undoing,
And ruined in my ruin,
Thirsty, cankered, goblin-ridden?"—
She clung about her sister,
Kissed and kissed and kissed her:
Tears once again
Refreshed her shrunken eyes,
Dropping like rain
90 After long sultry drouth;
Shaking with aguish fear, and pain,
She kissed and kissed her with a hungry mouth.

Her lips began to scorch,
That juice was wormwood to her tongue,
She loathed the feast:
Writhing as one possessed she leaped and sung,
Rent all her robe, and wrung
Her hands in lamentable haste,
And beat her breast.
00 Her locks streamed like the torch
Borne by a racer at full speed,
Or like the mane of horses in their flight,
Or like an eagle when she stems[14] the light
Straight toward the sun,
Or like a caged thing freed,
Or like a flying flag when armies run.

Swift fire spread through her veins, knocked
     at her heart,
Met the fire smouldering there
And overbore its lesser flame;
10 She gorged on bitterness without a name:
Ah fool, to choose such part
Of soul-consuming care!

[14] Stems: moves up against.

Sense failed in the mortal strife:
Like the watch-tower of a town
Which an earthquake shatters down,
Like a lightning-stricken mast,
Like a wind-uprooted tree
Spun about,
Like a foam-topped waterspout
Cast down headlong in the sea,   520
She fell at last;
Pleasure past and anguish past,
Is it death or is it life?

Life out of death.
That night long Lizzie watched by her,
Counted her pulse's flagging stir,
Felt for her breath,
Held water to her lips, and cooled her face
With tears and fanning leaves.
But when the first birds chirped about their
     eaves,   530
And early reapers plodded to the place
Of golden sheaves,
And dew-wet grass
Bowed in the morning winds so brisk to pass,
And new buds with new day
Opened of cup-like lilies on the stream,
Laura awoke as from a dream,
Laughed in the innocent old way,
Hugged Lizzie but not twice or thrice;
Her gleaming locks showed not one thread of
     grey,   540
Her breath was sweet as May,
And light danced in her eyes.

Days, weeks, months, years
Afterwards, when both were wives
With children of their own;
Their mother-hearts beset with fears,
Their lives bound up in tender lives;
Laura would call the little ones
And tell them of her early prime,
Those pleasant days long gone   550
Of not-returning time:
Would talk about the haunted glen,
The wicked quaint fruit-merchant men,
Their fruits like honey to the throat
But poison in the blood
 (Men sell not such in any town) :
Would tell them how her sister stood
In deadly peril to do her good,
And win the fiery antidote:
Then joining hands to little hands   560
Would bid them cling together,—

"For there is no friend like a sister
In calm or stormy weather;
To cheer one on the tedious way,
To fetch one if one goes astray,
To lift one if one totters down,
To strengthen whilst one stands."

(1859) 1862

Twice

I took my heart in my hand,
    (O my love, O my love),
I said: Let me fall or stand,
    Let me live or die,
But this once hear me speak—
    (O my love, O my love)—
Yet a woman's words are weak;
    You should speak, not I.

10 You took my heart in your hand
    With a friendly smile,
With a critical eye you scanned,
    Then set it down,
And said: It is still unripe,
    Better wait awhile;
Wait while the skylarks pipe,
    Till the corn grows brown.

As you set it down it broke—
    Broke, but I did not wince;
I smiled at the speech you spoke,
20 At your judgment that I heard:
But I have not often smiled
    Since then, nor questioned since,
Nor cared for corn-flowers wild,
    Nor sung with the singing bird.

I take my heart in my hand,
    O my God, O my God,
My broken heart in my hand:
    Thou hast seen, judge Thou.
My hope was written on sand,
30 O my God, O my God:
Now let Thy judgment stand—
    Yea, judge me now.

This contemned of a man,
    This marred one heedless day,
This heart take Thou to scan
    Both within and without:
Refine with fire its gold,
    Purge Thou its dross away—
Yea hold it in Thy hold,
40 Whence none can pluck it out.

I take my heart in my hand—
    I shall not die, but live—
Before Thy face I stand;
    I, for Thou callest such:
All that I have I bring,
    All that I am I give;
Smile Thou and I shall sing,
    But shall not question much.

(1864) 1866

Long Barren

Thou who didst hang upon a barren tree,
My God, for me;
    Though I till now be barren, now at length,
    Lord, give me strength
To bring forth fruit to Thee.

Thou who didst bear for me the crown of
        thorn,
Spitting and scorn;
    Though I till now have put forth thorns,
        yet now
    Strengthen me Thou
That better fruit be borne.

Thou Rose of Sharon, Cedar of broad roots,
Vine of sweet fruits,
    Thou Lily of the vale with fadeless leaf,
    Of thousands Chief,
Feed Thou my feeble shoots.

(1865) 1866

A Dirge

Why were you born when the snow was
        falling?
You should have come to the cuckoo's calling,
Or when grapes are green in the cluster,
Or at least when lithe swallows muster
    For their far off flying
    From summer dying.

Why did you die when the lambs were
        cropping?
You should have died at the apples' dropping,
When the grasshopper comes to trouble,
And the wheat-fields are sodden stubble,
    And all winds go sighing
    For sweet things dying.

(1865) 1874; 1875

The fourteen sonnets of "Monna Innominata"—
the unnamed lady—are supposed to be spoken by
the woman traditionally addressed in love sonnets.
"Had such a lady spoken for herself," Christina
Rossetti wrote in a preface to the poem, "the por-
trait left us might have appeared more tender, if
less dignified, than any drawn even by a devoted
friend. Or had the Great Poetess of our day and
nation only been unhappy instead of happy, her
circumstances would have invited her to bequeath
to us, in lieu of the 'Portuguese Sonnets', an inimi-
table 'donna innominata' drawn not from fancy but
from feeling."

In his notes in the collected edition of his sister's
poems William Michael Rossetti writes that "it is
not merely probable but certain that this 'sonnet of
sonnets' was a personal utterance—an intensely
personal one. The introductory prose-note . . . is
a blind—not an untruthful blind, for it alleges
nothing that is not reasonable, . . . but still a blind
interposed to draw off attention from the writer in
her proper person" (p. 462). The personal circum-
stances of the sonnets were, in her brother's opinion,
Christina Rossetti's relationship with Charles Cayley
(1823–1883), a friend of the Rossettis and a
translator of Dante, whose proposal of marriage was
refused because, according to William, Cayley's re-
ligious beliefs were incompatible with Christina's.
Lona Mosk Packer in her biography argues that at
least some of the sonnets express the difficulties of
a relationship she tries to document between Chris-
tina Rossetti and William Bell Scott (1811–1890),
a painter, poet, and intimate of the Rossetti circle.
Scott was married when he first met Christina Ros-
setti, and by the time these sonnets were written
after 1866 he had been for some years comfortably
established in a liaison with another woman which
endured until his death.

Monna Innominata

A Sonnet of Sonnets

1

Lo di che han detto a' dolci amici addio.   DANTE
Amor, con quanto sforzo oggi mi vinci!   PETRARCA[1]

Come back to me, who wait and watch for
    you:—
  Or come not yet, for it is over then,
  And long it is before you come again,
So far between my pleasures are and few.
While, when you come not, what I do I do
  Thinking "Now when he comes," my
    sweetest "when":
  For one man is my world of all the men
This wide world holds; O love, my world is
    you.
Howbeit, to meet you grows almost a pang
  Because the pang of parting comes so soon;   10
  My hope hangs waning, waxing, like a moon
  Between the heavenly days on which we
    meet:
Ah me, but where are now the songs I sang
  When life was sweet because you called
    them sweet?

2

Era già l'ora che volge il desio.   DANTE
Ricorro al tempo ch' io vi vidi prima.   PETRARCA[2]

I wish I could remember that first day,
  First hour, first moment of your meeting me,
  If bright or dim the season, it might be
Summer or Winter for aught I can say;
So unrecorded did it slip away,
  So blind was I to see and to foresee,
  So dull to mark the budding of my tree
That would not blossom yet for many a May.
If only I could recollect it, such
  A day of days! I let it come and go
  As traceless as a thaw of bygone snow;
It seemed to mean so little, meant so much;
If only now I could recall that touch,
  First touch of hand in hand—Did one but
    know!

3

O ombre vane, fuor che ne l'aspetto!   DANTE
Immaginata guida la conduce.   PETRARCA[3]

---

[1] In the notes to the collected edition of Christina Rossetti's poems William Michael Rossetti translates, without citing the sources of, the epigraphs to each of the sonnets. The epigraphs are all from Dante's *Divine Comedy* (c. 1320) and the *Canzoniere*, a collection of sonnets and other lyrics by Petrarch (1304–1374). "The day that they have said adieu to their sweet friends" (*Purgatorio*, VIII). "Love, with how great a stress dost thou vanquish me to-day!" (*Canzoniere*, 85).

[2] "It was already the hour which turns back the desire" (*Purgatorio*, VIII). "I recur to the time when I first saw thee" (*Canzoniere*, 20).

[3] "Oh shades, empty save in semblance!" (*Purgatorio*, II). "An imaginary guide conducts her" (*Canzoniere*, 277).

I dream of you, to wake: would that I might
  Dream of you and not wake but slumber on;
  Nor find with dreams the dear companion
      gone,
As, Summer ended, Summer birds take flight.
In happy dreams I hold you full in sight,
  I blush again who waking look so wan;
  Brighter than sunniest day that ever shone,
In happy dreams your smile makes day of
      night.
Thus only in a dream we are at one,
10   Thus only in a dream we give and take
      The faith that maketh rich who take or
        give;
  If thus to sleep is sweeter than to wake,
    To die were surely sweeter than to live,
Though there be nothing new beneath the sun.

4

Poca favilla gran fiamma seconda.   DANTE
Ogni altra cosa, ogni pensier va fore,
E sol ivi con voi rimansi amore.   PETRARCA[4]

I loved you first: but afterwards your love,
  Outsoaring mine, sang such a loftier song
As drowned the friendly cooings of my dove.
    Which owes the other most? My love was
      long,
    And yours one moment seemed to wax more
      strong;
I loved and guessed at you, you construed me
And loved me for what might or might not
    be—
    Nay, weights and measures do us both a
      wrong.
For verily love knows not "mine" or "thine,"
  With separate "I" and "thou" free love has
10   done,
    For one is both and both are one in love:
Rich love knows nought of "thine that is not
    mine";

Both have the strength and both the length
    thereof,
Both of us, of the love which makes us one.

5

Amor che a nullo amato amar perdona.   DANTE
Amor m'addusse in si gioiosa spene.   PETRARCA[5]

O my heart's heart, and you who are to me
  More than myself myself, God be with you,
  Keep you in strong obedience leal[6] and true
To Him whose noble service setteth free;
Give you all good we see or can foresee,
  Make your joys many and your sorrows few,
  Bless you in what you bear and what you do,
Yea, perfect you as He would have you be.
So much for you; but what for me, dear friend?
  To love you without stint and all I can,
To-day, to-morrow, world without an end;
To love you much and yet to love you more,
  As Jordan at his flood sweeps either shore;
  Since woman is the helpmeet made for man.[7]

6

Or puoi la quantitate
Comprender de l'amor che a te mi scalda.   DANTE
Non vo' che da tal nodo amor mi scioglia.   PETRARCA[8]

Trust me, I have not earned your dear
      rebuke,—
  I love, as you would have me, God the most;
  Would lose not Him, but you, must one be
    lost,
Nor with Lot's wife cast back a faithless look,[9]
Unready to forego what I forsook;
  This say I, having counted up the cost,
  This, though I be the feeblest of God's host,
The sorriest sheep Christ shepherds with His
    crook.[10]
Yet while I love my God the most, I deem
  That I can never love you over-much;
    I love Him more, so let me love you too;
  Yea, as I apprehend it, love is such

---

[4] "A small spark fosters a great flame" (*Paradiso*, I). "Every other thing, every other thought goes off, and love alone remains there with you" (*Canzoniere*, 72).

[5] "Love, who exempts no loved one from loving" (*Inferno*, V). "Love led me into such joyous hope" (*Canzoniere*, 56).   [6] Leal: loyal.

[7] "And the Lord God said, It is not good that the man should be alone: I will make him a help meet for him" (Genesis 2:18).

[8] "Now canst thou comprehend the quantity of the love which glows in me towards thee" (*Purgatorio*, XXI). "I do not choose that Love should release me from such a tie" (*Canzoniere*, 59).

[9] As Lot and his family fled from the destruction of Sodom and Gomorrah, "his wife looked back from behind him, and she became a pillar of salt" (Genesis 19:26).

[10] The parable of the Good Shepherd is in John 10.

I cannot love you if I love not Him,
   I cannot love Him if I love not you.

7

Qui primavera sempre ed ogni frutto.   DANTE
Ragionando con meco ed io con lui.   PETRARCA[11]

"Love me, for I love you"—and answer me,
   "Love me, for I love you": so shall we stand
   As happy equals in the flowering land
Of love, that knows not a dividing sea.
Love builds the house on rock and not on sand,
   Love laughs what while the winds rave desperately;
And who hath found love's citadel unmanned?
   And who hath held in bonds love's liberty?—
My heart's a coward though my words are brave—
   We meet so seldom, yet we surely part
   So often; there's a problem for your art!
Still I find comfort in his Book who saith,
Though jealousy be cruel as the grave,
And death be strong, yet love is strong as death.[12]

8

Come dicesse a Dio, D'altro non calme.   DANTE
Spero trovar pietà non che perdono.   PETRARCA[13]

"I, if I perish, perish"—Esther spake:
   And bride of life or death she made her fair
   In all the lustre of her perfumed hair
And smiles that kindle longing but to slake.
She put on pomp of loveliness, to take
   Her husband through his eyes at unaware;
   She spread abroad her beauty for a snare,
Harmless as doves and subtle as a snake.
She trapped him with one mesh of silken hair,
   She vanquished him by wisdom of her wit,
     And built her people's house that it should stand:[14]—
   If I might take my life so in my hand,

And for my love to Love put up my prayer,
   And for love's sake by Love be granted it!

9

O dignitosa coscienza e netta!   DANTE
Spirto più acceso di virtuti ardenti.   PETRARCA[15]

Thinking of you, and all that was, and all
   That might have been and now can never be,
   I feel your honoured excellence, and see
Myself unworthy of the happier call:
For woe is me who walk so apt to fall,
   So apt to shrink afraid, so apt to flee,
   Apt to lie down and die (ah woe is me!)
Faithless and hopeless turning to the wall.
And yet not hopeless quite nor faithless quite,
   Because not loveless; love may toil all night,
But take at morning; wrestle till the break
   Of day, but then wield power with God and man:—
   So take I heart of grace as best I can,
Ready to spend and be spent for your sake.

10

Con miglior corso e con migliore stella.   DANTE
La vita fugge e non s'arresta un' ora.   PETRARCA[16]

Time flies, hope flags, life plies a wearied wing;
   Death following hard on life gains ground apace;
   Faith runs with each and rears an eager face,
Outruns the rest, makes light of everything,
Spurns earth, and still finds breath to pray and sing;
   While love ahead of all uplifts his praise,
   Still asks for grace and still gives thanks for grace,
Content with all day brings and night will bring.
Life wanes; and when love folds his wings above

---

[11] "Here always Spring and every fruit" (*Purgatorio,* XXVIII). "Conversing with me, and I with him" (*Canzoniere,* 35).

[12] "For love is as strong as death; jealousy is cruel as the grave" (Song of Solomon 8:6).

[13] "As if he were to say to God, 'I care for nought else'" (*Purgatorio,* VIII). "I hope to find pity, and not only pardon" (*Canzoniere,* 1).

[14] The book of Esther in the Old Testament recounts how the daughter of a Jew, married to a king, used her influence with the king to turn a persecution of the Jews upon their enemies, who were violently defeated.

[15] "O dignified and pure conscience!" (*Purgatorio,* III). "Spirit more lit with burning virtues" (*Canzoniere,* 283).

[16] "With better course and with better star" (*Paradiso,* I). "Life flees, and stays not an hour" (*Canzoniere,* 272).

Tired hope, and less we feel his conscious
    pulse,
  Let us go fall asleep, dear friend, in peace:
    A little while, and age and sorrow cease;
A little while, and life reborn annuls
Loss and decay and death, and all is love.

11

Vien dietro a me e lascia dir le genti.   DANTE
Contando i casi della vita nostra   PETRARCA[17]

Many in aftertimes will say of you
  "He loved her"—while of me what will they
    say?
Not that I loved you more than just in play,
For fashion's sake as idle women do.
Even let them prate; who know not what we
    knew
  Of love and parting in exceeding pain,
  Of parting hopeless here to meet again,
Hopeless on earth, and heaven is out of view.
But by my heart of love laid bare to you,
  My love that you can make not void nor
    vain,
Love that foregoes you but to claim anew
Beyond this passage of the gate of death,
  I charge you at the Judgment make it plain
My love of you was life and not a breath.

12

Amor che ne la mente mi ragiona.   DANTE
Amor vien nel bel viso di costei.   PETRARCA[18]

If there be any one can take my place
  And make you happy whom I grieve to
    grieve,
  Think not that I can grudge it, but believe
I do commend you to that nobler grace,
That readier wit than mine, that sweeter face;
  Yea, since your riches make me rich, conceive
  I too am crowned, while bridal crowns I
    weave,
And thread the bridal dance with jocund pace.

For if I did not love you, it might be
  That I should grudge you some one dear
    delight;
  But since the heart is yours that was mine
    own,
  Your pleasure is my pleasure, right my right,
Your honourable freedom makes me free,
  And you companioned I am not alone.

13

E drizzeremo gli occhi al Primo Amore.   DANTE
Ma trovo peso non da le mie braccia.   PETRARCA[19]

If I could trust mine own self with your fate,
  Shall I not rather trust it in God's hand?
  Without Whose Will one lily doth not stand,
Nor sparrow fall at his appointed date;[20]
  Who numbereth the innumerable sand,
Who weighs the wind and water with a weight,
To Whom the world is neither small nor great,
  Whose knowledge foreknew every plan we
    planned.
Searching my heart for all that touches you,
  I find there only love and love's goodwill
Helpless to help and impotent to do,
Of understanding dull, of sight most dim;
And therefore I commend you back to Him
  Whose love your love's capacity can fill.

14

E la Sua Volontade è nostra pace.   DANTE
Sol con questi pensier, con altre chiome.   PETRARCA[21]

Youth gone, and beauty gone if ever there
  Dwelt beauty in so poor a face as this;
  Youth gone and beauty, what remains of
    bliss?
I will not bind fresh roses in my hair,
To shame a cheek at best but little fair,—
  Leave youth his roses, who can bear a
    thorn,—
I will not seek for blossoms anywhere,
  Except such common flowers as blow with
    corn.[22]

[17] "Come after me, and leave folk to talk" (*Purgatorio,* V). "Relating the casualties of our life" (*Canzoniere,* 285).
[18] "Love, who speaks within my mind" (*Purgatorio,* II). "Love comes in the beautiful face of this lady" (*Canzoniere,* 13).
[19] "And we will direct our eyes to the Primal Love" (*Paradiso,* XXXII). "But I find a burden to which my arms suffice not" (*Canzoniere,* 20).
[20] "Are not two sparrows sold for a farthing? and one of them shall not fall on the ground without your Father" (Matthew 10:29).
[21] "And His will is our peace" (*Paradiso,* III). "Only with these thoughts, with different locks" (*Canzoniere,* 30).
[22] Blow with corn: bloom in autumn at the time of harvest.

Youth gone and beauty gone, what doth re-
    main?
10 The longing of a heart pent up forlorn,
    A silent heart whose silence loves and
      longs;
    The silence of a heart which sang its songs
  While youth and beauty made a summer
    morn,
Silence of love that cannot sing again.

                  1881

Ash Wednesday

My God, my God, have mercy on my sin,
For it is great; and if I should begin
To tell it all, the day would be too small
    To tell it in.

My God, Thou wilt have mercy on my sin
For Thy Love's sake: yea, if I should begin

To tell This all, the day would be too small
    To tell it in.

                  1893

Advent[1]

Earth grown old, yet still so green,
  Deep beneath her crust of cold
Nurses fire unfelt, unseen:
  Earth grown old.

  We who live are quickly told:
Millions more lie hid between
  Inner swathings of her fold.

When will fire break up her screen?
  When will life burst thro' her mould?
Earth, earth, earth, thy cold is keen,
  Earth grown old.

                  1893

Dante Gabriel Rossetti
1828–1882

DANTE GABRIEL ROSSETTI came forward as an aggressively unconventional painter and poet at about the same time. He exhibited his first painting, a scene of the girlhood of the mother of Christ, in 1849. He had been writing poetry and imaginative prose since his adolescence, and in the same year he published a story and some poems, including the first version of "The Blessed Damozel," in *The Germ,* a short-lived literary magazine he had helped to found. Then for twenty years he made his reputation and his living as a painter in watercolors and oils. He did not publish a volume of his poems until 1870, and he published only one other volume of poems in his lifetime. Yet Rossetti is a figure of considerable standing in the history of nineteenth-century British poetry. One reason is the quality of his verse, in

which there is a remarkably high proportion of strikingly accomplished to relatively undistinguished poems. Another reason is that Rossetti's life as well as his work describe an idea of art and the artist that exercised a large, palpable, and persistent effect on poets who began to write after mid-century. Rossetti's style of being an artist proclaimed that, for better or worse, art was something out of the ordinary, an intensely individual way of living in and expressing a reality not only apart but in some measure alienated from the pleasures and values of common experience.

Rossetti gave this style one of its names. In 1848, which they noted as a year of revolutions, he and some other painters restless with their training in conventional art schools began signing their pictures "P. R. B.": Pre-

[1] The name of the liturgical season preceding Christmas.

Raphaelite Brotherhood. It is not necessary to take the name literally in order to take it seriously. The revolutionary overtones of the term "Brotherhood," and its conspiratorial initials, are art student jokes. Nevertheless, the name clearly attests that some artists of a new generation found an identity in their desire to do something different. What they intended to do was articulated less clearly, and the most notable talents in the group—Rossetti, John Everett Millais (1829–96), and Holman Hunt (1827–1910)—soon became quite different kinds of painters. But they agreed at the beginning about what they wanted to leave behind. "Raphael" to them meant the iconography, rules of composition, and dramatic lights and shadows of conventional academic painting; "Pre-Raphaelite" meant the natural lighting and accurate rendering of detail and figure they admired in Italian religious painters of the fourteenth and fifteenth centuries. Whatever else it might be in its subject and purpose, an art engendered by the originally rebellious Pre-Raphaelite gesture would be strong and clear in outline and coloring, and full of precisely depicted detail.

In his poetry as well as in his painting, Rossetti used these external features of color, line, and detail in ways that emphasized the artifice of his work and on subjects that emphasized the distance between art and ordinary experience. He sought unusual words (he called them "stunners") for his poems; he liked verse forms with refrains and emphatic rhyme schemes; he decorated the surfaces of his poems and his paintings with jewels, armor, aureoles, banners, flowers, and other sources of gleaming light and color. The subjects of his early paintings and of many of his poems throughout his life were medieval. Like that of William Morris, who was excited by Rossetti's early poems and who was engaged with him in the painting of frescoes on Arthurian subjects at Oxford in 1857, Rossetti's medievalism had less to do with the contemporary than Tennyson's did. Love, loss, isolation, and death in his poems and paintings tend to stand in their own clear air, purged of the moral and political references through which Tennyson in the *Idylls of the King* was making statements about the claims of duty in the war between soul and sense. When Rossetti moved from the remote to the eerie, as he did in poems like "Sister Helen" and in

paintings like that for which his sonnet "Body's Beauty" was written, the resonances of his poems were enigmatic and disturbing. It was poems such as these that excited Swinburne, who met him at Oxford in 1857, and that helped to continue a flourishing tradition of poems (see, for example, William Bell Scott's "The Witches' Ballad" and Thomas Gordon Hake's poem "The Snake Charmer," both in Part Four) in which the material world is haunted not by glimpses of the divine but by witches, goddesses of pagan rites, and other preternatural presences whose force seems to come from some exceptional depravity of flesh and human spirit. Finally, the sensuousness of Rossetti's attention to surfaces created an extraordinary intensity that seemed unnatural and even unhealthy to many of his contemporaries. The bosom of the Blessed Damozel warming the railing over which she leans from heaven; the large eyes, full nose and lips, and loose, dense hair of the women in his paintings of the 1860s and 1870s; the details of poems like "Nuptial Sleep" and "Silent Noon" and the private, inward stress of many of the other sonnets of "The House of Life": these characteristics announced a commitment, liberating or subversive of convention, not just to physical, individual existence but also to its extreme boundaries and possibilities.

Such a commitment later in the century was to be described as estheticism or art for art's sake, and associated with a decadence in art and history—phrases even less precise than "Pre-Raphaelite." Again, however, the ground idea is clear enough. It was stated most importantly by Walter Pater in the "Preface" and "Conclusion" to *The Renaissance,* a series of essays on painting he collected in 1873. One who feels the pleasure of art, he wrote in the "Preface," "has no need to trouble himself with the abstract question of what beauty is in itself, or what its exact relation to truth or experience—metaphysical questions, as unprofitable as metaphysical questions elsewhere." For we cannot really know, he continued in the "Conclusion," anything but that which we experience within our separate consciousnesses. Wisdom therefore lies in seeking experiences which amplify and intensify consciousness, and of this passionate wisdom "the poetic passion, the desire of beauty, the love of art for its own sake has most. For art comes to you professing frankly to give nothing but the highest quality to your moments as they pass, and simply for those moments' sake."

Rossetti's conceptions of the nature and purposes of art do not entirely fit Pater's formulation. From his father's elaborately allegorical commentary on Dante and from his own translations of early Italian poets, Rossetti learned how to read and make a highly formalized poetry in which physical reality consistently referred to something more. Millais and Hunt from the beginning gave Pre-Raphaelitism a habit of using precisely delineated detail to depict episodes and objects which quite explicitly pointed a moral or some other generalized meaning: Hunt especially became known for his illustrations of scriptural passages (Christ with a lantern lighting the world) which were nearly allegorical in the reference of their conventional emblems. Rossetti also often told stories in his pictures and poems. In his last volume of poems, for example, he published three long narrative poems, one of them "The White Ship," and he arranged the sonnets of "The House of Life" so that they more clearly marked the stages of a love affair and its consequences. Further, "The 'life' involved," he wrote on a manuscript of "The House of Life," "is life representative"; Rossetti's sonnet-sequence, like some of his other poems, especially those for pictures, is full of personified abstractions which move to extend the resonance of the episodes and action he depicts. Rossetti, in short, shared even if he did not characteristically realize some of the ambitions and large conceptions of mid-century poets who wrote continuous narratives and connected sequences of lyric poems as a means of establishing and enforcing the general meaning and effect of their poems.

On the other hand, there is a tonality in Rossetti's poems that does connect them with the poetry of later writers who thought of themselves as living in isolated moments of pleasure within a history winding down toward decadence. Despite his competence in long forms like "The White Ship" at the end of his life, his characteristic poetry is in short lyric and narrative forms that fix certain intense passages of experience. The episodes and moods that make up "The House of Life," for example, are connected by the movement of the whole poem from love to loss to a gesture toward solace. But each episode and mood is usually rendered in a sonnet or short sequence ("Willowwood") which emphatically completes its own movement within an insistently formal artifice. The power of Rossetti's style, and the principal source of his effect on other nineteenth-century poets, lies in this concentration, in the quality his poems typically possess of having been shaped and ornamented under a great and deliberate pressure of form. At the same time, there is often a sadness in the very repose of these poems. Those fixed images of desire stopped or gone perverse, of a sensuous energy turned down into stasis and toward pain—Sister Helen and the woman of "The Orchard Pit," Our Lady of the Rocks and Lilith in "Body's Beauty"—are the emblems of Rossetti's dominant theme of a wish for consummation and permanence which is framed and frustrated by time. The function of artifice for Rossetti was to fix these images, to transfigure life and hold its most intensely pleasurable moments against change. By "its flowering crest impearled and orient," he wrote in the introductory sonnet to "The House of Life," poetry will achieve its difference from natural objects whose flowers fall more quickly. But, as in the caught, consummated moment of a poem like "Silent Noon," Rossetti's poems usually and explicitly stand in and are defined against the fact of time out of which their artifice tries to hold them. One interest of his poetry, then, is that it shows a largeness of conception and purpose like that of Tennyson, Browning, and other mid-century poets, while it also shows the tones, themes, and insistent, self-preserving artifice common in the poetry of the last decades of the century. Again and again, Rossetti committed his craft to bound the space and to ornament the surface of episodes in which particular detail is pushed toward an expanded reference and resolution it hints at, wishes for, but expresses only in a recognition that the finally painful meaning of each moment is that its impulse toward completeness and permanence will not be fulfilled.

CHRONOLOGY

1828 Born in London. His father was a political exile from Italy who earned his living by teaching Italian; he also wrote, in Italian, commentaries on the work of Dante, and he was later professor of Italian at King's College, University of London. Rossetti's mother was of an Anglo-Italian family and a devout member of the Church of England; she had worked as a governess.

1836–45 Rossetti attended schools in London, including art classes.

1845–48 Rossetti entered the art school of the Royal Academy of Art in London, where he met Holman Hunt, John Everett Millais, and other painters who were to come together in a company they called the Pre-Raphaelite Brotherhood.

1849–50 Rossetti exhibited his first painting and published his first imaginative writing, including the prose sketch "Hand and Soul" and the poem "The Blessed Damozel," in *The Germ,* published by the circle of painters and writers who called themselves pre-Raphaelite.

1850 The Pre-Raphaelites were attacked by art critics on the occasion of an exhibition which included some of their paintings; in 1851 their painting was defended by John Ruskin (1819–1900), who was just entering his eminence as a writer on art. Later in the 1850s Ruskin helped to support Rossetti by means of an annual commission paid to Elizabeth Siddal, whom Rossetti met in 1850 and who under his influence began to draw and paint.

1850s Rossetti worked in London, painting watercolors and oils, usually on subjects drawn from Dante and the Arthurian stories. He taught art classes at the Working Men's College in London in 1854. In 1857, a year in which he and his associates confirmed their notoriety by staging a Pre-Raphaelite Exhibition, Rossetti organized a group commissioned to paint the frescoes for a new building at Oxford, where Swinburne met Rossetti and where Rossetti met Jane Burden, who was later to marry William Morris.

1860 Rossetti married Elizabeth Siddal; their only child was stillborn in 1861.

1861 *The Early Italian Poets,* Rossetti's translations from Dante and other writers, published.

1862 Elizabeth Siddal Rossetti died from an overdose of laudanum; remorsefully, because he thought their composition had distracted him from attending to his wife's despondence and poor health, Rossetti buried the manuscript of his poems with her.

1863 Rossetti helped to complete a life of the painter and poet William Blake, by Alexander Gilchrist, published in this year.

1866–68 Rossetti resumed the writing of poetry, including the writing of some of the sonnets of "The House of Life," in which the feelings, difficulties, and some of the episodes of his love for and relationship with Jane Burden Morris are described. Rossetti no longer exhibited his paintings but worked on a relatively steady flow of commissions; in the 1860s he painted mostly in oils and produced a series of female figures in mythological identities.

1869 The manuscript of Rossetti's earlier poems was exhumed from his wife's grave.

1870 *Poems,* Rossetti's first volume of poetry, a collection of some early poems, some revisions of early poems, and recent verse, was published.

1871–74 Troubled by poor health, delusions of a conspiracy against him, and some actual attacks on the alleged immorality of his writing (including Robert Buchanan's essay, "The Fleshly School of Poetry," first published in 1871), Rossetti lived with the Morrises at Kelmscott Manor outside London. In 1872 he attempted suicide.

1876 After an estrangement from the Morrises and a short stay in another house in the country outside London, Rossetti returned to London, his health still uncertain and his habits of work increasingly dilatory.

1881 *Ballads and Sonnets,* Rossetti's second volume of verse, was published, including many of the sonnets of "The House of Life." A two-volume edition of his poetry was published in the same year.

1882 Rossetti died at a resort outside London.

EDITIONS

The text of the poems reprinted here is that of the *Works* of Dante Gabriel Rossetti, edited by his brother William Michael Rossetti (1911). An early, privately printed poem, *Sir Hugh the Heron* (1843), is excluded from W. M. Rossetti's edition, and has not been reprinted. Another narrative poem, "Jan Van Hunks," first published in 1909, has been republished in a text edited by J. R. Wahl (1952). J. R. Wahl and Oswald Doughty have edited Rossetti's *Letters* in four volumes (1965–67).

BIOGRAPHY AND CRITICISM

The standard biography of Rossetti is Oswald Doughty's *Dante Gabriel Rossetti: A Victorian Romantic* (second edition, 1960), in which Rossetti's relationship with Jane Morris is patiently and persuasively reconstructed. William Michael Rossetti published several volumes of reminiscences and family papers useful for biographical study: *Dante Gabriel Rossetti: His Family Letters, with a Memoir* (1895); *Ruskin: Rossetti: Pre-Raphaelitism: Papers 1854–62* (1899); *Preraphaelite Diaries and Letters* (1900); *Rossetti Papers 1862–70* (1903); and *Some Reminiscences* (1906). Helen Rossetti Angeli, William Michael Rossetti's daughter, published *Dante Gabriel Rossetti: His Friends and Enemies* in 1949. Gail Pedrick's *Life with Rossetti* (1964) contains letters by Rossetti not included in the four-volume edition of Doughty and Wahl. William E. Fredeman's *Prelude to the Last Decade* (1971) studies Rossetti's life and work in 1872.

OTHER USEFUL BOOKS AND ESSAYS ON PRE-RAPHAELITISM

Boase, T. S. R. *English Art, 1800–1870* (1959).

Cook, E. T., and Wedderburn, Alexander, eds. *The Works of Ruskin.* 12 vols. (1903–12). John Ruskin's defense of the Pre-Raphaelites in 1851 is published in Vol. 12.

Fleming, G. H. *Rossetti and the Pre-Raphaelite Brotherhood* (1967); also a succeeding study by Fleming, *That Ne'er Shall Meet Again* (1971).

Fredeman, William E., ed. *The PRB Journal: William Michael Rossetti's Diary of the Pre-Raphaelite Brotherhood, 1849–1853, Together With Other Pre-Raphaelite Documents* (1975).

Hunt, Holman. *Pre-Raphaelitism and the Pre-Raphaelite Brotherhood* (1905; revised edition, 1913).

Ironside, Robin. *Pre-Raphaelite Painters* (1948).

Welby, T. E. *The Victorian Romantics 1850–1870* (1929).

Welland, D. S. R. *The Pre-Raphaelites in Literature and Art* (1953).

OTHER BOOKS AND ESSAYS

Baum, Paull F., ed. *The House of Life: A Sonnet Sequence* (1928). Includes an introductory essay.

Charlesworth, Barbara. *Dark Passages: The Decadent Consciousness in Victorian Literature* (1965).

Cooper, Robert M. *Lost on Both Sides: Dante Gabriel Rossetti, Critic and Poet* (1971).

Fraser, Robert S., ed. *Essays on the Rossettis* (1971).

Fredeman, William E. "Rossetti's 'In Memoriam': An Elegiac Reading of the House of Life," *Bulletin of John Rylands Library,* 47 (1965).

Hamilton, Walter. *The Aesthetic Movement in England* (1882).

Howard, Ronnalie Roper. *The Dark Glass: Vision and Technique in the Poetry of Dante Gabriel Rossetti* (1972).

Sonstroem, David. *Rossetti and the Fair Lady* (1970).

Vogel, Joseph F. *Dante Gabriel Rossetti's Versecraft* (1971).

William Michael Rossetti published a bibliography of Rossetti's writings in 1905. See also William E. Fredeman's *Pre-Raphaelitism: A Bibliocritical Study* (1965), and Ehrsam, Deily, and Smith (General Bibliography). Virginia Surtees has catalogued Rossetti's graphic art in *Dante Gabriel Rossetti: 1828–1882. The Paintings and Drawings: A Catalogue Raisonné* (1971).

The Blessed Damozel[1]

The blessed damozel leaned out
    From the gold bar of Heaven;
Her eyes were deeper than the depth
    Of waters stilled at even;
She had three lilies in her hand,
    And the stars in her hair were seven.

Her robe, ungirt from clasp to hem,
    No wrought flowers did adorn,
But a white rose of Mary's gift,
    For service meetly worn;
Her hair that lay along her back
    Was yellow like ripe corn.

Herseemed she scarce had been a day
    One of God's choristers;

10

---

[1] "The Blessed Damozel" was first published in *The Germ* in 1850; it was written three years earlier. Versions of the poem, similar to one another, were also published in 1856 and in Rossetti's 1870 volume of poems. The poem was not significantly revised after 1870. Paull Franklin Baum's edition, *Dante Gabriel Rossetti, The Blessed Damozel* (Chapel Hill, 1937), presents the texts of all four versions of the poem, including the manuscript version of 1847.

The wonder was not yet quite gone
  From that still look of hers;
Albeit, to them she left, her day
  Had counted as ten years.

(To one, it is ten years of years.
20   . . . Yet now, and in this place,
Surely she leaned o'er me—her hair
  Fell all about my face. . . .
Nothing: the autumn-fall of leaves.
  The whole year sets apace.)

It was the rampart of God's house
  That she was standing on;
By God built over the sheer depth
  The which is Space begun;
So high, that looking downward thence
30 She scarce could see the sun.

It lies in Heaven, across the flood
  Of ether, as a bridge.
Beneath, the tides of day and night
  With flame and darkness ridge
The void, as low as where this earth
  Spins like a fretful midge.[2]

Around her, lovers, newly met
  Mid deathless love's acclaims,
Spoke evermore among themselves
40 Their heart-remembered names;
And the souls mounting up to God
  Went by her like thin flames.

And still she bowed herself and stooped
  Out of the circling charm;
Until her bosom must have made
  The bar she leaned on warm,
And the lilies lay as if asleep
  Along her bended arm.

From the fixed place of Heaven she saw
  Time like a pulse shake fierce   50
Through all the worlds. Her gaze still strove
  Within the gulf to pierce
Its path; and now she spoke as when
  The stars sang in their spheres.

The sun was gone now; the curled moon[3]
  Was like a little feather
Fluttering far down the gulf; and now
  She spoke through the still weather.
Her voice was like the voice the stars
  Had when they sang together.   60

(Ah sweet! Even now, in that bird's song,
  Strove not her accents there,
Fain to be hearkened? When those bells
  Possessed the mid-day air,
Strove not her steps to reach my side
  Down all the echoing stair?)

"I wish that he were come to me,
  For he will come," she said.
"Have I not prayed in Heaven?—on earth,
  Lord, Lord, has he not pray'd?   70
Are not two prayers a perfect strength?
  And shall I feel afraid?

"When round his head the aureole[4] clings,
  And he is clothed in white,
I'll take his hand and go with him
  To the deep wells of light;
As unto a stream we will step down,
  And bathe there in God's sight.

"We two will stand beside that shrine,
  Occult, withheld, untrod,   80
Whose lamps are stirred continually
  With prayer sent up to God;

[2] Midge: gnat. In the first published version of this poem in *The Germ* in 1850 the poem continues after line 36:

    But in those tracts, with her, it was
      The peace of utter light
    And silence. For no breeze may stir
      Along the steady flight
    Of Seraphim; no echo there,
      Beyond all depth or height.

    Heard hardly, some of her new friends,
      Playing at holy games,
    Spake, gentle-mouthed, among themselves,
      Their virginal chaste names;
    And the souls, mounting up to God,
      Went by her like thin flames.

[3] Lines 55–66 do not appear in the 1850 version.
[4] Aureole: radiance around a body or object.

And see our old prayers, granted, melt
  Each like a little cloud.[5]

"We two will lie i' the shadow of
  That living mystic tree
Within whose secret growth the Dove[6]
  Is sometimes felt to be,
While every leaf that His plumes touch
  Saith His Name audibly.

"And I myself will teach to him,
  I myself, lying so,
The songs I sing here; which his voice
  Shall pause in, hushed and slow,
And find some knowledge at each pause,
  Of some new thing to know."

(Alas! We two, we two, thou say'st![7]
  Yea, one wast thou with me
That once of old. But shall God lift
  To endless unity
The soul whose likeness with thy soul
  Was but its love for thee?)

"We two," she said, "will seek the groves
  Where the lady Mary is,
With her five handmaidens, whose names
  Are five sweet symphonies,

Cecily, Gertrude, Magdalen,
  Margaret and Rosalys.

"Circlewise sit they, with bound locks
  And foreheads garlanded;   110
Into the fine cloth white like flame
  Weaving the golden thread,
To fashion the birth-robes for them
  Who are just born, being dead.

"He shall fear, haply, and be dumb:
  Then will I lay my cheek
To his, and tell about our love,
  Not once abashed or weak:
And the dear Mother will approve
  My pride, and let me speak.   120

"Herself shall bring us, hand in hand,
  To Him round whom all souls
Kneel, the clear-ranged unnumbered heads
  Bowed with their aureoles:
And angels meeting us shall sing
  To their citherns and citoles.[8]

"There will I ask of Christ the Lord
  Thus much for him and me:—
Only to live as once on earth[9]
  With Love—only to be,   130

[5] 1850: "And where each need, revealed, expects / Its patient period."
[6] The Dove: a conventional emblem of the Holy Ghost, one of the three persons of God.
[7] In the 1850 version these two stanzas appeared in the place of lines 97–102:

(Alas! to *her* wise simple mind
  These things were all but known
Before: they trembled on her sense,—
  Her voice had caught their tone.
Alas for lonely Heaven! Alas
  For life wrung out alone!

Alas, and though the end were reached? . . . . .
  Was *thy* part understood
Or borne in trust? And for her sake
  Shall this too be found good?—
May the close lips that knew not prayer
  Praise ever, though they would?)

[8] Citherns and citoles: medieval musical instruments, the first a lute or guitar, the second a box-shaped string instrument.
[9] 1850:

"To have more blessing than on earth
  In no wise; but to be
As then we were,—being as then
  At peace. Yea verily.

Yea, verily; when he is come
  We will do thus and thus:
Till this my vigil seems quite strange
  And almost fabulous;
We two will live at once, one life;
  And peace shall be with us."

The 1850 version of the poem then concludes with slightly varied versions of the last two stanzas of the final version.

As then awhile, for ever now
    Together, I and he."

She gazed and listened and then said,
    Less sad of speech than mild,—
"All this is when he comes." She ceased.
    The light thrilled towards her, fill'd
With angels in strong level flight.[10]
    Her eyes, prayed, and she smil'd.

(I saw her smile.) But soon their path
    Was vague in distant spheres:[11]
And then she cast her arms along
    The golden barriers,
And laid her face between her hands,
    And wept. (I heard her tears.)
                        (1847) 1850; 1870

My Sister's Sleep[1]

She fell asleep on Christmas Eve.
    At length the long-ungranted shade
    Of weary eyelids overweigh'd
The pain nought else might yet relieve.

Our mother, who had leaned all day
    Over the bed from chime to chime,
    Then raised herself for the first time,
And as she sat her down, did pray.

10 Her little work-table was spread
        With work to finish. For the glare
        Made by her candle, she had care
    To work some distance from the bed.

Without, there was a cold moon up,
    Of winter radiance sheer and thin;
    The hollow halo it was in
Was like an icy crystal cup.

Through the small room, with subtle sound
    Of flame, by vents the fireshine drove
    And reddened. In its dim alcove
20 The mirror shed a clearness round.

I had been sitting up some nights,
    And my tired mind felt weak and blank;
    Like a sharp strengthening wine it drank
The stillness and the broken lights.

Twelve struck. That sound, by dwindling years
    Heard in each hour, crept off; and then
    The ruffled silence spread again,
Like water that a pebble stirs.

Our mother rose from where she sat:
    Her needles, as she laid them down,
    Met lightly, and her silken gown
Settled: no other noise than that.

"Glory unto the Newly Born!"
    So, as said angels, she did say,
    Because we were in Christmas Day,
Though it would still be long till morn.

Just then in the room over us
    There was a pushing back of chairs,
    As some who had sat unawares
So late, now heard the hour, and rose.

With anxious softly-stepping haste
    Our mother went where Margaret lay,
    Fearing the sounds o'erhead—should they
Have broken her long watched-for rest!

She stopped an instant, calm, and turned;
    But suddenly turned back again;
    And all her features seemed in pain
With woe, and her eyes gazed and yearned.

For my part, I but hid my face,
    And held my breath, and spoke no word:
    There was none spoken; but I heard
The silence for a little space.

Our mother bowed herself and wept:
    And both my arms fell, and I said,
    "God knows I knew that she was dead."
And there, all white, my sister slept.

Then kneeling, upon Christmas morn
    A little after twelve o'clock,
    We said, ere the first quarter struck,
"Christ's blessing on the newly born!"
                        (1847) 1850; 1870

The Sea-Limits[1]

Consider the sea's listless chime:
    Time's self it is, made audible,—
    The murmur of the earth's own shell.

---

[10] 1850: "With Angels, in strong level lapse."
[11] 1850: ". . . But soon their flight / Was vague 'mid the poised spheres."
[1] In a note in the 1870 edition of his poems Rossetti pointed out that this poem was written in 1847 and published in *The Germ* in 1850 before Tennyson's *In Memoriam*, whose stanzaic form it shares, was published.
[1] First published (as "From the Cliffs") in *The Germ* in 1850.

Secret continuance sublime
　Is the sea's end: our sight may pass
　No furlong further. Since time was,
This sound hath told the lapse of time.

No quiet, which is death's,—it hath
　The mournfulness of ancient life,
　Enduring always at dull strife.
As the world's heart of rest and wrath,
　Its painful pulse is in the sands.
　Last utterly, the whole sky stands,
Grey and not known, along its path.

Listen alone beside the sea,
　Listen alone among the woods;
　Those voices of twin solitudes
Shall have one sound alike to thee:
　Hark where the murmurs of thronged men
　Surge and sink back and surge again,—
Still the one voice of wave and tree.

Gather a shell from the strown beach
　And listen at its lips: they sigh
　The same desire and mystery,
The echo of the whole sea's speech.
　And all mankind is thus at heart
　Not anything but what thou art:
And Earth, Sea, Man, are all in each.
　　　　　　　(1849)　1850; 1870

World's Worth

'Tis of the Father Hilary.
　He strove, but could not pray; so took
　The steep-coiled stair, where his feet shook
A sad blind echo. Ever up
　He toiled. 'Twas a sick sway of air
　That autumn noon within the stair,
As dizzy as a turning cup.
　His brain benumbed him, void and thin;
　He shut his eyes and felt it spin;
　The obscure deafness hemmed him in.
He said: "O world, what world for me?"

He leaned unto the balcony
　Where the chime keeps the night and day;
　It hurt his brain, he could not pray.

He had his face upon the stone:
　Deep 'twixt the narrow shafts, his eye
　Passed all the roofs of the stark sky,
Swept with no wing, with wind alone.
　Close to his feet the sky did shake
　With wind in pools that the rains make: 20
　The ripple set his eyes to ache.
He said: "O world, what world for me?"

He stood within the mystery
　Girding God's blessed Eucharist:
　The organ and the chaunt had ceas'd.
The last words paused against his ear
　Said from the altar: drawn round him
　The gathering rest was dumb and dim.
And now the sacring-bell[1] rang clear
　And ceased; and all was awe,—the breath 30
　Of God in man that warranteth
　The inmost utmost things of faith.
He said: "O God, my world in Thee!"[2]
　　　　　　　1850; 1881

Antwerp and Bruges[1]

I climbed the stair in Antwerp church,
　What time the circling thews of sound
　At sunset seem to heave it round.
Far up, the carillon did search
　The wind, and the birds came to perch
　Far under, where the gables wound.

In Antwerp harbour on the Scheldt[2]
　I stood alone,[3] a certain space
　Of night. The mist was near my face;
Deep on, the flow was heard and felt. 10
The carillon kept pause, and dwelt
　In music through the silent place.

John Memmeling and John van Eyck[4]
　Hold state at Bruges. In sore shame
　I scanned the works that keep their name.
The carillon, which then did strike
Mine ears, was heard of theirs alike:
　It set me closer unto them.

I climbed at Bruges all the flight
　The belfry has of ancient stone. 20
　For leagues I saw the east wind blown;

[1] Sacring-bell: the bell rung at the elevation of the host during the mass.
[2] When this poem was first published in *The Germ* in 1850 the last two lines read: "Wholly the inner things of faith. / He said: "There is the world outside.' "
[1] First published in *The Germ* in 1850 but not republished in Rossetti's lifetime.
[2] Scheldt: a river.　[3] Misprinted as "along" in the standard text.
[4] Hans Memling (c. 1440–1494) and Jan van Eyck (c. 1389–1441) were Flemish religious painters.

The earth was grey, the sky was white.
I stood so near upon the height
  That my flesh felt the carillon.

1850

For *Our Lady of the Rocks* by Leonardo da Vinci[1]

Mother, is this the darkness of the end,
  The Shadow of Death? and is that outer sea
Infinite imminent Eternity?
And does the death-pang by man's seed
    sustain'd
In Time's each instant cause thy face to bend
  Its silent prayer upon the Son, while he
  Blesses the dead with His hand silently
To His long day which hours no more offend?

Mother of grace, the pass is difficult,
  Keen as these rocks, and the bewildered souls
    Throng it like echoes, blindly shuddering
    through.
    Thy name, O Lord, each spirit's voice extols,
  Whose peace abides in the dark avenue
Amid the bitterness of things occult.

1870

For *A Venetian Pastoral* by Giorgione

(*In the Louvre*)[1]
Water, for anguish of the solstice:—nay,
  But dip the vessel slowly,—nay, but lean
  And hark how at its verge the wave sighs in
Reluctant. Hush! Beyond all depth away

The heat lies silent at the brink of day:
  Now the hand trails upon the viol-string
  That sobs, and the brown faces cease to sing,
Sad with the whole of pleasure. Whither stray
Her eyes now, from whose mouth the slim
    pipes creep
  And leave it pouting, while the shadowed
    grass
    Is cool against her naked side? Let be:—
Say nothing now unto her lest she weep,
  Nor name this ever. Be it as it was,—
    Life touching lips with Immortality.

1850; 1870

For *An Allegorical Dance of Women* by Andrea Mantegna

(*In the Louvre*)[1]
Scarcely, I think; yet it indeed *may* be
  The meaning reached him, when this music
    rang
  Clear through his frame, a sweet possessive
    pang,
And he beheld these rocks and that ridged sea.
But I believe that, leaning tow'rds them, he
  Just felt their hair carried across his face
  As each girl passed him; nor gave ear to
    trace
How many feet; nor bent assuredly
His eyes from the blind fixedness of thought
  To know the dancers. It is bitter glad
    Even unto tears. Its meaning filleth it,
    A secret of the wells of Life: to wit:—
  The heart's each pulse shall keep the sense
    it had
With all, though the mind's labour run to
    nought.

1850; 1870

[1] *The Virgin of the Rocks* by Leonardo da Vinci (1452–1519) depicts the Virgin against a dark background of sharply pointed rocks. Light enters through a jagged opening through which the sea is visible. This poem and the following "Sonnets for Pictures" are here arranged in the sequence in which Rossetti placed them when he published them under that title in his 1870 volume.
[1] The painting, sometimes attributed to Giorgione (c. 1477–1510) and sometimes to the sixteenth-century painter Titian, is now called *Concert Champêtre* (*Pastorale*) It is a group of four principal figures. Two male figures are clothed, and two female figures, probably nymphs, are nude: one has turned from the group to pour water from a pitcher, and the other has paused in her playing of a flute. The poem was first published in *The Germ* in 1850.
[1] The painting is probably that usually called "Parnassus." In it women dance to the music of Orpheus, the son of Apollo and a great musician of classical legend, to honor Mars and Venus, who preside over the ceremony. A figure representing the god Mercury stands to one side watching the dancers. Mantegna (c. 1431–1506) was an Italian painter. This poem was first published in *The Germ* in 1850.

For *Ruggiero and Angelica* by Ingres[1]

I

A remote sky, prolonged to the sea's brim:
  One rock-point standing buffeted alone,
  Vexed at its base with a foul beast unknown,
Hell-birth of geomaunt and teraphim:[2]
A knight, and a winged creature bearing him,
  Reared at the rock: a woman fettered there,
  Leaning into the hollow with loose hair
And throat let back and heartsick trail of limb.

The sky is harsh, and the sea shrewd and salt:
  Under his lord the griffin-horse ramps[3] blind
    With rigid wings and tail. The spear's lithe
      stem
    Thrills in the roaring of those jaws: behind,
That evil length of body chafes at fault.
    She doth not hear nor see—she knows of
      them.

II

Clench thine eyes now,—'tis the last instant,
    girl:
  Draw in thy senses, set thy knees, and take
  One breath for all: thy life is keen awake,—
Thou mayst not swoon. Was that the scattered
    whirl
Of its foam drenched thee?—or the waves that
    curl
  And split, bleak spray wherein thy temples
    ache?
  Or was it his the champion's blood to flake
Thy flesh?—or thine own blood's anointing,
    girl?

Now, silence: for the sea's in such a sound
  As irks not silence; and except the sea,
    And now is still. Now the dead thing doth
      cease

To writhe, and drifts. He turns to her: and
    she,
Cast from the jaws of Death, remains there,
    bound,
  Again a woman in her nakedness.

  1850; 1870

For *The Wine of Circe* by Edward Burne-Jones[1]

Dusk-haired and gold-robed o'er the golden
    wine
  She stoops, wherein, distilled of death and
    shame,
  Sink the black drops; while, lit with fragrant
    flame,
Round her spread board the golden sunflowers
    shine.
Doth Helios here with Hecatè combine
  (O Circe, thou their votaress?) to proclaim
  For these thy guests all rapture in Love's
    name,
Till pitiless Night gave Day the countersign?

Lords of their hour, they come. And by her
    knee
  Those cowering beasts, their equals hereto-
    fore,
Wait; who with them in new equality
  To-night shall echo back the sea's dull roar
  With a vain wail from passion's tide-strown
    shore
Where the dishevelled seaweed hates the sea.

  1870

The Card-Dealer[1]

Could you not drink her gaze like wine?
  Yet though its splendour swoon

---

[1] In Ariosto's *Orlando Furioso* (1516) the pagan Angelica is sent to sow discord among the Christians who contemplate crusades to the Holy Land. She is discovered and left to die, but is saved by Rogero or Ruggiero. Jean Auguste Dominique Ingres (1780–1867) was a French painter especially remarkable for nude figures and for his draughtmanship. This poem was first published in *The Germ* in 1850.

[2] Geomaunt: one who practices divination by reading patterns made by thrown objects or random writing. Teraphim: images or idols also used for divination among ancient Hebrews.

[3] Griffin: a creature half-eagle and half-lion. Ramps: rears.

[1] Edward Burne-Jones (1833–1898) was one of the early associates of Rossetti in the Pre-Raphaelite group. Circe in classical mythology was a magician who turned men into beasts. Her father was the sun (Helios). Hecate is variously the goddess of the underworld and of the moon, and thus of night.

[1] "The Card-Dealer" was first published in a magazine in 1852, and Rossetti included a note: "The picture is one painted by the late Theodore von Holst; and represents a beautiful woman,

Into the silence languidly
    As a tune into a tune,
Those eyes unravel the coiled night
    And know the stars at noon.

The gold that's heaped beside her hand,
    In truth rich prize it were;
And rich the dreams that wreathe her brows
10   With magic stillness there;
And he were rich who should unwind
    That woven golden hair.

Around her, where she sits, the dance
    Now breathes its eager heat;
And not more lightly or more true
    Fall there the dancers' feet
Than fall her cards on the bright board
    As 'twere an heart that beat.

Her fingers let them softly through,
20   Smooth polished silent things;
And each one as it falls reflects
    In swift light-shadowings,
Blood-red and purple, green and blue,
    The great eyes of her rings.

Whom plays she with? With thee, who lov'st
    Those gems upon her hand;
With me, who search her secret brows;
    With all men, bless'd or bann'd.
We play together, she and we,
30   Within a vain strange land:

A land without any order,—
    Day even as night, (one saith,) —
Where who lieth down ariseth not
    Nor the sleeper awakeneth;
A land of darkness as darkness itself
    And of the shadow of death.

What be her cards, you ask? Even these:—
    The heart, that doth but crave
More, having fed; the diamond,
40   Skilled to make base seem brave;
The club, for smiting in the dark;
    The spade, to dig a grave.

And do you ask what game she plays?
    With me 'tis lost or won;

With thee it is playing still; with him
    It is not well begun;
But 'tis a game she plays with all
    Beneath the sway o' the sun.

Thou seest the card that falls,—she knows
    The card that followeth:
Her game in thy tongue is called Life,
    As ebbs thy daily breath:
When she shall speak, thou'lt learn her tongue
    And knows she calls it Death.

                                          1852; 1870

Sister Helen[1]

"Why did you melt your waxen man,
                        Sister Helen?
To-day is the third since you began."
"The time was long, yet the time ran,
                        Little   brother."
            (O Mother, Mary Mother,
Three days to-day, between Hell and Heaven!)

"But if you have done your work aright,
                        Sister Helen,
You'll let me play, for you said I might."
"Be very still in your play to-night,
                        Little   brother."
            (O Mother, Mary Mother,
Third night, to-night, between Hell and
    Heaven!)

"You said it must melt ere vesper-bell,[2]
                        Sister Helen;
If now it be molten, all is well."
"Even so,—nay, peace! you cannot tell,
                        Little brother."
            (O Mother, Mary Mother,
O what is this, between Hell and Heaven?)

"Oh the waxen knave was plump to-day,
                        Sister Helen;
How like dead folk he has dropped away!"
"Nay now, of the dead what can you say,
                        Little   brother?"
            (O Mother, Mary Mother,
What of the dead, between Hell and Heaven?)

---

richly dressed, who is sitting at a lamp-lit table, dealing out cards, with a peculiar fixedness of
expression." Von Holst (1810–1844) was a British painter who was, according to W. M. Rossetti
in the *Family-Letters*, "greatly addicted to supernatural subjects, which he treated with imagina-
tive impulse and considerable pictorial skill" (I, 117) .
    [1] This poem was written in the late 1840s and first published in a magazine in 1853.
    [2] Vesper-bell: a call to evening prayer.

"See, see, the sunken pile of wood,
             Sister Helen,
Shines through the thinned wax red as blood!"
"Nay now, when looked you yet on blood,
             Little brother?"
        (O Mother, Mary Mother,
How pale she is, between Hell and Heaven!)

"Now close your eyes, for they're sick and sore,
             Sister Helen,
And I'll play without the gallery door."
"Aye, let me rest,—I'll lie on the floor,
             Little brother."
        (O Mother, Mary Mother,
What rest to-night, between Hell and Heaven?)

"Here high up in the balcony,
             Sister Helen,
The moon flies face to face with me."
"Aye, look and say whatever you see,
             Little brother."
        (O Mother, Mary Mother,
What sight to-night, between Hell and Heaven?)

"Outside it's merry in the wind's wake,
             Sister Helen;
In the shaken trees the chill stars shake."
"Hush, heard you a horse-tread as you spake,
             Little brother?"
        (O Mother, Mary Mother,
What sound to-night, between Hell and Heaven?)

"I hear a horse-tread, and I see,
             Sister Helen,
Three horsemen that ride terribly."
"Little brother, whence come the three,
             Little brother?"
        (O Mother, Mary Mother,
Whence should they come, between Hell and Heaven?)

"They come by the hill-verge from Boyne Bar,[3]
             Sister Helen,
And one draws nigh, but two are afar."
"Look, look, do you know them who they are,
             Little brother?"
        (O Mother, Mary Mother,
Who should they be, between Hell and Heaven?)

"Oh, it's Keith of Eastholm rides so fast,
             Sister Helen,

For I know the white mane on the blast."
"The hour has come, has come at last,
             Little brother!"
        (O Mother, Mary Mother,
Her hour at last, between Hell and Heaven!)

"He has made a sign and called Halloo!
             Sister Helen,
And he says that he would speak with you."   80
"Oh tell him I fear the frozen dew,
             Little brother."
        (O Mother, Mary Mother,
Why laughs she thus, between Hell and
     Heaven?)

"The wind is loud, but I hear him cry,
             Sister Helen,
That Keith of Ewern's like to die."
"And he and thou, and thou and I,
             Little brother."
        (O Mother, Mary Mother,   90
And they and we, between Hell and Heaven!)

"Three days ago, on his marriage-morn,[4]
             Sister Helen,
He sickened, and lies since then forlorn."
"For bridegroom's side is the bride a thorn,
             Little brother?"
        (O Mother, Mary Mother,
Cold bridal cheer, between Hell and Heaven!)

"Three days and nights he has lain abed,
             Sister Helen,   100
And he prays in torment to be dead."
"The thing may chance, if he have prayed,
             Little brother!"
        (O Mother, Mary Mother,
If he have prayed, between Hell and Heaven!)

"But he has not ceased to cry to-day,
             Sister Helen,
That you should take your curse away."
"*My* prayer was heard,—he need but pray,
             Little brother!"   110
        (O Mother, Mary Mother,
Shall God not hear, between Hell and Heaven?)

"But he says, till you take back your ban,
             Sister Helen,
His soul would pass, yet never can."
"Nay then, shall I slay a living man,
             Little brother?"

---

[3] Like Keith, Boyne is a topographical name on the North Sea coast of Scotland.
[4] This stanza did not appear in 1870; it was added in the 1881 edition of Rossetti's poems.

(O Mother, Mary Mother,
A living soul, between Hell and Heaven!)

120 "But he calls for ever on your name,
               Sister Helen,
And says that he melts before a flame."
"My heart for his pleasure fared the same,
               Little brother."
         (O Mother, Mary Mother,
Fire at the heart, between Hell and Heaven!)

"Here's Keith of Westholm riding fast,
               Sister Helen,
For I know the white plume on the blast."
130 "The hour, the sweet hour I forecast,
               Little brother!"
         (O Mother, Mary Mother,
Is the hour sweet, between Hell and Heaven?)

"He stops to speak, and he stills his horse,
               Sister Helen;
But his words are drowned in the wind's
    course."
"Nay hear, nay hear, you must hear perforce,
               Little brother!"
         (O Mother, Mary Mother,
What word now heard, between Hell and
140   *Heaven?)*

"Oh he says that Keith of Ewern's cry,
               Sister Helen,
Is ever to see you ere he die."
"In all that his soul sees, there am I,
               Little brother!"
         (O Mother, Mary Mother,
The soul's one sight, between Hell and
    Heaven!)

"He sends a ring and a broken coin,
               Sister Helen,
150 And bids you mind the banks of Boyne."
"What else he broke will he ever join,
               Little brother?"
         (O Mother, Mary Mother,
No, never joined, between Hell and Heaven!)

"He yields you these and craves full fain,
               Sister Helen,
You pardon him in his mortal pain."
"What else he took will he give again,
               Little brother?"
160   *(O Mother, Mary Mother,*
Not twice to give, between Hell and Heaven!)

[5] Lines 204–245 were added in 1881.

"He calls your name in an agony,
               Sister Helen,
That even dead Love must weep to see."
"Hate, born of Love, is blind as he,
               Little brother!"
         (O Mother, Mary Mother,
Love turned to hate, between Hell and
    Heaven!)

"Oh it's Keith of Keith now that rides fast,
               Sister Helen,   17
For I know the white hair on the blast."
"The short short hour will soon be past,
               Little brother!"
         (O Mother, Mary Mother,
Will soon be past, between Hell and Heaven!)

"He looks at me and he tries to speak,
               Sister Helen,
But oh! his voice is sad and weak!"
"What here should the mighty Baron seek,
               Little brother?"
         (O Mother, Mary Mother,   18
Is this the end, between Hell and Heaven?)

"Oh his son still cries, if you forgive,
               Sister Helen,
The body dies but the soul shall live."
"Fire shall forgive me as I forgive,
               Little brother!"
         (O Mother, Mary Mother,
As she forgives, between Hell and Heaven!)

"Oh he prays you, as his heart would rive,
               Sister Helen,   1ç
To save his dear son's soul alive."
"Fire cannot slay it, it shall thrive,
               Little brother!"
         (O Mother, Mary Mother,
Alas, alas, between Hell and Heaven!)

"He cries to you, kneeling in the road,
               Sister Helen,
To go with him for the love of God!"
"The way is long to his son's abode,
               Little brother."   2(
         (O Mother, Mary Mother,
The way is long, between Hell and Heaven!)

"A lady's here, by a dark steed brought,[5]
               Sister Helen,
So darkly clad, I saw her not."

"See her now or never see aught,
                Little brother!"
            (*O Mother, Mary Mother,*
210 *What more to see, between Hell and Heaven?*)

"Her hood falls back, and the moon shines
    fair,
                Sister Helen,
On the Lady of Ewern's golden hair."
"Blest hour of my power and her despair,
                Little brother!"
            (*O Mother, Mary Mother,*
Hour blest and bann'd, between Hell and
    Heaven!)

"Pale, pale her cheeks, that in pride did glow,
                Sister Helen,
220 'Neath the bridal-wreath three days ago."
"One morn for pride and three days for woe,
                Little brother!"
            (*O Mother, Mary Mother,*
Three days, three nights, between Hell and
    Heaven!)

"Her clasped hands stretch from her bending
    head,
                Sister Helen;
With the loud wind's wail her sobs are wed."
"What wedding-strains hath her bridal-bed,
                Little brother?"
230   (*O Mother, Mary Mother,*
What strain but death's, between Hell and
    Heaven!)

"She may not speak, she sinks in a swoon,
                Sister Helen,—
She lifts her lips and gasps on the moon."
"Oh! might I but hear her soul's blithe tune,
                Little brother!"
            (*O Mother, Mary Mother,*
Her woe's dumb cry, between Hell and
    Heaven!)

"They've caught her to Westholm's saddle-
    bow,
240   Sister Helen,
And her moonlit hair gleams white in its
    flow."
"Let it turn whiter than winter snow,
                Little brother!"
            (*O Mother, Mary Mother,*
Woe-withered gold, between Hell and
    Heaven!)

[6] Lines 267–273 were added in 1881.

"O Sister Helen, you heard the bell,
                Sister Helen!
More loud than the vesper-chime it fell."
"No vesper-chime, but a dying knell,
                Little brother!"   250
            (*O Mother, Mary Mother,*
His dying knell, between Hell and Heaven!)

"Alas! but I fear the heavy sound,
                Sister Helen;
Is it in the sky or in the ground?"
"Say, have they turned their horses round,
                Little brother?"
            (*O Mother, Mary Mother,*
What would she more, between Hell and
    Heaven?)

"They have raised the old man from his knee,   260
                Sister Helen,
And they ride in silence hastily."
"More fast the naked soul doth flee,
                Little brother!"
            (*O Mother, Mary Mother,*
The naked soul, between Hell and Heaven!)

"Flank to flank are the three steeds gone,[6]
                Sister Helen,
But the lady's dark steed goes alone."
"And lonely her bridegroom's soul hath flown,   270
                Little brother."
            (*O Mother, Mary Mother,*
The lonely ghost, between Hell and Heaven!)

"Oh the wind is sad in the iron chill,
                Sister Helen,
And weary sad they look by the hill."
"But he and I are sadder still,
                Little brother!"
            (*O Mother, Mary Mother,*
Most sad of all, between Hell and Heaven!)   280

"See, see, the wax has dropped from its place,
                Sister Helen,
And the flames are winning up apace!"
"Yet here they burn but for a space,
                Little brother!"
            (*O Mother, Mary Mother,*
Here for a space, between Hell and Heaven!)

"Ah! what white thing at the door has cross'd,
                Sister Helen?
Ah! what is this that sighs in the frost?"   290

"A soul that's lost as mine is lost,
          Little brother!"
  (*O Mother, Mary Mother,*
Lost, lost, all lost, between Hell and Heaven!)
                                        1853; 1870

Sudden Light[1]

  I have been here before,
      But when or how I cannot tell:
  I know the grass beyond the door,
      The sweet keen smell,
The sighing sound, the lights around the shore.

      You have been mine before,—
          How long ago I may not know:
      But just when at that swallow's soar
          Your neck turned so,
10 Some veil did fall,—I knew it all of yore.

      Has this been thus before?
          And shall not thus time's eddying flight
      Still with our lives our love restore
          In death's despite,
      And day and night yield one delight once
                  more?[2]
                                        1870

The Portrait

  This is her picture as she was:
      It seems a thing to wonder on,
  As though mine image in the glass
      Should tarry when myself am gone.
  I gaze until she seems to stir,—
  Until mine eyes almost aver
      That now, even now, the sweet lips part
  To breathe the words of the sweet heart:—
  And yet the earth is over her.

10 Alas! even such the thin-drawn ray
      That makes the prison-depths more rude,—

The drip of water night and day
      Giving a tongue to solitude.
Yet only this, of love's whole prize,
Remains; save what in mournful guise
      Takes counsel with my soul alone,—
      Save what is secret and unknown,
Below the earth, above the skies.

  In painting her I shrined her face   2
      'Mid mystic trees, where light falls in
  Hardly at all; a covert place
      Where you might think to find a din
  Of doubtful talk, and a live flame
  Wandering, and many a shape whose name
      Not itself knoweth, and old dew,
      And your own footsteps meeting you,
  And all things going as they came.[1]

  A deep dim wood; and there she stands
      As in that wood that day: for so   3
  Was the still movement of her hands
      And such the pure line's gracious flow.
  And passing fair the type must seem,
  Unknown the presence and the dream.
      'Tis she: though of herself, alas!
      Less than her shadow on the grass
  Or than her image in the stream.

  That day we met there, I and she
      One with the other all alone;
  And we were blithe; yet memory
      Saddens those hours, as when the moon   4
  Looks upon daylight. And with her
  I stooped to drink the spring-water,
      Athirst where other waters sprang:
      And where the echo is, she sang,—
  My soul another echo there.

  But when that hour my soul won strength
      For words whose silence wastes and kills,
  Dull raindrops smote us, and at length
      Thundered the heat within the hills.

---

[1] First published in a magazine in 1863.
[2] In the 1870 volume the last stanza read:

          Then, now,—perchance again!
              O round mine eyes your tresses shake!
          Shall we not lie as we have lain
              Thus for Love's sake,
          And sleep, and wake, yet never break the chain?

[1] Rossetti began this poem in the late 1840s and reworked it considerably later. In 1860 he also reworked an early design into a pen-and-ink sketch, "How They Met Themselves," in which a pair of lovers meet their doubles in a wood. The superstition is that such a meeting is an omen of death.

That eve I spoke those words again
Beside the pelted window-pane;
   And there she hearkened what I said.
   With under-glances that surveyed
The empty pastures blind with rain.

Next day the memories of these things,
   Like leaves through which a bird has flown,
Still vibrated with Love's warm wings;
   Till I must make them all my own
And paint this picture. So, 'twixt ease
Of talk and sweet long silences,
   She stood among the plants in bloom
At windows of a summer room,
To feign the shadow of the trees.

And as I wrought, while all above
   And all around was fragrant air,
In the sick burthen of my love
   It seemed each sun-thrilled blossom there
Beat like a heart among the leaves.
O heart that never beats nor heaves,
   In that one darkness lying still,
   What now to thee my love's great will
Or the fine web the sunshine weaves?

For now doth daylight disavow
   Those days,—nought left to see or hear.
Only in solemn whispers now
   At night-time these things reach mine ear;
When the leaf-shadows at a breath
Shrink in the road, and all the heath,
   Forest and water, far and wide,
   In limpid starlight glorified,
Lie like the mystery of death.

Last night at last I could have slept,
   And yet delayed my sleep till dawn,
Still wandering. Then it was I wept:
   For unawares I came upon
Those glades where once she walked with me:
And as I stood there suddenly,
   All wan with traversing the night,
   Upon the desolate verge of light
Yearned loud the iron-bosomed sea.

Even so, where Heaven holds breath and hears
   The beating heart of Love's own breast,—
Where round the secret of all spheres
   All angels lay their wings to rest,—
How shall my soul stand rapt and awed,
When, by the new birth borne abroad
   Throughout the music of the suns,

It enters in her soul at once
And knows the silence there for God!

Here with her face doth memory sit
   Meanwhile, and wait the day's decline.
Till other eyes shall look from it,
Eyes of the spirit's Palestine,[2]
Even than the old gaze tenderer:
While hopes and aims long lost with her
   Stand round her image side by side,
   Like tombs of pilgrims that have died
About the Holy Sepulchre.

1870

Penumbra

I did not look upon her eyes,
   (Though scarcely seen, with no surprise,
'Mid many eyes a single look),
Because they should not gaze rebuke,
At night, from stars in sky and brook.

I did not take her by the hand,
   (Though little was to understand
From touch of hand all friends might take),
Because it should not prove a flake
Burnt in my palm to boil and ache.

I did not listen to her voice,
   (Though none had noted, where at choice
All might rejoice in listening),
Because no such a thing should cling
In the wood's moan at evening.

I did not cross her shadow once,
   (Though from the hollow west the sun's
Last shadow runs along so far,)
Because in June it should not bar
My ways, at noon when fevers are.

They told me she was sad that day,
   (Though wherefore tell what love's soothsay,[1]
Sooner than they, did register?)
And my heart leapt and wept to her,
And yet I did not speak nor stir.

So shall the tongues of the sea's foam
   (Though many voices therewith come
From drowned hope's home to cry to me),
Bewail one hour the more, when sea
And wind are one with memory.

1870

---

[2] Palestine: as a destination of pilgrimage.   [1] Soothsay: prophecy.

The Woodspurge[1]

The wind flapped loose, the wind was still,
Shaken out dead from tree and hill:
I had walked on at the wind's will,—
I sat now, for the wind was still.

Between my knees my forehead was,—
My lips, drawn in, said not Alas!
My hair was over in the grass,
My naked ears heard the day pass.

My eyes, wide open, had the run
Of some ten weeds to fix upon;
Among those few, out of the sun,
The woodspurge flowered, three cups in one.

From perfect grief there need not be
Wisdom or even memory:
One thing then learnt remains to me,—
The woodspurge has a cup of three.

                                                    1870

A Little While

A little while a little love
    The hour yet bears for thee and me
    Who have not drawn the veil to see
If still our heaven be lit above.
Thou merely, at the day's last sigh,
    Hast felt thy soul prolong the tone;
And I have heard the night-wind cry
    And deemed its speech mine own.

A little while a little love
    The scattering autumn hoards for us
    Whose bower is not yet ruinous
Nor quite unleaved our songless grove.
Only across the shaken boughs
    We hear the flood-tides seek the sea,
And deep in both our hearts they rouse
    One wail for thee and me.

A little while a little love
    May yet be ours who have not said
    The word it makes our eyes afraid
To know that each is thinking of.
Not yet the end: be our lips dumb
In smiles a little season yet:
I'll tell thee, when the end is come,
    How we may best forget.

                                                    1870

Even So

    So it is, my dear.
All such things touch secret strings
    For heavy hearts to hear.
    So it is, my dear.

    Very like indeed:
Sea and sky, afar, on high,
    Sand and strewn seaweed,—
    Very like indeed.

    But the sea stands spread
As one wall with the flat skies,
Where the lean black craft like flies
    Seem well-nigh stagnated,
    Soon to drop off dead.

    Seemed it so to us
When I was thine and thou wast mine,
    And all these things were thus,
    But all our world in us?

    Could we be so now?
Not if all beneath heaven's pall
    Lay dead but I and thou,
    Could we be so now!

                                                    1870

Aspecta Medusa[1]

Andromeda, by Perseus saved and wed,
Hankered each day to see the Gorgon's head:
Till o'er a fount he held it, bade her lean,
And mirrored in the wave was safely seen
That death she lived by.

                        Let not thine eyes know
Any forbidden thing itself, although
It once should save as well as kill: but be
Its shadow upon life enough for thee.

                                                    1870

---

[1] The woodspurge is a common plant, many varieties of which have medicinal properties.
[1] Written for a drawing by Rossetti. Andromeda in classical mythology was chained to a rock on the seashore as an offering to appease Poseidon, the god of the sea. She was saved and later wed by Perseus, who was returning from the adventure in which he cut off and preserved the head of one of the Gorgons. The Gorgons were women whose direct gaze, even from a severed head, turned living creatures to stone.

On Refusal of Aid Between Nations

Not that the earth is changing, O my God!
  Nor that the seasons totter in their walk,—
  Not that the virulent ill of act and talk
Seethes ever as a winepress ever trod,—
Not therefore are we certain that the rod
  Weighs in thine hand to smite thy world;
    though now
Beneath thine hand so many nations bow,
So many kings:—not therefore, O my God!—

But because Man is parcelled out in men
  To-day; because, for any wrongful blow,
    No man not stricken asks, "I would be told
Why thou dost thus" but his heart whispers
    then,
  "He is he, I am I." By this we know
    That the earth falls asunder, being old.

1870

A Match with the Moon[1]

Weary already, weary miles to-night
  I walked for bed: and so, to get some ease,
  I dogged the flying moon with similes.
And like a wisp she doubled on my sight
In ponds; and caught in tree-tops like a kite;
  And in a globe of film all liquorish
Swam full-faced like a silly silver fish;—
Last like a bubble shot the welkin's height[2]
Where my road turned, and got behind me,
    and sent
  My wizened shadow craning round at me, 10
  And jeered, "So, step the measure,—one two
    three!"—
And if I faced on her, looked innocent.
  But just at parting, halfway down a dell,
  She kissed me for good-night. So you'll not
    tell.

1870

On the *Vita Nuova* of Dante[1]

As he that loves oft looks on the dear form
  And guesses how it grew to womanhood,
  And gladly would have watched the beauties
    bud
And the mild fire of precious life wax warm:
So I, long bound within the threefold charm
  Of Dante's love sublimed to heavenly mood,
  Had marvelled, touching his Beatitude,
How grew such presence from man's shameful
    swarm.

At length within this book I found pourtrayed
  Newborn that Paradisal Love of his,
And simple like a child; with whose clear aid
  I understood. To such a child as this,
Christ, charging well His chosen ones, forbade
  Offence: "for lo! of such my kingdom is."[2]

1870

The Orchard-Pit[1]

Piled deep below the screening apple-branch
  They lie with bitter[2] apples in their hands:
And some are only ancient bones that blanch,
And some had ships that last year's wind did
    launch,
  And some were yesterday the lords of lands.

In the soft dell, among the apple-trees,
  High up above the hidden pit she stands,
And there for ever sings, who gave to these,
That lie below, her magic hour of ease,
  And those her apples holden in their hands. 10

This in my dreams is shown me; and her hair
  Crosses my lips and draws my burning
    breath;
Her song spread golden wings upon the air,
Life's eyes are gleaming from her forehead fair,

<hr>

[1] Dante's *Vita Nuova* (The New Life) describes his meeting with and love for the girl he idealized as Beatrice, the emblem of perfect human love and beauty who greets him when in *The Divine Comedy* he enters Paradise.
[2] Mark 10: 14–15.
[1] Match: used here to suggest a contest between poets who compete by alternately offering lines of verse.
[2] Welkin: the sky.
[1] Rossetti worked on this poem in the late 1860s, but he never completed it, and it was published posthumously as a fragment.
[2] In a note to his edition of Rossetti's poems (1957) Oswald Doughty offers evidence to support his suggestion that this word should be "bitten."

And from her breasts the ravishing eyes of
Death.

Men say to me that sleep hath many dreams,
   Yet I knew never but this dream alone:
There, from a dried-up channel, once the
   stream's,
The glen slopes up; even such in sleep it seems

20   As to my waking sight the place well known.

    *   *   *   *   *   *   *

My love I call her, and she loves me well:
   But I love her as in the maelstrom's cup
The whirled stone loves the leaf inseparable
That clings to it round all the circling swell,
And that the same last eddy swallows up.

from The House of Life

When Rossetti first published sixteen of the son-
nets of "The House of Life" in a magazine in 1869
—including the "Willowwood" sequence and those
ultimately numbered LXIII, XCI, and XCVII—he
titled the group of poems "Of Life, Love, and
Death." In his first volume of verse in 1870 he in-
cluded a section titled "Sonnets and Songs Towards
a Work to be Called 'The House of Life.'" Fifty
sonnets were published in this section, and eleven
songs, including "Sudden Light," "The Wood-
spurge," "Penumbra," "A Little While," and "The
Sea-Limits." Among the other sonnets published in
the 1870 volume were six later incorporated in "The
House of Life," including those now numbered
LXXIV, LXXVII, and LXXVIII.

The poem took its present form and title when it
was published in Rossetti's second volume of verse
in 1881. The songs were dropped, along with one
sonnet ("Nuptial Sleep"). Forty-seven new sonnets
(including the introductory poem) were added, in
addition to the six previously published sonnets
now taken into the sequence. The poem was given
its present title, described as "A Sonnet Sequence,"
and divided into two sections.

Rossetti's first intention seems to have imagined
a collection of lyric poems held together by com-
mon themes. In that sense "The House of Life"
completes his intention as a collection of poems on
love, loss, change, death, and art. Although there is
no marked narrative continuity in the sequence, es-
pecially between Parts I and II, the themes contin-
ued and developed in Part II do proceed from a
kind of story told in Part I. The story is that of a
love described at first often in its sensual episodes.
The poet tries in the idealizing elaborations of
memory and art to transform or transfigure this love
so that he can hold it out from the mortal losses he
fears. The love is lost at the end of Part I, and
movement of Part II is that of a more general con-
tention between the hope that love and its tran-
scendent meanings are preserved in memory and
song, and increasingly bleak episodes in a life deso-
lated by loss and the sense of chances missed and
gone.

Oswald Doughty in his biography of Rossetti
carefully traces an autobiographical thread that also
runs through the poem. The lost love is both that
of Elizabeth Siddall, Rossetti's dead wife, and that
of Jane Morris, the wife of William Morris whom
Rossetti first met in the mid-1850s and saw and
painted frequently after 1868. Most of the poems
written between 1868 and 1871—the dates of com-
position cited below are those suggested by Doughty,
who usually accepts the dates given by William
Michael Rossetti—are memorials of his love for
Mrs. Morris, sometimes crossed (as in sonnet
XXXVI) by reflections on the qualities and fate of
his dead wife.

"A Sonnet is a moment's monument"

A Sonnet is a moment's monument,—
   Memorial from the Soul's eternity
   To one dead deathless hour. Look that it be,
Whether for lustral rite[1] or dire portent,
Of its own arduous fulness reverent:
   Carve it in ivory or in ebony,
   As Day or Night may rule; and let Time see
Its flowering crest impearled and orient.

A Sonnet is a coin: its face reveals
   The soul,—its converse, to what Power 'tis
     due:—
Whether for tribute to the august appeals
   Of Life, or dower in Love's high retinue,
It serve; or, 'mid the dark wharf's cavernous
     breath,
In Charon's palm it pay the toll to Death.[2]
                (1880) 1881

---

[1] Lustral: a Roman rite of purification.
[2] Charon: the ferryman who conducts souls into the realm of the dead in classical mythology.

PART I
YOUTH AND CHANGE

IV

Lovesight

When do I see thee most, beloved one?
  When in the light the spirits of mine eyes
  Before thy face, their altar, solemnize
The worship of that Love through thee made
  known?
Or when in the dusk hours, (we two alone,)
  Close-kissed and eloquent of still replies
  Thy twilight-hidden glimmering visage lies,
And my soul only sees thy soul its own?

O love, my love! if I no more should see
Thyself, nor on the earth the shadow of thee,
  Nor image of thine eyes in any spring,—
How then should sound upon Life's darkening
  slope
The ground-whirl of the perished leaves of
  Hope,
  The wind of Death's imperishable wing?

(1869) 1870

VI

The Kiss

What smouldering senses in death's sick delay
  Or seizure of malign vicissitude
  Can rob this body of honour, or denude
This soul of wedding-raiment worn to-day?
For lo! even now my lady's lips did play
  With these my lips such consonant interlude
  As laurelled Orpheus longed for when he
  wooed
The half-drawn hungering face with that last
  lay.[3]

I was a child beneath her touch,—a man
  When breast to breast we clung, even I and
  she,—
  A spirit when her spirit looked through
  me,—

A god when all our life-breath met to fan
Our life-blood, till love's emulous ardours ran,
  Fire within fire, desire in deity.

(1869) 1870

Nuptial Sleep[4]

At length their long kiss severed, with sweet
  smart:
  And as the last slow sudden drops are shed
  From sparkling eaves when all the storm has
  fled,
So singly flagged the pulses of each heart.
Their bosoms sundered, with the opening start
  Of married flowers to either side outspread
  From the knit stem; yet still their mouths,
  burnt red,
Fawned on each other where they lay apart.

Sleep sank them lower than the tide of dreams,
  And their dreams watched them sink, and
  slid away.
Slowly their souls swam up again, through
  gleams
  Of watered light and dull drowned waifs of
  day;
Till from some wonder of new woods and
  streams
  He woke, and wondered more: for there she
  lay.

(1869) 1870

X

The Portrait: II

O Lord of all compassionate control,
  O Love! let this my lady's picture glow
  Under my hand to praise her name, and
  show
Even of her inner self the perfect whole:
That he who seeks her beauty's furtherest goal,
  Beyond the light that the sweet glances
  throw
  And refluent wave of the sweet smile, may
  know
The very sky and sea-line of her soul.

---

[3] Orpheus: in classical mythology the musician Orpheus, a son of Apollo and one of the muses of song, descends to the underworld and by his music wins permission to take his dead wife back to the world of the living. Before they step onto the earth, however, Orpheus violates a condition of the return by looking back, and his wife is carried back to the underworld. Orpheus is later torn to pieces by Bacchanalian revelers as he sings his laments for his wife.

[4] This sonnet was strongly attacked after its appearance in the volume of poems Rossetti published in 1870, and he did not reprint it in the 1881 volume.

Lo! it is done. Above the enthroning throat
  The mouth's mould testifies of voice and
10   kiss,
    The shadowed eyes remember and foresee.
Her face is made her shrine. Let all men note
That in all years (O Love, thy gift is this!)
    They that would look on her must come
      to me.
                                    (1868) 1870

XIII

Youth's Antiphony

"I love you, sweet: how can you ever learn
  How much I love you?" "You I love even so,
  And so I learn it." "Sweet, you cannot know
How fair you are." "If fair enough to earn
Your love, so much is all my love's concern."
    "My love grows hourly, sweet." "Mine too
      doth grow,
    Yet love seemed full so many hours ago!"
Thus lovers speak, till kisses claim their turn.

Ah! happy they to whom such words as these
  In youth have served for speech the whole
10   day long,
    Hour after hour, remote from the world's
      throng,
Work, contest, fame, all life's confederate
    pleas,—
What while Love breathed in sighs and
    silences
  Through two blent souls one rapturous
    undersong.
                                    (1871) 1881

XIV

Youth's Spring-Tribute

On this sweet bank your head thrice sweet and
    dear
  I lay, and spread your hair on either side,
  And see the newborn woodflowers bashful-
    eyed
Look through the golden tresses here and
    there.
On these debateable borders of the year
  Spring's foot half falters; scarce she yet may
    know

The leafless blackthorn-blossom from the
    snow;
And through her bowers the wind's way still is
    clear.

But April's sun strikes down the glades to-day;
  So shut your eyes upturned, and feel my kiss
Creep, as the Spring now thrills through every
    spray,
    Up your warm throat to your warm lips: for
      this
Is even the hour of Love's sworn suitservice,[6]
With whom cold hearts are counted castaway.
                                    (1870) 1881

XVI

A Day of Love

Those envied places which do know her well,
  And are so scornful of this lonely place,
  Even now for once are emptied of her grace:
Nowhere but here she is: and while Love's
    spell
From his predominant presence doth compel
  All alien hours, an outworn populace,
  The hours of Love fill full the echoing space
With sweet confederate music favourable.

Now many memories make solicitous
  The delicate love-lines of her mouth, till, lit
  With quivering fire, the words take wing
    from it;
As here between our kisses we sit thus
  Speaking of things remembered, and so sit
Speechless while things forgotten call to us.
                                    1870

XIX

Silent Noon

Your hands lie open in the long fresh grass,—
  The finger-points look through like rosy
    blooms:
  Your eyes smile peace. The pasture gleams
    and glooms
'Neath billowing skies that scatter and amass.
All round our nest, far as the eye can pass,
  Are golden kingcup-fields with silver edge

---

[6] Suitservice: attendance due to a lord from his tenant.

Where the cow-parsley skirts the hawthorn-
    hedge.
'Tis visible silence, still as the hour-glass.

Deep in the sun-searched growths the dragon-
    fly
Hangs like a blue thread loosened from the
    sky:—
  So this wing'd hour is dropt to us from
    above.
Oh! clasp we to our hearts, for deathless
    dower,
This close-companioned inarticulate hour
  When twofold silence was the song of love.

                 (1871) 1881

XXXI

Her Gifts[7]

High grace, the dower of Queens; and there-
    withal
  Some wood-born wonder's sweet simplicity;
  A glance like water brimming with the sky
Or hyacinth-light where forest-shadows fall;
Such thrilling pallor of cheek as doth enthral
  The heart; a mouth whose passionate forms
    imply
  All music and all silence held thereby;
Deep golden locks, her sovereign coronal;
A round reared neck, meet column of Love's
    shrine
  To cling to when the heart takes sanctuary;
  Hands which for ever at Love's bidding be,
And soft-stirred feet still answering to his
    sign:—
  These are her gifts, as tongue may tell them
    o'er.
  Breathe low her name, my soul; for that
    means more.

                 (1871) 1881

XXXVI

Life-in-Love

Not in thy body is thy life at all,
  But in this lady's lips and hands and eyes;

Through these she yields thee life that
    vivifies
What else were sorrow's servant and death's
    thrall.
Look on thyself without her, and recall
  The waste remembrance and forlorn surmise
  That lived but in a dead-drawn breath of
    sighs
O'er vanished hours and hours eventual.

Even so much life hath the poor tress of hair
  Which, stored apart, is all love hath to show   10
  For heart-beats and for fire-heats long ago;
Even so much life endures unknown, even
    where,
'Mid change the changeless night environeth,
Lies all that golden hair undimmed in death.[8]

              (1869–70) 1870

XLVIII

Death-in-Love

There came an image in Life's retinue
  That had Love's wings and bore his
    gonfalon:[9]
  Fair was the web, and nobly wrought
    thereon,
O soul-sequestered face, thy form and hue!
Bewildering sounds, such as Spring wakens to,
  Shook in its folds; and through my heart its
    power
  Sped trackless as the immemorable hour
When birth's dark portal groaned and all was
    new.

But a veiled woman followed, and she caught
  The banner round its staff, to furl and
    cling,—   10
  Then plucked a feather from the bearer's
    wing,
And held it to his lips that stirred it not,
  And said to me, "Behold, there is no breath:
  I and this Love are one, and I am Death."

               (1869) 1870

---

    [7] This sonnet is one of six in "The House of Life" which do not divide octave from sestet.
    [8] Rossetti kept a tress of Elizabeth Siddal's hair, and he undoubtedly heard the story that the friends who retrieved his poems from her coffin discovered that her hair had grown after her death and was still luxuriant.
    [9] Gonfalon: a banner, often with streamers.

XLIX–LII

Willowwood

I

I sat with Love upon a woodside well,
　　Leaning across the water, I and he;
　　Nor ever did he speak nor looked at me,
But touched his lute wherein was audible
The certain secret thing he had to tell:
　　Only our mirrored eyes met silently
　　In the low wave; and that sound came to be
The passionate voice I knew; and my tears fell.

And at their fall, his eyes beneath grew hers;
And with his foot and with his wing-feathers
　　He swept the spring that watered my heart's
　　　drouth.
Then the dark ripples spread to waving hair,
And as I stooped, her own lips rising there
　　Bubbled with brimming kisses at my mouth.

II

And now Love sang: but his was such a song,
　　So meshed with half-remembrance hard to
　　　free,
　　As souls disused in death's sterility
May sing when the new birthday tarries long.
And I was made aware of a dumb throng
　　That stood aloof, one form by every tree,
　　All mournful forms, for each was I or she,
The shades of those our days that had no
　　tongue.

They looked on us, and knew us and were
　　known;
　　While fast together, alive from the abyss,
　　Clung the soul-wrung implacable close kiss;
And pity of self through all made broken
　　moan
Which said, "For once, for once, for once
　　alone!"
　　And still Love sang, and what he sang was
　　this:—

III

"O ye, all ye that walk in Willowwood,
　　That walk with hollow faces burning white;
What fathom-depth of soul-struck widowhood,
　　What long, what longer hours, one lifelong
　　night,

Ere ye again, who so in vain have wooed
　　Your last hope lost, who so in vain invite
Your lips to that their unforgotten food,
　　Ere ye, ere ye again shall see the light!

Alas! the bitter banks in Willowwood,
　　With tear-spurge wan, with blood-wort
　　　burning red:[10]
Alas! if ever such a pillow could
　　Steep deep the soul in sleep till she were
　　　dead,—
Better all life forget her than this thing,
That Willowwood should hold her
　　wandering!"

IV

So sang he: and as meeting rose and rose
　　Together cling through the wind's wellaway
　　Nor change at once, yet near the end of day
The leaves drop loosened where the heart-stain
　　glows,—
So when the song died did the kiss unclose;
　　And her face fell back drowned, and was as
　　grey
　　As its grey eyes; and if it ever may
Meet mine again I know not if Love knows.

Only I know that I leaned low and drank
A long draught from the water where she sank,
　　Her breath and all her tears and all her soul:
And as I leaned, I know I felt Love's face
Pressed on my neck with moan of pity and
　　grace,
　　Till both our heads were in his aureole.[11]
　　　　　　　　　(1868) 1869; 1870

LIII

Without Her

What of her glass without her? the blank grey
　　There where the pool is blind of the moon's
　　face.
　　Her dress without her? the tossed empty
　　space
Of cloud-rack[12] whence the moon has passed
　　away.
Her paths without her? Day's appointed sway

---

[10] Tear-spurge; blood-wort: spurge and wort are kinds of common plants; Rossetti apparently
invented these varieties.
[11] Aureole: radiance around a body.　　[12] Cloud-rack: mass of clouds.

Usurped by desolate night. Her pillowed
    place
Without her! Tears, ah me! for love's good
    grace
And cold forgetfulness of night or day.

What of the heart without her? Nay, poor
    heart,
    Of thee what word remains ere speech be
    still?
    A wayfarer by barren ways and chill,
Steep ways and weary, without her thou art,
Where the long cloud, the long wood's
    counterpart,
    Sheds doubled darkness up the labouring
    hill.

                                        (1871) 1881

LIX

Love's Last Gift

Love to his singer held a glistening leaf,
    And said: "The rose-tree and the apple-tree
    Have fruits to vaunt or flowers to lure the
    bee;
And golden shafts are in the feathered sheaf
Of the great harvest-marshal, the year's chief,
    Victorious Summer; aye, and, 'neath warm
    sea
    Strange secret grasses lurk inviolably
Between the filtering channels of sunk reef.

All are my blooms; and all sweet blooms of
    love
    To thee I gave while Spring and Summer
    sang;
But Autumn stops to listen, with some pang
From those worse things the wind is moaning
    of.
    Only this laurel[13] dreads no winter days:
    Take my last gift; thy heart hath sung my
    praise."

                                        (1871) 1881

PART II
CHANGE AND FATE

LX

Transfigured Life

As growth of form or momentary glance
    In a child's features will recall to mind
    The father's with the mother's face
    combin'd,—
Sweet interchange that memories still enhance:
And yet, as childhood's years and youth's
    advance,
    The gradual mouldings leave one stamp
    behind,
    Till in the blended likeness now we find
A separate man's or woman's countenance:—

So in the Song, the singer's Joy and Pain,
    Its very parents, evermore expand   10
To bid the passion's fullgrown birth remain,
    By Art's transfiguring essence subtly
    spann'd;
    And from that song-cloud shaped as a man's
    hand
There comes the sound as of abundant rain.[1]
                                                   1881

LXI

The Song-Throe

By thine own tears thy song must tears beget,
    O Singer! Magic mirror thou hast none
    Except thy manifest heart; and save thine
    own
Anguish or ardour, else no amulet.
Cisterned in Pride, verse is the feathery jet
    Of soulless air-flung fountains; nay, more
    dry
    Than the Dead Sea for throats that thirst
    and sigh,
That song o'er which no singer's lids grew wet.

The Song-god—He the Sun-god—is no slave
    Of thine: thy Hunter he,[2] who for thy soul   10
    Fledges his shaft: to no august control

---

[13] Laurel: an emblem of poetry.
    [1] The prophet Elijah, contesting with priests of another deity in a famine-plagued land, calls
attention to "a sound of abundance of rain," and has his prayers answered when God sends "a
little cloud out of the sea, like a man's hand" (I Kings 18:41–44).
    [2] Song-god: Apollo, also identified with the sun and as a hunter.

Of thy skilled hand his quivered store he gave:
   But if thy lips' loud cry leap to his smart,
   The inspir'd recoil shall pierce thy brother's
     heart.

                   (1880) 1881

LXIII

Inclusiveness

The changing guests, each in a different mood,
   Sit at the roadside table and arise:
   And every life among them in likewise
Is a soul's board set daily with new food.
What man has bent o'er his son's sleep, to
     brood
   How that face shall watch his when cold it
     lies?—
   Or thought, as his own mother kissed his
     eyes,
Of what her kiss was when his father wooed?

May not this ancient room thou sitt'st in dwell
   In separate living souls for joy or pain?
   Nay, all its corners may be painted plain
Where Heaven shows pictures of some life
10   spent well;
   And may be stamped, a memory all in vain,
Upon the sight of lidless eyes in Hell.

            (1868) 1869; 1870

LXX

The Hill Summit

This feast-day of the sun, his altar there
   In the broad west has blazed for vesper-
     song;[3]
   And I have loitered in the vale too long
And gaze now a belated worshipper.
Yet may I not forget that I was 'ware,
   So journeying, of his face at intervals
   Transfigured where the fringed horizon
     falls,—
A fiery bush with coruscating hair.

And now that I have climbed and won this
   height,

I must tread downward through the sloping
   shade
And travel the bewildered tracks till night.
   Yet for this hour I still may here be stayed
   And see the gold air and the silver fade
And the last bird fly into the last light.

               (1853) 1870

LXXIV–LXXV

Old and New Art
1. Saint Luke the Painter[4]

(For a Drawing)

Give honour unto Luke Evangelist;
   For he it was (the aged legends say)
   Who first taught Art to fold her hands and
     pray.
Scarcely at once she dared to rend the mist
Of devious symbols: but soon having wist
   How sky-breadth and field-silence and this
     day
   Are symbols also in some deeper way,
She looked through these to God and was God's
     priest.

And if, past noon, her toil began to irk,
And she sought talismans, and turned in vain
   To soulless self-reflections of man's skill,—
   Yet now, in this the twilight, she might still
Kneel in the latter grass to pray again,
Ere the night cometh and she may not work.[5]

               (1849) 1870

2. Not as These

"I am not as these are," the poet saith
   In youth's pride, and the painter, among
     men
   At bay, where never pencil comes nor pen,
And shut about with his own frozen breath.
To others, for whom only rhyme wins faith
   As poets,—only paint as painters,—then
   He turns in the cold silence; and again
Shrinking, "I am not as these are," he saith.

And say that this is so, what follows it?
   For were thine eyes set backwards in thine
     head,

---

[3] Vesper-song: evening song.

[4] One of the legends about the apostle Luke was that he painted a picture of the Virgin.

[5] "I must work the works of him that sent me, while it is day: the night cometh, when no man can work" (John 9:4).

Such words were well; but they see on, and
 far.
Unto the lights of the great Past, new-lit
 Fair for the Future's track, look thou
 instead,—
 Say thou instead, "I am not as *these* are."
                               (1849) 1881

LXXVII

Soul's Beauty[6]

Under the arch of life, where love and death,
 Terror and mystery, guard her shrine, I saw
 Beauty enthroned; and though her gaze
 struck awe,
I drew it in as simply as my breath.
Hers are the eyes which, over and beneath
 The sky and sea bend on thee,—which can
 draw,
 By sea or sky or woman, to one law,
The allotted bondman of her palm and wreath

This is that Lady Beauty, in whose praise
 Thy voice and hand shake still,—long
 known to thee
 By flying hair and fluttering hem,—the
 beat
 Following her daily of thy heart and feet,
How passionately and irretrievably,
In what fond flight, how many ways and days!
                               (1866) 1870

LXXVIII

Body's Beauty

Of Adam's first wife, Lilith,[7] it is told
 (The witch he loved before the gift of Eve,)
 That, ere the snake's, her sweet tongue could
 deceive,
And her enchanted hair was the first gold.
And still she sits, young while the earth is old,
 And, subtly of herself contemplative,

Draws men to watch the bright web she can
 weave,
Till heart and body and life are in its hold.

The rose and poppy[8] are her flowers; for where
 Is he not found, O Lilith, whom shed scent   10
And soft-shed kisses and soft sleep shall snare?
 Lo! as that youth's eyes burned at thine, so
 went
 Thy spell through him, and left his straight
 neck bent,
And round his heart one strangling golden
 hair.
                               (1867) 1870

LXXXIII

Barren Spring

Once more the changed year's turning wheel
 returns:
 And as a girl sails balanced in the wind,
 And now before and now again behind
Stoops as it swoops, with cheek that laughs and
 burns,—
So Spring comes merry towards me here, but
 earns
 No answering smile from me, whose life is
 twin'd
 With the dead boughs that winter still must
 bind,
And whom to-day the Spring no more concerns.

Behold, this crocus is a withering flame;
 This snowdrop, snow; this apple-blossom's
 part   10
 To breed the fruit that breeds the serpent's
 art.
Nay, for these Spring-flowers, turn thy face
 from them,
Nor stay till on the year's last lily-stem
 The white cup shrivels round the golden
 heart.
                                           1870

---

[6] "Soul's Beauty" and "Body's Beauty" were published in Rossetti's 1870 volume of poems, but not as a part of "The House of Life." The first was then titled "Sibylla Palmifera"; the second, "Lilith." These original titles were also those of the paintings for which Rossetti first wrote the sonnets. "Sibylla Palmifera" means "palm-bearing sibyl." Sibyls were female sorcerers and prophets; one of them, the sibyl of Cumae, wrote her prophecies on palm leaves, some of which —the Sibylline leaves—were preserved and consulted in a temple in Rome.
 [7] Lilith is the name for a demon in the Old Testament; medieval rabbinical commentators proposed that Lilith was Adam's first wife, who fled from him to become a witch.
 [8] Rose and poppy: emblems of love and sleep.

LXXXV

Vain Virtues

What is the sorriest thing that enters Hell?
  None of the sins,—but this and that fair
    deed
  Which a soul's sin at length could supersede.
These yet are virgins, whom death's timely
    knell
Might once have sainted; whom the fiends
    compel
  Together now, in snake-bound shuddering
    sheaves
  Of anguish, while the pit's pollution leaves[9]
Their refuse maidenhood abominable.

Night sucks them down, the tribute of the pit,[10]
  Whose names, half entered in the book of
10   Life,
    Were God's desire at noon. And as their
      hair
And eyes sink last, the Torturer deigns no
    whit
  To gaze, but, yearning, waits his destined
    wife,[11]
    The Sin still blithe on earth that sent them
      there.
                                        (1869) 1870

XCI

Lost on Both Sides

As when two men have loved a woman well,
  Each hating each, through Love's and
    Death's deceit;
  Since not for either this stark marriage-
    sheet
And the long pauses of this wedding-bell;
  Yet o'er her grave the night and day dispel
  At last their feud forlorn, with cold and heat;
  Nor other than dear friends to death may
    fleet
The two lives left that most of her can tell:—

So separate hopes, which in a soul had wooed
  The one same Peace, strove with each other
10   long,
    And Peace before their faces perished
      since:

So through that soul, in restless brotherhood,
  They roam together now, and wind among
    Its bye-streets, knocking at the dusty inns.
                                (1853) 1869; 1870

XCVII

A Superscription

Look in my face; my name is Might-have-been;
  I am also called No-more, Too-late,
    Farewell;
  Unto thine ear I hold the dead-sea shell
Cast up thy Life's foam-fretted feet between;
Unto thine eyes the glass where that is seen
  Which had Life's form and Love's, but by
    my spell
  Is now a shaken shadow intolerable,
Of ultimate things unuttered the frail screen.

Mark me, how still I am! But should there dart
  One moment through thy soul the soft
    surprise
  Of that winged Peace which lulls the breath
    of sighs,—
Then shalt thou see me smile, and turn apart
Thy visage to mine ambush at thy heart
  Sleepless with cold commemorative eyes.
                                (1869) 1869; 1870

CI

The One Hope

When vain desire at last and vain regret
  Go hand in hand to death, and all is vain,
  What shall assuage the unforgotten pain
And teach the unforgetful to forget?
Shall Peace be still a sunk stream long
    unmet,—
  Or may the soul at once in a green plain
  Stoop through the spray of some sweet life-
    fountain
And cull the dew-drenched flowering amulet?

Ah! when the wan soul in that golden air
  Between the scriptured petals softly blown
  Peers breathless for the gift of grace
    unknown,—
Ah! let none other alien spell soe'er[12]

---

[9] In 1870: "the scorching bridegroom leaves."   [10] In 1870: "the garbage of the pit."
[11] In 1870: "waits his worthier wife."   [12] 1870: "none other written spell."

But only the one Hope's one name be there,—
Not less nor more, but even that word alone.
                                        1870

*Henry I (1068–1135), called a "clerk" because he
was relatively well educated, was the son of William
the Conqueror. He was crowned king of England
in 1100, ruled the country with harsh justice, and
spent a good deal of time fighting to hold his pos-
sessions in France. In 1120, after concluding a peace
that would enable his son to succeed to his fiefs in
France, he sailed for England. The details of the
drowning of his son are as Rossetti recounts them,
including the name of the ship, the survival of a
butcher of Rouen, and the fact that his courtiers
withheld the news of the prince's death and an-
nounced it to the king through a young boy.*

The White Ship

Henry I of England.–25th November 1120

By none but me can the tale be told,
The butcher of Rouen, poor Berold.
    (*Lands are swayed by a King on a throne.*)
'Twas a royal train put forth to sea,
Yet the tale can be told by none but me.
    (*The sea hath no King but God alone.*)

King Henry held it as life's whole gain
That after his death his son should reign.

'Twas so in my youth I heard men say,
And my old age calls it back to-day.

King Henry of England's realm was he,
And Henry Duke of Normandy.

The times had changed when on either coast
"Clerkly Harry" was all his boast.

Of ruthless strokes full many an one
He had struck to crown himself and his son;
And his elder brother's eyes were gone.[1]

And when to the chase his court would crowd,
The poor flung ploughshares on his road,
And shrieked: "Our cry is from King to God!"

But all the chiefs of the English land
Had knelt and kissed the Prince's hand.

And next with his son he sailed to France
To claim the Norman allegiance:

And every baron in Normandy
Had taken the oath of fealty.

'Twas sworn and sealed, and the day had come
When the King and the Prince might journey
    home:

For Christmas cheer is to home hearts dear,
And Christmas now was drawing near.   30

Stout Fitz-Stephen came to the King,—
A pilot famous in seafaring;

And he held to the King, in all men's sight,
A mark of gold for his tribute's right.

"Liege Lord! my father guided the ship
From whose boat your father's foot did slip
When he caught the English soil in his grip,

"And cried: 'By this clasp I claim command
O'er every rood of English land!'

"He was borne to the realm you rule o'er now   40
In that ship with the archer carved at her prow:

"And thither I'll bear, an' it be my due,
Your father's son and his grandson too.

"The famed White Ship is mine in the bay;
From Harfleur's[2] harbour she sails to-day,

"With masts fair-pennoned as Norman spears
And with fifty well-tried mariners."

Quoth the King: "My ships are chosen each
    one,
But I'll not say nay to Stephen's son.

"My son and daughter and fellowship   50
Shall cross the water in the White Ship."

The King set sail with the eve's south wind,
And soon he left that coast behind.

The Prince and all his, a princely show,
Remained in the good White Ship to go.

[1] One of the stories, later discredited, about Henry was that he caused his elder brother to be blinded.
[2] Like Honfleur (line 163) a seaport in France on the English Channel.

With noble knights and with ladies fair,
With courtiers and sailors gathered there,
Three hundred living souls we were:

And I Berold was the meanest hind[3]
In all that train to the Prince assign'd.

The Prince was a lawless shameless youth;
From his father's loins he sprang without ruth:

Eighteen years till then he had seen,
And the devil's dues in him were eighteen.

And now he cried: "Bring wine from below;
Let the sailors revel ere yet they row:

"Our speed shall o'ertake my father's flight
Though we sail from the harbour at
    mid-night."

The rowers made good cheer without check;
The lords and ladies obeyed his beck;
The night was light, and they danced on the
    deck.

But at midnight's stroke they cleared the bay,
And the White Ship furrowed the water-way.

The sails were set, and the oars kept tune
To the double flight of the ship and the moon:

Swifter and swifter the White Ship sped
Till she flew as the spirit flies from the dead:

As white as a lily glimmered she
Like a ship's fair ghost upon the sea.

And the Prince cried, "Friends, 'tis the hour to
    sing!
Is a songbird's course so swift on the wing?"

And under the winter stars' still throng,
From brown throats, white throats, merry and
    strong,
The knights and the ladies raised a song.

A song,—nay, a shriek that rent the sky,
That leaped o'er the deep!—the grievous cry
Of three hundred living that now must die.

An instant shriek that sprang to the shock
As the ship's keel felt the sunken rock.

[3] Meanest hind: lowest servant.

'Tis said that afar—a shrill strange sigh—
The King's ships heard it and knew not why.

Pale Fitz-Stephen stood by the helm
'Mid all those folk that the waves must whelm.

A great King's heir for the waves to whelm,
And the helpless pilot pale at the helm!

The ship was eager and sucked athirst,
By the stealthy stab of the sharp reef pierc'd:

And like the moil round a sinking cup,
The waters against her crowded up.

A moment the pilot's senses spin,—
The next he snatched the Prince 'mid the din,
Cut the boat loose, and the youth leaped in.

A few friends leaped with him, standing near.
"Row! the sea's smooth and the night is clear!"

"What! none to be saved but these and I?"
"Row, row as you'd live! All here must die!"

Out of the churn of the choking ship,
Which the gulf grapples and the waves strip,
They struck with the strained oars' flash and
    dip.

'Twas then o'er the splitting bulwarks' brim
The Prince's sister screamed to him.

He gazed aloft, still rowing apace,
And through the whirled surf he knew her face.

To the toppling decks clave one and all
As a fly cleaves to a chamber-wall.

I Berold was clinging anear;
I prayed for myself and quaked with fear,
But I saw his eyes as he looked at her.

He knew her face and he heard her cry,
And he said, "Put back! she must not die!"

And back with the current's force they reel
Like a leaf that's drawn to a water-wheel.

'Neath the ship's travail they scarce might
    float,
But he rose and stood in the rocking boat.

Low the poor ship leaned on the tide:
O'er the naked keel as she best might slide,
The sister toiled to the brother's side.

He reached an oar to her from below,
And stiffened his arms to clutch her so.

30 But now from the ship some spied the boat,
And "Saved!" was the cry from many a throat.

And down to the boat they leaped and fell:
It turned as a bucket turns in a well,
And nothing was there but the surge and swell.

The Prince that was and the King to come,
There in an instant gone to his doom,

Despite of all England's bended knee
And maugre[4] the Norman fealty!

40 He was a Prince of lust and pride;
He showed no grace till the hour he died.

When he should be King, he oft would vow,
He'd yoke the peasant to his own plough.
O'er him the ships score their furrows now.

God only knows where his soul did wake,
But I saw him die for his sister's sake.

By none but me can the tale be told,
The butcher of Rouen, poor Berold.
        (*Lands are swayed by a King on a throne.*)
'Twas a royal train put forth to sea,
50 Yet the tale can be told by none but me.
        (*The sea hath no King but God alone.*)

And now the end came o'er the water's womb
Like the last great Day that's yet to come.

With prayers in vain and curses in vain,
The White Ship sundered on the mid-main:

And what were men and what was a ship
Were toys and splinters in the sea's grip.

I Berold was down in the sea;
And passing strange though the thing may be,
60 Of dreams then known I remember me.

Blithe is the shout on Harfleur's strand
When morning lights the sails to land:

And blithe is Honfleur's echoing gloam
When mothers call the children home:

And high do the bells of Rouen beat
When the Body of Christ goes down the street.[5]

These things and the like were heard and
        shown
In a moment's trance 'neath the sea alone;

And when I rose, 'twas the sea did seem,
And not these things, to be all a dream.   170

The ship was gone and the crowd was gone,
And the deep shuddered and the moon shone:

And in a strait grasp my arms did span
The mainyard rent from the mast where it ran;
And on it with me was another man.

Where lands were none 'neath the dim sea-sky,
We told our names, that man and I.

"O I am Godefroy de l'Aigle hight,
And son I am to a belted knight."[6]

"And I am Berod the butcher's son   180
Who slays the beasts in Rouen town."

Then cried we upon God's name, as we
Did drift on the bitter winter sea.

But lo! a third man rose o'er the wave,
And we said, "Thank God! us three may He
        save!"

He clutched to the yard with panting stare,
And we looked and knew Fitz-Stephen there.

He clung, and "What of the Prince?" quoth he.
"Lost, lost!" we cried. He cried, "Woe on me!"
And loosed his hold and sank through the sea.   190

And soul with soul again in that space
We two were together face to face:

And each knew each, as the moments sped,
Less for one living than for one dead:

And every still star overhead
Seemed an eye that knew we were but dead.

---

[4] Maugre: in spite of.   [5] Body of Christ: procession of the Eucharist.
[6] Hight: called. A "belted knight" is a reference to the belt worn to designate this title.

And the hours passed; till the noble's son
Sighed, "God be thy help! my strength's fore-
    done!

"O farewell, friend, for I can no more!"
"Christ take thee!" I moaned; and his life was
200   o'er.

Three hundred souls were all lost but one.
And I drifted over the sea alone.

At last the morning rose on the sea
Like an angel's wing that beat tow'rds me.

Sore numbed I was in my sheepskin coat;
Half dead I hung, and might nothing note,
Till I woke sun-warmed in a fisher-boat.

The sun was high o'er the eastern brim
As I praised God and gave thanks to Him.

210 That day I told my tale to a priest,
Who charged me, till the shrift[7] were releas'd,
That I should keep it in mine own breast.

And with the priest I thence did fare
To King Henry's court at Winchester.

We spoke with the King's high chamberlain,
And he wept and mourned again and again,
As if his own son had been slain:

And round us ever there crowded fast
Great men with faces all aghast:

220 And who so bold that might tell the thing
Which now they knew to their lord the King?
Much woe I learnt in their communing.

The King had watched with a heart sore stirred
For two whole days, and this was the third:

And still to all his court would he say,
"What keeps my son so long away?"

And they said: "The ports lie far and wide
That skirt the swell of the English tide;

"And England's cliffs are not more white
230 Than her women are, and scarce so light
Her skies as their eyes are blue and bright;

"And in some port that he reached from
    France
The Prince has lingered for his pleasaùnce."

But once the King asked: "What distant cry
Was that we heard 'twixt the sea and sky?"

And one said: "With suchlike shouts, pardie![8]
Do the fishers fling their nets at sea."

And one: "Who knows not the shrieking quest
When the sea-mew[9] misses its young from the
    nest?"

'Twas thus till now they had soothed his dread, 240
Albeit they knew not what they said:

But who should speak to-day of the thing
That all knew there except the King?

Then pondering much they found a way,
And met round the King's high seat that day:

And the King sat with a heart sore stirred,
And seldom he spoke and seldom heard.

'Twas then through the hall the King was
    'ware
Of a little boy with golden hair,

As bright as the golden poppy is 250
That the beach breeds for the surf to kiss:

Yet pale his cheek as the thorn[10] in Spring,
And his garb black like the raven's wing.

Nothing heard but his foot through the hall,
For now the lords were silent all.

And the King wondered, and said, "Alack!
Who sends me a fair boy dressed in black?

"Why, sweet heart, do you pace through the
    hall
As though my court were a funeral?"

Then lowly knelt the child at the dais, 260
And looked up weeping in the King's face.

"O wherefore black, O King, ye may say,
For white is the hue of death to-day.

---

[7] Shrift: penance.
[8] Pardie: a mild oath (by God).   [9] Sea-mew: gull.
[10] Thorn: the hawthorne or whitethorn.

"Your son and all his fellowship
Lie low in the sea with the White Ship."

King Henry fell as a man struck dead;
And speechless still he stared from his bed
When to him next day my rede[11] I read.

There's many an hour must needs beguile
A King's high heart that he should smile,—

Full many a lordly hour, full fain
Of his realm's rule and pride of his reign:—

But this King never smiled again.

By none but me can the tale be told,
The butcher of Rouen, poor Berold.
    (*Lands are swayed by a King on a throne.*)
'Twas a royal train put forth to sea,
Yet the tale can be told by none but me.
    (*The sea hath no King but God alone.*)

1881

A Sea-Spell

(*For a Picture*)

Her lute hangs shadowed in the apple-tree,
    While flashing fingers weave the sweet-strung
        spell
    Between its chords; and as the wild notes
        swell,
The sea-bird for those branches leaves the sea.
But to what sound her listening ear stoops she?
    What netherworld gulf-whispers doth she
        hear,
    In answering echoes from what planisphere,[1]
Along the wind, along the estuary?

She sinks into her spell: and when full soon
    Her lips move and she soars into her song,
    What creatures of the midmost main shall
        throng
In furrowed surf-clouds to the summoning
        rune:[2]
    Till he, the fated mariner, hears her cry,
    And up her rock, bare-breasted, comes to
        die?

1881

William Morris
1834–1896

WILLIAM MORRIS' father was a London broker who came into a moderate fortune through an increase in the value of some mining stock. His mother was the daughter of a family of merchants and landowners. Morris grew up on a small country estate near the Epping Forest south of London. One image from his boyhood, of Morris riding through the forest wearing a miniature suit of armor, epitomizes the juncture of natural landscape and retrieved medievalism that is the crux of many of the structures of value and wish he wrote about in his poetry and imaginative prose and worked for in his politics and in his career as a designer. After his early schooling he entered Oxford in 1853, where his early tastes were decisively confirmed. He was a member of a group of undergraduates, including Richard Watson Dixon (see Part Four) and Edward Burne-Jones, who was to become an important painter, brought together by their enthusiasms for the tales of Malory, Tennyson's poetry, and the first paintings of Dante Gabriel Rossetti and the Pre-Raphaelites (see pp. 559–561). Morris read John Ruskin's "On the Nature of Gothic" in *The Stones of Venice*

---

[11] Rede: story.
[1] Planisphere: a plane projection of a sphere, as a chart of the heavens.
[2] Rune: a poem of northern European people.

(1853), from which he learned and never forgot two lessons: that the degraded architecture and decorative art of the nineteenth century were the inevitable expressions of social and economic systems that exploit and deaden the capacities of workers; and that no society would produce an art as great as that of the Gothic until it was as healthily ordered as medieval society. Morris began to write poems and short romances at Oxford. But he decided to become an architect, and in 1856, after inheriting a comfortable income when he came of age, he moved to London to work and study in an architect's office.

In London he met and was strongly influenced by Dante Gabriel Rossetti, some of whose poems were published along with some of his own writing in *The Oxford and Cambridge Magazine,* a monthly journal Morris helped to found and largely financed. For a while Morris tried to be a painter, and he helped Rossetti with the frescoes he and others painted at Oxford in 1857. The next year Morris published his first collection of poems, *The Defence of Guinevere,* and he began planning and writing a series of poems on episodes in the Trojan War. In 1859 he married Jane Burden, the daughter of a livery stable groom he had met in Oxford when she began serving as a model for the painters in Rossetti's group. Morris had begun to design furniture for his lodgings in London, and after his marriage he started to design the furnishings and interior decoration of a house he was having built outside London. In 1861 he finally entered his principal profession when he, Burne-Jones, Rossetti, and some others founded what was later to become Morris and Company, a firm which offered to design carving, stained glass, metalwork, furniture, and later wallpaper and textiles for churches, public buildings, and private houses.

Morris worked as a designer and craftsman until his death. He learned and revived methods of weaving and dying that had been nearly extinguished by machinery and the introduction of chemical dyes. His flowing or formally patterned designs for wallpapers and textiles, always based on the natural forms of plants and birds described in clear colors and line, helped to reduce or at least to relieve the clutter of mid-Victorian decoration. His furniture and the rooms he designed and decorated were also relatively simple and straight-lined, and his ideas about allowing the character of the material and the hand of the workman to show in the object were part of the movement which went into twentieth-century functionalism. Near the end of his life his several interests, including one in the illumination of books and medieval manuscripts, came together again in the founding of the Kelmscott Press, for whose hand presses he designed the types to reprint some of his own poems and prose romances, the writing of Chaucer, some medieval romances, Tennyson's "Maud," Swinburne's "Atlanta in Calydon," poetry by Dante Gabriel Rossetti, Shelley, and Coleridge, and Ruskin's essay on the Gothic.

Ruskin's essay helped to prepare not only Morris' occupation but also his socialism. Like Ruskin, he came to believe that the ugliness of mid-nineteenth-century Britain was an index of a perversely inhumane economics and social organization. He cared about art, if art is defined not as a special order of craft and experience, but as a quality in work and objects which testifies that the maker was in an honest, useful, happy relationship with the material and with others in the society. Morris wanted art in this sense to flourish, to drive out the idea that art is the possession of a coterie of wealth and fashion, and to replace the debased, mass-produced art and decoration available to the middle and lower classes. But because art expressed rather than acted on society, its regeneration was not an aesthetic but a political and economic question. Art will not make a social revolution. It will rather be made anew by a social revolution. This conviction, which, as he wrote in an account of "How I Became a Socialist" (1894), saved him from a "fine pessimistic end of life," brought Morris into the membership of the socialist Social Democratic Federation in 1883. He was a socialist to the end of his life, persevering through several factional splinterings of the Federation and finally founding his own Socialist Society in 1890. He read Marx, lectured on art and socialism, spoke at open-air meetings and on street corners (for which he was once arrested), and supported, wrote for, and sometimes edited two socialist journals, *Justice* and *The Commonweal.* To these journals he contributed his "Chants for Socialists," *The Pilgrims of Hope,* a poem about English socialists during the Paris commune of 1870, and, most important, his two utopian romances, *A Dream of John Ball* (1888), and *News from Nowhere* (1890).

Morris confronted the paradox that, not only was he a wealthy socialist, himself a a capitalist and an employer, but that his services and products were expensive and purchased as luxuries by members of the social and economic classes he thought ought to be dissolved. In *News from Nowhere* he resolved the anomaly in a violent revolution after which everyone has a chance to live as he tried to live—in small communities within the countryside, doing work and making useful and beautiful objects in which they took pleasure, with some machines performing functions that release rather than enslave human energies but without large-scale industrialism and its associated structures of capitalism and the nineteenth-century city. In some of his lectures (see Part Ten) Morris was ready to propose, although he was unable actually to describe, a postrevolutionary future that had no place either for someone like him or for an art and society made on the pattern of a new medievalism. He was sure that in the apocalypse to come art must go under. Whether it emerged in forms he would recognize was unimportant. What mattered was that the inequity and misery he saw in late-century England be replaced by a society that permitted a self-fulfillment and pleasure like those he, in a grotesquely malproportioned system, had had the luck and privilege to find and exercise in art.

In these schemes of value and hope, the place of poetry was lower and its function less certain than those of even the arts to which Morris gave most of his time and craft. "Well, if this is poetry, it is very easy to write," he said in 1854 after he showed his friends some of the poems which appeared in *The Defence of Guinevere* volume. His habit, once Morris and Company was in business, was to write while weaving or dying or in the intervals of his other occupations. The simple bulk of his imaginative writing, even if it were his first interest, is prodigious. In addition to his two utopian romances and eight other prose romances written in the last decade of his life, he published translations of Norse sagas, Virgil, and Homer, the 42,000 rhymed lines of the narratives of *The Earthly Paradise* (1868–70), and two other long poetic narratives, *The Life and Death of Jason* (1867) and *The Story of Sigurd the Volsung* (1876). He also published a curious morality play, *Love Is Enough* (1872), and a late volume of *Poems*

By the Way (1891), in addition to *The Pilgrims of Hope* and his socialist songs.

This body of verse has its own worth as craft, as pleasing objects made by a talented writer. But Morris habitually put his poetry in the service of his own psychic needs or, late in his life, in the service of his politics. One of the interests of his verse, therefore, is that it is representative of a kind of poetry written in the last decades of the Victorian period by poets who no longer believed that their words and forms would alone change a reality alien to their sensibilities and desires.

Morris' first poems use the colors and details of remote environments and medieval objects as they are used in Tennyson's early poems and in Pre-Raphaelite writing and painting. His medieval reality is chivalric, its violence and treachery met by heroism and the settled, clear perspectives of speakers who are competent to the worst of their worlds. Many of these poems—"The Eve of Crecy," for example—are shadowed by a sense of time that will end this reality and its pleasures. In the late 1860s and in the 1870s Morris' own life was shadowed by his perception of the social and visual ruin that he believed England was becoming, and by his apparent awareness that Jane Morris and Dante Gabriel Rossetti, who for a while shared a house with the Morrises, were in love with one another. The whole gesture of *The Earthly Paradise,* its narratives set within a framing story of travelers fleeing pestilence and time, is to imagine a world apart from the disappointments of love and wish. Yet most of these stories are sad, and the entire long poem is bound in its pattern of a calendar of the months. One of the pleasures of this and similar late-century poems that place sadness in the distances of poetic form must be that not only do such poems give a vent to sadness, but they also enable sadness to be borne by permitting it to be safely regarded in the pleasing costumes and compositions of antique narrative, natural landscape, and the refined, special melodies of poetic language.

While he was writing and publishing *The Earthly Paradise,* which was to become his most popular poem, Morris first visited Iceland and began translating some of the Norse sagas with an Icelandic scholar. "Iceland First Seen" suggests the harshly stirring landscape and verse line, different from what Rossetti called the "trailing style" of his early poems, into which Morris put his telling of *The Story of*

Sigurd the Volsung (1876), a fine poem whose relentless movement cannot be demonstrated in extracts. In this landscape and line, and in the northern myth of the destruction of the gods and the subsequent regeneration of the earth, Morris found a promise in pain and desolation which probably brought him solace and certainly enlivened his poetry. When he found a political analogue to the myth in the socialist idea of a history that moved toward a regenerating revolution, he also found new forms for his energy in political speaking, organizing, and writing. His poetry then became an adjunct to his politics, or very late in his life, a means of expressing particular moments of pleasure and loss in those reaches of his private life he did not transform into politics. When William Butler Yeats met him late in Morris' life, he thought of him as "the happiest English poet" and envied the easy executive ability displayed in his verse. Morris' life and even his poetry were more troubled than Yeats knew. But Morris did take pleasure in the exercise of his poetic talent. He also took poetry seriously, insofar as he took seriously all work that gave pleasure and made shapely things. He was, therefore, a responsible steward of some of the means of nineteenth-century poetry in decades when, like many other late-century poets, he believed that the fabricated pleasures of poetry were at best a cry or stay against an unhappy reality that had to be changed by other means.

EDITIONS

The texts reprinted here are those of the original editions of Morris' poems; they are consistent with the texts of the standard edition, *The Collected Works of William Morris*, edited by May Morris (1910–1915). Some additional writing by Morris is included in *William Morris: Artist, Writer, Socialist* (1936), edited by May Morris. Eugene D. LeMire has edited *The Unpublished Lectures of William Morris* (1969). Philip Henderson has edited *The Letters of William Morris to His Family and Friends* (1950).

BIOGRAPHY AND CRITICISM

Philip Henderson's *William Morris: His Life, Work and Friends* (1967) has replaced J. W. Mackail's *The Life of William Morris* (1899) as the standard biography, although Mackail's book holds a place as a fine, representative Victorian biography. R. Page Arnot,

William Morris, the Man and the Myth (1964), James W. Hulse, *Revolutionists in London* (1970), and E. P. Thompson, *William Morris, Romantic and Revolutionary* (revised edition 1961) are studies of Morris' politics. Ray Watkinson has published a study of *William Morris as Designer* (1967). Paul Thompson's *The Work of William Morris* (1967) is a useful study of Morris' entire career and achievement.

OTHER USEFUL BOOKS AND ESSAYS

Dunlap, Joseph R. *The Book That Never Was* (1971). An account of the plans of Morris and Edward Burne-Jones to make *The Earthly Paradise* a grandly illustrated and printed book.

Evans, B. Ifor. *William Morris and His Poetry* (1925).

Faulkner, Peter. *William Morris and W. B. Yeats* (1962).

Goode, John. "William Morris and the Dream of Revolution," in *Literature and Politics*, edited by John Lucas (1972).

Grennan, Margaret R. *William Morris, Medievalist and Revolutionary* (1945). A study of Morris' uses of history.

Hoare, D. M. *The Work of Morris and Yeats in Relation to Early Saga Literature* (1937).

Sparling, Henry Halliday. *The Kelmscott Press and William Morris* (1924).

Transactions and Publications of the William Morris Society. Include G. D. H. Cole, *Morris as a Socialist* (1960); Jack Lindsay, *William Morris, Writer* (1961); J. N. Swannell, *William Morris and Old Norse Literature* (1961); and E. P. Thompson, *The Communism of William Morris* (1965).

Bibliographies of Morris' writing are included in H. B. Forman's *The Books of Morris Described* (1897) and Aymer Vallance's *William Morris: His Art, His Writing, His Public Life* (1898). For bibliographies of writing about Morris see William E. Fredeman, *Pre-Raphaelitism: A BiblioCritical Study* (1965); Philip Henderson's pamphlet, *William Morris*, in the Writers and Their Work series (1964); and Ehrsam, Deily, and Smith (see General Bibliography). Peter Faulkner has edited *William Morris: The Critical Heritage* (1973).

In this poem Morris adapts two stories from Thomas Malory's fifteenth-century compilation of

romances about King Arthur and the knights of his round table, Le Morte Darthur. *When she speaks the poem Guinevere, the wife of Arthur, is being tried for adultery on the accusation of Gawain, Arthur's trusted counselor, and some knights who have surprised Lancelot and the queen in her chambers. During her monologue Guinevere remembers (lines 168–221) an earlier accusation of adultery brought by Meliagrance, a knight who kidnapped her and brought her to his castle. Lancelot rescued her from the castle, and appeared at her earlier trial to fight as her champion, kill Meliagrance, and so vindicate her of the charges. In Malory's account Lancelot also appears at this second trial, kills many of Arthur's knights, flees with Guinevere to his own castle, and so begins a long war of painful and shifting allegiances which ends with the dissolution of Arthur's order.*

The Defence of Guenevere

But, knowing now that they would have her
   speak,
She threw her wet hair backward from her
   brow,
Her hand close to her mouth touching her
   cheek,

As though she had had there a shameful blow,
And feeling it shameful to feel aught but
   shame
All through her heart, yet felt her cheek
   burned so,

She must a little touch it; like one lame
She walked away from Gauwaine, with her
   head
Still lifted up; and on her cheek of flame

The tears dried quick; she stopped at last and
   said:
"O knights and lords, it seems but little skill
To talk of well-known things past now and
   dead.

"God wot I ought to say, I have done ill,
And pray you all forgiveness heartily!
Because you must be right, such great lords—
   still

"Listen, suppose your time were come to die,
And you were quite alone and very weak;
Yea, laid a dying while very mightily

"The wind was ruffling up the narrow streak
Of river through your broad lands running
   well:

Suppose a hush should come, then some one
   speak:

" 'One of these cloths is heaven, and one is hell,
Now choose one cloth for ever; which they be,
I will not tell you, you must somehow tell

" 'Of your own strength and mightiness; here,
   see!'
Yea, yea, my lord, and you to ope your eyes,
At foot of your familiar bed to see

"A great God's angel standing, with such dyes,
Not known on earth, on his great wings, and
   hands
Held out two ways, light from the inner skies   30

"Showing him well, and making his commands
Seem to be God's commands, moreover, too,
Holding within his hands the cloths on wands;

"And one of these strange choosing cloths was
   blue,
Wavy and long, and one cut short and red;
No man could tell the better of the two.

"After a shivering half-hour you said:
'God help! heaven's colour, the blue;' and he
   said: 'hell.'
Perhaps you then would roll upon your bed,

"And cry to all good men that loved you well,   40
'Ah Christ! if only I had known, known,
   known;'
Launcelot went away, then I could tell,

"Like wisest man how all things would be,
   moan,
And roll and hurt myself, and long to die,
And yet fear much to die for what was sown.

"Nevertheless you, O Sir Gauwaine, lie,
Whatever may have happened through these
   years,
God knows I speak truth, saying that you lie."

Her voice was low at first, being full of tears,
But as it cleared, it grew full loud and shrill,   50
Growing a windy shriek in all men's ears,

A ringing in their startled brains, until
She said that Gauwaine lied, then her voice
   sunk,
And her great eyes began again to fill,

Though still she stood right up, and never
   shrunk,
But spoke on bravely, glorious lady fair!
Whatever tears her full lips may have drunk,

She stood, and seemed to think, and wrung her
   hair,
Spoke out at last with no more trace of shame,
60   With passionate twisting of her body there:

"It chanced upon a day that Launcelot came
To dwell at Arthur's court: at Christmas-time
This happened; when the heralds sung his
   name,

" 'Son of King Ban of Benwick,'[1] seemed to
   chime
Along with all the bells that rang that day,
O'er the white roofs, with little change of
   rhyme.

"Christmas and whitened winter passed away,
And over me the April sunshine came,
Made very awful with black hail-clouds, yea

70   "And in the Summer I grew white with flame,
And bowed my head down—Autumn, and the
   sick
Sure knowledge things would never be the
   same,

"However often Spring might be most thick
Of blossoms and buds, smote on me, and I
   grew
Careless of most things, let the clock tick, tick,

"To my unhappy pulse, that beat right
   through
My eager body; while I laughed out loud,
And let my lips curl up at false or true,

"Seemed cold and shallow without any cloud.
Behold my judges, then the cloths were
80   brought;
While I was dizzied thus, old thoughts would
   crowd,

"Belonging to the time ere I was bought
By Arthur's great name and his little love;
Must I give up for ever then, I thought,

"That which I deemed would ever round me
   move

Glorifying all things; for a little word,
Scarce ever meant it all, must I now prove

"Stone-cold for ever? Pray you, does the Lord
Will that all folks should be quite happy and
   good?
I love God now a little, if this cord   90

"Were broken, once for all what striving could
Make me love anything in earth or heaven?
So day by day it grew, as if one should

"Slip slowly down some path worn smooth and
   even,
Down to a cool sea on a summer day;
Yet still in slipping there was some small leaven

"O stretched hands catching small stones by
   the way,
Until one surely reached the sea at last,
And felt strange new joy as the worn head lay

"Back, with the hair like sea-weed; yea all past   100
Sweat of the forehead, dryness of the lips,
Washed utterly out by the dear waves o'ercast,

"In the lone sea, far off from any ships!
Do I not know now of a day in Spring?
No minute of that wild day ever slips

"From out my memory; I hear thrushes sing,
And wheresoever I may be, straightway
Thoughts of it all come up with most fresh
   sting:

"I was half mad with beauty on that day,
And went without my ladies all alone,   110
In a quiet garden walled round every way;

"I was right joyful of that wall of stone,
That shut the flowers and trees up with the
   sky,
And trebled all the beauty: to the bone,

"Yea right through to my heart, grown very
   shy
With weary thoughts, it pierced, and made me
   glad;
Exceedingly glad, and I knew verily,

"A little thing just then had made me mad;
I dared not think, as I was wont to do,
Sometimes, upon my beauty; if I had   120

---

[1] King Ban of Benwick: a king of Brittany and Lancelot's father.

"Held out my long hand up against the blue,
And, looking on the tenderly darken'd fingers,
Thought that by rights one ought to see quite
    through,

"There, see you, where the soft still light yet
    lingers,
Round by the edges; what should I have done,
If this had joined with yellow spotted singers,

"And startling green drawn upward by the
    sun?
But shouting, loosed out, see now! all my hair,
And trancedly stood watching the west wind
    run

130 "With faintest half-heard breathing sound—
    why there
I lose my head e'en now in doing this;
But shortly listen—In that garden fair

"Came Launcelot walking; this is true, the kiss
Wherewith we kissed in meeting that spring
    day,
I scarce dare talk of the remember'd bliss,

"When both our mouths went wandering in
    one way,
And aching sorely, met among the leaves;
Our hands being left behind strained far away.

140 "Never within a yard of my bright sleeves
Had Launcelot come before—and now, so nigh!
After that day why is it Guenevere grieves?

"Nevertheless you, O Sir Gauwaine, lie,
Whatever happened on through all those years,
God knows I speak truth, saying that you lie.

"Being such a lady could I weep these tears
If this were true? A great queen such as I
Having sinn'd this way, straight her conscience
    sears;

"And afterwards she liveth hatefully,
Slaying and poisoning, certes never weeps,—
150 Gauwaine, be friends now, speak me lovingly.

"Do I not see how God's dear pity creeps
All through your frame, and trembles in your
    mouth?
Remember in what grave your mother sleeps,

"Buried in some place far down in the south,
Men are forgetting as I speak to you;
By her head sever'd in that awful drouth

"Of pity that drew Agravaine's fell blow,[2]
I pray your pity! let me not scream out
For ever after, when the shrill winds blow

"Through half your castle-locks! Let me not
    shout
For ever after in the winter night   160
When you ride out alone! in battle-rout

"Let not my rusting tears make your sword
    light!
Ah! God of mercy, how he turns away!
So, ever must I dress me to the fight;

"So—let God's justice work! Gauwaine, I say,
See me hew down your proofs: yea, all men
    know
Even as you said how Mellyagraunce one day,[3]

"One bitter day in *la Fausse Garde,* for so
All good knights held it after, saw—   170
Yea, sirs, by cursed unknightly outrage; though

"You, Gauwaine, held his word without a flaw,
This Mellyagraunce saw blood upon my bed—
Whose blood then pray you? is there any law

"To make a queen say why some spots of red
Lie on her coverlet? or will you say:
'Your hands are white, lady, as when you wed,

"'Where did you bleed?' and must I stammer
    out: 'Nay,
I blush indeed, fair lord, only to rend
My sleeve up to my shoulder, where there lay   180

---

[2] Malory recounts that Gawain's mother was beheaded by his brother Gaheris, not by his
brother Agrivain, because she had committed adultery.
[3] After Lancelot entered Meliagrance's castle—*la Fausse Garde* (the false or treacherous castle)
—and rescued Guinevere, she asked that the wounded knights who defended her be brought
to her room. During the night Lancelot climbed to her room, cutting his hand as he did so, and
spent the night in her bed. When Meliagrance found Lancelot's blood in Guinevere's bed, he ac-
cused her of adultery with one of the wounded knights. Lancelot offered to defend her, but
Meliagrance sprung a trap through which Lancelot fell into a dungeon. He freed himself in time
to confront Meliagrance during Guinevere's trial, and when Meliagrance begged for mercy,
fought and killed him with one arm tied behind him and one side of his body unarmored.

" 'A knife-point last night:' so must I defend
The honour of the lady Guenevere?
Not so, fair lords, even if the world should end

"This very day, and you were judges here
Instead of God. Did you see Mellyagraunce
When Launcelot stood by him? what white fear

"Curdled his blood, and how his teeth did
    dance,
His side sink in? as my knight cried and said:
'Slayer of unarm'd men, here is a chance!

190 " 'Setter of traps, I pray you guard your head,
By God I am so glad to fight with you,
Stripper of ladies, that my hand feels lead

" 'For driving weight; hurrah now! draw and
    do,
For all my wounds are moving in my breast,
And I am getting mad with waiting so.'

"He struck his hands together o'er the beast,
Who fell down flat and grovell'd at his feet,
And groan'd at being slain so young—'at least.'

"My knight said: 'Rise you, sir, who are so
    fleet
200 At catching ladies, half-arm'd will I fight,
My left side all uncovered!' then I weet,[4]

"Up sprang Sir Mellyagraunce with great
    delight
Upon his knave's face; not until just then
Did I quite hate him, as I saw my knight

"Along the lists look to my stake and pen[5]
With such a joyous smile, it made me sigh
From agony beneath my waist-chain, when

"The fight began, and to me they drew nigh;
Ever Sir Launcelot kept him on the right,
210 And traversed warily, and ever high

"And fast leapt caitiff's[6] sword, until my knight
Sudden threw up his sword to his left hand,
Caught it, and swung it; that was all the fight,

"Except a spout of blood on the hot land;
For it was hottest summer; and I know
I wonder'd how the fire, while I should stand,

"And burn, against the heat, would quiver so,
Yards above my head; thus these matters went;
Which things were only warnings of the woe

"That fell on me. Yet Mellyagraunce was
    shent,[7]   220
For Mellyagraunce had fought against the
    Lord;
Therefore, my lords, take heed lest you be
    blent

"With all this wickedness; say no rash word
Against me, being so beautiful; my eyes,
Wept all away to grey, may bring some sword

"To drown you in your blood; see my breast
    rise,
Like waves of purple sea, as here I stand;
And how my arms are moved in wonderful
    wise,

"Yea also at my full heart's strong command,
See through my long throat how the words go
    up   230
In ripples to my mouth; how in my hand

"The shadow lies like wine within a cup
Of marvellously colour'd gold; yea now
This little wind is rising, look you up,

"And wonder how the light is falling so
Within my moving tresses: will you dare,
When you have looked a little on my brow,

"To say this thing is vile? or will you care
For any plausible lies of cunning woof,[8]
When you can see my face with no lie there   240

"For ever? am I not a gracious proof—
'But in your chamber Launcelot was found'—
Is there a good knight then would stand aloof,

"When a queen says with gentle queenly
    sound:
'O true as steel, come now and talk with me,
I love to see your step upon the ground

" 'Unwavering, also well I love to see
That gracious smile light up your face, and
    hear
Your wonderful words, that all mean verily

---

[4] Weet: know.
[5] Stake and pen: where Guinevere awaits her execution by fire if Lancelot fails to defeat
Meliagrance.
[6] Caitiff: base person.   [7] Shent: disgraced.   [8] Woof: horizontal threads in a woven web.

" 'The thing they seem to mean: good friend,
250   so dear
To me in everything, come here to-night,
Or else the hours will pass most dull and drear;

" 'If you come not, I fear this time I might
Get thinking over much of times gone by,
When I was young, and green hope was in
    sight:

" 'For no man cares now to know why I sigh;
And no man comes to sing me pleasant songs,
Nor any brings me the sweet flowers that lie

" 'So thick in the gardens; therefore one so
    longs
260 To see you, Launcelot; that we may be
Like children once again, free from all wrongs

" 'Just for one night.' Did he not come to me?
What thing could keep true Launcelot away
If I said, 'Come?' There was one less than three

"In my quiet room that night, and we were
    gay;
Till sudden I rose up, weak, pale, and sick,
Because a bawling broke our dream up, yea

"I looked at Launcelot's face and could not
    speak,
For he looked helpless too, for a little while;
270 Then I remember how I tried to shriek,

"And could not, but fell down; from tile to tile
The stones they threw up rattled o'er my head
And made me dizzier; till within a while

"My maids were all about me, and my head
On Launcelot's breast was being soothed away
From its white chattering, until Launcelot
    said—

"By God! I will not tell you more to-day,
Judge any way you will—what matters it?
You know quite well the story of that fray,

"How Launcelot still'd their bawling, the mad
280   fit
That caught up Gauwaine—all, all, verily,
But just that which would save me; these
    things flit.

"Nevertheless you, O Sir Gauwaine, lie,
Whatever may have happen'd these long years,
God knows I speak truth, saying that you lie!

"All I have said is truth, by Christ's dear
    tears."
She would not speak another word, but stood
Turn'd sideways; listening, like a man who
    hears

His brother's trumpet sounding through the
    wood
Of his foes' lances. She lean'd eagerly,   290
And gave a slight spring sometimes, as she
    could

At last hear something really; joyfully
Her cheek grew crimson, as the headlong speed
Of the roan charger drew all men to see,
The Knight who came was Launcelot at good
    need.
                                                           1858

Old Love

"You must be very old, Sir Giles,"
    I said; he said: "Yea, very old:"
Whereat the mournfullest of smiles
    Creased his dry skin with many a fold.

"They hammer'd out my basnet point
    Into a round salade," he said,
"The basnet being quite out of joint,
    Natheless the salade rasps my head."[1]

He gazed at the great fire awhile:
    "And you are getting old, Sir John;"   10
(He said this with that cunning smile
    That was most sad) "we both wear on,

"Knights come to court and look at me,
    With eyebrows up, except my lord
And my dear lady, none I see
    That know the ways of my old sword."

(My lady! at that word no pang
    Stopp'd all my blood). "But tell me, John,
Is it quite true that Pagans hang
    So thick about the east, that on   20

---

[1] Basnet; salade: kinds of helmets.

"The eastern sea no Venice flag
   Can fly unpaid for?" "True," I said,
"And in such way the miscreants drag
   Christ's cross upon the ground, I dread

"That Constantine[2] must fall this year."
   Within my heart: "These things are small;
This is not small, that things outwear
   I thought were made for ever, yea, all

"All things go soon or late," I said.
30   I saw the duke in court next day;
Just as before, his grand great head
   Above his gold robes dreaming lay,

Only his face was paler; there
   I saw his duchess sit by him;
And she—she was changed more; her hair
   Before my eyes that used to swim,

And make me dizzy with great bliss
   Once, when I used to watch her sit—
Her hair is bright still, yet it is
40   As though some dust were thrown on it.

Her eyes are shallower, as though
   Some grey glass were behind; her brow
And cheeks the straining bones show through,
   Are not so good for kissing now.

Her lips are drier now she is
   A great duke's wife these many years;
They will not shudder with a kiss
   As once they did, being moist with tears.

Also her hands have lost that way
50   Of clinging that they used to have;
They look'd quite easy; as they lay
   Upon the silken cushions brave

With broidery of the apples green
   My Lord Duke bears upon his shield.
Her face, alas! that I have seen
   Look fresher than an April field,

This is all gone now; gone also
   Her tender walking; when she walks
She is most queenly I well know,
60   And she is fair still—as the stalks

Of faded summer-lilies are,
   So is she grown now unto me

This spring-time, when the flowers star
   The meadows, birds sing wonderfully.

I warrant once she used to cling
   About his neck, and kiss'd him so,
And then his coming step would ring
   Joy-bells for her,—some time ago.

Ah! sometimes like an idle dream
   That hinders true life overmuch,   70
Sometimes like a lost heaven, these seem—
   This love is not so hard to smutch.[3]
                            1858

Shameful Death

There were four of us about that bed;
   The mass-priest knelt at the side,
   I and his mother stood at the head,
   Over his feet lay the bride;
We were quite sure that he was dead,
   Though his eyes were open wide.

He did not die in the night,
   He did not die in the day,
But in the morning twilight
   His spirit pass'd away,   10
When neither sun nor moon was bright,
   And the trees were merely grey.

He was not slain with the sword,
   Knight's axe, or the knightly spear,
Yet spoke he never a word
   After he came in here;
I cut away the cord
   From the neck of my brother dear.

He did not strike one blow,
   For the recreants came behind,   20
In a place where the hornbeams[1] grow,
   A path right hard to find,
For the hornbeam boughs swing so,
   That the twilight makes it blind.

They lighted a great torch then,
   When his arms were pinion'd fast,
Sir John the knight of the Fen,
   Sir Guy of the Dolorous Blast,
With knights threescore and ten,
   Hung brave Lord Hugh at last.   30

I am threescore and ten,
   And my hair is all turn'd grey,

---

[2] Constantine: Constantinople, which fell to the Turks in 1422 and again in 1453.
[3] Smutch: stain.
[1] Hornbeam: a small tree with tough wood, often planted close together to make a hedge.

But I met Sir John of the Fen
  Long ago on a summer day,
And am glad to think of the moment when
  I took his life away.

I am threescore and ten,
  And my strength is mostly pass'd,
But long ago I and my men,
  When the sky was overcast,
And the smoke roll'd over the reeds of the fen,
  Slew Guy of the Dolorous Blast.

And now, knights all of you,
I pray you pray for Sir Hugh,
A good knight and a true,
And for Alice, his wife, pray too.

1858

The Eve of Crecy[1]

Gold on her head, and gold on her feet,
And gold where the hems of her kirtle[2] meet,
And a golden girdle round my sweet;—
  Ah! qu'elle est belle La Marguerite.

Margaret's maids are fair to see,
Freshly dress'd and pleasantly;
Margaret's hair falls down to her knee;—
  Ah! qu'elle est belle La Marguerite.

If I were rich I would kiss her feet,
I would kiss the place where the gold hems
    meet,
And the golden girdle round my sweet—
  Ah! qu'elle est belle La Marguerite.

Ah me! I have never touch'd her hand;
When the arriere-ban[3] goes through the land,
Six basnets under my pennon[4] stand;—
  Ah! qu'elle est belle La Marguerite.

And many an one grins under his hood:
"Sir Lambert du Bois, with all his men good,
Has neither food nor firewood."—
  Ah! qu'elle est belle La Marguerite.

If I were rich I would kiss her feet,
And the golden girdle of my sweet,
And thereabouts where the gold hems meet;
  Ah! qu'elle est belle La Marguerite.

Yet even now it is good to think,
While my few poor varlets grumble and drink
In my desolate hall, where the fires sink,—
  Ah! qu'elle est belle La Marguerite.

Of Margaret sitting glorious there,
In glory of gold and glory of hair,
And glory of glorious face most fair;
  Ah! qu'elle est belle La Marguerite.

Likewise to-night I make good cheer,
Because this battle draweth near:
For what have I to lose or fear?—
  Ah! qu'elle est belle La Marguerite.

For, look you, my horse is good to prance
A right fair measure in this war-dance,
Before the eyes of Philip of France;[5]—
  Ah! qu'elle est belle La Marguerite.

And sometime it may hap, perdie,[6]
While my new towers stand up three and
    three,
And my hall gets painted fair to see—
  Ah! qu'elle est belle La Marguerite.

That folks may say: "Times change, by the
    rood,[7]
For Lambert, banneret[8] of the wood,
Has heaps of food and firewood;—
  Ah! qu'elle est belle La Marguerite;

"And wonderful eyes, too, under the hood
Of a damsel of right noble blood."
St. Ives, for Lambert of the Wood!
  Ah! qu'elle est belle La Marguerite.

1858

---

[1] The battle of Crecy was fought in France in 1346. The French were routed, largely because the mounted knights of chivalric warfare were beaten by English archers and foot soldiers.

[2] Kirtle: skirt.

[3] Arriere-ban: the summons from a king to one of his feudal lords to join him in a military campaign.

[4] Basnets; pennon: helmets; narrow banner or streamer. As a lord of small estate, he brings the king only six other men.

[5] Philip VI, king of France from 1328 to 1350.   [6] Perdie: by God.

[7] Rood: the cross of Christ.

[8] Banneret: a knight who can bring men with him to a battle; a rank more elevated than that of a knight, but below that of a baron.

The Blue Closet

THE DAMOZELS

    Lady Alice, Lady Louise,
    Between the wash of the tumbling seas
    We are ready to sing, if so ye please;
    So lay your long hands on the keys;
            Sing: *"Laudate pueri."*[1]

    And ever the great bell overhead
    Boom'd in the wind a knell for the dead,
    Though no one toll'd it, a knell for the dead.

LADY LOUISE

    Sister, let the measure swell
10   Not too loud; for you sing not well
    If you drown the faint boom of the bell;
            He is weary, so am I.

    And ever the chevron[2] *overhead*
    Flapp'd on the banner of the dead;
    (Was he asleep, or was he dead?)

LADY ALICE

    Alice the Queen, and Louise the Queen,
    Two damozels wearing purple and green,
    Four lone ladies dwelling here
    From day to day and year to year;
20   And there is none to let us go;
    To break the locks of the doors below,
    Or shovel away the heaped-up snow;
    And when we die no man will know
    That we are dead; but they give us leave,
    Once every year on Christmas-eve,
    To sing in the Closet Blue one song;
    And we should be so long, so long,
    If we dared, in singing; for dream on dream,
    They float on in a happy stream;
    Float from the gold strings, float from the
30   keys,
    Float from the open'd lips of Louise;
    But, alas! the sea-salt oozes through
    The chinks of the tiles of the Closet Blue;
    And ever the great bell overhead
    Booms in the wind a knell for the dead,
    The wind plays on it a knell for the dead.

          They sing all together

How long ago was it, how long ago,
He came to this tower with hands full of snow?

"Kneel down, O love Louise, kneel down!" he
    said,
And sprinkled the dusty snow over my head.   40

He watch'd the snow melting, it ran through
    my hair,
Ran over my shoulders, white shoulders and
    bare.

"I cannot weep for thee, poor love Louise,
For my tears are all hidden deep under the
    seas;

"In a gold and blue casket she keeps all my
    tears,
But my eyes are no longer blue, as in old years;

"Yea, they grow grey with time, grow small
    and dry,
I am so feeble now, would I might die."

    And in truth the great bell overhead
    Left off his pealing for the dead,   50
    Perchance, because the wind was dead.

Will he come back again, or is he dead?
O! is he sleeping, my scarf round his head?

Or did they strangle him as he lay there,
With the long scarlet scarf I used to wear?

Only I pray thee, Lord, let him come here!
Both his soul and his body to me are most
    dear.

Dear Lord, that loves me, I wait to receive
Either body or spirit this wild Christmas-eve.

    Through the floor shot up a lily red,   60
    With a patch of earth from the land of the
    dead,
    For he was strong in the land of the dead.

What matter that his cheeks were pale,
    His kind kiss'd lips all grey?
"O, love Louise, have you waited long?"
    "O, my lord Arthur, yea."

What if his hair that brush'd her cheek
    Was stiff with frozen rime?[3]
His eyes were grown quite blue again,
    As in the happy time.   70

---

[1] *Laudate pueri:* let the children praise—words from a version of the Latin hymn "Te Deum."
[2] Chevron: a device on a banner.   [3] Rime: frost.

"O, love Louise, this is the key
    Of the happy golden land!
O, sisters, cross the bridge with me,
    My eyes are full of sand.
What matter that I cannot see,
    If ye take me by the hand?"

And ever the great bell overhead,
And the tumbling seas mourn'd for the
    dead;
For their song ceased, and they were dead.
                       1858

The Haystack in the Floods

Had she come all the way for this,
To part at last without a kiss?
Yea, had she borne the dirt and rain
That her own eyes might see him slain
Beside the haystack in the floods?

Along the dripping leafless woods,
The stirrup touching either shoe,
She rode astride as troopers do;
With kirtle[1] kilted to her knee,
To which the mud splash'd wretchedly;
And the wet dripp'd from every tree
Upon her head and heavy hair,
And on her eyelids broad and fair;
The tears and rain ran down her face.
By fits and starts they rode apace,
And very often was his place
Far off from her; he had to ride
Ahead, to see what might betide
When the roads cross'd; and sometimes, when
There rose a murmuring from his men,
Had to turn back with promises;
Ah me! she had but little ease;
And often for pure doubt and dread
She sobb'd, made giddy in the head
By the swift riding; while, for cold,
Her slender fingers scarce could hold
The wet reins; yea, and scarcely, too,
She felt the foot within her shoe
Against the stirrup: all for this,
To part at last without a kiss
Beside the haystack in the floods.

For when they near'd that old soak'd hay,
They saw across the only way
That Judas, Godmar, and the three
Red running lions dismally
Grinn'd from his pennon, under which
In one straight line along the ditch,
They counted thirty heads.

                So then,
While Robert turn'd round to his men,   40
She saw at once the wretched end,
And, stooping down, tried hard to rend
Her coif the wrong way from her head,
And hid her eyes; while Robert said:
"Nay, love, 'tis scarcely two to one,
At Poictiers where we made them run
So fast—why, sweet my love, good cheer,
The Gascon frontier[2] is so near,
Nought after this."

             But, "O!" she said,
"My God! my God! I have to tread   50
The long way back without you; then
The court at Paris; those six men;
The gratings of the Chatelet;[3]
The swift Seine on some rainy day
Like this, and people standing by
And laughing, while my weak hands try
To recollect how strong men swim.
All this, or else a life with him,
For which I should be damned at last.
Would God that this next hour were past!"   60

He answer'd not, but cried his cry,
"St. George for Marny!" cheerily;
And laid his hand upon her rein.
Alas! no man of all his train
Gave back that cheery cry again;
And, while for rage his thumb beat fast
Upon his sword-hilts, some one cast
About his neck a kerchief long,
And bound him.

           Then they went along
To Godmar; who said: "Now, Jehane,   70
Your lover's life is on the wane
So fast, that, if this very hour

---

[1] Kirtle: long skirt.

[2] Gascony is a province in the southwest of France. During the fourteenth-century wars between England and France, Gascony remained under leaders loyal to England. The battle of Poitiers in 1356 was an English victory in which the French king was taken prisoner.

[3] Chatelet: a fortress-prison in Paris. Jehane will be held there awaiting a trial in which, as in a trial of witches, she will be thrown into the river Seine; if she remains afloat, she will be judged guilty.

You yield not as my paramour,
He will not see the rain leave off—
Nay, keep your tongue from gibe and scoff,
Sir Robert, or I slay you now."

She laid her hand upon her brow,
Then gazed upon the palm, as though
She thought her forehead bled, and—"No!"
80   She said, and turn'd her head away,
As there were nothing else to say,
And everything were settled: red
Grew Godmar's face from chin to head:
"Jehane, on yonder hill there stands
My castle, guarding well my lands:
What hinders me from taking you,
And doing that I list to do
To your fair wilful body, while
Your knight lies dead?"

                    A wicked smile
Wrinkled her face, her lips grew thin,
90   A long way out she thrust her chin:
"You know that I should strangle you
While you were sleeping; or bite through
Your throat, by God's help—ah!" she said,
"Lord Jesus, pity your poor maid!
For in such wise they hem me in,
I cannot choose but sin and sin,
Whatever happens: yet I think
They could not make me eat or drink,
100 And so should I just reach my rest."
"Nay, if you do not my behest,
O Jehane! though I love you well,"
Said Godmar, "would I fail to tell
All that I know?" "Foul lies," she said.
"Eh? lies, my Jehane? by God's head,
At Paris folks would deem them true!
Do you know, Jehane, they cry for you:
'Jehane the brown! Jehane the brown!
Give us Jehane to burn or drown!'—
110 Eh—gag me Robert!—sweet my friend,
This were indeed a piteous end
For those long fingers, and long feet,
And long neck, and smooth shoulders sweet;
An end that few men would forget
That saw it—So, an hour yet:
Consider, Jehane, which to take
Of life or death!"

                    So, scarce awake,
Dismounting, did she leave that place,
And totter some yards: with her face
120 Turn'd upward to the sky she lay,
Her head on a wet heap of hay,
And fell asleep: and while she slept,

And did not dream, the minutes crept
Round to the twelve again; but she,
Being waked at last, sigh'd quietly,
And strangely childlike came, and said:
"I will not." Straightway Godmar's head,
As though it hung on strong wires, turn'd
Most sharply round, and his face burn'd.

For Robert—both his eyes were dry,   130
He could not weep, but gloomily
He seem'd to watch the rain; yea, too,
His lips were firm; he tried once more
To touch her lips; she reach'd out, sore
And vain desire so tortured them,
The poor grey lips, and now the hem
Of his sleeve brush'd them.

                    With a start
Up Godmar rose, thrust them apart;
From Robert's throat he loosed the bands
Of silk and mail; with empty hands   140
Held out, she stood and gazed, and saw
The long bright blade without a flaw
Glide out from Godmar's sheath, his hand
In Robert's hair; she saw him bend
Back Robert's head; she saw him send
The thin steel down; the blow told well,
Right backward the knight Robert fell,
And moaned as dogs do, being half dead,
Unwitting, as I deem: so then
Godmar turn'd grinning to his men,
Who ran, some five or six, and beat
His head to pieces at their feet.

Then Godmar turn'd again and said:
"So, Jehane, the first fitte is read!
Take note, my lady, that your way
Lies backward to the Chatelet!"
She shook her head and gazed awhile
At her cold hands with a rueful smile,
As though this thing had made her mad.

This was the parting that they had
Beside the haystack in the floods.

                                        1858

Two Red Roses Across the Moon

There was a lady lived in a hall,
Large of her eyes, and slim and tall;
And ever she sung from noon to noon,
Two red roses across the moon.

There was a knight came riding by
In early spring, when the roads were dry;

And he heard that lady sing at the noon,
Two red roses across the moon.

Yet none the more he stopp'd at all,
But he rode a-gallop past the hall;
And left that lady singing at noon,
Two red roses across the moon.

Because, forsooth, the battle was set,
And the scarlet and blue had got to be met,
He rode on the spur till the next warm
    noon:—
Two red roses across the moon.

But the battle was scatter'd from hill to hill,
From the windmill to the watermill;
And he said to himself, as it near'd the noon,
Two red roses across the moon.

You scarce could see for the scarlet and blue,
A golden helm[1] or a golden shoe;
So he cried, as the fight grew thick at the noon,
Two red roses across the moon!

Verily then the gold bore through
The huddled spears of the scarlet and blue;
And they cried, as they cut them down at the
    noon,
Two red roses across the moon!

I trow he stopp'd when he rode again
By the hall, though draggled sore with the
    rain;
And his lips were pinch'd to kiss at the noon
Two red roses across the moon.

Under the may[2] she stoop'd to the crown,
All was gold, there was nothing of brown;
And the horns blew up in the hall at noon,
Two red roses across the moon.

1858

from The Earthly Paradise

The Earthly Paradise *is a collection of twenty-four verse tales (two for each month of the year)* which Morris published in 1868 (Parts 1 and 2) and in 1870 (Parts 3 and 4). The tales are told by the survivors of a group of Norsemen who fled a plague in their homeland to find a fabled earthly paradise, and by the inhabitants of a city in which, old and resigned to failure, the Norsemen finally settle. The stories themselves are retellings of classical, medieval, and Norse myths and legends, most of them sad stories of human disappointment. In addition to this prologue Morris also interpolated lyrics before and after the tales of each month.*

Prologue

Of Heaven or Hell I have no power to sing,
I cannot ease the burden of your fears,
Or make quick-coming death a little thing,
Or bring again the pleasure of past years,
Nor for my words shall ye forget your tears,
Or hope again for aught that I can say,
The idle singer of an empty day.

But rather, when aweary of your mirth,
From full hearts still unsatisfied ye sigh,
And, feeling kindly unto all the earth,   10
Grudge every minute as it passes by,
Made the more mindful that the sweet days
    die—
Remember me a little then I pray,
The idle singer of an empty day.

The heavy trouble, the bewildering care
That weighs us down who live and earn our
    bread,
These idle verses have no power to bear;
So let me sing of names remember'd,
Because they, living not, can ne'er be dead,
Or long time take their memory quite away   20
From us poor singers of an empty day.

Dreamer of dreams, born out of my due
    time,
Why should I strive to set the crooked straight?
Let it suffice me that my murmuring rhyme
Beats with light wing against the ivory gate,[1]
Telling a tale not too importunate
To those who in the sleepy region stay,
Lulled by the singer of an empty day.

Folk say, a wizard to a northern king
At Christmas-tide such wondrous things did
    show,   30

---

[1] Helm: helmet.   [2] Under the may: under the blossoms of the hawthorne tree.
[1] Ivory gate: in classical mythology false dreams come into the world through an ivory gate, and true dreams through a gate of horn.

That through one window men beheld the
    spring,
And through another saw the summer glow,
And through a third the fruited vines a-row,
While still, unheard, but in its wonted way,
Piped the drear wind of that December day.

    So with this Earthly Paradise it is,
If ye will read aright, and pardon me,
Who strive to build a shadowy isle of bliss
Midmost the beating of the steely sea,
40   Where tossed about all hearts of men must be;
Whose ravening monsters mighty men shall
    slay,
Not the poor singer of an empty day.

                    1868

Written in a Copy of *The Earthly Paradise*, Dec. 25, 1870

So many stories written here
And none among them but doth bear
Its weight of trouble and of woe!
Well may you ask why it is so;
For surely neither sour nor dull
In such a world, of fair things full,
Should folk be.
              Ah, my dears, indeed
My wisdom fails me at my need
To tell why tales that move the earth
10   Are seldom of content and mirth.
Yet think if it may come of this—
That lives fulfilled of ease and bliss
Crave not for aught that we can give,
And scorn the broken lives we live;
Unlike to us they pass us by,
A dying laugh their history.
But those that struggled sore, and failed
Had one thing left them, that availed
When all things else were nought—
                  E'en Love–
20   Whose sweet voice, crying as they strove,
Begat sweet pity, and more love still,
Waste places with sweet tales to fill;
Whereby we, living here, may learn
Our eyes toward very Love to turn,
And all the pain it bringeth meet
As nothing strange amid the sweet:
Whereby we too may hope to be
Grains in the great world's memory
Of pain endured, and nobleness
30   That life ill-understood doth bless.
Words over-grave and sad for you
Maybe: but rime will still be true

Unto my heart—most true herein
In wishing, dear hearts, you may win
A life of every ill so clear,
That little tale for folk to hear
It may be: yet so full of love,
That e'en these words your hearts may move,
Years and years hence, when unto me
Life is a waste and windless Sea.

                (1870)   40

March

    He ended; and midst those who heard were
      some
Who, midst his tale, half dreamed they were at
    home
Round the great fire upon the winter night;
And, with the memory of the fresh delight
Wherewith they first had heard that story told,
Forgetting not they were grown weak and old,
Yet felt as if they had at least grown grey
Within the land left for so many a day.
He, with the gestures they were wont to see,
So told his tale, so strange with eld was he,   10
Just so he stammered, and in just such wise
He sighed, beginning fresh, as their young eyes,
Their ears, in happy days passed long ago,
Had ever noted other old men do,
When they, full filled with their quick-coming
    joys,
Would gaze on old folk as on carven toys.

    But he being silent, silently awhile
They mused on these things, masking with a
    smile
The vain regrets that in their hearts arose,
The while with eager talk the young folk chose   20
The parts that pleased them; but their elder
    hosts
Falling to talk, yet noted well the ghosts
Of old desires within their wasted eyes,
Till one by one the fresh-stirred memories,
So bitter-sweet, flickered and died away;
And as old men may do, whose hopes grew
    grey
Before their beards, they made a little mirth
Until the great moon rose upon the earth.

                    1868

May

    O Love, this morn when the sweet night-
      ingale
Had so long finished all he had to say,

That thou hadst slept, and sleep had told his
  tale;
And midst a peaceful dream had stolen away
In fragrant dawning of the first of May,
Didst thou see aught? didst thou hear voices
  sing
Ere to the risen sun the bells 'gan ring?

For then methought the Lord of Love went
  by
To take posssssion of his flowery throne,
Ringed round with maids, and youths, and
  minstrelsy;
A little while I sighed to find him gone,
A little while the dawning was alone,
And the light gathered; then I held my breath,
And shuddered at the sight of Eld and Death.

Alas! Love passed me in the twilight dun,
His music hushed the wakening ousel's[1] song;
But on these twain shone out the golden sun,
And o'er their heads the brown bird's tune was
  strong,
As shivering, 'twixt the trees they stole along;
None noted aught their noiseless passing by,
The world had quite forgotten it must die.

1868

October

Ah, these, with life so done with now, might
  deem
That better is it resting in a dream,
Yea, e'en a dull dream, than with outstretched
  hand,
And wild eyes, face to face with life to stand,
No more the master now of anything,
Through striving of all things to be the king—
Than waking in a hard taskmaster's grasp
Because we strove the unsullied joy to clasp—
Than just to find our hearts the world, as we
Still thought we were and ever longed to be,
To find nought real except ourselves, and find
All care for all things scattered to the wind,
Scarce in our hearts the very pain alive.
Compelled to breathe indeed, compelled to
  strive,
Compelled to fear, yet not allowed to hope—
For e'en as men laid on a flowery slope
'Twixt inaccessible cliffs and unsailed sea,

Painless, and waiting for eternity
That will not harm, were these old men now
  grown.
The seed of unrest, that their hearts had sown,   20
Sprung up, and garnered, and consumed, had
  left
Nought that from out their treasure might be
  reft;
All was a picture in these latter days,
That had been once, and they might sit and
  praise
The calm, wise heart that knowth how to rest,
The man too kind to snatch out at the best,
Since he is part of all, each thing a part,
Beloved alike of his wide-loving heart.

Ah, how the night-wind raved, and wind
  and sea
Clashed wildly in their useless agony,   30
But dulled not or made weak the minstrel's
  song
That through the hall bemocked the lost year's
  wrong!

1870

from Love Is Enough

The Music as the Emperor and Empress Enter

Invocation[1]

Love is enough: though the World be a-waning
  And the woods have no voice but the voice
  of complaining,
Though the sky be too dark for dim eyes to
  discover
The gold-cups and daisies fair blooming there-
  under,
Though the hills be held shadows, and the sea
  a dark wonder,
  And this day draw a veil over all deeds
  passed over,
Yet their hands shall not tremble, their feet
  shall not falter;
The void shall not weary, the fear shall not
  alter

---

[1] Ousel: blackbird.

[1] *Love Is Enough* is a dramatic poem—Morris called it a "morality"—about an emperor who leaves his people and his responsibilities to seek an ideal love, finds it in his love for a humble woman, and abdicates to live in obscurity with her.

These lips and these eyes of the loved and the lover.

1872

from The Pilgrims of Hope

The Pilgrims of Hope is a long narrative poem which Morris published in thirteen installments in the socialist magazine The Commonweal *in 1885–86. It is the story of a couple from the country who come to London, are persuaded by its display of social misery and political inequity to become socialists, and eventually leave to fight by the side of the Communards who set up a brief-lived republic in Paris when the second French Empire collapsed with its defeat in the Franco-Prussian War of 1870. Like many of Morris' stories,* The Pilgrims of Hope *includes a love-affair between a woman and a close friend of her husband's. Both the wife and the friend are killed on the barricades in Paris, and the husband lives on, putting hope against his disappointment: "I cling to the love of the past and the love of the day to be, / And the present, it is but the building of the man to be strong in me" (Book XIII: "The Story's Ending").*

III

Sending to the War

It was down in our far-off village that we
heard of the war[1] begun,
But none of the neighbours were in it save the
squire's thick-lipped son,
A youth and a fool and a captain, who came
and went away,
And left me glad of his going. There was little
for us to say
Of the war and its why and wherefore—and
we said it often enough;
The papers gave us our wisdom, and we used
it up in the rough.
But I held my peace and wondered; for I
thought of the folly of men,
The fair lives ruined and broken that ne'er
could be mended again;

And the tale by lies bewildered, and no cause
for a man to choose;
Nothing to curse or to bless—just a game to
win or to lose.

But here were the streets of London—strife
stalking wide in the world;
And the flag of an ancient people to the battle-
breeze unfurled.
And who was helping or heeding? The gaudy
shops displayed
The toys of rich men's folly, by blinded labour
made;
And still from naught to nothing the bright-
skinned horses drew
Dull men and sleek-faced women with never a
deed to do;
While all about and around them the street-
flood ebbed and flowed,
Worn feet, grey anxious faces, grey backs
bowed 'neath the load.
Lo the sons of an ancient people! And for this
they fought and fell
In the days by fame made glorious, in the tale
that singers tell.

We two we stood in the street in the midst of
a mighty crowd,
The sound of its mingled murmur in the
heavens above was loud,
And earth was foul with its squalor—that
stream of every day,
The hurrying feet of labour, the faces worn
and grey,
Were a sore and grivous sight, and enough and
to spare had I seen
Of hard and pinching want midst our quiet
fields and green;
But all was nothing to this, the London holi-
day throng.
Dull and with hang-dog gait they stood or
shuffled along,
While the stench from the lairs they had lain
in last night went up in the wind,
And poisoned the sun-lit spring: no story men
can find
Is fit for the tale of their lives; no word that
man hath made
Can tell the hue of their faces, or their rags by
filth o'er-laid:
For this hath our age invented—these are the
sons of the free,

[1] The uncertain chronology of the story of *The Pilgrims of Hope* makes it uncertain which war Morris refers to in this passage. If the passage does have a specific reference, it is perhaps to one of the expeditions sent out to India in the late 1850s and 1860s.

Who shall bear our name triumphant o'er
    every land and sea.
Read ye their souls in their faces, and what
    shall help you there?
Joyless, hopeless, shameless, angerless, set is
    their stare:
This is the thing we have made, and what shall
    help us now,
For the field hath been laboured and tilled and
    the teeth of the dragon shall grow.

But why are they gathered together? what is
    this crowd in the street?
This is a holiday morning, though here and
    there we meet
The hurrying tradesman's broadcloth, or the
    workman's basket of tools.
Men say that at last we are rending the snares
    of knaves and fools;
That a cry from the heart of the nation against
    the foe is hurled,
And the flag of an ancient people to the battle-
    breeze unfurled.
The soldiers are off to the war, we are here to
    see the sight,
And all our griefs shall be hidden by the
    thought of our country's might.
'Tis the ordered anger of England and her
    hope for the good of the Earth
That we to-day are speeding, and many a gift
    of worth
Shall follow the brand[2] and the bullet, and
    our wrath shall be no curse,
But a blessing of life to the helpless—unless
    we are liars and worse—
And these that we see are the senders; these are
    they that speed
The dread and the blessing of England to help
    the world at its need.

Sick unto death was my hope, and I turned
    and looked on my dear,
And beheld her frightened wonder, and her
    grief without a tear,
And knew how her thought was mine—when,
    hark! o'er the hubbub and noise,
Faint and a long way off, the music's measured
    voice,
And the crowd was swaying and swaying, and
    somehow, I knew not why,
A dream came into my heart of deliverance
    drawing anigh.

       [2] Brand: sword.

Then with roll and thunder of drums grew
    the music louder and loud,
And the whole street tumbled and surged, and
    cleft was the holiday crowd,   60
Till two walls of faces and rags lined either
    side of the way.
Then clamour of shouts rose upward, as bright
    and glittering gay
Came the voiceful brass of the band, and my
    heart beat fast and fast,
For the river of steel came on, and the wrath
    of England passed
Through the want and the woe of the town,
    and strange and wild was my thought,
And my clenched hands wandered about as
    though a weapon they sought.

Hubbub and din was behind them, and the
    shuffling haggard throng,
Wandering aimless about, tangled the street
    for long;
But the shouts and the rhythmic noise we still
    heard far away,
And my dream was become a picture of the
    deeds of another day.   70
Far and far was I borne, away o'er the years to
    come,
And again was the ordered march, and the
    thunder of the drum,
And the bickering points of steel, and the
    horses shifting about
'Neath the flashing swords of the captains—
    then the silence after the shout—
Sun and wind in the street, familiar things
    made clear,
Made strange by the breathless waiting for the
    deeds that are drawing anear.
For woe had grown into will, and wrath was
    bared of its sheath,
And stark in the streets of London stood the
    crop of the dragon's teeth.
Where then in my dream were the poor and
    the wall of faces wan?   80
Here and here by my side, shoulder to
    shoulder of man,
Hope in the simple folk, hope in the hearts of
    the wise,
For the happy life to follow, or death and the
    ending of lies,
Hope is awake in the faces angerless now no
    more,
Till the new peace dawn on the world, the
    fruit of the people's war.

War in the world abroad a thousand leagues
  away,
While custom's wheel goes round and day
  devoureth day.
Peace at home!—what peace, while the rich
  man's mill is strife,
And the poor is the grist that he grindeth, and
  life devoureth life?

                                        1885–86

The Day of Days

Each eve earth falleth down the dark,
  As though its hope were o'er;
Yet lurks the sun when day is done
  Behind to-morrow's door.

Grey grows the dawn while men-folk sleep,
  Unseen spreads on the light,
Till the thrush sings to the coloured things,
  And earth forgets the night.

No otherwise wends on our Hope:
10 E'en as a tale that's told
Are fair lives lost, and all the cost
  Of wise and true and bold.

We've toiled and failed; we spake the word;
  None hearkened; dumb we lie;
Our Hope is dead, the seed we spread
  Fell o'er the earth to die.

What's this? For joy our hearts stand still,
  And life is loved and dear,
The lost and found the Cause hath crowned,
20 The Day of Days is here.

                                        1890; 1891

Iceland First Seen

Lo from our loitering ship a new land at last
  to be seen;
Toothed rocks down the side of the firth on
  the east guard a weary wide lea,[1]
And black slope the hillsides above, striped
  adown with their desolate green:
And a peak rises up on the west from the
  meeting of cloud and of sea,
Foursquare from base unto point like the
  building of Gods that have been,

The last of that waste of the mountains all
  cloud-wreathed and snow-flecked and grey,
And bright with the dawn that began just now
  at the ending of day.

Ah! what came we forth for to see that our
  hearts are so hot with desire?
Is it enough for our rest, the sight of this
  desolate strand,
And the mountain-waste voiceless as death but
  for winds that may sleep not nor tire?
Why do we long to wend forth through the
  length and breadth of a land,
Dreadful with grinding of ice, and record of
  scarce hidden fire,[2]
But that there 'mid the grey grassy dales sore
  scarred by the ruining streams
Lives the tale of the Northland of old and the
  undying glory of dreams?

O land, as some cave by the sea where the
  treasures of old have been laid,
The sword it may be of a king whose name was
  the turning of fight:
Or the staff of some wise of the world that
  many things made and unmade,
Or the ring of a woman maybe whose woe is
  grown wealth and delight.
No wheat and no wine grows above it, no
  orchard for blossom and shade;
The few ships that sail by its blackness but
  deem it the mouth of a grave;
Yet sure when the world shall awaken, this too
  shall be mighty to save.

Or rather, O land, if a marvel it seemeth that
  men ever sought
Thy wastes for a field and a garden fulfilled of
  all wonder and doubt,
And feasted amidst of the winter when the
  fight of the year had been fought,
Whose plunder all gathered together was little
  to babble about;
Cry aloud from thy wastes, O thou land, "Not
  for this nor for that was I wrought.
Amid waning of realms and of riches and
  death of things worshipped and sure,
I abide here the spouse of a God, and I made
  and I make and endure."

O Queen of the grief without knowledge, of
  the courage that may not avail,

---

[1] Firth: an estuary or inlet. Lea: pasture.   [2] Scarce hidden fire: volcanoes.

Of the longing that may not attain, of the love
that shall never forget,
More joy than the gladness of laughter thy
voice hath amidst of its wail:
More hope than of pleasure fulfilled amidst of
thy blindness is set;
More glorious than gaining of all thine
unfaltering hand that shall fail:
For what is the mark on thy brow but the
brand that thy Brynhild[3] doth bear?
Lone once, and loved and undone by a love
that no ages outwear.

Ah! when thy Balder[4] comes back, and bears
from the heart of the Sun
Peace and the healing of pain, and the wisdom
that waiteth no more;
And the lilies are laid on thy brow 'mid the
crown of the deeds thou hast done;
And the roses spring up by thy feet that the
rocks of the wilderness wore:
Ah! when thy Balder comes back and we
gather the gains he hath won,
Shall we not linger a little to talk of thy
sweetness of old,
Yea, turn back awhile to thy travail when the
Gods stood aloof to behold?

1891

All for the Cause

Hear a word, a word in season, for the day is
drawing nigh,
When the Cause shall call upon us, some to
live, and some to die!

He that dies shall not die lonely, many an one
hath gone before,
He that lives shall bear no burden heavier
than the life they bore.

Nothing ancient is their story, e'en but
yesterday they bled,
Youngest they of earth's beloved, last of all the
valiant dead.

E'en the tidings we are telling was the tale they
had to tell,

E'en the hope that our hearts cherish, was the
hope for which they fell.

In the grave where tyrants thrust them, lies
their labor and their pain,
But undying from their sorrow springeth up
the hope again.   10

Mourn not therefore, nor lament it that the
world outlives their life;
Voice and vision yet they give us, making
strong our hands for strife.

Some had name, and fame, and honor, learned
they were, and wise, and strong;
Some were nameless, poor, unlettered, weak in
all but grief and wrong.

Named and nameless all live in us; one and all
they lead us yet,
Every pain to count for nothing, every sorrow
to forget.

Hearken how they cry, "O happy, happy ye
that ye were born
In the sad slow night's departing, in the
rising of the morn.

"Fair the crown the Cause hath for you, well
to die or well to live
"Through the battle, through the tangle, peace
to gain or peace to give."   20

Ah, it may be! Oft meseemeth, in the days that
yet shall be,
When no slave of gold abideth 'twixt the
breadth of sea to sea,

Oft, when men and maids are merry, ere the
sunlight leaves the earth,
And they bless the day beloved, all too short
for all their mirth,

Some shall pause awhile and ponder on the
bitter days of old,
Ere the toil of strife and battle overthrew the
curse of gold;

Then 'twixt lips of loved and lover solemn
thoughts of us shall rise;

---

[3] Brynhild: in Norse mythology one of the Valkyries, the protectors of warriors. Because she
helped a king against one of the friends of the gods, Brynhild was confined asleep within a ring
of fire, to be awakened only by the great warrior who would penetrate the fire.

[4] Balder: the god of light and harmony in the pantheon of Norse mythology. His death was a
great sorrow to the gods, but after the gods themselves and the universe dissolve in the
apocalypse of Norse myths, Balder will return to a newly formed earth and universe.

We who once were fools and dreamers,[1] then
   shall be the brave and wise.

There amidst the world new-builded shall our
   earthly deeds abide,
Though our names be all forgotten, and the
30   tale of how we died.

Life or death then, who shall heed it, what we
   gain or what we lose?
Fair flies amid the struggle, and the Cause for
   each shall choose.

Hear a word, a word in season, for the day is
   drawing nigh,
When the cause shall call upon us, some to live
   and some to die!

                       1884; 1891

Thunder in the Garden

When the boughs of the garden hang heavy
   with rain
And the blackbird reneweth his song,
And the thunder departing yet rolleth again,
I remember the ending of wrong.

When the day that was dusk while his death
   was aloof
Is ending wide-gleaming and strange
For the clearness of all things beneath the
   world's roof,
I call back the wild chance and the change.

For once we twain sat through the hot after-
   noon
10 While the rain held aloof fore a while,
Till she, the soft-clad, for the glory of June
Changed all with the change of her smile.

For her smile was of longing, no longer of glee,
And her fingers, entwined with mine own,
With caresses unquiet sought kindness of me
For the gift that I never had known.

Then down rushed the rain, and the voice of
   the thunder

Smote dumb all the sound of the street,
And I to myself was grown nought but a
   wonder,
As she leaned down my kisses to meet.   20

That she craved for my lips that had craved
   her so often,
And the hand that had trembled to touch,
That the tears filled her eyes I had hoped not
   to soften
In this world was a marvel too much.

It was dusk 'mid the thunder, dusk e'en as the
   night,
When first brake out our love like the storm,
But no night-hour was it, and back came the
   light
While our hands with each other were warm.

And her smile killed with kisses, came back as
   at first
As she rose up and led me along,   30
And out to the garden, where nought was
   athirst,
And the blackbird renewing his song.

Earth's fragrance went with her, as in the wet
   grass
Her feet little hidden were set;
She bent down her head, 'neath the roses to
   pass,
And her arm with the lily was wet.

In the garden we wandered while day waned
   apace
And the thunder was dying aloof;
Till the moon o'er the minster-wall[1] lifted his
   face,
And grey gleamed out the lead of the roof.   40

Then we turned from the blossoms, and cold
   were they grown
In the trees the wind westering moved;
Till over the threshold back fluttered her
   gown,
And in the dark house was I loved.

                              1891

---

[1] In May Morris' collected edition this line reads: "We who once were fools defeated."
[1] Minster-wall: wall of a church or churchyard.

Algernon Charles Swinburne
1837–1909

SWINBURNE was the last nineteenth-century British poet to create a major body of poetry in forms traditionally associated with important poetry and commanded by an idea, dominant in England since the generations of Wordsworth, Coleridge, and Shelley, that the poet was the maker of a new reality and the prophet of a universal truth unknown to common apprehension. He was also the first poet of the Victorian period who tried and realized such large ambitions in a poetry that broke from conceptions of material existence as a sign or incarnation of the spiritual or divine. These conceptions had made the poetry of Tennyson and Browning at least consistent with conventional religious belief and the ethics of conventional morality. Swinburne's denial in his early poems of the existence of a divine or transcendent reality, and his attempt in later poems like "Hertha" and the "Hymn of Man" to invest mortal and material reality with the attributes once given to the divine, made him something startling in mid-Victorian England: a poet who wanted fundamentally to change how people thought of themselves, and who set himself not only apart from but in opposition to conventional ideas of human identity and possibility.

There were of course nineteenth-century antecedents for Swinburne's early idea of himself as a poet in society. Among the models— he called them "masters"—of his early poetry were William Blake, Shelley, Victor Hugo, and Walt Whitman, poets who wrote in large literary forms and who wanted to effect philosophical, social, and political change by their words. The first poem by Swinburne to bring him into relatively wide and favorable notice, *Atalanta in Calydon* (1865), was a treatment of a classical myth in the form of Greek tragedy. Until the end of his life he wrote in the familiarly grand forms of Elizabethan as well as classical drama, long narratives, elegies, ceremonial odes, and a peculiarly nineteenth-century kind of long meditative lyric, in the tradition of Wordsworth's "Tintern Abbey" and Shelley's "Mont Blanc," of which "On the Cliffs" is an exceptionally complex example. At the climax of his powers as a poet in the 1860s and 1870s he made the new mythologies of "Hertha" and "Hymn of Man," in which he articulated the doctrine that the redemption of an exhausted time would come not from an incursion of the divine but from a fulfillment of the capacities of the human. He also made a style in which he pushed beyond their customary limits the capacities of mid-nineteenth-century poetic language for melody, color, and picture. He exploited the tolerance of poetic language and form in his time for metrical variety, syntactical complexity, and loose sequences of stanzas and rhymed lines. Swinburne from the beginning was, in a word, extreme. He wanted to perform the entire office of the nineteenth-century romantic poet as prophet. He entrusted his perception of a world radically different from that of orthodox belief to a poetic idiom that strained to be more vivid and intense than that of the poets on whom he modeled, and against whom he measured, his practice.

Swinburne's contemporaries often thought him not only extreme but excessive. He often seems to have sought this judgment. At Oxford he was a member of a group of undergraduates of advanced taste and opinions, a "revolutionary set," according to their Oxford contemporaries, who read Browning and doubted God. Swinburne's meeting with Dante Gabriel Rossetti and William Morris at Oxford in 1857 kindled his enthusiasm for the medieval subjects and decorated style of the early Pre-Raphaelites. When he came to London in 1861 to be a literary man—"poetry," he said, "is quite work enough for any one man" —he kept up his connections with Rossetti and his associates. Among the writings Swinburne published in an undergraduate magazine while he was at Oxford was "Queen Yseult," written in the first reflex of his response to the poems of Morris' *The Defence of Guenevere* volume, and the first volumes he published in London, *The Queen-Mother* and *Rosamond,* were in a style elaborated from Morris. But in the early 1860s Swinburne was reading and writing about the poetry of Charles Baudelaire, and he was also writing "The Triumph of Time," "Laus Veneris," "Dolores," and other poems that were to appear in the first series of *Poems and Ballads* in 1866. The sensuality and what seemed to be the atheism or blasphemous paganism of this volume were attacked, and its withdrawal from publication gave Swinburne a chance to increase his notoriety as well as his fame by his reply, *Notes on Poems and Reviews* (see Part Ten), before the volume was brought out again in the same year by another publisher. Stories of Swinburne's excited indulgence in alcohol, his occasional fits in public, and his reading and writing of erotica about flogging and other unconventional pleasures enlarged his notoriety in the 1860s and 1870s. He knew and enjoyed these perceptions of him as a kind of exultant dervish of the immoral, and he played to them. "I have a character to keep up as a scandalous poet," he wrote to one of his friends as he prepared the poems he published in *Songs Before Sunrise* (1871). He promised that when "Hymn of Man" appeared, Shelley's philosophically and politically radical *Queen Mab* would seem to be "an archdeacon's charge, and my own previous blasphemies . . . models of Catholic devotion."

But beneath these diversions of scandalizing proper readers and reviewers there runs through Swinburne's first three volumes of poems a coherent and profound line of development, one of whose culminations is the "Hymn of Man." In *Atalanta in Calydon* (1865) Swinburne used his thorough classical knowledge and sympathy with classical Greek literature to turn a Greek myth and tragic form into a fundamentally lyric enactment of a reality in which love, beauty, human consciousness, and the capacity for speech itself are painful ironies in a world governed by accident and doomed by time and death. In the first series of *Poems and Ballads* (1866) he continued to explore this world and, like Baudelaire in his poems, registered a moral disgust at the exhaustions and perversions of mortal flesh pushed to its limits by wishes for a wholeness and health that material existence cannot satisfy. In these poems time itself is

running down, the fabric of things is unraveling, and gods as well as men are dead or dying, or, as in "Laus Veneris," themselves bound in rock and flesh beyond knowledge of redemption.

Then, to complete the signal achievement of his poetic career, Swinburne in *Songs Before Sunrise* (1871) converted these transient sensual ecstasies and their disappointment into mythologies and proclamations of their fulfillment. He had been reading and writing about Hugo, Blake, and Whitman all through the 1860s. In 1867 he met Mazzini, the exiled Italian nationalist, who urged him to be "the apostle of a crusade" and to write of large political and national dreams rather than of the narrow sadness of individuals. Swinburne had already written *A Song of Italy* (1867), and his sympathy with the cause of Italian liberation was encouraged by his admiration for Walter Savage Landor, whom he met in Florence in 1864, and by his chronic rage at the forms of political oppression. But the politics of *Songs Before Sunrise* are not as important as the occasion the volume gave him to rise to the aspirations of his masters and write poems whose rhythms, words, and myths were intended literally to change the world by altering his readers' perceptions of it. He wrote in "Hertha" of flesh made transcendent by its own human meaning, in "Hymn of Man" of a religion that exalted without lying and disappointing, and in "To Walt Whitman" of a poetry that freshened life rather than recorded its decline. When the poems of *Songs Before Sunrise* are put with those of the first series of *Poems and Ballads,* they constitute Swinburne's accession to the most ambitious of the regenerative prophetic offices claimed by nineteenth-century poets. They also mark, interestingly, a passage from despair to hope common in such mid-Victorian testaments as *In Memoriam,* a passage that in Swinburne's poetry is exceptional because the energies of human salvation lie wholly in humanity itself.

During the 1870s the disorderly excesses of Swinburne's personal life continued, resulting in periods of dangerously poor health. He wrote a great deal of prose and poetry during this decade. But in 1879, after his father's death, Swinburne's inability to care for himself brought him into an illness from which he probably would have died had not his friend Theodore Watts-Dunton intervened and taken Swinburne to live with him, and after 1905 with his wife, in a house in one of the outlying districts of London. Swinburne's last three decades at The Pines, the name of the house he shared with Watts-Dunton, were remarkably prolific. He contributed over 200 reviews and poems to periodicals during these years, and published twenty volumes of prose, poetry, and verse dramas on historical and classical subjects. He gradually outlasted, in a sense he outwrote, the notoriety he had once courted, and he rose to an eminence as a learned man of letters and a poet on the old, grand scale, a master of his craft and the creator of a distinctive voice and presence. His political interests became fitful and were expressed in invective against continental kings and English and Irish politicians he disliked, or in patriotic paeans to the British navy and the union of England and Ireland. As early as the poems of the second series of *Poems and Ballads* (1878), which contained elegies to his father, Baudelaire, and other writers as well as "The Forsaken Garden" and similarly subdued poems, an autumnal mood entered his poetry. It is a mood not of the residue of energies desperately spent or fearfully thwarted, but rather of the slow encroachment of time, the sea eroding the shore, the night darkening the sea.

This mood persisted in his late poetry, especially in those poems in which he tried to discipline his style in versions he devised for himself of intricate French stanzas. In the most interesting of his late poems, however, often when as in "A Channel Passage" and "The Lake of Gaube" he wrote of events that occurred years earlier, he resurrects his sense of the mystery, power, and ecstasy of sensual existence. These late poems are more than simply recollections of his achievement during the climatic years between the publication of *Atalanta in Calydon* and *Songs Before Sunrise*. They are themselves achievements in the modes in which Swinburne made good his ambition to be a great poet in the way of his masters. In these poems Swinburne leaves the desolate landscapes and quiet tonalities characteristic of late-century verse to penetrate again the deep, dense life of things and to find again words, rhythms, and forms that will make or manifest realities whose power and meaning none will know until a poet speaks them.

CHRONOLOGY

1837   Born in London: his father was a captain in the navy, his mother the daughter of the Earl of Ashburnham. His mother's family was of great antiquity and had held land in the south of England since before the Norman invasion in the eleventh century. His father was of an old family in the north of England; in the seventeenth and eighteenth centuries the family had been Roman Catholic and supporters of the Stuart kings and pretenders to the throne of England.

1838–49   Swinburne grew up mostly in a family home in the Isle of Wight in the south of England, occasionally visiting a family house in the north. He was educated at home by tutors and his mother.

1849–53   Swinburne continued his education at Eton, studying Greek and Latin, reading Victor Hugo, and beginning his own writing by composing imitations of early seventeenth-century tragedies in verse.

1853–55   Swinburne was again tutored at home, perhaps originally in preparation for entrance into the army, and later in preparation for entrance to Oxford and possibly a career in clerical orders. He visited Germany in 1855.

1856   Swinburne entered Oxford, where he was one of the founding members of an undergraduate club soon known for its radical politics, skeptical freethinking in religious matters, and readings to one another of texts in British literature, then not formally studied as part of the curriculum.

1857   Dante Gabriel Rossetti, William Morris, and other associates in the Pre-Raphaelite Brotherhood came to Oxford to decorate a new building with frescoes, and Swinburne met them. He began writing a verse drama on the Arthurian story of Iseult which was published in a publication of an undergraduate club.

1859–60   Because his neglect of his studies endangered the possibility of his earning a degree, Swinburne left Oxford temporarily to be tutored privately. In 1860 he finally left Oxford without taking a degree. Two of his verse dramas, *The Queen-Mother* and *Rosamond*, were published in 1860 in editions paid for by Swinburne's father; they were reissued in 1865 and 1866.

1861–64   Swinburne settled in London on an allowance from his father. For a time he shared a house with Rossetti and George Meredith, and he helped Rossetti with his contributions to a life of the painter and poet William Blake, which was published in 1863. Swinburne published reviews, including reviews of the work of the French writers Victor Hugo and Charles Baudelaire, and he also wrote and published in magazines some of the poems which later appeared in *Poems and Ballads.*

1865 *Atalanta in Calydon* published, at his own expense; it received very favorable reviews. Another verse drama, *Chastelard,* was published in this year.

1866 *Poems and Ballads* was published, and then withdrawn by its publisher. After Swinburne wrote and published his pamphlet, *Notes on Poems and Reviews,* the volume was reissued by another publisher.

1867 Swinburne met the Italian nationalist Giuseppe Mazzini, who encouraged him to write political verse in the cause of Italian nationalism. *A Song of Italy,* begun in 1866, published.

1868–69 *William Blake,* a long study that includes an exposition of the mythology of Blake's long prophetic poems, published at the end of 1867; Swinburne began writing *Tristam of Lyonesse,* a poem on one of the stories in the Arthurian legends.

1871 *Songs Before Sunrise* published.

1872 *Under the Microscope,* a prose attack on the critics who judged his own poetry and Rossetti's to be unhealthily erotic, published. Swinburne in these years sometimes became so ill as a result of the unregulated habits of his life that he had to be taken to his parents' house to recuperate.

1874 *Bothwell,* another verse drama concerning the story of Mary Queen of Scots, published.

1875 Two books of literary criticism, *Essays and Studies* and *George Chapman,* and *Songs of Two Nations* published.

1876 *Erecthus,* a verse play on the model of classical Greek drama, published.

1877 Swinburne's father died, leaving him a modest inheritance. Swinburne published a novel, *Love's Cross-Currents,* in a magazine; he had begun writing fiction in the 1860s. He had another novel, *Lesbia Brandon,* set in galleys; it was not published, however, until 1952.

1878 *Poems and Ballads, Second Series,* published.

1879 Swinburne became very ill in his London lodgings, and he was taken to live in Putney, a London suburb, by Theodore Watts (later Watts-Dunton), a friend of Rossetti, Swinburne, and other writers, who had once practiced law and was now on the staff of a London weekly journal of literature and politics. For the rest of Swinburne's life Watts-Dunton managed all the details of his domestic life and of the publication of his books and essays.

1880 Two volumes of poems published, *Songs of the Springtides* and *Studies in Song.* Swinburne also published a collection of his parodies of contemporary poets which he had been circulating in manuscript for some time, *Specimens of Modern Poets: The Heptalogia.*

1881–87 In these years Swinburne published at least one book a year, most of them verse dramas—*Mary Stuart* (1881), *Marino Faliero* (1885), and *Locrine* (1887)—and volumes of poetry: *Tristam of Lyonesse and Other Poems* (1882); *A Century of Rondels* (1883), *A Midsummer Holiday and Other Poems* (1884). He published two volumes of prose, *Miscellanies* and *A Study of Victor Hugo,* in 1886. In 1888 he had his poems and a prose sketch on the erotic pleasures of flogging privately printed in *The Whippingham Papers.* In this decade he had grown deaf and lived in carefully regulated tranquillity at The Pines, the house he shared with Watts-Dunton, leaving England only once (and for the last time in his life) to meet Victor Hugo in Paris.

1889 *Poems and Ballads, Third Series* published. A prose *Study of Ben Jonson* also published.

1892 *The Sisters,* a blank verse play set in the nineteenth century, published.

1894 *Astrophel and Other Poems* published, and another volume of literary criticism, *Studies in Prose and Poetry,* also published.

1896 *The Tale of Balen,* another poetic treatment of a story from the Arthurian legends, published.

1899 *Rosamund, Queen of the Lombards,* a verse drama, published.

1901 *Love's Cross-Currents,* a novel in letters which was completed in 1866 and published in a magazine in 1877, published in the United States. In 1905 an edition was published in England.

1904 *A Channel Passage and Other Poems* published.

1908 *The Duke of Gandia,* a part of a projected verse tragedy on the Borgia family, published.

1909 Swinburne died at The Pines.

EDITIONS

The texts of the poems reprinted here are those of a collected edition of Swinburne's poems published in 1904; the texts of this edition are more accurate than those of the standard Bonchurch edition (1925–27). Some writing not included in Swinburne's collected editions, including some of his satires and literary hoaxes, are published in *New Writings by Swinburne* (1964), edited by Cecil Y. Lang. Swinburne's two novels have been republished in *The Novels of A. C. Swinburne: Love's Cross-Currents and Lesbia Brandon* (1962), with an introduction by Edmund Wilson. Cecil Y. Lang has edited *The Swinburne Letters*, in six volumes (1959–62). Clyde K. Hyder has edited two collections of Swinburne's literary criticism, *Swinburne Replies* (1966), and *Swinburne as Critic* (1972).

BIOGRAPHY AND CRITICISM

The most recent biography is Philip Henderson's *Swinburne: Portrait of a Poet* (1974). Edmund Gosse, a friend of Swinburne, wrote a reticent *The Life of Swinburne* (1917). Georges Lafourcade in *La jeunesse de Swinburne* (1928) and *Swinburne: A Literary Biography* (1932) was more open about the character of Swinburne's life in London. See also Samuel C. Chew's *Swinburne* (1929), Jean Overton Fuller's *Swinburne: A Critical Biography* (1968), and Cecil Y. Lang, "Swinburne's Lost Love," *Publications of the Modern Language Association*, 74 (1959). Jerome McGann's *Swinburne: An Experiment in Criticism* (1972) is an estimate of Swinburne's several claims to attention, written as a debate between opinions and responses named for literary friends and colleagues of Swinburne.

OTHER USEFUL BOOKS AND ESSAYS

Beerbohm, Max. "No. 2, The Pines," in *And Even Now* (1921).

Connolly, T. E. *Swinburne's Theory of Poetry* (1964).

Hyder, Clyde K. *Swinburne's Literary Career and Fame* (1931).

Panter-Downes, Mollie. *At the Pines: Swinburne and Watts-Dunton in Putney* (1971).

Peters, Robert L. *The Crowns of Apollo: Swinburne's Principles of Life and Art* (1965).

Raymond, Meredith B. *Swinburne's Poetics* (1971).

Rudman, H. W. *Italian Nationalism and English Letters* (1940).

Rutland, W. R. *Swinburne: A Nineteenth-Century Hellene* (1931).

Victorian Poetry, 9 (1971). A double issue devoted entirely to essays on Swinburne's poems.

The final volume of the Bonchurch edition of Swinburne's writing is a bibliography by T. J. Wise (1927). See also Ian Fletcher's pamphlet, *Swinburne* (1973), in the Writers and Their Work series; William E. Fredeman, *Pre-Raphaelitism: A Bibliocritical Study* (1965); and Ehrsam, Deily, and Smith (General Bibliography). Clyde T. Hyder has compiled *Swinburne: The Critical Heritage* (1970).

"Laus Veneris"—"In Praise of Venus"—is a treatment of the medieval legend of Tannhäuser, a knight who lives with Venus in her court in the mountain Horsel, leaves her to seek absolution from the Pope, but is told that he will not be forgiven until the Pope's wooden staff puts forth leaves and flowers. After Tannhäuser's return to the Horsel, the staff does miraculously blossom, but the knight is now lost in his despair and waits the end of the world and the last judgment of God.

Richard Wagner's opera Tannhäuser, first performed in 1845, was presented in Paris in 1861 in a performance famous for the hostility and controversy it aroused. The opera was not presented in England until 1876. The German ballad of Tannhäuser had been translated or retold by nineteenth-century British writers—for example, by Thomas Carlyle (translating a version by the German writer Johann Ludwig Tieck) in 1827. In Notes on Poems and Reviews, a pamphlet Swinburne published in 1866 as his contribution to the controversy aroused by the publication of the first series of Poems and Ballads, he wrote that in the poem "my first aim was to rehandle the old story in a new fashion. To me it seemed that the tragedy began with the knight's return to Venus—began at the point where hitherto it had seemed to leave off. The immortal agony of a man lost after all repentance—cast down from fearful hope into fearless despair—believing in Christ and bound to Venus—desirous of penitential pain, and damned to joyless pleasure—this, in my eyes, was the kernel and nucleus" of the myth. As he did frequently in this pamphlet, Swinburne insisted on the dramatic character of poems such as these. Readers must grant the premise of the knight who speaks the poem that Christ exists: "Once accept or admit the least admixture of pagan worship, or of modern thought, and the whole story collapses into froth and smoke."

Swinburne also remarks on a pamphlet by the French poet Charles Baudelaire on Wagner's Tannhäuser. He read the pamphlet after he wrote the poem, but he found that "I concur with the great musician and his great panegyrist" in proposing the medieval conception of Venus as a "fallen goddess, grown diabolic among ages that would not accept her as divine"; and in making "Venus the one love of her knight's whole life . . . ; I have sent him, poet and soldier, fresh to her fierce embrace. Thus only both legend and symbol appear to me noble and significant. Light loves and harmless errors must not touch the elect of heaven or of hell. The queen of evil, the lady of lust, will endure no rival but God; and when the vicar of God rejects him, to her only can he return to abide the day of judgment in weariness and sorrow and fear."

Laus Veneris

Asleep or waking is it? for her neck,
Kissed over close, wears yet a purple speck
    Wherein the pained blood falters and goes
      out;
Soft, and stung softly—fairer for a fleck.

But though my lips shut sucking on the place,
There is no vein at work upon her face;
    Her eyelids are so peaceable, no doubt
Deep sleep has warmed her blood through all
      its ways.

Lo, this is she that was the world's delight;
10   The old grey years were parcels of her might;
    The strewings of the ways wherein she trod
Were the twain seasons of the day and night.

Lo, she was thus when her clear limbs enticed
All lips that now grow sad with kissing Christ,
    Stained with blood fallen from the feet of
      God,
The feet and hands whereat our souls were
      priced.

Alas, Lord, surely thou art great and fair.
But lo her wonderfully woven hair!
    And thou didst heal us with thy piteous kiss;
20   But see now, Lord; her mouth is lovelier.

She is right fair; what hath she done to thee?
Nay, fair Lord Christ, life up thine eyes and
    see;

Had now thy mother such a lip—like this?
Thou knowest how sweet a thing it is to me.

Inside the Horsel here the air is hot;
Right little peace one hath for it, God wot;
    The scented dusty daylight burns the air,
And my heart chokes me till I hear it not.

Behold, my Venus, my soul's body, lies
With my love laid upon her garment-wise,
    Feeling my love in all her limbs and hair
And shed between her eyelids through her
      eyes.

She holds my heart in her sweet open hands
Hanging asleep; hard by her head there stands,
    Crowned with gilt thorns and clothed with
      flesh like fire,
Love, wan as foam blown up the salt burnt
      sands—

Hot as the brackish waifs of yellow spume
That shift and steam—loose clots of arid fume
    From the sea's panting mouth of dry desire;
There stands he, like one labouring at a loom.

The warp holds fast across; and every thread
That makes the woof up has dry specks of red;
    Always the shuttle cleaves clean through,
      and he
Weaves with the hair of many a ruined head.

Love is not glad nor sorry, as I deem;
Labouring he dreams, and labours in the
    dream,
    Till when the spool is finished, lo I see
His web, reeled off, curls and goes out like
      steam.

Night falls like fire; the heavy lights run low,
And as they drop, my blood and body so
    Shake as the flame shakes, full of days and
      hours
That sleep not neither weep they as they go.

Ah yet would God this flesh of mine might be
Where air might wash and long leaves cover
    me,
    Where tides of grass break into foam of
      flowers,
Or where the wind's feet shine along the sea.

Ah yet would God that stems and roots were
    bred
Out of my weary body and my head,

That sleep were sealed upon me with a seal,
And I were as the least of all his dead.

Would God my blood were dew to feed the
    grass,
Mine ears made deaf and mine eyes blind as
    glass,
My body broken as a turning wheel,
And my mouth stricken ere it saith Alas!

Ah God, that love were as a flower or flame,
That life were as the naming of a name,
    That death were not more pitiful than
    desire,
That these things were not one thing and the
    same!

Behold now, surely somewhere there is death:
For each man hath some space of years, he
    saith,
    A little space of time ere time expire,
A little day, a little way of breath.

And lo, between the sundawn and the sun,
His day's work and his night's work are
    undone;
    And lo, between the nightfall and the light,[1]
He is not, and none knoweth of such an one.

Ah God, that I were as all souls that be,
As any herb or leaf of any tree,
    As men that toil through hours of labouring
    night,
As bones of men under the deep sharp sea.

Outside it must be winter among men;
For at the gold bars of the gates again
    I heard all night and all the hours of it
The wind's wet wings and fingers drip with
    rain.

Knights gather, riding sharp for cold; I know
The ways and woods are strangled with the
    snow;
    And with short song the maidens spin and
    sit
Until Christ's birthnight, lily-like, arow.[2]

The scent and shadow shed about me make
The very soul in all my senses ache;
    The hot hard night is fed upon my breath,
And sleep beholds me from afar awake.

Alas, but surely where the hills grow deep,
Or where the wild ways of the sea are steep,
    Or in strange places somewhere there is
    death,
And on death's face the scattered hair of sleep.

There lover-like with lips and limbs that meet
They lie, they pluck sweet fruit of life and eat;
    But me the hot and hungry days devour,
And in my mouth no fruit of theirs is sweet.   100

No fruit of theirs, but fruit of my desire,
For her love's sake whose lips through mine
    respire;
    Her eyelids on her eyes like flower on flower,
Mine eyelids on mine eyes like fire on fire.

So lie we, not as sleep that lies by death,
With heavy kisses and with happy breath;
    Not as man lies by woman, when the bride
Laughs low for love's sake and the words he
    saith.

For she lies, laughing low with love; she lies
And turns his kisses on her lips to sighs,   110
    To sighing sound of lips unsatisfied,
And the sweet tears are tender with her eyes.

Ah, not as they, but as the souls that were
Slain in the old time, having found her fair;
    Who, sleeping with her lips upon their eyes,
Heard sudden serpents hiss across her hair.

Their blood runs round the roots of time like
    rain:
She casts them forth and gathers them again;
    With nerve and bone she weaves and
    multiplies
Exceeding pleasure out of extreme pain.   120

Her little chambers drip with flower-like red,
Her girdles, and the chaplets of her head,
    Her armlets and her anklets; with her feet
She tramples all that winepress of the dead.

Her gateways smoke with fume of flowers and
    fires,
With loves burnt out and unassuaged desires;
    Between her lips the steam of them is sweet,
The languor in her ears of many lyres.

Her beds are full of perfume and sad sound,
Her doors are made with music, and barred
    round   130

[1] In the first edition of the poem this line read: "between the nightfall and the night." So too in the first edition line 79 read: "hours of labouring light."
[2] Arow: in a row.

With sighing and with laughter and with
    tears,
With tears whereby strong souls of men are
    bound.

There is the knight Adonis[3] that was slain;
With flesh and blood she chains him for a
    chain;
    The body and the spirit in her ears
Cry, for her lips divide him vein by vein.

Yea, all she slayeth; yea, every man save me;
Me, love, thy lover that must cleave to thee
    Till the ending of the days and ways of
      earth,
140   The shaking of the sources of the sea.

Me, most forsaken of all souls that fell;
Me, satiated with things insatiable;
    Me, for whose sake the extreme hell makes
      mirth,
Yea, laughter kindles at the heart of hell.

Alas thy beauty! for thy mouth's sweet sake
My soul is bitter to me, my limbs quake
    As water, as the flesh of men that weep,
As their heart's vein whose heart goes nigh to
    break.

Ah God, that sleep with flower-sweet finger-tips
150 Would crush the fruit of death upon my lips;
    Ah God, that death would tread the grapes
      of sleep
And wring their juice upon me as it drips.

There is no change of cheer for many days,
But change of chimes high up in the air, that
    sways
    Rung by the running fingers of the wind;
And singing sorrows heard on hidden ways.

Day smiteth day in twain, night sundereth
    night,
And on mine eyes the dark sits as the light;
    Yea, Lord, thou knowest I know not, having
      sinned,
If heaven be clean or unclean in thy sight.

Yea, as if earth were sprinkled over me,
Such chafed harsh earth as chokes a sandy sea,

Each pore doth yearn, and the dried blood
    thereof
Gasps by sick fits, my heart swims heavily,

There is a feverish famine in my veins;
Below her bosom, where a crushed grape
    stains
    The white and blue, there my lips caught
      and clove
An hour since, and what mark of me remains?

I dare not always touch her, lest the kiss
Leave my lips charred. Yea, Lord, a little bliss,   170
    Brief bitter bliss, one hath for a great sin;
Nathless thou knowest how sweet a thing it is.

Sin, is it sin whereby men's souls are thrust
Into the pit? yet had I a good trust
    To save my soul before it slipped therein,
Trod under by the fire-shod feet of lust.

For if mine eyes fail and my soul takes breath,
I look between the iron sides of death
    Into sad hell where all sweet love hath end,
All but the pain that never finisheth.   180

There are the naked faces of great kings,
The singing folk with all their lute-playings;
    There when one cometh he shall have to
      friend
The grave that covets and the worm that clings.

There sit the knights that were so great of
    hand,
The ladies that were queens of fair green land,
    Grown grey and black now, brought unto
      the dust,
Soiled, without raiment, clad about with sand.

There is one end for all of them; they sit
Naked and sad, they drink the dregs of it,   19
    Trodden as grapes in the wine-press of lust,
Trampled and trodden by the fiery feet.[4]

I see the marvellous mouth whereby there fell
Cities and people whom the gods loved well,[5]
    Yet for her sake on them the fire gat hold,
And for their sakes on her the fire of hell.

---

[3] Adonis: a young man loved by Venus who was killed while hunting. Venus caused a flower,
the anemone, to grow from his blood, but it too is short-lived.

[4] "I have trodden the winepress alone; and of the people there was none with me: for I will
tread them in mine anger, and trample them in my fury. . . . For the day of vengeance is in
mine heart, and the year of the redeemed is come" (Isaiah 63:3-4).

[5] The marvellous mouth: Helen, whose seduction by Paris was the cause of the Trojan War.

And softer than the Egyptian lote-leaf is,
The queen whose face was worth the world to
    kiss,
    Wearing at breast a suckling snake of gold;
200 And large pale lips of strong Semiramis,[6]

Curled like a tiger's that curl back to feed;
Red only where the last kiss made them bleed;
    Her hair most thick with many a carven
    gem,
Deep in the mane, great-chested, like a steed.

Yea, with red sin the faces of them shine;
But in all these there was no sin like mine;
    No, not in all the strange great sins of them
That made the wine-press froth and foam with
    wine.

For I was of Christ's choosing, I God's knight,
210 No blinkard heathen stumbling for scant light;
    I can well see, for all the dusty days
Gone past, the clean great time of goodly fight.

I smell the breathing battle sharp with blows,
With shriek of shafts and snapping short of
    bows;
    The fair pure sword smites out in subtle
    ways,
Sounds and long lights are shed between the
    rows

Of beautiful mailed men; the edged light slips,
Most like a snake that takes short breath and
    dips
    Sharp from the beautifully bending head,
220 With all its gracious body lithe as lips

That curl in touching you; right in this wise
My sword doth, seeming fire in mine own eyes,
    Leaving all colours in them brown and red
And flecked with death; then the keen breaths
    like sighs,

The caught-up choked dry laughters following
    them,
When all the fighting face is grown a flame
    For pleasure, and the pulse that stuns the
    ears,
And the heart's gladness of the goodly game.

Let me think yet a little; I do know
These things were sweet, but sweet such years
230   ago,

Their savour is all turned now into tears;
Yea, ten years since, where the blue ripples
    blow,

The blue curled eddies of the blowing Rhine,
I felt the sharp wind shaking grass and vine
    Touch my blood too, and sting me with
    delight
Through all this waste and weary body of mine

That never feels clear air; right gladly then
I rode alone, a great way off my men,
    And heard the chiming bridle smite and
    smite,
And gave each rhyme thereof some rhyme
    again,   240

Till my song shifted to that iron one;
Seeing there rode up between me and the sun
    Some certain of my foe's men, for his three
White wolves across their painted coats did
    run.

The first red-bearded, with square cheeks—
    alack,
I made my knave's blood turn his beard to
    black;
    The slaying of him was a joy to see:
Perchance too, when at night he came not
    back,

Some woman fell a-weeping, whom this thief
Would beat when he had drunken; yet small
    grief   250
    Hath any for the ridding of such knaves;
Yea, if one wept, I doubt her teen[7] was brief.

This bitter love is sorrow in all lands,
Draining of eyelids, wringing of drenched
    hands,
    Sighing of hearts and filling up of graves;
A sign across the head of the world he stands,

An one that hath a plague-mark on his brows;
Dust and spilt blood do track him to his house
    Down under earth; sweet smells of lip and
    cheek,
Like a sweet snake's breath made more
    poisonous   260

With chewing of some perfumed deadly grass,
Are shed all round his passage if he pass,

---

[6] The queen: Cleopatra; Semiramis: a legendary queen of Babylon.
[7] Teen: grief.

And their quenched savour leaves the whole
    soul weak,
Sick with keen guessing whence the perfume
    was.

As one who hidden in deep sedge and reeds
Smells the rare scent made where a panther
    feeds,
    And tracking ever slotwise[8] the warm smell
Is snapped upon by the sweet mouth and
    bleeds,

His head far down the hot sweet throat of
    her—
270 So one tracks love, whose breath is deadlier,
    And lo, one springe and you are fast in hell,
Fast as the gin's[9] grip of a wayfarer.

I think now, as the heavy hours decease
One after one, and bitter thoughts increase
    One upon one, of all sweet finished things;
The breaking of the battle; the long peace

Wherein we sat clothed softly, each man's hair
Crowned with green leaves beneath white
    hoods of vair;[10]
    The sounds of sharp spears at great tourney-
    ings,
280 And noise of singing in the late sweet air.

I sang of love too, knowing nought thereof;
"Sweeter," I said, "the little laugh of love
    Than tears out of the eyes of Magdalen,[11]
Or any fallen feather of the Dove.

"The broken little laugh that spoils a kiss,
The ache of purple pulses, and the bliss
    Of blinded eyelids that expand again—
Love draws them open with those lips of his,

"Lips that cling hard till the kissed face has
    grown
290 Of one same fire and colour with their own;
    Then ere one sleep, appeased with sacrifice,
Where his lips wounded, there his lips atone."

I sang these things long since and knew them
    not;

"Lo, here is love, or there is love, God wot,
    This man and that finds favour in his eyes,"
I said, "but I, what guerdon have I got?

"The dust of praise that is blown everywhere
In all men's faces with the common air;
    The bay-leaf that wants chafing to be sweet
Before they wind it in a singer's hair."[12]   300

So that one dawn I rode forth sorrowing;
I had no hope but of some evil thing,
    And so rode slowly past the windy wheat
And past the vineyard and the water-spring,

Up to the Horsel. A great elder-tree
Held back its heaps of flowers to let me see
    The ripe tall grass, and one that walked
    therein,
Naked, with hair shed over to the knee.

She walked between the blossom and the grass;
I knew the beauty of her, what she was,   310
    The beauty of her body and her sin,
And in my flesh the sin of hers, alas!

Alas! for sorrow is all the end of this.
O sad kissed mouth, how sorrowful it is!
    O breast whereat some suckling sorrow
    clings,
Red with the bitter blossom of a kiss!

Ah, with blind lips I felt for you, and found
About my neck your hands and hair enwound,
    The hands that stifle and the hair that stings,
I felt them fasten sharply without sound.   320

Yea, for my sin I had great store of bliss:
Rise up, make answer for me, let thy kiss
    Seal my lips hard from speaking of my sin,
Lest one go mad to hear how sweet it is.

Yet I waxed faint with fume of barren bowers,
And murmuring of the heavy-headed hours;
    And let the dove's beak fret and peck within
My lips in vain, and Love shed fruitless flowers.

So that God looked upon me when your hands
Were hot about me; yea, God brake my bands   330

---

[8] Slotwise: along the track. It was a traditional belief that the panther lured victims by the sweet smell of its breath.
[9] Springe: a mechanical trap. Gin: a noose used to trap birds and small animals.
[10] Vair: squirrel fur.
[11] Magdalen: a sinful woman who is forgiven by Christ because of her repentance and faith (Luke 7:37–50).
[12] Bay-leaf: a crown of bay leaves was a traditional adornment and prize for poets.

To save my soul alive, and I came forth
Like a man blind and naked in strange lands

That hears men laugh and weep, and knows
    not whence
Nor wherefore, but is broken in his sense;
    Howbeit I met folk riding from the north
Towards Rome, to purge them of their souls'
    offence,

And rode with them, and spake to none; the
    day
Stunned me like lights upon some wizard way,
    And ate like fire mine eyes and mine eye-
    sight;
So rode I, hearing all these chant and pray,   340

And marvelled; till before us rose and fell
White cursed hills, like outer skirts of hell
    Seen where men's eyes look through the day
    to night,
Like a jagged shell's lips, harsh, untunable,

Blown in between by devils' wrangling breath;
Nathless we won well past that hell and death,
    Down to the sweet land where all airs are
    good,
Even unto Rome where God's grace tarrieth.

Then came each man and worshipped at his
    knees
Who in the Lord God's likeness bears the keys   350
    To bind or loose,[13] and called on Christ's
    shed blood,
And so the sweet-souled father gave him ease.

But when I came I fell down at his feet,
Saying, "Father, though the Lord's blood be
    right sweet,
    The spot it takes not off the panther's skin,
Nor shall an Ethiop's stain be bleached with
    it.[14]

"Lo, I have sinned and have spat out at God,
Wherefore his hand is heavier and his rod
    More sharp because of mine exceeding sin,
And all his raiment redder than bright blood   360

"Before mine eyes; yea, for my sake I wot
The heat of hell is waxen seven times hot
    Through my great sin." Then spake he some
    sweet word,
Giving me cheer; which thing availed me not;

Yea, scarce I wist if such indeed were said;
For when I ceased—lo, as one newly dead
    Who hears a great cry out of hell, I heard
The crying of his voice across my head.

"Until this dry shred staff, that hath no whit
Of leaf nor bark, bear blossom and smell sweet,   370
    Seek thou not any mercy in God's sight,
For so long shalt thou be cast out from it."

Yea, what if dried-up stems wax red and green,
Shall that thing be which is not nor has been?
    Yea, what if sapless bark wax green and
    white,
Shall any good fruit grow upon my sin?

Nay, though sweet fruit were plucked of a dry
    tree,
And though men drew sweet waters of the sea,
    There should not grow sweet leaves on this
    dead stem,
This waste wan body and shaken soul of me.   380

Yea, though God search it warily enough,
There is not one sound thing in all thereof;
    Though he search all my veins through,
    searching them
He shall find nothing whole therein but love.

For I came home right heavy, with small cheer,
And lo my love, mine own soul's heart, more
    dear
    Than mine own soul, more beautiful than
    God,
Who hath my being between the hands of
    her—

Fair still, but fair for no man saving me,
As when she came out of the naked sea[15]   390

[13] The first pope, the apostle Peter, was given the power to forgive sins at the same time he was named by Christ as the head of his church: "And I say also unto thee, That thou art Peter, and upon this rock I will build my church; and the gates of hell shall not prevail against it. And I will give unto thee the keys of the kingdom of heaven: and whatsoever thou shalt bind on earth shall be bound in heaven: and whatsoever thou shalt loose on earth shall be loosed in heaven" (Matthew 16:18–19).

[14] "Can the Ethiopian change his skin, or the leopard his spots? then may ye also do good, that are accustomed to evil" (Jeremiah 13:23).

[15] Venus was born from the foam of the sea.

Making the foam as fire whereon she trod,
And as the inner flower of fire was she.

Yea, she laid hold upon me, and her mouth
Clove unto mine as soul to body doth,
    And, laughing, made her lips luxurious;
Her hair had smells of all the sunburnt south,

Strange spice and flower, strange savour of
        crushed fruit,
And perfume the swart kings tread underfoot
    For pleasure when their minds wax amorous,
400 Charred frankincense and grated sandal-root.

And I forgot fear and all weary things,
All ended prayers and perished thanksgivings,
    Feeling her face with all her eager hair
Cleave to me, clinging as a fire that clings

To the body and to the raiment, burning
        them;
As after death I know that such-like flame
    Shall cleave to me for ever; yea, what care,
Albeit I burn then, having felt the same?

Ah love, there is no better life than this;
410 To have known love, how bitter a thing it is,
    And afterward be cast out of God's sight:
Yea, these that know not, shall they have such
        bliss

High up in barren heaven before his face
As we twain in the heavy-hearted place,
    Remembering love and all the dead delight,
And all that time was sweet with for a space?

For till the thunder in the trumpet be,
Soul may divide from body, but not we
    One from another; I hold thee with my
        hand,
420 I let mine eyes have all their will of thee,

I seal myself upon thee with my might,
Abiding alway out of all men's sight
    Until God loosen over sea and land
The thunder of the trumpets of the night.

                EXPLICIT LAUS VENERIS.[16]

                                            1866

The Triumph of Time[1]

Before our lives divide for ever,
    While time is with us and hands are free,
(Time, swift to fasten and swift to sever
    Hand from hand, as we stand by the sea)
I will say no word that a man might say
Whose whole life's love goes down in a day;
For this could never have been; and never,
    Though the gods and the years relent, shall
    be.

Is it worth a tear, is it worth an hour,
    To think of things that are well outworn?   10
Of fruitless husk and fugitive flower,
    The dream foregone and the deed forborne?
Though joy be done with and grief be vain,
Time shall not sever us wholly in twain;
Earth is not spoilt for a single shower;
    But the rain has ruined the ungrown corn.[2]

It will grow not again, this fruit of my heart,
    Smitten with sunbeams, ruined with rain.
The singing seasons divide and depart,
    Winter and summer depart in twain.   20
It will grow not again, it is ruined at root,
The bloodlike blossom, the dull red fruit;
Though the heart yet sickens, the lips yet
        smart,
    With sullen savour of poisonous pain.

I have given no man of my fruit to eat;
    I trod the grapes, I have drunken the wine.
Had you eaten and drunken and found it
        sweet,
    This wild new growth of the corn and vine,
This wine and bread without lees or leaven,
We had grown as gods, as the gods in heaven, 30
Souls fair to look upon, goodly to greet,
    One splendid spirit, your soul and mine.

In the change of years, in the coil of things,
    In the clamour and rumour of life to be,
We, drinking love at the furthest springs,
    Covered with love as a covering tree,

---

[16] Here ends the praise of Venus.
[1] Swinburne's early biographers assumed that the occasion of this poem was a rejected pro-
posal of marriage. Cecil Lang, in an essay in *Publications of the Modern Language Association*,
74 (1959), 123–30, suggests more plausibly that the poem deals with his love for and separation
from his cousin Mary Gordon, who married an army colonel in 1865. Lang's suggestion is greatly
elaborated in Jean Overton Fuller's biography, *Swinburne* (London, 1968).
[2] Corn: grain.

We had grown as gods, as the gods above,[3]
Filled from the heart to the lips with love,
Held fast in his hands, clothed warm with his
    wings,
40   O love, my love, had you loved but me!

We had stood as the sure stars stand, and
    moved
    As the moon moves, loving the world; and
      seen
Grief collapse as a thing disproved,
    Death consume as a thing unclean.
Twain halves of a perfect heart, made fast
Soul to soul while the years fell past;
Had you loved me once, as you have not loved;
    Had the chance been with us that has not
      been.

I have put my days and dreams out of mind,
50   Days that are over, dreams that are done.
Though we seek life through, we shall surely
    find
    There is none of them clear to us now, not
      one.
But clear are these things; the grass and the
    sand,
Where, sure as the eyes reach, ever at hand,
With lips wide open and face burnt blind,
    The strong sea-daisies feast on the sun.

The low downs lean to the sea; the stream,
    One loose thin pulseless tremulous vein,
Rapid and vivid and dumb as a dream,
    Works downward, sick of the sun and the
60   rain;
No wind is rough with the rank rare flowers;
The sweet sea, mother of loves and hours,
Shudders and shines as the grey winds gleam,
    Turning her smile to a fugitive pain.

Mother of loves that are swift to fade,
    Mother of mutable winds and hours.
A barren mother, a mother-maid,
    Cold and clean as her faint salt flowers.
I would we twain were even as she,
70 Lost in the night and the light of the sea,
Where faint sounds falter and wan beams
    wade,
    Break, and are broken, and shed into
      showers.

The loves and hours of the life of a man,
    They are swift and sad, being born of the
      sea.
Hours that rejoice and regret for a span,
    Born with a man's breath, mortal as he;
Loves that are lost ere they come to birth,
Weeds of the wave, without fruit upon earth.
I lose what I long for, save what I can,
    My love, my love, and no love for me!   80

It is not much that a man can save
    On the sands of life, in the straits of time,
Who swims in sight of the great third wave[4]
    That never a swimmer shall cross or climb.
Some waif washed up with the strays and spars
That ebb-tide shows to the shore and the stars;
Weed from the water, grass from a grave,
    A broken blossom, a ruined rhyme.

There will no man do for your sake, I think,
    What I would have done for the least word
      said.   90
I had wrung life dry for your lips to drink,
    Broken it up for your daily bread:
Body for body and blood for blood,
As the flow of the full sea risen to flood
That yearns and trembles before it sink,
    I had given, and lain down for you, glad and
      dead.

Yea, hope at highest and all her fruit,
    And time at fullest and all his dower,
I had given you surely, and life to boot,
    Were we once made one for a single hour.   100
But now, you are twain, you are cloven apart,
Flesh of his flesh, but heart of my heart;
And deep in one is the bitter root,
    And sweet for one is the lifelong flower.

To have died if you cared I should die for you,
    clung
    To my life if you bade me, played my part
As it pleased you—these were the thoughts that
    stung,
    The dreams that smote with a keener dart
Than shafts of love or arrows of death;
These were but as fire is, dust, or breath,   110
Or poisonous foam on the tender tongue
    Of the little snakes that eat my heart.

---

[3] "And the serpent said unto the woman, Ye shall not surely die: For God doth know that in the day ye eat thereof, then your eyes shall be opened, and ye shall be as gods, knowing good and evil" (Genesis 3:4–5).

[4] Great third wave: in popular belief every third wave was larger than the two preceding.

I wish we were dead together to-day,
   Lost sight of, hidden away out of sight,
Clasped and clothed in the cloven clay,
   Out of the world's way, out of the light,
Out of the ages of worldly weather,
Forgotten of all men altogether,
As the world's first dead, taken wholly away,
120   Made one with death, filled full of the night.

How we should slumber, how we should sleep,
   Far in the dark with the dreams and the
     dews!
And dreaming, grow to each other, and weep,
   Laugh low, live softly, murmur and muse;
Yea, and it may be, struck through by the
   dream,
Feel the dust quicken and quiver, and seem
Alive as of old to the lips, and leap
   Spirit to spirit as lovers use.

Sick dreams and sad of a dull delight;
130   For what shall it profit when men are dead
To have dreamed, to have loved with the
   whole soul's might,
   To have looked for day when the day was
     fled?
Let come what will, there is one thing worth,
To have had fair love in the life upon earth:
To have held love safe till the day grew night,
   While skies had colour and lips were red.

Would I lose you now? would I take you then,
   If I lose you now that my heart has need?
And come what may after death to men,
   What thing worth this will the dead years
140   breed?
Lose life, lose all; but at least I know,
O sweet life's love, having loved you so,
Had I reached you on earth, I should lose not
   again,
   In death nor life, nor in dream or deed.

Yea, I know this well: were you once sealed
   mine,
   Mine in the blood's beat, mine in the breath,
Mixed into me as honey in wine,
   Not time, that sayeth and gainsayeth,
Nor all strong things had severed us then;
150   Not wrath of gods, nor wisdom of men,

Nor all things earthly, nor all divine,
   Nor joy nor sorrow, nor life nor death.

I had grown pure as the dawn and the dew,
   You had grown strong as the sun or the sea.
But none shall triumph a whole life through:
   For death is one, and the fates are three.[5]
At the door of life, by the gate of breath,
There are worse things waiting for men than
   death;
Death could not sever my soul and you,
   As these have severed your soul from me.   160

You have chosen and clung to the chance they
   sent you,
   Life sweet as perfume and pure as prayer.
But will it not one day in heaven repent you?
   Will they solace you wholly, the days that
     were?
Will you lift up your eyes between sadness and
   bliss,
Meet mine, and see where the great love is,
And tremble and turn and be changed?
   Content you;
   The gate is strait; I shall not be there.[6]

But you, had you chosen, had you stretched
   hand,
   Had you seen good such a thing were done,   170
I too might have stood with the souls that
   stand
   In the sun's sight, clothed with the light of
     the sun;
But who now on earth need care how I live?
Have the high gods anything left to give,
Save dust and laurels and gold and sand?
   Which gifts are goodly; but I will none.

O all fair lovers about the world,
   There is none of you, none, that shall
    comfort me.
My thoughts are as dead things, wrecked and
   whirled
   Round and round in a gulf of the sea;   180
And still, through the sound and the straining
   stream,
Through the coil and chafe, they gleam in a
   dream,
The bright fine lips so cruelly curled,

---

[5] In classical mythology three fates spun the thread of human events, cutting it when they
pleased.

[6] "Strive to enter in at the strait gate: for many, I say unto you, will seek to enter in, and shall
not be able. When once the master of the house is risen up, and hath shut to the door, and ye
begin to stand without, and to knock at the door, saying, Lord, Lord, open unto us; and he shall
answer and say unto you, I know not whence ye are" (Luke 13:24-25).

And strange swift eyes where the soul sits
free.

Free, without pity, withheld from woe,
  Ignorant; fair as the eyes are fair.
Would I have you change now, change at a
  blow,
  Startled and stricken, awake and aware?
Yea, if I could, would I have you see
190 My very love of you filling me,
And know my soul to the quick, as I know
  The likeness and look of your throat and
  hair?

I shall not change you. Nay, though I might,
  Would I change my sweet one love with a
  word?
I had rather your hair should change in a
  night,
  Clear now as the plume of a black bright
  bird;
Your face fail suddenly, cease, turn grey,
Die as a leaf that dies in a day.
I will keep my soul in a place out of sight,
200 Far off, where the pulse of it is not heard.

Far off it walks, in a bleak blown space,
  Full of the sound of the sorrow of years.
I have woven a veil for the weeping face,
  Whose lips have drunken the wine of tears;
I have found a way for the failing feet,
A place for slumber and sorrow to meet;
There is no rumour about the place,
  Nor light, nor any that sees or hears.

I have hidden my soul out of sight, and said
210 "Let none take pity upon thee, none
Comfort thy crying: for lo, thou art dead,
  Lie still now, safe out of sight of the sun.
Have I not built thee a grave, and wrought
Thy grave-clothes on thee of grievous thought,
With soft spun verses and tears unshed,
  And sweet light visions of things undone?

"I have given thee garments and balm and
  myrrh,
  And gold, and beautiful burial things.
But thou, be at peace now, make no stir;
220 Is not thy grave as a royal king's?
Fret not thyself though the end were sore;
Sleep, be patient, vex me no more.
Sleep; what hast thou to do with her?

The eyes that weep, with the mouth that
  sings?"

Where the dead red leaves of the years lie
  rotten,
  The cold old crimes and the deeds thrown
  by,
The misconceived and the misbegotten,
  I would find a sin to do ere I die,
Sure to dissolve and destroy me all through,
That would set you higher in heaven, serve
  you   230
And leave you happy, when clean forgotten,
  As a dead man out of mind, am I.

Your lithe hands draw me, your face burns
  through me,
  I am swift to follow you, keen to see;
But love lacks might to redeem or undo me;
  As I have been, I know I shall surely be;
"What should such fellows as I do?"[7] Nay,
My part were worse if I chose to play;
For the worst is this after all; if they knew me,
  Not a soul upon earth would pity me.   240

And I play not for pity of these; but you,
  If you saw with your soul what man am I,
You would praise me at least that my soul all
  through
  Clove to you, loathing the lives that lie;
The souls and lips that are bought and sold,
The smiles of silver and kisses of gold,
The lapdog loves that whine as they chew,
  The little lovers that curse and cry.

There are fairer women, I hear; that may be;
  But I, that I love you and find you fair,   250
Who are more than fair in my eyes if they be,
  Do the high gods know or the great gods
  care?
Though the swords in my heart for one were
  seven,
Would the iron hollow of doubtful heaven,
That knows not itself whether night-time or
  day be,
  Reverberate words and a foolish prayer?

I will go back to the great sweet mother,
  Mother and lover of men, the sea.
I will go down to her, I and none other,
  Close with her, kiss her and mix her with
  me;   260

---

[7] "What should such fellows as I do": from *Hamlet,* III, i. Spoken by Hamlet as he tells
Ophelia to part from him, though he loved her once.

Cling to her, strive with her, hold her fast:
O fair white mother, in days long past
Born without sister, born without brother,
    Set free my soul as thy soul is free.

O fair green-girdled mother of mine,
    Sea, that art clothed with the sun and the
    rain,
Thy sweet hard kisses are strong like wine,
    Thy large embraces are keen like pain.
Save me and hide me with all thy waves,
270   Find me one grave of thy thousand graves,
Those pure cold populous graves of thine
    Wrought without hand in a world without
    stain.

I shall sleep, and move with the moving ships,
    Change as the winds change, veer in the tide;
My lips will feast on the foam of thy lips,
    I shall rise with thy rising, with thee subside;
Sleep, and not know if she be, if she were,
Filled full with life to the eyes and hair,
As a rose is fulfilled to the roseleaf tips
    With splendid summer and perfume and
280   pride.

This woven raiment of nights and days,
    Were it once cast off and unwound from me,
Naked and glad would I walk in thy ways,
    Alive and aware of thy ways and thee;
Clear of the whole world, hidden at home,
Clothed with the green and crowned with the
    foam,
A pulse of the life of thy straits and bays,
    A vein in the heart of the streams of the sea.

Fair mother, fed with the lives of men,
290   Thou are subtle and cruel of heart, men say.
Thou hast taken, and shalt not render again;
    Thou art full of thy dead, and cold as they.
But death is the worst that comes of thee;
Thou art fed with our dead, O mother, O sea,
But when hast thou fed on our hearts? or when,
    Having given us love, hast thou taken away?

O tender-hearted, O perfect lover,
    Thy lips are bitter, and sweet thine heart.
The hopes that hurt and the dreams that
    hover,
300   Shall they not vanish away and apart?
But thou, thou art sure, thou art older than
    earth;[8]

Thou art strong for death and fruitful of birth;
Thy depths conceal and thy gulfs discover;
    From the first thou wert; in the end thou art.

And grief shall endure not for ever, I know.
    As things that are not shall these things be;
We shall live through seasons of sun and of
    snow,
    And none be grievous as this to me.
We shall hear, as one in a trance that hears,
The sound of time, the rhyme of the years;   310
Wrecked hope and passionate pain will grow
    As tender things of a spring-tide sea.

Sea-fruit that swings in the waves that hiss,
    Drowned gold and purple and royal rings.
And all time past, was it all for this?
    Times unforgotten, and treasures of things?
Swift years of liking and sweet long laughter,
That wist not well of the years thereafter
Till love woke, smitten at heart by a kiss,
    With lips that trembled and trailing wings?   320

There lived a singer in France of old
    By the tideless dolorous midland sea.
In a land of sand and ruin and gold
    There shone one woman, and none but she.
And finding life for her love's sake fail,
Being fain to see her, he bade set sail,
Touched land, and saw her as life grew cold,
    And praised God, seeing; and so died he.[9]

Died, praising God for his gift and grace:
    For she bowed down to him weeping, and
        said   330
"Live;" and her tears were shed on his face
    Or ever the life in his face was shed.
The sharp tears fell through her hair, and stung
Once, and her close lips touched him and clung
Once, and grew one with his lips for a space;
    And so drew back, and the man was dead.

O brother, the gods were good to you.
    Sleep, and be glad while the world endures.
Be well content as the years wear through;
    Give thanks for life, and the loves and lures;   340
Give thanks for life, O brother, and death,
For the sweet last sound of her feet, her breath,
For gifts she gave you, gracious and few,
    Tears and kisses, that lady of yours.

[8] In Genesis 1:1–10 the existence of the waters precedes the creation of the dry land.
[9] Geoffrey Rudel, a twelfth-century Provençal poet, according to legend fell in love with a countess upon hearing her praises, and he sailed to see her before he died.

Rest, and be glad of the gods; but I,
 How shall I praise them, or how take rest?
There is not room under all the sky
 For me that know not of worst or best,
50 Dream or desire of the days before,
Sweet things or bitterness, any more.
Love will not come to me now though I die,
 As love came close to you, breast to breast.

I shall never be friends again with roses;
 I shall loathe sweet tunes, where a note
  grown strong
Relents and recoils, and climbs and closes,
 As a wave of the sea turned back by song.
There are sounds where the soul's delight takes
 fire,
Face to face with its own desire;
A delight that rebels, a desire that reposes;
60 I shall hate sweet music my whole life long.

The pulse of war and passion of wonder,
 The heavens that murmur, the sounds that
  shine,
The stars that sing and the loves that thunder,
 The music burning at heart like wine,
An armed archangel whose hands raise up
All senses mixed in the spirit's cup
Till flesh and spirit are molten in sunder—
 These things are over, and no more mine.

These were a part of the playing I heard
 Once, ere my love and my heart were at
70 strife;
Love that sings and hath wings as a bird,
 Balm of the wound and heft of the knife.
Fairer than earth is the sea, and sleep
Than overwatching of eyes that weep,
Now time has done with his one sweet word,
 The wine and leaven of lovely life.

I shall go my ways, tread out my measure,
 Fill the days of my daily breath
With fugitive things not good to treasure,
80 Do as the world doth, say as it saith;
But if we had loved each other—O sweet,
Had you felt, lying under the palms of your
 feet,
The heart of my heart, beating harder with
 pleasure
 To feel you tread it to dust and death—

Ah, had I not taken my life up and given
 All that life gives and the years let go,
The wine and honey, the balm and leaven,
 The dreams reared high and the hopes
  brought low?

Come life, come death, not a word be said;
Should I lose you living, and vex you dead?   390
I never shall tell you on earth; and in heaven,
 If I cry to you then, will you hear or know?
    1866

A Leave-Taking

Let us go hence, my songs; she will not hear.
Let us go hence together without fear;
Keep silence now, for singing-time is over,
And over all old things and all things dear.
She loves not you nor me as all we love her.
Yea, though we sang as angels in her ear,
 She would not hear.

Let us rise up and part; she will not know.
Let us go seaward as the great winds go,
Full of blown sand and foam; what help is
 here?   10
There is no help, for all these things are so,
And all the world is bitter as a tear.
And how these things are, though ye strove to
 show,
 She would not know.

Let us go home and hence; she will not weep.
We gave love many dreams and days to keep,
Flowers without scent, and fruits that would
 not grow,
Saying "If thou wilt, thrust in thy sickle and
 reap."
All is reaped now; no grass is left to mow;
And we that sowed, though all we fell on sleep,   20
 She would not weep.

Let us go hence and rest; she will not love.
She shall not hear us if we sing hereof,
Nor see love's ways, how sore they are and
 steep.
Come hence, let be, lie still; it is enough.
Love is a barren sea, bitter and deep;
And though she saw all heaven in flower
 above,
 She would not love.

Let us give up, go down; she will not care.
Though all the stars made gold of all the air,   30
And the sea moving saw before it move
One moon-flower making all the foam-flowers
 fair;
Though all those waves went over us, and
 drove

Deep down the stifling lips and drowning hair,
    She would not care.

Let us go hence, go hence; she will not see.
Sing all once more together; surely she,
She too, remembering days and words that
    were,
Will turn a little toward us, sighing; but we,
We are hence, we are gone, as though we had
40   not been there.
Nay, and though all men seeing had pity on
    me,
    She would not see.

                   1866

Hymn to Proserpine[1]

(After the Proclamation in Rome of the Christian Faith)

Vicisti, Galilæe

I have lived long enough, having seen one
    thing, that love hath an end;
Goddess and maiden and queen, be near me
    now and befriend.
Thou art more than the day or the morrow,
    the seasons that laugh or that weep;
For these give joy and sorrow; but thou,
    Proserpina, sleep.
Sweet is the treading of wine, and sweet the
    feet of the dove;
But a goodlier gift is thine than foam of the
    grapes or love.
Yea, is not even Apollo,[2] with hair and
    harpstring of gold,
A bitter God to follow, a beautiful God to be-
    hold?
I am sick of singing: the bays[3] burn deep and
    chafe: I am fain
To rest a little from praise and grievous
10   pleasure and pain.
For the Gods we know not of, who give us our
    daily breath,
We know they are cruel as love or life, and
    lovely as death.

O Gods dethroned and deceased, cast forth,
    wiped out in a day
From your wrath is the world released,
    redeemed from your chains, men say.
New Gods are crowned in the city; their
    flowers have broken your rods;
They are merciful, clothed with pity, the young
    compassionate Gods.
But for me their new device is barren, the days
    are bare;
Things long past over suffice, and men
    forgotten that were.
Time and the Gods are at strife; ye dwell in the
    midst thereof,
Draining a little life from the barren breasts
    of love.
I say to you, cease, take rest; yea, I say to you
    all, be at peace,
Till the bitter milk of her breast and the
    barren bosom shall cease.
Wilt thou yet take all, Galilean? but these
    thou shalt not take,
The laurel, the palms and the pæan, the breasts
    of the nymphs in the brake;[4]
Breasts more soft than a dove's, that tremble
    with tenderer breath;
And all the wings of the Loves, and all the joy
    before death;
All the feet of the hours that sound as a single
    lyre,
Dropped and deep in the flowers, with strings
    that flicker like fire.
More than these wilt thou give, things fairer
    than all these things?
Nay, for a little we live, and life hath mutable
    wings.
A little while and we die; shall life not thrive
    as it may?
For no man under the sky lives twice,
    outliving his day.
And grief is a grievous thing, and a man hath
    enough of his tears:
Why should he labour, and bring fresh grief to
    blacken his years?

---

[1] Proserpine (Persephone) was the classical goddess of growing things. She was carried into the underworld by Pluto, but the entreaties of her mother Ceres (Demeter), the goddess of agriculture and fertility, won an agreement that Proserpine could return to the surface of the earth for six months each year.
   The epigraph of the poem means "Thou hast conquered, Galilean," words attributed to the Roman emperor Julian the Apostate (331–363), who had abandoned Christianity and tried to resist its advances after it was recognized by the emperor Constantine in 313.
  [2] Apollo: the classical god of song.
  [3] Bays: a crown of bay leaves was a traditional prize and adornment of a poet.
  [4] Brake: fern.

Thou hast conquered, O pale Galilean; the
world has grown grey from thy breath;
We have drunken of things Lethean,[5] and fed
on the fullness of death.
Laurel is green for a season, and love is sweet
for a day;
But love grows bitter with treason, and laurel
outlives not May.
Sleep, shall we sleep after all? for the world is
not sweet in the end;
For the old faiths loosen and fall, the new years
ruin and rend.
Fate is a sea without shore, and the soul is a
rock that abides;
But her ears are vexed with the roar and her
face with the foam of the tides.
O lips that the live blood faints in, the leavings
of racks and rods![6]
O ghastly glories of saints, dead limbs of
gibbeted Gods!
Though all men abase them before you in
spirit, and all knees bend,
I kneel not neither adore you, but standing,
look to the end.
All delicate days and pleasant, all spirits and
sorrows are cast
Far out with the foam of the present that
sweeps to the surf of the past:
Where beyond the extreme sea-wall, and
between the remote sea-gates,
Waste water washes, and tall ships founder,
and deep death waits:
Where, mighty with deepening sides, clad
about with the seas as with wings,
And impelled of invisible tides, and fulfilled
of unspeakable things,
White-eyed and poisonous-finned, shark-
toothed and serpentine-curled,
Rolls, under the whitening wind of the future,
the wave of the world.
The depths stand naked in sunder behind it,
the storms flee away;
In the hollow before it the thunder is taken
and snared as a prey;
In its sides is the north-wind bound; and its
salt is of all men's tears;
With light of ruin, and sound of changes, and
pulse of years:
With travail of day after day, and with trouble
of hour upon hour;

And bitter as blood is the spray; and the crests
are as fangs that devour:
And its vapour and storm of its steam as the
sighing of spirits to be;
And its noise as the noise in a dream; and its
depth as the roots of the sea:
And the height of its heads as the height of
the utmost stars of the air:
And the ends of the earth at the might thereof
tremble, and time is made bare.
Will ye bridle the deep sea with reins, will ye
chasten the high sea with rods?
Will ye take her to chain her with chains, who
is older than all ye Gods?
All ye as a wind shall go by, as a fire shall ye
pass and be past;
Ye are Gods, and behold, ye shall die, and the
waves be upon you at last.
In the darkness of time, in the deeps of the
years, in the changes of things,
Ye shall sleep as a slain man sleeps, and the
world shall forget you for kings.
Though the feet of thine high priests tread
where thy lords and our forefathers trod,
Though these that were Gods are dead, and
thou being dead art a God,
Though before thee the throned Cytherean[7] be
fallen, and hidden her head,
Yet thy kingdom shall pass, Galilean, thy dead
shall go down to thee dead.
Of the maiden thy mother men sing as a
goddess with grace clad around;
Thou art throned where another was king;
where another was queen she is crowned.
Yea, once we had sight of another: but now
she is queen, say these.
Not as thine, not as thine was our mother, a
blossom of flowering seas,
Clothed round with the world's desire as with
raiment, and fair as the foam,
And fleeter than kindled fire, and a goddess,
and mother of Rome.
For thine came pale and a maiden, and sister
to sorrow; but ours,
Her deep hair heavily laden with odour and
colour of flowers,
White rose of the rose-white water, a silver
splendour, a flame,
Bent down unto us that besought her, and
earth grew sweet with her name.

[5] Lethean: a river in the underworld whose waters when drunk cause forgetfulness.
[6] Racks and rods: instruments of torture; references here, and in "gibbeted Gods" in the next line, to the persecutions of the Christians in Rome and to the crucifixion of Christ.
[7] Cytherean: Venus (Aphrodite), the goddess of love, born of sea-foam off the island of Cythera in the Ionian sea. Venus was the mother of Aeneas, the founder of Rome (line 8o).

For thine came weeping, a slave among slaves,
and rejected; but she
Came flushed from the full-flushed wave, and
imperial, her foot on the sea.
And the wonderful waters knew her, the winds
and the viewless ways,
And the roses grew rosier, and bluer the
sea-blue stream of the bays.
Ye are fallen, our lords, by what token? we wist
that ye should not fall.
90 Ye were all so fair that are broken; and one
more fair than ye all.
But I turn to her still, having seen she shall
surely abide in the end;
Goddess and maiden and queen, be near me
now and befriend.
O daughter of earth, of my mother, her crown
and blossom of birth,
I am also, I also, thy brother; I go as I came
unto earth.
In the night where thine eyes are as moons are
in heaven, the night where thou art,
Where the silence is more than all tunes, where
sleep overflows from the heart,
Where the poppies are sweet as the rose in our
world, and the red rose is white,
And the wind falls faint as it blows with the
fume of the flowers of the night,
And the murmur of spirits that sleep in the
shadow of Gods from afar
100 Grows dim in thine ears and deep as the deep
dim soul of a star,
In the sweet low light of thy face, under
heavens untrod by the sun,
Let my soul with their souls find place, and
forget what is done and undone.
Thou art more than the Gods who number the
days of our temporal breath;
For these give labour and slumber; but thou,
Proserpina, death.
Therefore now at thy feet I abide for a season
in silence. I know
I shall die as my fathers died, and sleep as they
sleep; even so.
For the glass of the years is brittle wherein we
gaze for a span;

A little soul for a little bears up this corpse
which is man.[8]
So long I endure, no longer; and laugh not
again, neither weep.
For there is no God found stronger than death;
and death is a sleep.

1866

Hermaphroditus[1]

I

Lift up thy lips, turn round, look back for love,
   Blind love that comes by night and casts out
    rest;
   Of all things tired thy lips look weariest,
Save the long smile that they are wearied of.
Ah sweet, albeit no love be sweet enough,
   Choose of two loves and cleave unto the best;
   Two loves at either blossom of thy breast
Strive until one be under and one above.
Their breath is fire upon the amorous air,
   Fire in thine eyes and where thy lips suspire:
And whosoever hath seen thee, being so fair,
   Two things turn all his life and blood to fire;
A strong desire begot on great despair,
   A great despair cast out by strong desire.

II

Where between sleep and life some brief space
   is,
   With love like gold bound round about the
    head,
   Sex to sweet sex with lips and limbs is wed,
Turning the fruitful feud of hers and his
To the waste wedlock of a sterile kiss;
   Yet from them something like as fire is shed
   That shall not be assuaged till death be
    dead,
Though neither life nor sleep can find out this.
Love made himself of flesh that perisheth
   A pleasure-house for all the loves his kin;
But on the one side sat a man like death,
   And on the other a woman sat like sin.[2]
So with veiled eyes and sobs between his breath
   Love turned himself and would not enter in.

[8] Swinburne glossed this line with a sentence in Greek from the first-century philosopher Epictetus; its translation is, "Thou art a little soul bearing up a corpse."

[1] Swinburne appended a tag to this poem, "Au Musée du Louvre, Mars, 1863." Originally Hermaphroditus was a classical emblem of the union of sexes in marriage. The Roman poet Ovid in the first century before Christ told the story in which a creature with two sexes is the result of a union between a son of the gods Hermes and Aphrodite and a nymph, Salmacis. There were two statues of the Hermaphroditus in the Louvre in Paris.

[2] In Book II of Milton's *Paradise Lost* the entrance to hell is flanked by the monstrous shapes of Sin and Death.

III

Love, is it love or sleep or shadow or light
    That lies between thine eyelids and thine
        eyes?
Like a flower laid upon a flower it lies,
Or like the night's dew laid upon the night.
Love stands upon thy left hand and thy right,
    Yet by no sunset and by no moonrise
    Shall make thee man and ease a woman's
        sighs,
Or make thee woman for a man's delight.
To what strange end hath some strange god
        made fair
    The double blossom of two fruitless flowers?
Hid love in all the folds of all thy hair,
    Fed thee on summers, watered thee with
        showers,
Given all the gold that all the seasons wear
    To thee that art a thing of barren hours?

IV

Yea, love, I see; it is not love but fear.
    Nay, sweet, it is not fear but love, I know;
    Or wherefore should thy body's blossom blow
So sweetly, or thine eyelids leave so clear
Thy gracious eyes that never made a tear—
    Though for their love our tears like blood
        should flow,
    Though love and life and death should come
        and go,
So dreadful, so desirable, so dear?
Yea, sweet, I know; I saw in what swift wise
    Beneath the woman's and the water's kiss
    Thy moist limbs melted into Salmacis,
And the large light turned tender in thine
        eyes,
And all thy boy's breath softened into sighs;
    But Love being blind, how should he know
        of this?

                                            1866

A Song in Time of Order 1852[1]

Push hard across the sand,
    For the salt wind gathers breath;
Shoulder and wrist and hand,
    Push hard as the push of death.

The wind is as iron that rings,
    The foam-heads loosen and flee;
It swells and welters and swings,
    The pulse of the tide of the sea.

And up on the yellow cliff
    The long corn flickers and shakes;   10
Push, for the wind holds stiff,
    And the gunwale dips and rakes.

Good hap to the fresh fierce weather,
    The quiver and beat of the sea!
While three men hold together,
    The kingdoms are less by three.

Out to the sea with her there,
    Out with her over the sand;
Let the kings keep the earth for their share!
    We have done with the sharers of land.   20

They have tied the world in a tether,
    They have bought over God with a fee;
While three men hold together,
    The kingdoms are less by three.

We have done with the kisses that sting,
    The thief's mouth red from the feast,
The blood on the hands of the king
    And the lie at the lips of the priest.

Will they tie the winds in a tether,
    Put a bit in the jaws of the sea?   30
While three men hold together,
    The kingdoms are less by three.

Let our flag run out straight in the wind!
    The old red shall be floated again
When the ranks that are thin shall be thinned,
    When the names that were twenty are ten;

When the devil's riddle is mastered
    And the galley-bench creaks with a Pope,
We shall see Buonaparte the bastard
    Kick heels with his throat in a rope.   40

While the shepherd sets wolves on his sheep
    And the emperor halters his kine,
While Shame is a watchman asleep
    And Faith is a keeper of swine,

[1] This poem was probably written in the late 1850s. Its reference to 1852 is to the period of repression and consolidation of authority which followed the Continental revolutions of 1848. Specifically, Swinburne refers to the return of the pope to Italy in 1850, after fleeing the nationalist revolutionary forces in 1849, and to the election of Louis Napoleon ("Buonaparte the Bastard") as emperor of France in 1852. Louis Napoleon was the son of the brother of the first emperor Napoleon.

Let the wind shake our flag like a feather,
    Like the plumes of the foam of the sea!
While three men hold together,
    The kingdoms are less by three.

All the world has its burdens to bear,
50   From Cayenne to the Austrian whips;[2]
Forth, with the rain in our hair
    And the salt sweet foam in our lips;

In the teeth of the hard glad weather,
    In the blown wet face of the sea;
While three men hold together,
    The kingdoms are less by three.
                  1862; 1866

A Song in Time of Revolution 1860

The heart of the rulers is sick, and the
    high-priest covers his head:
For this is the song of the quick that is heard
    in the ears of the dead.

The poor and the halt and the blind are keen
    and mighty and fleet:
Like the noise of the blowing of wind is the
    sound of the noise of their feet.

The wind has the sound of a laugh in the
    clamour of days and of deeds:
The priests are scattered like chaff, and the
    rulers broken like reeds.

The high-priest sick from qualms, with his
    raiment bloodily dashed;
The thief with branded palms, and the liar
    with cheeks abashed.

They are smitten, they tremble greatly, they
    are pained for their pleasant things:
For the house of the priests made stately, and
10   the might in the mouth of the kings.

They are grieved and greatly afraid; they are
    taken, they shall not flee:
For the heart of the nations is made as the
    strength of the springs of the sea.

They were fair in the grace of gold, they walked
    with delicate feet:

They were clothed with the cunning of old,
    and the smell of their garments was sweet.

For the breaking of gold in their hair they halt
    as a man made lame:
They are utterly naked and bare; their mouths
    are bitter with shame.

Wilt thou judge thy people now, O king that
    wast found most wise?
Wilt thou lie any more, O thou whose mouth
    is emptied of lies?

Shall God make a pact with thee, till his hook
    be found in thy sides?
Wilt thou put back the time of the sea, or the
    place of the season of tides?   20

Set a word in thy lips, to stand before God with
    a word in thy mouth:
That "the rain shall return in the land, and
    the tender dew after drouth."

But the arm of the elders is broken, their
    strength is unbound and undone:
They wait for a sign of a token; they cry, and
    there cometh none.

Their moan is in every place, the cry of them
    filleth the land:
There is shame in the sight of their face, there
    is fear in the thews of their hand.

They are girdled about the reins with a curse
    for the girdle thereon:
For the noise of the rending of chains the face
    of their colour is gone.

For the sound of the shouting of men they are
    grievously stricken at heart:
They are smitten asunder with pain, their
    bones are smitten apart.   30

There is none of them all that is whole; their
    lips gape open for breath;
They are clothed with sickness of soul, and the
    shape of the shadow of death.

The wind is thwart in their feet; it is full of
    the shouting of mirth;
As one shaketh the sides of a sheet, so it shaketh
    the ends of the earth.

[2] Cayenne: a town in French Guiana in South America to which French political prisoners
were taken. Austrian whips: The Austrian government exercised authority in much of Italy until
about 1860.

The sword, the sword is made keen; the iron
    has opened its mouth;
The corn is red that was green; it is bound for
    the sheaves of the south.

The sound of a word was shed, the sound of
    the wind as a breath,
In the ears of the souls that were dead, in the
    dust of the deepness of death;

Where the face of the moon is taken, the ways
    of the stars undone,
The light of the whole sky shaken, the light of
    the face of the sun:

Where the waters are emptied and broken, the
    waves of the waters are stayed;
Where God has bound for a token the
    darkness that maketh afraid;

Where the sword was covered and hidden, and
    dust had grown in its side,
A word came forth which was bidden, the
    crying of one that cried:

The sides of the two-edged sword shall be bare,
    and its mouth shall be red,
For the breath of the face of the Lord that is
    felt in the bones of the dead.

              1862; 1866

In the pamphlet he published explaining the poems of the first series of Poems and Ballads, Notes on Poems and Reviews *(1866), Swinburne wrote of "Dolores": "I have striven here to express that transient state of spirit through which a man may be supposed to pass, foiled in love and weary of loving, but not yet in sight of rest; seeking refuge in those 'violent delights' which 'have violent ends,' in fierce and frank sensualities which at least profess to be no more than they are. . . . She is the darker Venus, fed with burnt-offering and blood-sacrifice; the veiled image of that pleasure which men impelled by satiety and perverted by power have sought through ways as strange as Nero's before and since his time; the daughter of lust and death . . . ; Our Lady of Pain, antagonist alike of trivial sins and virtues: no Virgin, and unblessed of men; no mother of the Gods or God."*

The Latin name of the central figure of the poem means "sorrows." The sorrows of Mary, the mother of Christ, were also seven, all associated with the ministry and death of her son.

Dolores

(Notre-Dame des Sept Douleurs)

Cold eyelids that hide like a jewel
    Hard eyes that grow soft for an hour;
The heavy white limbs, and the cruel
    Red mouth like a venomous flower;
When these are gone by with their glories,
    What shall rest of thee then, what remain,
O mystic and sombre Dolores,
    Our Lady of Pain?

Seven sorrows the priests give their Virgin;
    But thy sins, which are seventy times seven,   10
Seven ages would fail thee to purge in,
    And then they would haunt thee in heaven:
Fierce midnights and famishing morrows,
    And the loves that complete and control
All the joys of the flesh, all the sorrows
    That wear out the soul.

O garment not golden but gilded,
    O garden where all men may dwell,
O tower not of ivory,[1] but builded
    By hands that reach heaven from hell;   20
O mystical rose of the mire,
    O house not of gold but of gain,
O house of unquenchable fire,
    Our Lady of Pain!

O lips full of lust and of laughter,
    Curled snakes that are fed from my breast,
Bite hard, lest remembrance come after
    And press with new lips where you pressed.
For my heart too springs up at the pressure,
    Mine eyelids too moisten and burn;   30
Ah, feed me and fill me with pleasure,
    Ere pain come in turn.

In yesterday's reach and to-morrow's,
    Out of sight though they lie of to-day,
There have been and there yet shall be sorrows
    That smite not and bite not in play.
The life and the love thou despisest,
    These hurt us indeed, and in vain,
O wise among women, and wisest,
    Our Lady of Pain.   40

Who gave thee thy wisdom? what stories
    That stung thee, what visions that smote?
Wert thou pure and a maiden, Dolores,
    When desire took thee first by the throat?

[1] "Thy neck is as a tower of ivory" (Solomon 7:4).

What bud was the shell of a blossom
   That all men may smell to and pluck?
What milk fed thee first at what bosom?
   What sins gave thee suck?

We shift and bedeck and bedrape us,
50   Thou art noble and nude and antique;
Libitina thy mother, Priapus[2]
   Thy father, a Tuscan and Greek.
We play with light loves in the portal,
   And wince and relent and refrain;
Loves die, and we know thee immortal,
   Our Lady of Pain.

Fruits fail and love dies and time ranges;
   Thou art fed with perpetual breath,
And alive after infinite changes,
60   And fresh from the kisses of death;
Of languors rekindled and rallied,
   Of barren delights and unclean,
Things monstrous and fruitless, a pallid
   And poisonous queen.

Could you hurt me, sweet lips, though I hurt
    you?
   Men touch them, and change in a trice
The lilies and languors of virtue
   For the raptures and roses of vice;
Those lie where thy foot on the floor is;
70   These crown and caress thee and chain,
O splendid and sterile Dolores,
   Our Lady of Pain.

There are sins it may be to discover,
   There are deeds it may be to delight.
What new work wilt thou find for thy lover,
   What new passions for daytime or night?
What spells that they know not a word of
   Whose lives are as leaves overblown?
What tortures undreamt of, unheard of,
80   Unwritten, unknown?

Ah beautiful passionate body
   That never has ached with a heart!
On thy mouth though the kisses are bloody,
   Though they sting till it shudder and smart,
More kind than the love we adore is,
   They hurt not the heart or the brain,
O bitter and tender Dolores,
   Our Lady of Pain.

As our kisses relax and redouble,
   From the lips and the foam and the fangs   90
Shall no new sin be born for men's trouble,
   No dream of impossible pangs?
With the sweet of the sins of old ages
   Wilt thou satiate thy soul as of yore?
Too sweet is the rind, say the sages,
   Too bitter the core.

Hast thou told all thy secrets the last time,
   And bared all thy beauties to one?
Ah, where shall we go then for pastime,
   If the worst that can be has been done?   100
But sweet as the rind was the core is;
   We are fain of thee still, we are fain,
O sanguine and subtle Dolores,
   Our Lady of Pain.

By the hunger of change and emotion,
   By the thirst of unbearable things,
By despair, the twin-born of devotion,
   By the pleasure that winces and stings,
The delight that consumes the desire,
   The desire that outruns the delight,   110
By the cruelty deaf as a fire
   And blind as the night,

By the ravenous teeth that have smitten
   Through the kisses that blossom and bud,
By the lips intertwisted and bitten
   Till the foam has a savour of blood,
By the pulse as it rises and falters,
   By the hands as they slacken and strain,
I adjure thee, respond from thine altars,
   Our Lady of Pain.   120

Wilt thou smile as a woman disdaining
   The light fire in the veins of a boy?
But he comes to thee sad, without feigning,
   Who has wearied of sorrow and joy;
Less careful of labour and glory
   Than the elders whose hair has uncurled;
And young, but with fancies as hoary
   And grey as the world.

I have passed from the outermost portal
   To the shrine where a sin is a prayer;   130
What care though the service be mortal?
   O our Lady of Torture, what care?
All thine the last wine that I pour is,
   The last in the chalice we drain,

---

[2] Libitina: an ancient Italian goddess of burial, later associated with Proserpine, the goddess
of fertility and growing things, and thus with sexual pleasure. Priapus: a classical god of male
generative potency, often depicted in phallic forms.

O fierce and luxurious Dolores,
  Our Lady of Pain.

All thine the new wine of desire,
  The fruit of four lips as they clung
Till the hair and the eyelids took fire,
140 The foam of a serpentine tongue,
The froth of the serpents of pleasure,
  More salt than the foam of the sea,
Now felt as a flame, now at leisure
  As wine shed for me.

Ah thy people, thy children, thy chosen,
  Marked cross from the womb and perverse!
They have found out the secret to cozen
  The gods that constrain us and curse;
They alone, they are wise, and none other;
150 Give me place, even me, in their train,
O my sister, my spouse, and my mother,
  Our Lady of Pain.

For the crown of our life as it closes
  Is darkness, the fruit thereof dust;
No thorns go as deep as a rose's,
  And love is more cruel than lust.
Time turns the old days to derision,
  Our loves into corpses or wives;
And marriage and death and division
160 Make barren our lives.

And pale from the past we draw nigh thee,
  And satiate with comfortless hours;
And we know thee, how all men belie thee,
  And we gather the fruit of thy flowers;
The passion that slays and recovers,
  The pangs and the kisses that rain
On the lips and the limbs of thy lovers,
  Our Lady of Pain.

The desire of thy furious embraces
170 Is more than the wisdom of years,
On the blossom though blood lie in traces,
  Though the foliage be sodden with tears.
For the lords in whose keeping the door is
  That opens on all who draw breath
Gave the cypress to love, my Dolores,
  The myrtle to death.[3]

And they laughed, changing hands in the
    measure,
  And they mixed and made peace after strife;
Pain melted in tears, and was pleasure;

Death tingled with blood, and was life.   180
Like lovers they melted and tingled,
  In the dusk of thine innermost fane;[4]
In the darkness they murmured and mingled,
  Our Lady of Pain.

In a twilight where virtues are vices,
  In thy chapels, unknown of the sun,
To a tune that enthralls and entices,
  They were wed, and the twain were as one.
For the tune from thine altar hath sounded
  Since God bade the world's work begin,   190
And the fume of thine incense abounded,
  To sweeten the sin.

Love listens, and paler than ashes,
  Through his curls as the crown on them
    slips,
Lifts languid wet eyelids and lashes,
  And laughs with insatiable lips.
Thou shalt hush him with heavy caresses,
  With music that scares the profane;
Thou shalt darken his eyes with thy tresses,
  Our Lady of Pain.   200

Thou shalt blind his bright eyes though he
    wrestle,
  Thou shalt chain his light limbs though he
    strive;
In his lips all thy serpents shall nestle,
  In his hands all thy cruelties thrive.
In the daytime thy voice shall go through him,
  In his dreams he shall feel thee and ache;
Thou shalt kindle by night and subdue him
  Asleep and awake.

Thou shalt touch and make redder his roses
  With juice not of fruit nor of bud;   210
When the sense in the spirit reposes,
  Thou shalt quicken the soul through the
    blood.
Thine, thine the one grace we implore is,
  Who would live and not languish or feign,
O sleepless and deadly Dolores,
  Our Lady of Pain.

Dost thou dream, in a respite of slumber,
  In a lull of the fires of thy life,
Of the days without name, without number,
  When thy will stung the world into strife;   220
When, a goddess, the pulse of thy passion
  Smote kings as they revelled in Rome;

---

[3] Conventionally the cypress is associated with death, and the myrtle with Venus and love.
[4] Fane: temple.

And they hailed thee re-risen, O Thalassian,[5]
   Foam-white, from the foam?

When thy lips had such lovers to flatter;
   When the city lay red from thy rods,
And thine hands were as arrows to scatter
   The children of change and their gods;[6]
When the blood of thy foemen made fervent
230   A sand never moist from the main,
As one smote them, their lord and thy servant,
   Our Lady of Pain.

On sands by the storm never shaken,
   Nor wet from the washing of tides;
Nor by foam of the waves overtaken,
   Nor winds that the thunder bestrides;
But red from the print of thy paces,
   Made smooth for the world and its lords,
Ringed round with a flame of fair faces,
240   And splendid with swords.

There the gladiator, pale for thy pleasure,
   Drew bitter and perilous breath;
There torments laid hold on the treasure
   Of limbs too delicious for death;
When thy gardens were lit with live torches;
   When the world was a steed for thy rein;
When the nations lay prone in thy porches,
   Our Lady of Pain.

When, with flame all around him aspirant,
250   Stood flushed, as a harp-player stands,
The implacable beautiful tyrant,
   Rose-crowned, having death in his hands;
And a sound as the sound of loud water
   Smote far through the flight of the fires,
And mixed with the lightning of slaughter
   A thunder of lyres.

Dost thou dream of what was and no more is,
   The old kingdoms of earth and the kings?
Dost thou hunger for these things, Dolores,
260   For these, in a world of new things?
But thy bosom no fasts could emaciate,
   No hunger compel to complain

Those lips that no bloodshed could satiate,
   Our Lady of Pain.

As of old when the world's heart was lighter,
   Through thy garments the grace of thee
     glows,
The white wealth of thy body made whiter
   By the blushes of amorous blows,
And seamed with sharp lips and fierce fingers,
   And branded by kisses that bruise;   270
When all shall be gone that now lingers,
   Ah, what shall we lose?

Thou wert fair in the fearless old fashion,
   And thy limbs are as melodies yet,
And move to the music of passion
   With lithe and lascivious regret.
What ailed us, O gods, to desert you
   For creeds that refuse and restrain?
Come down and redeem us from virtue,
   Our Lady of Pain.   280

All shrines that were Vestal are flameless,[7]
   But the flame has not fallen from this;
Though obscure be the god, and though name-
     less
   The eyes and the hair that we kiss;
Low fires that love sits by and forges
   Fresh heads for his arrows and thine;
Hair loosened and soiled in mid orgies
   With kisses and wine.

Thy skin changes country and colour,
   And shrivels or swells to a snake's.   290
Let it brighten and bloat and grow duller,
   We know it, the flames and the flakes,
Red brands on it smitten and bitten,
   Round skies where a star is a stain,
And the leaves with thy litanies written,
   Our Lady of Pain.

On thy bosom though many a kiss be,
   There are none such as knew it of old.
Was it Alciphron once or Arisbe,[8]
   Male ringlets or feminine gold,   300

---

[5] Thalassian: a name for Venus (Aphrodite), meaning "born of the sea": Venus was born from sea-foam.

[6] Children of change: the early Christians. In the following stanzas Swinburne refers to their persecution in Rome in gladiatorial combats and by being burned to light the gardens of the emperor Nero, the first-century Roman emperor who as legend has it played music while his city burned.

[7] Vesta was the Roman goddess of the hearth. A fire in her temple was tended by virgin priestesses, called Vestals.

[8] Alciphron: a second-century Greek author of a series of letters supposed to be by famous courtesans; Arisbe: the wife of Priam, king of Troy.

That thy lips met with under the statue,
    Whence a look shot out sharp after thieves
From the eyes of the garden-god at you
    Across the fig-leaves?[9]

Then still, through dry seasons and moister,
    One god had a wreath to his shrine;
Then love was the pearl of his oyster,[10]
    And Venus rose red out of wine.
We have all done amiss, choosing rather
310   Such loves as the wise gods disdain;
Intercede for us thou with thy father,
    Our Lady of Pain.

In spring he had crowns of his garden,
    Red corn[11] in the heat of the year,
Then hoary green olives that harden
    When the grape-blossom freezes with fear;
And milk-budded myrtles with Venus
    And vine-leaves with Bacchus[12] he trod;
And ye said, "We have seen, he hath seen us,
320   A visible God."

What broke off the garlands that girt you?
    What sundered you spirit and clay?
Weak sins yet alive are as virtue
    To the strength of the sins of that day.
For dried is the blood of thy lover,
    Ipsithilla,[13] contracted the vein;
Cry aloud, Will he rise and recover,
    Our Lady of Pain?"

Cry aloud; for the old world is broken:
330   Cry out; for the Phrygian[14] is priest,
And rears not the bountiful token
    And spreads not the fatherly feast.
From the midmost of Ida,[15] from shady
    Recesses that murmur at morn,
They have brought and baptized her, Our
    Lady,
    A goddess new-born.

And the chaplets of old are above us,
    And the oyster-bed teems out of reach;
Old poets outsing and outlove us,
    And Catullus makes mouths at our speech.   340
Who shall kiss, in thy father's own city,
    With such lips as he sang with, again?
Intercede for us all of thy pity,
    Our Lady of Pain.

Out of Dindymus[16] heavily laden
    Her lions draw bound and unfed
A mother, a mortal, a maiden,
    A queen over death and the dead.
She is cold, and her habit is lowly,
    Her temple of branches and sods;   350
Most fruitful and virginal, holy,
    A mother of gods.

She hath wasted with fire thine high places,
    She hath hidden and marred and made sad
The fair limbs of the Loves, the fair faces
    Of gods that were goodly and glad.
She slays, and her hands are not bloody;
    She moves as a moon in the wane,
White-robed, and thy raiment is ruddy,
    Our Lady of Pain.   360

They shall pass and their places be taken,
    The gods and the priests that are pure.
They shall pass, and shalt thou not be shaken?
    They shall perish, and shalt thou endure?
Death laughs, breathing close and relentless
    In the nostrils and eyelids of lust,
With a pinch in his fingers of scentless
    And delicate dust.

But the worm shall revive thee with kisses;
    Thou shalt change and transmute as a god,   370
As the rod to a serpent that hisses,
    As the serpent again to a rod.
Thy life shall not cease though thou doff it;
    Thou shalt live until evil be slain,

[9] Garden-god: Priapus was associated with gardens through his associations with fertility. His often phallic representations were placed in gardens as a charm against thieves. The fig is also a conventional emblem for the female genitalia.

[10] Swinburne glossed this line with a quotation in Latin from Catullus, a Roman poet of the first century: the quotation refers to the prevalent worship of Priapus in cities of the Hellespontian coast, abundant in oysters.

[11] Corn: grain.

[12] Bacchus: the classical god of wine and revelry, associated with vine leaves as Venus is associated with myrtle.

[13] Ipsithilla: a version of the name of a lover in one of Catullus' poems.

[14] Phrygian: Cybele (Rhea), the mother of the principal gods.

[15] Ida: a mountain in Greece at which Cybele was worshipped.

[16] Dindymus: a mountain in Asia Minor, also sacred to Cybele, from which she comes in a chariot drawn by lions.

And good shall die first, said thy prophet,
  Our Lady of Pain.

Did he lie? did he laugh? does he know it,
  Now he lies out of reach, out of breath,
Thy prophet, thy preacher, thy poet,
  Sin's child by incestuous Death?[17]
Did he find out in fire at his waking,
  Or discern as his eyelids lost light,
When the bands of the body were breaking
  And all came in sight?

Who has known all the evil before us,
  Or the tyrannous secrets of time?
Though we match not the dead men that bore
      us
  At a song, at a kiss, at a crime—
Though the heathen outface and outlive us,
390   And our lives and our longings are twain—
Ah, forgive us our virtues, forgive us,
  Our Lady of Pain.

Who are we that embalm and embrace thee
  With spices and savours of song?
What is time, that his children should face
      thee?
  What am I, that my lips do thee wrong?
I could hurt thee—but pain would delight
      thee;
  Or caress thee—but love would repel;
And the lovers whose lips would excite thee
400   Are serpents in hell.

Who now shall content thee as they did,
  Thy lovers, when temples were built
And the hair of the sacrifice braided
  And the blood of the sacrifice spilt,
In Lampsacus fervent with faces,
  In Aphaca[18] red from thy reign,
Who embraced thee with awful embraces,
  Our Lady of Pain?

Where are they, Cotytto or Venus,
410   Astarte or Ashtaroth, where?[19]

Do their hands as we touch come between us?
  Is the breath of them hot in thy hair?
From their lips have thy lips taken fever,
  With the blood of their bodies grown red?
Hast thou left upon earth a believer
  If these men are dead?

They were purple of raiment and golden,
  Filled full of thee, fiery with wine,
Thy lovers, in haunts unbeholden,
  In marvellous chambers of thine.   420
They are fled, and their footprints escape us,
  Who appraise thee, adore, and abstain,
O daughter of Death and Priapus,
  Our Lady of Pain.

What ails us to fear overmeasure,
  To praise thee with timorous breath,
O mistress and mother of pleasure,
  The one thing as certain as death?
We shall change as the things that we cherish,
  Shall fade as they faded before,   430
As foam upon water shall perish,
  As sand upon shore.

We shall know what the darkness discovers,
  If the grave-pit be shallow or deep;
And our fathers of old, and our lovers,
  We shall know if they sleep not or sleep.
We shall see whether hell be not heaven,
  Find out whether tares be not grain,[20]
And the joys of thee seventy times seven,
  Our Lady of Pain.   440
                                        1866

The Garden of Proserpine[1]

Here, where the world is quiet;
  Here, where all trouble seems
Dead winds' and spent waves' riot
  In doubtful dreams of dreams;
I watch the green field growing

[17] In Book II of *Paradise Lost* Milton tells of the birth of Sin from the head of the still glorious angel Satan, and then of the later birth of Death, the child of Sin and Satan.
[18] Priapus was worshipped in Lampsacus on the Hellespontian coast in Asia Minor; Venus was worshipped at Aphaca in Palestine.
[19] Cotytto was a goddess of ancient Thrace who was worshipped in licentious revels. Astarte and Ashtaroth are names for the ancient Phoenician goddess of fertility and sexuality.
[20] Tares: a weed referred to in one of the parables told by Christ (Matthew 13:24–30), in which an enemy sows tares among the good seeds of wheat in a field whose master says: "Let both grow together until the harvest: and in the time of harvest I will say to the reapers, Gather ye together first the tares, and bind them in bundles to burn them: but gather the wheat into my barn" (Matthew 13:30).
[1] Proserpine: see note to "Hymn to Proserpine."

For reaping folk and sowing,
For harvest-time and mowing,
   A sleepy world of streams.

I am tired of tears and laughter,
   And men that laugh and weep;
Of what may come hereafter
   For men that sow to reap:
I am weary of days and hours,
Blown buds of barren flowers,
Desires and dreams and powers
   And everything but sleep.

Here life has death for neighbour,
   And far from eye or ear
Wan waves and wet winds labour,
   Weak ships and spirits steer;
They drive adrift, and whither
They wot not who make thither;
But no such winds blow hither,
   And no such things grow here.

No growth of moor or coppice,
   No heather-flower or vine,
But bloomless buds of poppies,
   Green grapes of Proserpine,
Pale beds of blowing rushes
Where no leaf blooms or blushes
Save this whereout she crushes
   For dead men deadly wine.

Pale, without name or number,
   In fruitless fields of corn,[2]
They bow themselves and slumber
   All night till light is born;
And like a soul belated,
In hell and heaven unmated,
By cloud and mist abated
   Comes out of darkness morn.

Though one were strong as seven,
   He too with death shall dwell,
Nor wake with wings in heaven,
   Nor weep for pains in hell;
Though one were fair as roses,
His beauty clouds and closes;
And well though love reposes,
   In the end it is not well.

Pale, beyond porch and portal,
   Crowned with calm leaves, she stands

Who gathers all things mortal
   With cold immortal hands;
Her languid lips are sweeter
Than love's who fears to greet her
To men that mix and meet her
   From many times and lands.

She waits for each and other,
   She waits for all men born;
Forgets the earth her mother,[3]
   The life of fruits and corn;
And spring and seed and swallow   60
Take wing for her and follow
Where summer song rings hollow
   And flowers are put to scorn.

There go the loves that wither,
   The old loves with wearier wings;
And all dead years draw thither,
   And all disastrous things;
Dead dreams of days forsaken,
Blind buds that snows have shaken,   70
Wild leaves that winds have taken,
   Red strays of ruined springs.

We are not sure of sorrow,
   And joy was never sure;
To-day will die to-morrow;
   Time stoops to no man's lure;
And love, grown faint and fretful,
With lips but half regretful
Sighs, and with eyes forgetful
   Weeps that no loves endure.   80

From too much love of living,
   From hope and fear set free,
We thank with brief thanksgiving
   Whatever gods may be
That no life lives for ever;
That dead men rise up never;
That even the weariest river
   Winds somewhere safe to sea.

Then star nor sun shall waken,
   Nor any change of light: 90
Nor sound of waters shaken,
   Nor any sound or sight:
Nor wintry leaves nor vernal,
Nor days nor things diurnal;
Only the sleep eternal
   In an eternal night.

1866

[2] Corn: grain.
[3] Her mother: Ceres (Demeter), the goddess of agriculture, was the mother of Proserpine.

The Sundew

A little marsh-plant, yellow green,
And pricked at lip with tender red.
Tread close, and either way you tread
Some faint black water jets between
Lest you should bruise the curious head.

A live thing maybe; who shall know?
The summer knows and suffers it;
For the cool moss is thick and sweet
Each side, and saves the blossom so
10   That it lives out the long June heat.

The deep scent of the heather burns
About it; breathless though it be,
Bow down and worship; more than we
Is the least flower whose life returns,
Least weed renascent in the sea.

We are vexed and cumbered in earth's sight
With wants, with many memories;
These see their mother what she is,
Glad-growing, till August leave more bright
20   The apple-coloured cranberries.

Wind blows and bleaches the strong grass,
Blown all one way to shelter it
From trample of strayed kine,[1] with feet
Felt heavier than the moorhen was,
Strayed up past patches of wild wheat.

You call it sundew: how it grows,
If with its colour it have breath,
If life taste sweet to it, if death
Pain its soft petal, no man knows:
30   Man has no sight or sense that saith.

My sundew, grown of gentle days,
In these green miles the spring begun
Thy growth ere April had half done
With the soft secret of her ways
Or June made ready for the sun.

O red-lipped mouth of marsh-flower,
I have a secret halved with thee.
The name that is love's name to me
Thou knowest, and the face of her
40   Who is my festival to see.

The hard sun, as thy petals knew,
Coloured the heavy moss-water:
Thou wert not worth green midsummer

Nor fit to live to August blue,
O sundew, not remembering her.

                                              1862; 1866

Hendecasyllabics[1]

In the month of the long decline of roses
I, beholding the summer dead before me,
Set my face to the sea and journeyed silent,
Gazing eagerly where above the sea-mark
Flame as fierce as the fervid eyes of lions
Half divided the eyelids of the sunset;
Till I heard as it were a noise of waters
Moving tremulous under feet of angels
Multitudinous, out of all the heavens;
Knew the fluttering wind, the fluttered foliage,   10
Shaken fitfully, full of sound and shadow;
And saw, trodden upon by noiseless angels,
Long mysterious reaches fed with moonlight,
Sweet sad straits in a soft subsiding channel,
Blown about by the lips of winds I knew not,
Winds not born in the north nor any quarter,
Winds not warm with the south nor any
     sunshine;
Heard between them a voice of exultation,
"Lo, the summer is dead, the sun is faded,
Even like as a leaf the year is withered,   20
All the fruits of the day from all her branches
Gathered, neither is any left to gather.
All the flowers are dead, the tender blossoms,
All are taken away; the season wasted,
Like an ember among the fallen ashes.
Now with light of the winter days, with moon-
     light,
Light of snow, and the bitter light of hoarfrost,
We bring flowers that fade not after autumn,
Pale white chaplets and crowns of latter
     seasons,
Fair false leaves (but the summer leaves were
     falser),   30
Woven under the eyes of stars and planets
When low light was upon the windy reaches
Where the flower of foam was blown, a lily
Dropt among the sonorous fruitless furrows
And green fields of the sea that make no
     pasture:
Since the winter begins, the weeping winter,
All whose flowers are tears, and round his
     temples
Iron blossom of frost is bound for ever."

                                              1866

---

[1] Kine: cattle.
[1] Hendecasyllabics: a line of eleven syllables, principally used in classical Latin poetry.

Love and Sleep

Lying asleep between the strokes of night
  I saw my love lean over my sad bed,
  Pale as the duskiest lily's leaf or head,
Smooth-skinned and dark, with bare throat
    made to bite,
Too wan for blushing and too warm for white,
  But perfect-coloured without white or red.
And her lips opened amorously, and said—
I wist not what, saving one word—Delight.
And all her face was honey to my mouth,
  And all her body pasture to mine eyes;
    The long lithe arms and hotter hands than
      fire,
The quivering flanks, hair smelling of the
    south,
  The bright light feet, the splendid supple
    thighs
    And glittering eyelids of my soul's desire.
                        1866

May Janet

        (*Breton*) [1]
"Stand up, stand up, thou May Janet,
  And go to the wars with me."
He's drawn her by both hands
  With her face against the sea.

"He that strews red shall gather white,
  He that sows white reap red,
Before your face and my daughter's
  Meet in a marriage-bed.

"Gold coin shall grow in the yellow field,
  Green corn in the green sea-water,
And red fruit grow of the rose's red,
  Ere your fruit grow in her."

"But I shall have her by land," he said,
  "Or I shall have her by sea,
Or I shall have her by strong treason
  And no grace go with me."

Her father's drawn her by both hands,
  He's rent her gown from her,
He's ta'en the smock round her body,
  Cast in the sea-water. 20

The captain's drawn her by both sides
  Out of the fair green sea;
"Stand up, stand up, thou May Janet,
  And come to the war with me."

The first town they came to
  There was a blue bride-chamber;
He clothed her on with silk
  And belted her with amber.

The second town they came to
  The bridesmen feasted knee to knee; 30
He clothed her on with silver,
  A stately thing to see.

The third town they came to
  The bridesmaids all had gowns of gold;
He clothed her on with purple,
  A rich thing to behold.

The last town they came to
  He clothed her white and red,
With a green flag either side of her
  And a gold flag overhead.
             1866 40

Dedication[1]

      1865
The sea gives her shells to the shingle,[2]
  The earth gives her streams to the sea;
They are many, but my gift is single,
  My verses, the firstfruits of me.
Let the wind take the green and the grey leaf,
  Cast forth without fruit upon air;
Take rose-leaf and vine-leaf and bay-leaf
  Blown loose from the hair.

The night shakes them round me in legions,
  Dawn drives them before her like dreams; 10

[1] One of the forms of the medieval poetry composed and sung in the north of France in Breton, a Celtic language, was a *lay* or narrative, often dealing with elements of the fairy or supernatural. Swinburne may intend in this poem a suggestion of the fairy lover who transports a woman to another realm.

[1] Swinburne dedicated the first series of *Poems and Ballads* to Edward Burne-Jones (1833–1898), whom he first met when Burne-Jones, with Dante Gabriel Rossetti and William Morris, was in Oxford in 1857 to decorate the walls of a new building. Burne-Jones was a prolific and successful painter in the Pre-Raphaelite school; his paintings are decorative and patiently detailed, highly colored, and usually on mythological or literary subjects.

[2] Shingle: beaches of coarse gravel or stone.

Time sheds them like snows on strange regions,
   Swept shoreward on infinite streams;
Leaves pallid and sombre and ruddy,
   Dead fruits of the fugitive years;
Some stained as with wine and made bloody,
   And some as with tears.

Some scattered in seven years' traces,
   As they fell from the boy that was then;
Long left among idle green places,
   Or gathered but now among men;
On seas full of wonder and peril,
   Blown white round the capes of the north;
Or in islands where myrtles are sterile
   And loves bring not forth.[3]

O daughters of dreams and of stories
   That life is not wearied of yet,
Faustine, Fragoletta, Dolores,
   Félise and Yolande and Juliette,[4]
Shall I find you not still, shall I miss you,
   When sleep, that is true or that seems,
Comes back to me hopeless to kiss you,
   O daughters of dreams?

They are past as a slumber that passes,
   As the dew of a dawn of old time;
More frail than the shadows on glasses,
   More fleet than a wave or a rhyme.
As the waves after ebb drawing seaward,
   When their hollows are full of the night,
So the birds that flew singing to me-ward
   Recede out of sight.

The songs of dead seasons, that wander
   On wings of articulate words;
Lost leaves that the shore-wind may squander,
   Light flocks of untameable birds;
Some sang to me dreaming in class-time
   And truant in hand as in tongue;
For the youngest were born of boy's pastime,
   The eldest are young.

Is there shelter while life in them lingers,
   Is there hearing for songs that recede,
Tunes touched from a harp with man's fingers
   Or blown with boy's mouth in a reed?
Is there place in the land of your labour,
   Is there room in your world of delight,

Where change has not sorrow for neighbour
   And day has not night?

In their wings though the sea-wind yet quivers,
   Will you spare not a space for them there
Made green with the running of rivers
   And gracious with temperate air;
In the fields and the turreted cities,
   That cover from sunshine and rain
Fair passions and bountiful pities
   And loves without stain?

In a land of clear colours and stories,
   In a region of shadowless hours,
Where earth has a garment of glories
   And a murmur of musical flowers;
In woods where the spring half uncovers
   The flush of her amorous face,
By the waters that listen for lovers,
   For these is there place?

For the song-birds of sorrow, that muffle
   Their music as clouds do their fire:
For the storm-birds of passion, that ruffle
   Wild wings in a wind of desire;
In the stream of the storm as it settles
   Blown seaward, borne far from the sun,
Shaken loose on the darkness like petals
   Dropt one after one?

Though the world of your hands be more
    gracious
   And lovelier in lordship of things
Clothed round by sweet art with the spacious
   Warm heaven of her imminent wings,
Let them enter, unfledged and nigh fainting,
   For the love of old loves and lost times;
And receive in your palace of painting
   This revel of rhymes.

Though the seasons of man full of losses
   Make empty the years full of youth,
If but one thing be constant in crosses,
   Change lays not her hand upon truth;
Hopes die, and their tombs are for token
   That the grief as the joy of them ends
Ere time that breaks all men has broken
   The faith between friends.

[3] The myrtle is associated with Venus. One of the islands on which the myrtle is sterile is Lesbos, the home of the Greek poet Sappho (c. 650 B.C.) whose poems to lesbian love Swinburne celebrated in one of the poems in *Poems and Ballads.*

[4] These are names of women in Swinburne's poems, except for Juliette, who is the heroine of one of the novels of the Marquis de Sade (1740–1814). Swinburne began to read de Sade's erotic fiction in the 1860s.

Though the many lights dwindle to one light,
　There is help if the heaven has one;
Though the skies be discrowned of the sunlight
　And the earth dispossessed of the sun,
They have moonlight and sleep for repayment,
　When, refreshed as a bride and set free,
With stars and sea-winds in her raiment,
　Night sinks on the sea.

1866

The poems of Songs Before Sunrise *(1871) were
written while Swinburne was strongly influenced by
Guiseppe Mazzini (1805–1872), the Italian repub-
lican whom he met in 1867. About that time Maz-
zini wrote to Swinburne acknowledging the gift of a
copy of* Atalanta in Calydon *(1865) but urging him
to write no more "songs of egotistical love and idola-
try of physical beauty": "the poet ought to be the
apostle of a crusade, his word the watchword of the
fighting nations and the dirge of the oppressors"
(quoted in Lafourcade, p. 149). The crusade in
which Swinburne enlisted the poems of* Songs Be-
fore Sunrise *was not only that of a unified Italian
nation free of the political control Austria and
France had exercised through most of the nine-
teenth century but also of an Italian republic. By
1870 this latter hope was fading as Italy began to
unify under a king, Victor Emmanuel II (1820–
1878), who in that year ended the possibility of a
republic with Rome as its capital when he added
Rome to his kingdom.*

Prelude

Between the green bud and the red
Youth sat and sang by Time, and shed
　From eyes and tresses flowers and tears,
　From heart and spirit hopes and fears,
Upon the hollow stream whose bed
　Is channeled by the foamless years;
And with the white the gold-haired head
　Mixed running locks, and in Time's ears
Youth's dreams hung singing, and Time's truth
Was half not harsh in the ears of Youth.

Between the bud and the blown flower
Youth talked with joy and grief an hour,
　With footless joy and wingless grief
　And twin-born faith and disbelief
Who share the seasons to devour;
　And long ere these made up their sheaf
Felt the winds round him shake and shower
　The rose-red and the blood-red leaf,

Delight whose germ grew never grain,
And passion dyed in its own pain.　　　20

Then he stood up, and trod to dust
Fear and desire, mistrust and trust,
　And dreams of bitter sleep and sweet,
　And bound for sandals on his feet
Knowledge and patience of what must
　And what things may be, in the heat
And cold of years that rot and rust
　And alter; and his spirit's meat
Was freedom, and his staff was wrought
Of strength, and his cloak woven of thought.　30

For what has he whose will sees clear
To do with doubt and faith and fear,
　Swift hopes and slow despondencies?
　His heart is equal with the sea's
And with the sea-wind's, and his ear
　Is level to the speech of these,
And his soul communes and takes cheer
　With the actual earth's equalities,
Air, light, and night, hills, winds, and streams,
And seeks not strength from strengthless
　　dreams.　　　40

His soul is even with the sun
Whose spirit and whose eye are one,
　Who seeks not stars by day, nor light
　And heavy heat of day by night.
Him can no God cast down, whom none
　Can lift in hope beyond the height
Of fate and nature and things done
　By the calm rule of might and right
That bids men be and bear and do,
And die beneath blind skies or blue.　　　50

To him the lights of even and morn
Speak no vain things of love or scorn,
　Fancies and passions miscreate
　By man in things dispassionate.
Nor holds he fellowship forlorn
　With souls that pray and hope and hate,
And doubt they had better not been born,
　And fain would lure or scare off fate
And charm their doomsman from their doom
And make fear dig its own false tomb.　　　60

He builds not half of doubts and half
Of dreams his own soul's cenotaph,[1]
　Whence hopes and fears with helpless eyes,
　Wrapt loose in cast-off cerecloths,[2] rise

---

[1] Cenotaph: an empty tomb erected to honor a person buried elsewhere.
[2] Cerecloths: burial cloths.

And dance and wring their hands and laugh,
  And weep thin tears and sigh light sighs,
And without living lips would quaff
  The living spring in man that lies,
And drain his soul of faith and strength
70 It might have lived on a life's length.

He hath given himself and hath not sold
To God for heaven or man for gold,
  Or grief for comfort that it gives,
  Or joy for grief's restoratives.
He hath given himself to time, whose fold
  Shuts in the mortal flock that lives
On its plain pasture's heat and cold
  And the equal year's alternatives.
Earth, heaven, and time, death, life, and he,
80 Endure while they shall be to be.

"Yet between death and life are hours
To flush with love and hide in flowers;
  What profit save in these?" men cry:
  "Ah, see, between soft earth and sky,
What only good things here are ours!"
  They say, "what better wouldst thou try,
What sweeter sing of? or what powers
  Serve, that will give thee ere thou die
More joy to sing and be less sad,
90 More heart to play and grow more glad?"

Play then and sing; we too have played,
We likewise, in that subtle shade.
  We too have twisted through our hair
  Such tendrils as the wild Loves wear,
And heard what mirth the Mænads[3] made,
  Till the wind blew our garlands bare
And left their roses disarrayed,
  And smote the summer with strange air,
And disengirdled and discrowned
100 The limbs and locks that vine-wreaths bound.

We too have tracked by star-proof trees
The tempest of the Thyiades
  Scare the loud night on hills that hid
  The blood-feasts of the Bassarid,
Heard their song's iron cadences
  Fright the wolf hungering from the kid,
Outroar the lion-throated seas,
  Outchide the north-wind if it chid,
And hush the torrent-tongued ravines
110 With thunders of their tambourines.

But the fierce flute whose notes acclaim
Dim goddesses of fiery fame,
  Cymbal and clamorous kettledrum,
  Timbrels and tabrets, all are dumb
That turned the high chill air to flame;
  The singing tongues of fire are numb
That called on Cotys[4] by her name
  Edonian, till they felt her come
And maddened, and her mystic face
Lightened along the streams of Thrace.   1:

For Pleasure slumberless and pale,
And Passion with rejected veil,
  Pass, and the tempest-footed throng
  Of hours that follow them with song
Till their feet flag and voices fail,
  And lips that were so loud so long
Learn silence, or a wearier wail;
  So keen is change, and time so strong,
To weave the robes of life and rend
And weave again till life have end.   1

But weak is change, but strengthless time,
To take the light from heaven, or climb
  The hills of heaven with wasting feet.
  Songs they can stop that earth found meet,
But the stars keep their ageless rhyme;
  Flowers they can slay that spring thought
    sweet,
But the stars keep their spring sublime;
  Passions and pleasures can defeat,
Actions and agonies control,
And life and death, but not the soul.   1

Because man's soul is man's God still,
What wind soever waft his will
  Across the waves of day and night
  To port or shipwreck, left or right,
By shores and shoals of good and ill;
  And still its flame at mainmast height
Through the rent air that foam-flakes fill
  Sustains the indomitable light
Whence only man hath strength to steer
Or helm to handle without fear.   1

Save his own soul's light overhead,
None leads him, and none ever led,
  Across birth's hidden harbour-bar,
  Past youth where shoreward shallows are,

---

[3] Mænads: like the Thyiades and the Bassarid named below (lines 102 and 104) celebrants
in the orgiastic rituals of Bacchus or Dionysus, the classical god of wine and revelry.
[4] Cotys: a goddess of ancient Thrace equivalent to Cybele, the classical mother of the gods
who was sometimes worshipped as a goddess of fertility. Edonia was a part of Thrace, the old
name for the region of the Balkans north of the Aegean Sea.

Through age that drives on toward the red
   Vast void of sunset hailed from far,
To the equal waters of the dead;
   Save his own soul he hath no star,
And sinks, except his own soul guide,
Helmless in middle turn of tide.

No blast of air or fire of sun
Puts out the light whereby we run
   With girded loins our lamplit race,
   And each from each takes heart of grace
And spirit till his turn be done,
   And light of face from each man's face
In whom the light of trust is one;
   Since only souls that keep their place
By their own light, and watch things roll,
And stand, have light for any soul.

A little time we gain from time
To set our seasons in some chime,
   For harsh or sweet or loud or low,
   With seasons played out long ago
And souls that in their time and prime
   Took part with summer or with snow,
Lived abject lives out or sublime,
   And had their chance of seed to sow
For service or disservice done
To those days dead and this their son.

A little time that we may fill
Or with such good works or such ill
   As loose the bonds or make them strong
   Wherein all manhood suffers wrong.
By rose-hung river and light-foot rill
   There are who rest not; who think long
Till they discern as from a hill
   At the sun's hour of morning song,
Known of souls only, and those souls free,
The sacred spaces of the sea.

               (1870) 1871

Super Flumina Babylonis[1]

By the waters of Babylon we sat down and
      wept,
   Remembering thee,
That for ages of agony hast endured, and slept,
   And wouldst not see.

By the waters of Babylon we stood up and
      sang,
   Considering thee,
That a blast of deliverance in the darkness
      rang,
   To set thee free.

And with trumpets and thunderings and with
      morning song
   Came up the light;   10
And thy spirit uplifted thee to forget thy wrong
   As day doth night.

And thy sons were dejected not any more, as
      then
   When thou wast shamed;
When thy lovers went heavily without heart,
      as men
   Whose life was maimed.

In the desolate distances, with a great desire,
   For thy love's sake,
With our hearts going back to thee, they were
      filled with fire,
   Were nigh to break.   20

It was said to us: "Verily ye are great of heart,
   But ye shall bend;
Ye are bondmen and bondwomen, to be
      scourged and smart,
   To toil and tend."

And with harrows men harrowed us, and
      subdued with spears,
   And crushed with shame;
And the summer and winter was, and the
      length of years,
   And no change came.

By the rivers of Italy, by the sacred streams,
   By town, by tower,   30
There was feasting with revelling, there was
      sleep with dreams,
   Until thine hour.

And they slept and they rioted on their
      rose-hung beds,
   With mouths on flame,

---

[1] "By the rivers of Babylon, there we sat down, yea, we wept, when we remembered Zion" (Psalms 137:1). Swinburne uses the captivity of the Hebrews in Babylon as a metaphor for the oppression of Italy by the governments of other European nations, and, more generally, for the constraints placed by kings and by the papacy of the Roman Catholic Church on political liberty and moves toward a republic in Italy.

And with love-locks vine-chapleted, and with
    rose-crowned heads
      And robes of shame.

And they knew not their forefathers, nor the
    hills and streams
      And words of power,
Nor the gods that were good to them, but with
    songs and dreams
40   Filled up their hour.

By the rivers of Italy, by the dry streams' beds,
      When thy time came,
There was casting of crowns from them, from
    their young men's heads,
      The crowns of shame.

By the horn of Eridanus, by the Tiber mouth,[2]
      As thy day rose,
They arose up and girded them to the north
    and south,
      By seas, by snows.

As a water in January the frost confines,
50   Thy kings bound thee;
As a water in April is, in the new-blown vines,
      Thy sons made free.

And thy lovers that looked for thee, and that
    mourned from far,
      For thy sake dead,
We rejoiced in the light of thee, in the signal
    star
      Above thine head.

In thy grief had we followed thee, in thy
    passion loved,
      Loved in thy loss;
In thy shame we stood fast to thee, with thy
    pangs were moved,
60   Clung to thy cross.

By the hillside of Calvary we beheld thy blood,
      Thy bloodred tears,
As a mother's in bitterness, an unebbing flood,
      Years upon years.

And the north was Gethsemane, without leaf
    or bloom,
      A garden sealed;
And the south was Aceldama,[3] for a sanguine
    fume
      Hid all the field.

By the stone of the sepulchre we returned to
    weep,
      From far, from prison;
And the guards by it keeping it we beheld
    asleep,
      But thou wast risen.

And an angel's similitude by the unsealed
    grave,
      And by the stone:
And the voice was angelical, to whose words
    God gave
      Strength like his own.

"Lo, the graveclothes of Italy that are folded up
    In the grave's gloom![4]
And the guards as men wrought upon with a
    charmed cup,
      By the open tomb.

"And her body most beautiful, and her shining
    head,
      These are not here;
For your mother, for Italy, is not surely dead:
      Have ye no fear.

"As of old time she spake to you, and you
    hardly heard,
      Hardly took heed,
So now also she saith to you, yet another word,
      Who is risen indeed.

"By my saying she saith to you, in your ears she
    saith,
      Who hear these things,
Put no trust in men's royalties, nor in great
    men's breath,
      Nor words of kings.

---

    [2] Eridanus is the Greek name for the river Po, whose delta (horn) forms a part of the
Adriatic coast of northern Italy. The Tiber is a river of central Italy whose mouth is on its
southwestern coast.
    [3] Gethsemane was the name of the place in which Christ awaited his arrest; Aceldama was
the name of the place of Judas' suicide.
    [4] Swinburne in lines 78–120 paraphrases and elaborates the words of the angel to the women
who have come to visit the tomb of the risen Christ. See Matthew 28, Mark 16, and Luke 24.

"For the life of them vanishes and is no more
     seen,
     Nor no more known;
Nor shall any remember if a crown hath been,
     Or where a throne.

"Unto each man his handiwork, unto each his
     crown,
     The just Fate gives;
Whoso takes the world's life on him and his
     own lays down,
     He, dying so, lives.[5]

"Whoso bears the whole heaviness of the
     wronged world's weight
     And puts it by,
It is well with him suffering, though he face
     man's fate;
     How should he die?

"Seeing death has no part in him any more, no
     power
     Upon his head;
He has bought his eternity with a little hour,
     And is not dead.

"For an hour, if ye look for him, he is no more
     found,
     For one hour's space;
Then ye lift up your eyes to him and behold
     him crowned,
     A deathless face.

"On the mountains of memory, by the world's
     wellsprings,
     In all men's eyes,
Where the light of the life of him is on all past
     things,
     Death only dies.

"Not the light that was quenched for us, nor
     the deeds that were,
     Nor the ancient days,
Nor the sorrows not sorrowful, nor the face
     most fair
     Of perfect praise."

So the angel of Italy's resurrection said,
     So yet he saith;

So the son of her suffering, that from breasts
     nigh dead
     Drew life, not death.

That the pavement of Golgotha[6] should be
     Not red, but white;
That the waters of Babylon should no longer
     flow,
     And men see light.

                    1869; 1871

Hertha[1]

     I am that which began;
       Out of me the years roll;
       Out of me God and man;
       I am equal and whole;
God changes, and man, and the form of them
     bodily; I am the soul.

     Before ever land was,
       Before ever the sea,
     Or soft hair of the grass,
       Or fair limbs of the tree,
Or the flesh-coloured fruit of my branches, I
     was, and thy soul was in me.   10

     First life on my sources
       First drifted and swam;
     Out of me are the forces
       That save it or damn;
Out of me man and woman, and wild-beast
     and bird; before God was, I am.

     Beside or above me
       Nought is there to go;
     Love or unlove me,
       Unknow me or know,
I am that which unloves me and loves; I am
     stricken, and I am the blow.   20

     I the mark that is missed
       And the arrows that miss,
     I the mouth that is kissed
       And the breath in the kiss,
The search, and the sought, and the seeker, the
     soul and the body that is.

---

[5] "For whosoever will save his life shall lose it: and whosoever will lose his life for my sake shall find it" (Matthew 16:25).

[6] Golgotha: Calvary, the site of Christ's crucifixion.

[1] The first-century Roman historian Tacitus identified Hertha as a goddess of the earth in the religion of the Germanic people.

I am that thing which blesses
    My spirt elate;
That which caresses
    With hands uncreate
My limbs unbegotten that measure the length
30   of the measure of fate.

But what thing dost thou now,
    Looking Godward, to cry
"I am I, thou art thou,
    I am low, thou art high"?
I am thou, whom thou seekest to find him; find
    thou but thyself, thou art I.

I the grain and the furrow,
    The plough-cloven clod
And the ploughshare drawn thorough,
    The germ and the sod,
The deed and the doer, the seed and the sower,
40   the dust which is God.

Hast thou known how I fashioned thee,
    Child, underground?
Fire that impassioned thee,
    Iron that bound,
Dim changes of water, what thing of all these
    hast thou known of or found?

Canst thou say in thine heart
    Thou hast seen with thine eyes
With what cunning of art
    Thou wast wrought in what wise,
By what force of what stuff thou wast shapen,
50   and shown on my breast to the skies?

Who hath given, who hath sold it thee,
    Knowledge of me?[2]
Hath the wilderness told it thee?
    Hast thou learnt of the sea?
Hast thou communed in spirit with night? have
    the winds taken counsel with thee?

Have I set such a star
    To show light on thy brow
That thou sawest from afar
    What I show to thee now?
Have ye spoken as brethren together, the sun
60   and the mountains and thou?

What is here, dost thou know it?
    What was, hast thou known?
Prophet nor poet
    Nor tripod[3] nor throne
Nor spirit nor flesh can make answer, but only
    thy mother alone.

Mother, not maker,
    Born, and not made;
Though her children forsake her,
    Allured or afraid,
Praying prayers to the God of their fashion, she
    stirs not for all that have prayed.

A creed is a rod,
    And a crown is of night;
But this thing is God,
    To be man with thy might,
To grow straight in the strength of thy spirit,
    and live out thy life as the light.

I am in thee to save thee,
    As my soul in thee saith;
Give thou as I gave thee,
    Thy life-blood and breath,
Green leaves of thy labour, white flowers of
    thy thought, and red fruit of thy death.[4]

Be the ways of thy giving
    As mine were to thee;
The free life of thy living,
    Be the gift of it free;
Not as servant to lord, nor as master to slave,
    shalt thou give thee to me.

O children of banishment,
    Souls overcast,
Were the lights ye see vanish meant
    Alway to last,
Ye would know not the sun overshining the
    shadows and stars overpast.

I that saw where ye trod
    The dim paths of the night
Set the shadow called God
    In your skies to give light;
But the morning of manhood is risen, and the
    shadowless soul is in sight.

---

[2] In these lines Swinburne recalls the questions with which God demonstrates the ignorance of Job about the causes and means of creation (Job:38–39).

[3] Tripod: an instrument of religious ceremony, especially those of the priestesses of Apollo.

[4] Green, white, and red are the colors of the Italian flag; Swinburne displays them frequently in the poems of *Songs Before Sunrise*.

The tree many-rooted
  That swells to the sky
With frondage red-fruited,
  The life-tree am I;[5]
In the buds of your lives is the sap of my leaves:
  ye shall live and not die.

But the Gods of your fashion
  That take and that give,
In their pity and passion
  That scourge and forgive,
They are worms that are bred in the bark that
  falls off; they shall die and not live.

My own blood is what stanches
  The wounds in my bark;
Stars caught in my branches
  Make day of the dark,
And are worshipped as suns till the sunrise
  shall tread out their fires as a spark.

Where dead ages hide under
  The live roots of the tree,
In my darkness the thunder
  Makes utterance of me;
In the clash of my boughs with each other ye
  hear the waves sound of the sea.

That noise is of Time,
  As his feathers are spread
And his feet set to climb
  Through the boughs overhead,
And my foliage rings round him and rustles,
  and branches are bent with his tread.

The storm-winds of ages
  Blow through me and cease,
The war-wind that rages,
  The spring-wind of peace,
Ere the breath of them roughen my tresses, ere
  one of my blossoms increase.

All sounds of all changes,
  All shadows and lights
On the world's mountain-ranges
  And stream-riven heights,
Whose tongue is the wind's tongue and
  language of storm-clouds on earth-shaking
  nights;

All forms of all faces,
  All works of all hands

In unsearchable places
  Of time-stricken lands,
All death and all life, and all reigns and all
  ruins, drop through me as sands.

Though sore be my burden
  And more than ye know,
And my growth have no guerdon
  But only to grow,
Yet I fail not of growing for lightnings above
  me or deathworms below.   140

These too have their part in me,
  As I too in these;
Such fire is at heart in me,
  Such sap is this tree's,
Which hath in it all sounds and all secrets of
  infinite lands and of seas.

In the spring-coloured hours
  When my mind was as May's,
There brake forth of me flowers
  By centuries of days,
Strong blossoms with perfume of manhood,
  shot out from my spirit as rays.   150

And the sound of them springing
  And smell of their shoots
Were as warmth and sweet singing
  And strength to my roots;
And the lives of my children made perfect with
  freedom of soul were my fruits.

I bid you but be;
  I have need not of prayer;
I have need of you free
  As your mouths of mine air;
That my heart may be greater within me, be-
  holding the fruits of me fair.   160

More fair than strange fruit is
  Of faiths ye espouse;
In me only the root is
  That blooms in your boughs;
Behold now your God that ye made you, to
  feed him with faith of your vows.

In the darkening and whitening
  Abysses adored,
With dayspring and lightning
  For lamp and for sword,
God thunders in heaven, and his angels are
  red with the wrath of the Lord.   170

---

[5] Life-tree: Ydragsil is a tree of life, binding earth, heaven, and hell, in Norse mythology.

O my sons, O too dutiful
  Towards Gods not of me,
Was not I enough beautiful?
  Was it hard to be free?
For behold, I am with you, am in you and of
  you; look forth now and see.

Lo, winged with world's wonders,
  With miracles shod,
With the fires of his thunders
  For raiment and rod,
God trembles in heaven, and his angels are
180   white with the terror of God.

For his twilight is come on him,
  His anguish is here;
And his spirits gaze dumb on him,
  Grown grey from his fear;
And his hour taketh hold on him stricken, the
  last of his infinite year.

Thought made him and breaks him,
  Truth slays and forgives;
But to you, as time takes him,
  This new thing it gives,
Even love, the beloved Republic, that feeds
190   upon freedom and lives.

For truth only is living,
  Truth only is whole,
And the love of his giving
  Man's polestar and pole;
Man, pulse of my centre, and fruit of my body,
  and seed of my soul.

One birth of my bosom;
  One beam of mine eye;
One topmost blossom
  That scales the sky;
Man, equal and one with me, man that is made
200   of me, man that is I.

                                    1871

In 1869 Pius IX convened an Ecumenical or Vati-
can Council of members of the hierarchy of the
Roman Catholic Church. Its two principal purposes
and products were the enunciation of the doctrine
of papal infallibility—the dogma that the pope
cannot err when he speaks on matters of religious
belief and conduct, and the associated principle that
the pope is supreme in matters of discipline within
the church—and the condemnation of political and
intellectual liberalism. An Anti-Catholic Council
was convened in Rome about the same time, to
which Swinburne sent a letter of endorsement. He
imagined that the "Hymn of Man" might be read

at such a council. He also described the poem as a
companion piece to the "Hymn to Proserpine."

Hymn of Man

(During the Session in Rome of the
Œcumenical Council)

In the grey beginning of years, in the twilight
  of things that began,
The word of the earth in the ears of the world,
  was it God? was it man?
The word of the earth to the spheres her sisters,
  the note of her song,
The sound of her speech in the ears of the
  starry and sisterly throng,
Was it praise or passion or prayer, was it love
  or devotion or dread,
When the veils of the shining air first wrapt
  her jubilant head?
When her eyes new-born of the night saw yet
  no star out of reach;
When her maiden mouth was alight with the
  flame of muscial speech;
When her virgin feet were set on the terrible
  heavenly way,
And her virginal lids were wet with the dew of
  the birth of the day:
Eyes that had looked not on time, and ears
  that had heard not of death;
Lips that had learnt not the rhyme of change
  and passionate breath,
The rhythmic anguish of growth, and the
  motion of mutable things,
Of love that longs and is loth, and plume-
  plucked hope without wings,
Passions and pains without number, and life
  that runs and is lame,
From slumber again to slumber, the same race
  set for the same,
Where the runners outwear each other, but
  running with lampless hands
No man takes light from his brother till blind
  at the goal he stands:
Ah, did they know, did they dream of it,
  counting the cost and worth?
The ways of her days, did they seem then good
  to the new-souled earth?
Did her heart rejoice, and the might of her
  spirit exult in her then,
Child yet no child of the night, and mother-
  less mother of men?
Was it Love brake forth flower-fashion, a bird
  with gold on his wings,

Lovely, her firstborn passion, and impulse of
firstborn things?
Was Love that nestling indeed that under the
plumes of the night
Was hatched and hidden as seed in the furrow,
and brought forth bright?
Was it Love lay shut in the shell world-shaped,
having over him there
Black world-wide wings thas impel the might
of the night through air?
And bursting his shell as a bird, night shook
through her sail-stretched vans,
And her heart as a water was stirred, and its
heat was the firstborn man's.
For the waste of the dead void air took form
of a world at birth,
And the waters and firmaments were, and light,
and the life-giving earth.
The beautiful bird unbegotten that night
brought forth without pain
In the fathomless years forgotten whereover
the dead gods reign,
Was it love, life, godhead, or fate? we say the
spirit is one
That moved on the dark to create out of
darkness the stars and the sun.
Before the growth was the grower, and the
seed ere the plant was sown;
But what was seed of the sower? and the grain
of him, whence was it grown?
Foot after foot ye go back and travail and
make yourselves mad;
Blind feet that feel for the track where high-
way is none to be had.
Therefore the God that ye make you is
grievous, and gives not aid,
Because it is but for your sake that the God of
your making is made.
Thou and I and he are not gods made men for
a span,
But God, if a God there be, is the substance of
men which is man.
Our lives are as pulses or pores of his manifold
body and breath;
As waves of his sea on the shores where birth
is the beacon of death.
We men, the multiform features of man, what-
soever we be,
Recreate him of whom we are creatures, and
all we only are he.
Not each man of all men is God, but God is the
fruit of the whole;
Indivisible spirit and blood, indiscernible body
from soul.

Not men's but man's is the glory of godhead,
the kingdom of time,
The mountainous ages made hoary with snows
for the spirit to climb.
A God with the world inwound whose clay to
his footsole clings;
A manifold God fast-bound as with iron of
adverse things.
A soul that labours and lives, an emotion, a
strenuous breath,
From the flame that its own mouth gives
reillumed, and refreshed with death.
In the sea whereof centuries are waves the live
God plunges and swims;
His bed is in all men's graves, but the worm
hath not hold on his limbs.
Night puts out not his eyes, nor time sheds
change on his head;
With such fire as the stars of the skies are the
roots of his heart are fed.
Men are the thoughts passing through it, the
veins that fulfil it with blood,
With spirit of sense to renew it as springs
fulfilling a flood.
Men are the heartbeats of man, the plumes
that feather his wings,
Storm-worn, since being began, with the wind
and thunder of things.
Things are cruel and blind; their strength
detains and deforms:
And the wearying wings of the mind still beat
up the stream of their storms.
Still, as one swimming up stream, they strike
out blind in the blast,
In thunders of vision and dream, and light-
nings of future and past.
We are baffled and caught in the current and
bruised upon edges of shoals;
As weeds or as reeds in the torrent of things
are the wind-shaken souls.
Spirit by spirit goes under, a foam-bell's
bubble of breath,
That blows and opens in sunder and blurs not
the mirror of death.
For a worm or a thorn in his path is a man's
soul quenched as a flame;
For his lust of an hour or his wrath shall the
worm and the man be the same.
O God sore stricken of things! they have
wrought him a raiment of pain;
Can a God shut eyelids and wings at a touch on
the nerves of the brain?
O shamed and sorrowful God, whose force goes
out at a blow!

What world shall shake at his nod? at his
coming what wilderness glow?
What help in the work of his hands? what
light in the track of his feet?
His days are snowflakes or sands, with cold to
consume him and heat.
He is servant with Change for lord, and for
wages he hath to his hire
Folly and force, and a sword that devours,
and a ravening fire.
From the bed of his birth to his grave he is
driven as a wind at their will;
Lest Change bow down as his slave, and the
storm and the sword be still;
Lest earth spread open her wings to the
sunward, and sing with the spheres;
Lest man be master of things, to prevail on
their forces and fears.
By the spirit are things overcome; they are
stark, and the spirit hath breath;
It hath speech, and their forces are dumb; it is
living, and things are of death.
But they know not the spirit for master, they
feel not force from above,
While man makes love to disaster, and woos
desolation with love.
Yea, himself too hath made himself chains, and
his own hands plucked out his eyes;
For his own soul only constrains him, his own
mouth only denies.
The herds of kings and their hosts and the
flocks of the high priests bow
To a master whose face is a ghost's; O thou
that wast God, is it thou?
Thou madest man in the garden; thou
temptedst man, and he fell;
Thou gavest him poison and pardon for blood
and burnt-offering to sell.
Thou hast sealed thine elect to salvation, fast
locked with faith for the key;
Make now for thyself expiation, and be thine
atonement for thee.
Ah, thou that darkenest heaven—ah, thou that
bringest a sword[1]—
By the crimes of thine hands unforgiven they
beseech thee to hear them, O Lord.
By the balefires of ages that burn for thine
incense, by creed and by rood,[2]

By the famine and passion that yearn and that
hunger to find of thee food,
By the children that asked at thy throne of the
priests that were fat with thine hire
For bread, and thou gavest a stone;[3] for light,
and thou madest them fire;
By the kiss of thy peace like a snake's kiss, that
leaves the soul rotten at root;
By the savours of gibbets and stakes thou hast
planted to bear to thee fruit;
By torture and terror and treason, that make to
thee weapons and wings;
By thy power upon men for a season, made out
of the malice of things;
O thou that hast built thee a shrine of the
madness of man and his shame,
And hast hung in the midst for a sign of his
worship the lamp of thy name;
That hast shown him for heaven in a vision a
void world's shadow and shell,
And hast fed thy delight and derision with fire
of belief as of hell;
That hast fleshed on the souls that believe thee
the fang of the death-worm fear,
With anguish of dreams to deceive them whose
faith cries out in thine ear;
By the face of the spirit confounded before thee
and humbled in dust,
By the dread wherewith life was astounded
and shamed out of sense of its trust,
By the scrouges of doubt and repentance that
fell on the soul at thy nod,
Thou art judged, O judge, and the sentence is
gone forth against thee, O God.
Thy slave that slept is awake; thy slave but
slept for a span;
Yea, man thy slave shall unmake thee, who
made thee lord over man.
For his face is set to the east, his feet on the
past and its dead;
The sun rearisen is his priest, and the heat
thereof hallows his head.
His eyes take part in the morning; his spirit
out-sounding the sea
Asks no more witness or warning from temple
or tripod or tree.[4]
He hath set the centuries at union; the night
is afraid at his name;

---

[1] "Think not that I am come to send peace on earth: I came not to send peace, but a sword"
(Matthew 10:34).
[2] Balefires: funeral pyres; rood: the crucifix.
[3] "Or what man is there of you, whom if his son ask bread, will he give him a stone?"
(Matthew 7:9).
[4] Tripod or tree: the tripod was one of the instruments used by the priestesses of Apollo; the
tree is the cross of Christ.

Equal with life, in communion with death, he
  hath found them the same.
Past the wall unsurmounted that bars out our
  vision with iron and fire
He hath sent forth his soul for the stars to
  comply with and suns to conspire.
His thought takes flight for the centre where-
  through it hath part in the whole;
The abysses forbid it not enter: the stars make
  room for the soul.
Space is the soul's to inherit; the night is hers
  as the day;
Lo, saith man, this is my spirit; how shall not
  the worlds make way?
Space is thought's, and the wonders thereof,
  and the secret of space;
Is thought not more than the thunders and
  lightnings? shall thought give place?
Is the body not more than the vesture, the life
  not more than the meat?[5]
The will than the word or the gesture, the
  heart than the hands or the feet?
Is the tongue not more than the speech is? the
  head not more than the crown?
And if higher than is heaven be the reach of the
  soul, shall not heaven bow down?
Time, father of life, and more great than the
  life it begat and began,
Earth's keeper and heaven's and their fate,
  lives, thinks, and hath substance in man.
Time's motion that throbs in his blood is the
  thought that gives heart to the skies,
And the springs of the fire that is food to the
  sunbeams are light to his eyes.
The minutes that beat with his heart are the
  words to which worlds keep chime,
And the thought in his pulses is part of the
  blood and the spirit of time.
He saith to the ages, Give; and his soul fore-
  goes not her share;
Who are ye that forbid him to live, and would
  feed him with heavenlier air?
Will ye feed him with poisonous dust, and
  restore him with hemlock for drink,
Till he yield you his soul up in trust, and have
  heart not to know or to think?
He hath stirred him, and found out the flaw
  in his fetters, and cast them behind;

His soul to his soul is a law, and his mind is a
  light to his mind.
The seal of his knowledge is sure, the truth and
  his spirit are wed;
Men perish, but man shall endure; lives die,
  but the life is not dead.
He hath sight of the secrets of season, the roots
  of the years and the fruits;
His soul is at one with the reason of things
  that is sap to the roots.
He can hear in their changes a sound as the
  conscience of consonant spheres;
He can see through the years flowing round
  him the law lying under the years.
Who are ye that would bind him with curses
  and blind him with vapour of prayer?
Your might is as night that disperses when
  light is alive in the air.
The bow of your godhead is broken, the arm
  of your conquest is stayed;
Though ye call down God to bear token, for
  fear of you none is afraid.
Will ye turn back times, and the courses of
  stars, and the season of souls?
Shall God's breath dry up the sources that feed
  time full as it rolls?
Nay, cry on him then till he show you a sign,
  till he lift up a rod;
Hath he made not the nations to know him of
  old if indeed he be God?
Is no heat of him left in the ashes of thousands
  burnt up for his sake?
Can prayer not rekindle the flashes that shone
  in his face from the stake?
Cry aloud; for your God is a God and a
  Saviour; cry, make yourselves lean;
Is he drunk or asleep, that the rod of his wrath
  is unfelt and unseen?[6]
Is the fire of his old loving-kindness gone out
  that his pyres are acold?
Hath he gazed on himself unto blindness, who
  made men blind to behold?
Cry out, for his kingdom is shaken; cry out, for
  the people blaspheme;
Cry aloud till his godhead awaken; what doth
  he to sleep and to dream?
Cry, cut yourselves, gash you with knives and
  with scourges, heap on to you dust;

---

[5] "Is not the life more than meat, and the body more than raiment?" (Matthew 6:25) : spoken
by Christ.
[6] "And it came to pass at noon, that Elijah mocked them, and said, Cry aloud: for he is a
god; either he is talking, or he is pursuing, or he is in a journey, or peradventure he sleepeth,
and must be awaked. And they cried aloud, and cut themselves after their manner with knives
and lancets, till the blood gushed out upon them" (1 Kings 18:27-28) : Elijah is speaking to the
priests of the pagan god Baal.

Is his life but as other gods' lives? is not this
   the Lord God of your trust?
Is not this the great God of your sires, that
   with souls and with bodies was fed,
And the world was on flame with his fires? O
   fools, he was God, and is dead.
He will hear not again the strong crying of
   earth in his ears as before,
And the fume of his multitudes dying shall
   flatter his nostrils no more.
By the spirit he ruled as his slave is he slain
   who was mighty to slay,
And the stone that is sealed on his grave he
180   shall rise not and roll not away.
Yea, weep to him, lift up your hands; be your
   eyes as a fountain of tears;
Where he stood there is nothing that stands; if
   he call, there is no man that hears.
He hath doffed his king's raiment of lies now
   the wane of his kingdom is come;
Ears hath he, and hears not; and eyes, and he
   sees not; and mouth, and is dumb.[7]
His red king's raiment is ripped from him
   naked, his staff broken down;
And the signs of his empire are stripped from
   him shuddering; and where is his crown?
And in vain by the wellsprings refrozen ye cry
   for the warmth of his sun—
O God, the Lord God of thy chosen, thy will
   in thy kingdom be done.
Kingdom and will hath he none in him left
   him, nor warmth in his breath;
Till his corpse be cast out of the sun will ye
190   know not the truth of his death?
Surely, ye say, he is strong, though the times
   be against him and men;
Yet a little, ye say, and how long, till he come
   to show judgment again?
Shall God then die as the beasts die? who is it
   hath broken his rod?
O God, Lord God of thy priests, rise up now
   and show thyself God.
They cry out, thine elect, thine aspirants to
   heavenward, whose faith is as flame;

O thou the Lord God of our tyrants, they call
   thee, their God, by thy name.
By thy name that in hell-fire was written, and
   burned at the point of thy sword,
Thou art smitten, thou God, thou art smitten;
   thy death is upon thee, O Lord.
And the love-song of earth as thou diest
   resounds through the wind of her wings—
Glory to Man in the highest![8] for Man is the
   master of things.   200

                                                     1871

To Walt Whitman in America[1]

Send but a song oversea for us,
   Heart of their hearts who are free,
Heart of their singer, to be for us
   More than our singing can be;
Ours, in the tempest at error,
With no light but the twilight of terror;
   Send us a song oversea!

Sweet-smelling of pine-leaves and grasses,
   And blown as a tree through and through
With the winds of the keen mountain-passes,   1
   And tender as sun-smitten dew;
Sharp-tongued as the winter that shakes
The wastes of your limitless lakes,
   Wide-eyed as the sea-line's blue.

O strong-winged soul with prophetic
   Lips hot with the bloodbeats of song,
With tremor of heartstrings magnetic,
   With thoughts as thunders in throng,
With consonant ardours of chords   2
That pierce men's souls as with swords
   And hale them hearing along,

Make us too music, to be with us
   As a word from a world's heart warm,
To sail the dark as a sea with us,
   Full-sailed, outsinging the storm,
A song to put fire in our ears

---

[7] "Their idols are silver and gold, the work of men's hands. They have mouths, but they
speak not: eyes have they, but they see not: They have ears, but they hear not" (Psalms 115:
4–6).
   [8] "Glory to God in the highest" (Luke 2:14): an angel is speaking who announces the birth
of Christ.
   [1] Swinburne in the 1860s was greatly moved by the poetry of Walt Whitman, as he was by
that of Victor Hugo and William Blake. He said of *Songs Before Sunrise* that he wanted to
make it "a book of political and national poems as complete and coherent in its way as the
Châtiments [of Hugo] or Drum Taps," the latter a volume of poems about the American Civil
War published by Whitman in 1865. (*Letters*, I, 268).

Whose burning shall burn up tears,
  Whose sign bid battle reform;

A note in the ranks of a clarion,
  A word in the wind of cheer,
To consume as with lightning the carrion
  That makes time foul for us here;
In the air that our dead things infest
A blast of the breath of the west,
  Till east way as west way is clear.

Out of the sun beyond sunset,
  From the evening whence morning shall be,
With the rollers in measureless onset,
  With the van of the storming sea,
With the world-wide wind, with the breath
That breaks ships driven upon death,
  With the passion of all things free,

With the sea-steeds footless and frantic,
  White myriads for death to bestride
In the charge of the ruining Atlantic
  Where deaths by regiments ride,
With clouds and clamours of waters,
With a long note shriller than slaughter's
  On the furrowless fields world-wide,

With terror, with ardour and wonder,
  With the soul of the season that wakes
When the weight of a whole year's thunder
  In the tidestream of autumn breaks,
Let the flight of the wide-winged word
Come over, come in and be heard,
  Take form and fire for our sakes.

For a continent bloodless with travail
  Here toils and brawls as it can,
And the web of it who shall unravel
  Of all that peer on the plan;
Would fain grow men, but they grow not,
And fain be free, but they know not
  One name for freedom and man?

One name, not twain for division;
  One thing, not twain, from the birth;
Spirit and substance and vision,
  Worth more than worship is worth;
Unbeheld, unadored, undivined,
The cause, the centre, the mind,
  The secret and sense of the earth.

Here as a weakling in irons,
  Here as a weanling in bands,[2]

As a prey that the stake-net environs,
  Our life that we looked for stands;
And the man-child naked and dear,
Democracy, turns on us here
  Eyes trembling with tremulous hands.

It sees not what season shall bring to it
  Sweet fruit of its bitter desire;
Few voices it hears yet sing to it,   80
  Few pulses of hearts reaspire;
Foresees not time, nor forehears
The noises of imminent years,
  Earthquake, and thunder, and fire:

When crowned and weaponed and curbless
  It shall walk without helm or shield
The bare burnt furrows and herbless
  Of war's last flame-stricken field,
Till godlike, equal with time,
It stand in the sun sublime,   90
  In the godhead of man revealed.

Round your people and over them
  Light like raiment is drawn,
Close as a garment to cover them
  Wrought not of mail nor of lawn;
Here, with hope hardly to wear,
Naked nations and bare
  Swim, sink, strike out for the dawn.

Chains are here, and a prison,
  Kings, and subjects, and shame;   100
If the God upon you be arisen,
  How should our songs be the same?
How, in confusion of change,
How shall we sing, in a strange
  Land, songs praising his name?

God is buried and dead to us,
  Even the spirit of earth,
Freedom; so have they said to us,
  Some with mocking and mirth,
Some with heartbreak and tears;   110
And a God without eyes, without ears,
  Who shall sing of him, dead in the birth?

The earth-god Freedom, the lonely
  Face lightening, the footprint unshod,
Not as one man crucified only
  Nor scourged with but one life's rod;
The soul that is substance of nations,
Reincarnate with fresh generations;
  The great god Man, which is God.

[2] Bands: leashes or restraints put on children or small animals.

120 But in weariest of years and obscurest
    Doth it live not at heart of all things,
The one God and one spirit, a purest
    Life, fed from unstanchable springs?
Within love, within hatred it is,
And its seed in the stripe as the kiss,
    And in slaves is the germ, and in kings.

Freedom we call it, for holier
    Name of the soul's there is none;
Surelier it labours, if slowlier,
130   Than the metres of star or of sun;
Slowlier than life into breath,
Surelier than time into death,
    It moves till its labour be done.

Till the motion be done and the measure
    Circling through season and clime,
Slumber and sorrow and pleasure,
    Vision of virtue and crime;
Till consummate with conquering eyes,
A soul disembodied, it rise
140   From the body transfigured of time.

Till it rise and remain and take station
    With the stars of the worlds that rejoice;
Till the voice of its heart's exultation
    Be as theirs an invariable voice;
By no discord of evil estranged,
By no pause, by no breach in it changed,
    By no clash in the chord of its choice.

It is one with the world's generations,
    With the spirit, the star, and the sod;
150 With the kingless and king-stricken nations,
    With the cross, and the chain, and the rod;
The most high, the most secret, most lonely,
The earth-soul Freedom, that only
    Lives, and that only is God.

                    1871

Siena

Inside this northern summer's fold
The fields are full of naked gold,

Broadcast from heaven on lands it loves;
The green veiled air is full of doves;
Soft leaves that sift the sunbeams let
Light on the small warm grasses wet
Fall in short broken kisses sweet,
And break again like waves that beat
Round the sun's feet.

But I, for all this English mirth   10
Of golden-shod and dancing days,
And the old green-girt sweet-hearted earth,
Desire what here no spells can raise.
Far hence, with holier heavens above,
The lovely city of my love
Bathes deep in the sun-satiate air
That flows round no fair thing more fair
Her beauty bare.

There the utter sky is holier, there
More pure the intense white height of air,   20
More clear men's eyes that mine would meet,
And the sweet springs of things more sweet.
There for this one warm note of doves
A clamour of a thousand loves
Storms the night's ear, the day's assails,
From the tempestuous nightingales,
And fills, and fails.

O gracious city well-beloved,
    Italian, and a maiden crowned,
Siena, my feet are no more moved   30
    Toward thy strange-shapen mountain-
        bound:[1]
But my heart in me turns and moves,
O lady loveliest of my loves,
Toward thee, to lie before thy feet
And gaze from thy far fountain-seat
Up the sheer street;

And the house midway hanging see
That saw Saint Catherine bodily,[2]
Felt on its floors her sweet feet move,
And the live light of fiery love   40
Burn from her beautiful strange face,
As in the sanguine sacred place
Where in pure hands she took the head

---

[1] Siena is on a plateau near the Chianti mountains in northwestern Italy.

[2] St. Catherine of Siena (1347–1380) was an ascetic and visionary who undertook the practical tasks of nursing the sick and helping the poor, and who also was charged with important political missions of conciliation. In one of these she went to Avignon in France, to which the papacy had moved from Rome, to persuade the pope to return to Italy. In a note to this poem Swinburne calls this pilgrimage "the central act of St. Catherine's life, the great abiding sign of the greatness of spirit and genius of heroism which distinguished this daughter of the people . . . ; but there is no less significance in the story which tells how she succeeded in humanizing a criminal under sentence of death, . . . ; how the man thus raised and melted out of his fierce and brutal despair besought her to sustain him to the last by her presence; how,

Severed, and with pure lips still red
Kissed the lips dead.

For years through, sweetest of the saints,
    In quiet without cease she wrought,
Till cries of men and fierce complaints
    From outward moved her maiden thought;
And prayers she heard and sighs toward
        France,
"God, send us back deliverance,
Send back thy servant, lest we die!"
With an exceeding bitter cry
They smote the sky.

Then in her sacred saving hands
She took the sorrows of the lands,
With maiden palms she lifted up
The sick time's blood-embittered cup,
And in her virgin garment furled
The faint limbs of a wounded world.
Clothed with calm love and clear desire.
She went forth in her soul's attire,
A missive fire.

Across the might of men that strove
    It shone, and over heads of kings;
And molten in red flames of love
    Were swords and many monstrous things;
And shields were lowered, and snapt were
        spears,
And sweeter-tuned the clamorous years;
And faith came back, and peace, that were
Fled; for she bade, saying, "Thou, God's heir,
Hast thou no care?

"Lo, men lay waste thine heritage
Still, and much heathen people rage
Against thee, and devise vain things.
What comfort in the face of kings,
What counsel is there? Turn thine eyes
And thine heart from them in like wise;
Turn thee unto thine holy place
To help us that of God for grace
Require thy face.

"For who shall hear us if not thou
    In a strange land? what doest thou there?

Thy sheep are spoiled, and the ploughers
        plough
    Upon us; why hast thou no care
For all this, and beyond strange hills
Liest unregardful what snow chills
Thy foldless flock, or what rains beat?
Lo, in thine ears, before thy feet,
Thy lost sheep bleat.   90

"And strange men feed on faultless lives,
And there is blood, and men put knives,
Shepherd, unto the young lamb's throat;
And one hath eaten, and one smote,
And one had hunger and is fed
Full of the flesh of these, and red
With blood of these as who drinks wine.
And God knoweth, who hath sent thee a sign,
If these were thine."

But the Pope's heart within him burned,   100
    So that he rose up, seeing the sign,
And came among them; but she turned
    Back to her daily way divine,
And fed her faith with silent things,
And lived her life with curbed white wings,
And mixed herself with heaven and died:
And now on the sheer city-side
Smiles like a bride.

You see her in the fresh clear gloom,
Where walls shut out the flame and bloom   110
Of full-breathed summer, and the roof
Keeps the keen ardent air aloof
And sweet weight of the violent sky:
There bodily beheld on high,
She seems as one hearing in tune
Heaven within heaven, at heaven's full noon,
In sacred swoon:

A solemn swoon of sense that aches
    With imminent blind heat of heaven,
While all the wide-eyed spirit wakes,   120
    Vigilant of the supreme Seven,[3]
Whose choral flames in God's sight move,
Made unendurable with love,
That without wind or blast of breath

---

having accompanied him with comfort and support to the very scaffold, and seen his head fall, she took it up, and turning to the spectators who stood doubtful whether the poor wretch could be 'saved', kissed it in sign of her faith that his sins were forgiven him." Swinburne closes his note by emphasizing "the strength and breadth of patriotic thought and devotion which sent this girl across the Alps to seek the living symbol of Italian hope and unity. . . . The rapturous visionary and passionate ascetic was in plain matters of this earth as pure and practical a heroine as Joan of Arc."

[3] Supreme Seven: the spheres that are the abode of the saints in Dante's *Paradiso*.

Compels all things through life and death
Whither God saith.

There on the dim side-chapel wall[4]
Thy mighty touch memorial,
Razzi,[5] raised up, for ages dead,
130   And fixed for us her heavenly head:
And, rent with plaited thorn and rod,
Bared the live likeness of her God
To men's eyes turning from strange lands,
Where, pale from thine immortal hands,
Christ wounded stands;

And the blood blots his holy hair
   And white brows over hungering eyes
That plead against us, and the fair
   Mute lips forlorn of words or sighs
140   In the great torment that bends down
His bruised head with the bloomless crown,
White as the unfruitful thorn-flower,
A God beheld in dreams that were
Beheld of her.

In vain on all these sins and years
Falls the sad blood, fall the slow tears;
In vain poured forth as watersprings,
Priests, on your altars, and ye, kings,
About your seats of sanguine gold;
150   Still your God, spat upon and sold,
Bleeds at your hands; but now is gone
All his flock from him saving one;
Judas alone.

Surely your race it was that he,
   O men signed backward with his name,[6]
Beholding in Gethsemane
   Bled the red bitter sweat of shame,
Knowing how the word of Christian should
Mean to men evil and not good,
160   Seem to men shameful for your sake,
Whose lips, for all the prayers they make,
Man's blood must slake.

But blood nor tears ye love not, you
That my love leads my longing to,

Fair as the world's old faith of flowers,
O golden goddesses of ours!
From what Idalian rose-pleasance
Hath Aphrodite bidden glance
The lovelier lightnings of your feet?
From what sweet Paphian[7] sward or seat   170
Led you more sweet?

O white three sisters, three as one,[8]
   With flowerlike arms for flowery bands
Your linked limbs glitter like the sun,
   And time lies beaten at your hands.
Time and wild years and wars and men
Pass, and ye care not whence or when;
With calm lips over sweet for scorn,
Ye watch night pass, O children born
Of the old-world morn.   180

Ah, in this strange and shrineless place,
What doth a goddess, what a Grace,
Where no Greek worships her shrined limbs
With wreaths and Cytherean[9] hymns?
Where no lute makes luxurious
The adoring airs in Amathus,
Till the maid, knowing her mother near,
Sobs with love, aching with sweet fear?
What do ye here?

For the outer land is sad, and wears   19●
   A raiment of a flaming fire;
And the fierce fruitless mountain stairs
   Climb, yet seem wroth and loth to aspire,
Climb, and break, and are broken down,
And through their clefts and crests the town
Looks west and sees the dead sun lie,
In sanguine death that stains the sky
With angry dye.

And from the war-worn wastes without
In twilight, in the time of doubt,   20
One sound comes of one whisper, where
Moved with low motions of slow air
The great trees nigh the castle swing
In the sad coloured evening;
"*Ricorditi di me, che son*

---

    4 Swinburne's note: "In the church of San Domenico."
    5 Razzi: Giovanni Antonia Razzi (1477–1549)—Il Sodama—painted a picture of Christ bound
and tortured which Swinburne had seen and admired in Siena.
    6 Signed backward: marked perversely.
    7 Idalian; Paphian: Idalium and Paphos, like Amathus (line 186), were cities on Cyprus
sacred to the worship of Aphrodite, the goddess of love.
    8 White three sisters: the three Graces, goddess of the banquet, the dance, and social enjoy-
ments. In his note to the poem Swinburne remarks that he had also seen and admired in Siena
a sculpture of the Graces whose beauty refreshed "beyond expression a sense wholly wearied and
well-nigh nauseated with contemplation of endless sanctities and agonies attempted by medieval
art."
    9 Cytherean: an epithet of Aphrodite, referring to her birth from the sea-foam.

La Pia"[10]—that small sweet word alone
Is not yet gone.

"*Ricorditi di me*"—the sound
   Sole out of deep dumb days remote
210 Across the fiery and fatal ground
   Comes tender as a hurt bird's note
To where, a ghost with empty hands,
A woe-worn ghost, her palace stands
In the mid city, where the strong
Bells turn the sunset air to song,
And the towers throng.

With other face, with speech the same,
A mightier maiden's likeness came
Late among mourning men that slept,
220 A sacred ghost that went and wept,
White as the passion-wounded Lamb,
Saying, "Ah, remember me, that am
Italia." (From deep sea to sea
Earth heard, earth knew her, that this was she.)
"*Ricorditi*.

"Love made me of all things fairest thing,
   And Hate unmade me; this knows he
Who with God's sacerdotal ring
   Enringed mine hand, espousing me."
230 Yea, in thy myriad-mooded woe,
Yea, Mother, hast thou not said so?
Have not our hearts within us stirred,
O thou most holiest, at thy word?
Have we not heard?

As this dead tragic land that she
Found deadly, such was time to thee;
Years passed thee withering in the red
Maremma, years that deemed thee dead,
Ages that sorrowed or that scorned;
240 And all this while though all they mourned
Thou sawest the end of things unclean,
And the unborn that should see thee a queen.
Have we not seen?

The weary poet, thy sad son,[11]
   Upon thy soil, under thy skies,

Saw all Italian things save one—
   Italia; this thing missed his eyes;
The old mother-might, the breast, the face,
That reared, that lit the Roman race;
This not Leopardi saw; but we,   250
What is it, Mother, that we see,
What if not thee?

Look thou from Siena southward home,
Where the priest's pall hangs rent on Rome,
And through the red rent swaddling-bands[12]
Towards thine she strains her labouring hands.
Look thou and listen, and let be
All the dead quick, all the bond free;
In the blind eyes let there be sight;
In the eighteen centuries of the night   260
Let there be light.

Bow down the beauty of thine head,
   Sweet, and with lips of living breath
Kiss thy sons sleeping and thy dead,
   That there be no more sleep or death.
Give us thy light, thy might, thy love,
Whom thy face seen afar above
Drew to thy feet; and when, being free,
Thou hast blest thy children born to thee,
Bless also me.   270

Me that when others played or slept
Sat still under thy cross and wept;
Me who so early and unaware
Felt fall on bent bared brows and hair
(Thin drops of the overflowing flood!)
The bitter blessing of thy blood;
The sacred shadow of thy pain,
Thine, the true maiden-mother, slain
And raised again.

Me consecrated, if I might,   280
   To praise thee, or to love at least,
O mother of all men's dear delight,
   Thou madest a choral-souled boy-priest,
Before my lips had leave to sing,
Or my hands hardly strength to cling

---

[10] "*Ricorditi . . .*": Remember me who am Pia": spoken in the fifth canto of Dante's *Purgatorio*. Pia was a woman of Siena who was imprisoned in the Maremma (line 238) by her husband and finally murdered by him. Her speech continues in lines that Swinburne paraphrases in lines 227–229: "He knows of it who, first plighting his troth, wedded me with his gem."

[11] The weary poet: Giacomo Leopardi (1798–1837). In a note to this poem Swinburne quoted (in Italian) lines of Leopardi's which lament that he sees around him the buildings and statues, but not the glory of art and power, which graced the lives of his ancestors.

[12] "Siena" was first published in 1868, after the defeat of Garibaldi in what turned out to be his last attempt to establish a republican government in Rome, but before France withdrew from Rome in 1870 and left it to the control of the monarchy of Victor Emmanuel and the papacy. Swaddling-bands: leashes or restraints placed on infants.

About the intolerable tree
Whereto they had nailed my heart and thee
And said, "Let be."

For to thee too the high Fates gave
290   Grace to be sacrificed and save,
That being arisen, in the equal sun,
God and the People should be one;
By those red roads thy footprints trod,
Man more divine, more human God,
Saviour; that where no light was known
But darkness, and a daytime flown,
Light should be shown.

Let there be light, O Italy!
   For our feet falter in the night.
300   O lamp of living years to be,
   O light of God, let there be light!
Fill with a love keener than flame
Men sealed in spirit with thy name,
The cities and the Roman skies,
Where men with other than man's eyes
Saw thy sun rise.

For theirs thou wast and thine were they
Whose names outshine thy very day;
For they are thine and theirs thou art
310   Whose blood beats living in man's heart,
Remembering ages fled and dead
Wherein for thy sake these men bled;
They that saw Trebia, they that see
Mentana,[13] they in years to be
That shall see thee.

For thine are all of us, and ours
   Thou; till the seasons bring to birth
A perfect people, and all the powers
   Be with them that bear fruit on earth;
320   Till the inner heart of man be one
With freedom, and the sovereign sun;
And Time, in likeness of a guide,
Lead the Republic as a bride
Up to God's side.

                                        1868; 1871

Cor Cordium[1]

O heart of hearts, the chalice of love's fire,
   Hid round with flowers and all the bounty
      of bloom;
   O wonderful and perfect heart, for whom
The lyrist liberty made life a lyre;
O heavenly heart, at whose most dear desire
   Dead love, living and singing, cleft his tomb,
   And with him risen and regent in death's
      room
All day thy choral pulses rang full choir;
O heart whose beating blood was running song,
   O sole thing sweeter than thine own songs
      were,   10
      Help us for thy free love's sake to be free,
True for thy truth's sake, for thy strength's
      sake strong,
   Till very liberty make clean and fair
      The nursing earth as the sepulchral sea.
                                        1871

The Oblation[1]

Ask nothing more of me, sweet;
   All I can give you I give.
      Heart of my heart, were it more,
More would be laid at your feet:
   Love that should help you to live,
      Song that should spur you to soar.

All things were nothing to give
   Once to have sense of you more,
      Touch you and taste of you sweet,
Think you and breathe you and live,   10
   Swept of your wings as they soar,
      Trodden by chance of your feet.

I that have love and no more
   Give you but love of you, sweet:
      He that hath more, let him give;
He that hath wings, let him soar;
   Mine is the heart at your feet
      Here, that must love you to live.
                                        1871

---

[13] Trebia was the site of Hannibal's defeat of a Roman army in 218 B.C. Mentana was the
site of the defeat of Garibaldi's forces in 1867 by the French in support of the papacy.
   [1] Cor cordium—heart of hearts—is an inscription on the tomb of Percy Bysshe Shelley in
Rome.
   [1] The Oblation: an offering; in this poem, to liberty.

A Year's Burden

1870[1]

Fire and wild light of hope and doubt and fear,
Wind of swift change, and clouds and hours
  that veer
As the storm shifts of the tempestuous year;
  Cry wellaway, but well befall the right.

Hope sits yet hiding her war-wearied eyes,
Doubt sets her forehead earthward and denies,
But fear brought hand to hand with danger
  dies,
  Dies and is burnt up in the fire of fight.

Hearts bruised with loss and eaten through
  with shame
10 Turn at the time's touch to devouring flame;
Grief stands as one that knows not her own
  name,
  Nor if the star she sees bring day or night.

No song breaks with it on the violent air,
But shrieks of shame, defeat, and brute despair;
Yet something at the star's heart far up there
  Burns as a beacon in our shipwrecked sight.

O strange fierce light of presage, unknown star,
Whose tongue shall tell us what thy secrets are,
What message trembles in thee from so far?
20   Cry wellaway, but well befall the right.

From shores laid waste across an iron sea
Where the waifs drift of hopes that were to be,
Across the red rolled foam we look for thee,
  Across the fire we look up for the light.

From days laid waste across disastrous years,
From hopes cut down across a world of fears,
We gaze with eyes too passionate for tears,
  Where faith abides though hope be put to
  flight.

Old hope is dead, the grey-haired hope grown
  blind
30 That talked with us of old things out of mind,
Dreams, deeds and men the world has left
  behind;
  Yet, though hope die, faith lives in hope's
  despite.

Ay, with hearts fixed on death and hopeless
  hands
We stand about our banner while it stands
Above but one field of the ruined lands;
  Cry wellaway, but well befall the right.

Though France were given for prey to bird and
  beast,
Though Rome were rent in twain of king and
  priest,
The soul of man, the soul is safe at least
  That gives death life and dead men hands to
  smite.   40

Are ye so strong, O kings, O strong men? Nay,
Waste all ye will and gather all ye may,
Yet one thing is there that ye shall not slay,
  Even thought, that fire nor iron can affright.

The woundless and invisible thought that goes
Free throughout time as north or south wind
  blows,
Far throughout space as east or west sea flows,
  And all dark things before it are made
  bright.

Thy thought, thy word, O soul republican,
O spirit of life, O God whose name is man: 50
What sea of sorrows but thy sight shall span?
  Cry wellaway, but well befall the right.

With all its coils crushed, all its rings uncurled,
The one most poisonous worm[2] that soiled the
  world
Is wrenched from off the throat of man, and
  hurled
  Into deep hell from empire's helpless height.

Time takes no more infection of it now;
Like a dead snake divided of the plough,
The rotten thing lies cut in twain; but thou,
  Thy fires shall heal us of the serpent's bite.   60

Ay, with red cautery and a burning brand
Purge thou the leprous leaven of the land;
Take to thee fire, and iron in thine hand,
  Till blood and tears have washed the soiled
  limbs white.

We have sinned against thee in dreams and
  wicked sleep;

---

[1] In 1870 the Second Empire of Louis Napoleon was ended with the defeat of France in the
Franco-Prussian War; and the last hopes of a republican Rome were extinguished with the
addition of Rome to the kingdom of Victor Emmanuel, king of Italy.
[2] Most poisonous worm: Louis Napoleon, Napoleon III of the Second Empire of France.

Smite, we will shrink not; strike, we will not
    weep;
Let the heart feel thee; let thy wound go deep;
    Cry wellaway, but well befall the right.

Wound us with love, pierce us with longing,
    make
70 Our souls thy sacrifices; turn and take
Our hearts for our sin-offerings lest they break,
    And mould them with thine hands and give
    them might.

Then, when the cup of ills is drained indeed,
Will we come to thee with our wounds that
    bleed,
With famished mouths and hearts that thou
    shalt feed,
    And see thee worshipped as the world's
    delight.

There shall be no more wars nor kingdoms
    won,
But in thy sight whose eyes are as the sun
All names shall be one name, all nations one,
80   All souls of men in man's one soul unite.

O sea whereon men labour, O great sea
That heaven seems one with, shall these things
    not be?
O earth, our earth, shall time not make us free?
    Cry wellaway, but well befall the right.
                         1871

A Dead King

[*Ferdinand II. entered Malebolge*
May 22nd, 1859.][1]
Go down to hell. This end is good to see;
    The breath is lightened and the sense at ease
    Because thou art not; sense nor breath there
    is
In what thy body was, whose soul shall be
Chief nerve of hell's pained heart eternally.
    Thou art abolished from the midst of these

That are what thou wast: Pius[2] from his
    knees
Blows off the dust that flecked them, bowed for
    thee.
Yea, now the long-tongued slack-lipped litanies
    Fail, and the priest has no more prayer to
    sell—   10
Now the last Jesuit found about thee is
    The beast that made thy fouler flesh his
    cell—
Time lays his finger on thee, saying, "Cease;
    Here is no room for thee; go down to hell."
                         1873; 1875

Apologia

If wrath embitter the sweet mouth of song,
    And make the sunlight fire before those eyes
    That would drink draughts of peace from
    the unsoiled skies,
The wrongdoing is not ours, but ours the
    wrong,
Who hear too loud on earth and see too long
    The grief that dies not with the groan that
    dies,
    Till the strong bitterness of pity cries
Within us, that our anger should be strong.
For chill is known by heat and heat by chill,
And the desire that hope makes love to still   10
    By the fear flying beside it or above,
    A falcon fledged to follow a fledgeling dove,
And by the fume and flame of hate of ill
    The exuberant light and burning bloom of
    love.
                         1873; 1875

A Forsaken Garden

In a coign of the cliff between lowland and
    highland,
    At the sea-down's edge between windward
    and lee,
Walled round with rocks as an inland island,
    The ghost of a garden fronts the sea.

[1] This and the following sonnet are part of a series titled "Diræ," curses or imprecations. Swinburne published the sonnets in magazines in 1869 and 1873 and collected them in *Songs of Two Nations* in 1875, in which he celebrated the potential republics of France and Italy.
    Ferdinand II (1810–1859) was a king of the two Sicilies, an entity created in 1815 which joined the kingdoms of Naples and Sicily and stood until 1860 as an impediment to Italian unity. He suppressed a rebellion in Sicily at mid-century by bombarding cities and subsequent prosecutions, and he was ridiculed in England as "King Bomba." Malebolge is the place in which the fraudulent are punished in Dante's *Inferno*.
[2] Pius: Pius IX, elected pope in 1846 and established in Rome with the support of France in 1849, ending a short-lived Roman republic.

A girdle of brushwood and thorn encloses
  The steep square slope of the blossomless bed
Where the weeds that grew green from the
      graves of its roses
    Now lie dead.

The fields fall southward, abrupt and broken,[1]
10 To the low last edge of the long lone land.
If a step should sound or a word be spoken,
  Would a ghost not rise at the strange guest's
      hand?
So long have the grey bare walks lain guestless,
  Through branches and briars if a man make
      way,
He shall find no life but the sea-wind's, restless
    Night and day.

The dense hard passage is blind[2] and stifled
  That crawls by a track none turn to climb
To the strait waste place that the years have
      rifled
  Of all but the thorns that are touched not of
20   time.
The thorns he spares when the rose is taken;
  The rocks are left when he wastes the plain.
The wind that wanders, the weeds wind-
      shaken,
    These remain.

Not a flower to be pressed of the foot that falls
      not;
  As the heart of a dead man the seed-plots are
      dry;
From the thicket of thorns whence the night-
      ingale calls not,
  Could she call, there were never a rose to
      reply.
Over the meadows that blossom and wither
30   Rings but the note of a sea-bird's song;
Only the sun and the rain come hither
    All year long.

The sun burns sere and the rain dishevels
  One gaunt bleak blossom of scentless breath.
Only the wind here hovers and revels
  In a round where life seems barren as death.
Here there was laughing of old, there was
      weeping,
  Haply, of lovers none ever will know,
Whose eyes went seaward a hundred sleeping
40   Years ago.

Heart handfast in heart as they stood, "Look
      thither,"
  Did he whisper? "look forth from the flowers
      to the sea;
For the foam-flowers endure when the rose-
      blossoms wither,
  And men that love lightly may die—but we?"
And the same wind sang and the same waves
      whitened,
  And or ever the garden's last petals were
      shed,
In the lips that had whispered, the eyes that
      had lightened,
    Love was dead.

Or they loved their life through, and then went
      whither?
  And were one to the end—but what end who
      knows?   50
Love deep as the sea as a rose must wither,
  As the rose-red seaweed that mocks the rose.
Shall the dead take thought for the dead to
      love them?
  What love was ever as deep as a grave?
They are loveless now as the grass above them
    Or the wave.

All are at one now, roses and lovers.
  Not known of the cliffs and the fields and the
      sea.
Not a breath of the time that has been hovers
  In the air now soft with a summer to be.   60
Not a breath shall there sweeten the seasons
      hereafter
  Of the flowers or the lovers that laugh now or
      weep,
When as they that are free now of weeping and
      laughter
    We shall sleep.

Here death may deal not again for ever;
  Here change may come not till all change
      end.
From the graves they have made they shall rise
      up never,
  Who have left nought living to ravage and
      rend.
Earth, stones, and thorns of the wild ground
      growing,
  While the sun and the rain live, these shall
      be;   70

---

[1] Fall southward: the setting of the poem is most likely on or near the Isle of Wight off the southern coast of England, where land was often reclaimed by the sea.
[2] Blind: dimly traced.

Till a last wind's breath upon all these blowing
 Roll the sea.

Till the slow sea rise and the sheer cliff
  crumble,
 Till terrace and meadow the deep gulfs
  drink,
Till the strength of the waves of the high tides
  humble
 The fields that lessen, the rocks that shrink,
Here now in his triumph where all things falter,
 Stretched out on the spoils that his own hand
  spread,
As a god self-slain on his own strange altar,
  Death lies dead.

          1876; 1878

80

At a Month's End

The night last night was strange and shaken:
 More strange the change of you and me.
Once more, for the old's love forsaken,
 We went out once more toward the sea.

For the old love's love-sake dead and buried,
 One last time, one more and no more,
We watched the waves set in, the serried
 Spears of the tide storming the shore.

Hardly we saw the high moon hanging,
 Heard hardly through the windy night
Far waters ringing, low reefs clanging,
 Under wan skies and waste white light.

10

With chafe and change of surges chiming,
 The clashing channels rocked and rang
Large music, wave to wild wave timing,
 And all the choral water sang.

Faint lights fell this way, that way floated,
 Quick sparks of sea-fire keen like eyes
From the rolled surf that flashed, and noted
 Shores and faint cliffs and bays and skies.

20

The ghost of sea that shrank up sighing
 At the sand's edge, a short sad breath
Trembling to touch the goal, and dying
 With weak heart heaved up once in death—

The rustling sand and shingle[1] shaken
 With light sweet touches and small sound—

These could not move us, could not waken
 Hearts to look forth, eyes to look round.

Silent we went an hour together,
 Under grey skies by waters white.
Our hearts were full of windy weather,
 Clouds and blown stars and broken light.

30

Full of cold clouds and moonbeams drifted
 And streaming storms and straying fires,
Our souls in us were stirred and shifted
 By doubts and dreams and foiled desires.

Across, aslant, a scudding sea-mew[2]
 Swam, dipped, and dropped, and grazed the
  sea:
And one with me I could not dream you;
 And one with you I could not be.

40

As the white wing the white wave's fringes
 Touched and slid over and flashed past—
As a pale cloud a pale flame tinges
 From the moon's lowest light and last—

As a star feels the sun and falters,
 Touched to death by diviner eyes—
As on the old gods' untended altars
 The old fire of withered worship dies—

(Once only, once the shrine relighted
 Sees the last fiery shadow shine,
Last shadow of flame and faith benighted,
 Sees falter and flutter and fail the shrine)

50

So once with fiery breath and flying
 Your winged heart touched mine and went,
And the swift spirits kissed, and sighing,
 Sundered and smiled and were content.

That only touch, that feeling only,
 Enough we found, we found too much;
For the unlit shrine is hardly lonely
 As one the old fire forgets to touch.

60

Slight as the sea's sight of the sea-mew,
 Slight as the sun's sight of the star:
Enough to show one must not deem you
 For love's sake other than you are.

Who snares and tames with fear and danger
 A bright beast of a fiery kin,
Only to mar, only to change her
 Sleek supple soul and splendid skin?

---

[1] Shingle: course rounded stone similar to but larger than gravel. [2] Sea-mew: sea gull.

Easy with blows to mar and maim her,
  Easy with bonds to bind and bruise;
What profit, if she yield her tamer
  The limbs to mar, the soul to lose?

Best leave or take the perfect creature,
  Take all she is or leave complete;
Transmute you will not form or feature,
  Change feet for wings or wings for feet.

Strange eyes, new limbs, can no man give her;
  Sweet is the sweet thing as it is.
No soul she hath, we see, to outlive her;
  Hath she for that no lips to kiss?

So may one read his weird,[3] and reason,
  And with vain drugs assuage no pain.
For each man in his loving season
  Fools and is fooled of these in vain.

Charms that allay not any longing,
  Spells that appease not any grief;
Time brings us all by handfuls, wronging
  All hurts with nothing of relief.

Ah, too soon shot, the fool's blot misses!
  What help? the world is full of loves;
Night after night of running kisses,
  Chirp after chirp of changing doves.

Should Love disown or disesteem you
  For loving one man more or less?
You could not tame your light white sea-mew,
  Nor I my sleek black pantheress.

For a new soul let whoso please pray,
  We are what life made us, and shall be.
For you the jungle and me the sea-spray,
  And south for you and north for me.

But this one broken foam-white feather
  I throw you off the hither wing,
Splashed stiff with sea-scurf[4] and salt weather,
  This song for sleep to learn and sing—

Sing in your ear when, daytime over,
  You, couched at long length on hot sand
With some sleek sun-discoloured lover,
  Wince from his breath as from a brand:

Till the acrid hour aches out and ceases,
  And the sheathed eyeball sleepier swims,   110
The deep flank smoothes its dimpling creases,
  And passion loosens all the limbs:

Till dreams of sharp grey north-sea weather
  Fall faint upon your fiery sleep,
As on strange sands a strayed bird's feather
  The wind may choose to lose or keep.

But I, who leave my queen of panthers,
  As a tired honey-heavy bee
Gilt with sweet dust from gold-grained anthers
  Leaves the rose-chalice, what for me?   120

From the ardours of the chaliced centre,
  From the amorous anthers' golden grime,
That scorch and smutch all wings that enter,
  I fly forth hot from honey-time.

But as to a bee's gilt thighs and winglets
  The flower-dust with the flower-smell clings;
As a snake's mobile rampant[5] ringlets
  Leave the sand marked with print of rings;

So to my soul in surer fashion
  Your savage stamp and savour hangs;   130
The print and perfume of old passion,
  The wild-beast mark of panther's fangs.
                                    1871; 1878

Sestina[1]

I saw my soul at rest upon a day
  As a bird sleeping in the nest of night,
Among soft leaves that give the starlight way
  To touch its wings but not its eyes with light;
So that it knew as one in visions may,
  And knew not as men waking, of delight.

This was the measure of my soul's delight;
  It had no power of joy to fly by day,
Nor part in the large lordship of the light;
  But in a secret moon-beholden way   10
Had all its will of dreams and pleasant night,
  And all the love and life that sleepers may.

But such life's triumph as men waking may
  It might not have to feed its faint delight

[3] Weird: fate.   [4] Sea-scurf: scum.   [5] Rampant: coiled and raised.
[1] The sestina, one of the forms of French verse which became popular in England in the latter decades of the nineteenth century, is a poem of six six-line stanzas and a three-line envoy or concluding stanza. Its principal feature is that the six end words are repeated in each stanza and in the envoy.

Between the stars by night and sun by day,
   Shut up with green leaves and a little light;
Because its way was as a lost star's way,
   A world's not wholly known of day or night.

All loves and dreams and sounds and gleams of
     night
20   Made it all music that such minstrels may,
And all they had they gave it of delight;
   But in the full face of the fire of day
What place shall be for any starry light,
   What part of heaven in all the wide sun's
     way?

Yet the soul woke not, sleeping by the way,
   Watched as a nursling of the large-eyed
     night,
And sought no strength nor knowledge of the
     day,
   Nor closer touch conclusive of delight,
Nor mightier joy nor truer than dreamers may,
   Nor more of song than they, nor more of
30   light.

For who sleeps once and sees the secret light
   Whereby sleep shows the soul a fairer way
Between the rise and rest of day and night,
   Shall care no more to fare as all men may,
But be his place of pain or of delight,
   There shall he dwell, beholding night as day.

Song, have thy day and take thy fill of light
   Before the night be fallen across thy way;
Sing while he may, man hath no long delight.
                    1872; 1878

*Swinburne, hearing a report of Baudelaire's
death, completed this poem before the French poet
actually died in 1867. Baudelaire's most important
volume of poems,* Les Fleurs du Mal, *was published
in 1857, and Swinburne corresponded with him
after the publication of the first series of* Poems and
Ballads *(1866). The title of the poem means "Hail
and farewell"; it is taken from a poem by the
first-century* B.C. *Roman poet Catullus. The epi-
graph is from Baudelaire's "La Servante au Grand
Coeur," a poem about the death of a generous ser-
vant: "We ought to take her some flowers. The
dead, the poor dead, have great sorrows, and when
October, the stripper of old trees, whistles its sad*

*wind around their marbles, surely, they must think
the living very ungrateful."*

Ave Atque Vale

In Memory of Charles Baudelaire

*Nous devrions pourtant lui porter quelques fleurs;
Les morts, les pauvres morts, ont de grandes douleurs,
Et quand Octobre souffle, émondeur des vieux arbres,
Son vent mélancolique à l'entour de leurs marbres,
Certe, ils doivent trouver les vivants bien ingrats.*
                    LES FLEURS DU MAL

I

Shall I strew on thee rose or rue or laurel,[1]
   Brother, on this that was the veil of thee?
   Or quiet sea-flower moulded by the sea,
Or simplest growth of meadow-sweet or sorrel,
   Such as the summer-sleepy Dryads[2] weave,
   Waked up by snow-soft sudden rains at
     eve?
Or wilt thou rather, as on earth before,
   Half-faded fiery blossoms, pale with heat
   And full of bitter summer, but more sweet
To thee than gleanings of a northern shore   10
   Trod by no tropic feet?

II

For always thee the fervid languid glories
   Allured of heavier suns in mightier skies;
   Thine ears knew all the wandering watery
     sighs
Where the sea sobs round Lesbian promonto-
     ries,[3]
   The barren kiss of piteous wave to wave
   That knows not where is that Leucadian
     grave
Which hides too deep the supreme head of
     song.
   Ah, salt and sterile as her kisses were,
   The wild sea winds her and the green gulfs
     bear   20
Hither and thither, and vex and work her
     wrong,
   Blind gods that cannot spare.

III

Thou sawest, in thine old singing season,
     brother

[1] Rose or rue or laurel: signifying love, sorrow, and the accomplishment of poetry.
[2] Dryads: wood nymphs.
[3] Lesbian: Baudelaire's "Lesbos" is about the death of the seventh-century B.C. poet Sappho, who lived on the island of Lesbos and according to legend threw herself into the sea from Mount Leucadia (line 17) because of a futile love.

Secrets and sorrows unbeheld of us:
    Fierce loves, and lovely leaf-buds
        poisonous,
Bare to thy subtler eye, but for none other
    Blowing by night in some unbreathed-in
        clime;
    The hidden harvest of luxurious time,
Sin without shape, and pleasure without
        speech;
    And where strange dreams in a tumultuous
30   sleep
    Make the shut eyes of stricken spirits weep;
And with each face thou sawest the shadow on
        each,
    Seeing as men sow men reap.

IV

O sleepless heart and sombre soul unsleeping,
    That were athirst for sleep and no more
        life
    And no more love, for peace and no more
        strife!
Now the dim gods of death have in their
        keeping
    Spirit and body and all the springs of song,
    Is it well now where love can do no wrong,
40 Where stingless pleasure has no foam or fang
    Behind the unopening closure of her lips?
    Is it not well where soul from body slips
And flesh from bone divides without a pang
    As dew from flower-bell drips?

V

It is enough; the end and the beginning
    Are one thing to thee, who are past the
        end.
    O hand unclasped of unbeholden friend,
For thee no fruits to pluck, no palms for
        winning,
    No triumph and no labour and no lust,
50   Only dead yew-leaves and a little dust.
O quiet eyes wherein the light saith nought,
    Whereto the day is dumb, nor any night
    With obscure finger silences your sight,
Nor in your speech the sudden soul speaks
        thought,
    Sleep, and have sleep for light.

VI

Now all strange hours and all strange loves are
        over,
    Dreams and desires and sombre songs and
        sweet,
    Hast thou found place at the great knees
        and feet
Of some pale Titan-woman[4] like a lover,
    Such as thy vision here solicited,   60
    Under the shadow of her fair vast head,
The deep division of prodigious breasts,
    The solemn slope of mighty limbs asleep,
    The weight of awful tresses that still keep
The savour and shade of old-world pine-forests
    Where the wet hill-winds weep?

VII

Hast thou found any likeness for thy vision?
    O gardener of strange flowers, what bud,
        what bloom,
    Hast thou found sown, what gathered in
        the gloom?
What of despair, of rapture, of derision,   70
    What of life is there, what of ill or good?
    Are the fruits grey like dust or bright like
        blood?
Does the dim ground grow any seed of ours,
    The faint fields quicken any terrene[5] root,
    In low lands where the sun and moon are
        mute
And all the stars keep silence? Are there flowers
    At all, or any fruit?

VIII

Alas, but though my flying song flies after,
    O sweet strange elder singer, thy more
        fleet   80
    Singing, and footprints of thy fleeter feet,
Some dim derision of mysterious laughter
    From the blind tongueless warders of the
        dead,
    Some gainless glimpse of Proserpine's[6]
        veiled head,
Some little sound of unregarded tears
    Wept by effaced unprofitable eyes,
    And from pale mouths some cadence of
        dead sighs—
These only, these the hearkening spirit hears,
    Sees only such things rise.

---

[4] Titan-woman: Baudelaire's poem "La Géante" describes a wish for an enormous woman whose knees are like mountain slopes and under whose breast one can sleep, secure as a village at the base of a mountain.

[5] Terrene: of the earth.

[6] Proserpine: the classical goddess of growing things, kidnapped by the god of the underworld and required to spend half the year with him in his realm.

IX

Thou art far too far for wings of words to
    follow,
90   Far too far off for thought or any prayer.
    What ails us with thee, who art wind and
    air?
What ails us gazing where all seen is hollow?
      Yet with some fancy, yet with some desire,
      Dreams pursue death as winds a flying fire,
Our dreams pursue our dead and do not find.
      Still, and more swift than they, the thin
      flame flies,
      The low light fails us in elusive skies,
Still the foiled earnest ear is deaf, and blind
      Are still the eluded eyes

X

100 Not thee, O never thee, in all time's changes,
      Not thee, but this the sound of thy sad
      soul,
      The shadow of thy swift spirit, this shut
      scroll
I lay my hand on, and not death estranges
      My spirit from communion of thy song—
      These memories and these melodies that
      throng
Veiled porches of a Muse funereal—
      These I salute, these touch, these clasp and
      fold
      As though a hand were in my hand to
      hold,
Or through mine ears a mourning musical
110   Of many mourners rolled.

XI

I among these, I also, in such station
      As when the pyre was charred, and piled
      the sods,[7]
      And offering to the dead made, and their
      gods,
The old mourners had, standing to make
      libation,
      I stand, and to the gods and to the dead
      Do reverence without prayer or praise, and
      shed
Offering to these unknown, the gods of gloom,

And what of honey and spice my seedlands
    bear,
      And what I may of fruits in this chilled
      air,
And lay, Orestes-like, across the tomb   120
      A curl of severed hair.[8]

XII

But by no hand nor any treason stricken,
      Not like the low-lying head of Him, the
      King,[9]
      The flame that made of Troy a ruinous
      thing,
Thou liest, and on this dust no tears could
      quicken
      There fall no tears like theirs that all men
      hear
      Fall tear by sweet imperishable tear
Down the opening leaves of holy poets' pages.
      Thee not Orestes, not Electra[10] mourns;
      But bending us-ward with memorial urns   130
The most high Muses that fulfil all ages
      Weep, and our God's heart yearns.

XIII

For, sparing of his sacred strength, not often
      Among us darkling here the lord of light
      Makes manifest his music and his might
In hearts that open and in lips that soften
      With the soft flame and heat of songs that
      shine.
      Thy lips indeed he touched with bitter
      wine,
And nourished them indeed with bitter bread;
      Yet surely from his hand thy soul's food
      came,   140
      The fire that scarred thy spirit at his flame
Was lighted, and thine hungering heart he fed
      Who feeds our hearts with fame.

XIV

Therefore he[11] too now at thy soul's sunsetting,
      God of all suns and songs, he too bends
      down
      To mix his laurel with thy cypress crown,[12]
And save thy dust from blame and from
      forgetting.

---

[7] Sods: peat used as fuel.

[8] Orestes: the son of the Greek hero Agamemmon, who, in *The Libation Bearers* of the Greek tragedian Aeschylus, offers his dead father the sacrifice of a lock of his hair.

[9] Agamemnon, who was killed by his wife and her lover upon his victorious return from the Trojan War.

[10] Electra: the sister of Orestes.

[11] Lord of light: Apollo, the classical god of song, sometimes also associated with the sun.

[12] Cypress: associated with death.

Therefore he too, seeing all thou wert and
    art,
    Compassionate, with sad and sacred heart,
150 Mourns thee of many his children the last dead,
        And hallows with strange tears and alien
            sighs
        Thine unmelodious mouth and sunless
            eyes,
    And over thine irrevocable head
        Sheds light from the under skies.

XV

And one weeps with him in the ways Lethean,[13]
    And stains with tears her changing bosom
        chill:
    That obscure Venus of the hollow hill,[14]
    That thing transformed which was the
        Cytherean,
        With lips that lost their Grecian laugh
            divine
        Long since, and face no more called
160   Erycine;[15]
    A ghost, a bitter and luxurious god.
        Thee also with fair flesh and singing spell
        Did she, a sad and second prey, compel
    Into the footless places once more trod,
        And shadows hot from hell.

XVI

And now no sacred staff shall break in blossom,
    No choral salutation lure to light
    A spirit sick with perfume and sweet night
And love's tired eyes and hands and barren
    bosom.
    There is no help for these things; none to
170   mend
    And none to mar; not all our songs, O
        friend,
Will make death clear or make life durable.
    Howbeit with rose and ivy and wild vine
    And with wild notes about this dust of
        thine
At least I fill the place where white dreams
    dwell
    And wreath an unseen shrine.

XVII

Sleep; and if life was bitter to thee, pardon,
    If sweet, give thanks; thou has no more to
        live;
    And to give thanks is good, and to forgive.
Out of the mystic and the mournful garden   180
    Where all day through thine hands in
        barren braid
    Wove the sick flowers of secrecy and shade,
Green buds of sorrow and sin, and remnants
    grey,
    Sweet-smelling, pale with poison, sanguine-
        hearted,
    Passions that sprang from sleep and
        thoughts that started,
Shall death not bring us all as thee one day
    Among the days departed?

XVIII

For thee, O now a silent soul, my brother,
    Take at my hands this garland, and
        farewell.
    Thin is the leaf, and chill the wintry smell,   190
And chill the solemn earth, a fatal mother,
    With sadder than the Niobean womb,[16]
    And in the hollow of her breasts a tomb.
Content thee, howsoe'er, whose days are done;
    There lies not any troublous thing before,
    Nor sight nor sound to war against thee
        more,
For whom all winds are quiet as the sun,
    All waters as the shore.

                                    1868, 1878

Before Sunset

In the lower lands of day
    On the hither side of night,
There is nothing that will stay,
    There are all things soft to sight;
    Lighted shade and shadowy light
In the wayside and the way,
    Hours the sun has spared to smite,
Flowers the rain has left to play.

---

13 Lethean: of the river Lethe, a river in the underworld of classical mythology whose waters when drunk cause forgetfulness.

14 Venus of the hollow hill: the Venus of the Tannhäuser legend: see the introductory note to Swinburne's "Laus Veneris."

15 Cytherean, Erycine: names of the classical goddess of love, Venus or Aphrodite, the first referring to her birth from the sea-foam, and the second deriving from her worship at Mount Eryx in Sicily.

16 Niobean: because she compared the nobility and beauty of her family with those of the gods, Niobe in classical legend was punished by the deaths of her children.

Shall these hours run down and say
10   No good thing of thee and me?
Time that made us and will slay
     Laughs at love in me and thee;
But if here the flowers may see
One whole hour of amorous breath,
     Time shall die, and love shall be
Lord as time was over death.

                                        1878

Translations from the French of Villon[1]

The Complaint of the Fair Armouress

I

Meseemeth I heard cry and groan
     That sweet who was the armourer's maid;
For her young years she made sore moan,
     And right upon this wise she said;
     "Ah fierce old age with foul bald head,
To spoil fair things thou art over fain;
     Who holdeth me? who? would God I were
          dead!
Would God I were well dead and slain!

II

"Lo, thou hast broken the sweet yoke
10   That my high beauty held above
All priests and clerks and merchant-folk;
     There was not one but for my love
     Would give me gold and gold enough,
Though sorrow his very heart had riven,
     To win from we such wage thereof
As now no thief would take if given.

III

"I was right chary of the same,
     God wot it was my great folly,
For love of one sly knave of them,
20   Good store of that same sweet had he;
     For all my subtle wiles, perdie,
God wot I loved him well enow;
     Right evilly he handled me,
But he loved well my gold, I trow.

IV

"Though I gat bruises green and black,
     I loved him never the less a jot;
Though he bound burdens on my back,
     If he said 'Kiss me and heed it not'
     Right little pain I felt, God wot,
When that foul thief's mouth, found so sweet,   30
     Kissed me—Much good thereof I got!
I keep the sin and the same of it.

V

"And he died thirty year agone.
     I am old now, no sweet thing to see;
By God, though, when I think thereon,
     And of that good glad time, woe's me,
     And stare upon my changed body
Stark naked, that has been so sweet,
     Lean, wizen, like a small dry tree,
I am nigh mad with the pain of it.   40

VI

"Where is my faultless forehead's white,
     The lifted eyebrows, soft gold hair,
Eyes wide apart and keen of sight,
     With subtle skill in the amorous air;
     The straight nose, great nor small, but fair,
The small carved ears of shapeliest growth,
     Chin dimpling, colour good to wear,
And sweet red splendid kissing mouth?

VII

"The shapely slender shoulders small,
     Long arms, hands wrought in glorious wise,   50
Round little breasts, the hips withal
     High, full of flesh, not scant of size,
     Fit for all amorous masteries;
*** ***** *****, *** *** ****** **** ***
     ****** ***** ** **** ***** ******
** * ***** ***** ** **** *****?[2]

VIII

"A writhled forehead, hair gone grey,
     Fallen eyebrows, eyes gone blind and red,
Their laughs and looks all fled away,
     Yea, all that smote men's hearts are fled;   60
     The bowed nose, fallen from goodlihead;

---

[1] François Villon was a fifteenth-century French poet who lived and wrote about a dangerous life among urban criminals and adventurers. Swinburne translated and published several of his ballads. Villon's title of this poem seems to have been "The Old Woman's Longing for the Days of Her Youth."

[2] Three lines suppressed in both *Poems and Ballads: Second Series* (1878) and in 1904 collected edition of Swinburne's poems are printed from the manuscript in Wise's *Bibliography* (I, 292):

          The large loins, and the flower that was
          Planted above my strong, round thighs
          In a small garden of soft grass?

Foul flapping ears like water-flags;
   Peaked chin, and cheeks all waste and dead,
And lips that are two skinny rags:

IX

"Thus endeth all the beauty of us.
   The arms made short, the hands made lean,
The shoulders bowed and ruinous,
    The breasts, alack! all fallen in;
    The flanks too, like the breasts, grown thin;
70 ** *** *** **** *****, *** ** **¦³
For the lank thighs, no thighs but skin,
They are specked with spots like sausage-meat.

X

"So we make moan for the old sweet days,
   Poor old light women, two or three
Squatting above the straw-fire's blaze,
    The bosom crushed against the knee,
    Like faggots on a heap we be,
Round fires soon lit, soon quenched and done;
   And we were once so sweet, even we!
Thus fareth many and many an one."

1878

Dedication[1]

1878

Some nine years gone, as we dwelt together
In the sweet hushed heat of the south French
    weather
    Ere autumn fell on the vine-tressed hills
Or the season had shed one rose-red feather,

Friend, whose fame is a flame that fills
All eyes it lightens and hearts it thrills
    With joy to be born of the blood which
    bred
From a land with the grey sea girds and chills

The heart and spirit and hand and head
10 Whose might is as light on a dark day shed,

On a day now dark as a land's decline
Where all the peers of your praise are dead,

In a land and season of corn[2] and vine
I pledged you a health from a beaker of mine
    But halfway filled to the lip's edge yet
With hope for honey and song for wine.

Nine years have risen and eight years set
Since there by the wellspring our hands on it
    met:
    And the pledge of my songs that were then
    to be,
I could wonder not, friend, though a friend
    should forget.   20

For life's helm rocks to the windward and lee,
And time is as wind, and as waves are we;
    And song is as foam that the sea-winds fret,
Though the thought at its heart should be
    deep as the sea.

1878

Dedication

To Edward John Trelawny[1]

A sea-mew[2] on a sea-king's wrist alighting,
    As the north sea-wind caught and strained
    and curled
The raven-figured flag that led men fighting
    From field to green field of the water-world,
Might find such brief high favour at his hand
    For wings imbrued with brine, with foam
    impearled,
As these my songs require at yours on land,
    That durst not save for love's free sake
    require,
Being lightly born between the foam and sand,
    But reared by hope and memory and desire
Of lives that were and life that is to be,

³ In 1878 lines 70–72 were suppressed; in the 1904 collected edition the final two of these three lines were restored. Wise (I, 292) prints the remaining line from manuscript: "As for the sweet place, out on it!"

¹ Swinburne dedicated *Poems and Ballads: Second Series* (1878) to Richard Burton (1821–1890), an explorer and diplomat as well as the translator of the *Arabian Nights* (1885–1888). Swinburne had traveled with Burton in the south of France in 1869.

² Corn: grain.

¹ Edward John Trelawny (1792–1881) is best remembered for his friendships with Shelley and Byron, which he recounted in *Recollections of the Last Days of Shelley and Byron* (1858). He also served in the British navy, sailed in the East, and fought in Greece in the 1820s in the Greek insurrections against the Turks. He arranged for the cremation of Shelley's body after his drowning in Italy in 1822. Swinburne met Trelawny in the 1860s. This poem is the dedicatory poem to *Songs of the Springtides* (1880).

² Sea-mew: sea gull.

Even such as filled his[3] heavenlier song with
  fire
Whose very voice, that sang to set man free,
  Was in your ears as ever in ours his lyre,
Once, ere the flame received him from the sea.

1880

Thalassius[1]

Upon the flowery forefront of the year,
One wandering by the grey-green April sea[2]
Found on a reach of shingle[3] and shallower
  sand
Inlaid with starrier glimmering jewellery
Left for the sun's love and the light wind's
  cheer
Along the foam-flowered strand
Breeze-brightened, something nearer sea than
  land
Though the last shoreward blossom-fringe was
  near,
A babe asleep with flower-soft face that gleamed
To sun and seaward as it laughed and dreamed,   10
Too sure of either love for either's fear,
Albeit so birdlike slight and light, it seemed
Nor man nor mortal child of man, but fair
As even its twin-born tenderer spray-flowers
  were,
That the wind scatters like an Oread's hair.[4]

For when July strewed fire on earth and sea
The last time ere that year,
Out of the flame of morn Cymothoe[5]
Beheld one brighter than the sunbright sphere
Move toward her from its fieriest heart, whence
  trod   20
The live sun's very God,[6]
Across the foam-bright water-ways that are
As heavenlier heavens with star for answering
  star,

And on her eyes and hair and maiden mouth
Felt a kiss falling fierier than the South
And heard above afar
A noise of songs and wind-enamoured wings
And lutes and lyres of milder and mightier
  strings,
And round the resonant radiance of his car
Where depth is one with height,   30
Light heard as music, music seen as light.
And with that second moondawn of the spring's
That fosters the first rose,
A sun-child whiter than the sunlit snows
Was born out of the world of sunless things
That round the round earth flows and ebbs
  and flows.

But he that found the sea-flower by the sea[7]
And took to foster like a graft of earth
Was born of man's most highest and heaven-
  liest birth,
Free-born as winds and stars and waves are free;   40
A warrior grey with glories more than years,
Though more of years than change the quick
  to dead
Had rained their light and darkness on his
  head;
A singer that in time's and memory's ears
Should leave such words to sing as all his peers
Might praise with hallowing heat of rapturous
  tears
Till all the days of human flight were fled.
And at his knees his fosterling was fed
Not with man's wine and bread
Nor mortal mother-milk of hopes and fears,   50
But food of deep memorial days long sped;
For bread with wisdom and with song for wine
Clear as the full calm's emerald hyaline.[8]
And from his grave glad lips the boy would
  gather
Fine honey of song-notes goldener than gold,

---

3 His: Shelley's.
1 "Thalasius" means "the sea-born." The poem is a metaphorical version of Swinburne's
career as a poet.
2 Swinburne was born in April.
3 Shingle: course rounded stones similar to but somewhat larger than gravel.
4 Oread: nymph of mountains and hills.
5 Cymothoe: a sea-spirit, one of the daughters of Nereus and Doris, deities of the sea in
classical mythology.
6 Live sun's very God: Apollo, classical god of song and of the sun.
7 He that found: probably an allusion to Walter Savage Landor (1775–1864), whom Swin-
burne visited in Italy in 1864. Swinburne had venerated Landor since his own adolescence,
extravagantly admiring the classical learning and finish of his lyric poetry, the fierce con-
tentiousness of his liberal politics, and his high disdain for the patterns and decorous civilities
of conventional English life.
8 Hyaline: a transparent object.

More sweet than bees make of the breathing
    heather,
That he, as glad and bold,
Might drink as they, and keep his spirit from
    cold.
And the boy loved his laurel-laden hair[9]
As his own father's risen on the eastern air,
And that less white brow-binding bayleaf
    bloom
More than all flowers his father's eyes relume;
And those high songs he heard,
More than all notes of any landward bird,
More than all sounds less free
Than the wind's quiring[10] to the choral sea.

  High things the high song taught him; how
    the breath
Too frail for life may be more strong than
    death;
And this poor flash of sense in life, that gleams
As a ghost's glory in dreams,
More stabile than the world's own heart's root
    seems,
By that strong faith of lordliest love which gives
To death's own sightless-seeming eyes a light
Clearer, to death's bare bones a verier might,
Than shines or strikes from any man that lives.
How he that loves life overmuch shall die
The dog's death, utterly:
And he that much less loves it than he hates
All wrongdoing that is done
Anywhere always underneath the sun
Shall live a mightier life than time's or fate's.
One fairer thing he shewed him, and in might
More strong than day and night
Whose strengths build up time's towering
    period:
Yea, one thing stronger and more high than
    God,
Which if man had not, then should God not be:
And that was Liberty.
And gladly should man die to gain, he said,
Freedom: and gladlier, having lost, lie dead.[11]
For man's earth was not, nor the sweet
    sea-waves
His, nor his own land, nor its very graves,
Except they bred not, bore not, hid not slaves:
But all of all that is,
Were one man free in body and soul, were his.

And the song softened, even as heaven by
    night
Softens, from sunnier down to starrier light,
And with its moonbright breath
Blessed life for death's sake, and for life's sake
    death.
Till as the moon's own beam and bread
    confuse
In one clear hueless haze of glimmering hues   100
The sea's line and the land's line and the sky's,
And light for love of darkness almost dies,
As darkness only lives for light's dear love,
Whose hands the web of night is woven of,
So in that heaven of wondrous words were life
And death brought out of strife;
Yea, by that strong spell of serene increase
Brought out of strife to peace.

  And the song lightened, as the wind at morn
Flashes, and even with lightning of the wind   110
Night's thick-spun web is thinned
And all its weft unwoven and overworn
Shrinks, as might love from scorn.
And as when wind and light on water and land
Leap as twin gods from heavenward hand in
    hand,
And with the sound and splendour of their
    leap
Strike darkness dead, and daunt the spirit of
    sleep,
And burn it up with fire;
So with the light that lightened from the lyre
Was all the bright heat in the child's heart
    stirred   120
And blown with blasts of music into flame
Till even his sense became
Fire, as the sense that fires the singing bird[12]
Whose song calls night by name.
And in the soul within the sense began
The manlike passion of a godlike man,
And in the sense within the soul again
Thoughts that make men of gods and gods of
    men.

  For love the high song taught him: love that
    turns
God's heart toward man as man's to Godward;
    love   130

---

[9] Laurel: like bayleaf (line 61), conventionally worn by and awarded to poets.

[10] Quiring: singing.

[11] And gladly: a paraphrase of Landor's Latin epitaph for Spaniards who resisted Napoleon in the early years of the nineteenth century.

[12] Singing bird: nightingale.

That life and death and life are fashioned of,
From the first breath that burns
Half kindled on the flowerlike yeanling's lip,
So light and faint that life seems like to slip,
To that yet weaklier drawn
When sunset dies of night's devouring dawn.
But the man dying not wholly as all men dies
If aught be left of his in live men's eyes
Out of the dawnless dark of death to rise;
140 If aught of deed or word
Be seen for all time or of all time heard.
Love, that though body and soul were over-
  thrown
Should live for love's sake of itself alone,
Though spirit and flesh were one thing
  doomed and dead,
Not wholly annihilated.
Seeing even the hoariest ash-flake that the pyre
Drops, and forgets the thing was once afire
And gave its heart to feed the pile's full flame
Till its own heart its own heat overcame,
150 Outlives its own life, though by scarce a span,
As such men dying outlive themselves in man,
Outlive themselves for ever; if the heat
Outburn the heart that kindled it, the sweet
Outlast the flower whose soul it was, and flit
Forth of the body of it
Into some new shape of a strange perfume
More potent than its light live spirit of bloom,
How shall not something of that soul relive,
That only soul that had such gifts to give
160 As lighten something even of all men's doom
Even from the labouring womb
Even to the seal set on the unopening tomb?
And these the loving light of song and love
Shall wrap and lap round and impend above,
Imperishable; and all springs born illume
Their sleep with brighter thoughts than wake
  the dove
To music, when the hillside winds resume
The marriage-song of heather-flower and broom
And all the joy thereof.

170 And hate the song too taught him: hate of all
That brings or holds in thrall
Of spirit or flesh, free-born ere God began,
The holy body and sacred soul of man.
And wheresoever a curse was or a chain,
A throne for torment or a crown for bane
Rose, moulded out of poor men's molten pain,
There, said he, should man's heaviest hate be
  set
Inexorably, to faint not or forget
Till the last warmth bled forth of the last vein
180 In flesh that none should call a king's again,

Seeing wolves and dogs and birds that plague-
  strike air
Leave the last bone of all the carrion bare.

 And hope the high song taught him: hope
  whose eyes
Can sound the seas unsoundable, the skies
Inaccessible of eyesight; that can see
What earth beholds not, heard what wind and
  sea
Hear not, and speak what all these crying in
  one
Can speak not to the sun.
For in her sovereign eyelight all things are
Clear as the closest seen and kindlier star 190
That marries morn and even and winter and
  spring
With one love's golden ring.
For she can see the days of man, the birth
Of good and death of evil things on earth
Inevitable and infinite, and sure
As present pain is, or herself is pure.
Yea, she can hear and see, beyond all things
That lighten from before Time's thunderous
  wings
Through the awful circle of wheel-winged
  periods,
The tempest of the twilight of all Gods: 200
And higher than all the circling course they
  ran
The sundrawn of the spirit that was man.

 And fear the song too taught him; fear to be
Worthless the dear love of the wind and sea
That bred him fearless, like a sea-mew reared
In rocks of man's foot feared,
Where nought of wingless life may sing or
  shine.
Fear to wax worthless of that heaven he had
When all the life in all his limbs was glad
And all the drops in all his veins were wine 21
And all the pulses music; when his heart,
Singing, bade heaven and wind and sea bear
  part
In one live song's reiterance, and they bore:
Fear to go crownless of the flower he wore
When the winds loved him and the waters
  knew,
The blithest life that clove their blithe life
  through
With living limbs exultant, or held strife
More amorous than all dalliance aye anew
With the bright breath and strength of their
  large life,

With all strong wrath of all sheer winds that
    blew,
All glories of all storms of the air that fell
Prone, ineluctable,
With roar from heaven of revel, and with hue
As of a heaven turned hell.
For when the red blast of their breath had
    made
All heaven aflush with light more dire than
    shade,
He felt it in his blood and eyes and hair
Burn as if all the fires of the earth and air
Had laid strong hold upon his flesh, and stung
The soul behind it as with serpent's tongue,
Forked like the loveliest lightnings: nor could
    bear
But hardly, half distraught with strong delight,
The joy that like a garment wrapped him
    round
And lapped him over and under
With raiment of great light
And rapture of great sound
At every loud leap earthward of the thunder
From heaven's most furthest bound:
So seemed all heaven in hearing and in sight,
Alive and mad with glory and angry joy,
That something of its marvellous mirth and
    might
Moved even to madness, fledged as even for
    flight,
The blood and spirit of one but mortal boy.

So, clothed with love and fear that love
    makes great,
And armed with hope and hate,
He set first foot upon the spring-flowered ways
That all feet pass and praise.
And one dim dawn between the winter and
    spring,
In the sharp harsh wind harrying heaven and
    earth
To put back April that had borne his birth
From sunward on her sunniest shower-struck
    wing,
With tears and laughter for the dew-dropt
    thing,
Slight as indeed a dew-drop, by the sea
One met him lovelier than all men may be,
God-featured, with god's eyes; and in their
    might
Somewhat that drew men's own to mar their
    sight,
Even of all eyes drawn toward him: and his
    mouth
Was as the very rose of all men's youth,

One rose of all the rose-beds in the world:
But round his brows the curls were snakes that
    curled,
And like his tongue a serpent's; and his voice
Speaks death, and bids rejoice.
Yet then he spake no word, seeming as dumb,
A dumb thing mild and hurtless; nor at first
From his bowed eyes seemed any light to come,
Nor his meek lips for blood or tears to thirst:
But as one blind and mute in mild sweet wise
Pleading for pity of piteous lips and eyes,
He strayed with faint bare lily-lovely feet
Helpless, and flowerlike sweet:
Nor might man see, not having word hereof,
That this of all gods was the great god Love.

And seeing him lovely and like a little child
That wellnigh wept for wonder that it smiled
And was so feeble and fearful, with soft speech
The youth bespake him softly; but there fell
From the sweet lips no sweet word audible
That ear or thought might reach:
No sound to make the dim cold silence glad,
No breath to thaw the hard harsh air with
    heat;
Only the saddest smile of all things sweet,
Only the sweetest smile of all things sad.

And so they went together one green way
Till April dying made free the world for May;
And on his guide suddenly Love's face turned,
And in his blind eyes burned
Hard light and heat of laughter; and like
    flame
That opens in a mountain's ravening mouth
To blear and sear the sunlight from the south,
His mute mouth opened, and his first word
    came:
"Knowest thou me now by name?"
And all his stature waxed immeasurable,
As of one shadowing heaven and lightening
    hell;
And statelier stood he than a tower that stands
And darkens with its darkness far-off sands
Whereon the sky leans red;
And with a voice that stilled the winds he said:
"I am he that was thy lord before thy birth,
I am he that is thy lord till thou turn earth:
I make the night more dark, and all the
    morrow
Dark as the night whose darkness was my
    breath:
O fool, my name is sorrow;
Thou fool, my name is death."

And he that heard spake not, and looked
    right on
Again, and Love was gone.

Through many a night toward many a
    wearier day
His spirit bore his body down its way.
Through many a day toward many a wearier
    night
His soul sustained his sorrows in her sight.
And earth was bitter, and heaven, and even
310   the sea
Sorrowful even as he.
And the wind helped not, and the sun was
    dumb;
And with too long strong stress of grief to be
His heart grew sere and numb.

And one bright eve ere summer in autumn
    sank
At stardawn standing on a grey sea-bank
He felt the wind fitfully shift and heave
As toward a stormier eve;
And all the wan wide sea shuddered; and earth
320 Shook underfoot as toward some timeless birth,
Intolerable and inevitable; and all
Heaven, darkling, trembled like a stricken
    thrall.[13]
And far out of the quivering east, and far
From past the moonrise and its guiding star,
Began a noise of tempest and a light
That was not of the lightning; and a sound
Rang with it round and round
That was not of the thunder; and a flight
As of blown clouds by night,
330 That was not of them; and with songs and cries
That sang and shrieked their soul out at the
    skies
A shapeless earthly storm of shapes began
From all ways round to move in on the man,
Clamorous against him silent; and their feet
Were as the wind's are fleet,
And their shrill songs were as wild birds are
    sweet.

And as when all the world of earth was
    wronged
And all the host of all men driven afoam

By the red hand of Rome,[14]
Round some fierce amphitheatre overthronged   340
With fair clear faces full of bloodier lust
Than swells and stings the tiger when his mood
Is fieriest after blood
And drunk with trampling of the murderous
    must[15]
That soaks and stains the tortuous close-coiled
    wood
Made monstrous with its myriad-mustering
    brood,
Face by fair face panted and gleamed and
    pressed,
And breast by passionate breast
Heaved hot with ravenous rapture, as they
    quaffed
The red ripe full fume of the deep live
    draught,   350
The sharp quick reek of keen fresh bloodshed,
    blown
Through the dense deep drift up to the
    emperor's throne
From the under steaming sands
With clamour of all-applausive throats and
    hands,
Mingling in mirthful time
With shrill blithe mockeries of the lithe-limbed
    mime:
So from somewhere far forth of the
    unbeholden,
Dreadfully driven from over and after and
    under,
Fierce, blown through fifes of brazen blast and
    golden,
With sound of chiming waves that drown the
    thunder   360
Or thunder that strikes dumb the sea's own
    chimes,
Began the bellowing of the bull-voiced mimes,[16]
Terrible; firs bowed down as briars or palms
Even at the breathless blast as of a breeze
Fulfilled with clamour and clangour and storms
    of psalms;
Red hands rent up the roots of old-world trees,
Thick flames of torches tossed as tumbling seas
Made mad the moonless and infuriate air
That, ravening, revelled in the riotous hair
And raiment of the furred Bassarides.[17]   3

---

[13] Thrall: servant slave.
    [14] Rome: these lines refer to the political and religious persecutions by the emperors of Rome
in the first centuries of the Christian era, and perhaps as well to the mid-nineteenth-century
struggles for Italian freedom and a republic whose capital would be Rome.
    [15] Must: new wine.   [16] Bull-voiced mimes: tragic actors.
    [17] Bassarides: orgiastic worshippers of Bacchus or Dionysus, the classical god of revelry and
wine.

So came all those in on him; and his heart,
As out of sleep suddenly struck astart,
Danced, and his flesh took fire of theirs, and grief
Was as a last year's leaf
Blown dead far down the wind's way; and he set
His pale mouth to the brightest mouth it met
That laughed for love against his lips, and bade
Follow; and in following all his blood grew glad
And as again a sea-bird's; for the wind
Took him to bathe him deep round breast and brow
Not as it takes a dead leaf drained and thinned,
But as the brightest bay-flower blown on bough,
Set springing toward it singing: and they rode
By many a vine-leafed, many a rose-hung road,
Exalt with exultation; many a night
Set all its stars upon them as for spies
On many a moon-bewildering mountain-height
Where he rode only by the fierier light
Of his dread lady's hot sweet hungering eyes.
For the moon wandered witless of her way,
Spell-stricken by strong magic in such wise
As wizards use to set the stars astray.
And in his ears the music that makes mad
Beat always; and what way the music bade,
That alway rode he; nor was any sleep
His, nor from height nor deep.
But heaven was as red iron, slumberless,
And had no heart to bless;
And earth lay sere and darkling as distraught,
And help in her was nought.

Then many a midnight, many a morn and even,
His mother,[18] passing forth of her fair heaven,
With goodlier gifts than all save gods can give
From earth or from the heaven where sea-things live,
With shine of sea-flowers through the bay-leaf braid
Woven for a crown her foam-white hands had made
To crown him with land's laurel[19] and sea-dew,
Sought the sea-bird that was her boy: but he

Sat panther-throned beside Erigone,[20]
Riding the red ways of the revel through   410
Midmost of pale-mouthed passion's crownless crew.
Till on some winter's dawn of some dim year
He let the vine-bit on the panther's lip
Slide, and the green rein slip,
And set his eyes to seaward, nor gave ear
If sound from landward hailed him, dire or dear;
And passing forth of all those fair fierce ranks
Back to the grey sea-banks,
Against a sea-rock lying, aslant the steep,
Fell after many sleepless dreams on sleep.   420

And in his sleep the dun green light was shed
Heavily round his head
That through the veil of sea falls fathom-deep,
Blurred like a lamp's that when the night drops dead
Dies; and his eyes gat grace of sleep to see
The deep divine dark dayshine of the sea,
Dense water-walls and clear dusk water-ways,
Broad-based, or branching as a sea-flower sprays
That side or this dividing; and anew
The glory of all her glories that he knew.   430
And in sharp rapture of recovering tears
He woke on fire with yearnings of old years,
Pure as one purged of pain that passion bore,
Ill child of bitter mother; for his own
Looked laughing toward him from her midsea throne,
Up toward him there ashore.

Thence in his heart the great same joy began,
Of child that made him man:
And turned again from all hearts else on quest,
He communed with his own heart, and had rest.   440
And like sea-winds upon loud waters ran
His days and dreams together, till the joy
Burned in him of the boy.
Till the earth's great comfort and the sweet sea's breath
Breathed and blew life in where was heartless death,
Death spirit-stricken of soul-sick days, where strife

[18] Mother: the sea-spirit Cymothe, one of the daughters of Nereus and Doris, deities of the sea in classical mythology.
[19] Laurel conventionally worn by and awarded to poets.
[20] Erigone: in classical mythology a young girl who killed herself after her father was murdered by some shepherds who thought he had given them poisonous wine. She was transformed into a star. The panther is associated with Bacchus or Dionysus.

Of thought and flesh made mock of death and
    life.
And grace returned upon him of his birth
Where heaven was mixed with heavenlike sea
    and earth;
And song shot forth strong wings that took the
450   sun
From inward, fledged with might of sorrow
    and mirth
And father's fire made mortal in his son.
Nor was not spirit of strength in blast and
    breeze
To exalt again the sun's child and the sea's;
For as wild mares in Thessaly grow great[21]
With child of ravishing winds, that violate
Their leaping length of limb with manes like
    fire
And eyes outburning heaven's
With fires more violent than the lightning
    levin's[22]
And breath drained out and desperate of
460   desire,
Even so the spirit in him, when winds grew
    strong,
Grew great with child of song.
Nor less than when his veins first leapt for joy
To draw delight in such as burns a boy,
Now too the soul of all his senses felt
The passionate pride of deep sea-pulses dealt
Through nerve and jubilant vein
As from the love and largess of old time,
And with his heart again
470 The tidal throb of all the tides keep rhyme
And charm him from his own soul's separate
    sense
With infinite and invasive influence
That made strength sweet in him and sweet-
    ness strong,
Being now no more a singer, but a song.

Till one clear day when brighter sea-wind
    blew
And louder sea-shine lightened, for the waves
Were full of godhead and the light that saves,
His father's,[23] and their spirit had pierced him
    through,
He felt strange breath and light all round him
    shed
That bowed him down with rapture; and he
480   knew

His father's hand, hallowing his humbled
    head,
And the old great voice of the old good time,
    that said:

"Child of my sunlight and the sea, from
    birth
A fosterling and fugitive on earth;
Sleepless of soul as wind or wave or fire,
A manchild with an ungrown God's desire;
Because thou hast loved nought mortal more
    than me,
Thy father, and thy mother-hearted sea;
Because thou hast set thine heart to sing, and
    sold
Life and life's love for song, God's living gold; 490
Because thou hast given thy flower and fire of
    youth
To feed men's hearts with visions, truer than
    truth;
Because thou hast kept in those world-wander-
    ing eyes
The light that makes me music of the skies;
Because thou hast heard with world-unwearied
    ears
The music that puts light into the spheres;
Have therefore in thine heart and in thy
    mouth
The sound of song that mingles north and
    south,
The song of all the winds that sing of me,
And in thy soul the sense of all the sea." 500
                              1880

*The translation of the epigraph for "On the
Cliffs" is "Nightingale of lovely song." The night-
ingale becomes, through a sequence of identities and
associations, a complex emblem of song born out of
pain. Fundamentally, Swinburne draws on the myth
of Philomela, who is desired or raped by her sister's
husband, kills her son in vengeance, and is trans-
formed to a nightingale in order to protect her from
further vengeance. Swinburne also identifies the
nightingale with Sappho, the sixth century B.C.
Greek lyric poet who, according to legend, killed
herself because of disappointment in love. The
nightingale is also associated with Cassandra, who
was loved by the god Apollo and given the gift of
prophecy, and finally was killed in a catastrophe
she foresaw but could not prevent. Swinburne also
refers to the nightingale as immortal and divine,
associating it with Apollo, the god of poetry, and*

[21] Boreas, the north wind, fell in love with the beautiful mares of Thessaly, a region in Greece,
came among them as a horse and sired twelve colts who could run on the sea and on the land
without touching the grass. Homer recounts this myth in Book 20 of the *Iliad.*
[22] Levin's: flashes of.   [23] His father: Apollo, classical god of song and of the sun.

Aphrodite, the goddess of love. Finally, this complex symbol becomes the vehicle of a meditation on Swinburne's own life and identity as a poet.

The poem was written in 1879, when Swinburne was at his family home before it was sold and he moved with Watts-Dunton to the Pines. In this twilight between what turned out to be two passages in his life, physically ill and deeply troubled, he considers not the chronology of his career as a poet, as he did a year later in "Thalassius," but its meaning, the relationship between the beauty, order, and persistence of song and the painful knowledge of confusion, transience, and loss out of which song comes.

On the Cliffs

ἱμερόφωνος ἀηδών.

SAPPHO

Between the moondrawn and the sundown
  here
The twilight hangs half starless; half the sea
Still quivers as for love or pain or fear
Or pleasure mightier than these all may be
A man's live heart might beat
Wherein a God's with mortal blood should
  meet
And fill its pulse too full to bear the strain
With fear or love or pleasure's twin-born,
  pain.
Fiercely the gaunt woods to the grim soil cling
That bears for all fair fruits
Wan wild sparse flowers of windy and wintry
  spring
Between the tortive[1] serpent-shapen roots
Wherethrough their dim growth hardly strikes
  and shoots
And shews one gracious thing
Hardly, to speak for summer one sweet word
Of summer's self scarce heard.
But higher the steep green sterile fields, thick-
  set
With flowerless hawthorn even to the upward
  verge
Whence the woods gathering watch new cliffs
  emerge
Higher than their highest of crowns that sea-
  winds fret,
Hold fast, for all that night or wind can say,

Some pale pure colour yet,
Too dim for green and luminous for grey.
Between the climbing inland cliffs above
And these beneath that breast and break the
  bay,
A barren peace too soft for hate or love
Broods on an hour too dim for night or day.

O wind, O wingless wind that walk'st the sea,
Weak wind, wing-broken, wearier wind than
  we,
Who are yet not spirit-broken, maimed like
  thee,
Who wail not in our inward night as thou   30
In the outer darkness now,
What word has the old sea given thee for mine
  ear
From thy faint lips to hear?
For some word would she send me, knowing
  not how.

Nay, what far other word
Than ever of her was spoken, or of me
Or all my winged white kinsfolk of the sea
Between fresh wave and wave was ever heard,
Cleaves the clear dark enwinding tree with tree   40
Too close for stars to separate and to see
Enmeshed in multitudinous unity?
What voice of what strong God hath stormed
  and stirred
The fortressed rock of silence, rent apart
Even to the core Night's all-maternal heart?
What voice of God grown heavenlier in a bird,
Made keener of edge to smite
Than lightning—yea, thou knowest, O mother
  Night,[2]
Keen as that cry from thy strange children sent
Wherewith the Athenian judgment-shrine was
  rent,   50
For wrath that all their wrath was vainly spent,
Their wrath for wrong made right
By justice in her own divine despite
That bade pass forth unblamed
The sinless matricide and unashamed?
Yea, what new cry is this, what note more
  bright
Than their song's wing of words was dark of
  flight,
What word is this thou hast heard,

---

[1] Tortive: twisting.

[2] Lines 48–55 refer to the Furies, the daughters of Night, who pursued Orestes after he had killed his mother in vengeance for her murder of Agamemnon, his father. Eventually, Orestes sought sanctuary in a shrine in Athens, and he was released from the prosecution of the Furies by a judgment of Athena, the goddess of wisdom.

Thine and not thine or theirs, O Night, what
    word
More keen than lightning and more sweet
60   than light?
As all men's hearts grew godlike in one bird
And all those hearts cried on thee, crying with
    might,
Hear us, O mother Night.

Dumb is the mouth of darkness as of death:
Light, sound and life are one
In the eyes and lips of dawn that draw the
    sun
To hear what first child's word with glimmer-
    ing breath
Their weak wan weanling child the twilight
    saith;
But night makes answer none.

70   God, if thou be God,—bird, if bird thou be,—
Do thou then answer me.
For but one word, what wind soever blow,
Is blown up usward ever from the sea.
In fruitless years of youth dead long ago
And deep beneath their own dead leaves and
    snow
Buried, I heard with bitter heart and sere
The same sea's word unchangeable, nor knew
But that mine own life-days were changeless
    too
And sharp and salt with unshed tear on tear
80   And cold and fierce and barren; and my soul,
Sickening, swam weakly with bated breath
In a deep sea like death,
And felt the wind buffet her face with brine
Hard, and harsh thought on thought in long
    bleak roll
Blown by keen gusts of memory sad as thine
Heap the weight up of pain, and break, and
    leave
Strength scarce enough to grieve
In the sick heavy spirit, unmanned with strife
Of waves that beat at the tired lips of life.

90   Nay, sad may be man's memory, sad may be
The dream he weaves him as for shadow of
    thee,
But scarce one breathing-space, one heartbeat
    long,
Wilt thou take shadow of sadness on thy song.
Not thou, being more than man or man's
    desire,
Being bird and God in one,

With throat of gold and spirit of the sun;
The sun whom all our souls and songs call
    sire,[3]
Whose godhead gave thee, chosen of all our
    quire,
Thee only of all that serve, of all that sing
Before our sire and king,   100
Borne up some space on time's world-wander-
    ing wing,
This gift, this doom, to bear till time's wing
    tire—
Life everlasting of eternal fire.

Thee only of all; yet can no memory say
How many a night and day
My heart has been as thy heart, and my life
As thy life is, a sleepless hidden thing,
Full of the thirst and hunger of winter and
    spring,
That seeks its food not in such love or strife
As fill men's hearts with passionate hours and
    rest.   11
From no loved lips and on no loving breast
Have I sought ever for such gifts as bring
Comfort, to stay the secret soul with sleep.
The joys, the loves, the labours, whence men
    reap
Rathe[4] fruit of hopes and fears,
I have made not mine; the best of all my days
Have been as those fair fruitless summer strays,
Those water-waifs that but the sea-wind steers,
Flakes of glad foam or flowers on footless ways
That take the wind in season and the sun,   12
And when the wind wills is their season done.

For all my days as all thy days from birth
My heart as thy heart was in me as thee,
Fire; and not all the fountains of the sea
Have waves enough to quench it, nor on earth
Is fuel enough to feed,
While day sows night and night sows day for
    seed.

We were not marked for sorrow, thou nor I,
For joy nor sorrow, sister, were we made,
To take delight and grief to live and die,   1
Assuaged by pleasures or by pains affrayed
That melt men's hearts and alter; we retain
A memory mastering pleasure and all pain,
A spirit within the sense of ear and eye,
A soul behind the soul, that seeks and sings
And makes our life move only with its wings
And feed but from its lips, that in return

---

[3] Sire: Apollo, the god of the sun and of poetry.   [4] Rathe: early.

Feed of our hearts wherein the old fires that
    burn
Have strength not to consume
40 Nor glory enough to exalt us past our doom.

Ah, ah, the doom (thou knowest whence rang
    that wail)
Of the shrill nightingale!
(From whose wild lips, thou knowest, that wail
    was thrown)
For round about her have the great gods cast
A wing-borne body, and clothed her close and
    fast
With a sweet life that hath no part in moan.
But me, for me (how hadst thou heart to
    hear?)
Remains a sundering with the two-edged
    spear.[5]

Ah, for her doom! so cried in presage then
50 The bodeful bondslave of the king of men,
And might not win her will.
Too close the entangling dragnet woven of
    crime,
The snare of ill new-born of elder ill,
The curse of new time for an elder time,
Had caught, and held her yet,
Enmeshed intolerably in the intolerant net,
Who thought with craft to mock the God most
    high,
And win by wiles his crown of prophecy
From the Sun's hand sublime,
60 As God were man, to spare or to forget.[6]

But thou,[7]—the gods have given thee and
    forgiven thee
More than our master[8] gave
That strange-eyed spirit-wounded
    strange-tongued slave
There questing houndlike where the roofs
    red-wet
Reeked as a wet red grave.
Life everlasting has their strange grace given
    thee,

Even hers[9] whom thou wast wont to sing and
    serve
With eyes, but not with song, too swift to
    swerve;
Yet might not even thine eyes estranged
    estrange her,
Who seeing thee too, but inly, burn and bleed   170
Like that pale princess-priest of Priam's seed,
For stranger service gave thee guerdon
    stranger;
If this indeed be guerdon, this indeed
Her mercy, this thy meed[10]—
That thou, being more than all we born, being
    higher
Than all heads crowned of him that only gives
The light whereby man lives,
The bay[11] that bids man moved of God's desire
Lay hand on lute or lyre,
Set lip to trumpet or deflowered green reed—   180
If this were given thee for a grace indeed,
That thou, being first of all these, thou alone
Shouldst have the grace to die not, but to live
And lose nor change one pulse of song, one
    tone
Of all that were thy lady's and thine own,
Thy lady's whom thou criedst on to forgive,
Thou, priest and sacrifice on the altar-stone
Where none may worship not of all that live,
Love's priestess, errant on dark ways diverse;
If this were grace indeed for Love to give,   190
If this indeed were blessing and no curse.

Love's priestess, mad with pain and joy of
    song,
Song's priestess, mad with joy and pain of love,
Name above all names that are lights above,
We have loved, praised, pitied, crowned and
    done thee wrong,
O thou past praise and pity; thou the sole
Utterly deathless, perfect only and whole
Immortal, body and soul.
For over all whom time hath overpast
The shadow of sleep inexorable is cast,   200
The implacable sweet shadow of perfect sleep

---

[5] These words are spoken by Cassandra in the *Agamemnon* of Aeschylus (525–456 B.C.). Cassandra, the daughter of Priam, the king of Troy, is brought home as a captive by the victorious Greek king Agamemnon. Cassandra foretells that Agamemnon will be snared in a net and killed by his wife Clytemnestra, who has been unfaithful during his absence. Cassandra also foresees that she will be killed by the same sword or spear that kills Agamemnon.

[6] Apollo, the god of the sun, granted Cassandra the gift of prophecy, but when she refused to yield to him, decreed that no one would believe her prophecies.

[7] Thou: the nightingale; also (lines 215 f.) Sappho.   [8] Our master: Apollo.

[9] Hers: the rest of this passage suggests that the reference is to Aphrodite, the goddess of love: the nightingale thus becomes the agent of both Apollo (song) and Aphrodite (love).

[10] Meed: like guerdon, a reward.

[11] Bay: poets were rewarded in classical times with triumphal wreaths of bay.

That gives not back what life gives death to
   keep;
Yea, all that lived and loved and sang and
   sinned
Are all borne down death's cold sweet sound-
   less wind
That blows all night and knows not whom its
   breath,
Darkling, may touch to death:
But one that wind hath touched and changed
   not,—one
Whose body and soul are parcel of the sun;
One that earth's fire could burn not, nor the
   sea
Quench; nor might human doom take hold
210   on thee;
All praise, all pity, all dreams have done thee
   wrong,
All love, with eyes love-blinded from above;
Song's priestess, mad with joy and pain of
   love,
Love's priestess, mad with pain and joy of song.

Hast thou none other answer then for me
Than the air may have of thee,
Or the earth's warm woodlands girdling with
   green girth
Thy secret sleepless burning life on earth,
Or even the sea that once, being woman
   crowned
220 And girt with fire and glory of anguish round,
Thou wert so fain to seek to, fain to crave
If she would hear thee and save
And give thee comfort of thy great green
   grave?
Because I have known thee always who thou
   art,
Thou knowest, have known thee to thy heart's
   own heart,
Nor ever have given light ear to storied song
That did thy sweet name sweet unwitting
   wrong,
Nor ever have called thee nor would call for
   shame,
Thou knowest, but inly by thine only name,
Sappho—because I have known thee and loved,
230   hast thou
None other answer now?
As brother and sister were we, child and bird,
Since thy first Lesbian[12] word
Flamed on me, and I knew not whence I knew

This was the song that struck my whole soul
   through,
Pierced my keen spirit of sense with edge more
   keen,
Even when I knew not,—even ere sooth[13] was
   seen,—
When thou wast but the tawny sweet winged
   thing
Whose cry was but of spring.

And yet even so thine ear should hear me—yea,   240
Hear me this nightfall by this northland bay,
Even for their sake whose loud good word I
   had,
Singing of thee in the all-beloved clime
Once, where the windy wine of spring makes
   mad
Our sisters of Majano, who kept time
Clear to my choral rhyme.
Yet was the song acclaimed of these aloud
Whose praise had made mute humbleness
   misproud,
The song with answering song applauded thus,
But of that Daulian dream of Itylus.[14]   250
So but for love's love haply was it—nay,
How else?—that even their song took my
   song's part,
For love of love and sweetness of sweet heart,
Or god-given glorious madness of mid May
And heat of heart and hunger and thirst to
   sing,
Full of the new wine of the wind of spring.

Or if this were not, and it be not sin
To hold myself in spirit of thy sweet kin,
In heart and spirit of song;
If this my great love do thy grace no wrong,   260
Thy grace that gave me grace to dwell therein;
If thy gods thus be my gods, and their will
Made my song part of thy song—even such
   part
As man's hath of God's heart—
And my life like as thy life to fulfil;
What have our gods then given us? Ah, to thee,
Sister, much more, much happier than to me,
Much happier things they have given, and
   more of grace
Than falls to man's light race;
For lighter are we, all our love and pain   27?
Lighter than thine, who knowest of time or
   place

---

[12] Lesbian: Sappho lived on Lesbos, an island in the Aegean off Greece.   [13] Sooth: truth.
[14] Daulian; Itylus: Itylus was the son of the king of Daulus, in ancient Thrace; he was the boy
whom Philomela killed.

Thus much, that place nor time
Can heal or hurt or lull or change again
The singing soul that makes his soul sublime
Who hears the far fall of its fire-fledged rhyme
Fill darkness as with bright and burning rain
Till all the live gloom inly glows, and light
Seems with the sound to cleave the core of
    night.

The singing soul that moves thee, and that
    moved
280 When thou wast woman, and their songs divine
Who mixed for Grecian mouths heaven's lyric
    wine
Fell dumb, fell down reproved
Before one sovereign Lesbian song of thine.
That soul, though love and life had fain held
    fast,
Wind-winged with fiery music, rose and past
Through the indrawn hollow of earth and
    heaven and hell,
As through some strait sea-shell
The wide sea's immemorial song,—the sea
That sings and breathes in strange men's ears
    of thee
290 How in her barren bride-bed, void and vast,
Even thy soul sang itself to sleep at last.

To sleep? Ah, then, what song is this, that here
Makes all the night one ear,
One ear fulfilled and mad with music, one
Heart kindling as the heart of heaven, to hear
A song more fiery than the awakening sun
Sings, when his song sets fire
To the air and clouds that build the dead
    night's pyre?
*O thou of divers-coloured mind, O thou
Deathless, God's daughter subtle-souled*[15]—lo,
300   now,
Now too the song above all songs, in flight
Higher than the day-star's height,
And sweet as sound the moving wings of night!
Thou of the divers-coloured seat[16]—behold,
Her very song of old!—
O deathless, O God's daughter subtle-souled!
That same cry through this boskage[17] overhead

Rings round reiterated,
Palpitates as the last palpitated,
The last that panted through her lips and died   310
Not down this grey north sea's half sapped
    cliff-side
That crumbles toward the coastline, year by
    year
More near the sands and near;
The last loud lyric fiery cry she cried,
Heard once on heights Leucadian[18]—heard not
    here.

Not here; for this that fires our northland night,
This is the song that made
Love fearful, even the heart of love afraid,
With the great anguish of its great delight.
No swan-song, no far-fluttering half-drawn
    breath,   320
No word that love of love's sweet nature saith,
No dirge that lulls the narrowing lids of death,
No healing hymn of peace-prevented strife,—
This is her song of life.

I loved thee,—hark, one tenderer not than all—
Atthis, of old time, once[19]—one low long fall,
Sighing—one long low lovely loveless call,
Dying—one pause in song so flamelike fast—
Atthis, long since in old time overpast—
One soft first pause and last.   330
One,—then the old rage of rapture's fieriest
    rain
Storms all the music-maddened night again.

*Child of God, close craftswoman, I beseech
    thee,
Bid not ache nor agony break nor master,
Lady, my spirit*[20]—
O thou her mistress, might her cry not reach
    thee?
Our Lady of all men's loves, could Love go
    past her,
Pass, and not hear it?

She hears not as she heard not; hears not me,
O treble-natured mystery[21]—how should she   340
Hear, or give ear?—who heard and heard not
    thee;

[15] These lines are from one of Sappho's poems to Aphrodite.
[16] Seat: Aphrodite's throne, inlaid with various woods and ornaments.
[17] Boskage: thicket of trees and shrubs.
[18] Leucadian: Sappho is supposed to have thrown herself to her death from the cliffs of the island Leucadia.
[19] Atthis: lines from a poem by Sappho to Atthis, a woman whom she loved.
[20] Lines from another poem by Sappho to Aphrodite.
[21] Treble-natured mystery: the nightingale, now conceived as bird, woman (Philomela and Sappho), and a god.

Heard, and went past, and heard not; but all
    time
Hears all that all the ravin[22] of his years
Hath cast not wholly out of all men's ears
And dulled to death with deep dense funeral
    chime
Of their reiterate rhyme.
And now of all songs uttering all her praise,
All hers who had thy praise and did thee
    wrong,
Abides one song yet of her lyric days,
350   Thine only, this thy song.

O soul triune, woman and god and bird,
Man, man at least has heard.
All ages call thee conqueror, and thy cry
The mightiest as the least beneath the sky
Whose heart was ever set to song, or stirred
With wind of mounting music blown more
    high
Than wildest wing may fly,
Hath heard or hears,—even Æschylus as I.
But when thy name was woman, and thy word
360   Human,—then haply, surely then meseems
This thy bird's note was heard on earth of
    none,
Of none save only in dreams.
In all the world then surely was but one
Song; as in heaven at highest one sceptred sun
Regent, on earth here surely without fail
One only, one imperious nightingale.
Dumb was the field, the woodland mute, the
    lawn
Silent; the hill was tongueless as the vale
Even when the last fair waif of cloud that felt
370   Its heart beneath the colouring moonrays melt,
At high midnoon of midnight half withdrawn,
Bared all the sudden deep divine moondawn.
Then, unsaluted by her twin-born tune,
That latter timeless morning of the moon
Rose past its hour of moonrise; clouds gave way
To the old reconquering ray,
But no song answering made it more than day;
No cry of song by night
Shot fire into the cloud-constraining light.
380   One only, one Æolian[23] island heard
Thrill, but through no bird's throat,
In one strange manlike maiden's godlike note,
The song of all these as a single bird.
Till the sea's portal was as funeral gate
For that sole singer in all time's ageless date

Singled and signed for so triumphal fate,
All nightingales but one in all the world
All her sweet life were silent; only then,
When her life's wing of womanhood was
    furled,
Their cry, this cry of thine was heard again,   390
As of me now, of any born of men.

Through sleepless clear spring nights filled full
    of thee,
Rekindled here, thy ruling song has thrilled
The deep dark air and subtle tender sea
And breathless hearts with one bright sound
    fulfilled.
Or at midnoon to me
Swimming, and birds about my happier head
Skimming, one smooth soft way by water and
    air,
To these my bright born brethren and to me
Hath not the clear wind borne or seemed to
    bear   400
A song wherein all earth and heaven and sea
Were molten in one music made of thee
To enforce us, O our sister of the shore,
Look once in heart back landward and adore?
For songless were we sea-mews,[24] yet had we
More joy than all things joyful of thee—more,
Haply, than all things happiest; nay, save thee,
In thy strong rapture of imperious joy
Too high for heart of sea-borne bird or boy,
What living things were happiest if not we?   410
But knowing not love nor change nor wrath
    nor wrong,
No more we knew of song.

Song, and the secrets of it, and their might,
What blessings curse it and what curses bless,
I know them since my spirit had first in sight,
Clear as thy song's words or the live sun's light,
The small dark body's Lesbian loveliness
That held the fire eternal; eye and ear
Were as a god's to see, a god's to hear,
Through all his hours of daily and nightly
    chime,   420
The sundering of the two-edged spear of time:
The spear that pierces even the sevenfold
    shields
Of mightiest Memory,[25] mother of all songs
    made,
And wastes all songs as roseleaves kissed and
    frayed

---

[22] Ravin: rapine, ravage.   [23] Æolian: the name of the tribe that populated Lesbos.
[24] Sea-mews: sea gulls.
[25] Memory: Mnemosyne, mother of the Muses of science, history, and the arts.

As here the harvest of the foam-flowered fields;
But thine the spear may waste not that he
    wields
Since first the God whose soul is man's live
    breath,
The sun whose face hath our sun's face for
    shade,
Put all the light of life and love and death
430 Too strong for life, but not for love too strong,
Where pain makes peace with pleasure in thy
    song,
And in thine heart, where love and song make
    strife,
Fire everlasting of eternal life.

                (1879) 1880

from By the North Sea

I

1
A land that is lonelier than ruin;
   A sea that is stranger than death:
Far fields that a rose never blew in,
   Wan waste where the winds lack breath;
Waste endless and boundless and flowerless
   But of marsh-blossoms fruitless as free:
Where earth lies exhausted, as powerless
       To strive with the sea.

2
Far flickers the flight of the swallows,
10   Far flutters the weft of the grass
Spun dense over desolate hollows
   More pale than the clouds as they pass:
Thick woven as the weft of a witch is
   Round the heart of a thrall that hath sinned,
Whose youth and the wrecks of its riches
       Are waifs on the wind.

3
The pastures are herdless and sheepless,
   No pasture or shelter for herds:
The wind is relentless and sleepless,
20   And restless and songless the birds;
Their cries from afar fall breathless,
   Their wings are as lightnings that flee;
For the land has two lords that are deathless:
       Death's self, and the sea.

4
These twain, as a king with his fellow,
   Hold converse of desolate speech:

      ¹ Fortalice: outwork of a fort, or a small fort.

And her waters are haggard and yellow
   And crass with the scurf of the beach:
And his garments are grey as the hoary
   Wan sky where the day lies dim;   30
And his power is to her, and his glory,
       As hers unto him.

5
In the pride of his power she rejoices,
   In her glory he glows and is glad:
In her darkness the sound of his voice is,
   With his breath she dilates and is mad:
"If thou slay me, O death, and outlive me,
   Yet thy love hath fulfilled me of thee."
"Shall I give thee not back if thou give me,
       O sister, O sea?"   40

6
And year upon year dawns living,
   And age upon age drops dead:
And his hand is not weary of giving,
   And the thirst of her heart is not fed:
And the hunger that moans in her passion,
   And the rage in her hunger that roars,
As a wolf's that the winter lays lash on,
       Still calls and implores.

7
Her walls have no granite for girder,
   No fortalice¹ fronting her stands: 50
But reefs the bloodguiltiest of murder
   Are less than the banks of her sands:
These number their slain by the thousand;
   For the ship hath no surety to be,
When the bank is abreast of her bows and
       Aflush with the sea.

8
No surety to stand, and no shelter
   To dawn out of darkness but one,
Out of waters that hurtle and welter
   No succour to dawn with the sun,   60
But a rest from the wind as it passes,
   Where, hardly redeemed from the waves,
Lie thick as the blades of the grasses
       The dead in their graves.

9
A multitude noteless of numbers,
   As wild weeds cast on an heap:
And sounder than sleep are their slumbers,
   And softer than song is their sleep;

And sweeter than all things and stranger
70   The sense, if perchance it may be,
That the wind is divested of danger
        And scatheless the sea.

10

That the roar of the banks they breasted
    Is hurtless as bellowing of herds,
And the strength of his wings that invested
    The wind, as the strength of a bird's;
As the sea-mew's[2] might or the swallow's
    That cry to him back if he cries,
As over the graves and their hollows
80   Days darken and rise.

11

As the souls of the dead men disburdened
    And clean of the sins that they sinned,
With a lovelier than man's life guerdoned
    And delight as a wave's in the wind,
And delight as the wind's in the billow,
    Birds pass, and deride with their glee
The flesh that has dust for its pillow
        As wrecks have the sea.

12

When the ways of the sun wax dimmer,
90   Wings flash through the dusk like beams;
As the clouds in the lit sky glimmer,
    The bird in the graveyard gleams;
As the cloud at its wing's edge whitens
    When the clarions of sunrise are heard,
The graves that the bird's note brightens
        Grow bright for the bird.

13

As the waves of the numberless waters
    That the wind cannot number who guides
Are the sons of the shore and the daughters
100   Here lulled by the chime of the tides:
And here in the press of them standing
    We know not if these or if we
Live truliest, or anchored to landing
        Or drifted to sea.

14

In the valley he named of decision[3]
    No denser were multitudes met
When the soul of the seer in her vision
    Saw nations for doom of them set;
Saw darkness in dawn, and the splendour
110   Of judgment, the sword and the rod;

But the doom here of death is more tender
    And gentler the god.

15

And gentler the wind from the dreary
    Sea-banks by the waves overlapped,
Being weary, speaks peace to the weary
    From slopes that the tide-stream hath
        sapped;
And sweeter than all that we call so
    The seal of their slumber shall be
Till the graves that embosom them also
        Be sapped of the sea.   120

VII

1

But afar on the headland exalted,
    But beyond in the curl of the bay,
From the depth of his dome deep-vaulted
    Our father is lord of the day.
Our father and lord that we follow,
    For deathless and ageless is he;
And his robe is the whole sky's hollow,
        His sandal the sea.

2

Where the horn of the headland is sharper,
    And her green floor glitters with fire,   10
The sea has the sun for a harper,
    The sun has the sea for a lyre.
The waves are a pavement of amber,
    By the feet of the sea-winds trod
To receive in a god's presence-chamber
        Our father, the God.

3

Time, haggard and changeful and hoary,
    Is master and God of the land:
But the air is fulfilled of the glory
    That is shed from our lord's right hand.   20
O father of all of us ever,
    All glory be only to thee
From heaven, that is void of thee never,
        And earth, and the sea.

4

O Sun, whereof all is beholden,
    Behold now the shadow of this death,
This place of the sepulchres, olden
    And emptied and vain as a breath.

2 Sea-mew: seagull.
3 "Multitudes, multitudes in the valley of decision: the day of the Lord is near in the valley
of decision" (Joel 3:14).

The bloom of the bountiful heather
30   Laughs broadly beyond in thy light
As dawn, with her glories to gather,
   At darkness and night.

5

Though the Gods of the night lie rotten
   And their honour be taken away
And the noise of their names forgotten,
   Thou, Lord, art God of the day.
Thou art father and saviour and spirit,
   O Sun, of the soul that is free
And hath grace of thy grace to inherit
40   Thine earth and thy sea.

6

The hills and the sands and the beaches,
   The waters adrift and afar,
The banks and the creeks and the reaches,
   How glad of thee all these are!
The flowers, overflowing, overcrowded,
   Are drunk with the mad wind's mirth:
The delight of thy coming unclouded
   Makes music of earth.

7

I, last least voice of her voices,
50   Give thanks that were mute in me long
To the soul in my soul that rejoices
   For the song that is over my song.
Time gives what he gains for the giving
   Or takes for his tribute of me;
My dreams to the wind everliving,
   My song to the sea.

1880

In Harbour[1]

I

Goodnight and goodbye to the life whose signs
   denote us
As mourners clothed with regret for the life
   gone by;
To the waters of gloom whence winds of the
   day-spring float us
   Goodnight and goodbye.

A time is for mourning, a season for grief to
   sigh;

But were we not fools and blind, by day to
   devote us
As thralls to the darkness, unseen of the sun-
   dawn's eye?

We have drunken of Lethe at length, we have
   eaten of lotus;[2]
What hurts it us here that sorrows are born
   and die?
We have said to the dream that caressed and
   the dread that smote us
   Goodnight and goodbye.

II

Outside of the port ye are moored in, lying
Close from the wind and at ease from the
   tide,
What sounds come swelling, what notes fall
   dying
   Outside?
They will not cease, they will not abide:
Voices of presage in darkness crying
Pass and return and relapse aside.

Ye see not, but hear ye not wild wings flying
To the future that wakes from the past that
   died?
Is grief still sleeping, is joy not sighing
   Outside?

1883

Plus Ultra

Far beyond the sunrise and the sunset rises
Heaven, with worlds on worlds that lighten
   and respond:
Thought can see not thence the goal of hope's
   surmises
   Far beyond.

Night and day have made an everlasting bond
Each with each to hide in yet more deep
   disguises
Truth, till souls of men that thirst for truth
   despond.

All that man in pride of spirit slights or prizes,
All the dreams that make him fearful, fain, or
   fond,

---

[1] This poem and "Plus Ultra" are roundels, a form developed by Swinburne from one of the forms of French verse. As used by Swinburne, the roundel is an eleven-line stanza which contains only two rhymes. The fourth and the final lines are a refrain which repeats the first words of the poem.

[2] Lethe; lotus: the waters of the river Lethe in the underworld cause forgetfulness; so does the lotus plant.

Fade at forethought's touch of life's unknown
    surprises
        Far beyond.

                                                1883

*Guernsey is an island in the English Channel;
Swinburne first visited it in 1876. Victor Hugo lived
in Guernsey from 1852 to 1870, banished there by
the regime of Napoleon III.*
*Walter Theodore Watts, later Watts-Dunton
(1832–1914), was a lawyer, literary critic, poet, and
novelist who first met Swinburne when he advised
him in his relationships with publishers. When
Swinburne's health broke down in 1879, Watts be-
gan to administer Swinburne's personal life as well,
moving with him into a house in one of the
peripheral districts of London, managing the house-
hold and regulating the schedule and mode of its
life.*
*Each stanza of this poem except the sixth is a
roundel: see note on "In Harbour."*

In Guernsey

To Theodore Watts

I

The heavenly bay, ringed round with cliffs and
        moors,
Storm-stained ravines, and crags that lawns
        inlay,
Soothes as with love the rocks whose guard
        secures
            The heavenly bay.

O friend, shall time take ever this away,
This blessing given of beauty that endures,
This glory shown us, not to pass but stay?

Though sight be changed for memory, love
        ensures
What memory, changed by love to sight, would
        say—
10   The word that seals for ever mine and yours
            The heavenly bay.

II

My mother sea, my fostress, what new strand,
What new delight of waters, my this be,
The fairest found since time's first breezes
        fanned
            My mother sea?

Once more I give me body and soul to thee,
Who hast my soul for ever: cliff and sand
Recede, and heart to heart once more are we.

My heart springs first and plunges, ere my hand
Strike out from shore: more close it brings to
        me,   20
More near and dear than seems my fatherland,
        My mother sea.

III

Across and along, as the bay's breadth opens,
        and o'er us
Wild autumn exults in the wind, swift rapture
        and strong
Impels us, and broader the wide waves brighten
        before us
            Across and along.

The whole world's heart is uplifted, and knows
        not wrong;
The whole world's life is a chant to the sea-
        tide's chorus;
Are we not as waves of the water, as notes of
        the song?

Like children unworn of the passions and toils
        that wore us,   30
We breast for a season the breadth of the seas
        that throng,
Rejoicing as they, to be borne as of old they
        bore us
            Across and along.

IV

On Dante's track[1] by some funereal spell
Drawn down through desperate ways that lead
        not back
We seem to move, bound forth past flood and
        fell
            On Dante's track.

The grey path ends: the gaunt rocks gape: the
        black
Deep hollow tortuous night, a soundless shell,
Glares darkness: are the fires of old grown
        slack?   40

Nay, then, what flames are these that leap and
        swell
As 'twere to show, where earth's foundations
        crack,

---

[1] Dante's track: the path Dante takes as he descends to the underworld in the *Inferno*.

The secrets of the sepulchres of hell
    On Dante's track?

V

By mere men's hands the flame was lit, we
    know,
From leaps of dry waste whin[2] and casual
    brands:
Yet, knowing, we scarce believe it kindled so
    By mere men's hands.

Above, around, high-vaulted hell expands,
Steep, dense, a labyrinth walled and roofed
50   with woe,
Whose mysteries even itself not understands.

The scorn in Farinata's eyes aglow
Seems visible in this flame: there Geryon
    stands:[3]
No stage of earth's is here, set forth to show
    By mere men's hands.

VI

Night, in utmost noon forlorn and strong,
    with heart athirst and fasting,
Hungers here, barred up for ever, whence as
    one whom dreams affright
Day recoils before the low-browed lintel threat-
    ening doom and casting Night.

All the reefs and islands, all the lawns and
    highlands, clothed with light,
Laugh for love's sake in their sleep outside:
60   but here the night speaks, blasting
Day with silent speech and scorn of all things
    known from depth to height.

Lower than dive the thoughts of spirit-stricken
    fear in souls forecasting
Hell, the deep void seems to yawn beyond
    fear's reach, and higher than sight
Rise the walls and roofs that compass it about
    with everlasting Night.

VII

The house accurst, with cursing sealed and
    signed,

Heeds not what storms about it burn and
    burst:
No fear more fearful than its own may find
    The house accurst.

Barren as crime, anhungered and athirst,
Blank miles of moor sweep inland, sere and
    blind,   70
Where summer's best rebukes not winter's
    worst.

The low bleak tower with nought save wastes
    behind
Stares down the abyss whereon chance reared
    and nursed
This type and likeness of the accurst mans'
    mind,
    The house accurst.

VIII

Beloved and blest, lit warm with love and
    fame,
The house that had the light of the earth for
    guest
Hears for his name's sake all men hail its name
    Beloved and blest.

This eyrie was the homeless eagle's nest[4]   80
When storm laid waste his eyrie: hence he
    came
Again, when storm smote sore his mother's
    breast.

Bow down men bade us, or he clothed with
    blame
And mocked for madness: worst, they sware,
    was best:
But grief shone here, while joy was one with
    shame,
    Beloved and blest.

    1883

Envoi

Fly, white butterflies, out to sea,
Frail pale wings for the winds to try,
Small white wings that we scarce can see
    Fly.

---

[2] Whin: an evergreen herb.
[3] Farinata; Geryon: Farinata degli Uberti was a thirteenth-century political opponent of the faction to which Dante was aligned in Florence; Dante describes his tormented state in Canto 10 of the *Inferno*. Geryon is a monster who guards and represents the sins and punishments of fraud (Canto 17 of the *Inferno*).
[4] Homeless eagle: Victor Hugo.

Here and there may a chance-caught eye
Note in a score of you twain or three
Brighter or darker of tinge or dye.

Some fly light as a laugh of glee,
Some fly soft as a low long sigh:
All to the haven where each would be
   Fly.

                1883

from A Midsummer Holiday

VI

The Cliffside Path

Seaward goes the sun, and homeward by the
   down
We, before the night upon his grave be sealed.
Low behind us lies the bright steep murmuring
   town,
High before us heaves the steep rough silent
   field.
Breach by ghastlier breach, the cliffs collapsing
   yield:
Half the path is broken, half the banks divide;
Flawed and crumbled, riven and rent, they
   cleave and slide
Toward the ridged and wrinkled waste of
   girdling sand
Deep beneath, whose furrows tell how far and
   wide
Wind is lord and change is sovereign of the
   strand.   10

Star by star on the unsunned waters twiring[1]
   down.
Golden spear-points glance against a silver
   shield.
Over banks and bents,[2] across the headland's
   crown,
As by pulse of gradual plumes through twilight
   wheeled,
Soft as sleep, the waking wind awakes the
   weald.[3]
Moor and copse and fallow, near or far
   described,
Feel the mild wings move, and gladden where
   they glide:
Silence, uttering love that all things
   understand,

Bids the quiet fields forget that hard beside
Wind is lord and change is sovereign of the
   strand.   20

Yet may sight, ere all the hoar[4] soft shade grow
   brown,
Hardly reckon half the rifts and rents unhealed
Where the scarred cliffs downward sundering
   drive and drown,
Hewn as if with stroke of swords in tempest
   steeled,
Wielded as the night's will and the wind's may
   wield.
Crowned and zoned in vain with flowers of
   autumn-tide,
Soon the blasts shall break them, soon the
   waters hide;
Soon, where late we stood, shall no man ever
   stand.
Life and love seek harbourage on the landward
   side:
Wind is lord and change is sovereign of the
   strand.   30

Friend, though man be less than these, for all
   his pride,
Yet, for all his weakness, shall not hope abide?
Wind and change can wreck but life and waste
   but land:
Truth and trust are sure, though here till all
   subside
Wind is lord and change is sovereign of the
   strand.

                1884

To a Seamew[1]

When I had wings, my brother,
   Such wings were mine as thine:
Such life my heart remembers
In all as wild Septembers
As this when life seems other,
   Though sweet, than once was mine;
When I had wings, my brother,
   Such wings were mine as thine.

Such life as thrills and quickens
   The silence of thy flight,   10
Or fills thy note's elation
With lordlier exultation
Than man's, whose faint heart sickens
   With hopes and fears that blight

[1] Twiring: peering.   [2] Bents: slopes or hills.   [3] Weald: wooded land.
[4] Hoar: whitish gray.   [1] Seamew: sea gull.

Such life as thrills and quickens
  The silence of thy flight.

Thy cry from windward clanging
  Makes all the cliffs rejoice;
Though storm clothe seas with sorrow,
Thy call salutes the morrow;
While shades of pain seem hanging
  Round earth's most rapturous voice,
Thy cry from windward clanging
  Makes all the cliffs rejoice.

We, sons and sires of seamen,
  Whose home is all the sea,
What place man may, we claim it;
But thine—whose thought may name it?
Free birds live higher than freemen,
  And gladlier ye than we—
We, sons and sires of seamen,
  Whose home is all the sea.

For you the storm sounds only
  More notes of more delight
Than earth's in sunniest weather:
When heaven and sea together
Join strengths against the lonely
  Lost bark borne down by night,
For you the storm sounds only
  More notes of more delight.

With wider wing, and louder
  Long clarion-call of joy,
Thy tribe salutes the terror
Of darkness, wild as error,
But sure as truth, and prouder
  Than waves with man for toy;
With wider wing, and louder
  Long clarion-call of joy.

The wave's wing spreads and flutters,
  The wave's heart swells and breaks;
One moment's passion thrills it,
One pulse of power fulfils it
And ends the pride it utters
  When, loud with life that quakes,
The wave's wing spreads and flutters,
  The wave's heart swells and breaks.

But thine and thou, my brother,
  Keep heart and wing more high
Than aught may scare or sunder;
The waves whose throats are thunder
Fall hurtling each on other,
  And triumph as they die;

But thine and thou, my brother,
  Keep heart and wing more high.

More high than wrath or anguish,
  More strong than pride or fear,
The sense or soul half hidden
In thee, for us forbidden,
Bids thee nor change nor languish,
  But live thy life as here,   70
More high than wrath or anguish,
  More strong than pride or fear.

We are fallen, even we, whose passion
  On earth is nearest thine;
Who sing, and cease from flying;
Who live, and dream of dying:
Grey time, in time's grey fashion,
  Bids wingless creatures pine:
We are fallen, even we, whose passion
  On earth is nearest thine.   80

The lark knows no such rapture,
  Such joy no nightingale,
As sways the songless measure
Wherein thy wings take pleasure:
Thy love may no man capture,
  Thy pride may no man quail;
The lark knows no such rapture,
  Such joy no nightingale.

And we, whom dreams embolden,
  We can but creep and sing   90
And watch through heaven's waste hollow
The flight no sight may follow
To the utter bourne beholden
  Of none that lack thy wing:
And we, whom dreams embolden,
  We can but creep and sing.

Our dreams have wings that falter,
  Our hearts bear hopes that die;
For thee no dream could better
A life no fears may fetter,   100
A pride no care can alter,
  That wots not whence or why
Our dreams have wings that falter,
  Our hearts bear hopes that die.

With joy more fierce and sweeter
  Than joys we deem divine
Their lives, by time untarnished,
Are girt about and garnished,
Who match the wave's full metre
  And drink the wind's wild wine   110

With joy more fierce and sweeter
   Than joys we deem divine.

Ah, well were I for ever,
   Wouldst thou change lives with me,
And take my song's wild honey,
And give me back thy sunny
Wide eyes that weary never,
   And wings that search the sea;
Ah, well were I for ever,
120   Wouldst thou change lives with me.

                           1889

A Nympholept[1]

Summer, and noon, and a splendour of silence,
   felt,
   Seen, and heard of the spirit within the
     sense.
Soft through the frondage the shades of the
   sunbeams melt,
   Sharp through the foliage the shafts of them,
     keen and dense,
   Cleave, as discharged from the string of the
     God's bow, tense
As a war-steed's girth, and bright as a warrior's
   belt.
   Ah, why should an hour that is heaven for
     an hour pass hence?

I dare not sleep for delight of the perfect hour,
   Lest God be wroth that his gift should be
     scorned of man.
The face of the warm bright world is the face
10   of a flower,
   The word of the wind and the leaves that
     the light winds fan
   As the word that quickened at first into
     flame, and ran,
Creative and subtle and fierce with invasive
   power,
Through darkness and cloud, from the breath
   of the one God, Pan.[2]

The perfume of earth possessed by the sun
   pervades

The chaster air that he soothes but with
   sense of sleep.
Soft, imminent, strong as desire that prevails
   and fades,
   The passing noon that beholds not a cloudlet
     weep
   Imbues and impregnates life with delight
     more deep
Than dawn or sunset or moonrise on lawns
   or glades
   Can shed from the skies that receive it and
     may not keep.

The skies may hold not the splendour of
   sundown fast;
   It wanes into twilight as dawn dies down
     into day.
And the moon, triumphant when twilight is
   overpast,
   Takes pride but awhile in the hours of her
     stately sway.
   But the might of the noon, though the light
     of it pass away,
Leaves earth fulfilled of desires and of dreams
   that last;
   But if any there be that hath sense of them
     none can say.

For if any there be that hath sight of them,
   sense, or trust
   Made strong by the might of a vision, the
     strength of a dream,
His lips shall straiten and close as a dead man's
   must,
   His heart shall be sealed as the voice of a
     frost-bound stream.
   For the deep mid mystery of light and of
     heat that seem
To clasp and pierce dark earth, and enkindle
   dust,
   Shall a man's faith say what it is? or a man's
     guess deem?

Sleep lies not heavier on eyes that have watched
   all night
   Than hangs the heat of the noon on the hills
     and trees.

---

[1] A nympholept is one caught or possessed by the spirit of a nymph. In the "Dedicatory Epistle" to the collected edition of his poems published in 1904, Swinburne describes a class of poems in which he attempts to render his sense of a place, including those "as try to render the effect of inland or woodland solitude—the splendid oppression of nature at noon which found utterance of old in words of such singular and everlasting significance as panic and nympholepsy."

[2] Pan: the classical god of fields and wild nature; later, he became a kind of universal pagan god, the embodiment of the spirit of the universe and of the attributes of the other gods.

Why now should the haze not open, and yield
  to sight
   A fairer secret than hope or than slumber
   sees?
   I seek not heaven with submission of lips
   and knees,
With worship and prayer for a sign till it leap
  to light:
   I gaze on the gods about me, and call on
   these.

I call on the gods hard by, the divine dim
  powers
   Whose likeness is here at hand, in the breath-
   less air,
In the pulseless peace of the fervid and silent
  flowers,
   In the faint sweet speech of the waters that
   whisper there.
   Ah, what should darkness do in a world so
   fair?
The bent-grass heaves not, the couch-grass
  quails not or cowers;[3]
   The wind's kiss frets not the rowan's or
   aspen's hair.

But the silence trembles with passion of sound
  suppressed,
   And the twilight quivers and yearns to the
   sunward, wrung
With love as with pain; and the wide wood's
  motionless breast
   Is thrilled with a dumb desire that would
   fain find tongue
   And palpitates, tongueless as she whom a
   man-snake stung,[4]
Whose heart now heaves in the nightingale,
  never at rest
   Nor satiated ever with song till her last be
   sung.

Is it rapture or terror that circles me round,
  and invades
   Each vein of my life with hope—if it be not
   fear?
Each pulse that awakens my blood into rapture
  fades,
   Each pulse that subsides into dread of a
   strange thing near
   Requickens with sense of a terror less dread
   than dear.

Is peace not one with light in the deep green
  glades
   Where summer at noonday slumbers? Is
   peace not here?

The tall thin stems of the firs, and the roof
  sublime
   That screens from the sun the floor of the
   steep still wood,
Deep, silent, splendid, and perfect and calm as
  time,
   Stand fast as ever in sight of the night they
   stood,
   When night gave all that moonlight and
   dewfall could.
The dense ferns deepen, the moss glows warm
  as the thyme:
   The wild heath quivers about me: the world
   is good.   70

Is it Pan's breath, fierce in the tremulous
  maidenhair,[5]
   That bids fear creep as a snake through the
   woodlands, felt
In the leaves that it stirs not yet, in the mute
  bright air,
   In the stress of the sun? For here has the
   great God dwelt:
   For hence were the shafts of his love or his
   anger dealt.
For here has his wrath been fierce as his love
  was fair,
   When each was as fire to the darkness its
   breath bade melt.

Is it love, is it dread, that enkindles the
  trembling noon,
   That yearns, reluctant in rapture that fear
   has fed,
As man for woman, as woman for man? Full
  soon,   80
   If I live, and the life that may look on him
   drop not dead,
   Shall the ear that hears not a leaf quake hear
   his tread,
The sense that knows not the sound of the
  deep day's tune
   Receive the God, be it love that he brings or
   dread.

---

[3] Bent-grass; couch-grass: the first a stiff, coarse grass; the second a creeping grass.
[4] She whom a man-snake stung: Philomela, raped by her sister's husband, and then turned
into a nightingale by the gods to protect her from further violence.
[5] Maidenhair: a fern.

The naked noon is upon me: the fierce dumb
    spell,
    The fearful charm of the strong sun's
      imminent might,
Unmerciful, steadfast, deeper than seas that
    swell,
    Pervades, invades, appals me with loveless
      light,
    With harsher awe than breathes in the
      breath of night.
Have mercy, God who art all! For I know thee
90   well,
    How sharp is thine eye to lighten, thine
      hand to smite.

The whole wood feels thee, the whole air fears
    thee: but fear
    So deep, so dim, so sacred, is wellnigh sweet.
For the light that hangs and broods on the
    woodlands here,
    Intense, invasive, intolerant, imperious, and
      meet[6]
    To lighten the works of thine hands and the
      ways of thy feet,
Is hot with the fire of the breath of thy life,
    and dear
    As hope that shrivels or shrinks not for frost
      or heat.

Thee, thee the supreme dim godhead, approved
    afar,
    Perceived of the soul and conceived of the
100   sense of man,
We scarce dare love, and we dare not fear: the
    star
    We call the sun, that lit us when life began
    To brood on the world that is thine by his
      grace for a span,
Conceals and reveals in the semblance of things
    that are
    Thine immanent presence, the pulse of thy
      heart's life, Pan.

The fierce mid noon that wakens and warms
    the snake
    Conceals thy mercy, reveals thy wrath: and
      again
The dew-bright hour that assuages the twilight
    brake[7]
    Conceals thy wrath and reveals thy mercy:
      then
110   Thou art fearful only for evil souls of men

That feel with nightfall the serpent within
    them wake,
    And hate the holy darkness of glade and
      glen.

Yea, then we know not and dream not if ill
    things be,
    Or if aught of the work of the wrong of the
      world be thine.
We hear not the footfall of terror that treads
    the sea,
    We hear not the moan of winds that assail
      the pine:
    We see not if shipwreck reign in the storm's
      dim shrine;
If death do service and doom bear witness to
    thee
    We see not,—know not if blood for thy lips
      be wine.

But in all things evil and fearful that fear may
    scan,   12
    As in all things good, as in all things fair
      that fall,
We know thee present and latent, the lord of
    man;
    In the murmuring of doves, in the clamour-
      ing of winds that call
    And wolves that howl for their prey; in the
      midnight's pall,
In the naked and nymph-like feet of the dawn,
    O Pan,
    And in each life living, O thou the God who
      art all.

Smiling and singing, wailing and wringing of
    hands,
    Laughing and weeping, watching and
      sleeping, still
Proclaim but and prove but thee, as the shifted
    sands
    Speak forth and show but the strength of the
      sea's wild will   1
    That sifts and grinds them as grain in the
      storm-wind's mill.
In thee is the doom that falls and the doom
    that stands:
    The tempests utter thy word, and the stars
      fulfil.

Where Etna shudders with passion and pain
    volcanic

---

[6] Meet: fit.   [7] Brake: thicket.

That rend her heart as with anguish that
rends a man's,
Where Typho labours, and finds not his thews
Titanic,[8]
  In breathless torment that ever the flame's
  breath fans,
  Men felt and feared thee of old, whose
  pastoral clans
Were given to the charge of thy keeping; and
soundless panic
  Held fast the woodland whose depths and
  whose heights were Pan's.

And here, though fear be less than delight, and
awe
  Be one with desire and with worship of earth
  and thee,
So mild seems now thy secret and speechless
law,
  So fair and fearless and faithful and godlike
  she,
  So soft the spell of thy whisper on stream and
  sea,
Yet man should fear lest he see what of old
men saw
  And withered: yet shall I quail if thy breath
  smite me.

Lord God of life and of light and of all things
fair,
  Lord God of ravin[9] and ruin and all things
  dim,
Death seals up life, and darkness the sunbright
air,
  And the stars that watch blind earth in the
  deep night swim
  Laugh, saying, "What God is your God, that
  ye call on him?
What is man, that the God who is guide of
our way should care
  If day for a man be golden, or night be
  grim?"

But thou, dost thou hear? Stars too but abide
for a span,
  Gods too but endure for a season; but thou,
  if thou be
God, more than shadows conceived and adored
of man,
  Kind Gods and fierce, that bound him or
  made him free,

The skies that scorn us are less in thy sight
than we,
Whose souls have strength to conceive and
perceive thee, Pan,
  With sense more subtle than senses that hear
  and see.

Yet may not it say, though it seek thee and
think to find
  One soul of sense in the fire and the frost-
  bound clod,
What heart is this, what spirit alive or blind,
  That moves thee: only we know that the
  ways we trod
  We tread, with hands unguided, with feet
  unshod,
With eyes unlightened; and yet, if with stead-
fast mind,
  Perchance may we find thee and know thee
  at last for God.

Yet then should God be dark as the dawn is
bright,
  And bright as the night is dark on the
  world—no more.
Light slays not darkness, and darkness absorbs
not light;
  And the labour of evil and good from the
  years of yore
  Is even as the labour of waves on a sunless
  shore.
And he who is first and last, who is depth and
height,
  Keeps silence now, as the sun when the
  woods wax hoar.[10]

The dark dumb godhead innate in the fair
world's life
  Imbues the rapture of dawn and of noon
  with dread,
Infects the peace of the star-shod night with
strife,
  Informs with terror the sorrow that guards
  the dead.
  No service of bended knee or of humbled
  head
May soothe or subdue the God who has change
to wife:
  And life with death is as morning with
  evening wed.

---

[8] Etna: a volcanic mountain in Sicily. The classical myth is that the Titan Typho, vanquished
in his challenge to the gods of Olympus, is imprisoned beneath the mountain.
[9] Ravin: preying.   [10] Wax hoar: grow white or old.

160

170

180

40

50

And yet, if the light and the life in the light
  that here
    Seem soft and splendid and fervid as sleep
    may seem
Be more than the shine of a smile or the flash
  of a tear,
    Sleep, change, and death are less than a
    spell-struck dream,
    And fear than the fall of a leaf on a starlit
    stream.
And yet, if the hope that hath said it absorb
  not fear,
    What helps it man that the stars and the
    waters gleam?

What helps it man, that the noon be indeed
  190   intense,
    The night be indeed worth worship? Fear
    and pain
Were lords and masters yet of the secret sense,
    Which now dares deem not that light is as
    darkness, fain
    Though dark dreams be to declare it, crying
    in vain.
For whence, thou God of the light and the
  darkness, whence
    Dawns now this vision that bids not the sun-
    beams wane?

What light, what shadow, diviner than dawn
  or night,
    Draws near, makes pause, and again—or I
    dream—draws near?
More soft than shadow, more strong than the
  strong sun's light,
    More pure than moonbeams—yea, but the
  200   rays run sheer
    As fire from the sun through the dusk of
    the pine-wood, clear
And constant; yea, but the shadow itself is
  bright
    That the light clothes round with love that
    is one with fear.

Above and behind it the noon and the wood-
  land lie,
    Terrible, radiant with mystery, superb and
    subdued,
Triumphant in silence; and hardly the sacred
  sky
    Seems free from the tyrannous weight of the
    dumb fierce mood
    Which rules as with fire and invasion of
    beams that brood

The breathless rapture of earth till its hour
  pass by
    And leave her spirit released and her peace
    renewed.   21

I sleep not: never in sleep has a man beholden
    This. From the shadow that trembles and
    yearns with light
Suppressed and elate and reluctant—obscure
  and golden
    As water kindled with presage of dawn or
    night—
    A form, a face, a wonder to sense and sight,
Grows great as the moon through the month;
  and her eyes embolden
    Fear, till it change to desire, and desire to
    delight.

I sleep not: sleep would die of a dream so
    strange;
    A dream so sweet would die as a rainbow
    dies,
As a sunbow laughs and is lost on the waves
    that range   22
    And reck not of light that flickers or spray
    that flies.
    But the sun withdraws not, the woodland
    shrinks not or sighs,
No sweet thing sickens with sense or with fear
  of change;
    Light wounds not, darkness blinds not, my
    steadfast eyes.

Only the soul in my sense that receives the soul
    Whence now my spirit is kindled with
    breathless bliss
Knows well if the light that wounds it with
  love makes whole,
    If hopes that carol be louder than fears that
    hiss,
    If truth be spoken of flowers and of waves
    that kiss,
Of clouds and stars that contend for a sun-
  bright goal.   2
    And yet may I dream that I dream not indeed
    of this?

An earth-born dreamer, constrained by the
  bonds of birth,
    Held fast by the flesh, compelled by his veins
    that beat
And kindle to rapture or wrath, to desire or to
  mirth,
    May hear not surely the fall of immortal
    feet,

May feel not surely if heaven upon earth be
  sweet;
And here is my sense fulfilled of the joys of
  earth,
  Light, silence, bloom, shade, murmur of
  leaves that meet.

Bloom, fervour, and perfume of grasses and
  flowers aglow,
  Breathe and brighten about me: the
  darkness gleams,
The sweet light shivers and laughs on the
  slopes below,
  Made soft by leaves that lighten and change
  like dreams;
  The silence thrills with the whisper of secret
  streams
That well from the heart of the woodland:
  these I know:
  Earth bore them, heaven sustained them with
  showers and beams.

I lean my face to the heather, and drink the
  sun
  Whose flame-lit odour satiates the flowers:
  mine eyes
Close, and the goal of delight and of life is one:
  No more I crave of earth or her kindred
  skies.
  No more? But the joy that springs from
  them smiles and flies:
The sweet work wrought of them surely, the
  good work done,
  If the mind and the face of the season be
  loveless, dies.

Thee, therefore, thee would I come to, cleave
  to, cling,
  If haply thy heart be kind and thy gifts be
  good,
Unknown sweet spirit, whose vesture is soft in
  spring,
  In summer splendid, in autumn pale as the
  wood
  That shudders and wanes and shrinks as a
  shamed thing should,
In winter bright as the mail of a war-worn
  king
  Who stands where foes fled far from the face
  of him stood.

My spirit or thine is it, breath of thy life or of
  mine,

Which fills my sense with a rapture that
  casts out fear?
Pan's dim frown wanes, and his wild eyes
  brighten as thine,
  Transformed as night or as day by the
  kindling year.
  Earth-born, or mine eye were withered that
  sees, mine ear
That hears were stricken to death by the
  sense divine,
  Earth-born I know thee: but heaven is about
  me here.

The terror that whispers in darkness and
  flames in light,
  The doubt that speaks in the silence of earth
  and sea,
The sense, more fearful at noon than in mid-
  most night,
  Of wrath scarce hushed and of imminent ill
  to be,   270
  Where are they? Heaven is as earth, and as
  heaven to me
Earth: for the shadows that sundered them
  here take flight;
  And nought is all, as am I, but a dream of
  thee.

                                    1891; 1894

Hawthorn Dyke

All the golden air is full of balm and bloom
  Where the hawthorns line the shelving dyke[1]
  with flowers.
  Joyous children born of April's happiest
  hours,
High and low they laugh and lighten, knowing
  their doom
Bright as brief—to bless and cheer they know
  not whom,
  Heed not how, but washed and warmed
  with suns and showers
  Smile, and bid the sweet soft gradual banks
  and bowers
Thrill with love of sunlit fire or starry gloom.
All our moors and lawns all round rejoice; but
  here
All the rapturous resurrection of the year   10
  Finds the radiant utterance perfect, sees the
  word
Spoken, hears the light that speaks it. Far and
  near,

---

[1] Shelving: sloping.

All the world is heaven: and man and flower
    and bird
Here are one at heart with all things seen
    and heard.

1893; 1894

A Channel Passage

1855[1]

Forth from Calais, at dawn of night, when
    sunset summer on autumn shone,
Fared the steamer alert and loud through seas
    whence only the sun was gone:
Soft and sweet as the sky they smiled, and bade
    man welcome: a dim sweet hour
Gleamed and whispered in wind and sea, and
    heaven was fair as a field in flower.
Stars fulfilled the desire of the darkling world
    as with music: the starbright air
Made the face of the sea, if aught may make
    the face of the sea, more fair.

Whence came change? Was the sweet night
    weary of rest? What anguish awoke in the
    dark?
Sudden, sublime, the strong storm spake: we
    heard the thunders as hounds that bark.
Lovelier if aught may be lovelier than stars,
    we saw the lightnings exalt the sky,
Living and lustrous and rapturous as love that
10   is born but to quicken and lighten and die.
Heaven's own heart at its highest of delight
    found utterance in music and semblance in
    fire:
Thunder on thunder exulted, rejoicing to live
    and to satiate the night's desire.

And the night was alive and anhungered of
    life as a tiger from toils cast free:
And a rapture of rage made joyous the spirit
    and strength of the soul of the sea.
All the weight of the wind bore down on it,
    freighted with death for fraught:
And the keen waves kindled and quickened as
    things transfigured or things distraught.
And madness fell on them laughing and
    leaping; and madness came on the wind:
And the might and the light and the darkness
    of storm were as storm in the heart of Ind.[2]

Such glory, such terror, such passion, as lighten
    and harrow the far fierce East,
Rang, shone, spake, shuddered around us: the
    night was an altar with death for priest. 2
The channel that sunders England from shores
    where never was man born free
Was clothed with the likeness and thrilled with
    the strength and the wrath of a tropic sea.
As a wild steed ramps in rebellion, and rears
    till it swerves from a backward fall,
The strong ship struggled and reared, and her
    deck was upright as a sheer cliff's wall.
Stern and prow plunged under, alternate: a
    glimpse, a recoil, a breath,
And she sprang as the life in a god made man
    would spring at the throat of death.
Three glad hours, and it seemed not an hour of
    supreme and supernal joy,
Filled full with delight that revives in
    remembrance a sea-bird's heart in a boy.
For the central crest of the night was cloud
    that thundered and flamed, sublime
As the splendour and song of the soul
    everlasting that quickens the pulse of time. 3
The glory beholden of man in a vision, the
    music of light overheard,
The rapture and radiance of battle, the life
    that abides in the fire of a word,
In the midmost heaven enkindled, was
    manifest far on the face of the sea,
And the rage in the roar of the voice of the
    waters was heard but when heaven breathed
    free.
Far eastward, clear of the covering of cloud,
    the sky laughed out into light
From the rims of the storm to the sea's dark
    edge with flames that were flowerlike and
    white.
The leaping and luminous blossoms of live
    sheet lightning that laugh as they fade
From the cloud's black base to the black wave's
    brim rejoiced in the light they made.
Far westward, throned in a silent sky, where
    life was in lustrous tune,
Shone, sweeter and surer than morning or
    evening, the steadfast smile of the moon.
The limitless heaven that enshrined them was
    lovelier than dreams may behold, and deep
As life or as death, revealed and transfigured,
    may shine on the soul through sleep.

---

[1] In 1855 Swinburne accompanied one of his uncles, who had himself traveled in the east, on
a journey to the Continent. On their return they crossed the English Channel in a storm whose
violence was remarkable enough to be reported in the newspapers of the day—a storm whose
violence, his uncle said, was as great as that of a tropical storm (see line 18).
[2] Ind: India.

All glories of toil and of triumph and passion
  and pride that it yearns to know
Bore witness there to the soul of its likeness
  and kinship, above and below.
The joys of the lightnings, the songs of the
  thunders, the strong sea's labour and rage,
Were tokens and signs of the war that is life
  and is joy for the soul to wage.
No thought strikes deeper or higher than the
  heights and the depths that the night made
  bare,
Illimitable, infinite, awful and joyful, alive in
  the summit of air—
Air stilled and thrilled by the tempest that
  thundered between its reign and the sea's,
Rebellious, rapturous, and transient as faith or
  as terror that bows men's knees.
No love sees loftier and fairer the form of its
  godlike vision in dreams
Than the world shone then, when the sky and
  the sea were as love for a breath's length
  seems—
One utterly, mingled and mastering and
  mastered and laughing with love that sub-
  sides
As the glad mad night sank panting and satiate
  with storm, and released the tides.
In the dense mid channel the steam-souled ship
  hung hovering, assailed and withheld
As a soul born royal, if life or if death be
  against it, is thwarted and quelled.
As the glories of myriads of glowworms in
    lustrous grass on a boundless lawn
Were the glories of flames phosphoric that
  made of the water a light like dawn.
A thousand Phosphors, a thousand Hespers,[3]
  awoke in the churning sea,
And the swift soft hiss of them living and dying
  was clear as a tune could be;
As a tune that is played by the fingers of death
  on the keys of life or of sleep,
Audible alway alive in the storm, too fleet for
  a dream to keep:
Too fleet, too sweet for a dream to recover
  and thought to remember awake:
Light subtler and swifter than lightning, that
  whispers and laughs in the live storm's wake,
In the wild bright wake of the storm, in the
  dense loud heart of the labouring hour,

A harvest of stars by the storm's hand reaped,
  each fair as a star-shaped flower.
And sudden and soft as the passing of sleep is
  the passing of tempest seemed
When the light and the sound of it sank, and
  the glory was gone as a dream half dreamed.
The glory, the terror, the passion that made of
  the midnight a miracle, died,
Not slain at a stroke, nor in gradual reluctance
  abated of power and of pride;
With strong swift subsidence, awful as power
  that is wearied of power upon earth,
As a God that were wearied of power upon
  heaven, and were fain of a new God's birth,
The might of the night subsided: the tyranny
  kindled in darkness fell:
And the sea and the sky put off them the
  rapture and radiance of heaven and of hell.
The waters, heaving and hungering at heart,
  made way, and were wellnigh fain,
For the ship that had fought them, and
  wrestled, and revelled in labour, to cease
  from her pain.
And an end was made of it: only remembrance
  endures of the glad loud strife;
And the sense that a rapture so royal may come
  not again in the passage of life.

                                    1899; 1904

The Lake of Gaube[1]

The sun is lord and god, sublime, serene,
  And sovereign on the mountains: earth and
  air
Lie prone in passion, blind with bliss unseen
  By force of sight and might of rapture, fair
  As dreams that die and know not what they
  were.
The lawns, the gorges, and the peaks, are one
Glad glory, thrilled with sense of unison
In strong compulsive silence of the sun.

Flowers dense and keen as midnight stars
  aflame
  And living things of light like flames in
  flower[2]
That glance and flash as though no hand
  might tame

---

[3] Phosphor; Hesper: the morning and evening stars.
  [1] The Lake of Gaube is in the Pyrenees, which Swinburne visited in 1862. The local super-
stition was that anyone who swam in the lake courted death.
  [2] Living things of light: In a collection of essays, *Studies in Prose and Poetry* (1894), Swin-
burne recalled in prose the salamanders he saw during his visit to the Lake of Gaube: "the
salamanders glide like creeping flames, radiant and vivid, up to the skirt of the tragic little pine-

Lightnings whose life outshone their storm-
    lit hour
  And played and laughed on earth, with all
    their power
Gone, and with all their joy of life made long
And harmless as the lightning life of song,
Shine sweet like stars when darkness feels them
    strong.

The deep mild purple flaked with moonbright
    gold
  That makes the scales seem flowers of
    hardened light,
The flamelike tongue, the feet that noon leaves
    cold,
  The kindly trust in man, when once the
    sight
  Grew less than strange, and faith bade fear
    take flight,
Outlive the little harmless life that shone
And gladdened eyes that loved it, and was gone
Ere love might fear that fear had looked
    thereon.

Fear held the bright thing hateful, even as
    fear,
  Whose name is one with hate and horror,
    saith
That heaven, the dark deep heaven of water
    near,
  Is deadly deep as hell and dark as death.
  The rapturous plunge that quickens blood
    and breath
With pause more sweet than passion, ere they
    strive
To raise again the limbs that yet would dive
Deeper, should there have slain the soul alive.

As the bright salamander in fire of the noon-
    shine exults and is glad of his day,
The spirit that quickens my body rejoices to
    pass from the sunlight away,
To pass from the glow of the mountainous
    flowerage, the high multitudinous bloom,
Far down through the fathomless night of the
    water, the gladness of silence and gloom.
Death-dark and delicious as death in the dream
    of a lover and dreamer may be,

It clasps and encompasses body and soul with
    delight to be living and free:
Free utterly now, though the freedom endure
    but the space of a perilous breath,
And living, though girdled about with the
    darkness and coldness and strangeness
    of death:
Each limb and each pulse of the body rejoicing,
    each nerve of the spirit at rest,
All sense of the soul's life rapture, a passionate
    peace in its blindness blest.
So plunges the downward swimmer, embraced
    of the water unfathomed of man,
The darkness unplummeted, icier than seas in
    mid-winter, for blessing or ban;
And swiftly and sweetly, when strength and
    breath fall short, and the dive is done,
Shoots up as a shaft from the dark depth shot,
    sped straight into sight of the sun;
And sheer through the snow-soft water, more
    dark than the roof of the pines above,
Strikes forth, and is glad as a bird whose flight
    is impelled and sustained of love.
As a sea-mew's[3] love of the sea-wind breasted
    and ridden for rapture's sake
Is the love of his body and soul for the
    darkling delight of the soundless lake:
As the silent speed of a dream too living to live
    for a thought's space more
Is the flight of his limbs through the still strong
    chill of the darkness from shore to shore.
Might life be as this is and death be as life that
    casts off time as a robe,
The likeness of infinite heaven were a symbol
    revealed of the lake of Gaube.

  Whose thought has fathomed and
    measured
    The darkness of life and of death,
  The secret within them treasured,
    The spirit that is not breath?
  Whose vision has yet beholden
    The splendour of death and of life?
  Though sunset as dawn be golden,
    Is the word of them peace, not strife?
  Deep silence answers: the glory
    We dream of may be but a dream,
  And the sun of the soul wax hoary
    As ashes that show not a gleam.

---

wood at whose heart the fathomless lake lies silent, with a dark dull gleam on it as if of half-tarnished steel." He wrote of catching and taming a salamander, and of "the beauty of its purple-black coat of scaled armour inlaid with patches of dead-leaf gold, its shining eyes and flashing tongue."

[3] Sea-mew: sea gull.

But well shall it be with us ever
    Who drive through the darkness here,
If the soul that we live by never,
    For aught that a lie saith, fear.

                        1899; 1904

Delphic Hymn to Apollo

(B.C. 280)

Done into English[1]

I

    Thee, the son of God most high,
    Famed for harping song, will I
Proclaim, and the deathless oracular word
From the snow-topped rock that we gaze on
    heard,
    Counsels of thy glorious giving
    Manifest for all men living,
How thou madest the tripod of prophecy thine
Which the wrath of the dragon kept guard on,
    a shrine
    Voiceless till thy shafts could smite
    All his live coiled glittering might.[2]

II

    Ye that hold of right alone
    All deep woods on Helicon,

Fair daughters of thunder-girt God, with your
    bright
White arms uplift as to lighten the light,
    Come to chant your brother's praise,
    Gold-haired Phœbus, loud in lays,
Even his, who afar up the twin-topped seat
Of the rock Parnassian whereon we meet
    Risen with glorious Delphic maids
    Seeks the soft spring-sweetened shades   20
Castalian, fain of the Delphian peak
Prophetic, sublime as the feet that seek.[3]
    Glorious Athens, highest of state,
    Come, with praise and prayer elate,
O thou that art queen of the plain unscarred
That the warrior Tritonid[4] hath alway in
    guard,
    Where on many a sacred shrine
    Young bulls' thigh-bones burn and shine
As the god that is fire overtakes them, and fast
The smoke of Arabia[5] to heavenward is cast,   30
    Scattering wide its balm: and shrill
    Now with nimble notes that thrill
The flute strikes up for the song, and the harp
    of gold
Strikes up to the song sweet answer: and all
    behold,
    All, aswarm as bees, give ear,
    Who by birth hold Athens dear.

                        1894; 1904

Gerard Manley Hopkins
1844–1889

WHEN GERARD MANLEY HOPKINS decided in 1868 to enter the priesthood of the Society of Jesus, he destroyed (as he thought: some working drafts remain) all the poems he had written. He did not resume the writing of poetry for seven years. Although events during the rest of his life were to complement and complicate the meaning of this gesture, it was

---

[1] Upon its first publication in a magazine in 1894 this poem was described as a rendering of two inscriptions found during the excavation of the temple to Apollo at Delphi in the 1890s.

[2] The sacred site of Delphi was guarded by a serpent that was slain by Apollo. The site then became famous for the oracles of its priestesses, who spoke while entranced. They spoke seated on a tripod.

[3] Helicon: a mountain in Greece which was the abode of Apollo and the Muses of song and history. Parnassus is a mountain near the oracle at Delphi and sacred to Apollo and the Muses. Phoebus is one of the names of Apollo, especially in his association with the sun. Castalia is the name of a spring on Parnassus in which the priestess bathed before she prophesied. Fain: fond.

[4] Tritonid: associated with Triton, a god of the sea.   [5] Smoke of Arabia: fragrant smoke.

fundamentally a true one. Hopkins accepted the Jesuit principle that the purpose of his life was to serve and praise God, and so to save his soul. He did not see a general and necessary conflict between the vocation of a priest and that of a poet, or of any artist. He was later to believe that all work serves and praises God. He came to recognize poetry as a social act by which poets did good, and he wrote to his friends and fellow poets that for them publication and fame were desirable, the air and setting in which their genius flourished and completed itself. He himself wrote "The Wreck of the *Deutschland*" for publication in 1876, although it, like a companion poem "The Loss of the Eurydice," was refused by the Jesuit magazine to which he submitted it. Only a few of his poems were published during his lifetime. But he continued to write them, and he seems to have regarded his friend Robert Bridges as a kind of proto-public for them. He wrote Bridges long letters adjuring him to preserve the poems and preparing him to explain them to others. Once Hopkins even wrote a preface (see Part Ten) to the manuscript volume in which Bridges kept the poems. There is, in short, nothing peripheral or casual about the character of Hopkins' poems, as if he composed them in the relaxed intervals of another occupation, and there is nothing accidental about their survival and later publication. Hopkins fully and deliberately engaged his very complicated identity in his poems. He wanted them to be understood and to act on their readers, and he helped to prepare the day when their publication would enlarge the extremely limited circle of their readers during his lifetime.

At the same time, Hopkins was a painfully self-scrutinizing man. However he honored poets and poetry as instruments in the service of God, he seems always to have been sure that for him the primary terms of his service lay in the duties of a priest and teacher. In a letter to R. W. Dixon in 1881 (see pp. 744–746), the year in which he completed the long Jesuit course of study, work, and self-examination, Hopkins wrote that literature has not often been a "serviceable" means to the end to which his priesthood was given. In any event, he will not, he wrote, put himself forward as poet until he has received guidance from his superiors and his own inspiration to do so. "Now if you value what I write, if I do myself, much more does our Lord. And if he chooses to avail him-

self of what I leave at his disposal he can do so with a felicity and with a success which I could never command. And if he does not, then two things follow; one that the reward I shall nevertheless receive from him will be all the greater; the other that then I shall know how much a thing contrary to his will and even to my own best interests I should have done if I had taken things into my own hands and forced on publication." Hopkins, in short, placed the imperatives of his priesthood not above but around those of his poetic gifts.

It was for that reason that he wrote no poetry during the first seven years of study leading to his ordination. When he was a parish priest in the late 1870s he worked very hard at writing sermons and the other duties of his parish; when he was a university professor in the 1880s, he set himself to various scholarly projects he thought appropriate, and he labored scrupulously at lecturing and grading examinations. The commanding, circumscribing status of his priesthood is also the reason that one line of the development of his poetry follows the course of his concern about how to live in the mortal world and remain in a proper, dutiful, and fulfilling relationship with a God whom Hopkins wanted always to be intensely and personally present. In the early poem "The Habit of Perfection" Hopkins closes his senses to material creation: from his schooldays, when he once tried to abstain from water for a week because he thought people drank more liquids than they needed, he was given to acts of renunciation. Then, in "The Wreck of the *Deutschland*" and the poems which followed in the 1870s, he finds God, often in the persons of Christ and the Holy Ghost, in the storms and dawns of sensible existence, and he celebrates his presence in "God's Grandeur," "Pied Beauty," "The Windhover," and similar poems. In the so-called "terrible sonnets" of the mid-1880s Hopkins lives for a time in a self he yearns and fears to contemn, and with a divine presence who requires him not to seek ecstatic communion in the flashing light and color of the world but to struggle with the sour fact of his own heavy, dark imperfection. Finally, in poems like "Tom's Garland" and "That Nature Is a Heraclitean Fire," Hopkins comes again into a perception of man and nature made whole and glorious, perhaps in a social or political apocalypse in which the social order of the commonweal incarnates the entire order of spiritual and mundane existence, per-

haps in the already historical fact of the in-
carnation in which

I am all at once what Christ is since he was
    what I am, and
This Jack, joke, poor potshard, patch, match-
    wood, immortal diamond
    Is immortal diamond.

Hopkins' development of the singular style
of his poetry is connected to the personal
spiritual history that may be traced in his
poems. The relatively early "The Habit of
Perfection" (1866), with its clearly ordered if
complicated figure, conventional syntax, and
short, firmly closed lines and stanzas, is recog-
nizably in the idiom of mid-nineteenth-century
religious poems, like those of Christina Ros-
setti, that recall in turn the practices of hymns
and some seventeenth-century religious poets.
Beginning in the 1870s, a few years before he
began to write "The Wreck of the *Deutsch-
land*," Hopkins was working out some ideas
about the structures of created things, includ-
ing ideas about *inscape* and *instress*. To put it
very simply, by *inscape* Hopkins meant the
principle of organization of a thing, the lines
of its form as they flow out from and are held
by the principle that makes it one thing. *In-
stress* is the energy or presence that shows the
inscape, as the lines of force converging on the
arch in a barn show its structure, or the wind
causes a bluebell, a leaf, or a tree to show how
it arranges force to make its form. Later, Hop-
kins pondered a conception of *self* as an expres-
sion of inscape. Self became the note of in-
dividual being in a series or on a scale, the
particular pitch of each form that announces
itself and at the same time establishes its rela-
tionship to the notes or pitches of other forms.
In their elucidations of these ideas W. H.
Gardner and Alan Heuser (see below) fit them
into Hopkins' ideas of the whole creation in
which the order within each material thing
and the order of its relation to other things is
the type and expression of an ideal order. That
idea is consistent with a prevalent nineteenth-
century British esthetic that maintained that
poems held the ideal in the material, the uni-
versal in the particular, by explicating or body-
ing forth the transcendental meanings of the
material world. Hopkin's notions of inscape
and self also put a peculiar emphasis on the
particularity of objects. During the early 1870s,
when Hopkins was teaching rhetoric in a
Jesuit seminary, he began to think about the

stresses and patterns of verse as revealing the
inscape of speech. He looked for a way to write
that would display at once the inscapes of
speech and of the objects he perceived, of his
medium and his matter. In the poetry he began
to write in 1875 he tried to show the patterns,
the rays and waves and burls, of things in flux
and motion, pied and dappled, in broken light
and shadow. He wanted to delineate these ob-
jects in a freshly seen, immediate, authentic
particularity, and he also wanted to break his
reader, and himself, into a new perception of
the form of the poem as a particular thing, an
individuated self. One result of these attempts
was sprung rhythm, which Hopkins claimed
was a return to a native and natural system
of stress in verse. Another result was a bat-
tery of devices—assonance, alliteration, inter-
nal rhymes, the matching of syllables within
a line, echoes of sound from line to line, ex-
periments with the proportion of octave to
sestet in sonnets—which were the means by
which the clots and centrifugal tumble of his
syntax, rhythms, and sounds were made to
chime and express the unique form of each
poem, its emphatic singularity, the pitch that
showed it was related to other forms but iden-
tical with none.

Even though hardly more than a dozen of
these poems were published during the Vic-
torian era proper, the style and premises of
the poetry Hopkins wrote after 1875 make him
a Victorian poet. As a young man he knew and
liked the strong colors and emblematic images
of poems and paintings sponsored by Pre-
Raphaelite ideas: one of the projects he aban-
doned when he decided to enter the Jesuit
order was a review of William Morris' *The
Earthly Paradise*. One of his tutors at Oxford
was Walter Pater, who was beginning to formu-
late his doctrine that one of the characteristics
(Pater would say the defining characteristic)
of art was its intense enactment and preserva-
tion of the particulars of a moment in which
individual consciousness made a pleasing order
of the impressions pouring in on it from the
sensible world. By the time he went to school
to Pater, Hopkins had also read John Ruskin's
Modern Painters (1843–60). Ruskin too urged
that art be responsible to the particular, and
that artists break free of conventions which
reduced experience and perception to familiar
patterns. For Ruskin, however, as for Hopkins,
the issue of a fresh, responsible perception was
an art that proclaimed the reality of the spir-

itual and divine. Seen rightly, natural existence incarnated the supernatural, and an art that caught and celebrated this sacramental identity was a praise of God—a phrase used by Ruskin and exactly apt to one of the purposes to which Hopkins committed his life as a priest. Hopkins later went to Greek philosophy and mathematics, and to the writing of Duns Scotus and other medieval theologians, to elaborate his conceptions of how the visible world manifested God. But in its most simple statement, his belief that a poem rendered the particular in a way that caught it out of flux and opened to intimations and testaments of infinity was an idea fundamental to the most common and powerful conceptions of poetry in nineteenth-century England.

Hopkins' mature poetic style also evolved out of opinions about poetry he shared with other poets in the second half of the nineteenth century. Like his friends Coventry Patmore and Robert Bridges, he wanted to renew the force of the available idioms of poetry. He understood what Browning, Swinburne (whom he thought entombed in a "high head music"), and Rossetti were trying when they roughened or intensified the standard poetic rhythms of the period and added surprising words to the lexicon of poetry. He also understood and admired William Barnes' attempt to make a language of Saxon words, although he thought as a dialect poet Barnes was too limited in the stock of words he used. Hopkins was thoroughly grounded in the quantitative measures of classical verse and interested in the prosody of Milton and in other metrical experiments. In his correspondence with Bridges and Patmore he participated in important late-century reconsiderations of the proper measure of verse in English. In his own attempts to institute a meter he thought to be native to English and to restock the lexicon of poetry with native words, he so refined the language of his poetry that it often seems to be wilfully artificial, recondite, and obscure. Nonetheless, his desire was to make poetry of authentic contemporary language so that the character of the vernacular, its inscape, would be opened to its speakers.

As it turned out, only a few of his contemporaries read his poems. Nor did he, even for posterity, write enough poems to constitute the bulk he thought a significant poet should give to readers so that poetry could work its effects largely. The reasons he limited the audi-ence and number of his poems have to do with his sense of his vocation as a priest and with a punishing scrupulosity that compelled him to refine everything he did. Like many poets of his generation, he wrote poems to hold moments of pleasure and solace against time, and he wrote in a poetic idiom that insisted on its special status and concentrated force. More important, although he did not publish his poems, he wrote them, like the principal poets of the nineteenth-century romantic tradition, to open the natural to the supernatural, and he created his own forms and idiom so that his poetry would return their own language to his contemporaries in a way that made it and their common experience large and fresh and new.

CHRONOLOGY

1844　Born in Essex in the east of England. Hopkins' father was a specialist in shipping laws and insurance who served as Counsel-General or agent for the Hawaiian Islands in Great Britain; he wrote on marine insurance, a history of Hawaii, and published some of his poetry. Hopkins' mother was the daughter of a physician; she was interested in art, music, and philosophy.

1852–63　Hopkins attended schools near London when the family moved to a house just outside London proper; one of his teachers was Richard Watson Dixon (see pp. 744–746).

1863　One of Hopkins' early poems, "Winter with the Gulf Stream," was published in a weekly London magazine. He entered Oxford on a scholarship, where he was to meet Robert Bridges (see 763–771).

1866　After conversations with some of his contemporaries at Oxford and a short correspondence and interview with John Henry Newman, Hopkins converted from the Church of England to Roman Catholicism.

1867–68　Following his graduation from Oxford in 1867, he began teaching classics in a school in Birmingham attached to the religious order and house administered by Newman. In 1868 Hopkins decided to enter the order of the Society of Jesus. He burned many copies—he thought that he had destroyed them all—of his early poems.

1868–70　Hopkins was engaged at Roehampton in the first two years of the Jesuit course of study, the novitiate, given largely to prayer, self-examination, and menial tasks.

He began his Journal in 1868 and continued it until 1875, when he resumed the writing of poetry.

1870–73 Hopkins continued his study of philosophy, classics, and other subjects at Stonyhurst, a Jesuit seminary. He became very much interested in music during these years.

1873–74 As part of his training as a Jesuit, Hopkins taught at Roehampton; among his courses was one in poetry in which he began to work out some of his ideas about stress and chiming sound in verse.

1874–77 Hopkins studied theology at a Jesuit college in Wales. In 1875 he resumed the writing of poetry by beginning "The Wreck of the *Deutschland.*" He was ordained into the Jesuit priesthood in 1877.

1877–81 Hopkins served as a parish priest in London, Oxford, near Manchester, in Liverpool, and in Glasgow.

1881–82 Hopkins returned to Roehampton for his tertianship, a final year of self-examination and prayer before he finally reaffirmed and renewed the vows of his priesthood. He published a Latin rendering of an epigram by John Dryden in a Jesuit magazine.

1882–84 While teaching classics at Stonyhurst, Hopkins met and begain a correspondence with Coventry Patmore (see pp. 489–496). He published some humorous triolets in a Jesuit magazine (1883) and some letters in a scientific journal describing certain effects in the skies over Britain of an enormous volcanic eruption in the Pacific.

1884–89 Hopkins was appointed Professor of Greek in University College, Dublin, a Catholic university in whose founding Newman had played a part. A stanza of one of his poems was published in an anthology of religious poetry edited by R. W. Dixon in 1887, and two of his translations of Shakespeare's songs into Latin were published in Jesuit magazines in 1886 and 1887. He also began to plan to write some papers in literary scholarship.

1889 Hopkins died of a fever in Dublin.

1890–95 Several of Hopkins' poems, or parts of poems, were published, most notably, ten poems in a selection introduced by Robert Bridges in Alfred H. Miles' *The Poets and Poetry of the Century* (1893), and five poems in *Lyra Sacra: A Book of Religious Verse,* edited by Henry Beeching (1895).

1916 Six of Hopkins' poems were published in an anthology, *The Spirit of Man,* edited by Robert Bridges.

1918 First edition of the *Poems of Gerard Manley Hopkins,* edited by Bridges, published.

EDITIONS

The texts of the poems printed below are those of *The Poems of Gerard Manley Hopkins,* fourth edition, edited by W. H. Gardner and N. H. McKenzie (1967). The last date cited for each poem is that of its first publication, usually in Bridges' or subsequent editions. *The Sermons and Devotional Writings of Gerard Manley Hopkins* have been edited by Christopher Devlin (1959); Humphry House and Graham Storey have edited *The Journals and Papers of Gerard Manley Hopkins* (1959). C. C. Abbott has edited three collections of Hopkins' correspondence: *Letters of Gerard Manley Hopkins to Robert Bridges* (1935); *The Correspondence of Gerard Manley Hopkins and R. W. Dixon* (1935); and *Further Letters* (second edition, 1956).

BIOGRAPHY AND CRITICISM

The most useful biographical accounts are G. F. Lahey, *Gerard Manley Hopkins* (1930); Austin Warren's introductory essay in *Gerard Manley Hopkins by the Kenyon Critics* (1945); and the biographical sections of John Pick's *Gerard Manley Hopkins: Priest and Poet* (1942) and W. H. Gardner's two-volume study, *Gerard Manley Hopkins* (1944, 1949).

The books by Pick and Gardner are essentially studies of certain features of Hopkins' writing and thinking. Alan Heuser's *The Shaping Vision of Gerard Manley Hopkins* (1958) is a study of Hopkins' aesthetic, especially its nineteenth-century sources and analogues. Elisabeth W. Schneider, *The Dragon in the Gate: Studies in the Poetry of G. M. Hopkins* (1968) contains strong chapters on "The Wreck of the Deutschland" and sprung rhythm. Alfred Thomas, *Hopkins the Jesuit: The Years of Training* (1969) is an informed account of the nature and effect of Hopkins' studies for the priesthood.

OTHER USEFUL BOOKS AND ESSAYS

Ball, Patricia M. *The Science of Aspects: The Changing Role of Fact in the Work of Coleridge, Ruskin and Hopkins* (1971).

Bender, Todd K. *Gerard Manley Hopkins:*

The Classical Background and Critical Reception of His Work (1966).

Boyle, Robert. *Metaphor in Hopkins* (1961).

Cotter, James Finn. *Inscape: The Christology and Poetry of Gerard Manley Hopkins* (1972).

Davie, Donald. "Hopkins as a Decadent Critic," in *Purity of Diction in English Verse* (1957).

Downes, David A. *Gerard Manley Hopkins: A Study of His Ignation Spirit* (1959).

Gerald Manley Hopkins by the Kenyon Critics (1945). Includes Austin Warren's biographical sketch (see above) and an essay on sprung rhythm by Harold Whitehall.

Hartman, Geoffrey H. *The Unmediated Vision: An Interpretation of Wordsworth, Hopkins, Rilke, and Valery* (1954).

Holloway, M. M. *The Prosodic Theory of Gerard Manley Hopkins* (1947).

Johnson, Wendell Stacey. *Gerard Manley Hopkins: The Poet as Victorian* (1968).

Keating, Joseph E. *The Wreck of the Deutschland: An Essay and Commentary* (1963).

Mariani, Paul L. *A Commentary on the Complete Poems of Gerard Manley Hopkins* (1970).

Martin, Philip M. *Mastery and Mercy: A Study of Two Religious Poems, The Wreck of the Deutschland by Gerard Manley Hopkins and Ash Wednesday by T. S. Eliot* (1957).

Miller, J. Hillis. *The Disappearance of God* (1963). Includes a chapter on Hopkins' poetry.

Peters, W. A. M. *Gerard Manley Hopkins: A Critical Essay Toward an Understanding of His Works* (1948).

Ritz, Jean-Georges. *Le Poète Gérard Manley Hopkins* (1963); and *Robert Bridges and Gerard Hopkins* (1960).

Sulloway, Allison. *Gerard Manley Hopkins and the Victorian Temper* (1972).

Weyand, Norman, ed. *Immortal Diamond: Studies in Gerard Manley Hopkins* (1949). Includes an essay on sprung rhythm by Walter Ong.

Several short, general, introductory commentaries on Hopkins' poetry have been published: Donald McChesney, *A Hopkins Commentary* (1968); Norman Mackenzie, *Hopkins* (1968); J. F. J. Russell, *A Critical Commentary on Gerard Manley Hopkins' "Poems"* (1971); R. K. R. Thornton, *Gerard Manley Hopkins: The Poems* (1973); and Peter Millward, *A Commentary on the Sonnets of G. M. Hopkins* (1970). Geoffrey H. Hartman has edited *Hopkins: A Collection of Critical Essays* (1966). Edward B. Cohen has compiled a bibliography of *Works and Criticism of Gerard Manley Hopkins* (1969). *Immortal Diamond* (see above) and Geoffrey Grigson's pamphlet, *Hopkins* (1955), in the Writers and Their Work series, also contain useful bibliographies.

Winter with the Gulf Stream[1]

The boughs, the boughs are bare enough
But earth has never felt the snow.
Frost-furred[2] our ivies are and rough

With bills of rime[3] the brambles shew.
The hoarse leaves crawl on hissing ground
Because the sighing wind is low.[4]

But if the rain-blasts be unbound
And from dank feathers wring the drops
The clogged brook runs with choking sound

Kneading the mounded mire that stops   10
His channel under clammy coats
Of foliage fallen in the copse.

A simple[5] passage of weak notes
Is all the winter bird dare try.
The bugle moon by daylight floats[6]

So glassy white about the sky,
So like a berg of hyaline,[7]
And pencilled blue[8] so daintily,

I never saw her so divine.
But through black branches, rarely drest   20
In scarves of silky shot and shine,[9]

---

[1] First published in *Once a Week*, February 14, 1863.   [2] 1863: "Frost-fringed."
[3] 1863: "With spikéd rime." Bills of rime: frost in spiked patterns like birds' bills.
[4] 1863: "What time the sighing wind is low."   [5] 1863: "single."
[6] 1863: "The moon, half-orb'd, ere sunset floats." Bugle moon: crescent moon: shaped like a horn.
[7] Hyaline: a transparent substance.   [8] 1863: "Pencill'd with blue."
[9] 1863: "In streaming scarfs that smoothly shine." Silky shot and shine: cloth woven of different colored threads so that it changes color when light strikes it at different angles.

The webbed and the watery west
Where yonder crimson fireball sits
Looks laid for feasting and for rest.

I see long reefs of violets
In beryl-covered fens so dim,
A gold-water Pactolus[10] frets

Its brindled[11] wharves and yellow brim,
The waxen colours weep and run,
And slendering to his burning rim

Into the flat blue mist the sun
Drops out and all our day is done.[12]
1863; revised 1871

Heaven-Haven

A Nun Takes the Veil

I have desired to go
Where springs not fail,
To fields where flies no sharp and sided hail
And a few lilies blow.

And I have asked to be
Where no storms come,
Where the green swell is in the havens dumb,
And out of the swing of the sea.
(Revised from 1864 version) 1918

"I am like a slip of comet"

—I am like a slip of comet,
Scarce worth discovery, in some corner seen
Bridging the slender difference of two stars,
Come out of space, or suddenly engender'd
By heady elments, for no man knows:
But when she sights the sun she grows and sizes
And spins her skirts out, while her central star
Shakes its cocooning mists; and so she comes
To fields of light; millions of travelling rays
Pierce her; she hangs upon the flame-cased sun,   10
And sucks the light as full as Gideon's fleece:[1]
But then her tether calls her; she falls off,
And as she dwindles shreds her smock of gold
Amidst the sistering planets, till she comes
To single Saturn, last and solitary;
And then goes out into the cavernous dark.
So I go out: my little sweet is done:
I have drawn heat from this contagious sun:
To not ungentle death now forth I run.
(1864) 1935

The Beginning of the End[1]

(I)
My love is lessened and must soon be past.
I never promised such persistency
In its condition. No, the tropic tree
Has not a charter that its sap shall last

---

[10] Pactolus: in classical mythology Midas, cursed with a touch which turns all things to gold, cures himself by bathing in the river Pactolus, whose sands then turned golden.
[11] Brindled: streaked or flecked with darker tones on a gray or tawny ground.
[12] 1863:

> "Shot o'er with lights—the emblazon'd west,
> Where yonder crimson fire-ball sets,
> Trails forth a purfled silken vest.
> [Purfled: with an ornamented border]
>
> Long beds I see of violets
> In beryl lakes which they reef o'er:
> A Pactolean river frets
>
> Against its tawny golden shore:
> All ways the molten colours run:
> Till, sinking ever more and more
>
> Into an azure mist, the sun
> Drops down engulf'd, his journey done."
> 1863; revised 1871

[1] Gideon's fleece: to assure himself that God had chosen him as the instrument with which to save the nation of Israel, Gideon asked God to give him a sign by one night drenching a fleece with dew, and the next night drenching the ground and leaving the fleece dry (Judges 6:36–40).
[1] In one of the manuscripts these sonnets are subtitled, "A neglected lover's address to his mistress." Two of the sonnets were rejected by *Cornhill Magazine,* a monthly publication.

Into all seasons, though no Winter cast
  The happy leafing. It is so with me:
  My love is less, my love is less for thee.
I cease the mourning and the abject fast,

And rise and go about my works again
10 And, save by darting accidents, forget.
  But ah! if you could understand how then

That *less* is heavens higher even yet
  Than treble-fervent *more* of other men,
  Even your unpassion'd eyelids might be wet.

    (II)
I must feed Fancy. Show me any one
  That reads or holds the astrologic lore,
  And I'll pretend the credit given of yore;
And let him prove my passion was begun

In the worst hour that's measured by the sun,
20 With such malign conjunctions as before
  No influential heaven ever wore;
That no recorded devilish thing was done

With such a seconding, nor Saturn took
  Such opposition to the Lady-star[2]
  In the most murderous passage of his book;

And I'll love my distinction: Near or far
  He says his science helps him not to look
  At hopes so evil-heaven'd as mine are.

    (III)
You see that I have come to passion's end;
  This means you need not fear the storms, the
30   cries,
  That gave you vantage when you would
    despise:
My bankrupt heart has no more tears to
    spend.

Else I am well assured I should offend
  With fiercer weepings of these desperate eyes
  For poor love's failure than his hopeless rise.
But now I am so tired I soon shall send

Barely a sigh to thought of hopes forgone.
  Is this made plain? What have I come across
  That here will serve me for comparison?

The sceptic disappointment and the loss   40
  A boy feels when the poet he pores upon
  Grows less and less sweet to him, and knows
    no cause.
             (Revised from 1865 version) 1935

"Let me be to Thee as the circling bird"[1]

Let me be to Thee as the circling bird,
Or bat with tender and air-crisping wings
That shapes in half-light his departing rings,
From both of whom a changeless note is heard.
I have found my music in a common word,
Trying each pleasurable throat that sings
And every praisèd sequence of sweet strings,
And know infallibly which I preferred.
The authentic cadence was discovered late
Which ends those only strains that I approve,   10
And other science all gone out of date
And minor sweetness scarce made mention of:
I have found the dominant[2] of my range and
    state—
Love, O my God, to call Thee Love and Love.
                    (1865) 1918

The Habit of Perfection

Elected Silence, sing to me
And beat upon my whorlèd ear,
Pipe me to pastures still and be
The music that I care to hear.

Shape nothing, lips; be lovely-dumb:
It is the shut, the curfew sent
From there where all surrenders come
Which only makes you eloquent.

Be shellèd, eyes, with double dark
And find the uncreated light:[1]   10

---

   [2] Lady-star: Venus. One of the tenets of astrology is that events are influenced by relationships ("conjunctions") of stars to one another at the time of the events.
   [1] In a note in his journal in 1865, a year before his conversion to Roman Catholicism, Hopkins wrote that before he could leave the Anglican church he would first have to study and reject the example of those "Romanizing" heirs of the Oxford Movement who did remain within the doctrines and rituals of the Church of England.
   [2] Dominant: the fifth note in the scale of a key which is of special importance in establishing its harmonies.
   [1] Uncreated light: a figure in medieval theology for the primal energy of God.

This ruck and reel which you remark
Coils, keeps,[2] and teases simple sight.

Palate, the hutch of tasty lust,
Desire not to be rinsed with wine:
The can must be so sweet, the crust
So fresh that come in fasts divine!

Nostrils, your careless breath that spend
Upon the stir and keep[3] of pride,
What relish shall the censers[4] send
Along the sanctuary side!

O feel-of-primrose hands, O feet
That want the yield of plushy sward,
But you shall walk the golden street
And you unhouse and house the Lord.[5]

And, Poverty, be thou the bride
And now the marriage feast begun,
And lily-coloured clothes provide
Your spouse not laboured-at nor spun.[6]

(Revised from 1866 version) 1893

The German ship Deutschland *went aground and was wrecked during a storm at the mouth of the Thames. Among the passengers who drowned were five nuns who had been forced to leave Germany because of the passage of the May or Falk Laws of 1873–75, laws sponsored by Adalbert Falk, one of Bismarck's ministers, which extended state control over ecclesiastical matters and sharply restricted the rights of Roman Catholics and the activities of certain religious orders, such as the Jesuits and the Franciscans.*

In 1875 Hopkins had been a member of the Jesuit order for seven years and was studying in Wales. He had written no poetry since his entrance into the order. In a letter of 1878 he wrote that he read a newspaper account of the wreck of the Deutschland *and was moved by it: ". . . happening to say so to my rector he said that he wished someone would write a poem on the subject. On this hint I set to work and, though my hand was out at first, produced one. I had long had haunting my ear the echo of a new rhythm which now I realized on paper." Hopkins offered the poem to the Jesuit magazine* The Month, *but because of its strange rhythms "and a great many more oddnesses which could not but dismay an editor's eye," the magazine "dared not print it."*

Hopkins named his new rhythm "Sprung Rhythm," and he described it in an essay which Robert Bridges printed as an "Author's Preface" to the 1918 edition of Hopkins' poems. Hopkins' explanation, which makes use of several marks indicating how syllables are to be stressed or elided which are not reproduced in the printed versions of his poems, is not entirely satisfying. But it does set out one of the ground principles of sprung rhythm: that each line will have a specified and consistent number of stressed syllables and a varying number of unstressed syllables, but that lines with the same number of stressed syllables should be read in about the same time. For extensive analyses of sprung rhythm see Gardner's two chapters on "The New Rhythm" in the second volume of his study (pp. 98–178); and chapters 2 and 3 of Elizabeth W. Schneider's The Dragon in the Gate *(pp. 11–82): an earlier version of these chapters was published in* PMLA, 80 *(1965), 237–253.*

The individual feet of "The Wreck of the Deutschland" *contain from one to four syllables. The stress commonly falls on the first syllable of each foot. In Part I the number of stresses in each line of the eight-line stanza is 2/3/4/3/5/5/4/6. In Part II the pattern is the same, except that the first line of each stanza contains three stresses.*

Hopkins thought of his poem as an ode, a meditation on God's terrible power, love, and providence. In Part I he considers how God must be known through terror and suffering, and in the sacrifice of Christ, as well as through beauty and bliss. In Part II he describes the wreck, articulates the response of one of the nuns who recognizes her exile and death as God's means to accomplish her redemption, and then closes with a return to the meditations of Part I.

The Wreck of the *Deutschland*

To the
happy memory of five Franciscan nuns
exiles by the Falck Laws
drowned between midnight and morning of
Dec. 7th, 1875

PART THE FIRST

1

Thou mastering me
God! giver of breath and bread;

---

[2] Keeps: withholds from.   [3] Keep: upkeep.

[4] Censers: containers in which incense is burned during a religious ceremony.

[5] Unhouse and house: take the Communion Host from the tabernacle in the Roman Catholic ritual of Communion, and receive it.

[6] "Consider the lilies of the field, how they grow; they toil not, neither do they spin: And yet I say unto you, that not even Solomon in all his glory was arrayed like one of these" (Matthew 6:28–29).

World's strand, sway of the sea;
    Lord of living and dead;
Thou hast bound bones and veins in me,
    fastened me flesh,
And after it almost unmade, what with
    dread,
    Thy doing: and dost thou touch me afresh?
Over again I feel thy finger and find thee.

2

    I did say yes
    O at lightning and lashed rod;
Thou heardst me truer than tongue confess
    Thy terror, O Christ, O God;
Thou knowest the walls, altar and hour and
    night:
The swoon of a heart that the sweep and the
    hurl of thee trod
    Hard down with a horror of height:
And the midriff astrain with leaning of, laced
    with fire of stress.

3

    The frown of his face
    Before me, the hurtle of hell
Behind, where, where was a, where was a
    place?
    I whirled out wings that spell[1]
And fled with a fling of the heart to the heart
    of the Host.[2]
My heart, but you were dovewinged, I can
    tell,
    Carrier-witted,[3] I am bold to boast,
To flash from the flame to the flame then,
    tower from the grace to the grace.

4

    I am soft sift
    In an hourglass—at the wall
Fast, but mined with a motion, a drift,
    And it crowds and it combs to the fall;

I steady as a water in a well, to a poise, to a
    pane,
But roped with, always, all the way down
    from the tall
    Fells or flanks of the voel,[4] a vein
Of the gospel proffer, a pressure, a principle,
    Christ's gift.

5

    I kiss my hand
    To the stars, lovely-asunder
Starlight, wafting him out of it; and
    Glow, glory in thunder;
Kiss my hand to the dappled-with-damson
    west:
Since, tho' he is under the world's splendour
    and wonder,
    His mystery must be instressed, stressed;[5]
For I greet him the days I meet him, and bless
    when I understand.

6

    Not out of his bliss
    Springs the stress felt
Nor first from heaven (and few know this)
    Swings the stroke dealt—
Stroke and a stress that stars and storms
    deliver,
That guilt is hushed by, hearts are flushed
    by and melt—
    But it rides time like riding a river[6]
(And here the faithful waver, the faithless fable
    and miss) .

7

    It dates from day
    Of his going in Galilee;
Warm-laid grave of a womb-life grey;
    Manger, maiden's knee;
The dense and the driven Passion, and
    frightful sweat:

---

[1] That spell: in that brief moment.   [2] Host: the wafer of the sacrament of the Eucharist.

[3] Carrier-witted: with the intelligence of a carrier or homing pigeon.

[4] Voel: a Welsh word for bare hill or mountain; pronounced "voil." "Fell" is also a word for hill or mountain (usually Scottish or in the north of England); here, the words seems to refer to the sides of the mountain down which or through which water flows to the well, which is thus connected ("roped") to them.

[5] Instressed: as Hopkins used this word, the instress of an object or being is its essential nature, its individuality. God's nature is a mystery, and that fact creates the stress of faith in the existence and love of a being whose nature and actions—especially his coming to man in suffering, as in the passion of Christ—are ultimately incomprehensible.

[6] It rides time like riding a river: in stanzas 6–8 Hopkins states that the suffering which creates a stress exists from the beginning. It may be dated from the birth and passion of Christ, when it expressed itself in time. But suffering is not something that a God who precedes it creates or permits; like the sour and sweet taste of the sloe, the possibility of suffering exists in the existence of God.

Thence the discharge of it, there its swelling
    to be,
  Though felt before, though in high flood
    yet—
What none would have known of it, only the
    heart, being hard at bay,

8

     Is out with it! Oh,
    We lash with the best or worst
   Word last! How a lush-kept plush-capped
     sloe[7]
    Will, mouthed to flesh-burst,
  Gush!—flush the man, the being with it, sour
    or sweet,
  Brim, in a flash, full!—Hither then, last or
    first,
    To hero of Calvary, Christ's feet—
Never ask if meaning it, wanting it, warned of
    it—men go.

9

     Be adored among men,
    God, three-numberèd form;[8]
   Wring thy rebel, dogged in den,[9]
    Man's malice, with wrecking and storm.
  Beyond saying sweet, past telling of tongue,
  Thou art lightning and love, I found it, a
    winter and warm;
  Father and fondler of heart thou hast
    wrung:
Hast thy dark descending and most art
    merciful then.

10

     With an anvil-ding
    And with fire in him forge thy will
   Or rather, rather then, stealing as Spring
    Through him, melt him but master him
    still:

    Whether at once, as once at a crash Paul,
  Or as Austin,[10] a lingering-out swéet skíll,
   Make mercy in all of us, out of us all
Mastery, but be adored, but be adored King.   80

PART THE SECOND

11

     "Some find me a sword; some
    The flange and the rail;[1] flame,
   Fang, or flood" goes Death on drum,
    And storms bugle his fame.
But wé dream we are rooted in earth—Dust!
Flesh falls within sight of us, we, though our
    flower the same,
  Wave with the meadow, forget that there
    must
The sour scythe cringe, and the blear share[2]
    come.

12

     On Saturday sailed from Bremen,
    American-outward-bound,   90
   Take settler and seamen, tell[3] men with
    women,
    Two hundred souls in the round—
  O Father, not under thy feathers[4] nor ever
    as guessing
  The goal was a shoal, of a fourth the doom
    to be drowned;
   Yet did the dark side of the bay[5] of thy
    blessing
Not vault them, the million of rounds of thy
    mercy not reeve[6] even them in?

13

     Into the snows she sweeps,
    Hurling[7] the haven behind,
   The Deutschland, on Sunday; and so the
    sky keeps,[8]

---

[7] Sloe: the astringent fruit of the blackthorn.

[8] Three-numberèd form: the doctrine of the three persons of God, Father, Son, and Holy Ghost.

[9] Dogged in den: perhaps, penned by dogs as a hunted animal; perhaps, stubbornly persisting in a narrow existence.

[10] Paul; Austin: the first-century apostle Paul was converted to Christianity by a sudden vision of the crucifixion of Christ; the fourth-century bishop and theologian Augustine was converted to Christianity after a long study of philosophy and the Bible.

[1] Flange and rail: the wheels and tracks of a railroad train.

[2] Cringe: cause to cringe; blear share: stained plowshare.   [3] Tell: count.

[4] Feathers: Gardner in his notes (p. 259) cites Matthew 23:37, in which Christ laments the destruction of prophets by Jerusalem: "how often would I have gathered thy children together, even as a hen gathereth her chickens under her wings." The third person of the Trinity, the Holy Ghost, is also often emblemized as a dove.

[5] Bay: a protrusion, as in bay window.   [6] Reeve: a nautical term meaning "rope together."

[7] Hurling: hurling from.   [8] Keeps: stays the same.

100   For the infinite air is unkind,
     And the sea flint-flake, black-backed in the
          regular blow,
     Sitting Eastnortheast, in cursed quarter, the
          wind;
     Wiry and white-fiery and whirlwind-
          swivelled snow
Spins to the widow-making unchilding
     unfathering deeps.

          14
     She drove in the dark to leeward,
     She struck—not a reef or a rock
     But the combs of a smother of sand: night
          drew her
     Dead to the Kentish Knock;[9]
     And she beat the bank down with her bows
          and the ride of her keel:
     The breakers rolled on her beam with
110   ruinous shock;
     And canvas and compass, the whorl[10] and
          the wheel
Idle for ever to waft her or wind[11] her with,
     these she endured.

          15
     Hope had grown grey hairs,
     Hope had mourning on,
     Trenched with tears, carved with cares,
     Hope was twelve hours gone;
     And frightful a nightfall folded rueful a day
     Nor rescue, only rocket and lightship, shone,
     And lives at last were washing away:
To the shrouds they took,—they shook in the
120   hurling and horrible airs.

          16
     One stirred from the rigging to save
     The wild woman-kind below,
     With a rope's end round the man, handy
          and brave—
     He was pitched to his death at a blow,
     For all his dreadnought breast and braids of
          thew:
     They could tell[12] him for hours, dandled the
          to and fro
     Through the cobbled foam-fleece. What
          could he do

With the burl[13] of the fountains of air, buck
     and the flood of the wave?

          17
     They fought with God's cold—
     And they could not and fell to the deck   130
          (Crushed them) or water (and drowned
          them) or rolled
     With the sea-romp over the wreck.
Night roared, with the heart-break hearing a
     heart-broke rabble,
The woman's wailing, the crying of child
          without check—
     Till a lioness arose breasting the babble,
A prophetess towered in the tumult, a virginal
     tongue told.

          18
     Ah, touched in your bower of bone,
     Are you! turned for an exquisite smart,
     Have you! make words break from me here
          all alone,
     Do you!—mother of being in me, heart.   140
O unteachably after evil, but uttering truth,
Why, tears! is it? tears; such a melting, a
          madrigal start!
     Never-eldering revel and river of youth,
What can it be, this glee?[14] the good you have
     there of your own?

          19
     Sister, a sister calling
     A master, her master and mine!—
     And the inboard seas run swirling and
          hawling;[15]
     The rash smart sloggering brine
Blinds her; but she that weather[16] sees one
     thing, one;
Has one fetch[17] in her: she rears herself to
     divine   150
     Ears, and the call of the tall nun
To the men in the tops and the tackle[18] rode
     over the storm's brawling.

          20
     She was first of a five and came
     Of a coifèd sisterhood.
     (O Deutschland, double a desperate name!
     O world wide of its good!

[9] Dead to the Kentish Knock: the Kentish Knock is a sandbar near the mouth of the Thames.
"Dead" means "directly to," or dead in the sense of a ship no longer controlled.
[10] Whorl: the propeller of the ship.   [11] Wind: steer.   [12] Tell: discern.
[13] Burl: a full roundness.   [14] Glee: like madrigal, a kind of song.
[15] Hawling: perhaps "howling"; perhaps "hauling."
[16] That weather: analogous to "that day"; or, "in that weather."
[17] Fetch: expedient.   [18] Tops and tackle: masts and rigging.

But Gertrude, lily, and Luther, are two of a
    town,
Christ's lily and beast of the waste wood:[19]
From life's dawn it is drawn down,
Abel is Cain's brother and breasts they have
    sucked the same.) [20]

21

Loathed for a love men knew in them,
Banned by the land of their birth,
Rhine refused them, Thames would ruin
    them;
Surf, snow, river and earth
Gnashed: but thou art above, thou Orion of
    light;[21]
Thy unchancelling[22] poising palms were
    weighing the worth,
Thou martyr-master: in thy sight
Storm flakes were scroll-leaved flowers, lily
    showers—sweet heaven was astrew
    in them.

22

Five! the finding and sake[23]
And cipher of suffering Christ.[24]
Mark, the mark is of man's make
And the word of it Sacrificed.
But he scores it in scarlet himself on his own
    bespoken,
Before-time-taken, dearest prizèd and
    priced—

Stigma, signal, cinquefoil[25] token
For lettering of the lamb's fleece, ruddying of
    the rose-flake.[26]

23

Joy fall to thee, father Francis,[27]
Drawn to the Life that died;
With the gnarls of the nails in thee, niche
    of the lance, his
    Lovescape[28] crucified   180
And seal of his seraph-arrival![29] and these thy
    daughters
And five-livèd and leavèd favour and pride,
Are sisterly sealed in wild waters,
To bathe in his fall-gold mercies, to breathe in
    his all-fire glances.

24

Away in the loveable west,
On a pastoral forehead of Wales,[30]
I was under a roof here, I was at rest,
And they the prey of the gales;
She to the black-about air, to the breaker,
    the thickly
Falling flakes, to the throng that catches and
    quails   190
Was calling "O Christ, Christ, come
    quickly":[31]
The cross to her she calls Christ to her,
    christens her wild-worst Best.

[19] Gertrude; Luther: Gertrude (1256–c. 1302) was a Roman Catholic nun and mystic who lived near the birthplace of Martin Luther (1483–1546), the great leader of the Protestant Reformation; Beast of the waste wood: Psalm 80 is a parable of the transplanting of the vine of a true faith from Egypt to Israel, where it flourishes until "The boar out of the wood doth waste it, and the wild beast of the field doth devour it" (13).
[20] Genesis 4:1–16.
[21] Orion: a constellation named for Orion in one of his identities in classical mythology, that of a hunter.
[22] Unchancelling: unchurching, a reference to the exile of the nuns by means of prohibiting their order and its authority over its churches and congregations. The hands of God have done this unchurching, as a means of hunting the nuns to their finally redemptive fate.
[23] Finding and sake: "Finding" is the mark by which something is known or found. In a letter of 1879 Hopkins wrote: "*Sake* is a word I find it convenient to use: . . . It is the *sake* of 'for the sake of', *forsake, namesake, keepsake.* I mean by it the being a thing has outside itself, as a voice by its echo, a face by its reflection, a body by its shadow, a man by his name, fame, or memory, *and also* that in the thing by virtue of which especially it has this being abroad, and that is something distinctive, marked, specifically or individually speaking" (*Letters*, I, 83).
[24] Cipher of suffering Christ: the five wounds of the crucified Christ, on the hands and feet and in the side, pierced by a lance.
[25] Cinquefoil: a five-leaved plant or design.
[26] Lamb and rose are traditional emblems of martyrdom.
[27] Francis: Francis of Assisi (1182–1226), the founder of the Franciscan order whose body displayed the stigmata, the five wounds of Christ.
[28] Lovescape: the pattern of wounds expressing love.   [29] Seraph-arrival: salvation.
[30] Pastoral forehead: the college at which Hopkins was studying is situated on a hill.
[31] Hopkins drew the details of the wreck—the state of the ship, the efforts of the heroic sailor, and this cry of one of the nuns, a strikingly tall, gaunt woman—from newspaper accounts.

25

The majesty! what did she mean?
Breathe, arch[32] and original Breath.
Is it love in her of the being as her lover[33]
    had been?
Breathe, body of lovely Death.
They were else-minded then, altogether, the
    men
Woke thee with a *We are perishing* in the
    weather of Gennesareth.[34]
Or is it that she cried for the crown[35] then,
The keener to come at the comfort for feeling
    the combating keen?

26

For how to the heart's cheering
The down-dugged[36] ground-hugged grey
Hovers off, the jay-blue heavens appearing
Of pied and peeled May![37]
Blue-beating and hoary-glow[38] height; or
    night, still higher,
With belled fire[39] and the moth-soft Milky
    Way,
What by your measure is the heaven of
    desire,
The treasure never eyesight got, nor was ever
    guessed what for the hearing?[40]

27

No, but it was not these.
The jading and jar of the cart,[41]
Time's tasking, it is fathers that asking for
    ease

Of the sodden-with-its-sorrowing heart,
Not danger, electrical horror; then further it
    finds
The appealing of the Passion is tenderer in
    prayer apart:
Other, I gather, in measure her mind's
Burden, in wind's burly and beat of endrag-
    onèd seas.[42]

28

But how shall I . . . make me room
    there:
Reach me a . . . Fancy, come faster—
Strike you the sight of it? look at it loom
    there,
Thing that she . . . There then! the
    Master,
Ipse,[43] the only one, Christ, King, Head:
He was to cure the extremity where he had
    cast her;
Do, deal, lord it with living and dead;
Let him ride, her pride, in his triumph,
    despatch and have done with his
    doom[44] there.

29

Ah! there was a heart right!
There was single eye![45]
Read the unshapeable shock[46] night
And knew the who and the why;
Wording it how but by him that present and
    past,
Heaven and earth are word of, worded by?—

---

[32] Arch: from the Greek word meaning "first cause." "And the Lord God formed man of the dust of the ground, and breathed into his nostrils the breath of life; and man became a living soul" (Genesis 2:7).

[33] Lover: Christ; Roman Catholic nuns are imagined as marrying Christ. Hopkins asks if the nun's call is a wish to sacrifice herself as Christ sacrificed himself.

[34] When Christ and his disciples were in a ship on the Lake of Gennesareth, a great storm arose which frightened the disciples unil they called on Christ to save them. "Then he arose, and rebuked the winds and the sea; and there was a great calm" (Matthew 8:23–26).

[35] Crown: of martyrdom.

[36] Down-dugged: perhaps storm clouds hanging down like dugs.

[37] Pied: parti-colored or variegated; peeled: stripped to a freshness.

[38] Hoary-glow: glowing white.   [39] Belled: swelling out.

[40] "Eye hath not seen, nor ear heard, neither have entered into the heart of men, the things which God hath prepared for them that love him" (1 Corinthians 2:9).

[41] Jading and jar of the cart: the ordinary jars and difficulties of life.

[42] Measure; burden: in the musical meanings of these words, the cadence or tune of the refrain or undersong of her mind's thinking. Burly: bristle.

[43] *Ipse*: His very self. The word is used during the Roman Catholic mass at the elevation of the Host which is the actual presence of God. In Schneider's reading of the poem she argues that this stanza thus describes the actual coming of Christ to the nun (*The Dragon in the Gate*, p. 29).

[44] Doom: judgment.

[45] "The light of the body is the eye: therefore when thine eye is single [that is, focused entirely on God], thy whole body is also full of light" (Luke 11:34).

[46] Shock: here used as an adjective.

The Simon Peter of a soul! to the blast
Tarpeïan-fast,[47] but a blown beacon of light.

30

Jesu, heart's light,
Jesu, maid's son,
What was the feast followed the night
Thou hadst glory of this nun?—
Feast of the one woman without stain.[48]
For so conceivèd, so to conceive thee is done;
But here was heart-throe, birth of a brain,
Word, that heard and kept thee and uttered
thee outright.

31

Well, she has thee for the pain, for the
Patience; but pity of the rest of them!
Heart, go and bleed at a bitterer vein for
the
Comfortless unconfessed of them—
No not uncomforted: lovely-felicitous
Providence
Finger of a tender of, O of a feathery
delicacy, the breast of the
Maiden could obey so, be a bell to, ring of
it, and
Startle the poor sheep back! is the shipwrack
then a harvest, does tempest carry
the grain for thee?

32

I admire thee, master of the tides,
Of the Yore-flood,[49] of the year's fall;
The recurb and the recovery of the gulf's
sides,
The girth of it and the wharf of it and
the wall;

Stanching, quenching ocean of a motionable
mind;
Ground of being, and granite of it: past all
Grasp God, throned behind
Death with a sovereignty that heeds but hides,
bodes[50] but abides;

33

With a mercy that outrides
The all of water, an ark
For the listener; for the lingerer with a
love glides
Lower than death and the dark;[51]
A vein for the visitng of the past-prayer, pent
in prison,[52]
The-last-breath penitent spirits—the
uttermost mark
Our passion-plungèd giant risen,
The Christ of the Father compassionate,
fetched[53] in the storm of his strides.

34

Now burn, new born to the world,
Double-naturèd name,[54]
The heaven-flung, heart-fleshed, maiden-
furled
Miracle-in-Mary-of-flame,
Mid-numberèd[55] he in three of the thunder-
throne!
Not a dooms-day dazzle in his coming nor
dark as he came;
Kind, but royally reclaiming his own;
A released shower, let flash to the shire,[56] not
a lightning of fire hard-hurled.

35

Dame, at our door
Drowned, and among our shoals,

---

[47] ". . . thou art Peter, and upon this rock I will build my church; and the gates of hell shall not prevail against it" (Matthew 16:18). The Tarpeian rock was an elevation in Rome from which traitors to the Roman government were thrown to their deaths.

[48] December 8, the day following the wreck, is the feast of the Immaculate Conception, which celebrates the birth of Mary, the mother of Christ, without the stain of original sin.

[49] Yore-flood: the deluge of the Old Testament (Genesis 6–9).

[50] Bodes: knows and is poised to act.

[51] Lower than death: Gardner in his notes (p. 262) suggests that this line refers to the harrowing of hell, the descent of Christ after the crucifixion into purgatory to release the souls of those awaiting his redemptive act.

[52] "For Christ also hath once suffered for sins, the just for the unjust, that he might bring us to God, being put to death in the flesh, but quickened by the Spirit: By which also he went and preached unto the spirits in prison" (1 Peter 3:18-19).

[53] Fetched: the fetch of a wave is the distance it runs before the wind. "Fetch" here also has the meaning of fetched out of.

[54] Double-naturèd name: that of Christ.

[55] Mid-numbèred: Christ is the second person of the Trinity.

[56] Shire: a political division of land, such as a county.

Remember us in the roads,[57] the heaven-
    haven of the reward:
    Our King back, Oh, upon English
      souls![58]
Let him easter in us, be a dayspring to the
    dimness of us, be a crimson-cresseted
    east,
    More brightening her, rare-dear Britain, as
      his reign rolls,
    Pride, rose, prince, hero of us, high-priest,
Our hearts' charity's hearth's fire, our thoughts'
280   chivalry's throng's Lord.
                      (1876) 1918

God's Grandeur

The world is charged with the grandeur of
    God.
    It will flame out, like shining from shook
    foil;[1]
It gathers to a greatness, like the ooze of oil[2]
Crushed. Why do men then now not reck his
    rod?
Generations have trod, have trod, have trod;
    And all is seared with trade; bleared, smeared
      with toil;
    And wears man's smudge and shares man's
      smell: the soil
Is bare now, nor can foot feel, being shod.

And for all this, nature is never spent;
    There lives the dearest freshness deep down
10   things;
And though the last lights off the black West
    went

Oh, morning, at the brown brink eastward,
    springs—
Because the Holy Ghost[3] over the bent
    World broods with warm breast and with ah!
    bright wings.
                      (1877) 1918

The Starlight Night[1]

Look at the stars! look, look up at the skies!
    O look at all the fire-folk sitting in the air!
    The bright boroughs, the circle-citadels
    there![2]
Down in dim woods the diamond delves![3] the
    elves'-eyes!
The grey lawns cold where gold, where quick-
    gold lies!
    Wind-beat whitebeam! airy abeles set on a
    flare![4]
    Flake-doves sent floating forth at a farmyard
    scare!—
Ah well! it is all a purchase, all is a prize.[5]

Buy then! bid then!—What?—Prayer, patience,
    alms, vows.
Look, look: a May-mess, like on orchard
    boughs!   10
    Look! March-bloom, like on mealed-with-
    yellow sallows![6]
These are indeed the barn; withindoors house
The shocks. This piece-bright paling shuts the
    spouse[7]
    Christ home, Christ and his mother and all
    his hallows.[8]
                (1877) 1893; 1918

---

[57] Roads: sheltered water near shore.

[58] Our King back: the coming of Christ to the nun taken as a portent of the return of the English church to the Roman Catholic church.

[1] In a letter in 1883 Hopkins wrote: "I mean foil in its sense of leaf or tinsel. . . . Shaken gold-foil gives off broad glares like sheet lightning and . . . owing to its zigzag dints and creasings and network of small many cornered facets, a sort of fork lightning too."

[2] Oil: as in the making of olive oil.   [3] Holy Ghost: conventionally emblemized as a dove.

[1] First published in a somewhat different version in 1893.

[2] In 1893 lines 3-5 read:

"The bright bóroughs, the quivering citadels there!
The dim woods quick with diamond wells; the elf-eyes!
The grey lawns cold where quaking gold-dew lies!"

[3] Delves: dells, small hollows or valleys.

[4] Whitebeam: a small tree whose leaves are white on the underside. Abeles: white poplar trees.

[5] 1893: "Ah well! it is a purchase and a prize."

[6] Sallows: willows, here with yellow leaves like meal.

[7] Shocks: sheaves of grain. Paling: fence made of poles or stakes.

[8] 1893: "Christ, and the mother of Christ and all his hallows." Hallows: saints.

Spring

Nothing is so beautiful as Spring—
  When weeds, in wheels, shoot long and lovely
    and lush;
  Thursh's eggs look little low heavens, and
    thrush
Through the echoing timber does so rinse and
    wring[1]
The ear, it strikes like lightnings to hear him
    sing;
  The glassy peartree leaves and blooms, they
    brush
  The descending blue; that blue is all in a
    rush
With richness; the racing lambs too have fair
    their fling.

What is all this juice and all this joy?
  A strain of the earth's sweet being in the
    beginning
In Eden garden.—Have, get, before it cloy,

  Before it cloud, Christ, lord, and sour with
    sinning,
Innocent mind and Mayday in girl and boy,
  Most, O maid's child, thy choice and worthy
    the winning.

               (1877) 1893

The Windhover:[1]

To Christ our Lord

I caught this morning morning's minion, king-
  dom of daylight's dauphin,[2] dapple-dawn-
  drawn Falcon, in his riding
Of the rolling level underneath him steady
  air, and striding
High there, how he rung upon the rein of a
  wimpling wing[3]
In his ecstasy! then off, off forth on swing,
  As a skate's heel sweeps smooth on a bow-
  bend:[4] the hurl and gliding
  Rebuffed the big wind. My heart in hiding[5]
Stirred for a bird,—the achieve of, the mastery
  of the thing!

Brute beauty and valour and act, oh, air, pride,
  plume, here
  Buckle![6] AND the fire that breaks from thee
  then, a billion   10
Times told lovelier, more dangerous, O my
  chevalier!

  No wonder of it: shéer plód makes plough
  down sillion[7]
Shine, and blue-bleak embers, ah my dear,
  Fall, gall[8] themselves, and gash gold-
  vermilion.

              (1877) 1918

Pied Beauty

Glory be to God for dappled things—
  For skies of couple-colour as a brinded[1] cow;
    For rose-moles all in stipple upon trout
    that swim;
Fresh-firecoal chestnut-falls;[2] finches' wings;
    Landscape plotted and pieced—fold, fallow,
    and plough;[3]
      And áll trádes, their gear and tackle and
      trim.[4]

---

  [1] Rinse and wring: acts of cleansing, as in doing a washing.   [1] A windhover is a small falcon.

  [2] Dauphin: the title of the eldest son of the king of France. Gardner in his notes (p. 267) quotes a passage spoken by the Dauphin in Shakespeare's *Henry V* in praise of his horse: "When I bestride him I soar, I am a *hawk:* he trots the air" (III, vii, 11). The Dauphin and the falcon are the first of several chivalric references in this sonnet in which Hopkins pays homage to his lord and love.

  [3] Rung upon the rein: circling on a tether. Wimpling: rippling, pleated.

  [4] Bow-bend: the long turn of a skater.

  [5] In hiding: perhaps, passive or apathetic; perhaps, in its obscure service.

  [6] Buckle: the attributes of line 9 are bound together; perhaps, the bird puts (buckles) them on, as a Christian knight dons armor. The word also describes the sight of the bird's plumage as its force meets that of the wind, and at the point of meeting the forces buckle into the light that shoots from the ruffled wings and breast of the bird.

  [7] Sillion: a ploughed furrow; here worn smooth with plodding.

  [8] Gall: to break the surface of.

  [1] Brinded: streaked with different hues.

  [2] Chestnut-falls: freshly fallen chestnuts, bright as coals of fire.

  [3] Pieced: parceled out into fields used as pastures (fold), lying fallow, and under cultivation (plough).

  [4] Gear and tackle and trim: various kinds of tools and equipment.

All things counter, original, spare, strange;
   Whatever is fickle, freckled (who knows
      how?)
      With swift, slow; sweet, sour; adazzle,
      dim;
He fathers-forth whose beauty is past
      change:
          Praise him.
             (1877)   1918

Hurrahing in Harvest

Summer ends now; now, barbarous in beauty,
   the stooks[1] rise
Around; up above, what wind-walks! what
   lovely behaviour
Of silk-sack clouds! has wilder, wilful-wavier
Meal-drift[2] moulded ever and melted across
   skies?

I walk, I lift up, I lift up heart, eyes,
Down all that glory in the heavens to glean our
   Saviour;
And, éyes, heárt, what looks, what lips yet gave
   you a
Rapturous love's greeting of realer, of rounder
   replies?

And the azurous hung hills are his world-
   wielding shoulder
Majestic—as a stallion stalwart, very-violet-
10   sweet!—
These things, these things were here and but
   the beholder
Wanting;[3] which two when they once meet,
The heart rears wings bold and bolder
And hurls for him, O half hurls earth for him
   off under his feet.
             (1877)   1918

The Lantern Out of Doors

Sometimes a lantern moves along the night,
   That interests our eyes. And who goes there?

I think; where from and bound, I wonder,
   where,
With, all down darkness wide, his wading
   light?[1]

Men go by me whom either beauty bright
   In mould or mind or what not else makes
   rare:
   They rain against our much-thick and marsh
   air
Rich beams, till death or distance buys them
   quite.

Death or distance soon consumes them: wind[2]
   What most I may eye after, be in at the end   10
I cannot, and out of sight is out of mind.

Christ minds: Christ's interest, what to avow
   or amend
   There, éyes them, heart wánts, care haúnts,
   foot fóllows kínd,
   Their ránsom, théir rescue, ánd first, fást, last
   friénd.
             (1877)   1918

The May Magnificat

May is Mary's month, and I
Muse at that and wonder why:
   Her feasts follow reason,
   Dated due to season—

Candlemas, Lady Day;[1]
But the Lady Month, May,
   Why fasten that upon her,
   With a feasting in her honour?

Is it only its being brighter
Than the most are must delight her?   10
   Is it opportunest
   And flowers finds soonest?

Ask of her, the mighty mother:
Her reply puts this other
   Question: What is Spring?—
   Growth in everything—

---

[1] Stooks: sheaves of grain.   [2] Meal-drift: the dust of harvested or milled grain.
[3] Wanting: lacking.   [1] Wading light: the light imagined as wading in the darkness.
[2] Wind: a verb: I wind my eye after the light as far as I can.
[1] Candlemas: a feast day in February celebrating the presentation of Christ as a boy in the Temple at Jerusalem and the purification of Mary; Lady Day: a feast day in March celebrating the annunciation to Mary that she was to be the mother of Christ.

Flesh and fleece, fur and feather,
Grass and greenworld all together;
    Star-eyed strawberry-breasted
20   Throstle above her nested

Cluster of bugle blue² eggs thin
Forms and warms the life within;
    And bird and blossom swell
    In sod or sheath or shell.

All things rising, all things sizing³
Mary sees, sympathising
    With that world of good,
    Nature's motherhood.

Their magnifying of each its kind
30 With delight calls to mind
    How she did in her stored
    Magnify the Lord.

Well but there was more than this:
Spring's universal bliss
    Much, had much to say
    To offering Mary May.

When drop-of-blood-and-foam-dapple
Bloom lights the orchard-apple
    And thicket and thorp⁴ are merry
40   With silver-surfèd cherry⁵

And azuring-over greybell⁶ makes
Wood banks and brakes⁷ wash wet like lakes
    And magic cuckoocall
    Caps, clears, and clinches all—

This ecstasy all through mothering earth
Tells Mary her mirth till Chirst's birth
    To remember and exulation
    In God who was her salvation.
                  (1878) 1918

Binsey Poplars¹

felled 1879

My aspens dear, whose airy cages quelled,
Quelled or quenched in leaves the leaping
               sun,
All felled, felled, are all felled;
    Of a fresh and following folded rank²
      Not spared, not one
      That dandled a sandalled
    Shadow that swam or sank
On meadow and river and wind-wandering
      weed-winding bank.

O if we but knew what we do
    When we delve or hew—   10
  Hack and rack the growing green!
    Since country is so tender
To touch, her being só slender,
That, like this sleek and seeing ball
But a prick will make no eye at all,

Where we, even where we mean
    To mend her we end her,
  When we hew or delve:
After-comers cannot guess the beauty been.
  Ten or twelve, only ten or twelve   20
    Strokes of havoc únselve
      The sweet especial scene,³
  Rural scene, a rural scene,
  Sweet especial rural scene.
                (1879) 1918

Duns Scotus's Oxford

*Duns Scotus (c. 1265–1308) was a Franciscan
theologian whose thought was attractive to Hopkins
because he emphasized the variety of being in crea-
tion, the distinctive character, the* thisness, *which
makes individual existences singular. At the same
time Duns Scotus maintained that individual beings
participate in and ultimately may be seen to reveal
a common nature and the single being of God. Duns*

² Bugle blue: the plant called the bugle blooms in May.   ³ Sizing: preparing.
⁴ Thorp: village or hamlet.
⁵ Silver-surfèd cherry: the white blossoms of cherry trees like a surf.
⁶ Greybell: the opening of the bluebell flower.   ⁷ Brakes: thickets.
¹ Binsey is a town near Oxford. The trees whose felling Hopkins laments in this poem were
lined along a river bank.
² Following folded rank: the line of trees seeming to unfold to the eye.
³ Unselve; especial: Hopkins' idea of selving, acts that express the singular, individual char-
acter of a being, is closely related to his idea of inscape, the distinctive design or pattern of a
scene or thing. To alter the pattern by felling the trees is to deprive the scene of its individual
being. See note to "Duns Scotus's Oxford."

Scotus was born in Scotland, and lectured in Oxford and Paris; it was in the latter city that he is said to have been the first to defend the idea of the Immaculate Conception, that Mary was born without original sin, an idea that did not become a dogma of the Roman Catholic church until the middle of the nineteenth century.

Towery city and branchy between towers;
Cuckoo-echoing, bell-swarmèd, lark-charmèd,
  rook-racked,[1] river-rounded;
The dapple-eared lily below thee; that country
  and town did
Once encounter in, here coped and poisèd
  powers;[2]

Thou hast a base and brickish skirt there,[3]
  sours
That neighbour-nature thy grey beauty is
  grounded
Best in; graceless growth, thou hast confounded
Rural rural keeping—folk, flocks, and flowers.

Yet ah! this air I gather and I release
He lived on; these weeds and waters, these
10   walls are what
He haunted who of all men most sways my
  spirits to peace;

Of realty[4] the rarest-veinèd unraveller; a not
Rivalled insight, be rival Italy or Greece;
Who fired France for Mary without spot.

                                        (1879)   1918

Henry Purcell (1659–1695) was a musician and composer who held a variety of official court appointments as an organist and composer of hymns and odes for public occasions. His heresy, for Hopkins, is simply that he was a Protestant and served a Protestant British king.

In a letter of 1883 Hopkins wrote: "The Sonnet on Purcell means this: 1–4. I hope Purcell is not damned for being a Protestant, because I love his genius. 5–8. And that not so much for gifts he shares, even though it shd. be in higher measure,

with other musicians as for his own individuality. 9–14. So that while he is aiming only at impressing me his hearer with the meaning in hand I am looking out meanwhile for his specific, his individual markings and mottlings, 'the sakes of him.' It is as when a bird thinking only of soaring spreads its wings: a beholder may happen then to have his attention drawn by the act to the plumage displayed" (Letters, *I, 170*). *See also Hopkins' remarks on "sake" in the note on stanza 22 of "The Wreck of the* Deutschland."

Henry Purcell

The poet wishes well to the divine genius of Purcell and praises him that, whereas other musicians have given utterance to the moods of man's mind, he has, beyond that, uttered in notes the very make and species of man as created both in him and in all men generally.

Have fair fallen, O fair, fair have fallen,[1] so
  dear
To me, so arch-especial a spirit as heaves in
  Henry Purcell,
An age is now since passed,[2] since parted; with
  the reversal
Of the outward sentence[3] low lays him, listed
  to a heresy, here.

Not mood in him nor meaning, proud fire or
  sacred fear,
Or love or pity or all that sweet notes not his
  might nursle:[4]
It is the forgèd feature finds me; it is the
  rehearsal
Of own, of abrúpt sélf[5] there so thrusts on, so
  throngs the ear.

Let him oh! with his air of angels then lift me,
  lay me! only I'll
Have an eye to the sakes of him, quaint moon-
  marks,[6] to his pelted plumage under   10
Wings: so some great stormfowl, whenever he
  has walked his while

---

[1] Rook: crow.   [2] Coped and poisèd: set off against one another.
[3] Base and brickish: the nineteenth-century buildings that surround the medieval stone buildings of Oxford.
[4] Realty: reality.
[1] Hopkins intended "have fair fallen" to be singular past imperative; that is, let fair (fortune) have befallen.
[2] Since passed . . . : modifies "spirit"; a spirit since passed for an age.
[3] Outward sentence: as a Protestant, Purcell is ostensibly damned.   [4] Nursle: foster.
[5] Sélf: see note on "Binsey Poplars."
[6] Moonmarks: in a letter of Hopkins': "By *moonmarks* I mean crescent shaped markings on the quill feathers" (Letters, I, 83) .

The thunder-purple seabeach plumèd purple-
of-thunder,
If a wuthering⁷ of his palmy snow-pinions
scatter a colossal smile
Off him, but meaning motion fans fresh our
wits with wonder.

(1879) 1918

*In classical mythology Andromeda was a king's
daughter who was to be sacrificed to a sea-monster
in order to appease the gods of the sea. She is
chained to a rock, where she is seen from above by
the hero Perseus, returning on his winged horse
from his beheading of the gorgon Medusa, whose
gaze can turn living things to stone. A generally
accepted reading of Hopkins' treatment of the myth
is that "Time's Andromeda"—the Andromeda of
this time—is the Roman Catholic church in Eng-
land, "the wilder beast from West" is the anti-
Christ of the secular, rationalist modern age, and
Perseus is Christ in his second coming.*

Andromeda

Now Time's Andromeda on this rock rude,
With not her either beauty's equal or
Her injury's, looks off by both horns of shore,¹
Her flower, her piece of being, doomed dragon
food.

Time past she has been attempted and pursued
By many blows and banes;² but now hears roar
A wilder beast from West than all were, more
Rife in her wrongs, more lawless, and more
lewd.

Her Perseus linger and leave her tó her
extremes?—
Pillowy air he treads a time and hangs
His thoughts on her, forsaken that she seems,

All while her patience, morselled into pangs,
Mounts; then to alight disarming, no one
dreams,³
With Gorgon's gear and barebill/thongs and
fangs.⁴

(1879) 1918

Felix Randal

Felix Randal the farrier,¹ O is he dead then?
my duty all ended,
Who have watched his mould of man, big-
boned and hardy-handsome
Pining, pining, till time when reason rambled
in it and some
Fatal four disorders, fleshed there, all
contended?

Sickness broke him. Impatient, he cursed at
first, but mended
Being anointed² and all; though a heavenlier
heart began some
Months earlier, since I had our sweet reprieve
and ransom³
Tendered to him. Ah well, God rest him all
road⁴ ever he offended!

This seeing the sick endears them to us, us too
it endears.
My tongue had taught thee comfort, touch had
quenched thy tears,
Thy tears that touched my heart, child, Felix,
poor Felix Randal;

How far from then forethought of, all thy
more boisterous years,
When thou at the random⁵ grim forge, power-
ful amidst peers,
Didst fettle⁶ for the great grey drayhorse his
bright and battering sandal!

(1880) 1918

---

⁷ Wuthering: blustering, the rush of wind: a dialect word of northern England.
¹ Horns of shore: promontories that make a bay.   ² Banes: poisonous evils.
³ No one dreams: ". . . the day of the Lord will come as a thief in the night" (2 Peter 3:10).
⁴ Barebill/thongs and fangs: in Bridges' 1918 edition, the unusual slant mark (/) was replaced by a comma; the mark exists in some manuscripts of the poem, and in one draft there is no punctuation at all between "barebill" and "thongs." "Barebill" is a sword. Gardner thinks that the present punctuation of these last words suggests that "thongs and fangs" is part of the phrase "to alight disarming thongs and fangs" (pp. 277–278). If the words are part of the phrase "With Gorgon's gear . . . ", they may refer to the head of Medusa, still capable of turning living things to stone, which Perseus carried with him in a sack as a weapon.
¹ Farrier: shoer of horses.   ² Anointed: in Extreme Unction, the sacrament of the dying.
³ Reprieve and ransom: the sacraments of penance and communion.
⁴ All road ever: a dialect phrase: however; in whatever way.
⁵ Random: built with stones of irregular size.   ⁶ Fettle: make ready.

Spring and Fall:

to a young child

Márgarét, áre you gríeving
Over Goldengrove unleaving?
Leáves, líke the things of man, you
With your fresh thoughts care for, can you?
Áh! ás the heart grows older
It will come to such sights colder
By and by, nor spare a sigh
Though worlds of wanwood leafmeal[1] lie;
And yet you *will* weep and know why.
10 Now no matter, child, the name:
Sórrow's springs áre the same.
Nor mouth had, no nor mind, expressed
What heart heard of, ghost[2] guessed:
It ís the blight man was born for,
It is Margaret you mourn for.

(1880) 1893

"As kingfishers catch fire"

As kingfishers catch fire, dragonflies draw
   flame;
   As tumbled over rim in roundy[1] wells
   Stones ring; like each tucked[2] string tells,
   each hung bell's
Bow[3] swung finds tongue to fling out broad its
   name;
Each mortal thing does one thing and the
   same:
   Deals out that being indoors each one dwells;
   Selves[4]—goes itself; *myself* it speaks and
   spells,
Crying *What I do is me: for that I came.*

Í say more: the just man justices;[5]
10   Keeps[6] gráce: thát keeps all his goings graces;
Acts in God's eye what in God's eye he is—
   Christ. For Christ plays in ten thousand
   places,

Lovely in limbs, and lovely in eyes not his
   To the Father through the features of men's
   faces.

(c. 1881) 1918

The Blessed Virgin Compared to the Air We Breathe[1]

Wild air, world-mothering air,
Nestling me everywhere,
That each eyelash or hair
Girdles; goes home betwixt
The fleeciest, frailest-flixed[2]
Snowflake; that's fairly mixed
With, riddles, and is rife
In every least thing's life;
This needful, never spent,
And nursing element;   10
My more than meat and drink,
My meal at every wink;
This air, which, by life's law,
My lung must draw and draw
Now but to breathe its praise,
Minds[3] me in many ways
Of her who not only
Gave God's infinity
Dwindled to infancy
Welcome in womb and breast,   20
Birth, milk, and all the rest
But mothers each new grace
That does now reach our race—
Mary Immaculate,
Merely a woman, yet
Whose presence, power is
Great as no goddess's
Was deemèd, dreamèd; who
This one work has to do—
Let all God's glory through,   30
God's glory which would go
Through her and from her flow
Off, and no way but so.
   I say that we are wound
With mercy round and round

---

[1] Wanwood leafmeal: wan forests lie scattered in leaves.   [2] Ghost: spirit, soul.
[1] Roundy: as usual in Hopkins' verse, "round" means a full roundness, filled space.
[2] Tucked: plucked.   [3] Bow: the yoke from which bells are suspended.
[4] One thing and the same; selves: see notes on "Binsey Poplars" and "Duns Scotus's Oxford" on these ideas of the particular and common identities of things.
[5] Justices: a verb.   [6] Keeps: maintains.
[1] Hopkins wrote this poem during the last years of his study for the Jesuit priesthood to be displayed in the seminary with other poems in honor of Mary. He thought it "partly a compromise with popular taste" (*Letters*, I, 179). It was first printed in 1895 in an anthology of Christmas verse.
[2] Flixed: furred.   [3] Minds: brings to mind.

As if with air: the same
Is Mary, more by name.
She, wild web, wondrous robe,
Mantles the guilty globe,
Since God has let dispense
Her prayers his providence:
Nay, more than almoner,[4]
The sweet alms' self is her
And men are meant to share
Her life as life does air.

　　If I have understood,[5]
She holds high motherhood
Towards all our ghostly good
And plays in grace her part
About man's beating heart,
Laying, like air's fine flood,
The deathdance in his blood;
Yet no part but what will
Be Christ our Saviour still.
Of her flesh he took flesh:
He does take fresh and fresh,
Though much the mystery how,
Not flesh but spirit now
And makes, O marvellous!
New Nazareths in us,
Where she shall yet conceive
Him, morning, noon, and eve;
New Bethlems, and he born
There, evening, noon, and morn—
Bethlem or Nazareth,
Men here may draw like breath
More Christ and baffle death;
Who, born so, comes to be
New self and nobler me
In each one and each one
More makes, when all is done,
Both God's and Mary's Son.

　　Again, look overhead
How air is azurèd;
O how! Nay do but stand
Where you can lift your hand
Skywards: rich, rich it laps
Round the four fingergaps.
Yet such a sapphire-shot,
Charged, steepèd sky will not
Stain light. Yea, mark you this:

It does no prejudice.
The glass-blue days are those
When every colour glows,
Each shape and shadow shows.
Blue be it: this blue heaven
The seven or seven times seven
Hued sunbeam will transmit
Perfect, not alter it.
Or if there does some soft,[6]
On things aloof, aloft,
Bloom breathe, that one breath more
Earth is the fairer for.
Whereas did air not make
This bath of blue and slake
His fire, the sun would shake,
A blear and blinding ball
With blackness bound, and all
The thick stars round him roll
Flashing like flecks of coal,
Quartz-fret,[7] or sparks of salt,
In grimy vasty vault.

　　So God was god of old:
A mother came to mould
Those limbs like ours which are
What must make our daystar[8]
Much dearer to mankind;
Whose glory bare would blind
Or less would win man's mind.
Through her we may see him
Made sweeter, not made dim,
And her hand leaves his light
Sifted to suit our sight.

　　Be thou then, O thou dear
Mother, my atmosphere;
My happier world, wherein
To wend and meet no sin;
Above me, round me lie
Fronting my froward eye
With sweet and scarless sky;
Stir in my ears, speak there
Of God's love, O live air,
Of patience, penance, prayer:
World-mothering air, air wild,
Wound with thee, in thee isled,
Fold home, fast fold thy child.

(1883) 1895

---

[4] Almoner: the distributor of alms for a monastery or a great household.

[5] The doctrine of lines 46–72 is that Mary is now also mother to human spiritual (ghostly) good, interceding to bring grace which ultimately (lines 53–54) is from Christ. Christ thus can continually come into the mortal world, not in flesh now but in spirit, as through Mary's agency he and the new selves of humans may continually be born in new Nazareths and Bethlehems.

[6] Soft: modifies bloom (line 92).　　[7] Quartz-fret: with particles of quartz on the surface.

[8] Daystar: the sun.

"No worst, there is none"

No worst, there is none. Pitched past pitch of
   grief,
More pangs will, schooled at forepangs, wilder
   wring.
Comforter, where, where is your comforting?
Mary, mother of us, where is your relief?
My cries heave, herds-long; huddle in a main,[1]
   a chief-
woe, world-sorrow; on an age-old anvil wince
   and sing—
Then lull, then leave off. Fury had shrieked
   "No ling—
ering! Let me be fell: force I must be brief."[2]

O the mind, mind has mountains; cliffs of fall
Frightful, sheer, no-man-fathomed. Hold them
10   cheap
May who ne'er hung there. Nor does long our
   small
Durance deal with that steep[3] or deep. Here!
   creep,
Wretch, under a comfort serves in a whirl-
   wind: all
Life death does end and each day dies with
   sleep.

                            (1885?) 1918

"I wake and feel the fell of dark, not day"

I wake and feel the fell[1] of dark, not day.
What hours, O what black hoürs we have spent
This night! what sights you, heart, saw; ways
   you went!
And more must, in yet longer light's delay.

With witness I speak this. But where I say
Hours I mean years, mean life. And my lament
Is cries countless, cries like dead letters sent
To dearest him that lives alas! away.

I am gall, I am heartburn. God's most deep
   decree
Bitter would have me taste: my taste was me;   10
Bones built in me, flesh filled, blood brimmed
   the curse.

Selfyeast[2] of spirit a dull dough sours. I see
The lost are like this, and their scourge to be
As I am mine, their sweating selves; but worse.

                      (c. 1885) 1918

"My own heart let me more have pity on"

My own heart let me more have pity on; let
Me live to my sad self hereafter kind,
Charitable; not live this tormented mind
With this tormented mind tormenting yet.

I cast for comfort I can no more get
By groping round my comfortless, than blind
Eyes in their dark can day[1] or thirst can find
Thirst's all-in-all in all a world of wet.[2]

Soul, self; come, poor Jackself,[3] I do advise
You, jaded, let be; call off thoughts awhile   1
Elsewhere; leave comfort root-room; let joy
   size[4]

At God knows when to God knows what; whose
   smile
's not wrung,[5] see you; unforseen times rather
   —as skies
Betweenpie[6] mountains—lights a lovely mile.

                     (1885?) 1918

(Ashboughs) [1]

a.

Not of all my eyes see, wandering on the world,
Is anything a milk to the mind so, so sighs deep

---

   [1] Main: large host.   [2] Fell: fierce, keen. Force: perforce.
   [3] Steep: nearly perpendicular hill or mountain.   [1] Fell: the pelt of an animal.
   [2] Selfyeast: the "selving" energy of individual being (see notes to "Binsey Poplars" and "As kingfishers catch fire") is damaging when its medium makes it into the energy of aberrent beings, creatures, like the damned, grown apart from the integral being of God.
   [1] Day: make a light.   [2] Thirst's all-in-all: what thirst seeks, and cannot itself create.
   [3] Jackself: ordinary self.   [4] Size: prepare.   [5] Wrung: forced out.
   [6] Betweenpie: a verb; variegate, as here the sky variegates the colors of the landscape by shining between the dark masses of mountains.
   [1] When Bridges published this poem in the first collected edition of Hopkins' poems, he described the first version as complete, a curtal sonnet of eleven lines; and the variant another version in thirteen lines. Bridges bracketed certain words to indicate words he would delete to return this second version to the eleven-line form.

Poetry tó it, as a tree whose boughs break in the
　　sky.
Say it is áshboughs: whether on a December
　　day and furled
Fast ór they in clammyish lashtender combs
　　creep
Apart wide and new-nestle at heaven most
　　high.

They touch heaven, tabour[2] on it; how their
　　talons sweep
The smouldering enormous winter welkin![3]
　　May
Mells[4] blue and snowwhite through them, a
　　fringe and fray
Of greenery: it is old earth's groping towards
　　the steep
　　Heaven whom she childs us by.

(Variant from line 7.)   *b.*
They touch, they tabour on it, hover on it
　　[; here, there hurled],
　　　　　　　　With talons sweep
The smouldering enormous winter welkin. [Eye,
　　　　　　　But more cheer is when] May
Mells blue with snowwhite through their fringe
　　and fray
Of greenery and old earth gropes for, grasps at
　　steep
　　Heaven with it whom she childs
　　things by.

　　　　　　　　　　　　(1885?) 1918

"Thee, God, I come from, to thee go"

Thee, God, I come from, to thee go,
All dáy long I like fountain flow
From thy hand out, swayed about
Mote-like in thy mighty glow.

What I know of thee I bless,
As acknowledging thy stress
On my being and as seeing
Something of thy holiness

Once I turned from thee and hid,
Bound on what thou hadst forbid;
Sow the wind I would; I sinned:
I repent of what I did.

Bad I am, but yet thy child.
Father, be thou reconciled.
Spare thou me, since I see
With thy might that thou art mild.

I have life left with me still
And thy purpose to fulfil;
Yea a debt to pay thee yet:
Help me, sir, and so I will.   20

But thou bidst, and just thou art,
Me shew mercy from my heart
Towards my brother, every other
Man my mate and counterpart.

　　·　　·　　·　　·　　·　　·
　　　　　　　　　　　　(1885?) 1918

*In a letter to Bridges in 1888 Hopkins wrote: "I
laughed outright and often, but very sardonically,
to think you and the Canon [R. W. Dixon] could
not construe my last sonnet; . . . if you and he
cannot understand me who will? Yet, declaimed,
the strange constructions would be dramatic and
effective. . . . It means then that . . . the com-
monwealth or well ordered human society is like
one man; a body with many members and each its
function; some higher, some lower, but all honour-
able, from the honour which belongs to the whole.
The head is the sovereign, who has no superior but
God and from heaven receives his or her authority.
. . . The foot is the day-labourer, and this is
armed with hobnail boots, because it has to wear
and be worn by the ground. . . . And the 'garlands'
of nails they wear are therefore the visible badge
of the place they fill, the lowest in the common-
wealth. But this place still shares the common hon-
our, and if it wants one advantage, glory or public
fame, makes up for it by another, ease of mind, ab-
sence of care; and these things are symbolized by
the gold and iron garlands. (O, once explained,
how clear it all is!)" (Letters, I, 272–274).*
　　*Hopkins goes on to explain that the poem is set
in the evening, when the laborers are returning
from work, striking out sparks from the earth with
the nails of their boots. Tom reflects on his place
and its exemption from care, and then lightheart-
edly ("Little I reck ho!") dismisses the question.
"But," Hopkins continues, "presently I remember
that this is all very well for those who are in, how-
ever low in, the Commonwealth and share in any
way the Common weal; but that the curse of our
times is that many do not share it, that they are
outcasts from it and have neither security nor
splendour; that they share care with the high and
obscurity with the low, but wealth nor comfort with*

[2] Tabour: drum (verb).　　[3] Welkin: sky.　　[4] Mells: mixes.

neither. And this state of things, I say, is the origin of Loafers, Tramps, Cornerboys, Roughs, Socialists, and other pests of society. And I think that it is a very pregnant sonnet and in point of execution very highly wrought. Too much so, I am afraid" (Letters, I, 272–274).

Tom's Garland:

upon the Unemployed

Tom—garlanded with squat and surly steel
Tom; then Tom's fallowbootfellow[1] piles pick
By him and rips out rockfire[2] homeforth—
    sturdy Dick;
Tom Heart-at-ease, Tom Navvy:[3] he is all for
    his meal
Sure, 's bed now. Low be it: lustily he his low
    lot (feel
That ne'er need hunger, Tom; Tom seldom
    sick,
Seldomer heartsore; that treads through, prick-
    proof, thick
Thousands of thorns, thoughts) swings though.
    Commonweal
Little I reck ho! lacklevel[4] in, if all had bread:
What! Country is honour enough in all us—
10   lordly head,
With heaven's lights high hung round, or,
    mother-ground
That mammocks,[5] mighty foot. But nó way
    sped,[6]
Nor mind nor mainstrength; gold go garlanded
With, perilous, O nó; nor yet plod safe shod
    sound;
        Undenizened, beyond bound
Of earth's glory, earth's ease, all; no one,
    nowhere,

In wide the world's weal; rare gold, bold steel,
    bare[7]
        In both; care, but share care[8]—
This, by Despair, bred Hangdog dull; by Rage,
Manwolf, worse; and their packs infest the age.
                    (1887) 1918

That Nature Is a Heraclitean Fire and of the Comfort of the Resurrection[1]

Cloud-puffball, torn tufts, tossed pillows ' flaunt
    forth, then chevy[2] on an air-
built thoroughfare: heaven-roysterers, in gay-
    gangs ' they throng; they glitter in marches.[3]
Down roughcast, down dazzling whitewash,[4] '
    wherever an elm arches,
Shivelights and shadowtackle[5] in long ' lashes
    lace, lance, and pair.
Delightfully the bright wind boisterous ' ropes,
    wrestles, beats earth bare
Of yestertempest's creases; ' in pool and rutpeel
    parches[6]
Squandering ooze to squeezed ' dough, crust,
    dust; stanches, starches
Squadroned masks and manmarks[7] ' treadmire
    toil there
Footfretted in it. Million-fuelèd, ' nature's
    bonfire burns on.
But quench her bonniest, dearest ' to her, her
    clearest-selvèd[8] spark
Man, how fast his firedint, ' his mark on mind,
    is gone!
Both are in an unfathomable, all is in an
    enormous dark
Drowned. O pity and indig ' nation! Manshape,
    that shone

---

[1] Fallowbootfellow: his fellow worker, now quitting for the day (and thus fallow).
[2] Rips out rockfire: the sparks struck by their nailed boots as they walk home.
[3] Navvy: a manual laborer on the canals or railways.   [4] Lacklevel: a society without levels.
[5] Mammocks: shreds, breaks up. "Foot" is the subject of this verb.
[6] But no way sped: encouraged in neither way: Hopkins here begins his remarks on those who are outcast from the Commonwealth.
[7] Bare: lacking.   [8] Share care: have the cares of both high and low.
[1] The sixth-century B.C. Greek philosopher Heraclitus proposed that the primary element of creation was fire and that the first principle of existence was ceaseless change: all forms and identities endlessly dissolve into other forms and identities.
[2] Chevy: scamper.   [3] Marches: borders.
[4] Roughcast; whitewash: terms used to describe the surfaces of walls.
[5] Shivelights and shadowtackle: strips of light; and shadows of branches imagined as the rigging of a ship.
[6] Yestertempest's creases: marks made by yesterday's storm. Rutpeel: ruts described as peeled places in the earth. Parches: the subject of this verb is "wind."
[7] Squadroned masks and manmarks; footfretted: the patterned marks man has put on the earth by walking and working on it.
[8] Clearest-selvèd: most self-consciously individual.

Sheer off, disseveral,[9] a star, ' death blots black
out; nor mark
                    Is any of him at all so stark
But vastness blurs and time ' beats level.
    Enough! the Resurrection,
A heart's-clarion! Away grief's gasping, ' joyless
days, dejection.
                    Across my foundering deck shone
A beacon, an eternal beam. ' Flesh fade, and
mortal trash
Fall to the residuary worm; ' world's wildfire,
leave but ash:
                    In a flash, at a trumpet crash,
I am all at once what Christ is, ' since he was
what I am, and
This Jack, joke, poor potsherd, ' patch, match-
wood,[10] immortal diamond,
                    Is immortal diamond.
                              (1888) 1918

In honour of

St. Alphonsus Rodriguez

Laybrother of the Society of Jesus[1]

Honour is flashed off exploit, so we say;
And those strokes once that gashed flesh or
galled[2] shield
Should tongue that time now, trumpet now
that field,
And, on the fighter, forge his glorious day.
On Christ they do and on the martyr may;
But be the war within, the brand[3] we wield
Unseen, the heroic breast not outward-steeled,
Earth hears no hurtle[4] then from fiercest fray.
Yet God (that hews mountain and continent,
Earth, all, out; who, with trickling increment,
Veins violets and tall trees makes more and
more)
Could crowd career with conquest while there
went
Those years and years by of world without
event

That in Majorca Alfonso watched the door.
                              (1888) 1918

Epithalamion[1]

Hark, hearer, hear what I do; lend a thought
now, make believe
We are leafwhelmed somewhere with the hood
Of some branchy bunchy bushybowered wood,
Southern dean or Lancashire clough or Devon
cleave,[2]
That leans along the loins of hills, where a
candycoloured, where a gluegold-brown
Marbled river, boisterously beautiful, between
Roots and rocks is danced and dandled, all in
froth and waterblowballs, down.
We are there, when we hear a shout
That the hanging honeysuck, the dogeared
hazels in the cover
Makes dither, makes hover   10
And the riot of a rout
Of, it must be, boys from the town
Bathing: it is summer's sovereign good.

By there comes a listless stranger: beckoned by
the noise
He drops towards the river: unseen
Sees the bevy of them, how the boys
With dare and with downdolphinry and bell-
bright bodies huddling out,
Are earthworld, airworld, waterworld thorough
hurled, all by turn and turn about.

This garland of their gambol flashes in his
breast
Into such a sudden zest   20
Of summertime joys
That he hies to a pool neighbouring; sees it is
the best
There; sweetest, freshest, shadowiest;
Fairyland; silk-beech, scrolled ash, packed
sycamore, wild wychelm, hornbeam fretty[3]
overstood
By. Rafts and rafts of flake leaves light, dealt
so, painted on the air,

[9] Disseveral: separate.
[10] Jack; patch: an ordinary man; a paltry fellow. Matchwood: kindling wood.
[1] Hopkins wrote this sonnet "to order on the occasion of the first feast since his canonization proper of St. Alphonsus Rodriguez, a laybrother of our Order, who for 40 years acted as hall-porter to the College of Palma in Majorca: he was, it is believed, much favoured by God with heavenly lights and much persecuted by evil spirits" (note on manuscript quoted in Gardner's edition, p. 295).
[2] Galled: broke open.   [3] Brand: sword.   [4] Hurtle: rushing, rumbling noise.
[1] This poem was begun to celebrate the marriage of one of Hopkins' brothers in 1888.
[2] Dean: dell or valley. Clough: ravine. Cleave: cleft.
[3] Hornbeam fretty: a hedge of small trees (hornbeam) like a trellis.

Hang as still as hawk or hawkmoth, as the stars
    or as the angels there,
Like the thing that never knew the earth, never
    off roots
Rose. Here he feasts: lovely all is! No more:
    off with—down he dings[4]
His bleachèd both and woolwoven wear:
30   Careless these in coloured wisp
All lie tumbled-to; then with loop-locks
Forward falling, forehead frowning, lips crisp
Over finger-teasing task, his twiny boots
Fast he opens, last he off wrings
Till walk the world he can with bare his feet
And come where lies a coffer,[5] burly all of
    blocks
Built of chancequarrièd, selfquainèd,[6] hoar-
    huskèd rocks
And the water warbles over into, filleted ¹ with
    glassy grassy quicksilvery shivès[7] and shoots
And with heavenfallen freshness down from
    moorland still brims,
Dark or daylight on and on. Here he will then,
40   here he will the fleet
Flinty kindcold element let break across his
    limbs
Long. Where we leave him, froliclavish, while
    he looks about him, laughs, swims.

Enough now; since the sacred matter that I
    mean
I should be wronging longer leaving it to float
Upon this only gamboling and echoing-of-earth
    note—

What is . . . . the delightful dean?
Wedlock. What the water? Spousal love.

   .   .   .   .

   .   .   .   .

                         turns
Father, mother, brothers, sisters, friends
50   Into fairy trees, wildflowers, woodferns
Rankèd round the bower

   .   .   .   .
                   (1888) 1918

"Thou art indeed just, Lord, if I contend"

Justus quidem tu es, Domine, si disputem tecum; verum-
tamen justa loquar ad te: Quare via impiorum pros-
peratur? &c.¹

Thou art indeed just, Lord, if I contend
With thee; but, sir, so what I plead is just.
Why do sinners' ways prosper? and why must
Disappointment all I endeavour end?

Wert thou my enemy, O thou my friend,
How wouldst thou worse, I wonder, than thou
    dost
Defeat, thwart me? Oh, the sots and the thralls
    of lust
Do in spare hours more thrive than I that
    spend,

Sir, life upon thy cause. See, banks and brakes[2]
Now, leavèd how thick! lacèd they are again   10
With fretty chervil,[3] look, and fresh wind
    shakes

Them; birds build—but not I build; no, but
    strain,
Time's eunuch, and not breed one work that
    wakes.
Mine, O thou lord of life, send my roots rain.
                  (1889) 1918

To R. B.¹

The fine delight that fathers thought; the
    strong
Spur, live and lancing like the blowpipe flame,
Breathes once and, quenchèd faster than it
    came,
Leaves yet the mind a mother of immortal
    song.

Nine months she then, nay years, nine years
    she long
Within her wears, bears, cares and combs the
    same:

---

   ⁴ Dings: throws violently.   ⁵ Coffer: boxlike basin of water, here in a quarry.
   ⁶ Selfquainèd: lying at angles to one another.   ⁷ Shivès: splinters.
   ¹ "Righteous art thou, O Lord, when I plead with thee: yet let me talk with thee of thy
judgments: Wherefore doth the way of the wicked prosper?" (Jeremiah 12:1) .
   ² Brakes: thickets.   ³ Fretty chervil: a kind of parsley.
   ¹ R. B.: Robert Bridges. Printed in 1893 in a selection prepared by Bridges under the title
"To ———." Bridges changed "combs" in line 6 to "moulds," added a comma after "fire"
in line 9, and printed the fourteen lines as one stanza without a break.

The widow of an insight lost she lives, with
  aim
Now known and hand at work now never
  wrong.

Sweet fire the sire of muse, my soul needs this;
I want the one rapture of an inspiration.
O then if in my lagging lines you miss

The roll, the rise, the carol, the creation,
My winter world, that scarcely breathes that
  bliss
Now, yields you, with some sighs, our
  explanation.

                 (1889) 1893

PART FOUR

Mid-Victorian Poems 1850-1880

Robert Stephen Hawker
1803–1875

Robert Stephen Hawker was born into a clerical family of Devon and Cornwall in the southwest of England. He graduated from Oxford in 1828, was ordained in the Church of England in 1831, and became vicar of a parish in Cornwall in 1834, where he remained for the rest of his life. He published a poem for which he had won a prize at Oxford in 1827, and in 1832 and 1836 he published the two series of Records of the Western Shore, *poems that are often about places or stories of his native district. He also published volumes of religious poetry in the 1840s. But his most distinctive writing was* The Quest of the Sangraal, *which he began to write in 1863 and published unfinished in 1864, and the poetry of* Cornish Ballads, *published in 1869 and including a second edition of* The Quest. *In these poems he joined his sometimes quirky antiquarian interest in language, myth, and folklore to an ability to see and tell these stories, not as revivals of a quaint past, but as they might be told by poets who know them as part of the current life of their community. Hawker's poems were collected in 1879, and collected again in an edition edited by Alfred Wallis in 1899. The texts printed here are those of this latter edition. Sabine Baring Gould published a life of Hawker in 1875 (revised 1876); C. E. Byles published the life and letters of Hawker in 1905; and Margaret F. Burrows published* Hawker: A Study of His Thought and Poetry *in 1926.*

The Doom-Well of St. Madron[1]

"Plunge thy right hand in St. Madron's spring,
If true to its troth be the palm you bring:
But if a false sigil[2] thy fingers bear,
Lay them the rather on the burning share."[3]

Loud laughed King Arthur whenas he heard
That solemn friar his boding word:
And blithely he sware as a king he may
"We tryst for St. Madron's at break of day."

"Now horse and hattock, both but and ben,"[4]
Was the cry at Lauds, with Dundagel men;[5]   10
And forth they pricked upon Routorr side[6]
As goodly a raid as a king could ride.

Proud Gwennivar rode like a queen of the
     land,
With page and with squire at her bridle hand;
And the twice six knights of the stony ring,
They girded and guarded their Cornish king.

Then they halted their steeds at St. Madron's
     cell:
And they stood by the monk of the cloistered
     well;
"Now off with your gauntlets," King Arthur
     he cried,
"And glory or shame for our Tamar side." [7]   20

'Twere sooth to sing how Sir Gauvain smiled,
When he grasped the waters so soft and mild;
How Sir Lancelot dashed the glistening spray
O'er the rugged beard of the rough Sir Kay.

Sir Bevis he touched and he found no fear:
'Twas a *bénitée* stoup[8] to Sir Belvidere,
How the fountain flashed o'er King Arthur's
     Queen
Say, Cornish dames, for ye guess the scene.

---

[1] St. Madron: or St. Madern, a Breton and Cornish saint who was associated with miracles said to be worked by the properties of the water of a well named after him in Cornwall. This poem was first printed in a magazine in 1855.

[2] Sigil: sign or ring as token.   [3] Share: a sharp-edged piece of metal.

[4] Horse and hattock, but and ben: men who ride and who work the fields, who belong to the butlery and to the hall.

[5] Lauds: prayers in the early morning. Dundagel: an old name for Tintagel, the castle in the southwest of England where Arthur was begotten.

[6] Routorr: Red Hill.   [7] Tamar: a river in Devon and Cornwall.

[8] *Bénitée* stoup: good drink.

"Now rede me my riddle, Sir Mordred,[9] I pray,
30 My kinsman, mine ancient, my *bien-aimé;*
Now rede me my riddle, and rede it aright,
Art thou traitorous knave or my trusty knight?"

He plunged his right arm in the judgment well,
It bubbled and boiled like a cauldron of hell:
He drew and he lifted his quivering limb,
Ha! Sir Judas, how Madron had sodden him!

Now let Uter Pendragon[10] do what he can,
Still the Tamar river will run as it ran:
Let King or let Kaiser be fond or be fell,
40 Ye may harowe their troth[11] in St. Madron's
    well.

              (1851) 1855; 1869

from The Quest of the Sangraal[1]

[The Coming of the Sangraal]

Then saw they that the mighty Quest was won!
The Sangraal swoon'd along the golden air:
The sea breathed balsam, like Gennesaret:[2]
The streams were touched with supernatural
  light:
And fonts of Saxon rock, stood, full of God!
Altars arose, each like a kingly throne,
Where the royal chalice, with its lineal blood,
The Glory of the Presence, ruled and reigned.
This lasted long: until the white horse fled,[3]
440 The fierce fangs of the libbard[4] in his loins:
Whole ages glided in that blink of time,
While Merlin and the King, looked, wonder-
  ing, on.

But see! once more the wizard-wand arise,
To cleave the air with signals, and a scene.

Troops of the demon-north, in yellow garb,
The sickly hue of vile Iscariot's hair,[5]
Mingle with men, in unseen multitudes!
Unscared, they throng the valley and the hill;
The shrines were darkened and the chalice
  void:
That which held God was gone: Maran-atha![6]   45
The awful shadows of the Sangraal, fled!
Yet giant-men arose, that seemed as gods,
Such might they gathered from the swarthy
  kind:
The myths were rendered up: and one by one,
The Fire—the Light—the Air—were tamed
  and bound
Like votive vassals at their chariot-wheel.
Then learnt they War: yet not that noble
  wrath,
That brings the generous champion face to
  face
With equal shield, and with a measured
  brand,[7]
To peril life for life; and do or die;   4
But the false valour of the lurking fiend
To hurl a distant death from some deep den:
To wing with flame the metal of the mine:
And, so they rend God's image, reck not who!
"Ah! haughty England! lady of the wave!"
Thus said pale Merlin to the listening King,
"What is thy glory in the world of stars?
To scorch and slay: to win demoniac fame,
In arts and arms; and then to flash and die!
Thou art the diamond of the demon-crown,
Smitten by Michael upon Abarim,[8]   4
That fell; and glared, an island of the sea.
Ah! native England! wake thine ancient cry;
Ho! for the Sangraal! vanish'd Vase of Heaven,
That held, like Christ's own heart, an hin[9] of
  blood!"

---

[9] Mordred: a nephew of Arthur who finally betrayed and rose against him.
[10] Uter Pendragon: Arthur's father.   [11] Harowe their troth: test their truth or loyalty.
[1] The Sangraal is the Holy Grail, the vessel used by Christ in celebrating the supper of the evening before his crucifixion. It was then lost, or hid itself from men, and if it were found, men and society would again be whole and good.
[2] Gennesaret: a valley near the sea of Galilee.
[3] White horse: perhaps a reference to the white horse of Westbury, a figure carved on a hillside in the west of England during pre-Christian times. See note to Charles Tennyson Turner's "The White Horse of Westbury" (p. 742).
[4] Libbard: leopard; another antique word that Hawker used quite self-consciously.
[5] Iscariot: Judas, the betrayer of Christ.
[6] Maran-atha: Our Lord has come: used by Paul (1 Corinthians 16:22).   [7] Brand: sword.
[8] Abarim: a place at which earlier in the poem the archangel Michael is described fighting a "tournay" with Satan.
[9] Hin: a Hebrew measure; a little over a gallon.

He ceased; and all around was dreamy night:
There stood Dundagel,[10] throned: and the
    great sea

Lay, a strong vassal at his master's gate,
And, like a drunken giant, sobb'd in sleep!

                        (1863) 1864; 1869

Alexander Smith
1829–1867

Alexander Smith was born in Scotland, the son of a designer of lace patterns. For a while he studied and practiced his father's occupation, living and working in Glasgow. He began publishing poems in magazines in 1851, and in 1853 he published Poems, *a volume consisting mostly of a long poem,* A Life-Drama. *The ambition, pretension, and ornateness of this poem caused a considerable stir among readers and reviewers. The poem was attacked for its vulgarity, combed through to support charges of plagiarism against Smith, ridiculed, defended, and went through four editions by 1856. Smith wrote for and briefly edited a magazine until in 1854 he became secretary to the university at Edinburgh. In Edinburgh he wrote poems, reviews, essays, and some fiction for magazines and encyclopedias. He published another volume of verse,* City Poems, *in 1857, and a historical dramatic poem,* Edwin of Deira, *in 1861. A book of essays,* Dreamthorp, *was published in 1863. The text printed here is that of an edition of Smith's poems published in Boston in 1855.*

from A Life-Drama

From Scene VI

[The Poet's Hope]

EDWARD
                 What hope is that?

WALTER
To set this Age to music—The great work

Before the Poet now—I do believe
When it is fully sung, its great complaint,
Its hope, its yearning, told to earth and heaven,
Our troubled age shall pass, as doth a day
That leaves the west all crimson with the
    promise
Of the diviner morrow, which even then
Is hurrying up the world's great side with light.
Father! if I should live to see that morn,   10
Let me go upward, like a lark, to sing
One song in the dawning!

EDWARD
               Oh, you'd patch with song
The ragged mantle of the beggar earth!
Most hopeless, truly, this of all the tasks
You could put hands to. No, my ardent friend!
You need not tinker at this leaking world,
'Tis ruined past all cure.

WALTER
              Edward, for shame!
Not on a path of reprobation runs   20
The trembling earth. God's eye doth follow her
With far more love than doth her maid, the
    moon.
Speak no harsh words of Earth, she is our
    mother,
And few of us, her sons, who have not added
A wrinkle to her brow. She gave us birth,
We drew our nurture from her ample breast,
And there is coming, for us both, an hour
When we shall pray that she will ope her arms
And take us back again. Oh, I would pledge
My heart, my blood, my brain, to ease the earth   30
Of but one single pang!

[10] Dundagel: Tintagel, the castle in which Arthur was begotten.

EDWARD

                        So would not I.
Because the pangs of earth shall ne'er be eased.
We sleep on velvets now, instead of leaves;
The land is covered with a net of iron,
Upon whose spider-like, far-stretching lines,
The trains are rushing, and the peevish sea
Frets 'gainst the bulging bosoms of the ships
Whose keels have waked it from its hour's
    repose.
40 Walter! this height of civilization's tide
Measures our wrong. We've made the immortal
    Soul
Slave to the Body. 'T is the Soul has wrought
And laid the iron roads, evoked a power
Next mightiest to God, to drive the trains,
That bring the country butter up to town;
Has drawn the terrible lightning from its
    cloud,

And tamed it to an eager Mercury,[1]
Running with messages of news and grain;
And still the Soul is tasked to harder work,
For Paradise, according to the world,   5
Is scarce a league a-head. . . .
    The truly great
Rest in the knowledge of their own deserts,
Nor seek the confirmation of the world.
Wouldst thou be calm and still?

WALTER

                        I'd be as lieve
A minnow to leviathan,[2] that draws
A furrow like a ship. Away! away!
You'd make the world a very oyster-bed.
I'd rather be the glad, bright-leaping foam,
Than the smooth sluggish sea. O let me live   6
To love, and flush, and thrill—or let me die!

                                        1853

Sydney Dobell
1824–1874

Sydney Dobell was the son of a wine merchant, and early and later in his life he helped to conduct his father's business. He was privately educated and a precocious poet. He published a declamation in the cause of Italian nationalism, The Roman, in 1850, and won the attention of similarly sympathetic writers and readers. He then won yet more attention with Balder, a heroic poem published in the same year (1853) as Alexander Smith's "A Life-Drama" and associated with it to make a school of "Spasmodic" poets of autobiographical poetic structures and highly decorated language. Dobell never completed a promised second part of Balder. He wrote some sonnets with Alexander Smith on the Crimean War in 1855, and published them and other poems in England in Time of War (1856). Some of his lectures on poetry were published after his death, and his poetical works were collected in 1875 by John Nichol, who also wrote a memoir for this edition. The text printed here is that of the 1875 collected edition.

from Sonnets on the War
L'Avenir[1]

I saw the human millions as the sand
Unruffled on the starlit wilderness.
The day was near, and every star grew less
In universal dawn. Then woke a band
Of wheeling winds, and made a mighty stress
Of morning weather; and still wilder went
O'er shifting plains, till, in their last excess,
A whirlwind whirled across the whirling land.
Heaven blackened over it; a voice of woes
Foreran it; the great noise of clanging foes
Hurtled behind; beneath the earth was rent,
And howling Death, like an uncaverned beast,
Leaped from his lair. Meanwhile morn oped
    the East,
And thro' the dusty tumult God arose.

                                        1856

---

[1] Mercury: the messenger of the gods in Greek mythology.   [2] Leviathan: whale.
[1] L'Avenir: the future.

Daft Jean

Daft Jean,
The waesome wean,[1]
She cam' by the cottage, she cam' by the ha',[2]
The laird's ha' o' Wutherstanelaw,
The cottar's cot by the birken shaw;[3]
An' aye she gret,
To ilk ane she met,
For the trumpet had blawn an' her lad was
    awa'.

"Black, black," sang she,
"Black, black my weeds shall be,
My love has widowed me!
Black, black!" sang she.

Daft Jean,
The waesome wean,
She cam' by the cottage, she cam' by the ha',
The laird's ha' o' Wutherstanelaw,
The cottar's cot by the birken shaw;
Nae mair she creepit,
Nae mair she weepit,
She stept 'mang the lasses the queen o' them a',
The queen o' them a',
The queen o' them a',
She stept 'mang the lasses the queen o' them a'.
For the fight it was fought i' the fiel' far awa',
An' claymore[4] in han' for his love an' his lan',
The lad she lo'ed best he was foremost to fa'.

"White, white," sang she,
"White, white, my weeds shall be,
I am no widow," sang she,
"White, white, my wedding shall be,
White, white!" sang she.

Daft Jean,
The waesome wean,

She gaed na' to cottage, she gaed na' to ha',
But forth she creepit,
While a' the house weepit,
Into the snaw i' the eerie night-fa'.

At morn we found her,
The lammies[5] stood round her
The snaw was her pillow, her sheet was the
    snaw;   40
Pale she was lying,
Singing and dying,
A' for the laddie wha fell far awa'.

"White, white," sang she,
"My love has married me,
White, white, my weeds shall be,
White, white, my wedding shall be,
White, white," sang she!

        1856

The Botanist's Vision

The sun that in Breadalbane's lake doth fall
Was melting to the sea down golden Tay,[1]
When a cry came along the peopled way,
"Sebastopol is ours!"[2] From that wild call
I turned, and leaning on a time-worn wall
Quaint with the touch of many an ancient day,
The mappèd mould and mildewed marquetry
Knew with my focussed soul; which bent down
    all
Its sense, power, passion, to the sole regard
Of each green minim, as it were but born   10
To that one use. I strode home stern and hard;
In my hot hands I laid my throbbing head,
And all the living world and all the dead
Began a march which did not end at morn.
        1856

---

[1] Waesome wean: woesome child.   [2] Ha': hall.   [3] Birken shaw: a small birchwood.
[4] Claymore: a two-edged sword.   [5] Lammies: lambs, kids.
[1] Breadalbane: a range of mountains in Scotland. Tay: the principal river in Scotland.
[2] Sebastopol fell to the British and French in September 1855, effectively ending the Crimean War.

William Johnson Cory

1823–1892

William Johnson Cory entered Cambridge from
Eton, graduated in 1845, and was appointed a fel-
low in his Cambridge college and an assistant mas-
ter at Eton in the same year. He remained at Eton
teaching classics until 1872, when he came into an
inheritance, added the surname Cory to his own,
and retired to travel, write, and tutor private pu-
pils. He published two small collections of verse
under the title Ionica, one in 1858 and the other
in 1877. With a few additions and deletions, the
two volumes were published together in 1891; it is
from that edition that the texts printed here are
taken. Cory also published exercises for Latin com-
position and a guide to nineteenth-century English
history. R. B. Brett published a biography of Cory,
Ionicus, in 1923; Faith Compton Mackenzie's
William Cory (1950) includes some previously un-
published poems.

Mimnermus in Church

You promise heavens free from strife,
    Pure truth, and perfect change of will;
But sweet, sweet is this human life,
    So sweet, I fain would breathe it still;
Your chilly stars I can forego,
This warm kind world is all I know.

You say there is no substance here,
    One great reality above:
Back from that void I shrink in fear,
    And child-like hide myself in love:
Show me what angels feel. Till then,
I cling, a mere weak man, to men.

You bid me lift my mean desires
    From faltering lips and fitful veins
To sexless souls, ideal quires,[1]
    Unwearied voices, wordless strains:
My mind with fonder welcome owns
One dear dead friend's remembered tones.

Forsooth the present we must give
    To that which cannot pass away;
All beauteous things for which we live
    By laws of time and space decay.
But oh, the very reason why
I clasp them, is because they die.

                                                    1858

Heraclitus[1]

They told me, Heraclitus, they told me you
    were dead,
They brought me bitter news to hear and bitter
    tears to shed.
I wept, as I remembered, how often you and I
Had tired the sun with talking and sent him
    down the sky.

And now that thou art lying, my dear old
    Carian[2] guest,
A handful of grey ashes, long long ago at rest,
Still are thy pleasant voices, thy nightingales,
    awake;
For Death, he taketh all away, but them he
    cannot take.

                                        (1845) 1858

---

[1] Quires: choirs.
[1] Johnson wrote this poem as a model for students who were doing simple Greek translations.
[2] Carian: from a region in southwest Asia Minor.

Charles Tennyson Turner

1808–1879

Charles Tennyson Turner was an elder brother of Alfred Tennyson. He entered Cambridge with Alfred in 1827, and in the same year published some of his poems along with his brother in Poems by Two Brothers *(a third brother, Frederick, also contributed to this volume). After his graduation in 1832, he was ordained and was appointed to a curacy in his native district of Lincolnshire in 1835. He had published a volume of sonnets in 1830, but illness and a consequent addiction to opium severely disrupted his life throughout much of the 1830s and 1840s. He assumed the surname of Turner upon the death of a relative from whom he inherited some property in 1835, and late in the 1840s he settled to a diligent conduct of his pastoral duties which continued for the rest of his life. He published a collection of nearly one hundred of his sonnets in 1864, another volume of verse in 1868, and an enlarged collection of* Sonnets, Lyrics, and Translations *in 1873. His sonnets were collected in one edition in 1880, from which the texts printed here are taken. An account of his boyhood and young manhood is included in Charles Tennyson's "The Somersby Tennysons,"* Victorian Studies, **7** *(1963), Christmas supplement.*

The Lion's Skeleton

How long, O lion, hast thou fleshless lain?
What wrapt thy fierce and thirsty eyes away?
First came the vulture: worms, heat, wind, and
   rain
Ensued, and ardors of the tropic day.
I know not—if they spared it thee—how long
The canker sate within thy monstrous mane,

Till it fell piecemeal and bestrewed the plain;
Or, shredded by the storming sands, was flung
Again to earth; but now thine ample front,
Whereon the great frowns gather'd, is laid
   bare;   10
The thunders of thy throat, which erst were
   wont
To scare the desert, are no longer there;
The claws remain, but worms, wind, rain, and
   heat
Have sifted out the substance of thy feet.

                   1864

The Steam Threshing Machine

With the Straw Carrier [1]

Did any seer of ancient time forbode
This mighty engine, which we daily see
Accepting our full harvests, like a god,
With clouds about his shoulders,—it might be
Some poet-husbandman, some lord of verse,
Old Hesiod, or the wizard Mantuan [2]
Who catalogued in rich hexameters,
The Rake, the Roller, and the mystic Van:
Or else some priest of Ceres, [3] it might seem,
Who witness'd, as he trod the silent fane, [4]   10
The notes and auguries of coming change,
Of other ministrants in shrine and grange,—
The sweating statue, and her sacred wain [5]
Low-booming with the prophecy of steam!

                   1868

---

[1] This is the second of two connected sonnets on the subject.

[2] Hesiod: an eighth-century B.C. Greek poet who wrote an account of the creation of the gods and the world; tradition has it that he worked as a farmer. The wizard Mantuan is Baptista Spagnuoli (1448–1516), who wrote eclogues in Latin which were commonly used as textbooks in Elizabethan schools in England.

[3] Ceres: the god of growing things, in classical mythology.

[4] Fane: temple.   [5] Wain: wagon.

The White Horse of Westbury[1]

As from the Dorset shore I travell'd home,
I saw the charger of the Wiltshire wold;
A far-seen figure, stately to behold,
Whose groom the shepherd is, the hoe his
  comb;
His wizard-spell even sober daylight own'd;
That night I dream'd him into living will;
He neigh'd—and, straight, the chalk pour'd
  down the hill;
He shook himself, and all beneath was stoned;
Hengist and Horsa shouted o'er my sleep,
Like fierce Achilles;[2] while that storm-blanch'd
10 horse
Sprang to the van of all the Saxon force,
And push'd the Britons to the Western deep;
Then, dream-wise, as it were a thing of course,
He floated upwards, and regain'd the steep.[3]

1868

A Country Dance

He has not woo'd, but he has lost his heart.
That country dance is a sore test for him;
He thinks her cold; his hopes are faint and
  dim;
But though with seeming mirth she takes her
  part
In all the dances and the laughter there,
And though to many a youth, on brief demand,
She gives a kind assent and courteous hand,
She loves but him, for him is all her care.
With jealous heed her lessening voice he hears
Down that long vista, where she seems to move   10
Among fond faces and relays of love,
And sweet occasion, full of tender fears:
Down those long lines he watches from above,
Till with the refluent dance she reappears.

1880

John Byrne Leicester Warren, Third Baron de Tabley

1835–1895

Lord de Tabley graduated from Oxford in 1859, after spending much of his childhood on the Continent. He briefly served in a diplomatic post in Constantinople, and was called to the bar in 1860 but never practiced law. He lived for most of his mature life in London, studying and publishing monographs on Greek coins, two novels, and a dozen volumes of verse and verse tragedies which he sometimes published under the pseudonyms of G. F. Preston and William Lancaster. Not a single copy was sold of a verse tragedy, The Soldier of Fortune, which he published in 1876, and he published no more new volumes of poetry during his lifetime. But the inclusion of some of his poems in

A. H. Miles' collection, The Poets and Poetry of the Century (1891–97), created an interest in his writing, especially in some of the long dramatic monologues for which he was best known at the end of the century. He published two selections of Poems Dramatic and Lyrical in 1893 and 1895. The texts printed here are those of these two volumes.

Circe[1]

This is the house of Circe, queen of charms—
A kind of beacon-cauldron poised on high,
Hooped round with ember-clasping iron bars,

---

[1] White Horse of Westbury: the figure of a horse is cut into a hill in the west of England; the turf has been removed so that the chalky rock beneath the soil is exposed. The figure predates the settling of England by the Saxons in the fifth century.
[2] Hengist and Horsa: brothers who led the Saxon invasion of England in the fifth century. Achilles was a warrior hero of the Trojan War.
[3] Steep: hill.
[1] Circe: a magician in Homer's *Odyssey*, and in classical mythology, who turns men into beasts.

Sways in her palace porch, and smoulderingly
Drips out in blots of fire and ruddy stars;
But out behind that trembling furnace air,
The lands are ripe and fair,
Hush are the hills and quiet to the eye.
The river's reach goes by
With lamb and holy tower and squares of
  corn,²
And shelving interspace
Of holly bush and thorn,
And hamlets happy in an Alpine morn,
And deep-bowered lanes with grace
Of woodbine newly born.

But inward o'er the hearth a torch-head stands
Inverted, slow green flames of fulvous hue,
Echoed in wave-like shadows over her.
A censer's swing-chain set in her fair hands
Dances up wreaths of intertwisted blue
In clouds of fragrant frankincense and myrrh.
A giant tulip head and two pale leaves
Grew in the midmost of her chamber there,
A flaunting bloom, naked and undivine,
Rigid and bare,
Gaunt as a tawny bond-girl born to shame,
With freckled cheeks and splotched side
  serpentine,
A gipsy among flowers,
Unmeet for bed or bowers,
Virginal where pure-handed damsels sleep:
Let it not breathe a common air with them,
Lest when the night is deep,
And all things have their quiet in the moon,
Some birth of poison from its leaning stem
Waft in between their slumber-parted lips,
And they cry out or swoon,
Deeming some vampire sips,
Where riper Love may come for nectar boon!

And near this tulip, reared across a loom,
Hung a fair web of tapestry half done,
Crowding with folds and fancies half the room:
Men eyed as gods and damsels still as stone,
Pressing their brows alone,
In amethystine³ robes,
Or reaching at the polished orchard globes,
Or rubbing parted love-lips on their rind,
While the wind
Sows with sere apple leaves their breast and
  hair.
And all the margin there
Was arabesqued and bordered intricate
With hairy spider things

That catch and clamber,
And salamander in his dripping cave
Satanic ebon-amber;
Blind worm, and asp, and eft⁴ of cumbrous gait,
And toads who love rank grasses near a grave,
And the great goblin moth, who bears
Between his wings the ruined eyes of death;
And the enamelled sails
Of butterflies, who watch the morning's breath.   60
And many an emerald lizard with quick ears
Asleep in rocky dales.
And for an outer fringe embroidered small,
A ring of many locusts, horny-coated,
A round of chirping tree-frogs merry-throated,
And sly, fat fishes sailing, watching all.

                      1893

The Study of a Spider

From holy flower to holy flower
Thou weavest thine unhallowed bower.
The harmless dewdrops, beaded thin,
Ripple along thy ropes of sin.
Thy house a grave, a gulf thy throne
Affright the fairies every one.
Thy winding sheets are grey and fell,
Imprisoning with nets of hell
The lovely births that winnow by,
Winged sisters of the rainbow sky: 10
Elf-darlings, fluffy, bee-bright things,
And owl-white moths with mealy wings,
And tiny flies, as gauzy thin
As e'er were shut electrum¹ in.
These are thy death spoils, insect ghoul,
With their dear life thy fangs are foul.
Thou felon anchorite of pain
Who sittest in a world of slain.
Hermit, who tunest song unsweet
To heaving wing and writhing feet.   20
A glutton of creation's sighs,
Miser of many miseries.
Toper, whose lonely feasting chair
Sways in inhospitable air.
The board is bare, the bloated host
Drinks to himself toast after toast.
His lip requires no goblet brink,
But like a weasel must he drink.
The vintage is as old as time
And bright as sunset, pressed and prime.   30

Ah, venom mouth and shaggy thighs
And paunch grown sleek with sacrifice,

---

² Corn: grain.   ³ Amethystine: purple.   ⁴ Eft: a small aquatic salamander.
¹ Electrum: amber.

Thy dolphin back and shoulders round
Coarse-hairy, as some goblin hound
Whom a hag rides to sabbath on,
While shuddering stars in fear grow wan.
Thou palace priest of treachery,
Thou type of selfish lechery,
I break the toils around thy head
40   And from their gibbets take thy dead.

                                                    1893

The Knight in the Wood

The thing itself was rough and crudely done,
Cut in coarse stone, spitefully placed aside
As merest lumber, where the light was worst
On a back staircase. Overlooked it lay
In a great Roman palace crammed with art.
It had no number in the list of gems,
Weeded away long since, pushed out and
   banished,
Before insipid Guidos over-sweet
And Dolce's rose sensationalities,[1]
10   And curly chirping angels spruce as birds.
And yet the motive of this thing ill-hewn
And hardly seen *did* touch me. O, indeed,
The skill-less hand that carved it had belonged
To a most yearning and bewildered brain:
There was such desolation in the work;
And through its utter failure the thing spoke
With more of human message, heart to heart.

Than all these faultless, smirking, skin-deep
   saints,
In artificial troubles picturesque,
And martyred sweetly, not one curl awry—   20
Listen; a clumsy knight, who rode alone
Upon a stumbling jade in a great wood
Belated. The poor beast with head low-bowed
Snuffing the treacherous ground. The rider
   leant
Forward to sound the marish[2] with his lance.
You saw the place was deadly; that doomed
   pair,
The wretched rider and the hide-bound steed,
Feared to advance, feared to return—That's
   all!
                                                    1893

The Power of Interval

A fair girl tripping out to meet her love,
Trimmed in her best, fresh as a clover bud.
An old crone leaning at an ember'd fire,
Short-breath'd in sighs and moaning to
   herself—
And all the interval of stealing years
To make that this, and one by one detach
Some excellent condition; till Despair
Faint at the vision, sadly, fiercely blinds
Her burning eyes on her forgetful hands.
                                                    1893

Richard Watson Dixon

1833–1900

Richard Watson Dixon was the son of a clergy-man. Dixon was at Oxford with Edward Burne-Jones (1833–98) and William Morris, helped to put out the Oxford and Cambridge Magazine *which contained some of Morris' early writing, and helped too in the decoration of a new building in Oxford which was directed by Dante Gabriel Rossetti. Dixon graduated in 1857, was ordained in the Church of England in the following year, and began a long series of ecclesiastical appointments, mostly in the north of England, which extended through the rest of his life. He maintained his interest in the work*

[1] Guido: probably Guido Reni (c. 1574–1642), who painted highly finished pictures of saints.
Dolce: Carlo Dolce (1616–1686), a Florentine painter whose work was also mannered and senti-mental.
[2] Marish: marsh.

of the writers and painters he knew at Oxford, and he won the interest of Gerard Manley Hopkins and others with his own poetry, which he began to publish in 1861. The principal labor of his life was a History of the Church of England from the Abolition of the Roman Jurisdiction, published in six volumes between 1878 and 1902. He published five volumes of verse during his lifetime, and Robert Bridges published an edition of his Songs and Odes in 1896 and some late poems in 1905. Bridges also published a selection of Dixon's poems in 1909; the texts printed here are those of Bridges' selected edition. J. A. Sambrook published a biography of Dixon, The Poet Hidden, in 1962.

Dream

I

With camel's hair I clothed my skin,
   I fed my mouth with honey wild;
And set me scarlet wool to spin,
   And all my breast with hyssop[1] filled;
Upon my brow and cheeks and chin
   A bird's blood spilled.

I took a broken reed to hold,
   I took a sponge of gall to press;
I took weak water-weeds to fold
   About my sacrifical dress.

I took the grasses of the field,
   The flax was bolled upon my crine;[2]
And ivy thorn and wild grapes healed
   To make good wine.

I took my scrip[3] of manna sweet,
   My cruse of water did I bless;
I took the white dove by the feet,
   And flew into the wilderness.

II

The tiger came and played;
Uprose the lion in his mane;
The jackal's tawny nose
And sanguine dripping tongue
Out of the desert rose
And plunged its sands among;
The bear came striding o'er the desert plain.

Uprose the horn and eyes
And quivering flank of the great unicorn,
And galloped round and round;
Uprose the gleaming claw
Of the leviathan,[4] and wound   30
In steadfast march did draw
Its course away beyond the desert's bourn.
I stood within a maze
Woven round about me by a magic art,
And ordered circle-wise:
The bear more near did tread,
And with two fiery eyes,
And with a wolfish head,
Did close the circle round in every part.

III

With scarlet corded horn,   40
With frail wrecked knees and stumbling pace,
The scapegoat came:[5]
His eyes took flesh and spirit dread in flame
At once, and he died looking towards my face.

                             1861

The Wizard's Funeral

For me, for me, two horses wait,
Two horses stand before my gate:
Their vast black plumes on high are cast,
Their black manes swing in the midnight blast,
Red sparkles from their eyes fly fast.
But can they drag the hearse behind,
Whose black plumes mystify the wind?
What a thing for this heap of bones and hair!
Despair, despair!
Yet think of half the world's winged shapes   10
Which have come to thee wondering:
At thee the terrible idiot gapes,
At thee the running devil japes,
And angels stoop to thee and sing
From the soft midnight that enwraps
Their limbs, so gently, sadly fair;—
Thou seest the stars shine through their hair.
The blast again, ho, ho, the blast!
I go to a mansion that shall outlast;
And the stoled priest who steps before   20
Shall turn and welcome me at the door.

                             1861

---

[1] Hyssop: an aromatic herb.   [2] Crine: hair.   [3] Scrip: scrap.

[4] Leviathan: usually an aquatic monster, often associated with Satan.

[5] Scapegoat: Holman Hunt (1827–1910), one of the Pre-Raphaelite circle of painters to which Dixon's friend Burne-Jones also belonged, exhibited in 1856 a painting of *The Scapegoat* dying in a desert which became immediately famous for its stark lines and strong coloring.

Song

Oh, bid my tongue be still,
  Oh, bid mine eyes be dry:
And I will force them till
  They seem to mean a lie.

But bid me not forget:
  Thought is nor tongue nor eye:
Or, if thou bid me yet,
  Then dost thou bid me die.

1909

Jean Ingelow
1820–1897

Jean Ingelow was the daughter of a banker in Lincolnshire. She published a book of poems in 1850, a novel in the following year, and another collection of prose tales in 1860, none of which attracted unusual attention. Then in 1863 she published Poems, *a collection that was immediately and strongly popular; it went through four editions in its first year, and twenty-three editions by 1879. "Divided" was the first poem in this volume, and its highly colored imagery and parabolic structure were widely admired, even by Charles Stuart Calverley, who parodied the poem (see* Part Seven*). Ingelow moved to London and began to earn a comfortable living as a writer. She wrote and published novels and collections of stories, contributed fiction and poems to magazines, and published several more volumes of verse, including a two-volume collection (with additions) of all her poems in 1880 and* Poems: Third Series *in 1885. The text printed here is that of the Oxford edition of her poems (1913).*

Divided

I
An empty sky, a world of heather,
  Purple of foxglove, yellow of broom;
We two among them, wading together,
  Shaking out honey, treading perfume.

Crowds of bees are giddy with clover,
  Crowds of grasshoppers skip at our feet,
Crowds of larks at their matins hang over,
  Thanking the Lord for a life so sweet.

Flusheth the rise with her purple favour,
  Gloweth the cleft with her golden ring,
'Twixt the two brown butterflies waver,
  Lightly settle, and sleepily swing.

We two walk till the purple dieth
  And short dry grass under foot is brown;
But one little streak at a distance lieth
  Green like a ribbon to prank[1] the down.

II
Over the grass we stepped unto it,
  And God He knoweth how blithe we were!
Never a voice to bid us eschew it:
  Hey the green ribbon that showed so fair!

Hey the green ribbon! we kneeled beside it,
  We parted the grasses dewy and sheen;
Drop over drop there filtered and slided
  A tiny bright beck[2] that trickled between.

Tinkle, tinkle, sweetly it sung to us,
  Light was our talk as of faëry bells—
Faëry wedding-bells faintly rung to us
  Down in their fortunate parallels.

Hand in hand, while the sun peered over,
  We lapped the grass on that youngling
    spring;
Swept back its rushes, smoothed its clover,
  And said, "Let us follow it westering."

---

[1] Prank: decorate, spangle.   [2] Beck: brook or stream.

III

A dappled sky, a world of meadows,
  Circling above us the black rooks[3] fly
Forward, backward; lo, their dark shadows
  Flit on the blossoming tapestry—

Flit on the beck, for her long grass parteth
  As hair from a maid's bright eyes blown
      back:
And, lo, the sun like a lover darteth
  His flattering smile on her wayward track.

Sing on! we sing in the glorious weather
  Till one steps over the tiny strand,
So narrow, in sooth, that still together
  On either brink we go hand in hand.

The beck grows wider, the hands must sever.
  On either margin, our songs all done,
We move apart, while she singeth ever,
  Taking the course of the stooping sun.

He prays, "Come over"—I may not follow;
  I cry, "Return"—but he cannot come:
We speak, we laugh, but with voices hollow;
  Our hands are hanging, our hearts are numb.

IV

A breathing sigh, a sigh for answer,
  A little talking of outward things:
The careless beck is a merry dancer,
  Keeping sweet time to the air she sings.

A little pain when the beck grows wider;
  "Cross to me now—for her wavelets swell,"
"I may not cross"—and the voice beside her
  Faintly reacheth, though heeded well.

No backward path; ah! no returning;
  No second crossing that ripple's flow:
"Come to me now, for the west is burning
  Come ere it darkens;" "Ah, no! ah, no!"

Then cries of pain, and arms outreaching—
  The beck grows wider and swift and deep:
Passionate words as of one beseeching—
  The loud beck drowns them; we walk, and
      weep.

V

A yellow moon in splendour drooping,
  A tired queen with her state oppressed,

Low by rushes and swordgrass stooping,
  Lies she soft on the waves at rest.

The desert heavens have felt her sadness;
  Her earth will weep her some dewy tears;
The wild beck ends her tune of gladness,
  And goeth stilly as soul that fears.

We two walk on in our grassy places
  On either marge of the moonlit flood,
With the moon's own sadness in our faces,
  Where joy is withered, blossom and bud.   80

VI

A shady freshness, chafers whirring,
  A little piping of leaf-hid birds;
A flutter of wings, a fitful stirring,
  A cloud to the eastward snowy as curds.

Bare grassy slopes, where kids are tethered;
  Round valleys like nests all ferny lined;
Round hills, with fluttering tree-tops feathered,
  Swell high in their freckled robes behind.

A rose-flush tender, a thrill, a quiver,
  When golden gleams to the tree-tops glide;   90
A flashing edge for the milk-white river,
  The beck, a river—with still sleek tide.

Broad and white, and polished as silver,
  On she goes under fruit-laden trees
Sunk in leafage cooeth the culver,[4]
  And 'plaineth of love's disloyalties.

Glitters the dew and shines the river,
  Up comes the lily and dries her bell;
But two are walking apart for ever,
  And wave their hands for a mute farewell.   100

VII

A braver swell, a swifter sliding;
  The river hasteth, her banks recede:
Wing-like sails on her bosom gliding
  Bear down the lily and drown the reed.

Stately prows are rising and bowing
  (Shouts of mariners winnow the air) ,
And level sands for banks endowing
  The tiny green ribbon that showed so fair.

While, O my heart! as white sails shiver,
  And crowds are passing, and banks stretch
    wide   110

---

[3] Rooks: crows.   [4] Culver: dove.

How hard to follow, with lips that quiver,
  That moving speck on the far-off side!

Farther, farther—I see it—know it—
  My eyes brim over, it melts away:
Only my heart to my heart shall show it
  As I walk desolate day by day.

        VIII
And yet I know past all doubting, truly—
  A knowledge greater than grief can dim—

I know, as he loved, he will love me duly—
  Yea, better—e'en better than I love him.

And as I walk by the vast calm river,
  The awful river so dread to see,
I say "Thy breadth and thy depth for ever
  Are bridged by his thoughts that cross to
    me."

                                        1863

Joseph Skipsey
1832–1903

Joseph Skipsey, the son of a miner in the north of England, went to work in the mines when he was seven years old. He taught himself to read and write, and as a young man went to London for a while and worked in the construction of a railway. But he returned to the north, sometimes working in the mines, more often working in a string of marginally paid but genteel jobs: sublibrarian to a literary society in Newcastle-on-Tyne, caretaker of some schools in Newcastle, custodian (with his wife) of Shakespeare's birthplace. He first left the mines when he published some of his poems in a volume in 1859. He published two other volumes in the 1860s, and finally won the attention of London literary critics with a collection of Poems *in 1871. A* Book of Miscellaneous Lyrics *(1878) brought him the esteem and acquaintance of Dante Gabriel Rossetti and others associated with the Pre-Raphaelite school. He published two more volumes of poems, including an edition in 1892 in which he collected many of his previously published poems. Skipsey often in his late verse especially used the fanciful conceptions and decorated language of the kind of poetry which was popular in the middle and late decades of the Victorian period. But at his best his poetry is marked by a simplicity of event and a just, sure use of ordinary language which also pleased one of the tastes of decades dominated by poets like, or trying to be like, Swinburne. The texts printed below are those of* Songs and Lyrics, *the collection of old and new verse Skipsey published in 1892.*

Willy to Jinny

Duskier than the clouds that lie
  'Tween the coal-pit and the sky,
Lo, how Willy whistles by
    Right cheery from the colliree.

Duskier might the laddie be,
Save his coaxing coal-black e'e,
Nothing dark could Jinny see
    A-coming from the colliree.

                                        1892

"Get Up!"

"Get up!" the caller calls, "Get up!"
  And in the dead of night,
To win the bairns their bite and sup,
  I rise a weary wight.

My flannel dudden[1] donn'd, thrice o'er
  My birds are kiss'd, and then

---

[1] Dudden: clothes.

I with a whistle shut the door,
   I may not ope again.

1892

Mother Wept

Mother wept, and father sighed;
   With delight a-glow
Cried the lad, "To-morrow," cried,
   "To the pit I go."

Up and down the place he sped,—
   Greeted old and young;
Far and wide the tidings spread;
   Clapt his hands and sung.

Came his cronies; some to gaze
10   Wrapt in wonder; some
Free with counsel; some with praise;
   Some with envy dumb.

"May he," many a gossip cried,
   "Be from peril kept."
Father hid his face and sighed,
   Mother turned and wept.

1892

A Golden Lot

In the coal-pit, or the factory,
   I toil by night and day,
And still to the music of labour
   I lilt my heart-felt lay;

I lilt my heart-felt lay—
   And the gloom of the deep, deep mine,
Or the din of the factory dieth away,
   And a Golden Lot is mine.

1892

The Time Hath Been

The time hath been when they have laugh'd
   And danced, like them she laugh'd and
      danced;
That was ere his sweet vows she quaft,
   And wore the wreath, her heart entranced.

Those vows she proved a poison'd draught;
   That wreath a poison'd anadem;[1]
And next when danced the rest and laugh'd,
   She laugh'd and danced—but not like them.

1892

Francis Hastings Doyle
1810–1888

Sir Francis Hastings Doyle, who succeeded to a baronetcy in 1839, was born into a family of military distinction. Doyle graduated from Oxford in 1832, and was admitted to the practice of law in 1837. For most of his life he worked as a government official; he was first Receiver-General of Customs and then Commissioner of Customs. He published a volume of poems in 1834, which he enlarged and reissued in 1840. He also published a translation of Sophocles' Oedipus Rex in 1849, a poem on the funeral of the Duke of Wellington in 1852, and two other poems in volume form around the turn of the half-century. He was not well known as a poet, however, when in the mid-1860s he de-cided that he would like to succeed Matthew Arnold as Professor of Poetry at Oxford. He therefore collected the best of his early poems, added some new ones—including the immediately popular "The Private of the Buffs"—to them, and published The Return of the Guards and Other Poems in 1866. He was elected to the professorship at Oxford, and he published two series of his lectures on poetry, one in 1868 and the second in 1877, the year in which the second of his five-year appointments as professor of poetry expired. Doyle also published an autobiography in 1886. The text printed here is that of his 1866 volume.

[1] Anadem: a literary word for wreath, or a band to tie up hair.

The Private of the Buffs

"Some Sikhs, and a private of the Buffs[1] having remained behind with the grog-carts, fell into the hands of the Chinese. On the next morning they were brought before the authorities, and commanded to perform the *kotou*. The Sikhs obeyed; but Moyse, the English soldier, declaring that he would not prostrate himself before any Chinaman alive, was immediately knocked upon the head, and his body thrown on a dung-hill."—*See China Correspondent of the "Times."*

Last night, among his fellow roughs,
  He jested, quaffed, and swore;
A drunken private of the Buffs,
  Who never looked before.
To-day, beneath the foeman's frown,
  He stands in Elgin's[2] place,
Ambassador from Britain's crown,
  And type of all her race.

Poor, reckless, rude, low-born, untaught,
  Bewildered, and alone,
A heart, with English instinct fraught,
  He yet can call his own.
Ay, tear his body limb from limb,
  Bring cord, or axe, or flame:
He only knows, that not through *him*
  Shall England come to shame.

Far Kentish hop-fields round him seem'd,
  Like dreams, to come and go;
Bright leagues of cherry-blossom gleam'd,
  One sheet of living snow;
The smoke, above his father's door,
  In grey soft eddyings hung:
Must he then watch it rise no more,
  Doom'd by himself, so young?

Yes, honour calls!—with strength like steel
  He put the vision by.
Let dusky Indians whine and kneel;
  An English lad must die.
And thus, with eyes that would not shrink,
  With knee to man unbent,
Unfaltering on its dreadful brink,
  To his red grave he went.

Vain, mightiest fleets, of iron framed;
  Vain, those all-shattering guns;
Unless proud England keep, untamed,
  The strong heart of her sons.
So, let his name through Europe ring—
  A man of mean estate,
Who died, as firm as Sparta's king,
  Because his soul was great.

1866

William Bell Scott
1811–1890

William Bell Scott was best known in his lifetime as a painter in the highly decorated style and of the historical and legendary subjects associated with Dante Gabriel Rossetti and the Pre-Raphalites. Scott was born in Edinburgh, the son of an engraver, and he studied painting in Edinburgh and London. He began to publish poems in magazines in Edinburgh in the 1830s, and he also published two relatively long philosophical poems in Edinburgh in 1838 and 1846. For most of the 1830s and early 1840s he was painting, latterly in London, and in 1843 he accepted a commission to organize government art schools in the north of England. He spent the rest of his life in the north, frequently visiting London and friends and associates such as Swinburne and the Rossettis. He published volumes of poetry in 1854 and 1875; the latter volume is his own selection, with some additions (including "The Witch's Ballad"), from all his poetry to that date. He published a final volume of verse in 1882. Lona Mosk Packer's Christina Rossetti *(1963) contains a good deal of biographical infor-*

---

[1] Sikhs: Indian troops. The Buffs were an old, famous regiment from Kent.
[2] Elgin's place: James Bruce, eighth Earl of Elgin, was envoy to China in 1857 and 1860–61.

mation about Scott's mature life, useful even though it is presented to support a doubtful claim that Scott was Christina Rossetti's lover. The text printed below is that of the 1875 edition of Scott's Poems.

The Witch's Ballad

O, I hae come from far away,
  From a warm land far away,
A southern land across the sea,
With sailor-lads about the mast,
Merry and canny, and kind to me.

And I hae been to yon town
  To try my luck in yon town;
Nort, and Mysie, Elspie too.
Right braw[1] we were to pass the gate,
10 Wi' gowden clasps on girdles blue.

Mysie smiled wi' miminy[2] mouth,
  Innocent mouth, miminy mouth;
Elspie wore her scarlet gown,
Nort's grey eyes were unco' gleg,[3]
My Castile comb was like a crown.

We walked abreast all up the street,
  Into the market up the street;
Our hair with marigolds was wound,
Our bodices with love-knots[4] laced,
20 Our merchandise with tansy[5] bound.

Nort had chickens, I had cocks,
  Gamesome cocks, loud-crowing cocks;
Mysie ducks, and Elspie drakes,—
For a wee groat[6] or a pound;
We lost nae time wi' gives and takes.

Lost nae time, for well we knew,
  In our sleeves full well we knew,
When the gloaming came that night,
Duck nor drake nor hen nor cock
30 Would be found by candle-light.

And when our chaffering all was done,
  All was paid for, sold and done,
We drew a glove on ilka[7] hand,

We sweetly curtsied each to each,
And deftly danced a saraband.

The market-lasses looked and laughed,
  Left their gear and looked and laughed;
They made as they would join the game,
But soon their mithers, wild and wud,[8]   40
With whack and screech they stopped the same.

Sae loud the tongues o' randies grew,
  The flitin' and the skirlin'[9] grew,
At all the windows in the place,
Wi' spoons or knives, wi' needle or awl,
Was thrust out every hand and face.

And down each stair they thronged anon,
  Gentle, semple,[10] thronged anon;
Souter[11] and tailor, frowsy Nan,
The ancient widow young again,
Simpering behind her fan.   50

Without a choice, against their will,
  Doited,[12] dazed, against their will,
The market lassie and her mither,
The farmer and his husbandman,
Hand in hand dance a' thegether.

Slow at first, but faster soon,
  Still increasing wild and fast,
Hoods and mantles, hats and hose,
Blindly doffed and cast away,
Left them naked, heads and toes.   60

They would have torn us limb from limb,
  Dainty limb from dainty limb;
But never one of them could win
Across the line that I had drawn
With bleeding thumb a-widdershin.[13]

But there was Jeff the provost's[14] son,
  Jeff the provost's only son;
There was Father Auld himsel',
The Lombard[15] frae the hostelry,
And the lawyer Peter Fell.   70

All goodly men we singled out,
  Waled[16] them well, and singled out,

[1] Braw: fine, handsome.   [2] Miminy: prim.   [3] Unco' gleg: very sharp, clever.
[4] Love-knots: laces tied in a peculiar way.   [5] Tansy: a plant with a sharp aromatic scent.
[6] Groat: a small sum of money.   [7] Ilka: each.   [8] Wud: mad.
[9] Randies: frolics. Flitin' and skirlin': shrill, contentious noises.
[10] Semple: simple, foolish.   [11] Souter: shoemaker.
[12] Doited: stupified.   [13] A-widdershin: opposite.   [14] Provost: Scottish name for mayor.
[15] Lombard: people from Lombardy were popularly associated with the business of banking.
[16] Waled: chose.

And drew them by the left hand in;
Mysie the priest, and Elspie won
The Lombard, Nort the lawyer carle,[17]
I mysel' the provost's son.

Then, with cantrip[18] kisses seven,
    Three times round with kisses seven,
Warped and woven there spun we,
Arms and legs and flaming hair,
80 Like a whirlwind on the sea.

Like a wind that sucks the sea,
    Over and in and on the sea,
Good sooth it was a mad delight;
And every man of all the four
Shut his eyes and laughed outright.

Laughed as long as they had breath,
    Laughed while they had sense or breath;
And close about us coiled a mist
Of gnats and midges, wasps and flies,
90 Like the whirlwind shaft it rist.

Drawn up I was right off my feet,
    Into the mist and off my feet;
And, dancing on each chimney-top,
I saw a thousand darling imps
Keeping time with skip and hop.

And on the provost's brave ridge-tile,
    On the provost's grand ridge-tile,
The Blackamoor first to master me
I saw,—I saw that winsome smile,
The mouth that did my heart beguile,
And spoke the great Word over me,
100 In the land beyond the sea.

I called his name, I called aloud,
    Alas! I called on him aloud;
And then he filled his hand with stour,[19]

And threw it towards me in the air;
My mouse flew out,[20] I lost my pow'r!

My lusty strength, my power, were gone;
    Power was gone, and all was gone.
He will not let me love him more!
Of bell and whip and horse's tail[21]
He cares not if I find a store.   110

But I am proud if he is fierce!
    I am as proud as he is fierce;
I'll turn about and backward go,
If I meet again that Blackamoor,
And he'll help us then, for he shall know
I seek another paramour.

And we'll gang once more to yon town,
    Wi' better luck to yon town;
We'll walk in silk and cramoisie,[22]
And I shall wed the provost's son;
My-lady of the town I'll be!   120

For I was born a crowned king's child,
    Born and nursed a king's child,
King o' a land ayont the sea,
Where the Blackamoor kissed me first,
And taught me art and glamourie.[23]

Each one in her wame[24] shall hide
    Her hairy mouse, her wary mouse,
Fed on madwort and agramie,[25]
Wear amber beads between her breasts,
And blind-worm's skin about her knee.   130

The Lombard shall be Elspie's man,
    Elspie's gowden husband-man;
Nort shall take the lawyer's hand;
The priest shall swear another vow:
We'll dance again the saraband!

                                                               1875

---

[17] Carle: fellow, with connotations of low or mean fellow.
[18] Cantrip: magical, as in a spell.   [19] Stour: flying dust.
[20] My mouse flew out: in folklore the soul is often supposed to leave the body in the shape of a mouse or some other small animal.
[21] Bell and whip and horse's tail: instruments of exorcism.
[22] Cramoisie: crimson cloth.   [23] Glamourie: magic.   [24] Wame: belly.
[25] Madwort and agramie: herbs, the first supposed to cure anger and the bite of mad dogs.

Thomas Gordon Hake

1809–1895

Thomas Gordon Hake was a physician who studied medicine in Edinburgh, Glasgow, and Paris and finally settled to practice near London. He published two volumes of verse early in his life, including a tragedy whose subject matter was the mysteries of the Egyptian goddess Isis, and he also published Vates *(1840), a disquisition on the philosophy of madness. His interest in his own poetic talent was stimulated again when he met and began to treat Dante Gabriel Rossetti as a patient in the 1860s. He published four volumes of poems in the 1870s, each of which, as Hake's biographer in the* Dictionary of National Biography *puts it, "wanted every quality of popularity." He published three more volumes during his lifetime, including a collection of sonnets in 1890, and he won a small reputation as a poet with strong and curious gifts for fable and odd, entrancing settings and situations. He also published some novels and his* Memoirs *(1892). A selection from his poems was edited by Alice Meynell in 1894. The text printed below is that of* New Symbols, *a collection he published in 1876.*

The Snake-Charmer

I

The forest rears on lifted arms
    Its leafy dome, whence verdurous light
Shakes through the shady depths and warms
    Proud tree and stealthy parasite,
There where those cruel coils enclasp
The trunks they strangle in their grasp.

II

An old man creeps from out the woods,
    Breaking the vine's entangling spell;
He thrids[1] the jungle's solitudes
    O'er bamboos rotting where they fell;
Slow down the tiger's path he wends
Where at the pool the jungle ends.

III

No moss-greened alley tells the trace
    Of his lone step, no sound is stirred,

Even when his tawny hands displace
    The boughs, that backward sweep unheard:
His way as noiseless as the trail
Of the swift snake and pilgrim snail.

IV

The old snake-charmer,—once he played
    Soft music for the serpent's ear,   20
But now his cunning hand is stayed;
    He knows the hour of death is near.
And all that live in brake[2] and bough,
All know the brand is on his brow.

V

Yet where his soul is he must go:
    He crawls along from tree to tree.
The old snake-charmer, doth he know
    If snake or beast of prey he be?
Bewildered at the pool he lies
And sees as through a serpent's eyes.   30

VI

Weeds wove with white-flowered lily crops
    Drink of the pool, and serpents hie
To the thin brink as noonday drops,
    And in the froth-daubed rushes lie.
There rests he now with fastened breath
'Neath a kind sun to bask in death.

VII

The pool is bright with glossy dyes
    And cast-up bubbles of decay:
A green death-leaven overlies
    Its mottled scum, where shadows play   40
As the snake's hollow coil, fresh shed,
Rolls in the wind across its bed.

VIII

No more the wily note is heard
    From his full flute—the riving[3] air
That tames the snake, decoys the bird,
    Worries the she-wolf from her lair.

---

[1] Thrids: threads.   [2] Brake: thicket.
[3] Riving: cleaving.

Fain would he bid its parting breath
Drown in his ears the voice of death.

IX

Still doth his soul's vague longing skim
50   The pool beloved: he hears the hiss
That siffles at the sedgy⁴ rim,
     Recalling days of former bliss,
And the death-drops, that fall in showers,
Seem honied dews from shady flowers.

X

There is a rustle of the breeze
     And twitter of the singing bird;
He snatches at the melodies
     And his faint lips again are stirred:
The olden sounds are in his ears;
60   But still the snake its crest uprears.

XI

His eyes are swimming in the mist
     That films the earth like serpent's breath;
And now, as if a serpent hissed,—
     The husky whisperings of Death
Fill ear and brain—he looks around—
Serpents seem matted o'er the ground.

XII

Soon visions of past joys bewitch
     His crafty soul; his hands would set
Death's snare, while now his fingers twitch
70   At tasselled reed as 'twere his net.
But his thin lips no longer fill
The woods with song; his flute is still.

XIII

Those lips still quaver to the flute,
     But fast the life-tide ebbs away;
Those lips now quaver and are mute,
     But nature throbs in breathless play:
Birds are in open song, the snakes
Are watching in the silent brakes.

XIV

In sudden fear of snares unseen
80   The birds like crimson sunset swarm,
All gold and purple, red and green,
     And seek each other for the charm.
Lizards dart up the feathery trees
Like shadows of a rainbow breeze.

XV

The wildered birds again have rushed
     Into the charm,—it is the hour

⁴ Sedgy: covered with marsh plants.

When the shrill forest-note is hushed,
     And they obey the serpent's power,—
Drawn to its gaze with troubled whirr,
As by the thread of falconer.   90

XVI

As 'twere to feed, on slanting wings
     They drop within the serpent's glare:
Eyes flashing fire in burning rings
     Which spread into the dazzled air;
They flutter in the glittering coils;
The charmer dreads the serpent's toils.

XVII

While Music swims away in death
     Man's spell is passing to his slaves:
The snake feeds on the charmer's breath,
     The vulture screams, the parrot raves,   100
The lone hyena laughs and howls,
The tiger from the jungle growls.

XVIII

Then mounts the eagle—flame-flecked folds
     Belt its proud plumes; a feather falls:
He hears the death-cry, he beholds
     The king-bird in the serpent's thralls,
He looks with terror on the feud,—
And the sun shines through dripping blood.

XIX

The deadly spell a moment gone—
     Birds, from a distant Paradise,   110
Strike the winged signal and have flown,
     Trailing rich hues through azure skies:
The serpent falls; like demon wings
The far-out branching cedar swings.

XX

The wood swims round; the pool and skies
     Have met; the death-drops down that cheek
Fall faster; for the serpent's eyes
     Grow human, and the charmer's seek.
A gaze like man's directs the dart
Which now is buried at his heart.   120

XXI

The monarch of the world is cold:
     The charm he bore has passed away:
The serpent gathers up its fold
     To wind about its human prey.
The red mouth darts a dizzy sting,
And clenches the eternal ring.

1876

Austin Dobson
1840–1921

When he was sixteen years old Austin Dobson began to work as a clerk in the Board of Trade, a government agency responsible for the regulation of commerce and industry. He remained in this occupation until his retirement in 1901, rising to a responsible administrative position. In the 1860s he began a second career by publishing literary criticism and poems in magazines. His poems were first collected into a volume, Vignettes in Rhyme, *in 1873. A second collection,* Proverbs in Porcelain, *was published in 1877, and then an extremely popular selection from both volumes was published as* Old World Idylls *in 1883. Dobson had been educated in France, and both as a poet and as a literary critic he helped to create and please a taste for French literature and the graceful artifice of French verse forms. He also was one of the principal sponsors of a late-century taste for the imagined order and grace of eighteenth-century life and letters. He wrote books on Hogarth, Fielding, Steele, Goldsmith, Richardson, and Burney, along with three series of* Eighteenth-Century Vignettes *(1892, 1894, 1896): in all, he edited, wrote, or wrote introductions to about fifty books having to do with eighteenth-century British literature. He published three more volumes of poems before the end of the century, including* The Ballad of Beau Brocade and Other Poems of the XVIIIth Century *(1892). His poetry was first collected in 1897; the texts printed are those of the ninth edition (1920) of his* Collected Poems.

To "Lydia Languish"

'Il me faut des émotions.'—   BLANCHE AMORY.[1]

You ask me, Lydia, "whether I,
If you refuse my suit, shall die."

(Now pray don't let this hurt you!)
Although the time be out of joint,
I should not think a bodkin's point[2]
   The sole resource of virtue;
Nor shall I, though your mood endure,
Attempt a final Water-cure
   Except against my wishes;
For I respectfully decline   10
To dignify the Serpentine,[3]
   And make *hors-d'œuvres* for fishes;
But if you ask me whether I
   Composedly can go,
Without a look, without a sigh,
   Why, then I answer—No.

"You are assured," you sadly say
(If in this most considerate way
   To treat my suit your will is),
That I shall "quickly find as fair   20
Some new Neæra's tangled hair—
   Some easier Amaryllis."[4]
I cannot promise to be cold
If smiles are kind as yours of old
   On lips of later beauties;
Nor can I, if I would, forget
The homage that is Nature's debt,
   While man has social duties;
But if you ask shall I prefer
   To you I honour so,
A somewhat visionary Her,   30
   I answer truly—No.

You fear, you frankly add, "to find
In me too late the altered mind
   That altering Time estranges."

---

[1] Lydia Languish is a character in *The Rivals* (1775), a play by Richard Brinsley Sheridan (1751–1816), who is addicted to sensationally romantic fiction. Blanche Amory is a shallow young woman in *Pendennis* (1858–50), by William Makepeace Thackeray (1811–63). Her epigraph: "I need emotions."

[2] Bodkin: dagger: one of the ways in which Hamlet contemplates suicide in Shakespeare's play (III, i).

[3] Serpentine: an artificial body of water in London's Hyde Park.

[4] Neæra; Amaryllis: conventional names of young women in pastoral poetry. Dobson's allusion here is directly to Milton's "Lycidas" ("To sport with Amaryllis in the shade,/Or with the tangles of Neæra's hair"); Milton in turn takes the names over from classical pastoral poetry.

To this I make response that we
  (As physiologists agree)
    Must have septennial changes;
This is a thing beyond control,
40 And it were best upon the whole
    To try and find out whether
We could not, by some means, arrange
This not-to-be-avoided change
    So as to change together:
But, had you asked me to allow
  That you could ever grow
Less amiable than you are now,—
    Emphatically—No.

But—to be serious—if you care
50 To know how I shall really bear
    This much-discussed rejection,
I answer you. As feeling men
Behave, in best romances, when
    You outrage their affection;—
With that gesticulatory woe,
By which, as melodramas show,
    Despair is indicated;
Enforced by all the liquid grief
Which hugest pocket-handkerchief
60   Has ever simulated;
And when, arrived so far, you say
  In tragic accents "Go,"
Then, Lydia, then . . . I still shall stay,
    And firmly answer—No.

                  1872; 1873

Ars Victrix

    (Imitated from Théophile Gautier) [1]
YES; when the ways oppose—
  When the hard means rebel,
Fairer the work out-grows,—
  More potent far the spell.

O POET, then, forbear
  The loosely-sandalled verse,
Choose rather thou to wear
  The buskin—strait and terse; [2]

Leave to the tyro's [3] hand
  The limp and shapeless style,   10
See that thy form demand
  The labour of the file.

SCULPTOR, do thou discard
  The yielding clay,—consign
To Paros marble hard [4]
  The beauty of thy line;—

Model thy Satyr's face
  For bronze of Syracuse; [5]
In the veined agate trace
  The profile of thy Muse.   20

PAINTER, that still must mix
  But transient tints anew,
Thou in the furnace fix
  The firm enamel's hue;

Let the smooth tile receive
  Thy dove-drawn Erycine; [6]
Thy Sirens [7] blue at eve
  Coiled in a wash of wine.

All passes. ART alone
  Enduring stays to us;   30
The Bust outlasts the throne,—
  The Coin, Tiberius. [8]

Even the gods must go;
  Only the lofty Rhyme
Not countless years o'erthrow,—
  Not long array of time.

Paint, chisel, then, or write;
  But, that the work surpass,
With the hard fashion fight,—
  With the resisting mass.   40

                  1876; 1877

---

[1] An imitation of "L'Art" by the French poet Théophile Gautier (1811–72).
[2] Loosely-sandalled; buskin: footwear worn by Greek actors in comedy and tragedy respectively.
[3] Tyro: beginner.   [4] Paros: an island in the Aegean famous for its white marble.
[5] Syracuse: the site of an early Greek colony in Sicily.
[6] Erycine: a name for Venus, goddess of love in classical mythology, whose chariot was drawn by doves.
[7] Sirens: women who in classical legend (and in Homer's *Odyssey*) lured mariners to shipwreck and death by alluring song.
[8] Tiberius: emperor of Rome in the first century.

"With Pipe and Flute"

(*To E. G.*)[1]

With pipe and flute the rustic Pan
Of old made music sweet for man;
  And wonder hushed the warbling bird,
  And closer drew the calm-eyed herd,—
The rolling river slowlier ran.

Ah! would—ah! would, a little span,
Some air of Arcady[2] could fan

This age of ours, too seldom stirred
    With pipe and flute!

But now for gold we plot and plan;   10
And from Beersheba unto Dan,[3]
  Apollo's self might pass unheard,
  Or find the night-jar's note preferred:[4]—
Not so it fared, when time began,
    With pipe and flute!

1877

Philip Bourke Marston
1850–1887

Philip Bourke Marston was the son of John Westland Marston (1819–90), a poet, novelist, and especially a playwright of some success and distinction in the 1850s and 1860s. Philip Marston was accidentally blinded when he was three years old, and the rest of his life was troubled by other calamities, including the death of the young woman whom he was to marry. Marston grew up in the literary and artistic circles of London—one of his sisters married the poet Arthur O'Shaughnessy— and he published his first book of poems when he was twenty-one years old. He published two other collections of his poems during his lifetime, in 1875 and 1883. Marston's talent and style moved toward intense, highly wrought statement, and he also learned from Dante Gabriel Rossetti the benefits of holding such statement within the form of the sonnet. Each of his volumes contained many sonnets, some of them arranged, like Rossetti's "The House of Life," in sequences of mood if not of event. Two volumes of his poems were published after his death, and a collection of all his verse appeared in 1892, edited by Louise Chandler Moulton, who also wrote a memoir for this edition. The texts reprinted here are those of the 1892 edition.

Speechless:

Upon the Marriage of Two Deaf and Dumb Persons

Their lips upon each other's lips are laid;
  Strong moans of joy, wild laughter, and short
    cries
  Seem uttered in the passion of their eyes.
He sees her body fair, and fallen head,
And she the face whereon her soul is fed;
  And by the way her white breasts sink and
    rise,
  He knows she must be shaken by sweet sighs;
Though all delight of sound for them be dead.

They dance a strange, weird measure, who
    know not
  The tune to which their dancing feet are led;   10
Their breath in kissing is made doubly hot
  With flame of pent-up speech; strange light
    is shed

---

[1] E. G. is Edmund Gosse (1849–1928), who worked with Dobson at the Board of Trade and was as prolific as Dobson as a poet and literary critic. The poem is a rondeau, a French form which Gosse also helped to make popular in his own poetry.

[2] Arcady: a conventional name for the untroubled countryside of pastoral poetry.

[3] Beersheba unto Dan: the extent of the territory of the Israelites (Judges 20:1).

[4] Apollo: the god of poetry and song in classical mythology. Night-jar: a common bird that makes a whirring noise.

About their spirits, as they mix and meet
In passion-lighted silence, 'tranced and
    sweet.

                                        1871

Wedded Memories

And if my memory live when I am dead:
    When all whereby men knew me turns to
        dust;
    When deaf and dumb, and sightless, I am
        thrust
Into dank darkness, where the worms are fed
By Death's gaunt hand, that breed in my cold
    bed;
    When I, at last, with life and love break
        trust;
    When the soul's yearnings and the body's
        lust,
Are ended wholly, as a tune out-played,—

If then, men name my name, and from these
10   lays
    The depth and glory of thy soul divine,
    Shall not, beloved, my memory live in
        thine?—
Our memories moveless 'mid the moving days,
    Intense and sad, like changeless stars that
        shine
On ruined towers of a predestined race.

                                        1875

The Two Burdens

Over the deep sea Love came flying;
Over the salt sea Love came sighing—
    Alas, O Love, for thy journeying wings!
Through turbid light and sound of thunder,
When one wave lifts and one falls under,

Love flew, as a bird flies, straight for warm
    Springs.

Love reached the Northland, and found his
    own;
With budding roses, and roses blown,
    And wonderful lilies, he wove their wreath;
His voice was sweet as a tune that wells,
Gathers and thunders, and throbs and swells,
    And fails, and lapses in rapturous death.

His hands divided the tangled boughs;
They sat and loved in a moist, green house,
    With bird-songs and sunbeams faltering
        through;
One note of wind to each least light leaf:
O Love, those days they were sweet but brief,—
    Sweet as the rose is, and fleet as the dew!

Over the deep sea Death came flying;
Over the salt sea Death flew sighing:
    Love heard from afar the rush of his wings,
Felt the blast of them over the sea,
And turned his face where the shadows be,
    And wept for a sound of disastrous things.

Death reached the Northland, and claimed his
    own;
With pale, sweet flowers, by wet winds blown,
    He wove for the forehead of one a wreath;
His voice was sad as the wind that sighs
Through cypress trees under rainy skies,
    When the dead leaves drift on the path be-
        neath.

His hands divided the tangled boughs.
One lover he bore to a dark, deep house.
    Where never a bridegroom may clasp his
        bride,—
A place of silence, of dust, and sleep;
What vigil there shall the loved one keep,
    What cry of longing the lips divide?

                                        1883

Arthur O'Shaughnessy
1844–1881

Arthur O'Shaughnessy was born and educated privately in London. When he was seventeen years old he took an appointment in the British Museum, and he later worked in the natural history department of the museum, where he became an expert in studies of reptiles. He also knew a great deal about French literature, and at the end of his life was the British correspondent of a French literary magazine. He published his first book of poems in 1870, and two others (Lays of France: 1872; Music and Moonlight: 1874) during his lifetime; a fourth book, Songs of a Worker, was published the year of his death. His poems and his marriage to the daughter of the poet and dramatist John Westland Marston (1819–90) made him a familiar of the literary scene dominated by Dante Gabriel Rossetti and other writers who had grown up in the Pre-Raphaelite tonalities of the 1860s and 1870s. Like some poets of the last decades of the century, however, O'Shaughnessy joined to the themes and colors he took from Rossetti and Swinburne an elegance of form which gave his work a fragile grace and quiet more common at the end than it is in the middle of the Victorian period. The texts printed here are those of the original editions of his volumes of poems.

Ode

We are the music makers,
    And we are the dreamers of dreams,
Wandering by lone sea-breakers,
    And sitting by desolate streams;—
World-losers and world-forsakers,
    On whom the pale moon gleams:
Yet we are the movers and shakers
    Of the world for ever, it seems.

With wonderful deathless ditties
We build up the world's great cities,
    And out of a fabulous story
    We fashion an empire's glory:

One man with a dream, at pleasure,
    Shall go forth and conquer a crown;
And three with a new song's measure
    Can trample a kingdom down.

We, in the ages lying
    In the buried past of the earth,
Built Nineveh[1] with our sighing,
    And Babel[2] itself in our mirth;   20
And o'erthrew them with prophesying
    To the old of the new world's worth;
For each age is a dream that is dying,
    Or one that is coming to birth.

A breath of our inspiration
Is the life of each generation;
    A wondrous thing of our dreaming
    Unearthly, impossible seeming—
The soldier, the king, and the peasant
    Are working together in one,   30
Till our dream shall become their present,
    And their work in the world be done.

They had no vision amazing
Of the goodly house they are raising;
    They had no divine foreshowing
    Of the land to which they are going:
But on one man's soul it hath broken,
    A light that doth not depart;
And his look, or a word he hath spoken,
    Wrought flame in another man's heart.   40

And therefore to-day is thrilling
With a past day's late fulfilling;
    And the multitudes are enlisted
    In the faith that their fathers resisted,
And, scorning the dream of to-morrow,
    Are bringing to pass, as they may,
In the world, for its joy or its sorrow,
    The dream that was scorned yesterday.

[1] Nineveh: rebuilt into a splendid capital of the Assyrian empire by Sennacherib in the seventh century B.C.

[2] Babel: the city whose inhabitants tried to build a tower to reach to heaven; they were confounded by God, who gave them different languages to speak and dispersed them over the earth (Genesis 11).

But we, with our dreaming and singing,
   Ceaseless and sorrowless we!
The glory about us clinging
   Of the glorious futures we see,
Our souls with high music ringing:
   O men! it must ever be
That we dwell, in our dreaming and singing,
   A little apart from ye.

For we are afar with the dawning
   And the suns that are not yet high,
And out of the infinite morning
   Intrepid you hear us cry—
How, spite of your human scorning,
   Once more God's future draws nigh,
And already goes forth the warning
   That ye of the past must die.

Great hail! we cry to the comers
   From the dazzling unknown shore;
Bring us hither your sun and your summers,
   And renew our world as of yore;
You shall teach us your song's new numbers,
   And things that we dreamed not before:
Yea, in spite of a dreamer who slumbers,
   And a singer who sings no more.

                   1874

Silences

To ————

'Tis a world of silences. I gave a cry
   In the first sorrow my heart could not withstand;
I saw men pause, and listen, and look sad,
As though an answer in their hearts they had;
   Some turned away, some came and took my hand,
For all reply.

I stood beside a grave. Years had passed by;
   Sick with unanswered life I turned to death,
And whispered all my question to the grave,
And watched the flowers desolately wave,
   And grass stir on it with a fitful breath,
For all reply.

I raised my eyes to heaven; my prayer went high
   Into the luminous mystery of the blue;
My thought of God was purer than a flame
And God it seemed a little nearer came,

¹ Ellipsis in the original text.

Then passed; and greater still the silence grew,
For all reply.

But you! If I can speak before I die,
   I spoke to you with all my soul, and when
I look at you 'tis still my soul you see.
Oh, in your heart was there no word for me?
   All would have answered had you answered then
With even a sigh.

                   1881

Living Marble

When her large, fair, reluctant eyelids fell,
   And dreams o'erthrew her blond head mutinous,
That lollingly surrendered to the spell
   Of sleep's warm death, whose tomb is odorous
   And made of recent roses; then unchid
I gazed more rapturously than I may tell
On that vain-hearted queen with whom I dwell,
   The wayward Venus who for days hath hid
   Her peerless, priceless beauty, and forbid,
With impious shames and child-like airs perverse,
   My great, fond soul from worshipping the sight
   That gives religion to my day and night—
Her shape sublime that should be none of hers.

          *   *   *   *¹

The wonder of her nakedness, unspoiled
   By fear or feigning, showed each passionate limb
In reckless grace that failed not nor recoiled;
   And all the sweet, rebellious body, slim,
   Exuberant, lay abandoned to the whim
And miracle of unabashed repose.
   I joyed to see her glorious side left bare,
   Each snow-born flow'ret of her breast displayed,
One white hand vaguely touching one red rose,
   One white arm gleaming through thick golden hair.
   I gazed; then broke the marble I had made,
And yearned, restraining heart and holding breath,
That sleep indeed were endless, even as death.

                   1881

PART FIVE

Principal Victorian Poets 1880-1900

Robert Bridges

1844–1930

ROBERT BRIDGES was born into a family that had owned and farmed land in the south of England for several centuries. His father was a gentleman farmer of some station and substance; his mother was the daughter of a baronet who was ordained in the Church of England. After Bridges' father died in 1853, his mother married a clergyman and moved to the north of England. By that time Bridges was ready to enter school, first at Eton and then in 1863 at Oxford, where he began his lifelong friendship with Gerard Manley Hopkins. After his graduation in 1867 he traveled in Egypt, Syria, and Europe. He wanted to be a poet, and his inherited income would have enabled him to pursue that vocation alone. But he was interested in science and wanted to acquire a profession. He began the study of medicine in London in 1869. He received his degree five years later, and until 1881 he practiced medicine in London. An illness in that year led to his retirement with his mother to a country house in Berkshire, in the west of England. He married in 1882, and for the rest of his years he lived a finely tempered life as a poet, scholar, man of letters, proficient amateur in music, and country gentleman in Berkshire and, after 1907, in a house outside Oxford. He wrote and published poems and verse dramas and applied his interest in music to the editing of a hymnal. General and continuing explorations in classical, Continental, and British literature did not deter him from publishing essays and lectures on prosody, pronunciation, spelling, and hymn singing as well as on literary topics.

Bridges published his first volume of poems, to which he assigned his name, in 1873. Beginning in 1876 he published a series of anonymous pamphlets at a private press, some of which included poems that went into his sonnet sequence *The Growth of Love*. In the 1880s he started to publish a series of dramatic poems, the first (*Prometheus the Firegiver*) and most of the others concerning subjects in classical mythology and history, written in imita-

tions of classical dramatic forms or Elizabethan masques. In 1890 he collected the lyrics and descriptive poems he had been publishing in limited editions since 1873 in a volume of *Shorter Poems*. In the same year he published a limited edition of seventy-nine (he later eliminated ten of these poems) sonnets of *The Growth of Love*. Between 1898 and 1905 he culminated the first passage of his development as a poet by publishing a six-volume collected edition of his plays and poems.

Bridges had become interested, in these years, in writing poetry in the quantitative measures of classical verse. He published some of these poems in an additional volume of his poetical works in 1912. In the following year he was appointed poet laureate, an office that after Tennyson's death (his successor had been the almost entirely undistinguished Alfred Austin) did not necessarily imply that large numbers of his countrymen knew the laureate's poetry and thought it conspicuously valuable. But in the 1920s, after he had written some patriotic and ceremonial poems on occasions during World War I, Bridges did attain a certain popularity. He began to experiment with a prosody he thought would advance his persistent interest in founding the measure of poetry on the natural rhythms of speech. In 1926 he began writing a long philosophic poem, *The Testament of Beauty,* in a line measured by stress rather than by syllable and falling into measures he called "loose Alexandrines." When the poem was published in 1929, on Bridges' eighty-fifth birthday, its sales (into five figures, he noted in a letter) and the response of readers who received it as a book of wisdom gave him an identity as a bard or prophet, on a somewhat diminished scale, like that accorded to Tennyson and Browning in the mid-Victorian decades of his young manhood.

In one way, the idea of Bridges as a prophet or bard was just. He thought that the effect of poetry ought finally to be moral. In "The Ne-

763

cessity of Poetry," a lecture he delivered in 1917, he described beauty as an ideal existence associated with truth and good. Poetry is a vehicle that works on the senses to arouse a love of beauty; this love is morally elevating because it too is necessarily associated with the love of truth and good. Confident that there is a relationship between poetry and morals, the poet can then attend to the vehicle and make sure that beauty is fitly rendered for his readers by craft. What attracted him to poetry in the beginning, Bridges wrote in a memoir of one of his friends at Oxford, was not its use to express doctrine or emotion. He was rather attracted by the "inexhaustible satisfaction of form, the magic of speech, lying as it seemed to me in the masterly control of the material."

Bridges' definition of a moral office for poetry distinguishes him from those late-nineteenth-century poets who insisted that the end of art was only esthetic pleasure. On the other hand, his emphasis on craft, and, more important, the means by which he displayed his craft, connect the poems he wrote in the nineteenth century with a kind of deliberately artificial poetry commonly written in his time. Bridges had very little to do with contemporary poets. He once admired the early poems of Tennyson, and he encouraged the poetry of his friends R. W. Dixon and Hopkins. For the most part, however, the poets he kept in view as he wrote and thought about poetry were Keats and Shelley, Milton, the lyricists of the English renaissance, and the poets of classical Greece and Rome. The craft and quality of his nineteenth-century poems are founded in the lessons he learned from these models. The topics and precise descriptions of his lyrics and poems of landscape, for example, are familiar in the nineteenth century. But even in the autobiographical *The Growth of Love* Bridges obscures and objectifies an observing or discovering self in his lyrics, and he modulates the strong energies and large meanings instinct in the particulars of his landscapes. His poems, in short, do not burst into discoveries of self and ecstasies of communion with another life; their effect is always one of control, command, a clearly arranged passage to a resolution satisfying because it has been so artfully prepared by a poet who is most remarkably present in the poem in the craft he has spent on it.

Similarly, Bridges was one of several poets in the second half of the nineteenth century, among them Hopkins and Coventry Patmore, who wanted to break English verse free of lines measured by the number of syllables they contain. In poems such as "London Snow" Bridges tried to make a more natural rhythm for poetry by measuring the line by the number of its stresses. He also regulated the length of his lines by paying close attention to the quantity of its syllables, the amount of time required to say them, which he saw as another way to capture and refine the rhythm and phrasing of natural speech. Behind this highly self-conscious and technically learned attempt to return English to his conception of its natural music was Bridges' long study of classical metrics and Milton's prosody. To these ideas he added his opinion that the vocabulary of poetry ought to be refined and rare, his taste for the finely turned figures of the elegies, sonnets, and songs of the English renaissance, and his imitations of classical drama and Elizabethan masque in some of the verse dramas he wrote in the 1880s and after. The result, in the words of the poet Lionel Johnson in a review of Bridges' poetry published in 1891, was a poetry of "dainty luxury," a kind of "scholarship of poetry."

That opinion too is just. At the end of the nineteenth century Bridges was properly perceived as a rather special poet of an exceptionally refined craft and deliberately achieved effects. One interest of the poems that won Bridges this reputation is that they were written and published in the last decades of the nineteenth century by a poet who defined the moral agency of poetry in the grand terms advanced by poets earlier in the century. His artifice, therefore, like that of Hopkins, is not simply a pleasure or stay against time, but also the vehicle and emblem of an ideal order that redeems time. But at least in the shorter poems he wrote before 1900, Bridges did not work the enlarging moral effects of his poems widely. Like other poets of his generation, he went, if not into retreat, then certainly into retirement from the prominent public identity and its attendant social concerns and commitments sought or accepted by those of his predecessors who thought as he did about the moral responsibilities of poetry. Even in his longer dramatic verse he settled for trying to perfect, with the learned elegance of a court poet, an instrument whose rare music was best heard by the relatively small audience of poets and readers who were themselves schooled in the techniques and antique conventions he was adapting to make a contemporary but deliberately unusual poetry.

EDITIONS

The texts of the poems republished here are those of the collected *Poetical Works* (1898–1905); they are consistent with those of the Oxford edition of his poetry (third edition, 1953). Bridges' essays and lectures are published in *Collected Essays* (1927–36); some of his prose is more conveniently republished in John Sparrow's edition of Bridges' *Poetry and Prose* (1955), which also includes appreciations by some of Bridges' contemporaries and friends. *The Correspondence of Robert Bridges and Henry Bradley 1900–1927* was published in 1940. C. C. Abbott's edition of *The Letters of Gerard Manley Hopkins to Robert Bridges* (1935) is pertinent; and so is Bridges' compilation of *The Yattendon Hymnal* (1895–99).

BIOGRAPHY AND CRITICISM

Edward Thompson's *Robert Bridges, 1844–1930* (1944) is a heavily anecdotal biography. Albert Guerard, *Bridges: A Study of Traditionalism in Poetry* (1942) is the most useful general study. F. E. Brett Young's *Bridges: A Critical Study* (1914) is interesting because it is an estimate and study of Bridges' poetry before the publication of *The Testament of Beauty*.

OTHER USEFUL ESSAYS

J. M. Cohen, "The Road Not Taken: A Study in the Poetry of Bridges," *Cambridge Journal*, 4 (1951).

Derek Patmore, "Three Poets Discuss New Verse Forms: The Correspondence of Hopkins, Bridges, and Patmore," *Month* (August 1951)

Ritz, Jean-Georges. *Robert Bridges and Gerard Hopkins, 1863–1889* (1960).

George L. Mackay has compiled *A Bibliography of Robert Bridges* (1933) which describes only writings by Bridges. John Sparrow's pamphlet, *Robert Bridges,* in the Writers and Their Work series (1962), contains a select bibliography of writings about Bridges.

Elegy

On a Lady Whom Grief for the Death of Her Betrothed Killed

Assemble, all ye maidens, at the door,
And all ye loves, assemble; far and wide

Proclaim the bridal, that proclaimed before
Has been deferred to this late eventide:
    For on this night the bride,
    The days of her betrothal over,
  Leaves the parental hearth for evermore;
To-night the bride goes forth to meet her lover.

Reach down the wedding vesture, that has lain
  Yet all unvisited, the silken gown: 10
Bring out the bracelets, and the golden chain
  Her dearer friends provided: sere and brown
    Bring out the festal crown,
    And set it on her forehead lightly:
  Though it be withered, twine no wreath
    again;
This only is the crown she can wear rightly.

Cloke her in ermine, for the night is cold,
And wrap her warmly, for the night is long,
In pious hands the flaming torches hold,
While her attendants, chosen from among   20
    Her faithful virgin throng,
  May lay her in her cedar litter,
  Decking her coverlet with sprigs of gold,
Roses, and lilies white that best befit her.

Sound flute and tabor, that the bridal be
Not without music, nor with these alone;
But let the viol lead the melody,
With lesser intervals, and plaintive moan
    Of sinking semitone;
    And, all in choir, the virgin voices   30
  Rest not from singing in skilled harmony
The song that aye the bridegroom's ears
    rejoices.

Let the priests go before, arrayed in white,
And let the dark-stoled minstrels follow slow,
Next they that bear her, honoured on this
    night,
And then the maidens, in a double row,
    Each singing soft and low,
    And each on high a torch upstaying:
Unto her lover lead her forth with light,
With music, and with singing, and with
    praying.   40

'Twas at this sheltering hour he nightly came,
And found her trusty window open wide,
And knew the signal of the timorous flame,
That long the restless curtain would not hide
    Her form that stood beside;
    As scarce she dared to be delighted,
  Listening to that sweet tale, that is no shame
To faithful lovers, that their hearts have
    plighted.

But now for many days the dewy grass
50   Has shown no markings of his feet at morn:
And watching she has seen no shadow pass
The moonlit walk, and heard no music borne
     Upon her ear forlorn.
    In vain has she looked out to greet him;
    He has not come, he will not come, alas!
So let us bear her out where she must meet him.

    Now to the river bank the priests are come:
The bark is ready to receive its freight:
Let some prepare her place therein, and some
60   Embark the litter with its slender weight:
     The rest stand by in state,
    And sing her a safe passage over;
   While she is oared across to her new home,
Into the arms of her expectant lover.

And thou, O lover, that art on the watch,
Where, on the banks of the forgetful streams,
The pale indifferent ghosts wander, and snatch
The sweeter moments of their broken
      dreams,—
    Thou, when the torchlight gleams,
70   When thou shalt see the slow procession,
   And when thine ears the fitful music catch,
Rejoice, for thou art near to thy possession.
                    1873

[Song] "I have loved flowers that fade"

I have loved flowers that fade,
Within whose magic tents
Rich hues have marriage made
With sweet unmemoried scents:
A honeymoon delight,—
A joy of love at sight,
That ages in an hour:—
My song be like a flower!

I have loved airs, that die
10   Before their charm is writ
Along a liquid sky
Trembling to welcome it.
Notes, that with pulse of fire
Proclaim the spirit's desire,
Then die, and are nowhere:—
My song be like an air!

Die, song, die like a breath,
And wither as a bloom:

¹ Shires: counties.

Fear not a flowery death,
Dread not an airy tomb!   2●
Fly with delight, fly hence!
'Twas thine love's tender sense
To feast; now on thy bier
Beauty shall shed a tear.
                    1879

Indolence

We left the city when the summer day
Had verged already on its hot decline,
And charmèd Indolence in languor lay
In her gay gardens, 'neath her towers divine:
"Farewell," we said, "dear city of youth and
    dream!"
And in our boat we stepped and took the
    stream.

  All through that idle afternoon we strayed
Upon our proposed travel well begun,
As loitering by the woodland's dreamy shade,
Past shallow islets floating in the sun,   1
Or searching down the banks for rarer flowers
We lingered out the pleasurable hours.

  Till when that loveliest came, which mowers
    home
Turns from their longest labour, as we steered
Along a straitened channel flecked with foam,
We lost our landscape wide, and slowly neared
An ancient bridge, that like a blind wall lay
Low on its buried vaults to block the way.

  Then soon the narrow tunnels broader
    showed,
Where with its arches three it sucked the mass   2●
Of water, that in swirl thereunder flowed,
Or stood piled at the piers waiting to pass;
And pulling for the middle span, we drew
The tender blades aboard and floated through.

  But past the bridge what change we found
    below!
The stream, that all day long had laughed and
    played
Betwixt the happy shires,¹ ran dark and slow,
And with its easy flood no murmur made:
And weeds spread on its surface, and about
The stagnant margin reared their stout heads
    out.   3●

  Upon the left high elms, with giant wood
Skirting the water-meadows, interwove

Their slumbrous crowns, o'ershadowing where
    they stood
The floor and heavy pillars of the grove:
And in the shade, through reeds and sedges[2]
    dank,
A footpath led along the moated bank.

    Across, all down the right, an old brick wall,
Above and o'er the channel, red did lean;
Here buttressed up, and bulging there to fall,
Tufted with grass and plants and lichen green;
And crumbling to the flood, which at its base
Slid gently nor disturbed its mirrored face.

    Sheer on the wall the houses rose, their backs
All windowless, neglected and awry,
With tottering coigns,[3] and crooked chimney
    stacks;
And here and there an unused door, set high
Above the fragments of its mouldering stair,
With rail and broken step led out on air.

    Beyond, deserted wharfs and vacant sheds,
With empty boats and barges moored along,
And rafts half-sunken, fringed with weedy
    shreds,
And sodden beams, once soaked to season
    strong.
No sight of man, nor sight of life, no stroke,
No voice the somnolence and silence broke.

    Then I who rowed leant on my oar, whose
    drip
Fell without sparkle, and I rowed no more;
And he that steered moved neither hand nor
    lip,
But turned his wondering eye from shore to
    shore;
And our trim boat let her swift motion die,
Between the dim reflections floating by.

                   1880

London Snow

When men were all asleep the snow came
    flying,
In large white flakes falling on the city brown,
Stealthily and perpetually settling and loosely
    lying,
    Hushing the latest traffic of the drowsy
      town;
Deadening, muffling, stifling its murmurs
    failing;

Lazily and incessantly floating down and down;
    Silently sifting and veiling road, roof and
      railing;
Hiding difference, making unevenness even,
Into angles and crevices softly drifting and
    sailing.
    All night it fell, and when full inches seven
It lay in the depth of its uncompacted
    lightness,
The clouds blew off from a high and frosty
    heaven;
    And all woke earlier for the unaccustomed
    brightness
Of the winter dawning, the strange unheavenly
    glare:
The eye marvelled—marvelled at the dazzling
    whiteness;
    The ear hearkened to the stillness of the
      solemn air;
No sound of wheel rumbling nor of foot
    falling,
And the busy morning cries came thin and
    spare.
    Then boys I heard, as they went to school,
      calling,
They gathered up the crystal manna to freeze
Their tongues with tasting, their hands with
    snowballing;
    Or rioted in a drift, plunging up to the
      knees;
Or peering up from under the white-mossed
    wonder,
"O look at the trees!" they cried, "O look at
    the trees!"
    With lessened load a few carts creak and
      blunder,
Following along the white deserted way,
A country company long dispersed asunder:
    When now already the sun, in pale display
Standing by Paul's high dome,[1] spread forth
    below
His sparkling beams, and awoke the stir of the
    day.
    For now doors open, and war is waged with
      the snow;
And trains of sombre men, past tale of number,
Tread long brown paths, as toward their toil
    they go:
But even for them awhile no cares encumber
Their minds diverted; the daily word is
    unspoken,

[2] Sedges: marsh plants.   [3] Coign: projecting corners.
[1] Paul's high dome: the dome of St. Paul's cathedral.

The daily thoughts of labour and sorrow
    slumber
At the sight of the beauty that greets them,
    for the charm they have broken.

1880

from The Growth of Love

The Growth of Love *is a sonnet sequence whose Petrarchan form, language, and ground conception are consistent and deliberate references to Elizabethan traditions of love sonnets. The sequence contained twenty-four sonnets in its first issue in 1876. When it was published again in London in 1890 (an edition had been published in Oxford the previous year), ten of the original sonnets were omitted, and the total of sonnets was seventy-nine. Bridges in turn omitted ten of these later sonnets from his collected poems. Increasingly as it enlarged, the sequence became less narrative and more meditative as Bridges used it not to record events in a growing love but to speculate on love and other matters. The sonnets printed here were all first published in 1889–90 and survived in Bridges' collected works.*

"The whole world now is but the minister"

3

The whole world now is but the minister
Of thee to me: I see no other scheme
But universal love, from timeless dream
Waking to thee his joy's interpreter.
I walk around and in the fields confer
Of love at large with tree and flower and
    stream,
And list the lark descant upon my theme,
Heaven's musical accepted worshipper.

Thy smile outfaceth ill: and that old feud
'Twixt things and me is quash'd in our new
    truce;
And nature now dearly with thee endued
No more in shame ponders her old excuse,
But quite forgets her frowns and antics rude,
So kindly hath she grown to her new use.

1889–90

"For beauty being the best of all we know"

8

For beauty being the best of all we know
Sums up the unsearchable and secret aims
Of nature, and on joys whose earthly names
Were never told can form and sense bestow;
And man hath sped his instinct to outgo
The step of science; and against her shames
Imagination stakes out heavenly claims,
Building a tower above the head of woe.

Nor is there fairer work for beauty found
Than that she win in nature her release
From all the woes that in the world abound:
Nay with his sorrow may his love increase,
If from man's greater need beauty redound,
And claim his tears for homage of his peace.

1889–90

"Spring hath her own bright days of calm and peace"

24

Spring hath her own bright days of calm and
    peace;
Her melting air, at every breath we draw,
Floods heart with love to praise God's gracious
    law:
But suddenly—so short is pleasure's lease—
The cold returns, the buds from growing cease,
And nature's conquer'd face is full of awe;
As now the trait'rous north with icy flaw
Freezes the dew upon the sick lamb's fleece,

And 'neath the mock sun searching every-
    where
Rattles the crispèd leaves with shivering din:
So that the birds are silent with despair
Within the thickets; nor their armour thin
Will guady flies adventure in the air,
Nor any lizard sun his spotted skin.

1889–90

"I will be what God made me, nor protest"

62

I will be what God made me, nor protest
Against the bent of genius in my time,

That science of my friends robs all the best,
While I love beauty, and was born to rhyme.
  Be they our mighty men, and let me dwell
In shadow among the mighty shades of old,
With love's forsaken palace for my cell;
Whence I look forth and all the world behold,

  And say, These better days, in best things
    worse,
This bastardy of time's magnificence,
Will mend in fashion and throw off the curse,
To crown new love with higher excellence.
  Curs'd tho' I be to live my life alone,
My toil is for man's joy, his joy my own.

1889–90

Song

I love my lady's eyes
Above the beauties rare
She most is wont to prize,
Above her sunny hair,
And all that face to face
Her glass repeats of grace.

For those are still the same
To her and all that see:
But oh! her eyes will flame
When they do look on me:
And so above the rest
I love her eyes the best.

Now say, [*Say, O say! saith the music*]
  who likes my song?—
I knew you by your eyes,
That rest on nothing long,
And have forgot surprise;
And stray [*Stray, O stray! saith the music*]
  as mine will stray,
The while my love's away.

(c. 1880)   1890

"The upper skies are palest blue"

The upper skies are palest blue
Mottled with pearl and fretted[1] snow:
With tattered fleece of inky hue
Close overhead the storm-clouds go.

Their shadows fly along the hill
And o'er the crest mount one by one:

The whitened planking of the mill
Is now in shade and now in sun.

1890

"Say who is this with silvered hair"

Say who is this with silvered hair,
  So pale and worn and thin,
Who passeth here, and passeth there,
  And looketh out and in?

That useth not our garb nor tongue
  And knoweth things untold:
Who teacheth pleasure to the young,
  And wisdom to the old?

No toil he maketh his by day,
  No home his own by night;
But wheresoe'er he take his way,
  He killeth our delight.

Since he is come there's nothing wise
  Nor fair in man or child,
Unless his deep divining eyes
  Have looked on it and smiled.

Whence came he hither all alone
  Among our folk to spy?
There's nought that we can call our own,
  Till he shall hap to die.

And I would dig his grave full deep
  Beneath the churchyard yew,
Lest thence his wizard eyes might peep
  To mark the things we do.

1890

Laus Deo[1]

Let praise devote thy work, and skill employ
Thy whole mind, and thy heart be lost in joy.
Well-doing bringeth pride, this constant
    thought
Humility, that thy best done is nought.
Man doeth nothing well, be it great or small,
Save to praise God; but that hath savèd all:
For God requires no more than thou hast done,
And takes thy work to bless it for his own.

1890

---

[1] Fretted: carved patterns.   [1] Laus Deo: Praise of God.

The Palm Willow[1]

See, whirling snow sprinkles the starvèd fields,
    The birds have stayed to sing;
No covert yet their fairy harbour yields.
    When cometh Spring?
Ah! in their tiny throats what songs unborn
    Are quenched each morn.

The lenten lilies, through the frost that push,
    Their yellow heads withhold:
The woodland willow stands a lonely bush
10   Of nebulous gold;
There the Spring-goddess cowers in faint attire
    Of frightened fire.
                                        1893

Nightingales

Beautiful must be the mountains whence ye
        come,
And bright in the fruitful valleys the streams,
        wherefrom
    Ye learn your song:
Where are those starry woods? O might I
        wander there,
Among the flowers, which in that heavenly
        air
    Bloom the year long!

Nay, barren are those mountains and spent
        the streams:
Our song is the voice of desire, that haunts
        our dreams,
    A throe of the heart,
Whose pining visions dim, forbidden hopes
10   profound,
No dying cadence nor long sigh can sound,
    For all our art.

Alone, aloud in the raptured ear of men
We pour our dark nocturnal secret; and
        then,
    As night is withdrawn
From these sweet-springing meads and bursting
        boughs of May,
Dream, while the innumerable choir of day
    Welcome the dawn.
                                        1893

North Wind in October

In the golden glade the chestnuts are fallen all;
From the sered boughs of the oak the acorns
    fall:
The beech scatters her ruddy fire;
The lime hath stripped to the cold,
And standeth naked above her yellow attire:
The larch thinneth her spire
To lay the ways of the wood with cloth of gold.

    Out of the golden-green and white
Of the brake[1] the fir-trees stand upright
In the forest of flame, and wave aloft   10
To the blue of heaven their blue-green tuftings
    soft.

But swiftly in shuddering gloom the splendours
    fail,
As the harrying North-wind beareth
A cloud of skirmishing hail
The grievèd woodland to smite:
In a hurricane through the trees he teareth,
Raking the boughs and the leaves rending,
And whistleth to the descending
Blows of his icy flail.
Gold and snow he mixeth in spite,   20
And whirleth afar; as away on his winnowing
    flight
He passeth, and all again for awhile is bright.
                                        1893

"Riding adown the country lanes"

Riding adown the country lanes
    One day in spring,
Heavy at heart with all the pains
    Of man's imagining:—

The mist was not yet melted quite
    Into the sky:
The small round sun was dazzling white,
    The merry larks sang high:

The grassy northern slopes were laid
    In sparkling dew,   10
Out of the slow-retreating shade
    Turning from sleep anew:

Deep in the sunny vale a burn[1]
    Ran with the lane,

---

[1] Palm willow: a willow whose branches may be used as palms in celebrations like that of
Palm Sunday, celebrating Christ's entry to Jerusalem before his crucifixion.
[1] Brake: rough undergrowth.   [1] Burn: stream or brook.

O'erhung with ivy, moss and fern
    It laughed in joyful strain:

And primroses shot long and lush
    Their cluster'd cream;
Robin and wren and amorous thrush
    Carol'd above the stream:

The stillness of the lenten air
    Call'd into sound
The motions of all life that were
    In field and farm around:

So fair it was, so sweet and bright,
    The jocund Spring
Awoke in me the old delight
    Of man's imagining,

Riding adown the country lanes:
    The larks sang high.—   30
O heart! for all thy griefs and pains
    Thou shalt be loth to die.

                    1898

"Since we loved"

Since we loved,— (the earth that shook
As we kissed, fresh beauty took) —
Love hath been as poets paint,
Life as heaven is to a saint;

All my joys my hope excel,
All my work hath prosper'd well,
All my songs have happy been,
O my love, my life, my queen.

                    1898

William Ernest Henley
1849–1903

WILLIAM ERNEST HENLEY worked industriously all his adult life at nearly all the means by which late-nineteenth-century men and women of letters made their livings. He was the editor of several periodicals, including two, the weekly *Scots* (later *National*) *Observer* and the monthly *New Review,* in which he published the early writing of Robert Louis Stevenson, Rudyard Kipling, William Butler Yeats, H. G. Wells, Henry James, and Joseph Conrad. He wrote articles for encyclopedias, edited literary anthologies, and put together collections of the writing of (among others) Robert Burns, Byron, Fielding, and Wilfred Scawen Blunt (see Part Six). He also edited a thirty-two volume reprinting of sixteenth-century English translations of famous books, and he helped to compile a dictionary of slang. He wrote dramatic and art criticism as well as literary reviews and long essays of literary appreciation. He collaborated with Stevenson on four plays

and wrote another farce on his own; these plays were written for performance, and some of them were performed in England and in the United States. He first came to the attention of London editors and reviewers when some of the poems of "In Hospital" were published in 1875 in the *Cornhill,* a monthly magazine of considerable standing. He would have liked to concentrate on the writing of poetry, but it was only through literary journalism and editing that he could earn enough money to support himself. Nevertheless, after neglecting his poetry for a while in the 1880s when he was establishing himself as an editor and reviewer, he wrote poetry up to the year of his death, and he published five small volumes of poems between 1888 and 1901.

Henley's father was a marginally successful bookseller in the southwest of England who finally died penniless in 1867. Henley's mother was a descendant of Joseph Warton, an eighteenth-century man of letters. This heritage, his reading in his father's stock, and his early education—one of his teachers was the poet Thomas Edward Brown (see Part Six)—prepared Henley for a literary life. He left school when his father died and went to London to live a penurious, somewhat bohemian life as a journalist. While he was in school one of his legs had been amputated below the knee to arrest a form of tubercular arthritis. He became sick again in 1872, and to avoid another amputation he went to Edinburgh, where the surgeon Joseph Lister was practicing new doctrines of antiseptic surgery and treatment which in Henley's case did make further amputation unnecessary. Henley was in a hospital in Edinburgh for nearly two years. He taught himself several languages during this time, met Stevenson and his own future wife, and became acquainted with a circle of Edinburgh writers, literary journalists, book collectors, and others who were simply interested in literature. He remained in Edinburgh for a time after his discharge from the hospital, and then he returned to London in 1876 to become editor of a weekly magazine.

Henley worked in London for the next twelve years as an editor and journalist before he returned to Edinburgh to assume the editorship of the *Scots Observer,* which had been founded as a literary and political weekly by some of his Edinburgh friends. Two years before the magazine failed in 1894, its editorial office was moved to London (and its name changed). Henley now became the center of one of the sets of writers and literary journalists then common in London. He had published his first volume of verse in 1888, *A Book of Verse,* which included the entire series of poems "In Hospital" he had begun to publish in 1875. In 1890 he published a collection of his literary criticism, and a second volume of poems, *The Song of the Sword and Other Verses,* appeared in 1892 (it was republished in 1893 as *London Voluntaries*). As an editor, critic, poet, playwright, and as a forceful personality, he continued to play a magisterial role in London literary life until about 1896, when a move to the suburbs of London, his resignation from the editorship of the *New Review,* and then ill health gradually attenuated his presence. He published a collected edition of his poems in 1898, separate volumes in 1899 and 1900, and a pamphlet containing his last poem, *The Song of Speed,* a celebration

of the excitement of the motor car, in the year of his death.

One of Henley's roles in the literary London of the 1890s was as an advocate of a healthy realism and of the energy of the present. He was therefore also an antagonist of the lassitude and preciosity of writers who called or revealed themselves as decadent. The principal controversy over the alleged perversity of Oscar Wilde's *The Picture of Dorian Gray* (1891), for example, was conducted in the *Scots Observer* during Henley's editorship. Henley admired Fielding, Byron, Burns, and other writers who, as he saw it, directly and honestly engaged the mixed matter of living. He was generous but proprietary toward the young writers he helped, an aggressive controversialist in person and in print, strongly Tory, nationalist, and imperialist in his politics. In all his opinions and attitudes there was a strain of self-assertion, an insistence on the necessity of individual will and action in a reality that offered no recompense for pain and loss except the pleasure of defining oneself against the powerful forces that buffeted and would eventually extinguish individual consciousness.

One of the most important modes of this self-assertion was art. Henley wrote in the preface to *Lyra Heroica,* an anthology of poems he edited in 1892, that art was valuable because it "set forth the beauty and joy of living, the beauty and blessedness of death, the glory of battle and adventure, the nobility of devotion, . . . the dignity of resistance." Henley expressed this beauty and joy in the deliberately unsettling literalism of the "In Hospital" poems, in the declamation of the poem popularly known as "Invictus" ("I. M. R. Hamilton Bruce"), and in the excitement of the "London Voluntaries." In one way or another, all these poems testify that consciousness is competent to perceptions that could persuade it to despair, that if necessary the poet can improvise an unconventional poetic idiom and form to witness that he finds life, pleasure, and, quite literally, self-assurance in struggles with realities that seem hostile or indifferent to his existence. The same witness is borne in another way in those poems by Henley in the elegant forms of French verse, and in poems that describe less dramatic manifestations of the powers of nature, such as "At Queensferry." These poems too say more quietly not only that life can be a pleasurable excitement, but that the poet is there, asserting himself in the words and form that make a pleasure of what he sees, feels, and thrusts himself against.

Henley is a representative writer of his generation in his versatile, wholly professional literary occupations, in his eclectic use of several poetic styles, and in his acceptance of a reality that holds neither the solace nor the threat of the supernatural. Despite his opposition to some of the extreme forms of estheticism, he is also representative in his apparent acceptance of a limited function for poetry. His poems do not offer to alter the forces of a reality that threatens to overwhelm him, nor do they resolve themselves in a communion with nature that saves the self in a kind of transcendence. The triumphant access of these forms is not transcendence but survival. They state, sometimes militantly, sometimes sadly, that all that is to be won by an unillusioned regard of the world is the knowledge that human form and being can shape and speak themselves against its enormous and finally obliterating energies.

EDITIONS

The texts of the poems reprinted below are those of the original editions of Henley's poems, which are consistent with those of *The Works of W. E. Henley,* published in seven volumes in 1908. Twenty-five previously unpublished poems by Henley were edited from their manuscripts by W. M. Parker in the *Poetry Review* in 1949.

BIOGRAPHY AND CRITICISM

The most complete biography is *W. E. Henley,* by John Connell (John Henry Robertson) (1949). Horace Gregory includes an essay on "William Ernest Henley's Editorial Career" in *The Shield of Achilles* (1944). Jerome H. Buckley's *William Ernest Henley: A Study in the "Counter-Decadence" of the 'Nineties* (1945) is a study of Henley's entire career and presence in late-century British literature. Morris U. Schappes, "William Ernest Henley's Principles of Criticism," *Publications of the Modern Language Association,* **46** (1931); and Joseph M. Flora's *William Ernest Henley* (1970), a short study which includes a bibliography of writing about Henley, are also useful. See also Edward H. Cohen,

The Henley-Stevenson Quarrel (1974), and Andre Guillaume, *William Ernest Henley et son Groupe* (1973).

from In Hospital

II

Waiting

A square, squat room (a cellar on promotion),
  Drab to the soul, drab to the very daylight;
  Plasters astray in unnatural-looking tinware;
  Scissors and lint and apothecary's jars.

Here, on a bench a skeleton would writhe from,
  Angry and sore, I wait to be admitted:
  Wait till my heart is lead upon my stomach,
  While at their ease two dressers[1] do their
    chores.

One has a probe—it feels to me a crowbar.
  A small boy sniffs and shudders after blue-
    stone.[2]   10
  A poor old tramp explains his poor old
    ulcers.
  Life is (I think) a blunder and a shame.
            (1873–75) 1875; 1888

IV

Before

Behold me waiting—waiting for the knife.
A little while, and at a leap I storm
The thick, sweet mystery of chloroform,
The drunken dark, the little death-in-life.
The gods are good to me: I have no wife,
No innocent child, to think of as I near
The fateful minute; nothing all-too dear
Unmans me for my bout of passive strife.
Yet am I tremulous and a trifle sick,
And, face to face with chance, I shrink a little: 10
My hopes are strong, my will is something
  weak.
Here comes the basket? Thank you. I am
  ready.

---

[1] Dressers: surgeon's assistants.

[2] Bluestone: sulphate of copper, or vitriol, used for medicinal purposes.

But, gentlemen my porters, life is brittle:
You carry Cæsar and his fortunes—steady!
                                        (1873–75) 1875; 1888

XIII

Casualty

As with varnish red and glistening
    Dripped his hair; his feet looked rigid;
    Raised, he settled stiffly sideways:
    You could see his hurts were spinal.

He had fallen from an engine,
    And been dragged along the metals.[1]
    It was hopeless, and they knew it;
    So they covered him, and left him.

As he lay, by fits half sentient,
10   Inarticulately moaning,
    With his stockinged soles protruded
    Stark and awkward from the blankets,

To his bed there came a woman,
    Stood and looked and sighed a little,
    And departed without speaking,
    As himself a few hours after.

I was told it was his sweetheart.
    They were on the eve of marriage.
    She was quiet as a statue,
20   But her lip was gray and writhen.
                                        (1873–75) 1888

Ballade   (Double Refrain)

of Youth and Age

I. M.
Thomas Edward Brown[1]
(1829–1896)

Spring at her height on a morn at prime,
Sails that laugh from a flying squall,

Pomp of harmony, rapture of rhyme—
Youth is the sign of them, one and all.
Winter sunsets and leaves that fall,
An empty flagon, a folded page,
A tumble-down wheel, a tattered ball—
These are a type of the world of Age.

Bells that clash in a gaudy chime,
Swords that clatter in onsets tall,   1[0]
The words that ring and the fames that climb—
Youth is the sign of them, one and all.
Hymnals old in a dusty stall,
A bald, blind bird in a crazy cage,
The scene of a faded festival—
These are a type of the world of Age.

Hours that strut as the heirs of time,
Deeds whose rumour's a clarion-call,
Songs where the singers their souls sublime—
Youth is the sign of them, one and all.   2[0]
A staff that rests in a nook of wall,
A reeling battle, a rusted gage,[2]
The chant of a nearing funeral—
These are a type of the world of Age.

Envoy

Struggle and turmoil, revel and brawl—
Youth is the sign of them, one and all.
A smouldering hearth and a silent stage—
These are a type of the world of Age.
                                                            1888

At Queensferry

To W. G. S.[1]

The blackbird sang, the skies were clear and
    clean;
We bowled along a road that curved a spine
Superbly sinuous and serpentine
Thro' silent symphonies of summer green.
Sudden the Forth came on us—sad of mien,
No cloud to colour it, no breeze to line:
A sheet of dark, dull glass, without a sign

---

[1] Metals: rails.
[1] Ballade: a form of French verse consisting of three eight-line stanzas and a concluding quatrain, all twenty-eight lines using only three rhymes. The double refrain of this ballade is first stated in lines 4 and 8. For a brief account of the life and writings of Thomas Edward Brown, see Part Six. Henley was once Brown's pupil.
[2] Gage: here a mailed glove.
[1] Queensferry is a town near Edinburgh on the Firth of Forth, where the river Forth meets the sea. W. G. S. was Sir Walter Grindlay Simpson (1843–98), a friend of Robert Louis Stevenson and other writers in Edinburgh.

Of life or death, two spits of sand between.
Water and sky merged blank in mist together,
The Fort loomed spectral, and the Guardship's
    spars
Traced vague, black shadows on the shimmery
    glaze:
We felt the dim, strange years, the grey, strange
    weather,
The still, strange land, unvexed of sun or stars,
Where Lancelot rides clanking thro' the haze.
                          1888

I. M.

R. T. Hamilton Bruce[1]

(1846–1899)

Out of the night that covers me,
    Black as the Pit from pole to pole,
I thank whatever gods may be
    For my unconquerable soul.

In the fell clutch of circumstance
    I have not winced nor cried aloud.
Under the bludgeonings of chance
    My head is bloody, but unbowed.

Beyond this place of wrath and tears
    Looms but the Horror of the shade,
And yet the menace of the years
    Finds, and shall find, me unafraid.

It matters not how strait the gate,
    How charged with punishments the scroll,
I am the master of my fate:
    I am the captain of my soul.
                (1875) 1888

To W. R.[1]

Madam Life's a piece in bloom[2]
    Death goes dogging everywhere:

She's the tenant of the room,
    He's the ruffian on the stair.

You shall see her as a friend,
    You shall bilk him once and twice;
But he'll trap you in the end,
    And he'll stick you for her price.

With his kneebones at your chest,
    And his knuckles in your throat,   10
You would reason—plead—protest!
    Clutching at her petticoat;

But she's heard it all before,
    Well she knows you've had your fun,
Gingerly she gains the door,
    And your little job is done.
               (1877) 1893

Prologue[1]

Something is dead . . .
The grace of sunset solitudes, the march
Of the solitary moon, the pomp and power
Of round on round of shining soldier-stars
Patrolling space, the bounties of the sun—
Sovran, tremendous, unimaginable—
The multitudinous friendliness of the sea,
Possess no more—no more.

Something is dead . . .
The Autumn rain-rot deeper and wider soaks   10
And spreads, the burden of Winter heavier
    weighs,
His melancholy close and closer yet
Cleaves, and those incantations of the Spring
That made the heart a centre of miracles
Grow formal, and the wonder-working hours
Arise no more—no more.

Something is dead . . .
'Tis time to creep in close about the fire
And tell grey tales of what we were, and dream
Old dreams and faded, and as we may rejoice   20
In the young life that round us leaps and
    laughs,

---

[1] This poem is more generally known as "Invictus," the unconquered. R. T. Hamilton Bruce was one of the founders of the *Scots Observer,* later continued in London as the *National Observer,* a weekly magazine founded in Edinburgh in 1888 and edited by Henley until 1894.

[1] W. R.: probably Walter Raleigh (1861–1922), a literary critic and historian who contributed to magazines and anthologies edited by Henley in the 1890s.

[2] Piece: a sexually experienced woman; here, a prostitute whose pimp is death.

[1] Prologue to "Rhymes and Rhythms," a section of the volume of verse Henley published in 1892.

A fountain in the sunshine, in the pride
Of God's best gift that to us twain returns,
Dear Heart,[2] no more—no more.

                 1892

from London Voluntaries

Largo e mesto[1]

IV

Out of the poisonous East,
Over a continent of blight,
Like a maleficent Influence released
From the most squalid cellarage of hell,
The Wind-Fiend, the abominable—
The Hangman Wind that tortures temper and
     light—
Comes slouching, sullen and obscene,
Hard on the skirts of the embittered night;
And in a cloud unclean
Of excremental humours, roused to strife   10
By the operation of some ruinous change,
Wherever his evil mandate run and range,
Into a dire intensity of life,
A craftsman at his bench, he settles down
To the grim job of throttling London Town.

So, by a jealous lightlessness beset
That might have oppressed the dragons of old
     time
Crunching and groping in the abysmal slime,
A cave of cut-throat thoughts and villainous
     dreams,
Hag-rid and crying with cold and dirt and wet,   20
The afflicted City, prone from mark to mark
In shameful occultation, seems
A nightmare labyrinthine, dim and drifting,
With wavering gulfs and antic heights, and
     shifting,
Rent in the stuff of a material dark,
Wherein the lamplight, scattered and sick and
     pale,
Shows like the leper's living blotch of bale:[2]
Uncoiling monstrous into street on street
Paven with perils, teeming with mischance,
Where man and beast go blindfold and in
     dread,   30

Working with oaths and threats and faltering
     feet
Somewhither in the hideousness ahead;
Working through wicked airs and deadly dews
That make the laden robber grin askance
At the good places in his black romance,
And the poor, loitering harlot rather choose
Go pinched and pined to bed
Than lurk and shiver and curse her wretched
     way
From arch to arch, scouting some threepenny
     prey.

Forgot his dawns and far-flushed afterglows,   40
His green garlands and windy eyots[3] forgot,
The old Father-River flows,
His watchfires cores of menace in the gloom,
As he came oozing from the Pit, and bore,
Sunk in his filthily transfigured sides,
Shoals of dishonoured dead to tumble and rot
In the squalor of the universal shore:
His voices sounding through the gruesome air
As from the Ferry where the Boat of Doom[4]
With her blaspheming cargo reels and rides: 50
The while his children, the brave ships,
No more adventurous and fair,
Nor tripping it light of heel as home-bound
     brides,
But infamously enchanted,
Huddle together in the foul eclipse,
Or feel their course by inches desperately,
As through a tangle of alleys murder-haunted,
From sinister reach to reach out—out—to sea.

And Death the while—
Death with his well-worn, lean, professional
     smile,
Death in his threadbare working trim—   60
Comes to your bedside, unannounced and
     bland,
And with expert, inevitable hand
Feels at your windpipe, fingers you in the lung,
Or flicks the clot well into the labouring heart:
Thus signifying unto old and young,
However hard of mouth or wild of whim,
'Tis time—'tis time by his ancient watch—to
     part
From books and women and talk and drink and
     art.

---

    [2] Dear Heart: Henley's sister Margaret, who died in 1886.
    [1] A voluntary is a piece of music, often extemporized and often played on an organ at the beginning or end of a religious service. *Largo e mesto:* slowly and sadly.
    [2] Bale: a cause of ruin or sorrow.   [3] Eyots: small islands.
    [4] Boat of Doom: the boat that ferries the souls of the dead across the river which is the boundary of the underworld.

70 And you go humbly after him
To a mean suburban lodging: on the way
To what or where
Not Death, who is old and very wise, can say:
And you—how should you care
So long as, unreclaimed of hell,
The Wind-Fiend, the insufferable,
Thus vicious and thus patient, sits him down
To the black job of burking[5] London Town?

     1893

Two Days

(February 15–September 28, 1894)

To V.G.[1]

That day we brought our Beautiful One to lie
In the green peace within your gates, he came

To give us greeting, boyish and kind and shy,
And, stricken as we were, we blessed his name:
Yet, like the Creature of Light that had been
    ours,
Soon of the sweet Earth disinherited,
He too must join, even with the Year's old
    flowers,
The unanswering generations of the Dead.
So stand we friends for you, who stood our
    friend
Through him that day; for now through him
    you know   10
That though where love was, love is till the
    end,
Love, turned of death to longing, like a foe,
    Strikes: when the ruined heart goes forth to
    crave
Mercy of the high, austere, unpitying Grave.

     (1894) 1901

William Butler Yeats
1865–1939

BY 1895, the year in which he reached the age of thirty and published the first collected edition of his poems, William Butler Yeats had become an unusually accomplished poet in the subdued, wistful tonalities and minor modes then prevalent in British poetry. He was to go on to become a major twentieth-century poet, the winner of a Nobel prize for literature in 1923, a member of the Irish senate, a confident and imperious literary presence, and a man of large and very public enterprises and distinctions. The difference, for Yeats, was a development rather than a transformation. Some of the terms of his development can be marked in changes in the style and conception of his poems, especially in those changes he empha-

sized when in 1895 he began a series of revisions of his early poems. The interest of Yeats' development for this anthology is that terms of development also describe some of the characteristics of the kind of poetry Yeats and others wrote in the last decades of the nineteenth century, some of the effects a very good poet could achieve in this idiom, and some of the effects Yeats, at least, believed could not be achieved unless he moved out from the style of his early maturity.

Yeats was born in Ireland. His father was the son of a landowning Protestant clergyman; his mother was the daughter of a merchant. Yeats' father studied law and was admitted to its practice. But he decided instead to make

[5] Burking: strangling; after William Burke, who was executed in 1829 for murdering victims in order to obtain bodies to sell to doctors for dissection.
[1] V. G.: Violet Granby, later Duchess of Rutland. Her children attended the funeral of Henley's daughter Margaret, who died when she was five years old, and her own eldest son died a few months later.

his living as a painter, and he moved his family to London shortly after Yeats' birth. Yeats went to school in England and then in Dublin after his family's return to Ireland in 1880. In 1883 he entered art school in Dublin, but he soon began a literary career, publishing his first poems in a university literary magazine in 1885 and writing literary journalism for other Dublin journals. When his family moved back to London in 1887, Yeats went with them, and he became a familiar in the life of literary London. He published his first volume of poems, *The Wanderings of Oisin and Other Poems,* in 1889, and another volume containing a play as well as some poems—*The Countless Cathleen and Various Legends and Lyrics* —in 1892. He continued to write literary journalism, including articles he wrote as the literary correspondent of some American newspapers. He published a volume containing two short fictions (*John Sherman* and *Dhoya:* 1891), coedited a collection of the poems of William Blake (1893), put together a collection of tellings of Irish folktales and fairy tales (*The Celtic Twilight:* 1893), which also contained some of his poems, and edited an anthology of Irish poetry (1895). He met Oscar Wilde and William Morris; he was a member of the Rhymers' Club, where he knew Lionel Johnson, Ernest Dowson, and Arthur Symons. He was also a member of the group of writers who gathered around William Ernest Henley, who published some of Yeats' poems in one of the magazines he edited. This first passage in Yeat's career ended almost exactly with the century, with the publication of *The Wind Among the Reeds,* a volume of poems, in 1899, and his return to live in Ireland and serve as one of the founders and the first president of a society for a national Irish theater.

Most of the poems of *The Wind Among the Reeds* volume and the volumes which preceded it are fairly described in the phrases Yeats used in his essay "The Autumn of the Body" (1898) to characterize the poetry of the end of nineteenth century. He imagined his entire generation reacting against the declamation, discursiveness, and acquiescence in the externality of things he saw epitomized in the poetry of Tennyson and Browning. He claimed that poets and painters were turning instead to a "spiritual and unemphatic" poetry of essences, symbols, still moments out of time, faint colors and outlines, and what he called in another essay "those wavering, meditative,

organic rhythms, which are the embodiment of the imagination . . . because it has done with time, and only wishes to gaze upon some reality, some beauty" ("The Symbolism of Poetry", 1900). In Dublin in the 1880s and in London in the 1890s Yeats studied magic and joined magical societies. At the same time he became interested in Irish folktales and fairy tales and in old Irish poems and myths of heroes, out of which he hoped to make a national literature which would further the aims of political nationalism by giving Ireland an identity and voice. When in the poems before 1900 Yeats uses the symbolism of the occult ("To the Rose" and "The Two Trees," for example) or of Irish myth and legend ("Fergus and the Druid"), he is in his way using poetry to work effects on the consciousness and in the moral and political reality of his contemporaries. Through these symbols the poem is an act, a manifestation of the great cosmic spirit and national identity they bring into common experience in order to change it. But despite their implications for everyday, circumstantial experience, these poems usually feel and sound like "An Indian Song" and "The Lake Isle of Innisfree"—poems whose themes, tones, language, and rhythms register not action but passivity and retreat, a yearning to be out of time and ordinary experience and, often, a sad recognition that these quiet, static, strangely colored places of refuge are also subject to the erosion of time.

By the time he published the poems of *The Wind Among the Reeds,* however, Yeats was already beginning to change their style. In the revisions of his early poems he made for the collected edition of 1895—in the revision of "An Indian Song" into "The Indian to His Love," for example—he tended to move toward a more common syntax, more definite images, and a more distinct and explicit movement of the poem through its stanzas. Shortly after he published the volume of essays containing "The Autumn of the Body" and "The Symbolism of Poetry" in 1903, he decided that the esthetic moment he described in these essays was a preparation for but not a prediction of the art to come, which would not try to escape form and definiteness but would rather try to create them. The principal sponsor of these opinions was Yeats' experience in the theater. From the performance of his plays in 1899 and after, Yeats learned that what he recognized as the stasis and the "all-pervading rhythm" of his verse were inappropriate in a medium in which distinctions had to be established between characters and the discourse had to occur in time and in sensible, visible circumstance. When in the first decade of the twentieth century he began to write for the Irish theater he helped to found, he set himself to make an idiom which, as he put it in the preface to an edition of *Poems 1899–1905* (1906), displayed a "manful energy," followed a logic of events, showed clear outlines rather than moments "blurred with desire and vague regret," and which, above all, admitted and openly engaged the temporal existences from which in his earlier poems he had tried to retreat into a dream of timeless essences.

What replaced the dream in Yeats' poetry in the twentieth century was the explicit drama of the conflict his earlier poems had muted. The difference between "Adam's Curse," say, and "The Pity of Love," or between the early version of "The Lamentation of the Old Pensioner" and the entirely new poem Yeats made when he revised it in the 1920s, is not that the terms of the argument have changed. It is rather that the poles of its tension have been made pointed, particular, and dramatic in their engagement with one another. The tension between beauty and time, between the self who dreams beauty and the self who labors in the body to make it, exists in Yeats' poetry from the beginning. But rather than admit opposites into his early poetry he tried for tones and an impersonal symbolism that obscured the confrontations which are the exact and central point of his later poetry. Yeats did not write many poems during the decade in which he was writing for the theater. He published one volume of poetry, *In the Seven Woods* (which contained "Adam's Curse") in 1903, and another, *The Green Helmet and Other Poems,* in 1910. In the poems of *Responsibilities* (1914) he fully emerged in his mature style, and his further development, especially in *The Wild Swans at Coole* (1917), *Michael Robartes and the Dancer* (1920), and *The Tower* (1928), was in the poetic language to which he had carefully made his way.

It was a very formal, measured language, based on speech, it is true, and open to the vocabularies and rhythms of a wide range of common experience, but fundamentally tuned to the high, strong speech of oratory and theater, or even to the kind of poetry chanted to musical accompaniment (see "The Players Ask for a Blessing"). Its rhythms were emphatic, its lines and stanzas firmly modeled, its tensions often enunciated in dialogue or in the address of a speaker not musing on his situation but directly engaged in working through its hard, mundane difficulties. Yeats elaborated his early studies in the occult into an entire cosomology and system of symbolism which he used in his poems and set out in *A Vision* (1937). But he was not a symbolist poet in the way in which he understood that word in the 1890s. He no longer refined images to the nearly bodiless, evocative objects of his late nineteenth-century poems. He rather brought, as he believed, precise and definite signs out of the *anima mundi,* out of the stock of images and meanings common to all humanity.

All of these changes are continuous with Yeats' conception and practice of poetry before 1900. Poetry for him was always, as it was for nineteenth-century poets (like Blake) of similar ambitions, an act of magic and mastery, a control and transformation of circumstance that elucidated and brought into play the great powers of a fundamentally spiritual reality. The difference for Yeats was that he came to think the language of the late-century poetry in which he began attained the control of art by eliding and evading forces that threatened it. If his judgment was not entirely valid—it does not seem to hold, for example, for the poetry of Thomas Hardy—it was true for Yeats, and it is true as well for other poets of his generation like Arthur Symons, Lionel Johnson, and Ernest Dowson, who remained in the late-century idiom whose limitations Yeats sharply throws into relief in his will to move out from them.

EDITIONS

The texts reprinted here are those of the original editions, the collected edition of 1895, or *The Poems of W. B. Yeats* (1949). Yeats' many revisions of his published poems are recorded in *The Variorum Edition of the Poems of W. B. Yeats,* edited by Paul Allt and Russell K. Alspach (revised edition 1966). *The Collected Plays of W. B. Yeats* was published in 1953; Alspach has also edited a variorum edition of the plays (1966). Yeats' *Autobiographies,* its several parts published separately between 1917 and 1936, were published together in 1955; his *Memoirs,* earlier or alternative versions of some of his autobiographical writings, were published in 1972. *A Vision,* first published in 1937, was republished with Yeats' final corrections in 1956 and 1962. Three collections of his essays have been published: *Essays and Introductions* (1961), *Explorations* (1962), and *Mythologies* (1959); John P. Frayne has also edited the first volume of Yeats' *Uncollected Prose: First Articles and Reviews 1886–1896* (1970). Allen Wade has edited *The Letters of W. B. Yeats* (1954); Donald Pearce has edited Yeats' *Senate Speeches* (1960). Richard J. Finneran has edited Yeats' two early fictions, *John Sherman and Dhoya* (1969).

BIOGRAPHY AND CRITICISM
Standard biographical accounts are Joseph Hone, *W. B. Yeats 1865–1939* (1943; revised 1962); A. N. Jeffares, *W. B. Yeats, Man and Poet* (1949); and Richard Ellman, *Yeats, The Man and the Masks* (1948).

John Unterecker's *A Reader's Guide to William Butler Yeats* (1959) and A. N. Jeffares' *A Commentary on the Collected Poems of W. B. Yeats* (1968) are general and complete commentaries on Yeats' poetry. Among the standard studies of Yeats' ideas and writing are T. R. Henn, *The Lonely Tower* (1950); Richard Ellmann, *The Identity of Yeats* (1954); A. Stock, *Yeats: His Poetry and Thought* (1961); and Harold Bloom, *Yeats* (1970). The best of several short introductions of Yeats is Denis Donoghue's *Yeats* (1971).

Yeats is the central figure in Frank Kermode's *Romantic Image* (1957), a study of the idea of an autonomous art in the nineteenth and twentieth centuries. Some studies of Yeats' relationships with nineteenth-century writers and ideas about literature are: Philip L. Marcus, *Yeats and the Beginning of the Irish Renaissance* (1970); Dwight Eddins, *Yeats: The Nineteenth-Century Matrix* (1971); the first volume of *Yeats Studies* (1970), which contains essays on Yeats and the 1890s; Peter Faulkner, *Yeats and William Morris* (1962); D. Hoare, *The Works of Morris and Yeats in Relation to Early Saga Literature* (1937); Richard Ellmann, *Eminent Domain* (1967), which includes remarks on Yeats and Oscar Wilde; Allen R. Grossman, *Poetic Knowledge in the Early Yeats: A Study of The Wind Among the Reeds* (1969); and Harold Orel, *The Development of William Butler Yeats: 1885–1900* (1968). Herbert Howarth's *Irish Writers: Literature and Nationalism 1880–1939* (1958) includes a discussion of Yeats'

connections with Irish politics. See also William Irwin Thompson's *The Imagination of an Insurrection, Dublin, Easter, 1916* (1967); and Malcolm Brown, *The Politics of Irish Literature* (1972).

Among the many studies of Yeats' revisions of his poems are: Peter Allt, "Yeats and the Development of His Early Verse," *Hermanthea,* 64–65 (1944–45); Thomas Parkinson, *Yeats: Self-Critic* (1951), a study of the revisions of his early poems, and *Yeats: The Later Poetry* (1964); Jon Stallworthy, *Between the Lines: Yeats's Poems in the Making* (1963); and Curtis Bradford, *Yeats at Work* (1965).

OTHER USEFUL BOOKS AND ESSAYS
Adams, Hazard. *Blake and Yeats* (1955).

Beum, Robert. *The Poetic Art of William Butler Yeats* (1969).

Bornstein, George. *Yeats and Shelley* (1970).

Bushrui, S. *Yeats's Verse Plays: The Revisions 1900–10* (1965).

Harper, George M. *Yeats' Golden Dawn* (1974). Account of magical society of which Yeats was a member.

Moore, Virginia. *The Unicorn: Yeats's Search for Reality* (1954). A study of Yeats' use of the occult.

Shmiefsky, Marvel. "Yeats and Browning: The Shock of Recognition," *Studies in English Literature,* **10** (1970).

Sidnell, Michael J., Mayhew, George P., and Clark, David R., eds. *Druid Craft: The Writing of The Shadowy Waters* (1971). Reproduction of and commentary on the manuscript of a play published in 1900.

Whitaker, Thomas. *Swan and Shadow: Yeats's Dialogue with History* (1964).

Among the most generally useful of several collections of essays about Yeats are *The Permanence of Yeats,* edited by J. Hall and Martin Steinmann (1950); *W. B. Yeats: A Critical Anthology,* edited by W. H. Pritchard (1972); and *Yeats: A Collection of Critical Essays,* edited by John Unterecker (1963). Allen Wade and Russell K. Alspach have compiled *A Bibliography of the Writings of W. B. Yeats* (revised edition, 1968). J. I. M. Stewart's volume in the Oxford History of English Literature, *Eight Modern Writers* (1963) contains a select bibliography of writing about Yeats. K. G. W. Cross and R. T. Dunlop have compiled *A Bibliography of Yeats Criticism 1887–1965* (1971).

An Indian Song (1889)

Oh wanderer in the southern weather,
    Our isle awaits us; on each lea[1]
The pea-hens dance, in crimson feather
    A parrot swaying on a tree
    Rages at his own image in the enamelled sea.

There dreamy Time lets fall his sickle
    And Life the sandals of her fleetness,
And sleek young Joy is no more fickle,
    And Love is kindly and deceitless,
    And all is over save the murmur and the
        sweetness.

There we will moor our lonely ship
    And wander ever with woven hands,
Murmuring softly, lip to lip,
    Along the grass, along the sands—
    Murmuring how far away are all earth's
        feverish lands:

How we alone of mortals are
    Hid in the earth's most hidden part,
While grows our love an Indian star,
    A meteor of the burning heart,
    One with the waves that softly round us
        laugh and dart;

One with the leaves; one with the dove
    That moans and sighs a hundred days;
—How when we die our shades will rove,
    Dropping at eve in coral bays
    A vapoury footfall on the ocean's sleepy
        blaze.

                                        1886; 1889

The Indian to His Love (1895)

The island dreams under the dawn
    And great boughs drop tranquillity;
The peahens dance on a smooth lawn,
    A parrot sways upon a tree,
    Raging at his own image in the dim[1]
        enamelled sea.

Here we will moor our lonely ship
    And wander ever with woven hands,
Murmuring softly lip to lip,
    Along the grass, along the sands,
    Murmuring gently how far off are the
        unquiet lands: 10

How we alone of mortals are
    Hid under quiet boughs apart,
While our love grows an Indian star,
    A meteor of the burning heart,
    One with the glimmering tide, the wings
        that glimmer and gleam and dart;[2]

The great boughs,[3] and the burnished dove
    That moans and sighs a hundred days:
How when we die our shades will rove,
    Where eve has hushed the feathered ways,
    And drop a vapoury footfall in the water's
        drowsy blaze.[4]   20

                                            1895

*When this poem first appeared in a Dublin maga-
zine in 1885 its title was "An Epilogue. To 'The
Island of Statues' and 'The Seeker.' Spoken by a
Satyr, carrying a sea-shell." The two poems named
in this title, the first of them a short lyrical and
allegorical drama, were excluded by Yeats from the
1895 collection of his poems and never reprinted in
his collected works. The poem was titled "Song of
the Last Arcadian" when it was printed in* The
Wanderings of Oisin and Other Poems *in 1889. It
was revised and received its present title when it
was published in the 1895 collection. It was not
significantly revised after 1895.*

The Song of the Happy Shepherd

The woods of Arcady[1] are dead,
And over is their antique joy;
Of old the world on dreaming fed;
Gray Truth is now her painted toy;
Yet still she turns her restless head:
But O, sick children of the world,
Of all the many changing things
In dreary dancing past us whirled,
To the cracked tune that Chronos[2] sings,

---

[1] Lea: pasture.
[1] In an edition of his poems published in 1901 Yeats dropped the word "dim" from this line.
[2] After 1901: One with the tide that gleams, the wings that gleam and dart.
[3] After 1901: The heavy bough . . .
[4] 1901: With vapoury footsole among [later, "by"] the water's drowsy blaze.
[1] Arcady: a region in Greece conventionally named as the site of pastoral idylls.
[2] Chronos: one of the Titans in Greek mythology who was overthrown by his son Zeus as the
chief of the gods and the ruler of the universe. In 1889 the phrase read "old cracked tune."

10   Words alone are certain good.
     Where are now the warring kings,
     Word be-mockers?—By the Rood[3]
     Where are now the warring kings?
     An idle word is now their glory,
     By the stammering schoolboy said,
     Reading some entangled story:
     The kings of the old time are fled.[4]
     The wandering earth herself may be
     Only a sudden flaming word,
20   In clanging space a moment heard,
     Troubling the endless reverie.

     Then no wise worship dusty deeds,
     Nor seek—for this is also sooth[5]—
     To hunger fiercely after truth,
     Lest all thy toiling only breeds
     New dreams, new dreams; there is no truth,
     Saving in thine own heart. Seek, then,
     No learning from the starry men,
     Who follow with the optic glass
30   The whirling ways of stars that pass—
     Seek, then, for this is also sooth,
     No word of theirs—the cold star-bane[6]
     Has cloven and rent their hearts in twain,[7]
     And dead is all their human truth.
     Go gather by the humming sea
     Some twisted, echo-harbouring shell,

And to its lips thy story tell,
And they thy comforters will be,
Rewording in melodious guile
Thy fretful words a little while,   40
Till they shall singing fade in ruth,
And die a pearly brotherhood;[8]
For words alone are certain good:
Sing then, for this is also sooth.

I must be gone—there is a grave
Where daffodil and lily wave,
And I would please the hapless faun,[9]
Buried under the sleepy ground,
With mirthful songs before the dawn.
His shouting days with mirth were crowned;   50
And still I dream he treads the lawn,
Walking ghostly in the dew,
Pierced by my glad singing through,
My songs of old earth's dreamy youth:
But ah! she dreams not now—dream thou!
For fair are poppies on the brow:
Dream, dream, for this is also sooth.

                              1885; 1889; 1895

The Falling of the Leaves[1]

Autumn is over the long leaves that love us,
    And over the mice in the barley sheaves;

---

[3] Rood: the cross of Christ.

[4] In 1927 Yeats changed the last word of this line to "dead." In 1895 he had thoroughly re-vised lines 13–21 from the 1889 version:

> Where are now the old kings hoary?
> They were of no wordy mood;
> An idle word is now their glory,
> By the stammering schoolboy said,
> In the verse of Attic story
> Chronicling chimaeras fled.
> The very world itself may be
> Only a sudden flaming word,
> 'Mid clanging space a moment heard
> In the universe's reverie.

[5] Sooth: truth.   [6] Bane: poison, evil.   [7] 1889: Has torn and rent. . . .
[8] 1889: lines 42–44:

> For ruth and joy have brotherhood,
> And words alone are certain good—
> Sing then, for this is also sooth.

[9] 1889: lines 47–49:

> And downy bees have ambuscade,
> And birdly iteration is
> Through all the well-beloved glade.
> Farewell; I must be gone, I-wis,
> That I may soothe that hapless faun
> (Who 's buried in the sleepy ground),
> With mirthful songs till rise the dawn.

[1] Except that the title was changed from "Falling of the Leaves" after 1889, this poem was not revised.

Yellow the leaves of the rowan[2] above us,
  And yellow the wet wild-strawberry leaves.

The hour of the waning of love has beset us,
  And weary and worn are our sad souls now;
Let us part, ere the season of passion forget us,
  With a kiss and a tear on thy drooping brow.

1889; 1895

To the Rose upon the Rood of Time[1]

Red Rose, proud Rose, sad Rose of all my days,
Come near me, while I sing the ancient ways:
Cuhoolin[2] battling with the bitter tide;
The Druid, gray, wood nurtured, quiet eyed,
Who cast round Fergus dreams, and ruin
    untold;
And thine own sadness, whereof stars, grown
    old
In dancing silver sandalled on the sea,
Sing in their high and lonely melody.
Come near, that no more blinded by man's
    fate,
I find under the boughs of love and hate,
In all poor foolish things that live a day,
Eternal Beauty wandering on her way.

Come near, come near, come near—Ah, leave
    me still
A little space for the rose-breath to fill!
Lest I no more hear common things that crave;
The weak worm hiding down in its small cave,
The field mouse running by me in the grass,
And heavy mortal hopes that toil and pass;
But seek alone to hear the strange things said
By God to the bright hearts of those long dead,
And learn to chaunt a tongue men do not
    know.

Come near—I would, before my time to go,
Sing of old Eri and the ancient ways:
Red Rose, proud Rose, sad Rose of all my days.

1892; 1895

Fergus and the Druid[1]

FERGUS
The whole day have I followed in the rocks,
And you have changed and flowed from shape
    to shape.
First as a raven on whose ancient wings
Scarcely a feather lingered, then you seemed
A weasel moving on from stone to stone,
And now at last you take on human shape—
A thin gray man half lost in gathering night.

DRUID
What would you, king of the proud Red Branch
    kings?

FERGUS
This would I say, most wise of living souls:
Young subtle Concobar[2] sat close by me   10
When I gave judgment, and his words were
    wise,
And what to me was burden without end,
To him seemed easy, so I laid the crown
Upon his head to cast away my care.[3]

DRUID
What would you, king of the proud Red Branch
    kings?

FERGUS
I feast amid my people on the hill,[4]
And pace the woods, and drive my chariot
    wheels
In the white border of the murmuring sea;
And still I feel the crown upon my head.

[2] Rowan: a tree that bears white flowers and red fruit.
[1] Yeats used the rose in his poetry of the 1890s as a symbol for spiritual and eternal (as opposed to material) beauty, and as a symbol of Ireland. The rose on the cross (rood) is also a symbol borrowed from the mystical Rosicrucian order, symbolizing for Yeats both the marriage of masculine (cross) and feminine (rose) qualities and the presence of the spiritual and eternal in the temporal order. The poem was not substantively revised after 1892.
[2] Cuhoolin: one of Yeats' several spellings of the name of the central hero of the Red Branch cycle of stories about the heroes of early Ireland. One of the legends about Cuchulain was that of a battle with the tides of the sea.
[1] Yeats' note in the 1895 edition: "*Fergus*. He was the poet of the Red Branch cycle. . . . He was once king of all Ireland, but gave up his throne that he might live at peace hunting in the woods." The Red Branch cycle is a collection of legends about heroes of Ireland in the first centuries of the Christian era. A Druid is a priest of pagan and magical ritual.
[2] Concobar: the king of Ireland.   [3] In 1925 this word was changed to "sorrow."
[4] In 1925 Yeats added a line before line 16: "A king and proud! and that is my despair."

DRUID

20 What would you?

FERGUS

          I would be no more a king,
But learn the dreaming wisdom that is yours.

DRUID

Look on my thin gray hair and hollow cheeks,
And on these hands that may not lift the sword,
This body trembling like a wind-blown reed.
No maiden loves me, no man seeks my help,[5]
Because I be not of the things I dream.

FERGUS

A wild and foolish labourer is a king,
To do and do and do and never dream.[6]

DRUID

Take, if you must, this little bag of dreams,[7]
Unloose the cord, and they will wrap you
30   round.

FERGUS

I see my life go dripping like a stream[8]
From change to change; I have been many
   things—
A green drop in the surge, a gleam of light
Upon a sword, a fir-tree on a hill,
An old slave grinding at a heavy quern,[9]
A king sitting upon a chair of gold,
And all these things were wonderful and great;
But now I have grown nothing, being all,
And the whole world weighs down upon my
   heart—[10]

Ah! Druid, Druid, how great webs of sorrow   4(
Lay hidden in the small slate-coloured thing!
                   1892; 1895

The Ballad of Father O'Hart[1]

Good Father John O'Hart
   In penal days[2] rode out
To a shoneen[3] who had free lands
   And his own snipe and trout.

In trust took he John's lands;
   Sleiveens[4] were all his race;
And he gave them as dowers to his daughters,
   And they married beyond their place.

But Father John went up,
   And Father John went down;   1(
And he wore small holes in his shoes,
   And he wore large holes in his gown.

All loved him, only[5] the shoneen,
   Whom the devils have by the hair,
From the wives, and the cats, and the children,
   To the birds in the white of the air.

The birds, for he opened their cages
   As he went up and down;
And he said with a smile, "Have peace now,"
   And went his way with a frown.   2(

But if when any one died
   Came keeners[6] hoarser than rooks,

---

[5] In 1925 this line was changed to read "No woman's loved me, no man sought my help"; and the following line was dropped.

[6] 1925:

    A king is but a foolish labourer
    Who wastes his blood to be another's dream.

[7] 1892: "Take then this small slate-coloured bag of dreams."

[8] 1925: ". . . go drifting like a river."   [9] Quern: a hand mill for grinding grain.

[10] The ending of the poem was frequently revised. When it was first published in a magazine in 1892, line 39 was followed by these lines:

    And in my heart the daemons and the gods
    Wage an eternal battle, and I feel
    The pain of wounds, the labour of the spear,
    But have no share in loss or victory.

In Yeats' 1892 volume these four lines were dropped, and the present final two lines of the poem were added. In 1925 line 38 was ended with a period, and line 39 was dropped.

[1] In several notes to this poem Yeats wrote that it is based on stories of an eighteenth-century priest of Coloony in the northwest of Ireland in the county of Sligo, where Yeats' grandparents lived.

[2] Penal days: the days in which Roman Catholics were forbidden to own land. Yeats notes that the law was evaded by transferring nominal ownership to a Protestant.

[3] Shoneen: Yeats' note: "upstart."   [4] Sleiveen: Yeats' note: "mean fellow."   [5] Only: except.

[6] Keeners: professional mourners.

He bade them give over their keening;
   For he was a man of books.

All these were the works of John,
   When weeping score by score,
People came into Coloony,
   For he'd died at ninety-four.

There was no human keening;
   The birds from Knocknarea[7]
And the world round Knocknashee
   Came keening in that day.

The young birds and old birds
   Came flying, heavy, and sad;
Keening in from Tiraragh,
   Keening from Ballinafad;

Keening from Innismurry,
   Nor stayed for bite or sup;
This way were all reproved
   Who dig old customs up.

               1888; 1892; 1895

The Sorrow of Love

The quarrel of the sparrows in the eaves,
   The full round moon and the star-laden sky,
And the loud song of the ever-singing leaves,
   Had hid away earth's old and weary cry.

And then you came with those red mournful
   lips,
   And with you came the whole of the world's
   tears,
And all the sorrows of her labouring ships,
   And all the burden of her myriad years.[1]

And now the sparrows warring in the eaves,
   The curd-pale[2] moon, the white stars in the
   sky,   10
And the loud chaunting of the unquiet leaves,
   Are shaken with earth's old and weary cry.

                   1892; 1895

The Pity of Love (1892)

A pity beyond all telling,
   Is hid in the heart of love;
The folk who are buying and selling,
   The stars of God where they move,
The mouse-grey waters on flowing,
   The clouds on their journey above,
And the cold wet winds ever blowing,
   All threaten the head that I love.

                         1892

The Pity of Love (1895)

A pity beyond all telling
   Is hid in the heart of love:
The folk who are buying and selling;
   The clouds on their journey above;
The cold wet winds ever blowing;
   And the shadowy hazel grove
Where mouse-gray waters are flowing,
   Threaten the head that I love.

                         1895

The Lake Isle of Innisfree[1]

I will arise and go now, and go to Innisfree,
   And a small cabin build there, of clay and
   wattles[2] made;

---

[7] Knocknarea: a hill in Sligo; all the other places named in the poem are also in Sligo, except for Innismurry (line 37), which is an island in the Atlantic.

[1] Yeats so revised this poem for a 1925 edition of his poetry that it became a new poem. His revision of the second stanza indicates that in the earlier version he had in mind the story of Helen's abduction and the subsequent Trojan War:

> A girl arose that had red mournful lips
> And seemed the greatness of the world in tears,
> Doomed like Odysseus and the labouring ships
> And proud as Priam murdered with his peers;

In 1899 Yeats changed the word "burden" in the last line of this stanza to "trouble."

[2] In 1892 this word was "crumbling."

[1] Innisfree is an island in an inlet off Sligo Bay in the northwest of Ireland. Yeats in his *Autobiographies* called the poem "my first lyric with anything in its rhythm of my own music. I had begun to loosen rhythm as an escape from rhetoric and from that emotion of the crowd rhetoric brings, but I only understood vaguely and occasionally that I must for my special purpose use nothing but the common syntax. A couple of years later I would not have written that first line with its conventional archaism, . . . nor the inversion in the last stanza" (p. 153).

[2] Wattles: panels of interwoven poles.

Nine bean rows will I have there, a hive for
    the honey bee,
And live alone in the bee-loud glade.

And I shall have some peace there, for peace
    comes dropping slow,
    Dropping from the veils of the morning to
    where the cricket sings;
There midnight's all a glimmer, and noon a
    purple glow,
    And evening full of the linnet's wings.

I will arise and go now, for always night and
    day
    I hear lake water lapping with low sounds
10   by the shore;
While I stand on the roadway or on the
    pavements gray,[3]
    I hear it in the deep heart's core.
                     1890; 1892; 1895

The Lamentation of the Old Pensioner

I had a chair at every hearth,
    When no one turned to see,
With "Look at that old fellow there,
    And who may he be?"
And therefore do I wander now,
    And the fret[1] lies on me.

The road-side trees keep murmuring.
    Ah, wherefore murmur ye,
As in the old days long gone by,
10   Green oak and poplar tree?

The well-known faces are all gone:
    And the fret lies on me.[2]
                  1890; 1892; 1895

Yeats drew on his studies in magic for the idea of the tree which is fundamental to this poem. In the Cabbala, a supposedly medieval collection of rituals for magic, both the universe and man as a microcosm of the universe are described as organized like a tree whose different areas (head, heart, etc.) or branches are dominated or characterized by different human qualities and different states of purification in the universe. Each area or branch may also be dominated by beneficent or malign spirits. It is the purpose of the magician to keep the tree of his or her own being flourishing and in balance, and to work his or her way up the tree of the universe to higher states of knowledge and being, by invoking good spirits and by keeping malign spirits at bay.

The Two Trees

Beloved, gaze in thine own heart,
    The holy tree is growing there;
From joy the holy branches start,
    And all the trembling flowers they bear.
The changing colours of its fruit
    Have dowered the stars with merry light;
The surety of its hidden root
    Has planted quiet in the night;
The shaking of its leafy head
    Has given the waves their melody,
And made my lips and music wed,
    Murmuring a wizard song for thee.
There, through bewildered branches, go[1]
    Winged Loves borne on in gentle strife,
Tossing and tossing to and fro
    The flaming circle of our life.

---

[3] The poem was written in London during a bout of homesickness when Yeats saw a fountain in a commercial display and heard the fall of water.
    [1] Fret: doom, destiny.
    [2] In 1925 Yeats revised this lyric into a wholly new poem. The last stanza, for example, now reads:

> There's not a woman turns her face
> Upon a broken tree,
> And yet the beauties that I loved
> Are in my memory;
> I spit into the face of Time
> That has transfigured me.

  [1] In 1929 Yeats revised lines 13–18 to read:

> There the Loves a circle go,
> The flaming circle of our days,
> Gyring, spiring to and fro
> In those great ignorant leafy ways;
> Remembering all that shaken hair
> And how the winged sandals dart,

When looking on their shaken hair,
   And dreaming how they dance and dart,
Thine eyes grow full of tender care:
   Beloved, gaze in thine own heart.

Gaze no more in the bitter glass
   The demons, with their subtle guile,
Lift up before us when they pass,
   Or only gaze a little while;
For there a fatal image grows,
   With broken boughs, and blackened leaves,[2]
And roots half hidden under snows
   Driven by a storm that ever grieves.
For all things turn to barrenness
   In the dim glass the demons hold,
The glass of outer weariness,
   Made when God slept in times of old.
There, through the broken branches, go
   The ravens of unresting thought;
Peering and flying to and fro,[3]
   To see men's souls bartered and bought.
When they are heard upon the wind,
   And when they shake their wings; alas!
Thy tender eyes grow all unkind:
   Gaze no more in the bitter glass.

                1892; 1895

The Moods

Time drops in decay,
Like a candle burnt out,
And the mountains and woods
Have their day, have their day;
What one in the rout[1]

Of the fire-born moods
Has fallen away?

                1893; 1899

Aedh Tells of the Rose in His Heart[1]

All things uncomely and broken, all things
   worn out and old,
The cry of a child by the roadway, the creak
   of a lumbering cart,
The heavy steps of the ploughman, splashing
   the wintry mould,
Are wronging your image that blossoms a rose
   in the deeps of my heart.

The wrong of unshapely things is a wrong too
   great to be told;   10
I hunger to build them anew and sit on a
   green knoll apart,
With the earth and the sky and the water,
   remade, like a casket of gold
For my dreams of your image that blossoms a
   rose in the deeps of my heart.

                1892; 1899

The Song of Wandering Aengus[1]

I went out to the hazel wood,
Because a fire was in my head,
And cut and peeled a hazel wand,[2]
And hooked a berry to a thread;
And when white moths were on the wing,
And moth-like stars were flickering out,

---

[2] 1929: lines 26–28:

      That the stormy night receives,
      Roots half hidden under snows,
      Broken boughs and blackened leaves.

[3] 1929: lines 35–38:

      Flying, crying, to and fro,
      Cruel claw and hungry throat,
      Or else they stand and sniff the wind,
      And shake their ragged wings; alas!

[1] In 1893 these lines read:

      But, kindly old rout
      Of the fire-born moods,
      You pass not away.

[1] Yeats later changed the title of this poem and others spoken by Aedh to substitute "He" or "The Lover" for the speaker's name. As Yeats explained in a note to *The Wind Among the Reeds*, Aedh is a name for a principle of the mind: "Michael Robartes is the pride of imagination brooding upon the greatness of its possessions, or the adoration of the Magi; while Aedh is the myrrh and frankincense that the imagination continually offers before all that it loves" (*Variorum*, p. 803).

[1] Aengus was a figure in Celtic mythology, a god of youth, love, and poetry.

[2] The hazel was associated with Aengus by Yeats, and with the Tree of Life or Knowledge.

I dropped the berry in a stream
And caught a little silver trout.

When I had laid it on the floor
10   I went to blow the fire a-flame,
But something rustled on the floor,
And someone called me by my name:
It had become a glimmering girl
With apple blossom in her hair
Who called me by my name and ran
And faded through the brightening air.

Though I am old with wandering
Through hollow lands and hilly lands,
I will find out where she has gone,
20   And kiss her lips and take her hands;
And walk among long dappled grass,
And pluck till time and times are done,
The silver apples of the moon,
The golden apples of the sun.

                              1897; 1899

Mongan Laments the Change That Has Come upon Him and His Beloved[1]

Do you not hear me calling, white deer with no horns![2]
I have been changed to a hound with one red ear;
I have been in the Path of Stones and the Wood of Thorns,
For somebody hid hatred and hope and desire and fear
Under my feet that they follow you night and day.
A man with a hazel wand came without sound;[3]
He changed me suddenly; I was looking another way;

And now my calling is but the calling of a hound;
And Time and Birth and Change are hurrying by.
I would that the boar without bristles had come from the West[4]
And had rooted the sun and moon and stars out of the sky
And lay in the darkness, grunting, and turning to his rest.

                              1897; 1899

Aedh Hears the Cry of the Sedge[1]

I wander by the edge
Of this desolate lake
Where wind cries in the sedge
Until the axle break
That keeps the stars in their round
And hands hurl in the deep
The banners of East and West
And the girdle of light is unbound,
Your head will not lie on the breast
Of your beloved in sleep.

                              1898; 1899

Aedh Thinks of Those Who Have Spoken Evil of His Beloved[1]

Half close your eyelids, loosen your hair,
And dream about the great and their pride;
They have spoken against you everywhere,
But weigh this song with the great and their pride;
I made it out of a mouthful of air,
Their children's children shall say they have lied.

                              1898; 1899

[1] Yeats later changed the title of this poem to "He Mourns for the Change that Has Come upon Him and His Beloved, and Longs for the End of the World." Mongan was a magician and king in Celtic mythology.
[2] In a note in *The Wind Among the Reeds* Yeats wrote that he found the images of the hound and the deer in a story of the Celtic hero Oisin, who followed a hornless deer on his journey to a country of eternal youth. The hound and the deer, Yeats added, "seem plain images of the desire of the man 'which is for the woman,' and 'the desire of the woman which is for the desire of the man'."
[3] Yeats in his note suggests that this person may have been Aengus, a Celtic god of youth, beauty, and poetry.
[4] A reference to a legend of an apocalyptic battle in the west to be fought in the Valley of the Black Pig.
[1] Aedh: see note to "Aedh Tells of the Rose." Sedge: marsh plants.
[1] Aedh: see note to "Aedh Tells of the Rose in His Heart."

The Folly of Being Comforted

One that is ever kind said yesterday:
"Your well beloved's hair has threads of grey
And little shadows come about her eyes;[1]
Time can but make it easier to be wise
Though now it's hard, till trouble is at an end;
And so be patient, be wise and patient friend."
But heart, there is no comfort, not a grain.[2]
Time can but make her beauty over again
Because of that great nobleness of hers;
10 The fire that stirs about her, when she stirs
Burns but more clearly; O she had not these
  ways,
When all the wild summer was in her gaze.
O heart O heart if she'd but turn her head,[3]
You'd know the folly of being comforted.

                              1902; 1903

Adam's Curse

We sat together at one summer's end
That beautiful mild woman your close friend
And you and I, and talked of poetry.

I said "a line will take us hours maybe,
Yet if it does not seem a moment's thought
Our stitching and unstitching has been naught.
Better go down upon your marrow bones
And scrub a kitchen pavement, or break stones
Like an old pauper in all kinds of weather;
10 For to articulate sweet sounds together
Is to work harder than all these and yet
Be thought an idler by the noisy set
Of bankers, schoolmasters, and clergymen
The martyrs call the world."

                    That woman then
Murmured with her young voice, for whose
  mild sake

There's many a one shall find out all heartache
In finding that it's young and mild and low.
"There is one thing that all we women know
Although we never heard of it at school,[1]
That we must labour to be beautiful."   20

I said, "It's certain there is no fine thing
Since Adam's fall but needs much labouring.
There have been lovers who thought love
  should be
So much compounded of high courtesy
That they would sigh and quote with learned
  looks
Precedents out of beautiful old books;
Yet now it seems an idle trade enough."

We sat grown quiet at the name of love.
We saw the last embers of daylight die
And in the trembling blue-green of the sky   30
A moon, worn as if it had been a shell
Washed by time's waters as they rose and fell
About the stars and broke in days and years.

I had a thought for no one's but your ears;
That you were beautiful and that I strove
To love you in the old high way of love;
That it had all seemed happy, and yet we'd
  grown
As weary hearted as that hollow moon.

                              1902; 1903

The Players Ask for a Blessing on the Psalteries and Themselves[1]

THREE VOICES *together*.   Hurry to bless
  the hands that play
The mouths that speak, the notes and strings

---

[1] In 1902 this line read: "And there are little creases about her eyes."
[2] Yeats' final revision of lines 5–7:

> "Though now it seem impossible, and so
> All that you need is patience."
>   Heart cries, "No,
> I have not a crumb of comfort, not of grain"

[3] In 1906: O heart! O heart! . . .
[1] Yeats' final revision of lines 14–19:

> And thereupon
> That beautiful mild woman for whose sake
> There's many a one shall find out all heartache
> On finding that her voice is sweet and low
> Replied: "To be born woman is to know—
> Although they do not talk of it at school—

[1] Psalterie: a stringed instrument: Yeats had one made for him which was like a combination
of zither and lyre, and tuned to the intervals of a speaking voice so that poetry could be chanted
to it.

O masters[2] of the glittering town!
O! lay the shrilly trumpet down,
Though drunken with the flags that sway
Over the ramparts and the towers,
And with the waving of your wings.

    FIRST VOICE.   Maybe they linger by the way;
10 One gathers up his purple gown;
One leans and mutters by the wall;
He dreads the weight of mortal hours.

    SECOND VOICE.   O no, O no, they hurry down
Like plovers that have heard the call.

    THIRD VOICE.   O, kinsmen of the Three in
      One,
O, kinsmen bless the hands that play.
The notes they waken shall live on
When all this heavy history's done.
Our hands, our hands must ebb away.

    THREE VOICES *together*.   The proud and
      careless notes live on
But bless our hands that ebb away.   20

                                    1903

Rudyard Kipling
1865–1936

RUDYARD KIPLING was superbly fitted, by birth, experience, talent, and inclination, to make the most of two sets of circumstances in late nineteenth-century England. The first was that a great many English-speaking people were engaged in the imperial enterprise of extending the mercantile and industrial presence of Great Britain and America all over the world. The second was that publishing and journalism had become large and well-organized businesses that could efficiently retail accounts of these imperial adventures to the even larger number of people who wanted to read about them. By the end of the nineteenth century Kipling's accounts of the British outside Great Britain made him rich and famous, the most popular British writer since Dickens. His writing was not popular in the sense that it was a simple reduction of prevailing sentiment, an uncomplicated exaltation of white men and western machines in remote places. The short stories and poems that first made him a popular writer seemed rather to be clear-eyed, authentic accounts of the soldiers, engineers, administrators, and technicians who were really doing the hard, common, usually constructive work of Empire. More important, Kipling wrote about these people in a language appropriate to their character and experience. Especially in his first volumes of poetry he wrote an English full of the strange vocabularies of far places and contemporary occupations, sometimes quick and funny in its dialects, sometimes as sonorous as a sermon in its elevated periods, often memorably sententious in its phrases, and usually running bouyantly to the tunes and meters of such common forms as hymns, street ballads, the songs of music halls, parlors, and soldiers' barracks, and the kind of declamatory set-pieces familiar in the stand-up recitations of nineteenth-century students and elocution masters.

Kipling was born in India, where his father was a professor of sculptural architecture at the University of Bombay. Like his father, his mother was the child of a Methodist clergyman, and she too had close connections among London artists of the mid-nineteenth century: one of Kipling's uncles was the Pre-Raphaelite painter Edward Burne-Jones. As was common in Anglo-Indian families, Kipling was sent to England for his education. He lived for a

---

2 Masters: Jeffares (p. 98) notes that in 1902 Yeats wrote that he was engaged with a poem to the "Seven Archangels to Bless the Seven Notes." The angels are then "kinsmen" to the "Three in One," the Trinity (line 14).

while with an uncomfortably strict Calvinist family, and he completed his education at a school patronized by army officers and imperial administrators whose sons were preparing for the same careers. In 1882, when he was seventeen years old, Kipling returned to India to work as a journalist. In addition to reporting, he began to contribute narrative sketches and poems to the newspapers for which he wrote. Some of his poems, including "Giffen's Debt," were collected and published in India as *Departmental Ditties* in 1886. In 1888 he published a similar collection of narrative prose sketches, *Plain Tales from the Hills,* short, pointed pieces, most of them written to fit the requirements of newspaper publication. In the same year some other prose narratives and a few poems, most of them also first printed in Indian newspapers, were published in a series of cheap editions sold for reading on railways. By this time Kipling, at the age of twenty-three, was a popular writer in India, and his popularity was building in England and the United States. *Departmental Ditties* (in its third edition of 1888) and *Plain Tales from the Hills* were distributed in England by their Indian publishers, and in 1890 the six volumes of the Indian Railway Library, including the collections titled *Soldiers Three, The Phantom 'Rickshaw,* and *Wee Willie Winkie,* were published in Great Britain in editions of 7000 copies each.

By then Kipling was in London, having sailed east from India and traveled west to east through the United States to arrive in London at the end of 1889. During the next two years he published poems and fiction in British magazines that established the fact and style of his fame. When his poems appeared in magazines, they were often immediately talked about and quoted: "The Ballad of East and West" ("Oh, East is East, and West is West, and never the twain shall meet"), "Danny Deever," "Gunga Din," "The Widow's Party." When these poems and others were collected as *Barrack Room Ballads* in 1892, the volume went into three editions in the year of its publication and fifty more editions in the next thirty years. He also serialized a short novel, *The Light That Failed,* in a magazine in 1891, the same year in which he published a collection of short stories with Indian settings, also first published in magazines. In 1892 Kipling married an American, and after once again traveling eastward around the world he settled in

Vermont for four years. His writing was soon as popular in the United States as it was in Great Britain. During his residence in Vermont he published the two series of *Jungle Books* (1894, 1895), published another collection of stories from magazines in 1893, and the poems of *The Seven Seas* volume in 1896, whose first printing in Great Britain was 22,000 copies, a figure that recalled the printing orders of the mid-Victorian years of Tennyson's eminence.

When Kipling returned to England from the United States in 1896 he was a public figure of considerable eminence. He began a series of annual visits to South Africa, where he lived in a house given to him by the colonial statesman Cecil Rhodes. He corresponded with Theodore Roosevelt, whom he had met in the United States, and lived for a time in a house in Scotland put at his use by the industrialist Andrew Carnegie. He knew other powerful politicians and generals in America, South Africa, and England. His politics were deeply conservative and nationalistic, and he spoke and wrote frequently on topical political issues. During the last years of the nineteenth century the London *Times* printed on its editorial page anything he sent to them on public affairs, and he sent such statements as "The White Man's Burden" and "Recessional." During the South African War at the beginning of the nineteenth century he published similar statements and exhortations in other newspapers, and one of his poems ("The Absent-Minded Beggar"), set to a tune by Arthur Sullivan that Kipling said was "guaranteed to pull the teeth out of barrel-organs," raised £250,000 in performers' fees for a fund to purchase comforts for soldiers in South Africa. In 1899 he refused the first of several offers of knighthoods (all of them were refused), and in 1907 he was the first British writer to be awarded a Nobel prize for literature.

After the publication of *The Seven Seas* the bulk of Kipling's writing was fiction: novels (*Captains Courageous* in 1897, *Stalky and Co.* in 1899, *Kim* in 1901), the fables of the *Just So Stories* (1902), and then more than a half dozen collections of short narratives between 1898 and 1932. All of his fiction, even his novels, was written in relatively short forms, and almost all of it first appeared in magazines. He published a collection of verse, including his newspaper poems on the South African War, in 1903 (*The Five Nations*), and another collection in 1919, the same year in which he published the first of several editions of his collected poetry. Almost all of his collections of fiction in the twentieth century contained poems. In the twentieth century his verse became less frequently narrative and more often declamatory or fabulistic ("The Dykes," for example), often because the verse was written to comment on current political matters or to gloss and explicate the messages of his prose narratives. The messages of his verse itself were often perceptions and warnings about the state of civilization. Civilization to Kipling meant the engines of the present: bridges and roads, ships and deep-sea cables, books, magazines, and other agents of literacy and rational, technological enlightenment. He saw these civilizing elements as at once expressing and creating order and law. He knew the cost, at least to white men, of this civilizing work, and he knew the hypocrisy of those who stayed at home and either ignored the cost or deplored it while enjoying the benefits of empire. He also knew, and was fascinated by, what happened when the culture he called civilization met other, older, different cultures, by the revelation in this meeting of the relativity of cultural and moral values and the temporality of political and social systems.

But for Kipling the foundations of order and law lay deeper than the systems through which they were at one time or another expressed, and the excitement of advancing the culture of white Europeans cut through hypocrisy and validated its cost. Order and law existed in human experience because humans made them. Like McAndrew, Kipling did not make a god of a machine. He rather found God in the machine, as other nineteenth-century poets had found God in mountains and trees. For Kipling the joy was that this time the evidence was manifested in things humans had made. Kipling's celebration of human capacity to order and advance from the present was congenial to a popular late-nineteenth-century mood that did not get expressed in the languors and retreats of late-century aestheticism, and Kipling's themes are therefore one cause of his popularity as a writer. More important to the popularity of his poems, however, and to the place of his poetry at the end of the history of Victorian poetry, is that at the end of the century he brought into poetry some of the sounds and rhythms with which people who sang hymns and sentimental or heroic parlor songs, who heard sermons and read newspaper editorials, commonly found their beliefs stated and the content of their lives given form and force. More important yet, and the most significant measure of his achievement, is that the bright sounds, emphatic rhythms, short forms, and telling, memorable phrases of Kipling's verse, all perfectly fit to the journalism in which they first made their effect, again made a finely crafted body of poetry written in the nineteenth century something like a common literary and cultural possession of large numbers of his contemporaries.

EDITIONS

The texts of the poems printed here are those of the original editions. The texts of the standard edition, *Kipling's Verse: Definitive Edition* (1940), are sometimes slightly different, usually in their punctuation. The most complete of many collected editions of Kipling's writing are the Sussex (1937–39) and Burwash (1941) editions. Some of Kipling's letters are published in Morton N. Cohen's *Kipling to Rider Haggard: The Record of a Friendship* (1965).

BIOGRAPHY AND CRITICISM

The standard biography is C. E. Carrington's *Kipling: His Life and Work* (1955), now complemented by Philip Mason's *Kipling: The Glass, the Shadow and the Fire* (1975). Louis L. Cornell's *Kipling in India* (1966) is an account of Kipling's early journalistic career. J. M. S. Tompkins' *The Art of Rudyard Kipling* (1959), C. A. Bodelsen's *Aspects of Kipling's Art* (1964), J. I. M. Stewart's *Rudyard Kipling* (1966), and Bonamy Dobrée's *Rudyard Kipling: Realist and Fabulist* (1967) all consider (Tompkins rather lightly) Kipling's poetry. Edward Shanks' *Rudyard Kipling: A Study in Literature and Political Ideas* (1940; reprinted 1970) and Noel Annan's essay, "Kipling's Place in the History of Ideas," *Victorian Studies*, 3 (1960) discuss Kipling's ideas about politics and culture. In *The Eighteen Nineties* (revised edition, 1922) Holbrook Jackson discusses Kipling's place and presence in late-nineteenth-century literary life.

OTHER USEFUL BOOKS AND ESSAYS

Brown, Hilton. *Kipling: A New Appreciation* (1945).

Eliot, T. S. "Introduction" to *A Choice of Kipling's Verse* (1943).

Gross, John, ed. *Rudyard Kipling: The Man, His Work, and His World* (1972; American title: *The Age of Kipling*). Includes essays on Kipling's poetry, his imperialism, his knowledge of music halls, his response to the South African War, and his reputation.

Henn, T. R. *Kipling* (1967).

Rao, K. Bhaskara. *Rudyard Kipling's India* (1967).

Weygandt, A. M. *Kipling's Reading and Its Influence on His Poetry* (1939).

Wilson, Edmund. "The Kipling Nobody Knew", in *The Wound and the Bow* (1941).

Ralph A. Durand's *A Handbook to the Poetry of Rudyard Kipling* (1914) glosses many of the Indian words and military and technical terms of the poems.

There are two useful collections of critical essays on Kipling's writing: *Kipling's Mind and Art*, edited by Andrew Rutherford (1964), and *Kipling and the Critics*, edited by Eliot L. Gilbert (1965). Roger Lancelyn Green has compiled *Kipling: The Critical Heritage* (1971).

F. V. Livingstone has prepared *A Bibliography of the Works of Rudyard Kipling* (1927: supplement, 1938); her bibliography is partly corrected and enlarged by James McG. Stewart's *Rudyard Kipling: A Bibliographical Catalogue* (1959). Helmut E. Gerber and Edward Lauterbach have compiled "Kipling: An Annotated Bibliography of Writings About Him," *English Fiction in Transition*, 3 (1960), to which they added further items in a "Supplement" published in volume 8 (1965) of that periodical. J. I. M. Stewart's *Eight Modern Writers* (1963), a volume in the Oxford History of English Literature, contains a select annotated bibliography of writing about Kipling as well as a long essay on his writing. The *Kipling Journal* (1927–   ) records and reviews recent commentary on its subject.

Arithmetic on the Frontier[1]

A great and glorious thing it is
    To learn, for seven years or so,

The Lord knows what of that and this,
    Ere reckoned fit to face the foe—
The flying bullet down the Pass,
    That whistles clear: "All flesh is grass."

Three hundred pounds per annum spent
    On making brain and body meeter
For all the murderous intent
    Comprised in "villainous saltpetre"!   10
And after?—Ask the Yusufzaies[2]
What comes of all our 'ologies.

A scrimmage in a Border Station—
    A canter down some dark defile—
Two thousand pounds of education
    Drops to a ten-rupee *jezail*—
The Crammer's boast,[3] the Squadron's pride,
Shot like a rabbit in a ride![4]

No proposition Euclid wrote,
    No formulæ the text-books know,   20
Will turn the bullet from your coat,
    Or ward the tulwar's[5] downward blow.
Strike hard who cares—shoot straight who can—
The odds are on the cheaper man.

One sword-knot stolen from the camp
    Will pay for all the school expenses
Of any Kurrum Valley[6] scamp
    Who knows no word of moods and tenses,
But, being blessed with perfect sight,
Picks off our messmates left and right.   30

With home-bred hordes the hillsides teem.
    The troopships bring us one by one,
At vast expense of time and steam,
    To slay Afridis[7] where they run.
The "captives of our bow and spear"
Are cheap, alas! as we are dear.
                                   1886; 1890

Giffen's Debt

Imprimis[1] he was "broke." Thereafter left
His Regiment and, later, took to drink;
Then, having lost the balance of his friends,

---

[1] The texts of this and the following poem are those of the first edition of *Departmental Ditties* printed in London (1890).

[2] Yusufzaies: inhabitants of Afghanistan, northwest of India.

[3] Jezail: a heavy gun. Crammer: tutor who prepares students for examinations.

[4] Ride: road.   [5] Tulwar: a curved, decorated sword.

[6] Kurrum Valley: valley of a river in eastern Afghanistan.

[7] Afridis: an Indian tribe against whom the British fought nine campaigns in the second half of the nineteenth century.

[1] Imprimis: first of all.

"Went Fantee"—joined the people of the land,
Turned three parts Mussulman and one
        Hindu,
And lived among the Gauri villagers,
Who gave him shelter and a wife or twain,
And boasted that a thorough, full-blood *sahib*
Had come among them. Thus he spent his
        time,
Deeply indebted to the village *shroff*[2]
(Who never asked for payment) always drunk,
Unclean, abominable, out-at-heels;
Forgetting that he was an Englishman.

You know they dammed the Gauri with a dam,
And all the good contractors scamped their
        work,
And all the bad material at hand
Was used to dam the Gauri—which was cheap,
And, therefore, proper. Then the Gauri burst,
And several hundred thousand cubic tons
Of water dropped into the valley, *flop*,
And drowned some five-and-twenty villagers,
And did a lakh or two[3] of detriment
To crops and cattle. When the flood went down
We found him dead, beneath an old dead
        horse,
Full six miles down the valley. So we said
He was a victim to the Demon Drink,
And moralised upon him for a week,
And then forgot him. Which was natural.

But, in the valley of the Gauri, men
Beneath the shadow of the big new dam,
Relate a foolish legend of the flood,
Accounting for the little loss of life
(Only those five-and-twenty villagers)
In this wise:—On the evening of the flood,
They heard the groaning of the rotten dam,
And voices of the Mountain Devils. Then
An incarnation of the local God,
Mounted upon a monster-neighing horse,
And flourishing a flail-like whip, came down,
Breathing ambrosia, to the villages,
And fell upon the simple villagers
With yells beyond the power of mortal throat,
And blows beyond the power of mortal hand,
And smote them with his flail-like whip, and
        drove
Them clamorous with terror up the hill,
And scattered, with the monster-neighing steed,

Their crazy cottages about their ears,
And generally cleared those villages.
Then came the water, and the local God,
Breathing ambrosia, flourishing his whip,
And mounted on his monster-neighing steed,
Went down the valley with the flying trees
And residue of homesteads, while they watched
Safe on the mountain-side these wondrous
        things,
And knew that they were much beloved of
        Heaven.

Wherefore, and when the dam was newly built,
They raised a temple to the local God,
And burnt all manner of unsavoury things
Upon his altar, and created priests,
And blew into a conch and banged a bell,
And told the story of the Gauri flood
With circumstance and much embroidery.

So he, the whiskified Objectionable,
Unclean, abominable, out-at-heels,
Became the Tutelary Deity
Of all the Gauri valley villages;
And may in time become a Solar Myth.[4]
                                    1886; 1890

Prelude

(To Departmental Ditties) [1]
I have eaten your bread and salt.
    I have drunk your water and wine,
The deaths ye died I have watched beside,
    And the lives ye led were mine.

Was there aught that I did not share
    In vigil or toil or ease,—
One joy or woe that I did not know,
    Dear hearts across the seas?

I have written the tale of our life
    For a sheltered people's mirth,
In jesting guise—but ye are wise,
    And ye know what the jest is worth.
                                    1890

Danny Deever

"What are the bugles blowin' for?" said Files-
        on-Parade.
"To turn you out, to turn you out," the Colour-
        Sergeant[1] said.

---

[2] *Shroff:* moneylender.   [3] *Lakh:* a large measure of value.
[4] This line was added in 1888 in the third Indian edition.
[1] First published in the first English edition.
[1] Files-on-Parade is a common soldier; the Colour-Sergeant is the ranking noncommissioned
officer of a company.

"What makes you look so white, so white?"
  said Files-on-Parade.
"I'm dreadin' what I've got to watch," the
  Colour-Sergeant said.
  For they're hangin' Danny Deever, you
    can hear the Dead March play,
  The regiment's in 'ollow square²—they're
    hangin' him to-day;
  They've taken of his buttons off an' cut his
    stripes away,
  An' they're hangin' Danny Deever in the
    mornin'.

"What makes the rear-rank breathe so 'ard?"
  said Files-on-Parade.
"It's bitter cold, it's bitter cold," the Colour-
  Sergeant said.   10
"What makes that front-rank man fall down?"
  said Files-on-Parade.
"A touch o' sun, a touch o' sun," the Colour
  Sergeant said.
  They are hangin' Danny Deever, they are
    marchin' of 'im round,
  They 'ave 'alted Danny Deever by 'is coffin
    on the ground;
  An' 'e'll swing in 'arf a minute for a
    sneakin' shootin' hound—
  O they're hangin' Danny Deever in the
    mornin'!

" 'Is cot was right-'and cot to mine," said Files-
  on-Parade.
" 'E's sleepin' out an' far to-night," the Colour-
  Sergeant said.
"I've drunk 'is beer a score o' times," said Files-
  on-Parade.
" 'E's drinkin' bitter beer alone," the Colour-
  Sergeant said.   20
  They are hangin Danny Deever, you must
    mark 'im to 'is place,
  For 'e shot a comrade sleepin'—you must
    look 'im in the face;
  Nine 'undred of 'is county³ an' the
    Regiment's disgrace,
  While they're hangin' Danny Deever in
    the mornin'.

"What's that so black agin the sun?" said Files-
  on-Parade.

"It's Danny fightin' 'ard for life," the Colour-
  Sergeant said.
"What's that that whimpers over'ead?" said
  Files-on-Parade.
"It's Danny's soul that's passin' now," the
  Colour-Sergeant said.
  For they're done with Danny Deever, you
    can 'ear the quickstep play,
  The regiment's in column, an' they're
    marchin' us away;   30
  Ho! the young recruits are shakin', an'
    they'll want their beer to-day,
  After hangin' Danny Deever in the
    mornin'!

                                    1890; 1892

Gunga Din

You may talk o' gin and beer
When you're quartered safe out 'ere,
An' you're sent to penny-fights an' Aldershot¹
  it;
But when it comes to slaughter
You will do your work on water,
An' you'll lick the bloomin' boots of 'im that's
  got it.
Now in Injia's sunny clime,
Where I used to spend my time
A-servin' of 'Er Majesty the Queen,
Of all them black-faced crew   10
The finest man I knew
Was our regimental bhisti,² Gunga Din.
        He was "Din! Din! Din!
  "You limpin' lump o' brick-dust, Gunga Din!
        "Hi! Slippy *hitherao!*³
        "Water, get it! *Panee lao*⁴
  "You squidgy-nosed old idol, Gunga Din."

The uniform 'e wore
Was nothin' much before,
An' rather less than 'arf o' that be'ind,   20
For a piece o' twisty rag
An' a goatskin water-bag
Was all the field-equipment 'e could find.
When the sweatin' troop-train lay
In a sidin' through the day,
Where the 'eat would make your bloomin'
  eyebrows crawl,

---

² 'ollow square: a formation used for ceremonial occasions.
  ³ County: in the British army regiments were often recruited from and named after specific English counties.
    ¹ Aldershot: a permanent military camp in southern England. ² Bhisti: water carrier.
  ³ Slippy *hitherao*: quickly here. ⁴ *Panee lao*: bring water quickly.

We shouted "Harry By!"[5]
Till our throats were bricky-dry,
Then we wopped 'im 'cause 'e couldn't serve
      us all.
30   It was "Din! Din! Din!
   "You 'eathen, where the mischief 'ave you
         been?
      "You put some *juldee*[6] in it
      "Or I'll marrow[7] you this minute
      "If you don't fill up my helmet, Gunga
         Din!"

'E would dot an' carry one[8]
Till the longest day was done;
An' 'e didn't seem to know the use o' fear.
If we charged or broke or cut,
You could bet your bloomin' nut,[9]
40 'E'd be waitin' fifty paces right flank rear.
With 'is mussick[10] on 'is back,
'E would skip with our attack,
An' watch us till the bugles made "Retire,"
An' for all 'is dirty 'ide
'E was white, clear white, inside
When 'e went to tend the wounded under fire!
         It was "Din! Din! Din!"
   With the bullets kickin' dust-spots on the
         green
      When the cartridges ran out,
50   You could hear the front-ranks shout,
   "Hi! ammunition-mules an' Gunga Din!"

I sha'n't forgit the night
When I dropped be'ind the fight
With a bullet where my belt-plate should 'a'
      been.
I was chokin' mad with thirst,
An' the man that spied me first
Was our good old grinnin', gruntin' Gunga
      Din.
'E lifted up my 'ead,
An' he plugged me where I bled,
60 An' 'e guv me 'arf-a-pint o' water green.
It was crawlin' and it stunk,
But of all the drinks I've drunk,
I'm gratefullest to one from Gunga Din.
      It was "Din! Din! Din!

" 'Ere's a beggar with a bullet through 'is
      spleen;
   " 'E's chawin' up the ground,
      "An' 'e's kickin' all around:
   "For Gawd's sake git the water, Gunga Din!"

'E carried me away
To where a dooli[11] lay,   70
An' a bullet come an' drilled the beggar clean.
'E put me safe inside,
An' just before 'e died,
"I 'ope you liked your drink," sez Gunga Din.
So I'll meet 'im later on
At the place where 'e is gone—
Where it's always double drill and no canteen;
'E'll be squattin' on the coals
Givin' drink to poor damned souls,
An' I'll get a swig in hell from Gunga Din!   80
      Yes, Din! Din! Din!
   You Lazarushian-leather[12] Gunga Din!
      Though I've belted you and flayed
         you,
      By the livin' Gawd that made you,
   You're a better man than I am, Gunga Din!
                                          1890; 1892

The Widow's Party

"Where have you been this while away,
      Johnnie, Johnnie?"
Out with the rest on a picnic lay.[1]
      Johnnie, my Johnnie, aha!
They called us out of the barrack-yard
To Gawd knows where from Gosport Hard,[2]
And you can't refuse when you get the card,
      And the Widow gives the party.
      (*Bugle:* Ta—rara—ra-ra-rara!)

"What did you get to eat and drink,
      Johnnie, Johnnie?"   10
Standing water as thick as ink,
      Johnnie, my Johnnie, aha!
A bit o' beef that were three year stored,

---

    [5] "Harry By!": O brother!   [6] *Juldee:* be quick; quickness.   [7] Marrow: hit.
    [8] Dot and carry one: a schoolboy term referring to arithmetic exercises; here, work mechanically and industriously.
    [9] Nut: head.   [10] Mussick: water skin.   [11] Dooli: litter.
    [12] Lazarushian: apparently a coinage from "lazar," an outcast, and Russian leather, referring to the color and texture of Gunga Din's skin.
    [1] Lay: a slang word meaning trade or occupation.
    [2] Gosport: a naval and military depot on the southern coast of England.

A bit o' mutton as tough as a board,
And a fowl we killed with a sergeant's sword,
     When the Widow give the party.

"What did you do for knives and forks,
     Johnnie, Johnnie?"
We carries 'em with us wherever we walks,
     Johnnie, my Johnnie, aha!
And some was sliced and some was halved,
And some was crimped and some was carved,
And some was gutted and some was starved,
     When the Widow give the party.

"What ha' you done with half your mess,
     Johnnie, Johnnie?"
They couldn't do more and they wouldn't do
     less.
     Johnnie, my Johnnie, aha!
They ate their whack[3] and they drank their fill,
And I think the rations has made them ill,
For half my comp'ny's lying still
     Where the Widow give the party.

"How did you get away—away,
     Johnnie, Johnnie?"
On the broad o' my back at the end o' the day,
     Johnnie, my Johnnie, aha!
I comed away like a bleedin' toff,[4]
For I got four niggers to carry me off,
As I lay in the bight[5] of a canvas trough,
     When the Widow give the party.

"What was the end of all the show,
     Johnnie, Johnnie?"
Ask my Colonel, for I don't know,
     Johnnie, my Johnnie, aha!
We broke a King and we built a road—
A court-house stands where the reg'ment goed.
And the river's clean where the raw blood
  flowed
     When the Widow give the party.
     (*Bugle*: Ta—rara—ra-ra-rara!)
                  1892

The Deep-Sea Cables

The wrecks dissolve above us;[1] their dust drops
    down from afar—
Down to the dark, to the utter dark, where the
    blind white sea-snakes are.
There is no sound, no echo of sound, in the
    deserts of the deep,
Or the great grey level plains of ooze where
    the shell-burred cables creep.

Here in the womb of the world—here on the
    tie-ribs of earth
  Words, and the words of men, flicker and
    flutter and beat—
Warning, sorrow, and gain, salutation and
    mirth—
  For a Power troubles the Still that has
    neither voice nor feet.

They have wakened the timeless Things; they
    have killed their father Time;
  Joining hands in the gloom, a league from
    the last of the sun.
Hush! Men talk to-day o'er the waste of the
    ultimate slime,
  And a new Word runs between: whispering,
    "Let us be one!"
                  1896

M'Andrews' Hymn

Lord, Thou hast made this world below the
    shadow of a dream,
An', taught by time, I tak' it so—exceptin'
    always Steam.
From coupler-flange to spindle-guide I see Thy
    Hand, O God—
Predestination in the stride o' yon connectin'-
    rod.
John Calvin might ha' forged the same—
    enorrmous, certain, slow—
Ay, wrought it in the furnace-flame—*my*
    "Institutio."[1]

---

[3] Whack: share, portion.   [4] Toff: stylish person.   [5] Bight: hollow.

[1] Dissolve above us: a reference to the belief that sunken ships may never reach the ocean floor of very deep water because of its density.

[1] John Calvin (1509–1564), born in France and dominant at mid-century in the government of a theocracy he established in Switzerland at Geneva, influenced the religion of Scotland through John Knox (c. 1513–1572), who was with Calvin in Geneva in the 1550s and returned to Scotland at the end of that decade to lead the Protestant reformers. Both Calvin and Knox preached a religion rigorous in its demands that men and women work hard and forswear the sensuous pleasures of the world. Both also preached a doctrine that humans were predestined or elected to salvation, and that knowledge of one's election came in a sudden illumination like that described by M'Andrews in lines 79–89. Calvin's *Christianae Religionis Institutio* was published in 1536.

I cannot get my sleep to-night; old bones are
    hard to please;
I'll stand the middle watch up here—alone wi'
    God an' these
My engines, after ninety days o' race[2] an' rack
    an' strain
Through all the seas of all Thy world, slam-
10   bangin' home again.
Slam-bang too much—they knock a wee—the
    crosshead-gibs are loose;
But thirty thousand mile o' sea has gied them
    fair excuse. . . .
Fine, clear an' dark—a full-draught breeze,[3]
    wi' Ushant[4] out o' sight,
An' Ferguson relievin' Hay. Old girl, ye'll walk
    to-night!
His wife's at Plymouth. . . . Seventy—One—
    Two—Three[5] since he began—
Three turns for Mistress Ferguson . . . and
    who's to blame the man?
There's none at any port for me, by drivin' fast
    or slow,
Since Elsie Campbell went to Thee, Lord,
    thirty years ago.
(The year the *Sarah Sands*[6] was burned. Oh
    roads we used to tread,
Fra' Maryhill to Pollokshaws—fra' Govan to
20   Parkhead!)[7]
Not but they're ceevil on the Board. Ye'll hear
    Sir Kenneth say:
"Good morrn, McAndrews! Back again? An'
    how's your bilge to-day?"
Miscallin' technicalities but handin' me my
    chair
To drink Madeira wi' three Earls—the auld
    Fleet Engineer,
That started as a boiler-whelp—when steam
    and he were low.
I mind the time we used to serve a broken pipe
    wi' tow.[8]
Ten pound was all the pressure then—Eh!
    Eh!—a man wad drive;

An' here, our workin' gauges give one hunder
    fifty-five!
We're creepin' on wi' each new rig—less weight
    an' larger power:
There'll be the loco-boiler next an' thirty miles
    an hour!   3C
Thirty an' more. What I ha' seen since ocean-
    steam began
Leaves me na doot for the machine: but what
    about the man?
The man that counts, wi' all his runs, one
    million mile o' sea:
Four time the span from earth to moon. . . .
    How far, O Lord, from Thee?
That wast beside him night an' day. Ye mind
    my first typhoon?
It scoughed the skipper on his way to jock wi'
    the saloon.[9]
Three feet were on the stokehold-floor—just
    slappin' to an' fro—
An' cast me on a furnace-door. I have the
    marks to show.
Marks! I ha' marks o' more than burns—deep
    in my soul an' black,
An' times like this, when things go smooth, my
    wickudness comes back.   4●
The sins o' four an' forty years, all up an'
    down the seas,
Clack an' repeat like valves half-fed. . . .
    Forgie's our trespasses.
Nights when I'd come on deck to mark, wi'
    envy in my gaze,
The couples kittlin'[10] in the dark between the
    funnel-stays;
Years when I raked the ports wi' pride to fill
    my cup o' wrong—
Judge not, O Lord, my steps aside at Gay Street
    in Hong-Kong!
Blot out the wastrel hours of mine in sin when
    I abode—
Jane Harrigan's an' Number Nine, The
    Reddick an' Grant Road![11]

---

[2] Race: the running of a ship's propeller at excessive speed when it is lifted free of the water because of heavy seas.

[3] Durand notes (p. 110), in one of several specifications of the accuracy of Kipling's knowledge of marine engineering, that a ship's engines are affected by the direction and force of the wind because their furnaces burn more or less efficiently depending on the draft the wind enables them to draw.

[4] Ushant: an island off the northwest coast of France, marking an entrance to the English Channel.

[5] Seventy-One, etc.: revolutions per minute.   [6] *Sarah Sands:* a troopship that burned in 1857.

[7] Maryhill, Pollokshaws, Govan, Parkhead: villages near Glasgow.

[8] Serve with tow: repair with flaxen or hempen fiber; or a rope.

[9] Jock wi' the saloon: ride the storm in a large parlor for passengers.   [10] Kittlin': tickling.

[11] Jane Harrigan's an' Number Nine, The Reddick an' Grant Road: the names of actual houses of prostitution.

An' waur than all—my crownin' sin—rank
    blasphemy an' wild.
I was not four and twenty then—Ye wadna
    judge a child?
I'd seen the Tropics first that run—new fruit,
    new smells, new air—
How could I tell—blind-fou[12] wi' sun—the Deil
    was lurkin' there?
By day like playhouse-scenes the shore slid past
    our sleepy eyes;
By night those soft, lasceevious stars leered
    from those velvet skies,
In port (we used no cargo-steam) I'd daunder
    down the streets—
An ijjit grinnin' in a dream—for shells an'
    parrakeets,
An' walkin'-sticks o' carved bamboo an' blow-
    fish stuffed an' dried—
Fillin' my bunk wi' rubbishry the Chief put
    overside.
Till, off Sambawa Head,[13] Ye mind, I heard a
    land-breeze ca',
Milk-warm wi' breath o' spice an' bloom:
    "McAndrew, come awa'!"
Firm, clear an' low—no haste, no hate—the
    ghostly whisper went,
Just statin' eevidential facts beyon' all
    argument:
"Your mither's God's a graspin' deil, the
    shadow o' yoursel',
"Got out o' books by meenisters clean daft on
    Heaven an' Hell.
"They mak' him in the Broomielaw,[14] o'
    Glasgie cold an' dirt,
"A jealous, pridefu' fetich,[15] lad, that's only
    strong to hurt.
"Ye'll not go back to Him again an' kiss His
    red-hot rod,
"But come wi' Us" (Now, who were *They?*)
    "an' know the Leevin' God,
"That does not kipper[16] souls for sport or break
    a life in jest,
"But swells the ripenin' cocoanuts an' ripes the
    woman's breast."

An' there it stopped: cut off: no more; that
    quiet, certain voice—
For me, six months o' twenty-four, to leave or
    take at choice.
'Twas on me like a thunderclap—it racked me
    through an' through—
Temptation past the show o' speech, unname-
    able an' new—
The Sin against the Holy Ghost? . . . An'
    under all, our screw.[17]
That storm blew by but left behind her
    anchor-shiftin' swell,
Thou knowest all my heart an' mind, Thou
    knowest, Lord, I fell.
Third[18] on the *Mary Gloster* then, and first
    that night in Hell!
Yet was Thy Hand beneath my head, about my
    feet Thy care—
Fra' Deli clear to Torres Strait,[19] the trial o'
    despair,
But when we touched the Barrier Reef[20] Thy
    answer to my prayer!
We dared na run that sea by night but lay an'
    held our fire,
An' I was drowsin' on the hatch—sick—sick
    wi' doubt an' tire:
"Better the sight of eyes that see than wanderin'
    o' desire!"[21]
Ye mind that word? Clear as our gongs—again,
    an' once again,
When rippin' down through coral-trash ran
    out our moorin'-chain;
An' by Thy Grace I had the Light to see my
    duty plain.
Light on the engine-room—no more—bright as
    our carbons burn.
I've lost it since a thousand times, but never
    past return!

.   .   .   .

Obsairve! Per annum we'll have here two thou-
    sand souls aboard—

---

[12] Blind-fou: crazy.
[13] Sambawa Head: in the Malay Archipelago.   [14] Broomielaw: a part of the port of Glasgow.
[15] Fetich: fetish, idol.   [16] Kipper: to cure by smoking.
[17] "Wherefore I say unto you, All manner of sin and blasphemy shall be forgiven unto men:
but the blasphemy against the Holy Ghost shall not be forgiven unto men" (Matthew 24:31).
The screw is the ship's propeller.
[18] Third: Third engineer.
[19] Deli: an island off Java. Torres Strait: between Australia and New Guinea.
[20] Barrier Reef: a thousand-mile coral reef off the eastern coast of Australia.
[21] Ecclesiastes 6:9.

Think not I dare to justify myself before the
    Lord,
But—average fifteen hunder souls safe-borne
    fra' port to port—
I *am* o' service to my kind. Ye wadna blame the
    thought?
Maybe they steam from grace to wrath—to sin
    by folly lead,
It isna mine to judge their path—their lives
    are on my head.
Mine at the last—when all is done it all comes
    back to me,
The fault that leaves six thousand ton a log
    upon the sea.
We'll tak' one stretch—three weeks an' odd by
    any road ye steer—
Fra' Cape Town east to Wellington[22]—ye
    need an engineer.
Fail there—ye've time to weld your shaft—ay,
100   eat it, ere ye're spoke;
Or make Kerguelen under sail—three jiggers
    burned wi' smoke![23]
An' home again, the Rio run:[24] it's no child's
    play to go
Steamin' to bell for fourteen days o' snow an'
    floe an' blow—[25]
The bergs like kelpies overside that girn an'
    turn an' shift[26]
Whaur, grindin' like the Mills o' God, goes by
    the big South drift.
(Hail, snow and ice that praise the Lord: I've
    met them at their work,
An' wished we had anither route or they
    anither kirk.)
Yon's strain, hard strain, o' head an' hand, for
    though Thy Power brings
All skill to naught, Ye'll understand a man
    must think o' things.
Then, at the last, we'll get to port an' hoist
110   their baggage clear—

The passengers, wi' gloves an' canes—an' this
    is what I'll hear:
"Well, thank ye for a pleasant voyage. The
    tender's comin' now."
While I go testin' follower-bolts an' watch the
    skipper bow.
They've words for every one but me—shake
    hands wi' half the crew,
Except the dour Scots engineer, the man they
    never knew.
An' yet I like the wark for all we've dam' few
    pickin's here—
No pension, an' the most we'll earn's four
    hunder pound a year.
Better myself abroad? Maybe. *I'd* sooner starve
    than sail
Wi' such as call a snifter-rod *ross*.[27] . . . French
    for nightingale.
Commeesion on my stores? Some do; but I
    cannot afford   12
To lie like stewards wi' patty-pans—[28] I'm
    older than the Board.
A bonus on the coal I save? Ou ay, the Scots are
    close,
But when I grudge the strength Ye gave I'll
    grudge their food to *those*.
(There's bricks that I might recommend—an'
    clink[29] the fire-bars cruel.
No! Welsh—Wangarti[30] at the worst—an'
    damn all patent fuel!)
Inventions? Ye must stay in port to mak' a
    patent pay.
My Deeferential Valve-Gear taught me how
    that business lay,
I blame no chaps wi' clearer head for aught
    they make or sell.
I found that I could not invent an' look to
    these—as well.
So, wrestled wi' Apollyon[31]—Nah!—fretted like
    a bairn—   1

[22] Cape Town east to Wellington: from the lower tip of South Africa to New Zealand. Durand notes (p. 114) that this route lies far south and close to the Antartic; if the ship's engines failed, it would be a long time, time to repair even the main shaft, before it was "spoke" (sighted).

[23] Kerguelen: an archipelago in the Indian Ocean. Jiggers: vertical shafts.

[24] The Rio run: the homeward journey from New Zealand is eastward around Cape Horn at the tip of South America.

[25] Steamin' to bell: slowing and reversing engines in response to signals from the bridge in treacherous water.

[26] Kelpies: water spirits. Girn: snarl.

[27] *Ross:* the French word for a snifter-rod is *rossignol*, which is also the word for nightingale.

[28] Patty-pans: equipment for cooking and serving food: M'Andrew refers to an arrangement in which a steward will receive less equipment than he orders, and receive from the supplier a part of the money the company pays to him.

[29] Clink: make clinkers, pieces of unburnable coal.   [30] Wangarti: Australian coal.

[31] Apollyon: a monster whom Christian must conquer on his way to the Celestial City in John Bunyan's *The Pilgrim's Progress* (1678).

But burned the workin'-plans last run wi' all
    I hoped to earn.
Ye know how hard an Idol dies, an' what that
    meant to me—
E'en tak' it for a sacrifice acceptable to
    Thee. . . .
Below there! Oiler! What's your wark? Ye find
    it runnin' hard?
Ye needn't swill the cup wi' oil—this isn't the
    Cunard!
Ye thought? Ye are not paid to think. Go, sweat
    that off again!
Tck! Tck! It's deeficult to sweer nor tak' The
    Name in vain!
Men, ay an' women, call me stern. Wi' these to
    oversee
Ye'll note I've little time to burn on social
    repartee.
The bairns see what their elders miss; they'll
    hunt me to an' fro,   40
Till for the sake of—well, a kiss—I tak' 'em
    down below.
That minds me of our Viscount loon—Sir
    Kenneth's kin—the chap
Wi' Russia leather tennis-shoon an' spar-decked
    yachtin'-cap.
I showed him round last week, o'er all—an' at
    the last says he:
"Mister McAndrews, don't you think steam
    spoils romance at sea?"
Damned ijjit! I'd been doon that morn to see
    what ailed the throws,
Manholin', on my back—the cranks three
    inches off my nose.
Romance! Those first-class passengers they like
    it very well,
Printed an' bound in little books; but why
    don't poets tell?
I'm sick of all their quirks an' turns—the loves
    an' doves they dream—   50
Lord, send a man like Robbie Burns to sing
    the Song o' Steam!
To match wi' Scotia's noblest speech yon
    orchestra sublime
Whaurto—uplifted like the Just—the tail-rods
    mark the time.
The crank-throws give the double-bass, the
    feed-pump sobs an' heaves,
An' now the main eccentrics start their
    quarrel on the sheaves:
Her time, her own appointed time, the rocking
    link-head bides,
Till—hear that note?—the rod's return whings
    glimmerin' through the guides.
They're all awa'! True beat, full power, the
    clangin' chorus goes
Clear to the tunnel where they sit, my purrin'
    dynamoes.
Interdependence absolute, foreseen, ordained,
    decreed,   160
To work, Ye'll note, at ony tilt an' every rate
    o' speed.
Fra' skylight-lift to furnace-bars, backed,
    bolted, braced an' stayed,
An' singin' like the Mornin' Stars for joy that
    they are made;[32]
While, out o' touch o' vanity, the sweatin'
    thrust-block says:
"Not unto us the praise, or man—not unto us
    the praise!"[33]
Now, a' together, hear them lift their lesson—
    theirs an' mine:
"Law, Orrder, Duty an' Restraint, Obedience,
    Discipline!"
Mill, forge an' try-pit[34] taught them that when
    roarin' they arose,
An' whiles I wonder if a soul was gied them wi'
    the blows.
Oh for a man to weld it then, in one trip-
    hammer strain,   170
Till even first-class passengers could tell the
    meanin' plain!
But no one cares except mysel' that serve an'
    understand
My seven thousand horse-power here. Eh,
    Lord! They're grand—they're grand!
Uplift am I? When first in store the new-
    made beasties stood,
Were Ye cast down that breathed the Word
    declarin' all things good?[35]
Not so! O' that warld-liftin' joy no after-fall
    could vex,
Ye've left a glimmer still to cheer the Man—
    the Arrtifex!

---

[32] A reference to the joy of created things upon their creation: "When the morning stars sang together, and all the sons of God shouted for joy" (Job 38:7).
[33] "Not unto us, O Lord, not unto us, but unto thy name give glory, for thy mercy, and for thy truth's sake" (Psalm 115:1).
[34] Try-pit: a pit for testing engines.
[35] "And God saw every thing that he had made, and, behold, it was very good" (Genesis 1:31).

That holds, in spite o' knock and scale, o'
    friction, waste an' slip,[36]
An' by that light—now, mark my word—we'll
    build the Perfect Ship.
I'll never last to judge her lines or take her
180   curve—not I.
But I ha' lived an' I ha' worked. Be thanks to
    Thee, Most High!
An' I ha' done what I ha' done—judge Thou
    if ill or well—
Always Thy Grace preventin' me. . . .
                Losh! Yon's the "Stand-by" bell.
Pilot so soon? His flare it is. The mornin'-
    watch is set.
Well, God be thanked, as I was sayin', I'm no
    Pelagian[37] yet.
Now I'll tak' on. . . .
    'Morrn, Ferguson. Man, have ye ever thought
What your good leddy costs in coal? . . . I'll
    burn 'em down to port.
                      1894; 1896

The King

"Farewell, Romance!" the Cave-men said;
    "With bone well carved he went away.
"Flint arms the ignoble arrowhead,
    "And jasper tips the spear to-day.
"Changed are the Gods of Hunt and Dance,
    "And He with these. Farewell, Romance!"

"Farewell, Romance!" the Lake-folk sighed;
    "We lift the weight of flatling years;
"The caverns of the mountain-side
10   "Hold Him who scorns our hutted piers.
"Lost hills whereby we dare not dwell,
    "Guard ye His rest. Romance, Farewell!"

"Farewell, Romance!" the Soldier spoke;
    "By sleight of sword we may not win,
"But scuffle 'mid uncleanly smoke
    "Of arquebus and culverin.[1]
"Honour is lost, and none may tell
    "Who paid good blows. Romance, farewell!"

"Farewell, Romance!" the Traders cried;
20   "Our keels have lain with every sea;

"The dull-returning wind and tide
    "Heave up the wharf where we would be;
"The known and noted breezes swell
    "Our trudging sails. Romance, farewell!"

"Good-bye, Romance!" the Skipper said;
    "He vanished with the coal we burn.
"Our dial marks full-steam ahead,
    "Our speed is timed to half a turn.
"Sure as the ferried barge we ply
    " 'Twixt port and port. Romance, good-bye!"

"Romance!" the season-tickets[2] mourn,
    "He never ran to catch his train,
"But passed with coach and guard and horn—
    "And left the local—late again!"
Confound Romance! . . . And all unseen
Romance brought up the nine-fifteen.

His hand was on the lever laid,
    His oil-can soothed the worrying cranks,
His whistle waked the snowbound grade,
    His fog-horn cut the reeking Banks;[3]
By dock and deep and mine and mill
The Boy-god reckless laboured still!

Robed, crowned and throned, he wove his
    spell,
    Where heart-blood beat or hearth-smoke
        curled,
With unconsidered miracle,
    Hedged in a backward-gazing world;
Then taught his chosen bard to say:
"Our King was with us—yesterday!"
                    1894; 1896

The Song of the Banjo

You couldn't pack a Broadwood[1] half a mile—
    You mustn't leave a fiddle in the damp—
You couldn't raft an organ up the Nile,
    And play it in an Equatorial swamp.
I travel with the cooking-pots and pails—
    I'm sandwiched 'tween the coffee and the
        pork—
And when the dusty column checks and tails,[2]
    You should hear me spur the rearguard to a
        walk!

---

[36] Scale: incrustations on a ship's boilers. Slip: loss of power when a ship's propeller lifts from the water.
[37] Pelagian: a believer in a doctrine that holds that humans may earn salvation through the efforts of their own wills, as opposed to the doctrine of predestination.
    [1] Arquebus and culverin: early firearms.   [2] Season-tickets: commuters.
    [3] Banks: the Newfoundland Banks are shoals in the Atlantic; fogs are frequent in this area.
    [1] Broadwood: a piano.   [2] Checks and tails: reins and straggles out of line.

With my *"Pilly-willy-winky-winky-popp!"*
   [Oh, it's any tune that come into my
     head!]
So I keep 'em moving forward till they
   drop;
   So I play 'em up to water and to bed.

In the silence of the camp before the fight,
   When it's good to make your will and say
     your prayer,
You can hear my *strumpty-tumpty* overnight,
   Explaining ten to one was always fair.
I'm the Prophet of the Utterly Absurd,
   Of the Patently Impossible and Vain—
And when the Thing that Couldn't has
     occurred,
   Give me time to change my leg and go again.

     With my *"Tumpa-tumpa-tumpa-tumpa-*
       tump!"
       In the desert where the dung-fed camp-
        smoke curled
       There was never voice before us till I led
        our lonely chorus,
       I—the war-drum of the White Man
        round the world!

By the bitter road the Younger Son must tread,
   Ere he win to hearth and saddle of his own,—
'Mid the riot of the shearers at the shed,
   In the silence of the herder's hut alone—
In the twilight, on a bucket upside down,
   Hear me babble what the weakest won't con-
     fess—
I am Memory and Torment—I am Town!
   I am all that ever went with evening dress!

     With my *"Tunka-tunka-tunka-tunka-*
       tunk!"
       [So the lights—the London Lights—
        grow near and plain!]
       So I rowel[3] 'em afresh towards the Devil
        and the Flesh,

       Till I bring my broken rankers[4] home
        again.

In desire of many marvels over sea,
   Where the new-raised tropic city sweats and
     roars,
I have sailed with Young Ulysses from the quay
   Till the anchor rumbled down on stranger
     shores.   40
He is blooded[5] to the open and the sky,
   He is taken in a snare that shall not fail,
He shall hear me singing strongly, till he die,
   Like the shouting of a backstay[6] in a gale.

     With my *"Hya! Heeya! Heeya! Hullah!*
      Haul!"[7]
       [O the green that thunders aft along
        the deck!]
       Are you sick o' towns and men? You must
        sign and sail again,
        For it's "Johnny Bowlegs, pack your kit
        and trek!"[8]

Through the gorge that gives the stars at noon-
     day clear—
   Up the pass that packs the scud[9] beneath our
     wheel—   50
Round the bluff that sinks her thousand fathom
     sheer—
   Down the valley with our guttering brakes
     asqueal:
Where the trestle groans and quivers in the
     snow,
   Where the many-shedded levels[10] loop and
     twine.
So I lead my reckless children from below
   Till we sing the Song of Roland[11] to the
     pine!

     With my *Tinka-tinka-tinka-tinka-tink!"*
       [And the axe has cleared the mountain,
        croup[12] and crest!]

---

[3] Rowel: spur.   [4] Rankers: enlisted men in the army.
[5] Blooded: initiated.   [6] Backstay: wire rope that supports the mast of a ship.
[7] Hya! Heeya!: a sailor's chant.
[8] Johnny Bowlegs: Durand (p. 136) cites a reference to a South African song, "Pack your kit
and trek, Johnny with the limping leg." "Kit" is equipment.
[9] Scud: loose vapory clouds.
[10] Many-shedded levels: stretches of railroad track protected from snow and avalanches by
being enclosed in sheds.
[11] Song of Roland: a ninth- or tenth-century French epic poem about a chivalric hero. Durand
notes (p. 137) that there is a legend that the song was sung by a minstrel of William the Con-
queror as he rode into the battle of Hastings which was to determine William's sovereignty in
England.
[12] Croup: rump.

So we ride the iron stallions down to
            drink,
        Through the cañons to the waters of the
            West!

And the tunes that mean so much to you
            alone—
        Common tunes that make you choke and
            blow your nose—
    Vulgar tunes that bring the laugh that brings
            the groan—
        I can rip your very heartstrings out with
            those;
    With the feasting, and the folly, and the fun—
        And the lying, and the lusting, and the
            drink,
    And the merry play that drops you, when
            you're done,
        To the thoughts that burn like irons if you
            think.

        With my *"Plunka-lunka-lunka-lunka-
            lunk!"*
            Here's a trifle on account of pleasure
            past,
        Ere the wit that made you win gives you
            eyes to see your sin
            And the heavier repentance at the last!

    Let the organ moan her sorrow to the roof—
        I have told the naked stars the Grief of Man!
    Let the trumpets snare the foeman to the
            proof—
        I have known Defeat, and mocked it as we
            ran!
    My bray ye may not alter nor mistake
        When I stand to jeer the fatted Soul of
            Things,
    But the Song of Lost Endeavour that I make,
        Is it hidden in the twanging of the strings?

        With my *"Ta-ra-rara-rara-ra-ra-rrrp!"*
            [Is it naught to you that hear and pass
            me by?]
        But the word—the word is mine, when the
            order moves the line
            And the lean, locked ranks go roaring
            down to die!

The grandam of my grandam was the Lyre——
        [O the blue below the little fisher-huts!]
    That the Stealer[13] stooping beachward filled
            with fire,
        Till she bore my iron head and ringing guts!
    By the wisdom of the centuries I speak—
        To the tune of yestermorn I set the truth—
    I, the joy of life unquestioned—I, the Greek—
        I, the everlasting Wonder Song of Youth!

        With my *"tinka-tinka-tinka-tinka-tink!"*
            [What d'ye lack, my noble masters!
            What d'ye lack?]
        So I draw the world together link by link:
            Yea, from Delos up to Limerick and
            back![14]

                                                        1895; 1896

When Earth's Last Picture Is Painted[1]

When Earth's last picture is painted and the
        tubes are twisted and dried,
    When the oldest colours have faded, and the
        youngest critic has died,
    We shall rest, and, faith, we shall need it—lie
        down for an æon or two,
    Till the Master of All Good Workmen shall
        put us to work anew!

And those that were good shall be happy: they
        shall sit in a golden chair;
    They shall splash at a ten-league canvas with
        brushes of comets' hair;
    They shall find real saints to draw from—
        Magdalene, Peter, and Paul;
    They shall work for an age at a sitting and
        never be tired at all!

And only The Master shall praise us, and only
        The Master shall blame;
    And no one shall work for money, and no one
        shall work for fame,
    But each for the joy of the working, and each,
        in his separate star,
    Shall draw the Thing as he sees It for the God
        of Things as They Are!

                                                        1892; 1896

---

[13] The Stealer: the classical god Hermes, who stole some of the cattle of Apollo, and made
reparation by giving Apollo the lyre, which he had invented.
[14] Delos: an island off Greece, the birthplace of Apollo, classical god of poetry. Limerick is a
town and county in Ireland, and the name of a popular five-line verse form.
[1] Printed as "L'Envoi" in *The Seven Seas* (1896).

Recessional

1897[1]

God of our fathers, known of old,
  Lord of our far-flung battle-line,
Beneath whose awful Hand we hold
  Dominion over palm and pine—
Lord God of Hosts, be with us yet,
Lest we forget—lest we forget![2]

The tumult and the shouting dies;
  The Captains and the Kings depart:
Still stands Thine ancient sacrifice,
  An humble and a contrite heart.
Lord God of Hosts, be with us yet,
Lest we forget—lest we forget!

Far-called, our navies melt away;
  On dune and headland sinks the fire:
Lo, all our pomp of yesterday
  Is one with Nineveh and Tyre![3]
Judge of the Nations, spare us yet,
Lest we forget—lest we forget!

If, drunk with sight of power, we loose
  Wild tongues that have not Thee in awe,
Such boastings as the Gentiles use,
  Or lesser breeds without the Law[4]—
Lord God of Hosts, be with us yet,
Lest we forget—lest we forget!

For heathen heart that puts her trust
  In reeking tube and iron shard,
All valiant dust that builds on dust,
  And guarding, calls not Thee to guard,
For frantic boast and foolish word—
Thy mercy on Thy people, Lord!

                          1897; 1903

The Dykes

We have no heart for the fishing, we have no
  hand for the oar—

All that our fathers taught us of old pleases us
  now no more;
All that our own hearts bid us believe we
  doubt where we do not deny—
There is no proof in the bread we eat or rest
  in the toil we ply.

Look you, our foreshore stretches far through
  sea-gate, dyke, and groin—
Made land all, that our fathers made, where
  the flats and the fairway join.
They forced the sea a sea-league back. They
  died, and their work stood fast.
We were born to peace in the lee of the dykes,
  but the time of our peace is past.

Far off, the full tide clambers and slips,
  mouthing and testing all,
Nipping the flanks of the water-gates, baying
  along the wall;   10
Turning the shingle,[1] returning the shingle,
  changing the set of the sand . . .
We are too far from the beach, men say, to
  know how the outworks stand.

So we come down, uneasy, to look; uneasily
  pacing the beach
These are the dykes our fathers made: we have
  never known a breach.
Time and again has the gale blown by and we
  were not afraid;
Now we come only to look at the dykes—at the
  dykes our fathers made.

O'er the marsh where the homesteads cower
  apart the harried sunlight flies,
Shifts and considers, wanes and recovers,
  scatters and sickens and dies—
An evil ember bedded in ash—a spark blown
  west by the wind . . .
We are surrendered to night and the sea—the
  gale and the tide behind!   20

At the bridge of the lower saltings[2] the cattle
  gather and blare,

---

[1] 1897 was the Diamond Jubilee of Victoria, a celebration of the sixtieth anniversary of her coronation. Statesmen and troops from many of Britain's colonies convened in London to mark the occasion. A recessional is a hymn sung at the close of a ceremony. The poem was first published in the London *Times*.

[2] "Then beware lest thou forget the Lord, which brought thee forth from out of the land of Egypt, from the house of bondage" (Deuteronomy 6:12).

[3] Nineveh and Tyre: seats of ancient empires in Asia Minor.

[4] Another identification of the British people with the chosen people of the Old Testament. "Without the Law" seems to mean lacking the law: "The Gentiles, which have not the law" (Romans 2:14).

[1] Shingle: a beach of small, round stones.   [2] Saltings: land behind a dike.

Roused by the feet of running men, dazed by
   the lantern glare.
Unbar and let them away for their lives—the
   levels drown as they stand,
Where the flood-wash forces the sluices aback
   and the ditches deliver inland.

Ninefold deep[3] to the top of the dykes the
   galloping breakers stride,
And their overcarried spray is a sea—a sea on
   the landward side.
Coming, like stallions they paw with their
   hooves, going they snatch with their teeth,
Till the bents and the furze[4] and the sand are
   dragged out, and the old-time wattles
   beneath!

Bid men gather fuel for fire, the tar, the oil
   and the tow[5]—
Flame we shall need, not smoke, in the dark if
   the riddled sea-banks go.
Bid the ringers watch in the tower (who knows
   how the dawn shall prove?)
Each with his rope between his feet and the
   trembling bells above.

Now we can only wait till the day, wait and
   apportion our shame.
These are the dykes our fathers left, but we
   would not look to the same.
Time and again were we warned of the dykes,
   time and again we delayed:
Now, it may fall, we have slain our sons, as our
   fathers we have betrayed.

.   .   .   .   [6]

Walking along the wreck of the dykes, watching
   the work of the seas,
These were the dykes our fathers made to our
   great profit and ease;
But the peace is gone and the profit is gone,
   with the old sure days withdrawn . . .

That our own houses show as strange when we
   come back in the dawn!

                            1903

Chant-Pagan[1]

      [English Irregular: '99–02]
Me that 'ave been what I've been,
Me that 'ave gone where I've gone,
Me that 'ave seen what I've seen—
   'Ow can I ever take on
With awful old England again,
An' 'ouses both sides of the street,
And 'edges two sides of the lane,
And the parson an' gentry between,
An' touchin' my 'at when we meet—
   Me that 'ave been what I've been?

Me that 'ave watched 'arf a world
'Eave up all shiny with dew,
Kopje on kop to the sun,[2]
An' as soon as the mist let 'em through
Our 'elios[3] winkin' like fun—
Three sides of a ninety-mile square,
Over valleys as big as a shire[4]——
Are ye there? Are ye there? Are ye there?
An' then the blind drum of our fire. . .
An' I'm rollin' 'is lawns for the Squire,
                  Me!

Me that 'ave rode through the dark
Forty mile, often, on end,
Along the Ma'ollisberg Range,[5]
With only the stars for my mark
An' only the night for my friend,
An' things runnin' off as you pass,
An' things jumpin' up in the grass,
An' the silence, the shine an' the size
Of the 'igh, unexpressible skies . . .
I am takin' some letters almost
As much as a mile, to the post,
An' "mind you come back with the change!"
                  Me!

---

[3] Ninefold deep: in popular belief each ninth wave is larger than its predecessors.
[4] Bents and furze: stiff grass and evergreen shrubs, laid down on a panel of stakes (wattles),
to form the foundation over which sand drifts and holds to form a dike.
[5] Tow: flaxen or hempen fiber; a rope.
[6] Ellipsis in Kipling's text.
[1] Pagan: from *paganus*, a Latin word for an irregular or conscripted soldier, as opposed to a
regular soldier of a professional army.
[2] Kopje: hill. Kop: mountain. Both are South African Dutch words.
[3] 'Elios: heliograph, a device used to signal by flashing light reflected from the sun.
[4] Shire: county.   [5] Ma'ollisberg: the Magaliesberg mountains in South Africa.

Me that saw Barberton[6] took
When we dropped through the clouds on their
  'ead,
An' they 'ove the guns over and fled—
Me that was through Di'mond 'Ill,
An' Pieters an' Springs an' Belfast—
From Dundee to Vereeniging all!
Me that stuck out to the last
(An' five bloomin' bars on my chest)[7]—
I am doin' my Sunday-school best,
By the 'elp of the Squire an' 'is wife
(Not to mention the 'ousemaid an' cook) ,
To come in an' 'ands up an' be still,
An' honestly work for my bread,
My livin' in that state of life
To which it shall please God to call
                                    Me!

Me that 'ave followed my trade
In the place where the Lightnin's[8] are made,
'Twixt the Rains and the Sun and the Moon;
Me that lay down an' got up
Three years with the sky for my roof—
That 'ave ridden my 'unger an' thirst
Six thousand raw mile on the hoof,
With the Vaal and the Orange for cup,
An' the Brandwater Basin for dish,[9]—
Oh! it's 'ard to be'ave as they wish
(Too 'ard, an' a little too soon) ,
I'll 'ave to think over it first—
                                    Me!

I will arise an' get 'ence—
I will trek[10] South and make sure
If it's only my fancy or not
That the sunshine of England is pale,
And the breezes of England are stale,
An' there's somethin' gone small with the lot;
For *I* know of a sun an' a wind,
An' some plains and a mountain be'ind,
An' some graves by a barb-wire fence;
An' a Dutchman I've fought 'oo might give
Me a job were I ever inclined,
To look in an' offsaddle an' live
Where there's neither a road nor a tree—

But only my Maker an' me,
And I think it will kill me or cure,
So I think I will go there an' see.[11]

                                    1903

"Cities and Thrones and Powers"

Cities and Thrones and Powers
  Stand in Time's eye,
Almost as long as flowers,
  Which daily die:
But, as new buds put forth
  To glad new men,
Out of the spent and unconsidered Earth,
  The Cities rise again.

This season's Daffodil,
  She never hears,   10
What change, what chance, what chill,
  Cut down last year's;
But with bold countenance,
  And knowledge small,
Esteems her seven days' continuance
  To be perpetual.

So Time that is o'er-kind
  To all that be,
Ordains us e'en as blind,
  As bold as she: 20
That in our very death,
  And burial sure,
Shadow to shadow, well persuaded, saith,
  "See how our works endure!"

                                    1906

The Way Through the Woods

They shut the road through the woods
  Seventy years ago.
Weather and rain have undone it again,
  And now you would never know
There was once a road through the woods
  Before they planted the trees.

---

[6] Like the other place-names in this stanza, Barberton was the site of a battle in the South African War. Dundee was the site of the first battle of the war; Vereeniging was the site of the signing of an armistice in 1902.

[7] Five bloomin' bars: denoting action in five major engagements.

[8] Lightnin's: a reference to the violent storms of South Africa.

[9] Vaal and Orange: South African rivers. Brandwater Basin: a large valley, also the site of a British victory.

[10] Trek: originally a South African Dutch word meaning to draw (as with horses or oxen) ; Boer wagoners used it to call to their teams as they began a journey, and it thus came to mean a journey.

[11] In later versions of this poem Kipling ended it with a final "Me!"

It is underneath the coppice[1] and heath,
     And the thin anemones.
     Only the keeper sees
10 That, where the ring-dove broods,
     And the badgers roll at ease,
There was once a road through the woods.

Yet, if you enter the woods
     Of a summer evening late,
When the night-air cools on the trout-ringed
     pools

Where the otter whistles his mate,
(They fear not men in the woods,
     Because they see so few.)
You will hear the beat of a horse's feet,
     And the swish of a skirt in the dew,   2
     Steadily cantering through
The misty solitudes,
     As though they perfectly knew
The old lost road through the woods. . . .
But there is no road through the woods.

                                                         1910

Arthur Symons
1865–1945

ARTHUR SYMONS was born in Wales, the son of a Methodist clergyman who moved every two or three years to a different circuit of preaching, most of them in the west of England. Symons' schooling was therefore geographically discontinuous, and his formal education was over in 1882, when he was seventeen years old. He had already written several manuscript volumes (which he later destroyed) of what he called his "Poetical Works," and he was determined to earn a living in literature. For the remainder of the 1880s he lived mostly with his parents, studying languages and writing great quantities of poetry and literary criticism, working especially hard to attain the supple intricacy and polish of style he admired in the prose of Walter Pater's literary criticism and essays on painting. Another admiration for the poetry of Robert Browning brought Symons into the London Browning Society and to the attention of its founder, the literary scholar and critic F. J. Furnivall. Furnivall invited Symons to write introductions to some of the volumes in an edition of the work of Shakespeare he was supervising, and he also encouraged the publication of Symons' *An Introduction to the Study of Browning* in 1886. In 1889 Symons published his first volume of poems, *Days and Nights*. Two years later he

settled in London, and he began to work industriously within the pattern of the late-century man of letters he had prepared so diligently to become.

During the 1890s, and for most of the rest of his life, Symons edited and wrote introductions for other standard texts in British literature. He first visited Paris in 1889 and 1890 and met Paul Verlaine, J. K. Huysmans, and other French writers, and his essays on French literature were one of the most important connections between French and British writing in the 1890s. He published some of his poems in the two anthologies prepared by the poets associated in the Rhymers' Club, where he met William Butler Yeats, Lionel Johnson, Ernest Dowson, and John Davidson. He contributed to *The Yellow Book*, an aggressively provocative journal of new writing, and he edited its successor, *The Savoy*, in 1896. He published the drawings of Aubrey Beardsley in *The Savoy*, and he later wrote about Beardsley's art as well as adding criticism of performances in ballet and the music halls to his literary occupations. There were certain consistent qualities in all his writing and associations in the 1890s, qualities that were also expressed in the four volumes of poetry Symons published during the decade: *Silhouettes*

[1] Coppice: grove of trees.

(1892), *London Nights* (1895), *Amoris Victima* (1897), and *Images of Good and Evil* (1899). Symons himself gave two names to the qualities of the kind of art he wrote about and practiced—decadent and symbolist.

In an essay he published in 1893 Symons used the word decadent to describe the self-consciousness common in the literature of the end of any historical period. Such a literature, he wrote, will be oversubtle, elaborate, even perverse in its attempts to create a voice that was human yet disembodied, wholly defined in art and free of the common ruck of life. This art will also be, as he learned from the slender sales of his volumes of poetry and the failures of *The Yellow Book* and *The Savoy,* the literature of an esthetic elite whose morality and taste are suspect by the majority. As it is represented in the poetry Symons published in the 1890s, decadent literature is a literature of exquisite effects and distinctions, of artificial light and scent, of the stylized patterns of costume and dance and the manufactured excitements of cafes, music halls, and theaters. In Symons' poems and in poetry like them landscape itself is consciously rendered as in a painting, its detail seen and composed as color and shape, its objects still and fixed. Below the superficial motive of shocking by the mannered perversity of some of its pleasures, the fundamental gesture of this kind of poetry is to fix images and moods. Its recurrent sadness is a recognition that this art does happen at the end of time, and that even the moments it holds out from the shapeless blur of ordinary perception are nonetheless shadowed by a knowledge of the transitoriness of pleasure and all human creations.

Another and more interesting word Symons used to describe the literature of the end of the century was *symbolist.* In the essays he collected in three books around the turn of the century—*Studies in Two Literatures* (1897), *The Symbolist Movement in Literature* (1899), and *Studies in Prose and Verse* (1904)—Symons worked out an esthetic which gave a deeper resonance to some of the features he called decadent in the art of the 1890s. Like Walter Pater, Symons conceived art to be an intensification of experience. "Art begins," he wrote in the conclusion to *Studies in Prose and Verse,* "when a man wishes to immortalise the most vivid moment he has ever lived." Like Pater too, Symons named the reason late-nineteenth-century art was often sad when in

the conclusion to *The Symbolist Movement* he put art among those agencies humans have invented in the "great silent conspiracy between us to forget death." Symons was also interested in the peculiar intensity and possible transcendence of religious experience. Yeats, to whom he dedicated *The Symbolist Movement,* introduced him to how magic used symbols in order to know a reality of spirit and essence. Symons also wrote on or translated the writings of Augustine and the mystics Theresa and John of the Cross. He wrote a book on William Blake, helped the young James Joyce to find a publisher for his poems and fiction, and responded deeply to the fiction of Thomas Hardy and Joseph Conrad. In short, the definite, tightly composed structures of images with which artists held objects and events out of the common might also be symbols that opened to a reality or an ecstasy beyond the human, or, for Symons as well as for Hardy and Conrad the more likely issue, touched a dark mystery against which art heroically made and held its human order.

Symons did not enact in his poetry the implications of his ideas about symbolism. After his marriage in 1901 and the publication of a two-volume collection of his poems in the next year, he concentrated on the writing of books and essays on music, theater, the plastic arts, and literature in order to assure his income. In 1908 a manic-depressive disorder overwhelmed him, and he was for a time confined to a sanitarium. He recuperated slowly for the next decade. He became interested in the theater, and after 1916 he published several volumes of plays. Much of his writing when he resumed some of his remarkably industrious habits after 1920 was retrospective: translations of the poetry of Charles Baudelaire, essays on Dante Gabriel Rossetti, Swinburne, Wilde, Pater, the painters, dancers, and actors of the pre–World War I generation, and on the Cafe Royal in London, where they all used to meet before the war. He saw how the literature he practiced and advocated in the 1890s connected to the audacious, ambitious use of the symbolist esthetic in the generation that followed his own. His own talents as a poet could not create a literature like the one whose character and premises he had intuited. The achievement and interests of his literary criticism, therefore, and of his services in introducing French writers and literary ideas to late-nineteenth-century England, are greater than those of his poetry. But if it is not just to estimate Symons as a writer solely by the poems he wrote in the 1890s, it is accurate to take these poems as distillations of the themes and extreme formal compression of a kind of late-century literature that pulled into its artifice and away from common experience as it waited for the end.

EDITIONS

The texts reprinted here, unless otherwise noted, are those of a collected edition of his poems Symons published in 1902. They incorporate revisions of his early verse and are consistent (except in the wording of a few titles) with the texts of the standard but incomplete edition, *The Works of Arthur Symons* (1924).

BIOGRAPHY AND CRITICISM

Roger Lhombréaud's *Symons: A Critical Biography* (1963) is the most recent and complete account of Symons' life and career. William Butler Yeats in his *Autobiographies* (1955) and Ruth Z. Temple in *The Critic's Alchemy* (1953) discuss Symons' role in the literary culture of the turn of the century, especially (in Temple) his advertising of French writers and literary ideas in England. T. E. Welby's *Symons* (1925) is an appreciation of the poetry and criticism.

See also Karl Beckson and John M. Munro, "Symons, Browning and the Development of the Modern Aesthetic," *Studies in English Literature*, 10 (1970); Jean Wilson, "The Nineties' Movement in Poetry: Myth or Reality," *Yearbook of English Studies*, 1 (1927); and Tom H. Gibbons, *Rooms in the Darwin Hotel: Studies in English Literary Criticism and Ideas, 1880–1920* (1973).

John M. Munro's short book, *Arthur Symons* (1969), contains a bibliography of Symons' writing and of writings about him. See also Wendell V. Harris' account of the commentary on Symons, especially on his literary criticism, in *Victorian Prose: A Guide to Research*, edited by David DeLaura (1973); and Carol Simpson Stern's annotated bibliography of writings about Symons in *English Literature in Transition*, 17 (1974).

from At Dieppe[1]

II. ON THE BEACH

Night, a grey sky, a ghostly sea,
The soft beginning of the rain;
Black on the horizon, sails that wane
Into the distance mistily.

The tide is rising, I can hear
The soft roar broadening far along;
It cries and murmurs in my ear
A sleepy old forgotten song.[2]

Softly the stealthy night descends,
The black sails fade into the sky:
Is not this, where the sea-line ends,
The shore-line of infinity?

I cannot think or dream; the grey
Unending waste of sea and night,
Dull, impotently infinite,
Blots out the very hope of day.
                            (1890)   1892;   1896

Maquillage[1]

The charm of rouge on fragile cheeks,
Pearl-powder, and, about the eyes,
The dark and lustrous eastern dyes;
A voice of violets that speaks
Of perfumed hours of day, and doubtful night
Of alcoves curtained close against the light.

Gracile[2] and creamy white and rose,
Complexioned like the flower of dawn,
Her fleeting colours are as those
That, from an April sky withdrawn,
Fade in a fragrant mist of tears away
When weeping noon leads on the altered day.
                            (1891)   1892;   1896

Javanese Dancers

Twitched strings, the clang of metal, beaten
    drums,

---

[1] Dieppe is a French town on the English Channel.
[2] In the 1892 edition of *Silhouettes* these lines read: "As, deep through depths of sleep, a song/ Borne inward to a dreamy ear."
[1] Maquillage: makeup.   [2] Gracile: thin.

Dull, shrill, continuous, disquieting;
And now the stealthy dancer comes
Undulantly with cat-like steps that cling;

Smiling between her painted lids a smile,
Motionless, unintelligible, she twines
Her fingers into mazy lines,
The scarves across her fingers twine the while.

One, two, three, four glide forth, and, to and
    fro,
Delicately and imperceptibly,
Now swaying gently in a row,
Now interthreading slow and rhythmically,

Still, with fixed eyes, monotonously still,
Mysteriously, with smiles inanimate,
With lingering feet that undulate,
With sinuous fingers, spectral hands that thrill

In measure while the gnats of music whirr,
The little amber-coloured dancers move,
Like painted idols seen to stir
By the idolators in a magic grove.[1]

(1889)   1892;   1896

from City Nights

I. IN THE TRAIN

The train through the night of the town,
Through a blackness broken in twain
By the sudden finger of streets;
Lights, red, yellow, and brown,
From curtain and window-pane,
The flashing eyes of the streets.

Night, and the rush of the train,
A cloud of smoke through the town,
Scaring the life of the streets;
And the leap of the heart again,
Out into the night, and down
The dazzling vista of streets!

1892;   1896

Prologue [to *London Nights*]
In the Stalls

My life is like a music-hall,
Where, in the impotence of rage,
Chained by enchantment to my stall,
I see myself upon the stage
Dance to amuse a music-hall.

'Tis I that smoke this cigarette,
Lounge here, and laugh for vacancy,
And watch the dancers turn; and yet
It is my very self I see
Across the cloudy cigarette.   10

My very self that turns and trips,
Painted, pathetically gay,
An empty song upon the lips
In make-believe of holiday:
I, I, this thing that turns and trips!

The light flares in the music-hall,
The light, the sound, that weary us;
Hour follows hour, I count them all,
Lagging, and loud, and riotous:
My life is like a music-hall.   20

(1893)   1895

from Intermezzo: Pastoral

IV. AT GLAN-Y-WERN[1]: *White and Rose*

White-robed against the threefold white
Of shutter, glass, and curtains' lace,
She flashed into the evening light
The brilliance of her gipsy face:
I saw the evening in her light.

Clear, from the soft hair to the mouth,
Her ardent face made manifest
The sultry beauty of the South:
Below, a red rose, climbing, pressed
Against the roses of her mouth.   10

So, in the window's threefold white,
O'ertrailed with foliage like a bower,

---

[1] In 1892:

"The little amber-coloured dancers move,
    Like little painted figures on a screen,
    Or phantom-dancers haply seen
Among the shadows of a magic grove."

[1] Glan-y-Wern is in Wales.

She seemed, against the evening light,
Among the flowers herself a flower,
A tiger-lily sheathed in white.

(1892)   1895

from Bianca

I. BIANCA

Her cheeks are hot, her cheeks are white;
The white girl hardly breathes to-night,
So faint the pulses come and go,
That waken to a smouldering glow
The morbid faintness of her white.

What drowsing heats of sense, desire
Longing and languorous, the fire
Of what white ashes, subtly mesh
The fascination of her flesh
10   Into a breathing web of fire?

Only her eyes, only her mouth,
Live, in the agony of drouth,
Athirst for that which may not be:
The desert of virginity
Aches in the hotness of her mouth.

I take her hands into my hands,
Silently, and she understands;
I set my lips upon her lips;
Shuddering to her finger-tips
20   She strains my hands within her hands.

I set my lips on hers; they close
Into a false and phantom rose;
Upon her thirsting lips I rain
A flood of kisses, and in vain;
Her lips inexorably close.

Through her closed lips that cling to mine,
Her hands that hold me and entwine
Her body that abandoned lies,
Rigid with sterile ecstasies,
30   A shiver knits her flesh to mine.

Life sucks into a mist remote
Her fainting lips, her throbbing throat;
Her lips that open to my lips,
And, hot against my finger-tips,
The pulses leaping in her throat.

(1894)   1895

from Amoris Exsul

XI. Arques[1]

I. NOON
The shadows of the rooks[2] fly up the hill,
Up the green grass, and over the white wall;
The trees drowse in the sunlight; all is still;
Only the black rooks cry and call.

Out of the ruined castle, a slow crowd,
Their sultry wings against the sunlight beat;
They float across the valley like a cloud
Across the blue sky's cloudless heat.

Idly I watch them indolently fly,
And idly, like their wings, across my brain,
Drunken with sunlight, black-winged thoughts
    float by,
Pass, and return, and pass, and turn again.

II. AFTERNOON
Gently a little breeze begins to creep
Into the valley, and the sleeping trees
Are stirred, and breathe a little in their sleep,
And nod, half-wakened, to the breeze.

Cool little quiet shadows wander out
Across the fields, and dapple with dark trails
The snake-grey road coiled stealthily about
The green hill climbing from the vales.

And faintlier, in this cooler peace of things,
My brooding thoughts, a scattered flock grown
    few,
Withdrawn upon their melancholy wings,
Float farther off against the blue.

III. NIGHT
The darkness fills the hollows of the moat,
And rises up the valley, and comes down
From the low hills, and wicked white mists float
Like floods about the little town.

The night is all about me, crawling dark
Meshes the doubtful shadows of the way,
And all the woods and all the vales of Arques
Fade as the lamps put out the day.

[1] Arques is a town in northern France.   [2] Rooks: crows.

Then in the darkness, face to face at last
With those winged thoughts that gather to
   their goal,
I feel their beaks and talons taking fast
Hold on my shivering soul.

                 (1896) 1897

from In Ireland

II. BY THE POOL AT THE THIRD ROSSES[1]

I heard the sighing of the reeds
In the grey pool in the green land,
The sea-wind in the long reeds sighing
Between the green hill and the sand.

I heard the sighing of the reeds
Day after day, night after night;
I heard the whirring wild ducks flying,
I saw the sea-gull's wheeling flight.

I heard the sighing of the reeds
Night after night, day after day,
And I forgot old age, and dying,
And youth that loves, and love's decay.

I heard the sighing of the reeds
At noontide and at evening,
And some old dream I had forgotten
I seemed to be remembering.

I hear the sighing of the reeds:
Is it in vain, is it in vain
That some old peace I had forgotten
Is crying to come back again?

                 (1896) 1899

The Loom of Dreams

I broider the world upon a loom,
I broider with dreams my tapestry;
Here in a little lonely room
I am master of earth and sea,
And the planets come to me.

I broider my life into the frame,
I broider my love, thread upon thread;
The world goes by with its glory and shame,
Crowns are bartered and blood is shed:
I sit and broider my dreams instead.   10

And the only world is the world of my dreams,
And my weaving the only happiness;
For what is the world but what it seems?
And who knows but that God, beyond our
   guess,
Sits weaving worlds out of loneliness?

                 (1900) 1901

By Loe Pool[1]

The pool glitters, the fishes leap in the sun
With joyous fins, and dive in the pool again;
I see the corn in sheaves, and the harvestmen,
And the cows coming down to the water one by
   one.
Dragon-flies mailed in lapis and malachite[2]
Flash through the bending reeds and blaze on
   the pool;
Sea-ward, where trees cluster, the shadow is
   cool;
I hear a sighing, where the sea is, out of sight;
It is noontide, and the fishes leap in the pool.

                 (1903) 1906

The Andante of Snakes[1]

They weave a slow andante as in sleep,
Scaled yellow, swampy black, plague-spotted
   white;
With blue and lidless eyes at watch they keep
A treachery of silence; infinite

Ancestral angers brood in these dull eyes
Where the long-lineaged venom of the snake
Meditates evil; woven intricacies
Of Oriental arabesque awake,

Unfold, expand, contract, and raise and sway
Swoln heart-shaped heads, flattened as by a
   heel,   10

---

   [1] Third Rosses: Rosses is a town in Ireland near the sea.
   [1] Loe Pool: or Loo Pool, the estuary of a river in Cornwall in the Southwest of England. The texts of this and the following poem are those of the volume in which they were first published.
   [2] Lapis and malachite: blue and green stones.
   [1] Andante: a dance or piece of music in a moderately slow tempo.

Erect to suck the sunlight from the day,
And stealthily and gradually reveal

Dim cabalistic signs of spots and rings
Among their folds of faded tapestry;

Then these fat, foul, unbreathing, moving
  things
Droop back to stagnant immobility.

(1904) 1906

Lionel Johnson
1867–1902

LIONEL JOHNSON was born in the west of England, a fact which in his later sympathies with Irish nationalism he exaggerated to furnish himself with a Celtic heritage. His father was an army officer; his grandfather was a baronet, and his great-grandfather was both titled and a general. This heritage, too, was influential, for Johnson carried with him throughout his life an idea of himself as a gentleman and a code of formal, disciplined, austere manners he thought appropriate to that identity. He won prizes for his poems at school, and he entered Oxford in 1886 already displaying the affectations and deliberately uncommon tastes of a late-century esthete. When he graduated and went to live in London in 1890, he had no thought but to live a literary life. He furnished his room with his extensive library, reviewed for London literary journals and newspapers, joined the poets who formed the Rhymers' Club and published some of his first poems in the two collections of verse put out by this group of poets, and worked on a study of the fiction of Thomas Hardy, which he published in 1894. His tastes and style, from his classical learning to elaborate ideas about punctuation, were fastidious and bookish. In 1891 Johnson became a Roman Catholic. To the reclusiveness of a life he intended to live in books and words he now added an asceticism which defined itself against the evils of flesh and excess and took pleasure in what Johnson called

"catholic puritanism," the niceties of ritual and apologetics. He wanted, as he said, to live life as a ritual, and he found the orders of his literature and religious belief endlessly refined ritual in the forms and grammars in which the tones without touching the fundament of their statements.

There were other, much more unhappy and disorderly reasons for Johnson's reclusiveness. He was an alcoholic and an insomniac. His physical development was arrested during adolescence, and he was always delicate and in uncertain health. He published a volume of *Poems* in 1895, and another, *Ireland and Other Poems,* in 1897. He became very much interested in the mid-1890s in the political cause of home rule for Ireland, and, sometimes through the agency of Yeats, he traveled several times to Ireland to lecture and speak to public meetings. But even before the publication of his second volume of poems the physical circumstances of Johnson's life were increasingly slipping from his control. He wrote more prose than poetry in the last years of the century, probably in order to make a living. In the last few years of his life he was too ill and too addicted to alcohol to write much at all. He died as a result of a fall in which he fractured his skull, but the fall itself and his last illnesses were probably the results of a series of cerebral strokes.

When Yeats wrote of Johnson in his *Auto-*

biographies as one of the "Tragic Generation" who did not survive the 1890s as a writer, or at all, he thought that part of the explanation for Johnson's dissipation and the misfortune of his life lay in a despair that the rituals of art and dogma to which he had withdrawn could not satisfy him. There was also, Yeats suggests, a surrender to disorder that was a reflex of his discipline. Johnson was not simply fascinated by the evil and disorder, by the dark angels he summoned into his poems in order to command them. He was also vulnerable and finally helpless before these antithetical energies, which he refined from his poetry but could not purge from his life. In a way, that formulation says more about what Yeats thought necessary for the survival of a poet in the twentieth century than it says about Johnson's life and poetry. Nor can the collapse of Johnson's life be explained by an esthetic which is itself a piece rather than a cause of the pattern of his entire life and art. But the formulation does properly emphasize Johnson's attempt to maintain the equilibrium of his poetry by calling on the rigorously policed formal order of his poems not to transform but simply to suppress the force of disorder, flux, and strong emotion.

There were gains and costs in this attempt. Very little in Johnson's poetry moves. He characteristically achieved a carefully wrought simplicity and rightness of effect through a controlled passage within a poem to an eventual, resolving stillness. Each series of words, images, lines, clauses, stanzas is firmly closed off and set in place before a new series is begun. The feeling of enclosure is very strong in his poems—they are set in the sanctuaries of woods, for example, and in rooms or empty city spaces in which the poet is alone with Plato or the statue of King Charles. It is within these strongly enforced limits that Johnson confronts the intimations of dissolution in "Mystic and Cavalier" and "The Dark Angel." These poems triumph over dissolution. But the triumph is not the climax of a conflict but the last, resolving term of a series in which the poems have not so much engaged the antitheses of threat and assurance as shuttled back and forth between them. Such poems lack the plangency or rage, the carefully prepared-for closing cry, that gave Housman's similarly finished poems their remarkable popularity, and they lack too the drama with

which Thomas Hardy's poems or Robert Bridges' rise to and test their perceptions of the world's order. In his poetry Johnson kept current a worthy tradition of an austere craft that, within the bounds of this anthology, moves from the poetry of Walter Savage Landor and is important in the poetry of Tennyson, Matthew Arnold, and Swinburne. Johnson's poems are also, however, representative of a prevalent kind of late-nineteenth-century poetry in that their craft is the mark of their difference from other experience, and not the agency of their power on it. His poetry is a rhetoric of denials and defenses as well as one of deftly satisfying control. Literally and historically Johnson's poetry goes no place. It rather seeks for a repose by which it can distinguish and withhold itself from all that is not itself, from all that is not art, as it defines art within the stringently formal identities of its own existence.

EDITIONS
The texts reprinted here are those of the original editions; they are consistent with those of *The Complete Poems of Lionel Johnson,* edited by Ian Fletcher (1953). (See also Fletcher's "Amendments and Additions to *The Complete Poems of Lionel Johnson,*" *Victorian News Letter,* No. 33, Spring, 1968.) Some of Johnson's critical essays have been collected in *Post Linimium,* edited by T. Whittemore (1911), and *Reviews and Critical Papers,* edited by R. Shafer (1921).

BIOGRAPHY AND CRITICISM
The only extensive study of Johnson's life and writing is a dissertation in French by Arthur W. Patrick, *Lionel Johnson* (1939). William Butler Yeats in his *Autobiographies* (1955) and T. E. Welby in *Second Impressions* (1933) recall and reflect on features of Johnson's life and art. Barbara Charlesworth in *Dark Passages: The Decadent Consciousness in Victorian Literature* (1965); John Pick in "Divergent Disciples of Walter Pater," *Thought,* 23 (1948); and Jean Wilson in "The 'Nineties' Movement in Poetry: Myth or Reality," *Yearbook of English Studies,* 1 (1972) consider Johnson's poetry in the context of late-century British literature. See also Ian Fletcher's discussion of "The Dark Angel" in *Interpretations: Essays on Twelve English Poets,* edited by John Wain (1955).

Plato in London

To Campbell Dodgson[1]

The pure flame of one taper fall
Over the old and comely page:
No harsher light disturb at all
This converse with a treasured sage.
Seemly, and fair, and of the best,
    If Plato be our guest,
    Should things befall.

Without, a world of noise and cold:
Here, the soft burning of the fire.
And Plato walks, where heavens unfold,
About the home of his desire.
From his own city of high things,
    He shows to us, and brings,
    Truth of fine gold.

The hours pass; and the fire burns low;
The clear flame dwindles into death:
Shut then the book with care; and so,
Take leave of Plato, with hushed breath
A little, by the falling gleams,
    Tarry the gracious dreams:
    And they too go.

Lean from the window to the air:
Hear London's voice upon the night!
Thou hast held converse with things rare:
Look now upon another sight!
The calm stars, in their living skies:
    And then, these surging cries,
    This restless glare!

That starry music, starry fire,
High above all our noise and glare:
The image of our long desire,
The beauty, and the strength, are there.
And Plato's thought lives, true and clear,
    In as august a sphere:
    Perchance, far higher.

(1889) 1892; 1895

By the Statue of King Charles at Charing Cross

To William Watson[1]

Sombre and rich, the skies;
Great glooms, and starry plains.
Gently the night wind sighs;
Else a vast silence reigns.

The splendid silence clings
Around me: and around
The saddest of all kings
Crowned, and again discrowned.

Comely and calm, he rides
Hard by his own Whitehall:
Only the night wind glides:
No crowds, nor rebels, brawl.

Gone, too, his Court: and yet,
The stars his courtiers are:
Stars in their stations set;
And every wandering star.

Alone he rides, alone,
The fair and fatal king:
Dark night is all his own,
That strange and solemn thing.

Which are more full of fate:
The stars; or those sad eyes?
Which are more still and great:
Those brows; or the dark skies?

Although his whole heart yearn
In passionate tragedy:
Never was face so stern
With sweet austerity.

Vanquished in life, his death
By beauty made amends:
The passing of his breath
Won his defeated ends.

Brief life, and hapless? Nay:
Through death, life grew sublime.

---

[1] First printed in the first *Book of the Rhymers' Club* (1892). Campbell Dodgson (1867–1948) was a friend of Johnson's during school and college; he later was curator of prints and drawings in the British Museum in London.
[1] Charing Cross is in the center of London, near the Whitehall, the name of a series of royal residences the most recent of which was built in the seventeenth century. Charles I (1600–1649) was executed by the government of the Commonwealth in front of Whitehall. For a brief account of the life and writing of William Watson, see Part Six.

Speak after sentence?[2] Yea:
And to the end of time.

Armoured he rides, his head
Bare to the stars of doom:
He triumphs now, the dead,
40   Beholding London's gloom.

Our wearier spirit faints,
Vexed in the world's employ:
His soul was of the saints;
And art to him was joy.

King, tried in fires of woe!
Men hunger for thy grace:
And through the night I go,
Loving thy mournful face.

Yet, when the city sleeps;
50   When all the cries are still:
The stars and heavenly deeps
Work out a perfect will.

                (1889)   1892; 1895

The Precept of Silence

I know you: solitary griefs,
Desolate passions, aching hours!
I know you: tremulous beliefs,
Agonized hopes, and ashen flowers!

The winds are sometimes sad to me;
The starry spaces, full of fear:
Mine is the sorrow on the sea,
And mine the sigh of places drear.

Some players upon plaintive strings
10   Publish their wistfulness abroad:
I have not spoken of these things,
Save to one man,[1] and unto God.

                   (1893) 1895

Mystic and Cavalier

To Herbert Percy Horne[1]

Go from me: I am one of those, who fall.
What! hath no cold wind swept your heart at
    all,

In my sad company? Before the end,
    Go from me, dear my friend!

Yours are the victories of light: your feet
Rest from good toil, where rest is brave and
    sweet.
But after warfare in a mourning gloom,
    I rest in clouds of doom.

Have you not read so, looking in these eyes?
Is it the common light of the pure skies,   10
Lights up their shadowy depths? The end is
    set:
    Though the end be not yet.

When gracious music stirs, and all is bright,
And beauty triumphs through a courtly night;
When I too joy, a man like other men:
    Yet, am I like them, then?

And in the battle, when the horsemen sweep
Against a thousand deaths, and fall on sleep:
Who ever sought that sudden calm, if I
    Sought not? Yet, could not die.   20

Seek with thine eyes to pierce this crystal
    sphere:
Canst read a fate there, prosperous and clear?
Only the mists, only the weeping clouds:
    Dimness, and airy shrouds.

Beneath, what angels are at work? What powers
Prepare the secret of the fatal hours?
See! the mists tremble, and the clouds are
    stirred:
    When comes the calling word?

The clouds are breaking from the crystal ball,
Breaking and clearing: and I look to fall.   30
When the cold winds and airs of portent sweep,
    My spirit may have sleep.

O rich and sounding voices of the air!
Interpreters and prophets of despair:
Priests of a fearful sacrament! I come,
    To make with you mine home.

             (1889) 1894; 1895

---

[2] *Speak after sentence:* Charles was not permitted to speak in the court after he was sentenced to death. He did speak from the scaffold at the site of his execution.

[1] One man: his confessor.

[1] This poem first appeared in the second *Book of the Rhymers' Club* (1894). Herbert Percy Horne (1865–1916) was an editor, poet, architect, and art historian. He helped to design the typography of Johnson's 1895 volume of poems.

from Sancta Silvarum

II

The moon labours through black cloud,
Through the vast night, dark and proud:
　　The windy wood dances.
Still the massed heavens drive along:
And, of all night's fiery throng,
　　The moon alone glances.

How the lights are wild and strange!
Only one light doth not change,
　　From living fires flowing:
10　Where, on fragrant banks of fern,
Steadily and stilly burn
　　The greenwood worms glowing.

Going down the forest side,
The night robs me of all pride,
　　By gloom and by splendour.
High, away, alone, afar,
Mighty wills and workings are:
　　To them I surrender.

The processions of the night,
20　Sweeping clouds and battling light,
　　And wild winds in thunder,
Care not for the world of man,
Passionate on another plan:
　　O twin worlds of wonder!

Ancients of dark majesty!
Priests of splendid mystery!
　　The Powers of Night cluster:
In the shadows of the trees,
Dreams, that no man lives and sees,
30　　The dreams! the dreams! muster.

Move not! for the night wind stirs:
And the night wind ministers
　　To dreams, and their voices:
Ah! the wild moon earthward bowed
From that tyranny of cloud:
　　The dim wood rejoices.

What do I here? What am I,
Who may comprehend nor sky,
　　Nor trees, nor dreams thronging?
40　Over moonlight dark clouds drive:
The vast midnight is alive
　　With magical longing.
　　　　　　　　　　(1889)　1895

III

Through the fresh woods there fleet
Fawns, with bright eyes, light feet:

Bright eyes, and feet that spurn
　　The pure green fern.

Headed by leaping does,
The swift procession goes
Through thickets, over lawns:
　　Followed by fawns.

Over slopes, over glades,
Down dells and leafy shades,   1●
Away the quick deer troop:
　　A wildwood group.

Under the forest airs,
A life of grace is theirs:
Courtly their look; they seem
　　Things of a dream.

Some say, but who can say?
That a charmed troop are they:
Once youths and maidens white!
　　These may be right.   2●
　　　　　　　　　　(1889)　1895

IV

Over me, beeches broad beneath blue sky
In light winds through their cooling leaves
　　rejoice:
Now, the red squirrel, lithe and wild, runs by;
Anon the wood dove from deep glades, with
　　voice
　　Of mellow music, lulls the air:
All murmurs of the forest, stirs and cries,
Come stilly down green coverts; the high fern
Smells of rich earth aglow from burning skies.
Hither my greenwood ways love best to turn:
　　Hither my lone hours gladliest fare.   1

But not for melancholy solitude;
Not for the fond delight of loneliness:
Though here nor voice, nor alien feet, intrude.
Lone am I: but what lone dreams dare repress
　　High presences of vanished days?
Long billowy reaches of unnumbered trees
Roll downward from this haunt, and break at
　　length
Against such walls, as no man unmoved sees,
But hails the past of splendour and of strength:
　　And heights of immemorial praise.   2●

That Castle gray, marvellous with mighty
　　years,
Crowning the forest deeps in pride of place:
Towers, royal in their histories of tears,

And royal in their chronicles of grace:
   Am I alone, beholding those?
The solitary forest bowers me round:
Yet companies august go through the glade,
Crowned and resplendent! stately and
   discrowned!
All, solemn from the tragedies they played:
   Remembering, each the doom, the close.

Alone! Nay, but almost, would that I were
Alone: too high are these great things for me.
Immeasurable glooms and splendours here
Usurp the calm noon, where my rest should
   be:
   O proud, O ancient Towers! farewell.
I turn from you, and take the world of men:
Gladly I mix me with the common day:
But should they vex me with their tumult:
   then,
Hither my feet will find the accustomed way;
   Then cast once more your heightening spell.
                           (1889) 1895

Bagley Wood

To Percy Addleshaw[1]

The night is full of stars, full of magnificence:
Nightingales hold the wood, and fragrance
   loads the dark.
Behold, what fires august, what lights eternal!
   Hark,
What passionate music poured in passionate
   love's defence!
Breathe but the wafting wind's nocturnal
   frankincense!
Only to feel this night's great heart, only to
   mark
The splendours and the glooms, brings back
   the patriarch,
Who on Chaldæan wastes[2] found God through
   reverence.
Could we but live at will upon this perfect
   height,
Could we but always keep the passion of this
   peace,
Could we but face unshamed the look of this
   pure light,

Could we but win earth's heart, and give
   desire release:
Then were we all divine, and then were ours
   by right
These stars, these nightingales, these scents:
   then shame would cease.
                          (1890) 1895

The Dark Angel

Dark Angel, with thine aching lust
To rid the world of penitence:
Malicious Angel, who still dost
My soul such subtile violence!

Because of thee, no thought, no thing,
Abides for me undesecrate:
Dark Angel, ever on the wing,
Who never reaches me too late!

When music sounds, then changest thou
Its silvery to a sultry fire:
Nor will thine envious heart allow
Delight untortured by desire.

Through thee, the gracious Muses turn
To Furies, O mine Enemy!
And all the things of beauty burn
With flames of evil ecstasy.

Because of thee, the land of dreams
Becomes a gathering place of fears:
Until tormented slumber seems
One vehemence of useless tears.

When sunlight glows upon the flowers,
Or ripples down the dancing sea:
Thou, with thy troop of passionate powers,
Beleaguerest, bewilderest, me.

Within the breath of autumn woods,
Within the winter silences:
Thy venomous spirit stirs and broods,
O Master of impieties!

The ardour of red flame is thine,
And thine the steely soul of ice:
Thou poisonest the fair design
Of nature, with unfair device.

---

[1] Bagley Wood is near Oxford. Johnson knew Percy Addleshaw (1866–1916) at Oxford and later in London; Addleshaw published a volume of verse in 1896.

[2] Chaldæan wastes: Chaldea is the Old Testament name for the desert regions in Asia west of the land of the Israel. The patriarch Abraham was from Ur in Chaldea.

Apples of ashes, golden bright;
Waters of bitterness, how sweet!
O banquet of a foul delight,
Prepared by thee, dark Paraclete![1]

Thou art the whisper in the gloom,
The hinting tone, the haunting laugh:
Thou art the adorner of my tomb,
40   The minstrel of mine epitaph.

I fight thee, in the Holy Name!
Yet, what thou dost, is what God saith:
Tempter! should I escape thy flame,
Thou wilt have helped my soul from Death:

The second Death, that never dies,
That cannot die, when time is dead:
Live Death, wherein the lost soul cries,
Eternally uncomforted.

Dark Angel, with thine aching lust!
50   Of two defeats, of two despairs:
Less dread, a change to drifting dust,
Than thine eternity of cares.

Do what thou wilt, thou shalt not so,
Dark Angel! triumph over me:
Lonely, unto the Lone[2] I go;
Divine, to the Divinity.

                                   (1893) 1894; 1895

Magic

To John Myres[1]

I

Because I work not, as logicians work,
Who but to ranked and marshalled reason
     yield:
But my feet hasten through a faery field,
Thither, where underneath the rainbow lurk
Spirits of youth, and life, and gold, concealed:

Because by leaps I scale the secret sky,
Upon the motion of a cunning star:

Because I hold the winds oracular,
And think on airy warnings, when men die:
Because I tread the ground, where shadows
     are: 10

Therefore my name is grown a popular scorn,
And I a children's terror! Only now,
For I am old! O Mother Nature! thou
Leavest me not: wherefore, as night turns
     morn,
A magian[2] wisdom breaks beneath my brow.

These painful toilers of the bounded way,
Chaired within cloister halls: can they renew
Ashes to flame? Can they of moonlit dew
Prepare the immortalizing draughts? Can they
Give gold for refuse earth, or bring to view   20

Earth's deepest doings? Let them have their
     school,
Their science, and their safety! I am he,
Whom Nature fills with her philosophy,
And takes for kinsman. Let me be their fool,
And wise man in the winds' society.

                                   (1887) 1897

II

They wrong with ignorance a royal choice,
Who cavil at my loneliness and labour:
For them, the luring wonder of a voice,
The viol's cry for them, the harp and tabour:
          For me divine austerity,
          And voices of philosophy.

Ah! light imaginations, that discern
No passion in the citadel of passion:
Their fancies lie on flowers; but my thoughts
     turn
To thoughts and things of an eternal fashion:
          The majesty and dignity
          Of everlasting verity.

Mine is the sultry sunset, when the skies
Tremble with strange, intolerable thunder:
And at the dead of an hushed night, these eyes
Draw down the soaring oracles winged with
     wonder:

---

[1] Paraclete: the spirit of divinity as it intercedes in human affairs; here, its inversion.
[2] Fletcher notes (p. 347) the occurrence of this phrase in a late-eighteenth-century translation of the *Enneads* of the third century neoplatonic philosopher Plotinus: the life of the gods, and of divine and happy men, is "a life unaccompanied with human pleasures, and a flight of the alone to the alone" (*Enneads*, VI, 9, translated by Thomas Taylor).
[1] Sir John Linton Myres (1869–1954) knew Johnson at school and at Oxford; he was later a professor of ancient history at Oxford and an archaeologist.
[2] Magian: of a magi, a seer or magician.

From the four winds they come to me,
The Angels of Eternity.

Men pity me; poor men, who pity me!
Poor, charitable, scornful souls of pity!
I choose laborious loneliness: and ye
Lead Love in triumph through the dancing
    city:
    While death and darkness girdle me,
    I grope for immortality.

                  (1887) 1897

III

50 Pour slowly out your holy balm of oil,
Within the grassy circle: let none spoil
Our favourable silence. Only I,
Winding wet vervain[3] round mine eyes, will
    cry
Upon the powerful Lord of this our toil;
Until the first lark sing, the last star die.

Proud Lord of twilight, Lord of midnight,
    hear!
Thou hast forgone us; and hast drowsed thine
    ear,
When haggard voices hail thee: thou hast
    turned
Blind eyes, dull nostrils, when our vows have
    burned
60 Herbs on the moonlit flame, in reverent fear:
Silence is all, our love of thee hath earned.

Master! we call thee, calling on thy name!
Thy savoury laurel crackles: the blue flame
Gleams, leaps, devours apace the dewy leaves.
Vain! for nor breast of labouring midnight
    heaves,
Nor chilled stars fall: all things remain the
    same,
Save this new pang, that stings, and burns, and
    cleaves.

Despising us, thou knowest not! We stand,
Bared for thine adoration, hand in hand:
70 Steely our eyes, our hearts to all but thee
Iron: as waves of the unresting sea,
The wind of thy least Word is our command:
And our ambition hails thy sovereignty.

Come, Sisters! for the King of night is dead:
Come! for the frailest star of stars hath sped:
And though we waited for the waking sun,
Our King would wake not. Come! our world is
    done:
For all the witchery of the world is fled,
And lost all wanton wisdom long since won.

                  (1888) 1897

Songs

I

Now in golden glory goes
Autumn toward the time of snows:
Ere white winter come indeed,
Speed the hours, with music speed.

Heed not winter's mournful breath,
Sighing at the thought of death:
Make but music, dearly sad;
Make but music, gravely glad.

Music is a king of kings,
Mightiest of immortal things: 10
Music is a lord of lords,
Ruling all with royal chords.

Though the woodland ways be chill,
Though the woodland choirs be still:
Music moves the starry choir,
Music sets the soul on fire.

II

Country singers, leave not mute
Music of the voice and lute:
Country singers, come and sing;
Voice with viol rivalling.   20

Chaunt to Pales,[1] chaunt to Pan,
Gods of country maid and man:
They have blessed the shepherd's fold,
Filled the fields with waves of gold.

On the lawns, fair lovers all!
Dance, till Hesper[2] homeward call;
Lapped in dreamland, you will keep
Safely your delightful sleep.

---

[3] Vervain: an herb known for its medicinal properties.
[1] Pales: a divinity in Roman mythology, sometimes imagined as male and sometimes as female, who is the god or goddess of shepherds. Pan is a classical divinity who is the god of forests and pastures, or sometimes the spirit of nature in general.
[2] Hesper: the evening star.

But the red sun lingers yet:
30 While you sing, he will not set.
He is lord of light and song:
Hail him, and both joys prolong.

1893 (1897)

A Stranger

To Will Rothenstein[1]

Her face was like sad things: was like the lights
Of a great city, seen from far off fields,
Or seen from sea: sad things, as are the fires
Lit in a land of furnaces by night:
Sad things, as are the reaches of a stream
Flowing beneath a golden moon alone.
And her clear voice, full of remembrances,
Came like faint music down the distant air.
As though she had a spirit of dead joy
10 About her, looked the sorrow of her ways:

If light there be, the dark hills are to climb
First: and if calm, far over the long sea.
Fallen from all the world apart she seemed,
Into a silence and a memory.
What had the thin hands done, that now they
    strained
Together in such passion? And those eyes,
What saw they long ago, that now they
    dreamed
Along the busy streets, blind but to dreams?
Her white lips mocked the world, and all
    therein:
She had known more than this; she wanted not   20
This, who had known the past so great a thing.
Moving about our ways, herself she moved
In things done, years remembered, places gone.
Lonely, amid the living crowds, as dead,
She walked with wonderful and sad regard:
With us, her passing image: but herself
Far over the dark hills and the long sea.

(1889) 1897

Ernest Dowson

1867–1900

ERNEST DOWSON was born near London, where his father administered a dry dock that he had inherited. Both of Dowson's parents had literary and artistic interests and family traditions. His father tried unsuccessfully to publish some of his writing in magazines, and one of his father's uncles was Alfred Domett, a poet and friend of Robert Browning (who made him the hero of "Waring"; see pp. 214–217). Both of Dowson's parents also had symptoms of tuberculosis or a similar disease which required them to spend most of their winters out of England. Dowson's education was therefore irregular and conducted mostly by tutors, from whom he learned a great deal about French and Latin literature and very little about what did not interest him, which was almost everything else, including science, history, and the general matter of large political and social cultures. In 1886, when Dowson was nineteen years old, he entered Oxford, where he enlarged his education in Latin poetry, met Lionel Johnson (see pp. 814–815), indulged in some mild experiments with alcohol and hashish, and wrote some short stories and poems. He left Oxford in 1888 without a degree to return to London and work in his father's business.

Dowson had published two poems and a short story in magazines before he left Oxford, and in London he began to move on the circuit of pubs, restaurants, and music halls that were the settings of the city's literary and artistic bohemia. He was never able to earn an ample living from his writing. But between 1890 and 1896 he established himself as a poet, writer of fiction, and translator of exceptional talent among the editors, publishers, literary

[1] Sir William Rothenstein (1872–1945) was a British painter.

critics, and other writers and artists who promoted and practiced the styles of late-century estheticism and decadence. In 1891 and 1892 Dowson published some of his best-known poems, including the lyric to Cynara, in magazines and in the first anthology of the Rhymers' Club, a gathering of young poets in which Dowson renewed his acquaintance with Lionel Johnson and met William Butler Yeats. He wrote a short, impressionistic play, *The Pierrot of the Minute,* which was performed to small audiences in 1892 and after. He also published short stories in magazines, and in 1893 he published a novel, *A Comedy of Masks,* written in collaboration with Arthur Moore, whom he knew at Oxford. His translation of a novel by the French naturalistic novelist Émile Zola was published in 1894, and a collection of his own short fiction, *Dilemmas,* in 1895. He published poems and fiction in both *The Yellow Book* and *The Savoy,* which in the middle of the decade were ostentatious in their display of the new and unconventional sensibility of the writers and artists with whom Dowson was now prominently associated. In 1896 Dowson published his first book of poems, *Verses.*

By this time, however, the difficulties of Dowson's personal life were compromising the exercise of his literary profession. In 1891 he had fallen in love with the twelve-year-old daughter of the proprietor of a restaurant. This desire, nearly impossible to consummate, provided Dowson an emblem of remote innocence to be wished for but never possessed, and also caused him a great deal of confused personal pain. He was a convert to Roman Catholicism in his young manhood, and that gesture too, as he shows in poems like "Extreme Unction" and "Carthusians," was at least in part a sad wish for a comfort and completion unlikely of realization in mortal life. Dowson continued in the early years of the 1890s to work in the family business, but it was failing. His father died in 1894, and six months later his mother hanged herself. Dowson's own health was now uncertain. In 1895 he went to live in France. In France and during his occasional visits to England he sometimes, especially in 1898–99, set himself to bouts of relatively productive work. He published some more translations, including one of the eighteenth-century French novel *Les Liaisons Dangereuses,* published a second novel in collaboration with Arthur Moore

(Adrian Rome: 1899), and collected a second and final volume of verse and short prose pieces, *Decorations,* in 1899. But he was addicted to alcohol, especially to absinthe; his health was poor; he had very little money; and the shifts and disorder of his life among the down and out gradually unstitched the fabric of his talent and industry. Everything—his health, his will, his mind, his physical appearance—began to deteriorate. During his final visit to London at the end of the century an acquaintance found him sick, pathologically suspicious of doctors, and about to be evicted from his rooms. Dowson was taken into the house of his acquaintance, where he died in 1900 at the age of thirty-two.

In his poems Dowson tried for what he and some of his contemporaries conceived to be a classic finish of clearly lined stanzas, unexceptional words placed with a simple, elegant decorum, uncomplicated syntax, and a steady, delicate music that never swelled into sweetness or passionate utterance. The restraint and refinement of Dowson's verse are like that of Lionel Johnson's and A. E. Housman's. But Dowson's poems are not marked by the sense of rigorous exclusion manifested in Johnson's verse, nor do they characteristically open into the ease or turn to the bitter wit of which Housman is capable. It is revealing of Dowson's talent that his short prose poems create much the same effect as his verse. For all its formal order, what holds a Dowson poem together is tone, a prevailing note of longing as wish gives way to disappointment. Dowson does not often engage the actualities that frustrate his wish. He usually lingers rather on the result and not on the contest, on the sad, softly lit quiet after desire and act have subsided. The technical gifts with which he expressed these themes and created this tone deliberately forswear the excitement of experiment, advance, and even of much variety. Nonetheless, Dowson's talents made a minor, satisfying canon of verse in which, as in the poems of many of his contemporaries, the order and lucidity of poetic language and verse form are cherished because they can make a small and solacing music out of sadness.

EDITIONS

The texts of the poems printed below are those of the original editions. They are consistent with the texts of *The Poems of Ernest Dow-*

son, edited by Mark Longaker (1963) and Desmond Flowers' edition of Dowson's *Poetical Works* (third edition, 1967), which contains some unpublished poems not included in Longaker's edition. Desmond Flowers and Henry Maas have edited *The Letters of Ernest Dowson* (1967).

BIOGRAPHY AND CRITICISM

Mark Longaker has written the most complete biography, *Ernest Dowson* (1944). John Gawsworth (T. I. F. Armstrong) in "The Dowson Legend," *Essays by Divers Hands,* new series 17 (1938), and Russell Goldfarb in "The Dowson Legend Today," *Studies in English Literature,* 4 (1964) have corrected and reflected on over-simple and still-current conceptions of the dissipation, perverse idealism, and eventual squalor of Dowson's life. See also Jean Wilson, "The 'Nineties' Movement in Poetry: Myth or Reality," *Yearbook of English Studies,* 1 (1972); and James G. Nelson, "The Nature of Esthetic Experience in the Poetry of the Nineties: Ernest Dowson, Lionel Johnson, and John Gray," *English Literature in Transition,* 17 (1974).

Thomas Swann's short study, *Ernest Dowson* (1964), contains a bibliography of writing about Dowson. Jonathan Ramsey, "Ernest Dowson: An Annotated Bibliography of Writings About Him," *English Literature in Transition,* 14 (1971), is a more complete bibliography.

Vitae summa brevis spem nos vetat incohare longam[1]

They are not long, the weeping and the
　　laughter,
　　Love and desire and hate:
I think they have no portion in us after
　　We pass the gate.

They are not long, the days of wine and roses:
　　Out of a misty dream

Our path emerges for a while, then closes
　　Within a dream.

　　　　　　　　　　　　1896

To One in Bedlam

For Henry Davray[1]

With delicate, mad hands, behind his sordid
　　bars,
Surely he hath his posies, which they tear and
　　twine;
Those scentless wisps of straw, that miserably
　　line
His strait, caged universe, whereat the dull
　　world stares,

Pedant and pitiful. O, how his rapt gaze wars
With their stupidity! Know they what dreams
　　divine
Lift his long, laughing reveries like
　　enchaunted wine,
And make his melancholy germane to the
　　stars'?

O lamentable brother! if those pity thee,
Am I not fain of all thy lone eyes promise me;
Half a fool's kingdom, far from men who sow
　　and reap,
All their days, vanity? Better than mortal
　　flowers,
Thy moon-kissed roses seem: better than love
　　or sleep,
The star-crowned solitude of thine oblivious
　　hours!

　　　　　　　　　　　　1892; 1896

Non sum qualis eram bonae sub regno Cynarae[1]

Last night, ah, yesternight, betwixt her lips
　　and mine
There fell thy shadow, Cynara! thy breath was
　　shed

---

[1] The title is from the fourth ode of the first book of odes by the first-century B.C. Roman poet Horace: "The short span of life forbids us to consider a long hope."

[1] First published in a magazine and then in the second *Book of the Rhymers' Club* (1894). Bedlam is the name of a hospital for the insane (Bethelem Hospital) which has existed on one site or another in London from the fourteenth century. Henry Davray was an editor and writer who translated and advertised the work of young British poets in France in the 1890s.

[1] The title is from the first ode of the fourth book of the *Odes* by the first-century B.C. Roman poet Horace: "I am not what I formerly was under the reign of the good Cynara." This poem, and the following, were also published in the second *Book of the Rhymes' Club* (1894).

Upon my soul between the kisses and the
   wine;
And I was desolate and sick of an old passion,
   Yea, I was desolate and bowed my head:
I have been faithful to thee, Cynara! in my
   fashion.

All night upon mine heart I felt her warm
   heart beat,
Night-long within mine arms in love and sleep
   she lay;
Surely the kisses of her bought red mouth
   were sweet;
But I was desolate and sick of an old passion,
   When I awoke and found the dawn was
   grey:
I have been faithful to thee, Cynara! in my
   fashion.

I have forgot much, Cynara! gone with the
   wind,
Flung roses, roses riotously with the throng,
Dancing, to put thy pale, lost lilies out of
   mind;
But I was desolate and sick of an old passion,
   Yea, all the time, because the dance was
   long:
I have been faithful to thee, Cynara! in my
   fashion.

I cried for madder music and for stronger
   wine,
But when the feast is finished and the lamps
   expire,
Then falls thy shadow, Cynara! the night is
   thine;
And I am desolate and sick of an old passion,
   Yea hungry for the lips of my desire:
I have been faithful to thee, Cynara! in my
   fashion.

                                   1891; 1896

Extreme Unction

For Lionel Johnson[1]

Upon the eyes, the lips, the feet,
   On all the passages of sense,

The atoning oil is spread with sweet
   Renewal of lost innocence.

The feet, that lately ran so fast
   To meet desire, are soothly sealed;
The eyes, that were so often cast
   On vanity, are touched and healed.

From troublous sights and sounds set free;
   In such a twilight hour of breath,   10
Shall one retrace his life, or see,
   Through shadows, the true face of death?

Vials of mercy! Sacring oils!
   I know not where nor when I come,
Nor through what wanderings and toils,
   To crave of you Viaticum.[2]

Yet, when the walls of flesh grow weak,
   In such an hour, it well may be,
Through mist and darkness, light will break,
   And each anointed sense will see.   20
                                   1894; 1896

Carthusians[1]

Through what long heaviness, assayed in what
   strange fire,
   Have these white monks been brought into
   the way of peace,
Despising the world's wisdom and the world's
   desire,
   Which from the body of this death bring no
   release?

Within their austere walls no voices penetrate;
   A sacred silence only, as of death, obtains;
Nothing finds entry here of loud or passionate;
   This quiet is the exceeding profit of their
   pains.

From many lands they came, in divers fiery
   ways;
   Each knew at last the vanity of earthly joys;   10
And one was crowned with thorns, and one
   was crowned with bays,[2]

---

[1] Extreme Unction: the sacrament administered to the dying in the rites of the Roman Catholic church in which each of the five senses is anointed. For a brief account of the life and writings of Lionel Johnson, see pp. 814–815.
[2] Viaticum: Communion Host.
[1] Carthusians: a monastic order founded in the eleventh century; its best-known monastery is Le Grande Chartreuse in the French Alps.
[2] Crowned with bays: honored with a triumphal wreath.

And each was tired at last of the world's
  foolish noise.

It was not theirs with Dominic to preach God's
  holy wrath,
  They were too stern to bear sweet Francis'
  gentle sway;[3]
Theirs was a higher calling and a steeper path,
  To dwell alone with Christ, to meditate and
  pray.

A cloistered company, they are companionless,
  None knoweth here the secret of his brother's
  heart:
They are but come together for more
  loneliness,
  Whose bond is solitude and silence all their
20   part.

O beatific life! Who is there shall gainsay,
  Your great refusal's victory, your little loss,
Deserting vanity for the more perfect way,
  The sweeter service of the most dolorous
  Cross.

Ye shall prevail at last! Surely ye shall prevail!
  Your silence and austerity shall win at last:
Desire and mirth, the world's ephemeral lights
  shall fail,
  The sweet star of your queen is never
  overcast.

We fling up flowers and laugh, we laugh across
  the wine;
  With wine we dull our souls and careful
30   strains of art;
Our cups are polished skulls round which the
  roses twine:
  None dares to look at Death who leers and
  lurks apart.

Move on, white company, whom that has not
  sufficed!

Our viols cease, our wine is death, our roses
  fail:
Pray for our heedlessness, O dwellers with the
  Christ!
  Though the world fall apart, surely ye shall
  prevail.

                                   (1891) 1899

Villanelle of Acheron[1]

By the pale marge of Acheron,
  Methinks we shall pass restfully,
Beyond the scope of any sun.

There all men hie them one by one,
  Far from the stress of earth and sea,
By the pale marge of Acheron.

'Tis well when life and love is done,
  'Tis very well at last to be,
Beyond the scope of any sun.

No busy voices there shall stun
  Our ears: the stream flows silently
By the pale marge of Acheron.

There is the crown of labour won,
  The sleep of immortality,
Beyond the scope of any sun.

Life, of thy gifts I will have none,
  My queen is that Persephone,[2]
By the pale marge of Acheron,
  Beyond the scope of any sun.

                                          1899

Jadis[1]

Erewhile, before the world was old,
When violets grew and celandine,
In Cupid's train we were enrolled:
  Erewhile!

[3] Dominic: founder of the Dominicans in the twelfth century, an order dedicated to rigorous fasting and preaching to win converts. Francis of Assisi was the founder of the Franciscan order in the thirteenth century; he was best known for his communion with all forms of life.
[1] Villanelle: a form of French verse consisting of five triplets and a quatrain. The first and third lines of the first triplet furnish refrains for the entire poem, which uses only two rhymes. Acheron is a river of the underworld in classical mythology.
[2] Persephone: the goddess of growing things in classical mythology who was kidnapped by the god of the underworld and required to spend half the year with him in his realm.
[1] Jadis: formerly, in the old days. The poem is a roundel, an English imitation of one of the demanding forms of French verse; its eleven lines use only two rhymes, and its refrain is the first word or words of the first line (which is also supposed to, but in this poem does not, rhyme with the last word of the second line).

Your little hands were clasped in mine,
Your head all ruddy and sun-gold
Lay on my breast which was your shrine,
And all the tale of love was told:
Ah, God, that sweet things should decline,
And fires fade out which were not cold,
    Erewhile.

1899

A Last Word[1]

Let us go hence: the night is now at hand;
The day is overworn, the birds all flown;
And we have reaped the crops the gods have
    sown;
Despair and death; deep darkness o'er the
    land,
Broods like an owl; we cannot understand
Laughter or tears, for we have only known
Surpassing vanity: vain things alone
Have driven our perverse and aimless band.
Let us go hence, somewhither strange and cold,
To Hollow Lands where just men and unjust
Find end of labour, where's rest for the old,
Freedom to all from love and fear and lust.
Twine our torn hands! O pray the earth enfold
Our life-sick hearts and turn them into dust.

1895; 1899

The Princess of Dreams

Poor legendary princess! In her enchaunted tower of ivory, the liberator thought that she awaited him.

For once in a dream he had seen, as they were flowers de luce,[1] the blue lakes of her eyes, had seemed to be enveloped in a tangle of her golden hair.

And he sought her through the countless windings of her forest for many moons, sought her through the morasses, sparing not his horse nor his sword. On his way he slew certain evil magicians and many of his friends, so that at his journey's end his bright sword was tarnished and his comeliness swart with mud. His horses he had not spared: their bones made a white track behind him in the windings of the forest: but he still bore her ransom, all the costly, graceful things stored in a cypress chest: massed pearls and amethysts and silks from Samarcand, Valance[2] of Venice, and fine tapestry of Tyre. All these he brought with him to the gates of her ivory tower.

Poor legendary princess.

For he did not free her and the fustian[3] porter took his treasure and broke his stained sword in two.

And who knows where he went, horseless and disarmed, through the morasses and the dark windings of her forest under the moonless night, dreaming of those blue lakes which were flowers de luce, her eyes? Who knows? For the fustian porter says nothing, being slow of wit.

But there are some who say that she had no wish to be freed, and that those flowers de luce, her eyes, are a stagnant, dark pool, that her glorious golden hair was only long enough to reach her postern gate.

Some say, moreover, that her tower is not of ivory and that she is not even virtuous nor a princess.

1899

---

[1] First published in *The Yellow Book*. Longaker (p. 250) thinks that the poem was written as early as 1886.
[1] Flowers de luce: fleur-de-lis, an iris.   [2] Valance: drapery.
[3] Fustian: a common cotton fabric.

A. E. Housman

1859–1936

ALFRED EDWARD HOUSMAN was born in the west of England, near Birmingham and the county in which he placed the poems of *A Shropshire Lad*. His father owned land and practiced law, but after the death of Housman's mother in 1871 his father allowed his abilities and substance to drift away in despondence, improvidence, and drink. Housman was raised in the doctrines of the Church of England, but a faith in the providential rightness of things was eroded, or more likely frustrated from the beginning, by the illness and death of his mother and the slow waste of his father. Housman went to school near his home, and won a scholarship to the Oxford college he entered in 1877. There he met Moses Jackson, a conventionally handsome young man who excelled in science and athletics and with whom Housman formed a close friendship. Housman was already on guard against gestures that made him vulnerable to rejection, and already contemptuous of his need to win approval. The strength of his friendship with Jackson was therefore probably painfully confusing to him. For that reason this important friendship played its part not only in helping to engender the poetry Housman wrote in the mid-1890s, but also in enforcing the discipline and reticence with which Housman supervised his emotional life. At Oxford Housman continued to read and write poetry, and he began the scholarly and textual study of Latin poetry. Although he was expected to take honors in his final examinations, he failed them in 1881, closing for the time the possibility of a career as an academic and scholar.

After leaving Oxford without a degree (he later qualified to receive one), Housman in 1882 passed a civil service examination that won him an appointment as a clerk in the patent office in London, where Jackson also worked before he married at the end of the decade and went out to India to administer a school. Housman remained in the patent of-fice for the next decade, and at the same time he set himself to prepare a series of rigorously argued papers in the textual scholarship of Greek and Latin writers. The first of these papers was published in 1882, and he began to publish others regularly after 1888. In 1892 he applied for and won appointment as the professor of Latin in University College of the University of London, a post he held until 1911. He published his edition and commentary on the first book of the *Astromicon* of the first-century Roman writer Manilius in 1903; subsequent books in what was to be nearly a life's work were published in 1912, 1916, 1920, and 1930. He also published an edition of the satires of Juvenal in 1905, and in 1911 he moved to a chair of Latin in Cambridge. He spent the rest of his life in Cambridge, personally aloof and reticent, an unbendingly formal teacher and lecturer, industrious and scrupulous in his own elucidations and emendations of the texts of classical literature, and fiercely witty in his attacks on the works of other scholars. It was a life lived within tightly drawn boundaries—the conventions and cloisters of a British university, and the recondite disputes of the yet smaller realm of classical scholarship. It was also a life which Housman had retrieved from failure by intelligence, a gift for intuiting and restoring the meaning of classical texts, very hard work, and a personal discipline that was extraordinary, continual, and finally habitual.

Housman published only two volumes of his own poetry in his lifetime, *A Shropshire Lad* in 1896 and *Last Poems* in 1922. Together the two books contain only a little more than 100 poems. He left four manuscript books of poems, from which his brother Laurence published forty-nine lyrics as *More Poems* in 1936, and another twenty or so poems in a memoir in 1937. The rest of the manuscripts, which at A. E. Housman's direction were destroyed after his brother had selected for survival those texts good enough to stand with the published poems, were apparently fragmentary or working drafts of published poems. The poems of *A Shropshire Lad* were written in the 1890s, most of them in 1895. Whatever the causes of this flare of poetry, they subsided, and Housman wrote more slowly thereafter. Only a few of the poems in *Last Poems* were recent, and a number of the poems published in that volume and posthumously were written in the 1890s or were revisions of poems written in that decade.

A Shropshire Lad itself moved gradually into its exceptional popularity. The first edition of the book, published at Housman's expense, was sparsely reviewed, and the 500 copies of the first printing sold slowly. A second edition was brought out in 1898 by a new publisher. By 1907, after three other issues, the volume was published in England in an edition of 5000 copies, and it had also grown into an equivalent popularity in the United States. Sales and reviews of *Last Poems* were of course more ample. But it is as the author of *A Shropshire Lad* that Housman was and remains best known. Like the poems of Edward FitzGerald's *Rubáiyát*, Housman's verse is remembered because it continues to fit and express a certain mood or strand of sensibility in which the pleasures of love, drink, youth, landscape, and the fact of individual being are made poignant by a knowledge of transience. Their anger and self-pity please, when they please, because they are rigorously controlled, transmuted by measure, rhyme, and a carefully chosen diction into an understated eloquence whose courage is to complete its form in a cosmos careless of its existence.

When Housman was asked permission to include some of his poems in an anthology of 1890s verse, he refused, saying that it was as incorrect to put his poems in that company as it was to place Lot among the Sodomites. It is true that in his academic seclusion Housman met other writers rarely, and that his knowledge of contemporary poetry was narrow. Among the models he named for his poems were the songs of Shakespeare and the English ballads, and he surely had also before him the precision and terse point of Latin lyric and epigrammatic verse. But for all his remoteness from the normal traffic of writers with one another in his own time, the mood, themes, style, and very idea of his poetry are like those of other late-century British poets. Housman was affected by the elegiac poetry of Tennyson, Arnold, and Robert Bridges. His interest in verse that was sung or spoken to a pronounced rhythm did not extend as far as that of Bridges and William Butler Yeats (or, to a very different music, that of Kipling). His interest did, however, open his verse to simple words, common syntax, and spare, straight-line narratives that sometimes give it a vernacular ease within its extremely compressed metrical and stanzaic forms. Like Thomas Hardy, Housman sometimes ("The Immortal Part") looked beyond economically rendered details of landscape and event to the lineaments of a universe indifferent to losses that terrified and annihilated individual being. Like Kipling, he sometimes ("1887") counted these losses in social and political terms. Most important, like the poets of the *fin de siècle* from whom on other grounds he correctly dissociated himself, he regarded the artifice of verse as an insulation from, and not as an instrument upon, the enormously troubling matter of human existence in a universe full of silence and emptiness. The deliberately framed feeling and statement of his poems, each, as he says in "Terence, This Is Stupid Stuff", a shrewdly calibrated measure of poison, are analogous to the vigilance and reticence he exercised in his own life. His poems end always in the same perception. The knowing never itself changes or develops, nor does it ever change anything else. His poems say just enough, and say it just often enough, to remind us that the very saying of poetry is an assertion of self and an act of order. But in his view the poem does not, as Housman's high romantic predecessors would have it, alter the conditions and relations of being; it only assists us to endure them.

EDITIONS

The texts of the poems reprinted here are, unless otherwise noted, those of the original edition of *A Shropshire Lad;* they are consistent with those of the standard edition, *The Collected Poems of A. E. Housman,* edited by John Carter (1965). Carl J. Weber's edition of *A Shropshire Lad* (1946) contains useful notes. Carter has also edited a collection of Housman's *Selected Prose* (1961). Some of Housman's lectures have been published separately, principally, *The Name and Nature of Poetry* (1933), *The Confines of Criticism* (1969), and a lecture on Swinburne which has been published in *American Scholar,* **39** (1969).

Henry Maas has edited *The Letters of A. E. Housman* (1971). *The Classical Papers of A. E. Housman*, from 1882 to 1936, have been published in three volumes, edited by J. Diggle and F. R. D. Goodyear (1972–73).

Laurence Housman's *A. E. H.: Some Poems, Some Letters, and a Personal Memoir* (1937), and Grant Richards' (who was Housman's publisher) memoir, *Housman, 1897–1936* (1942), are standard sources of biographical information. The biographical sections of Norman Marlow's *A. E. Housman: Scholar and Poet* (1958) and Ian Scott-Kilvert's pamphlet on Housman in the Writers and Their Work series (1955) are succinct. George L. Watson's *A. E. Housman: A Divided Life* (1957) is very speculative, especially about Housman's relationship with Moses Jackson and its consequences in his poetry.

Marlow's *Housman* is fundamentally a study of Housman's use of the conventions and language of the classical, Continental, and British writers he echoes in his poetry. See also B. J. Leggett, *Housman's Land of Lost Content: A Critical Study of A Shropshire Lad* (1970).

Housman's methods of composition and revision are studied in William White, "*A Shropshire Lad* In Process: The Textual Evolution of Some A. E. Housman Poems," *Library*, 5th series, 9 (1954); and in Tom Burns Haber's *The Making of a Shropshire Lad: A Manuscript Variorum* (1966). Haber's interpretation and transcription of Housman's manuscripts have engendered considerable dispute: see John Sparrow's "The Housman Dilemma," first published in the *Times Literary Supplement* (29 April 1955) and reprinted in Sparrow's *Controversial Essays* (1966) and in Ricks' collection (see below).

Housman's published poems and the surviving manuscripts are described in John Carter and John Sparrow, *A. E. Housman: An Annotated Hand-List* (1952). Bibliographies of writing about Housman were published by R. W. Stallman in *Publications of the Modern Language Association*, **60** (1945), and William White in *Journal of English and Germanic Philology*, **61** (1959). Tom Burns Haber's short study, *A. E. Housman* (1967) contains a bibliography of writing about Housman. Christo-

pher Ricks has edited *A. E. Housman: A Collection of Critical Essays* (1968) which contains important essays by Edmund Wilson, Cyril Connolly, John Sparrow, J. P. Sullivan, and Ricks himself.

New Year's Eve

The end of the year fell chilly
   Between a moon and a moon;
Thorough the twilight shrilly
   The bells rang, ringing no tune.

The windows stained with story,
   The walls with miracle scored,
Were hidden for gloom and glory
   Filling the house of the Lord.

Arch and aisle and rafter
   And roof-tree dizzily high   10
Were full of weeping and laughter
   And song and saying good-bye.

There stood in the holy places
   A multitude none could name,
Ranks of dreadful faces
   Flaming, transfigured in flame.

Crown and tiar and mitre
   Were starry with gold and gem;
Christmas never was whiter
   Than fear on the face of them.   20

In aisles that emperors vaulted
   For a faith the world confessed,
Abasing the Host exalted,[1]
   They worshipped towards the west.

They brought with laughter oblation;
   They prayed, not bowing the head;
They made without tear lamentation,
   And rendered me answer and said:

"O thou that seest our sorrow,
   It fares with us even thus: 30
To-day we are gods, to-morrow
   Hell have mercy on us.

"Lo, morning over our border
   From out of the west comes cold;
Down ruins the ancient order
   And empire builded of old.

[1] Abasing the Host: kneeling before the Host of the Eucharist elevated during the Roman Catholic mass.

"Our house at even is queenly
   With psalm and censers[2] alight:
Look thou never so keenly
   Thou shalt not find us to-night.   40

"We are come to the end appointed
   With sands not many to run;
Divinities disanointed
   And kings whose kingdom is done.

"The peoples knelt down at our portal,
   All kindreds under the sky;
We were gods and implored and immortal
   Then; and to-day we die."

They turned them again to their praying,
   They worshipped and took no rest,   50
Singing old tunes and saying
   "We have seen his star in the west,"[3]

Old tunes of the sacred psalters,
   Set to wild farewells;
And I left them there at their altars
   Ringing their own dead knells.

               (1881)

from A Shropshire Lad

I

1887[1]

From Clee to heaven the beacon burns,
   The shires[2] have seen it plain,
From north and south the sign returns
   And beacons burn again.

Look left, look right, the hills are bright,
   The dales are light between,

Because 'tis fifty years to-night
   That God has saved the Queen.

Now, when the flame they watch not towers
   About the soil they trod,   10
Lads, we'll remember friends of ours
   Who shared the work with God.

To skies that knit their heartstrings right,
   To fields that bred them brave,
The saviours come not home to-night:
   Themselves they could not save.

It dawns in Asia, tombstones show
   And Shropshire names are read;
And the Nile spills his overflow
   Beside the Severn's dead.   20

We pledge in peace by farm and town
   The Queen they served in war,
And fire the beacons up and down
   The land they perished for.

"God save the Queen" we living sing,
   From height to height 'tis heard;
And with the rest your voices ring,
   Lads of the Fifty-third.[3]

Oh, God will save her, fear you not:
   Be you the men you've been,   30
Get you the sons your fathers got,
   And God will save the Queen.

             1896

II

"Loveliest of trees, the cherry now"

Loveliest of trees, the cherry now
Is hung with bloom along the bough,
And stands about the woodland ride[1]
Wearing white for Eastertide.

Now, of my threescore years and ten,
Twenty will not come again,

2 Censers: containers in which incense is burned.
3 His star: the star that announced the birth of Christ, and thus the end of the Eastern religions, deities, and kingdoms.
1 The jubilee of Queen Victoria, the fiftieth anniversary of her coronation, was celebrated by the lighting of signal fires from one end of the island to the other.
2 Shire: a political division, such as a county.
3 Fifty-Third: a Shropshire regiment.
1 Ride: road.

And take from seventy springs a score,
It only leaves me fifty more.

And since to look at things in bloom
10   Fifty springs are little room,
About the woodlands I will go
To see the cherry hung with snow.

                                        1896

XII

"When I watch the living meet"

When I watch the living meet,
    And the moving pageant file
Warm and breathing through the street
    Where I lodge a little while,

If the heats of hate and lust
    In the house of flesh are strong,
Let me mind the house of dust
    Where my sojourn shall be long.

In the nation that is not
10   Nothing stands that stood before;
There revenges are forgot,
    And the hater hates no more;

Lovers lying two and two
    Ask not whom they sleep beside,
And the bridegroom all night through
    Never turns him to the bride.

                                        1896

XIX

To an Athlete Dying Young

The time you won your town the race
We chaired you through the market-place;
Man and boy stood cheering by,
And home we brought you shoulder-high.

To-day, the road all runners come,
Shoulder-high we bring you home,
And set you at your threshold down,
Townsman of a stiller town.

Smart lad, to slip betimes away
From fields where glory does not stay   1（
And early though the laurel grows
It withers quicker than the rose.[1]

Eyes the shady night has shut
Cannot see the record cut,
And silence sounds no worse than cheers
After earth has stopped the ears:

Now you will not swell the rout
Of lads that wore their honours out,
Runners whom renown outran
And the name died before the man.   2（

So set, before its echoes fade,
The fleet foot on the sill of shade,
And hold to the low lintel up
The still-defended challenge-cup.

And round that early-laurelled head
Will flock to gaze the strengthless dead,
And find unwithered on its curls
The garland briefer than a girl's.

                                        1896

XXI

Bredon Hill

In summertime on Bredon
    The bells they sound so clear;
Round both the shires[1] they ring them
    In steeples far and near,
    A happy noise to hear.

Here of a Sunday morning
    My love and I would lie,
And see the coloured counties,
    And hear the larks so high
    About us in the sky.   1（

The bells would ring to call her
    In valleys miles away:
"Come all to church, good people;
    Good people, come and pray."
    But here my love would stay.

[1] Laurel; rose: conventional emblems of triumph and beauty.
[1] Both the shires: Bredon Hill (pronounced Bree-don) is in Worcestershire near the border of Gloucestershire in the central southwestern section of England. Housman said that he wrote this poem before he thought of putting together a book of Shropshire poems.

And I would turn and answer
  Among the springing thyme,
"Oh, peal upon our wedding,
  And we will hear the chime,
  And come to church in time."

But when the snows at Christmas
  On Bredon top were strown,
My love rose up so early
  And stole out unbeknown
  And went to church alone.

They tolled the one bell only,
  Groom there was none to see,
The mourners followed after,
  And so to church went she,
  And would not wait for me.

The bells they sound on Bredon,
  And still the steeples hum.
"Come all to church, good people,"—
  Oh, noisy bells, be dumb;
  I hear you, I will come.

(1891) 1896

XXIII

"The lads in their hundreds to Ludlow come in for the fair"

The lads in their hundreds to Ludlow come in
  for the fair,
  There's men from the barn and the forge and
  the mill and the fold,
The lads for the girls and the lads for the
  liquor are there,
  And there with the rest are the lads that will
  never be old.

There's chaps from the town and the field and
  the till[1] and the cart,
  And many to count are the stalwart, and
  many the brave,
And many the handsome of face and the hand-
  some of heart,
  And few that will carry their looks or their
  truth to the grave.

I wish one could know them, I wish there
  were tokens to tell

[1] Till: a money drawer in a shop.

The fortunate fellows that now you can
  never discern; 10
And then one could talk with them friendly
  and wish them farewell
  And watch them depart on the way that they
  will not return.

But now you may stare as you like and there's
  nothing to scan;
  And brushing your elbow unguessed-at and
  not to be told
They carry back bright to the coiner the
  mintage of man,
  The lads that will die in their glory and
  never be old.

1896

XXIV

"Say, lad, have you things to do?"

Say, lad, have you things to do?
  Quick then, while your day's at prime.
Quick, and if 'tis work for two,
  Here am I, man: now's your time.

Send me now, and I shall go;
  Call me, I shall hear you call;
Use me ere they lay me low
  Where a man's no use at all;

Ere the wholesome flesh decay,
  And the willing nerve be numb, 10
And the lips lack breath to say,
  "No, my lad, I cannot come."

1896

XXVII

" 'Is my team ploughing' "

"Is my team ploughing,
  That I was used to drive
And hear the harness jingle
  When I was man alive?"

Ay, the horses trample,
  The harness jingles now;

No change though you lie under
  The land you used to plough.

"Is football playing
  Along the river shore,
With lads to chase the leather,
  Now I stand up no more?"

Ay, the ball is flying,
  The lads play heart and soul;
The goal stands up, the keeper
  Stands up to keep the goal.

"Is my girl happy,
  That I thought hard to leave,
And has she tired of weeping
  As she lies down at eve?"

Ay, she lies down lightly,
  She lies not down to weep:
Your girl is well contented.
  Be still, my lad, and sleep.

"Is my friend hearty,
  Now I am thin and pine,
And has he found to sleep in
  A better bed than mine?"

Yes, lad, I lie easy,
  I lie as lads would choose;
I cheer a dead man's sweetheart,
  Never ask me whose.

                    1896

XXXI

"On Wenlock Edge the wood's in trouble"

On Wenlock Edge[1] the wood's in trouble;
  His forest fleece the Wrekin heaves;
The gale, it plies the saplings double,
  And thick on Severn snow the leaves.

'Twould blow like this through holt and
    hanger[2]
  When Uricon[3] the city stood:
'Tis the old wind in the old anger,
  But then it threshed another wood.

Then, 'twas before my time, the Roman
  At yonder heaving hill would stare:
The blood that warms an English yeoman,
  The thoughts that hurt him, they were there.

There, like the wind through woods in riot,
  Through him the gale of life blew high;
The tree of man was never quiet:
  Then 'twas the Roman, now 'tis I.

The gale, it plies the saplings double,
  It blows so hard, 'twill soon be gone:
To-day the Roman and his trouble
  Are ashes under Uricon.
                (1895) 1896

XLIII

The Immortal Part

When I meet the morning beam,
Or lay me down at night to dream,
I hear my bones within me say,
"Another night, another day.

"When shall this slough of sense be cast,
  This dust of thoughts be laid at last,
The man of flesh and soul be slain
  And the man of bone remain?

"This tongue that talks, these lungs that shout,
  These thews that hustle us about,
This brain that fills the skull with schemes,
  And its humming hive of dreams,—

"These to-day are proud in power
  And lord it in their little hour:
The immortal bones obey control
  Of dying flesh and dying soul.

" 'Tis long till eve and morn are gone:
  Slow the endless night comes on,
And late to fulness grows the birth
  That shall last as long as earth.

"Wanderers eastward, wanderers west,
  Know you why you cannot rest?
  'Tis that every mother's son
  Travails with a skeleton.

"Lie down in the bed of dust;
  Bear the fruit that bear you must;

---

[1] Edge: hill.   [2] Holt: a wood or grove. Hanger: a wood on the side of a steep hill.
[3] Uricon: a Roman city in what is now Shropshire.

Bring the eternal seed to light,
And morn is all the same as night.

"Rest you so from trouble sore,
Fear the heat o' the sun no more,
Nor the snowing winter wild,
Now you labour not with child.

"Empty vessel, garment cast,
We that wore you long shall last.
—Another night, another day."
So my bones within me say.

Therefore they shall do my will
To-day while I am master still,
And flesh and soul, now both are strong,
Shall hale the sullen slaves along,

Before this fire of sense decay,
This smoke of thought blow clean away,
And leave with ancient night alone
The stedfast and enduring bone.

1896

LXII

" 'Terence, this is stupid stuff' "

"Terence,[1] this is stupid stuff:
You eat your victuals fast enough;
There can't be much amiss, 'tis clear,
To see the rate you drink your beer.
But oh, good Lord, the verse you make,
It gives a chap the belly-ache.
The cow, the old cow, she is dead;
It sleeps well, the horned head:
We poor lads, 'tis our turn now
To hear such tunes as killed the cow.
Pretty friendship 'tis to rhyme
Your friends to death before their time
Moping melancholy mad:
Come, pipe a tune to dance to, lad."

Why, if 'tis dancing you would be,
There's brisker pipes than poetry.
Say, for what were hop-yards meant,
Or why was Burton built on Trent?[2]
Oh many a peer of England brews
Livelier liquor than the Muse,

And malt does more than Milton can
To justify God's ways to man.
Ale, man, ale's the stuff to drink
For fellows whom it hurts to think:
Look into the pewter pot
To see the world as the world's not.
And faith, 'tis pleasant till 'tis past:
The mischief is that 'twill not last.
Oh I have been to Ludlow fair
And left my necktie God knows where,
And carried half-way home, or near,
Pints and quarts of Ludlow beer:
Then the world seemed none so bad
And I myself a sterling lad;
And down in lovely muck I've lain,
Happy till I woke again.
Then I saw the morning sky:
Heigho, the tale was all a lie;
The world, it was the old world yet,
I was I, my things were wet,
And nothing now remained to do
But begin the game anew.

Therefore, since the world has still
Much good, but much less good than ill,
And while the sun and moon endure
Luck's a chance, but trouble's sure,
I'd face it as a wise man would,
And train for ill and not for good.
'Tis true, the stuff I bring for sale
Is not so brisk a brew as ale:
Out of a stem that scored the hand
I wrung it in a weary land.
But take it: if the smack is sour,
The better for the embittered hour;
It should do good to heart and head
When your soul is in my soul's stead;
And I will friend you, if I may,
In the dark and cloudy day.

There was a king reigned in the East:[3]
There, when kings will sit to feast,
They get their fill before they think
With poisoned meat and poisoned drink.
He gathered all that springs to birth
From the many-venomed earth;
First a little, thence to more,
He sampled all her killing store;
And easy, smiling, seasoned sound,

[1] Housman's original title for *A Shropshire Lad* was *The Poems of Terence Hearsay.*
[2] Burton-on-Trent: a city famous for its breweries.
[3] A king: Mithridates VI, a first-century B.C. king of Pontus, an ancient name for the region of northeastern Asia Minor which borders on the Black Sea. Mithridates was in his sixties when he died; one legend is that faced with defeat by rebellious forces led by his son, he tried to poison himself, but could not, and had himself killed by one of his mercenaries.

Sate the king when healths went round.
They put arsenic in his meat
70 And stared aghast to watch him eat;
They poured strychnine in his cup
And shook to see him drink it up:
They shook, they stared as white's their shirt:
Them it was their poison hurt.
—I tell the tale that I heard told.
Mithridates, he died old.

1896

LXIII

"I hoed and trenched and weeded"

I hoed and trenched and weeded,
  And took the flowers to fair:

I brought them home unheeded;
  The hue was not the wear.

So up and down I sow them
  For lads like me to find,
When I shall lie below them,
  A dead man out of mind.

Some seed the birds devour,
  And some the season mars,
But here and there will flower
  The solitary stars,

And fields will yearly bear them
  As light-leaved spring comes on,
And luckless lads will wear them
  When I am dead and gone.

1896

Thomas Hardy
1840–1928

THOMAS HARDY did not publish his first volume of poetry, *Wessex Poems,* until 1898. He was fifty-eight years old in that year, and he had completed a twenty-five-year career as a novelist that had placed him among the most distinguished living British writers. Hardy began to write verse in the 1860s, and he had wanted to make a profession and literary reputation as a poet. After he resumed the writing of poetry in the 1890s, he made and published a remarkably large and various canon. There are over 900 poems in the final collected edition of 1930, in addition to the three parts, eighteen acts, and over 100 scenes of Hardy's verse drama of the Napoleonic wars, *The Dynasts* (1903–8). Among his poems are lyrics of particularized scene and emotion, like "Neutral Tones"; lyrics of philosophical questioning and statement, like "Nature's Questioning"; dramatic poems; short fables like "Heiress and Architect"; narratives, some, like "The Tramp-woman's Tragedy" in the form of old ballads;

and the dramatic sequences of *The Dynasts.*

The themes of Hardy's poetry are often the large themes of his fiction. In his poetry as in his novels he regards the irony of human consciousness which makes its own pain by imagining possibilities the nature of things will not yield, and which is therefore driven to conclude that only an indifferent, cruel, or bungling God would have put sentient beings in a universe in which thought is a mistake and misfortune. The reality of his poems, like that of his novels, is full of lesser ironies and other sources of pain—unhappy coincidence, hard work and hard weather, human vice, error, and infidelity, the punishing obtuseness of social codes and structures, death. Much more extensively than in his novels, and more explicitly in *The Dynasts* than in his lyrics, Hardy also wonders whether things might not be getting better, whether the universe might now also be taking thought and evolving toward conditions in which the wasteful ironies humans know will be alleviated. The scale of these themes, and the bulk and quality of the poetic canon in which they are articulated, raise the question of whether Hardy is a major poet as well as a major novelist. The facts that his poetry continues to exercise a decisive effect on the writing of British poetry, and that much of it was written and almost all of it was published in the twentieth century, raise another question, whether he is really a nineteenth-century poet. This brief introduction and the small selection from Hardy's poetry that follows it do not provide appropriate occasions even to engage these questions. They are to the point, however, because when Hardy in his fifties went back to his beginnings as a writer to take up again the writing of poetry, he went back to mid-Victorian decades in which ambitious poets habitually committed themselves to large themes and to the making of a body of writing whose size and weight were earnest of intentions to create extensive and persistent effects.

Before he was a novelist, Hardy was an architect. He was born in the southwest of England in Dorset, the Wessex of his fiction and poetry. His father was a mason and building contractor who played and loved music and who taught Hardy to play the violin, on which he performed at country dances. His mother was of a family of farmers and small landowners in which literary interests had been common for several generations. Hardy attended local schools until 1856, when he was apprenticed to an architect in Dorchester. He had already studied French and Latin, and he now began to study Greek on his own. He also met the poet William Barnes (see pp. 337–339), who conducted a school in Dorchester, and Horace Moule, the son of a clergyman who was then a student in a Cambridge college and who introduced Hardy to current and often skeptical historical and theological writing. In 1862 Hardy went to London to work in an architectural office. He continued to read scientific and philosophical writing as well as the poetry of Browning, Swinburne, and others. He tried to publish some of his early poems in the 1860s, but his first published work was a short story in a magazine in 1865. In 1867, because of poor health, he returned to work as an architect in Dorchester, and he soon began to take up the writing of fiction in earnest.

Hardy's first extended fiction, *Desperate Remedies*, was published in 1871. He still made his living as an architect, in Dorchester and later again in London, often working on the restoration of churches. He became engaged to one of his cousins, but he broke the engagement in 1872. By that time he had met Emma Gifford in Cornwall, whom he married in 1874. His second novel, *Under the Greenwood Tree*, was published in 1872, and the serialization of another novel, *A Pair of Blue Eyes*, was begun in the same year. In 1874 the serialization of *Far From the Madding Crowd* brought Hardy his first notable recognition as a novelist. In the next twenty years he wrote and published, usually at first as serials or contributions in magazines, ten novels and three collections of short fiction, including *The Return of the Native* (1878), *The Mayor of Casterbridge* (1886), *The Woodlanders* (1887), *Tess of the D'Urbervilles* (1891), and *Jude the Obscure* (1896).

Although Hardy's fiction was esteemed and sufficiently popular to enable him to live comfortably on his income as a writer, its dark questioning of the indifferent or malevolent will of the universe and its strong physicality were persistently troubling to some late-century readers and reviewers. Hardy frequently agreed to excise some of the disturbing passages from his novels when they were first published in magazines. But the publication of *Tess of the D'Urbervilles* and *Jude the Obscure,* very dark stories of aspirations brutally frustrated by chance, social conventions, and the confusions and desolating consequences of several kinds of human desire, evoked larger than usual measures of shock and censure. Hardy decided that his fiction had made its statement and that it was profitless to provoke responses that confused and missed his point. In 1897 he published an earlier fiction, *The Well-Beloved*, in book form. But he was by this time arranging some of the poems he had written in the 1860s and some of his current poems to make up his first volume of verse. His second volume, *Poems of the Past and Present* (1901), also contained poems that were written or planned in the 1860s.

Hardy continued this practice of making a volume of verse by mixing poems written at different times in his life. He frequently revised his poems, both before and after publication. Sometimes a poem was rewritten from a version written in the 1860s or 1870s; sometimes, "When I Set Out for Lyonnesse," for example, the poem is written from a prose sketch or simply a memory dating from the decades of his early manhood. His habit of storing and using the impulses, matter, and texts of his poetry complicates the question of his development as a poet, for it is often difficult to fix the dates of the composition of Hardy's poems. But the ease with which all his life he returned to and used memories and texts out of his own past does suggest one answer to the question of whether, and how, he is a poet of the Victorian period. The ambitious themes and conceptions of poems that are often revelations or intimations of the very fundament of the universe, and certain habits of Hardy's often compressed, strongly particular style, are interesting when they are seen as the writing of a man who wrote poetry in the 1860s while listening to Tennyson, Browning, and Swinburne.

One of Hardy's responses to the writing of the poets he read in the 1860s seems to have been a reaction, common among his late-century contemporaries, against the prolixity of much mid-century poetry. From the beginning, Hardy's poems are very clearly ordered within stanzaic forms and self-consciously spare in their imagery. He is often at his most telling when his compression holds a poem within the particulars of a moment ("One We Knew," for example) which is memorable because important, yet its import is unexplicated, and remains bound in its circumstances. Again, like other late-nineteenth-century poets, Hardy wanted to write a poetic language more natural than the ornate, melodious, recondite idioms he heard in the poetry of major mid-century writers. He tried, although not consistently, to use common words and the rhythms of vernacular syntax. His use of ballad forms was related to his wish, also common in the last decades of the century, to work out a measure of verse based on stress rather than syllable, a measure like that of hymns and other sung verse as well as that of ballad.

The economy of Hardy's forms and the spare, particular images he used in poems like "Neutral Tones" are apt to his perception of a world drained of transcendental presence and poised on sharp turns of ironic recognition. But Hardy in his poems is as likely to enlarge the general, even cosmic significance of these perceptions as he is to compress them within particulars. Early poems like "Hap," for example, introduce into Hardy's poetry the spiritual personages, abstract vocabulary, and large, generalizing metaphors that are the most evident features of what can be called Hardy's "philosophic" style, and in which he wrote poetry all during his career. In other poems, such as "The Darkling Thrush" and "Shelley's Skylark," he moves explicitly in the poem from a particular scene to a meditation on its meaning; and in still others, like "Heiress and Architect," he tells a story or fable openly directed to a discovery of the general conditions of life.

In short, unlike many of his late-century contemporaries, Hardy as a poet (and as a novelist, for that matter) did not pull back from the discursiveness of his predecessors. He did not inhabit the spiritual universe common to Wordsworth, Tennyson, and Browning. He could not summon the ecstasy with which Swinburne in the 1860s and 1870s consecrated the hope of a reality quickened by entirely human possibility. In an "Apology" for a volume of his poetry (*Late Lyrics and Earlier*) published in 1922 he wrote that the "grave, positive [that is, particular or material], stark delineations" of some of his poems will still disturb readers who hold more conventionally hopeful and sacramental conceptions of the structure of the universe. But Hardy then quoted a line from the "In Tenebris" poems, which he conceived in 1895–96 and published in 1901: "If way to the Better there be, it exacts a full look at the Worst." He had come by the 1920s to believe that the will or forces that drive the universe might themselves be coming to a consciousness that will enlarge kindness, keep down pain, and intelligently direct "the modicum of free will conjecturally possessed by organic life when the mighty necessitating forces—unconscious or other—that have 'the balancings of the clouds', happen to be in equilibrium, which may or may not be often."

Hardy's name for this very guarded hope was "evolutionary meliorism," life growing better because growing more aware. What is to the point here is that poetry, because it is at once an expression and an occasion of consciousness, can therefore be an ameliorating act. Hardy wanted it to be such an act. In the "Apology" he called on Matthew Arnold and Wordsworth to give words to his hope that poetry will serve as a "criticism of life" by fusing religion and rationality, by rescuing truth from dogma and narrow utility and breathing into the world "the breath and finer spirit of all knowledge." That last phrase is Wordsworth's, from the preface to an edition of *Lyrical Ballads* published in 1800. Its hope, in one form or another, encouraged many British poets after 1800. Hardy's trust in the effectiveness of any human act was heavily qualified, and the terse, dry, ironic lyrics with which he often tried to educate the consciousness of his contemporaries were quite different from the grand, mobile lyricism of Wordsworth, Shelley, Tennyson, even of Arnold. But in the themes and motives of the poems he wrote and published in the nineteenth century Hardy implicitly put himself in this company, and one interest of these poems is that they suggest what a poet who created an important poetic achievement made of the nineteenth-century poetic traditions and idioms in which he grew but, unlike Yeats, did not outgrow.

EDITIONS

The poems reprinted below either were published in one of Hardy's first three volumes of poetry—*Wessex Poems* (1898), *Poems of the Past and the Present* (1901), or *Time's Laughingstocks and Other Verses* (1909)—or they were written in the nineteenth century or founded in sketches or memories dating from Hardy's life in the nineteenth century. The texts of the poems are those of the original editions. Hardy occasionally revised his poems; the standard edition of the final version of his poems is *The Collected Poems of Thomas Hardy* (1930). Some of Hardy's letters are published in an edition by Carl J. Weber (1963) and in *"Dearest Emmie": Hardy's Letters to His First Wife,* also edited by Weber (1963). Evelyn Hardy and F. B. Pinion have edited Hardy's letters to Florence Henniker between 1893 and 1922 in *One Rare Fair Woman* (1972). Evelyn Hardy is also the editor of *Hardy's Notebooks* (1955), and of some unpublished poems by Hardy in the *London Magazine* (January 1956) and in the *Times Literary Supplement* (2 June 1966). Harold Orel has collected some of Hardy's prefaces to his own writing, his reviews and remarks on the work of other writers—including his preface to a selection from the poems of William Barnes he published in 1908—and some of his reminiscences in *Hardy's Personal Writings* (1966).

BIOGRAPHY AND CRITICISM

Florence Emily Hardy, his second wife, put her name on the two-volume *The Life of Thomas Hardy* she first published in 1928 and 1930 (republished 1962). But the book was largely written or dictated by Thomas Hardy himself. Evelyn Hardy has edited, with Robert Gittings, the reminiscences of Hardy's first wife, *Some Recollections* (1961). Carl J. Weber's *Hardy of Wessex* (revised 1965), J. I. M. Stewart's *Thomas Hardy: A Critical Biography* (1971), and Robert Gittings, *Young Thomas Hardy* (1975) are the most generally useful biographical accounts. Lois Deacon, *Tryphena and Hardy* (1962), describes and speculates on Hardy's early engagement to one of his cousins and the possibility that she bore Hardy's illegitimate child.

J. O. Bailey's *The Poetry of Thomas Hardy: A Handbook and Commentary* (1970) is an indispensable compendium of information about the composition and publication of Hardy's poetry. Samuel Hynes, *The Patterns of Hardy's Poetry* (1961), Kenneth Marsden, *The Poems of Thomas Hardy: A Critical Introduction* (1969), and Paul Zietlow, *Moments of Vision: The Poetry of Thomas Hardy* (1974) are comprehensive studies of the language and kinds of Hardy's poetry. Donald Davie's *Thomas Hardy and British Poetry* (1972) is a study of the character of Hardy's poetry and how and why it has been centrally important as an influence on twentieth-century British poetry. Irving Howe's *Thomas Hardy* (1967) is a strong study of Hardy as a writer of fiction and poetry. Evelyn Hardy's *Thomas Hardy* (1954) establishes the relationships between Hardy's poems and his personal life.

R. G. Cox has compiled *Hardy: The Critical Heritage* (1970); and Laurence Lerner has compiled *Thomas Hardy and His Readers: A Selection of Contemporary Reviews* (1968). See also *Hardy: A Collection of Critical Essays,* edited by Albert J. Guerard (1963). Richard L. Purdy's *Thomas Hardy: A Bibliographical Study* (1954) is a description of writing by Hardy. Helmut Gerber and W. Eugene Davis have edited *Thomas Hardy: An Annotated Bibliography of Writings About Him* (1973). J. I. M. Stewart's *Eight Modern Writers* (1963) contains a select bibliography of writing about Hardy as well as Stewart's essay on the poetry and fiction.

OTHER USEFUL BOOKS AND ESSAYS

Bailey, J. O. *Thomas Hardy and the Cosmic Mind* (1956).

Brooks, Jean A. *Thomas Hardy: The Poetic Structure* (1972).

Chakravarty, Amiya C. *"The Dynasts" and the Post-War Age in Poetry* (1938).

Chew, Samuel. *Thomas Hardy: Poet and Novelist* (revised edition 1928).

Guerard, Albert J. *Thomas Hardy: The Novels and Stories* (1964). Includes an essay on the shorter poems.

Hickson, E. C. *The Versification of Hardy* (1931).

Miller, J. Hillis. *Thomas Hardy: Distance and Desire* (1970).

Orel, Harold. *Thomas Hardy's Epic Drama: A Study of "The Dynasts"* (1963).

Pinion, F. B. *A Hardy Companion* (1968).

Rutland, W. R. *Thomas Hardy: A Study of His Writings and Their Background* (1938).

Southern Review, 6 (1940). Contains an issue given wholly to essays on Hardy's poetry, including important essays by Allen Tate, R. P. Blackmur, F. R. Leavis, and Morton Dauwen Zabel.

Southworth, James G. *The Poetry of Thomas Hardy* (1947).

Webster, Harvey C. *On a Darkling Plain: The Art and Thought of Thomas Hardy* (1947).

Williams, Merryn. *Thomas Hardy and Rural England* (1972).

Williams, Raymond. "Thomas Hardy," *Critical Quarterly,* 6 (1964).

Wright, Walter F. *The Shaping of "The Dynasts"* (1967).

Zietlow, Paul. "Thomas Hardy and William Barnes: Two Dorset Poets," *Publications of the Modern Language Association,* 84 (1969).

Hap[1]

If but some vengeful god would call to me
    From up the sky, and laugh: "Thou
      suffering thing,
Know that thy sorrow is my ecstasy,
    That thy love's loss in my hate's profiting!"

Then would I bear it, clench myself, and die,
    Steeled by the sense of ire unmerited;

Half-eased in that a Powerfuller than I
    Had willed and meted me the tears I shed.

But not so. How arrives it joy lies slain,
    And why unblooms the best hope ever
      sown?   10
    —Crass Casualty[2] obstructs the sun and
      rain,
    And dicing Time for gladness casts a
      moan. . . .
    These purblind Doomsters had as readily
      strown
Blisses about my pilgrimage as pain.
                    (1866)   1898

Neutral Tones

We stood by a pond that winter day,
And the sun was white, as though chidden of
      God,
And a few leaves lay on the starving sod,
    —They had fallen from an ash, and were
      gray.

Your eyes on me were as eyes that rove
Over tedious riddles of years ago;
And some words played between us to and fro
    On which lost the more by our love.

The smile on your mouth was the deadest
    thing
Alive enough to have strength to die;   1(
And a grin of bitterness swept thereby
    Like an ominous bird a-wing. . . .

Since then, keen lessons that love deceives,
And wrings with wrong, have shaped to me
Your face, and the God-curst sun, and a tree,
    And a pond edged with grayish leaves.
                    (1867)   1898

She

At His Funeral[1]

They bear him to his resting-place—
In slow procession sweeping by;
I follow at a stranger's space;

---

[1] Hap: chance.

[2] Bailey notes (p. 52) that in response to a French translation of this word as "stupide" Hardy protested that "insensible" would be a more apt word. He elsewhere insisted that he had not intended to describe the governing principles of the universe as crude or malign, but simply indifferent to man.

[1] Bailey suggests (p. 57) that the occasion of this poem was the funeral of Hardy's friend Horace Mosley Moule, who committed suicide in 1873.

His kindred they, his sweetheart I.
Unchanged my gown of garish dye,
Though sable-sad is their attire;
But they stand round with griefless eye,
Whilst my regret consumes like fire!

(1873) 1898

The Ivy-Wife

I longed to love a full-boughed beech[1]
    And be as high as he:
I stretched an arm within his reach,
    And signalled unity.
But with his drip he forced a breach,
    And tried to poison me.

I gave the grasp of partnership
    To one of other race—
A plane: he barked him strip by strip
    From upper bough to base;
And me therewith; for gone my grip,
    My arms could not enlace.

In new affection next I strove
    To coll[2] an ash I saw,
And he in trust received my love;
    Till with my soft green claw
I cramped and bound him as I wove . . .
    Such was my love: ha-ha!

By this I gained his strength and height
    Without his rivalry.
But in my triumph I lost sight
    Of afterhaps. Soon he,
Being bark-bound, flagged, snapped, fell out-
    right,
    And in his fall felled me!

1898

Friends Beyond

William Dewy, Tranter Reuben, Farmer Led-
    low late at plough,
    Robert's kin, and John's, and Ned's,[1]

And the Squire, and Lady Susan, lie in Mell-
    stock churchyard now!

"Gone," I call them, gone for good, that group
    of local hearts and heads;
    Yet at mothy curfew-tide,[2]
And at midnight when the noon-heat breathes
    it back from walls and leads,[3]

They've a way of whispering to me—fellow-
    wight[4] who yet abide—
    In the muted, measured note
Of a ripple under archways, or a lone cave's
    stillicide:[5]

"We have triumphed: this achievement turns
    the bane[6] to antidote,   10
    Unsuccesses to success,
Many thought-worn eves and morrows to a
    morrow free of thought.

"No more need we corn and clothing, feel of
    old terrestial stress;
    Chill detraction stirs no sigh;
Fear of death has even bygone us: death gave
    all that we possess."

W. D.—"Ye mid[7] burn the old bass-viol that
    I set such valie by."
Squire.—"You may hold the manse in fee,[8]
    You may wed my spouse, may let my
    children's memory of me die."

Lady S.—"You may have my rich brocades,
    my laces; take each household key;
    Ransack coffer,[9] desk, bureau;   20
    Quiz the few poor treasures hid there, con
    the letters kept by me."[10]

Far.—"Ye mid zell my favourite heifer, ye
    mid let the charlock[11] grow,
    Foul the grinterns,[12] give up thrift."
Wife.—"If ye break my best blue china,
    children, I shan't care or ho."[13]

---

[1] Beech trees resist ivy; so do plane trees, on whose shedding bark the ivy cannot climb.
[2] Coll: hug, embrace.
[1] William Dewey and his son Reuben, a teamster or carter, also appear in Hardy's novel *Under the Greenwood Tree* (1872), as does Farmer Ledlow. Lady Susan was a member of a Dorset family who was buried in Stinsford, to which Hardy gave the name Mellstock in his poems and novels.
[2] One of the Dorset folk-beliefs is that at curfew or dusk the souls of the dead emerge as moths.
[3] Leads: roofs.   [4] Wight: an archaic word for creature.
[5] Stillicide: a continual dripping of water.   [6] Bane: poison.   [7] Mid: may.
[8] In fee: in absolute right of possession.   [9] Coffer: box.   [10] Quiz: scrutinize. Con: read.
[11] Charlock: wild mustard.   [12] Grinterns: compartments in a granary.   [13] Ho: long for.

ALL.—"We've no wish to hear the tidings,
    how the people's fortunes shift;
      What your daily doings are;
    Who are wedded, born, divided; if your
      lives beat slow or swift.

"Curious not the least are we if our intents
    you make or mar,
      If you quire to our old tune,
    If the City stage still passes, if the weirs[14] still
30   roar afar."

—Thus, with very gods' composure, freed those
    crosses late and soon
      Which, in life, the Trine[15] allow
(Why, none witteth), and ignoring all that
    haps beneath the moon,

William Dewy, Tranter Reuben, Farmer
    Ledlow late at plough,
      Robert's kin, and John's, and Ned's,
And the Squire, and Lady Susan, murmur
    mildly to me now.

                  1898

In a Wood

See "The Woodlanders"[1]

Pale beech and pine so blue,
    Set in one clay,
Bough to bough cannot you
    Live out your day?
When the rains skim and skip,
Why mar sweet comradeship,
Blighting with poison-drip
    Neighbourly spray?

Heart-halt and spirit-lame,
10   City-opprest,
Unto this wood I came
    As to a nest;
Dreaming that sylvan peace
Offered the harrowed ease—

Nature a soft release
    From men's unrest.

But, having entered in,
    Great growths and small
Show them to men akin—
    Combatants all!
Sycamore shoulders oak,
Bines[2] the slim sapling yoke,
Ivy-spun halters choke
    Elms stout and tall.

Touches from ash, O wych,[3]
    Sting you like scorn!
You, too, brave hollies, twitch
    Sidelong from thorn.
Even the rank poplars bear
Illy a rival's air,[4]
Cankering in black despair
    If overborne.

Since, then, no grace I find
    Taught me of trees,
Turn I back to my kind,
    Worthy as these.
There at least smiles abound,
There discourse trills around,
There, now and then, are found
    Life-loyalties.

          (1887; 1896) 1898

Nature's Questioning[1]

When I look forth at dawning, pool,
    Field, flock, and lonely tree,
      All seem to gaze at me
Like chastened children sitting silent in a
    school;

Their faces dulled, constrained, and worn,
    As though the master's ways
      Through the long teaching days
Their first terrestial zest had chilled and
    overborne.[2]

---

[14] Weirs: dams.   [15] Trine: Trinity.

[1] This poem, begun in 1887 and completed in 1896, does not appear in Hardy's novel *The Woodlanders* (1887). Chapter 7 of that novel includes a description of trees and vegetation strangling and injuring one another.

[2] Bines: plants with twining stems or shoots.   [3] Wych: elm.

[4] In his *Collected Poems* Hardy changed the first word of this line to "Lothly."

[1] Bailey quotes a letter from Hardy in 1920 (p. 102): "A poem often quoted against me . . . is the one called 'Nature's Questioning,' containing the words 'some Vast Imbecility,' etc.—as if these definitions were my creed. But they are merely enumerated in the poem as fanciful alternatives to several others, having nothing to do with my own opinion."

[2] Hardy later revised this line to read: "Had cowed them till their early zest was overborne."

And on them stirs in lippings mere
    (As if once clear in call,
    But now scarce breathed at all) —
"We wonder, ever wonder, why we find us here!

"Has some Vast Imbecility,
    Mighty to build and blend,
    But impotent to tend,
Framed us in jest, and left us now to hazardry?

"Or come we of an Automaton
    Unconscious of our pains? . . .
    Or are we live remains
Of Godhead dying downwards, brain and eye
    now gone?

"Or is it that some high Plan betides,
    As yet not understood,
    Of Evil stormed by Good,
We the Forlorn Hope over which Achievement
    strides?"

Thus things around. No answerer I . . .
    Meanwhile the winds, and rains,
    And Earth's old glooms and pains
Are still the same, and Life and Death are
    neighbours nigh.

              1898

Heiress and Architect

For A. W. B.[1]

She sought the Studios, beckoning to her side
An arch-designer, for she planned to build.
He was of wise contrivance, deeply skilled
In every intervolve of high and wide—
    Well fit to be her guide.

    "Whatever it be,"
    Responded he,
With cold, clear voice, and cold, clear view,
"In true accord with prudent fashionings
For such vicissitudes as living brings,
And thwarting not the law of stable things,
    That will I do."

"Shape me," she said, "high halls with tracery
And open ogive-work,[2] that scent and hue

Of buds, and travelling bees, may come in
    through,
The note of birds, and singings of the sea,
    For these are much to me."

    "An idle whim!"
    Broke forth from him
Whom nought could warm to gallantries:
"Cede all these buds and birds, the zephyr's
    call,
And scents, and hues, and things that falter all,
And choose as best the close and surly wall,
    For winters freeze."

"Then frame," she cried, "wide fronts of crystal
    glass,
That I may show my laughter and my light—
Light like the sun's by day, the stars' by night—
Till rival heart-queens, envying, wail, 'Alas,
    Her glory!' as they pass."

    "O maid misled!"
    He sternly said
Whose facile foresight pierced her dire;
"Where shall abide the soul when, sick of glee,
It shrinks, and hides, and prays no eye may see?
Those house them best who house for secrecy,
    For you will tire."

"A little chamber, then, with swan and dove
Ranged thickly, and engrailed[3] with rare device
Of reds and purples, for a Paradise
Wherein my Love may greet me, I my Love,
    When he shall know thereof?"

    "This, too, is ill,"
    He answered still,
The man who swayed her like a shade.
"An hour will come when sight of such sweet
    nook
Would bring a bitterness too sharp to brook,
When brighter eyes have won away his look;
    For you will fade."

Then said she faintly: "O, contrive some way—
Some narrow winding turret, quite mine own,
To reach a loft where I may grieve alone!
It is a slight thing; hence do not, I pray,
    This last dear fancy slay!"

---

[1] Arthur William Blomfield was the architect for whom Hardy worked as a draftsman from 1862 to 1867.

[2] Tracery and ogive-work: decoration within pointed arches which will serve for windows.

[3] Engrailed: decorated with an edge of concave indentations.

"Such winding ways
        Fit not your days,"
Said he, the man of measuring eye;
"I must even fashion as the rule declares,
To wit: Give space (since life ends unawares)
To hale a coffined corpse adown the stairs;
60   For you will die."

                                        (1867) 1898

"I look into my glass"

I look into my glass,
And view my wasting skin,
And say, "Would God it came to pass
My heart had shrunk as thin!"

For then, I, undistrest
By hearts grown cold to me,
Could lonely wait my endless rest
With equanimity.

But Time, to make me grieve,
10   Part steals, lets part abide;
And shakes this fragile frame at eve
With throbbings of noontide.

                                        1898

Drummer Hodge[1]

        I

They throw in Drummer Hodge, to rest
        Uncoffined—just as found:
His landmark is a kopje-crest[2]
        That breaks the veldt around;
And foreign constellations west
        Each night above his mound.

        II

Young Hodge the Drummer never knew—
        Fresh from his Wessex home—
The meaning of the broad Karoo,[3]
10   The Bush, the dusty loam,
And why uprose to nightly view
        Strange stars amid the gloom.

        III

Yet portion of that unknown plain
        Will Hodge for ever be;
His homely Northern breast and brain
        Grow up a Southern tree,
And strange-eyed constellations reign
        His stars eternally.

                                        1899; 1902

Shelley's Skylark

        (*The Neighbourhood of Leghorn: March
                1887*)[1]

Somewhere afield here something lies
In Earth's oblivious eyeless trust
That moved a poet to prophecies—
A pinch of unseen, unguarded dust:

The dust of the lark that Shelley heard,
And made immortal through times to be;—
Though it only lived like another bird,
And knew not its immortality.

Lived its meek life; then, one day, fell—
A little ball of feather and bone;   10
And how it perished, when piped farewell,
And where it wastes, are alike unknown.

Maybe it rests in the loam I view,
Maybe it throbs in a myrtle's green,
Maybe it sleeps in the coming hue
Of a grape on the slopes of yon inland scene.

Go find it, faeries, go and find
That tiny pinch of priceless dust,
And bring a casket silver-lined,
And framed of gold that gems encrust;   20

And we will lay it safe therein,
And consecrate it to endless time;
For it inspired a bard to win
Ecstatic heights in thought and rhyme.

                                        1902

---

[1] Hodge is a conventional name for a rustic. The title of this poem when it was first published was "The Dead Drummer."
[2] Kopje: a Boer word for a small hill on the veldt, the grassy plain of South Africa.
[3] Karoo: a Boer word for a dry tableland.
[1] Percy Bysshe Shelley (1792–1822) wrote "To a Skylark" in 1820 when he was living near Leghorn in Italy. In Shelley's poem the bird is a symbol of a soaring, far-seeing penetration toward the realm of ideal order: "Like a poet hidden/In the light of thought,/Singing hymns unbidden,/Till the world is wrought/To sympathy with hopes and fears it heeded not."

Rome

Building a New Street in the Ancient Quarter

(April 1887)

These umbered cliffs and gnarls of masonry
Outskeleton Time's central city, Rome;
Whereof each arch, entablature, and dome
Lies bare in all its gaunt anatomy.

And cracking frieze and rotten metope[1]
Express, as though they were an open tome
Top-lined with caustic monitory gnome;
"Dunces, Learn here to spell Humanity!"

And yet within these ruins' very shade
The singing workmen shape and set and join
Their frail new mansion's stuccoed cove and
    quoin[2]
With no apparent sense that years abrade,
Though each rent wall their feeble works in-
    vade
Once shamed all such in power of pier and
    groin.[3]

                                        1902

The Subalterns[1]

I

"Poor wanderer," said the leaden sky,
    "I fain would lighten thee,
But there are laws in force on high
    Which say it must not be."

II

—"I would not freeze thee, shorn one," cried
    The North, "knew I but how
To warm my breath, to slack my stride;
    But I am ruled as thou."

III

—"To-morrow I attack thee, wight,"[2]
    Said Sickness. "Yet I swear

I bear thy little ark no spite,
    But am bid enter there."

IV

—"Come hither, Son," I heard Death say;
    "I did not will a grave
Should end thy pilgrimage to-day,
    But I, too, am a slave!"

V

We smiled upon each other then,
    And life to me had less
That fell contour it wore ere when
    They owned their passiveness.   20

                                        1902

On a Fine Morning

I

Whence comes Solace?—Not from seeing
What is doing, suffering, being,
Not from noting Life's conditions,
Nor from heeding Time's monitions;
    But in cleaving to the Dream,
    And in gazing at the gleam
    Whereby gray things golden seem.

II

Thus do I this heyday, holding
Shadows but as lights unfolding,
As no specious show this moment   10
With its irisèd embowment;
    But as nothing other than
    Part of a benignant plan;
    Proof that earth was made for man.

                            (1899) 1902

At a Hasty Wedding

(Triolet) [1]

If hours be years the twain are blest,
For now they solace swift desire
By bonds of every bond the best,

---

[1] Metope: the space, often decorated, between the tablets of a frieze.

[2] Cove: concave recesses in an external wall. Quoin: the blocks forming the angle of an external wall.

[3] Pier: the wall between openings. Groin: the curved line along which intersecting vaults meet.

[1] Bailey notes (p. 147) that this poem is written in the "common measure" of hymns.

[2] Wight: archaic word for creature.

[1] A triolet is one of the mannered forms of French verse—eight lines with only two rhymes. Hardy first published the poem in a short story in 1900, in which it was spoken by a cynical character.

If hours be years. The twain are blest
Do eastern stars slope never west,
Nor pallid ashes follow fire:
If hours be years the twain are blest,
For now they solace swift desire.

1900; 1902

The Dream-Follower

A dream of mine flew over the mead[1]
    To the halls where my old Love reigns;
And it drew me on to follow its lead:
    And I stood at her window-panes;

And I saw but a thing of flesh and bone
    Speeding on to its cleft in the clay;
And my dream was scared, and expired on a
    moan,
    And I whitely hastened away.

1902

Wives in the Sere

I
Never a careworn wife but shows,
    If a joy suffuse her,
Something beautiful to those
    Patient to peruse her,
Some one charm the world unknows
    Precious to a muser,
Haply what, ere years were foes,
    Moved her mate to choose her.

II
But, be it a hint of rose
10   That an instant hues her,
Or some early light or pose
    Wherewith thought renews her—
Seen by him at full, ere woes
    Practised to abuse her—
Sparely comes it, swiftly goes,
    Time again subdues her.

1901; 1902

The Darkling Thrush[1]

I leant upon a coppice[2] gate
    When Frost was spectre-gray,

And Winter's dregs made desolate
    The weakening eye of day.
The tangled bine-stems[3] scored the sky
    Like strings of broken lyres,
And all mankind that haunted nigh
    Had sought their household fires.

The land's sharp features seemed to be
    The Century's corpse outleant,   1
His crypt the cloudy canopy,
    The wind his death-lament.
The ancient pulse of germ and birth
    Was shrunken hard and dry,
And every spirit upon earth
    Seemed fervourless as I.

At once a voice arose among
    The bleak twigs overhead
In a full-hearted evensong
    Of joy illimited;   2
An aged thrush, frail, gaunt, and small,
    In blast-beruffled plume,
Had chosen thus to fling his soul
    Upon the growing gloom.

So little cause for carolings
    Of such ecstatic sound
Was written on terrestrial things
    Afar or nigh around,
That I could think there trembled through
    His happy good-night air   3
Some blessed Hope, whereof he knew
    And I was unaware.

1900; 1902

The Comet at Yalbury or Yell'ham[1]

I
It bends far over Yell'ham Plain,
    And we, from Yell'ham Height,
Stand and regard its fiery train,
    So soon to swim from sight.

II
It will return long years hence, when
    As now its strange swift shine
Will fall on Yell'ham; but not then
    On that sweet form of thine.

1902

---

[1] Mead: meadow.
[1] This poem was first published on December 29, 1900, under the title "By the Century's Deathbed." It was perhaps written somewhat earlier and dated for the occasion of its first publication.
[2] Coppice: grove of small trees.   [3] Bine-stems: stems of twining plants.
[1] Hardy remembered seeing Encke's comet from the top of Yellowham hill in Dorset in 1858.

The following poem refers to a mid-nineteenth-century Biblical scholarship that sometimes disputed the dates and authenticity of events in Scripture by studying it with the newly rigorous practices of history and philology. In addition to the stories of Adam and the Flood, the events alluded to are the slaying of the giant Goliath by David (I Samuel 17); the celebration of love (customarily read as an allegory of Christ's love for the church) in the Song of Solomon; the triumphant influence of the beautiful Esther, daughter of Mordecai, over a king who was about to slaughter the Jews (Esther 2–5); Joshua's command that the sun stand still to assure his triumph in battle (Joshua 10); the trials of Job; the miraculous story in which Balaam's ass talks him out of his journey to make war on the Israelites (Numbers 22); the preservation of Daniel and his companions when they are thrust into a fiery furnace by the king Nebuchadnezzar (Daniel 3:10–28) and Daniel's preservation in the den of lions (Daniel 6:16–23); the raising of Lazarus, son of Nain, from the dead by Christ (Luke 7:11–15); the murder of a tyrant by Jael (Judges 4:17–22); and the conduct of Pontius Pilate, the Roman ruler of Jerusalem, and the apostle Peter, who cut off the ear of one of the men who took Christ in the garden, during the passion of Christ.

The Respectable Burgher

On "The Higher Criticism"

Since Reverend Doctors now declare
That clerks and people must prepare
To doubt if Adam ever were;
To hold the flood a local scare;
To argue, though the stolid stare,
That everything had happened ere
The prophets to its happening sware;
That David was no giant-slayer,
Nor one to call a God-obeyer
In certain details we could spare,
But rather was a debonair
Shrewd bandit, skilled as banjo-player:
That Solomon sang the fleshly Fair,
And gave the Church no thought whate'er;
That Esther with her royal wear,
And Mordecai, the son of Jair,

And Joshua's triumphs, Job's despair,
And Balaam's ass's bitter blare;
Nebuchadnezzar's furnace-flare,
And Daniel and the den affair,   20
And other stories rich and rare,
Were writ to make old doctrine wear
Something of a romantic air:
That the Nain widow's only heir,
And Lazarus with cadaverous glare
(As done in oils by Piombo's care)[1]
Did not return from Sheol's[2] lair:
That Jael set a fiendish snare,
That Pontius Pilate acted square,
That never a sword cut Malchus' ear;   30
And (but for shame I must forbear)
That —— —— did not reappear! . . .
—Since thus they hint, nor turn a hair,
All churchgoing will I forswear,
And sit on Sundays in my chair,
And read that moderate man Voltaire.

1902

The Self-Unseeing

Here is the ancient floor,
Footworn and hollowed and thin,
Here was the former door
Where the dead feet walked in.

She sat here in her chair,
Smiling into the fire;
He who played stood there,
Bowing it higher and higher.[1]

Childlike, I danced in a dream;
Blessings emblazoned that day;   10
Everything glowed with a gleam;
Yet we were looking away!

1902

In Tenebris

II

Considerabam ad dexteram, et videbam; et non erat qui cognosceret me. . . . Non est qui requirat animam meam.[1]

---

[1] Piombo: Sebastian del Piombo (1485–1547), an Italian painter whose masterpiece is a depiction of the raising of Lazarus.
[2] Sheol: the land of the dead in Hebrew mythology.
[1] "He" is Hardy's father, who played the fiddle.
[1] Hardy's first title for a series of three poems he later called "In Tenebris" (in the darkness) was "De Profundis" (from the depths). The epigraph is: "I looked on my right hand, and beheld, but there was no man that would know me: . . . no man cared for my soul" (Psalm 142:4).

When the clouds' swoln bosoms echo back the
    shouts of the many and strong
That things are all as they best may be, save a
    few to be right ere long,
And my eyes have not the vision in them to
    discern what to these is so clear,
The blot seems straightway in me alone; one
    better he were not here.

The stout upstanders say, All's well with us:
    ruers have nought to rue!
And what the potent say so oft, can it fail to be
    somewhat true?
Breezily go they, breezily come; their dust
    smokes around their career,
Till I think I am one born out of due time,
    who has no calling here.

Their dawns bring lusty joys, it seems; their
    eves exultance sweet;
Our times are blessed times, they cry: Life
10   shapes it as is most meet,
And nothing is much the matter; there are
    many smiles to a tear;
Then what is the matter is I, I say. Why should
    such an one be here? . . .

Let him in whose ears the low-voiced Best
    seems stilled[2] by the clash of the First,
Who holds that if way to the Better there be,
    it exacts a full look at the Worst,
Who feels that delight is a delicate growth
    cramped by crookedness, custom, and fear,
Get him up and be gone as one shaped awry;
    he disturbs the order here.

                                    (1895–96) 1902

A Trampwoman's Tragedy[1]

(182–)

I

From Wynyard's Gap the livelong day,
        The livelong day,
We beat afoot the northward way
        We had travelled times before.
The sun-blaze burning on our backs,

Our shoulders sticking to our packs,
By fosseway,[2] fields, and turnpike tracks
        We skirted sad Sedge-Moor.

II

Full twenty miles we jaunted on,
        We jaunted on,—   10
My fancy-man,[3] and jeering John,
        And Mother Lee, and I.
And, as the sun drew down to west,
We climbed the toilsome Poldon crest,
And saw, of landskip sights the best,
        The inn that beamed thereby.

III

For months we had padded side by side,
        Ay, side by side
Through the Great Forest, Blackmoor wide,
        And where the Parret ran.   20
We'd faced the gusts on Mendip ridge,
Had crossed the Yeo unhelped by bridge,
Been stung by every Marshwood midge,
        I and my fancy-man.

IV

Lone inns we loved, my man and I,
        My man and I;
"King's Stag," "Windwhistle" high and dry,
        "The Horse" on Hintock Green.
The cosy house at Wynyard's Gap,
"The Hut" renowned on Bredy Knap,   30
And many another wayside tap
        Where folk might sit unseen.

V

Now as we trudged—O deadly day,
        O deadly day!—
I teased my fancy-man in play
        And wanton idleness.
I walked alongside jeering John,
I laid his hand my waist upon;
I would not bend my glances on
        My lover's dark distress.   40

VI

Thus Poldon top at last we won,
        At last we won,
And gained the inn at sink of sun
        Far-famed as "Marshal's Elm."

---

[2] Hardy's later revision: "is killed."
[1] This poem, which Hardy once judged to be on the whole his most successful, was first published in an American magazine in 1903, having been declined by a British magazine because of its subject matter. The geographical details are those of the countryside of Dorset and Somerset in the west of England.
[2] Fosseway: ditch or moat.   [3] Fancy-man: lover.

Beneath us figured tor and lea,[4]
From Mendip to the western sea—
I doubt if finer sight there be
    Within this royal realm.

VII

Inside the settle[5] all a-row—
    All four a-row
We sat, I next to John, to show
    That he had wooed and won.
And then he took me on his knee,
And swore it was his turn to be
My favoured mate, and Mother Lee
    Passed to my former one.

VIII

Then in a voice I had never heard,
    I had never heard,
My only Love to me: "One word,
    My doxy, if you please!
Whose is the child you are like to bear?—
His? After all my months o' care?"
God knows 'twas not! But, O despair!
    I nodded—still to tease.

IX

Then up he sprung, and with his knife—
    And with his knife
He let out jeering Johnny's life,
    Yes; there, at set of sun.
The slant ray through the window nigh
Gilded John's blood and glazing eye,
Ere scarcely Mother Lee and I
    Knew that the deed was done.

X

The taverns tell the gloomy tale,
    The gloomy tale,
How that at Ivel-chester jail
    My Love, my sweetheart swung;
Though stained till now by no misdeed
Save one horse ta'en in time o' need;
(Blue Jimmy stole right many a steed
    Ere his last fling he flung.) [6]

XI

Thereaft I walked the world alone,
    Alone, alone!
On his death-day I gave my groan
    And dropt his dead-born child.

'Twas nigh the jail, beneath a tree,
None tending me; for Mother Lee
Had died at Glaston, leaving me
    Unfriended on the wild.

XII

And in the night as I lay weak,
    As I lay weak,   90
The leaves a-falling on my cheek,
    The red moon low declined—
The ghost of him I'd die to kiss
Rose up and said: "Ah, tell me this!
Was the child mine, or was it his?
    Speak, that I rest may find!"

XIII

O doubt not but I told him then,
    I told him then,
That I had kept me from all men
    Since we joined lips and swore.   100
Whereat he smiled, and thinned away
As the wind stirred to call up day . . .
—'Tis past! And here alone I stray
    Haunting the Western Moor.

            (1902) 1903; 1909

The Rejected Member's Wife[1]

We shall see her no more
    On the balcony,
Smiling, while hurt, at the roar
    As of surging sea
From the stormy sturdy band
    Who have doomed her lord's cause,
Though she waves her little hand
    As it were applause.

Here will be candidates yet,
    And candidates' wives,   10
Fervid with zeal to set
    Their ideals on our lives:
Here will come market-men
    On the market-days,
Here will clash now and then
    More such party assays.

And the balcony will fill
    When such times are renewed,
And the throng in the street will thrill
    With to-day's mettled mood;   20

[4] Tor: a high craggy hill. Lea: pasture. [5] Settle: a high-backed bench.
[6] In a note to the poem Hardy identifies Blue Jimmy as a notorious horse thief in the early decades of the nineteenth century who was hanged at Ivel-chester (Ilchester).
[1] Member: Member of Parliament.

But she will no more stand
    In the sunshine there,
With that wave of her white-gloved hand,
    And that chestnut hair.
              (1906) 1906; 1909

The Farm-Woman's Winter

I

If seasons all were summers,
    And leaves would never fall,
And hopping casement-comers
    Were foodless not at all,
And fragile folk might be here
    That white winds bid depart;
Then one I used to see here
    Would warm my wasted heart!

II

One frail, who, bravely tilling
10   Long hours in gripping gusts,
Was mastered by their chilling,
    And now his ploughshare rusts.
So savage winter catches
    The breath of limber things,
And what I love he snatches,
    And what I love not, brings.
              1905; 1909

In the Crypted Way[1]

In the crypted way, where the passage turned
To the shadowy corner that none could see,
You paused to part from me,—plaintively;
Though overnight had come words that burned
My fond frail happiness out of me.

And then I kissed you,—despite my thought
That our spell must end when reflection came
On what you had deemed me, whose one long
    aim
Had been to serve you; that what I sought
Lay not in a heart that could breathe such
10   blame.

But yet I kissed you; whereon you again
As of old kissed me. Why, why was it so?
Do you cleave to me after that light-tongued
    blow?

If you scorned me at eventide, how love then?
The thing is dark, Dear. I do not know.
              (1870) 1909

The Minute Before Meeting

The grey gaunt days dividing us in twain
Seemed hopeless hills my strength must faint
    to climb,
But they are gone; and now I would detain
The few clock-beats that part us; rein back
    Time,

And live in close expectance never closed
In change for far expectance closed at last,
So harshly has expectance been imposed
On my long need while these slow blank
    months passed.

And knowing that what is now about to be
Will all *have been* in O, so short a space!
I read beyond it my despondency
When more dividing months shall take its
    place,
Thereby denying to this hour of grace
A full-up measure of felicity.
              (1871) 1909

from At Casterbridge Fair[1]

I. The Ballad-Singer

Sing, Ballad-singer, raise a hearty tune;
Make me forget that there was ever a one
I walked with in the meek light of the moon
    When the day's work was done.

Rhyme, Ballad-rhymer, start a country song;
Make me forget that she whom I loved well
Swore she would love me dearly, love me long,
    Then—what I cannot tell!

Sing, Ballad-singer, from your little book;
Make me forget those heart-breaks, achings,
    fears;

[1] In his *Collected Poems* Hardy titled this poem "In the Vaulted Way."
[1] Casterbridge is Hardy's name for Dorchester.

Make me forget her name, her sweet sweet
  look—
  Make me forget her tears.
                              (1902) 1902; 1909

III. After the Club-Dance

Black'on frowns east on Maidon,
  And westward to the sea,
But on neither is his frown laden
  With scorn, as his frown on me!

At dawn my heart grew heavy,
  I could not sip the wine,
I left the jocund bevy
  And that young man o' mine.

The roadside elms pass by me,—
  Why do I sink with shame
When the birds a-perch there eye me?
  They, too, have done the same!
                              (1902) 1909

VII. After the Fair

The singers are gone from the Cornmarket-
  place
  With their broadsheets of rhymes,
The street rings no longer in treble and bass
  With their skits on the times,
And the Cross, lately thronged, is a dim naked
  space
  That but echoes the stammering chimes.

From Clock-corner steps, as each quarter ding-
  dongs,
  Away the folk roam
By the "Hart" and Grey's Bridge into byways
  and "drongs,"[1]
  Or across the ridged loam;
The younger ones shrilling the lately heard
  songs,
  The old saying, "Would we were home."

The shy-seeming maiden so mute in the fair
  Now rattles and talks,
And that one who looked the most swaggering
  there
  Grows sad as she walks,
And she who seemed eaten by cankering care
  In statuesque sturdiness stalks.

And midnight clears High Street of all but the
  ghosts
  Of its buried burghees,   20
From the latest far back to those old Roman
  hosts
  Whose remains one yet sees,
Who loved, laughed, and fought, hailed their
  friends, drank their toasts
  At their meeting-times here, just as these!
                              (1902) 1909

The Dark-Eyed Gentleman

I
I pitched my day's leazings[1] in Crimmercrock
  Lane,
To tie up my garter and jog on again,
When a dear dark-eyed gentleman passed there
  and said,
In a way that made all o' me colour rose-red,
  "What do I see—
  O pretty knee!"
And he came and he tied up my garter for me.

II
'Twixt sunset and moonrise it was, I can mind:
Ah, 'tis easy to lose what we nevermore find!—
Of the dear stranger's home, of his name, I
  knew nought,   10
But I soon knew his nature and all that it
  brought.
  Then bitterly
  Sobbed I that he
Should ever have tied up my garter for me!

III
Yet now I've beside me a fine lissom lad,
And my slip's nigh forgot, and my days are not
  sad;
My own dearest joy is he, comrade, and friend,
He it is who safe-guards me, on him I depend;
  No sorrow brings he,
  And thankful I be   20
That his daddy once tied up my garter for me!
                              1909

A Church Romance[1]

(Mellstock: circa 1835)

She turned in the high pew, until her sight
Swept the west gallery, and caught its row

---

[1] Drongs: narrow paths.   [1] Leazings: a bundle of gleaned grain.
[1] This poem is a memory of the meeting of Hardy's mother and father in Stinsford Church,
which Hardy calls Mellstock.

Of music-men with viol, book, and bow
Against the sinking sad tower-window light.

She turned again; and in her pride's despite
One strenuous viol's inspirer seemed to throw
A message from his string to her below,
Which said: "I claim thee as my own forth-
right!"

Thus their hearts' bond began, in due time
signed.
And long years thence, when Age had scared
10   Romance,
At some old attitude of his or glance
That gallery-scene would break upon her mind,
With him as minstrel, ardent, young, and trim,
Bowing "New Sabbath" or "Mount Ephraim."
                                        1906; 1909

After the Last Breath

(J. H. 1813–1904)[1]

There's no more to be done, or feared, or
hoped;
None now need watch, speak low, and list, and
tire;
No irksome crease outsmoothed, no pillow
sloped
        Does she require.

Blankly we gaze. We are free to go or stay;
Our morrow's anxious plans have missed their
aim;
Whether we leave to-night or wait till day
        Counts as the same.

The lettered vessels of medicaments
10 Seem asking wherefore we have set them here;
Each palliative its silly face presents
        As useless gear.

And yet we feel that something savours well;
We note a numb relief withheld before;
Our well-beloved is prisoner in the cell
        Of Time no more.

We see by littles now the deft achievement
Whereby she has escaped the Wrongers all,

In view of which our momentary bereavement
        Outshapes but small.   20
                                        (1904) 1909

One We Knew

(M. H. 1772–1857)[1]

She told how they used to form for the country
        dances—
        "The Triumph," "The New-rigged Ship"—
To the light of the guttering wax in the
        panelled manses,
        And in cots to the blink of a dip.[2]

She spoke of the wild "poussetting" and
        "allemanding"[3]
        On carpet, on oak, and on sod;
And the two long rows of ladies and gentlemen
        standing,
        And the figures the couples trod.

She showed us the spot where the maypole was
        yearly planted,
        And where the bandsmen stood   10
While breeched and kerchiefed partners
        whirled, and panted
        To choose each other for good.

She told of that far-back day when they learnt
        astounded
        Of the death of the King of France:[4]
Of the Terror; and then of Bonaparte's un-
        bounded
        Ambition and arrogance.

Of how his threats woke warlike preparations
        Along the southern strand,
And how each night brought tremors and
        trepidations
        Lest morning should see him land.   20

She said she had often heard the gibbet creak-
        ing
        As it swayed in the lightning flash,
Had caught from the neighbouring town a
        small child's shrieking
        At the cart-tail under the lash. . . .

---

[1] J. H.: Jemima Hardy, Hardy's mother. Hardy added this dedication after the first publica-
tion of the poem.
[1] M. H.: Mary Head Hardy, Hardy's grandmother.   [2] Cots: cottages. Dip: cheap candles.
[3] Poussetting and allemanding: dance figures.
[4] King of France: Louis XVI, executed in Paris in 1793.

With cap-framed face and long gaze into the
    embers—
  We seated around her knees—
She would dwell on such dead themes, not as
    one who remembers,
  But rather as one who sees.

She seemed one left behind of a band gone
    distant
30 So far that no tongue could hail:
Past things retold were to her as things existent,
  Things present but as a tale.

              (1902) 1903; 1909

"When I Set Out for Lyonnesse"[1]

When I set out for Lyonnesse,
  A hundred miles away,

The rime was on the spray,
And starlight lit my lonesomeness
When I set out for Lyonnesse
  A hundred miles away.

What would bechance at Lyonnesse
  While I should sojourn there
  No prophet durst declare,
Nor did the wisest wizard guess   10
What would bechance at Lyonnesse
  While I should sojourn there.

When I came back from Lyonnesse
  With magic in my eyes,
  None managed to surmise
What meant my godlike gloriousness[2]
When I came back from Lyonnesse
  With magic in my eyes!

              1914

[1] This poem is a memory of Hardy's trip to Cornwall in 1870 and his meeting with the woman who was to become his wife. Lyonnesse is the name of the land, now submerged, in the south-west of England in which Tristam of the Arthurian legends was born. Its associations are therefore with high romance. Hardy called the form of the poem a version of a rondel, which it resembles mostly in its use of a refrain.

[2] Hardy later revised these lines to read: "All marked with mute surmise/My radiance rare and fathomless."

PART SIX

Late-Victorian Poems 1880-1900

James Thomson

1834–1882

James Thomson was born in Scotland. His father was an officer in the merchant marine who was paralyzed while Thomson was a child. After his mother's death in 1840, Thomson was educated in an orphanage and then trained to be an army schoolteacher, a profession he practiced until 1862, when he was discharged for a minor breach of discipline. He had already published some poems in magazines, and he began to work in London as a journalist, contributing especially to the National Reformer, a journal of the secularist, free-thought movement, under the initials "B. V." (Bysshe Vanolis, for Percy Bysshe Shelley and the German philosopher Novalis). Thomson published "The City of Dreadful Night" in the National Reformer in 1874; the poem appeared in a volume of poetry, his first, in 1880. He published a second volume, Vane's Story and Other Poems, in 1881; the title poem of this volume had also been written many years earlier. Thomson was by this time in precarious mental and physical health, and addicted to alcohol. After leaving London for a while to attempt a recovery, he returned shortly before his death.

Henry S. Salt published a biography of Thomson in 1889 (revised in 1914), and Bertram Dobell, who edited a two-volume collection of his poems in 1895, published a study in 1910. The most recent study of Thomson's writing is William D. Schaefer's James Thomson (B. V.): Beyond "The City" (1965), which includes a calendar of the composition and publication of Thomson's poems. Anne Ridler's edition of Poems and Some Letters (1963) contains some unpublished poetry. The text printed here is that of the 1880 volume of Thomson's poems.

"The City of Dreadful Night" is a hallucinatory vision of London in twenty-one relatively disconnected sections as its speaker wanders from one section of the city to another. Some of its literary models are suggested by its epigraphs from Dante and the poetry of Giacomo Leopardi (1798–1837), some of whose pessimistic verse Thomson had translated and published in the National Reformer in 1867.

from The City of Dreadful Night

"Per me si va nella città dolente."

—DANTE

"Poi di tanto adoprar, di tanti moti
D'ogni celeste, ogni terrena cosa,
Girando senza posa,
Per tornar sempre là donde son mosse;
Uso alcuno, alcun frutto
Indovinar non so."

"Sola nel mondo eterna, a cui si volve
Ogni creata cosa,
In te, morte, si posa
Nostra ignuda natura;
Lieta no, ma sicura
Dell' antico dolor. . . .
Però ch' esser beato
Nega ai mortali e nega a' morti il fato."

—LEOPARDI.[1]

---

[1] The first epigraph is the first line of Canto 3 of The Inferno in Dante's Divine Comedy, written early in the fourteenth century. The lines are among the words inscribed over the entrance to hell: "Through me is the way to the woeful city."

The second and third epigraphs are from the poems of Giacomo Leopardi (1798–1837), some of whose poems Thomson had translated in the National Reformer. The first passage is from the twenty-third of Leopardi's Canti. The sense of the passage is: "Of the mazy toil and movement of all celestial and earthly things, ceaselessly circling, always returning to where they began, I can discern no use, no fruit." The second passage from Leopardi is from "Chorus of the Dead in the Laboratory of Frederick Ruysch": Ruysch was a seventeenth-century anatomist who devised a method of embalming. The sense of the passage is: "Alone eternal one, with whom the being of every creature ends. In you, death, reposes our denuded nature; not happy, but safe from the old pain . . . because assured that fate denies bliss to the living and the dead.

Proem

Lo, thus, as prostrate, "In the dust I write
  My heart's deep languor and my soul's sad
    tears."
Yet why evoke the spectres of black night
  To blot the sunshine of exultant years?
Why disinter dead faith from mouldering
    hidden?
Why break the seals[2] of mute despair
    unbidden,
  And wail life's discords into careless ears?

Because a cold rage seizes one at whiles
  To show the bitter old and wrinkled truth
10 Stripped naked of all vesture that beguiles,
    False dreams, false hopes, false masks and
      modes of youth;
Because it gives some sense of power and
    passion
In helpless impotence to try to fashion
  Our woe in living words howe'er uncouth.

Surely I write not for the hopeful young,
  Or those who deem their happiness of worth,
Or such as pasture and grow fat among
    The shows of life and feel nor doubt nor
      dearth,
Or pious spirits with a God above them
20 To sanctify and glorify and love them,
    Or sages who foresee a heaven on earth.

For none of these I write, and none of these
  Could read the writing if they deigned to try:
So may they flourish, in their due degrees,
    On our sweet earth and in their unplaced
      sky.
If any cares for the weak words here written,
It must be some one desolate, Fate-smitten,
    Whose faith and hope are dead, and who
      would die.

Yes, here and there some weary wanderer
30   In that same city of tremendous night,
Will understand the speech, and feel a stir
    Of fellowship in all-disastrous fight;
"I suffer mute and lonely, yet another
Uplifts his voice to let me know a brother
    Travels the same wild paths though out of
      sight."

O sad Fraternity, do I unfold
  Your dolorous mysteries shrouded from of
    yore?
Nay, be assured; no secret can be told
  To any who divined it not before:
None uninitiate by many a presage   40
Will comprehend the language of the message,
  Although proclaimed aloud for evermore.
                (1873) 1874; 1880

I

The City is of Night; perchance of Death,
  But certainly of Night; for never there
Can come the lucid morning's fragrant breath
  After the dewy dawning's cold grey air;
The moon and stars may shine with scorn or
    pity;
The sun has never visited that city,
  For it dissolveth in the daylight fair.

Dissolveth like a dream of night away;
  Though present in distempered gloom of
    thought
And deadly weariness of heart all day.   10
  But when a dream night after night is
    brought
Throughout a week, and such weeks few or
    many
Recur each year for several years, can any
  Discern that dream from real life in aught?

For life is but a dream whose shapes return,
  Some frequently, some seldom, some by night
And some by day, some night and day: we
    learn,
  The while all change and many vanish quite,
In their recurrence with recurrent changes
A certain seeming order; where this ranges   20
  We count things real; such is memory's
    might.

A river girds the city west and south,
  The main north channel of a broad lagoon,
Regurging with the salt tides from the mouth;
  Waste marshes shine and glister to the moon
For leagues, then moorland black, then stony
    ridges;
Great piers and causeways, many noble bridges,
  Connect the town and islet suburbs strewn.

---

[2] Break the seals: in Revelation the book that holds the vision of the end of the world is closed with seven seals: "And I saw a strong angel proclaiming with a loud voice, Who is worthy to open the book, and to loose the seals thereof?" (Revelation 5:2).

Upon an easy slope it lies at large,
30   And scarcely overlaps the long curved crest
Which swells out two leagues from the river
        marge.
    A trackless wilderness rolls north and west,
Savannahs, savage woods, enormous mountains,
Bleak uplands, black ravines with torrent
        fountains;
    And eastward rolls the shipless sea's unrest.

The city is not ruinous, although
    Great ruins of an unremembered past,
With others of a few short years ago
    More sad, are found within its precincts vast.
The street-lamps always burn; but scarce a
40   casement
In house or palace front from roof to basement
    Doth glow or gleam athwart the mirk air
        cast.

The street-lamps burn amidst the baleful
        glooms,
    Amidst the soundless solitudes immense
Of rangèd mansions dark and still as tombs.
    The silence which benumbs or strains the
        sense
Fulfils with awe the soul's despair unweeping:
Myriads of habitants are ever sleeping,
    Or dead, or fled from nameless pestilence!

50 Yet as in some necropolis you find
    Perchance one mourner to a thousand dead,
So there; worn faces that look deaf and blind
    Like tragic masks of stone. With weary tread,
Each wrapt in his own doom, they wander,
        wander,
Or sit foredone and desolately ponder
    Through sleepless hours with heavy drooping
        head.

Mature men chiefly, few in age or youth,
    A woman rarely, now and then a child:
A child! If here the heart turns sick with ruth
60   To see a little one from birth defiled,
Or lame or blind, as preordained to languish
Through youthless life, think how it bleeds
        with anguish
    To meet one erring in that homeless wild.

They often murmur to themselves, they speak
    To one another seldom, for their woe

Broods maddening inwardly and scorns to
        wreak
    Itself abroad; and if at whiles it grow
To frenzy which must rave, none heeds the
        clamour,
Unless there waits some victim of like glamour,
    To rave in turn, who lends attentive show.   70

The City is of Night, but not of Sleep;
    There sweet sleep is not for the weary brain;
The pitiless hours like years and ages creep,
    A night seems termless hell. This dreadful
        strain
Of thought and consciousness which never
        ceases,
Or which some moments' stupor but increases,
    This, worse than woe, makes wretches there
        insane.

They leave all hope behind who enter there:[3]
    One certitude while sane they cannot leave,
One anodyne for torture and despair;   80
    The certitude of Death, which no reprieve
Can put off long; and which, divinely tender,
But waits the outstretched hand to promptly
        render
    That draught whose slumber nothing can
        bereave.

                    (1870) 1874; 1880

XX

I sat me weary on a pillar's base,
    And leaned against the shaft; for broad
        moonlight
O'erflowed the peacefulness of cloistered space,
    A shore of shadow slanting from the right:
The great cathedral's western front stood there,
A wave-worn rock in that calm sea of air.

Before it, opposite my place of rest,
    Two figures faced each other, large, austere;
A couchant sphinx in shadow to the breast,
    An angel standing in the moonlight clear;   10
So mighty by magnificence of form,
They were not dwarfed beneath that mass
        enorm.

Upon the cross-hilt of a naked sword
    The angel's hands, as prompt to smite, were
        held;
His vigilant intense regard was poured

---

[3] Leave all hope behind: a paraphrase of another part of the motto over the entrance to hell
in Dante's *Inferno.*

Upon the creature placidly unquelled,
Whose front was set at level gaze which took
No heed of aught, a solemn trance-like look.

And as I pondered these opposèd shapes
20   My eyelids sank in stupor, that dull swoon
Which drugs and with a leaden mantle drapes
    The outworn to worse weariness. But soon
A sharp and clashing noise the stillness broke,
And from the evil lethargy I woke.

The angel's wings had fallen, stone on stone,
    And lay there shattered; hence the sudden
      sound:
A warrior leaning on his sword alone
    Now watched the sphinx with that regard
      profound;
The sphinx unchanged look forthright, as
    aware
30 Of nothing in the vast abyss of air.

Again I sank in that repose unsweet,
    Again a clashing noise my slumber rent;
The warrior's sword lay broken at his feet:
    An unarmed man with raised hands
      impotent
Now stood before the sphinx, which ever kept
Such mien as if with open eyes it slept.

My eyelids sank in spite of wonder grown;
    A louder crash upstartled me in dread:
The man had fallen forward, stone on stone,
    And lay there shattered, with his trunkless
40   head
Between the monster's large quiescent paws,
Beneath its grand front changeless as life's
    laws.

The moon had circled westward full and
    bright,
    And made the temple-front a mystic dream,
And bathed the whole enclosure with its light,
    The sworded angel's wrecks, the sphinx
      supreme:
I pondered long that cold majestic face
Whose vision seemed of infinite void space.
                  (1870) 1874; 1880

XXI
Anear the centre of that northern crest
    Stands out a level upland bleak and bare,

From which the city east and south and west
    Sinks gently in long waves; and thronèd there
An Image sits, stupendous, superhuman,
The bronze colossus of a wingèd Woman,
    Upon a graded granite base foursquare.[1]

Low-seated she leans forward massively,
    With cheek on clenched left hand, the
      forearm's might
Erect, its elbow on her rounded knee;   1
    Across a clasped book in her lap the right
Upholds a pair of compasses; she gazes
With full set eyes, but wandering in thick mazes
    Of sombre thought beholds no outward sight.

Words cannot picture her; but all men know
    That solemn sketch the pure sad artist
      wrought
Three centuries and threescore years ago,
    With phantasies of his peculiar thought:
The instruments of carpentry and science
Scattered about her feet, in strange alliance   2
    With the keen wolf-hound sleeping undis-
      traught;

Scales, hour-glass, bell, and magic-square above;
    The grave and solid infant perched beside,
With open winglets that might bear a dove,
    Intent upon its tablets, heavy-eyed;
Her folded wings of a mighty eagle,
But all too impotent to lift the regal
    Robustness of her earth-born strength and
      pride;

And with those wings, and that light wreath
    which seems
    To mock her grand head and the knotted
      frown   3
Of forehead charged with baleful thoughts and
    dreams,
    The household bunch of keys, the house-
      wife's gown
Voluminous, indented, and yet rigid
As if a shell of burnished metal frigid,
    The feet thick-shod to tread all weakness
      down;

The comet hanging o'er the waste dark seas,
    The massy rainbow curved in front of it

[1] The image is that of "Melancholia," a famous engraving published by Albrecht Dürer (1471–1528) in 1514. In addition to the figure of Melancholia, in an attitude and setting like that reproduced by Thomson, the engraving depicts St. Jerome cloistered in a study and busy, presumably, at his translation of Scriptures. An earlier version of this passage is printed in Anne Ridler's edition of Thomson's poems.

Beyond the village with the masts and trees;
  The snaky imp, dog-headed, from the Pit,
Bearing upon its batlike leathern pinions
Her name unfolded in the sun's dominions,
  The "Melencolia" that transcends all wit.

Thus has the artist copied her, and thus
  Surrounded to expound her form sublime,
Her fate heroic and calamitous;
  Fronting the dreadful mysteries of Time,
Unvanquished in defeat and desolation,
Undaunted in the hopeless conflagration
  Of the day setting on her baffled prime.

Baffled and beaten back she works on still,
  Weary and sick of soul she works the more,
Sustained by her indomitable will:
  The hands shall fashion and the brain shall pore,
And all her sorrow shall be turned to labour,
Till Death the friend-foe piercing with his sabre
  That mighty heart of hearts ends bitter war.

But as if blacker night could dawn on night,
  With tenfold gloom on moonless night unstarred,
A sense more tragic than defeat and blight,
  More desperate than strife with hope debarred,
More fatal than the adamantine Never

Encompassing her passionate endeavour,
  Dawns glooming in her tenebrous regard:

The sense that every struggle brings defeat
  Because Fate holds no prize to crown success;
That all the oracles are dumb or cheat
  Because they have no secret to express;
That none can pierce the vast black veil uncertain
Because there is no light beyond the curtain;
  That all is vanity and nothingness. 70

Titanic from her high throne in the north,
  That City's sombre Patroness and Queen,
In bronze sublimity she gazes forth
  Over her Capital of teen and threne,[2]
Over the river with its isles and bridges,
The marsh and moorland, to the stern rock-ridges,
  Confronting them with a coëval mien.

The moving moon and stars from east to west
  Circle before her in the sea of air;
Shadows and gleams glide round her solemn rest. 80
  Her subjects often gaze up to her there:
The strong to drink new strength of iron endurance,
The weak new terrors; all, renewed assurance
  And confirmation of the old despair.

                    (1873) 1874; 1880

Edwin Arnold
1832–1904

Edwin Arnold graduated from Oxford in 1854 after having won a prize for his poetry and having published a volume of poems in 1853. In 1856 he accepted an appointment as principal of a government school in India, where he remained until 1861. He returned to become an editorial writer on the Daily Telegraph *of London, and he became editor of the paper in 1873. While in India he*

studied Indian and other Eastern languages, religions, and literature. In 1879 he published The Light of Asia, *which quickly became very popular, going through about sixty editions in Britain and about eighty in the United States in the next fifty years. Arnold later published some other reworkings of Indian poetry, and a sequel to his famous poem,* The Light of the World (1891). *He also*

---

[2] Teen and threne: woe and a song of lamentation.

wrote many editorials and pamphlets on questions of Indian and colonial politics. He retired from the editorship of the Telegraph *in 1888 and spent the rest of his life writing, lecturing, and traveling, especially in Japan and the United States. The text printed here is that of the 1885 edition of Arnold's poems; he revised* The Light of Asia *before but not after that date.*

The Light of Asia *is a poem in eight books retelling some stories of Siddhartha or Gotama, the founder of the Buddhist religion and one of the Buddhas or teachers who according to Buddhist belief appear from time to time to revive and purify the principles and life of religion. Siddhartha, who lived in the sixth century* B.C., *was the son of a king or tribal chief. After his own marriage, Prince Siddhartha was so struck by the pain and suffering of all life that he left his family and luxurious palace to wander, learn, and meditate. He finally attained the state of Nirvana or enlightenment and began to teach the truths he had seen and felt. Arnold's poem is based principally on translations of the texts of Sanskrit scriptures. The poem follows Siddhartha from his early life of luxury through his perception of the pain of creation to his final enlightenment and the teachings that issue from it.*

from The Light of Asia

From Book I [The Deep Disease of Life]

. . . So they rode
Into a land of wells and gardens, where,
All up and down the rich red loam, the steers
Strained their strong shoulders in the creaking
    yoke
Dragging the ploughs; the fat soil rose and
    rolled
In smooth long waves back from the plough;
    who drove
Planted both feet upon the leaping share
To make the furrow deep; among the palms

The tinkle of the rippling water rang,
And where it ran the glad earth 'broidered it   10
With balsams and the spears of lemon-grass.
Elsewhere were sowers who went forth to sow;
And all the jungle laughed with nesting-songs,
And all the thickets rustled with small life
Of lizard, bee, beetle, and creeping things
Pleased at the spring-time. In the mango-sprays
The sun-birds flashed; alone at his green forge
Toiled the loud coppersmith; bee-eaters hawked
Chasing the purple butterflies; beneath,
Striped squirrels raced, the mynas perked and
    picked,   20
The seven brown sisters chattered in the thorn,
The pied fish-tiger[1] hung above the pool,
The egrets stalked among the buffaloes,
The kites[2] sailed circles in the golden air;
About the painted temple peacocks flew,
The blue doves cooed from every well, far off
The village drums beat for some marriage-
    feast:
All things spoke peace and plenty, and the
    Prince
Saw and rejoiced. But, looking deep, he saw
The thorns which grow upon this rose of life: 30
How the swart peasant sweated for his wage,
Toiling for leave to live; and how he urged
The great-eyed oxen through the flaming
    hours,
Goading their velvet flanks: then marked he,
    too,
How lizard fed on ant, and snake on him,
And kite on both; and how the fish-hawk
    robbed
The fish-tiger of that which it had seized;
The shrike chasing the bulbul,[3] which did chase
The jewelled butterflies; till everywhere
Each slew a slayer and in turn was slain,   40
Life living upon death. So the fair show
Veiled one vast, savage, grim conspiracy
Of mutual murder, from the worm to man,
Who himself kills his fellow; seeing which—
The hungry ploughman and his laboring kine,[4]
Their dewlaps blistered with the bitter yoke,
The rage to live which makes all living strife—
The Prince Siddârtha sighed. "Is this," he said,
"That happy earth they brought me forth to
    see?
How salt with sweat the peasant's bread! how
    hard   50

---

[1] Fish-tiger: a bird that preys on fish.   [2] Kites: hawks, birds of prey.
[3] Bulbul: a tropical bird, sometimes a name for a nightingale. Shrike: a bird that often impales its prey on thorns.
[4] Kine: cattle.

The oxen's service! in the brake⁵ how fierce
The war of weak and strong! i' th' air what
  plots!
No refuge e'en in water. Go aside
A space, and let me muse on what ye show."

So saying the good Lord Buddha seated him
Under a jambu-tree,⁶ with ankles crossed—
As holy statues sit—and first began
To meditate this deep disease of life,
What its far source and whence its remedy.
So vast a pity filled him, such wide love
For living things, such passion to heal pain,
That by their stress his princely spirit passed
To ecstasy, and, purged from mortal taint
Of sense and self, the boy attained thereat
Dhyâna,⁷ first step of "the path."

From Book VIII [The Teachings of Siddhartha]

If we lay bound upon the wheel of change,
  And no way were of breaking from the chain,
The Heart of boundless Being is a curse,
  The Soul of Things fell Pain.

Ye are not bound! the Soul of Things is sweet,
  The Heart of Being is celestial rest;
Stronger than woe is will: that which was Good
  Doth pass to Better—Best.

I, Buddh, who wept with all my brothers' tears,
  Whose heart was broken by a whole world's
    woe,
Laugh and am glad, for there is Liberty!
  Ho! ye who suffer! know

Ye suffer from yourselves. None else compels,
  None other holds you that ye live and die,
And whirl upon the wheel, and hug and kiss
  Its spokes of agony,

Its tire of tears, its nave of nothingness.
  Behold, I show you Truth! Lower than hell,
Higher than heaven, outside the utmost stars,
  Farther than Brahm¹ doth dwell,

Before beginning, and without an end,
  As space eternal and as surety sure,

Is fixed a Power divine which moves to good,
  Only its laws endure.

This is its touch upon the blossomed rose,
  The fashion of its hand shaped lotus-leaves;
In dark soil and the silence of the seeds
  The robe of Spring it weaves;

That is its painting on the glorious clouds,
  And these its emeralds on the peacock's train;   30
It hath its stations in the stars; its slaves
  In lightning, wind, and rain.

Out of the dark it wrought the heart of man,
  Out of dull shells the pheasant's pencilled
    neck;
Ever at toil, it brings to loveliness
  All ancient wrath and wreck.

·   ·   ·

The ordered music of the marching orbs
  It makes in viewless canopy of sky;
In deep abyss of earth it hides up gold,
  Sards,² sapphires, lazuli.   40

Ever and ever fetching secrets forth,
  It sitteth in the green of forest-glades
Nursing strange seedlings at the cedar's root,
  Devising leaves, blooms, blades.

It slayeth and it saveth, nowise moved
  Except unto the working out of doom;
Its threads are Love and Life; and Death and
    Pain
  The shuttles of its loom.

It maketh and unmaketh, mending all;
  What it hath wrought is better than hath
    been;   50
Slow grows the splendid pattern that it plans
  Its wistful hands between.

This is its work upon the things ye see,
  The unseen things are more; men's hearts
    and minds,
The thoughts of peoples and their ways and
    wills,
  Those, too, the great Law binds.

⁵ Brake: marshy land or rough undergrowth.   ⁶ Jambu-tree: fruit-bearing tree.
⁷ Dhyâna: the word means meditation as a means toward enlightenment.
¹ Brahm: heavenly abode, a state of virtue.   ² Sards: red or brown stones.

Unseen it helpeth ye with faithful hands,
   Unheard it speaketh stronger than the storm.
Pity and Love are man's because long stress
60   Moulded blind mass to form.

Such is the Law which moves to righteousness,
   Which none at last can turn aside or stay;
The heart of it is Love, the end of it
   Is Peace and Consummation sweet. Obey!

1879; 1885

. . .

Wilfred Scawen Blunt
1840–1922

Wilfred Scawen Blunt was the son of an army officer who was himself educated at Stonyhurst, a school which traditionally prepared young men for military careers. Blunt entered the diplomatic service when he was eighteen years old and served in Europe and South America until 1869. After inheriting some property, he began to travel in the Near East and India with his wife, Lady Anne Blunt, the granddaughter of the poet Byron, who herself achieved a considerable reputation with her books on her travels. This experience helped to make him strongly and outspokenly anti-imperial, and in 1887 he was imprisoned for two months for speaking in Ireland against its ties to England. Blunt lived, hunted, and raised horses on a country estate in England, wintered in a house he had built in Egypt, and continuously wrote poetry and his versions of imperial history in Egypt and Ireland. He published two collections of sonnets and lyrics by Proteus, his name for a sometimes autobiographical persona, in 1875 and 1880. These collections were enlarged, revised, and republished in 1892, the same year in which he published "Esther," a sonnet sequence, in a volume with some other lyrics. He also published two volumes of poems in 1889, one of them, In Vinculis, a collection of sonnets about his imprisonment in Ireland. He published a novel in verse (Griselda) in 1893, and a long poem, Satan Absolved: A Victorian Mystery, in 1899.

Blunt was never a popular or even a well-known poet. But his use of the sonnet form especially, and his readiness to enact a skeptical, contemporary sensibility in it, made him an interesting poet to late-century readers and to their successors who had learned from Meredith's Modern Love *how the traditions of the sonnet sequence can be played against to bespeak the ironic deflations of love. Blunt's poems were collected in two volumes in 1914; the texts printed here are those of this com-*

plete edition. Blunt published his Diaries *in 1919–20 and 1922. His grandson, the Earl of Lytton, published a biography,* Wilfred Scawen Blunt, *in 1961; Edith Finch published an earlier biography (1938) under the same title. Thomas J. Assad has described Blunt's eastern travels in* Three Victorian Travellers *(1964).*

from The Love Sonnets of Proteus

XVII

Joy's Treachery

I had a live joy once and pampered her,
For I had brought her from the "golden East,"
To lie when nights were cold upon my breast
And sit beside me the long days and purr,
Until her whole soul should be lapped in fur,
Deep as her claws; a beautiful sleek beast,
Which I might love.—But, when I deemed it least,
Her topaz eyes were on my stomacher,
Athirst for blood. Thus, for I loathed her since
I learned her guile, one night I had her slain
And thrown upon a dunghill to the flies,
Who bred in her fair limbs a pestilence,
Whereof I sickened.—Thus it ever is:
Dead joys unburied breed us death and pain.

1880; 1892

XXXVI

Fear Has Cast Out Love

'Tis not that love is less or sorrow more
Than in the days when first these things began.
Even then you doubted, and our hearts were
    sore
And you rebelled because I was a man.
Even then you fought and wrestled with my
    plan
Of earthly bliss. What bitter anguish too
When at the hour decreed our passion ran
Out of our keeping and love claimed its due!
'Tis not love's fault we part, or grief's. Alas,
One mightier now compels us with His nod.
The fire of Heaven has touched us, and we pass
From pleasure's chastenings to a fiercer rod;
And fear has cast our love, for flesh is grass
And we are withered with the wrath of God.

                                    1880; 1892

LXXIV

The Mockery of Life

God! What a mockery is this life of ours!
Cast forth in blood and pain from our mother's
    womb,
Most like an excrement, and weeping showers
Of senseless tears: unreasoning, naked, dumb,
The symbol of all weakness and the sum:
Our very life a sufferance.—Presently,
Grown stronger, we must fight for standing-
    room
Upon the earth, and the bare liberty
To breathe and move. We crave the right to
    toil.
We push, we strive, we jostle with the rest.
We learn new courage, stifle our old fears,
Stand with stiff backs, take part in every broil.
It may be that we love, that we are blest.
It may be, for a little space of years,
We conquer fate and half forget our tears.

LXXV

The Same Continued

And then fate strikes us. First our joys decay.
Youth, with its pleasures, is a tale soon told.

We grow a little poorer day by day.
Old friendships falter. Loves grow strangely
    cold.
In vain we shift our hearts to a new hold
And barter joy for joy, the less for less.
We doubt our strength, our wisdom, and our
    gold.
We stand alone, as in a wilderness
Of doubts and terrors. Then, if we be wise,
We make our terms with fate and, while we
    may,   10
Sell our life's last sad remnant for a hope.
And it is wisdom thus to close our eyes.
But for the foolish, those who cannot pray,
What else remains of their dark horoscope
But a tall tree and courage and a rope?

                                    1880; 1892

from An Idler's Calender

January

Cover Shooting[1]

The week at Whinwood next to Christmas
    week.
    Six guns, no more, but all good men and
        true,
Of the clean-visaged sort, with ruddy cheek
    Which knows not care. Light-hearted
        Montagu[2]
    At the cover's end, as down the wind they
        flew,
Has stopped his score of pheasants, every beak,
    Without more thought of Juliet than of you;
And still I hear his loud-mouthed Purdeys[3]
    speak.

Tybalt and Paris, with a bet on hand,
    Have fired at the same woodcock. "Truce,"
        say I,   10
"To civil jars." For look, as by command,

---

[1] Cover shooting: hunting for game in woods or undergrowth.
[2] Like Juliet, Tybalt, and Paris, a name from Shakespeare's *Romeo and Juliet*.
[3] Purdeys: a kind of fine gun made by James Purdey, a nineteenth-century London gunsmith.

Bunch following bunch, a hundred
    pheasants fly.
Now battle, murder, death on every side!
    Right, left, left, right, we pile up agony,

Till night stops all. Then home in chastened
    pride,
With aching heads, our slaughter satisfied.

1889

Oscar Wilde
1854–1900

*After creating an anticipatory reputation as a wit
and arbiter of new and exceptionally refined taste
while an undergraduate at Oxford, Oscar Wilde
made his first appearance as a writer by publishing
poems in magazines and collecting them in a vol-
ume of* Poems *in 1881. He was the son of a surgeon
and Irish antiquary in Dublin; his mother had
written for nationalist journals in the 1840s, pub-
lished her poetry in Dublin in the 1860s, and pre-
sided over literary salons in Dublin and in London.
After the publication of his poems, which went
into five editions before the end of 1882, Wilde
lectured in the United States, and then returned to
England to spend his talent in fiction* (The Picture
of Dorian Gray *was published in 1891*), *literary
criticism* (Intentions *1891*), *and especially the
theater. His four comedies produced between 1892
and 1895—*Lady Windemere's Fan, A Woman of
No Importance, An Ideal Husband, *and* The Im-
portance of Being Earnest—*were great successes.*

*In 1895 he brought an action for libel against the
father of Lord Alfred Douglas, one of his friends,
and Wilde was in consequence tried and impris-
oned for two years for homosexual practices. After
his release from prison he published a long poem,*
The Ballad of Reading Gaol (*1898*), *and wrote* De
Profundis (*1905*), *a volume of meditative, confes-
sional prose. Wilde lived in France after his release
from prison, and he died in Paris.*

*Wilde's talent as a poet, and his own interest in
his poetic talent, were peripheral to his large gifts
as a critic and dramatist. But the finish and wistful
sadness of his poetry caught and advertised early in
the last two decades of the century the qualities of
a kind of literary sensibility which was to become
important in them.*

*Biographies of Wilde have been written by,
among others, Frank Harris (1918), Lord Alfred
Douglas (1940), Hesketh Pearson (1946), his son,
Vyvyan Holland (1960), H. Montgomery Hyde
(1963), and Philippe Jullian (1969). Rupert Hart-
Davis has edited a collection of Wilde's letters
(1962). Karl Beekson has edited* Wilde: The Criti-
cal Heritage (*1971*). *The texts printed here are
those of the first collected edition of Wilde's writ-
ing (1908).*

Hélas!

To drift with every passion till my soul
Is a stringed lute on which all winds can play,
Is it for this that I have given away
Mine ancient wisdom, and austere control?
Methinks my life is a twice-written scroll
Scrawled over on some boyish holiday
With idle songs for pipe and virelay,[1]
Which do but mar the secret of the whole.
Surely there was a time I might have trod
The sunlit heights, and from life's dissonance
Struck one clear chord to reach the ears of God:
Is that time dead? lo! with a little rod
I did but touch the honey of romance—
And must I lose a soul's inheritance?

1881

Theoretikos[1]

This mighty empire hath but feet of clay:
    Of all its ancient chivalry and might
    Our little island is forsaken quite:

---

[1] Virelay: a French verse form.
[1] Theoretikos: having to do with a spectator, fond of contemplating, speculative.

Some enemy hath stolen its crown of bay,
And from its hills that voice hath passed away
  Which spake of Freedom: O come out of it,
  Come out of it, my Soul, thou art not fit
For this vile traffic-house, where day by day
  Wisdom and reverence are sold at mart,
  And the rude people rage with ignorant cries
Against an heritage of centuries.
  It mars my calm: wherefore in dreams of Art
  And loftiest culture I would stand apart,
Neither for God, nor for his enemies.

                         1881

Impression du Matin[1]

The Thames nocturne of blue and gold
  Changed to a Harmony in grey:
  A barge with ochre-coloured hay
Dropt from the wharf: and chill and cold

The yellow fog came creeping down
  The bridges, till the houses' walls
  Seemed changed to shadows and St. Paul's
Loomed like a bubble o'er the town.

Then suddenly arose the clang
  Of waking life; the streets were stirred

With country waggons: and a bird
Flew to the glistening roofs and sang.

But one pale woman all alone,
  The daylight kissing her wan hair,
  Loitered beneath the gas lamps' flare,
With lips of flame and heart of stone.

                         1881

Impressions: II. La Mer[1]

A white mist drifts across the shrouds,
  A wild moon in this wintry sky
  Gleams like an angry lion's eye
Out of a mane of tawny clouds.

The muffled steersman at the wheel
  Is but a shadow in the gloom;—
  And in the throbbing engine room
Leap the long rods of polished steel.

The shattered storm has left its trace
  Upon this huge and heaving dome,
  For the thin threads of yellow foam
Float on the waves like ravelled lace.

                   1882; 1908

Thomas Edward Brown
1830–1897

Thomas Edward Brown was born, the son of a clergyman, on the Isle of Man in the Irish Sea. He graduated from Oxford in 1853 after distinguishing himself in two subjects—classics, and law and history—and he was elected to a fellowship in the same year. He was ordained in the Church of England two years later, and returned to Man to become vice-principal of a school. He taught in schools, on Man and in the west of England, for the rest of his life. In 1873 he published one of his best-known poems, "Betsy Lee," in a monthly magazine. Like many of his poems it was a narrative in a literary version of Manx dialect about an event familiar in the lore of the community. Brown collected his poems in Fo'c'sle Yarns in 1881; a new edition was published in 1889. He published three other volumes of verse during his lifetime, not all of it in dialect, although it was for his narrative dialect poems that he was best known. His poems were collected in 1900 in a volume that includes a

---

[1] First published in a slightly different version in a magazine in 1881.
[1] First published in a magazine and not collected in a volume until the first edition of the collected works.

brief biographical tribute by W. E. Henley, who had been one of Brown's pupils. A volume of reminiscences by some of Brown's friends, Thomas Edward Brown *(1930), contains a bibliography that dates the composition and publication of his poems. The texts printed here are those of the 1900 edition.*

from In the Coach[1]

Conjergal Rights

Conjergal rights! conjergal rights!
I don't care for the jink of her and I don't care
　for the jaw[2] of her,
But I'll have the law of her.
Conjergal rights! yis, yis, I know what I'm
　sayin'
Fuss-rate, Misthress Corkhill, fuss-rate, Misther
　Cain,
And all the people in the coach—is there a
　man or a woman of the lot of ye—
Well now, that's what I wudn' have thought
　of ye,
I wudn' raelly—No, I *haven' got a little sup*,
Not me—is there one of ye that wudn' stand
　up
10　For conjergal rights?
No, ma'am, *tight's*
Not the word, not a drop since yesterday. But
　lizzen, good people, lizzen!
I'll have her in the coorts, I'll have her in
　prison—
It's the most scandalous thing you ever—
　What! this woman and her daughter—
It's clane murder, it's abslit[3] manslaughter,
Aye, and I wudn' trus' but beggamy, that's
　what it is—Married yesterday mornin'
In Kirk Breddhan Church, and not the
　smallest taste of warnin',
Takes her to her house in Castletown,
And jus' for I axed a quashtin[4]—and I'll be
　boun'
It's a quashtin any one of you wud have axed
20　—picks a quarrel, makes a row,
The two of them, aye, the two of them—
　bow-wow!

Hammer and tungs! sends for a pleeceman,
　puts me to the door—
But I'll owe her! I'll owe her!
Aisy, Mr. Cretney? No, I'll not be aisy;
It's enough to make a body crazy,
That's what it is, and the supper on the table,
And the hoss in the stable.
And I said nothin', nor I done nothin'. Aw, if
　there's law in the land,
Law or justice, I'll have it, d'ye understand?
Do ye see the thing? My grayshurs! married is
　married,
Isn' it? what? and me that carried
The woman's box. And that isn' all; what
　raison? what sense?
Think of the expense! think of the expense!
Don't ye know? God bless me! The certif'cake,
　that's hafe-a-crown,
And the licence, that's five shillin', money
　down, money down!
And not a farlin' off for cash, these Pazons, not
　a farlin';[5]
And said she was my darlin'
And all to that, guy heng![6] it's thrue! it's
　thrue!
And look at me now! boo-hoo-oo-oo!
Yis, cryin' I am, and no wondher—
You don't see me it's that dark in the coach.
　By the livin' thundher
I'm kilt mos'ly, that's what I am, almos' kilt
With throuble and disthress and all. *A jilt*,
You say, *a jilt*? But married, married, married,
　d'ye hear?
Married, Misthress Creer,
Married afore twelve at Kirk Breddhan,
Married, a reg'lar proper weddin'
And no mistake,
And this woman . . . O my gough![7] don't
　spake of her! don't spake!
It's me that's spakin'? Yis, and I will! I will!
Who's to spake if I amn'? But still—
It's lek you don't see, the coach is so dark, and
　no light from these houses,
But feel of this new coat, and the pair of new
　trousis,
Bought o' puppose, o' puppose! what else?
Bran new; and the shirt and the frells,
And the cuffs and the collar, every d—— thing
As bran and as new as a gull's wing—
And all to plaze her, and to look accordin'

---

[1] "In the Coach" is a series of six dramatic monologues spoken by one or another of the riders of an omnibus.
　[2] Jink and jaw: perhaps, money and argument.　　[3] Abslit: absolute.　　[4] Quashtin: question.
　[5] Farlin': farthing. Pazons: parsons.　　[6] Guy heng: go hang.　　[7] My gough: my god.

To the occasion, and to do her credit, and
  ho'rdin'
The teens of months.[8] And O, if I'd only
  borrowed them from a neighbour!
That's the thing, but bought them, bought
  them! and even so they might ha' been
  chaber,[9]
Yis, they might, at another shop. But you don'
  see the way I'm goin',
No, no, you don'—
But I'd lek you to—the tears! I'm jus' slushin'
  the sthraw
With the tears, makin' the coach all damp for
  the people—yis, I know I am, but I'll have
  the law, I'll have the law.
Just a quashtin about a bit of proppity,
The house, in fac', the very house we come
  into, d'ye see?
The house, her house! Of coorse! of coorse!
  But goodness grayshurs!
Who doesn' know the law about a thing like
  that? the iggorant! the ordashurs![10]
If ever there was a thing on God's earth
That was mine, it was yandhar house! But it
  isn' worth
Talkin'—no! There's people that'll go against
  anything.
      But what! no suttlement goin' a-makin',[11]
Nor nothin', jus' everything goin' a-takin'
Undher the common law of matrimony theer—
At my massy![12] at my massy! With your lave,
  Mr. Tear,
At my massy, sir. You'll 'scuse me.
But you know the law. Married—my chree!
  my chree![13]
What *iss* "married," if that isn'? it's as plain as
  a dus'bin—
Your own dear lovin' husbin'
As kind as kind!
See the beauty of it! And "all that's thine is
  mine,"
Isn' it sayin' that in the Bible?
And surely the woman is li'ble
As well as the man; and to "love, honour, and
  obey,"
Isn' that what they say?
But it's my heart, that's it! my poor broken
  heart! aw dear! aw dear!
And my feelin's! my feelin's! and that son of
  mine girnin' from ear to ear,

And his lip, and his imprince,[14] and his
  disrespeck,
And the waste and the neglec'—
O, it't awful! it's awful! O, the wounds that
  there's no healin's!
O, my feelin's! my feelin's!
But I'll see aburt,[15] I will, I'll see aburt—
The dirt!
The wife of my bosom! Don't be mockin'!
I heard a woman laughing: its shockin'
That a woman'd laugh at the lek of such doin's,
  yis, it is,
Downright wickedness—
A woman that I could name—
Fie for shame! fie for shame!
But I'll have law. Look here! Is James Gell a
  lawyer? You'll hardly uphould me
He isn', will ye? James Gell—the Attorney-
  Gineral: well, that's the man that tould me.
*Did I spake to him about it? was I axin' him
  afore*
I was anything to her?
Sartinly! my gough! was I goin' to run my neck
  into a noose,
And navar no 'pinion nor . . . I'm not such
  a goose
As yandhar ither, I've gorrit[16] in writin', yis, I
  have,
I've gorrit here—aw, you'll get lave! you'll get
  lave!
Not aisy to read, but God bless me! where's my
  specs? But lar't! lar't![17]
It's my feelin's: O, my heart! my heart!
My poor heart! my poor heart! boo-hoo-oo-oo!
  Aye, and you'd think there'd be
Some semperthy,
Some . . . Crow, open this door and let me
  out! there's no regard with ye
For a man's . . . I'll not ride another yard
  with ye . . .
Theer then! theer! No, I'll have none of your
  goodnights . . .
Congergal rights! conjergal rights!

(1891) 1893

Disguises

High stretched upon the swinging yard,
I gather in the sheet;[1]

---

[8] Ho'rdin' the teens of months: hoarding for tens of months.   [9] Chaber: cheaper.
[10] Ordashurs: Audacious.   [11] Goin' a-makin': to be made.   [12] Massy: mercy.
[13] My chree: my heart.   [14] Imprince: impertinence.   [15] Aburt: about it.
[16] Gorrit: got it.   [17] Lar't: let it be.   [1] Sheet: canvas of a sail.

But it is hard
And stiff, and one cries haste.
Then He that is most dear in my regard
Of all the crew gives aidance meet;
But from His hands, and from His feet,
A glory spreads wherewith the night is starred:
Moreover of a cup most bitter-sweet
10 With fragrance as of nard,
And myrrh, and cassia[2] spiced,
He proffers me to taste.
Then I to Him:—"Art Thou the Christ?"
He saith—"Thou say'st."

Like to an ox
That staggers 'neath the mortal blow,
She grinds upon the rocks:—
Then straight and low

Leaps forth the levelled line, and in our
    quarter locks.
The cradle's rigged;[3] with swerving of the blast
We go,   20
Our Captain last—
Demands
"Who fired that shot?" Each silent stands—
Ah, sweet perplexity!
This too was He.

I have an arbour wherein came a toad
Most hideous to see—
Immediate, seizing staff or goad,
I smote it cruelly.   30
Then all the place with subtle radiance
    glowed—
I looked, and it was He!

                                                    (1875) 1893

William Watson
1858–1935

William Watson was the son of a merchant who encouraged and supported Watson's precocious gifts in poetry. Watson began to publish poems in newspapers when he was fourteen years old, and his father paid for the publication of his first volume of verse in 1880. Watson then wrote and published poetry for the next decade without attracting any attention until he published Wordsworth's Grave and Other Poems in 1890, the title-poem of which became one of his best-known poems. Before the end of the century he published seven more volumes of verse, and he collected his poems in two volumes in 1898 and again in 1905. (A final collection was published in 1936.) Much of Watson's verse was political and topical, and even in "Wordsworth's Grave," an elegiac form which he made something of a speciality (he also wrote memorial poems to Tennyson, Shelley, and Burns), he characteristically turns to comment on the languid state of British letters and culture in his time. Watson was once considered for appointment to the laureateship of England, and he was knighted in 1917. A study of his work was published by James G. Nelson in 1966. The texts printed below are those of the collected edition of 1905.

from Wordsworth's Grave

I

The old rude church, with bare, bald tower, is
    here;
    Beneath its shadow high-born Rotha[1] flows;
Rotha, remembering well who slumbers near,
    And with cool murmur lulling his repose.

Rotha, remembering well who slumbers near.
    His hills, his lakes, his streams are with him
    yet.

[2] Nard: a fragrant oil. Cassia: coarse cinnamon.
[3] Cradle: a device to carry men from a ship gone aground to the shore on a line that has been shot with an explosive charge from the ship to the land.
[1] Rotha: a river that flows down from the hills of the Lake District in which Wordsworth lived.

Surely the heart that read her own heart clear
    Nature forgets not soon: 'tis we forget.

We that with vagrant soul his fixity
    Have slighted; faithless, done his deep faith
      wrong;
Left him for poorer loves, and bowed the knee
    To misbegotten strange new gods of song.

Yet, led by hollow ghost or beckoning elf
    Far from her homestead to the desert bourn,
The vagrant soul returning to herself
    Wearily wise, must needs to him return.

To him and to the powers that with him
      dwell:—
    Inflowings that divulged not whence they
      came;
And that secluded Spirit unknowable,
    The mystery we make darker with a name;

The Somewhat which we name but cannot
    know,
    Ev'n as we name a star and only see
His quenchless flashings forth, which ever show
    And ever hide him, and which are not he.

II
Poet who sleepest by this wandering wave!
    When thou wast born, what birth-gift hadst
      thou then?
To thee what wealth was that the Immortals
      gave,
    The wealth thou gavest in thy turn to men?

Not Milton's keen, translunar music thine;
    Not Shakespeare's cloudless, boundless
      human view;
Not Shelley's flush of rose on peaks divine;
    Nor yet the wizard twilight Coleridge knew.

What hadst thou that could make so large
      amends
    For all thou hadst not and thy peers
      possessed,
Motion and fire, swift means to radiant ends?—
    Thou hadst, for weary feet, the gift of rest.

From Shelley's dazzling glow or thunderous
      haze,
    From Byron's tempest-anger, tempest-mirth,

Men turned to thee and found—not blast and
      blaze,
    Tumult of tottering heavens, but peace on
      earth.

Nor peace that grows by Lethe,[2] scentless
      flower,
    There in white languors to decline and
      cease;
But peace whose names are also rapture, power,
    Clear sight, and love: for these are parts of
      peace.   20

III
I hear it vouched the Muse is with us still;—
    If less divinely frenzied than of yore,
In lieu of feelings she has wondrous skill
    To simulate emotion felt no more.

Not such the authentic Presence pure, that
      made
    This valley vocal in the great days gone!—
In *his* great days, while yet the spring-time
      played
    About him, and the mighty morning shone.

No word-mosaic artificer, he sang
    A lofty song of lowly weal and dole.   10
Right from the heart, right to the heart it
      sprang,
    Or from the soul leapt instant to the soul.

He felt the charm of childhood, grace of youth,
    Grandeur of age, insisting to be sung.
The impassioned argument was simple truth
    Half-wondering at its own melodious tongue.

Impassioned? ay, to the song's ecstatic core!
    But far removed were clangour, storm and
      feud;
For plenteous health was his, exceeding store
    Of joy, and an impassioned quietude.   20

.   .   .

V
Peace—peace—and rest! Ah, how the lyre is
      loth,
    Or powerless now, to give what all men seek!
Either it deadens with ignoble sloth
    Or deafens with shrill tumult, loudly weak.

[2] Lethe: the river in the underworld of classical mythology whose waters when drunk obliterate memory.

Where is the singer whose large notes and clear
　Can heal, and arm, and plenish, and sustain?
Lo, one with empty music floods the ear,
　And one, the heart refreshing, tires the
　　brain.[3]

And idly tuneful, the loquacious throng
10　Flutter and twitter, prodigal of time,
And little masters make a toy of song
　Till grave men weary of the sound of rhyme.

And some go prankt[4] in faded antique dress,
　Abhorring to be hale and glad and free;
And some parade a conscious naturalness,
　The scholar's not the child's simplicity.

Enough;—and wisest who from words forbear.
　The gentle river rails not as it glides;
And suave and charitable, the winsome air
20　Chides not at all, or only him who chides.

　　VI
Nature! we storm thine ear with choric notes.
　Thou answerest through the calm great
　　nights and days,
"Laud me who will: not tuneless are your
　　throats;
　Yet if ye paused I should not miss the
　　praise."

We falter, half-rebuked, and sing again.
　We chant thy desertness and haggard gloom,
Or with thy splendid wrath inflate the strain,
　Or touch it with thy colour and perfume.

One, his melodious blood aflame for thee,
　Wooed with fierce lust, his hot heart world-
10　　defiled.
One, with the upward eye of infancy,
　Looked in thy face, and felt himself thy
　　child.

Thee he approached without distrust or
　　dread—
　Beheld thee throned, an awful queen,
　　above—
Climbed to thy lap and merely laid his head
　Against thy warm wild heart of mother-love.

He heard that vast heart beating—thou didst
　press

Thy child so close, and lov'dst him unaware.
Thy beauty gladdened him; yet he scarce less
　Had loved thee, had he never found thee
　　fair!   20

For thou wast not as legendary lands
　To which with curious eyes and ears we
　　roam.
Nor wast thou as a fane[5] 'mid solemn sands,
　Where palmers[6] halt at evening. Thou wast
　　home.

And here, at home, still bides he; but he sleeps;
　Not to be wakened even at thy word;
Though we, vague dreamers, dream he some-
　　where keeps
　An ear still open to thy voice still heard,—

Thy voice, as heretofore, about him blown,
　For ever blown about his silence now;   30
Thy voice, though deeper, yet so like his own
　That almost, when he sang, we deemed 'twas
　　thou!

　　VII
Behind Helm Crag and Silver Howe[7] the sheen
　Of the retreating day is less and less.
Soon will the lordlier summits, here unseen,
　Gather the night about their nakedness.

The half-heard bleat of sheep comes from the
　　hill.
　Faint sounds of childish play are in the air.
The river murmurs past. All else is still.
　The very graves seem stiller than they were.

Afar though nation be on nation hurled,
　And life with toil and ancient pain
　　depressed,
Here one may scarce believe the whole wide   10
　　world
　Is not at peace, and all man's heart at rest.

Rest! 'twas the gift *he* gave; and peace! the
　　shade
　He spread, for spirits fevered with the sun.
To him his bounties are come back—here laid
　In rest, in peace, his labour nobly done.
　　　　　　　　　　　　　　　　(1884–87) 1890

---

[3] References probably to Swinburne and Meredith.   [4] Prankt: decorated.
[5] Fane: church, temple.   [6] Palmers: persons making a pilgrimage.
[7] Helm Crag and Silver Howe: hills in the Lake District.

John Davidson

1857–1909

John Davidson was born in Scotland, the son of an evangelical minister. At the age of thirteen he was placed as an assistant in a chemical laboratory. Later he trained to be a teacher and taught in several schools in Scotland. In the 1880s he published some verse plays and a novel in Glasgow, and in 1890 he went to London to support himself as a journalist and writer. He published a volume of poems, In a Music Hall, *in 1891, and the first of a series of* Fleet Street Eclogues *in 1893; the second series was published in 1896. His most popular book was a collection of* Ballads and Songs *he published in 1895. He continued to write and publish fiction, including* Earl Lavender *(1895), a burlesque of the esthetic movement. But his interest began to move away from the vernacular energy and particularity of his short poems toward the discursive, dramatic forms of his early work. In a series of blank verse "Testaments," culminating in* The Testament of John Davidson *(1908), and in his unfinished* God and Mammon *(1907), Davidson was trying to work out a kind of materialistic optimism which found in the consciousness of man the most complete expression of the will and idea of the universe, and which therefore charged humans with entire responsibility for its direction and salvation. Davidson was always pressed for money, even after being awarded a small government grant for his writing in 1906. In 1908 he moved out of London to live near the sea, and in the next year he committed suicide by drowning.*

R. D. Macleod's Davidson: A Study in Personality *(1957) is the first book-length biography; J. B. Townsend's* Davidson: Poet of Armageddon *(1961) is the most recent extensive study. A selection of Davidson's poems was published in 1961 with prefatory remarks by T. S. Eliot and Hugh McDiarmid; Andrew Turnbull has edited a two-volume collected edition (1973). The texts printed here are those of the original editions of Davidson's poems.*

Thirty Bob a Week[1]

I couldn't touch a stop[2] and turn a screw,
  And set the blooming world a-work for me,
Like such as cut their teeth—I hope, like you—

On the handle of a skeleton gold key;
I cut mine on a leek, which I eat it every week:
  I'm a clerk at thirty bob as you can see.

But I don't allow it's luck and all a toss;
  There's no such thing as being starred and
    crossed;
It's just the power of some to be a boss,
  And the bally power of others to be bossed: 10
I face the music, sir; you bet I ain't a cur;
  Strike me lucky if I don't believe I'm lost!

For like a mole I journey in the dark,
  A-travelling along the underground
From my Pillar'd Halls and broad Suburbean
  Park,
  To come the daily dull official round;
And home again at night with my pipe all
  alight,
  A-scheming how to count ten bob a pound.

And it's often very cold and very wet,
  And my missis stitches towels for a hunks;[3]   20
And the Pillar'd Halls is half of it to let—
  Three rooms about the size of travelling
    trunks.
And we cough, my wife and I, to dislocate a
  sigh,
  When the noisy little kids are in their bunks.

But you never hear her do a growl or whine,
  For she's made of flint and roses, very odd;
And I've got to cut my meaning rather fine,
  Or I'd blubber, for I'm made of greens and
    sod:
So p'r'aps we are in Hell for all that I can tell,
  And lost and damn'd and served up hot to
    God.   30

I ain't blaspheming, Mr. Silver-tongue;
  I'm saying things a bit beyond your art:
Of all the rummy starts you ever sprung,
  Thirty bob a week's the rummiest start!

---

[1] Bob: shilling   [2] Stop: a mechanism that starts and stops a machine.   [3] Hunks: miser.

With your science and your books and your
   the'ries about spooks,
   Did you ever hear of looking in your heart?

I didn't mean your pocket, Mr., no:
   I mean that having children and a wife,
With thirty bob on which to come and go,
40   Isn't dancing to the tabor and the fife:
When it doesn't make you drink, by Heaven! it
   makes you think,
   And notice curious items about life.

I step into my heart and there I meet
   A god-almighty devil singing small,
Who would like to shout and whistle in the
   street,
   And squelch the passers flat against the wall;
If the whole world was a cake he had the power
   to take,
   He would take it, ask for more, and eat it all.

And I meet a sort of simpleton beside,
50   The kind that life is always giving beans;
With thirty bob a week to keep a bride
   He fell in love and married in his teens:
At thirty bob he stuck; but he knows it isn't
   luck:
   He knows the seas are deeper than tureens.

And the god-almighty devil and the fool
   That meet me in the High Street on the
   strike,
When I walk about my heart a-gathering wool,
   Are my good and evil angels if you like.
And both of them together in every kind of
   weather
60   Ride me like a double-seated bike.

That's rough a bit and needs its meaning
   curled.
   But I have a high old hot un in my mind—
A most engrugious notion of the world,
   That leaves your lightning 'rithmetic behind:
I give it at a glance when I say "There ain't no
   chance,
   Nor nothing of the lucky-lottery kind."

And it's this way that I make it out to be:
   No fathers, mothers, countries, climates—
   none;
Not Adam was responsible for me,

Nor society, nor systems, nary one: 70
A little sleeping seed, I woke—I did, indeed—
   A million years before the blooming sun.

I woke because I thought the time had come;
   Beyond my will there was no other cause;
And everywhere I found myself at home,
   Because I chose to be the thing I was;
And in whatever shape of mollusc or of ape
   I always went according to the laws.

I was the love that chose my mother out;
   I joined two lives and from the union burst;   80
My weakness and my strength without a doubt
   Are mine alone for ever from the first:
It's just the very same with a difference in the
   name
   As "Thy will be done." You say it if you
   durst!

They say it daily up and down the land
   As easy as you take a drink, it's true;
But the difficultest go to understand,
   And the difficultest job a man can do,
Is to come it brave and meek with thirty bob a
   week,
   And feel that that's the proper thing for you.   90

It's a naked child against a hungry wolf;
   It's playing bowls upon a splitting wreck;
It's walking on a string across a gulf
   With millstones fore-and-aft about your
   neck;
But the thing is daily done by many and many
   a one;
   And we fall, face forward, fighting, on the
   deck.
                                                        1895

A Cinque Port[1]

Below the down the stranded town,
   What may betide forlornly waits,
With memories of smoky skies,
   When Gallic navies crossed the straits;
When waves with fire and blood grew bright,
And cannon thundered through the night.

With swinging stride the rhythmic tide
   Bore to the harbour barque and sloop;
Across the bar the ship of war,

---

[1] Cinque Port: one of five seaports on the southern coast of England; the land below one of
them, Romney, in particular, was once covered by the sea and is now used for grazing sheep.

In castled stern and lanterned poop,
Came up with conquests on her lee,
The stately mistress of the sea.

Where argosies have wooed the breeze,
    The simple sheep are feeding now;
And near and far across the bar
    The ploughman whistles at the plough;
Where once the long waves washed the shore,
Larks from their lowly lodgings soar.

Below the down the stranded town
    Hears far away the rollers beat;
About the wall the seabirds call;
    The salt wind murmurs through the street;
Forlorn the sea's forsaken bride,
Awaits the end that shall betide.

1895

A Frosty Morning

From heaven's high embrasure
    The sun with tufted rays
Illum'd the wandering azure
    And all the world's wide ways.

Usurping in its olden
    Abode the fog's demesne,
In watchet[1] weeds and golden
    The still air sparkled keen.

On window-sill and door-post,
    On rail and tramway rust,
Embroidery of hoar-frost
    Was sewn like diamond dust.

Unthronged, or crowded densely
    By people business-led,
The pavements, tuned intensely,
    Rang hollow to the tread.

The traffic hurled and hammered
    Down every ringing street;
Like gongs the causeys clamoured,
    Like drums the asphalt beat.

While ruling o'er the olden
    Abode of fog unclean,

In watchet weeds and golden
    The still air sparkled keen.

1897

In the Isle of Dogs[1]

While the water-wagon's ringing showers
Sweetened the dust with a woodland smell,
"Past noon, past noon, two sultry hours,"
Drowsily fell
From the schoolhouse clock
In the Isle of Dogs by Millwall Dock.

Mirrored in shadowy windows draped
With ragged net or half-drawn blind
Bowsprits, masts, exactly shaped
To woo or fight the wind,   10
Like monitors of guilt
By strength and beauty sent,
Disgraced the shameful houses built
To furnish rent.

From the pavements and the roofs
In shimmering volumes wound
The wrinkled heat;
Distant hammers, wheels and hoofs,
A turbulent pulse of sound,
Southward obscurely beat,   20
The only utterance of the afternoon,
Till on a sudden in the silent street
An organ-man drew up and ground
The Old Hundredth tune.[2]

Forthwith the pillar of cloud that hides the
        past
Burst into flame,
Whose alchemy transmuted house and mast,
Street, dockyard, pier and pile:
By magic sound the Isle of Dogs became
A northern isle—   30
A green isle like a beryl set
In a wine-coloured sea,
Shadowed by mountains where a river met
The ocean's arm extended royally.

There also in the evening on the shore
An old man ground the Old Hundredth tune,

---

¹ Watchet: blue.   ¹ The Isle of Dogs: a place in the dock district of London.
² Old Hundreth: the old metrical version of the 100th Psalm ("All people that on earth do
dwell/Sing to the Lord, with cheerful voice") popular in English psalters and hymnals since the
sixteenth century.

An old enchanter steeped in human lore,
Sad-eyed, with whitening beard, and visage
    lank:
40 Not since and not before,
Under the sunset or the mellowing moon,
Has any hand of man's conveyed
Such meaning in the turning of a crank.

Sometimes he played
As if his box had been
An organ in an abbey richly lit;
For when the dark invaded day's demesne,
And the sun set in crimson and in gold;
When idlers swarmed upon the esplanade,
And a late steamer wheeling towards the quay
50 Struck founts of silver from the darkling sea,
The solemn tune arose and shook and rolled
Above the throng,
Above the hum and tramp and bravely knit
All hearts in common memories of song.

Sometimes he played at speed;
Then the Old Hundredth like a devil's mass
Instinct with evil thought and evil deed,
Rang out in anguish and remorse. Alas!
That men must know both Heaven and Hell!
Sometimes the melody   60
Sang with the murmuring surge;
And with the winds would tell
Of peaceful graves and of the passing bell.
Sometimes it pealed across the bay
A high triumphal dirge,
A dirge
For the departing undefeated day.

A noble tune, a high becoming mate
Of the capped mountains and the deep broad
    firth;[3]
A simple tune and great,   70
The fittest utterance of the voice of earth.

                                                   1899

John Gray
1866–1934

---

*John Gray worked in government offices in London in the 1890s, published his first volume of poems (*Silverpoints*) in 1893, and a play in 1894. He was converted to Roman Catholicism in his boyhood, and relatively late in his life he was ordained a Roman Catholic priest at the age of thirty-five. He spent most of the rest of his life in Edinburgh, where he built a church and helped to found the Edinburgh zoo. His poetry after the verse of his first volume was religious. He published* Spiritual Poems, *including many translations, in 1896;* Ad Matrem *in 1904; and a final collection of* Poems *in 1931. The texts printed below are those of* An Anthology of 'Nineties Verse, *edited by A. J. A. Symons (1928).*

Les Demoiselles de Sauve[1]

Beautiful ladies through the orchard pass;
Bend under crutched-up branches, forked and
    low;
Trailing their samet palls[2] o'er dew-drenched
    grass.

Pale blossoms, looking on proud Jacqueline,
Blush to the colour of her finger tips,
And rosy knuckles, laced with yellow lace.

High-crested Berthe discerns, with slant,
    clinched eyes,
Amid the leaves pink faces of the skies;
She locks her plaintive hands Sainte-
    Margotwise.

Ysabeau follows last, with languorous pace;   1̣0
Presses, voluptuous, to her bursting lips,
With backward stoop, a branch of eglantine.

Courtly ladies through the orchard pass;
Bow low, as in lords' halls; and springtime
    grass
Tangles a snare to catch the tapering toe.

                                                   1893

---

[3] Firth: a common Scottish term for a body of water where the sea meets a river.
[1] Les Demoiselles de Sauve: the gentlewomen of Sauve, a French village.
[2] Samet palls: cloaks or wraps made of a rich fabric, sometimes interwoven with gold.

Mishka

Mishka is poet among the beasts.
When roots are rotten, and rivers weep,
The bear is at play in the land of sleep.
Though his head be heavy between his fists.
The bear is poet among the beasts.

The Dream:

Wide and large are the monster's eyes,
Nought saying, save one word alone:
Mishka! Mishka, as turned to stone,
Hears no word else, nor in anywise
10 Can see aught save the monster's eyes.
Honey is under the monster's lips;
And Mishka follows into her lair,
Dragged in the net of her yellow hair,

Knowing all things when honey drips
On his tongue like rain, the song of the hips.[1]

Of the honey-child, and of each twin mound.
Mishka! there screamed a far bird-note,
Deep in the sky, when round his throat
The triple coil of her hair she wound.
And stroked his limbs with a humming sound.   20

Mishka is white like a hunter's son;
For he knows no more of the ancient south
When the honey-child's lips are on his mouth,
When all her kisses are joined in one,
And his body is bathed in grass and sun.

1893

Theodore Wratislaw
1871–1933

Theodore William Graf Wratislaw was a member of a noble family of Bohemia who was educated in England and entered the practice of law. He published privately two volumes of poetry in 1892, and then he published another volume of verse and a verse tragedy before the mid-1890s. He also began to contribute to The Yellow Book *and* The Savoy, *and he attained something of a reputation with the publication of* Orchids *in 1896. By that time he had taken an appointment in a government office, and except for some translations of the fifteenth-century French poet Villon he published in 1933, Wratislaw apparently wrote no more poetry. His study of Swinburne appeared in 1900, and a selection of his poems in 1935. The text printed below is that of the first edition of* Orchids.

Orchids

Orange and purple, shot with white and
  mauve,

Such in a greenhouse wet with tropic heat
One sees these delicate flowers whose parents
  throve
In some Pacific island's hot retreat.

Their ardent colours that betray the rank
Fierce hotbed of corruption whence they rose
Please eyes that long for stranger sweets than
  prank[1]
Wild meadow-blooms and what the garden
  shows.

Exotic flowers! How great is my delight
To watch your petals curiously wrought,   10
To lie among your splendours day and night
Lost in a subtle dream of subtler thought.

Bathed in your clamorous orchestra of hues,
The palette of your perfumes, let me sleep
While your mesmeric presences diffuse

[1] Hips: fruit of rose plant.   [1] Prank: decorate, spangle.

Weird dreams: and then bizarre sweet rhymes
shall creep

Forth from my brain and slowly form and make
Sweet poems as a weaving spider spins,

A shrine of loves that laugh and swoon and
ache,
A temple of coloured sorrows and perfumed
sins!   20

         1896

Aubrey Beardsley
1872–1898

Aubrey Beardsley went from his early schooling to an architect's office, and from there to a clerkship in a London insurance office. He began a short, full, and very influential career as an illustrator with a set of over 500 drawings for an edition of the Morte d'Arthur *in 1891–92, and he followed this beginning by illustrating editions of Wilde's* Salome, *Pope's* The Rape of the Lock, *Jonson's* Volpone, *and posters and illustrations for* The Yellow Book *and* The Savoy, *important if short-lived journals of new art and writing in the mid-1890s. He published "The Three Musicians" in* The Savoy, *where he also published portions of* Under the Hill, *his novel based on the story of Tannhaüser, in 1896. The line of mockery that runs through "The Three Musicians" is also a central element in his drawings, which were celebrated and attacked for their cool, mannered surface and suggestion of elegant, epicene corruption. Arthur Symons (1897) and Stanley Weintraub (1967) have published studies of Beardsley's life and art. See also Osbert Burdett's* The Beardsley Period *(1925), and Malcolm Easton's* Aubrey and the Dying Lady *(1972) for accounts of Beardsley's professional and personal relationships. Those portions of* Under the Hill *which appeared in* The Savoy, *and a few of Beardsley's essays and poems, were collected in 1904; the text printed here is taken from this edition. An unexpurgated version of* Under the Hill *was published in 1967.*

The Three Musicians

Along the path that skirts the wood,
    The three musicians wend their way,
Pleased with their thoughts, each other's
    mood,
    Franz Himmel's[1] latest roundelay,
The morning's work, a new-found theme,
    their breakfast and the summer day.

One's a soprano, lightly frocked
    In cool, white muslin that just shows
Her brown silk stockings gaily clocked,
    Plump arms and elbows tipped with
    rose,
And frills of petticoats and things, and outlines
    as the warm wind blows.   10

Beside her a slim, gracious boy
    Hastens to mend her tresses' fall,
And dies her favour to enjoy,
    And dies for *réclame*[2] and recall
At Paris and St Petersburg, Vienna and St
    James's Hall.

The third's a Polish Pianist
    With big engagements everywhere,
A light heart and an iron wrist,
    And shocks and shoals of yellow hair,
And fingers that can trill on sixths and fill be-
    ginners with despair.   20

The three musicians stroll along
    And pluck the ears of ripened corn,
Break into odds and ends of song,
    And mock the woods with Siegfried's
    horn,[3]

---

[1] Franz Himmel: perhaps Frederich Himmel (1765–1814), like Christoph Willibald Gluck (1714–87), line 25, an eighteenth-century German composer.
[2] *Réclame:* publicity, renown.
[3] Siegfried: a hero of medieval German romance and of a series of mid-nineteenth-century operas by Richard Wagner (1813–83).

And fill the air with Gluck, and fill the tweeded
　　tourist's soul with scorn.

The Polish genius lags behind,
　　And, with some poppies in his hand,
Picks out the strings and wood and wind
　　Of an imaginary band,
Enchanted that for once his men obey his beat
　　and understand.

The charming cantatrice reclines
　　And rests a moment where she sees

Her château's roof that hotly shines
　　Amid the dusky summer trees,
And fans herself, half shuts her eyes, and
　　smoothes the frock about her knees.

The gracious boy is at her feet,
　　And weighs his courage with his chance;
His fears soon melt in noonday heat.
　　The tourist gives a furious glance,
Red as his guide-book grows, moves on, and
　　offers up a prayer for France.　　40

1896; 1904

Henry Newbolt
1862–1938

Drake's Drum[1]

Drake he's in his hammock an' a thousand
　　mile away,
　　(Capten, art tha sleepin' there below?),
Slung atween the round shot in Nombre Dios
　　Bay,[2]
　　An' dreamin' arl the time o' Plymouth Hoe.[3]
Yarnder lumes the Island, yarnder lie the ships,
　　Wi' sailor lads a-dancin' heel-an'-toe,
An' the shore-lights flashin', an' the night-tide
　　dashin',
　　He sees et arl so plainly as he saw et long ago.

Drake he was a Devon man, an' rüled the
　　Devon seas,
　　(Capten, art tha sleepin' there below?),　　10
Rovin' tho' his death fell, he went wi' heart at
　　ease,
　　An' dreamin' arl the time o' Plymouth Hoe.
"Take my drum to England, hang et by the
　　shore,
　　Strike et when your powder's runnin' low;

[1] Francis Drake (c. 1545–1596) was one of the most famous of the captains commissioned to harry Spanish shipping during Britain's conflicts with Spain in the last years of the sixteenth century.

[2] Nombre Dios: a town in the West Indies, the site of one of Drake's early victories and also the place where he died.

[3] Plymouth Hoe: the land on the northern edge of Plymouth Sound on the southern coast of England.

If the Dons[4] sight Devon, I'll quit the port o'
    Heaven,
  An' drum them up the Channel as we
    drummed them long ago."

Drake he's in his hammock till the great
    Armadas come,
  (Capten, art tha sleepin' there below?) ,
Slung atween the round shot, listenin' for the
    drum,
10   An' dreamin' arl the time o' Plymouth Hoe.
Call him on the deep sea, call him up the
    Sound,
  Call him when ye sail to meet the foe;
Where the old trade's plyin' an' the old flag
    flyin'
  They shall find him ware an' wakin', as they
    found him long ago!
                          1897

Admiral Death

Boys, are ye calling a toast to-night?
  (Hear what the sea-wind saith)
Fill for a bumper strong and bright,
  And here's to Admiral Death!
He's sailed in a hundred builds o' boat,
He's fought in a thousand kinds o' coat,

He's the senior flag of all that float,
  And his name's Admiral Death!

Which of you looks for a service free?
  (Hear what the sea-wind saith)   10
The rules o' the service are but three
  When ye sail with Admiral Death.
Steady your hand in time o' squalls,
Stand to the last by him that falls,
And answer clear to the voice that calls,
  "Ay, ay! Admiral Death!"

How will ye know him among the rest?
  (Hear what the sea-wind saith)
By the glint o' the stars that cover his breast
  Ye may find Admiral Death.   20
By the forehead grim with an ancient scar,
By the voice that rolls like thunder far,
By the tenderest eyes of all that are,
  Ye may know Admiral Death.

Where are the lads that sailed before?
  (Hear what the sea-wind saith)
Their bones are white by many a shore,
  They sleep with Admiral Death.
Oh! but they loved him, young and old,
For he left the laggard, and took the bold,   30
And the fight was fought, and the story's told,
  And they sleep with Admiral Death.
                          1898

[4] Dons: Spaniards.

PART SEVEN

Comic Poems

HE POEMS included in this section were all published in books during the Victorian period, some of them collected in a volume after their original publication in another form, others (the poems of Edward Lear and C. S. Calverley) first published in a book. In that sense they, and many other Victorian comic poems that appeared in bound volumes during the period, are exceptional. They are the accessible tip of a great mass of Victorian comic verse that did not make its way out of its first publication in periodicals and other ephemeral modes. The lyrics of many street ballads, for example, were comic. So were those of many of the songs performed in night-houses, pubs, minstrel shows, and music halls and then published as street ballads or in songbooks and sheet music (see Part Eight). Some of the many burlesques and pantomimes of the Victorian theater were written in a verse full of puns and comically forced rhymes, and many theatrical songs, from "Villikins and His Dinah" to the songs of Gilbert and Sullivan's Savoy Operas (see Part Eight), were comic.

Early Victorian newspapers sometimes printed lightly satirical poems and political squibs like those of Winthrop Mackworth Praed (see pp. 363–365). In the first decades of the Victorian period monthly magazines that printed essays and fiction intended to attract readers of general and diverse interests frequently published comic verse: Thomas Hood, Richard Harris Barham, "Bon Gaultier" (W. E. Aytoun and Theodore Martin), and Thackeray published some of their comic poems in such magazines. After the founding and success of the comic weekly *Punch* in 1841, scores of specifically comic journals, most of them also weeklies, were published during the remainder of the century, and they printed thousands of poems like those Thackeray wrote for *Punch,* W. S. Gilbert wrote for *Fun,* and Lewis Carroll contributed to comic journals early in his career. Finally, the kind of comic annual in which Thomas Hood published most of his writing in the 1830s evolved in the mid-Victorian decades into an annual, usually published at Christmas, which was sometimes a selection of the prose, verse, and cartoons of a comic weekly, and sometimes a collection of fiction and entertaining verse, usually fit for the season and innocent of ambitions, and bereft of means, to survive it.

In at least one extremely significant way, however, the comic poems re-published in this section are representative of the mass from which their survival distinguishes them. Like a great many other Victorian comic poems, they very often exist in a direct relationship to the literature their readers presumably took seriously. The most prevalent form of Victorian comic verse was literary parody and burlesque. These poems play with the language and forms of individual poems, with the styles of individual poets, with the idioms and conventions of certain kinds of poetry, and often with identities and attitudes common in nineteenth-century literature: for example, with the introspective, desolated, sensitive, and frequently self-pitying sensibility who appears in poems as different in their tones as Bon Gaultier's derisive "The Lay of the Lovelorn" and Lear's plangent "The Dong with the Luminous Nose." These two poems also represent two of the means by which comic poets turned the features of earnest literature into their joke on it. One way was to confront the high-flown styles and attitudes of earnest literature with the language, actualities, and responses of the contemporary and everyday. Thus Bon Gaultier accounts for Tennyson's maudlin hero by making him drunk, Barham puts the romance associated with medievalism on the ground of his unrelenting emphasis on carnality, and Thackeray requires the sorrows of Werther to yield to the durable priority of bread and butter. Another means of writing comic poetry was not to deflate but to exaggerate the uses other poets made of language. Comic poets often achieved their effects by straining the properties of sound in language. They forced rhymes and called attention to meter, made puns, used words entirely for their sound, and even made up words to make a rhyme or fill a measure. In the nonsense verse of Lear and Carroll, and in the poems of Gilbert, Calverley, and J. K. Stephen, these effects are maintained in their own rigorous decorum. These poems are funny, not because they interrupt high periods with unmannerly sounds and incongruous matter, but because they begin in a precisely false key or an absurd premise and then move imperturbedly through measures and rhymes and images consonant with one another. The joke of "The Dong with a Luminous Nose" is that it looks and sounds like the kind of poem of quest and loss which it burlesques, and much of the humor of Gilbert's Bab ballads is founded in the coherent logic and structure with which the poems work out the consequences of accidental or arbitrary premises (the code of "Etiquette") that the principals of the poems take just as seriously as the heroes of serious poems take the premises of their existences.

The proper audience for such comic poems—that is, the audience that could fully respond to their humor—knew or at least knew about the literature and literary attitudes against which the poems were playing. Why did these readers enjoy verse that very often quite literally made light of the idioms, forms, conventions, themes, and pretensions of the other poetry they knew? Sometimes Victorian readers found poems comic because the poems mocked and offered to change important political and social actualities. Robert Brough's verbal caricatures, the anti-Romanist bias of Barham's burlesques, "The Coming K———," and Gilbert's "Etiquette" could be enjoyed as doing the work other Victorian poems were supposed to do, including some poems by Thomas Hood, Arthur Hugh Clough ("The Latest Decalogue"), Browning, and Tennyson ("The Northern Farmer") which use comic means to earnest ends. Occasionally too, comic poets were in earnest about their mockery of literature and ridiculed dominant literary idioms and pretensions because they thought poetry ought to be written differently. Both Thackery and Aytoun, for example, advocated and wrote a more robust literature than that whose mannered and self-indulgent styles they burlesqued.

But the prevailing conceptions of poetry all through the Victorian period emphasized its elevated and unambiguously earnest character. Readers, literary critics, and most poets most of the time were therefore uneasy about the seriousness of poems that made them laugh. Further, most writers of verse parody and burlesque habitually testified that they really admired the poets and poetic modes they made fun of, and that they did not really mean anything by their travesties. And that in fact seems to have been the pleasure most usually offered by poems which made Victorians laugh: that they did not really mean anything. Early in the period, in the broad farce and rude sound of poems like Barham's, comic poems offered a kind of licensed breaking out, a temporary release into irreverence and exuberance from the dominion of conventionally solemn responses to literary language and to the topics properly treated in it. Later in the period the joke on literature became much more literary in those deftly managed structures in which the features of literary styles and forms were made into a discourse written like a poem, often indeed as well written as a poem, but which was yet not really a poem, not as most of its readers understood the meaning of that word. One of the most interesting issues of its relationship to literature, then, is that, early and late, Victorian comic poetry offered a holiday by being something that looked like literature but was not, not as literature was usually defined and practiced in the period as an unmistakably earnest enterprise. In another definition, however, it is because these comic poems offer pleasure that they are themselves literature, and are also a significant part of Victorian literature. Comic poems, like other poems, are words put in order by extraordinary attentions to their sound and to the form of their discourse. The pleasures created by these attentions served a purpose, as other Victorian poems were intended to do, in the lives and sensibilities of the contemporary readers who gladly took them in because they wanted and enjoyed the usually equable responses and satisfying resolutions of an artful language which was often content, for a change, to do no more than to please.

EDITIONS

Three collections of nineteenth-century comic verse are useful and representative: Walter Hamilton's four-volume collection of *Parodies of the Works of English and American Authors* (1884–87), *A Century of Parody and Imitation*, edited by Walter Jerrold and R. M. Leonard (1913), and the volume of *Humour, Society, and Occasional Verse* in *The Poets and Poetry of the Century*, edited by Alfred H. Miles (1891–97). George Kitchin's *A Survey of Burlesque and Parody in English* (1931) and the chapter on "Lighter Verse" in B. Ifor Evans' *English Poetry in the Later Nineteenth Century* (second edition, 1966) are general descriptions of certain kinds of comic poetry.

The comic traditions and practices of the Victorian theater are discussed in V. C. Clinton-Baddeley, *The Burlesque Tradition in the English Theatre After 1660* (1952); Maurice Willson Disher, *Clowns and Pantomimes* (1925); Ernest Reynolds, *Early Victorian Drama* (1936); George Rowell, *The Victorian Theatre* (1967); and two volumes in Allardyce Nicoll's *A History of English Drama:* Volume IV, *Early Nineteenth-Century Drama 1800–1850* (1955), and Volume V, *Late Nineteenth-Century Drama 1850–1900* (second edition 1959). Something of the practice of comic journalism is described in two standard accounts of *Punch:* M. H. Spielmann, *The History of Punch* (1895), and R. G. G. Price, *A History of Punch* (1957).

W. H. Auden, in his introduction to *The Oxford Book of Light Verse* (1949), and Dwight Macdonald in the introduction to his collection of *Parodies: An Anthology from Chaucer to Beerbohm—And After* (1960), consider the motives and effects of comic poetry in the nineteenth century as well as in other periods. Stuart Tave's *The Amiable Humorist* (1960) is a study of the changing idea of humor and its functions in the eighteenth and early nineteenth centuries in Great Britain. Elizabeth Sewell's *The Field of Nonsense* (1952), a study of the comic writing of Lear and Carroll, works out some broadly useful ideas about how and why comic verse pleases. See also Donald J. Gray, "The Uses of Victorian Laughter," and Max Keith Sutton, " 'Inverse Sublimity' in Victorian Humor," both in *Victorian Studies,* **10** (1966); and Robert M. Martin, *The Triumph of Wit: A Study of Victorian Comic Theory* (1974).

Richard Harris Barham
1788–1845

Richard Harris Barham was ordained in the Church of England in 1813, two years after his graduation from Oxford. His first curacy was in the south of England, but in 1821 he became a canon of St. Paul's Cathedral in London, and he held ecclesiastical appointments in London for the rest of his life. He had published a novel before he moved to London, and he continued steadily to contribute poems, essays, and occasionally fiction to periodicals in the 1820s and 1830s. In 1837 he began a series of stories in prose and verse in Bentley's Miscellany, a new monthly magazine heavily committed to the publication of fiction. In the second of these stories its authorship was attributed to Thomas Ingoldsby, a gentleman of antiquarian habits and orthodox opinions who lived in the south of England and retold stories found in his family's papers. In fact, most of Barham's stories were retellings of local or medieval legends, and the sturdily conservative, soundly Church of England (if not antipapist) social and ecclesiastical opinions were his own.

The Ingoldsby Legends were immediately popular, and Barham continued to publish them in magazines until his death. They were collected in three series, in 1840, 1842, and 1847, and they remained in print throughout the remainder of the century, keeping in play the physical humor and rough surfaces of a comic tradition different from that of the literary jokes and polished whimsy which Charles Stuart Calverley and others made popular in the second half of the century.

Barham's Life and Letters was written and edited by his son, R. H. Dalton Barham, in 1870. A biography and estimate of his writing, Richard Harris Barham, was published by William G. Lane in 1967. Lane's book is the occasion of an essay by Edmund Wilson republished in The Devils and Canon Barham (1973). The texts printed below are those of the 1840 edition of the first series of Ingoldsby Ballads.

from The Ingoldsby Legends

The Jackdaw of Rheims

The Jackdaw sat on the Cardinal's chair!
Bishop and abbot and prior were there;
    Many a monk, and many a friar,
    Many a knight, and many a squire,
With a great many more of lesser degree,—
In sooth a goodly company;
And they served the Lord Primate on bended
    knee.
    Never, I ween,
    Was a prouder seen,
Read of in books, or dreamt of in dreams!   10
Than the Cardinal Lord Archbishop of
    Rheims!

    In and out,
    Through the motley rout,
That little Jackdaw kept hopping about;
    Here and there,
    Like a dog in a fair,
    Over comfits and cakes,
    And dishes and plates,
Cowl and cope, and rochet and pall,
Mitre and crosier![1] he hopp'd upon all!   20
    With saucy air,
    He perch'd on the chair
Where in state the great Lord Cardinal sat
In the great Lord Cardinal's great red hat;
    And he peer'd in the face
    Of his Lordship's Grace,

---

[1] Cowl . . . crosier: the first four items are part of the vestments of an archbishop; the mitre is a tall hat, and the crosier the archbishop's staff.

With a satisfied look, as if he would say,
"We two are the greatest folks here to-day!"
        And the priests, with awe,
30   As such freaks they saw,
Said, "The Devil must be in that little Jack-
        daw!"

The feast was over, the board was clear'd,
The flawns[2] and the custards, had all
        disappear'd,
And six little singing-boys,—dear little souls!
In nice clean faces, and nice white stoles,
        Came, in order due,
        Two by two,
Marching that grand refectory through!
A nice little boy held a golden ewer,
40 Emboss'd, and fill'd with water as pure
As any that flows between Rheims and Namur,
Which a nice little boy stood ready to catch
In a fine golden hand-basin made to match.
Two nice little boys, rather more grown,
Carried lavender-water, and eau de Cologne;
And a nice little boy had a nice cake of soap,
Worthy of washing the hands of the Pope.
        One little boy more
        A napkin bore,
50 Of the best white diaper, fringed with pink,
And a Cardinal's Hat mark'd in permanent
        ink.

The great Lord Cardinal turns at the sight
Of these nice little boys dress'd all in white:
        From his finger he draws
        His costly turquoise;
And, not thinking at all about little Jackdaws,
        Deposits it straight
        By the side of his plate,
While the nice little boys on his Eminence
        wait;
60 Till, when nobody's dreaming of any such
        thing,
That little Jackdaw hops off with the ring!

        There's a cry and a shout,
        And a deuce of a rout,
And nobody seems to know what they're about,
But the monks have their pockets all turn'd in-
        side out;
        The friars are kneeling,
        And hunting, and feeling
The carpet, the floor, and the walls, and the
        ceiling.

        The Cardinal drew
        Off each plum-colour'd shoe,   7
And left his red stockings exposed to the view;
        He peeps, and he feels
        In the toes and the heels,
They turn up the dishes, they turn up the plates,
They take up the poker and poke out the
        grates,
        —They turn up the rugs,
        They examine the mugs:—
        But, no!—no such thing;
        They can't find the ring!
And the Abbot declared that, "when nobody
        twigg'd it,   8
Some rascal or other had popp'd in, and prigg'd
        it!"[3]

The Cardinal rose with a dignified look,
He call'd for his candle, his bell, and his book![4]
        In holy anger, and pious grief,
        He solemnly cursed that rascally thief!
        He cursed him at board, he cursed him in
        bed;
        From the sole of his foot to the crown of his
        head;
        He cursed him in sleeping, that every night
        He should dream of the devil, and wake in a
        fright:
        He cursed him in eating, he cursed him in
        drinking,   9
        He cursed him in coughing, in sneezing, in
        winking;
        He cursed him in sitting, in standing, in
        lying;
        He cursed him in walking, in riding, in
        flying,
        He cursed him in living, he cursed him
        dying!—
Never was heard such a terrible curse!
        But what gave rise
        To no little surprise,
Nobody seem'd one penny the worse!

        The day was gone,
        The night came on,   10
The monks and the friars they search'd till
        dawn;
        When the Sacristan saw,
        On crumpled claw,
Come limping a poor little lame Jackdaw!
        No longer gay,
        As on yesterday;

---

[2] Flawns: custard-cakes.   [3] Twigg'd: saw. Prigg'd: stolen.
[4] Candle, bell, and book: used in rites of exorcism.

His feathers all seem'd to be turned the wrong
    way;
His pinions droop'd, he could hardly stand,
His head was as bald as the palm of your hand;
10   His eyes so dim,
     So wasted each limb,
That, heedless of grammar, they all cried,
    "That's him!—
That's the scamp that has done this scandalous
    thing!
That's the thief that has got my Lord Cardi-
    nal's Ring!"
    The poor little Jackdaw,
    When the monks he saw,
Feebly gave vent to the ghost of a caw;
And turn'd his bald head, as much as to say,
"Pray be so good as to walk this way!"
20   Slower and slower
    He limp'd on before,
Till they came to the back of the belfry door,
    When the first thing they saw,
    'Midst the sticks and the straw,
Was the ring in the nest of that little Jackdaw!

Then the great Lord Cardinal call'd for his
    book,
And off that terrible curse he took;
    The mute expression
    Served in lieu of confession,
30 And, being thus coupled with full restitution,
The Jackdaw got plenary absolution.[5]
    —When those words were heard,
    That poor little bird
Was so changed in a moment, 'twas really
    absurd:
    He grew sleek, and fat;
    In addition to that,
A fresh crop of feathers came thick as a mat!
    His tail waggled more
    Even than before;
40 But no longer it wagg'd with an impudent air,
No longer he perch'd on the Cardinal's chair.
    He hopp'd now about
    With a gait devout;
At Matins, at Vespers[6] he never was out;
And, so far from any more pilfering deeds,
He always seem'd telling the Confessor's beads.

If any one lied, or if any one swore,
Or slumber'd in prayer-time and happen'd to
    snore,
    That good Jackdaw
    Would give a great "caw,"   150
As much as to say, "Don't do so any more!"
While many remark'd, as his manners they saw,
That they never had known such a pious
    Jackdaw!
    He long lived the pride
    Of that country side,
And at last in the odour of sanctity died;
    When, as words were too faint
    His merits to paint,
The Conclave determined to make him a Saint;
And on newly-made Saints and Popes, as you
    know,   160
It's the custom, at Rome, new names to bestow,
So they cannonized him by the name of Jem
    Crow![7]

                          1837; 1840

Gengulphus is a worthy citizen who returns from a pilgrimage to the Holy Land only to be murdered by his wife and the young clerk she has taken as her lover during her husband's absence. To conceal the murder, they dissect Gengulphus' body, distribute the pieces around the house and town, and stuff his beard (shaved off to disguise the corpse's identity) into the cushion of a chair.

from A Lay of St. Gengulphus

But to see now how strangely things sometimes
    turn out,
    And that in a manner the least expected!
Who could surmise a man ever could rise
    Who'd been thus carbonado'd,[1] cut up, and
     dissected?

No doubt 'twould surprise the pupils at Guy's;[2]
    I am no unbeliever—no man can say that o'
    me—

---

[5] Plenary absolution: a remission of all punishment.

[6] Matins; Vespers: morning and evening prayers.

[7] Jem Crow: the American minstrel entertainer Thomas D. Rice had made "Jump, Jim Crow" an extremely popular song in England in the mid-1830s (see Part Eight).

[1] Carbonado'd: hacked.

[2] Guy's: a London hospital named for its founder, Thomas Guy (1645?–1724). St. Thomas is the name of an adjacent hospital that, like Guy's, was used in the education of medical students. Barham also plays on the name of the apostle who doubted that Christ had risen from the dead until he saw him (John 20).

But St. Thomas himself would scarce trust his
    own eyes,
  If he saw such a thing in his School of
    Anatomy.

You may deal as you please with Hindoos or
    Chinese,
  Or a Mussulman making his heathen salaam,
    or
A Jew or a Turk, but it's other guess work
  When a man has to do with a Pilgrim or
    Palmer.

                    .   .   .   .   .³

By chance the Prince Bishop, a Royal Divine,
  Sends his cards round the neighbourhood
    next day, and urges his
Wish to receive a snug party to dine
  Of the resident clergy, the gentry, and
    burgesses.

At a quarter past five they are all alive
  At the palace, for coaches are fast rolling in;
And to every guest his card had expressed
  "Half past" as the hour for "a greasy chin."

Some thirty are seated, and handsomely treated
  With the choicest Rhine wines in his
    Highness's stock;
When a Count of the Empire, who felt himself
    heated,
  Requested some water to mix with his Hock.

The Butler, who saw it, sent a maid out to
    draw it,
  But scarce had she given the windlass a twirl,
Ere Gengulphus's head from the well's bottom
    said
  In mild accents, "Do help us out, that's a
    good girl!"

Only fancy her dread when she saw a great head
  In her bucket;—with fright she was ready to
    drop:—
Conceive, if you can, how she roar'd and she
    ran,
  With the head rolling after her bawling out
    "Stop!"

She ran and she roar'd till she came to the
    board

Where the Prince Bishop sat with his party
    around,
When Gengulphus's poll,⁴ which continued to
    roll
  At her heels, on the table bounced up with a
    bound.

Never touching the cates,⁵ or the dishes or
    plates,
  The decanters or glasses, the sweetmeats or
    fruits,
The head smiles, and begs them to bring his
    legs,
  As a well-spoken gentleman asks for his
    boots.

Kicking open the casement, to each one's
    amazement,
  Straight a right leg steps in, all impediment
    scorns,
And near the head stopping, a left follows
    hopping
  Behind,—for the left Leg was troubled with
    corns.

Next, before the beholders, two great brawny
    shoulders,
  And arms on their bent elbows dance
    through the throng,
While two hands assist, though nipped off at
    the wrist,
  The said shoulders in bearing a body along.

They march up to the head, not one syllable
    said,
  For the thirty guests all stare in wonder and
    doubt,
As the limbs in their sight arrange and unite,
  Till Gengulphus, though dead, looks as
    sound as a trout.

I will venture to say, from that hour to this
    day,
  Ne'er did such an assembly behold such a
    scene;
Or a table divide fifteen guests of a side
  With a dead body placed in the centre
    between.

Yes, they stared—well they might at so novel a
    sight:
  No one uttered a whisper, a sneeze, or a hem,

³ Ellipsis in original text.   ⁴ Poll: head.   ⁵ Cates: delicacies.

But sat all bolt upright, and pale with affright;
   And they gazed at the dead man, the dead
     man at them.

The Prince Bishop's Jester, on punning intent,
   As he view'd the whole thirty, in jocular
     terms
Said, "They put him in mind of a Council of
     Trente
   Engaged in reviewing the Diet of Worms."[6]

.   .   .   .   .

[*The officials of the town begin an investigation
to learn the identity of the dismembered corpse.*]

But now, while on all sides they rode and they
     ran,
   Trying all sorts of means to discover the
     caitiffs,
Losing patience, the holy Gengulphus began
   To think it high time to "astonish the
     natives."

First, a Rittmeister's[7] Frau, who was weak in
     both eyes,
   And supposed the most short-sighted
     woman in Holland,
Found greater relief, to her joy and surprize,
   From one glimpse of his "squint" than from
     glasses by Dollond.[8]

By the slightest approach to the tip of his Nose,
   Meagrims, headach, and vapours were put to
     the rout;
And one single touch of his precious Great
     Toes
   Was a certain specific for chilblains and
     gout.

Rheumatics, sciatica, tic-douloureux!
   Apply to his shin-bones—not one of them
     lingers; —
All bilious complaints in an instant withdrew,
   If the patient was tickled with one of his
     fingers.

Much virtue was found to reside in his thumbs;
   When applied to the chest, they cured
     scantness of breathing,
Sea-sickness, and colick; or, rubbed on the
     gums,
   Were remarkably soothing to infants in
     teething.

Whoever saluted[9] the nape of his neck,
   Where the mark remained visible still of the
     knife,
Notwithstanding east winds perspiration might
     check,
   Was safe from sore-throat for the rest of his
     life.

Thus, while each acute, and each chronic
     complaint,
   Giving way, proved an influence clearly
     divine,   90
They perceived the dead Gentleman must be a
     Saint,
   So they lock'd him up, body and bones, in a
     shrine.

Through country and town his new Saintship's
     renown,
   As a first-rate physician, kept daily
     increasing,
Till, as Alderman Curtis told Alderman
     Brown,
   It seemed as if "wonders had never *done
     ceasing.*"

The Three Kings of Cologne[10] began, it was
     known,
   A sad falling off in their off'rings to find;
His feats were so many—still the greatest of
     any,—
   In every sense of the word, was—behind;   100

For the German Police were beginning to
     cease
   From exertions which each day more fruitless
     appear'd,

---

[6] The Council of Trent was convened in that city in Italy in 1545 to articulate the response of the Roman Catholic Church to the doctrines of Martin Luther and the reformation. The Diet of Worms was a meeting of the leaders of that German city and estate; Luther appeared before the Diet in 1521.

[7] Rittmeister: master of horse.

[8] Dollond: a family whose members from the eighteenth century on conducted a business in London in the making of optical and scientific instruments.

[9] Saluted: kissed.

[10] Three Kings of Cologne: a famous shrine in Cologne to the Magi, the kings who journeyed to see the infant Christ.

When Gengulphus himself, his fame still to
    increase,
      Unravell'd the whole by the help of—his
      beard!

If you look back you'll see the aforesaid *barbe
    gris,*
      When divorced from the chin of its murder'd
      proprietor,
Had been stuffed in the seat of a kind of
    settee,
      Or double-arm'd chair, to keep the thing
      quieter.

It may seem rather strange, that it did not
    arrange
      Itself in its place when the limbs join'd
110   together;
P'rhaps it could not get out, for the cushion
    was stout,
      And constructed of good, strong, maroon-
      colour'd leather.

Or, what is more likely, Gengulphus might
    choose,
      For Saints, e'en when dead, still retain their
      volition,
It should rest there, to aid some particular
    views
      Produced by his very peculiar position.

Be that as it may, the very first day
    That the widow Gengulphus sat down on
    that settee,
What occurr'd almost frighten'd her senses
    away,
      Beside scaring her hand-maidens, Gertrude
120   and Betty.

They were telling their mistress the wonderful
    deeds
      Of the new Saint, to whom all the Town
      said their orisons;
And especially how, as regards invalids,
      His miraculous cures far outrivall'd Von
      Morison's.[11]

"The cripples," said they, "fling their crutches
    away,
      And people born blind now can easily see
      us!"—

But she, (we presume, a disciple of Hume,)
    Shook her head, and said angrily, "*Credat
    Judæus!*"[12]

"Those rascally liars, the Monks and the Friars,
    To bring grist to their mill, these devices
    have hit on.—   130
He works miracles!—pooh!—I'd believe it of
    you
      Just as soon, you great Geese, or the chair
      that I sit on!"

The Chair!—at that word—it seems really
    absurd,
      But the truth must be told,—what
      contortions and grins
Distorted her face!—She sprang up from the
    place
      Just as though she'd been sitting on needles
      and pins!

For, as if the Saint's beard the rash challenge
    had heard
      Which she utter'd, of what was beneath her
      forgetful,
Each particular hair stood on end in the chair,
      Like a porcupine's quills when the animal's
      fretful.   140

That stout maroon leather, they pierced
    altogether,
      Like tenter-hooks holding when clenched
      from within,
And the maids cried "Good gracious! how very
    tenacious!"—
      —They as well might endeavour to pull off
      her skin!

She shriek'd with the pain, but all efforts were
    vain;
      In vain did they strain every sinew and
      muscle,—
The cushion stuck fast!—From that hour to
    her last
      She could never get rid of that comfortless
      "Bustle!"

And e'en as Macbeth, when devising the death
    Of his King, heard "the very stones prate of
    his whereabouts;"[13]   150

[11] Von Morison: James Morison (1770–1840) was a British merchant who made and vigorously
advertised a pill that was supposed to cure many physical disorders.
[12] *Credat Judæus:* "Tell it to the Jews": an expression of disbelief; from the *Satires* of the
first-century B.C. Roman poet Horace.
[13] *Macbeth:* II, 1.

So this shocking bad wife heard a voice all her
   life
   Crying "Murder!" resound from the cushion,
      —or thereabouts.

With regard to the Clerk, we are left in the
   dark,
   As to what his fate was; but I cannot imagine
   he
Got off scot-free, though unnoticed it be
   Both by Ribadaneira and Jacques de
   Voragine:[14]

For cut-throats, we're sure, can be never secure,
   And "History's Muse" still to prove it her
   pen holds,
As you'll see, if you look in a rather scarce
   book,
   "God's Revenge against Murder," by one
   Mr. Reynolds.[15]

MORAL

Now you grave married Pilgrims, who wander
   away,

Like Ulysses of old (*vide* Homer and
   Naso[16]),
Don't lengthen your stay to three years and a
   day!
   And when you *are* coming home, just write
   and say so!

And you, learned Clerks, who're *not* given to
   roam,
   Stick close to your books, nor lose sight of
   decorum;
Don't visit a house when the master's from
   home!
   Shun drinking,—and study the *Vitæ Sancto-*
   rum![17]

Above all, you gay ladies, who fancy neglect
   In your spouses, allow not your patience to
   fail;
But remember Gengulphus's wife!—and reflect
   On the moral enforced by her terrible tale!

1839; 1840

William Edmondstoune Aytoun
1813–1865
and Theodore Martin
1816–1909

The comic poems of "Bon Gaultier" were pub-
lished in magazines all through the 1840s and col-
lected first in 1845 and again, in two editions in
the same year, in 1849. The poems were written by
Theodore Martin (1816–1909), a Scottish lawyer
and translator who later practiced successfully in
London and was commissioned by Queen Victoria

to write the biography of the Prince Consort, and
by William Edmondstoune Aytoun. Like Martin a
lawyer, Aytoun energetically pursued a career as a
man of letters and was well known as the author
of the Lays of the Scottish Cavaliers, *which he*
published in 1849 (see Part Two). In 1845 he
added to his practice of law the duties of the chair

[14] Pedro Ribadaneira (1527–1611) and James (or Giacomo) de Voragine (1230–1298) wrote
collections of saints' lives.

[15] John Reynolds' *The Triumph of God's Revenge against the Crying and Execrable Sin of*
Murder (1621) is a collection of "Tragical Histories" of murderers and their punishment.

[16] Naso: Publius Ovidus Naso, known as Ovid, a Roman poet (43 B.C.?–A.D. 17) who retold
many of the heroic and mythic stories of the past.

[17] *Vitæ Sanctorum* is a name for a kind of medieval book of edifying lives of saints.

of rhetoric and belles lettres in the University of Edinburgh, and he published translations of Goethe and a long poem Bothwell (1856), as well as contributing sometimes humorous, sometimes earnest verse and sketches to magazines.

The Bon Gaultier Ballads are parodies of contemporary poems or burlesques of forms common in the 1840s. They were popular at mid-century; the fourth edition of 1855, which contained fifty-four ballads, went through four more editions within the next ten years. The texts printed below are those of the 1845 edition of the ballads printed in London.

from The Bon Gaultier Ballads

from The Lay of the Lovelorn[1]

Comrades, you may pass the rosy.[2] With
   permission of the chair,
I shall leave you for a little, for I'd like to take
   the air.

Whether 't was the sauce at dinner, or that
   glass of ginger beer,
Or these strong cheroots, I know not, but I
   feel a little queer.

Let me go. Now Chuckster,[3] blow me, 'pon my
   soul, this is too bad!
When you want me, ask the waiter, he knows
   where I'm to be had.

Whew! This is a great relief now! Let me but
   undo my stock,[4]
Resting, here beneath the porch, my nerves will
   steady like a rock.

In my ears I hear the singing of a lot of
   favourite tunes—
Bless my heart, how very odd! Why, surely,
   there's a brace of moons!

See, the stars, how bright they twinkle, winking
   with a frosty glare,
Like my faithless cousin Amy, when she drove
   me to despair.

10

Oh, my cousin, spider-hearted! Oh, my Amy!
   No, confound it!
I must wear the mournful willow,—all around
   my hat I've bound it.[5]

Falser than the Bank of Fancy,—frailer than a
   shilling glove,
Puppet to a father's anger,—minion to a
   nabob's love!

Is it well to wish thee happy? Having known
   me, could you ever
Stoop to marry half a heart, and little more
   than half a liver?

Happy! Damme! Thou shalt lower, day by day,
   to suit thy lot—
Thy China clay all turning to the common
   kind of gallipot.

As the husband is, the wife is,—he is stomach-
   plagued and old;
And his curry soups will make thy cheek the
   colour of his gold.

When his feeble love is sated, he will hold thee
   surely, then,
Something lower than his hookah,—something
   less than his cayenne.

.   .   .

Hark, my merry comrades call me, bawling for
   another jorum;
They would mock me in derision, should I thus
   appear before 'em;

Womankind no more shall vex me, such at
   least as go arrayed
In the most expensive satins and the newest
   silk brocade.

I'll to Afric, lion-haunted, where the giant
   forest yields
Rarer robes and finer tissue than are sold at
   Spitalfields.[6]

Or to burst all chains of habit, flinging habit's
   self aside,
I shall walk the tangled jungle in mankind's
   primæval pride.

---

[1] A parody of Alfred Tennyson's "Locksley Hall" (see pp. 95–100).   [2] Rosy: wine.
[3] Chuckster: bouncer.   [4] Stock: scarf or necktie.
[5] "All round my hat I wears a green willow" was one of the most popular of the street songs of the 1830s; originally an Irish song of separated lovers, it was often burlesqued.
[6] Spitalfields: a district in London known as the residence of silkweavers.

Feeding on the luscious berries and the rich
cassava root,
Lots of dates and lots of guavas, clusters of
forbidden fruit.

Never comes the trader thither, never o'er the
purple main
Sounds the oath of British commerce, or the
accents of Cockaigne.[7]

There, methinks, would be enjoyment, where
no envious rule prevents,
Sink the steam-boats! cuss the railways! rot, O
rot the Three per Cents![8]

There the passions, cramped no longer, shall
have space to breathe, my cousin!
I will take some savage woman—nay, I'll take
at least a dozen.

They shall rear my young mulattoes, as no
Bond Street brats are reared,
They shall dive for alligators, catch the wild
goats by the beard—

Whistle to the cockatoos, and mock the hairy-
faced baboon,
Worship mighty Mumbo Jumbo in the
Mountains of the moon.

I myself, in far Timbuctoo, leopard's blood
will daily quaff,
Ride a tiger-hunting mounted on a thorough-
bred giraffe.

Fiercely shall I shout the war-whoop, as some
sullen stream he crosses,
Startling from their noon-day slumbers iron-
bound rhinoceroses.

Fool! again the dream, the fancy! But I know
my words are mad,
For I hold the grey barbarian lower than the
Christian cad. 50

. . . .

Stuff and nonsense! let me never fling a single
chance away,
Maids ere now, I know, have loved me, and
another maiden may.

"Morning Post"[9] ("The Times" won't trust
me) help me, as I know you can;
I will pen an advertisement,—that's a never-
failing plan.

"WANTED.—By a bard in wedlock, some young
interesting woman:
Looks are not so much an object, if the shiners
be forthcoming!
"Hymen's chains the advertiser vows shall be
but silken fetters,
Please address to A. T., Chelsea. N.B.—You
must pay the letters."[10]

That's the sort of thing to do it. Now I'll go
and taste the balmy,—
Rest thee with thy yellow nabob, spider-
hearted cousin Amy! 60

1845

Edward Lear
1812–1888

Edward Lear was trained and earned his living as an artist. His first important commission was to *draw the birds in the menagerie owned by the Earl of Derby, who helped to establish him as an artist*

[7] Cockaigne: Cockney.
[8] Three per Cents: government bonds, an unusually secure investment.
[9] *Morning Post:* a conservative daily newspaper especially known for its deferential reporting of events in the lives of the aristocracy and other socially prominent people.
[10] Pay the letters: pay the postage.

in Rome. For the rest of his life Lear traveled and published books of sketches and views of such places as Rome, Italy, Albania and Greece, southern Calabria, the Ionian Islands, and Corsica. He also contributed illustrations to several books of natural history, including The Zoology of the Voyage of HMS Beagle, *edited by Charles Darwin (1838–43). Lear also illustrated an edition of poems by his friend Alfred Tennyson which was published the year after Lear's death.*

While Lear was drawing the birds of Derby's menagerie, he entertained the children of the estate by composing and illustrating poems in the then uncommon form of limericks. These poems and illustrations were published as A Book of Nonsense *in 1846. The collection was enlarged in 1861 and again in 1863; by the end of the century it was in its twenty-seventh edition.* Nonsense Songs, Stories, Botany, and Alphabets *was published in 1871;* More Nonsense *in 1872, and* Laughable Lyrics *in 1877.*

The most recent biography of Lear is Vivien Noakes' well-illustrated Edward Lear: The Life of a Wanderer *(1968). Angus Davidson published an earlier study,* Edward Lear: Landscape Painter and Nonsense Poet *(1938). Elizabeth Sewell's* The Field of Nonsense *(1952) is an important study of the means and satisfactions of the nonsense writing of Lear and Lewis Carroll. See also Joanna Richardson's pamphlet in the Writers and Their Work series (1965). Unless otherwise noted, the texts printed below are those of the original editions of Lear's verse. The most conveniently available collection is* The Complete Nonsense of Edward Lear, *edited by Holbrook Jackson (1947).*

Limericks

There was an Old Person of Gretna,
Who rushed down the crater of Etna;
When they said, "Is it hot?" He replied, "No, it's not!"
That mendacious Old Person of Gretna.

1846; 1861

There was an Old Man of the Nile,
Who sharpened his nails with a file;
Till he cut off his thumbs, and said calmly,
"This comes—
Of sharpening one's nails with a file!"

1846; 1861

There was an Old Man of Whitehaven,
Who danced a quadrille with a Raven;

But they said—"It's absurd, to encourage this bird!"
So they smashed that Old Man of Whitehaven.

1861

There was an old person of Bow,
Whom nobody happened to know;
So they gave him some soap, and said coldly, "We hope
You will go back directly to Bow!"

1872

There was an old man whose despair
Induced him to purchase a hare:
Whereon one fine day, he rode wholly away,
Which partly assuaged his despair.

1872

The Dong with a Luminous Nose

When awful darkness and silence reign
Over the great Gromboolian plain,
    Through the long, long wintry nights;—
When the angry breakers roar
As they beat on the rocky shore;—
    When Storm-clouds brood on the towering heights
Of the Hills of the Chankly Bore:—

Then, through the vast and gloomy dark,
There moves what seems a fiery spark,
    A lonely spark with silvery rays   10
    Piercing the coal-black night,—
    A Meteor strange and bright:—
Hither and thither the vision strays,
    A single lurid light.

Slowly it wanders,—pauses,—creeps,—
Anon it sparkles,—flashes and leaps;
And ever as onward it gleaming goes
A light on the Bong-tree stems it throws.
And those who watch at that midnight hour
From Hall or Terrace, or lofty Tower,   20
Cry, as the wild light passes along,—
    "The Dong!—the Dong!
    The wandering Dong through the forest goes!
        The Dong! the Dong!
    The Dong with a luminous Nose!"

Long years ago
The Dong was happy and gay,
Till he fell in love with a Jumbly Girl
Who came to those shores one day,
30 For the Jumblies came in a sieve, they did,—
Landing at eve near the Zemmery Fidd
Where the Oblong Oysters grow,
And the rocks are smooth and gray.
And all the woods and the valleys rang
With the Chorus they daily and nightly sang,—
"Far and few, far and few,
Are the lands where the Jumblies live;
Their heads are green, and their hands
are blue
And they went to sea in a sieve."

40 Happily, happily passed those days!
While the cheerful Jumblies staid;
They danced in circlets all night long,
To the plaintive pipe of the lively Dong,
In moonlight, shine, or shade.
For day and night he was always there
By the side of the Jumbly Girl so fair,
With her sky-blue hands, and her sea-green
hair.
Till the morning came of that hateful day
When the Jumblies sailed in their sieve away,
50 And the Dong was left on the cruel shore
Gazing—gazing for evermore,—
Ever keeping his weary eyes on
That pea-green sail on the far horizon,—
Singing the Jumbly Chorus still
As he sate all day on the grassy hill,—
"Far and few, far and few,
Are the lands where the Jumblies live;
Their heads are green, and their hands
are blue,
And they went to sea in a sieve."

60 But when the sun was low in the West,
The Dong arose and said;—
—"What little sense I once possessed
Has quite gone out of my head!"—
And since that day he wanders still
By lake and forest, marsh and hill,
Singing—'O somewhere, in valley or plain
'Might I find my Jumbly Girl again!
'For ever I'll seek by lake and shore
'Till I find my Jumbly Girl once more!'

Playing a pipe with silvery squeaks,   70
Since then his Jumbly Girl he seeks,
And because by night he could not see,
He gathered the bark of the Twangum
Tree
On the flowery plain that grows.
And he wove him a wondrous Nose,—
A Nose as strange as a Nose could be!
Of vast proportions and painted red,
And tied with cords to the back of his head.
—In a hollow rounded space it ended
With a luminous Lamp within suspended,   80
All fenced about
With a bandage stout
To prevent the wind from blowing it
out;—
And with holes all round to send the light,
In gleaming rays on the dismal night.

And now each night, and all night long,
Over those plains still roams the Dong;
And above the wail of the Chimp and Snipe
You may hear the squeak of his plaintive pipe
While ever he seeks, but seeks in vain   90
To meet with his Jumbly Girl again;
Lonely and wild—all night he goes,—
The Dong with a luminous Nose!
And all who watch at the midnight hour,
From Hall or Terrace, or lofty Tower,
Cry, as they trace the Meteor bright,
Moving along through the dreary night,—
"This is the hour when forth he goes,
The Dong with a luminous Nose!
Yonder—over the plain he goes;   100
He goes!
He goes;
The Dong with a luminous Nose!"
1871

"How pleasant to know Mr. Lear!"[1]

How pleasant to know Mr. Lear!
Who has written such volumes of stuff!
Some think him ill-tempered and queer,
But a few think him pleasant enough.

His mind is concrete and fastidious,
His nose is remarkably big;
His visage is more or less hideous,
His beard it resembles a wig.

[1] Noakes writes (p. 279) that this poem was written one day in collaboration with a Miss Bevan, a neighbor who lived near the villa Lear owned in San Remo on the French Riveria. The poem was not published during his lifetime. Text from Jackson's collection.

He has ears, and two eyes, and ten fingers,
10   Leastways if you reckon two thumbs;
Long ago he was one of the singers,
    But now he is one of the dumbs.

He sits in a beautiful parlour,
    With hundreds of books on the wall;
He drinks a great deal of Marsala,
    But never gets tipsy at all.

He has many friends, laymen and clerical;
    Old Foss is the name of his cat;
His body is perfectly spherical,
20   He weareth a runcible hat.

When he walks in a waterproof white,
    The children run after him so!
Calling out, "He's come out in his night-
    Gown, that crazy old Englishman, oh!"

He weeps by the side of the ocean,
    He weeps on the top of the hill;
He purchases pancakes and lotion,
    And chocolate shrimps from the mill.

He reads but he cannot speak Spanish,
    He cannot abide ginger-beer:
Ere the days of his pilgrimage vanish,   30
    How pleasant to know Mr. Lear!

(1879)

Cold Are the Crabs[1]

Cold are the crabs that crawl on yonder hills,
Colder the cucumbers that grow beneath,
And colder still the brazen chops that wreathe
    The tedious gloom of philosophic pills!
For when the tardy film of nectar fills
The ample bowls of demons and of men,
There lurks the feeble mouse, the homely hen,
    And there the porcupine with all her
        quills.
Yet much remains—to weave a solemn strain
That lingering sadly—slowly dies away,
Daily departing with departing day.
A pea green gamut on a distant plain
When wily walrusses in congress meet—
    Such such is life—

William Makepeace Thackeray
1811–1863

Before the publication of Vanity Fair *in monthly parts (1847–48) established him as a novelist, William Makepeace Thackeray served a long and prolific apprenticeship as a journalist, art critic, and contributor of fiction, drawings, travel sketches, and comic sketches and verse to the monthly magazine* Fraser's *and the comic weekly* Punch. *He continued to write for* Punch *until 1851, principally prose sketches such as* The Snobs of England *(1846–47: collected as* The Book of Snobs *in 1848), the burlesques of* Punch's Prize Novelists *(1847), and the diary of Jeames de la Pluche (1845–46), a footman made rich through speculation in railway shares.*

Thackeray's comic poems exhibit the themes, assumptions, and habits of his prose. They are often topical and full of the objects of ordinary urban

life, acute in their representation of the rhythms of dialect and the vernacular, disdainful of social pretension and amused by the inflations of conventional literary forms and attitudes. Many of his comic poems were first collected in a volume of miscellanies published in 1855.

The texts printed below are those of a volume of Ballads and Miscellanies *published in 1899 as part of an edition of Thackeray's works edited by his daughter, Anne Ritchie. The authoritative account of Thackeray's writing in periodicals is in Gordon N. Ray's two-volume biography,* Thackeray: The Uses of Adversity 1811–1846 *(1955), and* Thackeray: The Age of Wisdom 1847–1863 *(1958).*

---

[1] A fragment unpublished until it appeared in a collection of Lear's writings and drawings taken from manuscripts, *Teapots and Quails,* edited by Angus Davidson and Philip Hofer (1954).

Jeames of Buckley Square[1]

A Heligy

Come all ye gents vot cleans the plate,
   Come all ye ladies' maids so fair—
Vile I a story vill relate
   Of cruel Jeames of Buckley Square.
A tighter[2] lad, it is confest,
   Neer valked with powder in his air,
Or vore a nosegay in his breast,
   Than andsum Jeames of Buckley Square.

O Evns! it vas the best of sights,
   Behind his Master's coach and pair,
To see our Jeames in red plush tights,
   A driving hoff from Buckley Square.
He vel became his hagwilletts,[3]
   He cocked his at with *such* a hair;
His calves and viskers *vas* such pets,
   That hall loved Jeames of Buckley Square.

He pleased the hupstairs folks as vell,
   And o! I vithered vith despair,
Missis *vould* ring the parler bell,
   And call up Jeames in Buckley Square.
Both beer and sperrits he abhord
   (Sperrits and beer I can't a bear),
You would have thought he vas a lord
   Down in our All in Buckley Square.

Last year he visper'd, "Mary Ann,
   Ven I've an under'd pound to spare,
To take a public[4] is my plan,
   And leave this hojous[5] Buckley Square."
O how my gentle heart did bound,
   To think that I his name should bear!
"Dear Jeames," says I, "I've twenty pound,"
   And gev them him in Buckley Square.

Our master vas a City gent,
   His name's in railroads everywhere,
And lord, vot lots of letters vent
   Betwigst his brokers and Buckley Square:
My Jeames it was the letters took,
   And read them all (I think it's fair),
And took a leaf from Master's book,
   As *hothers* do in Buckley Square.

Encouraged with my twenty pound,
   Of which poor *I* was unavare,
He wrote the Companies all round,
   And signed hisself from Buckley Square.
And how John Porter used to grin,
   As day by day, share after share,
Came railvay letters pouring in,
   "J. Plush, Esquire, in Buckley Square."

Our servants' All was in a rage—
   Scrip, stock, curves, gradients, bull and bear,   50
Vith butler, coachman, groom and page,
   Vas all the talk in Buckley Square.
But O! imagine vot I felt
   Last Vensday veek as ever were;
I gits a letter, which I spelt
   "Miss M. A. Hoggins, Buckley Square."

He sent me back my money true—
   He sent me back my lock of air,
And said, "My dear, I bid ajew
   To Mary Hann and Buckley Square.   60
Think not to marry, foolish Hann,
   With people who your betters are:
James Plush is now a gentleman,
   And you—a cook in Buckley Square.

"I've thirty thousand guineas won,
   In six short months, by genus rare;
You little thought, what Jeames was on,
   Poor Mary Hann, in Buckley Square.
I've thirty thousand guineas net,
   Powder and plush I scorn to vear;   70
And so, Miss Mary Hann, forget
   For hever Jeames of Buckley Square."
          1845; 1853

Sorrows of Werther[1]

Werther had a love for Charlotte
   Such as words could never utter;
Would you know how first he met her?
   She was cutting bread and butter.

Charlotte was a married lady,
   And a moral man was Werther,
And, for all the wealth of Indies,
   Would do nothing for to hurt her.

---

[1] Buckley Square: Berkeley Square, in a fashionable district of London. This poem was first published in *Punch*.
   [2] Tighter: neat, well-turned out.   [3] Hagwilletts: habiliments.
   [4] Public: public house, tavern.   [5] Hojous: odious.
   [1] *The Sorrows of Young Werther* (1774; revised 1787) is a short novel by Johann Wolfgang von Goethe (1749–1832) in which a romantic, idealistic young man, disappointed in his grand ambitions and in his love for a quite conventional young woman, finally shoots himself.

So he sighed and pined and ogled,
   And his passion boiled and bubbled,
Till he blew his silly brains out,
   And no more was by it troubled.

Charlotte, having seen his body
   Borne before her on a shutter,
Like a well-conducted person,
   Went on cutting bread and butter.

1855

Robert Brough
1828–1860

Robert Brough worked as a journalist and dramatist in Liverpool and London. By himself or in collaboration, often with his brother William (1826–70), he wrote nearly two dozen burlesques and farces for the London stage. He wrote for newspapers and comic journals, and published a novel, Marston Lynch *(1860). In 1855 he published* Songs of the Governing Classes, *a collection of political poems which articulated some of the disgust engendered, among other causes, by the mismanagement of titled officers during the Crimean War. Brough dedicated the collection to Edward M. Whitty (1827–60), a journalist whose satiric prose sketches of politicians in* The Governing Classes of Great Britain *(1854) gave Brough his title, the idea for his form, and his conviction: "I believe in the revolution you have said is coming," he wrote in the dedication to his poems, "—however slowly."*

The text printed below is that of an edition of the Songs of the Governing Classes *published in London in 1890.*

from Songs of the Governing Classes

My Lord Tomnoddy

My Lord Tomnoddy's the son of an Earl,
His hair is straight, but his whiskers curl;
His Lordship's forehead is far from wide,
But there's plenty of room for the brains inside.
He writes his name with indifferent ease,
He's rather uncertain about the "d's,"—

But what does it matter, if three or one,
To the Earl of Fitzdotterel's eldest son?

My Lord Tomnoddy to college went,
Much time he lost, much money he spent;   10
Rules, and windows, and heads, he broke—
Authorities wink'd—young men will joke!
He never peep'd inside of a book—
In two years' time a degree he took;
And the newspapers vaunted the honours won
By the Earl of Fitzdotterel's eldest son.

My Lord Tomnoddy came out in the world,
Waists were tighten'd, and ringlets curl'd.
Virgins languish'd, and matrons smil'd—
'Tis true, his Lordship is rather wild;   20
In very queer places he spends his life;
There's talk of some children, by nobody's
   wife—
But we mustn't look close into what is done
By the Earl of Fitzdotterel's eldest son.

My Lord Tomnoddy must settle down—
There's a vacant seat in the family town!
('Tis time he should sow his eccentric oats) —
He hasn't the wit to apply for votes:
He cannot e'en learn his election speech,
Three phrases he speaks—a mistake in each!   30
And then breaks down—but the borough is
   won
For the Earl of Fitzdotterel's eldest son.

My Lord Tomnoddy prefers the Guards,
(The House is a bore!) so—it's on the cards!
My Lord's a Lieutenant at twenty-three,
A Captain at twenty-six is he—
He never drew sword, except on drill;

The tricks of parade he has learnt but ill—
A full-blown Colonel at thirty-one
Is the Earl of Fitzdotterel's eldest son!

My Lord Tomnoddy is thirty-four;
The Earl can last but a few years more.
My Lord in the Peers will take his place:
Her Majesty's councils his words will grace.
Office he'll hold, and patronage sway;
Fortunes and lives he will vote away—
And what are his qualifications?—ONE!
He's the Earl of Fitzdotterel's eldest son!

1855

Sir Menenius Agrippa, The Friend of the People[1]

1st Citizen. Soft: who comes here?
2nd Cit. Worthy Menenius Agrippa; one that hath always loved the people.
1st Cit. He's one honest enough; would all the rest were so.
Men. What work's my countrymen in hand? Where go you with bats and clubs? The matter? Speak, I pray you.
1st Cit. Our business is not unknown to the senate; they have had inkling this fortnight what we intend to do, which now we'll show 'em in deeds. They say poor suitors have strong breaths; they shall know we have strong arms too.
Men. Why, masters, my good friends, mine honest neighbours, Will you undo yourselves?
1st Cit. We cannot, sir; we are undone already.
Men. I tell you, friends, most charitable care Have the patricians of you—
CORIOLANUS, ACT 1, SCENE 1

Sir Menenius Agrippa's a Radical stout,
With a rental of sixty-five thousand about,
Of opinions the lowest though lofty in grade,
A Sir Walter Fitz-Tyler, a Lord John de Cade.[2]
You may call him a Leveller—Do, 'tis his pride;
Nay, a stark staring Democrat—True! of the tide
He's a wave; you may stem him, my Lord, if you can;
Sir Menenius Agrippa's a popular man!
    Reform! Vote by ballot! Short Parliaments—cry!

Down—down, with each bishop, church, pulpit, and steeple! 10
The Peerage? Um! Ha! Well, we'll see by and bye?
Sir Menenius Agrippa's the friend of the people.

He sits for a borough remote from his home,
(Where he reigns like a slave-girt Patrician of Rome).
He goes on the hustings in very old coats—
(He's a change at the club) when soliciting votes,
His beard he neglects, and his nails he begrimes,
(His jokes on clean collars are killing at times);
Hang your wine? give him *beer* from the pewter or can;
Sir Menenius Agrippa's a popular man! 20
    Reform! Vote by ballot! Short Parliaments—cry!
        Down—down, with each bishop, church, pulpit, and steeple!
        The Peerage?—Um! Ha! Well, we'll see by and bye!
        Sir Menenius Agrippa's the friend of the people.

He hates all routine—lift the cart from the mud!
But the drivers are failing—new blood, sir! new blood!
Though the Lords have such pow'r—mind in principle quite
Constitutional—oh, most undoubtedly right!
But the men! an exclusive and arrogant class—
All behind in ideas—not a throb with the mass! 30
If we *could* to their ranks—Well! we'll do what we can—
Sir Menenius Agrippa's a popular man!
    Reform! Vote by ballot! Short Parliaments—cry!
        Down—down, with each bishop, church, pulpit, and steeple!
        The Peerage?—Um! Ha! Well, we'll see by and bye!
        Sir Menenius Agrippa's the friend of the people.

[1] Menenius Agrippa was a Roman of the sixth century B.C. who mediated a conflict between the plebeians and the patricians. In Shakespeare's *Coriolanus* he is a sensible man who is finally overborne and neglected by the scale of the politics he tries to manage.

[2] Wat Tyler was a leader of a peasant's revolt in fourteenth-century England. Jack Cade led a fifteenth-century insurrection which for a time succeeded in taking the city of London.

'Tis said Sir Menenius will soon be a peer,
(He annoyed the Queen's government sadly
        last year) ;
They've a service of plate[3] for him—tarrying
        but
To make sure if plain "Sir" or "His Lordship"
40   to cut.
His constituents hiccup, "Oh! just wait a bit
Till *we're* rais'd to the peerage—then see how
        things fit—
If oppress us much longer the Oligarch can!"

Sir Menenius Agrippa's a popular man.
    Reform! Vote by ballot! Short Parliaments—
        cry!
    Down—down, with each bishop, church,
        pulpit, and steeple!
    The Peerage? Um! Ha! Well, we'll see by
        and bye!
    Sir Menenius Agrippa's the friend of the
        people.

                                                            1855

Charles Stuart Calverley
1831–1884

Charles Stuart Calverley, the son of a clergyman, won academic honors—including a prize for his Latin poetry—as an undergraduate first at Oxford and then at Cambridge. He was elected to a fellowship in a Cambridge college and for a while worked as a tutor. After his marriage, which required him to resign his fellowship, he studied law and was admitted to its practice in 1865. The next year, however, an accident while ice-skating permanently impaired his health, and for the rest of his life he lived in a kind of semiretirement, writing, translating Virgil and other classical poets, and only occasionally employing his remarkable intellectual gifts in the practice of his profession.

Almost all of Calverley's comic poems are parodies and burlesques of well-known poems or literary forms and styles. Their effect usually depends upon a commonsense deflation of the grand gestures and earnest situations of the conventionally romantic literature of the century. But the sensibility they address is not an ordinary one. A reader fully commissioned in Calverley's humor has a taste and ear for the forms and measures of classical verse which find Browning's exotic choices of words and dissonances as foolish as the insipidities of Jean Ingelow. Calverley's humor, in short, is highly literate; it depends more on references to the events and standards of a literary tradition than it

does upon references to events and attitudes in the more general experience of mid-century Britain.

Calverley's first volume of Verses and Translations *(1862) contained comic poems and some of his Latin verse. It was in its fourth edition within a decade. He published another volume of translations of Latin verse into English, and English into Latin, in 1866, a translation of some of the poems by the Greek pastoral poet Theocritus in 1869, and* Fly Leaves, *a collection of parodies and burlesques, in 1872. The texts printed here are those of* The Complete Works of C. S. Calverley, *edited by Walter J. Sendall (1901), which contains a memoir. See also R. B. Ince,* Calverley and Some Cambridge Wits of the Nineteenth Century *(1929).*

Ballad[1]

The auld wife sat at her ivied door,
    (*Butter and eggs and a pound of cheese*)
A thing she had frequently done before;
    And her spectacles lay on her apron'd knees.

The piper he piped on the hill-top high,
    (*Butter and eggs and a pound of cheese*)

---

[3] Service of plate: a customary testimonial gift.
[1] A burlesque of literary ballads like those of Dante Gabriel Rossetti's "Sister Helen" (pp. 570–574) .

Till the cow said "I die," and the goose ask'd
   "Why?"
   And the dog said nothing, but search'd for
   fleas.

The farmer he strode through the square farm-
   yard;
   (*Butter and eggs and a pound of cheese*)
His last brew of ale was a trifle hard—
   The connexion of which with the plot one
   sees.

The farmer's daughter hath frank blue eyes;
   (*Butter and eggs and a pound of cheese*)
She hears the rooks[2] caw in the windy skies,
   As she sits at her lattice and shells her peas.

The farmer's daughter hath ripe red lips;
   (*Butter and eggs and a pound of cheese*)
If you try to approach her, away she skips
   Over tables and chairs with apparent ease.

The farmer's daughter hath soft brown hair;
   (*Butter and eggs and a pound of cheese*)
And I met with a ballad, I can't say where,
   Which wholly consisted of lines like these.

PART II

She sat with her hands 'neath her dimpled
   cheeks,
   (*Butter and eggs and a pound of cheese*)
And spake not a word. While a lady speaks
   There is hope, but she didn't even sneeze.

She sat, with her hands 'neath her crimson
   cheeks,
   (*Butter and eggs and a pound of cheese*)
She gave up mending her father's breeks,[3]
   And let the cat roll in her new chemise.

She sat, with her hands 'neath her burning
   cheeks,
   (*Butter and eggs and a pound of cheese*)
And gazed at the piper for thirteen weeks;
   Then she follow'd him out o'er the misty
   leas.[4]

Her sheep follow'd her, as their tails did them.
   (*Butter and eggs and a pound of cheese*)

And this song is consider'd a perfect gem,
   And as to the meaning, it's what you please.   40
                                   1872

Lovers, and a Reflection[1]

In moss-prankt dells which the sunbeams flatter
   (And heaven it knoweth what that may
   mean;
Meaning, however, is no great matter)
   Where woods are a-tremble, with rifts
   atween;

Thro' God's own heather we wonn'd together,
   I and my Willie (O love my love) :
I need hardly remark it was glorious weather,
   And flitterbats waver'd alow, above:

Boats were curtseying, rising, bowing,
   (Boats in that climate are so polite),   10
And sands were a ribbon of green endowing,
   And O the sundazzle on bark and bight![2]

Thro' the rare red heather we danced together,
   (O love my Willie!) and smelt for flowers:
I must mention again it was gorgeous weather,
   Rhymes are so scarce in this world of ours:—

By rises that flush'd with their purple favours,
   Thro' becks[3] that brattled o'er grasses sheen,
We walked and waded, we two young shavers.
   Thanking our stars we were both so green.   20

We journeyed in parallels, I and Willie,
   In fortunate parallels! Butterflies,
Hid in weltering shadows of daffodilly
   Or marjoram, kept making peacock eyes:

Songbirds darted about, some inky
   As coal, some snowy (I ween) as curds;
Or rosy as pinks, or as roses pinky—
   They reck of no eerie To-come, those birds!

But they skim over bents[4] which the millstream
   washes,
   Or hang in the lift 'neath a white cloud's
   hem;   30
They need no parasols, no goloshes;
   And good Mrs. Trimmer she feedeth them.

---

[2] Rooks: crows.   [3] Breeks: breeches.   [4] Leas: meadows on a seacoast.
[1] A parody of Jean Ingelow's "Divided" (pp. 746–748).   [2] Bight: bay.
[3] Becks: brooks.   [4] Bents: coarse, reedy grasses.

Then we thrid[5] God's cowslips (as erst His
    heather)
    That endowed the wan grass with their
        golden blooms;
And snapt— (it was perfectly charming
    weather) —
    Our fingers at Fate and her goddess-glooms:

And Willie 'gan sing (O, his notes were fluty;
    Wafts fluttered them out to the white-wing'd
        sea) —
Something made up of rhymes that have done
    much duty,
40   Rhymes (better to put it) of "ancientry:"

Bowers of flowers encounter'd showers
    In William's carol— (O love my Willie!)
Then he bade sorrow borrow from blithe
    tomorrow
    I quite forget what—say a daffodilly:

A nest in a hollow, "with buds to follow,"
    I think occurred next in his nimble strain;
And clay that was "kneaden" of course in
    Eden—
    A rhyme most novel, I do maintain:

Mists, bones, the singer himself, love-stories,
50   And all least furlable things got "furled;"
Not with any design to conceal their "glories,"
    But simply and solely to rhyme with "world."

      *   *   *   *   *   *[6]

O if billows and pillows and hours and flowers,
    And all the brave rhymes of an elder day,
Could be furled together, this genial weather,
    And carted, or carried on "wafts" away,
Nor ever again trotted out—ah me!
How much fewer volumes of verse there'd be!
                        1872

from The Cock and the Bull[1]

You see this pebble-stone? It's a thing I bought
Of a bit of a chit of a boy i' the mid o' the day—

I like to dock the smaller parts-o'-speech,
As we curtail the already cur-tail'd cur
(You catch the paronomasia, play 'po' words?)
Did, rather, i' the pre-Landseerian days.[2]
Well, to my muttons. I purchased the concern,
And clapt it i' my poke, having given for same
By way o' chop, swop, barter or exchange—
"Chop" was my snickering dandiprat's own
    term[3]—   1○
One shilling and fourpence, current coin o' the
    realm.
O-n-e one and f-o-u-r four
Pence, one and fourpence—you are with me,
    sir?—
What hour it skills not: ten or eleven o' the
    clock,
One day (and what a roaring day it was
Go shop or sight-see—bar a spit o' rain!)
In February, eighteen sixty nine,
Alexandrina Victoria, Fidei
Hm—hm—how runs the jargon? being on
    throne.

    Such, sir, are all the facts, succinctly put,   2○
The basis or substratum—what you will—
Of the impending eighty thousand lines.
"Not much in 'em either," quote perhaps
    simple Hodge.[4]
But there's a superstructure. Wait a bit.

Mark first the rationale of the thing:
Hear logic rivel and levigate[5] the deed.
That shilling—and for matter o' that, the
    pence—
I had o' course upo' me—wi' me say—
(Mecum's the Latin, make a note o' that)
When I popp'd pen i' stand, scratch'd ear,   3○
    wiped snout,
(Let everybody wipe his own himself)
Sniff'd—tch!—at snuffbox; tumbled up, he-
    heed,
Haw-haw'd (not hee-haw'd, that's another guess
    thing:)
Then fumbled at, and stumbled out of, door,
I shoved the timber ope wi' my omoplat;[6]

---

     [5] Thrid: threaded.   [6] Ellipsis in original.
    [1] A parody of the first book of Browning's *The Ring and the Book* (1868–69), in which the
poet meditates on the transformation of the matter of a book he has purchased into the form
of his poem.
    [2] Pre-Landseerian: Edwin Landseer (1802–73) was a British painter especially known for his
painting of animals, especially dogs.
    [3] Chop: barter. Dandiprat: seventeenth-century word for urchin.
    [4] Hodge: a conventional name for a rustic.
    [5] Rivel and levigate: wrinkle and make smooth.   [6] Omoplat: shoulder blade.

And *in vestibulo,* i' the lobby to-wit,
(Iacobi Facciolati's[7] rendering, sir,)
Donn'd galligaskins, antigropeloes,[8]
And so forth; and, complete with hat and gloves,
40 One on and one a-dangle i' my hand,
And ombrifuge[9] (Lord love you!), case o' rain,
I flopp'd forth, 'sbuddikins! on my own ten toes,
(I do assure you there be ten of them).
And went clump-clumping up hill and down dale
To find myself o' the sudden i' front o' the boy,
Put case I hadn't 'em on me, could I ha' bought
This sort-o'-kind-o'-what-you-might-call toy,
This pebble-thing, o' the boy-thing? Q. E. D.
That's proven without aid from mumping Pope,
50 Sleek porporate[10] or bloated Cardinal.
(Isn't it, old Fatchaps? You're in Euclid now.)
So, having the shilling—having i' fact a lot—
And pence and halfpence, ever so many o' them,
I purchased, as I think I said before,
The pebble (*lapis, lapidis, -di, -dem, -de*—

What nouns 'crease short i' the genitive, Fatchaps, eh?)
O' the boy, a bare-legg'd beggarly son of a gun,
For one-and-fourpence. Here we are again.

．　．　．

Where was I with my trope 'bout one in a quag?[11]
I did once hitch the syntax into verse: 60
Verbum personale, a verb personal,
Concordat—ay, "agrees," old Fatchaps—*cum Nominativo,* with its nominative,
Genere, i' point o' gender, *numero,*
O' number, *et persona,* and person. *Ut,*
Instance: *Sol ruit,* down flops sun, *et* and,
Montes umbrantur, out flounce mountains. Pah!
Excuse me, sir, I think I'm going mad.
You see the trick on't though, and can yourself
Continue the discourse *ad libitum.*[12] 70
It takes up about eighty thousand lines,
A thing imagination boggles at:
And might, odds-bobs, sir! in judicious hands,
Extend from here to Mesopotamy.

1872

Charles Lutwidge Dodgson (Lewis Carroll)
1832–1898

Charles Lutwidge Dodgson was the son of a clergyman in the Church of England who had himself won extraordinary academic honors as an undergraduate at Oxford and rose to become an archdeacon and then a canon in the church. Dodgson entered Oxford on a scholarship and graduated with honors in mathematics in 1855. For the rest of his life he remained in Oxford as a mathematical lecturer and tutor. In 1861 he was ordained as a deacon in the Church of England. But partly because of a stammer which made preaching difficult, he never took the next step of being fully ordained as a priest and he did not habitually perform the offices of a clergyman. His life was full of other interests and enterprises: the teaching of mathematics, on which he published papers and text-

[7] Iacobi Facciolati: an eighteenth-century Italian philologist.
[8] Galligaskins and antigropeloes: breeches and leggings.
[9] Ombrifuge: umbrella: a shelter from rain. The *OED* cites Calverley as the only source of this word in the nineteenth century.
[10] Porporate: clothed in purple.　[11] Quag: a marshy place.　[12] Ad libitum: at pleasure.

books during his mature life; the theater, to which he was addicted; photography, which he took up as a hobby in the 1850s and at which he became extraordinarily proficient; the invention of linguistic and logical games and puzzles, many of which he published; and, most important, the writing of comic and fantastic verse and prose, often to entertain the children with whom he made close friendships.

Dodgson began to publish comic poems, all of them in the then popular forms of parody and burlesque, in newspapers and London comic journals in the mid-1850s. It was to sign these latter publications that he adopted the name "Lewis Carroll," derived from his first two names. In 1865 he published Alice's Adventures in Wonderland, a greatly elaborated version of a story he had first told three years earlier to the children of one of his colleagues in Oxford. He published the sequel, Through the Looking-Glass, in 1872, and in 1876 he published The Hunting of the Snark, a strange and disquieting poem of over 500 lines about a quest that ends in personal extinction. In addition to his mathematical publications and essays and pamphlets describing puzzles and games, Dodgson published a collection of comic and earnest verse, Phantasmagoria, in 1869. He republished many of these poems in two later collections, one of his comic poems in 1883 and one of his sentimentally earnest poems in 1898. In his last two long books, Sylvie and Bruno (1889) and Sylvie and Bruno Concluded (1893), he tried without success to make again fictions in which familiar words, objects, poems, and attitudes slip or are driven from the security of their usual meanings, to reconstitute that mixture of irreason and tightly controlled language and literary form through which the Alice books especially make their unsettling and yet satisfying effects.

The Alice books were extremely popular in the nineteenth century. About 110,000 copies of Alice's Adventures in Wonderland, and 61,000 copies of its sequel, were published during Dodgson's lifetime. The poems especially were frequently themselves parodied and occasionally set to music. Dodgson's nephew, S. D. Collingwood, published The Life and Letters of Lewis Carroll in 1898. Derek Hudson's Lewis Carroll (1954) is the best recent biography; Roger Lancelyn Green published The Diaries of Lewis Carroll in 1953. Elizabeth Sewell's The Field of Nonsense (1952) is the most intelligent of many studies of Dodgson's nonsense writing. Kathleen Blake in Play, Games, and Sport: The Literary Works of Lewis Carroll (1974) studies his comic writing in the light of nineteenth- and

twentieth-century ideas about play and games. The texts printed here are those of Rhyme? and Reason?, a collection of his verse Dodgson published in 1883, and of corrected editions of the two Alice books he prepared in 1897. The most convenient (although incomplete) collection of his comic writing is The Complete Works of Lewis Carroll (1939), printed in England as the Nonesuch edition and in the United States as the Modern Library edition.

from The Three Voices[1]

The Third Voice

Not long this transport held its place:
Within a little moment's space
Quick tears were raining down his face.

His heart stood still, aghast with fear;
A wordless voice, nor far nor near,
He seemed to hear and not to hear.

"Tears kindle not the doubtful spark.
If so, why not? Of this remark
The bearings are profoundly dark."

"Her speech," he said, "hath caused this pain.   1
Easier I count it to explain
The jargon of the howling main,

"Or, stretched beside some babbling brook,
To con, with inexpressive look,
An unintelligible book."

Low spake the voice within his head,
In words imagined more than said,
Soundless as ghost's intended tread:

"If thou art duller than before,
Why quittedst thou the voice of lore?   2
Why not endure, expecting more?"

"Rather than that," he groaned aghast,
"I'd writhe in depths of cavern vast,
Some loathly vampire's rich repast."

---

[1] A parody of Tennyson's "The Two Voices" (1842), a poem about a man torn between religious faith and doubt. Tennyson's poem ends in scenes of domestic harmony and natural bounty which resolve his doubt. The poem was printed in a magazine Dodgson wrote for his family, and then in 1856 in a comic monthly published in London.

" 'Twere hard," it answered, "themes immense
To coop within the narrow fence
That rings *thy* scant intelligence."

"Not so," he urged, "nor once alone:
But there was something in her tone
30　That chilled me to the very bone.

"Her style was anything but clear,
And most unpleasantly severe;
Her epithets were very queer.

"And yet, so grand were her replies,
I could not choose but deem her wise;
I did not dare to criticise;

"Nor did I leave her, till she went
So deep in tangled argument
That all my powers of thought were spent."

40　A little whisper inly slid,
"Yet truth is truth: you know you did."
A little wink beneath the lid.

And, sickened with excess of dread,
Prone to the dust he bent his head,
And lay like one three-quarters dead.

The whisper left him—like a breeze
Lost in the depths of leafy trees—
Left him by no means at his ease.

Once more he weltered in despair,
50　With hands, through denser-matted hair,
More tightly clenched than then they were.

When, bathed in Dawn of living red,
Majestic frowned the mountain head,
"Tell me my fault," was all he said.

When, at high Noon, the blazing sky
Scorched in his head each haggard eye,
Then keenest rose his weary cry.

And when at Eve the unpitying sun
Smiled grimly on the solemn fun,
60　"Alack," he sighed, "what *have* I done?"

But saddest, darkest was the sight,
When the cold grasp of leaden Night
Dashed him to earth, and held him tight.

Tortured, unaided, and alone,
Thunders were silence to his groan,
Bagpipes sweet music to its tone:

"What? Ever thus, in dismal round,
Shall Pain and Mystery profound
Pursue me like a sleepless hound,

"With crimson-dashed and eager jaws,　70
Me, still in ignorance of the cause,
Unknowing what I broke of laws?"

The whisper to his ear did seem
Like echoed flow of silent stream,
Or shadow of forgotten dream,

The whisper trembling in the wind:
"Her fate with thine was intertwined,"
So spake it in his inner mind:

"Each orbed on each a baleful star:
Each proved the other's blight and bar:　80
Each unto each were best, most far:

"Yea, each to each was worse than foe:
Thou, a scared dullard, gibbering low,
AND SHE, AN AVALANCHE OF WOE!"

1856; 1869

from Alice's Adventures in Wonderland

The Mock Turtle's Song

[Early Version][1]
Beneath the waters of the sea
Are lobsters thick as thick can be—
They love to dance with you and me,
　My own, my gentle Salmon!

Chorus
Salmon come up! Salmon go down!
Salmon come twist your tail around!

[1] From *Alice's Adventures Under Ground,* a manuscript version of the story which Dodgson prepared in 1862–63. The manuscript was published in facsimile in 1886. This poem is a parody of a popular minstrel song, "Sally Come Up."

Of all the fishes of the sea
    There's none so good as Salmon!
                    (1862–63)

The Mock Turtle's Song

[*Later Version*][1]

"Will you walk a little faster?" said a whiting[2]
    to a snail.
"There's a porpoise close behind us, and he's
    treading on my tail.
See how eagerly the lobsters and the turtles all
    advance!
They are waiting on the shingle[3]—will you
    come and join the dance?
    Will you, wo'n't you, will you, wo'n't you,
      will you join the dance?
    Will you, wo'n't you, will you, wo'n't you,
      wo'n't you join the dance?

"You can really have no notion how delightful
    it will be,
When they take us up and throw us, with the
    lobsters, out to sea!"
But the snail replied "Too far, too far!" and
    gave a look askance—
Said he thanked the whiting kindly, but he
    would not join the dance.
    Would not, could not, would not, could not,
      would not join the dance.
    Would not, could not, would not, could not,
      could not join the dance.

"What matters it how far we go?" his scaly
    friend replied.
"There is another shore, you know, upon the
    other side.
The further off from England the nearer is to
    France—
Then turn not pale, beloved snail, but come
    and join the dance.
    Will you, wo'n't you, will you, wo'n't you,
      wo'n't you join the dance?
    Will you, wo'n't you, will you, wo'n't you,
      wo'n't you join the dance?
                  1865

from Through the Looking-Glass

Dodgson published an early version of "Jabberwocky" in a magazine he prepared for his family in 1855; it is reprinted in The Rectory Umbrella and Mischmasch, *edited by Florence Milner (1932). The original title of the poem was "Stanza of Anglo-Saxon Poetry." Dodgson also included a mock gloss of the vocabulary of the poem in this first version, and he later incorporated the gloss into Humpty Dumpty's explanation of the poem:*

"'Brillig' means four o'clock in the afternoon—the time when you begin broiling things for dinner."

"That'll do very well," said Alice: "and 'slithy'?"

"Well, 'slithy' means 'lithe and slimy.' 'Lithe' is the same as 'active.' You see it's like a portmanteau—there are two meanings packed up into one word."

"I see it now," Alice remarked thoughtfully: "and what are 'toves'?"

"Well, 'toves' are something like badgers—they're something like lizards—and they're something like corkscrews."

"They must be very curious-looking creatures."

"They are that," said Humpty Dumpty: "also they make their nests under sun-dials—also they live on cheese."

"And what's to 'gyre' and to 'gimble'?"

"To 'gyre' is to go round and round like a gyroscope. To 'gimble' is to make holes like a gimblet."

"And 'the wabe' is the grass-plot round a sundial, I suppose?" said Alice, surprised at her own ingenuity.

"Of course it is. It's called 'wabe,' you know, because it goes a long way before it, and a long way behind it——"

"And a long way beyond it on each side," Alice added.

"Exactly so. Well then, 'mimsy' is 'flimsy and miserable' (there's another portmanteau for you). And a 'borogove' is a thin shabby-looking bird with its feathers sticking out all round—something like a live mop."

"And then 'mome raths'?" said Alice. "I'm afraid I'm giving you a great deal of trouble."

"Well, a 'rath' is a sort of green pig: but 'mome' I'm not certain about. I think it's short for 'from

---

[1] The poem is a parody of "The Spider and the Fly" (1834), by Mary Howitt (1799–1888), a writer of children's books. In Howitt's poem the fly is enticed into the spider's parlor and devoured.
[2] Whiting: a common food fish.
[3] Shingle: beach.

10

home'—meaning that they'd lost their way, you know."

"And what does 'outgrabe' mean?"

"Well, 'outgribing' is something between bellowing and whistling, with a kind of sneeze in the middle: however, you'll hear it done, maybe—down in the wood yonder—and, when you've once heard it you'll be quite *content." (Chapter 6)*

Jabberwocky

'Twas brillig, and the slithy toves
    Did gyre and gimble in the wabe;
All mimsy were the borogoves,
    And the mome raths outgrabe.

"Beware the Jabberwock, my son!
    The jaws that bite, the claws that catch!
Beware the Jubjub bird, and shun
    The frumious Bandersnatch!"

He took his vorpal sword in hand:
    Long time the manxome foe he sought—
So rested he by the Tumtum tree,
    And stood awhile in thought.

And as in uffish thought he stood,
    The Jabberwock, with eyes of flame,
Came whiffling through the tulgey wood,
    And burbled as it came!

One, two! One, two! And through and through
    The vorpal blade went snicker-snack!
He left it dead, and with its head
    He went galumphing back.

"And hast thou slain the Jabberwock?
    Come to my arms, my beamish boy!
O frabjous day! Callooh! Callay!"
    He chortled in his joy.

'Twas brillig, and the slithy toves
    Did gyre and gimble in the wabe;
All mimsy were the borogoves,
    And the mome raths outgrabe.

1872

The White Knight's Ballad[1]

I'll tell thee everything I can;
    There's little to relate.

I saw an aged aged man,
    A-sitting on a gate.
"Who are you, aged man?" I said.
    "And how is it you live?"
And his answer trickled through my head
    Like water through a sieve.

He said "I look for butterflies
    That sleep among the wheat: 10
I make them into mutton-pies,
    And sell them in the street.
I sell them unto men," he said,
    "Who sail on stormy seas;
And that's the way I get my bread—
    A trifle, if you please."

But I was thinking of a plan
    To dye one's whiskers green,
And always use so large a fan
    That they could not be seen.   20
So, having no reply to give
    To what the old man said,
I cried "Come, tell me how you live!"
    And thumped him on the head.

His accents mild took up the tale:
    He said "I go my ways,
And when I find a mountain-rill,
    I set it in a blaze;
And thence they make a stuff they call
    Rowland's Macassar Oil[2]—   30
Yet twopence-halfpenny is all
    They give me for my toil."

But I was thinking of a way
    To feed oneself on batter,
And so go on from day to day
    Getting a little fatter.
I shook him well from side to side,
    Until his face was blue:
"Come, tell me how you live," I cried
    "And what it is you do!"   40

He said "I hunt for haddocks' eyes
    Among the heather bright,
And work them into waistcoat-buttons
    In the silent night.
And these I do not sell for gold
    Or coin of silvery shine,

---

[1] This poem is a burlesque of Wordsworth's "Resolution and Independence" (1807), in which a man is relieved of his sadness by a conversation with a resolute and resourceful old man. The form of the poem, however, parodies "My Heart and Lute," a poem by Thomas Moore (1779–1852).

[2] Rowland's Macassar Oil: a widely advertised hair dressing.

But for a copper halfpenny,
   And that will purchase nine.

"I sometimes dig for buttered rolls,
50   Or set limed twigs[3] for crabs;
I sometimes search the grassy knolls
   For wheels of Hansom-cabs.[4]
And that's the way" (he gave a wink)
   "By which I get my wealth—
And very gladly will I drink
   Your Honour's noble health."

I heard him then, for I had just
   Completed my design
To keep the Menai bridge[5] from rust
60   By boiling it in wine.
I thanked him much for telling me
   The way he got his wealth,
But chiefly for his wish that he
   Might drink my noble health.

And now, if e'er by chance I put
   My fingers into glue,
Or madly squeeze a right-hand foot
   Into a left-hand shoe,

Or if I drop upon my toe
   A very heavy weight,   70
I weep, for it reminds me so
Of that old man I used to know—
Whose look was mild, whose speech was slow,
Whose hair was whiter than the snow,
Whose face was very like a crow,
With eyes, like cinders, all aglow,
Who seemed distracted with his woe,
Who rocked his body to and fro,
And muttered mumblingly and low,
As if his mouth were full of dough,   80
Who snorted like a buffalo—
That summer evening long ago
   A-sitting on a gate.

                   1872

"Yet what are all such gaities to me"[1]

Yet what are all such gaieties to me
   Whose thoughts are full of indices and surds?

$$x^2 + 7x + 53 = \frac{11}{3}.$$

                   1869

William Schwenck Gilbert
1836–1911

William Schwenck Gilbert was educated at London University, studied law and was called to the bar in London. At about the same time that he committed himself to the study and practice of law he began to contribute poems and illustrations to Fun, *one of the most successful of the many comic weeklies engendered by the success of* Punch *early in the Victorian period. In 1865 he began to publish in both* Fun *and* Punch *a series of ballads, signed "Bab," which he also illustrated. He soon restricted the series to* Fun, *and he continued to publish ballads in the series regularly until 1871,*

by which time he had written more than 125 such poems. During the 1860s he had also been writing farces and burlesques for the stage, and in 1871 he collaborated for the first time with Arthur Sullivan and began the string of Savoy operas which were to be his principal work and achievement (see Part Eight).

A first series of Bab ballads was collected and published in 1868, a second series in 1871, and further selections in 1876, 1882, and 1898. The text printed is that of the 1898 edition, which has been generally adopted in James Ellis' useful edition of

[3] Limed twigs: twigs covered with bird lime, used to catch birds.
[4] Hansom-cab: a two-wheeled cab common as a means of hired transportation in London in the last half of the century.
[5] Menai Bridge: a suspension bridge in Wales.   [1] Published as a part of a rhymed riddle.

The Bab Ballads *(1970). The standard biography of Gilbert is that of Sidney Dark and Rowland Grey,* W. S. Gilbert: His Life and Letters *(1923). See also John Bush Jones,* W. S. Gilbert: A Century of Scholarship and Commentary *(1970).*

The Yarn of the *Nancy Bell*[1]

'Twas on the shores that round our coast
  From Deal to Ramsgate span,
That I found alone on a piece of stone
  An elderly naval man.

His hair was weedy, his beard was long,
  And weedy and long was he,
And I heard this wight on the shore recite,
  In a singular minor key:

"Oh, I am a cook and a captain bold,
  And the mate of the *Nancy* brig,
And a bo'sun tight, and a midshipmite,
  And the crew of the captain's gig."

And he shook his fists and he tore his hair,
  Till I really felt afraid,
For I couldn't help thinking the man had been
    drinking,
  And so I simply said:

"Oh, elderly man, it's little I know
  Of the duties of men of the sea,
But I'll eat my hand if I understand
  How you can possibly be

"At once a cook, and a captain bold,
  And the mate of the *Nancy* brig,
And a bo'sun tight, and a midshipmite,
  And the crew of the captain's gig."

Then he gave a hitch to his trousers, which
  Is a trick all seamen larn,
And having got rid of a thumping quid,
  He spun this painful yarn:

" 'Twas in the good ship *Nancy Bell*
  That we sailed to the Indian sea,
And there on a reef we come to grief,
  Which has often occurred to me.

"And pretty nigh all o' the crew was drowned
  (There was seventy-seven o' soul),

And only ten of the *Nancy's* men
  Said 'Here!' to the muster-roll.

"There was me and the cook and the captain
    bold,
  And the mate of the *Nancy* brig,
And the bo'sun tight, and a midshipmite,
  And the crew of the captain's gig.   40

"For a month we'd neither wittles nor drink,
  Till a-hungry we did feel,
So we drawed a lot, and accordin' shot
  The captain for our meal.

"The next lot fell to the *Nancy's* mate,
  And a delicate dish he made;
Then our appetite with the midshipmite
  We seven survivors stayed.

"And then we murdered the bo'sun tight,
  And he much resembled pig;   50
Then we wittled free, did the cook and me,
  On the crew of the captain's gig.

"Then only the cook and me was left,
  And the delicate question, 'Which
Of us two goes to the kettle?' arose,
  And we argued it out as sich.

"For I loved that cook as a brother, I did,
  And the cook he worshipped me;
But we'd both be blowed if we'd either be
    stowed
  In the other chap's hold, you see.   60

" 'I'll be eat if you dines off me,' says TOM,
  'Yes, that,' says I, 'you'll be,'—
'I'm boiled if I die, my friend,' quoth I,
  And 'Exactly so,' quoth he.

"Says he, 'Dear JAMES, to murder me
  Were a foolish thing to do,
For don't you see that you can't cook *me*,
  While I can—and will—cook *you!*'

"So he boils the water, and takes the salt
  And the pepper in portions true   70
(Which he never forgot), and some chopped
    shalot,
  And some sage and parsley too.

---

[1] Gilbert first submitted this poem to *Punch,* whose editor refused it because of its subject. The situation of the poem burlesques that of Samuel Taylor Coleridge's "The Rime of the Ancient Mariner" (1798).

" 'Come here,' says he, with a proper pride,
  Which his smiling features tell,
' 'Twill soothing be if I let you see
  How extremely nice you'll smell.'

"And he stirred it round and round and round,
  And he sniffed at the foaming froth;
When I ups with his heels, and smothers his
      squeals
80   In the scum of the boiling broth.

"And I eat that cook in a week or less,
  And—as I eating be
The last of his chops, why, I almost drops,
  For a wessel in sight I see!

                *   *   *   *²

"And I never grieve, and I never smile,
  And I never larf nor play,
But I sit and croak, and a single joke
  I have—which is to say:

"Oh, I am a cook and a captain bold,
90   And the mate of the *Nancy* brig,
And a bo'sun tight, and a midshipmite,
  And the crew of the captain's gig!"
                                          1866

Ben Allah Achmet

Or, The Fatal Tum

I once did know a Turkish man
  Whom I upon a two-pair-back met,
His name it was EFFENDI KHAN
  BACKSHEESH PASHA BEN ALLAH ACHMET.

A DOCTOR BROWN I also knew—
  I've often eaten of his bounty;
The Turk and he they lived at Hooe,
  In Sussex, that delightful county!

I knew a nice young lady there,
10   Her name was EMILY MACPHERSON,
And though she wore another's hair,
  She was an interesting person.

The Turk adored the maid of Hooe
  (Although his harem would have shocked
      her).

But BROWN adored that maiden too:
  He was a most seductive doctor.

They'd follow her where'er she'd go—
  A course of action most improper;
She neither knew by sight, and so
  For neither of them cared a copper.   20

BROWN did not know that Turkish male,
  He might have been his sainted mother:
The people in this simple tale
  Are total strangers to each other.

One day that Turk he sickened sore,
  And suffered agonies oppressive;
He threw himself upon the floor
  And rolled about in pain excessive.

It made him moan, it made him groan,
  And almost wore him to a mummy.   30
Why should I hesitate to own
  That pain was in his little tummy?¹

At length a doctor came, and rung
  (As ALLAH ACHMET had desired),
Who felt his pulse, looked up his tongue,
  And hemmed and hawed, and then inquired:

"Where is the pain that long has preyed
  Upon you in so sad a way, sir?"
The Turk he giggled, blushed, and said:
  "I don't exactly like to say, sir."   40

"Come, nonsense!" said good DOCTOR BROWN.
  "So this is Turkish coyness, is it?
You must contrive to fight it down—
  Come, come, sir, please to be explicit."

The Turk he shyly bit his thumb,
  And coyly blushed like one half-witted,
"The pain is in my little tum,"
  He, whispering, at length admitted.

"Then take you this, and take you that—
  Your blood flows sluggish in its channel—   50
You must get rid of all this fat,
  And wear my medicated flannel.

"You'll send for me when you're in need—
  My name is BROWN—your life I've saved it."

---

² Ellipsis in original.
¹ Tummy: Gilbert was apparently the first writer to use this word in print.

"My rival!" shrieked the invalid,
    And drew a mighty sword and waved it:

"This to thy weazand,[2] Christian pest!"
    Aloud the Turk in frenzy yelled it,
And drove right through the doctor's chest
60   The sabre and the hand that held it.

The blow was a decisive one,
    And DOCTOR BROWN grew deadly pasty.
"Now see the mischief that you've done—
    You Turks are so extremely hasty.

"There are two DOCTOR BROWNS in Hooe—
    He's short and stout, *I'm* tall and wizen;
You've been and run the wrong one through,
    That's how the error has arisen."

The accident was thus explained,
70   Apologies were only heard now:
"At my mistake I'm really pained—
    I am, indeed—upon my word now.

"With me, sir, you shall be interred,
    A mausoleum grand awaits me."
"Oh, pray don't say another word,
    I'm sure that more than compensates me.

"But p'raps, kind Turk, you're full inside?"[3]
    "There's room," said he, "for any number."
And so they laid them down and died.
80   In proud Stamboul they sleep their slumber.
                      1867

The Rival Curates[1]

List while the poet trolls
    Of MR. CLAYTON HOOPER,
Who had a cure of souls
    At Spiffton-extra-Sooper.

He lived on curds and whey,
    And daily sang their praises,
And then he'd go and play
    With buttercups and daisies.

Wild croquet HOOPER banned,
    And all the sports of Mammon,   10
He warred with cribbage, and
    He exorcised backgammon.

His helmet was a glance
    That spoke of holy gladness;
A saintly smile his lance,
    His shield a tear of sadness.[2]

His Vicar smiled to see
    This armour on him buckled;
With pardonable glee
    He blessed himself and chuckled: 20

"In mildness to abound
    My curate's sole design is,
In all the country round
    There's none so mild as mine is!"

And HOOPER, disinclined
    His trumpet to be blowing,
Yet didn't think you'd find
    A milder curate going.

A friend arrived one day
    At Spiffton-extra-Sooper,   30
And in this shameful way
    He spoke to MR. HOOPER:

"You think your famous name
    For mildness can't be shaken,
That none can blot your fame—
    But, HOOPER, you're mistaken!

"Your mind is not as blank
    As that of HOPLEY PORTER,
Who holds a curate's rank
    At Assesmilk-cum-Worter.   40

"*He* plays the airy flute,
    And looks depressed and blighted,
Doves round about him 'toot,'
    And lambkins dance delighted.

"*He* labours more than you
    At worsted work, and frames it;

---

[2] Weazand: windpipe or throat.

[3] Full inside: the conventional cry of an omnibus driver when all inside seats are taken.

[1] Gilbert used the situation of this poem as the plot of *Patience*, which he wrote to Sullivan's music in 1881. The rivals in the Savoy Opera are poets rather than curates. In the Church of England clerical livings are in the award of the state or landowners. A curate is a clergyman who assists or serves in the place of the person to whom the living is awarded.

[2] "Wherefore take unto you the whole armour of God. . . . Above all, taking the shield of faith, . . . and the helmet of salvation, and the sword of the Spirit, which is the word of God." (Ephesians 6: 13–17)

In old maids' albums, too,
    Sticks seaweed—yes, and names it!"

The tempter said his say,
50   Which pierced him like a needle—
He summoned straight away
    His sexton and his beadle.

These men were men who could
    Hold liberal opinions:
On Sundays they were good—
    On week-days they were minions.

"To HOPLEY PORTER go,
    Your fare I will afford you—
Deal him a deadly blow,
60   And blessings shall reward you.

"But stay—I do not like
    Undue assassination,
And so, before you strike,
    Make this communication:

"I'll give him this one chance—
    If he'll more gaily bear him,
Play croquêt, smoke, and dance,
    I willingly will spare him."

They went, those minions true,
70   To Assesmilk-cum-Worter,
And told their errand to
    The REVEREND HOPLEY PORTER.

"What?" said that reverend gent,
    "Dance through my hours of leisure?
Smoke?—bathe myself with scent?—
    Play croquêt? Oh, with pleasure!

"Wear all my hair in curl?
    Stand at my door, and wink—so—
At every passing girl?
80   My brothers, I should think so!

"For years I've longed for some
    Excuse for this revulsion:
Now that excuse has come—
    I do it on compulsion!!!"

He smoked and winked away—
    This REVEREND HOPLEY PORTER—

The deuce there was to pay
    At Assesmilk-cum-Worter.

And HOOPER holds his ground,
    In mildness daily growing—   90
They think him, all around,
    The mildest curate going.

                                                        1867

Etiquette

The Ballyshannon foundered off the coast of
    Cariboo,
And down in fathoms many went the captain
    and the crew;
Down went the owners—greedy men whom
    hope of gain allured:
Oh, dry the starting tear, for they were heavily
    insured.

Besides the captain and the mate, the owners
    and the crew,
The passengers were also drowned, excepting
    only two:
Young PETER GRAY, who tasted teas for BAKER,
    CROOP, AND CO.,
And SOMERS, who from Eastern shores imported
    indigo.

These passengers, by reason of their clinging
    to a mast,
Upon a desert island were eventually cast.   10
They hunted for their meals, as ALEXANDER
    SELKIRK[1] used,
But they couldn't chat together—they had not
    been introduced.

For PETER GRAY, and SOMERS too, though
    certainly in trade,
Were properly particular about the friends
    they made;
And somehow thus they settled it without a
    word of mouth—
That GRAY should take the northern half,
    while SOMERS took the south.

On PETER's portion oysters grew—a delicacy
    rare,

---

[1] Alexander Selkirk: a sailor who was marooned in 1704 at his own request on a deserted
island, where he lived for over four years. His adventures are suggested as one of the sources
for Daniel Defoe's *Robinson Crusoe* (1719–20).

But oysters were a delicacy PETER couldn't
   bear.
On SOMERS' side was turtle, on the shingle[2]
   lying thick,
Which SOMERS couldn't eat, because it always
20   made him sick.

GRAY gnashed his teeth with envy as he saw a
   mighty store
Of turtle unmolested on his fellow-creature's
   shore:
The oysters at his feet aside impatiently he
   shoved,
For turtle and his mother were the only things
   he loved.

And SOMERS sighed in sorrow as he settled in
   the south,
For the thought of PETER's oysters brought the
   water to his mouth.
He longed to lay him down upon the shelly
   bed, and stuff:
He had often eaten oysters, but had never had
   enough.

How they wished an introduction to each other
   they had had
When on board *The Ballyshannon!* And it
30   drove them nearly mad
To think how very friendly with each other
   they might get,
If it wasn't for the arbitrary rule of etiquette!

One day, when out a-hunting for the *mus
   ridiculus,*[3]
GRAY overheard his fellow-man soliloquising
   thus:
"I wonder how the playmates of my youth are
   getting on,
McCONNELL, S. B. WALTERS, PADDY BYLES, and
   ROBINSON?"

These simple words made PETER as delighted
   as could be,
Old chummies at the Charterhouse[4] were
   ROBINSON and he!
He walked straight up to SOMERS, then he
   turned extremely red,
Hesitated, hummed and hawed a bit, then
40   cleared his throat, and said:

"I beg your pardon—pray forgive me if I
   seem too bold,
But you have breathed a name I knew
   familiarly of old.
You spoke aloud of ROBINSON—I happened to
   be by—
You know him?" "Yes, extremely well." "Allow
   me—so do I!"

It was enough: they felt they could more
   sociably get on,
For (ah, the magic of the fact!) they each
   knew ROBINSON!
And Mr. SOMERS' turtle was at PETER's service
   quite,
And Mr. SOMERS punished PETER's oyster-beds
   all night.

They soon became like brothers from
   community of wrongs:
They wrote each other little odes and sang
   each other songs;
They told each other anecdotes disparaging
   their wives;   50
On several occasions, too, they saved each
   other's lives.

They felt quite melancholy when they parted
   for the night,
And got up in the morning soon as ever it was
   light;
Each other's pleasant company they reckoned
   so upon,
And all because it happened that they both
   knew ROBINSON!

They lived for many years on that inhospitable
   shore,
And day by day they learned to love each
   other more and more.
At last, to their astonishment, on getting up
   one day,
They saw a vessel anchored in the offing of the
   bay!   60

To PETER an idea occurred. "Suppose we cross
   the main?
So good an opportunity may not occur again."
And SOMERS thought a minute, then ejaculated,
   "Done!

---

[2] Shingle: beach.
[3] *Mus ridiculus:* trifling mouse: part of a line from the first-century Roman poet Horace
which in its entirety mocks pretension by observing that mountains labor to bring forth a
mouse.
[4] Charterhouse: a school in London.

I wonder how my business in the City's[5]
   getting on?"

"But stay," said MR. PETER: "when in England,
   as you know,
I earned a living tasting teas for BAKER, CROOP,
   AND CO.,
I may be superseded—my employers think me
   dead!"
"Then come with me," said SOMERS, "and
   taste indigo instead."

But all their plans were scattered in a moment
   when they found
70 The vessel was a convict ship from Portland,[6]
   outward bound!
When a boat came off to fetch them, though
   they felt it very kind,
To go on board they firmly but respectfully
   declined.

As both the happy settlers roared with laughter
   at the joke,
They recognised an unattractive fellow pulling
   stroke:
'Twas ROBINSON—a convict, in an unbecoming
   frock!
Condemned to seven years for misappropriat-
   ing stock!!!

They laughed no more, for SOMERS thought he
   had been rather rash
In knowing one whose friend had misappropri-
   ated cash;
And PETER thought a foolish tack he must have
   gone upon
In making the acquaintance of a friend of
   ROBINSON.   80

At first they didn't quarrel very openly, I've
   heard;
They nodded when they met, and now and
   then exchanged a word:
The word grew rare, and rarer still the nodding
   of the head,
And when they meet each other now, they cut
   each other dead.

To allocate the island they agreed by word of
   mouth,
And PETER takes the north again, and SOMERS
   takes the south;
And PETER has the oysters, which he loathes
   with horror grim,
And SOMERS has the turtle—turtle disagrees
   with him.

                              1869

By the Staff of

Beeton's Christmas Annual

from The Coming K———

    The Coming K——— *was published in 1872 as
the first of a series of comic, sometimes scurrilous
attacks on the hedonistic habits of the Prince of
Wales (the Coming King), members of his circle,
and other wealthy Englishmen indifferent to social
and ethical responsibilities. The publisher of the
series was Samuel Orchart Beeton (1831–77), an*

*enterprising London publisher who had been the
first to publish Harriet Beecher Stowe's* Uncle
Tom's Cabin *in England and whose wife was the
compiler of a widely used cookbook,* The Book of
Household Management *(1861). Beeton had been
publishing a series of Christmas annuals, collections
of seasonally entertaining verse, fiction, and il-
lustrations. In 1872 he converted the series to the
political and social commentary of* The Coming
K———, *and continued the attack in seven other*

---

[5] City: the name of the London financial district.
[6] Portland: the site of a prison on the southern coast of England.

similar annuals. The tone of these attacks was shrill and intended to shock. But despite occasional invocations of the threat of a revolution which would abolish the monarchy, the burden was finally that the Prince should put away his wasteful habits and companions and come forth as an example of the sober, manly rectitude which was really fundamental to him and to England.

The annuals were probably written by several persons in Beeton's employ. Most of them are loose burlesques in the topical, punning style then current on the comic stage. The Coming K—— is a direct parody of Tennyson's The Idylls of the King, which Tennyson began to publish in 1859. This parody remained popular throughout the 1870s; in 1877, when the series ended, Beeton was still advertising copies of The Coming K——, some of them bound to match the binding of Tennyson's Idylls.

In this episode, one of eight in the parody, Sir Loosealot spends the night under the roof of Brown, a socially ambitious merchant whose daughter is the fair Delaine. Loosealot is on his way to a shooting match on the estate of Guelpho, the heir to the throne, and he agrees to take Delaine's brother Sam with him to witness the match.

And Sam he looked again, and Sam he saw
It was a rare and noble company;
For half *Debrett*[1] was there. You could have made
A quorum of the Lower House; and Peers
Were thick as pink-tipped daisies in the grass;
Lords jostled Dukes; and Dukes on Barons trod;
And German Princes mustered in great force.
Moreover, 'neath a tent pitched in the shade,
Sam, warned by Loosealot, saw the coming K——,   10
In suit complete of Shetland homespun robed.
His open face, his laughing, bright blue eye
Told of no trouble, no official care;
But loud he laughed him with his fav'rite Knight,
What time he sucked a cobbler[2] through a straw,
Nor thought he of the coming conflict dread.
"There," said great Loosealot to his young friend,

"There is our chief, there is the Coming K——,
The worthy leader of our every game.
He sets our fashions. He a brother has
Who has invented for us a new drink.   20
He has a lion heart; he has no fear
When Knight meets dove, and comes the pull of string;
The pull's for us, you see, and not for them.
He knocks the billiard balls about unmoved,
And watches polo with a calm, brave face;
His courage such, it carries him well through
The thickest mazes of a crowded ball;
He sits out plays with unmatched hardihood;
He dines with valour full of fearlessness;
He lays large sums, and numberless first stones,[3]   30
(Though he throws none) with mason's skill and trowel.
He is indeed a pattern knight to us.
There is the man." And young Brown gazed upon him
As on a thing miraculous. But, anon,
A gun was fired, and then did either side—
They that assail'd and they that were attack'd—
Prepare the war. The pigeons in their traps;
The Knights about a post, with guns in hand.
A serving-man, in velveteen arrayed,
With many strings his fingers twisted round,   40
Pulls one. A trap is opened, and flies out
A pigeon, yearning, straining to be free.
Skyward it mounts, as though to plead its cause
At heaven's gate. Such orisons are naught.
A Knight is at the firing peg; the stock
Is at his shoulder. Suddenly he fires:
There is a flash, a crack; the hard earth shakes,
And falls the dove down dead—a mangled mass.
So is the Tournament commenced, and so
It does go on, with variation small.   50
Sometimes the bird is missed, sometimes so hit
That it just gets away to linger on
A few sharp hours of pain amongst the ferns.
And all the while the swell of music sounds,
And dresses *frou-frou,* and the ladies talk,
And ices pass around, and beauty smiles
Upon the *pigeontry* of Guelpho's Knights.

1872

---

[1] *Debrett:* one of the sources of information about members of the peerage and others who held aristocratic titles.

[2] Cobbler: an American word for a drink made of wine, sugar, and lemon.

[3] First stones: the ceremonial laying of foundation stones.

J. K. Stephen
1859–1892

*James Kenneth Stephen was elected to a fellowship in a Cambridge college after his graduation in 1882, served as a tutor to one of the members of the royal family, and entered the practice of law in London in 1885. He wrote for newspapers and edited a magazine in London before he returned to Cambridge as a tutor. He published studies in international law as well as two books of parodies and light verse—*Lapsus Calami *and* Quo Musa Tendis?—*both in 1891. The texts printed below are those of the original edition of* Lapsus Calami.

To R. K.[1]

*As long as I dwell on some
    stupendous
And tremendous (Heaven defend
    us!)
Monstr'-inform-ingens-
    Horrendous
Demoniaco-seraphic
Penman's latest piece of graphic.*
    —BROWNING ["Waring"]

Will there never come a season
  Which shall rid us from the curse
Of a prose which knows no reason
  And an unmelodious verse:
When the world shall cease to wonder
  At the genius of an Ass,
And a boy's eccentric blunder
  Shall not bring success to pass:

When mankind shall be delivered
  From the clash of magazines,
And the inkstand shall be shivered
  Into countless smithereens:
When there stands a muzzled stripling,
  Mute, beside a muzzled bore:

10

When the Rudyards cease from kipling
  And the Haggards Ride no more.[2]

1891

The Ballade of the Incompetent Ballade-Monger

I am not ambitious at all:
  I am not a poet, I know
(Though I do love to see a mere scrawl
  To order and symmetry grow).
  My muse is uncertain and slow,
I am not expert with my tools.
  I lack the poetic *argot:*
But I hope I have kept to the rules.[1]

When your brain is undoubtedly small,
  'Tis hard, sir, to write in a row,
Some five or six rhymes to Nepaul,
  And more than a dozen to Joe:
  And metre is easier though,
Three rhymes are sufficient for "ghouls,"
  My lines are deficient in go,
But I hope I have kept to the rules.

10

Unable to fly let me crawl,
  Your patronage kindly bestow:
I am not the author of Saul,[2]
  I am not Voltaire or Rousseau:
  I am not desirous, oh no!
To rise from the ranks of the fools,
  To shine with Gosse, Dobson, and Co.:[3]
But I hope I have kept to the rules.

20

Dear Sir, though my language is low,
  Let me dip in Pierian[4] pools:
My verses are only so so,
  But I hope I have kept to the rules.

1891

---

[1] Rudyard Kipling.

[2] Rider Haggard (1856–1925) was an author of popular books of adventure, including *King Solomon's Mines* (1885) and *She* (1887).

[1] The rules of a ballade require three stanzas of eight lines each, and a four-line envoy, each ending in the same refrain and all of them using only three rhymes. No rhyme word may be repeated.

[2] Browning.

[3] Edmund Gosse (1849–1928) and Austin Dobson (1840–1921) wrote frequently in the forms of ballade, rondeau, and other technically demanding French forms.

[4] Pierian: a conventional reference to an area sacred to the muses of classical mythology.

PART EIGHT

Songs

Street Ballads and Broadsides, Stage and Parlor Songs, Political Songs

T HE PRINCIPAL settings of the performance of Victorian songs were the streets, in which broadsheet ballads were sung and sold; the stages of theaters, night houses, and music halls, from which popular songs often moved into the repertories of street singers and amateurs who played and sang to please themselves and their friends; and the parlors and recital rooms in which relatively refined, often sentimental songs were sung and listened to. The oldest of these modes of performance was that of the street ballad, and it did not survive the century. Throughout the first half of the nineteenth century, broadsheet ballads and other forms of street literature were very popular. One late-nineteenth-century collector assembled about 12,000 titles, most of them published in the nineteenth century, and the most successful publisher of street ballads, James Catnach, claimed to have sold two and a half million copies of the ballads he published on the occasion of two executions for murder in the 1820s and 1830s. But after mid-century the broadsheet ballad gradually yielded to cheap newspapers and magazines, and by the end of the century it was no longer a significant form of popular entertainment.

The traditions of the street ballad were those of print, as opposed to the oral traditions of the ballads that were still sung and sometimes composed in the countryside. Chapbooks, closely printed 24-page pamphlets usually containing prose narratives, and broadsheets, single large sheets printed on one side with a story or topical commentary, often in verse, had been sold in Great Britain since the sixteenth century. At the beginning of the nineteenth century a trade in the printing and distribution of street ballads was well established. The most famous printers—James Catnach (1792–1841) and John Pitts (1765–1844), for example—were in London, but other cities in England, Scotland, and Ireland had their counterparts. The ballads usually sold for a penny. Each was illustrated with a woodcut which almost always had been used often before to decorate a ballad on a similar topic. The sheet contained no music, but the tune to which the ballad was to be sung was often named. Peddlers took strings of ballads into the countryside. In the pubs and streets of the cities ballad-mongers often put on a show, introducing the ballads with a patter and then singing them as a way of advertising them. The topics of the ballads were those of newspapers: the births, marriages, and deaths of royal and other national personages; great battles; current political disputes; and, above all, murders and executions. Their fundamental audience was poor and working-class, people who could not afford newspapers (which until mid-century cost six and seven times as much). The audience was not necessarily literate, although it is likely that most purchasers of a street ballad bought it because they wanted to read it. Finally, the audience was predominantly urban, and the topics and tones of most nineteenth-century street ballads—their sometimes wry, sometimes pious (but not sectarian), sometimes angry responses to the durable realities of work, poverty, domesticity, political impotence, and death—are those of people who were learning and saying how to live in an increasingly urban and industrialized culture.

Songs had also been sung in the theater since the sixteenth century, and to that tradition nineteenth-century performers added songs that were first sung on the stages of night houses and clubs, minstrel shows, and, most important, music halls. Until 1843 the performance of drama was restricted by law to a few "patent" theaters. The law was circumvented in other theaters by the presentation of plays which included music and dance. Even after the law was rescinded, a sturdy theatrical tradition continued to flourish in which burlesques, farces, pantomimes, melodramas, and operas were either interspersed with songs or sometimes carried by their music, as were the operas (really more like operetta or musical comedy) produced by Alfred Bunn in the 1840s and the Savoy Operas of Gilbert and Sullivan in the 1870s and 1880s. In the early Victorian decades popular songs also began to come from other kinds of stage. Performers in London night houses and in the working-class clubs in northern cities—W. G. Ross, for example, and George Ridley—made themselves at least locally famous by their singing of songs they took from the theater, the stock of traditional ballads, or wrote themselves. These songs often were sung and sold on the streets, and some of them, especially those sung by London performers, were also published in the sheet music purchased presumably by people who wanted to sing the songs in their own homes. The songs of the American minstrel troupes, whose performances were enormously popular in London and other cities in England in the 1840s and after, were also sold as street ballads, reprinted in songbooks and as sheet music, and sung and known by large numbers of mid-Victorians as a source of common amusement: one of the best-known poems in Lewis Carroll's *Alice* books, for example, "The Mock-Turtle's Song" (see pp. 905–906), began as a parody of a minstrel song. Most important, after mid-century the structure of music-hall performances, and of the music-hall theaters themselves, began to emerge from organized concerts of songs, recitations, and comic turns that had been staged in pubs. Originally the music halls were a predominantly working-class entertainment, and their origins are not only preserved but celebrated in the subjects, settings, and perspectives of such extremely popular and representative songs as Albert Chevalier's "My Old Dutch" and "Ta-Ra-Ra-Boom-De-Ay." By the late 1870s, however, the music halls were becoming a genuinely national medium of entertainment, capable of putting the political meaning of the word "jingoism" into the language through the currency of the refrain of a song G. W. Hunt wrote and sang in music halls in 1878:

> We don't want to fight,
> But by jingo if we do,
> We've got the men, we've got the ships, we've got
> the money too.

By the end of the century music-hall performances in the cities of Great Britain were regularly reviewed in newspapers and patronized by a large and heterogeneous audience who took them and their songs as one of the common pleasures of urban life.

Songs from the theaters and music halls frequently and easily made their way into the literature of what may be called Victorian parlor songs. In part, the term describes a kind of song, often a song from a play or opera, sometimes a setting of a well-known poem (Tennyson's lyrics were frequently set to music), sometimes associated with a performer who sang the song in recitals. The subjects and tones of these songs were often sentimental. There were a great many songs about leaving home, for example, or being disappointed in love, dying young, or growing old. The minstrel songs which at mid-century began to show up in the repertory of parlor performances were, however, more rousing and often comic, and so were the music-hall songs that moved into parlors later in the century. The presence of these songs in the literature of parlor music requires that this kind of entertainment also be defined as a mode of publication. Typically, parlor songs, whatever their origins, were published as sheet music, their covers elaborately illustrated, which sold for three or four shillings (more than thirty or forty times as much as a street ballad). Less frequently, these songs were collected in songbooks that included the music of the songs and were often expensively printed and illustrated. Presumably the Victorians who could afford this music had also acquired the parlors, pianos, musical education, and social customs requisite and customary to the performance of the songs. Presumably too purchasers of sheet music bought the song literally to make it their own and because its subject and tone, words and sound, moved or amused them and people like them who, again quite literally, came together to please one another.

The social character of the ways in which these songs were performed and enjoyed is important. Political songs, to take the most evident example, were explicitly intended to bring people together in a militant identity of class or interest. Songs were written to advance the causes of Chartism, Corn-Law repeal, temperance, and socialism; to organize unions, win elections, break strikes and intimidate strikebreakers; to rally one part of the nation and threaten another with the images and sounds of revolution. Their lyrics were written by journalists, workers, clergymen, political agents and organizers, and poets: in the early years of his laureateship Alfred Tennyson thought it natural to help to arm the country against a threat of invasion from France by contributing songs to newspapers. The verses were published in newspapers, on broadsheets, and in cheap songbooks; and the songs themselves were sung, usually to traditional tunes, in public meetings. Like hymns, to whose tunes they were sometimes sung, political songs were intended to inspirit as well as to express. The street ballad "The Workhouse Boy," for example, articulates a response to the callousness that created and administered workhouses. But Ernest Jones' "The Song of the Lower Classes" and the chants that William Morris wrote for socialist organizations (see pp. 610–612) were written to try to enlist people in the service of ideas which would do something about the society that permits or causes this oppression.

Other kinds of Victorian popular songs were social not because they urged concerted social action but because they drew people together in discourses of words and feelings they all knew. Popular songs are one of the elements that made contemporaries of many Victorians. They are, therefore, important parts of Victorian literature and culture because they come out of and were part of common knowledges and experiences, sets of feelings and assumptions shared by large numbers of people who used the songs to talk to and simply to be with one another. In a sentence, popular songs are a poetry that is already, by the nature of the acts that make them popular, in the lives of its audiences. In the nineteenth century, and in the twentieth as well, some poets and critics of literature and culture regret the presence of such artifices of a popular culture, for they see them as impediments to the rightful sway of the agents of a higher culture. But popular songs are interesting because they serve a purpose in the lives that so readily took them in, because they show a little of the content, tones, and needs of those lives, and because they verify the possibility many nineteenth-century poets hoped for when they sent their poems out to express, enliven, alter, and be knit into the common consciousness of at least some of their contemporaries.

EDITIONS

Unless otherwise indicated, the texts of the songs printed below are contained in collections edited by John Ashton, *Modern Street Ballads* (1888); Charles Hindley, *Curiosities of Street Literature* (1871, reprinted 1970); Harold Scott, *The English Song Book* (1926); A. L. Lloyd, *Come All Ye Bold Miners* (1952); and Lloyd's *Folk Song in England* (1967). Other useful collections are edited by William Henderson, *Victorian Street Ballads* (1938); Michael Pollard, *Ballads and Broadsides* (1969); and Ewen MacColl, *The Shuttle and the Cage: Industrial Folk Ballads* (1954). Some nineteenth-century songs are also included in *The Common Muse: An Anthology of Popular British Ballad Poetry*, edited by V. de Sola Pinto and A. E. Rodway (1957), and in *The Oxford Book of Light Verse*, edited by W. H. Auden (1949).

A. L. Lloyd's *Folk Song in England* (1967) is the most comprehensive study of songs which became the property of large numbers of people. Harold Scott's *The Early Doors* (1946) is a useful, general account of the origins of music halls. Maurice Willson Disher's *Victorian Song, From Dive to Drawing Room* (1955) is uneven in its emphases but full of titles. Robert Collison's *The Story of Street Literature* (1973) is a brief, general history given largely to the nineteenth century. Martha Vicinus' *The Industrial Muse: A Study of Nineteenth Century British Working-Class Literature* (1974) includes strong chapters on street literature and club and music hall songs.

OTHER USEFUL BOOKS AND ESSAYS

Hindley, Charles. *The Life and Time of James Catnach (late of Seven Dials)* (1878; reprinted 1968).

Holloway, John. "Cherry Girls and Crafty Maidens," "Broadside Verse Traditions" and "The Irish Ballads," *Listener*, **83** (1970).

Mellor, G. J. *Northern Music Hall* (1970).

Nettel, Reginald. *Seven Centuries of Popular Song* (1956).

Pearsall, Ronald. *Victorian Popular Music* (1973), and *Victorian Sheet Music Covers* (1972).

"The Poetry of Seven Dials," *Quarterly Review*, **122** (1867). An illuminating discussion of street ballads, unusual because it discusses them extensively and representative because it disapproves of their vulgarity.

Shepard, Leslie. *John Pitts, Ballad Printer of Seven Dials* (1969).

Street Ballads and Broadsides

Jone o' Grinfield[1]

I'm a poor cotton weaver as many one knows.
I've nowt to eat i' th' house an' I've wore out
    my cloas.
You'd hardly give sixpence for all I have on.
My clugs they are brossen[2] an' stockins I've
    none.
    You'd think it wur hard to be sent into
        th'world
    To clem[3] an' do th'best ot you con.

Our church parson kept tellin' us long,
We should have better times if we'd but hold
    our tongues.
I've houden my tongue till I can hardly draw
    breath.
I think i' my heart he means to clem me to
    death.
    I know he lives weel by backbitin' the de'il,
    But he never picked o'er[4] in his life.

We tarried six week an' thought every day were
    t'last.
We tarried an' shifted till now we're quite fast.
We lived on nettles while nettles were good,
An' Waterloo porridge[5] were best of us food.
    I'm tellin' you true, I can find folks enew
    That er livin' no better than me.

Old Bill o' Dan's sent bailiffs one day,
For a shop score I owed him that I couldn't
    pay,
But he wur too late, for old Bill o' Bent
Had sent tit an' cart and taen goods for rent.

We had nowt bur a stoo', that wur a seat for
    two;
An' on it cowered Margit an' me.

The bailiffs looked round as sly as a mouse,
When they saw aw things wur taen out o'
    t'house.
Says one to the other: All's gone, thou may see.
Aw sed: Lads, never fret, you're welcome to me.
    They made no more ado, but nipped up
        t'owd stoo',
    An' we both went wack upo' t'flags.[6]   30

I geet howd o' Margit, for hoo're[7] stricken sick.
Hoo sed hoo ne'er had such a bang sin hoo
    wur wick.[8]
The bailiffs scoured off wi' owd stoo' on their
    backs.
They would not have cared had they brokken
    our necks.
    They're mad at owd Bent cos he's taen goods
        for rent,
    An' wur ready to flay us alive.

I sed to our Margit as we lay upo' t'floor:
We shall never be lower in this world, I am
    sure.
But if we alter, I'm sure we mun mend,
For I think i' my heart we are both at far end,   40
    For meat we have none, nor looms to weave
        on,
    Egad, they're as weel lost as found.

Then I geet up my piece,[9] an' I took it 'em
    back.
I scarcely dare speak, mester lookit so black.
He said: You wur o'erpaid last time you coom.
I said: If I wur, 'twas for weavin' bout[10] loom.

---

[1] This song, often sold as a broadside in the midlands and north of England, is in a tradition of songs written in a northern dialect about a poor weaver. This version, sometimes titled "The Four-Loom Weaver," was written early in the nineteenth century when weavers often worked at home rather than in factories (see "Poverty Knock"). But the version remained very popular throughout the century; the text reprinted here is that of a broadside published around 1860. For an account and analysis of the poem see Martha Vicinus, "The Study of Nineteenth-Century British Working-Class Poetry," *College English*, 32 (1970–71), 548–562; and Lloyd's *Folk Song in England*, from which this text is reprinted.

[2] Clugs: wooden-soled shoes. Brossen: broken.   [3] Clem: starve.   [4] Picked oe'r: wove.

[5] Waterloo porridge: thin porridge.   [6] Flags: stones of the floor.   [7] Hoo're: she was.

[8] Wick: born.   [9] Piece: the length of cloth he is weaving.   [10] Bout: without.

In the mind as I'm in, I'll ne'er pick o'er
    again,
For I've woven mysel to th'fur end.

Then aw coom out o' t'warehouse, an' left him
    to chew that.
When aw thought again, aw wur vext till aw
    50   sweat.
To think we mun work to keep him an' aw
    th'set,[11]
All the days o' my life, an' then die in their
    debt!
    But I'll give o'er this trade, an' work with a
        spade,
    Or go an' break stones upo' th'road.

Our Margit declares if hoo'd cloas to put on,
Hoo'd go up to Lundun an' see the young
    Queen,
An' if things didn't alter when hoo had been,
Hoo swears hoo would fight, blood up to
    th'een.
    Hoo's nought agen t'queen, but hoo likes a
        fair thing,
    An' hoo says hoo can tell when hoo's hurt.
                                                    c. 1860

The Workhouse Boy[1]

The cloth was laid in the Vorkhouse hall,
The great-coats hung on the white-wash'd wall;
The paupers all were blithe and gay,
Keeping their Christmas holiday,
When the Master he cried with a roguish leer,
"You'll all get fat on your Christmas cheer!"
When one by his looks did seem to say,
"I'll have some more soup on this Christmas-
    day."
    Oh the poor Vorkhouse Boy, etc.

    10   At length, all on us to bed vos sent,
The boy vos missing—in search ve vent:
Ve sought him above, ve sought him below,
Ve sought him with faces of grief and woe;
Ve sought him that hour, ve sought him that
    night;

Ve sought him in fear, and ve sought him in
    fright,
Ven a young pauper cried "I knows ve shall
Get jolly vell vopt for losing our pal."
    Oh the poor Vorkhouse Boy, etc.

Ve sought in each corner, each crevice ve knew;   20
Ve sought down the yard, ve sought up the flue;
Ve sought in each kettle, each saucepan, each
    pot,
In the water-butt look'd, but found him not.
And veeks roll'd on;—ve vere all of us told,
That somebody said, he'd been burk'd[2] and
    sold;
Ven our master goes out, the Parishioners vild
Cry "There goes the cove that burk'd the poor
    child."
    Oh the poor Vorkhouse Boy, etc.

At length the soup copper repairs did need,
The Coppersmith came, and there he seed,
A dollop of bones lay a grizzling there,
In the leg of the breeches the poor boy did   30
    vear!
To gain his fill the boy did stoop,
And dreadful to tell, he was boil'd in the soup!
And ve all of us say, and ve say it sincere,
That he was push'd in there by an overseer.
    Oh the poor Vorkhouse Boy, etc.
                                                    1840s

A New Song on the Birth of the Prince of Wales[1]

There's a pretty fuss and bother both in
    country and in town,
Since we have got a present, and an heir unto
    the Crown,
A little Prince of Wales so charming and so sly,
And the ladies shout with wonder, What a
    pretty little boy!

He must have a little musket, a trumpet and a
    kite,
A little penny rattle, and silver sword so bright,

---

[11] To keep him an' aw th'set: support him and others like him.
[1] A London street ballad that parodies Thomas Haynes Bayley's "The Mistletoe Bough" (see p. 931). Reprinted from Ashton.
[2] Burk'd: strangled or suffocated so that his body could be sold to a medical school for dissection. William Burke (1792–1829) was hanged for this practice.
[1] Albert Edward, later Edward VII, was born in 1841. This London street ballad is reprinted from Ashton.

A little cap and feather with scarlet coat so
  smart,
And a pretty little hobby horse to ride about
  the park.

Prince Albert he will often take the young
  Prince on his lap,
And fondle him so lovingly while he stirs
  about the pap,
He will pin on his flannel before he takes his
  nap,
Then dress him out so stylish with his little
  clouts[2] and cap.

He must have a dandy suit to strut about the
  town,
John Bull must rake together six or seven
  thousand pound,[3]
You'd laugh to see his daddy, at night he home-
  wards runs,
With some peppermint or lollipops, sweet
  cakes and sugar plums.

He will want a little fiddle, and a little German
  flute,
A little pair of stockings and a pretty pair of
  boots,
With a handsome pair of spurs, and a golden
  headed cane,
And a stick of barley sugar, as long as Drury
  Lane.

An old maid ran through the palace, which
  did the nobs surprize,
Bawling out, he's got his daddy's mouth, his
  mammy's nose and eyes,
He will be as like his daddy as a frigate to a
  ship,
If he'd only got mustachios upon his upper lip.

Now to get these little niceties the taxes must
  be rose,
For the little Prince of Wales wants so many
  suits of clothes,
So they must tax the frying pan, the windows
  and the doors,
The bedsteads and the tables, kitchen pokers,
  and the floors.

1840s

The Way to Live[1]

Chorus
A man and a woman got married one day,
And thus unto each other did say,
As we the world must now begin,
We will deal in every following thing.

SHE.   We will deal in apples, plums and
  pears,
HE.   We will mend old bellows and bottom
  old chairs,
SHE.   We will buy old metal, rope and bags,
HE.   Yes, and I'll go out a gathering rags.

SHE.   We will sell red herrings and ginger
  pop,
HE.   Hot baked sheep's head and taters hot,
SHE.   We'll keep a school of high degree,
HE.   And learn the children A. B. C,
SHE.   We'll salt fat bacon, butter and lard,
HE.   And great long songs for a penny a
  yard,
SHE.   I'll sell potash, starch and blues,[2]
HE.   And I'll go sweeping the chimney flues.

SHE.   I'll make bustles and lady's frills,
HE.   And I'll sell mussels and pickled eels,
SHE.   We'll deal in razors, strops and hones,
HE.   And I'll go out a picking up bones,
SHE.   We'll deal in paper, take in the news,
HE.   And I'll go a cobbling ladies' shoes,
BOTH.   { And we'll learn the ladies all
  complete,
  To dance the Polka at threepence
  a week.[3]

SHE.   We'll deal in lollipops, sugar and figs,
HE.   We'll buy a donkey, ducks, hens, and
  pigs,
SHE.   We'll have a mangle, and buy old
  clothes,
HE.   And I'll make salve for the ladies' toes.
SHE.   We'll deal in pickled cabbage and
  eggs,
HE.   And make tin dishes and wooden legs.
SHE.   We'll deal in sausages, tripe and lard,
HE.   And if we can't live, 'twill be devilish
  hard.

---

[2] Clouts: swaddling clothes.
[3] The amount of money appropriated by Parliament for the expenses of the monarchy was increased because of the birth of a son.
[1] A London street ballad of the 1840s. Reprinted from Ashton.
[2] Blues: a powder used in laundering.
[3] The polka was extremely popular in England in the 1840s.

SHE.   We'll deal in Oils, sperm, train and
       neat,[4]
HE.   And I'll make stockings for children's
       feet,
SHE.   We will sell hot muffins and home
       baked bread,
HE.   Pins and needles, cotton and thread.
SHE.   We'll grind old razors, scissors and
       knives,
HE.   And keep lodgings for single men and
       their wives,
SHE.   We'll deal in lobsters, shrimps and
       sprats,
HE.   And I'll sell meat for the ladies' cats.

SHE.   We'll deal in fish, fresh, boiled, and
       fried,
HE.   And let out donkeys a penny a ride,
SHE.   I will the ladies fortune tell,
HE.   And I'll cry, Old umbrellas to sell,
SHE.   We will take in the blooming ladies
       bright,
HE.   And sleep in the garret at threepence
       a night,
SHE.   I'll sing, Come buy my Crockery ware,
HE.   And I'll go dressing the ladies hair.

SHE.   We'll sell ripe Cherries, pea soup and
       milk,
HE.   Oranges, lemons and pickled wilks,
SHE.   Wooden rolling-pins at the Royal
       Exchange,
HE.   And if we can't get on we may think
       it strange,
                    (Chorus repeated)
                                        1840s

The Bermondsey Tragedy[1]

Come all you good people of every degree,
I pray you give attention and listen to me,
'Twas in the county of Somersetshire where I
was bred and born,
And my wife she is a foreigner,—with her
must die in scorn.

For the murder of O'Connor we are condemned
to die;

My wife she said I'm innocent of that sad
tragedy,
But 'twas she who shot O'Connor and swore
she would shoot me,
Unless I would assist her to bury his body.

Four months before his murder his doom was
ready sealed,
His grave made ready under ground his body
to receive,
He little thought his death so near when to the
house he came,
But his death was plann'd all by our hands his
money to obtain.

For murder and plunder they both were fully
bent,
They shot him with a pistol, and to his lodgings
went,
They got his cash and jewels and quickly did
repair,
To hide the guilt for the blood they'd spilt—
oh! what a wretched pair.

At the Old Bailey, London, the trial it came on,
They were arraigned before the judge and
English jurymen,
The counsel for the prisoners they nobly did
defend,
And tried to prove their innocence, this point
they did contend.

After the trial, Mrs. Manning said,
I do protest I'm innocent and been unfairly
tried,
Though you've pronounced me guilty, and
doom'd me to be hung,
More like a dog than Christian, to a being thus
undone.

With rage and desperation the keepers by them
stood,
And to their gloomy prison they quickly were
removed,
The coolness and courage which they before
displayed,
Had now forsook them for a time, and they
look'd quite dismay'd.

---

[4] Train oil is whale oil; neat oil is made from the hooves of cattle.
[1] In 1849 Frederick George Manning and his wife Maria were convicted of the murder of
Patrick O'Connor, an acquaintance whom they murdered for money and buried beneath the
floor of their kitchen in Bermondsey, a district in London. According to Hindley, this ballad
and that on the execution of James Bloomfield Rush each sold two and a half million copies.
The text is reprinted from Hindley; the copy he reprints was published and sold in Carlisle in
the northwest of England.

This wicked woman taken was unto
   Horsemonger Gaol,
Her husband followed after, and very soon did
   feel
Contrition for his guilty deeds, and to his wife
   he wrote,
Begging of her to think how soon she was to
   meet her fate.

The end of poor O'Connor will long in
   memory reign,
And shew the vice and folly which followed in
   its train.
Oh! may it thus a warning prove to shun bad
   company,
Never like the Mannings commit such a
   tragedy.

Now in their gloomy prisons bound down in
   irons strong,
Awaiting for the fatal morn when they will
   meet their doom,
For the murder of O'Connor—oh! what a
   horrid crime,
Now they are both cut off in the height of their
   prime.

1849

A Ballad from the Seven Dials Press[1]

*together with "the 'gag' and 'patter' of a man
formerly well-known as 'Tragedy Bill' "*

Now, my friends, here you have, just printed
and published, a full, true, and pertickler ac-
count of the life, trial, character, confession,
behaviour, condemnation, and hexecution of
that unfortunate malefactor, Richard Wilby-
force, who was hexecuted on Monday last, for
the small charge of one ha'penny, and for the
most horrible, dreadful, and wicked murder of
Samuel—I means Sarah Spriggens, a lady's
maid, young, tender, and handsome. You have
here every pertickler, of that which he did, and
that which he didn't. It's the most foul and
horrible murder that ever graced the annals of
British history (?) Here, my customers, you may
read his hexecution on the fatal scaffold. You
may also read how he met his victim in a dark
and lonesome wood, and what he did to her
—for the small charge of a ha'penny; and,
further, you read how he brought her to Lon-
don,—after that comes the murder, which is
worth all the money. And you read how the
ghost appeared to him and then to her parents.
Then comes the capture of the *willain;* also the
trial, sentence, and hexecution, showing how
the ghost was in the act of pulling his leg on
one side, and the "old gentleman"[2] a pulling
on the other, waiting for his victim (my good
friends excuse my tears!) But as Shakespeare
says, "Murder most foul and unnatural," but
you'll find this more foul and unnatural than
that or the t'other—for the small charge of a
ha'penny! Yes, my customers, to which is added
a copy of serene and beautiful werses, pious
and immoral, as wot he wrote with his own
blood and skewer the night after—I mean the
night before his hexecution, addressed to young
men and women of all sexes—I beg pardon, but
I mean classes (my friends its nothing to laugh
at), for I can tell you the werses is made three
of the hard-heartedest things cry as never was
—to wit, that is to say, namely—a overseer, a
broker,[3] and a policeman. Yes, my friends, I
sold twenty thousand copies of them this here
morning, and could of sold twenty thousand
more than that if I could of but kept from
crying—only a ha'penny!—but I'll read the
werses.

Come all you blessed Christians dear,
   That's a-tender, kind, and free,
While I a story do relate
   Of a dreadful tragedy,
Which happened in London town,
   As you shall all be told;
But when you hear the horrid deed
   'Twill make your blood run cold.—
    For the small charge of a ha'penny!

'Twas in the merry month of May,
   When my true love I did meet;
She look'd all like an angel bright,
   So beautiful and sweet.
I told her I loved her much,
   And she could not say nay;

---

[1] Seven Dials was the name of a poor district in London. The publishers of street ballads and broadsides, among them James Catnach (1792–1841) and his successors, published from or near Seven Dials, which thus gave its name to this kind of street literature. Reprinted from Hindley.

[2] Old gentleman: the devil.   [3] Overseer: foreman in a factory. Broker: of a pawnshop.

'Twas then I strung her tender heart,
    And led her all astray.—
        Only a ha'penny!

I brought her up to London town,
20   To make her my dear wife;
But an evil spirit tempted me,
    And so I took her life!
I left the town all in the night,
    When her ghost in burning fire,
Saying, "Richard," I am still with you,
    Whenever you retire.—
        Only a ha'penny!

And justice follow'd every step,
    Though often I did cry;
30 And the cruel Judge and Jury
    Condemned me for to die.
And in a cell as cold as death,
    I always was afraid,
For Sarah she was with me,
    Although I killed her dead.—
        For the small charge of a ha'penny!

My tender-hearted Christians,
    Be warned by what I say,
And never prove unkind or false
40   To any sweet la'-dy.
Though some there, who wickedness
    Oft leads 'em to go astray;
So pray attend to what you hear.
    And a warning take I pray.

                                            1840s

Railroad to Hell,

*From Dissipation to Poverty, and from
Poverty to Desperation*

THIS LINE BEGINS IN THE BREWERY, AND RUNS
THROUGH ALL PUBLIC-HOUSES, DRAM-SHOPS, AND
JERRY-SHOPS, IN A ZIGZAG DIRECTION, UNTIL IT
LANDS IN THE KINGDOM OF HELL.[1]

If you are determined and wishful to go,
With blind debauchees to the regions of woe,
Then go to the Tap without any delay,
And drink both your reason and money away,
But never mind care, for if you despair,
It is the first train that will carry you there.

You've nothing to do but to guzzle and swill,
As long as the Landlord is willing to fill,
For this is the Line and the Railroad to Hell,
Where Drunkards and Devils for ever must
    dwell;   1
So drink all you can, it is the chief plan,
That e'er was invented by Devil for man.

This Railroad it runs thro' Parlours and
    Snugs,[2]
And here you can sit round glasses and jugs,
And have what you please, such as Ale, Gin, or
    Rum,
To please an old friend, or an old drunken
    chum;
And this is the way to drink all the day,
And then stagger home when you've swallowed
    your pay.

Such Taverns as these are Railroads to Hell,
Their barrels are engines which make men
    rebel;   2
Their jugs and their glasses which furnish their
    Trains,
Will empty their pockets and muddle their
    brains.
And thus drunkards ride to Hell in their pride,
With nothing but steam from the barrels
    inside.

We've Railroads to Heaven, and Railroads to
    Hell,
There good men can ride, and where Devils
    can dwell;
We've Taverns for drunkards and Churches
    for Saints,
And quacks of all sorts to heal our complaints;
So now we can ride to Hell in our pride,
On Railroads of sin with blue Devils inside.   3

Old Swilltub the doctor and guard of the
    Trains,
He filches your pockets and fuddles your
    brains;
But when he's got all from the poor silly man,
He then sends him home to do as he can,
With all his old chums, his badgers and bums,
Who sue him for money he owes in great sums.

But let us not ride on these Railroads of sin,
Nor drink either Brandy, Ale, Porter, or Gin;

---

[1] A London street ballad reprinted from Hindley. Jerry-shops were cheap beer shops.
[2] Snugs: parlors in taverns.

And then we shall ride into Heaven with joy,
Where no drunken quacks can our vitals
  destroy
With poisonous drugs, sold to us in jugs,
In either their Bars, their Parlours, or Snugs.

The number of vaults which we have in Town,
Have robbed the poor lass of her bonnet and
  gown,
Her topknots and feathers have gone to the
  Pop,[3]
And many have lost both credit and shop;
Both young men and maids of very good trades,
Have drunk all they earned, and gone down to
  the shades.

We've plenty of signs, both Horses and Bulls,
Of Lions and Dragons, to serve drunken
  Trulls;
We've signs too of Angels, of Warriors and
  Kings—
Yes, plenty of signs of good and bad things.
But what's their design? Why Gin, Rum, and
  Wine,
Sold here to intoxicate puppies and swine.

We've White and Black Bulls and two Suns in
  one street,
One Swan and two Lions which never taste
  meat,
And here you see women with bottles and jugs,
Roll into these taverns and dram-drinking
  snugs,
As brazen as brass to get an odd glass.
In some of these shops where a fool cannot
  pass.

No wonder that Pop-ticket women and wags,
Are dressed up in nothing but patches and
  rags.
Their dresses and shawls for strong liquor
  they'll swop,
Yes, Tagrag and Bobtail must go to the pop;
And when this is done, away they will run,
To either a Lion, a Bull, or a Sun.

Such poor sorry women who pledge their old
  rags,

Are known by their petticoats hanging in jags;
You'll see them at night with their heads wrapt
  in shawls
Not far from the Dram-shop, or sign of Three
  Balls,   70
With bonnets and hats, old dresses and brats,
Made up into bundles as you have seen Pat's.

                                    1840s/1850s

Poverty Knock[1]

Poverty knock, poverty knock!
Me loom is a-sayin' all day.
Poverty knock, poverty knock!
Gaffer's too skinny to pay.[2]
Poverty knock, poverty knock!
Keepin' one eye on the clock.
Ah know ah can guttle[3]
When ah hear me shuttle
Go: Poverty, poverty knock![4]

Up every mornin' at five.   10
Ah wonder that we keep alive.
Tired an' yawnin' on the cold mornin',
It's back to the dreary old drive.

Oh dear, we're goin' to be late.
Gaffer is stood at the gate.
We're out o' pocket, our wages they're docket;
We'll 'a' to buy grub on the slate.

An' when our wages they'll bring,
We're often short of a string.[5]
While we are fratchin'[6] wi' gaffer for snatchin', 20
We know to his brass[7] he will cling.

We've got to wet our own yarn
By dippin' it into the tarn.[8]
It's wet an' soggy an' makes us feel groggy,
An' there's mice in that dirty old barn.

Oh dear, me poor 'ead it sings.
Ah should have woven three strings,
But threads are breakin' and my back is achin'.
Oh dear, ah wish ah had wings.

---

[3] Gone to the Pop: pawned.
[1] Lloyd heard this song from an old weaver in 1965, who had learned it sixty years earlier. The song is earlier yet; "poverty knock" reproduces the sound of a nineteenth-century mechanical loom. Reprinted from Lloyd's *Folk Song in England*.
[2] Gaffer: the foreman. Skinny: tight-fisted.   [3] Guttle: eat.
[4] The first nine lines are repeated as a refrain after each stanza.
[5] String: length of cloth.   [6] Fratchin': quarreling.   [7] Brass: money.
[8] Tarn: a pool.

30 Sometimes a shuttle flies out,
    Gives some poor woman a clout.
    Ther she lies bleedin', but nobody's 'eedin'.[9]
    Who's goin' t'carry her out?

    Tuner[10] should tackle me loom.
    'E'd rather sit on his bum.
    'E's far too busy a-courtin' our Lizzie,
    An' ah cannat get 'im to come.

    Lizzie is so easy led.
    Ah think that 'e teks her to bed.

    She allus was skinny, now look at her pinny.[11]   40
    It's just about time they was wed.

    Poverty, poverty knock!
    My loom is a-sayin' all day.
    Poverty, poverty knock!
    Gaffer's too skinny to pay.
    Poverty, poverty knock!
    Keepin' one eye on the clock.
    Ah know ah can guttle
    When ah hear me shuttle
    Go: Poverty, poverty knock!

                            Mid-nineteenth century

Stage and Parlor Songs

Thomas D. Rice (1806–1860) was an American minstrel entertainer who first appeared in London in 1836. The version he sang then of his song "Jim Crow" became enormously popular; according to Ashton, it was also sung and sold on the streets as the "most popular of all modern street ballads" (p. 350). This text is reprinted from Scott's The Early Doors.

Jim Crow
by Thomas D. Rice

I came from ole Kentucky
A long time ago
Where I first learn to wheel about
And jump Jim Crow,

Chorus:
Wheel about, turn about and do jes so,
Eb'ry time I wheel about, I jump Jim Crow.

I us'd to take him fiddle,
Eb'ry morn and afternoon
And charm the old Buzzard
10 And dance to the Racoon.
    Chorus:

I landed first at Liverpool
Dat place of ships and docks,
I strutted down Lord Street
And as'd the price of stocks,
Chorus:

I paid my fare den up to town
On de coach to cut a dash,
De axletree soon gave way
And split us wid a smash,
Chorus: 20

I lighted den upon my head
All in de nassy dirt,
Dey all thought dat I war dead
But I laughed and wasn't hurt,
Chorus:

Dis head you know am putty tick,
Cause dere it made a hole,
On de dam macadmis road
Much bigger dan a
Chorus: 30

When I got into Lunnon
Dey took me for a savage,

---

[9] Nobody's 'eedin': no one helps her because the workers cannot afford to take time from their own looms.
[10] Tuner: the person who maintains the looms.   [11] Pinny: pinafore.

But I war putty well behaved
So I gazed with Massa Davidge,[1]
Chorus:

Den Johnny Jim Crow's 'bout de street
More like a raven rader,
Pray good people don't mistake
Indeed I'm not dare fader,
Chorus:

Dem urchins what sing my song
Had better mind dar looks,
For anyhow dey can't be crows,
You see d'ar only rooks,
Chorus:

1836

Thomas Haynes Bayley (1797–1839) was a drama-tist and one of the most popular writers of song in the 1820s and 1830s. "The Mistletoe Bough" was sung in a play of the same title which was first per-formed in 1834. The music for the lyric was written by Sir Henry Bishop (1786–1855), a composer of theatrical and operatic music. The text is from a selection of Bayley's lyrics, Songs of the Affections, *edited by W. L. Hanchant (1932).*

The Mistletoe Bough
by Thomas Haynes Bayley

The mistletoe hung in the castle hall,
The holly branch shone on the old oak wall;
And the baron's retainers were blithe and gay,
And keeping their Christmas holiday.
The baron beheld, with a father's pride,
His beautiful child, young Lovell's bride;
While she, with her bright eyes, seem'd to be
The star of the goodly company.

"I'm weary of dancing now," she cried;
"Here tarry a moment—I'll hide—I'll hide!
And, Lovell, be sure thou'rt first to trace
The clue to my secret lurking place."
Away she ran—and her friends began
Each tower to search, and each nook to scan;
And young Lovell cried, "Oh! where dost thou
    hide?
I'm lonesome without thee, my own dear
    bride."

They sought her that night! and they sought
    her next day!
And they sought her in vain, when a week
    pass'd away!
In the highest—the lowest—the loneliest spot,
Young Lovell sought wildly—but found her
    not.
And years flew by, and their grief at last
Was told as a sorrowful tale long past;
And when Lovell appear'd the children cried,
"See! the old man weeps for his fairy bride."

At length an oak chest, that had long lain hid
Was found in the castle—they raised the lid—
And a skeleton form lay mouldering there,
In the bridal wreath of that lady fair!
Oh! sad was her fate!—in sportive jest
She hid from her lord in the old oak chest,
It closed with a spring!—and, dreadful doom,
The bride lay clasp'd in her living tomb!

1834

The vogue of this song began with the revival of The Wandering Minstrel, *a play by Henry Mayhew (1812–87), in 1853. The song was apparently writ-ten for the revival by E. L. Blanchard (1820–89), like Mayhew a journalist and dramatist. It was sung in the play by the comic actor Frederick Rob-son (1821–64), picked up by Sam Cowell (1820–64), a singer in one of best-known London night houses, and moved from there to the early music halls and as a ballad to the streets of mid-Victorian London. Reprinted from Ashton.*

Vilikins and His Dinah
by Edward Laman Blanchard

Oh! 'tis of a rich merchant,
In London did dwell,
He had but one daughter,
An uncommon nice young gal!
Her name it was Dinah,
Scarce sixteen years old,
She had a large fortune
In silver and gold.
    Singing Too-ral-loo, etc.

As Dinah was valking
In the garden vun day,

10

Spoken—(*It was the front garden, not the back garden.*)

---

[1] Davidge was the manager of the Surrey theater, at which Rice appeared in 1836.

Her papa came up to her,
And thus he did say,
Go, dress yourself, Dinah,
In gor-ge-ous array
And I'll get you a husband,
Both val-ly-ant and gay.
    Singing Too-ral-loo, etc.

Spoken—*This is what the infant progeny
said to the author of her being.*
20   Oh, papa! oh, papa!
I've not made up my mind,
To marry just yet
I do not feel inclined,
And all my large fortune,
I'll freely give o'er,
If you'll let me stay single
A year or two more.
    Singing Too-ral-loo, etc.

*This is what the indignant parient replied—
I represent the father.*
30   Then go, boldest daughter,
The parient replied,
If you don't consent to be
This here young man's bride,
I'll leave your large fortune
To the nearest of kin,
And you shan't have the benefit
Of one single pin.
    Singing Too-ral-loo, etc.

*Now comes the epiflabbergastrinum of the
lovier.*
40   As Vilikins vas valking
The garden around—
(The aforesaid front garden,)
He spied his dear Dinah
Lying dead on the ground,
A cup of cold pison
It laid by her side,
And a billy dux stating
By pison she died.
50   *Taken inwardly,* Singing Too-ral-loo, etc.

This is what the lovier did.
Then he kissed her cold corpus
A thousand times o'er,
He called her his Dinah—
Though she was no more!
He swallowed the pison
Like a true lovier brave,

And Vilikins and his Dinah
Lie a-buried in one grave.
Both on 'em Singing Too-ral-loo, etc.   60

MORAL
Now all you young vimmen,
Take a warning by her,
And never by any means
Disobey the guv'ner:
And all you young fellers,
Mind who you clap eyes on,
Think on Vilikins and Dinah
And the cup of cold pison.
Else you'll be singing Too-ral-loo, etc.   70
                    1853

*Charles Kingsley (1819–1875) is best remembered
as a novelist. "The Sands of Dee" was published in
his first successful novel,* Alton Locke *(1850), the
fictional autobiography of a tailor and poet which
advertised the oppressive conditions of the London
tailoring trade. John Ruskin (1819–1900) cited
lines 20–21 in the third volume of* Modern Painters
*(1856: Part 4, chapter 12) as an example of the
pathetic fallacy. That allusion is one sign of the
currency of the song, which was set to music by at
least two composers and frequently sung in recitals.
The text is reprinted from the 1901–3 edition of
Kingsley's writing. The version in* Alton Locke *is
marked by a few gestures toward the vernacular—
"The Sands o' Dee," for example.*

The Sands of Dee
by Charles Kingsley

'O Mary, go and call the cattle home,
   And call the cattle home,
   And call the cattle home
  Across the sands of Dee;
The western wind was wild and dank with
   foam,
  And all alone went she.

The western tide crept up along the sand,[1]
   And o'er and o'er the sand,
   And round and round the sand,
  As far as eye could see.   10
The rolling mist came down and hid the land:
  And never home came she.

'Oh! is it weed, or fish, or floating hair—
   A tress of golden hair,
   A drownèd maiden's hair
  Above the nets at sea?

[1] In *Alton Locke:* "The creeping tide came up along the sand."

Was never salmon yet that shone so fair
　　Among the stakes on Dee.'

20　They rowed her in across the rolling foam,
　　The cruel crawling foam,
　　The cruel hungry foam,
To her grave beside the sea:
But still the boatmen hear her call the cattle
　　home
　　Across the sands of Dee.

(1849)　1850

Wellington Guernsey (1817–1885) was born in Ireland, worked as a journalist, and served as an officer in the British army. Disher writes that "Alice, Where Art Thou?" was "so well known that a greater degree of popularity cannot be imagined" (Victorian Song, p. 139). The music of the song was written by J. Ascher. The text is reprinted from Disher's Victorian Song.

Alice, Where Art Thou?
by Wellington Guernsey

The birds sleeping gently,
　　Sweet Lyra beameth bright;
Her rays tinge the forest,
　　And all seems glad tonight,
The winds sighing by me,
　　Cooling my fever'd brow,
The stream flows as ever,
　　Yet, Alice, where art thou?
One year back this even,
　　And thou wert by my side,
Vowing to love me, Alice,
　　Whate'er might betide.

The silver rain falling,
　　Just as it falleth now,
And all things slept gently,
　　Ah, Alice, where art thou?
I've sought thee by lakelet,
　　I've sought thee on the hill,
And in the pleasant wild-wood,
　　Where winds blew cold and chill;
I've sought thee in forest,
　　I'm looking heav'nward now,
Oh! there amid the starshine,
　　Alice, I know art thou!

1850s

Adelaide Anne Procter (1825–1864) was the daughter of Bryan Waller Procter (1787–1874), who under the name "Barry Cornwall" wrote plays, songs, and frequent contributions to the literary journals of London. Adelaide Procter began to contribute to magazines in the 1850s, especially to Charles Dickens' Household Words. *Her first collection of poems,* Legends and Lyrics, *was published in 1858; a second volume under the same title was published in 1861. She published one more collection of verse, in 1862, before her death. "A Lost Chord" became an extremely popular song in Victorian parlors and recitals after it was set to music in 1877 by Arthur Sullivan (1842–1900). The text printed here is that of the Oxford edition of Procter's poems (1914).*

A Lost Chord
by Adelaide Anne Procter

Seated one day at the Organ,
　　I was weary and ill at ease,
And my fingers wandered idly
　　Over the noisy keys.

I do not know what I was playing,
　　Or what I was dreaming then;
But I struck one chord of music,
　　Like the sound of a great Amen.

It flooded the crimson twilight
　　Like the close of an Angel's Psalm,　　　10
And it lay on my fevered spirit
　　With a touch of infinite calm.

It quieted pain and sorrow,
　　Like love overcoming strife;
It seemed the harmonious echo
　　From our discordant life.

It linked all perplexed meanings
　　Into one perfect peace,
And trembled away into silence
　　As if it were loth to cease.　　　　　　20

I have sought, but I seek it vainly,
　　That one lost chord divine,
Which came from the soul of the Organ,
　　And entered into mine.

It may be that Death's bright angel
　　Will speak in that chord again,—
It may be that only in Heaven
　　I shall hear that grand Amen.

1861

The Ballad of Sam Hall[1]
as sung by W. G. Ross

Oh my name it is Sam Hall, it is Sam Hall,
Oh, my name it is Sam Hall, it is Sam Hall,
My name it is Sam Hall, and I hate you one
    and all,
You're a gang of muckers all—
                    Damn your eyes!
10

Oh, I killed a man, they said, so they said,
Oh, I killed a man, they said, so they said,
Oh, I killed a man, they said, for I hit him on
    the head,
And I left him there for dead—
                    Damn his eyes!

Oh, they put me in the quad, in the quad,
Oh, they put me in the quad, in the quad,
Oh, they put me in the quad, and they tied me
    to a log,
And they left me there, by God—
                    Damn their eyes!

Oh, the parson he did come, he did come,
Oh, the parson he did come, he did come,
Oh, the parson he did come, and he looked so
    mighty glum,
And he talked of Kingdom Come—
20
                    Damn his eyes!

Oh, the Sheriff he came too, he came too,
Oh, the Sheriff he came too, he came too,
Oh, the Sheriff he came too, with his boys all
    dressed in blue.
There'll be bloody work to do,—
                    Damn their eyes!

So up the rope I go, up I go,
So up the rope I go, up I go,
So up the rope I go, with my friends all down
    below,
Saying, "Sam, we told you so!"
30
                    Damn their eyes!

I saw Molly in the crowd, in the crowd,
I saw Molly in the crowd, in the crowd,
I saw Molly in the crowd, so I hollered right
    out loud,

"Molly, ain't yer bloody proud?"
                    Damn your eyes!

So this shall be my knell, be my knell,
So this shall be my knell, be my knell,
So this shall be my knell, and I'll meet you all
    in Hell,
And I hope you sizzle well—
                    Damn your eyes!
                          1850s

Joseph Philip Robson (1808–1870) was a mechanic and schoolmaster who published several volumes of verse with Scottish and northern presses in the 1850s and later, among them a translation of the "Song of Solomon" into the Northumberland dialect. "California" was sung to a traditional tune. The text is reprinted from Lloyd's Come All Ye Bold Miners.

California
by J. P. Robson

MOLLY.   Oh hinny,[1] Geordie, canny man,
           Thou kens aw loves thou
              dearly!
           For thee aw turned off Baggy
             Crooks,
             An' used Tim Targit queerly;
           Billy Benson coaxed me sair to
             wed,
             But man, aw cuddent spurn
             thee!
           Oh hinny, canst thou think o'
             this,
             An' gan te Californy?
           Oh, Californy, fuilish Californy!
           Like honey blobs my heart'll brust
             If thou gans te Californy.
                                    1

GEORDIE.   Hoots, Mally, haud yor whinging
             gob,[2]
           Maw mind's myed up for sartin.
           Maw picks and spyeds is i' my
             kist,[3]
           The morn aw's sure be startin'.
           Aw'll seun be hikin' on the sea,
             An' fleein' roond Cape Horney;

---

[1] W. G. Ross, a singer in one of the famous London night houses, made this version of a traditional ballad famous at mid-century. Reprinted from Scott, *The English Song Book*.
    [1] Hinny: a term of endearment; honey.   [2] Whinging gob: whining mouth.
    [3] Kist: trunk or chest.

Aw kens the seam to hew for gold,
  When aw gets te Californy.
Oh, Californy, bonny Californy,
  The very clairts[4] upon the street
  Is goold in Californy.

MOLLY. Thou's mevies rue,[5] maw collier
    lad,
  When in the waves thou's
    sprawlin',
  When crocidiles and unicorns
  Is at thaw hoggers[6] haulin'.
  Thou's not had luck like Joney,[7]
    man,
  In some whale's guts to turn
    thee;
  Thou'll lang to be wi' me at
    hyem,
  An' far frae Californy.
  Oh, Californy, shem on Californy!
  Bob Stackers swears thor's nowt
    but fules
  Wad gan te Californy.

GEORDIE. Thou's wrang, aw tell thee, Mally
    lass,
  Just read the papers, hinny.
  The place is verra like the Mint,
  Another Coast o' Guinea!
  Though mind thee, yence aw
    heerd it telled,
  The cannibals wad burn ye,
  And make goold ointment of yor
    byens[8]
  When ye get te Californy.
  Oh, Californy, whei noo,
    Californy,
  Hoots, Mally, aw can thresh[9]
    them a',
  Aw'll conquer Californy!

MOLLY. Consider, Geordie, aw's thee wife,
  Aw diven't gan contrary,

If thou mun gan, thous' tyek the
    lass
  Thou caws thaw bonny Mary!
But weel aw kens afore thou gans,
  Thou's trim'lin at the journey;   50
Sea-sarpints tee may cowp[10] the
    boat,
  Then where's thaw Californy?
Oh, Californy, 'ticin' Californy!
Aw wish that folks wes not se
    poor,
  To want thee, Californy!

GEORDIE. Cheer up, maw duck, thou'll gan
    wi' me,
  Aw niver heeds the danger!
  Poor collier lads works hard for
    nowt
  An' still te death's ne stranger.
  Like Whittin'ton, aw hears the
    bells   60
  That says, "Come on your
    journey!"[11]
  Goold's better far than howkin'[12]
    coals—
  Oh dear, this Californy!
  Oh, Californy we're comin',
    Californy!
  Farewell to splint, choke damp
    and blast![13]
  Hurrah, for Californy!

        1860s

George Ridley (1834–1864) was a northern coal miner who by the time of his death was performing as a professional singer and comedian. His songs, some of which remained popular throughout the century (one of them, "Blaydon Races," is still sung), are properly stage rather than street songs, although printed versions were sung and sold on the streets of Newcastle, Durham, and other northern cities. This text is reprinted from Lloyd's Come All Ye Bold Miners.

---

[4] Clairts: clots of dirt or mud.   [5] Mevies rue: perhaps regret.
[6] Hoggers: stockings with the feet cut out and worn as gaiters or leggings.
[7] Joney: Jonah.   [8] Byens: bones.   [9] Thresh: thrash.   [10] Cowp: capsize.
[11] The legend of Richard Whittington, a fifteenth-century mayor of London, is that when he ran away as a boy because of mistreatment, he heard the bells of the city calling him back with a promise that he should be mayor.
[12] Howkin': digging.
[13] Splint: a kind of hard, stony coal, or a sliver of coal and rock that can wound a miner hacking at a coal face. Choke damp: carbonic acid gas which accumulates in old coal workings; after an explosion it mixes with steam and dust and causes suffocation. Blast: an explosion of firedamp, the carburetted hydrogen given off by coal.

Cushie Butterfield
by George Ridley

Aa's a broken-hairted keelman,[1] and aa's
 ower heid in love
Wiv a young lass in Gyetside an' aa caal hor me
dove.
Hor nyem's Cushie Butterfield, an' she sells
yaller clay,[2]
An' hor cousin is a muckman,[3] an' they caal
him Tom Grey.

> She's a big lass, an' a bonny lass,
>   An' she likes hor beor,
> An' they caal hor Cushie Butterfield,
>   An' aa wish she wes heor.

Hor eyes is like two holes in a blanket bornt
through,
Hor broos in a mornin wad spyen a young
coo,[4]
An' when aa hear hor shoutin: 'Will ye buy
ony clay?'
Like a candyman's[5] trumpet, it steals me heart
away.

Ye'll oft see her doon at Sangit[6] when the fresh
harrin comes in.
She's like a bag full o' sawdust, tied roond wiv
a string.
She wears big galoshes tee, an' hor stockins
once wes white,
An' hor bedgoit's laelock,[7] on an' hor hat's
nivor strite.

When aa axed hor te marry me she started te
laugh;
"Noo, nyen o' yer monkey tricks, for aa like ne
sich chaff."
Then she started a-blubbin, an' she roared like
a bull,
An' the cheps on the Quay says aa's nowt but
a fyeul.

She says the chep that gets hor must wark ivory
day,

An' when he comes hyem at neets he must gan
an' seek clay;
An' when he's away seekin, she'll myel baals[8]
an' sing:
O weel may the keel row that ma laddie's in.

> She's a big lass, an' a bonny lass,
>   An' she likes hor beor,
> An' they caal hor Cushie Butterfield,
>   An' aa wish she wes heor.

1860s

*Thomas Armstrong (1848–1919) was a Durham
miner who wrote and performed many popular
songs. The cages of this song are the platforms on
which miners are transported down into and up
from the mine shafts. Reprinted from Lloyd's* Come
All Ye Bold Miners.

The Row Between the Cages
by Thomas Armstrong

Ane mornin when aw went te wark,
  The sight wes most excitin,
Aw heard a noise an' looked aroond,
  An' whe d'ye think was fightin?
Aw stood amazed, an' at 'em gazed,
  To see 'em in such rages
For aw never seed a row like that
  Between the Brockwell cages.

Wor aud cage says: "Come ower the gates,
  Because its my intention
To let thee see whether thoo or me
  Is the best invention."
The new'un bein raised, took off his claes,
  Then at it they went dabbin;
The blood was runnin doon the skeets[1]
  An' past the weighman's cabin.

Wor aud cage says: "Lets hae me claes,
  Thoo thought that thoo could flay me,
But if aw'd been as young as thoo,
  Aw's certain aw could pay thee."

---

[1] Keelman: a worker on a flat-bottomed boat used to transport coal.
[2] Yaller clay: yellow clay containing oxides of iron used in household cleaning.
[3] Muckman: scavenger.
[4] Broos . . . wad sypen a young coo: brows would span a young cow.
[5] Candyman: a bailiff or process server who serves notices of eviction or repossession of furniture or other property.
[6] Sangit: Sandgate, a waterfront street or district in Newcastle.
[7] Bedgoit' laelock: petticoat is lilac.
[8] Myel baals: perhaps, prepare something to eat by rolling it in ground corn or grain.
[1] Skeets: the vertical frame on which the cages run.

The patent knocked his ankle off,
  An' they both had cutten faces;
The shifters rapped through for to ride,[2]
  So they both went to their places.

When gannin up and doon the shaft,
  The patent cage did threaten
For to take wor aud 'un's life
  If they stopped it meetin.
Wor aud cage bawled oot as it passed:
  "Thoo nasty dorty patent,
Rub thee eyes again the skeets—
  Aw think thoo's hardly wakenet."

The patent to wor aud cage says:
  "Although aw be a stranger,
Aw kin wark me wark as well as thoo,
  An' free the men frae danger.
Noo, if the rope should break wi' me,
  Aud skinny jaws, just watch us—
Thoo'll see me clag on to the skeets,
  For aw's full o' springs an' catches."

Wor aud cage to the patent says:
  "Aw warrant thoo think thoo's clever
Because they've polished thoo wi' paint,
  But thoo'll not last for ever.
The paint on thoo will wear away,
  And then thoo's lost thy beauty;
They never painted me at all,
  An' still aw've deun my duty."

The brakesman brought them both to bank
  The mischief for to settle.
They fit frae five o'clock to six,
  An' the patent won the battle,
It took the brakeman half a shift
  To clag them up wi' plaisters.
Wor aud cage sent his notice in,
  Just to vex the maisters.

Spoken: They're matched to fight again, but not under Queensbury Rules. Wor aud cage fancies fightin wi' the bare fist. Aw'll let ye knaw when it comes off. It'll hae to be kept quiet; if the bobby gets to knaw, they'll be both ta'en, because they winnet allow bare fist fightin noo. Keep on lookin in the *Christian 'Arald,* an' ye'll see when it comes off, an' where. There's six to fower on the aud 'un

noo. Bet nowt till the day, an' aw'll see ye in the field; it's a cheet.

                         1880s

Arthur Lloyd was an entertainer and songwriter who was one of the first popular stars of the early music halls in the 1860s. This song was performed by G. H. Macdermott (1845–1901), another famous comic singer of the early music halls. Macdermott also made famous the song with the refrain "We don't want to fight, but by jingo if we do," which established the word "jingo" as a synonym for fierce, manly patriotism. Reprinted from Scott's The English Song Book.

I'll Strike You with a Feather
by Arthur Lloyd

I'll sing of Hildebrand Montrose
  (His proper name is Charlie),
He speaks as tho' with a "cold id his
    dose,"
  Bad French he tries to "parley."
His hair is in Barber's ringlets,
  His eyes are made up dark,
He walks upon his uppers
  While strolling in the park.

Chorus:
  Au revoir, ta ta! you'll hear him say
  To the Marchioness Clerkenwell while bid-
    ding her good day,   10
  I'll strike you with a feather, I'll stab you
    with a rose,
  For the darling of the ladies is Hildebrand
    Montrose.

His scarf, unlike himself, is green,
  His gloves, "no kid," are "yaller,"
His washed-out pants are well-strapp'd
    down,
  He carries a "fake" umbrella;[1]
He never pays his tradesmen,
  To him they'll give no trust,
He drinks dry Champagne "cider"   20
  Until he's fit to "bust."

Chorus:
  His "stock in trade" of socks count three,
  He chalks his paper collars,
  He always pays his taxes
    For his income's just two dollars;

---

[2] Rapped through: signaled for the cages.
[1] "Fake" had a connotation of modish gadgetry in mid-century slang.

He swears he'll wed a "Duchess"
   Tho' he waits till "all is blue,"[2]
Tho' he goes to bed a beggar
   Wakes up "the Lord knows who."

30 Chorus:

1870s

Albert Chevalier (1816–1923) became the best known of the cockney music-hall singers who performed in the pearly-buttoned costumes of costermongers. Typically, his songs were in a stage version of cockney dialect and were humorous or sentimental treatments of events in London working-class life. Reprinted from sheet music in the Lilly Library.

My Old Dutch: A Cockney Song
by Albert Chevalier

I've got a pal
A reglar out an' outer,
She's a dear old gal,
I'll tell yer all about 'er.
It's many years since fust we met,
'Er 'air was then as black as jet,
It's white now, but she don't fret,
Not my old gal!

Chorus:
We've been together now for forty years,
10 An' it don't seem a day too much.
There ain't a body livin' in the land
As I "swop" for my dear old Dutch!

I calls 'er Sal,
'Er proper name is Sairer,
An' yer may find a gal
As you'd consider fairer.
She ain't an angel—she can start
A-jawin' till it makes yer smart,
She's just a *woman*, bless 'er heart,
20 Is my old gal!

Chorus:

Sweet fine old gal,
For worlds I wouldn't lose 'er,
She's a dear good old gal,
An' that's what made me choose 'er.
She's stuck to me through thick and thin,

When luck was out, when luck was in,
Ah! Wot a wife to me she's been,
An' wot a pal!

Chorus:

I sees yer Sal—
Yer pretty ribbons sportin'!
Many years now, old gal,
Since them young days of courtin'.
I ain't a coward, still I trust
When we've to part, as part we must
That Death may come and take me fust
To wait . . . my pal!

Chorus

1890s

The first of the Savoy Operas, named after the London theater in which they were produced after 1882, was performed in 1875. Arthur Sullivan (1842–1900), who was later to compose an opera, several oratorios (including one based on a well-known religious poem by Henry Hart Gilman), and several well-known hymn tunes, had already made a reputation in the theater by composing incidental music to a performance of Shakespeare's The Tempest and the music for a ballet, a comic opera, and a very popular farce. Gilbert (1836–1911) was as well known as the author of the Bab Ballads (see Part Seven) and nearly two dozen farces, burlesques, pantomimes, and comedies. Gilbert and Sullivan first collaborated in 1871. After the success of Trial by Jury in 1875, they launched on a series of extremely successful comic operas—fourteen in all—which did not end until 1896. Sullivan's music, which is often melodious and affecting even when as in "The Suicide's Grave" it parodies the forms of sentimental ballads, is a necessary element in the effect of Savoy Opera. But Gilbert's lyrics by themselves at least represent the quick, light topicality, confident pace, and clever playing with sound which are characteristic of the plots, words, and music of Gilbert and Sullivan.

There are several guides and dictionaries to the Savoy Operas: by George F. Dunn (1936), Frank Ledlie Moore (1962), and Michael Hardwick (1972). In addition to biographies of Gilbert by Sidney Dark and Rowland Grey (1923) and Hesketh Pearson (1957), Françoise Cellier and Cunningham Bridgman (1914), Percy Fitzgerald (1894), and W. A. Darlington (1950) have written accounts of the Savoy Opera and the D'Oyley Carte Company which performed them. See also John Bush Jones, W. S. Gilbert: A Century of Scholarship and Commentary (1970). The texts of the lyrics printed here is that of Songs of a Savoyard (1890).

[2] All is blue: to the limit, until the last minute.

Songs from the Savoy Operas by W. S. Gilbert

The Æsthete[1]

If you're anxious for to shine in the high
  æsthetic line, as a man of culture rare,
You must get up all the germs of the
  transcendental terms, and plant them
  everywhere.
You must lie upon the daisies and discourse in
  novel phrases of your complicated state of
  mind,
The meaning doesn't matter if it's only idle
  chatter of a transcendental kind.
        And everyone will say,
        As you walk your mystic way,
"If this young man expresses himself in terms
  too deep for *me*,
Why, what a very singularly deep young man
  this deep young man must be!"

Be eloquent in praise of the very dull old days
  which have long since passed away,
And convince 'em, if you can, that the reign of
  good QUEEN ANNE[2] was Culture's palmiest
  day.
Of course you will pooh-pooh whatever's fresh
  and new, and declare it's crude and mean,
And that Art stopped short in the cultivated
  court of the EMPRESS JOSEPHINE.[3]
        And everyone will say,
        As you walk your mystic way,
"If that's not good enough for him which is
  good enough for *me*,
Why, what a very cultivated kind of youth this
  kind of youth must be!"

Then a sentimental passion of a vegetable
  fashion must excite your lanquid spleen,
An attachment *à la* Plato for a bashful young
  potato, or a not-too-French French bean.
Though the Philistines may jostle, you will
  rank as an apostle in the high æsthetic band,
If you walk down Piccadilly with a poppy or a
  lily in your mediæval hand.
        And everyone will say,   20
        As you walk your flowery way,
"If he's content with a vegetable love which
  would certainly not suit *me*,
Why, what a most particularly pure young man
  this pure young man must be!"
                                          1881

They'll None of 'Em Be Missed[1]

As some day it may happen that a victim must
  be found,
  I've got a little list—I've got a little list
Of social offenders who might well be under-
  ground,
  And who never would be missed—who never
  would be missed!
There's the pestilential nuisances who write for
  autographs—
All people who have flabby hands and
  irritating laughs—
All children who are up in dates, and floor you
  with 'em flat—
All persons who in shaking hands, shake hands
  with you like *that*—
And all third persons who on spoiling *tête-à-
  têtes* insist—
  They'd none of 'em be missed—they'd none
  of 'em be missed!   10

There's the nigger serenader, and the others of
  his race,
  And the piano organist—I've got him on the
  list!
And the people who eat peppermint and puff
  it in your face,
  They never would be missed—they never
  would be missed!

---

[1] From *Patience* (1881). Sung by Reginald Bunthorne, a young man of extreme but in 1881 already conventional esthetic taste and poses.
[2] Queen Anne: some literary critics, poets, designers, and even architects had in the last decades of the century endorsed the order and elegance of the literature and domestic design of the reign of Queen Anne (1707–14). See, for example, some of the poems of Austin Dobson (pp. 755–757).
[3] Josephine: the wife of Napoleon and empress of France even after their marriage was dissolved in 1809.
[1] From *The Mikado* (1885). Sung by Ko-Ko, the Lord High Executioner who is himself under sentence of death for flirting.

Then the idiot who praises, with enthusiastic
    tone,
All centuries but this, and every country but
    his own;
And the lady from the provinces, who dresses
    like a guy,[2]
And who doesn't think she waltzes, but would
    rather like to try;
And that singular anomaly, the lady novelist—
    I don't think she'd be missed—I'm *sure* she'd
20   not be missed!

And that *Nisi Prius*[3] nuisance, who just now is
    rather rife,
    The Judicial humorist—I've got *him* on the
    list!
All funny fellows, comic men, and clowns of
    private life—
    They'd none of 'em be missed—they'd none
    of 'em be missed.
And apologetic statesmen of the compromising
    kind,
Such as—What-d'ye-call-him—Thing'em-Bob,
    and likewise—Never-mind
And 'St—'st—'st—and What's-his-name, and
    also—You-know-who—
(The task of filling up the blanks I'd rather
    leave to *you!*)
But it really doesn't matter whom you put
    upon the list,
    For they'd none of 'em be missed—they'd
30   none of 'em be missed!
                                                    1885

The Suicide's Grave[1]

On a tree by a river a little tomtit
        Sang "Willow, titwillow, titwillow!"
And I said to him, "Dicky-bird, why do you sit
        Singing 'Willow, titwillow, titwillow'?
Is it weakness of intellect, birdie?" I cried,
"Or a rather tough worm in your little inside?"
With a shake of his poor little head he replied,
        "Oh, willow, titwillow, titwillow!"

He slapped at his chest, as he sat on that bough,
        Singing "Willow, titwillow,
10   titwillow!"

And a cold perspiration bespangled his brow,
        Oh, willow, titwillow, titwillow!
He sobbed and he sighed, and a gurgle he gave,
Then he threw himself into the billowy wave,
And an echo arose from the suicide's grave—
        "Oh, willow, titwillow, titwillow!"

Now I feel just as sure as I'm sure that my
        name
        Isn't Willow, titwillow, titwillow,
That 'twas blighted affection that made him
        exclaim,
        "Oh, willow, titwillow, titwillow!"   20
And if you remain callous and obdurate, I
Shall perish as he did, and you will know why,
Though I probably shall not exclaim as I die,
        "Oh, willow, titwillow, titwillow!"
                                                    1885

*A version of this song was written by an Ameri-
can minstrel entertainer, Henry Sayers, for* Tuxedo,
*a farce performed in the United States in 1891. It
was made famous in London by Lottie Collins
(1866–1910), a music-hall singer who sang versions
of the song in several burlesques and pantomimes
in 1891 and after. Lottie Collins accompanied the
song with an exuberant dance which was part of
the innocent insouciance of her performance.
Disher in* Victorian Song *identifies B. M. Batchelor
as the author of a British version of the song. The
text reprinted here is from sheet music in the Lilly
Library on which Richard Morton is identified as
the author of the lyric; Angelo Asher is identified
as the composer.*

Ta-Ra-Ra-Boom-De-Ay
*by Richard Morton; as performed by
Lottie Collins*

A smart and stylish girl you see
Belle of good society;
Not too strict, but rather free,
Yet as right as right can be!
Never forward, never bold—
Not too hot and not too cold,
But the very thing I'm told,
That in your arms you'd like to hold!
    Ta-ra-ra boom-de-ay:
    (repeated eight times)

---

        [2] Guy: a grotesquely dressed dummy burned at celebrations of Guy Fawkes Day in the
autumn.
        [3] *Nisi Prius:* a legal term meaning "unless before."
        [1] From *The Mikado* (1885). Sung, to a very pretty tune, by Ko-Ko.

I'm not extravagantly shy
When a nice young man is nigh,
For his heart I have a try—
And faint away with tearful cry!
When the good young man, in haste,
Will support me round the waist;
I don't come to, while thus embraced,
Till of my lips he steals a taste!
    Refrain

I'm a timid flower of innocence,
Pa says that I have no sense—
I'm one eternal big expense;
But men say that I'm just immense!
Ere my verse I conclude
I'd like it known and understood,
Tho' free as air, I'm never rude,
I'm not too bad and not too good!
    Refrain

You should see me out with Pa,
Prim, and most particular;
Then young men say, "Ah, there you are!"
And Pa says, "That's peculiar."
"It's like their cheek," I say, and so
Off again with Pa I go—
He's quite satisfied—although
When his back's turned—well, you know—
    Refrain

When with swells I'm out to dine,
All my hunger I resign;
Taste the food, sip the wine—
No such daintiness as mine!
But when I am all alone,
For shortcomings I atone!
No old frumps to stare like stone—
Chops and chicken on my own!
    Refrain

Sometimes Pa says, with a frown,
"Soon you'll have to settle down—
Have to wear your wedding gown—
Be the strickest wife in town."
Well, it must come by-and-by—
When wed, to keep quiet, I'll try;
But till then I shall not sigh,
I shall still go for my
    Refrain

                  1891

This song was performed by Dan Leno (1860–1904), a music-hall singer whose stage presence

¹ Blucher: shoe or boot.

and costume anticipated that of Chaplin's tramp. The matter of his songs is typically that of the small defeats and ineffectualities of ordinary men, and the manner, especially in his spoken patter, was often characterized by a remarkable stream of linguistic association and invention. Fred Gilbert was a prolific composer of popular songs; he also wrote "The Man Who Broke the Bank at Monte Carlo", which was still well-known in the early decades of the twentieth-century. The text is reprinted from sheet music in the Lilly Library.

The Midnight March
by Fred Gilbert; as performed by Dan Leno

Plain it is to you that I am tir'd
    Nearly worn away to skin and bone,
Not the sort of man to be admir'd,
    Even by the misses all alone.
Here have I been spoutin' to the workin'
    classes,
Tellin' them as 'ow they are downright asses;
Tryin' to improve 'em such a bootless farce is,
    I haven't got a Blucher¹ fit to own.

Spoken.—It is my intention to hold a meeting here to-day and say a few speaks. Working men of England, you must rally round me. Working men, you don't seem to understand yourselves. You must rouse yourselves, get behind yourselves, and push yourselves forward. Don't stand about the place and stand about just for the sake of standing. No! Now is the time and the only time. When time is time you can't get away from facts. What did Mr. Gladstone say the other day? Ah, what did he say? I again ask you, working men of England, what did he say? You know some people see things when they look at 'em: you can't eat soap and wash with it. Well, that proves what I have just said, that the working men of England at the present day are nothing more or less than—than—than working men! You can't get away from facts! Again, is the working man going to be scrunched into the earth? No; why should he be scrunched? No more scrunching, and down with the scruncher! Now, working men, look at me. I love the working man; and I love to see him work. Work never killed any man yet; and it shall never kill me! Why have I organised myself here to-day? Simply to ask one question. What are you going to do with your money? Now I ask you working men, what are you going to do with your money and your children? I'll tell you what to do with it. Simply bring it to me! and what will I do with it? Do you think I'd give it to a lot of people what are nothing more nor less than a lot of people? No! I'd keep it myself! My dear people, what I've suffered for the working man no-one knows. I've had black eyes, broken noses, smashed heads, and torn clothes.

And all through joining in the midnight march
With the pals of Tillett and the friends of
   Arch;[2]
   You've read it thro' in Lloyds,[3]
   The so-call'd unemploy'ds
Had rare hard work to do the midnight march.

   Simply to display my iron will
      (And anxious Mr. Copper to defy) ,
   I took a noble stand on Tower Hill,
      And asked a lot o' fools to tell me why
The Prince o' Wales should ride, when such as
      us was walkin'.
I told 'em it was time to be like heroes stalkin';
The Square of Great Trafalgar I had sworn to
      talk in
   We went—and look at this discolored eye!

   Well, it's all through joining in the
      Midnight March,

With the pals of Tillett and the friends of
   Arch;
   You've read it all in Lloyd's,
   The so-called Un-Employeds
Had rare hard work along the Midnight
March.

We ventured past the Mansion House and
   Bank,
   We sallied round the Dome of old St.
   Paul's,
When someone shouted, "Stop yer blooming
   hank!
   Or soon you'll be in Bow Street's marble
   halls."
I waved my gingham bravely on the midnight
   breezes,
Cracked a lot of Reynold's unearthly wheezes,[4]
Got a bang on that with which a poor bloke
   sneezes,
   And then a Bobby kicked my overalls!

It was all through joining in the Midnight
   March
With the pals of Tillett and the friends of
   Arch;
   You've read it all in Lloyd's,
   How we noble Un-Employeds
Had rare hard work to do the Midnight
March.

                                          1893

Political Songs

Charles Mackay (1814–1889) was a poet and journalist. He published nearly a dozen books of poems, edited the Illustrated London News *and was a correspondent for the* London Times *during the American Civil War, wrote several books on American history and an interesting collection,* Memoirs of Extraordinary Popular Delusions *(1841) , which is still occasionally reprinted. "The*

Good Time Coming" was first published in the London Daily News, *and reprinted in a volume of poems Mackay published in 1846. It was immediately set to music by Henry Russell (1812–1900) , an entertainer and songwriter who was also well known for songs about the sorrow and hope of emigration. The text is that of* The Poetical Works of Charles Mackay *(London, 1857) .*

[2] Ben Tillett (1860–1943) was one of the founders of the dockers' union and a leader in the London dock strike in 1889. Joseph Arch (1826–1919) was a farm laborer, and later a member of Parliament, who founded a union of agricultural workers.

[3] Lloyd's: an illustrated weekly paper with a working-class readership.

[4] Reynold's: a weekly paper, also with a working-class readership.

The Good Time Coming
by Charles Mackay

There's a good time coming, boys,
  A good time coming:
We may not live to see the day,
But earth shall glisten in the ray
  Of the good time coming.
Cannon-balls may aid the truth,
  But thought's a weapon stronger;
We'll win a battle by its aid;—
  Wait a little longer.

There's a good time coming, boys,
  A good time coming:
The pen shall supersede the sword,
And Right, not Might, shall be the lord,
  In the good time coming.
Worth, not Birth, shall rule mankind,
  And be acknowledged stronger;
The proper impulse has been given;—
  Wait a little longer.

There's a good time coming, boys,
  A good time coming:
War in all men's eyes shall be
A monster of iniquity
  In the good time coming.
Nations shall not quarrel then,
  To prove which is the stronger;
Nor slaughter men for glory's sake;—
  Wait a little longer.

There's a good time coming, boys,
  A good time coming.
Hateful rivalries of creed
Shall not make their martyrs bleed
  In the good time coming.
Religion shall be shorn of pride,
  And flourish all the stronger;
And Charity shall trim her lamp;—
  Wait a little longer.

There's a good time coming, boys,
  A good time coming:
And a poor man's family
Shall not be his misery
  In the good time coming.
Every child shall be a help,
  To make his right arm stronger;
The happier he, the more he has;—
  Wait a little longer.

There's a good time coming, boys,
  A good time coming:

Little children shall not toil,
Under, or above the soil,
  In the good time coming;
But shall play in healthful fields
  Till limbs and mind grow stronger;
And every one shall read and write;—
  Wait a little longer.

There's a good time coming, boys,
  A good time coming:
The people shall be temperate,
And shall love instead of hate,
  In the good time coming.
They shall use, and not abuse,
  And make all virtue stronger.
The reformation has begun;—
  Wait a little longer.

There's a good time coming, boys,
  A good time coming:
Let us aid it all we can,
Every woman, every man,
  The good time coming.
Smallest helps, if rightly given,
  Make the impulse stronger;
'Twill be strong enough one day;—
  Wait a little longer.

1846

Ernest Jones (1819–69) was the son of an army officer who served in the court of a German king, after whom Jones was named. After completing a distinguished academic career in German schools, he studied law in England and was admitted to the bar. During the Chartist agitation of the mid-1840s, however, he enlisted his talents in the Chartist cause, and in 1848 he was imprisoned for sedition. After his release in 1850 he edited and wrote for radical newspapers, unsuccessfully contested several parliamentary seats, and in the last years of his life returned to the successful practice of law, including the defense of persons indicted for political activities.
"The Song of the Lower Classes" was published as one of a series of Songs of Democracy *in 1856. It was set to music by John Lowry, and also sung to a traditional air. It was also sold as a street ballad; the text is reprinted from Ashton.*

The Song of the Lower Classes
by Ernest Jones

We plough and sow—we're so very, very low
  That we delve in the dirty clay,
Till we bless the plain—with the golden grain,
  And the vale with the fragrant hay.

Our place we know,—we're so very low,
    'Tis down at the landlord's feet:
We're not too low—the bread to grow,
    But too low the bread to eat.

Down, down we go,—we're so very low,
10   To the hell of the deep sunk mines,
But we gather the proudest gems that glow,
    When the crown of a despot shines.
And whenever he lacks—upon our backs
    Fresh loads he deigns to lay:
We're far too low to vote the tax,
    But not too low to pay.

We're low—we're low—mere rabble, we know,
    But, at our plastic power,
The mould at the lordling's feet will grow
20   Into palace and church and tower.
Then prostrate fall—in the rich man's hate,
    And cringe at the rich man's door;
We're not too low to build the wall,
    But too low to tread the floor.

We're low—we're low—we're very very low,
    Yet from our fingers glide
The silken flow—and the robes that glow
    Round the limbs of the sons of pride.
And what we get—and what we give—
30   We know, and we know our share;
We're not too low the cloth to weave,
    But too low the Cloth to wear!

We're low—we're low—we're very very low,
    And yet when the trumpets ring,
The thrust of a poor man's arm will go
    Thro' the heart of the proudest King.
We're low—we're low—our place we know,
    We're only the rank and file,
We're not too low—to kill the foe,
40   But too low to touch the spoil.
                                    1840s; 1856

*Jim Connell was an Irish journalist who wrote
this lyric during the London dock strike of 1889.
The song was later adopted as the official anthem
of the British Labour Party. Its tune is that known
in the United States as "Maryland, My Maryland."
The text printed here is from Wanda Willson Whit-
man's compilation,* Songs That Changed the World
(1969).

The Red Flag
by Jim Connell

The people's flag is deepest red,
It shrouded oft our martyred dead,
And ere their limbs grew stiff and cold
Their hearts' blood dyed its ev'ry fold.

Chorus:
Then raise the scarlet standard high
Within its shade we'll live or die.
Though cowards flinch and traitors sneer,
We'll keep the red flag flying here.

It waved above our infant might
When all ahead seemed dark as night;   10
It witnessed many a deed and vow:
We must not change its color now.

Chorus:

It well recalls the triumphs past;
It gives the hope of peace at last—
The banner bright, the symbol plain
Of human right and human gain.

Chorus:

With heads uncovered swear we all
To bear it onward till we fall.
Come dungeon dark or gallows grim,
This song shall be our parting hymn.   20

Chorus:
                                            1889

The Blackleg Miners[1]

Oh, early in the evenin', just after dark,
The blackleg miners creep te wark,
Wi' their moleskin trousers an' dorty short,
There go the backleg miners!

They take their picks an' doon they go
Te dig the coal that lies belaw,
An' there's not a woman in this toon-raw[2]
Will look at a blackleg miner.

[1] A song composed during a strike in Durham late in the nineteenth century. A blackleg
miner is one who returns to work before a strike is settled. Deleval and Seghill are names of
mines in the Durham region. The text is reprinted from Lloyd's Folk Song in England.
[2] Toon-raw: town-row.

Oh, Delaval is a terrible place.
They rub wet clay in a blackleg's face,
An' roond the pit-heaps they run a foot-race
Wi' the dorty blackleg miners.

Now, don't go near the Seghill mine.
Across the way they stretch a line,
Te catch the throat an' break the spine
O' the dorty backleg miners.

They'll take your tools an' duds as well,
An' hoy[3] them doon the pit o' hell.
It's doon ye go, an' fare ye well,
Ye dorty blackleg miners!

Se join the union while ye may.
Don't wait till your dyin' day,
For that may not be far away,
Ye dorty blackleg miners!

1890s

[3] Hoy: heave.

PART NINE

Religious Poems and Hymns

I

N ITS MOST extensive definition Victorian religious poetry would encompass, to offer only a suggestive list of titles included in this anthology, Tennyson's *In Memoriam,* Clough's "Easter Day" poems, and Robert Browning's "Caliban upon Setebos;" some of the lyrics of Christina Rossetti and all of the lyrics of Gerard Manley Hopkins; Elizabeth Barrett Browning's "The Dead Pan," Swinburne's "Hymn of Man," Meredith's "Ode to the Spirit of Earth in Autumn," and some of Hardy's philosophical lyrics. The poems included in this section have important relationships with these and similar poems, but they have been selected by a more narrow principle. Except for Francis Thompson, the writers of these poems were known as poets almost entirely because of their religious and devotional poems. The poems were also published in one of the three forms that in the Victorian period were strongly associated with verse on religious subjects and intended for devotional purposes.

The first form is that of John Keble's *The Christian Year* (1827), the first and most popular of many nineteenth-century collections of poems arranged in a calendar of church seasons and feasts. The extracts from Robert Montgomery's *The Omnipresence of the Deity* (1828) and John Henry Newman's "The Dream of Gerontius," and Thompson's "The Hound of Heaven," represent, less exactly, a second kind of religious poetry popular in the first half of the century. Part of the appeal of big poems like Montgomery's—and of others such as James Montgomery's *The World Before the Flood* (1813), Henry Hart Milman's *The Fall of Jerusalem* (1820), Robert Pollok's *The Course of Time* (1827), and John Abraham Heraud's *The Judgement of the Flood* (1834)—was their scale. These were pious poems of first and last things, epic, scriptural, and (most obviously) Miltonic in their apocalyptic scenarios, their elevated imagery and language, and their sweep through the entire cosmos and chronology of human and divine history. The poems of Newman and Thompson are in the smaller dimensions of drama and ode, and they invite comparison not to Milton and the Old Testament but to other poems in these forms, especially, for Thompson, to the poems of Shelley. But within their forms the settings, actions, and imagery of these poems are on the cosmic scale of the religious epics esteemed in the early decades of the Victorian period. They were also popular with readers who liked them for their doctrine at least as much as for their poetry. But certainly one reason for this popularity was that the grand style in which in these poems Newman and Thompson engaged questions of religious belief and salvation excited sensibilities like those which earlier in the century had sent Montgomery's poem through twenty-eight editions in the thirty years after its publication.

The third kind of religious verse represented here is that of the hymn, by far the most prevalent form of devotional writing in the nineteenth century. Thousands of hymns were written in the century. Some (the hymns made from Keble's "Evening," for example, and John Henry Newman's "Lead, Kindly Light") were first published in collections of poems; others were published in newspapers and religious magazines. Eventually, if a hymn was to attain the currency and use for which it was intended, it was included in one or more of the hundreds of hymn books published during the century.

Most of the hymns in this selection were written for or included in services of the Church of England. The most important model of nineteenth-century hymns were those of the dissenting minister Isaac Watts (1674–1748) and those of Charles Wesley (1707–1788), who thought of himself as a member of the Church of England but helped to found a large evangelical party not always at ease within it. The hymns of Watts and Wesley were very widely used in Methodist and evangelical churches in the eighteenth and nineteenth centuries, and they were also taken into the hymnals of the established Church of England. At the beginning of the nineteenth century, however, congregations in the Anglican church were still usually "lining out" psalms, a practice in which the clergyman recited two lines of a psalm and the congregation replied by singing it to settings that had been in use for over a century. The hierarchy of the Church of England was still, in the first decades of the century, uncertain about the use of hymns in worship. It was not until after the posthumous publication in 1827 of a collection of hymns Reginald Heber had made when he was bishop of Calcutta that the Established Church unambiguously endorsed the publication of hymnals and the practice of hymn singing. By mid-century so many Anglican hymn books were being published—over 200 appeared during the century—that a committee of the Church of England moved to establish some authority by the publication in 1861 of the first edition of *Hymns Ancient and Modern*. This collection of texts and tunes, many of the latter composed for the hymnal, was in its original edition and subsequent revisions one of the most influential collections of verse published in Victorian England.

Some of the hymns of Watts and Wesley were included in *Hymns Ancient and Modern*, along with hymns (their texts sometimes altered to make them doctrinally suitable) by James Montgomery, Josiah Conder, Frederick Faber, and others who were not members of the Church of England or who, like Wesley and John Keble, were of parties different from the moderate

High Church sympathies of the editors of the hymnal. This readiness to take in hymns from many sources is important because it demonstrates that certain hymns were part of the common experience of contemporaries in different churches and liturgies. There were, of course, hymns whose statements, images, and assumptions were peculiarly apt to the beliefs of one church or sect—Thomas Toke Lynch's "Lift up your heads," for example, and the Quaker Bernard Barton's "Walking in the Light." There were also two movements in the history of Victorian religion that created significant differences in how their hymns were written and sung. One was the Tractarian or Oxford Movement, that in the 1830s and after aroused interest in the early and medieval Church. One issue of Tractarianism and the High Church movement in general was a relatively sophisticated style of hymn writing and translation represented here by John Mason Neale's translation of a medieval text, "For thee, O dear Country," from which one of the most popular hymns of the century was taken. The other movement, quite different in its origins and tonality, was the evangelical or revival movement given great impetus among working- and lower-middle-class members of nonconformist churches by the meetings held by the American evangelists Dwight Moody and Ira Sankey in the 1870s and 1880s. In their mass meetings in the cities of England and Scotland Moody and Sankey, and evangelists who emulated them, popularized a strongly rhythmic and emotional style of "gospel" singing whose accent and lift can be heard in Horatius Bonar's "A Little While" and Elizabeth Cecilia Clephane's "There were ninety and nine," British texts that fitted and were often used in the revival style of hymn singing.

Victorian hymns are important documents in the history of nineteenth-century British religion and in the social history of the period. For these histories the differences between hymns are a central matter. The differences between the hymns most often sung in Anglican and in Methodist and other dissenting congregations were founded on important differences in doctrine, liturgy, and conceptions of the social character and function of a church. There were also differences in the social class and entire lives, in their ideas of God and themselves, of the congregations which customarily sang, say, Christopher Wordsworth's "Hark! the sound of holy voices" and those who sang "There were ninety and nine." These differences also matter when hymns are placed in the literary history of the Victorian period, for they can be used to mark and suggest the appeals and audiences of different texts and styles in one of the most popular forms of poetry in the century. But the most significant aspect of Victorian hymns as poems is that so many of them were the common, often the most persistent, literary experience of the hundreds of thousands of people who used them. Their usual features—short lines, strong rhythms and rhymes, relatively simple syntax, firmly closed four- and six-line stanzas, the powerful and familiar figures of journeys, battles, and harvests, seas, mountains, cities, and stars: these features show up everywhere in Victorian poetry, in political songs and devotional lyrics, for example, in the invocation to *In Memoriam* (which was sung as a hymn) and in the sounds and shapes of poems by Hardy and Kipling. More to the point, many Victorians who rarely or never read poetry had this poetry in their lives. Hymns were a literature that pleased and moved by meter, rhyme, images, and form, as all nineteenth-century poetry was supposed to do; and they were also, as some nineteenth-century poems aspired to be, a poetry that was actually, demonstrably, and continually used to express and enlarge perceptions and feelings which those who used the poetry took very seriously.

Some of the standard histories of religion in nineteenth-century Great Britain are: L. E. Elliott-Binns, *Religion in the Victorian Era* (second edition, 1964) ; Owen Chadwick, *The Victorian Church* (1966, 1970) ; K. S. Latourette, *Christianity in a Revolutionary Age: A History of Christianity in the Nineteenth and Twentieth Centuries* (1959–63) ; Volumes Three and Four of H. Davies' *Worship and Theology in England* (1961–62) ; and Alec R. Vidler, *The Church in an Age of Revolution: 1789 to the Present Day* (1962). Erik Routley in *English Religious Dissent* (1960) discusses nonconforming religions; R. G. Cowherd in *The Politics of English Dissent* (1956) and E. P. Thompson in *The Making of the English Working Class* (1963) discuss the role religion, and hymns, played in the politics and social consciousness of the working class. See also W. R. Ward, *Religion and Society, 1790–1850* (1973).

Volumes Four and Five, covering the years 1830–1920, of Hoxie N. Fairchild's *Religious Trends in English Poetry* (1957, 1962) are a useful source of information about nineteenth-century religious poems. James G. Nelson in *The Sublime Puritan: Milton and the Victorians* (1963) considers the religious epics of the first decades of the period; James Benzinger in *Images of Eternity: Studies in the Poetry of Religious Vision from Wordsworth to T. S. Eliot* (1962) considers the religious character and function of better-known poems. J. Hillis Miller in *The Disappearance of God* (1963) considers the writing of, among others, Emily Brontë and Hopkins as attempts to recall or to make God in material reality.

A Dictionary of Hymnology, edited by John Julian (revised edition 1907, reprinted 1957) is an indispensable source of information about hymns and hymn writers. L. F. Benson, *The English Hymn* (1915), E. E. Ryder, *The Story of Christian Hymnody* (1959), and Erik Routley, *Hymns and Human Life* (1952) are all useful general histories of hymns. The volume titled "Sacred, Moral, and Religious Verse" in Alfred Miles' collection, *The Poets and the Poetry of the Century* (1891–97), contains many hymns and brief biographies of their writers. *Hymns Ancient and Modern, Historical Edition* (1909) and *The English Hymnal, with Tunes* (1906) both contain useful information about the texts and tunes of hymns sung during the Victorian period. *The Yattendon Hymnal* (1899), compiled by Robert Bridges (see pp. 763–765) is an interesting expression of a highly literary taste making decisions within a popular form of literature.

The introduction to *Hymns as Poetry,* compiled by Tom Ingram and Douglas Newton (1956), is a brief history of hymn writing in England, and the anthology itself is excellently chosen. Arthur Pollard's *English Hymns* (1960), a pamphlet in the Writers and Their Work series, is also a succinct history of hymn writing and contains useful bibliographies of works about hymns and of the best-known English hymns themselves. J. B. Reeves' *The Hymn as Literature* (1924) is a general survey.

John Keble

1792–1866

John Keble was the son of a clergyman in the Church of England. After a distinguished undergraduate career at Oxford, he was elected to a fellowship in 1811 and for the next twelve years served as an examiner and tutor in the university. He was ordained in 1816, and in the 1820s he assisted his father in several parishes. In 1831 he was elected professor of poetry at Oxford, although he continued throughout his life to perform the duties of a parish priest. Two years later he delivered a sermon on the relationships between the Church of England and the historical Christian church which emphasized the spiritual identity and historical continuity of the English church with that founded by Christ. This sermon initiated the series of sermons and tracts of the Tractarian or Oxford Movement, which in the 1830s and 1840s emphasized those elements of doctrine and liturgy in the Church of England which seemed to confirm its continuity with the early Christian church. Keble was also interested in opening the university to students from working-class or lower-middle-class families, an interest that culminated after his death in the foundation of a college in Oxford which bears his name.

In 1827 Keble published The Christian Year, a series of poems organized by the occasions of the church calendar. The volume was extremely popular; ninety-five editions were published during his lifetime. He published one other volume of verse, Lyra Innocentium (1846), as well as several tracts in the Tractarian series, an edition of the writings of the sixteenth-century divine Richard Hooker, and volumes of sermons and other theological writing. A posthumous collection of previously unpublished poetry was published in 1869. The standard nineteenth-century biography is by Walter Lock (1893); the currently definitive biography is Georgina Battiscombe's John Keble: A Study in Limitations (1963). For standard studies of the Oxford Movement see the introductory note to the poems of John Henry Newman below. The text of the poems printed below is that of the Oxford edition of The Christian Year and Other Poems (1914).

from The Christian Year

Evening[1]

Abide with us: for it is toward evening, and the day is far spent.

—LUKE 24:29.

'Tis gone, that bright and orbèd blaze,
Fast fading from our wistful gaze;
Yon mantling cloud has hid from sight
The last faint pulse of quivering light.

In darkness and in weariness
The traveller on his way must press,
No gleam to watch on tree or tower,
Whiling away the lonesome hour.

Sun of my soul! Thou Saviour dear,[2]
It is not night if Thou be near: 10
Oh! may no earth-born cloud arise
To hide Thee from Thy servant's eyes.

When round Thy wondrous works below
My searching rapturous glance I throw,
Tracing out Wisdom, Power, and Love,
In earth or sky, in stream or grove;—

Or by the light Thy words disclose
Watch Time's full river as it flows,
Scanning Thy gracious Providence,
Where not too deep for mortal sense:—   20

When with dear friends sweet talk I hold,
And all the flowers of life unfold;

---

[1] With a companion poem, "Morning," this poem served as an introduction to *The Christian Year*.

[2] Lines 9–28 were sung as a popular hymn; they appear in the revised edition of *Hymns Ancient and Modern* (1875) with a setting by John Bacchus Dykes (1823–76), a composer and clergyman who was one of the editors of the collection.

Let not my heart within me burn,
Except in all I Thee discern.

When the soft dews of kindly sleep
My wearied eyelids gently steep,
Be my last thought, how sweet to rest
For ever on my Saviour's breast.

Abide with me from morn till eve,
30   For without Thee I cannot live:
Abide with me when night is nigh,
For without Thee I dare not die.

Thou Framer of the light and dark,
Steer through the tempest Thine own ark:
Amid the howling wintry sea
We are in port if we have Thee.[3]

The Rulers of this Christian land,
'Twixt Thee and us ordain'd to stand,—
Guide Thou their course, O Lord, aright,
40   Let all do all as in Thy sight.

Oh! by Thine own sad burthen, borne
So meekly up the hill of scorn,
Teach Thou Thy Priests their daily cross
To bear as Thine, nor count it loss!

If some poor wandering child of Thine
Have spurn'd, to-day, the voice divine,
Now, Lord, the gracious work begin;
Let him no more lie down in sin.

Watch by the sick: enrich the poor
50   With blessings from Thy boundless store:
Be every mourner's sleep to-night
Like infants' slumbers, pure and light.

Come near and bless us when we wake,
Ere through the world our way we take;
Till in the ocean of Thy love
We lose ourselves in Heaven above.

                                        1827

Third Sunday in Lent

When a strong man armed keepeth his palace, his goods are in peace: but when a stronger than he shall come upon him, and overcome him, he taketh from him all his armour wherein he trusted, and divideth his spoils.

—LUKE 11:21–22.

See Lucifer like lightning fall,
    Dash'd from his throne of pride;
While, answering Thy victorious call,
    The Saints his spoils divide;
This world of Thine, by him usurp'd too
    long,
Now opening all her stores to heal Thy
    servants' wrong.

So when the first-born of Thy foes
    Dead in the darkness lay,
When Thy redeem'd at midnight rose
    And cast their bonds away,
The orphan'd realm threw wide her gates,
    and told
Into freed Israel's lap her jewels and her gold.[1]   1

And when their wondrous march was o'er,
    And they had won their homes,
Where Abraham fed his flock of yore,
    Among their fathers' tombs;—
A land that drinks the rain of Heaven at will,
Whose waters kiss the feet of many a vine-clad
    hill;—

Oft as they watch'd, at thoughtful eve,
    A gale from bowers of balm   2
Sweep o'er the billowy corn, and heave
    The tresses of the palm,
Just as the lingering Sun had touch'd with
    gold,
Far o'er the cedar shade, some tower of giants
    old;

It was a fearful joy, I ween,
    To trace the Heathen's toil,

---

[3] Keble's note: "Then they willingly received Him into the ship: and immediately the ship was at the land whither they went." John 6,21.

[1] Told: counted. Israel: Keble here uses a figure common in the typological reading of the Old Testament, in which its events were taken to predict or prefigure events in Christian history: thus, the salvation of the Israelite households when the Lord struck down the eldest sons of Egyptian families (Exodus 11–12), the exodus from Egypt, and the entrance of the Israelites into the promised land of Canaan prefigure the entrance of the blessed into heaven after the final judgment of God. The Israelite conquest of Canaan is recounted in the Old Testament Book of Joshua.

The limpid wells, the orchards green,
    Left ready for the spoil,
The household stores untouch'd, the roses
    bright
Wreath'd o'er the cottage walls in garlands of
    delight.

And now another Canaan yields
    To Thine all-conquering ark;—
Fly from the "old poetic" fields,[2]
    Ye Paynim[3] shadows dark!
Immortal Greece, dear land of glorious lays,
Lo! here the "unknown God" of thy uncon-
    scious praise![4]

The olive-wreath, the ivied wand,
    "The sword in myrtles drest,"
Each legend of the shadowy strand
    Now wakes a vision blest;
As little children lisp, and tell of Heaven,
So thoughts beyond their thought to those
    high Bards were given.

And these are ours: Thy partial grace
    The tempting treasure lends:
These relics of a guilty race
    Are forfeit to Thy friends;
What seem'd an idol hymn, now breathes of
    Thee,
Tun'd by Faith's ear to some celestial melody.

There's not a strain to Memory dear,
    Nor flower in classic grove,
There's not a sweet note warbled here,
    But minds us of Thy Love.
O Lord, our Lord, and spoiler of our foes,
There is no light but Thine: with Thee all
    beauty glows.

                1827

Eleventh Sunday After Trinity[1]

Is it a time to receive money, and to receive gar-
ments, and oliveyards, and vineyards, and sheep, and
oxen, and menservants, and maidservants?
                —2 KINGS 5:26.

Is this a time to plant and build,
Add house to house, and field to field,
When round our walls the battle lowers,
When mines are hid beneath our towers,
And watchful foes are stealing round
To search and spoil the holy ground?

Is this a time for moonlight dreams
Of love and home by mazy streams,
For Fancy with her shadowy toys,
Aerial hopes and pensive joys,   10
While souls are wandering far and wide,
And curses swarm on every side?

No—rather steel thy melting heart
To act the martyr's sternest part,
To watch, with firm unshrinking eye,
Thy darling visions as they die,
Till all bright hopes, and hues of day,
Have faded into twilight gray.

Yes—let them pass without a sigh,
And if the world seem dull and dry,   20
If long and sad thy lonely hours,
And winds have rent thy sheltering bowers,
Bethink thee what thou art and where,
A sinner in a life of care.

The fire of God is soon to fall
(Thou know'st it) on this earthly ball;
Full many a soul, the price of blood,
Mark'd by th' Almighty's hand for good,
To utter death that hour shall sweep—
And will the Saints in Heaven dare weep?   30

Then in His wrath shall GOD uproot
The trees He set, for lack of fruit,
And drown in rude tempestuous blaze
The towers His hand had deign'd to raise;
In silence, ere that storm begin,
Count o'er His mercies and thy sin.

Pray only that thine aching heart,
From visions vain content to part,
Strong for Love's sake its woe to hide,
May cheerful wait the Cross beside,   40

---

    [2] Keble's note: "Where each old poetic mountain / Inspiration breathed around": Thomas Gray, "The Progress of Poetry" (1757), ll. 73–74.
    [3] Paynim: pagan.
    [4] It was also common in theological writing since the renaissance to interpret events in classical poems as foreshadowing the birth of Christ or other events in Christian history.
    [1] The eighth Sunday after Easter.

Too happy if, that dreadful day,
Thy life be given thee for a prey.[2]

Snatch'd sudden from th' avenging rod,
Safe in the bosom of thy GOD,
How wilt thou then look back, and smile
On thoughts that bitterest seem'd erewhile,
And bless the pangs that made thee see
This was no world of rest for thee!

1827

Holy Matrimony[1]

The voice that breathed o'er Eden,
  That earliest wedding day,
The primal marriage blessing,
  It hath not passed away:

Still in the pure espousal
  Of Christian man and maid
The Holy Three are with us,
  The threefold grace is said.

For dower of blessèd children,
10   For love and faith's sweet sake,

For high mysterious union
  Which nought on earth may break.

Be present, awful Father,
  To give away this bride,
As Eve Thou gav'st to Adam
  Out of his own pierced side:

Be present, Son of Mary,
  To join their loving hands,
As Thou didst bind two natures
  In Thine Eternal bands: 2[0]

Be present, Holiest Spirit,
  To bless them as they kneel,
As Thou for Christ, the Bridegroom,
  The heavenly Spouse dost seal.

O spread Thy pure wing o'er them,
  Let no ill power find place,
When onward to Thine Altar
  The hallowed path they trace.

To cast their crowns before Thee
  In perfect sacrifice,   3[0]
Till to the home of gladness
  With Christ's own Bride they rise. Amen.

(1857) 1857; 1869

Robert Montgomery
1807–1855

Robert Montgomery was the illegitimate son of a theatrical clown. He was educated in private schools and encouraged in a florid and precocious turn for verse by his father. He published a volume of poems in 1825, two satiric poems (The Age Reviewed, 1827; The Puffiad, 1828) in an eighteenth-century tradition, and The Omnipresence of the Deity in 1828. The latter was a very popular poem, still in print in its twenty-eighth edition in 1855,

even though Montgomery's rhetoric was often derided, most famously by Thomas Babington Macaulay in a review in the Edinburgh Review in 1830. Montgomery entered Oxford in 1830, graduated in 1833, and was ordained in the Church of England in 1835. He wrote other grandly conceived poems —Satan (1830), The Messiah (1832), Luther (1842)—which were moderately popular, and he also achieved a considerable reputation as a theo-

[2] Keble's note refers to Jeremiah 45:4–5—"Thus shalt thou say unto him, the Lord saith thus; Behold, that which I have built will I break down, and that which I have planted I will pluck up, even this whole land. And seekest thou great things for thyself? seek them not: for, behold, I will bring evil upon all flesh, saith the Lord: but thy life will I give unto thee for a prey in all places whither thou goest."

[1] This poem was written for a hymnal published in 1857; it is sung to a tune by C. Steggell.

logical writer and preacher in Glasgow and London. The text of the extract reprinted here is that of a second edition of the poem published in 1828.

from The Omnipresence of the Deity

Stupendous God! how shrinks our bounded
    sense
To track the triumphs of Omnipotence;
From sky-clad mountain, to the deepest den,
From the mean insects, to immortal men;
Bless'd with Thy brightest smile, dare we
    confine
Paternal Providence, supreme as thine?
Far as the fancy flies, or life-stream flows,
From Georgia's desert to the Greenland snows,
Where space exists, Thine eyes of mercy see,—
Creation lives, and moves, and breathes *in
    Thee!*
Unseen, but felt, Thine interfused control
Works in each atom, and pervades the whole;
Expands the blossom, and erects the tree,
Conducts each vapour, and commands each
    sea;
The Laws of Nature Thy decree fulfil,
And all Her powers but personate Thy will.

    .   .   .

Then boast not thou, whose eye alone can see
In nature's glass reflected Deity;
From whence does moral elevation flow,
What pang is mute, what balm prepared for
    wo,
Though ocean, mountain, sky, and air impress
Full on the soul a felt Almightiness?
Can ocean teach magnificence of mind?
Is truth made vocal by the deep-voiced wind?

Can flowers their bloom of innocence impart,
Or tempt one weed of vileness from the heart?
Can thy benevolence, all bounteous Sun,
Thou burning shadow of the brightest ONE!
Array our souls with emulative beam
Like thine, to glad life's universal stream?   30
From yon pale stars does purity descend,
And their chaste beauty with our spirit blend?—
Alas, oh, God! if thou *alone* art found
When most creation with thy smile is crown'd;
Rather in blindness let this outward eye
Be dead to nature, than Thy throne deny,
Raised on the pillars of Redemption's might,
And dazzling angels with too deep a light!

There is a PRESENCE spiritually vast
Around Thy church, arisen Saviour! cast;   40
A holy Effluence, an unspoken Awe,
A sanctity which carnal eye ne'er saw,
A pure, impalpable, almighty sense
Of peace, by reconciled Omnipotence,
That hallows, haunts, and makes a Christian
    mind
Rich in all grace, celestially refined:
Mere Nature's worshippers can never feel
The fulness of that high seraphic zeal
Which veileth all things with religious light,
And works unwearied in Jehovah's sight: 50
Thought, dream, and action,—ev'ry pulse of
    soul
The awe of Christ will solemnly control;
Girt by THE SPIRIT, whereso'er we rove,
True Faith is feeding on His word of love.
Nature is now a more than nature far;
Each miracle of sun, or moon, or star,
Each sight, and sense, and sound of outward
    things
Seems haunted by august imaginings;
A dream of Calvary around her floats,
And oft the dew of those delicious notes
By angels once in Bethlehem's valley pour'd
Descends, with all their melody restored,
Till—peace on earth! to pardon'd man—good
    will!
With tones of heaven the ear of fancy fill.
        1828

John Henry Newman
1801–1890

John Henry Newman was educated at Oxford and elected to a fellowship in one of its colleges in 1822. He was ordained in the priesthood of the Church of England in 1824, and he served as a tutor in the university and as one of its preachers in the 1820s and 1830s. He was one of the founders, with John Keble, of the Tractarian Movement, and his tract in 1841, arguing the compatibility of the articles of faith of the Church of England with the doctrines of the Roman Catholic church, resulted in a ban on the series by church and university authorities. In 1845 Newman became a member of the Roman Catholic church, and in the next year he was ordained into its priesthood. He established a house of the clerical order of which he was a member in Birmingham, delivered a series of lectures on university education as rector of the Catholic university in Dublin, published two novels, and wrote polemical and explicatory essays and books on ecclesiastical and theological topics. In 1864, in response to an attack on his character, he wrote and published Apologia pro Vita Sua, an autobiographical account of his religious conversion and belief. He published some of his poems in a collection titled Lyra Apostolica (1836), to which John Keble and others also contributed, and he included many of these earlier published poems in Verses on Various Occasions (1868), a collection that was several times reprinted during the remainder of the century. Newman also published a long dramatic poem, The Dream of Gerontius, in 1865–66. The texts below are those published in the 1868 edition of Verses on Various Occasions.

Wilfred Ward (two volumes, 1921), Maisie Ward (Young Mr. Newman: 1948), Louis Boyer (translated 1958), and Meriol Trevor (two volumes, 1962) have written biographies of Newman. Wilfred Ward has also written a history of the Oxford Movement (1912); other histories have been written by Richard Church (1922, reprinted 1970), Geoffrey Faber (second edition, 1936), Marvin R. O'Connell (1969), and Raymond Chapman (1970). C. S. Dessain has edited the Letters and Diaries in 28 volumes (1961–75); Martin J. Svaglic has edited the Apologia (1967); C. F. Harrold has edited a volume of Newman's essays (1948), including an important essay on the nature and function of poetry. J. M. Cameron's pamphlet in the Writers and Their Work series (1956), and Americo D. Lapati's short study of Newman (1972) contain bibliographies of writing about him.

The Pillar of the Cloud[1]

Lead, Kindly Light, amid the encircling gloom,
    Lead Thou me on!
The night is dark, and I am far from home—
    Lead Thou me on!
Keep Thou my feet; I do not ask to see
The distant scene—one step enough for me.

I was not ever thus, nor pray'd that Thou
    Shouldst lead me on.
I loved to choose and see my path, but now
    Lead Thou me on!
I loved the garish day, and, spite of fears,
Pride ruled my will: remember not past years.

So long Thy power hath blest me, sure it still
    Will lead me on,
O'er moor and fen, o'er crag and torrent, till
    The night is gone;
And with the morn those angel faces smile
Which I have loved long since, and lost awhile.

                  (1833) 1834; 1836

[1] Newman wrote this poem in 1833 while traveling in Italy and Sicily. He published it in a magazine in 1834, in Lyra Apostolica in 1836, and in his collection of verse in 1868. The poem had been sung as a hymn before 1865, but Newman himself attributed its great popularity as a hymn to the setting written for the poem by John Bacchus Dykes (1823–76), one of the editors of Hymns Ancient and Modern, who included the hymn in the first edition of this collection in 1861. The appropriate scriptural text of the hymn is: "And the Lord went before them by day in a pillar of a cloud, to lead them the way; and by night in a pillar of fire, to give them light" (Exodus 13:21).

Matins—Sunday[1]

Let us arise, and watch by night,
    And meditate always;
And chant, as in our Maker's sight,
    United hymns of praise.

So, singing with the Saints in bliss,
    With them we may attain
Life everlasting after this,
    And heaven for earthly pain.

Grant this, O Father, Only Son,   10
    And Spirit, God of grace,
To whom all worship shall be done
    In every time and place.

                                    1868

Matins—Friday

May the dread Three in One, who sways
    All with His sovereign might,
Accept us for this hymn of praise,
    His watchers in the night.

For in the night, when all is still,
    We spurn our bed and rise,
To find the balm for ghostly ill,
    His bounteous hand supplies.

If e'er by night our envious foe   10
    With guilt our souls would stain,
May the deep streams of mercy flow,
    And make us white again;

That so with bodies braced and bright,
    And hearts awake within,
All fresh and keen may burn our light,
    Undimm'd, unsoil'd by sin.

Shine on Thine own, Redeemer sweet!
    Thy radiance increate[1]

Through the long day shall keep our feet
    In their pure morning state.   20

Grant this, O Father, etc.

                                    1868

from The Dream of Gerontius[1]

"O Lord, how wonderful in depth and height"

Angel

O Lord, how wonderful in depth and height,
    But most in man, how wonderful Thou
    art!
With what a love, what soft persuasive might
    Victorious o'er the stubborn fleshly heart,
    Thy tale complete of saints Thou dost
        provide,
    To fill the throne which angels lost through
        pride!

He lay a grovelling babe upon the ground,
    Polluted in the blood of his first sire,
With his whole essence shatter'd and unsound,
    And coil'd around his heart a demon dire,   10
    Which was not of his nature, but had skill
    To bind and form his op'ning mind to ill.

Then was I sent from heaven to set right
    The balance in his soul of truth and sin,
And I have waged a long relentless fight,
    Resolved that death-environ'd spirit to
        win,
    Which from its fallen state, when all was lost,
    Had been repurchased at so dread a cost.

---

[1] Matins are morning prayers in the daily offices of devotion recited by members of a priesthood or religious order.

[1] Increate: uncreated.

[1] Newman wrote this poem in 1865 during a time when he was still engaged in the controversy which engendered and followed the publication of *Apologia pro Vita Sua*. During this time he was strongly persuaded of the imminence of his own death. The poem is a colloquy between the soul of the mortal Gerontius and the spirits who surround him at the moment of his death. His soul is finally transported to purgatory, where it will suffer in the consolation, even the joy, of its eventual entrance into heaven. Newman first published the poem in a magazine in 1865, and then as a book in the same year. It was very popular, going through thirty-two editions by the end of the century. Edward Elgar (1857–1934) converted the poem to an oratorio in 1900.

O what a shifting parti-colour'd scene
    Of hope and fear, of triumph and dismay,
Of recklessness and penitence, has been
    The history of that dreary, life-long fray!
    And O the grace to nerve him and to lead,
    How patient, prompt, and lavish at his need!

O man, strange composite of heaven and earth!
    Majesty dwarf'd to baseness! fragrant
        flower
Running to poisonous seed! and seeming worth
    Cloking corruption! weakness mastering
        power!
    Who never art so near to crime and shame,
    As when thou hast achieved some deed of
        name;—

How should ethereal natures comprehend
    A thing made up of spirit and of clay,
Were we not task'd to nurse it and to tend,
    Link'd one to one throughout its mortal
        day?
    More than the Seraph in his height of place,
The Angel-guardian knows and loves the
        ransom'd race.

       ·   ·   ·

All praise to Him, at whose sublime decree
    The last are first, the first become the last;
By whom the suppliant prisoner is set free,
    By whom proud first-borns from their
        thrones are cast;
Who raises Mary to be Queen of heaven,
While Lucifer is left, condemn'd and
        unforgiven.

       ·   ·   ·

[Conclusion: "Now let the golden prison ope its gates"]

Angel

Now let the golden prison ope its gates,
Making sweet music, as each fold revolves
Upon its ready hinge. And ye, great powers,
Angels of Purgatory, receive from me
My charge, a precious soul, until the day,
When, from all bond and forfeiture released,
I shall reclaim it for the courts of light.

Souls in Purgatory

1. Lord, Thou hast been our refuge: in every
   generation;
2. Before the hills were born, and the world
   was: from age to age Thou art God.
3. Bring us not, Lord, very low: for Thou

hast said, Come back again, ye sons of
Adam.
4. A thousand years before Thine eyes are but
   as yesterday: and as a watch of the night
   which is come and gone.
5. The grass springs up in the morning: at
   evening-tide it shrivels up and dies.
6. So we fail in Thine anger: and in Thy
   wrath are we troubled.
7. Thou has set our sins in Thy sight: and
   our round of days in the light of Thy
   countenance.
8. Come back, O Lord! how long: and be en-
   treated for Thy servants.
9. In Thy morning we shall be filled with
   Thy mercy: we shall rejoice and be in
   pleasure all our days.
10. We shall be glad according to the days of
    our humiliation: and the years in which
    we have seen evil.
11. Look, O Lord, upon Thy servants and on
    Thy work: and direct their children.
12. And let the beauty of the Lord our God be
    upon us: and the work of our hands, estab-
    lish Thou it.

Glory be to the Father, and to the Son: and to
    the Holy Ghost.
As it was in the beginning, is now, and ever
    shall be: world without end. Amen.

Angel

Softly and gently, dearly-ransom'd soul,
    In my most loving arms I now enfold thee,
And, o'er the penal waters, as they roll,
    I poise thee, and I lower thee, and hold
        thee.

And carefully I dip thee in the lake,
    And thou, without a sob or a resistance,
Dost through the flood thy rapid passage take,
    Sinking deep, deeper, into the dim dis-
        tance.

Angels, to whom the willing task is given,
    Shall tend, and nurse, and lull thee, as
        thou liest;
And Masses on the earth, and prayers in
       heaven,
    Shall aid thee at the Throne of the Most
        Highest.

Farewell, but not for ever! brother dear,
    Be brave and patient on thy bed of sorrow;
Swiftly shall pass thy night of trial here,
    And I will come and wake thee on the
        morrow.

                (1865) 1865; 1866

Reginald Heber

1783–1826

Reginald Heber, the son of a clergyman, was edu-cated at Oxford, where he won prizes for his Latin and English verse. He was elected to a fellowship in one of Oxford's colleges, took orders in the Church of England in 1807, and served in several ecclesiastical appointments in England before being named Bishop of Calcutta in 1822. He died in India.

Heber published his prize poem in English in 1807, and a volume of poems and translations in 1812. He began publishing his hymns in magazines in 1811, and before he left England he tried but failed to persuade the church hierarchy to authorize a hymnal containing some of his hymns for use in services of the Church of England. His hymns were collected and published in 1827, and appeared in twelve editions before mid-century. George Smith published a biography of Heber in 1895; R. H. Cholomondeley has edited a collection of family letters (1950). The texts printed here are those of The Poetical Works of Reginald Heber (London, 1841).

"From Greenland's icy mountains"[1]

From Greenland's icy mountains,
    From India's coral strand,
Where Afric's sunny fountains
    Roll down their golden sand;
From many an ancient river,
    From many a palmy plain,
They call us to deliver
    Their land from error's chain.

What though the spicy breezes
    Blow soft o'er Ceylon's isle,
Though every prospect pleases
    And only man is vile;

In vain with lavish kindness
    The gifts of God are strown,
The heathen in his blindness
    Bows down to wood and stone!

Can we, whose souls are lighted
    With wisdom from on high,
Can we to men benighted
    The lamp of life deny?   20
Salvation! oh, Salvation!
    The joyful sound proclaim,
Till each remotest nation
    Has learnt Messiah's name!

Waft, waft, ye winds, His story,
    And you, ye waters, roll,
Till, like a sea of glory,
    It spreads from pole to pole!
Till o'er our ransomed nature
    The Lamb for sinners slain,—   30
Redeemer, King, Creator,—
    In bliss returns to reign.

                 (1819) 1821; 1827

"Holy, holy, holy, Lord God Almighty!"[1]

Holy, holy, holy, Lord God Almighty!
    Early in the morning our song shall rise to
        Thee;
Holy, holy, holy! merciful and mighty!
    God in three persons, blessèd Trinity!

Holy, holy, holy! all the saints adore Thee,
    Casting down their golden crowns around
        the glassy sea;

---

[1] Heber wrote this hymn for a service during which a collection to support missions was to be taken. It was published first in a magazine; it is sung to several settings.

[1] Heber's hymns, like the poems of Keble's *Christian Year*, were arranged by the church calendar. This hymn was titled "Trinity Sunday": the appropriate text is the description of God in Revelation 4, seated on a throne set upon "a sea of glass like unto crystal" and sur-rounded by four beasts who "rest not day and night, saying, Holy, holy, holy, Lord God Almighty, which was, and is, and is to come" (6–8). The best-known setting of the hymn is by John Bacchus Dykes (1823–76), one of the editors of *Hymns Ancient and Modern* who wrote the tune for the first edition of the collection in 1861.

Cherubim and seraphim falling down before
    Thee,
Which wert and art and evermore shalt be!

Holy, holy, holy! though the darkness hide
    Thee,
10   Though the eye of sinful man Thy glory
      may not see,

Only Thou art holy, there is none beside Thee,
    Perfect in power, in love, and purity!

Holy, holy, holy, Lord God Almighty!
    All Thy works shall praise Thy name, in
      earth, and sky, and sea.
Holy, holy, holy! merciful and mighty!
    God in three persons, blessèd Trinity!

                            1827

James Montgomery
1771–1854

James Montgomery was the son of a preacher and missionary of the Moravian Brethren, a church which in medieval Germany set itself against the authority of the state as well as the pope. After its renewal in the eighteenth century the church emphasized evangelical and missionary enterprises and the primacy of the Scripture as a guide to conscience and conduct. Montgomery became a radical journalist and editor in Sheffield in the 1790s—he was twice fined and briefly imprisoned, once for selling a ballad describing the fall of the Bastille during the French Revolution—and he continued to work as a journalist until 1825. He began publishing his poems at the turn of the century; among his ten volumes of poems are two collections of his hymns and The World Before the Flood *(1813), a narrative of the Biblical patriarchs which was often republished during his lifetime. Montgomery published his hymns in magazines and collected them in* Songs of Zion *(1822), metrical imitations of the psalms, and in* Original Hymns *(1853). He also edited two popular hymnals which included his own hymns,* The Christian Psalmist *(1825), and a revision of the hymnal of the Moravian Brethren in 1849.*

"Lift up your heads, ye gates of brass!"[1]

I

Lift up your heads, ye gates of brass!
    Ye bars of iron! yield;
And let the King of Glory pass,—
    The cross is in the field.

That banner, brighter than the star,
    That leads the train of night,
Shines on their march and guides from far
    His servants to the fight.

A holy war those servants wage;
    —Mysteriously at strife,
The powers of heaven and hell engage   10
    For more than death or life.

Earth's rankest soil they see outspread;
    So thronged, it seems within,
One city of the living dead,
    Dead while alive to sin.

---

[1] The title Montgomery gave this hymn was "China Evangelized." This version of nineteen stanzas was first published in a magazine in 1843 and then in a collection of Montgomery's hymns in 1853. Stanzas 1, 2, 3, 7, 14, 16, 18, and 19 were commonly sung as a hymn, with some alterations. The hymn was sung to several tunes. The appropriate scriptural text is Psalms 24:9: "Lift up your heads, O ye gates; even lift them up, ye everlasting doors; and the King of glory shall come in." The text printed here is from an edition of Montgomery's poems published in Boston in 1860.

The forms of life are everywhere,
The spirit nowhere found;
Like vapors kindling in the air,
Then sinking in the ground.

No hope have these above the dust,
No being but a breath;
In vanity and lies they trust,
Their very life is death.

II
Ye armies of the living God,
His sacramental host!
Where hallowed footstep never trod,
Take your appointed post.

Follow the cross, the ark of peace
Accompany your path,
To slaves and rebels bring release
From bondage and from wrath.

A barley-cake o'erthrew the camp
Of Midian, tent by tent,
Ere morn the trumpet and the lamp
Through all in triumph went.

Though China's sons like Midian's fill
As grasshoppers the vale,
The sword of God and Gideon[2] still
To conquer cannot fail.

As Jericho[3] before the blast
Of sounding rams' horns fell,
Sin's strongholds here shall be down cast,
Down cast these gates of hell.

Truth error's legions must o'erwhelm
And China's thickest wall,
(The wall of darkness round her realm,)
At your loud summons fall.

Though few and small and weak your bands,
Strong in your captain's strength,
Go to the conquest of all lands,
All must be his at length.

The closest sealed between the poles
Is opened to your toils;

Where thrice a hundred million souls
Are offered you for spoils.

Those spoils, at his victorious feet,
You shall rejoice to lay,
And lay yourselves, as trophies meet,
In his great judgment-day.

III
No carnal weapon those ye bear,
To lay the aliens low;
Then strike amain, and do not spare,
There's life in every blow.

Life!—more than life on earth can be;
All in this conflict slain
Die but to sin,—eternally
The crown of life to gain.

O fear not, faint not, halt not now;
Quit you like men, be strong;
To Christ shall Buddhu's votaries bow
And sing with you this song:

"Uplifted are the gates of brass,
The bars of iron yield;
Behold the King of Glory pass;
The cross hath won the field."

1843

At Home in Heaven[1]

PART I
"For ever with the Lord!"
—Amen; so let it be;
Life from the dead is in that word,
'Tis immortality.

Here in the body pent,
Absent from Him I roam;
Yet nightly pitch my moving tent
A day's march nearer home.

My Father's house on high,
Home of my soul, how near,
At times, to faith's foreseeing eye,
Thy golden gates appear!

---

[2] Midian; Gideon: the army of the Midians was defeated by Gideon in the battles in which the Israelites gained control of Canaan: Judges 6–8.
[3] Jericho: one of the cities that fell to the Israelites in their conquest of Canaan (Joshua 2–6).
[1] Part I of this poem of twenty-two stanzas was sung as a hymn to a traditional hymn tune. The poem was published in a magazine and in a volume of verse in the same year. The text is reprinted from Miles. The appropriate scriptural text is 2 Thessalonians 4:17—"Then we which are alive and remain shall be caught up together with them in the clouds, to meet the Lord in the air; and so shall we ever be with the Lord."

Ah! then my spirit faints
   To reach the land I love,
The bright inheritance of saints,
   Jerusalem above.

Yet clouds will intervene,
   And all my prospect flies;
Like Noah's dove, I flit between
20   Rough seas and stormy skies.

Anon the clouds dispart,
   The winds and waters cease,
While sweetly o'er my gladden'd heart
   Expands the bow of peace.

Beneath its glowing arch,
   Along the hallow'd ground,
I see cherubic armies march,
   A camp of fire around.

I hear at morn and even,
30   At noon and midnight hour,
The choral harmonies of heaven
   Earth's Babel-tongues o'erpower.

Then, then I feel that He,
   (Remember'd or forgot,)
The Lord, is never far from me,
   Though I perceive Him not.

PART II
IN darkness as in light
   Hidden alike from view,
I sleep, I wake within *His* sight
40   Who looks all nature through.

From the dim hour of birth,
   Through every changing state
Of mortal pilgrimage on earth,
   Till its appointed date;

All that I am, have been,
   All that I yet may be,
He sees at once, as He hath seen
   And shall for ever see.

How can I meet His eyes?
50   Mine on the cross I cast,

And own my life a Saviour's prize,
   Mercy from first to last.

"For ever with the Lord!"
   —Father, if 'tis Thy will,
The promise of that faithful word,
   Even here to me fulfil.

Be Thou at my right hand,
   Then can I never fail;
Uphold Thou me, and I shall stand,
   Fight, and I must prevail.   60

So when my latest breath
   Shall rend the veil in twain,
By death I shall escape from death,
   And life eternal gain.

Knowing as I am known,
   How shall I love that word,
And oft repeat before the throne,
   "For ever with the Lord!"

Then, though the soul enjoy
   Communion high and sweet,   70
While worms this body must destroy,
   Both shall in glory meet.

The trump of final doom
   Will speak the self-same word,
And Heaven's voice thunder through the tomb,
   "For ever with the Lord!"

The tomb shall echo deep
   That death-awakening sound;
The saints shall hear it in their sleep
   And answer from the ground.   80

Then, upward as they fly,
   That resurrection-word
Shall be their shout of victory,
   "For ever with the Lord!"

The resurrection-word,
   That shout of victory,
Once-more,—"For ever with the Lord!
   Amen; so let it be.

1835

Bernard Barton

1784–1849

Bernard Barton was a Quaker who worked as a dealer in coal and grain and eventually as a clerk in a bank. He published over a dozen volumes of poetry, including a collection of his poems in 1820, a collection of Devotional Verses *in 1826, and* Household Verses *(1845). He was a friend of Charles Lamb and Edward FitzGerald; his books of pastoral, religious, and occasional verse were reviewed by, and he corresponded with, some of the principal literary men of his generation; and in 1846 he was honored for his poetry by the award of a government pension. His correspondence with other writers has been edited by James E. Barcus (1966). "Walking in the Light" was published in* Devotional Verses *(1826); the text reprinted here is that of the original edition.*

Walking in the Light

Walk in the light! So shalt thou know
  That fellowship of love,
His spirit only can bestow,
  Who reigns in light above.

Walk in the light! and, sin abhorr'd,
  Shall ne'er defile again;

The blood of Jesus Christ, thy Lord
  Shall cleanse from every stain.

Walk in the light!—and thou shalt find
  Thy heart made truly His,
Who dwells in cloudless light enshrin'd,   10
  In whom no darkness is.

Walk in the light!—and thou shalt own
  Thy darkness passed away,
Because that Light hath on thee shone
  In which is perfect day.

Walk in the light!—and e'en the tomb
  No fearful shade shall wear;
Glory shall chase away its gloom,
  For Christ hath conquer'd there!

Walk in the light!—and thine shalt be
  A path, though thorny, bright;
For God, by grace, shall dwell in Thee,
  And God himself is Light!

        1826

Josiah Conder

1789–1855

Josiah Conder was the grandson of a teacher in a nonconformist theological college, and the son of a bookseller, in which business Conder joined when he was seventeen. He later conducted the business himself, edited for forty years two important magazines of the nonconformist churches, compiled and mostly wrote a thirty-volume trav-eler's companion to every area of the world, and wrote many religious tracts and hymns. In 1836 he compiled The Congregational Hymnbook, *in which he published many of his own hymns; many of his hymns were also collected in an edition published in 1856. "Bread of heaven" was published first in a slightly different version in 1824, and re-*

vised by one of the editors of a hymnal in 1853. The text printed here is that which was most popular in nineteenth-century hymnals, including Hymns Ancient and Modern, into which it was incorporated in 1861. The text is printed in Julian, along with the text of the original version. The version printed here of "Day by day the manna fell" is that printed in Miles.

"Bread of heaven, on Thee we feed"[1]

Bread of heaven, on Thee we feed,
For Thy Flesh is meat indeed;
Ever may our souls be fed
With this true and living Bread;
Day by day with strength supplied
Through the life of Him Who died.

Vine of heaven! Thy Blood supplies
This blest cup of Sacrifice;
LORD, Thy Wounds our healing give,
10 To Thy Cross we look and live:
JESU! may we ever be
Grafted, rooted, built in Thee. Amen.

1824, 1853

"Day by day the manna fell"[1]

Day by day the manna fell;
Oh, to learn this lesson well!

Still, by constant mercy fed,
Give me, Lord, my daily bread.

"Day by day," the promise reads;
Daily strength for daily needs:
Cast foreboding fears away;
Take the manna of to-day.

Lord, my times are in Thy hand.
All my sanguine hopes have planned   10
To Thy wisdom I resign,
And would make Thy purpose mine.

Thou my daily task shalt give:
Day by day to Thee I live:
So shall added years fulfil,
Not my own,—my Father's will.

Fond ambition, whisper not;
Happy is my humble lot.
Anxious, busy cares, away;
I'm provided for to-day.   20

Oh, to live exempt from care
By the energy of prayer;
Strong in faith, with mind subdued,
Yet elate with gratitude.

1836

Charlotte Elliott
1789–1871

Charlotte Elliott was the niece of John Venn (1759–1813), one of the leaders of the evangelical movement in the Church of England in the early decades of the nineteenth century. She was an invalid for most of her life, edited annuals of religious verse in the 1830s and after, and collected the hymns of successive editions of The Invalid's Hymn Book *(1834–41), to which she also contributed her own hymns. "Just as I am" was one of the most popular hymns of the period. It was sung to several tunes, and incorporated into almost every hymnal in English in the last half of the*

---

[1] The appropriate scriptural texts are from John: "I am the living bread, which came down from heaven. . . . Whoso eateth my flesh, and drinketh my blood, hath eternal life (6:51, 54); and "I am the true vine" (15:1).
[1] The appropriate text is that of the Lord's Prayer. Manna is the bread-like food miraculously furnished the Israelites during their years in the wilderness (Exodus 16).

century, *including one of the editions of* Hymns Ancient and Modern *(1875)*. *The text printed here is that of a hymnal,* Church Hymns, *published in 1871, which includes the sometimes omitted second stanza, added by Elliott in the year of the first publication of the hymn (1836)*.

"Just as I am—without one plea"

Him that cometh unto me I will in no wise cast out.
— JOHN 6:37.

Just as I am—without one plea,
But that thy blood was shed for me,
And that thou bid'st me come to thee,
  O Lamb of God, I come!

Just as I am—and waiting not
To rid my soul of one dark blot,
To thee, whose blood can cleanse each spot,
  O Lamb of God, I come!

Just as I am—though tossed about
With many a conflict—many a doubt,
"Fightings and fears within, without,"[1]
  O Lamb of God, I come!

Just as I am—poor, wretched, blind;
Sight, riches, healing of the mind,
Yea, all I need, in thee to find,
  O Lamb of God, I come!

Just as I am—thou wilt receive,
Wilt welcome, pardon, cleanse, relieve:
Because thy promise I believe,
  O Lamb of God, I come!

Just as I am—thy love unknown
Has broken every barrier down,
Now, to be thine, yea, thine alone,
  O Lamb of God, I come!

Just as I am, of that free love
The breadth, length, depth, and height to prove,
Here for a season, then above—
  O Lamb of God, I come!

1836

Sarah Flower Adams
1805–1848

Sarah Flower Adams was born into a family of independent ministers. Her father established a radical newspaper and was briefly imprisoned for criticizing the hierarchy of the Established Church. In the 1820s and 1830s, when her family lived in London, she and her sister Eliza were part of an intellectual circle which included John Stuart Mill and Robert Browning. She began writing for magazines in the 1830s, briefly tried to make a career as an actress, and published a dramatic poem in 1841. She was a member of the congregation of William Johnson Fox (1786–1864), one of the founders of the radical quarterly Westminster Review *and a powerful preacher whose Christianity had some points in common with American Unitarianism in its emphasis on the ethical rather than on the doctrinal imperatives of Christian belief. "Nearer, My God, to Thee," the best known of Adams' several hymns, was written in 1841 for a hymnal Fox compiled for the use of his congregation. Its appropriate scriptural text is the dream of Jacob of a ladder reaching to heaven in Genesis 28:10–22. The hymn was included in the first edition of* Hymns Ancient and Modern *(1861) with a setting by one of the compilers of the collection, John Bacchus Dykes (1823–76); it has also been set to a tune by Arthur Sullivan (1842–1900). It appeared very often in nineteenth-century hymnals, sometimes without the final stanza. The text is that of Fox's collection,* Hymns and Anthems *(1841).*

[1] "For when we were come into Macedonia, our flesh had no rest, but we were troubled on every side; without were fightings, within were fears" (II Corinthians 7:5).

"Nearer, my God, to thee"

Nearer, my God, to thee,
        Nearer to thee!
E'en though it be a cross
        That raiseth me:
Still all my song would be,
Nearer, my God, to thee—
        Nearer to thee!

Though like the wanderer,
        The sun gone down,
Darkness be over me,
        My rest a stone;
Yet in my dreams I'd be
Nearer, my God, to thee—
        Nearer to thee!

There let the way appear,
        Steps unto heaven;
All that thou send'st to me
        In mercy given;

Angels to beckon me
Nearer, my God, to thee—
        Nearer to thee!

Then with my waking thoughts
        Bright with thy praise,
Out of my stony griefs
        Bethel[1] I'll raise:
So by my woes to be
Nearer, my God, to thee—
        Nearer to thee!

Or if on joyful wing
        Cleaving the sky,
Sun, moon, and stars forgot,
        Upwards I fly:
Still all my song shall be,
Nearer, my God, to thee—
        Nearer to thee!

1841

Henry Francis Lyte
1793–1847

Henry Francis Lyte was educated at Trinity College, Dublin, ordained in the Church of England in 1815, and served as a cleryman in England. He published a volume of Poems, Chiefly Religious *in 1833, a metrical version of some psalms in 1834, and an edition of the poems of the seventeenth-century religious poet Henry Vaughan in 1847. "Abide with me" was composed in 1847 and published in a posthumous collection of his writing in 1850. Its most common setting is by William Henry Monk (1823–89), an organist and composer who was one of the editors of the first edition of* Hymns Ancient and Modern *and composed the tune for the first edition of that collection in 1861. The appropriate scriptural text of the hymn is Luke 24:29: "Abide with us; for it is toward evening, and the day is far spent." The version printed below is that printed in the historical edition of* Hymns Ancient and Modern *(1909).*

"Abide with me; fast falls the eventide"

Abide with me; fast falls the eventide;
The darkness deepens; Lord, with me abide!
When other helpers fail, and comforts flee,
Help of the helpless, O abide with me.

Swift to its close ebbs out life's little day;
Earth's joys grow dim, its glories pass away;

---

[1] Bethel: a place sanctified by God's presence.

Change and decay in all around I see;
O Thou Who changest not, abide with me.[1]

I need Thy presence every passing hour;
What but Thy grace can foil the tempter's
    power?
Who like Thyself my guide and stay can be?
Through cloud and sunshine, Lord, abide
    with me.

I fear no foe with Thee at hand to bless;
Ills have no weight, and tears no bitterness;

Where is death's sting? where, grave, Thy
    victory?
I triumph still, if Thou abide with me.

Hold Thou Thy Cross before my closing eyes;
Shine through the gloom, and point me to the
    skies;
Heav'n's morning breaks, and earth's vain
    shadows flee;
In life, in death, O Lord, abide with me. Amen.   20
    (1847) 1850

Cecil Frances Alexander
1823–1895

Cecil Frances Alexander was born and lived in Ireland, the daughter of a military officer and landowner. Her husband was a clergyman in the Church of England who became a bishop of an Irish diocese. Alexander published more than half a dozen volumes of religious poems and hymns, including Hymns for Little Children *(1848), of which about a quarter million copies were sold. "Maker of Heaven and Earth" was sung to several tunes, including one by William Henry Monk (1823–89), who wrote a setting for a hymnal in 1887. The text printed here is that of the first edition of* Hymns for Little Children, *published in London in 1848.*

Maker of Heaven and Earth

All things bright and beauteous,
    All creatures great and small,
All things wise and wondrous,
    The Lord God made them all.

Each little flower that opens,
    Each little bird that sings,
He made their glowing colours,
    He made their tiny wings.

The rich man in his castle,
    The poor man at his gate,   10

[1] In Lyte's original manuscript version three stanzas intervened between stanzas 2 and 3 of the present version:

Not a brief glance I beg, a passing word:
But as Thou dweltst with Thy disciples, Lord,
Familiar, condescending, patient, free,
Come not to sojurn, but abide with me.

Come not in terror, as the King of Kings,
But kind and good, with healing in Thy wings,
Tears for all woes, a heart for every plea,—
Come, Friend of sinners, and thus bide with me.

Thou on my head in early youth didst smile:
And, though rebellious and perverse meanwhile,
Thou hast not left me, oft as I left Thee,
On to the close, O Lord, abide with me!

God made them, high or lowly,
And ordered their estate.

The purple-headed mountain,
The river running by,
The sunset and the morning,
That brightens up the sky,

The cold wind in the winter,
The pleasant summer sun,
The ripe fruits in the garden,
20   He made them every one.

The tall trees in the greenwood,
The meadows where we play,
The rushes in the water,
We gather every day;—

He gave us eyes to see them,
And lips that we might tell,
How great is God Almighty,
Who has made all things well.

1848

Frederick William Faber
1814–1863

Frederick Faber was born into a clerical family; his father was steward to a bishop, and his grandfather was a vicar in the Church of England. At Oxford in the 1830s, where he won prizes for his poetry, Faber came under the influence of John Henry Newman, and after his ordination as a priest in the Church of England in 1839 he followed Newman into the Roman Catholic Church in 1845. In 1849 he became superior of the London house of the order of which Newman was also a member. Faber published volumes of poetry in the 1840s, and five increasingly larger collections of his hymns between 1848 and 1862. The most recent life of Faber is by Ronald Chapman (1961). Raleigh Addington has edited a selection from Faber's letters (1974). The text printed here is that of a collection by Faber published in London in 1862.

Come to Jesus[1]

Souls of men! why will ye scatter
Like a crowd of frightened sheep?
Foolish hearts! why will ye wander
From a love so true and deep?

Was there ever kindest shepherd
Half so gentle, half so sweet

As the Saviour who would have us
Come and gather round His Feet?

It is God: His love looks mighty,
But is mightier than it seems: 10
'Tis our Father: and His fondness
Goes far out beyond our dreams.

There's a wideness in God's mercy,
Like the wideness of the sea:
There's a kindness in His justice,
Which is more than liberty.

There is no place where earth's sorrows
Are more felt than up in heaven;
There is no place where earth's failings
Have such kindly judgment given.   20

There is welcome for the sinner,
And more graces for the good;
There is mercy with the Saviour;
There is healing in His Blood.

There is grace enough for thousands
Of new worlds as great as this;
There is room for fresh creations
In that upper home of bliss.

[1] First published in a version of eight stanzas in 1854.

For the love of God is broader
    Than the measures of man's mind;
And the Heart of the Eternal
    Is most wonderfully kind.

But we make His love too narrow
    By false limits of our own;
And we magnify His strictness
    With a zeal He will not own.

There is plentiful redemption
    In the Blood that has been shed;
There is joy for all the members
    In the sorrows of the Head.

'Tis not all we owe to Jesus;
    It is something more than all;
Greater good because of evil,
    Larger mercy through the fall.

Pining Souls! come nearer Jesus,
    And oh come not doubting thus,
But with faith that trusts more bravely
    His huge tenderness for us.

If our love were but more simple,
    We should take Him at His word;
And our lives would be all sunshine
    In the sweetness of our Lord.

1854; 1862

John Mason Neale

1818–1866

John Mason Neale was the son of a clergyman in the Church of England. He was educated at Cambridge, won prizes for his English and classical poetry, and was ordained in the priesthood of the Church of England in 1842. He was a part of the movement in the Anglican church which tried to restore some of the rituals and liturgy of the pre-Reformation church, and he wrote a five-volume history of the Eastern church (1847–73). He wrote and published several volumes of original hymns, but his best, and best-known, hymns were translations of medieval Latin and Greek texts, most of them published in Mediaeval Hymns and Sequences *(1851, enlarged 1863) and* Hymns of the Eastern Church *(1862).*

The sequence below, from which two often-sung hymns were taken, is a translation of part of the Hora Novissima *of Bernard of Cluny, a twelfth-century abbot of a monastary in France. The hymns were often sung to tunes by Alexander Ewing (1830–95), who wrote a setting for the first edition of* Hymns Ancient and Modern *(1861). The text printed below is that of the enlarged version of* Mediaeval Hymns and Sequences *(1863).*

from Hora Novissima

"For thee, O dear dear Country!" [Jerusalem the Golden]

For thee, O dear dear Country!
    Mine eyes their vigils keep;
For very love, beholding
    Thy happy name, they weep:
The mention of thy glory
    Is unction to the breast,
And medicine in sickness,
    And love, and life, and rest.
O one, O onely Mansion!
    O Paradise of Joy!
Where tears are ever banished,
    And smiles have no alloy;
Beside thy living waters
    All plants are, great and small,
The cedar of the forest,
    The hyssop[1] of the wall:

[1] Hyssop: an aromatic plant used in rites of purification by the Hebrews.

With jaspers glow thy bulwarks;
    Thy streets with emeralds blaze;
The sardius[2] and the topaz
20   Unite in thee their rays:
Thine ageless walls are bonded
    With amethyst unpriced:
Thy Saints build up its fabric,[3]
    And the corner-stone is CHRIST.
The Cross is all thy splendour,
    The Crucified thy praise:
His laud and benediction
    Thy ransomed people raise:
JESUS, the Gem of Beauty,
30   True GOD and Man, they sing:
The never-failing Garden,
    The ever-golden Ring:
The Door, the Pledge, the Husband,
    The Guardian of His Court:
The Day-star of Salvation,
    The Porter and the Port.
Thou hast no shore, fair ocean!
    Thou has no time, bright day!
Dear fountain of refreshment
40   To pilgrims far away!
Upon the Rock of Ages
    They raise thy holy tower:
Thine is the victor's laurel,
    And thine the golden dower:
Thou feel'st in mystic rapture,
    O Bride that know'st no guile,
The Prince's sweetest kisses,
    The Prince's loveliest smile:
Unfading lilies, bracelets
50   Of living pearl thine own;
The LAMB is ever near thee,
    The Bridegroom thine alone:
The Crown is He to guerdon,
    The Buckler to protect,
And He Himself the Mansion,
    And He the Architect.

The only art thou needest,
    Thanksgiving for thy lot:
The only joy thou seekest,
    The Life where Death is not: 60
And all thine endless leisure
    In sweetest accents sings,
The ill that was thy merit,—
    The wealth that is thy King's!

JERUSALEM THE GOLDEN,
    WITH MILK AND HONEY BLEST,
BENEATH THY CONTEMPLATION
    SINK HEART AND VOICE OPPRESSED:
I KNOW NOT, O I KNOW NOT,
    WHAT SOCIAL JOYS ARE THERE!   70
WHAT RADIANCY OF GLORY,
    WHAT LIGHT BEYOND COMPARE!

And when I fain would sing them
    My spirit fails and faints,
And vainly would it image
    The assembly of the Saints.

THEY STAND, THOSE HALLS OF SYON,
    CONJUBILANT WITH SONG,
AND BRIGHT WITH MANY AN ANGEL,
    AND ALL THE MARTYR THRONG: 80
THE PRINCE IS EVER IN THEM;
    THE DAYLIGHT IS SERENE:
THE PASTURES OF THE BLESSED
    ARE DECKED IN GLORIOUS SHEEN.

THERE IS THE THRONE OF DAVID,—
    AND THERE, FROM CARE RELEASED,
THE SONG OF THEM THAT TRIUMPH,
    THE SHOUT OF THEM THAT FEAST;
AND THEY WHO, WITH THEIR LEADER,
    HAVE CONQUERED IN THE FIGHT,   90
FOR EVER AND FOR EVER
    ARE CLAD IN ROBES OF WHITE!

1851; 1863

---

[2] Sardius: an orange-red stone.
[3] Fabric: framework.

Thomas Toke Lynch

1818–1871

Thomas Toke Lynch was an independent minister, the son of a surgeon, who won a reputation for preaching to a small congregation in London in the 1860s. He published a collection of meditative and religious verse in 1850, and in 1855 he edited a hymnal titled The Rivulet. *In the second edition of this collection, published in 1856, he published some of his hymns, including "Lift up your heads," which were attacked by other ministers and adherents of the Congregational and other independent churches as pantheistic and even atheistic in their emphasis on the presence of God in creation. His hymns remained popular in independent churches, however, and the author of a memoir of Lynch in Miles claimed that their popularity was still growing at the end of the century. The text below is that printed in Miles.*

"Lift up your heads, rejoice"

Lift up your heads, rejoice,
  Redemption draweth nigh;
Now breathes a softer air,
  Now shines a milder sky;
The early trees put forth
  Their new and tender leaf;
Hushed is the moaning wind
  That told of winter's grief.

Lift up your heads, rejoice,
  Redemption draweth nigh;   10
Now mount the laden clouds,
  Now flames the darkening sky;
The early scattered drops
  Descend with heavy fall,
And to the waiting earth
  The hidden thunders call.

Lift up your heads, rejoice,
  Redemption draweth nigh;
O, note the varying signs
  Of earth, and air, and sky;   20
The God of Glory comes
  In gentleness and might,
To comfort and alarm,
  To succour and to smite.

He comes the wide world's king,
  He comes the true heart's friend,
New gladness to begin,
  And ancient wrong to end;
He comes to fill with light
  The weary, waiting eye: 30
Lift up your heads, rejoice,
  Redemption draweth nigh.

                    1856

Horatius Bonar

1808–1889

Horatius Bonar was born into a Scots family of ministers and was himself ordained in 1837 as a minister in the established church of Scotland. In 1843, however, he broke with the church and assisted in the founding of the independent Free Church of Scotland. He published several volumes of hymns, principally Hymns Original and Selected *(1846) and three series of* Hymns of Faith and Hope *(1857–66). "A Little While" is more rhythmic than some of Bonar's more conventional hymns, including some which were taken into* Hymns Ancient and Modern. *It is more like the gospel hymns made popular in England by the meetings of the American evangelists Dwight Moody (1837–99) and Ira Sankey (1840–1908) in the 1870s and 1880s; the hymn was in fact more popular in America than in England. The versions printed here are those of a selection published by Bonar's son in 1904.*

A Little While

Beyond the smiling and the weeping
    I shall be soon;
Beyond the waking and the sleeping,
Beyond the sowing and the reaping,
10   I shall be soon.
    Love, rest, and home!
    Sweet hope!
Lord, tarry not, but come.

Beyond the blooming and the fading
    I shall be soon;
Beyond the shining and the shading,
Beyond the hoping and the dreading,
    I shall be soon.
    Love, rest, and home!
    Sweet hope!
Lord, tarry not, but come.

Beyond the rising and the setting
    I shall be soon!
Beyond the calming and the fretting,
20 Beyond remembering and forgetting,

    I shall be soon.
    Love, rest, and home!
    Sweet hope!
Lord, tarry not, but come.

Beyond the gathering and the strewing
    I shall be soon!
Beyond the ebbing and the flowing,
Beyond the coming and the going,
    I shall be soon.
    Love, rest, and home!   30
    Sweet hope!
Lord, tarry not, but come.

Beyond the parting and the meeting
    I shall be soon!
Beyond the farewell and the greeting,
Beyond this pulse's fever beating,
    I shall be soon.
    Love, rest, and home!
    Sweet hope!
Lord, tarry not, but come.   40

Beyond the frost-chain and the fever
    I shall be soon!
Beyond the rock-waste and the river,
Beyond the ever and the never,
    I shall be soon.
    Love, rest, and home!
    Sweet hope!
Lord, tarry not, but come.

                            1857

William Whiting
1825–1878

William Whiting was the master of a chorister's school who published a volume of verse in 1851 and wrote about a dozen hymns. None attained the currency of "Eternal Father, strong to save," which became one of the best-known hymns of the century. Whiting first wrote the hymn in 1860, and it was revised for the first edition of Hymns Ancient and Modern *in 1861. John Bacchus Dykes (1823–76) wrote its setting for this edition, of which he was* one of the editors. *The text is that of the historical edition of* Hymns Ancient and Modern *(1909).*

"Eternal Father, strong to save"

Eternal Father, strong to save,
Whose arm hath bound the restless wave,
Who bidd'st the mighty ocean deep

Its own appointed limits keep;
O hear us when we cry to Thee
For those in peril on the sea.

O Christ, Whose voice the waters heard
And hushed their raging at Thy word,
Who walkedst on the foaming deep,
And calm amid the storm didst sleep;
O hear us when we cry to Thee
For those in peril on the sea.

O Holy Spirit, Who didst brood
Upon the waters dark and rude,

And bid their angry tumult cease,
And give, for wild confusion, peace;
O hear us when we cry to Thee
For those in peril on the sea.

O Trinity of love and power,
Our brethren shield in danger's hour;   20
From rock and tempest, fire and foe,
Protect them whersoe'er they go;
Thus evermore shall rise to Thee
Glad hymns of praise from land and sea.

Amen.
1860; 1861

Sabine Baring-Gould
1834–1924

Sabine Baring-Gould was educated at Cambridge and ordained into the priesthood of the Church of England in 1865. He served as a curate in Yorkshire, Essex, and Devon, where, among other antiquarian pursuits, he collected many rural folk songs and other folklore. He wrote voluminously: a seventeen-volume Lives of the Saints (1872–89), some novels, books for children, a life of the poet and clergyman Robert Stephen Hawker, devotional and theological works; an incomplete listing of his publications in the Cambridge Bibliography of English Literature records 101 titles. He published his hymns in newspapers, magazines, and hymnals. "Onward, Christian soldiers" was first published in 1865, taken into Hymns Ancient and Modern in 1868, and given its best-known setting, by Arthur Sullivan (1842–1900), in 1872. Baring-Gould published his memoirs in 1923 and 1925; William E. Purcell has published a biography (1957). The text printed below is that of the historical edition of Hymns Ancient and Modern (1909).

"Onward, Christian soldiers"

Onward, Christian soldiers,
Marching as to war,
With the Cross of Jesus
Going on before.
Christ the Royal Master

Leads against the foe;
Forward into battle,
See, His banners go!
Onward, Christian soldiers,
Marching as to war,   10
With the Cross of Jesus
Going on before.

At the sign of triumph
Satan's host doth flee;
On then, Christian soldiers,
On to victory.
Hell's foundations quiver
At the shout of praise;
Brothers, lift your voices,
Loud your anthems raise.   20
Onward, Christian soldiers, etc.

Like a mighty army
Moves the Church of God;
Brothers, we are treading
Where the Saints have trod;
We are not divided,
All one body we,
One in hope and doctrine,
One in charity.
Onward, Christian soldiers, etc.   30

Crowns and thrones may perish,
  Kingdoms rise and wane,
But the Church of Jesus
  Constant will remain;
Gates of hell can never
  'Gainst that Church prevail;
We have Christ's own promise,
  And that cannot fail.
    Onward, Christian soldiers, etc.

Onward, then, ye people,   40
  Join our happy throng,
Blend with ours your voices
  In the triumph song;
Glory, laud, and honour
  Unto Christ the King,
This through countless ages
  Men and Angels sing.
    Onward, Christian soldiers, etc.

1865

Samuel John Stone
1839–1900

Samuel John Stone, the son of a clergyman in the Church of England, graduated from Oxford in 1862 and was ordained in the same year. He published a volume of religious and other poems in 1872, and several books of hymns and other religious verse, including Sonnets of the Christian Year *(1875), a service with hymns for children (1883), and two collections of hymns in 1866 and 1886. "The Church's one Foundation," with its epigraph from the creed of the church, is a response to theological and historical studies and controversies which in the 1860s questioned the validity of those grounds for belief which depended on the increasingly dubious authority of conventional history and scriptural texts. The hymn was first published in 1866 and expanded in 1885. It was sung to a tune by S. S. Wesley (1810–76). The text is that printed in Julian.*

"The Church's one Foundation"

"I Believe in the Holy Catholic Church, the Communion of Saints."

The Church's one Foundation
  Is Jesus Christ her Lord:
She is His new creation
  By water and the word;
From heaven He came and sought her
  To be His Holy Bride,
With His own blood He bought her,
  And for her life He died.

Elect from every nation,
  Yet one o'er all the earth,   10
Her charter of salvation
  One Lord, one Faith, one Birth;
One Holy Name she blesses,
  Partakes one holy Food,
And to one hope she presses,
  With every grace endued.

The Church shall never perish!
  Her dear Lord to defend,
To guide, sustain, and cherish,
  Is with her to the end;   20
Though there be those who hate her,
  And false sons in her pale,
Against or foe or traitor
  She ever shall prevail.

Though with a scornful wonder
  Men see her sore opprest,
By schisms rent asunder,
  By heresies distrest;
Yet saints their watch are keeping,
  Their cry goes up "How long?"   30
And soon the night of weeping
  Shall be the morn of song.

'Mid toil and tribulation,
  And tumult of her war,
She waits the consummation
  Of peace for evermore;

Till with the vision glorious
  Her longing eyes are blest,
And the great Church victorious
40   Shall be the Church at rest.

So, Lord, she stands before Thee,
  For evermore thine own;
No merit is her glory,
  Her boasting this alone:
That she who did not choose Thee
  Come, chosen, at Thy call,
Never to leave or lose Thee
  Or from Thy favour fall.

For Thy true word remaineth;
50   No creature far or nigh,
No friend of ill who reigneth
  In hell or haunted sky;
No doubting world's derision
  That holds her in despite,
Shall hide her from Thy vision,
  Shall lure her from Thy light.

Thine, Thine! in bliss or sorrow,
  As well in shade as shine:

Of old, to-day, to-morrow,
  To all the ages, Thine!   60
Thine in her great commission,
  Baptized into Thy Name,
And in her last fruition
  Of all her hope and aim.

As she on earth hath union,
  With God, the Three in One,
So hath she sweet communion
  With those whose rest is won;
With all her sons and daughters,
  Who by the Master's Hand   70
Led through the deathly waters,
  Repose in Eden-Land.

Oh, happy ones and holy!
  Lord, give us grace that we
Like them, the meek and lowly,
  On high may dwell with Thee;
There past the border mountains,
  Where, in sweet vales, the Bride
With Thee, by living fountains,
  For ever shall abide. Amen.   80

1866; 1885

Henry Alford
1810–1871

Henry Alford was educated at Cambridge, where he knew Tennyson, was ordained in 1833, and ended his ecclesiastical career as Dean of Canterbury. He published several volumes of verse, an edition of the poetry of John Donne, and an edition of the Greek testament. His religious and other verse was published in magazines as well as collected in two volumes of hymns, including a hymnal organized on the church calendar which Alford published in 1867. "Ten thousand times ten thousand" was written for the twenty-first Sunday after Trinity; it was often sung to a tune by John Bacchus Dykes (1823–76), one of the editors of Hymns Ancient and Modern *who wrote the setting for the revised edition in 1875. The text is that of the historical edition of* Hymns Ancient and Modern *(1909); it includes a fourth stanza Alford added in 1870.*

The title is from the book of Daniel, part of a passage in which Daniel recounts his vision of the end of the world: "I beheld till the thrones were cast down, and the Ancient of days did sit, whose garment was white as snow, and the hair of his head was like the pure wool: his throne was like the fiery flame, and his wheels as burning fire. A fiery stream issued and came forth from before him: thousand thousands ministered unto him, and ten thousand times ten thousand stood before him: the judgment was set, and the books were opened" (Daniel 7:9–10).

"Ten thousand times ten thousand"

Ten thousand times ten thousand,
  In sparkling raiment bright,
The armies of the ransom'd Saints
  Throng up the steeps of light:

'Tis finish'd! all is finish'd,
    Their fight with death and sin;
Fling open wide the golden gates,
    And let the victors in.

What rush of Alleluias
10   Fills all the earth and sky!
What ringing of a thousand harps
    Proclaims the triumph nigh!
O day, for which creation
    And all its tribes were made!
O joy, for all the former woes
    A thousand-fold repaid!

Oh, then what raptured greetings
    On Canaan's happy shore,

What knitting sever'd friendships up,
    Where partings are no more!   20
Then eyes with joy shall sparkle
    That brimm'd with tears of late;
Orphans no longer fatherless,
    Nor widows desolate.

Bring near Thy great salvation,
    Thou LAMB for sinners slain,
Fill up the roll of Thine elect,
    Then take Thy power and reign:
Appear, Desire of nations;
    Thine exiles long for home;   30
Show in the heav'ns Thy promised sign:
    Thou Prince and Saviour, come. Amen.
                                    1867; 1870

Elizabeth Cecilia Clephane
1830–1869

Elizabeth Cecilia Clephane lived in Scotland. Like her other poems, "There were ninety and nine" first appeared in a magazine and was republished in an annual of religious verse; the text printed here is that of a religious annual published in 1874. The American evangelist Ira Sankey (1840–1908) was given a clipping of the poem during one of his tours in Great Britain in the 1870s, and when during a meeting he was asked to sing something, he improvised a tune to Clephane's poem. The hymn became extremely popular among evangelists and their congregations. The appropriate scriptural text is Matthew 18:12—"How think ye? if a man have a hundred sheep, and one of them be gone astray, doth he not leave the ninety and nine, and goeth into the mountains, and seek that which is gone astray?"

"There were ninety and nine that safely lay"

There were ninety and nine that safely lay
    In the shelter of the fold;

And one was out on the hills, away
    Far off from the gates of gold—
Away on the mountains wild and bare,
    Away from the tender Shepherd's care.

Lord, thou hast here thy ninety and nine,
    Are they not enough for thee?
But the Shepherd made answer, "This of mine
    Has wandered away from me.   10
And although the road be rough and steep,
    I go to the desert to find my sheep."

But none of the ransomed ever knew
    How deep were the waters crossed,
Nor how dark the night that the Lord passed
        through,
    Ere he found his sheep that was lost
    Out in the desert he heard its cry,
    Sick and helpless and ready to die.

Lord, whence are those blood-drops all the way
    That mark out the mountain track?   20
They were shed for one that had gone astray
    Ere the Shepherd could bring him back.

Lord, whence are thy hands so rent and
    torn?
They are pierced to-night by many a thorn.

And all through the mountains, thunder-riven,
    And up from the rocky steep,

There rose a cry to the gates of heaven,
    "Rejoice, I have found my sheep!"
And the Angels echoed around the throne,
    "Rejoice, for the Lord hath found his
    own."   30

1868; 1874

Christopher Wordsworth
1807–1885

Christopher Wordsworth was the nephew of William Wordsworth; in 1851 he prepared the family Memoir *of his uncle. He was educated at Cambridge, where his father was Master of Trinity College. He himself was elected to a fellowship at Trinity, and he held other academic posts, including the headmastership of Harrow. In 1844 he accepted the first of a series of ecclesiastical appointments, which culminated in 1869 when he was installed as the Bishop of Lincoln. In addition to the memoir of William Wordsworth, he published* The Holy Year *in 1862, a collection of hymns for the feasts of the liturgical year. The text of the hymn reprinted here is that of* The Holy Year; *the hymn was included, with a tune by J. Langran, in the 1868 edition of* Hymns Ancient and Modern.

All Saints' Day, Nov. 1

Hark the sound of holy voices, chanting at the
    crystal sea[1]
Hallelujah! Hallelujah! Hallelujah! Lord to
    Thee.
Multitude, which none can number, like the
    stars, in glory stands
Cloth'd in white apparel, holding palms of
    Victory in their hands.

Patriarch, and holy Prophet, who prepar'd the
    Way of Christ,

King, Apostle, Saint, and Martyr, Confessor,
    Evangelist,
Saintly Maiden, godly Matron, Widows who
    have watch'd to prayer,
Join'd in holy concert singing to the Lord of
    all are there.

They have come from tribulation, and have
    wash'd their robes in Blood,
Wash'd them in the Blood of Jesus; tried they
    were, and firm they stood;   10
Mock'd, imprison'd, ston'd, tormented, sawn
    asunder, slain with sword,
They have conquer'd Death and Satan, by the
    might of Christ the Lord.

Marching with Thy Cross their banner, they
    have triumph'd, following
Thee the Captain of Salvation, Thee their
    Saviour and their King;
Gladly, Lord, with Thee they suffer'd; gladly,
    Lord, with Thee they died;
And by Death to Life immortal they were born
    and glorified.

Now they reign in heavenly glory, now they
    walk in golden light,
Now they drink, as from a river, holy bliss and
    infinite;

[1] "And before the throne there was a sea of glass like unto crystal" (Revelation 4:2).

Love and Peace they taste for ever; and all
    Truth and Knowledge see
20 In the beatific vision of the Blessed Trinity.

God of God, the One-begotten, Light of Light,
    Emmanuel,

In Whose Body join'd together all the Saints
    for ever dwell,
Pour upon us of Thy fulness, that we may for
    evermore
God the Father, God the Son, and God the
    Holy Ghost adore.

                                                                1862

Francis Thompson
1859–1907

Both the father and mother of Francis Thompson were fervent converts to Roman Catholicism, and Thompson entered a seminary at the age of twelve to study for the Roman Catholic priesthood. He left seven years later, upon the advice of his teachers, and spent the next six years studying medicine. He was by then addicted to drugs, and he abandoned his ambition and went to London, where he lived for over two years as a derelict. In 1887 he sent some poems to a Roman Catholic magazine edited by the poet Alice Meynell (1847–1922) and her husband. The Meynells sought to meet him, and they arranged that Thompson be cared for in hospitals and monasteries. He spent the last ten years of his life in London, working as a journalist and writing a life of Ignatius Loyola. Three volumes of his poems were published during his lifetime: Poems *(1893),* Sister Songs *(1895), and* New Poems *(1897). "The Hound of Heaven" was first published in the Meynells' magazine in 1890. Biographies of Thompson and studies of his writing have been published by Everard Meynell (1913, revised 1926), R. L. Megroz (1927), J. C. Reid (1960), Paul vanK. Thomson (1961), and John E. Walsh (1967). Myrtle Pihlman Pope has prepared a bibliography of Thompson's writings and of writings about him (1959); see also Paul Butter's pamphlet in the Writers and Their Work series (1961). The standard edition is the three-volume* Works of Francis Thompson *(1913); the text printed here is that of the 1893 edition of* Poems, *which is consistent with the text of the standard edition.*

The Hound of Heaven

I fled Him, down the nights and down the
        days;
I fled Him, down the arches of the years;
I fled Him, down the labyrinthine ways
    Of my own mind; and in the mist of tears
I hid from Him, and under running laughter.
            Up vistaed hopes I sped;
            And shot, precipitated,
    Adown Titanic glooms of chasmèd fears,
    From those strong Feet that followed, fol-
        lowed after.
            But with unhurrying chase,   10
            And unperturbèd pace,
        Deliberate speed, majestic instancy,
            They beat—and a Voice beat
            More instant than the Feet—
    "All things betray thee, who betrayest Me."

            I pleaded, outlaw-wise,
By many a hearted casement, curtained red,
    Trellised with intertwining charities;
(For, though I knew His love Who followèd,
            Yet was I sore adread   20
Lest, having Him, I must have naught beside.)
But, if one little casement parted wide,
    The gust of His approach would clash it to:
Fear wist[1] not to evade, as Love wist to
        pursue.

---

[1] Wist: knew.

Across the margent of the world I fled,
　And troubled the gold gateways of the stars,
　Smiting for shelter on their clangèd bars;
　　Fretted to dulcet jars
And silvern chatter the pale ports[2] o' the moon.
30　I said to Dawn: Be sudden—to Eve: Be soon;
　　With thy young skiey blossoms heap me over
　　　From this tremendous Lover—
Float thy vague veil about me, lest He see!
I tempted all His servitors, but to find
My own betrayal in their constancy,
In faith to Him their fickleness to me,
　Their traitorous trueness, and their loyal
　　deceit.
To all swift things for swiftness did I sue;
　Clung to the whistling mane of every wind.
40　　But whether they swept, smoothly fleet,
　　The long savannahs of the blue;
　　　Or whether, Thunder-driven,
　　They clanged his chariot 'thwart a
　　　heaven,
Plashy with flying lightnings round the spurn
　　o' their feet:—
　Fear wist not to evade as Love wist to
　　pursue.
　　Still with unhurrying chase,
　　And unperturbèd pace,
　Deliberate speed, majestic instancy,
　　Came on the following Feet,
　　And a Voice above their beat—
　"Naught shelters thee, who wilt not shelter
50　　Me."

I sought no more that after which I strayed
　　In face of man or maid;
But still within the little children's eyes
　　Seems something, something that replies,
They at least are for me, surely for me!
I turned me to them very wistfully;
But just as their young eyes grew sudden fair
　With dawning answers there,
60　Their angel plucked them from me by the hair.
"Come then, ye other children, Nature's—share
With me" (said I) "your delicate fellowship;
　Let me greet you lip to lip,
　Let me twine with you caresses,
　　Wantoning
　　With our Lady-Mother's vagrant tresses,
　　Banqueting
　With her in her wind-walled palace,
　Underneath her azured daïs,
70　Quaffing, as your taintless way is,
　　From a chalice

　　　　²Ports: gates.

Lucent-weeping out of the dayspring."
　So it was done:
I in their delicate fellowship was one—
Drew the bolt of Nature's secrecies.
　I knew all the swift importings
　On the wilful face of skies;
　I knew how the clouds arise
　Spumèd of the wild sea-snortings;
　　All that's born or dies　　　　　　80
　Rose and drooped with; made them
　　shapers
Of mine own moods, or wailful or divine;
　With them joyed and was bereaven.
　I was heavy with the even,
　When she lit her glimmering tapers
　Round the day's dead sanctities.
　I laughed in the morning's eyes.
I triumphed and I saddened with all weather,
　Heaven and I wept together,
And its sweet tears were salt with mortal mine;　90
Against the red throb of its sunset-heart
　I laid my own to beat,
　And share commingling heat;
But not by that, by that, was eased my human
　　smart.
In vain my tears were wet on Heaven's grey
　　cheek.
For ah! we know not what each other says,
　These things and I; in sound *I* speak—
Their sound is but their stir, they speak by
　　silences.
Nature, poor stepdame, cannot slake my
　　drouth;
　Let her, if she would owe me,　　　　100
Drop yon blue bosom-veil of sky, and show me
　The breasts o' her tenderness:
Never did any milk of hers once bless
　　My thirsting mouth.
　　Nigh and nigh draws the chase,
　　With unperturbèd pace,
　Deliberate speed, majestic instancy;
　　And past those noisèd Feet
　　A voice comes yet more fleet—
　"Lo! naught contents thee, who
　　content'st not Me."　　　　　　110

Naked I wait Thy love's uplifted stroke!
My harness piece by piece Thou hast hewn
　　from me,
　　And smitten me to my knee;
　I am defenceless utterly.
　I slept, methinks, and woke,
And, slowly gazing, find me stripped in sleep.

In the rash lustihead of my young powers,
    I shook the pillaring hours[3]
And pulled my life upon me; grimed with
    smears,
120 I stand amid the dust o' the mounded years—
My mangled youth lies dead beneath the heap.
My days have crackled and gone up in smoke,
Have puffed and burst as sun-starts on a stream.
      Yea, faileth now even dream
The dreamer, and the lute the lutanist;
Even the linked fantasies, in whose blossomy
    twist
I swung the earth a trinket at my wrist,
Are yielding; cords of all too weak account
For earth with heavy griefs so overplussed.
130   Ah! is Thy love indeed
A weed, albeit an amaranthine weed,
Suffering no flowers except its own to mount?
      Ah! must—
      Designer infinite!—
Ah! must Thou char the wood ere Thou canst
    limn with it?
My freshness spent its wavering shower i' the
    dust;
And now my heart is as a broken fount,
Wherein tear-drippings stagnate, split down
    ever
      From the dank thoughts that shiver
140 Upon the sighful branches of my mind.
      Such is; what is to be?
The pulp so bitter, how shall taste the rind?
I dimly guess what Time in mists confounds;
Yet ever and anon a trumpet sounds
From the hid battlements of Eternity;
Those shaken mists a space unsettle, then
Round the half-glimpsèd turrets slowly wash
    again.
      But not ere him who summoneth
      I first have seen, enwound

With glooming robes purpureal,[4] cypress-
    crowned;   150
His name I know, and what his trumpet saith.
Whether man's heart or life it be which yields
      Thee harvest, must Thy harvest-fields
      Be dunged with rotten death?

      Now of that long pursuit
      Comes on at hand the bruit;[5]
That Voice is round me like a bursting
    sea:
      "And is thy earth so marred,
      Shattered in shard on shard?
Lo, all things fly thee, for thou fliest Me! 160
Strange, piteous, futile thing!
Wherefore should any set thee love apart?
Seeing none but I makes much of naught" (He
    said),
"And human love needs human meriting:
    How hast thou merited—
Of all man's clotted clay the dingiest clot?
    Alack, thou knowest not
How little worthy of any love thou art!
Whom wilt thou find to love ignoble thee,
    Save Me, save only Me?   170
All which I took from thee I did but take,
    Not for thy harms,
But just that thou might'st seek it in My arms.
    All which thy child's mistake
Fancies as lost, I have stored for thee at home:
    Rise, clasp My hand, and come!"
    Halts by me that footfall:
    Is my gloom, after all,
Shade of His hand, outstretched caressingly?
    "Ah, fondest, blindest, weakest,   180
    I am He Whom thou seekest!
Thou dravest love from thee, who dravest Me."
                   1890; 1893

---

[3] A reference to the story of Samson who redeemed his strength by pulling a building down
on himself and his captors (Judges 16:23–30).
[4] Purpureal: purple.   [5] Bruit: noise, clamor.

PART TEN

Victorian Poetics

Arthur Henry Hallam
1811–1833

Arthur Henry Hallam was the son of Henry Hallam, the author of standard political histories of England and of medieval Europe. Arthur Hallam entered Cambridge in 1828, met Alfred Tennyson the following year, and began the friendship which is memorialized in Tennyson's In Memoriam. *Hallam wrote poems which he privately circulated in 1830, translated some of Dante's sonnets, and won a reputation as one of the most promising intelligences of his generation. He published this review of Tennyson's 1830 volume of poems in the monthly* Englishman's Magazine *in 1831; the publisher of the journal was Edward Moxon, an acquaintance of Hallam's and later to be the publisher of Tennyson's poems. After Hallam's death, the essay was republished in 1834 in a collection of* Remains *edited by his father. The text here is that reprinted in* The Writings of Arthur Henry Hallam, *edited by T. H. Vail Motter (New York, 1943).*

from On Some of the Characteristics of Modern Poetry, and on the Lyrical Poems of Alfred Tennyson

[*Hallam begins his essay by advancing the idea, for which he invokes the authority of Wordsworth, that the established taste of literary critics is not necessarily a proper standard by which to judge the worth of contemporary poetry. This idea, he suggests, can now be used to advance the interests of a poetry different from Wordsworth's.*]

. . . It is not true, as his exclusive admirers would have it, that the highest species of poetry is the reflective; it is a gross fallacy, that because certain opinions are acute or profound, the expression of them by the imagination must be eminently beautiful. Whenever the mind of the artist suffers itself to be occupied, during its periods of creation, by any other predominant motive than the desire of beauty, the result is false in art.

Now there is undoubtedly no reason why he may not find beauty in those moods of emotion, which arise from the combinations of reflective thought; and it is possible that he may delineate these with fidelity, and not be led astray by any suggestions of an unpoetical mood. But though possible, it is hardly probable; for a man whose reveries take a reasoning turn, and who is accustomed to measure his ideas by their logical relations rather than the congruity of the sentiments to which they refer, will be apt to mistake the pleasure he has in knowing a thing to be true, for the pleasure he would have in knowing it to be beautiful, and so will pile his thoughts in a rhetorical battery, that they may convince, instead of letting them flow in a natural course of contemplation, that they may enrapture.

It would not be difficult to shew, by reference to the most admired poems of Wordsworth, that he is frequently chargeable with this error; and that much has been said by him which is good as philosophy, powerful as rhetoric, but false as poetry. Perhaps this very distortion of the truth did more in the peculiar juncture of our literary affairs to enlarge and liberalize the genius of our age, than could have been effected by a less sectarian temper.

However this may be, a new school of reformers soon began to attract attention, who, professing the same independence of immediate favor, took their stand on a different region of Parnassus from that occupied by the

Lakers,[1] and one, in our opinion, much less liable to perturbing currents of air from ungenial climates. We shall not hesitate to express our conviction, that the cockney school (as it was termed in derision from a cursory view of its accidental circumstances) contained more genuine inspiration, and adhered more steadily to that portion of truth which it embraced, than any *form* of art that has existed in this country since the days of Milton. Their *caposetta*[2] was Mr. Leigh Hunt, who did little more than point the way, and was diverted from his aim by a thousand personal predilections and political habits of thought.

But he was followed by two men of very superior make; men who were born poets, lived poets, and went poets to their untimely graves. Shelley and Keats were indeed of opposite genius; that of the one was vast, impetuous, and sublime, the other seemed to be "fed with honeydew," and to have "drunk the milk of Paradise."[3] Even the softness of Shelley comes out in bold, rapid, comprehensive strokes; he has no patience for minute beauties, unless they can be massed into a general effect of grandeur. On the other hand, the tenderness of Keats cannot sustain a lofty flight; he does not generalize or allegorize Nature; his imagination works with few symbols, and reposes willingly on what is given freely.

Yet in this formal opposition of character there is, it seems to us, a groundwork of similarity sufficient for the purposes of classification, and constituting a remarkable point in the progress of literature. They are both poets of sensation rather than reflection. Susceptible of the slightest impulse from external nature, their fine organs trembled into emotion at colours, and sounds, and movements, unperceived or unregarded by duller temperaments. Rich and clear were their perceptions of visible forms; full and deep their feelings of music. So vivid was the delight attending the simple

exertions of eye and ear, that it became mingled more and more with their trains of active thought, and tended to absorb their whole being into the energy of sense. Other poets *seek* for images to illustrate their conceptions; these men had no need to seek; they lived in a world of images; for the most important and extensive portion of their life consisted in those emotions which are immediately conversant with the sensation. Like the hero of Goethe's novel, they would hardly have been affected by what is called the pathetic parts of a book; but the *merely beautiful* passages, "those from which the spirit of the author looks clearly and mildly forth,"[4] would have melted them to tears. Hence they are not descriptive, they are picturesque. They are not smooth and *negatively* harmonious; they are full of deep and varied melodies.

This powerful tendency of imagination to a life of immediate sympathy with the external universe, is not nearly so liable to false views of art as the opposite disposition of purely intellectual contemplation. For where beauty is constantly passing before "that inward eye, which is the bliss of solitude;"[5] where the soul seeks it as a perpetual and necessary refreshment to the sources of activity and intuition; where all the other sacred ideas of our nature, the idea of good, the idea of perfection, the idea of truth, are habitually contemplated through the medium of this predominant mood, so that they assume its colour, and are subject to its peculiar laws, there is little danger that the ruling passion of the whole mind will cease to direct its creative operations, or the energetic principle of love for the beautiful sink, even for a brief period, to the level of a mere notion in the understanding.

We do not deny that it is, on other accounts, dangerous for frail humanity to linger with fond attachment in the vicinity of sense. Minds of this description are especially liable to

---

[1] Parnassus: a mountain in Greece sacred to the Muses and Apollo, god of poetry. Wordsworth was sometimes described as the leader of the "Lake school" of poets who resided in or wrote about the Lake District in the north of England. Hallam added a note in which he puns on a word in a classical Greek play to force a mock heritage for the contemptuous use of the term "Lakist."

[2] *Caposetta:* leader of a sect. Leigh Hunt (1784–1859) was the editor of the *Examiner* in the first decades of the century, in which he published his own poetry and that of Keats and Shelley.

[3] The phrases are from "Kubla Khan," published in 1816, by Samuel Taylor Coleridge (1772–1834).

[4] From Goethe's *Wilhelm Meister's Apprenticeship,* published in German in 1796. Thomas Carlyle published an English translation in 1824.

[5] From Wordsworth's "I Wandered Lonely as a Cloud" (1807).

moral temptations; and upon them, more than any, it is incumbent to remember, that their mission as men, which they share with their fellow-beings, is of infinitely higher interest than their mission as artists, which they possess by rare and exclusive privilege. But it is obvious that, critically speaking, such temptations are of slight moment. Not the gross and evident passions of our nature, but the elevated and less separable desires, are the dangerous enemies which misguide the poetic spirit in its attempts at self-cultivation. That delicate sense of fitness which grows with the growth of artist feelings, and strengthens with their strength, until it acquires a celerity and weight of decision hardly inferior to the correspondent judgments of conscience, is weakened by every indulgence of heterogeneous aspirations, however pure they may be, however lofty, however suitable to human nature.

We are therefore decidedly of opinion that the heights and depths of art are most within the reach of those who have received from nature the "fearful and wonderful" constitution we have described, whose poetry is a sort of magic, producing a number of impressions, too multiplied, too minute, and too diversified to allow of our tracing them to their causes, because just such was the effect, even so boundless and so bewildering, produced on their imaginations by the real appearance of Nature.

.   .   .

. . . Undoubtedly the true poet addresses himself, in all his conceptions, to the common nature of us all. Art is a lofty tree, and may shoot up far beyond our grasp, but its roots are in daily life and experience. Every bosom contains the elements of those complex emotions which the artist feels, and every head can, to a certain extent, go over in itself the process of their combination, so as to understand his expressions and sympathize with his state. But this requires exertion; more or less, indeed, according to the difference of occasion, but always some degree of exertion. For since the emotions of the poet, during composition, follow a regular law of association, it follows that to accompany their progress up to the harmonious prospect of the whole, and to perceive the proper dependence of every step on that which preceded, it is absolutely necessary *to start from the same point*, i.e. clearly to apprehend that leading sentiment of the

poet's mind, by their conformity to which the host of suggestions are arranged.

Now this requisite exertion is not willingly made by the large majority of readers. It is so easy to judge capriciously, and according to indolent impulse! For very many, therefore, it has become *morally* impossible to attain the author's point of vision, on account of their habits, or their prejudices, or their circumstances; but it is never *physically* impossible, because nature has placed in every man the simple elements, of which art is the sublimation. Since then this demand on the reader for activity, when he wants to peruse his author in a luxurious passiveness, is the very thing that moves his bile, it is obvious that those writers will be always most popular who require the least degree of exertion. Hence, whatever is mixed up with art, and appears under its semblance, is always more favorably regarded than art free and unalloyed. Hence, half the fashionable poems in the world are mere rhetoric, and half the remainder are, perhaps, not liked by the generality for their substantial merits. Hence, likewise, of the really pure compositions, those are most universally agreeable which take for their primary subject the *usual* passions of the heart, and deal with them in a simple state, without applying the transforming powers of high imagination. Love, friendship, ambition, religion, &c., are matters of daily experience even amongst unimaginative tempers. The forces of association, therefore, are ready to work in these directions, and little effort of will is necessary to follow the artist.

.   .   .

What, then, some may be ready to exclaim, is the pleasure derived by most men, from Shakespeare, or Dante, or Homer, entirely false and factitious? If these are really masters of their art, must not the energy required of the ordinary intelligences that come in contact with their mighty genius, be the greatest possible? How comes it then, that they are popular? Shall we not say, after all, that the difference is in the power of the author, not in the tenor of his meditations? Those eminent spirits find no difficulty in conveying to common apprehensions their lofty sense and profound observation of Nature. They keep no aristocratic state, apart from the sentiments of society at large; they speak to the hearts of all, and by the magnetic force of their conceptions, elevate inferior intellects into a higher and purer atmosphere.

The truth contained in this observation is undoubtedly important; geniuses of the most universal order, and assigned by destiny to the most propitious era of a nation's literary development, have a clearer and a larger access to the minds of their compatriots than can ever open to those who are circumscribed by less fortunate circumstances. In the youthful periods of any literature there is an expansive and communicative tendency in mind which produces unreservedness of communion, and reciprocity of vigour between different orders of intelligence.

·   ·   ·

But the age in which we live comes late in our national progress. That first raciness and juvenile vigour of literature, when nature "wantoned as in her prime, and played at will her virgin fancies"[6] is gone, never to return. Since that day we have undergone a period of degradation. "Every handicraftsman has worn the mask of Poesy."[7] It would be tedious to repeat the tale so often related of the French contagion and the heresies of the Popian school.

With the close of the last century came an era of reaction, an era of painful struggle to bring our over-civilised condition of thought into union with the fresh productive spirit that brightened the morning of our literature. But repentance is unlike innocence; the laborious endeavor to restore has more complicated methods of action than the freedom of untainted nature. Those different powers of poetic disposition, the energies of Sensitive,[8] of Reflective, of Passionate Emotion, which in former times were intermingled, and derived from mutual support an extensive empire over the feelings of men, were now restrained within separate spheres of agency. The whole

system no longer worked harmoniously, and by intrinsic harmony acquired external freedom; but there arose a violent and unusual action in the several component functions, each for itself, all striving to reproduce the regular power which the whole had once enjoyed.

Hence the melancholy which so evidently characterises the spirit of modern poetry; hence that return of the mind upon itself and the habit of seeking relief in idiosyncrasies rather than community of interest. In the old times the poetic impulse went along with the general impulse of the nation; in these it is a reaction against it, a check acting for conservation against a propulsion towards change.

We have indeed seen it urged in some of our fashionable publications, that the diffusion of poetry must be in the direct ratio of the diffusion of machinery, because a highly civilised people must have new objects of interest, and thus a new field will be open to description. But this notable argument forgets that against this *objective* amelioration may be set the decrease of *subjective* power, arising from a prevalence of social activity, and a continual absorption of the higher feelings into the palpable interests of ordinary life. The French Revolution may be a finer theme than the war of Troy; but it does not so evidently follow that Homer is to find his superior.

Our inference, therefore, from this change in the relative position of artists to the rest of the community is, that modern poetry in proportion to its depth and truth is likely to have little immediate authority over public opinion. Admirers it will have; sects consequently it will form; and these strong undercurrents will in time sensibly affect the principal stream. Those writers whose genius, though great, is not strictly and essentially poetic, become mediators between the votaries of art and the careless cravers for excitement.[9] Art herself, less manifestly glorious than in her periods of undisputed supremacy, retains her essential

[6] Phrases from Wordsworth's *Descriptive Sketches* (1793).

[7] From John Keats' "Sleep and Poetry" (1817).

[8] Hallam's note: We are aware that this is not the right word, being appropriated by common use to a different signification. Those who think the caution given by Caesar should not stand in the way of urgent occasion, may substitute "sensuous;" a word in use amongst our elder divines, and revived by a few bold writers in our own time.

[9] Hallam's note: May we not compare them to the bright but unsubstantial clouds which, in still evenings, girdle the sides of lofty mountains, and seem to form a natural connexion between the lowly vallies spread out beneath, and those isolated peaks above that hold the "last parley with the setting sun?" [Hallam misquotes a line from Wordsworth's "There is an eminence" (1800): "The last that parleys with the setting sun."]

prerogatives, and forgets not to raise up chosen spirits who may minister to her state and vindicate her title.

One of the faithful Islâm, a poet in the truest and highest sense, we are anxious to present to our readers. He has yet written little and published less; but in these "preludes of a loftier strain"[10] we recognize the inspiring god. Mr. Tennyson belongs decidedly to the class we have already described as Poets of Sensation. He sees all the forms of nature with the "eruditus oculus,"[11] and his ear has a fairy fineness. There is a strange earnestness in his worship of beauty which throws a charm over his impassioned song, more easily felt than described, and not to be escaped by those who have once felt it. We think he has more definiteness and roundness of general conception than the late Mr. Keats, and is much more free from blemishes of diction and hasty capriccios of fancy. He has also this advantage over that poet and his friend Shelley, that he comes before the public unconnected with any political party or peculiar system of opinions. Nevertheless, true to the theory we have stated, we believe his participation in their characteristic excellences is sufficient to secure him a share of their unpopularity.

. . .

We have remarked five distinctive excellencies of his own manner. First, his luxuriance of imagination, and at the same time his control over it. Secondly his power of embodying himself in ideal characters, or rather moods of character, with such extreme accuracy of adjustment, that the circumstances of the narration seem to have a natural correspondence with the predominant feeling, and, as it were, to be evolved from it by assimilative force. Thirdly his vivid, picturesque delineation of objects, and the peculiar skill with which he holds all of them *fused*, to borrow a metaphor from science, in a medium of strong emotion. Fourthly, the variety of his lyrical measures, and exquisite modulation of harmonious words and cadences to the swell and fall of the feelings expressed. Fifthly, the elevated habits of thought, implied in these compositions, and imparting a mellow soberness of tone, more impressive, to our minds, than if the author had drawn up a set of opinions in verse, and sought to instruct the understanding rather than to communicate the love of beauty to the heart. . . .

1831

[10] From Shelley's "The Revolt of Islam" (1818).   [11] Eruditus oculus: educated eye.

Robert Browning

1812–1889

Browning wrote this essay in 1852 to serve as the introduction to a collection of Shelley's letters. The letters were found to be spurious, and the collection was not published; the essay itself was first published in 1881. The text printed here is that published in the Papers of the London Browning Society, I *(1881).*

from An Essay on Percy Bysshe Shelley

[*Browning begins the essay with a description of the kind of poet he calls a "fashioner," a poet of externalities who makes poetry of the objects around and outside him. A knowledge of the biography and personality of this kind of poet, Browning writes, is interesting because we learn what and how he learned of the objects he takes into his poetry.*]

We turn with stronger needs to the genius of an opposite tendency—the subjective poet of modern classification. He, gifted like the objective poet with the fuller perception of nature and man, is impelled to embody the thing he perceives, not so much with reference to the many below as to the One above him, the supreme Intelligence which apprehends all things in their absolute truth,—an ultimate view ever aspired to, if but partially attained, by the poet's own soul. Not what man sees, but what God sees—the *Ideas* of Plato, seeds of creation lying burningly on the Divine Hand[1]—it is toward these that he struggles. Not with the combination of humanity in action, but with the primal elements of humanity he has to do; and he digs where he stands,—preferring to seek them in his own soul as the nearest reflex of that absolute Mind, according to the intuitions of which he desires to perceive and speak. Such a poet does not deal habitually with the picturesque groupings and tempestuous tossings of the forest-trees, but with their roots and fibres naked to the chalk and stone. He does not paint pictures and hang them on the walls, but rather carries them on the retina of his own eyes: we must look deep into his human eyes, to see those pictures on them. He is rather a seer, accordingly, than a fashioner, and what he produces will be less a work than an effluence. That effluence cannot be easily considered in abstraction from his personality,—being indeed the very radiance and aroma of his personality, projected from it but not separated. Therefore, in our approach to the poetry, we necessarily approach the personality of the poet; in apprehending it we apprehend him, and certainly we cannot love it without loving him. Both for love's and for understanding's sake we desire to know him, and as readers of his poetry must be readers of his biography also.

I shall observe, in passing, that it seems not so much from any essential distinction in the faculty of the two poets or in the nature of the objects contemplated by either, as in the more immediate adaptability of these objects to the distinct purpose of each, that the objective poet, in his appeal to the aggregate human mind, chooses to deal with the doings of men, (the result of which dealing, in its pure form, when even description, as suggesting a describer, is dispensed with, is what we call dramatic poetry), while the subjective poet, whose study has been himself, appealing through himself to the absolute Divine mind, prefers to dwell upon those external scenic appearances which strike out most abundantly and uninterruptedly his inner light and power, selects that silence of the earth and sea in which he can best hear the beating of his individual heart, and leaves the noisy, complex,

[1] Plato's most extensive elaboration of a myth in which the material world is created on models of the ideal forms of things is in the dialogue *Timaeus.*

yet imperfect exhibitions of nature in the manifold experience of man around him, which serve only to distract and suppress the working of his brain. These opposite tendencies of genius will be more readily descried in their artistic effect than in their moral spring and cause. Pushed to an extreme and manifested as a deformity, they will be seen plainest of all in the fault of either artist, when subsidiarily to the human interest of his work his occasional illustrations from scenic nature are introduced as in the earlier works of the originative painters—men and women filling the foreground with consummate mastery, while mountain, grove and rivulet show like an anticipatory revenge on that succeeding race of landscape-painters whose "figures" disturb the perfection of their earth and sky. It would be idle to inquire, of these two kinds of poetic faculty in operation, which is the higher or even rarer endowment. If the subjective might seem to be the ultimate requirement of every age, the objective, in the strictest state, must still retain its original value. For it is with this world, as starting point and basis alike, that we shall always have to concern ourselves: the world is not to be learned and thrown aside, but reverted to and relearned. The spiritual comprehension may be infinitely subtilised, but the raw material it operates upon, must remain. There may be no end of the poets who communicate to us what they see in an object with reference to their own individuality; what it was before they saw it, in reference to the aggregate human mind, will be as desirable to know as ever. Nor is there any reason why these two modes of poetic faculty may not issue hereafter from the same poet in successive perfect works, examples of which, according to what are now considered the exigences of art, we have hitherto possessed in distinct individuals only. A mere running in of the one faculty upon the other, is, of course, the ordinary circumstance. Far more rarely it happens that either is found so decidedly prominent and superior, as to be pronounced comparatively pure: while of the perfect shield, with the gold and the silver side set up for all comers to challenge, there has as yet been no instance.[2] Either faculty in its eminent state is doubtless conceded by

Providence as a best gift to men, according to their especial want. There is a time when the general eye has, so to speak, absorbed its fill of the phenomena around it, whether spiritual or material, and desires rather to learn the exacter significance of what it possesses, than to receive any augmentation of what is possessed. Then is the opportunity for the poet of loftier vision, to lift his fellows, with their half-apprehensions, up to his own sphere, by intensifying the import of details and rounding the universal meaning. The influence of such an achievement will not soon die out. A tribe of successors (Homerides[3]) working more or less in the same spirit, dwell on his discoveries and reinforce his doctrine; till, at unawares, the world is found to be subsisting wholly on the shadow of a reality, on sentiments diluted from passions, on the tradition of a fact, the convention of a moral, the straw of last year's harvest. Then is the imperative call for the appearance of another sort of poet, who shall at once replace this intellectual rumination of food swallowed long ago, by a supply of the fresh and living swathe; getting at new substance by breaking up the assumed wholes into parts of independent and unclassed value, careless of the unknown laws for recombining them (it will be the business of yet another poet to suggest those hereafter), prodigal of objects for men's outer and not inner sight, shaping for their uses a new and different creation from the last, which it replaces by the right of life over death,—to endure until, in the inevitable process, its very sufficiency to itself shall require, at length, an exposition of its affinity to something higher,—when the positive yet conflicting facts shall again precipitate themselves under an harmonising law, and one more degree will be apparent for a poet to climb in that mighty ladder, of which, however cloud-involved and undefined may glimmer the topmost step, the world dares no longer doubt that its gradations ascend.

Such being the two kinds of artists, it is naturally, as I have shown, with the biography of the subjective poet that we have the deeper concern. Apart from his recorded life altogether, we might fail to determine with satisfactory precision to what class his productions belong, and what amount of praise is assign-

---

[2] A medieval fable tells of two knights who approached such a shield from opposite sides and argued whether the shield was made of gold or silver.
[3] Homerides: lesser poets who followed Homer.

able to the producer. Certainly, in the face of any conspicuous achievement of genius, philosophy, no less than sympathetic instinct, warrants our belief in a great moral purpose having mainly inspired even where it does not visibly look out of the same. Greatness in a work suggests an adequate instrumentality; and none of the lower incitements, however they may avail to initiate or even effect many considerable displays of power, simulating the nobler inspiration to which they are mistakenly referred, have been found able, under the ordinary conditions of humanity, to task themselves to the end of so exacting a performance as a poet's complete work. As soon will the galvanism that provokes to violent action the muscles of a corpse, induce it to cross the chamber steadily: sooner. The love of displaying power for the display's sake, the love of riches, of distinction, of notoriety,—the desire of a triumph over rivals, and the vanity in the applause of friends,—each and all of such whetted appetites grow intenser by exercise and increasingly sagacious as to the best and readiest means of self-appeasement,—while for any of their ends, whether the money, or the pointed finger of the crowd, or the flattery and hate to heart's content, there are cheaper prices to pay, they will all find soon enough, than the bestowment of a life upon a labour, hard, slow, and not sure. Also, assuming the proper moral aim to have produced a work, there are many and various states of an aim: it may be more intense than clear-sighted, or too easily satisfied with a lower field of activity than a steadier aspiration would reach. All the bad poetry in the world (accounted poetry, that is, by its affinities) will be found to result from some one of the infinite degrees of discrepancy between the attributes of the poet's soul, occasioning a want of correspondency between his work and the verities of nature,—issuing in poetry, false under whatever form, which shows a thing not as it is to mankind generally, nor as it is to the particular describer, but as it is supposed to be for some unreal neutral mood, midway between both and of value to neither, and living its brief minute simply through the indolence of whoever accepts it or his incapacity to denounce a cheat. . . . An absolute vision is not for this world, but we are permitted a continual approximation to it, every degree of which in the individual, provided it exceed the attainment of the masses, must

procure him a clear advantage. Did the poet ever attain to a higher platform than where he rested and exhibited a result? Did he know more than he spoke of?

.   .   .

[*Browning argues that Shelley's writings in the last decade of his life*]

present us with the complete enginery of a poet, as signal in the excellence of its several adaptitudes as transcendent in the combination of its effects,—examples, in fact, of the whole poet's function of beholding with an understanding keenness the universe, nature and man, in their actual state of perfection in imperfection,—of the whole poet's virtue of being untempted by the manifold partial developments of beauty and good on every side, into leaving them the ultimates he found them,—induced by the facility of the gratification of his own sense of those qualities, or by the pleasure of acquiescence in the short-comings of his predecessors in art, and the pain of disturbing their conventionalisms,—the whole poet's virtue, I repeat, of looking higher than any manifestation yet made of both beauty and good, in order to suggest from the utmost actual realisation of the one a corresponding capability in the other, and out of the calm, purity and energy of nature, to reconstitute and store up for the forthcoming stage of man's being, a gift in repayment of that former gift, in which man's own thought and passion had been lavished by the poet on the else-incompleted magnificence of the sunrise, the else-uninterpreted mystery of the lake,—so drawing out, lifting up, and assimilating this ideal of a future man, thus descried as possible, to the present reality of the poet's soul already arrived at the higher state of development, and still aspirant to elevate and extend itself in conformity with its still-improving perceptions of, no longer the eventual Human, but the actual Divine. In conjunction with which noble and rare powers, came the subordinate power of delivering these attained results to the world in an embodiment of verse more closely answering to and indicative of the process of the informing spirit, (failing as it occasionally does, in art, only to succeed in highest art),—with a diction more adequate to the task in its natural and acquired richness, its material colour and spiritual transparency,

—the whole being moved by and suffused with a music at once of the soul and the sense, expressive both of an external might of sincere passion and an internal fitness and consonancy, —than can be attributed to any other writer whose record is among us. Such was the spheric poetical faculty of Shelley, as its own self-sufficing central light, radiating equally through immaturity and accomplishment, through many fragments and occasional completion, reveals it to a competent judgment.

.   .   .

[*Browning concludes with a tribute to Shelley's "noblest and predominating characteristic."*]

This I call his simultaneous perception of Power and Love in the absolute, and of Beauty and Good in the concrete, while he throws, from his poet's station between both, swifter, subtler, and more numerous films for the connexion of each with each, than have been thrown by any modern artificer of whom I have knowledge; proving how, as he says,

The spirit of the worm within the sod,
In love and worship blends itself with God.[4]

I would rather consider Shelley's poetry as a sublime fragmentary essay towards a presentment of the correspondency of the universe to Deity, of the natural to the spiritual, and of the actual to the ideal, than I would isolate and separately appraise the worth of many detachable portions which might be acknowledged as utterly perfect in a lower moral point of view, under the mere conditions of art. It would be easy to take my stand on successful instances of objectivity in Shelley: there is the unrivalled "Cenci;" there is the "Julian and Maddalo" too; there is the magnificent "Ode to Naples:" why not regard, it may be said, the less organised matter as the radiant elemental foam and solution, out of which would have been evolved, eventually, creations as perfect even as those? But I prefer to look for the highest attainment, not simply the high,—and, seeing it, I hold by it. There is surely enough

of the work "Shelley" to be known enduringly among men, and, I believe, to be accepted of God, as human work may; and around the imperfect proportions of such, the most elaborated productions of ordinary art must arrange themselves as inferior illustrations.

(1852) 1881

Letter to John Ruskin[1]

PARIS, *December* 10, 1855

MY DEAR RUSKIN,—for so you let me begin, with the honest friendliness that befits,—You never were more in the wrong than when you professed to say "your unpleasant things" to me. This is pleasant and proper at all points, over-liberal of praise here and there, kindly and sympathetic everywhere, and with enough of yourself in even—what I fancy—the misjudging, to make the whole letter precious indeed. I wanted to thank you thus much at once,—that is, when the letter reached me; but the strife of lodging-hunting was too sore, and only now that I can sit down for a minute without self-reproach do I allow my thoughts to let go southaspects, warm bedrooms, and the like, and begin as you see. For the deepnesses you think you discern,—may they be more than mere blacknesses! For the hopes you entertain of what may come of subsequent readings,—all success to them! For your bewilderment more especially noted—how shall I help *that*? We don't read poetry the same way, by the same law; it is too clear. I cannot begin writing poetry till my imaginary reader has conceded licenses to me which you demur at altogether. I *know* that I don't make out my conception by my language; all poetry being a putting the infinite within the finite. You would have me paint it all plain out, which can't be; but by various artifices I try to make shift with touches and bits of outlines which *succeed* if they bear the conception from me to you. You ought, I think, to keep pace with the thought tripping from ledge to ledge of my "glaciers," as you call them; not stand poking

---

[4] From Shelley's *Epispychidion* (1821).

[1] John Ruskin (1819–1900), well established by the mid-1850s as an authority on the moral and social meanings of art and architecture, had written to Browning after the publication of *Men and Women* in 1855. Ruskin's criticisms of Browning's poetic manner, especially of his obscurity, may easily be derived from Browning's reply; Ruskin's complaints were common among Browning's critics. The letter is printed in W. G. Collingwood, *The Life and Work of John Ruskin* (Boston, 1893) I, 232–235.

your alpenstock into the holes and demonstrating that no foot could have stood there; suppose it sprang over there? In *prose* you may criticise so—because that is the absolute representation of portions of truth, what chronicling is to history—but in asking for more *ultimates* you must accept less *mediates,* nor expect that a Druid stone-circle will be traced for you with as few breaks to the eye as the North Crescent and South Crescent that go together so cleverly in many a suburb.[2] Why, you look at my little song as if it were Hobbs' or Nobbs'[3] lease of his house, or testament of his devisings, wherein, I grant you, not a "then and there," "to him and his heirs," "to have and to hold," and so on, would be superfluous; and so you begin: "Stand still,—why?" For the reason indicated in the verse, to be sure—*to let me draw him*— and because he is at present going his way, and fancying nobody notices him,—and moreover, "going on" (as we say) against the injustice of that,—and lastly, inasmuch as one night he'll fail us, as a star is apt to drop out of heaven, in authentic astronomic records, and I want to make the most of my time. So much may be in "stand still." And how much more was (for instance) in that "stay!" of Samuel's (I. xv. 16).[4] So could I twit you through the whole series of your objurgations, but the declaring my own notion of the law on the subject will do. And why,—I prithee, friend and fellow-student,—why, having told the Poet what you read,—may I not turn to the bystanders, and tell them a bit of my own mind about their own stupid thanklessness and mistaking? Is the jump too much there? The whole is all but a simultaneous feeling with me.

The other hard measure you deal me I won't bear—about my requiring you to pronounce words short and long, exactly as I like. Nay, but exactly as the language likes, in this case. *Fold-skirts* not a trochee?[5] A spondee possible in English? Two of the "longest monosyllables" continuing to be each of the old length when in junction? Sentence: let the delinquent be forced to supply the stone-cutter with a thousand companions to "Affliction sore —long time he bore," after the fashion of "He lost his life—by a pen-knife," "He turned to clay—last Good Friday," "Departed hence— nor owed six-pence," and so on—so would pronounce a jury accustomed from the nipple to say lord and landlord, bridge and Cambridge, Gog and Magog, man and woman, house and workhouse, coal and charcoal, cloth and broadcloth, skirts and fold-skirts, more and once more,—in short! Once *more* I prayed! —is the confession of a self-searching professor! "I stand here for law!"

The last charge I cannot answer, for you may be right in preferring it, however unwitting I am of the fact. I *may* put Robert Browning into Pippa and other men and maids. If so, *peccavi:*[6] but I don't see myself in them, at all events.

Do you think poetry was ever generally understood—or can be? Is the business of it to tell people what they know already, as they know it, and so precisely that they shall be able to cry out—"Here you should supply *this* —*that,* you evidently pass over, and I'll help you from my own stock"? It is all teaching, on the contrary, and the people hate to be taught. They say otherwise,—make foolish fables about Orpheus[7] enchanting stocks and stones, poets standing up and being worshiped,—all nonsense and impossible dreaming. A poet's affair is with God, to whom he is accountable, and

---

[2] North Crescent and South Crescent: common names for streets in new housing developments built to imitate the imitative classical elegances of early nineteenth-century residential architecture.

[3] Derisive names in Browning's poem "Popularity" for poets who attain fame by diluting the fresh elements of stronger and more difficult poets. The first line of the poem, one of those in *Men and Women,* is "Stand still, true poet that you are!" The type of the true poet in the poem is John Keats.

[4] Samuel tells Saul to "Stay" so that he may tell him of God's anger because Saul has disobeyed a command of the Lord's.

[5] Browning uses "fold-skirts" as a trochee ($\acute{\smile}$) twice in "Saul," one of the poems of *Men and Women.*

[6] *Peccavi:* I have sinned. Pippa is the central character of *Pippa Passes,* which Browning published in 1841.

[7] Orpheus: according to Greek myth, Orpheus could make inanimate things dance to his music.

of whom is his reward: look elsewhere, and you find misery enough. Do you believe people understand *Hamlet?* The last time I saw it acted, the heartiest applause of the night went to a little by-play of the actor's own—who, to simulate madness in a hurry, plucked forth his handkerchief and flourished it hither and thither: certainly a third of the play, with no end of noble things, had been (as from time immemorial) suppressed, with the auditory's amplest acquiescence and benediction. Are these wasted, therefore? No—they act upon a very few, who react upon the rest: as Goldsmith says, "some lords, my acquaintance, that settle the nation, are pleased to be kind."[8]

Don't let me lose *my* lord by any seeming self-sufficiency or petulance: I look on my own shortcomings too sorrowfully, try to remedy them too earnestly: but I shall never change

my point of sight, or feel other than disconcerted and apprehensive when the public, critics and all, begin to understand and approve me. But what right have *you* to disconcert me in the other way? Why won't you ask the next perfumer for a packet of *orris*-root?[9] Don't everybody know 't is a corruption of *iris*-root—the Florentine lily, the *giaggolo,* of world-wide fame as a good savor? And because "iris" means so many objects already, and I use the old word, you blame me! But I write in the blind-dark and bitter cold, and past post-time as I fear. Take my truest thanks, and understand at least this rough writing, and, at all events, the real affection with which I venture to regard you. And "I" means my wife as well as

> Yours ever faithfully,
> ROBERT BROWNING

Matthew Arnold
1822–1888

Arnold published some new poems and a selection of poems from his first two volumes in 1853. In his preface to this collection he repudiates some of the characteristics of his own earlier poetry as he tries to counter some of the excesses of contemporary poetry by advocating tenets he takes from Aristotle and a model of measured, entire achievement he finds in Goethe. The text printed here is that of the 1853 edition; it is reprinted in On the Classical Tradition, *edited by R. H. Super (1960), the first volume of* The Complete Prose Works of Matthew Arnold. *Super's excellent notes to the text specify many of Arnold's levies on the ideas and words of Aristotle and Goethe.*

from Preface to First Edition of Poems (1853)

In two small volumes of Poems, published anonymously, one in 1849, the other in 1852, many of the Poems which compose the present

---

[8] Oliver Goldsmith (1728–74), *The Haunch of Venison* (1776).

[9] *Orris*-root: Browning uses the phrase in "Fra Lippo Lippi," another of the poems of *Men and Women.*

volume have already appeared. The rest are now published for the first time.

I have, in the present collection, omitted the Poem[1] from which the volume published in 1852 took its title. I have done so, not because the subject of it was a Sicilian Greek born between two and three thousand years ago, although many persons would think this a sufficient reason. Neither have I done so because I had, in my own opinion, failed in the delineation which I intended to effect. I intended to delineate the feelings of one of the last of the Greek religious philosophers, one of the family of Orpheus and Musaeus,[2] having survived his fellows, living on into a time when the habits of Greek thought and feeling had begun fast to change, character to dwindle, the influence of the Sophists[3] to prevail. Into the feelings of a man so situated there entered much that we are accustomed to consider as exclusively modern; how much, the fragments of Empedocles himself which remain to us are sufficient at least to indicate. What those who are familiar only with the great monuments of early Greek genius suppose to be its exclusive characteristics, have disappeared; the calm, the cheerfulness, the disinterested objectivity have disappeared: the dialogue of the mind with itself has commenced; modern problems have presented themselves; we hear already the doubts, we witness the discouragement, of Hamlet and of Faust.

The representation of such a man's feelings must be interesting, if consistently drawn. We all naturally take pleasure, says Aristotle, in any imitation or representation whatever: this is the basis of our love of Poetry: and we take pleasure in them, he adds, because all knowledge is naturally agreeable to us; not to the philosopher only, but to mankind at large.[4] Every representation therefore which is consistently drawn may be supposed to be interesting, inasmuch as it gratifies this natural interest in knowledge of all kinds. What is *not*

interesting, is that which does not add to our knowledge of any kind; that which is vaguely conceived and loosely drawn; a representation which is general, indeterminate, and faint, instead of being particular, precise, and firm.

Any accurate representation may therefore be expected to be interesting; but, if the representation be a poetical one, more than this is demanded. It is demanded, not only that it shall interest, but also that it shall inspirit and rejoice the reader: that it shall convey a charm, and infuse delight. For the Muses, as Hesiod says, were born that they might be "a forgetfulness of evils, and a truce from cares":[5] and it is not enough that the Poet should add to the knowledge of men, it is required of him also that he should add to their happiness. "All Art," says Schiller, "is dedicated to Joy, and there is no higher and no more serious problem, than how to make men happy. The right Art is that alone, which creates the highest enjoyment."[6]

A poetical work, therefore, is not yet justified when it has been shown to be an accurate, and therefore interesting representation; it has to be shown also that it is a representation from which men can derive enjoyment. In presence of the most tragic circumstances, represented in a work of Art, the feeling of enjoyment, as is well known, may still subsist: the representation of the most utter calamity, of the liveliest anguish, is not sufficient to destroy it: the more tragic the situation, the deeper becomes the enjoyment; and the situation is more tragic in proportion as it becomes more terrible.

What then are the situations, from the representation of which, though accurate, no poetical enjoyment can be derived? They are those in which the suffering finds no vent in action; in which a continuous state of mental distress is prolonged, unrelieved by incident, hope, or resistance; in which there is everything to be endured, nothing to be done. In such

---

[1] "Empedocles on Etna." Arnold restored the poem to his collected works in 1867.

[2] Orpheus is a poet of Greek myth whose song could charm beasts and move inanimate objects. Musaeus was his son, also a poet of sacred songs and oracles.

[3] The Sophists were teachers and rhetoricians who were reputed to honor the means and success of an argument more than the truth to which discourse was traditionally directed.

[4] In the *Poetics*, IV, 1–5.

[5] Hesiod: an eighth-century B.C. poet whose *Theogony* is a mythical account of the origin of the universe and the history of the gods. Arnold's quotation is from line 55 of Hesiod's poem.

[6] Johann Christoph Friedrich von Schiller (1759–1805) was a German poet and dramatist. The sentences Arnold quotes are from Schiller's preface to his drama *Die Braut von Messina* (1803).

situations there is inevitably something morbid, in the description of them something monotonous. When they occur in actual life, they are painful, not tragic; the representation of them in poetry is painful also.

To this class of situations, poetically faulty as it appears to me, that of Empedocles, as I have endeavoured to represent him, belongs; and I have therefore excluded the Poem from the present collection.

And why, it may be asked, have I entered into this explanation respecting a matter so unimportant as the admission or exclusion of the Poem in question? I have done so, because I was anxious to avow that the sole reason for its exclusion was that which has been stated above; and that it has not been excluded in deference to the opinion which many critics of the present day appear to entertain against subjects chosen from distant times and countries: against the choice, in short, of any subjects but modern ones.

"The Poet," it is said, and by an intelligent critic, "the Poet who would really fix the public attention must leave the exhausted past, and draw his subjects from matters of present import, and *therefore* both of interest and novelty."[7]

Now this view I believe to be completely false. It is worth examining, inasmuch as it is a fair sample of a class of critical dicta everywhere current at the present day, having a philosophical form and air, but no real basis in fact; and which are calculated to vitiate the judgment of readers of poetry, while they exert, so far as they are adopted, a misleading influence on the practice of those who make it.

What are the eternal objects of Poetry, among all nations and at all times? They are actions; human actions; possessing an inherent interest in themselves, and which are to be communicated in an interesting manner by the art of the Poet. Vainly will the latter imagine that he has everything in his own power; that he can make an intrinsically inferior action equally delightful with a more excellent one by

his treatment of it. He may indeed compel us to admire his skill, but his work will possess, within itself, an incurable defect.

The Poet, then, has in the first place to select an excellent action; and what actions are the most excellent? Those, certainly, which most powerfully appeal to the great primary human affections: to those elementary feelings which subsist permanently in the race, and which are independent of time. These feelings are permanent and the same; that which interests them is permanent and the same also. The modernness or antiquity of an action, therefore, has nothing to do with its fitness for poetical representation; this depends upon its inherent qualities. To the elementary part of our nature, to our passions, that which is great and passionate is eternally interesting; and interesting solely in proportion to its greatness and to its passion. A great human action of a thousand years ago is more interesting to it than a smaller human action of to-day, even though upon the representation of this last the most consummate skill may have been expended, and though it has the advantage of appealing by its modern language, familiar manners, and contemporary allusions, to all our transient feelings and interests. These, however, have no right to demand of a poetical work that it shall satisfy them; their claims are to be directed elsewhere. Poetical works belong to the domain of our permanent passions: let them interest these, and the voice of all subordinate claims upon them is at once silenced.

Achilles, Prometheus, Clytemnestra, Dido[8] —what modern poem presents personages as interesting, even to us moderns, as these personages of an "exhausted past"? We have the domestic epic dealing with the details of modern life which pass daily under our eyes; we have poems representing modern personages in contact with the problems of modern life, moral, intellectual, and social; these works have been produced by poets the most distinguished of their nation and time; yet I fearlessly assert that *Hermann and Dorothea,*

---

[7] Arnold's note: "In *The Spectator* of April 2nd, 1853. The words quoted were not used with reference to poems of mine." The review was by R. S. Rintoul, the editor of the magazine; he was reviewing a volume of poems by Edwin Arnold.

[8] Achilles appears in Homer's *Iliad;* Prometheus and Clytemnestra in tragedies of the fifth-century B.C. Greek dramatist Aeschylus; the episode of Dido, a queen of Carthage who immolates herself when she is abandoned by the hero Aeneas, is in the fourth book of the *Aeneid* of the Roman poet Virgil (70–19 B.C.).

Childe Harold, Jocelyn, The Excursion,[9] leave the reader cold in comparison with the effect produced upon him by the latter books of the *Iliad,* by the *Oresteia,* or by the episode of Dido. And why is this? Simply because in the three last-named cases the action is greater, the personages nobler, the situations more intense: and this is the true basis of the interest in a poetical work, and this alone.

It may be urged, however, that past actions may be interesting in themselves, but that they are not to be adopted by the modern Poet, because it is impossible for him to have them clearly present to his own mind, and he cannot therefore feel them deeply, nor represent them forcibly. But this is not necessarily the case. The externals of a past action, indeed, he cannot know with the precision of a contemporary; but his business is with its essentials. The outward man of Oedipus or of Macbeth, the houses in which they lived, the ceremonies of their courts, he cannot accurately figure to himself; but neither do they essentially concern him. His business is with their inward man; with their feelings and behaviour in certain tragic situations, which engage their passions as men; these have in them nothing local and casual; they are as accessible to the modern Poet as to a contemporary.

The date of an action, then, signifies nothing: the action itself, its selection and construction, this is what is all-important. This the Greeks understood far more clearly than we do. The radical difference between their poetical theory and ours consists, as it appears to me, in this: that, with them, the poetical character of the action in itself, and the conduct of it, was the first consideration; with us, attention is fixed mainly on the value of the separate thoughts and images which occur in the treatment of an action. They regarded the whole; we regard the parts. With them, the action predominated over the expression of it; with us, the expression predominates over the action. Not that they failed in expression, or were inattentive to it; on the contrary, they are the highest models of expression, the unapproached masters of the *grand style.*[10] But their expression is so excellent because it is so admirably kept in its right degree of prominence; because it is so simple and so well subordinated; because it draws its force directly from the pregnancy of the matter which it conveys. For what reason was the Greek tragic poet confined to so limited a range of subjects? Because there are so few actions which unite in themselves, in the highest degree, the conditions of excellence: and it was not thought that on any but an excellent subject could an excellent Poem be constructed. A few actions, therefore, eminently adapted for tragedy, maintained almost exclusive possession of the Greek tragic stage. Their significance appeared inexhaustible; they were as permanent problems, perpetually offered to the genius of every fresh poet. This too is the reason of what appears to us moderns a certain baldness of expression in Greek tragedy; of the triviality with which we often reproach the remarks of the chorus, where it takes part in the dialogue: that the action itself, the situation of Orestes, or Merope, or Alcmaeon,[11] was to stand the central point of interest, unforgotten, absorbing, principal; that no accessories were for a moment to distract the spectator's attention from this; that the tone of the parts was to be perpetually kept down, in order not to impair the grandiose effect of the whole. The terrible old mythic story on which the drama was founded stood, before he entered the theatre, traced in its bare outlines upon the spectator's mind; it stood in his memory, as a group of statuary, faintly seen, at the end of a long and dark vista: then came the Poet, embodying outlines, developing situations, not a word wasted, not a sentiment capriciously thrown in: stroke upon stroke, the drama proceeded: the light deepened upon the group; more and more it revealed itself to the rivetted gaze of the spectator: until at last, when the final

[9] The first is a poem by Goethe published in 1797; *Jocelyn* was published in 1836 by the French poet Alphonse de Lamartine (1790–1869). Byron's sometimes autobiographical *Childe Harold's Pilgrimage* was published between 1812 and 1818; Wordsworth's philosophical *The Excursion* was published in 1814.

[10] ". . . the grand style arises in poetry, *when a noble nature, poetically gifted, treats with simplicity or severity a serious subject*": "Last Words," *On Translating Homer* (1861). Arnold's example in this lecture of the grand style simple was Homer, of the grand style severe, Milton, and of a combination of both, Dante.

[11] Only the first of these three figures in Greek mythology is the subject of a Greek tragedy. Arnold published his poetic treatment of the tragedy of Merope in 1858.

words were spoken, it stood before him in broad sunlight, a model of immortal beauty.

This was what a Greek critic demanded; this was what a Greek poet endeavoured to effect. It signified nothing to what time an action belonged. We do not find that the *Persae*[12] occupied a particularly high rank among the dramas of Aeschylus, because it represented a matter of contemporary interest: this was not what a cultivated Athenian required. He required that the permanent elements of his nature should be moved; and dramas of which the action, though taken from a long-distant mythic time, yet was calculated to accomplish this in a higher degree than that of the *Persae,* stood higher in his estimation accordingly. The Greeks felt, no doubt, with their exquisite sagacity of taste, that an action of present times was too near them, too much mixed up with what was accidental and passing, to form a sufficiently grand, detached, and self-subsistent object for a tragic poem. Such objects belonged to the domain of the comic poet, and of the lighter kinds of poetry. For the more serious kinds, for *pragmatic* poetry, to use an excellent expression of Polybius,[13] they were more difficult and severe in the range of subjects which they permitted. Their theory and practice alike, the admirable treatise of Aristotle, and the unrivalled works of their poets, exclaim with a thousand tongues—"All depends upon the subject; choose a fitting action, penetrate yourself with the feeling of its situations; this done, everything else will follow."

But for all kinds of poetry alike there was one point on which they were rigidly exacting; the adaptability of the subject to the kind of poetry selected, and the careful construction of the poem.

How different a way of thinking from this is ours! We can hardly at the present day understand what Menander meant, when he told a man who inquired as to the progress of his comedy that he had finished it, not having yet written a single line, because he had constructed the action of it in his mind.[14] A modern critic would have assured him that the merit of his piece depended on the brilliant things which arose under his pen as he went along. We have poems which seem to exist merely for the sake of single lines and passages; not for the sake of producing any total-impression. We have critics who seem to direct their attention merely to detached expressions, to the language about the action, not to the action itself. I verily think that the majority of them do not in their hearts believe that there is such a thing as a total-impression to be derived from a poem at all, or to be demanded from a poet; they think the term a common-place of metaphysical criticism. They will permit the Poet to select any action he pleases, and to suffer that action to go as it will, provided he gratifies them with occasional bursts of fine writing, and with a shower of isolated thoughts and images. That is, they permit him to leave their poetical sense ungratified, provided that he gratifies their rhetorical sense and their curiosity. Of his neglecting to gratify these, there is little danger. He needs rather to be warned against the danger of attempting to gratify these alone; he needs rather to be perpetually reminded to prefer his action to everything else; so to treat this, as to permit its inherent excellences to develop themselves, without interruption from the intrusion of his personal peculiarities: most fortunate, when he most entirely succeeds in effacing himself, and in enabling a noble action to subsist as it did in nature.

But the modern critic not only permits a false practice; he absolutely prescribes false aims.—"A true allegory of the state of one's own mind in a representative history," the Poet is told, "is perhaps the highest thing that one can attempt in the way of poetry."[15] —And accordingly he attempts it. An allegory of the state of one's own mind, the highest problem of an art which imitates actions! No assuredly, it is not, it never can be so: no great

---

[12] The topic of Aeschylus's *Persae* is the triumph of the Athenians over the Persians.

[13] Polybius: a Greek historian of the second century B.C.

[14] Menander was a Greek dramatist of the fourth century B.C. The anecdote is recounted in Plutarch, a first-century Greek historian and biographer.

[15] The sentence appears in a review of Alexander Smith's *A Life-Drama* (see Part Four) in the *North British Review* for 1853. One of the principal currents of contemporary poetic taste and practice against which Arnold sets this preface to his poems is the emphasis of poets like Smith (and the admirers of Keats) on intensity, verbal color and force, and personal authenticity at the expense of what Arnold will later in the preface call the "architectonics" of a poem.

poetical work has ever been produced with such an aim. Faust[16] itself, in which something of the kind is attempted, wonderful passages as it contains, and in spite of the unsurpassed beauty of the scenes which relate to Margaret, Faust itself, judged as a whole, and judged strictly as a poetical work, is defective: its illustrious author, the greatest poet of modern times, the greatest critic of all times, would have been the first to acknowledge it; he only defended his work, indeed, by asserting it to be "something incommensurable."

The confusion of the present times is great, the multitude of voices counselling different things bewildering, the number of existing works capable of attracting a young writer's attention and of becoming his models, immense. What he wants is a hand to guide him through the confusion, a voice to prescribe to him the aim which he should keep in view, and to explain to him that the value of the literary works which offer themselves to his attention is relative to their power of helping him forward on his road towards this aim. Such a guide the English writer at the present day will nowhere find. Failing this, all that can be looked for, all indeed that can be desired, is, that his attention should be fixed on excellent models; that he may reproduce, at any rate, something of their excellence, by penetrating himself with their works and by catching their spirit, if he cannot be taught to produce what is excellent independently.

Foremost among these models for the English writer stands Shakespeare: a name the greatest perhaps of all poetical names; a name never to be mentioned without reverence. I will venture, however, to express a doubt, whether the influence of his works, excellent and fruitful for the readers of poetry, for the great majority, has been of unmixed advantage to the writers of it. Shakespeare indeed chose excellent subjects; the world could afford no better than Macbeth, or Romeo and Juliet, or Othello: he had no theory respecting the necessity of choosing subjects of present import, or the paramount interest attaching to allegories of the state of one's own mind; like all great poets, he knew well what constituted a poetical

action; like them, wherever he found such an action, he took it; like them, too, he found his best in past times. But to these general characteristics of all great poets he added a special one of his own; a gift, namely, of happy, abundant, and ingenious expression, eminent and unrivalled: so eminent as irresistibly to strike the attention first in him, and even to throw into comparative shade his other excellences as a poet. Here has been the mischief. These other excellences were his fundamental excellences *as a poet;* what distinguishes the artist from the mere amateur, says Goethe, is *Architectonicè* in the highest sense; that power of execution, which creates, forms, and constitutes: not the profoundness of single thoughts, not the richness of imagery, not the abundance of illustration. But these attractive accessories of a poetical work being more easily seized than the spirit of the whole, and these accessories being possessed by Shakespeare in an unequalled degree, a young writer having recourse to Shakespeare as his model runs great risk of being vanquished and absorbed by them, and, in consequence, of reproducing, according to the measure of his power, these, and these alone. Of this preponderating quality of Shakespeare's genius, accordingly, almost the whole of modern English poetry has, it appears to me, felt the influence. To the exclusive attention on the part of his imitators to this it is in a great degree owing, that of the majority of modern poetical works the details alone are valuable, the composition worthless. In reading them one is perpetually reminded of that terrible sentence on a modern French poet—*il dit tout ce qu'il veut, mais malheureusement il n'a rien à dire.*[17]

.   .   .

I have said that the imitators of Shakespeare, fixing their attention on his wonderful gift of expression, have directed their imitation to this, neglecting his other excellences. These excellences, the fundamental excellences of poetical art, Shakespeare no doubt possessed them—possessed many of them in a splendid degree; but it may perhaps be doubted whether

[16] The first part of Goethe's *Faust* was published in 1808, the second part in 1832.
[17] "He says all he wishes, but unfortunately he has nothing to say." Super (p. 221) remarks that the sentence is a fair summary of a review published in a French journal in 1852 of a book by Théophile Gautier (1811–72), but that this sentence itself does not appear in the review.

even he himself did not sometimes give scope to his faculty of expression to the prejudice of a higher poetical duty. For we must never forget that Shakespeare is the great poet he is from his skill in discerning and firmly conceiving an excellent action, from his power of intensely feeling a situation, of intimately associating himself with a character; not from his gift of expression, which rather even leads him astray, degenerating sometimes into a fondness for curiosity of expression, into an irritability of fancy, which seems to make it impossible for him to say a thing plainly, even when the press of the action demands the very directest language, or its level character the very simplest. Mr. Hallam,[18] than whom it is impossible to find a saner and more judicious critic, has had the courage (for at the present day it needs courage) to remark, how extremely and faultily difficult Shakespeare's language often is. It is so: you may find main scenes in some of his greatest tragedies, *King Lear* for instance, where the language is so artificial, so curiously tortured, and so difficult, that every speech has to be read two or three times before its meaning can be comprehended. This over-curiousness of expression is indeed but the excessive employment of a wonderful gift—of the power of saying a thing in a happier way than any other man; nevertheless, it is carried so far that one understands what M. Guizot meant,[19] when he said that Shakespeare appears in his language to have tried all styles except that of simplicity. He has not the severe and scrupulous self-restraint of the ancients, partly no doubt, because he had a far less cultivated and exacting audience. He has indeed a far wider range than they had, a far richer fertility of thought; in this respect he rises above them. In his strong conception of his subject, in the genuine way in which he is penetrated with it, he resembles them, and is unlike the moderns. But in the accurate limitation of it, the conscientious rejection of superfluities, the simple and rigorous development of it from the first line of his work to the last, he falls below them, and comes nearer to the moderns. In his chief works, besides what he has of his own, he has the elementary soundness of the ancients; he has their important action and their large

and broad manner: but he has not their purity of method. He is therefore a less safe model; for what he has of his own is personal, and inseparable from his own rich nature; it may be imitated and exaggerated, it cannot be learned or applied as an art. He is above all suggestive; more valuable, therefore, to young writers as men than as artists. But clearness of arrangement, rigour of development, simplicity of style —these may to a certain extent be learned: and these may, I am convinced, be learned best from the ancients, who although infinitely less suggestive than Shakespeare, are thus, to the artist, more instructive.

What, then, it will be asked, are the ancients to be our sole models? the ancients with their comparatively narrow range of experience, and their widely different circumstances? Not, certainly, that which is narrow in the ancients, nor that in which we can no longer sympathize. An action like the action of the *Antigone* of Sophocles, which turns upon the conflict between the heroine's duty to her brother's corpse and that to the laws of her country, is no longer one in which it is possible that we should feel a deep interest. I am speaking too, it will be remembered, not of the best sources of intellectual stimulus for the general reader, but of the best models of instruction for the individual writer. This last may certainly learn of the ancients, better than anywhere else, three things which it is vitally important for him to know:—the all-importance of the choice of a subject; the necessity of accurate construction; and the subordinate character of expression. He will learn from them how unspeakably superior is the effect of the one moral impression left by a great action treated as a whole, to the effect produced by the most striking single thought or by the happiest image. As he penetrates into the spirit of the great classical works, as he becomes gradually aware of their intense significance, their noble simplicity, and their calm pathos, he will be convinced that it is this effect, unity and profoundness of moral impression, at which the ancient Poets aimed; that it is this which constitutes the grandeur of their works, and which makes them immortal. He will desire to direct his own efforts towards producing the same effect. Above all, he

---

[18] Henry Hallam (1777–1859) in volume 3 of *Introduction to the Literature of Europe in the Fifteenth, Sixteenth, and Seventeenth Centuries* (1837–39).

[19] François Guizot (1787–1874), a French historian and politician, published a book on Shakespeare in France in 1852.

will deliver himself from the jargon of modern criticism, and escape the danger of producing poetical works conceived in the spirit of the passing time, and which partake of its transitoriness.

The present age makes great claims upon us: we owe it service, it will not be satisfied without our admiration. I know not how it is, but their commerce with the ancients appears to me to produce, in those who constantly practise it, a steadying and composing effect upon their judgment, not of literary works only, but of men and events in general. They are like persons who have had a very weighty and impressive experience: they are more truly than others under the empire of facts, and more independent of the language current among those with whom they live. They wish neither to applaud nor to revile their age: they wish to know what it is, what it can give them, and whether this is what they want. What they want, they know very well; they want to educe and cultivate what is best and noblest in themselves: they know, too, that this is no easy task —χαλεπόν, as Pittacus said, χαλεπὸν ἐσθλὸν ἔμμεναι [20]—and they ask themselves sincerely whether their age and its literature can assist them in the attempt. If they are endeavouring to practise any art, they remember the plain and simple proceedings of the old artists, who attained their grand results by penetrating themselves with some noble and significant action, not by inflating themselves with a belief in the pre-eminent importance and greatness of their own times. They do not talk of their mission, nor of interpreting their age, nor of the coming Poet; all this, they know, is the mere delirium of vanity; their business is not to praise their age, but to afford to the men who live in it the highest pleasure which they are capable of feeling. If asked to afford this by means of subjects drawn from the age itself, they ask what special fitness the present age has for supplying them. They are told that it is an era of progress, an age commissioned to carry out the great ideas of industrial development and social amelioration. They reply that with all this they can do nothing; that the elements they need for the exercise of their art are great actions, calculated powerfully and delightfully to affect what is permanent in the human soul; that so far as the present age can supply such actions, they will gladly make use of them; but that an age wanting in moral grandeur can with difficulty supply such, and an age of spiritual discomfort with difficulty be powerfully and delightfully affected by them.

A host of voices will indignantly rejoin that the present age is inferior to the past neither in moral grandeur nor in spiritual health. He who possesses the discipline I speak of will content himself with remembering the judgments passed upon the present age, in this respect, by the two men, the one of strongest head, the other of widest culture, whom it has produced; by Goethe and by Niebuhr.[21] It will be sufficient for him that he knows the opinions held by these two great men respecting the present age and its literature; and that he feels assured in his own mind that their aims and demands upon life were such as he would wish, at any rate, his own to be; and their judgment as to what is impeding and disabling such as he may safely follow. He will not, however, maintain a hostile attitude towards the false pretensions of his age; he will content himself with not being overwhelmed by them. He will esteem himself fortunate if he can succeed in banishing from his mind all feelings of contradiction, and irritation, and impatience; in order to delight himself with the contemplation of some noble action of a heroic time, and to enable others, through his representation of it, to delight in it also.

I am far indeed from making any claim, for myself, that I possess this discipline; or for the following Poems, that they breathe its spirit. But I say, that in the sincere endeavour to learn and practise, amid the bewildering confusion of our times, what is sound and true in poetical art, I seemed to myself to find the only sure guidance, the only solid footing, among the ancients. They, at any rate, knew what they wanted in Art, and we do not. It is this uncertainty which is disheartening, and not

[20] "It is hard to be good." Pittacus (c. 650–570 B.C.) was one of the seven sages of Greece whose aphorisms were recorded, among other sources, by Plato and Diogenes Laertius, a second-century compiler of *Lives of the Greek Philosophers*. An edition of the latter text was published in 1850.

[21] Barthold Georg Niebuhr (1776–1831) was a German historian and philologist. Like Goethe, he thought the literature which followed that of the first decades of the nineteenth-century to be barren and torpid.

hostile criticism. How often have I felt this when reading words of disparagement or of cavil: that it is the uncertainty as to what is really to be aimed at which makes our difficulty, not the dissatisfaction of the critic, who himself suffers from the same uncertainty. *Non me tua fervida terrent Dicta: Dii me terrent, et Jupiter hostis.*[22]

Two kinds of *dilettanti*, says Goethe, there are in poetry: he who neglects the indispensable mechanical part, and thinks he has done enough if he shows spirituality and feeling; and he who seeks to arrive at poetry merely by mechanism, in which he can acquire an artisan's readiness, and is without soul and matter. And he adds, that the first does most harm to Art, and the last to himself. If we must be *dilettanti:* if it is impossible for us, under the circumstances amidst which we live, to think clearly, to feel nobly, and to delineate firmly: if we cannot attain to the mastery of the great artists—let us, at least, have so much respect for our Art as to prefer it to ourselves: let us not bewilder our successors: let us transmit to them the practice of Poetry, with its boundaries and wholesome regulative laws, under which excellent works may again, perhaps, at some future time, be produced, not yet fallen into oblivion through our neglect, not yet condemned and cancelled by the influence of their eternal enemy, Caprice.

1853

from The Study of Poetry

Arnold wrote this essay as the introduction to an anthology of English poetry edited by T. H. Ward and published in 1880. He is concerned in the essay to educate readers in the means of establishing the "real estimate" of the value of a poem by comparing its finest passages to the finest passages in the whole of literature (Arnold's touchstones) and by correcting misvaluations based upon historical estimates (the poet's eminence in his or her own time) and personal taste. The text is that of the 1880 volume; it is reprinted in Volume 9 of Super's edition of Arnold's prose (1973).

. . . We should conceive of poetry worthily, and more highly than it has been the custom to conceive of it. We should conceive of it as capable of higher uses, and called to higher destinies, than those which in general men have assigned to it hitherto. More and more mankind will discover that we have to turn to poetry to interpret life for us, to console us, to sustain us. Without poetry, our science will appear incomplete; and most of what now passes with us for religion and philosophy will be replaced by poetry. Science, I say, will appear incomplete without it. For finely and truly does Wordsworth call poetry "the impassioned expression which is in the countenance of all science"; and what is a countenance without its expression? Again, Wordsworth finely and truly calls poetry "the breath and finer spirit of all knowledge":[1] our religion, parading evidences such as those on which the popular mind relies now; our philosophy, pluming itself on its reasonings about causation and finite and infinite being; what are they but the shadows and dreams and false shows of knowledge? The day will come when we shall wonder at ourselves for having trusted to them, for having taken them seriously; and the more we perceive their hollowness, the more we shall prize "the breath and finer spirit of knowledge" offered to us by poetry.

But if we conceive thus highly of the destinies of poetry, we must also set our standard for poetry high, since poetry, to be capable of fulfilling such high destinies, must be poetry of a high order of excellence. We must accustom ourselves to a high standard and to a strict judgment. Sainte-Beuve relates that Napoleon one day said, when somebody was spoken of in his presence as a charlatan: "Charlatan as much as you please; but where is there *not* charlatanism?"—"Yes," answers Sainte-Beuve,[2] "in politics, in the art of governing mankind, that is perhaps true. But in the order of thought, in art, the glory, the eternal honour is that charlatanism shall find no entrance; herein lies the inviolableness of that noble

---

[22] "Your hot words do not frighten me; the gods frighten me, and Jupiter's enmity." From Virgil's *Aeneid*, XII, 894–95.

[1] Wordsworth uses these phrases in his "Preface" to the 1800 edition of *Lyrical Ballads*.

[2] Charles Augustin Sainte-Beuve (1804–69) was a French critic. The anecdote is recounted in his notebooks, published in Paris in 1876.

portion of man's being." It is admirably said, and let us hold fast to it. In poetry, which is thought and art in one, it is the glory, the eternal honour, that charlatanism shall find no entrance; that this noble sphere be kept inviolate and inviolable. Charlatanism is for confusing or obliterating the distinctions between excellent and inferior, sound and unsound or only half-sound, true and untrue or only half-true. It is charlatanism, conscious or unconscious, whenever we confuse or obliterate these. And in poetry, more than anywhere else, it is unpermissible to confuse or obliterate them. For in poetry the distinction between excellent and inferior, sound and unsound or only half-sound, true and untrue or only half-true, is of paramount importance. It is of paramount importance because of the high destinies of poetry. In poetry, as a criticism of life under the conditions fixed for such a criticism by the laws of poetic truth and poetic beauty, the spirit of our race will find, we have said, as time goes on and as other helps fail, its consolation and stay. But the consolation and stay will be of power in proportion to the power of the criticism of life. And the criticism of life will be of power in proportion as the poetry conveying it is excellent rather than inferior, sound rather than unsound or half-sound, true rather than untrue or half-true.

The best poetry is what we want; the best poetry will be found to have a power of forming, sustaining, and delighting us, as nothing else can. A clearer, deeper sense of the best in poetry, and of the strength and joy to be drawn from it, is the most precious benefit which we can gather from a poetical collection such as the present. And yet in the very nature and conduct of such a collection there is inevitably something which tends to obscure in us the consciousness of what our benefit should be, and to distract us from the pursuit of it. We should therefore steadily set it before our minds at the outset, and should compel ourselves to revert constantly to the thought of it as we proceed. . . .

The specimens I have quoted differ widely from one another, but they have in common this: the possession of the very highest poetical quality. If we are thoroughly penetrated by their power, we shall find that we have acquired a sense enabling us, whatever poetry may be laid before us, to feel the degree in which a high poetical quality is present or wanting there. Critics give themselves great labour to draw out what in the abstract constitutes the characters of a high quality of poetry. It is much better simply to have recourse to concrete examples;—to take specimens of poetry of the high, the very highest quality, and to say: The characters of a high quality of poetry are what is expressed *there*. They are far better recognised by being felt in the verse of the master, than by being perused in the prose of the critic. Nevertheless if we are urgently pressed to give some critical account of them, we may safely, perhaps, venture on laying down, not indeed how and why the characters arise, but where and in what they arise. They are in the matter and substance of the poetry, and they are in its manner and style. Both of these, the substance and matter on the one hand, the style and manner on the other, have a mark, an accent, of high beauty, worth, and power. But if we are asked to define this mark and accent in the abstract, our answer must be: No, for we should thereby be darkening the question, not clearing it. The mark and accent are as given by the substance and matter of that poetry, by the style and manner of that poetry, and of all other poetry which is akin to it in quality.

Only one thing we may add as to the substance and matter of poetry, guiding ourselves by Aristotle's profound observation that the superiority of poetry over history consists in its possessing a higher truth and a higher seriousness ($\phi\iota\lambda o\sigma o\phi\dot\omega\tau\epsilon\rho o\nu$ $\kappa\alpha\dot\iota$ $\sigma\pi o\upsilon\delta\alpha\iota\dot o\tau\epsilon\rho o\nu$) .[3] Let us add, therefore, to what we have said, this: that the substance and matter of the best poetry acquire their special character from possessing, in an eminent degree, truth and seriousness. We may add yet further, what is in itself evident, that to the style and manner of the best poetry their special character, their accent, is given by their diction, and, even yet more, by their movement. And though we distinguish between the two characters, the two accents, of superiority, yet they are nevertheless vitally connected one with the other. The superior character of truth and seriousness, in the matter and substance of the best poetry, is inseparable from the superiority of diction and movement marking its style and manner. The two superiorities are closely related, and are in steadfast proportion one to the other. So far as

[3] *Poetics*, IX.

high poetic truth and seriousness are wanting to a poet's matter and substance, so far also, we may be sure, will a high poetic stamp of diction and movement be wanting to his style and manner. In proportion as this high stamp of diction and movement, again, is absent from a poet's style and manner, we shall find, also, that high poetic truth and seriousness are absent from his substance and matter.

. . .

[*Arnold closes his essay by showing how to correct overgenerous historical estimates of the principal poets in the several chronological periods of British literature, deciding, for example, that for all their power and eminence Chaucer and Burns alike lack "high seriousness," and for all the masterful craft with which they expressed an age of prose and reason, Dryden and Pope are "not classics of our poetry, they are classics of our prose."*]

But we enter on burning ground as we approach the poetry of times so near to us—poetry like that of Byron, Shelley, and Wordsworth—of which the estimates are so often not only personal, but personal with passion. For my purpose, it is enough to have taken the single case of Burns, the first poet we come to of whose work the estimate formed is evidently apt to be personal, and to have suggested how we may proceed, using the poetry of the great classics as a sort of touchstone, to correct this estimate, as we had previously corrected by the same means the historic estimate where we

met with it. A collection like the present, with its succession of celebrated names and celebrated poems, offers a good opportunity to us for resolutely endeavoring to make our estimates of poetry real. I have sought to point out a method which will help us in making them so, and to exhibit it in use so far as to put any one who likes in a way of applying it for himself.

At any rate the end to which the method and the estimate are designed to lead, and from leading to which, if they do lead to it, they get their whole value,—the benefit of being able clearly to feel and deeply to enjoy the best, the truly classic, in poetry,—is an end, let me say it once more at parting, of supreme importance. We are often told that an era is opening in which we are to see multitudes of a common sort of readers, and masses of a common sort of literature; that such readers do not want and could not relish anything better than such literature, and that to provide it is becoming a vast and profitable industry. Even if good literature entirely lost currency with the world, it would still be abundantly worth while to continue to enjoy it by oneself. But it never will lose currency with the world, in spite of momentary appearances; it never will lose supremacy. Currency and supremacy are insured to it, not indeed by the world's deliberate and conscious choice, but by something far deeper,—by the instinct of self-preservation in humanity.

1880

Algernon Charles Swinburne
1837–1909

Upon its first publication in 1866 Swinburne's Poems and Ballads *was denounced as obscene and blasphemous by many reviewers, including one whom Swinburne respected, John Morley (1838–1923), a journalist, politician, and later the author of biographies of Edmund Burke and Voltaire, who attacked the volume in a review in the* Saturday Review. *The first publisher of the book withdrew it from publication, and its subsequent publisher asked Swinburne to answer his critics.* Notes on Poems and Reviews *was published as a pamphlet late in 1866. The text printed here is that reprinted in the Bonchurch edition of Swinburne's writing, and in* Swinburne Replies, *edited by Clyde Kenneth Hyder (1966).*

from Notes on Poems and Reviews

. . . Certain poems of mine, it appears, have been impugned by judges, with or without a name, as indecent or as blasphemous. To me, as I have intimated, their verdict is a matter of infinite indifference: it is of equally small moment to me whether in such eyes as theirs I appear moral or immoral, Christian or pagan. But, remembering that science must not scorn to investigate animalcules and infusoria, I am ready for once to play the anatomist.

With regard to any opinion implied or expressed throughout my book, I desire that one thing should be remembered: the book is dramatic, many-faced, multifarious; and no utterance of enjoyment or despair, belief or unbelief, can properly be assumed as the assertion of its author's personal feeling or faith. Were each poem to be accepted as the deliberate outcome and result of the writer's conviction, not mine alone but most other men's verses would leave nothing behind them but a sense of cloudy chaos and suicidal contradiction. Byron and Shelley, speaking in their own persons, and with what sublime effect we know, openly and insultingly mocked and reviled what the English of their day held most sacred. I have not done this. I do not say that, if I chose, I would not do so to the best of my power; I do say that hitherto I have seen fit to do nothing of the kind.

It remains then to inquire what in that book can be reasonably offensive to the English reader. In order to resolve this problem, I will not fish up any of the ephemeral scurrilities born only to sting if they can, and sink as they must. I will take the one article that lies before me; the work (I admit) of an enemy, but the work (I acknowledge) of a gentleman. I cannot accept it as accurate; but I readily and gladly allow that it neither contains nor suggests anything false or filthy. To him therefore, rather than to another, I address my reclamation. Two among my poems, it appears, are in his opinion "especially horrible." Good.

Though the phrase be somewhat "inexpressive," I am content to meet him on this ground. It is something—nay, it is much—to find an antagonist who has sufficient sense of honesty and honour to mark out the lists in which he, the challenger, is desirous to encounter the challenged.

.   .   .

[*The first of his poems Swinburne defends is "Anactoria," which he describes as an attempt to render in English the spirit of a poem by the Greek poet Sappho.*]

Next on the list of accusation stands the poem of *Dolores*. The gist and bearing of this I should have thought evident enough, viewed by the light of others which precede and follow it. I have striven here to express that transient state of spirit through which a man may be supposed to pass, foiled in love and weary of loving, but not yet in sight of rest; seeking refuge in those "violent delights" which "have violent ends,"[1] in fierce and frank sensualities which at least profess to be no more than they are. This poem, like *Faustine*, is so distinctly symbolic and fanciful that it cannot justly be amenable to judgment as a study in the school of realism. The spirit, bowed and discoloured by suffering and by passion (which are indeed the same thing and the same word), plays for awhile with its pleasures and its pains, mixes and distorts them with a sense half-humorous and half-mournful, exults in bitter and doubtful emotions:

Moods of fantastic sadness, nothing worth[2]

It sports with sorrow, and jests against itself; cries out for freedom and confesses the chain; decorates with the name of goddess, crowns anew as the mystical Cotytto,[3] some woman, real or ideal, in whom the pride of life with its companion lusts is incarnate. In her lover's half-shut eyes, her fierce unchaste beauty is transfigured, her cruel sensual eyes have a meaning and a message; there are memories and secrets in the kisses of her lips. She is the darker Venus, fed with burnt-offering and blood-sacrifice; the veiled image of that pleasure which men impelled by satiety and perverted by power have sought through ways as

---

[1] From Shakespeare's *Romeo and Juliet,* II, vi.
[2] From Matthew Arnold's poem "To a Gipsy Child by the Seashore" (1849).
[3] Cotytto: a goddess worshipped in ancient Thrace in Asia Minor in orgiastic rites.

strange as Nero's before and since his time; the daughter of lust and death, and holding of both her parents; Our Lady of Pain, antagonist alike of trivial sins and virtues: no Virgin, and unblessed of men; no mother of the Gods or God; no Cybele, served by sexless priests or monks, adored of Origen or Atys; no likeness of her in Dindymus or Loreto.[4]

The next act in this lyrical monodrama of passion represents a new stage and scene. The worship of desire has ceased; the mad commotion of sense has stormed itself out; the spirit, clear of the old regret that drove it upon such violent ways for a respite, healed of the fever that wasted it in the search for relief among fierce fancies and tempestuous pleasures, dreams now of truth discovered and repose attained. Not the martyr's ardour of selfless love, an unprofitable flame that burnt out and did no service—not the rapid rage of pleasure that seemed for a little to make the flesh divine, to clothe the naked senses with the fiery raiment of faith; but a stingless love, an innocuous desire. "Hesperia," the tenderest type of woman or of dream, born in the westward "islands of the blest,"[5] where the shadows of all happy and holy things live beyond the sunset a sacred and a sleepless life, dawns upon his eyes a western dawn, risen as the fiery day of passion goes down, and risen where it sank. Here, between moonrise and sunset, lives the love that is gentle and faithful, neither giving too much nor asking—a bride rather than a mistress, a sister rather than a bride. But not at once, or not forever, can the past be killed and buried; hither also the huntress follows her flying prey, wounded and weakened, still fresh from the fangs of passion; the cruel hands, the amorous eyes, still glitter and allure. *Qui a bu boira:*[6] the feet are drawn back towards the ancient ways. Only by lifelong flight, side by side with the goddess that redeems, shall her slave of old escape from the goddess that consumes: if even thus one may be saved, even thus distance the bloodhounds.

This is the myth or fable of my poem; and it is not without design that I have slipped in, between the first and the second part, the verses called *The Garden of Proserpine,* expressive, as I meant they should be, of that brief total pause of passion and of thought, when the spirit, without fear or hope of good things or evil, hungers and thirsts only after the perfect sleep. Now, what there is in all this unfit to be written—what there is here indecent in manner or repulsive in matter—I at least do not yet see; and before I can see it, my eyes must be purged with the euphrasy and rue[7] which keep clear the purer eyes of professional virtue. The insight into evil of chaste and critical pressmen, their sharp scent for possible or impossible impurities, their delicate ear for a sound or a whisper of wrong—all this knowledge "is too wonderful and excellent for me; I cannot attain unto it."[8] In one thing, indeed, it seems I have erred: I have forgotten to prefix to my work the timely warning of a great poet and humorist:

J'en préviens les mères des familles,
Ce que j'écries n'est pas pour les petites filles
Dont on coupe le pain et tartines; mes vers
Sont des vers de jeune homme.[9]

I have overlooked the evidence which every day makes clearer, that our time has room only for such as are content to write for children and girls. But this oversight is the sum of my offence.

It would seem indeed as though to publish a book were equivalent to thrusting it with vio-

---

[4] Nero, a first-century emperor of Rome, was infamous for his sensuality and cruelty. Cybele is a name for the mother of gods who was associated with several female divinities in Greek and Roman religions. Origen (185–254) was a theologian of the early Christian church; Atys in classical mythology was loved by Cybele but castrated himself. Dindymus is a site sacred to Cybele; Loreto in Italy boasted a church to which the house of the Virgin Mary was supposed to have been carried by angels.

[5] Hesperia: islands of the blest, used here to denote the beauty of twilight, repose, retreat, death—stasis after action.

[6] *Qui a bu boira:* who has drunk will drink.

[7] Euphrasy and rue: in John Milton's *Paradise Lost* (XI, line 414) Adam's eyes are washed in a distillation of these herbs to enable him to see the future.

[8] "Such knowledge is too wonderful for me: It is high, I cannot attain to it" (Psalm 139:6). *The Book of Common Prayer* of the Church of England translates the sentence in the words Swinburne uses.

[9] "I warn the mothers of families that I do not write for little girls, for whom one makes bread and butter; my verses are the verses of a young man": Théophile Gautier (1811–72), from a poem ("Albertus") published in 1833.

lence into the hands of every mother and nurse in the kingdom as fit and necessary food for female infancy. Happily there is no fear that the supply of milk for babes will fall short of the demand for some time yet. There are moral milkmen enough, in all conscience, crying their ware about the streets and byways; fresh or stale, sour or sweet, the requisite fluid runs from a sufficiently copious issue. In due time, perhaps, the critical doctors may prescribe a stronger diet for their hypochondriac patient, the reading world; or the gigantic *malade imaginaire* called the public may rebel against the weekly draught or the daily drug of MM. Purgon and Diafoirus.[10] We, meanwhile, who profess to deal neither in poison nor in pap, may not unwillingly stand aside. Let those read who will, and let those who will abstain from reading. *Caveat emptor.* No one wishes to force men's food down the throats of babes and sucklings. The verses last analysed were assuredly written with no moral or immoral design; but the upshot seems to me moral rather than immoral, if it must needs be one or the other, and if (which I cannot be sure of) I construe aright those somewhat misty and changeable terms.

. . .

Of the poem in which I have attempted once more to embody the legend of Venus and her knight, I need say only that my first aim was to rehandle the old story in a new fashion. To me it seemed that the tragedy began with the knight's return to Venus—began at the point where hitherto it had seemed to leave off. The immortal agony of a man lost after all repentance—cast down from fearful hope into fearless despair—believing in Christ and bound to Venus—desirous of penitential pain, and damned to joyless pleasure—this, in my eyes, was the kernel and nucleus of a myth comparable only to that of the foolish virgins and bearing the same burden. The tragic touch of the story is this: that the knight who has renounced Christ believes in him; the lover who

has embraced Venus disbelieves in her. Vainly and in despair would he make the best of that which is the worst—vainly remonstrate with God, and argue on the side he would fain desert. Once accept or admit the least admixture of pagan worship, or of modern thought, and the whole story collapses into froth and smoke. It was not till my poem was completed that I received from the hands of its author the admirable pamphlet of Charles Baudelaire on Wagner's *Tannhäuser.*[11] If any one desires to see, expressed in better words than I can command, the conception of the mediæval Venus which it was my aim to put into verse, let him turn to the magnificent passage in which M. Baudelaire describes the fallen goddess, grown diabolic among ages that would not accept her as divine. In another point, as I then found, I concur with the great musician and his great panegyrist. I have made Venus the one love of her knight's whole life, as Mary Stuart of Chastelard's;[12] I have sent him, poet and soldier, fresh to her fierce embrace. Thus only both legend and symbol appear to me noble and significant. Light loves and harmless errors must not touch the elect of heaven or of hell. The queen of evil, the lady of lust, will endure no rival but God; and when the vicar of God rejects him, to her only can he return to abide the day of judgment in weariness and sorrow and fear.

These poems do not seem to me condemnable, unless it be on the ground of bad verse; and to any charge of that kind I should of course be as unable as reluctant to reply. But I certainly was even less prepared to hear the batteries of virtue open fire in another quarter. Sculpture I knew was a dead art; buried centuries deep out of sight, with no angel keeping watch over the sepulchre; its very grave-clothes divided by wrangling and impotent sectaries, and no chance anywhere visible of a resurrection. I knew that belief in the body was the secret of sculpture, and that a past age of ascetics could no more attempt or attain it than the present age of hypocrites; I knew that modern moralities and recent religions were, if

[10] Purgon and Diafoirus: quack doctors in *Le Malade imaginaire* (*The Imaginary Invalid*, 1673) by Jean Baptiste Molière (1622–73).
[11] Richard Wagner (1813–83) produced *Tannhäuser,* his treatment of the legend on which Swinburne bases "Laus Veneris," in 1845. Charles Baudelaire (1821–67) published his pamphlet on Wagner in 1861.
[12] Chastelard: a nobleman and page in the court of Mary, Queen of Scots (1542–87), who was hanged when his love for the queen impelled him to secret himself in her apartments. Swinburne published a verse tragedy, *Chastelard,* in 1865.

possible, more averse and alien to this purely physical and pagan art than to the others; but how far averse I did not know. There is nothing lovelier, as there is nothing more famous, in later Hellenic art, than the statue of Hermaphroditus. No one would compare it with the greatest works of Greek sculpture. No one would lift Keats on a level with Shakespeare. But the Fates have allowed us to possess at once Othello and Hyperion, Theseus and Hermaphroditus.[13] At Paris, at Florence, at Naples, the delicate divinity of this work has always drawn towards it the eyes of artists and poets.[14] A creature at once foul and dull enough to extract from a sight so lovely, from a thing so noble, the faintest, the most fleeting idea of impurity, must be, and must remain, below comprehension and below remark. It is incredible that the meanest of men should derive from it any other than the sense of high and grateful pleasure. Odour and colour and music are not more tender or more pure. How favourite and frequent a vision among the Greeks was this of the union of sexes in one body of perfect beauty, none need be told. In Plato the legend has fallen into a form coarse, hard, and absurd. The theory of God splitting in two the double archetype of man and woman, the original hermaphrodite which had to get itself bisected into female and male, is repulsive and ridiculous enough.[15] But the idea thus incarnate, literal or symbolic, is merely beautiful. I am not the first who has translated into written verse this sculptured poem: another before me, as he says, has more than once "caressed it with a sculptor's love."[16] It is, indeed, among statues as a lyric among tragedies; it stands below the Niobe as Simonides below Æschylus, as Correggio beneath Titian.[17] The sad and subtle moral of this myth, which I have desired to indicate in verse, is that perfection once attained on all sides is a thing thenceforward barren of use or fruit; whereas the divided beauty of separate woman and man —a thing inferior and imperfect—can serve all turns of life. Ideal beauty, like ideal genius, dwells apart, as though by compulsion; supremacy is solitude. But leaving this symbolic side of the matter, I cannot see why this statue should not be the text for yet another poem. Treated in the grave and chaste manner as a serious "thing of beauty,"[18] to be for ever applauded and enjoyed, it can give no offence but to the purblind and the prurient. For neither of these classes have I ever written or will I ever write. "Loathsome and abominable" and full of "unspeakable foulnesses"[19] must be that man's mind who could here discern evil; unclean and inhuman the animal which could suck from this mystical rose of ancient liveli-

---

[13] Hyperion is the hero and title of a late, unfinished poem by John Keats (1820). Theseus, a legendary king of ancient Greece, was often depicted in sculpture; a figure of Theseus from the decoration of the Parthenon was in the British Museum in the nineteenth century.

[14] Swinburne's note: Witness Shelley's version:

> A sexless thing it was, and in its growth
> It seemed to have developed no defect
> Of either sex, yet all the grace of both;
> In gentleness and strength its limbs were decked;
> The bosom lightly swelled with its full youth,
> The countenance was such as might select
> Some artist, that his skill should never die,
> Imaging forth such perfect purity.
> *Witch of Atlas,* XXXVI [1820; 1824]

But Shelley had not studied purity in the school of reviewers. It is well for us that we have teachers able to enlighten our darkness, or Heaven knows into what error such as he, or such as I, might not fall. We might even, in time, come to think it possible to enjoy the naked beauty of a statue or a picture without any virtuous vision behind it of a filthy fancy; which would be immoral.

[15] Plato recounts the legend in the *Symposium,* a late philosophical dialogue on love.

[16] Swinburne refers to Shelley, although the words he quotes are not Shelley's.

[17] Niobe: probably a Roman copy of a Greek statue which was displayed in Florence in the nineteenth century. Simonides was a sixth-century B.C. Greek poet, the contemporary of the dramatist Aeschylus, whose poetry won him many prizes and honors. Correggio and Titian were also contemporaries, sixteenth-century Italian painters of large, strongly colored, often religious pictures.

[18] "A thing of beauty is a joy forever": the first line of John Keats' *Endymion* (1818).

[19] These phrases were used by Morley in his review.

ness the foul and rancid juices of an obscene
fancy. It were a scavenger's office to descend
with torch or spade into such depths of mental
sewerage, to plunge or peer into subterranean
sloughs of mind impossible alike to enlighten
or to cleanse.

I have now gone over the poems which, as I
hear, have incurred most blame; whether
deservedly or not, I have shown. For the terms
in which certain critics have clothed their
sentiments I bear them no ill-will: they are
welcome for me to write unmolested, as long
as they keep to simple ribaldry. I hope it gives
them amusement; I presume it brings them
profit; I know it does not affect me. Absolute
falsehood may, if it be worth while, draw
down contradiction and disproof; but the
mere calling of bad names is a child's trick, for
which the small fry of the press should have a
child's correction at the hands of able editors;
standing as these gentlemen ought to do in a
parental or pedagogic relation to their tender
charges. They have, by all I see and hear, been
sufficiently scurrilous—one or two in partic-
ular:

However, from one crime they are exempt;
They do not strike a brother, striking me.[20]

I will only throw them one crumb of advice
in return; I fear the alms will be of no avail,
but it shall not be withheld:

Why grudge them lotus-leaf and laurel,
    O toothless mouth or swinish maw,
Who never grudged you bells and coral,
    Who never grudged you troughs and straw?

Lie still in kennel, sleek in stable,
    Good creatures of the stall or sty;
Shove snouts for crumbs below the table;
    Lie still; and rise not up to lie.[21]

To all this, however, there is a grave side.
The question at issue is wider than any be-
tween a single writer and his critics, or it
might well be allowed to drop. It is this:
whether or not the first and last requisite of art
is to give no offence; whether or not all that
cannot be lisped in the nursery or fingered in
the schoolroom is therefore to be cast out of
the library; whether or not the domestic circle
is to be for all men and writers the outer limit
and extreme horizon of their world of work.
For to this we have come; and all students of
art must face the matter as it stands. Who has
not heard it asked, in a final and triumphant
tone, whether this book or that can be read
aloud by her mother to a young girl? whether
such and such a picture can properly be ex-
posed to the eyes of young persons? If you reply
that this is nothing to the point, you fall at
once into the ranks of the immoral. Never till
now, and nowhere but in England, could so
monstrous an absurdity rear for one moment
its deformed and eyeless head. In no past cen-
tury were artists ever bidden to work on these
terms; nor are they now, except among us. The
disease, of course, afflicts the meanest members
of the body with most virulence. Nowhere is
cant at once so foul-mouthed and so tight-
laced as in the penny, twopenny, threepenny,
or sixpenny press. Nothing is so favourable to
the undergrowth of real indecency as this over-
shadowing foliage of fictions, this artificial net-
work of proprieties. *L'Arioste rit au soleil,
l'Arétin ricane à l'ombre.*[22] The whiter the
sepulchre without, the ranker the rottenness
within.[23] Every touch of plaster is a sign of ad-
vancing decay. The virtue of our critical jour-
nals is a dowager of somewhat dubious anteced-
ents: every day that thins and shrivels her
cheek thickens and hardens the paint on it;
she consumes more chalk and ceruse than
would serve a whole courtful of crones. "It is to
be presumed," certainly, "that in her case "all
is not sweet, all is not sound."[24] The taint on
her fly-blown reputation is hard to overcome
by patches and perfumery. Literature, to be
worthy of men, must be large, liberal, sincere;
and cannot be chaste if it be prudish. Purity

[20] From "Appendix to the *Hellenics*" by Walter Savage Landor (1775–1864). Landor pub-
lished revised and enlarged editions of the *Hellenics* in 1847 and 1859.
[21] Swinburne's own verse, apparently composed for the occasion.
[22] "Ariosto laughs in the sun; Aretino sniggers in the shade." Arisosto (1474–1533) was the
author of the Italian epic poem *Orlando Furioso;* Aretino (1492–1557) was known as the author
of prurient, obscene verse.
[23] "Woe unto you, scribes and Pharisees, hypocrites! for ye are like unto whited sepulchres,
which indeed appear beautiful outward, but are within full of dead men's bones, and of all
uncleanness" (Matthew 24:27).
[24] From the song "Still to be neat, still to be dressed" in *Epicœne, or The Silent Woman,* by
Ben Jonson (1573?–1637).

and prudery cannot keep house together. Where free speech and fair play are interdicted, foul hints and evil suggestions are hatched into fetid life. And if literature indeed is not to deal with the full life of man and the whole nature of things, let it be cast aside with the rods and rattles of childhood. Whether it affect to teach or to amuse, it is equally trivial and contemptible to us; only less so than the charge of immorality. Against how few really great names has not this small and dirt-encrusted pebble been thrown! A reputation seems imperfect without this tribute also: one jewel is wanting to the crown. It is good to be praised by those whom all men should praise; it is better to be reviled by those whom all men should scorn.

Various chances and causes must have combined to produce a state of faith or feeling which would turn all art and literature "into the line of children." One among others may be this: where the heaven of invention holds many stars at once, there is no fear that the highest and largest will either efface or draw aside into its orbit all lesser lights. Each of these takes its own way and sheds its proper lustre. But where one alone is dominant in heaven, it is encircled by a pale procession of satellite moons, filled with shallow and stolen radiance. Thus, with English versifiers now, the idyllic form is alone in fashion. The one great and prosperous poet of the time[25] has given out the tune, and the hoarser choir takes it up. His highest lyrical work remains unimitated, being in the main inimitable. But the trick of tone which suits an idyl is easier to assume; and the note has been struck so often that the shrillest songsters can affect to catch it up. We have idyls good and bad, ugly and pretty; idyls of the farm and the mill; idyls of the dining-room and the deanery; idyls of the gutter and the gibbet. If the Muse of the minute will not feast with "gig-men"[26] and their wives, she must mourn with costermongers and their trulls. I fear the more ancient Muses are guests at neither house of mourning nor house of feasting.[27]

.   .   .

I need not be over-careful to justify my ways in other men's eyes; it is enough for me that

they also work after their kind, and earn the suffrage, as they labour after the law, of their own people. The idyllic form is best for domestic and pastoral poetry. It is naturally on a lower level than that of tragic or lyric verse. Its gentle and maidenly lips are somewhat narrow for the stream and somewhat cold for the fire of song. It is very fit for the sole diet of girls; not very fit for the sole sustenance of men.

When England has again such a school of poetry, so headed and so followed, as she has had at least twice before, or as France has now; when all higher forms of the various art are included within the larger limits of a stronger race; then, if such a day should ever rise or return upon us, it will be once more remembered that the office of adult art is neither puerile nor feminine, but virile; that its purity is not that of the cloister or the harem; that all things are good in its sight, out of which good work may be produced. Then the press will be as impotent as the pulpit to dictate the laws and remove the landmarks of art; and those will be laughed at who demand from one thing the qualities of another—who seek for sermons in sonnets and morality in music. Then all accepted work will be noble and chaste in the wider masculine sense, not truncated and curtailed, but outspoken and full-grown; art will be pure by instinct and fruitful by nature, no clipped and forced growth of unhealthy heat and unnatural air; all baseness and all triviality will fall off from it, and be forgotten; and no one will then need to assert, in defence of work done for the work's sake, the simple laws of his art which no one will then be permitted to impugn.

1866

from L'Année Terrible [by Victor Hugo]

Victor Hugo (1802–85), French dramatist, poet, and novelist whose achievement and political commitment were extravagantly and consistently ad-

---

[25] Tennyson. [26] Gig-men: respectable men who keep carriages.

[27] "It is better to go to the house of mourning, than to go to the house of feasting: for that is the end of all men; and the living will lay it to his heart" (Ecclesiastes 7:2).

mired by Swinburne, was exiled from France in 1852 by Louis Napoleon. He returned to Paris in 1870, during the short-lived Commune and the Franco-Prussian War which ended Napoleon's Second Empire. In 1872 he published L'Année Terrible, *a poem concerned with the events of 1870. Swinburne published this essay first as a review in a magazine in 1872; he republished it in a collection of his critical essays in 1875. The text printed here is that of the Bonchurch edition of Swinburne's writings.*

A poem having in it any element of greatness is likely to arouse many questions with regard to the poetic art in general, and certain in that case to illustrate them with fresh lights of its own. This of Victor Hugo's at once suggests two points of frequent and fruitless debate between critics of the higher kind. The first, whether poetry and politics are irreconcilable or not; the second, whether art should prefer to deal with things immediate or with things remote. Upon both sides of either question it seems to me that even wise men have ere now been led from errors of theory to errors of decision. The well-known formula of art for art's sake, opposed as it has ever been to the practice of the poet who was so long credited with its authorship, has like other doctrines a true side to it and an untrue. Taken as an affirmative, it is a precious and everlasting truth. No work of art has any worth or life in it that is not done on the absolute terms of art; that is not before all things and above all things a work of positive excellence as judged by the laws of the special art to whose laws it is amenable. If the rules and conditions of that art be not observed, or if the work done be not great and perfect enough to rank among its triumphs, the poem, picture, statue, is a failure irredeemable and inexcusable by any show or any proof of high purpose and noble meaning. The rule of art is not the rule of morals; in morals the action is judged by the intention, the doer is applauded, excused, or condemned, according to the motive which induced his deed; in art, the one question is not what you mean but what you do. Therefore, as I have said elsewhere, the one primary requisite of art is artistic worth; "art for art's sake first, and then all things shall be added to her—or if not, it is a matter of quite secondary importance; but from him that has not this one indispensable quality of the artist, shall be taken away even that which he has; whatever merit of aspiration, sentiment, sincerity, he may naturally possess, admirable and serviceable as in other lines of work it might have been and yet may be, is here unprofitable and unpraiseworthy."[1] Thus far we are at one with the preachers of "art for art"; we prefer for example Goethe to Körner and Sappho to Tyrtæus;[2] we would give many patriots for one artist, considering that civic virtue is more easily to be had than lyric genius, and that the hoarse monotony of verse lowered to the level of a Spartan understanding,[3] however commendable such verse may be for the doctrine delivered and the duty inculcated upon all good citizens, is of less than no value to art, while there is a value beyond price and beyond thought in the Lesbian[4] music which spends itself upon the record of fleshly fever and amorous malady. We admit then that the worth of a poem has properly nothing to do with its

---

[1] Swinburne wrote in his study of *William Blake* (1867): "Art is not like fire or water, a good servant and bad master; rather the reverse. She will help in nothing, of her own knowledge or freewill: upon terms of service you will get worse than nothing out of her. Handmaid of religion, exponent of duty, servant of fact, pioneer of morality, she cannot in any way become; she would be none of these things though you were to bray her in a mortar. . . . The contingent result of having good art about you and living in a time of noble writing or painting may no doubt be this: that the spirit and mind of men then living will receive on some points a certain exaltation and insight caught from the influence of such forms and colours of verse or painting; will become for one thing incapable of tolerating bad work, and capable therefore of reasonably relishing the best; which of course implies and draws with it many other advantages of a sort you may call moral or spiritual. But if the artist does his work with an eye to such results or for the sake of bringing about such improvements, he will too probably fail even of them. Art for art's sake first of all," etc. The phrase "all things shall be added to her" is from Matthew 6:33; it is an injunction to seek not the goods of the world, but the kingdom of God, "and all these things shall be added unto you."

[2] Theodore Körner (1791–1813) was a German writer of tendentious patriotic poetry; so was Tyrtæus, a contemporary of the seventh-century B.C. Greek poet Sappho.

[3] Spartan understanding: Tyrtæus' poems were written to encourage the Spartans, known for their hard, practical abilities, in their wars.

[4] Sappho resided on the island of Lesbos in the Aegean sea.

moral meaning or design; that the praise of a Cæsar as sung by Virgil, of a Stuart as sung by Dryden, is preferable to the most magnanimous invective against tyranny which love of country and of liberty could wring from a Bavius or a Settle;[5] but on the other hand we refuse to admit that art of the highest kind may not ally itself with moral or religious passion, with the ethics or the politics of a nation or an age. It does not detract from the poetic supremacy of Æschylus and of Dante, of Milton and of Shelley, that they should have been pleased to put their art to such use: nor does it detract from the sovereign greatness of other poets that they should have had no note of song for any such theme. In a word, the doctrine of art for art is true in the positive sense, false in the negative; sound as an affirmation, unsound as a prohibition. If it be not true that the only absolute duty of art is the duty she owes to herself, then must art be dependent on the alien conditions of subject and of aim; whereas she is dependent on herself alone, and on nothing above her or beneath; by her own law she must stand or fall, and to that alone she is responsible; by no other law can any work of art be condemned, by no other plea can it be saved. But while we refuse to any artist on any plea the licence to infringe in the least article the letter of this law, to overlook or overpass it in the pursuit of any foreign purpose, we do not refuse to him the liberty of bringing within the range of it any subject that under these conditions may be so brought and included within his proper scope of work. This liberty the men who take "art for art" as their motto, using the words in an exclusive sense, would refuse to concede; they see with perfect clearness and accuracy that art can never be a "handmaid" of any "lord," as the moralist, pietist, or politician would fain have her be; and therefore they will not allow that she can properly be even so much as an ally of anything else. So on the one side we have the judges who judge of art by her capacity to serve some other good end than the production of good work; these would leave us for instance *King John,* but would assuredly deprive us of *As You Like It;* the national devotion and patriotic fire of *King Henry V.* would suffice in their estimation to set it far above the sceptic and inconclusive meditations of *Hamlet,* the pointless and aimless beauty of *A Midsummer Night's Dream.* On the other side we have the judges who would ostracise every artist found guilty of a moral sense, of the political faith or the religious emotion of patriots and heroes; whose theory would raze the *Persæ*[6] from the scroll of Æschylus, and leave us nothing of Dante but the *Vita Nuova,* of Milton but the *Allegro* and *Penseroso,* of Shelley but the *Skylark* and the *Cloud.* In consistency the one order of fanatics would expel from the poetic commonwealth such citizens as Coleridge and Keats, the other would disfranchise such as Burns and Byron. The simple truth is that the question at issue between them is that illustrated by the old child's parable of the gold and silver shield.[7] Art is one, but the service of art is diverse. It is equally foolish to demand of a Goethe, a Keats, or a Coleridge, the proper and natural work of a Dante, a Milton, or a Shelley, as to invert the demand; to arraign the *Divina Commedia* in the name of *Faust,* the *Sonnet on the Massacres in Piedmont* in the name of the *Ode on a Grecian Urn,* or the *Ode to Liberty* in the name of *Kubla Khan.*[8] I know nothing stranger in the history of criticism than the perversity even of eminent and exquisite critics in persistent condemnation of one great artist for his deficiency in the qualities of another. . . . Art knows nothing of choice between the two kinds of preference of the one to the other; she asks only that the artist shall "follow his star" with the faith and the fervour of Dante, whether it lead him on a path like or unlike

---

[5] Bavius was a first-century Roman poet, mocked in his own time and since as the type of an inferior poet; Elkanah Settle (1648–1724), who wrote declamatory verse to commemorate state and civic occasions, was similarly mocked by poets of his time. John Dryden (1631–1700) appointed poet laureate in 1668, published poems celebrating the return of Charles II to the throne of England in 1660.

[6] The *Persæ* of the sixth-century B.C. Greek dramatist Æschylus celebrates the contemporary triumph of the Athenians over the Persians.

[7] A medieval fable about two knights who approach from opposite sides a shield that is silver on one side and golden on the other, and argue whether the shield is gold or silver.

[8] Dante's poem, Milton's sonnet (published in 1666), and Shelley's "Ode to Liberty" (1820) all have political content and point, as opposed to the less explicit or topical matter and tone of Goethe's *Faust* (1808; 1832), Keats' "Ode to a Grecian Urn" (1819), and Coleridge's "Kubla Khan" (1816).

the way of Dante's work; the ministers of either tribe, the savours of either sacrifice, are equally excellent in her sight.

The question whether past or present afford the highest matter for high poetry and offer the noblest reward to the noble workman has been as loudly and as long debated, but is really less debatable on any rational ground than the question of the end and aim of art. It is but lost labour that the champions on one side summon us to renounce the present and all its works, and return to bathe our spirits in the purer air and living springs of the past; it is but waste of breath for the champions of the other party to bid us break the yoke and cast off the bondage of that past, leave the dead to bury their dead, and turn from the dust and rottenness of old-world themes, epic or romantic, classical or feudal, to face the age wherein we live and move and have our being, to send forth our souls and songs in search of the wonderful and doubtful future. Art knows nothing of time; for her there is but one tense, and all ages in her sight are alike present; there is nothing old in her sight, and nothing new. It is true, as the one side urges, that she fears not to face the actual aspect of the hour, to handle if it please her the immediate matters of the day; it is true, as the other side insists, that she is free to go back when she will to the very beginnings of tradition and fetch her subject from the furthest of ancient days; she cannot be vulgarised by the touch of the present or deadened by the contact of the past. In vain, for instance, do the first poetess of England and the first poet of America[9] agree to urge upon their fellows or their followers the duty of confronting and expressing the spirit and the secret of their own time, its

meaning and its need; such work is worthy of a poet, but no worthier than any other work that has in it the principle of life. And a poem of the past, if otherwise as good, has in it as much of this principle as a poem of the present. If a poem cast in the mould of classic or feudal times, of Greek drama or mediæval romance, be lifeless and worthless, it is not because the subject or the form was ancient, but because the poet was inadequate to his task, incompetent to do better than a flat and feeble imitation; had he been able to fill the old types of art with new blood and breath, the remoteness of subject and the antiquity of form would in no wise have impaired the worth and reality of his work; he would have brought close to us the far-off loveliness and renewed for us the ancient life of his models, not by mechanical and servile transcript as of a copying clerk, but by loving and reverent emulation as of an original fellow-craftsman. No form is obsolete, no subject out of date, if the right man be there to rehandle it. To the question "Can these bones live?"[10] there is but one answer; if the spirit and breath of art be breathed upon them indeed, and the voice prophesying upon them be indeed the voice of a prophet, then assuredly will the bones "come together, bone to his bone"; and the sinews and the flesh will come up upon them, and the skin cover them above, and the breath come into them, and they will live. For art is very life itself, and knows nothing of death; she is absolute truth, and takes no care of fact; she sees that Achilles and Ulysses are even now more actual by far than Wellington and Talleyrand;[11] not merely more noble and more interesting as types and figures, but more positive and real. . . .

1872; 1875

[9] Elizabeth Barrett Browning and Walt Whitman.
[10] The words of God to the prophet Ezekiel: "So I prophesied as he commanded me, and the breath came into them, and they lived, and stood up upon their feet, an exceeding great army" (Ezekiel 37:1–10).
[11] The British general, politician, and hero Wellington died in 1852; the French politician Talleyrand died in 1838. Both were among the most powerful men in Europe during the Napoleonic and post-Napoleonic decades early in the century.

Gerard Manley Hopkins

1844–1889

Hopkins kept a journal during his years at Oxford (1863–67) and during his first years of study in the Jesuit order, which he entered in 1868. His journal entries are typically verbal sketches of natural effects, and notes and meditations on the sound and etymology of curious words, and on the idea of inscape, central to his idea of poetry and to his conception of the order and meaning of the created world. The standard edition of the journals is Journals and Papers of Gerard Manley Hopkins, edited by Humphry House and G. Storey (1959), from which the texts printed here are taken.

from Journals

1864

The sky minted into golden sequins.
Stars like gold tufts.
   — golden bees.
   — golden rowels.
Sky peak'd with tiny flames.
Stars like tiny-spoked wheels of fire.
Lantern of night pierced in eyelets, (or eye lets, which avoids ambiguity.)
Altogether peak is a good word. For sunlight through shutter, locks of hair, rays in brass knobs etc. Meadows peaked with flowers.

   His gilded rowels
   Now stars of blood.

Saw a curious thing on, I think, Oct 1.—A cloud hid the sun and its edges were so brilliant that the lustre prevented one seeing outlines which swam in the light. Happening to look in a pond, I saw the cloud reflected and therefore with much diminution of light, of course, and the outlines of the lightest part of the cloud were distinct and touched here and there with spots of colours.

.   .   .

Tuncks is a good name.
Gerard Manley Tuncks. Poor Tuncks.

1865

Sunrise at Chagford.[1] There was a remarkable fan of clouds traced in fine horizontals, which afterwards lost their levels, some becoming oblique. Below appearing bright streaks which crowded up one after another. A white mist in the churchyard, trees ghostly in it.

Sunset here also. Over the nearest ridge of Dartmoor. Sky orange, trail of Bronze-lit clouds, stars and streaks of brilliant electrum underneath, but not for this, but effect of dark intensified foreground. Long rounded ridge of Dartmoor deep purple then trees on the descending hill, and a field with an angle so that the upper level was lighter green the lower darker, then a purplish great brown field, then the manufactory with grey white timbers (it is built of wood) and grey shingle (?) roofs. Grey sky at Hampstead[2] lately. Clouds showing beautiful and rare curves like curds, comparable to barrows, arranged of course in parallels.

Rain railing off something.

The butterfly perching in a cindery dusty road and pinching his scarlet valves. Or wagging, one might say. And also valved eyes.
   Mallowy red of sunset and sunrise clouds.

   Brush and comb (how vastly absurd it is!) both apply to . . . of water ribs.
Ash clusters like grapes.
Water rushing over a sunken stone and hol-

---

[1] Chagford: like the Dartmoor forest or tract also mentioned in this description, a locality in Devon in the south of England.
[2] Hampstead: near London; Hopkins' parents moved to Hampstead in 1852, and Hopkins went to school there.

lowing itself to rise again seems to be de-
voured by the wave before which it forces up,
      Reverted, with thrown back and tossing
cape.
Bossy water, bosses.
Oak roots are silvery, smooth, solid and
muscular.
      Glazed water vaulted o'er a drowsy
stone.

1866

Drops of rain hanging on rails etc seen with
only the lower rim lighted like nails (of fin-
gers). Screws of brooks and twines. Soft
chalky look with more shadowy middles of the
globes of cloud on a night with a moon faint or
concealed. Mealy clouds with a not brilliant
moon. Blunt buds of the ash. Pencil buds of the
beech. Lobes of the trees. Cups of the eyes,
Gathering back the lightly hinged eyelids.
Bows of the eyelids. Pencil of eyelashes. Juices
of the eyeball. Eyelids like leaves, petals, caps,
tufted hats, handkerchiefs, sleeves, gloves. Also
of the bones sleeved in flesh. Juices of the sun-
rise. Joints and veins of the same. Vermilion
look of the hand held against a candle with the
darker parts as the middles of the fingers and
especially the knuckles covered with ash.

1870

March 12—A fine sunset: the higher sky dead
clear blue bridged by a broad slant causeway
rising from right to left of wisped or grass
cloud, the wisps lying across; the sundown
yellow, moist with light but ending at the top
in a foam of delicate white pearling and
spotted with big tufts of cloud in colour russet
between brown and purple but edged with
brassy light. But what I note it all for is this:
before I had always taken the sunset and the
sun as quite out of gauge with each other, as
indeed physically they are for the eye after
looking at the sun is blunted to everything else
and if you look at the rest of the sunset you
must cover the sun, but today I inscaped them
together and made the sun the true eye and
ace of the whole, as it is. It was all active and
tossing out light and started as strongly for-
ward from the field as a long stone or a boss in

³ The brackets are Hopkins'.

the knop of the chalice-stem: it is indeed by
stalling it so that it falls into scape with the sky.

.   .   .

One day when the bluebells were in bloom
I wrote the following. I do not think I have
ever seen anything more beautiful than the
bluebell I have been looking at. I know the
beauty of our Lord by it. It[s inscape]³ is
[mixed of] strength and grace, like an ash
[tree]. The head is strongly drawn over [back-
wards] and arched down like a cutwater [draw-
ing itself back from the line of the keel]. The
lines of the bells strike and overlie this, rayed
but not symmetrically, some lie parallel. They
look steely against [the] paper, the shades lying
between the bells and behind the cockled petal-
ends and nursing up the precision of their dis-
tinctness, the petal-ends themselves being deli-
cately lit. Then there is the straightness of the
trumpets in the bells softened by the slight
entasis and [by] the square splay of the mouth.
One bell, the lowest, some way detached and
carried on a longer footstalk, touched out with
the tips of the petals an oval / not like the rest
in a plane perpendicular to the axis of the bell
but a little atilt, and so with [the] square-in-
rounding turns of the petals.

.   .   .

Sept. 24—First saw the Northern Lights. My
eye was caught by beams of light and dark very
like the crown of horny rays the sun makes be-
hind a cloud. At first I thought of silvery cloud
until I saw that these were more luminous and
did not dim the clearness of the stars in the
Bear. They rose slightly radiating thrown out
from the earth-line. Then I saw soft pulses of
light one after another rise and pass upwards
arched in shape but waveringly and with the
arch broken. They seemed to float, not follow-
ing the warp of the sphere as falling stars look
to do but free though concentrical with it. This
busy working of nature wholly independent of
the earth and seeming to go on in a strain of
time not reckoned by our reckoning of days and
years but simpler and as if correcting the pre-
occupation of the world by being preoccupied
with and appealing to and dated to the day of
judgment was like a new witness to God and
filled me with delightful fear

Oct. 20—Laus Deo—the river today and yesterday. Yesterday it was a sallow glassy gold at Hodder Roughs[4] and by watching hard the banks began to sail upstream, the scaping unfolded, the river was all in tumult but not running, only the lateral motions were perceived, and the curls of froth where the waves overlap shaped and turned easily and idly.—I meant to have written more.—Today the river was wild, very full, glossy brown with mud, furrowed in permanent billows through which from head to head the water swung with a great down and up again. These heads were scalped with rags of jumping foam. But at the Roughs the sigh was the burly water-backs which heave after heave kept tumbling up from the broken foam and their plump heap turning open in ropes of velvet

act falls into an order as well as purpose: looking out of my window I caught it in the random clods and broken heaps of snow made by the cast of a broom. The same of the path trenched by footsteps in ankledeep snow across the fields leading to Hodder wood through which we went to see the river. The sun was bright, the broken brambles and all boughs and banks limed and cloyed with white, the brook down the clough pulling its way by drops and by bubbles in turn under a shell of ice

In March there was much snow

April 8—The ashtree growing in the corner of the garden was felled. It was lopped first: I heard the sound and looking out and seeing it maimed there came at that moment a great pang and I wished to die and not to see the inscapes of the world destroyed any more

1872

Stepped into a barn of ours, a great shadowy barn, where the hay had been stacked on either side, and looking at the great rudely arched timberframes—principals (?) and tie-beams, which make them look like bold big A*s* with the cross-bar high up—I thought how sadly beauty of inscape was unknown and buried away from simple people and yet how near at hand it was if they had eyes to see it and it could be called out everywhere again

1873

Feb. 24—In the snow flat-topped hillocks and shoulders outlined with wavy edges, ridge below ridge, very like the grain of wood in line and in projection like relief maps. These the wind makes I think and of course drifts, which are in fact snow waves. The sharp nape of a drift is sometimes broken by slant flutes or channels. I think this must be when the wind after shaping the drift first has changed and cast waves in the body of the wave itself. All the world is full of inscape and chance left free to

from Letters

To Alexander Baillie[1]

Sept. 10. 1864

. . . Do you know, a horrible thing has happened to me. I have begun to *doubt* Tennyson. (Baillejus ap. Hopk.)[2] It is a great *argumentum*, a great clue, that our minds jump together even if it be a leap into the dark. I cannot tell you how amused and I must say pleased and comforted by this coincidence I am. A little explanation first. You know I do not mistrust my judgment so soon as you do; I say it to the praise of your modesty. Therefore I do not think myself "getting into my dotage" for that, and I will shew why. I think (I am assuming a great deal in saying this I fear) I may shew, judging from my own mind, how far we are both of us right in this, and on what, if I may use the word, more enlightened ground we may set our admiration of Tennyson. I have been thinking about this on and off since I read *Enoch Arden*[3] and the other new poems,

[4] Hodder: a river in the north of England near Stonyhurst, where Hopkins studied for the Jesuit priesthood.

[1] Alexander Baillie (1843–1921) was a friend of Hopkins' at Oxford. He later became a barrister, traveled, and studied Egyptian archaeology and philology. The text of this letter is that printed in *Further Letters of Gerard Manley Hopkins*, edited by C. C. Abbott (1956).

[2] Ap.: according to, in the works of.

[3] Tennyson's *Enoch Arden and Other Poems* was published in 1864.

so that my judgment is more digested than if the ideas had only struck me while answering you. I was shaken too you know by Addis,[4] which makes a good deal of difference.

I am meditating an essay, perhaps for the *Hexameron,*[5] on some points of poetical criticism, and it is with reference to this a little that I have composed my thoughts on Tennyson. I think then the language of verse may be divided into three kinds. The first and highest is poetry proper, the language of inspiration. The word inspiration need cause no difficulty. I mean by it a mood of great, abnormal in fact, mental acuteness, either energetic or receptive, according as the thoughts which arise in it seem generated by a stress and action of the brain, or to strike into it unasked. This mood arises from various causes, physical generally, as good health or state of the air or, prosaic as it is, length of time after a meal. But I need not go into this; all that it is needful to mark is, that the poetry of inspiration can only be written in this mood of mind, even if it only last a minute, by poets themselves. Everybody of course has like moods, but not being poets what they then produce is not poetry. The second kind I call *Parnassian.* It can only be spoken by poets, but is not in the highest sense poetry. It does not require the mood of mind in which the poetry of inspiration is written. It is spoken *on and from the level* of a poet's mind, not, as in the other case, when the inspiration which is the gift of genius raises him above himself. For I think it is the case with genius that it is not when quiescent so very much above mediocrity as the difference between the two might lead us to think, but that it has the power and privilege of rising from that level to a height utterly far from mediocrity: in other words that its greatness is *that it can be* so great. You will understand. *Parnassian* then is that language which genius speaks as fitted to its exaltation, and place among other genius, but does not sing (I have been betrayed into the whole hog of a metaphor) in its flights. Great men, poets I mean, have each their own dialect as it were of Parnassian, formed generally as they go on writing, and at last,—this is the point to be marked,—they can see things in this Parnassian way and describe them in this Parnassian tongue, without fur-

ther effort of inspiration. In a poet's particular kind of Parnassian lies most of his style, of his manner, of his mannerism if you like. But I must not go farther without giving you instances of Parnassian. I shall take one from Tennyson, and from *Enoch Arden,* from a passage much quoted already and which will be no doubt often quoted, the description of Enoch's tropical island.

The mountain wooded to the peak, the lawns
And winding glades high up like ways to Heaven,
The slender coco's drooping crown of plumes,
The lightning flash of insect and of bird,
The lustre of the long convolvuluses
That coil'd around the stately stems, and ran
Ev'n to the limit of the land, the glows
And glories of the broad belt of the world,
All these he saw.

[lines 568–76]

Now it is a mark of Parnassian that one could conceive oneself writing it if one were the poet. Do not say that *if* you were Shakespear you can imagine yourself writing Hamlet, because that is just what I think you can*not* conceive. In a fine piece of inspiration every beauty takes you as it were by surprise, not of course that you did not think the writer could be so great, for that is not it,—indeed I think it is a mistake to speak of people admiring Shakespear more and more as they live, for when the judgment is ripe and you have read a good deal of any writer including his best things, and carefully, then, I think, however high the place you give him, that you must have rated him equally with his merits however great they be; so that all after admiration cannot increase but keep alive this estimate, make his greatness stare into your eyes and din it into your ears, as it were, but not make it greater,—but to go on with the broken sentence, every fresh beauty could not in any way be predicted or accounted for by what one has already read. But in Parnassian pieces you feel that if you were the poet you could have gone on as he has done, you see yourself doing it, only with the difference that if you actually try you find you cannot write his Parnassian. . . .

.   .   .

I think one had got into the way of thinking, or had not got out of the way of thinking, that

---

[4] William Addis (1844–1917), another of Hopkins' friends at Oxford, also became a Roman Catholic priest, but later returned to the Church of England.
[5] Probably an undergraduate club whose members read essays to one another.

Tennyson was always new, *touching*, beyond other poets, not pressed with human ailments, never using Parnassian. So at least I used to think. Now one sees he uses Parnassian; he is, one must see it, what we used to call Tennysonian. But the discovery of this must not make too much difference. When puzzled by one's doubts it is well to turn to a passage like this. Surely your maturest judgment will never be fooled out of saying that this is divine, terribly beautiful—the stanza of *In Memoriam* beginning with the quatrain

O Hesper o'er the buried sun,
  And ready thou to die with him,
  Thou watchest all things ever dim
And dimmer, and a glory done.[6]

I quote from memory. Inconsequent conclusion: Shakespear is and must be utterly the greatest of poets.

Just to end what I was saying about poetry. There is a higher sort of Parnassian which I call *Castalian,* or it may be thought the lowest kind of inspiration. Beautiful poems may be written wholly in it. Its peculiarity is that though you can hardly conceive yourself having written in it, if in the poet's place, yet it is too characteristic of the poet, too so-and-so-all-over-ish, to be quite inspiration. E.g.

                    Yet despair
Touches me not, though pensive as a bird
Whose vernal coverts winter hath laid bare.[7]

This is from Wordsworth, beautiful, but rather too essentially Wordsworthian, too persistently his way of looking at things. The third kind is merely the language of verse as distinct from that of prose, Delphic, the tongue of the Sacred *Plain,* I may call it, used in common by poet and poetaster. Poetry when spoken is spoken in it, but to speak it is not necessarily to speak poetry. I may add there is also *Olympian.* This is the language of strange masculine genius which suddenly, as it were, forces its

way into the domain of poetry, without naturally having a right there. Milman's[8] poetry is of this kind I think, and Rossetti's *Blessed Damozel.* But unusual poetry has a tendency to seem so at first. . . .

And now at last goodbye. Believe me, my dear friend, yours affectionately,
                    Gerard Manley Hopkins

To Richard Watson Dixon[1]

. . . Jan. 14 [1880] 8 Salisbury Street, Liverpool—The new prosody, Sprung Rhythm, is really quite a simple matter and as strict as the other rhythm. Bridges[2] treats it in theory and practice as something informal and variable without any limit but ear and taste, but this is not how I look at it. We must however distinguish its εἶναι and its εὖ εἶναι the writing it somehow and the writing it as it should be written; for written anyhow it is a shambling business and a corruption, not an improvement. In strictness then and simple εἶναι it is a matter of accent only, like common rhythm, and not of quantity at all. Its principle is that all rhythm and all verse consists of feet and each foot must contain one stress or verse-accent: so far is common to it and Common Rhythm; to this it adds that the stress alone is essential to a foot and that therefore even one stressed syllable may make a foot and consequently two or more stresses may come running, which in common rhythm can, regularly speaking, never happen. But there may and mostly there does belong to a foot an unaccented portion of "slack": now in common rhythm, in which less is made of stress, in which less stress is laid, the slack must be always one or else two syllables, never less than one and never more than two, and in most measures fixedly one or fixedly two, but in sprung rhythm, the stress being more *of* a stress, being more important, allows of greater

---

[6] Stanza 121. It begins "Sad Hesper"; and "thou" in the second line is set off by commas.

[7] The last lines of a sonnet "Composed near Calais, on the Road Leading to Ardres, August 7, 1802."

[8] Henry Hart Milman (1791–1868), a poet and clergyman whose strongly dramatic religious poems were popular from the early decades of the century.

[1] For a brief sketch of Dixon's life, see Part Six. Dixon came to correspond with Hopkins when the latter wrote to him in 1878 praising his poems. Hopkins had once been Dixon's pupil in a school at which Dixon had taught in 1861. This letter to Dixon was begun December 22, 1879. Its text and that of the following letter are those printed in *The Correspondence of Gerard Manley Hopkins and Richard Watson Dixon,* edited by C. C. Abbott (1955).

[2] Robert Bridges (see pp. 763–765), to whom Hopkins sent and corresponded about his poetry.

variation in the slack and this latter may range from three syllables to none at all—*regularly,* so that paeons (three short syllables and one long or three slack and one stressy) are regular in sprung rhythm, but in common rhythm can occur only by licence; moreover may in the same measure have this range. Regularly then the feet in sprung rhythm consist of one, two, three, or four syllables and no more, and if for simplicity's sake we call feet by Greek names, taking accent for quantity, and also scan always as for rising rhythm (I call *rising rhythm* that in which the slack comes first, as in iambs and anapaests, *falling* that in which the stress comes first, as in trochees and dactyls), scanning thus, the feet in sprung rhythm will be monosyllables, iambs, anapaests, and fourth paeons, and no others. But for particular rhythmic effects it is allowed, and more freely than in common rhythm, to use any number of slack syllables, limited only by ear. And though it is the virtue of sprung rhythm that it allows of "dochmiac" or "antipastic" effects or cadences,[3] when the verse suddenly changes from a rising to a falling movement, and this too is strongly felt by the ear, yet no account of it is taken in scanning and no irregularity caused, but the scansion always treated, conventionally and for simplicity, as rising. Thus the line "She had cóme from a crúise, tráining séamen" has a plain reversed rhythm, but the scanning is simply "She had cóme | from a crúise | tráin | ing séa | men"—that is rising throughout, having one monosyllabic foot and an overlapping syllable which is counted to the first foot of the next line. Bridges in the preface to his last issue[4] says something to the effect that all sorts of feet may follow one another, an anapaest a dactyl for instance (which would make four slack syllables running): so they may, if we look at the real nature of the verse; but for simplicity it is much better to recognize, in scanning this new rhythm, only one movement, either the rising (which I choose as being commonest in English verse) or the falling (which

is perhaps better in itself), and always keep to that.

In lyric verse I like sprung rhythm also to be *over-rove,* that is, the scanning to run on from line to line to the end of the stanza. But for dramatic verse, which is looser in form, I should have the lines "free-ended" and each scanned by itself.

Sprung rhythm does not properly require or allow of counterpoint. It does not require it, because its great variety amounts to a counterpointing, and it scarcely allows of it, because you have scarcely got in it that conventionally fixed form which you can mentally supply at the time when you are actually reading another one—I mean as when in reading "Bý the wá-ters of life where'er they sat" you mentally supply "By thé watérs," which is the normal rhythm. Nevertheless in dramatic verse I should sparingly allow it at the beginning of a line and after a strong caesura, and I see that Bridges does this freely in *London Snow* for instance.[5] However by means of the "outrides" or looped half-feet you will find in some of my sonnets and elsewhere I secure a strong effect of double rhythm, of a second movement in the verse besides the primary and essential one, and this comes to the same thing or serves the same purpose as counterpointing by reversed accents as in Milton.

But for the εὖ εἶναι of the new rhythm great attention to quantity[6] is necessary. And since English quantity is very different from Greek or Latin a sort of prosody ought to be drawn up for it, which would be indeed of wider service than for sprung rhythm only. We must distinguish strength (or gravity) and length. About length there is little difficulty: plainly *bidst* is longer than *bids* and *bids* than *bid.* But it is not recognized by everybody that *bid,* with a flat dental, is graver or stronger than *bit,* with a sharp. The strongest and, other things being alike, the longest syllables are those with the circumflex, like *fire.* Any syllable ending in *ng,* though *ng* is only a single sound, may be made as long as you like by prolonging

---

[3] Dochmiac: a measure in classical Greek poetry made of three long and two short syllables, commonly ⌒ – – ⌒ –. Antipastic: a measure of four syllables, commonly ⌒ – – ⌒.

[4] Of his poems.   [5] Pp. 767–768.

[6] Verse measured by its quantity is that in which the prosodic rhythm is determined by the time required to pronounce a syllable, as opposed to the measures of English verse, which are determined by a pattern of stressed and unstressed syllables without taking into account the time required to pronounce them. Hopkins' argument here is that because English sounds are different from those of classical Greek and Latin, a quantitative English prosody cannot be made out of classical meters but must have new measures devised for the sound of English.

the nasal. So too *n* may be prolonged after a long vowel or before a consonant, as in *soon* or *and*. In this way a great number of observations might be made: I have put these down at random as samples. You will find that Milton pays much attention to consonant-quality or gravity of sound in his line endings. Indeed every good ear does it naturally more or less in composing. The French too say that their feminine ending is graver than the masculine and that pathetic or majestic lines are made in preference to end with it. One may even by a consideration of what the music of the verse requires restore sometimes the pronunciation of Shakspere's time where it has changed and shew for instance that *cherry* must have been *cher-ry* (like *her, stir, spur*) or that *heavy* was *heave-y* in the lines "Now the heavy ploughman snores All with weary task foredone."[7] You speak of the word *over*. The *o* is long no doubt, but long *o* is the shortest of the long vowels and may easily be used in a weak place; I do not however find that Tennyson uses it so in the Ode to Memory: in the line "Over the dewy dark [or 'dark dewy'] earth forlorn"[8] it seems to be in a strong place. . . .

I do not despair of our coming to meet, for business might perhaps bring you here. Meanwhile believe me your affectionate friend

Gerard Manley Hopkins, S.J.

To Richard Watson Dixon

Manresa House, Roehampton, S. W.
Dec. 1 1881

(the very day 300 years ago of Father Campion's martyrdom).[1]

MY DEAR FRIEND,—I am heartily glad you did not make away with, as you say you thought of doing, so warm and precious a letter as your last. It reached me on the first break or day of repose in our month's retreat;[2] I began answering it on the second, but could not finish; and this is the third and last of them.

When a man has given himself to God's service, when he has denied himself and followed Christ, he has fitted himself to receive and does receive from God a special guidance, a more particular providence. This guidance is conveyed partly by the action of other men, as his appointed superiors, and partly by direct lights and inspirations. If I wait for such guidance, through whatever channel conveyed, about anything, about my poetry for instance, I do more wisely in every way than if I try to serve my own seeming interests in the matter. Now if you value what I write, if I do myself, much more does our Lord. And if he chooses to avail himself of what I leave at his disposal he can do so with a felicity and with a success which I could never command. And if he does not, then two things follow; one that the reward I shall nevertheless receive from him will be all the greater; the other that then I shall know how much a thing contrary to his will and even to my own best interests I should have done if I had taken things into my own hands and forced on publication. This is my principle and this in the main has been my practice: leading the sort of life I do here it seems easy, but when one mixes with the world and meets on every side its secret solicitations, to live by faith is harder, is very hard; nevertheless by God's help I shall always do so.

Our Society values, as you say, and has contributed to literature, to culture; but only as a means to an end. Its history and its experience shew that literature proper, as poetry, has seldom been found to be to that end a very serviceable means. We have had for three centuries often the flower of the youth of a country in numbers enter our body: among these how many poets, how many artists of all sorts, there must have been! But there have been very few Jesuit poets and, where they have been, I believe it would be found on examination that there was something exceptional in their circumstances or, so to say, counterbalancing in their career. For genius attracts fame and individual fame St. Ignatius[3] looked on as the most dangerous and dazzling of all attractions. . . . In England we had Fr. South-

---

[7] "Whilst the heavy ploughman snore,/ All with early task foredone" (*Midsummer Night's Dream*, V, 1).

[8] "Over the dark dewy earth forlorn": Tennyson's "Ode to Memory" was included in his 1830 volume of poems.

[1] Edmund Campion (1540–81) was an English Jesuit who was tortured and hanged for his attempts to preserve the Roman church in England.

[2] Retreat: a period of prayer and meditation.

[3] St. Ignatius: Ignatius Loyola (1491–1556) was the founder of the Society of Jesus.

well[4] a poet, a minor poet but still a poet; but he wrote amidst a terrible persecution and died a martyr, with circumstances of horrible barbarity: this is the counterpoise in his career. Then what a genius was Campion himself! was not he a poet? perhaps a great one, if he had chosen. His History of Ireland, written in hiding and hurrying from place to place, Mr. Simpson in his Life says,[5] and the samples prove it, shews an eloquence like Shakspere's; and in fact Shakspere made use of the book. He had all and more than all the rhetoric of that golden age and was probably the most vigorous mind and eloquent tongue engaged in theological strife then in England, perhaps in Europe. It seems in time he might have done anything. But his eloquence died on the air, his genius was quenched in his blood after one year's employment in his country. Music is more professional than poetry perhaps and Jesuits have composed and well, but none has any fame to speak of. We had one painter who reached excellence, I forget his name, he was a lay-brother; but then he only painted flower pieces. You see then what is against me, but since, as Solomon says, there is a time for everything,[6] there is nothing that does not some day come to be, it may be that the time will come for my verses. . . .

Earnestly thanking you for your kindness and wishing you all that is best I remain your affectionate friend

Gerard M. Hopkins, S.J.

from Author's Preface[1]

The poems in this book are written some in Running Rhythm, the common rhythm in English use, some in Sprung Rhythm, and some in a mixture of the two. And those in the common rhythm are some counterpointed, some not.

Common English rhythm, called Running Rhythm above, is measured by feet of either two or three syllables and (putting aside the imperfect feet at the beginning and end of lines and also some unusual measures, in which feet seem to be paired together and double or composite feet to arise) never more or less.

Every foot has one principal stress or accent, and this or the syllable it falls on may be called the Stress of the foot and the other part, the one or two unaccented syllables, the Slack. Feet (and the rhythms made out of them) in which the stress comes first are called Falling Feet and Falling Rhythms, feet and rhythm in which the slack comes first are called Rising Feet and Rhythms, and if the stress is between two slacks there will be Rocking Feet and Rhythms. These distinctions are real and true to nature; but for purposes of scanning it is a great convenience to follow the example of music and take the stress always first, as the accent or the chief accent always comes first in a musical bar. If this is done there will be in common English verse only two possible feet— the so-called accentual Trochee [ˊ˘] and Dactyl, [ˊ˘˘] and correspondingly only two possible uniform rhythms, the so-called Trochaic and Dactylic. But they may be mixed and then what the Greeks called a Logaoedic Rhythm[2] arises. These are the facts and according to these the scanning of ordinary regularly-written English verse is very simple indeed and to bring in other principles is here unnecessary.

But because verse written strictly in these feet and by these principles will become same and tame the poets have brought in licences and departures from rule to give variety, and especially when the natural rhythm is rising, as in the common ten-syllable or five-foot verse, rhymed or blank. These irregularities are chiefly Reversed Feet and Reversed or Counterpoint Rhythm, which two things are two steps or degrees of licence in the same kind. By a reversed foot I mean the putting the stress where, to judge by the rest of the measure, the

---

[4] Robert Southwell (1561?–95) was imprisoned and tortured for three years before his execution. Many of his poems were written in prison.

[5] Richard Simpson (1820–76) was a writer and editor of the Roman Catholic magazine *The Rambler;* his life of Campion was published in 1867.

[6] "To every thing there is a season, and a time to every purpose under heaven" (Ecclesiastes 3:1).

[1] Hopkins wrote this preface about 1883 for the manuscript book of his poems in the possession of Robert Bridges. The preface has been published in Bridges' (1918) and subsequent editions of Hopkins' poems.

[2] Logaoedic Rhythm: a mixed rhythm of anapest and iamb (rising), or dactyl and trochee (falling).

slack should be and the slack where the stress, and this is done freely at the beginning of a line and, in the course of a line, after a pause; only scarcely ever in the second foot or place and never in the last, unless when the poet designs some extraordinary effect; for these places are characteristic and sensitive and cannot well be touched. But the reversal of the first foot and of some middle foot after a strong pause is a thing so natural that our poets have generally done it, from Chaucer down, without remark and it commonly passes unnoticed and cannot be said to amount to a formal change of rhythm, but rather is that irregularity which all natural growth and motion shews. If however the reversal is repeated in two feet running, especially so as to include the sensitive second foot, it must be due either to great want of ear or else is a calculated effect, the super-inducing or *mounting* of a new rhythm upon the old; and since the new or mounted rhythm is actually heard and at the same time the mind naturally supplies the natural standard foregoing rhythm, for we do not forget what the rhythm is that by rights we should be hearing, two rhythms are in some manner running at once and we have something answerable to counterpoint in music, which is two or more strains of tune going on together, and this is Counterpoint Rhythm. Of this kind of verse Milton is the great master and the choruses of *Samson Agonistes* are written throughout in it —but with the disadvantage that he does not let the reader clearly know what the ground-rhythm is meant to be and so they have struck most readers as merely irregular. And in fact if you counterpoint throughout, since only one of the counter rhythms is actually heard, the other is really destroyed or cannot come to exist, and what is written is one rhythm only and probably Sprung Rhythm, of which I now speak.

Sprung Rhythm, as used in this book, is measured by feet of from one to four syllables, regularly, and for particular effects any number of weak or slack syllables may be used. It has one stress, which falls on the only syllable, if there is only one, or, if there are more, then scanning as above, on the first, and so gives

rise to four sorts of feet, a monosyllable and the so-called accentual Trochee, Dactyl, and the First Paeon.[3] And there will be four corresponding natural rhythms; but nominally the feet are mixed and any one may follow any other. And hence Sprung Rhythm differs from Running Rhythm in having or being only one nominal rhythm, a mixed or "logaoedic" one, instead of three, but on the other hand in having twice the flexibility of foot, so that any two stresses may either follow one another running or be divided by one, two, or three slack syllables. But strict Sprung Rhythm cannot be counterpointed. In Sprung Rhythm, as in logaoedic rhythm generally, the feet are assumed to be equally long or strong and their seeming inequality is made up by pause or stressing.

Remark also that it is natural in Sprung Rhythm for the lines to be *rove over*, that is for the scanning of each line immediately to take up that of the one before, so that if the first has one or more syllables at its end the other must have so many less at its beginning; and in fact the scanning runs on without a break from the beginning, say, of a stanza to the end and all the stanza is one long strain, though written in lines asunder.

Two licences are natural to Sprung Rhythm. The one is rests, as in music; but of this an example is scarcely to be found in this book, unless in the *Echos,* second line.[4] The other is *hangers* or *outrides,* that is one, two, or three slack syllables added to a foot and not counting in the nominal scanning. They are so called because they seem to hang below the line or ride forward or backward from it in another dimension than the line itself, according to a principle needless to explain here. . . .

Note on the nature and history of Sprung Rhythm—Sprung Rhythm is the most natural of things. For (1) it is the rhythm of common speech and of written prose, when rhythm is perceived in them. (2) It is the rhythm of all but the most monotonously regular music, so that in the words of choruses and refrains and in songs written closely to music it arises. (3) It is found in nursery rhymes, weather saws, and so on; because, however these may have

---

[3] Paeon: a foot of one long and three short syllables; the first Paeon is marked $-\smile\smile\smile$. *The Encyclopedia of Poetry and Poetics,* edited by Alex Preminger (1965), cites as an example of a Paeonic foot a line from "The Wreck of the Deutschland": "The appéaling/of the Pássion/is ténderer/in práyer apárt."

[4] "Back beauty, keep it, beauty, beauty, beauty, . . . from vanishing away": "The Leaden Echo and the Golden Echo." The ellipsis is a part of the line.

been once made in running rhythm, the terminations having dropped off by the change of language, the stresses come together and so the rhythm is sprung. (4) It arises in common verse when reversed or counterpointed, for the same reason.

But nevertheless in spite of all this and though Greek and Latin lyric verse, which is well known, and the old English verse seen in "Pierce Ploughman"[5] are in sprung rhythm, it has in fact ceased to be used since the Elizabethan age, Greene[6] being the last writer who can be said to have recognised it. For perhaps there was not, down to our days, a single, even short, poem in English in which sprung rhythm is employed—not for single effects or in fixed places—but as the governing principle of the scansion. I say this because the contrary has been asserted: if it is otherwise the poem should be cited.

Some of the sonnets in this book are in five-foot, some in six-foot or Alexandrine lines. ["Pied Beauty" and "Peace"] are Curtal-Sonnets, that is they are constructed in proportions resembling those of the sonnet proper, namely, 6 + 4 instead of 8 + 6, with however a half-line tailpiece (so that the equation is rather

$$\frac{12}{2} + \frac{9}{2} = \frac{21}{2} = 10\frac{1}{2}.$$

c. 1883

William Morris
1834–1896

---

from The Lesser Arts[1]

[*Early in the lecture Morris describes the purpose of decorative art: "To give people pleasure in the things they must perforce use, that is one great office of decoration; to give people pleasure in the things they must perforce make, that is the other use of it." He then considers how the decorative arts of the past express its life.*]

And now let me recapitulate a little before I go further, before we begin to look into the condition of the arts at the present day. These arts, I have said, are part of a great system invented for the expression of a man's delight in beauty: all peoples and times have used them; they have been the joy of free nations, and the solace of oppressed nations; religion has used and elevated them, has abused and degraded them; they are connected with all history, and are clear teachers of it; and, best of all, they are the sweeteners of human labour, both to the handicraftsman, whose life is spent in working in them, and to people in general who are influenced by the sight of them at every turn of the day's work: they make our toil happy, our rest fruitful.

And now if all I have said seems to you but mere open-mouthed praise of these arts, I must say that it is not for nothing that what I have hitherto put before you has taken that form.

It is because I must now ask you this question: All these good things—will you have them? will you cast them from you?

Are you surprised at my question—you, most

---

[5] *The Vision Concerning Piers Plowman*, a fourteenth-century poem in Middle English traditionally attributed to William Langland, is written in a meter in which the number of unstressed syllables in a foot may vary.

[6] Robert Greene (1560?–92), an Elizabethan playwright.

[1] This lecture was delivered 1877 and published as a pamphlet (under the title "The Decorative Arts") in 1878. It was republished in a volume of lectures in 1882. The text printed here, like that of the following selection from Morris's prose writing, is that of *The Collected Works of William Morris*, edited by May Morris (1910–15).

of whom, like myself, are engaged in the actual practice of the arts that are, or ought to be, popular?

In explanation, I must somewhat repeat what I have already said. Time was when the mystery and wonder of handicrafts were well acknowledged by the world, when imagination and fancy mingled with all things made by man; and in those days all handicraftsmen were *artists,* as we should now call them. But the thought of man became more intricate, more difficult to express; art grew a heavier thing to deal with, and its labour was more divided among great men, lesser men, and little men; till that art, which was once scarce more than a rest of body and soul, as the hand cast the shuttle or swung the hammer, became to some men so serious a labour, that their working lives have been one long tragedy of hope and fear, joy and trouble. This was the growth of art: like all growth, it was good and fruitful for a while; like all fruitful growth, it grew into decay; like all decay of what was once fruitful, it will grow into something new.

Into decay; for as the art sundered into the greater and the lesser, contempt on one side, carelessness on the other arose, both begotten of ignorance of that *philosophy* of the Decorative Arts, a hint of which I have tried just now to put before you. The artist came out from the handicraftsmen, and left them without hope of elevation, while he himself was left without the help of intelligent, industrious sympathy. Both have suffered; the artist no less than the workman. It is with art as it fares with a company of soldiers before a redoubt, when the captain runs forward full of hope and energy, but looks not behind him to see if his men are following, and they hang back, not knowing why they are brought there to die. The captain's life is spent for nothing, and his men are sullen prisoners in the redoubt of Unhappiness and Brutality.

I must in plain words say of the Decorative Arts, of all the arts, that it is not so much that we are inferior in them to all who have gone before us, but rather that they are in a state of anarchy and disorganization, which makes a sweeping change necessary and certain.

So that again I ask my question, All that good fruit which the arts should bear, will you have it? will you cast it from you? Shall that sweeping change that must come, be the change of loss or of gain?

We who believe in the continuous life of the

world, surely we are bound to hope that the change will bring us gain and not loss, and to strive to bring that gain about.

Yet how the world may answer my question, who can say? A man in his short life can see but a little way ahead, and even in mine, wonderful and unexpected things have come to pass. I must needs say that therein lies my hope rather than in all I see going on round about us. Without disputing that if the imaginative arts perish, some new thing, at present unguessed of, *may* be put forward to supply their loss in men's lives, I cannot feel happy in that prospect, nor can I believe that mankind will endure such a loss for ever: but in the meantime the present state of the arts and their dealings with modern life and progress seem to me to point, in appearance at least, to this immediate future; that the world, which has for a long time busied itself about other matters than the arts, and has carelessly let them sink lower and lower, till many not uncultivated men, ignorant of what they once were, and hopeless of what they might yet be, look upon them with mere contempt; that the world, I say, thus busied and hurried, will one day wipe the slate, and be clean rid in her impatience of the whole matter with all this tangle and trouble.

And then—what then?

Even now amid the squalor of London it is hard to imagine what it will be. Architecture, Sculpture, Painting, with the crowd of lesser arts that belong to them, these, together with Music and Poetry, will be dead and forgotten, will no longer excite or amuse people in the least: for, once more, we must not deceive ourselves; the death of one art means the death of all; the only difference in their fate will be that the luckiest will be eaten the last—the luckiest, or the unluckiest: in all that has to do with beauty the invention and ingenuity of man will have come to a dead stop; and all the while Nature will go on with her eternal recurrence of lovely changes—spring, summer, autumn, and winter; sunshine, rain, and snow; storm and fair weather; dawn, noon, and sunset; day and night—ever bearing witness against man that he has deliberately chosen ugliness instead of beauty, and to live where he is strongest amidst squalor or blank emptiness.

You see, sirs, we cannot quite imagine it; any more, perhaps, than our forefathers of ancient London, living in the pretty, carefully whitened houses, with the famous church and its huge spire rising above them—than they, passing about the fair gardens running down to the broad river, could have imagined a whole county or more covered over with hideous hovels, big, middle-sized, and little, which should one day be called London.

Sirs, I say that this dead blank of the arts that I more than dread is difficult even now to imagine; yet I fear that, I must say that if it does not come about, it will be owing to some turn of events which we cannot at present foresee: but I hold that if it does happen, it will only last for a time, that it will be but a burning up of the gathered weeds, so that the field may bear more abundantly. I hold that men would wake up after a while, and look round and find the dullness unbearable, and begin once more inventing, imitating, and imagining, as in earlier days.

That faith comforts me, and I can say calmly, if the blank space must happen, it must, and amidst its darkness the new seed must sprout. So it has been before: first comes birth, and hope scarcely conscious of itself; then the flower and fruit of mastery, with hope more than conscious enough, passing into insolence, as decay follows ripeness; and then—the new birth again.

Meantime it is the plain duty of all who look seriously on the arts to do their best to save the world from what at the best will be a loss, the result of ignorance and unwisdom; to prevent, in fact, that most discouraging of all changes, the supplying the place of an extinct brutality by a new one; nay, even if those who really care for the arts are so weak and few that they can do nothing else, it may be their business to keep alive some tradition, some memory of the past, so that the new life when it comes may not waste itself more than enough in fashioning wholly new forms for its new spirit.

To what side then shall those turn for help, who really understand the gain of a great art in the world, and the loss of peace and good life that must follow from the lack of it? I think that they must begin by acknowledging that the ancient art, the art of unconscious intelligence, as one should call it, which began without a date, at least so long ago as those strange and masterly scratchings on mammoth-bones and the like found but the other day in the drift[2]—that this art of unconscious intelligence

is all but dead; that what little of it is left lingers among half-civilized nations, and is growing coarser, feebler, less intelligent year by year; nay, it is mostly at the mercy of some commercial accident, such as the arrival of a few shiploads of European dye-stuffs or a few dozen orders from European merchants: this they must recognize, and must hope to see in time its place filled by a new art of conscious intelligence, the birth of wiser, simpler, freer ways of life than the world leads now, than the world has ever led.

I said, *to see* this in time; I do not mean to say that our own eyes will look upon it: it may be so far off, as indeed it seems to some, that many would scarcely think it worth while thinking of: but there are some of us who cannot turn our faces to the wall, or sit heedless because our hope seems somewhat dim; and, indeed, I think that while the signs of the last decay of the old art with all the evils that must follow in its train are only too obvious about us, so on the other hand there are not wanting signs of the new dawn beyond that possible night of the arts, of which I have before spoken; this sign chiefly, that there are some few at least, who are heartily discontented with things as they are, and crave for something better, or at least some promise of it—this best of signs: for I suppose that if some half-dozen men at any time earnestly set their hearts on something coming about which is not discordant with nature, it will come to pass one day or other; because it is not by accident that an idea comes into the heads of a few; rather they are pushed on, and forced to speak or act by something stirring in the heart of the world which would otherwise be left without expression.

.   .   .

Unless something or other is done to give all men some pleasure for the eyes and rest for the mind in the aspect of their own and their neighbours' houses, until the contrast is less disgraceful between the fields where beasts live and the streets where men live, I suppose that the practice of the arts must be mainly kept in the hands of a few highly cultivated men, who can go often to beautiful places, whose education enables them, in the contemplation of the past glories of the world, to shut out from their view the everyday squalors that the most of men move in. Sirs, I believe that art has

[2] Drift: rock deposits.

such sympathy with cheerful freedom, open-heartedness and reality, so much she sickens under selfishness and luxury, that she will not live thus isolated and exclusive. I will go further than this and say that on such terms I do not wish her to live. I protest that it would be a shame to an honest artist to enjoy what he had huddled up to himself of such art, as it would be for a rich man to sit and eat dainty food among starving soldiers in a beleaguered fort.

I do not want art for a few, any more than education for a few, or freedom for a few.

No, rather than art should live this poor thin life among a few exceptional men, despising those beneath them for an ignorance for which they themselves are responsible, for a brutality that they will not struggle with—rather than this, I would that the world should indeed sweep away all art for awhile, as I said before I thought it possible she might do; rather than the wheat should rot in the miser's granary, I would that the earth had it, that it might yet have a chance to quicken in the dark.

I have a sort of faith, though, that this clearing away of all art will not happen, that men will get wiser, as well as more learned; that many of the intricacies of life, on which we now pride ourselves more than enough, partly because they are new, partly because they have come with the gain of better things, will be cast aside as having played their part, and being useful no longer. I hope that we shall have leisure from war—war commercial, as well as war of the bullet and the bayonet; leisure from the knowledge that darkens counsel; leisure above all from the greed of money, and the craving for that overwhelming distinction that money now brings; I believe that as we have even now partly achieved LIBERTY, so we shall one day achieve EQUALITY, which, and which only, means FRATERNITY, and so have leisure from poverty and all its griping, sordid cares.[3]

Then having leisure from all these things, amidst renewed simplicity of life we shall have leisure to think about our work, that faithful daily companion, which no man any longer will venture to call the Curse of labour: for surely then we shall be happy in it, each in his place, no man grudging at another; no one

bidden to be any man's *servant*, everyone scorning to be any man's *master:* men will then assuredly be happy in their work, and that happiness will assuredly bring forth decorative, noble, *popular* art.

That art will make our streets as beautiful as the woods, as elevating as the mountain-sides: it will be a pleasure and a rest, and not a weight upon the spirits to come from the open country into a town; every man's house will be fair and decent, soothing to his mind and helpful to his work: all the works of man that we live among and handle will be in harmony with nature, will be reasonable and beautiful: yet all will be simple and inspiriting, not childish nor enervating; for as nothing of beauty and splendour that man's mind and hand may compass shall be wanting from our public buildings, so in no private dwelling will there be any signs of waste, pomp, or insolence, and every man will have his share of the *best*.

It is a dream, you may say, of what has never been and never will be; true, it has never been, and therefore, since the world is alive, and moving yet, my hope is the greater that it one day will be: true, it is a dream; but dreams have before now come about of things so good and necessary to us, that we scarcely think of them more than of the daylight, though once people had to live without them, without even the hope of them.

Anyhow, dream as it is, I pray you to pardon my setting it before you, for it lies at the bottom of all my work in the Decorative Arts, nor will it ever be out of my thoughts: and I am here with you to-night to ask you to help me in realizing this dream, this *hope*.

1878; 1882

from How I Became a Socialist[1]

. . . Apart from the desire to produce beautiful things, the leading passion of my life has been and is hatred of modern civilisation. What shall I say of it now, when the

---

[3] Liberty, Equality, Fraternity: one of the mottoes of the French Revolution.
[1] Published in 1894 in *Justice,* the newspaper of the Social Democratic Federation which Morris helped to found in 1884.

words are put into my mouth, my hope of its destruction—what shall I say of its supplanting by Socialism?

What shall I say concerning its mastery of and its waste of mechanical power, its commonwealth so poor, its enemies of the commonwealth so rich, its stupendous organisation—for the misery of life! Its contempt of simple pleasures which everyone could enjoy but for its folly? Its eyeless vulgarity which has destroyed art, the one certain solace of labour? All this I felt then as now, but I did not know why it was so. The hope of the past times was gone, the struggles of mankind for many ages had produced nothing but this sordid, aimless, ugly confusion; the immediate future seemed to me likely to intensify all the present evils by sweeping away the last survivals of the days before the dull squalor of civilisation had settled down on the world. This was a bad lookout indeed, and, if I may mention myself as a personality and not as a mere type, especially so to a man of my disposition, careless of metaphysics and religion, as well as of scientific analysis, but with a deep love of the earth and the life on it, and a passion for the history of the past of mankind. Think of it! Was it all to end in a counting-house on the top of a cinder-heap, with Podsnap's[2] drawing-room in the offing, and a Whig[3] committee dealing out champagne to the rich and margarine to the poor in such convenient proportions as would make all men contented together, though the pleasure of the eyes was gone from the world, and the place of Homer was to be taken by Huxley?[4] Yet, believe me, in my heart, when I really forced myself to look towards the future, that is what I saw in it, and, as far as I could tell, scarce anyone seemed to think it worth while to struggle against such a consummation of civilisation. So there I was in for a fine pessimistic end of life, if it had not somehow dawned on me that amidst all this filth of civilisation the seeds of a great change, what we others call Social-Revolution, were beginning to germinate. The whole face of things was changed to me by that discovery, and all I

had to do then in order to become a Socialist was to hook myself on to the practical movement, which, as before said, I have tried to do as well as I could.

To sum up, then the study of history and the love and practice of art forced me into a hatred of the civilisation which, if things were to stop as they are, would turn history into inconsequent nonsense, and make art a collection of the curiosities of the past, which would have no serious relation to the life of the present.

But the consciousness of revolution stirring amidst our hateful modern society prevented me, luckier than many others of artistic perceptions, from crystallising into a mere railer against "progress" on the one hand, and on the other from wasting time and energy in any of the numerous schemes by which the quasi-artistic of the middle classes hope to make art grow when it has no longer any root, and thus I became a practical Socialist.

A last word or two. Perhaps some of our friends will say, what have we to do with these matters of history and art? We want by means of Social-Democracy to win a decent livelihood, we want in some sort to live, and that at once. Surely any one who professes to think that the question of art and cultivation must go before that of the knife and fork (and there are some who do propose that) does not understand what art means, or how that its roots must have a soil of a thriving and unanxious life. Yet it must be remembered that civilisation has reduced the workman to such a skinny and pitiful existence, that he scarcely knows how to frame a desire for any life much better than that which he now endures perforce. It is the province of art to set the true ideal of a full and reasonable life before him, a life to which the perception and creation of beauty, the enjoyment of real pleasure that is, shall be felt to be as necessary to man as his daily bread, and that no man, and no set of men, can be deprived of this except by mere opposition, which should be resisted to the utmost.

1894

---

[2] Podsnap: an insular, complacent, materialistic man of business in Charles Dickens' *Our Mutual Friend* (1865).

[3] Earlier in this essay Morris defines the "Whig frame of mind" as that of "prosperous middle-class men" who are "quite contented with the civilisation of this century" and see "nothing to do but to perfect the said civilisation by getting rid of a few ridiculous survivals of the barbarous ages."

[4] Thomas Henry Huxley (1825–95) wrote prolifically and persuasively of the benefits of science and its empirical set of mind.

Oscar Wilde
1854–1900

---

from Intentions

The Decay of Lying: An Observation[1]

A Dialogue
Persons: CYRIL *and* VIVIAN.
Scene: the library of a country house in Nottinghamshire

CYRIL (*coming in through the open window from the terrace*). My dear Vivian, don't coop yourself up all day in the library. It is a perfectly lovely afternoon. The air is exquisite. There is a mist upon the woods, like the purple bloom upon a plum. Let us go and lie on the grass, and smoke cigarettes, and enjoy Nature.

VIVIAN. Enjoy Nature! I am glad to say that I have entirely lost that faculty. People tell us that Art makes us love Nature more than we loved her before; that it reveals her secrets to us; and that after a careful study of Corot and Constable[2] we see things in her that had escaped our observation. My own experience is that the more we study Art, the less we care for Nature. What Art really reveals to us is Nature's lack of design, her curious crudities, her extraordinary monotony, her absolutely unfinished condition. Nature has good intentions, of course, but, as Aristotle once said, she cannot carry them out. When I look at a landscape I cannot help seeing all its defects. It is fortunate for us, however, that Nature is so imperfect, as otherwise we should have had no art at all. Art is our spirited protest, our gallant attempt to teach Nature her proper place.

As for the infinite variety of Nature, that is a pure myth. It is not to be found in Nature herself. It resides in the imagination, or fancy, or cultivated blindness of the man who looks at her.

. . .

[*Vivian then discusses the content of literature which appropriates and reproduces the externalities of experience, "dull facts under the guise of fiction"; and then he goes on to condemn as well "modernity of form," literature which tries to reproduce the shape and tone of ordinary experience.*]

CYRIL. Do you object to modernity of form, then?

VIVIAN. Yes. It is a huge price to pay for a very poor result. Pure modernity of form is always somewhat vulgarising. It cannot help being so. The public imagine that, because they are interested in their immediate surroundings, Art should be interested in them also, and should take them as her subject-matter. But the mere fact that they are interested in these things makes them unsuitable subjects for Art. The only beautiful things, as somebody once said, are the things that do not concern us. As long as a thing is useful or necessary to us, or affects us in any way, either for pain or for pleasure, or appeals strongly to our sympathies, or is a vital part of the environment in which we live, it is outside the proper sphere of art. To art's subject-matter we should be more or less indifferent. We should, at any rate, have no preferences, no prejudices, no partisan feeling of any kind. It is exactly because Hecuba is nothing to us[3] that her sorrows

---

[1] "The Decay of Lying" was first printed in a magazine in 1889. It was reprinted as one of four essays under the title *Intentions* in 1891. In the dialogue Vivian reads from an essay he calls "The Decay of Lying: A Protest." The text, which Wilde revised from its first magazine publication, is that of the first collected edition of Wilde's writing, published in 1908.

[2] The French painter Jean Baptiste Corot (1796–1875) and the English painter John Constable (1776–1837) were both painters of landscape.

[3] "What's Hecuba to him, or he to Hecuba, / That he should weep for her?": Hamlet's words about an actor who is moved by the role he is playing (*Hamlet*, II, 2).

are such an admirable motive for a tragedy.
. . . Believe me, my dear Cyril, modernity of
form and modernity of subject-matter are en-
tirely and absolutely wrong. We have mistaken
the common livery of the age for the vesture
of the Muses, and spend our days in the sordid
streets and hideous suburbs of our vile cities
when we should be out on the hillside with
Apollo.[4] Certainly we are a degraded race, and
have sold our birthright for a mess of facts.

CYRIL. There is something in what you
say, and there is no doubt that whatever
amusement we may find in reading a purely
modern novel, we have rarely any artistic
pleasure in re-reading it. And this is perhaps
the best rough test of what is literature and
what is not. If one cannot enjoy reading a book
over and over again, there is no use reading it
at all. But what do you say about the return
to Life and Nature? This is the panacea that
is always being recommended to us.

VIVIAN. I will read you what I say on that
subject. The passage comes later on in the
article, but I may as well give it to you now:—

"The popular cry of our time is 'Let us re-
turn to Life and Nature; they will recreate Art
for us, and send the red blood coursing through
her veins; they will shoe her feet with swift-
ness and make her hand strong.' But, alas! we
are mistaken in our amiable and well-meaning
efforts. Nature is always behind the age. And
as for Life, she is the solvent that breaks up
Art, the enemy that lays waste her house."

CYRIL. What do you mean by saying that
Nature is always behind the age?

VIVIAN. Well, perhaps that is rather cryptic.
What I mean is this. If we take Nature to mean
natural simple instinct as opposed to self-
conscious culture, the work produced under
this influence is always old-fashioned, anti-
quated, and out of date. One touch of Nature
may make the whole world kin, but two
touches of Nature will destroy any work of Art.
If, on the other hand, we regard Nature as the
collection of phenomena external to man, peo-
ple only discover in her what they bring to her.
She has no suggestions of her own. Wordsworth
went to the lakes, but he was never a lake poet.
He found in stones the sermons he had already
hidden there.[5] He went moralizing about the
district, but his good work was produced when
he returned not to Nature but to poetry. . . .

CYRIL. I think that view might be ques-
tioned. I am rather inclined to believe in the
"impulse from a vernal wood,"[6] though of
course the artistic value of such an impulse
depends entirely on the kind of temperament
that receives it, so that the return to Nature
would come to mean simply the advance to a
great personality. You would agree with that, I
fancy. However, proceed with your article.

VIVIAN (reading). "Art begins with abstract
decoration with purely imaginative and pleas-
urable work dealing with what is unreal and
non-existent. This is the first stage. Then Life
becomes fascinated with this new wonder, and
asks to be admitted into the charmed circle.
Art takes life as part of her rough material,
recreates it, and refashions it in fresh forms, is
absolutely indifferent to fact, invents, imagines,
dreams, and keeps between herself and reality
the impenetrable barrier of beautiful style, of
decorative or ideal treatment. The third stage
is when Life gets the upper hand, and drives
Art out into the wilderness. This is the true
decadence, and it is from this that we are now
suffering.

"Take the case of the English drama. At
first in the hands of the monks Dramatic Art
was abstract, decorative, and mythological.
Then she enlisted Life in her service, and using
some of life's external forms, she created an
entirely new race of beings, whose sorrows
were more terrible than any sorrow man has
ever felt, whose joys were keener than lover's
joys, who had the rage of the Titans and the
calm of the gods, who had monstrous and
marvellous sins, monstrous and marvellous
virtues. To them she gave a language different
from that of actual use, a language full of
resonant music and sweet rhythm, made stately
by solemn cadence, or made delicate by fanci-
ful rhyme, jewelled with wonderful words, and
enriched with lofty diction. She clothed her
children in strange raiment and gave them
masks, and at her bidding the antique world
rose from its marble tomb. A new Cæsar
stalked through the streets of risen Rome, and
with purple sail and flute-led oars another
Cleopatra passed up the river to Antioch. Old

---

[4] Apollo: the classical god of song.
[5] "One touch of Nature": *Troilus and Cressida,* III, 3; Sermons in stones: *As You Like It,* II, 1.
[6] "One impulse from a vernal wood / May teach you more of man; / Of moral evil and of good, / Than all the sages can": Wordsworth, "The Tables Turned" (1798).

myth and legend and dream took shape and substance. History was entirely re-written, and there was hardly one of the dramatists who did not recognize that the object of Art is not simple truth but complex beauty. In this they were perfectly right. Art itself is really a form of exaggeration; and selection, which is the very spirit of art, is nothing more than an intensified mode of over-emphasis.

"But Life soon shattered the perfection of the form. Even in Shakespeare we can see the beginning of the end. It shows itself by the gradual breaking up of the blank-verse in the later plays, by the predominance given to prose, and by the over-importance assigned to characterisation. The passages in Shakespeare— and they are many—where the language is uncouth, vulgar, exaggerated, fantastic, obscene even, are entirely due to Life calling for an echo of her own voice, and rejecting the intervention of beautiful style, through which alone should Life be suffered to find expression. Shakespeare is not by any means a flawless artist. He is too fond of going directly to life, and borrowing life's natural utterance. He forgets that when Art surrenders her imaginative medium she surrenders everything. Goethe says, somewhere—

In der Beschränkung zeigt sich erst der Meister,[7]

'It is in working within limits that the master reveals himself,' and the limitation, the very condition of any art is style. However, we need not linger any longer over Shakespeare's realism. *The Tempest* is the most perfect of palinodes. All that we desired to point out was, that the magnificent work of the Elizabethan and Jacobean artists contained within itself the seeds of its own dissolution, and that, if it drew some of its strength from using life as rough material, it drew all its weakness from using life as an artistic method. As the inevitable result of this substitution of an imitative for a creative medium, this surrender of an imaginative form, we have the modern English melodrama. The characters in these plays talk on the stage exactly as they would talk off it; they have neither aspirations nor aspirates;

they are taken directly from life and reproduce its vulgarity down to the smallest detail; they present the gait, manner, costume, and accent of real people; they would pass unnoticed in a third-class railway carriage. And yet how wearisome the plays are! They do not succeed in producing even that impression of reality at which they aim, and which is their only reason for existing. As a method, realism is a complete failure.

. . . .

"That some change will take place before this century has drawn to its close we have no doubt whatsoever. Bored by the tedious and improving conversation of those who have neither the wit to exaggerate nor the genius to romance, tired of the intelligent person whose reminiscences are always based upon memory, whose statements are invariably limited by probability, who is at any time liable to be corroborated by the merest Philistine[8] who happens to be present, Society sooner or later must return to its lost leader, the cultured and fascinating liar. Who he was who first, without ever having gone out to the rude chase, told the wondering cavemen at sunset how he had dragged the Megatherium[9] from the purple darkness of its jasper cave, or slain the Mammoth in single combat and brought back its gilded tusks, we cannot tell, and not one of our modern anthropologists, for all their much-boasted science, has had the ordinary courage to tell us. Whatever was his name or race, he certainly was the true founder of social intercourse. For the aim of the liar is simply to charm, to delight, to give pleasure. He is the very basis of civilized society, and without him a dinner party, even at the mansions of the great, is as dull as a lecture at the Royal Society, or a debate at the Incorporated Authors, or one of Mr. Burnand's farcical comedies.[10]

"Nor will he be welcomed by society alone. Art, breaking from the prison-house of realism, will run to greet him, and will kiss his false, beautiful lips, knowing that he alone is in possession of the great secret of all her mani-

[7] From *Was wir bringen* (1802).
[8] Philistine: used in the nineteenth century, especially by Matthew Arnold in *Culture and Anarchy* (1869), to denote someone deficient in the refinements of high culture.
[9] Megatherium: a gigantic slothlike animal.
[10] Francis C. Burnand (1836–1917) was a prolific writer of theatrical farce and burlesque and a frequent contributor to the comic weekly *Punch*, which he edited from 1880 to 1906.

festations, the secret that Truth is entirely and absolutely a matter of style; while Life—poor, probable, uninteresting human life—tired of repeating herself for the benefit of Mr. Herbert Spencer,[11] scientific historians, and the compilers of statistics in general, will follow meekly after him, and try to produce, in her own simple and untutored way, some of the marvels of which he talks. . . .

"Art finds her own perfection within, and not outside of, herself. She is not to be judged by any external standard of resemblance. She is a veil, rather than a mirror. She has flowers that no forests know of, birds that no woodland possesses. She makes and unmakes many worlds, and can draw the moon from heaven with a scarlet thread. Hers are the 'forms more real than living man,'[12] and hers the great archetypes of which things that have existence are but unfinished copies. Nature has, in her eyes, no laws, no uniformity. She can work miracles at her will, and when she calls monsters from the deep they come.[13] She can bid the almond tree blossom in winter, and send the snow upon the ripe cornfield. At her word the frost lays its silver finger on the burning mouth of June, and the winged lions creep out from the hollows of the Lydian hills. The dryads peer from the thicket as she passes by, and the brown fauns smile strangely at her when she comes near them. She has hawk-faced gods that worship her, and the centaurs gallop at her side. . . ."

CYRIL. . . . I can quite understand your objection to art being treated as a mirror. You think it would reduce genius to the position of a cracked looking-glass. But you don't mean to say that you seriously believe that Life imitates Art, that Life in fact is the mirror, and Art the reality?

VIVIAN. Certainly I do. Paradox though it may seem—and paradoxes are always dangerous things—it is none the less true that Life imitates art far more than Art imitates life.

We have all seen in our own day in England how a certain curious and fascinating type of beauty, invented and emphasised by two imaginative painters, has so influenced Life that whenever one goes to a private view or to an artistic salon one sees, here the mystic eyes of Rossetti's dream, the long ivory throat, the strange square-cut jaw, the loosened shadowy hair that he so ardently loved, there the sweet maidenhood of "The Golden Stair," the blossom-like mouth and weary loveliness of the "Laus Amoris," the passion-pale face of Andromeda, the thin hands and lithe beauty of the Vivien in "Merlin's Dream." And it has always been so. A great artist invents a type, and Life tries to copy it, to reproduce it in a popular form, like an enterprising publisher. Neither Holbein nor Vandyck[14] found in England what they have given us. They brought their types with them, and Life with her keen imitative faculty set herself to supply the master with models. . . .

However, I do not wish to dwell any further upon individual instances. Personal experience is a most vicious and limited circle. All that I desire to point out is the general principle that Life imitates Art far more than Art imitates Life, and I feel sure that if you think seriously about it you will find that it is true. Life holds the mirror up to Art, and either reproduces some strange type imagined by painter or sculptor, or realizes in fact what has been dreamed in fiction. Scientifically speaking, the basis of life—the energy of life, as Aristotle would call it—is simply the desire for expression, and Art is always presenting various forms through which this expression can be attained. Life seizes on them and uses them, even if they be to her own hurt. Young men have committed suicide because Rolla did so, have died by their own hand because by his own hand Werther died.[15] Think of what we owe to the imitation of Christ, of what we owe to the imitation of Cæsar.

---

[11] Herbert Spencer (1820–1903) wrote on scientific and philosophical subjects, trying especially to induce an ethical system from human observation and understanding of physical phenomena.

[12] Shelley, *Prometheus Unbound* (1820), Act I, line 748.

[13] Monsters from the deep: *I Henry IV*, III, 1.

[14] Hans Holbein (1497–1543) visited in England in the 1520s and 1530s, and was appointed court painter to the English king in 1536; many of his portraits are of British eminences. Anthony Van Dyck (1599–1641) was knighted by the English king in 1632 and also painted many portraits of English royalty and other personages.

[15] Rolla is the hero of a poem, which bears his name, by Alfred Musset (1810–57), a French poet and dramatist. Werther is the hero of Goethe's *The Sorrows of Young Werther* (1774).

CYRIL. The theory is certainly a very curious one, but to make it complete you must show that Nature, no less than Life, is an imitation of Art. Are you prepared to prove that?

VIVIAN. My dear fellow, I am prepared to prove anything.

CYRIL. Nature follows the landscape painter then, and takes her effects from him?

VIVIAN. Certainly. Where, if not from the Impressionists, do we get those wonderful brown fogs that come creeping down our streets, blurring the gas-lamps and changing the houses into monstrous shadows? To whom, if not to them and their master, do we owe the lovely silver mists that brood over our river, and turn to faint forms of fading grace curved bridge and swaying barge? The extraordinary change that has taken place in the climate of London during the last ten years is entirely due to this particular school of Art. You smile. Consider the matter from a scientific or a metaphysical point of view, and you will find that I am right. For what is Nature? Nature is no great mother who has borne us. She is our creation. It is in our brain that she quickens to life. Things are because we see them, and what we see, and how we see it, depends on the Arts that have influenced us. To look at a thing is very different from seeing a thing. One does not see anything until one sees its beauty. Then, and then only, does it come into existence. At present, people see fogs, not because there are fogs, but because poets and painters have taught them the mysterious loveliness of such effects. There may have been fogs for centuries in London. I dare say there were. But no one saw them, and so we do not know anything about them. They did not exist till Art had invented them. Now, it must be admitted, fogs are carried to excess. They have become the mere mannerism of a clique, and the exaggerated realism of their method gives dull people bronchitis. Where the cultured catch an effect, the uncultured catch cold. . . . Art creates an incomparable and unique effect, and, having done so, passes on to other things. Nature, upon the other hand, forgetting that imitation can be made the sincerest form of insult, keeps on repeating this effect until we all become absolutely wearied of it. Nobody of any real culture, for instance, ever talks now-a-days about the beauty of a sunset. Sunsets are quite old-fashioned. They belong to the time when Turner[16] was the last note in art. To admire them is a distinct sign of provincialism of temperament. Upon the other hand they go on. Yesterday evening Mrs. Arundel insisted on my going to the window, and looking at the glorious sky, as she called it. Of course I had to look at it. She is one of those absurdly pretty Philistines, to whom one can deny nothing. And what was it? It was simply a very second-rate Turner, a Turner of a bad period, with all the painter's worst faults exaggerated and overemphasised. . . .

CYRIL. . . . But even admitting this strange imitative instinct in Life and Nature, surely you would acknowledge that Art expresses the temper of its age, the spirit of its time, the moral and social conditions that surround it, and under whose influence it is produced.

VIVIAN. Certainly not! Art never expresses anything but itself. This is the principle of my new æsthetics; and it is this, more than that vital connection between form and substance, on which Mr. Pater dwells, that makes music the type of all the arts.[17] Of course, nations and individuals, with that healthy natural vanity which is the secret of existence, are always under the impression that it is of them that the Muses are talking, always trying to find in the calm dignity of imaginative art some mirror of their own turbid passions, always forgetting that the singer of life is not Apollo, but Marsyas.[18] Remote from reality, and with her eyes turned away from the shadows of the cave, Art reveals her own perfection, and the wondering crowd that watches the opening of the marvellous, many-petalled rose fancies that it is its own history that is being told to it, its own spirit that is finding

[16] J. M. W. Turner (1775–1851) was a British painter whose large paintings of light on clouds, sky, and water were enthusiastically advocated in the early volumes of *Modern Painters* (1843–60) by John Ruskin (1819–1900).

[17] "I have spoken of a certain interpenetration of the matter or subject of a work of art with the form of it, a condition realised absolutely only in music, as the condition to which every form of art is perpetually aspiring": Walter Pater (1839–94), "The School of Giorgione" (1877; reprinted in the third edition of *The Renaissance*, 1888).

[18] Marsyas: a satyr who in classical legend challenged Apollo, the god of song, to a flute contest, lost, and was tied to a tree and flayed in consequence.

expression in a new form. But it is not so. The highest art rejects the burden of the human spirit, and gains more from a new medium or a fresh material than she does from any enthusiasm for art, or from any lofty passion, or from any great awakening of the human consciousness. She develops purely on her own lines. She is not symbolic of any age. It is the ages that are her symbols.

Even those who hold that Art is representative of time and place and people, cannot help admitting that the more imitative an art is, the less it represents to us the spirit of its age. The evil faces of the Roman emperors look out at us from the foul porphyry and spotted jasper in which the realistic artists of the day delighted to work, and we fancy that in those cruel lips and heavy sensual jaws we can find the secret of the ruin of the Empire. But it was not so. The vices of Tiberius could not destroy that supreme civilization, any more than the virtues of the Antonines[19] could save it. It fell for other, for less interesting reasons. The sibyls and prophets of the Sistine[20] may indeed serve to interpret for some that new birth of the emancipated spirit that we call the Renaissance; but what do the drunken boors and brawling peasants of Dutch art tell us about the great soul of Holland? The more abstract, the more ideal an art is, the more it reveals to us the temper of its age. If we wish to understand a nation by means of its art, let us look at its architecture or its music.

CYRIL. I quite agree with you there. The spirit of an age may be best expressed in the abstract ideal arts, for the spirit itself is abstract and ideal. Upon the other hand, for the visible aspect of an age, for its look, as the phrase goes, we must of course go to the arts of imitation.

VIVIAN. I don't think so. After all, what the imitative arts really give us are merely the various styles of particular artists, or of certain schools of artists. Surely you don't imagine that the people of the Middle Ages bore any resemblance at all to the figures on mediæval stained glass, or in mediæval stone and wood carving, or on mediæval metal-work, or tapestries, or illuminated MSS. They were probably very ordinary-looking people, with nothing grotesque, or remarkable, or fantastic in their appearance. The Middle Ages, as we know them in art, are simply a definite form of style, and there is no reason at all why an artist with this style should not be produced in the nineteenth century. No great artist ever sees things as they really are. If he did, he would cease to be an artist. Take an example from our own day. I know that you are fond of Japanese things. Now, do you really imagine that the Japanese people, as they are presented to us in art, have any existence? If you do, you have never understood Japanese art at all. The Japanese people are the deliberate self-conscious creation of certain individual artists. If you set a picture by Hokusai, or Hokkei,[21] or any of the great native painters, beside a real Japanese gentleman or lady, you will see that there is not the slightest resemblance between them. The actual people who live in Japan are not unlike the general run of English people; that is to say, they are extremely commonplace, and have nothing curious or extraordinary about them. In fact the whole of Japan is a pure invention. There is no such country, there are no such people. . . .

CYRIL. . . . I want you to tell me briefly the doctrines of the new æsthetics.

VIVIAN. Briefly, then, they are these. Art never expresses anything but itself. It has an independent life, just as Thought has, and develops purely on its own lines. It is not necessarily realistic in an age of realism, nor spiritual in an age of faith. So far from being the creation of its time, it is usually in direct opposition to it, and the only history that it preserves for us is the history of its own progress. Sometimes it returns upon its footsteps, and revives some antique form, as happened in the archaistic movement of late Greek Art, and in the pre-Raphaelite movement of our own day. At other times it entirely anticipates its age, and produces in one century work that it takes another century to understand, to appreciate, and to enjoy. In no case does it reproduce its age. To pass from the art of a time to the time

[19] Tiberius Claudius Nero, an emperor of Rome in the first century, retired from the capitol to indulge his sensual vices. The Antonines (Antonius Pius and Marcus Aurelius Antonius) were Roman emperors of the second century.

[20] Figures in the frescoes of the Sistine Chapel, painted by Michelangelo in the 1530s.

[21] Hokusai (1760–1849) was a great Japanese draftsman and artist. Hokkei, who worked in the early decades of the nineteenth century, was his student.

itself is the great mistake that all historians commit.

The second doctrine is this. All bad art comes from returning to Life and Nature, and elevating them into ideals. Life and Nature may sometimes be used as part of Art's rough material, but before they are of any real service to art they must be translated into artistic conventions. The moment Art surrenders its imaginative medium it surrenders everything. As a method Realism is a complete failure, and the two things that every artist should avoid are modernity of form and modernity of subject-matter. To us, who live in the nineteenth century, any century is a suitable subject for art except our own. The only beautiful things are the things that do not concern us. It is, to have the pleasure of quoting myself, exactly because Hecuba is nothing to us that her sorrows are so suitable a motive for a tragedy. Besides, it is only the modern that ever becomes old-fashioned. M. Zola[22] sits down to give us a picture of the Second Empire. Who cares for the Second Empire now? It is out of date. Life goes faster than Realism, but Romanticism is always in front of Life.

The third doctrine is that Life imitates Art far more than Art imitates Life. This results not merely from Life's imitative instinct, but from the fact that the self-conscious aim of Life is to find expression, and that Art offers it certain beautiful forms through which it may realize that energy. It is a theory that has never been put forward before, but it is extremely fruitful, and throws an entirely new light upon the history of Art.

It follows, as a corollary from this, that external Nature also imitates Art. The only effects that she can show us are effects that we have already seen through poetry, or in paintings. This is the secret of Nature's charm, as well as the explanation of Nature's weakness.

The final revelation is that Lying, the telling of beautiful untrue things, is the proper aim of Art. But of this I think I have spoken at sufficient length. And now let us go out on the terrace, where "droops the milk-white peacock like a ghost," while the evening star "washes the dusk with silver." At twilight nature becomes a wonderfully suggestive effect, and is not without loveliness, though perhaps its chief use is to illustrate quotations from the poets. Come! We have talked long enough.

1889; 1891

William Butler Yeats
1865–1939

from The Symbolism of Poetry[1]

II

In "Symbolism in Painting,"[2] I tried to describe the element of symbolism that is in pictures and sculpture, and described a little the symbolism in poetry, but did not describe at all the continuous indefinable symbolism which is the substance of all style.

There are no lines with more melancholy beauty than these by Burns:—

The white moon is setting behind the white wave,
And Time is setting with me, O![3]

[22] Émile Zola (1840–1902) was a French novelist who set some of his detailed, naturalistic fictions in the bourgeois life of the Second Empire of Louis Napoleon, which ended in 1870.

[1] First published in a magazine in 1900, and then collected in a volume of critical essays in 1903. The text is that of the collected edition of his works that Yeats published in 1908.

[2] An earlier essay also published in *Ideas of Good and Evil*, the volume of critical essays Yeats published in 1903.

[3] "The wan moon is setting behind the white wave, / And Time is setting with me, Oh": in "Open the Door Oh," published in a collection of Robert Burns' poems in 1793.

and these lines are perfectly symbolical. Take from them the whiteness of the moon and of the wave, whose relation to the setting of Time is too subtle for the intellect, and you take from them their beauty. But, when all are together, moon and wave and whiteness and setting Time and the last melancholy cry, they evoke an emotion which cannot be evoked by any other arrangement of colours and sounds and forms. We may call this metaphorical writing, but it is better to call it symbolical writing, because metaphors are not profound enough to be moving, when they are not symbols, and when they are symbols they are the most perfect of all, because the most subtle, outside of pure sound, and through them one can best find out what symbols are. If one begins the reverie with any beautiful lines that one can remember, one finds they are like those by Burns. Begin with this line by Blake:—

The gay fishes on the wave when the moon sucks
    up the dew;[4]

or these lines by Nash:—

Brightness falls from the air,
Queens have died young and fair,
Dust hath closed Helen's eye;[5]

or these lines by Shakespeare:—

Timon hath made his everlasting mansion
Upon the beached verge of the salt flood;
Who once a day with his embossed froth
The turbulent surge shall cover;[6]

or take some line that is quite simple, that gets its beauty from its place in a story, and see how it flickers with the light of the many symbols that have given the story its beauty, as a sword-blade may flicker with the light of burning towers.

All sounds, all colours, all forms, either because of their preordained energies or because of long association, evoke indefinable and yet precise emotions, or, as I prefer to think, call down among us certain disembodied powers, whose footsteps over our hearts we call emotions; and when sound, and colour, and form are in a musical relation, a beautiful relation to one another, they become, as it were, one sound, one colour, one form, and evoke an emotion that is made out of their distinct evocations and yet is one emotion. The same relation exists between all portions of every work of art, whether it be an epic or a song, and the more perfect it is, and the more various and numerous the elements that have flowed into its perfection, the more powerful will be the emotion, the power, the god it calls among us. Because an emotion does not exist, or does not become perceptible and active among us, till it has found its expression, in colour or in sound or in form, or in all of these, and because no two modulations or arrangements of these evoke the same emotion, poets and painters and musicians, and in a less degree because their effects are momentary, day and night and cloud and shadow, are continually making and unmaking mankind. It is indeed only those things which seem useless or very feeble that have any power, and all those things that seem useful or strong, armies, moving wheels, modes of architecture, modes of government, speculations of the reason, would have been a little different if some mind long ago had not given itself to some emotion, as a woman gives herself to her lover, and shaped sounds or colours or forms, or all of these, into a musical relation, that their emotion might live in other minds. A little lyric evokes an emotion, and this emotion gathers others about it and melts into their being in the making of some great epic; and at last, needing an always less delicate body, or symbol, as it grows more powerful, it flows out, with all it has gathered, among the blind instincts of daily life, where it moves a power within powers, as one sees ring within ring in the stem of an old tree. This is maybe what Arthur O'Shaughnessy meant when he made his poets say they had built Nineveh with their sighing;[7] and I am certainly never sure, when I hear of some war, or of some religious excitement, or of some new manufacture, or of anything else that fills the ear of the world, that it has not all happened because of something that a boy piped in Thessaly.[8] I remember once telling a seeress to ask one among the gods who, as she believed, were standing about her in their symbolic bodies, what would come of a charm-

[4] From *Europe*, which William Blake completed in 1794.
[5] From "In Time of Pestilence," by Thomas Nashe (1567–1601).
[6] From *Timon of Athens* (c. 1607), V, 1.
[7] In "Ode: We are the music makers"; see pp. 759–760.
[8] Thessaly: a region in Greece associated with pastoral poetry.

ing but seeming trivial labour of a friend, and the form answering, "the devastation of peoples and the overwhelming of cities." I doubt indeed if the crude circumstance of the world, which seems to create all our emotions, does more than reflect, as in multiplying mirrors, the emotions that have come to solitary men in moments of poetical contemplation; or that love itself would be more than an animal hunger but for the poet and his shadow the priest, for unless we believe that outer things are the reality, we must believe that the gross is the shadow of the subtle, that things are wise before they become foolish, and secret before they cry out in the market-place. . . .

III

The purpose of rhythm, it has always seemed to me, is to prolong the moment of contemplation, the moment when we are both asleep and awake, which is the one moment of creation, by hushing us with an alluring monotony, while it holds us waking by variety, to keep us in that state of perhaps real trance, in which the mind liberated from the pressure of the will is unfolded in symbols. If certain sensitive persons listen persistently to the ticking of a watch, or gaze persistently on the monotonous flashing of a light, they fall into the hypnotic trance; and rhythm is but the ticking of a watch made softer, that one must needs listen, and various, that one may not be swept beyond memory or grow weary of listening; while the patterns of the artist are but the monotonous flash woven to take the eyes in a subtler enchantment. I have heard in meditation voices that were forgotten the moment they had spoken; and I have been swept, when in more profound meditation, beyond all memory but of those things that came from beyond the threshold of waking life. I was writing once at a very symbolical and abstract poem, when my pen fell on the ground; and as I stooped to pick it up, I remembered some fantastic adventure that yet did not seem fantastic, and then another like adventure, and when I asked myself when these things had happened, I found that I was remembering my dreams for many nights. I tried to remember what I had done the day before, and then what I had done that morning; but all my waking life had perished from me, and it was only

after a struggle that I came to remember it again, and as I did so that more powerful and startling life perished in its turn. Had my pen not fallen on the ground and so made me turn from the images that I was weaving into verse, I would never have known that meditation had become trance, for I would have been like one who does not know that he is passing through a wood because his eyes are on the pathway. So I think that in the making and in the understanding of a work of art, and the more easily if it is full of patterns and symbols and music, we are lured to the threshold of sleep, and it may be far beyond it, without knowing that we have ever set our feet upon the steps of horn or of ivory.[9]

. . .

V

If people were to accept the theory that poetry moves us because of its symbolism, what change should one look for in the manner of our poetry? A return to the way of our fathers, a casting out of descriptions of nature for the sake of nature, of the moral law for the sake of the moral law, a casting out of all anecdotes and of that brooding over scientific opinion that so often extinguished the central flame in Tennyson, and of that vehemence that would make us do or not do certain things; or, in other words, we should come to understand that the beryl stone was enchanted by our fathers that it might unfold the pictures in its heart, and not to mirror our own excited faces, or the boughs waving outside the window. With this change of substance, this return to imagination, this understanding that the laws of art, which are the hidden laws of the world, can alone bind the imagination, would come a change of style, and we would cast out of serious poetry those energetic rhythms, as of a man running, which are the invention of the will with its eyes always on something to be done or undone; and we would seek out those wavering, meditative, organic rhythms, which are the embodiment of the imagination, that neither desires nor hates, because it has done with time, and only wishes to gaze upon some reality, some beauty; nor would it be any longer possible for anybody to deny the importance of form, in all its kinds, for although you can

[9] In classical mythology true dreams issue into the world through gates of horn, and false dreams through gates of ivory.

expound an opinion, or describe a thing, when your words are not quite well chosen, you cannot give a body to something that moves beyond the senses, unless your words are as subtle, as complex, as full of mysterious life, as the body of a flower or of a woman. The form of sincere poetry, unlike the form of the "popular poetry," may indeed be sometimes obscure, or ungrammatical as in some of the best of the *Songs of Innocence and Experience*,[10] but it must have the perfections that escape analysis, the subtleties that have a new meaning every day, and it must have all this whether it be but a little song made out of a moment of dreamy indolence, or some great epic made out of the dreams of one poet and of a hundred generations whose hands were never weary of the sword.

1900; 1903

from Autobiography

The Trembling of the Veil[1]

[*In the chapters of his autobiography titled "Four Years: 1887–1891" and "The Tragic Generation," Yeats recounts the organization and dissolution of the Rhymers' Club, a society of poets who met in the Cheshire Cheese, a London pub, read their poems to one another, and published two collections of these poems in 1892 and 1894. Lionel Johnson, Ernest Dowson, Arthur Symons, John Davidson, and other poets of the 1890s were associated in the Rhymers' Club.*]

We read our poems to one another and talked criticism and drank a little wine. I sometimes say when I speak of the club, "We had such and such ideas, such and such a quarrel with the great Victorians, we set before us such and such aims", as though we had many philosophical ideas. I say this because I am ashamed to admit that I had these ideas and that whenever I began to talk of them a gloomy silence fell upon the room. A young Irish poet, who wrote excellently but had the worst manners, was to say a few years later, "You do not talk like a poet, you talk like a man of letters", and if all the Rhymers had not been polite, if most of them had not been to Oxford or Cambridge, the greater number would have said the same thing. I was full of thought, often very abstract thought, longing all the while to be full of images, because I had gone to the art school instead of a university. Yet even if I had gone to a university, and learned all the classical foundations of English literature and English culture, all that great erudition which once accepted frees the mind from restlessness, I should have had to give up my Irish subject-matter, or attempt to found a new tradition. Lacking sufficient recognised precedent I must needs find out some reason for all I did. I knew almost from the start that to overflow with reasons was to be not quite well-born; and when I could I hid them, as men hide a disagreeable ancestry; and that there was no help for it seeing that my country was not born at all. I was of those doomed to imperfect achievement, and under a curse, as it were, like some race of birds compelled to spend the time, needed for the making of the nest, in argument as to the convenience of moss and twig and lichen. Le Gallienne[2] and Davidson, and even Symons, were provincial at their setting out, but their provincialism was curable, mine incurable; while the one conviction shared by all the younger men, but principally by Johnson and Horne,[3] who imposed their personalities upon us, was an opposition to all ideas, all generalisations that can be explained and debated. Symons fresh from Paris would sometimes say, "We are concerned with nothing but impressions", but that itself was a generalisation and met but stony silence. Conversation constantly dwindled into "Do you like so and so's last book?" "No, I prefer the book before it", and I think that but for its Irish members, who

---

[10] Blake completed *Songs of Innocence* in 1789, *Songs of Experience* in 1794, and published them together after the latter date.

[1] Yeats began to publish his autobiography in 1915, with *Reveries Over Childhood and Youth*. Eventually the *Autobiography,* collected under that title in 1938, comprised six separately titled sections, which had been previously published in three different volumes. *The Trembling of the Veil* was first published in 1922. The text printed here is that of the 1953 edition.

[2] Richard Le Gallienne (1866–1947) published his first volumes of poems in the late 1880s.

[3] Herbert Percy Horne (1846–1916) was a translator and art historian.

said whatever came into their heads, the club would not have survived its first difficult months. I saw—now ashamed that I saw "like a man of letters", now exasperated at the indifference of these poets to the fashion of their own river-bed—that Swinburne in one way, Browning in another, and Tennyson in a third, had filled their work with what I called "impurities", curiosities about politics, about science, about history, about religion; and that we must create once more the pure work.

. . .

The Rhymers had begun to break up in tragedy, though we did not know that till the play had finished. I have never found a full explanation of that tragedy; sometimes I have remembered that, unlike the Victorian poets, almost all were poor men, and had made it a matter of conscience to turn from every kind of money-making that prevented good writing, and that poverty meant strain, and for the most part, a refusal of domestic life. Then I have remembered that Johnson had private means, and that others who came to tragic ends had wives and families. Another day I think that perhaps our form of lyric, our insistence upon emotion which has no relation to any public interest, gathered together overwrought, unstable men; and remember, the moment after, that the first to go out of his mind had no lyrical gift, and that we valued him mainly because he seemed a witty man of the world; and that a little later another who seemed, alike as man and writer, dull and formless, went out of his mind, first burning poems which I cannot believe would have proved him, as the one man who saw them claims, a man of genius. The meetings were always decorous and often dull; some one would read out a poem and we would comment, too politely for the criticism to have great value; and yet that we read out our poems, and thought that they could be so tested, was a definition of our aims. *Love's Nocturne*[4] is one of the most beautiful poems in the world, but no one can find out its beauty, so intricate its thought and metaphor, till he has read it over several times, or stopped several times to re-read a passage, and the

Faustine of Swinburne, where much is powerful and musical, could not, were it read out, be understood with pleasure, however clearly it were read, because it has no more logical structure than a bag of shot. I shall, however, remember all my life that evening when Lionel Johnson read or spoke aloud in his musical monotone, where meaning and cadence found the most precise elocution, his poem suggested "by the Statue of King Charles at Charing Cross." It was as though I listened to a great speech. Nor will that poem be to me again what it was that first night. For long I only knew Dowson's *O Mors*, to quote but the first words of its long title, and his *Villanelle of Sunset* from his reading, and it was because of the desire to hold them in my hand that I suggested the first *Book of The Rhymers' Club*. They were not speech but perfect song, though song for the speaking voice. It was perhaps our delight in poetry that was, before all else, speech or song, and could hold the attention of a fitting audience like a good play or good conversation, that made Francis Thompson, whom we admired so much—before the publication of his first poem I had brought to the Cheshire Cheese the proof sheets of his *Ode to the Setting Sun,* his first published poem—come but once and refuse to contribute to our book. Preoccupied with his elaborate verse, he may have seen only that which we renounced, and thought what seemed to us simplicity, mere emptiness. To some members this simplicity was perhaps created by their tumultuous lives, they praised a desired woman and hoped that she would find amid their praise her very self, or at worst, their very passion; and knew that she, ignoramus that she was, would have slept in the middle of *Love's Nocturne,* lofty and tender though it be. Woman herself was still in our eyes, for all that, romantic and mysterious, still the priestess of her shrine, our emotions remembering the *Lilith* and the *Sybilla Palmifera*[5] of Rossetti; for as yet that sense of comedy, which was soon to mould the very fashion plates, and, in the eyes of men of my generation, to destroy at last the sense of beauty itself, had scarce begun to show here and there, in slight subordinate touches among the designs of great painters and craftsmen. It could not be other-

[4] A poem by Dante Gabriel Rossetti.
[5] Dante Gabriel Rossetti gave these titles to two of his paintings and to the sonnets (p. 585) written to accompany them.

wise, for Johnson's favourite phrase, that life is ritual, expressed something that was in some degree in all our thoughts, and how could life be ritual if woman had not her symbolical place? . . .

Why should men who spoke their opinions in low voices, as though they feared to disturb the readers in some ancient library, and timidly as though they knew that all subjects had long since been explored, all questions long since decided in books whereon the dust settled, live lives of such disorder and seek to rediscover in verse the syntax of impulsive common life? Was it that we lived in what is called "an age of transition" and so lacked coherence, or did we but pursue antithesis?

1922

General Bibliography

General Histories of Victorian Britain

Briggs, Asa. *The Age of Improvement* (1962).

Buckley, Jerome. *The Victorian Temper* (1951).

Burn, W. L. *The Age of Equipoise: A Study of the Mid-Victorian Generation* (1964).

Clark, G. Kitson. *The Making of Victorian England* (1962).

Ensor, R. C. K. *England, 1870–1914* (1936).

Hammond, J. L., and Hammond, Barbara. *The Age of the Chartists, 1832–1854* (1930).

Houghton, Walter. *The Victorian Frame of Mind, 1830–1870* (1957).

Hynes, Samuel. *The Edwardian Turn of Mind* (1968).

Nowell-Smith, Simon, ed. *Edwardian England, 1901–1914* (1964).

Schneewind, J. B. *Backgrounds of English Victorian Literature* (1970). Essays on social, political, intellectual, religious, and other aspects of Victorian culture.

Woodward, E. L. *The Age of Reform, 1815–1870*, 2nd ed. (1962).

Young, G. M., ed. *Early Victorian England, 1830–65* (1934).

General Histories of Victorian Literature

Bowra, C. M. *The Romantic Imagination* (1949). Includes essays on the fortunes of the romantic idea of imagination in the Victorian period, and on the poetry of the Rossettis and Swinburne.

Drinkwater, John. *Victorian Poetry* (1923).

Elton, Oliver. *A Survey of English Literature, 1780–1880* (1920).

Evans, B. Ifor. *English Poetry in the Later Nineteenth Century* (1933; revised, 1966).

Grierson, H. J. C. *Lyrical Poetry of the Nineteenth Century* (1929).

Heath-Stubbs, John. *The Darkling Plain: A Study of the Later Fortunes of Romanticism in English Poetry from George Darley to W. B. Yeats* (1950).

Hough, Graham. *The Last Romantics* (1949). Yeats and other poets of the last decades of the century.

Johnson, E. D. H. *The Alien Vision of Victorian Poetry* (1952). Includes chapters on Tennyson, Browning, and other major poets.

Lester, J. A. *Journey Through Despair 1800–1914: Transformations in British Literary Culture* (1968).

Pinto, Vivian de Sola. *Crisis in English Poetry, 1880–1940* (1951).

Saintsbury, George. *A History of Nineteenth-Century Literature, 1780–1900* (1901).

Stedman, E. C. *Victorian Poets* (1876; 28th ed., 1896).

Symons, Arthur. *The Romantic Movement in English Poetry* (1909).

Walker, Hugh. *The Age of Tennyson* (1897).

Accounts of Particular Schools in Victorian Poetry

Bergonzi, Bernard. *The Turn of a Century* (1973). Essays on writing and writers around 1900.

Charlesworth, Barbara. *Dark Passages: The Decadent Consciousness in Victorian Literature* (1965).

Clarke, Austin. *The Celtic Twilight and the Nineties* (1969).

Croft-Cooke, Rupert. *Feasting with Panthers* (1967). Essays on Swinburne, Wilde, and their associates among Pre-Raphaelite and late-century writers and artists.

Farmer, A. J. *Le mouvement esthétique et décadent en Angleterre* (1931).

Hamilton, Walter. *The Aesthetic Movement in England* (1882).

Hunt, John Dixon. *The Pre-Raphaelite Imagination, 1848–1900* (1968).

Jackson, Holbrook. *The Eighteen Nineties* (1913).

Nelson, James G. *The Early Nineties: The View from the Bodley Head* (1971). Study of one of the important publishers of the new writers of the 1890s.

Rosenblatt, Louise. *L'Idée de l'art pour l'art dans la littérature anglais pendant la periode victorienne* (1931).

Starkie, Enid. *From Gautier to Eliot: The Influence of France on English Literature, 1851–1939* (1960).

Stevenson, Lionel. *The Pre-Raphaelite Poets* (1972).

Temple, Ruth Z. *The Critics' Alchemy: A Study of the Introduction of French Symbolism into England* (1953).

Wilson, Edmund. *Axel's Castle: A Study in the Imaginative Literature of 1870–1930* (1931).

THE ROMANTIC AND VICTORIAN ESTHETIC

Abrams, M. H. *The Mirror and the Lamp: Romantic Theory and the Critical Tradition* (1953). Ideas about poetry to about 1840. See also Abrams' *Natural Supernaturalism: Tradition and Revolution in Romantic Literature* (1971).

Ball, Patricia M. *The Central Self: A Study in Romantic and Victorian Imagination* (1968). Tennyson, Browning, Arnold, Hopkins, Yeats, and the Victorian idea of "sincerity" in poetry.

Bloom, Harold. *The Ringers in the Tower* (1971). Essays on Tennyson, Browning, Ruskin and Pater, the internalization of quest romance in nineteenth-century British poetry, and A. H. Hallam and the young Tennyson in the romantic tradition.

Bloom, Harold, ed. *Romanticism and Consciousness* (1970); and Robert F. Gleckner and Gerald E. Enscoe, eds., *Romanticism: Points of View*, second edition (1970). Both collections contain essays setting out some currently central definitions of and formulations about nineteenth-century British romanticism, including: in Bloom, his own essay on the internalization of quest romance, Geoffrey Hartman's "Romanticism and Anti-Self-Consciousness," Josephine Miles' "The Romantic Mode," M. H. Abrams' "Style and Structure in the Greater Romantic Lyric," and "English Romanticism: The Spirit of the Age"; and in Gleckner and Enscoe, Arthur J. Lovejoy's "On the Discrimination of Romanticisms," René Wellek's "The Concept of Romanticism in Literary History," Northrop Frye's "The Drunken Boat: The Revolutionary Element in Romanticism, "Earl Wasserman's "The English Romantics: The Grounds of Knowledge," and essays by Morse Peckham and Raymond Williams.

Christ, Carol. *The Finer Optic: The Aesthetic of Particularity in Victorian Poetry* (1975).

Gibbons, Tom. *Rooms in the Darwin Hotel: Studies in English Literary Criticism and Ideas, 1880–1920* (1973).

Kaplan, Fred. *Miracles of Rare Device: The Poet's Sense of Self in Nineteenth-Century Poetry* (1972). Tennyson, Browning, and Arnold, among others.

Kermode, Frank. *Romantic Image* (1957).

Ladd, Henry. *The Victorian Morality of Art* (1932). Ruskin's ideas about art.

Langbaum, Robert. *The Poetry of Experience: The Dramatic Monologue in Modern Literature Tradition* (1957). See also Langbaum's collection of his own essays, *The Modern Spirit: Essays on the Continuity of Nineteenth- and Twentieth-Century Literature* (1970), which includes essays on Browning, Tennyson, the Victorian idea of culture, and the relationship between nineteenth- and twentieth-century nature poetry.

Miller, J. Hillis. *The Disappearance of God: Five Nineteenth-Century Writers* (1963). Browning, Arnold, Emily Brontë, and Hopkins are among the five.

Nicolson, Marjorie H. *Mountain Gloom and Mountain Glory: The Development of the Aesthetics of the Infinite* (1959). From the renaissance into the nineteenth century.

Peckham, Morse. *Beyond the Tragic Vision: The Quest for Identity in the Nineteenth Century* (1962), and *Victorian Revolutionaries: Speculations on Some Heroes of a Culture Crisis* (1970). The first book considers Wagner, Nietzsche, and other nineteenth-century European artists and thinkers as well as some British nineteenth-century writers; the second book contains studies of Browning, Tennyson, Swinburne, and Carlyle, and an essay on the relationship between subject and object in nineteenth-century art and thought. See also Peckham's collection of his own essays, including definitions of romanticism and the term "Victorian," *The Triumph of Romanticism* (1970).

Praz, Mario. *The Romantic Agony*, translated by Angus Davidson (1933).

Rosenberg, John D. *The Darkening Glass: A Portrait of Ruskin's Genius* (1961).

Warren, Alba. *English Poetic Theory, 1825–1865* (1950).

Wellek, René. *A History of Modern Criticism, 1750–1950.* Vols. 2, 3, and 4 (1955–65).

Williams, Raymond. *Culture and Society, 1780–1950* (1958). See also Williams' *The Long Revolution* (1961) and *The Country and the City* (1973).

Wimsatt, W. K., and Brooks, Cleanth. *Literary Criticism: A Short History* (1957).

VICTORIAN READERS AND REVIEWERS

Altick, Richard D. *The English Common Reader: A Social History of the Mass Reading Public, 1800–1900* (1957).

Armstrong, Isobel, ed. *Victorian Scrutinies: Reviews of Poetry 1830–1870* (1972). Principally reviews of important volumes by Tennyson, Browning, Arnold, and Clough, and a useful introductory essay about the premises and practices of Victorian literary reviewing.

Cox, R. G. "Victorian Criticism of Poetry: The Minority Tradition," *Scrutiny*, 18 (1951).

Cruse, Amy. *The Victorians and Their Reading* (1935).

Dodds, John W. *The Age of Paradox* (1952). Includes an account of how poetry was received in the 1840s.

Gross, John. *The Rise and Fall of the Man of Letters* (1969).

Jump, J. D. "Weekly Reviewing in the Eighteen Sixties," *Review of English Studies*, n.s., 3 (1952).

Orel, Harold and Worth, George, eds. *The Nineteenth-Century Writer and His Audience: Selected Problems in Theory, Form, and Content* (1969).

SPECIAL TOPICS

Baker, William. *Syntax in English, 1870–1930* (1967).

Bateson, F. W. *English Poetry and the English Language* (1934; 3rd edition, 1973).

Beach, Joseph Warren. *The Concept of Nature in Nineteenth-Century English Poetry* (1936).

Benn, A. W. *History of English Rationalism in the Nineteenth Century* (1910).

Brinton, Crane. *English Political Thought in the Nineteenth Century* (1949).

Buckley, Jerome H. *The Triumph of Time: A Study of Victorian Concepts of Time, History, Progress, and Decadence* (1966).

Bush, Douglas. *Mythology and the Romantic Tradition in English Poetry* (1937; rev. ed., 1963).

Chadwick, Owen. *The Victorian Church* (1966–70).

Clark, Kenneth. *The Gothic Revival* (1928; enlarged edition 1950).

Colville, Derek. *Victorian Poetry and the Romantic Religion* (1970).

Elliott-Binns, L. E. *Religion in the Victorian Era* (1936).

Fairchild, Hoxie Neal. *Religious Trends in English Poetry*, volumes 4 and 5, 1830–1880, and 1880–1920 (1957; 1962).

Foakes, R. A. *The Romantic Assertion: A Study of the Language of Nineteenth-Century Poets* (1958).

Friedman, A. B. *The Ballad Revival: Studies in the Influence of Popular on Sophisticated Poetry* (1961).

Gross, Harvey. *Sound and Form in Modern Poetry: A Study of Prosody from Thomas Hardy to Robert Lowell* (1964).

Kroeber, Karl. *Romantic Narrative Art* (1960).

Miles, Josephine. *Eras and Modes in English Poetry* (1957). Contains essays on the romantic mode, the classical mode of the late nineteenth century, and the poetry of Hopkins and Yeats. See also Miles' *The Continuity of Poetic Language: The Primary Language of Poetry from the 1540's to the 1940's* (1951; reprinted 1965), and *Pathetic Fallacy in the Nineteenth Century: A Study of a Changing Relationship Between Object and Emotion* (1942; reprinted 1965).

Passmore, J. A. *A Hundred Years of Philosophy* (1966).

Roppen, Georg. *Evolution and Poetic Belief* (1956).

Smith, Timothy d'Arch. *Love in Earnest: Some Notes on the Lives and Writings of English "Uranian" Poets from 1889 to 1930* (1970). Poetry of homoerotic relationships.

Somervell, D. C. *English Thought in the Nineteenth Century* (1929).

Stevenson, Lionel. *Darwin Among the Poets* (1932).

Thompson, J. A. K. *Classical Influences on English Poetry* (1951).

Vicinus, Martha. *The Industrial Muse: A Study of British Working-Class Literature* (1974).

Willey, Basil. *Nineteenth-Century Studies* (1949) and *More Nineteenth-Century Studies* (1956). Studies of skeptical and liberal thinkers in the century, including, in the latter book, Tennyson.

Wilkie, Brian. *Romantic Poets and the Epic Tradition* (1965).

Wolff, Michael, and Dyos, H. J., eds. *The Victorian City: Images and Realities* (1973).

Includes an essay by G. Robert Stange on poets and the city.

Woodring, Carl. *Politics in English Romantic Poetry* (1970).

COLLECTIONS OF ESSAYS

Armstrong, Isobel, ed. *The Major Victorian Poets: Reconsiderations* (1969). Tennyson, Browning, Arnold, Clough, and Hopkins.

Bradbury, Malcolm, and Palmer, David, eds. *Victorian Poetry* (1973). Essays on Arnold, Tennyson, Browning, the Pre-Raphaelites, Morris, Hopkins, Yeats, Hardy, the use of the past in Victorian poetry, and historical modes in the nineteenth century.

Kumar, Shiv, ed. *British Victorian Literature* (1969). Includes an essay by Kingsley Amis on the audience of Victorian poets, and essays on Tennyson, Browning, Arnold, Kipling, Swinburne, Hopkins, and the Pre-Raphaelites.

Lucas, F. L. *Ten Victorian Poets* (1948). Tennyson, Browning, Arnold, Clough, Dante Gabriel Rossetti, Swinburne, Morris, Hardy, Patmore, and Christina Rossetti.

ANTHOLOGIES OF HISTORICAL OR SPECIALIZED INTEREST

Aldington, Richard D., ed. *The Religion of Beauty: Selections from the Aesthetes* (1950).

Auden, W. H., ed. *Nineteenth-Century British Minor Poets* (1966).

Fairweather, Eugene R., ed. *The Oxford Movement* (1964). A collection of tracts, sermons, essays, etc.

Heath-Stubbs, John, and Wright, David, eds. *The Forsaken Garden: An Anthology of Poetry, 1824–1909* (1950). A fine collection of poems by minor poets, and of poems in subdued tonalities.

Hoffman, Daniel G., and Hynes, Samuel, eds. *English Literary Criticism, Romantic and Victorian* (1963).

Jones, E. D., ed. *English Critical Essays* (Nineteenth Century) (1916).

Lang, Cecil Y., ed. *The Pre-Raphaelites and Their Circle* (1968).

Levine, George, ed. *The Emergence of Victorian Consciousness* (1967). A collection of essays on culture by early Victorian writers.

Miles, A. H., ed. *The Poets and Poetry of the Century*, 10 vols. (1891–97); 12 vols. (1905–7).

Palmer, Roy, ed. *A Touch on the Times*

(1975). A collection of working-class and music-hall songs.

Peters, Robert L., ed. *Victorians on Literature and Art* (1961).

Stanford, Derek, ed. *Poets of the Nineties: A Biographical Anthology* (1965); and *Pre-Raphaelite Writing* (1973).

Stedman, E. C. *A Victorian Anthology* (1895).

Thornton, R. K. R., ed. *Poetry of the 'Nineties* (1970).

Williams, Charles. *A Book of Victorian Narrative Verse* (1927).

BIBLIOGRAPHIES

Altholz, Josef L., ed. *Victorian England 1837–1900* (1970). A bibliography arranged by kinds of history: general, political, social, scientific and technological, etc.

Altick, Richard D., and Matthews, William R., eds. *A Guide to Doctoral Dissertations in Victorian Literature, 1886–1958* (1960).

Annual bibliographies of studies in Victorian Literature appear in *Victorian Studies* (1958–) and the *Publications of the Modern Language Association* (1957–). The periodical *Victorian Poetry* publishes an annual survey of scholarship and criticism on topics in Victorian poetry (1963–). *Studies in English Literature* publishes an annual survey of books published on topics in nineteenth-century British literature (1961–). The annual bibliographies of studies in Victorian literature which now appear in *Victorian Studies* have been cumulated in three separate volumes: studies published 1932–44 in a volume edited by William D. Templeman (1945); 1945–54 in a volume edited by Austin Wright (1956); and 1955–64 in a volume edited by Robert C. Slack (1967). Bibliographies of writing about late-century writers are published annually in *English Literature* (originally . . . *Fiction*) *in Transition* (1957–).

Buckley, Jerome, ed. *Victorian Poets and Prose Writers* (1966).

DeLaura, David J., ed. *Victorian Prose: A Guide to Research* (1973).

Ehrsam, T. G., Deily, R. H., and Smith, R. M., eds. *Bibliographies of Twelve Victorian Authors* (1936). Includes Elizabeth Barrett Browning, FitzGerald, the Rossettis, Clough, Arnold, Tennyson, Morris, Stevenson, Swinburne, Hardy, and Kipling. A supplement was published by J. G. Fucilla in *Modern Philology*, **37** (1939).

Faverty, Frederic E., ed. *The Victorian Poets: A Guide to Research,* second edition (1968).

Houghton, Walter E. *The Wellesley Index to Victorian Periodicals, 1824–1900,* Vols. 1 and 2 (1966, 1972). Identifies the authors of essays and reviews in twenty principal Victorian quarterly and monthly magazines.

Howard-Hill, T. H. *Bibliography of British Literary Bibliographies* (1969).

Jordan, Frank, Jr., ed. *The English Romantic Poets: A Review of Research and Criticism,* third edition (1972).

Kunitz, Stanley J., and Haycraft, H. *British Authors of the Nineteenth Century* (1936).

Lauterbach, Edward S., and Davis, Eugene, eds., *The Transitional Age: British Literature 1800–1920* (1973). Bibliographies of writings about literary forms, and of writings by and about individual writers.

Madden, Lionel. *How to Find Out About the Victorian Period: A Guide to Sources of Information* (1970).

Watson, George, ed. *The New Cambridge Bibliography of English Literature,* vol. 3, 1800–1900 (1969).

Index to First Lines

This index includes only the first line of the first verse of long poems that are made up of short poems and are reprinted in the anthology in their entirety (for example, *In Memoriam, Modern Love*) or in relatively long extracts (*The House of Life, The Angel in the House*).

Index to Authors and Titles